SCIENCE FICTION

AND

FANTASY

LITERATURE

1975 - 1991

SCIENCE FICTION
AND
FANTASY
LITERATURE
1975 - 1991

A Bibliography of Science Fiction,
Fantasy, and Horror Fiction Books
and Nonfiction Monographs

by **Robert Reginald**
California State University,
San Bernardino

Associate Editors:
Mary A. Burgess, Daryl F. Mallett

Editorial Assistants and Advisors:
Scott Alan Burgess, John Clute,
William G. Contento,
John Hansen Gurley,
Douglas Menville, Paul David Seldis

 Gale Research Inc. • *DETROIT* • *WASHINGTON, D.C.* • *LONDON*

The paper used in this publication meets the minimum requirements of the American National Standard for Information Sciences—Permanence Paper for Printing Library Materials, ANSI Z39.48-1984.

∞™

Grateful acknowledgment of previous publication of selected material in *Science Fiction and Fantasy Literature* is made to the following publications: *Stella Nova: The Contemporary Science Fiction Authors*, by Robert Reginald, published 1970 by Unicorn & Son, Publishers. *Contemporary Science Fiction Authors, First Edition*, by Robert Reginald, published 1975 by Arno Press. *Science Fiction and Fantasy Literature: A Checklist, 1700-1974; with, Contemporary Science Fiction Authors II*, by Robert Reginald, published 1979 by Gale Research Co. *Science Fiction and Fantasy Awards*, by Robert Reginald, published 1981 by The Borgo Press. *Reginald's Science Fiction and Fantasy Awards, Second Edition*, by Robert Reginald and Daryl F. Mallett, published 1991 by The Borgo Press. *Reginald's Science Fiction and Fantasy Awards, Third Edition*, by Robert Reginald and Daryl F. Mallett, published 1992 by The Borgo Press. Used by permission of R. Reginald, The Borgo Press and Gale Research Inc.

Printed in the United States of America.

Published simultaneously in the United Kingdom by Gale Research International Limited
(an affiliated company of Gale Research Inc.)

Library of Congress Cataloging-in-Publication Data

Reginald, R.
    Science fiction and fantasy literature, 1975-1991 : a bibliography of science fiction, fantasy, and horror fiction books and nonfiction monographs / Robert Reginald ; associate editors, Mary A. Burgess, Daryl F. Mallett ; editorial assistants and advisors, Scott Alan Burgess ... [et al.].
       p. cm.
    Continues the author's Science fiction and fantasy literature : a checklist, 1700-1974.
    Includes indexes.
    ISBN 0-8103-1825-3 : $199
      1. Science fiction—Bio-bibliography. 2. Fantastic fiction—Bio-bibliography. 3. Horror tales—Bio-bibliography. 4. Authors—20th century—Biography. I. Burgess, Mary Wickizer, 1938- . II. Mallett, Daryl F. (Daryl Furumi), 1969- . III. Title.
Z5917.S36R4212 1992
[PN3448.S45]
016.80883'876—dc20
                                            92-28219
                                               CIP

CONTENTS

Once Again for Mary:

When in disgrace with fortune and men's eyes
I all alone beweep my outcast state
And trouble deaf heaven with my bootless cries
And look upon myself and curse my fate,
Wishing me like to one more rich in hope,
Featur'd like him, like him with friends possess'd,
Desiring this man's art, and that man's scope,
With what I most enjoy contented least;
Yet in these thoughts myself almost despising,
Haply I think on thee,—and then my state,
Like to the lark at break of day arising
From sullen earth, sings hymns at heaven's gate;
    For thy sweet love remember'd such wealth brings
    That then I scorn to change my state with kings.

—William Shakespeare

INTRODUCTION

It all started on the bus. I was a bright, eager, somewhat serious twenty-year-old college senior attending my first science-fiction convention (Baycon) at the end of August, 1968, being held in an old hotel above Berkeley, California. It was my first grand adventure. I couldn't afford to stay in the hotel, so I camped at my aunt's place in San Francisco, and commuted back and forth to Berkeley by bus. And there I met the first author I had ever encountered, Emil Petaja, who was gracious enough to talk to me without condescension, to treat me as an equal, even to invite me to visit his home, where he showed me dozens of original paintings and drawings by his deceased friend, Hannes Bok. Over the next few days I talked to Edmond Hamilton and Leigh Brackett, met Randall Garrett and Gene Roddenberry, literally ran into Mark Lenard (Spock's father Sarek on *Star Trek*), and saw and sometimes talked to dozens of other men and women who had previously been just names on brightly colored book covers. I was overwhelmed. And it occurred to me, as I was riding back on the bus that evening to San Francisco, that there had never been a biographical directory of SF authors, and that I could do it.

From that inspiration sprang my first book, *Stella Nova*, self-published in 1970, and from *Stella Nova* grew *Science Fiction and Fantasy Literature* in its several incarnations, as well as an interesting life as publisher and author and librarian. The original idea—a "who's who" of science fiction—gradually metamorphosized over the past two decades into *Science Fiction and Fantasy Literature: A Checklist, 1700-1974*, a comprehensive bibliography of fantastic literature, with the biographical portions being relegated to a much smaller second volume, and being removed altogether from this new checklist.

The bibliography that remains has grown with the genre of fantastic literature, which has itself branched into three distinct modern publishing categories: science fiction, fantasy, and horror (or dark fantasy) fiction. During the last seventeen years more than a thousand original works of fantastic literature have been published annually in the English language. In other words, more original titles of science fiction, fantasy, and supernatural horror were published between 1975 and 1991 than were issued in the entire previous history of the genre through 1974. Altogether, the two editions of *Science Fiction and Fantasy Literature* record some 38,000 unique SF monographs of 2,000 authors, with many additional thousands of variant titles and other such anomalies.

The purpose of this new volume remains the same as the original: to record all monographs of fantastic literature in their first appearances in the English language, plus all significant variations in content or title or byline. The definitions used in the original bibliography (Gale Research Co., 1979) remain the same (see also the lengthy Afterword in Volume 2 of that set for further elaboration), but the method of compilation has changed as the field itself has changed, and the world of information along with it. The data in the original set were organized onto 3" x 5" cards, checked manually through the massive *National Union* and *British Library* catalogs, and typed onto oversized masters. This new bibliography was input directly into a computer data base, and checked through OCLC and other media, including some printed sources, before being transferred and formatted into word-processed copy for final printout on a laser printer.

The genre of fantastic literature has changed markedly in the seventeen years since the cut-off of the original data base (1974). The fantasy genre became almost a separate publishing category in the mid-1970s, and the horror category exploded in the 1980s, developing its own set of authors and its own unique cover packages. Similarly, the British SF scene generated its own group of writers during the 1980s, many of whose works have never been reprinted in the United States. Series novels proliferated, game tie-ins and novelizations became extraordinarily popular, "shared world" fictions were developed, and multiple-ending stories grew like weeds in the adolescent paperback market. Sub-genres (Christian-world fantasies, for example) proliferated, and small-run, small-press productions were made possible by changes in the printing industry and the wide availability of cheap computer technology. The thousands of peripheral items generated by these processes have been extraordinarily difficult to capture, and undoubtedly some few have been missed and will be added to subsequent editions of this ongoing project. Still, the 22,000 unique records recorded herein comprise at least 98% of the SF, fantasy, and horror books actually published during the last seventeen years in the English language, and include more than a thousand retrospective additions to the original data base (many with new pseudonym identifications). Corrections and additions are always welcome, and should be sent to Box 2845, San Bernardino, CA 92406.

The primary source for the materials listed herein remains (as before) my personal collection of fantastic literature, now approaching 35,000 volumes, supplemented by the resources of the J. Lloyd Eaton Collection of Science Fiction and Fantasy Literature at the Tomás Rivera Library, University of California, Riverside, and the collection at the Texas A&M University Libraries; plus my extensive personal collection of SF reference sources; and the general literary resources of the Pfau Library, California State University, San Bernardino. Thanks to all these institutions. Other major sources include the annual volumes of Brown and Contento's *Science Fiction, Fantasy, and Horror*, the forthcoming Second Edition of Peter Nicholls and John Clute's *Encyclopedia of Science Fiction*, Gale Research Inc.'s *Biography and Genealogy Master Index*, and many hundreds of other reference works. Where specific publication data are lacking (usually paginations for British books), I have been able to verify the content of the book without actually examining the first edition (although I may have examined an American reprint), and no known source provides that information (the British Library listings in OCLC and in the *British National Bibliography* have become notoriously deficient in recent years, rarely being updated to include paginations); estimated paginations are provided for such works in brackets.

The SF field is extraordinarily rich in bibliographies and indexes, with some 550 volumes having been produced in the short history of the field. A tip of the hat, then, to those earlier men and women who labored so mightily to categorize a very difficult and diffuse literature, particularly to Everett Bleiler, whose pioneering 1948 work, *The Checklist of Fantastic Literature*, was the first serious attempt to provide bibliographical control of the genre. His efforts and those of the other pioneering bibliographers in the field made a difficult task significantly easier.

Many hands also assisted in the erection of this new bibliographical edifice. Gracious thanks to: **Mary Burgess**, who formatted much of the book; **Daryl Mallett**, who transcribed the final two years of data from my collection, formatted significant portions of the text, and phoned and phoned hundreds of authors to ask them questions; **John Clute**, good friend and good researcher, who noted many additions and corrections to the original data base during the past decade, critiqued a printout of this new bibliography prior to publication, checked titles at the British Library, and generously supplied an advance copy of his own work; **Bill Contento** and **Charlie Brown** of *Locus* Publications, who provided a cumulative printout of the entire data base of their annual bibliography of fantastic literature from 1984-1991; **Andy Porter** at *Science Fiction Chronicle*, for helping with dates and addresses; **Doug Menville**, my oldest friend, who has added so many strange and offbeat titles to the data base that I have often wondered whether he was printing single copies in his garage; **Hal Hall**, for his constant support and advice; **Barry** and **Sally Levin**, who provided cards on vanity press titles; **Lloyd Currey**, always a sound resource on obscure bibliographical points; **Neil Barron**, for his continuing interest and support; **Leslie Kay Swigart**, friend and colleague; **Darrell Schweitzer**, who sent numerous postcards with addenda; **Tony Lewis**, who provided a complete checklist of NESFA Press publications and its authors; **Marty Greenberg**, whose personal bibliography is nearly as long as this volume; **Ken Johnson** (the bibliographer, not the novelist), for adding during the final months over a hundred strange and unknown SF paperbacks; **Don D'Ammassa, Dave Hartwell, Lydia Marano** and **Art Cover** of Dangerous Visions, **John Peel, Ed Gorman, Tim Underwood**, for confirming last-minute IDs; **Will Murray**, who generously supplied numerous identifications of the real authors behind several house pseudonyms; **andy offutt**, who helped with penname identification; **Phil Harbottle** and **Stephen Holland**, for additional pseudonym identifications for the early 1950s British pulp paperbacks; **Chet Cunningham, Mark Roberts**, and **Bill Johnstone**, for material on the modern men's adventure series; **Forrest J Ackerman**, for helping with much-needed addresses and phone numbers, and for tapping his fount of knowledge about the field; **Zayra Kabot** at *Star Trek: The Next Generation* (Paramount Pictures), and **Scott Shannon, David Stern**, and **Kevin Ryan** at the Pocket Books *Star Trek* program, for help with addresses and other information on their writers; **Dean Wesley Smith, Debra Gray Cook**, and **O'Neil De Noux** at Pulphouse Publishing; **Bud Plant**; the many writers who responded, especially **Sheila Finch, Arthur C. Clarke**, and **Jon Gustafson**; and **Scott Burgess, Paul Seldis**, and **John Gurley**, editors at The Borgo Press, who checked and verified data from a variety of sources, and assisted greatly with the proofreading. Finally, thanks to those writers who took time from their busy schedules to respond to our calls and letters. Without the help of all of these individuals, and the many persons I do not have space to list, this book would be much less complete.

My thanks also to **Arthur E. Nelson, Marty Bloomberg, Johnnie Ann Ralph**, and **Dr. William Aguilar**, directors and acting directors at the Pfau Library, California State University, San Bernardino, during the decade this book was being compiled, and to **Buckley Barrett**, my direct supervisor, for their continuing support of my research projects; to **George Slusser, Cliff Wurfel, Gladys L. Murphy, Shoshona Stocking, Sid Berger**, and **Daryl Mallett** of the Eaton Collection, University of California, Riverside, for allowing me free access to the largest publicly accessible library of fantastic literature; and to **Don Dyal** and **Hal Hall** of the Texas A&M University Libraries, for opening the doors of that august institution's fine collection of fantastic literature.

Finally, thanks to my editors and contacts at Gale Research Inc., especially **Jim Ethridge, Dedria Bryfonski, Amy Marcaccio**, and **Peter Gareffa**, for their patience and generous support. This book could not have been produced without them, or without the willingness of my wife, Mary, to share me with the computer on so many sleepless nights.

Ave.

—Robert Reginald
(Professor Michael Burgess)
California State University, San Bernardino
12 June 1992

HOW TO USE THIS BOOK

Authors are listed in the first section of this book alphabetically by surname, with each writer's works being arranged under his or her name in alphabetical order by title, giving (when known) the following data: title (in italics), city of publication of the first English-language edition, publisher, year of publication, pagination, binding (paper or cloth), type (novel, collection, anthology, television or movie adaptation, nonfiction work [about fantastic literature]), series information (in small caps), and other bibliographical notes (where applicable).

Titles are referenced in the **Title Index** by title and author only; one must look to the main entry under the author's name to find complete bibliographical data. The **Series Index** correlates series name, author, series number, title (in italics), and year of publication; specific author identifications of individual titles are provided where necessary. The **Doubles Index** is arranged by publisher, then by publication number, with numbers, titles, and authors. The **Awards Index** provides complete information on the major SF awards, alphabetically by name of award, then chronologically by award date, giving: year, award name, title, and author (where applicable). Awards have also been cross-indexed in the Author Index to specific winning book titles, as noted at the end of those monographs' entries.

Although it can stand on its own, this bibliography is best used in tandem with *Science Fiction and Fantasy Literature: a Checklist, 1700-1974* (Gale Research Co., 1979). For the convenience of users, some entries from the original two-volume set have been repeated in this new book in lieu of "see" references, as have the several hundred entries that originally constituted the "Addendum" to the 1700-1974 work. In addition, some author entries from the first edition have also been amended with new dates of birth and/or death or with middle names, without, however, the repetition of the bibliographical data for their books; such records include a star before the author's surname, with new material (usually death dates) underlined for easy identification. Finally, some bibliographical records from the 1979 edition have been repeated when new information has been discovered. Item numbers used in the previous book have been reproduced here when entries are repeated; the numbering for new records begins where the previous set ended, #15885 being the first book noted in this supplement. As before, jointly authored works generate only one unique bibliographical number, that number being repeated as many times as necessary throughout the book; newly revised or expanded versions of previous books (of which they are many) are considered new works, and receive new numbers. I have also added considerably more bibliographic notes to entries than in the previous set.

This book includes monographs of fantastic prose literature published in the English language between the years 1975-1991, plus works published between 1700-1974 which were not covered in the original set. As in the original set, I have excluded stage plays, poetry, songs, and graphic novels or comic books, but have added nonfiction works about the field, plus compilations of SF art. Coverage includes science fiction, fantasy, supernatural horror, works set in a definite future, fictions set in the science-fiction or SF fan world (even when they are not in themselves fantastic), fictional "nonfiction" works (*The Dune Encyclopedia*, for example), fantasy gamebooks (but not instruction books for fantasy games), criticism on SF or fantasy authors or subjects, bibliographies and other reference works, and miscellanea about the genre. Actually applying or even identifying these definitions has become very tricky as genre lines have blurred, and I have thus tended to include more borderline items in this bibliography than in my previous work.

ABBREVIATIONS AND DEFINITIONS

anth. A compilation of works by more than one author.
art A work consisting primarily of artwork.
cloth A hardcover book.
coll. A compilation of works by one author.
ed. An edition of a work (e.g., rev. ed. =revised edition).
fiction A work of fiction that does not fit any other category.
movie An adaptation in fictional form of a screenplay.
nonf. A nonfiction work, usually about fantastic literature or film.
paper A softcover book.
pseud. A pen name; a "house pseud." is a name used individually by more than one author.
radio An adaptation in fictional form of a radio play.
rev. Revised edition.
S.l. No place of publication is known for this book.
s.n. No publisher is known for this book.
story A work of short fiction published in monograph form.
tele. An adaptation in fictional form of a teleplay.

The names of the American states have been abbreviated to the two-letter codes used by the United States Postal Service. The names of Australian, British, and Canadian states, counties, and provinces have been written out in full.

AUTHOR INDEX

A

?, pseud.—SEE: Miller, George Noyes

AAKHUS, Patricia

15885 *The voyage of Mael Duin's curragh.* Santa Cruz, CA: Story Line Press, 1989, 227 p., cloth, novel.

AAMODT, Donald

15886 *A name to conjure with.* New York: Avon Books, 1989, 265 p., paper, novel. NAME TO CONJURE WITH #1.
15887 *A troubling along the border.* New York: AvoNova, 1991, 275 p., paper, novel. NAME TO CONJURE WITH #2.

AARON, Chester (Norman), 1923-

15888 *Out of sight, out of mind.* Philadelphia, PA: J. B. Lippincott Co., 1985, 184 p., cloth, novel.

AARONOVITZ, Ben

15889 *Doctor Who: Remembrance of the Daleks.* London: A Target Book, W. H. Allen & Co., 1990, 160 p., paper, tele. DOCTOR WHO #148.
Remembrance of the Daleks—SEE: *Doctor Who: Remembrance of the Daleks.*

AARONS, Edward S(idney), 1916-1975

15890 *Assignment Unicorn.* Greenwich, CT: A Fawcett Gold Medal Book, Fawcett Publications, 1976, 191 p., paper, novel. SAM DURELL SERIES.

AB HUGH, Dafydd [legalized name], 1960-

15891 *Heroing; or, How he wound down the world.* New York: Baen Books, 1987, 345 p., paper, novel.
15892 *Warriorwards.* Riverdale, NY: Baen Fantasy, 1990, 344 p., paper, novel.

ABBEY, Edward, 1927-1989

15893 *Good news.* New York: E. P. Dutton & Co., 1980, 242 p., cloth, novel.

ABBEY, Lloyd (Robert), 1943-

15894 *The last whales.* New York: Grove Weidenfeld, 1989, 358 p., cloth, novel.

ABBEY, Lynn [i.e., Marilyn Lorraine Abbey], 1948-

15895 *The Black Flame.* New York: Ace Books, 1980, 376 p., paper, novel. RIFKIND #2.
15896 *Conquest.* New York: A Byron Preiss Book, Avon, 1988, 262 p., paper, novel. UNICORN & DRAGON #2.
15896A retitled: *The green man.* London: Headline, 1989, 262 p., paper, novel. UNICORN & DRAGON #2.
15897 *Daughter of the bright moon.* New York: Ace Books, 1979, 410 p., paper, novel. RIFKIND #1.
15898 *The forge of virtue.* New York: Popular Library, 1991, 312 p., paper, novel. [A novelization of the *Ultima Saga* game].
The green man—SEE: *Conquest.*
15899 *The guardians.* New York: Ace Books, 1982, 380 p., paper, novel.
15900 *Unicorn & dragon.* London: Headline, 1987, 230 p., paper, novel. UNICORN & DRAGON #1.
15901 *The wooden sword.* New York: Ace Books, 1991, 247 p., paper, novel.

with Robert Lynn Asprin

15902 *Aftermath.* New York: Ace Books, 1987, xiv+273 p., paper, anth. THIEVES' WORLD #10.
15903 *Blood ties.* New York: Ace Fantasy Books, 1986, xiv+238 p., paper, anth. THIEVES' WORLD #9.
15904 *Cross-currents.* Garden City, NY: Nelson Doubleday, 1984, 628 p., cloth, anth. THIEVES' WORLD #4-6. [Includes *Storm season, The face of chaos, Wings of omen*].
15905 *The dead of winter.* New York: Ace Fantasy Books, 1985, xiv+273 p., paper, anth. THIEVES' WORLD #7.
15906 *The face of chaos.* New York: Ace Fantasy Books, 1983, 242 p., paper, anth.

21645 *The price of victory.* Garden City, NY: Nelson Doubleday, 1990, [750] p., cloth, anth. THIEVES' WORLD #10-12. [Includes *Aftermath*; *Uneasy alliances*; *Stealers' sky*].

15907 *The shattered sphere.* Garden City, NY: Nelson Doubleday, 1986, 728 p., cloth, anth. THIEVES' WORLD #7-9. [Includes *The dead of winter, Soul of the city, Blood ties*].

15908 *Soul of the city.* New York: Ace Fantasy Books, 1986, xiii+242 p., paper, anth. THIEVES' WORLD #8.

15909 *Stealers' sky.* New York: Ace Books, 1989, xv+240 p., paper, anth. THIEVES' WORLD #12.

15910 *Uneasy alliances.* New York: Ace Books, 1988, xiii+258 p., paper, anth. THIEVES' WORLD #11.

15911 *Wings of omen.* New York: Ace Fantasy Books, 1984, 277 p., paper, anth. THIEVES' WORLD #6.

with Robert Lynn Asprin and Richard Pini

15912 *The blood of ten chiefs.* New York: Tor SF, A Tom Doherty Associates Book, 1986, 314 p., cloth, anth. ELFQUEST #1.

15913 *Elfquest: Wolfsong: The blood of ten chiefs.* New York: Tor SF, A Tom Doherty Associates Book, 1988, 307 p., paper, anth. ELFQUEST #2.
Wolfsong—SEE: *Elfquest: Wolfsong: The blood of ten chiefs.*

with others unknown

15914 *Game master's guide for Sanctuary.* [S.l.]: Midkemia Press, 1981, 64 p., paper, nonf.

ABBEY, Marilyn L.—SEE: Abbey, Lynn

ABBOTT, Keith (George), 1944-

15915 *Gush.* Berkeley, CA: Blue Wind Press, 1975, 140 p., cloth, novel.

15916 *Rhino Ritz: an American mystery.* Berkeley, CA: Blue Wind Press, 1979, 166 p., cloth, novel.

ABE, Kobo, 1924-

15917 *The ark Sakura.* New York: Alfred A. Knopf, 1988, 333 p., cloth, novel. [Translation by Juliet Winters Carpenter of *Hakobune Sakura Maru*].

15918 *Beyond the curve: (and other stories).* Tokyo: Kodansha, 1991, 247 p., cloth, coll. [Translation by Juliet Winters Carpenter].

ABELLA, Alex, 1950-

15919 *The killing of the saints.* New York: Crown Publishers, 1991, 308 p., cloth, novel.

ABERCROMBIE, Nora, 1960- , with Candas Dorsey

18237 *Hardwired angel.* Vancouver, British Columbia, Canada: Arsenal Pulp Press, 1987, 113 p., paper, novel.

ABRAHAMS, Doris—SEE: Brahms, Caryl

ABRAHAMS, William (Miller), 1919-, with Peter Stansky

15920 *Orwell: the transformation.* London: Constable, 1979, xi+240 p., cloth, nonf.

15921 *The unknown Orwell.* London: Constable, 1972, xvi+271 p., cloth, nonf.

*ABRAMOV, Aleksandr (Sergeevich), 1904-1985

ABRAMS, R. Vaughan, 1949-

15922 *Para.* Fairfield, IA: Seven Suns Publications, 1986, x+372 p., cloth, novel.

ABRASH, Merritt (G.), 1930-

15923 *Utopia in a scientific age.* Troy, NY: Center for the Study of the Human Dimensions of Science and Technology, Rensselaer Polytechnic Institute, 1979, v+178 p., paper, anth. [Includes some nonfiction].

ABRASHKIN, Raymond, 1911-1960, with Jay Williams

15924 *Danny Dunn and the universal glue.* New York: McGraw-Hill Book Co., 1977, 160 p., cloth, novel. DANNY DUNN #15. [The final book in the series].

15925 *Danny Dunn, scientific detective.* New York: McGraw-Hill Book Co., 1975, 172 p., cloth, novel. DANNY DUNN #14.

ABSHIRE, Richard K., with William R. Clair

15926 *Gants.* Los Angeles: SOS Publications, 1985, 334 p., paper, novel. GANTS #1.

15927 *The shaman tree.* New York: A Thomas Dunne Book, St. Martin's Press, 1989, [256] p., cloth, novel. GANTS #2.

ACHILLEOS, Chris, 1947-

15928 *Beauty and the beast: a collection of heroic fantasy illustrations.* Limpsfield, Surrey, England: Dragon's World, 1978, 92 p., paper, art.

15929 *Medusa: the third book of illustrations.* Limpsfield, Surrey, England: Paper Tiger, 1988, 143 p., cloth, art.

15930 *Sirens: the second book of illustrations.* Limpsfield, Surrey, England: Dragon's World, 1986, 125 p., cloth, art.

ACKER, Kathy, 1948-

18238 *Don Quixote which was a dream: a novel.* New York: Grove Press, 1986, 207 p., cloth, novel.

15931 *Empire of the senseless.* New York: Grove Press, 1988, 227 p., cloth, novel.

ACKERMAN, Forrest J(ames), 1916-

15932 *Close encounters of the third kind.* New York: Warren Publishing Co., 1977, 38 p., paper, nonf.
   Fantastic movie memories—SEE: *Forrest J Ackerman's Fantastic movie memories.*

15933 *Forrest J Ackerman, famous monster of filmland.* Pittsburgh, PA: Imagine, 1985, 151 p., paper, nonf.

15934 *Forrest J Ackerman presents Mr. Monster's movie gold.* Virginia Beach, VA: Donning Co., 1985, 205 p., paper, nonf.

15935 *Forrest J Ackerman's Fantastic movie memories.* Canoga Park, CA: New Media Books, 1985, 100 p., paper, nonf.

15936 *Gosh! Wow! (sense of wonder) science fiction.* Toronto, New York: Bantam Books, 1982, xxii+561 p., paper, anth.

15937 *J. R. R. Tolkien's The lord of the rings: a fantasy film.* New York: Warren Publishing Co., 1979, 47 p., paper, nonf.

15938 *Lon of 1000 faces.* Beverly Hills, CA: Morrison, Raven-Hill Co., 1983, 286 p., cloth, nonf.
   Mr. Monster's movie gold—SEE: *Forrest J Ackerman presents Mr. Monster's movie gold.*

15939 *Souvenir book of Mr. Science Fiction's fantasy museum.* Tokyo: Tsurumoto Book Room, 1978, 76 p., paper, nonf.

as ANONYMOUS EDITOR

15940 *The Gernsback awards, 1926.* Los Angeles: Triton Books, 1982, v+309 p., cloth, anth.

with Philip J. Riley

"The bride of Frankenstein"—SEE: *MagicImage Filmbooks presents "The bride of Frankenstein".*
   "Frankenstein"—SEE: *MagicImage Filmbooks presents "Frankenstein".*

15941 *MagicImage Filmbooks presents "The bride of Frankenstein".* Absecon, NJ: MagicImage Filmbooks, 1989, [177] p., paper, nonf. anth. [Includes screenplay plus commentary].

15942 *MagicImage Filmbooks presents "Frankenstein".* Absecon, NJ: MagicImage Filmbooks, 1989, [192] p., paper, nonf. anth. [Includes screenplay plus commentary].

with Clark Ashton Smith & H. P. Lovecraft & others

15943 *The boiling point.* West Warwick, RI: Necronomicon Press, 1985, [9] p., paper, nonf.

with A. W. Strickland

15944 *A reference guide to American science fiction films, volume 1.* Bloomington, IN: T.I.S. Publications, 1981, xvii+397 p., cloth, nonf. [Only volume published].

ACKROYD, Peter (Warwick), 1949-

15945 *First light.* New York: Grove Weidenfeld, 1989, 328 p., cloth, novel.

15946 *Hawksmoor.* London: Hamish Hamilton, 1985, [217] p., cloth, novel.

ACRES, Mark (Douglas), 1949-

15947 *Combat command in the world of Jerry E. Pournelle's Janissaries: Lord of lances.* New York: Ace Books, 1988, xvi+183 p., paper, novel. COMBAT COMMAND #7.

15948 *Combat command in the world of Robert A. Heinlein's Starship troopers: Shines the name.* New York: Ace Books, 1987, xix+[293] p., paper, novel. COMBAT COMMAND #2.

15949 *Dark divide.* New York: Ace Books, 1991, 183 p., paper, novel. RUNESWORD #5.
   Lord of lances—SEE: *Combat command in the world of Jerry E. Pournelle's Janissaries: Lord of lances.*
   Shines the name—SEE: *Combat command in the world of Robert A. Heinlein's Starship troopers: Shines the name.*

ACTON, Harold (Mario Mitchell), Sir, 1904-

19135 *Cornelian.* London: Chatto & Windus, 1928, 90 p., cloth, novel.

ACWORTH, Andrew

19265 *A new Eden.* London: Ward & Lock, 1896, 134 p., cloth, novel.

ADAIR, Gilbert

15950 *Alice through the needle's eye.* London: Macmillan, 1984, v+184 p., cloth, novel. ALICE IN WONDERLAND SEQUEL.

ADAIR, James B.

15951 *DeepCore.* New York: Berkley Books, 1991, 280 p., paper, novel. DEEPCORE #1.

with Gordon Rottman

Target Iran—SEE: *WWIII: Behind the lines: Target Iran.*
Target nuke—SEE: *WWIII: Behind the lines: Target nuke.*
Target Texas—SEE: *WWIII: Behind the lines: Target Texas.*

15952 *WWIII: Behind the lines: Target Iran.* New York: Berkley Books, 1991, 282 p., paper, novel. WWIII: BEHIND THE LINES #3.

15953 *WWIII: Behind the lines: Target nuke.* New York: Berkley Books, 1990, 321 p., paper, novel. WWIII: BEHIND THE LINES #2.

15954 *WWIII: Behind the lines: Target Texas.* New York: Berkley Books, 1990, 294 p., paper, novel. WWIII: BEHIND THE LINES #1.

ADAM, Auguste Villiers de L'Isle—SEE: Villiers de L'Isle Adam, Auguste

ADAMS, Anthony

15955 *Edgar Allan Poe and Ambrose Bierce.* London: Harrap, 1976, 214 p., cloth, anth.

ADAMS, Bill [i.e., William Adams], *with Cecil Brooks*

15956 *The unwound way.* New York: A Del Rey Book, Ballantine Books, 1991, 339 p., paper, novel.

ADAMS, Douglas (Noel), 1952-

15957 *Dirk Gently's holistic detective agency.* New York: Simon & Schuster, 1987, 247 p., cloth, novel. DIRK GENTLY #1.

15958 *The hitch hiker's guide to the galaxy.* London & Sydney: Pan Books, 1979, 159 p., paper, radio. HITCHHIKER SERIES #1.

15958A retitled: *The hitchhiker's guide to the galaxy.* New York: Harmony Books, 1980, 215 p., cloth, novel. HITCHHIKER SERIES #1.

The hitchhiker's guide to the galaxy—SEE: *The hitch hiker's guide to the galaxy.*

15959 *The hitchhiker's guide to the galaxy: a trilogy in four parts.* London: Heinemann, 1986, 590 p., cloth, coll. HITCHHIKER SERIES #1-4.

15959A retitled: *The hitchhiker's quartet.* New York: Harmony Books, 1986, xi+624 p., cloth, coll. HITCHHIKER SERIES #1-4.

The hitchhiker's quartet—SEE: *The hitchhiker's guide to the galaxy: a trilogy in four parts.*

15960 *The hitchhiker's trilogy.* New York: Harmony Books, 1983, xi+468 p., cloth, coll. HITCHHIKER SERIES #1-3.

15961 *Life, the universe and everything.* London & Sydney: Pan Books, 1982, 162 p., paper, novel. HITCHHIKER SERIES #3.

15962 *The long dark tea-time of the soul.* London: Heinemann, 1988, 246 p., cloth, novel. DIRK GENTLY #2.

15963 *The more than complete Hitchhiker's guide: five stories.* New York: Longmeadow Press, 1987, [200] p., cloth, coll. HITCHHIKER SERIES #1-4. [Also includes "Young Zaphod plays it safe"].

15964 *The original Hitchhiker radio scripts.* London & Sydney: Pan Books, 1985, [160] p., paper, coll. [Includes some commentary].

15965 *The Restaurant at the End of the Universe.* London & Sydney: Pan Books, 1980, 187 p., paper, novel. HITCHHIKER SERIES #2.

15966 *So long, and thanks for all the fish.* London & Sydney: Pan Books, 1984, 191 p., cloth, novel. HITCHHIKER SERIES #4.

*ADAMS, Francis A(lexandre), 1874-1975

*ADAMS, Fred C(alvin Jr.), 1949-

ADAMS, Glenda (Emilie), 1939-

15967 *Games of the strong.* London, Sydney: Angus & Robertson, 1982, 150 p., cloth, novel.

ADAMS, Harriet Stratemeyer, 1892-1982, *as* VICTOR APPLETON

00420 *Tom Swift and the planet stone; or, Discovering the secret of another world.* New York: Grosset & Dunlap, 1935, 203 p., cloth, novel. TOM SWIFT #38.

*ADAMS, Hazard (Simeon), 1926-

ADAMS, Hunter, pseud.—SEE: Lawrence, Jim

ADAMS, Ian, 1937-

15968 *The Trudeau papers: a novel.* Toronto: McClelland & Stewart, 1971, 108 p., cloth, novel.

*ADAMS, Jack [pseud. of Alcanoan O. Grigsby & Mary P. Lowe]

ADAMS, John, pseud.—SEE: Glasby, John

ADAMS, Nicholas, house pseud.

Final curtain—SEE: *Horror High: Final curtain.*
Hard rock—SEE: *Horror High: Hard rock.*
Heartbreaker—SEE: *Horror High: Heartbreaker.*

15969 *Horror High: Final curtain.* New York: HarperPaperbacks, 1991, 156 p., paper, novel. HORROR HIGH #8. [By Sherwood Smith].

15970 *Horror High: Hard rock.* New York: HarperPaperbacks, 1991, 156 p., paper, novel. HORROR HIGH #5. [By Clay Coleman].

15971 *Horror High: Heartbreaker.* New York: HarperPaperbacks, 1991, 154 p., paper, novel. HORROR HIGH #3. [By Clay Coleman].

15972 *Horror High: Mr. Popularity.* New York: HarperPaperbacks, 1990, 153 p., paper, novel. HORROR HIGH #1. [By Clay Coleman].

15973 *Horror High: New kid on the block.* New York: HarperPaperbacks, 1991, 151 p., paper, novel. HORROR HIGH #4. [By Clay Coleman].

15974 *Horror High: Pep rally.* New York: HarperPaperbacks, 1991, 155 p., paper, novel. HORROR HIGH #7. [By Debra Doyle & James D. Macdonald].

15975 *Horror High: Resolved, you're dead.* New York: HarperPaperbacks, 1990, 153 p., paper, novel. HORROR HIGH #2. [By Clay Coleman].

15976 *Horror High: Sudden death.* New York: HarperPaperbacks, 1991, 151 p., paper, novel. HORROR HIGH #6. [By Bruce Fretts].

15977 *I.O.U.* New York: HarperPaperbacks, 1991, 187 p., paper, novel. [By John Peel].

Mr. Popularity—SEE: *Horror High: Mr. Popularity.*
New kid on the block—SEE: *Horror High: New kid on the block.*
Pep rally—SEE: *Horror High: Pep rally.*
Resolved, you're dead—SEE: *Horror High: Resolved, you're dead.*

15978 *Santa claws.* New York: HarperPaperbacks, 1991, 187 p., paper, novel. [By John Peel].

Sudden death—SEE: *Horror High: Sudden death.*

ADAMS, Pamela Crippen, 1961- , *with Robert Adams*

15979 *Alternatives.* New York: Baen Fantasy, 1989, 312 p., paper, novel.

15980 *Friends of the Horseclans.* New York: A Signet Book, New American Library, 1987, 284 p., paper, anth.

Friends of the Horseclans II—SEE: *Horseclans: Friends of the Horseclans II.*

15981 *Horseclans: Friends of the Horseclans II.* New York: A Signet Book, New American Library, 1989, 287 p., paper, anth.

with Robert Adams & Martin H. Greenberg

15982 *Barbarians II.* New York: A Signet Book, New American Library, 1988, xi+364 p., paper, anth. [Charles Waugh was an uncredited co-editor for this book].

Book of alternate worlds—SEE: *Robert Adams' Book of alternate worlds.*
Book of soldiers—SEE: *Robert Adams' Book of soldiers.*

15983 *Hunger for horror.* New York: DAW Books, 1988, ix+256 p., paper, anth.

15984 *Phantom regiments.* New York: Baen Books, 1990, 271 p., paper, novel.

15985 *Robert Adams' Book of alternate worlds.* New York: A Signet Book, New American Library, 1987, 366 p., paper, anth.

15986 *Robert Adams' Book of soldiers.* New York: A Signet Book, New American Library, 1988, 348 p., paper, anth.

ADAMS, Richard (George), 1920-

15987 *The day gone by: an autobiography.* London: Century Hutchinson, 1990, xiii+398 p., cloth, nonf.

15988 *The girl in a swing.* London: Allen Lane, 1980, 397 p., cloth, novel.

15989 *The iron wolf, and other stories.* London: Allen Lane, 1980, 141 p., cloth, coll.

15989A retitled: *The unbroken web: stories & fables.* New York: Crown Publishers, 1980, 141 p., cloth, coll.

15990 *Maia.* Harmondsworth, Middlesex, England, New York: Viking, 1984, 1055 p., cloth, novel. BEKLAN EMPIRE #2.

15991 *The plague dogs.* London: Allen Lane, Rex Collings, 1977, xiii+461 p., cloth, novel.

15992 *Sinister and supernatural stories.* London: Ward Lock, 1978, 135 p., cloth, anth.

15993 *Traveller.* New York: Alfred A. Knopf, 1988, 270 p., cloth, novel.

The unbroken web: stories & fables—SEE: *The iron wolf, and other stories.*

15994 *The Watership Down film book.* New York: Macmillan, 1978, p., cloth, nonf.

ADAMS, (Franklin) Robert, 1932-1990

15995 *Bili the Axe: a Horseclans novel.* New York: A Signet Book, New American Library, 1983, 185 p., paper, novel. HORSECLANS #10.

15996 *Castaways in time.* Virginia Beach, VA: Starblaze Editions, Donning Co., 1979, 221 p., paper, novel. CASTAWAYS IN TIME #1.

15997 *A cat of silvery hue: A Horseclans novel.* New York: A Signet Book, New American Library, 1979, 166 p., paper, novel. HORSECLANS #4.

15998 *Champion of the last battle: a Horseclans novel.* New York: A Signet Book, New American Library, 1983, 201 p., paper, novel. HORSECLANS #11.

15999 *The Clan of the Cats.* New York: A Signet Book, New American Library, 1988, 221 p., paper, novel. HORSECLANS #18.

16000 *The coming of the Horseclans.* New York: Pinnacle Books, 1975, 180 p., paper, novel. HORSECLANS #1.

16001 *The coming of the Horseclans: a Horseclans novel.* New York: A Signet Book, New American Library, 1982, 200 p., paper, novel. HORSECLANS #1. [Expanded edition].

16002 *The death of a legend.* New York: A Signet Book, New American Library, 1981, 185 p., paper, novel. HORSECLANS #8.

16003 *Horseclans odyssey: a Horseclans novel.* New York: A Signet Book, New American Library, 1981, 241 p., paper, novel. HORSECLANS #7.

16004 *Horses of the north.* New York: A Signet Book, New American Library, 1985, 253 p., paper, novel. HORSECLANS #13.

16005 *Madman's army.* New York: A Signet Book, New American Library, 1987, 222 p., paper, novel. HORSECLANS #17.

16006 *A man called Milo Morai.* New York: A Signet Book, New American Library, 1986, 221 p., paper, novel. HORSECLANS #14.

16007 *The memories of Milo Morai.* New York: A Signet Book, New American Library, 1986, 221 p., paper, novel. HORSECLANS #15.

16008 *Monsters and magicians.* New York: Baen, 1989, 311 p., paper, novel. STAIRWAY TO FOREVER #2.

16009 *Of beginnings and endings.* New York: A Signet Book, New American Library, 1989, 238 p., paper, novel. CASTAWAYS IN TIME #6.

16010 *Of chiefs and champions.* New York: A Signet Book, New American Library, 1987, 238 p., paper, novel. CASTAWAYS IN TIME #4.

16011 *Of myths and monsters.* New York: A Signet Book, New American Library, 1988, 237 p., paper, novel. CASTAWAYS IN TIME #5.

16012 *Of quests and kings.* New York: A Signet Book, New American Library, 1986, 237 p., paper, novel. CASTAWAYS IN TIME #3.

16013 *The patrimony: a Horseclans novel.* New York: A Signet Book, New American Library, 1980, 184 p., paper, novel. HORSECLANS #6.

16014 *Revenge of the Horseclans.* Los Angeles: Pinnacle Books, 1977, 182 p., paper, novel. HORSECLANS #3.

16015 *The savage mountains: a Horseclans novel.* New York: A Signet Book, New American Library, 1980, 165 p., paper, novel. HORSECLANS #5.

16016 *The seven magical jewels of Ireland.* New York: A Signet Book, New American Library, 1985, 254 p., paper, novel. CASTAWAYS IN TIME #2.

16017 *Stairway to forever.* New York: Baen Books, 1988, 265 p., paper, novel. STAIRWAY TO FOREVER #1.

16018 *Swords of the Horseclans.* New York: Pinnacle Books, 1977, 182 p., paper, novel. HORSECLANS #2.

16019 *Tales of the Horseclans: collectors' edition, books 1, 2, 3.* New York: A Plume Book, New American Library, 1985, 578 p., paper, coll. HORSECLANS SERIES #1-3. [Includes *The coming of the Horse-*

clans; *Swords of the Horseclans; Revenge of the Horseclans*].

16020 *Trumpets of war.* New York: A Signet Book, New American Library, 1987, 223 p., paper, novel. HORSECLANS #16.

16021 *The witch goddess.* New York: A Signet Book, New American Library, 1982, 201 p., paper, novel. HORSECLANS #9.

16022 *A woman of the Horseclans: a Horseclans novel.* New York: A Signet Book, New American Library, 1983, 197 p., paper, novel. HORSECLANS #12.

with Pamela Crippen Adams

15979 *Alternatives.* New York: Baen Fantasy, 1989, 312 p., paper, novel.

15980 *Friends of the Horseclans.* New York: A Signet Book, New American Library, 1987, 284 p., paper, anth. HORSECLANS SERIES.
Friends of the Horseclans II—SEE: *Horseclans: Friends of the Horseclans II.*

15981 *Horseclans: Friends of the Horseclans II.* New York: A Signet Book, New American Library, 1989, 287 p., paper, anth. HORSECLANS SERIES.

with Pamela Crippen Adams & Martin H. Greenberg

15982 *Barbarians II.* New York: A Signet Book, New American Library, 1988, xi+364 p., paper, anth. [Charles Waugh was an uncredited co-editor for this book].
Book of alternate worlds—SEE: *Robert Adams' Book of alternate worlds.*
Book of soldiers—SEE: *Robert Adams' Book of soldiers.*

15983 *Hunger for horror.* New York: DAW Books, 1988, ix+256 p., paper, anth.

15984 *Phantom regiments.* New York: Baen Books, 1990, 271 p., paper, novel.

15985 *Robert Adams' Book of alternate worlds.* New York: A Signet Book, New American Library, 1987, 366 p., paper, anth.

15986 *Robert Adams' Book of soldiers.* New York: A Signet Book, New American Library, 1988, 348 p., paper, anth.

with Martin H. Greenberg & Charles G. Waugh

16023 *Barbarians.* New York: A Signet Book, New American Library, 1986, 368 p., paper, anth.

with Andre Norton

16024 *Magic in Ithkar.* New York: Tor SF, A Tom Doherty Associates Book, 1985, 317 p., paper, anth.

16024A retitled: *Magic in Ithkar 1.* New York: Tor SF, A Tom Doherty Associates Book, 1988, 317 p., paper, anth.

16025 *Magic in Ithkar 2.* New York: Tor SF, A Tom Doherty Associates Book, 1985, 306 p., paper, anth.

16026 *Magic in Ithkar 3.* New York: Tor SF, A Tom Doherty Associates Book, 1986, 319 p., paper, anth.

16027 *Magic in Ithkar 4.* New York: Tor SF, A Tom Doherty Associates Book, 1987, 278 p., paper, anth.

ADAMS, Terry A.

16028 *The master of chaos.* New York: DAW Books, 1989, 496 p., paper, novel. SENTIENCE #2.

16029 *Sentience: a novel of first contact.* New York: DAW Books, 1986, 381 p., paper, novel. SENTIENCE #1.

*ADDEO, Edmund G., 1907-1980

ADDER, Dr, pseud.—SEE: Jeter, K. W.

*ADDERLEY, Joseph James (Granville), 1861-1942

ADDINGTON, Sarah, 1891-1940

03939 *Hound of Heaven.* New York: D. Appleton-Century, 1935, 50 p., cloth, story.

ADDISON, Joseph

16030 *Tesseract.* New York: A Del Rey Book, Ballantine Books, 1988, 246 p., paper, novel.

ADKINS, Patrick H., 1948-

16031 *Lord of the crooked paths.* New York: Ace Books, 1987, 216 p., paper, novel. TITANS #1.

16032 *Master of the fearful depths.* New York: Ace Books, 1989, 218 p., paper, novel. TITANS #2.

16033 *Sons of the titans.* New York: Ace Books, 1990, 264 p., paper, novel. TITANS #3.

ADKINSON, Robert K., *with Allen Eyles & Nicholas Fry*

16034 *The house of horror: the complete story of Hammer Films, 2nd ed.* London: Lorrimer, 1981, 144 p., cloth, nonf.

ADLARD, Mark [i.e., Peter Marcus Adlard], 1932-

16035 *Multiface: science fiction.* London: Sidgwick & Jackson, 1975, 184 p., cloth, novel. T-CITY TRILOGY #3.

ADLARD, Peter M.—SEE: Adlard, Mark

*ADLEMAN, Robert H., 1916-1989

ADLER, Alan (Michael), 1951-

16036 *Science-fiction and horror movie posters in full color.* New York: Dover Publications, 1977, viii+40 p., paper, nonf.

*ADLER, Allen A., 1916-1964

ADLER, C(arole) S(chwerdtfeger), 1932-

16037 *Eddie's blue winged dragon.* New York: G. P. Putnam's Sons, 1988, 144 p., cloth, novel.
16038 *Footsteps on the stairs: a novel.* New York: Delacorte Press, 1982, 151 p., cloth, novel.
16039 *Ghost brother.* New York: Clarion Books, 1990, 150 p., cloth, novel.
16040 *Goodbye, Pink Pig.* New York: G. P. Putnam's Sons, 1985, 176 p., cloth, novel. PINK PIG #1.
16041 *Help, Pink Pig.* New York: G. P. Putnam's Sons, 1990, 160 p., cloth, novel. PINK PIG #2.
 The magical coach—SEE: *The silver coach.*
16042 *The silver coach.* New York: Coward, McCann & Geoghegan, 1979, 122 p., cloth, novel.
16042A retitled: *The magical coach.* Middletown, CT: Weekly Reader Books, 1983, 122 p., paper, novel.

ADLER, Paul

16043 *Saucer Hill.* New York: Avon, 1979, 203 p., paper, novel.

ADOFF, Virginia—SEE: Hamilton, Virginia

ADRIAN, Jack [pseud. of Christopher Lowder], 1945-

16044 *Deathlands: Pilgrimage to Hell.* Toronto, New York: A Gold Eagle Book, Worldwide, 1986, 380 p., paper, novel. DEATHLANDS #1.
 Pilgrimage to Hell—SEE: *Deathlands: Pilgrimage to Hell.*

16045 *Strange tales from the Strand Magazine.* Oxford, England, New York: Oxford University Press, 1991, xxiii+373 p., cloth, anth.

as Jack Hamilton Teed

35461 *The blood of Dracula.* London, Sydney: Mills & Boon, 1977, 94 p., paper, novel. DRACULA SERIES.

ADRIAN, Werner

16046 *Freaks: cinema of the bizarre.* London: Lorrimer Publishing, 1976, 110 p., paper, nonf.

*ADRIEL, Jeanne, 1892-1984

AELLEN, Richard

16047 *Redeye: a novel.* New York: Donald I. Fine, 1988, 374 p., cloth, novel.

AESCHLIMAN, Michael D(avid), 1948-

16048 *The restitution of man: C. S. Lewis and the case against scientism.* Grand Rapids, MI: William B. Eerdmans Publishing Co., 1983, 94 p., paper, nonf.

AFFABEE, Eric, pseud.—SEE: Stine, R. L.

AGNEW, Spiro T(heodore), 1918-

16049 *The Canfield decision.* Chicago: Playboy Press, 1976, 344 p., cloth, novel.

AGOSIN, Marjorie [i.e., Marjorie Stela Agosin Halpern], 1955-

16050 *The secret weavers: stories of the fantastic by women of Argentina and Chile.* Buffalo, NY: White Pine Press, 1991, 339 p., paper, anth.

AGUILERA MALTA, Demetrio, 1909-1981

16051 *Seven serpents and seven moons.* Austin, TX: University of Texas Press, 1979, 305 p., cloth, novel. [Translation by Gregory Rabassa of *Siete lunas y siete serpientes*].

AGUIRRE, Manuel, 1948-

16052 *The closed space: horror literature and western symbolism.* Manchester, England, New York: Manchester University Press, 1990, vi+234 p., cloth, nonf.

AHERN, Jerome M.—SEE: Ahern, Jerry

AHERN, Jerry [i.e., Jerome Morrell Ahern], 1946-

16053 *The arsenal.* New York: Zebra Books, Kensington Publishing Corp., 1988, 236 p., paper, novel. SURVIVALIST #16.

16054 *The awakening.* New York: Zebra Books, Kensington Publishing Corp., 1984, 235 p., paper, novel. SURVIVALIST #10.

16055 *The battle begins.* New York: A Dell Book, 1988, 245 p., paper, novel. DEFENDER #1.

16056 *Brutal conquest.* New York: Zebra Books, Kensington Publishing Corp., 1991, 254 p., paper, novel. SURVIVALIST #22.

16057 *The challenge.* New York: A Dell Book, 1990, 183 p., paper, novel. DEFENDER #11.

16058 *Death grip.* New York: A Dell Book, 1990, 293 p., paper, novel. DEFENDER #9.

16059 *Decision time.* New York: A Dell Book, 1989, 192 p., paper, novel. DEFENDER #4.

16060 *The doomsayer.* New York: Zebra Books, Kensington Publishing Corp., 1981, 222 p., paper, novel. SURVIVALIST #4.

16061 *Earth fire.* New York: Zebra Books, Kensington Publishing Corp., 1984, 237 p., paper, novel. SURVIVALIST #9.

16062 *The end is coming.* New York: Zebra Books, Kensington Publishing Corp., 1984, 234 p., paper, novel. SURVIVALIST #8.

16063 *Entrapment.* New York: A Dell Book, 1989, 183 p., paper, novel. DEFENDER #5.

16064 *Escape.* New York: A Dell Book, 1989, 180 p., paper, novel. DEFENDER #6.

16065 *Final rain.* New York: Zebra Books, Kensington Publishing Corp., 1989, 220 p., paper, novel. SURVIVALIST #19.

16066 *Firestorm.* New York: Zebra Books, Kensington Publishing Corp., 1990, 192 p., paper, novel. SURVIVALIST #20.

16067 *The good fight.* New York: A Dell Book, 1990, 184 p., paper, novel. DEFENDER #10.

16068 *Justice denied.* New York: A Dell Book, 1989, 183 p., paper, novel. DEFENDER #8.

16069 *The killing wedge.* New York: A Dell Book, 1988, 183 p., paper, novel. DEFENDER #2.
The legend—SEE: *The Survivalist: The legend.*

Mid-wake—SEE: *The Survivalist: Mid-wake.*

16070 *The nightmare begins.* New York: Zebra Books, Kensington Publishing Corp., 1981, 240 p., paper, novel. SURVIVALIST #2.

16071 *No survivors.* New York: A Dell Book, 1990, 185 p., paper, novel. DEFENDER #12.

16072 *The ordeal.* New York: Zebra Books, Kensington Publishing Corp., 1988, 220 p., paper, novel. SURVIVALIST #17.

16073 *Out of control.* New York: A Dell Book, 1988, 183 p., paper, novel. DEFENDER #3.

16074 *Overlord.* New York: Zebra Books, Kensington Publishing Corp., 1987, 252 p., paper, novel. SURVIVALIST #15.

16075 *The prophet.* New York: Zebra Books, Kensington Publishing Corp., 1984, 239 p., paper, novel. SURVIVALIST #7.

16076 *Pursuit.* New York: Zebra Books, Kensington Publishing Corp., 1986, 240 p., paper, novel. SURVIVALIST #13.

16077 *The quest.* New York: Zebra Books, Kensington Publishing Corp., 1981, 239 p., paper, novel. SURVIVALIST #3.

16078 *The rebellion.* New York: Zebra Books, Kensington Publishing Corp., 1985, 252 p., paper, novel. SURVIVALIST #12.

16079 *The reprisal.* New York: Zebra Books, Kensington Publishing Corp., 1985, 224 p., paper, novel. SURVIVALIST #11.

16080 *The savage horde.* New York: Zebra Books, Kensington Publishing Corp., 1983, 208 p., paper, novel. SURVIVALIST #6.

16081 *The struggle.* New York: Zebra Books, Kensington Publishing Corp., 1989, 223 p., paper, novel. SURVIVALIST #18.

16082 *The survivalist: Mid-wake.* New York: Zebra Books, Kensington Publishing Corp., 1988, 476 p., paper, novel. SURVIVALIST (UNNUMBERED).

16083 *The survivalist: The legend.* New York: Zebra Books, Kensington Publishing Corp., 1991, 383 p., paper, novel. SURVIVALIST (UNNUMBERED).

16084 *The survivalist: Total war.* New York: Zebra Books, Kensington Publishing Corp., 1981, 218 p., paper, novel. SURVIVALIST #1.

16085 *The terror.* New York: Zebra Books, Kensington Publishing Corp., 1987, 222 p., paper, novel. SURVIVALIST #14.

16086 *To end all war.* New York: Zebra Books, Kensington Publishing Corp., 1990, 223 p., paper, novel. SURVIVALIST #21.
Total war—SEE: *The survivalist: Total war.*

16087 *Vengeance.* New York: A Dell Book, 1989, 185 p., paper, novel. DEFENDER #7.

16088 *The web.* New York: Zebra Books, Kensington Publishing Corp., 1983, 222 p., paper, novel. SURVIVALIST #5.

as NICK CARTER

16089 *Deathlight.* New York: Charter Books, 1982, 212 p., paper, novel. NICK CARTER SERIES.

with Sharon Ahern

16090 *The freeman.* Toronto, New York: Bantam Books, 1986, 372 p., paper, novel.

16091 *The kamikaze legacy.* New York, London: Pocket Books, 1990, 274 p., paper, novel.

16092 *Miamigrad.* New York: Pocket Books, 1987, 373 p., paper, novel.

River of gold—SEE: *The takers: River of gold.*

16093 *The takers.* Toronto, New York: A Gold Eagle Book, Worldwide, 1984, 382 p., paper, novel. TAKERS #1. [Sharon Ahern's contribution is anonymous].

16094 *The takers: River of gold.* Toronto, New York: A Gold Eagle Book, Worldwide, 1985, 378 p., paper, novel. TAKERS #2.

16095 *WerewolveSS* [Nazi insignia]. New York: Pinnacle Books, Windsor Publishing Corp., 1990, 383 p., paper, novel.

AHERN, S. A.—SEE: Ahern, Sharon A.

AHERN, Sharon A(nn), 1948- , *with Jerry Ahern*

16090 *The freeman.* Toronto, New York: Bantam Books, 1986, 372 p., paper, novel.

16091 *The kamikaze legacy.* New York, London: Pocket Books, 1990, 274 p., paper, novel.

16092 *Miamigrad.* New York: Pocket Books, 1987, 373 p., paper, novel.

River of gold—SEE: *The takers: River of gold.*

16093 *The takers.* Toronto, New York: A Gold Eagle Book, Worldwide, 1984, 382 p., paper, novel. TAKERS #1. [Sharon Ahern's contribution is anonymous].

16094 *The takers: River of gold.* Toronto, New York: A Gold Eagle Book, Worldwide, 1985, 378 p., paper, novel. TAKERS #2.

16095 *WerewolveSS* [Nazi insignia]. New York: Pinnacle Books, Windsor Publishing Corp., 1990, 383 p., paper, novel.

AHO, Gary L(awrence), 1935-

16096 *William Morris: a reference guide.* Boston: G. K. Hall & Co., 1985, xliii+428 p., cloth, nonf.

AICKMAN, Robert (Fordyce), 1914-1981

16097 *Cold hand in mine: strange stories.* London: Victor Gollancz, 1975, 252 p., cloth, coll.

16098 *Intrusions: strange tales.* London: Victor Gollancz, 1980, 216 p., cloth, coll.

16099 *The late breakfasters.* London: Victor Gollancz, 1964, 252 p., cloth, novel.

16100 *The model.* New York: Arbor House, 1987, 138 p., cloth, novel.

16101 *Night voices: strange stories.* London: Victor Gollancz, 1985, 185 p., cloth, coll.

16102 *Painted devils: strange stories.* New York: Charles Scribner's Sons, 1979, 234 p., cloth, coll.

16103 *Tales of love and death.* London: Victor Gollancz, 1977, 192 p., cloth, coll.

16104 *The unsettled dust.* London: Mandarin, 1990, 301 p., paper, coll.

16105 *The wine-dark sea.* New York: Arbor House, 1988, 388 p., cloth, coll.

AIGNER, Kurt W.

16106 *Allistar: journey through a mind.* New York, Washington: Vantage Press, 1985, 101 p., cloth, novel.

AIKEN, Joan (Delano), 1924-

16107 *All & more.* London: Jonathan Cape, 1971, 360 p., cloth, coll. [Includes *All you've ever wanted* and *More than you bargained for*].

16108 *All you've ever wanted, and other stories.* London: Jonathan Cape, 1953, 191 p., cloth, coll.

16109 *Authors' choice 2: stories.* London: Hamilton, 1973, ix+246 p., cloth, anth.

12961 *Black hearts in Battersea.* Garden City, NY: Doubleday & Co., 1964, 240 p., cloth, novel. DIDO TWITE #2.

16110 *Bridle the wind.* London: Jonathan Cape, 1983, 270 p., cloth, novel.

16111 *A bundle of nerves: stories of horror, suspense, and fantasy.* London: Victor Gollancz, 1976, 220 p., cloth, coll.

13593 *The cuckoo tree.* London: Jonathan Cape, 1971, 250 p., cloth, novel. DIDO TWITE #5.

16112 *Dido and Pa.* London: Jonathan Cape, 1986, 251 p., cloth, novel. DIDO TWITE #6.

16113 *Faithless lollybird, and other stories.* London: Jonathan Cape, 1977, 223 p., cloth, coll.

16114 *The far forests: tales of romance, fantasy, and suspense.* New York: Viking Press, 1977, 154 p., cloth, coll.

16115 *A fit of shivers.* London: Victor Gollancz, 1990, 140 p., cloth, coll.

16116 *Fog hounds, wind cat, sea mice.* London: Macmillan, 1984, 64 p., cloth, coll.

16117 *Give yourself a fright: thirteen tales of the supernatural.* New York: Delacorte Press, 1989, 180 p., cloth, coll.

16118 *A goose on your grave.* London: Victor Gollancz, 1987, 159 p., cloth, coll.

16119 *A harp of fishbones, and other stories.* London: Jonathan Cape, 1972, 229 p., cloth, coll.

16120 *The haunting of Lamb House.* London: Jonathan Cape, 1991, 200 p., cloth, novel.

16121 *The kingdom under the sea, and other stories.* London: Jonathan Cape, 1971, 104 p., cloth, coll.

16122 *The last slice of the rainbow, and other stories.* London: Jonathan Cape, 1985, 127 p., cloth, coll.

16123 *Midnight is a place.* London: Jonathan Cape, 1974, 303 p., cloth, novel.

16124 *More than you bargained for, and other stories.* London: Jonathan Cape, 1955, 190 p., cloth, coll.

16125 *Necklace of raindrops, and other stories.* London: Jonathan Cape, 1968, 107 p., cloth, coll.

16126 *Night fall.* London & Sydney: Pan Books, 1969, 126 p., paper, novel.

13756 *Nightbirds on Nantucket.* Garden City, NY: Doubleday & Co., 1966, 216 p., cloth, novel. DIDO TWITE #3.

16127 *Past eight o'clock: goodnight stories.* London: Jonathan Cape, 1986, 128 p., cloth, coll.

16128 *The shadow guests.* London: Jonathan Cape, 1980, 169 p., cloth, novel.

16129 *A small pinch of weather, and other stories.* London: Jonathan Cape, 1969, 190 p., cloth, coll.

16130 *The stolen lake.* London: Jonathan Cape, 1981, 272 p., cloth, novel. DIDO TWITE #4. [A direct sequel to *Nightbirds on Nantucket*].

16131 *Tale of a one-way street, and other stories.* London: Jonathan Cape, 1978, 127 p., cloth, coll.

16132 *A touch of chill: stories of horror, suspense & fantasy.* London: Victor Gollancz, 1979, 191 p., cloth, coll.

16133 *Up the chimney down, and other stories.* London: Jonathan Cape, 1984, 268 p., cloth, coll.

16134 *Voices.* London: Hippo, 1988, 109 p., paper, novel.

16135 *Voices in an empty house: a novel.* London: Victor Gollancz, 1975, 349 p., cloth, novel.

16136 *A whisper in the night: stories of horror, suspense, and fantasy.* London: Victor Gollancz, 1982, 189 p., cloth, coll.

15784 *The wolves of Willoughby Chase.* London: Jonathan Cape, 1962, 159 p., cloth, novel. DIDO TWITE #1.

with Jan Pienkowski

16137 *A foot in the grave.* London: Jonathan Cape, 1989, 128 p., cloth, coll.

*AIKEN, John (Kempton), 1913-<u>1990</u>

AIKIN, James D.—SEE: Aikin, Jim

AIKIN, Jim [i.e., James Douglas Aikin], 1948-

16138 *Walk the Moons Road.* New York: A Del Rey Book, Ballantine Books, 1985, 340 p., paper, novel.

AIMÉ, Albert du—SEE: Wharton, William

AINSWORTH, Ruth [i.e., Ruth Gallard Ainsworth Gilbert], 1908-

The phantom carousel, and other ghostly tales—SEE: The phantom runabout, and other ghostly tales.

16139 *The phantom runabout, and other ghostly tales.* London: André Deutsch, 1977, 173 p., cloth, coll.

16139A retitled: *The phantom carousel, and other ghostly tales.* Chicago: Follett Publishing Co., 1978, 176 p., cloth, coll.

16140 *Up the airy mountain: stories of magic.* London: Heinemann, 1977, 132 p., cloth, coll.

AINSWORTHY, Roy, pseud.—SEE: Paine, Lauren

AIREY, Jean

16141 *The doctor and the Enterprise.* Canoga Park, CA: New Media Books, 1986, [64] p., paper, novel. STAR TREK SERIES; DOCTOR WHO SERIES.

with Laurie Haldeman

16142 *Travel without the Tardis.* London: A Target Book, W. H. Allen & Co., 1986, 160 p., paper, nonf.

AITMATOV, Chingiz (Torekulovich), 1928-

16143 *The day lasts more than a hundred years.* Bloomington, IN: Indiana University Press, 1983, xix+352 p., cloth, novel. [Translation by John French of *I dol'she veka dlitsia den'*].

AJEMIAN, Diran

16144 *The edge of immortality.* Liverpool, NY: Arcadia Books, 1978, 269 p., paper, novel.

AKERS, Alan Burt, pseud.—SEE: Bulmer, Kenneth

AKSENOV, Vasilii—SEE: Aksyonov, Vassily

AKSYONOV, Vassily [i.e., Vasilii Pavlovich Aksenov], 1932-

16145 *The island of Crimea: a novel.* New York: Random House, 1983, 369 p., cloth, novel. [Translation by Michael Henry Heim of *Ostrov Krym*].

ALBANO, Peter, 1940?-

16146 *Attack of the seventh carrier.* New York: Zebra Books, Kensington Publishing Corp., 1989, 400 p., paper, novel. SEVENTH CARRIER #5.
16147 *Quest of the seventh carrier.* New York: Zebra Books, Kensington Publishing Corp., 1989, 381 p., paper, novel. SEVENTH CARRIER #4.
16148 *Return of the seventh carrier.* New York: Zebra Books, Kensington Publishing Corp., 1987, 397 p., paper, novel. SEVENTH CARRIER #3.
16149 *The second voyage of the seventh carrier.* New York: Zebra Books, Kensington Publishing Corp., 1986, 398 p., paper, novel. SEVENTH CARRIER #2.
16150 *The seventh carrier.* New York: Zebra Books, Kensington Publishing Corp., 1983, 397 p., paper, novel. SEVENTH CARRIER #1.
16151 *Tides of valor.* New York: Popular Library, 1990, 326 p., paper, novel.
16152 *Trial of the seventh carrier.* New York: Zebra Books, Kensington Publishing

Corp., 1990, 382 p., paper, novel. SEVENTH CARRIER #6.
16153 *Waves of glory.* New York: Popular Library, 1989, 322 p., paper, novel.

ALBERTAZZIE, Ralph (Dayton), 1923- , *with David E. Fisher*

16154 *Hostage one.* New York: Random House, 1989, 448 p., cloth, novel.

ALBINSKI, Nan Bowman, 1934-

16155 *Women's utopias in nineteenth and twentieth century fiction.* London: Routledge & Kegan Paul, 1988, 204 p., cloth, nonf.

ALCOCK, Vivien (Dolores), 1924-

16156 *Ghostly companions.* London: Methuen, 1984, 123 p., cloth, coll.
16157 *The haunting of Cassie Palmer.* London: Methuen, 1980, 155 p., cloth, novel.
16158 *The monster garden.* London: Methuen, 1988, 121 p., cloth, novel.
16159 *The stonewalkers.* London: Methuen's Children Books, 1981, 142 p., cloth, novel.
16160 *The Sylvia game.* London: Methuen, 1982, 157 p., cloth, novel.
16161 *The thing in the woods.* London: Methuen, 1989, [96] p., cloth, novel.

ALD, Roy A.—SEE: Mann, A. Philo

ALDERMAN, Gill(ian), 1941-

16162 *The archivist: a black romance.* London, Sydney: Unwin Hyman, 1989, 380 p., cloth, novel. GUNA #1.
16163 *The land beyond.* London, Sydney: Unwin Hyman, 1990, 306 p., cloth, novel. GUNA #2.

ALDISS, Brian W(ilson), 1925-

16164 *...And the lurid glare of the comet: articles and autobiography.* Seattle, WA: Serconia Press, 1986, 123 p., cloth, nonf. coll.
16165 *Best SF stories of Brian W. Aldiss, 2nd rev. ed.* London: Victor Gollancz, 1988, 328 p., cloth, coll.
16165A retitled: *Man in his time: best SF stories.* London: Victor Gollancz, 1989, 328 p., paper, coll.
16166 *Bodily functions: stories, poems, and a letter on the subject of bowel movement addressed to Sam J. Lundwall on the occasion of his birthday, February 24th, A.D. 1991.* London: Avernus, 1991, 106 p.,

cloth, coll. [Includes verse and nonfiction; limited to 100 copies].

16167 *Brothers of the head.* London: Pierrot Publishing, 1977, 119 p., cloth, novel.

16168 *Brothers of the head; and, Where the lines converge.* London: Panther, 1979, 156 p., paper, coll.

16169 *Bury my heart at W. H. Smith's: a writing life.* London: Avernus, 1990, 280 p., cloth, nonf. [Limited to 250 copies].

Cracken at critical—SEE: *The year before yesterday.*

16170 *Dracula unbound.* Norwalk, CT: Easton Press, 1991, 196 p., cloth, novel. DRACULA SEQUEL.

16171 *Enemies of the system: a tale of Homo uniformis.* London: Jonathan Cape, 1978, 119 p., cloth, novel.

16172 *Equator; and, Segregation.* London: New English Library, 1977, 127 p., paper, coll.

16173 *Evil earths: an anthology of way-back-when futures.* London: Weidenfeld & Nicholson, 1975, x+322 p., cloth, anth.

16174 *Foreign bodies: stories.* Singapore: Chopmen, 1981, v+99 p., cloth, coll.

16175 *Galactic empires: an anthology of way-back-when futures.* London: Futura Publications, An Orbit Book, 1976, 2 v. [I-xii+338 p.; II-viii+296 p.], paper, anth.

16176 *Helliconia spring.* London: Jonathan Cape, 1982, 361 p., cloth, novel. HELLICONIA #1. [Winner of the John W. Campbell Jr. Memorial Award for Best Novel, 1982 (1983)].

16177 *Helliconia summer.* London: Jonathan Cape, 1983, 398 p., cloth, novel. HELLICONIA #2.

16178 *Helliconia winter.* London: Jonathan Cape, 1985, 281 p., cloth, novel. HELLICONIA #3.

16179 *An island called Moreau: a novel.* New York: Simon & Schuster, 1981, 173 p., cloth, novel.

16180 *Journey to the goat star.* Eugene, OR: Pulphouse Publishing, 1991, 47 p., paper, story. SHORT STORY PAPERBACKS #22.

Last orders—SEE: *Last orders, and other stories.*

16181 *Last orders, and other stories.* London: Jonathan Cape, 1977, 223 p., cloth, coll.

16181A retitled: *Last orders.* New York: Carroll & Graf, 1989, 223 p., cloth, coll.

16182 *The magic of the past.* Worcester Park, Surrey, England: Kerosina Books, 1987, 48 p., paper, coll.

16183 *The Malacia tapestry.* London: Jonathan Cape, 1976, 313 p., cloth, novel.

Man in his time—SEE: *Best SF stories of Brian W. Aldiss, 2nd rev. ed.*

16184 *Moreau's other island: a novel.* London: Jonathan Cape, 1980, 174 p., cloth, novel. ISLAND OF DR. MOREAU SEQUEL.

16185 *New arrivals, old encounters: twelve stories.* London: Jonathan Cape, 1979, 223 p., cloth, coll.

16186 *The pale shadow of science: recent essays.* Seattle, WA: Serconia Press, 1985, 128 p., cloth, nonf. coll.

16187 *Perilous planets: an anthology of way-back-when futures.* London: Weidenfeld & Nicolson, 1978, 367 p., cloth, anth.

16188 *A romance of the equator: best fantasy stories of Brian W. Aldiss.* London: Victor Gollancz, 1989, 345 p., cloth, coll.

16189 *Ruins.* London: Hutchinson, 1987, 85 p., cloth, story.

16190 *The saliva tree.* New York: Tor SF, A Tom Doherty Associates Book, 1988, 87 p., paper, story. [Bound with *Born with the dead* / by Robert Silverberg].

16191 *Science fiction art.* London: New English Library, 1975, 128 p., paper, art.

16192 *Science fiction as science fiction.* Frome, Somerset, England: Bran's Head Books, 1978, 39 p., paper, nonf.

16193 *Science fiction blues.* London: Avernus, 1988, 159 p., paper, coll.

16194 *Science fiction quiz.* London: Weidenfeld & Nicolson, 1983, 128 p., paper, nonf.

16195 *Seasons in flight.* London: Jonathan Cape, 1984, 157 p., cloth, coll.

16196 *Sex and the black machine: the first Aldiss cutup.* London: Avernus, 1990, 21 p., cloth, coll.

16197 *Space odysseys: an anthology of way-back-when futures.* London: Weidenfeld & Nicolson, 1975, 324 p., cloth, anth.

16198 *This world and nearer ones: essays exploring the familiar.* London: Weidenfeld & Nicolson, 1979, 261 p., cloth, nonf. coll.

16199 *The year before yesterday.* New York: Franklin Watts, 1987, 227 p., cloth, novel. [Includes *Equator* and "The Impossible Smile" in a framing story].

16199A retitled: *Cracken at critical.* Worcester Park, Surrey, England: Kerosina Books, 1987, 192 p., cloth, novel.

as INTRODUCER

16540 *Gollancz-'Sunday Times' best SF stories.* London: Victor Gollancz, 1975, 317 p., cloth, anth.

16540A retitled: *Let's go to Golgotha: the Gollancz-'Sunday Times' best SF stories.*

London, Toronto: Panther, Granada Publishing, 1979, 220 p., paper, anth.

with Harry Harrison

00164 *Best SF: 1973.* New York: G. P. Putnam's Sons, 1974, 238 p., cloth, anth.
00164A retitled: *The year's best science fiction, no. 7.* London: Sphere Books, 1975, 174 p., paper, anth.
16200 *Best SF: 1974.* Indianapolis, New York: Bobbs-Merrill Co., 1975, 253 p., cloth, anth.
16200A retitled: *The year's best science fiction, no. 8.* London: Sphere Books, 1976, 253 p., paper, anth.
Best SF: 75—SEE: *The ninth annual best SF: 75.*
16201 *Decade, the 1940s.* London: Macmillan, 1975, 213 p., cloth, anth.
16202 *Decade, the 1950s.* London: Macmillan, 1976, 219 p., cloth, anth.
16203 *Decade, the 1960s.* London: Macmillan, 1977, 287 p., cloth, anth.
16204 *Hell's cartographers: some personal histories of science fiction writers.* London: An SF Horizons Production, Weidenfeld & Nicolson, 1975, 246 p., cloth, nonf. anth.
16205 *The ninth annual best SF: 75.* Indianapolis, New York: Bobbs-Merrill Co., 1976, 240 p., cloth, anth.
16205A retitled: *The year's best science fiction, no. 9.* London: Weidenfeld & Nicolson, 1976, 206 p., cloth, anth.
16206 *SF Horizons.* New York: Arno Press, 1975, 64+64 p., cloth, nonf. anth. [The republication in one volume of two magazine issues].
The year's best science fiction, no. 7—SEE: *Best SF: 1973.*
The year's best science fiction, no. 8—SEE: *Best SF: 1974.*
The year's best science fiction, no. 9—SEE: *The ninth annual best SF: 75.*

with Sam J. Lundwall

16207 *The Penguin world omnibus of science fiction.* Harmondsworth, Middlesex, England: Penguin Books, 1986, 320 p., paper, anth.

with David Wingrove

16208 *Trillion year spree: the history of science fiction.* London: Victor Gollancz, 1986, 511 p., cloth, nonf. [An expansion of *Billion year spree* (see #00123); winner of the Hugo Award for Best Nonfiction Book, 1986 (1987); winner of the *Locus* Award for Best Nonfiction, 1986 (1987); winner of the J. Lloyd Eaton Award for Best Nonfiction Book of the Year, 1986 (1988)].

ALDISS, Margaret (Christie Manson), 1933- , with Frank Hatherley & Malcolm Edwards

16209 *A is for Brian: a 65th birthday present for Brian W. Aldiss.* London: Avernus, 1988, 128 p., paper, anth. [A festschrift for Brian W. Aldiss which includes some nonfiction; limited to 500 copies].

ALDRIDGE, Alan, 1943-

16210 *Phantasia of Dockland, Rockland, and Dodos.* New York: Ballantine Books, 1981, [74] p., paper, art. [Includes some fiction].

with Steven R. Boyett

16211 *The gnole.* London: Heinemann, 1991, 503 p., cloth, novel.

ALDRIDGE, Alexandra (Bertash), 1940-

16212 *The scientific world view in dystopia.* Ann Arbor, MI: UMI Research Press, 1984, x+97 p., cloth, nonf. STUDIES IN SPECULATIVE FICTION #3.

ALDRIDGE, Ray(mon Huebert), 1948-

16213 *The pharoah contract.* New York, Toronto: Spectra, Bantam Books, 1991, 290 p., paper, novel. THE EMANCIPATOR #1.

ALEXANDER, C. M.

16214 *Alien atlas.* New York: Manor Books, 1979, 239 p., paper, novel.
16215 *Biodroids 2300.* New York: Manor Books, 1979 (i.e., 1980?), 238 p., paper, novel.

ALEXANDER, David

Dark messiah—SEE: *Phoenix: Dark messiah.*
Death quest—SEE: *Phoenix: Death quest.*
Ground zero—SEE: *Phoenix: Ground zero.*
Metalstorm—SEE: *Phoenix: metalstorm.*
16216 *Phoenix: Dark messiah.* New York: Leisure Books, 1987, 221 p., paper, novel. PHOENIX #1.

16217 *Phoenix: Death quest.* New York: Leisure Books, 1988, 224 p., paper, novel. PHOENIX #3.

16218 *Phoenix: Ground zero.* New York: Leisure Books, 1987, 224 p., paper, novel. PHOENIX #2.

16219 *Phoenix: Metalstorm.* New York: Leisure Books, 1988, 192 p., paper, novel. PHOENIX #4.

16220 *Whirlwind.* New York: Leisure Books, 1988, 191 p., paper, novel. PHOENIX #5.

as JAN SIEVERT

16221 *Death zone attack.* New York: Zebra Books, Kensington Publishing Corp., 1991, 176 p., paper, novel. C.A.D.S. #11.

16222 *Recon by fire.* New York: Zebra Books, Kensington Publishing Corp., 1990, 222 p., paper, novel. C.A.D.S. #10.

16223 *Suicide attack.* New York: Zebra Books, Kensington Publishing Corp., 1990, 224 p., paper, novel. C.A.D.S. #9.

16224 *Tech assassins.* New York: Zebra Books, Kensington Publishing Corp., 1991, 192 p., paper, novel. C.A.D.S. #12.

ALEXANDER, David M(ichael), 1945-

16225 *The chocolate spy.* New York: Coward, McCann & Geoghegan, 1978, 223 p., cloth, novel.

16226 *Fane.* New York: A Timescape Book, Pocket Books, 1981, 311 p., paper, novel.

*ALEXANDER, Holmes (Moss), 1906-1985

ALEXANDER, Jan [pseud. of Victor Jerome Banis], 1937-

16227 *Blood moon.* New York: Lancer Books, 1970, 224 p., paper, novel.

16228 *Blood ruby.* New York: Ballantine Books, 1975, 154 p., paper, novel. BIRTHSTONE GOTHIC #7.

16229 *The glass painting.* New York: Popular Library, 1972, 319 p., paper, novel.

19281 *Shadows, together with Blood moon and The wolves of Graywood.* New York: Lancer Books, 1972, 205+224+189 p., paper, coll.

ALEXANDER, Karl, 1944-

16230 *The curse of the vampire.* New York: Pinnacle Books, 1982, 310 p., paper, novel.

16231 *Time after time: a novel.* New York: Delacorte Press, 1979, 341 p., cloth, novel.

ALEXANDER, Katherine

16232 *A dream of things that were.* New York: Manor Books, 1979, 220 p., paper, novel.

ALEXANDER, Lloyd (Chudley), 1924-

16233 *The beggar queen.* New York: E. P. Dutton, 1984, 237 p., cloth, novel. WESTMARK #3.

16234 *The Drackenberg adventure.* New York: E. P. Dutton, 1988, 152 p., cloth, novel. VESPER HOLLY #3.

16235 *The El Dorado adventure.* New York: E. P. Dutton, 1987, 164 p., cloth, novel. VESPER HOLLY #2.

16236 *The first chronicles of Prydain.* London: Fontana Books, 1986, 472 p., paper, coll. PRYDAIN #1-3. [Includes *The Book of Three*; *The Black Cauldron*; *The castle of Llyr*].

16237 *The first two lives of Lukas-Kasha.* New York: E. P. Dutton, 1978, 213 p., cloth, novel.

16238 *The Illyrian adventure.* New York: E. P. Dutton, 1986, 132 p., cloth, novel. VESPER HOLLY #1.

16239 *The Jedera adventure.* New York: E. P. Dutton, 1989, 152 p., cloth, novel. VESPER HOLLY #4.

16240 *The Kestrel.* New York: E. P. Dutton, 1982, 244 p., cloth, novel. WESTMARK #2.

16241 *The Philadelphia adventure.* New York: E. P. Dutton, 1990, 150 p., cloth, novel. VESPER HOLLY #5.

16242 *The Prydain chronicles.* New York: Guild America Books, 1991, 767 p., cloth, coll. PRYDAIN #1-5. [Includes *The Book of Three*; *The Black Cauldron*; *The castle of Llyr*; *Taran wanderer*; *The high king*; *The foundling, and other tales*].

16243 *The remarkable journey of Prince Jen.* New York: E. P. Dutton, 1991, 273 p., cloth, novel.

16244 *The second chronicles of Prydain.* London: Fontana Books, 1986, 413 p., paper, coll. PRYDAIN #4-5. [Includes *Taran wanderer*; *The high king*].

16245 *The town cats, and other tales.* New York: E. P. Dutton, 1977, 126 p., cloth, coll.

16246 *Westmark.* New York: E. P. Dutton, 1981, 184 p., cloth, novel. WESTMARK #1.

16247 *The wizard in the tree.* New York: E. P. Dutton, 1975, 137 p., cloth, novel.

ALEXANDER, Lynne, 1958-

16248 *Resonating bodies.* London: Macmillan, 1988, 229 p., cloth, novel.

ALEXANDER, Marc (Elward), 1929-

16249 *Ancient dreams.* London: Headline, 1988, 338 p., paper, novel. WELLS OF YTHAN #1.
16250 *Magic casements.* London: Headline, 1989, 342 p., paper, novel. WELLS OF YTHAN #2.
16251 *Not after midnight: thirteen stories to haunt your dreams.* London: Viking Kestrel, 1985, 142 p., cloth, coll.
16252 *Shadow realm.* London: Headline, 1991, 438 p., paper, novel. WELLS OF YTHAN #3.

as MARK RONSON

32638 *The Beaver book of horror stories.* London: Beaver Books, 1981, 157 p., paper, anth.
Blood-thirst—SEE: *Bloodthirst.*
32639 *Bloodthirst.* Feltham, England: Hamlyn Paperbacks, 1979, 210 p., paper, novel.
32639A retitled: *Blood-thirst.* New York: A Critic's Choice Paperback from Lorevan Publishing, 1986, 210 p., paper, novel.
32640 *The dark domain.* London: Century, 1984, [346] p., cloth, novel.
32641 *Ghoul.* Feltham, England: Hamlyn Paperbacks, 1980, 202 p., paper, novel.
32642 *Ogre.* Feltham, England: Hamlyn Paperbacks, 1980, 198 p., paper, novel.
32643 *Plague pit.* Feltham, England: Hamlyn Paperbacks, 1981, 191 p., paper, novel.
32644 *Whispering corner.* London: Arrow Books, 1989, 351 p., paper, novel.

with Stella Whitelaw & Judy Gardiner

23659 *Grimalkin's tales: strange and wonderful cat stories.* London: Hamlyn Paperbacks, 1983, 160 p., paper, anth.

ALEXANDER, Marsha

16253 *Demon fire.* New York: Pinnacle Books, 1982, 215 p., paper, novel.

ALEXANDER, Patrick (James), 1926-

16254 *Show me a hero.* London: Macmillan, 1979, 271 p., cloth, novel.

ALEXANDER, Paul, *with Laurie Bridges*

16255 *Devil wind.* Toronto, New York: Bantam Books, 1983, 152 p., paper, novel. DARK FORCES #4.
16256 *Magic show.* Toronto, New York: Bantam Books, 1983, 135 p., paper, novel. DARK FORCES #2.
16257 *Swamp witch.* Toronto, New York: Bantam Books, 1983, 153 p., paper, novel. DARK FORCES #6.

ALEXANDER, Peter, 1917- , *with Roger Gill*

16258 *Utopias.* London: Duckworth, 1984, xx + 218 p., cloth, nonf. anth.

ALEXANDER, Robert (William), 1905-1980

20202 *Back to nature.* London: Stanley Paul & Co., 1945, 192 p., cloth, novel.
20710 *Mariners' rest.* London: Stanley Paul & Co., 1943, 256 p., cloth, novel.

as JOAN BUTLER

21268 *Bed and breakfast.* London: Stanley Paul & Co., 1933, 288 p., cloth, novel.
21269 *Cloudy weather.* London: Stanley Paul & Co., 1940, 286 p., cloth, novel.
22080 *Full house.* London: Stanley Paul & Co., 1947, 240 p., cloth, novel.
22514 *Home run.* London: Jarrolds, 1958, 240 p., cloth, novel.
23055 *The old firm.* London: Stanley Paul & Co., 1947, 236 p., cloth, novel.
23210 *Sheet lightning.* London: Stanley Paul & Co., 1950, 223 p., cloth, novel.
23698 *Space to let.* London: Stanley Paul & Co., 1955, 191 p., cloth, novel.

ALEXANDER, Thea

11545 *2150: "the macro love story"* / by Don and Thea Plym. Grosse Pointe, MI: Macro Development Center, 1971, 281 p., paper, novel
16259 retitled: *2150 A.D.* / by Thea Alexander. Tempe, AZ: Macro Books, 1976, 350 p., cloth, novel. [Revised and expanded edition].

ALEXIS, Athena

16260 *Along came a spider.* New York: A Dell Book, 1991, 322 p., paper, novel.

ALEXIS, Katina [pseud. of Katina Parthemos Strauch], 1946-

16261 *Scorpion.* New York: Leisure Books, 1986, 287 p., paper, novel.
16262 *Witch.* New York, London: Pocket Books, 1990, 343 p., paper, novel.
16263 *Young blood.* New York: Tor, A Tom Doherty Associates Book, 1982, 283 p., paper, novel.

ALFAU, Felipe, 1902-

16264 *Locos: a comedy of gestures.* New York: Farrar & Rinehart, 1936, xiv+306 p., cloth, novel.

ALGOZIN, Bruce

16265 *Blood knot.* New York: Zebra Books, Kensington Publishing Corp., 1982, 235 p., paper, novel.
16266 *Claw of the dragon.* Lake Geneva, WI: TSR Inc., 1986, 159 p, paper, novel. ENDLESS QUEST #34.
16267 *Invisible rival.* Lake Geneva, WI: TSR Inc., 1987, 128 p., paper, novel. LAZER TAG ADVENTURE #3.
16268 *Lair of the Lich.* Lake Geneva, WI: TSR Inc., 1985, 157 p., paper, novel. ENDLESS QUEST #27.
16269 *Prisoner of Elderwood.* Lake Geneva, WI: TSR Inc., 1986, 157 p., paper, novel. ENDLESS QUEST #32.

as NICK CARTER

16270 *The last samurai.* New York: Charter Books, 1982, 197 p., paper, novel. NICK CARTER SERIES.

ALGUIRE, Judith, 1946-

16271 *Zeta base.* Tallahassee, FL: Naiad Press, 1991, 191 p., paper, novel.

ALI, Jaffer, *with Matthew White*

16272 *The official Prisoner companion.* New York: Warner Books, 1988, ix+244 p., paper, nonf.

ALKON, Paul K(ent), 1935-

16273 *Origins of futuristic fiction.* Athens, GA: University of Georgia Press, 1987, xii+341 p., cloth, nonf. [Winner of the J. Lloyd Eaton Award for Best Nonfiction Book of the Year, 1987 (1989)].

ALLABY, (John) Michael, 1933- , *with James Lovelock*

16274 *The greening of Mars.* London: André Deutsch, 1984, 165 p., cloth, novel.

ALLAN, Jim

16275 *An extrapolation on the 'Silmarillion'.* Liverpool, England: Tolkien Society, 1975, 35 p., paper, nonf.
16276 *A glossary of the Eldarin tongues.* Toronto: [s.n.], 1972, p., paper, nonf.
16277 *A speculation on the Silmarillion.* Baltimore, MD: T-K Graphics, 1977, [22] p., paper, nonf. [Probably adapted from *An extrapolation on 'The Silmarillion'*].

with Nina Carson

16278 *An introduction to Elvish, and to other tongues and proper names and writing systems of the Third Age of the western lands of Middle-Earth, as set forth in the published writings of Professor John Ronald Reuel Tolkien.* Hayes, Middlesex, England: Bran's Head Books, 1978, xxxi+303 p., paper, nonf. anth.

ALLAN, Mabel E(sther), 1915-

16279 *Hunger Moss.* New York: Dodd, Mead & Co., 1983, 188 p., cloth, novel.
16280 *Romansgrove.* New York: Atheneum, 1975, 217 p., cloth, novel.

*ALLAN, Mea, 1909-<u>1982</u>

ALLAN, Ted—SEE: Maxwell, Edward

ALLBEURY, Ted [i.e., Theodore Edward le Bouthillier Allbeury], 1917-

16281 *All our tomorrows.* London, New York: Granada, 1982, 248 p., cloth, novel.
OMEGA-MINUS—SEE: *Palomino blonde.*
16282 *Palomino blonde.* London: Peter Davies, 1975, 150 p., cloth, novel.
16282A retitled: *OMEGA-MINUS.* New York: Ballantine Books, 1976, 168 p., paper, novel.

ALLBEURY, Theodore—SEE: Allbeury, Ted

ALLCOCK, Phil

16283 *In search of the golden sceptre.* Eastbourne, East Sussex, England: Kingsway Publications, 1991, 287 p., paper, novel. STORIES OF THE REALM #2.

16284 *The will of Dargan.* Eastbourne, East Sussex, England: Kingsway Publications, 1989, 224 p., paper, novel. STORIES OF THE REALM #1.

ALLDRITT, Keith, 1935-

16285 *The making of George Orwell: an essay in literary history.* London: Edward Arnold, 1969, 181 p., cloth, nonf.

*ALLEN, Arthur Bruce, 1903-1975

*ALLEN, Barbara Jo, 1904?-1974

ALLEN, Derek, pseud.—SEE: Farmer, Derek

ALLEN, Dick [i.e., Richard Stanley Allen], 1939-

16286 *Science fiction: the future, 2nd ed.* New York: Harcourt Brace Jovanovich, 1983, x+432 p., paper, anth.

with Lori Allen

16287 *Looking ahead: the vision of science fiction.* New York: Harcourt Brace Jovanovich, 1975, viii+408 p., paper, anth.

ALLEN, F. M. [pseud. of Edmund Downey], 1856-1937

24054 *The little green man.* London: Downey & Co., 1895, 152 p., cloth, novel.
24507 *The round tower of Babel.* London: Ward & Downey, 1891, 121 p., cloth, novel.

ALLEN, Harold W. G.

16288 *The edge of the universe: what is our destiny? is there life after death? what incredible secret lies in the depths of space?* Downsview, Ontario, Canada: Allen Book Publishing, 1975, 268 p., cloth, novel.

*ALLEN, Henry Wilson, 1912-1991

ALLEN, Hervey, 1889-1949

16289 *Israfel: the life and times of Edgar Allan Poe.* New York: George H. Doran, 1926, 2 v., cloth, nonf.

*ALLEN, Johannes, 1916-1973

ALLEN, Judy, *with Jeanne Griffiths*

16290 *The book of the dragon.* London: Orbis Books, 1979, 128 p., cloth, fiction.

ALLEN, L(ouis) David, 1940-

16291 *Asimov's Foundation trilogy and other works: notes, including life of the author, an overview of Asimov's science fiction, categories of science fiction, analyses of the works.* Lincoln, NE: Cliffs Notes, 1977, 90 p., paper, nonf.
16292 *The Ballantine teachers' guide to science fiction.* New York: Ballantine Books, 1975, 346 p., paper, nonf.
16293 *Herbert's Dune and other works: notes.* Lincoln, NE: Cliffs Notes, 1975, 101 p., paper, nonf.

ALLEN, Lori (Negridge), 1939- , *with Dick Allen*

16287 *Looking ahead: the vision of science fiction.* New York: Harcourt Brace Jovanovich, 1975, viii+408 p., paper, anth.

*ALLEN, M. C. [i.e., Marion Carroll Allen], 1914-

ALLEN, Marilyn

16294 *White mambo.* New York: A Berkley Medallion Book, Berkley Publishing Corp., 1977, 249 p., paper, novel.

ALLEN, Martin

Sky lord—SEE: *Steve Jackson and Ian Livingstone present Sky lord.*
16295 *Steve Jackson and Ian Livingstone present Sky lord.* Harmondsworth, Middlesex, England: Puffin Books, 1988, 27+[225] p., paper, fiction. FIGHTING FANTASY GAMEBOOK SERIES.

ALLEN, Mary Ann, pseud.—SEE: Pardoe, Rosemary

ALLEN, Mary C(harlotte Chocqueel), 1909-

16296 *Great ghost stories in large print.* Boston: G. K. Hall & Co., 1988, x+390 p., cloth, anth.

ALLEN, Michael L.

16297 *Poe and the British magazine tradition.* New York: Oxford University Press, 1969, x+255 p., cloth, nonf.

ALLEN, Ralph, 1913-1966

16298 *The chartered libertine.* Toronto: Macmillan, 1954, 270 p., cloth, novel.

ALLEN, Richard S.—SEE: Allen, Dick

ALLEN, Roger MacBride, 1957-

16299 *Farside cannon.* New York: Baen Books, 1988, 406 p., paper, novel.
16300 *Orphan of creation.* New York: Baen Books, 1988, 345 p., paper, novel.
16301 *The Ring of Charon.* New York: Tor SF, A Tom Doherty Associates Book, 1990, 500 p., paper, novel. HUNTED EARTH #1.
16302 *Rogue powers.* New York: Baen Science Fiction Books, 1986, 403 p., paper, novel. TORCH #2.
16303 *The torch of honor.* New York: A Baen Book, 1985, 339 p., paper, novel. TORCH #1.

with David Drake

16304 *The war machine.* New York: Baen Books, 1989, 338 p., paper, novel. CRISIS OF EMPIRE #3.

with Eric Kotani

16305 *Supernova.* New York: Avon Books, 1991, 345 p., paper, novel.

ALLEN, Sheila Rosalynd, 1942-

16306 *The helpful ghost.* New York: Walker & Co., 1990, 214 p., cloth, novel. LOVERS OF STEADFORD ABBEY #3.
16307 *The meddlesome ghost.* New York: Walker & Co., 1989, 224 p., cloth, novel. LOVERS OF STEADFORD ABBEY #2.
16308 *The passionate ghost.* New York: Walker & Co., 1991, 199 p., cloth, novel. LOVERS OF STEADFORD ABBEY #4.
16309 *The reluctant ghost.* New York: Walker & Co., 1989, 242 p., cloth, novel. LOVERS OF STEADFORD ABBEY #1.

ALLEN, Tom, 1938?-1988, *with Mitchell Galin*

16310 *Tales from the darkside, volume one.* New York: Berkley Books, 1988, 248 p., paper, anth. [Only volume published].

ALLEN, William Rodney, 1952-

16311 *Conversations with Kurt Vonnegut.* Jackson, MS: University Press of Mississippi, 1988, xix+305 p., cloth, nonf. anth.
16312 *Understanding Kurt Vonnegut.* Columbia, SC: University of South Carolina Press, 1991, xi+192 p., cloth, nonf.
16313 *Walker Percy, a Southern wayfarer.* Jackson, MS: University Press of Mississippi, 1986, xx+160 p., cloth, nonf.

ALLENDE, Isabel, 1942-

16314 *The house of the spirits.* New York: Alfred A. Knopf, 1985, 368 p., cloth, novel. [Translation by Magda Bogin of *La casa de los espíritus*].

ALLHOFF, Fred, 1904-1988

16315 *Lightning in the night.* Englewood Cliffs, NJ: Prentice-Hall, 1979, 198 p., cloth, novel.

ALLNUTT, Frank(lin L.)

16316 *After the Omen.* Van Nuys, CA: Bible Voice, 1976, 154 p., paper, nonf.
16317 *The force of Star Wars.* Van Nuys, CA: Bible Voice, 1977, 200 p., paper, nonf.

ALLOTT, Kenneth, 1912-1973

16318 *Jules Verne.* London: The Cresset Press, 1940, xvi+283 p., cloth, nonf.

ALLSBURG, Chris Van—SEE: Van Allsburg, Chris

ALLSTON, Aaron (Dale), 1960-

16319 *Web of danger.* Lake Geneva, WI: TSR Inc., 1988, 318 p., paper, novel. [Bound with *Agent 13: acolytes of darkness* / by Flint Dille and David Marconi].

ALMEDINGEN, E. M. [pseud. of Martha Edith von Almedingen], 1898-1971

24763 *Stand fast, beloved city.* London: Hutchinson, 1954, 264 p., cloth, novel.

ALMOND, Jocelyn, *with Keith Seldon*

16320 *The faceless tarot.* London: Dunscaith Publishing, 1989, 155 p., paper, novel.

ALMQUIST, Gregg (Andrew), 1948-

16321 *Beast rising.* New York: Pocket Books, 1987, 256 p., paper, novel.
16322 *Wolf kill.* New York, London: Pocket Books, 1990, 273 p., paper, novel.

ALMQUIST, John, *as* VICTOR APPLETON II

00445 *Tom Swift and his jetmarine.* New York: Grosset & Dunlap, 1954, 208 p., cloth, novel. TOM SWIFT JR. #A2.
00450 *Tom Swift and his rocket ship.* New York: Grosset & Dunlap, 1954, 208 p., cloth, novel. TOM SWIFT JR. #A3.

ALOK Rai

16323 *Orwell and the politics of despair: a critical study of the writings of George Orwell.* Cambridge, England, New York: Cambridge University Press, 1988, xi+ 192 p., cloth, nonf.

ALPHIN, Elaine Marie, 1955-

16324 *The ghost cadet.* New York: Henry Holt & Co., 1991, 182 p., cloth, novel.

ALTENA, Arnaud d'—SEE: de Borchgrave, Arnaud

ALTERTON, Margaret, 1877-1934

16325 *Origins of Poe's critical theory.* Iowa City, IA: University of Iowa, 1925, 191 p., cloth, nonf.

ALTMAN, Mark A.

16326 *Twin Peaks behind-the-scenes: an unofficial visitors guide to Twin Peaks.* Las Vegas, NV: Pioneer Books, 1990, 145 p., paper, nonf.

ALTMAN, Thomas, pseud.—SEE: Black, Campbell

ALTON, Andrea I(nez M.), 1946-

16327 *Demon of undoing.* New York: Baen Books, 1988, 308 p., paper, novel.

AL'TOV, Genrikh [pseud. of Genrikh Saulovich Altshuller], *with Valentina Zhuravleva*

16328 *Ballad of the stars.* New York: Macmillan, 1982, 280 p., cloth, coll.

ALTSHULLER, Genrikh—SEE: Al'tov, Genrikh

ALVARADO, Manuel, 1948- , *with John Tulloch*

16329 *Doctor Who: the unfolding text.* London: Macmillan Press, 1983, xi+342 p., cloth, nonf.

ALVERSON, Charles (E.), 1935-

16330 *Time bandits.* London: Sparrow Books, 1981, 124 p., paper, movie.

AMADO, Jorge (Luis), 1912-

16331 *Dona Flor and her two husbands: a moral and amorous tale.* New York: Alfred A. Knopf, 1969, 553 p., cloth, novel. [Translation by Harriet de Onís of *Dona Flor e seus dois maridos*].
16332 *The two deaths of Quincas Wateryell.* New York: Alfred A. Knopf, 1965, 97 p., cloth, novel. [Translation Barbara Shelby of *A morte e a morte de Quincas Berro D'agua*].

AMANO, Yoshitaka

16333 *Hiten: the art of Yoshitaka Amano: acrylic, watercolor, pen and ink.* Tokyo: Asahi Sonorama, 1991, unpaginated, paper, art.

AMARE, Rothayne, pseud.—SEE: Byrne, Stuart J.

AMBROSE, Lottie F.—SEE: Biagi, L. D.

AMES, J(ohn) Edward, 1949-

16334 *The death crystal.* New York: Leisure Books, 1990, 396 p., paper, novel.
16335 *The force.* New York: Leisure Books, 1987, 400 p., paper, novel.
16336 *Spellcaster.* New York: Zebra Books, Kensington Publishing Corp., 1989, 347 p., paper, novel.

AMES, Lee J(udah), 1921-

16337 *Draw 50 beasties and yugglies and turnover uglies and things that go bump in the night.* New York: Doubleday & Co., 1988, [64] p., cloth, art.
16338 *Draw 50 monsters, creeps, superheroes, demons, dragons, nerds, dirts, ghouls, giants, vampires, zombies, & other curiosa.* Garden City, NY: Doubleday & Co., 1983, [62] p., cloth, art.

16339 *How to draw Star Wars heroes, creatures, space-ships, and other fantastic things.* New York: Random House, 1984, 80 p., paper, nonf.

AMES, Mildred (Walsh), 1919-

16340 *Anna to the infinite power.* New York: Charles Scribner's Sons, 1981, 198 p., cloth, novel.
16341 *Conjuring summer in.* New York: Harper & Row, 1986, 217 p., cloth, novel.
16342 *Is there life on a plastic planet?* New York: E. P. Dutton, 1975, 134 p., cloth, novel.
16343 *The silver link, the silken tie.* New York: Charles Scribner's Sons, 1984, 215 p., cloth, novel.

AMIS, Kingsley (William, Sir), 1922-

16344 *The alteration.* London: Jonathan Cape, 1976, 208 p., cloth, novel. [Winner of the John W. Campbell Jr. Memorial Award for Best Novel, 1976 (1977)].
16345 *The golden age of science fiction.* London: Hutchinson, 1981, 370 p., cloth, anth.
16346 *Memoirs.* London: Hutchinson, 1991, xvi+346 p., cloth, nonf.
16347 *Russian hide-and-seek: a melodrama.* London: Hutchinson, 1980, 239 p., cloth, novel.

AMIS, Martin (Louis), 1949-

16348 *Dead babies.* London: Jonathan Cape, 1975, 254 p., cloth, novel.
16349 *Einstein's monsters.* London: Jonathan Cape, 1987, 127 p., cloth, coll.
16350 *London fields.* London: Jonathan Cape, 1989, 470 p., cloth, novel.
24781 *Other people: a mystery story.* London: Jonathan Cape, 1981, 223 p., cloth, novel.
16351 *Time's arrow; or, The nature of the offence.* London: Jonathan Cape, 1991, 176 p., cloth, novel.

AMORY, Mark, 1941-

16352 *Biography of Lord Dunsany.* London: Collins, 1972, 288 p., cloth, nonf. [Cover says *Lord Dunsany: a biography*]. *Lord Dunsany: a biography*—SEE: *Biography of Lord Dunsany.*

AMPRIMOZ, Alexandre L(aurent Antoine), 1948- , *with John Robert Colombo & John Bell & Michael Richardson*

16353 *CDN SF & F: a bibliography of Canadian science fiction and fantasy.* Toronto: Hounslow Press, 1979, viii+85 p., paper, nonf.

AMTHOR, Terry K.

16354 *Middle-Earth quest: A spy in Isengard.* London: Unwin Hyman, 1988, [204] p., paper, fiction. MIDDLE-EARTH QUEST. *A spy in Isengard*—SEE: *Middle-Earth quest: A spy in Isengard.*

ANASTOS, Andrea L.—SEE: Melrose, Andrea LaSonde

ANDERS, Agnetha

16355 *Pleasurehouse 13.* London: Nexus, 1991, 249 p., paper, novel.

ANDERSON, Betty

16356 *Isle of illusion.* Encino, CA: World-Wide Publishing Co., 1980, 184 p., paper, novel.

***ANDERSON, Chester (Valentine John), 1932-1991**

***ANDERSON, Colin (Skelton), Sir, 1904-1980**

ANDERSON, Craig W(orden), 1945-

16357 *Science fiction films of the seventies.* Jefferson, NC & London: McFarland & Co., 1985, ix+261 p., paper, nonf.

ANDERSON, Don(ald), 1939-

16358 *Heatshield.* London & Sydney: Pan Books, 1990, 288 p., paper, novel.

ANDERSON, Jack(son Northman), 1922- , *with John Kidner*

16359 *Alice in Blunderland.* Washington, DC: Acropolis Books, 1983, 183 p., paper, fiction. ALICE IN WONDERLAND SEQUEL.

ANDERSON, James (Arthur), 1955-

16360 *The illustrated Bradbury.* Center Harbor, NH: Niekas Publications, 1990, 56 p., paper, nonf.

ANDERSON, Jani, 1949-

16361   *Bringing down the Moon: 15 tales of fantasy and terror.* New York: Space & Time, 1985, 251 p., cloth, anth.

ANDERSON, June M.—SEE: Anderson, Karen

ANDERSON, Karen [i.e., June Millichamp "Karen" Kruse Anderson], 1932-

15785   *Henry Kuttner: a memorial symposium.* Berkeley, CA: Sevagram Enterprises, 1958, 34 p., paper, nonf. anth.

with Poul Anderson

16362   *Dahut.* New York: Baen Books, 1988, 398 p., paper, novel. KING OF YS #3.
16363   *The dog and the wolf.* New York: Baen Books, 1988, 531 p., paper, novel. KING OF YS #4.
16364   *Gallicenae.* New York: Baen Books, 1987, 374 p., paper, novel. KING OF YS #2.
16365   *The king of Ys.* Garden City, NY: Nelson Doubleday, 1988, 655 p., cloth, coll. KING OF YS #1-2. [Includes *Roma mater*; *Gallicenae*].
16366   *The king of Ys, volume 2.* Garden City, NY: Nelson Doubleday, 1988, 784 p., cloth, coll. KING OF YS #3-4. [Includes *Dahut*; *The dog and the wolf*].
16367   *The king of Ys: Roma mater.* New York: Baen Books, 1986, 461 p., paper, novel. KING OF YS #1.
           Roma mater—SEE: *The king of Ys: Roma mater.*
16368   *The unicorn trade.* New York: A Tom Doherty Associates Book, 1984, 284 p., paper, coll. [Includes some verse].

ANDERSON, Kay, *with Edward Gross & Wendy Rathbone & Ron Magid & Sheldon Teitelbaum*

16369   *The making of the Trek films.* East Meadow, NY: Image Publishing, 1991, 172 p., paper, nonf.

ANDERSON, Kevin J(ames), 1962-

16370   *Gamearth.* New York: A Signet Book, New American Library, 1989, 335 p., paper, novel. GAMEARTH TRILOGY #1.
16371   *Gameplay.* New York: A Signet Book, New American Library, 1989, 325 p., paper, novel. GAMEARTH TRILOGY #2.
16372   *Game's end.* New York: A Roc Book, 1990, 333 p., paper, novel. GAMEARTH TRILOGY #3.

16373   *Resurrection, Inc.* New York: A Signet Book, New American Library, 1988, 304 p., paper, novel.

with Doug Beason

16374   *Lifeline.* New York, Toronto: Spectra, Bantam Books, 1990, 460 p., paper, novel.
16375   *The trinity paradox.* New York, Toronto: Spectra, Bantam Books, 1991, 325 p., paper, novel.

ANDERSON, Margaret J(ean), 1931-

16376   *The brain on Quartz Mountain.* New York: Alfred A. Knopf, 1982, 114 p., cloth, novel.
16377   *The druid's gift.* New York: Alfred A. Knopf, 1989, x+211 p., cloth, novel.
16378   *The ghost inside the monitor.* New York: Bullseye Books, Alfred A. Knopf, 1990, 119 p., cloth, novel.
16379   *In the circle of time.* New York: Alfred A. Knopf, 1979, 181 p., cloth, novel. TIME #2.
16380   *In the keep of time.* New York: Alfred A. Knopf, 1977, 149 p., cloth, novel. TIME #1.
16381   *The mists of time.* New York: Alfred A. Knopf, 1984, 179 p., cloth, novel. TIME #3.
16382   *To nowhere and back.* New York: Alfred A. Knopf, 1975, 141 p., cloth, novel.

*ANDERSON, Mary, 1872-1964

ANDERSON, Mary, 1929-

16383   *The haunting of Hillcrest.* New York: A Yearling Book, 1987, 128 p., paper, novel. MOSTLY GHOSTS #1.
16384   *The Leipzig vampire.* New York: A Yearling Book, 1987, 122 p., paper, novel. MOSTLY GHOSTS #2.
16385   *Terror under the tent.* New York: A Yearling Book, 1987, 123 p., paper, novel. MOSTLY GHOSTS #3.
16386   *The three spirits of Vandermeer Manor.* New York: A Yearling Book, 1987, 124 p., paper, novel. MOSTLY GHOSTS #4.

ANDERSON, Michael Falconer

16387   *Black trinity.* London: Robert Hale, 1988, 256 p., cloth, novel.
           Blood rite—SEE: *The woodsmen.*
16388   *The clan of Golgotha Scalp.* London: Robert Hale, 1989, 255 p., cloth, novel.

16389 *The covenant.* London: Robert Hale, 1988, 208 p., cloth, novel.

16390 *God of a thousand faces.* London: Robert Hale, 1987, 249 p., cloth, novel.

16391 *The unholy.* London: Robert Hale, 1987, 223 p., cloth, novel.

16392 *The woodsmen.* London: Robert Hale, 1986, 156 p., cloth, novel.

16392A retitled: *Blood rite.* New York: St. Martin's Press, 1988, 156 p., paper, novel.

ANDERSON, Paul Dale, 1944-

16393 *Claw hammer.* New York: Pinnacle Books, Windsor Publishing Corp., 1989, 288 p., paper, novel.

16394 *Daddy's home.* New York: Pinnacle Books, Windsor Publishing Corp., 1990, 320 p., paper, novel.

16395 *The devil made me do it! twenty tales of subtle horror.* Madison, WI: Miskatonic University Press Publication of The Strange Co., 1985, 40 p., paper, coll.

ANDERSON, Poul (William), 1926-

16396 *Alight in the void.* New York: Tor SF, A Tom Doherty Associates Book, 1991, xiii+242 p., paper, coll. [Includes some verse].

16397 *Annals of the Time Patrol: The guardians of Time and The time patrolman.* Garden City, NY: Nelson Doubleday, 1984, 312 p., cloth, coll. TIME PATROL #1-2.

16398 *Avatar.* New York: Berkley Publishing Corp., 1978, 380 p., cloth, novel.

16399 *The best of Poul Anderson.* New York: Pocket Books, 1976, xvi+287 p., paper, coll.

16400 *The boat of a million years.* Norwalk, CT: Easton Press, 1989, 468 p., cloth, novel.

The book of Poul Anderson—SEE: *Many worlds of Poul Anderson.*

Cold victory—SEE: *The Psychotechnic League: Cold victory.*

16401 *Conan the rebel.* Toronto, New York: Bantam Books, 1980, 208 p., paper, novel. CONAN SERIES.

16402 *Conflict.* New York: A Jim Baen Presentation, Tor, A Tom Doherty Associates Book, 1983, 284 p., paper, coll.

Conquests—SEE: *Seven conquests.*

16403 *The dark between the stars.* New York: Berkley Books, 1981, 207 p., paper, novel.

16404 *The day of their return.* New York: A Signet Book, New American Library, 1975, 185 p., paper, novel.

16405 *The devil's game.* New York: Pocket Books, 1980, 255 p., paper, novel.

16406 *Dialogue with darkness.* New York: Tor, A Tom Doherty Associates Book, 1985, 320 p., paper, coll.

16407 *The Earth book of Stormgate.* New York: Berkley Publishing Corp., 1978, 390 p., cloth, coll. POLESOTECHNIC LEAGUE SERIES.

16408 *The enemy stars.* New York: Tor, A Tom Doherty Associates Book, 1987, 218 p., paper, coll. [Expanded from the original edition (see #00272) to include the story, "The ways of love"].

16409 *Explorations.* New York: Tor, A Tom Doherty Associates Book, 1981, 317 p., paper, coll.

16410 *Fantasy.* New York: Tor, A Tom Doherty Associates Book, 1981, 334 p., paper, coll.

16411 *The game of empire.* New York: Baen Science Fiction Books, 1985, 278 p., paper, novel. FLANDRY SERIES.

16412 *The gods laughed.* New York: Tor, A Tom Doherty Associates Book, 1982, 320 p., paper, coll.

16413 *The guardians of time.* New York: Tor, A Tom Doherty Associates Book, 1981, 254 p., paper, coll. TIME PATROL #1. [Expanded from the original edition (see #00276)].

16414 *Homebrew.* Cambridge, MA: A Boskone Book, NESFA Press, 1976, ii+75 p., cloth, coll. [Includes some nonfiction and verse].

16415 *Homeward and beyond.* Garden City, NY: Doubleday & Co., 1975, 204 p., cloth, coll.

16416 *Inconstant star.* New York: Baen Books, 1991, 314 p., paper, coll. MAN-KZIN WARS.

16417 *Kinship with the stars.* New York: Tor SF, A Tom Doherty Associates Book, 1991, vii+276 p., paper, coll.

Knight Flandry—SEE: *A knight of ghosts and shadows.*

00280 *A knight of ghosts and shadows.* Garden City, NY: Nelson Doubleday, 1974, 184 p., cloth, novel. FLANDRY SERIES.

00280A retitled: *Knight Flandry.* London: Severn House, 1980, 221 p., cloth, novel. FLANDRY SERIES.

00281 *Let the spacemen beware!* New York: Ace Books, 1963, 98 p., paper, novel. POLESOTECHNIC LEAGUE SERIES. [Bound with *The wizard of Starship Poseidon* / by Kenneth Bulmer].

00281A retitled: *The night face.* New York: Ace Books, 1978, vi+145 p., paper, novel. POLESOTECHNIC LEAGUE SERIES. [Not the same as the Gregg Press book of the same title].

16418 *The long night.* New York: A Jim Baen Presentation, Tor, A Tom Doherty Associates Book, 1983, 317 p., paper, coll. POLESOTECHNIC LEAGUE SERIES— NICHOLAS VAN RIJN.

The long way home—SEE: *No world of their own.*

16419 *The longest voyage.* New York: Tor SF, A Tom Doherty Associates Book, 1991, p. 1-52, paper, story. [Bound with *Slow lightning* / by Steven Popkes].

16420 *Losers' night.* Eugene, OR: Pulphouse Publishing, 1991, 42 p., cloth, story. SHORT STORY HARDBACKS #1; SHORT STORY PAPERBACKS #1.

The man who counts—SEE: *War of the wing-men.*

00283 *The many worlds of Poul Anderson.* Radnor, PA: Chilton Book Co., 1974, 324 p., cloth, coll.

00283A retitled: *The book of Poul Anderson.* New York: DAW Books, 1975, 284 p., paper, coll.

16421 *Maurai & Kith.* New York: Tor, A Tom Doherty Associates Book, 1982, 239 p., paper, coll.

16422 *The merman's children.* New York: Berkley Publishing Corp., 1979, 319 p., cloth, novel.

16423 *Mirkheim.* New York: Berkley Publishing Corp., 1977, 218 p., cloth, novel. POLESOTECHNIC LEAGUE #6—VAN RIJN.

16424 *New America.* New York: Tor, A Tom Doherty Associates Book, 1982, 287 p., paper, coll.

The night face—SEE: *Let the spacemen beware!*

16425 *The night face, and other stories.* Boston: Gregg Press, 1978, xii+221 p., cloth, coll. [Not the same as the Ace book of the same title].

16426 *No truce with kings.* New York: Tor SF, A Tom Doherty Associates Book, 1989, 104 p., paper, novel. [Bound with *Ship of shadows* / by Fritz Leiber].

00287 *No world of their own.* New York: Ace Books, 1955, 158 p., paper, novel. [Bound with *The 1,000 Year Plan* / by Isaac Asimov].

16427 retitled: *The long way home.* Boston: Gregg Press, 1978, vi+245 p., paper, novel. [Expanded edition].

16428 *Orion shall rise.* Huntington Woods, MI: Phantasia Press, 1983, 463 p., cloth, novel. [Limited to 600 copies].

16429 *Past times.* New York: Tor, A Tom Doherty Associates Book, 1984, 288 p., paper, coll.

16430 *The people of the wind; and, The day of their return.* New York: A Signet Book, New American Library, 1982, 176+185 p., paper, coll.

The Peregrine—SEE: *Star ways.*

00292 *Planet of no return.* New York: Ace Books, 1957, 105 p., paper, novel. [Bound with *Star Guard* / by Andre Norton].

00292A retitled: *Question and answer.* New York: Ace Books, 1978, 147 p., paper, novel.

16431 *The Psychotechnic League.* New York: A Tom Doherty Associates Book, Tor Science Fiction, Pinnacle Books, 1981, 285 p., paper, coll. PSYCHOTECHNIC LEAGUE #1.

16432 *The Psychotechnic League: Cold victory.* New York: Tor, A Tom Doherty Associates Book, 1982, 284 p., paper, coll. PSYCHOTECHNIC LEAGUE #2.

Question and answer—SEE: *Planet of no return.*

16433 *The Saturn game.* New York: Tor SF, A Tom Doherty Associates Book, 1989, 85 p., paper, novel. [Bound with *Iceborn* / by Gregory Benford & Paul A. Carter].

00296 *Seven conquests: an adventure in science fiction.* New York: Macmillan Co., 1969, 224 p., cloth, coll.

00296A retitled: *Conquests.* London, Toronto: A Panther Book, Granada, 1981, 250 p., paper, coll.

16434 *The shield of time.* New York: Tor, A Tom Doherty Associates Book, 1990, 359 p., cloth, coll. TIME PATROL #4.

16435 *Space folk.* New York: Baen Books, 1989, 303 p., paper, coll.

00300 *Star ways.* NY: Avalon Books, 1956, 224 p., cloth, novel.

00300A retitled: *The Peregrine.* New York: Ace Books, 1978, 184 p., paper, novel.

16436 *Starship.* New York: Tor, A Tom Doherty Associates Books, 1982, 281 p., paper, coll. PSYCHOTECHNIC LEAGUE #3.

16437 *A stone in heaven.* New York: Ace Books, 1979, 255 p., paper, novel. FLANDRY SERIES.

16438 *There will be time; and, The dancer from Atlantis.* New York: A Signet Book, New American Library, 1982, 176+192 p., paper, coll.

16439 *Time Patrol.* New York: Tor, A Tom Doherty Associates Book, 1991, 458 p., cloth, coll. TIME PATROL #1-3. [Includes *The guardians of time*, *Time patrolman*, *The year of the ransom*, and "Star of the sea"].

16440 *Time Patrolman.* New York: A Jim Baen Presentation, A Tom Doherty Associates Book, 1983, 254 p., paper, novel. TIME PATROL #2.

16441 *Two worlds*. Boston: Gregg Press, 1978, 237 p., cloth, coll. [Includes *Planet of no return*; *World without stars*].

00314 *War of the wing-men*. New York: Ace Books, 1958, 160 p., paper, novel. [Bound with *The snows of Ganymede* / by Poul Anderson].

00314A retitled: *The man who counts*. New York: Ace Books, 1978, vii+209 p., paper, novel. POLESOTECHNIC LEAGUE— NICHOLAS VAN RIJN SERIES.

16442 *Winners*. New York: Tor, A Tom Doherty Associates Book, 1981, 299 p., paper, coll.

16443 *The winter of the world*. Garden City, NY: Nelson Doubleday, 1975, 182 p., cloth, novel.

16444 *The winter of the world; and, The queen of air and darkness, and other stories*. New York: A Signet Book, New American Library, 1982, 190+149 p., paper, coll.

16445 *The year of the ransom*. New York: Millennium, A Byron Preiss Book, Walker & Co., 1988, 169 p., cloth, novel. TIME PATROL #3.

with Karen Anderson

16362 *Dahut*. New York: Baen Books, 1988, 398 p., paper, novel. KING OF YS #3.

16363 *The dog and the wolf*. New York: Baen Books, 1988, 531 p., paper, novel. KING OF YS #4.

16364 *Gallicenae*. New York: Baen Books, 1987, 374 p., paper, novel. KING OF YS #2.

16365 *The king of Ys*. Garden City, NY: Nelson Doubleday, 1988, 655 p., cloth, coll. KING OF YS #1-2. [Includes *Roma mater*; *Gallicenae*].

16366 *The king of Ys, volume 2*. Garden City, NY: Nelson Doubleday, 1988, 784 p., cloth, coll. KING OF YS #3-4. [Includes *Dahut*; *The dog and the wolf*].

16367 *The king of Ys: Roma mater*. New York: Baen Books, 1986, 461 p., paper, novel. KING OF YS #1.
   Roma mater—SEE: *The king of Ys: Roma mater*.

16368 *The unicorn trade*. New York: A Tom Doherty Associates Book, 1984, 284 p., paper, coll. [Includes some verse].

with Mildred Downey Broxon

16446 *The demon of Scattery*. New York: Ace Books, 1979, 207 p., paper, novel.

with Gordon R. Dickson

16447 *Hoka!* New York: A Wallaby Book, Simon & Schuster, 1983, 219 p., paper, coll. HOKA #3.

16448 *Star prince Charlie*. New York: G. P. Putnam's Sons, 1975, 190 p., cloth, novel. HOKA #2.

with Stephen L. Gillett

16449 *How to build a planet*. Eugene, OR: Writer's Notebook Press, Pulphouse Publishing, 1991, 25 p., paper, nonf.

with Martin H. Greenberg & Charles G. Waugh

16450 *Mercenaries of tomorrow*. New York: A Critic's Choice Paperback from Lorevan Publishing, 1985, xi+372 p., paper, anth.

16451 *Space wars*. New York: Tor SF, A Tom Doherty Associates Book, 1988, 372 p., paper, anth.

16452 *Terrorists of tomorrow*. New York: A Critic's Choice Paperback from Lorevan Publishing, 1986, 376 p., paper, anth.

16453 *Time wars*. New York: Tor SF, A Tom Doherty Associates Book, 1986, 374 p., paper, anth.

with Larry Niven & Dean Ing

16454 *The Man-Kzin wars*. New York: Baen Books, 1988, 289 p., paper, coll. MAN-KZIN WARS #1.

with Jerry Pournelle, S. M. Stirling, & Larry Niven

16455 *The Man-Kzin wars III*. New York: Baen Books, 1990, 310 p., paper, coll. MAN-KZIN WARS #3.

ANDERSON, Rex

16456 *My dead brother*. New York: St. Martin's, 1990, 213 p., cloth, novel.

ANDERSON, Roberta (Cuomo), 1942- , with Mary Kuczkir as FERN MICHAELS

16457 *Without warning*. New York: Pocket Books, 1981, 224 p., paper, novel.

ANDERSON, Susan Janice [i.e., Susan Janice Rubinyi-Anderson], with Vonda N. McIntyre

16458 *Aurora: beyond equality*. Greenwich, CT: A Fawcett Gold Medal Book, Fawcett Publications, 1976, 222 p., paper, anth.

ANDERSSON, C. Dean

16459 *Raw pain Max* / by Dean Andersson. New York: Popular Library, 1988, 260 p., paper, novel.
16460 *Torture tomb.* New York: Popular Library, 1987, 325 p., paper, novel.

as ASA DRAKE

16461 *Death Riders of Hel.* New York: Popular Library, Warner Books, 1986, 263 p., paper, novel. HEL #2.
16462 *Warrior Witch of Hel.* New York: Popular Library, Warner Books, 1985, 218 p., paper, novel. HEL #1.
16463 *Werebeasts of Hel.* New York: Popular Library, Warner Books, 1986, 250 p., paper, novel. HEL #3.

with Nina Romberg as ASA DRAKE

16464 *Crimson kisses.* New York: Avon, 1981, 292 p., paper, novel. DRACULA SEQUEL.
16465 *The lair of ancient dreams.* New York: Avon, 1982, 239 p., paper, novel.

ANDERSSON, Nina R.—SEE: Romberg, Nina

ANDRADE, Mário (Raúl) de (Morais), 1893-1945

16466 *Macunaíma.* New York: Random House, 1984, 168 p., cloth, novel. [Translation by E. A. Goodland of *Macunaíma*].

ANDREISSEN, David, pseud.—SEE: Poyer, David C.

ANDREOPOULOS, Spyros (George), 1929- , *with Eugene Dong*

16467 *Heart beat: a novel.* New York: Coward, McCann & Geoghegan, 1978, 352 p., cloth, novel.

ANDREWS, Allen, 1913-

16468 *Castle Crespin.* London: Hutchinson, 1982, 238 p., cloth, novel. PIG PLANTAGENET #2.
16469 *The pig Plantagenet.* London: Hutchinson, 1980, 199 p., cloth, novel. PIG PLANTAGENET #1.

ANDREWS, Bart, 1945-

with Howard Davenport

16470 *From The Blob to Star Wars: the science fiction movie quiz book: 1001 trivia teasers for sci-fi fans.* New York: A Signet Book, New American Library, 1977, 154 p., paper, nonf.

with Brad Dunning

16471 *Star Trek quiz book: 1,001 trivia teasers for trekkies.* New York: A Signet Book, New American Library, 1977, 150 p., paper, nonf.
16471A retitled: *The trekkie quiz book: 1,001 teasers for trekkies.* New York: A Signet Book, New American Library, 1978, 150 p., paper, nonf.
The trekkie quiz book—SEE: *Star Trek quiz book.*

with Bernie Zuber

16472 *The Tolkien quiz book: 1001 questions about Tolkien's tales of Middle-Earth and other fantasies.* New York: A Signet Book, New American Library, 1979, 154 p., paper, nonf.

ANDREWS, Cecily—SEE: West, Rebecca

ANDREWS, Claire, 1940- , *with Keith Andrews as* KEITH CLAIRE

16473 *The otherwise girl.* New York: Holt, Rinehart & Winston, 1976, 147 p., cloth, novel.

*ANDREWS, F(rank) Emerson, 1902-1978

ANDREWS, Felicia, pseud.—SEE: Grant, Charles L.

ANDREWS, Graham

16474 *Darkness audible.* London: Excalibur Press, 1991, 213 p., paper, novel.

ANDREWS, Keith, 1930- , *with Claire Andrews as* KEITH CLAIRE

16473 *The otherwise girl.* New York: Holt, Rinehart & Winston, 1976, 147 p., cloth, novel.

ANDREWS, Keith William, house pseud.

16475 *Freedom's rangers.* New York: Berkley Books, 1989, 311 p., paper, novel. FREEDOM'S RANGERS #1. [By William H. Keith Jr.].
16476 *Freedom's rangers: Raiders of the Revolution.* New York: Berkley Books, 1989,

202 p., paper, novel. FREEDOM'S RANGERS #2. [By William H. Keith Jr.].

16477 *Freedom's rangers: Search and destroy.* New York: Berkley Books, 1990, 203 p., paper, novel. FREEDOM'S RANGERS #3. [By William H. Keith Jr.].

16478 *Freedom's rangers: Sink the armada.* New York: Berkley Books, 1990, 217 p., paper, novel. FREEDOM'S RANGERS #5. [By William H. Keith Jr.].

16479 *Freedom's rangers: Snow kill.* New York: Berkley Books, 1991, 204 p., paper, novel. FREEDOM'S RANGERS #6. [By William H. Keith Jr.].

16480 *Freedom's rangers: Treason in time.* New York: Berkley Books, 1990, 219 p., paper, novel. FREEDOM'S RANGERS #4. [By William H. Keith Jr.].

Raiders of the Revolution—SEE: *Freedom's rangers: Raiders of the Revolution.*

Search and destroy—SEE: *Freedom's rangers: Search and destroy.*

Sink the armada—SEE: *Freedom's rangers: Sink the armada.*

Snow kill—SEE: *Freedom's rangers: Snow kill.*

Treason in time—SEE *Freedom's rangers: Treason in time.*

*ANDREWS, Lewis M(arshall), 1946-

ANDREWS, Mark

16481 *Bomb squad.* New York: Leisure Books, 1977, 224 p., paper, novel.

16482 *Satan's manor.* New York: Leisure Books, 1977, 287 p., paper, novel.

ANDREWS, Nicola

16483 *Rules of the game.* New York: Berkley Books, 1984, 182 p., paper, novel.

ANDREWS, Nigel

16484 *Horror films.* New York: Gallery Books, 1985, 95 p., cloth, nonf.

ANGELL, Judie [i.e., Judie Angell Gaberman], 1937-

16485 *The weird disappearance of Jordan Hall.* New York: A Richard Jackson Book, Orchard Books, 1987, 121 p., cloth, novel.

ANGELO, Ivan, 1936-

16486 *The tower of glass.* New York: A Bard Book, Avon, 1986, 195 p., paper, coll.

[Translation by Eileen Watson of *Casa de vidro*].

ANGLO, Michael

16487 *Penny dreadfuls and other Victorian horrors.* London: Jupiter Books, 1977, 124 p., cloth, nonf.

*ANGOFF, Charles, 1902-1979

ANNAN, David

16488 *Ape: monster of the movies.* New York: Bounty Books, 1975, 93 p., cloth, nonf.

16489 *Catastrophe: the end of the cinema?* London: Lorrimer Publishing, 1975, 110 p., paper, nonf.

00348 *Cinefantastique: beyond the dream machine.* London: Lorrimer Publishing, 1974, 132 p., paper, nonf.

00348A retitled: *Movie fantastic: beyond the dream machine.* New York: Bounty Books, 1975, 132 p., paper, nonf.

00348B retitled: *Cinema of mystery and fantasy.* London: Lorrimer Publishing, 1984, 135 p., cloth, nonf.

Cinema of mystery and fantasy—SEE: *Cinefantastique.*

Movie fantastic: beyond the dream machine—SEE: *Cinefantastique.*

16490 *Robot: the mechanical monster.* London: Lorrimer Publishing, 1978, 111 p., paper, nonf.

ANNAN, Ralph

16491 *The spider-men: a science-fantasy adventure.* New York, Washington: Vantage Press, 1979, 56 p., cloth, story.

ANNE, David, 1930-

Day of the mad dogs—SEE: *Rabid.*

16492 *The folly.* London: W. H. Allen & Co., 1978, 168 p., cloth, novel.

16493 *Rabid.* London: W. H. Allen, 1977, 249 p., cloth, movie.

16493A retitled: *Day of the mad dogs.* London: Corgi Books, 1978, 249 p., paper, movie.

ANOBILE, Richard J(oseph), 1947-

16494 *The Wizard scrapbook.* New York: A Berkley Windhover Book, 1978, 144 p., paper, nonf.

ANONYMOUS WORKS

NOTE: Works in this section are listed alphabetically by title. Those books whose anonymous authors or editors have been positively identified are listed under those authors in the main section of the author index, with appropriate see references given below; if no editor of an anthology is known, such works may be listed under introducers, translators, or any other unique authorial element mentioned in the front matter of the book, as indicated.

14 top SF stories—SEE: *Isaac Asimov's choice: 14 top SF stories.*

16495 *100 magical stories.* London: Hamlyn, 1981, 157 p., cloth, anth.

16496 *After midnight.* Belmont, CA: Lake, 1989, 137 p., paper, anth.

16497 *Alfred Hitchcock's Witch's brew.* New York: Random House, 1977, 171 p., cloth, anth.

Aliens, travelers, and other strangers—SEE: **DeGaris, Roger**

16498 *Analog: The best of science fiction.* New York: Galahad Books, 1985, 621 p., cloth, anth.

The angel—SEE: **Weinberg, Robert**

16499 *The anthology of fear: 20 haunting stories for winter nights.* London: Marshall Cavendish, 1988, 368 p., cloth, anth.

16500 *Anticipations: a short history of the future: an exhibition of science fiction imagery.* Wolverhampton, England: Faculty of Art & Design, The Polytechnic, 1974, 19 p., paper, nonf.

16501 *Arabian nights entertainments.* Closter, NJ: Sharon Publications, 1981, 215 p., paper, anth.

Arrival—SEE: *Buck Rogers: Arrival.*

16502 *The art of Return of the Jedi, Star Wars: including the complete script of the film by Lawrence Kasdan and George Lucas.* New York: Ballantine Books, 1983, 151 p., cloth, art.

Asimov's choice: 14 top SF stories—SEE: *Isaac Asimov's Choice: 14 top SF stories.*

Asimov's choice: Astronauts & androids—SEE: **Scithers, George H.**

Astronauts & androids—SEE: **Scithers, George H.**

16503 *Avon Books presents: Haunting love stories.* New York: Avon Books, 1991, 467 p., paper, anth.

Bart science fiction triplet #1—SEE: **Greenberg, Martin H.**

16504 *Begotten of the demon.* New York: Star Distributors, 1978, 180 p., paper, novel.

16505 *Beloved of Satan.* New York: Star Distributors, 1979, 180 p., paper, novel.

16506 *Berlinguer and the professor: chronicles of the next Italy.* New York: A Richard Seaver Book, Viking Press, 1976, 117 p., cloth, novel. [Translation by John Shepley of *Berlinguer e il professore*].

The best ghost stories—SEE: **Fowkes, Charles**

16507 *The best ghost stories.* New York: Mallard Press, 1990, 397 p., cloth, anth.

The best horror stories—SEE: **Picknett, Lynn**

16508 *The best horror stories.* New York: Mallard Press, 1990, 398 p., cloth, anth.

The best of science fiction—SEE: *Analog: The best of science fiction.*

16509 *The best of SF: an international exhibition of science fiction literature, May 17-31.* London: National Book League and The Science Fiction Foundation, 1971, 50 p., paper?, nonf.

The best science fiction stories—SEE: **Stapledon, Michael**

16510 *Beyond the horizon: an anthology of science fact and science fiction.* Sunderland, England: Coelfrith 24, 1973, 146 p., paper, anth. [Includes some nonfiction].

Binary star no. 1: Destiny times three / Fritz Leiber ; Riding the torch / Norman Spinrad—SEE: **Frenkel, James**

Binary star no. 2: The twilight river / Gordon Eklund ; The tery / F. Paul Wilson—SEE: **Frenkel, James**

Binary star no. 3: Dr. Scofflaw / Ron Goulart ; Outerworld / Isidore Haiblum—SEE: **Frenkel, James**

Binary star no. 4: Legacy / Joan D. Vinge ; The Janus equation / Steven G. Spruill—SEE: **Frenkel, James**

Binary star no. 5: Nightflyers / George R. R. Martin ; True names / Vernor Vinge—SEE: **Frenkel, James**

16511 *The black hole.* New York: Golden Press; Racine, WI: Western Publishing Co., 1979, 48 p., paper, movie.

The bone yard—SEE: **Koontz, Dean R. & Mikol, Paul**

The book of the Sixth World Fantasy Convention—SEE: **Underwood, Tim & Miller, Chuck**

Boskone XVI filksong book—SEE: **Raskind, Lisa**

16512 *Buck Rogers: Arrival.* Lake Geneva, WI: TSR Inc., 1989, 316 p., paper, anth.

16513 *Buster book of spooky stories.* London: IPC Magazines, 1975, 128 p., paper, anth.

16514 *Cafe Purgatorium: three original novels of horror and the supernatural.* New York:

Tor Horror, A Tom Doherty Associates Book, 1991, 279 p., cloth, anth.

The chair where terror sat—SEE: **Weinberg, Robert**

16515 *Chamber of horrors.* London: Octopus, 1984, 349 p., cloth, anth.

16516 *Chamber of horrors.* Belmont, CA: Fearon Educational, 1991, 233 p., paper, anth.

Citadels on Earth—SEE: **Hagberg, David**

Citadels under attack—SEE: **Hagberg, David**

16519 *Classic ghost stories.* New York: Dover Publications, 1975, 330 p., paper, anth.

Claws & feathers—SEE: **Brandner, Gary**

Colymbia—SEE: **Dudgeon, Robert Ellis**

The corpse factory—SEE: **Weinberg, Robert**

Crisis on Citadel II—SEE: **Hagberg, David**

16521 *Criticism—who needs it?* Baltimore, MD: Science Fiction Writers of America, 1968, 15 p., paper, nonf. anth.

The cruise of the anti-torpedo—SEE: **Payn, James**

The dance of the skeletons—SEE: **Weinberg, Robert**

The death dealers—SEE: **Weinberg, Robert**

Death orchids, & other bizarre tales—SEE: **Weinberg, Robert**

16522 *Demon bitch's punishment.* New York: Satan's Library, 1979, 180 p., paper, novel.

16523 *Devil's handmaiden.* New York: Star Distributors, 1979, 180 p., paper, novel.

16524 *Devil's incest daughter.* New York: Star distributors, 1979, 180 p., paper, novel.

16525 *Devil's sex slaves.* New York: Star Distributors, 1979, 180 p., paper, novel.

16526 *The devil's torture.* New York: Star Distributors, 1978, 180 p., paper, novel.

Dictionary catalogue of the J. Lloyd Eaton Collection of Science Fiction and Fantasy Literature—SEE: **Slusser, George Edgar**

16527 *Dune.* South Norwalk, CT: Paradise Press, 1984, 61 p., paper, nonf.

16528 *Edges of reality: confrontations with the uncanny, the macabre, and the mad.* Glenview, IL: Scott, Foresman & Co., 1972, 295 p., paper, anth.

Edmond Dantès: a sequel to The Count of Monte-Cristo—SEE: **Flagg, Edmund**

The emperor of death—SEE: **Weinberg, Robert**

16529 *Enterprise: log entries 60.* Strathmartine by Dundee, Scotland: ScoTpress, 1984, 51 p., paper, tele. anth. STAR TREK SERIES.

Exciting stories of fantasy and the future—SEE: **Frey, Oliver**

Experiment perilous—SEE: **Porter, Andrew**

Exploring Cordwainer Smith—SEE: **Porter, Andrew**

24915 *The fairies return; or, New tales for old by several hands: with reverent apologies to the memory of Perrault, the Brothers Grimm, Hans Andersen, the author of the Thousand and one nights, &c.* London: Peter Davies, 1934, v+350 p., cloth, anth.

Famous fantastic classics #1—SEE: **Weinberg, Robert**

Famous fantastic classics #2—SEE: **Weinberg, Robert**

Famous pulp classics #1—SEE: **Weinberg, Robert**

16530 *Fantasy Review: 1984 index to the reviews, volume 7, no.'s 1-11, whole numbers 64-74.* Boca Raton, FL: College of Humanities, Florida Atlantic University, 1985?, 14 p., paper, nonf. [Cover title].

Fantasy voices: great science fiction from the Saturday Evening Post—SEE: **Miranda, Vincent**

16531 *A Federation trivia book.* [S.l.: s.n., n.d.], 29 p., paper, nonf.

Flash Gordon: Massacre in the 22nd century—SEE: **Hagberg, David**

16533 *Forbidden lines: science fiction, fantasy, essays.* Chapel Hill, NC: Science Fiction Writers' Group, 1989, 202 p., paper, anth. [Includes some nonfiction].

Forces from the Federation—SEE: **Hagberg, David**

16535 *Frankenstein; Dracula; Dr. Jekyll and Mr. Hyde.* New York: A Signet Classic, New American Library, 1978, xiii+xiv+211+382+70 p., paper, anth.

16536 *The future: science fiction book exhibit.* Houston, TX: Houston Public Library in Connection with Houston Arts Festival, 1968, unpaginated, paper, nonf.

Futurelove: a science fiction triad—SEE: **Elwood, Roger**

16537 *Galactic adventures.* Chicago: Rand McNally, 1980, 188 p., cloth, anth.

16538 *George Orwell & Nineteen Eighty-Four: the man and the book: a conference at the Library of Congress, April 30 and May 1, 1984, presented under the auspices of the Gertrude Clarke Whittall Poetry and Literature Fund.* Washington, DC: Library of Congress, 1985, ix+150 p., paper, nonf. anth.

The Gernsback awards 1926—SEE: **Ackerman, Forrest J**

16539 *Ghost and horror stories: a selection of classic tales of apparitions, werewolves, diabolism, divination, possession, occult, magic, fantasy, and destiny.* Thornhall, Scotland: Tynron Press, 1990, 579 p., paper, anth.

Ghosts & scholars: stories in the tradition of M. R. James—SEE: **Dalby, Richard & Rosemary Pardoe**

Gollancz-'Sunday Times' best SF stories. London: Victor Gollancz, 1975, 317 p., cloth, anth.—SEE: **Aldiss, Brian W.**

Gollancz/Sunday Times SF competition stories—SEE: **Edwards, Malcolm**

16541 *The great ghost story book.* Bedford, Bedfordshire, England: Bedfordshire County Library, 1980?, 47 p., paper, anth.

16542 *Great science fiction stories: 2001: a space odyssey* / Arthur C. Clarke ; *The demolished man* / Alfred Bester; *The day of the triffids* / John Wyndham; *I, robot* / Isaac Asimov. London: Octopus Books, 1979, 702 p., cloth, anth.

16543 *Great short tales of mystery and terror.* Pleasantville, NY: Reader's Digest Association, 1982, 639 p., cloth, anth.

16544 *Great stories from The Twilight Zone Magazine.* New York: Twilight Zone Publications, 1982, [96] p., paper, anth.

Guide to SF, horror, and fantasy movies 1991-92—SEE: *Hoffman's Guide to SF, horror, and fantasy movies 1991-92.*

16545 *H. P. Lovecraft: a symposium.* Los Angeles: Riverside Quarterly & Los Angeles Science Fantasy Society, 1964, 17 p., paper, nonf.

16546 *The H. P. Lovecraft memorial plaque.* West Warwick, RI: Necronomicon Press, 1991, 28 p., paper, nonf.

Hardshell—SEE: **Barker, Clive & Mikol, Paul**

16547 *Haunting Christmas tales.* London: Scholastic, 1991, 269 p., cloth, anth.

Haunting love stories—SEE: *Avon Books presents: Haunting love stories.*

16548 *Hell's bitch.* New York: Satan's Library, 1979, 180 p., paper, novel.

16549 *Her master was Satan.* New York: Star Distributors, 1978, 180 p., paper, novel.

16550 *Hoffman's Guide to SF, horror, and fantasy movies 1991-92.* London: Corgi Books, 1991, 432 p., paper, nonf. [Despite the title, the supposed author "Hoffman" appears to be fictitious].

Illusions—SEE: **Brandner, Gary**

16551 *In the wake of man: a science fiction triad.* Indianapolis, IN: Bobbs-Merrill Co., 1975, 229 p., cloth, anth.

16552 *Index to fantasy & science fiction in Munsey publications.* [S.l.: s.n., n.d.], 36 p., paper, nonf.

16553 *Indiana Jones and the Temple of Doom.* South Norwalk, CT: Paradise Press, 1984, 64 p., paper, nonf.

16554 *Isaac Asimov's Choice: 14 top SF stories.* London: Robert Hale, 1986, 255 p., cloth, anth. [This may be a reprint of a title previously published in the United States].

Isaac Asimov's Science fiction anthology, volume 1—SEE: **Scithers, George**

16555 *Isaac Asimov's Tomorrow's voices.* New York: Dial Press, Davis Publications, 1984, 287 p., cloth, anth.

Jenny Ewing: my diary—SEE: **Blumenfeld, Yorick**

The lake of life—SEE: **Weinberg, Robert**

Let's go to Golgotha: the Gollancz-'Sunday Times' best SF stories—SEE: **Aldiss, Brian W.**

16556 *Letters from home: stories.* London: The Women's Press, 1991, xv+233 p., paper, anth.

16557 *Lilith's daughter.* New York: Star Distributors, 1978, 180 p., paper, novel.

Lost fantasies #4—SEE: **Weinberg, Robert**

Lost fantasies #5—SEE: **Weinberg, Robert**

Lost fantasies #6—SEE: **Weinberg, Robert**

16558 *Love and the unexplained: stories of romance, mystery, and the occult.* London: IPC Magazines, 1983, 74 p., paper, anth.

16559 *Lucifer's altar girl.* New York: Satan's Library, 1979, 180 p., paper, novel.

16560 *The man in black: macabre stories from "Fear on Four".* London: BBC Books, 1990, 413 p., paper, tele. anth.

Massacre in the 22nd century—SEE: **Hagberg, David**

The master sinner: a romance—SEE: **Vivian, Herbert**

16561 *Masters of horror & suspense: The interlopers, The specter, The tell-tale heart, The cask of Amontillado.* Boston: Houghton Mifflin Co., 1989, 64 p., paper?, anth.

The molecular cafe: science-fiction stories—SEE: **Strugatsky, Arkady & Strugatsky, Boris**

More ghosts & scholars: ghost stories in the tradition of M. R. James—SEE: **Pardoe, Rosemary**

16563 *The mound, and other SF stories from the Low Lands.* Netherlands?: Babel Productions, 1990, 84 p., paper, anth.

16564 *Necon stories.* Providence, RI: Three Bobs Press, 1990, 160 p., paper, anth. [Includes some nonfiction].

New Soviet science fiction—SEE: **De-Garis, Roger**

The new visions: a collection of modern science fiction art—SEE: **Pohl, Frederik**

Night fears—SEE: **Barker, Clive & Mikol, Paul**

Night visions 4: all original stories—SEE: **Barker, Clive & Mikol, Paul**

Night visions 6: all original stories—SEE: **Koontz, Dean R. & Mikol, Paul**

Night visions 8: all original stories—SEE: **McCammon, Robert R. & Mikol, Paul**

Night visions 9: all original stories—SEE: **Wilson, F. Paul & Mikol, Paul**

Night visions: Hardshell—SEE: **Barker, Clive & Mikol, Paul**

No frills science fiction—SEE: **Silbersack, John**

16565 *Official correspondence between the Honorable the First Minister of Duffy and His Exalted Majesty Night Blooming Ceres, Monarch of the Moon, Emperor of the Starry Isles, etc., etc., relative to the construction of the Imperial, Lunar, Grand, Mid-Air, Lunatic Governmental Railway, also the reports of the Chief Engineer, and the draft treaty in relation to same, with the speech from the throne.* Ottawa: Citizen Printing & Publishing Co., 1875, 14 p., paper?, fiction. [At the head of the title: "House of the Gallery, 2nd Session, 3d Parliament"].

16566 *The official price guide to Star Trek and Star Wars collectibles.* Orlando, FL: House of Collectibles, 1983, [200] p., paper, nonf.

16567 *The official price guide to Star Trek and Star Wars collectibles, 2nd ed.* Orlando, FL: House of Collectibles, 1984, 236 p., paper, nonf.

16568 *The official price guide to Star Trek and Star Wars collectibles, 3rd ed.* Orlando, FL: House of Collectibles, 1985, 257 p., paper, nonf.

16569 *The only eleven-year cumulative index to Galaxy Magazine, by author and by title, Oct. 1950-Dec. 1961: complete, including a listing-by-subject of Willy Ley's science articles.* [S.l.: s.n., 1962?, 22 leaves], paper, nonf.

16570 *The Orbit poster book.* London: Orbit Books, 1987, 32 p., paper, art.

16571 *Over the rainbow: tales of fantasy and imagination.* London: Octopus Books, 1983, 288 p., cloth, anth.

16572 *Paranoia and science fiction.* Baltimore, MD: Science Fiction Writers of America, 1967, 11 p., paper, nonf. anth.

16573 *Princess of darkness.* New York: Star Distributors, 1979, 180 p., paper, novel.

16574 *Purnell's book of horror stories.* Bristol, Avon, England: Purnell, 1983, 192 p., cloth, anth.

16575 *Quantum science fiction special (1): In the ocean of night* / Gregory Benford ; *The Ophiuchi hotline* / John Varley. London: Sidgwick & Jackson, 1979, 333+ 237 p., cloth, anth.

16576 *Quantum special (2): The far call* / Gordon R. Dickson ; *In the hall of the Martian kings* / John Varley. London: Sidgwick & Jackson, 1981, 316+xvii+316 p., cloth, anth.

16577 *Radical utopias.* New York: Book-of-the-Month Club, 1991, 832 p., cloth, anth. [Includes *The Female Man* / by Joanna Russ ; *Triton* / by Samuel R. Delany ; *Walk to the End of the World* / by Suzy McKee Charnas].

16578 *Raped by the devil.* New York: Star Distributors, 1979, 180 p., paper, novel.

Romanian fantastic tales—SEE: **Cartianu, Ana**

16579 *Satanic virgin.* New York: Satan's Library, 1979, 180 p., paper, novel.

Satan's roadhouse—SEE: **Weinberg, Robert**

16580 *Schooled by the devil.* New York: Star Distributors, 1979, 180 p., paper, novel.

Science fiction—SEE: **Silbersack, John**

16581 *Science fiction: a bibliography.* Regina, Saskatchewan, Canada: Saskatchewan Provincial Library, 1973, 33 p., paper, nonf.

16582 *Science fiction: a selected list of books that have appeared in Talking book topics and Braille book review.* Washington, DC: Library of Congress, 1979, 61 p., paper, nonf.

16583 *Science fiction book reviews, 1969-1972.* Sydney, Australia: Australian Science Fiction Association, 1973, 60 p., paper, nonf.

Science fiction by the rivals of H. G. Wells—SEE: **Russell, Alan K.**

Science fiction: English and American short stories—SEE: **Murav'ev, V. S.**

16584 *Science Fiction Foundation Library holdings: (additional to the BSFA Catalogue of 1970).* Dagenham, Essex, England: Science Fiction Foundation, 1975, 92 p., paper, nonf.

16585 *Science fiction special (12): Volteface* / Mark Adlard ; *Night of the robots* / Brian N. Ball ; *The anvil of time* / Robert Silverberg. London: Sidgwick & Jackson, 1975, 210+235+192 p., cloth, anth.

16586 *Science fiction special (13): The probability man* / Brian N. Ball ; *Age of miracles* / John Brunner ; *A choice of gods* / Clifford D. Simak. London: Sidgwick & Jackson, 1975, 175+190+190 p., cloth, anth.

16587 *Science fiction special (14): The world shuffler* / Keith Laumer ; *The invincible* / Stanislaw Lem ; *Beyond control* / Robert Silverberg. London: Sidgwick & Jackson, 1975, 185+221+219 p., cloth, anth.

16588 *Science fiction special (15): The best of John W. Campbell* / John W. Campbell ; *The far-out worlds of A. E. van Vogt* / A. E. van Vogt ; *Bright new universe* / Jack Williamson. London: Sidgwick & Jackson, 1975, 278+223+192 p., cloth, anth.

16589 *Science fiction special (16): Bedlam planet* / John Brunner ; *The Fingalnan conspiracy* / John Rankine ; *The three eyes of evil; and, Earth's last fortress* / A. E. van Vogt. London: Sidgwick & Jackson, 1976, 159+190+218 p., cloth, anth.

16590 *Science fiction special (17): Flight from time* / Deane Romano ; *Dying inside* / Robert Silverberg ; *The darkness on Diamondia* / A. E. van Vogt. London: Sidgwick & Jackson, 1976, 251+245+254 p., cloth, anth.

16591 *Science fiction special (18): The house in November* / Keith Laumer ; *Planet probability* / Brian N. Ball ; *The eternal frontiers* / James H. Schmitz. London: Sidgwick & Jackson, 1976, 192+188+190 p., cloth, anth.

16592 *Science fiction special (19): The parasaurians* / Robert Wells ; *The star treasure* / Keith Laumer ; *Operation Umanaq* / John Rankine. London: Sidgwick & Jackson, 1976, 190+176+188 p., cloth, anth.

16593 *Science fiction special (20): Orbit unlimited* / Poul Anderson ; *Singularity station* / Brian N. Ball ; *The best of John W. Campbell* / John W. Campbell. London: Sidgwick & Jackson, 1977, 158+176+278 p., cloth, anth.

16594 *Science fiction special (21): Enchanted pilgrimage* / Clifford D. Simak ; *The portals* / Edward Andrew Mann ; *The man with a thousand names* / A. E. van Vogt. London: Sidgwick & Jackson, 1977, 218+204+159 p., cloth, anth.

16595 *Science fiction special (22): To live again* / Robert Silverberg ; *Cemetery world* / Clifford D. Simak ; *Multiface* / Mark

Adlard. London: Sidgwick & Jackson, 1977, 231+191+184 p., cloth, anth.

16596 *Science fiction special (23): Our children's children* / Clifford D. Simak ; *The secret galactics* / A. E. van Vogt. London: Sidgwick & Jackson, 1978, 186+215 p., cloth, anth.

16597 *Science fiction special (24): Future glitter* / A. E. van Vogt ; *The Telzey toy* / James H. Schmitz ; *Candle in the Sun* / Robert Wells. London: Sidgwick & Jackson, 1978, 216+175+158 p., cloth, anth.

16598 *Science fiction special (25): A choice of gods* / Clifford D. Simak ; *Age of miracles* / John Brunner ; *The Fingalnan conspiracy* / John Rankine. London: Sidgwick & Jackson, 1978, 190+190+190 p., cloth, anth.

16599 *Science fiction special (26): The three eyes of evil, and, Earth's last fortress* / A. E. van Vogt ; *Bedlam planet* / John Brunner. London: Sidgwick & Jackson, 1978, 218+159 p., cloth, anth.

16600 *Science fiction special (27): The lion game* / James H. Schmitz ; *The universe maker; and, The proxy intelligence* / A. E. van Vogt ; *Merlin's mirror* / Andre Norton. London: Sidgwick & Jackson, 1978, 157+196+205 p., cloth, anth.

16601 *Science fiction special (28): Master of life and death* / Robert Silverberg ; *Shakespeare's planet* / Clifford D. Simak ; *Healer* / F. Paul Wilson. London: Sidgwick & Jackson, 1978, 144+188+183 p., cloth, anth.

16602 *Science fiction special (29): The best of Harry Harrison* / Harry Harrison ; *The best of Frederik Pohl* / Frederik Pohl. London: Sidgwick & Jackson, 1978, 315+xvi+363 p., cloth, anth.

Science fiction special (30): Invaders from Earth ; The best of Robert Silverberg—SEE: **Silverberg, Robert**

16603 *Science fiction special (31): Mind of my mind* / Octavia E. Butler ; *The magicians* / James Gunn ; *Star bridge* / Jack Williamson and James Gunn. London: Sidgwick & Jackson, 1979, xvii+169+197+vii+213 p., cloth, anth.

16604 *Science fiction special (32): Survivor* / Octavia E. Butler ; *Under a calculating star* / John Morressy ; *The anarchistic colossus* / A. E. van Vogt. London: Sidgwick & Jackson, 1981, 185+186+248 p., cloth, anth.

Science fiction special (34): Hiero's journey ; The war for the Lot—SEE: **Lanier, Sterling E.**

16605 *Science fiction special (35): The peculiar exploits of Brigadier ffellows* / Sterling E.

Lanier ; *Xeno* / D. F. Jones ; *Frostworld and Dreamfire* / John Morressy. London: Sidgwick & Jackson, 1981, 159+267+vi+186, cloth, anth.

16606 *Science fiction special (37): Blind voices* / Tom Reamy ; *The ultimax man* / Keith Laumer. London: Sidgwick & Jackson, 1981, 254+217 p., cloth, anth.

16607 *Science fiction special (38): Gateway to Limbo* / Chris Lampton ; *Wheels within wheels* / F. Paul Wilson ; *The planet masters* / Allen Wold. London: Sidgwick & Jackson, 1981, 184+xiii+177+230 p., cloth, anth.

16608 *Science fiction special (39): Leviathan's deep* / Jayge Carr ; *How the gods wove in Kyrannon* / Ardath Mayhar ; *The ravens of the Moon* / Charles L. Grant. London: Sidgwick & Jackson, 1981, 213+181+184 p., cloth, anth.

16609 *Science fiction stories.* London: Macmillan, 1975, x+118 p., paper, anth.

16610 *Science fiction stories selected from Young world magazine.* Indianapolis, IN: Youth Publications, The Saturday Evening Post Co., 1975, 34 p., paper, anth.

The second book of After midnight stories—SEE: **Myers, Amy**

SF introduction—SEE: *Supernova 1.*

16611 *SF reprise 3.* London: Compact Books, 1966, [256] p., paper, anth.

16612 *SF reprise 4.* London: Compact Books, 1966, [256] p., paper, anth.

16613 *SF reprise 6.* London: Compact Books, 1967, [256] p., paper, anth.

The sin eaters—SEE: **Weinberg, Robert**

Slaves of the blood wolves—SEE: **Weinberg, Robert**

16614 *Space odyssey.* London: Octopus, 1983, 349 p., cloth, anth.

16615 *Spectra: a galaxy of bestsellers.* New York: Bantam Books, 1991, 54 p., paper, anth. [May have been edited by Lou Aronica].

Spiderwomon's lesbian fairy tales—SEE: **Marion**

16616 *Spinechilling tales for the dead of night.* London: Hamlyn, 1984, 256 p., cloth, anth.

16617 *Spread for Satan.* New York: Star Distributors, 1979, 180 p., paper, novel.

16618 *The Star Wars album: the incredible behind-the-scenes story of the most extraordinary motion picture of our time.* New York: Ballantine Books, 1977, 75 p., paper, nonf.

16619 *Stories about not being afraid of ghosts.* Peking, China: Foreign Languages Press, 1961, 88 p., paper, anth. [Selections from: *Pu p'a kuei ti ku shih*].

16620 *Stories about not being afraid of ghosts, 2nd ed.* Peking, China: Foreign Languages Press, 1979, 92 p., paper, anth. [Selections from: *Pu p'a kuei ti ku shih*].

16621 *Strange world of science fiction.* London: New English Library, 1977?, 71 p., cloth, anth.

16622 *A study guide to Watership down: a novel by Richard Adams.* New York: Avon Books Education Dept., 1980?, [12] p., paper, nonf.

16623 *Supernova 1: SF introduction.* London: Faber & Faber, 1976, xii+225 p., cloth, anth. [Only volume published].

16624 *Sweeping beauties: fairytales for feminists.* Dublin, Ireland: Attic Press, 1989, 64 p., paper, anth.

16625 *Sword & sorcery annual, special—1975.* Flushing, NY: Ultimate Publishing Co., 1974, 129 p., paper, anth. [Only volume published].

15868 *Tales of mystery and horror.* [S.l.]: World Society Editions, 1966, 210 p., paper, anth.

Tales of the Cthulhu Mythos—SEE: **Derleth, August & Turner, James**

16626 *Tales of the uncanny.* Pleasantville, NY: Reader's Digest Association, 1983, 606 p., cloth, anth.

Their immortal hearts—SEE: **McAllister, Bruce**

Time dreams—SEE: **Carson, David M.**

16627 *The Times anthology of ghost stories.* London: Jonathan Cape, 1975, 195 p., cloth, anth.

Tomorrow's voices—SEE: *Isaac Asimov's Tomorrow's voices.*

16628 *A treasury of gothic and supernatural.* New York: Avenel Books, 1981, 707 p., cloth, anth.

The twelfth ghost book—SEE: **Parkin, Patricia**

16629 *Twin souls: a romance of duality* / by the author of 'Fallen Angels'. London: Gay & Bird, 1906, 332 p., cloth, novel.

University of California, Riverside dictionary catalogue of the J. Lloyd Eaton Collection of Science Fiction and Fantasy Literature—SEE: **Slusser, George Edgar**

16630 *Unnatural causes: based on the Central television series.* Poole, England: Blandford, 1986, 267 p., cloth, tele. anth.

16631 *Vulcan language guide.* [S.l.]: April Publications, 1977, 16 p., paper, nonf.

War of the Citadels—SEE: **Hagberg, David**

16633 *William Hope Hodgson: a centenary tribute, 1877-1977.* Dagenham, Essex,

England: British Fantasy Society, 1977, 15 p., paper, anth. [Includes two pieces by Hodgson and a tribute by Peter Tremayne].

16634 *William Morris and Kelmscott.* London: The Design Council, 1981, 190 p., paper, nonf.

Witch's brew—SEE: *Alfred Hitchcock's Witch's brew.*

WomanSpace—SEE: **Lamperti, Claudia**

16635 *The work of William Morris: an exhibition arranged by the William Morris Society.* London: William Morris Society, 1975, 62 p., paper, nonf.

16636 *World of The Neverending Story.* Limpsfield, Surrey, England: Paper Tiger, 1984, 126 p., cloth, nonf.

Worlds within worlds—SEE: **Dikty, Thaddeus**

ANSLE, Dorothy—SEE: Conway, Laura

ANSON, Barbara

16637 *Golem.* New York: Leisure Books, 1978, 184 p., paper, novel.

*ANSON, Capt. [i.e., Charles Vernon Anson], 1841-

ANSON, Jay, 1921-1980

16638 *666.* New York: Simon & Schuster, 1981, 283 p., cloth, novel.

ANTCZAK, Janice, 1947-

16639 *Science fiction: the mythos of a new romance.* New York, London: Neal-Schuman Publishers, 1985, xxiii+233 p., paper, nonf.

ANTHONY, Dee, *with Robert Stigwood*

16640 *The official "Sgt. Pepper's Lonely Hearts Club Band" scrapbook: the making of a hit movie musical.* New York: A Wallaby Book, Pocket Books, 1978, 80 p., paper, nonf.

ANTHONY, Mark (Russell Lee), 1966- , *with Ellen Porath*

16641 *Kindred spirits.* Lake Geneva, WI: TSR Inc., 1991, 307 p., paper, novel. DRAGONLANCE SAGA—MEETINGS SEXTET #1.

ANTHONY, Piers [pseud. of Piers Anthony Dillingham Jacob], 1934-

16642 *And eternity.* New York: William Morrow & Co., 1990, 369 p., cloth, novel. INCARNATIONS OF IMMORTALITY #7.

16643 *Anthonology.* New York: Tor, A Tom Doherty Associates Book, 1985, 381 p., cloth, coll.

16644 *Balook.* Novato, CA, Lancaster, PA: Underwood-Miller, 1990, 197 p., cloth, novel.

16645 *Battle circle: a trilogy: Sos the Rope; Var the Stick; Neq the Sword.* New York: Avon, 1978, 537 p., paper, coll. BATTLE CIRCLE #1-3.

16646 *Bearing an hourglass.* New York: A Del Rey Book, Ballantine Books, 1984, v+292 p., cloth, novel. INCARNATIONS OF IMMORTALITY #2.

16647 *Being a green mother.* New York: A Del Rey Book, Ballantine Books, 1987, 313 p., cloth, novel. INCARNATIONS OF IMMORTALITY #5.

16648 *Bio of an ogre: the autobiography of Piers Anthony.* New York: Ace Books, 1988, 297 p., cloth, nonf.

16649 *Blue adept.* New York: A Del Rey Book, Ballantine Books, 1981, 327 p., cloth, novel. APPRENTICE ADEPT #2.

16650 *But what of Earth? a novel rendered into a bad example.* New York: Tor SF, A Tom Doherty Associates Book, 1989, 282 p., paper, novel. [Restores the original uncut text, the first edition having been published as a "collaboration" with Robert Coulson (see #16708)].

16651 *Castle Roogna.* New York: A Del Rey Book, Ballantine Books, 1979, 329 p., paper, novel. XANTH #3.

16652 *Centaur Aisle.* New York: A Del Rey Book, Ballantine Books, 1982, 294 p., paper, novel. XANTH #4.

16653 *Chaining the lady.* New York: Avon, 1978, 342 p., paper, novel. CLUSTER #2.

16654 *Cluster.* New York: Avon, 1977, 254 p., paper, novel. CLUSTER #1.

16654A retitled: *Vicinity cluster.* London: Millington, 1979, 254 p., cloth, novel. CLUSTER #1.

16655 *Crewel lye: a caustic yarn.* New York: A Del Rey Book, Ballantine Books, 1985, 309 p., paper, novel. XANTH #8.

16656 *Double exposure.* Garden City, NY: Nelson Doubleday, 1982, 790 p., cloth, coll. APPRENTICE ADEPT #1-3.

16657 *Dragon on a pedestal.* New York: A Del Rey Book, Ballantine Books, 1983, 306 p., paper, novel. XANTH #7.

16658 *Executive.* New York: Avon, 1985, 330 p., paper, novel. BIO OF A SPACE TYRANT #4.

16659 *Faith of Tarot.* New York: A Berkley Book, Berkley Publishing Corp., 1980, viii+246 p., paper, novel. TAROT #3.

16660 *Firefly.* New York: William Morrow & Co., 1990, 384 p., cloth, novel.

16661 *For love of evil.* New York: William Morrow & Co., 1988, 383 p., cloth, novel. INCARNATIONS OF IMMORTALITY #6.

16662 *Ghost.* New York: Tor, A Tom Doherty Associates Book, 1986, 279 p., cloth, novel.

16663 *God of Tarot.* New York: A Jove/HBJ Book, 1979, 288 p., paper, novel. TAROT #1.

16664 *Golem in the gears.* New York: A Del Rey Book, Ballantine Books, 1986, 327 p., paper, novel. XANTH #9.

16665 *Hard sell.* Houston, TX: Tafford Publishing Co., 1990, 187 p., cloth, coll.
Hasan—SEE: *Piers Anthony's Hasan.*

16666 *Heaven cent.* New York: Avon Books, 1988, 324 p., paper, novel. XANTH #11.

16667 *Index to book reviews in science fiction magazines, 1926-1963.* Gainesville, FL: Phyrne Bacon, [1966?], xvi+119 p., paper, nonf.

16668 *Isle of view.* New York: William Morrow & Co., 1990, 344 p., cloth, novel. XANTH #13.

16669 *Juxtaposition.* New York: A Del Rey Book, Ballantine Books, 1982, 358 p., cloth, novel. APPRENTICE ADEPT #3.

16670 *Kirlian quest.* New York: Avon, 1978, 313 p., paper, novel. CLUSTER #3.

16671 *The magic of Xanth.* Garden City, NY: Nelson Doubleday, 1981, 660 p., cloth, coll. XANTH #1-3.

16672 *Man from Mundania.* New York: Avon Books, 1989, 361 p., paper, novel. XANTH #12.

16673 *Mercenary.* New York: Avon, 1984, 373 p., paper, novel. BIO OF A SPACE TYRANT #2.

16674 *Mer-cycle.* Houston, TX: Tafford Publishing, 1991, 262 p., cloth, novel.

16675 *Mute.* New York: Avon, 1981, 440 p., paper, novel.

16676 *Neq the sword.* London: Corgi Books, 1975, 191 p., paper, novel. BATTLECIRCLE #3.

16677 *Night mare.* New York: A Del Rey Book, Ballantine Books, 1983, 307 p., paper, novel. XANTH #6.

16678 *Of man and mantra: a trilogy: Omnivore, Orn, OX.* London: Corgi Books, 1986, 622 p., paper, coll. ORN #1-3.

16679 *Ogre, ogre.* New York: A Del Rey Book, Ballantine Books, 1982, 307 p., paper, novel. XANTH #5.

16680 *On a pale horse.* New York: A Del Rey Book, Ballantine Books, 1983, 249 p., cloth, novel. INCARNATIONS OF IMMORTALITY #1.

16681 *Out of Phaze.* New York: An Ace/Putnam Book, 1987, 288 p., cloth, novel. APPRENTICE ADEPT #4.

16682 *OX.* Garden City, NY: Nelson Doubleday, 1976, 216 p., cloth, novel. ORN #3.

16683 *Phaze doubt.* New York: An Ace/Putnam Book, 1990, 303 p., cloth, novel. APPRENTICE ADEPT #7.

16684 *Phthor.* New York: A Berkley Medallion Book, Berkley Publishing Corp., 1975, 198 p., paper, novel. CHTHON #2.

16685 *Piers Anthony's Hasan.* San Bernardino, CA: R. Reginald, The Borgo Press, 1977, 190 p., paper, novel.

16685A retitled: *Hasan.* New York: A Dell Book, 1979, 271 p., paper, novel.

16686 *Politician.* New York: Avon, 1985, 345 p., paper, novel. BIO OF A SPACE TYRANT #3.

16687 *Pornucopia.* Houston, TX: Tafford Publishing, 1989, 187 p., cloth, novel.

16688 *Question quest.* New York: William Morrow & Co., 1991, 359 p., cloth, novel. XANTH #14.

16689 *Refugee.* New York: Avon, 1983, 312 p., paper, novel. BIO OF A SPACE TYRANT #1.

16690 *Robot adept.* New York: An Ace/Putnam Book, 1988, 286 p., cloth, novel. APPRENTICE ADEPT #5.

16691 *Shade of the tree.* New York: Tor, A Tom Doherty Associates Book, 1986, 348 p., cloth, novel.

16692 *The source of magic.* New York: A Del Rey Book, Ballantine Books, 1979, 326 p., paper, novel. XANTH #2.

16693 *A spell for Chameleon.* New York: A Del Rey Book, Ballantine Books, 1977, 344 p., paper, novel. XANTH #1.

16694 *Split infinity.* New York: A Del Rey Book, Ballantine Books, 1980, v+372 p., cloth, novel. APPRENTICE ADEPT #1.

16695 *Statesman.* New York: Avon, 1986, 312 p., paper, novel. BIO OF A SPACE TYRANT #5.

16696 *Steppe.* London: Millington, 1976, 158 p., cloth, novel.

16697 *Tarot.* New York: Ace Books, 1987, xxiii+616 p., paper, coll. TAROT #1-3.

16698 *Tatham Mound.* New York: William Morrow & Co., 1991, 522 p., cloth, novel.

16699 *Thousandstar.* New York: Avon, 1980, 294 p., paper, novel. CLUSTER #4.

16700 *Total recall.* New York: William Morrow & Co., 1989, 246 p., cloth, movie.

16701 *Unicorn point.* New York: An Ace/ Putnam Book, 1989, 303 p., cloth, novel. APPRENTICE ADEPT #6.

16702 *Vale of the vole.* New York: Avon, 1987, 324 p., paper, novel. XANTH #10.

Vicinity cluster—SEE: *Cluster.*

16703 *Virtual mode.* New York: An Ace/Putnam Book, 1991, 304 p., cloth, novel. MODE SERIES #1.

16704 *Viscous circle.* New York: Avon, 1982, 266 p., paper, novel. CLUSTER #5.

16705 *Vision of Tarot.* New York: A Berkley Book, Berkley Publishing Corp., 1980, ix + 260 p., paper, novel. TAROT #2.

16706 *Wielding a red sword.* New York: A Del Rey Book, Ballantine Books, 1986, 297 p., cloth, novel. INCARNATIONS OF IMMORTALITY #4.

16707 *With a tangled skein.* New York: A Del Rey Book, Ballantine Books, 1985, 280 p., cloth, novel. INCARNATIONS OF IMMORTALITY #3.

with Robert Coulson

16708 *But what of Earth?* Toronto, New York: Laser Books, 1976, 190 p., paper, novel. [Cut without the author's permission; the original version was published intact in 1989 (see #16650)].

with Roberto Fuentes

16709 *Amazon slaughter.* New York: A Berkley Medallion Book, Berkley Publishing Corp., 1976, 204 p., paper, novel. JASON STRIKER #5.

16710 *Dead morn.* Houston, TX: Tafford Publishing, 1990, 265 p., cloth, novel.

16711 *Ninja's revenge.* New York: A Berkley Medallion Book, Berkley Publishing Corp., 1975, 188 p., paper, novel. JASON STRIKER #4.

with Frances Hall

16712 *Pretender: science fiction.* San Bernardino, CA: R. Reginald, The Borgo Press, 1979, 159 p., cloth, novel.

with Robert Kornwise

16713 *Through the ice.* Novato, CA, Lancaster, PA: Underwood-Miller, 1989, 203 p., cloth, novel.

with Barry Malzberg & Martin H. Greenberg & Charles G. Waugh

16714 *Uncollected stars.* New York: Avon, 1986, vii + 312 p., paper, anth.

with Robert Margroff

16715 *Chimaera's copper.* New York: Tor, A Tom Doherty Associates Book, 1990, 311 p., cloth, novel. DRAGON #3.

16716 *Dragon's gold.* New York: Tor SF, A Tom Doherty Associates Book, 1987, 282 p., paper, novel. DRAGON #1.

16717 *Orc's opal.* New York: Tor, A Tom Doherty Associates Book, 1990, 280 p., cloth, novel. DRAGON #4.

16718 *Serpent's silver.* New York: Tor, A Tom Doherty Associates Book, 1988, 313 p., cloth, novel. DRAGON #2.

with Jody Lynn Nye

16719 *Piers Anthony's Visual guide to Xanth.* New York: Avon, 1989, 236 p., paper, fiction.

Visual guide to Xanth—SEE: *Piers Anthony's Visual guide to Xanth.*

ANTIEAU, Kim

16720 *Blossoms.* Eugene, OR: Pulphouse Publishing, 1991, 38 p., paper, story. SHORT STORY PAPERBACKS #5.

ANTILL, (Alick) Keith, 1929-

16721 *Moon in the ground.* Carlton, Victoria, Australia: Norstrilia Press, 1979, 220 p., cloth, novel.

ANTON, Uwe

16722 *Welcome to reality: the nightmares of Philip K. Dick.* Cambridge, MA: Broken Mirrors Press, 1991, 208 p., cloth, anth. [An anthology of stories influenced by Dick or featuring him as character; translated by James M. Young].

ANVIC, Frank, pseud.—SEE: Sherman, Jory

ANVIE, Frank, pseud.—SEE: Sherman, Jory

ANVIL, Christopher [pseud. of Harry C. Crosby Jr.]

16723 *The steel, the mist, and the blazing sun.* New York: Ace Books, 1980, 282 p., paper, novel.

16724 *Warlord's world.* New York: DAW Books, 1975, 207 p., paper, novel.

APEL, D. Scott

16725 *Philip K. Dick: the dream connection.* San Jose, CA: Permanent Press, 1987, 296 p., cloth, nonf. anth.

APOSTOLOU, John L., 1930- , with Martin H. Greenberg

16726 *The best Japanese science fiction stories.* New York: Dembner Books, 1989, 176 p., cloth, anth.

APPEL, Allen

16727 *Till the end of time.* New York: Doubleday, 1990, 405 p., cloth, novel. ALEX BALFOUR #3.
16728 *Time after time.* New York: Carroll & Graf, 1985, 372 p., cloth, novel. ALEX BALFOUR #1.
16729 *Twice upon a time: a novel.* New York: Carroll & Graf, 1988, 351 p., cloth, novel. ALEX BALFOUR #2.

APPEL, Benjamin, 1907-1977

16730 *The devil and W. Kaspar.* New York: Popular Library, 1977, 176 p., paper, novel.

APPIGNANESI, Lisa, 1946- , with Sara Maitland

16731 *The Rushdie file.* London: ICA, Fourth Estate, 1989, x+258 p., cloth, nonf. anth.

APPLEBY, Ken(neth Philip), 1953-

16732 *The voice of Cepheus.* New York: A Del Rey Book, Ballantine Books, 1989, 267 p., paper, novel.

APPLEFORD, R. Duncan, 1938-

16733 *SF: inventing the future.* Scarborough, Ontario, Canada: Bellhaven House, 1972, ix+227 p., paper, anth. [Includes some verse and nonfiction].

APPLEGATE, John

16734 *Deadly sleep.* New York: Pinnacle Books, Windsor Publishing Corp., 1988, 285 p., paper, novel.

APPLEMAN, Philip (Dean), 1926-

16735 *Shame the devil: a novel.* New York: A Herbert Michelman Book, Crown Publishers, 1981, 152 p., cloth, novel.

APPLETON, Victor, house pseud.

The alien probe—SEE: *Tom Swift: The alien probe.*
16736 *Aquatech warriors.* New York, London: An Archway Paperback, Pocket Books, 1991, 154 p., paper, novel. TOM SWIFT #C6. [By James D. Macdonald and Debra Doyle].
16737 *Ark Two.* New York: Wanderer Books, Simon & Schuster, 1982, 206 p., paper, novel. TOM SWIFT #B7. [By Neal Barrett, Jr.?].
16738 *The astral fortress.* New York: Wanderer Books, Simon & Schuster, 1981, 191 p., paper, novel. TOM SWIFT #B5. [By Sharman DiVono and William Rotsler].
16739 *The black dragon.* New York, London: An Archway Paperback, Pocket Books, 1991, 165 p., paper, novel. TOM SWIFT #C1. [By Bill McCay].
16740 *The city in the stars.* New York: Wanderer Books, Simon & Schuster, 1981, 191 p., paper, novel. TOM SWIFT #B1. [By Sharman DiVono and William Rotsler].
Crater of mystery—SEE: *Tom Swift: Crater of mystery.*
16741 *Cyborg kickboxer.* New York, London: An Archway Paperback, Pocket Books, 1991, 166 p., paper, novel. TOM SWIFT #C3. [By Steven Grant].
16742 *The DNA disaster.* New York, London: An Archway Paperback, Pocket Books, 1991, 154 p., paper, novel. TOM SWIFT #C4. [By F. Gwynplaine MacIntyre].
15786 *Don Sturdy in the port of lost ships; or, Adrift in the Sargasso Sea.* New York: Grosset & Dunlap, 1926, 214 p., cloth, novel. DON STURDY #6. [By Edward L. Stratemeyer].
16743 *The invisible force.* New York: Wanderer Books, Simon & Schuster, 1983, 175 p., paper, novel. TOM SWIFT #B10. [By Neal Barrett Jr.?].
16744 *Monster machine.* New York, London: An Archway Paperback, Pocket Books, 1991, 154 p., paper, novel. TOM SWIFT #C5. [By James D. Macdonald and Debra Doyle].
16745 *The negative zone.* New York, London: An Archway Paperback, Pocket Books, 1991, 151 p., paper, novel. TOM SWIFT #C2. [By Bill McCay].
16746 *Planet of nightmares.* New York: Wanderer Books, Simon & Schuster, 1984,

174 p., paper, novel. Tom Swift #B11. [By Mike McQuay].

16747 *The rescue mission.* New York: Wanderer Books, Simon & Schuster, 1981, 188 p., paper, novel. Tom Swift #B6. [By Sharman DiVono and William Rotsler].

Terror on the moons of Jupiter—SEE: *Tom Swift: Terror on the moons of Jupiter.*

00420 *Tom Swift and the planet stone; or, Discovering the secret of another world.* New York: Grosset & Dunlap, 1935, 203 p., cloth, novel. Tom Swift #38. [By Harriet Adams].

16748 *Tom Swift: Crater of mystery.* New York: Wanderer Books, Simon & Schuster, 1983, 191 p., cloth, novel. Tom Swift #B8. [By Mike McQuay].

16749 *Tom Swift: Gateway to doom.* New York: Wanderer Books, Simon & Schuster, 1983, 175 p., paper, novel. Tom Swift #B9. [By Robert E. Vardeman].

16750 *Tom Swift: Terror on the moons of Jupiter.* New York: Wanderer Books, Simon & Schuster, 1981, 185 p., paper, novel. Tom Swift #B2. [By Sharman DiVono and William Rotsler].

16751 *Tom Swift: The alien probe.* New York: Wanderer Books, Simon & Schuster, 1981, 186 p., paper, novel. Tom Swift #B3. [By Sharman DiVono and William Rotsler].

16752 *Tom Swift: The war in outer space.* New York: Wanderer Books, Simon & Schuster, 1981, 171 p., paper, novel. Tom Swift #B4. [By Sharman DiVono and William Rotsler].

The war in outer space—SEE: *Tom Swift: The war in outer space.*

APPLETON, Victor II, house pseud.

00435 *Tom Swift and his aquatomic tracker.* New York: Grosset & Dunlap, 1964, 178 p., cloth, novel. Tom Swift Jr. #A23. [By Jim Lawrence].

00436 *Tom Swift and his atomic earth blaster.* New York: Grosset & Dunlap, 1954, 210 p., cloth, novel. Tom Swift Jr. #A5. [By Jim Lawrence].

00437 *Tom Swift and his Cosmotron Express.* New York: Grosset & Dunlap, 1970, 180 p., cloth, novel. Tom Swift Jr. #A32. [By Richard McKenna].

00438 *Tom Swift and his deep-sea hydrodome.* New York: Grosset & Dunlap, 1958, 184 p., cloth, novel. Tom Swift Jr. #A11. [By Jim Lawrence].

00439 *Tom Swift and his diving seacopter.* New York: Grosset & Dunlap, 1956, 214 p.,

cloth, novel. Tom Swift Jr. #A7. [By Jim Lawrence].

00440 *Tom Swift and his Dyna-4 capsule.* New York: Grosset & Dunlap, 1969, 175 p., cloth, novel. Tom Swift Jr. #A31. [By Richard McKenna].

00441 *Tom Swift and his electronic retroscope.* New York: Grosset & Dunlap, 1959, 184 p., cloth, novel. Tom Swift Jr. #A14. [By Jim Lawrence].

00441A retitled: *Tom Swift in the jungle of the Mayas.* New York: Grosset & Dunlap, 1972, 184 p., paper, novel. Tom Swift Jr. #A14. [By Jim Lawrence].

00442 *Tom Swift and his flying lab.* New York: Grosset & Dunlap, 1954, 208 p., cloth, novel. Tom Swift Jr. #A1. [By William Dougherty].

00443 *Tom Swift and his G-force inverter.* New York: Grosset & Dunlap, 1968, 175 p., cloth, novel. Tom Swift Jr. #A30. [By Jim Lawrence].

00444 *Tom Swift and his giant robot.* New York: Grosset & Dunlap, 1954, 211 p., cloth, novel. Tom Swift Jr. #A4. [By Richard Sklar].

00445 *Tom Swift and his jetmarine.* New York: Grosset & Dunlap, 1954, 208 p., cloth, novel. Tom Swift Jr. #A2. [By John Almquist].

00446 *Tom Swift and his megascope space prober.* New York: Grosset & Dunlap, 1962, 176 p., cloth, novel. Tom Swift Jr. #A20. [By Jim Lawrence].

00447 *Tom Swift and his outpost in space.* NY: Grosset & Dunlap, 1955, 210 p., cloth, novel. Tom Swift Jr. #A6. [By Jim Lawrence].

00447A retitled: *Tom Swift and his sky wheel.* New York: Tempo Books, Grosset & Dunlap Publishers, 1977, 210 p., paper, novel. Tom Swift Jr. #A5 (RENUMBERED). [By Jim Lawrence].

00448 *Tom Swift and his polar-ray dynasphere.* New York: Grosset & Dunlap, 1965, 177 p., cloth, novel. Tom Swift Jr. #A25. [By Jim Lawrence].

00449 *Tom Swift and his repelatron skyway.* New York: Grosset & Dunlap, 1963, 179 p., cloth, novel. Tom Swift Jr. #A22. [By Jim Lawrence].

00450 *Tom Swift and his rocket ship.* New York: Grosset & Dunlap, 1954, 208 p., cloth, novel. Tom Swift Jr. #A3. [By John Almquist].

Tom Swift and his sky wheel—SEE: *Tom Swift and his outpost in space.*

00451 *Tom Swift and his sonic boom trap.* New York: Grosset & Dunlap, 1965, 178 p., cloth, novel. TOM SWIFT JR. #A26. [By Jim Lawrence].

00452 *Tom Swift and his space solartron.* New York: Grosset & Dunlap, 1958, 183 p., cloth, novel. TOM SWIFT JR. #A13. [By Jim Lawrence].

00453 *Tom Swift and his spectromarine selector.* New York: Grosset & Dunlap, 1960, 184 p., cloth, novel. TOM SWIFT JR. #A15. [By Jim Lawrence].

00453A retitled: *Tom Swift and the city of gold.* New York: Grosset & Dunlap, 1972, 184 p., paper, novel. TOM SWIFT JR. #A15. [By Jim Lawrence].

00454 *Tom Swift and his subocean geotron.* New York: Grosset & Dunlap, 1966, 178 p., cloth, novel. TOM SWIFT JR. #A27. [By Jim Lawrence].

00455 *Tom Swift and his 3-D telejector.* New York: Grosset & Dunlap, 1964, 177 p., cloth, novel. TOM SWIFT JR. #A24. [By Jim Lawrence].

00456 *Tom Swift and his triphibian atomicar.* New York: Grosset & Dunlap, 1962, 188 p., cloth, novel. TOM SWIFT JR. #A19. [By Jim Lawrence].

00457 *Tom Swift and his ultrasonic cycloplane.* New York: Grosset & Dunlap, 1957, 182 p., cloth, novel. TOM SWIFT JR. #A10. [By Jim Lawrence].

00458 *Tom Swift and the asteroid pirates.* New York: Grosset & Dunlap, 1963, 178 p., cloth, novel. TOM SWIFT JR. #A21. [By Jim Lawrence].

00459 *Tom Swift and the captive planetoid.* New York: Grosset & Dunlap, 1967, 174 p., cloth, novel. TOM SWIFT JR. #A29. [By Jim Lawrence].

Tom Swift and the city of gold—SEE: *Tom Swift and his spectromarine selector.*

00460 *Tom Swift and the cosmic astronauts.* New York: Grosset & Dunlap, 1960, 178 p., cloth, novel. TOM SWIFT JR. #A16. [By Jim Lawrence].

00461 *Tom Swift and the electric hydrolung.* New York: Grosset & Dunlap, 1961, 188 p., cloth, novel. TOM SWIFT JR. #A18. [By Jim Lawrence].

00462 *Tom Swift and the galaxy ghosts.* New York: Grosset & Dunlap, 1971, 180 p., cloth, novel. TOM SWIFT JR. #A33. [By Richard McKenna; last book in the series].

00463 *Tom Swift and the mystery comet.* New York: Grosset & Dunlap, 1966, 178 p., cloth, novel. TOM SWIFT JR. #A28. [By Jim Lawrence].

00464 *Tom Swift and the visitor from Planet X.* New York: Grosset & Dunlap, 1961,

184 p., cloth, novel. TOM SWIFT JR. #A17. [By Jim Lawrence].

00465 *Tom Swift in the caves of nuclear fire.* New York: Grosset & Dunlap, 1956, 214 p., cloth, novel. TOM SWIFT JR. #A8. [By Thomas Mulvey].

Tom Swift in the jungle of the Mayas—SEE: *Tom Swift and his electronic retroscope.*

00466 *Tom Swift in the race to the Moon.* New York: Grosset & Dunlap, 1958, 180 p., cloth, novel. TOM SWIFT JR. #A12. [By Jim Lawrence].

00467 *Tom Swift on the phantom satellite.* New York: Grosset & Dunlap, 1957, 214 p., cloth, novel. TOM SWIFT JR. #A9. [By Jim Lawrence].

APTER, T(erri) E(ve), 1949-

16753 *Fantasy literature: an approach to reality.* London: Macmillan, 1982, 161 p., cloth, nonf.

AQUINO, John (Thomas), 1949-

16754 *Fantasy in literature.* Washington, DC: National Education Association, 1977, 63 p., paper, nonf.

16755 *Science fiction as literature.* Washington, DC: National Education Association, 1976, 64 p., paper, nonf.

ARAI, Motoko, 1960-

16756 *Green requiem.* Tokyo: Kodansha, 1984, 151 p., paper, novel. [Translation by Naomi Anderson of *Guriin rekuiemu*].

25814 *A ship to the stars.* Tokyo: Kodansha, 1984, 150 p., paper, novel. [Translation by Naomi Anderson of *Hoshi e iku fune*].

ARANA, Ric, pseud.—SEE: Sellers, Con

ARBUCCI, John

16757 *Blood of innocents.* New York: An Onyx Book, 1990, 304 p., paper, novel.

ARBUR, Rosemarie, 1944-

16758 *Leigh Brackett, Marion Zimmer Bradley, Anne McCaffrey: a primary and secondary bibliography.* Boston: G. K. Hall, 1982, xlviii+277 p., cloth, nonf. MASTERS OF SCIENCE FICTION AND FANTASY.

16759 *Marion Zimmer Bradley.* Mercer Island, WA: Starmont House, 1985, 138 p., cloth, nonf. STARMONT READER'S GUIDES #27.

ARCHER, Jeffrey (Howard), 1940-

16760 *The prodigal daughter.* New York: Linden Press/Simon & Schuster, 1982, 464 p., cloth, novel.
16761 *Shall we tell the president?* New York: Viking Press, 1977, x+241 p., cloth, novel.

ARCHITECTS ADVENTURE—SEE: Scammell, Bill & Jamieson, Evan & Hunt, Lisa & Hunt, Walter & Meyer, Richard S. & Bloom, Mark & Ivey, Christine

ARDAI, Charles, 1969-

16762 *Great tales of madness & the macabre.* New York: Galahad Books, 1990, 518 p., cloth, anth.

with Sheila Williams

16763 *Why I left Harry's All-Night Hamburgers, and other stories from Isaac Asimov's Science Fiction Magazine.* New York: Delacorte Press, 1990, ix+285 p., cloth, anth.

*ARDREY, Robert, 1908-1980

ARENAS, Reinaldo, 1943-1990

16764 *The ill-fated peregrinations of Fray Servando.* New York: Avon Books, 1987, xxii+246 p., paper, novel. [Translation by Andrew Hurley of *El mundo alucinante*].

ARIAS, Ron(ald Francis), 1941-

26037 *The road to Tamazunchale.* Albuquerque, NM: Pajarito Publications, 1978, 127 p., cloth, novel.

ARKHAM, Candice, pseud.—SEE: Alice Ramirez

ARKIN, Alan (Wolf), 1934-

16765 *The clearing.* San Francisco: A Charlotte Zolotow Book, Harper & Row, Publishers, 1986, 186 p., cloth, novel.

ARMITT, Lucie, 1962-

16766 *Where no man has gone before: women and science fiction.* London, New York:

Routledge, 1991, 234 p., cloth, nonf. anth.

ARMSTRONG, Anthony [pseud. of George Anthony Armstrong Willis], 1897-1976

16767 *The prince who hiccupped, and other tales: being some fairy tales for grown-ups.* London: Ernest Benn, 1932, 216 p., cloth, coll.

ARMSTRONG, Campbell, pseud.—SEE: Black, Campbell

ARMSTRONG, Charles W(icksteed), 1871-1951+

26806 *Paradise found; or, Where the sex problem has been solved: a story from South America.* London: J. Bale Sons & Danielsson, 1936, 211 p., cloth, novel.

ARMSTRONG, F. W., pseud.—SEE: Wright, T. M.

*ARMSTRONG, (Terence Ian) Fytton, 1912-1970

ARMSTRONG, Michael (Allan), 1956-

16768 *After the zap.* New York: Popular Library, 1987, 246 p., paper, novel.
16769 *Agviq: the whale.* New York: Popular Library, 1990, 275 p., paper, novel.

ARMSTRONG, Sarah

16770 *Blood red roses.* New York: Twilight/Dell, 1982, 154 p., paper, novel. TWILIGHT #8.

ARMYTAGE, Walter (Harry Green), 1915-

26038 *Yesterday's tomorrows: a historical survey of future societies.* London: Routledge & Kegan Paul, 1968, 288 p., cloth, nonf.

ARNASON, Eleanor (Atwood), 1942-

16771 *Daughter of the bear king.* New York: Avon, 1987, 239 p., paper, novel.
16772 *The sword smith.* New York: Condor, 1978, 208 p., paper, novel.
16773 *To the resurrection station.* New York: Avon, 1986, 276 p., paper, novel.
16774 *A woman of the iron people.* New York: William Morrow & Co., 1991, 525 p., cloth, novel.

ARNESON, D(on) J(on), 1935-

16775 *Sometimes in the dead of night.* New York: Wanderer Books, Simon & Schuster, 1983, 124 p., paper, coll.

16776 *Strange ghost stories.* Old Tappan, NJ: D. J. Arneson/Andor Publishing Co., 1979, 64 p., paper, coll.

16777 *Strange monster stories.* Old Tappan, NJ: D. J. Arneson/Andor Publishing Co., 1979, 64 p., paper, coll.

with Tony Tallarico

16778 *The aliens are here!* Mahwah, NJ: Watermill Press, 1980, 64 p., paper, coll.

16779 *Beware of the supernatural.* Mahwah, NJ: Watermill Press, 1980, 63 p., paper, coll.

16780 *Black Star chronicles.* Mahwah, NJ: Watermill Press, 1981, 96 p., paper, coll.

16781 *Ghost horse mystery.* Mahwah, NJ: Watermill Press, 1981, 96 p., paper, novel.

16782 *The haunted planet.* Mahwah, NJ: Watermill Press, 1980, 96 p., paper, coll.

16783 *Monster madness.* Mahwah, NJ: Watermill Press, 1980, 64 p., paper, coll.

16784 *The secret drawing guide to creating space creatures / by "Dr. Drew".* Mahwah, NJ: Watermill Press, 1981, 48 p., paper, nonf.

ARNETT, Jack, pseud.—SEE: McQuay, Mike

ARNOLD, Alan, 1922-

16785 *Once upon a galaxy: a journal of the making of Star Wars: The Empire strikes back.* New York: A Del Rey Book, Ballantine Books, 1980, vii+277 p., paper, nonf.

ARNOLD, Edwin Lester (Linden), 1857-1935

00505 *Lieut. Gullivar Jones: his vacation.* London: S. C. Brown, Langham, 1905, 301 p., cloth, novel

00505B retitled: *Lieut Gulliver Jones: his vacation.* London: New English Library, 1976, 206 p., paper, novel.
Lieut Gulliver Jones—SEE: Lieut. Gullivar Jones.

*ARNOLD, Frank Edward, 1914-1987

ARNOLD, Margot [pseud. of Petronelle Marguerite Mary Cook], 1925-

16786 *Death of a voodoo doll.* New York: Playboy Press, 1982, 220 p., paper, novel.

PENNY SPRING & TOBY GLENDOWER SERIES.

16787 *Death on the dragon's tongue.* New York: Playboy Press, 1982, 224 p., paper, novel. PENNY SPRING & TOBY GLENDOWER SERIES.

16788 *Marie.* New York: Pocket Books, 1979, 486 p., paper, novel.

ARNOLD, Mark Alan, *with Terri Windling*

16789 *Borderland.* New York: A Signet Book, New American Library, 1986, 252 p., paper, anth. BORDERLANDS #1.

16790 *Bordertown: a chronicle of the Borderlands.* New York: A Signet Book, New American Library, 1986, 253 p., paper, anth. BORDERLANDS #2.

16791 *Elsewhere.* New York: Ace Books, 1981, 366 p., paper, anth. [Winner of the World Fantasy Award for Best Fantasy Anthology/Collection, 1981 (1982)].

16792 *Elsewhere: tales of fantasy, vol. II.* New York: Ace Books, 1982, 388 p., paper, anth.

16793 *Elsewhere: tales of fantasy, vol. III.* New York: Ace Fantasy Books, 1984, 404 p., paper, anth.

ARNSTON, Harrison

16794 *The big one: a novel.* New York: Zebra Books, Kensington Publishing Corp., 1990, 430 p., paper, novel.

ARON, Elaine (N.)

16795 *Samraj.* London: New English Library, 1989, 499 p., cloth, novel. MAHABARATA #1.

ARONICA, Lou(is Michael), 1958-

16796 *The Bantam Spectra sampler.* Toronto, New York: Bantam Books, 1985, 93 p., paper, anth.

with Shawna McCarthy

16797 *Full spectrum.* Toronto, New York: Spectra, Bantam Books, 1988, 483 p., paper, anth. [Winner of the *Locus* Award for Best Anthology, 1988 (1989)].

with Shawna McCarthy, Amy Stout, & Patrick LoBrutto

16798 *Full spectrum 2.* New York: A Foundation Book, Doubleday, 1989, xi+464 p., cloth, anth.

with Amy Stout & Betsy Mitchell

16799 *Full spectrum 3.* New York: A Foundation Book, Doubleday, 1991, x+535 p., cloth, anth. [Winner of the *Locus* Award for Best Anthology, 1991 (1992)].

*ARONIN, Ben, 1904-1980

ARONOVITZ, David, 1947-

16800 *Ballantine Books: the first decade: a bibliographical guide & history of the publisher's early years.* Rochester, MI: Bailiwick Books, 1987, x+107 p., cloth, nonf.

AROUET, François-Marie—SEE: Voltaire

ARQUETTE, Lois Duncan—SEE: Duncan, Lois

*ARRIGHI, Mel(vin), 1933-1986

ARROW, Jay, pseud.

Angel of passion—SEE: *The occult coxsman.*
16801 *The occult coxsman.* New York: Orpheus Books, 1976, 251 p., paper, novel.
16801A retitled: *Angel of passion* / by Gordon Bradford. New York: Tigress Books, 1981, 251 p., paper, novel.

ARROW, William, house pseud.

16802 *Escape from Terror Lagoon.* New York: Ballantine Books, 1976, 138 p., paper, tele. RETURN TO THE PLANET OF THE APES #2. [By Donald J. Pfeil].
16803 *Man, the hunted animal.* New York: Ballantine Books, 1976, 184 p., paper, tele. RETURN TO THE PLANET OF THE APES #3. [By William Rotsler].
16804 *Visions from nowhere.* New York: Ballantine Books, 1976, 183 p., paper, tele. RETURN TO THE PLANET OF THE APES #1. [By William Rotsler].

ARSCOTT, David, *with David Marl*

16805 *A flight of bright birds.* London: George Allen & Unwin, 1985, 229 p., cloth, novel.
16806 *The frozen city.* London: George Allen & Unwin, 1984, 231 p., cloth, novel.

ARTHUR, David Stuart

16807 *The Oasis Project.* Los Angeles: Sword & Stone Press, 1981, 440 p., cloth, novel.

ARTHUR, Ruth M. [i.e., Ruth Mabel Arthur Huggins], 1905-1979

16808 *Miss Ghost.* New York: Atheneum, 1979, 119 p., cloth, novel.
16809 *An old magic.* New York: Atheneum, 1977, 175 p., cloth, novel.
16810 *On the wasteland.* New York: Atheneum, 1975, 159 p., cloth, novel.
15787 *Requiem for a princess.* New York: Atheneum, 1967, 182 p., cloth, novel.

ARTHURS, Bruce D(ouglas), 1952-

16811 *Copper star.* Tucson, AZ: 1991 World Fantasy Convention, 1991, 221 p., cloth, anth.

ARVEN, Andrea

16812 *Wicked.* London: Nexus, 1991, 224 p., paper, novel.

ARVONEN, Helen

16813 *The witches of Brimstone Hill.* New York: Fawcett, 1971, 160 p., paper, novel.

ASCH, Frank (Edward), 1946-

16814 *Journey to Terezor.* New York: Holiday House, 1989, vi+160 p., cloth, novel. ORB TRILOGY #1.

ASCHER, Eugene, pseud.—SEE: Kelly, Harold Ernest

ASCHER, Sheila, 1944- , *with Dennis Straus* as ASCHER/STRAUS

16815 *The other planet: a novel.* Kingston, NY: McPherson, 1988, 244 p., cloth, novel.
26090 *Red moon/red lake.* New York: Top Stories, 1984, 28 p., paper, story.
16816 *Red moon, red lake: stories.* Kingston, NY: McPherson, 1988, 128 p., cloth, coll.

ASCHER/STRAUS, pseud.—SEE: Ascher, Sheila & Straus, Dennis

*ASH, Alan, 1908-

ASH, Brian, 1936-

16817 *Faces of the future: the lessons of science fiction.* London: Elek/Pemberton, 1975, 213 p., cloth, nonf.

16818 *The visual encyclopedia of science fiction.* London & Sydney: Pan Books, 1977, 352 p., paper, nonf.

16819 *Who's who in H. G. Wells.* London: Elm Tree Books, 1979, xvii + 299 p., cloth, nonf.

16820 *Who's who in science fiction.* London: Elm Tree Books, 1976, 220 p., cloth, nonf.

ASH, Cay Van—SEE: Van Ash, Cay

ASH, Constance (Lee), 1950-

16821 *The horsegirl.* New York: Ace Books, 1988, 232 p., paper, novel. HORSEGIRL #1.

16822 *The stalking horse: an evening-length opera ballet in five acts.* New York: Ace Books, 1990, 295 p., paper, novel. HORSEGIRL #2.

ASHBY, Ruth

16823 *Quest for King Arthur.* Toronto, New York: A Byron Preiss Book, Bantam Books, 1988, 124 p., paper, novel. TIME MACHINE #23.

ASHE, Gordon, pseud.—SEE: Creasey, John

ASHE, Rosalind [pseud. of Rosalind Dale-Harris]

16824 *Dark runner.* London: Sphere Books, 1985, 235 p., paper, novel.

16825 *The hurricane wake.* London: Hutchinson, 1977, 239 p., cloth, novel.

16826 *The laying of the Noone Walker.* London: Bantam Books, 1987, 314 p., cloth, novel.

16827 *Moths.* London: Hutchinson, 1976, 239 p., cloth, novel.

16828 *Starcrossed.* Toronto, New York: Bantam Books, 1979, 278 p., paper, novel.

ASHER, Martin—SEE: Asher, Marty

ASHER, Marty [i.e., Martin Asher]

16829 *Shelter.* New York: Arbor House, 1986, 136 p., cloth, novel.

ASHERMAN, Allan, 1947-

16830 *The making of Star Trek II, the Wrath of Khan.* New York: Pocket Books, 1982, 223 p., paper, nonf.

16831 *The Star Trek compendium.* New York: A Wallaby Book, Simon & Schuster, 1981, 187 p., paper, nonf.

16832 *The Star Trek compendium.* London: A Star Book, W. H. Allen, 1983, 194 p., paper, nonf. [Expanded edition].

16833 *The Star Trek compendium.* New York: Pocket Books, 1986, 184 p., paper, nonf. [Expanded edition].

16834 *The Star Trek compendium, revised and updated edition.* New York: Pocket Books, 1989, 182 p., paper, nonf. [Expanded edition].

16835 *The Star Trek inverview book.* New York: Pocket Books, 1988, 278 p., paper, nonf.

16836 *Who's who in Star Trek.* New York: D.C. Comics, 1987, 2 v., paper, nonf.

with Jonathon Green & Doug Murray

16837 *Star Wars: the full story.* [S.l.]: Paradise Press, 1977, 62 p., paper, nonf.

ASHLEE, Ted, 1914-

16838 *Night of the sasquatch.* Toronto: Holt, Rinehart & Winston, 1973, vii + 182 p., cloth, novel.

ASHLEY, Michael—SEE: Ashley, Mike

ASHLEY, Mike [i.e., Michael Raymond Donald Ashley], 1948-

16839 *Algernon Blackwood: a bio-bibliography.* New York, Westport, CT: Greenwood Press, 1987, xx + 349 p., cloth, nonf.

16840 *The best of British SF 1.* London: Futura Publications, An Orbit Book, 1977, 411 p., paper, anth.

16841 *The best of British SF 2.* London: Futura Publications, An Orbit Book, 1977, 378 p., paper, anth.

16842 *A complete index and annotated commentary to the John Spencer fantasy publications (1950-66)* / by Michael Ashley. Wallsend, Tyne & Wear, England: Cosmos Literary Agency, 1979, 54 p., paper, anth. FANTASY READERS GUIDE #2. [Includes two stories by E. C. Tubb & John Glasby; cover title].

16843 *Fantasy readers guide to Ramsey Campbell.* Wallsend, Tyne & Wear, England: Cosmos Literary Agency, 1980, 62 p., paper, anth. FANTASY READERS GUIDE #1.

16844 *The history of the science fiction magazine, part 2, 1936-1945.* London: New English Library, 1975, 298 p., cloth, anth.

16845 *The history of the science fiction magazine, part 3, 1946-1955.* London: New English Library, 1976, 349 p., cloth, anth.

16846 *The history of the science fiction magazine, part 4, 1956-1965.* London: New English Library, 1978, 288 p., cloth, anth.

16847 *The illustrated book of science fiction lists.* London: Virgin Books, 1982, 190 p., paper, nonf.

16848 *Jewels of wonder: an anthology of heroic fantasies.* London: William Kimber, 1981, 203 p., cloth, anth.

16849 *The mammoth book of short horror novels.* London: Robinson, 1988, x+518 p., paper, anth.

16850 *The Pendragon chronicles: heroic fantasy from the time of King Arthur.* London: Robinson Books, 1990, 417 p., paper, anth.

16851 *SF choice 77.* London, Melbourne: Quartet Books, 1977, 137 p., paper, anth.

16852 *Souls in metal: an anthology of robot futures.* New York: St. Martin's Press; London: Robert Hale, 1977, 207 p., cloth, anth.

16853 *Weird legacies.* London: A Star Book, W. H. Allen, 1977, 157 p., paper, anth.

16854 *When spirits talk.* England: Ghost Story Society, 1990, 32 p., paper, anth.

16855 *Who's who in horror and fantasy fiction.* London: Elm Tree Books, 1977, 240 p., cloth, nonf.

16856 *The writings of Barrington J. Bayley: a bibliography prepared specially for Beccon.* [Harold Wood, Essex, England: Beccon Committee], 1981, [7] p., paper, nonf.

with Terry Jeeves

16857 *The complete index to Astounding/Analog: being an index to the 50 years of Astounding stories—Astounding SF & Analog: January 1930-December 1979, together with the Analog annual, the Analog yearbook, & the John W. Campbell memorial anthology.* Oak Forest, IL: Robert Weinberg Publications, 1981, 253 p., cloth, nonf.

with Frank H. Parnell

16858 *Monthly terrors: an index to the weird fantasy magazines published in the United States and Great Britain.* Westport, CT, London: Greenwood Press, 1985, xxvii+602 p., cloth, nonf.

with Marshall B. Tymn

16859 *Science fiction, fantasy, and weird fiction magazines.* Westport, CT, London: Greenwood Press, 1985, xxx+970 p., cloth, nonf. anth.

ASHLEY, Steven [pseud. of Donald McCaig], 1940-

16860 *Love out of time.* New York: Berkley Books, 1985, 263 p., paper, novel.

ASHMAN, Howard (Elliott), 1950-1991

16861 *Mandrake the magician.* New York: Ace Books, 1979, 156 p., paper, movie.

ASHMEAD, John (XIII), 1950- , *with Darrell Schweitzer & George Scithers*

16862 *Constructing scientifiction & fantasy.* Lake Geneva, WI: TSR Inc., 1982, 31 p., paper, nonf.

ASHTON, Charles

16863 *Jet Smoke and the dragon fire.* London: Walker Books, 1991, 214 p., cloth, novel.

ASHTON, Jay

16864 *Looking for Ilyriand.* Oxford, England: Oxford University Press, 1990, 256 p., cloth, novel.

ASHTON, Marvin, pseud.—SEE: Hughes, Dennis Talbot

ASHTON, Winifred—SEE: Dane, Clemence

ASIMOV, Isaac [anglicized from Isaak Iudich Azimov], 1920-1992

16865 *3 by Asimov: three science fiction tales.* New York: Targ Editions, 1981, 18 p., paper?, coll. [Limited to 250 copies].

16866 *The adventures of Lucky Starr.* Garden City, NY: Nelson Doubleday, 1985?, viii+340 p., cloth, coll. LUCKY STARR #1-3.

16867 *The alternate Asimovs.* Garden City, NY: Doubleday & Co., 1986, xii+272 p., cloth, coll.

16868 *The Asimov chronicles: fifty years of Isaac Asimov.* Arlington Heights, IL: Dark Harvest, 1989, 678 p., cloth, coll. [Edited by Martin H. Greenberg; includes some nonfiction].

16869 *Asimov on science fiction.* Garden City, NY: Doubleday & Co., 1981, 334 p., cloth, nonf. coll.

16870   *Asimov's galaxy: reflections on science fiction.* New York: Doubleday, 1989, 318 p., cloth, nonf. coll.

16871   *Azazel.* New York: A Foundation Book, Doubleday, 1988, 221 p., cloth, coll.

16872   *The best science fiction of Isaac Asimov.* Garden City, NY: Doubleday & Co., 1986, xiv+320 p., cloth, coll.

      Beyond the stars—SEE: *The Hugo winners, volume 4.*

16873   *The bicentennial man, and other stories.* Garden City, NY: Doubleday & Co., 1976, 211 p., cloth, coll.

16874   *Buy Jupiter, and other stories.* Garden City, NY: Doubleday & Co., 1975, 206 p., cloth, coll.

16875   *Cal.* New York: Doubleday, 1991, 30 p., paper, story.

16876   *The complete robot.* Garden City, NY: Doubleday & Co., 1982, xiv+557 p., cloth, coll. ROBOT SERIES.

16877   *The complete stories, volume one.* New York: A Foundation Book, Doubleday, 1990, 614 p., cloth, coll. [Includes: *Earth is room enough, Nine tomorrows, Nightfall and other stories*].

      The dark void—SEE: *The Hugo winners, volume 4.*

      Destination brain—SEE: *Fantastic voyage II.*

16878   *"The dream," "Benjamin's dream," and "Benjamin's bicentennial blast".* New York: "Privately Printed," 1976, 50 p., paper?, coll.

16879   *The edge of tomorrow.* New York: Tor, A Tom Doherty Associates Book, 1985, xiv+462 p., cloth, coll. [Includes some nonfiction].

16880   *Fantastic voyage II: Destination brain.* Garden City, NY: Doubleday & Co., 1987, 332 p., cloth, novel. FANTASTIC VOYAGE #2.

16881   *The far ends of time and Earth.* Garden City, NY: Doubleday & Co., 1979, xiv+538 p., cloth, coll. [Includes *Pebble in the sky, Earth is room enough, The end of eternity*].

16882   *Foundation and Earth.* Garden City, NY: Doubleday & Co., 1986, 356 p., cloth, novel. FOUNDATION #5.

16883   *Foundation; I, robot.* London: Octopus Books, 1984, 298 p., cloth, coll.

16884   *The Foundation trilogy: Foundation, Foundation and Empire, Second Foundation; The stars, like dust; The naked sun; I, robot.* London: Octopus/Heinemann, 1981, 864 p., cloth, coll.

16885   *Foundation's edge.* Garden City, NY: Whispers Press, 1982, xi+366 p., cloth, novel. FOUNDATION #4. [Winner of the Hugo Award for Best Novel, 1982 (1983); winner of the *Locus* Award for Best Science Fiction Novel, 1982 (1983)].

16886   *The further adventures of Lucky Starr.* Garden City, NY: Nelson Doubleday, 1985?, viii+341 p., cloth, coll. LUCKY STARR #4-6.

16887   *Futuredays: a nineteenth-century vision of the year 2000.* New York: A Lucy-Carroll Book, An Owl Book, Henry Holt & Co., 1986, 96 p., paper, nonf.

16888   *Good taste: a story.* Topeka, KS: Apocalypse Press, 1976, 36 p., paper, story. [Limited to 500 copies].

16889   *The heavenly host.* New York: Walker & Co., 1975, 79 p., cloth, novel.

16890   *The Hugo winners, volume 3.* Garden City, NY: Doubleday & Co., 1977, xvi+603 p., cloth, anth.

16891   *The Hugo winners, volume 4.* Garden City, NY: Doubleday & Co., 1985, xiv+561 p., cloth, anth.

16891A retitled: *Dark void.* London: Severn House, 1987, 239 p., cloth, anth. [The first half of the original book].

16891B retitled: *Beyond the stars.* London: Severn House, 1987, 321 p., cloth, anth. [The second half of the original book].

16892   *The Hugo winners, volume 5, 1980-1982.* Garden City, NY: Doubleday & Co., 1986, 372 p., cloth, anth.

16893   *In joy still felt: the autobiography of Isaac Asimov, 1954-1978.* Garden City, NY: Doubleday & Co., 1980, x+828 p., cloth, nonf. [Winner of the *Locus* Award for Best Nonfiction, 1980 (1981)].

16894   *In memory yet green: the autobiography of Isaac Asimov, 1920-1954.* Garden City, NY: Doubleday & Co., 1979, vii+732 p., cloth, nonf.

16895   *Little lost robot.* Cambridge, England: Cambridge University Press, 1977, 30 p., paper, story.

16896   *Nemesis.* New York: A Foundation Book, Doubleday, 1989, 364 p., cloth, novel.

16897   *Opus 200.* Boston: Houghton Mifflin Co., 1979, xiii+329 p., cloth, coll. [Includes some nonf.].

16898   *Opus 300.* Boston: Houghton Mifflin Co., 1984, xv+377 p., cloth, coll. [Includes some nonfiction].

16899   *Opus: a selection from the first 200 books.* London: André Deutsch, 1980, 669 p., cloth, coll. [Includes: *Opus 100; Opus 200*].

16900   *Other worlds of Isaac Asimov.* New York: Avenel Books, 1987, xi+651 p., cloth, coll. [Edited by Martin H. Greenberg].

16901 *Prelude to Foundation.* New York: A Foundation Book, Doubleday, 1988, 403 p., cloth, novel. FOUNDATION #6.

16902 *Prisoners of the stars.* Garden City, NY: Doubleday & Co., 1979, xiv+538 p., cloth, coll. [Includes *The stars like dust*; *The Martian way*; *The currents of space*].

16903 *The robot collection: the robot novels.* Garden City, NY: Doubleday & Co., 1983, 557 p., cloth, coll. ROBOT SERIES. [Includes *The caves of steel*; *The naked sun*; *The complete robot*].

16904 *Robot dreams.* New York: A Byron Preiss Visual Productions Presentation, Berkley Books, 1986, 349 p., cloth, coll. ROBOT SERIES.

16905 *The robot novels.* New York: A Del Rey Book, Ballantine Books, 1988, 671 p., paper, coll. ROBOT SERIES. [Not the same as 1971 book of the same title; includes *The caves of steel*; *The naked sun*; *The robots of Dawn*].

16906 *Robot visions.* New York: A Byron Preiss Visual Publications Inc. Book, A Roc Book, 1990, 482 p., cloth, coll. ROBOT SERIES.

16907 *Robots and empire.* West Bloomfield, MI: Phantasia Press, 1985, 349 p., cloth, novel. ROBOT SERIES; FOUNDATION SERIES. [Limited to 650 copies].

16908 *The robots of dawn.* Huntington Woods, MI: Phantasia Press, 1983, 336 p., cloth, novel. LIJE BALEY #3; ROBOT SERIES. [Limited to 750 copies].

16909 *Science fiction masterpieces.* New York: Galahad Books, 1986, 633 p., cloth, anth.

16910 *The ugly little boy.* New York: Tor SF, A Tom Doherty Associates Book, 1989, 60 p., paper, story. [Bound with *The [widget], the [wadget], and boff* / by Theodore Sturgeon].

16911 *The winds of change, and other stories.* Garden City, NY: Doubleday & Co., 1983, 269 p., cloth, coll.

ISAAC ASIMOV, *with Janet Jeppson Asimov*

16912 *Laughing space: funny science fiction chuckled over* / edited by Isaac Asimov and J. O. Jeppson. Boston: Houghton Mifflin Co., 1982, xvi+520 p., cloth, anth.

16913 *Norby and the court jester.* New York: Walker & Co., 1991, 118 p., cloth, novel. NORBY #10.

16914 *Norby and the invaders.* New York: Walker & Co., 1985, 138 p., cloth, novel. NORBY #4.

16915 *Norby and the lost princess.* New York: Walker & Co., 1985, 129 p., cloth, novel. NORBY #3.

16916 *Norby and the oldest dragon.* New York: Walker & Co., 1990, 110 p., cloth, novel. NORBY #9.

16917 *Norby and the queen's necklace.* New York: Walker & Co., 1986, 136 p., cloth, novel. NORBY #5.

16918 *Norby and Yobo's great adventure.* New York: Walker & Co., 1989, 100 p., cloth, novel. NORBY #8.

16919 *The Norby chronicles.* New York: Ace Science Fiction Books, 1986, 185 p., paper, coll. NORBY #1-2.

16920 *Norby down to Earth.* New York: Walker & Co., 1989, 107 p., cloth, novel. NORBY #7.

16921 *Norby finds a villain.* New York: Walker & Co., 1987, 102 p., cloth, novel. NORBY #6.

16922 *Norby: robot for hire.* New York: Ace Science Fiction Books, 1987, 203 p., paper, coll. NORBY #3-4.

16923 *Norby, the mixed-up robot.* New York: Walker & Co., 1983, 96 p., cloth, novel. NORBY #1.

16924 *Norby through space and time.* New York: Ace Books, 1988, 202 p., paper, coll. NORBY #5-6.

16925 *Norby's other secret.* New York: Walker & Co., 1984, 138 p., cloth, novel. NORBY #2.

ISAAC ASIMOV, *with Rosemary Border*

16926 *The caves of steel.* Cambridge, England: Cambridge University Press, 1978, viii+117 p., paper, novel. [Abridged and modernized from the original edition].

ISAAC ASIMOV, *with Terry Carr & Martin H. Greenberg*

16927 *100 great fantasy short short stories.* Garden City, NY: Doubleday & Co., 1984, xviii+311 p., cloth, anth.

ISAAC ASIMOV, *with David Fickling*

16928 *I, robot.* Oxford, England: Alpha Books, Oxford University Press, 1979, 95 p., paper, novel. [Adapted by Fickling from Asimov's original novel].

ISAAC ASIMOV, *with Martin H. Greenberg*

16929 *Amazing stories: 60 years of the best science fiction.* Lake Geneva, WI: TSR Inc., 1985, 255 p., paper, anth.

16930 *Atlantis.* New York: A Signet Book, New American Library, 1988, 349 p., paper, anth. ISAAC ASIMOV'S MAGICAL WORLDS OF FANTASY #9.

16931 *Cosmic critiques: how & why ten science fiction stories work.* Cincinnati, OH: Writer's Digest Books, 1990, 197 p., paper, anth. [Includes some nonfiction].

16932 *Devils.* New York: A Signet Book, New American Library, 1987, 351 p., paper, anth. ISAAC ASIMOV'S MAGICAL WORLDS OF FANTASY #8.

16933 *Election day 2084: a science fiction anthology on the politics of the future.* Buffalo, New York: Prometheus Books, 1984, 301 p., cloth, anth.

The golden years of science fiction—SEE: *Isaac Asimov presents: The golden years of science fiction.*

The great science fiction stories—SEE: *Isaac Asimov presents: The great science fiction stories.*

16934 *Isaac Asimov presents The golden years of science fiction.* New York: Bonanza Books, 1983, 432, 350 p., cloth, anth. GREAT SF STORIES #1-2.

16935 *Isaac Asimov presents The golden years of science fiction, 2nd series: 28 stories and novellas.* New York: Bonanza Books, 1983, 723 p., cloth, anth. GREAT SF STORIES #3-4.

16936 *Isaac Asimov presents The golden years of science fiction, 3rd series: 20 stories and novellas.* New York: Bonanza Books, 1984, 633 p., cloth, anth. GREAT SF STORIES #5-6.

16937 *Isaac Asimov presents The golden years of science fiction, fourth series: 26 stories and novellas.* New York: Bonanza Books, 1984, 632 p., cloth, anth. GREAT SF STORIES #7-8.

16938 *Isaac Asimov presents The golden years of science fiction, fifth series: 33 stories and novellas.* New York: Bonanza Books, 1985, 641 p., cloth, anth. GREAT SF STORIES #9-10.

16939 *Isaac Asimov presents The golden age of science fiction, sixth series: 33 stories and novellas.* New York: Bonanza Books, 1988, 624 p., cloth, anth. GREAT SF STORIES #11-12.

16940 *Isaac Asimov presents The great science fiction stories, volume 1, 1939.* New York: DAW Books, 1979, 432 p., paper, anth.

16941 *Isaac Asimov presents The great science fiction stories, volume 2, 1940.* New York: DAW Books, 1979, 350 p., paper, anth.

16942 *Isaac Asimov presents The great science fiction stories, volume 3, 1941.* New York: DAW Books, 1980, 352 p., paper, anth.

16943 *Isaac Asimov presents The great science fiction stories, volume 4, 1942.* New York: DAW Books, 1980, 448 p., paper, anth.

16944 *Isaac Asimov presents The great science fiction stories, volume 5, 1943.* New York: DAW Books, 1981, 380 p., paper, anth.

16945 *Isaac Asimov presents The great science fiction stories, volume 6, 1944.* New York: DAW Books, 1981, 368 p., paper, anth.

16946 *Isaac Asimov presents The great science fiction stories, volume 7, 1945.* New York: DAW Books, 1982, 368 p., paper, anth.

16947 *Isaac Asimov presents The great science fiction stories, volume 8, 1946.* New York: DAW Books, 1982, 368 p., paper, anth.

16948 *Isaac Asimov presents The great SF stories, volume 9, 1947.* New York: DAW Books, 1983, 366 p., paper, anth.

16949 *Isaac Asimov presents The great science fiction stories, volume 10, 1948.* New York: DAW Books, 1983, 287 p., paper, anth.

16950 *Isaac Asimov presents The great science fiction stories, volume 11, 1949.* New York: DAW Books, 1984, 317 p., paper, anth.

16951 *Isaac Asimov presents The great SF stories 12 (1950).* New York: DAW Books, 1984, 319 p., paper, anth.

16952 *Isaac Asimov presents The great SF stories #13 (1951).* New York: DAW Books, 1985, xii+337 p., paper, anth.

16953 *Isaac Asimov presents The great SF stories #14 (1952).* New York: DAW Books, 1986, 352 p., paper, anth.

16954 *Isaac Asimov presents The great SF stories #15 (1953).* New York: DAW Books, 1986, 352 p., paper, anth.

16955 *Isaac Asimov presents The great SF stories #16 (1954).* New York: DAW Books, 1987, 350 p., paper, anth.

16956 *Isaac Asimov presents The great SF stories #17 (1955).* New York: DAW Books, 1988, 349 p., cloth, anth.

16957 *Isaac Asimov presents The great SF stories #18 (1956).* New York: DAW Books, 1988, 366 p., cloth, anth.

16958 *Isaac Asimov presents The great SF stories #19 (1957).* New York: DAW Books, 1989, 350 p., paper, anth.

16959 *Isaac Asimov presents The great SF stories #20 (1958).* New York: DAW Books, 1990, 351 p., paper, anth.

16960 *Isaac Asimov presents The great SF stories #21 (1959).* New York: DAW Books, 1990, 347 p., paper, anth.

16961 *Isaac Asimov presents The great SF stories #22 (1959)* [sic]. New York: DAW Books, 1991, 351 p., paper, anth. [Cover title gives the correct year (1960)].

16962 *Isaac Asimov presents The great SF stories #23 (1961).* New York: DAW Books, 1991, 367 p., paper, anth.

16963 *The new Hugo winners: award-winning science fiction stories.* New York: Wynwood Press, 1989, 320 p., cloth, anth.

16964 *Science fiction and fantasy story-a-month 1989 calendar.* Petaluma, CA: Pomegranate, 1988, [12] p., paper, anth. [A calendar with a short story for each month].

16965 *Visions of fantasy: tales from the masters.* New York: Doubleday, 1989, ix+180 p., cloth, anth.

ISAAC ASIMOV, *with Martin H. Greenberg & Joseph D. Olander*

16966 *100 great science fiction short short stories.* Garden City, NY: Doubleday & Co., 1978, xvi+270 p., cloth, anth.

16967 *The future I.* New York: Fawcett Crest, 1980, 381 p., paper, anth.

16968 *The future in question.* New York: Fawcett Crest, 1980, 381 p., paper, anth.

16969 *Isaac Asimov's Science fiction treasury.* New York: Bonanza Books, 1980, 786 p., cloth, anth. [Includes *The future in question* and *Space mail*].

16970 *Microcosmic tales: 100 wondrous science fiction short-short stories.* New York: Taplinger Publishing Co., 1980, 325 p., cloth, anth.

Science fiction treasury—SEE: *Isaac Asimov's Science fiction treasury.*

16971 *Space mail.* New York: Fawcett Crest, 1980, 416 p., paper, anth.

ISAAC ASIMOV, *with Martin H. Greenberg & Patricia S. Warrick*

16972 *Machines that think: the best science fiction stories about robots and computers.* New York: Holt, Rinehart & Winston, 1984, 627 p., cloth, anth.

ISAAC ASIMOV, *with Martin H. Greenberg & Carol-Lynn Rössel Waugh*

16973 *13 horrors of Halloween.* New York: Avon, 1983, 175 p., paper, anth.

ISAAC ASIMOV, *with Martin H. Greenberg & Charles G. Waugh*

16974 *The 13 crimes of science fiction.* Garden City, NY: Doubleday & Co., 1979, 455 p., cloth, anth.

16975 *After the end.* Milwaukee, WI: Raintree Publishers, 1981, 48 p., cloth, anth.

Asimov's extraterrestrials—SEE: *Young extraterrestrials.*

Asimov's ghosts—SEE: *Young ghosts.*

16976 *Asimov's ghosts & monsters.* London: Armada, 1988, 413 p., paper, anth. [Includes *Young ghosts* and *Young monsters*].

Asimov's monsters—SEE: *Young monsters.*

Asimov's mutants—SEE: *Young mutants.*

16977 *Baker's dozen: thirteen short fantasy novels.* New York: Greenwich House, 1984, ix+612 p., cloth, anth.

16977A retitled: *The mammoth book of short fantasy novels.* London: Robinson Publishing, 1986, 612 p., paper, anth.

16978 *Baker's dozen: thirteen short science fiction novels.* New York: Bonanza Books, 1985, ix+574 p., cloth, anth.

16978A retitled: *The mammoth book of short science fiction novels.* London: Robinson Publishing, 1986, 612 p., paper, anth.

The best fantasy of the 19th century—SEE: *Isaac Asimov presents the best fantasy of the 19th century.*

The best horror and supernatural of the 19th century—SEE: *Isaac Asimov presents The best horror and supernatural of the 19th century.*

The best science fiction firsts—SEE: *Isaac Asimov presents The best science fiction firsts.*

The best science fiction of the 19th century—SEE: *Isaac Asimov presents The best science fiction of the 19th century.*

16979 *Bug awful.* Milwaukee, WI: Raintree Publishers, 1984, 48 p., cloth, anth.

16980 *Catastrophes!* New York: Fawcett Crest, 1981, 413 p., paper, anth.

16981 *Caught in the organ draft: biology in science fiction.* New York: Farrar Straus Giroux, 1983, xi+276 p., cloth, anth.

16982 *Children of the future.* Milwaukee, WI: Raintree Publishers, 1984, 48 p., cloth, anth.

16983 *Comets.* New York: A Signet Book, New American Library, 1986, xii+339 p., paper, anth. ISAAC ASIMOV'S WONDERFUL WORLDS OF SCIENCE FICTION #4.

16984 *Computer crimes and capers.* Chicago: Academy Chicago Publishers, 1983, 235 p., cloth, anth.

16985 *Cosmic knights.* New York: A Signet Book, New American Library, 1985, 339 p., paper, anth. ISAAC ASIMOV'S MAGICAL WORLDS OF FANTASY #3.

16986 *Curses.* New York: A Signet Book, New American Library, 1989, 350 p., paper, anth. ISAAC ASIMOV'S MAGICAL WORLDS OF FANTASY #11.

16987 *The deadly sins and cardinal virtues of science fiction.* New York: Bonanza Books, 1982, 317, 350 p., cloth, anth. [Includes both books].

16988 *Dragon tales.* New York: Fawcett Crest, 1982, 318 p., paper, anth.

16989 *Earth invaded.* Milwaukee, WI: Raintree Publishers, 1982, 46 p., cloth, anth.

16990 *Encounters.* London: Headline, 1988, 399 p., paper, anth.

Extraterrestrials—SEE: *Young extraterrestrials.*

16991 *Faeries: Isaac Asimov's magical worlds of fantasy.* New York: A Roc Book, 1991, 374 p., paper, coll. ISAAC ASIMOV'S MAGICAL WORLDS OF FANTASY (UNNUMBERED).

16992 *Fantastic creatures: an anthology of fantasy and science fiction.* New York: Franklin Watts, 1981, 155 p., cloth, anth.

16993 *Flying saucers.* New York: Fawcett Crest, 1982, 349 p., paper, anth.

16994 *Ghosts.* New York: A Signet Book, New American Library, 1988, 347 p., paper, anth. ISAAC ASIMOV'S MAGICAL WORLDS OF FANTASY #10.

Ghosts & monsters—SEE: *Asimov's Ghosts & monsters.*

16995 *Giants.* New York: A Signet Books, New American Library, 1985, 351 p., paper, anth. ISAAC ASIMOV'S MAGICAL WORLDS OF FANTASY #5.

16996 *Great science fiction stories by the world's great scientists.* New York: Donald I. Fine, 1985, 400 p., cloth, anth.

Great tales of classic science fiction—SEE: *The mammoth book of classic science fiction: short novels of the 1930s.*

16997 *Hallucination orbit: psychology in science fiction.* New York: Farrar Straus Giroux, 1983, 279 p., cloth, anth.

16998 *The immortals.* Milwaukee, WI: Raintree Publishers, 1984, 48 p., cloth, anth.

16999 *Intergalactic empires.* New York: A Signet Book, New American Library, 1983, 303 p., paper, anth. ISAAC ASI-

MOV'S WONDERFUL WORLDS OF SCIENCE FICTION #1.

17000 *Invasions.* New York: A Roc Book, 1990, 382 p., paper, anth. ISAAC ASIMOV'S WONDERFUL WORLDS OF SCIENCE FICTION #10.

17001 *Isaac Asimov presents Tales of the occult: stories.* Buffalo, NY: Prometheus Books, 1989, 354 p., cloth, anth.

17002 *Isaac Asimov presents The best fantasy of the 19th century.* New York: Beaufort Books, 1982, 368 p., cloth, anth.

17003 *Isaac Asimov presents The best horror and supernatural of the 19th century.* New York: Beaufort Books, 1983, 368 p., cloth, anth.

17004 *Isaac Asimov presents The best science fiction firsts.* New York: Beaufort Books, 1984, 249 p., cloth, anth.

17005 *Isaac Asimov presents The best science fiction of the 19th century.* New York: Beaufort Books, 1981, 316 p., cloth, anth.

17006 *Isaac Asimov's Magical worlds of fantasy: Witches & Wizards.* New York: Bonanza Books, 1985, 649 p., cloth, anth. [Includes *Witches* and *Wizards*].

17007 *The last man on Earth.* New York: Fawcett Crest, 1982, 350 p., paper, anth.

17008 *Mad scientists.* Milwaukee, WI: Raintree Publishers, 1982, 48 p., cloth, anth.

17009 *Magical wishes.* New York: A Signet Book, New American Library, 1986, 350 p., paper, anth. ISAAC ASIMOV'S MAGICAL WORLDS OF FANTASY #7.

Magical worlds of fantasy—SEE: *Isaac Asimov's Magical worlds of fantasy.*

17010 *The Mammoth book of classic science fiction: short novels of the 1930s.* London: Robinson, 1988, xiii+572 p., paper, anth.

17010A retitled: *Great tales of classic science fiction.* New York: Galahad, 1990, 498 p., cloth, anth.

17011 *The mammoth book of golden age science fiction: short novels of the 1940s.* New York: Carroll & Graf, 1989, 504 p., paper, anth.

17012 *The mammoth book of new world science fiction: short novels of the 1960s.* New York: Carroll & Graf, 1991, 506 p., paper, anth.

The mammoth book of short fantasy novels—SEE: *Baker's dozen: thirteen short fantasy novels.*

The mammoth book of short science fiction novels—SEE: *Baker's dozen: thirteen short science fiction novels.*

17013 *The mammoth book of vintage science fiction: short novels of the 1950s.* London: Robinson, 1990, 503 p., paper, anth.

17014 *Monsters.* New York: A Signet Book, New American Library, 1988, 349 p., paper, anth. ISAAC ASIMOV'S WONDERFUL WORLDS OF SCIENCE FICTION #8.

17015 *Mutants.* Milwaukee, WI: Raintree Publishers, 1982, 46 p., cloth, anth.

Mutants—SEE: Young mutants.

Mythic beasts—SEE: Mythical beasties.

17016 *Mythical beasties.* New York: A Signet Book, New American Library, 1986, 343 p., paper, anth. ISAAC ASIMOV'S MAGICAL WORLDS OF FANTASY #6.

17016A retitled: *Mythic beasts.* London: Robinson, 1988, 343 p., paper, anth.

17017 *Robots.* New York: A Signet Book, New American Library, 1989, 351 p., paper, anth. ISAAC ASIMOV'S WONDERFUL WORLDS OF SCIENCE FICTION #9.

17018 *Science fiction A to Z: a dictionary of great S.F. themes.* Boston: Houghton Mifflin Co., 1982, xvii+651 p., cloth, anth.

17019 *The science fictional Olympics.* New York: A Signet Book, New American Library, 1984, 356 p., paper, anth. ISAAC ASIMOV'S WONDERFUL WORLDS OF SCIENCE FICTION #2.

17020 *The science fictional solar system.* New York: Harper & Row, 1979, ix+317 p., cloth, anth.

17021 *The seven cardinal virtues of science fiction.* New York: Fawcett Crest, 1981, 350 p., paper, anth.

17022 *The seven deadly sins of science fiction.* New York: Fawcett Crest, 1980, 317 p., paper, anth.

17023 *Sherlock Holmes through time and space.* New York: Bluejay Book, 1984, 355 p., cloth, anth.

17024 *Space mail, volume II.* New York: Fawcett Crest, 1982, 380 p., paper, anth.

17025 *Space shuttles.* New York: A Signet Book, New American Library, 1987, 384 p., paper, anth. ISAAC ASIMOV'S WONDERFUL WORLDS OF SCIENCE FICTION #7.

17026 *Spells.* New York: A Signet Book, New American Library, 1985, 350 p., paper, anth. ISAAC ASIMOV'S MAGICAL WORLDS OF FANTASY #4.

17027 *Starships.* New York: Fawcett Crest, 1983, 342 p., paper, anth.

17028 *Supermen.* New York: A Signet Book, New American Library, 1984, 350 p., paper, anth. ISAAC ASIMOV'S WONDERFUL WORLDS OF SCIENCE FICTION #3.

Tales of the occult—SEE: Isaac Asimov presents Tales of the occult.

17029 *Thinking machines.* Milwaukee, WI: Raintree Publishers, 1981, 48 p., cloth, anth.

17030 *Those amazing electronic thinking machines: an anthology of robot and computer stories* / by Isaac Asimov, Martin S. Greenberg & Charles H. Waugh [sic]. New York: Franklin Watts, 1983, 147 p., cloth, anth.

17031 *Time warps.* Milwaukee, WI: Raintree Publishers, 1984, 48 p., cloth, anth.

17032 *Tin stars.* New York: A Signet Book, New American Library, 1986, 351 p., paper, anth. ISAAC ASIMOV'S WONDERFUL WORLDS OF SCIENCE FICTION #5.

17033 *Tomorrow's TV.* Milwaukee, WI: Raintree Publishers, 1982, 48 p., cloth, anth.

17034 *Travels through time.* Milwaukee, WI: Raintree Publishers, 1981, 47 p., cloth, anth.

17035 *TV: 2000.* New York: Fawcett Crest, 1982, 352 p., paper, anth.

17036 *The twelve frights of Christmas.* New York: Avon, 1986, 263 p., paper, anth.

17037 *Wild inventions.* Milwaukee, WI: Raintree Publishers, 1981, 46 p., cloth, anth.

17038 *Witches.* New York: A Signet Book, New American Library, 1984, 350 p., paper, anth. ISAAC ASIMOV'S MAGICAL WORLDS OF FANTASY #2.

17039 *Wizards.* New York: A Signet Book, New American Library, 1983, 303 p., paper, anth. ISAAC ASIMOV'S MAGICAL WORLDS OF FANTASY #1.

17040 *Young extraterrestrials.* New York: Harper & Row, 1984, xiv+240 p., cloth, anth.

17040A retitled: *Asimov's extraterrestrials.* London: Dragon Books, 1986, 204 p., paper, anth.

17040B retitled: *Extraterrestrials.* New York: Harper & Row, 1988, xiv+240 p., paper, anth.

17041 *Young ghosts.* New York: Harper & Row, 1985, xiv+210 p., cloth, anth.

17041A retitled: *Asimov's ghosts.* London: Dragon Books, 1986, 202 p., paper, anth.

17042 *Young immortals.* New York: Harper & Row, 1985, vii+213 p., cloth, anth.

17043 *Young monsters.* New York: Harper & Row, 1985, 213 p., cloth, anth.

17043A retitled: *Asimov's monsters.* London: Dragon Books, 1986, 203 p., paper, anth.

17044 *Young mutants.* New York: Harper & Row, 1984, 256 p., cloth, anth.

17044A retitled: *Asimov's mutants.* London: Dragon Books, 1986, 201 p., paper, anth.

17044B retitled: *Mutants*. New York: Harper & Row, 1988, 256 p., paper, anth.

17045 *Young star travelers*. New York: Harper & Row, 1986, xiii+209 p., cloth, anth.

17046 *Young witches & warlocks*. New York: Harper & Row, 1987, xvi+207 p., cloth, anth.

ISAAC ASIMOV, *with Martin H. Greenberg & David Clark Yeager*

17047 *Fantastic reading: stories and activities for grades 5-8*. Glenview, IL: A Goodyear Book, Scott, Foresman & Co., 1984, xiii+169 p., paper?, anth.

ISAAC ASIMOV, *with Alice Laurance*

17048 *Speculations*. Boston: Houghton Mifflin Co., 1982, xiii+288 p., cloth, anth.

ISAAC ASIMOV, *with George R. R. Martin & Martin H. Greenberg*

17049 *The science fiction weight-loss book*. New York: Crown Publishers, 1983, v+249 p., cloth, anth.

ISAAC ASIMOV, *with Robert Silverberg*

17050 *Child of time*. London: Victor Gollancz, 1991, 302 p., cloth, novel.

17051 *Nightfall*. London: Victor Gollancz, 1990, 352 p., cloth, novel.

ISAAC ASIMOV, *with George Zebrowski & Martin H. Greenberg*

17052 *Creations: the quest for origins in story and science*. New York: Crown Publishers, 1983, xii+351 p., cloth, anth.

ASIMOV, Janet (Opal) Jeppson, 1926-

17053 *Mind transfer*. New York: Walker & Co., 1988, 312 p., cloth, novel.

17054 *A package in hyperspace*. New York: Walker & Co., 1988, 84 p., cloth, novel.

as **J. O. JEPPSON**

17055 *The last immortal*. Boston: Houghton Mifflin Co., 1980, 278 p., cloth, novel.

17056 *The mysterious cure, and other stories of Pshrinks Anonymous*. Garden City, NY: Doubleday & Co., 1985, viii+180 p., cloth, coll.

17056A retitled: *Pshrinks Anonymous: the mysterious cure, and other stories* / by Janet Jeppson Asimov. New York: A Roc Book, 1990, 203 p., paper, coll.

Pshrinks Anonymous—SEE: *The mysterious cure and other stories of Pshrinks Anonymous*.

with Isaac Asimov

16912 *Laughing space: funny science fiction chuckled over* / edited by Isaac Asimov and J. O. Jeppson. Boston: Houghton Mifflin Co., 1982, xvi+520 p., cloth, anth.

16913 *Norby and the court jester*. New York: Walker & Co., 1991, 118 p., cloth, novel. NORBY #10.

16914 *Norby and the invaders*. New York: Walker & Co., 1985, 138 p., cloth, novel. NORBY #4.

16915 *Norby and the lost princess*. New York: Walker & Co., 1985, 129 p., cloth, novel. NORBY #3.

16916 *Norby and the oldest dragon*. New York: Walker & Co., 1990, 110 p., cloth, novel. NORBY #9.

16917 *Norby and the queen's necklace*. New York: Walker & Co., 1986, 136 p., cloth, novel. NORBY #5.

16918 *Norby and Yobo's great adventure*. New York: Walker & Co., 1989, 100 p., cloth, novel. NORBY #8.

16919 *The Norby chronicles*. New York: Ace Science Fiction Books, 1986, 185 p., paper, coll. NORBY #1-2.

16920 *Norby down to Earth*. New York: Walker & Co., 1989, 107 p., cloth, novel. NORBY #7.

16921 *Norby finds a villain*. New York: Walker & Co., 1987, 102 p., cloth, novel. NORBY #6.

16922 *Norby: robot for hire*. New York: Ace Science Fiction Books, 1987, 203 p., paper, coll. NORBY #3-4.

16923 *Norby, the mixed-up robot*. New York: Walker & Co., 1983, 96 p., cloth, novel. NORBY #1.

16924 *Norby through space and time*. New York: Ace Books, 1988, 202 p., paper, coll. NORBY #5-6.

16925 *Norby's other secret*. New York: Walker & Co., 1984, 138 p., cloth, novel. NORBY #2.

ASIMOW, Morris, 1906-1982

17057 *Tale of two planets*. [S.l.]: Plantian Press, 1981, 278 p., cloth, novel.

ASIRE, Nancy, 1945-

17058 *Twilight's kingdoms.* New York: Baen, 1987, 376 p., paper, novel.

with C. J. Cherryh

17059 *Wizard spawn.* New York: Baen, 1989, 275 p., paper, novel. SWORD OF KNOWLEDGE #2.

ASNIN, Scott

17060 *A cold wind from Orion: a novel.* New York: A Del Rey Book, Ballantine Books, 1980, 280 p., paper, novel.

ASPLER, Tony, 1939- , *with Gordon Pape*

17061 *Chain reaction.* New York: Viking Press, 1978, 284 p., cloth, novel.

ASPRIN, Robert Lynn, 1946-

17062 *Another fine myth...* / by Robert Asprin. Norfolk, VA: Starblaze Editions/ Donning, 1978, 159 p., paper, novel. SKEEVE #1.

17063 *The bug wars* New York: St. Martin's Press, 1979, 234 p., cloth, novel.

17064 *The cold cash war* / by Robert Asprin. New York: St. Martin's Press, 1977, 170 p., cloth, novel.

17065 *Hit or myth* / by Robert Asprin. Norfolk, Virginia Beach, VA: Donning, 1983, 127 p., paper, novel. SKEEVE #4.

17066 *Little Myth Marker* / by Robert Asprin. Norfolk, Virginia Beach, VA: The Donning Company, Starblaze Editions, 1985, 172 p., cloth, novel. SKEEVE #6.

17067 *Myth adventures.* Garden City, NY: Nelson Doubleday, 1984, 599 p., cloth, coll. SKEEVE #1-4.

17068 *Myth alliances.* Garden City, NY: Nelson Doubleday, 1987, 375 p., cloth, coll. SKEEVE #5-7.

17069 *Myth conceptions* / by Robert Asprin. Virginia Beach, VA: Starblaze Editions/Donning, 1980, 158 p., paper, novel. SKEEVE #2.

17070 *Myth directions* / by Robert Asprin. Norfolk/Virginia Beach, VA: Starblaze Editions/Donning, 1982, 169 p., paper, novel. SKEEVE #3.

17071 *M.Y.T.H. Inc. in action.* Norfolk & Virginia Beach, VA: The Donning Co., Publishers, Starblaze Editions, 1990, 236 p., cloth, novel. SKEEVE #9.

17072 *M.Y.T.H. Inc. link.* Norfolk, VA: Donning Co., 1986, x+150 p., cloth, novel. SKEEVE #7.

17073 *Myth-ing persons.* Norfolk/Virginia Beach, VA: Starblaze Editions, The Donning Company/Publishers, 1984, 170 p., cloth, novel. SKEEVE #5.

17074 *Myth-nomers and im-pervections.* Norfolk & Virginia Beach, VA: The Donning Co., Publishers, 1987, 189 p., cloth, novel. SKEEVE #8.

17075 *Phule's company.* New York: Ace Books, 1990, 232 p., cloth, novel. PHULE #1.

17076 *Sanctuary.* Garden City, NY: Nelson Doubleday, 1982, 600 p., cloth, anth. THIEVES' WORLD #1-3.

17077 *Shadows of Sanctuary.* New York: Ace Books, 1981, 338 p., paper, anth. THIEVES' WORLD #3. [Winner of the *Locus* Award for Best Anthology, 1981 (1982)].

17078 *Storm season.* New York: Ace Books, 1982, 305 p., paper, anth. THIEVES' WORLD #4.

17079 *Tales from the Vulgar Unicorn.* New York: Ace Books, 1980, 299 p., paper, anth. THIEVES' WORLD #2.

17080 *Tambu.* New York: Ace Books, 1979, 195 p., paper, novel.

17081 *Thieves' world* / by Robert Asprin. New York: Ace Books, 1979, 308 p., paper, anth. THIEVES' WORLD #1.

with Lynn Abbey

15902 *Aftermath.* New York: Ace Books, 1987, xiv+273 p., paper, anth. THIEVES' WORLD #10.

15903 *Blood ties.* New York: Ace Fantasy Books, 1986, xiv+238 p., paper, anth. THIEVES' WORLD #9.

15904 *Cross-currents.* Garden City, NY: Nelson Doubleday, 1984, 628 p., cloth, anth. THIEVES' WORLD #4-6. [Includes *Storm season*, *The face of chaos*, *Wings of omen*].

15905 *The dead of winter.* New York: Ace Fantasy Books, 1985, xiv+273 p., paper, anth. THIEVES' WORLD #7.

15906 *The face of chaos.* New York: Ace Fantasy Books, 1983, 242 p., paper, anth.

21645 *The price of victory.* Garden City, NY: Nelson Doubleday, 1990, [750] p., cloth, anth. THIEVES' WORLD #10-12. [Includes *Aftermath*; *Uneasy alliances*; *Stealers' sky*].

15907 *The shattered sphere.* Garden City, NY: Nelson Doubleday, 1986, 728 p., cloth, anth. THIEVES' WORLD #7-9. [Includes

The dead of winter; Soul of the city; Blood ties].

15908 *Soul of the city.* New York: Ace Fantasy Books, 1986, xiii+242 p., paper, anth. THIEVES' WORLD #8.

15909 *Stealers' sky.* New York: Ace Books, 1989, xv+240 p., paper, anth. THIEVES' WORLD #12.

15910 *Uneasy alliances.* New York: Ace Books, 1988, xiii+258 p., paper, anth. THIEVES' WORLD #11.

15911 *Wings of omen.* New York: Ace Fantasy Books, 1984, 277 p., paper, anth. THIEVES' WORLD #6.

with Lynn Abbey & Richard Pini

15912 *The blood of ten chiefs.* New York: Tor SF, A Tom Doherty Associates Book, 1986, 314 p., cloth, anth. ELFQUEST #1.

15913 *Elfquest: Wolfsong: The blood of ten chiefs.* New York: Tor SF, A Tom Doherty Associates Book, 1988, 307 p., paper, anth. ELFQUEST #2.
Wolfsong—SEE: *Elfquest: Wolfsong: The blood of ten chiefs.*

with Bill Fawcett

Cold cash warrior—SEE: *Combat command in the world of Robert Asprin's Cold cash war: Cold cash warrior.*

17082 *Combat command in the world of Robert Asprin's Cold cash war: Cold cash warrior* / by Robert Asprin.... New York: Ace Books, 1989, x+132 p., paper, novel. COMBAT COMMAND #9.

with George Takei

17083 *Mirror friend, mirror foe.* Chicago: Playboy Press Paperbacks, 1979, 223 p., paper, novel.

ASSANTE, Allison

17084 *Moon lady.* Haddon Heights, NJ: Allison Assante, 1968, 41 p., paper, story.

ASSELINEAU, Roger (Maurice), 1915-

17085 *Edgar Allan Poe.* Minneapolis, MN: University of Minnesota Press, 1970, 48 p., paper, nonf.

ASTEN, Gail Van—SEE: **Van Asten, Gail**

*ATKEY, Bertram, 1880-1952

ATKINS, Frank—SEE: **Aubrey, Frank**

ATKINS, John (Alfred), 1916-

17086 *Aldous Huxley: a literary study.* London: John Calder, 1953, 224 p., cloth, nonf.

17087 *George Orwell: a literary study.* London: John Calder, 1954, 348 p., cloth, nonf.

17088 *Walter de la Mare: an exploration.* London: C. & J. Temple, 1947, 45 p., paper, nonf.

ATKINS, Margaret E.—SEE: **Atkins, Meg Elizabeth**

ATKINS, Meg Elizabeth [i.e., Margaret Elizabeth Atkins]

17089 *By the north door.* New York: Harper & Row, Publishers, 1975, 180 p., cloth, novel.

17090 *Samain.* New York: Harper & Row, Publishers, 1976, 213 p., cloth, novel.

ATKINS, Thomas R(adcliffe), 1939-

17091 *Science fiction films.* New York: Monarch Press, 1976, ix+101 p., paper, nonf. anth.

ATKINSON, Stuart

17092 *Journey into space.* New York: Viking Kestrel, 1988, 80 p., cloth, fiction. [Includes some nonfiction].

ATKINSON-KEEN, Susan

17093 *Weekend in the Jurassic.* Halifax, Nova Scotia, Canada: Nimbus, 1990, 144 p., paper, novel.

ATTANASIO, A. A., 1951-

17094 *Arc of the dream.* Toronto, New York: Bantam Books, 1986, 262 p., paper, novel. RADIX TETRAD #3.

17095 *Beastmarks.* Willimantic, CT: Mark V. Ziesing, 1984, 120 p., cloth, coll.

17096 *Hunting the ghost dancer.* New York: HarperCollinsPublishers, 1991, xxviii+371 p., cloth, novel.

17097 *In other worlds.* New York: William Morrow & Co., 1984, 211 p., cloth, novel. RADIX TETRAD #2.

17098 *The last legends of Earth.* Norwalk, CT: Easton Press, 1989, 481 p., cloth, novel. RADIX TETRAD #4.

17099 *Radix.* New York: William Morrow & Co., 1981, 467 p., cloth, novel. RADIX TETRAD #1.

17100 *Wyvern*. New York: Ticknor & Fields, 1988, 422 p., cloth, novel.

ATTEBERY, Brian (Leonard), 1951-

17101 *The fantasy tradition in American literature from Irving to Le Guin*. Bloomington, IN: Indiana University Press, 1980, viii+212 p., cloth, nonf.

ATTIAS, Diana, *with Lindsay Smith*

17102 *The Empire Strikes Back notebook*. New York: Ballantine Books, 1980, 127 p., paper, nonf.

ATTWOOD, Tony, 1947-

Afterlife—SEE: *Terry Nation's Blake's 7: Afterlife.*

17103 *The companions of Doctor Who: Turlough and the Earthlink dilemma*. London: W. H. Allen & Co., 1985, 221 p., cloth, tele. DOCTOR WHO SERIES.

17104 *Terry Nation's Blake's 7: Afterlife.* London: A Target Book, W. H. Allen & Co., 1984, 217 p., paper, tele. BLAKE'S 7 #4.

17105 *Terry Nation's Blake's 7: the programme guide*. London: A Target Book, W. H. Allen, 1983, 192 p., paper, nonf.

Turlough and the Earthlink dilemma—SEE: *The companions of Doctor Who: Turlough and the Earthlink dilemma.*

ATWOOD, Margaret (Eleanor Killian), 1939-

17106 *The handmaid's tale*. Toronto: McClelland & Stewart, 1985, 324 p., cloth, novel.

AUBIN, Horace de Saint- —SEE: Balzac, Honoré de

AUBREY, Crispin, 1946- , *with Paul Chilton*

17107 *Nineteen Eighty-Four in 1984: autonomy, control, and communication*. London: Comedia Publishing Group in Association with Marion Boyars, 1983, 120 p., cloth, nonf. anth.

*AUBREY, Frank [pseud. of Francis Henry "Frank" Atkins], 1840-1927

*AUDEN, Renée [pseud. of Uta West], 1928-

AUEL, Jean M(arie), 1936-

17108 *The Clan of the Cave Bear: a novel.* New York: Crown Publishers, 1980, 468 p., cloth, novel. EARTH'S CHILDREN #1.

17109 *Earth's children*. London: Hodder & Stoughton, 1987, 491+571+639 p., cloth, coll. EARTH'S CHILDREN #1-3. [Includes *The Clan of the Cave Bear*; *The valley of horses*; *The mammoth hunters*].

17110 *The mammoth hunters*. New York: Crown Publishers, 1985, ix+645 p., cloth, novel. EARTH'S CHILDREN #3.

17111 *The plains of passage*. New York: Crown Publishers, 1990, 760 p., cloth, novel. EARTH'S CHILDREN #4.

17112 *The valley of horses: a novel*. New York: Crown Publishers, 1982, 502 p., cloth, novel. EARTH'S CHILDREN #2.

AUERBACH, Jonathan, 1954-

17113 *The romance of failure: first-person fictions of Poe, Hawthorne, and James*. New York: Oxford University Press, 1989, 201 p., cloth, nonf.

AULICH, Chris

17114 *IT*. Sydney: Wild & Woolley, 1977, 111 p., cloth, novel.

AULT, O(rvill) E., 1899-

17115 *Johnny Transplant: a novel*. New York: A Geneva Book, Carlton Press, 1972, 155 p., cloth, novel.

AULTMAN, Mark

17116 *Nightfire*. New York, Ramsey, NJ: Paulist Press, 1976, 155 p., cloth, novel.

AUSTER, Paul, 1947-

17117 *In the country of last things*. New York: Viking, 1987, 188 p., cloth, novel.

17118 *Moon palace*. New York: Viking, 1989, 307 p., cloth, novel.

*AUSTIN, Alex, 1925-1985

AUSTIN, Alicia, 1942-

17119 *Alicia Austin's age of dreams*. West Kingston, RI: Donald M. Grant, Publisher, 1978, 143 p., cloth, art.

AUSTIN, R. G. [pseud. of Rita Golden Gelman], 1937-

17120 *The castle of no return.* New York: An Archway Paperback, Pocket Books, 1982, 116 p., paper, novel. WHICH WAY BOOKS #1.

17121 *Cosmic encounters.* New York: An Archway Paperback, Pocket Books, 1982, 118 p., paper, novel. WHICH WAY BOOKS #8.

17122 *Creatures of the dark.* New York: An Archway Paperback, Pocket Books, 1982, 118 p., paper, novel. WHICH WAY BOOKS #9.

17123 *Curse of the sunken treasure.* New York: An Archway Paperback, Pocket Books, 1982, 119 p., paper, novel. WHICH WAY BOOKS #7.

17124 *Famous and rich.* New York: An Archway Paperback, Pocket Books, 1982, 136 p., paper, novel. WHICH WAY BOOKS #4.

17125 *Invasion of the black slime, and other tales of horror.* New York: An Archway Paperback, Pocket Books, 1983, 118 p., paper, novel. WHICH WAY BOOKS #10.

17126 *Islands of terror.* New York: An Archway Paperback, Pocket Books, 1985, 117 p., paper, novel. WHICH WAY BOOKS #18.

17127 *Lost in a strange land.* New York: An Archway Paperback, Pocket Books, 1982, 133 p., paper, novel. WHICH WAY BOOKS #5.

17128 *Poltergeists, ghosts, and psychic encounters.* New York: An Archway Book, Pocket Books, 1984, 118 p., paper, novel. WHICH WAY BOOKS #14.

17129 *The shadow stealers.* New York: An Archway Paperback, Pocket Books, 1984, 118 p., paper, novel. WHICH WAY BOOKS #16.

17130 *The spell of the black raven.* New York: An Archway Paperback, Pocket Books, 1982, 120 p., paper, novel. WHICH WAY BOOKS #3.

17131 *Ten-ton monster.* New York: An Archway Paperback, Pocket Books, 1985, 117 p., paper, novel. WHICH WAY BOOKS #21.

17132 *Trapped in the black box.* New York: An Archway Paperbacks, Pocket Books, 1983, 118 p., paper, novel. WHICH WAY BOOKS #12.

17133 *Vampires, spies, and alien beings.* New York: An Archway Paperback, Pocket Books, 1982, 120 p., paper, novel. WHICH WAY BOOKS #2.

AUSTIN, Richard, pseud.—SEE: Milán, Victor

AUTHOR of "The Realm of the Ice King", pseud.—SEE: Frost, Thomas

AVALLONE, Michael (Angelo Jr.), 1924-

17134 *Friday the 13th, part 3, 3-D.* New York: Leisure Books, 1982, 200 p., paper, movie. FRIDAY THE 13TH #3.

00661 *The Man from U.N.C.L.E.* New York: Ace Books, 1965, 160 p., paper, tele. THE MAN FROM U.N.C.L.E. #1. [Running title reads: *The thousand coffins affair.* According to Terry Carr's obituary, Carr rewrote the book before its publication].

17135 *One more time.* New York: Popular Library, 1970, 144 p., paper, movie.

17136 *Where monsters walk: terror tales for people afraid of the dark and the unknown.* New York, Toronto: Scholastic Book Services, 1978, 121 p., paper, coll.

as DOROTHEA NILE

17137 *The vampire cameo.* New York: Lancer Books, 1968, 190 p., paper, novel.

AVERY, Richard, pseud.—SEE: Cooper, Edmund

AVI [pseud. of Edward Irving Wortis], 1937-

17138 *Bright shadow.* New York: Bradbury Press, 1985, 167 p, cloth, novel.

17139 *Devil's race.* New York: J. P. Lippincott, 1984, 152 p., cloth, novel.

17140 *The man who was Poe: a novel.* New York: A Richard Jackson Book, Orchard Books, 1989, 208 p., cloth, novel.

17141 *No more magic.* New York: Pantheon Books, 1975, 138 p., cloth, novel.

17142 *Something upstairs: a tale of ghosts.* New York: A Richard Jackson Book, Orchard Books, 1988, 120 p., cloth, novel.

AVICE, Claude—SEE: Barbet, Pierre

AWLINSON, Richard, house pseud.

Dragonwall—SEE: Forgotten realms fantasy adventure: Dragonwall.

17143 *Forgotten realms fantasy adventure: Dragonwall.* Lake Geneva, WI: TSR Inc., 1990, 311 p., paper, novel. EMPIRES TRILOGY #2. [By Troy Denning].

17144 *Forgotten realms fantasy adventure: Shadowdale.* Lake Geneva, WI: TSR Inc., 1989, 335 p., paper, novel. AVATAR TRILOGY #1. [By Scott Ciencin].

17145 *Forgotten realms fantasy adventure: Tantras.* Lake Geneva, WI: TSR Inc., 1989, 338 p., paper, novel. AVATAR TRILOGY #2. [By Scott Ciencin & James Lowder].

17146 *Forgotten realms fantasy adventure: The parched sea.* Lake Geneva, WI: TSR Inc., 1991, 310 p., paper, novel. THE HARPERS #1. [By Troy Denning].

17147 *Forgotten realms fantasy adventure: Waterdeep.* Lake Geneva, WI: TSR Inc., 1989, 341 p., paper, novel. AVATAR TRILOGY #3. [By Troy Denning].

The parched sea—SEE: *Forgotten realms fantasy adventure: The parched sea.*

Shadowdale—SEE: *Forgotten realms fantasy adventure: Shadowdale.*

Tantras—SEE: *Forgotten realms fantasy adventure: Tantras.*

Waterdeep—SEE: *Forgotten realms fantasy adventure: Waterdeep.*

AXELROD, Alan (David), 1952-

17148 *Charles Brockden Brown: an American tale.* Austin, TX: University of Texas Press, 1983, xx+203 p., cloth, nonf.

AXLER, James, pseud.—SEE: James, Laurence

AYCLIFFE, Jonathan, pseud.—SEE: Easterman, Daniel

AYCOCK, Dale, 1930?-

17149 *Stardrifter.* New York: Leisure Books, 1981, 216 p., paper, novel.

17150 *Starspinner.* New York: Leisure Books, 1981, 239 p., paper, novel.

AYCOCK, Roger D.—SEE: Dee, Roger

AYLESWORTH, Thomas G(ibbons), 1927-

17151 *Monster and horror movies.* New York: A Bison Book, Gallery Books, 1986, 192 p., cloth, nonf.

17152 *Movie monsters.* Philadelphia, PA: J. B. Lippincott, 1975, 79 p., cloth, nonf.

AYRAUD, Pierre—SEE: Narcejac, Thomas

AYRTON, Elisabeth Walshe, 1918-1991

26045 *Day eight.* London: Hutchinson, 1978, 271 p., cloth, novel.

AZIMOV, Isaak I.—SEE: Asimov, Isaac

B

'B', pseud.

17153 *When the door is shut, and other ghost stories.* Runcorn, Cheshire, England: Haunted Library, Rosemary Pardoe, 1986, 33 p., paper, coll.

BABBITT, Lucy Cullyford

17154 *Children of the Maker.* New York: Farrar, Straus & Giroux, 1988, 231 p., cloth, novel. MELDE #2.
17155 *The Oval amulet.* New York: Harper & Row, 1985, 243 p., cloth, novel. MELDE #1.

BABBITT, Natalie (Moore), 1932-

17156 *Tuck everlasting.* New York: Farrar Straus Giroux, 1975, 139 p., cloth, novel.

BACH, Richard (David), 1936-

17157 *The bridge across forever: a lovestory.* New York: William Morrow & Co., 1984, 315 p., cloth, novel.
17158 *Illusions: the adventures of a reluctant messiah.* New York: Delacorte Press/Eleanor Friede, 1977, 143 p., cloth, novel.
17159 *One: a novel.* New York: Silver Arrow Books, William Morrow & Co., 1988, 284 p., cloth, novel.
17160 *There's no such place as far away.* New York: Delacorte Press/Eleanor Friede, 1979, [47] p., cloth, story.

BACHMAN, Richard, pseud.—SEE: King, Stephen

BACKMAN, Diana, *with Christopher Nicole as* MAX MARLOW

17161 *Meltdown.* London: New English Library, 1991, 286 p., cloth, novel.
17162 *The red death.* London: New English Library, 1989, 347 p., cloth, novel.

BACON, Donald

17163 *The midnight hour.* New York: Pinnacle Books, Windsor Publishing Corp., 1988, 380 p., paper, novel.

BACON, Martha [i.e., Martha Sherman Bacon Oliver-Smith], 1917-1981

17164 *Moth Manor: a gothic tale.* Boston: An Atlantic Monthly Book, Little, Brown & Co., 1978, 148 p., cloth, novel.

BACON, Peggy [i.e., Margaret Frances Bacon Brook], 1895-1987

17165 *The magic touch.* Boston: Little, Brown & Co., 1968, 112 p., cloth, novel.

BADDELEY, Pam

17166 *Fall of night.* Strathmartine by Dundee, Scotland: ScoTpress, 1984, 104 p., paper, tele. STAR TREK SERIES.
17167 *The mark of Cain.* Strathmartine by Dundee, Scotland: ScoTpress, 1984, 54 p., paper, tele. STAR TREK SERIES.
17168 *Spinner of nightmares.* Strathmartine by Dundee, Scotland: ScoTpress, 1986, 118 p., paper, tele. STAR TREK SERIES.
17169 *Weaver of dreams.* Strathmartine by Dundee, Scotland: ScoTpress, 1981, 46 p., paper, tele. STAR TREK SERIES.

BADE, Thomas M.—SEE: Bade, Tom

BADE, Tom [i.e., Thomas Michael Bade], 1946-

as T. M. MINTON

17170 *Offerings.* New York: Leisure Books, 1986, 395 p., paper, novel.

with Robin Stevenson

17171 *Switchback.* New York: Pinnacle Books, Windsor Publishing Corp., 1988, 447 p., paper, novel.

BADENOCH, Lindsay

17172 *The daughter of the runes.* London, New York: Arkana, 1989, 229 p., paper, novel.

BAEN, James Patrick, 1943-

17173 *The best from Galaxy, volume III* / by James Baen. New York: Award Books, 1975, 219 p., paper, anth.

17174 *The best from Galaxy, volume IV* / by James Baen. New York: Award Books, 1976, 218 p., paper, anth.

17175 *The best from If, volume III* / by James Baen. New York: Award Books, 1976, 220 p., paper, anth.

17176 *The best of Destinies.* New York: Ace Books, 1980, 335 p., paper, anth.

17177 *Destinies: the paperback magazine of science fiction and speculative fact, November-December, 1978.* New York: Ace Books, 1978, 308 p., paper, anth.

17178 *Destinies: the paperback magazine of science fiction and speculative fact, February-March, 1979.* New York: Ace Books, 1979, 318 p., paper, anth.

17179 *Destinies: the paperback magazine of science fiction and speculative fact, April-June, 1979.* New York: Ace Books, 1979, 320 p., paper, anth.

17180 *Destinies: the paperback magazine of science fiction and speculative fact, August-September, 1979.* New York: Ace Books, 1979, 320 p., paper, anth.

17181 *Destinies: the paperback magazine of science fiction and speculative fact, October-December, 1979.* New York: Ace Books, 1979, 320 p., paper, anth.

17182 *Destinies: the paperback magazine of science fiction and speculative fact: February-March, 1980.* New York: Ace Books, 1980, 320 p., paper, anth.

17183 *Destinies: the paperback magazine of science fiction and speculative fact: Spring edition, 1980.* New York: Ace Books, 1980, 320 p., paper, anth.

17184 *Destinies: the paperback magazine of science fiction and speculative fact: Summer edition, 1980.* New York: Ace Books, 1980, 351 p., paper, anth.

17185 *Destinies: the paperback magazine of science fiction and speculative fact: Fall edition, 1980.* New York: Ace Books, 1980, 320 p., paper, anth.

17186 *Destinies: the paperback magazine of science fiction and speculative fact, Spring edition, 1981.* New York: Ace Books, 1981, 286 p., paper, anth.

17187 *Destinies: the paperback magazine of science fiction and speculative fact: vol. 3, no. 2.* New York: Ace Books, 1981, 349 p., paper, anth. [Last volume].

17188 *Galaxy: the best of my years.* New York: Ace Books, 1980, 306 p., paper, anth.

17189 *New destinies, vol. 1, Spring 1987* / by Jim Baen. New York: Baen Books, 1987, 288 p., paper, anth.

17190 *New destinies, vol. 2, Fall 1987* / by Jim Baen. New York: Baen Books, 1987, 232 p., paper, anth.

17191 *New destinies, vol. III* / by Jim Baen. New York: Baen Books, 1988, 273 p., paper, anth.

17192 *New destinies, vol. IV* / by Jim Baen. New York: Baen Books, 1988, 287 p., paper, anth.
[*New Destinies, vol. V* does not exist].

17193 *New destinies, vol. VI* / by Jim Baen. New York: Baen Books, 1988, 284 p., paper, anth.

17194 *New destinies, vol. VII* / by Jim Baen. New York: Baen Books, 1989, 287 p., paper, anth.

17195 *New destinies, vol. VIII* / by Jim Baen. New York: Baen Books, 1989, 283 p., paper, anth.

17196 *New destinies, vol. IX* / by Jim Baen. New York: Baen Books, 1990, 286 p., paper, anth. [Last volume in series].

with Barney Cohen

17197 *The taking of Satcon Station* / by Jim Baen.... New York: Tor, A Tom Doherty Associates Book, 1982, 287 p., paper, novel.

with Jerry Pournelle

17198 *Far frontiers* / by Jim Baen.... New York: A Baen Book, 1985, 315 p., paper, anth. [Includes some nonfiction].

17199 *Far frontiers, volume II, Spring 1985* / by Jim Baen.... New York: Baen Science Fiction Books, 1985, 319 p., paper, anth. [Includes some nonfiction].

17200 *Far frontiers, Fall edition 1985 [vol. III]* / by Jim Baen.... New York: Baen Science Fiction Books, 1985, 319 p., paper, anth.

17201 *Far frontiers, Winter edition 1985 [vol. IV]* / by Jim Baen. New York: Baen Publishing Enterprises, 1986, 278 p., paper, anth.

17202 *Far frontiers, Summer edition 1986 [vol. V]* / by Jim Baen. New York: Baen Science Fiction Books, 1986, iv+284 p., paper, anth.

17203 *Far frontiers, volume VI, Fall 1986* / by Jim Baen.... New York: Baen Science Fiction Books, 1986, 270 p., paper, anth.

17204 *Far frontiers, Fall edition, 1986 [vol. VII]* / by Jim Baen.... New York: Baen Books, 1986, 279 p., paper, anth. [Last volume in series].

with Jerry Pournelle & John F. Carr

17205 *The science fiction yearbook.* New York: Baen Science Fiction Books, 1985, 344 p., cloth, anth. [Includes some nonfiction].

BAEN, Jim—SEE: Baen, James Patrick

BAGDON, Paul, *as* TONY PHILLIPS

City of glass—SEE: Turbo Cowboys: City of glass.
Night riders—SEE: Turbo Cowboys: Night riders.
Speed shift—SEE: Turbo Cowboys: Speed shift.
Super charge—SEE: Turbo Cowboys: Super charge.

17206 *Turbo Cowboys: City of glass.* New York: Ballantine Books, 1989, 140 p., paper, novel. TURBO COWBOYS #10.

17207 *Turbo Cowboys: Night riders.* New York: Ballantine Books, 1989, 134 p., paper, novel. TURBO COWBOYS #7.

17208 *Turbo Cowboys: Speed shift.* New York: Ballantine Books, 1989, 135 p., paper, novel. TURBO COWBOYS #8.

17209 *Turbo Cowboys: Super charge.* New York: Ballantine Books, 1989, 138 p., paper, novel. TURBO COWBOYS #5.

BAGLEY, Desmond, 1923-1983

17210 *The enemy.* London: Collins, 1977, 322 p., cloth, novel.

BAGLIO, Ben M.

17211 *The first Olympics.* Toronto, New York: An Edward Packard Book, Bantam Books, 1988, 116 p., paper, novel. CHOOSE YOUR OWN ADVENTURE #77.

BAGNALL, R(obert) D(avid), 1945-

17212 *Fourth connection.* London: Dennis Dobson, 1975, 160 p., cloth, coll.

BAHLKE, Valerie—SEE: Worth, Valerie

BAHRENBURG, Bruce

17213 *The creation of Dino De Laurentiis' King Kong.* New York: Pocket Books, 1976, ix+273 p., paper, nonf.

BAILEY, Albert Edward, 1871-1951

15788 *The wise man's story: a Christmas tale for dreamers.* Boston: Pilgrim Press, 1916, 54 p., cloth, story.

BAILEY, Dennis R., *with David F. Bischoff*

17214 *Tin woodman.* Garden City, NY: Doubleday & Co., 1979, 182 p., cloth, novel.

BAILEY, Gerald Earl, 1929-

17215 *The sword of Poyana.* New York: A Berkley Book, Berkley Publishing Corp., 1979, 197 p., paper, novel. SAGA OF THORGRIM #2.

17216 *Sword of the Nurlingas.* New York: A Berkley Book, Berkley Publishing Corp., 1979, 180 p., paper, novel. SAGA OF THORGRIM #1.

BAILEY, Hilary, 1936-

17217 *New worlds 8: the science fiction quarterly.* London: Sphere Books, 1975, 221 p., paper, anth.

17218 *New worlds 9.* London: Corgi Books, 1975, 219 p., paper, anth.

17219 *New worlds 10.* London: Corgi Books, 1976, 238 p., paper, anth.

17220 *A stranger to herself.* London: Macmillan, 1989, 474 p., cloth, novel.

with Charles Platt

New worlds #6—SEE: New worlds 7.
00709 *New worlds 7.* London: Sphere Books, 1974, 213 p., paper, anth.
00709A retitled: *New worlds #6.* New York: Equinox Books, Avon, 1975, 233 p., paper, anth.

*BAILEY, J(ames) O(liver), 1903-1979

BAILEY, John, 1944-

17221 *The moon baby.* Sydney, Australia: Angus & Robertson, 1978, 220 p., paper, novel.

BAILEY, Nancy

17222 *Bound for Australia.* Toronto, New York: A Byron Preiss Book, Bantam Books,

1987, 125 p., paper, novel. TIME MA-CHINE #20.

*BAILEY, Paul (Dayton), 1906-<u>1987</u>

BAILEY, Robert W.—SEE: Bailey, Robin W.

BAILEY, Robin W. [i.e., Robert Wayne Bailey], 1952-

17223 *Bloodsongs.* New York: Tor SF, A Tom Doherty Associates Book, 1986, 314 p., paper, novel. FROST #3.
17224 *Enchanter.* New York: A Byron Preiss Book, An Infocom Book, Avon Books, 1989, 315 p., paper, novel.
17225 *Frost.* New York: A Timescape Book, Pocket Books, 1983, 208 p., paper, novel. FROST #1.
17226 *The lake of fire.* New York, Toronto: A Byron Preiss Book, Bantam Books, 1989, xii+281 p., paper, novel. PHILIP JOSE FARMER'S THE DUNGEON #4.
17227 *The lost city of Zork.* New York: A Byron Preiss Book, An Infocom Book, Avon Books, 1991, 299 p., paper, novel. ZORK SERIES. [Based on the computer game, *Zork*].
17228 *Nightwatch* / by Robin Wayne Bailey. Lake Geneva, WI: TSR Inc., 1990, 311 p., paper, novel.
17229 *Skull Gate.* New York: Tor SF, A Tom Doherty Associates Book, 1985, 288 p., paper, novel. FROST #2.

BAINBRIDGE, William Sims, 1940-

17230 *Dimensions of science fiction.* Cambridge, MA & London: Harvard University Press, 1986, 278 p., cloth, nonf.
17231 *The spaceflight revolution: a sociological study.* New York: John Wiley, 1976, x+294 p., cloth, nonf.

*BAINES, Cuthbert Edward, <u>1879-</u>

BAIR, Patrick—SEE: Gurney, David

BAIRD, Newton D(anforth), 1928-

17232 *A key to Fredric Brown's wonderland: a study and an annotated bibliographical checklist.* Georgetown, CA: Talisman Literary Research, 1981, 63 p., cloth, nonf.

BAIRD, Thomas P., 1923-1990

17233 *Smart rats: a novel.* New York: Harper & Row, 1990, 199 p., cloth, novel.

17234 *Where time ends: a novel.* New York: Harper & Row, 1988, 230 p., cloth, novel.

BAKER, Betty [i.e., Betty Lou Baker Venturo], 1928-1987

17235 *Save Sirrushany! also Agotha, Princess Gwyn, and all the fearsome beasts.* New York: Macmillan, 1978, 134 p., cloth, novel.
17236 *Seven spells to farewell.* New York: Macmillan Publishing Co.; London: Collier Macmillan Publishers, 1982, 123 p., cloth, novel.

BAKER, Denys Val, 1917-1984

17237 *Cornish ghost stories, and other tales of the macabre.* London: William Kimber, 1981, 196 p., cloth, anth.
17238 *Ghosts in country houses.* London: William Kimber, 1981, 192 p., cloth, anth.
17239 *Ghosts in country villages: stories of mystery and the supernatural.* London: William Kimber, 1983, 189 p., cloth, anth.
17240 *Phantom lovers.* London: William Kimber, 1984, 206 p., cloth, anth.
17241 *Stories of fear.* London: William Kimber, 1980, 237 p., cloth, anth.
17242 *Stories of haunted inns.* London: William Kimber, 1983, 173 p., cloth, anth.
17243 *Stories of horror and suspense: an anthology.* London: William Kimber, 1977, 192 p., cloth, anth.
17244 *Stories of the macabre.* London: William Kimber, 1976, 221 p., cloth, anth.
17245 *Stories of the night: an anthology.* London: William Kimber, 1976, 204 p., cloth, anth.
17246 *Stories of the occult, and other tales of mystery.* London: William Kimber, 1978, 208 p., cloth, anth.
17247 *Stories of the supernatural.* London: William Kimber, 1979, 192 p., cloth, anth.
17248 *When churchyards yawn: an anthology of ghostly and supernatural stories.* London: William Kimber, 1982, 186 p., cloth, anth.

BAKER, Elliott, 1922-

17249 *Klynt's law: a novel.* New York: Harcourt Brace Jovanovich, 1976, 264 p., cloth, novel.

*BAKER, Emerson <u>(Woods), 1882-1934</u>

BAKER, Frank (Edgar), 1908-1982

17250 *Stories of the strange & sinister.* London: William Kimber, 1983, 186 p., cloth, coll.

BAKER, Howard, 1947-

17251 *All the gods are dead.* London: Robert Hale, 1983, 191 p., cloth, novel.

BAKER, Isadore (Lewis)

17252 *George Orwell: Animal farm.* London: James Brodie, 1961, 71 p., paper, nonf.

BAKER, Jane, *with Pip Baker*

17253 *Doctor Who: Race against time.* New York: Ballantine Books, 1986, [127] p., paper, novel. FIND YOUR FATE—DOCTOR WHO #6.
17254 *Doctor Who: Terror of the Vervoids.* London: W. H. Allen & Co., 1987, 144 p., cloth, tele. DOCTOR WHO #125.
17255 *Doctor Who: The mark of the Rani.* London: W. H. Allen, 1986, 135 p., cloth, tele. DOCTOR WHO #107.
17256 *Doctor Who: The ultimate foe.* London: W. H. Allen & Co., 1988, 126 p., cloth, tele. DOCTOR WHO #131.
17257 *Doctor Who: Time and the Rani.* London: W. H. Allen & Co., 1987, 143 p., cloth, tele. DOCTOR WHO #127.
 The mark of the Rani—SEE: Doctor Who: The mark of the Rani.
 Race against time—SEE: Doctor Who: Race against time.
 Terror of the Vervoids—SEE: Doctor Who: Terror of the Vervoids.
 Time and the Rani—SEE: Doctor Who: Time and the Rani.
 The ultimate foe—SEE: Doctor Who: The ultimate foe.
17258 *Watt on Earth.* London: BBC Books, 1991, 144 p., paper, novel.

BAKER, Mike

17259 *Adam!* London, Sydney: Mills & Boon, 1977, 96 p., paper, novel.

BAKER, Nick

17260 *Split second.* London: Collins, 1989, 176 p., cloth, novel.

BAKER, Nina Brown, 1888-1957

15789 *Inca gold.* Boston: W. A. Wilde Co., 1938, 320 p., cloth, novel.

BAKER, Pip, *with Jane Baker*

17253 *Doctor Who: Race against time.* New York: Ballantine Books, 1986, [127] p., paper, novel. FIND YOUR FATE—DOCTOR WHO #6.
17254 *Doctor Who: Terror of the Vervoids.* London: W. H. Allen & Co., 1987, 144 p., cloth, tele. DOCTOR WHO #125.
17255 *Doctor Who: The mark of the Rani.* London: W. H. Allen, 1986, 135 p., cloth, tele. DOCTOR WHO #107.
17256 *Doctor Who: The ultimate foe.* London: W. H. Allen & Co., 1988, 126 p., cloth, tele. DOCTOR WHO #131.
17257 *Doctor Who: Time and the Rani.* London: W. H. Allen & Co., 1987, 143 p., cloth, tele. DOCTOR WHO #127.
 The mark of the Rani—SEE: Doctor Who: The mark of the Rani.
 Race against time—SEE: Doctor Who: Race against time.
 Terror of the Vervoids—SEE: Doctor Who: Terror of the Vervoids.
 Time and the Rani—SEE: Doctor Who: Time and the Rani.
 The ultimate foe—SEE: Doctor Who: The ultimate foe.
17258 *Watt on Earth.* London: BBC Books, 1991, 144 p., paper, novel.

BAKER, Robert S., 1940-

17261 *Brave new world: history, science, and dystopia.* Boston: Twayne Publishers, 1990, x+155 p., cloth, nonf.

BAKER, Scott (MacMartin), 1947-

17262 *Dhampire.* New York: A Timescape Book, Pocket Books, 1982, 260 p., paper, novel.
17263 *Drink the fire from the flames.* New York: Tor SF, A Tom Doherty Associates Book, 1987, 343 p., paper, novel. ASHLU CYCLE #3.
17264 *Firedance.* New York: Tor SF, A Tom Doherty Associates Book, 1986, 380 p., paper, novel. ASHLU CYCLE #2.
17265 *Nightchild.* New York: Berkley Publishing Corp., 1979, 273 p., cloth, novel. ASHLU CYCLE #1.
17266 *Nightchild.* New York: A Timescape Book, Pocket Books, 1983, 255 p., paper, novel. ASHLU CYCLE #1. [Revised edition].

17267 *Symbiote's crown.* New York: A Berkley Book, Berkley Publishing Corp., 1978, 214 p., paper, novel.

17268 *Webs.* New York: Tor Horror, A Tom Doherty Associates Book, 1989, 310 p., paper, novel.

BAKER, Sharon (Sklensky), 1938-1991

17269 *Burning tears of Sassurum.* New York: Avon Books, 1988, 280 p., paper, novel. NAPHAR #3.

17270 *Journey to Membliar.* New York: Avon Books, 1987, 247 p., paper, novel. NAPHAR #2.

17271 *Quarreling, they met the dragon.* New York: Avon, 1984, 268 p., paper, novel. NAPHAR #1.

BAKER, W(illiam Arthur) Howard, 1925-1991

00751 *The Guardians.* London: Mayflower Books, 1967, 144 p., paper, novel. GUARDIANS SERIES.

with various co-authors as PETER SAXON

12719 *Black Honey.* London: Mayflower Books, 1968, 157 p., paper, novel. [Sole author].

12721 *The curse of Rathlaw.* New York: Lancer Books, 1968, 190 p., paper, novel. GUARDIANS SERIES. [With Martin Thomas].

12722 *Dark ways to death.* London: Howard Baker, 1968, 176 p., cloth, novel. GUARDIANS #2. [With Wilfred G. McNeilly].

00753 *The darkest night.* London: Mayflower Books, 1966, 157 p., paper, novel. [With Wilfred G. McNeilly].

12723 *The disorientated man.* London: Mayflower Books, 1966, 126 p., paper, novel. [With Stephen D. Frances].

12723A retitled: *Scream and scream again.* New York: Paperback Library, 1967, 158 p., paper, novel. [With Stephen D. Frances].

12725 *The haunting of Alan Mais.* New York: Berkley Books, 1969, 143 p., paper, novel. GUARDIANS #3. [With Wilfred G. McNeilly].

12724 *The killing bone.* New York: Berkley Books, 1969, 159 p., paper, novel. GUARDIANS #1. [Sole author].

Scream and scream again—SEE: *The disorientated man.*

00755 *The Torturer.* London: Mayflower Books, 1966, 159 p., paper, novel. [With Wilfred G. McNeilly].

12728 *Vampire's moon.* New York: Belmont Books, 1970, 176 p., paper, novel. [Sole author].

BAKER, W. J.—SEE: Churchward, John

BAL, Sant Singh, 1942-

17274 *George Orwell: the ethical imagination.* New Delhi: Gulab Vazirani, Arnold-Heinemann, 1981, 254 p., cloth, nonf.

BALABAN, Bob, 1945-

17275 *Close encounters of the third kind diary.* New York: A Paradise Press Book, 1978, 177 p., paper, nonf.

BALCH, Frank, 1880-1937

35633 *A submarine tour.* New York: Broadway Publishing Co., 1905, 179 p., cloth, novel.

BALDICK, Chris(topher Giles), 1954-

17276 *In Frankenstein's shadow: myth, monstrosity, and nineteenth-century writing.* Oxford, England: Oxford University Press, 1987, 207 p., cloth, nonf.

BALDRY, Cherith

17277 *The book and the phoenix.* Eastbourne, East Sussex, England: Kingsway Publications, 1989, 160 p., paper, novel. STORIES OF SIX WORLDS #1.

17277A retitled: *A rush of golden wings.* Wheaton, IL: Crossway Books, 1991, 160 p., paper, novel. STORIES OF SIX WORLDS #1.

17278 *Hostage of the sea.* Eastbourne, East Sussex, England: Kingsway Publications, 1990, 158 p., paper, coll. STORIES OF SIX WORLDS #2.

A rush of golden wings—SEE: *The book and the phoenix.*

*BALDWIN, Bee [i.e., Beatrice Lillian Baldwin]

BALDWIN, Bill [i.e., Merl William Baldwin Jr.], 1935-

17279 *Galactic convoy.* New York: Popular Library, 1987, 332 p., paper, novel. HELMSMAN #2.

17280 *The helmsman.* New York: Popular Library, 1985, 311 p., paper, novel. HELMSMAN #1. [Cover byline gives author's name as Merl Baldwin].

17281 *The mercenaries*. New York: Warner Books, 1991, 313 p., paper, novel. HELMSMAN #4.

17282 *The trophy*. New York: Popular Library, 1990, 315 p., paper, novel. HELMSMAN #3.

BALDWIN, Merl—SEE: Baldwin, Bill

BALE, G. F., pseud.—SEE: Wellbrock, Gladys Bale & Cox, Patricia Bale

BALFOUR, B. Gabriel

17283 *Escalator down*. Appalachia, VA: Young Publications, 1965, 159 p., paper, novel.

*BALINT, Emery, 1892-1982

BALIOL, Alexander de, 1953-

17284 *The magefire*. London: Headline, 1990, 436 p., cloth, novel. AMULETS OF DARKNESS #1.

BALIZET, Carol, 1933-

17285 *The seven last years*. Lincoln, VA: Chosen Books, 1978, 376 p., cloth, novel.

BALL, Brian (Neville), 1932-

The evil at Monteine—SEE: Witch finder: The evil at Monteine.
The mark of the beast—SEE: Witchfinder: The mark of the beast.

17286 *The quest for Queenie*. London: Macdonald & Co., 1988, 95 p., cloth, novel.

17287 *The space guardians*. London: Futura Publications, An Orbit Book, 1975, 142 p., paper, tele. SPACE: 1999 #3.

17288 *The Starbuggy: a space adventure*. London: Heinemann, 1983, 127 p., cloth, novel.

17289 *Stone age magic*. London: Antelope Books, Hamilton Children's Books, 1989, [96] p., cloth, novel.

17290 *Truant from space*. London: Antelope Books, Hamilton, 1985, 82 p., cloth, novel.

17291 *Witch finder: The evil at Monteine* / by Brian N. Ball. St Albans, Hertfordshire, England: Mayflower, 1977, 171 p., paper, novel. WITCHFINDER #2.

17292 *Witchfinder: the mark of the beast*. St Albans, Hertfordshire, England: Mayflower, 1976, 156 p., paper, novel. WITCHFINDER #1.

BALL, Donna, 1951-

17293 *A cry in the woods*. New York: Pinnacle Books, Windsor Publishing Corp., 1991, 319 p., paper, novel.

as REBECCA FLANDERS

17294 *Earthbound*. Toronto, New York: Harlequin Books, 1990, 252 p., paper, novel.

BALL, Duncan, 1941-

17295 *The ghost and the gogglebox*. London, Sydney: Angus & Robertson, 1984, 85 p., cloth, novel. GHOST #1.

17296 *The ghost and the gory story*. London, Sydney: Angus & Robertson, 1987, 110 p., cloth, novel. GHOST #2.

BALL, Florence E.

17297 *Zero plus ten*. New York: Exposition Press, 1965, 131 p., cloth, novel.

*BALL, John (Dudley Jr.), 1911-1988

BALL, Margaret (Elizabeth), 1947-

17298 *Flameweaver*. Riverdale, NY: Baen Fantasy, 1991, 374 p., paper, novel.

17299 *The shadow gate*. Riverdale, NY: Baen Fantasy, 1991, 346 p., paper, novel.

BALLANTYNE, David (Watt), 1924-1986

17300 *The penfriend*. Palmerston North, New Zealand: Dunmore Press; London: Robert Hale, 1980, 223 p., cloth, novel.

BALLARD, J(ames) G(raham), 1930-

17301 *The atrocity exhibition*. San Francisco: Re/Search Publications, 1990, 127 p., cloth, novel. [Expanded edition].

17302 *The best of J. G. Ballard*. London: Futura Publications, An Orbit Book, 1977, 411 p., paper, coll. [Cover title: *The best science fiction of J. G. Ballard*].
The best science fiction of J. G. Ballard—SEE: The best of J. G. Ballard.

17303 *The best short stories of J. G. Ballard*. New York: Holt, Rinehart & Winston, 1978, ix+302 p., cloth, coll.

17304 *The crystal world; Crash; Concrete island*. New York: Book-of-the-Month Club, 1991, 610 p., paper, coll.

17305 *The four-dimensional nightmare*. Harmondsworth, Middlesex, England: Penguin Books, 1977, 210 p., paper, coll. [Two stories are replaced in this edition].

17305A retitled: *The voices of time.* London: J. M. Dent & Sons, 1984, 197 p., paper, coll.

17306 *Hello America.* London: Jonathan Cape, 1981, 224 p., cloth, novel.

17307 *Low-flying aircraft, and other stories.* London: Jonathan Cape, 1976, 191 p., cloth, coll.

17308 *Memories of the space age.* Sauk City, WI: Arkham House Publishers, 1988, 216 p., cloth, coll.

17309 *Myths of the near future.* London: Jonathan Cape, 1982, 205 p., cloth, coll.

17310 *News from the sun.* London: Interzone, 1982, 180 p., paper, nonf. [Limited to 750 copies].

17311 *Running wild.* London: Hutchinson, 1988, 72 p., cloth, novel.

17312 *The unlimited dream company.* London: Jonathan Cape, 1979, 223 p., cloth, novel.

17313 *The Venus hunters.* London, Toronto: A Panther Book, Granada, 1980, 144 p., paper, coll.

17314 *The voices of time.* London: Victor Gollancz, 1985, 197 p., cloth, coll. [Contents differ from earlier collections of the same title].

The voices of time—SEE: *The four-dimensional nightmare.*

17315 *War fever.* London: Collins, 1990, 176 p., cloth, coll.

BALLARD, S. M.

17316 *Fool's gold.* New York: Ballantine Books, 1988, 122 p., paper, novel. G.I. JOE #3.

17317 *G.I. Joe: Operation: killer comet.* New York: Ballantine Books, 1987, 89 p., paper, novel. FIND YOUR FATE—G.I. JOE #18.

Operation: killer comet—SEE: *G.I. Joe: Operation: killer comet.*

BALLENTINE, Lee (Kenney), 1954-

17318 *Poly: new speculative writing.* Mountain View, CA: Ocean View Press, 1989, 319 p., cloth, anth. [Includes some nonfiction and verse].

BALLINGER, Bill S. [i.e. William Sanborn Ballinger], 1912-1980

17319 *The ultimate warrior: a novel.* New York: Warner Books, 1975, 142 p., paper, movie.

BALLINGER, William S.—SEE: Ballinger, Bill

*BALLOU, Arthur W., 1915-1981

BALUN, Chas. [i.e., Charles Balun]

17320 *The gore score: ultraviolent horror in the '80s.* Albany, NY: FantaCo Enterprises, 1987, unpaginated, paper, nonf.

BALZAC, Honoré de, 1799-1850

15790 *The quest of the absolute; Séraphita.* New York: McKinlay, Stone & MacKenzie, 1915, 341 p., cloth, coll.

as HORACE DE SAINT-AUBIN

17321 *The Centenarian; or, The two Béringhelds.* New York: Arno Press, 1976, vi+454 p., cloth, novel. [Translation by George Edgar Slusser of *Le centenaire; or, Les deux Béringheld*].

BANDY, (Eugene) Franklin, 1914-1987

17322 *Athena.* New York: Tor, A Tom Doherty Associates Book, 1987, 309 p., cloth, novel.

17323 *The farewell party.* New York: Charter, 1980, 313 p., paper, novel.

BANEHAM, Sam, 1947-

17324 *Cloud of desolation.* Dublin: Wolfhound Press, 1982, 302 p., cloth, novel.

BANERJI, Sara (Ann), 1932-

17325 *Cobwebwalking.* London: Victor Gollancz, 1986, 176 p., cloth, novel.

17326 *The tea-planter's daughter.* London: Victor Gollancz, 1988, 190 p., cloth, novel.

BANIS, Victor J.—SEE: Alexander, Jan

*BANISTER, Manly (Miles), 1914-1986

BANKS, David

Cyberman—SEE: *Doctor Who: Cybermen.*

17327 *Doctor Who: Cybermen.* London: W. H. Allen & Co., 1990, 144 p., cloth, nonf. DOCTOR WHO SERIES.

BANKS, Iain M(enzies), 1954-

17328 *The bridge* / by Iain Banks. Basingstoke, Hamptonshire, England: Macmillan, 1986, 259 p., cloth, novel.

17329 *Canal dreams* / by Iain Banks. London: Macmillan, 1989, 198 p., cloth, novel.

26048 *Cleaning up.* Birmingham, England: Birmingham Science Fiction Group, 1987, 20 p., paper, story?

17330 *Consider Phlebas.* London: Macmillan, 1987, 471 p., cloth, novel. THE CULTURE #1.

17331 *The player of games.* London: Macmillan, 1988, 309 p., cloth, novel. THE CULTURE #2.

17332 *The state of the art.* Willimantic, CT: Mark V. Ziesing, 1989, 136 p., cloth, novel. THE CULTURE #3.

17333 *The state of the art.* London: Orbit, 1991, 182 p., cloth, coll. [Includes the novel plus additional stories].

17334 *Use of weapons.* London: Orbit, 1990, 371 p., cloth, novel. THE CULTURE #4.

17335 *Walking on glass* / by Iain Banks. London: Macmillan, 1985, 239 p., cloth, novel.

BANKS, John, *with Richard Covell & Lee Clarke & Jay Clarke as* MICHAEL SLADE

17336 *Ghoul.* New York: Beech Tree Books, 1987, 417 p., cloth, novel.

BANKS, Lynne Reid—SEE: Reid Banks, Lynne

BANKS, Michael A. [pseud. of Alan Gould], 1951-

17337 *Understanding science fiction.* Morristown, NJ, Glenview, IL: Silver Burdett Co., 1982, xi+180 p., paper, anth. [Includes some nonfiction].

with Dean R. Lambe

17338 *The Odysseus solution.* New York: Baen Science Fiction Books, 1986, 279 p., paper, novel.

with Mack Reynolds

17339 *Joe Mauser, mercenary from tomorrow* / by Michael Banks... New York: Baen Science Fiction Books, 1986, 280 p., paper, novel. JOE MAUSER #1-2. [Previously published in different form as "Mercenary" and "Frigid Fracas" (i.e., *Mercenary from tomorrow* and *The earth war* in book form)].

17340 *Sweet dreams, sweet princes* / by Michael Banks... New York: Baen Books, 1986, 269 p., paper, novel. JOE MAUSER #4. [Revised edition of *Time gladiator* (see #12183)].

BANKS, R(onald) A(lfred), 1930-

17341 *Ten ghost stories.* London: Hodder & Stoughton, 1978, xv+141 p., paper, anth.

17342 *Ten science fiction stories.* London: Hodder & Stoughton, 1977, 156 p., paper, anth.

BANKS, Ramond E.—SEE: Banks, Raymond E.

BANKS, Raymond E., 1918-

17343 *Daryk, Skull Keep of the primal clans.* Wilmington, DE: Orchid Publishing Co., 1978, 192 p., paper, novel.

17343A retitled: *The savage princess.* Encino, CA: World-Wide Publishing Co., 1980, 192 p., paper, novel. [Bound with *Penetrators of time* / by Merlin Kaye].

17344 *The moon rapers* / by Ramond E. Banks. Encino, CA: World-Wide Publishing Co., 1980, 190 p., paper, novel.

The savage princess—SEE: *Daryk, Skull Keep of the primal clans.*

BANNISTER, Jo, 1951-

17345 *A cactus garden.* London: Robert Hale, 1983, 203 p., cloth, novel.

17346 *The matrix.* London: Robert Hale, 1981, 191 p., cloth, novel.

17347 *The winter plain.* London: Robert Hale, 1982, 191 p., cloth, novel.

BANNON, Mark, pseud.—SEE: King, Albert

BARAKET, Mark

17348 *Scream gems.* New York: Drake Press, 1977, 143 p., cloth, nonf.

BARBA, Harry, 1922-

17349 *The day the world went sane.* Saratoga Springs, NY: Harian Creative Press, 1979, 140 p., cloth, coll.

17350 *Round trip to Byzantium.* Metroland-Ballston Spa, NY: Harian Creative Press, 1985, 371 p., cloth, novel.

***BARBEAU, Clayton C(harles), 1930-**

BARBER, Dulan—SEE: Brookes, Owen

BARBER, Richard (William), 1941-

17351 *The Arthurian legends: an illustrated anthology.* Woodbridge, Suffolk, England:

Boydell Press, 1979, 224 p., cloth, anth.
[Includes some nonfiction].

BARBERO, Yves—SEE: François, Yves Regis

BARBET, Pierre [pseud. of Claude Pierre Marie Avice], 1925-

17352 *Cosmic crusaders: Two complete novels: Baphomet's meteor; Cosmic crusade.* New York: DAW Books, 1980, 286 p., paper, coll. BAPHOMET #1-2. [Translation by Bernard Kay of *L'Empire du Baphomet*; and by C. J. Cherryh of *Croisade stellaire*].

17353 *The emperor of Eridanus.* New York: DAW Books, 1983, 160 p., paper, novel. ERIDANUS #2. [Translation by Stanley Hochman of *L'Empereur d'Éridan*].

17354 *The enchanted planet.* New York: DAW Books, 1975, 159 p., paper, novel. [Translation by C. J. Richards of *La planète enchantée*].

17355 *The Joan-of-Arc replay.* New York: DAW Books, 1978, 189 p., paper, novel. [Translation by Stanley Hochman of *Liane de Noldaz*]

17356 *The Napoleons of Eridanus.* New York: DAW Books, 1976, 157 p., paper, novel. ERIDANUS #1. [Translation by Stanley Hochman of *Les grognards d'Éridan*].

*BARBOR, H(erbert) R(eginald), <u>1893-1933</u>

BARBOUR, Alan G., 1933-

17357 *Fantastic: a new collection of scenes from all-time favorite films featuring Boris Karloff.* [S.l.]: Screen Facts Press, 1971, [49] p., paper, nonf.

17358 *Lugosi.* [S.l.]: Screen Facts Press, 1971, [48] p., paper, nonf.

with James Robert Parish & Alvin H. Marill

17359 *Karloff.* Kew Gardens, NY: Cinefax, 1969, [64] p., paper, nonf.

BARBOUR, Douglas (Fleming), 1940-

17360 *Worlds out of words: the SF novels of Samuel R. Delany.* Frome, Somerset, England: Bran's Head, 1979, 171 p., paper, nonf.

with Phyllis Gotlieb

17361 *Tesseracts².* Victoria, British Columbia, Canada: A Tesseract Book, Porcépic Books, 1987, 295 p., paper, anth.

BARBREE, Jay

17362 *Pilot error: a novel.* New York: Warner Paperback Library, 1975, 158 p., paper, tele. SIX MILLION DOLLAR MAN #4.

BARCLAY, Alan [pseud. of George B. Tait], 1910-

17363 *The city and the desert.* London: Robert Hale, 1976, 190 p., cloth, novel.

17364 *The cruel years of winter.* London: Robert Hale, 1978, 192 p., cloth, novel.

17365 *The guardian at sunset.* London: Robert Hale, 1979, 188 p., cloth, novel.

17366 *No magic carpet.* London: Robert Hale, 1976, 171 p., cloth, novel.

BARCLAY, Ben

17367 *The empty palace.* London: Arthur Barker, 1976, 187 p., cloth, novel.

BARCLAY, (A.) Bernice, 1922-

17368 *Guide to reference sources of science fiction materials in the collections of San Diego State University Library.* San Diego, CA: San Diego State University Library, 1978, iv+39 p., paper, nonf.

17369 *Guide to reference sources of science fiction materials in the collections of the SDSUL, 2nd ed.* San Diego, CA: San Diego State University Library, 1981, xii+51 p., paper, nonf.

BARCLAY, Glen St John, 1930-

17370 *Anatomy of horror: the masters of occult fiction.* London: Weidenfeld & Nicolson, 1978, 144 p., paper, nonf.

*BARJAVEL, René (Gustave Henri), 1911-<u>1985</u>

BARK, Conrad Voss—SEE: Voss Bark, Conrad

BARKER, Clive, 1952-

17371 *The books of blood.* Los Angeles: Scream/Press, 1985, xiv+455 p., cloth, coll. BOOKS OF BLOOD #1-3. [Winner of the World Fantasy Award for Best Fantasy Anthology/Collection, 1984 (1985)].
Books of blood V—SEE: Clive Barker's Books of blood, volume V.
Books of blood VI—SEE: Clive Barker's Books of blood, volume VI.
Books of blood, volume I—SEE: Clive Barker's Books of blood, volume I.

Books of blood, volume II—SEE: Clive Barker's Books of blood, volume II.

Books of blood, volume III—SEE: Clive Barker's Books of blood, volume III.

Books of blood, volume IV—SEE: Clive Barker's Books of blood, volume IV.

17372 *Books of blood, volumes IV, V & VI.* London: Weidenfeld & Nicolson, 1988, 452 p., cloth, coll. BOOKS OF BLOOD #4-6.

Books of blood, volume V—SEE: Clive Barker's Books of blood, volume V.

Books of blood, volume VI—SEE: Clive Barker's Books of blood, volume VI.

17373 *Cabal.* New York: Poseidon Press, 1988, 377 p., cloth, coll.

17373A retitled: *Cabal: the nightbreed.* Toronto: A Collins Paperback, 1989, 268 p., paper, novel. [Drops the short stories included in the US edition].

17374 *Clive Barker's Books of blood, volume I.* London: Sphere Books, 1984, 149 p., paper, coll. BOOKS OF BLOOD #1. [Winner of the World Fantasy Award for Best Fantasy Anthology/Collection, 1984 (1985)].

17375 *Clive Barker's Books of blood, volume II.* London: Sphere Books, 1984, 150 p., paper, coll. BOOKS OF BLOOD #2. [Winner of the World Fantasy Award for Best Fantasy Anthology/Collection, 1984 (1985)].

17376 *Clive Barker's Books of blood, volume III.* London: Sphere Books, 1984, 182 p., paper, coll. BOOKS OF BLOOD #3. [Winner of the World Fantasy Award for Best Fantasy Anthology/Collection, 1984 (1985)].

17377 *Clive Barker's Books of blood, volume IV.* London: Sphere Books, 1985, 151 p., paper, coll. BOOKS OF BLOOD #4.

17377A retitled: *The inhuman condition: tales of terror.* New York: Poseidon Press, 1986, 220 p., cloth, coll. BOOKS OF BLOOD #4. [Abridged edition].

17378 *Clive Barker's Books of blood, volume V.* London: Sphere Books, 1985, 149 p., paper, coll. BOOKS OF BLOOD #5.

17378A retitled: *In the flesh.* New York: Poseidon Press, 1986, 187 p., cloth, coll. BOOKS OF BLOOD #4.

17378B retitled: *The books of blood V.* Los Angeles: Scream/Press, 1988, 159 p., cloth, coll.

17379 *Clive Barker's Books of blood, volume VI.* London: Sphere Books, 1985, 152 p., paper, coll. BOOKS OF BLOOD #6.

17379A retitled: *Books of blood VI.* Los Angeles: Scream/Press, 1991, 158 p., cloth, coll.

17380 *Clive Barker's Nightbreed: the making of the film.* London: Fontana, 1990, 233 p., paper, nonf. anth.

17381 *The damnation game.* London: Weidenfeld & Nicolson, 1985, 374 p., cloth, novel.

17382 *The great and secret show: the first book of the art.* London: Collins, 1989, 689 p., cloth, novel. BOOK OF THE ART #1.

17383 *The hell-bound heart.* London: Fontana, 1991, 128 p., paper, novel.

17384 *Imajica.* London: HarperCollinsPublishers, 1991, 854 p., cloth, novel.

In the flesh—SEE: Clive Barker's books of blood, volume V.

The inhuman condition—SEE: Clive Barker's books of blood, volume IV.

Nightbreed—SEE: Clive Barker's Nightbreed.

17385 *The nightbreed chronicles.* London: Titan, 1990, 80 p., paper, nonf.

17386 *Weaveworld.* London: Collins, 1987, 721 p., cloth, novel.

with Fred Burke

17387 *Clive Barker, illustrator.* Forestville, CA: Arcane/Eclipse Books, 1991, iv+124 p., cloth, art. [Edited by Steve Niles].

with Stephen Jones

17388 *Clive Barker's Shadows in Eden.* Novato, CA, Lancaster, PA: Underwood-Miller, 1991, xv+465 p., cloth, nonf. anth. [Includes material by and about Barker; winner of the Bram Stoker Award for Best Horror Non-Fiction Book, 1991 (1992)].

with Paul Mikol

Hardshell—SEE: Night visions 4.

Night fears—SEE: Night visions 4.

Night visions: Hardshell—SEE: Night visions 4.

17389 *Night visions 4: all original stories.* Arlington Heights, IL: Dark Harvest, 1987, 275 p., cloth, anth.

17389A retitled: *Night visions: Hardshell.* New York: Berkley Books, 1988, 279 p., paper, anth.

17389B retitled: *Night fears.* London: Headline, 1990, 308 p., paper, anth.

BARKER, D(onald) A(ndrew), 1947-

17390 *A matter of evolution.* London: Robert Hale, 1975, 188 p., cloth, novel.

17391 *A question of reality.* London: Robert Hale, 1981, 205 p., cloth, novel.

BARKER, Dennis (Malcolm), 1929-

17392 *Winston three three three.* London: Grafton, 1987, 267 p., paper, novel.

BARKER, M. A. R. [i.e. Muhammad Abd al-Rahman Barker], 1929-

17393 *The book of ebon bindings.* Minneapolis, MN: Imperium Publishing Co., 1978, vi+83 p., paper, fiction.
17394 *Deeds of the ever-glorious: histories of the Tsolyani legions.* St. Paul, MN: Adventure Games, 1981, v+102 p., paper, fiction.
17395 *Flamesong.* New York: DAW Books, 1985, 412 p., paper, novel. TEKUMEL #2.
17396 *The man of gold.* New York: DAW Books, 1984, 367 p., paper, novel. TEKUMEL #1. [Based on the game, *Empire of the Petal Throne*].
17397 *The Tsolyani language.* St. Paul, MN: Adventure Games, 1978, iv+129 p. in 2 v., paper, nonf.

BARKER, Muhammad Abd al-Rahman—SEE: Barker, M. A. R.

BARKER, Nicholas (John), 1932- , *with Anthony Masters*

17398 *Red ice.* London: Constable, 1986, 250 p., cloth, novel.

***BARKER, Nugent, 1888-**

BARKER, Thomas W.

17399 *Five for infinity.* Chatsworth, CA: Major Books, 1976, 175 p., paper, novel.

BARKER, Wade, house pseud.—SEE: Meyers, Richard

BARLING, Tom

with Mary Shelley

17400 *Frankenstein.* London: Corgi Books, 1976, 96 p., paper, novel. [Adapted from the original novel by Shelley].

with Bram Stoker

17401 *Dracula.* London: Corgi Books, 1976, 96 p., paper, novel. [Adapted from the original novel by Stoker].

with Jules Verne

17402 *20,000 leagues under the sea.* London: Piccolo Adventure Library, 1977, 125 p., paper, novel. [Adapted from the original novel by Verne].

BARLOW, R(obert) H(ayward), 1918-1951

17403 *Annals of the jinns.* West Warwick, RI: Necronomicon Press, 1978, 30 p., paper, coll.
17404 *A dim-remembered story.* West Warwick, RI: Necronomicon Press, 1980, [20] p., paper, story.

with H. P. Lovecraft

17405 *Collapsing cosmoses.* West Warwick, RI: Necronomicon Press, 1977?, [7] p., paper, story.
17406 *The night ocean.* West Warwick, RI: Necronomicon Press, 1982, [23] p., paper, story.

BARLOWE, Wayne Douglas, 1958-

17407 *Expedition: being an account in words and artwork of the 2358 A.D. voyage to Darwin IV.* New York: Workman Publishing, 1991, 192 p., cloth, fiction/art.

with Ian Summers & Beth Meacham

17408 *Barlowe's Guide to extraterrestrials.* New York: Workman Publishing, 1979, 112+[32] p., cloth, art. [Meacham's contribution is uncredited; winner of the *Locus* Award for Best Art Book, 1979 (1980)].
17409 *Barlowe's Guide to extraterrestrials, 2nd ed.* New York: Workman Publishing, 1987, 112+[32] p., cloth, art.
    Guide to extraterrestrials—SEE: Barlowe's Guide to extraterrestrials.

BARNARD, Keith

17410 *The Betz cell.* London: Souvenir Press, 1991, 307 p., cloth, novel.
17411 *Embryo.* London: Souvenir Press, 1990, 298 p., cloth, novel.

BARNARD, Marjorie Faith—SEE: Eldershaw, M. Barnard

BARNES, Adrienne Martine- —SEE: Martine-Barnes, Adrienne

BARNES, John (Allen), 1957-

17412 *How to build a future.* Eugene, OR: Writer's Notebook Press, Pulphouse Publishing, 1991, 34 p., paper, nonf.

17413 *Isaac Asimov presents Sin of origin.* New York: Congdon & Weed, 1988, viii+269 p., cloth, novel.

17414 *Isaac Asimov presents The man who pulled down the sky.* New York: Congdon & Weed, 1986, xv+256 p., cloth, novel.
The man who pulled down the sky—SEE: *Isaac Asimov presents The man who pulled down the sky.*

17415 *Orbital resonance.* New York: Tor, A Tom Doherty Associates Book, 1991, 214 p., cloth, novel.
Sin of origin—SEE: *Isaac Asimov presents Sin of origin.*

BARNES, Julian (Patrick), 1946-

17416 *A history of the world in 10 ½ chapters.* London: Jonathan Cape, 1989, 309 p., cloth, novel.

17417 *Staring at the sun.* London: London Limited Editions, 1986, 195 p., cloth, novel.

BARNES, Linda (Joyce Appelblatt), 1949-

17418 *Blood will have blood.* New York: Avon, 1982, 191 p., paper, novel.

BARNES, Megan

17419 *Be careful what you wish for.* New York, Toronto: Scholastic Inc., 1988, 169 p., paper, novel. TEEN WITCH #2.

17420 *Gone with the witch.* New York, Toronto: Scholastic Inc., 1989, 166 p., paper, novel. TEEN WITCH #3.
Lucky 13—SEE: *Teen witch: Lucky 13.*

17421 *Teen witch: Lucky 13.* New York, Toronto: Scholastic Inc., 1988, 187 p., paper, novel. TEEN WITCH #1.

17422 *Witch switch.* New York, Toronto: Scholastic Inc., 1989, 172 p., paper, novel. TEEN WITCH #4.

BARNES, Myra Edwards, 1933-

17423 *Linguistics and languages in science fiction-fantasy.* New York: Arno Press, 1975, vi+196 p., cloth, nonf.

BARNES, (Keith) Rory, 1946- , *with Damien Broderick*

17424 *Valencies.* St. Lucia, Queensland, Australia, New York: University of Queensland Press, 1983, 230 p., paper, novel.

BARNES, Stephen E.—SEE: Barnes, Steven

BARNES, Steven [i.e., Stephen Emory Barnes], 1952-

17425 *Gorgon child.* New York: Tor SF, A Tom Doherty Associates Book, 1989, 345 p., paper, novel.

17426 *The Kundalini equation.* New York: Tor SF, A Tom Doherty Associates Book, 1986, 348 p., paper, novel.

17427 *Streetlethal.* New York: Ace Science Fiction Books, 1983, 310 p., paper, novel.

with Larry Niven

17428 *Achilles' choice.* New York: Tor, A Tom Doherty Associates Book, 1991, 214 p., cloth, novel.

17429 *The Barsoom project.* New York: Ace Books, 1989, 340 p., paper, novel. DREAM PARK #2.

17430 *The beehive game.* London & Sydney: Pan Books, 1991, 320 p., paper, novel.

17431 *The descent of Anansi.* New York: Tor, A Tom Doherty Associates Book, 1982, 278 p., paper, novel.

17432 *Dream Park.* Huntington Woods, MI: Phantasia Press, 1981, 434 p., cloth, novel. DREAM PARK #1. [Limited to 600 copies].

17433 *Dream Park: The voodoo game.* London & Sydney: Pan Books, 1991, 350 p., paper, novel. DREAM PARK #3.
The voodoo game—SEE: *Dream Park: The voodoo game.*

with Larry Niven & Jerry Pournelle

17434 *The legacy of Heorot.* London: Victor Gollancz, 1987, 352 p., cloth, novel. HEOROT SERIES.

BARNETT, Lisa A., *with Melissa Scott*

17435 *The armor of light.* New York: Baen Fantasy, 1988, 504 p., paper, novel.

BARNETT, Paul—SEE: Grant, John

BARNEY, pseud.

17436 *1876.* [S.l: s.n.], 1972, p., paper?, novel. [No other information].

*BARNEY, Natalie Clifford, <u>1876</u>-1972

BARNISH, Valerie L(ewis)

17437   *Notes on Ray Bradbury's science fiction.* London: Methuen Paperbacks, 1978, 88 p., paper, nonf.

BARNWELL, William (Curtis), 1943-

17438   *The Blessing Papers.* New York: Pocket Books, 1980, 354 p., paper, novel. BLESSING TRILOGY #1.
17439   *Imram.* New York: A Timescape Book, Pocket Books, 1981, 261 p., paper, novel. BLESSING TRILOGY #2.
17440   *The Sigma curve.* New York: A Timescape Book, Pocket Books, 1981, 239 p., paper, novel. BLESSING TRILOGY #3.

BARON, Nick, pseud.—SEE: Ciencin, Scott

BARR, Donald, 1921-

17441   *A planet in arms.* New York: Fawcett Crest, 1981, 285 p., paper, novel.

BARR, Elisabeth

17442   *Song of the black witch.* New York: Playboy Paperbacks, 1981, 302 p., paper, novel.

BARR, George, 1937-

17443   *Upon the winds of yesterday, and other explorations: the paintings of George Barr.* West Kingston, RI: Donald M. Grant, Publisher, 1976, 140 p., cloth, art.

BARR, Marleen S(andra), 1953-

17444   *Alien to femininity: speculative fiction and feminist theory.* New York, London: Greenwood Press, 1987, xxv+189 p., cloth, nonf. CONTRIBUTIONS TO THE STUDY OF SCIENCE FICTION AND FANTASY #27.
17445   *Future females: a critical anthology.* Bowling Green, OH: Bowling Green State University Popular Press, 1981, 191 p., cloth, nonf. anth.

with Ruth Salvaggio & Richard Law

17446   *Suzy McKee Charnas; Octavia Butler; Joan D. Vinge.* Mercer Island, WA: Starmont House, 1986, 52+44+72 p., cloth, nonf. coll. STARMONT READER'S GUIDE #23.

with Nicholas D. Smith

17447   *Women and utopia: critical interpretations.* Lanham, MD, New York: University Press of America, 1983, 171 p., cloth, nonf. anth.

BARRATT, David

17448   *C. S. Lewis and his world.* Basingstoke, Hampshire, England: Marshall Pickering; MI: William B. Eerdmans Publishing Co., 1987, 46 p., cloth, nonf.

BARRETT, David V(ickers), 1952-

17449   *Digital dreams.* London: New English Library, 1990, 347 p., paper, anth.

BARRETT, Dick

17450   *Time double.* New York: Lynx Books, 1989, 295 p., paper, novel.

*BARRETT, Ethel <u>(Cook), 1892?</u>-

BARRETT, G(eoffrey) J(ohn), 1928-

17451   *The bodysnatchers of Lethe.* London: Robert Hale, 1976, 174 p., cloth, novel.
17452   *City of the first time.* London: Robert Hale, 1975, 173 p., cloth, novel.
17453   *Earth watch.* London: Robert Hale, 1978, 176 p., cloth, novel.
17454   *The halls of the Evolvulus.* London: Robert Hale, 1977, 189 p., cloth, novel.
17455   *The night of the deathship.* London: Robert Hale, 1976, 195 p., cloth, novel.
17456   *The other side of red.* London: Robert Hale, 1977, 172 p., cloth, novel.
17457   *Overself.* London: Robert Hale, 1975, 152 p., cloth, novel.
17458   *The paradise zone.* London: Robert Hale, 1975, 191 p., cloth, novel.
17459   *Robotria.* London: Robert Hale, 1977, 172 p., cloth, novel.
17460   *Slaver from the stars.* London: Robert Hale, 1975, 192 p., cloth, novel.
17461   *Timeship to Thebes.* London: Robert Hale, 1976, 188 p., cloth, novel.

as EDWARD LEIGHTON

17462   *A light from tomorrow.* London: Robert Hale, 1977, 191 p., cloth, novel.
17463   *Lord of the lightning.* London: Robert Hale, 1977, 176 p., cloth, novel.
17464   *Out of Earth's deep.* London: Robert Hale, 1977, 180 p., cloth, novel.

as DENNIS SUMMERS

17465 *A madness from Mars.* London: Robert Hale, 1976, 173 p., cloth, novel.
17466 *Master of ghosts.* London: Robert Hale, 1977, 188 p., cloth, novel.
17467 *Robot in the glass.* London: Robert Hale, 1977, 190 p., cloth, novel.
17468 *Stalker of the worlds.* London: Robert Hale, 1976, 184 p., cloth, novel.

as JAMES WALLACE

17469 *The guardian of Krandor.* London: Robert Hale, 1977, 192 p., cloth, novel.
17470 *A man for tomorrow.* London: Robert Hale, 1976, 176 p., cloth, novel.
17471 *The plague of the golden rat.* London: Robert Hale, 1976, 183 p., cloth, novel.

BARRETT, Gerald R., *with Thomas L. Erskine*

17472 *From fiction to film: Ambrose Bierce's "An occurrence at Owl Creek Bridge."* Encino & Belmont, CA: Dickenson Publishing Co., 1973, 216 p., paper, nonf. anth.

BARRETT, Kevin, *with Saul Peters*

17473 *Treason at Helms Deep.* New York: Berkley Books, 1988, [214] p., paper, fiction. MIDDLE-EARTH QUEST.

*BARRETT, Laurence (Irwin), 1935-

BARRETT, Michael Dennis, 1947-

17474 *Asylum and circus.* New York: Manor Books, 1977, 335 p., paper, novel.

BARRETT, Neal Jr., 1929-

Across the misty sea—SEE: *Aldair, across the misty sea.*
17475 *Aldair, across the misty sea.* New York: DAW Books, 1980, 188 p., paper, novel. ALDAIR #3.
17476 *Aldair in Albion.* New York: DAW Books, 1976, 205 p., paper, novel. ALDAIR #1.
17477 *Aldair, master of ships.* New York: DAW Books, 1977, 158 p., paper, novel. ALDAIR #2.
17478 *Aldair: the legion of beasts.* New York: DAW Books, 1982, 174 p., paper, novel. ALDAIR #4.
17479 *Dawn's uncertain light.* New York: A Signet Book, New American Library,

1989, 252 p., paper, novel. DARKEST AMERICA #2.
17480 *The hereafter gang.* Shingletown, CA: Mark V. Ziesing, 1991, 348 p., cloth, novel.
17481 *Isaac Asimov presents Through darkest America.* New York: Congdon & Weed, 1986, vii+275 p., cloth, novel. DARKEST AMERICA #1.
17482 *The Karma Corps.* New York: DAW Books, 1984, 239 p., paper, novel.
The legion of beasts—SEE: *Aldair: The legion of beasts.*
Master of ships—SEE: *Aldair, master of ships.*
Through darkest America—SEE: *Isaac Asimov presents Through darkest America.*

BARRETT, Nicholas

17483 *Fledger.* London: Michael Joseph, 1985, 208 p., cloth, novel.

*BARRETT, William E(dmund), 1900-1986

BARRIE, J(ames) M(atthew), Sir, 1860-1937

17484 *Farewell, Miss Julie Logan: a wintry tale.* London: Hodder & Stoughton, 1932, 98 p., cloth, novel.

BARRIE, Monica, pseud.—SEE: Wind, David

BARRIOS, Enrique, 1945-

17485 *Ami, child of the stars.* Santa Fe, NM: Lotus Press, 1989, 113 p., paper, novel.

BARRON, (Richard) Neil, 1934-

17486 *Anatomy of wonder: science fiction.* New York, London: R. R. Bowker Co., A Xerox Education Co., 1976, xxi+471 p., cloth, nonf. anth.
17487 *Anatomy of wonder: a critical guide to science fiction, 2nd ed.* New York, London: R. R. Bowker Co., 1981, xiv+724 p., cloth, nonf. anth.
17488 *Anatomy of wonder: a critical guide to science fiction, 3rd ed.* New York, London: R. R. Bowker Co., 1987, xii+874 p., cloth, nonf. anth.
17489 *Fantasy literature: a reader's guide.* New York, London: Garland Publishing, 1990, xxvii+586 p., cloth, nonf. anth.
17490 *Horror literature: a reader's guide.* New York, London: Garland Publishing, 1990, xxvii+596 p., cloth, nonf. anth.

BARRON, T(om) A.

17491   *Heartlight.* New York: Philomel Books, 1990, 272 p., cloth, novel. HEARTLIGHT #1.

BARROW, Louis

17492   *Supernatural romance of Suzanne, The conquest of demon Cabeto, and Allen Mountain ghosts.* March, Cambridgeshire, England: Louis Barrow, 1991, 104 p., paper, coll.

BARRUS, Tim

17493   *Genocide: the anthology.* Stamford, CT: A Leather Lit Book, Knights Press, 1988, 210 p., paper, novel. [Despite the title, this is not an anthology].

*BARRY, Iris, 1895-<u>1969</u>

BARRY, Jonathan, pseud.—SEE: Strieber, Whitley

BARSHAY, Robert Howard

17494   *Philip Wylie: the man and his work.* Washington, DC: University Press of America, 1979, iii + 127 p., cloth, nonf.

BARTH, John (Simmons), 1930-

17495   *The last voyage of Somebody the Sailor.* Boston: Little, Brown & Co., 1991, 573 p., cloth, novel.

BARTHELME, Donald, 1931-1989

17496   *The king.* New York: An Edward Burlingame Book, Harper & Row, 1990, 157 p., cloth, novel.

BARTHOLOMEW, Barbara (G.), 1941-

17497   *The cereal box adventures.* Elgin, IL: Chariot Books, 1981, 138 p., paper, novel.
17498   *Child of tomorrow.* New York: A Signet Vista Book, New American Library, 1985, 192 p., paper, novel. TIME KEEPER #2.
17499   *Flight into the unknown.* Elgin, IL: Chariot Books, 1982, 138 p., paper, novel.
17500   *The great gradepoint mystery.* New York: Macmillan, 1983, 106 p., cloth, novel. MICROKID MYSTERY #1.

17501   *The time keeper.* New York: A Signet Vista Book, New American Library, 1985, 191 p., paper, novel. TIME KEEPER #1.
17502   *When dreams cease to dream.* New York: A Signet Vista Book, New American Library, 1985, 190 p., paper, novel. TIME KEEPER #3.

BARTKOWSKI, Frances, 1948-

17503   *Feminist utopias.* Lincoln, NE: University of Nebraska, 1989, x + 198 p., cloth, nonf.

*BARTLETT, Landell, <u>1897-1972</u>

BARTLETT, Lynn (M.)

17504   *Defy the eagle.* Toronto, New York: Worldwide, 1986, 415 p., paper, novel.

*BARTLETT, Vernon (Oldfield), 1894-<u>1983</u>

BARTON, Dan

17505   *Banshee.* Toronto, New York: Worldwide, 1988, 382 p., paper, novel.
17506   *Relife.* New York, London: Pocket Books, 1991, 296 p., paper, novel.

BARTON, James

17507   *Aftermath.* London: Granada, 1983, 128 p., paper, novel. WASTEWORLD #1.
17508   *Angels.* London: Granada, 1984, [128] p., paper, novel. WASTEWORLD #3.
17509   *My way.* London: Granada, 1984, 125 p., paper, novel. WASTEWORLD #4.
17510   *Resurrection.* London: Granada, 1983, 142 p., paper, novel. WASTEWORLD #2.

BARTON, S. W. [pseud. of Barton Stewart Whaley], 1928- , *with Michael Kurland*

17511   *The last president.* New York: A Bernard Geis Associates Book, William Morrow & Co., 1980, 357 p., cloth, novel.

*BARTON, Samuel, <u>1785-1858</u>

BARTON, William (Renald III), 1950-

17512   *A plague of all cowards.* New York: Ace Books, 1976, 147 p., paper, novel.

with Michael Capobianco

17513   *Fellow traveler, Sputnik Mira: a science fiction novel.* New York, Toronto:

Spectra, Bantam Books, 1991, 403 p., paper, novel. [*Sputnik Mira* is written in cyrillic letters]

17514 *Iris.* New York: A Foundation Book, Doubleday, 1990, 436 p., cloth, novel.

BARTRAM, George, pseud.—SEE: Cameron, Kenneth M.

BARTTER, Martha (Ann), 1932-

17515 *The way to ground zero: the atomic bomb in American science fiction.* New York, London: Greenwood Press, 1988, xii + 278 p., cloth, nonf. CONTRIBUTIONS TO THE STUDY OF SCIENCE FICTION AND FANTASY #33.

*BARZMAN, Ben, 1912-1989

*BASIL, Otto, 1901-1983

BASS, Eben E(dward), 1924-

17516 *Aldous Huxley: an annotated bibliography of criticism.* New York, London: Garland Publishing, 1981, xxiii + 221 p., cloth, nonf.

BASTRAW, Michael, 1954-

17517 *Fifty extremely SF stories.* Center Harbor, NH: Niekas Publications, 1982, 51 p., paper, anth.

BATCHELOR, John (Barham), 1942-

17518 *H. G. Wells.* Cambridge, England: Cambridge University Press, 1985, xii + 176 p., cloth, nonf.
17519 *Mervyn Peake: a biographical and critical exploration.* London: Duckworth, 1974, 176 p., paper, nonf.

BATCHELOR, John Calvin, 1948-

17520 *The birth of the People's Republic of Antarctica.* New York: The Dial Press, 1983, 401 p., cloth, novel.
17521 *The further adventures of Halley's Comet.* New York: Congdon & Lattes, 1980, 508 p., cloth, novel.

BATEMAN, Frederick—SEE: Paton, John

BATEMAN, John (MacArthur), 1918-

17522 *Loch Ness conspiracy.* New York: R. Speller & Sons, 1987, 196 p., cloth, novel.

BATES, Brian

17523 *A spectre in the hall: a novel.* London: Piatkus, 1984, 248 p., cloth, novel.
17524 *The way of wyrd: tales of an Anglo-Saxon sorcerer.* London: Century, 1983, 208 p., cloth, novel.

BATES, Harry—SEE: Gilmore, Anthony

BATES, Susannah (Vacella Church), 1941-

17525 *The PENDEX: an index of pen names and house names in fantastic, thriller, and series literature.* New York, London: Garland Publishing, 1981, xii + 233 p., cloth, nonf.

BATTEN, Ralph

17526 *In the kingdom of the carpet dragon.* Oxford, England, Batavia, IL: Lion Publishing, 1989, 142 p., paper, novel.
17527 *Under the golden throne.* Tring, Oxford, England: Lion Publishing, 1984, 95 p., paper, novel.

BATTIN, B(rinton) W(arner), 1941

17528 *The creep.* New York: Fawcett Gold Medal, 1987, 296 p., paper, novel.
17529 *Demented.* New York: Fawcett Gold Medal, 1988, 277 p., paper, novel.
17530 *Satan help me.* Canoga Park, CA: Major Books, 1980, 302 p., paper, novel.
17530A retitled: *Satan's servant.* Toronto, New York: PaperJacks Ltd., 1984, 302 p., paper, novel.
Satan's servant—SEE: Satan help me.
17531 *Smithereens.* New York: Fawcett Gold Medal, 1987, 309 p., paper, novel.

as WARNER LEE

17532 *Into the pit.* New York, London: Pocket Books, 1989, 278 p., paper, novel.
17533 *It's loose.* New York, London: Pocket Books, 1990, 312 p., paper, novel.

BATTLES, (Roxy) Edith (Baker), 1921-

17534 *The witch in room 6.* New York: Harper & Row, 1987, vii + 151 p., cloth, novel.

BAUDELAIRE, Charles (Pierre), 1821-1867

17535 *Baudelaire on Poe: critical papers.* State College, PA: Bald Eagle Press, 1952, 175 p., cloth, nonf. coll.

17536 *Fatal destinies: the Edgar Poe papers.* Woodhaven, NY: Cross Country Press, 1981, 85 p., cloth, nonf. coll.

17537 *Selected critical studies of Baudelaire.* Cambridge, England: Cambridge University Press, 1949, xxxii+224 p., cloth, nonf. coll. [Edited by D. Parmee].

BAUDINO, Gael, 1955?-

17538 *Dragon sword, volume I.* New York: A Byron Preiss Book, Lynx Omeiga Books, 1988, 452 p., paper, novel. DRAGONSWORD #1.

17538A retitled: *Dragonsword.* New York: A Roc Book, 1991, 383 p., paper, novel. DRAGONSWORD #1.

Dragonsword—SEE: *Dragon sword, volume I.*

17539 *Duel of dragons.* New York: A Roc Book, 1991, 383 p., paper, novel. DRAGONSWORD #2.

17540 *Gossamer axe.* New York: A Roc Book, 1990, 351 p., paper, novel.

17541 *Strands of starlight.* New York: A Signet Book, New American Library, 1989, 371 p., paper, novel.

BAUER, Steven (Albert), 1948-

Amazing stories—SEE: *Steven Spielberg's Amazing stories.*

17542 *Satyrday: a fable.* New York: Berkley Publishing Corp., 1980, 213 p., cloth, novel.

17543 *Steven Spielberg's Amazing stories.* New York: Charter Books, 1986, 234 p., paper, tele. coll.

17544 *Volume II of Steven Spielberg's Amazing stories.* New York: Charter Books, 1986, 225 p., paper, tele. coll.

BAUM, L(yman) Frank, 1856-1919, *with Michael Patrick Hearn*

17545 *The wizard of Oz.* New York: Schocken Books, 1983, 305 p., cloth, anth. [Includes text of the novel plus critical essays].

BAUM, Roger S.

17546 *Dorothy of Oz.* New York: Books of Wonder, 1989, 166 p., cloth, novel. OZ SERIES.

17547 *The Rewolf of Oz.* San Marcos, CA: Green Tiger Press, 1990, 32 p., cloth?, novel. OZ SERIES.

17548 *The SillyOZbuls of Oz.* Westlake Village, CA: Yellow Brick Road Press, 1991, 31 p., cloth?, novel. OZ SERIES.

BAUM, Thomas, 1940-

17549 *It looks alive to me!* New York: Harper & Row, 1976, 168 p., cloth, novel.

BAUSCH, Richard (Carl), 1945-

17550 *Spirits, and other stories.* New York: Linden Press, Simon & Schuster, 1987, 237 p., cloth, coll.

BAUSCH, Robert, 1945-

17551 *Almighty me.* Boston: Houghton Mifflin Co., 1991, 263 p., cloth, novel.

BAWDEN, Nina (Mary Mabey), 1925-

17552 *Devil by the sea.* London: Collins, 1957, 191 p., cloth, novel.

17553 *The witch's daughter.* London: Victor Gollancz, 1966, 160 p., cloth, novel.

BAX, Martin (Charles Owen), 1933-

17554 *The hospital ship.* New York: New Directions, 1974, 223 p., cloth, novel.

BAXTER, John, 1939-

The first Pacific book of science fiction—SEE: *The Pacific book of Australian SF.*

17555 *The Hermes fall.* New York: Simon & Schuster, 1978, 252 p., cloth, novel.

00955 *The Pacific book of Australian SF.* Sydney, Australia: Pacific Books, Angus & Robertson, 1968, 180 p., paper, anth.

00955A retitled: *The Pacific book of science fiction.* Sydney, Australia: Pacific Books, Angus & Robertson, 1969, 180 p., paper, anth.

00955B retitled: *The first Pacific book of science fiction.* Sydney, Australia: Arkon Books, 1973, 180 p., paper, anth.

***with John Brosnan as* JAMES BLACKSTONE**

18768 *Torched!* London: Grafton, 1986, 223 p., paper, novel.

BAXTER, Lorna

17556 *The eggchild.* London: Faber & Faber, 1978, 157 p., cloth, novel.

BAXTER, Stephen (M.), 1957-

17557 *Raft.* London: Grafton, 1991, 264 p., cloth, novel.

BAXTER, Terry

17558 *The URSA ultimatum.* New York: Zebra Books, Kensington Publishing Corp., 1988, 414 p., paper, novel.

BAYER, Sandra L.—SEE: Bayer, Sandy

BAYER, Sandy [i.e. Sandra Lee Bayer], 1945-

17559 *The crystal cage.* Boston: Alyson Publications, 1991, 216 p., paper, novel. CRYSTAL #2.
17560 *The crystal curtain.* Boston: Alyson Publications, 1988, 214 p., paper, novel. CRYSTAL #1.

BAYER-BERENBAU, Linda, 1948-

17561 *The gothic imagination: expansion in gothic literature and art.* Rutherford & Madison, NJ: Fairleigh Dickinson University Press; London & Toronto: Associated University Presses, 1982, 155 p., cloth, nonf.

BAYLEY, Barrington J(ohn), 1937-

00960 *Collision course.* New York: DAW Books, 1973, 175 p., paper, novel
00960A retitled: *Collision with Chronos: a novel.* London: Allison & Busby, 1977, 169 p., cloth, novel.
 Collision with chronos—SEE: Collision course.
17562 *The fall of Chronopolis; and, Collision with Chronos.* London: Pan Books, 1989, 399 p., paper, coll.
17563 *The forest of Peldain.* New York: DAW Books, 1985, 223 p., paper, novel.
17564 *The garments of Caean.* Garden City, NY: Doubleday & Co., 1976, 189 p., cloth, novel.
17565 *The garments of Caean.* London: A Fontana Paperback, Collins, 1978, 222 p., paper, novel. [Expanded edition].
17566 *The Grand Wheel.* New York: DAW Books, 1977, 176 p., paper, novel.
17567 *The knights of the limits.* London: Allison & Busby, 1978, 218 p., cloth, coll.
17568 *The pillars of eternity.* New York: DAW Books, 1982, 159 p., paper, novel.
17569 *The pillars of eternity; and, The garments of Caean.* London: Pan Books, 1989, 414 p., paper, coll.

17570 *The rod of light.* London: Allison & Busby, 1984, 193 p., cloth, novel. SOUL OF THE ROBOT #2.
17571 *The seed of evil.* London: Allison & Busby, 1979, 175 p., cloth, coll.
17572 *Star winds.* New York: DAW Books, 1978, 191 p., paper, novel.
17573 *The Zen gun.* New York: DAW Books, 1983, 159 p., paper, novel.

BAYLEY, Victor—SEE: Smith, Wayland

BAYLUS, Robert F(rederic), 1948-

17574 *The people exchange.* New York: Carlyle, 1980, 221 p., paper, novel.

BAYLY, Joseph (Tate), 1920-1986

17575 *The gospel blimp.* Havertown, PA: Windward Press, 1960, 85 p., cloth, novel
17576 *I saw Gooley fly, and other stories.* Old Tappan, NJ: Fleming H. Revell, 1968, 127 p., cloth, coll.
17577 *Winterflight: a novel.* Waco, TX: Word Books Publisher, 1981, 174 p., cloth, novel.

BAYNE, Neil (F.)

17578 *Inoculate!* New York: Leisure Books, 1979, 319 p., paper, novel.

BEACH, Lynn, pseud.—SEE: Lance, Kathryn

BEACHCROFT, (Ellinor) Nina, 1931-

17579 *Beyond world's end.* London: Heinemann, 1985, 139 p., cloth, novel.
17580 *Cold Christmas.* London: Heinemann, 1974, 120 p., cloth, novel.
17581 *The genie and her bottle.* London: Heinemann, 1983, 151 p., cloth, novel.
17582 *A spell of sleep.* London: Heinemann, 1976, 140 p., cloth, novel.
17583 *Under the enchanter.* London: Heinemann, 1974, 121 p., cloth, novel.
17584 *A visit to Folly Castle.* London: Heinemann, 1977, 140 p., cloth, novel.
17585 *The wishing people.* London: Heinemann, 1980, 138 p., cloth, novel.

BEAGLE, Peter S(oyer), 1939-

 The fantasy world of Peter S. Beagle—SEE: The fantasy worlds of Peter S. Beagle.
17586 *The fantasy worlds of Peter Beagle: Lila the werewolf; The last unicorn; Come,*

Lady Death; A fine and private place. New York: Viking Press, 1978, 430 p., cloth, coll.

17586A retitled: *The fantasy world of Peter S. Beagle.* London: Souvenir Press, 1980, 430 p., cloth, coll.

17587 *The folk of the air.* New York: A Del Rey Book, Ballantine Books, 1986, 330 p., cloth, novel.

17588 *The last unicorn; A fine and private place.* New York: Book-of-the-Month Club, 1991, 272+218 p., cloth, coll.

BEAHM, George W(illiam), 1953-

17589 *Grimoire.* Williamsburg, VA: GB Publishing, 1990, xvi+110 p., paper, nonf. anth.

17590 *The Stephen King companion.* Kansas City, MO: Andrews & McMeel, 1989, xiv+363 p., paper, nonf. anth.

17591 *The Stephen King story: a literary profile.* Kansas City, MO: Andrews & McMeel, 1991, 291 p., paper, nonf.

with Vaughn Bodé

17592 *Vaughn Bodé index.* Newport News, VA: C. W. Brooks, Jr., 1976, 64 p., paper, nonf.

with Tim Kirk

17593 *Kirk's works: an index to the art of Tim Kirk.* Newport News, VA: Heresy Press, 1980, 121 p., cloth, nonf.

BEAIRD, Richard F.

17594 *Death screen.* New York: Zebra Books, Kensington Publishing Corp., 1983, 382 p., paper, novel.

*BEAL, John Robinson, 1906-1985

*BEALS, Carleton, 1893-1979

BEAM, Alex

17595 *The Americans are coming!: a novel.* New York: St. Martin's Press, 1991, viii+342 p., cloth, novel.

BEAMER, (George) Charles (Jr.), 1942-

17596 *Charlcie Arrow & the magic red cape.* Grand Rapids, MI: Baker Book House, 1983, 132 p., cloth, novel.

17597 *Lightning in the bottle.* Nashville, TN: Thomas Nelson Publishers, 1981, 317 p., cloth, novel. LEGENDS OF EORTHE #2.

17598 *Magician's bane.* Nashville, TN: Thomas Nelson, 1980, 203 p., cloth, novel. LEGENDS OF EORTHE #1.

17599 *When the gods returned.* New York: A Del Rey Book, Ballantine Books, 1986, 231 p., paper, novel.

BEAR, David, 1949-

17600 *Keeping time.* New York: St. Martin's Press, 1979, 236 p., cloth, novel.

BEAR, Greg(ory Dale), 1951-

17601 *Beyond heaven's river.* New York: A Dell Book, 1980, 192 p., paper, novel.

17602 *Blood music.* New York: Arbor House, 1985, 262 p., cloth, novel.

17603 *Corona: a Star Trek novel.* New York: Pocket Books, 1984, 192 p., paper, novel. STAR TREK #15.

17604 *Early harvest.* Cambridge, MA: A Boskone Book, NESFA Press, 1988, vi+131 p., cloth, coll. [Includes some nonfiction; limited to 800 copies].

17605 *Eon.* New York: Bluejay International Edition, 1985, 504 p., cloth, novel. EON #1.

17606 *Eternity.* New York: Warner Books, 1988, 399 p., cloth, novel. EON #2.

17607 *The forge of God.* New York: Tor, A Tom Doherty Associates Book, 1987, 474 p., cloth, novel.

17608 *Hardfought.* New York: Tor SF, A Tom Doherty Associates Book, 1988, 97 p., paper, novel. [Bound with *Cascade Point* / by Timothy Zahn].

17609 *Heads.* London: Legend, 1990, 125 p., cloth, novel.

17610 *Hegira.* New York: A Dell Book, 1979, 240 p., paper, novel.

17611 *The infinity concerto.* New York: Berkley Books, 1984, 342 p., paper, novel. MICHAEL PERRIN #1.

Lost souls—SEE: *Psychlone.*

17612 *Psychlone.* New York: Ace Books, 1979, 311 p., paper, novel.

17612A retitled: *Lost souls.* New York: Charter, 1982, 311 p., paper, novel.

17613 *Queen of angels.* Norwalk, CT: Easton Press, 1990, 420 p., cloth, novel.

17614 *The Serpent Mage.* New York: Berkley Books, 1986, 343 p., paper, novel. MICHAEL PERRIN #2.

17615 *Sleepside story.* New Castle, VA: Cheap Street, 1988, 79 p., cloth, story. [Limited to 127 copies].

17616 *Strength of stones.* New York: Ace Books, 1981, 237 p., paper, novel.
17617 *Strength of stones, new rev. ed.* London: Victor Gollancz, Ltd., 1988, 221 p., paper, novel. [Revised edition].
17618 *Tangents.* New York: Warner Books, 1989, 290 p., cloth, coll.
17619 *The wind from a burning woman.* Sauk City, WI: Arkham House, 1983, xii + 270 p., cloth, coll.

BEARDSLEY, Aubrey (Vincent), 1872-1898, with *John Glassco*

17620 *Under the hill; or, The story of Venus and Tannhäuser, in which is set forth an exact account of state held by Madame Venus, Goddess and Meretrix, under the famous Hörselberg, and containing the adventures of Tannhäuser in that place, his journeying to Rome and return to the Loving Mountain.* London: New English Library, 1966, 125 p., cloth, novel. [Completed by Glassco].

BEASLEY, (William) Conger Jr., 1940-

17621 *Hidalgo's beard: a California fantasy.* Kansas City, MO: Andrews & McMeel, 1979, 146 p., cloth, novel.
17622 *The magic deer.* Union, OR: Wordcraft, 1989, 31 p., paper, coll.

BEASON, (James) Doug(las), 1953-

17623 *Assault on Alpha Base.* New York, London: Pocket Books, 1990, 236 p., paper, novel.
17624 *Return to honor.* New York, London: Pocket Books, 1989, 237 p., paper, novel.
17625 *Strike eagle.* New York: A Signet Book, 1991, 380 p., paper, novel

with *Kevin J. Anderson*

16374 *Lifeline.* New York, Toronto: Spectra, Bantam Books, 1990, 460 p., paper, novel.
16375 *The trinity paradox.* New York, Toronto: Spectra, Bantam Books, 1991, 325 p., paper, novel.

BEATTY, Jerome Jr., 1918-

17626 *Bob Fulton's amazing soda-pop stretcher: an international spy story.* New York: W. R. Scott, 1963, 239 p., cloth, novel. BOB FULTON #1.

17627 *Bob Fulton's terrific time machine: an adventure in space and time.* Toronto, New York: Bantam Books, 1982, 188 p., paper, novel. BOB FULTON #2.
17628 *Maria Looney and the cosmic circus.* New York: An Avon Camelot Book, 1978, 160 p., paper, novel. MARIA LOONEY #2.
17629 *Maria Looney and the remarkable robot.* New York: An Avon Camelot Book, 1979, 144 p., paper, novel. MARIA LOONEY #3.
17630 *Maria Looney on the red planet.* New York: A Camelot Book, Avon Books, 1977, 160 p., paper, novel. MARIA LOONEY #1.
17631 *The tunnel to yesterday.* New York: An Avon Camelot Book, 1983, 158 p., paper, novel.

BEAUCHAMP, Gorman (Lynn), 1938-

17632 *Jack London.* Mercer Island, WA: Starmont House, 1984, 96 p., cloth, nonf. STARMONT READER'S GUIDE #15.

with *Kenneth Roemer & Nicholas D. Smith*

17633 *Utopian studies 1.* Lanham, MD: University Press of America, 1987, v + 197 p., cloth, nonf. anth.

BEAUDRY, Antoinette

17634 *Jungle of desire.* New York: Pinnacle Books, 1982, 341 p., paper, novel.

BEAUJON, Paul [pseud. of Beatrice Lamberton Warde], 1900-1969

17635 *The shelter in bedlam.* London: The Author, 1937, [30] p., paper?, story.
00997 retitled: *Peace under earth: dialogues from the year 1946.* London: Megaw, 1938, 47 p., cloth, story. [Revised edition].

BEAUMONT, Charles [legalized from Charles Leroy Nutt], 1929-1967

17636 *Best of Beaumont.* Toronto, New York: Bantam Books, 1982, xvi + 238 p., paper, coll.
17637 *Charles Beaumont: selected stories.* Arlington Heights, IL: Dark Harvest, 1988, 404 p., cloth, coll. [Edited by Roger Anker; winner of the Bram Stoker Award for Best Horror Collection, 1988 (1989)]. *Selected stories*—SEE: *Charles Beaumont: selected stories.*

BEAUMONT, Roger (Alban), 1935- , with R. Snowden Ficks

17638 *Deep space processional.* London: Robert Hale, 1982, 190 p., cloth, novel.

BECHARD, Gorman

17639 *The second greatest story ever told: a novel.* New York: Carol Publishing Group, A Citadel Press Book, 1991, 291 p., cloth, novel.

BECK, Calvin Thomas, 1930-1989

17640 *Heroes of the horrors.* New York: Collier Books; London: Collier Macmillan Publishers, 1975, xiv+353 p., paper, nonf.
17641 *Scream queens: heroines of the horrors.* New York: Macmillan, 1978, viii+344 p., cloth, nonf.

BECKER, Alida, 1948-

17642 *The Tolkien scrapbook.* New York: Grosset & Dunlap, 1978, 192 p., cloth, nonf. anth.
17642A retitled: *The Tolkien treasury: stories, poems, and illustrations celebrating the author and his world.* Philadelphia, PA: Running Press, 1989, 192 p., cloth, nonf. anth.
The Tolkien treasury—SEE: *The Tolkien scrapbook.*

BECKER, Eve

17643 *Instant popularity.* New York, Toronto: A Bantam Skylark Book, 1990, 117 p., paper, novel. ABRACADABRA #5.
17644 *The love potion.* New York, Toronto: A Bantam Skylark Book, 1989, 116 p., paper, novel. ABRACADABRA #2.
17645 *The magic mix-up.* New York, Toronto: A Bantam Skylark Book, 1989, 116 p., paper, novel. ABRACADABRA #3.
17646 *The sneezing spell.* New York, Toronto: A Bantam Skylark Book, 1990, 112 p., paper, novel. ABRACADABRA #4.
17647 *Thirteen means magic.* New York, Toronto: A Bantam Skylark Book, 1989, 134 p., paper, novel. ABRACADABRA #1.
17648 *Too much magic.* New York, Toronto: A Bantam Skylark Book, 1990, 118 p., paper, novel. ABRACADABRA #6.

BECKER, Margot

17649 *Divide and conquer.* New York: Ballantine Books, 1988, 117 p., paper, novel. G.I. JOE #2.

BECKER, Muriel R(ogow), 1924-

17650 *Clifford D. Simak: a primary and secondary bibliography.* Boston: G. K. Hall & Co., 1980, xliii+149 p., cloth, nonf. MASTERS OF SCIENCE FICTION AND FANTASY.

BECKET, Jim

17651 *Inca gold.* Toronto, New York: An R. A. Montgomery Book, Bantam Books, 1988, 115 p., paper, novel. CHOOSE YOUR OWN ADVENTURE #85.

BECKETT, Jenifer

17652 *The echoing silence.* London: Hamlyn Paperbacks, 1982, 235 p., paper, novel.

BECKWITH, Henry L(yman) P(arsons) Jr., 1935-

17653 *Lovecraft's Providence, and adjacent parts.* West Kingston, RI: Donald M. Grant, Publisher, 1979, 89 p., cloth, nonf.
17654 *Lovecraft's Providence, & adjacent parts, second edition, revised and enlarged.* West Kingston, RI: Donald M. Grant, Publisher, 1986, 95 p., cloth, nonf.

BÉDARD, Michael (A.), 1949-

17655 *A darker magic.* New York: Atheneum, 1987, 183 p., cloth, novel.
17656 *Redwork.* Toronto: Lester & Orpen Dennys, 1990, 261 p., cloth, novel.

BEDFORD, Clive

17657 *Barbarian victim.* Wilmington, DE: A Bizarre Book, An Eros Goldstripe Publication, 1975, 182 p., paper, novel.
17658 *Mistress of torment.* Wilmington, DE: A Bizarre Book, An Eros Goldstripe Publication, 1975, 182 p., paper, novel.
17659 *Salome's slave.* Wilmington, DE: A Bizarre Book, An Eros Goldstripe Publication, 1975, 183 p., paper, novel.

BEDFORD, John, pseud.—SEE: Wiltshire, David

BEDFORD, Michael, *with Bruce Dettman*

17660 *The horror factory: the horror films of Universal, 1931 to 1955.* New York: Gordon Press, 1976, 193 p., cloth, nonf.

BEDFORD, Sybille, Dame, 1911-

17661 *Aldous Huxley: a biography, volume I: 1894-1939.* London: Chatto & Windus, 1973, 400 p., cloth, nonf.
17662 *Aldous Huxley: a biography, volume II: 1939-1962.* London: Chatto & Windus, 1974, 378 p., cloth, nonf.

BEEBEE, Chris

17663 *The hub.* London: Macdonald & Co., 1987, 249 p., cloth, novel. CIPOLA SEQUENCE #1.
17664 *The main event.* London: Macdonald & Co., 1989, [202] p., paper, novel. CIPOLA SEQUENCE #2.

BEECHCROFT, William [pseud. of William Finn Hallstead III], 1924-

17665 *Image of evil.* New York: Dodd, Mead & Co., 1985, 219 p., cloth, novel.

*BEECHING, Jack, 1922-

BEEKS, Graydon (Fisher), 1919-

17666 *Hosea Globe and the fantastical peg-legged chu.* New York: Atheneum, 1975, 170 p., cloth, novel.

BEERE, Peter

17667 *The crucifixion squad.* London: Arrow, 1984, 223 p., paper, novel. TRAUMA 2020 #2.
17668 *Silent slaughter.* London: Arrow, 1985, 202 p., paper, novel. TRAUMA 2020 #3.
17669 *Urban prey.* London: Arrow, 1984, 198 p., paper, novel. TRAUMA 2020 #1.

BEESE, P. J., 1946- , with Todd Cameron Hamilton

17670 *The guardsman.* New York: Pageant Books, 1988, 313 p., paper, novel.

BEESLEY, Charles, *with Michael Weldon & Bob Martin & Akira Fitton*

17671 *The psychotronic encyclopedia of film.* New York: Ballantine Books, 1983, xvi+815 p., paper, nonf.

BEHRENDS, Steve, 1959-

17672 *Clark Ashton Smith.* Mercer Island, WA: Starmont House, 1990, v+112 p., cloth, nonf. STARMONT READER'S GUIDE #49.

BEIZER, Boris—SEE: Shedley, Ethan I.

BELANGER, Sharlene, *with Steven Talley & Adrian Malone*

17673 *The secret.* Boston: Houghton Mifflin Co., 1984, 390 p., cloth, novel.

BELDEN, David (Corderoy), 1949-

17674 *Children of Arable.* New York: A Signet Book, New American Library, 1987, 289 p., paper, novel. GALACTIC CONNECTIVITY SEQUENCE #1.
17675 *To warm the Earth.* New York: A Signet Book, New American Library, 1988, 317 p., paper, novel. GALACTIC CONNECTIVITY SEQUENCE #2.

BELDEN, Wilanne Schneider, 1925-

17676 *Frankie!* San Diego, CA: Harcourt Brace Jovanovich, 1987, 163 p., cloth, novel.
17677 *Mind-call.* New York: An Argo Book, Atheneum, 1981, 246 p., cloth, novel. MIND #1.
17678 *Mind-find.* San Diego, CA: Harcourt Brace Jovanovich, 1988, 191 p., cloth, novel. MIND #3.
17679 *Mind-hold.* San Diego, CA: Harcourt Brace Jovanovich, 1987, 242 p., cloth, novel. MIND #2.
17680 *The rescue of Ranor.* New York: Atheneum, 1983, 173 p., cloth, novel.

BELGION, (Harold) Montgomery, 1892-1973

17681 *H. G. Wells.* London: Published for the British Council and the National Book League by Longmans, Green & Co., 1953, 43 p., paper, nonf.
17682 *H. G. Wells, rev. ed.* London: Published for the British Council and the National Book League by Longmans, Green & Co., 1964, 44 p., paper, nonf.

BELIAEV, Aleksandr (Romanovich), 1884-1942

17683 *Professor Dowell's head* / by Alexander Beliaev. New York: Macmillan Publishing Co.; London: Collier Macmillan Publishers, 1980, viii+157 p., cloth,

Science Fiction and Fantasy Literature, 1975-1991

novel. [Translation of *Golova Professora Douelia*].

BELL, Clare (Louise), 1952-

17684 *Clan ground.* New York: A Margaret K. McElderry Book, An Argo Book, Atheneum, 1984, 258 p., cloth, novel. RATHA #2.

17685 *People of the sky.* New York: Tor, A Tom Doherty Associates Book, 1989, 344 p., cloth, novel.

17686 *Ratha and Thistle-Chaser.* New York: Margaret K. McElderry Books, 1990, 232 p., cloth, novel. RATHA #3.

17687 *Ratha's creature.* New York: A Margaret K. McElderry Book, An Argo Book, Atheneum, 1983, 259 p., cloth, novel. RATHA #1.

17688 *Tomorrow's sphinx.* New York: Margaret K. McElderry Books, 1986, 292 p., cloth, novel.

BELL, Douglas

17689 *Mojo and the pickle jar.* New York: Tor Fantasy, A Tom Doherty Associates Book, 1991, 250 p., paper, novel.

BELL, Gordon B(ennett), 1934-

17690 *The Golden Troubadour.* New York: McGraw-Hill Book Co., 1980, 331 p., cloth, novel.

BELL, Ian

17691 *Virgil Finlay indexed: the eighth book of Virgil Finlay.* Chalgrove, Oxford, England: Bell & Sons, 1986, 40 p., paper, nonf.

17692 *William Hope Hodgson: voyages and visions.* Oxford, England: Bell & Sons, 1987, 64 p., paper, nonf. anth.

BELL, John (Charles), 1952-

with Lesley Choyce

17693 *Visions from the edge: an anthology of Atlantic Canadian science fiction and fantasy.* Porters Lake, Nova Scotia, Canada: Pottersfield Press, 1981, 215 p., cloth, anth.

with John Robert Colombo & Michael Richardson & Alexandre L. Amprimoz

16353 *CDN SF & F: a bibliography of Canadian science fiction and fantasy.* Toronto:

Hounslow Press, 1979, viii+85 p., paper, nonf.

BELL, Joseph, 1949-

17694 *The books of Clive Barker.* Toronto: Soft Books, 1988, [18] p., paper, nonf.

17695 *First editions: "a thousand and one nights of reading".* Toronto: Soft Books, 1988, 82 p. in 2 v., paper, nonf. [Limited to 200 numbered copies].

17696 *Howard Phillips Lovecraft: a chronology.* Toronto: Soft Books, 1984-87, 8 v., paper, nonf. [Title varies slightly from section to section].

17697 *Howard Phillips Lovecraft: the books, 1915-1981.* Toronto: Soft Books, 1981, 71 p., paper, nonf. [Limited to 100 copies].

17698 *Howard Phillips Lovecraft: the books, 1915-1986, 2nd ed.* Toronto: Soft Books, 1987, v+63 p., paper, nonf.

17699 *Howard Phillips Lovecraft: the books, addenda and auxiliary.* Toronto: Soft Books, 1983, 39 p., paper, nonf. [Limited to 100 copies].

17700 *Soft Book publications: the first five years, 1981-1986.* Toronto: Soft Books, 1986, 7 p., paper, nonf.

17701 *William Hope Hodgson, night pirate, volume one: an annotated bibliography of published works, 1902-1987.* Toronto: Soft Books, 1988?, viii+41 p., paper, nonf.

with Roy A. Squires

17702 *The books of Clark Ashton Smith.* Toronto: Soft Books, 1987, [10]+27 p., paper, nonf. [Limited to 300 copies].

BELL, M(ichael) Shayne, 1957-

17703 *Inuit.* Eugene, OR: Pulphouse Publishing, 1991, 45 p., paper, story. SHORT STORY PAPERBACKS #34.

17704 *Nicoji.* Riverdale, NY: Baen Books, 1991, 243 p., paper, novel.

*BELL, Neil [pseud. of Stephen Henry Critten], 1887-1964

*BELL, Paul W., 1933-

BELL, Rob

17705 *Narnia solo games: Return of the white witch.* Charlottesville, VA: Iron Crown Enterprises, 1988, [198] p., paper, fiction. NARNIA SOLO GAMES #5.

Return of the white witch—SEE: *Narnia solo games: Return of the white witch.*

BELL, Trudy E., *with Ben Bova*

17706   *Closeup: new worlds.* New York: St. Martin's Press, 1977, xv+222 p., cloth, nonf. anth.

*BELL, William Dixon, <u>1865-1951</u>

BELLAIRS, John (Anthony), 1938-1991

17707   *The chessmen of doom.* New York: Dial Books for Young Readers, 1989, 155 p., cloth, novel. JOHNNY DIXON #7.

17708   *The curse of the blue figurine.* New York: Dial Books for Young Readers, 1983, 200 p., cloth, novel. JOHNNY DIXON #1.

17709   *The dark secret of Weatherend.* New York: Dial Books for Young Readers, 1984, 182 p., cloth, novel. ANTHONY MONDAY #2.

17710   *The eyes of the killer robot.* New York: Dial Books for Young Readers, 1986, 167 p., cloth, novel. JOHNNY DIXON #5.

17711   *The figure in the shadows: sequel to The house with a clock in its walls.* New York: Dial Press, 1975, 155 p., cloth, novel. LEWIS #2.

17712   *The lamp from the warlock's tomb.* New York: Dial Books for Young Readers, 1988, 168 p., cloth, novel. ANTHONY MONDAY #3.

17713   *The letter, the witch, and the ring.* New York: Dial Press, 1976, 188 p., cloth, novel. LEWIS #3.

17714   *The mummy, the will, and the crypt.* New York: Dial Books for Young Readers, 1983, 168 p., cloth, novel. JOHNNY DIXON #2.

17715   *The pedant and the shuffly.* New York: Macmillan, 1968, 75 p., cloth, novel.

17716   *The revenge of the wizard's ghost.* New York: Dial Books for Young Readers, 1985, 147 p., cloth, novel. JOHNNY DIXON #4.

17717   *The secret of the underground room.* New York: Dial Books for Young Readers, 1990, 125 p., cloth, novel. JOHNNY DIXON #8.

17718   *The spell of the sorcerer's skull.* New York: Dial Books for Young Readers, 1984, 170 p., cloth, novel. JOHNNY DIXON #3.

17719   *The treasure of Alpheus Winterborn.* New York: Harcourt Brace Jovanovich, 1978, 180 p., cloth, novel. ANTHONY MONDAY #1.

17720   *The trolly to yesterday.* New York: Dial Books for Young Readers, 1989, 183 p., cloth, novel. JOHNNY DIXON #6.

BELLAMY, David, 1944- , *with Frank Bellamy*

17721   *Doctor Who: timeview: the Doctor Who illustrations.* Bournemouth, Dorset, England: Who Dares Publishing, 1985, 55 p., cloth, art.

BELLAMY, Edward, 1850-1898

17722   *Apparitions of things to come: tales of mystery & imagination.* Chicago: Charles H. Kerr Publishing Co., 1990, 175 p., cloth, coll. [Edited by Franklin Rosemont].

BELLAMY, Frank, 1917-1976, *with David Bellamy*

17721   *Doctor Who: timeview: the Doctor Who illustrations.* Bournemouth, Dorset, England: Who Dares Publishing, 1985, 55 p., cloth, art.

BELLAMY, William, 1942-

17723   *The novels of Wells, Bennett, and Galsworthy, 1890-1910.* London: Routledge & Kegan Paul, 1971, xi+257 p., cloth, nonf.

BELLINI, Tina—SEE: Forest, Salambo

BELLMORE, Cynthia, pseud.

17724   *Space lust.* Wilmington, DE: Eros Publishing Co., 1978, 191 p., paper, novel. [Bound with *Mixed doubles*, by Cynthia Bellmore].

*BELOVE, Benjamin, 1880-<u>1969</u>

BEMMANN, Hans

17725   *The stone and the flute.* Harmondsworth, Middlesex, England, New York: Viking, 1986, 855 p., cloth, novel. [Translation by Anthea Bell of *Stein und Flöte*].

BEN JELLOUN, Tahar, 1944-

17726   *The sacred night.* San Diego, CA: A Helen & Kurt Wolff Book, Harcourt Brace Jovanovich, 1989, vii+178 p., cloth, novel. SAND CHILD #2. [Translation by Alan Sheridan of *La nuit sacrée*].

17727 *The sand child.* San Diego, CA: Harcourt Brace Jovanovich, 1987, vi+165 p., cloth, novel. SAND CHILD #1. [Translation by Alan Sheridan of *L'Enfant de sable*].

BEN-YEHUDA, Nachman

17728 *Deviance and moral boundaries: witchcraft, the occult, science fiction, deviant sciences, and scientists.* Chicago: University of Chicago Press, 1985, 260 p., cloth, nonf.

*BENARY-ISBERT, Margot, 1889-1979

BENCHLEY, Nathaniel (Goddard), 1915-1981

17729 *Demo and the dolphin.* New York: Harper & Row, 1981, 88 p., cloth, novel.
17730 *Kilroy and the gull.* New York: Harper & Row, 1977, 118 p., cloth, novel.
15791 *The visitors.* New York: McGraw-Hill Book Co., 1964, 248 p., cloth, novel.

BENCHLEY, Peter (Bradford), 1940-

17731 *The island.* Garden City, NY: Doubleday & Co., 1979, 302 p., cloth, novel.

BENDAU, Clifford P(hillip), 1950-

17732 *Colin Wilson: the outsider and beyond.* San Bernardino, CA: R. Reginald, The Borgo Press, 1979, 63 p., cloth, nonf. THE MILFORD SERIES: POPULAR WRITERS OF TODAY #21.
17733 *Still worlds collide: Philip Wylie and the end of the American dream.* San Bernardino, CA: R. Reginald, The Borgo Press, 1980, 63 p., cloth, nonf. THE MILFORD SERIES: POPULAR WRITERS OF TODAY #30.

BENDERS, Kris, *with A. Joseph Ross*

17734 *Boskone 10 filksongbook.* Cambridge, MA: New England Science Fiction Association, 1973, 22 p., paper, nonf. anth.

BENDIXEN, Alfred, 1952-

17735 *Haunted women: the best supernatural stories by American women writers.* New York: Frederick Ungar Publishing Co., 1985, 276 p., cloth, anth.

*BENÉT, Laura, 1884-1979

BENFORD, Gregory (Albert), 1941-

17736 *Across the sea of suns.* New York: Timescape Books, 1984, 400 p., cloth, novel. OCEAN #2.
17737 *Across the sea of suns.* New York: Bantam Books, 1987, 353 p., paper, novel. OCEAN #2. [Revised and expanded edition].
17738 *Against infinity.* New York: Timescape Books, 1983, 215 p., cloth, novel.
17739 *Artifact.* New York: Tor, A Tom Doherty Associates Book, 1985, x+533 p., cloth, novel.
17740 *Centigrade 233.* New Castle, VA: Cheap Street, 1990, 23 p., cloth, story.
17741 *Deeper than the darkness.* New York: Berkley Publishing Corp., 1978, 291 p., cloth, novel. OCEAN #3. [*The stars in shroud* rewritten].
17742 *Great Sky River.* Toronto, New York: A Bantam Spectra Book, Bantam Books, 1987, x+326 p., cloth, novel. GREAT SKY RIVER #1.
17743 *In alien flesh.* New York: Tor, A Tom Doherty Associates Book, 1986, 280 p., cloth, coll.
17744 *In the ocean of night: a novel.* New York: Quantum Science Fiction, Dial Press/ James Wade, 1977, 333 p., cloth, novel. OCEAN #1.
17745 *Jupiter project.* Nashville, TN, New York: Thomas Nelson, 1975, 192 p., cloth, novel.
17746 *The Jupiter project.* New York: Berkley Books, 1980, 182 p., paper, novel. [Revised edition].
17747 *Matter's end.* New Castle, VA: Cheap Street, 1991, 76 p., cloth, story.
17748 *Of space/time and the river.* New Castle, VA: Cheap Street, 1985, 67 p., cloth, story. [Limited to 177 copies].
The stars in shroud—SEE: *Deeper than the darkness.*
17749 *Tides of light.* Toronto, New York: A Bantam Spectra Book, Bantam Books, 1989, 362 p., cloth, novel. GREAT SKY RIVER #2.
17750 *Time's rub.* New Castle, VA: Cheap Street, 1984, 20 p., cloth, story.
17751 *Timescape.* New York: Simon & Schuster, 1980, 412 p., cloth, novel. [Winner of the Nebula Award for Best Novel, 1980 (1981); winner of the John W. Campbell Jr. Memorial Award for Best Novel, 1980 (1981)].
17752 *We could do worse.* [Laguna Beach, CA]: Abbenford Associates, 1988, 18 p., paper?, story.

with David Brin

17753 *Heart of the comet.* Toronto, New York: Bantam Books, 1986, 468 p., cloth, novel.

with Paul A. Carter

17754 *Iceborn.* New York: Tor SF, A Tom Doherty Associates Book, 1989, 96 p., paper, novel. [Bound with *The Saturn Game* / by Poul Anderson].

with Arthur C. Clarke

Against the fall of night; and, Beyond the fall of night—SEE: *Beyond the fall of night.*

20114 *Beyond the fall of night.* New York: An Ace/Putnam Book, 1990, 298 p., cloth, coll. [Includes Clarke's *Against the fall of night* and Benford's sequel].

20114A retitled: *Against the fall of night; and, Beyond the fall of night.* London: Victor Gollancz, 1991, 239 p., cloth, coll.

with Gordon Eklund

17755 *Find the changeling.* New York: A Dell Book, 1980, 249 p., paper, novel.

17756 *If the stars are gods.* New York: Berkley Publishing Corp., 1977, 214 p., cloth, novel.

with Martin H. Greenberg

17757 *Alternate empires.* New York: Bantam Books, 1989, 291 p., paper, anth. WHAT MIGHT HAVE BEEN? #1.

17758 *Alternate heroes.* New York: Bantam Books, 1990, 354 p., paper, anth. WHAT MIGHT HAVE BEEN? #2.

17759 *Alternate wars.* New York, Toronto: Spectra, Bantam Books, 1991, viii+296 p., paper, anth. WHAT MIGHT HAVE BEEN? #3.

17760 *Hitler victorious: eleven stories of the German victory in World War II.* New York: Garland Publishing, 1986, 299 p., cloth, anth.

17761 *Nuclear war.* New York: Ace Books, 1988, 231 p., paper, anth.

17762 *What might have been? volumes I and II.* New York: Bantam Books, 1990, 542 p., cloth, anth. WHAT MIGHT HAVE BEEN? #1-2.

with William Rotsler

17763 *Shiva descending.* New York: Avon, 1980, 394 p., paper, novel.

BENFORD, Timothy B(artholomew), 1941-

17764 *The Ardennes tapes.* New York: Pinnacle Books, Windsor Publishing Corp., 1989, 382 p., paper, novel.

BENJAMIN, Jacob

17765 *Flight of the Sandpiper.* Davenport, FL: Laura Books, 1979, 219 p., paper, novel.

17766 *Walk the dark valley.* Davenport, FL: Laura Books, 1979, 217 p., paper, novel.

BENJAMIN, Michele, *with Jim Ridgway*

17767 *PsiFi: psychological theories and science fictions.* Leicester, England: British Psychological Society, 1987, ix+229 p., paper, nonf.

BENNET, Pamela Dyer- —SEE: Dean, Pamela

BENNET, Robert Ames, 1870-1954

17768 *The bowl of Baal.* West Kingston, RI: Donald M Grant, Publisher, 1975, 351 p., cloth, novel.

BENNETT, Barbara Curry

17769 *Berryhill.* New York: Manor Books, 1979 (i.e., 1980?), 218 p., paper, novel.

BENNETT, Gary L(ee), 1940-

17770 *The star sailors.* New York: St. Martin's Press, 1980, 312 p., cloth, novel.

BENNETT, Geoffrey M.—SEE: 'Sea-Lion'

BENNETT, Janice

17771 *A Christmas keepsake.* New York: Zebra Books, Kensington Publishing Corp., 1991, 319 p., paper, novel.

17772 *Forever in time.* New York: Zebra Books, Kensington Publishing Corp., 1990, 384 p., paper, novel.

BENNETT, Jay, 1922-

17773 *The haunted one.* New York: Franklin Watts, 1987, 175 p., cloth, novel.

BENNETT, Jeff, pseud.

01108   *Cosmic rape.* New York: Orpheus Series, 1974, 187 p., paper, novel.

01108A   retitled: *Orgy girl* / by Terrance Braun. New York: Late Night Library, 1977, 187 p., paper, novel.

01108B   retitled: *Lovers in paradise* / by Hannah Bronto. New York: A Beeline Double Novel, 1983, 187 p., paper, novel. [Bound with *Twice as nice vice* / by Don Tsuris].

01108C   retitled: *Gentlemen prefer nymphs* / by Lara Ross. New York: Late Night Library, 1984, 187 p., paper, novel.

01108D   retitled: *Rent-a-nymph* / by Hannah Bronto. New York: A Beeline Double Novel, 1985, 187 p., paper, novel. [Bound with *Desires for hire* / by Don Tsuris].

     Gentlemen prefer nymphs—SEE: *Cosmic rape.*

     Lovers in paradise—SEE: *Cosmic rape.*

     Orgy girl—SEE: *Cosmic rape.*

     Rent-a-nymph—SEE: *Cosmic rape.*

BENNETT, Jill, 1947-

17774   *Skylark ghost and monster stories.* London: Book Club Associates, 1980, 191 p., cloth, anth.

17775   *Skylark science fiction stories.* London: Book Club Associates, 1980, 191 p., cloth, anth.

BENNETT, Laura, *with Jean Gilmour Harvey as* LAURA GILMOUR BENNETT

     By all that is sacred—SEE: *A wheel of stars.*

17776   *A time and a place.* London: Viking, 1988, 409 p., cloth, novel.

17777   *A wheel of stars.* London: Viking, 1989, 432 p., cloth, novel.

17777a   retitled: *By all that is sacred.* New York: Avon Books, 1991, 385 p., paper, novel.

BENNETT, Laura Gilmour, pseud.—SEE: Bennett, Laura & Harvey, Jean Gilmour

BENNETT, M. J.—SEE: Bennett, Marcia J.

BENNETT, Marcia J(oanne), 1945-

17778   *Beyond the Draak's Teeth.* New York: A Del Rey Book, Ballantine Books, 1986, 278 p., paper, novel. NI-LACH #3.

17779   *Seeking the dream brother.* New York: A Del Rey Book, Ballantine Books, 1989, 279 p., paper, novel. NI-LACH #4.

17780   *Shadow singer.* New York: A Del Rey Book, Ballantine Books, 1984, 245 p., paper, novel. NI-LACH #2.

17781   *Where the Ni-lach* / by M. J. Bennett. New York: A Del Rey Book, Ballantine Books, 1983, 246 p., paper, novel. NI-LACH #1.

17782   *Yaril's children.* New York: A Del Rey Book, Ballantine Books, 1988, 277 p., paper, novel.

*BENNETT, Margot (M.), 1903-<u>1980</u>

BENNETT, Mike

17783   *A Cordwainer Smith checklist.* Polk City, IA: Chris Drumm, 1991, [28] p., paper, nonf. DRUMM BOOKLET #37.

BENNETT, Thea

17784   *The Gemini factor.* London: Methuen Children's Books in Association with Thames Television International, 1987, 168 p., paper, tele.

BENNI, Stefano, 1947-

17785   *Terra!* New York: Pantheon Books, 1985, 360 p., paper, novel. [Translation by Annapaola Cancogni of *Terra!*].

BENOIST, Elizabeth S(mith), 1901-

17786   *Doomsday clock.* San Antonio, TX: Naylor Co., 1975, viii+221 p., cloth, novel.

BENOIT, Hendra, pseud.—SEE: Crawford, Betty Anne

BENSEN, D(onald) R(oynold), 1927-

17787   *And having writ...: a science fiction novel.* Indianapolis, IN, New York: Bobbs-Merrill Co., 1978, 250 p., cloth, novel.

BENSINK, John—SEE: Robertson, John

BENSON, E(dward) F(rederic), 1867-1940

17788   *The flint knife.* Wellingborough, Northamptonshire, England: Equation, 1988, 184 p., paper, coll. [Edited by Jack Adrian].

17789   *The tale of the empty house, and other ghost stories.* London: Black Swan, 1986, 232 p., cloth?, coll.

BENSON, Gordon (Kent) Jr., 1936-

17790 *Arthur Bertram Chandler, master navigator of space: a working bibliography.* Albuquerque, NM: Galactic Central Publications, 1982, 14 p., paper, nonf. GALACTIC CENTRAL BIBLIOGRAPHIES FOR THE AVID READER #3.

17791 *Arthur Bertram Chandler, master navigator of space: a working bibliography, 2nd ed.* Leeds, West Yorkshire, England & Albuquerque, NM: Galactic Central Publications, 1989, v+43 p., paper, nonf. GALACTIC CENTRAL BIBLIOGRAPHIES FOR THE AVID READER #3.

17792 *Arthur Wilson "Bob" Tucker.* Albuquerque, NM: Galactic Central Publications, 1982, 5 p., paper, nonf. GALACTIC CENTRAL BIBLIOGRAPHIES FOR THE AVID READER #8.

17793 *Edgar Pangborn: a bibliography.* Albuquerque, NM: Galactic Central Publications, 1982, i+4 p., paper, nonf. GALACTIC CENTRAL BIBLIOGRAPHIES FOR THE AVID READER #5.

17794 *Fritz Leiber: a working bibliography.* Leeds, West Yorkshire, England & Albuquerque, NM: Galactic Central Publications, 1987, 34 p., paper, nonf. GALACTIC CENTRAL BIBLIOGRAPHIES FOR THE AVID READER #22.

17795 *Gordon Rupert Dickson, first Dorsai.* Albuquerque, NM: Galactic Central Publications, 1982, 20 p., paper, nonf. GALACTIC CENTRAL BIBLIOGRAPHIES FOR THE AVID READER #2.

17796 *Hal Clement (Harry Clement Stubbs).* Albuquerque, NM: Galactic Central Publications, 1982, 5 p., paper, nonf. GALACTIC CENTRAL BIBLIOGRAPHIES FOR THE AVID READER #4.

17797 *Hal Clement, scientist with a mission: a working bibliography.* Leeds, West Yorkshire, England & Albuquerque, NM: Galactic Central Publications, 1989, v+20 p., paper, nonf. GALACTIC CENTRAL BIBLIOGRAPHIES FOR THE AVID READER #4.

17798 *Harry Maxwell Harrison, stainless steel talent: a working bibliography.* Albuquerque, NM: Galactic Central Publications, 1982, 16 p., paper, nonf. GALACTIC CENTRAL BIBLIOGRAPHIES FOR THE AVID READER #9.

17799 *Henry Beam Piper.* Albuquerque, NM: Galactic Central Publications, 1982, 5 p., paper, nonf. GALACTIC CENTRAL BIBLIOGRAPHIES FOR THE AVID READER #6.

17800 *Jack (John Stewart) Williamson, child and father of wonder.* Albuquerque, NM: Galactic Central Publications, 1985, 14 p., paper, nonf. GALACTIC CENTRAL BIBLIOGRAPHIES FOR THE AVID READER #10.

17801 *James White, doctor to aliens: a working bibliography.* Albuquerque, NM: Galactic Central Publications, 1986, 9 p., paper, nonf. GALACTIC CENTRAL BIBLIOGRAPHIES FOR THE AVID READER #12.

17802 *John K. H. Brunner: a working bibliography.* NM: Galactic Central Publications, 1983, 24 p., paper, nonf. GALACTIC CENTRAL BIBLIOGRAPHIES FOR THE AVID READER #11.

17803 *Leigh Douglass Brackett and Edmond Hamilton: a working bibliography.* Leeds, West Yorkshire, England & Albuquerque, NM: Galactic Central Publications, 1986, i+25 p., paper, nonf. GALACTIC CENTRAL BIBLIOGRAPHIES FOR THE AVID READER #20.

17804 *Leigh Douglass Brackett and Edmond Hamilton: a working bibliography.* Leeds, West Yorkshire, England & Albuquerque, NM: Galactic Central Publications, 1988, i+25 p., paper, nonf. GALACTIC CENTRAL BIBLIOGRAPHIES FOR THE AVID READER #20. [Revised edition].

17805 *Manly Wade Wellman, the gentleman from Chapel Hill: a memorial working bibliography.* Albuquerque, NM: Galactic Central Publications, 1986, 18 p., paper, nonf. GALACTIC CENTRAL BIBLIOGRAPHIES FOR THE AVID READER #17.

17806 *Margaret St. Clair.* Albuquerque, NM: Galactic Central Publications, 1986, 10 p., paper, nonf. GALACTIC CENTRAL BIBLIOGRAPHIES FOR THE AVID READER #15.

17807 *Philip José Farmer: a working bibliography.* Leeds, West Yorkshire, England & Albuquerque, NM: Galactic Central Publications, 1987, 21 p., paper, nonf. GALACTIC CENTRAL BIBLIOGRAPHIES FOR THE AVID READER #23.

17808 *Philip Kindred Dick: a preliminary, working bibliography.* Leeds, West Yorkshire, England & Albuquerque, NM: Galactic Central Publications, 1986, 19 p., paper, nonf. GALACTIC CENTRAL BIBLIOGRAPHIES FOR THE AVID READER #18.

17809 *Poul Anderson, myth-master and wondermaker: an interim bibliography.* Albuquerque, NM: Galactic Central Publications, 1982, p., paper, nonf. GALACTIC CENTRAL BIBLIOGRAPHIES FOR THE AVID READER #1.

17810 *Poul Anderson, myth-master and wonder-maker: an interim bibliography (1947-1986), 4th rev. ed.* Leeds, West Yorkshire, England & Albuquerque, NM: Galactic Central Publications, 1986, 46 p., paper, nonf. GALACTIC CENTRAL BIBLIOGRAPHIES FOR THE AVID READER #1.

17811 *William Tenn (Philip Klass).* Albuquerque, NM: Galactic Central Publications, 1987, 7 p., paper, nonf. GALACTIC CENTRAL BIBLIOGRAPHIES FOR THE AVID READER #7.

with Chris Nelson

17812 *Bob Shaw: a working bibliography.* Albuquerque, NM: Galactic Central Publications, 1984, 8 p., paper, nonf.

with Phil Stephensen-Payne

17813 *Anne McCaffrey, dragonlady and more: a working bibliography.* Albuquerque, NM: Galactic Central Publications, 1984, 9 p., paper, nonf. GALACTIC CENTRAL BIBLIOGRAPHIES FOR THE AVID READER #13.

17814 *Anne McCaffrey, dragonlady and more: a working bibliography, 3rd rev. ed.* Leeds, West Yorkshire, England & Albuquerque, NM: Galactic Central Publications, 1989, 9+30 p., paper, nonf. GALACTIC CENTRAL BIBLIOGRAPHIES FOR THE AVID READER #13.

17815 *Bob Shaw, artist at ground zero, 4th rev. ed.* Leeds, West Yorkshire, England & Albuquerque, NM: Galactic Central Publications, 1989, 9+32 p., paper, nonf. GALACTIC CENTRAL BIBLIOGRAPHIES FOR THE AVID READER #14.

17816 *Cyril M. Kornbluth: a working bibliography.* Leeds, West Yorkshire, England & Albuquerque, NM: Galactic Central Publications, 1988, 28 p., paper, nonf. GALACTIC CENTRAL BIBLIOGRAPHIES FOR THE AVID READER #29.

17817 *Cyril M. Kornbluth, the cynical scrutineer: a working bibliography, 2nd rev. ed.* Leeds, West Yorkshire, England & Albuquerque, NM: Galactic Central Publications, 1990, 9+39 p., paper, nonf. GALACTIC CENTRAL BIBLIOGRAPHIES FOR THE AVID READER #29.

17818 *Eric Frank Russell: a working bibliography.* Leeds, West Yorkshire, England & Albuquerque, NM: Galactic Central Publications, 1986, 19 p., paper, nonf.

17819 *Frederik Pohl, merchant of excellence: a working bibliography.* Leeds, West Yorkshire, England & Albuquerque, NM: Galactic Central Publications, 1989, 9+109 p., paper, nonf. GALACTIC CENTRAL BIBLIOGRAPHIES FOR THE AVID READER #34.

17820 *Fritz Leiber, sardonic swordsman: a working bibliography, 2nd rev. ed.* Leeds, West Yorkshire, England & Albuquerque, NM: Galactic Central Publications, 1990, 9+90 p., paper, nonf. GALACTIC CENTRAL BIBLIOGRAPHIES FOR THE AVID READER #22.

17821 *Gordon Rupert Dickson, first Dorsai: a working bibliography, 4th rev. ed.* Leeds, West Yorkshire, England & Albuquerque, NM: Galactic Central Publications, 1990, 9+62 p., paper, nonf. GALACTIC CENTRAL BIBLIOGRAPHIES FOR THE AVID READER #2.

17822 *Harry Maxwell Harrison, stainless steel talent: a working bibliography, 4th rev. ed.* Leeds, West Yorkshire, England & Albuquerque, NM: Galactic Central Publications, 1989, 9+71 p., paper, nonf. GALACTIC CENTRAL BIBLIOGRAPHIES FOR THE AVID READER #9.

17823 *Jack Vance: a working bibliography.* Leeds, West Yorkshire, England & Albuquerque, NM: Galactic Central Publications, 1988, 46 p., paper, nonf. GALACTIC CENTRAL BIBLIOGRAPHIES FOR THE AVID READER #28.

17824 *Jack Vance, a fantasmic imagination: a working bibliography, 2nd rev. ed.* Leeds, West Yorkshire, England & Albuquerque, NM: Galactic Central Publications, 1990, 9+61 p., paper, nonf. GALACTIC CENTRAL BIBLIOGRAPHIES FOR THE AVID READER #28.

17825 *James Tiptree Jr., a lady of letters: a working bibliography.* Leeds, West Yorkshire, England & Albuquerque, NM: Galactic Central Publications, 1989, 9+26 p., paper, nonf. GALACTIC CENTRAL BIBLIOGRAPHIES FOR THE AVID READER #31.

17826 *John Brunner, shockwave writer: a working bibliography, 3rd ed.* Leeds, West Yorkshire, England & Albuquerque, NM: Galactic Central Publications, 1989, 9+79 p., paper, nonf. GALACTIC CENTRAL BIBLIOGRAPHIES FOR THE AVID READER #11.

17827 *John Wyndham Parkes Lucas Beynon Harris: a bibliography.* Leeds, West Yorkshire, England & Albuquerque, NM: Galactic Central Publications, 1985, 18 p., paper, nonf. GALACTIC CENTRAL BIBLIOGRAPHIES FOR THE AVID READER #16.

17828 *Keith Laumer, ambassador to space: a working bibliography,* 2nd rev. ed. Leeds, West Yorkshire, England & Albuquerque, NM: Galactic Central Publications, 1990, 9+41 p., paper, nonf. GALACTIC CENTRAL BIBLIOGRAPHIES FOR THE AVID READER #30.

17829 *Marion Zimmer Bradley, mistress of magic: a working bibliography.* Leeds, West Yorkshire, England & Albuquerque, NM: Galactic Central Publications, 1991, 9+51 p., paper, nonf. GALACTIC CENTRAL BIBLIOGRAPHIES FOR THE AVID READER #40.

17830 *Philip José Farmer, good-natured groundbreaker: a working bibliography,* 2nd rev. ed. Leeds, West Yorkshire, England & Albuquerque, NM: Galactic Central Publications, 1990, 9+63 p., paper, nonf. GALACTIC CENTRAL BIBLIOGRAPHIES FOR THE AVID READER #23.

17831 *Philip Kindred Dick, metaphysical conjurer: a working bibliography,* 3rd rev. ed. Leeds, West Yorkshire, England & Albuquerque, NM: Galactic Central Publications, 1990, 9+102 p., paper, nonf. GALACTIC CENTRAL BIBLIOGRAPHIES FOR THE AVID READER #18.

17832 *Poul Anderson, myth-master and wondermaker: a working bibliography,* 5th ed. Leeds, West Yorkshire, England & Albuquerque, NM: Galactic Central Publications, 1989, 9+123 p., paper, nonf. GALACTIC CENTRAL BIBLIOGRAPHIES FOR THE AVID READER #1.

17833 *Theodore Sturgeon, sculptor of love and hate: a working bibliography.* Leeds, West Yorkshire, England & Albuquerque, NM: Galactic Central Publications, 1989, 9+75 p., paper, nonf. GALACTIC CENTRAL BIBLIOGRAPHIES FOR THE AVID READER #32.

with Virgil S. Utter Jr.

17834 *Catherine Lucille Moore & Henry Kuttner, a marriage of souls and talent: a working bibliography.* Modesto, CA & Albuquerque, NM: Galactic Central Publications, 1986, 45 p., paper, nonf. GALACTIC CENTRAL BIBLIOGRAPHIES FOR THE AVID READER #21.

17835 *Catherine Lucille Moore & Henry Kuttner, a marriage of souls and talent: a working bibliography,* 3rd rev. ed. Leeds, West Yorkshire, England & Albuquerque, NM: Galactic Central Publications, 1989, v+92 p., paper, nonf. GALACTIC CENTRAL BIBLIOGRAPHIES FOR THE AVID READER #21.

BENSON, Michael

17836 *Vintage science fiction films, 1896-1949.* Jefferson, NC & London: McFarland & Co., 1985, ix+219 p., cloth, nonf.

BENSON, Nella

17837 *Amaranth.* New York: Avon, 1984, 172 p., paper, novel.

BENT, Jorj

17838 *Sometime after the equinox.* New York: Tower Books, 1981, 281 p., paper, novel.

BENTCLIFFE, Eric, 1927?-1992

17839 *Checklist of British science-fiction and fantasy, part 1: magazines, original & reprint.* Stockbridge, England: Northwest Science Fantasy Club, 1952?, 12 p., paper, nonf.

BENTHAM, (J.) Jeremy, 1956-

17840 *Doctor Who: the early years.* London: W. H. Allen & Co., 1986, 224 p., cloth, nonf.

BENTINE, Michael, 1922-

17841 *Lords of the levels: a novel of the paranormal.* London: Grafton Books, 1986, 302 p., cloth, novel.

BENTLEY, Peter [pseud. of Alan Moon]

17842 *Destined to survive.* London: Robert Hale, 1977, 155 p., cloth, novel.

BERBERICK, Nancy Varian, 1951-

17843 *The jewels of Elvish.* Lake Geneva, WI: TSR Inc., 1989, 343 p., paper, novel.

17844 *Shadow of the seventh moon.* New York: Ace Books, 1991, x+303 p., paper, novel.

17845 *Stormblade.* Lake Geneva, WI: TSR Inc., 1988, 347 p., paper, novel. DRAGONLANCE SAGA—HEROES #2.

BERBRICH, Joan D(olores), 1925-

17846 *Heaven and Hell.* New York, St. Louis, MO: McGraw-Hill Book Co., 1975, vii+268 p., paper, anth. [Includes some verse].

*BERCKMAN, Evelyn (Domenica), 1900-1978

BERDNYK, Oleksandr—SEE: Berdnyk, Oles

BERDNYK, Oles [i.e., Oleksandr Pavlovych Berdnyk], 1927-

17847 *Apostle of immortality: Ukrainian science fiction.* Toronto, Chicago: Bayda Books, 1984, 129 p., cloth, coll. [Translation by Yuri Tkach].

BERENBAU, Linda Bayer- —SEE: Bayer-Berenbau, Linda

BERESFORD, Elizabeth [pseud. of Inez McAlister Faber], 1897-

17848 *Hauntings: The wooden gun.* London: Hippo, Swift, 1989, 100 p., paper, novel.

BERESFORD, J(ohn) D(avys), 1873-1947

17849 *H. G. Wells.* London: Nisbet, 1915, 127 p., cloth, nonf.

BERESFORD, Leigh

17850 *Fantocine.* London: Robert Hale, 1981, 191 p., cloth, novel.

*BERESFORD, Leslie, 1891?-1937?

BERESFORD, Marcus—SEE: Brandel, Marc

BERGAMINI, David (Howland), 1928-1983

17851 *Venus development.* New York: Popular Library, 1976, 304 p., paper, novel.

BERGEN, James A(llen) Jr., 1948-

17852 *Price and reference guide to books written by Edgar Rice Burroughs, 2nd ed.* Beaverton, OR: Golden Lion, 1991, vii+214 p., paper, nonf.
17853 *A reference and price guide to U.S. books written by Edgar Rice Burroughs.* Tualatin, OR: James A. Bergen Jr., 1989, 46 p., paper, nonf.

BERGER, Harold L., 1923-

17854 *Science fiction and the new dark age.* Bowling Green, OH: Bowling Green University Popular Press, 1976, xi+231 p., cloth, nonf.

BERGER, Mel—SEE: Stein, Duffy

BERGER, Thomas (Louis), 1924-

17855 *Arthur Rex: a legendary novel.* New York: A Seymour Lawrence Book, Delacorte Press, 1978, ix+499 p., cloth, novel.
17856 *Being invisible: a novel.* Boston, Toronto: Little, Brown & Co., 1987, 262 p., cloth, novel.
17857 *Changing the past.* London: Weidenfeld & Nicolson, 1990, 285 p., cloth, novel.
17858 *Nowhere.* London: Methuen, 1986, 192 p., cloth, novel.

BERGER, Yves, 1934-

21360 *The garden.* New York: George Braziller, 1963, 226 p., cloth, novel. [Translation by Robert Baldick of *Le sud*].

BERGLUND, Edward P(aul), 1942-

17859 *The disciples of Cthulhu.* New York: DAW Books, 1976, 288 p., paper, anth. CTHULHU MYTHOS.

BERGONZI, Bernard, 1929-

17860 *The early H. G. Wells: a study of the scientific romances.* Toronto: University of Toronto Press, 1961, ix+226 p., cloth, nonf.
17861 *H. G. Wells: a collection of critical essays.* Englewood Cliffs, NJ: Prentice-Hall, 1976, 182 p., cloth, nonf. anth.

BERGSTEN, Staffan, 1932-

17862 *Mary Poppins and myth.* Stockholm, Sweden: Almquist & Wiksell, 1978, 79 p., paper?, nonf.

BERGSTROM, Elaine, 1946-

17863 *Blood alone.* New York: Jove Books, 1990, 325 p., paper, novel. AUSTRAS FAMILY #2.
17864 *Blood rites.* New York: Jove Books, 1991, 332 p., paper, novel. AUSTRAS FAMILY #3.
17865 *Shattered glass.* New York: Jove Books, 1989, 372 p., paper, novel. AUSTRAS FAMILY #1.

BERGSTROM, Janet, *with Constance Penley & Elisabeth Lyon & Lynn Spigel*

17866 *Close encounters: film, feminism, and science fiction.* Minneapolis, MN, Oxford, England: A Camera Obscura Book, Uni-

versity of Minnesota Press, 1991, xi +
298 p., cloth, nonf. anth.

BERGSTRÖM, K. Gunnar

17867 *An odyssey to freedom: four themes in
Colin Wilson's novels.* Uppsala, Sweden:
University of Uppsala, 1983, 160 p., pa-
per, nonf.

*BERK, Howard, 1926-

*BERKELEY, Edmund C(allis), 1912-

BERKEY, John, 1932- , with Sharon Berkey

17868 *John Berkey, painted space.* Pittsburgh,
PA: Friedlander Publishing Group,
1991, 95 p., paper, art.

BERKEY, Sharon, with John Berkey

17868 *John Berkey, painted space.* Pittsburgh,
PA: Friedlander Publishing Group,
1991, 95 p., paper, art.

BERKMAN, Edwina—SEE: Reed, Dana

BERLYN, Michael (Steven), 1949-

17869 *Crystal phoenix.* Toronto, New York:
Bantam Books, 1980, 214 p., paper,
novel.
17870 *The eternal enemy.* New York: William
Morrow & Co., 1990, 323 p., cloth,
novel.
17871 *The integrated man.* Toronto, New York:
Bantam Books, 1980, 214 p., paper,
novel.

as MARK SONDERS

17872 *Blight.* New York: Ace Books, 1981, 259
p., paper, novel.

BERMAN, Mitch, 1956-

17873 *Time capsule.* New York: G. P. Putnam's
Sons, 1987, 295 p., cloth, novel.

*BERMAN, Ruth (Amelia)

BERMANT, Chaim (Icyk), 1929-

17874 *Belshazzar: a cat's story for humans.* London, Boston: George Allen & Unwin,
1979, 67 p., cloth, novel.

*BERNA, Paul, 1910-

BERNANOS, Georges, 1888-1948

15792 *The star of Satan.* London: John Lane,
The Bodley Head, 1927, 339 p., cloth,
novel.
15792A retitled: *Under the sun of Satan: a novel.*
New York: Pantheon, 1949, 253 p.,
cloth, novel.

BERNAU, George, 1945-

17875 *Candle in the wind.* New York: Warner
Books, 1990, 499 p., cloth, novel.
17876 *Promises to keep.* New York: Warner
Books, 1988, 643 p., cloth, novel.

**BERNIERES, Louis de—SEE: de Bernières,
Louis**

***BERRIAULT, Gina [i.e., Georgianna], 1926-
1991**

*BERRIDGE, Jesse, 1874-1966

BERRY, Adrian (Michael), 1937-

17877 *Koyama's diamond: a novel of the future.*
New York, Washington: Vantage Press,
1982, 281 p., cloth, novel. KOYAMA #1.
17878 *Labyrinth of lies.* New York, Washington:
Vantage Press, 1984, xi + 165 p., cloth,
novel. KOYAMA #2.

*BERRY, Bryan, 1930-1955

BERRY, D(ouglas) Bruce

with Andrew J. Offutt

17879 *Genetic bomb.* New York: Warner Paperback Library, 1975, 207 p., paper, novel.

with Andrew J. Offutt as JOHN CLEVE

17880 *Pleasure us!* New York: Bee-Line Books,
1971, 187 p., paper, novel.

BERRY, James R(ussell), 1933-

17881 *The galactic invaders.* Toronto, New
York: Laser Books, 1976, 190 p., paper,
novel.
17882 *Magicians of Erianne.* New York: Harper
& Row, 1988, 246 p., cloth, novel.
17883 *Quas Starbrite / by James Berry.* Toronto,
New York: Bantam Books, 1981, 214 p.,
paper, novel.

BERRY, N. L.

17884 *Haunted: a first person space tale.* Bognor Regis, West Sussex, England: New Horizons, 1983, 205 p., cloth, novel.

BERRY, Shelley Dutton

17885 *The roots of fantasy: Myth, folklore & archetype.* Seattle, WA: World Fantasy Convention, 1989, 124 p., paper, anth.

BERRY, Stephen Ames, 1947-

17886 *The AI war.* New York: Tor SF, A Tom Doherty Associates Book, 1987, 249 p., paper, novel. JOHN HARRISON #3.
17887 *The battle for Terra Two.* New York: Tor SF, A Tom Doherty Associates Book, 1986, 247 p., paper, novel. JOHN HARRISON #2.
17888 *The biofab war.* New York: Ace Science Fiction Books, 1984, 175 p., paper, novel. JOHN HARRISON #1.
17889 *Final assault.* New York: Tor SF, A Tom Doherty Associates Book, 1988, 314 p., paper, novel. JOHN HARRISON #4.

BERTHA, Csilla, *with Donald E. Morse*

17890 *More real than reality: the fantastic in Irish literature and the arts.* New York, London: Greenwood Press, 1991, xi+266 p., cloth, nonf. anth. CONTRIBUTIONS TO THE STUDY OF SCIENCE FICTION AND FANTASY #45.

BES SHAHAR, Eluki, 1956-

17891 *Hellflower.* New York: DAW Books, 1991, 252 p., paper, novel.

BESAW, Vic—SEE: Besaw, Victor

BESAW, Victor (John), 1916-

17892 *The alien.* New York: Fawcett Gold Medal, 1979, 191 p., paper, novel.
17893 *The sword of Shandar* / by Vic Besaw. New York: Manor Books, 1978, 224 p., paper, novel.

*BEST, (Oswald) Herbert, 1894-<u>1980</u>

BESTER, Alfred, 1913-1987

17894 *The computer connection.* New York: Berkley Publishing Corp., 1975, 218 p., cloth, novel.

17894A retitled: *Extro.* London: Eyre Methuen, 1975, 218 p., cloth, novel.
17895 *The deceivers.* New York: A Wallaby Book, Simon & Schuster, 1981, 300 p., paper, novel.
    Extro—SEE: *The computer connection.*
17896 *Golem^{100}.* New York: Simon & Schuster, 1980, 384 p., cloth, novel.
17897 *The light fantastic: the great short fiction of Alfred Bester, volume I.* New York: Berkley Publishing Corp., 1976, 254 p., cloth, coll.
17898 *Star light, star bright: the great short fiction of Alfred Bester, volume II.* New York: Berkley Publishing Corp., 1976, 248 p., cloth, coll.
17899 *Starlight: the great short fiction of Alfred Bester: The light fantastic; Star light, star bright.* Garden City, NY: Nelson Doubleday, 1976, 409 p., cloth, coll. [Includes *The light fantastic* and *Star light, star bright*].

BETANCOURT, John Gregory, 1963-

17900 *The blind archer.* New York: Avon, 1988, 233 p., paper, novel.
17901 *The dragons of Komako.* New York: A Byron Preiss Visual Publications Inc. Book, Ace Books, 1989, 157 p., paper, novel. DR. BONES #4.
17902 *Johnny Zed* / by John Betancourt. New York: Popular Library, 1988, 213 p., paper, novel.
17903 *Rememory.* New York: Popular Library, 1990, 197 p., paper, novel.
17904 *Rogue pirate.* Lake Geneva, WI: Windwalker Books, TSR Inc., 1987, 219 p., paper, novel.
17905 *Slab's tavern, and other uncanny places.* Buffalo, NY: W. Paul Ganley, 1990, 96 p., cloth, coll.

as JEREMY KINGSTON

Caesar's time legions—SEE: *Robert Silverberg's Time Tours: Caesar's time legions.*
17906 *Robert Silverberg's Time Tours: Caesar's time legions.* New York: HarperPaperbacks, 1991, 139 p., paper, novel. ROBERT SILVERBERG'S TIME TOURS #6.

with *Arthur Byron Cover* and *Tim Sullivan* as THOMAS SHADWELL

The dinosaur trackers—SEE: *Robert Silverberg's Time tours: The dinosaur trackers.*

20683 *Robert Silverberg's Time tours: The dinosaur trackers.* New York: A Byron Preiss Book, HarperPaperbacks, 1991, 138 p., paper, novel. ROBERT SILVERBERG'S TIME TOURS #4.

with Byron Preiss & David Keller & Megan Miller

17907 *The ultimate Frankenstein.* New York: A Byron Preiss Book, A Dell Trade Paperback, 1991, viii+327 p., paper, anth.

17908 *The ultimate werewolf.* New York: A Byron Preiss Book, A Dell Trade Paperback, 1991, viii+357 p., paper, anth.

with Charles C. Ryan

17909 *Letters of the alien publisher.* Woburn, MA: First Books, 1991, 128 p., paper, nonf. coll.

BETCHOV, Robert, 1919-

17910 *The year of the Spiatnik: a novel.* Oakville, Ontario, Canada: CPRI Press, 1975, 278 p., cloth, novel.

BETHANCOURT, T. Ernesto [i.e., Tomás Ernesto Bethancourt Passailaigue], 1932-

17911 *The dog days of Arthur Cane.* New York: Holiday House, 1976, 160 p., cloth, novel.

17912 *Instruments of darkness.* New York: Holiday House, 1977, 159 p., cloth, novel. ODIN #2.

17913 *The mortal instruments.* New York: Holiday House, 1977, 157 p., cloth, novel. ODIN #1.

17914 *Nightmare town.* New York: Holiday House, 1979, 158 p., cloth, novel.

17915 *The tomorrow connection.* New York: Holiday House, 1984, 134 p., cloth, novel. YESTERDAY #2.

17916 *Tune in yesterday.* New York: Holiday House, 1978, 156 p., cloth, novel. YESTERDAY #1.

with Mary Shelley

17917 *Frankenstein.* Belmont, CA: David S. Lake, A Fearon Classic, 1986, v+74 p., paper, novel. [Adapted from Shelley's novel].

with Robert Louis Stevenson

17918 *Dr. Jekyll and Mr. Hyde.* Belmont, CA: Fearon Education, A Fearon Classic, 1985, 90 p., paper, novel. [Adapted from Stevenson's novella].

with H. G. Wells

17919 *The time machine.* Belmont, CA: David S. Lake, A Fearon Classic, 1986, vi+74 p., paper, novel. [Adapted from Wells's novel].

BETHELL, Jean (Frankenberry), 1922-

17920 *Pete's dragon.* New York: Wonder Books, Grosset & Dunlap, 1978, 94 p., paper, movie.

BETHKE, Bruce (Raymond), 1955-

17921 *Isaac Asimov's robot city: robots and aliens: Maverick.* New York: A Byron Preiss Visual Publications Inc. Book, Ace Books, 1990, xi+184 p., paper, novel. ISAAC ASIMOV'S ROBOT CITY: ROBOTS AND ALIENS #5.
Maverick—SEE: Isaac Asimov's robot city: robots and aliens: Maverick.

BETTELHEIM, Bruno, 1903-1990

17922 *The uses of enchantment: the meaning and importance of fairy tales.* New York: Alfred A. Knopf, 1976, vi+328+xi p., cloth, nonf.

*BEUF, Carlo (Maria Luigi), 1893-1981

BEUTTLER, Edward—SEE: Butler, Ivan

*BEYMER, William, 1881-1969

BEYNON, John, pseud.—SEE: Wyndham, John

BHATHAL, R(agbir) S(ingh), *with Dudley de Souza & Kirpal Singh*

17923 *Singapore science fiction.* Singapore: Rotary Club of Jurongtown, Singapore Science Centre, 1980, ix+116 p., cloth, anth.

*BIAGI, L. D. [pseud. of Lottie F. Ambrose]

BICKERTON, Derek, 1926-

17924 *King of the sea.* New York: Random House, 1979, 212 p., cloth, novel.

BICKHAM, Jack M(iles), 1930-

17925 *ARIEL.* New York: St. Martin's Press, 1984, 316 p., cloth, novel.
17926 *Day seven.* New York: Tor, A Tom Doherty Associates Book, 1988, 314 p., cloth, novel.

as JEFF CLINTON

17927 *Kane's odyssey.* Toronto, New York: Laser Books, 1976, 190 p., paper, novel.

BICKMORE, Deborah Talmadge- —SEE: Talmadge-Bickmore, Deborah

BICKNELL, Arthur

17928 *Scavenger's hunt.* New York: Twilight, Where Darkness Begins, 1987, 148 p., paper, novel. TWILIGHT #26.

BIDMEAD, Christopher H.

Castrovalva—SEE: *Doctor Who: Castrovalva*
17929 *Doctor Who: Castrovalva.* London: W. H. Allen, 1983, 118 p., cloth, tele. DOCTOR WHO #76.
17930 *Doctor Who: Frontios.* London: W. H. Allen, 1984, 143 p., cloth, tele. DOCTOR WHO #91.
17931 *Doctor Who: Logopolis.* London: W. H. Allen, 1982, 127 p., cloth, tele. DOCTOR WHO #41.
Frontios—SEE: *Doctor Who: Frontios.*
Logopolis—SEE: *Doctor Who: Logopolis.*

BIEDERSTADT, Lynn

17932 *The eye of the mind.* New York: Richard Marek Publishers, 1981, 298 p., cloth, novel.
17933 *Sleep: a horror story.* New York: St. Martin's Press/Richard Marek, 1986, 310 p., cloth, novel.

BIEGEL, Paul (Johannes), 1925-

17934 *The curse of the werewolf.* London: Blackie & Son, 1981, 143 p., cloth, novel. [Translation of *De vloek van woestewolf*]
17935 *The gardens of Dorr.* London: J. M. Dent & Sons, 1975, 240 p., cloth, novel. [Translation by Paul Biegel and Gillian Hume of *Tuinen van Dorr*].
17936 *The king of the Copper Mountains.* London: J. M. Dent & Sons, 1969, vi+176 p., cloth, novel. [Translation by Paul Biegel and Gillian Hume of *Sleutelkruid*].
17937 *The little captain.* London: J. M. Dent & Sons, 1971, 126 p., cloth, novel. [Translation of *Kleine kapitein*].
17938 *The twelve robbers.* London: J. M. Dent & Sons, 1974, 95 p., cloth, novel. [Translation by Patricia Crampton of *De twaalf rovers*].

BIEMILLER, Carl L(udwig), 1912-1979

17939 *The hydronaut adventures.* Garden City, NY: Doubleday & Co., 1981, 375 p., cloth, coll. HYDRONAUTS #1-3. [Includes *The hydronauts, Follow the whales,* and *The reunion* (i.e., *Escape from the crater*)].

BIERCE, Ambrose (Gwinett), 1842-1914?

17940 *The best of Ambrose Bierce.* Secaucus, NJ: Castle, 1984?, vi+484 p., cloth, coll.
17941 *The devil's advocate: an Ambrose Bierce reader.* San Francisco: Chronicle Books, 1987, 327 p., cloth, coll. [Edited by Brian St. Pierre].
17942 *The letters of Ambrose Bierce.* San Francisco: Book Club of California, 1922, xlvii+204 p., cloth, nonf. coll. [Limited to 415 copies; edited by Bertha Clark Pope].
17943 *Twenty-one letters of Ambrose Bierce.* Cleveland, OH: G. Kirk, 1922, 33 p., paper, coll. [Edited by Samuel Loveman].

BIFULCO, Michael (J).

17944 *Rocket men of the movies.* Grand Rapids, MI: Bifulco Books, 1991, 122 p., paper?, nonf.
17945 *Superman on television: a comprehensive viewer's guide to the daring exploits of Superman as presented in the TV series.* Canoga Park, CA: Bifulco Books, 1988, 109 p., paper?, nonf.

BIGGLE, Lloyd Jr., 1923-

17946 *A galaxy of strangers.* Garden City, NY: Doubleday & Co., 1976, xii+177 p., cloth, coll.
Out of the silent sky—SEE: *Rule of the door.*
01275 *The rule of the door, and other fanciful regulations.* Garden City, NY: Doubleday & Co., 1967, 206 p., cloth, coll.
01275A retitled: *Out of the silent sky.* New York: Belmont Tower Books, 1977, 176 p., pa-

per, coll. [Cover title reads: *The silent sky*].

01275B retitled: *The silent sky*. London: Robert Hale, 1979, 207 p., cloth, coll.

17947 *Silence is deadly*. Garden City, NY: Doubleday & Co., 1977, 184 p., cloth, novel. JAN DARZEK #4.

The silent sky—SEE: *The rule of the door*.

17948 *This darkening universe*. Garden City, NY: Doubleday & Co., 1976, 210 p., cloth, novel. JAN DARZEK #3.

17949 *The tunesmith*. New York: Tor SF, A Tom Doherty Associates Book, 1990, p. 97-186, paper, story. [Bound with *Eye for eye* / by Orson Scott Card].

17950 *The whirligig of time*. Garden City, NY: Doubleday & Co., 1979, 211 p., cloth, novel. JAN DARZEK #5.

with T. L. Sherred

17951 *Alien main*. Garden City, NY: Doubleday & Co., 1985, 182 p., cloth, novel. ALIEN ISLAND #2.

BIGGS, Cheryl

17952 *Yesterday's passion*. New York: Harper-Paperbacks, 1991, 311 p., paper, novel.

◆BIGGS, John Jr., 1895-1979

BIGLAND, Eileen [pseud. of Eileen Anne Carstairs Lilburn]

17953 *Marie Corelli: the woman and the legend: a biography*. London: Jarrolds Publishers, 1953, 274 p., cloth, nonf.

17954 *Mary Shelley*. London: Cassell, 1959, 269 p., cloth, nonf.

BILDERDIJK, Willem, 1756-1831

17955 *A short account of a remarkable aerial voyage and discovery of a new planet*. Paisley, Scotland: Wilfion Books, 1987, 88 p., paper, novel. [Translation by Paul Vincent of *Kor verhaal van eene aanmerklijke luchtreis en nieuwe planeetontdekking*].

BILENKIN, Dmitri(i Aleksandrovich), 1933-1987

17956 *The uncertainty principle*. New York: Macmillan Publishing Co.; London: Collier Macmillan Publishers, 1978, xii+163 p., cloth, coll. [Translated by Antonina W. Bouis].

BILES, Jack I., 1920-

with Robert O. Evans

17957 *William Golding: some critical considerations*. Lexington, KY: University Press of Kentucky, 1978, xi+283 p., cloth, nonf. anth.

with William Golding

17958 *Talk: conversations with William Golding*. New York: Harcourt Brace Jovanovich, 1970, xii+112 p., cloth, nonf. coll.

BILKER, Audrey (L.), with Harvey L. Bilker

17959 *Writing science fiction that sells*. Chicago: Contemporary Books, 1982, ix+159 p., cloth, nonf.

BILKER, Harvey L., with Audrey Bilker

17959 *Writing science fiction that sells*. Chicago: Contemporary Books, 1982, ix+159 p., cloth, nonf.

BILL, Andrew

17960 *Wrath of the ice sorcerer*. [S.l.]: Holland Studio Craft, 1989, 85 p., cloth, novel.

BILLIAS, Stephen

17961 *The American book of the dead*. New York: Popular Library, 1987, 213 p., paper, novel.

17962 *Deryni challenge: a Crossroads adventure in the world of Katherine Kurtz's Deryni*. New York: Tor, A Tom Doherty Associates Book, 1988, 27+[222] p., paper, novel. DERYNI SEQUEL; CROSSROADS ADVENTURE.

17963 *Horrible humes*. New York: Ace Books, 1991, 184 p., paper, novel. RUNESWORD #4.

17964 *The quest for the 36*. New York: Popular Library, 1988, 210 p., paper, novel.

BILLSON, Anne

17965 *Dream demon*. London: New English Library, 1989, 188 p., paper, movie.

BILYEU, Richard

17966 *The Tanelorn archives: a primary and secondary bibliography of the works of Michael Moorcock, 1949-1979*. Altona, Manitoba, Canada: Pandora's Books, 1981, 108 p., cloth, nonf.

*BINDER, Earl Andrew, 1904-1965

BINGEMAN, Alison, *with Gerry Davis*

    The Celestial Toymaker—SEE: *Doctor Who: The Celestial Toymaker.*

17967 *Doctor Who: The Celestial Toymaker.* London: W. H. Allen, 1986, 127 p., cloth, tele. DOCTOR WHO #111.

BINGHAM, Carson, pseud.—SEE: Cassiday, Bruce

BINGHAM, Roger, *with Raymond Hawkey*

17968 *Wild card.* London: Sphere Books, 1988, 283 p., paper, novel. PRESIDENTIAL TRILOGY #1. [Revised edition of #01309].

BINGLEY, Margaret, 1947-

17969 *After Alice died.* London: Piatkus, 1986, 234 p., cloth, novel.
17970 retitled: *After Alice.* New York: Popular Library, 1989, 234 p., paper, novel.
    After Alice—SEE: *After Alice died.*
17971 *Children of the night.* London: Piatkus, 1985, 292 p., cloth, novel.
    Deadtime story—SEE: *The unquiet dead.*
17972 *The devil's child.* Loughton: Piatkus, 1983, 253 p., cloth, novel.
17973 *Gateway to Hell.* London: Piatkus, 1991, 313 p., cloth, novel.
17974 *Seeds of evil.* London: Piatkus, 1988, 245 p., cloth, novel.
17975 *The unquiet dead.* London: Piatkus, 1987, 215 p., cloth, novel.
17975A retitled: *Deadtime story.* New York: Popular Library, 1990, 232 p., paper, novel.
17976 *Village of Satan.* London: Piatkus, 1990, 203 p., cloth, novel.
17977 *The waiting darkness.* London: Piatkus, 1984, 236 p., cloth, novel.

BINKIN, Irving, 1906?-1989?, *with Mark Owings*

17978 *A catalog of Lovecraftiana: the Grill/Binkin collection.* Baltimore, MD: Mirage Press, 1975, x+71 p., cloth, nonf.

*BINNS, Ottwell, 1872-

BIOY CASARES, Adolfo, 1914- , *with Jorge Luis Borges & Silvina Ocampo*

17979 *The book of fantasy.* London: Xanadu, 1988, 384 p., cloth, anth. [Translation of *Antología de la literatura fantástica*].

BIRD, Antoinette Kelsall

17980 *The daughters of Megwyn.* London: Headline, 1987, vi+250 p., cloth, novel.

BIRDSALL, Peter, 1948-, *with Delores Broten*

17981 *A science fiction teaching guide.* Victoria, British Columbia, Canada: CANLIT, 1978, 61 p., paper, nonf.

*BIRDWELL, Russell (J.), 1903-1977

*BIRKIN, Charles (Lloyd), Sir, 5th Bart., 1907-1985

BIRNBAUM, Alfred (T.), 1957-

17982 *Monkey brain sushi: new tastes in Japanese fiction.* Tokyo: Kodansha, 1991, 304 p., cloth, anth.

BIRNBAUM, Milton, 1919-

17983 *Aldous Huxley's quest for values.* Knoxville, TN: University of Tennessee Press, 1971, x+230 p., cloth, nonf.

BIRREN, Faber—SEE: Lang, Gregor

BISCHOFF, David (Fredrick), 1951-

17984 *Abduction: the UFO conspiracy.* New York: Warner Books, 1990, 328 p., paper, novel. UFO CONSPIRACY #1.
17985 *The blob: a novel.* New York: Bantam Books, 1988, 210 p., paper, movie.
17986 *The crunch bunch.* New York: Avon, 1985, 143 p., paper, novel.
17987 *Deception: the UFO conspiracy.* New York: Warner Books, 1991, 324 p., paper, novel. UFO CONSPIRACY #2.
17988 *The destiny dice.* New York: A Signet Book, New American Library, 1985, 238 p., paper, novel. GAMING MAGI #1.
17989 *Galactic warriors.* New York: Ace Science Fiction Books, 1985, 188 p., paper, novel. STAR HOUNDS #2.
17990 *Gremlins 2: the new batch.* New York: Avon Books, 1990, 225 p., paper, movie. GREMLINS #2.
17991 *The infinite battle.* New York: Ace Science Fiction Books, 1985, 171 p., paper, novel. STARHOUNDS #1.
17992 *The macrocosmic conflict.* New York: Ace Science Fiction Books, 1986, 202 p., paper, novel. STAR HOUNDS #3.
17993 *Mandala* / by David F. Bischoff. New York: Berkley Books, 1983, 232 p., paper, novel.

17994 *The Manhattan project.* New York: Avon, 1986, 216 p., paper, movie.

The new batch—SEE: *Gremlins 2: the new batch.*

17995 *Night of the living shark!* New York: A GLC Book, Ace Books, 1991, 153 p., paper, novel. DANIEL M. PINKWATER'S MELVINGE OF THE MEGAVERSE #1.

17996 *Nightworld.* New York: A Del Rey Book, Ballantine Books, 1979, 199 p., paper, novel. NIGHTWORLD #1.

17997 *Quest.* Milwaukee, WI: Raintree Editions, 1977, 64 p., cloth, anth.

17998 *Revelation: the UFO conspiracy.* New York: Warner Books, 1991, 355 p., paper, novel. UFO CONSPIRACY #3.

17999 *Search for dinosaurs.* Toronto, New York: Bantam Books, 1984, 120 p., paper, novel. TIME MACHINE #2.

18000 *Some kind of wonderer.* New York: Bantam Books, 1987, 192 p., paper, novel.

18001 *Star Fall: a space fantasy.* New York: Berkley Books, 1980, 233 p., paper, novel. STAR FALL #1.

18002 *Star spring: a space operetta.* New York: Berkley Books, 1982, 249 p., paper, novel. STAR FALL #2.

18003 *Strange encounters.* Milwaukee, WI: Raintree Editions, 1977, 64 p., cloth, anth.

18004 *The unicorn gambit.* New York: A Signet Book, New American Library, 1986, 237 p., paper, novel. GAMING MAGI #3.

18005 *Vampires of nightworld.* New York: A Del Rey Book, Ballantine Books, 1981, 182 p., paper, novel. NIGHTWORLD #2.

18006 *WarGames: a novel.* New York: A Dell Book, 1983, 220 p., paper, movie.

18007 *Wraith Board.* New York: A Signet Book, New American Library, 1985, 238 p., paper, novel. GAMING MAGI #2.

alone or with others as MARK GRANT

18008 *Holocaust horror.* New York: Avon Books, 1991, 196 p., paper, novel. MUTANTS AMOK #4.

18009 *Mutant hell.* New York: Avon Books, 1991, 216 p., paper, novel. MUTANTS AMOK #2.

18010 *Mutants amok.* New York: Avon Books, 1991, 216 p., paper, novel. MUTANTS AMOK #1. [With Tim Sullivan].

18011 *Rebel attack.* New York: Avon Books, 1991, 169 p., paper, novel. MUTANTS AMOK #3.

with Dennis R. Bailey

17214 *Tin woodman* / by David F. Bischoff & Dennis R. Bailey. Garden City, NY: Doubleday & Co., 1979, 182 p., cloth, novel.

with Rich Brown & Linda Richardson

18012 *A personal demon.* New York: A Signet Book, New American Library, 1985, 253 p., paper, novel.

with Harry Harrison

18013 *Bill, the galactic hero on the planet of tasteless pleasure.* New York: A Byron Preiss Book, Avon Books, 1991, 213 p., paper, novel. BILL, THE GALACTIC HERO #3.

18014 *Bill, the galactic hero on the planet of ten thousand bars.* New York: A Byron Preiss Book, Avon Books, 1991, 214 p., paper, novel. BILL, THE GALACTIC HERO #5.

with Christopher Lampton

18015 *The seeker.* Toronto, New York: Laser Books, 1976, 190 p., paper, novel.

with Thomas F. Monteleone

18016 *Day of the dragonstar.* New York: Berkley Books, 1983, 291 p., paper, novel. DRAGONSTAR TRILOGY #1.

18017 *Dragonstar destiny* / by David F. Bischoff. New York: Ace Books, 1989, 216 p., paper, novel. DRAGONSTAR TRILOGY #3.

18018 *Night of the Dragonstar* / by David F. Bischoff. New York: Berkley Books, 1985, 264 p., paper, novel. DRAGONSTAR TRILOGY #2.

with Charles Sheffield

18019 *The Selkie.* New York: Macmillan Publishing Co., 1982, 375 p., cloth, novel.

with Ted White

18020 *Forbidden world: a science fiction novel* / by Ted White and Dave Bischoff. New York: Popular Library, 1978, 224 p., paper, novel.

BISCHOFF, Heather Woodard, *with Edwin Woodard*

18021 *Storehouses of the snow.* New York: Leisure Books, 1980, 284 p, paper, novel.

BISHOP, Carly

18022 *Prince of dreams.* Toronto, New York: Harlequin Books, 1990, 252 p., paper, novel.

BISHOP, George (Victor), 1924-

18023 *The apparition.* Toronto, New York: Bantam Books, 1979, 211 p., paper, novel.

18024 *The shuttle people.* Toronto, New York: Bantam Books, 1983, 210 p., paper, novel.

BISHOP, Gerald (Vernon), 1949-

18025 *Science fiction books published in Britain, 1972 & 1973.* Winchester, England: Aardvark House, 1975, v+33 p., paper, nonf.

18000 *Science fiction books published in Britain, 1974-1978.* Winchester, England: Aardvark House, 1979, vi+82 p., paper, nonf.

BISHOP, Leonard, 1922-

18026 *The everlasting.* New York: Poseidon Press, 1982, 479 p., cloth, novel.

BISHOP, Michael (Lawson), 1945-

18027 *Ancient of days.* New York: Arbor House, 1985, 354 p., cloth, novel.

18028 *And strange at Ecbatan the trees: a novel.* New York: Harper & Row, 1976, 154 p., cloth, novel.

18028A retitled: *Beneath the shattered moons.* New York: DAW Books, 1977, 189 p., paper, novel.

20183 retitled: *Beneath the shattered moons; &, The white otters of childhood.* London: Sphere Books, 1978, 221 p., paper, coll. [Expanded edition].

18029 *Apartheid, superstrings, and Mordecai Thubana.* Eugene, OR: Axolotl Press, 1989, [18]+95 p., cloth, novel. AXOLOTL PRESS #10.

Beneath the shattered moons—SEE: *And strange at Ecbatan the trees.*

18030 *Blooded on Arachne.* Sauk City, WI: Arkham House, 1982, xiii+338 p., cloth, coll. [Includes some verse].

18031 *Catacomb years.* New York: Berkley Publishing Corp., 1979, 384 p., cloth, novel. URBAN NUCLEUS SERIES.

18032 *Close encounters with the deity: stories.* Atlanta, GA: Peachtree Publishers, 1986, vi+306 p., cloth, coll.

18033 *Emphatically not SF, almost.* Eugene, OR: Pulphouse Publishing, 1990 (i.e., 1991), 102 p., cloth, coll. AUTHOR'S CHOICE MONTHLY #15.

Eyes of fire—SEE: *A funeral for the eyes of fire.*

18034 *A funeral for the eyes of fire.* New York: Ballantine Books, 1975, 294 p., paper, novel.

18035 retitled: *Eyes of fire.* New York: Pocket Books, 1980, 262 p., paper, novel. [Revised edition].

18036 retitled: *A funeral for the eyes of fire.* Worcester Park, Surrey, England: Kerosina, 1989, 255 p., cloth, novel. [Substantially rewritten again].

18037 *Light years and dark: science fiction and fantasy of and for our time.* New York: Berkley Books, 1984, xiv+498 p., paper, anth. [Winner of the *Locus* Award for Best Anthology, 1984 (1985)].

18038 *A little knowledge.* New York: Berkley Publishing Corp., 1977, xxi+293 p., cloth, novel. URBAN NUCLEUS SERIES.

18039 *Nebula awards 23: SFWA's choices for the best science fiction & fantasy 1987.* San Diego, CA, New York: Harcourt Brace Jovanovich, Publishers, 1989, x+374 p., cloth, anth.

18040 *Nebula awards 24: SFWA's choices for the best science fiction & fantasy 1988.* San Diego, CA, New York: Harcourt Brace Jovanovich, Publishers, 1990, xv+302 p., cloth, anth.

18041 *Nebula awards 25: SFWA's choices for the best science fiction & fantasy 1989.* San Diego, CA, New York: Harcourt Brace Jovanovich, Publishers, 1991, xv+346 p., cloth, anth.

18042 *No enemy but time: a novel.* New York: Timescape Books, 1982, 397 p., cloth, novel. [Winner of the Nebula Award for Best Novel, 1982 (1983)].

18043 *One winter in Eden.* Sauk City, WI: Arkham House, 1984, xiv+273 p., cloth, coll.

Philip K. Dick is dead, alas—SEE: *The secret ascension.*

18044 *The quickening.* Eugene, OR: Pulphouse Publishing, 1991, 44 p., paper, story. SHORT STORY PAPERBACKS #12.

18045 *The secret ascension; or, Philip K. Dick is dead, alas.* New York: Tor, A Tom Doherty Associates Book, 1987, x+341 p., cloth, novel.

18045A retitled: *Philip K. Dick is dead, alas.* London: Grafton, 1988, 411 p., cloth, novel.

18046 *Stolen faces.* New York: Harper & Row, 1977, 176 p., cloth, novel.

18047 *Transfigurations.* New York: Berkley Publishing Corp., 1979, 362 p., cloth, novel.

18048 *Unicorn mountain.* New York: Arbor House, William Morrow & Co., 1988, x+367 p., cloth, novel.

18049 *Who made Stevie Crye? a novel of the American South.* Sauk City, WI: Arkham House, 1984, 309 p., cloth, novel.

with Ian Watson

18050 *Changes: stories of metamorphosis: an anthology of speculative fiction about startling metamorphoses, both psychological and physical.* New York: Ace Science Fiction Books, 1983, 259 p., paper, anth.

18051 *Under heaven's bridge.* London: Victor Gollancz, 1980 (i.e., 1981), 159 p., cloth, novel. URBAN NUCLEUS SERIES.

BISHOP, Morchard [pseud. of Oliver Stonor], 1903- , *with Arthur Machen*

18051 *Dreams and visions: a brief journey into the remarkable imagination of Arthur Machen, as recorded by Morchard Bishop, with a postscript from the unpublished portion of The secret glory.* Southampton, England: Caermaen Books, 1987, 7 p., paper, story.

*BISHOP, Zealia B(rown), 1897-1968

*BISS, Gerald, 1876-

BISSON, Terry (Ballantine), 1942-

18052 *Fire on the mountain.* New York: Arbor House, 1988, 167 p., cloth, novel.

18053 *Talking man.* New York: Arbor House, 1986, 192 p., cloth, novel.

18054 *Voyage to the red planet.* New York: William Morrow & Co., 1990, 236 p., cloth, novel.

18055 *Wyrldmaker: a heroic romance.* New York: A Timescape Book, Pocket Books, 1981, 176 p., paper, novel.

BITTNER, James W(arren), 1921-1977

18056 *Approaches to the fiction of Ursula K. Le Guin.* Ann Arbor, MI: UMI Research Press, 1984, xviii+161 p., cloth, nonf. STUDIES IN SPECULATIVE FICTION #4.

BITTNER, William (Robert), 1921-1977

18057 *Poe: a biography.* Boston: Little, Brown & Co., 1962, 306 p., cloth, nonf.

BIXBY, E. Rew, 1920?-

18058 *Ambush planet.* Canoga Park, CA: Major Books, 1978 (i.e., 1980?), 224 p., paper, novel.

18059 *Fire throne mountain.* New York: Tower Books, 1981, 206 p., paper, novel.

BIZAR, Scott, *with Lin Carter*

18060 *Royal armies of the Hyborean Age: a wargamers guide to the age of Conan.* Roslyn, NY: Fantasy Games Unlimited, 1975, vii+56 p., paper, nonf.

BJERKE, Odd, *with Meredith Motson*

18061 *The search for Trollhaven.* Boise, ID: Beatty Books, 1977, 172 p., cloth, novel.

BJORNSTAD, James, 1940- , *with John Weldon*

18062 *Playing with fire.* Chicago: Moody Press, 1984, 91 p., paper, nonf.

*BLACK, Angus, 1943

BLACK, Campbell (Armstrong?), 1944

18063 *Brainfire: a novel.* New York: William Morrow & Co., 1979, 360 p., cloth, novel.

18064 *Letters from the dead.* New York: Villard Books, 1985, 227 p., cloth, novel.

18065 *The piper.* New York: Pocket Books, 1986, 343 p., paper, novel.

18066 *Raiders of the lost Ark: novel.* New York: Ballantine Books, 1981, 181 p., paper, movie. INDIANA JONES #1.

18067 *The wanting.* New York: McGraw-Hill Book Co., 1986, 263 p., cloth, novel.

as THOMAS ALTMAN

18068 *The true bride: a novel.* Toronto, New York: Bantam Books, 1982, 214 p., paper, novel.

as CAMPBELL ARMSTRONG

18063A *Brainfire.* New York: Harper Paperbacks, 1990, 414 p., cloth, [Previously published under the name Campbell Black].

with Jeffrey Caine as JEFFREY CAMPBELL

18069   *The homing.* New York: G. P. Putnam's Sons, 1980, 275 p., cloth, novel.

BLACK, Christopher

18070   *The android invasion.* New York: A Yearling Book, 1984, 117 p., paper, fiction. STAR CHALLENGE #2.
18071   *The cosmic funhouse.* New York: A Yearling Book, 1984, 117 p., paper, fiction. STAR CHALLENGE #3.
18072   *Dimension of doom.* New York: A Yearling Book, 1985, 117 p., paper, fiction. STAR CHALLENGE #7.
18073   *The exploding suns.* New York: A Yearling Book, 1984, 117 p., paper, fiction. STAR CHALLENGE #4.
18074   *Galactic raiders.* New York: A Yearling Book, 1984, 117 p., paper, fiction. STAR CHALLENGE #5.
18075   *The haunted planet.* New York: A Yearling Book, 1985, 117 p., paper, fiction. STAR CHALLENGE #10.
18076   *The lost planet.* New York: A Yearling Book, 1985, 117 p., paper, fiction. STAR CHALLENGE #8.
18077   *Moons of mystery.* New York: A Yearling Book, 1985, 117 p., paper, fiction. STAR CHALLENGE #9.
18078   *Planets in peril.* New York: A Yearling Book, 1984, 117 p., paper, fiction. STAR CHALLENGE #1.
18079   *The weird zone.* New York: A Yearling Book, 1984, 117 p., paper, fiction. STAR CHALLENGE #6.

*BLACK, Dorothy (Delius), 1899-1985

BLACK, Ian Stuart, 1915-

18080   *Cry wolf.* London: Constable, 1990, 283 p., cloth, novel.
18081   *Doctor Who: The Macra terror.* London: W. H. Allen & Co., 1987, 138 p., cloth, tele. DOCTOR WHO #123.
18082   *Doctor Who: The savages.* London: W. H. Allen & Co., 1986, 127 p., cloth, tele. DOCTOR WHO #109.
18083   *Doctor Who: The war machines.* London: W. H. Allen & Co., 1988, 142 p., cloth, tele. DOCTOR WHO #136.
　　　　The Macra terror—SEE: Doctor Who: The Macra terror.
　　　　The savages—SEE: Doctor Who: The savages.
　　　　The war machines—SEE: Doctor Who: The war machines.

BLACK, Jeannie

18084   *Ring of the ruby dragon.* Lake Geneva, WI: TSR Inc., 1983, 157 p., paper, novel. HEARTQUEST #1.

BLACK, Malacai

18085   *On my honor.* New York: Pinnacle Books, Windsor Publishing Corp., 1989, 431 p., paper, novel.

BLACK, Robert, pseud.-SEE: Holdstock, Robert

BLACK, William D., *with Christopher Keane*

18086   *Christmas babies.* New York, London: Pocket Star Books, 1991, 280 p., paper, novel.

BLACKBURN, John (Fenwick Anderson), 1923-

18087   *Our lady of pain.* London: Jonathan Cape, 1974, 191 p., cloth, novel.

BLACKBURN, Susan Stone- —SEE: Stone-Blackburn, Susan

BLACKFORD, Jenny, 1957- , *with Russell Blackford & Lucy Sussex & Norman Talbot*

18088   *Contrary modes: proceedings of the World Science Fiction Conference, Melbourne, Australia, 1985.* Melbourne, Australia: Ebony Books in Association with Department of English, University of Newcastle, 1985, 154 p., paper, nonf. anth.

BLACKFORD, Russell (Kenneth), 1954-

18089   *The tempting of the witch king.* St. Kilda, Victoria, Australia: Cory & Collins, 1983, 265 p., paper, novel.

with Jenny Blackford & Lucy Sussex & Norman Talbot

18088   *Contrary modes: proceedings of the World Science Fiction Conference, Melbourne, Australia, 1985.* Melbourne, Australia: Ebony Books in Association with Department of English, University of Newcastle, 1985, 154 p., paper, nonf. anth.

with David King

18090   *Urban fantasies.* Melbourne, Australia: Ebony Books, 1985, 177 p., paper, anth.

BLACKLIN, Malcolm, pseud.—SEE: Chambers, Aidan

BLACKMOOR, Edmund, pseud.

18091 *Satanic orgy*. Sausalito, CA: Tiburon Publishing House, 1974, 183 p., paper, novel

BLACKMORE, Leigh (D.)

18092 *Brian Lumley: a new bibliography*. Penrith, New South Wales, Australia: Dark Press Publication, 1984, 53 p., paper, nonf.

with S. T. Joshi

18093 *H. P. Lovecraft and Lovecraft criticism: an annotated bibliography supplement, 1980-1984*. West Warwick, RI: Necronomicon Press, 1985, iv+72 p., paper, nonf.

*BLACKSTOCK, Charity [pseud. of Ursula Torday], 1888-

BLACKSTONE, James, pseud.—SEE: Brosnan, John & Baxter, John

BLACKWELDER, Richard E(liot), 1909-

18094 *Tolkien phraseology: a companion to A Tolkien thesaurus*. Milwaukee, WI: Tolkien Archives Fund, Marquette University, 1990, 15 p., paper, nonf.
18095 *A Tolkien thesaurus*. New York, London: Garland Publishing, 1990, 277 p., cloth, nonf.

BLACKWOOD, Algernon (Henry), 1869-1951

18096 *The magic mirror: lost supernatural and mystery stories*. London: William Kimber, 1989, 235 p., cloth, coll. [Edited by Mike Ashley].
18097 *The mysterious house*. Edinburgh, Scotland: Tregara Press, 1987, 22 p., paper, story. [Limited to 125 copies].
18098 *Tales of terror and darkness*. London, New York: Spring Books, 1977, 793 p., cloth, coll.
18099 *Tales of the supernatural*. Suffolk, England: Boydell Press, 1983, xi+240 p., paper, coll.

BLACKWOOD, Gary L.

18100 *Beyond the door*. New York: Atheneum; Toronto: Collier Macmillan Canada; NY: Maxwell Macmillan International Publishing Group, 1991, 166 p., cloth, novel.
18101 *The dying sun*. New York: Atheneum, 1989, 213 p., cloth, novel.

BLAINE, John [pseud. of Harold Leland "Hal" Goodwin], 1914-1990

18102 *The magic talisman*. Mountain Home, TN: Manuscript Press, 1990, vi+247 p., cloth, novel. RICK BRANT #24. [The last of the series, originally written in the 1960s].

*BLAIR, Andrew, d. 1885

BLAIR, Cynthia, 1953-

18103 *Freedom to dream*. New York: Fawcett Juniper, 1987, 139 p., paper, novel.

BLAIR, Eric—SEE: Orwell, George

BLAIR, John (M.), 1961-

18104 *A landscape of darkness*. New York: A Del Rey Book, Ballantine Books, 1990, 247 p., paper, novel.

BLAIR, Karin

18105 *Meaning in Star Trek*. Chambersburg, PA: Anima Books, 1977, vi+157 p., cloth, nonf.

BLAIR, Pauline Hunter—SEE: Clarke, Pauline

*BLAIR, Peter Hunter, 1912-1982

BLAKE, Katherine

18106 *The interior life*. New York: Baen Fantasy, 1990, 313 p., paper, novel.
18107 *Night stands at the door: a novel*. New York: Stein & Day, 1974, 236 p., cloth, novel.

*BLAKE, Stacey, 1878-1964

BLAKE, Stephanie, pseud.—SEE: Pearl, Jack

BLAKE, Susan

18108 *The haunted dollhouse*. New York: Dell/Twilight, 1984, 153 p., paper, novel. TWILIGHT #22.

BLAKE, William Dorsey

18109 *My time or yours.* New York: Manor Books, 1980, 220 p., paper, novel.

*BLAKEMORE, Felix J(ohn), 1872-

BLAKENEY, Jay D. [pseud. of Deborah Ann Chester], 1957-

18110 *The children of Anthi.* New York: Ace Science Fiction Books, 1985, 251 p., paper, novel. ANTHI #1.
18111 *The Goda war.* New York: Ace Books, 1989, 234 p., paper, novel.
18112 *The Omcri matrix.* New York: Ace Science Fiction Books, 1987, 203 p., paper, novel.
18113 *Requiem for Anthi.* New York: Ace Books, 1990, 202 p., paper, novel. ANTHI #2.

as SEAN DALTON

18114 *Beyond the void.* New York: Ace Books, 1991, 203 p., paper, novel. OPERATION STARHAWKS #3.
18115 *Code name Peregrine.* New York: Ace Books, 1990, 184 p., paper, novel. OPERATION STARHAWKS #2.
18116 *Destination: mutiny.* New York: Ace Books, 1991, 181 p., paper, novel. OPERATION STARHAWKS #5.
18117 *The Rostma lure.* New York: Ace Books, 1991, 169 p., paper, novel. OPERATION STARHAWKS #4.
18118 *Space hawks.* New York: Ace Books, 1990, 188 p., paper, novel. OPERATION STARHAWKS #1. [Title is correct as given].

BLAKESLEE, Mermer

18119 *Same blood.* Boston: Houghton Mifflin Co., 1989, xii+178 p., cloth, novel.

*BLANCHARD, Charles Elton, 1868-1945

BLANCHE, John, *with Ian Miller*

18120 *Ratspike.* Honesdale, PA: Games Workshop/GW Books, 1990, 140 p., cloth, art.

BLAND, Jay, 1945-

18121 *Lavington Pugh.* Carlton, Victoria, Australia: Norstrilia Press, 1982, 178 p., paper, novel.

BLANK, Karen [i.e., Karen Blank Ranade]

18122 *The Boskone 9 filk-song book.* Cambridge, MA: New England Science Fiction Association, 1972, 17 p., paper, nonf. anth.

BLANKENSHIP, William D(ouglas), 1934-

18123 *Blood stripe.* New York: Avon, 1987, 393 p., paper, novel.

BLANPIED, Pamela Wharton, 1937-

18124 *Dragons: an introduction to the modern infestation.* New York: Warner Books, 1980, 194 p., cloth, fiction.

BLASHFIELD, Jean

18125 *The art of Dragon Magazine.* Lake Geneva, WI: TSR Inc., 1988, 128 p., paper, art.
18126 *The ghost tower.* Lake Geneva, WI: TSR Inc., 1985, 189 p., paper, novel. SUPER ENDLESS QUEST ADVENTURE GAMEBOOK #2.
18127 *Master of Ravenloft.* Lake Geneva, WI: TSR Inc., 1986, 189 p., paper, novel. ADVANCED DUNGEONS & DRAGONS ADVENTURE GAMEBOOK #6.
18128 *Villains of Volturnus.* Lake Geneva, WI: TSR Inc., 1983, 157 p., paper, novel. ENDLESS QUEST #8.

with Beverly Charette

18129 *Star rangers and the spy.* Lake Geneva, WI: TSR Inc., 1984, 77 p., paper, novel. FANTASY FOREST BOOK #6.

with James M. Ward

18130 *Faerie mound of dragonkind.* Lake Geneva, WI: TSR Inc., 1987, 157 p., paper, novel. CATACOMBS BOOKS #1.
18131 *Gnomes-100, dragons-0.* Lake Geneva, WI: TSR, 1987, [156] p., paper, fiction. CATACOMBS BOOKS #2.

BLATTY, William Peter, 1928-

Exorcist III: Legion—SEE: *Legion: a novel.*
18132 *Legion: a novel.* New York: Simon & Schuster, 1983, 269 p., cloth, novel. LT. KINDERMAN #2.
18132A retitled: *Exorcist III: Legion.* New York, London: Pocket Books, 1990, 310 p., paper, novel. LT. KINDERMAN #2.
18133 *William Peter Blatty on The exorcist, from novel to film.* Toronto, New York:

Bantam Books, 1974, 375 p., paper, nonf.

BLAYLOCK, James P(aul), 1950-

18134 *The digging leviathan.* New York: Ace Science Fiction Books, 1984, 276 p., paper, novel.

18135 *The disappearing dwarf.* New York: A Del Rey Book, Ballantine Books, 1983, 275 p., paper, novel. JONATHAN BING #2.

18136 *The elfin ship.* New York: A Del Rey Book, Ballantine Books, 1982, 337 p., paper, novel. JONATHAN BING #1.

18137 *Homunculus.* New York: Ace Science Fiction Books, 1986, 247 p., paper, novel.

18138 *Land of dreams.* New York: Arbor House, 1987, 264 p., cloth, novel.

18139 *The last coin.* Willimantic, CT: Mark V. Ziesing, 1988, viii+330 p., cloth, novel. [Limited to 750 copies].

18140 *The magic spectacles.* Bath, Avon, England: Morrigan Publications, 1991, 186 p., cloth, novel. [The special edition (250 copies) includes an extra essay by Lewis Shiner; the trade edition (178 p.) is limited to 750 copies].

18141 *Paper dragons.* Seattle, WA: Axolotl Press, 1986, 26 p., cloth, story.

18142 *The paper grail.* Norwalk, CT: Easton Press, 1991, 371 p., cloth, novel.

18143 *The pink of fading neon.* Seattle, WA: Axolotl Press, 1986, 8 p., cloth, story. [Bound with *The way down the hill* / by Tim Powers].

18144 *The shadow on the doorstep.* Seattle, WA: Axolotl Press, 1987, 14 p., cloth, story. AXOLOTL DOUBLE #2; AXOLOTL PRESS #6. [Bound with *Trilobyte* / by Edward Bryant; limited to 300 copies].

18145 *The stone giant.* New York: Ace Books, 1989, 264 p., paper, novel. JONATHAN BING #3.

18146 *Two views of a cave painting; and, The idol's eye.* Seattle, WA: Axolotl Press, 1988, 22 p., cloth, coll. AXOLOTL DOUBLE #3; AXOLOTL PRESS #7. [Bound with *Escape from Kathmandu* / by Kim Stanley Robinson].

BLAYN, Hugo, pseud.—SEE: Fearn, John Russell

BLEICH, (Judah) David, 1936-

18147 *Utopia: the psychology of a cultural fantasy.* Ann Arbor, MI: UMI Research Press, 1984, 154 p., cloth, nonf. STUDIES IN SPECULATIVE FICTION #5.

BLEILER, E(verett) F(ranklin), 1920-

18148 *The checklist of science-fiction and supernatural fiction, 2nd ed.* Glen Rock, NJ: Firebell Books, 1978, xxii+266 p., cloth, nonf. [A revised and expanded edition of *The checklist of fantastic literature* (see #01465)].

18149 *The golem* / Gustav Meyrink ; *The man who was born again* / Paul Busson: *two German supernatural novels.* New York: Dover Publications, 1976, xxv+412 p., paper, anth.

18150 *The guide to supernatural fiction: a full description of 1,775 books from 1750 to 1960, including ghost stories, weird fiction, stories of supernatural horror, fantasy, gothic novels, occult fiction, and similar literature, with author, title, and motif indexes.* Kent, OH: Kent State University Press, 1983, ix+723 p., cloth, nonf.

18151 *Science fiction writers: critical studies of the major writers from the early nineteenth century to the present day.* New York: Charles Scribner's Sons, 1982, xv+623 p., cloth, nonf. anth.

18152 *Supernatural fiction writers: fantasy and horror.* New York: Charles Scribner's Sons, 1985, xix+1169 p. in 2 v., cloth, nonf. anth.

18153 *Three supernatural novels of the Victorian period.* New York: Dover Publications, 1975, xiii+325 p., paper, anth.

18154 *A treasury of Victorian ghost stories.* New York: Charles Scribner's Sons, 1981, viii+358 p., cloth, anth.

with Richard Bleiler

18155 *Science fiction: the early years: full description of more than 3,000 science-fiction stories from earliest times to the appearance of the genre magazines in 1930, with author, title, and motif indexes* / by Everett F. Bleiler.... Kent, OH, London: Kent State University Press, 1990, xxiii+998 p., cloth, nonf. [Winner of the *Locus* Award for Best Nonfiction, 1991 (1992)].

BLEILER, Richard (James), 1959-

18156 *The annotated index to The Thrill Book: complete indexes to and descriptions of everything published in Street & Smith's The Thrill Book.* Mercer Island, WA:

Starmont House, 1991, vii+256 p., cloth, nonf.   STARMONT REFERENCE GUIDE #18.

18157   *The index to Adventure Magazine.* Mercer Island, WA: Starmont House, 1990, 2 v. [I-xii, 505 p.; II-576 p.], cloth, nonf.

with Everett F. Bleiler

18155   *Science fiction: the early years: full description of more than 3,000 science-fiction stories from earliest times to the appearance of the genre magazines in 1930, with author, title, and motif indexes.* Kent, OH, London: Kent State University Press, 1990, xxiii+998 p., cloth, nonf. [Winner of the *Locus* Award for Best Nonfiction, 1991 (1992)].

BLISH, James (Benjamin), 1921-1975

18158   *After such knowledge.* London: Legend, 1991, 730 p., paper, coll. AFTER SUCH KNOWLEDGE #1-4. [Includes *Dr. Mirabilis, Black Easter, The day after judgment, A case of conscience*].

18159   *The best of James Blish.* New York: A Del Rey Book, Ballantine Books, 1979, xxi+358 p., paper, coll. [Edited by Robert A. W. Lowndes; not the same book as the 1973 title].

01484   *Best science fiction stories of James Blish, revised edition.* London: Faber & Faber, 1973, 216 p., cloth, coll.

01484A   retitled: *The testament of Andros.* London: Arrow Books, 1977, 216 p., paper, coll.

18160   *Black Easter; The day after judgment.* Boston: Gregg Press, 1980, x+165, 166 p., cloth, coll. AFTER SUCH KNOWLEDGE #2-3.

18161   *Cities in flight, volume 1.* Riverdale, NY: Baen Books, 1991, 309 p., paper, coll. CITIES IN FLIGHT #1-2. [Includes *They shall have stars; A life for the stars*].

18162   *Cities in flight, volume 2.* Riverdale, NY: Baen Books, 1991, 393 p., paper, coll. CITIES IN FLIGHT #3-4. [Includes *Earthman, Go Home; The Triumph of time*].
Day of the dove—SEE: *Star Trek 11.*

18163   *The devil's day.* New York: Baen Fantasy, 1990, 312 p., paper, coll. AFTER SUCH KNOWLEDGE #2-3. [Includes *Black Easter; The day after judgment*].

18164   *Get out of my sky; and, There shall be no darkness.* London, Toronto: Panther, 1980, 168 p., paper, coll.

18165   *The seeding stars; and, Galactic cluster.* New York: A Signet Book, New American Library, 1983, 158+176 p., paper, coll.

01504   *Star Trek.* Toronto, New York: Bantam Books, 1967, 136 p., paper, tele. coll. STAR TREK #1.

01504A   retitled: *Star Trek 1.* Toronto, New York: Bantam Books, 1975, 136 p., paper, tele. coll. STAR TREK #1.

18166   *Star Trek 11.* Toronto, New York: Bantam Books, 1975, 188 p., paper, tele. coll. STAR TREK #11.

18166A   retitled: *Day of the dove.* Toronto, New York: Bantam Books, 1985, 188 p., paper, tele. coll. STAR TREK #11.

18167   *The Star Trek reader.* New York: E. P. Dutton, 1976, 422 p., cloth, tele. coll. STAR TREK #2, 3, 8.

18168   *The Star Trek reader II.* New York: E. P. Dutton, 1977, 457 p., cloth, tele. coll. STAR TREK #1, 4, 9.

18169   *The Star Trek reader III.* New York: E. P. Dutton, 1977, 447 p., cloth, tele. coll. STAR TREK #5, 6, 7.

18170   *The Star Trek reader IV.* New York: E. P. Dutton, 1978, 472 p., cloth, tele. coll. STAR TREK #10, 11, and *Spock Must Die!*

18171   *Star Trek: the classic episodes 2.* New York, Toronto: Spectra, Bantam Books, 1991, vi+647 p., paper, tele. coll. STAR TREK SERIES.

18172   *The tale that wags the god.* Chicago: Advent:Publishers, 1987, 290 p., cloth, nonf. coll. [Edited by Cy Chauvin; includes a lengthy bibliography by J. A. Lawrence].
The testament of Andros—SEE: *Best science fiction stories of James Blish.*

with J. A. Lawrence

18173   *Mudd's angels.* Toronto, New York: Bantam Books, 1978, xii+177 p., paper, tele. STAR TREK SERIES. [Lawrence's contribution is anonymous].

18174   *Star Trek 12.* Toronto, New York: Bantam Books, 1977, x+177 p., paper, tele. coll. STAR TREK #12.

18175   *Star Trek: the classic episodes 1.* New York, Toronto: Spectra, Bantam Books, 1991, vi+646 p., paper, tele. coll. STAR TREK SERIES.

18176   *Star Trek: the classic episodes 3.* New York, Toronto: Spectra, Bantam Books, 1991, vi+627 p., paper, tele. coll. STAR TREK SERIES.

BLISHEN, Edward, 1920-

18177   *Science fiction stories.* London: Kingfisher, 1988, 253 p., cloth, anth.

102

*BLOCH, Bertram, <u>1892-1987</u>

BLOCH, Robert (Albert), 1917-

18178   *The best of Robert Bloch.* New York: A Del Rey Book, Ballantine Books, 1977, xvii+397 p., paper, coll. [Edited by Lester del Rey].

18179   *Bitter ends: the selected stories of Robert Bloch, volume 2.* Los Angeles, Columbia, PA: Underwood-Miller, 1987 (i.e., 1988), 368 p., cloth, coll.

18180   *Cold chills.* Garden City, New York: Nelson Doubleday, 1977, 178 p., cloth, coll.

18181   *Fear and trembling.* New York: Tor Horror, A Tom Doherty Associates Book, 1989, 309 p., paper, coll.

18182   *Final reckonings: the selected stories of Robert Bloch, volume 1.* Los Angeles, Columbia, PA: Underwood-Miller, 1987 (i.e., 1988), 376 p., cloth, coll.

      House of the hatchet—SEE: *The opener of the way.*

18183   *The kidnapper.* New York: Tor, A Tom Doherty Associates Book, 1988, 216 p., paper, novel.

18184   *The king of terrors: tales of madness and death.* New York: Mysterious Press, 1977, 202 p., cloth, coll.

18185   *Last rites: the selected stories of Robert Bloch, volume 3.* Los Angeles, Columbia, PA: Underwood-Miller, 1987 (i.e., 1988), 398 p., cloth, coll.

18186   *Lori.* New York: Tor Horror, A Tom Doherty Associates Book, 1989, 282 p., cloth, novel.

18187   *Lost in time and space with Lefty Feep.* Pacifica, CA: Creatures at Large, 1987, 258 p., cloth, coll.

18188   *Midnight pleasures.* Garden City, NY: Doubleday & Co., 1987, 177 p., cloth, coll.

18189   *Mysteries of the worm: all the Cthulhu Mythos stories of Robert Bloch.* New York: Zebra Books, Kensington Publishing Corp., 1981, 334 p., paper, coll. CTHULHU MYTHOS.

01546   *The opener of the way.* Sauk City, WI: Arkham House, 1945, 309 p., cloth, coll.

01546A   retitled: *House of the hatchet.* St Albans, England: Panther, 1976, 174 p., paper, coll. [Abridged edition].

18190   *Out of my head.* Cambridge, MA: A Boskone Book, NESFA Press, 1986, xi+193 p., cloth, nonf. [Limited to 800 copies].

18191   *Out of the mouths of graves.* New York: Mysterious Press, 1979, xiii+193 p., cloth, coll.

18192   *Psycho-house.* New York: Tor, A Tom Doherty Associates Books, 217 p., cloth, novel.

18193   *Strange eons.* Chapel Hill, NC: Whispers Press, 1978, v+194 p., cloth, novel. CTHULHU MYTHOS.

18194   *Such stuff as screams are made of.* New York: A Del Rey Book, Ballantine Books, 1979, xiii+287 p., paper, coll.

18195   *Twilight zone: the movie: a novel.* New York: Warner Books, 1983, 205 p., paper, movie.

18196   *Yours truly, Jack the Ripper.* Eugene, OR: Pulphouse Publishing, 1991, 40 p., cloth, story. SHORT STORY HARDBACKS #6; SHORT STORY PAPERBACKS #10.

with Andre Norton

18197   *The Jekyll legacy.* New York: Tor Horror, A Tom Doherty Associates Book, 1990, 248 p., cloth, novel. DR. JEKYLL & MR. HYDE SEQUEL.

with Martin H. Greenberg

18198   *Psycho-paths.* New York: Tor Horror, A Tom Doherty Associates Book, 1991, xxii+293 p., cloth, anth. [Greenberg's contribution is anonymous].

with Randall D. Larson

18199   *The Robert Bloch companion: collected interviews, 1969-1986.* Mercer Island, WA: Starmont House, 1989, 156 p., cloth, nonf. anth.

with T. E. D. Klein & Fritz Leiber

18200   *The first World Fantasy Convention: three authors remember.* West Warwick, RI: Necronomicon Press, 1980, 52 p., paper, nonf.

BLOCK, Bob

18201   *Galloping galaxies.* London: A Target Book, W. H. Allen & Co., 1987, 124 p., paper, tele.

BLOCK, Francesca Lia, 1962-

18202   *Weetzie Bat.* New York: A Charlotte Zolotow Book, Harper & Row, 1989, 88 p., cloth, novel. WEETZIE BAT #1.

18203   *Witch baby.* New York: A Charlotte Zolotow Book, HarperCollins, 1991, 103 p., cloth, novel. WEETZIE BAT #2.

BLOCK, Thomas H(arris), 1945-

18204 *Airship Nine.* New York: G. P. Putnam's Sons, 1984, 286 p., cloth, novel.
18205 *Orbit.* New York: Coward, McCann & Geoghegan, 1982, 297 p., cloth, novel.

BLOOM, Britton

18206 *Buck Rogers: Matrix cubed.* Lake Geneva, WI: TSR Inc., 1991, 278 p., paper, novel. BUCK ROGERS—INNER PLANETS Trilogy #3.
Matrix cubed—SEE: *Buck Rogers: Matrix cubed.*

BLOOM, Clive, 1953-

18207 *Reading Poe, reading Freud: the romantic imagination in crisis.* New York: St. Martin's Press, 1988, 138 p., cloth, nonf.

BLOOM, Harold, 1930-

18208 *Doris Lessing.* New York: Chelsea House Publishers, 1986, viii+224 p., cloth, nonf. anth.
18209 *Edgar Allan Poe.* New York: Chelsea House Publishers, 1985, 155 p., cloth, nonf. anth.
18210 *The flight to Lucifer: a gnostic fantasy.* New York: Farrar, Straus & Giroux, 1979, 240 p., cloth, novel.
18211 *George Orwell.* New York: Chelsea House Publishers, 1987, vii+166 p., cloth, nonf. anth.
18212 *George Orwell's 1984.* New York: Chelsea House Publishers, 1987, vii+135 p., cloth, nonf. anth.
18213 *Mary Shelley.* New York: Chelsea House Publishers, 1985, 205 p., cloth, nonf. anth.
18214 *Ursula K. Le Guin.* New York: Chelsea House Publishers, 1986, x+274 p., cloth, nonf. anth.
18215 *Ursula K. Le Guin's The left hand of darkness.* New York: Chelsea House Publishers, 1987, vii+150 p., cloth, nonf. anth.

BLOOM, John—SEE: Briggs, Joe Bob

BLOOM, Mark, *with Bill Scammell, Evan Jamieson, Lisa Hunt, Walter Hunt, Richard S. Meyer & Christine Ivey* as ARCHITECTS ADVENTURE

18216 *Dzurlord: a Crossroads adventure in the world of Steven Brust's Jhereg / by Architects Adventure.* New York: Tor, A Tom Doherty Associates Book, 1987, 24+[224] p., paper, novel. JHEREG SERIES; CROSSROADS ADVENTURE.

BLOOM, Robert, 1930-

18217 *Anatomies of realism: a reading of the last novels of H. G. Wells.* Lincoln, NE & London: University of Nebraska Press, 1977, ix+196 p., cloth, nonf.

*BLOOM, Ursula [i.e., Ursula Harvey Bloom Robinson], 1893-1984

BLOOM, William—SEE: W. W.

*BLOOMER, J(ames) M(oses), 1842-1923

BLOOMFIELD, Paul, 1898-

18218 *L. P. Hartley.* London: Published for the British Council by Longmans, Green & Co., 1961, 40 p., paper, nonf. [Bound with *Anthony Powell* / by Bernard Bergonzi].
18219 *L. P. Hartley.* Harlow, England: Longmans, 1970, 36 p., paper, nonf. [Revised edition].
18220 *The life and work of William Morris.* London: Royal Society of Arts, 1934, 27 p., paper, nonf.
18221 *William Morris.* London: Arthur Barker, 1934, x+314 p., cloth, nonf.

BLUE, Tyson, 1952-

18222 *The unseen King.* Mercer Island, WA: Starmont House, 1989, viii+200 p., cloth, nonf. STARMONT STUDIES IN LITERARY CRITICISM #26.

BLUEJAY [pseud. of Terry Woodrow]

18223 *It's time: a nuclear novel.* Little River, CA: Tough Dove Books, 1985, 190 p., paper, novel.

BLUM, Robert S(teven), 1958-

18224 *The girl from the Emeraline Island.* New York: A Del Rey Book, Ballantine Books, 1984, 274 p., paper, novel.

BLUMBERG, Rhoda, 1917-

18225 *The first travel guide to the moon: what to pack, how to go, and what to see when you get there.* New York: Four Winds Press, 1980, 83 p., cloth, fiction.

BLUMENFELD, (Frank) Yorick, 1932-

18226 *Jenny Ewing: my diary.* Sussex, England: Centaur Press, 1981, [91] p., cloth, novel. [Published anonymously].
18226A retitled: *Jenny: my diary.* Boston: Little Brown & Co., 1982, [96] p., cloth, novel.
Jenny: my diary—SEE: Jenny Ewing.

BLUMLEIN, Michael, 1948-

18227 *The brains of rats.* Los Angeles: Scream/Press, 1989, 209 p., paper, coll.
18228 *The movement of mountains.* New York: St. Martin's Press, 1987, viii+289 p., cloth, novel.

BLUNDERLAND Cartoonist

18229 *Jeannie Jemima Jones: the adventures of a runaway girl on a desert island.* London: Simpkin, Marshall, Hamilton, Kent, 1905, 195 p., cloth, novel.

BLUNT, Giles

18230 *Cold eye.* New York: Arbor House, 1989, 288 p., cloth, novel.

*BLUNT, Wilfrid (Jasper Walter), 1901-<u>1987</u>

BLYTHE, Ronald (George), 1922-

26654 *The stories of Ronald Blythe.* London: Chatto & Windus, Hogarth Press, 1985, 239 p., cloth, coll.

BOARD, Prudence F.—SEE: Foster, Prudence

BOARDMAN, Thomas—SEE: Boardman, Tom

BOARDMAN, Tom [i.e., Thomas Volney Boardman, Jr.], 1930-

18231 *Science fiction stories.* London: Octopus, 1979, 350 p., cloth, anth.

BOATMAN, Garrett

18232 *Stage fright.* New York: An Onyx Book, New American Library, 1988, 381 p., paper, novel.

BODÉ, Vaughn (Frederick), 1941-1975, *with George W. Beahm*

17592 *Vaughn Bodé index.* Newport News, VA: C. W. Brooks Jr., 1976, 64 p., paper, nonf.

BODENBURG, Angela Sommer- —SEE: Sommer-Bodenburg, Angela

BOEX-BOREL, Joseph—SEE: Rosny, J.-H., Aîné

BOGART, William G., 1903-1977

18233 *The crazy Indian.* Chicago: Tattered Pages Press, 1987, 60 p., paper, story. DOC SAVAGE PASTICHE.

as KENNETH ROBESON

18234 *The flying goblin: a Doc Savage adventure.* Toronto, New York: Bantam Books, 1977, 120 p., paper, novel. DOC SAVAGE #90.
18235 *Tunnel terror: a Doc Savage adventure.* Toronto, New York: Bantam Books, 1979, 122 p., paper, novel. DOC SAVAGE #93.

with Lester Dent as KENNETH ROBESON

18236 *The angry ghost: a Doc Savage adventure.* Toronto, New York: Bantam Books, 1977, 120 p., paper, novel. DOC SAVAGE #86.
21574 *Doc Savage: four complete adventures in one volume: The awful dynasty; The magic forest; Fire and ice; The disappearing lady.* Toronto, New York: Bantam Books, 1988, 378 p., paper, coll. DOC SAVAGE #148-151. [Cover title: *Doc Savage omnibus, volume 6*; *The magic forest* and *Fire and ice* by Lester Dent and William G. Bogart; *The disappearing lady* and *The awful dynasty* by William G. Bogart].
04154 *Hex: a Doc Savage adventure.* Toronto, New York: Bantam Books, 1969, 120 p., paper, novel. DOC SAVAGE #37.
18239 *The spotted men: a Doc Savage adventure.* Toronto, New York: Bantam Books, 1977, 121 p., paper, novel. DOC SAVAGE #87.
04199 *World's Fair goblin: a Doc Savage adventure.* Toronto, New York: Bantam Books, 1969, 122 p., paper, novel. DOC SAVAGE #39.

with Lester Dent and Harold A. Davis as KENNETH ROBESON

21568 *Doc Savage: five complete adventures in one volume: Bequest of evil; Death in little houses; Target for death; The death lady; The exploding lake.* New York,

Toronto: Bantam Books, 1990, 441 p., paper, coll. DOC SAVAGE #173-177. [Cover title: *Doc Savage omnibus, volume 12*; *Death in little houses* by Lester Dent and William G. Bogart; *The exploding lake* by Lester Dent and Harold A. Davis; *Target for death* and *The death lady* and *Bequest of evil* by William G. Bogart].

BOGAS, Ed, *with Michael Orkin*

18240 *Survival on Planet X with the Atari home computer*. Reston, VA: A Reston Computer Group Book, 1984, vii+151 p., paper, fiction.

BOGDANOV, Alexander [i.e., Aleksandr Aleksandrovich Malinovskii], 1873-1928

18241 *Red star: the first Bolshevik utopia: Red star, Engineer Menni, A Martian stranded on Earth* / by Alexander Bogdanov. Bloomington, IN: Indiana University Press, 1984, x+257 p., cloth, coll. [Edited by Loren R. Graham & Richard Stites; translated by Charles Rougle].

BOGGS, D. W.

18242 *Astounding story-key, 1930-1951*. Minneapolis, MN: D. W. Boggs, 1952, 18 p., paper, nonf.

BOGNER, Norman, 1935-

18243 *Snowman*. New York: A Dell Book, 1978, 221 p., paper, novel.

BOILEAU, Pierre (Louis), 1906- , *with Thomas Narcejac*

26826 *The evil eye*. London: Hutchinson, 1959, 207 p., cloth, coll. [Translation by Geoffrey Sainsbury and James Kirkup of *Le mauvais oeil*].

BOK, Hannes (Vajn) [pseud. of Wayne Woodard], 1914-1964

18244 *Beauty and the beasts: the art of Hannes Bok*. Saddle River, NJ: Gerry de la Ree, 1978, 127 p., cloth, art. [Edited by Gerry de la Ree].

18245 *The Hannes Bok memorial showcase of fantasy art*. San Francisco: SISU Publishers, 1974, 166 p., paper, art. [Edited by Emil Petaja].

18246 *A Hannes Bok sketchbook* Saddle River, NJ: Gerry de la Ree, 1976, 80 p., paper, art. [Edited by Gerry de la Ree and Gene Nigra].

with A. Merritt

18247 *The fox woman and the blue pagoda; and, The black wheel*. New York: Arno Press, 1976, 109+115 p., cloth, coll.

*BOLAND, (Bertram) John, 1913-1976

BOLT, Joe De—SEE: De Bolt, Joe

BOLTON, F. M.

37652 *Into the soundless deeps: a tale of wonder and adventure*. London: Boy's Own Paper, 1919, 390 p., cloth, novel.

37653 *Under the edge of the Earth: a story of three chums and a startling quest*. London: Religious Tract Society, 1913, 378 p., cloth, novel.

BOLTON, Johanna M.

18248 *The alien within*. New York: A Del Rey Book, Ballantine Books, 1989, 277 p., paper, novel.

18249 *Mission: Tori*. New York: A Del Rey Book, Ballantine Books, 1990, 232 p., paper, novel.

BOLTON, W(hitney) F(rench), 1930-

18250 *The language of 1984: Orwell's English and ours*. Knoxville, TN: University of Tennessee Press, 1984, 252 p., cloth, nonf.

*BOLTON, William W(orden), 1900-1966

*BOMBAL, Maria-Luisa, 1910-1980

BONANNO, Margaret Wander, 1950-

18251 *Dwellers in the crucible: a Star Trek novel*. New York: Pocket Books, 1985, 308 p., paper, novel. STAR TREK #25.

18252 *The others: a science fiction novel*. New York: A Thomas Dunne Book, St. Martin's Press, 1990, 370 p., cloth, novel. THE OTHERS #1.

18253 *Otherwhere*. New York: A Thomas Dunne Book, St. Martin's Press, 1991, ix+317 p., cloth, novel. THE OTHERS #2.

18254 *Star Trek: Strangers from the sky.* New York: Pocket Books, 1987, 402 p., paper, novel. STAR TREK (UNNUMBERED).
Strangers from the sky—SEE: *Star Trek: Strangers from the sky.*

as RICK NORTH

30810 *Citizens of Mars.* New York: Zebra Books, Kensington Publishing Corp., 1991, 158 p., paper, novel. YOUNG ASTRONAUTS #6.
30811 *Destination Mars.* New York: Zebra Books, Kensington Publishing Corp., 1991, 172 p., paper, novel. YOUNG ASTRONAUTS #4.

BOND, Edlyne

18255 *Miranda.* Lawndale, CA: Phantom Press, 1982, p., paper, novel.

BOND, Larry

18256 *Red phoenix.* New York: Warner Books, 1989, ix+588 p., cloth, novel.
18257 *Vortex.* Franklin Center, PA: Franklin Library, 1991, xiv+670 p., cloth, novel.

*BOND, Mary Dilgh, 1893-

BOND, Nancy (Barbara), 1945-

18258 *Another shore.* New York: Margaret K. McElderry Books, 1988, 308 p., cloth, novel.
18259 *A string in the harp.* New York: A Margaret K. McElderry Book, Atheneum, 1976, 370 p., cloth, novel.
18260 *The voyage begun.* New York: An Argo Book, A Margaret K. McElderry Book, Atheneum, 1981, 319 p., cloth, novel.

BOND, Nelson (Slade), 1908- , *with James N. Hall*

18261 *James Branch Cabell: a complete bibliography, with a supplement of current values of Cabell books by Nelson Bond.* New York: Revisionist Press, 1974, xi+245 p., cloth, nonf.

BONE, J(esse) F(ranklin), 1916-

18262 *Confederation matador.* Norfolk, VA: Starblaze Editions/Donning, 1978, 211 p., paper, novel.
18263 *Legacy.* Toronto, New York: Laser Books, 1976, 190 p., paper, novel.

18264 *The meddlers.* Toronto, New York: Laser Books, 1976, 190 p., paper, novel.

with Roy L. Meyers

18265 *Gift of the Manti.* Toronto, New York: Laser Books, 1977, 190 p., paper, novel.

BONESTELL, Chesley, 1888-1986, *with Ron Miller & Frederick C. Durant III*

22325 *Worlds beyond: the art of Chesley Bonestell.* Norfolk, Virginia Beach, VA: A Starblaze Special, Donning Co., 1983, 133 p., paper, art.

BONHAM, Frank, 1914-1988

18266 *The forever formula.* New York: E. P. Dutton, 1979, 181 p., cloth, novel.
18267 *The missing persons league.* New York: E. P. Dutton, 1976, 157 p., cloth, novel.
18268 *Premonitions.* New York: Holt, Rinehart & Winston, 1984, 166 p., cloth, novel.

BONIFER, Michael

18269 *The art of Tron.* New York: Little Simon, 1982, 63 p., paper, art.

BONTLY, Thomas (John), 1939-

18270 *Celestial chess.* New York: Harper & Row, Publishers, 1979, 279 p., cloth, novel.

BOORSTIN, Paul (Terry), 1944- , *with Sharon Boorstin*

18271 *The Glory Hand.* New York: Berkley Books, 1983, 289 p., paper, novel.

BOORSTIN, Sharon, 1945- , *with Paul Boorstin*

18271 *The Glory Hand.* New York: Berkley Books, 1983, 289 p., paper, novel.

BOOS, Florence S(aunders), 1943-

18272 *The design of William Morris' 'The earthly paradise'.* Lewiston, NY: Edwin Mellen Press, 1990, 530 p., cloth, nonf.

with Carole Silver

18273 *Socialism and the literary artistry of William Morris.* Columbia, MO: University of Missouri Press, 1990, vii+177 p., cloth, nonf. anth.

BOOTH, Bradford A(llen), 1909-1968, with Claude E. Jones

18274 *A concordance of the poetical works of Edgar Allan Poe.* Baltimore, MD: Johns Hopkins Press, 1941, xiv+211 p., cloth, nonf.

BOOTHBY, Guy (Newell), 1867-1905

01623 *A bid for fortune; or, Dr. Nikola's vendetta.* London: Ward, Lock & Bowden, 1895, 344 p., cloth, novel. DR. NIKOLA #1.

01623A retitled: *Enter Dr. Nikola!* Hollywood, CA: Newcastle Publishing Co., 1975, 256 p., paper, novel. DR. NIKOLA #1.

01625 *Doctor Nikola.* London: Ward, Lock & Co., 1896, 322 p., cloth, novel. DR. NIKOLA #2.

01625A retitled: *Dr. Nikola returns.* Van Nuys, CA: Newcastle Publishing Co., 1976, 256 p., paper, novel. DR. NIKOLA #2.
Dr. Nikola returns—SEE: *Doctor Nikola.*
Enter Dr. Nikola!—SEE: *A bid for fortune.*

BORCHGRAVE, Arnaud de—SEE: de Borchgrave, Arnaud

BORDER, Rosemary, 1943-

18275 *Ghost stories.* Oxford, England: Oxford University Press, 1989, 90 p., paper, coll.

with Isaac Asimov

16926 *The caves of steel.* Cambridge, England: Cambridge University Press, 1978, viii+117 p., paper, novel. [Abridged and modernized from the original edition by Asimov].

with Robert A. Heinlein

18276 *Space family Stone.* Cambridge, England: Cambridge University Press, 1978, viii+150 p., paper, novel. [Adapted from the original novel by Robert A. Heinlein].

with Frank Herbert

18277 *Dune.* Oxford, England: Oxford University Press, 1980, 144 p., paper, novel. [Adapted from the original novel by Herbert].

with Robert Louis Stevenson

18278 *Dr Jekyll and Mr Hyde.* Oxford, England: Oxford University Press, 1991, 75 p., paper, novel. [Adapted from the original novel by Stevenson].

BORDERS, Gary B(radford), 1955-

18279 *The adventure companion: hints, maps, and solutions to Wizard and the princess, Zork I, Adventureland, Transylvania, and Planetfall.* Hasbrouck Heights, NJ: Hayden Book Co., 1985, 207 p., paper, nonf.

BOREL, Joseph Boëx- —SEE: Rosny, J.-H., Aîné

BORGES, Jorge Luis, 1899-1986

18280 *Tlön, Uqbar, Orbis Tertius.* Scarborough, Ontario, Canada: The Porcupine's Quill, 1983, 22 p., paper, story. [Translation by James E. Irby of *Tlön, Uqbar, Orbis Tertius*].

with Adolfo Bioy Casares & Silvina Ocampo

17979 *The book of fantasy.* London: Xanadu, 1988, 384 p., cloth, anth. [Translation of *Antología de la literatura fantástica*].

*BORGHESE, Elisabeth Mann, <u>1918-</u>

BORISOFF, Norman

18281 *Bewitched and bewildered: a spooky love story.* New York: Laurel-Leaf Books, 1982, 107 p., paper, novel.

BORN, Franz, 1912-

18282 *Jules Verne: the man who invented the future.* Englewood Cliffs, NJ: Prentice-Hall, 1964, 102 p., cloth, nonf. [Translation by Juliana Biro of *Der mann der die zukunft erfand*].

BORRELLO, Alfred, 1931-

18283 *H. G. Wells: author in agony.* Carbondale & Edwardsville, IL: Southern Illinois University Press; London & Amsterdam: Feffer & Simon, 1972, xvii+137 p., cloth, nonf.

BORSHEIM, Roger M.

18284 *Earth watch.* Smithtown, NY: Exposition Press, 1980, 168 p., cloth, novel.

BORTON, Douglas (Child), 1960-

18285 *Deathsong.* New York: An Onyx Book, New American Library, 1989, 287 p., paper, novel.

18286 *Dreamhouse.* New York: An Onyx Book, New American Library, 1989, 285 p., paper, novel.

18287 *Kane.* New York: An Onyx Book, 1990, 350 p., paper, novel.

18288 *Manstopper.* New York: An Onyx Book, New American Library, 1988, 254 p., paper, novel.

18289 *Shadow dance.* New York: A Signet Book, 1991, 281 p., paper, novel.

BOSCO, Clyde

18290 *Dinosaur dilemma.* New York, London: An Archway Paperback, Pocket Books, 1991, 121 p., paper, novel. NINTENDO ADVENTURE BOOKS #7.

18291 *Double trouble.* New York, London: An Archway Paperback, Pocket Books, 1991, 121 p., paper, novel. NINTENDO ADVENTURE BOOKS #1.

18292 *Leaping lizards.* New York, London: An Archway Paperback, Pocket Books, 1991, 121 p., paper, novel. NINTENDO ADVENTURE BOOKS #2.

18293 *Pipe down!* New York, London: An Archway Paperback, Pocket Books, 1991, 121 p., paper, novel. NINTENDO ADVENTURE BOOKS #5.

*BOSHELL, Gordon, 1908-

*BOSSCHERE, Jean de, 1878-1953

BOSSE, Malcolm J(oseph Jr.), 1932-

18294 *Cave beyond time.* New York: Harper & Row, 1980, 187 p., cloth, novel.

18295 *Mister Touch.* Boston: Ticknor & Fields, 1991, 502 p., cloth, novel.

BOSSHARDT, Robert

18296 *Whom the gods destroy.* Canada: Maverick, 1987, 305 p., paper, novel.

BOSTON, Bruce (David), 1943-

18297 *After magic.* Boise, ID: Eotu Group, 1990, 54 p., paper, story.

18298 *All the clocks are melting.* Eugene, OR: Pulphouse Publishing, 1991, 38 p., paper, story. SHORT STORY PAPERBACKS #4.

18299 *Hypertales and metafictions.* Polk City, IA: Chris Drumm, 1990, 62 p., paper, coll. DRUMM BOOKLET

18300 *Jackbird: tales of illusion & identity.* Berkeley, CA: Berkeley Poets' Workshop & Press, 1976, 85 p., paper, coll.

18301 *She comes when you're leaving & other stories.* Berkeley, CA: Berkeley Poets' Workshop & Press, 1982, 62 p., paper, coll.

18302 *Short circuits.* Mountain View, CA: Ocean View, 1991, 38 p., cloth, coll. [Includes some verse; bound with a poetry collection, *Bad news from the stars* / by Steve Sneyd].

18303 *Skin trades.* Polk City, IA: Chris Drumm, 1988, 62 p., paper, coll. DRUMM BOOKLET #31.

BOSTON, L(ucy) M(aria Wood), 1892-1990

18304 *Guardians of the house.* London: Bodley Head, 1974, 53 p., cloth, novel. GREEN KNOWE #6.

18305 *The stones of Green Knowe.* London: Bodley Head, 1976, 118 p., cloth, novel. GREEN KNOWE #7.

BOTHELL, Diane J.

18306 *Rinim Poodor.* Seattle, WA: Three-Stones Publications, 1986, 284 p., paper, novel.

BOTTIGHEIMER, Ruth B., 1939-

18307 *Grimms' bad girls and bold boys: the moral and social vision of the tales.* New Haven, CT: Yale University Press, 1987, xv+211 p., cloth, nonf.

BOULLE, Pierre (François Marie-Louis), 1912-

18308 *The good leviathan.* New York: Vanguard Press, 1979, 204 p., cloth, novel. [Translation by Margaret Giovanelli of *Le bon léviathan*].

18309 *The marvelous palace, and other stories.* New York: Vanguard Press, 1977, 187 p., cloth, coll. [Translation by Margaret Giovanelli of *Histoires perfides*].

18310 *Trouble in paradise.* New York: Vanguard Press, 1985, 188 p., cloth, novel. [Translation by Patricia Wolf of *Les coulisses du ciel*].

18311 *The whale of the Victoria Cross.* New York: Vanguard Press, 1983, 182 p., cloth, novel. [Translation by Patricia Wolf of *La baleine des Malouines*].

BOULT, S. Kye, pseud.—SEE: Cochrane, William E.

*BOURNE, John [pseud. of Owen John], 1918-

BOURNS, Marsha, pseud.

18312 *The suculent witch.* Encino, CA: World-Wide Publishing Co., 1980, 183 p., paper, novel.

BOURQUIN, David Ray, 1941-

18313 *The work of Bruce McAllister: an annotated bibliography & guide.* San Bernardino, CA: R. Reginald, The Borgo Press, 1985, 30 p., cloth, nonf. BIBLIOGRAPHIES OF MODERN AUTHORS #10. [Edited by Boden Clarke].

18314 *The work of Bruce McAllister: an annotated bibliography & guide, rev. ed.* San Bernardino, CA: R. Reginald, The Borgo Press, 1986, 32 p., cloth, nonf. BIBLIOGRAPHIES OF MODERN AUTHORS #10. [Edited by Boden Clarke].

*BOUSFIELD, H(enry) T(homas) W(ishart), 1891-

*BOUTELL, C(larence) B(urley), 1908-1981

*BOUTELLE, Clarence M(iles), 1851-1903

BOVA, Ben(jamin William), 1932-

18315 *The alien within.* New York: Tor, A Tom Doherty Associates Book, 1986, 344 p., cloth, novel. VOYAGERS #2.

18316 *Aliens: 3 novellas.* New York: St. Martin's Press, 1978, 156 p., cloth, anth.

18317 *Analog annual.* New York: Pyramid Books, 1976, 256 p., paper, anth. [Includes some nonfiction].

18319 *The Analog yearbook.* New York: Baronet Publishing Co., 1978, 299 p., paper, anth.

18320 *The astral mirror.* New York: Tor SF, A Tom Doherty Associates Book, 1985, x + 274 p., paper, coll.

18321 *Battle station.* New York: Tor SF, A Tom Doherty Associates Book, 1987, 304 p., paper, coll. [Includes some nonfiction].

18322 *The best of Analog.* New York: Baronet Publishing Co., 1978, 418 p., paper, anth.

18323 *The best of the Nebulas.* New York: Tor, A Tom Doherty Doherty Associates, 1989, 593 p., cloth, anth.

18324 *City of darkness: a novel.* New York: Charles Scribner's Sons, 1976, 150 p., cloth, novel.

18325 *Colony.* New York: A Kangaroo Book, Pocket Books, 1978, 470 p., paper, novel.

18326 *Cyberbooks.* New York: Tor, A Tom Doherty Associates Book, 1989, 283 p., cloth, novel.

18327 *End of exile.* New York: E. P. Dutton, 1975, 214 p., cloth, novel. EXILES TRILOGY #3.

18328 *Escape plus.* New York: Tor, A Tom Doherty Associates Book, 1984, 285 p., paper, coll.

18329 *Exiles: 3 novellas.* New York: St. Martin's Press, 1978, 159 p., cloth, anth.

18330 *The exiles trilogy: three novels.* New York: Berkley Books, 1980, 441 p., paper, coll. EXILES #1-3. [Includes *Exiled from Earth*; *Flight of exiles*; *End of exile*].

18331 *Future crime.* New York: Tor SF, A Tom Doherty Associates Book, 1990, 374 p., paper, coll. [Includes the novel *City of darkness*].

18332 *Kinsman: a novel.* New York: A Quantum Novel, The Dial Press, 1979, 280 p., cloth, novel. KINSMAN #2.

18333 *The Kinsman saga.* New York: Tor, A Tom Doherty Associates Book, 1987, x+566 p., cloth, novel. KINSMAN #1-2. [Incorporates *Millennium* and *Kinsman*].

18334 *Maxwell's demons.* New York: Baronet Publishing Co., 1978, 321 p., paper, coll.

18335 *Millennium: a novel about people and politics in the year 1999.* New York: Random House, 1976, 277 p., cloth, novel. KINSMAN #1.

18336 *The multiple man: a novel of suspense.* Indianapolis, IN: Bobbs-Merrill Co., 1976, 210 p., cloth, novel.

18337 *Notes to a science fiction writer.* New York: Charles Scribner's Sons, 1975, 177 p., cloth, coll. [Includes nonf.].

18338 *Notes to a science fiction writer, 2nd ed.* Boston: Houghton Mifflin Co., 1981, 193 p., paper, coll. [Includes nonfiction; revised and expanded].

18339 *Orion.* New York: A Fireside Book, Simon & Schuster, 1984, 432 p., paper, novel. ORION #1.

18340 *Orion in the dying time.* New York: Tor, A Tom Doherty Associates Book, 1990, x+356 p., cloth, novel. ORION #3.

18341 *Out of the sun.* New York: A Tom Doherty Associates Book, 1984, 223 p., paper, novel. [Expanded to include the nonfiction book, *The amazing Lazar*].

18342 *Peacekeepers*. New York: Tor, A Tom Doherty Associates Book, 1988, 337 p., cloth, novel.

18343 *Privateers*. New York: Tor, A Tom Doherty Associates Book, 1985, 383 p., cloth, novel.

18344 *Prometheans*. New York: Tor SF, A Tom Doherty Associates Book, 1986, 278 p., paper, coll. [Includes some nonfiction].

18345 *Star brothers*. Norwalk, CT: Easton Press, 1990, 341 p., cloth, novel. VOYAGERS #3.

18346 *The starcrossed*. Radnor, PA: Chilton Book Co., 1975, 197 p., cloth, novel.

18347 *Test of fire*. New York: Tor, A Tom Doherty Associates Book, 1982, 317 p., paper, novel. [Expanded edition of *When the sky burns* (see #01693)].

18348 *Through the eyes of wonder: science fiction and science*. Reading, MA: An Addisonian Press Book, Addison-Wesley, 1975, 127 p., cloth, nonf.

18349 *Vengeance of Orion*. New York: Tor, A Tom Doherty Associates Book, 1988, 342 p., cloth, novel. ORION #2.

18350 *Viewpoint*. Cambridge, MA: A Boskone Book, The NESFA Press, 1977, ii+114 p., cloth, nonf. coll.

18351 *Vision of the future: the art of Robert McCall*. New York: Henry N. Abrams, 1982, 178 p., cloth, art.

18352 *Voyagers*. Garden City, NY: Doubleday & Co., 1981, 389 p., cloth, novel. VOYAGERS #1.

18353 *The winds of Altair*. New York: Tor, A Tom Doherty Associates Book, 1983, 317 p., paper, novel. [Expanded edition of #01694].

with Trudy E. Bell

17706 *Closeup: new worlds*. New York: St. Martin's Press, 1977, xv+222 p., cloth, nonf. anth.

with Don Myrus

18354 *The best of Omni science fiction*. New York: Omni Society, 1980, 143 p., paper, anth. [Includes some nonfiction].

18355 *The best of Omni science fiction, no. 2*. New York: Omni, 1981, 144 p., paper, anth. [Includes some nonfiction].

18356 *The best of Omni science fiction, no. 3*. New York: Omni Publications, 1982, 143 p., paper, anth. [Includes some nonfiction].

18357 *The best of Omni science fiction, no. 4*. New York: Omni Publications, 1982, 143 p., paper, anth. [Includes some nonfiction].

*BOWDEN, Etta, <u>1893-1973</u>

*BOWDEN, Phil(ip), <u>1906-1980</u>

BOWEN, Marjorie, pseud.—SEE: Campbell, Margaret

BOWER, Brock, 1931-

18358 *The late great creature*. New York: Atheneum, 1972, 295 p., cloth, novel.

BOWERING, Peter (Edwin), 1926-

18359 *Aldous Huxley: a study of the major novels*. London: Athlone Press, 1968, 242 p., cloth, nonf.

BOWERS, B. L., pseud.—SEE: Glasby, John

BOWES, Richard (Dirrane), 1944-

18360 *Feral cell*. New York: Popular Library, 1987, 220 p., paper, novel.

18361 *Goblin market*. New York: Popular Library, 1988, 250 p., paper, novel. WARCHILD #2.

18362 *Warchild*. New York: Popular Library, Warner Books, 1986, 248 p., paper, novel. WARCHILD #1.

BOWKER, Richard (John), 1950-

18363 *Dover Beach*. Toronto, New York: Bantam Books, 1987, 265 p., paper, novel.

18364 *Forbidden sanctuary*. New York: A Del Rey Book, Ballantine Books, 1982, 203 p., paper, novel.

18365 *Marlborough Street*. Garden City, NY: Doubleday & Co., 1987, 182 p., cloth, novel.

18366 *Replica*. Toronto, New York: Bantam Books, 1987, 300 p., paper, novel.

18367 *Summit*. New York, Toronto: Bantam Books, 1989, 313 p., paper, novel.

BOWKETT, Stephen, 1953-

18368 *Catch, and other stories*. London: Victor Gollancz, 1988, 123 p., cloth, coll.

18369 *Dualists*. London: Victor Gollancz, 1987, 152 p., cloth, novel.

18370 *Frontiersville High*. London: Victor Gollancz, 1990, 139 p., cloth, coll.

18371 *Gameplayers*. London: Victor Gollancz, 1986, 159 p., cloth, novel.

18372 *Spellbinder.* London: Victor Gollancz, 1985, [90] p., cloth, novel.

BOWLES, Steve

18373 *Twisters: stories of the sinister and macabre.* London: Collins, 1981, 121 p., cloth, anth.

BOYAJIAN, Jerel—SEE: Boyajian, Jerry

BOYAJIAN, Jerry [i.e., Jerel Michael Boyajian], 1953-

with Kenneth R. Johnson

18374 *Index to the science fiction magazines 1977.* Cambridge, MA: Twaci Press, 1982, 28 p., paper, nonf.
18375 *Index to the science fiction magazines 1978.* Cambridge, MA: Twaci Press, 1982, 28 p., paper, nonf.
18376 *Index to the science fiction magazines 1979.* Cambridge, MA: Twaci Press, 1981, 32 p., paper, nonf.
18377 *Index to the science fiction magazines 1980.* Cambridge, MA: Twaci Press, 1981, 27 p., paper, nonf.
18378 *Index to the science fiction magazines 1981.* Cambridge, MA: Twaci Press, 1982, 32 p., paper, nonf.
18379 *Index to the science fiction magazines 1982.* Cambridge, MA: Twaci Press, 1983, 35 p., paper, nonf.
18380 *Index to the science fiction magazines, 1983.* Cambridge, MA: Twaci Press, 1984, 31 p., paper, nonf.
18381 *Index to the science fiction magazines, 1984.* Cambridge, MA: Twaci Press, 1985, 31 p., paper, nonf.
18382 *Index to the science fiction magazines 1985.* Cambridge, MA: Twaci Press, 1985, 31 p., paper, nonf.
18383 *Index to the semi-professional fantasy magazines, 1982.* Cambridge, MA: Twaci Press, 1983, 27 p., paper, nonf. [First in series.]
18384 *Index to the semi-professional magazines, 1983.* Cambridge, MA: Twaci Press, 1984, 27 p., paper, nonf.

with David Stever

18385 *A John Schoenherr SF checklist.* Somerville, MA: Paratime Press, 1977, [36] p., paper, nonf.

BOYCE, (Joseph) Chris(topher), 1943-

18386 *Brainfix.* London: Panther, 1988, 254 p., paper, novel.
18387 *Catchworld.* London: Victor Gollancz, 1975, 255 p., cloth, novel.

BOYD, John [pseud. of Boyd Bradfield Upchurch], 1919-

18388 *Barnard's Planet.* New York: Berkley Publishing Corp., 1975, 216 p., cloth, novel.
18389 *The girl with the jade green eyes.* New York: Viking Press, 1978, 241 p., cloth, novel. [Edited by A(nson) Richard Barbour].

as BOYD UPCHURCH

18390 *Scarborough Hall.* New York: A Berkley Medallion Book, Berkley Publishing Corp., 1976, 316 p., paper, novel.

BOYER, Elizabeth (H.)

18391 *The curse of Slagfid* / by Elizabeth H. Boyer. New York: A Del Rey Book, Ballantine Books, 1989, 341 p., paper, novel. WIZARD'S WAR #2.
18392 *The dragon's carbuncle* / by Elizabeth H. Boyer. New York: A Del Rey Book, Ballantine Books, 1990, 311 p., paper, novel. WIZARD'S WAR #3.
18393 *The elves and the otterskin.* New York: A Del Rey Book, Ballantine Books, 1981, 297 p., paper, novel. WORLD OF ALFAR #2.
18394 *Lord of chaos* / by Elizabeth H. Boyer. New York: A Del Rey Book, Ballantine Books, 1991, 312 p., paper, novel. WIZARD'S WAR #4.
18395 *The sword and the satchel.* New York: A Del Rey Book, Ballantine Books, 1980, 311 p., paper, novel. WORLD OF ALFAR #1.
18396 *The thrall and the dragon's heart.* New York: A Del Rey Book, Ballantine Books, 1982, 294 p., paper, novel. WORLD OF ALFAR #3.
18397 *The troll's grindstone.* New York: A Del Rey Book, Ballantine Books, 1986, 342 p., paper, novel. WIZARD'S WAR #1.
18398 *The wizard and the warlord.* New York: A Del Rey Book, Ballantine Books, 1983, 278 p., paper, novel. WORLD OF ALFAR #4.

BOYER, Robert H., 1937-

with Marshall Tymn & Kenneth J. Zahorski

18399 *Fantasy literature: a core collection and reference guide.* New York, London: R. R. Bowker Co., 1979, xiii+273 p., cloth, nonf.

with Kenneth J. Zahorski

18400 *Dark imaginings: a collection of gothic fantasy.* New York: A Delta Book, 1978, 398 p., paper, anth.
18401 *Fantasists on fantasy: a collection of critical reflections.* New York: A Discus Book, Avon Books, 1984, 287 p., paper, nonf. anth.
18402 *The fantastic imagination: an anthology of high fantasy.* New York: Avon, 1977, ix+325 p., paper, anth.
18403 *The fantastic imagination II: an anthology of high fantasy.* New York: Avon, 1978, xi+307 p., paper, anth.
18404 *Lloyd Alexander, Evangeline Walton Ensley, Kenneth Morris: a primary and secondary bibliography.* Boston: G. K. Hall & Co., 1981, xvi+291 p., cloth, nonf. MASTERS OF SCIENCE FICTION AND FANTASY.
18405 *The phoenix tree: an anthology of myth fantasy.* New York: Avon, 1980, xxii+279 p., paper, anth.
18406 *Visions of wonder: an anthology of Christian fantasy.* New York: Avon, 1981, 240 p., paper, anth.

BOYETT, Steven R., 1960-

18407 *The architect of sleep.* New York: Ace Fantasy Books, 1986, 290 p., paper, novel.
18408 *Ariel: a book of the Change.* New York: Ace Fantasy Books, 1983, 325 p., paper, novel.

with Alan Aldridge

16211 *The gnole.* London: Heinemann, 1991, 503 p., cloth, novel.

BOYLAN, James Finney, 1958-

18409 *The planets.* New York: Poseidon Press, 1991, 265 p., cloth, novel.

BOYLE, Josephine

18410 *Maiden's end.* London: Piatkus, 1988, 265 p., cloth, novel.

BOYLE, T. Coraghessan, 1948-

18411 *Greasy Lake, and other stories.* New York: Viking, 1985, 229 p., cloth, coll.

BOYLL, (James) Randall, 1962-

18412 *After sundown.* New York: Charter Books, 1989, 299 p., paper, novel.
18413 *Darkman: a novel.* New York: Jove Books, 1990, 252 p., paper, movie. DARKMAN #1.
18414 *Mongster.* New York: Berkley Books, 1991, 280 p., paper, novel.
18415 *Shocker: a novel.* London: Corgi Books, 1990, 192 p., paper, movie.

BOZIC, Streten—SEE: Wongar, B.

BRACKETT, Leigh (Douglass), 1915-1978

18416 *The best of Leigh Brackett.* Garden City, NY: Nelson Doubleday, 1977, xii+363 p., cloth, coll. [Edited by Edmond Hamilton].
18417 *The best of Planet stories #1: strange adventures on other worlds.* New York: Ballantine Books, 1975, 212 p., paper, anth. [Only volume published].
18418 *The book of Skaith: the adventures of Eric John Stark.* Garden City, NY: Nelson Doubleday, 1976, 468 p., cloth, coll. ERIC JOHN STARK #1-3.
18419 *The jewel of Bas.* New York: Tor SF, A Tom Doherty Associates Book, 1990, p. 99-187, paper, story. [Bound with *Thieves' carnival* / by Karen Haber].
18420 *The reavers of Skaith.* New York: Ballantine Books, 1976, xv+208 p., paper, novel. ERIC JOHN STARK #3.
01752 *The starmen.* New York: Gnome Press, 1952, 213 p., cloth, novel.
01752A retitled: *The starmen of Llyrdis.* New York: Ballantine Books, 1976, 164 p., paper, novel.
The starmen of Llyrdis—SEE: The starmen.

BRADBURY, Ray (Douglas), 1920-

18421 *The April witch.* Mankato, MN: Creative Education, 1988, 37 p., cloth, story.
18422 *The aqueduct: (a Martian chronicle).* [Glendale, CA: Roy A. Squires], 1979, [12] p., paper, story. [Limited to 230 copies].
18423 *Beyond 1984: a remembrance of things future.* New York: Tary Editions, 1979,

22 p., paper?, nonf. [Limited to 350 copies].

18424 *Classic stories 1: selections from The golden apples of the sun and R is for rocket.* New York, Toronto: Bantam Books, 1990, viii + 342 p., paper, coll. [Incorporates most of the stories from *Golden Apples* and *R Is for Rocket*].

18425 *Classic stories 2: selections from A medicine for melancholy and S is for space.* New York, Toronto: Bantam Books, 1990, 341 p., paper, coll. [Incorporates most of the stories from *Medicine for Melancholy* and *S Is for Space*].

18426 *Dinosaur tales.* Toronto, New York: A Byron Preiss Book, Bantam Books, 1983, 144 p., paper, coll.

18427 *The dragon.* Round Top, NY: Footsteps Press, 1988, 15 p., paper, story.

18428 *Fahrenheit 451; The illustrated man; Dandelion wine; The golden apples of the sun; The Martian chronicles.* New York: Octopus/Heinemann, 1987, 798 p., cloth, coll.

18429 *Fever dream.* New York: St. Martin's Press, 1987, 32 p., cloth, story.

18430 *The fog horn.* Mankato, MN: Creative Education, 1989, 31 p., cloth, story.

18431 *The fog horn, and other stories.* Tokyo: Kinseido, 1977, 89 p., paper, coll. [An English-language reader; introduction and notes in Japanese].

18432 *The god in science fiction.* Northridge, CA: Santa Susana Press, 1977?, p. 37-43, paper, nonf.

18433 *The last circus; &, The electrocution.* Northridge, CA: Lord John Press, 1980, xx + 29 p., cloth, coll.

18434 *Long after midnight.* New York: Alfred A. Knopf, 1976, vii + 271 p., cloth, coll.

18435 *The novels of Ray Bradbury.* London: Granada, 1984, 647 p., cloth, coll. [Includes *Fahrenheit 451, Dandelion wine; Something wicked this way comes*].

18436 *The other foot.* Mankato, MN: Creative Education, 1987, 39 p., cloth, story.

18437 *Ray Bradbury.* London: Harrap, 1975, 188 p., paper, coll. [Edited by Anthony Adams; includes some nonfiction].

18438 *The stories of Ray Bradbury.* New York: Alfred A. Knopf, 1980, xx + 884 p., cloth, coll.

18439 *To sing strange songs.* Exeter, England: Wheaton, 1979, ix + 102 p., paper, coll.

18440 *The Toynbee convector.* New York: Alfred A. Knopf, 1988, 275 p., cloth, coll.

18441 *Zen and the art of writing; and, The joy of writing: two essays.* Santa Barbara, CA:

Capra Press, 1973, 34 p., cloth, nonf. coll.

18442 *Zen in the art of writing.* Santa Barbara, CA: Capra Press, A Joshua Odell Edition, 1990, 154 p., cloth, nonf. coll. [Expanded edition].

with Aldo Sessa

18443 *The bridge of forever.* New York: Rizzoli, 1981, 130 p., cloth, fiction.

BRADFIELD, J. C.

18444 *A dictionary of Quenya, and of Proto-Eldarin, with an index.* Cambridge, England: J. C. Bradfield, 1982, 40 leaves, paper, nonf.

BRADFIELD, Scott (Michael), 1955-

18445 *The secret life of houses.* London: Unwin Hyman, 1988, 166 p., cloth, coll.

18940 retitled: *Dream of the wolf: stories.* New York: Alfred A. Knopf, 1990, 239 p., cloth, coll. [Expanded edition].

*BRADFORD, Columbus, <u>1887-1975</u>

BRADFORD, Gordon, pseud.—SEE: Arrow, Jay

BRADFORD, Matthew C., pseud.—SEE: Jennison, John

BRADFORD, Robert, *with Ward Moore*

18446 *Caduceus wild.* Los Angeles: A Futorian Book, Pinnacle Books, 1978, 273 p., paper, novel.

BRADLEY, Christine

18447 *Memoirs of an astral vampire.* Culver City, CA: Unquiet Grave, 1989, p., paper, novel.

BRADLEY, David

18448 *The Lodestar project.* New York: Pocket Books, 1986, 279 p., paper, novel.

BRADLEY, Ian (Campbell), 1950-

18449 *William Morris and his world.* London: Thames & Hudson, 1978, 127 p., cloth, nonf.

BRADLEY, Marion (Eleanor) Zimmer, 1930-

18450 *The best of Marion Zimmer Bradley.* Chicago: Academy Chicago, 1985, 367 p., cloth, coll. [Edited by Martin H. Greenberg].

18451 *The bloody sun.* New York: Ace Books, 1979, 408 p., paper, coll. DARKOVER SERIES. [An expanded version of *The bloody sun* (see #01788), plus the short story, "To Keep the Oath"].

18451A retitled: *The bloody sun; and, "To keep the oath".* Boston: Gregg Press, 1979, xi+408 p., cloth, coll. DARKOVER SERIES.

18452 *Children of Hastur: The heritage of Hastur; Sharra's exile.* Garden City, NY: Nelson Doubleday, 1982, 691 p., cloth, coll. DARKOVER SERIES.

18453 *City of sorcery.* New York: DAW Books, 1984, 424 p., paper, novel. DARKOVER SERIES.

18454 *The colors of space.* Norfolk, Virginia Beach, VA: The Donning Company/ Publishers, 1983, 141 p., paper, novel. [Expanded edition of #01790].

18455 *Drums of darkness: an astrological gothic novel: Leo.* New York: Ballantine Books, 1976, 212 p., paper, novel.

Endless universe—SEE: *Endless voyage.*

18456 *Endless voyage.* New York: Ace Books, 1975, 189 p., paper, novel.

18456A retitled: *Endless universe.* New York: Ace Books, 1979, 341 p., paper, novel. [Expanded edition].

The fall of Atlantis—SEE: *Web of darkness.*

18457 *The firebrand: a novel.* New York: Simon & Schuster, 1987, 608 p., cloth, novel.

18458 *The forbidden Tower: a Darkover novel.* New York: DAW Books, 1977, 364 p., paper, novel. DARKOVER SERIES.

18459 *Greyhaven: an anthology of fantasy.* New York: DAW Books, 1983, 240 p., paper, anth.

18460 *Hawkmistress!* New York: DAW Books, 1982, 336 p., paper, novel. DARKOVER SERIES.

18461 *The heirs of Hammerfell.* New York: DAW Books, 1989, 300 p., cloth, novel. DARKOVER SERIES.

18462 *The heritage of Hastur.* New York: DAW Books, 1975, 381 p., paper, novel. DARKOVER SERIES.

18463 *The house between the worlds.* Garden City, NY: Doubleday & Co., 1980, 244 p., cloth, novel.

18464 *The house between the worlds.* New York: A Del Rey Book, Ballantine Books, 1981, 313 p., paper, novel. [Expanded and revised edition].

18465 *The inheritor.* New York: Tor, A Tom Doherty Associates Book, 1984, 414 p., paper, novel. LESLIE BARNES #2.

18466 *Lythande.* New York: DAW Books, 1986, 237 p., paper, coll. THIEVES' WORLD. [Includes one story by Vonda N. McIntyre].

18467 *The mists of Avalon.* New York: Alfred A. Knopf, 1982, xi+876 p., cloth, novel. [Winner of the *Locus* Award for Best Fantasy Novel, 1983 (1984)].

18468 *Night's daughter: a novel.* New York: A Del Rey Book, Ballantine Books, 1985, 249 p., paper, novel.

18469 *Oath of the renunciates.* Garden City, NY: Nelson Doubleday, 1984, 593 p., cloth, coll. DARKOVER SERIES. [Includes *The shattered chain* and *Thendara House*].

18470 *The planet savers.* New York: Ace Books, 1976, 116 p., paper, coll. DARKOVER SERIES. [Adds to the original novel (see #01801) the short story, "The Waterfall"].

18471 *The planet savers; The sword of Aldones.* New York: Ace Books, 1980, 359 p., paper, coll. DARKOVER SERIES.

18472 *The ruins of Isis.* Norfolk, VA: Starblaze Editions, Donning Co., 1978, 234 p., paper, novel.

18473 *Sharra's exile.* New York: DAW Books, 1981, 365 p., paper, novel. DARKOVER SERIES. [A recasting of *The sword of Aldones* (see #01806)].

18474 *The shattered chain: a Darkover novel.* New York: DAW Books, 1976, 287 p., paper, novel. DARKOVER SERIES.

18475 *The spells of wonder.* New York: DAW Books, 1989, 288 p., paper, anth.

18476 *Stormqueen! a Darkover novel.* New York: DAW Books, 1978, 364 p., paper, novel. DARKOVER SERIES.

18477 *Survey ship.* New York: Ace Books, 1980, 231 p., paper, novel.

18478 *Sword and sorceress: an anthology of heroic fantasy.* New York: DAW Books, 1984, 255 p., paper, anth.

18479 *Sword and sorceress II: an anthology of heroic fantasy.* New York: DAW Books, 1985, 287 p., paper, anth.

18480 *Sword and sorceress III: an anthology of heroic fantasy.* New York: DAW Books, 1986, 285 p., paper, anth.

18481 *Sword and sorceress IV: an anthology of heroic fantasy.* New York: DAW Books, 1987, 285 p., paper, anth.

18482 *Sword and sorceress V: an anthology of heroic fantasy.* New York: DAW Books, 1988, 284 p., paper, anth.

18483 *Sword and sorceress VI: an anthology of heroic fantasy.* New York: DAW Books, 1990, vi+286 p., paper, anth.

18484 *Sword and sorceress VII: an anthology of heroic fantasy.* New York: DAW Books, 1990, vi+288 p., paper, anth.

18485 *Sword and sorceress VIII: an anthology of heroic fantasy.* New York: DAW Books, 1991, vi+285 p., paper, anth.

18486 *Thendara House.* New York: DAW Books, 1983, 414 p., paper, novel. DARKOVER SERIES.

18487 *Two to conquer.* New York: DAW Books, 1980, 335 p., paper, novel. DARKOVER SERIES.

18488 *Warrior woman.* New York: DAW Books, 1985, 205 p., paper, novel.

18489 *Web of darkness.* Virginia Beach, Norfolk, VA: Donning Co., 1983, 200 p., paper, novel. ATLANTEAN CHRONICLES #2.

18490 *Web of darkness.* Glasgow, Scotland: Richard Drew, 1985, 369 p., cloth, coll. ATLANTEAN CHRONICLES #1-2.

18490A retitled: *The fall of Atlantis.* New York: Baen Books, 1987, 502 p., paper, novel. ALTANTEAN CHRONICLES #1-2.

18491 *Web of light.* Norfolk, Virginia Beach, VA: Donning Co., 1983, 190 p., paper, novel. ATLANTEAN CHRONICLES #1.

18492 *Witch hill.* New York: Tor, A Tom Doherty Associates Book, 1990, 244 p., paper, novel. LESLIE BARNES #3.

with Julian May & Andre Norton

18493 *Black Trillium.* New York: A Foundation Book, Doubleday, 1990, 409 p., cloth, novel. TRILLIUM #1.

with Paul Edwin Zimmer

18494 *The survivors.* New York: DAW Books, 1979, 238 p., paper, novel. RED MOON #2.

with the Friends of Darkover

18495 *Domain of Darkover.* New York: DAW Books, 1990, 254 p., paper, anth. DARKOVER SERIES.

18496 *Four moons of Darkover.* New York: DAW Books, 1988, 284 p., paper, anth. DARKOVER SERIES.

18497 *Free Amazons of Darkover: an anthology.* New York: DAW Books, 1985, 304 p., paper, anth. DARKOVER SERIES.

18498 *The Keeper's price, and other stories.* New York: DAW Books, 1980, 207 p., paper, anth. DARKOVER SERIES.

18499 *Leroni of Darkover.* New York: DAW Books, 1991, 334 p., paper, anth. DARKOVER SERIES.

18500 *The other side of the mirror, and other Darkover stories.* New York: DAW Books, 1987, 303 p., paper, anth. DARKOVER SERIES.

18501 *Red sun of Darkover.* New York: DAW Books, 1987, 287 p., paper, anth. DARKOVER SERIES.

18502 *Renunciates of Darkover.* New York: DAW Books, 1991, 317 p., paper, anth. DARKOVER SERIES.

18503 *Sword of chaos, and other stories.* New York: DAW Books, 1982, 240 p., paper, anth. DARKOVER SERIES.

BRADLEY, Michael (Anderson), 1944-

18504 *Imprint: a novel.* Toronto: Dorset Publishing, 1978, 233 p, cloth, novel.

BRADMAN, Tony, 1954-

18505 *The magic kiss, and other tales of princes and princesses.* London: Blackie, 1987, 94 p., cloth, anth.

BRADSHAW, Gillian (Marucha), 1956-

18506 *Down the long wind.* London: Methuen, 1988, 842 p., paper, coll. ARTHURIAN CYCLE #1-3.

18507 *The dragon and the thief.* New York: Greenwillow Books, 1991, 154 p., cloth, novel.

18508 *Hawk of May.* New York: Simon & Schuster, 1980, 313 p., cloth, novel. ARTHURIAN SAGA #1.

18509 *Horses of heaven.* New York: Doubleday, 1991, viii+448 p., cloth, novel.

18510 *In winter's shadow.* New York: Simon & Schuster, 1982, 379 p., cloth, novel. ARTHURIAN SAGA #3.

18511 *Kingdom of summer.* New York: Simon & Schuster, 1981, 283 p., cloth, novel. ARTHURIAN SAGA #2.

*BRADWELL, James [pseud. of Arthur William Charles Kent], 1925-

BRADY, Jane—SEE: White, Jane

BRADY, John Paul, 1928-

18512 *A voyage to Inshneefa: a first-hand account of the fifth voyage of Lemuel Gulliver.* Santa Barbara, CA: John Daniel, 1987, 103 p., paper, novel. GULLIVER SEQUEL.

BRADY, Michael, 1928-

18513 *American surrender*. London: Michael Joseph, 1979, 288 p., cloth, novel.

BRADY, Richard

18514 *The-land-where-the-sun-goes-down: a fantasy*. Menomonie, WI: Vagabond Press, 1972, [14] p., paper, story.

*BRAHMS, Caryl [pseud. of Doris Caroline Abrahams], 1901-1982

*BRAINE, Robert D., 1861-1943

*BRALEY, Berton, 1882-1966

BRAND, (Mary) Christianna (Milne Lewis), 1907-1988

18515 *The brides of Aberdar*. London: Michael Joseph, 1982, 252 p., cloth, novel.

BRAND, Kurt, 1917-

18516 *Agents of destruction*. Van Nuys, CA: Master Publications, 1979, 64 p., paper, novel. PERRY RHODAN #134. [Translation of *Agenten der vernichtung*]

18517 *Man in danger*. New York: Ace Books, 1975, 169 p., paper, novel. PERRY RHODAN #82. [Includes additional fiction and nonfiction].

18518 *Blitzkrieg galactica*. Van Nuys, CA: Master Publications, 1979, 64 p., paper, novel. PERRY RHODAN #129. [Translation of *Sturm auf die galaxis*].

18519 *Blockade: Lepso*. New York: Ace Books, 1976, 189 p., paper, novel. PERRY RHODAN #101. [Includes additional fiction and nonfiction].

18520 *Caller from eternity*. New York: Ace Books, 1976, 169 p., paper, novel. PERRY RHODAN #106. [Includes additional fiction and nonfiction].

18521 *The man with two faces*. New York: Ace Books, 1976, 186 p., paper, novel. PERRY RHODAN #104. [Includes additional fiction and nonfiction].

18522 *Peril unlimited*. Van Nuys, CA: Master Publications, 1979, 64 p., paper, novel. PERRY RHODAN #130. [Translation of *Risiko unendlich gross*].

18523 *Planet Topside, please reply!* New York: Ace Books, 1975, 159 p., paper, novel. PERRY RHODAN #75. [Includes additional fiction and nonfiction].

18524 *Power's price*. New York: Ace Books, 1976, 207 p., paper, novel. PERRY

RHODAN #89. [Includes additional fiction and nonfiction].

18525 *Pucky's greatest hour*. New York: Ace Books, 1975, 154 p., paper, novel. PERRY RHODAN #81. [Includes additional fiction and nonfiction].

18526 *Saboteurs in A-1*. New York: Ace Books, 1977, 117 p., paper, novel. PERRY RHODAN #115. [Bound with *The psycho duel* / by William Voltz].

18527 *The sinister power*. Van Nuys, CA: Master Publications, 1978, 62 p., paper, novel. PERRY RHODAN #124. [Translation of *Die macht der unheimlichen*].

18528 *Thora's sacrifice*. New York: Ace Books, 1975, 157 p., paper novel. PERRY RHODAN #70. [Includes additional fiction and nonfiction].

18529 *The Tigris leaps*. New York: Ace Books, 1975, 157 p., paper, novel. PERRY RHODAN #63. [Includes additional fiction and nonfiction].

18530 *Unleashed powers*. New York: Ace Books, 1976, 201 p., paper, novel. PERRY RHODAN #90. [Includes additional fiction and nonfiction].

18531 *Volunteers for Frago*. Van Nuys, CA: Master Publications, 1978, 63 p., paper novel. PERRY RHODAN #122. [Translation of *Freiwillige für Frago*].

BRAND, Larry

18532 *Birthpyre*. New York: Avon, 1980, 285 p., paper, novel.

BRAND, Max [pseud. of Frederick Schiller Faust], 1892-1944

18533 *The smoking land: a Max Brand popular classic*. Santa Barbara, CA: Capra Press, 1980, 112 p., paper, novel.

BRANDAO, Ignácio de Loyola (Lopes), 1936-

18534 *And still the Earth: an archival narration*. New York: A Bard Book, 1985, 374 p., paper, novel. [Translation by Ellen Watson of *Nao verás país nenhum*].

BRANDEL, Marc [legalized from Marcus Beresford], 1919-

The hand—SEE: *The lizard's tail*.

18535 *The lizard's tail*. New York: Simon & Schuster, 1979, 286 p., cloth, novel.

18535A retitled: *The hand*. New York: Berkley Books, 1981, 245 p., paper, novel.

18536 *Survivor*. New York: Simon & Schuster, 1976, 254 p., cloth, novel.

BRANDEN, Barbara

18537 *The passion of Ayn Rand.* Garden City, NY: Doubleday & Co., 1986, xiii+442 p., cloth, nonf.

with Nathaniel Branden

18538 *In answer to Ayn Rand.* New York: Nathaniel Branden Institute, 1968, 12 p., paper, nonf.

18539 *Who is Ayn Rand? an analysis of the novels of Ayn Rand* / by Nathaniel Branden ; *Biographical essay* / by Barbara Branden. New York: Random House, 1962, vi+239 p., cloth, nonf. coll.

BRANDEN, Nathaniel, 1930-

18540 *Judgment day: my years with Ayn Rand.* Boston: A Marc Jaffe Book, Houghton Mifflin Co., 1989, x+436 p., cloth, nonf.

with Barbara Branden

18538 *In answer to Ayn Rand.* New York: Nathaniel Branden Institute, 1968, 12 p., paper, nonf.

18539 *Who is Ayn Rand? an analysis of the novels of Ayn Rand* / by Nathaniel Branden ; *Biographical essay* / by Barbara Branden. New York: Random House, 1962, vi+239 p., cloth, nonf. coll.

BRANDER, Laurence, 1903-

18541 *Aldous Huxley: a critical study.* London: Rupert Hart-Davis, 1969, 244 p., cloth, nonf.

18542 *George Orwell.* London, New York: Longmans, Green & Co., 1954, 212 p., cloth, nonf.

BRANDEWYNE, (Mary) Rebecca (Wadsworth), 1955-

18543 *And gold was ours.* New York: Warner Books, 1984, 530 p., paper, novel.

18544 *Beyond the starlit frost.* New York, London: Pocket Star Books, 1991, 428 p., paper, novel. CHRONICLES OF TINTAGEL #2.

18545 *Forever my love.* New York: Warner Books, 1982, 556 p., paper, novel.

18546 *Passion moon rising.* New York: Pocket Books, 1988, 434 p., paper, novel. CHRONICLES OF TINTAGEL #1.

BRANDNER, Gary (Phil), 1933-

18547 *The aardvark affair.* New York: Zebra Books, Kensington Publishing Corp., 1975, 189 p., paper, novel. BIG BRAIN #1.

18547A retitled: *The big brain.* London: Severn House, 1991, 189 p., cloth, novel. BIG BRAIN #1.

18548 *The Beelzebub business.* New York: Zebra Books, Kensington Publishing Corp., 1975, 188 p., paper, novel. BIG BRAIN #2.

The big brain—SEE: *The aardvark affair.*

18549 *The brain eaters.* New York: Fawcett Gold Medal, 1985, 278 p., paper, novel.

18550 *Cameron's closet.* New York: Fawcett Gold Medal, 1987, 314 p., paper, novel.

18550A retitled: *Cameron's terror.* London: Severn House, 1988, 314 p., cloth, novel.

Cameron's terror—SEE: *Cameron's closet.*

18551 *Carrion.* New York: Fawcett Gold Medal, 1986, 265 p., paper, novel.

18552 *Cat people: a novel.* New York: Fawcett Gold Medal, 1982, 221 p., paper, movie.

Deathwalkers—SEE: *Walkers.*

18553 *Doomstalker.* New York: Fawcett Gold Medal, 1989, 234 p., paper, novel.

Echoes—SEE: *The howling III.*

18554 *The experiment.* Belmont, CA: Fearon, 1987, 58 p., paper, novel.

18555 *Floater.* New York: Fawcett Gold Medal, 1988, 295 p., paper, novel.

18556 *Hellborn.* New York: Fawcett Gold Medal, 1981, 224 p., paper, novel.

18557 *The howling.* Greenwich, CT: A Fawcett Gold Medal Book, Fawcett Publications, 1977, 223 p., paper, novel. HOWLING #1.

18558 *The howling II.* New York: Fawcett Gold Medal, 1978, 284 p., paper, novel. HOWLING #2.

18558A retitled: *Return of the howling.* Feltham, England: Hamlyn Paperbacks, 1979, 193 p., paper, novel.

18558B retitled: *The howling II: the return.* London: Severn House, 1987, 193 p., cloth, novel.

18559 *The howling III.* New York: Fawcett Gold Medal, 1985, 252 p., paper, novel. HOWLING #3.

18559A retitled: *The Howling III: Echoes.* London: Hamlyn Paperbacks, 1985, 254 p., paper, novel. HOWLING #3.

18560 *Mind grabber.* Belmont, CA: Fearon, 1987, 62 p., paper, novel.

18561 *Quintana Roo.* New York: Fawcett Gold Medal, 1984, 251 p., paper, novel.

The return—SEE: *The howling II.*

The return of the howling—SEE: *The howling II.*

18562 *Tribe of the dead.* London: Hamlyn Paperbacks, 1984, 251 p., paper, novel.

18563 *Walkers.* New York: Fawcett Gold Medal, 1980, 222 p., paper, novel.

18563A retitled: *Deathwalkers.* London: Severn House, 1989, 222 p., cloth, novel.

as ANONYMOUS EDITOR

18564 *Claws & feathers.* Belmont, CA: Lake Books, 1989, 135 p., cloth, anth.

18565 *Illusions.* Belmont, CA: Lake Books, 1988, 136 p., cloth, anth.

with Clayton Matthews (as uncredited co-author)

18556 *Energy zero.* New York: Zebra Books, Kensington Publishing Corp., 1976, 203 p., paper, novel. BIG BRAIN #3.

BRANDON, Ruth, 1943-

18557 *Mind out.* London: Collins, 1991, [200] p., cloth, novel.

18558 *Out of body, out of mind.* London: Macmillan, 1987, 234 p., cloth, novel.

BRANSFORD, Stephen (E.), 1949-

18559 *High places.* Wheaton, II.: Crossway Books, 1991, 443 p., paper, novel.

BRANTENBERG, Gerd, 1941-

18560 *The daughters of Egalia.* London, West Nyack, NY: Journeyman Press, 1985, 269 p., paper, novel. [Translation by Louis Mackay of *Egalias dotre*].

18560A retitled: *Egalia's daughters: a satire of the sexes.* Seattle, WA: The Seal Press, 1985, 269 p., cloth, novel. [Translation by Louis Mackay of *Egalias dotre*].
Egalia's daughters—SEE: *The daughters of Egalia.*

BRAUDE, Anne Janet

18561 *Andre Norton: fables & futures.* Center Harbor, NH: Niekas Publications, 1990, 52 p., paper, nonf. anth.

BRAUN, Matthew, 1932-

18562 *The second coming of Lucas Brokaw.* New York: A Dell/Bernard Geis Associates Book, 1977, 255 p., paper, novel.

as WARREN BURKE

18563 *The killing touch.* New York: Charter Books, 1983, viii+228 p., paper, novel.

BRAUN, Terrance, pseud.—SEE: **Bennett, Jeff**

*BRAUTIGAN, Richard (Gary), 1933-1984

BRAVARD, Robert S(taton), 1935- , *with Michael W. Peplow*

18564 *Samuel R. Delany: a primary and secondary bibliography, 1962-1979.* Boston: G. K. Hall & Co., 1980, xiv+178 p., cloth, nonf. MASTERS OF SCIENCE FICTION AND FANTASY.

BRAWN, Anna—SEE: **Livia, Anna**

BREDENBERG, Jeff(rey Ellis), 1953-

18565 *The dream compass.* New York: Avon Books, 1991, 180 p., paper, novel.

BREEN, Jon L(inn), 1943-

18566 *The gathering place.* New York: Walker & Co., 1984, 168 p., cloth, novel

BREEN, Walter (Henry), 1930-

18567 *The Darkover concordance: a reader's guide.* Berkeley, CA: Pennyfarthing Press, 1979, ix+163 p., cloth, nonf.

18568 *The Gemini problem: a study in Darkover.* Baltimore, MD: T-K Graphics, 1975, [39] p., paper, nonf. [Revised edition of #01855].

BREGENZER, Don (Marshall), 1888-1931

18569 *A list of Cabelliana belonging to Don Bregenzer of Cleveland.* Cleveland, OH: Privately Produced, 1925 (i.e., 1926), [22] leaves, paper, nonf.

with Samuel Loveman

18570 *A round-table in Poictesme.* Cleveland, OH: Privately Printed by Members of the Colophon Club, 1924, xi+126 p., cloth, nonf. anth.

BRELLEN, Marc [pseud. of Bruce Jack Freshman]

18571 *Crossbearers.* New York: Leisure Books, 1988, 362 p., paper, novel.

*BRENNAN, Elizabeth, 1922-

BRENNAN, J(ames) H(erbert), 1940-

18572 *Ancient evil.* London: A Fontana Book, Collins, 1985, 156 p., paper, novel. SAGAS OF THE DEMONSPAWN.

18573 *Barmy Jeffers and the Quasimodo walk.* London: Armada, 1988, 157 p., paper, novel. BARMY JEFFERS #1.

18574 *Barmy Jeffers and the shrinking potion.* London: Armada, 1989, 174 p., paper, novel. BARMY JEFFERS #3.

18575 *The castle of darkness.* London: Armada Books, 1984, [187] p., paper, novel. GRAILQUEST #1.

18576 *The crone.* London: Collins, 1990, 240 p., cloth, novel. SHIVA #2.

18576A retitled: *Shiva accused.* New York: HarperCollins, 1991, 275 p., cloth, novel. SHIVA #2.

18577 *The crypts of terror.* London: Fontana/Collins, 1984, 192 p., paper, novel. SAGAS OF THE DEMONSPAWN.

18578 *The curse of Frankenstein.* London: Armada, 1986, [210] p., paper, novel. FRANKENSTEIN SERIES.

18579 *Demonstration.* London: Fontana/Collins, 1985, 191 p., paper, novel. SAGAS OF THE DEMONSPAWN.

18580 *The den of dragons.* London: Armada, 1984, [219] p., paper, novel. GRAILQUEST #2.

18581 *Dracula's castle.* London: Armada, 1986, [200] p., paper, novel.

18582 *Fire wolf.* London: Fontana/Collins, 1984, 252 p., paper, novel. SAGAS OF THE DEMONSPAWN #1.

18583 *The gateway of doom.* London: Fontana, 1984, 223 p., paper, novel. GRAILQUEST #3.

18584 *Kingdom of horror.* London: Fontana, 1985, 223 p., paper, novel. GRAILQUEST #5.

18585 *Monster horrorshow.* London: Armada, 1987, 255 p., paper, novel.

18586 *Realm of chaos.* London: Fontana, 1986, 208 p., paper, novel. GRAILQUEST #6.

18587 *Return of Barmy Jeffers and the Quasimodo walk.* London: Armada, 1988, 157 p., paper, novel. BARMY JEFFERS #2.
Shiva accused—SEE: *The crone.*

18588 *Shiva: an adventure of the ice age.* London: Collins, 1989, 141 p., cloth, novel. SHIVA #1.

18589 *Voyage of terror.* London: Fontana, 1985, 237 p., paper, novel. GRAILQUEST #4.

as JAN BRENNAN

18590 *Dream of destiny.* Garden City, NY: Doubleday & Co., 1980, 332 p., cloth, novel.

18591 *The Greythorn woman.* London: Collins, 1979, 309 p., cloth, novel.

BRENNAN, Jan, pseud.—SEE: Brennan, J. H.

BRENNAN, Joseph Payne, 1918-1990

18592 *The adventures of Lucius Leffing.* Hampton Falls, NH: Donald M. Grant, Publisher, 1990, 223 p., cloth, coll. LUCIUS LEFFING SERIES.

18593 *The borders just beyond.* West Kingston, RI: Donald M. Grant, Publisher, 1986, 200 p., cloth, coll. [Limited to 750 copies].

18594 *The chronicles of Lucius Leffing.* West Kingston, RI: Donald M. Grant, Publisher, 1977, 253 p., cloth, coll. LUCIUS LEFFING SERIES.

18595 *Evil always ends.* West Kingston, RI: Donald M. Grant, Publisher, 1982, 123 p., cloth, novel.

18596 *The shapes of midnight: horror.* New York: Berkley Books, 1980, xvi+176 p., paper, coll.

with Donald Grant

18597 *Act of Providence.* West Kingston, RI: Donald M. Grant, Publisher, 1979, 122 p., cloth, novel. LUCIUS LEFFING SERIES.

BRENNAN, Noel-Anne (Gerson), 1948-

18598 *Winter reckoning.* West Kingston, RI: Donald M. Grant, Publisher, 1986, 253 p., cloth, novel. [Limited to 600 copies].

BRENNER, Mayer Alan, 1956-

18599 *Catastrophe's spell.* New York: DAW Books, 1989, 320 p., paper, novel. DANCE OF THE GODS #1.

18600 *Spell of intrigue.* New York: DAW Books, 1990, 336 p., paper, novel. DANCE OF THE GODS #2.

as RICK NORTH

30815 *Space pioneers.* New York: Zebra Books, Kensington Publishing Corp., 1991, 174 p., paper, novel. YOUNG ASTRONAUTS #5.

BRENNERT, Alan (Michael), 1954-

18601 *City of masques.* Chicago: Playboy Press Paperbacks, 1978, 206 p., paper, novel.

18602 *Her pilgrim soul, and other stories.* New York: Tor, A Tom Doherty Associates Book, 1990, 244 p., cloth, coll.

18603 *Kindred spirits.* New York: Tor, A Tom Doherty Associates Book, 1984, 320 p., paper, novel.

18604 *Ma Qui, and other phantoms.* Eugene, OR: Pulphouse Publishing, 1991, 103 p., cloth, coll. AUTHOR'S CHOICE MONTHLY #17.

18605 *Time and chance.* New York: Tor, A Tom Doherty Associates Book, Books, 1990, 281 p., cloth, novel.

BRENT, Peter L.—SEE: Peters, Ludovic

BRETNOR, Reginald [legalized from Alfred Reginald Kahn], 1911-1992

18606 *The craft of science fiction: a symposium on writing science fiction and science fantasy.* New York, Hagerstown, NJ: Harper & Row, Publishers, 1976, xi+321 p., cloth, nonf. anth.

18607 *Gilpin's space.* New York: Ace Science Fiction Books, 1986, 218 p., paper, novel.

18608 *Modern science fiction: its meaning and its future.* Chicago: Advent:Publishers, 1979, xvi+327 p., cloth, nonf. anth. [Revised from #01874]

18609 *Orion's sword: (war in interstellar and intergalactic space).* New York: Ace Books, 1980, 324 p., paper, anth. FUTURE AT WAR #3.

18610 *The Schimmelhorn file: memoirs of a dirty old genius.* New York: Ace Books, 1979, 280 p., paper, coll. PAPA SCHIMMELHORN #1.

18611 *Schimmelhorn's gold.* New York: Tor SF, A Tom Doherty Associates Book, 1986, 216 p., paper, novel. PAPA SCHIMMELHORN #2.

18612 *The spear of Mars.* New York: Ace Books, 1980, 408 p., paper, anth. FUTURE AT WAR #2.

18613 *Thor's hammer: on or near Earth.* New York: Ace Books, 1979, 391 p., paper, anth. FUTURE AT WAR #1. [Includes some nonfiction].

as GRENDEL BRIARTON

18614 *The compleat Feghoot: the many lives and greatest exploits of history's punniest space-time traveller.* Baltimore, MD: The Mirage Press, 1975, [124] p., paper, coll. FEGHOOT SERIES. [No cloth edition was issued despite a statement to that effect in the book; expanded from #01876].

18615 *The (even more) compleat Feghoot: the many lives and greatest exploits of history's punniest space-time traveler.* Baltimore, MD: Mirage Press, 1980, [137] p., paper, coll. FEGHOOT SERIES. [Expanded from the two previous editions].

BRETT, Brian, 1950-

18616 *The fungus garden.* Saskatoon, Saskatchewan, Canada: Thistledown Press, 1988, 127 p., cloth, novel.

BRETT, David, 1937-

18617 *Black folder.* London: Harrap, 1976, 155 p., cloth, novel.

BRETT, Stephen

18618 *The vampire chase.* New York: Manor Books, 1979, p., paper, novel.

BREUER, M(iles) J(ohn), 1888-1947, with Jack Williamson

18619 *The birth of a new republic.* New Orleans, LA: P.D.A. Enterprises, 1981, 80 p., paper, story.

BREWER, Frances Joan, 1913-1965

18620 *James Branch Cabell: a bibliography of his writings, biography, and criticism.* Charlottesville, VA: University of Virginia Press, 1957, 206 p., cloth, nonf.

BREWER, Jeutonne P(atten), 1939-

26959 *Anthony Burgess: a bibliography.* Metuchen, NJ: Scarecrow Press, 1980, xv+175 p., cloth, nonf.

BREWSTER, Dorothy, 1883-1979

18621 *Doris Lessing.* New York: Twayne Publishers, 1965, 173 p., cloth, nonf.

BRIANS, Paul, 1942-

18622 *Nuclear holocausts: atomic war in fiction, 1895-1984.* Kent, OH: Kent State University Press, 1987, xi+398 p., cloth, nonf.

BRIARTON, Grendel, pseud.—SEE: Bretnor, Reginald

BRICE, Martin H(ubert), 1935-

18623 *The witch in the cave.* London: George Allen & Unwin, 1986, 196 p., cloth, novel.

BRIDGES, Laurie [pseud. of Lorraine Bruck], 1921-

18624 *The Ashton horror.* Toronto, New York: Bantam Books, 1984, 150 p., paper, novel. DARK FORCES #12.

with Paul Alexander

16255 *Devil wind.* Toronto, New York: Bantam Books, 1983, 152 p., paper, novel. DARK FORCES #4.
16256 *Magic show.* Toronto, New York: Bantam Books, 1983, 135 p., paper, novel. DARK FORCES #2.
16257 *Swamp witch.* Toronto, New York: Bantam Books, 1983, 153 p., paper, novel. DARK FORCES #6.

*BRIDGES, T(homas) C(harles), 1868-1944

BRIDGWATER, Sue, *with Alistair McGechie*

18625 *Perian's journey.* London: Julia MacRae Books, 1989, 133 p., cloth, novel.

BRIENO, Linda

18626 *Brain dead.* New York: Leisure Books, 1985, 379 p., paper, novel.
18627 *Pacemaker.* New York: Leisure Books, 1987, 346 p., paper, novel.

BRIERY, Traci, *with Mara McCuniff*

18628 *The vampire memoirs.* New York: Zebra Books, Kensington Publishing Corp., 1991, 432 p., paper, novel.

BRIGG, Peter, 1942-

18629 *J. G. Ballard.* Mercer Island, WA: Starmont House, 1985, 138 p., cloth, nonf. STARMONT READER'S GUIDE #26.

BRIGGS, Ian

The curse of Fenric—SEE: *Doctor Who: The curse of Fenric.*

18630 *Doctor Who: Dragonfire.* London: W. H. Allen & Co., 1989, 144 p., cloth, tele. DOCTOR WHO #137.
18631 *Doctor Who: The curse of Fenric.* London: W. H. Allen & Co., 1990, 188 p., cloth, tele. DOCTOR WHO #151. [No author given on title page]. *Dragonfire*—SEE: *Doctor Who: Dragonfire.*

BRIGGS, Joe Bob [pseud. of John Bloom], 1953-

18632 *Joe Bob goes back to the drive-in.* New York: Delacorte Press, 1990, xxi+223 p., paper, nonf.
18633 *Joe Bob goes to the drive-in.* New York: Delacorte Press, 1987, 325 p., paper, nonf.

BRIGGS, Julia (Ruth), 1943-

18634 *Night visitors: the rise and fall of the English ghost story.* London: Faber & Faber, 1977, 238 p., cloth, nonf.
18635 *A woman of passion: the life of E. Nesbit, 1858-1924.* London: Hutchinson, 1987, xx+473 p., cloth, nonf.

with Don Crompton

18636 *A view from the spire: William Golding's later novels.* Oxford, England: Basil Blackwell, 1985, vi+199 p., cloth, nonf.

BRIGGS, K(atharine) M(ary), 1898-1980

18637 *The fairies in tradition and literature.* London: Routledge & Kegan Paul, 1967, x+261 p., cloth, nonf. anth.
18638 *Hobberdy Dick.* London: Eyre & Spottiswoode, 1955, 191 p., cloth, novel.
18639 *Kate Crackernuts.* Oxford, England: Alden Press, 1963, 252 p., cloth, novel.

*BRIGGS, Philip [pseud. of Phyllis Briggs], 1904-

BRIGGS, Phyllis—SEE: Briggs, Philip

BRIGHTFIELD, Glory, *with Rick Brightfield*

18640 *Outer space mazes.* New York: Harper Colophon Books, 1978, 58 p., paper, nonf.

BRIGHTFIELD, Richard, 1927-

18641 *The battle of Astar.* Toronto, New York: Bantam Books, 1987, 133 p., paper, novel. ESCAPE FROM THE KINGDOM OF FROME #4.

18642 *Battle of the dragons.* New York: Tor, A Tom Doherty Associates Book, 1986, 127 p., paper, novel. YOUR MAZE ADVENTURES #6.

18643 *The castle of doom.* New York: Tor, A Tom Doherty Associates Book, 1984, 127 p., paper, novel. YOUR AMAZING ADVENTURES #1.

18644 *The caverns of Mornas.* Toronto, New York: Bantam Books, 1987, 118 p., paper, novel. ESCAPE FROM THE KINGDOM OF FROME #3.

18645 *China: why was an army made of clay?* New York: McGraw-Hill Book Co., 1989, 102 p., paper, novel. EARTH INSPECTORS #7.

18646 *The curse of Batterslea Hall.* Toronto, New York: An Edward Packard Book, Bantam Books, 1984, 118 p., paper, novel. CHOOSE YOUR OWN ADVENTURE #30.

18647 *The deadly shadow.* Toronto, New York: An Edward Packard Book, Bantam Books, 1985, 118 p., paper, novel. CHOOSE YOUR OWN ADVENTURE #46.

18648 *The dragonmaster.* New York: Tor, A Tom Doherty Associates Book, 1985, 127 p., paper, novel. YOUR AMAZING ADVENTURES #4.

18649 *The dragons' den.* Toronto, New York: An Edward Packard Book, Bantam Books, 1984, 116 p., paper, novel. CHOOSE YOUR OWN ADVENTURE #33.

18650 *The forest of the king.* Toronto, New York: Bantam Books, 1987, 131 p., paper, novel. ESCAPE FROM THE KINGDOM OF FROME #2.

18651 *The gruesome guests, and other stories* / by Rick Brightfield. Mahwah, NJ: Troll Associates, 1990, 90 p., cloth, coll.

18652 *Hijacked!* New York, Toronto: An Edward Packard Book, Bantam Books, 1990, 116 p., paper, novel. CHOOSE YOUR OWN ADVENTURE #106.

18653 *Hurricane!* Toronto, New York: An Edward Packard Book, Bantam Books, 1988, 114 p., paper, novel. CHOOSE YOUR OWN ADVENTURE #82.

18654 *Invaders of the planet Earth* / by Rick Brightfield. Toronto, New York: An Edward Packard Book, Bantam Books, 1987, 115 p., paper, novel. CHOOSE YOUR OWN ADVENTURE #70.

18655 *Island of fear.* New York: Tor, A Tom Doherty Associates Book, 1984, 127 p., paper, novel. YOUR AMAZING ADVENTURES #2.

18656 *Master of karate.* New York, Toronto: An Edward Packard Book, A Bantam Skylark Book, 1990, 113 p., paper, novel. CHOOSE YOUR OWN ADVENTURE #108.

18657 *Master of kung fu.* New York, Toronto: An Edward Packard Book, Bantam Books, 1989, 113 p., paper, novel. CHOOSE YOUR OWN ADVENTURE #88.

18658 *Master of tae kwon do.* New York, Toronto: An Edward Packard Book, Bantam Books, 1990, 119 p., paper, novel. CHOOSE YOUR OWN ADVENTURE #102.

18659 *Murder comes to life, and other stories* / by Rick Brightfield. Mahwah, NJ: Troll Associates, 1990, 95 p., cloth, coll.

18660 *The phantom submarine.* Toronto, New York: An Edward Packard Book, Bantam Books, 1983, 111 p., paper, novel. CHOOSE YOUR OWN ADVENTURE #26.

18661 *Planet of the dragons.* Toronto, New York: An Edward Packard Book, A Bantam Skylark Book, 1988, 117 p., paper, novel. CHOOSE YOUR OWN ADVENTURE #75.

18662 *Revenge of the dragonmaster.* New York: Tor, A Tom Doherty Associates Book, 1985, 127 p., paper, novel. YOUR MAZE ADVENTURES #5.

18663 *Secret of the pyramids.* Toronto, New York: An Edward Packard Book, Bantam Books, 1983, 116 p., paper, novel. CHOOSE YOUR OWN ADVENTURE #19.

18664 *The secret treasure of Tibet.* Toronto, New York: An Edward Packard Book, Bantam Books, 1984, 117 p., paper, novel. CHOOSE YOUR OWN ADVENTURE #36.

18665 *Star system Tenopia.* Toronto, New York: Bantam Books, 1986, 131 p., paper, novel. ESCAPE FROM TENOPIA #4.

18666 *Terror on Kabran.* Toronto, New York: Bantam Books, 1986, 129 p., paper, novel. ESCAPE FROM TENOPIA #3.

18667 *Terror under the Earth.* New York: Tor, A Tom Doherty Associates Book, 1984, 127 p., paper, novel. YOUR AMAZING ADVENTURES #3.

18668 *Trapped in the sea kingdom.* Toronto, New York: Bantam Books, 1986, 134 p., paper, novel. ESCAPE FROM TENOPIA #2.

18669 *U.S.A.: what is the great American invention?* New York: McGraw-Hill Book Co., 1989, 105 p., paper, novel. EARTH INSPECTORS #8.

with Glory Brightfield

18640 *Outer space mazes.* New York: Harper Colophon Books, 1978, 58 p., paper, nonf.

with Jim Razzi & Jack Looney

18670 *Star games: with a space adventure* / by Rick Brightfield.... Toronto, New York: Bantam Books, 1978, 128 p., paper, nonf.

BRIGHTFIELD, Rick—SEE: Brightfield, Richard

BRIMACOMBE, Joseph, 1959-

18671 *The last rainforest.* Lewes, East Sussex, England: The Book Guild, 1991, 280 p., cloth, novel.

BRIN, (Glen) David, 1950-

18672 *Dr. Pak's preschool.* New Castle, VA: Cheap Street, 1989, 78 p., cloth, story. [Limited to 175 copies].
18673 *Earth.* New York, Toronto: A Bantam Spectra Book, Bantam Books, 1990, 601 p., cloth, novel.
18674 *Earthclan: Startide rising; The uplift war.* Garden City, NY: Nelson Doubleday, 1987, 985 p., cloth, coll. EARTHCLAN #1-2. [Includes *Startide rising*; *The uplift war*].
18675 *Piecework.* Eugene, OR: Pulphouse Publishing, 1991, 44 p., cloth, story. SHORT STORY HARDBACKS #15; SHORT STORY PAPERBACKS #23.
18676 *The postman.* Toronto, New York: Bantam Books, 1985, 294 p., cloth, novel. [Winner of the John W. Campbell Jr. Memorial Award for Best Novel, 1985 (1986); winner of the *Locus* Award for Best Science Fiction Novel, 1985 (1986)].
18677 *The practice effect.* Toronto, New York: Bantam Books, 1984, 277 p., paper, novel.
18678 *The river of time.* Niles, IL: Dark Harvest, 1986, 366 p., cloth, coll.
18679 *Startide rising.* Toronto, New York: Bantam Books, 1983, 462 p., paper, novel. EARTHCLAN #1. [Winner of the Hugo Award for Best Novel, 1983 (1984); winner of the Nebula Award for Best Novel, 1983 (1984); winner of the *Locus* Award for Best Science Fiction Novel, 1983 (1984)].].
18680 *Sundiver.* Toronto, New York: Bantam Books, 1980, 340 p., paper, novel.
18681 *The uplift war.* West Bloomfield, MI: Phantasia Press, 1987, vii+506 p., cloth, novel. EARTHCLAN #2. [Winner of the Hugo Award for Best Novel, 1987 (1988); winner of the *Locus* Award for Best Science Fiction Novel, 1987 (1988)].

with Gregory Benford

17753 *Heart of the comet.* Toronto, New York: Bantam Books, 1986, 468 p., cloth, novel.

with Arthur C. Clarke

18682 *Project Solar Sail.* New York: A Roc Book, 1990, 246 p., paper, anth.

BRINBERG, Sybil Wuletich- —SEE: Wuletich-Brinberg, Sybil

BRINDEL, June Rachuy, 1919-

18683 *Phaedra: a novel of ancient Athens.* New York: St. Martin's Press, 1985, 227 p., cloth, novel.

BRINEY, R(obert) E(dward), 1933- , *with D. W. Dickensheet & J. R. Christopher*

18684 *A Boucher bibliography.* [White Bear Lake, MN: Allen J. Hubin], 1969, [34] p., paper, nonf. [Bound with *A Boucher portrait: Anthony Boucher as seen by his friends and colleagues* / edited by Lenore Glen Offord].

BRINGSJORD, Selmer, 1958-

18685 *Soft wars.* New York: A Signet Book, 1991, 526 p., paper, novel.

*BRINIG, Myron, 1896-1991

*BRINK, Carol (Ryrie), 1895-1981

BRINKLEY, William (Clark), 1917-

18686 *The last ship: a novel.* New York: Viking, 1988, vii+616 p., cloth, novel.

*BRINSMADE, Herman Hine, 1876-1968

*BRINTON, Henry, 1901-1977

BRISCO, Pat A.—SEE: Matthews, Patricia

BRITTAIN, Bill [i.e. William E. Brittain], 1930-

18687 *All the money in the world.* New York: Harper & Row, 1979, 150 p., cloth, novel.

18688 *Devil's donkey.* New York: Harper & Row, 1981, vii+120 p., cloth, novel. COVEN TREE #1.

18689 *Dr. Dredd's wagon of wonders.* New York: Harper & Row, 1987, viii+179 p., cloth, novel. COVEN TREE #3.

18690 *The fantastic freshman: a novel.* New York: Harper & Row, 1988, 151 p., cloth, novel.

18691 *My buddy, the King: a novel.* New York: Harper & Row, 1989, 135 p., cloth, novel.

18692 *Professor Popkin's prodigious Polish: a tale of Coven Tree.* New York: Harper & Row, 1990, 152 p., cloth, novel. COVEN TREE #4.

18693 *Who knew there'd be ghosts?* New York: Harper & Row, 1985, 119 p., cloth, novel.

18694 *Wings: a novel.* New York: Harper-CollinsPublishers, 1991, 135 p., cloth, novel.

18695 *The wish giver: three tales of Coven Tree.* Cambridge, MA: Harper & Row, 1983, 181 p., cloth, coll. COVEN TREE #2.

BRITTAIN, C. Dale, 1948-

18696 *A bad spell in Yurt.* Riverdale, NY: Baen Fantasy, 1991, 314 p., paper, novel.

BRITTAIN, William E.—SEE: Brittain, Bill

BRITTON, David, 1945- , with Michael Butterworth

18697 *The Savoy book.* Manchester, England: Savoy Books, 1978, 144 p., paper, anth.

18698 *Savoy dreams.* Manchester, England: Savoy Books, 1984, 260 p., cloth, anth.

BRIZZI, Mary (A.) T(urzillo), 1940-

18699 *Anne McCaffrey.* Mercer Island, WA: Starmont House, 1986, 95 p., cloth, nonf. STARMONT READER'S GUIDE #30.

18700 *Philip José Farmer.* Mercer Island, WA: Starmont House, 1980, 80 p., paper, nonf. STARMONT READER'S GUIDE #3.

BRIZZOLARA, John

18701 *Empire's horizon.* New York: DAW Books, 1989, 320 p., paper, novel.

BROCK, A. Clutton- —SEE: Clutton-Brock, A.

BROCK, Darryl

18702 *If I never get back: a novel.* New York: Crown Publishers, 1990, 424 p., cloth, novel.

BROCKLEY, Fenton, pseud.—SEE: Rowland, Donald S.

*BROCKWAY, (Archibald) Fenner, Baron Brockway, 1888-1988

BRODERICK, Damien (Francis), 1944-

The black grail—SEE: *Sorcerer's world.*

18703 *The dark between the stars.* Port Melbourne, Victoria, Australia: Mandarin Australia, 1991, 252 p., paper, coll.

18704 *The dreaming dragons: a time opera.* New York: Pocket Books, 1980, 224 p., paper, novel.

18705 *The Judas mandala.* New York: A Timescape Book, Pocket Books, 1982, 189 p., paper, novel.

18706 *The Judas mandala.* Port Melbourne, Victoria, Australia: Mandarin Australia, 1990, 228 p., paper, novel. [Revised edition].

18707 *Matilda at the speed of light.* North Ryde, New South Wales: Australian Sirius, 1988, xv+263 p., paper, anth.

01906 *Sorcerer's world.* New York: A Signet Book, New American Library, 1970, 144 p., paper, novel

18708 retitled: *The black grail.* New York: Avon, 1986, 310 p., paper, novel. [Expanded edition].

18709 *Strange attractors: original Australian speculative fiction.* Sydney, New South Wales, Australia: Hale & Iremonger, 1985, 237 p., cloth, anth.

18710 *Striped holes.* New York: Avon Books, 1988, 179 p., paper, novel.

18711 *Transmitters: an imaginary documentary, 1969-1984.* Melbourne, Victoria, Australia: Ebony, 1984, 320 p., paper, novel.

18712 *The Zeitgeist machine: a new anthology of science fiction.* London & Sydney: Angus & Robertson, 1977, 200 p., cloth, anth.

with Rory Barnes

17424 *Valencies.* St. Lucia, Queensland, Australia, New York: University of Queensland Press, 1983, 230 p., paper, novel.

BRODERICK, Mick, 1959-

18713 *Nuclear movies: a filmography.* Northcote, Victoria, Australia: Post-Modern Publishing, 1988, 135 p., cloth?, nonf.

18714 *Nuclear movies: a critical analysis and filmography of international feature length films dealing with experimentation, aliens, terrorism, holocaust and other disaster scenarios, 1914-1989.* Jefferson, NC & London: McFarland & Co., Publishers, 1991, xix+219 p., cloth, nonf. [Expanded edition].

*BRODEUR, Arthur Gilchrist, 1888-1968?

*BRODHAY, O(tto) Chester, 1874-1954

*BRODIE-INNES, J(ohn) W(illiam), 1848-1923

BRODSKY, Stanley L(eon), 1939- , *with Kenneth B. Melvin & Raymond D. Fowler Jr.*

18715 *Psy-fi one: an anthology of psychology in science fiction.* New York: Random House, 1977, xiii+299 p., paper, anth.

BROER, Lawrence R(ichard), 1938-

18716 *Sanity plea: schizophrenia in the novels of Kurt Vonnegut.* Ann Arbor, MI: UMI Research Press, 1988, 216 p., cloth, nonf. STUDIES IN SPECULATIVE FICTION #18.

BROME, (Herbert) Vincent, 1910-

18717 *H. G. Wells.* London: Longmans, Green & Co., 1951, 255 p., cloth, nonf.

BROMLEY, Dudley (Lee), 1948-

18718 *Comet!* Belmont, CA: Fearon Education, 1982, 72 p., paper, novel.

18719 *Lost valley.* Belmont, CA: Fearon Education, 1982, 75 p., paper, novel.

BRONTE, Louisa—SEE: Roberts, Janet Louise

BRONTO, Hannah, pseud.—SEE: Bennett, Jeff

BROOK, Margaret—SEE: Bacon, Peggy

BROOKE, (Bernard) Jocelyn, 1908-1966

18720 *Aldous Huxley.* London: Published for the British Council and the National Book League by Longmans, Green & Co., 1954, 34 p., paper, nonf.

18721 *Aldous Huxley, rev. ed.* London: Published for the British Council and the National Book League by Longmans, Green & Co., 1958, 34 p., paper, nonf.

BROOKE, Keith, 1966-

18722 *Expatria.* London: Victor Gollancz, 1991, 252 p., cloth, novel.

18723 *Keepers of the peace.* London: Victor Gollancz, 1990, 216 p., cloth, novel.

BROOKE-ROSE, Christine, 1923-

18725 *Amalgamemnon.* Manchester, England: Carcanet, 1984, 144 p., cloth, novel.

26996 *The Christine Brooke-Rose omnibus: four novels.* Manchester, England, NY: Carcanet, 1986, 742 p., cloth, coll. [Includes *Out; Such; Between; Thru*].

18726 *The rhetoric of the unreal: studies in narrative and structure, especially of the fantastic.* Cambridge, England & London: Cambridge University Press, 1981, vi+446 p., cloth, nonf.

18727 *Verbivore.* Manchester, England: Carcanet, 1990, 196 p., cloth, novel. XORANDOR #2.

18728 *Xorandor.* Manchester, England: Carcanet, 1986, 211 p., cloth, novel. XORANDOR #1.

BROOKER, Wallace, pseud.—SEE: Daniels, Norman A.

BROOKES, Owen [pseud. of Dulan Friar Whilberton Barber], 1940-

18729 *Deadly communion.* New York: Holt, Rinehart & Winston, 1984, 272 p., cloth, novel.

18730 *Forget-me-knots.* London: Futura, 1986, 261 p., paper, novel.

18731 *Inheritance.* New York: Holt, Rinehart & Winston, 1980, 282 p., cloth, novel.

18732 *The widow of Ratchets.* New York: Holt, Rinehart & Winston, 1979, 318 p., cloth, novel.

BROOKINS, Dana (Lloyd Martin), 1931-

18733 *The manipulator.* New York: Zebra Books, Kensington Publishing Corp., 1989, 286 p., paper, novel. BOBBIE TOPPIN #2.

18734 *Soul-eater.* New York: Zebra Books, Kensington Publishing Corp., 1985, 318 p., paper, novel. BOBBIE TOPPIN #1.

*BROOKINS, Dewey C., 1904-1982

BROOKS, Bruce

18735 *No kidding.* New York: Harper & Row, 1989, 207 p., cloth, novel.

BROOKS, C(uyler) W(arnell "Ned") Jr.

18736 *Interim Hannes Bok illustration index.* Newport News, VA: Purple Mouth Press, 1967, [16] leaves, paper, nonf.

BROOKS, Cecil (J.), *with Bill Adams*

15956 *The unwound way.* New York: A Del Rey Book, Ballantine Books, 1991, 339 p., paper, novel.

BROOKS, Kate

18737 *The exhumation.* Davenport, FL: Laura Books, 1979, 223 p., paper, novel.

BROOKS, Terrence D.—SEE: Brooks, Terry

BROOKS, Terry [i.e., Terrence Dean Brooks], 1944-

18738 *The black unicorn.* New York: A Del Rey Book, Ballantine Books, 1987, x+287 p., cloth, novel. MAGIC KINGDOM OF LANDOVER #2.

18739 *The druid of Shannara.* New York: A Del Rey Book, Ballantine Books, 1991, 423 p., cloth, novel. SHANNARA #5.

18740 *The Elfstones of Shannara.* New York: A Del Rey Book, Ballantine Books, 1982, 469 p., cloth, novel. SHANNARA #2.

18741 *Hook.* London: Arrow Books, 1991, 273 p., cloth, movie.

18742 *Magic kingdom for sale—sold!* New York: A Del Rey Book, Ballantine Books, 1986, x+324 p., cloth, novel. MAGIC KINGDOM OF LANDOVER #1.

18743 *The scions of Shannara.* New York: A Del Rey Book, Ballantine Books, 1990, 465 p., cloth, novel. SHANNARA #4.

18744 *The sword of Shannara.* New York: Random House, 1977, 726 p., cloth, novel. SHANNARA #1.

18745 *The wishsong of Shannara.* New York: A Del Rey Book, Ballantine Books, 1985, 499 p., cloth, novel. SHANNARA #3.

18746 *Wizard at large.* New York: A Del Rey Book, Ballantine Books, 1988, 291 p., cloth, novel. MAGIC KINGDOM OF LANDOVER #3.

BROOKS, Van Wyck, 1886-1963

18747 *The world of H. G. Wells.* New York: Mitchell Kennerley, 1915, 189 p., cloth, nonf.

BROOKS, Walter R(ollin), 1886-1958

18748 *The clockwork twin.* New York: Alfred A. Knopf, 1937, 242 p., cloth, novel. FREDDY SERIES.

18749 *Ernestine takes over: a novel.* New York: William Morrow & Co., 1935, 265 p., cloth, novel.

18750 *The story of Freginald.* New York: Alfred A. Knopf, 1936, 249 p., cloth, novel. FREDDY SERIES.

BROOKS-JANOWIAK, Jean, 1955-

18751 *Winter lord.* New York: A Signet Book, New American Library, 1983, 186 p., paper, novel.

BROOMHEAD, Ann (Alleda), 1947-

18752 *The NESFA index to the science fiction magazines and original anthologies, 1983.* Cambridge, MA: NESFA Press, 1984, ii+68 p., paper, nonf.

as ANN MCCUTCHEN

18753 *The NESFA index to the science fiction magazines and original anthologies, 1977-1978.* Cambridge, MA: NESFA Press, 1983, vi+74 p., paper, nonf.

18754 *The NESFA index to the science fiction magazines and original anthologies, 1979-1980.* Cambridge, MA: NESFA Press, 1982, viii+90 p., paper, nonf.

18755 *The NESFA index to the science fiction magazines and original anthologies, 1981.* Cambridge, MA: NESFA Press, 1982, vi+60 p., paper, nonf.

18756 *The NESFA index to the science fiction magazines and original anthologies, 1982.* Cambridge, MA: NESFA Press, 1983, vi+64 p., paper, nonf.

BROPHY, Brigid (Antonia), 1929-

18757 *Palace without chairs.* London: Hamish Hamilton, 1978, 295 p., cloth, novel.

BROSNAN, John (Raymond), 1947-

18758 *The fall of the sky lords.* London: Victor Gollancz, 1991, 284 p., cloth, novel. SKY LORDS #3.

18759 *Future tense: the cinema of science fiction.* London: Macdonald & Jane's, 1978, 320 p., cloth, nonf. [Winner of the J. Lloyd Eaton Award for Best Nonfiction Book of the Year, 1978 (1980)].

18760 *The horror people.* London: Michael Joseph, 1976, vi+304 p., cloth, nonf.

18761 *Movie magic: the story of special effects in the cinema, rev. and updated ed.* New York: New American Library, 1976, 302 p., paper, nonf.

18762 *The primal screen: a history of science fiction film.* London: Orbit, 1991, xiii+402 p., cloth, nonf.

18763 *The sky lords: a novel.* London: Victor Gollancz, 1988, 317 p., cloth, novel. SKY LORDS #1.

18764 *Skyship.* London: Hamlyn Paperbacks, 1981, 333 p., paper, novel.

18765 *War of the sky lords.* London: Victor Gollancz, 1989, 252 p., cloth, novel. SKY LORDS #2.

as SIMON IAN CHILDER

18766 *Worm.* London: Grafton, 1987, 189 p., paper, novel.

as HARRY ADAM KNIGHT

18767 *Carnosaur.* London: A Star Book, W. H. Allen & Co., 1984, 214 p., paper, novel.

18766A *Worm.* New York: Bart Books, 1988, 189 p., paper, novel. [Previously published under the name Simon Ian Childer].

with John Baxter as JAMES BLACKSTONE

18768 *Torched!* London: Grafton, 1986, 223 p., paper, novel.

with Leroy Kettle as SIMON IAN CHILDER

18769 *Tendrils.* London: Grafton, 1986, 208 p., paper, novel.

with Leroy Kettle as HARRY ADAM KNIGHT

Death spore—SEE: *The fungus.*

18770 *The fungus.* London: A Star Book, W. H. Allen & Co., 1985, 220 p., paper, novel.

18770A retitled: *Death spore.* New York: Pinnacle Books, Windsor Publishing Corp., 1990, 256 p., paper, novel.

18771 *Slimer.* London: A Star Book, W. H. Allen & Co., 1983, 156 p., paper, novel.

BROTEN, Delores, 1948- , with Peter Birdsall

17981 *A science fiction teaching guide.* Victoria, British Columbia, Canada: CANLIT, 1978, 61 p., paper, nonf.

BROUGHTON, Jane, with Norma Brown & Di Williams

18772 *Herzone: fantasy short stories by women.* Manchester, England: Crocus, 1991, 103 p., paper, anth.

BROUSSARD, Louis, 1922-

18773 *The measure of Poe.* Norman, OK: University of Oklahoma Press, 1969, xi+168 p., cloth, nonf.

*BROWN, Alex (John Charles), 1900-1962

BROWN, Carter, pseud.—SEE: Yates, Alan

BROWN, Charles N(ikki), 1937-

18774 *Alien worlds: three novellas of science fiction by award winning authors.* London & Conn.: Mews Books, 1976, 144 p., paper, anth.

18775 *Far travellers: three science fiction novellas.* London & Conn.: Mews Books, 1976, 143 p., paper, anth.

18776 *Locus, the newspaper of the science fiction field, numbers 1-103, 1968-1971.* Boston: Gregg Press, 1978, [ca. 800] p., cloth, nonf. anth.

18777 *Locus, the newspaper of the science fiction field, numbers 104-207, 1972-1977.* Boston: Gregg Press, 1978, [ca. 800 p.], cloth, nonf. anth.

with William G. Contento

18778 *Science fiction, fantasy, & horror: 1984: a comprehensive bibliography of books and short fiction published in the English language.* Oakland, CA: Locus Press, 1990, viii+269 p., cloth, nonf.

18779 *Science fiction, fantasy, & horror: 1986: a comprehensive bibliography of books and short fiction published in the English language.* Oakland, CA: Locus Press; Westport, CT: Meckler Corp., 1987, xiii+347 p., cloth, nonf.

18780 *Science fiction, fantasy, & horror: 1987: a comprehensive bibliography of books and short fiction published in the English language.* Oakland, CA: Locus Press, 1988, ix+417 p., cloth, nonf.

18781 *Science fiction in print: 1985: a comprehensive bibliography of books and short fiction published in the English language.* Oakland, CA: Locus Press, 1986, x+237 p., cloth, nonf.

with William G. Contento & Hal W. Hall

18782 *Science fiction, fantasy, & horror: 1988: a comprehensive bibliography of books and short fiction published in the English language.* Oakland, CA: Locus Press, 1989, viii+463 p., cloth, nonf. [Winner of the J. Lloyd Eaton Award for Best Nonfiction Book of the Year, 1989 (1991)].

18783 *Science fiction, fantasy, & horror: 1989: a comprehensive bibliography of books and short fiction published in the English language.* Oakland, CA: Locus Press, 1990, viii+515 p., cloth, nonf.

18784 *Science fiction, fantasy, & horror: 1990: a comprehensive bibliography of books and short fiction published in the English language.* Oakland, CA: Locus Press, 1991, viii+587 p., cloth, nonf.

BROWN, Crosland [pseud. of A. W. Grey]

18785 *Tombley's walk.* New York: Avon Books, 1991, 407 p., paper, novel.

BROWN, Dale (Francis), 1956-

18786 *Day of the cheetah: a novel.* New York: Donald I. Fine, 1989, 504 p., cloth, novel.

18787 *Flight of the old dog: a novel.* New York: Donald I. Fine, 1987, 347 p., cloth, novel.

18788 *Silver tower.* New York: Donald I. Fine, 1988, 349 p., cloth, novel.

18789 *Sky masters.* New York: Donald I. Fine, G. P. Putnam's Sons, 1991, 510 p., cloth, novel.

BROWN, Dennis Phillip

18790 *Foxglove Hollow.* New York: Fawcett Gold Medal, 1982, 192 p., paper, novel.

BROWN, E(dward) J(ames), 1909-1991

18791 *Brave new world, 1984, and We: an essay on anti-utopia.* Ann Arbor, MI: Ardis Publishers, 1976, 61 p., cloth, nonf.

18792 *Brave new world, 1984, and We: an essay on anti-utopia, rev. ed.* New York: McDougal, Littell & Co., 1979, 254 p., paper, nonf.

BROWN, Eric, 1960-

18793 *The time-lapsed man, and other stories.* Birmingham, England: Drunken Dragon Press, 1990, 216 p., cloth, coll.

BROWN, Fredric (William), 1906-1972

18794 *And the gods laughed: a collection of science fiction and fantasy.* West Bloomfield, MI: Phantasia Press, 1987, xxii+431 p., cloth, coll.

18795 *The best of Fredric Brown.* Garden City, NY: Nelson Doubleday, 1977, viii+279 p., cloth, coll. [Edited by Robert Bloch].

18796 *The best short stories of Fredric Brown.* London: New English Library, 1982, 447 p., paper, coll. [Includes *Nightmares & geezenstacks* and *Space on my hands*].

27134 *Brother monster.* Miami Beach, FL: Dennis McMillan, 1987, 180 p., cloth, coll.

18797 *Happy ending.* Missoula, MT: Dennis McMillan, 1990, 230 p., cloth, coll. [Limited to 450 copies; includes some verse].

18798 *Sex life on the planet Mars.* Miami Beach, FL: Dennis McMillan, 1986, 190 p., cloth, coll. [Includes some nonfiction; limited to 400 copies].

18799 *The water-walker.* Missoula, MT: Dennis McMillan, 1990, 188 p., cloth, coll. [Limited to 425 copies].

BROWN, George Mackay, 1921-

18800 *Time in a red coat.* London: Chatto & Windus/Hogarth Press, 1984, 249 p., cloth, novel.

BROWN, George Sheldon, pseud.—SEE: Hughes, Dennis Talbot

*BROWN, Harrison (Scott), 1917-1986

BROWN, Himan, 1910-

18801 *Strange tales from CBS Radio Mystery Theater.* New York: Popular Library, 1976, 250 p., paper, anth.

*BROWN, James Cooke, 1921-1987

BROWN, James D.—SEE: Ryman, Ras

BROWN, Jerry Earl, 1940-

18802 *Darkhold.* New York: Ace Science Fiction Books, 1985, 342 p., paper, novel.

18803 *Earthfall.* New York: Ace Books, 1990, 278 p., paper, novel.

18804 *Under the City of Angels.* Toronto, New York: Bantam Books, 1981, 291 p., paper, novel.

BROWN, Katy

27445 *Spellcaster.* New York, Toronto: Scholastic Inc., 1984, 93 p., paper, fiction. TWISTAPLOT #15.

BROWN, Ken, *as anonymous co-author with David Pringle*

31900 *The ultimate guide to science fiction.* London, Glasgow: Grafton Books, 1990, xx+407 p., cloth, nonf.

BROWN, Mary, 1929-

18805 *The unlikely ones.* London: Century, 1986, 425 p., cloth, novel.

BROWN, Melissa Mather—SEE: Mather, Melissa

BROWN, Michael

18806 *Pandemonium.* Staten Island, NY: Eclipse Books, 1991, 104+liv p., cloth, nonf. anth. [Includes an unpublished play, artwork, and essays].

BROWN, Norma, *with Jane Broughton & Di Williams*

18772 *Herzone: fantasy short stories by women.* Manchester, England: Crocus, 1991, 103 p., paper, anth.

BROWN, Olivia—SEE: Caldecott, Moyra

BROWN, Rebecca, 1956-

18807 *The haunted house.* London: Picador, 1986, 138 p., paper, novel.

BROWN, Rebecca Bard—SEE: Ore, Rebecca

BROWN, Rich(ard W.), 1942- , *with David Bischoff & Linda Richardson*

18012 *A personal demon.* New York: A Signet Book, New American Library, 1985, 253 p., paper, novel.

BROWN, Rita Mae, 1944- , *with Sneaky Pie Brown*

18808 *Wish you were here.* New York, Toronto: Bantam Books, 1990, 242 p., cloth, novel. [Sneaky Pie Brown is her cat].

BROWN, Rupert, *with J. J. Llewellyn & Brian Froud*

18809 *The world of the Dark Crystal.* New York: Alfred A. Knopf, 1983, 128 p., paper, nonf.

BROWN, Sneaky Pie—SEE: Brown, Rita Mae

BROWN, Wenzell, 1911-1981

18810 *Possess & conquer.* New York: Warner Books, 1975, 175 p., paper, novel.

BROWN, William Glenn

18811 *The dynamo & the tree: my twins and I journeying in a technate in the year 1981.* Hicksville, NY: Exposition Press, 1977, 288 p., cloth, novel.

*BROWNE, Barum [pseud. of Hilary Aidan St. George Saunders], 1898-1951

BROWNE, C. J.

18812 *Escape Carthus.* North Hollywood, CA: A Carousel Star Edition, 1980, 159 p., paper, novel.

BROWNE, George Sheldon, pseud.—SEE: Jennison, John W.

BROWNE, Gerald A(ustin), 1928-

18813 *Stone 588.* New York: Arbor House, 1986, 465 p., cloth, novel.

BROWNE, Joseph, *with Bernard S. Oldsey*

18814 *Critical essays on George Orwell.* Boston: G. K. Hall & Co., 1986, viii+256 p., cloth, nonf. anth.

BROWNE, Nelson, 1908-

18815 *Sheridan Le Fanu.* London: Arthur Barker, 1951, 135 p., cloth, nonf.

BROWNE, Peter Francis

18816 *Land's end.* London: Secker & Warburg, 1981, 247 p., cloth, novel.

BROWNE, Ray B(roadus), 1922- , *with Gary Hoppenstand*

25937 *The gothic world of Stephen King: landscape of nightmares.* Bowling Green, OH: Bowling Green State University Popular Press, 1988, 143 p., cloth, nonf. anth.

BROWNE, Robert, pseud.—SEE: Karlins, Marvin

BROWNING, Daphne—SEE: du Maurier, Daphne

BROWNING, Dixie (Burrus), 1930- , *with Mary Williams as* BRONWYN WILLIAMS

18817 *White witch.* Toronto, New York: Harlequin Books, 1988, 301 p., paper, novel.

BROWNING, Pamela, 1942-

18818 *A man worth loving.* Toronto, New York: Harlequin Books, 1991, 253 p., paper, novel.

BROWNING, Robert, 1928-

18819 *No ordinary man.* Lewes, East Sussex, England: The Book Guild, 1991, 312 p., cloth, novel.

BROWNJOHN, Alan (Charles), 1931-

27705 *The way you tell them: a yarn of the nineties.* London: André Deutsch, 1990, 145 p., cloth, novel.

BROXON, Mildred Downey, 1944-

18820 *The SFWA handbook.* [S.l.]: Science Fiction Writers of America, 1976, 147 p., paper, nonf. anth.
18821 *Too long a sacrifice.* New York: A Dell Book, 1981, 251 p., paper, novel.

as SIGFRIOUR SKALDASPILLIR

18822 *A witch's welcome.* New York: Zebra Books, Kensington Publishing Corp., 1979, 319 p., paper, novel. ERIC BRIGHTEYES #2. [A sequel to the novel by H. Rider Haggard].

with Poul Anderson

16446 *The demon of Scattery.* New York: Ace Books, 1979, 207 p., paper, novel.

BROYLES, R(andall) L.

18823 *The man who could read cards.* New York: Manor Books, 1979, 200 p., paper, novel.

BRUCCOLI, Matthew J(oseph), 1931-

18824 *Notes on the Cabell Collection at the University of Virginia.* Charlottesville, VA: University of Virginia Press, 1957, 178 p., cloth, nonf. JAMES BRANCH CABELL: A BIBLIOGRAPHY, PART II.

BRUCE, Joanna—SEE: Simon, Jo Ann

BRUCK, Lorraine—SEE: Bridges, Laurie

BRULLER, Jean—SEE: Vercors

BRUMBAUGH, James (Drew), 1946-

18825 *Trail sinister.* Lake Geneva, WI: TSR Inc., 1987, 184 p., paper, fiction. ADVANCED DUNGEONS & DRAGONS ADVENTURE GAMEBOOK #14.

BRUMMELS, J. V.

18826 *Deus ex machina.* Toronto, New York: Spectra, Bantam Books, 1989, 277 p., paper, novel.

BRUNAS, John, 1949- , *with Tom Weaver & Michael Brunas*

18827 *Interviews with B science fiction and horror movie makers: writers, producers, directors, actors, moguls, and makeup.* Jefferson, NC & London: McFarland & Co., 1988, xi+413 p., cloth, nonf.
18828 *Science fiction stars and horror heroes: interviews with actors, producers, and writers of the 1940s through 1960s.* Jefferson, NC & London: McFarland & Co., 1991, xiii+448 p., cloth, nonf.
18829 *Universal horrors: the studio's classic films, 1931-1946.* Jefferson, NC & London: McFadden & Co., 1990, viii+616 p., cloth, nonf.

BRUNAS, Michael, 1952- , *with Tom Weaver & John Brunas*

18827 *Interviews with B science fiction and horror movie makers: writers, producers, directors, actors, moguls, and makeup.* Jefferson, NC & London: McFarland & Co., 1988, xi+413 p., cloth, nonf.
18828 *Science fiction stars and horror heroes: interviews with actors, producers, and writers of the 1940s through 1960s.* Jefferson, NC & London: McFarland & Co., 1991, xiii+448 p., cloth, nonf.
18829 *Universal horrors: the studio's classic films, 1931-1946.* Jefferson, NC & London: McFadden & Co., 1990, viii+616 p., cloth, nonf.

BRUNELLE, Jan

18830 *Death on tour: chill module.* Cleveland, OH: Pacesetter, 1985, p., cloth?, novel.

BRUNN, Robert

18831 *The initiation.* New York: Twilight/Dell, 1982, 154 p., paper, novel. TWILIGHT #3.

BRUNNER, John (Kilian Houston), 1934-

18832 *The best of John Brunner.* New York: A Del Rey Book, Ballantine Books, 1988, 288 p., paper, coll.

18833 *The book of John Brunner.* New York: DAW Books, 1976, 159 p., paper, coll.

18834 *A case of painter's ear.* Eugene, OR: Pulphouse Publishing, 1991, 34 p., cloth, story. SHORT STORY HARDBACKS #2; SHORT STORY PAPERBACKS #2.

18835 *Children of the thunder.* New York: A Del Rey Book, Ballantine Books, 1989, 340 p., paper, novel.

18836 *The compleat traveller in black.* New York: Bluejay Books, 1986, 250 p., paper, coll. [Adds one story to *The traveler in black* (see #02070)].

18837 *The crucible of time.* New York: A Del Rey Book, Ballantine Books, 1983, 288 p., cloth, novel.

18838 *Foreign constellations: the fantastic worlds of John Brunner.* New York: Everest House, 1980, 188 p., cloth, coll.

18839 *The infinitive of go.* New York: A Del Rey Book, Ballantine Books, 1980, 154 p., paper, novel.

18840 *Interstellar empire.* New York: DAW Books, 1976, 256 p., paper, coll. [Includes *The altar on Asconel*, *The space-time juggler*, and two other stories].

18841 *Manshape.* New York: DAW Books, 1982, 159 p., paper, novel. [A greatly expanded version of *Endless shadow* (see #02026)].

18842 *A maze of stars.* Norwalk, CT: Easton Press, 1991, 393 p., cloth, novel.

18843 *A new settlement of old scores.* Cambridge, MA: A ConStellation Book, NESFA Press, 1983, viii+68 p., paper, nonf. anth.

18844 *Players at the game of people.* Garden City, New York: Nelson Doubleday, 1980, 218 p., cloth, novel.

18845 *The shift key.* London: Methuen, 1987, 227 p., cloth, novel.

18846 *The shockwave rider.* New York: Harper & Row, Publishers, 1975, 288 p., cloth, novel.

18847 *The tides of time.* New York: A Del Rey Book, Ballantine Books, 1984, 235 p., paper, novel.

18848 *Tomorrow may be even worse: an alphabet of science fiction clichés.* Cambridge, MA: A Boskone Book, NESFA Press, 1978, [62] p., paper, nonf. coll.

18849 *Victims of the nova.* London: Arrow Books, 1989, 473 p., paper, coll. ZARATHUSTRA TRILOGY #1-3. [Includes *Polymath*; *The avengers of Carrig*; *The repairmen of Cyclops*].

18850 *While there's hope.* Richmond, England: Keepsake, 1982, 22 p., paper, story.

BRUSH, Karen A(lexandra), 1960-

18851 *The demon pig.* New York: AvoNova, 1991, xii+241 p., paper, novel. PIG #2.

18852 *The pig, the prince, & the unicorn.* New York: Avon, 1987, 216 p., paper, novel. PIG #1.

BRUSSEL, I(sidore) R(osenbaum), 1895-

18853 *A bibliography of the writings of James Branch Cabell: a revised bibliography, 2nd ed.* Philadelphia, PA: The Centaur Book Shop, 1932, 126 p., cloth, nonf.

BRUST, Steven (Karl Zoltán), 1955-

18854 *Brokedown palace.* New York: Ace Fantasy Books, 1986, xi+270 p., paper, novel.

18855 *Cowboy Feng's space bar and grille.* New York: Ace Books, 1990, 224 p., paper, novel.

18856 *Jhereg.* New York: Ace Fantasy Books, 1983, 239 p., paper, novel. JHEREG #1.

18857 *Phoenix.* New York: Ace Books, 1990, 245 p., paper, novel. JHEREG #5.

18858 *The phoenix guards.* New York: Tor, A Tom Doherty Associates Book, 1991, xv+331 p., cloth, novel.

18859 *The sun, the moon, and the stars.* New York: Ace Fantasy Books, 1987, v+210 p., cloth, novel.

18860 *Taltos.* New York: Ace Books, 1988, 181 p., paper, novel. JHEREG #4.

18860A retitled: *Taltos and the paths of the dead.* London & Sydney: Pan Books, 1991, 181 p., paper, novel. JHEREG #4.

Taltos and the paths of the dead—SEE: *Taltos.*

18861 *Taltos the assassin.* London & Sydney: Pan Books, 1991, 684 p., paper, coll.

JHEREG #1-3. [Includes *Jhereg, Yendi, Teckla*].

18862 *Teckla*. New York: Ace Fantasy Books, 1987, 214 p., paper, novel. JHEREG #3.

18863 *To reign in Hell*. Minneapolis, MN: Steel-Dragon Press, 1984, ix+257 p., cloth, novel. [Limited to 1000 copies].

18864 *Yendi*. New York: Ace Fantasy Books, 1984, 209 p., paper, novel. JHEREG #2.

BRYAN, Jessica [pseud. of Yaffa Chudnow]

18865 *Across a wine-dark sea*. New York, Toronto: Fanfare, Bantam Books, 1991, 355 p., paper, novel.

BRYANT, Dorothy (Mae), 1930-

02082 *The comforter: a mystical fantasy*. Berkeley, CA: Evan Press, 1971, 170 p., paper, novel

02082A retitled: *The kin of Ata are waiting for you*. Berkeley, CA & New York: Moon Books/Random House, 1976, 220 p., cloth, novel.
The kin of Ata are waiting for you—SEE: *The comforter*.

BRYANT, Edward (Winslow Jr.), 1945-

18866 *2076: the American Tricentennial*. New York: Pyramid Books, 1977, 255 p., paper, anth.

18867 *Cinnabar*. New York: Macmillan Publishing Co., 1976, xvi+186 p., cloth, coll.

18868 *The cutter*. Eugene, OR: Pulphouse Publishing, 1991, 52 p., cloth, story. SHORT STORY HARDBACKS #4; SHORT STORY PAPERBACKS #8.

18869 *Fetish*. Eugene, OR: Axolotl Press, Pulphouse Publishing, 1991, 132 p., cloth, novel. AXOLOTL PRESS #20.

18870 *The man of the future*. Arvada, CO: Roadkill Press, 1990, 25 p., paper, story. [Limited to 400 copies].

18871 *Neon twilight*. Eugene, OR: Pulphouse Publishing, 1990, 110 p., cloth, coll. AUTHOR'S CHOICE MONTHLY #7.

18872 *Particle theory*. New York: A Timescape Book, Pocket Books, 1981, 252 p., paper, coll.

18873 *Trilobyte: an Easter treasure*. Seattle, WA: Axolotl Press, 1987, 27 p., paper, coll. AXOLOTL DOUBLE #2; AXOLOTL PRESS #6. [Bound with *The shadow on the doorstep* / by James P. Blaylock].

18874 *Wyoming sun*. Laramie, WY: Jelm Mountain Press, 1980, 132 p., cloth, coll.

with Harlan Ellison

18875 *Phoenix without ashes: a novel of the starlost*. Greenwich, CT: A Fawcett Gold Medal Book, Fawcett Publications, 1975, 192 p., paper, tele.

*BRYHER [pseud. of Anna Winifred Ellerman], 1894-1983

BUCAR, Cary A.

18876 *Esper!* East Lansing, MI: T'Kuhtian Press, 1981?, 75 p., paper, novel. STAR WARS SERIES.

*BUCHAN, Bryan, 1945-

BUCHAN, John, Baron Tweedsmuir, 1875-1940

18877 *The best supernatural stories of John Buchan*. London: Robert Hale, 1991, 254 p., cloth, coll. [Edited by Peter Haining].

18878 *The far islands, and other tales of fantasy*. West Kingston, RI: Donald M. Grant, Publisher, 1984, 206 p., cloth, coll. [Edited by John Bell].

BUCHAN, John Stuart—SEE: Erskine, Douglas

BUCHANAN, Jessica—SEE: Horsting, Jessie

BUCHANAN, Marie [i.e., Eileen Marie Duell Buchanan], 1922-

18879 *The dark backward*. London: Hart-Davis, MacGibbon, 1975, 232 p., cloth, novel.

18880 *Morgana: a novel*. Garden City, New York: Doubleday & Co., 1977, 287 p., cloth, novel.

*BUCHANAN, Thomas G(ittings), 1919-1988

BUCHHOLZ, (Patricia) Suzanne

18881 *The Middle-Earth quiz book*. Boston: Houghton Mifflin Co., 1979, xii+146 p., cloth, nonf.

BUCK, Charles H(enry, Jr.), 1915-dead?

18882 *The master cure*. New York: Jove Books, 1989, 284 p., paper, novel. [Copyright by Ray Buck & Hugh Culik].

BUCKHOLTZ, Eileen (Garber), 1949- , with Ruth Glick

28518 *Captain Kid and the pirates.* New York, Toronto: Scholastic Inc., 1985, 79 p., paper, novel. MAGIC MICRO ADVENTURE #1.

18883 *The cats of Castle Mountain.* New York, Toronto: Scholastic Inc., 1985, 79 p., paper, novel. MAGIC MICRO ADVENTURE #4.

18884 *Doom stalker.* New York, Toronto: A Parachute Press Book, Scholastic Inc., 1985, 123 p., paper, novel. MICRO ADVENTURE #7.

18885 *Mindbenders.* New York, Toronto: A Parachute Press Book, Scholastic Inc., 1984, 126 p., paper, novel. MICRO ADVENTURE #5.

18886 *Mission of the secret spy squad.* New York, Toronto: Scholastic Inc., 1984, 93 p., paper, novel. TWISTAPLOT #10.

18887 *Space attack.* New York, Toronto: A Parachute Press Book, Scholastic Inc., 1984, 123 p., paper, novel. MICRO ADVENTURE #1.

with Ruth Glick as REBECCA YORK

18888 *Flight of the raven.* New York: A Dell Book, 1986, 218 p., paper, novel. PEREGRINE CONNECTION #2.

18889 *In search of the dove.* New York: A Dell Book, 1986, 220 p., paper, novel. PEREGRINE CONNECTION #3.

18890 *Tales of the falcon.* New York: A Dell Book, 1986, 223 p., paper, novel. PEREGRINE CONNECTION #1.

BUCKINGHAM, M. E. [pseud. of Agnes Mary Easton]

18891 *Argh: the tale of a tiger.* London: Country Life Ltd., 1935, x + 135 p., cloth, novel.

BUCKLEY, Christopher (Taylor), 1952-

18892 *The White House mess.* New York: Alfred A. Knopf, 1986, xxii + 224 p., cloth, novel.

BUCKLEY, Doug(las John), 1934-

18893 *State of play.* Sutherland, New South Wales, Australia: Albatross Books, 1990, 228 p., paper, novel.

BUCKLEY, Kathleen, *with Sharon Jarvis as* H. M. MAJOR

18894 *The alien trace.* New York: A Signet Book, New American Library, 1984, 222 p., paper, novel. ALIEN TRACE #1.

18895 *Time twister.* New York: A Signet Book, New American Library, 1984, 255 p., paper, novel. ALIEN TRACE #2.

*BUCKMASTER, Henrietta [pseud. of Henrietta Henkle Stephens], 1909-1983

BUCKNALL, Barbara J(ane), 1933-

18896 *Ursula K. Le Guin.* New York: Frederick Ungar Publishing Co., 1981, xv + 175 p., cloth, nonf.

*BUCKNER, Robert (Henry), 1906-1989

BUDD, Mike, 1944-

18897 *The cabinet of Dr. Caligari: texts, contexts, histories.* New Brunswick, NJ: Rutgers University Press, 1990, xii + 261 p., cloth, nonf. anth.

BUDDICOM, Jacintha (Laura May), 1901-

18898 *Eric and us: a remembrance of George Orwell.* London: Leslie Frewin of London, 1974, xxi + 165 p., cloth, nonf.

BUDRYS, Algirdas—SEE: Budrys, Algis

BUDRYS, Algis [i.e. Algirdas Jonas Budrys], 1931-

18899 *Benchmarks: Galaxy bookshelf.* Carbondale & Edwardsville, IL: Southern Illinois University Press, 1985, xxvi + 349 p., cloth, nonf. coll. [Winner of the *Locus* Award for Best Nonfiction, 1985 (1986)].

18900 *Blood & burning.* New York: A Berkley Book, Berkley Publishing Corp., 1978, 227 p., paper, coll.

18901 *Cerberus.* Eugene, OR: The Convention Series, Pulphouse Publishing, 1989, 24 p., cloth, story. [Limited to 147 copies].

18902 *Falling torch.* Riverdale, NY: Baen Books, 1991, viii + 211 p., paper, novel. [Expanded edition of #02108].

18903 *L. Ron Hubbard presents Writers of the future.* Los Angeles: Bridge Publications, 1985, 354 p., paper, anth.

18904 *L. Ron Hubbard presents Writers of the future, volume II.* Los Angeles: Bridge Publications, 1986, 391 p., paper, anth.

18905 *L. Ron Hubbard presents Writers of the future, volume III: 14 great new tales from the Writers of the Future Interna-*

tional Talent Search. Los Angeles: Bridge Publications, 1987, 429 p., paper, anth.

18906 *L. Ron Hubbard presents Writers of the future, volume IV: 16 new top-rated tales from his Writers of the Future International Talent Search.* Los Angeles: Bridge Publications, 1987, 425 p., paper, anth.

18907 *L. Ron Hubbard presents Writers of the future, volume V: the year's 14 best tales from his Writers of the Future International Writing-Talent Program.* Los Angeles: Bridge Publications, 1989, 427 p., paper, anth.

18908 *L. Ron Hubbard presents Writers of the future, volume VI: the year's 18 best tales from his Writers of the Future International Writing Program.* Los Angeles: Bridge Publications, 1990, 409 p., paper, anth.

18909 *L. Ron Hubbard presents Writers of the future, volume VII: the year's 15 best tales from his Writers of the Future International Writing Program.* Los Angeles: Bridge Publications, 1991, 461 p., paper, anth.

18910 *Michaelmas.* New York: Berkley Publishing Corp., 1977, 253 p., cloth, novel.

18911 *Non-literary influence on science fiction: (an essay).* Polk City, IA: Drumm Books, 1983, 24 p., paper, nonf. DRUMM BOOKLET #9.

18912 *Some will not die.* Norfolk, VA: The Donning Co., 1978, 179 p., paper, novel. [Expanded edition of #02110].

Writers of the future—SEE: *L. Ron Hubbard presents Writers of the future.*

18913 *Writing science fiction and fantasy.* Eugene, OR: Writer's Notebook Press, Pulphouse Publishing, 1990, 22 p., paper, nonf.

BUFFERY, Judith, 1943-

18914 *Gringol weed.* London: Dennis Dobson, 1980, 240 p., cloth, novel. STAR LORDS #4.

18915 *The iron clog.* London: Dennis Dobson, 1979, 185 p., cloth, novel. STAR LORDS #3.

18916 *Saffron.* London: Dennis Dobson, 1979, 185 p., cloth, novel. STAR LORDS #2.

18917 *The Sheeg.* London: Dennis Dobson, 1979, 192 p., cloth, novel. STAR LORDS #1.

BUFFIE, Margaret

18918 *The guardian circle.* Toronto: Kids Can Press, 1989, 220 p., cloth, novel.

18918A retitled: *The warnings.* New York: Scholastic Inc., 1991, 245 p., cloth, novel.

The haunting of Frances Rain—SEE: *Who is Frances Rain?*

The warnings—SEE: *The guardian circle.*

18919 *Who is Frances Rain?* Toronto: Kids Can Press, 1987, 192 p., cloth, novel.

18919A retitled: *The haunting of Frances Rain.* Toronto: Kids Can Press, 1987, 192 p., cloth, novel.

BUJOLD, Lois (Joy) McMaster, 1949-

18920 *Barrayar.* Norwalk, CT: Easton Press, 1991, 389 p., paper, novel. VORKOSIGAN SERIES. [Winner of the Hugo Award for Best Novel, 1991 (1992); winner of the *Locus* Award for Best Science Fiction Novel, 1991 (1992)].

18921 *Borders of infinity.* Norwalk, CT: Easton Press, 1989, 311 p., cloth, novel. VORKOSIGAN #1.

18922 *Brothers in arms: a Miles Vorkosigan adventure.* New York: Baen Books, 1989, 338 p., paper, novel. VORKOSIGAN #3.

18923 *Ethan of Athos.* New York: Baen Books, 1986, 237 p., paper, novel. NAISMITH SERIES.

18924 *Falling free.* New York: Baen Books, 1988, 307 p., paper, novel. [Winner of the Nebula Award for Best Novel, 1988 (1989)].

18925 *Shards of honor.* New York: Baen Science Fiction Books, 1986, 313 p., paper, novel.

18925A retitled: *Shards of honour.* London: Headline, 1988, 313 p., paper, novel.

Shards of honour—SEE: *Shards of honor.*

18926 *Test of honor.* Garden City, NY: Nelson Doubleday, 1987, 473 p., cloth, coll. [Includes *Shards of honor* and *The warrior's apprentice*].

18927 *The Vor game.* Norwalk, CT: Easton Press, 1990, 345 p., cloth, novel. VORKOSIGAN #2. [Winner of the Hugo Award for Best Novel, 1990 (1991)].

18928 *Vorkosigan's game.* New York: Guild America Books, 1990, 484 p., cloth, coll. VORKOSIGAN #1-2. [Includes *The Vor game*; *Borders of infinity*].

18929 *The warrior's apprentice.* New York: Baen Science Fiction Books, 1986, 315 p., paper, novel.

BUKIET, Melvin Jules

18930 *Sandman's dust.* New York: Arbor House, 1985, 234 p., cloth, novel.

BULL, Angela (Mary), 1936-

18931 *A wish at the baby's grave.* London: Hippo, 1988, 94 p., paper, novel. HAUNTINGS #5.

BULL, Emma [i.e., Emma Bull Shetterly], 1954-

18932 *Bone dance: a fantasy for technophiles.* New York: Ace Books, 1991, 278 p., paper, novel.

18933 *Falcon.* New York: Ace Books, 1989, 281 p., paper, novel.

18934 *War for the oaks.* New York: Ace Books, 1987, 309 p., paper, novel. [Winner of the *Locus* Award for Best First Novel, 1987 (1988)].

with Will Shetterly

Festival week—SEE: *Liavek: Festival week.*

18935 *Liavek.* New York: Ace Fantasy Books, 1985, 274 p., paper, anth.

18936 *Liavek: Festival week.* New York: Ace Books, 1990, 275 p., paper, anth. LIAVEK #5.

18937 *Liavek: Spells of binding.* New York: Ace Books, 1988, 245 p., paper, anth. LIAVEK #4.

18938 *Liavek: The players of luck.* New York: Ace Fantasy Books, 1986, 290 p., paper, anth. LIAVEK #2.

18939 *Liavek: Wizard's row.* New York: Ace Fantasy Books, 1987, 212 p., paper, anth. LIAVEK #3.

The players of luck—SEE: *Liavek: The players of luck.*

Spells of binding—SEE: *Liavek: Spells of binding.*

Wizard's row—SEE: *Liavek: Wizard's row.*

*BULLIVANT, Cecil H(enry), 1882-

BULLUCK, Vic, *with Valerie Hoffman*

18941 *The art of The Empire Strikes Back.* New York: Ballantine Books, 1980, 176 p., cloth, nonf.

BULMER, (Henry) Kenneth, 1921-

18942 *The Diamond Contessa.* New York: DAW Books, 1983, 174 p., paper, novel. KEYS TO THE DIMENSIONS #7.

18943 *New writings in SF (25).* London: Sidgwick & Jackson, 1975, 189 p., cloth, anth.

18944 *New writings in SF (26).* London: Sidgwick & Jackson, 1975, 191 p., cloth, anth.

18945 *New writings in SF (27).* London: Sidgwick & Jackson, 1975, 207 p., cloth, anth.

18946 *New writings in SF (28).* London: Sidgwick & Jackson, 1976, 189 p., cloth, anth.

18947 *New writings in SF (29).* London: Sidgwick & Jackson, 1976, 187 p., cloth, anth.

18948 *New writings in SF 30.* London: Corgi Books, 1977, 203 p., paper, anth.

18949 *New writings in SF special (2).* London: Sidgwick & Jackson, 1978, 191+187 p., cloth, anth. [Includes *New Writings in SF* #26 and #29].

18950 *New writings in SF special (3).* London: Sidgwick & Jackson, 1978, 207+189 p., cloth, anth. [Includes *New Writings in SF* #27 and #28].

Stained-glass world—SEE: *The ulcer culture.*

02166 *The ulcer culture.* London: Macdonald & Co., 1969, 160 p., cloth, novel.

02166A retitled: *Stained-glass world.* London: New English Library, 1976, 160 p., paper, novel.

as ALAN BURT AKERS

18951 *Armada of Antares.* New York: DAW Books, 1976, 223 p., paper, novel. DRAY PRESCOT #11?.

18952 *Avenger of Antares.* New York: DAW Books, 1975, 176 p., paper, novel. DRAY PRESCOT #10.

18953 *Bladesman of Antares.* New York: DAW Books, 1975, 192 p., paper, novel. DRAY PRESCOT #9.

18954 *Fliers of Antares.* New York: DAW Books, 1975, 207 p., paper, novel. DRAY PRESCOT #8.

18955 *Golden Scorpio.* New York: DAW Books, 1978, 207 p., paper, novel. DRAY PRESCOT #18.

18956 *Krozair of Kregan.* New York: DAW Books, 1977, 223 p., paper, novel. DRAY PRESCOT #14. [Title elsewhere in book listed as *Krozair of Kregen*].

18957 *Renegade of Kregen.* New York: DAW Books, 1976, 192 p., paper, novel. DRAY PRESCOT #13.

18958 *Savage Scorpio.* New York: DAW Books, 1978, 191 p., paper, novel. DRAY PRESCOT #16.

18959 *Secret Scorpio.* New York: DAW Books, 1977, 207 p., paper, novel. DRAY PRESCOT #15.

18960 *The tides of Kregen.* New York: DAW Books, 1976, 208 p., paper, novel. DRAY PRESCOT #12.

18961 *Captive Scorpio /* by Allan Burt Akers. New York: DAW Books, 1978, 190 p., paper, novel. DRAY PRESCOT #17.

as DRAY PRESCOT WITH ALAN BURT AKERS

18962 *Allies of Antares.* New York: DAW Books, 1981, 189 p., paper, novel. DRAY PRESCOT #26.

18963 *Beasts of Antares.* New York: DAW Books, 1980, 206 p., paper, novel. DRAY PRESCOT #23.

18964 *Delia of Vallia.* New York: DAW Books, 1982, 192 p., paper, novel. DRAY PRESCOT #28.

18965 *Fires of Scorpio.* New York: DAW Books, 1983, 173 p., paper, novel. DRAY PRESCOT #29.

18966 *A fortune for Kregen.* New York: DAW Books, 1979, 222 p., paper, novel. DRAY PRESCOT #21.

18967 *Legions of Antares.* New York: DAW Books, 1981, 192 p., paper, novel. DRAY PRESCOT #25.

18968 *A life for Kregen.* New York: DAW Books, 1979, 215 p., paper, novel. DRAY PRESCOT #19.

18969 *Manhounds of Antares; and, Arena of Antares.* New York: DAW Books, 1981, 185, 207 p., paper, coll. DRAY PRESCOT #6-7.

18970 *Masks of Scorpio.* New York: DAW Books, 1984, 175 p., paper, novel. DRAY PRESCOT #31—PANDAHEM CYCLE #4.

18971 *Mazes of Antares.* New York: DAW Books, 1982, 176 p., paper, novel. DRAY PRESCOT #27.

18972 *Omens of Kregen.* New York: DAW Books, 1985, 222 p., paper, novel. DRAY PRESCOT #36—WITCH WAR CYCLE #3.

18973 *Rebel of Antares.* New York: DAW Books, 1980, 191 p., paper, novel. DRAY PRESCOT #24.

18974 *Seg the bowman.* New York: DAW Books, 1984, 255 p., paper, novel. DRAY PRESCOT #32.

18975 *Storm over Valla.* New York: DAW Books, 1985, 254 p., paper, novel. DRAY PRESCOT #35.

18976 *A sword for Kregen.* New York: DAW Books, 1979, 206 p., paper, novel. DRAY PRESCOT #20.

18977 *Talons of Scorpio.* New York: DAW Books, 1983, 173 p., paper, novel. DRAY PRESCOT #30.

18978 *A victory for Kregen.* New York: DAW Books, 1980, 224 p., paper, novel. DRAY PRESCOT #22.

18979 *Warlord of Antares.* New York: DAW Books, 1988, 255 p., paper, novel. DRAY PRESCOT #37—WITCH WAR CYCLE #4. [The last volume of the series].

18980 *Werewolves of Kregen.* New York: DAW Books, 1985, 220 p., paper, novel. DRAY PRESCOT #33—WITCH WAR CYCLE #1.

18981 *Witches of Kregen.* New York: DAW Books, 1985, 223 p., paper, novel. DRAY PRESCOT #34—WITCH WAR CYCLE #2.

as MANNING NORVIL

18982 *Crown of the sword god.* New York: DAW Books, 1980, 175 p., paper, novel. ODAN THE HALF-GOD #3.

18983 *Dream chariots.* New York: DAW Books, 1977, 192 p., paper, novel. ODAN THE HALF-GOD #1.

18984 *Whetted bronze.* New York: DAW Books, 1978, 190 p., paper, novel. ODAN THE HALF-GOD #2.

as TULLY ZETFORD

18985 *Hook: Virility gene.* London: New English Library, 1975, 111 p., paper, novel. HOOK #4.
Virility gene—SEE: *Hook: Virility gene.*

with John Carnell

18986 *New writings in SF special (1).* London: Sidgwick & Jackson, 1975, 189+189+191 p., cloth, anth. [Includes *New Writings in SF #21-23*].

BULYCHEV, Kirill [pseud. of Igor Vsevelodovich Mozheiko], 1934-

18987 *Gusliar wonders.* New York: Macmillan; London: Collier Macmillan, 1983, 228 p., cloth, novel. [Translation by Roger DeGaris of *Chudesa v Gusliare*].

18988 *Half a life, and other stories.* New York: Macmillan Publishing Co.; London: Collier Macmillan Publishers, 1977, x+142 p., cloth, coll. [Translation by Helen Saltz Jacobson of stories from *Liudi* and *Chudesa v Gusliaru*].

with Mirra Ginsberg

18989 *Alice: some incidents in the life of a little girl of the twenty-first century, recorded by her father on the eve of her first day in school.* New York: Macmillan, 1977, 64 p., cloth, novel. [Translation and adaptation by Ginsberg of *Devochka s kotoroi nichego ne sluchitsa*].

BUNCH, Chris(topher R.), 1943- , with Allan Cole

18990 *The court of a thousand suns.* New York: A Del Rey Book, Ballantine Books, 1986, 275 p., paper, novel. STEN #3.

18991 *Fleet of the damned.* New York: A Del Rey Book, Ballantine Books, 1988, 340 p., paper, novel. STEN #4.

18992 *The return of the emperor.* New York: A Del Rey Book, Ballantine Books, 1990, 371 p., paper, novel. STEN #6.

18993 *Revenge of the damned.* New York: A Del Rey Book, Ballantine Books, 1989, 354 p., paper, novel. STEN #5.

18994 *Sten.* New York: A Del Rey Book, Ballantine Books, 1982, 279 p., paper, novel. STEN #1.

18995 *The wolf worlds.* New York: A Del Rey Book, Ballantine Books, 1984, 298 p., paper, novel. STEN #2.

BUNCH, David R(oosevelt), 1925?-

BUNDY, Ralph, pseud.—SEE: Easton, Thomas

BUNN, T. Davis, 1952-

18996 *The presence.* Minneapolis, MN: Bethany House Publishers, 1990, 349 p., paper, novel.

BUNTING, (Anne) Eve(lyn Bolton), 1928-

18997 *The Cloverdale switch.* Philadelphia, PA: Lippincott Junior Books, 1979, 119 p., cloth, novel.

18997A retitled: *Strange things happen in the woods.* New York: An Archway Paperback, Pocket Books, 1984, 106 p., paper, novel.

18998 *The creature of Cranberry Cove.* St. Paul, MN: EMC Corp., 1976, 39 p., cloth, story. DINOSAUR MACHINES SERIES.

18999 *The day of the dinosaurs.* St. Paul, MN: EMC Corp., 1975, 37 p., cloth, story. DINOSAUR MACHINES SERIES.

19000 *Day of the earthlings.* Mankato, MN: Creative Education, 1978, 25 p., cloth, story.

19001 *Death of a dinosaur.* St. Paul, MN: EMC Corp., 1975, 37 p., cloth, story. DINOSAUR MACHINES SERIES.

19002 *The demon.* St. Paul, MN: EMC Corp., 1976, 39 p., cloth, story. DINOSAUR MACHINES SERIES.

19003 *The dinosaur trap.* St. Paul, MN: EMC Corp., 1975, 39 p., cloth, story. DINOSAUR MACHINES SERIES.

19004 *Escape from tyrannosaurus.* St. Paul, MN: EMC Corp., 1975, 39 p., cloth, story. DINOSAUR MACHINES SERIES.

19005 *The followers.* Mankato, MN: Creative Education, 1978, 35 p., cloth, story.

19006 *The ghost.* St. Paul, MN: EMC Corp., 1976, 37 p., cloth, story. DINOSAUR MACHINES SERIES.

19007 *Ghost behind me.* New York: An Archway Paperback, Pocket Books, 1984, 169 p., paper, novel.

19008 *Ghost of summer.* New York: Frederick Warne, 1977, 192 p., cloth, novel.

19009 *The ghosts of Departure Point.* New York: J. B. Lippincott, 1982, 113 p., cloth, novel.

19010 *The haunting of SafeKeep.* New York: J. B. Lippincott, 1985, 153 p., cloth, novel.

19011 *The island of one.* Mankato, MN: Creative Education, 1978, 35 p., cloth, story.

19012 *The mask.* Mankato, MN: Creative Education, 1978, 35 p., cloth, story.

19013 *The mirror planet.* Mankato, MN: Creative Education, 1978, 35 p., cloth, story.

19014 *The robot birthday.* New York: E. P. Dutton, 1980, 80 p., cloth, novel.

19015 *The robot people.* Mankato, MN: Creative Education, 1978, 25 p., cloth, story.

19016 *The space people.* Mankato, MN: Creative Education, 1978, 27 p., cloth, story.

Strange things happen in the woods—SEE: The Cloverdale switch.

19017 *The tongue of the ocean.* St. Paul, MN: EMC Corp., 1976, 35 p., cloth, story. DINOSAUR MACHINES SERIES.

19018 *The undersea people.* Mankato, MN: Creative Education, 1978, 26 p., cloth, story.

BURANELLI, Vincent (John), 1919-

19019 *Edgar Allan Poe.* New York: Twayne Publishers, 1961, 157 p., cloth, nonf.

19020 *Edgar Allan Poe, second edition.* Boston: Twayne Publishers, 1977, 166 p., cloth, nonf. [Expanded edition].

BURCH, Ralph, pseud.

19021 *Duplicate lovers.* Encino, CA: World-Wide Publishing Co., 1980, 188 p., paper, novel.

BURCHETT, (Paul) Jay, *with M. Ann Evans*

19022 *Border to terrorism.* Newport Beach, CA: Newport Publishing House, 1988, 295 p., paper, novel.

BURCHILL, Julie, 1960-

19023 *Ambition.* London: The Bodley Head, 1989, 263 p., cloth, novel.

BURDEKIN, Katharine (Penelope) "Kay", 1896-1963

19024 *The end of this day's business.* Old Westbury, NY: The Feminist Press at the City University of New York, 1990, 190 p., paper, novel.

03323A *Swastika night.* London: Lawrence & Wishart, 1985, xv + 196 p., paper, novel. [Originally published under the name Murray Constantine].

as **MURRAY CONSTANTINE**

03321 *The devil, poor devil! a novel.* London: Boriswood, 1934, 256 p., cloth, novel.
03322 *Proud man.* London: Boriswood, 1934, 318 p., cloth, novel.
03323 *Swastika night.* London: Victor Gollancz, 1937, 288 p., cloth, novel.

BURDEKIN, Kay—SEE: Burdekin, Katharine

BURDICK, G. S.

19025 *The accursed.* New York: Playboy Paperbacks, 1982, 256 p., paper, novel.

*BURGER, Dionys, 1892-

BURGER, Joanne (Denise), 1938-

19026 *SF published in 1973.* Lake Jackson, TX: Joanne Burger, 1975, 46 p., paper, nonf.
19027 *SF published in 1974.* Lake Jackson, TX: Joanne Burger, 1977, 40 p., paper, nonf.
19028 *SF published in 1975.* Lake Jackson, TX: Joanne Burger, 1977, 45 p., paper, nonf.
19029 *SF published in 1976.* Lake Jackson, TX: Joanne Burger, 1977, 48 p., paper, nonf.
19030 *SF published in 1977.* Lake Jackson, TX: Joanne Burger, 1979, 61 p., paper, nonf.

BURGER, Neal R., *with George E. Simpson*

19031 *Ghostboat.* New York: A Dell Book, 1976, 412 p., paper, novel.
19032 *Thin air.* New York: A Dell Book, 1978, 318 p., paper, novel.

BURGESS, Anthony [pseud. of John Anthony Burgess Wilson], 1917-

19033 *1985.* London: Hutchinson, 1978, 240 p., cloth, novel.
28561 *Any old iron.* New York: Random House, 1989, 360 p., cloth, novel.
28582 *Beard's Roman women: a novel.* New York: McGraw-Hill Book Co., 1976, 155 p., cloth, novel.
19034 *The end of the world news: an entertainment.* London: Hutchinson, 1982, x + 388 p., cloth, novel.
19035 *Little Wilson and big God.* New York: Weidenfeld & Nicolson, 1986, ix + 460 p., cloth, nonf.
19036 *A long trip to teatime.* London: Dempsey & Squires, 1976, 120 p., cloth, novel.
19037 *You've had your time: being the second part of the Confessions of Anthony Burgess.* London: Heinemann, 1990, xi + 403 p., cloth, nonf.

BURGESS, Eric (Alexander), 1912- , *with Arthur Friggens*

19038 *The hounds of heaven.* London: Robert Hale, 1979, 186 p., cloth, novel.
19039 *The Mants of Myrmedon.* London: Robert Hale, 1977, 189 p., cloth, novel.
19040 *Mortorio two.* London: Robert Hale, 1975, 192 p., cloth, novel. MORTORIO #2.

BURGESS, Mary A(lice Wickizer), 1938- , *with Douglas Menville & R. Reginald*

19041 *Futurevisions: the new golden age of the science fiction film.* North Hollywood, CA: A Greenbriar Book, Newcastle Publishing Co., 1985, 192 p., paper, nonf. [A sequel to *Things to come* (see #29749)].

BURGESS, Mason [pseud. of Gregory Zawidoski]

19042 *Blood moon.* New York: Leisure Books, 1986, 352 p., paper, novel.
19043 *Child of demons.* New York: Leisure Books, 1985, 345 p., paper, novel.
19044 *Graveyard.* New York: Leisure Books, 1987, 320 p., paper, novel.

BURGESS, Michael—SEE: Reginald, Robert

BURGESS, Scott Alan, 1964-

19045 *The work of Dean Ing: an annotated bibliography & guide.* San Bernardino, CA: R. Reginald, The Borgo Press, 1990, 82 p., cloth, nonf. BIBLIOGRAPHIES OF MODERN AUTHORS #11. [Edited by Boden Clarke].
19046 *The work of Reginald Bretnor: an annotated bibliography & guide.* San Bernardino, CA: R. Reginald, The Borgo Press, 1989, 122 p., cloth, nonf. BIBLIOGRAPHIES OF MODERN AUTHORS #8. [Edited by Boden Clarke].

BURGIN, Victor, 1941- , with James Donald & Cora Kaplan

19047 *Formations of fantasy.* London, New York: Methuen, 1986, 221 p., paper, nonf. anth.

BURGO, Joseph

19048 *The Lights of Barbrin.* New York: Pocket Books, 1978, 192 p., paper, novel.

BURIAN, Zdenek

28876 *Jungle scenes of Tarzan.* Clinton, LA: Opar Press, (1973), 30 leaves, paper, art.

BURKE, Fred, 1965- , with Clive Barker

17387 *Clive Barker, illustrator.* Forestville, CA: Arcane/Eclipse Books, 1991, iv+124 p., cloth, art. [Edited by Steve Niles].

BURKE, George, Abbot, 1940-

19049 *The way of the chalice.* Spring Valley, NY: Saint George Publications, 1984, 164 p., paper, novel.

BURKE, John (Frederick), 1922-

19050 *The black charade: a Dr. Caspian story.* London: Weidenfeld & Nicolson, 1977, 186 p., cloth, novel. DR. CASPIAN & BRONWEN #2.
19051 *The devil's footsteps.* London: Weidenfeld & Nicolson, 1976, 181 p., cloth, novel. DR. CASPIAN & BRONWEN #1.
19052 *Dracula, prince of darkness.* London: Pan Books, 1967, [144] p., paper, movie.
19053 *Ladygrove: the third adventure of Dr Caspian and Bronwen.* London: Wei-denfeld & Nicolson, 1978, 190 p., cloth, novel. DR. CASPIAN & BRONWEN #3.
19054 *New tales of unease.* London & Sydney: Pan Books, 1976, 205 p., paper, anth.
30043 *Privilege.* London & Sydney: Pan Books, 1967, 155 p., paper, movie.

BURKE, Warren—SEE: Braun, Matthew

BURKHOLZ, Herbert, 1932-

19055 *The sensitives.* New York: Atheneum, 1987, 278 p., cloth, novel. SENSITIVES #1.
19056 *Strange bedfellows.* New York: Atheneum, 1988, 290 p., cloth, novel. SENSITIVES #2.

BURLESON, Donald R(ichard), 1941-

19057 *H. P. Lovecraft: a critical study.* Westport, CT, London: Greenwood Press, 1983, xi+243 p., cloth, nonf. CONTRIBUTIONS TO THE STUDY OF SCIENCE FICTION AND FANTASY #5.
19058 *Lovecraft: disturbing the universe.* Lexington, KY: University Press of Kentucky, 1990, xi+170 p., cloth, nonf.

BURLEY, W(illiam) J(ohn), 1914-

30169 *Charles and Elizabeth: a novel.* London: Victor Gollancz, 1979, 173 p., cloth, novel.
19059 *The sixth day.* London: Victor Gollancz, 1978, 174 p., cloth, novel.

*BURMAN, Ben Lucien, 1895-1984

BURMEISTER, Jon, 1933-

19060 *The protector conclusion.* London: Michael Joseph, 1977, 191 p., cloth, novel.

*BURNFORD, Sheila (Philip Cochrane), 1918-1984

BURNHAM, Jeremy, with Trevor Ray

19061 *Children of the stones.* London: Carousel Books, 1977, 189 p., paper, novel.
19062 *Raven.* London: Corgi Books, 1977, 222 p., paper, tele.

BURNIAUX, Robert—SEE: Muno, Jean

BURNS, Alan, 1929-

31044 *Dreamerika! a surrealistic fantasy.* London: Calder & Boyars, 1972, 135 p., cloth, novel.

BURNS, Christopher, 1944-

19064 *About the body.* London: Secker & Warburg, 1988, 193 p., cloth, coll.

BURNS, Cliff, 1963-

19065 *Sex and other acts of the imagination: a collection of short stories.* Regina, Saskatchewan, Canada: Harman Burns Publications, 1991, 115 p, paper, coll.

BURNS, Jim, 1948-

19066 *The Jim Burns portfolio.* Limpsfield, Surrey, England: Paper Tiger, 1990, [64] p., paper, art.

with Chris Evans

19067 *Lightship.* Limpsfield, Surrey, England: Paper Tiger, 1985, 125 p., cloth, art.

with Harry Harrison

19068 *Planet story.* New York: A&W Visual Library, 1979, 112 p., cloth, novel.

BURNS, Richard, 1958-1992

19069 *Khalindaine.* London: George Allen & Unwin, 1985, 268 p., cloth, novel. KHALINDAINE #1.
19070 *Troubadour.* London: Unwin Paperbacks, 1988, 250 p., paper, novel. KHALINDAINE #2.

*BURRAGE, A(thol) Harcourt, 1899-

BURRAGE, A(lfred) M(cLelland), 1889-1956

19071 *Warning whispers: new weird tales.* Wellingborough, Northamptonshire, England: Equation, 1988, 190 p., paper, coll. [Edited by Jack Adrian].

BURROUGHS, Edgar Rice, 1875-1950

19072 *Science fiction classics: Pellucidar; Thuvia, maid of Mars; Tanar of Pellucidar; Chessmen of Mars; Master mind of Mars.* Secaucus, NJ: Castle Books, 1982, 451 p., cloth, coll. MARS series.

19073 *Swords of Mars; and, Synthetic men of Mars.* Garden City, NY: Nelson Doubleday, 1975, 314 p., cloth, coll. MARS #8-9.
19074 *Tarzan of the apes: four volumes in one.* New York: Avenel Books, 1988, xvi+ 848 p., cloth, coll. TARZAN series. [Includes: *Tarzan of the apes*; *The son of Tarzan*; *Tarzan at the earth's core*; *Tarzan triumphant*].
02343 *The wizard of Venus.* New York: Ace Books, 1970, 158 p., paper, coll. VENUS #5.
02343A retitled: *The wizard of Venus; and, Pirate blood.* New York: Ace Books, 1979, 248 p., paper, coll. VENUS #5.

with Joan D. Vinge

19075 *Tarzan, king of the apes.* New York: Random House, 1983, 104 p., cloth, novel. [Adapted from the original novel by Burroughs].

*BURROUGHS, John Coleman, 1913-1979

BURROUGHS, William S(eward, Sr.), 1914-

19076 *The adding machine: collected essays.* London: John Calder, 1985, 201 p., cloth, nonf. coll.
19077 *Blade runner (a movie).* Berkeley, CA: Blue Wind Press, 1979, [80] p., cloth, movie.
19078 *Cities of the red night.* New York: Holt, Rinehart and Winston, 1981, xviii+332 p., cloth, novel.
19079 *The place of dead roads.* New York: Holt, Rinehart & Winston, 1984, 306 p., cloth, novel.
19080 *Port of saints.* London: Covent Garden Press; Ollon, Switzerland: America Here Books, 1973, 133 p., cloth. [Limited to 200 copies].
19081 *Port of saints.* Berkeley, CA: Blue Wind Press, 1980, 174 p., cloth, novel. [Expanded and rewritten edition].
19082 *The soft machine; Nova express; The wild boys: three novels.* New York: A Black Cat Book, A Grove Press Outrider Book, 1984, 182+155+184 p., paper, coll.

with Allen Ginsberg

19083 *Letters to Allen Ginsberg, 1953-1957.* New York: Full Court Press, 1982, 203 p., cloth, nonf. coll.
19084 *The Yage letters.* San Francisco: City Lights Books, 1975, 66 p., paper, nonf. coll.

with Daniel Odier

19085 *The job: interviews with William S. Burroughs.* New York: Grove Press, 1974, 224 p., cloth, nonf. coll.

BURTON, S(amuel) H(olroyd), 1919-

19086 *Eight ghost stories.* London: Longman, 1978, 73 p., paper, coll.

as SAM HOLROYD

19087 *Tibb's house.* London: New English Library, 1977, 112 p., paper, novel.

BUSBY, F(rancis) M(arion Jr.), 1921-

19088 *The alien debt.* Toronto, New York: Bantam Books, 1984, 226 p., paper, novel. BRAN TREGARE #2. [Sequel to *Rissa Kerguelen*].

19089 *All these Earths.* New York: A Berkley Book, Berkley Publishing Corp., 1978, 213 p., paper, novel.

19090 *The breeds of man.* Toronto, New York: Spectra, Bantam Books, 1988, 294 p., paper, novel.

19091 *The Demu trilogy.* New York: Pocket Books, 1980, 522 p., paper, coll. DEMU TRILOGY #1-3. [Includes *Cage a man*; *The proud enemy*; *End of the line*].

19092 *Getting home.* New York: Ace Books, 1987, xii+195 p., paper, coll.

19093 *The long view.* New York: Berkley Publishing Corp., 1976, 280 p., cloth, novel. RISSA KERGUELEN #2. [This novel was published in two volumes in cloth as *Rissa Kerguelen* and *The long view*, then in one volume in paper as *Rissa Kerguelen*, then again in three volumes in paper as *Rissa Kerguelen*, *Rissa and Tregare*, and *The long view*].

19094 *The long view.* New York: Berkley Books, 1984, xi+301 p., paper, novel. RISSA KERGUELEN #3.

19095 *The proud enemy.* New York: A Berkley Medallion Book, Berkley Publishing Corp., 1975, 187 p., paper, novel. DEMU TRILOGY.

19096 *The rebel dynasty, volume 1: Star rebel; Rebel's quest.* Toronto, New York: Bantam Books, 1987, 443 p., paper, coll. REBEL DYNASTY #1-2. [Includes *Star rebel*; *Rebel's quest*].

19097 *The rebel dynasty, volume 2: The alien debt; Rebel's seed.* Toronto, New York: Bantam Books, 1988, 475 p., paper, coll. REBEL DYNASTY #3-4. [Includes *The alien debt*; *Rebel's seed*].

19098 *Rebel's quest.* Toronto, New York: Bantam Books, 1985, 243 p., paper, novel. BRAN TREGARE #3. [Title correct].

19099 *Rebels' seed.* Toronto, New York: Bantam Books, 1986, 249 p., paper, novel. BRAN TREGARE #4. [Title correct].

19100 *Rissa and Tregare.* New York: Berkley Books, 1984, vi+249 p., paper, novel. RISSA KERGUELEN #2.

19101 *Rissa Kerguelen.* New York: Berkley Publishing Corp., 1976, 408 p., cloth, novel. RISSA KERGUELEN #1.

19102 *Rissa Kerguelen.* New York: A Berkley Medallion Book, Berkley Publishing Corp., 1977, x+630 p., paper, coll. RISSA KERGUELEN #1-2. [Published originally in two volumes as *Rissa Kerguelen* and *The long view*].

19103 *Slow freight.* New York, Toronto: Spectra, Bantam Books, 1991, 311 p., paper, novel.

19104 *Star rebel.* Toronto, New York: Bantam Books, 1984, 216 p., paper, novel. BRAN TREGARE #1, or HULZEIN FAMILY SAGA. [Sequel to *Rissa Kerguelen*].

19105 *Young Rissa.* New York: Berkley Books, 1984, 177 p., paper, novel. RISSA KERGUELEN #1.

19106 *Zelde M'Tana.* New York: A Dell Book, 1980, 316 p., paper, novel.

*BUSHNELL, Adelyn, <u>1894-</u>

BUSHYAGER, Linda E(yster), 1947-

19107 *Master of hawks.* New York: A Dell Book, 1979, 256 p., paper, novel.

19108 *The spellstone of Shaltus.* New York: A Dell Book, 1980, 204 p., paper, novel.

BÜSSING, Sabine, 1960-

19109 *Aliens in the home: the child in horror fiction.* New York, Westport, CT, London: Greenwood Press, 1987, xxi+203 p., cloth, nonf.

BUTCHER, (Charles) William, 1951-

19110 *Verne's journey to the centre of the self: space and time in the voyages extraordinaires.* London: Macmillan, 1990, xvii+206 p., cloth, nonf.

BUTLER, Beverly (Kathleen), 1932-

19111 *Ghost cat.* New York: Dodd, Mead & Co., 1984, 189 p., cloth, novel.

BUTLER, David, 1941-

19112 *The men who mastered time.* London: Heinemann, 1986, 262 p., cloth, novel.

BUTLER, Gwendoline—SEE: Melville, Jennie

BUTLER, Ivan [pseud. of Edward Ivan Oakley Beuttler], 1909-

19113 *Horror in the cinema, 3rd ed.* South Brunswick, NJ: A. S. Barnes, 1979, 162 p., cloth, nonf. [Expanded edition].

BUTLER, Jack (Armand), 1944-

19114 *Nightshade.* New York: Atlantic Monthly Press, 1989, x+276 p., cloth, novel.

BUTLER, Jimmie H.

19115 *The Iskra incident.* New York: E. P. Dutton, 1990, 377 p., cloth, novel.

BUTLER, Joan, pseud.—SEE: Alexander, Robert

BUTLER, Michael, *with Dennis Shryack*

19116 *The car: a novel.* New York: A Dell Book, 1977, 235 p., paper, movie.

BUTLER, Nathan, pseud.—SEE: Sohl, Jerry

BUTLER, Octavia E(stelle), 1947-

19117 *Adulthood rites: xenogenesis.* New York: Warner Books, 1988, 277 p., cloth, novel. XENOGENESIS #2.
19118 *Clay's ark.* New York: St. Martin's Press, 1984, 201 p., cloth, novel. PATTERNIST #5.
19119 *Dawn: xenogenesis.* New York: Warner Books, 1987, 264 p., cloth, novel. XENOGENESIS #1.
19120 *The evening and the morning and the night.* Eugene, OR: Pulphouse Publishing, 1991, 45 p., cloth, story. SHORT STORY HARDBACKS #23; SHORT STORY PAPERBACKS #38.
19121 *Imago.* New York: Warner Books, 1989, 264 p., cloth, novel. XENOGENESIS #3.
19122 *Kindred.* Garden City, NY: Doubleday & Co., 1979, 264 p., cloth, novel.
19123 *Mind of my mind.* Garden City, NY: Doubleday & Co., 1977, xvi+168 p., cloth, novel. PATTERNIST #2.
19124 *Patternmaster.* Garden City, NY: Doubleday & Co., 1976, 186 p., cloth, novel. PATTERNIST #1.

19125 *Survivor.* Garden City, NY: Doubleday & Co., 1978, 185 p., cloth, novel. PATTERNIST #3.
19126 *Wild seed.* Garden City, NY: Doubleday & Co., 1980, 248 p., cloth, novel. PATTERNIST #4.
19127 *Xenogenesis.* New York: Guild America Books, 1989, 726 p., cloth, coll. XENOGENESIS #1-3.

BUTTERFIELD, John H., *with Richard Siegel*

19128 *The extraterrestrial report.* New York: A&W Visual Library, 1978, 128 p., paper, fiction.

BUTTERS, Dorothy Gilman—SEE: Gilman, Dorothy

BUTTERWORTH, Michael, 1947-

19129 *The edge of the infinite.* New York: Warner Books, 1977, 174 p., paper, tele. SPACE: 1999, YEAR 2 #6.
Planets of peril—SEE: Space 1999: Planets of peril.
The psychomorph—SEE: Space 1999: The psychomorph.
19130 *Queens of Deltra.* London: A Star Book, W. H. Allen, 1977, 191 p., paper, novel. HAWKLORDS #2.
19131 *Space 1999: Planets of peril.* London: A Star Book, W. H. Allen, 1977, 159 p., paper, tele. SPACE 1999 YEAR 2 #1.
19132 *Space 1999: The psychomorph.* London: A Star Book, W. H. Allen, 1977, 156 p., paper, tele. SPACE 1999 YEAR 2 #4.
19133 *Space 1999: The space-jackers.* London: A Star Book, W. H. Allen, 1977, 158 p., paper, tele. SPACE 1999 YEAR 2 #3.
19134 *Space 1999: The time fighters.* London: A Star Book, W. H. Allen, 1977, 156 p., paper, tele. SPACE 1999 YEAR 2 #5.
The space-jackers—SEE: Space 1999: The space-jackers.
The time fighters—SEE: Space 1999: The time fighters.

with David Britton

18697 *The Savoy book.* Manchester, England: Savoy Books, 1978, 144 p., paper, anth.
18698 *Savoy dreams.* Manchester, England: Savoy Books, 1984, 260 p., cloth, anth.

with J. Jeff Jones

Mind-breaks of space—SEE: Space 1999: Mind-breaks of space.

19136 *Space 1999: Mind-breaks of space.* London: A Star Book, W. H. Allen, 1977, 157 p., paper, tele. SPACE 1999 YEAR 2 #2.

with Michael Moorcock

19137 *The time of the Hawklords.* Henley-on-Thames, England: Aidan Ellis, 1976, 255 p., cloth. HAWKLORDS #1. [Mostly written by Butterworth].

*BUTTERWORTH, Oliver, 1915-1990

BUTTERWORTH, William E(dmund III), 1929-

19138 *Next stop Earth.* New York: Walker & Co., 1978, 80 p., cloth, novel.

BUTTS, Jane—SEE: Roberts, Jane

BUXTON, James

19139 *Subterranean.* London: Orbit, 1989, 288 p., paper, novel.

BUXTON, Meg

19140 *No earthly reason: stories of the supernatural.* London: William Kimber, 1980, 190 p., cloth, coll.
19141 *One footprint in the sand: stories of the supernatural.* London: William Kimber, 1979, 206 p., cloth, coll.

BUZZELLI, Elizabeth Kane, 1936-

19142 *A gift of evil.* Toronto, New York: Bantam Books, 1983, xi+301 p., paper, novel.

BYARS, Betsy (Cromer), 1928-

19143 *The winged colt of Casa Mia.* New York: Viking Press, 1973, 128 p., cloth, novel.

BYERS, Edward A(dams), 1939-1989

19144 *The Babylon Gate.* New York: Baen Science Fiction Books, 1986, 246 p., paper, novel.
19145 *The long forgetting.* New York: Baen Science Fiction Books, 1985, 283 p., paper, novel.

BYERS, Richard Lee, 1950-

19146 *Deathward.* Lake Geneva, WI: New Infinities Productions, 1989, 326 p., paper, novel.

19147 *Fright line.* Lake Geneva, WI: New Infinities Productions, 1989, 330 p., paper, novel.

BYFIELD, Bruce (Allan), 1958-

19148 *Witches of the mind: a critical study of Fritz Leiber.* West Warwick, RI: Necronomicon Press, 1991, 76 p., paper, nonf.

BYRNE, Beverly

19149 *A matter of time.* New York: Villard Books, 1987, 564 p., cloth, novel.

BYRNE, John L.

Fear book—SEE: *John L. Byrne's Fear book.*
19150 *John L. Byrne's Fear book.* New York: Warner Books, 1988, 249 p., paper, novel.

BYRNE, Patrick F(rancis), 1919-

19151 *The bedside book of Irish ghost stories.* Dublin: Mercier, 1980, 112 p., cloth, anth.

BYRNE, Robert, 1930-

19152 *Mannequin.* New York: Atheneum, 1988, 273 p., cloth, novel.
19153 *The tunnel.* New York, London: Harcourt Brace Jovanovich, 1977, 214 p., cloth, novel.

BYRNE, Stuart J(ames), 1913-

19154 *The alpha trap.* Chatsworth, CA: Major Books, 1976, 192 p., paper, novel.
19155 *Star man 1-5 / by S. J. Byrne.* Van Nuys, CA: Master Publications, 1979, 60+64+64+64+67 p., paper, coll. STAR MAN #1-5. [Bound with PERRY RHODAN #137 / by Clark Darlton].
19156 *Star man 6-11 / by S. J. Byrne.* Van Nuys, CA: Master Publications, 1980, 384 p., paper, coll. STAR MAN #6-11.

as ROTHAYNE AMARE

19157 *The visitation.* Canoga Park, CA: Major Books, 1977, 208 p., paper, novel.

BYRON, Amanda

19158 *The warning.* New York: Twilight, 1985, 156 p., paper, novel. TWILIGHT #23.

C

CABELL, James Branch, 1879-1958

19159 *As I remember it: some epilogues in recollection.* New York: The McBride Co., 1955, ix+243 p., cloth, nonf.
19160 *Between friends: letters of James Branch Cabell and others.* New York: Harcourt, Brace & World, 1962, xvi+304 p., cloth, nonf. coll. [Edited by Padraic Colum and Margaret Freeman Cabell].
19161 *The letters of James Branch Cabell.* Norman, OK: University of Oklahoma Press, 1975, xvii+277 p., cloth, nonf. coll. [Edited by Edward Wagenknecht].

CABRAL, Ciruelo, *with Nigel Suckling*

19162 *Ciruelo.* Limpsfield, Surrey, England: Paper Tiger, 1990, 128 p., cloth, art.

CADIGAN, Pat(ricia Kearney), 1953-

19163 *Mindplayers.* Toronto, New York: Bantam Books, 1987, 276 p., paper, novel.
19164 *Patterns: stories.* Kansas City, MO: Ursus Imprints, 1989, xi+207 p., cloth, coll. [Winner of the *Locus* Award for Best Collection, 1989 (1990)].
19165 *Synners.* New York, Toronto: Spectra, Bantam Books, 1991, viii+435 p., paper, novel.

CADNUM, Michael, 1949-

19166 *Nightflight: a novel.* New York: St. Martin's Press, 1990, 198 p., cloth, novel.
19167 *Saint Peter's wolf.* New York: Carroll & Graf, 1991, 335 p., cloth, novel.
19168 *Sleepwalker.* New York: St. Martin's Press, 1991, 197 p., cloth, novel.

CADY, Jack (Andrew), 1932-

19169 *The Jonah watch: a true-life ghost story in the form of a novel.* New York: Arbor House, 1981, 224 p., cloth, novel.
19170 *The man who could make things vanish.* New York: Arbor House, 1983, 268 p., cloth, novel.
19171 *McDowell's ghost.* New York: Arbor House, 1982, 320 p., cloth, novel.

19172 *The well.* New York: Arbor House, 1980, 242 p., cloth, novel.

as PAT FRANKLIN

19173 *Dark dreaming.* New York: Diamond Books, 1991, 264 p., paper, novel.

CAIDIN, Martin (Karl von Strasser), 1927-

19174 *Aquarius mission: a novel.* Toronto, New York: Bantam Books, 1978, 312 p., paper, novel.
19175 *Beamriders!* New York: Baen Books, 1989, 411 p., paper, novel.
19176 *Cyborg IV.* New York: Arbor House, 1975, 205 p., cloth, novel. STEVE AUSTIN SERIES.
19177 *Dark messiah.* Riverdale, NY: Baen Books, 1990, 405 p., paper, novel. MESSIAH #2.
 Encounter three—SEE: *The Mendelov conspiracy.*
19178 *Exit Earth.* New York: Baen Books, 1987, 638 p., paper, novel.
19179 *The final countdown: a novel.* Toronto, New York: Bantam Books, 1980, 230 p., paper, movie.
19180 *Jericho 52.* New York: A Dell Book, 1979, 507 p., paper, novel.
19181 *Killer station.* New York: Baen Fiction Books, 1985, 370 p., paper, novel.
19181 *ManFac.* New York: A Dell Book, 1981, 384 p., paper, novel.
02432 *The Mendelov conspiracy.* New York: Hawthorn Books, 1969, 274 p., cloth, novel.
02432A retitled: *Encounter three.* Los Angeles: Pinnacle Books, 1978, 372 p., paper, novel.
19182 *The Messiah Stone.* New York: Baen Fiction Books, 1986, 407 p., paper, novel. MESSIAH #1.
19183 *Prison ship.* New York: Baen Books, 1989, 596 p., paper, novel.
19184 *Star Bright.* Toronto, New York: Bantam Books, 1980, 201 p., paper, novel.
19185 *Three corners to nowhere.* Toronto, New York: Bantam Books, 1975, 276 p., paper, novel.

19186 *Zoboa.* New York: Baen Science Fiction Books, 1986, 430 p., paper, novel.

*CAILLOIS, Roger, 1913-1978

CAIN, Robert, house pseud.

19187 *Cybernarc.* New York: HarperPaperbacks, 1991, 245 p., paper, novel. CYBERNARC #1. [By William H. Keith Jr.].

19188 *Cybernarc: Gold dragon.* New York: HarperPaperbacks, 1991, 218 p., paper, novel. CYBERNARC #2. [By William K. Keith Jr.].
Gold dragon—SEE: *Cybernarc: Gold dragon.*

CAINE, Geoffrey, pseud.—SEE: Walker, Robert W.

CAINE, Jeffrey (Andrew), 1944-

19189 *The cold room.* London: W. H. Allen, 1976, 189 p., cloth, novel.

with Campbell Black as JEFFREY CAMPBELL

18069 *The homing.* New York: G. P. Putnam's Sons, 1980, 275 p., cloth, novel.

CAINE, Peter

19190 *Virus.* New York: An Onyx Book, New American Library, 1989, 333 p., paper, novel.

CAINS, Josephine, pseud.—SEE: Goulart, Ron

CAIRD, Janet (Hinshaw), 1913-

19191 *The loch.* London: Geoffrey Bles, 1968, 223 p., cloth, novel.

CALDECOTT, Moyra [pseud. of Olivia Brown], 1927-

19192 *Adventures by leaf light.* La Jolla, CA: A Star & Elephant Book, Green Tiger Publishing Co., 1978, 46 p., paper, coll.

19193 *Daughter of Ra.* London: Arrow Books, 1990, 313 p., paper, novel. AMUN #3.

19194 *Etheldreda, Princess of East Anglia, Queen of Northumbria, saint of Ely, born AD 630, died AD679.* London: Arkana, 1987, 215 p., paper, novel.

19195 *Guardians of the tall stones: the sacred stones trilogy.* London: Arrow Books, 1986, 234+232+160 p., paper, coll. SACRED STONES #1-3.

19196 *The king of shadows.* London: Moyra Caldecott, 1981, 177 p., cloth, novel.

19197 *Shadow on the stones.* London: Rex Collings, 1978, 160 p., cloth, novel. SACRED STONES #3.

19198 *The silver vortex.* London: Arrow Books, 1987, 218 p., paper, novel. SACRED STONES #4.

19199 *The son of the sun.* London: Allison & Busby, 1986, 186 p., cloth, novel. AMUN #2.

19200 *The son of the sun.* London: Arrow Books, 1990, 297 p., paper, novel. AMUN #2. [Expanded edition].

19201 *The tall stones.* London: Rex Collings, 1977, 234 p., cloth, novel. SACRED STONES #1.

19202 *The Temple of the Sun.* London: Rex Collings, 1977, 232 p., cloth, novel. SACRED STONES #2.

19203 *The tower and the emerald.* London: Arrow Books, 1985, 348 p., paper, novel.

CALDER, Jenni, 1941-

19204 *Animal farm and Nineteen eighty-four.* Milton Keynes, England, Philadelphia: Open University Press, 1987, x+110 p., cloth, nonf.

19205 *Chronicles of conscience: George Orwell and Arthur Koestler.* London: Secker & Warburg, 1968, 303 p., cloth, nonf.

CALDER, Robert, pseud.—SEE: Mundis, Jerrold J.

CALDERONELLO, Alice (Helm), *with Thomas L. Wymer & Lowell P. Leland & Sara Jayne Steen & R. Michael Evers*

19206 *Intersections: the elements of science in science fiction.* Bowling Green, OH: The Popular Press, 1978, viii+130 p., paper, nonf.

CALDWELL, Steven, 1947-

19207 *Aliens in space: an illustrated guide to the inhabited galaxy.* Berkshire: Intercontinental Book Productions, 1979, 62 p., cloth, novel.

19208 *The fantastic planet: a world of magic and mystery.* New York: Crescent, 1980, 62 p., cloth, fiction.

19209 *Settlers in space: the fight for survival on distant worlds.* New York: Crescent, 1980, 60 p., cloth, fiction.

19210 *Space Patrol: the official guide to the Galactic Security Force.* New York: Crescent, 1980, 62 p., cloth, fiction.

19211 *Star quest: an incredible voyage into the unknown.* Berkshire, England: Intercontinental Book Productions, 1979, 62 p., cloth, novel.

19212 *Worlds at war: an illustrated study of interplanetary conflict.* New York: Crescent, 1980, 62 p., cloth, fiction.

CALDWELL, (Janet Miriam) Taylor (Holland), 1900-1985, with Jess Stearn

19213 *The romance of Atlantis.* New York: William Morrow & Co., 1975, 285 p., cloth, novel.

CALHOUN, (Catharine) Blue, 1936-

19214 *The pastoral vision of William Morris: the earthly paradise.* Athens, GA: University of Georgia Press, 1975, 263 p., cloth, nonf.

CALIF, R(uth) C., 1922-

19215 *Rust.* New York: Manor Books, 1980, 213 p., paper, novel.

CALIFIA, Pat, 1954-

19216 *Doc and Fluff: the dystopian tale of a girl and her biker.* Boston: Alyson Publications, 1990, 319 p., paper, novel.

CALLAHAN, Jay

19217 *Footprints of the dead.* New York: Twilight/Dell, 1983, 151 p., paper, novel. TWILIGHT #14.

19218 *Night of the wolf.* New York: Leisure Books, 1979, 208 p., paper, novel.

CALLENBACH, Ernest (William Jr.), 1929-

19219 *Ecotopia emerging.* Berkeley, CA: Banyan Tree Books, 1981, 326 p., cloth, novel. ECOTOPIA #1.

19220 *Ecotopia: the notebooks and reports of William Weston.* Berkeley, CA: Banyan Tree Books, 1975, 167 p., cloth, novel. ECOTOPIA #2.

CALLIN, Grant (David), 1941-

19221 *A lion on Tharthee.* New York: Baen Books, 1987, 342 p., paper, novel. SATURNALIA #2.

19222 *Saturnalia.* New York: Baen Science Fiction Books, 1986, 278 p., paper, novel. SATURNALIA #1.

CALLOW, A. J.

19223 *The chronicles of Moorcock.* Worcester, England: A. J. Callow, 1978, 43 p., paper, nonf.

CALMENSON, Stephanie (Lyn), 1952-

19224 *The Addams family: a novelization.* New York, Toronto: Scholastic Inc., 1991, 72 p., paper, movie. ADDAMS FAMILY.

with Joanna Cole

19225 *The scary book.* New York: Morrow Junior Books, 1991, 127 p., cloth, anth.

CALVERT, Mary—SEE: Danby, Mary

CALVINO, Italo, 1923-1985

19226 *The castle of crossed destinies.* New York, London: A Helen & Kurt Wolff Book, Harcourt Brace Jovanovich, 1977, 129 p., cloth, novel. [Translation by William Weaver of *Il castello dei destini incrociati*].

19227 *Our ancestors.* London: Picador, 1980, 302 p., paper, coll. [Includes *The cloven viscount*, *Baron in the trees*, *The non-existent knight*, and some nonfiction; translation by Archibald Colquhoun].

19228 *Under the jaguar sun.* San Diego, CA: A Helen and Kurt Wolff Book, Harcourt Brace Jovanovich, 1988, 86 p., cloth, coll. [Translation by William Weaver].

CAMBIAIRE, C(élestin) P(ierre), 1880-

19229 *The influence of Edgar Allan Poe in France.* New York: G. E. Stechert & Co., 1927, 332 p., cloth, nonf.

CAMERON, Barbara Anne—SEE: Hubert, Cam

CAMERON, Eleanor (Frances Butler), 1912-

19230 *Beyond silence.* New York: E. P. Dutton, 1980, 197 p., cloth, novel.

30749 *To the Green Mountains.* New York: E. P. Dutton, 1975, 180 p., cloth, novel. STONE CHILDREN #2.

CAMERON, Ian [pseud. of Donald Gordon Payne], 1924-

Devil country—SEE: The mountains at the bottom of the world.

11232 *The mountains at the bottom of the world: a novel of adventure.* New York:

William Morrow & Co., 1972, 212 p., cloth, novel.

11232A retitled: *Devil country.* London & Sydney: Pan Books, 1976, 188 p., paper, novel.

19231 *The white ship: a novel of adventure.* London: Hodder & Stoughton, 1975, 192 p., cloth, novel.

with George Erskine

Beware the Tektrons—SEE: *Counter force: Beware the Tektrons.*

19232 *Counter force: Beware the Tektrons.* London: Armada, 1988, 110 p., paper, novel. COUNTER FORCE SERIES.

19233 *Counter force: Find the Tektrons.* London: Armada, 1988, 125 p., paper, novel. COUNTER FORCE SERIES.

Find the Tektrons—SEE: *Counter force: Find the Tektrons.*

31220 *The official Counter Force reference book: the background on the Counter Force characters and the world they live in.* Glenrothes, Scotland: Dram Enterprises, 1986, [61] p., paper, nonf. COUNTER FORCE TIE-IN.

CAMERON, J. D., house pseud.

19234 *Blood tide.* New York: Avon Books, 1991, 219 p., paper, novel. OMEGA SUB #4. [By David Robbins].

19235 *City of fear.* New York: Avon Books, 1991, 215 p., paper, novel. OMEGA SUB #3. [By Michael Jahn].

19236 *Command decision.* New York: Avon Books, 1991, 246 p., paper, novel. OMEGA SUB #2. [By David Robbins].

19237 *Omega sub.* New York: Avon Books, 1991, 249 p., paper, novel. OMEGA SUB #1. [By Michael Jahn].

CAMERON, James (Francis), 1954- , with William Wisher

19238 *Terminator 2: Judgment day: the book of the film: an illustrated screenplay.* New York: Applause Books, 1991, 318 p., paper, anth.

CAMERON, Joan

with Robert Louis Stevenson

19239 *The strange case of Dr. Jekyll and Mr. Hyde.* Loughborough, England: Ladybird, 1986, 51 p., paper, novel. [Adapted from Stevenson's novel].

with Bram Stoker

19240 *Dracula.* Loughborough, England: Ladybird, 1984, 51 p., paper, novel. [Adapted from Stoker's novel].

CAMERON, Julie, pseud.—SEE: Cameron, Lou

CAMERON, Kate, pseud.—SEE: DuBreuil, Linda

CAMERON, Kate [pseud. of Beverly McGlamry], 1932-

19241 *As if they were gods.* New York: Ballantine Books, 1987, 463 p., paper, novel.

CAMERON, Kenneth M., 1931-

19242 *Power play.* New York: Popular Library, 1979, 351 p., paper, novel.

as GEORGE BARTRAM

19243 *The sunset gun.* New York: Pinnacle Books, 1983, 375 p., paper, novel.

CAMERON, Lou, 1924-

as JULIE CAMERON

19244 *The Darklings.* New York: A Berkley Medallion Book, Berkley Publishing Corp., 1975, 188 p., paper, novel.

as DAGMAR

31412 *The spy with the blue kazoo.* New York: Lancer Books, 1967, 160 p., paper, novel. SPY #1.

CAMERON, Marie, 1948- , with Patrick Macnee

19245 *Blind in one ear: the Avenger returns.* London: Harrap, 1988, 398 p., cloth, nonf.

*CAMMAERTS, Émile (Léon), 1878-1953

CAMP, Catherine Crook de—SEE: de Camp, Catherine Crook

CAMP, Deborah

19246 *Fire lily.* New York: Avon Books, 1991, 372 p., paper, novel.

CAMP, Joe [i.e., Joseph Shelton Camp, Jr.], 1939-

19247 *Oh heavenly dog.* New York, Toronto: Scholastic Book Services, 1980, 125 p., paper, movie.

CAMP, Joseph S.—SEE: Camp, Joe

CAMP, L. Sprague de—SEE: de Camp, L. Sprague

CAMPBELL, Clive S.

19248 *The day the Sun came through.* New York, Washington: Vantage Press, 1979, 50 p., cloth, novel.

CAMPBELL, H(erbert) J(ames), 1925-

CAMPBELL, Hope [pseud. of Geraldine June McDonald Wallis], 1925-

19249 *Looking for Hamlet: a haunting at Deeping Lake.* New York: Macmillan Publishing Co., 1987, 238 p., cloth, novel.

CAMPBELL, Jeffrey, pseud.—SEE: Black, Campbell & Caine, Jeffrey

CAMPBELL, John W(ood, Jr.), 1910-1971

19250 *The best of John W. Campbell.* Garden City, NY: Nelson Doubleday, 1976, 307 p., cloth, coll. [Edited by Lester del Rey; not the same as the 1973 edition of the same name].
19251 *The John W. Campbell letters, volume 1.* Franklin, TN: AC Projects, 1985, viii + 610 p., cloth, nonf. coll. [Edited by Perry A. Chapdelaine, Tony Chapdelaine, and George Hay; only volume published to date].
19252 *The moon is hell.* London: New English Library, 1975, 128 p., paper, novel. [Not the same as the 1951 collection of the same title, which did, however, include the novel as part of its contents].
19253 *The space beyond.* New York: Pyramid Books, 1976, 287 p., paper, coll. [Edited by Roger Elwood].
31773 *Who goes there?* Universal City, CA: Universal Studios, 1982, 31 p., paper, story. [Cover title reads: *John Carpenter's The thing*].

with Martin H. Greenberg

19254 *Astounding science fiction, July, 1939.* Carbondale & Edwardsville, IL: South-ern Illinois University Press, 1981, ix + 180 p., cloth, anth. [A facsimile reproduction of the original magazine issue, with notes and commentary by Greenberg].

CAMPBELL, Margaret [i.e., Gabrielle Margaret Vere Campbell Long], 1886-1952

01704B *The spectral bride.* New York: A Signet Book, New American Library, 1975, 240 p., paper, novel. [Originally published as *The fetch* under the name Joseph Shearing].

as MARJORIE BOWEN

19255 *Kecksies, and other twilight tales.* Sauk City, WI: Arkham House, 1976, xiii + 207 p., cloth, coll.

as JOSEPH SHEARING

01704 *The fetch.* London: Hutchinson, 1942, 184 p., cloth, novel.

CAMPBELL, (John) Ramsey, 1946-

19256 *Ancient images.* London: Legend, Century Hutchinson, 1989, 299 p., cloth, novel.
19257 *Cold print.* Santa Cruz, CA: Scream/Press, 1985, xxi + 217 p., cloth, coll.
19258 *Cold print.* New York: Tor Horror, A Tom Doherty Associates Book, 1987, 331 p., paper, coll. [Expanded edition].
19259 *The count of eleven.* London: Macdonald & Co., 1991, 374 p., cloth, novel
19260 *Dark companions.* London: Fontana/Collins, 1982, 255 p., paper, coll.
19261 *Dark feasts: the world of Ramsey Campbell.* London: Robinson, 1987, xii + 339 p., cloth, coll.
31774 *The doll who ate his mother.* London: Century, 1987, [288] p., cloth, novel. [Expanded edition].
19262 *The doll who ate his mother: a novel of modern terror.* Indianapolis, IN, New York: Bobbs-Merrill Co., 1976, 209 p., cloth, novel.
19263 *The face that must die.* London: Star Books, 1979, 175 p., paper, novel.
19264 *The face that must die.* Los Angeles: Scream/Press, 1983, xxxv + 213 p., cloth, novel. [Revised and expanded edition].
The far reaches of fear—SEE: *Superhorror*.
19266 *Fine frights: stories that scared me.* New York: Tor Horror, A Tom Doherty As-

sociates Book, 1988, ix+309 p., paper, coll.

19267 *The gruesome book.* London & Sydney: Piccolo, Pan Books, 1983, 109 p., paper, anth.

19268 *The height of the scream.* Sauk City, WI: Arkham House, 1976, xx+229 p., cloth, coll.

19269 *The hungry moon.* New York: Macmillan Publishing Co., 1986, 293 p., cloth, novel.

19270 *Incarnate.* New York: Macmillan Publishing Co., 1983, 368 p., cloth, novel.

19271 *The influence.* New York: Macmillan Publishing Co., 1988, 260 p., cloth, novel.

19272 *Medusa.* Round Top, NY: Footsteps Press, 1987, xi+61 p., cloth, story. [Limited to 300 copies].

19273 *Midnight sun.* London: Macdonald & Co., 1990, 312 p., cloth, novel.

19274 *The nameless.* London: Macmillan, 1981, 229 p., cloth, novel.

19275 *The nameless.* London: Panther, 1985, 272 p., paper, novel. [Revised edition].

19276 *Needing ghosts.* London: Legend, 1990, 80 p., cloth, story. [Limited to 300 copies].

19277 *New tales of the Cthulhu Mythos.* Sauk City, WI: Arkham House, 1980, xi+257 p., cloth, anth.

19278 *New terrors.* London & Sydney: Pan Books, 1980, 336 p., paper, anth. [Cover title states *New terrors 1*].

19278A retitled: *New terrors 1.* New York: Pocket Books, 1984, 262 p., paper, anth.

19279 *New terrors two.* London & Sydney: Pan Books, 1980, 333 p., paper, anth.

19292B *Night of the claw.* New York: Tor, A Tom Doherty Associates Book, 1985, 367 p., paper, novel. [Originally published under the name Jay Ramsay].

19280 *Obsession.* London: Granada, 1985, 280 p., cloth, novel.

The parasite—SEE: *To wake the dead.*

19282 *Scared stiff: tales of sex and death.* Los Angeles: Scream/Press, 1987, xii+173 p., cloth, coll.

19283 *Slow.* Round Top, NY: Footsteps Press, Bill Munster, Publisher, 1985, [28] p., paper, story.

19284 *Superhorror.* London: W. H. Allen, 1976, 187 p., cloth, anth.

19284A retitled: *The far reaches of fear.* London: W. H. Allen, 1980, 187 p., paper, anth.

19285 *Through the walls.* Rochdale, Lancashire, England: British Fantasy Society, 1981, [16] p., paper, story.

19286 *To wake the dead.* London: Millington, 1980, 316 p., cloth, novel.

31836 retitled: *The parasite.* New York: Macmillan Publishing Co., 1980, 267 p., cloth, novel. [Revised edition].

19287 *Waking nightmares.* New York: Tor, A Tom Doherty Associates Book, 1991, ix+273 p., cloth, coll.

19288 *Watch the birdie: a story.* Runcorn, Cheshire, England: Rosemary Pardoe, 1984, [8] p., paper, story.

as CARL DREADSTONE

19289 *The bride of Frankenstein.* New York: A Berkley Medallion Book, Berkley Publishing Corp., 1977, xiv+210 p., paper, movie. FRANKENSTEIN SERIES.

19290 *Dracula's daughter.* New York: A Berkley Medallion Book, Berkley Publishing Corp., 1977, xi+212 p., paper, movie. DRACULA SERIES. [Reprinted under the name E. K. Leyton].

19291 *The wolfman.* New York: A Berkley Medallion Book, Berkley Publishing Corp., 1977, xi+212 p., paper, movie.

as E. K. LEYTON

19290A *Dracula's daughter.* London: Star Books, 1980, x+182 p., paper, movie. DRACULA SERIES. [originally published under the name Carl Dreadstone].

as JAY RAMSAY

19292 *The claw.* London: Macdonald & Co., 1983, 367 p., cloth, novel.

19292A retitled: *Night of the claw.* New York: St. Martin's Press, 1983, 367 p., cloth, novel.

with Charles L. Grant

19293 *Black wine.* Niles, IL: Dark Harvest, 1986, 165 p., cloth, coll. [Edited by Douglas E. Winter].

with Stephen Jones

19294 *Best new horror.* London: Robinson Publishing, 1990, 390 p., paper, anth. [Winner of the World Fantasy Award for Best Fantasy Anthology, 1990 (1991)].

19295 *Best new horror 2.* London: Robinson Publishing, 1991, 433 p., paper, anth.

CAMPION, Sidney (Ronald), 1891-

19296 *The world of Colin Wilson: a biographical study.* London: Frederick Muller, 1962, xvii+254 p., cloth, nonf.

CAMPTON, David, 1924-

with John Polidori

19297   *The vampyre.* London: Hutchinson, 1986, 143 p., cloth, novel. FLESHCREEPERS. [A retelling of Polidori's "The Vampyre"].

with Mary Wollstonecraft Shelley

19298   *Frankenstein.* London: Hutchinson, 1987, 143 p., cloth, novel. [A retelling of Mary Shelley's novel].

CANARY, Brenda Brown

19299   *The voice of the clown.* New York: Avon, 1982, 282 p., paper, novel.

CANNADAY, Marilyn

19300   *Bigger than life: the creator of Doc Savage.* Bowling Green, OH: Bowling Green State University Popular Press, 1990, 201 p., cloth, nonf.

CANNELL, Charles H.—SEE: Vivian, E. Charles

CANNING, Victor, 1911-1986

19301   *The circle of the gods.* London: Heinemann, 1977, 178 p., cloth, novel. CRIMSON CHALICE #2.
19302   *The crimson chalice.* London: Heinemann, 1976, 179 p., cloth, novel. CRIMSON CHALICE #1.
19303   *The crimson chalice trilogy.* Harmondsworth, Middlesex, England: Penguin Books, 1980, 654 p., paper, coll. CRIMSON CHALICE #1-3.
19304   *The immortal wound.* London: Heinemann, 1978, 179 p., cloth, novel. CRIMSON CHALICE #3.

CANNON, Martin

19305   *Dark knight: an analysis.* Canoga Park, CA: Psi Fi Movie Press, 1987, 65 p., paper, nonf.
19306   *Files Magazine spotlight on The Howard the Duck files.* Canoga Park, CA: Psi Fi Movie Press, 1986, 63 p., paper, nonf.
          Green mansions—SEE: Swamp Thing: Green mansions.
          The Howard the Duck files—SEE: Files magazine spotlight on The Howard the Duck files.

19307   *Swamp Thing.* Canoga Park, CA: Psi Fi Movie Press, 1987, 45 p., paper, nonf.
19308   *Swamp Thing: Green mansions.* Canoga Park, CA: Psi Fi Movie Press, 1987, 53 p., paper, nonf.

CANNON, Peter (Hughes), 1951-

19309   *The chronology out of time: dates in the fiction of H. P. Lovecraft.* West Warwick, RI: Necronomicon Press, 1986, 33 p., paper, nonf.
19310   *H. P. Lovecraft.* Boston: Twayne Publishers, 1989, xv+153 p., cloth, nonf.
19311   *Pulptime: being a singular adventure of Sherlock Holmes, H. P. Lovecraft, and the Kalem Club, as if narrated by Frank Belknap Long, Jr. / by P. H. Cannon.* Buffalo, NY: Weirdbook Press, 1984, xiii+94 p., cloth, novel.
19312   *The sky garden.* Richmond, VA: Dementia Press, 1989, [12] p., paper, story.
19313   *"Sunset Terrace imagery in Lovecraft", and other essays.* West Warwick, RI: Necronomicon Press, 1990, 42 p., paper, nonf. coll.

CANNY, James R., *with Charles F. Heartman*

19314   *A bibliography of first printings of the writings of Edgar Allan Poe: together with a record of first and contemporary later printings of his contributions to annuals, anthologies, periodicals, and newspapers issued during his lifetime: also some spurious Poeana and fakes, revised edition.* Hattiesburg, MS: The Book Farm, 1943, x+294 p., cloth, nonf.

CANON, Jack, *as* NICK CARTER

19315   *The Poseidon target.* New York: Jove Books, 1987, 198 p., paper, novel. NICK CARTER #232.
19316   *Tunnel for traitors.* New York: Charter Books, 1986, 196 p., paper, novel. NICK CARTER #214.

CANTOR, Eli—SEE: Douglas, Gregory A.

CANTOR, Jay

19317   *Krazy Kat: a novel in five panels.* New York: Alfred A. Knopf, 1988, 245 p., cloth, novel.

CANTOR, Johanna T.

19318 *The trekker cookbook.* New York: Yeoman Press, 1977, 80 p., paper, nonf. anth.

CANTRELL, Lisa W(right), 1945-

19319 *The manse.* New York: Tor Horror, A Tom Doherty Associates Book, 1987, 341 p., paper, novel. THE MANSE #1. [Winner of the Bram Stoker Award for Best First Horror Novel, 1987 (1988)].
19320 *The ridge.* New York: Tor Horror, A Tom Doherty Associates Book, 1989, 338 p., paper, novel.
19321 *Torments.* New York: Tor Horror, A Tom Doherty Associates Book, 1990, 308 p., paper, novel. THE MANSE #2.

CANTWELL, Lois, 1951- , *as* MILO DENNISON

32463 *Blackstone's magical adventure: America's secret king* / by Milo Dennison and Lois Cantwell. New York: Tor, A Tom Doherty Associates Book, 1986, 64 p., paper, fiction. BLACKSTONE'S MAGICAL ADVENTURE #1.
33344 *Blackstone's magical adventure: The secrets of Stonehenge.* New York: Tor, A Tom Doherty Associates Book, 1986, 64 p., paper, fiction. BLACKSTONE'S MAGICAL ADVENTURE #2.

CANTY, Thomas

19323 *A monster at Christmas.* West Kingston, RI: Donald M. Grant, Publisher, 1985, 45 p., cloth, story.

CAPE, Judith—SEE: Page, P. K.

CAPEK, Karel, 1890-1938

19324 *Nine fairy tales and one more thrown in for good measure.* Evanston, IL: Northwestern University Press, 1990, 252 p., cloth, coll. [Translation by Dagmar Herrmann of *Devatero pohádek a jeste jedna*].
19325 *Three novels: Hordubal, Meteor, An ordinary life.* Highland Park, NJ: A Garrique Book, Catbird Press, 1990, 464 p., paper, coll. [Translation by M. and R. Weatherall of *Hordubal*; *Povetron*; *Obycejny*].
19326 *Toward the radical center: a Karel Capek reader.* Highland Park, NJ: A Garrique Book, Catbird Press, 1990, 408 p., pa-

per, coll. [Translation by Norma Comrada].

CAPELLA, Raul Garcia

19327 *The leopard of Poitain.* Philadelphia, PA: Celt Press, 1985, 209 p., cloth, novel. CONAN PASTICHE.

CAPES, Bernard (Edward Joseph), 1854-1918

19328 *The black reaper: tales of terror by Bernard Capes.* Wellingborough, Northamptonshire, England: William Kimber, 1989, 192 p., cloth, coll. [Edited by Hugh Lamb].

CAPOBIANCO, Michael (Victor), 1950-

19329 *Burster.* New York, Toronto: Spectra, Bantam Books, 1990, 247 p., paper, novel.

with William Barton

17513 *Fellow traveler, Sputnik Mira: a science fiction novel.* New York, Toronto: Spectra, Bantam Books, 1991, 403 p., paper, novel. [*Sputnik Mira* is written in cyrillic letters]
17514 *Iris.* New York: A Foundation Book, Doubleday, 1990, 436 p., cloth, novel.

CAPONEGRO, Candace

19330 *The breeze horror.* New York: An Onyx Book, New American Library, 1988, 316 p., paper, novel.

CAPPELLI, Mario

19331 *The great drake.* New York, Hagerstown, NJ: Barnes & Noble Books, 1979, 102 p., paper, novel.

CAPPS, Carroll M.—SEE: MacApp, C. C.

CAPRIO, Betsy [i.e., Elizabeth Blair Caprio], 1933-

19332 *Star Trek: good news in modern images.* Kansas City, KS: Sheed Andrews & McMeel, 1978, 156 p., cloth, nonf.

CAPRIO, Elizabeth B.—SEE: Caprio, Betsy

CARAKER, Mary

19333 *The faces of Ceti.* Boston: Houghton Mifflin Co., 1991, 201 p., cloth, novel.

19334 *I remember, I remember...* Eugene, OR: Pulphouse Publishing, 1991, 46 p., paper, story. SHORT STORY PAPERBACKS #24.

19335 *Seven worlds.* New York: A Signet Book, New American Library, 1986, 223 p., paper, novel. SEVEN WORLDS #1.

19336 *The snows of Jaspre.* Boston: Houghton Mifflin Co., 1989, 234 p., cloth, novel. SEVEN WORLDS #2.

19337 *Water song.* New York: Popular Library, 1987, 214 p., paper, novel.

CARAVELA, Jack

19338 *The gifted.* New York: Zebra Books, Kensington Publishing Corp., 1991, 288 p., paper, novel.

CARD, Orson Scott, 1951-

19339 *The abyss: a novel.* New York, London: Pocket Books, 1989, 363 p., paper, movie.

19340 *Capitol: the Worthing Chronicle.* New York: Ace Books, 1979, 278 p., paper, coll. WORTHING CHRONICLES.

19341 *Cardography.* Eugene, OR: Hypatia Press, 1987, vii+183+xv p., cloth, coll. [Limited to 1186 copies].

19342 *Dragons of darkness.* New York: Ace Books, 1981, 351 p., paper, anth.

19343 *Dragons of light.* New York: Ace Books, 1980, 317 p., paper, anth.

19344 *Ender's game.* New York: Tor, A Tom Doherty Associates Book, 1985, 357 p., cloth, novel. ENDER WIGGINS #1. [Winner of the Hugo Award for Best Novel, 1985 (1986); winner of the Nebula Award for Best Novel, 1985 (1986); winner of the *Science Fiction Chronicle* Award for Best Novel, 1985 (1986)].].

19345 *Ender's game.* New York: Tor, A Tom Doherty Associates Book, 1991, xxi+226 p., cloth, novel. ENDER WIGGINS #1. [Revised edition].

19346 *Ender's war.* Garden City, NY: Nelson Doubleday, 1986, 634 p., cloth, coll. ENDER WIGGINS #1-2. [Includes *Ender's war* and *Speaker for the dead*].

19347 *Eye for eye.* New York: Tor SF, A Tom Doherty Associates Book, 1990, p. 1-96, paper, story. [Bound with *The tunesmith* / by Lloyd Biggle Jr.].

19348 *The folk of the fringe.* West Bloomfield, MI: Phantasia Press, 1989, 243 p., cloth, coll.

19349 *Future on fire.* New York: Tor SF, A Tom Doherty Associates Book, 1991, viii+376 p., paper, anth.

19350 *Hart's hope.* New York: Berkley Books, 1983, 261 p., paper, novel.

19351 *Hatrack River: the tales of Alvin Maker, part one.* New York: Guild America Books, 1989, 792 p., cloth, coll. ALVIN MAKER #1-3. [Includes *Seventh son, Red prophet, Prentice Alvin*].

19352 *Hot sleep: the Worthing chronicle.* New York: Baronet Publishing Co., 1979, 309 p., paper, novel. WORTHING CHRONICLES.

19353 *How to write science fiction and fantasy.* Cincinnati, OH: Writer's Digest Books, 1990, 140 p., cloth, nonf. [Winner of the Hugo Award for Best Nonfiction Book, 1990 (1991)].

19354 *Maps in a mirror: the short fiction of Orson Scott Card.* Norwalk, CT: Easton Press, 1990, ix+675 p., cloth, coll. [Winner of the *Locus* Award for Best Collection, 1990 (1991)].

19355 *A planet called Treason.* New York: St. Martin's Press, 1979, 256 p., cloth, novel.

19356 retitled: *Treason.* New York: St. Martin's Press, 1988, 275 p., cloth, novel. [Expanded edition].

19357 *Prentice Alvin.* New York: Tor, A Tom Doherty Associates Book, 1989, x+310 p., cloth, novel. ALVIN MAKER #3. [Winner of the *Locus* Award for Best Fantasy Novel, 1989 (1990)].

19358 *Red prophet.* New York: Tor, A Tom Doherty Associates Book, 1988, 311 p., cloth, novel. ALVIN MAKER #2. [Winner of the *Locus* Award for Best Fantasy Novel, 1988 (1989)].

19359 *Seventh son.* New York: Tor, A Tom Doherty Associates Book, 1987, 241 p., cloth, novel. ALVIN MAKER #1. [Winner of the *Locus* Award for Best Fantasy Novel, 1987 (1988)].

19360 *Songmaster.* New York: A Quantum Book, The Dial Press, 1980, 338 p., cloth, novel.

19361 *Speaker for the dead.* New York: Tor, A Tom Doherty Associates Book, 1986, xiv+415 p., cloth, novel. ENDER WIGGINS #2. [Winner of the Hugo Award for Best Novel, 1986 (1987); winner of the Nebula Award for Best Novel, 1986 (1987); winner of the *Locus* Award for Best Science Fiction Novel, 1986 (1987); winner of the *Science Fiction Chronicle* Award for Best Novel, 1986 (1987)].

19362 *Speaker for the dead.* New York: Tor, A Tom Doherty Associates Book, 1991, xxii+280 p., cloth, novel. ENDER WIGGINS #2. [Revised edition].

Treason—SEE: *A planet called Treason.*

19363 *Unaccompanied sonata, & other stories.* New York: Quantum Science Fiction, Dial Press, 1980, 272 p., cloth, coll.

19364 *The Worthing chronicle.* New York: Ace Science Fiction Books, 1983, 264 p., paper, novel. WORTHING CHRONICLES. [Includes portions of *Capitol* and *Hot sleep*].

19365 *The Worthing saga.* New York: Tor SF, A Tom Doherty Associates Book, 1990, xiv+463 p., paper, coll. WORTHING CHRONICLES. [Includes *The Worthing chronicle* plus additional stories].

19366 *Wyrms.* New York: Arbor House, 1987, 263 p., cloth, novel.

19367 *Xenocide.* New York: Tor, A Tom Doherty Associates Book, 1991, x+394 p., cloth, novel. ENDER WIGGINS #3.

CARDEW, Christopher

19368 *Pellafino.* Ilfracombe, England: Arthur H. Stockwell, 1976, 132 p., cloth, novel.

CAREW, Jan R(ynveld Alwin), 1925-

19369 *Stranger than tomorrow: three stories of the future.* London: Longman, 1976, 80 p., cloth, coll.

CAREY, Diane (L.)

19370 *Battlestations! a Star Trek novel.* New York: Pocket Books, 1986, 274 p., paper, novel. STAR TREK #31. [A direct sequel to *Dreadnought!*].

19371 *Dreadnought!: a Star Trek novel.* New York: Pocket Books, 1986, 251 p., paper, novel. STAR TREK #29.
        Final frontier—SEE: *Star Trek: Final frontier.*

19372 *Ghost ship.* New York, London: Pocket Books, 1988, 258 p., paper, tele. STAR TREK: THE NEXT GENERATION #1.

19373 *Star Trek: Final frontier.* New York: Pocket Books, 1988, x+434 p., paper, tele. STAR TREK (UNNUMBERED).

CAREY, Mary (Virginia), 1925-

19374 *The Gremlins story book.* Racine, WI: A Golden Book, Western Publishing Co., 1984, [41] p., cloth, movie.

CAREY, Peter (Philip), 1943-

33436 *Bliss.* St. Lucia, Queensland, Australia: University of Queensland Press, 1981, 296 p., cloth, novel.

19375 *The fat man in history.* St. Lucia, Queensland, Australia: University of Queensland Press, 1974, 141 p., cloth, coll.

19376 *The fat man in history, and other stories.* New York: Random House, 1980, 186 p., cloth, coll. [Includes *The fat man in history* and *War crimes*].

19377 *Illywhacker.* St. Lucia, Queensland, Australia: University of Queensland Press, 1985, 600 p., paper, novel.

19378 *War crimes: short stories.* St. Lucia, Queensland, Australia: University of Queensland Press, 1979, 282 p., cloth, coll.

CARHART, Arthur H.—SEE: Van Sickle, V. A.

CARKEET, David (Corydon), 1946-

19379 *I been there before: a novel.* New York: Harper & Row, Publishers, 1985, 314 p., cloth, novel.

19380 *Quiver River.* New York: HarperCollinsPublishers, 1991, 236 p., cloth, novel.

CARL, Lillian Stewart, 1949-

19381 *Ashes to ashes.* New York: Charter/Diamond Books, 1990, 346 p., paper, novel.

19382 *Dust to dust.* New York: Diamond Books, 1991, 360 p., paper, novel.

19383 *Sabazel.* New York: Ace Fantasy Books, 1985, 251 p., paper, novel. SABAZEL #1.

19384 *Shadow dancers.* New York: Ace Books, 1987, 283 p., paper, novel. SABAZEL #3.

19385 *Wings of power.* New York: Ace Books, 1989, 309 p., paper, novel.

19386 *The winter king.* New York: Ace Fantasy Books, 1986, 283 p., paper, novel. SABAZEL #2.

CARL, Mary Jo

19387 *Science fiction: our heritage of the future.* Fort Lauderdale, FL: Broward Community College, 1972, 54 p., paper, nonf.

19388 *Science fiction: our heritage of the future.* Dubuque, IA: Kendall/Hunt Publishing Co., 1974, ix+62 p., paper?, nonf. [Revised edition].

CARLETON, Barbee Oliver, 1917-

19389 *The witches' bridge.* New York: Holt, Rinehart & Winston, 1967, 232 p., cloth, novel.

19389A retitled: *Mystery of the witches' bridge.* New York: An Apple Paperback, Scholastic Book Services, 1975?, 304 p., paper, novel.

CARLILE, Clancy [i.e., Clarence Carlile], 1930-

19390 *Spore 7.* New York: William Morrow & Co., 1979, 300 p., cloth, novel.

CARLILE, Clarence—SEE: Carlile, Clancy

CARLINSKY, Dan, 1944- , with Edwin Goodgold

19391 *The world's greatest monster quiz.* New York: A Berkley Medallion Book, Berkley Publishing Corp., 1975, 122 p., paper, nonf.

CARLISLE, Anne, 1956-

19392 *Liquid sky: the novel.* Garden City, NY: Doubleday & Co., 1987, 186 p., paper, movie.

CARLOCK, Lynn [pseud. of Marilyn Cunningham], 1927-

19393 *Daughter of the moon.* Toronto, New York: First Love from Silhouette, Silhouette Books, 1986, 155 p., paper, novel.

CARLSEN, Chris, pseud.—SEE: Holdstock, Robert

CARLSON, Dale (Elissa Bick), 1935-

19394 *The frog people.* New York: A Skinny Book, E. P. Dutton, 1982, 75 p., cloth, novel.
19395 *The mystery of the hidden trap.* New York: Grosset & Dunlap, 1983, 135 p., cloth, novel. JENNY DEAN #2.
19396 *The mystery of the shining children.* New York: Grosset & Dunlap, 1983, 136 p., cloth, novel. JENNY DEAN #1.
19397 *The plant people.* New York: A Triumph Book, Franklin Watts, 1977, 92 p., cloth, novel.
19398 *The secret of the invisible city.* New York: Grosset & Dunlap, 1984, 135 p., cloth, novel. JENNY DEAN #4.
19399 *The secret of the third eye.* New York: Grosset & Dunlap, 1983, 135 p., cloth, novel. JENNY DEAN #3.
19400 *The secret Operation Brain.* New York: Golden Book, 1984, 140 p., cloth, novel. JAMES BUDD #2. [The rest of this series is not SF].

with Danny Carlson

19401 *The shining pool.* New York: An Argo Book, Atheneum, 1979, 138 p., cloth, novel.

CARLSON, Daniel B.—SEE: Carlson, Danny

CARLSON, Danny [i.e., Daniel Bick Carlson], 1960- , with Dale Carlson

19401 *The shining pool.* New York: An Argo Book, Atheneum, 1979, 138 p., cloth, novel.

CARLSON, Eric W(alter), 1910-

19402 *The recognition of Edgar Allan Poe: selected criticism since 1829.* Ann Arbor, MI: University of Michigan Press, 1966, xv+316 p., cloth, nonf. anth.

CARLSON, Larry G.

19403 *Molecular ramjet, and other bedtime stories.* Seattle, WA: TadAleX, 1989, 212 p., paper, coll.

CARLSON, William K.

19404 *Elysium.* Garden City, NY: Doubleday & Co., 1982, 216 p., cloth, novel.
19405 *Sunrise west.* Garden City, NY: Doubleday & Co., 1981, 184 p., cloth, novel.

CARLTON, Ardith, with Kay Reynolds

19406 *Robotech art 1: from the animated series Robotech.* Norfolk, VA: Donning Co., 1986, ix+254 p., paper, art.

CARLTON, Roger, pseud.—SEE: Rowland, Donald S.

CARLYON, Richard

19407 *The Dark Lord of Pengersick.* London: G. Whizzard, André Deutsch, 1976, 130 p., cloth, novel.

CARMODY, Isobelle (Jane), 1958-

33500 *The farseekers.* Auckland, New Zealand, NY: Viking, 1990, 325 p., cloth, novel. OBERNEWTYN CHRONICLES #2.
35002 *Obernewtyn.* Auckland, New Zealand, NY: Viking, 1987, p., cloth, novel. OBERNEWTYN CHRONICLES #1.
35149 *Scatterlings.* Auckland, New Zealand, NY: Viking, 1991, p., cloth, novel. OBERNEWTYN CHRONICLES #3.

CARNELL, Corbin Scott, 1929-

19408 *Bright shadow of reality: C. S. Lewis & the feeling intellect.* Grand Rapids, MI: William B. Eerdmans Publishing Co., 1974, 182 p., cloth, nonf.

CARNELL, (Edward) John ("Ted"), 1912-1972, with Kenneth Bulmer

18986 *New writings in SF special (1).* London: Sidgwick & Jackson, 1975, 189+189+ 191 p., cloth, anth. [Includes *New Writings in SF #21-23*].

CARNES, Ralph L(ee), 1931- , with Valerie Carnes

19409 *The officers of the bridge.* New York: Star Trek 1976, 1976, 56 p., paper, nonf.

CARNES, Valerie (Folts-Bohanan), 1944- , with Ralph L. Carnes

19409 *The officers of the bridge.* New York: Star Trek 1976, 1976, 56 p., paper, nonf.

CARNEY, William M(ichael), 1950-

19410 *Devil's moon.* New York: Zebra Books, Kensington Publishing Corp., 1988, 480 p., paper, novel.
19411 *Hide and seek.* New York: Zebra Books, Kensington Publishing Corp., 1991, 384 p., paper, novel.

CARO, Dennis R., 1944-

19412 *Devine war.* New York: Arbor House, 1986, 276 p., cloth, novel.
19413 *The man in the darksuit: a futuristic mystery.* New York: Pocket Books, 1980, 188 p., paper, novel.

CARPELAN, Bo (Gustaf Berelsson), 1926-

19414 *Voices at the late hour: a novel.* Athens, GA: University of Georgia Press, 1988, xxxii+183 p., cloth, novel. [Translation by Irma Margareta Martin of *Rösterna i den sena timmen*].

CARPENTER, Christopher, pseud.—SEE: Evans, Chris

CARPENTER, Humphrey (William Bouverie), 1946-

19415 *The Inklings: C. S. Lewis, J. R. R. Tolkien, Charles Williams, and their friends.* London, Boston: George Allen & Unwin, 1978, xv+287 p., cloth, nonf.
19416 *J. R. R. Tolkien: a biography.* London: George Allen & Unwin, 1977, 287 p., cloth, nonf.
19416A retitled: *Tolkien: a biography.* Boston: Houghton Mifflin Co., 1977, 286 p., cloth, nonf.
19417 *Secret gardens: a study of the golden age of children's literature.* London: George Allen & Unwin, 1985, xi+235 p., cloth, nonf.
Tolkien: a biography—SEE: *J. R. R. Tolkien.*

CARPENTER, Leonard (Paul), 1948-

19418 *Conan the great.* New York: Tor SF, A Tom Doherty Associates Book, 1989 (i.e., 1990), 277 p., paper, novel. CONAN SERIES.
19419 *Conan the hero.* New York: Tor SF, A Tom Doherty Associates Book, 1989, 278 p., paper, novel. CONAN SERIES.
19420 *Conan the outcast.* New York: Tor SF, A Tom Doherty Associates Book, 1991, 274 p., paper, novel. CONAN SERIES.
19421 *Conan the raider.* New York: Tor SF, A Tom Doherty Associates Book, 1986, 276 p., paper, novel. CONAN SERIES.
19422 *Conan the renegade.* New York: Tor SF, A Tom Doherty Associates Book, 1986, 276 p., paper, novel. CONAN SERIES.
19423 *Conan the warlord.* New York: Tor SF, A Tom Doherty Associates Book, 1988, 273 p., paper, novel. CONAN SERIES.

CARPENTER, Lynette, 1951- , with Wendy K. Kolmar

19424 *Haunting the house of fiction: feminist perspectives on ghost stories by American women.* Knoxville, TN: University of Tennessee Press, 1991, x+266 p., cloth, nonf. anth.

CARPENTER, Richard, 1929-

19425 *Catweazle and the magic zodiac.* Harmondsworth, Middlesex, England: Puffin Books, 1971, 175 p., paper, novel.
19426 *Robin of Sherwood: The time of the wolf.* Harmondsworth, Middlesex, England: Puffin Books, 1988, 149 p., paper, tele. ROBIN OF SHERWOOD SERIES.
The time of the wolf—SEE: *Robin of Sherwood: The time of the wolf.*

CARPENTER, (Malcolm) Scott, 1925-

19427 *The steel albatross.* New York, London: Pocket Books, 1991, 371 p., cloth, novel.

*CARPENTIER (y Valmont), Alejo (F.), 1904-1980

CARPOZI, George Jr., 1920-

19428 *Sunstrike.* Los Angeles: Pinnacle Books, 1978, 372 p., paper, novel.

CARR, Barbara Comyns- —SEE: Comyns-Carr, Barbara

CARR, Bentley [pseud. of Keith Michael King], 1946-

19429 *The gateway of time.* London: Merlin, 1991, 72 p., paper, novel. TALES OF MAROTH #1.

CARR, Helen

19430 *From my guy to sci-fi: genre and women's writing in the postmodern world.* London: Pandora Books, 1989, 252 p., paper, nonf. anth.

CARR, Jayge [pseud. of Margery Krueger], 1940-

19431 *Leviathan's deep.* Garden City, NY: Doubleday & Co., 1979, 213 p., cloth, novel.
19432 *Navigator's sindrome.* Garden City, NY: Doubleday & Co., 1983, 187 p., cloth, novel. NAVIGATOR #1.
19433 *Rabelaisian reprise.* New York: Doubleday, 1988, 212 p., cloth, novel. NAVIGATOR #3.
19434 *The treasure in the heart of the maze.* Garden City, NY: Doubleday & Co., 1985, 183 p., cloth, novel. NAVIGATOR #2.

CARR, John F(rancis), 1944-

19435 *Carnifex Mardi Gras.* Los Angeles: Pequod Press, 1982, 218 p., cloth, novel.
19436 *The Ophidian conspiracy.* Chatsworth, CA: Major Books, 1976, 176 p., paper, novel.
19437 *Pain gain.* Canoga Park, CA: Major Books, 1977, 192 p., paper, novel.

with Roland Green

19455 *Great Kings' War.* New York: Ace Science Fiction Books, 1985, 357 p., paper,

novel. PARATIME POLICE—LORD KALVAN #2.

with Jerry Pournelle

19438 *After armageddon.* New York: Tor, A Tom Doherty Associates Book, 1990, 404 p., paper, anth. THERE WILL BE WAR #9.
19439 *Armageddon!* New York: Tor SF, A Tom Doherty Associates Book, 1989, 368 p., paper, anth. THERE WILL BE WAR #8.
19440 *Blood and iron.* New York: Tor, A Tom Doherty Associates Book, 1984, 383 p., paper, anth. THERE WILL BE WAR #3. [Includes some nonfiction].
19441 *Call to battle.* New York: Tor SF, A Tom Doherty Associates Book, 1988, 375 p., paper, anth. THERE WILL BE WAR #7.
19442 *Cities in space.* New York: Ace Books, 1991, 259 p., paper, anth. ENDLESS FRONTIER #3.
19443 *The crash of empire.* New York: Baen Books, 1989, 376 p., paper, anth. IMPERIAL STARS #3.
19444 *Day of the tyrant.* New York: Tor SF, A Tom Doherty Associates Book, 1985, xiv+370 p., paper, anth. THERE WILL BE WAR #4. [Includes some nonfiction].
19445 *The endless frontier, vol. II.* New York: Ace Books, 1982, 429 p., paper, anth. ENDLESS FRONTIER #2.
19446 *Guns of darkness.* New York: Tor SF, A Tom Doherty Associates Book, 1987, 406 p., paper, anth. THERE WILL BE WAR #6.
19447 *Nebula award stories sixteen.* New York: Holt, Rinehart & Winston, 1982, 286 p., cloth, anth.
19448 *Republic and empire.* New York: Baen Books, 1987, 399 p., paper, anth. IMPERIAL STARS #2.
19449 *Sauron dominion.* Riverdale, NY: Baen Books, 1991, 356 p., paper, anth. WAR WORLD #3.
19450 *The stars at war.* New York: Baen Books, 1986, 464 p., paper, anth. IMPERIAL STARS #1.
19451 *The survival of freedom.* New York: Fawcett Crest, 1981, 381 p., paper, anth.
19452 *There will be war.* New York: A Jim Baen Presentation, Tor, A Tom Doherty Associates Book, 1983, 352 p., paper, anth. THERE WILL BE WAR #1. [Includes some nonfiction and verse].
19453 *There will be war, volume V: [Warrior].* New York: Tor SF, A Tom Doherty Associates Book, 1986, 384 p., paper, anth. THERE WILL BE WAR #5.

with Jerry Pournelle & Jim Baen

17205 *The science fiction yearbook.* New York: Baen Science Fiction Books, 1985, 344 p., cloth, anth. [Includes some nonfiction].

with Jerry Pournelle & Roland Green

19454 *The burning eye.* New York: Baen Books, 1988, 366 p., paper, anth. WAR WORLD #1.

CARR, John L(eonard), 1945-

19456 *Leigh Brackett, American writer.* Polk City, IA: Drumm Books, 1986, 67 p., paper, nonf. DRUMM BOOKLET #22.

CARR, Kirby, pseud.—SEE: Platt, Kin

CARR, Michael—SEE: Carr, Mike

CARR, Mike [i.e., Michael Carr]

19457 *Keep of the ancient king* / by Mike Carr. Lake Geneva, WI: TSR Inc., 1983, 76 p., paper, fiction. FANTASY FOREST BOOK #4. [Author's name appears on book cover as Michael Carr].
19458 *Robbers and robots* / by Mike Carr. Lake Geneva, WI: TSR Inc., 1983, 157 p., paper, novel. ENDLESS QUEST #9.
19459 *Ruins of Rangar* / by Mike Carr. Lake Geneva, WI: TSR Inc., 1983, 76 p., paper, fiction. FANTASY FOREST BOOK #2. [Author's name appears on cover as Michael Carr].

CARR, Nick [i.e. Wooda Nicholas Carr]

19460 *The flying spy: a history of G-8.* Chicago: Robert Weinberg, 1978, 160 p., paper, nonf. PULP CLASSICS #18.

CARR, Terry (Gene), 1937-1987

19461 *The best from Universe.* Garden City, NY: Doubleday & Co., 1984, ix+209 p., cloth, anth.
19462 *The best science fiction novellas of the year #1.* New York: A Del Rey Book, Ballantine Books, 1979, viii+328 p., paper, anth.
19463 *The best science fiction novellas of the year #2.* New York: A Del Rey Book, Ballantine Books, 1980, ix+320 p., paper, anth.

19464 *The best science fiction of the year #4.* New York: Ballantine Books, 1975, xii+304 p., paper, anth.
19465 *The best science fiction of the year #5.* New York: Ballantine Books, 1976, xi+367 p., paper, anth. [Winner of the *Locus* Award for Best Reprint Anthology, 1976 (1977)].
19466 *The best science fiction of the year #6.* New York: Holt, Rinehart & Winston, 1977, viii+388 p., cloth, anth.
19467 *The best science fiction of the year #7.* New York: A Del Rey Book, Ballantine Books, 1978, xiii+365 p., paper, anth.
19468 *The best science fiction of the year #8.* New York: A Del Rey Book, Ballantine Books, 1979, xi+372 p., paper, anth.
19469 *The best science fiction of the year #9.* New York: A Del Rey Book, Ballantine Books, 1980, xi+369 p., paper, anth.
19470 *The best science fiction of the year #10.* New York: Pocket Books, 1981, viii+434 p., paper, anth.
19471 *The best science fiction of the year #11.* New York: A Timescape Book, Pocket Books, 1982, viii+438 p., paper, anth. [Winner of the *Locus* Award for Best Anthology, 1982 (1983)].
19472 *The best science fiction of the year #12.* New York: A Timescape Book, Pocket Books, 1983, viii+359 p., paper, anth. [Winner of the *Locus* Award for Best Anthology, 1983 (1984)].
19473 *The best science fiction of the year #13.* New York: A Baen Book Science Fiction, 1984, 384 p., paper, anth.
Best science fiction of the year [#14]—SEE: Terry Carr's best science fiction of the year [#14].
Best SF of the year 15—SEE: Terry Carr's best science fiction of the year #15.
Best SF of the year 16—SEE: Terry Carr's best science fiction and fantasy of the year #16.
19474 *Between two worlds.* Cambridge, MA: NESFA Press, 1986, vi+68 p., cloth, coll. [Includes some nonfiction; bound with *Messages found in an oxygen bottle* / by Bob Shaw].
19475 *Beyond reality: 8 stories of science fiction.* New York: Elsevier/Nelson, 1979, 214 p., cloth, anth.
19476 *Cirque: a novel of the far future.* Indianapolis & New York: Bobbs-Merrill Co., 1977, 187 p., cloth, novel.
19477 *Classic science fiction: the first golden age.* New York: Harper & Row, 1978, viii+445 p., cloth, anth.
19478 *Creatures from beyond: nine stories of science fiction and fantasy.* Nashville, TN

& New York: Thomas Nelson, 1975, 192 p., cloth, anth.

19479 *Dream's edge: science fiction stories about the future of the planet Earth.* San Francisco, CA: Sierra Club Books, 1980, v+313 p., cloth, anth.

19480 *Fandom harvest.* Solna, Sweden: Laissez Faire Produktion, 1986, 191 p., cloth, nonf. coll.

19481 *Fantasy annual III.* New York: A Timescape Book, Pocket Books, 1981, xi+291 p., paper, anth.

19482 *Fantasy annual IV.* New York: A Timescape Book, Pocket Books, 1981, 341 p., paper, anth.

19483 *Fantasy annual V.* New York: A Timescape Book, Pocket Books, 1982, 264 p., paper, anth.

19484 *The ides of tomorrow: original science fiction tales of horror.* Boston: Little, Brown & Co., 1976, x+229 p., cloth, anth.

19485 *The infinite arena: seven science fiction stories about sports.* Nashville, TN, New York: Thomas Nelson, 1977, 191 p., cloth, anth.

19486 *The light at the end of the universe.* New York: Pyramid Books, 1976, 304 p., paper, coll.

Nebula winners, 1970 1974—SEE: *The science fiction hall of fame, volume IV.*

19487 *Planets of wonder: a treasury of space opera.* New York: Thomas Nelson, 1976, 189 p., cloth, anth.

19488 *The science fiction hall of fame, volume IV: Nebula winners, 1970 1974.* New York: Avon, 1986, xiv+434 p., paper, anth.

19489 *Terry Carr's best science fiction of the year [#14].* New York: Tor SF, A Tom Doherty Associates Book, 1985, 384 p., paper, anth.

19490 *Terry Carr's best science fiction of the year #15.* New York: Tor SF, A Tom Doherty Associates Book, 1986, 379 p., paper, anth.

19490A retitled: *Best SF of the year 15.* London: Victor Gollancz, 1986, 365 p., cloth, anth.

19491 *Terry Carr's best science fiction and fantasy of the year #16.* New York: Tor, A Tom Doherty Associates Book, 1987, 402 p., paper, anth.

19491A retitled: *Best SF of the year 16.* London: Victor Gollancz, 1987, 388 p., paper, anth.

19492 *To follow a star: nine science fiction stories about Christmas.* New York: Thomas Nelson, 1977, 152 p., cloth, anth.

19493 *Universe 6.* Garden City, NY: Doubleday & Co., 1976, 184 p., cloth, anth.

19494 *Universe 7.* Garden City, NY: Doubleday & Co., 1977, 184 p., cloth, anth.

19495 *Universe 8.* Garden City, NY: Doubleday & Co., 1978, 185 p., cloth, anth.

19496 *Universe 9.* Garden City, NY: Doubleday & Co., 1979, 182 p., cloth, anth. [Winner of the *Locus* Award for Best Anthology, 1979 (1980)].

19497 *Universe 10.* Garden City, NY: Doubleday & Co., 1980, 182 p., cloth, anth.

19498 *Universe 11.* Garden City, NY: Doubleday & Co., 1981, 192 p., cloth, anth.

19499 *Universe 12.* Garden City, NY: Doubleday & Co., 1982, 181 p., cloth, anth.

19500 *Universe 13.* Garden City, NY: Doubleday & Co., 1983, 181 p., cloth, anth.

19501 *Universe 14.* Garden City, NY: Doubleday & Co., 1984, 182 p., cloth, anth.

19502 *Universe 15.* Garden City, NY: Doubleday & Co., 1985, 179 p., cloth, anth.

19503 *Universe 16.* Garden City, NY: Doubleday & Co., 1986, 181 p., cloth, anth.

19504 *Universe 17.* Garden City, NY: Doubleday & Co., 1987, 180 p., cloth, anth. [Last volume in the series].

19505 *Year's finest fantasy.* New York: A Berkley Book, Berkley Publishing Corp., 1978, 261 p., paper, anth.

19506 *The year's finest fantasy, volume 2.* New York: Berkley Publishing Corp., 1979, 277 p., cloth, anth.

with Isaac Asimov & Martin H. Greenberg

16927 *100 great fantasy short short stories.* Garden City, NY: Doubleday & Co., 1984, xviii+311 p., cloth, anth.

as uncredited co-author with Michael Avallone

00661 *The Man from U.N.C.L.E.* New York: Ace Books, 1965, 160 p., paper, tele. THE MAN FROM U.N.C.L.E. #1. [Running title reads: *The thousand coffins affair.* According to Carr's obituary, he extensively reworked this novel prior to publication].

with Martin Harry Greenberg

19507 *A treasury of modern fantasy.* New York: Avon, 1981, xvii+588 p., paper, anth.

CARR, Wooda N.—SEE: **Carr, Nick**

CARR RIBEIRO, Stella—SEE: **Ribeiro, Stella Carr**

*CARREL, Frederic, 1869-

CARREL, Mark, pseud.—SEE: Paine, Lauran

CARRERE, Emmanuel, 1957-

19508 *Gothic romance.* New York: Charles Scribner's Sons, 1990, 307 p., cloth, novel. [Translation by Lanie Goodman of *Bravoure*].

CARRINGTON, Grant, 1938-

35376 *Time's fool.* Garden City, NY: Doubleday & Co., 1981, 180 p., cloth, novel.

*CARRINGTON, Hereward (Hubert Lavington), 1880-1958

CARRINGTON, Leonora, 1917-

19509 *The hearing trumpet.* New York: St. Martin's Press, 1976, 158 p., cloth, novel. [Translation of *Le cornet acoustique*]
19510 *The house of fear: notes from Down below.* New York: E. P. Dutton, 1988, 216 p., cloth, coll. [Translation by Kathrine Talbot and Marina Warner; includes *The oval lady*].
19511 *The oval lady, other stories: six surreal stories.* Santa Barbara, CA: Capra Press, 1975, 52 p., paper, coll. [Translation by Rochelle Holt].
19512 *The seventh horse, and other stories.* New York: E. P. Dutton, 1988, 197 p., cloth, coll. [Translation by Kathrine Talbot and Anthony Kerrigan].
19513 *The stone door.* New York: St. Martin's Press, 1977, 118 p., cloth, novel. [Translation of *La porte de pierre*].

CARROLL, Jonathan (Samuel), 1949-

19514 *Black cocktail.* London: Legend, 1990, 76 p., cloth, story. [Limited to 300 copies].
19515 *Bones of the moon.* London: Century Publishing, 1987, 216 p., cloth, novel. BONES #1.
19516 *A child across the sky.* London, Sydney: Century, 1989, 268 p., cloth, novel. BONES #3.
19517 *The Land of Laughs.* New York: Viking Press, 1980, 241 p., cloth, novel.
19518 *Outside the Dog Museum.* London: Macdonald, 1991, 244 p., cloth, novel.
19519 *Sleeping in flame.* New York, London: Doubleday, 1988, 273 p., cloth, novel. BONES #2.
19520 *Voice of our shadow.* New York: Viking Press, 1983, 189 p., cloth, novel.

*CARROLL, Joy, 1924-

*CARROLL, (Archer) Latrobe, 1894-

CARROLL, Noël (E.), 1947-

19521 *The philosophy of horror; or, Paradoxes of the heart.* New York: Routledge, 1989, xi+256 p., cloth, nonf.

*CARROLL, Ruth (Crombie Robinson), 1899-

CARROLL, Theodus (Catherine), 1928-

19522 *Evil is a quiet word.* New York: Warner Books, 1975, 189 p., paper, novel.

CARSON, David, *with William Vernon & Daryl Lane*

19523 *The sound of wonder: interviews from "The science fiction radio show".* Phoenix, AZ: Oryx Press, 1985, 2 v. (I-xi+203 p.; II-vi+201 p.), paper, nonf. coll.

CARSON, David M., *as* ANONYMOUS AUTHOR

19524 *Time dreams.* Kansas City, KS: Kangam, 1979, 105 p., paper, coll.

*CARSON, John F(ranklin), 1920-

CARSON, Michael

19525 *Pain.* New York: A Signet Book, New American Library, 1982, 250 p., paper, novel.

CARSON, Nina, *with Jim Allan*

16278 *An introduction to Elvish, and to other tongues and proper names and writing systems of the Third Age of the western lands of Middle-Earth, as set forth in the published writings of Professor John Ronald Reuel Tolkien.* Hayes, Middlesex, England: Bran's Head Books, 1978, xxxi+303 p., paper, nonf. anth.

CARSTENSEN, Bernice, *with Sharry Michels as* SHARICE KENDYL

19526 *To share a sunset.* New York: Leisure Books, 1990, 368 p., paper, novel.

CARTER, Albert Howard III, 1943-

19527 *Italo Calvino: metamorphoses of fantasy.* Ann Arbor, MI: UMI Research Press,

1987, viii + 182 p., cloth, nonf. STUDIES IN SPECULATIVE FICTION #13.

CARTER, Angela (Olive Stalker), 1940-1992

19528 *Artificial fire.* Toronto: McClelland & Stewart, 1988, 236 p., cloth, coll. [Includes *Fireworks*; and, *Love*].

19529 *Black Venus.* London: Chatto & Windus, Hogarth Press, 1985, 121 p., cloth, coll.

19529A retitled: *Saints and strangers.* New York: Viking, 1986, 126 p., cloth, coll.

19530 *The bloody chamber, and other stories.* London: Victor Gollancz, 1979, 157 p., cloth, coll.

19531 *Fireworks, rev. ed.* London: Virago Press, 1987, 120 p., paper, coll.

19532 *Nights at the circus.* London: Chatto & Windus, 1984, 295 p., cloth, novel.

The old wives' fairy tale book—SEE: *The Virago book of fairy tales.*

19533 *The passion of new Eve.* London: Victor Gollancz, 1977, 191 p., cloth, novel.

Saints and strangers—SEE: *Black Venus.*

19534 *The Virago book of fairy tales.* London: Virago Press, 1990, xxii + 242 p., cloth, anth.

19534A retitled: *The old wives' fairy tale book.* New York: Book-of-the-Month Club, 1991, 242 p., paper, anth.

CARTER, Brian, 1937-

19535 *In the long dark.* London: Century, 1989, 256 p., cloth, novel.

19536 *Nightworld.* London: Century, 1987, [288] p., cloth, novel.

CARTER, Bruce [pseud. of Richard Alexander Hough], 1922-

19537 *Buzzbugs.* London: J. M. Dent & Sons, 1977, 119 p., cloth, novel.

35509 *The deadly freeze.* London: J. M. Dent & Sons, 1976, 128 p., cloth, novel.

CARTER, Carmen (Cecelia), 1954-

19538 *The children of Hamlin.* New York, London: Pocket Books, 1988, 252 p., paper, novel. STAR TREK: THE NEXT GENERATION #3.

19539 *Dreams of the raven: a Star Trek novel.* New York: Pocket Books, 1987, 255 p., paper, novel. STAR TREK #34.

19540 *The shy beast.* Brooklyn, NY: Bodle Books, 1984, [26] p., paper, story. [A miniature book].

with Michael Jan Friedman & Peter David & Robert Greenberger

19541 *Doomsday world.* New York, London: Pocket Books, 1990, xi + 276 p., paper, novel. STAR TREK: THE NEXT GENERATION #12.

*CARTER, George Goldsmith-, 1911-

CARTER, John

19542 *The Eagle's Nest.* London: Futura Publications, 1976, 190 p., paper, tele. NEW AVENGERS #2.

CARTER, Lin(wood Vrooman), 1930-1988

19543 *As the Green Star rises.* New York: DAW Books, 1975, 172 p., paper, novel. GREEN STAR #4.

19544 *The barbarian of world's end.* New York: DAW Books, 1977, 188 p., paper, novel. GONDWANE EPIC #4.

Barbarians and black magicians—SEE: *Flashing swords! #4.*

19545 *Callipygia: further adventures in Terra Magica.* New York: DAW Books, 1988, 252 p., cloth, novel. TERRA MAGICA #.

19546 *The city outside the world.* New York: A Berkley Medallion Book, Berkley Publishing Corp., 1977, viii + 215 p., paper, novel. MARS #3.

19547 *Darya of the bronze age.* New York: DAW Books, 1981, 173 p., paper, novel. ERIC CARSTAIRS #4.

Demons and daggers—SEE: *Flashing swords! no. 5.*

19548 *Down to a sunless sea.* New York: DAW Books, 1984, 174 p., paper, novel. MARS #4.

19549 *Dragonrouge: further adventures in Terra Magica.* New York: DAW Books, 1984, 222 p., paper, novel. TERRA MAGICA #2.

The Earth-shaker—SEE: *Zarkon, Lord of the Unknown, in The Earth-shaker.*

19550 *The enchantress of world's end.* New York: DAW Books, 1975, 192 p., paper, novel. GONDWANE EPIC #2.

19551 *Eric of Zanthodon.* New York: DAW Books, 1982, 176 p., paper, novel. ERIC CARSTAIRS #5.

19552 *Flashing swords! #3: Warriors and wizards.* New York: A Dell Book, 1976, 272 p., paper, anth.

19553 *Flashing swords! #4: Barbarians and black magicians.* Garden City, New York:

Nelson Doubleday, 1977, 183 p., cloth, anth.

19554 *Flashing swords! no. 5: Demons and daggers.* Garden City, New York: Nelson Doubleday, 1981, 184 p., cloth, anth.

19555 *Found wanting.* New York: DAW Books, 1985, 220 p., paper, novel.

35789 *History and chronology of the Book of Eibon.* New York: Charnel House, 1984, 8 p., paper, nonf.

19556 *Horror wears blue.* New York: Doubleday, 1987, 174 p., cloth, novel. PRINCE ZARKON #5.

19557 *Hurok of the stone age.* New York: DAW Books, 1981, 192 p., paper, novel. ERIC CARSTAIRS #3.

19558 *The immortal of world's end.* New York: DAW Books, 1976, 160 p., paper, novel. GONDWANE EPIC #3.

19559 *In the Green Star's glow.* New York: DAW Books, 1976, 192 p., paper, novel. GREEN STAR #5.

Invisible death—SEE: *Zarkon, Lord of the Unknown, in Invisible death.*

19560 *Journey to the underground world.* New York: DAW Books, 1979, 175 p., paper, novel. ERIC CARSTAIRS #1.

19561 *Kellory the warlock.* Garden City, NY: Doubleday & Co., 1984, 180 p., cloth, novel.

19562 *Kesrick.* New York: DAW Books, 1982, 176 p., paper, novel. TERRA MAGICA #1.

19563 *Kingdoms of sorcery.* Garden City, NY: Doubleday & Co., 1976, xv+218 p., cloth, anth.

19564 *Lankar of Callisto.* New York: A Dell Book, 1975, 203 p., paper, novel. JANDAR #6.

19565 *Lost worlds.* New York: DAW Books, 1980, 176 p., paper, coll. [Several stories are collaborations].

19566 *Mad empress of Callisto.* New York: A Dell Book, 1975, 191 p., paper, novel. JANDAR #4.

19567 *Mandricardo: new adventures in Terra Magica.* New York: DAW Books, 1987, 223 p., cloth, novel. TERRA MAGICA.

19568 *Mind wizards of Callisto.* New York: A Dell Book, 1975, 189 p., paper, novel. JANDAR #5.

Nemesis of evil—SEE: *Zarkon, Lord of the Unknown, in The nemesis of evil.*

19569 *Pirate of world's end.* New York: DAW Books, 1978, 173 p., paper, novel. GONDWANE EPIC #5.

19570 *Realms of wizardry.* Garden City, NY: Doubleday & Co., 1976, xv+269 p., cloth, anth.

19571 *Renegade of Callisto.* New York: A Dell Book, 1978, 218 p., paper, novel. JANDAR #8.

19572 *Tara of the twilight.* New York: Zebra Books, Kensington Publishing Corp., 1979, 288 p., paper, novel.

The volcano ogre—SEE: *Zarkon, Lord of the Unknown, in The volcano ogre.*

Warriors and wizards—SEE: *Flashing swords! #3.*

19573 *Weird tales #1.* New York: Zebra Books, Kensington Publishing Corp., 1980, 268 p., paper, anth.

19574 *Weird tales #2.* New York: Zebra Books, Kensington Publishing Corp., 1980, 265 p., paper, anth.

19575 *Weird tales #3.* New York: Zebra Books, Kensington Publishing Corp., 1981, 318 p., paper, anth.

19576 *Weird tales #4.* New York: Zebra Books, Kensington Publishing Corp., 1983, 288 p., paper, anth.

19577 *The wizard of Zao.* New York: DAW Books, 1978, 176 p., paper, novel. CHRONICLES OF KYLIX #2. [Sequel to *Quest of Kadji*].

19578 *The year's best fantasy stories.* New York: DAW Books, 1975, 175 p., paper, anth.

19579 *The year's best fantasy stories: 2.* New York: DAW Books, 1976, 192 p., paper, anth.

19580 *The year's best fantasy stories: 3.* New York: DAW Books, 1977, 237 p., paper, anth.

19581 *The year's best fantasy stories: 4.* New York: DAW Books, 1978, 208 p., paper, anth.

19582 *The year's best fantasy stories: 5.* New York: DAW Books, 1980, 204 p., paper, anth.

19583 *The year's best fantasy stories: 6.* New York: DAW Books, 1980, 191 p., paper, anth.

19584 *Ylana of Callisto.* New York: A Dell Book, 1977, 192 p., paper, novel. JANDAR #7.

19585 *Zanthodon.* New York: DAW Books, 1980, 188 p., paper, novel. ERIC CARSTAIRS #2.

19586 *Zarkon, Lord of the Unknown, in Invisible death, a case from the files of Omega.* Garden City, NY: Doubleday & Co., 1975, xii+173 p., cloth, novel. PRINCE ZARKON #2.

19586A retitled: *Zarkon, Lord of the Unknown and his Omega Crew: Invisible death.* New York: Popular Library, 1978, 192 p., paper, novel. PRINCE ZARKON #2.

19587 *Zarkon, Lord of the Unknown, in The Earth-shaker, a case from the files of*

Omega. Garden City, NY: Doubleday & Co., 1982, xii+175 p., cloth, novel. PRINCE ZARKON #4.

19588 *Zarkon, Lord of the Unknown, in The nemesis of evil, a case from the files of Omega*. Garden City, NY: Doubleday & Co., 1975, xiv+172 p., cloth, novel. PRINCE ZARKON #1.

19588A retitled: *The nemesis of evil*. New York: Popular Library, 1978, 219 p., paper, novel. PRINCE ZARKON #1.

19589 *Zarkon, Lord of the Unknown, in The volcano ogre, a case from the files of Omega*. Garden City, NY: Doubleday & Co., 1976, xii+177 p., cloth, novel. PRINCE ZARKON #3.

19589A retitled: *Zarkon, Lord of the Unknown and his Omega Crew: The volcano ogre*. New York: Popular Library, 1978, 224 p., paper, novel. PRINCE ZARKON #3.

with Scott Bizar

18060 *Royal armies of the Hyborean Age: a wargamers guide to the age of Conan*. Roslyn, NY: Fantasy Games Unlimited, 1975, vii+56 p., paper, nonf.

with L. Sprague de Camp

19590 *Conan the barbarian*. Toronto, New York: Bantam Books, 1982, ix+181 p., paper, movie. CONAN SERIES.

19591 *Conan the liberator*. Toronto, New York: Bantam Books, 1979, 214 p., paper, novel. CONAN SERIES.

with L. Sprague de Camp & Robert E. Howard

19592 *The Conan chronicles*. London: Orbit, 1989, 569 p., paper, coll. CONAN #1-3.

19593 *The Conan chronicles 2*. London: Orbit, 1990, 531 p., paper, coll. CONAN SERIES. [Includes *Conan the Wanderer*; *Conan the Adventurer*; *Conan the Buccaneer*.]

19594 *Conan of Aquilonia*. New York: Prestige Books, 1977, xii+171 p., paper, coll. CONAN #11.

with L. Sprague de Camp & Björn Nyberg

19595 *Conan the swordsman*. Toronto, New York: Bantam Books, 1978, 274 p., paper, novel. CONAN SERIES.

with David Wenzel

19596 *Middle Earth: the world of Tolkien illustrated*. New York: Centaur Books, 1977, 64 p., paper, nonf.

CARTER, Margaret L(ouise), 1948-

19597 *Dracula: the vampire and the critics*. Ann Arbor, MI & London: UMI Research Press, 1988, xviii+253 p., cloth, nonf. anth. STUDIES IN SPECULATIVE FICTION #19.

19598 *Shadow of a shade: a survey of vampirism in literature*. New York: Gordon Press, 1975, viii+176 p., cloth, nonf.

19599 *Specter or delusion? the supernatural in gothic fiction*. Ann Arbor, MI & London: UMI Research Press, 1987, 131 p., cloth, nonf. STUDIES IN SPECULATIVE FICTION #15.

19600 *Vampire bibliography annual update, no. 1 (January, 1990)*. Annapolis, MD: [Margaret L. Carter], 1990, 18 p., paper, nonf.

19601 *Vampire bibliography annual update, no. 2 (January, 1991)*. Annapolis, MD: [Margaret L. Carter], 1991, 30 p., paper, nonf.

19602 *The vampire in literature: a critical bibliography*. Ann Arbor, MI & London: UMI Research Press, 1989, viii+135 p., cloth, nonf. STUDIES IN SPECULATIVE FICTION #21.

CARTER, Nick, house pseud.

35806 *Code name: werewolf*. New York: Award Books, 1973, 167 p., paper, novel. NICK CARTER SERIES. [By Martin Cruz Smith].

36402 *The death strain*. New York: Award Books; London: Tandem Books, 1971, 156 p., paper, novel. NICK CARTER SERIES. [By Jon Messmann].

16089 *Deathlight*. New York: Charter Books, 1982, 212 p., paper, novel. NICK CARTER SERIES. [By Jerry Ahern].

31758 *The devil's dozen*. New York: Award Books, 1973, 184 p., paper, novel. NICK CARTER SERIES. [By Martin Cruz Smith].

19603 *Doctor DNA*. New York: Ace Charter Books, 1982, 196 p., paper, novel. NICK CARTER SERIES. [By Robert E. Vardeman].

19604 *The doomsday spore*. New York: Charter, 1979, 242 p., paper, novel. NICK CARTER SERIES. [By George Warren].

02747 *The human time bomb: a Killmaster spy chiller*. New York: Award Books; London: Tandem Books, 1969, 154 p., paper, novel. NICK CARTER SERIES. [By William L. Rohde].

34389 *The Inca death squad.* New York: Award Books, 1972, 169 p., paper, novel. NICK CARTER SERIES. [By Martin Cruz Smith].

16270 *The last samurai.* New York: Charter Books, 1982, 197 p., paper, novel. NICK CARTER SERIES. [By Jerry Ahern].

19605 *Living death.* New York: Award Books; London: Tandem Books, 1969, 153 p., paper, novel. NICK CARTER SERIES. [By Jon Messmann].

36631 *Operation Moon Rocket.* New York: Award Books; London: Tandem Books, 1968, 160 p., paper, novel. NICK CARTER SERIES. [By Lew Louderback].

19315 *The Poseidon target.* New York: Jove Books, 1987, 198 p., paper, novel. NICK CARTER #232. [By Jack Canon].

19606 *The Q-Man.* New York: Charter, 1981, 217 p., paper, novel. NICK CARTER SERIES. [By John Stevenson].

19607 *The red rays.* New York: Award Books; London: Tandem Books, 1969, 153 p., paper, novel. NICK CARTER SERIES. [By Manning Lee Stokes].

19608 *The samurai kill.* New York: Charter Books, 1986, 200 p., paper, novel. NICK CARTER #215. [By Dennis Lynds].

19609 *The sea trap.* New York: Award Books; London: Tandem Books, 1969, 156 p., paper, novel. NICK CARTER SERIES. [By Jon Messmann].

19610 *The solar menace.* New York: Charter, 1981, 215 p., paper, novel. NICK CARTER SERIES. [By Robert E. Vardeman].

19316 *Tunnel for traitors.* New York: Charter Books, 1986, 196 p., paper, novel. NICK CARTER #214. [By Jack Canon].

CARTER, Noël Vreeland

19611 *Moondragon.* New York: A Signet Book, New American Library, 1979, 277 p., paper, novel.

CARTER, Paul A(llen), 1926-

19612 *The creation of tomorrow: fifty years of magazine science fiction.* New York: Columbia University Press, 1977, x+318 p., cloth, nonf. [Winner of the J. Lloyd Eaton Award for Best Nonfiction Book of the Year, 1976/1977 (1979)].

with Gregory Benford

17754 *Iceborn.* New York: Tor SF, A Tom Doherty Associates Book, 1989, 96 p., paper, novel. [Bound with *The Saturn Game* / by Poul Anderson].

CARTER, R(ebecca) M(arie) H(unt), 1955-

19613 *The dream killers.* London: Robert Hale, 1981, 192 p., cloth, novel.

CARTER, Tonya R., *with Paul B. Thompson*

19614 *Darkness & light.* Lake Geneva, WI: TSR Inc., 1989, 377 p., paper, novel. DRAGONLANCE PRELUDES #1.

19615 *DragonLance saga: Firstborn.* Lake Geneva, WI: TSR Inc., 1991, 305 p., paper, novel. ELVEN NATIONS TRILOGY #1.

19615 *DragonLance saga: The Qualinesti.* Lake Geneva, WI: TSR Inc., 1991, 310 p., paper, novel. ELVEN NATIONS TRILOGY #3.

Firstborn—SEE: *DragonLance saga: Firstborn.*

The Qualinesti—SEE: *DragonLance saga: The Qualinesti.*

19616 *Red sands: an Arabian adventure.* Lake Geneva, WI: TSR Inc., 1988, 338 p., paper, novel.

19617 *Riverwind the plainsman.* Lake Geneva, WI: TSR Inc., 1990, 313 p., paper, novel. DRAGONLANCE PRELUDES II #1.

CARTIANU, Ana, *as* TRANSLATOR

19618 *Romanian fantastic tales.* Bucharest, Romania: Minerva Publishing House, 1981, xxxvi+340 p., cloth, anth.

CARTIER, Edd, 1914-

19619 *Edd Cartier: the known and the unknown.* Saddle River, NJ: Gerry de la Ree, 1977, 128 p., cloth, art. [Edited by Dean Cartier].

CARTLAND, Barbara [i.e., Barbara Hamilton Cartland McCorquodale], 1901-

19620 *The black panther.* London: Rich & Cowan, 1939, 320 p., cloth, novel.

19620A retitled: *Lost love.* New York: Pyramid Books, 1970, 239 p., paper, novel.

19621 *The ghost who fell in love.* New York: E. P. Dutton, 1978, 163 p., cloth, novel.

19622 *The ghost who fell in love.* New York: E. P. Dutton & Company, Inc., 1979, 246 p., cloth, coll. [Bound with *The chieftain without a heart* / by Barbara Cartland].

Lost love—SEE: *The black panther.*

CARTMILL, Cleve, 1908-1964

19623 *The space scavengers.* Chatsworth, CA: Major Books, 1975, 190 p., paper, novel.

CARVER, Jeffrey A(llan), 1949-

19624 *Clypsis.* Toronto, New York: A Byron Preiss Book, Bantam Books, 1987, xiii + 163 p., paper, novel. ROGER ZELAZNY'S ALIEN SPEEDWAY #1.

19625 *Down the stream of stars.* New York, Toronto: Spectra, Bantam Books, 1990, 355 p., paper, novel. CHANGELING STAR #2.

19626 *From a changeling star.* Toronto, New York: Spectra, Bantam Books, 1989, viii + 355 p., paper, novel. CHANGELING STAR #1.

19626 *The infinity link.* New York: Bluejay International Edition, 1984, 540 p., cloth, novel.

19627 *Panglor.* New York: A Dell Book, 1980, 268 p., paper, novel.

19628 *The rapture effect.* New York: Tor, A Tom Doherty Associates Book, 1987, 371 p., cloth, novel.

19629 *Seas of Ernathe* / by Jeffrey Carver. Toronto, New York: Laser Books, 1976, 190 p., paper, novel.

19630 *Star rigger's way.* Garden City, NY: Nelson Doubleday, 1978, 214 p., cloth, novel.

CASANOVA DE SEINGALT, Jacques [i.e., Giovanni Giacomo Jacopo Girolamo Casanova de Seingalt], 1725-1798

19631 *Casanova's "Icosameron"; or, The story of Edward and Elizabeth, who spent eighty-one years in the land of Megamicres, original inhabitants of Protocosmos in the interior of our globe.* New York: Jenna Press, 1986, 260 p., paper, novel. [Translation by Rachel Zurer of *Icosameron*].

CASARES, Adolfo Bioy—SEE: Bioy Casares, Adolfo

CASCIANI, Patricia Nada

19632 *The brains of Kalos.* Bognor Regis, West Sussex, England: New Horizons, 1983, 131 p., cloth, novel.

19633 *Ice planet.* Bognor Regis, West Sussex, England: New Horizons, 1982, 134 p., cloth, novel.

19634 *The lizards of Trianada.* New York, Washington: Vantage Press, 1983, 147 p., cloth, novel.

CASE, (Brian) David (Francis), 1937-

19635 *The third grave.* Sauk City, WI: Arkham House, 1981, 184 p., cloth, novel.

19636 *Wolf tracks.* New York: Belmont Tower Books, 1980, 240 p., paper, novel.

CASE, Tom [pseud. of Tony Knight]

19637 *Cook.* Reading, England: Tom Case, 1981, 190 p., paper, novel.

CASPER, Susan, 1947- , *with Gardner Dozois*

Jack the Ripper—SEE: Ripper!

19638 *Ripper!* New York: Tor Horror, A Tom Doherty Associates Book, 1988, xx + 427 p., paper, anth.

19638A retitled: *Jack the ripper.* London: Futura, 1988, 384 p., paper, anth.

with Gardner Dozois & Jack Dann & Jack C. Haldeman II & Michael Swanwick

19639 *Slow dancing through time.* Kansas City, MO: Ursus Imprints; Shingletown, CA: Mark V. Ziesing, 1990, xvii + 253 p., cloth, coll. [All the stories are collaborations by Dozois with other writers, the majority with Jack Dann].

CASPIAN, Jonatha Ariadne

19640 *The nightmare dream.* Honesdale, PA: West End Books, 1990, 314 p., paper, novel. TORG: THE POSSIBILITY WARS #3. [Novelization of a game].

CASS, DeLysle Ferree, 1887-1973

19641 *As it is written* / by Clark Ashton Smith. West Kingston, RI: Donald M. Grant, Publisher, 1982, 125 p., cloth, novel. [Originally thought to have been written by Smith, and published under his name, but later determined from payment records of the original pulp magazine publisher to have been penned by DeLysle Ferree Cass].

CASSABA, Carlos, pseud.—SEE: Parry, Michel

CASSEDY, Sylvia, 1930-1989

19642 *Behind the attic wall.* New York: Thomas Y. Crowell, 1983, 315 p., cloth, novel.

CASSIDAY, Bruce (Bingham), 1920-

as CARSON BINGHAM

19643 *Flash Gordon: The war of the Cybernauts.* New York: Avon, 1975, 143 p., paper, novel. FLASH GORDON #6.
The war of the Cybernauts—SEE: *Flash Gordon: The war of the Cybernauts.*

as ANNIE LAURIE MCALLISTER

19644 *Queen of the looking glass.* New York: A Berkley Medallion Book, Berkley Publishing Corp., 1978, 219 p., paper, novel.

as ANNIE LAURIE MCMURDIE

09955 *Nightmare hall.* New York: Lancer Books, 1973, 303 p., paper, novel.

with Dieter Wuckel

19645 *The illustrated history of science fiction.* New York: Ungar, 1989, viii+251 p., cloth, nonf. [Translation by Jenny Vowles of *Science fiction: eine illustrierte literaturgeschichte*].

CASSUTT, Michael (Joseph), 1954-

19646 *Dragon season.* New York: Tor Fantasy, A Tom Doherty Associates Book, 1991, 247 p., paper, novel.
19647 *The star country.* Garden City, NY: Doubleday & Co., 1986, 180 p., cloth, novel.

with Andrew M. Greeley

19648 *Sacred visions.* New York: Tor, A Tom Doherty Associates Book, 1991, xiv+363 p., cloth, anth.

CASTEVANO, Roman

19649 *Rites of the demon.* New York: Tempo Books, Grosset & Dunlap Publishers, 1976, 154 p., paper, novel. DEATH-WALKER #1.

CASTILLA, Clyde Andre, 1907-1983

CASTLE, Damon, pseud.—SEE: Reinsmith, Richard

CASTLE, Mort, 1946-

19650 *Cursed be the child.* New York: Leisure Books, 1990, 357 p., paper, novel.

19651 *The deadly election.* Canoga Park, CA: Major Books, 1976, 176 p., paper, novel.
19653 *The strangers.* New York: Leisure Books, 1984, 320 p., paper, novel.

CASTO, Jackie

19654 *Daughter of destiny.* New York: Leisure Books, 1990, 365 p., paper, novel.
19655 *Dreams of destiny.* New York: Leisure Books, 1990, 363 p., paper, novel.

CASTORO, Laura—SEE: Parker, Laura

CASTRO, Adolphe de—SEE: de Castro, Adolphe

CATES, Emily

The ghost ferry—SEE: *Haunting with Louisa: The ghost ferry.*
The ghost in the attic—SEE: *Haunting with Louisa: The ghost in the attic.*
19656 *Haunting with Louisa: The ghost ferry.* New York: Bantam Skylark, 1991, 152 p., paper, novel. HAUNTING WITH LOUISA #3.
19657 *Haunting with Louisa: The ghost in the attic.* New York: Bantam Skylark, 1990, 146 p., paper, novel. HAUNTING WITH LOUISA #1.
19658 *Haunting with Louisa: The mystery of Misty Island Inn.* New York: Bantam Skylark, 1990, 146 p., paper, novel. HAUNTING WITH LOUISA #2.
The mystery of Misty Island Inn—SEE: *Haunting with Louisa: The mystery of Misty Island Inn.*

CATLEY, Melanie

19659 *Moonlight and magic.* New York: A Dell Book, 1986, 283 p., paper, novel.

CATLING, Patrick Skene, 1925-

19660 *John Midas in the dreamtimes.* New York: William Morrow & Co., 1986, 119 p., cloth, novel.

CATRAN, Jack, 1933-

19661 *Walden Three.* Sherman Oaks, CA: Pygmalion Books, Jade Publications, 1988, 422 p., paper, novel.

CAUSETT, William

37654 *Pirates in space.* London: S. Baker, 1953, 63 p., paper, story.

CAUTHEN, Irby B(ruce) Jr., 1919- , with J. Lasley Dameron

19662 *Edgar Allan Poe: a bibliography of criticism, 1827-1967.* Charlottesville, VA: Published for the Bibliographical Society of the University of Virginia by the University Press of Virginia, 1974, xvi+386 p., cloth, nonf.

CAVALIERO, Glen (Tilburn), 1927-

19663 *Charles Williams: poet of theology.* Grand Rapids, MI: Wm. B. Eerdmans Publishing Co., 1983, x+199 p., cloth, nonf.

CAVANAUGH, Sara

19664 *A woman in space.* New York: Tiara Books, 1981, 192 p., paper, novel.

CAVE, Hugh B(arnett), 1910-

19665 *The corpse maker.* Mercer Island, WA: Starmont House, 1988, xii+156 p., cloth, coll. STARMONT POPULAR CULTURE STUDIES #2. [Edited by Sheldon Jaffery].
19666 *Disciples of dread.* New York: Tor, A Tom Doherty Associates Book, 1988, 376 p., cloth, novel.
19667 *The evil.* New York: Charter Books, 1981, 309 p., paper, novel.
19668 *Legion of the dead.* New York: Avon, 1979, 224 p., paper, novel.
19669 *The lower deep.* New York: Tor Horror, A Tom Doherty Associates Book, 1990, 378 p., paper, novel.
19670 *Lucifer's eye.* New York: Tor Horror, A Tom Doherty Associates Book, 1991, 284 p., paper, novel.
19671 *Murgunstrumm, and others.* Chapel Hill, NC: Carcosa House, 1977, x+475 p., cloth, coll. [Winner of the World Fantasy Award for Best Single Author Fantasy Collection/Anthology, 1977 (1978)].
19672 *The Nebulon horror.* New York: A Dell Book, 1980, 238 p., paper, novel.
19673 *Shades of evil.* New York: Charter, 1982, 307 p., paper, novel.

CAVE, Peter, 1940-

19674 *House of cards.* London: Arthur Barker, 1977, 160 p., cloth, tele. NEW AVENGERS SERIES.
19675 *The new Avengers: Last of the cybernauts.* London: Arthur Barker, 1977, 156 p., cloth, tele. NEW AVENGERS SERIES.

with Margaret Wredden

19676 *Pisces rising.* London: Sidgwick & Jackson, 1978, 189 p., cloth, novel.

CAVENEY, Philip (Richard), 1951-

19677 *The sins of Rachel Ellis.* New York: St. Martin's Press, 1978, 213 p., cloth, novel.

CAWTHORN, James (Philip), 1929-

with Michael Moorcock

19678 *Fantasy: the 100 best books.* London: Xanadu, 1988, 216 p., cloth, nonf. [Mostly written by Cawthorn].

as PHILIP JAMES, with Michael Moorcock

19679 *The distant suns.* Llanfynydd, Dyfed, Wales: Unicorn Bookshop, 1975, 45 p., paper, novel.

CAZEDESSUS, Camille Jr., with John F. Roy & John Harwood

19680 *ERB-dom: a guide to issues no. 1-25.* Evergreen, CO: Opar Press, 1964, 23 p., paper, nonf.

CEBULASH, Mel, 1937-

19681 *Ghost dad: a novel.* New York: Berkley Books, 1990, 118 p., paper, movie.
19682 *The strongest man in the world.* New York, Toronto: Scholastic Book Services, 1975, 93 p., paper, movie.

CERASINI, Marc A., 1952- , with Charles E. Hoffman

19683 *Robert E. Howard.* Mercer Island, WA: Starmont House, 1987, 156 p., cloth, nonf. STARMONT READER'S GUIDE #35.

CERF, Christopher (Bennett), 1941- , with Michael K. Frith as I*N FL*M*NG

19684 *Alligator.* Boston, MA: A Vanitas Book, Harvard Lampoon, 1963, 77 p., paper, novel.

CERNA, Zlata, 1905- , with Václav Cerny & Miroslav Novák

19685 *Tales of the uncanny.* London, New York: Hamlyn, 1976, 211 p., cloth, coll. [Translation by Helen Notzl].

CERNY, Václav, *with Zlata Cerná & Miroslav Novák*

19685 *Tales of the uncanny.* London, New York: Hamlyn, 1976, 211 p., cloth, coll. [Translation by Helen Notzl].

CHADWICK, Paul—SEE: House, Brant

*CHADWICK, Philip George, <u>1893-1955</u>

CHAKOO, B(ansi) L(al), 1946-

19686 *Aldous Huxley and eastern wisdom.* Delhi, India: Atma Ram, 1981, xii+308 p., cloth, nonf.
19687 *William Golding revisited: a collection of original essays.* Bangalore & Bombay, India: Arnold Publishers, 1989, 150 p., cloth, nonf. anth.

CHALK, Gary, 1952- , *with Joe Dever*

19688 *Castle Death.* London: Beaver Books, 1986, 37+[194] p., paper, novel. LONE WOLF #7.
19689 *The Caverns of Kalte.* London: Sparrow Books, 1984, [192] p., paper, novel. LONE WOLF #3.
19690 *The chasm of doom.* London: Sparrow Books, 1985, [350] p., paper, novel. LONE WOLF #4.
19691 *Creatures from the depths.* London: Knight, 1989, 64 p., paper, novel. PRINCE OF SHADOWS #2.
19692 *Fire on the water.* London: Sparrow Books, 1984, [219] p., paper, novel. LONE WOLF #2.
19693 *Flight from the dark.* London: Sparrow Books, 1984, [160] p., paper, novel. LONE WOLF #1.
19694 *The jungle of horrors.* London: Beaver Books, 1987, 39+[198] p., paper, novel. LONE WOLF #8.
19695 *The kingdoms of terror.* London: Beaver Books, 1985, 36+[196] p., paper, novel. LONE WOLF #6.
19696 *The Lone Wolf adventures.* London: Hutchinson, 1984, [27+184] p., cloth, coll. LONE WOLF #1-2. [Includes *Flight from the dark* and *Fire on the water*].
19697 *The Magnamund companion.* London: Beaver Books, 1986, 96 p., paper, nonf.
19698 *Mean streets.* Sevenoaks, Kent, England: Knight, 1988, 63 p., paper, novel. PRINCE OF SHADOWS #1.
19699 *Shadow on the sand: including two Lone Wolf adventures.* London: Beaver Books, 1985, [400] p., paper, novel. Lone Wolf #5.

CHALKER, Jack L(aurence), 1944-

19700 *And the devil will drag you under: a novel.* New York: A Del Rey Book, Ballantine Books, 1979, vii+273 p., paper, novel.
19701 *The birth of Flux & Anchor.* New York: Tor SF, A Tom Doherty Associates Book, 1985, viii+374 p., paper, novel. SOUL RIDER #4.
19702 *Cerberus: a wolf in the fold.* New York: A Del Rey Book, Ballantine Books, 1982, 243 p., paper, novel. FOUR LORDS OF THE DIAMOND #2.
19703 *Charon: a dragon at the gate.* New York: A Del Rey Book, Ballantine Books, 1982, 289 p., paper, novel. FOUR LORDS OF THE DIAMOND #3.
19704 *Children of Flux & Anchor.* New York: Tor SF, A Tom Doherty Associates Book, 1986, 350 p., paper, novel. SOUL RIDER #5.
19705 *Dance band on the Titanic.* New York: A Del Rey Book, Ballantine Books, 1988, 339 p., paper, coll.
19706 *Dancers in the afterglow.* New York: A Del Rey Book, Ballantine Books, 1978, 198 p., paper, novel.
19707 *The demons at Rainbow Bridge.* New York: Ace Books, 1989, 375 p., cloth, novel. QUINTARA MARATHON #1.
19708 *Demons of the Dancing Gods.* New York: A Del Rey Book, Ballantine Books, 1984, 257 p., paper, novel. DANCING GODS #2.
19709 *Downtiming the night side.* New York: Tor SF, A Tom Doherty Associates Book, 1985, 284 p., paper, novel.
19710 *Empires of Flux & Anchor.* New York: Tor, A Tom Doherty Associates Book, 1984, 320 p., paper, novel. SOUL RIDER #2.
19711 *Exiles of the Well of Souls.* New York: A Del Rey Book, Ballantine Books, 1978, xi+337 p., paper, novel. WELL WORLD #2.
19712 *Four lords of the diamond.* Garden City, NY: Nelson Doubleday, 1983, 755 p., cloth, coll. FOUR LORDS OF THE DIAMOND #1-4.
19713 *The identity matrix, The.* New York: A Timescape Book, Pocket Books, 1982, 254 p., paper, novel.
19714 *A jungle of stars.* New York: Ballantine Books, 1976, 217 p., paper, novel.
19715 *The labyrinth of dreams.* New York: Tor SF, A Tom Doherty Associates Book, 1987, 320 p., paper, novel. G.O.D. INC. #1.

19716 *Lilith: a snake in the grass*. New York: A Del Rey Book, Ballantine Books, 1981, v+248 p., paper, novel. FOUR LORDS OF THE DIAMOND #1.

19717 *Lords of the middle dark*. New York: A Del Rey Book, Ballantine Books, 1986, 357 p., paper, novel. RINGS OF THE MASTER #1.

19718 *Masks of the martyrs*. New York: A Del Rey Book, Ballantine Books, 1988, 340 p., paper, novel. RINGS OF THE MASTER #4.

19719 *Masters of Flux & Anchor*. New York: Tor, A Tom Doherty Associates Book, 1985, 429 p., paper, novel. SOUL RIDER #3.

19720 *The maze in the mirror*. New York: Tor SF, A Tom Doherty Associates Book, 1989, 403 p., paper, novel. G.O.D. INC. #3.

19721 *Medusa: a tiger by the tail*. New York: A Del Rey Book, Ballantine Books, 1983, 294 p., paper, novel. FOUR LORDS OF THE DIAMOND #4.

19722 *The messiah choice*. New York: Bluejay Books, 1985, 380 p., cloth, novel.

19723 *Midnight at the Well of Souls*. New York: A Del Rey Book, Ballantine Books, 1977, viii+360 p., paper, novel. WELL WORLD #1.

19724 *The ninety trillion Fausts*. New York: Ace Books, 1991, 263 p., cloth, novel. QUINTARA MARATHON #3.

19725 *On writing*. Eugene, OR: Writer's Notebook Press, Pulphouse Publishing, 1991, 26 p., paper, nonf.

19726 *Pirates of the thunder*. New York: A Del Rey Book, Ballantine Books, 1987, 307 p., paper, novel. RINGS OF THE MASTER #2.

19727 *Quest for the Well of Souls*. New York: A Del Rey Book, Ballantine Books, 1978, xii+302 p., paper, novel. WELL WORLD #3.

19728 *The return of Nathan Brazil*. New York: A Del Rey Book, Ballantine Books, 1980, ix+289 p., paper, novel. WELL WORLD #4.

19729 *Riders of the winds*. New York: Ace Books, 1988, 276 p., paper, novel. CHANGEWINDS #2.

19730 *The River of Dancing Gods*. New York: A Del Rey Book, Ballantine Books, 1984, 263 p., paper, novel. DANCING GODS #1.

19731 *The run to Chaos Keep*. New York: Ace Books, 1991, 359 p., cloth, novel. QUINTARA MARATHON #2.

19732 *The shadow dancers*. New York: Tor SF, A Tom Doherty Associates Book, 1987, 284 p., paper, novel. G.O.D. INC. #2.

19733 *Songs of the dancing gods*. New York: A Del Rey Book, Ballantine Books, 1990, 322 p., paper, novel. DANCING GODS #4.

19734 *Spirits of Flux & Anchor*. New York: A Tom Doherty Associates Book, 1984, 320 p., paper, novel. SOUL RIDER #1.

19735 *Twilight at the Well of Souls: the legacy of Nathan Brazil*. New York: A Del Rey Book, Ballantine Books, 1980, x+304 p., paper, novel. WELL WORLD #5.

19736 *Vengeance of the dancing gods*. New York: A Del Rey Book, Ballantine Books, 1985, 303 p., paper, novel. DANCING GODS #3.

19737 *A war of shadows*. New York: Ace Books, 1979, 314 p., paper, novel.

19738 *War of the maelstrom*. New York: Ace Books, 1988, 360 p., paper, novel. CHANGEWINDS #3.

19739 *Warriors of the storm*. New York: A Del Rey Book, Ballantine Books, 1987, 338 p., paper, novel. RINGS OF THE MASTER #3.

19740 *The web of the Chozen*. New York: A Del Rey Book, Ballantine Books, 1978, 212 p., paper, novel.

19741 *When the changewinds blow*. New York: Ace Books, 1987, 293 p., paper, novel. CHANGEWINDS #1.

with Mark Owings

19742 *The science-fantasy publishers: a critical and bibliographic history, 3rd ed., rev. and enlarged*. Westminster, MD: The Mirage Press, 1991, xxviii+744 p., cloth, nonf.

with Mike Resnick & George Alec Effinger

19743 *The red tape war*. New York: Tor, A Tom Doherty Associates Book, 1991, ix+244 p., cloth, novel.

CHALMERS, Garet

19744 *Homo-hetero*. London: Robert Hale, 1980, 189 p., cloth, novel.

19745 *A legend in his own deathtime*. London: Robert Hale, 1978, 192 p., cloth, novel.

*CHAMBERLAIN, (Edwin) William, 1903-<u>1969</u>?

CHAMBERS, Aidan, 1934-

19746 *The bumper book of ghost stories.* London & Sydney: Pan Books, 1976, 381 p., paper, anth. [Includes *The tenth ghost book* and *The eleventh ghost book*].

19747 *The eleventh ghost book.* London: Barrie & Jenkins, 1975, 190 p., cloth, anth.

19748 *Ghost after ghost.* Harmondsworth, Middlesex, England: Kestrel Books, 1982, 172 p., cloth, anth.

19749 *Ghost carnival: stories of ghosts in their haunts.* London: Heinemann, 1977, 152 p., cloth, coll.

19750 *Ghosts that haunt you.* Harmondsworth, Middlesex, England: Kestrel Books, 1980, 168 p., cloth, anth.

19751 *A haunt of ghosts*: stories. New York: A Charlotte Zolotow Book, Harper & Row, 1987, xi+177 p., cloth, anth.

19752 *Out of time: stories of the future.* London: Bodley Head, 1984, 155 p., paper, anth.

19753 *A quiver of ghosts.* London: Bodley Head, 1987, 136 p., paper, anth.

19754 *Shades of dark: ghost stories.* London: Hardy, 1984, 126 p., cloth, anth.

as MALCOLM BLACKLIN

19755 *Ghosts four.* Basingstoke, Hampshire, England: Macmillan, 1978, 121 p., paper, anth.

with Nancy Chambers

19756 *Ghosts.* London: M Books, Macmillan, 1990, [128] p., cloth, anth.

CHAMBERS, Jane, 1937-1983

19757 *Burning.* New York: A Jove/HBJ Book, 1978, 157 p., paper, novel.

CHAMBERS, Nancy, *with Aidan Chambers*

19756 *Ghosts.* London: M Books, Macmillan, 1990, [128] p., cloth, anth.

CHAMBERS, Robert W(illiam), 1865-1933, *with Arthur Machen*

19758 *Kings of horror.* North Hollywood, CA: Ken Krueger, 1975, 80 p., paper, coll.

CHAMBERS, Robin (Bernard), 1942-

19759 *The fight of neither century, and other stories.* Toronto: Granada, 1980, 121 p., cloth, coll.

19760 *The ice warrior, and other stories.* Harmondsworth, Middlesex, England: Kestrel Books, 1976, 142 p., cloth, coll.

19761 *Shadows in the pit.* London, Toronto: A Dragon Book, Granada, 1980, 94 p., paper, novel.

*CHAMBERS, (Elwyn) Whitman, 1896-1968

CHAMPIE, Channing K.

19762 *Worlds on fire.* New York, Washington: Vantage Press, 1979, 193 p., cloth, novel.

CHANADY, Amaryll Beatrice, 1954-

19763 *Magical realism and the fantastic: resolved versus unresolved antinomy.* New York: Garland Publishing, 1985, ix+183 p., cloth, nonf.

CHANCE, John Newton—SEE: Lymington, John

CHANCELLOR, Ann Laymon

19764 *Costumes, creatures, and characters.* Cambridge, MA: NESFA Press, 1980, 36 p., paper, nonf. anth.

CHANDLER, A(rthur) Bertram, 1912-1984

19765 *The anarch lords.* New York: DAW Books, 1981, 208 p., paper, novel. GRIMES SERIES.

19766 *The big black mark.* New York: DAW Books, 1975, 224 p., paper, novel. GRIMES SERIES.

19767 *The broken cycle.* London: Robert Hale, 1975, 158 p., cloth, novel. GRIMES SERIES.

19768 *The commodore at sea; [and, Spartan planet].* New York: Ace Books, 1979, 374 p., paper, coll. GRIMES DOUBLE #5.

19769 *The dark dimensions; [and, The Rim gods].* New York: Ace Books, 1978, 406 p., paper, coll. GRIMES DOUBLE #3.
The Far Traveler—SEE: *Far Traveler.*

19770 *Far Traveller.* London: Robert Hale, 1977, 188 p., cloth, novel. GRIMES SERIES.

19770A retitled: *The Far Traveler.* New York: DAW Books, 1979, 174 p., paper, novel. GRIMES SERIES.

19771 *From sea to shining star.* Fyshwick, Australian Capital Territory & Perth, Australia: Dreamstone, 1989, 342 p., cloth, coll. [Edited by Keith Curtis and Susan Chandler; limited to 500 copies].

19772 *Frontier of the dark.* New York: Ace Science Fiction Books, 1984, 233 p., paper, novel.

19773 *The inheritors; [and, Gateway to never].* New York: Ace Books, 1978, 377 p., paper, coll. GRIMES DOUBLE #2.

19774 *Into the alternate universe; [and, Contraband from otherspace].* New York: Ace Books, 1979, 309 p., paper, coll. GRIMES DOUBLE #4.

19775 *Kelly country.* Ringwood, Victoria, Australia: Penguin Books with the Assistance of the Literature Board of the Australian Council, 1983, 341 p., paper, novel.

19776 *The last Amazon.* New York: DAW Books, 1984, 156 p., paper, novel. GRIMES SERIES—SPARTAN PLANET #2.

19777 *Matilda's stepchildren.* London: Robert Hale, 1979, 208 p., cloth, novel. GRIMES SERIES.

02853 *Rendezvous on a lost world.* New York: Ace Books, 1961, 124 p., paper, novel. [Bound with *The door through space* / by Marion Zimmer Bradley].

02853A retitled: *When the dream dies.* London: Allison & Busby, 1981, 128 p., cloth, novel.

19778 *The rim of space; The ship from outside.* New York: Ace Books, 1979, 312 p., paper, coll. DEREK CALVER #1-2.

19779 *The road to the Rim; [and, The hard way up].* New York: Ace Books, 1978, 340 p., paper, coll. GRIMES DOUBLE #1.

19780 *Star courier.* New York: DAW Books, 1977, 142 p., paper, novel. GRIMES SERIES.

19781 *Star loot.* New York: DAW Books, 1980, 223 p., paper, novel. GRIMES SERIES.

19782 *To keep the ship.* New York: DAW Books, 1978, 175 p., paper, novel. GRIMES SERIES.

19783 *Up to the sky in ships.* Cambridge, MA: A Chicon IV Publication, NESFA Press, 1982, iv+94 p., cloth, novel. [Bound with *In and out of quandry* / by Lee Hoffman].

19784 *The way back.* London: Robert Hale, 1976, 149 p., cloth, novel. GRIMES SERIES.

When the dream dies—SEE: *Rendezvous on a lost world.*

19785 *The wild ones.* St. Kilda, Victoria, Australia: Paul Collins, 1984, 204 p., paper, novel. GRIMES SERIES.

CHANDLER, Bryn, 1945-

19786 *Dying light.* New York: A Signet Book, New American Library, 1979, 185 p., paper, novel.

19787 *Eve's rib.* New York: Pageant Books, 1989, 278 p., paper, novel.

CHANDLER, Glenn

19788 *The sanctuary.* London: Hamlyn Paperbacks, 1981, 171 p., paper, novel.

19789 *The tribe.* Feltham, England: Hamlyn Paperbacks, 1981, 187 p., paper, novel.

CHANDLER, Laurel, pseud.—SEE: Holder, Nancy

CHANG, Shi-Kuo, 1944-

19790 *Chess king: a novel.* Singapore: Asiapac, 1986, 182 p., paper, novel. [Translation by Ivan David Zimmerman of *Ch'i wang*].

*CHANNING, Mark, 1879-

CHANT, Joy [pseud. of Eileen Joyce Rutter], 1945-

19791 *Fantasy and allegory in literature for young people.* Aberystwyth, Wales: College of Librarianship, 1971, 31 p., paper, nonf.

19792 *The grey mane of morning.* London: George Allen & Unwin, 1977, 262 p., cloth, novel.

19793 *The high kings.* London: George Allen & Unwin, 1983, 237 p., cloth.

19794 *When Voiha wakes.* London: Unwin Paperbacks, 1983, 168 p., paper, novel.

CHAPDELAINE, Perry A(nthony Sr.), 1925-

19795 *The laughing Terran.* London: Robert Hale, 1977, 176 p., cloth, novel.

19796 *Spork of the Ayor.* London: Robert Hale, 1978, 208 p., cloth, novel.

CHAPLIN, Patrice, 1940-

19797 *Forget me not.* London: Methuen, 1989, 311 p., cloth, novel.

CHAPMAN, Andrew (Edward), 1960-

The rings of Kether—SEE: *Steve Jackson and Ian Livingstone presesnt The rings of Kether.*

19798 *Seas of blood.* Harmondsworth, Middlesex, England: Penguin Books, 1985, [249] p., paper, novel. FIGHTING FANTASY GAMEBOOK #16.

19799 *Space assassin.* Harmondsworth, Middlesex, England: Penguin Books, 1985,

[196] p., paper, novel. FIGHTING FANTASY GAMEBOOK #12.

19800 *Steve Jackson and Ian Livingstone presesnt The rings of Kether.* Harmondsworth, Middlesex, England: Penguin Books, 1986, [200] p., paper, novel. FIGHTING FANTASY GAMEBOOK #15.

CHAPMAN, Clodagh [pseud. of Clodagh Gibson-Jarvie], 1923-

19801 *The echoes answer.* London: Piatkus, 1989, 237 p., cloth, novel.

19802 *The night before dark.* London: Piatkus, 1988, 197 p., cloth, novel.

CHAPMAN, D. D., *with Deloris Lehman Tarzan*

19803 *Red tide.* New York: Ace Books, 1975, 239 p., paper, novel.

CHAPMAN, Edgar L(eon), 1936-

19804 *The magic labyrinth of Philip José Farmer.* San Bernardino, CA: R. Reginald, The Borgo Press, 1984, 96 p., cloth, nonf. THE MILFORD SERIES: POPULAR WRITERS OF TODAY #38.

CHAPMAN, John, 1947-

19805 *City war.* London: Robert Hale, 1979, 192 p., cloth, novel.

CHAPMAN, Vera, 1898-

19806 *Blaedud the birdman.* London: Rex Collings, 1978, 146 p., cloth, novel.

19807 *The green knight.* London: Rex Collings, 1975, 148 p., cloth, novel. THREE DAMOSELS SERIES #1.

19808 *King Arthur's daughter.* London: Rex Collings, 1976, 153 p., cloth, novel. THREE DAMOSELS #3.

19809 *The king's damosel.* London: Rex Collings, 1976, 123 p., cloth, novel. THREE DAMOSELS #2.

19810 *Miranty and the alchemist.* New York: An Avon Camelot Book, 1983, 95 p., paper, novel.

19811 *The three damosels.* London: Magnum Books, Methuen Paperbacks, 1978, 352 p., paper, coll. THREE DAMOSELS #1-3.

CHAPPELL, Fred (Davis), 1936-

19812 *Dagon.* New York: Harcourt, Brace & World, 1968, 177 p., cloth, novel. CTHULHU MYTHOS.

19813 *The Fred Chappell reader.* New York: St. Martin's Press, 1987, xx+491 p., cloth, coll. CTHULHU MYTHOS. [Includes *Dagon*].

19814 *More shapes than one.* New York: St. Martin's Press, 1991, 197 p., cloth, coll.

CHARBONNEAU, Eileen

19815 *The ghosts of Stony Clove.* New York: Orchard Books, 1988, 150 p., cloth, novel.

CHARBONNEAU, Louis (Henry), 1924-

19816 *Embryo: a novel.* New York: Warner Books, 1976, 191 p., paper, movie.

CHARBONNIER, Marc [pseud. of Vernon Coleman], 1946-

19817 *Tunnel.* London: Robert Hale, 1980, 174 p., cloth, novel.

CHARETTE, Beverly (Rae)

with Jean Blashfield

18129 *Star rangers and the spy.* Lake Geneva, WI: TSR Inc., 1984, 77 p., paper, novel. FANTASY FOREST BOOK #6.

with Mario D. Macari

37655 *Star rangers meet the solar robot.* Lake Geneva, WI: TSR Inc., 1984, 77 p., paper, novel. FANTASY FOREST BOOK #8.

CHARLES, Neil, house pseud.—SEE: Holloway, Brian & Hughes, Dennis Talbot

CHARLES, Robert [pseud. of Robert Charles Smith], 1938-

The comet—SEE: *Nightworld.*

19818 *Flowers of evil.* London: Macdonald Futura, 1981, 254 p., paper, novel.

19819 *Nightworld.* London: Corgi Books, 1984, 350 p., paper, novel.

19819A retitled: *The comet.* New York: Tor, A Tom Doherty Associates Book, 1985, 351 p., paper, novel.

CHARLES, Steven, pseud.—SEE: Grant, Charles L.

CHARLTON, William (E.), *with Aidan Reynolds*

19820 *Arthur Machen: a short account of his life and work.* London: John Baker for the

Richard Press, 1963, xiv+202 p., cloth, nonf.

CHARNAS, Suzy McKee, 1939-

19821 *The bronze king.* Boston: Houghton Mifflin Co., 1985, 196 p., cloth, novel. SORCERY HALL #1.

19822 *Dorothea dreams.* New York: Arbor House, 1986, 308 p., cloth, novel.

19823 *The golden thread.* New York, Toronto: Bantam Books, 1989, 209 p., cloth, novel. SORCERY HALL #3.

19824 *Listening to Brahms.* Eugene, OR: Pulphouse Publishing, 1991, 46 p., paper, story. SHORT STORY PAPERBACKS #19.

19825 *Motherlines.* New York: Berkley Publishing Corp., 1978, 273 p., cloth, novel. WALK #2.

19826 *The silver glove.* Toronto, New York: Bantam Books, 1988, 162 p., cloth, novel. SORCERY HALL #2.

19827 *The vampire tapestry.* New York: Simon & Schuster, 1980, 285 p., cloth, novel. VAMPIRE CHRONICLES #1.

19828 *Walk to the end of the world; and, Motherlines.* London: The Women's Press, 1989, 436 p., paper, coll. WALK #1-2.

*CHARQUES, Dorothy (Taylor), 1899-1976

CHARRETTE, Robert N.

19829 *Battletech: Heir to the dragon.* Delavan, WI: FASA, 1989, 338 p., paper, novel. BATTLETECH SERIES.

19830 *Battletech: Wolves on the border.* Delavan, WI: FASA, 1989, 337 p., paper, novel. BATTLETECH SERIES.

Choose your enemies carefully—SEE: *Shadowrun: Choose your enemies carefully.*

Find your own truth—SEE: *Shadowrun: Find your own truth.*

Heir to the dragon—SEE: *Battletech: Heir to the dragon.*

Never deal with a dragon—SEE: *Shadowrun: Never deal with a dragon.*

19831 *Shadowrun: Choose your enemies carefully.* New York: A Roc Book, 1991, 373 p., paper, novel. SECRETS OF POWER #2.

19832 *Shadowrun: Find your own truth.* New York: A Roc Book, 1991, 329 p., paper, novel. SECRETS OF POWER #3.

19833 *Shadowrun: Never deal with a dragon.* New York: A Roc Book, 1990, 377 p., paper, novel. SECRETS OF POWER #1. [Novelization of *Shadowrun* game].

Wolves on the border—SEE: *Battletech: Wolves on the border.*

CHARTAIR, Max, pseud.—SEE: Glasby, John

CHARTERIS, Leslie [legalized from Leslie Charles Bowyer Yin], 1907-

19834 *The fantastic Saint.* Garden City, NY: Doubleday & Co., 1982, x+180 p., cloth, coll. [Edited by Martin Harry Greenberg and Charles G. Waugh].

*CHARTERS, David Wilton, 1900-1972

CHARYN, Jerome, 1937-

37656 *Pinocchio's nose.* New York: Arbor House, 1983, 384 p., cloth, novel.

CHASE, Carol

19835 *Hawk's flight.* Riverdale, NY: Baen Books, 1991, 437 p., paper, novel.

CHASE, Glen, pseud.

23408 *The man who was God.* New York: Leisure Books, 1978, 190 p., paper, novel. CHERRY DELIGHT SERIES. [Possibly the work of Leonard Levinson (q.v.), who is known to have written books in this series].

*CHASE, James Hadley [pseud. of René Brabizon Raymond], 1906-1985

CHASE, Lewis (Nathaniel), 1873-1937

19836 *Poe and his poetry.* London: George G. Harrap & Co., 1913, 129 p., cloth, nonf.

CHASE, Mary (Coyle), 1907-1981

15793 *Loretta Mason Potts.* Philadelphia, PA: J. B. Lippincott, 1958, 221 p., cloth, novel.

CHASE, Robert R(eynolds), 1948-

19837 *Crucible.* New York: A Del Rey Book, Ballantine Books, 1991, 182 p., paper, novel. GAME #2.

19838 *The game of fox and lion.* New York: A Del Rey Book, Ballantine Books, 1986, 246 p., paper, novel. GAME #1.

19839 *Shapers.* New York: A Del Rey Book, Ballantine Books, 1989, 250 p., paper, novel.

CHATER, Elizabeth (Eileen Moore), 1910-

19840 *The Elsingham portrait.* New York: Fawcett Coventry, 1979, 223 p., paper, novel.
19841 *An introductory bibliography, giving a sampling of fantasy and science fiction* / by Elizabeth E. Chater. San Diego, CA: Friends of the Malcolm A. Love Library, San Diego State University, 1977, 17 p., paper, nonf.

CHATTERJEE, Sisir, 1919-

19842 *Aldous Huxley: a study.* Calcutta, India: Uttarayan, 1955, 132 p., cloth, nonf.
19843 *Aldous Huxley: a study, 2nd ed.* Calcutta, India: Firma K. L. Mukhopadhay, 1966, 117 p., cloth, nonf.

*CHATTERTON, E(dward) Keble, 1878-1944

CHAUVIN, Cy

19844 *A multitude of visions.* Baltimore, MD: T-K Graphics, 1975, 67 p., paper, nonf. anth.

CHAYEFSKY, Paddy [i.e., Sidney Aaron Chayefsky], 1923-1981

19845 *Altered states: a novel.* New York: Harper & Row, 1978, 184 p., cloth, novel.

CHAYEFSKY, Sidney A.—SEE: Chayefsky, Paddy

CHEETHAM, Ann

19846 *The beggar's curse.* London: Armada, 1984, 192 p., paper, novel. BLACK HARVEST #2.
19847 *Black harvest.* London: Armada, 1983, 143 p., paper, novel. BLACK HARVEST #1.
19848 *The pit.* London: Armada, 1987, 154 p., paper, novel. BLACK HARVEST #4.
19849 *The witch of Lagg.* London: Armada, 1985, 160 p., paper, novel. BLACK HARVEST #3.

CHENNEVIERE, Daniel—SEE: Rudhyar, Dane

CHERRY, Carolyn—SEE: Cherryh, C. J.

CHERRY, David A(lan), 1949-

19850 *Imagination: the art & technique of David A. Cherry.* Norfolk, VA: Donning Co., 1987, 110 p., cloth, art.

CHERRYH, C. J. [pseud. of Carolyn Janice Cherry], 1942-

19851 *Angel with the sword.* New York: DAW Books, 1985, 293 p., cloth, novel. MEROVINGEN NIGHTS #1.
19851A retitled: *Merovingen nights: Angel with the sword.* New York: DAW Books, 1986, 293 p., paper, novel. MEROVINGEN NIGHTS #1.
19852 *Arafel's saga.* Garden City, NY: Nelson Doubleday, 1983, 408 p., cloth, coll. EALDWOOD #1-2.
19852A retitled: *Ealdwood.* London: Victor Gollancz, 1991, 432 p., paper, coll. EALDWOOD #1-2.
The betrayal—SEE: *Cyteen: The betrayal.*
19853 *The book of Morgaine.* Garden City, NY: Nelson Doubleday, 1979, 633 p., cloth, coll. MORGAINE #1-3.
19853A retitled: *The chronicles of Morgaine.* London: Methuen, 1985, 682 p., cloth, coll. MORGAINE #1-3.
19854 *Brothers of Earth.* Garden City, New York: Nelson Doubleday, 1976, 246 p., cloth, novel.
19855 *Chanur's homecoming.* West Bloomfield, MI: Phantasia Press, 1986, 312 p., cloth, novel. CHANUR #4.
19856 *Chanur's venture.* Huntington Woods, MI: Phantasia Press, 1984, 201 p., cloth, novel. CHANUR #2.
19857 *Chernevog.* Norwalk, CT: Easton Press, 1990, 328 p., cloth, novel. RUSALKA #2.
The chronicles of Morgaine—SEE: *The book of Morgaine.*
19858 *Cuckoo's egg.* Huntington Woods, MI: Phantasia Press, 1985, 206 p., cloth, novel.
19859 *Cyteen.* New York: Warner Books, 1988, 680 p., cloth, novel. CYTEEN. [Broken into three parts for paperback reprint; winner of the Hugo Award for Best Novel, 1988 (1989); winner of the *Locus* Award for Best Science Fiction Novel, 1988 (1989); winner of the *Science Fiction Chronicle* Award for Best Novel, 1988 (1989)].
19859A retitled: *Cyteen: The betrayal.* New York: Popular Library, 1989, 359 p., paper, novel. CYTEEN #1-A. [The original book split into three parts].
19859B retitled: *Cyteen: The rebirth.* New York: Popular Library, 1989, 248 p., paper, novel. CYTEEN #1-B. [The original book split into three parts].
19859C retitled: *Cyteen: The vindication.* New York: Popular Library, 1989, 308 p.,

paper, novel. CYTEEN #1-C. [The original book split into three parts].

Divine right—SEE: *Merovingen nights: Divine right*.

19860 *Downbelow Station*. New York: DAW Books, 1981, 432 p., paper, novel. DOWNBELOW STATION #1. [Winner of the Hugo Award for Best Novel, 1981 (1982)].

19861 *The dreamstone*. New York: DAW Books, 1983, 192 p., paper, novel. EALDWOOD #1. [Part of this book was originally published as *Ealdwood*].

19862 *Ealdwood*. West Kingston, RI: Donald M. Grant, Publisher, 1981, 142 p., cloth, novel. EALDWOOD #0.

Ealdwood—SEE: *Arafel's saga*.

Endgame—SEE: *Merovingen nights: Endgame*.

19863 *Exile's gate*. New York: DAW Books, 1988, 414 p., paper, novel. MORGAINE #4.

19864 *The faded sun: Kesrith*. Garden City, New York: Nelson Doubleday, 1978, 248 p., cloth, novel. FADED SUN #1.

19865 *The faded sun: Kutath*. Garden City, NY: Nelson Doubleday, 1979, 280 p., cloth, novel. FADED SUN #3.

19866 *The faded sun: Shon'jir*. Garden City, New York: Nelson Doubleday, 1978, 243 p., cloth, novel. FADED SUN #2.

Festival moon—SEE: *Merovingen nights: Festival moon*.

Fever season—SEE: *Merovingen nights: Fever season*.

19867 *The faded sun trilogy*. London: Methuen, 1987, 756 p., paper, coll. FADED SUN #1-3.

19868 *Fires of Azeroth*. New York: DAW Books, 1979, 236 p., paper, novel. MORGAINE #3.

Flood tide—SEE: *Merovingen nights: Flood tide*.

19869 *Forty thousand in Gehenna*. Huntington Woods, MI: Phantasia Press, 1983, 316 p., cloth, novel. DOWNBELOW STATION #3.

19870 *Gate of Ivrel*. New York: DAW Books, 1976, 191 p., paper, novel. MORGAINE #1.

19871 *Glass and amber*. Cambridge, MA: A Boskone Book, NESFA Press, 1987, 212 p., cloth, coll. [Includes some nonfiction].

19872 *Heavy time*. Norwalk, CT: Easton Press, 1991, 330 p., cloth, novel. MERCHANTER SERIES.

19873 *Hestia*. New York: DAW Books, 1979, 160 p., paper, novel.

19874 *Hunter of worlds*. Garden City, NY: Nelson Doubleday, 1977, 214 p., cloth, novel.

Kesrith—SEE: *Faded sun: The Kesrith*.

19875 *The Kif strike back*. Huntington Woods, MI: Phantasia Press, 1985, 294 p., cloth, novel. CHANUR #3.

Kutath—SEE: *Faded sun: The Kutath*.

19876 *Legions of Hell*. New York: Baen Books, 1987, 407 p., paper, novel. HEROES IN HELL #6.

19877 *Merchanter's luck*. New York: DAW Books, 1982, 208 p., paper, novel. DOWNBELOW STATION #2.

Merovingen nights: Angel with the sword—SEE: *Angel with the sword*.

19878 *Merovingen nights: Divine right*. New York: DAW Books, 1989, 343 p., paper, anth. MEROVINGEN NIGHTS #5.

19879 *Merovingen nights: Endgame*. New York: DAW Books, 1991, 312 p., paper, anth. MEROVINGEN NIGHTS #7.

19880 *Merovingen nights: Festival moon*. New York: DAW Books, 1987, viii+300 p., paper, anth. MEROVINGEN NIGHTS #1.

19881 *Merovingen nights: Fever season*. New York: DAW Books, 1987, 297 p., paper, anth. MEROVINGEN NIGHTS #2.

19882 *Merovingen nights: Flood tide*. New York: DAW Books, 1990, viii+340 p., paper, anth. MEROVINGEN NIGHTS #6.

19883 *Merovingen nights: Smuggler's gold*. New York: DAW Books, 1988, 293 p., paper, anth. MEROVINGEN NIGHTS #4.

19884 *Merovingen nights: Troubled waters*. New York: DAW Books, 1988, 292 p., paper, anth. MEROVINGEN NIGHTS #3.

19885 *The paladin*. New York: Baen Books, 1988, 383 p., paper, novel.

19886 *Port Eternity*. New York: DAW Books, 1982, 191 p., paper, novel.

19887 *The Pride of Chanur*. New York: DAW Books, 1982, 224 p., paper, novel. CHANUR #1.

The rebirth—SEE: *Cyteen: The rebirth*.

19888 *Rimrunners*. New York: Warner Books, 1989, 327 p., cloth, novel.

19889 *Rusalka*. Norwalk, CT: Easton Press, 1989, 374 p., cloth, novel. RUSALKA #1.

19890 *Serpent's reach*. Garden City, NY: Nelson Doubleday, 1980, 312 p., cloth, novel.

Shon'jir—SEE: *Faded sun: Shon'jir*.

Smuggler's gold—SEE: *Merovingen nights: Smuggler's gold*.

19891 *Sunfall*. New York: DAW Books, 1981, 158 p., paper, coll.

19892 *The tree of swords and jewels*. New York: DAW Books, 1983, 254 p., paper, novel. EALDWOOD #2.

Troubled waters—SEE: *Merovingen nights: Troubled waters.*
The vindication—SEE: *Cyteen: The vindication.*

19893 *Visible light.* West Bloomfield, MI: Phantasia Press, 1986, 230 p., cloth, coll.

19894 *Voyager in night.* New York: DAW Books, 1984, 221 p., paper, novel.

19895 *Wave without a shore.* New York: DAW Books, 1981, 176 p., paper, novel.

19896 *Well of Shiuan.* New York: DAW Books, 1978, 253 p., paper, novel. MORGAINE #2.

19897 *Yvgenie.* New York: A Del Rey Book, Ballantine Books, 1991, 280 p., cloth, novel. RUSALKA #3.

with Nancy Asire

17059 *Wizard spawn.* New York: Baen, 1989, 275 p., paper, novel. SWORD OF KNOWLEDGE #2.

with Leslie Fish

19898 *A dirge for Sabis.* New York: Baen, 1989, 393 p., paper, novel. SWORD OF KNOWLEDGE #1.

with Mercedes Lackey

19899 *Reap the whirlwind.* New York: Baen, 1989, 273 p., paper, novel. SWORD OF KNOWLEDGE #3.

with Janet Morris

19900 *The gates of Hell.* New York: Baen Science Fantasy Books, 1986, 250 p., cloth, novel. HEROES IN HELL #3.

19901 *Kings in Hell.* New York: Baen Books, 1987, 375 p., paper, novel. HEROES IN HELL #4.

with Janet Morris & Jack Vance

37657 *Rhialto the Marvellous.* New York: Baen Books, 1985, 250 p., paper, anth. DYING EARTH #4; HEROES IN HELL. [Includes Vance's novel, plus the novella "Basileus" by Cherryh and Morris].

CHESBRO, George C(lark), 1940-

19902 *An affair of sorcerers.* New York: Simon & Schuster, 1979, 351 p., cloth, novel. MONGO #3.

19903 *The beasts of Valhalla.* New York: Atheneum, 1985, 329 p., cloth, novel. MONGO #4.

37658 *The city of whispering stone.* New York: Simon & Schuster, 1978, 236 p., cloth, novel. MONGO #2.

19904 *The cold smell of sacred stone.* New York: Atheneum, 1988, 297 p., cloth, novel. MONGO #6.

19905 *The fear in yesterday's rings.* New York: Mysterious Press, 1991, 214 p., cloth, novel. MONGO #10.

19906 *The golden child.* New York: Pocket Books, 1986, 221 p., paper, movie.

19907 *In the house of secret enemies.* New York: Mysterious Press, 1990, 234 p., cloth, coll. MONGO #9.

19908 *Jungle of steel & stone.* New York: Mysterious Press, 1988, 200 p., cloth, novel. VEIL KENDRY #2.

19909 *The language of cannibals.* New York: Mysterious Press, 1990, 200 p., cloth, novel. MONGO #8.

19910 *Second horseman out of Eden.* New York: Atheneum, 1989, 248 p., cloth, novel. MONGO #7.

19911 *Shadow of a broken man.* New York: Simon & Schuster, 1977, 252 p., cloth, novel. MONGO #1.

19912 *Two songs this archangel sings.* New York: Atheneum, 1986, 249 p., cloth, novel. MONGO #5.

19913 *Veil.* New York: Mysterious Press, 1986, 228 p., cloth, novel. VEIL KENDRY #1.

as DAVID CROSS

19914 *Chant.* New York: Jove Books, 1986, 231 p., paper, novel. CHANT #1.

19915 *Chant: Code of blood.* New York: Jove Books, 1987, 212 p., paper, novel. CHANT #3.

19916 *Chant: Silent killer.* New York: Jove Books, 1986, 217 p., paper, novel. CHANT #2.

Code of blood—SEE: *Chant: Code of blood.*
Silent killer—SEE: *Chant: Silent killer.*

CHESNEY, Marion [pseud. of Marion McChesney], 1936-

19917 *The ghost and Lady Alice.* New York: Fawcett Coventry, 1982, 222 p., paper, novel.

CHESTER, Deborah (A.)—SEE: Blakeney, Jay D.

CHESTER, Michael (Arthur), 1928-

19918   *The shores of the near past.* Hastings-on-Hudson, NY: School Street Press, 1986, 181 p., cloth, novel.

CHESTER, William L., 1907-1960?

19919   *Kioga of the unknown land.* New York: DAW Books, 1978, 222 p., paper, novel. KIOGA #4.

37659   *Kioga of the wilderness.* New York: DAW Books, 1976, 303 p., paper, novel. KIOGA #2.

19920   *One against a wilderness.* New York: DAW Books, 1977, 172 p., paper, novel. KIOGA #3.

CHESTERTON, G(ilbert) K(eith), 1874-1936

19921   *Daylight and nightmare: uncollected stories and fables.* London: Xanadu, 1986, 144 p., cloth, coll. [Edited by Marie Smith].

CHETWIN, Grace

19922   *The Atheling.* New York: Tor, A Tom Doherty Associates Book, 1988, 445 p., cloth, novel. LAST LEGACY #1.

19923   *Child of the air.* New York: Bradbury Press, 1991, 234 p., cloth, novel.

19924   *Collidescope.* New York: Bradbury Press, 1990, 221 p., cloth, novel.

19925   *The crystal stair.* New York: Bradbury Press, 1988, 225 p., cloth, novel. TALES OF GOM IN THE LEGENDS OF ULM #3.

19926   *Gom on Windy Mountain.* New York: Lothrop, Lee & Shepard Books, 1986, 206 p., cloth, novel. TALES OF GOM IN THE LEGENDS OF ULM #1.

19927   *On All Hollows' Eve.* New York: Lothrop, Lee & Shepard, 1984, 160 p., cloth, novel.

19928   *Out of the dark world.* New York: Lothrop, Lee & Shepard, 1985, 154 p., cloth, novel.

19929   *The riddle and the rune.* New York: Bradbury Press, 1987, 257 p., cloth, novel. TALES OF GOM IN THE LEGENDS OF ULM #2.

19930   *The starstone.* New York: Macmillan Publishing Co. 1989, 240 p., cloth, novel. TALES OF GOM IN THE LEGENDS OF ULM #4.

*CHETWYND, Bridget, 1910-

CHETWYND-HAYES, R(onald Henry Glynn), 1919-

    And love survived—SEE: *The dark man.*

19931   *The awakening: novelisation.* London: Magnum, 1980, 224 p., paper, movie.

19932   *The brats: a novel of the future.* London: William Kimber, 1979, 191 p., cloth, novel.

19933   *The cradle demon, and other stories of fantasy and terror.* London: William Kimber, 1978, 205 p., cloth, coll.

19934   *The curse of the snake god.* London: William Kimber, 1989, 191 p., cloth, novel.

02938   *The dark man.* London: Sidgwick & Jackson, 1964, 288 p., cloth, novel.

02938A   retitled: *And love survived.* New York: Zebra Books, Kensington Publishing Corp., 1979, 288 p., paper, novel.

19935   *Dominique.* New York: Belmont Tower Books, 1979, 172 p., paper, movie.

19936   *Doomed to the night: an anthology of ghost stories.* London: William Kimber, 1978, 207 p., cloth, anth.

19937   *Dracula's children.* London: William Kimber, 1987, 208 p., cloth, coll. DRACULA'S CHILDREN #1.

19938   *The eighteenth Fontana book of great ghost stories.* London: Fontana Paperbacks, 1982, 192 p., paper, anth.

19939   *The eleventh Fontana book of great ghost stories.* London: Fontana/Collins, 1975, 183 p., paper, anth.

19940   *The fantastic world of Kamtellar: a book of vampires and ghouls.* London: William Kimber, 1980, 189 p., cloth, coll.

19941   *The fifteenth Fontana book of great ghost stories.* London: Collins/Fontana, 1979, 191 p., paper, anth.

19942   *The fifth Armada monster book.* London: Armada, 1979, 127 p., paper, anth.

19943   *The first Armada monster book.* London: Armada, 1975, 125 p., paper, anth.

19944   *The fourteenth Fontana book of great ghost stories.* London: Collins/Fontana, 1978, 190 p., paper, anth.

19945   *The fourth Armada ghost book.* London: Armada, 1978, 125 p., paper, anth.

19946   *Gaslight tales of terror.* London: Collins, Fontana Books, 1976, 191 p., paper, anth.

37660   *Ghosts from the mist of time.* London: William Kimber, 1985, 205 p., cloth, coll. TALES OF CLAVERING GRANGE.

    The grange—SEE: *The king's ghost.*

19947   *The haunted grange.* London: William Kimber, 1988, 184 p., cloth, novel. TALES OF CLAVERING GRANGE.

19948   *The house of Dracula.* London: William Kimber, 1987, 206 p., cloth, coll. DRACULA'S CHILDREN #2.

19949 *The king's ghost.* London: William Kimber, 1985, 220 p., cloth, novel. TALES OF CLAVERING GRANGE.

19950 retitled: *The grange.* New York: Tor Horror, A Tom Doherty Associates Books, 1985, 249 p., paper, novel. TALES OF CLAVERING GRANGE.

19951 *The monster club.* London: New English Library, 1976, 192 p., paper, coll.

19952 *The night ghouls, and other grisly tales.* London: Fontana/Collins, 1975, 183 p., paper, coll.

19953 *The nineteenth Fontana book of great ghost stories.* London: Fontana Paperbacks, 1983, 191 p., paper, anth.

The other side—SEE: *Tales from the other side.*

19954 *The partaker: a novel of fantasy.* London: William Kimber, 1980, 224 p., cloth, novel.

19955 *A quiver of ghosts.* London: William Kimber, 1984, 207 p., cloth, coll.

19956 *The second Armada monster book.* London: Armada, 1976, 127 p., paper, anth.

19957 *The seventeenth Fontana book of great ghost stories.* London: Fontana/Collins, 1981, 190 p., paper, anth.

19958 *The sixteenth Fontana book of great ghost stories.* London: Fontana/Collins, 1980, 192 p., paper, anth.

19959 *The sixth Armada ghost book.* London: Armada, 1981, 128 p., paper, anth.

19960 *Tales from beyond.* London: William Kimber, 1982, 189 p., cloth, coll.

19961 *Tales from the dark lands.* London: William Kimber, 1984, 205 p., cloth, coll.

19962 *Tales from the haunted house.* London: William Kimber, 1986, 176 p., cloth, coll.

19963 *Tales from the hidden world.* London: William Kimber, 1988, 206 p., cloth, novel.

19964 *Tales from the other side.* London: William Kimber, 1983, 199 p., cloth, coll.

19964A retitled: *The other side.* New York: Tor Horror, A Tom Doherty Associates Book, 1988, xi+273 p., paper, coll.

19965 *Tales from the shadows.* London: William Kimber, 1986, 188 p., cloth, coll.

19966 *Tales of darkness.* London: William Kimber, 1981, 188 p., cloth, coll. TALES OF CLAVERING GRANGE.

19967 *Tales of fear and fantasy.* London: Fontana/Collins, 1977, 160 p., paper, coll.

19968 *Tales of terror from outer space.* London: Collins, Fontana Books, 1975, 190 p., paper, anth.

19969 *Tales of the hidden world.* London: William Kimber, 1988, 206 p., cloth, novel. TALES OF CLAVERING GRANGE.

19970 *The third Armada monster book.* London: Armada, 1977, 125 p., paper, anth.

19971 *The thirteenth Fontana book of great ghost stories.* London: Collins/Fontana, 1977, 189 p., paper, anth.

19972 *The twelfth Fontana book of great ghost stories.* London: Collins/Fontana, 1976, 190 p., paper, anth.

19973 *The twentieth Fontana book of great ghost stories.* London: Fontana/Collins, 1984, 190 p., paper, anth.

CHEW, Ruth, 1920-

19974 *Do-it-yourself magic.* New York, Toronto: Scholastic Inc., 1987, 127 p., paper, novel.

19975 *Earthstar magic.* New York, Toronto: Scholastic Book Services, 1979, 128 p., paper, novel.

19976 *The hidden cave.* New York: Scholastic Book Services, 1973, 128 p., paper, novel.

19976A retitled: *The magic cave.* New York: Holiday House, 1978, 128 p., cloth, novel.

The magic cave—SEE: *The hidden cave.*

19977 *The magic coin.* New York, Toronto: Scholastic Inc., 1983, 127 p., paper, novel.

19978 *Magic in the park.* New York: Scholastic Book Services, 1972, 127 p., paper, novel.

19979 *Magic of the black mirror.* New York, Toronto: A Little Apple Paperback, Scholastic Inc., 1990, 127 p., paper, novel.

19980 *Mostly magic.* New York, Toronto: Scholastic Book Services, 1982, 126 p., paper, novel.

19981 *No such thing as a witch.* New York: Scholastic Book Services, 1971, 112 p., paper, novel.

19982 *Royal magic.* New York, Toronto: Scholastic Inc., 1991, 127 p., paper, novel.

19983 *Secondhand magic.* New York, Toronto: Scholastic Book Services, 1981, 127 p., paper, novel.

19984 *Summer magic.* New York, Toronto: Scholastic Book Services, 1977, 112 p., paper, novel.

19985 *Trapped in time.* New York, Toronto: Scholastic Inc., 1986, 126 p., paper, novel.

19986 *The trouble with magic.* New York: Scholastic Book Services, 1976, 112 p., paper, novel.

19987 *The Wednesday witch.* New York: Scholastic Book Services, 1969, 128 p., paper, novel.

19988 *What the witch left.* New York: Scholastic Book Services, 1973, 128 p., paper, novel.

19989 *The wishing tree.* New York, Toronto: Scholastic Book Services, 1980, 141 p., paper, novel.

19990 *The witch and the ring.* New York, Toronto: Scholastic Inc., 1989, 126 p., paper, novel.

19991 *The witch at the window.* New York, Toronto: Scholastic Inc., 1984, 127 p., paper, novel.

19992 *Witch in the house.* New York: Scholastic Book Services, 1975, 112 p., paper, novel

19993 *Witch's broom.* New York, Toronto: Scholastic Book Services, 1977, 128 p., paper, novel.

19994 *The witch's buttons.* New York: Scholastic Book Services, 1974, 108 p., paper, novel.

19995 *The witch's garden.* New York, Toronto: Scholastic Book Services, 1978, 112 p., paper, novel.

19996 *The would-be witch.* New York: Scholastic Book Services, 1976, 112 p., paper, novel.

CHEYFITZ, Eric

19997 *The poetics of imperialism: translation and colonization from The tempest to Tarzan.* New York: Oxford University Press, 1991, xx+202 p., cloth, nonf.

CHIBA, Milan

19998 *Moonblaze.* New York: Leisure Books, 1981, 284 p., paper, novel.

CHILD, Lincoln

19999 *Dark banquet: a feast of twelve great ghost stories.* New York: St. Martin's Press, 1985, 255 p., cloth, anth.

20000 *Dark company: the ten greatest ghost stories.* New York: St. Martin's Press, 1984, x+334 p., cloth, anth.

20001 *Tales of the dark.* New York: St. Martin's Press, 1987, viii+184 p., paper, anth.

20002 *Tales of the dark #2.* New York: St. Martin's Press, 1987, x+181 p., paper, anth.

20003 *Tales of the dark #3.* New York: St. Martin's Press, 1988, x+179 p., paper, anth.

CHILD, Tim, *with Dave Morris*

20004 *Knightmare.* London: Young Corgi, 1988, 143 p., paper, novel. KNIGHTMARE SERIES.

CHILDER, Simon Ian, pseud.—SEE: Brosnan, John & Kettle, Leroy

CHILDERHOSE, R. J. "Chick", 1928-

20005 *The man who wanted to save Canada: a prophetic novel.* Victoria, British Columbia, Canada: Hoot Productions, 1975, 196 p., cloth, novel.

CHILSON, Rob(ert Dean), 1945-

20006 *Men like rats.* New York: Popular Library, 1989, 212 p., paper, novel.

20007 *Refuge.* New York: A Byron Preiss Visual Publications Inc. Book, Ace Books, 1988, xvi+163 p., paper, novel. ISAAC ASIMOV'S ROBOT CITY #5.

20008 *Rounded with sleep.* New York: Popular Library, 1990, 193 p., paper, novel.

20009 *The shores of Kansas* / by Robert Chilson. New York: Popular Library, 1976, 220 p., paper, novel.

20010 *The star-crowned kings* / by Robert Chilson. New York: DAW Books, 1975, 188 p., paper, novel.

*CHILTON, H(enry) Herman, 1863-

CHILTON, Paul (Anthony), 1944- , *with Crispin Aubrey*

17107 *Nineteen Eighty-Four in 1984: autonomy, control, and communication.* London: Comedia Publishing Group in Association with Marion Boyars, 1983, 120 p., cloth, nonf. anth.

CHIN, M. Lucie

20011 *The fairy of Ku-She.* New York: Ace Books, 1988, 265 p., paper, novel.

CHINN, Mike

20012 *Mystique: tales of wonder.* England: British Fantasy Society, 1988, 34 p., paper, anth.

CHITTENDEN, Margaret, 1935-

20013 *The scent of magic.* Toronto, New York: Harlequin Books, 1991, 300 p., paper, novel.
20014 *This time forever.* Toronto, New York: Harlequin Books, 1990, 252 p., paper, novel.

CHIU, Tony, 1945-

20015 *Realm seven.* Toronto, New York: Bantam Books, 1984, 279 p., paper, novel.

CHIVERS, Thomas Holley, 1807-1858

20016 *Life of Poe.* New York: E. P. Dutton, 1952, 127 p., cloth, nonf. [Edited by Richard Beale Davis].

CHIZMAR, Richard T(homas), 1965-

20017 *Cold blood.* Shingletown, CA: Mark V. Ziesing, 1991, xxi+401 p., cloth, anth.

CHOCHOLAK, Misha—SEE: Misha

CHODOS, Robert, 1946- , with Patrick Mac-Fadden & Rae Murphy

20018 *Your place or mine? an entertainment.* Ottawa, Ontario: Deneau & Greenberg, 1978, 240 p., paper, novel.

"CHOLA", pseud.

37661 *A new divinity, and other stories.* London: Longmans, Green & Co., 1899, 1899, viii+164 p., cloth, coll.

CHOLFIN, Bryan

20019 *Monochrome: the Readercon anthology.* Cambridge, MA: Broken Mirrors Press, 1990, 158 p., cloth, anth. [Includes some verse].

CHOWN, Marcus, 1959- , with John Gribbin

20020 *Double planet.* London: Victor Gollancz, 1988, 220 p., cloth, novel.
20021 *Reunion.* London: Victor Gollancz, 1991, 256 p., cloth, novel.

CHOYCE, Lesley (Willis), 1951-

20022 *The dream auditor: short stories.* Charlottetown, Prince Edward Island, Canada: Ragweed Press, 1986, 87 p., paper, coll.

with John Bell

17693 *Visions from the edge: an anthology of Atlantic Canadian science fiction and fantasy.* Porters Lake, Nova Scotia, Canada: Pottersfield Press, 1981, 215 p., cloth, anth.

CHRISTCHILD, Ravan

20023 *Agonies of time.* London: Dunscaith, 1989, 111 p., paper, coll.

*CHRISTIAN, Catherine (Mary), <u>1901-</u>

*CHRISTIAN, Emeline, <u>1909-1984</u>

*CHRISTIE, Douglas, <u>1894-</u>

CHRISTOPHER, Joe R(andall), 1935-

20024 *C. S. Lewis.* Boston: Twayne Publishers, 1987, 150 p., cloth, nonf.

with R. E. Briney and D. W. Dickensheet

18684 *A Boucher bibliography.* [White Bear Lake, MN: Allen J. Hubin], 1969, [34] p., paper, nonf. [Bound with *A Boucher portrait: Anthony Boucher as seen by his friends and colleagues* / edited by Lenore Glen Offord].

with Joan K. Ostling

20025 *C. S. Lewis: an annotated checklist of writings about him and his works.* Kent, OH: Kent State University Press, 1974?, xiii+389 p., cloth, nonf. THE SERIF SERIES #30.

CHRISTOPHER, John [pseud. of Christopher Samuel Youd], 1922-

20026 *In the beginning.* London: Longman, 1972, 63 p., paper, novel. [A brief, early version of *Dom and Va* (see #02975)].
Dragon dance—SEE: *Dragondance.*
20027 *Dragondance.* London: Viking Kestrel, 1986, 128 p., cloth, novel. FIREBALL #3.
20027A retitled; *Dragon dance.* New York: E. P. Dutton, 1986, 139 p., cloth, novel. FIREBALL #3.
20028 *Empty world.* London: Hamilton, 1977, 134 p., cloth, novel.
20029 *Fireball.* London: Victor Gollancz, 1981, 148 p., cloth, novel. FIREBALL #1.
In the beginning—SEE: *Dom and Va.*

20030 *New found land.* London: Victor Gollancz, 1983, 135 p., cloth, novel. FIREBALL #2.
20031 *The prince in waiting trilogy.* Harmondsworth, Middlesex, England: Puffin Books, 1983, 459 p., paper, coll. PRINCE IN WAITING #1-3. [Includes: *The prince in waiting; Beyond the burning lands; The sword of the spirits*].
20032 *When the tripods came.* New York: E. P. Dutton, 1988, 151 p., cloth, novel. TRIPODS SERIES PREQUEL.

as CHRISTOPHER YOUD

37662 *The winter swan.* London: Dennis Dobson, 1949, 268 p., cloth, novel.

with David Fickling

20033 *The death of grass.* Oxford, England: Alpha Books, Oxford University Press, 1979, 96 p., paper, novel. [Adapted by Fickling from Christopher's novel].

CHRISTOPHER, Matt(hew Frederick), 1917-

20034 *Devil pony.* Boston: Little, Brown & Co., 1977, 103 p., cloth, novel.
20035 *Favor for a ghost.* Philadelphia, PA: Westminster Press, 1983, 107 p., cloth, novel.
20036 *Ice magic.* Boston: Little, Brown & Co., 1973, 151 p., cloth, novel.

CHRISTOPHER, Paul

20037 *Beyond that river.* England: Pal Books, 1987, 288 p., paper, coll.
20038 *Galactic chronicles.* England: Pal Books, 1987, 128 p., paper, novel.

CHRONISTER, Alan B.

20039 *Cry wolf.* New York: Zebra Books, Kensington Publishing Corp., 1987, 320 p., paper, novel.

CHUDNOW, Yaffa—SEE: Bryan, Jessica

*CHURCH, Alfred J(ohn), 1861-

CHURCH, Ralph (Bruce), 1927-

20040 *Mork & Mindy.* New York: Pocket Books, 1979, 190 p., paper, tele. MORK & MINDY #1.

CHURCH, Richard, 1893-1972

20041 *Mary Shelley.* New York: Viking Press, 1928, 177 p., cloth, nonf.

CHURCHWARD, John [pseud. of W. J. Baker]

20042 *What beck'ning ghost?* London: New English Library, 1975, 199 p., cloth, novel.
20042A retitled: *What beckoning ghost.* New York: A Berkley Medallion Book, Berkley Publishing Corp., 1977, 214 p., paper, novel.
What beckoning ghost—SEE: *What beck'ning ghost.*

CHWAT, Aleksander—SEE: Wat, Aleksander

CIENCIN, (Malcolm) Scott, 1962-

as RICHARD AWLINSON

17144 *Forgotten realms fantasy adventure: Shadowdale.* Lake Geneva, WI: TSR Inc., 1989, 335 p., paper, novel. AVATAR TRILOGY #1. [Edited by James Lowder].
Shadowdale—SEE: *Forgotten realms fantasy adventure: Shadowdale.*

as RICHARD AWLINSON, *with James Lowder*

17145 *Forgotten realms fantasy adventure: Tantras.* Lake Geneva, WI: TSR Inc., 1989, 338 p., paper, novel. AVATAR TRILOGY #2.
Tantras—SEE: *Forgotten realms fantasy adventure: Tantras.*

as NICK BARON

Glory's end—SEE: *Robert Silverberg's Time Tours: Glory's end.*
20043 *Robert Silverberg's Time Tours: Glory's end.* New York: A Byron Preiss Book, HarperPaperbacks, 1990, 143 p., paper, novel. ROBERT SILVERBERG'S TIME TOURS #2. [Edited by Alice Alfonsi].

as NICK BARON, *with Greg Cox*

The pirate paradox—SEE: *Robert Silverberg's Time Tours: The Pirate paradox.*
20044 *Robert Silverberg's Time Tours: The Pirate paradox.* New York: A Byron Preiss Book, HarperPaperbacks, 1991, 139 p., paper, novel. ROBERT SILVERBERG'S TIME TOURS #5. [Edited by John Gregory Betancourt].

CIOFFI, Frank (L.), 1951-

20045 *Formula fiction? an anatomy of American science fiction, 1930-1940.* Westport, CT & London: Greenwood Press, 1982, xi+181 p., cloth, nonf. CONTRIBUTIONS TO THE STUDY OF SCIENCE FICTION AND FANTASY #3.

CIRILIUS, Marcus, pseud.

20046 *Prehistoric epic!* New York, Washington: Vantage Press, 1978, 178 p., cloth, novel.

CITRO, Joseph (A.)

20047 *Dark twilight.* New York: Warner Books, 1991, 211 p., paper, novel.
20048 *Guardian angels.* New York: Zebra Books, Kensington Publishing Corp., 1988, 411 p., paper, novel.
20049 *Shadow child* / by Joseph A. Citro. New York: Zebra Books, Kensington Publishing Corp., 1987, 367 p., paper, novel.
20050 *The unseen.* New York: Warner Books, 1990, 274 p., paper, novel.

CLAGETT, John (Henry), 1916-

20051 *The orange R.* New York: Popular Library, 1978, 256 p., paper, novel.
20052 *A world unknown.* New York: Popular Library, 1975, 238 p., paper, novel.

CLAIBORNE, Sybil, 1923-

20053 *Loose connections.* Chicago: Academy Chicago, 1988, 171 p., cloth, coll.

CLAIR, William R., *with Richard K. Abshire*

15926 *Gants.* Los Angeles: SOS Publications, 1985, 334 p., paper, novel. GANTS #1.
15927 *The shaman tree.* New York: A Thomas Dunne Book, St. Martin's Press, 1989, [256] p., cloth, novel. GANTS #2.

CLAIRE, Keith, pseud.—SEE: Andrews, Keith & Andrews, Claire

CLANCY, Judith S.

20054 *The ecotopian sketchbook: a book for drawing, coloring, writing, collaging, designing, thinking about & creating a new world.* Berkeley, CA: Banyan Tree Books, 1981, [48] p., paper, nonf. ECOTOPIA tie-in.

CLANCY, Thomas L.—SEE: Clancy, Tom

CLANCY, Tom [i.e., Thomas Leo Clancy Jr.], 1947-

20055 *Red storm rising.* New York: G. P. Putnam's Sons, 1986, 652 p., cloth, novel.
20056 *The sum of all fears.* New York: G. P. Putnam's Sons, 1991, 798 p., cloth, novel.

CLARE, John

20057 *The passionate invaders.* Garden City, NY: Doubleday & Co., 1965, 208 p., cloth, novel.

CLARE, Mariette

20058 *Doris Lessing and women's appropriation of science fiction.* Birmingham, England: Centre for Contemporary Cultural Studies, University of Birmingham, 1984, 52 p., paper, nonf.

CLAREMONT, Chris(topher Simon), 1950-

20059 *FirstFlight.* New York: Ace Books, 1987, 243 p., paper, novel. FIRSTFLIGHT #1.
20060 *Grounded!* New York: Ace Books, 1991, 323 p., paper, novel. FIRSTFLIGHT #2.

*CLARENS, Carlos (Figueredo y), 1936-<u>1987</u>

CLARESON, Thomas D(ean), 1926-

20061 *Frederik Pohl.* Mercer Island, WA: Starmont House, 1987, x+173 p., cloth, nonf. STARMONT READER'S GUIDE #39.
20062 *Many futures, many worlds: theme and form in science fiction.* Kent, OH: Kent State University Press, 1977, ix+303 p., cloth, nonf. anth.
20063 *Robert Silverberg.* Mercer Island, WA: Starmont House, 1983, 96 p., cloth, nonf. STARMONT READER'S GUIDE #18.
20064 *Robert Silverberg: a primary and secondary bibliography.* Boston: G. K. Hall, 1983, xxx+321 p., cloth, nonf. MASTERS OF SCIENCE FICTION AND FANTASY.
20065 *Science fiction in America, 1870s-1930s: an annotated bibliography of primary sources.* Westport, CT & London: Greenwood Press, 1984, xiv+305 p., cloth, nonf.
20066 *Some kind of paradise: the emergence of American science fiction.* Westport, CT & London: Greenwood Press, 1985, xiv+248 p., cloth, nonf. CONTRIBU-

TIONS TO THE STUDY OF SCIENCE FICTION AND FANTASY #16. [Winner of the J. Lloyd Eaton Award for Best Nonfiction Book of the Year, 1985 (1987)].

20067 *Understanding contemporary American science fiction: the formative period (1926-1970)*. Columbia, SC: University of South Carolina Press, 1990, vii+300 p., cloth, nonf.

20068 *Voices for the future: essays on major science fiction writers, volume I*. Bowling Green, OH: Bowling Green University Popular Press, 1976, 283 p., cloth, nonf. anth.

20069 *Voices for the future: essays on major science fiction writers, volume two*. Bowling Green, OH: Bowling Green University Popular Press, 1979, vii+208 p., cloth, nonf. anth.

with Thomas L. Wymer

20070 *Voices for the future, volume three*. Bowling Green, OH: Bowling Green University Popular Press, 1984, 220 p., cloth, nonf. anth.

CLARK, Beverly Lyon, 1948-

20071 *Lewis Carroll*. Mercer Island, WA: Starmont House, 1990, viii+96 p., cloth, nonf. STARMONT READER'S GUIDE #47.

20072 *Reflections of fantasy: the mirror-worlds of Carroll, Nabokov, and Pynchon*. New York, Berne: Peter Lang, 1986, x+195 p., cloth, nonf.

CLARK, Blair Foster—SEE: Foster, Blair

CLARK, Catherine Anthony (Smith), 1892-1977

20073 *The diamond feather; or, The door in the mountain: a magic tale for children*. Toronto: Macmillan of Canada, 1962, 224 p., cloth, novel.

20074 *The hunter and the medicine man*. Toronto: Macmillan of Canada, 1966, 183 p., cloth, novel.

20075 *The one-winged dragon*. Toronto: Macmillan of Canada, 1955, 271 p., cloth, novel.

20076 *The silver man*. Toronto: Macmillan of Canada, 1958, 231 p., cloth, novel.

20077 *The sun horse*. Toronto: Macmillan of Canada, 1951, 289 p., cloth, novel.

CLARK, Dale

20078 *Resolutions in time*. North Riverside, IL: Pandora Publications, 1980, 100 p., paper, novel.

CLARK, David Lee, 1887-1956

20079 *Brockden Brown and the rights of women*. Austin, TX: University of Texas, 1922, 48 p., paper?, nonf.

20080 *Charles Brockden Brown: pioneer voice of America*. Durham, NC: Duke University Press, 1952, xi+363 p., cloth, nonf.

CLARK, Douglas W.

20081 *Alchemy unlimited*. New York: Avon Books, 1990, 310 p., paper, novel.

CLARK, Joan, 1934-

20082 *Wild man of the woods*. Markham, Ontario, Canada: Viking Kestrel, 1985, 171 p., cloth, novel.

CLARK, Karen, 1960-

20083 *The synthetics*. London: Merlin, 1988, 52 p., paper, story.

CLARK, Leigh

20084 *Blood sabbath*. New York: Zebra Books, Kensington Publishing Corp., 1991, 416 p., paper, novel.

20085 *The feeding*. New York: Leisure Books, 1988, 352 p., paper, novel.

CLARK, Lydia Benson [pseud. of Eloise Meeker], 1915-

20086 *Demon cat*. New York: Zebra Books, Kensington Publishing Corp., 1975, 222 p., paper, novel.

20086A *Seance for Susan*. New York: Zebra Books, Kensington Publishing Corp., 1977, 222 p., paper, novel.

CLARK, Mark, 1946-

20087 *Ripper: a novel*. Kingston, Ontario, Canada: Byren House Publishing, 1987, 297 p., cloth, novel.

CLARK, Mary

37663 *Stop that witch!* Lake Geneva, WI: TSR Inc., 1985, 142 p., paper, novel. ENDLESS QUEST CRIMSON CRYSTAL ADVENTURE #4.

CLARK, Michael

20088 *The proteus vector.* New York: Pinnacle Books, Windsor Publishing Corp., 1991, 320 p., paper, novel.

CLARK, Ronald W(illiam), 1916-1987

20089 *The Huxleys.* London: Heinemann, 1968, xvi+398 p., cloth, nonf.

CLARK, Sheila

20090 *Enterprise incidents 2: stories.* Strathmartine by Dundee, Scotland: Star Trek Action Group, 1977, 59 p., paper, coll. STAR TREK SERIES.
20091 *Something hidden.* Strathmartine by Dundee, Scotland: Star Trek Action Group, 1979, [66] p., paper, tele. STAR TREK SERIES.
20092 *Something lost.* Strathmartine by Dundee, Scotland: ScoTpress, 1983, 69 p., paper, tele. STAR TREK SERIES.

with Valerie Piacentini

20093 *The wheel of fate.* Strathmartine by Dundee, Scotland: ScoTpress, 1980, 47 p., paper, tele. STAR TREK SERIES.

CLARK, Simon

20094 *Blood & grit.* Barnsley, South Yorkshire, England: BBR Books, 1990, 103 p., paper, coll.

CLARK, Virginia M(artha), 1953-

20095 *Aldous Huxley and film.* Metuchen, NJ & London: Scarecrow Press, 1987, xii+155 p., cloth, nonf.

CLARK, William (Donaldson), 1916-1985

20096 *Cataclysm: the North-South conflict of 1987.* London: Sidgwick & Jackson, 1984, 236 p., cloth, novel.

CLARKE, A(nthony) F(rederick) N(eville), 1948-

20097 *Collisions: a novel.* London: Secker & Warburg, 1986, 256 p., cloth, novel.

CLARKE, Arthur C(harles), 1917-

20098 *1984: Spring: a choice of futures.* New York: A Del Rey Book, Ballantine Books, 1984, x+259 p., cloth, nonf. coll.

20099 *2001: a space odyssey; The city and the stars; The deep range; A fall of moondust; Rendezvous with Rama.* London: Octopus, 1985, 747 p., cloth, coll.
20100 *2010: odyssey two.* Huntington Woods, MI: Phantasia Press, 1982, 303 p., cloth, novel. 2001 #2. [Limited to 650 copies].
20101 *2061: odyssey three.* London: Grafton, 1988, 254 p., cloth, novel. 2001 #3.
20102 *Astounding days: a science fictional autobiography.* London: Victor Gollancz, 1989, 224 p., cloth, nonf. [Includes some fiction].
20103 *The fountains of Paradise.* London: Victor Gollancz, 1979, 255 p., cloth, novel. [Winner of the Hugo Award for Best Novel, 1979 (1980); winner of the Nebula Award for Best Novel, 1979 (1980)].
20104 *Four great SF novels.* London: Victor Gollancz, 1978, 615 p., cloth, coll. [Includes *The city and the stars*; *The deep range*; *A fall of moondust*; *Rendezvous with Rama*].
20105 *The ghost from the Grand Banks.* London: Victor Gollancz, 1990, 253 p., cloth, novel.
20106 *Imperial Earth: a fantasy of love and discord.* London: Victor Gollancz, 1975, 287 p., cloth, novel.
20107 *A meeting with Medusa.* New York: Tor SF, A Tom Doherty Associates Book, 1988, 67 p., paper, novel. [Bound with *Green Mars* / by Kim Stanley Robinson].
20108 *More than one universe: the collected stories of Arthur C. Clarke.* New York, Toronto: Spectra, Bantam Books, 1991, ix+554 p., paper, coll. [Includes *Tales of ten worlds*; *The other side of the sky*; *The nine billion names of God*; *The wind from the sun*].
20109 *Project solar sail.* New York: A Roc Book, 1990, 246 p., paper, anth.
20110 *The sentinel.* New York: Berkley Books, 1983, 303 p., paper, coll.
20111 *The songs of distant Earth.* New York: A Del Rey Book, Ballantine Books, 1986, 256 p., cloth, novel.
20112 *Tales from planet Earth.* London: Century, A Legend Book, 1989, 313 p., cloth, coll.
20113 *The view from Serendip.* New York: Random House, 1977, 273 p., cloth, nonf. coll.

with Gregory Benford

Against the fall of night; and, Beyond the fall of night—SEE: *Beyond the fall of night.*

20114 *Beyond the fall of night.* New York: An Ace/Putnam Book, 1990, 298 p., cloth, coll. [Includes Clarke's *Against the fall of night* and Benford's sequel].

20114A retitled: *Against the fall of night; and, Beyond the fall of night.* London: Victor Gollancz, 1991, 239 p., cloth, coll.

with Suzan Davies

20115 *Islands in the sky.* Hong Kong, Oxford: Oxford University Press, 1976, 66 p., paper, novel. [Adapted from the novel by Clarke].

with David Fickling

20116 *Rendezvous with Rama.* Oxford, England: Alpha Books, Oxford University Press, 1979, 96 p., paper, novel. RAMA #1. [Adapted from the novel by Clarke].

with Peter Hyams

20117 *The Odyssey file.* London: Panther, 1985, xxv + 132 p., paper, nonf.

with Daniel Keyes

20118 *Dilemmas: The secret* / by Arthur C. Clarke ; *Flowers for Algernon* / by Daniel Keyes. Boston: Houghton Mifflin Co., 1989, 61 p., paper, anth.

with Gentry Lee

20119 *Cradle.* London: Victor Gollancz, 1988, 309 p., cloth, novel.

20120 *The garden of Rama.* New York: Bantam Books, 1991, 441 p., cloth, novel. RAMA #3.

20121 *Rama II.* London: Victor Gollancz, 1989, 377 p., cloth, novel. RAMA #2.

with Geo. W. Proctor

20122 *The science fiction hall of fame, volume III: Nebula winners, 1965-1969.* New York: Avon, 1982, xii + 672 p., paper, anth.

CLARKE, Boden, pseud.—SEE: Reginald, R.

CLARKE, I(gnatius) F(rederick "Ian"), 1918-

20123 *The pattern of expectation, 1644-2001.* London: Jonathan Cape, 1979, xi + 344 p., cloth, nonf.

20124 *Tale of the future, from the beginning to the present day, third edition: an annotated bibliography of those satires, ideal states, imaginary wars and invasions, coming catastrophes and end-of-the-world stories, political warnings and forecasts, inter-planetary voyages and scientific romances—all located in an imaginary future period—that have been published in the United Kingdom between 1644 and 1976.* London: The Library Association, 1978, xvii + 357 p., paper, nonf.

CLARKE, J(ames) Brian, 1928-

20125 *The expediter.* New York: DAW Books, 1990, 255 p., paper, novel.

CLARKE, Jay, with Richard Covell & John Banks & Lee Clarke as MICHAEL SLADE

17336 *Ghoul.* New York: Beech Tree Books, 1987, 417 p., cloth, novel.

CLARKE, Jeremy, 1958-

20126 *Necrotrivia vs. Skull.* London: The Fourth Estate, 1990, 184 p., paper, novel.

*CLARKE, Joan B., 1921-

CLARKE, Kevin

20127 *Doctor Who: Silver nemesis.* London: A Target Book, W. H. Allen & Co., 1989, 138 p., paper, tele. DOCTOR WHO #143. *Silver nemesis*—SEE: *Doctor Who: Silver nemesis.*

CLARKE, Lee, with Richard Covell & John Banks & Jay Clarke as MICHAEL SLADE

17336 *Ghoul.* New York: Beech Tree Books, 1987, 417 p., cloth, novel.

CLARKE, (Victor) Lindsay, 1939-

20128 *The chymical wedding: a romance.* London: Jonathan Cape, 1989, 542 p., cloth, novel.

CLARKE, Pauline [i.e., Pauline Clarke Hunter Blair], 1921-

15794 *The two faces of Silenus.* London: Faber & Faber, 1972, 162 p., cloth, novel.

CLARKE, Robert, pseud.—SEE: Platt, Charles

*CLARKE, T(homas) E(rnest) B(ennett), 1907-1989

CLARKK, Regor

20129 *The last of the sorcerer-dragons.* West Hempstead, NY: Grail Press, 1944, p., cloth, novel.

*CLARKSON, Helen [i.e., Helen Worrell Clarkson McCloy], 1904-

CLARO, Joe [i.e., Joseph Claro]

20130 *Condorman.* New York, Toronto: Scholastic Book Services, 1981, 126 p., paper, movie.

20131 *Herbie goes bananas: a novel.* New York, Toronto: Scholastic Book Services, 1980, 122 p., paper, movie. HERBIE SERIES.

20132 *Herbie the matchmaker: a novel.* New York, Toronto: Scholastic Book Services, 1982, 132 p., paper, movie. HERBIE SERIES.

20133 *SpaceCamp.* New York, Toronto: Scholastic Inc., 1986, 139 p., paper, movie.

20134 *Voyagers!* New York, Toronto: Scholastic Book Services, 1982, 76 p., paper, tele.

CLARO, Joseph—SEE: Claro, Joe

CLAUSEN, Dennis M(onroe), 1943-

20135 *Ghost lover.* Toronto, New York: Bantam Books, 1982, 263 p., paper, novel.

CLAVELL, James (duMaresq), 1925-

20136 *The children's story.* New York: An Eleanor Friede Book, Delacorte Press, 1981, [88] p., cloth, story.

CLAYTON, Donald D(elbert), 1935-

20137 *The Joshua factor.* Austin, TX: Texas Monthly Press, 1986, vi+250 p., cloth, novel.

CLAYTON, (Patricia) Jo, 1939-

20138 *A bait of dreams: a five-summer quest.* New York: DAW Books, 1985, 404 p., paper, novel.

20139 *Blue magic.* New York: DAW Books, 1988, 333 p., paper, novel. DRINKER OF SOULS #2.

20140 *Changer's moon.* New York: DAW Books, 1985, 352 p., paper, novel. DUEL OF SORCERY #3.

20141 *Diadem from the stars.* New York: DAW Books, 1977, 235 p., paper, novel. DIADEM #1.

20142 *Drinker of Souls.* New York: DAW Books, 1986, 335 p., paper, novel. DRINKER OF SOULS #1.

20143 *A gathering of stones.* New York: DAW Books, 1989, 368 p., paper, novel. DRINKER OF SOULS #3.

20144 *Ghosthunt.* New York: DAW Books, 1983, 189 p., paper, novel. DIADEM #7.

20145 *Irsud.* New York: DAW Books, 1978, 191 p., paper, novel. DIADEM #3.

20146 *Lamarchos.* New York: DAW Books, 1978, 224 p., paper, novel. DIADEM #2.

20147 *Maeve.* New York: DAW Books, 1979, 220 p., paper, novel. DIADEM #4.

20148 *Moongather.* New York: DAW Books, 1982, 240 p., paper, novel. DUEL OF SORCERY #1.

20149 *Moonscatter.* New York: DAW Books, 1983, 304 p., paper, novel. DUEL OF SORCERY #2.

20150 *The Nowhere Hunt.* New York: DAW Books, 1981, 208 p., paper, novel. DIADEM #6.

20151 *Quester's endgame: a novel of the Diadem.* New York: DAW Books, 1986, xi+372 p., paper, novel. DIADEM #9.

20152 *Shadow of the Warmaster.* New York: DAW Books, 1988, 398 p., paper, novel.

20153 *Shadowkill.* New York: DAW Books, 1991, 362 p., paper, novel. DIADEM #12; SHADITH'S QUEST #3.

20154 *Shadowplay.* New York: DAW Books, 1990, 396 p., paper, novel. DIADEM #10; SHADITH'S QUEST #1.

20155 *Shadowspeer.* New York: DAW Books, 1990, 342 p., paper, novel. DIADEM #11; SHADITH'S QUEST #2.

20156 *Skeen's leap.* New York: DAW Books, 1986, 320 p., paper, novel. SKEEN #1.

20157 *Skeen's return.* New York: DAW Books, 1987, 320 p., paper, novel. SKEEN #2.

20158 *Skeen's search.* New York: DAW Books, 1987, 303 p., paper, novel. SKEEN #3.

20159 *The snares of Ibex.* New York: DAW Books, 1984, 320 p., paper, novel. DIADEM #8.

20160 *The soul drinker.* New York: Guild America Books, 1989, 889 p., cloth, coll. DRINKER OF SOULS #1-3. [Includes *Drinker of Souls*; *Blue magic*; *A gathering of stones*].

20161 *Star hunters.* New York: DAW Books, 1980, 176 p., paper, novel. DIADEM #5.

20162 *Wild magic.* New York: DAW Books, 1991, 363 p., paper, novel. WILD MAGIC #1. [A sequel to the *Soul Magic Trilogy*].

CLAYTON, Sheena

20163 *Danielle, book two.* New York: Tigress Books, 1983, 251 p., paper, novel.
20164 *Tide of desire.* New York: Tigress Books, 1983, 252 p., paper, novel. CTHULHU MYTHOS.

CLEAR, Val(orous Bernard), 1915- , with Patricia Warrick & Martin Harry Greenberg & Joseph D. Olander

20165 *Marriage and the family through science fiction.* New York: St. Martin's Press, 1976, xiv+358 p., paper, anth.

CLEGG, Barbara

20166 *Doctor Who: Enlightenment.* London: W. H. Allen & Co., 1984, 127 p., paper, tele. DOCTOR WHO #85.
Enlightenment—SEE: *Doctor Who: Enlightenment.*

CLEGG, Douglas (Alan), 1958-

20167 *Breeder.* New York, London: Pocket Books, 1990, 310 p., paper, novel.
20168 *Goat dance.* New York, London: Pocket Books, 1989, 422 p., paper, novel.
20169 *Never land.* New York, London: Pocket Books, 1991, 373 p., paper, novel.

CLEM, Ralph (Scott), 1943- , with Martin H. Greenberg & Joseph D. Olander

20170 *The city: 2000 A.D.: urban life through science fiction.* Greenwich, CT: A Fawcett Crest Book, Fawcett Publications, 1976, 304 p., paper, anth.
20171 *No room for man: population and the future through science fiction.* Totowa, NJ: Rowman & Littlefield, 1979, 247 p., cloth, anth.

CLEMENCE, Bruce

20172 *No way street.* Eugene, OR: Pulphouse Publishing, 1991, 44 p., paper, story. SHORT STORY PAPERBACKS #15.

CLEMENS, Rodgers, pseud.—SEE: Lovin, Roger

CLEMENS, Samuel L.—SEE: Twain, Mark

CLEMENT, Aeron, 1936?-1989

20173 *The cold moons.* Llandeilo, Dyfed, Wales: Kindredson Publishing, 1987, 322 p., cloth, novel.

CLÉMENT, François

20174 *The birth of an island.* New York: Simon & Schuster, 1975, 346 p., cloth, novel. [Translation by Helen Weaver of *Naissance d'un île*].

CLEMENT, Hal [pseud. of Harry Clement Stubbs], 1922-

20175 *The best of Hal Clement.* New York: A Del Rey Book, Ballantine Books, 1979, xvii+379 p., paper, coll. [Edited by Lester del Rey].
20176 *Intuit.* Cambridge, MA: A CactusCon Book, NESFA Press, 1987, xx+164 p., cloth, coll. [Limited to 820 copies].
20177 *The nitrogen fix.* New York: Ace Books, 1980, 289 p., paper, novel.
20178 *Still river.* New York: A Del Rey Book, Ballantine Books, 1987, viii+280 p., cloth, novel.
20179 *Through the eye of a needle.* New York: A Del Rey Book, Ballantine Books, 1978, in 1 197 p., paper, novel. NEEDLE #2.

CLEMENT, Henry

20180 *The clairvoyant.* New York: Pinnacle Books, 1984, 215 p., paper, movie.
20181 *The hearse.* Los Angeles: Pinnacle Books, 1980, 213 p., paper, movie.
20182 *She waits.* New York: Popular Library, 1975, 173 p., paper, movie.

CLEMENTS, David

20184 *The backwater man.* London: Robert Hale, 1979, 191 p., cloth, novel.

CLEMENTS, Mark A.

20185 *6:02: a novel of horror.* New York: Popular Library, 1988, 252 p., paper, novel.

CLENDENEN, Bill

20186 *Stigma.* Toronto, New York: Bantam Books, 1988, 227 p., paper, novel.

CLERC, Charles, 1926-

20187　*Approaches to Gravity's Rainbow.* Columbus, OH: Ohio State University Press, 1983, 307 p., cloth, nonf. anth.

CLERY, (Reginald) Val(entine), 1924-

20188　*Ghost stories of Canada.* Willowdale, Ontario, Canada: Hounslow Press, 1985, 114 p., cloth?, coll.

with Peter Hogarth

20189　*Dragons.* New York: A Studio Book, A Jonathan-James Book, Viking Press, 1979, 208 p., cloth, novel.

CLEVE, John, pseud.—SEE: Offutt, Andrew J.

*CLEWES, Howard (Charles Vivian), 1912-1988

*CLIFFORD, Sarah, 1916-1976

CLIFTON, Mark Irvin, 1906-1963

20190　*The science fiction of Mark Clifton.* Carbondale & Edwardsville, IL: Southern Illinois University Press; London & Amsterdam: Feffer & Simons, 1980, xix+296 p., cloth, coll. [Edited by Barry N. Malzberg & Martin H. Greenberg].

CLIMO, Shirley, 1928-

20191　*T. J.'s ghost.* New York: Thomas Y. Crowell, 1989, 151 p., cloth, novel.

CLINE, C(harles) Terry, Jr., 1935-

20192　*Cross current.* Garden City, NY: Doubleday & Co., 1979, 299 p., cloth, novel.
20193　*Death knell.* New York: G. P. Putnam's Sons, 1977, 311 p. cloth, novel.
20194　*Mindreader.* Garden City, NY: Doubleday & Co., 1981, 325 p., cloth, novel

CLINE, Linda, 1941-

20195　*The miracle season.* New York: Berkley Publishing Corp., 1976, ix+182 p., cloth, novel.

CLINTON, Jeff, pseud.—SEE: Bickham, Jack M.

*CLOCK, Herbert, 1890-1979

CLOKE, Richard, 1916-

20196　*Vector-Lee.* Northridge, CA: Kent Publications, 1977, 261 p., cloth, novel.

CLOUGH, B(renda) W(ang), 1955-

20197　*The Crystal Crown.* New York: DAW Books, 1984, 223 p., paper, novel. AVERIDAN #1.
20198　*The dragon of Mishbil.* New York: DAW Books, 1985, 189 p., paper, novel. AVERIDAN #2.
20199　*The name of the sun.* New York: DAW Books, 1988, 304 p., paper, novel. AVERIDAN #4.
20200　*The realm beneath.* New York: DAW Books, 1986, 256 p., paper, novel. AVERIDAN #3.

CLOUGH, S(amuel) D(ennis) P(rocter), 1928-

20201　*The wandering Jew: an account of his last adventures, with an appendix of selected memoirs.* Malvern Wells, Worcestershire: S. D. P. Clough, 1983, 102 p., paper, novel. WANDERING JEW SERIES.

CLOWES, Carolyn (MacDonald), 1946-

　　　The pandora principle—SEE: *Star Trek: The pandora principle.*
20203　*Star Trek: The pandora principle.* New York, London: Pocket Books, 1990, 273 p., paper, novel. STAR TREK #49.

CLUTE, John (Frederick), 1940-

20204　*Strokes: essays and reviews, 1966-1986.* Seattle, WA: Serconia Press, 1988, xiii+178 p., cloth, nonf. coll.

with Colin Greenland & David Pringle

20205　*Interzone: the first anthology: new science fiction and fantasy writing.* London: J. M. Dent & Sons, 1985, 206 p., paper, anth.

with Peter Nicholls

20206　*The encyclopedia of science fiction: an illustrated A to Z.* London, Toronto: Granada, 1979, 672 p., cloth, nonf. anth. [Winner of the Hugo Award for Best Nonfiction Book, 1979 (1980); winner of the *Locus* Award for Best Nonfiction Book, 1979 (1980)].
20206A retitled: *The science fiction encyclopedia.* Garden City, NY: Doubleday & Co., 1979, 672 p., cloth, nonf. anth.

The science fiction encyclopedia—SEE: *The encyclopedia of science fiction.*

with David Pringle & Lee Montgomerie

20207 *Interzone: the 5th anthology: new science fiction and fantasy writing.* London: New English Library, 1991, 280 p., paper, anth.

with David Pringle & Simon Ounsley

20208 *Interzone: the 2nd anthology: new science fiction and fantasy writing.* London, Sydney: Simon & Schuster, 1987, x+ 208 p., cloth, anth.

20209 *Interzone: the 3rd anthology: new science fiction and fantasy writing.* London, Sydney: Simon & Schuster, 1988, viii+ 184 p., cloth, anth.

20210 *Interzone: the 4th anthology: new science fiction and fantasy writing.* London: Simon & Schuster, 1989, ix+208 p., cloth, anth.

CLUTHA, Janet Paterson Frame—SEE: **Frame, Janet**

CLUTTON-BROCK, A(rthur), 1868-1924

20211 *William Morris: his work and influence.* London: Williams & Norgate, 1914, viii+256 p., cloth, nonf.

COALE, Samuel (Chase), 1943-

37664 *Anthony Burgess.* New York: Frederick Unger Publishing Co., 1981, x+223 p., cloth, nonf.

COATES, Paul, 1953-

20212 *The gorgon's gaze: German cinema, expressionism, and the image of horror.* Cambridge, England, New York: Cambridge University Press, 1991, xiv+287 p., cloth, nonf.

*COATSWORTH, Elizabeth (Jane), 1893-1986

COBALT, Martin, pseud.—SEE: **Mayne, William**

COBB, Irvin S(hrewsbury), 1876-1944

20213 *Fishhead.* West Warwick, RI: Necronomicon Press, 1985, 9 p., paper, story.

*COBEY, Herbert T., 1917-1986

*COBLENTZ, Stanton A(rthur), 1896-1982

COBURN, Anthony, 1927-1977

20214 *Gargantua.* London: Futura Publications, A Futura Book, 1977, 394 p., paper, novel.

20215 *The tribe of Gum.* London: Titan Books, 1987, 125 p., paper, fiction. DOCTOR WHO SERIES. [Includes script of first *Doctor Who* series, plus commentary].

COCHRAN, Molly

with Warren Murphy

20216 *Grandmaster.* New York: Pinnacle Books, 1984, 427 p., paper, novel.

20217 *The hand of Lazarus.* New York: Pinnacle Books, Windsor Publishing Corp., 1988, 445 p., paper, novel.

20218 *High priest.* New York: NAL Books, New American Library, 1987, 354 p., cloth, novel.

as anonymous author or co-author with Warren Murphy & Richard Sapir and others (as indicated)

20218 *Balance of power.* New York: Pinnacle Books, 1981, viii+183 p., paper, novel. DESTROYER #44. [By Richard Sapir & Warren Murphy & Molly Cochran].

20219 *Date with death* / by Warren Murphy. New York: Pinnacle Books, 1984, 186 p., paper, novel. DESTROYER #57. [By Warren Murphy & Molly Cochran & Ed Hunsburger].

20220 *Dying space* / by Warren Murphy. New York: Pinnacle Books, 1982, 196 p., paper, novel. DESTROYER #47. [By Molly Cochran].

20221 *The eleventh hour.* New York: A Signet Book, New American Library, 1987, 222 p., paper, novel. DESTROYER #70. [By Warren Murphy & Will Murray & Molly Cochran].

20222 *Killing time* / by Warren Murphy. New York: Pinnacle Books, 1982, 199 p., paper, novel. DESTROYER #50. [By Molly Cochran].

20223 *Last drop* / by Warren Murphy. New York: Pinnacle Books, 1983, 199 p., paper, novel. DESTROYER #54. [By Molly Cochran].

20224 *Master's challenge.* New York: Pinnacle Books, 1984, 245 p., paper, novel. DESTROYER #55. [By Richard Sapir & Warren Murphy & Molly Cochran].

20225 *Next of kin* / by Warren Murphy. New York: Pinnacle Books, 1981, 183 p., paper, novel. DESTROYER #46. [By Molly Cochran].

20226 *Shock value* / by Warren Murphy. New York: Pinnacle Books, 1983, 199 p., paper, novel. DESTROYER #51. [By Molly Cochran].

20227 *Skin deep* / by Warren Murphy. New York: Pinnacle Books, 1982, 199 p., paper, novel. DESTROYER #49. [By Molly Cochran].

20228 *Spoils of war* / by Warren Murphy. New York: Pinnacle Books, 1981, 182 p., paper, novel. DESTROYER #45. [By Molly Cochran].

20229 *Time trial* / by Warren Murphy. New York: Pinnacle Books, 1983, 201 p., paper, novel. DESTROYER #53. [By Molly Cochran].

COCHRANE, William E(ugene), 1926-

20230 *Class six climb.* New York: Ace Books, 1980, 273 p., paper, novel.

as S. KYE BOULT

20231 *Solo kill.* New York: A Berkley Medallion Book, Berkley Publishing Corp., 1977, 244 p., paper, novel.

COCKBURN, Francis C.—SEE: Helvick, James

COCKBURN, Terry

20232 *The Altoran creed.* London: Dennis Dobson, 1980, 233 p., cloth, novel.

COCKCROFT, George—SEE: Rhinehart, Luke

COCKCROFT, T(homas) G. L.

20233 *The tales of Clark Ashton Smith: a bibliography, rev. ed.* Lower Hutt, New Zealand: Thomas G. L. Cockcroft, 1959, vii p., paper, nonf.

*COCKRELL, Marian (Brown), 1907-1972

COCKRUM, Kurt, *with Daniel J. H. Levack & Tim Underwood*

20234 *Fantasms II: a bibliography of the works of Jack Vance.* [S.l.: s.n.], 1979, xiii+83, 1, 118, 20 p., paper, nonf.

28244 *Fantasms II: a bibliography of the literature of Jack Vance.* Riverside, CA: Kurt Cockrum, 1979, vi+99 p. on 112 leaves, printout, nonf. [Revised edition].

COE, Ross Anton, pseud.—SEE: Renauld, Ron

COEN, Franklin, *with Edmund H. North*

20235 *Meteor.* New York: Warner Books, 1979, 236 p., paper, movie.

COFFEY, Brian, pseud.—SEE: Koontz, Dean R.

COFFEY, Frank, 1947-

20236 *Modern masters of horror.* New York: Coward, McCann & Geoghegan, 1981, 286 p., cloth, anth.

20237 *Night prayers.* New York: A Jove Book, 1986, 249 p., paper, novel.

20238 *The shaman.* New York: St. Martin's Press, 1980, 240 p., cloth, novel.

COFFMAN, Ardis

20239 *Terror at Octagon House.* New York: Manor Books, 1979, 189 p., paper, novel.

COFFMAN, C. C.

20240 *Spacedust one.* New York, Washington: Vantage Press, 1979, 129 p., cloth, coll.

COFFMAN, Virginia (Edith), 1914-

03145 *Chalet Diabolique.* New York: Lancer Books, 1971, 206 p., paper, novel. LUCIFER COVE #5.

03145A retitled: *Chalet of the devil.* London: Piatkus, 1988, 216 p., cloth, novel. LUCIFER COVE #5.

Chalet of the devil—SEE: *Chalet Diabolique.*

20241 *The vampyre of Moura.* New York: Ace Books, 1970, 220 p., paper, novel.

COGELL, Elizabeth Cummins—SEE: Cummins, Elizabeth

COGSWELL, Theodore R(ose), 1918-1987, *with Charles A. Spano, Jr.*

20242 *Spock, messiah!* Toronto, New York: Bantam Books, 1976, 182 p., paper, novel. STAR TREK SERIES.

COHAN, Anthony R.—SEE: Cohan, Tony

COHAN, Tony [i.e., Anthony Robert Cohan], 1939-

20243 *Nine ships: a book of tales.* Los Angeles: Acrobat Books, 1975, 90 p., paper, coll.

COHEN, Barbara (Ann), 1932-

20244 *Roses.* New York: Lothrop, Lee & Shepard, 1984, 221 p., cloth, novel.
20245 *Unicorns in the rain.* New York: An Argo Book, Atheneum, 1980, 164 p., cloth, novel.

COHEN, Barney [i.e., Bernard Halsband Cohen]

20246 *Blood on the moon.* New York: Tor, A Tom Doherty Associates Book, 1984, 254 p., paper, novel.
20247 *The night of the toy dragons.* New York: A Berkley Medallion Book, Berkley Publishing Corp., 1977, 218 p., paper, novel.

with Jim Baen

17197 *The taking of Satcon Station.* New York: Tor, A Tom Doherty Associates Book, 1982, 287 p., paper, novel.

COHEN, Bernard—SEE: Cohen, Barney

COHEN, Daniel (E.), 1936-

20248 *Hollywood dinosaur.* New York: An Archway Paperback, Pocket Books, 1987, 117 p., paper, nonf.
20249 *Horror in the movies.* Boston: Clarion Books, 1982, 118 p., cloth, nonf.
20250 *Horror movies.* New York: A Bison Book, Gallery Books, 1984, 80 p., cloth, nonf.
20251 *Masters of horror.* New York: Clarion Books, 1984, 119 p., cloth, nonf.
20252 *The monsters of Star Trek.* New York: An Archway Paperback, Pocket Books, 1980, 117 p., paper, nonf.
20253 *The restless dead: ghostly tales from around the world.* New York: Dodd, Mead & Co., 1984, 123 p., cloth, coll.
20254 *Science fiction's greatest monsters.* New York: Dodd, Mead & Co., 1980, 122 p., cloth, nonf.
20255 *Strange and amazing facts about Star Trek.* New York: An Archway Paperback, Pocket Books, 1986, 110 p., paper, nonf.

COHEN, James, 1956- , *with Peter Rubie*

20256 *Mindbender.* New York: Lynx Books, 1989, 279 p., paper, novel.

COHEN, Jamey

20257 *Dmitri.* New York: Seaview Books, 1980, 310 p., cloth, novel.

COHEN, Jon

20258 *Max Lakeman and the beautiful stranger: a novel.* New York: Warner Books, 1990, 210 p., cloth, novel.

COHEN, Matthew, 1942-

20259 *The colours of war.* Toronto: McClelland & Stewart, 1977, 234 p., cloth, novel.

COHEN, Morton N(orton), 1921-

20260 *Rider Haggard: his life and works.* London: Hutchinson of London, 1960, 327 p., cloth, nonf.
20261 *Rider Haggard: his life and work, 2nd ed.* London, Melbourne: Macmillan, 1968, 328 p., cloth, nonf.

COHEN, Sarah

20262 *Scoffing Marah.* Seattle, WA: Three-Stones Publications, 1986, ix+227 p., paper, novel. TALES OF THE NASHRAMH #1.

COHEN, Stephen Paul, *with Jake Garn*

20263 *Night launch.* New York: William Morrow & Co., 1989, 285 p., cloth, novel.

COHEN, Susan H.—SEE: St. Clair, Elizabeth

COHN, Nik, 1946-

37665 *King Death.* New York: Harcourt Brace Jovanovich, 1975, 143 p., cloth, novel.

COINS, Wally

20264 *Whispers of heavenly death.* New York: Manor Books, 1979, 251 p., paper, novel.

COLANDER, Valerie Nieman, 1955-

20265 *Neena gathering.* New York: Pageant Books, 1988, 270 p., paper, novel.

COLCHIE, Thomas

20266 *A hammock beneath the mangoes: stories from Latin America.* New York: E. P. Dutton, 1991, xiv+430 p., cloth, anth.

COLE, Adrian (Christopher Synnot), 1949-

20267 *Bane of nightmares.* New York: Zebra Books, Kensington Publishing Corp., 1976, 208 p., paper, novel. DREAM LORDS #3.

20268 *The coming of the Voidal.* Burton-on-Trent, Staffordshire, England: Spectre Press, 1977, 24 p., paper, story.

20269 *Dream Lords: Lord of nightmares.* New York: Zebra Books, Kensington Publishing Corp., 1975, 221 p., paper, novel. DREAM LORDS #2.

20270 *The gods in anger.* London: Unwin Paperbacks, 1988, 386 p., paper, novel. OMARAN SAGA #4.

20271 *The king of light and shadows.* London: Unwin Paperbacks, 1988, 388 p., paper, novel. OMARAN SAGA #3.

20272 *Labyrinth of worlds.* London: Unwin Paperbacks, 1990, 341 p., paper, novel. STAR REQUIEM #4.

20273 *Longborn the inexhaustible.* Dagenham, Essex, England: British Fantasy Society, 1978, [12] p., paper, story.

Lord of nightmares—SEE: *Dream Lords: Lord of nightmares.*

20274 *The LUCIFER experiment.* London: Robert Hale, 1981, 208 p., cloth, novel.

20275 *Madness emerging.* London: Robert Hale, 1976, 189 p., cloth, novel.

20276 *Moorstones.* Barnstaple, Devonshire, England: Spindlewood, 1982, 163 p., cloth, novel.

20277 *Mother of storms.* London: Unwin Paperbacks, 1989, 378 p., paper, novel. STAR REQUIEM #1.

20278 *Paths in darkness.* London: Robert Hale, 1977, 190 p., cloth, novel.

20279 *A place among the fallen.* London: George Allen & Unwin, 1986, 268 p., cloth, novel. OMARAN SAGA #1.

20279 *A plague of nightmares.* New York: Zebra Books, Kensington Publishing Corp., 1975, 176 p., paper, novel. DREAM LORDS #1.

20280 *The sleep of giants.* Barnstable, Devonshire, England: Spindlewood, 1983, 169 p., cloth, novel.

20281 *Thief of dreams.* London: Unwin Paperbacks, 1989, 366 p., paper, novel. STAR REQUIEM #2.

20282 *Throne of fools.* London: Unwin Paperbacks, 1987, 410 p., paper, novel. OMARAN SAGA #2.

20283 *Wargods of Ludorbis.* London: Robert Hale, 1981, 206 p., cloth, novel.

20284 *Warlord of Heaven.* London: Unwin Paperbacks, 1990, 356 p., paper, novel. STAR REQUIEM #3.

COLE, Allan, 1943- , *with Chris Bunch*

18990 *The court of a thousand suns.* New York: A Del Rey Book, Ballantine Books, 1986, 275 p., paper, novel. STEN #3.

18991 *Fleet of the damned.* New York: A Del Rey Book, Ballantine Books, 1988, 340 p., paper, novel. STEN #4.

18992 *The return of the emperor.* New York: A Del Rey Book, Ballantine Books, 1990, 371 p., paper, novel. STEN #6.

18993 *Revenge of the damned.* New York: A Del Rey Book, Ballantine Books, 1989, 354 p., paper, novel. STEN #5.

18994 *Sten.* New York: A Del Rey Book, Ballantine Books, 1982, 279 p., paper, novel. STEN #1.

18995 *The wolf worlds.* New York: A Del Rey Book, Ballantine Books, 1984, 298 p., paper, novel. STEN #2.

COLE, Burt [pseud. of Thomas Dixon], 1930-

20285 *The quick.* New York: William Morrow & Co., 1989, 307 p., cloth, novel.

COLE, Damaris

20286 *Token of dragonsblood.* Lake Geneva, WI: TSR Inc., 1991, 314 p., paper, novel.

COLE, Joanna, 1944- , *with Stephanie Calmenson*

19225 *The scary book.* New York: Morrow Junior Books, 1991, 127 p., cloth, anth.

COLE, Lee

20287 *Star Trek the motion picture peel-off graphics book.* New York: A Wallaby Book, Pocket Books, 1979, 242 p., paper, nonf.

COLEMAN, Clay [pseud. of Coleman Stokes]

Attack!—SEE: *Escape from Lost Island: Attack.*

Discovered!—SEE: *Escape from Lost Island: Discovered!*

20288 *Escape from Lost Island: Stranded!* New York: HarperPaperbacks, 1990, 152 p.,

paper, novel. ESCAPE FROM LOST IS-
LAND #1.

20289 *Escape from Lost Island: Attack!* New
York: HarperPaperbacks, 1990, 138 p.,
paper, novel. ESCAPE FROM LOST IS-
LAND #2.

20290 *Escape from Lost Island: Discovered!* New
York: HarperPaperbacks, 1991, 132 p.,
paper, novel. ESCAPE FROM LOST IS-
LAND #4.

20291 *Escape from Lost Island: Escape!* New
York: HarperPaperbacks, 1991, 140 p.,
paper, novel. ESCAPE FROM LOST IS-
LAND #6.

20292 *Escape from Lost Island: Mutiny!* New
York: HarperPaperbacks, 1991, 134 p.,
paper, novel. ESCAPE FROM LOST IS-
LAND #3.

20293 *Escape from Lost Island: Revenge!* New
York: HarperPaperbacks, 1991, 140 p.,
paper, novel. ESCAPE FROM LOST IS-
LAND #5.

Escape!—SEE: *Escape from Lost Island:
Escape!*

Mutiny!—SEE: *Escape from Lost Island:
Mutiny!*

Revenge!—SEE: *Escape from Lost Island:
Revenge!*

Stranded!—SEE: *Escape from Lost Island:
Stranded!*

as NICHOLAS ADAMS

Hard rock—SEE: *Horror High: Hard
rock.*

Heartbreaker—SEE: *Horror High: Heartbreaker.*

15970 *Horror High: Hard rock.* New York:
HarperPaperbacks, 1991, 156 p., paper,
novel. HORROR HIGH #5.

15971 *Horror High: Heartbreaker.* New York:
HarperPaperbacks, 1991, 154 p., paper,
novel. HORROR HIGH #3.

15972 *Horror High: Mr. Popularity.* New York:
HarperPaperbacks, 1990, 153 p., paper,
novel. HORROR HIGH #1.

15973 *Horror High: New kid on the block.* New
York: HarperPaperbacks, 1991, 151 p.,
paper, novel. HORROR HIGH #4.

15975 *Horror High: Resolved, you're dead.* New
York: HarperPaperbacks, 1990, 153 p.,
paper, novel. HORROR HIGH #2.

Mr. Popularity—SEE: *Horror High: Mr.
Popularity.*

New kid on the block—SEE: *Horror High:
New kid on the block.*

Resolved, you're dead—SEE: *Horror
High: Resolved, you're dead.*

COLEMAN, Joseph

20294 *First witch, and seven more stories of
demons, ghosts, and vampires.* Middletown, CT: A Pal Paperback, Xerox Education Publications, 1980, 93 p., paper,
coll.

20295 *Space wars, and six more tales of space
and time.* Middletown, CT: A Pal Paperback, Xerox Education Publications,
1980, 94 p., paper, coll.

COLEMAN, Vernon—SEE: Charbonnier, Marc

COLEMAN, Wim, *with Pat Perrin*

20296 *The jamais vu papers; or, Misadventures in
the worlds of science, myth, and magic.*
New York: Harmony Books, 1991, 327
p., cloth, fiction.

COLES, Lesley

20297 *Tomorrow is another day.* Strathmartine by
Dundee, Scotland: ScoTpress, 1979, 55
p., paper, tele. STAR TREK SERIES.

20298 *The world of difference.* Strathmartine by
Dundee, Scotland: ScoTpress, 1983, 49
p., paper, tele. STAR TREK SERIES.

COLIN, Veronica

20299 *The unusual genitals party, and other stories.* Glasgow, Scotland: CRM, 1991,
36 p., paper, anth.

**COLL, Joseph Clement, 1881-1921, *with Walt
Reed***

20300 *The magic pen of Joseph Clement Coll.*
West Kingston, RI: Donald M. Grant,
Publisher, 1978, 176 p., cloth, art.

COLLAS, Felix E.—SEE: Collas, Phil

COLLAS, Phil [i.e., Felix Edward Collas]

20301 *The inner domain.* Sydney, Australia:
Graham Stone, 1989, 32 p., cloth, story.

*COLLIER, Dwight A(ustin), 1932-

COLLIER, James Lincoln, 1928-

20302 *Planet out of the past.* New York: Macmillan Publishing Co.; London: Collier
Macmillan Publishers, 1983, 162 p.,
cloth, novel.

COLLIER, John (Henry Noyes), 1901-1980

The best of John Collier—SEE: *The John Collier reader.*

03188 *The John Collier reader.* New York: Alfred A. Knopf, 1972, 571 p., cloth, coll.

03188A retitled: *The best of John Collier.* New York: Pocket Books, 1975, xvii+492 p., paper, coll. [Abridged edition].

COLLIGAN, Douglas

37666 *The video avenger.* New York, Toronto: Scholastic Inc., 1983, 93 p., paper, fiction. TWISTAPLOT #7.

COLLINGS, Michael R(obert), 1947-

20303 *The annotated guide to Stephen King: a primary and secondary bibliography of the works of America's premier horror writer.* Mercer Island, WA: Starmont House, 1986, 176 p., cloth, nonf. STARMONT REFERENCE GUIDE #8.

20304 *Brian Aldiss.* Mercer Island, WA: Starmont House, 1986, 115 p., cloth, nonf. STARMONT READER'S GUIDE #28.

20305 *Card catalogue: the science fiction and fantasy of Orson Scott Card.* Eugene, OR: Hypatia Press, 1987, 15 p., cloth, nonf.

20306 *Dark transformations: deadly visions of change.* Mercer Island, WA: Starmont House, 1990, 95 p., cloth, coll. [Includes two stories with many poems].

20307 *The films of Stephen King.* Mercer Island, WA: Starmont House, 1986, 201 p., cloth, nonf. STARMONT STUDIES IN LITERARY CRITICISM #12.

20308 *In the image of God: theme, characterization, and landscape in the fiction of Orson Scott Card.* New York: Greenwood Press, 1990, ix+192 p., cloth, nonf. CONTRIBUTIONS TO THE STUDY OF SCIENCE FICTION AND FANTASY #42.

20309 *The many facets of Stephen King.* Mercer Island, WA: Starmont House, 1985, 190 p., cloth, nonf. STARMONT STUDIES IN LITERARY CRITICISM #11.

20310 *Piers Anthony.* Mercer Island, WA: Starmont House, 1983, 96 p., cloth, nonf. STARMONT READER'S GUIDE #20.

20311 *Reflections on the fantastic: selected essays from the Fourth International Conference on the Fantastic in the Arts.* New York: Greenwood Press, 1986, xi+113 p., cloth, nonf. anth. CONTRIBUTIONS TO THE STUDY OF SCIENCE FICTION AND FANTASY #24.

20312 *Stephen King as Richard Bachman.* Mercer Island, WA: Starmont House, 1985, 168 p., cloth, nonf. STARMONT STUDIES IN LITERARY CRITICISM #10.

20313 *The Stephen King phenomenon.* Mercer Island, WA: Starmont House, 1987, 144 p., cloth, nonf. STARMONT STUDIES IN LITERARY CRITICISM #14.

with David Engebretson

20314 *The shorter works of Stephen King.* Mercer Island, WA: Starmont House, 1985, 202 p., cloth, nonf. STARMONT STUDIES IN LITERARY CRITICISM #9.

COLLINS, Charles M.

03203 *Fright.* New York: Avon, 1963, 141 p., paper, anth.

03203A retitled: *Harvest of fear.* New York: Avon, 1975, 172 p., paper, anth.
Harvest of fear—SEE: *Fright.*

COLLINS, Erroll

37667 *Conquerors of space.* London: S. Baker, 1954, 60 p., paper, story.

COLLINS, Hunt, pseud.—SEE: **Hunter, Evan**

COLLINS, Jackson, 1939-

20315 *The Votan treasure.* New York: Avon Books, 1989, 281 p., paper, novel.

COLLINS, John L.—SEE: **Collins, Larry**

COLLINS, Larry [i.e., John Lawrence Collins Jr.], 1929-

20316 *Maze: a novel.* New York: Simon & Schuster, 1989, 432 p., cloth, novel.

COLLINS, Len

20317 *Science fiction collections index.* South Porcupine, Ontario, Canada: Arthur Hayes, 1970, 64 p., paper, nonf.

COLLINS, Nancy A(verill), 1959-

20318 *In the blood.* London: Kinnell, 1991, 301 p., cloth, novel.

20319 *Sunglasses after dark.* New York: An Onyx Book, New American Library, 1989, 253 p., paper, novel. SUNGLASSES #1. [Winner of the Bram Stoker Award for Best First Horror Novel, 1989 (1990)].

20320 *Tempter*. New York: An Onyx Book, 1990, 299 p., paper, novel. SUNGLASSES #2.

20321 *The Tortuga Hill Gang's last ride: the true story*. Arvada, CO: Roadkill Press, 1991, 25 p., paper, story. [Limited to 500 copies].

as NANZI REGALIA

20322 *Love throbbing Bob*. Berkeley, CA: Dark Carnival Press, 1990, 20 p., paper, story.

COLLINS, Paul, 1954-

20323 *Alien worlds*. St. Kilda, Victoria, Australia: Void Publications, 1979, 252 p., cloth, anth.

20324 *Distant worlds*. St. Kilda, Victoria, Australia: Cory & Collins, 1980, 242 p., cloth, anth.

20325 *Envisaged worlds: from the editor of Void, Australia's first original science fiction anthology*. St. Kilda, Victoria, Australia: Void Publications, 1978, 233 p., cloth, anth.

20326 *Frontier worlds*. St. Kilda, Victoria, Australia: Cory & Collins, 1983, 241 p., paper, anth.

Other worlds—SEE: Ron Graham presents Other worlds.

20327 *Ron Graham presents Other worlds*. St. Kilda, Victoria, Australia: Void Publications, 1978, 248 p., cloth, anth.

COLLINS, Randall, 1941- , *as* DR. JOHN H. WATSON

20328 *The case of the philosophers' ring / by Dr. John H. Watson*. New York: Crown Publishers, 1978, 152 p., cloth, novel. SHERLOCK HOLMES SERIES.

COLLINS, Robert A(rnold), 1929-

20329 *Thomas Burnett Swann: a brief critical biography and annotated bibliography*. Boca Raton, FL: The Thomas Burnett Swann Fund, College of Humanities, Florida Atlantic University, 1979, 29 p., paper, nonf.

with Howard D. Pearce

20330 *The scope of the fantastic: culture, biography, themes, children's literature: selected essays from the First International Conference on the Fantastic in Literature and Film*. Westport, CT & London: Greenwood Press, 1985, xii+284 p., cloth, nonf. anth. CONTRIBUTIONS TO THE STUDY OF SCIENCE FICTION AND FANTASY #11.

20331 *The scope of the fantastic: theory, practice, major authors: selected essays from the First International Conference on the Fantastic in Literature and Film*. Westport, CT & London: Greenwood Press, 1985, xii+295 p., cloth, nonf. anth. CONTRIBUTIONS TO THE STUDY OF SCIENCE FICTION AND FANTASY #10.

with Robert Latham

20332 *Science fiction & fantasy book review annual 1988*. Westport, CT, London: Meckler, 1988, ix+486 p., cloth, nonf. anth.

20333 *Science fiction & fantasy book review annual 1989*. Westport, CT, London: Meckler, 1989, ix+624 p., cloth, nonf. anth.

20334 *Science fiction & fantasy book review annual 1990*. New York, Westport, CT: Greenwood Press, 1991, ix+711 p., cloth, nonf. anth.

*COLLINS, V(ere) H(enry Gratz), 1872-

COLLINS, Warwick

20335 *Challenge*. London & Sydney: Pan Books, 1990, 400 p., cloth, novel. CHALLENGE #1.

20336 *New world*. London & Sydney: Pan Books, 1991, 432 p., cloth, novel. CHALLENGE #2.

COLLINS, (William) Wilkie, 1824-1889

20337 *The best supernatural stories of Wilkie Collins*. London: Robert Hale, 1990, 303 p., cloth, coll. [Edited by Peter Haining].

20338 *The illustrated Wilkie Collins: tales of mystery and the supernatural by the father of the detective novel*. Wellingborough, Northamptonshire, England: Equation, 1989, [256] p., cloth, coll. [Edited by Peter Haining].

COLMORE, G., pseud.—SEE: Dunn, Gertrude

COLOMBO, John Robert, 1936-

20339 *Blackwood's books: a bibliography devoted to Algernon Blackwood*. Toronto: Hounslow Press, 1981, 119 p., paper, nonf.

Book of marvels—SEE: Columbo's Book of marvels.

20340 *Friendly aliens: thirteen stories of the fantastic set in Canada by foreign authors.* Toronto: Hounslow Press, 1981, 81 p., paper, anth.

20341 *Other Canadas: an anthology of science fiction and fantasy.* Toronto: McGraw-Hill Ryerson, 1979, viii + 360 p., cloth, anth. [Includes some verse and nonfiction].

20342 *Windigo: an anthology of fact and fantastic fiction.* Saskatoon, Saskatchewan, Canada: Western Producer Prairie Books, 1982, viii + 208 p., cloth, anth. [Includes some nonfiction].

with Leslie A. Croutch

20343 *Years of light: a celebration of Leslie A. Croutch: a compilation and a commentary.* Toronto: Hounslow Press, 1982, 193 p., paper, nonf. coll.

with Michael Richardson

20344 *Not to be taken at night: thirteen classic Canadian tales of mystery and the supernatural.* Toronto: Lester & Orpen Dennys, 1981, 189 p., cloth, anth.

with Michael Richardson & John Bell & Alexandre L. Amprimoz

16353 *CDN SF & F: a bibliography of Canadian science fiction and fantasy.* Toronto: Hounslow Press, 1979, viii + 85 p., paper, nonf.

COLOMBO, Judith Woolcock

20345 *The fablesinger.* Freedom, CA: Crossing Press, 1989, 131 p., cloth, novel.

*COLVIN, Ian (Goodhope), 1912-1975

COMBES, Sharon (M.)

20346 *Caly.* New York: Zebra Books, Kensington Publishing Corp., 1980, 282 p., paper, novel.

20347 *Cherron.* New York: Zebra Books, Kensington Publishing Corp., 1980, 314 p., paper, novel.

COMBS, David, 1934-

20348 *The intrusion.* New York: Avon, 1981, 221 p., paper, novel.

20349 *The surrogate.* New York: Avon, 1982, 205 p., paper, novel.

COMBS, James (Everett), 1941- , with Robert L. Savage and Dan Nimmo

20350 *The Orwellian moment: hindsight and foresight in the post-1984 world.* Fayetteville, AR: University of Arkansas Press, 1989, viii + 180 p., cloth, nonf. anth.

COMERFORD, Sherna, with Devra M. Langsam

20351 *More Vulcan reflections: essays on Spock and his world.* Baltimore, MD: T-K Graphics, 1976, 26 p., paper, nonf. anth. [Cover title].

COMFORT, Alex(ander), 1920-

37668 *Come out to play.* London: Eyre & Spottiswoode, 1961, 220 p., cloth, novel.

37669 *The philosophers.* London: Duckworth, 1989, 176 p., cloth, novel.

20352 *Tetrarch.* Boulder, CO: Shambhala, 1980, 309 p., cloth, novel.

COMFORT, Daniel, 1950-

20353 *To the top of the mountain.* Tampa, FL: Bridges to the Sound Publishing Co., 1983, 226 p., cloth, novel.

COMFORT, Iris (Tracy), 1917-

20354 *Echoes of evil.* Garden City, NY: Doubleday & Co., 1977, 188 p., cloth, novel.

20355 *Shadow masque.* Garden City, NY: Doubleday & Co., 1980, 185 p., cloth, novel.

COMO, James T.

20356 *C. S. Lewis at the breakfast table, and other reminiscences.* New York: Macmillan Publishing Co., 1979, xxxiv + 299 p., cloth, nonf. anth.

COMPTON, D(avid) G(uy), 1930-

20357 *Ascendancies.* London: Victor Gollancz, 1980, 208 p., cloth, novel.
Chronicles—SEE: *Chronocules.*

03243 *Chronocules.* New York: Ace books, 1970, 255 p., paper, novel.

03243B retitled: *Chronicules.* London: Arrow Books, 1976, 205 p., paper, novel.
Death watch—SEE: *The unsleeping eye.*

20358 *Radio plays.* Worcester Park, Surrey, England: Kerosina Publications, 1988, 62 p., cloth, coll.

20359 *Scudder's game.* Worcester Park, Surrey, England: Kerosina Publications, 1988, 175 p., cloth, novel.

03250 *The unsleeping eye.* New York: DAW Books, 1974, 221 p., paper, novel. KATHERINE MORTENHOE #1.

03250B retitled: *Death watch.* London: Magnum Books, 1981, 255 p., paper, novel. KATHERINE MORTENHOE #1.

20360 *A usual lunacy.* San Bernardino, CA: R. Reginald, The Borgo Press, 1978, 191 p., cloth, novel.

20361 *Windows.* New York: Berkley Publishing Corp., 1979, 255 p., cloth, novel. KATHERINE MORTENHOE #2.

with John Gribbin

20362 *Ragnarok.* London: Victor Gollancz, 1991, 344 p., cloth, novel.

COMPTON, Sara

20363 *Amazon: where do fish swim through the treetops?* New York: McGraw-Hill Book Co., 1988, 101 p., paper, novel. EARTH INSPECTORS #2.

20364 *Europe: why was a city built to capture a castle?* New York: McGraw-Hill Book Co., 1989, [100] p., paper, novel. EARTH INSPECTORS #9.

20365 *Venice: who are the three?* New York: McGraw-Hill Book Co., 1989, 97 p., paper, novel. EARTH INSPECTORS #5.

with Spencer Compton

20366 *Daredevil park.* New York, Toronto: An Edward Packard Book, Bantam Books, 1991, 112 p., paper, novel. CHOOSE YOUR OWN ADVENTURE #114.

COMPTON, Spencer, *with Sara Compton*

20366 *Daredevil park.* New York, Toronto: An Edward Packard Book, Bantam Books, 1991, 112 p., paper, novel. CHOOSE YOUR OWN ADVENTURE #114.

COMPTON-RICKETT, Arthur, 1869-1937

20367 *William Morris: a study in personality.* London: Herbert Jenkins, 1913, xxii+ 325 p., cloth, nonf.

COMPTON-RICKETT, Joseph, Sir, 1847-1919

37670 *The quickening of Caliban: a modern story of evolution* / by J. Compton Rickett. London, Paris: Cassell & Co., 1893, 275 p., cloth, novel.

COMSTOCK, Jarrod, pseud.—SEE: Jarvis, Sharon & Kozak, Ellen M.

*COMYNS(-Carr), Barbara (Irene Veronica), 1909-1992

CONAWAY, J. C.

20368 *The magician's sleeve: a novel.* New York: Fawcett Gold Medal, 1979, 221 p., paper, novel.

20369 *Quarrel with the Moon.* New York: Tor, A Tom Doherty Associates Book, 1982, 319 p., paper, novel.

CONDÉ, Nicholas

The believers—SEE: *The religion.*

20370 *In the deep woods.* New York: St. Martin's Press, 1989, 306 p., cloth, novel.

20371 *The legend.* New York: A Signet Book, New American Library, 1984, 399 p., paper, novel.

20372 *The religion.* New York: NAL Books, New American Library, 1982, 375 p., cloth, novel.

20372A retitled: *The believers.* New York: A Signet Book, New American Library, 1987, 377 p., paper, novel.

CONDÉ, Phillip

20373 *The phantom pilot.* London: Mellifont Press, (1947?), 128 p., paper, novel.

CONDIT, Tom, *with Katherine MacLean*

20374 *Trouble with treaties.* [S.l.]: Lanthorne Press, 1975, 24 p., paper, story.

CONDON, Richard (Thomas), 1915-

20375 *Emperor of America.* New York: Simon & Schuster, 1990, 300 p., cloth, novel.

37671 *The final addiction.* New York: A Thomas Dunne Book, St. Martin's Press, 1991, 296 p., cloth, novel.

37672 *The star-spangled crunch.* Toronto, New York: Bantam Books, 1974, 130 p., paper, novel.

20376 *A talent for loving; or, The great cowboy race: a novel.* New York: McGraw-Hill Book Co., 1961, x+267 p., cloth, novel.

37673 *The whisper of the axe: a novel.* New York: Dial Press, 1976, 279 p., cloth, novel.

*CONDRAY, Bruno G. [pseud. of Leslie George Humphrys], 1921-

CONEY, Michael (Greatrex), 1932-

20377 *Brontomek!* London: Victor Gollancz, 1976, 254 p., cloth, novel.
20378 *Cat Karina.* New York: Ace Books, 1982, 294 p., paper, novel.
20379 *The celestial steam locomotive.* Boston: Houghton Mifflin Co., 1983, 302 p., cloth, novel. SONG OF EARTH #1.
20380 *Charisma.* London: Victor Gollancz, 1975, 224 p., cloth, novel.
20381 *Fang, the gnome* / by Michael Greatrex Coney. New York: NAL Books, 1988, 345 p., cloth, novel. SONG OF EARTH #3.
The girl with a symphony in her fingers—SEE: *The jaws that bite, the claws that catch.*
20382 *Gods of the Greataway.* Boston: Houghton Mifflin Co., 1984, vi+278 p., cloth, novel. SONG OF EARTH #2.
20383 *Hello summer, goodbye.* London: Victor Gollancz, 1975, 221 p., cloth, novel.
20383A retitled: *Rax.* New York: DAW Books, 1975, 189 p., paper, novel.
20383B retitled: *Pallahaxi tide.* Vancouver, British Columbia, Canada: A Tesseract Book, Porcépic Books, 1990, 237 p., paper, novel.
20384 *The jaws that bite, the claws that catch.* New York: DAW Books, 1975, 191 p., paper, novel.
20384A retitled: *The girl with a symphony in her fingers.* Morley, West Yorkshire, England: Elmfield Press, 1975, 199 p., cloth, novel.
20385 *King of the scepter'd isle* / by Michael Greatrex Coney. New York: NAL Books, New American Library, 1989, 399 p., cloth, novel. SONG OF EARTH #4.
20386 *Neptune's cauldron.* New York: Tower Books, 1981, 238 p., paper, novel.
Pallahaxi tide—SEE: *Hello summer, goodbye.*
Rax—SEE: *Hello summer, goodbye.*
20387 *The ultimate jungle.* London: Millington, 1979, 250 p., cloth, novel.

CONFORD, Ellen, 1942-

20388 *And this is Laura.* Boston: Little, Brown & Co., 1977, 179 p., cloth, novel.
20389 *Genie with the light blue hair.* New York: Bantam Books, 1989, 150 p., cloth, novel.

CONGER, Syndy M(cMillen), 1942-

20390 *Matthew G. Lewis, Charles Robert Maturin, and the Germans: an interpretative study of the influence of German literature on two Gothic novels.* Salzburg, Austria: Institut für Englische Sprache und Literatur, Universität Salzburg, 1977, iv+307 p., paper, nonf.

CONLY, Jane Leslie

20391 *Rasco and the rats of NIMH.* New York: Harper & Row, 1986, 278 p., cloth, novel. NIMH #2.
20392 *RT, Margaret, and the rats of NIMH.* New York: Harper & Row, 1990, 260 p., cloth, novel. NIMH #3.

CONLY, Robert—SEE: O'Brien, Robert C.

CONN, Phoebe (Jane), 1941-

20393 *Beyond the stars.* New York: Popular Library, 1988, 403 p., paper, novel.

CONNELLY, Mark, 1951-

20394 *The diminished self: Orwell and the loss of freedom.* Pittsburgh, PA: Duquesne University Press, 1987, 166 p., cloth, nonf.

CONNER, Jeff

20395 *Stephen King goes to Hollywood: a lavisly illustrated guide to all the films based on Stephen King's fiction.* New York: NAL Books, New American Library, 1987, xv+144 p., cloth, nonf.

CONNER, Michael, 1951-

20396 *Eye of the sun* / by Mike Conner. New York: Ace Books, 1988, 311 p., paper, novel.
20397 *Groupmind* / by Mike Conner. New York: Berkley Books, 1984, 217 p., paper, novel.
The Houdini detective—SEE: *I am not the other Houdini.*
20398 *I am not the other Houdini.* New York, Hagerstown, NJ: Harper & Row, Publishers, 1978, 186 p., cloth, novel.
20398A retitled: *The Houdini detective* / by Mike Conner. New York: Ace Books, 1989, 166 p., paper, novel.

CONNER, Mike—SEE: Conner, Michael

CONNERS, Bernard F., 1926-

20399 *The Hampton sisters: a novel.* New York: Donald I. Fine, 1987, 285 p., cloth, novel.

CONNOLLY, Eileen

20400 *Earthdance: a romance of reincarnation.* North Hollywood, CA: Newcastle Publishing Co., 1984, ix+246 p., paper, novel.

CONOVER, Willis (Jr.), 1920-

20401 *The old gent.* Arlington, VA: Carrollton Clark, 1977, [8] p., paper, nonf.
20402 *Science-fantasy correspondent: First World Fantasy Convention.* Arlington, VA: Carrollton Clark, 1976, 64+70 p., cloth, anth. [Includes some nonf.; incorporates *Science-fantasy correspondent one*; limited to 100 copies].
20403 *Science-fantasy correspondent one: an anthology of variations on a theme.* Arlington, VA: Carrollton Clark, 1975, 64 p., paper, anth.

with H. P. Lovecraft

20404 *Lovecraft at last.* Arlington, VA: Carrollton Clark, 1975, xxii+272 p., cloth, nonf. coll.

CONQUEST, Joan, 1883?-1941

37674 *Love's curse.* London: Jarrolds Ltd., 1936, 286 p., cloth, novel.
37675 *With the lid off.* London: T. Werner Laurie, 1935, 463 p., cloth, novel.

CONRAD, Allan

20405 *Glahmian shock.* North Hollywood, CA: Carousel Science Fantasy, 1980, 175 p., paper, novel.

CONRAD, Barnaby, Jr., 1922- , *with Nico Mastorakis*

20406 *Fire below zero.* New York: A Dell Book, 1981, 303 p., paper, novel.

*CONRAD, Earl, 1912-1986

CONRAD, Pam, 1947-

20407 *Stonewords: a ghost story.* New York: Harper & Row, 1990, 130 p., cloth, novel.

CONRAD, Paul, pseud.—SEE: King, Albert

CONSTANTINE, Murray, pseud.—SEE: Burdekin, Katharine

CONSTANTINE, Storm [legalized from her original name], 1956-

20408 *Aleph.* London: Orbit, 1991, 314 p., paper, novel. MONSTROUS REGIMENT #2.
20409 *The bewitchments of love and hate.* London: Macdonald & Co., 1988, 411 p., cloth, novel. BOOK OF WRAETHTHU #2.
20410 *The enchantments of flesh and spirit.* London: Macdonald & Co., 1987, 318 p., cloth, novel. BOOK OF WRAETHTHU #1.
20411 *The fulfilments of fate and desire.* London: Orbit, 1989, 424 p., paper, novel. BOOK OF WRAETHTHU #3.
20412 *Hermetech.* London: Headline, 1991, 372 p., cloth, novel.
20413 *The monstrous regiment.* London: Futura Orbit, 1990, 344 p., paper, novel. MONSTROUS REGIMENT #1.

CONTE, Edward Le—SEE: Le Conte, Edward

CONTE, Sol

20414 *Child's play.* New York: Leisure Books, 1986, 400 p., paper, novel.
20415 *The power.* New York: Leisure Books, 1989, 355 p., paper, novel.

CONTENTO, William G(uy), 1947-

20416 *Index to science fiction anthologies and collections.* Boston: G. K. Hall & Co., 1978, xii+608 p., cloth, nonf. REFERENCE PUBLICATION IN SCIENCE FICTION.
20417 *Index to science fiction anthologies and collections, 1977-1983.* Boston: G. K. Hall & Co., 1984, xvi+503 p., cloth, nonf. REFERENCE PUBLICATION IN SCIENCE FICTION.

with Charles N. Brown

18778 *Science fiction, fantasy, & horror: 1984: a comprehensive bibliography of books and short fiction published in the English language.* Oakland, CA: Locus Press, 1990, viii+269 p., cloth, nonf.
18779 *Science fiction, fantasy, & horror: 1986: a comprehensive bibliography of books and short fiction published in the English language.* Oakland, CA: Locus Press; Westport, CT: Meckler Corp., 1987, xiii+347 p., cloth, nonf.

18780 *Science fiction, fantasy, & horror: 1987: a comprehensive bibliography of books and short fiction published in the English language.* Oakland, CA: Locus Press, 1988, ix+417 p., cloth, nonf.

18781 *Science fiction in print: 1985: a comprehensive bibliography of books and short fiction published in the English language.* Oakland, CA: Locus Press, 1986, x+237 p., cloth, nonf.

with William G. Contento & Hal W. Hall

18782 *Science fiction, fantasy, & horror: 1988: a comprehensive bibliography of books and short fiction published in the English language.* Oakland, CA: Locus Press, 1989, viii+463 p., cloth, nonf. [Winner of the J. Lloyd Eaton Award for Best Nonfiction Book of the Year, 1989 (1991)].

18783 *Science fiction, fantasy, & horror: 1989: a comprehensive bibliography of books and short fiction published in the English language.* Oakland, CA: Locus Press, 1990, viii+515 p., cloth, nonf.

18784 *Science fiction, fantasy, & horror: 1990: a comprehensive bibliography of books and short fiction published in the English language.* Oakland, CA: Locus Press, 1991, viii+587 p., cloth, nonf.

*CONVERSE, Frank H., <u>d. 1889</u>

CONVERTITO, Bill

20418 *The Rombella shuttle.* Canoga Park, CA: Major Books, 1977, 158 p., paper, novel.

CONWAY, Gerard F., 1952- , as WALLACE MOORE

37676 *The blood stones.* New York: Pyramid Books, 1975, 190 p., paper, novel. BALZAN OF THE CAT PEOPLE #1.

37677 *The caves of madness.* New York: Pyramid Books, 1975, 159 p., paper, novel. BALZAN OF THE CAT PEOPLE #2.

37678 *The lights of Zetar.* New York: Pyramid Books, 1976, 144 p., paper, novel. BALZAN OF THE CAT PEOPLE #3.

CONWAY, Laura [pseud. of Dorothy Phoebe Ansle]

20419 *A link in the chain.* London: Collins, 1975, 156 p., cloth, novel.

20420A *Strange visitor.* London: Collins, 1973, 160 p., cloth, novel. [First published under the name Hebe Elsna].

03330A *Take heed of loving me.* New York: Saturday Review Press, E.P. Dutton, 1976, 160 p., cloth, novel. [Previously published under the name Hebe Elsna].

as HEBE ELSNA

20420 *Strange visitor.* London: Robert Hale, 1956, 191 p., cloth, novel.

CONWAY, Norman [pseud. of Lee Fleming]

20421 *Alpha death.* Chatsworth, CA: Canyon Books, 1975, 191 p., paper, novel. HUNTER #2.

20422 *The omega operation.* Chatsworth, CA: Canyon Books, 1974, 191 p., paper, novel. HUNTER #1.

COOK, David "Zeb", 1940?-

Beyond the moons—SEE: *Spelljammer: Beyond the moons.*

20423 *Dungeon master's guide, revised and updated edition.* Lake Geneva, WI: TSR Inc., 1989, 192 p., cloth, nonf.

20424 *Forgotten realms fantasy adventure: Horselords.* Lake Geneva, WI: TSR Inc., 1990, 312 p., paper, novel. EMPIRES TRILOGY #1.

Horselords—SEE: *Forgotten realms fantasy adventure: Horselords.*

20425 *Spelljammer: Beyond the moons.* Lake Geneva, WI: TSR Inc., 1991, 311 p., paper, novel. CLOAKMASTER CYCLE #1.

with Gary Gygax & François Marcela-Froideval

20426 *Oriental adventures.* Lake Geneva, WI: TSR Inc., 1985, 144 p., cloth, nonf. ADVANCED DUNGEONS & DRAGONS REFERENCE BOOKS.

COOK, Fred, with Sheldon R. Jaffery

20427 *The collector's guide to Weird tales.* Bowling Green, OH: Bowling Green State University Popular Press, 1985, 162 p., cloth, nonf.

COOK, Glen (Charles), 1944-

20428 *All darkness met.* New York: Berkley Books, 1980, 323 p., paper, novel. DREAD EMPIRE #3.

20429 *Annals of the Black Company.* Garden City, NY: Nelson Doubleday, 1986, 759 p., cloth, coll. CHRONICLES OF THE BLACK COMPANY #1-3.

20430 *Bitter gold hearts.* New York: A Signet Book, 1988, 253 p., paper, novel. GARRETT #2.

20431 *The Black Company.* New York: Tor, A Tom Doherty Associates Book, 1984, 319 p., paper, novel. CHRONICLES OF THE BLACK COMPANY #1.

20432 *Ceremony.* New York: Popular Library, Warner Books, 1986, 281 p., paper, novel. DARKWAR TRILOGY #3.

20433 *Cold copper tears.* New York: A Signet Book, 1988, 255 p., paper, novel. GARRETT #3.

20434 *Doomstalker.* New York: Popular Library, Warner Books, 1985, 264 p., paper, novel. DARKWAR Trilogy #1.

20435 *The dragon never sleeps.* New York: Popular Library, 1988, 422 p., paper, novel.

20436 *Dread brass shadows: from the files of Garrett, P.I.* New York: A Roc Book, 1990, 255 p., paper, novel. GARRETT #5.

20437 *Dreams of steel: second book of the South.* New York: Tor Fantasy, A Tom Doherty Associates Book, 1990, 346 p., paper, novel. CHRONICLES OF THE BLACK COMPANY #5.

20438 *The fire in his hands.* New York: A Timescape Book, Pocket Books, 1984, 224 p., paper, novel. DREAD EMPIRE #4.

20439 *The Garrett files.* Garden City, NY: Nelson Doubleday, 1989, 695 p., cloth, coll. GARRETT #1-3. [Includes *Sweet silver blues*; *Bitter gold hearts*; *Cold copper tears*].

20440 *An ill fate marshalling.* New York: Tor SF, A Tom Doherty Associates Book, 1988, 313 p., paper, novel. DREAD EMPIRE #7.

20441 *A matter of time.* New York: Ace Science Fiction Books, 1985, 268 p., paper, novel.

20442 *October's baby.* New York: A Berkley Book, Berkley Publishing Corp., 1980, 248 p., paper, novel. DREAD EMPIRE #2.

20443 *Old tin sorrows: from the files of Garrett, P.I.* New York: A Signet Book, New American Library, 1989, 252 p., paper, novel. GARRETT #4.

20444 *Passage at arms.* New York: Popular Library, 1985, 265 p., paper, novel.

20445 *Reap the east wind.* New York: Tor SF, A Tom Doherty Associates Book, 1987, 213 p., paper, novel. DREAD EMPIRE #6.

20446 *Red iron nights.* New York: A Roc Book, 1991, 270 p., paper, novel. GARRETT #6.

20447 *Shadow games: first book of the South.* New York: Tor Fantasy, A Tom Doherty Associates Book, 1989, 311 p., paper, novel. CHRONICLES OF THE BLACK COMPANY #4.

20448 *A shadow of all night falling.* New York: A Berkley Book, Berkley Publishing Corp., 1979, xii+240 p., paper, novel. DREAD EMPIRE #1.

20449 *Shadowline.* New York: Warner Books, 1982, 350 p., paper, novel. STARFISHERS TRILOGY #1.

20450 *Shadows linger.* New York: A Tom Doherty Associates Book, 1984, 319 p., paper, novel. CHRONICLES OF THE BLACK COMPANY #2.

20451 *The silver spike.* New York: Tor Fantasy, A Tom Doherty Associates Book, 1989, 313 p., paper, novel. CHRONICLES OF THE BLACK COMPANY #6.

20452 *Starfishers.* New York: Warner Books, 1982, 350 p., paper, novel. STARFISHERS TRILOGY #2.

20453 *Stars' End.* New York: Warner Books, 1982, 351 p., paper, novel. STARFISHERS TRILOGY #3.

20454 *Sung in blood.* Cambridge, MA: A Boskone Book, NESFA Press, 1990, 161 p., cloth, novel. [Limited to 800 copies; the author's name appears as "Glenn" Cook on the spine of the dustjacket].

20455 *Sweet silver blues.* New York: A Signet Book, 1987, 255 p., paper, novel. GARRETT #1.

20456 *The swordbearer.* New York: A Timescape Book, Pocket Books, 1982, 239 p., paper, novel.

20457 *The tower of fear.* New York: Tor Fantasy, A Tom Doherty Associates Book, 1989, 375 p., cloth, novel.

20458 *Warlock.* New York: Popular Library, Warner Books, 1985, 268 p., paper, novel. DARKWAR TRILOGY #2.

20459 *The White Rose.* New York: Tor, A Tom Doherty Associates Books, 1985, 317 p., paper, novel. CHRONICLES OF THE BLACK COMPANY #3.

20460 *With mercy toward none.* New York: Baen Books, 1985, 336 p., paper, novel. DREAM EMPIRE #5.

with Roger C. Schlobin

20461 *A Glen Cook bibliography.* [S.l.: s.n.], 1983, [4] p., paper, nonf.

COOK, Hugh (Walter Gilbert), 1956-

The hero's return—SEE: *The wordsmiths and the warguild.*
Lords of the sword—SEE: *The walrus and the warwolf.*

The oracle—SEE: *The women and the warlords.*

The questing hero—SEE: *The wordsmiths and the warguild.*

20461 *The shift.* London: Jonathan Cape, 1987, 215 p., cloth, novel.

20462 *The walrus and the warwolf.* London: Corgi Books, 1988, 779 p., paper, novel. CHRONICLES OF AN AGE OF DARKNESS #4.

20462A retitled: *Lords of the sword.* New York: A Roc Book, 1991, 272 p., paper, novel. CHRONICLES OF AN AGE OF DARKNESS #4. [Abridged edition].

20463 *The wazir and the witch.* Ealing, England: Corgi Books, 1990, 448 p., paper, novel. CHRONICLES OF AN AGE OF DARKNESS #7.

20464 *The werewolf and the wormlord.* London: Corgi Books, 1991, 352 p., paper, novel. CHRONICLES OF AN AGE OF DARKNESS #8.

20465 *The wicked and the witless.* London: Corgi Books, 1989, 458 p., paper, novel. CHRONICLES OF AN AGE OF DARKNESS #5.

20466 *The wishstone and the wonderworkers.* London: Corgi Books, 1990, 447 p., paper, novel. CHRONICLES OF AN AGE OF DARKNESS #6.

Wizard war—SEE: *Wizards and warriors.*

20467 *The wizards and the warriors.* Gerrards Cross, England: Colin Smythe, 1986, 351 p., cloth, novel. CHRONICLES OF AN AGE OF DARKNESS #1.

20467A retitled: *Wizard war.* New York: Popular Library, 1988, 447 p., paper, novel. WIZARD WAR CHRONICLES #1.

20468 *The women and the warlords.* London: Corgi Books, 1987, 428 p., paper, novel. CHRONICLES OF AN AGE OF DARKNESS #3.

20468A retitled: *The oracle.* New York: Popular Library, 1989, 346 p., paper, novel. WIZARD WAR CHRONICLES #4.

20469 *The wordsmiths and the warguild.* London: Corgi Books, 1987, 316 p., paper, novel. CHRONICLES OF AN AGE OF DARKNESS #2.

20469A retitled: *The questing hero.* New York: Popular Library, 1987, 200 p., paper, novel. WIZARD WAR CHRONICLES #2. [The original novel split into two parts].

20469B retitled: *The hero's return.* New York: Popular Library, 1988, 204 p., paper, novel. WIZARD WAR CHRONICLES #3. [The original novel split into two parts].

COOK, James R.—SEE: Cook, Rick

COOK, Michael L(ewis), 1929-1988

20470 *The ancient curse of the Baskervilles* / by "Michael Cooke". Bloomington, IN: Gaslight Publications, 1984, v+63 p., paper, novel.

20471 *Dime novel roundup: annotated index, 1931-1981.* Bowling Green, OH: Bowling Green State University Popular Press, 1983, 105 p., cloth, nonf.

20472 *Mystery fanfare: a composite annual index to mystery and related fanzines, 1963-1981.* Bowling Green, OH: Bowling Green State University Popular Press, 1983, 441 p., cloth, nonf.

COOK, Paul (Harlin), 1950-

20473 *The Alejandra variations.* New York: Ace Science Fiction Books, 1984, 248 p., paper, novel.

20474 *Duende meadow.* Toronto, New York: Bantam Books, 1985, 227 p., paper, novel.

20475 *Halo.* Toronto, New York: Bantam Books, 1986, 291 p., paper, novel.

20476 *On the rim of the mandala.* Toronto, New York: Bantam Books, 1987, 246 p., paper, novel.

20477 *Tintagel: a romance of the future* / by Paul H. Cook. New York: Berkley Books, 1981, 210 p., paper, novel.

COOK, Petronelle—SEE: Arnold, Margot

COOK, Rick [i.e., James Richard Cook], 1944-

20478 *Limbo system.* New York: Baen Books, 1989, 305 p., paper, novel.

20479 *The wizardry compiled.* New York: Baen Books, 1990, 307 p., paper, novel. WIZARD'S BANE #2.

20480 *The wizardry cursed.* Riverdale, NY: Baen Books, 1991, 394 p., paper, novel. WIZARD'S BANE #3.

20481 *Wizard's bane.* New York: Baen Books, 1989, 310 p., paper, novel. WIZARD'S BANE #1.

COOK, Robin, 1940-

20482 *Brain.* New York: G. P. Putnam's Sons, 1981, 283 p., cloth, novel.

20483 *Coma: a novel.* Boston: Little, Brown & Co., 1977, 306 p., cloth, novel.

20484 *Harmful intent.* New York: G. P. Putnam's Sons, 1990, 400 p., cloth, novel.

20485 *Mindbend.* New York: G. P. Putnam's Sons, 1985, 368 p., cloth, novel.

20486 *Mortal fear*. New York: G. P. Putnam's Sons, 1988, 364 p., cloth, novel.

20487 *Mutation*. New York: G. P. Putnam's Sons, 1989, 367 p., cloth, novel.

COOK, W(illiam) Paul, 1881-1948

20488 *In memoriam Howard Phillips Lovecraft: recollections, appreciations, estimates*. [North Montpelier, VT]: Driftwind Press, 1941, 75 p., paper, nonf. [Limited to 94 copies].

20489 *The recluse 1927*. Glenview, IL: Moshassuck Press, 1990, 78 p., paper, anth. [Limited to 125 copies; a reproduction of the 1927 magazine published by Cook's Recluse Press].

COOKE, Catherine [i.e., Catherine Marie Cooke Montrose], 1963-

20490 *The crimson goddess*. New York: Ace Books, 1989, 232 p., paper, novel. WINGED ASSASSIN #3.

20491 *The hidden temple*. New York: Tor SF, A Tom Doherty Associates Book, 1988, 306 p., paper, novel. MASK #3.

20492 *Mask of the wizard*. New York: Tor, A Tom Doherty Associates Book, 1985, 384 p., paper, novel. MASK #1.

20493 *Realm of the gods*. New York: Ace Books, 1988, 218 p., paper, novel. WINGED ASSASSIN #2.

20494 *Veil of shadow*. New York: Tor SF, A Tom Doherty Associates Book, 1987, 286 p., paper, novel. MASK #2.

20495 *The winged assassin*. New York: Ace Fantasy Books, 1987, 279 p., paper, novel. WINGED ASSASSIN #1.

*COOKE, Donald E(win), 1916-1985

COOKE, John Peyton, 1967-

20496 *The lake*. New York: Avon Books, 1989, 218 p., paper, novel.

20497 *Out for blood*. New York: Avon Books, 1991, 313 p., paper, novel.

COOKE, Michael—SEE: Cook, Michael L.

COOKSON, Catherine (Ann McMullen), 1906-

20498 *Mrs Flannagan's trumpet*. London: Macdonald & Jane's, 1976, 144 p., cloth, novel.

*COOLIDGE, Olivia (Ensor), 1908-

*COON, Merlin J(oseph), 1912-1956

COON, Susan [pseud. of Susan Irene Fassender Plunkett], 1945-

20499 *Cassilee*. New York: Avon, 1980, 250 p., paper, novel. LIVING PLANET SERIES #2.

20500 *Chiy-une*. New York: Avon, 1982, 312 p., paper, novel. LIVING PLANET SERIES #4.

20501 *Rahne*. New York: Avon, 1980, 206 p., paper, novel. LIVING PLANET SERIES #1.

20502 *The Virgin*. New York: Avon, 1981, 280 p., paper, novel. LIVING PLANET SERIES #3.

COONEY, Caroline B., 1947-

20503 *The cheerleader*. New York, Toronto: Point Fiction, Scholastic Inc., 1991, 179 p., paper, novel.

20504 *The fire*. New York, Toronto: Point Fiction, Scholastic Inc., 1990, 198 p., paper, novel. FOG #3.

20505 *The fog*. New York, Toronto: Scholastic Inc., 1989, 218 p., paper, novel. FOG #1.

20506 *The snow*. New York, Toronto: Point Fiction, Scholastic Inc., 1990, 201 p., paper, novel. FOG #2.

COONTZ, Otto, 1946-

20507 *Isle of the shapeshifters*. Boston: Houghton Mifflin Co., 1983, 209 p., cloth, novel.

20507A retitled: *The shapeshifters*. London: Methuen, 1987, 209 p., cloth, novel.

20508 *The night walkers*. Boston: Houghton Mifflin Co., 1982, 179 p., cloth, novel.

The shapeshifters—SEE: *Isle of the shapeshifters*.

20509 *Through the nightsea wall*. London: Methuen, 1989, 225 p., cloth, novel. AUSABLE ODYSSEYS #1.

COOPER, C. Everett, pseud.—SEE: Reginald, R.

COOPER, (Brenda) Clare, 1935-

20510 *Ashar of Qarius*. London: Sprint, Simon & Schuster, 1988, 160 p., paper, novel.

20511 *Earthchange*. London: Hodder & Stoughton, 1985, 96 p., cloth, novel.

20512 *The settlement on Planet B*. London: Hodder & Stoughton, 1987, 158 p., cloth, novel.

20513 *The skyrifters*. London: Sprint, Simon & Schuster, 1989, 141 p., paper, novel.

COOPER, Colin (Symons), 1926-

20514 *Dargason.* London: Dennis Dobson, 1977, 191 p., cloth, novel.

20515 *The Epping pyramid.* London: Robert Hale, 1978, 205 p., cloth, novel.

COOPER, Edmund, 1926-1982

20519A *The deathworms of Kratos.* London: Severn House, 1977, 142 p., cloth, novel. EXPENDABLES #1. [Originally published under the name Richard Avery].

20516 *Jupiter laughs, and other stories.* London, Sydney: Hodder & Stoughton, 1979, 220 p., cloth, coll.

20517 *Merry Christmas, Ms Minerva.* London: Robert Hale, 1978, 158 p., cloth, novel.

20521A *The rings of Tantalus.* London: Severn House, 1977, 157 p., cloth, novel. EXPENDABLES #2. [Originally published under the name Richard Avery].

20522A *The War Games of Zelos.* London: Coronet Books, Hodder & Stoughton, 1980, 192 p., paper, novel. EXPENDABLES #3. [Originally published under the name Richard Avery].

20518 *A world of difference.* London: Robert Hale, 1980, 192 p., cloth, novel.

as RICHARD AVERY

20519 *The death worms of Kratos.* London: Coronet Books, Hodder & Stoughton, 1975, 142 p., paper, novel. EXPENDABLES #1.

20520 *The Expendables: The venom of Argus.* London: Coronet Books, Hodder & Stoughton, 1976, 160 p., paper, novel. EXPENDABLES #4.

20521 *The rings of Tantalus.* London: Coronet Books, Hodder & Stoughton, 1975, 157 p., paper, novel. EXPENDABLES #2.

The venom of Argus—SEE: *The Expendables: The venom of Argus.*

20522 *The War Games of Zelos.* London: Coronet Books, Hodder & Stoughton, 1975, 192 p., paper, novel. EXPENDABLES #3.

COOPER, Hughes, pseud.—SEE: Leonard, George H.

COOPER, Jeffrey (B.), 1950-

20523 *The Nightmare on Elm Street companion: the official guide to America's favorite fiend.* New York: St. Martin's Press, 1987, 110 p., paper, nonf.

20524 *Nightmares on Elm Street, parts 1, 2, 3: the continuing story: a novel.* New York: St. Martin's Press, 1987, 216 p., paper, movie coll. NIGHTMARE ON ELM STREET #1-3.

COOPER, John R.

20525 *The Lord Falcon: the making of a legend.* Lewes, East Sussex, England: The Book Guild, 1991, 220 p., cloth, novel. REPOSITORS #1.

COOPER, Louise, 1952-

20526 *Avatar.* London: Grafton, 1991, xiii+299 p., paper, novel. INDIGO #6.

20527 *Blood summer.* London: New English Library, 1976, 127 p., paper, novel.

20528 *Crown of Horn.* London: Hamlyn Paperbacks, 1981, 256 p., paper, novel.

20529 *The deceiver.* New York, Toronto: Spectra, Bantam Books, 1991, 280 p., paper, novel. CHAOS GATE TRILOGY #1.

20530 *In memory of Louise Bailey.* London: New English Library, 1977, 143 p., paper, novel.

20531 *Infanta.* London: Unwin Paperbacks, 1989, 318 p., paper, novel. INDIGO #3.

20532 *Inferno.* London: Unwin Paperbacks, 1988, 241 p., paper, novel. INDIGO #2.

20533 *The initiate.* New York: Tor SF, A Tom Doherty Associates Book, 1985, 278 p., paper, novel. TIME MASTER TRILOGY #1.

20534 *Lord of no time.* London: Sphere Books, 1977, 221 p., paper, novel.

20535 *The master.* London: Unwin Paperbacks, 1987, 249 p., paper, novel. TIME MASTER TRILOGY #3.

20536 *Mirage.* London: Unwin Paperbacks, 1987, 343 p., paper, novel.

20537 *Nemesis.* London: Unwin Paperbacks, 1988, 246 p., paper, novel. INDIGO #1.

20538 *Nocturne.* London: Unwin Paperbacks, 1989, 291 p., paper, novel. INDIGO #4.

20539 *The outcast.* London: George Allen & Unwin, 1986, 301 p., cloth, novel. TIME MASTER TRILOGY #2.

20540 *The pretender.* New York, Toronto: Spectra, Bantam Books, 1991, 377 p., paper, novel. CHAOS GATE TRILOGY #2.

20541 *The sleep of stone.* New York: A Byron Preiss Visual Publications Book, Dragonflight Books, Atheneum; Toronto: Maxwell Macmillan Canada; New York: Maxwell Macmillan International, 1991, 138 p., cloth, novel.

20542 *The thorn key.* London: Orchard Books, 1988, 163 p., cloth, novel.

20542 *Troika.* London: Grafton, 1991, xi+268 p., paper, novel. INDIGO #5.

COOPER, Margaret C(hilvers)

20544   *Code name: Clone.* New York: Walker & Co., 1982, 121 p., cloth, novel. STEFAN & EVONN #2.

37679   *It's about time: a witches' brew of comedy, tragedy, and ghosts.* London: William Kimber, 1980, 192 p., cloth, coll.

20545   *Solution: escape.* New York: Walker & Co., 1981, 93 p., cloth, novel. STEFAN & EVONN #1.

COOPER, Parley J(oseph), 1937-

20546   *Reverend Mama.* New York: Pocket Books, 1975, 239 p., paper, novel.

20547   *Wreck.* New York: Ace Books, 1977, 311 p., paper, novel.

as ALEX NEBRENSKY

20548   *The unholy.* New York: A Signet Book, New American Library, 1982, 274 p., paper, novel.

COOPER, Peter L(ee), 1949-

20549   *Signs and symptoms: Thomas Pynchon and the contemporary world.* Berkeley, Los Angeles, CA: University of California Press, 1983, 238 p., cloth, nonf.

COOPER, Richard

20550   *Knights of God.* London: Lion, 1987, 228 p., paper, tele.

COOPER, Rick, *with Mark Davis as* NICHOLAS SARAZEN

20551   *Family reunion.* New York: Pinnacle Books, Windsor Publishing Corp., 1990, 287 p., paper, novel.

COOPER, Sandra L.—SEE: Cooper, Sonni

COOPER, Sonni [i.e., Sandra Lenore Cooper], 1934-

20552   *Black fire: a Star Trek novel.* New York: A Timescape Book, Pocket Books, 1983, 220 p., paper, novel. STAR TREK #8.

COOPER, Susan (Mary), 1935-

20553   *The dark is rising sequence.* Harmondsworth, Middlesex, England: Penguin Books, 1984, 786 p., paper, coll. DARK IS RISING #1-5.

20554   *The grey king.* London: Chatto & Windus, 1975, 208 p., cloth, novel. DARK IS RISING #4.

20555   *Seaward.* London: Bodley Head, 1976, 166 p., cloth, novel.

20556   *Silver on the tree.* London: Chatto & Windus, 1977, 269 p., cloth, novel. DARK IS RISING #5.

20557   *Stars in our hands.* Toronto: Toronto Public Library, 1977, iv+8 p., paper, nonf.

COOPER, Tom

20558   *War*Moon.* Toronto, New York: Worldwide Library, 1987, 381 p., paper, novel.

COOVER, Robert (Lowell), 1932-

20559   *Pinocchio in Venice.* New York: Simon & Schuster, Linden Press, 1991, 330 p., cloth, novel.

COPELAND, Lori

20560   *Out of this world.* New York: A Dell Book, 1986, 189 p., paper, novel.

COPP, DeWitt S.

20561   *A different kind of rain.* New York: W.W. Norton & Co., 1978, 224 p., cloth, novel.

COPPARD, Audrey (Jean), 1931- , with Bernard Crick

20562   *Orwell remembered.* London: British Broadcasting Corp., Ariel Books, 1984, 287 p., paper, nonf. anth.

COPPEL, Alfred (José de Araña-Marini y), 1921-

20563   *The burning mountain: a novel of the invasion of Japan.* San Diego, CA: Harcourt Brace Jovanovich, 1983, 438 p., cloth, novel.

20564   *The dragon.* New York, London: Harcourt Brace Jovanovich, 1977, 438 p., cloth, novel.

as ROBERT CHAM GILMAN

20565   *The Warlock of Rhada.* New York: Ace Science Fiction Books, 1985, 172 p., paper, novel. RHADA PREQUEL.

COPPER, Basil, 1924-

20566 *And afterward, the dark: seven tales.* Sauk City, WI: Arkham House, 1977, xii+ 222 p., cloth, coll.

20567 *The curse of the Fleers.* Blandford, England: Harwood-Smart, 1976, 140 p., cloth, novel.

20568 *Here be daemons: tales of horror and the uneasy.* London: Robert Hale, 1978, 219 p., cloth, coll.

20569 *The house of the wolf.* Sauk City, WI: Arkham House, 1983, vi+298 p., cloth, novel.

20570 *Into the silence.* London: Sphere Books, 1983, 243 p., paper, novel.

20571 *Necropolis.* Sauk City, WI: Arkham House, 1980, xii+352 p., cloth, novel.

20572 *The vampire in legend, fact, and art.* London: Robert Hale, 1973, 208 p., cloth, nonf.

20573 *Voices of doom: tales of terror and the uncanny.* London: Robert Hale, 1980, 190 p., cloth, coll.

20574 *The werewolf in legend, fact, & art.* London: Robert Hale, 1977, 240 p., cloth, nonf.

20575 *When footsteps echo: tales of terror and the unknown.* London: Robert Hale, 1975, 184 p., cloth, coll.

CORBETT, Fred, *with Gerry Goldberg & Stephen Storoschuk*

20576 *Nighttouch.* Don Mills, Ontario, Canada: General Publishing, 1977, 156 p., cloth, anth. [Includes some nonfiction and verse].

CORBETT, James, d. 1958?

20577 *Vampire of the skies.* London: Herbert Jenkins, 1932, vii+248 p., cloth, novel.

CORBETT, Lionel, *with Murray Stein*

20578 *Psyche's stories: modern Jungian interpretations of fairy tales, volume 1.* Wilmette, IL: Chiron Publications, 1991, viii+166 p., cloth, nonf. anth.

CORBETT, Scott, 1913-

20579 *Captain Butcher's body.* Boston: An Atlantic Monthly Book, Little, Brown & Co., 1976, 168 p., cloth, novel.

20580 *The deadly hoax.* New York: A Unicorn Book, E. P. Dutton, 1981, 86 p., cloth, novel.

20581 *The donkey planet.* New York: A Unicorn Book, E. P. Dutton, 1979, 89 p., cloth, novel.

with Oscar Wilde

20582 *The discontented ghost.* New York: A Unicorn Book, E. P. Dutton, 1980, 180 p., cloth, novel. [A retelling of Oscar Wilde's *The Canterville Ghost*].

CORBETT, W(illiam) J(esse), 1938-

20583 *Pentecost and the chosen one.* London: Methuen, 1984, v+237 p., cloth, novel. PENTECOST #2.

20584 *Pentecost of Lickey Top.* London: Methuen's Children's Books, 1987, xi+ 189 p., cloth, novel. PENTECOST #3.

20585 *The song of Pentecost.* London: Methuen, 1982, 215 p., cloth, novel. PENTECOST #1.

CORBY, (A.) Adam

20586 *The divine queen.* New York: A Timescape Book, Pocket Books, 1982, 313 p., paper, novel. DOOM-QUEST OF ARA-KARN #2.

20587 *The former king.* New York: A Timescape Book, Pocket Books, 1981, 224 p., paper, novel. DOOM-QUEST OF ARA-KARN #1.

CORBY, Michael, *with Michael Geare*

20588 *Dracula's diary.* London: Buchan & Enright, 1982, 153 p., cloth, novel.

*CORIELL, Vernell, <u>1918-1987</u>

CORLETT, William (Albert), 1938-

20589 *The dark side of the Moon.* London: Hamish Hamilton, 1976, 159 p., cloth, novel.

20590 *The door in the tree.* London: Bodley Head, 1991, 261 p., cloth, novel. MAGICIAN'S HOUSE #2.

20591 *The gate of Eden.* London: Hamish Hamilton, 1974, 175 p., cloth, novel. GATE TRILOGY #1.

20592 *The land beyond.* London: Hamish Hamilton, 1975, 184 p., cloth, novel. GATE TRILOGY #2.

20593 *Return to the gate.* London: Hamish Hamilton, 1975, 165 p., cloth, novel. GATE TRILOGY #3.

20594 *The steps up the chimney.* London: Bodley Head, 1990, 233 p., cloth, novel. MAGICIAN'S HOUSE #1.
20595 *The tunnel behind the waterfall.* London: Bodley Head, 1991, 280 p., cloth, novel. MAGICIAN'S HOUSE #3.

CORLEY, Edwin (Raymond), 1931-1981

20596 *The Genesis Rock.* Garden City, NY: Doubleday & Co., 1980, 253 p., cloth, novel.
20597 *Sargasso.* Garden City, NY: Doubleday & Co., 1977, 259 p., cloth, novel.

CORLEY, James, 1947-

20598 *Benedict's Planet.* Morley, Yorkshire, England: Elmfield Press, 1976, 170 p., cloth, novel.
20599 *Orsini Godbase.* London: Robert Hale, 1978, 176 p., cloth, novel.
20600 *Sundrinker.* London: Robert Hale, 1980, 192 p., cloth, novel.

*CORMACK, Maribelle (B.), 1902-1984

*CORMAN, Avery, 1935-

CORMIER, Robert (Edmund), 1925-

20601 *Fade.* New York: Delacorte Press, 1988, 310 p., cloth, novel.

CORN, Joseph J., *with Brian Horrigan*

20602 *Yesterday's tomorrows: past vision of the American future.* New York: Summit Books; Washington: Smithsonian Institution Traveling Exhibition Service, 1984, xvii+158 p., paper, nonf.

*CORNELL, Fred(erick) C(arruthers), 1867-1921

CORNELL, Paul

20603 *Timewyrm: Revelation.* London: Doctor Who Books, 1991, 220 p., paper, novel. TIMEWYRM #4.

CORNETT, Robert (Charles), 1952- , *with Kevin Randle*

20604 *The Aldebaran campaign.* New York: Ace Books, 1988, 202 p., paper, novel. SEEDS OF WAR #2.
20605 *The Aquarian attack.* New York: Ace Books, 1989, 188 p., paper, novel. SEEDS OF WAR #3.

20606 *Remember Gettysburg!* New York: Charter Books, 1988, 231 p., paper, novel. REMEMBER #2.
20607 *Remember the Alamo!* TA Publications, 1980, [160] p., paper?, novel. REMEMBER #1. [The 1986 Charter Books edition may be revised].
20608 *Remember the Little Bighorn!* New York: Charter Books, 1990, 188 p., paper, novel. REMEMBER #3.
20609 *Seeds of war.* New York: Ace Science Fiction Books, 1986, 265 p., paper, novel. SEEDS OF WAR #1.

*CORNWALL, Ian W(olfram), 1909-

CORNWELL, Neil, 1942-

20610 *The literary fantastic: from gothic to postmodernism.* London: Harvester/Wheatsheaf, 1990, xvii+269 p., cloth, nonf.

CORNWELL, Sue, *with Mike Kott*

20611 *The official price guide to the Star Trek and Star wars collectibles.* New York: House of Collectibles, 1986, 377 p., paper, nonf.
20612 *The official price guide to the Star Trek and Star wars collectibles, 2nd ed.* New York: House of Collectibles, 1987, 415 p., paper, nonf.
20613 *The official price guide to the Star Trek and Star wars collectibles, 3rd ed.* New York: House of Collectibles, 1991, 277 p., paper, nonf.

CORON, Hannah

15795 *Ten years hence?* London: J. M. Ouseley & Son, 1924, 255 p., cloth, novel.

CORREN, Grace, pseud.—SEE: Hoskins, Robert

CORREY, Lee, pseud—SEE: Stine, G. Harry

CORRICK, James A(dam Jr.), 1913-

20614 *Double your pleasure: the Ace SF double.* Brooklyn, NY: Gryphon Books, 1989, 85 p., paper, nonf.

CORRIGAN, Theresa, 1949- , *with Stephanie T. Hoppe*

20615 *And a deer's ear, eagle's song, & bear's game: animals and women.* Pittsburgh, PA: Cleis Press, 1990, 228 p., cloth, anth.

20616 *With a fly's eye, whale's wit, and woman's heart: animals and women.* San Francisco: Cleis Press, 1989, 234 p., cloth, anth.

CORRIN, Sara, 1918- , *with Stephen Corrin*

21567 *Imagine that! fifteen fantastic tales.* London: Faber & Faber, 1986, 176 p., cloth, coll.

CORRIN, Stephen, *with Sara Corrin*

21567 *Imagine that! fifteen fantastic tales.* London: Faber & Faber, 1986, 176 p., cloth, coll.

*CORTAZAR, Julio, 1914-<u>1984</u>

CORY, Vivian—SEE: Cross, Victoria

CORYDON, Bent, *with L. Ron Hubbard Jr.*

20617 *L. Ron Hubbard: messiah or madman?* Secaucus, NJ: Lyle Stuart, 1987, 402 p., cloth, nonf.

COSTA, Richard Hauer, 1921-

20618 *H. G. Wells.* New York: Twayne Publishers, 1967, 181 p., cloth, nonf.
20619 *H. G. Wells, revised edition.* Boston: Twayne Publishers, 1985, 177 p., cloth, nonf.

COSTELLO, Matthew J(ohn), 1948-

20620 *Beneath still waters.* New York: Berkley Books, 1989, 266 p., paper, novel.
20621 *Child's play 2: a novel.* New York: Jove Books, 1990, 250 p., paper, movie. Child's Play #2.
20622 *Child's play 3: a novel.* New York: Jove Books, 1991, 250 p., paper, movie. CHILD'S PLAY #3.
20623 *Hour of the scorpion.* New York: A Roc Book, 1991, 335 p., paper, novel. TIME WARRIOR #2.
20624 *Midsummer.* New York: Charter/Diamond Books, 1990, 307 p., paper, novel.
20625 *Revolt on Majipoor: a Crossroads adventure in the world of Robert Silverberg's Majipoor /* by Matt Costello. New York: Tor, A Tom Doherty Associates Book, 1987, 243 p., paper, novel. CROSSROADS ADVENTURES; MAJIPOOR TIE-IN].
20626 *Robert Heinlein's Glory road: Fate's trick /* by Matt Costello. New York: Tor, A Tom Doherty Associates Book, 1988, viii+22+[215] p., paper, novel. CROSS-

ROADS ADVENTURE; GLORY ROAD SEQUEL.

20627 *Sleep tight.* New York: Zebra Books, Kensington Publishing Corp., 1987, 302 p., paper, novel.
20628 *Time of the fox.* New York: A Roc Book, 1990, 331 p., paper, novel. TIME WARRIOR #1.
20630 *The wizard of Tizare.* New York: Bantam Books, 1990, 313 p., paper, novel. GUARDIANS OF THE THREE #3.
20631 *Wurm.* New York: Diamond Books, 1991, 360 p., paper, novel.

COSTELLO, Peter, 1946-

20632 *Jules Verne: inventor of science fiction.* London & Sydney: Hodder & Stoughton, 1978, 239 p., cloth, nonf.

COSTELLO, Sean

20633 *Captain Quad.* New York, London: Pocket Books, 1991, viii+370 p., paper, novel.
20634 *The cartoonist.* New York, London: Pocket Books, 1990, 248 p., paper, novel.
20635 *Eden's eyes.* New York, London: Pocket Books, 1989, 278 p., paper, novel.

COSTIKYAN, Greg(ory John), 1959-

20636 *Another day, another dungeon.* New York: Tor Fantasy, A Tom Doherty Associates Book, 1990, 341 p., paper, novel. CUPS AND SORCERY #1.
20637 *Star Wars—the roleplaying game.* New York: West End Games, 1987, 121 p., paper, fiction.

with Allen Varney

20638 *The Willow sourcebook.* New York: Tor, An Eric Goldberg Associates Sourcebook, 1988, 90 p., paper, nonf.

COTÉ, Denis, 1954-

37680 *The invisible empire.* Windsor, Ontario, Canada: Black Moss Press, 1990, 102 p., paper, novel. [Translation by David Homel of *L'Invisible puissance*].
37681 *Shooting for the stars.* Windsor, Ontario, Canada: Black Moss Press, 1990, 120 p., paper, novel. [Translation by Jane Brierley of *Hockeyeurs cybernétiques*].

COTT, Jonathan, 1942-

20639 *Wandering ghost: the odyssey of Lafcadio Hearn.* New York: Alfred A. Knopf, 1991, xxi + 438 p., cloth, nonf.

COTTER, John, pseud.—SEE: Couffer, Jack

COTTON, Donald

20640 *Doctor Who: The gunfighters.* London: W. H. Allen & Co., 1985, 152 p., cloth, tele. DOCTOR WHO #101.

20641 *Doctor Who: The myth makers.* London: W. H. Allen & Co., 1985, 142 p., cloth, tele. DOCTOR WHO #97.

20642 *Doctor Who: The myth makers; and, The gunfighters.* London: A Target Book, W. H. Allen & Co., 1988, 290 p., paper, tele. coll. DOCTOR WHO SERIES.

20643 *Doctor Who: The Romans.* London: W. H. Allen & Co., 1987, 128 p., cloth, tele. DOCTOR WHO #120.
    The gunfighters—SEE: Doctor Who: The gunfighters.
    The myth makers—SEE: Doctor Who: The myth makers.
    The myth makers; and, The gunfighters—SEE: Doctor Who: The myth makers; and, The gunfighters.
    The Romans—SEE: Doctor Who: The Romans.

COTTON, José Edmondson y—SEE: Edmondson, G. C.

COTTRILL, Tim, 1958- , *with Martin H. Greenberg & Charles G. Waugh*

20644 *Science fiction and fantasy series and sequels: a bibliography, volume 1: books.* New York, London: Garland Publishing, 1986, xix + 398 p., cloth, nonf. [Only volume published].

COUFFER, Jack (C.), 1924- , *as* JOHN COTTER, *with Judith Frankle*

20645 *Nights with Sasquatch.* New York: A Berkley Medallion Book, Berkley Publishing Corp., 1977, 182 p., paper, novel.

COULIANO, I. P.—SEE: Culianu, I. P.

COULSON, Juanita (Ruth Wellons), 1933-

20646 *Dark priestess.* New York: Ballantine Books, 1977, 444 p., paper, novel.

20647 *The death god's Citadel.* New York: A Del Rey Book, Ballantine Books, 1980, 386 p., paper, novel. KRANTIN #2.

20648 *Door into terror.* New York: A Berkley Medallion Book, 1972, 224 p., paper, novel.

20649 *Fear stalks the bayou.* New York: Ballantine Books, 1976, 212 p., paper, novel. ASTROLOGICAL GOTHIC NOVEL—ARIES.

20650 *Legacy of Earth.* New York: A Del Rey Book, Ballantine Books, 1989, 357 p., paper, novel. CHILDREN OF THE STARS #3.

20651 *Outward bound.* New York: A Del Rey Book, Ballantine Books, 1982, 371 p., paper, novel. CHILDREN OF THE STARS #2.

20652 *The past of forever.* New York: A Del Rey Book, Ballantine Books, 1989, 327 p., paper, novel. CHILDREN OF THE STARS #4.

20653 *The secret of Seven Oaks.* New York: A Berkley Medallion Book, 1972, 191 p., paper, novel.

20654 *Space trap.* Toronto, New York: Laser Books, 1976, 191 p., paper, novel.

20655 *Star sister.* New York: A Del Rey Book, Ballantine Books, 1990, 219 p., paper, novel.

20656 *Stone of blood.* New York: Ballantine Books, 1975, 182 p., paper, novel. BIRTHSTONE GOTHIC #3.

20657 *Tomorrow's heritage.* New York: A Del Rey Book, Ballantine Books, 1981, 372 p., paper, novel. CHILDREN OF THE STARS #1.

20658 *Unto the last generation.* Don Mills, Ontario: Laser Books, 1975, 190 p., paper, novel.

20659 *The web of wizardry.* New York: A Del Rey Book, Ballantine Books, 1978, 359 p., paper, novel. KRANTIN #1.

COULSON, Robert (Stratton), 1928-

20660 *High spy.* Lake Geneva, WI: TSR Inc., 1987, 128 p., paper, novel. LAZER TAG ADVENTURE #1.

20661 *To renew the ages.* Toronto, New York: Laser Books, 1976, 190 p., paper, novel.

with Piers Anthony

16708 *But what of Earth?* Toronto, New York: Laser Books, 1976, 190 p., paper, novel.

with Gene DeWeese

20662 *Charles Fort never mentioned wombats.* Garden City, NY: Doubleday & Co.,

1977, xv + 173 p., cloth, novel. JOE KARNS #2.

20663 *Gates of the universe*. Don Mills, Ontario: Laser Books, 1975, 190 p., paper, novel.

20664 *Nightmare universe*. Lake Geneva, WI: TSR Inc., 1985, 223 p., paper, novel.

20665 *Now you see it/him/them....* Garden City, NY: Doubleday & Co., 1975, 157 p., cloth, novel. JOE KARNS #1.

COUNSELMAN, Mary Elizabeth, 1911-

20666 *Half in shadow*. Sauk City, WI: Arkham House, 1978, ix + 212 p., cloth, coll.

COUPER, Stephen, pseud.—SEE: Gallagher, Stephen

COURLANDER, Harold, 1908-

20667 *The Bordeaux narrative*. Albuquerque, NM: University of New Mexico Press, 1990, ix + 192 p., cloth, novel.

COURTIER, S(idney) H(obson), 1904-1974

20668 *The smiling trip*. London: Robert Hale, 1975, 182 p., cloth, novel.

COURTNEY, Dayle, pseud.—SEE: Kimberly, Gail

COURTNEY, Vincent

20669 *Vampire beat*. New York: Pinnacle Books, Windsor Publishing Corp., 1991, 302 p., paper, novel.

COVELL, Ian

20670 *An index to DAW Books*. Albuquerque, NM: Galactic Central Publications, 1990, 58 p., paper, nonf. GALACTIC CENTRAL PUBLISHER CHECKLISTS #1.

20671 *J. T. McIntosh: memoir & bibliography*. Polk City, IA: Chris Drumm, 1987, 32 p., paper, nonf. [Includes a one-page insert update; cover title]. DRUMM BOOKLET #25.

COVELL, Richard, *with John Banks & Lee Clarke & Jay Clarke, as* MICHAEL SLADE

17336 *Ghoul*. New York: Beech Tree Books, 1987, 417 p., cloth, novel.

COVER, Arthur Byron, 1950-

20672 *American revolutionary*. Toronto, New York: A Byron Preiss Book, Bantam

Books, 1985, 125 p., paper, novel. TIME MACHINE #10.

20673 *Autumn angels*. New York: Pyramid Books, 1975, 191 p., paper, novel. AUTUMN ANGELS #1.

20674 *Blade of the guillotine*. Toronto, New York: A Byron Preiss Book, Bantam Books, 1986, 125 p., paper, novel. TIME MACHINE #14.

20675 *An east wind coming*. New York: A Berkley Book, Berkley Publishing Corp., 1979, 355 p., paper, novel. AUTUMN ANGELS #3.

20676 *Flash Gordon: a novel*. New York: A Jove Book, 1980, 220 p., paper, movie. FLASH GORDON SERIES.

20677 *Planetfall*. New York: A Byron Preiss Book, An Infocom Book, Avon Books, 1988, 298 p., paper, novel. PLANETFALL #1.

20678 *The Platypus of Doom, and other nihilists*. New York: Warner Books, 1976, 222 p., paper, coll. AUTUMN ANGELS #2.

20679 *Prodigy*. New York: A Byron Preiss Visual Publications Inc. Book, Ace Books, 1988, xiii + 177 p., paper, novel. ISAAC ASIMOV'S ROBOT CITY #4.

20680 *The rings of Saturn*. Toronto, New York: A Byron Preiss Book, Bantam Books, 1985, 125 p., paper, novel. TIME MACHINE #6.

20681 *The sound of winter*. New York: Pyramid Books, 1976, 156 p., paper, novel.

20682 *Stationfall*. New York: A Byron Preiss Book, An Infocom Book, Avon Books, 1989, 297 p., paper, novel. PLANETFALL #2.

with Tim Sullivan and John Gregory Betancourt as THOMAS SHADWELL

The dinosaur trackers—SEE: *Robert Silverberg's Time tours: The dinosaur trackers*.

20683 *Robert Silverberg's Time tours: The dinosaur trackers*. New York: A Byron Preiss Book, HarperPaperbacks, 1991, 138 p., paper, novel. ROBERT SILVERBERG'S TIME TOURS #4.

with Lynn Haney

20684 *The Flash Gordon book*. New York: G. P. Putnam's Sons, 1980, [58] p., cloth, movie. FLASH GORDON SERIES. [Adapted by Haney from Cover's novel].

COVER, James P.

20685 *Notes on Jurgen*. Easton: At the Sign of the Fired Typist, 1927, [78] p., cloth?, nonf. anth.

20686 *Notes on Jurgen*. New York: Robert M. McBride & Co., 1928, x+115 p., cloth, nonf. anth. [Expanded edition].

with John Philips Cranwell

20687 *Notes on Figures of Earth*. New York: Robert M. McBride & Co., 1929, xi+140 p., cloth, nonf. [Limited to 865 copies].

COVILLE, Bruce (Farrington), 1950-

20688 *Amulet of doom*. New York: Dell/Twilight, 1985, 156 p., paper, novel. TWILIGHT #24.

20689 *The dark abyss*. Toronto, New York: A Byron Preiss Book, Bantam Books, 1989, xiii+311 p., paper, novel. PHILIP JOSE FARMER'S THE DUNGEON #2.

20690 *The dinosaur that followed me home*. New York: A GLC Book, A Minstrel Book, Pocket Books, 1990, 121 p., paper, novel. CAMP HAUNTED HILLS #3.

20691 *Eyes of the tarot*. Toronto, New York: Bantam Books, 1983, 152 p., paper, novel. DARK FORCES #9.

20692 *Forever begins tomorrow*. New York: A Signet Vista Book, New American Library, 1986, 219 p., paper, novel. A.I. GANG #4.

20693 *The ghost in the big brass bed*. New York: A Bantam Skylark Book, 1991, 184 p., paper, novel.

20694 *The ghost in the third row*. Toronto, New York: Bantam Books, 1987, 134 p., paper, novel.

20695 *The ghost wore gray*. Toronto, New York: Bantam Books, 1988, 153 p., paper, novel.

20696 *How I survived my summer vacation*. New York: Pocket Books, 1988, 106 p., paper, novel. CAMP HAUNTED HILLS #1.

20697 *Jeremy Thatcher, dragon hatcher: a magic shop book*. San Diego, CA: Jane Yolen Books, Harcourt Brace Jovanovich, 1991, 148 p., cloth, novel.

20698 *Monster of the year*. New York: A GLC Book, A Minstrel Book, Pocket Books, 1989, 135 p., paper, novel.

20699 *The monster's ring*. New York: Pocket Books, 1987, 87 p., paper, novel.

Murder in orbit—SEE: *Space Station ICE-3*.

20700 *My teacher fried my brains*. New York, London: A GLC Book, A Minstrel Book, Pocket Books, 1991, 136 p., paper, novel. MY TEACHER IS AN ALIEN #2.

20701 *My teacher glows in the dark*. New York, London: A GLC Book, A Minstrel Book, Pocket Books, 1991, 137 p., paper, novel. MY TEACHER IS AN ALIEN #3.

20702 *My teacher is an alien*. New York, London: A GLC Book, A Minstrel Book, Pocket Books, 1989, 123 p., paper, novel. MY TEACHER IS AN ALIEN #1.

20703 *Operation Sherlock*. New York: A Signet Vista Book, 1986, 219 p., paper, novel. A.I. GANG #1.

20704 *Robot trouble*. New York: A Signet Vista Book, New American Library, 1986, 221 p., paper, novel. A.I. GANG #3.

20705 *Some of my best friends are monsters*. New York: Pocket Books, 1988, 108 p., paper, novel. CAMP HAUNTED HILLS #2.

20706 *Space Station ICE-3*. New York, Toronto: Scholastic Inc., 1987, 188 p., paper, novel. OMNI ODYSSEYS #2.

20706A retitled: *Murder in orbit*. London: Dragon Books, 1987, 187 p., paper, novel. OMNI ODYSSEYS #2.

20707 *Spirits and Spells*. New York: Twilight/Dell, 1983, 152 p., paper, novel. TWILIGHT #15.

20708 *The unicorn treasury: stories, poems, and unicorn lore*. New York: Doubleday, 1988, 166 p., cloth, anth. [Includes some verse].

20709 *Waiting spirits*. Toronto, New York: Bantam Books, 1984, 150 p., paper, novel. DARK FORCES #11.

as ROBYN TALLIS

20711 *Planet builders: Mountain of stolen dreams*. New York: Ivy Books, 1988, 185 p., paper, novel. PLANET BUILDERS #1.

20712 *Planet builders: Night of two new moons*. New York: Ivy Books, 1989, 183 p., paper, novel. PLANET BUILDERS #6.

COWAN, Dale

20713 *Deadly sleep*. New York: Twilight/Dell, 1982, 167 p., paper, novel. TWILIGHT #1.

*COWAN, James, 1870-1943

COWART, David (Guyland), 1947- , with Thomas L. Wymer

20714 *Twentieth-century American science-fiction writers.* Detroit, MI: A Bruccoli Clark Book, Gale Research Co., 1981, 2 v. [I-xv+306 p.; II-ix+346 p.], cloth, nonf.

COWERN, Roger W.—SEE: Perry, Roger

COWIE, Donald (John), 1911-

37682 *The indiscretions of an infant; or, The baby's revenge.* Malvern, England: The Tantivy Press, 1944?, 176 p., cloth, novel.

*COWLES, Frederick I(gnatius), 1900-1949

COWLEY, Stewart

20715 *Space: 2000 to 2100 A.D.* London: Hamlyn Publishing Group, 1979, 95 p., cloth, fiction.
20716 *The space warriors.* London: Dean, 1980, 122 p., cloth, novel.
20717 *Spacebase 2000.* London: Hamlyn Publishing Group, 1984, 192 p., cloth, coll. [Includes *Spacecraft, 2000-2100 A. D.* and *Great space battles*].
20718 *Spacecraft, 2000 to 2100 A.D.* London: Hamlyn Publishing Group, 1978, 95 p., cloth, fiction.
20719 *Spacewreck: ghostships and derelicts of space.* London: Hamlyn Publishing Group, 1979, 98 p., cloth, fiction.
20720 *Starliners: commercial spacetravel in 2200 A.D.* London: Hamlyn Publishing Group, 1980, 90 p., cloth, fiction.

with Charles Herridge

20721 *Great space battles.* London: Hamlyn, 1979, 96 p., cloth, coll.

with others

20722 *The tourist's guide to Transylvania.* London: Octopus Books, 1981, 78 p., cloth, fiction.

COWPER, Richard [pseud. of John "Colin" Middleton Murry Jr.], 1926-

20723 *The custodians, and other stories.* London; Victor Gollancz, 1976, 191 p., cloth, coll.
20724 *A dream of kinship.* London: Victor Gollancz, 1981, 239 p., cloth. BIRD OF KINSHIP #2.

20725 *The magic spectacles, and other tales.* Salisbury, Wiltshire, England: Kerosina Books, 1986, 37 p., paper, coll. [Limited to 350 copies].
20726 *The missing heart.* New Castle, VA: Cheap Street, 1982, 14 p., paper, story.
20727 *Out there where the big ships go.* New York: Pocket Books, 1980, 191 p., paper, coll.
20728 *Profundis.* London: Victor Gollancz, 1979, 171 p., cloth, novel.
20729 *The road to Corlay.* London: Victor Gollancz, 1978, 158 p., cloth, novel. BIRD OF KINSHIP #1.
37683 *The road to Corlay.* New York: Pocket Books, 1979, 239 p., paper, novel. [Expanded edition].
20730 *Shades of darkness: a novel.* Salisbury, Wiltshire, England: Kerosina Books, 1986, 143 p., cloth, novel.
20731 *The story of Pepita and Corindo.* New Castle, VA: Cheap Street, 1982, [28] p., paper, story.
20732 *A tapestry of time.* London: Victor Gollancz, 1982, 186 p., cloth, novel. BIRD OF KINSHIP #3.
20733 *The Tithonian factor, and other stories.* London: Victor Gollancz, 1984, 150 p., cloth, coll.
20734 *The unhappy princess.* New Castle, VA: Cheap Street, 1982, 28 p., paper, story.
20735 *The web of the Magi, and other stories.* London: Victor Gollancz, 1980, 160 p., cloth, coll.
20736 *The young student.* New Castle, VA: Cheap Street, 1982, [20] p., paper, story.

as COLIN MIDDLETON MURRY

I at the keyhole—SEE: One hand clapping.
20737 *One hand clapping: a memoir of childhood.* London: Victor Gollancz, 1975, 208 p., cloth, nonf.
20737A retitled: *I at the keyhole.* New York: Stein & Day, 1975, 208 p., cloth, nonf.
20000 *Shadows on the grass.* London: Victor Gollancz, 1977, 190 p., cloth, nonf.

COWPERTHWAITE, David

20738 *Transactions of the Doppelgänger Society.* New Duston, Northamptonshire, England: Doppelgänger Society, 1990, 47 p., paper, anth.

COX, (William) Greg(ory), 1959- , with Nick Baron (i.e., Scott Ciencin)

The pirate paradox—SEE: *Robert Silverberg's Time Tours: The Pirate paradox.*

20044 *Robert Silverberg's Time Tours: The Pirate paradox.* New York: A Byron Preiss Book, HarperPaperbacks, 1991, 139 p., paper, novel. ROBERT SILVERBERG'S TIME TOURS #5. [Edited by John Gregory Betancourt].

COX, J(ohn) Randolph, 1936- , with William J. Scheick

33289 *H. G. Wells: a reference guide.* Boston: G. K. Hall & Co., 1988, xxxiii+430 p., cloth, nonf. anth.

COX, Joan (Irene), 1942-

20739 *Mindsong.* New York: Avon, 1979, 282 p., paper, novel.
20740 *Star Web.* New York: Avon, 1980, 328 p., paper, novel.

*COX, Luther (Bigby), 1901-

COX, Michael (Andrew), 1948-

20741 *M. R. James: an informal portrait.* Oxford, New York: Oxford University Press, 1983, xiii+268 p., cloth, nonf.

with R. A. Gilbert

20742 *The Oxford book of English ghost stories.* Oxford, New York: Oxford University Press, 1986, xvii+504 p., cloth, anth.
20743 *Victorian ghost stories: an Oxford anthology.* Oxford, New York: Oxford University Press, 1991, xx+497 p., cloth, anth.

COX, Patricia Bale, with Gladys Bale Wellbrock as G. F. BALE

20744 *If thoughts could kill.* New York: Charter/Diamond Books, 1990, 291 p., paper, novel.

COX, Richard (Hubert Francis), 1931-

20745 *The ice raid.* London: Hutchinson, 1983, 318 p., cloth, novel.

COX, Stephen (LeRoy), 1966-

20746 *The Addams chronicles: everything you ever wanted to know about The Addams Fam-*

ily. New York: HarperCollinsPublishers, 1991, xviii+205 p., paper, nonf.

20747 *The Munchkins remember: "The Wizard of Oz" and beyond.* New York: E. P. Dutton, 1989, x+89 p., paper, nonf.
20748 *The Munsters: television's first family of fright.* Chicago: Contemporary Books, 1989, 174 p., paper, nonf.

COX, William—SEE: Trevor, William

COYLE, Harold W., 1952-

20749 *Bright star: a novel.* New York: Simon & Schuster, 1990, 432 p., cloth, novel.
20750 *Sword Point.* New York: Simon & Schuster, 1988, 397 p., cloth, novel.
20751 *Team Yankee: a novel of World War III.* Novato, CA: Presidio Press, 1987, xiii+313 p., cloth, novel. THIRD WORLD WAR #2. [A sequel to John Hackett's novel, *The third world war*].

COYLE, Wallace

20752 *Stanley Kubrick: a guide to references and sources.* Boston: G. K. Hall & Co., 1980, xv+155 p., cloth, nonf.

COYLE, William, 1917-

20753 *Aspects of fantasy: selected essays from the Second International Conference on the Fantastic in Literature and Film.* Westport, CT & London: Greenwood Press, 1986, ix+250 p., cloth, nonf. anth. CONTRIBUTIONS TO THE STUDY OF SCIENCE FICTION AND FANTASY #19.

COYNE, John (P.), 1937-

20754 *Child of shadows.* New York: Warner Books, 1990, xi+292 p., cloth, novel.
20755 *Fury.* New York: Warner Books, 1989, 280 p., cloth, novel.
20756 *Hobgoblin.* New York: G. P. Putnam's Sons, 1981, 304 p., cloth, novel.
20757 *The hunting season.* New York: Macmillan Publishing Co., 1987, 245 p., cloth, novel.
20758 *The legacy: a novel.* New York: Berkley Books, 1979, 264 p., paper, movie.
20759 *The piercing.* New York: G. P. Putnam's Sons, 1979, 274 p., cloth, novel.
20760 *The searing.* New York: G. P. Putnam's Sons, 1980, 223 p., cloth, novel.
20761 *The shroud.* New York: Berkley Books, 1983, 297 p., paper, novel.

CRABBE, Katharyn (F.) W., 1945-

20762 *J. R. R. Tolkien.* New York: Frederick Ungar Publishing Co., 1981, viii+192 p., cloth, nonf.
20763 *J. R. R. Tolkien.* New York: Continuum Books, 1988, x+233 p., cloth, nonf. [Expanded edition].

CRACE, Jim, 1946-

20764 *The gift of stones.* London: Secker & Warburg, 1988, 170 p., cloth, novel.

CRAIG, Brian, pseud.—SEE: Stableford, Brian

CRAIG, Randolph, pseud.—SEE: Page, Norvell W.

CRAIG, Robert (Charles), 1921-

20767 *Creepers.* New York: A Signet Book, New American Library, 1982, 251 p., paper, novel.
20768 *TRAUMA.* New York: A Signet Book, New American Library, 1984, 220 p., paper, novel.

*CRAIGIE, David [pseud. of Dorothy M. Craigie], 1908-

CRAIGIE, Dorothy M.—SEE: Craigie, David

*CRAM, Mildred, 1889-1985

CRAM, Ralph Adams, 1863-1942

20769 *The dead valley.* West Warwick, RI: Necronomicon Press, 1984, 8 p., paper, story.

CRAMER, John (Gleason Jr.), 1934-

20770 *Twistor.* New York: William Morrow & Co., 1989, 250 p., cloth, novel.

CRAMER, Kathryn (Elizabeth), 1962-

20771 *Walls of fear.* New York: William Morrow & Co., 1990, 395 p., cloth, anth.

with David G. Hartwell

20772 *Christmas ghosts.* New York: Arbor House, 1987, xv+284 p., cloth, anth.
20773 *Masterpieces of fantasy and enchantment.* New York: St. Martin's Press, 1988, xvi+622 p., cloth, anth.

20774 *Masterpieces of fantasy and wonder.* Garden City, NY: Doubleday Book and Music Clubs, 1989, xvi+656 p., cloth, anth.
20775 *Spirits of Christmas: twenty other-worldly tales.* New York: Wynwood Press, 1989, 284 p., cloth, anth.

with Peter D. Pautz

20776 *Architecture of fear.* New York: Arbor House, 1987, 304 p., cloth, anth.

*CRAMER, Maurice Browning, 1910-1990

CRANE, Caroline, 1930-

20777 *The foretelling.* New York: Dodd, Mead & Co, 1982, 234 p., cloth, novel.

CRANE, John K(enny), 1942-

20778 *T. H. White.* Boston: Twayne Publishers, 1974, 202 p., cloth, nonf.

CRANE, Lillie

37684 *The black and white house.* London: Digby, Long & Co., 1902, 192 p., cloth, novel.

CRANE, Martin

20779 *Sex slaves.* Chatsworth, CA: World-Wide Publishing Co., 1981, 182 p., paper, novel.

*CRANE, Robert [pseud. of Bernard Glemser], 1908-1990

CRANWELL, John Philips, 1904- , with James P. Cover

20687 *Notes on Figures of Earth.* New York: Robert M. McBride & Co., 1929, xi+140 p., cloth, nonf. [Limited to 865 copies].

CRAVENS, Gwyneth

20780 *Speed of light.* New York: A David Obst Book, Simon & Schuster, 1979, 352 p., cloth, novel.

with John S. Marr

20781 *The black death.* New York: Thomas Congdon Books, E.P. Dutton & Co., 1977, x+302 p., cloth, novel.

CRAWFORD, Betty Anne

as HENDRA BENOIT

20782 *Hendra's book.* New York, Toronto: Scholastic Inc., 1985, 137 p., paper, novel. PSI PATROL #2.

as LEE CREIGHTON

20783 *Two queens of Lochrin.* New York: Ace Books, 1990, 181 p., paper, novel.

as MAXWELL HURLEY

20784 *Max's book.* New York, Toronto: Scholastic Inc., 1985, 151 p., paper, novel. PSI PATROL #3.

as SAL LIQUORI

20785 *Sal's book.* New York, Toronto: Scholastic Inc., 1985, 148 p., paper, novel. PSI PATROL #1.

CRAWFORD, F(rancis) Marion, 1854-1909

20786 *The dead smile.* West Warwick, RI: Necronomicon Press, 1986, 18 p, paper, story.

CRAWFORD, Gary William, 1953-

20787 *Ramsey Campbell.* Mercer Island, WA: Starmont House, 1988, 74 p., cloth, nonf. STARMONT READER'S GUIDE #48.

with Frederick S. Frank & Benjamin Franklin Fisher IV & Kent Ljungquist

20788 *The 1980 bibliography of gothic studies.* Baton Rouge, LA: Gothic Press, 1983, ii+20 p., paper, nonf. [Limited to 275 copies].

CRAWFORD, James

20789 *Quinton.* Petersfield, Hampshire, England: Toad Publications, 1989, 424 p., paper, novel. HISTORICAL BEGINNINGS OF THE ADMARIAN EMPIRE #1.

CRAWFORD, Ned

20790 *Naming the animals: a haunting.* London, Boston: Faber & Faber, 1980, 190 p., cloth, novel.

CRAWLEY, Fenton, pseud.

37685 *The seeing knife.* London: Curtis Warren Ltd., 1954, 159 p., paper, novel.

CRAWLEY, Tony, 1938-

20791 *The Steven Spielberg story.* London: Zomba Books, 1983, 159 p., paper, nonf.

*CRAWFORD, William L(evi), 1911-<u>1984</u>

CRAYENCOUR, Marguerite de—SEE: Yourcenar, Marguerite

CRAZE, Anthony, 1944-

20792 *Harvest moon.* London: Futura Publications, An Orbit Book, 1975, 187 p., paper, novel.

CREASEY, John, 1908-1973

37686 *Dangerous quest.* London: John Long, 1944, 245 p., cloth, novel.
37687 *Dangerous quest.* London: John Long, 1965, 191 p., cloth, novel. [Revised edition].
15796 *The island of peril.* London: John Long, 1940, 224 p., cloth, novel. DEPT. Z SERIES.
37688 *Seven times seven.* London: John Long, 1932, 255 p., cloth, novel.
20793 *The thunder-maker: a new Dr Palfrey adventure.* London: Hodder & Stoughton, 1976, 189 p., cloth, novel. DR. PALFREY #33.
20794 *The whirlwind: the 34th Dr Palfrey adventure.* London: Hodder & Stoughton, 1979, 192 p., cloth, novel. DR. PALFREY #34.

as GORDON ASHE

20795 *A scream of murder.* London: John Long, 1969, 184 p., cloth, novel. PATRICK DAWLISH SERIES.
20796 *A shadow of death.* London: John Long, 1968, 184 p., cloth, novel. PATRICK DAWLISH SERIES.

CREESE, Irene—SEE: Ray, Rène

CREIGHTON, Lee, pseud.—SEE: Crawford, Betty Anne

CRESSWELL, Helen [i.e., Helen Cresswell Rowe], 1934-

20797 *Moondial.* London: Faber in Association with the National Trust, 1987, 214 p., cloth, novel.

20798 *The secret world of Polly Flint*. London: Faber & Faber, 1982, 176 p., cloth, novel.

Time out—SEE: *The Wilkses*.

20799 *The Wilkses*. London: British Broadcasting Corp. Publications, 1970, 79 p., cloth, novel.

20800 retitled: *Time out*. Cambridge, England: Lutterworth Press, 1987, 72 p., cloth, novel. [Revised edition].

20801 *The winter of the birds*. London: Faber & Faber, 1975, 204 p., cloth, novel.

CRICHTON, (John) Michael, 1942-

37689 *Congo*. Franklin Center, PA: Franklin Library, 1980, xx+336 p., cloth, novel.

20802 *Eaters of the dead: the manuscript of ibn Fadlan, relating his experiences with the Northmen in A.D. 922*. New York: Alfred A. Knopf, 1976, 193 p., cloth, novel.

20803 *Jurassic Park*. Franklin Center, PA: Franklin Library, 1990, xi+399 p., cloth, novel.

20804 *Sphere: a novel*. New York: Alfred A. Knopf, 1987, 385 p., cloth, novel.

20805 *Travels*. New York: Alfred A. Knopf, 1988, 377 p., cloth, nonf.

CRICHTON, Neil (McCollum), 1932-

20806 *Rerun: a novel*. Don Mills, Ontario, Canada: Musson Book Co., 1976, 213 p., cloth, novel.

CRICK, Bernard (Rowland), 1929-

20807 *George Orwell: a life*. Boston: Little, Brown & Co., An Atlantic Monthly Press Book, 1980, xxx+473 p., cloth, nonf.

with Audrey Coppard

20562 *Orwell remembered*. London: British Broadcasting Corp., Ariel Books, 1984, 287 p., paper, nonf. anth.

CRIDER, Allen Billy—SEE: Maclane, Jack

CRISP, Quentin, 1908-

20808 *Chog: a gothic fantasy*. London: Eyre Methuen, 1979, 164 p., cloth, novel.

CRISPIN, A(nn) C(arol), 1950-

20809 *The eyes of the beholder*. New York, London: Pocket Books, 1990, 243 p., paper, novel. STAR TREK: THE NEXT GENERATION #13.

20810 *Star Trek: Time for yesterday*. New York, London: Pocket Books, 1988, xv+303 p., paper, novel. STAR TREK #39. [A direct sequel to *Yesterday's Son*].

20811 *StarBridge, book one*. New York: Ace Books, 1989, 309 p., paper, novel. STARBRIDGE #1.

Time for yesterday—SEE: *Star Trek: Time for yesterday*.

20812 *V*. New York: Pinnacle Books, 1984, 402 p., paper, tele. V #1.

20813 *Yesterday's son: a Star Trek novel*. New York: A Timescape Book, Pocket Books, 1983, 191 p., paper, novel. STAR TREK #11.

with Jannean Elliott

20814 *Shadow world*. New York: Ace Books, 1991, 279 p., paper, novel. STARBRIDGE #3.

with Deborah A. Marshall

Death tide—SEE: *V: Death tide*.

20815 *V: Death tide*. New York: Pinnacle Books, 1985, xii+207 p., paper, tele. V #10.

with Andre Norton

20816 *Gryphon's eyrie*. New York: Tor, A Tom Doherty Associates Book, 1984, 248 p., cloth, novel. WITCH WORLD-KEROVAN #4.

with Kathleen O'Malley

20817 *Silent dances*. New York: Ace Books, 1990, vi+275 p., paper, novel. STARBRIDGE #2.

with Howard Weinstein

East Coast crisis—SEE: *V: East Coast crisis*.

20818 *V: East Coast crisis*. New York: Pinnacle Books, 1984, xi+305 p., paper, tele. V #2.

CRITTEN, Stephen H.—SEE: Bell, Neil

CROCCO, Kyle (Brendan)

20819 *Heroes, Inc*. New York: Ace Books, 1991, 226 p., paper, novel. HEROES INC. #1.

20820　*Heroes wanted.* New York: Ace Books, 1991, 244 p., paper, novel. HEROES INC. #2.

CROCKETT, Linda—SEE: Gray, Linda Crockett

CROGHAN, Antony

20821　*Science fiction and the universe of knowledge: the structure of an aesthetic form.* London: Coburgh, 1981, iv+47 p., cloth?, nonf.

CROMPTON, Anne (Eliot), 1930-

20822　*Warrior wives.* New York: Pinnacle Books, 1982, 314 p., paper, novel.

CROMPTON, Don (Walter), 1935?-1983, *with Julia Briggs*

18636　*A view from the spire: William Golding's later novels.* Oxford, England: Basil Blackwell, 1985, vi+199 p., cloth, nonf.

CRONE, Joni, *with Maeve Kelly & Mary Dorcy*

20823　*Mad and bad fairies: a collection of feminist fairytales.* Dublin: Attic Press, 1987, 60 p., paper, anth.

CRONIN, Bernard—SEE: North, Eric

CROOK, Compton N.—SEE: Tall, Stephen

CROSBY, Harry C. Jr.—SEE: Anvil, Christopher

CROSHER, Geoffrey—SEE: Casteven, G. R.

CROSS, David, pseud.—SEE: Chesbro, George C.

CROSS, Gilbert B., 1939-

20824　*A witch across time.* New York: Atheneum, 1990, 216 p., cloth, novel.

CROSS, Gillian (Clare), 1945-

20825　*Born of the sun.* New York: Holiday House, 1983, 229 p., cloth, novel.
20826　*The dark behind the curtain.* Oxford, England, New York: Oxford University Press, 1982, 159 p., cloth, novel.

CROSS, Robin, 1948-

20827　*Science fiction films.* New York: Gallery Books, 1985, 88 p., cloth, nonf.

CROSS, Ronald Anthony, 1937-

20828　*Prisoners of paradise.* New York, Toronto: Franklin Watts, 1988, 263 p., cloth, novel.

CROSS, Victoria [pseud. of Annie Sophie "Vivian" Cory], 1868-1952?

CROSSEN, Kendell Foster, 1910-1981, *with Frederick C. Davis*

20829　*The Green Lama: an amazing exploit taken right out of the case-book of the Green Lama, in which his unusual powers are put to the test.* Chicago: Robert Weinberg, 1976, 89 p., paper, coll. PULP CLASSICS #14.

CROSSLEY, Robert (Thomas), 1945-

20830　*H. G. Wells.* Mercer Island, WA: Starmont House, 1986, 79 p., cloth, nonf. STARMONT READER'S GUIDE #19.

CROUSE, Anne D.—SEE: Jordan, Anne

CROUTCH, Leslie A(lfred), 1915-1969, *with John Robert Colombo*

20343　*Years of light: a celebration of Leslie A. Crouch: a compilation and a commentary.* Toronto: Hounslow Press, 1982, 193 p., paper, nonf. coll.

CROW, Charles L(loyd), 1940- , *with Howard Kerr & John W. Crowley*

20831　*The haunted dusk: American supernatural fiction, 1820-1920.* Athens, GA: University of Georgia Press, 1983, vi+236 p., cloth, nonf. anth.

CROWCROFT, (William) Peter, 1922-

20832　*Monster.* North Hollywood, CA: A Carousel Star Edition, 1980, 192 p., paper, novel.

CROWDER, Fay

20833　*Edith and the mermaids.* London: Lutterworth Press, 1971, 125 p., cloth, novel.

CROWDER, Herbert (Alexander), 1925-

20834 *Weatherhawk.* New York: G. P. Putnam's Sons, 1990, 413 p., cloth, novel.

CROWLEY, Aleister [i.e., Edward Alexander Crowley], 1875-1947

20835 *The strategem, and other stories.* Brighton, England: Temple Press, 1990, 108 p., cloth, coll. [Adds one story to the original edition (see #03666)].

CROWLEY, Edward A.—SEE: Crowley, Aleister

CROWLEY, John (William), 1942-

20836 *Ægypt.* Toronto, New York: Bantam Books, 1987, 390 p., cloth, novel.
20837 *Beasts.* Garden City, NY: Doubleday & Co., 1976, 184 p., cloth, novel.
20838 *Beasts; Engine summer; Little, big.* New York: Book-of-the-Month Club, 1991, 184+182+627 p., paper, coll.
20839 *The Deep.* Garden City, NY: Doubleday & Co., 1975, 180 p., cloth, novel.
20840 *Engine summer.* Garden City, NY: Doubleday & Co., 1979, 182 p., cloth, novel.
20841 *Great work of time.* New York, Toronto: Spectra, Bantam Books, 1991, 136 p., paper, novel.
20842 *Little, big.* Toronto, New York: Bantam Books, 1981, 538 p., paper, novel. [Winner of the World Fantasy Award for Best Fantasy Novel, 1981 (1982)].
20843 *Novelty.* New York: A Foundation Book, Doubleday, 1989, 227 p., cloth, coll.

with Howard Kerr & Charles L. Crow

20831 *The haunted dusk: American supernatural fiction, 1820-1920.* Athens, GA: University of Georgia Press, 1983, vi+236 p., cloth, nonf. anth.

CRUGER, Julie—SEE: Gordon, Julien

CRUME, Vic

20844 *C.H.O.M.P.S..* New York, Toronto: Scholastic Book Services, 1979, 121 p., paper, movie.
20845 *Frankenstein and the whiz kid.* New York: Pyramid Books, 1975, 128 p., paper, novel.
20846 *The ghost that came alive.* New York: Scholastic Book Services, 1975, 126 p., paper, novel.

20847 *Herbie goes to Monte Carlo.* New York, Toronto: Scholastic Book Services, 1977, 139 p., paper, movie. HERBIE SERIES.
20848 *The mystery in Dracula's castle.* New York: Scholastic Book Services, 1973, 110 p., paper, movie.
20849 *The shaggy D.A.* Greenwich, CT: A Fawcett Gold Medal Book, Fawcett Publications, 1976, 128 p., paper, movie.
20850 *Unidentified flying oddball.* New York, Toronto: Scholastic Book Services, 1979, 120 p., paper, movie.
20851 *The whiz kid and the carnival caper.* New York: Pyramid Books, 1975, 128 p., paper, movie.

*CRUMP, (James) Irving, 1887-<u>1979</u>

*CRUSO, Solomon, <u>1887-1977</u>

CRUZ, Daniel da—SEE: da Cruz, Daniel

CRYPTON, Dr. [pseud. of Paul W. Hoffman], 1956- , with Sheldon Renan

20852 *Treasure: in search of the golden horse: a puzzle.* New York: An IntraVision Book, Warner Books, 1984, 81 p., paper, novel.

CUBITT, George (S.)

20853 *Darkly through a glass: ghost stories.* Norwich, England: George S. Cubitt, 1969, 73 p., paper, coll.

CUDDON, J(ohn) A(nthony Bowden), 1928-

20854 *The Penguin book of ghost stories.* Harmondsworth, Middlesex, England: Penguin Books, 1984, 512 p., paper, anth.
20855 *The Penguin book of horror stories.* Harmondsworth, Middlesex, England: Penguin Books, 1984, 607 p., paper, anth.

CUDLIP, David R., 1933-

20856 *Comprador.* New York: E. P. Dutton, 1984, 336 p., cloth, novel.

CULBREATH, Myrna (Lou), 1938- , with Sondra Marshak

20857 *The fate of the phoenix.* Toronto, New York: Bantam Books, 1979, 262 p., paper, novel. STAR TREK SERIES.
20858 *The price of the phoenix.* Toronto, New York: Bantam Books, 1977, 182 p., paper, novel. STAR TREK SERIES.

20859 *The Prometheus design: a Star Trek novel.* New York: A Timescape Book, Pocket Books, 1982, 190 p., paper, tele. STAR TREK #5.

20860 *Star Trek: the new voyages.* Toronto, New York: Bantam Books, 1976, xvi+237 p., paper, coll. STAR TREK SERIES.

20861 *Star Trek: the new voyages 2.* Toronto, New York: Bantam Books, 1978, xxvii+252 p., paper, anth. STAR TREK SERIES.

20862 *Triangle: a Star Trek novel.* New York: A Timescape Book, Pocket Books, 1983, 188 p., paper, tele. STAR TREK #9.

with William Shatner & Sondra Marshak

20863 *Shatner: where no man...: the authorized biography of William Shatner.* New York: A Tempo Star Book, Grosset & Dunlap, 1979, 327 p., paper, nonf.

CULIANU, I(oan) P(etru), 1950-1991

20864 *Out of this world: otherworldly journeys from Gilgamesh to Albert Einstein* / by I. P. Couliano. Boston: Shambhala Publications, 1991, xvi+287 p., paper, nonf.

CULLEN, Brian

20865 *What Niall saw: the unabridged testimony of a seven-year-old.* London: Sphere Books, 1985, 89 p., paper, novel.

CULLEN, Jean V., with Marjorie Housepian Dobkin

20866 *Inside out.* New York: Ivy Books, 1989, 267 p., paper, novel.

CULLEN, Seamus

20867 *Astra and Flondrix.* London: Allen Lane, 1976, 286 p., cloth, novel.

20868 *A noose of light.* London: An Orbit Book, Futura, 1986, 216 p., paper, novel. NOOSE #1.

20869 *The Sultan's turret.* London: An Orbit Book, 1986, 252 p., paper, novel. NOOSE #2.

CULLINAN, Thomas

20870 *The bedeviled.* New York: G. P. Putnam's Sons, 1978, 285 p., cloth, novel.

CULLINGWORTH, N(icholas) J(ohn)

20871 *Dodos of Einstein.* London: Robert Hale, 1976, 191 p., cloth, novel.

CULP, William Maurice

20872 *Tumba of Torrey Pines.* San Francisco: Harr Wagner Publishing Co., 1931, 115 p., cloth, novel.

CUMBOW, Robert C(harles), 1946-

20873 *Order in the universe: the films of John Carpenter.* Metuchen, NJ: Scarecrow Press, 1990, vi+241 p., cloth, nonf.

CUMMINGS, David George

20874 *An Edgar Rice Burroughs checklist.* [S.l.]: Savage Press in Association with Comma Publications, 1974, 31 p., paper, nonf.

*CUMMINGS, M(onette) A., 1914-

CUMMINGS, Michael S., 1943- , with Nicholas D. Smith

20875 *Utopian studies II.* Lanham, MD: University Press of America, 1989, 154 p., cloth, nonf. anth.

CUMMINGS, Ray(mond King), 1887-1957

20876 *Into the 4th dimension.* Oak Forest, IL: Robert Weinberg Publications, 1981, 80 p., paper, novel. INCREDIBLE ADVENTURES #3.

20877 *Tales of the Scientific Crime Club.* London: Ferret Fantasy, 1979, 45 p., paper, coll. [Limited to 100 copies].

CUMMINS, Elizabeth (Ann), 1939-

20878 *Understanding Ursula K. Le Guin.* Columbia, SC: University of South Carolina Press, 1990, 216 p., cloth, nonf.

as ELIZABETH CUMMINS COGELL

20879 *Ursula K. Le Guin: a primary and secondary bibliography.* Boston: G. K. Hall & Co., 1983, xl+244 p., cloth, nonf. MASTERS OF SCIENCE FICTION AND FANTASY.

CUNNINGHAM, Cathy, pseud.—SEE: Cunningham, Chet

CUNNINGHAM, Chester—SEE: Cunningham, Chet

CUNNINGHAM, Chet [i.e., Chester Grant Cunningham], 1928-

as CATHY CUNNINGHAM

20880 *Curse of Valkyrie House.* New York: Leisure Books, 1981, 176 p., paper, novel.
20881 *The demons of Highpoint House.* New York: Popular Library, 1973, 320 p., paper, novel.

as TONY PHILLIPS

Full throttle—SEE: *Turbo Cowboys: Full throttle.*
Jump start—SEE: *Turbo Cowboys: Jump start.*
Spark fire—SEE: *Turbo Cowboys: Spark fire.*
Spin out—SEE: Turbo Cowboys: *Spin out.*
20882 *Turbo Cowboys: Full throttle.* New York: Ballantine Books, 1989, 135 p., paper, novel. TURBO COWBOYS #4.
20883 *Turbo Cowboys: Jump start.* New York: Ballantine Books, 1988, 120 p., paper, novel. TURBO COWBOYS #1.
20884 *Turbo Cowboys: Spark fire.* New York: Ballantine Books, 1989, 130 p., paper, novel. TURBO COWBOYS #3.
20885 *Turbo Cowboys: Spin out.* New York: Ballantine Books, 1989, 136 p., paper, novel. TURBO COWBOYS #2.

CUNNINGHAM, Elaine

Elfshadow—SEE: *Forgotten realms fantasy adventure: Elfshadow.*
20886 *Forgotten realms fantasy adventure: Elfshadow.* Lake Geneva, WI: TSR Inc., 1991, 312 p., paper, novel. THE HARPERS #2.

CUNNINGHAM, Jere (Pearson Jr.), 1943-

20887 The abyss: a novel. New York: Wyndham Books, 1981, 286 p., cloth, novel.
20888 *Love object: a gothic fantasy.* Santa Cruz, CA: Dream/Press, 1985, 164 p., cloth, novel.
20889 *The visitor.* New York: St. Martin's Press, 1978, 282 p., cloth, novel.

CUNNINGHAM, Marilyn—SEE: Carlock, Lynn

CUNNINGHAM, Richard B(ryan), 1932-

20890 *C. S. Lewis, defender of the faith.* Philadelphia, PA: Westminster Press, 1967, 223 p., cloth, nonf.

CUNNINGHAM, Scott (Douglas), 1956-

20891 *Operation: death ray.* North Hollywood, CA: American Art Enterprises, 1982, 156 p., paper, novel.

CURLEY, Chris

20892 *The doorkeepers.* Oxford, England: Oxford University Press, 1989, 187 p., cloth, novel.

CURLOVICH, John—SEE: Paine, Michael

CURRAN, Ronald (Thomas), 1938-

20893 *The weird gathering, and other tales: "supernatural" women in American popular fiction, 1800-1850.* New York: Fawcett Crest, 1979, 574 p., paper, anth.

CURREY, L(loyd) W(esley), 1942-

20894 *Catalogue of the fantasy and science fiction library of the late P. Schuyler Miller.* Elizabethtown, NY: Dragon Press, 1977, x+270 p., paper, nonf.

with David G. Hartwell

20895 *The battle of the monsters, and other stories.* Boston: Gregg Press, 1976, xii+238 p., cloth, anth.
20896 *Science fiction and fantasy authors: a bibliography of first printings of their fiction and selected nonfiction.* Boston: G. K. Hall & Co., 1979, xxix+571 p., cloth, nonf.

with David G. Hartwell as KILGORE TROUT

20897 *SF-1: a selective bibliography.* Elizabethtown, NY: L. W. Currey, 1971, [32] leaves, paper, nonf.

with Marshall Tymn & Roger C. Schlobin

20898 *A research guide to science fiction studies: an annotated checklist of primary and secondary sources for fantasy and science fiction.* New York, London: Garland Publishing, 1977, ix+165 p., cloth, nonf.

with Marshall Tymn & Martin H. Greenberg & Joseph D. Olander

20899 *Index to stories in thematic anthologies of science fiction.* Boston: G. K. Hall &

Co., 1978, xiii+193 p., cloth, nonf. REFERENCE PUBLICATION IN SCIENCE FICTION.

CURRY, Chris [pseud. of Cheryl Curry Sayre], 1957?- , *with L. Dean James*

20900 *Winter scream.* New York, London: Pocket Books, 1991, 403 p., paper, novel.

CURRY, Graeme

20901 *Doctor Who: The happiness patrol.* London: W. H. Allen, 1989, 140 p., cloth, tele. DOCTOR WHO #146.
The happiness patrol—SEE: *Doctor Who: The happiness patrol.*

CURRY, Jane Louise, 1932-

20902 *The Bassumtyte treasure.* New York: A Margaret K. McElderry Book, Atheneum, 1978, 129 p., cloth, novel.
20903 *The birdstones.* New York: A Margaret K. McElderry Book, Atheneum, 1977, 204 p., cloth, novel. CALLIE #3.
20904 *The magical cupboard.* New York: A Margaret K. McElderry Book, Atheneum, 1976, 138 p., cloth, novel. ROSEMARY #2.
20905 *Me, myself, and I: a tale of time travel.* New York: Margaret K. McElderry Books, 1987, 184 p., cloth, novel.
20906 *Parsley Sage, Rosemary, & time.* New York: A Margaret K. McElderry Book, Atheneum, 1975, 108 p., cloth, novel. ROSEMARY #1.
20907 *Poor Tom's ghost.* New York: A Margaret K. McElderry Book, Atheneum, 1977, 178 p., cloth, novel.
20908 *Shadow dancers.* New York: A Margaret K. McElderry Book, Atheneum, 1983, 198 p., cloth, novel. LEK #2.
20909 *The watchers.* New York: Atheneum, 1975, 235 p., cloth, novel.
20910 *The wolves of Aam.* New York: An Argo Book, A Margaret K. McElderry Book, Atheneum, 1981, viii+192 p., cloth, novel. LEK #1.

CURTIES, Henry, Capt., 1860-

37690 *Tears of angels: a novel.* London: Sisley's Ltd., 1907, viii+262 p., cloth, novel.

*CURTIS, J(ean)-L(ouis) [pseud. of Louis Lafitte], 1917-

CURTIS, Jack, pseud., 1922-

20911 *Crows' parliament.* London, New York: Bantam Press, 1987, 348 p., cloth, novel.

*CURTIS, Monica (Mary), 1892-

CURTIS, Peter, pseud.—SEE: Lofts, Norah

CURTIS, Philip (Delacourt), 1920-

20912 *Beware of the Brain Sharpeners.* London: Andersen Press, 1983, 136 p., cloth, novel. BRAIN SHARPENERS #5.
20913 *Bewitched by the Brain Sharpeners.* London: Andersen Press, 1986, 128 p., cloth, novel. BRAIN SHARPENERS #8.
20914 *The Brain Sharpeners abroad.* London: Andersen Press, 1987, [128] p., cloth, novel. BRAIN SHARPENERS #9.
20915 *Chaos comes to Chivvy Chase.* London: Andersen Press, 1988, 120 p., cloth, novel. BRAIN SHARPENERS #10.
20916 *A gift from another galaxy.* London: Andersen Press, 1987, 120 p., cloth, novel.
Invasion from below the Earth—SEE: *Mr Browser meets the Burrowers.*
Invasion of the Brain Sharpeners—SEE: *Mr Browser and the Brain Sharpeners.*
Invasion of the comet people—SEE: *Mr Browser and the comet crisis.*
20917 *Mr Browser and the Brain Sharpeners.* London: Andersen Press, 1979, 96 p., cloth, novel. BRAIN SHARPENERS #1.
20917A retitled: *Invasion of the Brain Sharpeners.* New York: Alfred A. Knopf, 1981, 117 p., cloth, novel. BRAIN SHARPENERS #1.
20918 *Mr Browser and the comet crisis.* London: Andersen Press, 1981, 118 p., cloth, novel. BRAIN SHARPENERS #3.
20918A retitled: *Invasion of the comet people.* New York: Alfred A. Knopf, 1983, 122 p., cloth, novel. BRAIN SHARPENERS #3.
20919 *Mr Browser and the mini-meteorites.* London: Andersen Press, 1983, 127 p., cloth, novel. BRAIN SHARPENERS #6.
20920 *Mr Browser and the space maggots.* London: Andersen Press, 1989, 126 p., cloth, novel. BRAIN SHARPENERS #11.
20921 *Mr Browser in the space museum.* London: Andersen Press, 1985, 142 p., cloth, novel. BRAIN SHARPENERS #7.
20922 *Mr Browser meets the Burrowers.* London: Andersen Press, 1980, 128 p., cloth, novel. BRAIN SHARPENERS #2.
20922A retitled: *Invasion from below the Earth.* New York: Alfred A. Knopf, 1981, 121 p., cloth, novel. BRAIN SHARPENERS #2.
20923 *Mr Browser meets the mind shrinkers.* London: Andersen Press, 1989, 126 p., cloth, novel. BRAIN SHARPENERS #12.

20924 *Pen friend from another planet.* London: Andersen Press, 1990, [128] p., cloth, novel.

20925 *The quest of the Quidnuncs.* London: Andersen Press, 1985, [128] p., cloth, novel.

20926 *The revenge of the Brain Sharpeners.* London: Andersen Press, 1982, 120 p., cloth, novel. BRAIN SHARPENERS #4.

20927 *Welcome to the giants.* London: Andersen Press, 1991, 128 p., cloth, novel.

CURTIS, Richard (Alan), 1937-

20928 *Squirm: novelization.* New York: Ace Books, 1976, 184 p., paper, movie.

CURVAL, Philippe [pseud. of Philippe Tronche], 1929-

20929 *Brave old world.* London: Allison & Busby, 1981, 262 p., cloth, novel. [Translation by Steve Cox of *Cette chère humanité*].

CUSACK, Frank

20930 *Australian ghost stories.* Melbourne, Australia: William Heinemann, 1967, xiv+177 p., cloth, anth.

CUSH, Geoffrey, 1956-

20931 *God help the Queen.* London: Abacus, 1987, 147 p., paper, novel.

CUSHING, Peter (Wilton), 1913-

20932 *'Past forgetting': memoirs of the Hammer years.* London: Weidenfeld & Nicolson, 1988, 112 p., cloth, nonf.

20933 *Peter Cushing: an autobiography.* London: Weidenfeld & Nicolson, 1986, 157 p., cloth, nonf.

20934 *Tales of a monster hunter.* London: Arthur Barker, 1977, ix+208 p., cloth, anth.

CUSICK, Richie Tankersley, 1952-

20935 *April fools.* New York, Toronto: Point, Scholastic Inc., 1990, 218 p., paper, novel.

20936 *Evil on the bayou.* New York: Twilight/Dell, 1984, 148 p., paper, novel. TWILIGHT #21.

20937 *The lifeguard.* New York, Toronto: Scholastic Inc., Point Horror, 1988, 213 p., paper, novel.

20938 *Scarecrow.* New York, London: Pocket Books, 1990, 280 p., paper, novel.

20939 *Teacher's pet.* New York, Toronto: Point Fiction, Scholastic Inc., 1990, 214 p., paper, novel.

20940 *Trick or treat.* New York, Toronto: Scholastic Inc., Point Fiction, 1989, 209 p., paper, novel.

20941 *Vampire.* New York, London: An Archway Paperback, Pocket Books, 1991, 214 p., paper, novel.

CUSSLER, Clive (Eric), 1931-

20942 *Cyclops: a novel.* New York: Simon & Schuster, 1986, 475 p., cloth, novel. DIRK PITT #8.

20943 *Deep six: a novel.* New York: Simon & Schuster, 1984, 432 p., cloth, novel. DIRK PITT #7.

20944 *Dragon: a novel.* New York, London: Simon & Schuster, 1990, 542 p., cloth, novel. DIRK PITT #10.

20945 *Iceberg.* New York: Dodd, Mead & Co., 1975, 314 p., cloth, novel. DIRK PITT #3.

Mayday!—SEE: *The Mediterranean caper.*

20946 *The Mediterranean caper.* New York: Pyramid Books, 1973, p., paper, novel. DIRK PITT #2.

20946A retitled: *Mayday!* London: Sphere Books, 1977, 237 p., paper, novel. DIRK PITT #2. ?1st 1973?

20947 *Night probe!* Toronto, New York: Bantam Books, 1981, 344 p., cloth, novel. DIRK PITT #6.

20948 *Pacific vortex!* Toronto, New York: Bantam Books, 1983, xiii+270 p., paper, novel. DIRK PITT #1.

20949 *Raise the Titanic!* New York: Viking Press, 1976, 314 p., cloth, novel. DIRK PITT #4.

20950 *Treasure: a novel.* New York, London: Simon & Schuster, 1988, 539 p., cloth, novel. DIRK PITT #9.

20951 *Vixen 03.* New York: Viking Press, 1978, 286 p., cloth, novel. DIRK PITT #5.

CUTLER, Roland, 1938-

20952 *The firstborn: a novel.* New York: A Fawcett Gold Medal Book, 1978, 352 p., paper, novel.

CUTLER, Ron

20953 *The Medusa syndrome.* New York: A Signet Book, New American Library, 1983, 252 p., paper, novel.

*CUTT, W(illiam) Towrie, 1898-<u>1981</u>

CZEBATUL, Anthony A.

20954 *The legend of Protogonos.* New York,
Washington: Vantage Press, 1984, 84 p.,
cloth, novel.

D

D. N. J.—SEE: J., D. N.

DA CRUZ, Daniel (Jr.), 1921-1991

20955 *The ayes of Texas.* New York: A Del Rey Book, Ballantine Books, 1982, 246 p., paper, novel. FORTE FAMILY #1.

20956 *F-cubed.* New York: A Del Rey Book, Ballantine Books, 1987, 291 p., paper, novel.

20957 *The Grotto of the Formigans.* New York: A Del Rey Book, Ballantine Books, 1980, 185 p., paper, novel.

20958 *Mixed doubles.* New York: A Del Rey Book, Ballantine Books, 1989, 259 p., paper, novel.

20959 *Texas on the rocks.* New York: A Del Rey Book, Ballantine Books, 1986, 293 p., paper, novel. FORTE FAMILY #2.

20960 *Texas triumphant.* New York: A Del Rey Book, Ballantine Books, 1987, 301 p., cloth, novel. FORTE FAMILY #3.

DADEY, Debbie [i.e., Debra S. Dadey], *with Marcia Thornton Jones*

20961 *Santa Claus doesn't mop floors.* New York, Toronto: A Little Apple Book, Scholastic Inc., 1991, 70 p., paper, novel.

20962 *Vampires don't wear polka dots.* New York, Toronto: A Little Apple Book, Scholastic Inc., 1990, 78 p., paper, novel.

20963 *Werewolves don't go to summer camp.* New York, Toronto: A Little Apple Book, Scholastic Inc., 1991, 92 p., paper, novel.

DADEY, Debra S.—SEE: Dadey, Debbie

DAGMAR, pseud.—SEE: Cameron, Lou

DAGMAR, Peter, pseud.—SEE: Pinchin, Frank

DAGNOL, Jules N.

20964 *The Sandoval transmissions.* London: Robert Hale, 1980, 190 p., cloth, novel.

DAHL, Roald, 1916-1990

20965 *The best of Roald Dahl: stories from Over to you, Someone like you, Kiss kiss, Switch bitch.* New York: Vintage Books, Random House, 1978, xv+401 p., paper, coll.

Book of ghost stories—SEE: *Roald Dahl's Book of ghost stories.*

20966 *The collected short stories of Roald Dahl.* London: Michael Joseph, 1991, 762 p., cloth, coll. [Includes *Kiss, kiss*; *Over to you*; *Switch bitch*; *Someone like you*; plus eight other stories].

20967 *The complete adventures of Charlie and Mr. Willy Wonka.* London: Unwin Hyman, 1987, 316 p., cloth, coll.

Completely unexpected tales—SEE: *Roald Dahl's Completely unexpected tales.*

Further tales of the unexpected—SEE: *More Roald Dahl tales of the unexpected.*

20968 *Kiss, kiss; Over to you; Switch bitch; Someone like you; More tales of the unexpected; My uncle Oswald.* London: Heinemann/Octopus, 1986, 816 p., cloth, coll.

20969 *More Roald Dahl tales of the unexpected.* London: Michael Joseph, 1980, 127 p., cloth, coll.

20969A retitled: *More tales of the unexpected.* Harmondsworth, Middlesex, England: Penguin Books, 1980, 127 p., paper, coll.

20969B retitled: *Further tales of the unexpected.* London: Cedric Chivers, 1981, 228 p., cloth, coll. [A large print edition].

More tales of the unexpected—SEE: *More Roald Dahl tales of the unexpected.*

20970 *Roald Dahl's Book of ghost stories.* London: Jonathan Cape, 1983, 235 p., cloth, anth.

20971 *Roald Dahl's Completely unexpected tales.* Harmondsworth, Middlesex, England: Penguin Books, 1986, 404 p., paper, coll. [Includes *Tales of the unexpected* and *More tales of the unexpected*].

20972 *Roald Dahl's Tales of the unexpected.* London: Michael Joseph, 1979, 256 p., cloth, coll.

20973 *A second Roald Dahl selection: eight short stories.* Harlow, Essex, England: Longman, 1987, iii+150 p., paper, coll.

Tales of the unexpected—SEE: *Roald Dahl's Tales of the unexpected.*

20974 *Two fables.* Harmondsworth, Middlesex, England: Viking, 1986, 61 p., cloth, coll.

*DAIL, C(harles) C(urtis), <u>1851-1902</u>

DAKERS, Elaine K.—SEE: Lane, Jane

DALBY, Richard, 1949-

20975 *Bram Stoker: a bibliography of first editions.* London: Dracula Press, 1983, 81 p., paper, nonf.

20976 *Chillers for Christmas.* London: Michael O'Mara Books, 1989, 311 p., cloth, anth.

20977 *Crime for Christmas.* London: Michael O'Mara Books, 1991, 279 p., cloth, anth.

20978 *Dracula's brood: neglected vampire classics.* Wellingborough, Northamptonshire, England: Crucible, 1987, 348 p., paper, anth.

20979 *Ghosts for Christmas.* London: Michael O'Mara Books, 1988, 339 p., cloth, anth.

20980 *The mammoth book of ghost stories.* London: Robinson Publishing, 1990, xi+ 654 p., paper, anth.

20981 *The mammoth book of ghost stories 2.* London: Robinson Publishing, 1991, 658 p., paper, anth.

20982 *Mystery for Christmas.* London: Michael O'Mara Books, 1990, 292 p., cloth, anth.

20983 *Tales of witchcraft.* London: Michael O'Mara Books, 1991, 243 p., cloth, anth.

20984 *The town of a magic dream: Arthur Machen in Whitby.* Southampton, England: Mark Valentine, 1987, 15 p., paper, nonf. anth.

Victorian ghost stories by eminent women writers—SEE: *The Virago book of Victorian ghost stories.*

20985 *The Virago book of ghost stories: the twentieth century.* London: Virago Press, 1987, xvi+331 p., cloth, anth.

20986 *The Virago book of ghost stories: the twentieth century, volume two.* London: Virago Press, 1991, xv+318 p., cloth, anth.

20987 *The Virago book of Victorian ghost stories.* London: Virago Press, 1988, xvi+347 p., cloth, anth.

20987A retitled: *Victorian ghost stories by eminent women writers.* New York: Carroll & Graf, 1989, xvi+347 p., cloth, anth.

with Rosemary Pardoe

20988 *Ghosts and scholars: ghost stories in the tradition of M. R. James.* Wellingbor-

ough, Northamptonshire, England: Crucible, 1987, 270 p., cloth, anth.

DALE, Floyd D.

20989 *A hunter's fire.* New York: A Signet Book, New American Library, 1989, 271 p., paper, novel.

DALE-HARRIS, Rosalind—SEE: Ashe, Rosalind

DALEY, Brian (C.), 1947-

20990 *The doomfarers of Coramonde.* New York: A Del Rey Book, Ballantine Books, 1977, 344 p., paper, novel. CORAMONDE #1.

20991 *Fall of the white ship Avatar.* New York: A Del Rey Book, Ballantine Books, 1987, 340 p., paper, novel. ALACRITY FITZHUGH #3.

20992 *Han Solo and the lost legacy: from the adventures of Luke Skywalker.* New York: A Del Rey Book, Ballantine Books, 1980, 187 p., paper, novel. STAR WARS—HAN SOLO #3.

20993 *Han Solo at Star's End, from the adventures of Luke Skywalker.* New York: A Del Rey Book, Ballantine Books, 1979, 198 p., cloth, novel. STAR WARS—HAN SOLO #1.

20994 *Han Solo's revenge, from the adventures of Luke Skywalker.* New York: A Del Rey Book, Ballantine Books, 1979, 198 p., cloth, novel. STAR WARS—HAN SOLO #2.

20995 *Jinx on a Terran inheritance.* New York: A Del Rey Book, Ballantine Books, 1985, 403 p., paper, novel. ALACRITY FITZHUGH #2.

20996 *Requiem for a ruler of worlds.* New York: A Del Rey Book, Ballantine Books, 1985, 290 p., paper, novel. ALACRITY FITZHUGH #1.

20997 *The starfollowers of Coramonde.* New York: A Del Rey Book, Ballantine Books, 1979, 361 p., paper, novel. CORAMONDE #2.

20998 *A tapestry of magics.* New York: A Del Rey Book, Ballantine Books, 1983, 289 p., paper, novel.

20999 *Tron: a novel.* New York: A Del Rey Book, Ballantine Books, 1982, 173 p., paper, movie.

with James Luceno as JACK MCKINNEY

21001 *Artifact of the system.* New York: A Del Rey Book, Ballantine Books, 1991, 281 p., paper, novel. BLACK HOLE TRAVEL AGENCY #2.

21002 *Battle cry*. New York: A Del Rey Book, Ballantine Books, 1987, 216 p., paper, tele. ROBOTECH #2.

21003 *Battlehymn*. New York: A Del Rey Book, Ballantine Books, 1987, 212 p., paper, tele. ROBOTECH #4.

21004 *Dark powers*. New York: A Del Rey Book, Ballantine Books, 1988, 233 p., paper, tele. SENTINELS #2.

21005 *Death dance*. New York: A Del Rey Book, Ballantine Books, 1988, 185 p., paper, tele. SENTINELS #3.

21006 *The devil's hand*. New York: A Del Rey Book, Ballantine Books, 1988, 214 p., paper, tele. SENTINELS #1.

21007 *Doomsday*. New York: A Del Rey Book, Ballantine Books, 1987, 216 p., paper, tele. ROBOTECH #6.

The end of the circle—SEE: *Robotech: The end of the circle.*

21008 *Event horizon*. New York: A Del Rey Book, Ballantine Books, 1991, 310 p., paper, novel. BLACK HOLE TRAVEL AGENCY #1.

21009 *The final nightmare*. New York: A Del Rey Book, Ballantine Books, 1987, 248 p., paper, tele. ROBOTECH #9.

21010 *Force of arms*. New York: A Del Rey Book, Ballantine Books, 1987, 214 p., paper, tele. ROBOTECH #5.

21011 *Genesis*. New York: A Del Rey Book, Ballantine Books, 1987, 214 p., paper, tele. ROBOTECH #1.

21012 *Homecoming*. New York: A Del Rey Book, Ballantine Books, 1987, 214 p., paper, tele. ROBOTECH #3.

21013 *Invid invasion*. New York: A Del Rey Book, Ballantine Books, 1987, 212 p., paper, tele. ROBOTECH #10.

21014 *Kaduna memories*. New York: A Del Rey Book, Ballantine Books, 1990, 249 p., paper, novel.

21015 *Metal fire*. New York: A Del Rey Book, Ballantine Books, 1987, 216 p., paper, tele. ROBOTECH #8.

21016 *Metamorphosis*. New York: A Del Rey Book, Ballantine Books, 1987, 212 p., paper, tele. ROBOTECH #11.

21017 *Robotech: The end of the circle*. New York: A Del Rey Book, Ballantine Books, 1990, vi+343 p., paper, tele. ROBOTECH #13.

21018 *Rubicon*. New York: A Del Rey Book, Ballantine Books, 1988, 215 p., paper, tele. SENTINELS #5.

21019 *Southern cross*. New York: A Del Rey Book, Ballantine Books, 1987, 215 p., paper, tele. ROBOTECH #7.

21020 *Symphony of light*. New York: A Del Rey Book, Ballantine Books, 1987, 212 p., paper, tele. ROBOTECH #12.

21021 *World killers*. New York: A Del Rey Book, Ballantine Books, 1988, 279 p., paper, tele. SENTINELS #4.

DALKEY, Kara (Mia), 1953-

21022 *The curse of Sagamore*. New York: Ace Fantasy Books, 1986, 232 p., paper, novel. SAGAMORE #1.

21023 *Euryale*. New York: Ace Books, 1988, 217 p., paper, novel.

21024 *The nightingale*. New York: Ace Books, 1988, xv+221 p., cloth, novel.

21025 *The sword of Sagamore*. New York: Ace Books, 1989, 235 p., paper, novel. SAGAMORE #2.

DALMAS, John [pseud. of John Robert Jones], 1926-

21026 *Fanglith*. New York: Baen Science Fiction Books, 1985, 245 p., paper, novel. FANGLITH #1.

21027 *The general's president*. New York: Baen Books, 1988, 420 p., paper, novel.

21028 *Homecoming*. New York: Tor, A Tom Doherty Associates Book, 1984, 247 p., paper, novel. NILS JÄRNHAN #2.

21029 *The Kalif's war*. Riverdale, NY: Baen Books, 1991, 392 p., paper, novel. REGIMENT #3.

21030 *The lantern of God*. New York: Baen Books, 1989, 407 p., paper, novel.

21031 *The lizard war*. New York: Baen Books, 1989, 307 p., paper, novel.

21032 *The reality matrix*. New York: Baen Science Fiction Books, 1986, 310 p., paper, novel.

21033 *The regiment*. New York: Baen Books, 1987, 404 p., paper, novel. REGIMENT #1.

21034 *Return to Fanglith*. New York: Baen Books, 1987, 280 p., paper, novel. FANGLITH #2.

21035 *The scroll of man*. New York: Tor, A Tom Doherty Associates Book, 1985, 255 p., paper, novel.

21036 *The Varkaus conspiracy*. New York: Tor, A Tom Doherty Associates Book, 1983, 285 p., paper, novel.

21037 *The walkaway clause*. New York: Tor SF, A Tom Doherty Associates Book, 1986, 253 p., paper, novel.

21038 *The white regiment*. New York: Baen Books, 1990, 406 p., paper, novel. REGIMENT #2.

37691 *The yngling.* New York: Tor, A Tom Doherty Associates Book, 1984, 254 p., paper, novel. NILS JÄRNHAN #1. [Revised edition of #03757].

with Carl Martin

21039 *Touch the stars: emergence.* New York: A Tom Doherty Associates Book, 1983, 318 p., paper, novel.

with Rod Martin

21040 *The playmasters.* New York: Baen Books, 1987, 317 p., paper, novel.

DALOS, György (Alfred), 1943-

21041 *1985: a historical report (Hongkong 2036), from the Hungarian of ***.* London: Pluto Press, 1983, 118 p., paper, novel. 1984 SEQUEL. [Translation by Stuart Hood & Estella Schmid of *1985*].

D'ALTENA, Arnaud—SEE: de Borchgrave, Arnaud

DALTON, Annie, 1948?-

21042 *The afterdark princess.* London: Methuen Children's Books, 1990, 115 p., cloth, novel.
21043 *The alpha box.* London: Methuen Children's Books, 1991, 192 p., cloth, novel.
21044 *Demon-spawn.* London: Blackie Children's Books, 1991, 126 p., cloth, novel.
21045 *Night maze.* London: Methuen Children's Books, 1989, 256 p., cloth, novel.
21046 *Out of the ordinary.* London: Methuen Children's Books, 1988, 172 p., cloth, novel.

*DALTON, H(enry) R(obert) S(amuel), <u>1835-</u>

DALTON, John J.

21047 *The cattle mutilators.* New York: Manor Books, 1980, 252 p., paper, novel.

DALTON, Sean, pseud.—SEE: Blakeney, Jay D.

DALY, Carroll John, 1889-1958

21048 *The legion of the living dead.* London: Popular, 1947, p., cloth, novel.

DALY, Wally K.

21049 *Doctor Who: Ultimate evil.* London: A Target Book, W. H. Allen & Co., 1989, 144 p., paper, tele. DOCTOR WHO SERIES (UNNUMBERED).
Ultimate evil—SEE: *Doctor Who: Ultimate evil.*

D'AMELIO, Dan, 1927-

21050 *Silvabamba.* Belmont, CA: A Pacemaker Bestsellers Book, Fearon-Pitman Publishers, 1977, 60 p., paper, novel.

DAMERON, J(ohn) Lasley, 1925- , with Irby B. Cauthen Jr.

19662 *Edgar Allan Poe: a bibliography of criticism, 1827-1967.* Charlottesville, VA: Published for the Bibliographical Society of the University of Virginia by the University Press of Virginia, 1974, xvi+386 p., cloth, nonf.

D'AMMASSA, Don(ald Eugene), 1946-

21051 *Blood beast.* New York: Pinnacle Books, Windsor Publishing Corp., 1988, 384 p., paper, novel.

DAN, Uri, 1937- , with Peter Mann

21052 *Ultimatum: Pu 94.* New York: Leisure Books, 1977, 288 p., paper, novel.

DANBERG, Norman A.—SEE: Jones, G. Wayman

DANBY, Mary [i.e., Mary Heather Danby Calvert], 1941-

21053 *65 great spine chillers.* London: Octopus, 1982, 672 p., cloth, anth.
21054 *65 great tales of horror.* London: Octopus, 1981, 688 p., cloth, anth.
21055 *65 great tales of the supernatural.* London: Octopus, 1979, 704 p., cloth, anth.
21056 *The eighth Armada ghost book.* London: Armada, 1976, 127 p., paper, anth.
21057 *The eleventh Armada ghost book.* London: Armada, 1979, 125 p., paper, anth.
21058 *The eleventh Fontana book of great horror stories.* London: Collins/Fontana, 1978, 191 p., paper, anth.
21059 *The fifteenth Armada ghost book.* London: Armada, 1983, 128 p., paper, anth.
21060 *The fifteenth Fontana book of great horror stories.* London: Fontana/Collins, 1982, 192 p., paper, anth.
21061 *The fourteenth Armada ghost book.* London: Armada, 1982, 126 p., paper, anth.

21062 *The fourteenth Fontana book of great horror stories.* London: Collins/Fontana, 1981, 189 p., paper, anth.

21063 *Frighteners 2.* London: Fontana/Collins, 1976, 157 p., paper, anth.

21064 *The green ghost, and other stories.* London: Armada, 1989, 507 p., paper, anth.

21065 *Nightmares.* London: Fontana/Collins, 1983, 128 p., paper, anth.

21066 *Nightmares 2.* London: Armada, 1984, 157 p., paper, anth.

21067 *Nightmares 3.* London: Armada, 1985, 128 p., paper, anth.

21068 *The ninth Armada ghost book.* London: Armada, 1977, 125 p., paper, anth.

21069 *The ninth Fontana book of great horror stories.* London: Collins/Fontana, 1975, 192 p., paper, anth.

21070 *Realms of darkness.* London: Octopus Books, 1985, 796 p., cloth, anth.

21071 *The seventeenth Fontana book of great horror stories.* London: Fontana/Collins, 1984, 188 p., paper, anth.

21072 *The seventh Armada ghost book.* London: Armada, 1975, 126 p., paper, anth.

21073 *The sixteenth Fontana book of great horror stories.* London: Fontana Paperbacks, 1983, 190 p., paper, anth.

21074 *The tenth Armada ghost book.* London: Armada, 1978, 127 p., paper, anth.

21075 *The tenth Fontana book of great horror stories.* London: Collins/Fontana, 1977, 192 p., paper, anth.

21076 *The thirteenth Armada ghost book.* London: Armada, 1981, 128 p., paper, anth.

21077 *The thirteenth Fontana book of great horror stories.* London: Collins/Fontana, 1980, 191 p., paper, anth.

21078 *The twelfth Armada ghost book.* London: Armada, 1980, 126 p., paper, anth.

21079 *The twelfth Fontana book of great horror stories.* London: Collins/Fontana, 1979, 187 p., paper, anth.

DANE, Christopher, pseud.—SEE: DeBolt, Adriana

DANE, Clemence [pseud. of Winifred Ashton], 1888-1965

37692 *Legend.* London: William Heinemann, 1919, 193 p., cloth, novel.

D'ANGELO, Carr, *with David McDonnell*

21082 *Aliens: the official movie magazine.* New York: O'Quinn Studios, 1986, 66 p., paper, nonf. anth.

21083 *Star Trek IV, the voyage home official movie magazine.* New York: O'Quinn Studios, 1986, 65 p., paper, nonf. anth.

DANIEL, Colin—SEE: Windsor, Patricia

*DANIEL', IUlii (Markovich), 1925-1988

DANIEL, Mark [pseud. of Mark Daniel Fitzgeorge-Parker], 1954-

21084 *Chocky's challenge.* London: A Thames Magnet Book, Methuen Children's Books in Association with Thames Television, 1986, 141 p., paper, tele. CHOCKY #2. [Sequel to John Wyndham's *Chocky*, and a novelization of a TV serial].

21085 *Movie magic.* London: Carnival, 1988, 109 p., paper, tele. THE REAL GHOSTBUSTERS.

DANIEL, Yuli—SEE: Daniel, IUlii

DANIELS, Cora Lynn (Morrison), 1852-

21086 *Sardia: a story of love.* Boston: Lee & Shepard, 1891, 299 p., cloth, novel.

DANIELS, Dorothy (Smith), 1915-

21087 *House of silence.* New York: A Signet Book, New American Library, 1980, 168 p., paper, novel.

21088 *A mirror of shadows.* New York: Warner Books, 1977, 509 p., paper, novel.

21089 *The prisoner of Malville Hall.* New York: Warner Paperback Library, 1973, 191 p., paper, novel.

as ANGELA GRAY

21090 *Blackwell's ghost.* New York: Lancer Books, 1972, 255 p., paper, novel.

*DANIELS, Jonathan (Worth), 1902-1981

DANIELS, Les(lie Noel III), 1943-

21091 *The black castle: a novel of the macabre.* New York: Charles Scribner's Sons, 1978, 241 p., cloth, novel. DON SEBASTIEN #1.

21092 *Citizen vampire.* New York: Charles Scribner's Sons, 1981, 199 p., cloth, novel. DON SEBASTIEN #3.

21093 *Dying of fright: masterpieces of the macabre.* New York: Charles Scribner's Sons, 1976, x+271 p., cloth, anth. *Fear—SEE: Living in fear.*

21094 *Living in fear: a history of horror in the mass media.* New York: Charles Scriber's Sons, 1975, 248 p., cloth, nonf.

21094A retitled: *Fear: a history of horror in the mass media.* London: Paladin, 1977, 271 p., paper, nonf.

21095 *Marvel: five fabulous decades of the world's greatest comics.* New York: Henry N. Abrams, 1991, 287 p., cloth, nonf.

21096 *No blood spilled.* New York: Tor Horror, A Tom Doherty Associates Book, 1991, 218 p., paper, novel. DON SEBASTIEN #5.

21097 *The silver skull: a novel of sorcery.* New York: Charles Scribner's Sons, 1979, 222 p., cloth, novel. DON SEBASTIEN #2.

21098 *Yellow fog.* West Kingston, RI: Donald M. Grant, Publisher, 1986, 191 p., cloth, novel. DON SEBASTIEN #4.

21099 *Yellow fog.* New York: Tor Horror, A Tom Doherty Associates Book, 1988, 294 p., paper, novel. DON SEBASTIEN #4. [Expanded edition].

with Diane Thompson

21100 *Thirteen tales of terror.* New York: Charles Scribner's Sons, 1977, xviii+260 p., paper, anth.

DANIELS, Max [pseud. of Roberta Leah Jacobs Gellis], 1927-

21101 *Offworld.* New York: Pocket Books, 1979, 191 p., paper, novel.

21102 *The space guardian.* New York: A Kangaroo Book, Pocket Books, 1978, 174 p., paper, novel.

DANIELS, Norman A. [originally Norman Arthur Danberg], 1906- , as WALLACE BROOKER

18724 *Breathless island.* Chicago: Robert Weinberg, 1977, 96 p., paper, novel. PULP CLASSICS #16.

DANIELS, Philip [pseud. of Dennis John Andrew Phillips], 1924-

21103 *The Dracula murders.* London: Robert Hale, 1983, 190 p., cloth, novel.

DANIELSON, Henry

21104 *Arthur Machen: a bibliography.* London: Henry Danielson, 1923, x+59 p., cloth, nonf.

DANK, Gloria Rand, 1955-

21105 *The forest of App.* New York: Greenwillow Books, 1983, 154 p., cloth, novel.

with Milton Dank

21106 *A UFO has landed.* New York: Delacorte Press, 1983, 113 p., cloth, novel

DANK, Milton, 1920-, with Gloria Dank

21106 *A UFO has landed.* New York: Delacorte Press, 1983, 113 p., cloth, novel

DANN, Colin (Michael), 1943-

21107 *The animals of Farthing Wood.* London: Heinemann, 1979, 302 p., cloth, novel. FARTHING WOOD SERIES.

21108 *The beach dogs.* London: Hutchinson, 1988, [144] p., cloth, novel.

21109 *The city vagabonds.* London: Hutchinson, 1991, 135 p., cloth, novel. VAGABONDS #2.

21110 *A great escape.* London: Hutchinson, 1990, 164 p., cloth, novel.

21111 *In the grip of winter.* London: Hutchinson, 1981, 168 p., cloth, novel. FARTHING WOOD SERIES.

21112 *In the path of the storm.* London: Hutchinson Children's Books, 1989, 154 p., cloth, novel. FARTHING WOOD SERIES.

21113 *King of the vagabonds.* London: Hutchinson, 1987, [128] p., cloth, novel. VAGABONDS #1.

21114 *A legacy of ghosts.* London: Hutchinson, 1991, 154 p., cloth, novel.

21115 *The ram of Sweetriver.* London: Hutchinson, 1986, 214 p., cloth, novel.

DANN, Jack (Mayo), 1945-

21116 *Immortal: short novels of the transhuman future.* New York & Hagerstown, NJ: Harper & Row, Publishers, 1978, xiii+225 p., cloth, anth.

21117 *Junction.* New York: A Dell Book, 1981, 251 p., paper, novel.

21118 *The man who melted.* New York: A Bluejay International Edition, 1984, 280 p., cloth, novel.

21119 *More wandering stars: outstanding stories of Jewish fantasy and science fiction.* Garden City, NY: Doubleday & Co., 1981, x+180 p., cloth, anth.

21120 *Starhiker: a novel.* New York & Hagerstown, NJ: Harper & Row, Publishers, 1977, 164 p., cloth, novel.

21121 *Timetipping.* Garden City, NY: Doubleday & Co., 1980, xiii+236 p., cloth, coll.

with Gardner Dozois

21122 *Aliens!* New York: Pocket Books, 1980, xi+305 p., paper, anth.
21123 *Bestiary!* New York: Ace Fantasy Books, 1985, 306 p., paper, anth.
21124 *Demons!* New York: Ace Books, 1987, 281 p., paper, anth.
21125 *Dinosaurs!* New York: Ace Books, 1990, 226 p., paper, anth.
21126 *Dogtails!* New York: Ace Books, 1988, 274 p., paper, anth.
21127 *Future power: a science fiction anthology.* New York: Random House, 1976, xxviii+256 p., cloth, anth.
21128 *Little people!* New York: Ace Books, 1991, 221 p., paper, anth.
21129 *Magicats!* New York: Ace Fantasy Books, 1984, xvii+267 p., paper, anth.
21130 *Magicats II.* New York: Ace Books, 1991, 213 p., paper, anth.
21131 *Mermaids!* New York: Ace Fantasy Books, 1986, 260 p., paper, anth.
21132 *Seaserpents!* New York: Ace Books, 1989, xiii+226 p., paper, anth.
21133 *Sorcerers!* New York: Ace Fantasy Books, 1986, xi+244 p., paper, anth.
21134 *Unicorns!* New York: Ace Books, 1982, 310 p., paper, anth.

with Gardner Dozois & Susan Casper & Jack C. Haldeman II & Michael Swanwick

19639 *Slow dancing through time.* Kansas City, MO: Ursus Imprints; Shingletown, CA: Mark V. Ziesing, 1990, xvii+253 p., cloth, coll. [All the stories are collaborations by Dozois with other writers, the majority with Jack Dann].

with Jeanne Van Buren Dann

21135 *In the field of fire.* New York: Tor, A Tom Doherty Associates Book, 1987, 416 p., cloth, anth.

with Jack C. Haldeman II

21136 *Echoes of thunder.* New York: Tor SF, A Tom Doherty Associates Book, 1991, p. 91-184, paper, story. [Bound with *Run for the stars* / by Harlan Ellison].

with George Zebrowski

21137 *Faster than light: an original anthology about interstellar travel.* New York, Hagerstown, NJ: Harper & Row, Publishers, 1976, xviii+321 p., cloth, anth.

DANN, Jeanne (Helen) Van Buren, 1949- , with Jack Dann

21135 *In the field of fire.* New York: Tor, A Tom Doherty Associates Book, 1987, 416 p., cloth, anth.

DANN, Sam, 1918-

21138 *The third body.* New York: Popular Library, 1979, 255 p., paper, novel.

DANTZ, William R. [pseud. of William Rodman Philbrick]

21139 *Pulse.* New York: Avon Books, 1990, 284 p., paper, novel.
21140 *The seventh sleeper.* New York: William Morrow & Co., 1991, 363 p., cloth, novel.

DANVERS, Dennis (Howard), 1947-

21141 *Wilderness.* New York: Poseidon Press, 1991, 255 p., cloth, novel.

DANZIGER, Gustaf—SEE: de Castro, Adolphe

DANZIGER, Paula, 1944-

21142 *This place has no atmosphere.* New York: Delacorte Press, 1986, 156 p., cloth, novel.

DARBY, Catherine [pseud. of Maureen Peters], 1935-

21143 *A circle of Rowan.* London: Robert Hale, 1983, 187 p., cloth, novel.
21144 *Cobweb across the moon.* New York: Popular Library, 1978, 254 p., paper, novel. MOON CHALICE QUEST #5.
21145 *A dream of fair serpents.* New York: Popular Library, 1979, 318 p., paper, novel.
21146 *The flaunting moon.* New York: Popular Library, 1977, 221 p., paper, novel. MOON CHALICE QUEST #3.
21147 *Frost on the moon.* New York: Popular Library, 1977, 221 p., paper, novel. MOON CHALICE QUEST #2.
21148 *Moon in Pisces.* New York: Popular Library, 1978, 221 p., paper, novel. MOON CHALICE QUEST #6.

21149 *Sing me a moon.* New York: Popular Library, 1977, 221 p., paper, novel. MOON CHALICE QUEST #4.

21150 *Whisper down the moon.* New York: Popular Library, 1977, 240 p., paper, novel. MOON CHALICE QUEST #1.

as SHARON WHITBY

21151 *Children of the rainbow.* London: Robert Hale, 1983, 159 p., cloth, novel.

21152 *The savage web.* London: Robert Hale, 1982, 190 p., cloth, novel.

DARBY, Lyndan, pseud.—SEE: Grimsley, Ann & Kinnerley, Lynne

*DARDIS, Thomas A(loysius), 1926-

D'ARGENTEUIL, Paul, pseud.

37693 *The trembling of Borealis.* London & New York: F. Tennyson Neely, 1899, 316 p., cloth, novel.

DARK, James [pseud. of James Edmond Mac-Donnell], 1917-

15797 *The invisibles.* New York: A Signet Book, New American Library, 1969, 127 p., paper, novel. MARK HOOD SERIES.

DARK, Jon

21153 *Satan's victor.* Chatsworth, CA: GX, 1972, p., paper, novel.

DARK, Larry [i.e., Lawrence Charny Dark]

21153 *The literary ghost: great contemporary ghost stories.* New York: Atlantic Monthly Press, 1991, 369 p., cloth, anth.

DARK, Lawrence C.—SEE: Dark, Larry

DARKE, James, pseud.—SEE: James, Laurence

DARKE, Marjorie (Sheila), 1929-

21155 *Messages: a collection of shivery tales.* London: Viking Kestrel, 1984, 139 p., cloth, coll.

DARLTON, Clark, pseud.—SEE: Ernsting, Walter

DARNAY, Arsen (Julius), 1936-

21156 *A hostage for Hinterland.* New York: Ballantine Books, 1976, 248 p., paper, novel.

The karma affair—SEE: Karma.

21157 *Karma: a novel of retribution and transcendence.* New York: St. Martin's Press, 1978, 366 p., cloth, novel.

21157A retitled: *The karma affair.* New York: Ace Books, 1979, 366 p., paper, novel.

21158 *The purgatory zone.* New York: Ace Books, 1981, 240 p., paper, novel.

21159 *The siege of Faltara.* New York: Ace Books, 1978, ix+226 p., paper, novel.

21160 *The splendid freedom.* New York: Ace Books, 1980, 244 p., paper, coll.

DARROW, Paul

Avon: a terrible aspect—SEE: Terry Nation's Avon: a terrible aspect.

21161 *Terry Nation's Avon: a terrible aspect.* Secaucus, NJ: Citadel Press, 1989, 189 p., cloth, tele. BLAKE'S 7 #5.

DARVILL-EVANS, Peter

Beneath Nightmare Castle—SEE: Steve Jackson and Ian Livingstone present Beneath Nightmare Castle.

37694 *Portal of evil.* Harmondsworth, Middlesex, England: Puffin Books, 1989, [288] p., paper, fiction. FIGHTING FANTASY GAMEBOOK SERIES.

37695 *Spectral stalker.* Harmondsworth, Middlesex, England: Puffin Books, 1991, [400] p., paper, fiction. FIGHTING FANTASY GAMEBOOK SERIES.

21162 *Steve Jackson and Ian Livingstone present Beneath Nightmare Castle.* Harmondsworth, Middlesex, England: Puffin Books, 1987, [400] p., paper, fiction. FIGHTING FANTASY GAMEBOOK #25.

with Ian Marsh

21163 *Time lord.* London: Doctor Who Books, 1991, 287 p., paper, nonf.

DAS, Manoj, 1934-

21164 *Bulldozers; and, Fables and fantasies for adults.* Delhi, India: B.R. Publishing Co., 1990, viii+154 p., cloth, coll.

21165 *Fables and fantasies for adults.* New Delhi, India: Orient Paperbacks, 1978, 133 p., paper, coll.

21166 *The man who lifted the mountain, and other fantasies.* Fareham, Hampshire, England: Spectre Press, 1979, 22 p., paper, coll.

DATESH, John Nicholas, 1950-

21167 *The nightmare machine.* New York: Belmont Tower Books, 1979, 239 p., paper, novel.

DATLOW, Ellen (Sue), 1949-

21168 *Alien sex: 19 tales by the masters of science fiction and dark fantasy.* New York: E. P. Dutton, 1990, xvi+251 p., cloth, anth.

21169 *Blood is not enough: 17 stories of vampirism.* New York: William Morrow & Co., 1989, 319 p., cloth, anth.

21170 *The fifth Omni book of science fiction.* New York: Zebra Books, Kensington Publishing Corp., 1987, 381 p., paper, anth.

21171 *The first Omni book of science fiction.* New York: Zebra Books, Kensington Publishing Corp., 1984, 395 p., paper, anth.

21172 *The fourth Omni book of science fiction.* New York: Zebra Books, Kensington Publishing Corp., 1985, 397 p., paper, anth.

21173 *The second Omni book of science fiction.* New York: Zebra Books, Kensington Publishing Corp., 1984, 414 p., paper, anth.

21174 *The seventh Omni book of science fiction.* New York: Zebra Books, Kensington Publishing Corp., 1989, 408 p., paper, anth.

21175 *The sixth Omni book of science fiction.* New York: Zebra Books, Kensington Publishing Corp., 1989, 382 p., paper, anth.

21176 *The third Omni book of science fiction.* New York: Zebra Books, Kensington Publishing Corp., 1985, 479 p., paper, anth.

21177 *A whisper of blood.* New York: William Morrow & Co., 1991, 287 p., cloth, anth.

with Terri Windling

Demons and dreams—SEE: *The year's best fantasy: first annual collection.*
Demons and dreams 2—SEE: *The year's best fantasy: second annual collection.*

21178 *The year's best fantasy: first annual collection.* New York: St. Martin's Press, 1988, xxxv+491 p., cloth, anth. [Winner of the World Fantasy Award for Best Fantasy Anthology, 1988 (1989)].

21178A retitled: *Demons and dreams: the best fantasy and horror 1.* London: Legend, 1989, xxxiv+482 p., cloth, anth.

21179 *The year's best fantasy: second annual collection.* New York: St. Martin's Press, 1989, lvii+579 p., cloth, anth. [Winner of the World Fantasy Award for Best Fantasy Anthology, 1989 (1990)].

21179A retitled: *Demons and dreams: the best fantasy and horror 2.* London: Legend, 1989, lvii+579 p., paper, anth.

21180 *The year's best fantasy and horror: third annual collection.* New York: St. Martin's Press, 1990, liii+563 p., cloth, anth.

21181 *The year's best fantasy and horror: fourth annual collection.* New York: St. Martin's Press, 1991, liv+552 p., cloth, anth.

DAUD, David [pseud. of David Alexander Pennington], 1954-

21182 *The pulse of eternity.* Lewes, East Sussex, England: The Book Guild, 1991, 498 p., cloth, novel. STARMAKER #1.

DAVENPORT, Howard, *with Bart Andrews*

16470 *From The Blob to Star Wars: the science fiction movie quiz book: 1001 trivia teasers for sci-fi fans.* New York: A Signet Book, New American Library, 1977, 154 p., paper, nonf.

DAVENPORT, Roger (Hamilton), 1946-

21183 *Onlooker.* London: Bodley Head, 1989, 192 p., cloth, novel.

DAVENTRY, Leonard (John), 1915-

21184 *You must remember us—?* London: Robert Hale, 1980, 192 p., cloth, novel.

DAVEY, John, 1937-

21185 *Michael Moorcock: a reader's guide.* Sidcup, Kent, England: John Davey, 1991, 32 p., paper, nonf.

with Bram Stoker

21186 *Tales of horror.* London: Heinemann Educational, 1983, v+56 p., paper, coll. [Adapted by Davey from Stoker's original tales].

DAVID, Marjorie (S.), 1950-

21187 *Primavera.* New York: Poseidon Press, 1982, 206 p., cloth, novel.

DAVID, Peter (Allen), 1956-

21188 *The amazing Spider-Man: As the world burns.* Lake Geneva, WI: TSR Inc., 1987, 191 p., paper, fiction. MARVEL SUPERHEROES ADVENTURE GAMEBOOK #7.
As the world burns—SEE: *The amazing Spider-Man: As the world burns.*

21189 *Howling mad: a tale of relenting horror.* New York: Ace Books, 1989, 201 p., paper, novel.

21190 *Knight life.* New York: Ace Fantasy Books, 1987, 195 p., paper, novel.

21191 *Q-in-law.* New York, London: Pocket Books, 1991, xiii+252 p., paper, tele. STAR TREK, THE NEXT GENERATION #18.

21192 *The return of Swamp Thing: a novel.* New York: Jove Books, 1989, 239 p., paper, movie. SWAMP THING #2.
The rift—SEE: *Star trek: The rift.*

21193 *A rock and a hard place.* New York, London: Pocket Books, 1990, 244 p., paper, tele. STAR TREK THE NEXT GENERATION #10.

21194 *The rocketeer: a novel.* New York, Toronto: Falcon, Bantam Books, 1991, 245 p., paper, movie.

21195 *Star trek, the next generation: Vendetta: the giant novel.* New York, London: Pocket Books, 1991, xi+400 p., paper, tele. STAR TREK, THE NEXT GENERATION SERIES.

21196 *Star trek: The rift.* New York, London: Pocket Books, 1991, 274 p., paper, tele. STAR TREK #57.

21197 *Strike zone.* New York, London: Pocket Books, 1989, 275 p., paper, tele. STAR TREK THE NEXT GENERATION #5.
Vendetta—SEE: *Star trek, the next generation: Vendetta.*

as DAVID PETERS

The chaos kid—SEE: *Psi-Man: The chaos kid.*
Deathscape—SEE: *Psi-Man: Deathscape.*

21198 *Exile.* New York: Berkley Books, 1987, 152 p., paper, novel. PHOTON #5.

21199 *For the glory.* New York: Pacer Books for Young Adults, 1987, 155 p., paper, novel. PHOTON #1. [Novelization of a game].

21200 *High stakes.* New York: Pacer Books for Young Adults, 1987, 150 p., paper, novel. PHOTON #2.

21201 *In search of MOM.* New York: Pacer Books for Young Adults, 1987, 155 p., paper, novel. PHOTON #3.
Main Street D.O.A.—SEE: *Psi-Man: Main Street D.O.A.*

21202 *Psi-Man.* New York: Charter/Diamond Books, 1990, 202 p., paper, novel. PSI-MAN #1.

21203 *Psi-Man: Deathscape.* New York: Diamond Books, 1991, 185 p., paper, novel. PSI-MAN #2.

21204 *Psi-Man: Main Street D.O.A.* New York: Diamond Books, 1991, 185 p., paper, novel. PSI-MAN #3.

21205 *Psi-Man: Stalker.* New York: Diamond Books, 1991, 171 p., paper, novel. PSI-MAN #5.

21206 *Psi-Man: The chaos kid.* New York: Diamond Books, 1991, 170 p., paper, novel. PSI-MAN #4.

21207 *Skin deep.* New York: Pacer Books for Young Adults, 1988, 138 p., paper, novel. PHOTON #6.
Stalker—SEE: *Psi-Man: Stalker.*

21208 *This is your life, Bhodi Li.* New York: Pacer Books for Young Adults, 1987, 149 p., paper, novel. PHOTON #4.

with Carmen Carter & Michael Jan Friedman & Robert Greenberger

19541 *Doomsday world.* New York, London: Pocket Books, 1990, xi+276 p., paper, novel. STAR TREK: THE NEXT GENERATION #12.

DAVIDSON, Alan, 1943-

21209A *The bewitching of Alison Allbright.* London: Viking Kestrel, 1988, 156 p., cloth, novel. [Originally published under the name A. D. Langholm].

as A. D. LANGHOLM

21209 *The bewitching of Alison Allbright.* London: W. H. Allen & Co., 1979, 159 p., cloth, novel.

DAVIDSON, Angela, pseud.—SEE: Merwin, Sam

DAVIDSON, Avram (James), 1923-

21210 *The adventures of Doctor Eszterhazy.* Philadelphia, PA: Owlswick Press, 1991, xii+366 p., cloth, coll. [Adds six stories to *The enquiries of Doctor Eszterhazy*].

21211 *And don't forget the one red rose.* Seattle, WA: Dryad Press, 1986, 8 p., paper, story. [Limited to 200 copies].

21212 *The best of Avram Davidson.* Garden City, NY: Doubleday & Co., 1979, xii+210 p., cloth, coll. [Edited by Michael Kurland].

21213 *Collected fantasies.* New York: Berkley Books, 1982, xi+224 p., paper, coll. [Edited by John W. Silbersack].

21214 *The enquiries of Doctor Eszterhazy.* New York: Warner Books, 1975, 206 p., paper, coll. [Winner of the World Fantasy Award for Best Fantasy Single Author Collection/Anthology, 1975 (1976)].

21215 *The Kar-Chee reign; Rogue dragon.* New York: Ace Books, 1979, 377 p., paper, coll. KAR-CHEE #1-2.

21216 *Magic for sale.* New York: Ace Books, 1983, xiv+210 p., paper, anth.

21217 *Peregrine: secundus.* New York: Berkley Books, 1981, 166 p., paper, novel. PEREGRINE #2.

21218 *Polly charms the sleeping woman.* [Williamsburg, VA: English Dept., College of William & Mary], 1977, [20] p., paper, story. [Limited to 100 copies].

21219 *The Redward Edward papers.* Garden City, NY: Doubleday & Co., 1978, xiv+208 p., cloth, coll.

21220 *Virgil in Averno.* Garden City, NY: Doubleday & Co., 1987, 184 p., cloth, novel. VIRGIL MAGUS #2.

as ELLERY QUEEN

03804 *And on the eighth day.* New York: Random House, 1964, 191 p., cloth, novel.

with Grania Davis

21221 *Marco Polo and the sleeping beauty.* New York: Baen, 1988, 300 p., paper, novel.

DAVIDSON, Cathy N(otari), 1949-

21222 *The experimental fictions of Ambrose Bierce: structuring the ineffable.* Lincoln, NE & London: University of Nebraska Press, 1984, 166 p., cloth, nonf.

DAVIDSON, Edward H(utchins), 1912-

21223 *Poe: a critical study.* Cambridge, MA: Belknap Press of Harvard University Press, 1957, x+296 p., cloth, nonf.

DAVIDSON, Lionel, 1922-

37696 *The rose of Tibet.* London: Victor Gollancz, 1962, 320 p., cloth, novel.

37697 *The sun chemist.* London: Jonathan Cape, 1976, 273 p., cloth, novel.

21224 *Under Plum Lake.* London: Jonathan Cape, 1980, 144 p., cloth, novel.

as DAVID LINE

21224A *Under Plum Lake.* London: Heinemann Educational, 1982, 144 p, paper, novel. [Originally published under the name Lionel Davidson].

DAVIDSON, Michael

21225 *Daughter of Is: a science fiction epic: an "Else-when" parable.* New York: Popular Library, 1978, 351 p., paper, novel.

21226 *The karma machine.* New York: Popular Library, 1975, 285 p., paper, novel.

DAVIDSON, Robert K.

21227 *Great monsters of the movies.* New York: Pyramid Books, 1977, 128 p., paper, nonf.

DAVIES, Andrew (Wynford), 1936-

21228 *Conrad's war.* London: Blackie & Son, 1978, 127 p., cloth, novel.

21229 *Marmalade Atkins in space.* London: Abelard-Schuman, 1982, 87 p., cloth, novel.

*DAVIES, Hugh Sykes, 1909-1984

DAVIES, Joan—SEE: Lyngseth, Joan

DAVIES, L(eslie) P(urnell), 1914-

21236 *Possession.* Garden City, NY: The Crime Club, Doubleday & Co., 1976, 186 p., cloth, novel.

DAVIES, Paul (Charles William), 1946-

21237 *Fireball.* London: Heinemann, 1987, 178 p., cloth, novel.

DAVIES, Pete, 1959-

21238 *Dollarville.* New York: Random House, 1989, 211 p., cloth, novel.

21239 *The last election.* London: André Deutsch, 1986, 234 p., cloth, novel.

DAVIES, Philip John, 1948-

21240 *Science fiction, social conflict, and war.* Manchester, England: Manchester University Press; New York: St. Martin's Press, 1990, 185 p., cloth, nonf. anth.

DAVIES, (William) Robertson, 1913-

21241 *High spirits.* Harmondsworth, Middlesex, England: Penguin Books, 1982, iv+198 p., paper, coll. [Winner of the World Fantasy Award for Best Fantasy Anthology/Collection, 1983 (1984)].

21242 *The lyre of Orpheus: a novel.* Franklin Center, PA: Franklin Library, 1988, 472 p., cloth, novel. REBEL ANGELS #3.

21243 *Murther & walking spirits.* Toronto: A Douglas Gibson Book, McClelland & Stewart, 1991, 357 p., cloth, novel.

21244 *The rebel angels.* Toronto: Macmillan of Canada, 1981, 326 p., cloth, novel. REBEL ANGELS #1.

21245 *What's bred in the bone.* Toronto: Macmillan of Canada, 1985, 436 p., cloth, novel. REBEL ANGELS #2.

with J. Madison Davis

21246 *Conversations with Robertson Davies.* Jackson, MS: University Press of Mississippi, 1989, xxi+285 p., cloth, nonf. anth.

DAVIES, Suzan, *with Arthur C. Clarke*

20115 *Islands in the sky.* Hong Kong, Oxford: Oxford University Press, 1976, 66 p., paper, novel. [Adapted from the novel by Clarke].

DAVIES, Thomas—SEE: Davies, Tom

DAVIES, Tom [i.e., Thomas Davies], 1941-

21247 *The electric harvest.* Sevenoaks, Kent, England: New English Library, 1984, 256 p., cloth, novel.

DAVIES, W. X., pseud.

21248 *Countdown World War III: Operation Black Sea.* New York: Berkley Books, 1984, 234 p., paper, novel. COUNTDOWN WORLD WAR III #2.

21249 *Countdown WWIII: Operation choke point: a novel.* New York: Berkley Books, 1984, 240 p., paper, novel. COUNTDOWN WWIII #3.

21250 *Countdown WWIII: Operation North Africa: a novel.* New York: Berkley Books, 1984, 233 p., paper, novel. COUNTDOWN WWIII #1.

21251 *Countdown WWIII: Operation Persian Gulf: a novel.* New York: Berkley Books, 1984, x+228 p., paper, novel. COUNTDOWN WWIII #4.

Operation Black Sea—SEE: *Countdown World War III: Operation Black Sea.*

Operation choke point—SEE: *Countdown WWIII: Operation choke point.*

Operation North Africa—SEE: *Countdown WWIII: Operation North Africa.*

Operation Persian Gulf—SEE: *Countdown WWIII: Operation Persian Gulf.*

DAVIES, Wilfred, 1929- , *with Robin Waterfield*

21252 *The money spider.* Harmondsworth, Middlesex, England: Puffin Books, 1988, 280 p., paper, novel. FIGHTING FANTASY GAMEBOOK SERIES.

21253 *The water spider.* Harmondsworth, Middlesex, England: Puffin Books, 1988, 300 p., paper, novel. FIGHTING FANTASY GAMEBOOK SERIES.

DAVIS, Bart, 1950-

21254 *Blind Prophet.* Garden City, NY: Doubleday & Co., 1983, 334 p., cloth, novel.

*DAVIS, (G.) Brian, 1925-1988

DAVIS, Don(ald), *with Jay Davis*

21255 *Sins of the flesh.* New York: Tor Horror, A Tom Doherty Associates Book, 1989, 400 p., paper, novel.

DAVIS, Frederick C(lyde), 1902-1977

21230 *The complete adventures of the Moon Man: volume 1, The night nemesis.* Bowling Green, OH: Purple Prose Press, 1984, 469 p., cloth, coll. [Edited by Garyn G. Roberts & Gary Hoppenstand; only volume published].

21231 *The mole men want your eyes.* North Hollywood, CA: Shroud: Publishers, 1976, 38 p., paper, story. PULP READER #1.

21232 *The Moon Man.* Oak Lawn, IL: Robert Weinberg, 1974, 64 p., paper, coll. PULP CLASSICS #5.

The night nemesis—SEE: *The complete adventures of the Moon Man: volume 1, The night nemesis.*

as CURTIS STEELE

21233 *Cavern of the damned.* Oak Forest, IL: Dimedia/Pulp Press, 1980, [96] p., paper, novel. OPERATOR 5 SERIES.
21234 *Legions of starvation.* Oak Forest, IL: Dimedia/Pulp Press, 1980, [96] p., paper, novel. OPERATOR 5 SERIES.
21235 *Scourge of the invisible death.* Oak Forest, IL: Dimedia/Pulp Press, 1980, [96] p., paper, novel. OPERATOR 5 SERIES.

with Kendell Foster Crossen

20829 *The Green Lama: an amazing exploit taken right out of the case-book of the Green Lama, in which his unusual powers are put to the test.* Chicago: Robert Weinberg, 1976, 89 p., paper, coll. PULP CLASSICS #14.

DAVIS, Gerry, 1931-1991

21256 *Doctor Who and the tenth planet.* London: Longbow Series, Allan Wingate, 1976, 141 p., cloth, tele. DOCTOR WHO.
21257 *Doctor Who and the tomb of the cybermen.* London: W. H. Allen, 1978, 141 p., cloth, tele. DOCTOR WHO.
21258 *Doctor Who. The Highlanders.* London: W. H. Allen, 1984, 126 p., cloth, tele. DOCTOR WHO #90.
The highlanders—SEE: *Doctor Who: The Highlanders.*

with Alison Bingeman

The Celestial Toymaker—SEE: *Doctor Who: The Celestial Toymaker.*
17967 *Doctor Who: The Celestial Toymaker.* London: W. H. Allen, 1986, 127 p., cloth, tele. DOCTOR WHO #111.

with Kit Pedler

21259 *Doomwatch: The world in danger.* London: Longman, 1975, 90 p., paper, tele.
21260 *The Dynostar menace.* London: Souvenir Press, 1975, 271 p., cloth, novel.
The world in danger—SEE: *Doomwatch: The world in danger.*

DAVIS, Graeme

Midnight rogue—SEE: *Steve Jackson and Ian Livingstone present Midnight rogue.*
21261 *Steve Jackson and Ian Livingstone present Midnight rogue.* Harmondsworth, Middlesex, England: Puffin Books, 1987, 400 p., paper, fiction. FIGHTING FANTASY GAMEBOOK #29.

DAVIS, Grania (Eve), 1943-

21262 *Moonbird.* Garden City, NY: Doubleday & Co., 1986, 181 p., cloth, novel.
21263 *The rainbow annals.* New York: Avon, 1980, 208 p., paper, novel.

with Avram Davidson

21221 *Marco Polo and the sleeping beauty.* New York: Baen, 1988, 300 p., paper, novel.

DAVIS, Gwen, 1936-

21264 *The princess and the pauper: an erotic fairy tale.* Boston: Little, Brown & Co., 1989, 242 p., cloth, novel. [A retelling of *The prince and the pauper* / by Mark Twain].

DAVIS, Harold A., 1902-1955

as KENNETH ROBESON

04152 *The green death: a Doc Savage adventure.* Toronto, New York: Bantam Books, 1971, 138 p., paper, novel. DOC SAVAGE #65.
04158 *The living fire menace: a Doc Savage adventure.* Toronto, New York: Bantam Books, 1971, 120 p., paper, novel. DOC SAVAGE #61.
21266 *The mountain monster: a Doc Savage adventure.* Toronto, New York: Bantam Books, 1976, 122 p., paper, novel. DOC SAVAGE #84.
04171 *The munitions master: a Doc Savage adventure.* Toronto, New York: Bantam Books, 1971, 135 p., paper, novel. DOC SAVAGE #58.

with Lester Dent as KENNETH ROBESON

04134 *The crimson serpent: a Doc Savage adventure.* Toronto, New York: Bantam Books, 1974, 138 p., paper, novel. DOC SAVAGE #78.
04142 *Dust of death: a Doc Savage adventure.* Toronto, New York: Bantam Books, 1969, 139 p., paper, novel. DOC SAVAGE #32.
04151 *The golden peril: a Doc Savage adventure.* Toronto, New York: Bantam Books, 1970, 138 p., paper, novel. DOC SAVAGE #55.

21265 *The king maker.* Toronto, New York: Bantam Books, 1975, 170 p., paper, novel. DOC SAVAGE #80.

04156 *The land of fear: a Doc Savage adventure.* Toronto, New York: Bantam Books, 1973, 136 p., paper, novel. DOC SAVAGE #75.

04165 *Merchants of disaster: a Doc Savage adventure.* Toronto, New York: Bantam Books, 1969, 138 p., paper, novel. DOC SAVAGE #41.

21267 *The Purple Dragon: a Doc Savage adventure.* Toronto, New York: Bantam Books, 1978, 136 p., paper, novel. DOC SAVAGE #91.

with Lester Dent and William G. Bogart as KENNETH ROBESON

21568 *Doc Savage: five complete adventures in one volume: Bequest of evil; Death in little houses; Target for death; The death lady; The exploding lake.* New York, Toronto: Bantam Books, 1990, 441 p., paper, coll. DOC SAVAGE #173-177. [Cover title: *Doc Savage omnibus, volume 12*; *Death in little houses* by Lester Dent and William G. Bogart; *The exploding lake* by Lester Dent and Harold A. Davis; *Target for death* and *The death lady* and *Bequest of evil* by William G. Bogart].

with Alan Hathway as KENNETH ROBESON

21269 *Doc Savage: Devils of the deep; and, The headless men: two complete adventures in one volume.* Toronto, New York: Bantam Books, 1984, 228 p., paper, coll. DOC SAVAGE #123-124. [*Devils of the deep* by Harold A. Davis; *The headless men* by Alan Hathway].

DAVIS, Hazel K., 1941- , with James E. Davis

37698 *Presenting William Sleator.* New York: Twayne Publishers, Maxwell Macmillan International, 1991, xii+131 p., cloth, nonf.

DAVIS, J(ames) Madison (Jr.), 1951-

21270 *Stanislaw Lem.* Mercer Island, WA: Starmont House, 1990, ix+116 p., cloth, nonf. STARMONT READER'S GUIDE #32.

with Robertson Davies

21246 *Conversations with Robertson Davies.* Jackson, MS: University Press of Missis-

sippi, 1989, xxi+285 p., cloth, nonf. anth.

DAVIS, James, with Barbara Raifsnider

21271 *The fire crystal.* San Diego, CA: Infinity Books, 1978, 52 p., paper, novel.

DAVIS, James E., 1934- , with Hazel K. Davis

37698 *Presenting William Sleator.* New York: Twayne Publishers, Maxwell Macmillan International, 1991, xii+131 p., cloth, nonf.

DAVIS, Jay, with Don Davis

21255 *Sins of the flesh.* New York: Tor Horror, A Tom Doherty Associates Book, 1989, 400 p., paper, novel.

DAVIS, Joe Lee, 1906-1974

21272 *James Branch Cabell.* New York: Twayne Publishers, 1962, 174 p., cloth, nonf.

DAVIS, Maggie (Hill)

21273 *Forbidden objects.* New York: Tor Horror, A Tom Doherty Associates Book, 1986, 276 p., paper, novel.

DAVIS, Mark, with Rick Cooper as NICHOLAS SARAZEN

20551 *Family reunion.* New York: Pinnacle Books, Windsor Publishing Corp., 1990, 287 p., paper, novel.

DAVIS, Phil

21274 *Nemesis.* New York: Avon, 1979, 280 p., paper, novel.

DAVIS, Richard, 1945-

21275 *Animal ghosts: a new collection.* London: Hutchinson, 1980, 143 p., cloth, anth.

21276 *Armada sci-fi 1.* London: Armada, 1975, 127 p., paper, anth.

21276A retitled: *SF 1: science fiction stories.* London: Armada, 1980, 127 p., paper, anth.

21277 *Armada sci-fi 2.* London: Armada, 1975, 126 p., paper, anth.

21277A retitled: *SF 2: science fiction stories.* London: Armada, 1980, 126 p., paper, anth.

21278 *Armada sci-fi 3.* London: Armada, 1976, 127 p., paper, anth.

21279 *The encyclopedia of horror*. London: Octopus, 1981, 192 p., cloth, nonf. anth.

The first Orbit book of horror stories—SEE: *The year's best horror stories, series III.*

21280 *The Jon Pertwee book of monsters*. London: Methuen, 1978, 166 p., cloth, anth.

The price of fear—SEE: *Vincent Price presents The price of fear.*

SF 1—SEE: *Armada sci-fi 1.*

SF 2—SEE: *Armada sci-fi 2.*

21281 *SF 4: science fiction stories*. London: Armada, 1977, 128 p., paper, anth.

21282 *Space 3: a collection of science fiction stories*. London: Abelard-Schuman, 1976, 152 p., cloth, anth.

21283 *Space 4: a collection of science-fiction stories*. London: Abelard-Schuman, 1977, 132 p., cloth, anth.

21284 *Space 5: a collection of science fiction stories*. London: Hutchinson, 1979, 160 p., cloth, anth.

21285 *Space 6: a collection of science fiction stories*. London: Hutchinson, 1980, 168 p., cloth, anth.

21286 *Space 7: a collection of science fiction stories*. London: Hutchinson, 1981, 159 p., cloth, anth.

21287 *Space 8: a collection of science fiction stories*. London: Hutchinson, 1983, 108 p., cloth, anth.

21288 *Space 9: a collection of science fiction stories*. London: Hutchinson Children's Books, 1985, 95 p., cloth, anth.

21289 *Spectre 2: a collection of ghost stories*. London: Abelard-Schuman, 1975, 158 p., cloth, anth.

21290 *Spectre 3: a collection of ghost stories*. London: Abelard-Schuman, 1976, 138 p., cloth, anth.

21291 *Spectre 4: a collection of ghost stories*. London: Abelard-Schuman, 1977, 145 p., cloth, anth.

21292 *Vincent Price presents The price of fear*. London: Everest Books, 1976, 189 p., paper, anth.

21293 *The year's best horror stories, series III*. New York: DAW Books, 1975, 173 p., paper, anth.

21293A retitled: *The first Orbit book of horror stories*. London: Futura Publications, An Orbit Book, 1976, 192 p., paper, anth.

DAVIS, Sonia H. [i.e., Sonia Haft Davis Lovecraft Greene], 1883-1972

21294 *The private life of H. P. Lovecraft*. West Warwick, RI: Necronomicon Press, 1985, v+25 p., paper, nonf.

DAVIS, Tony

21295 *The best of South African science fiction, volume 1*. [South Africa: s.n.], 1981, [110] p., paper, anth.

21296 *The best of South African science fiction, volume 2*. [South Africa: s.n.], 1985, iii+116 p., paper, anth.

DAVISON, Jean

21297 *Dreaming witness*. New York: A Berkley Medallion Book, Berkley Publishing Corp., 1978, 218 p., paper, novel.

DAVISON, Peter, 1951-

Book of alien monsters—SEE: *Peter Davison's Book of alien monsters.*

Book of alien planets—SEE: *Peter Davison's Book of alien planets.*

21298 *Peter Davison's Book of alien monsters*. London: Hutchinson, 1982, 125 p., cloth, anth.

21299 *Peter Davison's Book of alien planets*. London: Hutchinson, 1983, 96 p., cloth, anth.

DAWIDZIAK, Mark, 1956-

21300 *Night stalking: a 20th anniversary Kolchak companion*. East Meadow, NY: Image Publishing, 1991, 155 p., paper, nonf.

DAWSON, Fielding, 1930-

21301 *The sun rises into the sky, and other stories*. Los Angeles: Black Sparrow Press, 1974, 134 p., cloth, coll.

*DAWSON, Forbes, 1860-

DAWSON, Les

21302 *A time before Genesis: a novel of the future's past*. London: Elm Tree Press, 1986, 179 p., cloth, novel.

DAWSON, Saranne (Hoover)

21303 *The enchanted land*. New York: Leisure Books, 1991, 361 p., paper, novel.

21304 *From the mist*. New York: Leisure Books, 1991, 368 p., paper, novel.

21305 *Greenfire*. New York: Leisure Books, 1990, 364 p., paper, novel. [Title page gives the author's name as Saranne Hoover].

DAY, A(rthur) Grove, 1904- , with Bacil F. Kirtley

21306 *Horror in paradise: grim and uncanny tales from Hawaii and the South Seas.* Honolulu, HI: Mutual Publishing Co., 1986, 285 p., paper, anth.

DAY, Bradford M(arshall), 1916-

21307 *Bibliography of adventure: Mundy, Burroughs, Rohmer, Haggard.* New York: Arno Press, 1978, 125 p., cloth, nonf. LOST RACE AND ADULT FANTASY FICTION. [Revised edition].

DAY, Chet

21308 *The hacker.* New York, London: Pocket Books, 1989, 310 p., paper, novel.
21309 *Halo.* New York: Pocket Books, 1987, 344 p., paper, novel.

DAY, David, 1947-

21310 *The Burroughs bestiary: an encyclopaedia of monsters and imaginary beings created by Edgar Rice Burroughs.* London: New English Library, 1978, 150 p., cloth, nonf.
21311 *A Tolkien bestiary.* London: Mitchell Beazley Publishers, 1979, 287 p., cloth, nonf.
21312 *Tolkien: the illustrated encyclopedia.* London: Mitchell Beazley Publishers, 1991, 279 p., cloth, nonf.

DAY, Donald B(ryne), 1909-1978

21313 *Index to the science fiction magazines, 1926-1950, revised edition.* Boston: G. K. Hall & Co., 1982, xv+289 p., cloth, nonf.

DAY, William Patrick, 1950-

21314 *In the circles of fear and desire: a study of gothic fantasy.* Chicago & London: University of Chicago Press, 1985, xi+208 p., cloth, nonf.

DAYAN, Joan, 1949-

21315 *Fables of mind: an inquiry into Poe's fiction.* New York: Oxford University Press, 1987, 273 p., cloth, nonf.

DE ANDRADE, Mario—SEE: Andrade, Mario de

DE BALIOL, Alexander—SEE: Baliol, Alexander de

DE BALZAC, Honore—SEE: Balzac, Honore de

DE BERNIERES, Louis, 1954-

37699 *Señor Vivo and the Coca Lord.* London: Secker & Warburg, 1991, 279 p., cloth, novel.

DE BOLT, Joe [i.e., Joseph Wayne de Bolt Sr.], 1939-

21316 *The happening worlds of John Brunner: critical explorations in science fiction.* Port Washington, NY & London: Kennikat Press, 1975, 216 p., cloth, nonf. anth.
21317 *Ursula K. Le Guin: voyager to inner lands and to outer space.* Port Washington, NY & London: National University Publications, Kennikat Press, 1979, 221 p., cloth, nonf. anth.

DE BOLT, Joseph W.—SEE: de Bolt, Joe

DE BORCHGRAVE, Arnaud [i.e., Arnaud Paul Charles Marie-Philippe de Borchgrave d'Altena], 1926- , with Robert Moss

21318 *The spike.* London: Weidenfeld & Nicolson, 1980, 374 p., cloth, novel.

DE BOSSCHERE, Jean—SEE: Bosschere, Jean de

DE CAMP, Catherine (Adelaide) Crook, 1907-

21319 *Creatures of the cosmos.* Philadelphia, PA: Westminster Press, 1977, 152 p., cloth, anth.

with L. Sprague de Camp

21320 *The bones of Zora.* Huntington Woods, MI: Phantasia Press, 1983, 239 p., cloth, novel. KRISHNA SERIES. [Limited to 650 copies].
21321 *Footprints on the sand: a literary sampler.* Chicago: Advent:Publishers, 1981, xvii+327 p., cloth, coll. [Includes some nonfiction].
21322 *The incorporated knight.* West Bloomfield, MI: Phantasia Press, 1987, 191 p., cloth, novel. INCORPORATED KNIGHT #1.
21323 *The pixilated peeress.* New York: A Del Rey Book, Ballantine Books, 1991, 208 p, cloth, novel. INCORPORATED KNIGHT #2.

21324 *Science fiction handbook, revised.* Philadelphia, PA: Owlswick Press, 1975, viii+220 p., cloth, nonf.

21325 *The stones of Nomuru.* Norfolk & Virginia Beach, VA: The Donning Co., Publishers, 1988, 215 p., paper, novel.

21326 *The swords of Zinjaban.* Riverdale, NY: Baen Fantasy, 1991, 309 p., paper, novel. KRISHNA SERIES.

with L. Sprague de Camp & Jane Whittington Griffin

21327 *Dark Valley destiny: the life of Robert E. Howard.* New York: Bluejay Books, 1983, 402 p., cloth, nonf.

DE CAMP, L(yon) Sprague, 1907-

21328 *The best of L. Sprague de Camp.* Garden City, NY: Nelson Doubleday, 1978, xv+301 p., cloth, anth.

21329 *The blade of Conan.* New York: Ace Books, 1979, ix+310 p., paper, nonf. anth.

21330 *Blond barbarians and noble savages.* Baltimore, MD: T-K Graphics, 1975, 46 p., paper, nonf. coll.

21331 *Conan and the spider god.* Toronto, New York: Bantam Books, 1980, xi+175 p., paper, novel. CONAN SERIES.

21332 *Divide and rule.* New York: Tor SF, A Tom Doherty Associates Book, 1990, 94 p., paper, story. [Bound with *The sword of Rhiannon* / by Leigh Brackett].

21333 *The great fetish.* Garden City, NY: Doubleday & Co., 1978, 177 p., cloth, novel.

21334 *The hand of Zei.* Philadelphia, PA: Owlswick Press, 1981, vi+276 p., cloth, novel. KRISHNA #2. [Incorporates *The search for Zei*].

21335 *The honorable barbarian.* Norwalk, CT: Easton Press, 1989, 240 p., cloth, novel.

21336 *The hostage of Zir.* New York: Berkley Publishing Corp., 1977, 213 p., cloth, novel. KRISHNA #3.

21337 *Literary swordsmen and sorcerers: the makers of heroic fantasy.* Sauk City, WI: Arkham House, 1976, xxix+313 p., cloth, nonf. coll.

21338 *Lovecraft: a biography.* Garden City, NY: Doubleday & Co., 1975, xvi+510 p., cloth, nonf.

21339 *The miscast barbarian: a biography of Robert E. Howard (1906-1936).* Saddle River, NJ: Gerry de la Ree, 1975, 43 p., paper, nonf.

21340 *The prisoner of Zhamanak.* Huntington Woods, MI: Phantasia Press, 1982, x+228 p., cloth, novel. KRISHNA SERIES.

21341 *The purple pterodactyls: the adventures of W. Wilson Newbury, ensorcelled financier.* Huntington Woods, MI: Phantasia Press, 1979, 228 p., cloth, coll.

21342 *The queen of Zamba.* New York: Davis Publications, 1977, 224 p., paper, coll.

21343 *The reluctant king.* Garden City, NY: Nelson Doubleday, 1985, 533 p., cloth, coll. JORIAN #1-3.

21344 *Sir Harold and the gnome king.* Newark, NJ: Wildside Press, 1991, 71 p., cloth, story. HAROLD SHEA #4.

21345 *The spell of Conan.* New York: Ace Books, 1980, x+244 p., paper, nonf. anth. [Includes some verse].

21346 *The unbeheaded king.* New York: A Del Rey Book, Ballantine Books, 1983, 185 p., cloth, novel. JORIAN #3.

21347 *The virgin & the wheels.* New York: Popular Library, 1976, 191 p., paper, coll. [Includes *The virgin of Zesh* and *The wheels of If*].

21348 *The virgin of Zesh; &, The tower of Zanid.* New York: Ace Books, 1983, 263 p., paper, coll. KRISHNA #4.

21349 *The wheels of if.* New York: Tor SF, A Tom Doherty Associates Book, 1990, p. 1-88, paper, story. [Bound with *The pugnacious peacemaker* / by Harry Turtledove].

with Lin Carter

19590 *Conan the barbarian.* Toronto, New York: Bantam Books, 1982, ix+181 p., paper, movie. CONAN SERIES.

19591 *Conan the liberator.* Toronto, New York: Bantam Books, 1979, 214 p., paper, novel. CONAN SERIES.

with Lin Carter & Robert E. Howard

19592 *The Conan chronicles.* London: Orbit, 1989, 569 p., paper, coll. CONAN #1-3.

19593 *The Conan chronicles 2.* London: Orbit, 1990, 531 p., paper, coll. CONAN SERIES. [Includes *Conan the Wanderer*; *Conan the Adventurer*; *Conan the Buccaneer*.]

19594 *Conan of Aquilonia.* New York: Prestige Books, 1977, xii+171 p., paper, coll. CONAN #11.

with Lin Carter & Björn Nyberg

19595 *Conan the swordsman.* Toronto, New York: Bantam Books, 1978, 274 p., paper, novel. CONAN SERIES.

with Catherine Crook de Camp

21320 *The bones of Zora.* Huntington Woods, MI: Phantasia Press, 1983, 239 p., cloth, novel. KRISHNA SERIES. [Limited to 650 copies].

21321 *Footprints on the sand: a literary sampler.* Chicago: Advent:Publishers, 1981, xvii+ 327 p., cloth, coll. [Includes some non-fiction].

21322 *The incorporated knight.* West Bloomfield, MI: Phantasia Press, 1987, 191 p., cloth, novel. INCORPORATED KNIGHT #1.

21323 *The pixilated peeress.* New York: A Del Rey Book, Ballantine Books, 1991, 208 p, cloth, novel. INCORPORATED KNIGHT #2.

21324 *Science fiction handbook, revised.* Philadelphia, PA: Owlswick Press, 1975, viii+220 p., cloth, nonf.

21325 *The stones of Nomuru.* Norfolk & Virginia Beach, VA: The Donning Co., Publishers, 1988, 215 p., paper, novel.

21326 *The swords of Zinjaban.* Riverdale, NY: Baen Fantasy, 1991, 309 p., paper, novel. KRISHNA SERIES.

with Catherine Crook de Camp & Jane Whittington Griffin

21327 *Dark Valley destiny: the life of Robert E. Howard.* New York: Bluejay Books, 1983, 402 p., cloth, nonf.

with David Drake

21350 *The undesired princess; & The enchanted bunny.* New York: Baen Fantasy, 1990, 263+13 p., paper, coll. [Includes Drake's sequel to de Camp's original novel].

with Robert E. Howard

Conan: the flame knife—SEE: *Tales of Conan.*
The flame knife—SEE: *Tales of Conan.*
03989 *Tales of Conan.* New York: Gnome Press, 1955, 219 p., cloth, coll. CONAN SERIES.
03989A retitled: *Conan: The flame knife.* New York: Ace Books, 1981, 158 p., paper, coll. CONAN SERIES.
21351 *The treasure of Tranicos.* New York: Ace Books, 1980, 191 p., paper, novel. CONAN SERIES.

with Fletcher Pratt

21352 *The compleat enchanter: the magical misadventures of Harold Shea.* Garden City,

NY: Nelson Doubleday, 1975, 341 p., cloth, coll. HAROLD SHEA #1-2. [Includes *The incomplete enchanter* and *The castle of iron*].
The complete compleat enchanter—SEE: *The intrepid enchanter.*
The enchanter compleated—SEE: *Wall of serpents.*
The incompleat enchanter—SEE: *The incomplete enchanter.*
03995 *The incomplete enchanter.* New York: Henry Holt, 1941, 326 p., cloth, novel. HAROLD SHEA #1.
03995A retitled: *The incompleat enchanter.* London: Sphere Books, 1979, xv+236 p., paper, novel. HAROLD SHEA #1.
21353 *The intrepid enchanter: the complete magical misadventures of Harold Shea.* London: Sphere Books, 1988, xiii+497 p., paper, coll. HAROLD SHEA #1-3.
21353A retitled: *The complete compleat enchanter.* New York: Baen Books, 1989, 532 p., paper, coll. HAROLD SHEA #1-3.
21354 *Tales from Gavagan's Bar.* Philadelphia, PA: Owlswick Press, 1978, ix+310 p., cloth, coll. [Expanded edition].
03998 *Wall of serpents.* New York: Avalon Books, 1960, 223 p., cloth, novel. HAROLD SHEA #3.
03998A retitled: *The enchanter compleated.* London: Sphere Books, 1980, 157 p., paper, novel. HAROLD SHEA #3.

DE CASTRO, Adolphe [i.e., Gustaf Adolf de Castro Danziger], 1859-1959

21355 *Portrait of Ambrose Bierce.* New York, London: The Century Co., 1929, xiii+ 339 p., cloth, nonf.

DE CRAYENCOUR, Marguerite—SEE: **Yourcenar, Marguerite**

DE FELITTA, Frank (Paul), 1921-

21356 *Audrey Rose: a novel.* New York: G. P. Putnam's Sons, 1975, 374 p., cloth, novel. AUDREY ROSE #1.

21357 *The entity: a novel.* New York: G. P. Putnam's Sons, 1978, 432 p., cloth, novel.

21358 *For love of Audrey Rose.* New York: Warner Books, 1982, 459 p., paper, novel. AUDREY ROSE #2.

21359 *Golgotha Falls: an assault on the fourth dimension.* New York: Simon & Schuster, 1984, 319 p., cloth, novel.

DE FORTIS, Paul

21361 *The Kingdom of Redonda, 1865-1990: a celebration.* Upton, Wirral, Cheshire, England: Aylesford Press, 1991, 105 p., cloth, nonf. anth.

DE GRAMONT, Sanche—SEE: Morgan, Ted

DE HAAN, Tom, pseud.

21362 *The child of good fortune.* London: Jonathan Cape, 1989, 251 p., cloth, novel. BRYNCHMACHRYE #2.

21363 *A mirror for princes.* London: Jonathan Cape, 1987, [576] p., cloth, novel. BRYNCHMACHRYE #1.

DE HARTOG, Jan, 1914-

21364 *The centurion.* Franklin Center, PA: Franklin Library, 1989, xxii+286 p., cloth, novel.

DE HAVEN, Tom, 1949-

21365 *The end-of-everything man.* New York: A Byron Preiss Book, A Foundation Book, Doubleday, 1991, 436 p., cloth, novel. CHRONICLES OF THE KING'S TRAMP #2.

21366 *Freaks' amour.* New York: William Morrow, 1979, 276 p., cloth, novel.

21367 *Joe Gosh.* New York: Millennium, A Byron Preiss Visual Productions Book, Walker & Co., 1988, 196 p., cloth, novel.

21368 *Sunburn Lake.* New York: Viking, 1988, 293 p., cloth, coll.

21369 *U.S.S.A., book 1.* New York: A GLC Book, Avon, 1987, 185 p., paper, novel. U.S.S.A. #1.

21370 *Walker of worlds.* New York: A Byron Preiss Book, A Foundation Book, Doubleday, 1990, 342 p., cloth, novel. CHRONICLES OF THE KING'S TRAMP #1.

DE LA REE, Gereaux—SEE: de la Ree, Gerry

DE LA REE, Gerry [i.e., Gereaux deForest de la Ree], 1924-

21371 *The art of the fantastic: an anthology of illustrations from the collection of the editor and publisher.* Saddle River, NJ: Gerry de la Ree, 1978, 128 p., cloth, art.

21372 *Bok: a tribute to the late fantasy artist on the 60th anniversary of his birth and the 10th anniversary of his death.* Saddle River, NJ: Gerry de la Ree, 1974, 74 p.,

cloth, nonf. anth. [Edited by Gerry de la Ree].

21373 *Fantasy collector's annual—1975.* Saddle River, NJ: Gerry de la Ree, 1975, 84 p., cloth, nonf. anth.

21374 *Selected fragments.* NJ: Gerry de la Ree, 1945, 10 p., paper, coll.

21375 *Virgil Finlay remembered: the seventh book of Virgil Finlay: his art and poetry: memoirs by Lail Finlay, Robert Bloch, Stephen E. Fabian, Sam Moskowitz, Harlan Ellison, Robert A. W. Lowndes.* Saddle River, NJ: Gerry de la Ree, 1981, 128 p., cloth, nonf. anth.

with Sam Moskowitz

21385 *After ten years: a tribute to the late Stanley G. Weinbaum.* Westwood, NJ: Gerry de la Ree, 1945, 28 p., paper, nonf. anth.

DE LARRABEITI, Michael

Across the dark metropolis—SEE: The Borribles: Across the dark metropolis.

21386 *The Borribles.* London: Bodley Head, 1976, 240 p., cloth, novel. BORRIBLES #1.

21387 *The Borribles: Across the dark metropolis.* London: Piccolo, 1986, 332 p., paper, novel. BORRIBLES #3.

21388 *The Borribles go for broke.* London: Bodley Head, 1981, 224 p., cloth, novel. BORRIBLES #2.

DE LINT, Charles (Henri Diederick Hoefsmit), 1951-

21389 *Ascian in rose.* Seattle, WA: Axolotl Press, 1987, 83 p., cloth, novel. MOONHEART #2.

21390 *The badger in the bag: a tale of Cerin Songweaver.* Ottawa, Ontario, Canada: Triskell Press, 1985, ii+15 p., cloth, story. [Limited to 100 copies].

21391 *Berlin.* Ottawa, Ontario, Canada: Fourth Avenue Press, 1989, 55 p., cloth, story. [Limited to 326 copies].

21392 *The dreaming place.* New York: A Byron Preiss Book, Atheneum, 1990, 138 p., cloth, novel.

21393 *Drink down the moon.* New York: Ace Books, 1990, 216 p., paper, novel. JACK #2.

21394 *The drowned man's reel.* Ottawa, Canada: Triskell Press, 1988, iii+16 p., paper, story. [Limited to 100 copies].

21395 *The fair in Emain Macha.* New York: Tor Fantasy, A Tom Doherty Associates Book, 1990, 104 p., paper, story.

[Bound with *Ill met in Lankhmar* / by Fritz Leiber].

21396 *Ghosts of wind and shadow.* Ottawa, Canada: Triskell Press, 1990, ii+42 p., cloth, story. [Limited to 100 copies].

21397 *Ghostwood.* Eugene, OR: Axolotl Press, Pulphouse Publishing, 1990, 226 p., cloth, novel. MOONHEART #4; AXOLOTL PRESS #14.

21398 *Glass eyes and cotton strings: a tale of Cerin Songweaver.* Ottawa, Ontario, Canada: Triskell Press, 1982, ii+19 p., cloth, story. [Limited to 100 copies].

21399 *Greenmantle.* New York: Ace Books, 1988, 328 p., paper, novel.

21400 *The harp of the Grey Rose.* Norfolk, VA: Donning Co., 1985, 207 p., paper, novel.

21401 *Hedgework and guessery.* Eugene, OR: Pulphouse Publishing, 1991, 118 p., cloth, coll. AUTHOR'S CHOICE MONTHLY #22. [Includes some verse].

21402 *The hidden city.* New York, Toronto: Spectra, Bantam Books, 1990, 261 p., paper, novel. PHILIP JOSE FARMER'S THE DUNGEON #5.

21403 *In mask and motley: a tale of Cerin Songweaver.* Ottawa, Ontario, Canada: Triskell Press, 1983, ii+21+iii p., cloth, story. [Limited to 100 copies].

21404 *Jack, the giant-killer.* New York: Ace Books, 1987, viii+202 p., cloth, novel. JACK #1.

21405 *The lark in the morning: a tale of Cerin Songweaver.* Ottawa, Ontario, Canada: Triskell Press, 1987, ii+15 p., paper, story. [Limited to 100 copies].

21406 *Laughter in the leaves: a tale of Cerin Songweaver.* Ottawa, Ontario, Canada: Triskell Press, 1984, ii+12 p., cloth, story. [Limited to 100 copies].

21407 *The little country.* New York: William Morrow & Co., 1991, 630 p., cloth, novel.

21408 *The moon is a meadow: a tale of Tam Tinkern.* Ottawa, Ontario, Canada: Triskell Press, 1980, ii+27 p., cloth, story. [Limited to 100 copies].

21409 *Moonheart: a romance.* New York: Ace Fantasy Books, 1984, 485 p., paper, novel. MOONHEART #1.

21410 *Mulengro: a Romany tale.* New York: Ace Fantasy Books, 1985, 357 p., paper, novel.

21411 *The oak king's daughter: a tale of Cerin Songweaver.* Ottawa, Ontario, Canada: Triskell Press, 1979, 30 p., cloth, story. [Limited to 100 copies].

21412 *Our lady of the harbour.* Eugene, OR: Axolotl Press, Pulphouse Publishing, 1991, 88 p., cloth, novel. AXOLOTL SPECIAL EDITION #3.

21413 *A pattern of silver strings: a tale of Cerin Songweaver.* Ottawa, Ontario, Canada: Triskell Press, 1981, ii+33+vi p., cloth, story. [Limited to 100 copies].

21414 *The rafters were singing: a tale of Cerin Songweaver.* Ottawa, Ontario, Canada: Triskell Press, 1986, ii+17 p., cloth, story. [Limited to 100 copies].

21415 *The riddle of the Wren.* New York: Ace Fantasy Books, 1984, 295 p., paper, novel.

21416 *The stone drum.* Ottawa, Ontario, Canada: Triskell Press, 1989, v+35 p., paper, story. [Limited to 100 copies].

21417 *Svaha.* New York: Ace Books, 1989, 275 p., paper, novel.

21418 *Three plusketeers and the garden slugs.* Ottawa, Ontario, Canada: Triskell Press, 1985, 9 p., cloth, story. [Limited to 26 copies].

21419 *Uncle Dobbin's parrot fair.* Eugene, OR: Pulphouse Publishing, 1991, 45 p., cloth, story. SHORT STORY HARDBACKS #11; SHORT STORY PAPERBACKS #17.

21420 *The valley of thunder.* New York, Toronto: A Byron Preiss Book, Bantam Books, 1989, xii+263 p., paper, novel. PHILIP JOSE FARMER'S THE DUNGEON #3.

21421 *Westlin wind.* Eugene, OR: Axolotl Press, Pulphouse Publishing, 1989, 92 p., cloth, story. MOONHEART #3; AXOLOTL PRESS #9.

21422 *Wolf moon.* New York: A Signet Book, New American Library, 1988, 252 p., paper, novel.

21423 *World Fantasy Convention 1984: fantasy, an international genre celebration: ten years of accomplishment, October 12-14, the Westin Hotel, Ottawa, Canada.* Ottawa: Triskell Press, 1984, 103 p., cloth, nonf. anth.

21424 *Yarrow: an autumn tale.* New York: Ace Fantasy Books, 1986, 244 p., paper, novel.

as SAMUEL M. KEY

21425 *Angel of darkness.* New York: Jove Books, 1990, 262 p., paper, novel.

DE L'ISLE ADAM, Auguste Villiers—SEE: Villiers de L'Isle Adam, Auguste

DE MARINIS, Rick, 1934-

21426 *Cinder.* New York: Farrar, Straus, Giroux, 1978, 209 p., cloth, novel.

21427 *A lovely monster: the adventures of Claude Rains and Dr. Tellenbeck: a novel.* New York: Simon & Schuster, 1975, 163 p., cloth, novel.

21428 *Scimitar: a novel.* New York: A Henry Robbins Book, E. P. Dutton, 1977, 314 p., cloth, novel.

DE MARINO, Lawrence (August), 1943-

21429 *The odyssey project.* New York: Pageant Books, 1989, 309 p., paper, novel.

DE MAUPASSANT, Guy—SEE: Maupassant, Guy de

*DE MENDELSSOHN, Peter, <u>1909-1982</u>

DE NOUX, O'Neil (Paul Jr.), 1950-

21431 *Grim reaper* / by O'Neil DeNoux. New York: Zebra Books, Kensington Publishing Corp., 1988, 300 p., paper, novel.

DE NOUX, O'Neill

21430 *Cadavers: stories of speculative fiction.* Larabi, LA: O'Neill De Noux, 1975, [100] p., paper, coll. [O'Neil Paul De Noux claims not to have written this book].

DE OVALLE, Pilar

21432 *Calabrinia falling: a fantasy.* Freedom, CA: Crossing Press, 1990, 194 p., cloth, novel.

DE PAUL, Don

21433 *Caterfly.* Wheaton, IL, Madras, India: A Quest Book, Theosophical Publishing House, 1977, 124 p., paper, novel.

DE PAUL, Edith [pseud. of Edith G. Delatush], 1921-1991

21434 *The viscount's witch.* New York: A Candlelight Regency Romance, A Dell Book, 1981, [144] p., paper, novel.

DE POLNAY, Peter, 1906-1984

21435 *The other shore of time.* London: W. H. Allen, 1978, 216 p., cloth, novel.

37700 *The stuffed dog.* London: W. H. Allen, 1976, 223 p., cloth, novel.

DE QUEIROZ, Eça—SEE: Queiros, Eça de

DE RICO, Ul [pseud. of Count Ulderico Gropplero di Troppenburg], 1944-

21436 *The rainbow goblins.* London: Mitchell Beazley Publishers, 1978, [35] p., cloth, fiction. [Translation of *Die Regenkobolde*].

DE REYNIAC, Maurice Druon—SEE: Druon, Maurice

DE SAINT-AUBIN, Horace, pseud.—SEE: Balzac, Honoré de

DE SEINGALT, Giacomo Casanova—SEE: Casanova de Seingalt, Jacques

DE SENA, Jorge—SEE: Sena, Jorge de

DE SOUZA, Dudley—SEE: Souza, Dudley de

DE STEFANO, Anthony—SEE: DeStefano, Anthony

DE TIMMES, Graeme—SEE: de Timms, Graeme

DE TIMMS, Graeme

Fringe—SEE: *Split.*
Plague—SEE: *Three-quarters.*

04256 *Split.* London: Digit Books, 1963, 160 p., paper, novel.

04256A *Split* / by Graeme de Timmes. Australia: Universal Paperbacks, 1972, 160 p., paper, novel.

04256B retitled: *The fringe* / by G. D. Timms. Australia: Bill Ewington Books, 1973, 160 p., paper, novel.

04257 *Three-quarters.* London: Digit Books, 1963, 158 p., paper, novel.

04257A retitled: *Plague* / by G. D. Timmes. Australia: Bill Ewington Books, 1973, 158 p., paper, novel.

DE VERE, V. C. [pseud. of Conrad Charles Rolf Vere-Hodge], 1931-

21438 *The motto excelsior, book I.* Braunton, Devon, England: Merlin Books, 1988, 212 p., paper, novel. MOTTO EXCELSIOR #1.

21439 *The motto excelsior, books II-IV.* Braunton, Devon, England: Merlin Books, 1988, 443 p., paper, novel. MOTTO EXCELSIOR #2.

21440 *The motto excelsior, books V-VIII.* Braunton, Devon, England: Merlin Books, 1990, 537 p., paper, novel. EXCELSIOR MOTTO #3.

as ROGER MASON

21441 *The idea: the motto excelsior, books I-VI.* Braunton, Devon, England: Merlin Books, 1991, 832 p., paper, novel. MOTTO EXCELSIOR #1-3.
21442 *The idea: the motto excelsior, books VII-XII.* Braunton, Devon, England: Merlin Books, 1991, 1028 p., paper, novel. MOTTO EXCELSIOR #4.

DE VET, Charles V(incent), 1911-

21443 *Special feature.* New York: Avon, 1975, 176 p., paper, novel.

with Katherine MacLean

04270 *Cosmic checkmate.* New York: Ace Books, 1962, 96 p., paper, novel. [Bound with *King of the fourth planet /* by Robert Moore Williams].
21444 retitled: *Second game.* New York: DAW Books, 1981, 158 p., paper, novel. [Expanded edition].
Second game—SEE: *Cosmic checkmate.*

DE VOS, Luk—SEE: Vos, Luk de

DEAKINS, John

21445 *Barrow.* New York: A Roc Book, 1990, 336 p., paper, novel.

DEAMER, Dulcie, 1890-1972

37701 *As it was in the beginning.* Melbourne, Australia: F. Wilmot, 1929, 64 p., cloth, story. [Limited to 500 copies].

DEAN, Lisa, pseud.—SEE: James, L. Dean

DEAN, Martyn

with Chris Evans

21446 *Dream makers: six fantasy artists at work.* Limpsfield, Surrey, England: Paper Tiger, 1988, 127 p., cloth, art.
21447 *The guide to fantasy art techniques.* Limpsfield, Surrey, England: Dragon's World, A Paper Tiger Book, 1984, 111 p., cloth, nonf.

with Colin Greenland & Roger Dean

21448 *Magnetic storm.* Limpsfield, Surrey, England: Dragon's Dream, 1984, 154 p., cloth, art.

DEAN, Pamela [i.e., Pamela Collins Dean Dyer-Bennet], 1953-

21449 *The Hidden Land.* New York: Ace Fantasy Books, 1986, 202 p., paper, novel. SECRET COUNTRY #2.
21450 *The Secret Country /* by Pamela C. Dean. New York: Ace Fantasy Books, 1985, 293 p., paper, novel. SECRET COUNTRY #1.
21451 *Tam Lin.* New York: Tor, A Tom Doherty Associates Book, 1991, xi+468 p., cloth, novel.
21452 *The whim of the dragon.* New York: Ace Books, 1989, 328 p., paper, novel. SECRET COUNTRY #3.

DEAN, Roger, 1944- , *with Colin Greenland & Martyn Dean*

21448 *Magnetic storm.* Limpsfield, Surrey, England: Dragon's Dream, 1984, 154 p., cloth, art.

DEAR, Ian (C. B.), 1935-

21453 *Village of blood.* London: New English Library, 1975, 128 p., paper, novel.

DEAREN, Patrick, 1951-

21454 *Starflight to Faroul.* New York: Tower Books, 1980, 247 p., paper, novel.

DEAVER, Jeffrey Wilds, 1950-

21455 *Voodoo.* Toronto, New York: PaperJacks Ltd., 1988, 265 p., paper, novel.

DEBAL, Swami Puja--SEE: Knight, Stephen

DeBOLT, Adriana

21456 *The alien within.* North Hollywood, CA: American Art Enterprises, 1980, 160 p., paper, novel.
21457 *The crystal of power.* North Hollywood, CA: American Art Enterprises, 1980, 159 p., paper, novel. MYRA MORGANA #1.
21458 *Voyage of the Trigon.* North Hollywood, CA: American Art Enterprises, 1981, 160 p., paper, novel.

as CHRISTOPHER DANE

21080 *The galactic arena.* North Hollywood, CA: American Art Enterprises, 1981, 159 p., paper, novel. MYRA MORGANA #2.

21081 *Riders of the Dragon.* North Hollywood, CA: American Art Enterprises, 1981, 160 p., paper, novel.

DECARNIN, Camilla, *with Eric Garber & Lyn Paleo*

21459 *Worlds apart: an anthology of lesbian and gay science fiction and fantasy.* Boston: Alyson Publications, 1986, 293 p., paper, anth.

DeCHANCIE, John, 1946-

21460 *Castle for rent.* New York: Ace Books, 1989, 195 p., paper, novel. CASTLE PERILOUS #2.
21461 *Castle kidnapped.* New York: Ace Books, 1989, 216 p., paper, novel. CASTLE PERILOUS #3.
21462 *Castle murders.* New York: Ace Books, 1991, 243 p., paper, novel. CASTLE PERILOUS #5.
21463 *Castle perilous.* New York: Ace Books, 1988, 249 p., paper, novel. CASTLE PERILOUS #1.
21464 *Castle war!* New York: Ace Books, 1990, 233 p., paper, novel. CASTLE PERILOUS #4
21465 *Paradox alley.* New York: Ace Science Fiction Books, 1987, 314 p., paper, novel. SKYWAY TRILOGY #3.
21466 *Red limit freeway.* New York: Ace Science Fiction Books, 1984, 280 p., paper, novel. SKYWAY TRILOGY #2.
21467 *Starrigger.* New York: Ace Science Fiction Books, 1983, 264 p., paper, novel. SKYWAY TRILOGY #1.

with Thomas F. Monteleone

21468 *Crooked house.* New York: Tor Horror, A Tom Doherty Associates Book, 1987, 346 p., paper, novel.

DECKER, Jake

21469 *Deadly snow.* New York: Pinnacle Books, 1984, 250 p., paper, novel. THE FORCE #1.
21470 *Death comes home.* New York: Pinnacle Books, 1985, 215 p., paper, novel. THE FORCE #4.
21471 *Death gambit.* New York: Pinnacle Books, 1984, 220 p., paper, novel. THE FORCE #3.
21472 *Death's little sister.* New York: Pinnacle Books, 1984, 218 p., paper, novel. THE FORCE #2.

DeCLEMENTS, Barthe, 1920-

21473 *No place for me.* New York: Viking Kestrel, 1987, 136 p., cloth, novel.

with Christopher Greimes

21474 *Double trouble.* New York: Viking Kestrel, 1987, 168 p., cloth, novel.

DeCLES, Jon [pseud. of Donald Valantine Studebaker], 1941-

21475 *The particolored unicorn: an entertainment.* New York: Ace books, 1987, 230 p., paper, novel.

as MASON POWELL

21476 *The brig.* San Francisco: Alternate Press, 1984, 167 p., paper, novel.

with Paul Edwin Zimmer

21477 *Blood of the Colyn Muir.* New York: Avon Books, 1988, 245 p., paper, novel.

DEE, John

21478 *Stagger Lee.* Atlanta, GA: IMAC Inc., 1973, 241 p., cloth, novel.

*DEE, Roger [pseud. of Roger Dee Aycock], 1914-

DEE, Ron(ald David), 1957-

21479 *Blood lust.* New York: A Dell Book, 1990, 264 p., paper, novel.
37702 *Boundaries.* Port Washington, NY: Ashley Books, 1979, 188 p., cloth, novel.
21480 *Brain fever.* New York: Pinnacle Books, Windsor Publishing Corp., 1989, 283 p., paper, novel.
21481 *Descent.* New York: A Dell Book, 1991, 354 p., paper, novel.
21482 *Dusk.* New York: A Dell Book, 1991, 369 p., paper, novel.

*DEE, Sylvia [pseud. of Josephine Moore Proffitt], 1914-1967

DeFELICE, Cynthia C.

21483 *The strange night writing of Jessamine Colter.* New York: Macmillan Publishing Co.; London: Collier Macmillan, 1988, 51 p., cloth, story.

DEFONTENAY, C(harlemagne) I(schir), 1814-1856

21484 *Star (Psi Cassiopeia).* New York: DAW Books, 1975, 191 p., paper, novel. [Translation by P. J. Sokolowski of *Star; ou, Psi de Cassiopée*].

DeGARIS, Roger

21485 *Earth and elsewhere.* New York: Macmillan; London: Collier Macmillan, 1985, 315 p., cloth, anth. [Translation by Roger DeGaris].

as ANONYMOUS EDITOR

21486 *Aliens, travelers, and other strangers.* New York: Macmillan; London: Collier Macmillan, 1984, 220 p., cloth, anth. [Translation by Roger DeGaris].

21487 *New Soviet science fiction.* New York: Macmillan Books, 1979, 297 p., paper, anth. [Translation by Allen Saltz Jacobson].

DEIGHTON, Len [i.e., Leonard Cyril Deighton], 1929-

21488 *SS-GB: Nazi-occupied Britain 1941.* London: Jonathan Cape, 1978, 349 p., cloth, novel.

DEIGHTON, Leonard C.—SEE: Deighton, Len

DEITZ, Thomas F.—SEE: Deitz, Tom

DEITZ, Tom [i.e., Thomas Franklin Deitz], 1952-

21489 *Darkthunder's way.* New York: Avon Books, 1989, 342 p., paper, novel. DAVID SULLIVAN #3.

21490 *Fireshaper's doom: a tale of vengeance.* New York: Avon, 1987, 306 p., paper, novel. DAVID SULLIVAN #2.

21491 *The gryphon king.* New York: Avon Books, 1989, 406 p., paper, novel.

21492 *Soulsmith.* New York: AvoNova, 1991, 449 p., paper, novel.

21493 *Stoneskin's revenge: a tale of Calvin McIntosh.* New York: Avon Books, 1991, 307 p., paper, novel. DAVID SULLIVAN #5.

21494 *Sunshaker's war: a tale of David Sullivan.* New York: Avon Books, 1990, 372 p., paper, novel. DAVID SULLIVAN #4.

21495 *Windmaster's bane.* New York: Avon, 1986, 279 p., paper, novel. DAVID SULLIVAN #1.

DEL MARTIA, Astron, house pseud.

04063 *Dawn of darkness.* London: Gaywood Press, 1951, 98 p., paper, novel.

04064 *Interstellar espionage.* London: Gaywood Press, 1952, 100 p., paper, novel. SPACE EXPRESS COMPANY #3. [By the same pseudonymous author who previously published as "Franz Harkon"].

04065A *One against time.* London: Mayflower Books, 1969, 140 p., paper, novel. [By Stephen Frances; previously published under the house name Hank Janson].

04066 *Space pirates.* London: Gaywood Press, 1951, 112 p., paper, novel. SPACE EXPRESS COMPANY #1. [By the same pseudonymous author who later published as "Franz Harkon"].

04067 *The trembling world.* London: S. D. Frances, 1949, 128 p., paper, novel. [By John Russell Fearn].

DEL REY, Judy-Lynn (Benjamin), 1943-1986

21496 *Stellar science-fiction stories #2.* New York: Ballantine Books, 1976, 209 p., paper, anth. [Winner of the *Locus* Award for Best Original Anthology, 1976 (1977)].

21500 *Stellar science-fiction stories #3.* New York: Ballantine Books, 1977, 244 p., paper, anth.

21501 *Stellar science-fiction stories #4.* New York: A Del Rey Book, Ballantine Books, 1978, 230 p., paper, anth.

21502 *Stellar science-fiction stories #5.* New York: A Del Rey Book, Ballantine Books, 1980, 246 p., paper, anth.

21503 *Stellar science-fiction stories #6.* New York: A Del Rey Book, Ballantine Books, 1981, 186 p., paper, anth.

21504 *Stellar science-fiction stories #7.* New York: A Del Rey Book, Ballantine Books, 1981, 213 p., paper, anth.

21505 *Stellar short novels.* New York: Ballantine Books, 1976, x+198 p., paper, anth.

DEL REY, Lester [i.e., Ramón Felipe San Juan Mario Silvio Enrico Smith Heathcourt-Brace Sierra y Alvarez-del Rey y de Los Uerdes], 1915-

21506 *The best of Lester del Rey.* New York: A Del Rey Book, Ballantine Books, 1978, xviii+366 p., paper, coll.

21507 *Best science fiction stories of the year, fourth annual collection.* New York: E. P. Dutton & Co., 1975, 254 p., cloth, anth.

21508 *Best science fiction stories of the year, fifth annual collection.* New York: E. P. Dutton & Co., 1976, 206 p., cloth, anth.

21509 *Early del Rey.* Garden City, NY: Doubleday & Co., 1975, 424 p., cloth, coll.

21510 *Fantastic science-fiction art, 1926-1954.* New York: Ballantine Books, 1975, [15, 40] p., paper, nonf.

04105A *The mysterious planet.* New York: A Del Rey Book, Ballantine Books, 1978, 183 p., paper, novel. [Previously published under the name Kenneth Wright].

21511 *Nerves.* New York: Ballantine Books, 1976, 180 p., paper, novel. [Revised edition].

04101B *Rocket jockey.* New York: A Del Rey Book, Ballantine Books, 1978, 166 p., paper, novel. [Previously published under name Philip St. John].

21512 *The world of science fiction: 1926-1976: the history of a subculture.* New York: A Del Rey Book, Ballantine Books, 1979, xiii+416 p., paper, nonf.

as LESTER DEL REY & ERIK VAN LHIN

21513 *Police your planet.* New York: Ballantine Books, 1975, 217 p., paper, novel. [Expanded edition; previously published under the name Erik van Lhin (see #04104)].

with Raymond F. Jones

21514 *Weeping may tarry.* Los Angeles: Pinnacle Books, 1978, 180 p., paper, novel.

with Risa Kessler

21515 *Once upon a time: a treasury of modern fairy tales.* New York: A Del Rey Book, Ballantine Books, 1991, ix+336 p., cloth, anth.

DELAHAYE, Michael (John), 1946-

21516 *On the third day.* New York: Macmillan Publishing Co., 1984, viii+360 p., cloth, novel.

37703 *Stalking horse.* New York & Los Angeles: Tudor Publishing Co., 1989, viii+353 p., paper, novel.

DELANEY, Joseph H(enry), 1932-

21517 *In the face of my enemy.* New York: Baen Science Fiction Books, 1985, 349 p., paper, novel.

21518 *Lords temporal.* New York: Baen Books, 1987, 374 p., paper, novel.

with Marc Stiegler

21519 *Valentina: soul in sapphire.* New York: A Baen Book, 1984, 318 p., paper, novel.

DELANEY, Laurence

21520 *The Triton ultimatum.* New York: Thomas Y. Crowell, 1977, 247 p., cloth, novel.

DELANEY, Michael (Clark)

21521 *Not your average Joe.* New York: E. P. Dutton, 1990, 136 p., cloth, novel.

DELANY, Samuel R(ay, Jr.), 1942-

21522 *The American shore: meditations on a tale of science fiction by Thomas M. Disch: Angouleme.* Elizabethtown, NY: Dragon Press, 1978, v+243 p., cloth, nonf.

21523 *The ballad of Beta-2; [and, Empire star].* New York: Ace Books, 1975, 126+114 p., paper, coll.

21523A retitled: *The ballad of Beta-2; and, Empire star.* London: Sphere, 1977, 157 p., paper, coll.

21524 *The bridge of lost desire.* New York: Arbor House, 1987, 310 p., cloth, coll. NEVERYON #4.

21524A retitled: *Return to Nevèrÿon.* London: Grafton, 1989, 399 p., paper, novel. NEVERYON #4.

21525 *The complete Nebula Award-winning fiction of Samuel R. Delany.* Toronto, New York: Bantam Books, 1986, 425 p., paper, coll. [Includes *Babel-17* and *The Einstein Intersection*, plus several stories].

21526 *Dhalgren.* Toronto, New York: Bantam Books, 1975, 879 p., paper, novel.

21527 *Distant stars.* Toronto, New York: Bantam Books, 1981, 352 p., paper, coll.

21528 *Flight from Nevèrÿon.* Toronto, New York: Bantam Books, 1985, 385 p., paper, novel. NEVERYON #3.

21529 *Heavenly breakfast: an essay on the winter of love.* Toronto, New York: Bantam Books, 1979, xi+127 p., paper, nonf.

21530 *The jewel-hinged jaw: notes on the language of science fiction.* Elizabethtown, NY: Dragon Press, 1977, 326 p., cloth, nonf.

21531 *The motion of light in water: sex and science fiction writing in the East Village, 1957-1965.* New York: Arbor House, William Morrow & Co., 1988, 302 p., cloth, nonf. [Winner of the Hugo Award for Best Nonfiction Book, 1988 (1989)].

21532 *The motion of light in water: sex and science fiction writing in the East Village, 1957-1965; with, The column at the market's edge.* London: Paladin, 1990, xxii+581 p., paper, nonf. [Expanded edition].

21533 *Nebula winners thirteen.* New York: Harper & Row, 1980, xiv+239 p., cloth, anth.

21534 *Neveryóna; or, The tale of signs and cities: some informal remarks toward the modular calculus, part four.* Toronto, New York: Bantam Books, 1983, ix+385 p., paper, novel. NEVERYON #2.

Return to Nevèryon—SEE: *The bridge of lost desire.*

21535 *The star pit.* New York: Tor SF, A Tom Doherty Associates Book, 1989, 82 p., paper, novel. [Bound with *Tango Charlie and Foxtrot Romeo* / by John Varley].

21536 *Starboard wine: more notes on the language of science fiction.* Pleasantville, NY: Dragon Press, 1984, 244 p., cloth, nonf.

21537 *Stars in my pocket like grains of sand.* Toronto, New York: Bantam Books, 1984, 368 p., cloth, novel.

21538 *The Straits of Messina.* Seattle, WA: Serconia Press, 1989, xiii+169 p., cloth, nonf. coll.

21539 *Tales of Nevèryon.* Toronto, New York: Bantam Books, 1979, 264 p., paper, coll. NEVERYON #1.

21540 *Triton.* Toronto, New York: Bantam Books, 1976, 369 p., paper, novel.

21541 *We, in some strange power's employ, move on a rigorous line.* New York: Tor SF, A Tom Doherty Associates Book, 1990, 84 p., paper, story. [Bound with *Home is the hangman* / by Roger Zelazny].

DELAP, Richard (Leon), 1942-1987, *with Walt Lee*

21542 *Shapes: a romance of horror.* New York: Charter Books, 1987, 324 p., paper, novel.

DELARO, Selina, *with Edward Heron-Allen*

07137 *The princess Daphne: a novel.* London: Henry J. Drane, 1885, 264 p., cloth, novel

DELATUSH, Edith G.—SEE: de Paul, Edith

DELIGHT, Cherry, pseud.

21543 *The virgin ring.* New York: Pleasure Books, 1977, 181 p., paper, novel.

DeLILLO, Don, 1936-

21544 *Ratner's Star.* New York: Alfred A. Knopf, 1976, 437 p., cloth, novel.

*DELL, Jeffrey, <u>1899-1985?</u>

*DELMONT, Joseph [pseud. of Karl Pick], 1873-1935

DELRAY, Chester, pseud.—SEE: Rayer, Francis G.

*DEMAITRE, Edmund, 1906-<u>1991</u>

DEMBO, L(awrence) S(anford), 1929- , *with Annis Pratt*

21545 *Doris Lessing: critical studies.* Madison, WI: University of Wisconsin Press, 1974, xi+172 p., cloth, nonf. anth.

DEMERS, Patricia, 1946-

21546 *P. L. Travers.* Boston: Twayne Publishers, 1991, xii+141 p., cloth, nonf.

DeMILLE, Nelson (Richard), 1943-

21547 *The quest.* New York: Manor Books, 1975, 255 p., paper, novel.

DEMING, Richard—SEE: Franklin, Max

DEMPSEY, Al

21548 *Dog kill.* Englewood Cliffs, NJ: Prentice-Hall, 1976, 203 p., cloth, novel.

with Joseph Van Winkle & Sidney Levine

21549 *Miss Finney kills now and then.* New York: Tor, A Tom Doherty Associates Book, 1982, 256 p., paper, movie.

DEMPSEY, Henry—SEE: Harrison, Harry

DENAERDE, Stefan

21550 *Operation survival Earth.* New York: Pocket Books, 1977, 159 p., paper, novel. [Translation by Jim Lodge of *Buitenaarse beschaving*].

DENIS, John, pseud.—SEE: Edwards, John & Frost, Denis

DENNING, Troy, 1958-

21551 *Combat command in the world of Keith Laumer's Star colony: The Omega rebellion.* New York: Ace Books, 1987, xv+[294] p., paper, novel. COMBAT COMMAND #3.

21552 *Dark sun: The verdant passage.* Lake Geneva, WI: TSR Inc., 1991, 341 p., paper, novel. PRISM PENTAD #1.

The Omega rebellion—SEE: *Combat command in the world of Keith Laumer's Star colony: The Omega rebellion.*

The verdant passage—SEE: *Dark sun: The verdant passage.*

as RICHARD AWLINSON

Dragonwall—SEE: *Forgotten realms fantasy adventure: Dragonwall.*

17143 *Forgotten realms fantasy adventure: Dragonwall.* Lake Geneva, WI: TSR Inc., 1990, 311 p., paper, novel. EMPIRES TRILOGY #2.

17146 *Forgotten realms fantasy adventure: The parched sea.* Lake Geneva, WI: TSR Inc., 1991, 310 p., paper, novel. THE HARPERS #1.

17147 *Forgotten realms fantasy adventure: Waterdeep.* Lake Geneva, WI: TSR Inc., 1989, 341 p., paper, novel. AVATAR TRILOGY #3.

The parched sea—SEE: *Forgotten realms fantasy adventure: The parched sea.*

Waterdeep—SEE: *Forgotten realms fantasy adventure: Waterdeep.*

with Gordon R. Dickson & Cory Glaberson

21553 *Dorsai's command.* New York: Ace Books, 1989, 246 p., paper, novel. COMBAT COMMAND #8; DORSAI SERIES.

with James Ward

21554 *Advanced Dungeons & Dragons, legends & lore, second edition.* Lake Geneva, WI: TSR Inc., 1990, 192 p., paper, nonf.

DENNIS, Carol L(arkey), 1938-

21555 *Dragon's knight.* New York: Popular Library, 1989, 198 p., paper, novel. DRAGON #2.

21556 *Dragon's pawn.* New York: Popular Library, 1987, 232 p., paper, novel. DRAGON #1.

21557 *Dragon's queen.* New York: Warner Books, 1991, 247 p., paper, novel. DRAGON #3.

*DENNIS, Clifford E., 1891-1979

DENNIS, Ian, 1952-

21558 *Bagdad.* Toronto: Macmillan Canada, 1985, 210 p., cloth, novel. PRINCE OF STARS IN THE CAVERN OF TIME #1.

21559 *The prince of stars.* Toronto: Macmillan of Canada, 1987, 221 p., paper, novel. PRINCE OF STARS IN THE CAVERN OF TIME #2.

21560 *The prince of stars in the cavern of time.* New York: Viking Overlook, 1989, 433 p., cloth, novel. PRINCE OF STARS IN THE CAVERN OF TIME #1-2.

DENNIS, K. C.

21561 *Blood red!* New York, Washington: Vantage Press, 1984, 156 p., paper, novel.

*DENNIS, Robert C., 1915-1983

DENNISON, Milo, pseud.—SEE: Cantwell, Lois

DeNOUX, O'Neil—SEE: De Noux, O'Neil

DENT, Lester, 1905-1959

21562 *The Doc Savage files.* Greenwood, MA: Odyssey Publications, 1986, 28 p., paper, coll. DOC SAVAGE SERIES.

21563 *The sinister ray.* Brooklyn, NY: Gryphon Publications, 1987, 175 p., paper, coll.

alone or with others as KENNETH ROBESON (as indicated)

The all-white elf—SEE: *Doc Savage: four complete adventures in one volume: The all-white elf; The running skeletons; The angry canary; and The swooning lady.*

The angry canary—SEE: *Doc Savage: four complete adventures in one volume: The all-white elf; The running skeletons; The angry canary; and The swooning lady.*

18236 *The angry ghost: a Doc Savage adventure.* Toronto, New York: Bantam Books, 1977, 120 p., paper, novel. DOC SAVAGE #86. [With William G. Bogart].

04132 *The annihilist: a Doc Savage adventure.* Toronto, New York: Bantam Books, 1968, 138 p., paper, novel. DOC SAVAGE #31.

The awful dynasty—SEE: *Doc Savage: four complete adventures in one volume: The awful dynasty; The magic forest; Fire and ice; The disappearing lady.*

21564   *The awful egg: a Doc Savage adventure.* Toronto, New York: Bantam Books, 1978, 120 p., paper, novel. DOC SAVAGE #92.

Bequest of evil—SEE: *Doc Savage: five complete adventures in one volume: Bequest of evil; Death in little houses; Target for death; The death lady; The exploding lake.*

Birds of death—SEE: *Doc Savage: four complete adventures in one volume: The invisible-box murders; Birds of death; The wee ones; Terror takes 7.*

The black, black witch—SEE: *Doc Savage: Jiu San; and, The black, black witch.*

21565   *The boss of terror: a Doc Savage adventure.* Toronto, New York: Bantam Books, 1976, 118 p., paper, novel. DOC SAVAGE #85.

04133   *Brand of the werewolf: a Doc Savage adventure.* Toronto, New York: Bantam Books, 1965, 138 p., paper, novel. DOC SAVAGE #5.

Cargo unknown—SEE: *Doc Savage: Satan black; and, Cargo unknown: two complete adventures in one volume.*

Cold death—SEE: *Doc Savage: The secret in the sky; and, Cold death: two complete adventures in one volume.*

Colors for murder—SEE: *Doc Savage: five complete adventures in one volume: Se-Pah-Poo; Colors for murder; Three times a corpse; Death is a round black spot; The devil is Jones.*

04134   *The crimson serpent: a Doc Savage adventure.* Toronto, New York: Bantam Books, 1974, 138 p., paper, novel. DOC SAVAGE #78. [With Harold A. Davis].

04135   *The czar of fear: a Doc Savage adventure.* Toronto, New York: Bantam Books, 1968, 140 p., paper, novel. DOC SAVAGE #22.

The czar of fear—SEE ALSO: *Doc Savage: The Czar of fear; and, Fortress of Solitude: two complete adventures in one volume.*

04136   *The dagger in the sky: a Doc Savage adventure.* Toronto, New York: Bantam Books, 1969, 120 p., paper, novel. DOC SAVAGE #40.

Danger lies east—SEE: *Doc Savage: four complete adventures in one volume: The men vanished; Five fathoms dead; The terrible stork; Danger lies east.*

04137   *The deadly dwarf: a Doc Savage adventure.* Toronto, New York: Bantam Books, 1968, 115 p., paper, novel. DOC SAVAGE #28.

Death had yellow eyes—SEE: *Doc Savage: The shape of terror; and, Death had yellow eyes: two complete adventures in one volume.*

Death in little houses—SEE: *Doc Savage: five complete adventures in one volume: Bequest of evil; Death in little houses; Target for death; The death lady; The exploding lake.*

04138   *Death in silver: a Doc Savage adventure.* Toronto, New York: Bantam Books, 1968, 134 p., paper, novel. DOC SAVAGE #26.

Death in silver—SEE ALSO: *Doc Savage: Death in silver; and, Mystery under the sea.*

Death is a round black spot—SEE: *Doc Savage: five complete adventures in one volume: Se-Pah-Poo; Colors for murder; Three times a corpse; Death is a round black spot; The devil is Jones.*

The death lady—SEE: *Doc Savage: five complete adventures in one volume: Bequest of evil; Death in little houses; Target for death; The death lady; The exploding lake.*

The derelict of Skull Shoal—SEE: *Doc Savage: five complete adventures in one volume: The derelict of Skull Shoal; Terror wears no shoes; The green master; Return from Cormoral; Up from Earth's center.*

04139   *The derrick devil: a Doc Savage adventure.* Toronto, New York: Bantam Books, 1973, 138 p., paper, novel. DOC SAVAGE #74.

04140   *The devil Genghis.* Toronto, New York: Bantam Books, 1974, 149 p., paper, novel. DOC SAVAGE #79.

The devil is Jones—SEE: *Doc Savage: five complete adventures in one volume: Se-Pah-Poo; Colors for murder; Three times a corpse; Death is a round black spot; The devil is Jones.*

04141   *Devil on the Moon: a Doc Savage adventure.* Toronto, New York: Bantam Books, 1970, 120 p., paper, novel. DOC SAVAGE #50.

The devil's black rock—SEE: *Doc Savage: four complete adventures in one volume: The devil's black rock; Waves of death; The too-wise owl; Terror and the lonely widow.*

The devil's playground—SEE: *Doc Savage: The green eagle; and, The devil's playground: two complete adventures in one volume.*

The disappearing lady—SEE: *Doc Savage: four complete adventures in one volume: The awful dynasty; The magic forest; Fire and ice; The disappearing lady.*

21566 *Doc Savage: Death in silver; and, Mystery under the sea: two complete adventures in one volume.* Toronto, New York: Bantam Books, 1983, 260 p., paper, coll. DOC SAVAGE #26-27.

21568 *Doc Savage: five complete adventures in one volume: Bequest of evil; Death in little houses; Target for death; The death lady; The exploding lake.* New York, Toronto: Bantam Books, 1990, 441 p., paper, coll. DOC SAVAGE #173-177. [Cover title: *Doc Savage omnibus, volume 12; Death in little houses* by Lester Dent and William G. Bogart; *The exploding lake* by Lester Dent and Harold A. Davis; *Target for death* and *The death lady* and *Bequest of evil* by William G. Bogart].

21569 *Doc Savage: five complete adventures in one volume: No light to die by; The monkey suit; Let's kill Ames; Once over lightly; I died yesterday.* Toronto, New York: Bantam Books, 1988, 407 p., paper, coll. DOC SAVAGE #143-147. [Cover title: *Doc Savage omnibus, volume 5*].

21570 *Doc Savage: five complete adventures in one volume: Se-Pah-Poo; Colors for murder; Three times a corpse; Death is a round black spot; The devil is Jones.* New York, Toronto: Bantam Books, 1990, 455 p., paper, coll. DOC SAVAGE #168-172. [Cover title: *Doc Savage omnibus, volume 11*].

21571 *Doc Savage: five complete adventures in one volume: The derelict of Skull Shoal; Terror wears no shoes; The green master; Return from Cormoral; Up from Earth's center.* New York, Toronto: Bantam Books, 1990, 441 p., paper, coll. DOC SAVAGE #178-182. [Cover title: *Doc Savage omnibus, volume 13*].

21572 *Doc Savage: four complete adventures in one volume: Mystery island; Men of fear; Rock sinister; The pure evil.* Toronto, New York: Bantam Books, 1987, 392 p., paper, coll. DOC SAVAGE #139-142. [Cover title: *Doc Savage omnibus, volume 4*].

21573 *Doc Savage: four complete adventures in one volume: The all-white elf; The running skeletons; The angry canary; and The swooning lady.* Toronto, New York: Bantam Books, 1986, 373 p., paper, coll. DOC SAVAGE #127-130. [Cover title: *Doc Savage omnibus, volume I*].

21574 *Doc Savage: four complete adventures in one volume: The awful dynasty; The magic forest; Fire and ice; The disappearing lady.* Toronto, New York:

Bantam Books, 1988, 378 p., paper, coll. DOC SAVAGE #148-151. [Cover title: *Doc Savage omnibus, volume 6; The magic forest,* and *Fire and ice* by Lester Dent and William G. Bogart; *The disappearing lady* and *The awful dynasty* by William G. Bogart].

21575 *Doc Savage: four complete adventures in one volume: The devil's black rock; Waves of death; The too-wise owl; Terror and the lonely widow.* New York, Toronto: Bantam Books, 1989, 425 p., paper, coll. DOC SAVAGE #164-167. [Cover title: *Doc Savage omnibus, volume 10*].

21576 *Doc Savage: four complete adventures in one volume: The invisible-box murders; Birds of death; The wee ones; Terror takes 7.* New York: Bantam Books, 1989, 404 p., paper, coll. DOC SAVAGE #160-163. [Cover title: *Doc Savage omnibus, volume 9*].

21577 *Doc Savage: four complete adventures in one volume: The men vanished; Five fathoms dead; The terrible stork; Danger lies east.* Toronto, New York: Bantam Books, 1988, 378 p., paper, coll. DOC SAVAGE #152-155. [Cover title: *Doc Savage omnibus, volume 7*]

21578 *Doc Savage: four complete adventures in one volume: The mental monster; The pink lady; Weird valley; Trouble on parade.* Toronto, New York: Bantam Books, 1989, 407 p., paper, coll. DOC SAVAGE #156-159. [Cover title: *Doc Savage omnibus, volume 8*].

21579 *Doc Savage: four complete adventures in one volume: The mindless monsters; The rustling death; King Joe Cay; The thing that pursued.* Toronto, New York: Bantam Books, 1987, 410 p., paper, coll. DOC SAVAGE #131-134. [Cover title: *Doc Savage omnibus, volume 2; The mindless monsters* and *The rustling death* by Alan Hathway; *King Joe Cay* and *The thing that pursued* by Lester Dent].

21580 *Doc Savage: four complete adventures in one volume: The spook of Grandpa Eben; Measures for a coffin; The three devils; Strange fish.* Toronto, New York: Bantam Books, 1987, 378 p., paper, coll. DOC SAVAGE #135-138. [Cover title: *Doc Savage omnibus, volume 3*].

21581 *Doc Savage: Hell below; and, The lost giant: two complete adventures in one volume.* Toronto, New York: Bantam Books, 1980, 214 p., paper, coll. DOC SAVAGE #99-100.

21582 *Doc Savage: Jiu San; and, The black, black witch: two complete adventures in one volume.* Toronto, New York: Bantam Books, 1981, 200 p., paper, coll. Doc Savage #107-108.

Doc Savage omnibus, volumes #1-13—SEE: *Doc Savage: five complete adventures in one volume,* and *Doc Savage: four complete adventures in one volume*—various volumes.

21583 *Doc Savage: One-eyed mystic; and, The man who fell up: two complete adventures in one volume.* Toronto, New York: Bantam Books, 1982, 213 p., paper, coll. Doc Savage #111-112.

21584 *Doc Savage: Pirate isle; and, The speaking stone: two complete adventures in one volume.* Toronto, New York: Bantam Books, 1983, 200 p., paper, coll. Doc Savage #115-116.

21585 *Doc Savage: Python Isle.* New York, Toronto: Falcon, Bantam Books, 1991, 207 p., paper, novel. Doc Savage (UNNUMBERED). [With Will Murray].

21586 *Doc Savage: Satan black; and, Cargo unknown: two complete adventures in one volume.* Toronto, New York: Bantam Books, 1980, 213 p., paper, coll. Doc Savage #97-98.

21587 *Doc Savage: The Czar of fear; and, Fortress of Solitude: two complete adventures in one volume.* Toronto, New York: Bantam Books, 1982, 274 p., paper, coll. Doc Savage #22-23.

21588 *Doc Savage: The goblins; and, The secret of the Su: two complete adventures in one volume.* Toronto, New York: Bantam Books, 1985, 214 p., paper, coll. Doc Savage #125-126.

21589 *Doc Savage: The golden man; and, Peril in the north: two complete adventures in one volume.* Toronto, New York: Bantam Books, 1984, 210 p., paper, coll. Doc Savage #117-118.

21590 *Doc Savage: The green eagle; and, The devil's playground: two complete adventures in one volume.* Toronto, New York: Bantam Books, 1983, 217 p., paper, coll. Doc Savage #24-25. [*The devil's playground* by Alan Hathway; *The green eagle* by Lester Dent].

21591 *Doc Savage: The laugh of death; and, The king of terror: two complete adventures in one volume.* Toronto, New York: Bantam Books, 1984, 216 p., paper, coll. Doc Savage #119-120.

21592 *Doc Savage: The pharaoh's ghost; and, The time terror: two complete adventures in one volume.* Toronto, New York: Bantam Books, 1981, 197 p., paper, coll. Doc Savage #101-102.

21593 *Doc Savage: The secret in the sky; and, Cold death: two complete adventures in one volume.* Toronto, New York: Bantam Books, 1982, 261 p., paper, coll. Doc Savage #20-21. [*The secret in the sky* by Lester Dent; *Cold death* by Laurence Donovan].

21594 *Doc Savage: The shape of terror; and, Death had yellow eyes: two complete adventures in one volume.* Toronto, New York: Bantam Books, 1982, 185 p., paper, coll. Doc Savage #109-110.

21595 *Doc Savage: The talking devil; and, The ten ton snakes: two complete adventures in one volume.* Toronto, New York: Bantam Books, 1982, 183 p., paper, coll. Doc Savage #113-114.

21596 *Doc Savage: The three wild men; and, The fiery menace: two complete adventures in one volume.* Toronto, New York: Bantam Books, 1984, 212 p., paper, coll. Doc Savage #121-122.

21597 *Doc Savage: The whisker of Hercules; and, The man who was scared: two complete adventures in one volume.* Toronto, New York: Bantam Books, 1981, 201 p., paper, coll. Doc Savage #103-104.

21598 *Doc Savage: They died twice; and, The screaming man: two complete adventures in one volume.* Toronto, New York: Bantam Books, 1981, 183 p., paper, coll. Doc Savage #105-106.

04142 *Dust of death: a Doc Savage adventure.* Toronto, New York: Bantam Books, 1969, 139 p., paper, novel. Doc Savage #32. [With Harold A. Davis].

21599 *The evil gnome: a Doc Savage adventure.* Toronto, New York: Bantam Books, 1976, 120 p., paper, novel. Doc Savage #82.

The exploding lake—SEE: *Doc Savage: five complete adventures in one volume: Bequest of evil; Death in little houses; Target for death; The death lady; The exploding lake.*

04143 *The fantastic island: a Doc Savage adventure.* Toronto, New York: Bantam Books, 1966, 135 p., paper, novel. Doc Savage #14. [With Ryerson Johnson].

04144 *Fear Cay: a Doc Savage adventure.* Toronto, New York: Bantam Books, 1966, 138 p., paper, novel. Doc Savage #11.

04145 *The Feathered Octopus: a Doc Savage adventure.* Toronto, New York: Bantam Books, 1970, 122 p., paper, novel. Doc Savage #48.

The fiery menace—SEE: *Doc Savage: The three wild men; and, The fiery menace: two complete adventures in one volume.*

Fire and ice—SEE: *Doc Savage: four complete adventures in one volume: The awful dynasty; The magic forest; Fire and ice; The disappearing lady.*

Five fathoms dead—SEE: *Doc Savage: four complete adventures in one volume: The men vanished; Five fathoms dead; The terrible stork; Danger lies east.*

04146 *The flaming falcons: a Doc Savage adventure.* Toronto, New York: Bantam Books, 1968, 118 p., paper, novel. DOC SAVAGE #30.

04147 *Fortress of Solitude: a Doc Savage adventure.* Toronto, New York: Bantam Books, 1968, 118 p., paper, novel. DOC SAVAGE #23.

Fortress of Solitude—SEE ALSO: *Doc Savage: The Czar of fear; and, Fortress of Solitude: two complete adventures in one volume.*

04148 *The freckled shark: a Doc Savage adventure.* Toronto, New York: Bantam Books, 1972, 139 p., paper, novel. DOC SAVAGE #67.

04149 *The giggling ghosts: a Doc Savage adventure.* Toronto, New York: Bantam Books, 1971, 123 p., paper, novel. DOC SAVAGE #56.

The goblins—SEE: *Doc Savage: The goblins; and, The secret of the Su: two complete adventures in one volume.*

04150 *The gold ogre: a Doc Savage adventure.* Toronto, New York: Bantam Books, 1969, 122 p., paper, novel. DOC SAVAGE #42.

The golden man—SEE: *Doc Savage: The golden man; and, Peril in the north: two complete adventures in one volume.*

04151 *The golden peril: a Doc Savage adventure.* Toronto, New York: Bantam Books, 1970, 138 p., paper, novel. DOC SAVAGE #55. [With Harold A. Davis].

04153 *The green eagle: a Doc Savage adventure.* Toronto, New York: Bantam Books, 1968, 114 p., paper, novel. DOC SAVAGE #24.

The green eagle—SEE ALSO: *Doc Savage: The green eagle; and, The devil's playground: two complete adventures in one volume.*

The green master—SEE: *Doc Savage: five complete adventures in one volume: The derelict of Skull Shoal; Terror wears no shoes; The green master; Return from Cormoral; Up from Earth's center.*

21601 *The hate genius: a Doc Savage adventure.* Toronto, New York: Bantam Books, 1979, 119 p., paper, novel. DOC SAVAGE #94.

Hell below—SEE: *Doc Savage: Hell below; and, The lost giant: two complete adventures in one volume.*

04154 *Hex: a Doc Savage adventure.* Toronto, New York: Bantam Books, 1969, 120 p., paper, novel. DOC SAVAGE #37. [With William G. Bogart].

I died yesterday—SEE: *Doc Savage: five complete adventures in one volume: No light to die by; The monkey suit; Let's kill Ames; Once over lightly; I died yesterday.*

21602 *The incredible radio exploits of Doc Savage, volume 1.* Greenwood, MA: Odyssey Publications, 1982, 128 p., paper, coll. DOC SAVAGE SERIES. [By Lester Dent; only volume published].

The invisible-box murders—SEE: *Doc Savage: four complete adventures in one volume: The invisible-box murders; Birds of death; The wee ones; Terror takes 7.*

Jiu San—SEE: *Doc Savage: Jiu San; and, The black, black witch: two complete adventures in one volume.*

King Joe Cay—SEE: *Doc Savage: four complete adventures in one volume: The mindless monsters; The rustling death; King Joe Cay; The thing that pursued.*

21265 *The king maker.* Toronto, New York: Bantam Books, 1975, 170 p., paper, novel. DOC SAVAGE #80. [With Harold A. Davis].

The king of terror—SEE: *Doc Savage: The laugh of death; and, The king of terror: two complete adventures in one volume.*

04155 *Land of always-night: a Doc Savage adventure.* Toronto, New York: Bantam Books, 1966, 138 p., paper, novel. DOC SAVAGE #13. [With Ryerson Johnson].

04156 *The land of fear: a Doc Savage adventure.* Toronto, New York: Bantam Books, 1973, 136 p., paper, novel. DOC SAVAGE #75. [With Harold A. Davis].

04157 *The land of terror: Doc Savage and his pals in a novel of unusual adventure.* New York: Street & Smith, 1933, 252 p., cloth, novel. DOC SAVAGE #2 (old series); DOC SAVAGE #8 (new series).

The laugh of death—SEE: *Doc Savage: The laugh of death; and, The king of terror: two complete adventures in one volume.*

Let's kill Ames—SEE: *Doc Savage: five complete adventures in one volume: No light to die by; The monkey suit; Let's kill Ames; Once over lightly; I died yesterday.*

The lost giant—SEE: *Doc Savage: Hell below; and, The lost giant.*

04159 *The lost oasis: a Doc Savage adventure.* Toronto, New York: Bantam Books,

1965, 123 p., paper, novel. DOC SAVAGE #6.

04160 *Mad Mesa: a Doc Savage adventure.* Toronto, New York: Bantam Books, 1972, 122 p., paper, novel. DOC SAVAGE #66.

The magic forest—SEE: *Doc Savage: four complete adventures in one volume: The awful dynasty; The magic forest; Fire and ice; The disappearing lady.*

21603 *The magic island: a Doc Savage adventure.* Toronto, New York: Bantam Books, 1977, 137 p., paper, novel. DOC SAVAGE #89.

04161 *The Majii: a Doc Savage adventure.* Toronto, New York: Bantam Books, 1971, 140 p., paper, novel. DOC SAVAGE #60.

04162 *The man of bronze: Doc Savage and his pals in a novel of unusual adventure.* New York: Street & Smith, 1933, 252 p., cloth, novel. DOC SAVAGE #1.

04163 *The man who shook the Earth: a Doc Savage adventure.* Toronto, New York: Bantam Books, 1969, 154 p., paper, novel. DOC SAVAGE #43.

The man who fell up—SEE: *Doc Savage: One-eyed mystic; and, The man who fell up: two complete adventures in one volume.*

The man who was scared—SEE: *Doc Savage: The whisker of Hercules; and, The man who was scared: two complete adventures in one volume.*

Measures for a coffin—SEE: *Doc Savage: four complete adventures in one volume: The spook of Grandpa Eben; Measures for a coffin; The three devils; Strange fish.*

Men of fear—SEE: *Doc Savage: four complete adventures in one volume: Mystery island; Men of fear; Rock sinister; The pure evil.*

The men vanished—SEE: *Doc Savage: four complete adventures in one volume: The men vanished; Five fathoms dead; The terrible stork; Danger lies east.*

The mental monster—SEE: *Doc Savage: four complete adventures in one volume: The mental monster; The pink lady; Weird valley; Trouble on parade.*

04164 *The mental wizard: a Doc Savage adventure.* Toronto, New York: Bantam Books, 1970, 135 p., paper, novel. DOC SAVAGE #53.

04165 *Merchants of disaster: a Doc Savage adventure.* Toronto, New York: Bantam Books, 1969, 138 p., paper, novel. DOC SAVAGE #41. [With Harold A. Davis].

04166 *The Metal Master: a Doc Savage adventure.* Toronto, New York: Bantam Books, 1973, 137 p., paper, novel. DOC SAVAGE #72.

04167 *Meteor menace: a Doc Savage adventure.* Toronto, New York: Bantam Books, 1964, 140 p., paper, novel. DOC SAVAGE #3.

04168 *The Midas man: a Doc Savage adventure.* Toronto, New York: Bantam Books, 1970, 121 p., paper, novel. DOC SAVAGE #46.

The mindless monsters—SEE: *Doc Savage: four complete adventures in one volume: The mindless monsters; The rustling death; King Joe Cay; The thing that pursued.*

The monkey suit—SEE: *Doc Savage: five complete adventures in one volume: No light to die by; The monkey suit; Let's kill Ames; Once over lightly; I died yesterday.*

04169 *The monsters: a Doc Savage adventure.* Toronto, New York: Bantam Books, 1965, 138 p., paper, novel. DOC SAVAGE #7.

04170 *The motion menace: a Doc Savage adventure.* Toronto, New York: Bantam Books, 1971, 123 p., paper, novel. DOC SAVAGE #64. [With Ryerson Johnson].

Mystery island—SEE: *Doc Savage: four complete adventures in one volume: Mystery island; Men of fear; Rock sinister; The pure evil.*

21604 *Mystery on Happy Bones: a Doc Savage adventure.* Toronto, New York: Bantam Books, 1979, 134 p., paper, novel. DOC SAVAGE #96.

04172 *The mystery on the snow: a Doc Savage adventure.* Toronto, New York: Bantam Books, 1972, 149 p., paper, novel. DOC SAVAGE #69.

04173 *Mystery under the sea: a Doc Savage adventure.* Toronto, New York: Bantam Books, 1968, 120 p., paper, novel. DOC SAVAGE #27.

Mystery under the sea—SEE ALSO: *Doc Savage: Death in silver; and, Mystery under the sea.*

04174 *The Mystic Mullah: a Doc Savage adventure.* Toronto, New York: Bantam Books, 1965, 137 p., paper, novel. DOC SAVAGE #9.

No light to die by—SEE: *Doc Savage: five complete adventures in one volume: No light to die by; The monkey suit; Let's kill Ames; Once over lightly; I died yesterday.*

Omnibus volumes—SEE: *Doc Savage omnibus volumes*

Once over lightly—SEE: *Doc Savage: five complete adventures in one volume: No light to die by; The monkey suit; Let's kill Ames; Once over lightly; I died yesterday.*

One-eyed mystic—SEE: *Doc Savage: One-eyed mystic; and, The man who fell up: two complete adventures in one volume.*

04175 *The other world: a Doc Savage adventure.* Toronto, New York: Bantam Books, 1968, 119 p., paper, novel. DOC SAVAGE #29.

Peril in the north—SEE: *Doc Savage: The golden man; and, Peril in the north: two complete adventures in one volume.*

04176 *The Phantom City: a Doc Savage adventure.* Toronto, New York: Bantam Books, 1966, 137 p., paper, novel. DOC SAVAGE #10.

The pharaoh's ghost—SEE: *Doc Savage: The pharaoh's ghost; and, The time terror: two complete adventures in one volume.*

The pink lady—SEE: *Doc Savage: four complete adventures in one volume: The mental monster; The pink lady; Weird valley; Trouble on parade.*

Pirate isle—SEE: *Doc Savage: Pirate isle; and, The speaking stone: two complete adventures in one volume.*

04177 *Pirate of the Pacific: a Doc Savage adventure.* Toronto, New York: Bantam Books, 1967, 136 p., paper, novel. DOC SAVAGE #19.

04178 *The pirate's ghost: a Doc Savage adventure.* Toronto, New York: Bantam Books, 1971, 135 p., paper, novel. DOC SAVAGE #62.

04179 *Poison island: a Doc Savage adventure.* Toronto, New York: Bantam Books, 1971, 118 p., paper, novel. DOC SAVAGE #57.

04180 *The polar treasure: a Doc Savage adventure.* Toronto, New York: Bantam Books, 1965, 122 p., paper, novel. DOC SAVAGE #4.

The pure evil—SEE: *Doc Savage: four complete adventures in one volume: Mystery island; Men of fear; Rock sinister; The pure evil.*

21267 *The Purple Dragon: a Doc Savage adventure.* Toronto, New York: Bantam Books, 1978, 136 p., paper, novel. DOC SAVAGE #91. [With Harold A. Davis].

Python Isle—SEE: *Doc Savage: Python Isle.*

04181 *Quest of Qui: a Doc Savage adventure.* Toronto, New York: Bantam Books, 1966, 119 p., paper, novel. DOC SAVAGE #12.

04182 *Quest of the Spider: Doc Savage and his pals in a novel of unusual adventure.* New York: Street & Smith, 1933, 252 p., cloth, novel. DOC SAVAGE #3 (old series; DOC SAVAGE #68 (new series).

04183 *The red skull: a Doc Savage adventure.* Toronto, New York: Bantam Books, 1967, 124 p., paper, novel. DOC SAVAGE #17.

04184 *Red snow: a Doc Savage adventure.* Toronto, New York: Bantam Books, 1969, 139 p., paper, novel. DOC SAVAGE #38.

21605 *The red spider: a Doc Savage adventure.* Toronto, New York: Bantam Books, 1979, 122 p., paper, novel. DOC SAVAGE #95.

21606 *The red terrors: a Doc Savage adventure.* Toronto, New York: Bantam Books, 1976, 136 p., paper, novel. DOC SAVAGE #83.

04185 *Resurrection day: a Doc Savage adventure.* Toronto, New York: Bantam Books, 1969, 119 p., paper, novel. DOC SAVAGE #36.

Return from Cormoral—SEE: *Doc Savage: five complete adventures in one volume: The derelict of Skull Shoal; Terror wears no shoes; The green master; Return from Cormoral; Up from Earth's center.*

21607 *The Roar Devil: a Doc Savage adventure.* Toronto, New York: Bantam Books, 1977, 153 p., paper, novel. DOC SAVAGE #88.

Rock sinister—SEE: *Doc Savage: four complete adventures in one volume: Mystery island; Men of fear; Rock sinister; The pure evil.*

The running skeletons—SEE: *Doc Savage: four complete adventures in one volume: The all-white elf; The running skeletons; The angry canary; and The swooning lady.*

The rustling death—SEE: *Doc Savage: four complete adventures in one volume: The mindless monsters; The rustling death; King Joe Cay; The thing that pursued.*

04186 *The Sargasso ogre: a Doc Savage adventure.* Toronto, New York: Bantam Books, 1967, 140 p., paper, novel. DOC SAVAGE #18.

Satan black—SEE: *Doc Savage: Satan black; and, Cargo unknown: two complete adventures in one volume.*

The screaming man—SEE: *Doc Savage: They died twice; and, The screaming man: two complete adventures in one volume.*

04187 *The Sea Angel: a Doc Savage adventure.* Toronto, New York: Bantam Books, 1970, 120 p., paper, novel. DOC SAVAGE #49.

04188 *The sea magician: a Doc Savage adventure.* Toronto, New York: Bantam Books, 1970, 137 p., paper, novel. Doc SAVAGE #44.

04189 *The secret in the sky: a Doc Savage adventure.* Toronto, New York: Bantam Books, 1967, 119 p., paper, novel. Doc SAVAGE #20.

The secret in the sky—SEE ALSO: *Doc Savage: The secret in the sky; and, Cold death: two complete adventures in one volume.*

The secret of the Su—SEE: *Doc Savage: The goblins; and, The secret of the Su: two complete adventures in one volume.*

Se-Pah-Poo—SEE: *Doc Savage: five complete adventures in one volume: Se-Pah-Poo; Colors for murder; Three times a corpse; Death is a round black spot; The devil is Jones.*

04190 *The seven agate devils: a Doc Savage adventure.* Toronto, New York: Bantam Books, 1973, 134 p., paper, novel. Doc SAVAGE #73.

The shape of terror—SEE: *Doc Savage: The shape of terror; and, Death had yellow eyes: two complete adventures in one volume.*

04191 *The South Pole terror: a Doc Savage adventure.* Toronto, New York: Bantam Books, 1974, 137 p., paper, novel. Doc SAVAGE #77.

The speaking stone—SEE: *Doc Savage: Pirate isle; and, The speaking stone: two complete adventures in one volume.*

04192 *Spook Hole: a Doc Savage adventure.* Toronto, New York: Bantam Books, 1972, 138 p., paper, novel. Doc SAVAGE #70.

04193 *The spook legion: a Doc Savage adventure.* Toronto, New York: Bantam Books, 1967, 122 p., paper, novel. Doc SAVAGE #16.

The spook of Grandpa Eben—SEE: *Doc Savage: four complete adventures in one volume: The spook of Grandpa Eben; Measures for a coffin; The three devils; Strange fish.*

18239 *The spotted men: a Doc Savage adventure.* Toronto, New York: Bantam Books, 1977, 121 p., paper, novel. Doc SAVAGE #87. [With William G. Bogart].

04194 *The Squeaking Goblin: a Doc Savage adventure.* Toronto, New York: Bantam Books, 1969, 138 p., paper, novel. Doc SAVAGE #35.

21608 *The stone man: a Doc Savage adventure.* Toronto, New York: Bantam Books, 1976, 119 p., paper, novel. Doc SAVAGE #81.

Strange fish—SEE: *Doc Savage: four complete adventures in one volume: The spook of Grandpa Eben; Measures for a coffin; The three devils; Strange fish.*

04195 *The submarine mystery: a Doc Savage adventure.* Toronto, New York: Bantam Books, 1971, 121 p., paper, novel. Doc SAVAGE #63.

The swooning lady—SEE: *Doc Savage: four complete adventures in one volume: The all-white elf; The running skeletons; The angry canary; and The swoon lady*

The talking devil—SEE: *Doc Savage: The talking devil; and, The ten ton snakes: two complete adventures in one volume.*

Target for death—SEE: *Doc Savage: five complete adventures in one volume: Bequest of evil; Death in little houses; Target for death; The death lady; The exploding lake.*

The ten ton snakes—SEE: *Doc Savage: The talking devil; and, The ten ton snakes: two complete adventures in one volume.*

The terrible stork—SEE: *Doc Savage: four complete adventures in one volume: The men vanished; Five fathoms dead; The terrible stork; Danger lies east.*

Terror and the lonely widow—SEE; *Doc Savage: four complete adventures in one volume: The devil's black rock; Waves of death; The too-wise owl; Terror and the lonely widow.*

04196 *The terror in the Navy: a Doc Savage adventure.* Toronto, New York: Bantam Books, 1969, 122 p., paper, novel. Doc SAVAGE #33.

Terror takes 7—SEE: *Doc Savage: four complete adventures in one volume: The invisible-box murders; Birds of death; The wee ones; Terror takes 7.*

Terror wears no shoes—SEE: *Doc Savage: five complete adventures in one volume: The derelict of Skull Shoal; Terror wears no shoes; The green master; Return from Cormoral; Up from Earth's center.*

They died twice—SEE: *Doc Savage: They died twice; and, The screaming man: two complete adventures in one volume.*

The thing that pursued—SEE: *Doc Savage: four complete adventures in one volume: The mindless monsters; The rustling death; King Joe Cay; The thing that pursued.*

04197 *The Thousand-headed Man: a Doc Savage adventure.* Toronto, New York: Bantam Books, 1964, 150 p., paper, novel. Doc SAVAGE #2.

The three devils—SEE: *Doc Savage: four complete adventures in one volume: The* spook of Grandpa Eben; Measures for a coffin; The three devils; Strange fish.

Three times a corpse—SEE: *Doc Savage: five complete adventures in one volume: Se-Pah-Poo; Colors for murder; Three times a corpse; Death is a round black spot; The devil is Jones.*

The three wild men—SEE: *Doc Savage: The three wild men; and, The fiery menace: two complete adventures in one volume.*

The time terror—SEE: *Doc Savage: The pharaoh's ghost; and, The time terror: two complete adventures in one volume.*

The too-wise owl—SEE: *Doc Savage: four complete adventures in one volume: The devil's black rock; Waves of death; The too-wise owl; Terror and the lonely widow.*

Trouble on parade—SEE: *Doc Savage: four complete adventures in one volume: The mental monster; The pink lady; Weird valley; Trouble on parade.*

Up from Earth's center—SEE: *Doc Savage: five complete adventures in one volume: The derelict of Skull Shoal; Terror wears no shoes; The green master; Return from Cormoral; Up from Earth's center.*

04198 *The vanisher; a Doc Savage adventure.* Toronto, New York: Bantam Books, 1970, 139 p., paper, novel. DOC SAVAGE #52.

Waves of death—SEE: *Doc Savage: four complete adventures in one volume: The devil's black rock; Waves of death; The too-wise owl; Terror and the lonely widow.*

The wee ones—SEE: *Doc Savage: four complete adventures in one volume: The invisible-box murders; Birds of death; The wee ones; Terror takes 7.*

Weird valley—SEE: *Doc Savage: four complete adventures in one volume: The mental monster; The pink lady; Weird valley; Trouble on parade.*

The whisker of Hercules—SEE: *Doc Savage: The whisker of Hercules; and, The man who was scared: two complete adventures in one volume.*

04199 *World's Fair goblin: a Doc Savage adventure.* Toronto, New York: Bantam Books, 1969, 122 p., paper, novel. DOC SAVAGE #39. [With William G. Bogart].

04200 *The yellow cloud: a Doc Savage adventure.* Toronto, New York: Bantam Books, 1971, 121 p., paper, novel. DOC SAVAGE #59.

DENTON, Bradley (Clayton), 1958-

21610 *Buddy Holly is alive and well on Ganymede.* New York: William Morrow & Co., 1991, 359 p., cloth, novel. [Winner of the John W. Campbell Jr. Memorial Award for Best Novel, 1991 (1992)].

21611 *Wrack & roll.* New York: Popular Library, Warner Books, 1986, 406 p., paper, novel.

DENZEL, Justin (Francis), 1917-

21612 *Boy of the painted cave.* New York: Philomel Books, 1988, 158 p., cloth, novel.

21613 *Hunt for the last cat.* New York: Philomel Books, 1991, 191 p., cloth, novel.

DERESKE, Jo

21614 *Glom gloom.* New York: A Jean Karl Book, Atheneum, 1985, 195 p., cloth, novel.

21615 *The lone sentinel.* New York: A Jean Karl Book, Atheneum, 1989, 169 p., cloth, novel.

DERLETH, August (William), 1909-1971

21616 *August Derleth: thirty years of writing, 1926-1956.* Sauk City, WI: Arkham House, 1956, 24 p., paper, nonf.

21617 *Dwellers in darkness.* Sauk City, WI: Arkham House, 1976, 203 p., cloth, coll.

21618 *Harrigan's file.* Sauk City, WI: Arkham House, 1975, 256 p., cloth, coll.

with James Turner as ANONYMOUS EDITORS

21619 *Tales of the Cthulhu Mythos* / by H. P. Lovecraft and divers hands. Sauk City, WI: Arkham House, 1989, xiv+529 p., cloth, anth. [Drops 4 stories from 1969 version (see #04228), and adds 7].

DERMAN, Martha

21620 *Tales from Academy Street.* New York, Toronto: Scholastic Inc., 1991, 103 p., cloth, novel.

DERRICK, Lionel, house pseud.

NOTE: Even-numbered books in this series were written by Chet Cunningham, odd numbers by Mark K. Roberts.

21621 *Black massacre.* Los Angeles: Pinnacle Books, 1980, 182 p., paper, novel. PENETRATOR #35. [By Mark K. Roberts].

21622 *Orphan army.* New York: Pinnacle Books, 1982, 196 p., paper, novel. PEN-ETRATOR #47. [By Mark K. Roberts].

21623 *Quaking terror.* New York: Pinnacle Books, 1982, 200 p., paper, novel. PEN-ETRATOR #45. [By Mark K. Roberts].

21624 *Satan's swarm.* New York: Pinnacle Books, 1983, 184 p., paper, novel. PEN-ETRATOR #49. [By Mark K. Roberts].

21625 *Satellite slaughter.* Los Angeles: Pinnacle Books, 1979, 174 p., paper, novel. PEN-ETRATOR #33. [By Mark K. Roberts].

21626 *The supergun mission.* New York: Pinnacle Books, 1977, 147 p., paper, novel. PENETRATOR #21. [By Mark K. Roberts].

DERRY, Charles, 1951-

21627 *Dark dreams: a psychological history of the modern horror film.* South Brunswick, NJ: A. S. Barnes & Co., 1977, 143 p., cloth, nonf.

DESJARLAIS, John (Joseph), 1953-

21628 *The throne of Tara.* Wheaton, IL: Crossway Books, 1990, 249 p., paper, novel.

DESMOND, Shaw, 1877-1960

37704 *World-birth.* London: Methuen, 1938, xv+404 p., cloth, novel.

DESPAIN, Dezra

37705 *Shadow over Nordmaar.* Lake Geneva, WI: TSR, 1988, 192 p., paper, novel. ADVANCED DUNGEONS & DRAGONS ADVENTURE GAMEBOOK #16.

DeSTEFANO, Anthony

21437 *The sorceress* / by Anthony de Stefano. New York: Manor Books, 1977, 172 p., paper, novel.

with John S. Littell as ANTHONY JOHN

21629 *The predator.* New York: Ballantine Books, 1983, 345 p., paper, novel.

*DETRE, L(ászló), 1874-1939 or 1906-1974

DETTMAN, Bruce, *with Michael Bedford*

17660 *The horror factory: the horror films of Universal, 1931 to 1955.* New York: Gordon Press, 1976, 193 p., cloth, nonf.

DEUKER, Carl

21630 *On the devil's court.* Boston: Joy Street Books, 1988, 252 p., cloth, novel.

DEUTSCHMAN, Deborah

21631 *Signals.* New York: Seaview Books, 1978, 357 p., cloth, novel.

DEVENPORT, Emily

21632 *Shade.* New York: A Roc Book, 1991, 246 p., paper, novel.

DEVER, Joe, 1956-

Black baron—SEE: *Combat heroes: Black baron.*

21633 *California countdown.* London: Beaver Books, 1989, 39+[264] p., paper, novel. FREEWAY WARRIOR #4.

21634 *The cauldron of fear.* London: Beaver Books, 1987, 41+[200] p., paper, novel. LONE WOLF #9.

21635 *Combat heroes: Black baron.* London: Beaver Books, 1986, 349 p., paper, novel. COMBAT HEROES.

21636 *Combat heroes: Emerald enchanter.* London: Beaver Books, 1986, 344 p., paper, novel. COMBAT HEROES.

21637 *Combat heroes: Scarlet sorcerer.* London: Beaver Books, 1986, 343 p., paper, novel. COMBAT HEROES: LONE WOLF #11.

21638 *Combat heroes: White warlord.* London: Beaver Books, 1986, 349 p., paper, novel. COMBAT HEROES.

21639 *The dungeons of Torgar.* London: Beaver Books, 1987, 41+[216] p., paper, novel. LONE WOLF #10.

Emerald enchanter—SEE: *Combat Heroes: Emerald enchanter.*

21640 *Highway holocaust.* London: Beaver Books, 1988, 35+[254] p., paper, novel. FREEWAY WARRIOR #1.

21641 *The masters of darkness.* London: Beaver Books, 1988, 42+[224] p., paper, novel. LONE WOLF #12.

Mountain run—SEE: *Slaughter Mountain run.*

21642 *The Omega Zone.* London: Beaver Books, 1989, 38+[283] p., paper, novel. FREEWAY WARRIOR #3.

21643 *The prisoners of time.* London: Beaver Books, 1987, 41+[299] p., paper, novel. LONE WOLF #11.

Scarlet sorcerer—SEE: *Combat heroes: Scarlet sorcerer.*

21644 *Slaughter Mountain run.* London: Beaver Books, 1988, 35+[246] p., paper, novel. FREEWAY WARRIOR #2.

21644A retitled: *Mountain run.* New York: Pacer Books for Young Adults, 1990, 35+[246] p., paper, novel. FREEWAY WARRIOR #2.

with Gary Chalk

19688 *Castle Death.* London: Beaver Books, 1986, 37+[194] p., paper, novel. LONE WOLF #7.

19689 *The Caverns of Kalte.* London: Sparrow Books, 1984, [192] p., paper, novel. LONE WOLF #3.

19690 *The chasm of doom.* London: Sparrow Books, 1985, [224] p., paper, novel. LONE WOLF #4.

19691 *Creatures from the depths.* London: Knight, 1989, 64 p., paper, novel. PRINCE OF SHADOWS #2.

19692 *Fire on the water.* London: Sparrow Books, 1984, [219] p., paper, novel. LONE WOLF #2.

19693 *Flight from the dark.* London: Sparrow Books, 1984, [160] p., paper, novel. LONE WOLF #1.

19694 *The Jungle of horrors.* London: Beaver Books, 1987, 39+[198] p., paper, novel. LONE WOLF #8.

19695 *The kingdoms of terror.* London: Beaver Books, 1985, 36+[196] p., paper, novel. LONE WOLF #6.

19696 *The Lone Wolf adventures.* London: Hutchinson, 1984, [224] p., cloth, coll. LONE WOLF #1-2.

19697 *The Magnamund companion.* London: Beaver Books, 1986, 96 p., paper, nonf.

19698 *Mean streets.* Sevenoaks, Kent, England: Knight, 1988, 63 p., paper, novel. PRINCE OF SHADOWS #1.

19699 *Shadow on the sand: including two Lone Wolf adventures.* London: Beaver Books, 1985, [224] p., paper, novel. Lone Wolf #5.

with John Grant

The claws of Helgedad—SEE: *Legends of Lone Wolf: The claws of Helgedad.*
The dark door opens—SEE: *Legends of Lone Wolf: The dark door opens.*
Eclipse of the Kai—SEE: *Legends of Lone Wolf: Eclipse of the Kai.*
Hunting Wolf—SEE: *Legends of Lone Wolf: Hunting Wolf.*

21646 *Legends of Lone Wolf: Eclipse of the Kai.* London: Beaver Books, 1989, 237 p., paper, novel. LEGENDS OF LONE WOLF #1.

21647 *Legends of Lone Wolf: Hunting Wolf.* London: Beaver Books, 1990, 226 p., paper, novel. LEGENDS OF LONE WOLF #4.

21648 *Legends of Lone Wolf: The claws of Helgedad.* London: Beaver Books, 1991, 268 p., paper, novel. LEGENDS OF LONE WOLF #5.

21649 *Legends of Lone Wolf: The dark door opens.* London: Beaver Books, 1989, 272 p., paper, novel. LEGENDS OF LONE WOLF #2.

21650 *Legends of Lone Wolf: The sacrifice of Ruanon.* London: Arrow Books, 1991, 366 p., paper, novel. LEGENDS OF LONE WOLF #6.

21651 *Legends of Lone Wolf: The sword of the sun.* London: Beaver Books, 1989, [400] p., paper, novel. LEGEND OF LONE WOLF #3.

21651A retitled: *The tides of treachery.* New York: Berkley Books, 1991, 182 p., paper, novel. LEGENDS OF LONE WOLF #3. [The first half of the British edition].

21651B retitled: *The sword of the sun.* New York: Berkley Books, 1991, 182 p., paper, novel. LEGENDS OF LONE WOLF #4. [The second half of the British edition].

The sacrifice of Ruanon—SEE: *Legends of Lone Wolf: The sacrifice of Ruanon.*
The sword of the sun—SEE: *Legends of Lone Wolf: The sword of the sun.*
The tides of treachery—SEE: *Legends of Lone Wolf: The sword of the sun.*

DEVERAUX, Jude [pseud. of Jude Gilliam White]

21652 *A knight in shining armor.* New York, London: Pocket Books, 1989, 341 p., cloth, novel.

21653 *The maiden.* New York, London: Pocket Books, 1988, 312 p., cloth, novel.

DEVIN, Flanna

21654 *Alien encounter.* New York: Leisure Books, 1981, 207 p., paper, novel.

DEVON, Gary, pseud.

21655 *Lost: a novel.* New York: Alfred A. Knopf, 1986, 355 p., cloth, novel.

DEVORE, Howard, 1925- , with Donald Franson

21656 *A history of the Hugo, Nebula, and International Fantasy awards.* Dearborn, MI:

Howard DeVore, 1975, 97 p., paper, nonf.

21657 *A history of the Hugo, Nebula, and International Fantasy awards.* Dearborn, MI: Howard DeVore, 1976, [114] p., paper, nonf. [Expanded edition].

21657 *A history of the Hugo, Nebula, and International Fantasy awards.* Dearborn, MI: Misfit Press, 1978, 112 p., paper, nonf. [Expanded edition].

21658 *A history of the Hugo, Nebula, and International Fantasy awards.* Dearborn, MI: Misfit Press, 1980, 129 p., paper, nonf. [Expanded edition].

21659 *A history of the Hugo, Nebula, and International Fantasy awards.* Dearborn, MI: Howard DeVore, 1981, 141 p., paper, nonf. [Expanded edition].

21660 *A history of the Hugo, Nebula, and International Fantasy awards, updated ed.* Dearborn, MI: Howard DeVore, 1985, 185 p., paper, nonf. [Expanded edition].

DEWDNEY, A(lexander) K(eewatin), 1941-

21661 *The planiverse: computer contact with a two-dimensional world.* Toronto: McClelland & Stewart, 1984, 267 p., cloth, novel.

DeWEESE, Gene [i.e., Thomas Eugene DeWeese], 1934-

21662 *The adventures of a two-minute werewolf.* Garden City, NY: Doubleday & Co., 1983, 132 p., cloth, novel.

Beepers from outer space—SEE: *Black suits from outer space.*

21663 *Black suits from outer space.* New York: G. P. Putnam's Sons, 1985, 144 p., cloth, novel. CALVIN WILLEFORD #1.

21663A retitled: *Beepers from outer space.* New York: G. P. Putnam's Sons; Columbus, OH: Weekly Reader Books, 1985, 144 p., paper, novel. CALVIN WILLEFORD #1.

21664 *The Calvin nullifier.* New York: G. P. Putnam's Sons, 1987, 142 p., cloth, novel. CALVIN WILLEFORD #3.

21665 *Chain of attack: a Star Trek novel.* New York: Pocket Books, 1987, 251 p., paper, novel. STAR TREK #32.

21666 *The dandelion caper.* New York: G. P. Putnam's Sons, 1986, 159 p., cloth, novel. CALVIN WILLEFORD #2.

21667 *A different darkness.* New York: Playboy Paperbacks, 1982, 301 p., paper, novel.

The final nexus—SEE: *Star Trek: The final nexus.*

21668 *Jeremy Case.* Toronto, New York: Laser Books, 1976, 190 p., paper, novel.

21669 *Major Corby and the unidentified flying object.* Garden City, NY: A Doubleday Signal Book, Doubleday & Co., 1979, 108 p., cloth, novel.

21670 *Nightmares from space.* New York: A Triumph Book, Franklin Watts, 1981, 88 p., cloth, novel.

21671 *The peacekeepers.* New York, London: Pocket Books, 1988, 310 p., paper, novel. STAR TREK: THE NEXT GENERATION #2.

Renegade—SEE: *Star Trek: Renegade.*

21672 *Something answered.* New York: A Dell Book, 1983, 315 p., paper, novel.

21673 *Star Trek: Renegade.* New York, London: Pocket Books, 1991, 276 p., paper, novel. STAR TREK #55.

21674 *Star Trek: The final nexus.* New York, London: Pocket Books, 1988, 282 p., paper, novel. STAR TREK #43. [A direct sequel to *Chain of attack*].

21675 *The wanting factor.* New York: Playboy Paperbacks, 1980, 303 p., paper, novel.

21676 *Whatever became of Aunt Margaret?* New York: G. P. Putnam's Sons, 1990, 172 p., cloth, novel.

as JEAN DeWEESE

21677 *The carnelian cat.* New York: Ballantine Books, 1975, 184 p., paper, novel. BIRTHSTONE GOTHIC #8.

21678 *The moonstone spirit.* New York: Ballantine Books, 1975, 183 p., paper, novel. BIRTHSTONE GOTHIC #6.

37706 *Nightmare in pewter.* Garden City, NY: Doubleday & Co., 1978, 181 p., cloth, novel.

21679 *The Reimann curse.* New York: Ballantine Books, 1975, 182 p., paper, novel.

with Robert Coulson

20662 *Charles Fort never mentioned wombats.* Garden City, NY: Doubleday & Co., 1977, xv+173 p., cloth, novel. JOE KARNS #2.

20663 *Gates of the universe.* Don Mills, Ontario: Laser Books, 1975, 190 p., paper, novel.

20664 *Nightmare universe.* Lake Geneva, WI: TSR Inc., 1985, 223 p., paper, novel.

20665 *Now you see it/him/them....* Garden City, NY: Doubleday & Co., 1975, 157 p., cloth, novel. JOE KARNS #1.

DeWEESE, Jean, pseud.—SEE: DeWeese, Gene

DeWEESE, Thomas E.—SEE: DeWeese, Gene

DEWEY, Joseph, 1957-

21680 *In a dark time: the apocalyptic temper in the American novel of the nuclear age.* West Lafayette, IN: Purdue University Press, 1990, 255 p., cloth, nonf.

DEWEY, Patrick R., 1949-

21681 *Adventure games for microcomputers: an annotated directory of interactive fiction.* Westport, CT: Meckler, 1991, xi+157 p., cloth, nonf.

21682 *Interactive fiction and adventure games for microcomputers: an annotated bibliography, 1988.* Westport, CT: Meckler, 1988, xvi+189 p., cloth, nonf.

DEXTER, Carmen

21683 *Beyond shattered illusions.* Omaha, NE: Vicki R. Kirklin, 1980, 79 p., paper, novel. STAR TREK SERIES.

DEXTER, Catherine [i.e., Catherine Dexter Martin]

21684 *Gertie's green thumb.* New York: Macmillan Publishing Co., London: Collier Macmillan Publishers, 1983, 118 p., cloth, novel.

21685 *Mazemaker.* New York: Morrow Junior Books, 1989, 202 p., cloth, novel.

21686 *The oracle doll.* New York: Four Winds Press; London: Collier Macmillan Publishing, 1985, 195 p., cloth, novel.

DEXTER, Susan (Elizabeth), 1955-

21687 *The Mountains of Channadran.* New York: A Del Rey Book, Ballantine Books, 1986, 367 p., paper, novel. WINTER KING'S WAR #3.

21688 *The ring of Allaire.* New York: A Del Rey Book, Ballantine Books, 1981, 232 p., paper, novel. WINTER KING'S WAR #1.

21689 *The sword of Calandra.* New York: A Del Rey Book, Ballantine Books, 1985, 341 p., paper, novel. WINTER KING'S WAR #2.

DEYO, David D(ean) Jr., 1962-

21690 *All the devils are here.* Atlanta, GA: Unnameable Press, 1986, ix+117 p., paper, anth. [Includes some verse].

DI TROPPENBURG, Ulderico—SEE: de Rico, Ul

DIAMAN, N(ickolas) A(nthony "Nikos"), 1936-

21691 *Ed Dean is queer: a novel.* San Francisco: Persona Press, 1978, 224 p., paper, novel.

21692 *The fourth wall.* San Francisco: Persona Press, 1980, 128 p., paper, novel.

DIAMOND, Graham (R.), 1945-

21693 *The beasts of Hades.* New York: Playboy Paperbacks, 1981, 255 p., paper, novel. THE HAVEN #5.

21694 *Captain Sinbad.* New York: Fawcett Gold Medal, 1980, 383 p., paper, novel.

21695 *Cinnabar.* New York: Fawcett Gold Medal, 1985, 291 p., paper, novel.

21696 *Dungeons of Kuba.* Chicago: Playboy Press Paperbacks, 1979, 254 p., paper, novel. THE HAVEN #3.

21697 *The Falcon of Eden.* New York: Playboy Press Paperbacks, 1980, 283 p., paper, novel. THE HAVEN #4.

21698 *The Haven.* Chicago: Playboy Press Paperbacks, 1977, 347 p., paper, novel. THE HAVEN #1.

21699 *Lady of the Haven: adventures of the Empire princess.* Chicago: Playboy Press Paperbacks, 1978, 382 p., paper, novel. THE HAVEN #2.

21700 *Marrakesh.* New York: Fawcett Gold Medal, 1981, 286 p., paper, novel. MARRAKESH #1.

21701 *Marrakesh nights.* New York: Fawcett Gold Medal, 1984, 310 p., paper, novel. MARRAKESH #2.

21702 *Samarkand.* New York: Playboy Press Paperbacks, 1980, 301 p., paper, novel. SAMARKAND #1.

21703 *Samarkand dawn.* New York: Playboy Paperbacks, 1981, 252 p., paper, novel. SAMARKAND #2.

21704 *The thief of Kalimar.* New York: Fawcett Gold Medal, 1979, 382 p., paper, novel.

DIAMOND, Jacqueline, pseud.—SEE: Hyman, Jackie

DIAMOND, Sander (A.), 1942- , with Jeff Rovin

21705 *Starik.* New York: E. P. Dutton, 1988, 309 p., cloth, novel. [*Starik* is spelled with a backward "r"].

DIAPER, John

21706 *The Arkham evil.* Kirkwood, NJ: Theatre of the Mind, 1983, 59 p., paper, story. CTHULHU MYTHOS.

with Bob Gallagher

21707 *Pursuit to Kadath.* Kirkwood, NJ: The-atre of the Mind, 1983, 71 p., paper, novel. CTHULHU MYTHOS.

DIBBLE, (James) Birney, 1925-

21708 *Brain child.* New York: Leisure Books, 1987, 368 p., paper, novel.
21709 *Pan.* New York: Leisure Books, 1980, 256 p., paper, novel.

DIBBLE, Nancy—SEE: Dibell, Ansen

DIBELL, Ansen [pseud. of Nancy Ann Dibble], 1942-

21710 *Circle, crescent, star.* New York: DAW Books, 1981, 252 p., paper, novel. KANTMORIE #2.
21711 *Pursuit of the Screamer.* New York: DAW Books, 1978, 270 p., paper, novel. KANTMORIE #1.
21712 *Summerfair.* New York: DAW Books, 1982, 272 p., paper, novel. KANTMORIE #3.

DiCARLANTONIO, Martin

21713 *Motherland.* Harris, IA: Ansuda Publica-tions, 1987, 112 p., paper, novel.

DiCHIARA, Robert

21714 *The dick and the devil.* New York: Tor, A Tom Doherty Associates Book, 1989, 374 p., cloth, novel.

DICK, Bernard F(rancis), 1935-

21715 *William Golding.* New York: Twayne Publishers, 1967, 119 p., cloth, nonf.
21716 *William Golding, revised edition.* Boston: Twayne Publishers, 1987, 168 p., cloth, nonf.

DICK, Kay, 1915-

37707 *They: a sequence of unease.* London: Allen Lane, 1977, 94 p., cloth, story.

DICK, Philip K(indred), 1928-1982

21717 *The best of Philip K. Dick.* New York: A Del Rey Book, Ballantine Books, 1977, xiv+450 p., paper, coll. [Edited by John Brunner].
21718 *Beyond lies the wub: the collected stories of Philip K. Dick, volume one.* Los Ange-les, Columbia, PA: Underwood-Miller, 1987, xxii+404 p., cloth, coll.
21718A retitled: *The short happy life of the brown Oxford.* Secaucus, NJ: A Citadel Twi-light Book, Carol Publishing Group, 1990, xxii+404 p., paper, coll.
Bladerunner—SEE: *Do androids dream of electric sheep?*
04286 *The book of Philip K. Dick.* New York: DAW Books, 1973, 187 p., paper, coll.
04286A retitled: *The turning wheel, and other sto-ries.* London: Coronet Books, Hodder & Stoughton, 1977, 189 p., paper, coll.
21719 *The dark-haired girl.* Willimantic, CT: Mark V. Ziesing, 1988, xx+246 p., cloth, nonf. coll. [Includes some verse].
21720 *The days of Perky Pat: the collected stories of Philip K. Dick, volume four.* Los An-geles-Columbia, PA: Underwood-Miller, 1987, x+380 p., cloth, coll.
21720A retitled: *The minority report.* New York: A Citadel Twilight Book, Carol Publish-ing Group, 1991, x+380 p., paper, coll.
21721 *The divine invasion.* New York: Time-scape Books, 1981, 239 p., cloth, novel.
04291 *Do androids dream of electric sheep?* Gar-den City, NY: Doubleday & Co., 1968, 210 p., cloth, novel.
04291A retitled: *Bladerunner: (Do androids dream of electric sheep).* New York: A Del Rey Book, Ballantine Books, 1982, 216 p., paper, novel.
21722 *The father-thing: the collected stories of Philip K. Dick, volume three.* Los An-geles, Columbia, PA: Underwood-Miller, 1987, xi+376 p., cloth, coll.
21723 retitled: *Second variety: the collected sto-ries of Philip K. Dick, volume three.* New York: A Citadel Twilight Book, Carol Publishing Group, 1991, 414 p., paper, coll. [Different contents from the original].
21724 *The golden man.* New York: A Berkley Book, Berkley Publishing Corp., 1980, xxviii+336 p., paper, coll. [Edited by Mark Hurst].
21725 *I hope I shall arrive soon.* Garden City, NY: Doubleday & Co., 1985, 179 p., cloth, coll. [Edited by Mark Hurst & Paul Williams].
21726 *In pursuit of VALIS: selections from the Ex-egesis.* Los Angeles, CA & Lancaster, PA: Underwood-Miller, 1991, xxxvi+278 p., cloth, nonf. coll. [Edited by Larry Sutin].
Lies, Inc.—SEE: *The unteleported man.*
21727 *The little black box: the collected stories of Philip K. Dick, volume five.* Los Ange-les, Columbia, PA: Underwood-Miller, 1987, xi+395 p., cloth, coll.

21727A retitled: *We can remember it for you wholesale.* London: Grafton, 1991, 400 p., paper, coll.
The minority report—SEE: *The days of Perky Pat: the collected stories of Philip K. Dick, volume four.*

21728 *Nick and the glimmung.* London: Victor Gollancz, 1988, 141 p., cloth, novel.

21729 *Radio Free Albemuth.* New York: Arbor House, 1985, 214 p., cloth, novel. [An early version of VALIS].

21730 *Robots, androids, and mechanical oddities: the science fiction of Philip K. Dick.* Carbondale & Edwardsville, IL: Southern Illinois University Press, 1984, ix+261 p., cloth, coll. [Edited by Patricia S. Warrick & Martin H. Greenberg].

21731 *A scanner darkly.* Garden City, NY: Doubleday & Co., 1977, 220 p., cloth, novel.
Second variety—SEE: *The father-thing: the collected stories of Philip K. Dick, volume three.*

21732 *Second variety: the collected stories of Philip K. Dick, volume two.* Los Angeles, Columbia, PA: Underwood-Miller, 1987, xii+395 p., cloth, coll.

21732A retitled: *We can remember it for you wholesale.* New York: A Citadel Twilight Book, Carol Publishing Group, 1990, xii+395 p., paper, coll.

21733 *Selected letters of Philip K. Dick: 1974.* Novato, CA, Lancaster, PA: Underwood-Miller, 1991, 314 p., cloth, nonf. coll. [Edited by Paul Williams].
The short happy life of the brown Oxford—SEE: *Beyond lies the wub: the collected stories of Philip K. Dick, volume one.*

21734 *The transmigration of Timothy Archer.* New York: Timescape Books, 1982, 255 p., cloth, novel.
The turning wheel, and other stories—SEE: *The book of Philip K. Dick.*

21735 *Ubik: the screenplay.* Minneapolis, MN: Corroboree Press, 1985, xiv+154 p., cloth, fiction.

21736 *The unteleported man.* New York: Berkley Books, 1983, 202 p., paper, novel. [Expanded edition of #04313; edited by John Sladek].

21736A retitled: *Lies, Inc.* London: Victor Gollancz, 1984, 199 p., cloth, novel.

21737 *VALIS.* Toronto, New York: Bantam Books, 1981, 227 p., paper, novel.

21738 *The VALIS trilogy.* New York: Quality Paperback Book Club, 1989, 241+238+255+[14] p., paper, coll. [Includes VALIS, The divine invasion, The transmigration of Timothy Archer].

21739 *We can remember it for you wholesale.* Berkeley, CA: Dark Carnival, 1990, 18 p., paper, story.
We can remember it for you wholesale—SEE: *The little black box: the collected stories of Philip K. Dick, volume five.*
We can remember it for you wholesale—SEE: *Second variety: the collected stories of Philip K. Dick, volume two.*

with Gregg Rickman

21740 *Philip K. Dick: in his own words.* Long Beach, CA: Fragments West/The Valentine Press, 1984, xxii+256 p., paper, nonf.

21741 *Philip K. Dick: in his own words, 2nd ed.* Long Beach, CA: Fragments West/Valentine Press, 1988, xxii+250 p., paper, nonf.

21742 *Philip K. Dick: the last testament.* Long Beach, CA: Fragments West/The Valentine Press, 1985, xxii+241 p., paper, nonf.

with Paul Williams

21743 *Only apparently real.* New York: Arbor House, 1986, viii+184 p., paper, nonf.

with Roger Zelazny

21744 *Deus irae.* Garden City, NY: Doubleday & Co., 1976, 182 p., cloth, novel.

*DICK-LAUDER, George (Andrew), Sir, Bart., 1917-1981

DICKENS, Charles (John Huffham), 1812-1870

21744 *A Christmas carol, and other Christmas stories.* New York: A Signet Book, New American Library, 1984, 223 p., paper, coll.

21745 *The complete ghost stories of Charles Dickens.* London: Michael Joseph, 1982, 341 p., cloth, coll. [Edited by Peter Haining].

21745A retitled: *The ghost stories of Charles Dickens.* Sevenoaks, Kent, England: Coronet Books, 1984-1985, 2 v., paper, coll.
The ghost stories of Charles Dickens—SEE: *The complete ghost stories of Charles Dickens.*

21746 *The haunted man; and, The haunted house.* Gloucester, England: Alan Sutton, 1985, vi+123 p., paper, coll.

21747 *The signalman, & other ghost stories*. Gloucester, England: Alan Sutton, 1984, x + 138 p., paper, coll.

21748 *The supernatural short stories of Charles Dickens*. London: John Calder; Dallas, TX: Riverrun Press, 1978, 159 p., cloth, coll. [Edited by Michael Hayes].

DICKENS, Monica [i.e., Monica Enid Dickens Stratton], 1915-

21749 *Ballad of favour*. London: Collins, 1985, 127 p., cloth, novel. THE MESSENGER SERIES #2.

21750 *Cry of a seagull*. London: Collins, 1986, 128 p., cloth, novel.

21751 *The haunting of Bellamy 4*. London: Collins, 1986, 123 p., cloth, novel. THE MESSENGER SERIES #3.

21752 *The messenger*. London: Collins, 1985, 155 p., cloth, novel. THE MESSENGER SERIES #1.

DICKENSHEET, D(ean) W., *with J. R. Christopher & R. E. Briney*

18684 *A Boucher bibliography*. [White Bear Lake, MN: Allen J. Hubin], 1969, [34] p., paper, nonf. [Bound with *A Boucher portrait: Anthony Boucher as seen by his friends and colleagues* / edited by Lenore Glen Offord].

DICKENSON, Sylvia

21753 *The Andromeda vein*. New York, Washington: Vantage Press, 1984, 182 p., cloth, novel.

DICKERSON, Marilyn K.

21754 *Lord Hap*. New York: Avon, 1980, 173 p., paper, novel.

DICKERSON, Matthew T., 1963-

21755 *The Finnsburg encounter*. Wheaton, IL: Crossway Books, 1991, 352 p., paper, novel.

DICKINSON, P(auline)

21756 *Index to the comics in the science fiction and fantasy collection, University of Sydney Library*. Sydney, Australia: The Library, University of Sydney, 1984, i+54 p., paper, nonf.

DICKINSON, Peter (Malcolm de Brissac), 1927-

21757 *Annerton Pit*. London: Victor Gollancz, 1977, 175 p., cloth, novel.

21758 *The Blue Hawk*. London: Victor Gollancz, 1976, 224 p., cloth, novel.

21759 *A box of nothing*. London: Victor Gollancz, 1985, 128 p., cloth, novel.

Changes trilogy—SEE: *The changes: a trilogy*.

21760 *The changes: a trilogy, comprising The devil's children, Heartsease, The weathermonger*. London: Victor Gollancz, 1975, 510 p., cloth, coll. THE CHANGES #1-3.

21760A retitled: *The changes trilogy*. Harmondsworth, Middlesex, England: Puffin Books, 1985, 348 p., paper, coll. THE CHANGES #1-3.

21761 *Eva*. London: Victor Gollancz, 1988, 207 p., cloth, novel.

21762 *The flight of dragons*. London: Pierrot Publishing, 1979, 137 p., cloth, nonf.

21763 *Healer*. London: Victor Gollancz, 1983, 184 p., cloth, novel.

21764 *King and joker*. London: Hodder & Stoughton, 1976, 222 p., cloth, novel. KING VICTOR #1.

21765 *Merlin dreams*. London: Victor Gollancz, 1988, 166 p., cloth, coll.

21766 *Skeleton-in-waiting*. London: The Bodley Head, 1989, 154 p, cloth, novel. KING VICTOR #2.

21767 *Tulku*. London: Victor Gollancz, 1979, 286 p., cloth, novel.

DICKS, Terrance

21768 *The adventures of Doctor Who: Doctor Who and the genesis of the Daleks; Doctor Who and the revenge of the cybermen; Doctor Who and the Loch Ness monster*. Garden City, NY: Nelson Doubleday, 1979, xii+307 p., cloth, coll. DOCTOR WHO SERIES.

21769 *The adventures of K9, and other mechanical creatures*. London: A Target Book, W. H. Allen, 1979, 94 p., paper, fiction. DOCTOR WHO SERIES.

The ambassadors of death—SEE: *Doctor Who: The ambassadors of death*.

Arc of infinity—SEE: *Doctor Who: Arc of infinity*.

The auton invasion—SEE: *Doctor Who and the auton invasion*.

The brain of Morbius—SEE: *Doctor Who and the brain of Morbius*.

The caves of Androzani—SEE: *Doctor Who: The caves of Androzani*.

21770 *Cry vampire!* Glasgow: Blackie & Son, 1981, 111 p., cloth, coll. SIMON & SALLY #1.

The dalek invasion of Earth—SEE: *Doctor Who and the Dalek invasion of Earth.*

The dalek invasion of Earth; and, The crusaders—SEE: *Doctor Who: The dalek invasion of Earth; and, The crusaders.*

The day of the Daleks—SEE: *Doctor Who and the day of the Daleks.*

Death to the Daleks—SEE: *Doctor Who: Death to the Daleks.*

21771 *Demon of the dark.* Glasgow: Blackie & Son, 1983, 120 p., cloth, novel.

Doctor Who: An unearthly child—SEE: *Doctor Who and an unearthly child.*

21772 *Doctor Who and an unearthly child.* London: W. H. Allen & Co., 1981, 128 p., cloth, tele. DOCTOR WHO #68.

21772A retitled: *Doctor Who: An unearthly child.* London: A Target Book, W. H. Allen & Co., 1990, 128 p., cloth, tele. DOCTOR WHO #68.

21773 *Doctor Who and the android invasion.* London: A Target Book, W. H. Allen, 1978, 126 p., paper, tele. DOCTOR WHO.

21774 *Doctor Who and the androids of Tara.* London: A Target Book, W. H. Allen, 1980, 128 p., cloth, tele. DOCTOR WHO.

21775 *Doctor Who and the armageddon factor.* London: Target, W. H. Allen, 1980, 127 p., paper, tele. DOCTOR WHO.

04343 *Doctor Who and the Auton invasion.* London: A Target Book, 1974, 156 p., paper, tele. DOCTOR WHO.

04343A retitled: *Doctor Who: The Auton invasion.* London: A Target Book, 1991, 156 p., paper, tele. DOCTOR WHO.

21776 *Doctor Who and the brain of Morbius.* London: A Longbow Book, Allan Wingate, 1977, 139 p., cloth, tele. DOCTOR WHO.

21776A retitled: *Doctor Who: The brain of Morbius.* London: A Target Book, 1991, 139 p., cloth, tele. DOCTOR WHO.

21777 *Doctor Who and the carnival of monsters.* London: A Longbow Book, Allan Wingate, 1977, 125 p., cloth, tele. DOCTOR WHO.

21778 *Doctor Who and the claws of Axos.* London: A Longbow Book, Allan Wingate, 1977, 141 p., cloth, tele. DOCTOR WHO.

21779 *Doctor Who and the Dalek invasion of Earth.* London: A Longbow Book, Allan Wingate, 1977, 142 p., cloth, tele. DOCTOR WHO #17.

21779A retitled: *Doctor Who: The Dalek invasion of Earth.* London: A Target Book, W. H. Allen & Co., 1990, 142 p., paper, tele. DOCTOR WHO #17.

04344 *Doctor Who and the day of the Daleks.* London: A Target Book, 1974, 140 p., paper, tele. DOCTOR WHO #18.

04344A retitled: *Doctor Who: The day of the Daleks.* London: A Target Book, 1991, 126 p., paper, tele. DOCTOR WHO #18.

21780 *Doctor Who and the deadly assassin.* London: A Longbow Book, Allan Wingate, 1977, 122 p., cloth, tele. DOCTOR WHO.

21781 *Doctor Who and the destiny of the Daleks.* London: A Target Book, W. H. Allen, 1979, 110 p., paper, tele. DOCTOR WHO.

21782 *Doctor Who and the face of evil.* London: Target, W. H. Allen, 1978, 126 p., paper, tele. DOCTOR WHO.

21783 *Doctor Who and the genesis of the Daleks.* London: A Longbow Book, Allan Wingate, 1976, 140 p., cloth, tele. DOCTOR WHO #27.

21783A retitled: *Doctor Who: The genesis of the Daleks.* London: A Target Book, 1991, 140 p., paper, tele. DOCTOR WHO #27.

21784 *Doctor Who and the giant robot.* London: Target, 1975, 124 p., paper, tele. DOCTOR WHO #14.

21785 *Doctor Who and the hand of fear.* London: A Target Book, W. H. Allen, 1979, 127 p., paper, tele. DOCTOR WHO.

21786 *Doctor Who and the horns of Nimon.* London: A Target Book, W. H. Allen, 1980, 111 p., paper, tele. DOCTOR WHO.

21787 *Doctor Who and the horror of Fang Rock.* London: Target, W. H. Allen, 1978, 126 p., paper, tele. DOCTOR WHO.

21788 *Doctor Who and the image of the Fendahl.* London: A Target Book, W. H. Allen, 1979, 109 p., paper, tele. DOCTOR WHO.

21789 *Doctor Who and the invasion of time.* London: A Target Book, W. H. Allen, 1980, 142 p., paper, tele. DOCTOR WHO.

21790 *Doctor Who and the invisible enemy.* London: A Target Book, W. H. Allen, 1979, 110 p., paper, tele. DOCTOR WHO.

21791 *Doctor Who and the Keeper of Traken.* London: A Target Book, W. H. Allen, 1982, 124 p., paper, tele. DOCTOR WHO.

21792 *Doctor Who and the Loch Ness monster.* London: A Longbow Book, Allan Wingate, 1976, 127 p., cloth, tele. DOCTOR WHO.

21793 *Doctor Who and the monster of Peladon.* London: W. H. Allen & Co., 1980, 124 p., cloth, tele. DOCTOR WHO #43.

21794 *Doctor Who and the mutants.* London: A Longbow Book, Allan Wingate, 1977, 127 p., cloth, tele. DOCTOR WHO.

21795 *Doctor Who and the nightmare of Eden.* London: A Target Book, W. H. Allen, 1980, 111 p., paper, tele. DOCTOR WHO #45.

21796 *Doctor Who and the planet of evil.* London: A Longbow Book, Allan Wingate, 1977, 126 p., cloth, tele. DOCTOR WHO.

21797 *Doctor Who and the planet of the Daleks.* London: A Longbow Book, Allan Wingate, 1976, 125 p., cloth, tele. DOCTOR WHO.

21798 *Doctor Who and the planet of the spiders.* London: Target, 1975, 121 p., paper, tele. DOCTOR WHO #15/48.

21798A retitled: *Doctor Who: The planet of the spiders.* London: A Target Book, 1991, 121 p., paper, tele. DOCTOR WHO #48.

21799 *Doctor Who and the power of Kroll.* London: A Target Book, W. H. Allen & Co., 1980, 128 p., paper, tele. DOCTOR WHO.

21800 *Doctor Who and the Pyramids of Mars.* London: A Longbow Book, Allan Wingate, 1976, 125 p., cloth, tele. DOCTOR WHO.

21801 *Doctor Who and the revenge of the Cybermen.* London: A Longbow Book, Allan Wingate, 1976, 128 p., cloth, tele. DOCTOR WHO #51.

21801A retitled: *Doctor Who: The revenge of the Cybermen.* London: A Target Book, 1991, 128 p., cloth, tele. DOCTOR WHO #51.

21802 *Doctor Who and the robots of death.* London: A Target Book, W. H. Allen, 1979, 108 p., paper, tele. DOCTOR WHO.

21803 *Doctor Who and the state of decay.* London: A Target Book, W. H. Allen, 1982, 125 p., paper, tele. DOCTOR WHO.

21804 *Doctor Who and the stones of blood.* London: A Target Book, W. H. Allen & Co., 1980, 124 p., paper, tele. DOCTOR WHO.

21805 *Doctor Who and the sunmakers.* London: W. H. Allen, 1982, 127 p., cloth, tele. DOCTOR WHO.

21806 *Doctor Who and the talons of Weng-Chiang.* London: A Longbow Book, Allan Wingate, 1977, 140 p., cloth, tele. DOCTOR WHO.

21807 *Doctor Who and the terror of the Autons.* London: A Target Book, W. H. Allen & Co., 1975, 127 p., paper, tele. DOCTOR WHO #13.

21808 *Doctor Who and the time warrior.* London: Target, W. H. Allen, 1978, 144 p., paper, tele. DOCTOR WHO.

21809 *Doctor Who and the underworld.* London: A Target Book, W. H. Allen, 1980, 123 p., paper, tele. DOCTOR WHO.

21810 *Doctor Who and the web of fear.* London: A Longbow Book, Allan Wingate, 1976, 127 p., cloth, tele. DOCTOR WHO.

21811 *Doctor Who: Arc of infinity.* London: W. H. Allen, 1983, 117 p., cloth, tele. DOCTOR WHO.

21812 *Doctor Who: Death to the Daleks.* London: Target, W. H. Allen, 1978, 125 p., paper, tele. DOCTOR WHO #20.

21813 *The Doctor Who dinosaur book.* London: A Target Book, W. H. Allen, 1976, 64 p., paper, nonf.

21814 *Doctor Who: Four to doomsday.* London: W. H. Allen, 1983, 128 p., cloth, tele. DOCTOR WHO #77.

21815 *Doctor Who: Inferno.* London: W. H. Allen & Co., 1984, 126 p., cloth, tele. DOCTOR WHO #89.

21816 *Doctor Who: Kinda.* London: W. H. Allen & Co., 1983, 126 p., cloth, tele. DOCTOR WHO #84.

21817 *Doctor Who: Meglos.* London: W. H. Allen, 1983, 126 p., cloth, tele. DOCTOR WHO.

21818 *The Doctor Who monster book.* London: A Target Book, W. H. Allen, 1975, 64 p., paper, nonf.

21819 *The Doctor Who omnibus.* London: W. H. Allen & Co., 1983, 362 p., cloth, tele. coll. DOCTOR WHO SERIES. [Includes *Doctor Who and the Dalek invasion of Earth*; *Doctor Who and the day of the Daleks*; *Doctor Who and the planet of the Daleks*].

21820 *Doctor Who: Planet of giants.* London: A Target Book, W. H. Allen & Co., 1990, 112 p., paper, tele. DOCTOR WHO #145.

21821 *Doctor Who: Snakedance.* London: W. H. Allen & Co., 1984, 124 p., cloth, tele. DOCTOR WHO #83.

21822 *Doctor Who: The ambassadors of death.* London: W. H. Allen & Co., 1987, 144 p., cloth, tele. DOCTOR WHO #121.

Doctor Who: The auton invasion—SEE: *Doctor Who and the auton invasion.*

Doctor Who: The brain of Morbius—SEE: *Doctor Who and the brain of Morbius.*

21823 *Doctor Who: The caves of Androzani.* London: W. H. Allen, 1984, 135 p., cloth, novel. DOCTOR WHO.

21824 *Doctor Who: The dalek invasion of Earth; and, The crusaders.* London: W. H. Allen & Co., 1988, 296 p., paper, tele. coll. DOCTOR WHO CLASSICS #1.

Doctor Who: The Dalek invasion of Earth—SEE: *Doctor Who and the Dalek invasion of Earth.*

Doctor Who: The day of the Daleks—SEE: *Doctor Who and the day of the Daleks.*

21825 *Doctor Who: The face of evil; and, The sunmakers.* London: A Star Book, W. H. Allen & Co., 1989, 251 p., paper, tele. coll. DOCTOR WHO CLASSICS #7.

21826 *Doctor Who: The faceless ones.* London: W. H. Allen & Co., 1986, 140 p., cloth, tele. DOCTOR WHO #116.

21827 *Doctor Who: The five doctors.* London: W. H. Allen, 1983, 126 p., cloth, tele. DOCTOR WHO #81.

Doctor Who: The genesis of the Daleks—SEE: Doctor Who and the genesis of the Daleks.

21828 *Doctor Who: The Krotons.* London: W. H. Allen & Co., 1985, 121 p., cloth, tele. DOCTOR WHO #99.

21829 *Doctor Who: The mind of evil.* London: W. H. Allen & Co., 1985, 144 p., cloth, tele. DOCTOR WHO #96.

21830 *Doctor Who: The mind of evil; and, The claws of Axos.* London: A Star Book, W. H. Allen & Co., 1989, 144+141 p., paper, tele. coll. DOCTOR WHO CLASSICS #4.

21831 *Doctor Who: The mysterious planet.* London: W. H. Allen & Co., 1987, 127 p., cloth, tele. DOCTOR WHO #127.

Doctor Who: The planet of the spiders—SEE: Doctor Who and the planet of the spiders.

Doctor Who: The revenge of the Cybermen—SEE: Doctor Who and the revenge of the Cybermen.

21832 *Doctor Who: The seeds of death.* London: W. H. Allen & Co., 1986, 149 p., cloth, tele. DOCTOR WHO #112.

21833 *Doctor Who: The smugglers.* London: W. H. Allen & Co., 1988, 128 p., cloth, tele. DOCTOR WHO #133.

21834 *Doctor Who: The space pirates.* London: A Target Book, W. H. Allen & Co., 1990, 132 p., paper, tele. DOCTOR WHO #147.

21835 *Doctor Who: The three doctors.* London: A Longbow Book, Allan Wingate, 1975, 127 p., cloth, tele. DOCTOR WHO #64.

21836 *Doctor Who: The time monster.* London: W. H. Allen & Co., 1985, 151 p., cloth, tele. DOCTOR WHO #102.

21837 *Doctor Who: The wheel in space.* London: W. H. Allen & Co., 1988, 143 p., cloth, tele. DOCTOR WHO #130.

21838 *Doctor Who: Warriors of the deep.* London: W. H. Allen & Co., 1984, 126 p., cloth, tele. DOCTOR WHO #87.

Exodus—SEE: The new Doctor Who adventures: Timewyrm: Exodus.

The face of evil; and, The sunmakers—SEE: Doctor Who: The face of evil; and, The sunmakers.

The faceless ones—SEE: Doctor Who: The faceless ones.

The five doctors—SEE: Doctor Who: The five doctors.

Four to doomsday—SEE: Doctor Who: Four to doomsday.

21839 *The further adventures of Doctor Who: Doctor Who and the deadly assassin; Doctor Who and the face of evil; Doctor Who and the robots of death.* Garden City, NY: Nelson Doubleday, 1986, 245 p., cloth, coll. DOCTOR WHO SERIES.

The genesis of the Daleks—SEE: Doctor Who and the genesis of the Daleks.

21840 *The ghosts of Gallows Cross.* Glasgow, Scotland: Blackie & Son, 1984, 119 p., cloth, novel.

Inferno—SEE: Doctor Who: Inferno.

Kinda—SEE: Doctor Who: Kinda.

The Krotons—SEE: Doctor Who: The Krotons.

21841 *Marvin's monster.* Glasgow: Blackie & Son, 1982, 114 p., cloth, novel.

Meglos—SEE: Doctor Who: Meglos.

The mind of evil—SEE: Doctor Who: The mind of evil.

The mind of evil; and, The claws of Axos—SEE: Doctor Who: The mind of evil; and, The claws of Axos.

21842 *The mind of evil; The claws of Axos.* London: W. H. Allen & Co., 1989, 140, p., paper, tele. coll. DOCTOR WHO CLASSICS.

21843 *My brother the vampire.* London: Piccadilly, 1990, 91 p., cloth, novel.

The mysterious planet—SEE: Doctor Who: The mysterious planet.

21844 *The new Doctor Who adventures: Timewyrm: Exodus.* London: A Target Book, 1991, 234 p., paper, tele. DOCTOR WHO: THE NEW ADVENTURES #2.

Planet of giants—SEE: Doctor Who: Planet of giants.

The planet of the spiders—SEE: Doctor Who and the planet of the spiders.

The revenge of the Cybermen—SEE: Doctor Who and the revenge of the Cybermen.

Roboworld—SEE: Star quest: Roboworld.

21845 *The second Doctor Who monster book.* London: A Target Book, 1977, 59 p., paper, nonf.

The seeds of death—SEE: Doctor Who: The seeds of death.

The smugglers—SEE: Doctor Who: The smugglers.

Snakedance—SEE: Doctor Who: Snakedance.

The space pirates—SEE: Doctor Who: The space pirates.

21846 *Spacejack!* London: A Longbow Book, W. H. Allen, 1978, 111 p., cloth, novel. STAR QUEST #1.

21847 *Star quest: Roboworld.* London: W. H. Allen, 1979, 119 p., cloth, novel. STAR QUEST #2.

21848 *Star quest: Terrorsaur!* London: W. H. Allen, 1981, 125 p., cloth, novel. STAR QUEST #3.

Terrorsaur!—SEE: *Space quest: Terrorsaur!*

21849 *Terry Nation's Dalek special.* London: A Target Book, W. H. Allen & Co., 1979, [86] p., paper, tele.

The three doctors—SEE: *Doctor Who: The three doctors.*

The time monster—SEE: *Doctor Who: The time monster.*

Timewyrm: Exodus—SEE: *The new Doctor Who adventures: Timewyrm: Exodus.*

An unearthly child—SEE: *Doctor Who and an unearthly child.*

21850 *War of the witches.* Glasgow: Blackie, 1983, 112 p., cloth, novel. SIMON & SALLY #2.

Warriors of the deep—SEE: *Doctor Who: Warriors of the deep.*

21851 *Wereboy!* Glasgow: Blackie & Son, 1982, 119 p., cloth, novel.

The wheel in space—SEE: *Doctor Who: The wheel in space.*

with Philip Hinchcliffe

21852 *The deadly assassin; The seeds of doom.* London: W. H. Allen, 1989, 128+121 p., paper, coll. DOCTOR WHO CLASSICS.

with Malcolm Hulke

21853 *The making of Doctor Who.* London: Target, 1976, 128 p., paper, nonf. [Revised edition].

with Barry Letts

The daemons; The time monster—SEE: *Doctor Who: The Daemons; The time monster.*

21854 *Doctor Who: The Daemons; The time monster.* London: W. H. Allen & Co., 1989, 151 p., paper, tele. coll. DOCTOR WHO CLASSICS #5.

DICKSON, Gordon R(upert), 1923-

21855 *Alien art; Arcturus landing.* New York: Ace Books, 1981, 339 p., paper, coll.

04347 *Alien from Arcturus.* New York: Ace Books, 1956, 150 p., paper, novel. [Bound with *The atom curtain* / by Nick B. Williams]

21856 retitled: *Arcturus landing.* New York: Ace Books, 1978, 213 p., paper, novel. [Expanded edition].

Arcturus landing—SEE: *Alien from Arcturus.*

21857 *Beginnings.* New York: Baen Books, 1988, 282 p., paper, coll.

21858 *Beyond the Dar al-Harb.* New York: Tor SF, A Tom Doherty Associates Book, 1985, 253 p., paper, coll.

21859 *The chantry guild.* New York: Ace Books, 1988, 428 p., cloth, novel. CHILDE CYCLE. [Direct sequel to *The final encyclopedia*].

21860 *Combat SF.* Garden City, NY: Doubleday & Co., 1975, ix+204 p., cloth, anth.

21861 *Dickson!* Boston: An L.A.con II Publication, NESFA Press, 1984, xii+193 p., cloth, coll. [Includes some nonfiction].

21862 retitled: *Steel brother.* New York: Tor SF, A Tom Doherty Associates Book, 1985, xvii+236 p., paper, coll. [Includes some nonfiction, and adds one story].

21863 *The Dorsai companion.* New York: Ace Science Fiction Books, 1986, xiv+231 p., paper, coll.

Dorsai!—SEE: *The genetic general.*

21864 *The dragon and the George.* Garden City, NY: Nelson Doubleday, 1976, 244 p., cloth, novel. DRAGON #1.

21865 *The dragon knight.* New York: Tor Fantasy, A Tom Doherty Associates Book, 1990, 409 p., cloth, novel. DRAGON #2.

21866 *The earth lords.* New York: Ace Books, 1989, 311 p., paper, novel.

21867 *Ends.* New York: Baen Books, 1988, 342 p., paper, coll.

21868 *The far call.* New York: Quantum Science Fiction, Dial Press/James Wade, 1978, 414 p., cloth, novel.

21869 *The final encyclopedia.* New York: A Tor Book, Tom Doherty Associates, 1984, 696 p., cloth, novel. CHILDE CYCLE.

21870 *The forever man.* New York: Ace Science Fiction Books, 1986, 375 p., cloth, novel.

21871 *Forward!* New York: Baen Science Fiction Books, 1985, 242 p., paper, coll. [Edited by Sandra Miesel].

04352 *The genetic general.* New York: Ace Books, 1960, 159 p., paper, novel. [Bound with *Time to teleport* / by Gordon R. Dickson].

21872 retitled: *Dorsai!* New York: DAW Books, 1976, 236 p., paper, novel. [Expanded edition].

21873 *Gordon R. Dickson's SF best.* New York: A Dell Book, 1978, 236 p., paper, coll. [Edited by James R. Frenkel].

21874 retitled: *In the bone: the best science fiction of Gordon R. Dickson.* New York:

Ace Science Fiction Books, 1987, 228 p., paper, coll. [Expanded edition].

21875   *Guided tour.* New York: Tor SF, A Tom Doherty Associates Book, 1988, 244 p., paper, coll.

21876   *The harriers.* Riverdale, NY: Baen Books, 1991, 258 p., paper, anth. WAR AND HONOR #1.

21877   *Home from the shore.* New York: Sunridge Press, 1978, 221 p., paper, novel.

21878   *In iron years.* Garden City, NY: Doubleday & Co., 1980, 250 p., cloth, coll.

  In the bone—SEE: *Gordon R. Dickson's SF best.*

21879   *Invaders!* New York: Baen Science Fiction Books, 1985, 253 p., paper, coll. [Edited by Sandra Miesel].

21880   *The last dream.* New York: Baen Fantasy Books, 1986, 263 p., paper, coll.

  The last master—SEE: *The R-master.*

21881   *Lost Dorsai.* New York: Ace Books, 1980, 287 p., paper, coll. CHILDE CYCLE.

21882   *Love not human.* New York: Ace Books, 1981, 249 p., paper, coll.

21883   *The man from Earth.* New York: A Jim Baen Presentation, Tor, A Tom Doherty Associates Book, 1983, 288 p., paper, coll.

21884   *The man the worlds rejected.* New York: Tor SF, A Tom Doherty Associates Book, 1986, 250 p., paper, coll.

04354   *Mankind on the run.* New York: Ace Books, 1956, 151 p., paper, novel. [Bound with *The crossroads of time* / by Andre Norton].

04354A retitled: *On the run.* New York: Ace Books, 1979, 213 p., paper, novel.

21885   *Masters of Everon.* Garden City, New York: Doubleday & Co., 1979, 213 p., cloth, novel.

21886   *Mindspan.* New York: Baen Science Fiction Books, 1986, 276 p., paper, coll. [Edited by Sandra Miesel].

21887   *Mission to universe.* New York: A Del Rey Book, Ballantine Books, 1977, 213 p., paper, novel. [Revised edition of #04355].

21888   *Naked to the stars; The alien way.* New York: Tor SF, A Tom Doherty Associates Book, 1991, 282 p., paper, coll.

21889   *Nebula winners twelve.* New York: Harper & Row, Publishers, 1978, xiii + 242 p., cloth, anth.

  On the run—SEE: *Mankind on the run.*

21890   *Pro.* New York: Ace Books, 1978, 185 p., paper, novel.

04362   *The R-Master.* Philadelphia: J. B. Lippincott Co., 1972, 214 p., cloth, novel.

21891   retitled: *The last master.* New York: A Tom Doherty Associates Book, 1984, 318 p., paper, novel. [Expanded edition].

21892   *Secrets of the deep.* New York: A Critic's Choice Paperback from Lorevan Publishing, 1985, 285 p., paper, coll. ROBBY HOENIG #1-3.

21893   *The spirit of Dorsai.* New York: Ace Books, 1979, 281 p., paper, coll. CHILDE CYCLE.

  Steel brother—SEE: *Dickson!*

21894   *Stranger.* New York: Tor SF, A Tom Doherty Associates Book, 1987, 254 p., paper, coll.

21895   *Survival!* New York: A Baen Book, 1984, 279 p., paper, coll.

21896   *Three to Dorsai! three novels from the Childe Cycle: Necromancer; Tactics of mistake; Dorsai!* Garden City, NY: Nelson Doubleday, 1975, ix + 532 p., cloth, coll. CHILDE CYCLE.

21897   *Time to teleport; Delusion world.* New York: Ace Books, 1981, 215 p., paper, coll.

21898   *Timestorm.* New York: St. Martin's Press, 1977, 342 p., cloth, novel.

21899   *Way of the pilgrim.* New York: Ace Science Fiction Books, 1987, 341 p., cloth, novel.

21900   *Wolf and iron.* Norwalk, CT: Easton Press, 1990, 477 p., cloth, novel.

21901   *Young Bleys.* New York: Tor, A Tom Doherty Associates Book, 1991, 456 p., cloth, novel. CHILDE CYCLE. [A prequel to *The final encyclopedia*].

as ROD SERLING

12890   *Rod Serling's Devils and demons: a collection.* Toronto, New York: Bantam Books, 1967, 213 p., paper, anth.

12891   *Rod Serling's Triple W: witches, warlocks, and werewolves: a collection.* Toronto, New York: Bantam Books, 1963, 181 p., paper, anth.

with Poul Anderson

16447   *Hoka!* New York: A Wallaby Book, Simon & Schuster, 1983, 219 p., paper, coll. HOKA #3.

16448   *Star prince Charlie.* New York: G. P. Putnam's Sons, 1975, 190 p., cloth, novel. HOKA #2.

with Troy Denning & Cory Glaberson

21553   *Dorsai's command.* New York: Ace Books, 1989, 246 p., paper, novel. COMBAT COMMAND #8; DORSAI SERIES.

with Roland Green

21903 *Jamie the Red.* New York: Ace Fantasy Books, 1984, 220 p., paper, novel. THIEVES' WORLD.

with Martin G. Greenberg & Charles G. Waugh

21904 *Robot warriors.* New York: Ace Books, 1991, x+240 p., paper, anth.

with Harry Harrison

    Lifeboat—SEE: *Lifeship.*
21905 *The lifeship.* New York & Hagerstown, NJ: Harper & Row, Publishers, 1976, 181 p., cloth, novel.
21905A retitled: *Lifeboat.* London: Dennis Dobson, 1978, 181 p., cloth, novel.

with Keith Laumer

21906 *Planet run, plus two bonus stories: "Once there was a giant,"* by Keith Laumer ; *"Call him Lord,"* by Gordon R. Dickson. New York: Tor, A Tom Doherty Associates Book, 1982, 287 p., paper, coll. [Includes *Planet run* (see #04377)].

DICKSON, (Horatio Henry) Lovat, 1902-1987

21907 *H. G. Wells: his turbulent life and times.* London: Macmillan, 1969, xi+330 p., cloth, nonf.

DIETZ, William C(orey), 1945-

21908 *Alien bounty.* New York: Ace Books, 1990, 214 p., paper, novel. SAM MCCADE #3.
21909 *Drifter.* New York: Ace Books, 1991, 200 p., paper, novel.
21910 *Freehold.* New York: Ace Science Fiction Books, 1987, 212 p., paper, novel.
21912 *Imperial bounty.* New York: Ace Books, 1988, 278 p., paper, novel. SAM MCCADE #2.
21913 *Matrix man.* New York: A Roc Book, 1990, 251 p., paper, novel.
21914 *McCade's bounty.* New York: Ace Books, 1990, 215 p., paper, novel. SAM MCCADE #4.
21915 *Prison planet.* New York: Ace Books, 1989, 250 p., paper, novel.
21916 *War world.* New York: Ace Science Fiction Books, 1986, 247 p., paper, novel. SAM MCCADE #1.

with David Drake

21917 *Cluster command /* by W. C. Dietz. New York: Baen Books, 1989, 276 p., paper, novel. CRISIS OF EMPIRE #2.

DIEUDONNÉ, Florence (Lucinda) Carpenter, 1850-

37708 *Xartella.* Washington, DC: Press of Gedney & Roberts, 1891, 28 p., paper, story.

DiFATE, Vincent, 1945- , *with Ian Summers & Beth Meacham*

    Catalog of science fiction hardware—SEE: *DiFate's Catalog of science fiction hardware.*
21918 *DiFate's Catalog of science fiction hardware.* New York: Workman Publishing, 1980, 135 p., cloth, art.

DIGBY, Anne, 1942?-

21919 *Ghostbusters: a storybook.* New York, Toronto: Scholastic Inc., 1984, [63] p., paper, movie. GHOSTBUSTERS #1.
21920 *Indiana Jones and the last crusade storybook.* New York, Toronto: Scholastic Inc., 1989, [63] p., paper, movie. INDIANA JONES SERIES.

D'IGNAZIO, (Silvio) Fred(erick III), 1949-

21921 *Escape from Robotropolis.* New York: Tor, A Tom Doherty Associates Book, 1988, 284 p., cloth, novel. ROBOT ODYSSEY #1. [Adapted from *Robot Odyssey I*, a software product].

DIKTY, Judy—SEE: May, Julian

DIKTY, Thaddeus (Maxim Eugene), 1920-1991

as ANONYMOUS EDITOR

21922 *Worlds within worlds: four classic Argosy tales of science fiction.* Mercer Island, WA: Starmont House, 1991, vii+122 p., cloth, anth. STARMONT FACSIMILE FICTION #12.

with R. Reginald

21923 *The work of Julian May: an annotated bibliography & guide.* San Bernardino, CA: R. Reginald, The Borgo Press, 1985, 66 p., cloth, nonf. BIBLIOGRAPHIES OF MODERN AUTHORS #3.

DILENBECK, John

21924 *A tour of the world.* New York, Washington: Vantage Press, 1980, xiv+265 p., cloth, novel.

DILLARD, J(eanne) M., 1954-

21925 *Bloodthirst: a Star Trek novel.* New York: Pocket Books, 1987, 264 p., cloth, novel. STAR TREK #37.
21926 *Demons: a Star Trek novel.* New York: Pocket Books, 1986, 271 p., paper, novel. STAR TREK #30.
The final frontier—SEE: *Star Trek V: the final frontier: a novel.*
The lost years—SEE: *Star Trek: The lost years.*
21927 *Mindshadow: a Star Trek novel.* New York: Pocket Books, 1986, 252 p., paper, novel. STAR TREK #27.
The resurrection—SEE: *War of the Worlds: The resurrection.*
21928 *Specters.* New York: A Dell Book, 1991, 374 p., paper, novel.
21929 *Star Trek V: the final frontier: a novel.* New York, London: Pocket Books, 1989, 311 p., cloth, movie. STAR TREK (unnumbered).
21930 *Star Trek: The lost years.* New York: Pocket Books, 1989, vii+307 p., cloth, novel. STAR TREK SERIES (unnumbered).
21931 *War of the Worlds: The resurrection: a novel.* New York, London: Pocket Books, 1988, 405 p., paper, tele.

DILLARD, R(ichard) H(enry) W(ilde), 1937-

21932 *The first man on the sun: a novel.* Baton Rouge, LA & London: Louisiana State University Press, 1983, 287 p., cloth, novel.
21933 *Horror films.* New York: Monarch Press, 1976, xi+129 p., paper, nonf.

DILLE, (Robert Nichols) Flint, 1955-

with Gary Gygax

21934 *The crimson sea.* New York: An Archway Paperback, Pocket Books, 1985, [186] p., paper, novel. SAGARD THE BARBARIAN #3.
21935 *The fire demon.* New York: An Archway Paperback, Pocket Books, 1986, [190] p., paper, novel. SAGARD THE BARBARIAN #4.
21936 *The green hydra.* New York: An Archway Paperback, Pocket Books, 1985, [190] p.,

paper, novel. SAGARD THE BARBARIAN #2.
21937 *The ice dragon.* New York: An Archway Paperback, Pocket Books, 1985, [186] p., paper, novel. SAGARD THE BARBARIAN #1.

with David Marconi

Acolytes of darkness—SEE: *Agent 13: Acolytes of darkness.*
21938 *Agent 13: Acolytes of darkness.* Lake Geneva, WI: TSR Inc., 1988, 318 p., paper, novel. AGENT 13, THE MIDNIGHT AVENGER #3. [Bound with *Web of danger* / by Aaron Allston].
21939 *The invisible empire.* Lake Geneva, WI: TSR Inc., 1986, 192 p., paper, novel. AGENT 13, THE MIDNIGHT AVENGER #1.
21940 *The serpentine assassin.* Lake Geneva, WI: TSR Inc., 1986, 192 p., paper, novel. AGENT 13, THE MIDNIGHT AVENGER #2.

DILLON, Diane (Claire Sorber), 1933- , *with Leo Dillon*

21941 *The art of Leo and Diane Dillon.* New York: Ballantine Books, 1981, [95] p., cloth, art. [Edited by Byron Preiss].

DILLON, John, 1923- , *with Gregory Fitz Gerald*

21942 *The late great future.* Greenwich, CT: A Fawcett Crest Book, Fawcett Publications, 1976, 288 p., paper, anth.

DILLON, Leo [i.e., Lionel John Dillon Sr.], 1933- , *with Diane Dillon*

21941 *The art of Leo and Diane Dillon.* New York: Ballantine Books, 1981, [95] p., cloth, art. [Edited by Byron Preiss].

DILLON, Lionel—SEE: Dillon, Leo

DILLON, Peter C.

21943 *An Ace alpha-numeric annotated science fiction checklist.* Richmond, CA: Peter C. Dillon, 1973, 29 p., paper, nonf.

DILLOW, Jeffrey C.

21944 *Adventures in high fantasy.* Reston, VA: Reston Publishing Co., 1981, 199 p., cloth, fiction.
21945 *Goldchester: more adventures in high fantasy.* Reston, VA: Reston Publishing Co., 1982, xxiv+245 p., cloth, fiction.

21946 *High fantasy.* Reston, VA: Reston Publishing Co., 1981, 196 p., cloth, fiction.

21947 *Murder in Irliss.* Reston, VA: Reston Publishing Co., 1982, xxv+145 p., cloth, fiction.

21948 *Wizards and warriors: two complete play-as-you-read fantasy games.* Reston, VA: Reston Publishing Co., 1982, xxv+145 p., cloth, coll.

DILSAVER, Paul, 1949-

21949 *Nurtz! nurtz!: novel.* Laramie, WY: Ghost Rocks Publishing, 1989, 206 p., paper, novel.

DIMENSTEIN, Catherine—SEE: Wells, Catherine

*DIMONDSTEIN, Boris, 1891-1973

DINBGO, Wu—SEE: Wu, Dingbo

DiPEGO, Gerald (F.), 1941-

21950 *Shadow of the beast.* New York: A Signet Book, New American Library, 1984, 286 p., paper, novel.

DISCH, Thomas M(ichael), 1940-

21951 *The brave little toaster.* Garden City, NY: Doubleday & Co., 1986, 79 p., cloth, story. BRAVE LITTLE TOASTER #1.

21952 *The brave little toaster goes to Mars.* Garden City, NY: Doubleday & Co., 1988, 72 p., cloth, story. BRAVE LITTLE TOASTER #2.

21953 *The businessman: a tale of terror.* New York: Harper & Row, Publishers, 1984, 292 p., cloth, novel.

21954 *The early science fiction stories of Thomas M. Disch.* Boston: Gregg Press, 1977, xxxii+334 p., cloth, coll. [Includes *102 H-bombs* and *Puppies of Terra*].

21955 *The fundamental Disch.* Toronto, New York: Bantam Books, 1980, xiii+398 p., paper, coll.

21956 *Getting into death, and other stories.* New York: Alfred A. Knopf, 1976, 227 p., cloth, coll.

21957 *The M.D.: a horror story.* New York: Alfred A. Knopf, 1991, 401 p., cloth, novel.

21958 *The man who had no idea: a collection of stories.* Toronto, New York: Bantam Books, 1982, 231 p., paper, coll.

04406 *Mankind under the leash: being a true and faithful account of the great upheavals of 2037, with portraits of many of the prin-cipals involved, as well as reflections by the authors of the nature of art, revolution & theology.* New York: Ace Books, 1966, 140 p., paper, novel. [Bound with *Planet of exile* / by Ursula K. Le Guin].

04406A retitled: *The puppies of Terra: being a true and faithful account of the great upheavals of 2037, with portraits of many of the principals involved, as well as reflections by the authors of the nature of art, revolution & theology.* London, Toronto: Panther, Granada Publishing, 1978, 142 p., paper, novel.

21959 *The new improved sun: an anthology of utopian S-F.* New York: Harper & Row, 1975, viii+208 p., cloth, anth.

21960 *On wings of song.* New York: St. Martin's Press, 1979, 359 p., cloth, novel. [Winner of the John W. Campbell Jr. Memorial Award for Best Novel, 1979 (1980)].

The puppies of Terra—SEE: *Mankind under the leash.*

21961 *Ringtime: a story.* West Branch, IA: Toothpaste Press, 1983, 40 p., cloth, story. [Limited to 975 copies].

21962 *The silver pillow: a tale of witchcraft.* Willimantic, CT: Mark V. Ziesing, 1987, 48 p., cloth, story.

21963 *Torturing Mr. Amberwell.* New Castle, VA: Cheap Street, 1985, 76 p., cloth, story. [Limited to 175 copies].

21964 *Triplicity.* Garden City, NY: Nelson Doubleday, 1980, 409 p., cloth, coll. [Includes *Echo round his bones*; *The genocides*; *The puppies of Terra*].

with Charles Naylor

21965 *New constellations: an anthology of tomorrow's mythologies.* New York: Harper & Row, 1976, xiii+192 p., cloth, anth.

21966 *Strangeness: a collection of curious tales.* New York: Charles Scribner's Sons, 1977, viii+309 p., cloth, anth.

DiSILVESTRO, Roger L., 1949-

21967 *Living with the reptiles.* New York: Donald I. Fine, 1990, 284 p., cloth, novel.

21968 *Ursula's gift: a novel.* New York: Donald I. Fine, 1988, 220 p., cloth, novel.

DISKIN, Lahna F(aga), 1932-

21969 *Theodore Sturgeon.* Mercer Island, WA: Starmont House, 1981, 72 p., paper, nonf. STARMONT READER'S GUIDE #7.

21970 *Theodore Sturgeon: a primary and secondary bibliography.* Boston: G. K.

Hall & Co., 1980, xxvii+105 p., cloth, nonf. MASTERS OF SCIENCE FICTION AND FANTASY.

*DIVINE, Arthur D(urham <u>David</u>), 1904-<u>1987</u>

DIVINEY, Jim, *with Shirl Diviney*

21971 *Index Astounding Analog, British edition, Nov. 53-Aug 63.* Brampton, Huntington, England: [Jim & Shirl Diviney?, 1963?], 41 p., paper, nonf.

DIVINEY, Shirl(ey), *with Jim Diviney*

21971 *Index Astounding Analog, British edition, Nov. 53-Aug 63.* Brampton, Huntington, England: [Jim & Shirl Diviney?, 1963?], 41 p., paper, nonf.

DiVONO, Sharman, *with William Rotsler as* **VICTOR APPLETON**

The alien probe—SEE: *Tom Swift: The aline probe.*

16738 *The astral fortress.* New York: Wanderer Books, Simon & Schuster, 1981, 191 p., paper, novel. TOM SWIFT #B5.

16740 *The city in the stars.* New York: Wanderer Books, Simon & Schuster, 1981, 191 p., paper, novel. TOM SWIFT #B1.

16747 *The rescue mission.* New York: Wanderer Books, Simon & Schuster, 1981, 188 p., paper, novel. TOM SWIFT #B6.

Terror on the moons of Jupiter—SEE: *Tom Swift: Terror on the moons of Jupiter.*

16750 *Tom Swift: Terror on the moons of Jupiter.* New York: Wanderer Books, Simon & Schuster, 1981, 185 p., paper, novel. TOM SWIFT #B2.

16751 *Tom Swift: The alien probe.* New York: Wanderer Books, Simon & Schuster, 1981, 186 p., paper, novel. TOM SWIFT #B3.

16752 *Tom Swift: The war in outer space.* New York: Wanderer Books, Simon & Schuster, 1981, 171 p., paper, novel. TOM SWIFT #B4.

The war in outer space—SEE: *Tom Swift: The war in outer space.*

DIXON, Chris

21972 *Winter in Aphelion: the adventures of Skarry the Dreamer.* London: Unwin Paperbacks, 1989, 220 p., paper, novel. SKARRY THE DREAMER #1.

DIXON, Dougal, 1947-

21973 *After man: a zoology of the future.* New York: St. Martin's Press, 1981, 124 p., cloth, fiction.

21974 *Ice age explorer.* Toronto, New York: A Byron Preiss Book, Bantam Books, 1985, 123 p., paper, novel. TIME MACHINE #7.

21975 *Man after man: an anthropology of the future.* New York: St. Martin's Press, 1990, 128 p., cloth, fiction.

DIXON, Franklin W., house pseud.

21976 *The Hardy Boys ghost stories.* New York: Wanderer Books, Simon & Schuster, 1984, 154 p., paper, coll.

DIXON, James

21977 *It lives again.* New York: Ballantine Books, 1978, 168 p., paper, movie. IT'S ALIVE #2.

DIXON, Jeanne—SEE: Stone, Josephine Rector

DIXON, Roger—SEE: Lewis, Charles

DIXON, Thomas—SEE: Cole, Burt

DIXON, William

21978 *A portfolio of drawings by William Dixon based on the novels of Edgar Rice Burroughs.* Philadelphia, PA: Oswald Train, 1971, 10 leaves, paper, art coll.

DIZER, John T(homas) Jr., 1921-

21979 *Tom Swift & company: 'boy's books' by Stratemeyer and others.* Jefferson, NC: McFarland & Co., 1982, viii+183 p., cloth, nonf.

DOBBIN, Muriel (Isabella)

21980 *A taste for power.* New York: Richard Marek, 1980, 238 p., cloth, novel.

DOBBS, Michael, 1950-

21981 *House of cards.* London: Collins, 1989, 383 p., cloth, novel.

DOBKIN, Kaye [pseud. of Kathleen Hamel Peifer], 1945-

21982 *The queen of hearts.* New York: A Dell/Banbury Book, 1982, 298 p., paper, novel.

21983 *The white rabbit.* New York: A Dell/ Banbury Book, 1983, 276 p., paper, novel.

DOBKIN, Marjorie Housepian, 1923- , *with Jean V. Cullen*

20866 *Inside out.* New York: Ivy Books, 1989, 267 p., paper, novel.

DOBSON, Margaret (June), 1931-

21984 *The soothsayer.* New York: A Dell Book, 1987, 187 p., paper, novel.

DOBSON, Roger, *with Mark Valentine*

21985 *Arthur Machen: apostle of wonder.* Oxford, England: Caermaen Books, 1985, ix+61 p., paper, nonf. anth.
21986 *Arthur Machen: artist and mystic.* Oxford, England: Caermaen Books, 1986, xii+ 54 p., paper, nonf. anth. [Limited to 300 copies].

DOCHERTY, Brian

21987 *American horror fiction: from Brockden Brown to Stephen King.* Basingstoke, Hampshire, England: Macmillan, 1990, ix+180 p., cloth, nonf. anth.

DODDERIDGE, Esmé, 1916-

21988 *The new Gulliver; or, The adventures of Lemuel Gulliver Jr. in Capovolta: a novel.* New York: Taplinger Publishing Co., 1979, 247 p., cloth, novel. GUL-LIVER SEQUEL.

DODGE, Jim

21989 *Stone Junction: an alchemical potboiler.* New York: Atlantic Monthly Press, 1990, 355 p., cloth, novel.

DODGE, Mary Louise

21990 *Sticks and stones.* New York: Manor Books, 1979 (i.e., 1980?), 189 p., paper, novel.

DODGE, Michael J., pseud.—SEE: Ford, John M.

DODSON, Fitzhugh (James), 1923- , *with Paula Reuben*

21991 *The carnival kidnap caper.* La Jolla, CA: Oak Tree Publications, 1979, v+129 p., cloth, novel.

*DOERR, Edd, 1930-

DOGBOLT, Barnaby [pseud. of Herbert Silvette], 1906-

15798 *The goose's tale.* New York: E. P. Dutton, 1947, 317 p., cloth, novel.

DOHERTY, Berlie, 1943-

21992 *Spellhorn.* London: Hamish Hamilton Children's Books, 1989, 132 p., cloth, novel.

DOLAN, Bill, pseud.—SEE: Willard, Tom

DOLLERUP, (Erik) Cay (Krebs), 1939-

21993 *Vølve: Scandinavian views on science fiction: selected papers from the Scandinavian Science-Fiction Festival, 1977.* Copenhagen, Denmark: B. Stougaard Jensen, 1977, 123 p., paper, nonf. anth.

DOLLNER, Karl

21994 *The Galaxy checklist: covering the period October 1950 to December 1958.* Cheltenham, Gloucester, England: British Science Fiction Association, 1961, 60 p., paper, nonf.

DOLPHIN, Reginald C.—SEE: Dolphin, Rex

DOLPHIN, Rex [i.e., Reginald Charles Dolphin], *as* PETER SAXON

12726 *The vampires of Finistère.* New York: A Berkley Medallion Book, 1970, 190 p., paper, novel. GUARDIANS #4.

DOMAN, David Alan, *with Terrence Lore Smith*

21995 *Yours truly, from Hell.* New York: St. Martin's Press, 1987, 336 p., cloth, novel.

DOMATILLA, John, 1936-

21996 *The last crime.* London: Heinemann, 1980, 155 p., cloth, novel.

DON, Ian

21997 *Baby: a novel.* London: A Star Book, W. H. Allen, 1985, 169 p., paper, movie.

21998 *My science project: a novel.* London: A Target Book, W. H. Allen, 1985, 158 p., paper, movie.

21999 *Splash: a novel.* London: A Star Book, W. H. Allen, 1984, 141 p., paper, movie.

DONABEDIAN, Bairj—SEE: Westerly, Daniel

DONALD, James, 1948-

22000 *Fantasy and the cinema.* London: BFI Publishing, 1989, 298 p., cloth, nonf. anth.

with Victor Burgin & Cora Kaplan

19047 *Formations of fantasy.* London, New York: Methuen, 1986, 221 p., paper, nonf. anth.

DONALDSON, D. J.

22001 *Cajun nights.* New York: St. Martin's Press, 1988, 234 p., cloth, novel.

DONALDSON, Stephen R(eeder), 1947-

22002 *Daughter of Regals.* West Kingston, RI: Donald M. Grant, Publisher, 1984, 125 p., cloth, novel.

22003 *Daughter of Regals, and other tales.* New York: A Del Rey Book, Ballantine Books, 1984, xi+337 p., cloth, coll.

22004 *Epic fantasy in the modern world: a few observations.* Kent, OH: Kent State University Libraries, 1986, [18] p., paper, nonf.

22005 *The first chronicles of Thomas Covenant the Unbeliever.* Glasgow, Scotland: Richard Drew Publishing, 1983, 3 v. in 1, cloth, coll. THOMAS COVENANT #1-3.

Forbidden knowledge—SEE: The gap into vision: forbidden knowledge.

22006 *The gap into conflict: the real story.* London: Collins, 1990, 173 p., cloth, novel. GAP INTO CONFLICT #1.

22007 *The gap into vision: forbidden knowledge.* New York: Bantam Books, 1991, 407 p., cloth, novel. GAP INTO CONFLICT #2.

22008 *Gilden-fire.* San Francisco, Columbia, PA: Underwood-Miller, 1981, 71 p., cloth, story. THOMAS COVENANT SERIES.

22009 *The Illearth war.* New York: Holt, Rinehart & Winston, 1977, xii+407 p., cloth, novel. THOMAS COVENANT #2.

22010 *Lord Foul's bane.* New York: Holt, Rinehart & Winston, 1977, 369 p., cloth, novel. THOMAS COVENANT #1.

22011 *A man rides through.* New York: A Del Rey Book, Ballantine Books, 1987, vi+661 p., cloth, novel. MORDANT'S NEED #2.

22012 *The mirror of her dreams.* London: Collins, 1986, 658 p., cloth, novel. MORDANT'S NEED #1.

22013 *The one tree.* New York: A Del Rey Book, Ballantine Books, 1982, xi+475 p., cloth, novel. THOMAS COVENANT, SECOND SERIES #2.

22014 *The power that preserves.* New York: Holt, Rinehart & Winston, 1977, xiii+379 p., cloth, novel. THOMAS COVENANT #3.

The real story—SEE: The gap into conflict: the real story.

22015 *White gold wielder.* New York: A Del Rey Book, Ballantine Books, 1983, xiii+485 p., cloth, novel. THOMAS COVENANT, SECOND SERIES #3.

22016 *The wounded land.* New York: A Del Rey Book, Ballantine Books, 1980, xi+497 p., cloth, novel. THOMAS COVENANT, SECOND SERIES #1.

DONG, Eugene, 1932- , *with Spyros Andreopoulos*

16467 *Heart beat; a novel.* New York: Coward, McCann & Geoghegan, 1978, 352 p., cloth, novel.

*DONIS, Miles, 1936-1979

DONNELLY, Joe

22017 *Bane.* London: Barrie & Jenkins, 1989, 381 p., cloth, novel.

22018 *The Shee.* London: Ebury Press, 1991, 384 p., cloth, novel.

22019 *Stone.* London: Barrie & Jenkins, 1990, 381 p., cloth, novel.

DONOHUE, Trevor

22020 *Savage tomorrow.* St. Kilda, Victoria, Australia: Cory & Collins, 1983, 154 p., paper, novel.

DONOSO, José [i.e., José Donoso Yanez], 1924-

22021 *The obscene bird of night.* New York: Alfred A. Knopf, 1973, 488 p., cloth, novel. [Translation by Hardie St. Martin and Leonard Mades of *El obsceno pájaro de la noche*].

22022 *Sacred families: three novellas.* New York: Alfred A. Knopf, 1977, 206 p., cloth, coll. [Translation by Andrée Conrad of *Tres novelitas burguesas*].

DONOVAN, John, 1928-

22023 *Family: a novel.* New York: An Ursula Nordstrom Book, Harper & Row, 1976, 116 p., cloth, novel.

DONOVAN, Laurence, d. 1950?

as KENNETH ROBESON

03794 *The black spot: a Doc Savage adventure.* Toronto, New York: Bantam Books, 1974, 152 p., paper, novel. DOC SAVAGE #76.

03795 *Cold death: a Doc Savage adventure.* Toronto, New York: Bantam Books, 1968, 121 p., paper, novel. DOC SAVAGE #21.

03796 *Haunted ocean: a Doc Savage adventure.* Toronto, New York: Bantam Books, 1970, 140 p., paper, novel. DOC SAVAGE #51.

03797 *He could stop the world: a Doc Savage adventure.* Toronto, New York: Bantam Books, 1970, 140 p., paper, novel. DOC SAVAGE #54.

03798 *Land of long juju: a Doc Savage adventure.* Toronto, New York: Bantam Books, 1970, 140 p., paper, novel. DOC SAVAGE #47.

03799 *Mad eyes: a Doc Savage adventure.* Toronto, New York: Bantam Books, 1969, 120 p., paper, novel. DOC SAVAGE #34.

03800 *The men who smiled no more: a Doc Savage adventure.* Toronto, New York: Bantam Books, 1970, 138 p., paper, novel. DOC SAVAGE #45.

03801 *Murder melody: a Doc Savage adventure.* Toronto, New York: Bantam Books, 1967, 138 p., paper, novel. DOC SAVAGE #15.

03802 *Murder mirage: a Doc Savage adventure.* Toronto, New York: Bantam Books, 1973, 153 p., paper, novel. DOC SAVAGE #71.

with Lester Dent as KENNETH ROBESON

21593 *Doc Savage: The secret in the sky; and, Cold death: two complete adventures in one volume.* Toronto, New York: Bantam Books, 1982, 261 p., paper, coll. DOC SAVAGE #20-21. [*The secret in the sky* by Lester Dent; *Cold death* by Laurence Donovan].

*DONSON, Cyril, 1919-<u>1986</u>

DOOLEY, Dennis, 1942- , *with Gary Engle*

22024 *Superman at fifty: the persistence of a legend.* Cleveland, OH: Octavia Press, 1987, 189 p., cloth, nonf.

DORCY, Mary, 1950- , *with Maeve Kelly & Joni Crone*

20823 *Mad and bad fairies: a collection of feminist fairytales.* Dublin: Attic Press, 1987, 60 p., paper, anth.

DOREN, Carl Van—SEE: Van Doren, Carl

DORER, Frances (Catherine)

with Nancy Dorer

22025 *By daybreak the Eagle.* New York: Manor Books, 1979 (i.e., 1980?), 224 p., paper, novel. EAGLE #1.

22026 *The eternal fountain.* Davenport, FL: Laura Books, 1979, 218 p., paper, novel.

22027 *Return of the Eagle.* New York: Manor Books, 1979 (i.e., 1980?), 229 p., paper, novel. EAGLE #2.

22028 *Two came calling.* New York: Manor Books, 1979, 271 p., paper, novel.

22029 *Where no man has trod.* New York: Manor Books, 1979, 217 p., paper, novel.

22030 *The wings of the Eagle* / by Francis Dorer... New York: Manor Books, 1979 (i.e., 1980?), 233 p., paper, novel. EAGLE #3.

with Nancy Dorer as FRANK DORN

22031 *Appointment with yesterday.* New York: Manor Books, 1979, 208 p., paper, novel.

22032 *Sunwatch.* New York: Manor Books, 1979, 247 p., paper, novel.

22033 *When next I wake.* New York: Manor Books, 1978, 261 p., paper, novel.

DORER, Nancy (Jane)

with Frances Dorer

22025 *By daybreak the Eagle.* New York: Manor Books, 1979 (i.e., 1980?), 224 p., paper, novel. EAGLE #1.

22026 *The eternal fountain.* Davenport, FL: Laura Books, 1979, 218 p., paper, novel.

22027 *Return of the Eagle.* New York: Manor Books, 1979 (i.e., 1980?), 229 p., paper, novel. EAGLE #2.

22028 *Two came calling.* New York: Manor Books, 1979, 271 p., paper, novel.

22029 *Where no man has trod.* New York: Manor Books, 1979, 217 p., paper, novel.

22030 *The wings of the Eagle.* New York: Manor Books, 1979 (i.e., 1980?), 233 p., paper, novel. EAGLE #3.

with Frances Dorer as FRANK DORN

22031 *Appointment with yesterday.* New York: Manor Books, 1979, 208 p., paper, novel.

22032 *Sunwatch.* New York: Manor Books, 1979, 247 p., paper, novel.

22033 *When next I wake.* New York: Manor Books, 1978, 261 p., paper, novel.

DORFMAN, Ariel, 1942-

22034 *Mascara: a novel.* New York: Viking, 1988, 158 p., cloth, cloth, novel.

DORMAN, Sonya (Hess), 1924-

22035 *Planet patrol.* New York: Coward, Mc-Cann & Geoghegan, 1978, 161 p., cloth, novel.

DORMAN, Thomas (Edwin), 1914

22036 *The days after.* New York: Vantage Press, 1969, 248 p., cloth, novel.

DORN, Frank, pseud.—SEE: Dorer, Frances & Dorer, Nancy

DORRE, Pamela

22037 *Wind over Stonehenge.* Belmont, CA: A Pacemaker Bestsellers Book, Fearon-Pitman Publishers, 1977, 59 p., paper, novel.

DORSEY, Candas Jane, 1952-

22038 *Machine sex, and other stories.* Victoria, British Columbia, Canada: A Tesseract Book, Porcépic Books, 1988, 141 p., paper, coll.

with Nora Abercrombie

18237 *Hardwired angel.* Vancouver, British Columbia, Canada: Arsenal Pulp Press, 1987, 113 p., paper, novel.

with Gerry Truscott

22039 *Tesseracts³.* Victoria, British Columbia, Canada: A Tesseract Book, Porcépic

Books, 1991, x+437 p., paper, coll. [Includes some verse].

DOSSOR, Howard F.

22040 *The Colin Wilson collection of Howard F. Dossor.* Melbourne, Australia: Privately Printed, 1986, 107 p., paper, nonf.

22041 *Colin Wilson: the man and his mind.* Shaftesbury, England: Element, 1990, [264] p., cloth, nonf.

DOTY, Jean Slaughter, 1924-

22042 *Can I get there by candlelight?* New York: Macmillan, 1980, 111 p., cloth, novel.

DOUGHERTY, Kathleen

22043 *Moth to the flame.* New York: Diamond Books, 1991, 323 p., paper, novel.

DOUGHERTY, William, as VICTOR APPLETON II

00442 *Tom Swift and his flying lab.* New York: Grosset & Dunlap, 1954, 208 p., cloth, novel. TOM SWIFT JR. #A1.

DOUGLAS, Carole Nelson, 1944-

22044 *Counterprobe.* New York: Tor, A Tom Doherty Associates Book, 1988, 344 p., cloth, novel. PROBE #2.

22045 *Cup of clay.* New York: Tor Fantasy, A Tom Doherty Associates Book, 1991, xix+329 p., cloth, novel. TALISWOMAN #1.

22046 *Exiles of the Rynth.* New York: A Del Rey Book, Ballantine Books, 1984, 343 p., paper, novel. KENDRIC & IRISSA #2.

22047 *Heir of Reingarth.* New York: Tor, A Tom Doherty Associates Book, 1988, 374 p., cloth, novel. SWORD & CIRCLET #2.

22048 *Keepers of Edanvant.* New York: Tor, A Tom Doherty Associates Book, 1987, 346 p., cloth, novel. SWORD & CIRCLET #1; KENDRIC & IRISSA #3.

22049 *Probe.* New York: Tor SF, A Tom Doherty Associates Book, 1985, 383 p., paper, novel. PROBE #1.

22050 *Seven of swords.* New York: Tor, A Tom Doherty Associates Book, 1989, 408 p., cloth, novel. SWORD & CIRCLET #3.

22051 *Six of Swords.* New York: A Del Rey Book, Ballantine Books, 1982, 276 p., paper, novel. KENDRIC & IRISSA #1.

DOUGLAS, Drake [pseud. of Werner Zimmerman]

22052 *Creature.* New York: Leisure Books, 1985, 396 p., paper, novel.
22053 *Horrors!* Woodstock, NY: Overlook Press, 1989, 418 p., cloth, nonf. [Expanded edition of #04478].
22054 *Undertow.* New York: Leisure Books, 1984, 398 p., paper, novel.

with Stephen Kent

22055 *Death song.* New York: Leisure Books, 1987, 368 p., paper, novel.

DOUGLAS, Garry, pseud.—SEE: Kilworth, Garry

DOUGLAS, Gregory A. [pseud. of Eli Cantor], 1913-

22056 *The nest.* New York: Zebra Books, Kensington Publishing Corp., 1980, 448 p., paper, novel.
22057 *The rite.* New York: Zebra Books, Kensington Publishing Corp., 1979, 336 p., paper, novel.
22057A retitled: *The unholy smile.* London: New English Library, 1986, 336 p., paper, novel.
    The unholy smile—SEE: *The rite.*

DOUGLAS, Iain

22058 *The hearth of Ruvaig.* London: Robert Hale, 1981, 192 p., cloth, novel.
22059 *Point of impact.* London: Robert Hale, 1979, 206 p., cloth, novel.
22060 *Saturn's missing rings.* London: Robert Hale, 1980, 173 p., cloth, novel.
22061 *The world of the sower.* London: Robert Hale, 1981, 160 p., cloth, novel.

DOUGLAS, Lauren Wright, 1947-

22062 *In the blood.* Tallahassee, FL: Naiad Press, 1989, 242 p., paper, novel.

*DOUGLASS, Ellsworth [pseud. of Elmer Dwiggins]

DOUGLASS, Keith, house pseud.

22063 *Carrier.* New York: Berkley Books, 1991, 325 p., paper, novel. CARRIER #1. [By William H. Keith Jr.].
22064 *Carrier: Viper strike.* New York: Berkley Books, 1991, 329 p., paper, novel. CARRIER #2. [By William H. Keith Jr.].

Viper strike—SEE: *Carrier: Viper strike.*

DOUGLIS, Marjie

22065 *Matrix witch.* Minneapolis, MN: Gemstone Books, Dillon Press, 1988, 285 p., cloth, novel.

DOWD, Tom, *with Chris Kubasik*

22066 *Virtual realities: a Shadowrun sourcebook.* Chicago: FASA Corp., 1991, 152 p., paper, fiction. SHADOWRUN SERIES.

DowDELL, Del

22067 *Spearmen of Arn.* New York: Belmont Tower Books, 1978, 223 p., paper, novel.
22068 *Torpedo alley.* New York: Pinnacle Books, Windsor Publishing Corp., 1988, 414 p., paper, novel.
22069 *Warlord of Ghandor.* New York: DAW Books, 1977, 253 p., paper, novel.

*DOWDING, Henry Wallace, 1888?-1967?

DOWLING, David (Hurst), 1950-

22070 *Fictions of nuclear disaster.* Iowa City, IA: University of Iowa Press, 1987, ix+239 p., cloth, nonf.

DOWLING, Kevin

22071 *Brodie's notes on H. G. Wells's The war of the worlds.* London & Sydney: Pan Books, 1986, 63 p., paper, nonf.

DOWLING, Terry, 1948-

22072 *Rynosseros.* North Adelaide, South Australia, Australia: Aphelion Publications, 1990, 228 p., paper, coll.
22073 *Wormwood.* North Adelaide, South Australia, Australia: Aphelion Publications, 1991, 251 p., cloth, coll.

DOWNER, Ann, 1960-

22074 *The glass salamander.* New York: A Lucas/Evans Book, Atheneum, 1989, 216 p., cloth, novel. CAITLIN #2.
22075 *The spellkey.* New York: A Lucas/Evans Book, Atheneum, 1987, 217 p., cloth, novel. CAITLIN #1.

DOWNEY, Edmund—SEE: Allen, F. M.

DOWNEY, Jack

22076   *Doomstar.* New York, Washington: Vantage Press, 1980, 97 p., cloth, novel.

DOWNIE, Gary

22077   *The Doctor Who cookbook.* London: W. H. Allen, 1985, 119 p., cloth, nonf.

DOWNIE, Jill, 1938-

22078   *The raven in the glass.* Toronto, New York: PaperJacks, 1987, 471 p., paper, novel.

DOWNING, David, 1946-

22079   *The Moscow option: an alternative Second World War.* London: New English Library, 1979, 254 p., cloth, novel.
22081   *Russian revolution 1985: a contemporary fable.* Sevenoaks, Kent, England: New English Library, 1983, 235 p., cloth, novel.

DOWNING, Paula E. [i.e., Paula Elaine Downing King], 1951-

22082   *Rinn's Star.* New York: A Del Rey Book, Ballantine Books, 1990, 229 p., paper, novel.

as PAULA KING

22083   *Mad Roy's light.* Riverdale, NY: Baen Books, 1990, 275 p., paper, novel.

DOWNING, Peggy (Louise), 1924-

22084   *Brill and the Dragators.* Wheaton, IL: Victor Books, 1987, 131 p., paper, novel. EXITORN ADVENTURES #1.
22085   *Brill and the puffire volcano.* Wheaton, IL: Victor Books, 1989, 128 p., paper, novel. EXITORN ADVENTURES #6.
22086   *Brill and the Zinders.* Wheaton, IL: Victor Books, 1988, 131 p., paper, novel. EXITORN ADVENTURES #4.
22087   *Help! I'm drowning! and other emergencies.* Elgin, IL: Chariot Books, 1985, 138 p., paper, novel.
22088   *Help! I'm shrinking!* Elgin, IL: Chariot Books, 1986, 152 p., paper, novel.
22089   *Segra and Stargull.* Wheaton, IL: Victor Books, 1987, 130 p., paper, novel. EXITORN ADVENTURES #2.
22090   *Segra and the magician.* Wheaton, IL: Victor Books, 1989, 132 p., paper, novel. EXITORN ADVENTURES #5.

22091   *Segra in diamond castle.* Wheaton, IL: Victor Books, 1988, 131 p., paper, novel. EXITORN ADVENTURES #3.

DOWNS, Gerry

22092   *Alternative: the epilog to Orion.* Anchorage, AK: [s.n.], 1976, p., paper, novel. STAR TREK SERIES.

DOWNS, Sally Gibson- —SEE: Gibson-Downs, Sally

DOWRICK, Stephanie

22093   *Classic tales of horror.* London: Constable, 1976, xiii+270 p., cloth, anth.
22093A retitled: *Great tales of the supernatural.* London, Melbourne, Australia: Everyman's Library, 1978, 207 p., paper, anth. [Abridged edition].
       Great tales of the supernatural—SEE: *Classic tales of horror.*

DOXEY, William (Sanford, Jr.), 1935-

22094   *ESPionage.* New York: Belmont Tower Books, 1979, 250 p., paper, novel.

DOYLE, Arthur Conan, (Sir), 1859-1930

22095   *The best horror stories of Arthur Conan Doyle.* Chicago: Academy Chicago, 1989, vi+294 p., paper, coll. [Edited by Martin H. Greenberg, Frank D. McSherry Jr., Charles G. Waugh].
22096   *The best science fiction of Arthur Conan Doyle.* Carbondale & Edwardsville, IL: Southern Illinois University Press, 1981, xix+190 p., cloth, coll. [Edited by Charles G. Waugh and Martin H. Greenberg].
22097   *The best supernatural tales of Arthur Conan Doyle.* New York: Dover Publications, 1979, xiv+302 p., paper, coll.
       The complete Professor Challenger—SEE: *The Professor Challenger stories.*
22098   *The Edinburgh stories.* Edinburgh, Scotland: Polygon Books, 1981, viii+86 p., cloth, coll.
04503   *The Professor Challenger stories: The lost world; The poison belt; The land of mist; The disintegration machine; When the world screamed.* London: John Murray, 1952, 577 p., cloth, coll. PROFESSOR CHALLENGER #1-3.
04503A retitled: *The complete Professor Challenger.* Ware, Hertfordshire, England: Wordsworth Editions, 1989, vi+577 p.,

cloth, coll. PROFESSOR CHALLENGER SERIES.

22099 *The supernatural tales of Sir Arthur Conan Doyle.* London, New York: W. Foulsham, 1987, 272 p., cloth, coll. [Edited by Peter Haining].

22100 *Tales of terror and mystery.* Harmondsworth, Middlesex, England: Penguin Books, 1979, 224 p., paper, coll.

22101 *When the world screamed, & other stories: the Professor Challenger adventures, volume 2.* San Francisco, CA: Chronicle Books, 1990, 233 p., paper, coll. [Includes *When the world screamed*; *The disintegration machine*; *The land of mist*]. PROFESSOR CHALLENGER SERIES.

DOYLE, Debra, 1952-

with James D. Macdonald

22102 *City by the sea.* Mahwah, NJ: Troll Associates, 1990, 132 p., cloth, novel. CIRCLE OF MAGIC #3.

22103 *The high king's daughter.* Mahwah, NJ: Troll Associates, 1990, 136 p., cloth, novel. CIRCLE OF MAGIC #6.

22104 *The prince's players.* Mahwah, NJ: Troll Associates, 1990, 133 p., cloth, novel. CIRCLE OF MAGIC #4.

22105 *The prisoners of Bell Castle.* Mahwah, NJ: Troll Associates, 1990, 137 p., cloth, novel. CIRCLE OF MAGIC #5.

22106 *Robert Silverberg's Time Tours: Timecrime, Inc.* New York: A Byron Preiss Book, HarperPaperbacks, 1991, 145 p., paper, novel. ROBERT SILVERBERG'S TIME TOURS #3.

22107 *School of wizardry.* Mahwah, NJ: Troll Associates, 1990, 139 p., cloth, novel. CIRCLE OF MAGIC #1.
Timecrime, Inc.—SEE: *Robert Silverberg's Time Tours: Timecrime, Inc.*.

22108 *Tournament and tower.* Mahwah, NJ: Troll Associates, 1990, 134 p., cloth, novel. CIRCLE OF MAGIC #2.

with James D. Macdonald as NICHOLAS ADAMS

15974 *Horror High: Pep rally.* New York: HarperPaperbacks, 1991, 155 p., paper, novel. HORROR HIGH #7. [By Debra Doyle & James D. Macdonald].
Pep rally—SEE: *Horror High: Pep rally.*

with James D. Macdonald as VICTOR APPLETON

16736 *Aquatech warriors.* New York, London: An Archway Paperback, Pocket Books, 1991, 154 p., paper, novel. TOM SWIFT

#C6. [By James D. Macdonald and Debra Doyle].

16744 *Monster machine.* New York, London: An Archway Paperback, Pocket Books, 1991, 154 p., paper, novel. TOM SWIFT #C5. [By James D. Macdonald and Debra Doyle].

with James D. Macdonald as ROBYN TALLIS

22109 *Planet builders: Night of ghosts and lightning.* New York: Ivy Books, 1989, 185 p., paper, novel. PLANET BUILDERS #2.

22110 *Planet builders: Zero-sum games.* New York: Ivy Books, 1989, 182 p., paper, novel. PLANET BUILDERS #5.

DOZOIS, Gardner (Raymond), 1947-

Aliens—SEE: *Isaac Asimov's Aliens.*

22111 *Another world: a science fiction anthology.* Chicago: Follett Publishing Co., 1977, 282 p., cloth, anth.
Best new SF 2—SEE: *The year's best science fiction: fifth annual collection.*
Best new SF 3—SEE: *The year's best science fiction: sixth annual collection.*
Best new SF 4—SEE: *The year's best science fiction: seventh annual collection.*
Best new SF 5—SEE: *The year's best science fiction: eighth annual collection.*

22112 *The best of Isaac Asimov's science fiction magazine.* New York: Ace Books, 1988, 258 p., paper, anth.

22113 *Best science fiction stories of the year, sixth annual collection.* New York: E. P. Dutton, 1977, xxii+184 p., cloth, anth.

22114 *Best science fiction stories of the year, seventh annual collection.* New York: E. P. Dutton, 1978, xvi+208 p., cloth, anth.

22115 *Best science fiction stories of the year, eighth annual collection.* New York: E. P. Dutton, 1979, xxi+234 p., cloth, anth.

22116 *Best science fiction stories of the year, ninth annual collection.* New York: E. P. Dutton, 1980, xxx+225 p., cloth, anth.

37709 *Best science fiction stories of the year, tenth annual collection.* New York: E. P. Dutton, 1981, 225 p., cloth, anth.

22117 *The fiction of James Tiptree, Jr.* New York: Algol Press, 1977, [36] p., paper, nonf.

22118 *Isaac Asimov's Aliens.* New York: Ace Books, 1991, 240 p., paper, anth.

22119 *Isaac Asimov's Mars.* New York: Ace Books, 1991, 225 p., paper, anth.

22120 *The Legend book of science fiction.* London: Legend, 1991, 672 p., paper, anth.

The mammoth book of best new science fiction—SEE: *Year's best science fiction, fourth annual collection.*

Mars—SEE: *Isaac Asimov's Mars.*

22121 *The peacemaker.* Eugene, OR: Pulphouse Publishing, 1991, 46 p., cloth, story. SHORT STORY HARDBACKS #21; SHORT STORY PAPERBACKS #39.

22122 *Strangers.* New York: Berkley Publishing Corp., 1978, 191 p., cloth, novel.

22123 *Time travelers: from Isaac Asimov's science fiction magazine.* New York: Ace Books, 1989, 275 p., paper, anth.

22124 *Transcendental tales from Isaac Asimov's science fiction magazine.* Norfolk, VA: Donning Co., 1989, 301 p., paper, anth.

22125 *The visible man.* New York: A Berkley Medallion Book, Berkley Publishing Corp., 1977, 312 p., paper, coll.

22126 *The year's best science fiction, first annual collection.* New York: Bluejay Books, 1984, 575 p., cloth, anth.

22127 *The year's best science fiction, second annual collection.* New York: Bluejay Books, 1985, 573 p., cloth, anth.

22128 *The year's best science fiction, third annual collection.* New York: Bluejay Books, 1986, 624 p., cloth, anth. [Winner of the *Locus* Award for Best Anthology, 1986 (1987)].

22129 *The year's best science fiction, fourth annual collection.* New York: St. Martin's Press, 1987, xxi+602 p., cloth, anth. [Winner of the *Locus* Award for Best Anthology, 1987 (1988)].

22129A retitled: *The mammoth book of best new science fiction.* London: Robinson, 1987, 615 p., paper, anth.

22130 *The year's best science fiction, fifth annual collection.* New York: St. Martin's Press, 1988, 678 p., cloth, anth.

22130A retitled: *Best new SF 2.* London: Robinson, 1988, 678 p., cloth, anth.

22131 *The year's best science fiction, sixth annual collection.* New York: St. Martin's Press, 1989, xxiv+596 p., cloth, anth. [Winner of the *Locus* Award for Best Anthology, 1989 (1990)].

22131A retitled: *Best new SF 3.* London: Robinson Publishing, 1989, xxiv+596 p., paper, anth.

22132 *The year's best science fiction, seventh annual collection.* New York: St. Martin's Press, 1990, xxvi+598 p., cloth, anth. [Winner of the *Locus* Award for Best Anthology, 1990 (1991)].

22132A retitled: *Best new SF 4.* London: Robinson Publishing, 1990, xxvi+598 p., paper, anth.

22133 *The year's best science fiction, eighth annual collection.* New York: St. Martin's Press, 1991, xxxii+624 p., cloth, anth.

22133A retitled: *Best new SF 5.* London: Robinson Publishing, 1991, xxxii+624 p., paper, anth.

with Susan Casper

Jack the Ripper—SEE: *Ripper!*

19638 *Ripper!* New York: Tor Horror, A Tom Doherty Associates Book, 1988, xx+427 p., paper, anth.

19638A retitled: *Jack the ripper.* London: Futura, 1988, 384 p., paper, anth.

with Jack Dann

21122 *Aliens!* New York: Pocket Books, 1980, xi+305 p., paper, anth.

21123 *Bestiary!* New York: Ace Fantasy Books, 1985, 306 p., paper, anth.

21124 *Demons!* New York: Ace Books, 1987, 281 p., paper, anth.

21125 *Dinosaurs!* New York: Ace Books, 1990, 226 p., paper, anth.

21126 *Dogtails!* New York: Ace Books, 1988, 274 p., paper, anth.

21127 *Future power: a science fiction anthology.* New York: Random House, 1976, xxviii+256 p., cloth, anth.

21128 *Little people!* New York: Ace Books, 1991, 221 p., paper, anth.

21129 *Magicats!* New York: Ace Fantasy Books, 1984, xvii+267 p., paper, anth.

21130 *Magicats II.* New York: Ace Books, 1991, 213 p., paper, anth.

21131 *Mermaids!* New York: Ace Fantasy Books, 1986, 260 p., paper, anth.

21132 *Seaserpents!* New York: Ace Books, 1989, xiii+226 p., paper, anth.

21133 *Sorcerers!* New York: Ace Fantasy Books, 1986, xi+244 p., paper, anth.

21134 *Unicorns!* New York: Ace Books, 1982, 310 p., paper, anth.

with Jack Dann & Susan Casper & Jack C. Haldeman II & Michael Swanwick

19639 *Slow dancing through time.* Kansas City, MO: Ursus Imprints; Shingletown, CA: Mark V. Ziesing, 1990, xvii+253 p., cloth, coll. [All the stories are collaborations by Dozois with other writers, the majority with Jack Dann].

with George Alec Effinger

22134 *Nightmare blue.* New York: A Berkley Medallion Book, Berkley Publishing Corp., 1975, 185 p., paper, novel.

with Sheila Williams

22135 *Isaac Asimov's Robots.* New York: Ace Books, 1991, xiv+209 p., paper, anth. *Robots*—SEE: *Isaac Asimov's Robots.*

with others

22136 *Writing science fiction and fantasy: twenty dynamic essays by today's top professionals.* New York: St. Martin's Press, 1991, viii+264 p., cloth, nonf. anth.

DRAINE, Betsy, 1945-

22137 *Substance under pressure: artistic coherence and evolving form in the novels of Doris Lessing.* Madison, WI: University of Wisconsin Press, 1983, xv+224 p., cloth, nonf.

DRAKE, Alexander W(ilson), 1843-1916

22138 *Three midnight stories.* New York: Century Co., 1916, 117 p., cloth, coll. [Limited to 500 copies].

DRAKE, Alison (Claire)

22139 *Lagoon.* New York: Ballantine Books, 1990, 375 p., paper, novel.

DRAKE, Asa, pseud.—SEE: Andersson, C. Dean & Romberg, Nina

DRAKE, David (Allen), 1945-

At any price—SEE: *Hammer's Slammers: At any price.*
22140 *Birds of prey.* New York: Baen Book, 1984, 348 p., cloth, novel.
22141 *Bluebloods.* New York: Baen Books, 1990, 279 p., paper, anth. STARHUNTERS #3.
22142 *Bridgehead.* New York: Tor SF, A Tom Doherty Associates Book, 1986, 279 p., paper, novel.
Counting the cost—SEE: *Hammer's Slammers: Counting the cost.*
22143 *Cross the stars.* New York: Tor, A Tom Doherty Associates Book, 1984, 342 p., paper, novel. HAMMER'S SLAMMERS #2.

22144 *Dagger.* New York: Ace Books, 1988, 250 p., paper, novel. THIEVES' WORLD NOVELS #5.
22145 *The dragon lord.* New York: Berkley Publishing Corp., 1979, 286 p., cloth, novel.
22146 *The forlorn hope.* New York: A Jim Baen Presentation, Tom Doherty Associates, 1984, 318 p., paper, novel.
22147 *Fortress.* New York: Tor Books, 1987, 311 p., cloth, novel.
22148 *From the heart of darkness.* New York: A Jim Baen Presentation, A Tom Doherty Associates Book, 1983, 320 p., paper, coll.
22149 *Hammer's Slammers.* New York: Ace Books, 1979, xiii+274 p., paper, coll. HAMMER'S SLAMMERS #1.
22150 *Hammer's Slammers.* New York: Baen Books, 1987, 318 p., paper, coll. HAMMER'S SLAMMERS #1. [Expanded; includes the original collection plus the short novel, "Tank Lords"].
22151 *Hammer's Slammers: At any price.* New York: Baen Science Fiction Books, 1985, 288 p., paper, novel. HAMMER'S SLAMMERS #3.
22152 *Hammer's Slammers: Counting the cost.* New York: Baen Books, 1987, 267 p., paper, novel. HAMMER'S SLAMMERS #4.
22153 *Hammer's Slammers: Rolling hot.* New York: Baen Books, 1989, 280 p., paper, novel. HAMMER'S SLAMMERS #5.
22154 *Hammer's Slammers: The warrior.* Riverdale, NY: Baen Books, 1991, 275 p., paper, novel. HAMMER'S SLAMMERS #6.
22155 *Lacey and his friends.* New York: Baen Books, 1986, 299 p., paper, coll.
22156 *Men hunting things.* New York: Baen Books, 1988, 271 p., paper, anth. STARHUNTERS #1.
22157 *The military dimension.* Riverdale, NY: Baen Books, 1991, 273 p., paper, coll.
22158 *Northworld.* New York: Ace Books, 1990, 250 p., paper, novel. NORTHWORLD #1.
22159 *Old Nathan.* Riverdale, NY: Baen Books, 1991, 228 p., paper, coll.
22160 *Ranks of bronze.* New York: Baen Science Fiction Books, 1986, 314 p., paper, novel.
Rolling hot—SEE: *Hammer's Slammers: Rolling hot.*
22161 *The sea hag.* New York: Baen Books, 1988, 334 p., paper, novel. WORLD OF CRYSTAL WALLS #1.
22162 *Skyripper.* New York: Tor, A Tom Doherty Associates Book, 1983, 352 p., paper, novel.

22163 *Surface action.* New York: Ace Books, 1990, 236 p., paper, novel.

22164 *Things hunting men.* New York: Baen Books, 1988, 307 p., paper, anth. STARHUNTERS #2.

22165 *Time safari.* New York: Tor, A Tom Doherty Associates Book, 1982, 278 p., paper, novel.

22166 *Vengeance.* New York: Ace Books, 1991, 330 p., paper, novel. NORTHWORLD #2.

22167 *Vettius and his friends.* New York: Baen, 1989, 304 p., paper, coll. [One story in collaboration with Karl Edward Wagner]. *The warrior*—SEE: *Hammer's Slammers: The warrior.*

with Roger MacBride Allen

16304 *The war machine.* New York: Baen Books, 1989, 338 p., paper, novel. CRISIS OF EMPIRE #3.

with L. Sprague de Camp

21350 *The undesired princess; & The enchanted bunny.* New York: Baen Fantasy, 1990, 263+13 p., paper, coll. [Includes Drake's sequel to de Camp's original novel].

with W. C. Dietz

21917 *Cluster command* / by W. C. Dietz. New York: Baen Books, 1989, 276 p., paper, novel. CRISIS OF EMPIRE #2.

with Bill Fawcett

22168 *Breakthrough.* New York: Ace Books, 1989, 294 p., paper, anth. THE FLEET #3.

22169 *Counterattack.* New York: Ace Books, 1988, 311 p., paper, anth. THE FLEET #2.

22170 *Crisis.* New York: Ace Books, 1991, 293 p., paper, anth. THE FLEET #6.

22171 *The fleet.* New York: Ace Books, 1988, 280 p., paper, anth. THE FLEET #1.

22172 *Sworn allies.* New York: Ace Books, 1990, 248 p., paper, anth. THE FLEET #4.

22173 *Total war.* New York: Ace Books, 1990, 278 p., paper, anth. THE FLEET #5.

with Martin H. Greenberg & Charles G. Waugh

22174 *The eternal city.* New York: Baen Books, 1990, 280 p., paper, anth.

22175 *Space dreadnoughts.* New York: Ace Books, 1990, xiii+220 p., paper, anth.

22176 *Space gladiators.* New York: Ace Books, 1989, 310 p., paper, anth.

22177 *Space infantry.* New York: Ace Books, 1989, xii+244 p., paper, anth.

with Jim Kjelgaard

22178 *The hunter returns.* Riverdale, NY: Baen Books, 1991, 275 p., paper, novel. [Expanded and adapted from *Fire-hunter* / by Jim Kjelgaard (see #08301)].

with Henry Kuttner

22179 *The jungle.* New York: Tor SF, A Tom Doherty Associates Book, 1991, 282 p., cloth, coll. [Includes *Clash by night* / by Henry Kuttner, plus Drake's sequel].

with Sandra Miesel

22180 *Heads to the storm.* New York: Baen Books, 1989, 273 p., paper, anth.

22181 *A separate star: a science fiction tribute to Rudyard Kipling.* New York: Baen Books, 1989, 278 p., paper, anth.

with Janet Morris

22182 *Active measures.* New York: Baen Science Fiction Books, 1985, 365 p., paper, novel.

22183 *Explorers in Hell.* New York: Baen Books, 1989, 312 p., paper, novel. HEROES IN HELL #11.

22184 *Kill ratio.* New York: Ace Books, 1987, 268 p., paper, novel.

22185 *Target.* New York: Ace Books, 1989, 312 p., paper, novel.

with S. M. Stirling

22186 *The forge.* Riverdale, NY: Baen Books, 1991, 323 p., paper, novel. GENERALS #1.

with Thomas T. Thomas

22187 *An honorable defense.* New York: Baen Books, 1988, 310 p., paper, novel. CRISIS OF EMPIRE #1.

with Karl Edward Wagner

22188 *Killer.* New York: A Baen Book, 1985, 270 p., paper, novel.

DRAKE, H. L.

22189 *The Null-A worlds of A. E. van Vogt.* Polk City, IA: Chris Drumm Books, 1989, 30 p., paper, nonf. DRUMM BOOKLET #32.

*DRAKE, H(enry) B(urgess), 1894-

DRAKE, Morgan [pseud. of James D. Ferguson]

22190 *Sacrifice.* New York: Leisure Books, 1990, 360 p., paper, novel.

DREADSTONE, Carl, house pseud.

19289 *The bride of Frankenstein.* New York: A Berkley Medallion Book, Berkley Publishing Corp., 1977, xiv+210 p., paper, movie. FRANKENSTEIN SERIES.

22191 *The classic library of horror omnibus.* London: Wingate, 1978, 280 p., cloth, movie coll. [Includes *The mummy* and *The werewolf of London*].

22192 *Creature from the black lagoon.* New York: A Berkley Medallion Book, Berkley Publishing Corp., 1977, x+194 p., paper, movie.

19290 *Dracula's daughter.* New York: A Berkley Medallion Book, Berkley Publishing Corp., 1977, xi+212 p., paper, movie. DRACULA SERIES. [Reprinted under the name E. K. Leyton].

22193 *The mummy.* New York: A Berkley Medallion Book, Berkley Publishing Corp., 1977, ix+166 p., paper, movie.

22194 *The werewolf of London.* New York: A Berkley Medallion Book, Berkley Publishing Corp., 1977, xi+194 p., paper, movie.

19291 *The wolfman.* New York: A Berkley Medallion Book, Berkley Publishing Corp., 1977, xi+212 p., paper, movie.

as E. K. LEYTON

22192A *Creature from the black lagoon.* London: Star Books, 1980, viii+168 p., paper, movie.

19290A *Dracula's daughter.* London: Star Books, 1980, x+182 p., paper, movie. DRACULA SERIES. [originally published under the name Carl Dreadstone].

DREHER, Sarah (Anne), 1937-

22195 *A captive in time: a Stoner McTavish mystery.* Norwich, VT: New Victoria Publishers, 1990, 246 p., paper, novel. STONER MCTAVISH #4.

22196 *Gray magic: a Stoner McTavish mystery.* Norwich, VT: New Victoria Publishers, 1987, 282 p., paper, novel. STONER MCTAVISH #3.

22197 *Something shady: a Stoner McTavish mystery.* Norwich, VT: New Victoria Publishers, 1986, 264 p., paper, novel. STONER MCTAVISH #2.

22198 *Stoner McTavish.* Lebanon, NH: New Victoria Publishers, 1985, 204 p., paper, novel. STONER MCTAVISH #1.

*DREIFUSS, Kurt, 1897-1991

DRENNAN, Paul, 1949-

22199 *Wooden Centauri: a science-fiction novel.* Morley, Yorkshire, England: Elmfield Press, 1975, 224 p., cloth, novel.

DRESSER, Norine, 1931-

22200 *American vampires: fans, victims, & practitioners.* New York: W. W. Norton & Co., 1989, 255 p., cloth, nonf.

DREW, Bernard A(lger), 1950-

22201 *Heroines: a bibliography of women series characters in mystery, espionage, action, science fiction, fantasy, horror, western, romance, and juvenile novels.* New York, London: Garland Publishing, 1989, 400 p., cloth, nonf.

DREW, Wayland, 1932-

22202 **batteries not included: a novel.* New York: Berkley Books, 1987, 213 p., paper, movie.

22203 *Dragonslayer: a novel.* New York: A Del Rey Book, Ballantine Books, 1981, 218 p., paper, movie.

22204 *The Erthring Cycle.* Garden City, NY: Nelson Doubleday, 1986, 657 p., cloth, coll. ERTHRING CYCLE #1-3.

22205 *The Gaian expedient.* New York: A Del Rey Book, Ballantine Books, 1985, 259 p., paper, novel. ERTHRING CYCLE #2.

22206 *Halfway man.* Ottawa, Ontario, Canada: Oberon Press, 1989, 219 p., cloth, novel.

22207 *The master of Norriya.* New York: A Del Rey Book, Ballantine Books, 1986, 243 p., paper, novel. ERTHRING CYCLE #3.

22208 *The memoirs of Alcheringia.* New York: A Del Rey Book, Ballantine Books, 1984, 239 p., paper, novel. ERTHRING CYCLE #1.

22209 *The Wabeno feast.* Toronto, Ontario, Canada: Anansi, 1973, 280 p., cloth, novel.

22210 *Willow: a novel.* New York: A Del Rey Book, Ballantine Books, 1988, 276 p., paper, movie.

*DREYFUSS, Ernst, 1910?-1976?

DRIVER, John

22211 *Hunger of the beast.* New York: Jove Books, 1991, 293 p., paper, novel.

DRUMM, Chris(topher Streit), 1949-

22212 *An Algis Budrys checklist.* Polk City, IA: Chris Drumm, 1983, 16 p., paper, nonf. DRUMM BOOKLET

22213 *A Hal Clement checklist.* Polk City, IA: Chris Drumm, 1983, 8 p., paper, nonf. DRUMM BOOKLET

22214 *A James Gunn checklist.* Polk City, IA: Chris Drumm, 1984, [24] p., paper, nonf. DRUMM BOOKLET

22215 *A John Sladek checklist: pre-publication version.* Polk City, IA: Chris Drumm, 1984, [26] p., paper, nonf. [Despite the title, no other edition was issued]. DRUMM BOOKLET

22216 *A Larry Niven checklist.* Polk City, IA: Chris Drumm, 1983, [24] p., paper, nonf. DRUMM BOOKLET

22217 *An R. A. Lafferty checklist: a bibliographical chronology with notes and index.* Polk City, IA: Chris Drumm, 1983 (i.e., 1984), [31] p., paper, nonf. DRUMM BOOKLET

22218 *A Richard Wilson checklist.* Polk City, IA: Drumm Books, 1986, 16 p., paper, nonf. [Bound with *Adventures in the space trade* / by Richard Wilson]. DRUMM BOOKLET

22219 *A Tom Disch checklist: notes toward a bibliography.* Polk City, IA: Chris Drumm, 1983, [22] p., paper, nonf. DRUMM BOOKLET

with George Flynn

22220 *A Mack Reynolds checklist: notes toward a bibliography.* Polk City, IA: Chris Drumm, 1983, 24 p., paper, nonf. DRUMM BOOKLET

with Paul Guptill

22221 *The many worlds of Larry Niven, 2nd ed.* Polk City, IA: Chris Drumm, 1989, ii+ 63 p., paper, nonf. DRUMM BOOKLET

DRUMM, D. B., house pseud.

22222 *Border war.* New York: A Dell Book, 1985, 172 p., paper, novel. TRAVELER #6. [By John Shirley].

22223 *The children's crusade.* New York: A Dell Book, 1987, 172 p., paper, novel. TRAVELER #11. [By Ed Naha].

22224 *First, you fight.* New York: A Dell Book, 1984, 175 p., paper, novel. TRAVELER #1. [By Ed Naha].

22225 *Ghost dancers.* New York: A Dell Book, 1987, 171 p., paper, novel. TRAVELER #13. [By Ed Naha].

22226 *Hell on Earth.* New York: A Dell Book, 1986, 171 p., paper, novel. TRAVELER #10. [By Ed Naha].

22227 *Kingdom come.* New York: A Dell Book, 1984, 176 p., paper, novel. TRAVELER #2. [By John Shirley].

22228 *The prey.* New York: A Dell Book, 1987, 170 p., paper, novel. TRAVELER #12. [By Ed Naha].

22229 *The road ghost.* New York: A Dell Book, 1985, 172 p., paper, novel. TRAVELER #7. [By Ed Naha].

22230 *Road war.* New York: A Dell Book, 1985, 158 p., paper, novel. TRAVELER #5. [By John Shirley].

22231 *The stalkers.* New York: A Dell Book, 1984, 176 p., paper, novel. TRAVELER #3. [By John Shirley].

22232 *The stalking time.* New York: A Dell Book, 1986, 174 p., paper, novel. TRAVELER #9. [By Ed Naha].

22233 *Terminal road.* New York: A Dell Book, 1986, 173 p., paper, novel. TRAVELER #8. [By John Shirley].

22234 *To kill a shadow.* New York: A Dell Book, 1984, 173 p., paper, novel. TRAVELER #4. [By John Shirley].

DRUON (de Reyniac), Maurice (Samuel Roger Charles), 1918-

15799 *Tistou of the green fingers.* London: Rupert Hart-Davis, 1958, 141 p., cloth, novel.

15799A retitled: *Tistou of the green thumbs.* New York: Charles Scribner's Sons, 1958, 178 p., cloth, novel.

DRURY, Allen (Stuart), 1918-

22235 *The hill of summer: a novel of the Soviet conquest.* Garden City, NY: Doubleday & Co., 1981, xvi+484 p., cloth, novel. HILL OF SUMMER #1.

22236 *The promise of joy.* Garden City, NY: Doubleday & Co., 1975, x+445 p., cloth, novel. ADVISE & CONSENT #6.

22237 *The roads of Earth: a novel.* Garden City, NY: Doubleday & Co., 1984, 368 p., cloth, novel. HILL OF SUMMER #2.

DU AIMÉ, Albert—SEE: Wharton, William

DU MAURIER, Daphne [i.e., Daphne du Maurier Browning, Dame], 1907-1989

22238 *The birds, and other stories.* Harlow, England: Longman, 1980, ix+138 p., cloth, coll. [Edited by Richard Adams].

Classics of the macabre—SEE: *Daphne du Maurier's Classics of the macabre.*

22239 *Daphne du Maurier's Classics of the macabre.* London: Victor Gollancz, 1987, 284 p., cloth, coll.

22240 *Don't look now, and other stories.* Harmondsworth, Middlesex, England: Penguin Books, 1981, 267 p., paper, coll.

22241 *Echoes from the macabre: selected stories.* London: Victor Gollancz, 1976, 348 p., cloth, coll.

37710 *The loving spirit.* London: William Heinemann, 1931, 399 p., cloth, novel.

22242 *Three complete novels and five short stories.* New York: Avenel books, 1981, 677 p., cloth, coll. [Includes *The king's general*, *The house on the strand*, *Don't look now and other stories*].

22243 *Three famous du Maurier novels.* London: Victor Gollancz, 1982, 664 p., cloth, coll. [Includes *The king's general*; *The flight of the falcon*; *The house on the strand*].

DU PONT, Denise

22244 *Women of vision.* New York: St. Martin's Press, 1988, xii+163 p., cloth, nonf. anth.

DU PONT, Diane

22245 *The emerald embrace.* New York: Fawcett Gold Medal, 1980, 319 p., paper, novel.

DUANE, Diane (Elizabeth), 1952-

22246 *Deep wizardry.* New York: Delacorte Press, 1985, 272 p., cloth, novel. NITA & KIT #2.

Doctor's orders—SEE: *Star Trek: Doctor's orders.*

22247 *The door into fire.* New York: A Dell Book, 1979, 304 p., paper, novel. EPIC TALES OF THE FIVE #1.

22248 *The door into shadow.* New York: Bluejay Books, 1984, xii+298 p., cloth, novel. EPIC TALES OF THE FIVE #2.

22249 *High wizardry.* New York: Delacorte Press, 1990, 269 p., cloth, novel. NITA & KIT #3.

22250 *My enemy, my ally: a Star Trek novel.* New York: Pocket books, 1984, 309 p., paper, novel. STAR TREK #18.

22251 *So you want to be a wizard?* New York: Delacorte Press, 1983, 226 p., cloth, novel. NITA & KIT #1.

Spock's world—SEE: *Star Trek: Spock's world.*

22252 *Star Trek: Doctor's orders.* New York, London: Pocket Books, 1990, 291 p., paper, novel. STAR TREK #50.

22253 *Star Trek: Spock's world: a novel.* New York, London: Pocket Books, 1988, 310 p., cloth, novel. STAR TREK (UNNUMBERED).

22254 *Support your local wizard.* New York: Guild America Books, 1990, 473 p., cloth, coll. NITA & KIT #1-3.

22255 *The wounded sky: a Star Trek novel.* New York: A Timescape Book, Pocket Books, 1983, 255 p., paper, novel. STAR TREK #13.

with Peter Morwood

22256 *Keeper of the city.* New York: Bantam Books, 1989, x+309 p., paper, novel. GUARDIANS OF THE THREE #2. [Created by Bill Fawcett].

Mindblast—SEE: *Space cops: Mindblast.*

22257 *The Romulan way: a Star Trek novel.* New York: Pocket Books, 1987, 254 p., paper, novel. STAR TREK #35.

22258 *Space cops: Mindblast.* New York: Avon Books, 1991, 250 p., paper, novel. SPACE COPS #1.

DUBAY, Sandra, 1954-

22259 *The Claverleigh curse.* New York: Zebra Books, Kensington Publishing Corp., 1982, 270 p., paper, novel.

DUBBS, Chris

22260 *Ms. Faust.* New York: Richardson & Steirman, 1985, 253 p., cloth, novel.

DUBOIS, D., *with K. S. T'Lan*

22261 *T'Zad'U, part 2.* Brackley, Northamptonshire, England: [s.n.], 1982, p., paper, novel. STAR TREK SERIES.

*DuBOIS, Gaylord, <u>1899-</u>

*DuBOIS, Theodora (McCormick), <u>1890-1986</u>

DUBOWSKI, Cathy East

22262 *The ring, the witch, and the crystal: an Ewok adventure, based on the television movie Ewoks.* New York: Random House, 1986, [32] p., cloth, movie. STAR WARS SERIES.

22263 *Willow: the storybook based on the movie.* New York: Random House, 1988, [58] p., cloth, movie.

DuBREUIL, Elizabeth L.—SEE: DuBreuil, Linda

DuBREUIL, Linda [i.e., Elizabeth Lorinda DuBreuil], 1924-1980

as KATE CAMERON

37711 *Deadly nightshade.* New York: Leisure Books, 1975, 165 p., paper, novel. HOLDERLY HALL #4.

37712 *The legend of Holderly Hall.* New York: Leisure Books, 1974, [192] p., paper, novel. HOLDERLY HALL #1.

22264 *Music from the past.* New York: Leisure Books, 1975, 201 p., paper, novel. HOLDERLY HALL #5.

22265 *Portraits of the past.* New York: Leisure Books, 1975, 215 p., paper, novel. HOLDERLY HALL #6.

37713 *Shadows of the past.* New York: Leisure Books, 1974, 198 p., paper, novel. HOLDERLY HALL #2.

37714 *Voices in the fog.* New York: Leisure Books, 1975, 192 p., paper, novel. HOLDERLY HALL #3.

as ELIZABETH L. GRIFFEN

06362 *The shaggy dog.* New York: Scholastic Book Services, 1967, 96 p., paper, movie.

as LORINDA HAGEN

22266 *Amy Jean.* New York: Belmont Tower Books, 1977, 252 p., paper, novel.

as ELIZABETH HANLEY

22267 *Ms. President.* New York: Belmont Tower Books, 1977, 214 p., paper, novel.

with Jeffrey Wallman as MARGARET MAITLAND

22268 *Love's golden circle.* New York: Leisure Books, 1978, 304 p., paper, novel.

DUCHACEK, Ivo—SEE: Duka, Ivo

DUCHAMP, L. Timmel

22269 *A case of mistaken identity.* Eugene, OR: Pulphouse Publishing, 1991, 46 p., paper, story. SHORT STORY PAPERBACKS #7.

DUDGEON, Robert Ellis, 1820-1904, *as* ANONYMOUS AUTHOR

37715 *Columbia.* London: Trübner, 1873, 255 p., cloth, novel.

DUDLEY, Terence

Black orchid—SEE: *Doctor Who: Black orchid.*

22270 *Doctor Who: Black orchid.* London: W. H. Allen, 1986, 143 p., cloth, tele. DOCTOR WHO #113.

22271 *Doctor Who: The king's demons.* London: W. H. Allen, 1986, 153 p., cloth, tele. DOCTOR WHO #108.

22272 *K9 and company.* London: A Target Book, W. H. Allen & Co., 1987, 160 p., paper, tele. COMPANIONS OF DR. WHO #3.

The king's demons—SEE: *Doctor Who: The king's demons.*

DUDLEY-SMITH, Trevor—SEE: Trevor, Elleston

DUFFY, Maureen (Patricia), 1933-

22273 *The erotic world of faery.* London: Hodder & Stoughton, 1972, 352 p., cloth, nonf.

22274 *Gor saga.* London: Eyre Methuen, 1981, 221 p., cloth, novel.

DUIGON, Lee

22275 *Lifeblood.* New York: Pinnacle Books, Windsor Publishing Corp., 1988, 432 p., paper, novel.

22276 *Mindstealer.* New York: Pinnacle Books, Windsor Publishing Corp., 1990, 286 p., paper, novel.

22277 *Precog.* New York: Pinnacle Books, Windsor Publishing Corp., 1990, 288 p., paper, novel.

22278 *Schoolhouse.* New York: Pinnacle Books, Windsor Publishing Corp., 1988, 317 p., paper, novel.

*DUKA, Ivo [pseud. of Ivo Maria Rudolf Duchacek], 1913-1988

DUKE, Madeleine [i.e., Elizabeth Madeleine Duke Macfarlane], 1919-

22279 *Flashpoint.* London: Michael Joseph, 1982, 286 p., cloth, novel.

DUNAWAY, David King, 1948-

22280 *Huxley in Hollywood.* New York: A Cornelia & Michael Bessie Book, Harper & Row, Publishers, 1989, xviii+458 p., cloth, nonf.

DUNBAR, Joyce

22281 *Mundo and the weather-child.* London: Heinemann, 1985, 158 p., cloth, novel.

DUNBAR, Robert

22282 *The pines.* New York: Leisure Books, 1989, 359 p., paper, novel.

DUNCAN, Dave [i.e., David John Duncan], 1933-

22283 *The coming of wisdom.* New York: A Del Rey Book, Ballantine Books, 1988, 337 p., paper, novel. SEVENTH SWORD #2.

22284 *The destiny of the sword.* New York: A Del Rey Book, Ballantine Books, 1988, 338 p., paper, novel. SEVENTH SWORD #3.

22285 *Faery lands forlorn.* New York: A Del Rey Book, Ballantine Books, 1991, 335 p., paper, novel. A MAN OF HIS WORD #2.

22286 *Hero!* New York: A Del Rey Book, Ballantine Books, 1991, 293 p., paper, novel.

22287 *Magic casement.* New York: A Del Rey Book, Ballantine Books, 1990, 307 p., paper, novel. A MAN OF HIS WORD #1.

22288 *Perilous seas.* New York: A Del Rey Book, Ballantine Books, 1991, 336 p., paper, novel. A MAN OF HIS WORD #3.

22289 *The reluctant swordsman.* New York: A Del Rey Book, Ballantine Books, 1988, 326 p., paper, novel. SEVENTH SWORD #1.

22290 *A rose-red city.* New York: A Del Rey Book, Ballantine Books, 1987, 230 p., paper, novel.

22291 *Shadow.* New York: A Del Rey Book, Ballantine Books, 1987, 276 p., paper, novel.

22292 *Strings.* New York: A Del Rey Book, Ballantine Books, 1990, 311 p., paper, novel.

22293 *West of January.* New York: A Del Rey Book, Ballantine Books, 1989, 343 p., paper, novel.

DUNCAN, David J.—SEE: Duncan, Dave

DUNCAN, Jody, *with Don Shay*

22294 *The making of T2, Terminator 2: Judgment day.* New York, Toronto: Bantam Books, 1991, 127 p., paper, nonf.

DUNCAN, Kirk, *with Rico Gusman*

22295 *Albatross.* England: Ithkos Publications, 1988, 119 p., paper, novel.

DUNCAN, Lois [i.e., Lois S. Duncan Arquette], 1934-

The eyes of Karen Connors—SEE: The third eye.

22296 *Locked in time.* Boston: Little, Brown & Co., 1985, 210 p., cloth, novel.

22297 *Stranger with my face.* Boston: Little, Brown & Co., 1981, 250 p., cloth, novel.

22298 *Summer of fear.* Boston: Little, Brown & Co., 1976, 217 p., cloth, novel.

22299 *The third eye.* Boston: Little, Brown & Co., 1984, 220 p., cloth, novel.

22299A retitled: *The eyes of Karen Connors.* London: Hamilton, 1985, 220 p., cloth, novel.

DUNCAN, Robert L(ipscomb), 1927-

22300 *The serpent's mark.* New York: St. Martin's Press, 1989, 289 p., cloth, novel.

*DUNCAN, Ronald (Frederick Henry), 1914-1982

DUNLAP, Joseph (Riggs), 1913-1984?, *with Carole Silver*

22301 *Studies in the late romances of William Morris: papers presented at the annual meeting of the Modern Language Association, December 1975.* New York: William Morris Society, 1976, 139 p., paper, nonf. anth.

DUNLOP, Eileen (Rhona), 1938-

22302 *The chip shop ghost.* London: Blackie Children's Books, 1991, 128 p., cloth, novel.

22303 *Clementina.* Oxford, England: Oxford University Press, 1985, [160] p., cloth, novel.

Elizabeth, Elizabeth—SEE: *Robinsheugh.*

22304 *The house on the hill.* Oxford, England: Oxford University Press, 1987, [160] p., cloth, novel.

22305 *The maze stone.* Oxford, England: Oxford University Press, 1982, 140 p., cloth, novel.

22306 *Robinsheugh.* London: Oxford University Press, 1975, v+185 p., cloth, novel.

22306A retitled: *Elizabeth, Elizabeth.* New York: Holt, Rinehart & Winston, 1977, 185 p., cloth, novel.

22307 *The Valley of Deer.* Oxford, England: Oxford University Press, 1989, [160] p., cloth, novel.

DUNMORE, Spencer (Sambrook), 1928-

22308 *The sound of wings.* London: Heinemann, 1984, 280 p., cloth, novel.

DUNN, Dawn (Pauline Hartzell), 1958- , with Susan Hartzell as PAULINE DUNN

22309 *The crawling dark.* New York: Zebra Books, Kensington Publishing Corp., 1991, 349 p., paper, novel. [Based on Dean Koontz's novel, *Phantoms*].

22310 *Demonic color.* New York: Zebra Books, Kensington Publishing Corp., 1990, 351 p., paper, novel. [Based on Dean Koontz's novel, *Phantoms*].

22311 *Flesh stealer.* New York: Zebra Books, Kensington Publishing Corp., 1990, 317 p., paper, novel.

DUNN, Dennis

22312 *The big trucker: a magical novel.* San Francisco: Dancing Rock Press, 1979, 222 p., cloth, novel.

***DUNN, Gertrude [pseud. of Gertrude Renton Weaver], 1884-1926**

DUNN, Katherine (Karen), 1945-

22313 *Geek love.* New York: Alfred A. Knopf, 1989, 347 p., cloth, novel.

DUNN, Pauline, pseud.—SEE: Dunn, Dawn & Hartzell, Susan

DUNN, Philip—SEE: Dunn, Saul

DUNN, Saul [i.e., Philip M. Dunn], 1946-

22314 *The black moon.* London: Corgi Books, 1978, 174 p., paper, novel. CABAL #2.

22315 *The Cabal.* London: Corgi Books, 1978, 175 p., paper, novel. CABAL #1.

22316 *The coming of Steeleye.* London: Coronet Books, Hodder & Stoughton, 1976, 142 p., paper, novel. STEELEYE #1.

22317 *The evangelist.* London: Corgi Books, 1979, 157 p., paper, novel. CABAL #3.

22318 *Steeleye: The Wideways.* London: Coronet Books, Hodder & Stoughton, 1976, 159 p., paper, novel. STEELEYE #2.

22319 *Steeleye: Waterspace.* London: Coronet Books, Hodder & Stoughton, 1976, 144 p., paper, novel. STEELEYE #3.

Waterspace—SEE: *Steeleye: Waterspace.*

The Wideways—SEE: *Steeleye: The Wideways.*

as PHILIP DUNN

22314A *The black moon.* New York: Berkley Books, 1982, 201 p., paper, novel. CABAL #2. [Originally published under the name Saul Dunn].

22315A *The Cabal.* New York: Berkley Books, 1981, 184 p., paper, novel. CABAL #1. [Originally published under the name Saul Dunn].

22317A *The evangelist.* New York: Berkley Books, 1982, 187 p., paper, novel. CABAL #3. [Originally published under the name Saul Dunn].

DUNN, Thomas P(eckham), 1940- , with Richard D. Erlich

22320 *Clockwork worlds: mechanized environments in SF.* Westport, CT, London: Greenwood Press, 1983, xiii+369 p., cloth, nonf. CONTRIBUTIONS TO THE STUDY OF SCIENCE FICTION AND FANTASY #7.

22321 *The mechanical god: machines in science fiction.* Westport, CT, London: Greenwood Press, 1982, xiv+284 p., cloth, nonf. anth. CONTRIBUTIONS TO THE STUDY OF SCIENCE FICTION AND FANTASY #1.

DUNNE, Thomas L(eo), 1946-

22322 *The scourge.* New York: Coward, McCann & Geoghegan, 1978, 312 p., cloth, novel.

DUNNING, Brad, 1957- , *with Bart Andrews*

16471 *Star Trek quiz book: 1,001 trivia teasers for trekkies.* New York: A Signet Book, New American Library, 1977, 150 p., paper, nonf.
16471A retitled: *The trekkie quiz book: 1,001 teasers for trekkies.* New York: A Signet Book, New American Library, 1978, 150 p., paper, nonf.
    The trekkie quiz book—SEE: *Star Trek quiz book.*

DUNSANY, Lord [i.e., Edward John Moreton Drax Plunkett, 18th Baron Dunsany], 1878-1957

22323 *The ghosts of the heaviside layers, and other fantasms.* Philadelphia, PA: Owlswick Press, 1980, x+354 p., cloth, coll. [Includes some nonfiction and plays].

DUPONT, Inge, *with Hope Mayo*

37716 *Morgan Library ghost stories.* New York: Fordham University Press, 1990, 107 p., cloth, anth.

DUPREY, Richard (Allen), 1929- , *with Brian O'Leary*

22324 *Spaceship Titanic.* New York: Dodd, Mead & Co., 1983, 230 p., cloth, novel.

DURANT, Frederick C(lark) III, 1916- , *with Ron Miller & Chesley Bonestell*

22325 *Worlds beyond: the art of Chesley Bonestell.* Norfolk, Virginia Beach, VA: A Starblaze Special, Donning Co., 1983, 133 p., paper, art.

DURHAM, Guy

22326 *Stealth.* New York: G. P. Putnam's Sons, 1989, 334 p., cloth, novel.

DURIE, Alistair (J. L.)

22327 *Weird tales.* London: Jupiter, 1979, 128 p., cloth, art.

DURIEZ, Colin

22328 *The C. S. Lewis handbook: a comprehensive guide to his life, thought, and writings.* Grand Rapids, MI: Baker Book House, 1990, 255 p., paper, nonf.

*DURKIN, Douglas (Leader), 1884-1967

DURRELL, Lawrence (George), 1912-1990

22329 *Balthazar.* London: Faber & Faber, 1958, 250 p., cloth, novel.
22330 *The revolt of Aphrodite.* London: Faber & Faber, 1974, 317+285 p., cloth, coll. [Includes *Tunc* and *Nunquam*].

DURWOOD, Thomas

22331 *Ariel.* Kansas City, MO: Morning Star Press; New York: Ballantine Books, 1977, 79 p., paper, anth.
22332 *Ariel, the book of fantasy, volume two.* Kansas City, MO: A Thomas Durwood/ Armand Eisen Publication, Ariel Books, 1977?, 79 p., paper, anth.
22333 *Ariel, the book of fantasy, volume three.* Kansas City, MO: A Thomas Durwood/ Armand Eisen Publication, Ariel Books, 1977?, 95 p., paper, anth.
22334 *Ariel, the book of fantasy, volume four.* Kansas City, MO: A Thomas Durwood/ Armand Eisen Publication, Ariel Books, 1978, 94 p., paper, anth.
22335 *Close Encounters of the Third Kind: a document of the film.* Kansas City, MO: Ariel Books, 1978, [147] p., paper, nonf.

with Armand Eisen

22336 *Masterpieces of science fiction.* Kansas City, MO: A Thomas Durwood/Armand Eisen Production, Ariel Books, 1978, 107 p., paper, anth.

DVORKIN, Daniel, 1969- , *with David Dvorkin*

22337 *The captains' honor.* New York, London: Pocket Books, 1989, 255 p., paper, novel. STAR TREK THE NEXT GENERATION #8.

DVORKIN, David, 1943-

22338 *Budspy.* New York, Toronto: Franklin Watts, 1987, 259 p., cloth, novel.
22339 *Central heat.* New York: Ace Books, 1988, 294 p., paper, novel.
22340 *The children of Shiny Mountain.* New York: A Kangaroo Book, Pocket Books, 1977, 279 p., paper, novel.
22340A retitled: *Shiny Mountain.* London: Magnum Books, 1978, viii+279 p., paper, novel.
22341 *The green god.* New York: Pocket Books, 1979, 238 p., paper, novel.
22342 *The seekers.* New York, Toronto: Franklin Watts, 1988, 283 p., cloth, novel.

Shiny Mountain—SEE: *The children of Shiny Mountain.*

22343 *Star Trek: Timetrap.* New York, London: Pocket Books, 1988, 221 p., paper, novel. STAR TREK #40.

22344 *Time for Sherlock Holmes: a novel.* New York: Dodd, Mead & Co., 1983, 200 p., cloth, novel.

Timetrap—SEE: *Star Trek: Timetrap.*

22345 *The Trellisane confrontation: a Star Trek novel.* New York: Pocket Books, 1984, 190 p., paper, novel. STAR TREK #14.

22346 *Ursus.* New York, Toronto: Franklin Watts, 1989, 379 p., cloth, novel.

with Daniel Dvorkin

22337 *The captains' honor.* New York, London: Pocket Books, 1989, 255 p., paper, novel. STAR TREK THE NEXT GENERATION #8.

DWIGGINS, Elmer—SEE: **Douglass, Ellsworth**

***DWINELL, Ralph M(ilton), 1894-<u>1978</u>**

DWINNELL, R(alph) M(ilton), 1894-

22347 *The gates of creation.* Boston: Bruce Humphries, 1934, 270 p., cloth, novel.

DWYER, James Francis, 1874-1952

22348 *Cold-Eyes.* London: Methuen & Co., 1934, vii+277 p., cloth, novel.

DYCKE, Ignatz Sahula- —SEE: **Sahula-Dycke, Ignatz**

DYER, Alfred

22349 *The Gabriel inheritance.* London: Robert Hale, 1981, 176 p., cloth, novel.

22350 *The symbiotic mind.* London: Robert Hale, 1980, 223 p., cloth, novel.

DYER, Wayne (Walter), 1940-

22351 *Gifts from Eykis.* New York: Simon & Schuster, 1983, 191 p., cloth, novel.

DYER-BENNET, Pamela—SEE: **Dean, Pamela**

DYKEWOMAN, Elana [pseud. of Elana Nachman/Dykewoman, originally Elana Nachman]

22352 *They will know me by my teeth: stories and poems of Lesbian struggle, celebration, and survival.* Northampton, MA: Magaera Press, 1976, 117 p., cloth?, coll.

DZIEMIANOWICZ, Stefan R(ichard), 1957-

22353 *The annotated guide to Unknown & Unknown Worlds.* Mercer Island, WA: Starmont House, 1991, 212 p., cloth, nonf. STARMONT STUDIES IN LITERARY CRITICISM #13.

with Robert Weinberg & Martin H. Greenberg

22354 *Famous fantastic mysteries: 30 great tales of fantasy and horror from the classic pulp magazines Famous fantastic mysteries & Fantastic novels.* New York: Gramercy Books, 1991, xiii+449 p., cloth, anth.

22355 *Rivals of Weird tales: 30 great fantasy & horror stories from the weird fiction pulps.* New York: Bonanza Books, 1990, xx+486 p., cloth, anth.

22356 *Weird tales: 32 unearthed terrors.* New York: Bonanza Books, 1988, xv+665 p., cloth, anth.

E

EAKINS, William (K.)

22357 *Key West, 2720 A.D.* Stamford, CT: Knights Press, 1989, 211 p., paper, novel.

EARLS, Bill [i.e., William Earls]

22358 *The gladiator.* New York: A Dell Book, 1981, 255 p., paper, novel.

EARLS, H. Clayton

22359 *Trying times.* New York, Washington: Vantage Press, 1989, 209 p., cloth, novel.

EARLS, William—SEE: Earls, Bill

EARNSHAW, Brian, 1924-

22360 *Dragonfall 5 and the haunted world.* London: Methuen, 1979, 159 p., cloth, novel. DRAGONFALL 5 #7.

22361 *Dragonfall 5 and the master mind.* London: Methuen Children Books, 1975, 175 p., cloth, novel. DRAGONFALL 5 #5.

22362 *Dragonfall 5 and the super horse.* London: Methuen Children's Books, 1977, 148 p., cloth, novel. DRAGONFALL 5 #6.

22363 *Starclipper and the galactic final.* London: Methuen Children's Books, 1987, 126 p., cloth, novel. STAR JAM PACK #3.

22364 *Starclipper and the song wars.* London: A Pied Piper Book, Methuen Children's Books, 1985, 124 p., cloth, novel. STAR JAM PACK #1.

22365 *Starclipper on the snowstone.* London: A Pied Piper Book, Methuen Children's Books, 1986, [128] p., cloth, novel. STAR JAM PACK #2.

EASTERMAN, Daniel [pseud. of Denis Mac-Eoin], 1949-

22366 *Night of the seventh darkness.* London: Grafton, 1991, 448 p., cloth, novel.

as JONATHAN AYCLIFFE

22367 *Naomi's room.* London: HarperCollins-Publishers, 1991, 173 p., cloth, novel.

EASTON, Agnes—SEE: Buckingham, M. E.

EASTON, Edward [pseud. of Edward P. Malerich], 1940-

22368 *The miscast gentleman.* New York: Manor Books, 1978, 365 p., paper, novel.

22369 *The pirate of Hitchfield.* New York: Manor Books, 1978, 285 p., paper, novel.

EASTON, M(alcolm) Coleman, 1942-

22370 *The fisherman's curse.* New York: Popular Library, 1987, 236 p., paper, novel. KYALA #2.

22371 *Iskiir.* New York: Popular Library, Warner Books, 1986, 259 p., paper, novel.

22372 *Masters of glass.* New York: Popular Library, Warner Books, 1985, 245 p., paper, novel. KYALA #1.

22373 *Spirits of cavern and hearth.* New York: St. Martin's Press, 1988, 294 p., cloth, novel.

22374 *Swimmers beneath the bright.* New York: Popular Library, 1987, 236 p., paper, novel.

EASTON, Thomas A(twood), 1944-

22375 *Greenhouse.* New York: Ace Books, 1991, 246 p., paper, novel. SPARROWHAWK #2.

22376 *Sparrowhawk.* New York: Ace Books, 1990, 230 p., paper, novel. SPARROWHAWK #1.

as RALPH BUNDY

22377 *Drugged sex.* North Hollywood, CA: Aquarius 7 Publishers, 1976?, 189 p., paper, novel.

ECA DE QUEIROZ—SEE: Queirós, Eça de

ECCARIUS, J. G.

22378 *The last days of Christ the vampire.* San Diego, CA: III Publishing, 1988, 180 p., paper, novel.

22379 *We should have killed the king.* San Diego, CA: III Publishing, 1990, 191 p., paper, novel.

ECCLES, W. H. T.

22380 *One house: Taurus.* London: Merlin, 1988, 146 p., paper, novel. ONE HOUSE #1.
Taurus—SEE: *One house: Taurus.*

ECKERT, Allan W(esley), 1931-

22381 *The dark green tunnel.* Boston: Little, Brown & Co., 1984, 216 p., cloth, novel. MESMERIAN ANNALS #1.

22382 *The HAB Theory: a novel.* Boston: Little, Brown, 1976, 566 p., cloth, novel.
The return to Mesmeria—SEE: *The wand: the return to Mesmeria.*

22383 *Song of the wild.* Boston: Little, Brown & Co., 1980, 225 p., cloth, novel.

22384 *The wand: the return to Mesmeria.* Boston, Toronto: Little, Brown & Co., 1985, 214 p., cloth, novel. MESMERIAN ANNALS #2.

ECKLAR, Julia (Marie), 1964-

The Kobayashi Maru—SEE: *Star Trek: The Kobayashi Maru.*

22385 *Star Trek: The Kobayashi Maru.* New York, London: Pocket Books, 1989, 254 p., paper, tele. STAR TREK #47.

ECKSTROM, Michael—SEE: Jade, Symon

ECO, Umberto, 1932-

22386 *Foucault's pendulum.* Franklin Center, PA: Franklin Library, 1989, 641 p., cloth, novel. [Translation by William Weaver of *Pendolo di Foucault*].

with Thomas A. Sebeok

22387 *The sign of three: Dupin, Holmes, Peirce.* Bloomington, IN: Indiana University Press, 1983, xi+236 p., cloth, nonf. anth.

ECORDIAN, G., pseud.

22388 *The eye of Argon.* Eugene, OR: Hypatia Press, 1987, iv+54 p., paper, story.

EDDINGS, David (Carroll), 1931-

22389 *The Belgariad.* Garden City, NY: Nelson Doubleday, 1985, 2 v. (I-759 p.; II-626 p.), cloth, coll. BELGARIAD #1-5. [Part one includes *Pawn of prophecy, Queen of sorcery, Magician's gambit*; part two includes *Castle of wizardry* and *Enchanters' end game*].

22390 *Castle of wizardry.* New York: A Del Rey Book, Ballantine Books, 1984, 373 p., paper, novel. BELGARIAD #4.

22391 *Demon lord of Karanda.* New York: A Del Rey Book, Ballantine Books, 1988, 422 p., cloth, novel. MALLOREON #3.

22392 *The diamond throne.* New York: A Del Rey Book, Ballantine Books, 1989, 448 p., cloth, novel. ELENIUM #1.

22393 *Enchanters' end game.* New York: A Del Rey Book, Ballantine Books, 1984, 372 p., paper, novel. BELGARIAD #5.

22394 *Guardians of the west.* New York: A Del Rey Book, Ballantine Books, 1987, 454 p., cloth, novel. MALLOREON #1.

22395 *King of the Murgos.* London: Bantam Press, 1988, 416 p., cloth, novel. MALLOREON #2.

22396 *Magician's gambit.* New York: A Del Rey Book, Ballantine Books, 1983, 305 p., paper, novel. BELGARIAD #3.

22397 *Pawn of prophecy.* New York: A Del Rey Book, Ballantine Books, 1982, 256 p., paper, novel. BELGARIAD #1.

22398 *Queen of sorcery.* New York: A Del Rey Book, Ballantine Books, 1982, 327 p., paper, novel. BELGARIAD #2.

22399 *The ruby knight.* London: Grafton, 1990, 347 p., cloth, novel. ELENIUM #2.

22400 *The sapphire rose.* London: Harper-Collins, 1991, 525 p., cloth, novel. ELENIUM #3.

22401 *The seeress of Kell.* New York: A Del Rey Book, Ballantine Books, 1991, xv+399 p., cloth, novel. MALLOREON #5.

22402 *Sorceress of Darshiva.* New York: A Del Rey Book, Ballantine Books, 1989, 406 p., cloth, novel. MALLOREON #4.

EDDINGS, Dennis W(ayne), 1938-

22403 *The naiad voice: essays on Poe's satiric hoaxer.* Port Washington, NY: National University Publications, Associated Faculty Press, 1983, xii+175 p., cloth, nonf. anth.

EDDY, C(lifford) M(artin) Jr., 1896-1967, with Muriel E. Eddy

37717 *Erased from exile.* Lamoni, IA: Stygian Isle Press, 1976, 31 p., paper, coll. [Cover title; limited to 300 copies; includes some verse].

EDDY, Muriel E., 1896-1978, with C. M. Eddy

37717 *Erased from exile.* Lamoni, IA: Stygian Isle Press, 1976, 31 p., paper, coll. [Cover title; limited to 300 copies; includes some verse].

EDELMAN, Scott (Jeffrey), 1955-

22404 *The gift.* New York: Space & Time, 1990, 178 p., paper, novel.

EDELSON, Edward, 1932-

Great science fiction from the movies— SEE: *Visions of tomorrow.*
22405 *Visions of tomorrow: great science fiction from the movies.* Garden City, NY: Doubleday & Co., 1975, 117 p., cloth, nonf.
22405A retitled: *Great science fiction from the movies.* New York: An Archway Paperback, Pocket Books, 1976, 149 p., paper, nonf.

EDELSTEIN, Scott (Samuel), 1954-

22406 *Future pastimes.* Nashville, TN & London: Aurora Publishers, 1977, viii+325 p., cloth, anth.

*EDGAR, Ken(neth Frank), 1925-

EDGERTON, Teresa (Ann), 1949-

22407 *Child of Saturn.* New York: Ace Books, 1989, 276 p., paper, novel. GREEN LION TRILOGY #1.
22408 *The gnome's engine.* New York: Ace Books, 1991, 265 p., paper, novel. GOBLIN #2.
22409 *Goblin moon.* New York: Ace Books, 1991, 293 p., paper, novel. GOBLIN #1.
22410 *The moon in hiding.* New York: Ace Books, 1989, 208 p., paper, novel. GREEN LION TRILOGY #2.
22411 *The work of the sun.* New York: Ace Books, 1990, 258 p., paper, novel. GREEN LION TRILOGY #3.

EDMONDS, Gill

22412 *The common.* London: Blond & Briggs, 1984, 167 p., cloth, novel.

EDMONDS, Harry (Moreton Southey), 1891-1989

37718 *The clockmaker of Heidelburg; or, The strange affair of Hugh Brodie, Englishman.* London: Macdonald & Co., 1949, 240 p., cloth, novel.

EDMONDS, Helen Woods—SEE: Kavan, Anna

EDMONDS, Walter D(umaux Jr.), 1903-

15801 *Hound dog Moses and the promised land.* New York: Dodd, Mead & Co., 1954, 81 p., cloth, story.

EDMONDSON, G. C. [i.e., José Mario Garry Ordoñez Edmondson y Cotton], 1922-

22413 *The aluminum man.* New York: A Berkley Medallion Book, Berkley Publishing Corp., 1975, 172 p., paper, novel.
22414 *The man who corrupted Earth.* New York: Ace Books, 1980, 312 p., paper, novel.
22415 *The ship that sailed the time stream.* New York: Ace Books, 1978, 274 p., paper, novel. SHIP THAT SAILED THE TIME STREAM #1. [Expanded edition of #04695].
22416 *To sail the century sea.* New York: Ace Books, 1981, 194 p., paper, novel. SHIP THAT SAILED THE TIME STREAM #2.

with C. M. Kotlan

22418 *The black magician.* New York: A Del Rey Book, Ballantine Books, 1986, 298 p., paper, novel. CUNNINGHAM #2.
22419 *The Cunningham equations.* New York: A Del Rey Book, Ballantine Books, 1986, 295 p., paper, novel. CUNNINGHAM #1.
22420 *Maximum effort.* New York: A Del Rey Book, Ballantine Books, 1987, 299 p., paper, novel. CUNNINGHAM #3.
22421 *The takeover.* New York: Ace Science Fiction Books, 1984, 284 p., paper, novel.

with Andrew J. Offutt as JOHN CLEVE

22417 *Star slaver.* New York: Berkley Books, 1983, 211 p., paper, novel. SPACEWAYS #12.

EDMONDSON Y COTTON, José—SEE: Edmondson, G. C.

EDSON, J(ohn) T(homas), 1928-

22422 *Bunduki.* London: Corgi Books, 1975, 204 p., paper, novel. BUNDUKI #1.

22423 *Bunduki and Dawn.* London: Corgi Books, 1976, 190 p., paper, novel. BUNDUKI #2.

22424 *The fast gun.* London: Sabre Books, Brown, Watson, 1967, 158 p., paper, novel.

22425 *Fearless master of the jungle.* London: Corgi Books, 1980, 220 p., paper, novel. BUNDUKI #4.

22426 *Sacrifice for the Quagga God.* London: Corgi Books, 1976, 205 p., paper, novel. BUNDUKI #3.

22427 *Set a-Foot.* London: Corgi Books, 1978, 205 p., paper, novel.

EDWARDS, Anne, 1927-

22428 *Child of night.* New York: Random House, 1975, 174 p., cloth, novel.

EDWARDS, Bruce L(ee Jr.), 1952-

22429 *The taste of the pineapple: essays on C. S. Lewis as reader, critic, and imaginative writer.* Bowling Green, OH: Bowling Green State University Popular Press, 1988, x+246 p., cloth, nonf. anth.

EDWARDS, Claudia J(ane), 1943-

22430 *Bright and shining tiger.* New York: Popular Library, 1988, 218 p., paper, novel. FOREST KING #3.

22431 *Eldrie the healer.* New York: Pageant Books, 1989, 237 p., paper, novel. BASTARD PRINCESS #1.

22432 *A horsewoman in Godsland.* New York: Popular Library, 1987, 219 p., paper, novel. FOREST KING #2.

22433 *Taming the Forest King.* New York: Popular Library, Warner Books, 1986, 215 p., paper, novel. FOREST KING #1.

EDWARDS, David, 1945?-

22434 *Dreams, tales, & lullabies: stories from my grandfather's house.* Newbury Park, CA: Lexicon Books, 1985, 123 p., cloth, coll.

EDWARDS, Dorothy, 1914-1982

22435 *Ghosts and shadows.* Guildford, England: Lutterworth Press, 1980, 160 p., cloth, anth.

22436 *Mists and magic.* Guildford, England: Lutterworth Press, 1983, 159 p., cloth, anth.

*EDWARDS, Gawain [pseud. of George Edward Pendray], 1901-1987

EDWARDS, Gene, 1932-

22437 *The birth: the chronicles of the door.* Wheaton, IL: Tyndale House Publishers, 1991, viii+135 p., paper, novel. THE CHRONICLES OF THE DOOR #1.

EDWARDS, Henry

22438 *Sgt. Pepper's Lonely Hearts Club Band: a novel.* New York: A Kangaroo Book, Pocket Books, 1978, 190 p., paper, movie.

EDWARDS, John, *with Denis Frost as* JOHN DENIS

22439 *Goliath.* London: Fontana, 1987, 284 p., cloth, novel.

EDWARDS, K. C.

22440 *G.I. Joe: Operation: thunderbolt.* New York: Ballantine Books, 1987, 88 p., paper, novel. FIND YOUR FATE—G.I. JOE #14.
Operation: thunderbolt—SEE: *G.I. Joe: Operation: thunderbolt.*

EDWARDS, Les

22441 *Blood and iron.* Honesdale, PA: Games Workshop, GW Books, 1990, 98 p., cloth, art.

EDWARDS, Malcolm (John), 1949-

22442 *Constellations: stories of the future.* London: Victor Gollancz, 1980, 188 p., cloth, anth.

as ANONYMOUS EDITOR

22443 *Gollancz/Sunday Times SF competition stories.* London: Victor Gollancz, 1987, 200 p., cloth, anth.

with Harry Harrison

22444 *Spacecraft in fact and fiction.* London: Orbis Books, 1979, 128 p., cloth, nonf.

with Frank Hatherley & Margaret Aldiss

16209 *A is for Brian: a 65th birthday present for Brian W. Aldiss.* London: Avernus, 1988, 128 p., paper, anth. [A festschrift for Brian W. Aldiss which includes some nonfiction; limited to 500 copies].

with Robert Holdstock

22445 *Alien landscapes.* London: Pierrot Publishing, 1979, 116 p., paper, art.
22446 *Lost realms.* Limpsfield, Surrey, England: Paper Tiger, 1984, 114 p., cloth, art.
22447 *Magician: the lost journals of the magus, Geoffrey Carlyle.* Limpsfield, Surrey, England: Paper Tiger, 1982, 127 p., paper, art.
22448 *Realms of fantasy.* Limpsfield, Surrey, England: Paper Tiger, 1983, 120 p., cloth, nonf.
22449 *Tour of the universe: the journey of a lifetime: the recorded diaries of Leio Scott and Caroline Luranski.* London: Pierrot Publishing, 1980, 141 p., cloth, novel.

with Maxim Jakubowski

22450 *The complete book of science fiction and fantasy lists.* London, Toronto: Granada, 1983, 350 p., paper, nonf.
22451 retitled: *The SF book of lists.* New York: Berkley Books, 1983, 384 p., paper, nonf. [Expanded edition].
The SF book of lists—SEE: *The complete book of science fiction and fantasy lists.*

EDWARDS, Marie A.—SEE: Landis, Marie

EDWARDS, Nicholas

22452 *Arachnaphobia: a novel.* New York, Toronto: Point Fiction, Scholastic Inc., 1990, 119 p., paper, movie.

EDWARDS, Nicky, 1958-

22453 *Stealing time.* London: Onlywomen Press, 1990, 190 p., paper, novel.

EDWARDS, Paul

22454 *The deadly cyborgs.* New York: Pyramid Books, 1975, 176 p., paper, novel. JOHN EAGLE, EXPEDITOR #9.
22455 *The green goddess.* New York: Pyramid Books, 1975, 188 p., paper, novel. JOHN EAGLE, EXPEDITOR #12.

22456 *Operation Weatherkill.* New York: Pyramid Books, 1975, 159 p., paper, novel. JOHN EAGLE, EXPEDITOR #13.

EDWARDS, Peter, 1946-

22457 *Terminus.* London: Macmillan; New York: St. Martin's Press, 1976, 336 p., cloth, novel.

EERDE, John A. Van—SEE: Van Eerde, John A.

EFFINGER, George Alec, 1947-

22458 *The bird of time.* Garden City, NY: Doubleday & Co., 1986, 176 p., cloth, novel. NICK OF TIME #2.
22459 *Death in Florence.* Garden City, NY: Doubleday & Co., 1978, 185 p., cloth, novel.
22459A retitled: *Utopia 3.* New York: Playboy Press Paperbacks, 1980, 192 p., paper, novel.
22460 *Dirty tricks.* Garden City, NY: Doubleday & Co., 1978, 179 p., cloth, coll.
22461 *Escape to tomorrow.* New York: Award Books, 1975, 158 p., paper, tele. PLANET OF THE APES #2.
22462 *The exile kiss.* Norwalk, CT: Easton Press, 1991, 265 p., cloth, novel. MARID AUDRAN #3.
22463 *Felicia.* New York: Berkley Publishing Corp., 1976, 243 p., cloth, novel.
22464 *A fire in the sun.* New York: A Foundation Book, Doubleday, 1989, 289 p., cloth, novel. MARID AUDRAN #2. [Winner of the *Science Fiction Chronicle* Award for Best Novel, 1989 (1990)].
22465 *Heroics.* Garden City, NY: Doubleday & Co., 1979, 181 p., cloth, novel.
22466 *Idle pleasures.* New York: Berkley Books, 1983, 197 p., paper, coll.
22467 *Irrational numbers.* Garden City, NY: Doubleday & Co., 1976, xiv+174 p., cloth, coll.
22468 *Journey into terror.* New York: Award Books, 1975, 157 p., paper, tele. PLANET OF THE APES #3.
22469 *Look away.* Eugene, OR: Axolotl Press, Pulphouse Publishing, 1990, 90 p., cloth, novel. AXOLOTL PRESS #12.
22470 *Lord of the apes.* New York: Award Books, 1976, 154 p., paper, tele. PLANET OF THE APES #4.
22471 *The nick of time.* Garden City, NY: Doubleday & Co., 1985, 180 p., cloth, novel. NICK OF TIME #1.

22472 *The old funny stuff.* Eugene, OR: Pulphouse Publishing, 1989, 116 p., cloth, coll. AUTHOR'S CHOICE MONTHLY #1.

22473 *Those gentle voices: a Promethean romance of the spaceways.* New York: Warner Books, 1976, 190 p., paper, novel.

Utopia 3—SEE: *Death in Florence.*

22474 *When gravity fails.* New York: Arbor House, 1987, 290 p., cloth, novel. MARID AUDRAN #1.

22475 *The wolves of memory.* New York: G. P. Putnam's Sons, 1981, 227 p., cloth, novel.

22476 *The Zork chronicles.* New York: A Byron Preiss Book, An Infocom Book, Avon Books, 1990, 290 p., paper, novel. ZORK SERIES. [Based on the Infocom game, *Zork*].

with Jack L. Chalker & Mike Resnick

19743 *The red tape war.* New York: Tor, A Tom Doherty Associates Book, 1991, ix+244 p., cloth, novel.

with Gardner Dozois

22134 *Nightmare blue.* New York: A Berkley Medallion Book, Berkley Publishing Corp., 1975, 185 p., paper, novel.

EFIMOV, Igor'—SEE: **Moscovit, Andrei**

EGAN, Doris

22477 *The gate of ivory.* New York: DAW Books, 1989, 319 p., paper, novel. GATE OF IVORY #1.

EGAN, Greg, 1961-

22478 *An unusual angle.* Carlton, Victoria, Australia: Norstrilia Press, 1983, 200 p., paper, novel.

EGAN, Kevin

22479 *The Perseus breed.* New York: Pageant Books, 1988, 206 p., paper, novel.

EGAN, Louise, *with Robert Egan*

22480 *Little shop of horrors.* New York: A Perigee Book, 1989, 79 p., paper, movie.

EGAN, Robert, 1945- , *with Louise Egan*

22480 *Little shop of horrors.* New York: A Perigee Book, 1989, 79 p., paper, movie.

EGLETON, Clive (Frederick), 1927-

37719 *State visit.* London: Hodder & Stoughton, 1976, 221 p., cloth, novel.

EGOFF, Sheila A., 1918-

22481 *Worlds within: children's fantasy from the Middle Ages to today.* Chicago & London: American Library Association, 1988, xi+339 p., cloth, nonf.

EGREMONT, Michael, pseud.—SEE: **Harrison, Michael**

EHLY, Ehren M. [i.e., Moreen Ehly]

22482 *Evil eye.* New York: Leisure Books, 1989, 359 p., paper, novel.

22483 *Obelisk.* New York: Leisure Books, 1988, 392 p., paper, novel.

22484 *Totem.* New York: Leisure Books, 1989, 391 p., paper, novel.

EHLY, Moreen—SEE: **Ehly, Ehren M.**

EHRENFELD, David (M.), *with Carol K. Mack*

22485 *The chameleon variant.* New York: Dial Press, 1980, 256 p., cloth, novel.

EHRHARDT, Eleanor, *with Terry Flanagan*

22486 *Trek or treat.* New York: Ballantine Books, 1977, [95] p., paper, nonf.

EHRLICH, Max (Simon), 1909-1983

The bond—SEE: *Reincarnation in Venice.*

22487 *Reincarnation in Venice.* New York: Simon & Schuster, 1979, 279 p., cloth, novel. PETER PROUD #2.

22487A retitled: *The bond.* London: Mayflower Books, 1980, 253 p., paper, novel.

22488 *Shaitan: a novel.* New York: Arbor House, 1981, 318 p., cloth, novel.

*EICHNER, Henry M., <u>1910</u>-1971

EILERS, Robert

22489 *The Hermes stone.* New York: Manor Books, 1979 (i.e., 1980?), 223 p., paper, novel.

EINSTEIN, Xavier, pseud.

22490 *Star Trek trivia mania.* New York: Zebra Books, Kensington Publishing Corp., 1985, 238 p., paper, nonf.

EISEN, Armand (Avram), 1952-

with Thomas Durwood

22336 *Masterpieces of science fiction.* Kansas City, MO: A Thomas Durwood/Armand Eisen Production, Ariel Books, 1978, 107 p., paper, anth.

with Bruce Jones

22491 *Sorcerers: a collection of fantasy art.* Kansas City, MO: An Armand Eisen/ Thomas Durwood Production, Ariel Books, 1978, [78] p., paper, art.

*EISENBERG, Lawrence B(enjamin)

*EISENBERG, Manuel (Bruce), 1946-

EISENSTEIN, Phyllis (Leah Kleinstein), 1946-

22492 *Born to exile.* Sauk City, WI: Arkham House, 1978, 202 p., cloth, coll. ALARIC THE MINSTREL #1.

22493 *The crystal palace.* New York: A Signet Book, New American Library, 1988, 382 p., paper, novel. SORCERER'S SON #2.

22494 *In the hands of glory.* New York: A Timescape Book, Pocket Books, 1981, 236 p., paper, novel.

22495 *In the red lord's reach.* New York: A Signet Book, New American Library, 1989, 268 p., paper, novel. ALARIC THE MINSTREL #2.

22496 *Shadow of Earth.* New York: A Dell Book, 1979, 329 p., paper, novel.

22497 *Sorcerer's son.* New York: A Del Rey Book, Ballantine Books, 1979, 387 p., paper, novel. SORCERER'S SON #1.

EISLER, Steven, pseud.—SEE: Holdstock, Robert

EISNER, Joel, 1959-

22500 *The official Batman batbook.* Chicago, New York: Contemporary Books, 1986, 171 p., paper, nonf.

EKLUND, Gordon (Stewart), 1945-

22501 *Dance of the apocalypse.* Toronto, New York: Laser Books, 1976, 190 p., paper, novel.

22502 *Devil world.* Toronto, New York: Bantam Books, 1979, 153 p., paper, novel. STAR TREK SERIES.

22503 *Falling toward forever.* Don Mills, Ontario, Canada: Laser Books, 1975, 190 p., paper, novel.

22504 *The garden of winter.* New York: Berkley Books, 1980, 199 p., paper, novel.

22505 *The Grayspace beast.* Garden City, NY: Doubleday & Co., 1976, 183 p., cloth, novel.

22506 *Serving in time.* Don Mills, Ontario, Canada: Laser Books, 1975, 190 p., paper, novel.

22507 *The starless world.* Toronto, New York: Bantam Books, 1978, 152 p., paper, novel. STAR TREK SERIES.

22508 *A thunder on Neptune.* New York: William Morrow & Co., 1989, 274 p., cloth, novel.

with Gregory Benford

17755 *Find the changeling.* New York: A Dell Book, 1980, 249 p., paper, novel.

17756 *If the stars are gods.* New York: Berkley Publishing Corp., 1977, 214 p., cloth, novel.

with E. E. Smith

Alien realms. SEE: Lord Tedric: Alien realms.

22509 *Black knight of the Iron Sphere.* New York: Baronet Publishing Co., 1979, 216 p., paper, novel. LORD TEDRIC #3.

22509A retitled: *Lord Tedric: The black knight of the Iron Sphere.* London: A Star Book, W. H. Allen, 1979, 140 p., paper, novel. LORD TEDRIC #3. [The British editions do not mention Eklund as author].

22510 *Lord Tedric.* New York: Baronet Publishing Co., 1978, 221 p., paper, novel. LORD TEDRIC #1.

22511 *Lord Tedric: Alien realms.* London: Star Books, 1980, 143 p., paper, novel. LORD TEDRIC #4.

22512 *Lord Tedric; Alien realms.* London: A Star Book, W. H. Allen, 1980, 159+143 p., paper, coll. LORD TEDRIC #1 & 4.

Lord Tedric: The black knight of the Iron Sphere—SEE: The black knight of the Iron Sphere.

22513 *Space pirates.* New York: Baronet Publishing Co., 1979, 223 p., paper, novel. LORD TEDRIC #2.

ELBOZ, Stephen

22515 *The house of rats.* Oxford, England: Oxford University Press, 1991, 135 p., cloth, novel.

ELDER, Michael (Aiken), 1931-

22516 *Centaurian quest*. London: Robert Hale, 1975, 189 p., cloth, novel.

22517 *Double time*. London: Robert Hale, 1976, 184 p., cloth, novel.

22518 *The island of the dead*. London: Robert Hale, 1975, 183 p., cloth, novel. BAR-CLAY #5.

22519 *Mindquest*. London: Robert Hale, 1978, 189 p., cloth, novel. MINDSLIP #2.

22520 *Mindslip*. London: Robert Hale, 1976, 173 p., cloth, novel. MINDSLIP #1.

22521 *Oil-planet*. London: Robert Hale, 1978, 175 p., cloth, novel. OIL-SEEKER #2.

22522 *Oil-seeker*. London: Robert Hale, 1977, 189 p., cloth, novel. OIL-SEEKER #1.

ELDERSHAW, M. Barnard [pseud. of Marjorie Faith Barnard, 1897-1987]

00879 *Tomorrow and tomorrow*. Melbourne, Australia: Georgian House, 1947, 466 p., cloth, novel.

22523 retitled: *Tomorrow and tomorrow and tomorrow*. London: Virago, 1983, xiv+ 456 p., paper, novel. [Expanded and uncensored edition].

Tomorrow and tomorrow and tomorrow—SEE: *Tomorrow and tomorrow*.

*ELDRIDGE, Paul, 1888-<u>1982</u>

ELDRIDGE, Roger

22524 *The fishers of Darksea*. London: Victor Gollancz, 1982, 214 p., cloth, novel.

22525 *The shadow of the Gloom-World*. London: Victor Gollancz, 1977, 191 p., cloth, novel.

ELFLANDSSON, Galad, 1951-

22526 *The black wolf*. West Kingston, RI: Donald M. Grant, Publisher, 1979, 172 p., cloth, novel.

ELFMAN, Blossom, 1925-

22527 *The ghost-sitter*. New York: A Fawcett Juniper Book, 1990, 105 p., paper, novel. MIKE & ALLY MYSTERY #3.

ELGIN, Don D(ean), 1944-

22528 *The comedy of the fantastic: ecological perspectives on the fantasy novel*. Westport, CT & London: Greenwood Press, 1985, 203 p., cloth, nonf. CONTRIBUTIONS TO THE STUDY OF SCIENCE FICTION AND FANTASY #15.

ELGIN, (Patricia Ann) Suzette (Wilkins) Haden, 1936-

22529 *And then there'll be fireworks*. Garden City, NY: Doubleday & Co., 1981, 185 p., cloth, novel. OZARK FANTASY TRILOGY #3.

22530 *Communipath worlds*. New York: Pocket Books, 1980, 348 p., paper, coll. COYOTE JONES #1-3.

22531 *First diction and grammar of Láadan*. Madison, WI: Society for the Furtherance and Study of Fantasy and Science Fiction, 1985, iv+104 p., paper?, fiction.

22532 *First diction and grammar of Láadan, second edition*. Madison, WI: Society for the Furtherance and Study of Fantasy and Science Fiction, 1988, iv+160 p., paper, fiction.

22533 *The grand Jubilee*. Garden City, NY: Doubleday & Co., 1981, 218 p., cloth, novel. OZARK FANTASY TRILOGY #2.

22534 *The Judas rose*. New York: DAW Books, 1987, 363 p., paper, novel. NATIVE TONGUE #2.

22535 *Native tongue*. New York: DAW Books, 1984, 301 p., paper, novel. NATIVE TONGUE #1.

22536 *The Ozark trilogy*. Garden City, NY: Nelson Doubleday, 1982, 535 p., cloth, coll. OZARK TRILOGY #1-3.

22537 *Star anchored, star angered*. Garden City, New York: Doubleday & Co., 1979, 182 p., cloth, novel. COYOTE JONES #4.

22538 *Twelve fair kingdoms*. Garden City, NY: Doubleday & Co., 1981, 183 p., cloth, novel. OZARK FANTASY TRILOGY #1.

22539 *Yonder comes the other end of time*. New York: DAW Books, 1986, 302 p., paper, novel. COYOTE JONES #5.

EL-HAJJAN, Mohammed—SEE: Mrabet, Mohammed

ELIADE, Mircea, 1907-1986

22540 *Tales of the sacred and the supernatural*. Philadelphia, PA: Westminster Press, 1981, 108 p., cloth, coll.

Two strange tales—SEE: *Two tales of the occult*.

04760 *Two tales of the occult*. New York: Herder & Herder, 1970, xiii+130 p., cloth, coll. [Translation by William Ames Coates of *Nopti la serampore* and *Secretul Doctorurlui Honigberger*].

04760A retitled: *Two strange tales.* Columbus, OH: Ohio State University Press, 1986, xiii+130 p., cloth, coll. [Translation by William Ames Coates of *Nopti la serampore and Secretul Doctorurlui Honigberger*].

22541 *Youth without youth, and other novellas.* London: Forest, 1989, xxxix+288 p., paper, coll. [Edited by Matei Calinescu; translation by Mac Linscott Ricketts].

ELIAS, Albert J., 1920-

22542 *The Bowman Test.* New York: A Dell Book, 1977, 222 p., paper, novel.

22543 *The Sonora mutation.* NY: Avon, 1978, 249 p., paper, novel.

ELIOT, Ethel Cook, 1890-1972

15802 *The Wind Boy.* Garden City, NY: Doubleday, Page & Co., 1923, 238 p., cloth, novel.

ELIOT, MARC, pseud.—SEE: Pedneau, Dave

ELKIN, Marsha

22544 *Lord of the Rings coloring book.* [Cambridge, MA: NESFA Press], 1972, 23 p., paper, art anth.

ELKIN, Stanley (Lawrence), 1930-

22545 *The living end.* New York: A Henry Dobbins Book, E. P. Dutton, 1979, 148 p., cloth, novel.

ELKINS, Charles (L.), 1940- , *with Patrick A. McCarthy & Martin Harry Greenberg*

22546 *The legacy of Olaf Stapledon: critical essays and an unpublished manuscript.* New York: Greenwood Press, 1989, x+132 p., cloth, nonf. anth. CONTRIBUTIONS TO THE STUDY OF SCIENCE FICTION AND FANTASY #34.

ELLERMAN, Anna—SEE: Bryher

ELLERN, William B(ert), 1933-

22547 *New lensman.* London: Futura Publications, An Orbit Book, 1976, 191 p., paper, novel. LENSMAN SERIES.

ELLIOT, Frances (Minton Dickinson), 1820-1898

37720 *The red cardinal: a romance.* Leipzig, Germany: Bernhard Tauchnitz, 1884, 272 p., cloth, novel.

ELLIOT, Jeffrey M., 1947-

22548 *Fantasy voices: interviews with American fantasy writers.* San Bernardino, CA: R. Reginald, The Borgo Press, 1982, 64 p., cloth, nonf. MILFORD SERIES: POPULAR WRITERS OF TODAY #31.

22549 *The future of the space program; Large corporations & society: discussions with 22 science-fiction writers.* San Bernardino, CA: R. Reginald, The Borgo Press, 1981, 64 p., cloth, nonf. anth. GREAT ISSUES OF THE DAY #1.

22550 *Kindred spirits: an anthology of gay and lesbian science fiction stories.* Boston: Alyson Publications, 1984, 262 p., paper, anth.

Large corporations & society—SEE: The future of the space program.

22551 *Literary voices #1.* San Bernardino, CA: R. Reginald, The Borgo Press, 1980, 64 p., cloth, nonf. MILFORD SERIES: POPULAR WRITERS OF TODAY #27.

22552 *Pulp voices; or, Science fiction voices #6: interviews with pulp magazine writers and editors.* San Bernardino, CA: R. Reginald, The Borgo Press, 1983, 63 p., cloth, nonf. MILFORD SERIES: POPULAR WRITERS OF TODAY #37.

22553 *Science fiction voices #2: interviews with science fiction writers.* San Bernardino, CA: R. Reginald, The Borgo Press, 1979, 62 p., cloth, nonf. MILFORD SERIES: POPULAR WRITERS OF TODAY #25.

22554 *Science fiction voices #3: interviews with science fiction writers.* San Bernardino, CA: R. Reginald, The Borgo Press, 1980, 64 p., cloth, nonf. MILFORD SERIES: POPULAR WRITERS OF TODAY #29.

22555 *Science fiction voices [#4]: interviews with modern science fiction writers.* San Bernardino, CA: R. Reginald, The Borgo Press, 1982, 63 p., cloth, nonf. MILFORD SERIES: POPULAR WRITERS OF TODAY #33.

22556 *The work of Jack Dann: an annotated bibliography & guide.* San Bernardino, CA: R. Reginald, The Borgo Press, 1990, 128 p., cloth, nonf. BIBLIOGRAPHIES OF MODERN AUTHORS #16. [Edited by Boden Clarke].

22557 *The work of Pamela Sargent: an annotated bibliography & guide.* San Bernardino, CA: R. Reginald, The Borgo Press, 1990, 80 p., cloth, nonf. BIBLIOGRA-

PHIES OF MODERN AUTHORS #13. [Edited by Boden Clarke].

with Michael Burgess

22558 *The work of R. Reginald: an annotated bibliography & guide.* San Bernardino, CA: The Borgo Press, 1985, 48 p., cloth, nonf. BIBLIOGRAPHIES OF MODERN AUTHORS #5.

with Raymond Z. Gallun

22559 *Starclimber: the literary adventures and autobiography of Raymond Z. Gallun.* San Bernardino, CA: R. Reginald, The Borgo Press, 1991, 168 p., cloth, nonf. BORGO BIOVIEWS #1.

with R(obert) Reginald

22560 *If J.F.K. had lived: a political scenario.* San Bernardino, CA: Borgo Press, 1978, 64 p., cloth, novel. BORGO POLITICAL SCENARIOS #1. [Expanded and rewritten version of *The attempted assassination of John F. Kennedy* / by Lucas Webb; mostly written by Reginald, with Elliot contributing only the introduction and minor copy editing].

22561 *The work of George Zebrowski: an annotated bibliography & guide.* San Bernardino, CA: R. Reginald, The Borgo Press, 1986, 54 p., cloth, nonf. BIBLIOGRAPHIES OF MODERN AUTHORS #4.

22562 *The work of George Zebrowski: an annotated bibliography & guide, second edition.* San Bernardino, CA: R. Reginald, The Borgo Press, 1990, 118 p., cloth, nonf. BIBLIOGRAPHIES OF MODERN AUTHORS #4.

*ELLIOTT, Bruce (Walter Gardner Lively Stacy), 1914-1973

ELLIOTT, Elton T., *with Richard E. Geis as* RICHARD ELLIOTT

22563 *The burnt lands.* New York: Fawcett Gold Medal, 1985, 263 p., paper, novel. JOHN NORRIS #2.

22564 *The Einstein legacy.* New York: Fawcett Gold Medal, 1987, 281 p., paper, novel.

22565 *The master file.* New York: Fawcett Gold Medal, 1986, 250 p., paper, novel.

22566 *The Sword of Allah.* New York: Fawcett Gold Medal, 1984, 281 p., paper, novel. JOHN NORRIS #1.

ELLIOTT, George P(aul), 1918-1980

22567 *An hour of last things, and other stories.* New York: Harper & Row, 1968, 292 p., cloth, coll.

ELLIOTT, Janice, 1931-

22568 *The empty throne.* London: Walker Books, 1988, 183 p., cloth, novel. SWORD AND THE DREAM #2.

22569 *The king awakes.* London: Walker Books, 1987, 188 p., cloth, novel. SWORD AND THE DREAM #1.

22570 *The sadness of witches.* London: Hodder & Stoughton, 1987, [192] p., cloth, novel.

37721 *Summer people.* London: Hodder & Stoughton, 1980, 188 p., cloth, novel.

ELLIOTT, Jannean (L.), *with A. C. Crispin*

20814 *Shadow world.* New York: Ace Books, 1991, 279 p., paper, novel. STARBRIDGE #3.

ELLIOTT, Nathan, pseud.—SEE: Evans, Chris

*ELLIOTT, Hettie, 1865-1926

ELLIOTT, Richard, pseud.—SEE: Geis, Richard E. & Elliott, Elton T.

ELLIOTT, Sumner Locke, 1917-1991

37722 *Eden's lost.* London: Michael Joseph, 1970, 270 p., cloth, novel.

22571 *Going.* New York: Harper & Row, 1975, 170 p., cloth, novel.

ELLIOTT, Tom

22572 *The dwelling.* New York: St. Martin's Press, 1989, 243 p., paper, novel.

ELLIS, Albert C(harles), 1947-

22573 *Worldmaker* / by A. C. Ellis. New York: Ace Science Fiction Books, 1985, 233 p., paper, novel.

with Jeff Slaten

22574 *Death jag.* New York: Manor Books, 1979, 235 p., paper, novel.

ELLIS, Amabel Williams- —SEE: Williams-Ellis, Amabel

ELLIS, Carol (R.), 1946-

22575 *A cry in the night.* New York, Toronto: An Apple Paperback, Scholastic Inc., 1990, 154 p., paper, novel.
22576 *My secret admirer.* New York, Toronto: Point, Scholastic Inc., 1989, 184 p., paper, novel.

ELLIS, D. E.

04801 *A thousand ages.* London: Digit Books, 1961, 156 p., paper, novel.
04801A retitled: *Space voyage.* Australia: Bill Ewington Books, 1973, 156 p., paper, novel.

ELLIS, Julie—SEE: Marvin, Susan

ELLIS, Kate Ferguson, 1938-

22577 *The contested castle: gothic novels and the subversion of domestic ideology.* Urbana & Chicago, IL: University of Illinois Press, 1989, xviii+226 p., cloth, nonf.

ELLIS, Leigh [pseud. of Louise Courtenay Rudeen], 1959-

22578 *The Quick.* New York: Avon, 1982, 205 p., paper, novel.

ELLIS, Novalyne Price, 1908-

22579 *Day of the stranger: further memories of Robert E. Howard.* West Warwick, RI: Necronomicon Press, 1989, 47 p., paper, nonf. [Edited by Rusty Burke].
22580 *One who walked alone: Robert E. Howard, the final years.* West Kingston, RI: Donald M. Grant, Publisher, 1986, 317 p., cloth, nonf.

ELLIS, Peter Berresford—SEE: Tremayne, Peter

ELLIS, R. J., 1949-, *with Rhys Garnett*

22581 *Science fiction roots and branches: contemporary critical approaches.* London: Macmillan, 1990, xi+210 p., cloth, nonf. anth.

ELLIS, Reed

22582 *Journey into darkness: the art of James Whale's horror films.* New York: Arno Press, 1980, 199 p., cloth, nonf.

ELLIS, S(tewart) M(arsh)

37723 *Wilkie Collins, Le Fanu, and others.* London: Constable & Co., 1931, 343 p., cloth, nonf.

ELLIS, T(homas) Mullett, 1850-1919

37724 *Zalma.* London: Tower Publishing Co., 1895, 438 p., cloth, novel.

ELLIS, Terry

22583 *Explorers of Willow Springs.* Santa Monica, CA: Roundtable Publishing, 1989, x+165 p., paper, novel. WILLOW WOOD SPRINGS #2.
22584 *Invasion of Willow Springs.* Santa Monica, CA: Roundtable Publishing, 1989, x+153 p., paper, novel. WILLOW WOOD SPRINGS #3.
22585 *Legend of Willow Springs.* Santa Monica, CA: Roundtable Publishing, 1989, x+165 p., paper, novel. WILLOW WOOD SPRINGS #1.

ELLISON, Harlan (Jay), 1934-

22586 *All the lies that are my life.* San Francisco, Columbia, PA: Underwood Miller, 1980, 130 p., cloth, novel. [Limited to 620 copies].
22587 *Angry candy.* Norwalk, CT: Easton Press, 1988, xxiv+324 p., cloth, coll. [Winner of the World Fantasy Award for Best Fantasy Collection, 1988 (1989); winner of the *Locus* Award for Best Collection, 1988 (1989)].
22588 *Deathbird stories: a pantheon of modern gods.* New York: Harper & Row, 1975, xv+334 p., cloth, coll.
22589 *Dreams with sharp teeth.* New York: Book-of-the-Month Club, 1991, 990 p., paper, coll. [Includes *Shatterday*; *Deathbird stories*; *I have no mouth and I must scream*, plus two new stories and an essay].
22590 *An edge in my voice.* Norfolk, Virginia Beach, VA: Donning Co., Publishers, 1985, 548 p., cloth, nonf. coll.
22591 *The essential Ellison: a 35-year retrospective.* Omaha, NE, Kansas City, MO: Nemo Press, 1987, xv+1019 p., cloth, coll. [Includes some nonfiction; edited by Terry Dowling, Richard Delap, and Gil Lamont; winner of the Bram Stoker Award for Best Horror Collection, 1987 (1988)].
22592 *The fantasies of Harlan Ellison.* Boston: Gregg Press, 1979, xxiv+316 p., cloth,

coll. [Includes *Paingod* and *I Have No Mouth*].

22593 *Footsteps.* Round Top, NY: Footsteps Press, 1989, 20 p., paper, story. [limited to 582 copies].

22594 *The Harlan Ellison hornbook.* New York: Penzler Books, 1990, xxviii+417 p., cloth, nonf. coll.

22595 *Harlan Ellison's movie.* Westminster, MD: Mirage Press, 1990, xi+151 p., cloth, fiction.

22596 *Harlan Ellison's watching.* Los Angeles, Lancaster, PA: Underwood-Miller, 1989, xxxvii+514 p., cloth, nonf. coll. [Winner of the Bram Stoker Award for Best Horror Nonfiction Book, 1989 (1990)].

Harlan's world—SEE: *Medea.*

22597 *The illustrated Harlan Ellison.* New York: Baronet Publishing Co., 1978, [96] p., cloth, coll. [Edited by Byron Preiss].

22598 *Love ain't nothing but sex misspelled.* New York: Pyramid Books, 1976, 380 p., paper, coll. [Drops nine stories and adds three from the original edition (see #04813)].

22599 *Medea: Harlan's world.* Huntington Woods, MI: Phantasia Press, 1985, 532 p., cloth, anth. [Winner of the *Locus* Award for Best Anthology, 1985 (1986)].

22600 *No doors, no windows.* New York: Pyramid, 1975, 223 p. coll.

22601 *Paingod, and other delusions.* New York: Pyramid, 1975, 176 p., paper, coll. ["This edition has added and revised front matter and an additional story"].

22602 *Run for the stars.* New York: Tor SF, A Tom Doherty Associates Book, 1991, p. 1-89, paper, story. [Bound with *Echoes of thunder* / by Jack Dann & Jack C. Haldeman II].

22603 *Shatterday.* Boston: Houghton Mifflin Co., 1980, xiii+332 p., cloth, coll.

22604 *Sleepless nights in the Procrustean bed: essays.* San Bernardino, CA: R. Reginald, The Borgo Press, 1984, 192 p., cloth, nonf. coll. I.O. EVANS STUDIES IN THE PHILOSOPHY & CRITICISM OF LITERATURE #5. [Edited by Marty Clark; winner of the *Locus* Award for Best Nonfiction, 1984 (1985)].

22605 *Stalking the nightmare.* Huntington Woods, MI: Phantasia Press, 1982, 332 p., cloth, coll.

22606 *Strange wine: fifteen new stories from the nightside of the world.* New York: Harper & Row, 1978, 262 p., cloth, coll.

with Edward Bryant

18875 *Phoenix without ashes: a novel of the star-lost.* Greenwich, CT: A Fawcett Gold Medal Book, Fawcett Publications, 1975, 192 p., paper, tele.

with Andrew Porter

22607 *The book of Ellison.* New York: Algol Press, 1978, 192 p., cloth, anth. [Material by and about Ellison].

ELLWOOD, Gracia Fay, 1938- , *with Doris Robin & Lee Vibber*

22608 *In a faraway galaxy: a literary approach to a film saga.* Pasadena, CA: Extequer Press, 1984, 149 p., paper, nonf.

*ELMORE, Ernest (Carpenter), 1901-1957

ELOUS, Marv, pseud.—SEE: Vardeman, Robert E. & Proctor, Geo. W.

ELPHINSTONE, Margaret, 1948-

22609 *The incomer.* London: The Women's Press, 1987, 229 p., paper, novel. THE INCOMER #1.

37725 *A sparrow's flight.* Edinburgh, Scotland: Polygon, 1989, 257 p., paper, novel. INCOMER #2.

ELRICK, George S(eefurth), 1921-

22610 *Science fiction handbook for readers and writers.* Chicago: Chicago Review Press, 1978, 315 p., paper, nonf.

ELROD, P(atricia) N(ead)

22611 *Art in the blood.* New York: Ace Books, 1991, 195 p., paper, novel. VAMPIRE FILES #4.

22612 *Bloodcircle.* New York: Ace Books, 1990, 202 p., paper, novel. VAMPIRE FILES #3.

22613 *Bloodlist.* New York: Ace Books, 1990, 200 p., paper, novel. VAMPIRE FILES #1.

22614 *Fire in the blood.* New York: Ace Books, 1991, 198 p., paper, novel. VAMPIRE FILES #5.

22615 *Lifeblood.* New York: Ace Books, 1990, 202 p., paper, novel. VAMPIRE FILES #2.

EL-SHATER, Safaa

22616 *The novels of Mary Shelley.* Salzburg, Austria: Institut für Englische Sprache und Literatur, 1977, 172 p., paper, nonf.

ELSNA, Hebe, pseud.—SEE: Conway, Laura

ELSON, Jenny

22617 *Worlds apart: a study of Earth and Vulcan in fiction and article.* Strathmartine by Dundee, Scotland: Star Trek Action Group, 1979, 57 p., paper, coll. [Includes some nonfiction].

ELTON, Ben(jamin Charles), 1959-

37726 *Gridlock.* London: Macdonald & Co., 1991, 340 p., cloth, novel.
22618 *Stark.* London: Sphere Books, 1989, 453 p., paper, novel.

ELWOOD, Roger (P.), 1943-

22619 *The 50-meter monsters, and other horrors: six tales of terror.* New York: An Archway Paperback, Pocket Books, 1976, 134 p., paper, anth.
22620 *Angelwalk: a modern fable.* Westchester, IL: Crossway Books, 1988, 189 p., paper, novel. ANGELWALK #1.
22621 *The christening.* Eugene, OR: Harvest House Publishers, 1989, 266 p., cloth?, novel.
22622 *Continuum 4.* New York: Berkley Publishing Corp., 1975, vi+186 p., cloth, anth.
22623 *Dark knight: the antichrist or just another madman?* Lake Mary, FL: Creation House, 1991, 120 p., paper, novel.
22624 *Dystopian visions.* Englewood Cliffs, NJ: Prentice-Hall, 1975, vi+197 p., cloth, anth.
22625 *Fallen angel: a novel.* Dallas, TX: Word Publishing, 1990, 288 p., paper, novel. ANGELWALK #2.
22626 *Fantasy Island.* Middletown, CT: Weekly Reader, 1981, 125 p., paper, tele. coll.
22627 *The Frankenstein project.* Dallas, TX: Word Publishing, 1991, 119 p., paper, novel.
22628 *Future corruption.* New York: Warner Paperback Library, 1975, 189 p., paper, anth.
22629 *The gifts of Asti, and other stories of science fiction.* Chicago: Follett Publishing Co., 1975, 216 p., cloth, anth.
22630 *SF sampler.* [S.l.]: Educational Progress, 197?, p., paper, anth.
22631 *Tomorrow: new worlds of science fiction.* New York: M. Evans & Co., 1975, 218 p., cloth, anth.
22632 *Visions of tomorrow.* New York: Pocket Books, 1976, viii+390 p., paper, anth.
37727 *Wise one.* Chicago: Moody Press, 1991, 245 p., paper, novel.
22633 *A world named Cleopatra.* New York: Pyramid Books, 1977, 192 p., paper, anth.

as ANONYMOUS EDITOR

22634 *Futurelove: a science fiction triad.* Indianapolis, IN, New York: Bobbs-Merrill Co., 1977, x+181 p., cloth, anth.

with Vic Ghidalia

22635 *Beware more beasts.* New York: Manor Books, 1975, 192 p., paper, anth.

with Howard Goldsmith

22636 *Spine-chillers: unforgettable tales of terror.* Garden City, NY: Doubleday & Co., 1978, viii+396 p., cloth, anth.

with Robert Silverberg

22637 *Epoch.* New York: Berkley Publishing Corp., 1975, viii+623 p., cloth, anth. [Winner of the *Locus* Award for Best Anthology, 1975 (1976)]

ELY, David [pseud. of David Eli Lilienthal], 1927-

37728 *Seconds: a novel.* New York: Pantheon Books, 1963, 181 p., cloth, novel.

ELY, Scott, 1944-

22638 *Starlight.* New York: Weidenfeld & Nicolson, 1987, 195 p., cloth, novel.

EMANUEL, Victor—SEE: Rousseau, Victor

EMECHETA, (Florence Onye) Buchi, 1944-

22639 *The rape of Shavi.* London, Nigeria: Ogwugwu Afor, 1983, 178 p., cloth, novel.

EMERSON, Ru, 1944-

22640 *Beauty and the beast: Masques: a novel.* New York: Avon Books, 1990, 279 p., paper, tele. BEAUTY AND THE BEAST #2.
22641 *The calling of the three.* New York: Ace Books, 1990, 248 p., paper, novel. NIGHT-THREADS #1.
22642 *In the caves of exile.* New York: Ace Books, 1988, 310 p., paper, novel. NEDAO #2.

Masques—SEE: *Beauty and the beast: Masques.*

22643 *On the seas of destiny.* New York: Ace Books, 1989, 280 p., paper, novel. NEDAO #3.

22644 *The Princess of Flames.* New York: Ace Fantasy Books, 1986, 327 p., paper, novel.

22645 *Spell bound.* New York: Ace Books, 1990, 243 p., paper, novel.

22646 *To the haunted mountains.* New York: Ace Fantasy Books, 1987, 314 p., paper, novel. NEDAO #1.

22647 *The two in hiding.* New York: Ace Books, 1991, 294 p., paper, novel. NIGHT-THREADS #2.

EMERY, Clayton, 1953-

22648 *Outcasts.* New York: Ace Books, 1990, 181 p., paper, novel. RUNESWORD #1.

22649 *Tales of Robin Hood.* New York: Baen Books, 1988, 309 p., paper, novel.

with Earl Wajenberg

22650 *4-D funhouse.* Lake Geneva, WI: TSR Inc., 1985, 219 p., paper, novel. AMAZING STORIES #1.

EMERY, Edith—SEE: Pattou, Edith

EMME, Eugene M(orlock), 1919-1985

22651 *Science fiction and space futures, past and present.* San Diego, CA: Published for the American Astronautical Society by Univelt, 1982, viii+270 p., cloth, nonf. anth.

EMMERTON, Anton

22652 *Blood red sky.* New York: Zebra Books, Kensington Publishing Corp., 1985, 382 p., paper, novel.

22653 *Ghost pilot.* New York: Zebra Books, Kensington Publishing Corp., 1987, 302 p., paper, novel.

22654 *High command.* New York: Zebra Books, Kensington Publishing Corp., 1986, 384 p., paper, novel.

EMMS, William

22655 *Doctor Who: Galaxy Four.* London: W. H. Allen & Co., 1985, 141 p., cloth, tele. DOCTOR WHO #104.

22656 *Doctor Who: Mission to Venus.* New York: Ballantine Books, 1986, [126] p.,

paper, novel. FIND YOUR FATE—DOCTOR WHO #4.

Galaxy Four—SEE: *Doctor Who: Galaxy Four.*

Mission to Venus—SEE: *Doctor Who: Mission to Venus.*

EMSHWILLER, Carol (Fries), 1921-

22657 *Carmen dog.* London: The Women's Press, 1988, 148 p., paper, novel.

22658 *The start of the end of it all.* San Francisco: Mercury House, 1991, 204 p., cloth, coll. [Drops four and adds four stories from the UK edition.]

22659 *The start of the end of it all, and other stories.* London: The Women's Press, 1990, 163 p., paper, coll. [Winner of the World Fantasy Award for Best Fantasy Collection, 1990 (1991)].

22660 *Verging on the pertinent: stories.* Minneapolis, MN: Coffee House Press, 1989, 130 p., paper, coll.

EMSHWILLER, Peter R(obert), 1959-

22661 *The host.* New York, Toronto: Spectra, Bantam Books, 1991, 358 p., paper, novel.

EMTSEV, Mikhail (Tikhonovich), 1930- , with Eremei Parnov

22662 *World soul.* New York: Macmillan Publishing Co.; London: Collier Macmillan Publishers, 1978, viii+178 p., cloth, novel. [Translation by Antonina W. Bouis of *Dusha mira*].

*ENCK, John Edward, d. 1980

ENDE, Michael (Andreas Helmuth), 1929-

22663 *The grey gentlemen.* London: Burke, 1974, 238 p., cloth, novel. [Translation by J. Michael Brownjohn of *Momo*].

22663A retitled: *Momo.* Garden City, NY: Doubleday & Co., 1985, 227 p., cloth, novel. [Translation by J. Michael Brownjohn of *Momo*].

22664 *Jim Button and Luke the engine driver.* Woodstock, NY: Overlook Press, 1990, 226 p., cloth, novel. [Translation by Maurice S. Dodd of *Jim Knopf & Lukas der lokomotivführer*].

22665 *Mirror in the mirror.* Harmondsworth, Middlesex, England: Viking, 1986, 224 p., cloth, coll. [Translation by J. Maxwell Brownjohn of *Der spiegel im spiegel*].

Momo—SEE: *The grey gentlemen.*

22666 *The neverending story.* London: Allen Lane, 1983, 396 p., cloth. [Translation by Ralph Manheim of *Undendliche geschichte*].

ENDERLE, Judith (Ann Ross), 1941-

22667 *Adrienne and the blob.* New York: Silhouette Books, 1986, 155 p., paper, novel.

with Stephanie Tessler as JEFFIE ROSS GORDON

22668 *A touch of genius.* New York: Silhouette Books, 1986, 157 p., paper, novel.
22669 *A touch of magic.* New York: Silhouette Books, 1987, 155 p., paper, novel.

ENFANTINO, Peter

22670 *Quick chills: the year's best horror stories from the small press, volume one.* San Jose, CA: Deadline Publications, 1990, 172 p., cloth, anth.

ENGDAHL, Sylvia Louise, 1933-

22671 *Anywhere, anywhen: stories of tomorrow.* New York: Atheneum, 1976, x+301 p., cloth, anth.
22672 *The doors of the universe.* New York: An Argo Book, Atheneum, 1981, 262 p., cloth, novel. NOREN #3.

with Rick Roberson

22673 *Universe ahead: stories of the future.* New York: Atheneum, 1975, 336 p., cloth, anth.

ENGEBRETSON, David, 1964- , with Michael R. Collings

20314 *The shorter works of Stephen King.* Mercer Island, WA: Starmont House, 1985, 202 p., cloth, nonf. STARMONT STUDIES IN LITERARY CRITICISM #9.

ENGEL, Alan [pseud. of Alan D. Engelberg], 1941-

22674 *Variant: a novel.* New York: Donald I. Fine, 1988, 269 p., cloth, novel.

ENGEL, Joel, 1952-

22675 *Rod Serling: the dreams and nightmares of life in the Twilight zone: a biography.*

Chicago: Contemporary Books, 1989, ix+353 p., cloth, nonf.

ENGEL, Theodore

22676 *Evolution of modern science fiction.* [New York: Hugo Gernsback?, 1952?], 12 p., paper, nonf.

ENGELBERG, Alan D.—SEE: Engel, Alan

ENGH, M(ary) J(ane), 1933-

22677 *Arslan.* New York: Warner Books, 1976, 318 p., paper, novel.
22677A retitled: *A wind from Bukhara.* London: Grafton, 1989, 365 p., paper, novel.
22678 *The house in the snow.* New York: A Richard Jackson Book, Orchard Books, 1987, 132 p., cloth, novel.
22679 *Wheel of the winds.* New York: Tor, A Tom Doherty Associates Book, 1988, 377 p., cloth, novel.
A wind from Bukhara—SEE: *Arslan.*

ENGLAND, James

22680 *The measured caverns.* London: Robert Hale, 1979, 173 p., cloth, novel.

ENGLAND, Wendy

22681 *In the shadow of the cat.* New York: Leisure Books, 1980, 251 p., paper, novel.

ENGLE, Gary (Dean), 1947- , with Dennis Dooley

22024 *Superman at fifty: the persistence of a legend.* Cleveland, OH: Octavia Press, 1987, 189 p., cloth, nonf.

ENGLEHART, Stephen

22682 *The point man.* New York: A Dell Book, 1981, 350 p., paper, novel.

ENGLING, Richard (David George Patrick), 1952-

22683 *Body mortgage.* New York: An Onyx Book, New American Library, 1989, 254 p., paper, novel.

ENGLISH, (Emma) Jean (Martin), 1937-

22684 *The devices of darkness.* Garden City, NY: Doubleday & Co., 1976, 181 p., cloth, novel.

ENGSTROM, Betsy L.—SEE: Engstrom, Elizabeth

ENGSTROM, Elizabeth [i.e., Betsy Lynn Gutzmer Engstrom], 1951-

22685 *Black ambrosia.* New York: Tor Horror, A Tom Doherty Associates Book, 1988, 341 p., paper, novel.
22686 *Lizzie Borden.* New York: Tor, A Tom Doherty Associates Book, 1991, 342 p., cloth, novel.
22687 *When darkness loves us.* New York: William Morrow & Co., 1985, 249 p., cloth, coll.

ENNIS, Catherine, 1937-

22688 *To the lightning.* Tallahassee, FL: Naiad Press, 1988, 191 p., paper, novel.

ENSLEY, Evangeline—SEE: Walton, Evangeline

ENSTROM, Robert (William), 1946-

22689 *Beta Colony.* Garden City, NY: Doubleday & Co., 1980, 177 p., cloth, novel.
22690 *Encounter program.* Garden City, NY: Doubleday & Co., 1977, 202 p., cloth, novel.

EPPERSON, Jerry, *with James M. Ward*

22691 *Night of the wolverine.* Lake Geneva, WI: TSR Inc., 1986, 190 p., paper, novel. MARVEL SUPERHEROES ADVENTURE GAMEBOOK #3.

ERDMAN, Paul (Emil), 1932-

22692 *The crash of '79.* New York: Simon & Schuster, 1976, 350 p., cloth, novel.
22693 *The last days of America.* New York: Simon & Schuster, 1981, 363 p., cloth, novel.
22694 *The panic of '89.* London: André Deutsch, 1986, 308 p., cloth, novel.

ERGAS, Elizabeth (L.)

22695 *Devil's gate.* New York: Pinnacle Books, Windsor Publishing Corp., 1991, 352 p., cloth, novel.
22696 *The shapechanger.* New York: Pinnacle Books, Windsor Publishing Corp., 1989, 348 p., cloth, novel.

ERICKSON, Paul

The Ark—SEE: Doctor Who: The Ark.
22697 *Doctor Who: The Ark.* London: W. H. Allen & Co., 1986, 144 p., cloth, tele. DOCTOR WHO #114.

ERICKSON, Stephen M.—SEE: Erickson, Steve

ERICKSON, Steve [i.e., Stephen Michael Erickson], 1950-

22698 *Days between stations: a novel.* New York, London: Poseidon Press, 1985, 253 p., cloth, novel.
22699 *Rubicon beach.* New York: Poseidon Press, 1986, 300 p., cloth, novel.
22700 *Tours of the black clock.* New York, London: Poseidon Press, 1989, 320 p., cloth, novel.

ERICSON, Eric, 1925-

22701 *Master of the temple.* Sevenoaks, Kent, England: New English Library, 1983, 422 p., paper, novel.
22702 *The sorcerer.* London: New English Library, 1978, 220 p., paper, novel.
22703 *The woman who slept with demons.* New York: St. Martin's Press, 1980, 240 p., cloth, novel.

ERLANGER, Ellen (Louise), 1950-

22704 *Isaac Asimov: scientist and storyteller.* Minneapolis, MN: Lerner Publications, 1986, 55 p., cloth, nonf.

ERLICH, Richard D(ee), 1943- , *with Thomas P. Dunn*

22320 *Clockwork worlds: mechanized environments in SF.* Westport, CT, London: Greenwood Press, 1983, xiii+369 p., cloth, nonf. CONTRIBUTIONS TO THE STUDY OF SCIENCE FICTION AND FANTASY #7.
22321 *The mechanical god: machines in science fiction.* Westport, CT, London: Greenwood Press, 1982, xiv+284 p., cloth, nonf. anth. CONTRIBUTIONS TO THE STUDY OF SCIENCE FICTION AND FANTASY #1.

ERNST, Kathryn F(itzgerald), 1942-

22705 *ESP McGee and the mysterious magician.* New York: An Avon Camelot Book, 1983, 124 p., paper, novel. ESP MCGEE #3.

ERNST, Paul (Frederick), 1899-1985, *as* KENNETH ROBESON

04915   *The Avenger: Death in slow motion.* New York: Warner Paperback Library, 1973, 158 p., paper, novel. AVENGER #18.

37729   *The Avenger: House of death.* New York: Warner Paperback Library, 1973, 158 p., paper, novel. AVENGER #15.

37730   *The Avenger: Justice, Inc.* New York: Paperback Library, 1972, 159 p., paper, novel. AVENGER #1.

37731   *The Avenger: Midnight murder.* New York: Warner Paperback Library, 1974, 158 p., paper, novel. AVENGER #24.

37732   *The Avenger: Murder on wheels.* New York: Warner Paperback Library, 1973, 158 p., paper, novel. AVENGER #13.

04916   *The Avenger: Nevlo.* New York: Warner Paperback Library, 1973, 159 p., paper, novel. AVENGER #17.

37733   *The Avenger: Pictures of death.* New York: Warner Paperback Library, 1973, 158 p., paper, novel. AVENGER #19.

04917   *The Avenger: River of ice.* New York: Warner Paperback Library, 1973, 157 p., paper, novel. AVENGER #11.

37734   *The Avenger: Stockholders in death.* New York: Warner Paperback Library, 1972, 158 p., paper, novel. AVENGER #7.

04918   *The Avenger: The black death.* New York: Warner Paperback Library, 1974, 158 p., paper, novel. AVENGER #22.

37735   *The Avenger: The blood ring.* New York: Warner Paperback Library, 1972, 158 p., paper, novel. AVENGER #6.

37736   *The Avenger: The devil's horns.* New York: Warner Paperback Library, 1972, 160 p., paper, novel. AVENGER #4.

04919   *The Avenger: The flame breathers.* New York: Warner Paperback Library, 1973, 157 p., paper, novel. AVENGER #12.

04920   *The Avenger: The frosted death.* New York: Warner Paperback Library, 1972, 157 p., paper, novel. AVENGER #5.

37737   *The Avenger: The glass mountain.* New York: Warner Paperback Library, 1973, 158 p., paper, novel. AVENGER #8.

04921   *The Avenger: The green killer.* New York: Warner Paperback Library, 1974, 158 p., paper, novel. AVENGER #20.

37738   *The Avenger: The happy killers.* New York: Warner Paperback Library, 1974, 158 p., paper, novel. AVENGER #21.

04922   *The Avenger: The hate master.* New York: Warner Paperback Library, 1973, 158 p., paper, novel. AVENGER #16.

04923   *The Avenger: The sky walker.* New York: Warner Paperback Library, 1972, 156 p., paper, novel. AVENGER #3.

37739   *The Avenger: The smiling dogs.* New York: Warner Paperback Library, 1973, 159 p., paper, novel. AVENGER #10.

37740   *The Avenger: The Wilder curse.* New York: Warner Paperback Library, 1974, 158 p., paper, novel. AVENGER #23.

37741   *The Avenger: The yellow hoard.* New York: Warner Paperback Library, 1972, 158 p., paper, novel. AVENGER #2.

37742   *The Avenger: Three gold crowns.* New York: Warner Paperback Library, 1973, 158 p., paper, novel. AVENGER #14.

04924   *The Avenger: Tuned for murder.* New York: Warner Paperback Library, 1973, 158 p., paper, novel. AVENGER #9.

The black death—SEE: *The Avenger: The black death.*

The blood ring—SEE: *The Avenger: The blood ring.*

Death in slow motion—SEE: *The Avenger: Death in slow motion.*

The devil's horns—SEE: *The Avenger: The devil's horns.*

The flame breathers—SEE: *The Avenger: The flame breathers.*

The frosted death—SEE: *The Avenger: The frosted death.*

The glass mountain—SEE: *The Avenger: The glass mountain.*

The green killer—SEE: *The Avenger: The green killer.*

The happy killers—SEE: *The Avenger: The happy killers.*

The hate master—SEE: *The Avenger: The hate master.*

House of death—SEE: *The Avenger: House of death.*

Justice, Inc.—SEE: *The Avenger: Justice, Inc.*

Midnight murder—SEE: *The Avenger: Midnight murder.*

Murder on wheels—SEE: *The Avenger: Murder on wheels.*

Nevlo—SEE: *The Avenger: Nevlo.*

Pictures of death—SEE: *The Avenger: Pictures of death.*

River of ice—SEE: *The Avenger: River of ice.*

The sky walker—SEE: *The Avenger: The sky walker.*

The smiling dogs—SEE: *The Avenger: The smiling dogs.*

Stockholders in death—SEE: *The Avenger: Stockholders in death.*

Three gold crowns—SEE: *The Avenger: Three gold crowns.*

Tuned for murder—SEE: *The Avenger: Tuned for murder.*

The Wilder curse—SEE: *The Avenger: The Wilder curse.*

The yellow hoard—SEE: *The Avenger: The yellow hoard.*

with Basil Wells

14962 *Dr. Satan.* Oak Lawn, IL: Robert Weinberg, 1974, 95 p, paper, coll. [Corrected entry; includes five Dr. Satan stories by Ernst, and one by Wells].

ERNSTING, Walter, 1920-

22706 *The day the gods died.* Toronto, New York: Bantam Books, 1976, 240 p., paper, novel.

as CLARK DARLTON

22707 *Atom fire on Mechanica.* Van Nuys, CA: Master Publications, 1978, 54 p., paper, novel. PERRY RHODAN #121. [Translation of *Atombrand auf Mechanica*].

22708 *Blazing sun.* New York: Ace Books, 1976, 171 p., paper, novel. PERRY RHODAN #86. [Includes additional fiction and nonfiction].

22709 *The bonds of eternity.* New York: Ace Books, 1975, 155 p., paper, novel. PERRY RHODAN #69. [Includes additional fiction and nonfiction].

22710 *Conflict center: Naator.* New York: Ace Books, 1975, 174 p., paper, novel. PERRY RHODAN #77. [Includes additional fiction and nonfiction].

22711 *Deadmen shouldn't die.* Van Nuys, CA: Master Publications, 1979, 64 p., paper, novel. PERRY RHODAN #132. [Translation of *Ein toter soll nicht sterben*].

22712 *Ernst Ellert returns!* New York: Ace Books, 1975, 172 p., paper, novel. PERRY RHODAN #83. [Includes additional fiction & nonfiction].

22713 *False front.* New York: Ace Books, 1976, 167 p., paper, novel. PERRY RHODAN #103. [Includes additional fiction and nonfiction].

22714 *Flight from Tarkihl.* New York: Ace Books, 1977, 111-251 p., paper, novel. ATLAN #2. [Bound with *Menace of atomigeddon* / by Kurt Mahr].

22715 *Heritage of the lizard people.* New York: Ace Books, 1977, 117 p., paper, novel. PERRY RHODAN #113. [Bound with *Death's demand* / by Kurt Mahr].

In the center of the galaxy—SEE: *Perry Rhodan: In the center of the galaxy.*

22716 *Perry Rhodan: In the center of the galaxy.* New York: Ace Books, 1978, 219 p., paper, novel. PERRY RHODAN SERIES.

22717 *Phantom fleet.* New York: Ace Books, 1976, 182 p., paper, novel. PERRY RHODAN #97. [Includes additional fiction and nonfiction].

22718 *The phantom horde.* Van Nuys, CA: Master Productions, 1979, 64 p., paper, novel. PERRY RHODAN #137. [Bound with *Star man* / by Stuart J. Byrne].

22719 *Recruits for Arkon.* New York: Ace Books, 1975, 155 p., paper, novel. PERRY RHODAN #76. [Includes additional fiction and nonfiction].

22720 *Sentinels of solitude.* Van Nuys, CA: Master Publications, 1979, 62 p., paper, novel. PERRY RHODAN #127. [Translation of *Wächter in der einsamkeit*].

22721 *The shadows attack.* New York: Ace Books, 1977, 133-255 p., paper, novel. PERRY RHODAN #118. [Bound with *Savior of the empire* / by K. H. Scheer].

22722 *Spaceship of ancestors.* New York: Ace Books, 1975, 160 p., paper, novel. PERRY RHODAN #73. [Includes additional fiction and nonfiction].

22723 *The starless realm.* New York: Ace Books, 1976, 166 p., paper, novel. PERRY RHODAN #87. [Includes additional fiction and nonfiction].

22724 *The stolen spacefleet.* New York: Ace Books, 1977, 123 p., paper, novel. PERRY RHODAN #109. [Includes some nonfiction; bound with *Sgt. Robot* / by Kurt Mahr].

22725 *Under the stars of Druufon.* New York: Ace Books, 1975, 158 p., paper, novel. PERRY RHODAN #68. [Includes additional fiction and nonfiction].

22726 *Vagabond of space.* New York: Ace Books, 1976, 203 p., paper, novel. PERRY RHODAN #93. [Includes additional fiction and nonfiction].

22727 *War of the ghosts.* New York: Ace Books, 1977, 133-250 p., paper, novel. ATLAN #5. [Bound with *The Crystal Prince* / by K. H. Scheer].

ERSKINE, Barbara, 1944-

22728 *Encounters.* London: Michael Joseph, 1990, viii+360 p., cloth, coll.

22729 *Kingdom of shadows.* London: Michael Joseph, 1988, 599 p., cloth, novel.

22730 *Lady of Hay.* London: Michael Joseph, 1986, 562 p., cloth, novel.

*ERSKINE, Douglas [pseud. of John Stuart Buchan]

ERSKINE, George, *with Ian Cameron*

Beware the Tektrons—SEE: *Counter force: Beware the Tektrons.*

19232 *Counter force: Beware the Tektrons.* London: Armada, 1988, 110 p., paper, novel. COUNTER FORCE SERIES.

19233 *Counter force: Find the Tektrons.* London: Armada, 1988, 125 p., paper, novel. COUNTER FORCE SERIES.

Find the Tektrons—SEE: *Counter force: Find the Tektrons.*

31220 *The official Counter Force reference book: the background on the Counter Force characters and the world they live in.* Glenrothes, Scotland: Dram Enterprises, 1986, [61] p., paper, nonf. COUNTER FORCE TIE-IN.

ERSKINE, Thomas L(eonard), 1939- , *with Gerald R. Barrett*

17472 *From fiction to film: Ambrose Bierce's "An occurrence at Owl Creek Bridge."* Encino & Belmont, CA: Dickenson Publishing Co., 1973, 216 p., paper, nonf. anth.

~~ERTZ, Susan, 1894 1985~~

ERWIN, Alan R.

22731 *The power exchange: a novel.* Austin, TX: Texas Monthly Press, 1979, 261 p., cloth, novel.

22732 *Skeleton dancer* / by Alan Erwin. New York: A Dell Book, 1989, 265 p., cloth, novel.

ESCHELBACH, Claire John, 1929- , *with Joyce Lee Shober*

22733 *Aldous Huxley: a bibliography, 1916-1959.* Berkeley & Los Angeles: University of California Press, 1961, x+150 p., cloth, nonf.

ESHBACH, Lloyd Arthur, 1910-

22734 *The armlet of the gods.* New York: A Del Rey Book, Ballantine Books, 1986, 261 p., paper, novel. GATES OF LUCIFER #2.

22735 *The elfin lights* / by L. A. Eshbach. [S.l.: s.n., n.d.], 12 p., paper, story.

22736 *The land beyond the gate.* New York: A Del Rey Book, Ballantine Books, 1984, 209 p., paper, novel. GATES OF LUCIFER #1.

22737 *Over my shoulder: reflections on a science fiction era.* Philadelphia, PA: Oswald Train: Publisher, 1983, 417 p., cloth, nonf.

22738 *The scroll of Lucifer.* New York: A Del Rey Book, Ballantine Books, 1990, 242 p., paper, novel. GATES OF LUCIFER #4.

22739 *The sorceress of Scath.* New York: A Del Rey Book, Ballantine Books, 1988, 241 p., paper, novel. GATES OF LUCIFER #3.

with E. E. "Doc" Smith

24074 *Subspace encounter.* New York: Berkley Books, 1983, 198 p., paper, novel. SUBSPACE EXPLORERS #2. ["Edited" (but actually completed) by Eshbach].

ESHLEMAN, Lloyd Wendell, 1902-1949

22740 *A Victorian rebel: the life of William Morris.* New York: Charles Scribner's Sons, 1940, xiv+386 p., cloth, nonf.

as LLOYD ERIC GREY

22740A retitled: *William Morris: prophet of England's new order.* London: Cassell, 1949, xiv+386 p., cloth, nonf.

ESLER, Anthony (James), 1934-

22741 *Babylon.* New York: William Morrow & Co., 1980, 416 p., cloth, novel.

22742 *Hellbane.* New York: William Morrow & Co., 1975, v+311 p., cloth, novel.

*****ESMOND, Sidney, 1893-**

ESSER, Kevin (Michael), 1953-

22743 *Dance of the warriors.* Amsterdam, Netherlands: Acolyte Press, 1988, 280 p., paper, novel.

*****ESSEX, Rosamund (Sibyl), 1900-1985**

ESSEX, William, pseud.—SEE: **Tigges, John**

*****ESTABROOKS, G(eorge) H(oben), 1895-1973**

*****ESTES, Eleanor (Ruth Rosenfeld), 1906-1988**

ESTES, Rose

22744 *Blood of the tiger.* Toronto, New York: Spectra, Bantam Books, 1987, 198 p., paper, novel. SAGA OF LOST LANDS #1.

22745 *Brother to the lion.* Toronto, New York: Spectra, Bantam Books, 1988, 212 p., paper, novel. SAGA OF LOST LANDS #2.

22746 *The children of the dragon.* New York: Random House, 1985, 183 p., cloth, novel.

22747 *Circus of fear.* Lake Geneva, WI: TSR Inc., 1983, 157 p., paper, novel. ENDLESS QUEST #10.

22748 *The demon hand: a journey to a land of wizards, demons, and magical gems.* Lake Geneva, WI: TSR Inc., 1988, 314 p., paper, novel. GREYHAWK ADVENTURES #5.

22749 *Dragon of doom.* Lake Geneva, WI: TSR Inc., 1983, 157 p., paper, novel. ENDLESS QUEST #13.

22750 *Dungeon of dread.* Lake Geneva, WI: TSR Inc., 1982, 128 p., paper, novel. ENDLESS QUEST #1.

22751 *The eyes have it: an adventure in a land of wizards, demons, and fire-breathing dragons.* Lake Geneva, WI: TSR Inc., 1989, 314 p., paper, novel. GREYHAWK ADVENTURES.

22752 *Hero of Washington Square.* Lake Geneva, WI: TSR Inc., 1983, 157 p., paper, novel. ENDLESS QUEST #7.

22753 *The hunter.* New York: Popular Library, 1990, 279 p., paper, novel. HUNTER #1.

22754 *The hunter on Arena.* New York: Warner Books, 1991, 267 p., paper, novel. HUNTER #2.

22755 *Indiana Jones and the lost treasure of Sheba.* New York: Ballantine Books, 1984, 115 p., paper, novel. FIND YOUR FATE ADVENTURE #2; INDIANA JONES SERIES.

22756 *Master Wolf: a novel of quest and romance, sorcery and death.* Lake Geneva, WI: TSR Inc., 1987, 314 p., paper, novel. GREYHAWK ADVENTURES #3.

22757 *Mountain of mirrors.* Lake Geneva, WI: TSR Inc., 1982, 153 p., paper, novel. ENDLESS QUEST #2.

22758 *The name of the game: a journey to a land of wizards, kings, and magical gems.* Lake Geneva, WI: TSR Inc., 1988, 311 p., paper, novel. GREYHAWK ADVENTURES #6.

22759 *Pillars of Pentegarn.* Lake Geneva, WI: TSR Inc., 1982, 153 p., paper, novel. ENDLESS QUEST #3.

22760 *The price of power: a journey into an incredible world of magic and peril.* Lake Geneva, WI: TSR Inc., 1987, 316 p., paper, novel. GREYHAWK ADVENTURES #4.

22761 *Return to Brookmere.* Lake Geneva, WI: TSR Inc., 1982, 153 p., paper, novel. ENDLESS QUEST #4.

22762 *Revenge of the rainbow dragons.* Lake Geneva, WI: TSR Inc., 1983, 157 p., paper, novel. ENDLESS QUEST #6.

22763 *Revolt of the dwarves.* Lake Geneva, WI: TSR Inc., 1983, 157 p., paper, novel. ENDLESS QUEST #5.

22764 *Spirit of the hawk.* Toronto, New York: Spectra, Bantam Books, 1988, 246 p., paper, novel. SAGA OF LOST LANDS #3.

with Tom Wham

22765 *Skryling's blade.* New York: Ace Books, 1990, 220 p., paper, novel. RUNESWORD #2.

ESTEY, Dale

Fortress island—SEE: *A lost tale.*

22766 *A lost tale.* London: W. H. Allen, 1980, 223 p., cloth, novel.

22766A retitled: *Fortress island.* London: A Star Book, W. H. Allen & Co., 1981, 223 p., paper, novel.

ESTLEMAN, Loren D., 1952- , as DR. JOHN H. WATSON

22767 *Dr. Jekyll and Mr. Holmes* / by Dr. John H. Watson, as edited by Loren D. Estleman. Garden City, NY: Doubleday & Co., 1979, 214 p., cloth, novel. SHERLOCK HOLMES SERIES.

22768 *Sherlock Holmes vs. Dracula; or, The adventure of the sanguinary count* / by John H. Watson, as edited by Loren D. Estleman. Garden City, New York: Doubleday & Co., 1978, 214 p., cloth, novel. SHERLOCK HOLMES SERIES; DRACULA SERIES.

ESTRADA, Patricia—SEE: Wallace, Patricia

ESTRIDGE, Robin—SEE: Loraine, Philip

ETCHEMENDY, Nancy (Elise Howell), 1952-

22769 *The crystal city.* New York: An Avon Camelot Book, 1985, 173 p., paper, novel. WATCHERS #2.

22770 *Stranger from the stars.* New York: An Avon Camelot Book, 1983, 150 p., paper, novel.

22771 *The watchers of space.* New York: An Avon Camelot Book, 1980, 124 p., paper, novel. WATCHERS #1.

ETCHISON, Dennis (William), 1943-

22772 *The blood kiss.* Los Angeles: Scream/Press, 1988, 216 p., cloth, coll.

22773 *The complete Masters of darkness.* Novato, CA, Lancaster, PA: Underwood-Miller, 1991, 766 p., cloth, anth. [Includes *Masters of Darkness*; *Masters of Darkness II*; *Masters of Darkness III* (the first appearance of the latter)].

22774 *Cutting edge.* Garden City, NY: Doubleday & Co., 1986, xv+290 p., cloth, anth.

22775 *The dark country.* Santa Cruz, CA: Scream/Press, 1982, vi+207 p., cloth, coll.

22776 *The dark country.* Eugene, OR: Pulphouse Publishing, 1991, 47 p., cloth, story. SHORT STORY HARDBACKS #13; SHORT STORY PAPERBACKS #21.

22777 *Darkside.* New York: Charter Books, 1986, 246 p., paper, novel.

22778 *The fog: a novel.* Toronto, New York: Bantam Books, 1980, 180 p., paper, movie.

22779 *Lord John ten: 10: a celebration.* Northridge, CA: Lord John Press, 1988, 240 p., cloth, anth. [Includes verse and nonfiction]

22780 *Masters of darkness.* New York: Tor Horror, A Tom Doherty Associates Book, 1986, xii+338 p., paper, anth.

22781 *Masters of darkness II.* New York: Tor Horror, A Tom Doherty Associates Book, 1988, x+338 p., paper, anth.

22782 *Masters of darkness III.* New York: Tor, A Tom Doherty Associates Book, 1991, xiii+332 p., paper, anth. [Previously included as the last third of *The complete masters of darkness*].

22783 *Red dreams.* Santa Cruz, CA: Scream/Press, 1984, 220 p., cloth, coll.

as JACK MARTIN

22784 *Halloween II.* New York: Zebra Books, Kensington Publishing Corp., 1981, 256 p., paper, movie. HALLOWEEN #2.

22785 *Halloween III: Season of the witch.* New York: A Jove Book, 1982, 228 p., paper, movie. HALLOWEEN #3.
Season of the witch—SEE: *Halloween III: Season of the witch.*

22786 *Videodrome: a novel.* New York: Zebra Books, Kensington Publishing Corp., 1983, 255 p., paper, movie.

ETHERINGTON, Norman (Alan), 1941-

22787 *Rider Haggard.* Boston: Twayne Publishers, 1984, 138 p., cloth, nonf.

ETKIN, Anne (Dunwoody Little), 1923-

22788 *Eglerio! in praise of Tolkien.* Greencastle, PA: Quest Communications, 1978, 100 p., paper, nonf. anth.

22789 *The magination.* Baltimore, MD: T-K Graphics, 1975?, 45 p., paper, fiction. MABINOGION PARODY.

22790 *Waterspout up.* Baltimore, MD: T-K Graphics, 1975, [63] p., paper, novel. WATERSHIP DOWN PARODY.

ETRA, Jonathan, 1952-1991, *with Stephanie Spinner*

22791 *Aliens for breakfast.* New York: A Stepping Stone Book, Random House, 1988, 62 p., paper, story. ALIENS #1.

22792 *Aliens for lunch.* New York: A Stepping Stone Book, Random House, 1991, 62 p., paper, story. ALIENS #2.

EULO, Elena Yates

22793 *Ice orchids.* New York: Berkley Books, 1984, 223 p., paper, novel.

EULO, Ken, 1939-

22794 *The bloodstone.* New York: Pocket Books, 1981, 326 p., paper, novel. CHANDAL #2.

22795 *The brownstone.* New York: Pocket Books, 1980, x+332 p., paper, novel. CHANDAL #1.

22796 *The deathstone.* New York: Pocket Books, 1982, 329 p., paper, novel. CHANDAL #3.

22797 *The ghost of Veronica Gray.* New York: Pocket Books, 1985, 279 p., paper, novel.

22798 *The house of Caine.* New York: Tor Horror, A Tom Doherty Associates Book, 1988, 501 p., paper, novel.

22799 *Nocturnal.* New York: Pocket Books, 1983, 294 p., paper, novel.

EVANS, Arthur B(ruce), 1946-

22800 *Jules Verne rediscovered: didacticism and the scientific novel.* New York, Westport, CT: Greenwood Press, 1988, xv+199 p., cloth, nonf. [Winner of the J. Lloyd Eaton Award for Best Nonfiction Book of the Year, 1988 (1990)].

EVANS, Bill [i.e., William Harrington Evans], 1921-1985

22801 *The Gernsback forerunners.* Brooklyn, New York: Julius Unger, 1944, 5 p., paper, nonf.

with Francis T. Laney

22802 *Howard Phillips Lovecraft (1890-1937): a tentative bibliography* / by Francis T. Laney and William H. Evans. Los Angeles: An "Acolyte" Publication, FAPA, 1943, 12 p., paper, nonf.

with Robert Pavlat

22803 *Fanzine index: listing most fanzines from the beginning through 1952, including titles, editors' names, and data on each issue.* Flushing, NY: Harold Palmer Piser, Worldfair Publications, 1965, 141 p., paper, nonf.

EVANS, Chris(topher D.), 1951-

22804 *Capella's Golden Eyes* / by C. D. Evans. London, Boston: Faber & Faber, 1980, 220 p., cloth, novel.
22805 *Conspiracy theories.* London: Chris Evans, 1987, 50 p., paper, nonf. anth.
22806 *The insider.* London, Boston: Faber & Faber, 1981, 215 p., cloth, novel.
22807 *Writing science fiction* / by Christopher Evans. New York: St. Martin's Press, 1988, 97 p., cloth, nonf.

as CHRISTOPHER CARPENTER

22808 *The twilight realm.* London: Arrow Books, 1985, 302 p., cloth, novel.

as NATHAN ELLIOTT

22809 *Earth invaded.* London: Grafton, 1986, 160 p., cloth, novel. HOOD'S ARMY TRILOGY #1.
      Innerspace—SEE: *Steven Spielberg's Innerspace.*
22810 *Kidnap in space.* London: Dragon, 1987, 155 p., paper, movie. STAR PIRATES #1.
22811 *The liberators.* London: Grafton, 1986, 144 p., cloth, novel. HOOD'S ARMY TRILOGY #3.
22812 *Plague moon.* London: Dragon, 1987, 160 p., paper, movie. STAR PIRATES #2.
22813 *Staveworld.* London: Grafton, 1986, 144 p., cloth, novel. HOOD'S ARMY TRILOGY #2.

22814 *Steven Spielberg's Innerspace.* London: Dragon, 1987, 141 p., paper, movie.
22815 *Treasure planet.* London: Dragon, 1987, 156 p., paper, movie. STAR PIRATES #3.

as ROBERT KNIGHT

22816 *Plasmid: a novelisation.* London: A Star Book, W. H. Allen & Co., 1980, 191 p., paper, movie.

as JOHN LYON

22817 *The summoning.* London: Panther, 1985, 207 p., paper, novel.

with Jim Burns

19067 *Lightship.* Limpsfield, Surrey, England: Paper Tiger, 1985, 125 p., cloth, art.

with Martyn Dean

21446 *Dream makers: six fantasy artists at work.* Limpsfield, Surrey, England: Paper Tiger, 1988, 127 p., cloth, art.
21447 *The guide to fantasy art techniques.* Limpsfield, Surrey, England: Dragon's World, A Paper Tiger Book, 1984, 111 p., cloth, nonf.

with Stan Gooch

22818 *Science fiction as religion* / by Christopher Evans... Frome, Somerset, England: Bran's Head Books, 1981, 15 p., paper, nonf.

with Robert Holdstock

22819 *Other Edens* / by Christopher Evans... London: Unwin Paperbacks, 1987, ix+ 237 p., paper, anth.
22820 *Other Edens II* / by Christopher Evans... London: Unwin Paperbacks, 1988, viii+ 266 p., paper, anth.
22821 *Other Edens III* / by Christopher Evans... London, Sydney: Unwin Paperbacks, 1989, viii+237 p., paper, anth.

*EVANS, Christopher (Riche), 1931-_1979_

EVANS, Dik, *with Hilary Evans*

22822 *Beyond the gaslight: science in popular fiction, 1895-1905.* London: Frederick Muller, 1976, 160 p., cloth, anth.

EVANS, Gerald, 1910-

37743 *Shadows in Landore: the collected short stories of Gerald Evans, volume 1.* Swansea, Wales: A Morfa Production, 1979, 78 p., paper, coll. [Only volume published].

as VICTOR LA SALLE

08633 *The black sphere.* London: John Spencer & Co., 1952, 108 p., paper, novel.

*EVANS, Gwyn, 1899-1938

EVANS, Hilary, 1929- , *with Dik Evans*

22822 *Beyond the gaslight: science in popular fiction, 1895-1905.* London: Frederick Muller, 1976, 160 p., cloth, anth.

EVANS, Ian, pseud.—SEE: Wells, Angus

EVANS, Lawrence Watt—SEE: Watt-Evans, Lawrence

EVANS, M(ary?) Ann, *with Jay Burchett*

10022 *Border to terrorism.* Newport Beach, CA: Newport Publishing House, 1988, 295 p., paper, novel.

EVANS, Mary Ann, *with H. G. Wells*

22824 *The war of the worlds.* New York: Random House, 1991, 94 p., cloth, novel. [Adapted from Wells's original novel].

EVANS, May Garrettson, 1866-1947

22825 *Music and Edgar Allan Poe: a bibliographical study.* Baltimore, MD: Johns Hopkins Press, 1939, 97 p., cloth, nonf.

EVANS, Peter Darvill- —SEE: Darvill-Evans, Peter

EVANS, Robert O(wen), 1919- , *with Jack I. Biles*

17957 *William Golding: some critical considerations.* Lexington, KY: University Press of Kentucky, 1978, xi+283 p., cloth, nonf. anth.

EVANS, William H.—SEE: Evans, Bill

EVARTS, Hal G(eorge) Jr., 1915-

22826 *Jay-Jay and the Peking monster.* New York: Charles Scribner's Sons, 1978, 185 p., cloth, novel.

*EVARTS, R(ichard) C(onover), 1890-1972

EVERETT, H(enrietta) D(orothy), 1851-1923

22827 *Malevola.* London: Heath Cranton & Ouseley, 1914, p., cloth, novel.

EVERETT, Percival (L.), 1937-

22828 *Zulus.* Sag Harbor, NY: Permanent Press, 1991, 247 p., cloth, novel.

EVERMAN, Welch D(uane), 1946-

22829 *Jerzy Kosinski: the literature of violation.* San Bernardino, CA: R. Reginald, The Borgo Press, 1991, 158 p., cloth, nonf. MILFORD SERIES: POPULAR WRITERS OF TODAY #47.

EVERS, R. Michael, *with Thomas L. Wymer & Alice Calderonello & Sara Jayne Steen & Lowell P. Leland*

10206 *Intersections: the elements of science in science fiction.* Bowling Green, OH: The Popular Press, 1978, viii+130 p., paper, nonf.

EVERSON, William K(eith), 1929-

22830 *More classics of the horror film.* Secaucus, NJ: Citadel Press, 1986, 256 p., cloth, nonf.

EVERTS, R. Alain

37744 *Lovecraft and Lord Dunsany.* [Madison, WI]: The Strange Company, 1979, [23] p., paper, nonf.

37745 *William Hope Hodgson, night pirate, volume two: Some facts in the case of William Hope Hodgson, master of phantasy.* Toronto: Soft Books, 1987, [40] p., paper, nonf.

with George Wetzel

37746 *Winifred Virginia Jackson, Lovecraft's lost romance.* Madison, WI: The Strange Company, 1975?, 13 p., paper, nonf.

EVSLIN, Bernard, 1922-

22831 *Jason and the Argonauts.* New York: William Morrow, 1986, 165 p., cloth, novel.

EWERS, Hanns Heinz, 1871-1943

22832 *Blood.* San Diego, CA: Valcour & Krueger, 1977, 80 p., paper, coll. [Limited to 1000 copies].

EYERS, John

Genesis of a hero—SEE: *Survivors: Genesis of a hero.*

22833 *Survivors: Genesis of a hero.* London: Weidenfeld & Nicolson, 1977, 189 p., cloth, novel. SURVIVORS #2. [Sequel to the novel by Terry Nation].

EYLES, Allen, 1941-

22834 *The world of Oz.* Harmondsworth, Middlesex, England: Viking, 1985, 96 p., cloth, nonf.

with R. K. Adkinson & Nicholas Fry

16034 *The house of horror: the complete story of Hammer Films, 2nd ed.* London: Lorrimer, 1981, 144 p., cloth, nonf.

F

FABER, Inez M.—SEE: Beresford, Elizabeth

FABIAN, Stephen E(mil Jr.), 1930-

22835 *The best of Stephen E. Fabian.* Mason, MI: Loompanics Unlimited, 1976, 50 leaves, paper, art.

22836 *Crystal of a hundred dreams: a portfolio.* San Francisco, Columbia, PA: Underwood-Miller, 1979, 16 leaves, paper, art coll.

37747 *Fabian in color.* Mercer Island, WA: Starmont House, 1980, [8] plates, cloth, art.

22837 *Fantastic nudes: a portfolio.* Saddle River, NJ: Gerry de la Ree, 1976, [10] leaves, paper, art. [Edited by Gerry de la Ree].

22838 *Fantastic nudes, second series.* Saddle River, NJ: Gerry de la Ree, 1976, [10] leaves, paper, art. [Edited by Gerry de la Ree].

21376 *Fantasy by Fabian: the art of Stephen E. Fabian.* Saddle River, NJ: Gerry de la Ree, 1978, 128 p., cloth, art. [Edited by Gerry de la Ree].

37748 *Letters Lovecraftian: an alphabet of illuminated letters inspired by the works of the late master of the weird tale, Howard Phillips Lovecraft (1890-1937).* Saddle River, NJ: Gerry de la Ree, 1974, [57] p., paper, art. [Limited to 400 copies].

21377 *More fantasy by Fabian: the art of Stephen E. Fabian.* Saddle River, NJ: Gerry de la Ree, 1979, 128 p., cloth, art. [Edited by Gerry de la Ree].

22839 *Portfolio.* West Linn, OR: FAX Collector's Editions, 1979, [8] leaves, cloth, art.

FAGIN, Nathan Bryllion, 1888-1972

22840 *The histrionic Mr. Poe.* Baltimore, MD: Johns Hopkins Press, 1949, xiii+289 p., cloth, nonf.

FAGUNDES TELLES, Lygia—SEE: Telles, Lygia Fagundes

FAHY, Christopher, 1937-

22841 *Dream house.* New York: Zebra Books, Kensington Publishing Corp., 1987, 350 p., paper, novel.

22842 *Eternal bliss.* New York: Zebra Books, Kensington Publishing Corp., 1988, 287 p., paper, novel.

22843 *The Lyssa syndrome.* New York: Zebra Books, Kensington Publishing Corp., 1990, 352 p., paper, novel.

22844 *Nightflyer.* New York: A Jove Book, 1982, 296 p., paper, novel.

FAIG, Kenneth W. Jr.

22845 *H. P. Lovecraft: his life, his work.* West Warwick, RI: Necronomicon Press, 1979, 36 p., paper, nonf.

22846 *In memoriam: Howard Phillips Lovecraft, Ethel M. Phillips Morrish.* Glenview, IL: Moshassuck Press, 1987, 14 p., paper, nonf. [Limited to 50 copies].

22847 *Life and death: a hoax and a retraction.* Glenview, IL: Moshassuck Press, 1989, 6 leaves, paper, nonf. [Limited to 19 copies].

22848 *The parents of Howard Phillips Lovecraft.* West Warwick, RI: Necronomicon Press, 1990, 46 p., paper, nonf.

22849 *Tales of the Lovecraft collectors.* Glenview, IL: Moshassuck Press, 1989, 77 p., paper, nonf. [Limited to 25 copies].

FAIR, Jeff, 1952-

22850 *The burning.* New York: Leisure Books, 1981, 287 p., paper, novel.

FAIRBAIRNS, Zoë (Ann), 1948-

22851 *Benefits: a novel.* London: Virago, 1979, 214 p., cloth, novel.

FAIRCLOTH, Cyril E(dward)

22852 *Escape from the city of gold.* Ilfracombe, England: Arthur H. Stockwell, 1980, 103 p., cloth, novel.

22853 *The midget planet.* Ilfracombe, England: Arthur H. Stockwell, 1974, 138 p., cloth, novel.

FAIRMAN, Paul W(arren), 1909-1977

22854 *The girl with something extra.* New York: Lancer Books, 1973, 192 p., paper, tele.

as IVAR JORGENSEN

　　　Ten deadly men--SEE: *Ten from infinity.*
05005 *Ten from infinity.* Derby, CT: Monarch Books, 1963, 139 p., paper, novel.
05005B retitled: *Ten deadly men.* New York: Pinnacle Books, 1976, 188 p., paper, novel.

FALCONAR, A. E. I.

22855 *Tales of myth and fantasy.* Douglas, Isle of Man, United Kingdom: Norris Modern Press, 1984, 89 p., paper, coll.

FALCONER, Lee N., pseud.—SEE: May, Julian

FALCONER, Sovereign, pseud.—SEE: Strete, Craig

FALK, Jonathan, *with Todd Mecklem*

22856 *The liquid retreats.* Union, OR: Wordcraft of Oregon, 1991, 43 p., paper, coll.

FALK, Margaret

22857 *Darkscope.* New York: Pinnacle Books, Windsor Publishing Corp., 1990, 382 p., paper, novel.

FALKNER, J(ohn) Meade, 1858-1932

37749 *A midsummer night's marriage.* Edinburgh, Scotland: Tragara Press, 1977, 35 p., paper, story. [Limited to 160 copies].

FALLINGSTAR, Cerridwen

22858 *The heart of the fire: a novel.* San Geronimo, CA: Cauldron Publications, 1990, xi+521 p., paper, novel.

FANCHER, Jane S(uzanne), 1952-

22859 *Groundties.* New York: Warner Books, 1991, 376 p., paper, novel.

FANE, Julian (Charles), 1927-

22860 *Revolution island.* London: Hamish Hamilton & St. George's Press, 1979, 216 p., cloth, novel.

FANTHORPE, (Robert) Lionel, 1935-

as L. P. KENTON

08175 *Destination Moon.* London: Badger Books, 1959, 157 p., paper, novel.

with Patricia Fanthorpe

22861 *The Black Lion.* Cardiff, Wales: Greystoke Mobray Ltd., 1979, 159 p., paper, novel.

FANTHORPE, Patricia (Alice Tooke), 1938- , *with Lionel Fanthorpe*

22861 *The Black Lion.* Cardiff, Wales: Greystoke Mobray Ltd., 1979, 159 p., paper, novel.

FANU, J. Sheridan Le—SEE: Le Fanu, J. Sheridan

FARADAY, M. M., pseud.—SEE: Rorvik, David

FARBER, James

22862 *Blood island.* New York: Pocket Books, 1981, 323 p., paper, novel.
22863 *Nightmare's child.* New York: Pocket Books, 1983, 297 p., paper, novel.

FARIGOULE, Louis—SEE: Romains, Jules

FARJEON, Eleanor, 1881-1965

15803 *The silver curlew.* London: Oxford University Press, 1953, 182 p., cloth, novel.

*FARLEY, Walter, 1915-<u>1989</u>

FARMER, Derek

with Bram Stoker

22864 *Blood from the mummy's tomb.* London: Fleshcreepers, Century Hutchinson, 1986, 144 p., cloth, novel. [An adaptation of Bram Stoker's *Jewel of seven stars*].

with Bram Stoker as DEREK ALLEN

22864A *Blood from the mummy's tomb.* New York: Barron's Educational Series, 1988, 138 p., cloth?, novel. [An adaptation of Stoker's *Jewel of seven stars*; previously published under the name Derek Farmer].

FARMER, Penelope (Jane), 1939-

22865 *Eve: her story*. London: Victor Gollancz, 1985, 188 p., cloth, novel.

22866 *Glasshouses*. London: Victor Gollancz, 1988, 215 p., cloth, novel.

22867 *The summer birds*. London: The Bodley Head, 1985, 107 p., cloth, novel. EMMA #1. [Revised edition of #05179].

22868 *Thicker than water*. London: Walker Books, 1989, 189 p., cloth, novel.

22869 *Year king*. London: Chatto & Windus, 1977, 232 p., cloth, novel.

FARMER, Philip José, 1918-

22870 *A barnstormer in Oz; or, A rationalization and extrapolation of the split-level continuum*. Huntington Woods, MI: Phantasia Press, 1982, 278 p., cloth, novel. OZ SERIES. [Limited to 600 copies].

22871 *Behind the walls of Terra*. Huntington Woods, MI: Phantasia Press, 1982, 222 p., cloth, novel. WORLD OF TIERS #4. [Revised edition of #05183].

22872 *The cache; includes two bonus stories: They twinkled like jewels and Rastignac the devil*. New York: Tor, A Tom Doherty Associates Book, 1981, 207 p., paper, coll. [Includes *The cache from outer space*].

22873 *The classic Philip José Farmer, 1952-1964*. New York: Crown SF Classics, Crown Publishers, 1984, xii+215 p., cloth, coll.

22874 *The classic Philip José Farmer, 1964-1973*. New York: Crown SF Classics, Crown Publishers, 1984, xv+207 p., cloth, coll.

22875 *The dark design*. New York: Berkley Publishing Corp., 1977, 412 p., cloth, novel. RIVERWORLD #3.

22876 *Dark is the sun*. New York: A Del Rey Book, Ballantine Books, 1979, 405 p., cloth, novel.

22877 *Dayworld*. New York: G. P. Putnam's Sons, 1985, 320 p., cloth, novel. DAYWORLD #1.

22878 *Dayworld breakup*. New York: Tor SF, A Tom Doherty Associates Book, 1990, iii+324 p., cloth, novel. DAYWORLD #3.

22879 *Dayworld rebel*. New York: An Ace/Putnam Book, 1987, 317 p., cloth, novel. DAYWORLD #2.

22880 *Doc Savage: Escape from Loki: Doc Savage's first adventure*. New York, Toronto: Falcon, Bantam Books, 1991, 214 p., paper, novel. DOC SAVAGE SERIES.

The empire of the nine—SEE: *Lord of the trees; and, The mad goblin*.

Escape from Loki—SEE: *Doc Savage: Escape from Loki*.

22881 *Father to the stars*. New York: A Tom Doherty Associates Book, Tor Science Fiction, Pinnacle Books, 1981, 319 p., paper, coll.

22882 *Flesh; and, Lord Tyger*. New York: A Signet Book, New American Library, 1981, 191+287 p., paper, coll.

22883 *Flight to Opar*. New York: DAW Books, 1976, 212 p., paper, novel. OPAR #2.

05195 *The gate of time*. New York: Belmont Productions, 1966, 176 p., paper, novel.

22884 retitled: *Two Hawks from Earth*. New York: Ace Books, 1979, 311 p., paper, novel. [Expanded edition].

22885 *The gates of creation*. Huntington Woods, MI: Phantasia Press, 1981, 192 p., cloth, novel. WORLD OF TIERS #2. [Revised edition of #05196].

22886 *Gods of Riverworld*. Huntington Woods, MI: Phantasia Press, 1983, 279 p., cloth, novel. RIVERWORLD #5. [Limited to 650 copies].

22887 *The grand adventure*. New York: Berkley Books, 1984, xvii+327 p., cloth, coll.

22888 *Greatheart Silver*. New York: Tor, A Tom Doherty Associates Book, 1982, 286 p., paper, novel.

22889 *Image of the beast*. Chicago: Playboy Press Paperbacks, 1979, 336 p., paper, coll. HERALD CHILDE #1-2. [Includes *Image of the beast* and *Blown*].

22890 *Jesus on Mars*. Los Angeles: Pinnacle Books, 1979, 256 p., paper, novel.

Keepers of the secrets—SEE: *The mad goblin*.

22891 *The lavalite world*. New York: Ace Books, 1977, 282 p., paper, novel. WORLD OF TIERS #5.

22892 *The lavalite world*. Huntington Woods, MI: Phantasia Press, 1983, 227 p., cloth, novel. WORLD OF TIERS #5. [Revised edition].

22893 *Lord of the trees; and, The mad goblin*. New York: Ace Books, 1980, 374 p., paper, coll. LORD GRANDITH #2; DOC CALIBAN #2.

22893A retitled: *The empire of the nine*. London: Sphere Books, 1988, 306 p., paper, coll. LORD GRANDITH #2; DOC CALIBAN #2.

22894 *The lovers*. New York: A Del Rey Book, Ballantine Books, 1979, 219 p., cloth, novel. [Revised and expanded edition of #05203].

05204 *The mad goblin*. New York: Ace Books, 1970, 130 p., paper, novel. DOC CALIBAN #2. [Bound with *Lord of the trees*].

05204A retitled: *Keepers of the secrets*. London: Sphere Books, 1983, 152 p., paper, novel. DOC CALIBAN #2.

22895 *The magic labyrinth*. New York: Berkley Publishing Corp., 1980, 339 p., cloth, novel. RIVERWORLD #4.

22896 *The maker of universes*. Huntington Woods, MI: Phantasia Press, 1980, 220 p., cloth, novel. WORLD OF TIERS #1. [Revised edition of #05205].

22897 *A private cosmos*. Huntington Woods, MI: Phantasia Press, 1981, 250 p., cloth, novel. WORLD OF TIERS #3. [Revised edition of #05209].

22898 *The purple book*. New York: Tor, A Tom Doherty Associates Book, 1982, 287 p., paper, coll.

22899 *Reap: the Baycon guest-of-honor speech*. Los Angeles: Philip José Farmer, 1968, 14 p., paper, nonf.

22900 *Red Orc's rage*. New York: Tor Fantasy, A Tom Doherty Associates Book, 1991, vi+282 p., cloth, novel.

22901 *River of eternity*. Huntington Woods, MI: Phantasia Press, 1983, 205 p., cloth, novel. RIVERWORLD SERIES. [The original Riverworld novel, written in the early 1950s, and very loosely corresponding to *The dark design*].

22902 *Riverworld: the great short fiction of Philip José Farmer*. New York: A Berkley Book, Berkley Publishing Corp., 1979, 264 p., paper, coll. RIVERWORLD SERIES.

22903 *Riverworld war: the suppressed fiction of Philip Jose Farmer*. Peoria, IL: Ellis Press, 1980, 107 p., paper, coll.

22904 *Stations of the nightmare*. New York: Tor, A Tom Doherty Associates Book, 1982, 256 p., paper, novel.
Two Hawks from Earth—SEE: *The gate of time*.

22905 *The unreasoning mask*. New York: G. P. Putnam's Sons, 1981, 293 p., cloth, novel.

22909A *Venus on the half-shell*. Toronto, New York: Spectra, Bantam Books, 1988, xii+178 p., paper, novel. [Previously published under the name Kilgore Trout].

22906 *The world of tiers*. Garden City, NY: Nelson Doubleday, 1981, 2 v. (I-312 p.; II- p.), cloth, coll. WORLD OF TIERS #1-5. [Includes (volume 1) *The maker of universes*, *The gates of creation*; (volume 2) *A private cosmos*, *Behind the walls of Terra*, *The lavalite world*].

22907 *World of tiers 1*. London: Sphere Books, 1986, 467 p., paper, coll. WORLD OF TIERS #1-3. [Includes *The maker of universes*; *The gates of creation*; *A private cosmos*].

22908 *World of tiers 2*. London: Sphere Books, 1986, 325 p., paper, coll. WORLD OF TIERS #4-5. [Includes *Behind the walls of Terra*; *The lavalite world*].

as KILGORE TROUT

22909 *Venus on the half-shell*. New York: A Dell Book, 1975, 204 p., paper, novel.

with J.-H. Rosny, Aîné

22910 *Ironcastle*. New York: DAW Books, 1976, 175 p., paper, novel. [Translation and adaptation by Farmer of *L'Etonnante aventure de Hareton Ironcastle*].

FARMER, Richard N(eil), 1928-

22911 *Islandia revisited*. Bloomington, IN: Cedarwood Press, 1983, 216 p., paper?, novel. ISLANDIA SEQUEL.

FARRAR, Stewart, 1916-

22912 *Backlash*. London: Robert Hale, 1988, 191 p., cloth, novel.

22913 *The dance of blood*. London: Arrow Books, 1977, 235 p., paper, novel.

22914 *Omega*. London: Arrow Books, 1980, 506 p., paper, novel.

22915 *The serpent of Lilith*. London: Arrow Books, 1976, 254 p., paper, novel.

22916 *The sword of Orley*. London: Michael Joseph, 1977, 235 p., cloth, novel.

FARRELL, Edmund J(ames), 1927- , with Thomas E. Gage & John Pfordresher & Raymond J. Rodrigues

22917 *Fantasy: shapes of things unknown*. Glenview, IL & Dallas, TX: Scott, Foresman & Co., 1974, 384 p., paper, anth. [Includes some nonfiction].

FARRELL, Jackson T., 1904-1978

22918 *The flight of the Endeavor*. New York: Manor Books, 1978, 224 p., paper, novel.

FARRELL, Robert T(homas), 1938- , with Mary Salvaggio

22919 *J. R. R. Tolkien, scholar and storyteller: essays in memoriam*. Ithaca, NY: Cornell University Press, 1979, 325 p., cloth, nonf. anth.

FARRELL, Simon, 1960- , *with Jon Sutherland*

22920 *Bardik the thief.* London: Magnet, 1987, [192] p., paper, fiction. CITY OF SHADOWS #2.

22921 *Coreus the prince.* London: Magnet, 1987, [192] p., paper, fiction. CITY OF SHADOWS #1.

22922 *Darian: master magician.* London: Magnet Books, 1987, [200] p., paper, fiction. GLADE OF DREAMS #1.

22923 *Issel: warrior king.* London: Magnet Books, 1987, [200] p., paper, fiction. GLADE OF DREAMS #2.

FARREN, David [pseud. of Douglass David McFerran], 1934-

22924 *Mendaga's morning.* London: Sphere Books, 1979, 176 p., paper, novel.

FARREN, Mick, 1943-

22925 *The Armageddon crazy.* New York: A Del Rey Book, Ballantine Books, 1989, 282 p., paper, novel.

Citizen Phaid—SEE: *The song of Phaid.*

22926 *Corpse.* Sevenoaks, Kent, England: New English Library, 1986, 304 p., paper, novel.

22926A retitled: *Vickers.* New York: Ace Books, 1988, 263 p., paper, novel.

Exit Funtopia—SEE: *The long orbit.*

22927 *The feelies.* London: Michael Dempsey, Big O Publishing, 1978, 158 p., paper, novel.

22928 *The feelies.* New York: A Del Rey Book, Ballantine Books, 1990, 197 p., paper, novel. [Revised edition].

22929 *The last stand of the DNA cowboys.* New York: A Del Rey Book, Ballantine Books, 1989, 283 p., paper, novel. JEB STUART HO #4.

22930 *The long orbit.* New York: A Del Rey Book, Ballantine Books, 1988, 264 p., paper, novel.

22930A retitled: *Exit Funtopia.* London: Sphere Books, 1989, 264 p., paper, novel.

22931 *Mars—the red planet.* New York: A Del Rey Book, Ballantine Books, 1990, 315 p., paper, novel.

22932 *Necrom.* New York: A Del Rey Book, Ballantine Books, 1991, 371 p., paper, novel.

22933 *The neural atrocity.* St Albans, Hertfordshire, England: Mayflower, 1977, 191 p., paper, novel. JEB STUART HO #3.

Phaid the gambler—SEE: *The song of Phaid the Gambler.*

22934 *Protectorate.* Sevenoaks, Kent, England: New English Library, 1984, 251 p., paper, novel.

22935 *The quest of the DNA cowboys.* St Albans, Hertfordshire, England: Mayflower, 1976, 223 p., paper, novel. JEB STUART HO #1.

22936 *The song of Phaid the Gambler.* London: New English Library, 1981, 537 p., paper, novel.

22937 retitled: *Phaid the Gambler, being part one of The song of Phaid the Gambler.* New York: Ace Science Fiction Books, 1986, 296 p., paper, novel. [A revised edition which splits the original version into two pieces, of which the second part is *Citizen Phaid*].

22938 retitled: *Citizen Phaid, being part two of The song of Phaid the gambler.* New York: Ace Science Fiction Books, 1987, 234 p., paper, novel. [A revised edition which splits the original version into two pieces, of which the first part is *Phaid the Gambler*].

22939 *Synaptic manhunt.* St Albans, Hertfordshire, England: Mayflower, 1976, 252 p., paper, novel. JEB STUART HO #2.

22940 *Their master's war.* New York: A Del Rey Book, Ballantine Books, 1987, 295 p., paper, novel.

Vickers—SEE: *Corpse.*

FARRINGTON, Geoffrey, 1955-

22941 *The acts of the apostates.* Sawtry, Cambridgeshire, England: Dedalus, 1990, viii+272 p., cloth, novel.

22942 *The revenants.* London: Dedalus, 1983, 168 p., cloth, novel.

FARRIS, John, 1936-

22943 *All heads turn when the hunt goes by.* Chicago: A Playboy Press Book, 1977, 364 p., cloth, novel.

22943A retitled: *Bad blood.* London: Victor Gollancz Horror, 1989, 350 p., paper, novel.

The axeman cometh—SEE: *The axman cometh.*

22944 *The axman cometh.* New York: Tor Horror, A Tom Doherty Associates Book, 1989, 269 p., paper, novel.

22944A retitled: *The axeman cometh.* London: Hodder & Stoughton, 1990, 160 p., cloth, novel.

Bad blood—SEE: *All heads turn when the hunt goes by.*

22945 *Catacombs.* New York: Delacorte Press, 1981, 439 p., cloth, novel.

22946 *Fiends: a novel.* Arlington Heights, IL: Dark Harvest, 1990, 314 p., cloth, novel.

22947 *The fury.* Chicago: Playboy Press, 1976, 341 p., cloth, novel.

22948 *King Windom.* New York: Trident Press, 1967, 635 p., cloth, novel.

22949 *Minotaur.* New York: Tor, A Tom Doherty Associates Book, 1985, 373 p., paper, novel.

22950 *Nightfall.* New York: Tor Horror, A Tom Doherty Associates Book, 1987, 311 p., paper, novel.

22951 *Scare tactics.* New York: Tor Books, 1988, 310 p., cloth, coll.

22952 *Scare tactics.* New York: Tor Horror, A Tom Doherty Associates Book, 1989, 343 p., paper, coll. [Expanded edition which includes two extra stories].

22953 *Sharp practice: a novel.* New York: Simon & Schuster, 1974, 286 p., cloth, novel.

22954 *Shatter.* London: W. H. Allen & Co., 1980, 283 p., cloth, novel.

22955 *Son of the endless night.* New York: St. Martin's Press, 1985, 509 p., cloth, novel.

22956 *The uninvited.* New York: Delacorte Press, 1982, 261 p., cloth, novel.

22957 *When Michael calls.* New York: Trident Press, 1967, 184 p., cloth, novel.

22958 *Wildwood.* New York: Tor, A Tom Doherty Associates Book, 1986, 445 p., cloth, novel.

FARSON, Daniel (Negley), 1927-

22959 *The Beaver book of horror.* London: Beaver Books, 1977, 206 p., paper, nonf.

22959A retitled: *The Hamlyn book of horror.* London: Hamlyn, 1979, 157 p., cloth, nonf.

22960 *Clifton House mystery: a modern ghost story.* London: Independent Television Books, Arrow Books, 1978, 160 p., paper, novel.

22961 *Curse.* Feltham, England: Hamlyn, 1980, ix+241 p., cloth, novel.

The Hamlyn book of horror—SEE: *The Beaver book of horror.*

22962 *The man who wrote Dracula: a biography of Bram Stoker.* London: Michael Joseph, 1975, 240 p., cloth, nonf.

FAST, Howard (Melvin), 1914-

The magic door—SEE: *Tony and the wonderful door.*

22963 *Time and the riddle: thirty-one zen stories.* Pasadena, CA: Ward Ritchie Press, 1975, xv+490 p., cloth, coll.

05232 *Tony and the wonderful door.* New York: Alfred A. Knopf, 1968, 80 p., cloth, novel.

05232A retitled: *The magic door.* Culver City, CA: Peace Press, 1979, 80 p., cloth, novel.

FAST, Jonathan (David), 1948-

37750 *The beast: a novel.* New York: Random House, 1981, 290 p., cloth, novel.

22964 *The Inner Circle.* New York: Delacorte Press, 1979, 274 p., cloth, novel.

22965 *Mortal gods: a novel.* New York: Harper & Row, 1978, 153 p., cloth, novel.

Prisoner of the planets—SEE: *Secrets of synchronicity.*

22966 *The secrets of synchronicity.* New York: A Signet Book, New American Library, 1977, 170 p., paper, novel.

22966A retitled: *Prisoner of the planets.* London, Toronto: Panther, 1980, 190 p., paper, novel.

FATOUT, Paul, 1897-1982

22967 *Ambrose Bierce and the Black Hills.* Norman, OK: University of Oklahoma Press, 1956, xi+180 p., cloth, nonf.

22968 *Ambrose Bierce: the devil's lexicographer.* Norman, OK: University of Oklahoma Press, 1951, xv+349 p., cloth, nonf.

FAUCHER, Elizabeth

22969 *The Addams family: a novelization.* New York, Toronto: Scholastic Inc., 1991, 141 p., paper, movie.

22970 *Honey, I shrunk the kids: a novel.* New York, Toronto: Scholastic Inc., 1989, 117 p., paper, movie.

FAULCON, Robert, pseud.—SEE: Holdstock, Robert

FAULKNER, Peter, 1933-

22971 *Against the age: an introduction to William Morris.* London, Boston: George Allen & Unwin, 1980, xi+193 p., cloth, nonf.

22972 *William Morris and Eric Gill.* London: William Morris Society, 1975, 31 p., paper, nonf.

22973 *William Morris and W. B. Yeats.* Dublin: Dolmen Press, 1962, 30 p., paper, nonf.

22974 *William Morris: the critical heritage.* London & Boston: Routledge & Kegan Paul, 1973, xiii+465 p., cloth, nonf. anth.

FAUST, Frederick—SEE: Brand, Max

FAUST, Joe Clifford, 1957-

22975 *The company man.* New York: A Del Rey Book, Ballantine Books, 1988, 327 p., paper, novel.

22976 *A death of honor.* New York: A Del Rey Book, Ballantine Books, 1987, 326 p., paper, novel.

22977 *Desperate measures.* New York: A Del Rey Book, Ballantine Books, 1989, 245 p., paper, novel. ANGEL'S LUCK #1.

22978 *The essence of evil.* New York: A Del Rey Book, Ballantine Books, 1990, 281 p., paper, novel. ANGEL'S LUCK #3.

22979 *Precious cargo.* New York: A Del Rey Book, Ballantine Books, 1990, 293 p., paper, novel. ANGEL'S LUCK #2.

FAVILLE, Barry

22980 *The return.* Auckland, New Zealand: Oxford University Press, 1987, 163 p., cloth, novel.

FAVORS, Jean M.

22981 *The big freeze.* New York: A Parachute Press Book, 1985, 126 p., paper, novel. MICRO ADVENTURES #8.

22982 *James Bond in Programmed for danger.* New York: Ballantine Books, 1985, 117 p., paper, novel. FIND YOUR FATE #13—JAMES BOND.

Programmed for danger—SEE: *James Bond in Programmed for danger.*

22983 *Time trap.* New York, Toronto: A Parachute Press Book, Scholastic Inc., 1984, 126 p., paper, novel. MICRO ADVENTURES #4.

FAVORS, Sarah

22984 *The ghost of Paradise Island.* Davenport, FL: Laura Books, 1979, 198 p., paper, novel.

FAWCETT, Bill [i.e., William Brian Fawcett], 1947-

22985 *The far stars war.* New York: A Roc Books, 1990, 255 p., paper, anth. WAR YEARS #1.

22986 *The Jupiter war.* New York: A Roc Book, 1991, 254 p., paper, anth. WAR YEARS #3.

Quest for the Demon Gate—SEE: *SwordQuest: Quest for Demon Gate.*

Quest for the dragon's eye—SEE: *SwordQuest: Quest for the dragon's eye.*

Quest for the elf king—SEE: *SwordQuest: Quest for the elf king.*

Quest for the unicorn's horn—SEE: *SwordQuest: Quest for the unicorn's horn.*

22987 *The siege of Arista.* New York: A Roc Book, 1991, 252 p., paper, anth. WAR YEARS #2.

22988 *SwordQuest: Quest for the Demon Gate.* New York: Ace Fantasy Books, 1986, [180] p., paper, novel. SWORDQUEST SERIES.

22989 *SwordQuest: Quest for the dragon's eye.* New York: Ace Fantasy Books, 1985, 24+[142] p., paper, novel. SWORD-QUEST SERIES.

22990 *SwordQuest: Quest for the elf king.* New York: Ace Fantasy Books, 1987, 20+[242] p., paper, novel. SWORDQUEST SERIES.

22991 *SwordQuest: Quest for the unicorn's horn.* New York: Ace Fantasy Books, 1985, 22+[146] p., paper, novel. SWORD-QUEST SERIES.

with Robert Asprin

Cold cash warrior—SEE: *Combat command in the world of Robert Asprin's Cold cash war: Cold cash warrior.*

17082 *Combat command in the world of Robert Asprin's Cold cash war: Cold cash warrior.* New York: Ace Books, 1989, x+132 p., paper, novel. COMBAT COMMAND #9.

with David Drake

22168 *Breakthrough.* New York: Ace Books, 1989, 294 p., paper, anth. THE FLEET #3.

22169 *Counterattack.* New York: Ace Books, 1988, 311 p., paper, anth. THE FLEET #2.

22170 *Crisis.* New York: Ace Books, 1991, 293 p., paper, anth. THE FLEET #6.

22171 *The fleet.* New York: Ace Books, 1988, 280 p., paper, anth. THE FLEET #1.

22172 *Sworn allies.* New York: Ace Books, 1990, 248 p., paper, anth. THE FLEET #4.

22173 *Total war.* New York: Ace Books, 1990, 278 p., paper, anth. THE FLEET #5.

with Neil Randall

22992 *Lord of Cragsclaw.* New York, Toronto: Bantam Books, 1989, 392 p., paper, novel. GUARDIANS OF THE THREE #1.

with Robert Silverberg

22993 *Time gate.* New York: Baen Books, 1989, 277 p., paper, anth. TIME GATE #1.

with Christopher Stasheff

22994 *The crafters.* New York: Ace Books, 1991, viii+246 p., paper, anth.

FAWCETT, Edgar, 1847-1904

37751 *A romance of two brothers.* New York: Minerva Publishing Co., 1891, 146 p., cloth?, novel.

FAWCETT, William B.—SEE: Fawcett, Bill

FEARN, John (Francis) Russell, 1908-1960

37752 *"Climate, Incorporated": classic science fiction.* Wallsend, Tyne and Wear, England: Philip Harbottle, 1987, 36 p., paper, story.
22995 *From afar.* Wallsend, Tyne and Wear, England: Cosmos Literary Agency, 1982, 28 p., paper, story.
22996 *Lord of Atlantis.* Marsh, Westbury, England: Zeon Books, 1991, 68 p., paper, story.
22997 *No grave need I.* Wallsend, Tyne and Wear, England: Philip Harbottle, 1984, 42 p., paper, story.
22998 *The slitherers.* Wallsend, Tyne & Wear, England: Philip Harbottle, 1984, [40] p., paper, story.
22999 *Survivor of Mars.* Wallsend, Tyne and Wear, England: Cosmos Literary Agency, 1982, 39 p., paper, story.
23001 *Tales of Wonder.* Wallsend, Tyne and Wear, England: Cosmos Literary Agency, 1983, 39 p., paper, coll.
23002 *Worlds within.* Wallsend, Tyne and Wear, England: Cosmos Literary Agency, 1982, 32 p., paper, coll.

as HUGO BLAYN

37753 *The silvered cage.* London: Dragon Books, 1955, 144 p., paper, novel.

as ASTRON DEL MARTIA

04067 *The trembling world.* London: S. D. Frances, 1949, 128 p., paper, novel.

FEDDUP, I. M., pseud.

23003 *Afternoon foreplay.* New York: A Beeline Double Novel, 1983, 186 p., paper, novel. [Bound with *Sex-crazed days* / by Hy Cocky].

FEDERBUSH, Arnold, 1935-

23004 *Ice!* Toronto, New York: Bantam Books, 1978, 309 p., paper, novel.

FEDERMAN, Raymond, 1928-

23005 *The two-fold vibration.* Bloomington, IN: Indiana University Press; Brighton, England: Harvester Press, 1982, 175 p., cloth, novel.

*FEDUCHA, Bertha, 1882-1968

FEELEY, Gregory (Patrick), 1955-

23006 *The oxygen barons.* New York: Ace Books, 1990, 264 p., paper, novel.

FEIGE, Otto—SEE: Traven, B.

FEIL, Hila, 1942-

23007 *Blue moon.* New York: A Jean Karl Book, Atheneum, 1990, 200 p., cloth, novel.

FEIST, Raymond E(lias), 1945-

Apprentice—SEE: Magician.
23008 *A darkness at Sethanon.* Garden City, NY: Doubleday & Co., 1986, 425 p., cloth, novel. RIFTWAR SAGA #3.
23009 *Faerie tale.* Garden City, NY: Doubleday & Co., 1988, 420 p., cloth, novel.
23010 *Magician.* Garden City, NY: Doubleday & Co., 1982, 545 p., cloth, novel. RIFTWAR SAGA #1.
23010A retitled: *Magician: apprentice.* Toronto, New York: Bantam Books, 1986, 323 p., paper, novel. RIFTWAR SAGA #1A. [The original novel split into two parts].
23010B retitled: *Magician: master.* Toronto, New York: Bantam Books, 1986, xiii+366 p., paper, novel. RIFTWAR SAGA #1B. [The original novel split into two parts].
Magician: apprentice—SEE: Magician.
Magician: master—SEE: Magician.
Master—SEE: Magician.
23011 *Prince of the blood.* New York: A Foundation Book, Doubleday, 1989, 293 p., cloth, novel. RIFTWAR SAGA #4.
23012 *Silverthorn.* Garden City, NY: Doubleday & Co., 1985, 352 p., cloth, novel. RIFTWAR SAGA #2.

with Janny Wurts

23013 *Daughter of the empire.* Garden City, NY: Doubleday & Co., 1987, 394 p., cloth, novel. EMPIRE #1.

23014 *Servant of the empire.* New York: A Foundation Book, Doubleday, 1990, 580 p., cloth, novel. EMPIRE #2.

FELICE, Cynthia (Lindgren), 1942-

23015 *Double Nocturne.* New York: A Bluejay International Edition, 1986, 330 p., cloth, novel.

23016 *Downtime.* New York: Bluejay Books, 1985, 246 p., cloth, novel.

23017 *Eclipses.* New York: A Timescape Book, Pocket Books, 1983, 298 p., paper, novel.

23018 *Godsfire.* New York: A Kangaroo Book, Pocket Books, 1978, 264 p., paper, novel.

23019 *Iceman.* New York: Ace Books, 1991, 185 p., paper, novel.

23020 *The Khan's persuasion.* New York: Ace Books, 1991, 284 p., cloth, novel.

23021 *The Sunbound.* New York: A Dell Book, 1981, 366 p., paper, novel.

with Connie Willis

23022 *Light raid.* New York: Ace Books, 1989, 229 p., cloth, novel.

23023 *Water witch: a novel.* New York: Ace Books, 1982, 216 p., paper, novel.

FELITTA, Frank De—SEE: De Felitta, Frank

FELKIN, Mrs. Alfred—SEE: Fowler, Ellen Thorneycroft

FENDALL, Percy

37754 *Lady Ermyntrude and the plumber: a love tale of MCMXX.* London: S. Swift, 1912, 275 p., cloth, novel.

FENLON, Peter C., *with John David Ruemmler*

23024 *The world of Vog Mur.* Charlottesville, VA: Iron Crown Enterprises, 1984, 33 p., paper, fiction.

FENN, Lionel, pseud.—SEE: Grant, Charles L.

FENNER, Phyllis R(eid), 1899-1982

23025 *Wide-angle lens: stories of time and space.* New York: William Morrow & Co., 1980, 223 p., cloth, anth.

FENTON, Edward, 1917-1988

15804 *The nine questions.* Garden City, NY: Doubleday & Co., 1959, 235 p., cloth, novel.

FERGUSON, Brad(ley Michael), 1953-

23026 *Crisis on Centaurus: a Star Trek novel.* New York: Pocket Books, 1986, 254 p., paper, novel. STAR TREK #28.
A flag full of stars—SEE: *Star Trek: A flag full of stars.*

23027 *Star Trek: A flag full of stars.* New York, London: Pocket Books, 1991, 241 p., paper, novel. STAR TREK #54.

23028 *The world next door.* New York: Tor SF, A Tom Doherty Associates Book, 1990, 342 p., paper, novel.

FERGUSON, James D.—SEE: Drake, Morgan

FERGUSON, Neil, 1947-

23029 *Double helix fall.* London: Abacus, 1990, 272 p., paper, novel.

23030 *Putting out.* London: Hamish Hamilton, 1988, 207 p., cloth, novel.

FERGUSON, Virginia (Sue), 1940- , *with Angela M. Ridsdale*

23031 *Ghost stories.* Melbourne, Australia: Thomas Nelson, 1977, 125 p., paper, anth.

FERGUSSON, Bruce (Chandler)

23032 *The mace of souls: a novel of the Six Kingdoms.* New York: William Morrow & Co., 1989, 321 p., cloth, novel. SIX KINGDOMS #2.

23033 *The shadow of his wings.* New York: Arbor House, 1987, 278 p., cloth, novel. SIX KINGDOMS #1.

FERMAN, Edward L(ewis), 1937-

23034 *The best fantasy stories from The magazine of fantasy & science fiction.* London: Octopus Books, 1985, 792 p., cloth, anth.

23035 *The best from Fantasy and science fiction, 22nd series.* Garden City, NY: Doubleday & Co., 1977, 273 p., cloth, anth.

23036 *The best from Fantasy & science fiction, 23rd series.* Garden City, NY: Doubleday & Co., 1980, 273 p., cloth, anth.

23037 *The best from Fantasy & science fiction, 24th series.* New York: Charles

Scriber's Sons, 1982, viii+311 p., cloth, anth.

23038 *The best from Fantasy & science fiction: a 40th anniversary anthology.* New York: St. Martin's Press, 1989, xix+376 p., cloth, anth.

23039 *The magazine of fantasy and science fiction: a 30-year retrospective.* Garden City, NY: Doubleday & Co., 1980, x+310 p., cloth, anth. [Winner of the *Locus* Award for Best Anthology, 1980 (1981)].

with Martin H. Greenberg

23040 *The Magazine of fantasy and science fiction, April 1965.* Carbondale & Edwardsville, IL: Southern Illinois University Press, 1981, x+157 p., cloth, anth. [A facsimile of the April 1965 issue of this magazine, with notes and commentary by Greenberg].

with Anne Jordan

23041 *The best horror stories from The magazine of fantasy & science fiction.* New York: St. Martin's Press, 1988, xi+403 p., cloth, anth.

23041A retitled: *The best of modern horror.* London: Viking, 1989, xi+403 p., cloth, anth.

23041B retitled: *The best horror stories from The magazine of fantasy and science fiction, volume 1.* New York: St. Martin's Press, 1989, 260 p., paper, anth. [The original book split into two volumes].

23041C retitled: *The best horror stories from The magazine of fantasy and science fiction, volume 2.* New York: St. Martin's Press, 1990, 269 p., paper, anth. [The original book split into two volumes].

The best of modern horror—SEE: The best horror stories from The magazine of fantasy & science fiction.

with Barry N. Malzberg

23042 *Arena: sports SF.* Garden City, New York: Doubleday & Co., 1976, x+223 p., cloth, anth.

23043 *Final stage: the ultimate SF anthology.* Baltimore: Penguin Books, 1975, 284 p., paper, anth. ["First complete edition of an original anthology published in 1974 with several stories cut" (see #05377)].

23044 *Graven images: three original novellas of science fiction.* Nashville, New York: Thomas Nelson Publishers, 1977, 151 p., cloth, anth.

FERNANDEZ, Fernando, *with Patrick Tilley*

23045 *Dark visions: an illustrated guide to the Amtrak wars.* London: Sphere, 1988, 64 p., paper, fiction. AMTRAK WARS SERIES.

FERNS, C(hristopher) S.

23046 *Aldous Huxley: novelist.* London: Athlone Press, 1980, v+240 p., cloth, nonf.

FERRARI, Mark J(oseph), 1956- , *with Sandy Petersen & Lynn Willis & Tom Sullivan*

Field guide to creatures of the dreamlands—SEE: Petersen's Field guide: creatures of the dreamlands.

23047 *Petersen's Field guide: creatures of the dreamlands: an album of entities from beyond the wall of sleep.* Albany, CA: Chaosium, 1989, 64 p., paper, art.

FERREIRA, Rick

23048 *A chill to the sunlight: tropical stories of the macabre.* London: William Kimber, 1978, 191 p., cloth, anth.

23049 *The darling fishes, and other tales of fantasy, horror, and the supernatural.* London: William Kimber, 1977, 204 p., cloth, coll.

FERRELL, Keith

23050 *George Orwell: the political pen.* New York: M. Evans & Co., 1985, 180 p., cloth, nonf.

23051 *H. G. Wells: first citizen of the future.* New York: M. Evans & Co., 1983, 121 p., cloth, nonf.

FERRIE, Richard

23052 *Bloodrock.* New York: Leisure Books, 1987, 400 p., paper, novel.

FERRING, David, pseud.—SEE: Garnett, David S.

FERRIS, Paul (Frederick), 1929-

23053 *A distant country: a novel.* London: Weidenfeld & Nicolson, 1983, 208 p., cloth, novel.

FERRON, Jacques, 1921-1985

23054 *Tales from the uncertain country.* Toronto: Anansi, 1972, v+101 p., cloth, coll. [Translation by Betty Bednarski of *Contes du pays incertain*].

*FESSIER, Michael, 1907-1988

FETZER, Leland (Alvin), 1930-

23056 *Pre-revolutionary Russian science fiction: (seven utopias and a dream).* Ann Arbor, MI: Ardis, 1982, 253 p., cloth, anth.

FEYDY, Anne—SEE: Lindbergh, Anne

*FEZANDIÉ, Clement, 1865-1959

FICHMAN, Frederick

23057 *SETI.* New York: A Roc Book, 1990, 336 p., paper, novel.

FICKLING, David

with Isaac Asimov

16928 *I, robot.* Oxford, England: Alpha Books, Oxford University Press, 1979, 95 p., paper, novel. [Adapted by Fickling from Asimov's original novel].

with John Christopher

20033 *The death of grass.* Oxford, England: Alpha Books, Oxford University Press, 1979, 96 p., paper, novel. [Adapted by Fickling from Christopher's novel].

with Arthur C. Clarke

20116 *Rendezvous with Rama.* Oxford, England: Alpha Books, Oxford University Press, 1979, 96 p., paper, novel. RAMA #1. [Adapted from the novel by Clarke].

with Robert A. Heinlein

23058 *The puppet masters.* Oxford, England: Alpha Books, Oxford University Press, 1979, 96 p., paper, novel. [Adapted from the novel by Heinlein].

with Perry Hinton

23059 *Helmquest.* Harmondsworth, Middlesex, England: Puffin Books, 1986, [32] p., paper, novel. FANTASY QUESTBOOK.

23060 *The path of peril.* Harmondsworth, Middlesex, England: Puffin Books, 1984, [32] p., paper, novel. FANTASY QUESTBOOK.

23061 *Starflight zero.* Harmondsworth, Middlesex, England: Puffin Books, 1985, [32] p., paper, novel. FANTASY QUESTBOOK.

23062 *Ten doors of doom.* Harmondsworth, Middlesex, England: Puffin Books, 1987, [32] p., paper, novel. FANTASY QUESTBOOK.

with Walter Tevis

23063 *The man who fell to Earth.* Oxford, England: Alpha Books, Oxford University Press, 1979, 94 p., paper, novel. [Adapted from the novel by Tevis].

with Craig Thomas

23064 *Firefox.* Oxford, England: Alpha Books, Oxford University Press, 1980, 96 p., paper, novel. [Adapted from the novel by Thomas].

FICKS, R. Snowden, *with Roger Beaumont*

17638 *Deep space processional.* London: Robert Hale, 1982, 190 p., cloth, novel.

*FIDLER, Kathleen [i.e., Kathleen Annie Goldie], 1899-1980

FIEDLER, Jean(nette Feldman), 1928- , *with Jim Mele*

23065 *Isaac Asimov.* New York: Frederick Ungar, 1982, viii+122 p., cloth, nonf.

FIEDLER, Leslie A(aron), 1917-

23066 *Olaf Stapledon: a man divided.* Oxford, New York: Oxford University Press, 1983, ix+236 p., cloth, nonf.

*FIELD, Ben, 1902?-1973?

FIELD, Lawrence, pseud.

23067 *Lullaby.* New York: St. Martin's Press, 1982, 337 p., cloth, novel.

FIELD, Ruth Baker

23068 *Wild violets.* New York: Zebra Books, Kensington Publishing Corp., 1980, 334 p., paper, novel.

FIELDING, Joy, 1945-

23069 *Trance.* Chicago: Playboy Press, 1977, 275 p., cloth, novel.

FIELDS, Morgan, pseud.—SEE: Morgan, J. M.

FIELDS, Terri, 1948-

23070 *Fourth-graders don't believe in witches.* New York, Toronto: An Apple Paperback, Scholastic Inc., 1989, 105 p., paper, novel.

*FIFIELD, William, 1916-1987

*FIGGIS, (M.) Darrell (Edmund), 1882-1925

FIGGIS, N. P., 1939-

23071 *The fourth mode.* London: Penguin Books, 1989, 210 p., cloth, novel.

FIGUEREDO Y CLARENS, Carlos—SEE: Clarens, Carlos

*FIGUEROA (Ramirez), Medardo, 1887-1981

FILBRUN, J. S.

23072 *Gemini rising.* New York: Fawcett Gold Medal, 1982, 183 p., paper, novel.

FILES, Meg, 1946-

23073 *Meridian 144.* New York: Soho Press, 1991, 264 p., cloth, novel.

FINCH, Christopher, 1939-

23074 *The making of The Dark Crystal: creating a unique film.* New York: Henry Holt & Co., 1983, 96 p., paper, nonf.
23075 *Of muppets & men: the making of The Muppet Show.* New York: Muppet Press/Alfred A. Knopf, 1981, 178 p., cloth, nonf.
23076 *Special effects: creating movie magic.* New York: Abbeville Press, 1984, 252 p., cloth, nonf.

FINCH, Phillip, 1948-

23077 *In a place dark and secret: a novel.* New York: Franklin Watts, 1985, 376 p., cloth, novel.

FINCH, Sheila (Rosemary), 1935-

23078 *The garden of the shaped.* Toronto, New York: Bantam Books, 1987, 217 p., paper, novel. SHAPER EXILE #1.
23079 *The garden of the shaped.* Toronto, New York: Bantam Books, 1988, 217 p., paper, novel. SHAPER EXILE #1. [Revised edition].
23080 *Infinity's web.* Toronto, New York: Bantam Books, 1985, 230 p., paper, novel.
23081 *Shaper's legacy.* New York, Toronto: Bantam Books, 1989, 279 p., paper, novel. SHAPER EXILE #2.
23082 *Shaping the dawn.* New York, Toronto: Spectra, Bantam Books, 1989, 309 p., paper, novel. SHAPER EXILE #3.
23083 *Triad.* Toronto, New York: Bantam Books, 1986, 233 p., paper, novel.

FINDER, Jan Howard, 1939-

23084 *Alien encounters.* New York: Taplinger Publishing Co., 1982, 232 p., cloth, anth.

FINDLEY, Nigel

Into the void—SEE: *Spelljammer: Into the void.*
23085 *Spelljammer: Into the void.* Lake Geneva, WI: TSR Inc., 1991, 311 p., paper, novel. CLOAKMASTER CYCLE #2.

FINDLEY, Timothy (Irving), 1930-

23086 *Not wanted on the voyage.* Markham, Ontario & New York: Viking, 1984, 352 p., cloth, novel.

FINE, Gary Alan, 1950-

23087 *Shared fantasies: role-playing games as social worlds.* Chicago & London: University of Chicago Press, 1983, xiv+283 p., cloth, nonf.

FINE, Stephen

23088 *Molly Dear: the autobiography of an android; or, How I came to my senses, was repaired, escaped my master, and was educated in the ways of the world.* New York: A Thomas Dunne Book, St. Martin's Press, 1988, xii+420 p., cloth, novel.

FINK, Howard

23089 *Animal farm: notes.* Toronto: Coles Publishing Co., 1965, 62 p., paper, nonf.

FINLAY, D. G.

23090 *Deadly relations*. London: Century, 1986, 310 p., cloth, novel. WATCHMAN CHRONICLES #3.

23091 *The edge of tomorrow*. London: A Star Book, W. H. Allen & Co., 1979, 334 p., paper, novel

23092 *Graven image*. London: Century, 1987, 255 p., cloth, novel. WATCHMAN CHRONICLES #4.

23093 *The grey regard*. London: Century, 1985, 304 p., cloth, novel. WATCHMAN CHRONICLES #2.

23094 *The killing glance*. London: Arrow Books, 1989, 646 p., paper, coll. WATCHMAN CHRONICLES #1-4. [Abridged edition].

23095 *Once around the Sun*. London: A Star Book, W. H. Allen & Co., 1978, 316 p., paper, novel.

23096 *Watchman*. London: Century, 1984, 283 p., cloth, novel. WATCHMAN CHRONICLES #1.

FINLAY, Virgil (Worden), 1914-1971

21378 *The book of Virgil Finlay: being the drawings of Virgil Finlay (1914 1971), from the collection of Gerry de la Ree*. Saddle River, NJ: Gerry de la Ree, 1975, 128 p., cloth, art. [Edited by Gerry de la Ree].

21379 *The fifth book of Virgil Finlay: the "Weird Tales" years*. Saddle River, NJ: Gerry de la Ree, 1979, 127 p., cloth, art. [Edited by Gerry de la Ree].

23097 *Finlay's femmes: a portfolio*. Chicago: Science Fiction Graphics, 1977, 8 leaves, paper, art coll.

21381 *Finlay's lost drawings*. Saddle River, NJ: Gerry de la Ree, 1975, 28 p., cloth, art. [Edited by Gerry de la Ree].

21380 *The fourth book of Virgil Finlay: the fantasy art of Virgil Finlay*. Saddle River, NJ: Gerry de la Ree, 1979, 127 p., cloth, art. [Edited by Gerry de la Ree].

21382 *The second book of Virgil Finlay*. Saddle River, NJ: Gerry de la Ree, 1978, 127 p., cloth, art. [Edited by Gerry de la Ree].

21383 *The sixth book of Virgil Finlay: the astrology years*. Saddle River, NJ: Gerry de la Ree, 1980, 128 p., cloth, art. [Edited by Gerry de la Ree].

21384 *The third book of Virgil Finlay: the fantasy art of Virgil Finlay*. Saddle River, NJ: Gerry de la Ree, 1979, 127 p., cloth, art. [Edited by Gerry de la Ree].

23098 *Virgil Finlay: a portfolio of his unpublished illustrations*. Saddle River, NJ: Gerry de la Ree, 1971, 20 leaves, paper, art coll. [Edited by Gerry de la Ree].

23099 *Virgil Finlay: an astrology sketchbook*. West Kingston, RI: Donald M. Grant, Publisher, 1975, 148 p., cloth, art coll.

FINLAY, Winifred (Lindsay Crawford McKissack), 1910-

23100 *Beadbonny ash*. London: G. G. Harrap, 1973, 126 p., cloth, novel.

23101 *Singing stones*. London: George G. Harrap, 1970, 186 p., cloth, novel.

23102 *Tales of fantasy and fear*. London: Kaye and Ward, 1981, 120 p., cloth, coll.

23103 *Tales of sorcery and witchcraft*. London: Kaye and Ward, 1980, 127 p., cloth, coll.

23104 *Vampires, werewolves, and phantoms of the night*. London: Methuen, 1983, 125 p., cloth, coll.

FINN, F(rederick) E(dward) S(impson), 1916-

23105 *Horror*. London: John Murray, 1978, 121 p., paper, anth.

FINN, Ralph L(eslie), 1912-

37755 *The lunatic, the lover, and the poet*. London: Hutchinson, 1948, 192 p., cloth, novel.

37756 *Twenty-seven stairs: a novel*. London: Hutchinson, 1949, 223 p., cloth, novel.

FINNEY, Charles (Grandison), 1905-1984

23106 *The magician out of Manchuria*. St Albans, England: Panther, 1976, 109 p., paper, novel.

FINNEY, Jack [i.e., Walter Braden Finney], 1911-

23107 *3 by Finney: The Woodrow Wilson dime; Marion's wall; The night people*. New York: A Fireside Book, Simon & Schuster, 1987, 416 p., paper, coll.

23108 *About time: twelve stories*. New York: Simon & Schuster, A Fireside Book, 1986, 219 p., paper, coll. [Includes *The Third Level; I Love Galesburg in the Springtime*].

37757 *Forgotten news: the crime of the century, and other lost stories*. Garden City, NY: Doubleday & Co., 1983, xiv+290 p., cloth, coll.

FINNEY, Walter B.—SEE: Finney, Jack

FINSTER, E. Burke

23109   *Walk with the dead.* Portland, OR: Dime Novels, 1991, 90 p., paper, novel.

FIRCHOW, Peter E(dgerly), 1937-

23110   *Aldous Huxley, satirist and novelist.* Minneapolis, MN: University of Minnesota Press, 1972, viii+203 p., cloth, nonf.

23111   *End of utopia: a study of Aldous Huxley's Brave new world.* Lewisburg, NJ: Bucknell University Press, 1984, 154 p., cloth, nonf.

FIRTH, N(orman) Wesley, 1920-1949

23112   *Spawn of the vampire.* London: Bear, 1946, [64] p., paper, novel.

FISCHER, Andrew, *with K. S. Salikof*

23113   *Children of darkness.* New York: Manor Books, 1977, 236 p., paper, novel.

FISCHER, Dennis (K.)

23114   *Horror film directors, 1931-1990.* Jefferson, NC & London: McFarland & Co. Publishers, 1991, xxii+877 p., cloth, nonf.

FISCHER, William B(aldwin)

23115   *The empire strikes out: Kurd Lasswitz, Hans Dominik, and the development of German science fiction.* Bowling Green, OH: Bowling Green State University Popular Press, 1984, 335 p., cloth, nonf.

FISETTE, James J.

23116   *The war of 1974.* Minneapolis, MN: Post Publishing Co., 1965, 272 p., paper, novel.

FISH, Leonard G.

as FYSH

05702   *Planet war.* London: Archer Press, 1952, 96 p., paper, novel.

as CLAUDE HALEY

06642   *Beyond the solar system.* London: Arc Press, 1954, 141 p., paper, novel. [Cover byline reads Claud Haley].

as VICTOR LA SALLE

08631   *After the atom.* London: John Spencer & Co., 1953, 108 p., paper, novel.

as JOHN RAYMOND

37758   *Zamba of the jungle.* London: John Spencer & Co., 1951, 114 p., paper, novel.

FISH, Leslie, *with C. J. Cherryh*

19898   *A dirge for Sabis.* New York: Baen, 1989, 393 p., paper, novel. SWORD OF KNOWLEDGE #1.

FISHBURN, Katherine (Richards), 1944-

23117   *Doris Lessing: life, work, and criticism.* Fredricton, New Brunswick, Canada: York Press, 1987, 33 p., paper, nonf.

23118   *The unexpected universe of Doris Lessing.* Westport, CT: Greenwood Press, 1985, 184 p., cloth, nonf. CONTRIBUTIONS TO THE STUDY OF SCIENCE FICTION AND FANTASY #17.

FISHER, Benjamin Franklin IV, 1940-

23119   *The gothic's gothic: study aids to the tradition of the tale of terror.* New York, London: Garland Publishing, 1988, xix+485 p., cloth, nonf.

23120   *Myths and realities: the mysterious Mr. Poe.* Baltimore, MD: Edgar Allan Poe Society, 1987, ix+89 p., paper, nonf. anth.

23121   *Poe and his times: the artist and his milieu.* Baltimore, MD: Edgar Allan Poe Society, 1990, xvi+290 p., cloth, nonf. anth.

with Frederick S. Frank & Gary William Crawford & Kent Ljungquist

20788   *The 1980 bibliography of gothic studies.* Baton Rouge, LA: Gothic Press, 1983, ii+20 p., paper, nonf. [Limited to 275 copies].

FISHER, Catherine

23122   *The conjuror's game.* London: Bodley Head Children's Books, 1990, 97 p., cloth, novel.

23123   *Fintan's tower.* London: Bodley Head Children's Books, 1991, 160 p., cloth, novel.

FISHER, David, 1929-

23124 *Doctor Who and the creature from the pit.* London: W. H. Allen, 1981, 121 p., cloth, tele. DOCTOR WHO.

23125 *Doctor Who and the Leisure Hive.* London: W. H. Allen, 1982, 127 p., cloth, tele. DOCTOR WHO.

FISHER, David E(limelech), 1932- , with Ralph Albertazzie

16154 *Hostage one.* New York: Random House, 1989, 448 p., cloth, novel.

FISHER, Gene—SEE: Lancour, Gene

FISHER, Leonard Everett, 1924-

23126 *Noonan: a novel about baseball, ESP, & time warps.* Garden City, NY: Doubleday & Co., 1978, 125 p., cloth, novel.

23127 *Sweeney's ghost.* Garden City, NY: Doubleday & Co., 1975, 133 p., cloth, novel.

FISHER, Lou, 1935-

23128 *The blue ice pilot.* New York: Popular Library, Warner Books, 1986, 247 p., paper, novel.

23129 *SunStop 8.* New York: A Dell Book, 1978, 222 p., paper, novel.

FISHER, M(ary) F(rances) K(ennedy), 1908-1992

23130 *Not now, but now.* New York: Viking Press, 1947, 256 p., cloth, novel.

FISHER, Paul R., 1960-

23131 *The ash staff.* New York: Atheneum, 1979, 179 p., cloth, novel. ASH STAFF TRILOGY #1.

23132 *The hawks of Fellheath.* New York: Atheneum, 1980, 211 p., cloth, novel. ASH STAFF TRILOGY #2.

23133 *Mont Cant gold.* New York: An Argo Book, Atheneum, 1981, 251 p., cloth, novel.

23134 *The princess and the thorn.* New York: Atheneum, 1980, 237 p., cloth, novel. ASH STAFF TRILOGY #3.

FISHER, R(obert) L(ynn)

23135 *The prince of whales: a fantasy adventure.* New York: Carroll & Graf; Hartsdale, NY: Quicksilver Books, 1985, 151 p., cloth, novel.

FISHER, Stephen G.—SEE: Fisher, Steve

*FISHER, Steve [i.e., Stephen Gould Fisher], 1912-1980

FISK, Nicholas [pseud. of David Lee Higginbottom], 1923-

23136 *Antigrav.* Harmondsworth, Middlesex, England: Kestrel Books, 1978, 125 p., cloth, novel.

23137 *Backlash.* London: Walker Books, 1988, 137 p., cloth, novel.

23138 *The back-yard war.* London: Macmillan Children's Books, 1990, 90 p., cloth, novel.

23139 *Bonkers clocks.* Harmondsworth, Middlesex, England: Viking Kestrel, 1985, [80] p., cloth, novel.

23140 *Catfang.* Sevenoaks, Kent, England: Knight Books, Hodder & Stoughton, 1981, 110 p., paper, novel. STARSTORMERS #3.

23141 *Dark sun, bright sun.* Glasgow, Scotland: Blackie, 1986, 124 p., cloth, novel.

23142 *Escape from Splatterbang.* London: Pelham, 1978, 96 p., cloth, novel.

23142A retitled: *Flamers.* Sevenoaks, Kent, England, Knight Books, Hodder & Stoughton, 1979, 95 p., paper, novel.

23143 *Evil eye.* London: Knight Books, Hodder & Stoughton, 1982, 102 p., paper, novel. STARSTORMERS #4.

23144 *Extraterrestrial tales.* Harmondsworth, Middlesex, England: Puffin Books, 1991, 386 p., paper, coll. [Includes *Space hostages*; *Trillions*; *On the flip side*].

Flamers—SEE: *Escape from Splatterbang.*

23145 *High way home.* London: Hamish Hamilton, 1973, 126 p., cloth, novel.

23146 *A hole in the head.* London: Walker Books, 1991, 139 p., cloth, novel.

23147 *Little green spaceman.* London: Heinemann, 1974, 38 p., cloth, story.

23148 *Living fire, and other S.F. stories.* London: Corgi Books, 1987, 188 p., paper, coll.

23149 *Mindbenders.* Harmondsworth, Middlesex, England: Viking Kestrel, 1987, 110 p., cloth, novel.

23150 *Monster maker.* London: Pelham, 1979, 141 p., cloth, novel.

23151 *On the flip side.* Harmondsworth, Middlesex, England: Viking Kestrel, 1983, 121 p., cloth, novel.

23152 *Pig ignorant.* London: Walker Books, 1991, [96] p., cloth, novel.

23153   *A rag, a bone, and a hank of hair.* Harmondsworth, Middlesex, England: Kestrel Books, 1980, 126 p., cloth, novel.

23154   *Robot revolt.* London: Pelham Books, 1981, 128 p., cloth, novel.

23155   *Starstormers.* Sevenoaks, Kent, England: Knight Books, Hodder & Stoughton, 1980, 109 p., paper, novel. STARSTORMERS #1.

23156   *Sunburst.* Sevenoaks, Kent, England: Knight Books, Hodder & Stoughton, 1980, 125 p., paper, novel. STARSTORMERS #2.

23157   *Sweets from a stranger, and other SF stories.* Harmondsworth, Middlesex, England: Kestrel Books, 1982, 155 p., cloth, coll.

23158   *The talking car.* London: Macmillan Children's Books, 1988, 85 p., cloth, novel. FIREFLY SERIES.

23159   *Time trap.* London: Victor Gollancz, 1976, 128 p., cloth, novel.

23160   *Volcano.* London: Knight Books, Hodder & Stoughton, 1983, 139 p., paper, novel. STARSTORMERS #5.

23161   *Wheelie in the stars.* London: Heinemann, 1976, 82 p., cloth, novel.

23162   *The worm charmers.* London: Walker Books, 1989, 186 p., cloth, novel.

23163   *You remember me!* Harmondsworth, Middlesex, England: Viking Kestrel, 1984, 152 p., cloth, novel.

FISK, Pauline, 1948-

23164   *Midnight blue.* Oxford, England, Batavia, IL: Lion Publishing, 1990, 217 p., cloth, novel.

FITCH, Ed, pseud.

23165   *Castle of deception: a novel of sorcery and swords and other-worldly matters.* St. Paul, MN: Llewellyn Publications, 1983, 289 p., paper, novel.

FITTON, Akira, *with Charles Beesley & Bob Martin & Michael Weldon*

17671   *The psychotronic encyclopedia of film.* New York: Ballantine Books, 1983, xvi+815 p., paper, nonf.

FITZ GERALD, Gregory, 1923-

23166   *Neutron stars.* Greenwich, CT: A Fawcett Gold Medal Book, Fawcett Publications, 1977, 480 p., paper, anth.

with John Dillon

21942   *The late great future.* Greenwich, CT: A Fawcett Crest Book, Fawcett Publications, 1976, 288 p., paper, anth.

FITZGEORGE-PARKER, Mark—SEE: Daniel, Mark

FITZGERALD, F(rancis) Scott (Key), 1896-1940

23167   *The fantasy and mystery stories of F. Scott Fitzgerald.* London: Robert Hale, 1991, 192 p., cloth, coll. [Edited by Peter Haining].

FITZGERALD, Julia [i.e., Julia Watson], 1943-

23168   *Beauty of the devil.* London: Century, 1988, 383 p., cloth, novel.

FITZGIBBON, (Robert Louis) Constantine (Lee-Dillon), 1919-1983

23169   *The golden age: a novel.* London: Hart-Davis, MacGibbon, 1975, 189 p., cloth, novel.

23170   *The rat report.* London: Constable, 1980, 183 p., cloth, novel.

*FITZGIBBON, Ralph Edgerton, <u>1904-</u>

FITZHARDINGE, Joan—SEE: Phipson, Joan

FITZPATRICK, Jim, 1948-

23171   *The book of conquests.* London: Dragon's World, 1978, [112] p., paper, novel.

23172   *Celtia: a collection of posters and drawings in the celtic style.* Dublin, Ireland: Dé Danann Press, 1975, [34] leaves, cloth, art.

23173   *Érinsaga: the mythological paintings of Jim Fitzpatrick.* Dublin, Ireland: Dé Danann Press, 1985, 111 p., paper, art.

23174   *The silver arm.* Limpsfield, Surrey, England: Paper Tiger, 1981, 112 p., cloth, art.

FIVELSON, Scott, 1954-

23175   *Guess what's coming to dinner? the extraterrestrial etiquette guide.* Toronto, New York: Bantam Books, 1983, xiv+113 p., paper, fiction.

FLAGG, Edmund, 1815-1890, as ANONYMOUS AUTHOR

15806   *Edmond Dantès: a sequel to The Count of Monte-Cristo.* Philadelphia: T. B. Peterson & Bros., 1878, 203 p., cloth, novel. COUNT OF MONTE-CRISTO #2.

15807 *Edmond Dantès: a sequel to Alexandre Dumas' celebrated novel, The Count of Monte-Cristo.* Philadelphia: T. B. Peterson & Bros., 1884, 378 p., cloth, novel. COUNT OF MONTE-CRISTO #2. [Expanded edition].

FLANAGAN, Graeme

23176 *Robert Bloch: a bio-bibliography.* Canberra City, Australia: Graeme Flanagan, 1979, 63 p., paper, nonf.

with Mark Rathbun

23177 *Richard Matheson: he is legend: an illustrated bio-bibliography.* Chico, CA: Mark Rathbun, 1984, 55 p., paper, nonf.

FLANAGAN, Terry, *with Eleanor Ehrhardt*

22486 *Trek or treat.* New York: Ballantine Books, 1977, [95] p., paper, nonf.

FLANDERS, Rebecca, pseud.—SEE: Ball, Donna

FLANERY, Karen "K-nut," *with Nana Grasmick*

23178 *Fandom is for the young; or, One convention too many.* New York, Washington: Vantage Press, 1981, xiii+160 p., cloth, nonf.

FLANNERY, Constance O'Day- —SEE: O'Day-Flannery, Constance

FLATON, Johan-Martijn

23179 *Confiction souvenir book.* Netherlands: Confiction, 1990, 152 p., paper, anth.

*FLECKER, (Herman) James Elroy, 1884-1915

FLEENOR, Juliann E(vans)

23180 *The female gothic.* Montréal: Eden Press, 1983, 311 p., paper, nonf. anth.

FLEETWOOD, Jenni

23181 *The intergalactic omniglot.* London: Orchard Books, 1988, 121 p., cloth, novel.

FLEISCHER, Leonore, 1932-

23182 *The fisher king: a novel.* New York: A Signet Book, 1991, 208 p., paper, movie.

23183 *Flatliners: a novel.* New York: Tor, A Tom Doherty Associates Book, 1990, 249 p., paper, movie.

23184 *Heaven can wait: a novel.* New York: Ballantine Books, 1978, 169 p., paper, movie.

*FLEISCHER, Max, 1889-1972

FLEISCHMAN, Paul, 1952-

23185 *Graven images: stories.* New York: A Charlotte Zolotow Book, Harper & Row, 1982, 85 p., cloth, coll.

FLEISCHMAN, (Albert) Sid(ney), 1920-

23186 *The ghost in the noonday sun.* Boston: An Atlantic Monthly Press Book, Little, Brown & Co., 1965, xi+173 p., cloth, novel.

23000 *The midnight horse.* New York: Greenwillow Books, 1990, 84 p., cloth, novel.

FLEISHER, Michael (Lawrence), 1942- , *with Joe Orlando*

23187 *DC Comics presents: Superman II, the movie magazine.* New York: DC Comics, 1981, 64 p., paper, nonf.
Superman II, the movie magazine—SEE: *DC Comics presents: Superman II, the movie magazine.*

FL*M*NG, I*n, pseud.—SEE: Frith, Michael K. & Cerf, Christopher Cerf

*FLEMING, (Jiles) Berry, 1899-1989

*FLEMING, Joan (Margaret), 1908-1980

FLEMING, Keith

37759 *By the night express: a psychological romance.* London: George Routledge & Sons, 1889, 185 p., cloth, coll.

FLEMING, Lee—SEE: Conway, Norman

FLEMING, Nigel

23188 *To love a vampire.* Encino, CA: World-Wide Publishing Co., 1980, 187 p., paper, novel.

FLEMING, Robert Loren

23189 *Back to the future: a story.* New York: Berkley Books, 1985, [48] p., paper, movie. [Adapted from George Gipe's novelization].

23190 *Justice League of America.* New York: An Archway Paperback, Pocket Books, 1984, 119 p., paper, novel. WHICH WAY BOOKS—SUPER POWERS #3.

*FLES, Barthold, 1902-1989

FLETCHER, Adrian [pseud. of Rosemary Ellen Guiley], *with Ryder Syvertsen*

23191 *Psychic spawn: a novel.* New York: Popular Library, 1987, 376 p., paper, novel.

FLETCHER, Jo(anna Louise Gould), 1958-

23192 *Peter Tremayne.* Wembley, Middlesex, England: British Fantasy Society, 1984, [20] p., paper, anth.

with Stephen Jones

23193 *Gaslight & ghosts.* Wembley, Middlesex, England: 1988 World Fantasy Convention in Association with Robinson Publishing, 1988, 258 p., cloth, anth. [Includes some nonfiction].

FLETCHER, Marilyn P(endleton), 1940-

23194 *Science fiction story index, 1950-1979, 2nd ed.* Chicago: American Library Association, 1981, xi+610 p., paper, nonf.

with James L. Thorson

23195 *Reader's guide to twentieth-century science fiction.* Chicago & London: American Library Association, 1989, xiv+673 p., cloth, nonf.

FLETCHER, Susan (Clemens), 1951-

23196 *Dragon's milk.* New York: A Jean Karl Book, Atheneum, 1989, 242 p., cloth, novel.

FLIEGEL, Hellmuth—SEE: Heym, Stefan

FLIEGER, Verlyn, 1933-

23197 *Splintered light: logos and language in Tolkien's world.* Grand Rapids, MI: William B. Eerdmans, 1983, xx+167 p., paper, nonf.

FLINDT, Homer—SEE: Flint, Homer

FLINN, Russell

23198 *Stirring within.* [England]: British Fantasy Society, 1991, 23 p., paper, coll.

*FLINT, Homer Eon [pseud. of Homer Eon Flindt], 1892?-1924

FLINT, Kenneth C(ovey)

23199 *Challenge of the clans.* Toronto, New York: Bantam Books, 1986, 328 p., paper, novel. FINN MACCUMHAL #1.
23200 *Champions of the Sidhe.* Toronto, New York: Bantam Books, 1984, 277 p., paper, novel. SIDHE #2.
23201 *Cromm.* New York: A Foundation Book, Doubleday, 1990, 387 p., cloth, novel.
23202 *The dark druid.* Toronto, New York: Bantam Books, 1987, 326 p., paper, novel. FINN MACCUMHAL #3.
The hound of Culain—SEE: *A storm upon Ulster.*
23203 *Isle of destiny: a novel of ancient Ireland.* Toronto, New York: Spectra, Bantam Books, 1988, 438 p., paper, novel.
23204 *Master of the Sidhe.* Toronto, New York: Bantam Books, 1985, 248 p., paper, novel. SIDHE #3.
23205 *The riders of the Sidhe.* Toronto, New York: Bantam Books, 1984, 260 p., paper, novel. SIDHE #1.
23206 *Storm shield.* Toronto, New York: Bantam Books, 1986, 310 p., paper, novel. FINN MACCUMHAL #2.
23207 *A storm upon Ulster.* Toronto, New York: Bantam Books, 1981, ix+309 p., paper, novel. SIDHE LEGENDS #1.
23207A retitled: *The hound of Culain.* Toronto, New York: Bantam Books, 1986, ix+309 p., paper, novel. SIDHE LEGENDS #1.

as CASEY FLYNN

23208 *The enchanted isles.* New York, Toronto: Spectra, Bantam Books, 1991, 275 p., paper, novel. GODS OF IRELAND #2.
23209 *Most ancient song.* New York, Toronto: Spectra, Bantam Books, 1991, 261 p., paper, novel. GODS OF IRELAND #1.

FLORA, Joseph M(artin), 1934-

23211 *Vardis Fisher.* New York: Twayne Publishers, 1965, 158 p., cloth, nonf.

*FLORES, Angel, 1900-1983?

FLORESCU, Radu R. N., 1925-

23212 *In search of Frankenstein.* Boston: New York Graphic Society, 1975, xi+244 p., cloth, nonf.

with Raymond T. McNally

23213 *Dracula, prince of many faces: his life and his times.* Boston: Little, Brown & Co., 1989, xxii+261 p., cloth, nonf.

FLOWERS, A(rthur) R.

23214 *De mojo blues: de quest of HighJohn de Conqueror.* New York: E. P. Dutton, 1986, 216 p., cloth, novel.

FLOWERS, T. J., pseud.—SEE: Forest, Salambo

FLUKE, Joanna, 1942-

23215 *The other child.* New York: A Dell Book, 1983, 250 p., paper, novel.

FLUTE, Molly, pseud.—SEE: Lottman, Eileen

FLYNN, Casey, pseud.—SEE: Flint, Kenneth C.

FLYNN, George (Patrick), 1936- , *with Chris Drumm*

22220 *A Mack Reynolds checklist: notes toward a bibliography.* Polk City, IA: Chris Drumm, 1983, 24 p., paper, nonf.

FLYNN, J. M.

23216 *Warlock.* New York: Pocket Books, 1976, 159 p., paper, novel.

FLYNN, John L.

23217 *Future threads: costume design for the science fiction world.* Studio City, CA: New Media Books, 1985, 80 p., cloth, nonf.

FLYNN, Michael (Francis), 1947-

23218 *In the country of the blind.* New York: Baen Books, 1990, 527 p., paper, novel. [Winner of the *Locus* Award for Best First Novel, 1990 (1991)].
23219 *The nanotech chronicles.* Riverdale, NY: Baen Books, 1991, 339 p., paper, coll.

with Larry Niven & Jerry Pournelle

23220 *Fallen angels.* Norwalk, CT: Easton Press, 1991, 394 p., cloth, novel.

FODOR, R(onald) V(ictor), 1944- , *with G. J. Taylor*

23221 *Impact!* New York: Leisure Books, 1979, 302 p., paper, novel.

FOERSTER, Valerie E(lizabeth)

23222 *Teacher's guide: worlds on worlds: journalistic writing.* Englewood Cliffs, NJ: Prentice-Hall, 1978, 50 p., paper, nonf.
23223 *Worlds on worlds: journalistic writing.* Englewood Cliffs, NJ: Prentice-Hall, 1978, xiv+274 p., cloth, anth.

FOGARTY, John

23224 *The haunt.* New York: Popular Library, 1990, 280 p., paper, novel.

FOGLIO, Phil, 1956- , *with Nick Pollotta*

23225 *Illegal aliens.* Lake Geneva, WI: TSR Inc., 1989, 336 p., paper, novel.

FOLEY, (Mary) Louise Munro, 1933-

23226 *Australia: find the flying foxes!* New York: McGraw-Hill Book Co., 1988, 101 p., paper, novel. EARTH INSPECTORS #4.
23227 *The cobra connection.* New York, Toronto: An Edward Packard Book, A Bantam Skylark Book, 1990, 118 p., paper, novel. CHOOSE YOUR OWN ADVENTURE #104.
37760 *Danger at Anchor Mine.* Toronto, New York: An Edward Packard Book, Bantam Books, 1985, 113 p., paper, novel. CHOOSE YOUR OWN ADVENTURE #49.
23228 *Forest of fear.* Toronto, New York: An Edward Packard Book, Bantam Books, 1986, 116 p., paper, novel. Choose Your Own Adventure #54.
37761 *The lost tribe.* Toronto, New York: An Edward Packard Book, Bantam Books, 1983, 116 p., paper, novel. Choose Your Own Adventure #23.
23229 *The Mardi Gras mystery.* Toronto, New York: An Edward Packard Book, Bantam Books, 1987, 118 p., paper, novel. CHOOSE YOUR OWN ADVENTURE #65.
37762 *The mystery of Echo Lodge.* Toronto, New York: An Edward Packard Book, Bantam Books, 1985, 118 p., paper, novel. CHOOSE YOUR OWN ADVENTURE #42.
23230 *The mystery of the Highland crest.* Toronto, New York: An Edward Packard

Book, Bantam Books, 1984, 117 p., paper, novel. CHOOSE YOUR OWN ADVENTURE #34.

23231 *Mystery of the sacred stones.* Toronto, New York: An Edward Packard Book, A Bantam Skylark Book, 1988, 118 p., paper, novel. CHOOSE YOUR OWN ADVENTURE #79.

37763 *The sinister studios of KESP-TV.* New York, Toronto: Scholastic Inc., 1983, 92 p., paper, fiction. TWISTAPLOT #5.

37764 *The train of terror.* New York, Toronto: Scholastic Book Services, 1982, 107 p., paper, fiction. TWISTAPLOT #2.

FOLLETT, James, 1939-

37765 *The doomsday ultimatum.* London: Weidenfeld & Nicolson, 1976, 224 p., cloth, novel.

37766 *The doomsday ultimatum.* London: Mandarin, 1991, 285 p., paper, novel. [Revised edition].

23232 *Earth search.* London: British Broadcasting Corp., 1981, 208 p., cloth, radio. EARTH SEARCH #1.

23233 *Ice.* London: Weidenfeld & Nicolson, 1978, 206 p., cloth, novel.

23234 *Torus.* London: Methuen, 1990, 404 p., cloth, novel. EARTH SEARCH #2.

23235 *Trojan.* London: Lime Tree, 1991, 490 p., cloth, novel.

FOLLETT, Ken(neth Martin), 1949-

as MARTIN MARTINSEN

23236 *The power twins and the worm puzzle: a science fantasy for young people.* London: A Grasshopper Book, Abelard-Schuman, 1976, 96 p., cloth, novel.

23236A retitled: *The power twins* / by Ken Follett. New York: Morrow Junior Books, 1990, 90 p., cloth, novel.

as BERNARD L. ROSS

23237 *Amok: king of legend.* London: Futura Publications, A Futura Book, 1976, 219 p., paper, novel.

23238 *Capricorn One.* London: Arthur Barker, 1978, 219 p., cloth, movie.

FONSTAD, Karen Wynn, 1945-

23239 *The atlas of Middle-Earth.* Boston: Houghton Mifflin Co., 1981, xiv+208 p., cloth, atlas.

23240 *The atlas of Middle-Earth, revised edition.* Boston: Houghton Mifflin Co., 1991, xii+210 p., cloth, atlas.

23241 *The atlas of Pern.* New York: A Del Rey Book, Ballantine Books, 1984, xvii+169 p., cloth, atlas.

23242 *The atlas of the DRAGONLANCE™ world.* Lake Geneva, WI & Cambridge, England: TSR Inc., 1987, xx+168 p., paper, atlas.

23243 *The atlas of the Land.* New York: A Del Rey Book, Ballantine Books, 1985, xix+201 p., cloth, atlas.

23244 *The Forgotten Realms atlas.* Lake Geneva, WI: TSR Inc., 1990, xi+176 p., paper, atlas.

FONTANA, D(orothy) C(atherine), 1939-

23245 *Star Trek: Vulcan's glory.* New York, London: Pocket Books, 1989, 252 p., paper, tele. STAR TREK #44.
Vulcan's glory—SEE: *Star Trek: Vulcan's glory.*

FONTES, Ron

23246 *Rocketeer: a novel.* New York: Disney Press, 1991, 76 p., paper, movie.

FOOTE, Bud [i.e., Irving Flint Foote], 1930-

23247 *The Connecticut Yankee in the twentieth century: travel to the past in science fiction.* New York, London: Greenwood Press, 1991, x+209 p., cloth, nonf. CONTRIBUTIONS TO THE STUDY OF SCIENCE FICTION AND FANTASY #43.

FOOTE, Irving F.—SEE: Foote, Bud

*FOOTMAN, David J(ohn), 1895-1983

FORBES, Caroline, 1952-

23248 *The needle on full: Lesbian feminist science fiction.* London: OnlyWomen Press, 1985, 267 p., paper, coll.

FORD, Adam, 1940-

23249 *The cuckoo plant.* London: Teens Mandarin, 1991, 237 p., paper, novel.

FORD, Henry, *with Simon Hendage*

23250 *Sidney Sime: master of the mysterious.* London: Thames & Hudson, 1980, 96 p., paper, art.

FORD, Jeffrey, 1955-

23251 *Vanitas.* New York: Space & Time, 1988, 167 p., paper, novel.

FORD, John M., 1957-

23252 *Casting fortune.* New York: Tor Fantasy, A Tom Doherty Associates Book, 1989, 249 p., paper, coll.

23253 *The dragon waiting: a masque of history.* New York: Timescape Books, 1983, 365 p., cloth, novel. [Winner of the World Fantasy Award for Best Fantasy Novel, 1983 (1984)].

23254 *The final reflection: a Star Trek novel.* New York: Pocket Books, 1984, 253 p., paper, novel. STAR TREK #16.

23255 *Fugue state.* New York: Tor SF, A Tom Doherty Associates Book, 1990, 121 p., paper, story. [Bound with *The death of Doctor Island* / by Gene Wolfe].

23256 *How much for just the planet? a Star Trek novel.* New York: Pocket Books, 1987, 253 p., paper, novel. STAR TREK #36.

23257 *The princes of the air.* New York: A Timescape Book, Pocket Books, 1982, 207 p., paper, novel.

23258 *Web of angels.* New York: Pocket Books, 1980, 256 p., paper, novel.

as MICHAEL J. DODGE

23259 *Star Trek: Voyage to adventure.* New York: An Archway Paperback, Pocket Books, 1984, 118 p., paper, novel. WHICH WAY BOOKS #15; STAR TREK SERIES.
Voyage to adventure—SEE: *Star Trek: Voyage to adventure.*

with George H. Scithers & Darrell Schweitzer

23260 *On writing science fiction: (the editors strike back!).* Philadelphia, PA: Owlswick Press, 1981, vii+227 p., cloth, nonf. anth.

FORD, Paul F(rancis Xavier), 1947-

23261 *Companion to Narnia.* New York: Harper & Row, Publishers, 1980, xxxii+313 p., cloth, nonf.

23262 *Companion to Narnia, 2nd ed.* San Francisco: Harper & Row, Publishers, 1983, xxxix+448 p., paper, nonf.

23263 *Companion to Narnia, 3rd ed.* New York: Collier Books, Macmillan Publishing Co., 1986, xli+450 p., paper, nonf.

FORD, Richard, 1948-

23264 *The children of Ashgaroth.* London: Grafton, 1986, 444 p., cloth, novel. FARADAWN TRILOGY #3.

23265 *Melvaig's vision.* London: Granada, 1984, 445 p., cloth, novel. FARADAWN TRILOGY #2.

23266 *Quest for the Faradawn.* London, Toronto: Granada, 1982, 310 p., cloth, novel. FARADAWN TRILOGY #1.

FORD, Robert Curry

23267 *Hex.* New York: Playboy Press Paperbacks, 1980, 288 p., paper, novel.

FORD, Williston—SEE: Merrick, Williston

FORDE, R. A., 1948-

23268 *Wise-woman.* London: New English Library, 1988, 351 p., cloth, novel.

FOREMAN, Bob [i.e., Roberto Foreman], *with Robin Moore*

23269 *Two Saturday Yankees; &, Ali in T.V. Land.* New York: Manor Books, 1976, 287 p., paper, coll.

FOREMAN, Roberto—SEE: Foreman, Bob

FOREMAN, Russell (Ralph), 1921-

23270 *The Ringway virus.* London: Millington, 1976, 294 p., cloth, novel.

FOREST, Regan

23271 *Moonspell.* Toronto, New York: Harlequin Books, 1990, 251 p., paper, novel. [Translated from the Italian].

FOREST, Salambo [pseud. of Tina Bellini (and possibly others?)]

05514 *Night of the wolf.* New York: Ophelia Press, 1969, 187 p., paper, novel.

05514A retitled: *Moonglow* / by T. J. Flowers. New York: Midwood Books, 1974, 215 p., paper, novel. [Previously listed as entry #05497].

FORESTAL, Sean

23272 *Dark angel.* New York: A Dell Book, 1982, 443 p., paper, novel.

FORESTER, Bruce (Michael), 1939-

23273 *Blood fever.* New York: Zebra Books, Kensington Publishing Corp., 1990, 350 p., paper, novel.

FORGEY, William W., 1942-

23274 *Campfire stories: things that go bump in the night.* Merrillville, IN: ICS Books, 1985, 176 p., paper, anth.

23275 *Campfire tales: ghoulies, ghosties, and long-leggety beasties.* Merrillville, IN: ICS Books, 1989, 163 p., paper, coll.

FORMAN, James D(ouglas), 1932-

23276 *Call back yesterday.* New York: Charles Scribner's Sons, 1981, 163 p., cloth, novel. DOOMSDAY #1.

23277 *Cry havoc.* New York: Charles Scribner's Sons, 1988, 199 p., cloth, novel.

23278 *Doomsday plus twelve.* New York: Charles Scribner's Sons, 1984, 230 p., cloth, novel. DOOMSDAY #2.

FORMAN, H(arry) Buxton, 1842-1917

23279 *The books of William Morris described, with some account of his doings in literature and in the allied crafts.* London: Frank Hollings, 1897, xv+224 p., cloth, nonf.

FORREST, Katherine V(irginia), 1939-

23280 *Daughters of a coral dawn.* Tallahassee, FL: Naiad Press, 1984, 226 p., paper, novel.

23281 *Dreams and swords.* Tallahassee, FL: Naiad Press, 1987, 175 p., paper, coll.

FORRESTER, John, 1943-

23282 *Bestiary Mountain.* New York: Bradbury Press, 1985, 140 p., cloth, novel. BESTIARY TRILOGY #1.

23283 *The forbidden beast.* New York: Bradbury Books, 1988, viii+135 p., cloth, novel. BESTIARY TRILOGY #3.

23284 *The secret of the round beast.* New York: Bradbury Press, 1986, 145 p., cloth, novel. BESTIARY TRILOGY #2.

FORSTCHEN, William R., 1950-

23285 *The Alexandrian ring.* New York: A Del Rey Book, Ballantine Books, 1987, 295 p., paper, novel. GAMESTER WARS #1.

23286 *The assassin gambit.* New York: A Del Rey Book, Ballantine Books, 1988, 306 p., paper, novel. GAMESTER WARS #2.

23287 *A darkness upon the ice.* New York: A Del Rey Book, Ballantine Books, 1985, 275 p., paper, novel. ICE PROPHET #3.

23288 *The flame upon the ice.* New York: A Del Rey Book, Ballantine Books, 1984, 279 p., paper, novel. ICE PROPHET #2.

23289 *Ice prophet.* New York: A Del Rey Book, Ballantine Books, 1983, 293 p., paper, novel. ICE PROPHET #1.

23290 *Into the sea of stars.* New York: A Del Rey Book, Ballantine Books, 1986, 231 p., paper, novel.

23291 *Rally cry.* New York: A Roc Book, 1990, 412 p., paper, novel. LOST REGIMENT #1.

23292 *Union forever.* New York: A Roc Book, 1991, 457 p., paper, novel. LOST REGIMENT #2.

with Greg Morrison

23293 *The crystal sorcerers.* New York: Avon Books, 1991, 291 p., paper, novel. CRYSTAL #2.

23294 *The crystal warriors.* New York: Avon Books, 1988, 308 p., paper, novel. CRYSTAL #1.

FORSYTH, Frederick, 1938-

23295 *The devil's alternative.* London: Hutchinson, 1979, 478 p., cloth, novel.

37767 *The negotiator.* London, New York: Bantam Press, 1989, 448 p., cloth, novel.

23296 *The shepherd.* London: Hutchinson, 1975, 55 p., cloth, novel.

FORSYTHE, Richard

23297 *Bishop's Landing.* New York: Leisure Books, 1980, 368 p., paper, novel.

23298 *Fangs.* New York: Leisure Books, 1988, 380 p., paper, novel.

FORTIER, Ron (J.), *with Ardath Mayhar*

23299 *Monkey station.* Lake Geneva, WI: TSR Inc., 1989, 311 p., paper, novel.

23300 *Trail of the seahawks.* Lake Geneva, WI: TSR Inc., 1987, 222 p., paper, novel. WINDWALKER SERIES.

FORTIS, Paul de—SEE: de Fortis, Paul

FORWARD, Robert (Dodson), 1958-

23301 *The owl.* New York: Pinnacle Books, 1984, 247 p., paper, novel. OWL #1.

23302 *The owl II: Scarlet serenade* / by Bob Forward. London: New English Library, 1990, 207 p., paper, novel. OWL #2.

FORWARD, Robert L(ull), 1932-

23303 *Dragon's Egg.* New York: A Del Rey Book, Ballantine Books, 1980, 345 p., cloth, novel. DRAGON'S EGG #1. [Winner of the *Locus* Award for Best First Novel, 1980 (1981)].

23304 *The flight of the Dragonfly.* New York: Timescape Books, 1984, 319 p., cloth, novel.

23305 *The flight of the Dragonfly.* New York: Baen Books, 1985, 376 p., paper, novel. [Expanded edition].

23306 retitled: *Rocheworld.* New York: Baen Books, 1990, 470 p., paper, novel. [Expanded edition].

23307 *Martian rainbow.* Norwalk, CT: Easton Press, 1991, 319 p., cloth, novel.

Rocheworld—SEE: *The flight of the Dragonfly.*

23308 *Starquake.* New York: A Del Rey Book, Ballantine Books, 1985, v+326 p., cloth, novel. DRAGON'S EGG #2.

FOSBURGH, Liza, 1930-

23309 *Bella Arabella.* New York: Four Winds Press, 1985, 102 p., cloth, novel.

FOSS, Chris(topher Frank), 1946-

23310 *21st century Foss.* Brighton, East Sussex, England: Dragon's Dream, 1978, 144 p., paper, art.

23311 *The Chris Foss portfolio.* Limpsfield, Surrey, England: Paper Tiger, 1990, [64] p., paper, art.

23312 *Diary of a spaceperson.* Limpsfield, Surrey, England: Paper Tiger, 1990, 143 p., cloth, art.

23313 *Science fiction art.* London: Hart-Davis, MacGibbon, 1976, [23] p., paper, art.

FOSTER, Alan Dean, 1946-

23314 *Alien.* New York: Warner Books, 1979, 270 p., paper, movie. ALIEN #1.

23315 *Alien nation: a novelization.* New York: Warner Books, 1988, 217 p., paper, movie.

23316 *Aliens: a novelization.* New York: Warner Books, 1986, 247 p., paper, movie. ALIEN #2.

23317 *The black hole: a novel.* New York: A Del Rey Book, Ballantine Books, 1979, 213 p., paper, movie.

23318 *Cachalot: a novel.* New York: A Del Rey Book, Ballantine Books, 1980, 275 p., paper, novel.

23319 *A call to arms.* Norwalk, CT: Easton Press, 1991, 341 p., cloth, novel. THE DAMNED #1.

23320 *Cat-a-Lyst.* New York: Ace Books, 1991, 325 p., paper, novel.

23321 *Clash of the titans: novelization.* New York: Warner Books, 1981, 304 p., paper, movie.

23322 *Cyber way.* New York: Ace Books, 1990, 306 p., paper, novel.

23323 *The day of the dissonance.* Huntington Woods, MI: Phantasia Press, 1984, 269 p., cloth, novel. SPELLSINGER #3.

23324 *The deluge drivers.* New York: A Del Rey Book, Ballantine Books, 1987, 311 p., paper, novel. THRANX #5; ICERIGGER #3.

23325 *The end of the matter.* New York: A Del Rey Book, Ballantine Books, 1977, 246 p., paper, novel. FLINX #4.

23326 *Flinx in flux.* New York: A Del Rey Book, Ballantine Books, 1988, 324 p., paper, novel. FLINX #6.

23327 *For love of Mother-not.* New York: A Del Rey Book, Ballantine Books, 1983, 247 p., paper, novel. FLINX #1.

23328 *Glory lane.* New York: Ace Books, 1987, 295 p., paper, novel.

23329 *The horror on the beach: a tale in the Cthulhu Mythos.* San Diego, CA: Valcour & Krueger, 1978, 46 p., paper, story. LIBRARY LOVECRAFTIAN #4; CTHULHU MYTHOS. [Limited to 1000 copies].

23330 *The hour of the gate.* New York: Warner Books, 1984, 300 p., paper, novel. SPELLSINGER #2.

23331 *The I inside.* New York: Warner Books, 1984, 311 p., paper, novel.

23332 *Into the Out Of.* New York: Warner Books, 1986, 293 p., cloth, novel.

23333 *Krull: a novel.* New York: Warner Books, 1983, 237 p., paper, movie.

23334 *The last starfighter.* New York: Berkley Books, 1984, 218 p., paper, movie.

23335 *The man who used the universe.* New York: Warner Books, 1983, 316 p., paper, novel.

23336 *Maori.* New York: Ace Books, 1988, 501 p., paper, novel.

23337 *The Metrognome, and other stories.* New York: A Del Rey Book, Ballantine Books, 1990, 243 p., paper, coll.

23338 *Midworld.* Garden City, NY: Nelson Doubleday, 1975, 179 p., cloth, novel. THRANX #2.

23339 *Mission to Moulokin.* Garden City, New York: Nelson Doubleday, 1979, vi+282 p., paper, novel. THRANX #4; ICERIGGER #2.

23340 *The moment of the magician.* Huntington Woods, MI: Phantasia Press, 1984, 266 p., cloth, novel. SPELLSINGER #4.

23341 *Nor crystal tears.* New York: A Del Rey Book, Ballantine Books, 1982, 231 p., paper, novel. THRANX #1.

23342 *Orphan star.* New York: A Del Rey Book, Ballantine Books, 1977, 234 p., paper, novel. FLINX #3.

23343 *Outland: novelization.* New York: Warner Books, 1981, 269 p., paper, movie.

23344 *Pale rider: a novelization.* New York: Warner Books, 1985, 218 p., paper, movie.

23345 *The paths of the perambulator.* West Bloomfield, MI: Phantasia Press, 1985, 204 p., cloth, novel. SPELLSINGER #5.

23346 *Quozl.* New York: Ace Books, 1989, 344 p., paper, novel.

23347 *Season of the spellsong.* Garden City, NY: Nelson Doubleday, 1985, 730 p., cloth, coll. SPELLSINGER #1-3. [Includes *Spellsinger, Hour of the gate, Day of the Dissonance*].

23348 *Sentenced to Prism.* New York: A Del Rey Book, Ballantine Books, 1985, 273 p., paper, novel. THRANX #7.

23349 *Shadowkeep.* New York: Warner Books, 1984, 243 p., paper, novel. [Based on the computer game *Shadowkeep*].

23350 *Slipt.* New York: Berkley Books, 1984, 265 p., paper, novel.

23351 *Spellsinger.* New York: Warner Books, 1983, 347 p., paper, novel. SPELLSINGER #1.

23352 *Spellsinger at the gate.* Huntington Woods, MI: Phantasia Press, 1983, 562 p., cloth, coll. SPELLSINGER #1-2. [Includes *Spellsinger* and *The hour of the gate*; limited to 450 copies].

23353 *Spellsinger's scherzo.* Garden City, NY: Nelson Doubleday, 1987, 661 p., cloth, coll. SPELLSINGER #4-6. [Includes *The moment of the magician, The paths of the perambulator, The time of the transference*].

23354 *Splinter of the mind's eye, from the adventures of Luke Skywalker.* New York: A Del Rey Book, Ballantine Books, 1978, 216 p., cloth, novel. STAR WARS SERIES.

23355 *Star Trek, log three.* New York: Ballantine Books, 1975, 215 p., paper, tele. coll. STAR TREK LOG #3.

23356 *Star Trek, log four.* New York: Ballantine Books, 1975, 215 p., paper, tele. coll. STAR TREK LOG #4.

23357 *Star Trek, log five.* New York: Ballantine Books, 1975, 195 p., paper, tele. coll. STAR TREK LOG #5.

23358 *Star Trek, log six.* New York: Ballantine Books, 1976, 195 p., paper, tele. coll. STAR TREK LOG #6.

23359 *Star Trek, log seven.* New York: Ballantine Books, 1976, 182 p., paper, tele. coll. STAR TREK LOG #7.

23360 *Star Trek, log eight.* New York: Ballantine Books, 1976, 183 p., paper, tele. coll. STAR TREK LOG #8.

23361 *Star Trek, log nine.* New York: Ballantine Books, 1977, 183 p., paper, tele. coll. STAR TREK LOG #9.

23362 *Star Trek, log ten.* New York: A Del Rey Book, Ballantine Books, 1978, 250 p., paper, tele. coll. STAR TREK LOG #10.

23363 *Starman: a novel.* New York: Warner Books, 1984, 280 p., paper, movie.

23364 *The Thing: a novel.* Toronto, New York: Bantam Books, 1982, 196 p., paper, movie.

23365 *The time of the transference.* West Bloomfield, MI: Phantasia Press, 1986, 253 p., cloth, novel. SPELLSINGER #6.

23366 *To the vanishing point.* New York: Warner Books, 1988, 310 p., cloth, novel.

23367 *Voyage to the city of the dead.* New York: A Del Rey Book, Ballantine Books, 1984, 243 p., paper, novel. THRANX #6.

23368 *...Who needs enemies?* New York: A Del Rey Book, Ballantine Books, 1984, x+257 p., paper, coll.

23369 *With friends like these....* New York: A Del Rey Book, Ballantine Books, 1977, xv+232 p., paper, coll.

with Lynn Haney

23370 *The last starfighter storybook.* New York: G. P. Putnam's Sons, 1984, [47] p., cloth, movie. [Adapted from Foster's novelization].

with Martin H. Greenberg

23371 *Smart dragons, foolish elves.* New York: Ace Books, 1991, xi+340 p., paper, anth.

FOSTER, Blair [pseud. of Blair Foster Clark], 1917-

23372 *Love's unearthly power.* New York: Leisure Books, 1983, 351 p., paper, novel.

FOSTER, D(avid) M(anning), 1944- , *with D. K. Lyall*

23373 *The empathy experiment.* Sydney: Wild & Woolley, 1977, 201 p., cloth, novel.

FOSTER, George C(ecil), 1893-

05544 *The change.* London: Digit Books, 1963, 160 p., paper, novel.
05544A retitled: *2001 A.D.* Australia: Bill Ewington Books, 1973, 160 p., paper, novel.

FOSTER, John L(ouis), 1941-

23374 *Science fiction stories.* London: Ward, Lock & Co., 1975, 152 p., cloth, anth.
23375 *Stories of terror.* London: Ward, Lock Educational, 1982, 122 p., cloth, anth.

FOSTER, M(ichael) A(nthony), 1939-

23376 *The day of the Klesh.* New York: DAW Books, 1979, 240 p., paper, novel. LER #3.
23377 *The gameplayers of Zan.* New York: DAW Books, 1977, 445 p., paper, novel. LER #1.
23378 *The Morphodite.* New York: DAW Books, 1981, 224 p., paper, novel. MORPHODITE TRILOGY #1.
23379 *Owl time: a collection of fictions.* New York: DAW Books, 1985, 251 p., paper, coll.
23380 *Preserver.* New York: DAW Books, 1985, 253 p., paper, novel. MORPHODITE TRILOGY #3.
23381 *Transformer.* New York: DAW Books, 1983, 255 p., paper, novel. MORPHODITE TRILOGY #2.
23382 *The warriors of Dawn.* New York: DAW Books, 1975, 278 p., paper, novel. LER #2.
23383 *Waves.* New York: DAW Books, 1980, 256 p., paper, novel.

FOSTER, P. T.—SEE: Foster, Prudence

FOSTER, Prudence [i.e., Prudence Foster Taylor Board], 1933-

23384 *Blood legacy.* New York, London: Pocket Books, 1989, 252 p., paper, novel.
23385 *The vow / by P. T. Foster.* New York: Leisure Books, 1989, 359 p., paper, novel. [No author name on title page].

FOSTER, Robert (Alfred), 1949-

23386 *The complete guide to Middle-Earth, from The hobbit to The Silmarillion, rev. and enlarged ed.* New York: A Del Rey Book, Ballantine Books, 1978, xvi+575 p., cloth, nonf. [Expanded edition of *The guide to Middle-Earth* (see #05551)].
23387 *Teacher's guide to The hobbit.* New York: Ballantine Books, 1981, 40 p., paper, nonf.

FOSTER, Ruth

23388 *Beware the child.* New York: A Dell Book, 1989, 293 p., paper, novel.

FOUST, Ronald, 1942-

23389 *A. Merritt.* Mercer Island, WA: Starmont House, 1989, v+104 p., cloth, nonf. STARMONT READER'S GUIDE #43.

FOWKES, Charles, *as* INTRODUCER

23390 *The best ghost stories.* London: Hamlyn, 1977, 750 p., cloth, anth.

FOWLER, Christopher, 1953-

23391 *The Bureau of Lost Souls.* London, Sydney: Century, 1989, 244 p., cloth, coll. [Includes seven stories from *More city jitters*, plus five additional tales].
23392 *City jitters.* London: Sphere Books, 1986, 164 p., paper, coll. CITY JITTERS #1.
23393 *More city jitters.* New York: A Dell Book, 1988, 212 p., paper, coll. CITY JITTERS #2.
23394 *Roofworld.* New York: A Del Rey Book, Ballantine Books, 1988, 333 p., paper, novel.
23395 *Roofworld.* London: Legend, 1988, 344 p., cloth, novel. [Expanded edition].
23396 *Rune.* London: Century, 1990, 368 p., cloth, novel.

FOWLER, D. A.

23397 *What's wrong with Valerie?* New York, London: Pocket Books, 1991, 247 p., paper, novel.

FOWLER, Douglas (Russell), 1940-

23398 *Ira Levin.* Mercer Island, WA: Starmont House, 1988, vii+87 p., cloth, nonf. STARMONT READER'S GUIDE #34.

FOWLER, Ellen Thorneycroft (Mrs. Alfred Felkin)

37768 *Signs and wonders.* London: Hodder & Stoughton, 1926, 316 p., cloth, coll.

FOWLER, Karen Joy, 1950-

23399 *Artificial things.* Toronto, New York: Bantam Books, 1986, 218 p., paper, coll.
23400 *Peripheral vision.* Eugene, OR: Pulphouse Publishing, 1990, 97 p., cloth, coll. AUTHOR'S CHOICE MONTHLY #6.
23401 *Sarah Canary.* New York: Henry Holt & Co., 1991, 290 p., cloth, novel.
23402 *The war of the roses.* Eugene, OR: Pulphouse Publishing, 1991, 43 p., cloth, story. SHORT STORY HARDBACKS #18; SHORT STORY PAPERBACKS #28.

FOWLER, Raymond D(alton) Jr., 1930- , with Kenneth B. Melvin & Stanley L. Brodsky

18715 *Psy-fi one: an anthology of psychology in science fiction.* New York: Random House, 1977, xiii+299 p., paper, anth.

FOWLES, John (Robert), 1926-

23403 *A maggot.* Boston: Little, Brown & Co., 1985, 455 p., cloth, novel.
37769 *The magus.* Boston: Little, Brown & Co., 1965, 606 p., cloth, novel.
37770 *The magus: a revised edition.* Boston: Little, Brown & Co., 1977, 656 p., cloth, novel. [Expanded edition].

FOX, Gardner F(rancis), 1911-1986

05560 *Escape across the cosmos.* New York: Paperback Library, 1964, 160 p., paper, novel
05560A retitled: *Titans of the universe* / by Moonchild. New York: Manor Books, 1978, 223 p., paper, novel. [A blatant plagiarism of Fox's original novel; cover byline reads "James Harvey"].
05560B retitled: *Star chase* / by Brian James Royal. New York: Elsevier/Nelson Books, 1979, 159 p., cloth, novel. [The same plagiarism resold; copyrighted by James Harvey].

23404 *Kyrik and the lost queen.* New York: Leisure Books, 1976, 175 p., paper, novel. KYRIK #4.
23405 *Kyrik and the wizard's sword.* New York: Leisure Books, 1976, 186 p., paper, novel. KYRIK #3.
23406 *Kyrik fights the demon world.* New York: Leisure Books, 1975, 159 p., paper, novel. KYRIK #2.
23407 *Kyrik, warlock warrior.* New York: Leisure Books, 1975, 153 p., paper, novel. KYRIK #1.
Star chase—SEE: *Escape across the cosmos.*
Titans of the universe—SEE: *Escape across the cosmos.*

as ROD GRAY

06270 *Blow my mind.* New York: Tower Books, 1970, 153 p., paper, novel. LADY FROM L.U.S.T. #12.
06271 *The copulation explosion.* New York: Tower Books, 1970, 159 p., paper, novel. LADY FROM L.U.S.T. #14.
06272 *Laid in the future.* New York: Tower Books, 1970, 157 p., paper, novel. LADY FROM L.U.S.T. #13.
06273 *The poisoned pussy.* New York: Tower Books, 1969, 154 p., paper, novel. LADY FROM L.U.S.T. #9.

FOX, Peter (F.), 1946-

23409 *Downtime.* London: Hodder & Stoughton, 1986, 254 p., cloth, novel.

FOX, Robert Elliot, 1944-

23410 *Conscientious sorcerers: the Black postmodernist fiction of LeRoi Jones/Amiri Baraka, Ishmael Reed, and Samuel R. Delany.* Westport, CT: Greenwood Press, 1987, xi+142 p., cloth, nonf.

FOX, W. Randolph

23411 *After the apocalypse.* New York: Manor Books, 1979, 218 p., paper, novel.

FOYE, Raymond, 1957-

23412 *Edgar Allan Poe: the unknown Poe.* San Francisco: City Lights Books, 1980, 117 p., cloth, nonf. anth.

FRAIL, Edward J.

23413 *Cult.* New York: An Onyx Book, 1990, 241 p., paper, novel.

FRAKES, Randall

Judgment day—SEE: *T2: The Terminator 2: Judgment day.*

23414 *T2: Terminator 2: Judgment day: a novel.* New York, Toronto: Spectra, Bantam Books, 1991, 240 p., paper, movie. TERMINATOR #2.
Terminator 2—SEE: *T2: Terminator 2: Judgment day: a novel.*

with W. H. Wisher

23415 *The Terminator: a novel.* Toronto, New York: Bantam Books, 1985, 240 p., paper, movie. TERMINATOR #1. [Completely different from the British novelization of the same title].

FRAME, Janet [i.e., Janet Paterson Frame Clutha], 1924-

23416 *The Carpathians.* London: Bloomsbury, 1988, 196 p., cloth, novel.

FRANCES, Stephen (Daniel), 1917-1989

as ASTRON DEL MARTIA

04065A *One against time.* London: Mayflower Books, 1969, 140 p., paper, novel. [Possibly rewritten from its earlier appearance in the Hank Janson series].

as HANK JANSON

04065 *One against time.* London: Alexander Moring, 1956, [160] p., paper, novel.
07850 *Tomorrow and a day.* London: Alexander Moring, 1955, 160 p., paper, novel.
07851 *The unseen assassin.* London: Top Fiction Press, 1953, 142 p., paper, novel.

with W. Howard Baker as PETER SAXON

12723 *The disorientated man.* London: Mayflower Books, 1966, 126 p., paper, novel.
12723A retitled: *Scream and scream again.* New York: Paperback Library, 1967, 158 p., paper, novel.
Scream and scream again—SEE: *The disorientated man.*

FRANCIS, Dorothy Brenner, 1926-

23417 *Blink of the mind.* New York: Twilight/Dell, 1982, 154 p., paper, novel. TWILIGHT #5.

FRANCIS, Gail K.—SEE: Kimberly, Gail

FRANCIS, Richard (H.), 1945-

23418 *Blackpool vanishes.* London, Boston: Faber & Faber, 1979, 191 p., cloth, novel.
23419 *Swansong.* London: Flamingo, 1986, 304 p., paper, novel.

FRANÇOIS, Yves Regis [pseud. of Yves Regis François Barbero], 1943-

23420 *The CTZ paradigm.* Garden City, NY: Doubleday & Co., 1975, 183 p., cloth, novel.

FRANE, Jeff

23421 *Fritz Leiber.* Mercer Island, WA: Starmont House, 1980, 64 p., paper, nonf. STARMONT READER'S GUIDE #8.

with Jack Rems

23422 *A fantasy reader: the seventh World Fantasy Convention book.* Berkeley, CA: Seventh World Fantasy Convention, 1991, x+197 p., cloth, anth.

FRANK, Alan (G.), 1937-

23423 *Galactic aliens.* London: Angus & Robertson, 1979, [98] p., cloth, fiction.
23424 *The horror film handbook.* London: B. T. Batsford, 1982, 194 p., cloth, nonf.
23425 *Horror films.* London, New York: Hamlyn, 1977, 189 p., cloth, nonf.
23426 *Monsters & vampires.* London: Octopus Books, 1976, 160 p., cloth, nonf.
23427 *The science fiction and fantasy film handbook.* London: B. T. Batsford, 1982, 187 p., cloth, nonf.
23428 *Sci-fi now: 10 exciting years of science fiction, from 2001 to Star wars and beyond....* London: Octopus, 1978, 80 p., paper, nonf.

FRANK, Frederick S(tilson), 1935-

23429 *The first gothics: a critical guide to the English gothic novel.* NY & London: Garland Publishing, 1987, xxxi+496 p., cloth, nonf.
23430 *Gothic fiction: a master list of twentieth century criticism and research.* Westport, CT: Meckler Corp., 1988, xv+193 p., cloth, nonf. MECKLER'S BIBLIOGRAPHIES ON SCIENCE FICTION, FANTASY, AND HORROR #3.

23431 *Guide to the gothic: an annotated bibliography of criticism.* Metuchen, NJ & London: Scarecrow Press, 1984, xvi+421 p., cloth, nonf.

23432 *Montague Summers: a bibliographical portrait.* Metuchen, NJ: Scarecrow Press, 1988, xviii+277 p., cloth, nonf.

23433 *Through the pale door: a guide to and through the American gothic.* New York: Greenwood Press, 1990, xvii+338 p., cloth, nonf.

with Gary William Crawford & Benjamin Franklin Fisher IV & Kent Ljungquist

20788 *The 1980 bibliography of gothic studies.* Baton Rouge, LA: Gothic Press, 1983, ii+20 p., paper, nonf. [Limited to 275 copies].

FRANK, Howard, *with Roy Torgeson*

23434 *The 1977 science fiction & fantasy magazine checklist & price guide, 1923-1976.* Port Washington, NY: Science Fiction Resources, 1977, 50 p., paper, nonf.

FRANKEL, Ellen, 1938- , *with Robin Stevenson*

23435 *George Washington and the Constitution.* Toronto, New York: A Byron Preiss Book, A Bantam Skylark Book, 1987, 80 p., paper, novel. TIME TRAVELER #6.

FRANKLE, Judith, pseud.—SEE: Couffer, Jack

FRANKLIN, Cheryl J(ean), 1955-

23436 *Fire crossing.* New York: DAW Books, 1991, 541 p., paper, novel. MAGICAL TALES OF THE TAORMIN #3.

23437 *Fire get.* New York: DAW Books, 1987, 338 p., paper, novel. MAGICAL TALES OF THE TAORMIN #1.

23438 *Fire lord.* New York: DAW Books, 1989, 348 p., paper, novel. MAGICAL TALES OF THE TAORMIN #2.

23439 *The light in exile.* New York: DAW Books, 1990, 334 p., paper, novel. NETWORK/CONSORTIUM #1.

FRANKLIN, H(oward) Bruce, 1934-

23440 *Countdown to midnight: twelve great stories about nuclear war.* New York: DAW Books, 1984, 287 p., paper, anth.

23441 *Future perfect: American science fiction of the nineteenth century, rev. ed.* New York: Oxford University Press, 1978, xi+404 p., cloth, anth. [Includes some nonf.].

23442 *Robert A. Heinlein: America as science fiction.* Oxford, England, New York: Oxford University Press, 1980, ix+232 p., cloth, nonf. [Winner of the J. Lloyd Eaton Award for Best Nonfiction Book of the Year, 1980 (1982)].

23443 *War stars: the superweapon and the American imagination.* New York, Oxford: Oxford University Press, 1988, 256 p., cloth, nonf.

FRANKLIN, K. D.

23444 *The worlds of Sector P.* London: Dennis Dobson, 1979, 185 p., cloth, novel.

FRANKLIN, Madeleine—SEE: L'Engle, Madeleine

FRANKLIN, Max [pseud. of Richard Deming], 1915-1983

23445 *The dark.* New York: A Signet Book, New American Library, 1978, 187 p., paper, movie.

FRANKLIN, Michael

with Baird Searles & Beth Meacham

23446 *A reader's guide to fantasy.* New York: Avon, 1982, 217 p., paper, nonf.

with Baird Searles & Beth Meacham & Martin Last

23447 *A reader's guide to science fiction.* New York: Avon, 1979, xv+266 p., paper, nonf.

FRANKLIN, Pat, pseud.—SEE: Cady, Jack

FRANKLIN, Stephen, 1922-

23448 *Knowledge Park.* Toronto: McClelland & Stewart, 1972, 191 p., cloth, novel.

FRANKOWSKI, Leo (A.), 1943-

23449 *Copernick's rebellion.* New York: A Del Rey Book, Ballantine Books, 1987, 202 p., paper, novel.

23450 *The cross-time engineer.* New York: A Del Rey Book, Ballantine Books, 1986, 259 p., paper, novel. ADVENTURES OF CONRAD STARGARD #1.

23451 *The flying warlord.* New York: A Del Rey Book, Ballantine Books, 1989, 232 p., paper, novel. ADVENTURES OF CONRAD STARGARD #4.

23452 *The high-tech knight.* New York: A Del Rey Book, Ballantine Books, 1989, 247 p., paper, novel. ADVENTURES OF CONRAD STARGARD #2.

23453 *Lord Conrad's lady.* New York: A Del Rey Book, Ballantine Books, 1990, 296 p., paper, novel. ADVENTURES OF CONRAD STARGARD #5.

23454 *The radiant Warrior.* New York: A Del Rey Book, Ballantine Books, 1989, 281 p., paper, novel. ADVENTURES OF CONRAD STARGARD #3.

FRANSON, Donald (Lewis), 1916-

23455 *An author index to Astounding/Analog, part II: vol. 36, n.1, Sept. 1945 to vol. 73, n.3, May, 1964.* North Hollywood, CA: Donald Franson, 1964, 7 p., paper, nonf.

with Howard DeVore

21656 *A history of the Hugo, Nebula, and International Fantasy awards.* Dearborn, MI: Howard DeVore, 1975, 97 p., paper, nonf.

21657 *A history of the Hugo, Nebula, and International Fantasy awards.* Dearborn, MI: Howard DeVore, 1976, [114] p., paper, nonf. [Expanded edition].

21657 *A history of the Hugo, Nebula, and International Fantasy awards.* Dearborn, MI: Misfit Press, 1978, 112 p., paper, nonf. [Expanded edition].

21658 *A history of the Hugo, Nebula, and International Fantasy awards.* Dearborn, MI: Misfit Press, 1980, 129 p., paper, nonf. [Expanded edition].

21659 *A history of the Hugo, Nebula, and International Fantasy awards.* Dearborn, MI: Howard DeVore, 1981, 141 p., paper, nonf. [Expanded edition].

21660 *A history of the Hugo, Nebula, and International Fantasy awards, updated ed.* Dearborn, MI: Howard DeVore, 1985, 185 p., paper, nonf. [Expanded edition].

FRANSON, Robert Wilfred, 1946-

23456 *The shadow of the ship.* New York: A Del Rey Book, Ballantine Books, 1983, 273 p., paper, novel.

FRANZ, Marie-Luise von, 1915-

23457 *Individuation in fairy tales.* Zürich, Switzerland: Spring Publications, 1977, 189 p., cloth, nonf.

23458 *Individuation in fairy tales, rev. ed.* Boston: A C. G. Jung Foundation Book, Shambhala, 1990, vii+230 p., cloth, nonf.

23459 *Shadow and evil in fairy tales.* Zürich, Switzerland: Spring Publications, 1974, 284 p., cloth, nonf.

FRASER, Anthea (Mary), 1930-

23560 *Whistler's Lane.* Aylesbury, England: Milton House Books, 1975, 206 p., cloth, novel.

FRASER, Christine Marion

23461 *Rhanna at war.* London: Blond & Briggs, 1980, 223 p., cloth, novel. RHANNA SERIES.

FRASER, David (William, General Sir), 1920-

23462 *August 1988.* London: Collins, 1983, 235 p., cloth, novel.

FRASER, Dorothy   SEE: Spicer, Dorothy

FRASER, (Arthur) Ronald, Sir, 1888-1974

37771 *The pen—the brush—the well: a work of imagination.* Gerrards Cross, England: Colin Smythe, 1973, 128 p., cloth, novel.

FRASER, W(illiam) A(lexander), 1859-1933

23463 *The Sa'-Zada tales.* New York: Charles Scribner's Sons, 1905, xii+231 p., cloth, novel.

FRAYLING, Christopher (John), 1946-

23464 *The vampyre: Lord Ruthven to Count Dracula.* London: Victor Gollancz, 1978, 336 p., cloth, anth.

23465 *Vampyres: Lord Byron to Count Dracula.* London: Faber & Faber, 1991, 528 p., cloth, anth.

FRAZER, Shamus [i.e., James Ian Arbuthnot Frazzer], 1912-

37772 *A shroud as well as a shirt.* London: Chapman & Hall, 1935, viii+344 p., cloth, novel.

FRAZETTA, Frank [originally Frank Frazzetta], 1928-

23466 *The fantastic art of Frank Frazetta.* New York, Toronto: Rufus Publications, Peacock Press, Bantam Books, 1975, [95] p., paper, art.
23467 *Frank Frazetta, book two.* New York, Toronto: Peacock Press, Bantam Books, 1977, [95] p., paper, art.
23468 *Frank Frazetta, book three.* New York, Toronto: Peacock Press, Bantam Books, 1978, [95] p., paper, art.
23469 *Frank Frazetta, book four.* New York, Toronto: Peacock Press, Bantam Books, 1980, 95 p., paper, art.
23470 *Frank Frazetta, book five.* Toronto, New York: Bantam Books, 1985, 95 p., paper, art.
23471 *Frank Frazetta: the living legend.* Marshall Creek, PA: Sun Litho-Print, 1981, 96 p., paper?, art.
23472 *Frazetta memory book.* Columbia, PA: Charles Miller, 1977, 40 leaves, paper, art coll.
23473 *The Frazetta treasury.* [S.l.: s.n., 1975?], [48] p., paper, art.
23474 *The rare Frazetta.* [S.l.: s.n., 1975?], 48 p., paper, art.

FRAZIER, Robert (Alexander), 1951- , *with Lucius Shepard*

23475 *Nantucket slayrides: three short novels.* Nantucket, MA: Eel Grass Press, 1989, 219 p., cloth, coll.

FRAZZETTA, Frank—SEE: Frazetta, Frank

FREAS, Frank Kelly, 1922-

23476 *Frank Kelly Freas: the art of science fiction.* Norfolk, VA: Donning, 1977, 119 p., cloth, art.
23477 *A separate star.* Virginia Beach, VA: Greenswamp Publications, 1984, 128 p., cloth, nonf.

FREDDI, Cris, 1955-

23478 *The elder: a novel.* New York: Alfred A. Knopf, 1985, 323 p., cloth, novel.

FREDERICKS, (Sigmund) Casey, 1943-

23479 *The future of eternity: mythologies of science fiction and fantasy.* Bloomington, IN: Indiana University Press, 1982, xvi+229 p., cloth, nonf.

with David A. Randall & Tim Mitchell

23480 *Science fiction and fantasy: an exhibition, January-April, 1975 /* by Sigmund Casey Fredericks and.... Bloomington, IN: Lilly Library, Indiana University, 1975, 71 p., paper, nonf.

FREDERICKSON, Anthony

23481 *The world of Star Wars: a compendium of fact and fantasy from Star Wars and The Empire Strikes Back.* New York: Paradise Press, 1981, p., paper, nonf.

FREED, L. A.

23482 *Blood thirst.* New York: Pinnacle Books, Windsor Publishing Corp., 1989, 384 p., paper, novel.

FREEMAN, Barbara C(onstance), 1906-

23483 *A haunting air.* London: Macmillan, 1976, 158 p., cloth, novel.
23484 *The other face.* London: Macmillan, 1975, 151 p., cloth, novel.
23485 *A pocket of silence.* London: Macmillan, 1977, 171 p., cloth, novel.

FREEMAN, Don L.

23486 *Children of the shadows.* New York: Zebra Books, Kensington Publishing Corp., 1990, 352 p., paper, novel.

FREEMAN, E. M., 1949-

23487 *Campfire chillers.* Charlotte, NC: East/Woods Press, 1980, 190 p., paper, anth.

FREEMAN, Gaail

23488 *Alien thunder.* Scarsdale, NY: Bradbury Press, 1982, 201 p., cloth, novel.

FREEMAN, Maggie

23489 *Danger! space pirates.* London: Hodder & Stoughton, 1987, 112 p., cloth, novel.
23490 *The spaceball.* London: Black, 1986, [64] p., cloth, novel.

FREEMAN, Simon (David), 1952- , *with H. G. Wells*

23491 *The country of the blind.* Cambridge, England: Cambridge University Press, 1977, 24 p., paper, story. [Adapted from Wells's story].

FREIBERG, Stanley K(enneth), 1923-

23492 *Nightmare tales*. Ottawa, Ontario: Borealis Press, 1980, 93 p., cloth, coll.

FREMONT, Eleanor

23493 *Tales from the crypt, volume 1*. New York: Random House, 1991, 96 p., paper, coll. [Adapted from the comic book].

23494 *Tales from the crypt, volume 2*. New York: Random House, 1991, 96 p., paper, coll. [Adapted from the comic book].

FRENCH, Laura, 1949-

23495 *The dragon's ransom*. Lake Geneva, WI: TSR Inc., 1984, 157 p., paper, novel. ENDLESS QUEST #16.

FRENCH, Michael (Raymond), 1944-

23496 *Indiana Jones and the temple of doom: a storybook based on the movie*. New York: Random House, 1984, [57] p., cloth, movie. INDIANA JONES SERIES.

FRENCH, Robert

23497 *Now, the gods*. New York: Manor Books, 1978, 267 p., paper, novel.

23498 *Them*. New York: Manor Books, 1979, 219 p., paper, novel.

FRENKEL, James (Raymond), 1948- , as ANONYMOUS EDITOR

23499 *Binary star no. 1: Destiny times three* / Fritz Leiber ; *Riding the torch* / Norman Spinrad. New York: A Dell Book, 1978, 251 p., paper, anth.

23500 *Binary star no. 2: The twilight river* / Gordon Eklund ; *The tery* / F. Paul Wilson. New York: A Dell Book, 1979, 268 p., paper, anth.

23501 *Binary star no. 3: Dr. Scofflaw* / Ron Goulart ; *Outerworld* / Isidore Haiblum. New York: A Dell Book, 1979, 303 p., paper, anth.

23502 *Binary star no. 4: Legacy* / Joan D. Vinge ; *The Janus equation* / Steven G. Spruill. New York: A Dell Book, 1980, 287 p., paper, anth.

23503 *Binary star no. 5: Nightflyers* / George R. R. Martin ; *True names* / Vernor Vinge. New York: A Dell Book, 1981, 239 p., paper, anth.

FRENKEL, Joan D.—SEE: Vinge, Joan D.

FRENTZEN, Jeffrey, 1956- , *with David J. Schow*

23504 *The Outer Limits: the official companion*. New York: Ace Science Fiction Books, 1986, 406 p., paper, nonf.

FRESHMAN, Bruce—SEE: Brellen, Marc

FRESHWATER, Mark Edwards, 1948-

23505 *C. S. Lewis and the truth of myth*. Lanham, MD: University Press of America, 1988, x + 147 p., cloth, nonf.

FRETTS, Bruce, *as* NICHOLAS ADAMS

15976 *Horror High: Sudden death*. New York: HarperPaperbacks, 1991, 151 p., paper, novel. HORROR HIGH #6.
Sudden death—SEE: *Horror High: Sudden death*.

FREY, Alexander M(oriz), 1881-1957

23506 *The stout-hearted cat: a fable for cat lovers*. New York: Henry Holt & Co., 1947, ix + 140 p., cloth, novel. [Translation by Richard Wilson and Clara Wilson of *Birl, die kühne katze*].

FREY, James N. [pseud. of Mark Washburn], 1948-

23507 *Circle of death*. New York: Zebra Books, Kensington Publishing Corp., 1988, 349 p., paper, novel.

23508 *The elixir*. New York: Zebra Books, Kensington Publishing Corp., 1986, 414 p., paper, novel.

23509 *U.S.S.A.: a novel*. New York: Zebra Books, Kensington Publishing Corp., 1987, 493 p., paper, novel.

FREY, Oliver, *as* ILLUSTRATOR

23510 *Exciting stories of fantasy and the future*. London, New York: Hamlyn, 1982, 256 p., cloth, anth.

FREZZA, Robert, 1956-

23511 *A small colonial war*. New York: A Del Rey Book, Ballantine Books, 1990, 289 p., paper, novel.

FRICKE, John, *with Jay Scarfone & William Stillman*

23512 *The Wizard of Oz: the official 50th anniversary pictorial history.* New York: Warner Books, 1989, 245 p., cloth, nonf.

*FRIEDBERG, Gertrude (Tonkonogy), 1908-1989

FRIEDLI, Emilie—SEE: Van Ith, Lily

FRIEDMAN, C(elia) S., 1955?-

23513 *Black sun rising.* New York: DAW Books, 1991, 489 p., cloth, novel.
23514 *In conquest born.* New York: DAW Books, 1987, 511 p., paper, novel.
23515 *The madness season.* New York: DAW Books, 1990, 495 p., paper, novel.

FRIEDMAN, David G.—SEE: Gerrold, David

FRIEDMAN, Harold Lee

23516 *Crib.* New York: Pocket Books, 1982, 293 p., paper, novel.

FRIEDMAN, Lenemaja (von Heister), 1924-

23517 *Mary Stewart.* Boston: Twayne Publishers, 1990, xv+137 p., cloth, nonf.
23518 *Shirley Jackson.* Boston: Twayne Publishers, 1975, 182 p., cloth, nonf.

FRIEDMAN, Michael Jan, 1955-

23519 *A call to darkness.* New York, London: Pocket Books, 1989, 274 p., paper, tele. STAR TREK, THE NEXT GENERATION #9.
Double, double—SEE: *Star Trek: Double, double.*
23520 *The fortress and the fire.* New York: Popular Library, 1988, 244 p., paper, novel. VIDAR #3.
23521 *Fortune's light.* New York, London: Pocket Books, 1991, 278 p., paper, tele. STAR TREK, THE NEXT GENERATION #15.
23522 *The glove of maiden's hair.* New York: Popular Library, 1987, 234 p., paper, novel.
23523 *The hammer and the horn.* New York: Popular Library, 1985, 297 p., paper, novel. VIDAR #1.
Legacy—SEE: *Star Trek: Legacy.*
Reunion—SEE: *Star Trek, the next generation: Reunion.*
23524 *The seekers and the sword.* New York: Popular Library, Warner Books, 1985, 263 p., paper, novel. VIDAR #2.

23525 *Star Trek: Double, double.* New York, London: Pocket Books, 1989, 308 p., paper, tele. STAR TREK #45.
23526 *Star Trek: Legacy.* New York, London: Pocket Books, 1991, 280 p., paper, tele. STAR TREK #56.
23527 *Star Trek, the next generation: Reunion.* New York, London: Pocket Books, 1991, viii+343 p., cloth, tele. STAR TREK, THE NEXT GENERATION [UNNUMBERED].

with Carmen Carter & Peter David & Robert Greenberger

19541 *Doomsday world.* New York, London: Pocket Books, 1990, xi+276 p., paper, novel. STAR TREK, THE NEXT GENERATION #12.

FRIEDMAN, Stuart

23528 *Maniac.* New York: Leisure Books, 1987, 365 p., paper, novel.

FRIEMAN, Joel, *with Robert Weinberg*

23529 *A tribute to Unknown worlds.* Newark, NJ: Joel Frieman, 1969, 22 p., paper, nonf.

FRIEND, Lonn, *with Jeff Gelb*

23530 *Hot blood: tales of provocative horror.* New York, London: Pocket Books, 1989, xiv+302 p., paper, anth.

*FRIEND, Oscar J(erome), 1897-1963

FRIENDS OF DARKOVER—SEE: Bradley, Marion Zimmer

FRIESNER, Esther M. [i.e., Esther Mona Friesner-Stutzman], 1951-

23531 *Demon blues* / by Esther Friesner. New York: Ace Books, 1989, 280 p., paper, novel. DEMONS #2
23532 *Druid's blood.* New York: A Signet Book, New American Library, 1988, 279 p., paper, novel.
23533 *Ecce hominid.* Eugene, OR: Pulphouse Publishing, 1991, 37 p., paper, story. SHORT STORY PAPERBACKS #16.
23534 *Elf defense.* New York: A Signet Book, New American Library, 1988, 234 p., paper, novel. NEW YORK #2.
23535 *Gnome man's land.* New York: Ace Books, 1991, 235 p., paper, novel. GNOME #1.

23536 *Harlot's ruse.* New York: Popular Library, Warner Books, 1986, 296 p., paper, novel.

23537 *Harpy High.* New York: Ace Books, 1991, 252 p., paper, novel. GNOME #2.

23538 *Here be demons* / by Esther Friesner. New York: Ace Books, 1988, 233 p., paper, novel. DEMONS #1.

23539 *Hooray for Hellywood* / by Esther Friesner. New York: Ace Books, 1990, 217 p., paper, novel. DEMONS #3.

23540 *It's been fun.* Eugene, OR: Pulphouse Publishing, 1991, 110 p., cloth, coll. AUTHOR'S CHOICE MONTHLY #23.

23541 *Mustapha and his wise dog.* New York: Avon, 1985, 175 p., paper, novel. CHRONICLES OF THE TWELVE KINGDOMS #1.

23542 *New York by knight* / by Esther Friedman. New York: A Signet Book, New American Library, 1986, 252 p., paper, novel. NEW YORK #1.

23543 *The Silver Mountain.* New York: Popular Library, Warner Books, 1986, 280 p., paper, novel.

23544 *Spells of mortal weaving.* New York: Avon, 1986, 215 p., paper, novel. CHRONICLES OF THE TWELVE KINGDOMS #2.

23545 *Sphynxes wild.* New York: A Signet Book, New American Library, 1989, 271 p., paper, novel. NEW YORK #3.

23546 *The water king's laughter.* New York: Avon Books, 1989, 283 p., paper, novel. CHRONICLES OF THE TWELVE KINGDOMS #4.

23547 *The witchwood cradle.* New York: Avon, 1987, 241 p., paper, novel. CHRONICLES OF THE TWELVE KINGDOMS #3.

FRIESNER-STUTZMAN, Esther—SEE: Friesner, Esther

FRIGGENS, Arthur (Henry), 1920- , *with Eric Burgess*

19038 *The hounds of heaven.* London: Robert Hale, 1979, 186 p., cloth, novel.

19039 *The Mants of Myrmedon.* London: Robert Hale, 1977, 189 p., cloth, novel.

19040 *Mortorio two.* London: Robert Hale, 1975, 192 p., cloth, novel. MORTORIO #2.

*FRINGS, Ketti, _1915-1981_

FRISBIE, Carol, *with Susan James*

23548 *Night visions.* Arlington, VA: Pulsar Press, 1979, p., paper, tele. STAR TREK SERIES.

FRISTER, Robert Allen, 1936-

23549 *Eclipse.* New York, Washington: Vantage Press, 1982, 207 p., cloth, novel.

FRISWELL, (James) Hain, 1825-1878

37773 *Ghost stories and phantom fancies.* London: Richard Bentley, 1858, vii+222 p., cloth, coll.

*FRITCH, Charles E(dward), 1927-

FRITH, Michael K., *with Christopher Cerf as* I*N FL*M*NG

19684 *Alligator.* Boston, MA: A Vanitas Book, Harvard Lampoon, 1963, 77 p., paper, novel.

FRITH, Nigel (Andrew Silver), 1941-

Asgard—SEE: *The spear of mistletoe.*

23550 *Dragon.* London: Unwin Paperbacks, 1987, 305 p., paper, novel. PANGAIA #2.

23551 *Jormundgand.* London: Unwin Paperbacks, 1986, 210 p., paper, novel. PANGAIA #1.

Krishna—SEE: *The legend of Krishna.*

23552 *The legend of Krishna.* London: Sheldon Press, 1975, 238 p., cloth, novel.

23552A retitled: *Krishna.* London: Unwin Paperbacks, 1985, 237 p., paper, novel.

23553 *Olympiad.* London: Unwin Paperbacks, 1988, 224 p., paper, novel. PANGAIA #3.

23554 *The spear of mistletoe: an epic.* London: Routledge & Kegan Paul, 1977, 293 p., cloth, novel.

23554A retitled: *Asgard.* London: Unwin Paperbacks, 1982, 293 p., paper, novel.

FRITTS, William

The house—SEE: *House of another kind.*

23555 *House of another kind.* New York: Tower Books, 1981, 238 p., paper, novel.

23555A retitled: *The house.* New York: Leisure Books, 1985, 238 p., paper, novel.

FRITZ, Jean (Guttery), 1915-

15808 *Magic to burn.* New York: Coward-McCann, 1964, 255 p., cloth, novel.

FRITZHAND, James, 1946- , *with Frank Glicksman*

23556 *The unicorn affair.* New York: A Signet Book, New American Library, 1981, 230 p., paper, novel.

FROESE, Robert, 1945-

23557 *The hour of blue.* Unity, ME: North Country Press, 1990, 252 p., cloth, novel.

FROIDEVAL, François Marcela- —SEE: Marcela-Froideval, François

FROME, Nils Helmer, 1918-1962, *with H. P. Lovecraft*

23558 *Howard Phillips Lovecraft and Nils Helmer Frome: a recollection of one of Canada's earliest science fiction fans.* Glenview, IL: Moshassuck Press, 1989, 167 leaves, spiral-bound paper, nonf. coll. [Limited to 110 copies; edited by Sam Moskowitz].

FROST, Alexander

Metal gear—SEE: *Worlds of power: Metal gear.*
23559 *Worlds of power: Metal gear: a novel based on the best-selling game by Ultragames.* New York, Toronto: A Seth Godin Production, Scholastic Inc., 1990, 120 p., paper, fiction. WORLDS OF POWER #2.

FROST, Brian J(ohn)

23560 *The monster with a thousand faces: guises of the vampire in myth and literature.* Bowling Green, OH: Bowling Green State University Popular Press, 1989, 152 p., cloth, nonf.

FROST, Denis, 1925- , *with John Edwards as* JOHN DENIS

22439 *Goliath.* London: Fontana, 1987, 284 p., cloth, novel.

FROST, Gregory (Dee), 1951-

23561 *Lyrec.* New York: Ace Fantasy Books, 1984, 267 p., paper, novel.
23562 *Remscéla.* New York: Ace Books, 1988, 278 p., paper, novel. TAIN #2.
23563 *Tain.* New York: Ace Fantasy Books, 1986, ix+386 p., paper, novel. TAIN #1.

FROST, Jason, house pseud.

23564 *Badland.* New York: Zebra Books, Kensington Publishing Corp., 1984, 254 p., paper, novel. WARLORD #3. [By Raymond Obstfeld].
23565 *The cutthroat.* New York: Zebra Books, Kensington Publishing Corp., 1984, 269 p., paper, novel. WARLORD #2. [By Raymond Obstfeld].
23566 *Invasion U.S.A.* New York: Pinnacle Books, 1985, 214 p., paper, movie. [By Raymond Obstfeld].
23567 *Killer's keep.* New York: Zebra Books, Kensington Publishing Corp., 1987, 236 p., paper, novel. WARLORD #6. [By Rich Rainey].
23568 *Prisonland.* New York: Zebra Books, Kensington Publishing Corp., 1985, 240 p., paper, novel. WARLORD #4. [By Raymond Obstfeld].
23569 *Terminal island.* New York: Zebra Books, Kensington Publishing Corp., 1985, 235 p., paper, novel. WARLORD #5. [By Raymond Obstfeld].
23570 *The warlord.* New York: Zebra Books, Kensington Publishing Corp., 1983, 398 p., paper, novel. WARLORD #1. [By Raymond Obstfeld].

FROST, Thomas, *as* AUTHOR OF "THE REALM OF THE ICE KING"

00650 *The North Pole, and Charlie Wilson's adventures in search of it.* London: Griffith Farran Browne, 1875, 284 p., cloth, novel.

FROUD, Brian, 1948-

23571 *Goblins.* New York: Macmillan Publishing Co., 1983, [10] p., cloth, art.
23572 *The land of Froud.* New York: Peacock Press, Bantam Books, 1977, [96] p., paper, art.

with Alan Lee & David Larkin

23573 *Faeries.* New York: Henry N. Abrams, 1978, [ca. 200] p., cloth, fiction.

with J. J. Llewellyn & Rupert Brown

18809 *The world of the Dark Crystal.* New York: Alfred A. Knopf, 1983, 128 p., paper, nonf.

with Terry Jones

23574   *The goblins of Labyrinth.* London: Pavilion, 1986, 137 p., cloth, art.

FROUD, Jane

23575   *The torn tapestry.* London: Century, 1989, 448 p., cloth, novel.

FRUCHTMAN, Joel—SEE: Richards, Joel

*FRUEH, A(lfred) J(oseph), 1880-1968

FRY, Nicholas, 1942- , *with R. V. Adkinson & Allen Eyles*

16034   *The house of horror: the complete story of Hammer Films, 2nd ed.* London: Lorrimer, 1981, 144 p., cloth, nonf.

FRYER, Donald Sidney—SEE: Sidney-Fryer, Donald

FUENTES, Carlos [i.e., Carlos Manuel Fuentes Macías], 1928-

23576   *Aura.* New York: Farrar, Straus & Giroux, 1965, 74 p., cloth, story. [Translation by Lysander Kemp of *Aura*].
23577   *Christopher unborn.* New York: Farrar Straus Giroux, 1989, xi+531 p., cloth, novel. [Translation by Alfred MacAdam and Carlos Fuentes of *Cristóbal nonato*].
37774   *The hydra head.* New York: Farrar Straus Giroux, 1978, 291 p., cloth, novel. [Translation by Margaret Sayres of *La cabeza de la hidra*].
37775   *Terra nostra.* New York: Farrar Straus Giroux, 1976, 777 p., cloth, novel. [Translation by Margaret Sayres of *Terra nostra*].

FUENTES, Roberto, 1934- , *with Piers Anthony*

16709   *Amazon slaughter.* New York: A Berkley Medallion Book, Berkley Publishing Corp., 1976, 204 p., paper, novel. JASON STRIKER #5.
16710   *Dead morn.* Houston, TX: Tafford Publishing, 1990, 265 p., cloth, novel.
16711   *Ninja's revenge.* New York: A Berkley Medallion Book, Berkley Publishing Corp., 1975, 188 p., paper, novel. JASON STRIKER #4.

FULGHAM, Steven Ray

23578   *The forsaken.* New York: Diamond Books, 1991, 292 p., paper, novel.

23579   *The summoned.* New York: Diamond Books, 1991, 323 p., paper, novel.

FULLER, John (Leopold), 1937-

23580   *Flying to nowhere: a tale.* Edinburgh, Scotland: The Salamander Press, 1983, 89 p., cloth, novel

FULLER, John G(rant Jr.), 1913-1990

23581   *The pack.* New York: St. Martin's Press, 1989, 282 p., paper, novel.

FULLERTON, Alexander (Fergus), 1924-

23582   *Regenesis: a novel.* London: Michael Joseph, 1983, 346 p., cloth, novel.

FULTON, Elizabeth G.—SEE: Fulton, Liz

FULTON, Liz [i.e., Elizabeth G. Fulton]

23583   *The palm dome.* New York, Toronto: Bantam Books, 1991, 266 p., paper, novel.

FULTON, Roger

23584   *The encyclopedia of TV science fiction.* London: Boxtree, TV Times, 1990, ix+596 p., paper, nonf.

FULTZ, Regina Oehler

23585   *Tower of darkness.* Lake Geneva, WI: TSR Inc., 1985, 157 p., paper, novel. ENDLESS QUEST #29.

*FUNARO, Sergio (F.), 1922-1986

FUNNELL, Augustine, 1952-

23586   *Brandyjack.* Toronto, New York: Laser Books, 1976, 190 p., paper, novel. BRANDYJACK #1.
23587   *Rebels of Merka.* Toronto, New York: Laser Books, 1976, 190 p., paper, novel. BRANDYJACK #2.

FURLONG, Monica (Teavis), 1930-

Juniper—SEE: *A year and a day.*
23588   *Wise child.* London: Victor Gollancz, 1987, 192 p., cloth, novel. WISE CHILD #2.
23589   *A year and a day.* London: Victor Gollancz, 1990, 175 p., cloth, novel. WISE CHILD #1.

23589A retitled: *Juniper*. New York: Alfred A. Knopf, 1991, 198 p., cloth, novel. WISE CHILD #1.

FURMAN, A(braham) L(oew), 1902-1972

More haunted stories—SEE: *More teen-age haunted stories*.

23590 *More teen-age haunted stories*. New York: Lantern Press, 1967, 189 p., cloth, anth.

23590A retitled: *More haunted stories*. New York: A Lantern Press Book, Pocket Books, 1975, 166 p., paper, anth.

FYSH, pseud.—SEE: Fish, Leonard G.

G

GABALDON, Diana [i.e., Diana Jean Gabaldon Watkins], 1952-

Cross stitch—SEE: *Outlander: a novel.*
23591 *Outlander: a novel.* New York: Delacorte Press, 1991, 627 p., cloth, novel. OUTLANDER #1.
23591A retitled: *Cross stitch.* London & Sydney: Century Random, 1991, 641 p., cloth, novel. OUTLANDER #1.

GABBARD, G(regory) N(orman), 1941-

23592 *Runes from an infant Edda.* New Boston, TX: Flea King, 1980, 20 p., paper, coll. [Limited to 300 copies].

GABERMAN, Judie—SEE: Angell, Judie

GABHART, Ann

23593 *Wish come true.* New York: An Avon Flare Book, 1988, 137 p., paper, novel.

GADALLAH, Leslie (Anne Payne), 1939-

23594 *Cat's gambit.* New York: A Del Rey Book, Ballantine Books, 1990, 247 p., paper, novel. CAT'S PAWN #2.
23595 *Cat's pawn.* New York: A Del Rey Book, Ballantine Books, 1987, 262 p., paper, novel. CAT'S PAWN #1.
23596 *The loremasters.* New York: A Del Rey Book, Ballantine Books, 1988, 280 p., paper, novel.

GADOL, Peter, 1964-

23597 *Coyote: a novel.* New York: Crown Publishers, 1990, 311 p., cloth, novel.

GAER, Joseph, 1897-1969

23598 *Ambrose Gwinnett Bierce: bibliography and biographical data.* [S.l.]: California Literary Research, 1935, 102 leaves, paper, nonf.

GAGE, Thomas E., with Edmund J. Farrell & John Pfordresher & Raymond J. Rodrigues

22917 *Fantasy: shapes of things unknown.* Glenview, IL & Dallas, TX: Scott, Foresman & Co., 1974, 384 p., paper, anth. [Includes some nonfiction].

GAGHAN, Gloria, with Michael Scott

23599 *Navigator: the voyage of Saint Brendan.* London: Methuen, 1988, 205 p., paper, novel.

GAGHER, John E.

23600 *The Peanut Butter Express.* New York, Washington: Vantage Press, 1982, xi+ 158 p., cloth, novel.

GAGNE, Paul R., 1956-

23601 *The zombies that ate Pittsburgh: the films of George A. Romero.* New York: Dodd, Mead & Co., 1987, xv+264 p., paper, nonf.

GAIDA, Davida

23602 *2084.* Chicago: Ringa Press, 1983, 106 p., paper, novel.

GAIL, Otto (Willi), 1896-1956

23603 *The shot into infinity.* New York: Garland Publishing, 1975, 77 p., cloth, story. [Translation by Francis Currier of *Der schuss ins all*].

GAIMAN, Neil (Richard), 1960-

23604 *Don't panic: the official Hitch-hiker's guide to the galaxy handbook.* London: Titan Books, 1988, 182 p., paper, nonf.

with Kim Newman

23605 *Ghastly beyond belief.* London: Arrow Books, 1985, 343 p., paper, anth.

with Terry Pratchett

23606 *Good omens: the nice and accurate prophecies of Agnes Nutter, witch.* London:

Victor Gollancz, 1990, [288] p., cloth, novel.

with Alex Stewart

23607 *Temps, volume 1.* London: A Roc Book, 1991, 353 p., paper, anth.

GAKOV, Vladimir [pseud. of Mikhail Andreevich Kovalchuk], 1951-

23608 *World's spring.* New York: Macmillan, 1981, xiv+297 p., cloth, anth.

GALEN, James, 1918-1987

23609 *The subsidy.* New York, Washington: Vantage Press, 1978, 122 p., cloth, novel.

GALFORD, Ellen, 1947-

23610 *The fires of bride.* London: The Women's Press, 1986, 240 p., cloth, novel.

GALIN, Mitchell, *with Tom Allen*

16310 *Tales from the darkside, volume one.* New York: Berkley Books, 1988, 248 p., paper, anth. [Only volume published].

GALL, Edward R. Home- —SEE: Home-Gall, Edward R.

GALLAGHER, Bob, *with John Diaper*

21707 *Pursuit to Kadath.* Kirkwood, NJ: Theatre of the Mind, 1983, 71 p., paper, novel. CTHULHU MYTHOS.

GALLAGHER, Diana G(race), 1946-

23611 *The alien dark.* Lake Geneva, WI: TSR Books, 1990, 309 p., paper, novel.

GALLAGHER, Edward J(oseph), 1940-

23612 *The annotated guide to Fantastic Adventures.* Mercer Island, WA: Starmont House, 1985, xxi+170 p., cloth, nonf. STARMONT REFERENCE GUIDE #2.

with Judith A. Mistichelli & John A. Van Eerde

23613 *Jules Verne: a primary and secondary bibliography.* Boston: G. K. Hall & Co., 1980, xxi+387 p., cloth, nonf. MASTERS OF SCIENCE FICTION AND FANTASY.

GALLAGHER, Stephen, 1954-

23614 *The boat house.* London: New English Library, 1991, 272 p., cloth, novel.

23615 *Chimera.* London: Sphere Books, 1982, 313 p., paper, novel.

37776 *Down river.* London: New English Library, 1989, [256] p., cloth, novel.

23616 *Follower.* London: Sphere Books, 1984, 313 p., paper, novel.

23617 *The last rose of summer* / by Steve Gallagher. London: Corgi Books, 1978, 204 p., paper, radio. PARADISE #1.

23618 *Oktober.* London: New English Library, 1989, 256 p., paper, novel.

37777 *Rain.* London: New English Library, 1990, 244 p., cloth, novel.

23619 *Saturn Three: a novelisation* / by Steve Gallagher. London: Sphere Books, 1980, 160 p., paper, movie.

23620 *Valley of lights.* London: New English Library, 1987, 191 p., cloth, novel.

as STEPHEN COUPER

23621 *Dying of paradise.* London: Sphere Books, 1982, 183 p., paper, novel. PARADISE #1. [An expanded and rewritten edition of *The last rose of summer*; previously published under the name Steve Gallagher].

23622 *The ice belt.* London: Sphere Books, 1983, 251 p., paper, novel. PARADISE #2.

as JOHN LYDECKER

23623 *Doctor Who and the warriors' gate.* London: A Target Book, W. H. Allen & Co., 1982, 124 p., paper, tele. DOCTOR WHO SERIES.

23624 *Doctor Who: Terminus.* London: W. H. Allen & Co., 1983, 159 p., paper, tele. *Doctor Who series.*
Terminus—SEE: *Doctor Who: Terminus.*

GALLAGHER, Steve—SEE: Gallagher, Stephen

GALLARDO, Gervasio [i.e., Gervasio Gallardo Villaseñor], 1934-

23625 *The fantastic world of Gervasio Gallardo.* New York, London: A Peacock Press/Ballantine Book, 1976, [95] p., paper, art.

*GALLERY, Daniel V(incent), 1901-<u>1977</u>

GALLICO, Paul (William), 1897-1976

23626 *The best of Paul Gallico.* London: Michael Joseph, 1988, 215 p., cloth, coll.
23627 *The house that wouldn't go away.* London: Heinemann, 1979, 222 p., cloth, novel.
23628 *Ludmila; and, The lonely.* Harmondsworth, Middlesex, England: Penguin Books, 1967, 189 p., paper, coll.
15809 *Manxmouse.* London: Heinemann, 1968, 191 p., cloth, novel.

GALLOWAY, Bruce, 1952-

23629 *Fantasy wargaming.* Cambridge, England: Stephens, 1981, 222 p., cloth, nonf. anth.

GALLUN, Raymond Z(inke), 1911-

23630 *The best of Raymond Z. Gallun.* New York: A Del Rey Book, Ballantine Books, 1978, xvi+336 p., paper, coll. [Edited by John J. Pierce].
23631 *Bioblast.* New York: Berkley Books, 1985, 236 p., paper, novel.
23632 *Skyclimber.* New York: Tower Books, 1981, 240 p., paper, novel.

with Jeffrey M. Elliot

22559 *Starclimber: the literary adventures and autobiography of Raymond Z. Gallun.* San Bernardino, CA: R. Reginald, The Borgo Press, 1991, 168 p., cloth, nonf. BORGO BIOVIEWS #1.

GAMMELL, Leon (L.), 1936-

23633 *The annotated guide to Startling Stories.* Mercer Island, WA: Starmont House, 1986, 90 p., cloth, nonf. STARMONT REFERENCE GUIDE #3.

GAMMON, Joy

23634 *The Doctor Who pattern book.* London: W. H. Allen & Co., 1986, 120 p., cloth, nonf.
23635 *Teenage Mutant Ninja Turtles knitting book.* London: Hippo Books, 1990, 32 p., paper, nonf.

GANDHI, Kishore, 1939-

23636 *Aldous Huxley: the search for perennial religion.* New Delhi, India: Arnold-Heinemann, 1980, 220 p., cloth, nonf.

GANLEY, W(illiam) Paul, 1934-

23637 *Toadstool wine.* Buffalo, NY: Weirdbook Press, 1975, 63 p., paper, anth. [Includes some verse].
23638 *The Weirdbook sampler.* Buffalo, NY: W. Paul Ganley, 1988, 32 p., paper, anth.

GANN, Ernest K(ellogg), 1910-1991

23639 *Brain 2000.* Garden City, NY: Doubleday & Co., 1980, 372 p., cloth, novel.

GANPAT [pseud. of Martin Louis Alan Gompertz], 1886-1951

23640 *Adventures in Sakaeland, comprising Harilek and Wrexham's romance.* New York: Arno Press, 1978, 336+316 p., cloth, coll. SAKAELAND #1-2.

GANSOVSKY, Sever [i.e., Sever Feliksovich Gansovskii], 1918-1990

37778 *The day of wrath.* Moscow: Mir Publishers, 1989, 367 p., cloth, coll. [Translation by Alexander Repyev].

GARBER, Eric

23641 *Embracing the dark.* Boston: Alyson Publications, 1991, 190 p., paper, anth.

with Lyn Paleo

23642 *Uranian worlds: a reader's guide to alternative sexuality in science fiction and fantasy.* Boston: G. K. Hall & Co., 1983, xxvi+177 p., cloth, nonf. REFERENCE PUBLICATION IN SCIENCE FICTION.
23643 *Uranian worlds: a reader's guide to alternative sexuality in science fiction and fantasy, 2nd ed.* Boston: G. K. Hall & Co., 1990, xxvi+286 p., cloth, nonf.

with Lyn Paleo & Camilla Decarnin

21459 *Worlds apart: an anthology of lesbian and gay science fiction and fantasy.* Boston: Alyson Publications, 1986, 293 p., paper, anth.

GARCIA, Mike

23644 *Lovecraft: five art studies.* Hollywood, CA: Ken Krueger, 1974, 5 leaves, paper, art coll. LIBRARY LOVECRAFTIAN #1.

GARCIA, Robert T(erence), 1958-

23645 *Chilled to the bone.* Niles, IL: Mayfair Games, 1991, 245 p., paper, anth.

*GARCIA MARQUEZ, Gabriel (José), 1928-

GARCIA Y ROBERTSON, R(odrigo), 1949-

23646 *The spiral dance.* New York: William Morrow & Co., 1991, 227 p., cloth, novel.

GARDAM, Jane (Mary), 1928-

23647 *Through the dolls' house door.* London: Julia MacRae Books, 1987, 121 p., cloth, novel.

GARDEN, Donald J(ohn)

23648 *Dawn chorus.* London: Robert Hale, 1975, 175 p., cloth, novel.

GARDEN, Nancy, 1938-

23649 *The door between.* New York: Farrar Straus Giroux, 1987, 183 p., cloth, novel. FOURS CROSSING #3.
23650 *Fours Crossing.* New York: Farrar Straus Giroux, 1981, 197 p., cloth, novel. FOURS CROSSING #1.
23651 *Mystery of the midnight menace.* New York: Farrar Straus Giroux, 1988, 193 p., cloth, novel. MONSTER HUNTERS #2.
23652 *Mystery of the night raiders.* New York: Farrar Straus Giroux, 1987, 167 p., cloth, novel. MONSTER HUNTERS #1.
23653 *Mystery of the secret marks.* New York: Farrar Straus Giroux, 1989, 225 p., cloth, novel. MONSTER HUNTERS #3.
23654 *Prisoner of vampires.* New York: Farrar Straus Giroux, 1984, vii+213 p., cloth, novel. DRACULA SERIES.
23655 *Watersmeet.* New York: Farrar Straus Giroux, 1983, 201 p., cloth, novel. FOURS CROSSING #2.

GARDETTE, Charles D(esmarais), 1830-1884

23656 *Golgotha: a phantasm.* Saddle River, NJ: Gerry de la Ree, 1973, [10] p., cloth, story. [Limited to 450 copies].

GARDINE, Michael

23657 *Lamia.* New York: A Dell Book, 1981, 186 p., paper, novel.

GARDINER, Judy, 1922-

23658 *The quick and the dead.* London: Hamlyn Paperbacks, 1981, 144 p., paper, novel.

with Stella Whitelaw & Mark Ronson

23659 *Grimalkin's tales: strange and wonderful cat stories.* London: Hamlyn Paperbacks, 1983, 160 p., paper, anth.

GARDINER-SCOTT, Tanya J., 1958-

23660 *Mervyn Peake: the evolution of a dark romantic.* New York: Peter Lang, 1989, 328 p., cloth, nonf.

GARDNER, Averil, 1937-

23661 *George Orwell.* Boston: Twayne Publishers, 1987, 157 p., cloth, nonf.

GARDNER, Craig Shaw, 1949-

23662 *Back to the future, part II: a novel.* New York: Berkley Books, 1989, 251 p., paper, movie. BACK TO THE FUTURE #2.
23663 *Back to the future, part III: a novel.* New York: Berkley Books, 1990, 248 p., paper, movie. BACK TO THE FUTURE #3.
23664 *A bad night for Ali Baba.* London: Headline, 1991, 280 p., cloth, novel. ARABIAN NIGHTS TRILOGY #2.
23665 *Batman.* New York: Warner Books, 1989, 225 p., paper, movie. BATMAN SERIES.
23666 *The Batman murders.* New York: Warner Books, 1990, 246 p., paper, novel. BATMAN SERIES.
23667 *Bride of the slime monster.* New York: Ace Books, 1990, 213 p., paper, novel. CINEVERSE CYCLE #2.
23668 *The Cineverse cycle.* New York: Guild America Books, 1991, 519 p., cloth, coll. CINEVERSE CYCLE #1-3.
23669 *A difficulty with dwarves.* New York: Ace Books, 1987, 188 p., paper, novel. BALLAD OF WUNTVOR #1; EBENEZUM #4.
23670 *A disagreement with death.* New York: Ace Books, 1989, 185 p., paper, novel. BALLAD OF WUNTVOR #3.
23671 *An excess of enchantments.* New York: Ace Books, 1988, 180 p., paper, novel. BALLAD OF WUNTVOR #2.
23672 *The exploits of Ebenezum.* Garden City, NY: Nelson Doubleday, 1987, 437 p., cloth, coll. EBENEZUM #1-3.
23673 *The lost boys: a novel.* New York: Berkley Books, 1987, 220 p., paper, movie.

23674 *A malady of magicks.* New York: Ace Fantasy Books, 1986, 235 p., paper, novel. EBENEZUM #1.

23675 *A multitude of monsters.* New York: Ace Fantasy Books, 1986, 201 p., paper, novel. EBENEZUM #2.

23676 *A night in the Netherhells.* New York: Ace Fantasy Books, 1987, 185 p., paper, novel. EBENEZUM #3.

23677 *The other Sinbad.* London: Headline, 1991, 277 p., cloth, novel. ARABIAN NIGHTS TRILOGY #1.

23678 *Revenge of the fluffy bunnies.* New York: Ace Books, 1990, 216 p., paper, novel. CINEVERSE CYCLE #3.

23679 *Slaves of the volcano god.* New York: Ace Books, 1989, 213 p., paper, novel. CINEVERSE CYCLE #1.

23680 *The wanderings of Wuntvor.* Garden City, NY: Nelson Doubleday, 1989, 505 p., cloth, coll. BALLAD OF WUNTVOR #1-3.

23681 *Wishbringer.* New York: A Byron Preiss Book, An Infocom Book, Avon Books, 1988, 248 p., paper, novel. [Novelization of fantasy game].

GARDNER, Delbert R(alph), 1923-

23682 *An "idle singer" and his audience: a study of William Morris's poetic reputation in England, 1858-1900.* The Hague, Paris: Mouton, 1975, vi+135 p., cloth, nonf.

GARDNER, Erle Stanley, 1889-1970

23683 *The human zero: the science fiction stories of Erle Stanley Gardner.* New York: William Morrow, 1981, 444 p., cloth, coll. [Edited by Martin H. Greenberg & Charles G. Waugh].

GARDNER, Gerald B.—SEE: Scrire. O.T.O. 4=7

*GARDNER, Gerald (C.), <u>1929-</u>

GARDNER, Jerome—SEE: Gilchrist, John

GARDNER, John (Champlin Jr.), 1933-1982

23684 *The art of living, and other stories.* New York: Alfred A. Knopf, 1981, 309 p., cloth, coll.

23685 *Freddy's book.* New York: Alfred A. Knopf, 1981, 245 p., cloth, novel.

23686 *In the Suicide Mountains.* New York: Alfred A. Knopf, 1977, 158 p., cloth, novel.

23687 *The king's Indian: stories and tales.* New York: Alfred A. Knopf, 1974, 323 p., cloth, coll.

23688 *Mickelsson's ghosts: a novel.* New York: Alfred A. Knopf, 1982, viii+590 p., cloth, novel.

GARDNER, John (Edmund), 1926-

37779 *Founder member.* London: Frederick Muller, 1969, 184 p., cloth, novel.

23689 *Golgotha.* London: W. H. Allen & Co., 1980, 253 p., cloth, novel.

23689A retitled: *The last trump.* New York: McGraw-Hill Book Co., 1980, 255 p., cloth, novel.

The last trump—SEE: *Golgotha.*

GARDNER, Martin, 1914-

23690 *The no-sided professor, and other tales of fantasy, humor, mystery, and philosophy.* Buffalo, New York: Prometheus Books, 1987, 224 p., cloth, coll.

23691 *Puzzles from other worlds: fantastic brain-teasers from Isaac Asimov's science fiction magazine.* New York: Vintage Books, 1984, xii+189 p., paper, nonf. coll.

23692 *Science fiction puzzle tales.* New York: Clarkson N. Potter, 1981, xii+148 p., cloth, nonf.

GARDNER, Philip, 1936-

23693 *Kingsley Amis.* Boston: Twayne Publishers, 1981, 174 p., cloth, nonf.

GARDNER, Richard [originally Richard Maurice Orth], 1931-

23694 *Mandrill.* New York: Pocket Books, 1975, 208 p., paper, novel.

GARDNER, Tonita S.

23695 *The Angriff technique.* New York: Lynx Books, 1988, 345 p., paper, novel.

GARFIELD, Leon, 1921-

23696 *Empty sleeve.* Harmondsworth, Middlesex, England: Viking Kestrel, 1988, 185 p., cloth, novel.

GARI, Roman—SEE: Gary, Romain

GARIS, Howard R(oger), 1873-1962, *with Edward L. Stratemeyer as* ROY ROCKWOOD

12339 *Five thousand miles underground; or, The mystery of the center of the Earth.* New York: Cupples & Leon, 1908, 242 p., cloth, novel. GREAT MARVEL SERIES #3.

12340 *Lost on the Moon; or, In quest of the field of diamonds.* New York: Cupples & Leon, 1911, 248 p., cloth, novel. GREAT MARVEL SERIES #5.

12341 *On a torn-away world; or, The captives of the great earthquake.* New York: Cupples & Leon, 1913, 246 p., cloth, novel. GREAT MARVEL SERIES #6.

12342 *Through space to Mars; or, The longest journey on record.* New York: Cupples & Leon, 1910, 248 p., cloth, novel. GREAT MARVEL SERIES #4.

12343 *Through the air to the North Pole; or, The wonderful cruise of the Electric Monarch.* New York: Cupples & Leon, 1906, 240 p., cloth, novel. GREAT MARVEL SERIES #1.

12344 *Under the ocean to the South Pole; or, The strange cruise of the submarine wonder.* New York: Cupples & Leon, 1907, 248 p., cloth, novel. GREAT MARVEL SERIES #2.

GARLICK, Nicholas

23697 *California dreaming.* London: Robert Hale, 1981, 188 p., cloth, novel.

GARN, Edwin J.—SEE: Garn, Jake

GARN, Jake [i.e., Edwin Jacob Garn], 1932- , *with Stephen Paul Cohen*

20263 *Night launch.* New York: William Morrow & Co., 1989, 285 p., cloth, novel.

GARNER, Graham, pseud.—SEE: Rowland, Donald S.

GARNETT, Bill [i.e., William John Garnett], 1941-

23699 *The crone.* London: Sphere Books, 1984, 215 p., paper, novel.

05790 *Down-bound train.* Garden City, NY: Doubleday, 1973, 189 p., cloth, novel.

23700 retitled: *Helltrain.* New York: St. Martin's Press, 1988, 186 p., paper, novel. [Revised edition].

Helltrain—SEE: *Down-bound train.*

23701 *The shadow.* London: Sphere, 1982, 146 p., paper, novel.

23702 *The unbegotten.* Feltham, England: Hamlyn Paperbacks, 1982, 160 p., paper, novel.

GARNETT, David, 1892-1981

23703 *The master cat: the true and unexpurgated story of Puss in Boots.* London: Macmillan, 1974, 137 p., cloth, novel.

GARNETT, David S., 1947-

23704 *Cosmic carousel.* London: Robert Hale, 1976, 192 p., cloth, coll.

23705 *The forgotten dimension.* London: Robert Hale, 1975, 182 p., cloth, novel.

23706 *New worlds 1.* London: Victor Gollancz, 1991, 267 p., paper, anth.

23707 *The Orbit science fiction yearbook 1.* London: Orbit Books, Futura, 1988, 336 p., paper, anth.

23708 *The Orbit science fiction yearbook two.* London: Orbit Books, Futura, 1989, 347 p., paper, anth.

23709 *The Orbit science fiction yearbook three.* London: Orbit Books, 1990, 361 p., paper, anth.

23710 *Phantom universe.* London: Robert Hale, 1975, 188 p., cloth, novel.

23711 *Zenith: the best in new British science fiction.* London: Sphere Books, 1989, 297 p., paper, anth.

23712 *Zenith 2: the best in new British science fiction.* London: Orbit Books, 1990, 320 p., paper, anth.

as DAVID FERRING

37780 *The hills have eyes, part 2: novelization.* London: Panther, 1984, 189 p., paper, movie.

Konrad—SEE: *Warhammer: Konrad.*
Shadowbreed—SEE: *Warhammer: Shadowbreed.*

23713 *Warhammer: Konrad.* Brighton, East Sussex, England: GW Books, 1990, 228 p., paper, novel. WARHAMMER SERIES—KONRAD #1.

23714 *Warhammer: Shadowbreed.* Brighton, East Sussex, England: GW Books, 1991, 239 p., paper, novel. WARHAMMER SERIES—KONRAD #2. [The concluding book of this trilogy, *Warblade*, was never published].

as DAVID LEE

08765 *Destiny past.* London: Robert Hale, 1974, 157 p., cloth, novel.

GARNETT, Rhys, 1935- , *with R. J. Ellis*

22581 *Science fiction roots and branches: contemporary critical approaches.* London: Macmillan, 1990, xi+210 p., cloth, nonf. anth.

GARNETT, William J.—SEE: Garnett, Bill

GARRETT, Dave

23715 *The seedseekers.* Chatsworth, CA: GX, 1973, p., paper, novel.

GARRETT, Michael, *with Jeff Gelb*

23716 *Hotter blood: more tales of erotic horror.* New York, London: Pocket Books, 1991, xii+336 p., paper, anth.

GARRETT, (Gordon) Randall (Phillip David), 1927-1987

23717 *The best of Randall Garrett.* New York: A Timescape Book, Pocket Books, 1982, 261 p., paper, coll. [Edited by Robert Silverberg].

23718 *Lord Darcy: a 3-in-1 volume.* Garden City, NY: Nelson Doubleday, 1983, 600 p., cloth, coll. LORD DARCY #1-3. [Includes *Too many magicians*; *Murder and magic*; *Lord Darcy investigates*].

23719 *Lord Darcy investigates.* New York: Ace Books, 1981, 229 p., paper, coll. LORD DARCY #3.

23720 *Murder and magic.* New York: Ace Books, 1979, 266 p., paper, coll. LORD DARCY #2.
Starship Death—SEE: *Unwise child.*

23721 *Takeoff!* / by Randall Garret [sic]. Virginia Beach, VA: Starblaze Editions/Donning, 1980, 247 p., paper, coll. [Includes some verse].

23722 *Takeoff too.* Norfolk & Virginia Beach, VA: The Donning Co., Publishers, Starblaze Editions, 1987, 311 p., paper, coll.

05805 *Unwise child.* Garden City, NY: Doubleday, 1962, 215 p., cloth, novel.

05805A retitled: *Starship Death.* New York: Leisure Books, 1982, 233 p., paper, novel.

with Vicki Ann Heydron

23723 *The bronze of Eddarta.* Toronto, New York: Bantam Books, 1983, 165 p., paper, novel. GANDALARA CYCLE #3.

23724 *The Gandalara cycle, volume 1.* Toronto, New York: Bantam Books, 1986, 515 p., paper, coll. GANDALARA CYCLE #1-3.

23725 *The Gandalara cycle, vol. 2.* Toronto, New York: Bantam Books, 1986, 439 p., paper, coll. GANDALARA CYCLE #4-6.

23726 *The glass of Dyskornis.* Toronto, New York: Bantam Books, 1982, 174 p., paper, novel. GANDALARA CYCLE #2.

23727 *Return to Eddarta.* Toronto, New York: Bantam Books, 1985, 149 p., paper, novel. GANDALARA CYCLE #6.

23728 *The river wall.* Toronto, New York: Bantam Books, 1986, 275 p., paper, novel. GANDALARA CYCLE #7.

23729 *The search for Kä.* Toronto, New York: Bantam Books, 1984, 180 p., paper, novel. GANDALARA CYCLE #5.

23730 *The steel of Raithskar.* Toronto, New York: Bantam Books, 1981, 180 p., paper, novel. GANDALARA CYCLE #1.

23731 *The well of darkness.* Toronto, New York: Bantam Books, 1983, 166 p., paper, novel. GANDALARA CYCLE #4.

GARRIDO, Mar

23732 *Once upon a kiss.* New York: Avon Flare, 1987, 170 p., paper, novel. EILEEN GOUDGE'S SWEPT AWAY #6.

GARTH, Will [possible pseud. of Alexander Samalman, 1904-1956]

08491 *Dr. Cyclops.* New York: Phoenix Press, 1940, 255 p., cloth, movie.

GARTON, Ray

Crucifax—SEE: *Crucifax autumn.*

23733 *Crucifax autumn: a novel.* Arlington Heights, IL: Dark Harvest, 1988, 326 p., cloth, novel.

23733A retitled: *Crucifax.* New York, London: Pocket Books, 1988, 387 p., paper, novel. [Abridged edition].

23734 *Darklings.* New York: Pinnacle Books, 1985, 309 p., paper, novel.

23735 *Invaders from Mars: a novel.* New York: Pocket Books, 1986, 221 p., paper, movie.

23736 *Live girls.* New York: Pocket Books, 1987, 311 p., paper, novel.

23737 *Lot lizards.* Shingletown, CA: Mark V. Ziesing, 1991, 188 p., cloth, novel.

23738 *Methods of madness: a collection.* Arlington Heights, IL: Dark Harvest, 1990, 243 p., cloth, coll.

23739 *The new neighbor.* Lynbrook, NY: Charnel House, 1991, 280 p., cloth, novel. [Limited to 500 copies].

23740 *Seductions.* New York: Pinnacle Books, 1984, 277 p., paper, novel.

23741 *Trade secrets.* Shingletown, CT: Mark V. Ziesing, 1990, 292 p., cloth, novel.
23742 *Warlock: a novel.* New York: Avon Books, 1989, 228 p., paper, movie.

as JOSEPH LOCKE

> *The dream child*—SEE: *Nightmares on Elm Street, part 4: The dream master; part 5: The dream child: a novel.*
> *The dream master*—SEE: *Nightmares on Elm Street, part 4: The dream master; part 5: The dream child: a novel.*

28472 *Nightmares on Elm Street, part 4: The dream master; part 5: The dream child: a novel.* New York: St. Martin's Press, 1989, 188 p., paper, movie coll. NIGHTMARE ON ELM STREET #4-5.

*GARVIN, Richard M(cClellan), 1934-1980

*GARY, Romain [pseud. of Roman Kassevgari], 1914-1980

GASCOIGNE, Marc

> *Battleblade Warnor*—SEE: *Steve Jackson and Ian Livingstone present Battleblade Warnor.*
> *Demonstealer*—SEE: *Steve Jackson and Ian Livingstone present Demonstealer.*

23743 *Steve Jackson and Ian Livingstone present Battleblade Warnor.* Harmondsworth, Middlesex, England: Puffin Books, 1988, 400 p., paper, fiction. FIGHTING FANTASY GAMEBOOK SERIES.
23744 *Steve Jackson and Ian Livingstone present Demonstealer.* Harmondsworth, Middlesex, England: Puffin Books, 1991, 227 p., paper, fiction. FIGHTING FANTASY GAMEBOOK SERIES.

with Pete Tamlyn

> *Blacksand!*—SEE: *Steve Jackson and Ian Livingstone present Blacksand!*
> *Dungeoneer*—SEE: *Steve Jackson and Ian Livingstone present Dungeoneer.*

23745 *Steve Jackson and Ian Livingstone present Blacksand!* Harmondsworth, Middlesex, England: Puffin Books, 1990, vi+362 p., paper, fiction. FIGHTING FANTASY GAMEBOOK.
23746 *Steve Jackson and Ian Livingstone present Dungeoneer.* Harmondsworth, Middlesex, England: Puffin Books, 1989, 394 p., paper, fiction. FIGHTING FANTASY GAMEBOOK.

GASCOIGNE, Toss, *with Jo Goodman & Margot Tyrrell*

23747 *Dream time: new stories by sixteen award-winning authors.* Ringwood, Victoria, Australia: Penguin Books, 1989, 184 p., paper, anth.

GASKELL, Jane [i.e., Jane Gaskell Lynch], 1941-

> *The dragon*—SEE: *The serpent.*
05833 *The serpent.* London: Hodder & Stoughton, 1963, 445 p., cloth, novel.
05833A retitled: *The dragon.* London: Tandem, 1975, 206 p., paper, novel. ATLAN SAGA #1B. [The original novel split into two parts].
05833B retitled: *The serpent.* London: Tandem, 1975, 317 p., paper, novel. ATLAN SAGA #1A. [The original novel split into two parts].
23748 *Some summer lands.* London: Hodder & Stoughton, 1977, 352 p., cloth, novel. ATLAN SAGA #4.
37781 *Sun bubble: a novel.* London: Weidenfeld & Nicolson, 1990, [224] p., cloth, novel.

GASKELL, Elizabeth C.—SEE: Gaskell, Mrs.

GASKELL, Mrs. [i.e., Elizabeth Cleghorn Stevenson Gaskell], 1810-1865

23749 *Mrs. Gaskell's tales of mystery and horror.* London: Victor Gollancz, 1978, 231 p., cloth, coll. [Edited by Mike Ashley].

GASKIN, Carol

23750 *Caravan to China.* Toronto, New York: A Byron Preiss Book, Bantam Books, 1987, 125 p., paper, novel. TIME MACHINE #21.
37782 *The first settlers.* Toronto, New York: A Byron Preiss Book, A Bantam Skylark Book, 1987, 80 p., paper, novel. TIME TRAVELER #3.
23751 *The forbidden towers.* Mahwah, NJ: Troll Associates, 1985, 124 p., cloth, novel. FORGOTTEN FOREST SERIES.
23752 *Journey to the center of the atom!* New York, Toronto: A Byron Preiss Book, Scholastic Inc., 1987, 115 p., paper, novel. EXPLORER #1.
37783 *The legend of Hiawatha.* Toronto, New York: A Byron Preiss Book, A Bantam Skylark Book, 1986, 80 p., paper, novel. TIME TRAVELER #2.

23753 *The magician's ring.* Mahwah, NJ: Troll Associates, 1985, 122 p., cloth, novel. FORGOTTEN FOREST SERIES.

23754 *The master of mazes.* Mahwah, NJ: Troll Associates, 1985, 122 p., cloth, novel. FORGOTTEN FOREST SERIES.

23755 *Secret of the royal treasure.* Toronto, New York: A Byron Preiss Book, Bantam Books, 1986, 126 p., paper, novel. TIME MACHINE #13.

23756 *Secrets of the samurai.* New York: A Byron Preiss Book, Avon Books, 1990, [100] p., paper, novel.

23757 *The war of the wizards.* Mahwah, NJ: Troll Associates, 1985, 122 p., cloth, novel. FORGOTTEN FOREST SERIES.

with George Guthridge

23758 *Death mask of Pancho Villa.* Toronto, New York: A Byron Preiss Book, Bantam Books, 1987, 125 p., paper, novel. TIME MACHINE #19.

GASPERINI, Jim, 1952-

23759 *The mystery of Atlantis.* Toronto, New York: A Byron Preiss Book, Bantam Books, 1985, 123 p., paper, novel. TIME MACHINE #8.

23760 *Sail with pirates.* Toronto, New York: A Byron Preiss Book, Bantam Books, 1984, 125 p., paper, novel. TIME MACHINE #4.

23761 *Secret of the knights.* Toronto, New York: A Byron Preiss Book, Bantam Books, 1984, 124 p., paper, novel. TIME MACHINE #1.

GATES, R(andy) Patrick, 1954-

23762 *Fear.* New York: An Onyx Book, New American Library, 1988, 318 p., paper, novel.

23763 *Grimm memorials.* New York: An Onyx Book, 1990, 367 p., paper, novel.

23764 *Tunnelvision.* New York: A Dell Book, 1991, xv+430 p., paper, novel.

GATTO, John Taylor

23765 *The major works of H. P. Lovecraft: a critical commentary.* New York: Monarch Press, 1977, 110 p., paper, nonf.

GAUGER, Richard C.—SEE: Gauger, Rick

GAUGER, Rick [i.e., Richard C. Gauger]

23766 *Charon's ark.* New York: A Del Rey Book, Ballantine Books, 1987, 375 p., paper, novel.

GAUNT, Eleanor

37784 *A romance of the imagination.* London: Digby, Long & Co., 1894, 64 p., cloth, story.

GAUTIER, Théophile, 1811-1872

23767 *My fantoms.* London: Quartet Books, 1976, 179 p., cloth, coll. [Translation of *Contes fantastiques*; edited and translated by Richard Holmes].

GAVIN, Jamila, 1941-

23768 *Ali and the robots.* London: Methuen Children's Books, 1986, 89 p., cloth, novel.

GAWRON, Jean Mark, 1953-

23769 *Algorithm.* New York: A Berkley Book, Berkley Publishing Corp., 1978, 211 p., paper, novel.

GAY, Anne, 1952-

23770 *The brooch of azure midnight.* London: Orbit, 1991, 455 p., cloth, novel.

23771 *Mindsail.* London: Orbit, 1990, 303 p., cloth, novel.

*GAZDANOV, Gaito [i.e., Georgii Gazdanov], 1903-<u>1971</u>

GAZDANOV, Georgii—SEE: Gazdanov, Gaito

GEAR, Kathleen (M.) O'Neal, 1954-

as KATHLEEN M. O'NEAL

23772 *An abyss of light.* New York: DAW Books, 1990, 464 p., paper, novel. POWERS OF LIGHT #1.

23773 *Redemption of light.* New York: DAW Books, 1991, 527 p., paper, novel. POWERS OF LIGHT #3.

23774 *Treasure of light.* New York: DAW Books, 1990, 544 p., paper, novel. POWERS OF LIGHT #2.

with W. Michael Gear

23775 *People of the fire.* New York: Tor, A Tom Doherty Associates Book, 1991, 467 p., paper, novel. PEOPLE #2.

23776 *People of the wolf.* New York: Tor, A Tom Doherty Associates Book, 1990, 435 p., paper, novel. PEOPLE #1.

GEAR, Marty, *with Peggy Kennedy*

23777 *The Kennedy masquerade compendium, revised and expanded edition.* Menands, NY: Firepearl Editions, 1984, v+110 p., paper, nonf.

GEAR, W(illiam) Michael, 1955-

23778 *The artifact.* New York: DAW Books, 1990, 526 p., paper, novel. SPIDER PREQUEL.

23779 *Requiem for the conqueror.* New York: DAW Books, 1991, 622 p., paper, novel. FORBIDDEN BORDERS #1.

23780 *Starstrike.* New York: DAW Books, 1990, 542 p., paper, novel.

23781 *The warriors of spider.* New York: DAW Books, 1988, 367 p., paper, novel. SPIDER #1.

23782 *The way of spider.* New York: DAW Books, 1989, 408 p., paper, novel. SPIDER #2.

23783 *The web of spider.* New York: DAW Books, 1989, 648 p., paper, novel. SPIDER #3.

with Kathleen O'Neal Gear

23775 *People of the fire.* New York: Tor, A Tom Doherty Associates Book, 1991, 467 p., paper, novel. PEOPLE #2.

23776 *People of the wolf.* New York: Tor, A Tom Doherty Associates Book, 1990, 435 p., paper, novel. PEOPLE #1.

GEARE, Michael, 1919- , *with Michael Corby*

20588 *Dracula's diary.* London: Buchan & Enright, 1982, 153 p., cloth, novel.

GEARHART, Sally Miller, 1931-

23777 *The Wanderground: stories of the hill women.* Watertown, MA: Persephone Press, 1978, 196 p., cloth, coll.

GEARY, Patricia (Carol), 1951-

23778 *Living in ether: a novel.* New York: Harper & Row, 1982, 212 p., cloth, novel.

23779 *Strange toys.* Toronto, New York: Bantam Books, 1987, 248 p., paper, novel.

GEASLAND, Jack [i.e., John Buchanan Geasland Jr.], 1944- , *with Bari Wood*

Dead ringers—SEE: *Twins: Dead ringers.*

23780 *Twins: a novel.* New York: G. P. Putnam's Sons, 1977, 316 p., cloth, novel.

23781A retitled: *Dead ringers.* London: Sphere Books, 1988, 346 p., paper, novel.

GEASLAND, John B.—SEE: Geasland, Jack

GED, Caer, pseud.—SEE: Proctor, George W.

GEDDES, Adrienne (Marie)

23782 *The rim of eternity.* Auckland, New Zealand: Collins, 1964, 175 p., cloth, novel.

GEDGE, Pauline (Alice), 1945-

Mirage—SEE: *Scroll of Saqqara.*

23783 *Scroll of Saqqara.* Markham, Ontario, Canada: Viking Penguin Canada, 1991, 460 p., cloth, novel.

23783A retitled: *Mirage.* New York: HarperCollinsPublishers, 1991, 460 p., cloth, novel.

23784 *Stargate.* Toronto: Macmillan of Canada, 1982, 341 p., cloth, novel.

GEDULD, Carolyn

23785 *Bernard Wolfe.* New York: Twayne Publishers, 1972, 155 p., cloth, nonf.

GEDULD, Harry M(aurice), 1931-

23786 *The definitive Dr. Jekyll and Mr. Hyde companion.* New York: Garland Publishing, 1983, xi+219 p., cloth, nonf.

with Ronald Gottesman

23787 *The girl in the hairy paw: King Kong as myth, movie, and monster.* New York: A Flare Book, Avon, 1976, 233 p., paper, nonf. anth.

23788 *Robots, robots, robots.* Boston: NY Graphic Society, 1978, vii+246 p., cloth, anth.

GEE, Maggie (Mary), 1948-

23789 *The burning book.* London: Faber & Faber, 1983, 303 p., cloth, novel.

37785 *Where are the snows?* London: William Heinemann, 1991, 376 p., cloth, novel.

GEE, Maurice (Gough), 1931-

23790 *The halfmen of O.* Auckland, New Zealand, New York: Oxford University Press, 1982, 204 p., cloth, novel. WORLD OF O #1.

23791 *Motherstone.* Auckland, New Zealand: Oxford University Press, 1985, 184 p., cloth, novel. WORLD OF O #3.

23792 *The priests of Ferris.* Auckland, New Zealand, Oxford: Oxford University Press, 1984, 180 p., cloth, novel. WORLD OF O #2.

37786 *Under the mountain.* Wellington, New Zealand: Oxford University Press, 1976, 155 p., cloth, novel.

37787 *The world around the corner.* Wellington, New Zealand: Oxford University Press, 1980, 72 p., cloth, novel.

GEIS, Richard E(rwin), 1927-

23793 *Canned meat: a science fiction novel.* Portland, OR: Richard E. Geis, 1978, 67 leaves, paper, novel.

23794 *The corporation strikes back.* Portland, OR: Richard E. Geis, 1981, 92 p., paper, novel. [Limited to 470 copies].

23795 *Star whores.* Portland, OR: Richard E. Geis, 1980, 93 p., paper, novel.

with Elton T. Elliott as RICHARD ELLIOTT

22563 *The burnt lands.* New York: Fawcett Gold Medal, 1985, 263 p., paper, novel. JOHN NORRIS #2.

22564 *The Einstein legacy.* New York: Fawcett Gold Medal, 1987, 281 p., paper, novel.

22565 *The master file.* New York: Fawcett Gold Medal, 1986, 250 p., paper, novel.

22566 *The Sword of Allah.* New York: Fawcett Gold Medal, 1984, 281 p., paper, novel. JOHN NORRIS #1.

GELB, Jeff

23796 *Specters.* New York: Bart Books, 1988, 241 p., paper, novel.

with Lonn Friend

23530 *Hot blood: tales of provocative horror.* New York, London: Pocket Books, 1989, xiv+302 p., paper, anth.

with Michael Garrett

23716 *Hotter blood: more tales of erotic horror.* New York, London: Pocket Books, 1991, xii+336 p., paper, anth.

GELFLAND, M. Howard

23797 *E.T., the extraterrestrial.* Mankato, MN: Creative Education, 1983, 32 p., cloth, movie.

GELLER, Stephen

23798 *Gad: a novel.* New York & Hagerstown, NJ: Harper & Row, Publishers, 1979, 241 p., cloth, novel.

GELLER, Uri, 1946-

23799 *Shawn.* England: Goodyer, 1990, 236 p., cloth, novel.

GELLIS, Roberta—SEE: Daniels, Max

GELMAN, Rita Golden—SEE: Austin, R. G.

GEMMELL, David A., 1948-

Against the horde—SEE: Legend.

23800 *Dark prince.* London: A Legend Book, Century Publishing, 1991, viii+451 p., cloth, novel. LION OF MACEDON #2.

23801 *Drenai tales.* London: Legend, 1991, viii+756 p., paper, coll. DRENAI SAGA #1-3. [Includes *Waylander, Legend, The king beyond the gate,* and the novelette "Druss the Legend"].

23802 *Ghost king.* London: A Legend Book, Century, 1988, 266 p., cloth, novel. SIPSTRASSI TALES #2.

The Jerusalem man—SEE: Wolf in shadow.

23803 *The king beyond the gate.* London: Century Publishing, 1985, x+308 p., cloth, novel. DRENAI SAGA #2 [*Legend* Trilogy].

23804 *Knights of dark renown.* London: A Legend Book, Century, 1989, 400 p., cloth, novel.

23805 *The last guardian.* London, Sydney: Century, A Legend Book, 1989, 279 p., cloth, novel. SIPSTRASSI TALES #4.

23806 *Last sword of power.* London: A Legend Book, 1988, xii+275 p., paper, novel. SIPSTRASSI TALES #3.

23807 *Legend.* London: Century Publishing, 1986, 383 p., cloth, novel. DRENAI SAGA #1 [*Legend* Trilogy].

23807A retitled: *Against the horde.* Delavan, WI: New Infinities Productions, 1988, 383 p., paper, novel. DRENAI SAGA #1 [*Legend* Trilogy].

23808 *Lion of Macedon.* London: A Legend Book, Century Publishing, 1990, ix+420 p., cloth, novel. LION OF MACEDON #1.

23809 *The lost crown.* London: Hutchinson Children's Books, 1989, [144] p., cloth, novel.

23810 *Quest for lost heroes.* London: A Legend Book, Century Publishing, 1990, 316 p., cloth, novel. DRENAI SAGA #4.

23811 *Waylander.* London: Century Publishing, 1986, ix+323 p., cloth, novel. DRENAI SAGA #3. [*Legend* Trilogy].

23812 *Wolf in shadow.* London: Century, A Legend Book, 1987, ix+326 p., cloth, novel. SIPSTRASSI TALES #1.

23812A retitled: *The Jerusalem man.* New York: Baen Books, 1988, 343 p., paper, novel.

GENDALL, Stuart

23813 *Weekend book of science fiction.* London: Published for Harmsworth by Associated Newspapers Group, 1981, 127 p., paper, anth.

GENTILE, Anthony

23814 *The Judas seed.* New York: A Dell Book, 1982, 299 p., paper, novel.

GENTILE, Gary, 1946-

23815 *Dragons past.* New York: Ace Books, 1990, 229 p., paper, novel. DRAGONS #2.

23816 *The lurking.* New York: Charter Books, 1989, 261 p., paper, novel.

23817 *No future for dragons.* New York: Ace Books, 1990, 247 p., paper, novel. DRAGONS #3.

23818 *A time for dragons.* New York: Ace Books, 1989, 232 p., paper, novel. DRAGONS #1.

GENTLE, Mary (Rosalyn), 1956-

23819 *Ancient light.* London: Victor Gollancz, 1987, 539 p., cloth, novel. ORTHE #2.

23820 *The architecture of desire.* London: Bantam Press, 1991, 192 p., cloth, novel. WHITE CROW #2.

23821 *Golden witchbreed.* London: Victor Gollancz, 1983, 476 p., cloth, novel. ORTHE #1.

23822 *A hawk in silver.* London: Victor Gollancz, 1977, 192 p., cloth, novel.

23823 *Rats and gargoyles.* London: Bantam Press, 1990, 414 p., cloth, novel. WHITE CROW #1.

23824 *Scholars and soldiers: a story collection.* London: Macdonald, 1989, 192 p., cloth, coll.

GENTRY, Christine [i.e., Christine Mary Gentry Rodriguez], 1954-

23825 *When spirits walk.* New York: A Critic's Choice Paperback from Lorevan Publishing, 1988, 279 p., paper, novel

with Sally Gibson-Downs

23826 *Encyclopedia of Trekkie memorabilia: identification and value guide.* Florence, AL: Books Americana, 1988, iii+269 p., paper, nonf.

23827 *Greenberg's guide to Star Trek collectibles.* Sykesville, MD: Greenberg Publishing, 1991, 3 v., paper, nonf.

GEORGE, Bill [i.e., William Francis George], 1951-

23828 *Eroticism in the fantasy cinema.* Pittsburgh, PA: Imagine, 1984, 128 p., paper, nonf.

GEORGE, Edward, pseud.—SEE: Vardeman, Robert E. & Proctor, Geo. W.

GEORGE, Sara, 1947-

23829 *Fatal shadows.* London: Macmillan, 1976, 191 p., cloth, novel.

GEORGE, Stephen R.

23830 *Beasts.* New York: Zebra Books, Kensington Publishing Corp., 1989, 350 p., paper, novel.

23831 *Brain child.* New York: Zebra Books, Kensington Publishing Corp., 1989, 352 p., paper, novel.

23832 *Dark miracle.* New York: Zebra Books, Kensington Publishing Corp., 1989, 416 p., paper, novel.

23833 *Dark reunion.* New York: Zebra Books, Kensington Publishing Corp., 1990, 320 p., paper, novel.

23834 *The forgotten.* New York: Zebra Books, Kensington Publishing Corp., 1991, 351 p., paper, novel.

23835 *Grandma's little darling.* New York: Zebra Books, Kensington Publishing Corp., 1990, 320 p., paper, novel.

GEORGE, William F.—SEE: George, Bill

GERALD, Gregory Fitz—SEE: Fitz Gerald, Gregory

GERANI, Gary

23836 *Batman official souvenir magazine.* Brooklyn, NY: Topps, 1989, 62 p., paper, nonf. anth. [Cover title].

23837 *Norman Jacobs and Kerry O'Quinn present TV episode guides: science fiction, adventure, and superheroes.* New York: Starlog Press, 1981-82, 2 vols., paper, nonf.
TV episode guides—SEE: *Norman Jacobs and Kerry O'Quinn present TV episode guides.*

with Paul H. Schulman

23838 *Fantastic television.* New York: Harmony Books, 1977, 192 p., cloth, nonf.

*GERBERG, Mort, 1931-

*GERMANO, Peter B., 1913-1983

GERRAND, Rob(ert)

23839 *Transmutations.* Collingwood, Victoria, Australia: Outback Press, 1979, 216 p., paper, anth.

GERRARE, Wirt [pseud. of William Oliver Greener], 1862-

37788 *Rufin's legacy: a theosophical romance.* London: Hutchinson & Co., 1892, viii+312 p., cloth, novel.

GERROLD, David [pseud. of Jerrold David Freidman], 1944-

23840 *Chess with a dragon.* New York: Millennium, A Byron Preiss Book, Walker & Co., 1987, 207 p., cloth, novel.

23841 *A day for damnation.* New York: Timescape Books, 1984, 382 p., cloth, novel. WAR AGAINST THE CHTORR #2.

23842 *A day for damnation, rev. ed.* Toronto, New York: Spectra, Bantam Books, 1989, 423 p., paper, novel. WAR AGAINST THE CHTORR #2.

23843 *Deathbeast.* New York: Popular Library, 1978, 255 p., paper, novel.
Encounter at farpoint—SEE: *Star Trek the Next Generation: Encounter at Farpoint: a novel.*

23844 *The galactic whirlpool: a Star Trek novel.* Toronto, New York: Bantam Books, 1980, ix+223 p., paper, novel. STAR TREK SERIES.
Invasion—SEE: *The war against the Chtorr: Invasion.*

23845 *A matter for men.* New York: Timescape Books, 1983, 399 p., cloth, novel. WAR AGAINST THE CHTORR #1.

23846 *A matter for men.* New York, Toronto: Spectra, Bantam Books, 1989, 435 p., paper, novel. WAR AGAINST THE CHTORR #1. [Expanded edition].

23847 *Moonstar odyssey.* New York: A Signet Book, New American Library, 1977, 159 p., paper, novel.

23848 *A rage for revenge.* New York, Toronto: Spectra, Bantam Books, 1989, vii+517 p., paper, novel. WAR AGAINST THE CHTORR #3.

23849 *Star Trek the Next Generation: Encounter at Farpoint: a novel.* New York: Pocket Books, 1987, 192 p., paper, tele. STAR TREK THE NEXT GENERATION (UNNUMBERED).
Starhunt—SEE: *Yesterday's children.*

23850 *Voyage of the Star Wolf.* New York, Toronto: Spectra, Bantam Books, 1990, 276 p., paper, novel.

23851 *The war against the Chtorr: Invasion.* Garden City, NY: Nelson Doubleday, 1984, 693 p., cloth, coll. WAR AGAINST THE CHTORR #1-2.

23852 *When HARLIE was one: (release 2.0).* Toronto, New York: Spectra, Bantam Books, 1988, xiii+287 p., paper, novel. [Expanded and rewritten version of *When HARLIE was one* (see #05908)].

23853 *World of Star Trek, revised edition.* New York: Bluejay Books, 1984, xx+209 p., paper, nonf. [Revised and expanded edition of #05910].

23854 *Yesterday's children.* New York: Fawcett Popular Library, 1980, 252 p., paper, novel. [Revised edition of #05911].

23854A retitled: *Starhunt.* London: Hamlyn Paperbacks, 1985, 252 p., paper, novel.

with Stephen Goldin

23855 *Ascents of wonder.* New York: Popular Library, 1977, 288 p., paper, anth.

with Barry B. Longyear

23856 *Enemy mine.* New York: Charter Books, 1985, 218 p., paper, movie. DRACON #1.

with Dave Truesdale

23857 *Norman Jacobs & Kerry O'Quinn present Starlog's science fiction yearbook, vol. 1.* New York: A Starlog Press Book, 1979, 111 p., paper, nonf. anth.

Starlog's science fiction yearbook, vol. 1—SEE: *Norman Jacobs & Kerry O'Quinn present Starlog's science fiction yearbook, vol. 1.*

GERSON, Jack

23858　*The evil thereof.* London: Piatkus, 1991, 348 p., cloth, novel.

*GERSON, Noel B(ertram), 1914-<u>1988</u>

GERSTNER, Nickolae

23859　*Dark veil.* New York: Ballantine Books, 1989, 213 p., paper, novel.

GERTZ, Elmer, 1906-

23860　*Odyssey of a barbarian: the biography of George Sylvester Viereck.* Buffalo, NY: Prometheus Books, 1978, vi+305 p., cloth, nonf.

GESTON, Mark S(ymington), 1946-

23861　*The siege of wonder.* Garden City, NY: Doubleday & Co., 1976, 180 p., cloth, novel.

GHIDALIA, Vic(tor Simon), 1926-

23862　*Feast of fear.* New York: Manor Books, 1977, 205 p., paper, anth.
23863　*Nightmare garden.* New York: Manor Books, 1976, 192 p., paper, anth.

with Roger Elwood

22635　*Beware more beasts.* New York: Manor Books, 1975, 192 p., paper, anth.

GHOLOSTON, J. N. [i.e., Homer N. Gholston]

23864　*The Koiec corollary.* New York: Manor Books, 1979 (i.e., 1980?), 215 p., paper, novel. [Cover byline states Homer N. Gholston].

GHOLSTON, Homer N.—SEE: Gholston, J. N.

GHOSE, Sisirkumar, 1919-

23865　*Aldous Huxley: a cynical salvationist.* New York: Asia Publishing House, 1962, ix+205 p., cloth, nonf.

GHOSE, Zulfikar (Ahmed), 1935-

23866　*Figures of enchantment.* London: Hutchinson, 1986, 256 p., cloth, novel.

GIANNONE, Richard (J.), 1934-

23867　*Vonnegut: a preface to his novels.* Port Washington, NY & London: National University Press Publications, Kennikat Press, 1977, 136 p., cloth, nonf.

GIBB, Jocelyn (Easton), 1907-

23868　*Light on C. S. Lewis.* London: Geoffrey Bles, 1965, 160 p., cloth, nonf. anth.

GIBBARD, T. S. J., pseud.—SEE: Vinter, Michael

GIBBERMAN, Susan R., 1958-

23869　*Star Trek: an annotated guide to resources on the development, the phenomenon, the people, the television series, the films, the novels, and the recordings.* Jefferson, NC & London: McFarland & Co., 1991, xii+434 p., cloth, nonf.

*GIBBS, Anthony, 1902-<u>1975</u>

*GIBBS, Henry (St. John Clair), <u>1913-</u>

GIBESON, Jacqueline—SEE: La Tourrette, Jacqueline

GIBSON, Colin (A.)

23870　*The pepper leaf: an episode.* London: Chatto & Windus, 1971, 231 p., cloth, novel.

GIBSON, Edward (George), 1936-

23871　*Reach: a novel.* New York, London: A Foundation Book, Doubleday, 1989, xi+334 p., cloth, novel.

GIBSON, Evan K(eith), 1909-1986

23872　*C. S. Lewis, spinner of tales: a guide to his fiction.* Grand Rapids, MI: Christian University Press, a Subsidiary of Christian College Consortium and Wm. B. Eerdmans Publishing Co., 1980, ix+284 p., paper, nonf.

GIBSON, Floyd, pseud.—SEE: King, Albert

GIBSON, James (Charles), 1919-

23873 *Science fiction.* London: John Murray, 1978, 120 p., paper, anth.

with Alan Ridout

23874 *Supernatural.* London: John Murray, 1978, 120 p., paper, anth.

GIBSON, Miles, 1947-

23875 *Dancing with mermaids.* London: Heinemann, 1985, 195 p., cloth, novel.

GIBSON, Walter B(rown), 1897-1985

Crime over Casco; &, The Mother Goose murders—SEE: *The Shadow: Crime over Casco & The Mother Goose murders.*

Jade dragon; &, House of ghosts—SEE: *The Shadow: Jade dragon & House of ghosts.*

The mask of Mephisto; &, Murder by magic—SEE: *The Shadow: The mask of Mephisto & Murder by magic.*

A quarter of eight; &, The freak show murders—SEE: *The Shadow: A quarter of eight & The freak show murders.*

23876 *Rod Serling's Twilight Zone.* New York: Bonanza Books, 1983, x+364 p., cloth, tele. coll. [Includes *Rod Serling's The twilight zone* and *Twilight zone revisited*].

23877 *The Shadow: A quarter of eight & The freak show murders.* Garden City, NY: Doubleday & Co., 1978, xv+248 p., cloth, coll. SHADOW SERIES.

23878 *The Shadow and the Golden Master.* New York: Mysterious Press, 1984, 130+114 p., cloth, coll. SHADOW SERIES. [Includes *The Golden Master; and, Shiwan Khan returns*].

23879 *The Shadow: Crime over Casco & The Mother Goose murders.* Garden City, NY: Doubleday & Co., 1979, xiii+197 p., cloth, coll. SHADOW SERIES.

23880 *The Shadow: Jade dragon & House of ghosts.* Garden City, NY: Doubleday & Co., 1981, iv+205 p., cloth, coll. SHADOW SERIES.

23881 *The Shadow scrapbook.* New York: An Original Harvest/HBJ Book, Harcourt Brace Jovanovich, 1979, 162 p., paper, coll. [Includes some nonf.].

23882 *The Shadow: The mask of Mephisto & Murder by magic.* Garden City, NY: Doubleday & Co., 1975, xi+179 p., cloth, coll. SHADOW SERIES.

as MAXWELL GRANT

23883 *Charg, monster: from the Shadow's private annals.* New York: A Jove/HBJ Book, 1977, 158 p., paper, novel. SHADOW #20.

23884 *The creeping death: from the Shadow's private annals.* New York: Pyramid Books, 1977, 144 p., paper, novel. SHADOW #14.

23885 *The crime cult: from the Shadow's private annals.* New York: Pyramid Books, 1975, 156 p., paper, novel. SHADOW #6.

23886 *The crime oracle; and, The teeth of the dragon: two adventures of the Shadow.* New York: Dover Publications, 1975, xxv+163 p., paper, coll. SHADOW SERIES.

23887 *The Death Giver: from the Shadow's private annals.* New York: A Jove/HBJ Book, 1978, 160 p., paper, novel. SHADOW #23.

23888 *Double Z: from the Shadow's private annals.* New York: Pyramid Books, 1975, 188 p., paper, novel. SHADOW #5.

23889 *Fingers of death: from the Shadow's private annals.* New York: A Jove/HBJ Book, 1977, 144 p., paper, novel. SHADOW #17.

23890 *Gray Fist: from the Shadow's private annals.* New York: Pyramid Books, 1977, 174 p., paper, novel. SHADOW #15.

23891 *Green Eyes: from the Shadow's private annals.* New York: Pyramid Books, 1977, 158 p., paper, novel. SHADOW #13.

23892 *Hands in the dark: from the Shadow's private annals.* New York: Pyramid Books, 1975, 187 p., paper, novel. SHADOW #4.

23893 *Kings of crime: from the Shadow's private annals.* New York: Pyramid Books, 1976, 160 p., paper, novel. SHADOW #11.

23894 *Mox: from the Shadow's private annals.* New York: Pyramid Books, 1975, 126 p., paper, novel. SHADOW #8.

23895 *Murder trail: from the Shadow's private annals.* New York: A Jove/HBJ Book, 1977, 159 p., paper, novel. SHADOW #18.

23896 *Norgil: more tales of prestidigitection.* New York: Mysterious Press, 1979, xi+207 p., cloth, coll. NORGIL #2.

23897 *Norgil the magician.* New York: Mysterious Press, 1977, 208 p., cloth, coll. NORGIL #1.

23898 *The red menace: from the Shadow's private annals.* New York: Pyramid Books, 1975, 176 p., paper, novel. SHADOW #7.

23899 *The Romanoff jewels: from the Shadow's private annals.* New York: Pyramid

Books, 1975, 142 p., paper, novel. SHADOW #9.

23900 *Shadowed millions: from the Shadow's private annals.* New York: Pyramid Books, 1976, 142 p., paper, novel. SHADOW #12.

23901 *The Shadow's shadow: from the Shadow's private annals.* New York: Pyramid Books, 1977, 173 p., paper, novel. SHADOW #16.

23902 *The silent death: from the Shadow's private annals.* New York: A Jove/HBJ Book, 1978, 160 p., paper, novel. SHADOW #22.

23903 *The Silent Seven: from the Shadow's private annals.* New York: Pyramid Books, 1975, 142 p., paper, novel. SHADOW #10.

23904 *The wealth seeker: from the Shadow's private annals.* New York: A Jove/HBJ Book, 1978, 158 p., paper, novel. SHADOW #21.

23905 *Zemba: from the Shadow's private annals.* New York: A Jove/HBJ Book, 1977, 160 p., paper, novel. SHADOW #19.

GIBSON, William (Ford), 1948-

23906 *Burning chrome.* New York: Arbor House, 1986, 200 p., cloth, coll.

23907 *Count Zero.* New York: Arbor House, 1986, 278 p., cloth, novel. NEUROMANCER #2.

23908 *Mona Lisa overdrive.* London: Victor Gollancz, 1988, 251 p., cloth, novel. NEUROMANCER #3.

23909 *Neuromancer.* New York: Ace Science Fiction Books, 1984, x+271 p., paper, novel. NEUROMANCER #1. [Winner of the Hugo Award for Best Novel, 1984 (1985); winner of the Nebula Award for Best Novel, 1984 (1985); winner of the *Science Fiction Chronicle* Award for Best Novel, 1984 (1985)].

as MINK MOLE, with Dr Adder (i.e., K. W. Jeter)

23910 *Alligator Alley.* Scotforth, Lancashire, England: Morrigan Publications, 1989, 295 p., cloth, novel.

with Bruce Sterling

23910 *The difference engine.* London: Victor Gollancz, 1990, 383 p., cloth, novel.

GIBSON-DOWNS, Sally (May), 1954- , with Christine Gentry

23826 *Encyclopedia of Trekkie memorabilia: identification and value guide.* Florence, AL: Books Americana, 1988, iii+269 p., paper, nonf.

23827 *Greenberg's guide to Star Trek collectibles.* Sykesville, MD: Greenberg Publishing, 1991, 3 v., paper, nonf.

GIBSON-JARVIE, Clodagh—SEE: Chapman, Clodagh

GIDDINGS, Robert (Lindsay), 1935-

23911 *J. R. R. Tolkien: this far land.* London: Vision; Totowa, NJ: Barnes & Noble, 1983, 206 p., cloth, nonf. anth.

with Elizabeth Holland

23912 *J. R. R. Tolkien: the shores of Middle-Earth.* London: Junction Books, 1981, x+289 p., cloth, nonf.

GIDEON, John, pseud.—SEE: Hoklin, Lonn

GIFALDI, David

23913 *Yours till forever.* New York: J. B. Lippincott, 1989, 90 p., cloth, novel.

GIFFORD, Denis, 1927-

23914 *Mad doctors, monsters, and mummies: lobby card posters from Hollywood horrors!* England: Blossom, 1991, [96] p., cloth, nonf.

23915 *Monsters of the movies.* London: Carousel Books, 1977, 95 p., paper, nonf.

23916 *A pictorial history of horror movies, rev. ed.* London, New York: Hamilton, 1983, 232 p., cloth, nonf.

23917 *Things, its, and aliens: lobby card posters from sci-fi schockers!* England: Blossom, 1991, [64] p., cloth, nonf.

GIFFORD, Thomas (Eugene), 1937-

23918 *The assassini.* New York, Toronto: Bantam Books, 1990, viii+600 p., cloth, novel.

GIGER, H. R. [i.e., Hansruedi Giger], 1940-

23919 *Giger's Alien: film design, 20th Century-Fox.* Basel, Switzerland: Sphinx-Verlag, 1979, 72 p., cloth, art.

37789 *H. R. Giger.* Frankfort, Germany: Sydow-Zirkwitz, 1976, 45 p., paper, art.

23920 *H. R. Giger ARh+.* Gurtendorff, Switzerland: W. Zürcher Verlag, 1971, 135 p., paper, art.
23921 *H. R. Giger's biomechanics.* Beverly Hills, CA: Morpheus International, 1990, 95 p., cloth, art.
23922 *H. R. Giger's Necronomicon.* Basel, Switzerland: Sphinx-Verlag, 1977, 72 p., cloth, art.
23923 *H. R. Giger's Necronomicon 2.* Zürich, Switzerland: Edition C, 1985, [90] p., cloth, art.

GIGER, Hansruedi—SEE: Giger, H. R.

GIKOW, Louise

23924 *Labyrinth: a storybook.* New York: Henry Holt & Co., 1986, [56] p., cloth, movie.

GILBERT, C. M.

23925 *The Ozine conquest.* New York: Leisure Books, 1981, 176 p., paper, novel.

GILBERT, Douglas (R.), 1942- , with Clyde S. Kilby

23926 *C. S. Lewis: images of his world.* Grand Rapids, MI: William B. Eerdmans Publishing Co., 1973, 192 p., cloth, nonf.

GILBERT, John

23927 *Aiki: a novel.* New York: Donald I. Fine, 1986, 286 p., cloth, novel.

GILBERT, Michael (Francis), 1912- , with Andre Norton

23928 *The day of the Ness.* New York: Walker & Co., 1975, 119 p., cloth, novel.

GILBERT, R(obert) A(ndrew), 1942- , with Michael Cox

20742 *The Oxford book of English ghost stories.* Oxford, New York: Oxford University Press, 1986, xvii+504 p., cloth, anth.
20743 *Victorian ghost stories: an Oxford anthology.* Oxford, New York: Oxford University Press, 1991, xx+497 p., cloth, anth.

GILBERT, Ruth—SEE: Ainsworth, Ruth

GILCHRIST, John [pseud. of Jerome Gardner], 1932-

23929 *Birdbrain.* London: Robert Hale, 1975, 176 p., cloth, novel.
23930 *The engendering.* London: Robert Hale, 1978, 187 p., cloth, novel.
23931 *The English corridor.* London: Robert Hale, 1976, 190 p., cloth, novel.
23932 *Lifeline.* London: Robert Hale, 1976, 176 p., cloth, novel.
23933 *Out north.* London: Robert Hale, 1975, 191 p., cloth, novel.

GILDEN, Mel, 1947-

23934 *Boogeymen.* New York, London: Pocket Books, 1991, 244 p., paper, tele. STAR TREK, THE NEXT GENERATION #17.
23935 *Born to howl.* New York: A GLC Book, An Avon Camelot Book, 1987, 90 p., paper, novel. FIFTH GRADE MONSTERS #2.
23936 *Harry Newberry and the raiders of the red drink.* New York: Henry Holt & Co., 1989, 151 p., cloth, novel
23937 *Hawaiian U.F.O. aliens.* New York: A Roc Book, A Byron Preiss Visual Publications Inc. Book, 1991, 272 p., paper, novel. ZOOT MARLOWE #2.
23938 *How to be a vampire in one easy lesson.* New York: A GLC Book, An Avon Camelot Book, 1990, 91 p., paper, novel. FIFTH GRADE MONSTERS #10.
23939 *Island of the weird.* New York: A GLC Book, An Avon Camelot Book, 1990, 90 p., paper, novel. FIFTH GRADE MONSTERS #11.
23940 *M is for monster.* New York: A GLC Book, An Avon Camelot Book, 1987, 89 p., paper, novel. FIFTH GRADE MONSTERS #1.
23941 *Monster boy.* New York: A GLC Book, An Avon Camelot Book, 1991, 90 p., paper, novel. FIFTH GRADE MONSTERS #13.
23942 *The monster in Creeps Head Bay.* New York: A GLC Book, An Avon Camelot Book, 1990, 91 p., paper, novel. FIFTH GRADE MONSTERS #9.
23943 *Monster mashers.* New York: A GLC Book, An Avon Camelot Book, 1989, 91 p., paper, novel. FIFTH GRADE MONSTERS #6.
23944 *Outer space and all that junk.* New York: J. B. Lippincott, 1989, 167 p., cloth, novel.
23945 *The pet of Frankenstein.* New York: A GLC Book, An Avon Camelot Book, 1988, 96 p., paper, novel. FIFTH GRADE MONSTERS #4.

23946 *The planetoid of amazement.* New York: HarperCollinsPublishers, 1991, 215 p., cloth, novel.

23947 *The return of Captain Conquer.* Boston: Houghton Mifflin Co., 1986, 153 p., cloth, novel.

23948 *The secret of Dinosaur Bog.* New York: A GLC Book, An Avon Camelot Book, 1991, 90 p., paper, novel. FIFTH GRADE MONSTERS #15.

23949 *Surfing samurai robots.* New York: Lynx Books, 1988, 246 p., paper, novel. ZOOT MARLOWE #1.

23950 *Things that go bark in the park.* New York: A GLC Book, An Avon Camelot Book, 1989, 88 p., paper, novel. FIFTH GRADE MONSTERS #7.

23951 *Troll patrol.* New York: A GLC Book, An Avon Camelot Book, 1991, 89 p., paper, novel. FIFTH GRADE MONSTERS #14.

23952 *Tubular android superheroes.* New York: A Byron Preiss Visual Publications Inc. Book, A Roc Book, 1991, 288 p., paper, novel. ZOOT MARLOWE #3.

23953 *Werewolf, come home.* New York: A GLC Book, An Avon Camelot Book, 1990, 87 p., paper, novel. FIFTH GRADE MONSTERS #12.

23954 *Yuckers!* New York: A GLC Book, An Avon Camelot Book, 1989, 91 p., paper, novel. FIFTH GRADE MONSTERS #8.

23955 *Z is for zombie.* New York: A GLC Book, An Avon Camelot Book, 1988, 89 p., paper, novel. FIFTH GRADE MONSTERS #5.

GILL, Richard, 1948-

23956 *Time keepers.* London: Merlin, 1989, 79 p., paper, coll.

GILL, Roger, *with Peter Alexander*

16258 *Utopias.* London: Duckworth, 1984, xx+ 218 p., cloth, nonf. anth.

GILL, Stephen (M.), 1932-

23957 *Scientific romances of H. G. Wells: a critical study.* Cornwall, Ontario, Canada: Vesta Publications, 1975, 155 p., paper, nonf.

23958 *Scientific romances of H. G. Wells: (a critical study), new edition.* / by Stephen M. Gill. Cornwall, Ontario, Canada: Vesta Publications, 1977, 160 p., paper, nonf.

GILLESPIE, Bruce, 1947-

23959 *Philip K. Dick: electric shepherd.* Melbourne, Australia: Norstrilia Press, 1975, 106 p., paper, nonf. anth. BEST OF SF COMMENTARY #1.

GILLETT, Stephen L(ee), 1953- , with Poul Anderson

16449 *How to build a planet.* Eugene, OR: Writer's Notebook Press, Pulphouse Publishing, 1991, 25 p., paper, nonf.

GILLIAM, Terry (Vance), 1940-

with Jack Mathews

23960 *The battle of Brazil: the authorized story and annotated screenplay of Terry Gilliam's landmark film.* New York: Crown Publishers, 1987, xi+228 p., cloth, nonf. anth.

with Charles McKeown

23961 *The adventures of Baron Munchausen.* London: Mandarin, 1989, 212 p., paper, movie.

GILLIGAN, Alison

23962 *The treasure of the Onyx Dragon.* New York, Toronto: An R. A. Montgomery Book, Bantam Books, 1990, 116 p., paper, novel. CHOOSE YOUR OWN ADVENTURE #105.

GILLIGAN, Shannon

37790 *The case of the silk king.* Toronto, New York: An R. A. Montgomery Book, Bantam Books, 1986, 114 p., paper, novel. CHOOSE YOUR OWN ADVENTURE #53.

37791 *The mystery of Ura Senke.* Toronto, New York: An R. A. Montgomery Book, Bantam Books, 1985, 116 p., paper, novel. CHOOSE YOUR OWN ADVENTURE #44.

23963 *Terror in Australia.* Toronto, New York: An R. A. Montgomery Book, Bantam Books, 1988, 113 p., paper, novel. CHOOSE YOUR OWN ADVENTURE #81.

23964 *The terrorist trap.* Toronto, New York: An R. A. Montgomery Book, Bantam Books, 1991, 112 p., paper, novel. CHOOSE YOUR OWN ADVENTURE #119.

GILLILAND, Alexis A(rnaldus), 1931-

23965　*The end of the Empire.*　New York:　A Del Rey Book, Ballantine Books, 1983, 169 p., paper, novel.

23966　*Long shot for Rosinante.*　New York:　A Del Rey Book, Ballantine Books, 1981, 181 p., paper, novel.　ROSINANTE #2.

23967　*The pirates of Rosinante.*　New York:　A Del Rey Book, Ballantine Books, 1982, 216 p., paper, novel.　ROSINANTE #3.

23968　*The revolution from Rosinante.*　New York:　A Del Rey Book, Ballantine Books, 1981, 185 p., paper, novel.　ROSINANTE #1.

23969　*The shadow Shaia.*　New York:　A Del Rey Book, Ballantine Books, 1990, 213 p., cloth, novel.　WIZENBEAK #2.

23970　*The waltzing wizard: cartoons.*　Mercer Island, WA:　Starmont House, 1989, 116 p., cloth, art.

23971　*Wizenbeak.*　New York:　Bluejay Books, 1986, 279 p., paper, novel.　WIZENBEAK #1.

GILLULY, Sheila

23972　*The boy from the burren.*　New York:　A Roc Book, 1990, 351 p., paper, novel. BOOK OF THE PAINTER #1.

23973　*The crystal keep.*　New York:　A Signet Book, New American Library, 1988, 348 p., paper, novel.　GREENBRIAR QUEEN #2.

23974　*Greenbriar queen.*　New York:　A Signet Book, New American Library, 1988, 330 p., paper, novel.　GREENBRIAR QUEEN #1.

23975　*Ritnym's daughter.*　New York:　A Signet Book, New American Library, 1989, 351 p., paper, novel.　GREENBRIAR QUEEN #3.

GILMAN, Charlotte (Anna) Perkins (Stetson), 1860-1935

23976　*The Charlotte Perkins Gilman reader: The yellow wallpaper, and other fiction.*　New York:　Pantheon Books, 1980, xiii+208 p., cloth, coll. [Edited by Ann J. Lane].

23977　*Herland.*　New York:　Pantheon, 1979, xxiv+147 p., cloth, novel.

23978　*The yellow wallpaper.*　Alexandria, VA:　Orchises, 1990, 16 p., paper?, story.

23979　*The yellow wallpaper, and other writings.*　New York, Toronto:　Bantam Books, 1989, xxvii+240 p., paper, coll.

GILMAN, Dorothy [i.e., Dorothy Gilman Butters], 1923-

23980　*The clairvoyant countess.*　Garden City, NY:　Doubleday & Co., 1975, 179 p., cloth, novel.

23981　*Incident at Badamyâ.*　New York:　Doubleday, 1989, 204 p., cloth, novel.

23982　*The maze in the heart of the castle.*　Garden City, NY:　Doubleday, 1983, 230 p., cloth, novel.

GILMAN, Greer Ilene, 1951-

23983　*Moonwise.*　New York:　A Roc Book, 1991, 373 p., paper, novel.

GILMAN, Robert Cham, pseud.—SEE:　Coppel, Alfred

*GILMORE, Anthony [pseud. of Hiram Gilmore "Harry" Bates III, 1900-<u>1981</u>, and of HALL, Desmond]

GILMORE, Kate

23984　*Enter three witches.*　Boston:　Houghton Mifflin Co., 1991, 210 p., cloth, novel.

GILMORE, Maeve (Peake), d. 1983

23985　*Mervyn Peake, 1911-1968: exhibition of manuscripts, drawings, illustrations.*　Oxford:　Bodleian Library, 1978, 21 p., paper, nonf.

23986　*A world away: a memoir of Mervyn Peake.*　London:　Victor Gollancz, 1970, 157 p., cloth, nonf.

GILMOUR, H(arriet) B., 1939-

23987　*Eyes of Laura Mars.*　Toronto, New York:　Bantam Books, 1978, 213 p., paper, movie.

GILMOUR, William

23988　*Lost on Jupiter.*　Peoria, IL:　House of Greystoke, 1962, [20] p., paper, story. MARS SEQUEL.

23989　*Tarzan and the lightning man.*　Kansas City, MO:　House of Greystoke, 1963, 20 p., paper, story.　TARZAN SEQUEL.

23990　*The undying land.*　West Kingston, RI:　Donald M. Grant, Publisher, 1985, 208 p., cloth, novel.

GINGOLD, Helene E. A., Baroness

23991　*Seven stories.*　London:　Remington & Co., 1893, 187 p., cloth, coll.

GINSBERG, Allen, 1926- , *with William S. Burroughs*

19083 *Letters to Allen Ginsberg, 1953-1957.* New York: Full Court Press, 1982, 203 p., cloth, nonf. coll.
19084 *The Yage letters.* San Francisco: City Lights Books, 1975, 66 p., paper, nonf. coll.

GINSBURG, Mirra, 1919-

23992 *The air of Mars, and other stories of time and space.* New York: Macmillan Publishing Co., 1976, ix+141 p., cloth, anth.

with Kirill Bulychev

18989 *Alice: some incidents in the life of a little girl of the twenty-first century, recorded by her father on the eve of her first day in school.* New York: Macmillan, 1977, 64 p., cloth, novel. [Translation and adaptation by Ginsberg of *Devochka s kotoroi nichego ne sluchitsa*].

GIPE, George, 1933-1986

23993 *Back to the future: a novel.* New York: Berkley Books, 1985, 248 p., paper, movie.
23994 *Explorers: a novel.* New York: Pocket Books, 1985, 250 p., paper, movie.
23995 *Gremlins.* New York: Avon, 1984, 278 p., paper, movie.
23996 *Resurrection: a novel.* New York: Pocket Books, 1980, 283 p., paper, movie.

GIRARD, Kenneth

23997 *Altered egos.* New York: Pinnacle Books, 1983, 276 p., paper, novel.
23998 *Fun house* / by Ken Girard. Belmont, CA: Fearon, 1987, 60 p., paper, story.
23999 *Weekend vacation* / by Ken Girard. Belmont, CA: Fearon, 1987, 58 p., paper, story.

*GIRAUDOUX, (Hippolyte) Jean, 1882-1944

GIROUX, Leo Jr.

24000 *Dark ashram.* London: Grafton, 1990, 411 p., paper, novel.
24001 *The rishi.* New York: M. Evans & Co., 1985, 355 p., cloth, novel.

GIRZONE, Joseph F(rancis), 1930-

24002 *Joshua.* Albany, NY: Richelieu Court, 1983, 310 p., paper, novel. JOSHUA #1.
24003 *Joshua and the children: a parable.* New York: Macmillan, 1989, 224 p., cloth, novel. JOSHUA #2.

GLABERSON, Cory, *with Troy Denning & Gordon R. Dickson*

21553 *Dorsai's command.* New York: Ace Books, 1989, 246 p., paper, novel. COMBAT COMMAND #8; DORSAI SERIES.

GLAD, John P(eter), 1941-

24004 *Extrapolations from dystopia: a critical study of Soviet science fiction.* Princeton, NJ: Kingston Press, 1982, 223 p., cloth, nonf.

GLADNEY, Heather (Jeanne), 1957-

24005 *Blood storm.* New York: Ace Books, 1989, 277 p., paper, novel. SONG OF NAGA TEOT #2.
24006 *Teot's war.* New York: Ace Books, 1987, 264 p., paper, novel. SONG OF NAGA TEOT #1.

GLADSTEIN, Mimi Reisel, 1936-

24007 *The Ayn Rand companion.* Westport, CT, London: Greenwood Press, 1984, xii+130 p., cloth, nonf.

GLASBY, John (Stephen), 1928-

as JOHN ADAMS

00048 *When the gods came.* London: Badger Books, 1960, 142 p., paper, novel.

as B. L. BOWERS

01715 *This second Earth.* London: Cobra Books, 1957, 158 p., paper, novel.

as VICTOR LA SALLE

06015 *Dawn of the half-gods.* London: John Spencer & Co., 1953, 128 p., paper, novel.
08636 *Twilight Zone.* London: John Spencer & Co., 1954, 130 p., paper, novel.
08637 *Twilight Zone.* London: Badger Books, 1959, 158 p., paper, coll. [Includes an additional story, "Point of no return," by "Max Chartair" (another pseudonym of Glasby)].

as JOHN C. MAXWELL

09844 *"The world makers"*. London: Badger Books, 1958, 160 p., paper, novel.

as JOHN MULLER

10493 *Alien*. London: Badger Books, 1961, 158 p., paper, novel.
10494 *Day of the beasts*. London: Badger Books, 1961, 158 p., paper, novel.
10499 *The unpossessed*. London: Badger Books, 1961, 158 p., paper, novel.

as KARL ZIEGFRIED

15761 *"Dark Centauri"*. London: John Spencer & Co., 1954, 130 p., paper, novel.
15762 *The uranium seekers*. London: John Spencer & Co., 1953, 128 p., paper, novel.

GLASS, Amanda, pseud.—SEE: Krentz, Jayne Ann

GLASS, Theodore—SEE: Theodamus

GLASSCO, John (Stinson), 1909-1981

24008 *The fatal woman: three tales*. Toronto: Anansi, 1974, iv+172 p., paper, coll.

with Aubrey Beardsley

17620 *Under the hill; or, The story of Venus and Tannhäuser, in which is set forth an exact account of state held by Madame Venus, Goddess and Meretrix, under the famous Hörselberg, and containing the adventures of Tannhäuser in that place, his journeying to Rome and return to the Loving Mountain*. London: New English Library, 1966, 125 p., cloth, novel. [Completed by Glassco].

GLASSER, Alan—SEE: Glasser, Allen

GLASSER, Allen, 1918-

37792 *The cavemen of Venus*. Jamaica, NY: Solar Publications, [1932], 17 p., paper, story.
24009 *The demon cosmos* / by Alan Glasser. Canoga Park, CA: Major Books, 1978 (i.e., 1980), 173 p., paper, novel.

GLASSFORD, Wilfred, pseud.—SEE: McNeilly, Wilfred G.

GLATZER, Richard (Mark)

24010 *Quest for the cities of gold*. Toronto, New York: A Byron Preiss Book, Bantam Books, 1987, 125 p., paper, novel. TIME MACHINE #16.

GLAZE, Eleanor, 1930-

24011 *Jaiyavara: a novel*. Memphis, TN: St. Lukes Press, 1988, 281 p., cloth, novel.

GLAZER, Mindy

24012 *The perfect object*. Bronx, NY: Yeoman Press, 1979, 108 p., paper, novel. STAR TREK SERIES.

GLEMSER, Bernard—SEE: Crane, Robert

GLENN, Lois (Ruth), 1941-

24013 *Charles W. S. Williams: a checklist*. Kent, OH: Kent State University Press, 1975, viii+128 p., cloth, nonf. SERIF SERIES: BIBLIOGRAPHIES AND CHECKLISTS #33.

GLENN, Nancy Tyler, 1938-

24014 *Clicking stones*. Tallahassee, FL: Naiad Press, 1989, 269 p., paper, novel.

GLICK, Ruth (Burtnick), 1942-

24015 *Invasion of the blue lights*. New York, Toronto: Scholastic Book Services, 1982, 126 p., paper, novel.

with Eileen Buckholtz

28518 *Captain Kid and the pirates*. New York, Toronto: Scholastic Inc., 1985, 79 p., paper, novel. MAGIC MICRO ADVENTURE #1.
18883 *The cats of Castle Mountain*. New York, Toronto: Scholastic Inc., 1985, 79 p., paper, novel. MAGIC MICRO ADVENTURE #4.
18884 *Doom stalker*. New York, Toronto: A Parachute Press Book, Scholastic Inc., 1985, 123 p., paper, novel. MICRO ADVENTURE #7.
18885 *Mindbenders*. New York, Toronto: A Parachute Press Book, Scholastic Inc., 1984, 126 p., paper, novel. MICRO ADVENTURE #5.
18886 *Mission of the secret spy squad*. New York, Toronto: Scholastic Inc., 1984, 93 p., paper, novel. TWISTAPLOT #10.
18887 *Space attack*. New York, Toronto: A Parachute Press Book, Scholastic Inc.,

1984, 123 p., paper, novel. MICRO ADVENTURE #1.

with Eileen Buckholtz as REBECCA YORK

18888 *Flight of the raven.* New York: A Dell Book, 1986, 218 p., paper, novel. PEREGRINE CONNECTION #2.
18889 *In search of the dove.* New York: A Dell Book, 1986, 220 p., paper, novel. PEREGRINE CONNECTION #3.
18890 *Tales of the falcon.* New York: A Dell Book, 1986, 223 p., paper, novel. PEREGRINE CONNECTION #1.

GLICKSMAN, Frank, *with James Fritzhand*

23556 *The unicorn affair.* New York: A Signet Book, New American Library, 1981, 230 p., paper, novel.

GLICKSOHN, Susan—SEE: Wood, Susan

GLOAG, John (Edwards), 1896-1981

37793 *Artorius Rex.* London: Cassell, 1977, ix + 197 p., cloth, novel.

GLOSS, Molly, 1944-

24016 *Outside the gates.* New York: Argo, Atheneum, 1986, 120 p., cloth, novel.

GLOVER, Donald E(llsworth), 1933-

24017 *C. S. Lewis: the art of enchantment.* Athens, OH: Ohio University Press, 1981, xii + 235 p., cloth, nonf.

GLOVER-WRIGHT, Geoffrey—SEE: Wright, Glover

GLUCKMAN, Janet (Doris Berliner), 1939-

24018 *Rite of the dragon.* Virginia Beach, VA: Donning Co., 1981, 310 p., cloth, novel.

GLUT, Donald F(rank), 1944-

24019 *Bones of Frankenstein.* London: New English Library, 1977, 109 p., paper, novel. NEW ADVENTURES OF FRANKENSTEIN #3.
24020 *Classic movie monsters.* Metuchen, NJ: Scarecrow Press, 1978, xviii + 442 p., cloth, nonf.
24021 *The Dracula book.* Metuchen, NJ: Scarecrow Press, 1975, xx + 388 p., cloth, nonf.
The Empire strikes back—SEE: *Star wars: The Empire strikes back.*

24022 *The Frankenstein catalog: being a complete listing of novels, translations, adaptations, stories, critical works, popular articles, series, fumetti, verse, stage plays, films, cartoons, puppetry, radio & television programs, comics, satire & humor, spoken & musical recordings, tapes, and sheet music featuring Frankenstein's monster and/or descended from Mary Shelley's novel.* Jefferson, NC & London: McFarland & Co., 1984, xiii + 525 p., cloth, nonf.
24023 *Frankenstein lives again.* London & Conn.: Mews Books, 1977, 110 p., paper, novel. NEW ADVENTURES OF FRANKENSTEIN #1.
24024 *Frankenstein lives again!* Norfolk, Virginia Beach, VA: Donning Company/Publishers, 1981, 157 p., cloth, novel. NEW ADVENTURES OF FRANKENSTEIN #1. [Expanded edition].
24025 *Frankenstein meets Dracula.* London: New English Library, 1977, 140 p., paper, novel. NEW ADVENTURES OF FRANKENSTEIN #4.
24026 *Spawn.* Toronto, New York: Laser Books, 1976, 192 p., paper, novel.
24027 *Star Wars: The Empire strikes back.* New York: A Del Rey Book, Ballantine Books, 1980, 214 p., paper, movie. STAR WARS #2.
24028 *Terror of Frankenstein.* London & Conn.: Mews Books, 1977, 128 p., paper, novel. NEW ADVENTURES OF FRANKENSTEIN #2.

with George Lucas & James Kahn

24029 *The Star Wars trilogy.* New York: A Del Rey Book, Ballantine Books, 1987, 471 p., paper, anth.

*GLUYAS, Constance, 1920-1983

GOBLE, Lou

24030 *The Kalevide.* Toronto, New York: Bantam Books, 1982, xiii + 397 p., paper, novel.

GODBOUT, Jacques, 1933-

24031 *Dragon Island.* Don Mills, Ontario: Musson Book Co., 1978, 118 p., cloth, novel. [Translation by David Ellis of *L'Isle au dragon*].

GODDARD, James, *with David Pringle*

24032 *J. G. Ballard: the first twenty years.* Hayes, Middlesex, England: Bran's

Head Books, 1976, [99] p., cloth, nonf. anth.

GODDIN, (Margaret) Jean, 1946- , *with Doreen Webbert*

24033 *Fantasy cookbook.* Tucson, AZ: World Fantasy Convention, 1991, 86 p., paper, nonf.

GODDIN, Jeffrey (Kim), 1950-

24034 *Blood of the wolf.* New York: Leisure Books, 1987, 366 p., paper, novel.
24035 *The living dead.* New York: Leisure Books, 1987, 383 p., paper, novel.

GODFREY, Martyn N., 1949-

37794 *Alien wargames.* Richmond Hill, Ontario, Canada: Scholastic-TAB, 1984, 142 p., paper, novel.
24036 *I spent my summer vacation kidnapped into space.* New York, Toronto: An Apple Paperback, Scholastic Inc., 1990, 133 p., paper, novel.
24037 *The last war.* Don Mills, Ontario, Canada: Collier Macmillan, 1986, 91 p., cloth, novel.
37795 *More than weird.* Don Mills, Ontario, Canada: Collier Macmillan Canada, 1987, 88 p., cloth, novel.
37796 *The Vandarian incident.* Richmond Hill, Ontario, Canada: Scholastic-TAB, 1981, 106 p., paper, novel.

GODWIN, Edward (F.), *with Stephani Godwin*

24038 *Warrior bard: the life of William Morris.* London: George G. Harrap, 1947, 175 p., cloth, nonf.

GODWIN, Parke, 1929-

24039 *Beloved exile.* Toronto, New York: Bantam Books, 1984, 422 p., paper, novel. ARTHURIAN CYCLE #2.
24040 *The fire when it comes.* Garden City, NY: Doubleday & Co., 1984, xiii+170 p., cloth, coll.
24041 *Firelord.* Garden City, NY: Doubleday & Co., 1980, 396 p., cloth, novel. ARTHURIAN CYCLE #1.
24042 *Invitation to Camelot: an Arthurian anthology of short stories.* New York: Ace Books, 1988, 258 p., paper, anth.
24043 *The last rainbow.* Toronto, New York: Bantam Books, 1985, 358 p., paper, novel. ARTHURIAN CYCLE #3.

24044 *Sherwood.* New York: William Morrow & Co., 1991, 526 p., cloth, novel.
24045 *The snake oil wars; or, Scheherazade Ginsberg strikes again.* New York: A Foundation Book, Doubleday, 1989, 212 p., cloth, novel. SNAKE OIL WARS #2.
24046 *A truce with time: (a love story with occasional ghosts).* Toronto, New York: Bantam Books, 1988, 310 p., cloth, novel.
24047 *Waiting for the galactic bus.* New York: Doubleday & Co., 1988, 229 p., cloth, novel. SNAKE OIL WARS #1.

with Marvin Kaye

24048 *A cold blue light.* New York: Charter Books, 1983, 294 p., paper, novel. COLD BLUE LIGHT #1.
24049 *The masters of solitude.* Garden City, NY: Doubleday & Co., 1978, 397 p., cloth, novel. SOLITUDE TRILOGY #1.
24050 *Wintermind.* Garden City, NY: Doubleday & Co., 1982, xiii+291 p., cloth, novel. SOLITUDE TRILOGY #2.

GODWIN, Stephani (Allfree), *with Edward Godwin*

24038 *Warrior bard: the life of William Morris.* London: George G. Harrap, 1947, 175 p., cloth, nonf.

GODWIN, Thomas—SEE: Godwin, Tom

*GODWIN, Tom [i.e., Thomas Godwin], 1915-1980

GOFFIN, Dallas Clive

24051 *Legends of Fogrophol.* [England]: British Fantasy Society, 1991, 30 p., paper, coll.

GOICOECHEA, Ana M.—SEE: Matute, Ana María

GOLD, E(ugene) J., 1941-

37797 *Creation story verbatim.* Nevada City, CA: Gateways/IDHHB, 1986, ix+267 p., paper, novel.

GOLD, Horace L(eonard), 1914-

24052 *"What will they think of last?": SF for fun and profit from the inside.* Crestline, CA: Institute for the Development of the Harmonious Human Being, 1976, 151 p., paper, nonf. coll. [Edited by Eugene J. Gold].

GOLD, Jerome

24053 *The inquisitor.* Seattle, WA: Black Heron Press, 1991, 290 p., cloth, novel.

GOLDBERG, Gerry

24055 *Strange glory.* Toronto: McClelland & Stewart, 1975, 148 p., cloth, anth. [Includes some nonfiction and verse].

with Stephen Storoschuk & Fred Corbett

20576 *Nighttouch.* Don Mills, Ontario, Canada: General Publishing, 1977, 156 p., cloth, anth. [Includes some nonfiction and verse].

GOLDBERG, (Elliott) Marshall, 1930-

24056 *Nerve.* New York: Coward, McCann & Geoghegan, 1981, 335 p., cloth, novel.

with Kenneth Kay

24057 *Disposable people.* New York: Tower Books, 1980, 316 p., paper, novel.

GOLDEN, Christie

24058 *Ravenloft: Vampire of the mists.* Lake Geneva, WI: TSR Inc., 1991, 341 p., paper, novel. RAVENLOFT #1.
Vampire of the mists—SEE: *Ravenloft: Vampire of the mists.*

GOLDIE, Kathleen—SEE: Fidler, Kathleen

GOLDIN, Stephen (Charles), 1947-

24059 *And not make dreams your master.* New York: Fawcett Gold Medal, 1981, 222 p., paper, novel.
24060 *Assault on the gods.* Garden City, NY: Doubleday & Co., 1977, 181 p., cloth, novel.
24061 *Caravan.* Don Mills, Ontario, Canada: Laser Books, 1975, 190 p., paper, novel.
24062 *Crystals of air and water.* Toronto, New York: Spectra, Bantam Books, 1989, 292 p., paper, novel. PARSINA SAGA #3.
24063 *The eternity brigade.* New York: Fawcett Gold Medal, 1980, 254 p., paper, novel.
24064 *Finish line.* Toronto, New York: Laser Books, 1976, 192 p., paper, novel. HONEY B #2.
24065 *Herds.* Don Mills, Ontario, Canada: Laser Books, 1975, 190 p., paper, novel.
24066 *Mindflight.* New York: A Fawcett Gold Medal Book, 1978, 224 p., paper, novel.

24067 *Scavenger hunt.* Toronto, New York: Laser Books, 1976, 190 p., paper, novel. HONEY B #1.
24068 *Shrine of the desert mage.* Toronto, New York: Spectra, Bantam Books, 1988, 243 p., paper, novel. PARSINA SAGA #1.
24069 *The storyteller and the Jann.* Toronto, New York: Spectra, Bantam Books, 1988, 277 p., paper, novel. PARSINA SAGA #2.
24070 *Trek to madworld: a Star Trek novel.* Toronto, New York: Bantam Books, 1979, xii + 177 p., paper, novel. STAR TREK SERIES.
24071 *A world called solitude.* Garden City, NY: Doubleday & Co., 1981, 187 p., cloth, novel.

with David Gerrold

23855 *Ascents of wonder.* New York: Popular Library, 1977, 288 p., paper, anth.

with Mary Mason

Jade Darcy and the affair of honor—SEE: *The rehumanization of Jade Darcy: Jade Darcy and the affair of honor.*
Jade Darcy and the zen pirates—SEE: *The rehumanization of Jade Darcy: Jade Darcy and the zen pirates.*
24072 *The rehumanization of Jade Darcy: Jade Darcy and the affair of honor.* New York: A Signet Book, New American Library, 1988, 254 p., paper, novel. REHUMANIZATION OF JADE DARCY #1.
24073 *The rehumanization of Jade Darcy: Jade Darcy and the zen pirates.* New York: A Roc Book, 1990, 293 p., paper, novel. REHUMANIZATION OF JADE DARCY #2.

with E. E. "Doc" Smith

24075 *Appointment at Bloodstar.* New York: A Jove/HBJ Book, 1978, 189 p., paper, novel. FAMILY D'ALEMBERT #5.
24075A retitled: *The Bloodstar conspiracy.* London: Panther, 1978, 158 p., paper, novel. FAMILY D'ALEMBERT SERIES.
The Bloodstar conspiracy—SEE: *Appointment at Bloodstar.*
24076 *The clockwork traitor.* New York: Pyramid Books, 1977, 158 p., paper, novel. FAMILY D'ALEMBERT #3.
24077 *Eclipsing binaries.* New York: Berkley Books, 1983, 184 p., paper, novel. FAMILY D'ALEMBERT #8.
24078 *Getaway world.* New York: Pyramid Books, 1977, 191 p., paper, novel. FAMILY D'ALEMBERT #4.

24079 *Imperial stars*. New York: Pyramid Books, 1976, 143 p., paper, novel. FAMILY D'ALEMBERT #1.

24080 *The Omicron invasion*. New York: Berkley Books, 1984, 184 p., paper, novel. FAMILY D'ALEMBERT #9.

24081 *Planet of treachery*. New York: Berkley Books, 1982, 199 p., paper, novel. FAMILY D'ALEMBERT #7.

24082 *The Purity plot*. New York: Berkley Books, 1980, 184 p., paper, novel. FAMILY D'ALEMBERT #6.

24083 *Revolt of the galaxy*. New York: Berkley Books, 1985, 186 p., paper, novel. FAMILY D'ALEMBERT SERIES #10.

24084 *Strangler's moon*. New York: Pyramid Books, 1976, 159 p., paper, novel. FAMILY D'ALEMBERT #2.

GOLDING, Louis, 1895-1958

37798 *Pale blue nightgown: a book of tales*. London: Hutchinson, 1944, 163 p., cloth, coll.

GOLDING, William (Gerald), 1911-

24085 *Lord of the flies; Pincher Martin; Rites of passage*. London: Faber & Faber, 1984, 517 p., cloth, coll.

with Jack I. Biles

17958 *Talk: conversations with William Golding*. New York: Harcourt Brace Jovanovich, 1970, xii+112 p., cloth, nonf. coll.

GOLDMAN, Stephen H., *with James Gunn*

24086 *Teacher's manual: The road to science fiction*. New York: New American Library, 1980, 45 p., paper, nonf.

GOLDMAN, William (W.), 1931-

24087 *Brothers*. New York: Warner Books, 1987, 310 p., cloth, novel. MARATHON MAN #2.

24088 *Magic*. New York: Delacorte Press, 1976, p., cloth, novel.

as S. MORGENSTERN

24089 *The silent gondoliers: a fable*. New York: A Del Rey Book, Ballantine Books, 1983, 110 p., cloth, novel.

GOLDNER, Orville (Charles), 1906-1985, *with George E. Turner*

24090 *The making of King Kong: the story behind a film classic*. South Brunswick, NJ: A. S. Barnes & Co., 1975, 271 p., cloth, nonf.

GOLDS, Cassandra (Mia), 1962-

24091 *Michael and the secret war*. Sydney: Angus & Robertson, 1985, [183] p., cloth, novel.

GOLDSBERRY, Steven (Taylor), 1949-

24092 *Maui: the demigod*. New York: Simon & Schuster, 1984, 410 p., cloth, novel.

GOLDSMITH, Arnold L(ouis), 1928-

24093 *The Golem remembered, 1909-1980: variations of a Jewish legend*. Detroit, MI: Wayne State University Press, 1981, 181 p., cloth, novel.

GOLDSMITH, Howard, 1943-

24094 *Invasion: 2200 A.D.* Garden City, NY: Doubleday & Co., 1979, 137 p., cloth, novel.

24095 *The shadow, and other strange tales*. Middletown, CT: Weekly Reader Books, Xerox Education Publications, 1977, 83 p., paper, coll.

24096 *Terror by night, and other strange tales*. Middletown, CT: Weekly Reader Books, 1977, 113 p., paper, coll.

24097 *The whispering sea*. Indianapolis, IN: Bobbs-Merrill Co., 1976, 131 p., cloth, novel.

with Roger Elwood

22636 *Spine-chillers: unforgettable tales of terror*. Garden City, NY: Doubleday & Co., 1978, viii+396 p., cloth, anth.

GOLDSTEIN, Fred (P.), *with Susan Sackett & Stan Goldstein*

24098 *Star Trek speaks*. New York: A Wallaby Book, Pocket Books, 1979, 160 p., paper, anth.

GOLDSTEIN, Lisa (Joy), 1953-

24099 *Daily voices*. Eugene, OR: Pulphouse Publishing, 1989, 99 p., cloth, coll. AUTHOR'S CHOICE MONTHLY #3.

24100 *The dream years*. Toronto, New York: Bantam Books, 1985, 181 p., cloth, novel.

24101 *A mask for the general.* Toronto, New York: Bantam Books, 1987, 201 p., cloth, novel.

24102 *The red magician.* New York: Pocket Books, 1982, 156 p., paper, novel.

24103 *Tourists: a novel.* New York: Simon & Schuster, 1989, 239 p., cloth, novel.

GOLDSTEIN, Stan

24104 *Star Trek spaceflight chronology.* New York: A Wallaby Book, Pocket Books, 1980, 192 p., paper, fiction.

with Susan Sackett & Fred Goldstein

24098 *Star Trek speaks.* New York: A Wallaby Book, Pocket Books, 1979, 160 p., paper, anth.

GOLDSTONE, Adrian (H.), 1897-1977, with Wesley Sweetser

24105 *A bibliography of Arthur Machen.* Austin, TX: University of Texas, 1965, 180 p., cloth, nonf.

35310 *Machen /* by Wesley Sweetser; *Men about Machen /* by Adrian H. Goldstone. Llandeilo, Wales: St. Alberts Press, 1960, 24 p., paper, nonf. coll.

GOLIS, Paul

24106 *A day in the life of Jay Peter Sweetly.* Rohnert Park, CA: Rohnert Park Publishing Co., 1974, iv+127 p., paper, novel.

GOM, Leona, 1946-

24107 *The Y chromosome.* Toronto: Second Story Press, 1990, 267 p., paper, novel.

GOMERY, Percy, 1881-

24108 *End of the circle.* Toronto: Macmillan of Canada, 1929, viii+266 p., cloth, novel.

GOMEZ, Jewelle, 1948-

24109 *The Gilda stories: a novel.* Ithaca, NY: Firebrand Books, 1991, 252 p., cloth, novel.

GOMPERTZ, Martin—SEE: Ganpat

GONDOSCH, Linda (Ann), 1944-

24110 *The witches of Hopper Street.* New York: Lodestar Books, 1986, 118 p., cloth, novel.

GONZALEZ, Gloria (María), 1940-

24111 *A deadly rhyme.* New York: Dell/ Twilight, 1986, 136 p., paper, novel. TWILIGHT #25.

GOOCH, Stan(ley Alfred), 1932-

24112 *Alternative persons: the entities of science fiction and myth.* Frome, Somerset, England: Bran's Head, 1979, 29 p., paper, nonf. [Edited by Grahaeme Barrasford Young].

with Christopher Evans

22818 *Science fiction as religion /* by Christopher Evans. Frome, Somerset, England: Bran's Head Books, 1981, 15 p., paper, nonf.

GOODCHILD, George, 1888-1969

37799 *The eye of Abu.* London: George Newnes, 1934, 255 p., cloth, novel.

GOODEN, Philip

24113 *Brodie's notes on John Wyndham's 'The Chrysalids'.* London & Sydney: Pan Books, 1980, 45 p., paper, nonf.

GOODGOLD, Edwin, 1944- , with Dan Carlinsky

19391 *The world's greatest monster quiz.* New York: A Berkley Medallion Book, Berkley Publishing Corp., 1975, 122 p., paper, nonf.

GOODMAN, Deborah Lerme, 1956-

24114 *The magic of the unicorn.* Toronto, New York: An R. A. Montgomery Book, Bantam Books, 1985, 114 p., paper, novel. CHOOSE YOUR OWN ADVENTURE #51.

24115 *The magic shuttle.* Washington: Smithsonian Institution, 1982, 24 p., paper, story.

24116 *The throne of Zeus.* Toronto, New York: An R. A. Montgomery Book, Bantam Books, 1985, 118 p., paper, novel. CHOOSE YOUR OWN ADVENTURE #40.

24117 *The trumpet of terror.* Toronto, New York: An R. A. Montgomery Book, Bantam Books, 1986, 114 p., paper, novel. CHOOSE YOUR OWN ADVENTURE #55.

24118 *Vanished!* Toronto, New York: An R. A. Montgomery Book, Bantam Books, 1986, 116 p., paper, novel. CHOOSE YOUR OWN ADVENTURE #60.

24119 *You see the future.* Toronto, New York: Bantam Books, 1988, 51 p., paper, fiction. CHOOSE YOUR OWN ADVENTURE #44.

GOODMAN, Jo(sephine Charlotte), 1940- , with Toss Gascoigne & Margot Tyrrell

23747 *Dream time: new stories by sixteen award-winning authors.* Ringwood, Victoria, Australia: Penguin Books, 1989, 184 p., paper, anth.

GOODMAN, Julius

24120 *The horror of High Ridge.* Toronto, New York: An R. A. Montgomery Book, Bantam Books, 1983, 116 p., paper, novel. CHOOSE YOUR OWN ADVENTURE #27.

24121 *Space patrol.* Toronto, New York: An R. A. Montgomery Book, Bantam Books, 1903, 110 p., paper, novel. CHOOSE YOUR OWN ADVENTURE #22.

37800 *Treasure diver.* Toronto, New York: An R. A. Montgomery Book, Bantam Books, 1984, 114 p., paper, novel. CHOOSE YOUR OWN ADVENTURE #32.

GOODMAN, Laurie (E.), 1962-

24122 *A spell of deceit.* New York: A Del Rey Book, Ballantine Books, 1989, 344 p., paper, novel.

GOODRICH, Clifford, pseud.—SEE: Hathway, Alan

GOODRICH, Richard

24124 *Science fiction: a resource unit for teachers and librarians.* Jacksonville, IL: Perma-Books, 1980, 16 p., paper, nonf.

GOODSTONE, Tony

24125 *The pulps: fifty years of American pop culture.* New York: Chelsea House, 1976, xvi+239 p., paper, anth.

GOODWIN, Hal—SEE: Blaine, John

GOODWIN, Marie D.

24126 *Where the towers pierce the sky.* New York: Four Winds Press, 1989, 185 p., cloth, novel.

GOODWIN, Michael (C.), 1951- , with Robert Teague

24127 *A guide to the Commonwealth: the official guide to Alan Dean Foster's Humanx Commonwealth universe.* Roy, UT: Galagraphics Press, 1985, 70 p., paper, nonf.

GOODWYN, Andrew (Cecil), 1954-

24128 *Fantasy stories.* Oxford, England: Oxford University Press, 1991, vi+151 p., paper, anth.

24129 *Science fiction stories.* Oxford, England: Oxford University Press, 1991, vi+154 p., paper, anth.

*GORDON, Caroline, Lady, 1895-<u>1981</u>

GORDON, Giles (Alexander Esmé), 1940-

24130 *A book of contemporary nightmares.* London: Michael Joseph, 1977, 192 p., cloth, anth.

24131 *Pictures from an exhibition.* London: Allison & Busby, 1970, 172 p., cloth, novel.

24132 *Prevailing spirits: a book of Scottish ghost stories.* London: Hamish Hamilton, 1976, 216 p., cloth, anth.

GORDON, Jeffie Ross, pseud.—SEE: Enderle, Judith & Tessler, Stephanie

GORDON, Joan (Lois), 1947-

24133 *Gene Wolfe.* Mercer Island, WA: Starmont House, 1986, iv+116 p., cloth, nonf. STARMONT READER'S GUIDE #29.

24134 *Joe Haldeman.* Mercer Island, WA: Starmont House, 1980, 64 p., paper, nonf. STARMONT READER'S GUIDE #4.

GORDON, John (William), 1925-

24135 *Catch your death, and other ghost stories.* London: Hardy, 1984, 120 p., cloth, coll.

24136 *The edge of the world.* London: Patrick Hardy Books, 1983, 186 p., cloth, novel.

24137 *The ghost on the hill.* Harmondsworth, Middlesex, England: Kestrel Books, 1976, 171 p., cloth, novel.

24138 *The quelling eye.* London: The Bodley Head, 1986, 140 p., cloth, novel.

24139   *Ride the wind.* London: The Bodley Head, 1989, 175 p., cloth, novel. GIANT UNDER THE SNOW #2.

GORDON, Julien [pseud. of Julie Grinnell Storrow Cruger], 1850?-1920

24140   *Vampires: Mademoiselle Réséda.* Philadelphia, PA: J. B. Lippincott, 1891, 299 p., cloth, novel.

GORDON, (Richard Alex) Stuart, 1947-

24141   *Achon!* London: Macdonald & Co., 1987, 316 p., cloth, novel. WATCHERS #1.
24142   *The 'Eyes' trilogy: science fiction.* London: Sidgwick & Jackson, 1978, 224+ 240+268 p., cloth, coll. EYES #1-3. [Includes *One-Eye*; *Two-Eyes*; *Three-Eyes*].
24143   *Fire in the abyss.* New York: Berkley Books, 1983, xiii+322 p., paper, novel.
24144   *The hidden world.* London: Macdonald & Co., 1988, 352 p., cloth, novel. WATCHERS #2.
24145   *The mask.* London: Orbit, 1990, 368 p., paper, novel. WATCHERS #3.
24146   *Smile on the void: the mythhistory of Ralph M'Botu Kitaj.* New York: Berkley Publishing Corp., 1981, 294 p., cloth, novel.
24147   *Suaine and the crow-god.* London: New English Library, 1975, 255 p., cloth, novel.
24148   *Three-Eyes.* New York: DAW Books, 1975, 268 p., paper, novel. EYES TRILOGY #3.

as ALEX R. STUART

37801   *The bike from Hell.* London: New English Library, 1973, 144 p., paper, novel.
37802   *The devil's rider.* London: New English Library, 1973, 141 p., paper, novel.
37803   *The outlaws.* London: New English Library, 1972, 142 p., paper, novel.

GORDON-WISE, Barbara Ann, 1946-

24149   *The reclamation of a queen: Guinevere in modern fantasy.* New York, London: Greenwood Press, 1991, x+174 p., cloth, nonf. CONTRIBUTIONS TO THE STUDY OF SCIENCE FICTION AND FANTASY #44.

*GORER, Geoffrey (Edgar Solomon), 1905-1985

GORES, Alida Van—SEE: Van Gores, Alida

GORHAM, Melvin (Ezell), 1910-

24150   *The curse of the ring: an archetypal translation of Richard Wagner's The rhinegold.* Rochester, WA: Sovereign Press, 1975, 95 p., paper, novel.
24151   retitled: *Rhinegold.* Rochester, WA: Sovereign Press, 1990, 127 p., paper, novel. [Revised edition].
24152   *The ring cycle.* Rochester, WA: Sovereign Press, 1979, 142 p., paper, coll. [Based on Wagner's *Ring Cycle*—includes two plays and one story].

GORMAN, Ed(ward Joseph), 1941-

as DANIEL RANSOM

24153   *The babysitter.* New York: St. Martin's Press, 1989, 214 p., paper, novel.
24154   *Daddy's little girl.* New York: Zebra Books, Kensington Publishing Corp., 1985, 333 p., paper, novel.
24155   *The forsaken.* New York: St. Martin's Press, 1988, 305 p., paper, novel.
24156   *Night caller.* New York: Zebra Books, Kensington Publishing Corp., 1987, 301 p., paper, novel.
24157   *Nightmare child.* New York: St. Martin's Press, 1990, 163 p., paper, novel.
24158   *Toys in the attic.* New York: Zebra Books, Kensington Publishing Corp., 1986, 317 p., paper, novel.

with Martin H. Greenberg

24159   *Stalkers: all new tales of terror and suspense.* Arlington Heights, IL: Dark Harvest, 1989, 310 p., cloth, anth.

GORMAN, Herbert (Sherman), 1893-1954

37804   *The place called Dagon.* New York: George H. Doran Co., 1927, 315 p., cloth, novel.

GORMLEY, Beatrice, 1942-

24160   *Best friend insurance.* New York: E. P. Dutton, 1983, 147 p., cloth, novel.
24161   *Fifth grade magic.* New York: E. P. Dutton, 1982, 131 p., cloth, novel. FIFTH GRADE MAGIC #1.
24161A   retitled: *Understudy magic.* London: Macdonald & Co., 1988, 128 p., cloth, novel. [Identification uncertain].
         Focus pocus—SEE: *The ghastly glasses.*
24162   *The ghastly glasses.* New York: E. P. Dutton, 1985, 117 p., cloth, novel.
24162A   retitled: *Focus pocus.* London: Macdonald & Co., 1987, 126 p., cloth, novel.

24163   *The magic mean machine.* New York: An Avon Camelot Book, 1989, 116 p., paper, novel.

24164   *Mail-order wings.* New York: E. P. Dutton, 1981, 164 p., cloth, novel.

24165   *More fifth grade magic.* New York: E. P. Dutton, 1989, 102 p., cloth, novel. FIFTH GRADE MAGIC #2.

24166   *Paul's volcano.* Boston: Houghton Mifflin Co., 1987, 143 p., cloth, novel.

24167   *Richard and the Vratch.* New York: An Avon Camelot Book, 1987, 134 p., paper, novel.

24168   *Sky guys to White Cat.* New York: Dutton's Children's Books, 1991, 137 p., cloth, novel.

         Understudy magic—SEE: *Fifth grade magic.*

24169   *Wanted: UFO.* New York: Dutton's Children's Books, 1990, 119 p., cloth, novel.

GOROG, Judith (Allen), 1938-

24170   *In a messy, messy room.* New York: Philomel Books, 1990, 48 p., cloth, coll.

24171   *No swimming in Dark Pond, and other chilling tales.* New York: Philomel Books, 1987, 111 p., cloth, coll.

24172   *On meeting witches at wells.* New York: Philomel Books, 1991, 119 p., cloth, coll.

24173   *A taste for quiet, and other disquieting tales.* New York: Philomel Books, 1982, 128 p., cloth, coll.

24173A retitled: *When flesh begins to creep.* London: Victor Gollancz, 1986, 128 p., cloth, coll.

24174   *Three dreams and a nightmare, and other tales of the dark.* New York: Philomel Books, 1988, 156 p., cloth, coll.

         When flesh begins to creep—SEE: *A taste for quiet.*

24175   *Winning Scheherezade.* New York: Atheneum; Toronto: Collier Macmillan Canada; New York: Maxwell Macmillan International Publishing Group, 1991, 101 p., cloth, novel. SCHEHEREZADE #2.

GORST, H(arold) E(dward), 1868-1950

24176   *Sketches of the future.* London: John MacQueen, 1898, 128 p., cloth, coll.

GORTON, Ron

24177   *The lawyers of hell.* New York: Frederick Fell Publishers, 1978, 225 p., cloth, novel.

24178   *The soul.* New York: Zebra Books, Kensington Publishing Corp., 1977, 443 p., paper, novel.

GOSE, Elliott B(ickley Jr.), 1926-

24179   *Imagination indulged: the irrational in the nineteenth-century novel.* Montréal: McGill-Queen's University Press, 1972, xii + 182 p., cloth, nonf.

24180   *Mere creatures: a study of modern fantasy tales for children.* Toronto, London: University of Toronto Press, 1988, x + 202 p., cloth, nonf.

GOSLING, Paula—SEE: Skinner, Ainslie

GOSWAMI, Amit, 1936- , *with Maggie Goswami*

24181   *The cosmic dancers: exploring the physics of science fiction.* New York: Harper & Row, 1983, xi + 292 p., cloth, nonf.

GOSWAMI, Maggie, 1937- , *with Amit Goswami*

24181   *The cosmic dancers: exploring the physics of science fiction.* New York: Harper & Row, 1983, xi + 292 p., cloth, nonf.

GOTH, Louis A.

24182   *Red-12.* New York: A Dell Book, 1980, 380 p., paper, novel.

GOTLIEB, Phyllis (Fay Bloom), 1926-

24183   *Emperor, swords, pentacles.* New York: Ace Books, 1982, 299 p., paper, novel. STARCATS #2.

24184   *Heart of red iron.* New York: St. Martin's Press, 1989, 235 p., cloth, novel. DAHLGREN #2.

24185   *A judgment of dragons.* New York: Berkley Books, 1980, 263 p., paper, coll. STARCATS #1.

24186   *The kingdom of the cats.* New York: Ace Science Fiction Books, 1985, 284 p., paper, novel. STARCATS #3.

24187   *O master Caliban! a novel.* New York: Harper & Row, 1976, 244 p., cloth, novel. DAHLGREN #1.

24188   *Son of the morning, and other stories.* New York: Ace Science Fiction Books, 1983, 228 p., paper, coll.

with Douglas Barbour

17361   *Tesseracts².* Victoria, British Columbia, Canada: A Tesseract Book, Porcépic Books, 1987, 295 p., paper, anth.

GOTSCHALK, Felix C. (Jr.), 1929-

24189 *Growing up in Tier 3000.* New York: Ace Books, 1975, 158 p., paper, novel.

GOTTESFELD, Gary

24190 *Blood harvest.* New York: Fawcett Gold Medal, 1990, 341 p., paper, novel.

GOTTESMAN, Ronald, 1933- , with Harry M. Geduld

23787 *The girl in the hairy paw: King Kong as myth, movie, and monster.* New York: A Flare Book, Avon, 1976, 233 p., paper, nonf. anth.
23788 *Robots, robots, robots.* Boston: NY Graphic Society, 1978, vii+246 p., cloth, anth.

GOTTFRIED, Chet (M.), 1947-

24191 *The steel eye.* New York: Space & Time, 1984, 151 p., paper, novel.

*GOTTHELF, Ezra Gerson, 1907-1981

GOTTLIEB, Hinko, 1886-1948

GOTTLIEB, Sherry (Maureen) Gershon, 1947?-

24192 *Hell no we won't go!: resisting the draft during the Vietnam War.* New York: Viking, 1991, xxvi+274 p., cloth, nonf. anth. [Includes interviews with a number of SF authors].

GOTTLIEB, Theodore—SEE: Theodore, Brother

GOUDGE, Eileen, 1950-

24193 *Gone with the wish.* New York: Avon Flare, 1986, 166 p., paper, novel. EILEEN GOUDGE'S SWEPT AWAY #1.

GOUDGE, Elizabeth (de Beauchamp), 1900-1984

15810 *Smoky-House.* London: Duckworth, 1940, 208 p., cloth, novel.
15811 *The Valley of Song.* London: University of London Press, 1951, 255 p., cloth, novel.

GOULART, Ron(ald Joseph), 1933-

24194 *The adventurous decade.* New Rochelle, NY: Arlington House, 1975, 224 p., cloth, nonf.

24195 *Big bang.* New York: DAW Books, 1982, 160 p., paper, novel. ODD JOBS SERIES.
24196 *Blood wedding.* New York: Warner Books, 1976, 140 p., paper, novel. VAMPIRELLA #4.
24197 *Bloodstalk.* New York: Warner Books, 1975, 141 p., paper, novel. VAMPIRELLA #1.
24198 *Brainz, Inc..* New York: DAW Books, 1985, 205 p., paper, novel. ODD JOBS SERIES.
24199 *Brinkman.* Garden City, NY: Doubleday & Co., 1981, 150 p., cloth, novel.
24200 *Calling Dr. Patchwork.* New York: DAW Books, 1978, 156 p., paper, novel. ODD JOBS SERIES.
24201 *Capricorn One.* New York: Fawcett Gold Medal, 1978, 189 p., paper, movie.
24202 *Challengers of the unknown.* New York: A Dell Book, 1977, 155 p., paper, novel.
24203 *Cowboy heaven.* Garden City, NY: Doubleday & Co., 1979, 185 p., cloth, novel.
24204 *Crackpot.* Garden City, NY: Doubleday & Co., 1977, 150 p., cloth, novel.
24205 *The curse of the obelisk.* New York: Avon, 1987, 139 p., paper, novel.
24206 *The cyborg king.* New York: Playboy Paperbacks, 1981, 190 p., paper, novel. STAR HAWKS #2; BARNUM SERIES.
24207 *Daredevils, Ltd.* New York: St. Martin's Press, 1987, 185 p., paper, novel. EXCHAMELEON #1; BARNUM SERIES.
24208 *Deadwalk.* New York: Warner Books, 1976, 144 p., paper, novel. VAMPIRELLA #3.
24209 *Deathgame.* New York: Warner Books, 1976, 141 p., paper, novel. VAMPIRELLA #5.
24210 *The Emperor of the Last Days.* New York: Popular Library, 1977, 189 p., paper, novel.
Empire 99—SEE: *Star Hawks: Empire 99.*
24211 *The encyclopedia of American comics.* New York: A Promised Land Production, Facts on File, 1990, viii+408 p., cloth, nonf. anth.
24212 *The enormous hourglass.* New York: Award Books, 1976, 154 p., paper, novel.
24213 *Everybody comes to Cosmo's.* New York: St. Martin's Press, 1988, 184 p., paper, novel. EXCHAMELEON #3.
24214 *Eye of the Vulture: a novel.* New York: Jove Books, 1977, 216 p., paper, novel. GYPSY #2; WEIRD HEROES #7.
24215 *Flux; The tin angel: two novels.* London: Millington, 1978, 251 p., cloth, coll.
24216 *Focus on Jack Cole.* Agoura, CA: Fantagraphics Books, 1986, 78 p., paper, nonf.

24217 *Galaxy Jane.* New York: Berkley Books, 1986, 168 p., paper, novel.

24218 *The great comic book artists.* New York: St. Martin's Press, 1986, vii+128 p., paper, nonf.

Great history of comic books—SEE: *Ron Goulart's Great history of comic books.*

24219 *Hail Hibbler.* New York: DAW Books, 1980, 157 p., paper, novel.

24220 *The hellhound project.* Garden City, New York: Doubleday & Co., 1975, 156 p., cloth, novel.

24221 *Hello, Lemuria, hello.* New York: DAW Books, 1979, 156 p., paper, novel. WILD TALENTS #2.

24222 *Hellquad.* New York: DAW Books, 1984, 158 p., paper, novel.

24223 *Nemo.* New York: A Berkley Medallion Book, Berkley Publishing Corp., 1977, 186 p., paper, novel.

24224 *Nutzenbolts, and more troubles with machines.* New York: Macmillan Publishing Co., 1975, 182 p., cloth, coll.

24225 *On alien wings.* New York: Warner Books, 1975, 138 p., paper, novel. VAMPIRELLA #2.

24226 *Over 50 years of American comic books.* Lincolnwood, IL: Mallard Press, 1991, 317 p., cloth, nonf.

24227 *The panchronicon plot.* New York: DAW Books, 1977, 156 p., paper, novel.

24228 *The prisoner of Blackwood Castle.* New York: Avon, 1984, 174 p., paper, novel.

24229 *Quest of the Gypsy: a novel.* New York: Pyramid Books, 1976, 213 p., paper, novel. WEIRD HEROES #3; GYPSY #1.

24230 *The robot in the closet.* New York: DAW Books, 1981, 160 p., paper, novel.

24231 *Ron Goulart's Great history of comic books.* Chicago: Contemporary books, 1986, vi+314 p., paper, nonf.

24232 *Skyrocket Steele.* New York: Pocket Books, 1980, 160 p., paper, novel. SKYROCKET STEELE #1.

24233 *Skyrocket Steele conquers the universe, and other media tales.* Eugene, OR: Pulphouse Publishing, 1990, 100 p., cloth, coll. AUTHOR'S CHOICE MONTHLY #11; SKYROCKET STEELE #2.

24234 *Snakegod.* New York: Warner Books, 1976, 139 p., paper, novel. VAMPIRELLA #6.

24235 *Star Hawks: Empire 99.* New York: Playboy Press Paperbacks, 1980, 191 p., paper, novel. STAR HAWKS #1; BARNUM SERIES.

24236 *Starpirate's brain.* New York: St. Martin's Press, 1987, 184 p., paper, novel. EXCHAMELEON #2.

24237 *Suicide, Inc.* New York: Berkley Books, 1985, 156 p., paper, novel.

24238 *Upside downside.* New York: DAW Books, 1982, 156 p., paper, novel.

24239 *When the waker sleeps.* New York: DAW Books, 1975, 157 p., paper, novel.

24240 *A whiff of madness.* New York: DAW Books, 1976, 156 p., paper, novel. BARNUM SYSTEM—JACK SUMMER.

24241 *The wicked cyborg.* New York: DAW Books, 1978, 156 p., paper, novel. BARNUM SYSTEM.

24242 *The year of the bat: the history of DC Comics: fifty years of fantastic imagination.* Las Vegas, NV: Pioneer Books, 1989, 100 p., paper, nonf. anth.

as JOSEPHINE KAINS

24243 *The witch's tower mystery.* New York: Zebra Books, Kensington Publishing Corp., 1979, 159 p., paper, novel.

as KENNETH ROBESON

06179 *The Avenger: Black chariots.* New York: Warner Paperback Library, 1974, 142 p., paper, novel. AVENGER #30.

24244 *The Avenger: Demon Island.* New York: Warner Paperback Library, 1975, 141 p., paper, novel. AVENGER #36.

24245 *The Avenger: Dr. Time.* New York: Warner Paperback Library, 1974, p., paper, novel. AVENGER #28.

06180 *The Avenger: Red moon.* New York: Warner Paperback Library, 1974, 158 p., paper, novel. AVENGER #26.

24246 *The Avenger: The blood countess.* New York: Warner Paperback Library, 1975, p., paper, novel. AVENGER #34.

24247 *The Avenger: The cartoon crimes.* New York: Warner Paperback Library, 1974, p., paper, novel. AVENGER #31.

24248 *The Avenger: The death machine.* New York: Warner Paperback Library, 1975, 142 p., paper, novel. AVENGER #32?.

24249 *The Avenger: The glass man.* New York: Warner Paperback Library, 1975, 142 p., paper, novel. AVENGER #34.

24250 *The Avenger: The Iron Skull.* New York: Warner Paperback Library, 1975, p., paper, novel. AVENGER #32.

24251 *The Avenger: The man from Atlantis.* New York: Warner Paperback Library, 1974, p., paper, novel. AVENGER #25.

24252 *The Avenger: The nightwitch devil.* New York: Warner Paperback Library, 1974, p., paper, novel. AVENGER #29.

06181 *The Avenger: The purple zombie.* New York: Warner Paperback Library, 1974, 141 p., paper, novel. AVENGER #27.

Black chariots—SEE: *The Avenger: Black chariots.*

The blood countess—SEE: *The Avenger: The blood countess.*

The cartoon crimes—SEE: *The Avenger: The cartoon crimes.*

The death machine—SEE: *The Avenger: The death machine.*

Demon Island—SEE: *The Avenger: Demon Island.*

Dr. Time—SEE: *The Avenger: Dr. Time.*

The glass man—SEE: *The Avenger: The glass man.*

The Iron Skull—SEE: *The Avenger: The Iron Skull.*

The man from Atlantis—SEE: *The Avenger: The man from Atlantis.*

The nightwitch devil—SEE: *The Avenger: The nightwitch devil.*

The purple zombie—SEE: *The Avenger: The purple zombie.*

Red moon—SEE: *The Avenger: Red moon.*

as JOSEPH SILVA

24253 *Holocaust for hire.* New York: Pocket Books, 1979, 191 p., paper, novel. CAPTAIN AMERICA; MARVEL SUPER-HEROES #4.

24254 *The island of Dr. Moreau: novelization.* New York: Ace Books, 1977, 180 p., paper, movie.

with Glen A. Larson

24255 *Experiment in Terra.* New York: Berkley Books, 1984, 151 p., paper, tele. BATTLESTAR GALACTICA #9.

24256 *Greetings from Earth: a novel.* New York: Berkley Books, 1983, 183 p., paper, tele. BATTLESTAR GALACTICA #8.

24257 *The long patrol: novel.* New York: Berkley Books, 1984, 171 p., paper, tele. BATTLESTAR GALACTICA #10.

as JOSEPH SILVA, with Lein Wein & Marv Wolfman

24258 *Stalker from the stars.* New York: Pocket Books, 1978, 174 p., paper, novel. INCREDIBLE HULK #1; MARVEL SUPER-HEROES #2.

GOULD, Alan—SEE: **Banks, Michael A.**

GOULD, F(rederick) J(ames), 1855-1938

37805 *The agnostic island.* London: Watts & Co., 1891, 124 p., cloth, novel.

GOULD, Joan [i.e., Joan Gould Kleinbard], 1927-

24259 *Otherborn: a novel.* New York: Coward, McCann & Geoghegan, 1980, 160 p., cloth, novel.

GOWAR, Michael R.—SEE: **Gowar, Mick**

GOWAR, Mick [i.e., Michael Robert Gowar], 1951-

24260 *Twisted circuits.* London: Beaver, 1987, 144 p., paper, anth.

GRABIEN, Deborah

Eyes in the fire—SEE: *Woman of fire.*

24261 *Fire queen.* New York, Toronto: Bantam Books, 1990, 319 p., paper, novel.

24262 *Plainsong.* New York: St. Martin's Press, 1990, 231 p., cloth, novel.

24263 *Woman of fire.* London: Piatkus, 1988, 250 p., cloth, novel.

24263A retitled: *Eyes in the fire.* New York: St. Martin's Press, 1989, 250 p., cloth, novel.

GRABO, Norman S(tanley), 1930-

24264 *The coincidental art of Charles Brockden Brown.* Chapel Hill, NC: University of North Carolina Press, 1981, xii+209 p., cloth, nonf.

GRABOWSKY, Nicholas, pseud.—SEE: **Randers, Nicholas**

GRAE, Camarin

24265 *Paz.* Chicago: Blazon Books, 1984, 326 p., paper, novel.

24266 *Soul snatcher: a novel.* Chicago: Blazon Books, 1986, 216 p., paper, novel.

24267 *Stranded.* Tallahassee, FL: Naiad Press, 1991, 307 p., paper, novel.

*GRAEME, Bruce [pseud. of Graham Montague Jeffries], 1900-1982

GRAHAM, David [pseud. of Evan Wright], 1919-

24268 *Down to a sunless sea.* London: Robert Hale, 1979, 320 p., cloth, novel.

24269 *Sidewall.* London: Robert Hale, 1982, 208 p., cloth, novel.

GRAHAM, Heather [i.e., Heather Elizabeth Graham Pozzessere]

24270   *Every time I love you.* New York: A Dell Book, 1988, 372 p., paper, novel.

GRAHAM, Jean

24271   *Dark angel.* Santa Clara, CA: Pentagram Publications, 1977, 84 p., paper?, novel. DARK ANGEL #1.
24272   *Dark lord.* San Diego, CA: Peacock Press, 1980, 48 p., paper?, novel. DARK ANGEL #2.

GRAHAM, Kenneth W(ayne), 1938-

24273   *Gothic fictions: prohibition/transgression.* New York: AMS Press, 1989, xvii+292 p., cloth, nonf. anth.
24274   *Vathek & the escape from time: bicentenary reevaluations.* New York: AMS Press, 1990, xiv+277 p., cloth, nonf. anth.

GRAHAM, Robert, pseud.—SEE: Haldeman, Joe

GRAHAM, Winifred [i.e., Matilda Winifred Muriel Graham Cory], d. 1950

37806   *The needlewoman.* London: Mills & Boon, 1911, 313 p., cloth, novel.

GRAHAME, Kenneth, 1859-1932

15812   *The wind in the willows.* London: Methuen, 1908, 302 p., cloth, novel.

GRAHAME-WHITE, Claude, 1879-1959, *with Harry Harper*

37807   *The air-king's treasure: a story of adventure with airship & aeroplane.* London, New York: Cassell, 1913, vi+312 p., cloth, novel.

GRAMONT, Sanche de—SEE: Morgan, Ted

GRANADOS, Onnie

24275   *Dark spirit.* Portland, OR: Dime Novels, 1991, 94 p., paper, novel.

GRAND, Rebecca

24276   *Labyrinth: the photo album.* London: Virgin Books, 1986, 63 p., paper, nonf.

GRANT, Aline

24277   *Ann Radcliffe: a biography.* Denver, CO: Alan Swallow, 1951, 153 p., xvii+388 p., cloth, nonf.

GRANT, Anthony [pseud. of Marion Stapylton Pares], 1914-

24278   *The mutant.* London: Robert Hale, 1980, 192 p., cloth, novel.

GRANT, Barry Keith, 1947-

24279   *Planks of reason: essays on the horror film.* Metuchen, NJ: Scarecrow Press, 1984, xiv+428 p., cloth, nonf. anth.

GRANT, Charles L(ewis), 1942-

24280   *After midnight.* New York: Tor, A Tom Doherty Associates Book, 1986, ix+276 p., paper, anth.
24281   *Ascension.* New York: A Berkley Medallion Book, Berkley Publishing Corp., 1977, 220 p., paper, novel. PARRIC FAMILY #2.
24282   *The best of Shadows.* New York, London: A Foundation Book, Doubleday, 1988, xiv+219 p., cloth, anth.
24283   *The bloodwind.* New York: Fawcett Popular Library, 1982, 223 p., paper, novel. OXRUN STATION SERIES.
24284   *The curse* / by C. L. Grant. Canoga Park, CA: Major Books, 1977, 192 p., paper, novel.
24285   *The dark cry of the Moon.* West Kingston, RI: Donald M. Grant, Publisher, 1985, 190 p., cloth, coll. OXRUN STATION SERIES. [Sequel to *Soft whisper*].
         Dead image—SEE: *Night visions 2.*
24286   *Dialing the wind.* New York: Tor Horror, A Tom Doherty Associates Book, 1988, 210 p., paper, novel.
24287   *The Dodd, Mead gallery of horror.* New York: Dodd, Mead & Co., 1983, 365 p., cloth, anth.
24287A   retitled: *Gallery of horror.* London: Robson, 1983, 365 p., cloth, anth.
24288   *Doom city.* New York: Tor Horror, A Tom Doherty Associates Book, 1987, 307 p., paper, anth. CHRONICLE OF GREYSTONE BAY #2.
24289   *Fears.* New York: Berkley Books, 1983, viii+280 p., paper, anth.
24290   *Final Shadows.* New York, London: A Foundation Book, Doubleday, 1991, xiv+490 p., cloth, anth. [12th and last volume in SHADOWS SERIES].
24291   *Fire mask.* New York, Toronto: Bantam Books, 1991, 202 p., cloth, novel.

24292 *The first chronicles of Greystone Bay.* New York: Tor, A Tom Doherty Associates Book, 1985, 274 p., paper, anth. CHRONICLE OF GREYSTONE BAY #1.

24293 *For fear of the night.* New York: Tor, A Tom Doherty Associates Book, 1988, 277 p., cloth, novel.

Gallery of horror—SEE: *The Dodd, Mead gallery of horror.*

24294 *A glow of candles, and other stories.* New York: Berkley Books, 1981, xi+211 p., paper, coll.

24295 *The grave.* New York: Fawcett Popular Library, 1981, 223 p., paper, novel. OXRUN STATION SERIES.

Greystone Bay—SEE: *The first chronicles of Greystone Bay.*

24296 *Horrors.* New York: Playboy Paperbacks, 1981, 223 p., paper, anth.

24297 *The hour of the Oxrun dead.* Garden City, NY: Doubleday & Co., 1977, 182 p., cloth, novel. OXRUN STATION SERIES.

24298 *In a dark dream.* New York: Tor, A Tom Doherty Associates Book, 1989, 310 p., cloth, novel.

24299 *The last call of mourning.* Garden City, NY: Doubleday & Co., 1979, 179 p., cloth, novel. OXRUN STATION SERIES.

24300 *Legion.* New York: A Berkley Book, Berkley Publishing Corp., 1979, 213 p., paper, novel. PARRIC FAMILY #3.

24301 *The long night of the grave.* West Kingston, RI: Donald M. Grant, Publisher, 1986, 187 p., cloth, novel. OXRUN STATION SERIES. [Direct sequel to *Dark cry*].

24302 *Midnight.* New York: Tor, A Tom Doherty Associates Books, 1985, 284 p., paper, anth.

24303 *The nestling.* New York: Pocket Books, 1982, 406 p., paper, novel.

24304 *Night songs.* New York: Pocket Books, 1984, 346 p., paper, novel.

Night terrors—SEE: *Night visions 2.*

Night visions: Dead image—SEE: *Night visions 2.*

24305 *Night visions 2: all original stories.* Niles, IL: Dark Harvest, 1985, 327 p., cloth, anth.

24305A retitled: *Night visions: Dead image.* New York: Berkley Books, 1987, 309 p., paper, anth.

24305B retitled: *Night terrors.* London: Headline, 1989, viii+308 p., paper, anth.

24306 *Nightmare seasons.* Garden City, NY: Doubleday & Co., 1982, 185 p., cloth, coll. OXRUN SERIES. [Winner of the World Fantasy Award for Best Fantasy Anthology/Collection, 1982 (1983)].

24307 *Nightmares.* Chicago: Playboy Press Paperbacks, 1979, 256 p., paper, anth.

24308 *The orchard.* New York: Tor Horror, A Tom Doherty Associates Book, 1986, 287 p., paper, novel. OXRUN STATION SERIES.

24309 *The pet.* New York: Tor, A Tom Doherty Associates Book, 1986, 343 p., cloth, novel.

24310 *A quiet night of fear.* New York: Berkley Books, 1981, 183 p., paper, novel.

24311 *The ravens of the moon.* Garden City, NY: Doubleday & Co., 1978, 184 p., cloth, novel.

24312 *The SeaHarp Hotel.* New York: Tor, A Tom Doherty Associates Book, 1990, 294 p., cloth, anth. CHRONICLE OF GREYSTONE BAY #3.

24313 *The shadow of alpha /* by C. L. Grant. New York: A Berkley Medallion Book, Berkley Publishing Corp., 1976, 215 p., paper, novel. PARRIC FAMILY #1.

24314 *Shadows.* Garden City, NY: Doubleday & Co., 1978, ix+182 p., cloth, anth. [Winner of the World Fantasy Award for Best Fantasy Single Author Collection/Anthology, 1978 (1979)].

24314A retitled: *Shadows II.* London: Headline, 1987, 223 p., cloth, anth.

Shadows—SEE: *Shadows 4.*

24315 *Shadows 2.* Garden City, NY: Doubleday & Co., 1979, viii+212 p., cloth, anth.

Shadows II—SEE: *Shadows.*

24316 *Shadows 3.* Garden City, NY: Doubleday & Co., 1980, ix+211 p., cloth, anth.

24317 *Shadows 4.* Garden City, NY: Doubleday & Co., 1981, vi+181 p., cloth, anth.

24318A retitled: *Shadows.* London: Headline, 1987, 216 p., cloth, anth.

24319 *Shadows 5.* Garden City, NY: Doubleday & Co., 1982, viii+182 p., cloth, anth.

24320 *Shadows 6.* Garden City, NY: Doubleday & Co., 1983, viii+180 p., cloth, anth.

24321 *Shadows 7.* Garden City, NY: Doubleday & Co., 1984, 181 p., cloth, anth.

24322 *Shadows 8.* Garden City, NY: Doubleday & Co., 1985, 191 p., cloth, anth.

24323 *Shadows 9.* Garden City, NY: Doubleday & Co., 1986, viii+182 p., cloth, anth.

24324 *Shadows 10.* Garden City, NY: Doubleday & Co., 1987, ix+178 p., cloth, anth.

24325 *The soft whisper of the dead.* West Kingston, RI: Donald M. Grant, Publisher, 1982, 205 p., cloth, novel. OXRUN STATION SERIES. [First in trilogy].

24326 *Something stirs.* New York: Tor, A Tom Doherty Associates Book, 1991, 275 p., cloth, novel.

24327 *The sound of midnight.* Garden City, NY: Doubleday & Co., 1978, 179 p., cloth, novel. OXRUN STATION SERIES.

24328 *Stunts.* New York: Tor Horror, A Tom Doherty Associates Book, 1990, 438 p., cloth, novel.

24329 *Tales from the nightside: dark fantasy.* Sauk City, WI: Arkham House, 1981, xii+228 p., cloth, coll.

24330 *The tea party.* New York: Pocket Books, 1985, 312 p., paper, novel.

24331 *Terrors.* New York: Playboy Paperbacks, 1982, 222 p., paper, anth.

24332 *Writing and selling science fiction* / by The Science Fiction Writers of American. Cincinnati: Writer's Digest Books, 1976, 195 p., cloth, nonf. anth.

as FELICIA ANDREWS

37808 *Mountain witch.* New York: A Jove Book, 1980, 349 p., paper, novel.

as STEVEN CHARLES

24333 *Academy of terror.* New York: A Byron Preiss Visual Publications Inc. Book, An Archway Paperback, Pocket Books, 1986, 150 p., paper, novel. PRIVATE SCHOOL #2.

24334 *The enemy within.* New York: A Byron Preiss Visual Publications Inc. Book, An Archway Paperback, Pocket Books, 1987, 147 p., paper, novel. PRIVATE SCHOOL #5.

24335 *The last alien.* New York: A Byron Preiss Visual Publications Inc. Book, An Archway Paperback, Pocket Books, 1987, 137 p., paper, novel. PRIVATE SCHOOL #6.

24336 *Nightmare session.* New York: A Byron Preiss Visual Publications Inc. Book, An Archway Paperback, Pocket Books, 1986, 151 p., paper, novel. PRIVATE SCHOOL #1.

24337 *Skeleton key.* New York: A Byron Preiss Visual Publications Inc. Book, An Archway Paperback, Pocket Books, 1986, 150 p., paper, novel. PRIVATE SCHOOL #4.

24338 *Witch's eye.* New York: A Byron Preiss Visual Publications Inc. Book, An Archway Paperback, Pocket Books, 1986, 149 p., paper, novel. PRIVATE SCHOOL #3.

as LIONEL FENN

24339 *Agnes day.* New York: Tor SF, A Tom Doherty Associates Book, 1987, 248 p., paper, novel. QUEST FOR THE WHITE DUCK #3.

24340 *Blood river down.* New York: Tor SF, A Tom Doherty Associates Book, 1986, 310 p., paper, novel. QUEST FOR THE WHITE DUCK #1.

24341 *Kent Montana and the once and future thing.* New York: Ace Books, 1991, 198 p., paper, novel. KENT MONTANA #3.

24342 *Kent Montana and the really ugly thing from Mars.* New York: Ace Books, 1990, 195 p., paper, novel. KENT MONTANA #1.

24343 *Kent Montana and the reasonably invisible man.* New York: Ace Books, 1991, 198 p., paper, novel. KENT MONTANA #2.

24344 *The seven spears of the W'dch'ck.* New York: Tor SF, A Tom Doherty Associates Book, 1988, 375 p., paper, novel.

24345 *Web of defeat.* New York: Tor SF, A Tom Doherty Associates Book, 1987, 284 p., paper, novel. QUEST FOR THE WHITE DUCK #2.

as GEOFFREY MARSH

24346 *The fangs of the hooded demon: a Lincoln Blackthorne adventure.* New York: Tor Books, 1988, 281 p., cloth, novel. LINCOLN BLACKTHORNE #4

24347 *The king of Satan's eyes.* Garden City, NY: Doubleday & Co., 1984, 185 p., cloth, novel. LINCOLN BLACKTHORNE #1.

24348 *The patch of the Odin soldier.* Garden City, NY: Doubleday & Co., 1987, 182 p., cloth, novel. LINCOLN BLACKTHORNE #3.

24349 *The tail of the Arabian, knight.* Garden City, NY: Doubleday & Co., 1986, 181 p., cloth, novel. LINCOLN BLACKTHORNE #2.

with Ramsey Campbell

19293 *Black wine.* Niles, IL: Dark Harvest, 1986, 165 p., cloth, coll. [Edited by Douglas E. Winter].

GRANT, Clay

24350 *The demon samurai.* New York: Belmont Tower Books, 1978, 158 p., paper, novel.

GRANT, David, pseud.—SEE: Thomas, Craig

GRANT, Donald M(etcalf), 1927-

24351 *Talbot Mundy, messenger of destiny.* West Kingston, RI: Donald M. Grant, Publisher, 1983, 253 p., cloth, nonf. anth.

with Joseph Payne Brennan

18597 *Act of Providence.* West Kingston, RI: Donald M. Grant, Publisher, 1979, 122 p., cloth, novel. LUCIUS LEFFING SERIES.

GRANT, Edward

24352 *The ultimate weapon.* New York: Pinnacle Books, 1976, 183 p., paper, novel.

GRANT, Gwen(doline Ellen), 1940-

24353 *Bonny Starr and the riddles of time.* London: Heinemann, 1987, 139 p., cloth, novel.

GRANT, James, 1822-1887

37809 *The queen's cadet, and other tales.* London, New York: George Routledge & Sons, 1874, 320 p., cloth, coll.

GRANT, John [pseud. of Paul Le Page Barnett], 1949-

24354 *Albion.* London: Headline, 1991, 310 p., cloth, novel.
24355 *Aries I.* Newton Abbot, England; North Pompret, VT: David & Charles, 1979, 191 p., cloth, anth. [Only volume published].

with Joe Dever

The claws of Helgedad—SEE: *Legends of Lone Wolf: The claws of Helgedad.*
The dark door opens—SEE: *Legends of Lone Wolf: The dark door opens.*
Eclipse of the Kai—SEE: *Legends of Lone Wolf: Eclipse of the Kai.*
Hunting Wolf—SEE: *Legends of Lone Wolf: Hunting Wolf.*
21646 *Legends of Lone Wolf: Eclipse of the Kai.* London: Beaver Books, 1989, 237 p., paper, novel. LEGENDS OF LONE WOLF #1.
21647 *Legends of Lone Wolf: Hunting Wolf.* London: Beaver Books, 1990, 226 p., paper, novel. LEGENDS OF LONE WOLF #4.
21648 *Legends of Lone Wolf: The claws of Helgedad.* London: Beaver Books,

1991, 268 p., paper, novel. LEGENDS OF LONE WOLF #5.
21649 *Legends of Lone Wolf: The dark door opens.* London: Beaver Books, 1989, 272 p., paper, novel. LEGENDS OF LONE WOLF #2.
21650 *Legends of Lone Wolf: The sacrifice of Ruanon.* London: Arrow Books, 1991, 366 p., paper, novel. LEGENDS OF LONE WOLF #6.
21651 *Legends of Lone Wolf: The sword of the sun.* London: Beaver Books, 1989, [400] p., paper, novel. LEGEND OF LONE WOLF #3.
21651A retitled: *The tides of treachery.* New York: Berkley Books, 1991, 182 p., paper, novel. LEGENDS OF LONE WOLF #3. [The first half of the British edition].
21651B retitled: *The sword of the sun.* New York: Berkley Books, 1991, 182 p., paper, novel. LEGENDS OF LONE WOLF #4 (U.S. edition). [The second half of the British edition].
The sacrifice of Ruanon—SEE: *Legends of Lone Wolf: The sacrifice of Ruanon.*
The sword of the sun—SEE: *Legends of Lone Wolf: The sword of the sun.*
The tides of treachery—SEE: *Legends of Lone Wolf: The sword of the sun.*

with David Langford

24356 *Earthdoom!* London: Grafton, 1987, 303 p., paper, novel.

GRANT, Kathryn—SEE: Ptacek, Kathryn

GRANT, Mark, house pseud.

24357 *Christmas slaughter.* New York: Avon Books, 1991, 181 p., paper, novel. MUTANTS AMOK #5. [By Bruce King].
18008 *Holocaust horror.* New York: Avon Books, 1991, 196 p., paper, novel. MUTANTS AMOK #4. [By David Bischoff].
18009 *Mutant hell.* New York: Avon Books, 1991, 216 p., paper, novel. MUTANTS AMOK #2. [By David Bischoff].
18010 *Mutants amok.* New York: Avon Books, 1991, 216 p., paper, novel. MUTANTS AMOK #1. [[By David Bischoff and Tim Sullivan].
18011 *Rebel attack.* New York: Avon Books, 1991, 169 p., paper, novel. MUTANTS AMOK #3. [By David Bischoff].

GRANT, Maxwell, house pseud.

23883 *Charg, monster: from the Shadow's private annals.* New York: A Jove/HBJ Book, 1977, 158 p., paper, novel. SHADOW #20. [By Walter B. Gibson].

23884 *The creeping death: from the Shadow's private annals.* New York: Pyramid Books, 1977, 144 p., paper, novel. SHADOW #14. [By Walter B. Gibson].

23885 *The crime cult: from the Shadow's private annals.* New York: Pyramid Books, 1975, 156 p., paper, novel. SHADOW #6. [By Walter B. Gibson].

23886 *The crime oracle; and, The teeth of the dragon: two adventures of the Shadow.* New York: Dover Publications, 1975, xxv + 163 p., paper, coll. SHADOW SERIES. [By Walter B. Gibson].

23887 *The Death Giver: from the Shadow's private annals .* New York: A Jove/HBJ Book, 1978, 160 p., paper, novel. SHADOW #23. [By Walter B. Gibson].

23888 *Double Z: from the Shadow's private annals.* New York: Pyramid Books, 1975, 188 p., paper, novel. SHADOW #5. [By Walter B. Gibson].

23889 *Fingers of death: from the Shadow's private annals.* New York: A Jove/HBJ Book, 1977, 144 p., paper, novel. SHADOW #17. [By Walter B. Gibson].

23890 *Gray Fist: from the Shadow's private annals.* New York: Pyramid Books, 1977, 174 p., paper, novel. SHADOW #15. [By Walter B. Gibson].

23891 *Green Eyes: from the Shadow's private annals.* New York: Pyramid Books, 1977, 158 p., paper, novel. SHADOW #13. [By Walter B. Gibson].

23892 *Hands in the dark: from the Shadow's private annals.* New York: Pyramid Books, 1975, 187 p., paper, novel. SHADOW #4. [By Walter B. Gibson].

23893 *Kings of crime: from the Shadow's private annals.* New York: Pyramid Books, 1976, 160 p., paper, novel. SHADOW #11. [By Walter B. Gibson].

23894 *Mox: from the Shadow's private annals.* New York: Pyramid Books, 1975, 126 p., paper, novel. SHADOW #8. [By Walter B. Gibson].

23895 *Murder trail: from the Shadow's private annals.* New York: A Jove/HBJ Book, 1977, 159 p., paper, novel. SHADOW #18. [By Walter B. Gibson].

23898 *The red menace: from the Shadow's private annals.* New York: Pyramid Books, 1975, 176 p., paper, novel. SHADOW #7. [By Walter B. Gibson].

23899 *The Romanoff jewels: from the Shadow's private annals.* New York: Pyramid Books, 1975, 142 p., paper, novel. SHADOW #9. [By Walter B. Gibson].

23900 *Shadowed millions: from the Shadow's private annals.* New York: Pyramid Books, 1976, 142 p., paper, novel. SHADOW #12. [By Walter B. Gibson].

23901 *The Shadow's shadow: from the Shadow's private annals.* New York: Pyramid Books, 1977, 173 p., paper, novel. SHADOW #16. [By Walter B. Gibson].

23902 *The silent death: from the Shadow's private annals.* New York: A Jove/HBJ Book, 1978, 160 p., paper, novel. SHADOW #22. [By Walter B. Gibson].

23903 *The Silent Seven: from the Shadow's private annals .* New York: Pyramid Books, 1975, 142 p., paper, novel. SHADOW #10. [By Walter B. Gibson].

23904 *The wealth seeker: from the Shadow's private annals.* New York: A Jove/HBJ Book, 1978, 158 p., paper, novel. SHADOW #21. [By Walter B. Gibson].

23905 *Zemba: from the Shadow's private annals.* New York: A Jove/HBJ Book, 1977, 160 p., paper, novel. SHADOW #19. [By Walter B. Gibson].

GRANT, Penelope (Anne), 1942- , *with Pat Hornsey*

24358 *Edgar Rice Burroughs.* London: New English Library, 1975, 30 p., paper, nonf. anth.

GRANT, Richard, 1952-

24359 *Rumors of spring.* Toronto, New York: Bantam Books, 1987, 439 p., cloth, novel.

24360 *Saraband of lost time.* New York: Avon, 1985, 327 p., paper, novel.

24361 *Views from the oldest house: a novel.* New York: A Foundation Book, Doubleday, 1989, 470 p., cloth, novel.

GRANT, Rob, *with Doug Naylor as* GRANT NAYLOR

24362 *Better than life.* Harmondsworth, Middlesex, England: Viking, 1990, 229 p., cloth, movie. RED DWARF #2.

24363 *Red dwarf.* Harmondsworth, Middlesex, England: Penguin Books, 1989, 298 p., paper, movie. RED DWARF #1.

GRANT, Steven, 1953- , *as* VICTOR APPLETON

16741 *Cyborg kickboxer.* New York, London: An Archway Paperback, Pocket Books, 1991, 166 p., paper, novel. TOM SWIFT #C3.

GRASMICK, Nana, *with Karen "K-nut" Flanery*

23178 *Fandom is for the young; or, One convention too many.* New York, Washington: Vantage Press, 1981, xiii+160 p., cloth, nonf.

GRASS, Günter (Wilhelm), 1927-

24364 *The flounder.* New York, London: A Helen and Kurt Wolff Book, Harcourt Brace Jovanovich, 1978, xi+547 p., cloth, novel. [Translation by Ralph Manheim of *Der Butt*].
24365 *The rat.* San Diego, CA: Harcourt Brace Jovanovich, 1987, 371 p., cloth, novel. [Translation by Ralph Manheim of *Die rättin*].

GRATTAN, C(linton) Hartley, 1902-1980

24366 *Bitter Bierce: a mystery of American letters.* Garden City, NY: Doubleday, Doran & Co., 1929, xi+291 p., cloth, nonf.

GRAVEL, Geary, 1951-

24367 *The alchemists.* New York: A Del Rey Book, Ballantine Books, 1984, 289 p., paper, novel. AUTUMN WORLD #1.
24368 *A key for the nonesuch.* New York: A Del Rey Book, Ballantine Books, 1990, 229 p., paper, novel. FADING WORLDS #1.
24369 *The Pathfinders.* New York: A Del Rey Book, Ballantine Books, 1986, 230 p., paper, novel. AUTUMN WORLD #2.
24370 *The return of the Breakneck Boys.* New York: A Del Rey Book, Ballantine Books, 1991, 217 p., paper, novel. FADING WORLDS #2.

GRAVER, Fred

24371 *Journey to Stonehenge.* Toronto, New York: An R. A. Montgomery Book, Bantam Books, 1984, 111 p., paper, novel. CHOOSE YOUR OWN ADVENTURE #35.

GRAVERSEN, Pat(ricia Ann Spears), 1935-

24372 *Dollies.* New York: Zebra Books, Kensington Publishing Corp., 1990, 288 p., paper, novel.
24373 *The Fagin: a novel.* New York: A&W Publishers, 1982, xiii+285 p., cloth, novel
24374 *Invisible fire.* New York: Fawcett Gold Medal, 1981, 222 p., paper, novel.
24375 *Stones.* New York: Zebra Books, Kensington Publishing Corp., 1991, 288 p., paper, novel.

*GRAVES, Gordon Harwood, 1884-1973

GRAVES, Robert (von Ranke), 1895-1985

37810 *The shout.* London: Elkin Mathews & Marrot, 1929, 31 p., cloth, story.

GRAY, Alasdair (James), 1934-

37811 *1982, Janine.* London: Jonathan Cape, 1984, 345 p., cloth, novel.
24376 *Alasdair Gray.* Edinburgh, Scotland: The Saltire Society, 1988, 19 p., paper, nonf. SALTIRE SELF-PORTRAITS #4.
24377 *Lanark: a life in four books.* Edinburgh, Scotland: Canongate Publishing, 1981, 560 p., cloth, novel.
24378 *Unlikely stories, mostly.* Edinburgh, Scotland: Canongate Publishing, 1983, 271 p., cloth, coll.

GRAY, Angela, pseud.—SEE: Daniels, Dorothy

*GRAY, Curme, 1910-1980

GRAY, Linda Crockett, 1943-

24379 *Dark window.* New York: A Signet Book, 1991, 463 p., paper, novel.
24380 *Mama's boy.* New York: An Onyx Book, New American Library, 1989, 352 p., paper, novel.
24381 *Satyr.* New York: Playboy Paperbacks, 1981, 224 p., paper, novel.
24382 *Scryer.* New York: Tor Horror, A Tom Doherty Associates Book, 1987, 346 p., paper, novel.
24383 *Siren.* New York: Playboy Paperbacks, 1982, 253 p., paper, novel.
24384 *Tangerine.* New York: Tor Horror, A Tom Doherty Associates Book, 1988, 344 p., paper, novel.

as LINDA CROCKETT

24385 *Sandman.* New York: Tor, A Tom Doherty Associates Book, 1990, 406 p., paper, novel.

GRAY, Michael

37812 *The lost wizard.* Lake Geneva, WI: TSR Inc., 1984, 76 p., paper, fiction. FANTASY FOREST BOOK #10.

37813 *Shadowcastle.* Lake Geneva, WI: TSR Inc., 1983, 76 p., paper, fiction. FANTASY FOREST BOOK #3.

GRAY, Nicholas Stuart, 1922-1981

24386 *The edge of evening.* London: Faber & Faber, 1976, 124 p., cloth, coll.

24387 *The garland of Filigree.* London: Dennis Dobson, 1979, 160 p., cloth, novel.

24388 *The wardens of the weir.* London: Dennis Dobson, 1978, 156 p., cloth, novel.

24389 *A wind from nowhere.* London: Faber & Faber, 1978, 155 p., cloth, coll.

*GRAY, Rod, pseud.—SEE: Fox, Gardner F.

*GRAYDON, William Murray, 1877?-1963?

GRAZIUNAS, Daina, 1953- , *with Jim Starlin*

24390 *Among madmen.* New York: A Roc Book, 1990, 268 p., paper, novel.

GREAVES, Margaret, 1914-

24391 *Cat's magic.* London: Methuen, 1980, 157 p., cloth, novel.

24392 *The dagger and the bird: a story of suspense.* London: Methuen, 1971, 143 p., cloth, novel.

GREBENS, G. V. [pseud. of George Vladimir Grebenschikov], 1943-

24393 *Ivan Efremov's theory of Soviet science fiction.* New York, Washington: Vantage Press, 1978, xviii + 135 p., cloth, nonf.

GREBENSCHIKOV, G. V.—SEE: Grebens, G. V.

GREELEY, Andrew M(oran), 1928-

24394 *Angel fire.* New York: Warner Books, 1988, 394 p., cloth, novel.

24395 *The final planet.* New York: Warner Books, 1987, 302 p., cloth, novel.

24396 *God game.* New York: Warner Books, 1986, 308 p., cloth, novel.

24397 *The magic cup: an Irish legend.* New York: McGraw-Hill Book Co., 1979, 246 p., cloth, novel.

24398 *Nora Maeve and Sebi.* New York, Ramsey, NJ: Paulist Press, 1976, [64] p., cloth, novel.

with Michael Cassutt

19648 *Sacred visions.* New York: Tor, A Tom Doherty Associates Book, 1991, xiv + 363 p., cloth, anth.

GREEN, Carl R., 1932- , *with William R. Sanford*

24399 *The black cat.* Mankato, MN: Crestwood House, 1987, 47 p., cloth, movie.

24400 *Black Friday.* Mankato, MN: Crestwood House, 1985, 48 p., cloth, movie.

24401 *Bride of Frankenstein.* Mankato, MN: Crestwood House, 1985, 48 p., cloth, movie.

24402 *Dracula's daughter.* Mankato, MN: Crestwood House, 1985, 48 p., cloth, movie.

24403 *Ghost of Frankenstein.* Mankato, MN: Crestwood House, 1985, 48 p., cloth, movie.

24404 *House of fear.* Mankato, MN: Crestwood House, 1987, 48 p., cloth, movie.

24405 *The house of the seven gables.* Mankato, MN: Crestwood House, 1987, 48 p., cloth, movie.

24406 *The invisible man.* Mankato, MN: Crestwood House, 1987, 47 p., cloth, movie.

24407 *The mole people.* Mankato, MN: Crestwood House, 1985, 48 p., cloth, movie.

24408 *The murders in the Rue Morgue.* Mankato, MN: Crestwood House, 1987, 47 p., cloth, movie.

24409 *The phantom of the opera.* Mankato, MN: Crestwood House, 1987, 47 p., cloth, movie.

24410 *The raven.* Mankato, MN: Crestwood House, 1985, 48 p., cloth, movie.

24411 *The revenge of the creature.* Mankato, MN: Crestwood House, 1987, 48 p., cloth, movie.

24412 *Tarantula.* Mankato, MN: Crestwood House, 1985, 48 p., cloth, movie.

24413 *Werewolf of London.* Mankato, MN: Crestwood House, 1985, 48 p., cloth, movie.

*GREEN, Edith Piñero, 1929-

*GREEN, Henry [pseud. of Henry Vincent Yorke], 1905-1974

GREEN, Hilary

24414 *Centrifuge.* London: Robert Hale, 1978, 160 p., cloth, novel.

GREEN, Jen, 1954- , with Sarah Lefanu

24415 *Despatches from the frontiers of the female mind: an anthology of original stories.* London: Women's Press, 1985, 248 p., paper, anth.

GREEN, Jonathon, 1948- , with Allan Asherman & Doug Murray

16837 *Star Wars: the full story.* [S.l.]: Paradise Press, 1977, 62 p., paper, nonf.

GREEN, Joseph (Lee), 1931-

24416 *The horde.* Toronto, New York: Laser Books, 1976, 191 p., paper, novel.
24417 *Star probe.* London: Millington Books, 1976, 162 p., cloth, novel.

GREEN, Kate, 1950-

24418 *Night angel.* New York: Delacorte Press, 1989, 282 p., cloth, novel. SHATTERED #2.
24419 *Shattered moon.* New York: A Dell Book, 1986, 352 p., paper, novel. SHATTERED #1.

GREEN, Martin (Burgess), 1927-

24420 *The Earth again redeemed: May 26 to July 1, 1984, on this Earth of ours and its alter ego: a science fiction novel.* New York: Basic Books, 1977, 359 p., cloth, novel.

GREEN, Maury, 1916-

24421 *The Delphi calculus.* New York: A Dell Book, 1979, 268 p., paper, novel.

GREEN, Michael (Jonathan), 1943-

24422 *De historia et veritate unicornis = On the history and truth of the unicorn.* Philadelphia, PA: Running Press Book Publishers, 1983, 64 p., cloth, fiction.
24423 *A Hobbit's travels: being hitherto unpublished travel sketches of Sam Gamgee.* Philadelphia, PA: Running Press, 1978, p., cloth, art.
On the history and truth of the unicorn—SEE: *De historia et veritate unicornis.*

GREEN, Roger J(ames), 1944-

24424 *The fear of Samuel Walton.* Oxford, England: Oxford University Press, 1984, 233 p., cloth, novel. SAMUEL WALTON #1.
24425 *The lengthening shadow.* Oxford, England: Oxford University Press, 1986, 215 p., cloth, novel. SAMUEL WALTON #2.

GREEN, Roger (Gilbert) Lancelyn, 1918-1987

24426 *Andrew Lang: a critical bibliography of the works of Andrew Lang.* Leicester, England: Edmund Ward, 1946, xi+265 p., cloth, nonf.
The Beaver book of other worlds—SEE: *The Hamish Hamilton book of other worlds.*
A book of magicians—SEE: *The Hamish Hamilton book of magicians.*
24427 *The Hamish Hamilton book of magicians.* London: Hamish Hamilton, 1973, xii+274 p., cloth, anth.
24427A retitled: *A book of magicians.* Harmondsworth, Middlesex, England: Puffin Books, 1977, 268 p., paper, anth.
24428 *The Hamish Hamilton book of other worlds.* London: Hamish Hamilton, 1976, xiii+239 p., cloth, anth.
24428A retitled: *The Beaver book of other worlds.* London: Beaver Books, 1978, 205 p., paper, anth.
37814 *The land beyond the north.* London: John Lane, 1958, 157 p., cloth, novel.

with Walter Hooper

24429 *C. S. Lewis: a biography.* London: Collins, 1974, 320 p., cloth, nonf.

GREEN, Roland (James), 1944-

24430 *Conan the guardian.* New York: Tor SF, A Tom Doherty Associates Book, 1991, 280 p., paper, novel. CONAN SERIES.
24431 *Conan the valiant.* New York: Tor SF, A Tom Doherty Associates Book, 1988, 280 p., paper, novel. CONAN SERIES.
24432 *Division of the spoils* / by Roland J. Green. New York: A Roc Book, 1990, 303 p., paper, novel. STARCRUISER SHENANDOAH #2.
24433 *The mountain walks: a Peace Company novel.* New York: Ace Books, 1989, 228 p., paper, novel. PEACE COMPANY #3.

24434 *Peace Company.* New York: Ace Science Fiction Books, 1985, 210 p., paper, novel. PEACE COMPANY #1.

Squadron alert—SEE: *Starcruiser Shenandoah: Squadron alert.*

24435 *Starcruiser Shenandoah: Squadron alert /* by Roland J. Green. New York: A Signet Book, New American Library, 1989, 316 p., paper, novel. STARCRUISER SHENANDOAH #1.

24436 *The sum of things /* by Roland J. Green. New York: A Roc Book, 1991, xiv+368 p., paper, novel. STARCRUISER SHENANDOAH #3.

24437 *These green foreign hills: a Peace Company novel.* New York: Ace Books, 1987, 188 p., paper, novel. PEACE COMPANY #2.

24438 *Wandor's flight.* New York: Avon, 1981, 357 p., paper, novel. WANDOR #4.

24439 *Wandor's journey.* New York: Avon, 1975, 188 p., paper, novel. WANDOR #2.

24440 *Wandor's voyage.* New York: Avon, 1979, 222 p., paper, novel. WANDOR #3.

as JEFFREY LORD

24441 *Blade: Champion of the gods.* New York: Pinnacle Books, 1976, 183 p., paper, novel. RICHARD BLADE #21.

24442 *Blade: City of the living dead.* Los Angeles: Pinnacle Books, 1978, 185 p., paper, novel. RICHARD BLADE #26.

24443 *Blade: Empire of blood.* New York: Pinnacle Books, 1977, 196 p., paper, novel. RICHARD BLADE #23.

24444 *Blade: Guardians of the coral throne.* New York: Pinnacle Books, 1976, 182 p., paper, novel. RICHARD BLADE #20.

24445 *Blade: Looters of Tharn.* New York: Pinnacle Books, 1976, 184 p., paper, novel. RICHARD BLADE #19.

24446 *Blade: The crystal seas.* New York: Pinnacle Books, 1975, 184 p., paper, novel. RICHARD BLADE #16.

24447 *Blade: The forests of Gleor.* New York: Pinnacle Books, 1977, 186 p., paper, novel. RICHARD BLADE #22.

24448 *Blade: The mountains of Brega.* New York: Pinnacle Books, 1976, 184 p., paper, novel. RICHARD BLADE #17.

24449 *Blade: The Torian pearls.* Los Angeles: Pinnacle Books, 1977, 186 p., paper, novel. RICHARD BLADE #25.

24450 *Blade: The towers of Melnon.* New York: Pinnacle Books, 1975, 183 p., paper, novel. RICHARD BLADE #15.

24451 *Blade: Warlords of Gaikon.* New York: Pinnacle Books, 1976, 185 p., paper, novel. RICHARD BLADE #18.

Champion of the gods—SEE: BLADE: CHAMPION OF THE GODS.

City of the living dead—SEE: *Blade: City of the living dead.*

The crystal seas—SEE: *Blade: The crystal seas.*

06298 *Dimension of dreams.* New York: Pinnacle Books, 1974, 181 p., paper, novel. RICHARD BLADE #11.

The dragons of Englor—SEE: *Richard Blade: The dragons of Englor.*

Empire of blood—SEE: *Blade: Empire of blood.*

The forests of Gleor—SEE: *Blade: The forests of Gleor.*

Gladiators of Hapanu—SEE: *Richard Blade: Gladiators of Hapanu.*

The golden steed—SEE: *Richard Blade: The golden steed.*

Guardians of the coral throne—SEE: *Blade: Guardians of the coral throne.*

06299 *Ice dragon: the Richard Blade series.* New York: Pinnacle Books, 1974, 183 p., paper, novel. RICHARD BLADE #10.

Killer plants of Binaark—SEE: *Richard Blade: Killer plants of Binaark.*

King of Zunga—SEE: *Richard Blade: King of Zunga.*

06300 *Kingdom of Royth: the Richard Blade series.* New York: Pinnacle Books, 1974, 188 p., paper, novel. RICHARD BLADE #9.

Looters of Tharn—SEE: *Blade: Looters of Tharn.*

The Lords of the Crimson River—SEE: *Richard Blade: The Lords of the Crimson River.*

Master of the Hashomi—SEE: *Richard Blade: Master of the Hashomi.*

The mountains of Brega—SEE: *Blade: The mountains of Brega.*

Pirates of Gohar—SEE: *Richard Blade: Pirates of Gohar.*

Return to Kaldak—SEE: *Richard Blade: Return to Kaldak.*

24452 *Richard Blade: Gladiators of Hapanu.* Los Angeles: Pinnacle Books, 1979, 187 p., paper, novel. RICHARD BLADE #31.

24453 *Richard Blade: Killer plants of Binaark.* Los Angeles: Pinnacle Books, 1980, 187 p., paper, novel. RICHARD BLADE #33.

24454 *Richard Blade: King of Zunga.* New York: Pinnacle Books, 1975, 181 p., paper, novel. RICHARD BLADE #12.

24455 *Richard Blade: Master of the Hashomi.* Los Angeles: Pinnacle Books, 1978, 182 p., paper, novel. RICHARD BLADE #27.

24456 *Richard Blade: Pirates of Gohar.* Los Angeles: Pinnacle Books, 1979, 181 p., paper, novel. RICHARD BLADE #32.

24457 *Richard Blade: Return to Kaldak.* New York: Pinnacle Books, 1983, 216 p., paper, novel. RICHARD BLADE #36.

24458 *Richard Blade: The dragons of Englor.* New York: Pinnacle Books, 1977, 182 p., paper, novel. RICHARD BLADE #24.

24459 *Richard Blade: The golden steed.* New York: Pinnacle Books, 1975, 182 p., paper, novel. RICHARD BLADE #13.

24460 *Richard Blade: The Lords of the Crimson River.* New York: Pinnacle Books, 1981, 182 p., paper, novel. RICHARD BLADE #35.

24461 *Richard Blade: The ruins of Kaldac.* New York: Pinnacle Books, 1981, 182 p., paper, novel. RICHARD BLADE #34.

24462 *Richard Blade: The temples of Ayocan.* New York: Pinnacle Books, 1975, 182 p., paper, novel. RICHARD BLADE #14.

24463 *Richard Blade: Treasure of the stars.* Los Angeles: Pinnacle Books, 1978, 183 p., paper, novel. RICHARD BLADE #29.

24464 *Richard Blade: Warriors of Latan.* New York: Pinnacle Books, 1984, 218 p., paper, novel. RICHARD BLADE #37.

24465 *Richard Blade: Wizard of Rentoro.* Los Angeles: Pinnacle Books, 1978, 185 p., paper, novel. RICHARD BLADE #28.

The ruins of Kaldac—SEE: *Richard Blade: The ruins of Kaldac.*

The temples of Ayocan—SEE: *Richard Blade: The temples of Ayocan.*

The Torian pearls—SEE: *Blade: The Torian pearls.*

The towers of Melnon—SEE: *Blade: The towers of Melnon.*

Treasure of the stars—SEE: *Richard Blade: Treasure of the stars.*

Warlords of Gaikon—SEE: *Blade: Warlords of Gaikon.*

Warriors of Latan—SEE: *Richard Blade: Warriors of Latan.*

Wizard of Rentoro—SEE: *Richard Blade: Wizard of Rentoro.*

with John F. Carr

19455 *Great Kings' War.* New York: Ace Science Fiction Books, 1985, 357 p., paper, novel. PARATIME POLICE—LORD KALVAN #2.

with Gordon R. Dickson

21903 *Jamie the Red.* New York: Ace Fantasy Books, 1984, 220 p., paper, novel. THIEVES' WORLD.

with Frieda A. Murray

The book of Kantela—SEE: *Throne of Sherran.*

24466 *Throne of Sherran: The Book of Kantela: a novel of high fantasy* / by Roland J. Green.... New York: A Bluejay International Edition, 1985, 340 p., paper, novel. THRONE OF SHERRAN TRILOGY #1.

with Andrew J. Offutt as JOHN CLEVE

24467 *Starship Sapphire.* New York: Berkley Books, 1984, 212 p., paper, novel. SPACEWAYS #15.

with Jerry E. Pournelle

Clan and crown—SEE: *Janissaries: Clan and crown.*

24468 *Janissaries: Clan and crown.* New York: Ace Books, 1982, 437 p., paper, novel. JANISSARIES #2.

24469 *Storms of victory.* New York: Ace Science Fiction Books, 1987, xiv, 359 p., cloth, novel. JANISSARIES #3.

with Jerry Pournelle & John F. Carr

19454 *The burning eye.* New York: Baen Books, 1988, 366 p., paper, anth. WAR WORLD #1.

GREEN, Scott E(lliott), 1951-

24470 *Contemporary science fiction, fantasy, and horror poetry: a resource guide and biographical dictionary.* New York, Westport, CT: Greenwood Press, 1989, xviii+216 p., cloth, nonf.

GREEN, Sharon, 1942-

24471 *Chosen of Mida.* New York: DAW Books, 1984, 365 p., paper, novel. JALAV, AMAZON WARRIOR #3.

24472 *The Crystals of Mida.* New York: DAW Books, 1982, 352 p., paper, novel. JALAV, AMAZON WARRIOR #1.

24473 *Dawn song.* New York: Avon Books, 1990, 373 p., paper, novel.

24474 *The far side of forever.* New York: DAW Books, 1987, 383 p., paper, novel. FAR SIDE OF FOREVER #1.

24475 *Gateway to Xanadu: a Diana Santee spaceways novel.* New York: DAW Books, 1985, 413 p., paper, novel. DIANA SANTEE, SPACEWAYS AGENT #2.

24476 *Haunted house.* Toronto, New York: Harlequin Books, 1990, 252 p., paper, novel.

24477 *Hellbound magic.* New York: DAW Books, 1989, 400 p., paper, novel. FAR SIDE OF FOREVER #2.

24478 *Lady blade, lord fighter.* New York: DAW Books, 1987, 366 p., paper, novel.

24479 *Mind guest: a Diana Santee spaceways novel.* New York: DAW Books, 1984, 415 p., paper, novel. DIANA SANTEE, SPACEWAYS AGENT #1.

24480 *Mists of the ages.* New York: DAW Books, 1988, 317 p., paper, novel. THIEF AND THE WARRIOR #1.

24481 *An oath to Mida.* New York: DAW Books, 1983, 397 p., paper, novel. JALAV, AMAZON WARRIOR #2.

24482 *The rebel prince.* New York: DAW Books, 1987, 367 p., paper, novel.

24483 *To battle the gods: a novel.* New York: DAW Books, 1986, 446 p., paper, novel. JALAV, AMAZON WARRIOR #5.

24484 *The warrior challenged.* New York: DAW Books, 1986, 382 p., paper, novel. TERRILIAN #4.

24485 *The warrior enchanted.* New York: DAW Books, 1983, 352 p., paper, novel. TERRILIAN #2.

24486 *The warrior rearmed.* New York: DAW Books, 1984, 253 p., paper, novel. TERRILIAN #3.

24487 *The warrior victorious.* New York: DAW Books, 1988, 415 p., paper, novel. TERRILIAN #5.

24488 *The warrior within.* New York: DAW Books, 1982, 224 p., paper, novel. TERRILIAN #1.

24489 *The will of the gods: a novel.* New York: DAW Books, 1985, 383 p., paper, novel. JALAV, AMAZON WARRIOR #4.

GREEN, Simon (R.), 1955-

24490 *Blue moon rising.* New York: A Roc Book, 1991, 476 p., paper, novel.
Devil take the hindmost—SEE: *Hawk & Fisher: Winner takes all.*
The god killer—SEE: *Hawk & Fisher: The god killer.*
Guard against dishonor—SEE: *Hawk & Fisher: Guard against dishonor.*

24491 *Hawk & Fisher.* New York: Ace Books, 1990, 213 p., paper, novel. HAWK & FISHER #1.

24491A retitled: *No haven for the guilty.* London: Headline, 1990, 213 p., paper, novel. HAWK & FISHER #1.

24492 *Hawk & Fisher: Guard against dishonor.* New York: Ace Books, 1991, 188 p., paper, novel. HAWK & FISHER #5.

24493 *Hawk & Fisher: The god killer.* New York: Ace Books, 1991, 187 p., paper, novel. HAWK & FISHER #3.

24493A retitled: *The god killer.* London: Headline, 1991, 187 p., paper, novel. HAWK & FISHER #3.

24494 *Hawk & Fisher: Winner takes all.* New York: Ace Books, 1991, 201 p., paper, novel. HAWK & FISHER #2.

24494A retitled: *Devil take the hindmost.* London: Headline, 1991, 201 p., paper, novel. HAWK & FISHER #2.

24495 *Hawk & Fisher: Wolf in the fold.* New York: Ace Books, 1991, 186 p., paper, novel. HAWK & FISHER #4.
No haven for the guilty—SEE: *Hawk & Fisher.*

24496 *Robin Hood, prince of thieves.* New York: Berkley Books, 1991, 234 p., paper, movie.
Winner takes all—SEE: *Hawk & Fisher: Winner takes all.*
Wolf in the fold—SEE: *Hawk & Fisher: Wolf in the fold.*

GREEN, Stephanie

24497 *The triple spiral.* London: Walker Books, 1989, 186 p., cloth, novel.

GREEN, Susan Kohn, 1941-

24498 *Self-portrait with wings.* Boston: Little, Brown & Co., 1989, x+206 p., cloth, novel.

GREEN, Terence M(ichael), 1947-

24499 *Barking dogs.* New York: St. Martin's Press, 1988, 214 p., cloth, novel.

24500 *The woman who is the midnight wind.* Porters Lake, Nova Scotia, Canada: Pottersfield Press, 1987, 137 p., paper, coll.

GREENAN, Russell H., 1925-

37815 *The bric-a-brac man.* New York: Random House, 1976, 211 p., cloth, novel.

24501 *The secret life of Algernon Pendleton.* New York: Random House, 1973, 247 p., paper, novel.

GREENAWAY, Peter Van—SEE: Van Greenaway, Peter

*GREENBERG, Martin (L.), 1918-

GREENBERG, Martin H(arry), 1941-

24502 *Amazing science fiction anthology: the war years, 1936-1945.* Lake Geneva, WI: TSR Inc., 1987, 331 p., paper, anth.

24503 *Amazing science fiction anthology: the wild years, 1946-1955.* Lake Geneva, WI: TSR Inc., 1987, 318 p., paper, anth.

24504 *Amazing science fiction anthology: the wonder years, 1926-1935.* Lake Geneva, WI: TSR Inc., 1987, 316 p., paper, anth.

24505 *Amazing stories: visions of other worlds.* Lake Geneva, WI: TSR Inc., 1986, 253 p., paper, anth.

24506 *Christmas on Ganymede, and other stories.* New York: Avon Books, 1990, viii+243 p., paper, anth. [Charles Waugh was an uncredited co-editor for this book].

The Diplomacy guild—SEE: *Isaac's universe, volume one: The diplomacy guild.*

24508 *The fantastic adventures of Robin Hood.* New York: A Signet Book, 1991, 285 p., paper, anth.

24509 *Fantastic Chicago.* Chicago: Chicon V, 1991, 136 p., paper, anth.

24510 *Fantastic lives: autobiographical essays by notable science fiction writers.* Carbondale & Edwardsville: Southern Illinois University Press, 1981, xi+215 p., cloth, nonf. anth.

24511 *Foundation's friends: stories in honor of Isaac Asimov.* New York: Tor SF, A Tom Doherty Associates Book, 1989, 403 p., cloth, anth.

24512 *The further adventures of Batman.* New York, Toronto: Bantam Books, 1989, 401 p., paper, anth. BATMAN SERIES.

24513 *The further adventures of the Joker.* New York, Toronto: Bantam Books, 1990, 462 p., paper, anth. BATMAN SERIES.

24514 *Isaac's universe, volume one: The diplomacy guild.* New York: Avon Books, 1991, xii+260 p., paper, anth.

24515 *Isaac's universe, volume two: Phases in chaos.* New York: Avon Books, 1991, xiv+273 p., paper, anth.

24516 *Mummy stories.* New York: Ballantine Books, 1990, 225 p., paper, anth.

24517 *New stories from The Twilight Zone.* New York: Avon Books, 1991, viii+295 p., paper, anth.

24518 *Nightmares on Elm Street: Freddy Krueger's seven sweetest dreams.* New York: St. Martin's Press, 1991, 289 p., paper, anth. NIGHTMARE ON ELM STREET.

Phases in chaos--SEE: *Isaac's universe, volume two: Phases in chaos.*

MARTIN H. GREENBERG, *as* ANONYMOUS EDITOR

24519 *Bart science fiction triplet #1.* New York: Bart, 1988, 285 p., paper, anth. [Only volume published].

NOTE: Anthologies compiled by Martin H. Greenberg with one or more other editors are listed in alphabetical order by the surname of the best-known co-editor of the group, then alphabetically by title.

MARTIN H. GREENBERG, *with Robert Adams & Pamela Crippen Adams*

15982 *Barbarians II.* New York: A Signet Book, New American Library, 1988, xi+364 p., paper, anth. [Charles Waugh was an uncredited co-editor for this book].

Book of alternate worlds—SEE: *Robert Adams' Book of alternate worlds.*

Book of soldiers—SEE: *Robert Adams' Book of soldiers.*

15983 *Hunger for horror.* New York: DAW Books, 1988, ix+256 p., paper, anth.

15984 *Phantom regiments.* New York: Baen Books, 1990, 271 p., paper, novel.

15985 *Robert Adams' Book of alternate worlds.* New York: A Signet Book, New American Library, 1987, 366 p., paper, anth.

15986 *Robert Adams' Book of soldiers.* New York: A Signet Book, New American Library, 1988, 348 p., paper, anth.

MARTIN H. GREENBERG, *with Robert Adams & Charles G. Waugh*

16023 *Barbarians.* New York: A Signet Book, New American Library, 1986, 368 p., paper, anth.

MARTIN H. GREENBERG, *with Poul Anderson & Charles G. Waugh*

16450 *Mercenaries of tomorrow.* New York: A Critic's Choice Paperback from Lorevan Publishing, 1985, xi+372 p., paper, anth.

16451 *Space wars.* New York: Tor SF, A Tom Doherty Associates Book, 1988, 372 p., paper, anth.

16452 *Terrorists of tomorrow.* New York: A Critic's Choice Paperback from Lorevan Publishing, 1986, 376 p., paper, anth.

16453 *Time wars.* New York: Tor SF, A Tom Doherty Associates Book, 1986, 374 p., paper, anth.

MARTIN H. GREENBERG, *with Piers Anthony & Barry Malzberg & Charles G. Waugh*

16714 *Uncollected stars.* New York: Avon, 1986, vii+312 p., paper, anth.

MARTIN H. GREENBERG, *with John L. Apostolou*

16726 *The best Japanese science fiction stories.* New York: Dembner Books, 1989, 176 p., cloth, anth.

MARTIN H. GREENBERG, *with Isaac Asimov*

16929 *Amazing stories: 60 years of the best science fiction.* Lake Geneva, WI: TSR Inc., 1985, 255 p., paper, anth.

16930 *Atlantis.* New York: A Signet Book, New American Library, 1988, 349 p., paper, anth. ISAAC ASIMOV'S MAGICAL WORLDS OF FANTASY #9.

16931 *Cosmic critiques: how & why ten science fiction stories work.* Cincinnati, OH: Writer's Digest Books, 1990, 197 p., paper, anth. [Includes some nonfiction].

16932 *Devils.* New York: A Signet Book, New American Library, 1987, 351 p., paper, anth. ISAAC ASIMOV'S MAGICAL WORLDS OF FANTASY #8.

16933 *Election day 2084: a science fiction anthology on the politics of the future.* Buffalo, New York: Prometheus Books, 1984, 301 p., cloth, anth.

The golden years of science fiction—SEE: *Isaac Asimov presents: The golden years of science fiction.*

The great science fiction stories—SEE: *Isaac Asimov presents: The great science fiction stories.*

16934 *Isaac Asimov presents The golden years of science fiction.* New York: Bonanza Books, 1983, 432, 350 p., cloth, anth. GREAT SF STORIES #1-2.

16935 *Isaac Asimov presents The golden years of science fiction, 2nd series: 28 stories and novellas.* New York: Bonanza Books, 1983, 723 p., cloth, anth. GREAT SF STORIES #3-4.

16936 *Isaac Asimov presents The golden years of science fiction, 3rd series: 20 stories and novellas.* New York: Bonanza Books, 1984, 633 p., cloth, anth. GREAT SF STORIES #5-6.

16937 *Isaac Asimov presents The golden years of science fiction, fourth series: 26 stories and novellas.* New York: Bonanza Books, 1984, 632 p., cloth, anth. GREAT SF STORIES #7-8.

16938 *Isaac Asimov presents The golden years of science fiction, fifth series: 33 stories and novellas.* New York: Bonanza Books, 1985, 641 p., cloth, anth. GREAT SF STORIES #9-10.

16939 *Isaac Asimov presents The golden age of science fiction, sixth series: 33 stories and novellas.* New York: Bonanza Books, 1988, 624 p., cloth, anth. GREAT SF STORIES #11-12.

16940 *Isaac Asimov presents The great science fiction stories, volume 1, 1939.* New York: DAW Books, 1979, 432 p., paper, anth.

16941 *Isaac Asimov presents The great science fiction stories, volume 2, 1940.* New York: DAW Books, 1979, 350 p., paper, anth.

16942 *Isaac Asimov presents The great science fiction stories, volume 3, 1941.* New York: DAW Books, 1980, 352 p., paper, anth.

16943 *Isaac Asimov presents The great science fiction stories, volume 4, 1942.* New York: DAW Books, 1980, 448 p., paper, anth.

16944 *Isaac Asimov presents The great science fiction stories, volume 5, 1943.* New York: DAW Books, 1981, 380 p., paper, anth.

16945 *Isaac Asimov presents The great science fiction stories, volume 6, 1944.* New York: DAW Books, 1981, 368 p., paper, anth.

16946 *Isaac Asimov presents The great science fiction stories, volume 7, 1945.* New York: DAW Books, 1982, 368 p., paper, anth.

16947 *Isaac Asimov presents The great science fiction stories, volume 8, 1946.* New York: DAW Books, 1982, 368 p., paper, anth.

16948 *Isaac Asimov presents The great SF stories, volume 9, 1947.* New York: DAW Books, 1983, 366 p., paper, anth.

16949 *Isaac Asimov presents The great science fiction stories, volume 10, 1948.* New York: DAW Books, 1983, 287 p., paper, anth.

16950 *Isaac Asimov presents The great science fiction stories, volume 11, 1949.* New York: DAW Books, 1984, 317 p., paper, anth.

16951 *Isaac Asimov presents The great SF stories 12 (1950).* New York: DAW Books, 1984, 319 p., paper, anth.

16952 *Isaac Asimov presents The great SF stories #13 (1951).* New York: DAW Books, 1985, xii+337 p., paper, anth.

16953 *Isaac Asimov presents The great SF stories #14 (1952).* New York: DAW Books, 1986, 352 p., paper, anth.

16954 *Isaac Asimov presents The great SF stories #15 (1953)*. New York: DAW Books, 1986, 352 p., paper, anth.

16955 *Isaac Asimov presents The great SF stories #16 (1954)*. New York: DAW Books, 1987, 350 p., paper, anth.

16956 *Isaac Asimov presents The great SF stsories #17 (1955)*. New York: DAW Books, 1988, 349 p., cloth, anth.

16957 *Isaac Asimov presents The great SF stsories #18 (1956)*. New York: DAW Books, 1988, 366 p., cloth, anth.

16958 *Isaac Asimov presents The great SF stories #19 (1957)*. New York: DAW Books, 1989, 350 p., paper, anth.

16959 *Isaac Asimov presents The great SF stories #20 (1958)*. New York: DAW Books, 1990, 351 p., paper, anth.

16960 *Isaac Asimov presents The great SF stories #21 (1959)*. New York: DAW Books, 1990, 347 p., paper, anth.

16961 *Isaac Asimov presents The great SF stories #22 (1959) [sic]*. New York: DAW Books, 1991, 351 p., paper, anth. [Cover title gives the correct year (1960)].

16962 *Isaac Asimov presents The great SF stories #23 (1961)*. New York: DAW Books, 1991, 367 p., paper, anth.

16963 *The new Hugo winners: award-winning science fiction stories*. New York: Wynwood Press, 1989, 320 p., cloth, anth.

16964 *Science fiction and fantasy story-a-month 1989 calendar*. Petaluma, CA: Pomegranate, 1988, [12] p., paper, anth. [A calendar with a short story for each month].

16965 *Visions of fantasy: tales from the masters*. New York: Doubleday, 1989, ix+180 p., cloth, anth.

MARTIN H. GREENBERG, *with Isaac Asimov & Terry Carr*

16927 *100 great fantasy short short stories*. Garden City, NY: Doubleday & Co., 1984, xviii+311 p., cloth, anth.

MARTIN H. GREENBERG, *with Isaac Asimov & George R. R. Martin*

17049 *The science fiction weight-loss book*. New York: Crown Publishers, 1983, v+249 p., cloth, anth.

MARTIN H. GREENBERG, *with Isaac Asimov & Joseph D. Olander*

16966 *100 great science fiction short short stories*. Garden City, NY: Doubleday & Co., 1978, xvi+270 p., cloth, anth.

16967 *The future I*. New York: Fawcett Crest, 1980, 381 p., paper, anth.

16968 *The future in question*. New York: Fawcett Crest, 1980, 381 p., paper, anth.

16969 *Isaac Asimov's Science fiction treasury*. New York: Bonanza Books, 1980, 786 p., cloth, anth. [Includes *The future in question* and *Space mail*].

16970 *Microcosmic tales: 100 wondrous science fiction short-short stories*. New York: Taplinger Publishing Co., 1980, 325 p., cloth, anth.

Science fiction treasury—SEE: *Isaac Asimov's Science fiction treasury*.

16971 *Space mail*. New York: Fawcett Crest, 1980, 416 p., paper, anth.

MARTIN H. GREENBERG, *with Isaac Asimov & Patricia S. Warrick*

16972 *Machines that think: the best science fiction stories about robots and computers*. New York: Holt, Rinehart & Winston, 1984, 627 p., cloth, anth.

MARTIN H. GREENBERG, *with Isaac Asimov & Carol-Lynn Rössel Waugh*

16973 *13 horrors of Halloween*. New York: Avon, 1983, 175 p., paper, anth.

MARTIN H. GREENBERG, *with Isaac Asimov & Charles G. Waugh*

16974 *The 13 crimes of science fiction*. Garden City, NY: Doubleday & Co., 1979, 455 p., cloth, anth.

16975 *After the end*. Milwaukee, WI: Raintree Publishers, 1981, 48 p., cloth, anth.

Asimov's extraterrestrials—SEE: *Young extraterrestrials*.

16976 *Asimov's ghosts & monsters*. London: Armada, 1988, 413 p., paper, anth. [Includes *Young ghosts* and *Young monsters*].

Asimov's ghosts—SEE: *Young ghosts*.

Asimov's monsters—SEE: *Young monsters*.

Asimov's mutants—SEE: *Young mutants*.

16977 *Baker's dozen: thirteen short fantasy novels*. New York: Greenwich House, 1984, ix+612 p., cloth, anth.

16977A retitled: *The mammoth book of short fantasy novels*. London: Robinson Publishing, 1986, 612 p., paper, anth.

16978 *Baker's dozen: thirteen short science fiction novels*. New York: Bonanza Books, 1985, ix+574 p., cloth, anth.

16978A retitled: *The mammoth book of short science fiction novels.* London: Robinson Publishing, 1986, 612 p., paper, anth.

The best fantasy of the 19th century—SEE: *Isaac Asimov presents the best fantasy of the 19th century.*

The best horror and supernatural of the 19th century—SEE: *Isaac Asimov presents The best horror and supernatural of the 19th century.*

The best science fiction firsts—SEE: *Isaac Asimov presents The best science fiction firsts.*

The best science fiction of the 19th century—SEE: *Isaac Asimov presents The best science fiction of the 19th century.*

16979 *Bug awful.* Milwaukee, WI: Raintree Publishers, 1984, 48 p., cloth, anth. Martin Harry.

16980 *Catastrophes!* New York: Fawcett Crest, 1981, 413 p., paper, anth.

16981 *Caught in the organ draft: biology in science fiction.* New York: Farrar Straus Giroux, 1983, xi+276 p., cloth, anth.

16982 *Children of the future.* Milwaukee, WI: Raintree Publishers, 1984, 48 p., cloth, anth.

16983 *Comets.* New York: A Signet Book, New American Library, 1986, xii+339 p., paper, anth. ISAAC ASIMOV'S WONDERFUL WORLDS OF SCIENCE FICTION #4.

16984 *Computer crimes and capers.* Chicago: Academy Chicago Publishers, 1983, 235 p., cloth, anth.

16985 *Cosmic knights.* New York: A Signet Book, New American Library, 1985, 339 p., paper, anth. ISAAC ASIMOV'S MAGICAL WORLDS OF FANTASY #3.

16986 *Curses.* New York: A Signet Book, New American Library, 1989, 350 p., paper, anth. ISAAC ASIMOV'S MAGICAL WORLDS OF FANTASY #11.

16987 *The deadly sins and cardinal virtues of science fiction.* New York: Bonanza Books, 1982, 317, 350 p., cloth, anth. [Includes both books].

16988 *Dragon tales.* New York: Fawcett Crest, 1982, 318 p., paper, anth.

16989 *Earth invaded.* Milwaukee, WI: Raintree Publishers, 1982, 46 p., cloth, anth.

16990 *Encounters.* London: Headline, 1988, 399 p., paper, anth.

Extraterrestrials—SEE: *Young extraterrestrials.*

16991 *Faeries: Isaac Asimov's magical worlds of fantasy.* New York: A Roc Book, 1991, 374 p., paper, coll. ISAAC ASIMOV'S MAGICAL WORLDS OF FANTASY (UNNUMBERED).

16992 *Fantastic creatures: an anthology of fantasy and science fiction.* New York: Franklin Watts, 1981, 155 p., cloth, anth.

16993 *Flying saucers.* New York: Fawcett Crest, 1982, 349 p., paper, anth.

16994 *Ghosts.* New York: A Signet Book, New American Library, 1988, 347 p., paper, anth. ISAAC ASIMOV'S MAGICAL WORLDS OF FANTASY #10.

Ghosts & monsters—SEE: *Asimov's Ghosts & monsters.*

16995 *Giants.* New York: A Signet Books, New American Library, 1985, 351 p., paper, anth. ISAAC ASIMOV'S MAGICAL WORLDS OF FANTASY #5.

16996 *Great science fiction stories by the world's great scientists.* New York: Donald I. Fine, 1985, 400 p., cloth, anth.

Great tales of classic science fiction—SEE: *The mammoth book of classic science fiction: short novels of the 1930s.*

16997 *Hallucination orbit: psychology in science fiction.* New York: Farrar Straus Giroux, 1983, 279 p., cloth, anth.

16998 *The immortals.* Milwaukee, WI: Raintree Publishers, 1984, 48 p., cloth, anth.

16999 *Intergalactic empires.* New York: A Signet Book, New American Library, 1983, 303 p., paper, anth. ISAAC ASIMOV'S WONDERFUL WORLDS OF SCIENCE FICTION #1.

17000 *Invasions.* New York: A Roc Book, 1990, 382 p., paper, anth. ISAAC ASIMOV'S WONDERFUL WORLDS OF SCIENCE FICTION #10.

17001 *Isaac Asimov presents Tales of the occult: stories.* Buffalo, NY: Prometheus Books, 1989, 354 p., cloth, anth.

17002 *Isaac Asimov presents The best fantasy of the 19th century.* New York: Beaufort Books, 1982, 368 p., cloth, anth.

17003 *Isaac Asimov presents The best horror and supernatural of the 19th century.* New York: Beaufort Books, 1983, 368 p., cloth, anth.

17004 *Isaac Asimov presents The best science fiction firsts.* New York: Beaufort Books, 1984, 249 p., cloth, anth.

17005 *Isaac Asimov presents The best science fiction of the 19th century.* New York: Beaufort Books, 1981, 316 p., cloth, anth.

17006 *Isaac Asimov's Magical worlds of fantasy: Witches & wizards.* New York: Bonanza Books, 1985, 649 p., cloth, anth. [Includes both volumes].

17007 *The last man on Earth.* New York: Fawcett Crest, 1982, 352 p., paper, anth.

17008 *Mad scientists.* Milwaukee, WI: Raintree Publishers, 1982, 48 p., cloth, anth.

17009 *Magical wishes.* New York: A Signet Book, New American Library, 1986, 350 p., paper, anth. ISAAC ASIMOV'S MAGICAL WORLDS OF FANTASY #7.

Magical worlds of fantasy—SEE: *Isaac Asimov's Magical worlds of fantasy.*

17010 *The Mammoth book of classic science fiction: short novels of the 1930s.* London: Robinson, 1988, xiii+572 p., paper, anth.

17010A retitled: *Great tales of classic science fiction.* New York: Galahad, 1990, 498 p., cloth, anth.

17011 *The mammoth book of golden age science fiction: short novels of the 1940s.* New York: Carroll & Graf, 1989, 504 p., paper, anth.

17012 *The mammoth book of new world science fiction: short novels of the 1960s.* New York: Carroll & Graf, 1991, 506 p., paper, anth.

The mammoth book of short fantasy novels—SEE: *Baker's dozen: thirteen short fantasy novels.*

The mammoth book of short science fiction novels—SEE: *Baker's dozen: thirteen short science fiction novels.*

17013 *The mammoth book of vintage science fiction: short novels of the 1950s.* London: Robinson, 1990, 503 p., paper, anth.

17014 *Monsters.* New York: A Signet Book, New American Library, 1988, 349 p., paper, anth. ISAAC ASIMOV'S WONDERFUL WORLDS OF SCIENCE FICTION #8.

17015 *Mutants.* Milwaukee, WI: Raintree Publishers, 1982, 46 p., cloth, anth.

Mutants—SEE: *Young mutants.*

Mythic beasts—SEE: *Mythical beasties.*

17016 *Mythical beasties.* New York: A Signet Book, New American Library, 1986, 343 p., paper, anth. ISAAC ASIMOV'S MAGICAL WORLDS OF FANTASY #6.

17016A retitled: *Mythic beasts.* London: Robinson, 1988, 343 p., paper, anth.

17017 *Robots.* New York: A Signet Book, New American Library, 1989, 351 p., paper, anth. ISAAC ASIMOV'S WONDERFUL WORLDS OF SCIENCE FICTION #9.

17018 *Science fiction A to Z: a dictionary of great S.F. themes.* Boston: Houghton Mifflin Co., 1982, xvii+651 p., cloth, anth.

17019 *The science fictional Olympics.* New York: A Signet Book, New American Library, 1984, 356 p., paper, anth. ISAAC ASIMOV'S WONDERFUL WORLDS OF SCIENCE FICTION #2.

17020 *The science fictional solar system.* New York: Harper & Row, 1979, ix+317 p., cloth, anth.

17021 *The seven cardinal virtues of science fiction.* New York: Fawcett Crest, 1981, 350 p., paper, anth.

17022 *The seven deadly sins of science fiction.* New York: Fawcett Crest, 1980, 317 p., paper, anth.

17023 *Sherlock Holmes through time and space.* New York: Bluejay Book, 1984, 355 p., cloth, anth.

17024 *Space mail, volume II.* New York: Fawcett Crest, 1982, 380 p., paper, anth.

17025 *Space shuttles.* New York: A Signet Book, New American Library, 1987, 384 p., paper, anth. ISAAC ASIMOV'S WONDERFUL WORLDS OF SCIENCE FICTION #7.

17026 *Spells.* New York: A Signet Book, New American Library, 1985, 350 p., paper, anth. ISAAC ASIMOV'S MAGICAL WORLDS OF FANTASY #4.

17027 *Starships.* New York: Fawcett Crest, 1983, 342 p., paper, anth.

17028 *Supermen.* New York: A Signet Book, New American Library, 1984, 350 p., paper, anth. ISAAC ASIMOV'S WONDERFUL WORLDS OF SCIENCE FICTION #3.

Tales of the occult—SEE: *Isaac Asimov presents Tales of the occult.*

17029 *Thinking machines.* Milwaukee, WI: Raintree Publishers, 1981, 48 p., cloth, anth.

17030 *Those amazing electronic thinking machines: an anthology of robot and computer stories* / by Isaac Asimov, Martin S. Greenberg & Charles H. Waugh [sic]. New York: Franklin Watts, 1983, 147 p., cloth, anth.

17031 *Time warps.* Milwaukee, WI: Raintree Publishers, 1984, 48 p., cloth, anth.

17032 *Tin stars.* New York: A Signet Book, New American Library, 1986, 351 p., paper, anth. ISAAC ASIMOV'S WONDERFUL WORLDS OF SCIENCE FICTION #5.

17033 *Tomorrow's TV.* Milwaukee, WI: Raintree Publishers, 1982, 48 p., cloth, anth.

17034 *Travels through time.* Milwaukee, WI: Raintree Publishers, 1981, 47 p., cloth, anth.

17035 *TV: 2000.* New York: Fawcett Crest, 1982, 352 p., paper, anth.

17036 *The twelve frights of Christmas.* New York: Avon, 1986, 263 p., paper, anth.

17037 *Wild inventions.* Milwaukee: Raintree Publishers, 1981, 46 p., cloth, anth.

17038 *Witches.* New York: A Signet Book, New American Library, 1984, 350 p., paper, anth. ISAAC ASIMOV'S MAGICAL WOR-LDS OF FANTASY #2.

17039 *Wizards.* New York: A Signet Book, New American Library, 1983, 303 p., paper, anth. ISAAC ASIMOV'S MAGICAL WOR-LDS OF FANTASY #1.

17040 *Young extraterrestrials.* New York: Harper & Row, 1984, xiv+240 p., cloth, anth.

17040A retitled: *Asimov's extraterrestrials.* London: Dragon Books, 1986, 204 p., paper, anth.

17040B retitled: *Extraterrestrials.* New York: Harper & Row, 1988, xiv+240 p., paper, anth.

17041 *Young ghosts.* New York: Harper & Row, 1985, xiv+210 p., cloth, anth.

17041A retitled: *Asimov's ghosts.* London: Dragon Books, 1986, 202 p., paper, anth.

17042 *Young immortals.* New York: Harper & Row, 1985, vii+213 p., cloth, anth.

17043 *Young monsters.* New York: Harper & Row, 1985, 213 p., cloth, anth.

17043A retitled: *Asimov's monsters.* London: Dragon Books, 1986, 203 p., paper, anth.

17044 *Young mutants.* New York: Harper & Row, 1984, 256 p., cloth, anth.

17044A retitled: *Asimov's mutants.* London: Dragon Books, 1986, 201 p., paper, anth.

17044B retitled: *Mutants.* New York: Harper & Row, 1988, 256 p., paper, anth.

17045 *Young star travelers.* New York: Harper & Row, 1986, xiii+209 p., cloth, anth.

17046 *Young witches & warlocks.* New York: Harper & Row, 1987, xvi+207 p., cloth, anth.

MARTIN H. GREENBERG, *with Isaac Asimov & David Clark Yeager*

17047 *Fantastic reading: stories and activities for grades 5-8.* Glenview, IL: A Goodyear Book, Scott, Foresman & Co., 1984, xiii+169 p., paper?, anth.

MARTIN H. GREENBERG, *with Isaac Asimov & George Zebrowski*

17052 *Creations: the quest for origins in story and science.* New York: Crown Publishers, 1983, xii+351 p., cloth, anth.

MARTIN H. GREENBERG, *with Gregory Benford*

17757 *Alternate empires.* New York: Bantam Books, 1989, 291 p., paper, anth. WHAT MIGHT HAVE BEEN? #1.

17758 *Alternate heroes.* New York: Bantam Books, 1990, 354 p., paper, anth. WHAT MIGHT HAVE BEEN? #2.

17759 *Alternate wars.* New York, Toronto: Spectra, Bantam Books, 1991, viii+296 p., paper, anth. WHAT MIGHT HAVE BEEN? #3.

17760 *Hitler victorious: eleven stories of the German victory in World War II.* New York: Garland Publishing, 1986, 299 p., cloth, anth.

17761 *Nuclear war.* New York: Ace Books, 1988, 231 p., paper, anth.

17762 *What might have been? volumes I and II.* New York: Bantam Books, 1990, 542 p., cloth, anth. WHAT MIGHT HAVE BEEN? #1-2.

MARTIN H. GREENBERG, *with Robert Bloch*

18198 *Psycho-paths.* New York: Tor Horror, A Tom Doherty Associates Book, 1991, xxii+295 p., cloth, anth. [Greenberg's contribution is anonymous].

MARTIN H. GREENBERG, *with John W. Campbell*

19254 *Astounding science fiction, July, 1939.* Carbondale & Edwardsville, Il: Southern Illinois University Press, 1981, ix+180 p., cloth, anth. [A facsimile reproduction of the original magazine issue, with notes and commentary by Greenberg].

MARTIN H. GREENBERG, *with Terry Carr*

19507 *A treasury of modern fantasy.* New York: Avon, 1981, xvii+588 p., paper, anth.

MARTIN H. GREENBERG, *with Ralph S. Clem & Joseph D. Olander*

20170 *The city: 2000 A.D.: urban life through science fiction.* Greenwich, CT: A Fawcett Crest Book, Fawcett Publications, 1976, 304 p., paper, anth.

20171 *No room for man: population and the future through science fiction.* Totowa, NJ: Rowman & Littlefield, 1979, 247 p., cloth, anth.

MARTIN H. GREENBERG, *with Tim Cottrill & Charles G. Waugh*

20644 *Science fiction and fantasy series and sequels: a bibliography, volume 1: books.* New York, London: Garland Publishing, 1986, xix+398 p., cloth, nonf. [Only volume published].

MARTIN H. GREENBERG, *with Gordon R. Dickson & Charles G. Waugh*

21904 *Robot warriors.* New York: Ace Books, 1991, x+240 p., paper, anth.

MARTIN H. GREENBERG, *with David Drake & Charles G. Waugh*

22174 *The eternal city.* New York: Baen Books, 1990, 280 p., paper, anth.
22175 *Space dreadnoughts.* New York: Ace Books, 1990, xiii+220 p., paper, anth.
22176 *Space gladiators.* New York: Ace Books, 1989, 310 p., paper, anth.
22177 *Space infantry.* New York: Ace Books, 1989, xii+244 p., paper, anth.

MARTIN H. GREENBERG, *with Charles Elkins & Patrick A. McCarthy*

22546 *The legacy of Olaf Stapledon: critical essays and an unpublished manuscript.* New York: Greenwood Press, 1989, x+132 p., cloth, nonf. anth. CONTRIBUTIONS TO THE STUDY OF SCIENCE FICTION AND FANTASY #34.

MARTIN H. GREENBERG, *with Edward L. Ferman*

23040 *The Magazine of fantasy and science fiction, April 1965.* Carbondale & Edwardsville, IL: Southern Illinois University Press, 1981, x+157 p., cloth, anth. [A facsimile of the April 1965 issue of this magazine, with notes and commentary by Greenberg].

MARTIN H. GREENBERG, *with Alan Dean Foster*

23371 *Smart dragons, foolish elves.* New York: Ace Books, 1991, xi+340 p., paper, anth.

MARTIN H. GREENBERG, *with Ed Gorman*

24159 *Stalkers: all new tales of terror and suspense.* Arlington Heights, IL: Dark Harvest, 1989, 310 p., cloth, anth.

MARTIN H. GREENBERG, *with Rosalind M. Greenberg*

24520 *Horse fantastic.* New York: DAW Books, 1991, xii+314 p., paper, anth.
24521 *Phantoms.* New York: DAW Books, 1989, 270 p., paper, anth.

MARTIN H. GREENBERG, *with Rosalind M. Greenberg & Charles G. Waugh*

24522 *14 vicious valentines.* New York: Avon Books, 1988, vii+196 p., paper, anth.

MARTIN H. GREENBERG, *with Joe Haldeman & Charles G. Waugh*

24523 *Body armor: 2000.* New York: Ace Science Fiction Books, 1986, 311 p., paper, anth.
24524 *Spacefighters.* New York: Ace Books, 1988, 296 p., paper, anth.
24525 *Supertanks.* New York: Ace Science Fiction Books, 1987, 262 p., paper, anth.

MARTIN H. GREENBERG, *with Harvey A. Katz & Patricia S. Warrick*

24526 *Introductory psychology through science fiction, 2nd ed.* Chicago: Rand McNally Publishing Co., 1977, vii+550 p., paper, anth.

MARTIN H. GREENBERG, *with Damon Knight & Joseph D. Olander*

08340 *First flight.* New York: Lancer, 1963, 160 p., paper, anth.
24527 retitled: *First voyages.* New York: Avon, 1981, 373 p., paper, anth. [An expanded and reworked version of Knight's *First flight* (see 08340)].

MARTIN H. GREENBERG, *with Barry N. Malzberg & Joseph D. Olander*

24528 *Neglected visions.* Garden City, NY: Doubleday & Co., 1979, ix+211 p., cloth, anth.

MARTIN H. GREENBERG, *with Richard Matheson & Charles G. Waugh*

24529 *The Twilight Zone: the original stories.* New York: Avon, 1985, 550 p., paper, anth.

MARTIN H. GREENBERG, *with Frank D. McSherry Jr. & Charles G. Waugh*

24530 *Baseball 3000.* New York: Elsevier/Nelson Books, 1981, vi+210 p., cloth, anth.
24531 *Cinemonsters.* Lake Geneva, WI: TSR Inc., 1987, 319 p., paper, anth.
24532 *Civil war ghosts.* Little Rock, AR: August House Publishers, 1991, 204 p., paper, anth.
24533 *Dixie ghosts: haunting, spine-chilling stories from the American South.* Nashville,

TN: Rutledge Hill Press, 1988, 208 p., paper, anth.

24534 *Eastern ghosts: haunting, spine-chilling stories from New York, Pennsylvania, New Jersey, Delaware, Maryland, and the District of Columbia.* Nashville, TN: Rutledge Hill Press, 1990, x+208 p., paper, anth.

24535 *Ghosts of the heartland: haunting, spine-chilling stories from the American midwest.* Nashville, TN: Rutledge Hill Press, 1990, 210 p., paper, anth.

24536 *Great American ghost stories.* Nashville, TN: Rutledge Hill Press, 1991, 512 p., cloth, anth.

24537 *Haunted New England: classic tales of the strange and supernatural.* Dublin, NH: Yankee Books, 1988, 287 p., cloth, anth.

24538 *Hollywood ghosts: haunting, spine-chilling stories from America's film capital.* Nashville, TN: Rutledge Hill Press, 1991, 210 p., paper, anth.

24539 *New England ghosts: haunting, spine-chilling stories from the New England states.* Nashville, TN: Rutledge Hill Press, 1990, 213 p., paper, anth.

24540 *Nightmares in Dixie: thirteen horror tales from the American South.* Little Rock, AR: August House, 1987, 260 p., cloth, anth.

24541 *Pirate ghosts of the American coast: stories of hauntings at sea.* Little Rock, AR: August House, 1988, 206 p., paper, anth.

24542 *Red Jack.* New York: DAW Books, 1988, 333 p., paper, anth.

24543 *Strange Maine.* Augusta, ME: Lance Tapley, 1986, 295 p., paper, anth.

24544 *Treasury of American horror stories.* New York: Bonanza Books, 1985, xii+670 p., cloth, anth.

24545 *Western ghosts: haunting, spine-chilling stories from the American West.* Nashville, TN: Rutledge Hill Press, 1990, 215 p., paper, anth.

24546 *Yankee witches.* Augusta, ME: Lance Tapley, Publisher, 1988, 315 p., paper, anth.

MARTIN H. GREENBERG, *with Walter M. Miller Jr.*

24547 *Beyond armageddon: twenty-one sermons to the dead.* New York: Donald I. Fine, 1985, 387 p., cloth, anth.

MARTIN H. GREENBERG, *with John W. Milstead & Joseph D. Olander & Patricia S. Warrick*

24548 *Social problems through science fiction.* New York: St. Martin's Press, 1975, xvi+356 p., cloth, anth.

MARTIN H. GREENBERG, *with Francis M. Nevins Jr.*

24549 *Hitchcock in prime time.* New York: Avon, 1985, 356 p., paper, anth.

MARTIN H. GREENBERG, *with William F. Nolan*

24550 *The Bradbury chronicles: stories in honor of Ray Bradbury.* New York: A Roc Book, 1991, viii+328 p., cloth, anth. [A festschrift honoring Ray Bradbury].

24551 *Science fiction origins.* New York: Fawcett Popular Library, 1980, 319 p., paper, anth.

24552 *Urban horrors.* Arlington Heights, IL: Dark Harvest, 1990, 246 p., cloth, anth.

MARTIN H. GREENBERG, *with Andre Norton*

24553 *Catfantastic: nine lives and fifteen tales.* New York: DAW Books, 1989, viii+320 p., paper, anth.

24554 *Catfantastic II.* New York: DAW Books, 1991, 318 p., paper, anth.

MARTIN H. GREENBERG, *with Joseph D. Olander*

24555 *Arthur C. Clarke.* New York: Taplinger Publishing Co., 1977, 254 p., cloth, nonf. anth.

24556 *Criminal justice through science fiction.* New York, London: New Viewpoints, 1977, xvi+239 p., cloth, anth.

24557 *International relations through science fiction.* New York: New Viewpoints, 1978, xviii+236 p., cloth, anth.

24558 *Isaac Asimov.* New York: Taplinger Publishing Co., 1977, 247 p., cloth, nonf. anth.

24559 *Philip K. Dick.* New York: Taplinger Publishing Co., 1983, 256 p., cloth, nonf. anth.

24560 *Ray Bradbury.* New York: Taplinger Publishing Co., 1980, 248 p., cloth, nonf. anth.

24561 *Robert A. Heinlein.* New York: Taplinger Publishing Co., 1978, 268 p., cloth, nonf. anth.

24562 *Science fiction of the fifties.* New York: Avon, 1979, xxiii+438 p., paper, anth.

24563 *Time of passage.* New York: Taplinger Publishing Co., 1978, 292 p., cloth, anth.

24564 *Tomorrow, Inc.: SF stories about business.* New York: Taplinger Publishing Co., 1976, 256 p., cloth, anth.

24565 *Ursula K. Le Guin.* New York: Taplinger Publishing Co., 1979, 258 p., cloth, nonf. anth.

MARTIN H. GREENBERG, *with Joseph D. Olander & Patricia S. Warrick*

24566 *Run to starlight: sports through science fiction.* New York: Delacorte Press, 1975, vi+383 p., cloth, anth.

24567 *Science fiction: contemporary mythology: the SFWA-SFRA anthology.* New York: Harper & Row, 1978, xviii+476 p., cloth, anth. [Includes some nonfiction].

MARTIN H. GREENBERG, *with Joseph D. Olander & Patricia S. Warrick & Val Clear*

20165 *Marriage and the family through science fiction.* New York: St. Martin's Press, 1976, xiv+358 p., paper, anth.

MARTIN H. GREENBERG, *with Joseph D. Olander & Charles G. Waugh*

24568 *Mysterious visions: great science fiction by masters of the mystery.* New York: St. Martin's Press, 1979, xxvi+516 p., cloth, anth.

MARTIN H. GREENBERG, *with Frederik Pohl & Joseph D. Olander*

24569 *Galaxy: thirty years of innovative science fiction.* Chicago: Playboy Press, 1980, xiii+465 p., cloth, anth.

24570 *The great science fiction series: stories from the best of the series from 1944 to 1980 by twenty all-time favorite writers.* New York: Harper & Row, 1980, x+419 p., cloth, anth.

24571 *Science fiction of the forties.* New York: Avon, 1978, 377 p., paper, anth.

24572 *Worlds of if.* New York: Bluejay Books, 1986, 438 p., cloth, anth.

MARTIN H. GREENBERG, *with Patrick L. Price*

24573 *Fantastic stories: tales of the weird & wondrous.* Lake Geneva, WI: TSR Inc., 1987, 253 p., paper, anth.

MARTIN H. GREENBERG, *with Bill Pronzini & Barry N. Malzberg*

24574 *The Arbor House treasury of horror and the supernatural.* New York: Arbor House, 1981, 599 p., paper, anth.

24574A retitled: *Great tales of horror & the supernatural.* Secaucus, NJ: Galahad Books, Castle Books, 1985, 597 p., cloth, anth. [Abridged edition].

24574B retitled: *Classic tales of horror and the supernatural.* New York: Quill, 1991, 599 p., paper, anth.

24574C retitled: *The giant book of horror stories.* ?: Magpie, 1991, 597 p., paper, anth. [Abridged edition].

Classic tales of horror and the supernatural—SEE: *The Arbor House treasury of horror and the supernatural.*

The giant book of horror stories—SEE: *The Arbor House treasury of horror and the supernatural.*

Great tales of horror & the supernatural—SEE: *The Arbor House treasury of horror and the supernatural.*

MARTIN H. GREENBERG, *with Eric S. Rabkin & Joseph D. Olander*

24575 *The end of the world.* Carbondale & Edwardsville, IL: Southern Illinois University Press, 1983, xv+204 p., cloth, nonf. anth.

24576 *No place else: explorations in utopian and dystopian fiction.* Carbondale & Edwardsville, IL: Southern Illinois University Press, 1983, 278 p., cloth, nonf. anth.

MARTIN H. GREENBERG, *with Fred Saberhagen*

24577 *Machines that kill.* New York: Ace Science Fiction Books, 1984, 326 p., paper, anth.

MARTIN H. GREENBERG, *with Stanley Schmidt*

24578 *Unknown worlds: tales from beyond.* New York: Galahad Books, 1988, 517 p., cloth, anth.

MARTIN H. GREENBERG, *with Carol Serling & Charles G. Waugh*

Night gallery reader—SEE: *Rod Serling's Night gallery reader.*

24579 *Rod Serling's Night gallery reader.* New York: Dembner Books, 1987, x+326 p., cloth, anth.

MARTIN H. GREENBERG, *with Robert Silverberg*

24580 *The horror hall of fame.* New York: Carroll & Graf, 1991, 416 p., cloth, anth.

MARTIN H. GREENBERG, *with Robert Silverberg & Joseph D. Olander*

24581 *The Arbor House treasury of great science fiction short novels.* New York: Arbor House, 1980, x+768 p., paper, anth.
24581A retitled: *Worlds imagined: 14 short science fiction novels.* New York: Avenel Books, 1989, x+704 p., cloth, anth.
24582 *The Arbor House treasury of modern science fiction.* New York: Priam Books, Arbor House, 1980, xii+754 p., paper, anth.
24582A retitled: *Great science fiction of the 20th century.* New York: Avenel Books, 1987, x+726 p., cloth, anth.
24583 *The Arbor House treasury of science fiction masterpieces.* New York: Arbor House, 1983, 538 p., cloth, anth.
24583A retitled: *Great tales of science fiction.* Secaucus, NJ: Galahad Books, Castle Books, 1985, 529 p., cloth, anth. [Abridged edition].
24584 *Car sinister.* New York: Avon, 1979, 253 p., paper, anth.
24585 *Dawn of time: prehistory through science fiction.* New York: Elsevier/Nelson, 1979, 224 p., cloth, anth.
24586 *The fantasy hall of fame.* New York: Arbor House, 1983, 431 p., cloth, anth.
24586A retitled: *The mammoth book of fantasy all-time greats.* London: Robinson, 1988, 431 p., paper, anth.
 Great science fiction of the 20th century—SEE: *The Arbor House treasury of modern science fiction.*
 Great tales of science fiction—SEE: *The Arbor House treasury of science fiction masterpieces.*
 The mammoth book of fantasy all-time greats—SEE: *The fantasy hall of fame.*
24587 *The time travelers: a science fiction quartet.* New York: Donald I. Fine, 1985, 284 p., cloth, anth.
 Worlds imagined—SEE: *The Arbor House treasury of great science fiction short novels.*

MARTIN H. GREENBERG, *with Robert Silverberg & Charles G. Waugh*

24588 *Neanderthals.* New York: A Signet Book, New American Library, 1987, 351 p., paper, anth. ISAAC ASIMOV'S WON-DERFUL WORLDS OF SCIENCE FICTION #6.

24589 *The science fictional dinosaur.* New York: An Avon Flare Book, 1982, 224 p., paper, anth.

MARTIN H. GREENBERG, *with S. M. Stirling & Frank D. McSherry Jr. & Charles G. Waugh*

24590 *The fantastic Civil War.* Riverdale, NY: Baen Books, 1991, 307 p., paper, anth.
24591 *Fantastic World War II.* New York: Baen Books, 1990, 281 p., paper, anth.

MARTIN H. GREENBERG, *with Marshall B. Tymn & L. W. Currey & Joseph D. Olander*

20899 *Index to stories in thematic anthologies of science fiction.* Boston: G. K. Hall & Co., 1978, xiii+193 p., cloth, nonf. REFERENCE PUBLICATION IN SCIENCE FICTION.

MARTIN H. GREENBERG, *with Patricia S. Warrick*

24592 *The new awareness: religion through science fiction.* New York: Delacorte Press, 1975, xii+485 p., cloth, anth.

MARTIN H. GREENBERG, *with Patricia S. Warrick & Charles G. Waugh*

24593 *Science fiction: the Science Fiction Research Association anthology.* New York: Harper & Row, 1988, xi+522 p., cloth, anth.

MARTIN H. GREENBERG, *with Charles G. Waugh*

24594 *Alternative histories: eleven stories of the world as it might have been.* New York & London: Garland Publishing, 1986, 363 p., cloth, anth.
24595 *The Arbor House celebrity book of horror stories.* New York: Arbor House, 1982, 448 p., cloth, anth.
24596 *Back from the dead.* New York: DAW Books, 1991, 364 p., paper, anth.
24597 *Baker's dozen: 13 short horror novels.* New York: Bonanza Books, 1987, ix+758 p., cloth, anth.
24598 *Battlefields beyond tomorrow: science fiction war stories.* New York: Bonanza Books, 1987, xiii+650 p., cloth, anth.
24599 *Cults! an anthology of secret societies, sects, and the supernatural.* New York: Beaufort Books, 1983, 358 p., cloth, anth.
24600 *Cults of horror.* New York: DAW Books, 1990, 350 p., paper, anth.

24601 *Devil .vorshippers.* New York: DAW Books, 1990, 348 p., paper, anth.

24602 *East Coast ghosts.* Wilmington, DE: Middle Atlantic Press, 1989, 310 p., paper, anth.

24603 *Hollywood unreel: fantasies about Hollywood and the movies.* New York: Taplinger Publishing Co., 1982, 308 p., cloth, anth.

24604 *House shudders: an anthology of haunted house stories.* New York: DAW Books, 1987, 332 p., paper, anth.

24605 *Love, 3000.* New York: Elsevier/Nelson Books, 1980, 240 p., cloth, anth.

24606 *Vamps: an anthology of female vampire stories.* New York: DAW Books, 1987, 365 p., paper, anth.

MARTIN H. GREENBERG, *with Charles G. Waugh & Jenny-Lynn Waugh*

24607 *101 science fiction stories.* New York: Avenel Books, 1986, xvii+651 p., cloth, anth.

MARTIN H. GREENBERG, *with Robert Weinberg*

24608 *Lovecraft's legacy.* New York: Tor, A Tom Doherty Associates Book, 1990, 334 p., cloth, anth.

MARTIN H. GREENBERG, *with Robert Weinberg & Stefan R. Dziemianowicz*

22354 *Famous fantastic mysteries: 30 great tales of fantasy and horror from the classic pulp magazines Famous fantastic mysteries & Fantastic novels.* New York: Gramercy Books, 1991, xiii+449 p., cloth, anth.

22355 *Rivals of Weird tales: 30 great fantasy & horror stories freom the weird fiction pulps.* New York: Bonanza Books, 1990, xx+486 p., cloth, anth.

22356 *Weird tales: 32 unearthed terrors.* New York: Bonanza Books, 1988, xv+665 p., cloth, anth.

MARTIN H. GREENBERG, *with Jane Yolen*

24609 *Things that go bump in the night: a collection of original stories.* New York: Harper & Row, 1989, 280 p., cloth, anth.

24610 *Vampires: a collection of original stories.* New York: HarperCollinsPublishers, 1991, xi+228 p., cloth, anth.

24611 *Werewolves: a collection of original stories.* New York: Harper & Row, 1988, xi+271 p., cloth, anth.

MARTIN H. GREENBERG, *with Jane Yolen & Charles G. Waugh*

24612 *Dragons & dreams: a collection of new fantasy and science fiction stories.* New York: Harper & Row, 1986, x+180 p., cloth, anth.

24613 *Spaceships & spells: a collection of new fantasy and science-fiction stories.* New York: Harper & Row, 1987, 182 p., cloth, anth.

GREENBERG, Rosalind (Elizabeth) M(orton), 1951-

with Martin H. Greenberg

24520 *Horse fantastic.* New York: DAW Books, 1991, xii+314 p., paper, anth.

24521 *Phantoms.* New York: DAW Books, 1989, 270 p., paper, anth.

with Martin H. Greenberg & Charles G. Waugh

24522 *14 vicious valentines.* New York: Avon Books, 1988, vii+196 p., paper, anth.

GREENBERGER, Robert (Edward), 1958- , *with Carmen Carter & Peter David & Michael Jan Friedman*

19541 *Doomsday world.* New York, London: Pocket Books, 1990, xi+276 p., paper, novel. STAR TREK: THE NEXT GENERATION #12.

GREENBLATT, Stephen (Jay), 1943-

24614 *Three modern satirists: Waugh, Orwell, and Huxley.* New Haven, CT: Yale University Press, 1965, xi+125 p., cloth, nonf.

GREENBURG, Dan, 1936-

The guardian—SEE: *The nanny.*

24615 *The nanny.* New York: Macmillan Publishing Co., 1987, 229 p., cloth, novel.

24615A retitled: *The guardian.* New York: Berkley Books, 1990, 231 p., paper, novel.

24616 *The witchfires of Leth: a Crossroads adventure in the world of C. J. Cherryh's Morgaine.* New York: Tor, A Tom Doherty Associates Book, 1987, 27+[224] p., paper, novel. CROSSROADS ADVENTURE; MORGAINE SEQUEL.

GREENE, David L(ouis), 1944- , with Dick Martin

24617 *The Oz scrapbook.* New York: Random House, 1977, 182 p., cloth, nonf.

GREENE, Douglas G(eorge), 1944- , with Peter E. Hanff

24618 *Bibliographia Oziana: a concise bibliographical checklist of the Oz books by L. Frank Baum and his successors.* Kinderhook, IL: International Wizard of Oz Club, 1976, 103 p., cloth?, nonf.

24619 *Bibliographia Oziana: a concise bibliographical checklist of the Oz books by L. Frank Baum and his successors, rev. and enl. ed.* Kinderhook, IL: International Wizard of Oz Club, 1988, 146 p., cloth?, nonf.

*GREENE, (Henry) Graham, 1904-1991

*GREENE, Jay E(lihu), 1914-1987

GREENE, Liz, 1946-

24620 *The dreamer of the vine.* New York: W. W. Norton & Co., 1980, 282 p., cloth, novel.
24620A retitled: *Nostradamus: a novel.* Toronto, New York: Bantam Books, 1983, 256 p., paper, novel.
　　Nostradamus: a novel—SEE: *The dreamer of the vine.*
24621 *The puppet master: a novel.* London, New York: Arkana, 1987, 305 p., paper, novel.

GREENE, Sonia—SEE: Davis, Sonia H.

GREENER, William O.—SEE: Gerrare, Wirt

GREENFIELD, Irving A., 1928-

24622 *Aton.* New York: Avon, 1975, 310 p., paper, novel.
24623 *Barracuda.* New York: Arbor House, 1978, 245 p., cloth, novel.
24624 *Battle stations.* New York: Zebra Books, Kensington Publishing Corp., 1985, 255 p., paper, novel. DEPTH FORCE #4.
24625 *Bloody seas.* New York: Zebra Books, Kensington Publishing Corp., 1985, 225 p., paper, novel. DEPTH FORCE #3.
24626 *Death cruise.* New York: Zebra Books, Kensington Publishing Corp., 1988, 253 p., paper, novel. DEPTH FORCE #10.

24627 *Death dive.* New York: Zebra Books, Kensington Publishing Corp., 1984, 235 p., paper, novel. DEPTH FORCE #2.
24628 *Deep kill.* New York: Zebra Books, Kensington Publishing Corp., 1986, 268 p., paper, novel. DEPTH FORCE #7.
24629 *Deep rescue.* New York: Zebra Books, Kensington Publishing Corp., 1990, 224 p., paper, novel. DEPTH FORCE #14. [No byline on title page].
24630 *Depth force.* New York: Zebra Books, Kensington Publishing Corp., 1984, 362 p., paper, novel. DEPTH FORCE #1.
24631 *Depth Force: Project discovery.* New York: Zebra Books, Kensington Publishing Corp., 1988, 397 p., paper, novel. DEPTH FORCE #9.
24632 *The face of Him.* New York: Manor Books, 1976, 186 p., paper, novel.
24633 *The fate of an eagle.* New York: Zebra Books, Kensington Publishing Corp., 1990, 349 p., paper, novel.
37816 *The gods' temptress.* New York: A Dell Book, 1978, 221 p., paper, novel.
24634 *Harbor of doom.* New York: Zebra Books, Kensington Publishing Corp., 1989, 253 p., paper, novel. DEPTH FORCE #12.
24635 *Ice island.* New York: Zebra Books, Kensington Publishing Corp., 1988, 254 p., paper, novel. DEPTH FORCE #11.
24636 *Julius Caesar is alive and well.* New York: Manor Books, 1977, 238 p., paper, novel.
24637 *Over the brink.* New York: Zebra Books, Kensington Publishing Corp., 1990, 287 p., paper, novel.
　　Project discovery—SEE: *Depth Force: Project discovery.*
24638 *Sea of flames.* New York: Zebra Books, Kensington Publishing Corp., 1986, 254 p., paper, novel. DEPTH FORCE #6.
　　Star trial—SEE: *The stars will judge.*
06329 *The stars will judge.* New York: A Dell Book, 1974, 160 p., paper, novel.
06329A retitled: *Star trial.* New York: Manor Books, 1977, 160 p., paper, novel.
24639 *Suicide run.* New York: Zebra Books, Kensington Publishing Corp., 1987, 254 p., paper, novel. DEPTH FORCE #8.
24640 *To savor the past.* New York: A Berkley Medallion Book, Berkley Publishing Corp., 1975, 220 p., paper, novel.
24641 *Torpedo tomb.* New York: Zebra Books, Kensington Publishing Corp., 1986, 236 p., paper, novel. DEPTH FORCE #5. [Cover title].
24642 *Torpedo treasure.* New York: Zebra Books, Kensington Publishing Corp.,

1991, 208 p., paper, novel. DEPTH FORCE #15. [No byline on title page].

24643 *Warmonger.* New York: Zebra Books, Kensington Publishing Corp., 1989, 255 p., paper, novel. DEPTH FORCE #13.

as CAMPO VERDE

24644 *Succubus.* New York: Manor Books, 1977, 205 p., paper, novel.

GREENHALGH, Zohra

24645 *Contrarywise.* New York: Ace Books, 1989, 290 p., paper, novel. TRICKSTER #1.
24646 *Trickster's touch.* New York: Ace Books, 1989, 236 p., paper, novel. TRICKSTER #2.

GREENHALL, Ken(neth R.)

24647 *Childgrave.* New York: Pocket Books, 1982, 295 p., paper, novel.
24648 *The companion.* New York, London: Pocket Books, 1988, 223 p., paper, novel.
24649 *Deathchain.* New York, London: Pocket Books, 1991, 251 p., paper, novel.
24650 *Hell hound.* New York: Zebra Books, Kensington Publishing Corp., 1977, 192 p., paper, novel.

as JESSICA HAMILTON

25099 *Baxter: a novel of inhuman evil.* London: George G. Harrap, 1977, 142 p., cloth, novel.
25100 *Elizabeth: a novel of the unnatural.* New York: Random House, 1976, 153 p., cloth, novel.

GREENHOUGH, Terence—SEE: Greenhough, Terry

GREENHOUGH, Terry [i.e., Terence Greenhough], 1944-

24651 *The alien contract.* London: Robert Hale, 1980, 159 p., cloth, novel.
24652 *Thoughtworld.* London: New English Library, 1977, 144 p., cloth, novel.
24653 *Time and Timothy Grenville.* London: New English Library, 1975, 221 p., cloth, novel.
24654 *The wandering worlds.* London: New English Library, 1976, 172 p., cloth, novel.

as ANDREW LESTER

24655 *The thrice-born.* London: New English Library, 1976, 158 p., cloth, novel.

GREENLAND, Colin, 1954-

24656 *Daybreak on a different mountain: a fantasy novel.* London: George Allen & Unwin, 1984, 246 p., cloth, novel. DAYBREAK #1.
24657 *The entropy exhibition: Michael Moorcock and the British "New Wave" in science fiction.* London & Boston: Routledge & Kegan Paul, 1983, xii+244 p., cloth, nonf. [Winner of the J. Lloyd Eaton Award for Best Nonfiction Book of the Year, 1983 (1985)].
24658 *The hour of the thin ox.* London: Unwin Paperbacks, 1987, 186 p., cloth, novel. DAYBREAK #2.
24659 *Other voices.* London: Unwin Hyman, 1988, 182 p., cloth, novel. DAYBREAK #3.
24660 *Take back plenty.* London: Unwin Paperbacks, 1990, 359 p., paper, novel.

with John Clute & David Pringle

20205 *Interzone: the first anthology: new science fiction and fantasy writing.* London: J. M. Dent & Sons, 1985, 206 p., paper, anth.

with Roger Dean & Martyn Dean

21448 *Magnetic storm.* Limpsfield, Surrey, England: Dragon's Dream, 1984, 154 p., cloth, art.

with Mervyn Peake

24661 *Titus unbound.* Oxford, England: Oxford University Press, 1977, 27 p., paper, story. [Adapted from the novel by Peake].

with George Slusser and Eric S. Rabkin

24662 *Storm warnings: science fiction confronts the future.* Carbondale & Edwardsville, IL: Southern Illinois University Press, 1987, xi+278 p., cloth, nonf. anth. PROCEEDINGS OF THE J. LLOYD EATON CONFERENCE ON SCIENCE FICTION AND FANTASY LITERATURE #6.

GREENLEAF, William

24663 *Clarion.* New York: Tor SF, A Tom Doherty Associates Book, 1988, 213 p., paper, novel.

24664 *The Pandora stone.* New York: Ace Science Fiction Books, 1984, 216 p., paper, novel.

24665 *Starjacked!* New York: Ace Science Fiction Books, 1987, 187 p., paper, novel. TARTARUS #2.

24666 *The Tartarus incident.* New York: Ace Science Fiction Books, 1983, 202 p., paper, novel. TARTARUS #1.

24667 *Timejumper.* New York: Leisure Books, 1980, 224 p., paper, novel.

GREENWALD, Harry J.

24668 *Chinaman's chance.* London: Robert Hale, 1981, 192 p., cloth, novel.

GREENWOOD, Ed

24669 *Forgotten realms fantasy adventure: Spellfire.* Lake Geneva, WI: TSR Inc., 1987, 382 p., paper, novel.
Spellfire—SEE: *Forgotten realms fantasy adventure: Spellfire.*

with Jeff Grubb

24670 *Adventures: an updated tour of the Heartlands AD&D 2nd edition game.* Lake Geneva, WI: TSR Inc., 1990, 154 p., paper, nonf.

GREENWOOD, James

24671 *The adventures of seven four-footed foresters narrated by themselves.* London: Ward & Lock, 1865, vii+390 p., cloth, novel.

GREER, Gery, *with Bob Ruddick*

24672 *Jason and the aliens down the street.* New York: HarperCollinsPublishers, 1991, 94 p., cloth, novel. JASON #1.

24673 *Let me off this spaceship!* New York: HarperCollinsPublishers, 1991, 54 p., cloth, story.

24674 *Max and me and the time machine.* San Diego, CA: Harcourt Brace Jovanovich, 1983, 114 p., cloth, novel. MAX AND ME #1.

24675 *Max and me and the Wild West.* San Diego, CA: Harcourt Brace Jovanovich, 1988, 138 p., cloth, novel. MAX AND ME #2.

*GREER, Tom, 1846?-1904

GREGORIAN, Joyce Ballou [i.e., Joyce Ballou Gregorian Hampshire], 1946-1991

24676 *The broken citadel.* New York: Atheneum, 1975, 373 p., cloth, novel. TREDANA TRILOGY #1.

24677 *Castledown.* New York: Atheneum, 1977, 371 p., cloth, novel. TREDANA TRILOGY #2.

24678 *The great wheel.* New York: Ace Fantasy Books, 1987, 307 p., paper, novel. TREDANA TRILOGY #3.

*GREGORY, Franklin (Long), 1905-1985

GREGORY, Guy, pseud.—SEE: Wright, Guier S. III & Wright, Gregory Scott Jr.

GREGORY, John, pseud.—SEE: Hoskins, Robert

GREGORY, Mary L.—SEE: Gregory, Mollie

GREGORY, Mollie [i.e., Mary Lawrence Gregory], 1940-

24679 *Making Mr. Right: a novel.* Toronto, New York: PaperJacks Ltd., 1987, 203 p., paper, movie.

GREGORY, Philippa, 1954-

24680 *The favored child.* New York: Pocket Books, 1989, 473 p., cloth, novel.

GREGORY, Stephen, 1952-

24681 *The cormorant.* London: Heinemann, 1986, 148 p., cloth, novel.

24682 *The woodwitch.* London: Heinemann, 1988, 231 p., cloth, novel.

GREGSON, Maureen

24683 *1990.* London: Sphere Books, 1977, 199 p., paper, tele.

GREIMES, Christopher, *with Barthe DeClements*

21474 *Double trouble.* New York: Viking Kestrel, 1987, 168 p., cloth, novel.

GRENANDER, M(ary) E(lizabeth), 1918-

24684 *Ambrose Bierce.* New York: Twayne Publishers, 1971, 193 p., cloth, nonf.

GRENNAN, Margaret R(ose), 1912-

24685 *William Morris, medievalist and revolutionary.* New York: King's Crown Press, 1945, x+173 p., cloth, nonf.

GRESHAM, Douglas H., 1945-

24686 *Lenten lands.* New York: Macmillan Publishing Co., 1988, x+225 p., cloth, nonf.

GRESHAM, Stephen (Leroy), 1947-

24687 *Abracadabra.* New York: Zebra Books, Kensington Publishing Corp., 1988, 381 p., paper, novel.

24688 *Blood wings.* New York: Zebra Books, Kensington Publishing Corp., 1990, 383 p., paper, novel.

24689 *Demon's eye.* New York: Zebra Books, Kensington Publishing Corp., 1989, 328 p., paper, novel.

24690 *Dew claws.* New York: Zebra Books, Kensington Publishing Corp., 1986, 335 p., paper, novel.

24691 *Half Moon down.* New York: Zebra Books, Kensington Publishing Corp., 1985, 364 p., paper, novel.

24692 *The living dark.* New York: Zebra Books, Kensington Publishing Corp., 1991, 335 p., paper, novel.

24693 *Midnight boy.* New York: Zebra Books, Kensington Publishing Corp., 1987, 396 p., paper, novel.

24694 *Moon Lake.* New York: Zebra Books, Kensington Publishing Corp., 1982, 302 p., paper, novel.

24695 *Night touch.* New York: Zebra Books, Kensington Publishing Corp., 1988, 351 p., paper, novel.

24696 *Runaway.* New York: Zebra Books, Kensington Publishing Corp., 1988, 447 p., paper, novel.

24697 *The Shadow Man.* New York: Zebra Books, Kensington Publishing Corp., 1986, 363 p., paper, novel.

GREVE, Felix—SEE: Grove, Frederick Philip

GREY, A. W.—SEE: Brown, Crosland

GREY, Lloyd Eric, pseud.—SEE: Eshleman, Lloyd Wendell

GREY, M. Cameron

24698 *Angels and awakenings: stories of the miraculous by great modern writers.* Garden City, NY: Doubleday & Co., 1980, xxii+402 p., cloth, anth.

GREY, Michael, 1937-

24699 *The room.* Ealing, England: Corgi Books, 1990, 238 p., paper, novel.

GREYWHISKERS, Fifi—SEE: Lobsang Rampa, T.

GRIBBIN, John (R.), 1946-

24700 *Father to the man.* London: Victor Gollancz, 1989, 221 p., cloth, novel.

with Marcus Chown

20020 *Double planet.* London: Victor Gollancz, 1988, 220 p., cloth, novel.

20021 *Reunion.* London: Victor Gollancz, 1991, 256 p., cloth, novel.

with D. G. Compton

20362 *Ragnarok.* London: Victor Gollancz, 1991, 344 p., cloth, novel.

with Douglas Orgill

24701 *Brother Esau.* London: Bodley Head, 1982, 220 p., cloth, novel.

24702 *The sixth winter.* London: Bodley Head, 1979, 315 p., cloth, novel.

GRIBBON, William L.—SEE: Mundy, Talbot

GRICE, Julia (A. Haughey), 1940-

24703 *Cry for the demon.* New York: Warner Books, 1980, 397 p., paper, novel.

24704 *Daughters of the flame.* New York: Pocket Books, 1979, 506 p., paper, novel.

*GRIERSON, Francis D(urham), 1888-1972

GRIFFEN, Elizabeth L., pseud.—SEE: DuBreuil, Lorinda

GRIFFIN, Brian, 1941-

24705 *The nucleation.* London: Robert Hale, 1977, 191 p., cloth, novel.

24706 *The OMEGA Project.* London: Robert Hale, 1978, 190 p., cloth, novel.

with David Wingrove

24707 *Apertures: a study of the writings of Brian W. Aldiss.* Westport, CT & London: Greenwood Press, 1984, xvi+261 p., cloth, nonf. CONTRIBUTIONS TO THE STUDY OF SCIENCE FICTION AND FANTASY #8.

GRIFFIN, Gerald G(ehrig), 1933- , *with Robin Moore*

24708   *The death disciple.* Westport, CT: Condor, 1977, 249 p., paper, novel.
24709   *The last coming.* Westport, CT: Condor Books, 1978 (i.e., 1979?), 328 p., paper, novel.

GRIFFIN, Jane Whittington, 1916-1979, *with L. Sprague de Camp & Catherine Crook de Camp*

21327   *Dark Valley destiny: the life of Robert E. Howard.* New York: Bluejay Books, 1983, 402 p., cloth, nonf.

GRIFFIN, John

24710   *Animal farm, George Orwell.* Harlow, England: Longman, 1989, 48 p., paper, nonf.
24711   *Brave new world, Aldous Huxley.* Harlow, England: Longman, 1990, 48 p., paper, nonf.

with Nigel Grimshaw & Paul Groves

24712   *13 sinister stories.* London: Edward Arnold, 1987, 100 p., paper, coll.

GRIFFIN, P(auline) M(argaret), 1947-

   Call to arms—SEE: *Star Commandos: Call to arms.*
   Colony in peril—SEE: *Star Commandos: Colony in peril.*
   Death planet—SEE: *Star Commandos: Death planet.*
   Fire planet—SEE: *Star Commandos: Fire planet.*
   Jungle assault—SEE: *Star Commandos: Jungle assault.*
   Mind slaver—SEE: *Star Commandos: Mind slaver.*
   Mission underground—SEE: *Star Commandos: Mission underground.*
   Return to war—SEE: *Star Commandos: Return to war.*
24713   *Star Commandos.* New York: Ace Science Fiction Books, 1986, 228 p., paper, novel. STAR COMMANDOS #1.
24714   *Star Commandos: Call to arms.* New York: Ace Books, 1991, 197 p., paper, novel. STAR COMMANDOS #9.
24715   *Star Commandos: Colony in peril.* New York: Ace Science Fiction Books, 1987, 199 p., paper, novel. STAR COMMANDOS #2.

24716   *Star Commandos: Death planet.* New York: Ace Books, 1989, 201 p., paper, novel. STAR COMMANDOS #4.
24717   *Star Commandos: Fire planet.* New York: Ace Books, 1990, 186 p., paper, novel. STAR COMMANDOS #7.
24718   *Star Commandos: Jungle assault.* New York: Ace Books, 1991, 186 p., paper, novel. STAR COMMANDOS #8.
24719   *Star Commandos: Mind slaver.* New York: Ace Books, 1990, 231 p., paper, novel. STAR COMMANDOS #5.
24720   *Star Commandos: Mission underground.* New York: Ace Books, 1988, 201 p., paper, novel. STAR COMMANDOS #3.
24721   *Star Commandos: Return to war.* New York: Ace Books, 1990, 247 p., paper, novel. STAR COMMANDOS #6.

with Andre Norton

   The turning: storms of victory—SEE: *Witch World: The turning: Storms of victory.*
24722   *Witch World: The turning: Storms of victory.* New York: Tor Fantasy, A Tom Doherty Associates Book, 1991, 432 p., cloth, novel. WITCH WORLD SERIES.

GRIFFIN, Peni R(ae), 1961-

24723   *A dig in time.* New York: Margaret K. McElderry Books; Toronto: Collier Macmillan Canada; New York: Maxwell Macmillan International Publishing Group, 1991, 186 p., cloth, novel.
24724   *Otto from otherwhere.* New York: Margaret K. McElderry Books, 1990, 182 p., cloth, novel.

GRIFFIN, Russell M(organ), 1943-1986

24725   *The blind men and the elephant.* New York: Timescape Books, 1982, 295 p., paper, novel.
24726   *Century's end.* Toronto, New York: Bantam Books, 1981, 260 p., paper, novel.
24727   *The makeshift god.* New York: A Dell Book, 1979, 315 p., paper, novel.
24728   *The timeservers.* New York: Avon, 1985, 238 p., paper, novel.

GRIFFIN, (Henry) William, 1935-

24729   *Clive Staples Lewis: a dramatic life.* San Francisco: Harper & Row, 1986, xxv + 507 p., cloth, nonf.
24730   *The Fleetwood correspondence: a devilish tale of temptation.* New York: Doubleday, 1989, 166 p., cloth, novel.

GRIFFITH, Clem

24731 *Four thaumastic tales.* London: Excalibur Press, 1989, 156 p., paper, coll.

GRIFFITH, Kathryn (Ann) Meyer, 1950-

24732 *Blood forge.* New York: Leisure Books, 1989, 392 p., paper, novel.
24733 *Evil stalks the night.* New York: Leisure Books, 1984, 368 p., paper, novel.
24734 *Vampire blood.* New York: Zebra Books, Kensington Publishing Corp., 1991, 285 p., paper, novel.

*GRIFFITH, Mary, 1800?-1877

GRIFFITH, Nancy Snell, 1946-

24735 *Edward Bellamy: a bibliography.* Metuchen, NJ: Scarecrow Press, 1986, xi + 185 p., cloth, nonf.

GRIFFITH, William, 1921-

24736 *Fantasies two.* Millbrae, CA: Dawne-Leigh Publications, 1980, 158 p., cloth, coll.

GRIFFITHS, David Arthur, *as* KING LANG

08599 *Projectile war.* London: Curtis Warren, 1951, 111 p., paper, novel.

GRIFFITHS, Jeanne, *with Judy Allen*

16290 *The book of the dragon.* London: Orbis Books, 1979, 128 p., cloth, fiction.

GRIFFITHS, John (Charles), 1934-

24737 *Three tomorrows: American, British, and Soviet science fiction.* London: Macmillan, 1980, 217 p., cloth, nonf.

GRIFFITHS, Paul (Anthony), 1947-

24738 *Myself and Marco Polo.* London: Chatto & Windus, 1989, [224] p., cloth, novel.

GRIFFITHS, Vivien

24739 *Ghostly encounters.* London: National Book League, 1978?, 24 p., paper, nonf.

GRIGSBY, Alcanoan O.—SEE: Adams, Jack

GRIMM, Cherry—SEE: Wilder, Cherry

GRIMSHAW, Nigel (Gilroy), 1925-

24740 *Bluntstone and the wildkeepers.* London: Faber & Faber, 1974, 152 p., cloth, novel.

with Paul Groves

24741 *10 ghosts.* London: Edward Arnold, 1984, 79 p., paper, coll.
24742 *10 strange tales.* London: Edward Arnold, 1985, 96 p., paper, coll.
24743 *13 ghosts: a collection of original ghost stories with suggestions for varied work in English.* London: Edward Arnold, 1976, 90 p., paper, coll.
24744 *13 horror stories.* London: Edward Arnold, 1978, 107 p., paper, coll.
24745 *13 sci-fi stories.* London: Edward Arnold, 1979, 92 p., paper, coll.
24746 *13 weird tales: a collection of original strange stories with suggestions for varied work in English.* London: Edward Arnold, 1977, 108 p., paper, coll.

with Paul Groves & John Griffin

24712 *13 sinister stories.* London: Edward Arnold, 1987, 100 p., paper, coll.

GRIMSLEY, Ann, *with Lynne Kinnerley as* LYNDAN DARBY

24747 *Bloodseed.* London: Unwin Paperbacks, 1988, 262 p., paper, novel. EYE OF TIME TRILOGY #2.
24748 *Crystal and steel.* London: Unwin Paperbacks, 1988, 340 p., paper, novel. EYE OF TIME TRILOGY #1.
24749 *Phoenix fire.* London: Unwin Paperbacks, 1989, 202 p., paper, novel. EYE OF TIME TRILOGY #3.

GRIMWADE, Peter

24750 *Doctor Who: Mawdryn undead.* London: W. H. Allen & Co., 1983, 119 p., cloth, tele. DOCTOR WHO #82.
24751 *Doctor Who: Planet of fire.* London: A Target Book, W. H. Allen, 1984, 143 p., paper, tele. DOCTOR WHO #93.
24752 *Doctor Who: Time flight.* London: A Target Book, W. H. Allen, 1983, 128 p., paper, tele. DOCTOR WHO #.
Mawdryn undead—SEE: Doctor Who: Mawdryn undead.
Planet of fire—SEE: Doctor Who: Planet of fire.
24753 *Robot.* London: A Star Book, W. H. Allen & Co., 1987, 144 p., paper, novel.

Time flight—SEE: *Doctor Who: Time flight.*

GRIMWOOD, Ken

24754 *Breakthrough.* Garden City, NY: Doubleday & Co., 1976, 233 p., cloth, novel.
24755 *Replay.* New York: Arbor House, 1986, 310 p., cloth, novel. [Winner of the World Fantasy Award for Best Fantasy Novel, 1987 (1988)].

GRIPE, Maria (Kristina), 1923-

24756 *Agnes Cecilia.* New York: Harper & Row, 1990, 282 p., cloth, novel. [Translation by Rika Lesser of *Agnes Cecilia*].
24757 *In the time of the bells.* New York: Delacorte Press, A Seymour Lawrence/ Merloyd Lawrence Book, 1976, 208 p., cloth, novel. [Translation by Sheila La Farge of *Klockornas tid*].

GRIXTI, Joseph, 1950-

24758 *Terrors of uncertainty: the cultural contexts of horror fiction.* London & New York: Routledge, 1989, xviii+214 p., cloth, nonf.

GROCOTT, Ann (Oenone), 1938-

24759 *Danni's desperate journey.* Sydney: Angus & Robertson, 1987, 170 p., cloth, novel.

*GROH, Irwin (William), 1894-1985

GRONAU, Mary Ellen

24760 *Passionate warriors.* New York, Toronto: Bantam Books, 1989, 311 p., paper, novel.

GRONMARK, Scott—SEE: Sharman, Nick

GRONOWSKI, Paul

24761 *The secret in the Argentine jungle.* Santee, CA: The Blueboy Library, 1977, 184 p., paper, novel.

GROSS, Edward, 1960-

24762 *Above & below: a guide to Beauty and the Beast.* New York: Image Publishing, 1990, 110 p., paper, nonf.
Conclusion—SEE: *Files magazine spotlight on The V files, book five: Conclusion.*

24764 *Dark Shadows: a 20th anniversary tribute.* Canoga Park, CA: Psi Fi Movie Press, 1986, 57 p., paper, nonf.
24765 *Dark Shadows: The secret of Barnabas.* Canoga Park, CA: Psi Fi Movie Press, 1986, 57 p., paper, nonf. [Cover title].
24766 *Dark Shadows: The terror begins.* Canoga Park, CA: Psi Fi Movie Press, 1986, 56 p., paper, nonf. [Cover title].
24767 *Files magazine spotlight on Star Trek IV, the voyage home.* Canoga Park, CA: Psi Fi Movie Press, 1986, 58 p., paper, nonf.
24768 *Files magazine spotlight on The V files, book four: They're back.* Canoga Park, CA: New Media Books, 1986, 55 p., paper, nonf.
24769 *Files magazine spotlight on The V files, book five: Conclusion.* Canoga Park, CA: New Media Books, 1986, [51] p., paper, nonf.
24770 *Files magazine spotlight on The Star Trek III files, The search for Spock.* Canoga Park, CA: Psi Fi Movie Press, 1985, 51 p., paper, nonf.
24771 *The making of the Next generation.* Las Vegas, NV: Pioneer Books, 1989, 124 p., paper, nonf.
The motion picture—SEE: *The Star Trek movie files: The motion picture.*
A new beginning—SEE: *The V files, book six: A new beginning.*
The search for Spock—SEE: *Files magazine spotlight on The Star Trek III files, The search for Spock.*
The secret of Barnabas—SEE: *Dark Shadows: The secret of Barnabas.*
The Star Trek III files, The search for Spock—SEE: *Files magazine spotlight on The Star Trek III files, The search for Spock.*
Star Trek IV, the voyage home—SEE: *Files magazine spotlight on Star Trek IV, the voyage home.*
24772 *The Star Trek movie files: The motion picture.* Canoga Park, CA: Psi Fi Movie Press, 1986, 57 p., paper, nonf.
24773 *The Star Trek movie files: The wrath of Khan* / by Ed Gross. Canoga Park, CA: Psi Fi Movie Press, 1986, 54 p., paper, nonf.
24774 *Superheroes on screen* / by Ed Gross. Canoga Park, CA: Psi Fi Movie Press, 1986, 55 p., paper, nonf.
24775 *The superheroes on screen files: Superman and Spider-Man* / by Ed Gross. Canoga Park, CA: Psi Fi Movie Press, 1986, 64 p., paper, nonf. [Not the same as the other book of the same title].

24776 *The Superheroes on screen files: Superman and Spider-Man.* Canoga Park, CA: Psi Fi Movie Press, 1986, 51 p., paper, nonf. [Not the same as the other book of the same title].
Superman and Spider-Man—SEE: *The superheroes on screen files: Superman and Spider-Man.*
The terror begins—SEE: *Dark Shadows: The terror begins.*
They're back—SEE: *Files magazine spotlight on The V files, book four: They're back.*

24777 *Trek: the lost years.* Las Vegas, NV: Pioneer Books, 1989, 121 p., paper, nonf. [Title page credit says James Van Hise (q.v.)].

24778 *The unofficial tale of Beauty and the Beast.* Las Vegas, NV: Pioneer Books, 1988, 130 p., paper, nonf.

24779 *The unofficial tale of Beauty and the Beast, 2nd ed.* Las Vegas, NV: Pioneer Books, 1990?, 153 p., paper, nonf.
The V files, book four: They're back—SEE: *Files magazine spotlight on The V files, book four: They're back.*
The V files, book five: Conclusion—SEE: *Files magazine spotlight on The V files, book five: Conclusion.*

24780 *The V files, book six: A new beginning.* Canoga Park, CA: Psi Fi Movie Press, 1986, 49 p., paper, nonf.
The Wrath of Khan—SEE: *The Star Trek movie files: The wrath of Khan.*

with James Van Hise

24782 *The Dark Shadows tribute book.* Las Vegas, NV: Pioneer Books, 1990, 144 p., paper, nonf.

with Kay Anderson & Wendy Rathbone & Ron Magid & Sheldon Teitelbaum

16369 *The making of the Trek films.* East Meadow, NY: Image Publishing, 1991, 172 p., paper, nonf.

GROSS, Louis S., 1954-

24783 *Redefining the American gothic: from Wieland to Day of the Dead.* Ann Arbor, MI: UMI Research Press, 1989, 112 p., cloth, nonf. STUDIES IN SPECULATIVE FICTION #20.

GROSS, Michael, 1957- , with Paul Scanlon

24784 *The book of Alien.* New York: Heavy Metal Communications, 1979, [12] p., paper, nonf.

GROSS, Miriam, 1936?-

24785 *The world of George Orwell.* London: Weidenfeld & Nicolson, 1971, 182 p., cloth, nonf. anth.

GROSSBACH, Robert (Alvin), 1941-

24786 *The devil and Max Devlin: a novel.* New York: Ballantine Books, 1980, 185 p., paper, movie.

24787 *Never say die: an autonecrographical novel.* New York, Hagerstown, NJ: Harper & Row, Publishers, 1979, 263 p., cloth, novel.

*GROSSER, Morton, <u>1931-</u>

GROSSMAN, Arnold, *with Richard Lamm*

24788 *1988.* New York: St. Martin's Press, 1985, 264 p., cloth, novel.

GROSSMAN, Gary H(oward), 1948-

24789 *Superman, serial to cereal.* New York: Big Apple Books, Popular Library, 1976, 188 p., paper, nonf.

GROSSMAN, Josephine—SEE: **Merril, Judith**

GROTTA-KURSKA, Daniel, 1944-

The biography of J. R. R. Tolkien—SEE: *J. R. R. Tolkien.*

24790 *J. R. R. Tolkien: architect of Middle Earth: a biography.* Philadelphia, PA: Running Press, 1976, 165 p., cloth, nonf. [Edited by Frank Wilson].

24791 retitled: *The biography of J. R. R. Tolkien: architect of Middle Earth, 2nd ed.* Philadelphia, PA: Running Press, 1978, 197 p., cloth, nonf. [Expanded edition].

GROVE, Frederick Philip [originally Felix Paul Greve], 1879-1948

24792 *Consider her ways.* Toronto: Macmillan Co. of Canada, 1947, xxxii+298 p., cloth, novel.

GROVE, Peter J.

24793 *The Levellers.* London: Robert Hale, 1981, 189 p., cloth, novel.

GROVER, Dorys C(row), 1921-

24794   *A solitary voice: Vardis Fisher: a collection of essays.* New York: The Revisionist Press, 1973, iv+72 p., cloth, nonf. coll.

24795   *Vardis Fisher: the novelist as poet.* New York: The Revisionist Press, 1973, vii+140 p., cloth, nonf.

GROVES, Ann

24796   *Tales of science fiction and the supernatural.* Lewes, East Sussex, England: The Book Guild, 1990, 115 p., paper, coll.

GROVES, Paul, 1930-

with Nigel Grimshaw

24741   *10 ghosts.* London: Edward Arnold, 1984, 79 p., paper, coll.

24742   *10 strange tales.* London: Edward Arnold, 1985, 96 p., paper, coll.

24743   *13 ghosts: a collection of original ghost stories with suggestions for varied work in English.* London: Edward Arnold, 1976, 90 p., paper, coll.

24744   *13 horror stories.* London: Edward Arnold, 1978, 107 p., paper, coll.

24745   *13 sci-fi stories.* London: Edward Arnold, 1979, 92 p., paper, coll.

24746   *13 weird tales: a collection of original strange stories with suggestions for varied work in English.* London: Edward Arnold, 1977, 108 p., paper, coll.

with Nigel Grimshaw & John Griffin

24712   *13 sinister stories.* London: Edward Arnold, 1987, 100 p., paper, coll.

GRUBB, Davis (Alexander), 1919-1980

24797   *Ancient lights.* New York: Viking Press, 1982, 540 p., cloth, novel.

24798   *The siege of 318: thirteen mystical stories.* Webster Springs, WV: Back Fork Books, 1978, vii+180 p., cloth, coll.

24799   *You never believe me, and other stories.* New York: A Thomas Dunne Book, St. Martin's Press, 1989, xi+259 p., cloth, coll.

GRUBB, Jeff

The amazing Spider-Man: City in darkness—SEE: *City in darkness.*

24800   *City in darkness.* Lake Geneva, WI: TSR Inc., 1986, 188 p., paper, novel. MAR-VEL SUPERHEROES ADVENTURE GAMEBOOK #1.

24800A   retitled: *The amazing Spider-Man: City in darkness.* Harmondsworth, Middlesex, England: Puffin Books, 1987, 188 p., paper, novel.

with Ed Greenwood

24670   *Adventures: an updated tour of the Heartlands AD&D 2nd edition game.* Lake Geneva, WI: TSR Inc., 1990, 154 p., paper, nonf.

with Kate Novak

Azure bonds—SEE: *Forgotten realms: Azure bonds.*

24801   *Forgotten realms: Azure bonds.* Lake Geneva, WI: TSR Inc., 1988, 380 p., paper, novel. FINDER'S STONE TRILOGY #1; FORGOTTEN REALMS FANTASY ADVENTURE.

24802   *Forgotten realms: Song of the saurials.* Lake Geneva, WI: TSR Inc., 1991, 315 p., paper, novel. FINDER'S STONE TRILOGY #3; FORGOTTEN REALMS FANTASY ADVENTURE.

Song of the saurials—SEE: *Forgotten realms: Song of the saurials.*

24803   *The wyvern's spur.* Lake Geneva, WI: TSR Inc., 1990, 313 p., paper, novel. FINDER'S STONE TRILOGY #2; FORGOTTEN REALMS FANTASY ADVENTURE.

GRUEN, Von, pseud.—SEE: **Holloway, Brian**

*GRUHN, Carrie E. (Myers), 1907-<u>1990</u>

GRUSKIN, Edward

24804   *The invincible Doc Savage.* Greenwood, MA: Odyssey Publications, 1983, 52 p., paper, coll. DOC SAVAGE SERIES.

GRYLLS, Rosalie Glynn [i.e., Mary Rosalie Glynn Grylls Mander], 1905-1988

24805   *Mary Shelley: a biography.* Oxford, England: Oxford University Press, 1938, xvi+345 p., cloth, nonf.

GRZIMEK, Martin, 1950-

24806   *Shadowlife: a novel.* New York: New Directions, 1991, 207 p., cloth, novel. [Translation by Breon Mitchell of *Die beschattung*].

GUADALUPI, Gianni, 1945- , *with Alberto Manguel*

24807 *The dictionary of imaginary places.* New York: Macmillan Publishing Co., 1980, 438 p., cloth, nonf.
24808 *The dictionary of imaginary places.* San Diego, CA: Harcourt Brace Jovanovich, 1987, 454 p., paper, nonf. [Expanded edition].

GUARD, David, 1934-1991

24809 *Deirdre: a Celtic legend.* Millbrae, CA: Celestial Arts, 1977, 118 p., paper, novel.

GUEST, Diane

24810 *Forbidden garden.* New York: A Bernard Geiss Associates Book, Bantam Books, 1987, 265 p., paper, novel.
24811 *Lullaby.* New York: A Bernard Geis Associates Book, G. P. Putnam's Sons, 1990, 220 p., cloth, novel.

GUEST, Lynn, 1939-

24812 *The sword of Hachiman: a novel of early Japan.* New York: McGraw-Hill Book Co., 1981, 309 p., cloth, novel.

GUFFEY, George R(obert), 1932- , *with George E. Slusser & Mark Rose*

24813 *Bridges to science fiction.* Carbondale & Edwardsville, IL: Southern Illinois University Press; London & Amsterdam: Feffer & Simons, 1980, viii+168 p., cloth, nonf. anth. PROCEEDINGS OF THE J. LLOYD EATON CONFERENCE ON SCIENCE FICTION AND FANTASY LITERATURE #1.

GUHA, Anton-Andreas, 1937-

24814 *Ende: a diary of the Third World War.* London: Corgi Books, 1986, 173 p., paper, novel. [Translation by Fred Taylor of *Ende*].

GUIGONNAT, Henri

24815 *Daemon in Lithuania.* New York: New Directions, 1985, 136 p., cloth, novel. [Translation by Erika Weihs of *Démone en Lituanie*].

GUILEY, Rosemary—SEE: Fletcher, Adrian

GUIN, Ursula K. Le—SEE: Le Guin, Ursula K.

*GUIN, Wyman (Woods), 1915-1989

*GUIRDHAM, Arthur, 1905-

GÜN, Güneli

24816 *On the road to Baghdad: a picaresque novel of magical adventures, begged, borrowed, and stolen from The thousand and one nights.* Claremont, CA: Hunter House, 1991, xviii+377 p., cloth, novel.

GUNDEN, Kenneth Von—SEE: Von Gunden, Kenneth

GUNDERLOY, Mike

24817 *How to publish a fanzine.* Port Townsend, WA: Loompanics Unlimited, 1988, 91 p., paper, nonf.

GUNN, A. J., 1945-

24818 *The Shon warrior.* Bognor Regis, England: New Horizons, 1983, 237 p., cloth, novel.

GUNN, James (Edwin), 1923-

24819 *Alternate worlds: the illustrated history of science fiction.* Englewood Cliffs, NJ: Prentice-Hall, 1975, 256 p., cloth, nonf. [Winner of the *Locus* Award for Best Associational Item, 1975 (1976)].
24820 *Crisis!* New York: Tor SF, A Tom Doherty Associates Book, 1986, 219 p., paper, coll.
24821 *The discovery of the future: the ways science fiction developed.* College Station, TX: Texas A&M University Library, 1975, 17 leaves, paper, nonf.
24822 *The dreamers.* New York: Simon & Schuster, 1980, 166 p., cloth, novel.
24822A retitled: *The mind master.* New York: A Timescape Book, Pocket Books, 1982, 174 p., paper, novel.
24823 *The end of the dreams: three short novels about space, happiness, and immortality.* New York: Charles Scribner's Sons, 1975, xv+202 p., cloth, coll.
24824 *Isaac Asimov: the foundations of science fiction.* Oxford, New York: Oxford University Press, 1982, ix+236 p., cloth, nonf. [Winner of the Hugo Award for Best Nonfiction Book, 1982 (1983)].
24825 *Kampus: a novel.* Toronto, New York: Bantam Books, 1977, 308 p., paper, novel.

24826 *The magicians.* New York: Charles Scribner's Sons, 1976, 197 p., cloth, novel.
The mind master—SEE: *The dreamers.*
24827 *Nebula award stories ten.* New York: Harper & Row, 1975, xiii+254 p., cloth, anth.
24828 *The new encyclopedia of science fiction.* New York: Viking, 1988, xix+524 p., cloth, nonf. anth.
24829 *The road to science fiction: from Gilgamesh to Wells.* New York: A Mentor Book, New American Library, 1977, 404 p., paper, anth.
24830 *The road to science fiction #2: from Wells to Heinlein.* New York: A Mentor Book, New American Library, 1979, 535 p., paper, anth.
24831 *The road to science fiction #3: from Heinlein to here.* New York: A Mentor Book, New American Library, 1979, xi+656 p., paper, anth.
24832 *The road to science fiction #4: from here to forever.* New York: A Mentor Book, New American Library, 1982, 531 p., paper, anth.
24833 *Tiger! tiger!* Polk City, IA: Chris Drumm, 1984, 55 p., paper, story. DRUMM BOOKLET #17.

with Stephen H. Goldman

24086 *Teacher's manual: The road to science fiction.* New York: New American Library, 1980, 45 p., paper, nonf.

GUNN, Neil M(iller), 1891-1973

37817 *The serpent.* London: Faber & Faber, 1943, 255 p., cloth, novel.

GUNNARSSON, Olafur—SEE: Olafur Gunnarsson

GUNNARSSON, Thorarinn, 1957-

Battle of the ring—SEE: *Starwolves: Battle of the ring.*
24834 *Human, beware!* New York: Ace Books, 1990, 263 p., paper, novel. DRAGONS #2.
24835 *Make way for dragons!* New York: Ace Books, 1990, 215 p., paper, novel. DRAGONS #1.
24836 *Revenge of the Valkyrie.* New York: Ace Books, 1989, 202 p., paper, novel. SONG #2.
24837 *Song of the dwarves.* New York: Ace Books, 1988, 214 p., paper, novel. SONG #1.

24838 *The starwolves.* New York: Popular Library, 1988, 281 p., paper, novel. STARWOLVES #1.
24839 *Starwolves: Battle of the ring.* New York: Popular Library, 1989, 235 p., paper, novel. STARWOLVES #2.
24840 *Starwolves: Tactical error.* New York: Popular Library, 1991, vii+231 p., paper, novel. STARWOLVES #3.
Tactical error—SEE: *Starwolves: Tactical error.*

GUNTHER, Max, 1927-

24841 *Doom wind: a novel.* Chicago: Contemporary Books, 1986, 346 p., cloth, novel.

GUON, Ellen (Sue), 1964- , *with Mercedes Lackey*

24842 *Knight of ghosts and shadows: an urban fantasy.* New York: Baen Fantasy, 1990, 345 p., paper, novel.

GUPTILL, Paul, *with Chris Drumm*

22221 *The many worlds of Larry Niven, 2nd ed.* Polk City, IA: Chris Drumm, 1989, ii+63 p., paper, nonf. DRUMM BOOKLET #33.

GURNEY, David [pseud. of Patrick Bair]

06497 *The conjurers.* London: New English Library, 1972, 285 p., cloth, novel. CONJURERS #1.
06497a retitled: *The demonists.* New York: Manor Books, 1977, 285 p., paper, novel. CONJURERS #1.
The demonists—SEE: *The conjurers.*
24843 *The devil in the Atlas: a study of modern satanism.* London: New English Library, 1976, 190 p., paper, novel. CONJURERS #2.
24844 *The evil under the water.* London: New English Library, 1977, 189 p., paper, novel.

GUSMAN, Rico, *with Kirk Duncan*

22295 *Albatross.* England: Ithkos Publications, 1988, 119 p., paper, novel.

GUSTAFSON, Jon (Martin), 1945-

with Alex Schomburg

24845 *Chroma: the art of Alex Schomburg.* Poughkeepsie, NY: Father Tree Press, 1986, 108 p., cloth, art.

with Dean Wesley Smith as SMITH GUSTAFSON

24846 *The Moscow Moffia presents Rat tales.* Eugene, OR: Hyratia Press [sic], 1987, v+114 p., cloth, anth. [Limited to 144 copies].
  Rat tales—SEE: *The Moscow Mafia presents Rat tales.*

GUSTAFSON, Smith, pseud.—SEE: Smith, Dean Wesley & Gustafson, Jon

GUSTAFSON, Victoria—SEE: Mitchell, V. E.

GUTHKE, Karl S(iegfried), 1933-

24847 *The last frontier: imagining other worlds, from the Copernican revolution to modern science fiction.* Ithaca, NY: Cornell University Press, 1990, xiv+ 402 p., cloth, nonf. [Translation by Helen Atkins of *Der mythos der neuzeit*; winner of the J. Lloyd Eaton Award for Best Nonfiction Book of the Year, 1990 (1992)].].

GUTHRIDGE, George (Lloyd), 1948- , *with Carol Gaskin*

23758 *Death mask of Pancho Villa.* Toronto, New York: A Byron Preiss Book, Bantam Books, 1987, 125 p., paper, novel. TIME MACHINE #19.

GUTTENBERG, Elyse (Margaret), 1952-

24848 *Sunder, Eclipse & Seed.* New York: A Roc Book, 1990, 351 p., paper, novel.

GUTTERIDGE, (Thomas Gordon) Lindsay, 1923-

24849 *Fratricide is a gas.* London: Jonathan Cape, 1975, 192 p., cloth, novel. MATTHEW DILKE #3.

GYGAX, (Ernest) Gary, 1938-

24850 *Advanced Dungeons & Dragons: Dungeon Masters guide: special reference work: a compiled volume of information primarily used by Advanced Dungeons & Dragons game referees, including combat tables; monster lists and encounters; treasury and magic tables and descriptions; random dungeon generation; random wilderness terrain generation; suggestions on gamemastering; and more.* Lake Geneva, WI: TSR Inc., 1979, 236 p., cloth, nonf. ADVANCED DUNGEONS & DRAGONS REFERENCE BOOKS.

24851 *Advanced Dungeons & Dragons: Dungeon Masters guide: special reference work: a compiled volume of information primarily used by Advanced Dungeons & Dragons game referees, including combat tables; monster lists and encounters; treasury and magic tables and descriptions; random dungeon generation; random wilderness terrain generation; suggestions on gamemastering; and more.* Lake Geneva, WI: TSR Inc., 1979, 238 p., cloth, nonf. [Revised edition]. ADVANCED DUNGEONS & DRAGONS REFERENCE BOOKS.

24852 *Advanced Dungeons & Dragons: Dungeon Masters guide: special reference work: a compiled volume of information primarily used by Advanced Dungeons & Dragons referees, including combat tables; monster lists and encounters; treasury and magic tables and descriptions; random dungeon generation; random wilderness terrain generation; suggestions on gamemastering; and more, 2nd ed.* Lake Geneva, WI: TSR Inc., 1989, 192 p., cloth, nonf. ADVANCED DUNGEONS & DRAGONS REFERENCE BOOKS.

24853 *Advanced Dungeons & Dragons: Monster manual: an alphabetical compendium of all the monsters found in Advanced Dungeons & Dragons, including attacks, damage, special abilities, and descriptions.* Lake Geneva, WI: TSR Inc., 1977, 112 p., cloth, nonf. ADVANCED DUNGEONS & DRAGONS REFERENCE BOOKS.

24854 *Advanced Dungeons & Dragons: Monster manual II: an alphabetical listing of monsters found in Advanced Dungeons & Dragons adventures, including attacks, damage, special abilities, descriptions, and random encounter tables.* Lake Geneva, WI: TSR Inc., 1983, 160 p., cloth, nonf. ADVANCED DUNGEONS & DRAGONS REFERENCE BOOKS.

24855 *Advanced Dungeons & Dragons: Players handbook: a compiled volume of information for players of Advanced Dungeons & Dragons, including: character races, classes, and level abilities; spell tables and descriptions; equipment costs; weapons data; and information on adventuring.* Lake Geneva, WI: TSR Inc., 1978, 127 p., cloth, nonf. ADVANCED DUNGEONS & DRAGONS REFERENCE BOOKS.

24856 *Artifact of evil: a novel of fantastic action in a world where magic is law.* Lake Geneva, WI: TSR Inc., 1986, 352 p., paper, novel. GREYHAWK ADVENTURES #2.

24857 *City of hawks*. Lake Geneva, WI: New Infinities Productions, 1987, 400 p., paper, novel. GORD THE ROGUE #3.

24858 *Come endless darkness*. Delavan, WI: New Infinities Productions, 1988, 379 p., paper, novel. GORD THE ROGUE #4.

24859 *Dance of demons*. Delavan, WI: New Infinities Productions, 1988, 428 p., paper, novel. GORD THE ROGUE #5.

24860 *Master of the game*. New York: Perigee Books, 1989, 174 p., paper, nonf.

24861 *Night arrant: a collection of short stories featuring Gord, his friends, and his foes*. Lake Geneva, WI: New Infinities Productions, 1987, 398 p., paper, coll. GORD THE ROGUE #2.

24862 *Official Advanced Dungeons & Dragons Unearthed arcana: a compendium of new ideas and new discoveries for AD&D campaigns, of benefit to players and dungeon masters alike*. Lake Geneva, WI: TSR Inc., 1985, 128 p., cloth, nonf. ADVANCED DUNGEONS & DRAGONS REFERENCE BOOKS.

24863 *Role-playing mastery*. New York: Perigee Books, 1987, 176 p., paper, nonf.

24864 *Saga of old city: a novel of swordplay, thievery, and magic*. Lake Geneva, WI: TSR Inc., 1985, 352 p., paper, novel. GREYHAWK ADVENTURES #1.

24865 *Sea of death*. Lake Geneva, WI: New Infinities Productions, 1987, 394 p., paper, novel. GORD THE ROGUE #1.

with David Cook and François Marcela-Froideval

20426 *Oriental adventures*. Lake Geneva, WI: TSR Inc., 1985, 144 p., cloth, nonf. ADVANCED DUNGEONS & DRAGONS REFERENCE BOOKS.

with Flint Dille

21934 *The crimson sea*. New York: An Archway Paperback, Pocket Books, 1985, [186] p., paper, novel. SAGARD THE BARBARIAN #3.

21935 *The fire demon*. New York: An Archway Paperback, Pocket Books, 1986, [190] p., paper, novel. SAGARD THE BARBARIAN #4.

21936 *The green hydra*. New York: An Archway Paperback, Pocket Books, 1985, [190] p., paper, novel. SAGARD THE BARBARIAN #2.

21937 *The ice dragon*. New York: An Archway Paperback, Pocket Books, 1985, [186] p., paper, novel. SAGARD THE BARBARIAN #1.

with Frank Mentzer

24866 *The temple of elemental evil*. Lake Geneva, WI: TSR Inc., 1985, 128 p., paper, novel.

GYSIN, Brion, 1916-1986

24867 *The last museum*. New York: Grove Press, 1986, 186 p, cloth, novel.

H

H., D. E. W.

24868 *Götterdämmerung on Tety's Delta, being an account of a visit to that planet, reporting sundry particulars of the lives, customs, religious beliefs, history, and sad fate of its late inhabitants, observations on the present condition of that world, some speculations on the writing of science fiction, and weaknesses of human nature, an examination of an instance of parallel evolution of religious mythology on another world, together with some reflections on life in general, and concluding with an interview with the deity; all perfectly proper to be read in respectable families and especially suitable for the consideration of boys interested in theology, and theologians who are boys at heart.* Portsmouth, England: Meeting House Press, 1978, 20 leaves, paper, novel.

H. G. WELLS SOCIETY

24869 *H. G. Wells: a comprehensive bibliography.* Edgware, England: H. G. Wells Society, 1966, viii+61 p., paper, nonf.
24870 *H. G. Wells: a comprehensive bibliography, 2nd ed.* London: H. G. Wells Society, 1968, vi+69 p., paper, nonf.
24871 *H. G. Wells: a comprehensive bibliography, 3rd ed.* London: H. G. Wells Society, 1972, vi+74 p., paper, nonf.

with Patrick Parrinder & A. H. Watkins & J. R. Hammond

24872 *H. G. Wells: a comprehensive bibliography, 4th ed.* London: H. G. Wells Society, 1986, 58 p., paper, nonf.

HAAF, Beverly T(erhune), 1936-

24873 *The chanting.* New York: Popular Library, 1991, 263 p., paper, novel.

HAAN, Tom de—SEE: de Haan, Tom

HAAS, Dorothy (F.)

24874 *The secret life of Dilly McBean.* New York: Bradbury Press, 1986, 202 p., cloth, novel.

HABER, Karen [i.e., Karen Lee Haber Silverberg], 1955-

24875 *The mutant prime.* New York: A Byron Preiss Book, A Foundation Book, Doubleday, 1990, xi+250 p., cloth, novel. MUTANT #2.
24876 *Thieves' carnival.* New York: Tor SF, A Tom Doherty Associates Book, 1990, p. 1-97, paper, story. [Bound with *The jewel of Bas* / by Leigh Brackett].

with Robert Silverberg

24877 *The mutant season.* New York: A Foundation Book, Doubleday, 1989, xi+289 p., cloth, novel. MUTANT #1.
24878 *Universe 1.* New York: A Foundation Book, Doubleday, 1990, xiii+449 p., cloth, anth.

HACKETT, John (Winthrop, General Sir), 1910-

24879 *The third world war: a future history (August 1985).* London: Simon & Schuster, 1978, 368 p., cloth, fiction. THIRD WORLD WAR #1.
24880 *The third world war: the untold story.* London: Sidgwick & Jackson, 1982, xvii+446 p., cloth, fiction. THIRD WORLD WAR #2.

HACKETT, Martin

24881 *Fantasy wargaming: games with magic & monsters.* Wellingborough, Northamptonshire, England: Patrick Stephens Ltd., 1990, 232 p., cloth, nonf.

*HADER, (Ro)Berta (Hoerner), 1890-1976

*HADER, Elmer (Stanley), 1889-1973

HADFIELD, A(lice) M(ary Smith), 1908-

24882 *Charles Williams: an exploration of his life and work.* New York: Oxford University Press, 1983, ix+268 p., cloth, nonf.

HAGAN, Chet, 1922-

24883 *Bon marché.* New York: Tor, A Tom Doherty Associates Book, 1988, 437 p., cloth, novel. DEWEY ANNALS #1.
24884 *From the ashes.* New York: Tor, A Tom Doherty Associates Book, 1989, 563 p., cloth, novel. DEWEY ANNALS #2.
24885 *Redemption.* New York: Richardson & Steirman, 1987, 263 p., cloth, novel.
24886A *The witching.* New York: Leisure Books, 1985, 331 p., paper, novel. [Previously published under the name Colin John].

as COLIN JOHN

24886 *The witching.* New York: Tower Books, 1982, 331 p., paper, novel.

HAGBERG, David (James), 1942-

24887 *The capsule.* New York: A Dell Book, 1976, 268 p., paper, novel.
24888 *Heartland.* New York: Tor, A Tom Doherty Associates Book, 1983, 409 p., paper, novel.
24889 *Last come the children.* New York: Tor, A Tom Doherty Associates Book, 1982, 347 p., paper, novel.

as ANONYMOUS AUTHOR

16517 *Citadels on Earth.* New York: Tempo Books, Grosset & Dunlap, 1981, 200 p., paper, novel. FLASH GORDON #6.
16518 *Citadels under attack.* New York: Tempo Books, Grosset & Dunlap, 1981, 185 p., paper, novel. FLASH GORDON #5.
16520 *Crisis on Citadel II.* New York: Tempo Books, Grosset & Dunlap, 1980, 197 p., paper, novel. FLASH GORDON #3.
16532 *Flash Gordon: Massacre in the 22nd century.* New York: Tempo Books, Grosset & Dunlap, 202 p., paper, novel. FLASH GORDON #1.
16534 *Forces from the Federation.* New York: Tempo Books, Grosset & Dunlap, 1981, 210 p., paper, novel. FLASH GORDON #4.
16632 *War of the Citadels.* New York: Tempo Books, Grosset & Dunlap, 1980, 203 p., paper, novel. FLASH GORDON #2.

as DAVID JAMES

26446 *Croc'.* New York: Belmont Books, 1976, 211 p., paper, novel.

HAGEN, Lorinda, pseud.—SEE: DuBreuil, Linda

HAGGARD, H(enry) Rider, Sir, 1856-1925

06520 *Allan Quatermain: being an account of his further adventures and discoveries in company with Sir Henry Curtis, Bart., Commander John Good, R.N., and one Umslopogaas.* London: Longmans, Green & Co., 1887, 278 p., cloth, novel. ALLAN QUATERMAIN #18.
06520A retitled: *Allan Quatermain and the lost city of gold.* London: Arrow Books, 1986, 176 p., paper, novel. [Abridged by Sarah Litvinoff].
24890 *The annotated She: a critical edition of H. Rider Haggard's Victorian romance, with introduction and notes.* Bloomington & Indianapolis, IN: Indiana University Press, 1991, xliii+241 p., cloth, novel. [Edited by Norman Etherington; includes the novel *She* (see #06563), with commentary and notes].
24891 *The best short stories of Rider Haggard.* London: Michael Joseph, 1981, 254 p., cloth, coll. [Edited by Peter Haining].
24892 *The classic adventures.* Poole, England, New York: New Orchard, 1986, 335 p., cloth, coll. [Includes *Ayesha* and *Benita*].
24893 *Collected novels: King Solomon's mines, Maiwa's revenge, Cleopatra, She.* Secaucus, NJ: Castle Books, 1987, 449 p., cloth, coll.
24894 *King Solomon's mines; She; Allan Quatermain.* London: Octopus Books, 1979, 638 p., cloth, coll.
24895 *The private diaries of Sir H. Rider Haggard, 1914-1925.* London: Cassell, 1980, xvi+299 p., cloth, nonf. [Edited by D. S. Higgins].

HAGGARD, Lilias (Margetson) Rider, 1892-1968

24896 *The cloak that I left: a biography of the author Henry Rider Haggard, K.B.E., by his daughter.* London: Hodder & Stoughton, 1951, 287 p., cloth, nonf.

HAHN, Mary Downing, 1937-

24897 *The doll in the garden: a ghost story.* New York: Clarion Books, 1989, 128 p., cloth, novel.
24898 *Time of the witch.* New York: Clarion Books, 1982, 171 p., cloth, novel.

24899 *Wait till Helen comes: a ghost story.* New York: Clarion Books, 1986, 184 p., cloth, novel.

HAHN, Steve, pseud.—SEE: Robinett, Stephen

HAIBLUM, Isidore, 1935-

24900 *The hand of Ganz: a science fiction novel.* New York: A Signet Book, New American Library, 1985, 238 p., paper, novel. SISCOE & BLOCK #2.

24901 *The identity plunderers.* New York: A Signet Book, New American Library, 1984, 207 p., paper, novel. SISCOE & BLOCK #1.

24902 *Interworld.* New York: A Dell Book, 1977, 256 p., paper, novel. GUNJER #1.

24903 *The mutants are coming.* Garden City, NY: Doubleday & Co., 1984, 183 p., cloth, novel. MUTANTS #1.

24904 *Nightmare express.* New York: Fawcett Gold Medal, 1979, 284 p., paper, novel.

24905 *Out of sync.* New York: A Del Rey Book, Ballantine Books, 1990, 184 p., paper, novel. MUTANTS #2.

24906 *Specterworld.* New York: Avon Books, 1991, 215 p., paper, novel. GUNJER #2.

24907 *The milk are among us.* Garden City, NY: Doubleday & Co., 1975, 210 p, cloth, novel.

HAICH, Elisabeth, 1897-

24908 *Initiation.* London: George Allen & Unwin, 1965, 366 p., cloth, novel. [Translation by John P. Robertson of *Einweihung*].

HAIGH, Richard

24909 *The city.* London: Grafton, 1986, 191 p., paper, novel. FARM #2.

24910 *The farm.* London: Grafton, 1984, 188 p., paper, novel. FARM #1.

24911 *The golden astronauts.* London: Robert Hale, 1980, 191 p., cloth, novel.

HAIGH, Sheila

24912 *Watch for the ghost.* London: Methuen, 1975, 128 p., cloth, novel.

HAILE, Terence

06593 *Space train.* London: Digit Books, 1962, 159 p., paper, novel.

06593A retitled: *The claw.* Australia: Bill Ewington Books, 1973, 160 p., paper, novel.

HAILEY, Johanna, pseud.—SEE: Jarvis, Sharon & Howl, Marcia Yvonne

HAINING, Peter (Alexander), 1940-

24913 *The ancient mysteries reader.* Garden City, NY: Doubleday & Co., 1975, xi+321 p., cloth, anth.

The art of horror stories—SEE: *Terror!*

Black magic 1—SEE: *The black magic omnibus.*

Black magic 2—SEE: *The black magic omnibus.*

24914 *The black magic omnibus.* London: Robson Books, 1976, 413 p., cloth, anth.

24914A retitled: *Black magic 1.* London: Futura Publications, An Orbit Book, 1977, 230 p., paper, anth. [The original book split into two volumes].

24914B retitled: *Black magic 2.* London: Futura Publications, An Orbit Book, 1977, 183 p., paper, anth. [The original book split into two volumes].

24916 *Christmas spirits: ghost stories of the festive season.* London: William Kimber, 1983, 192 p., cloth, anth.

06597 *Christopher Lee's New chamber of horrors.* London: Souvenir Press, 1974, 316 p., cloth, anth.

06597A retitled: *More of Christopher Lee's New chamber of horrors.* St Albans, Hertfordshire, England: Mayflower, 1976, 159 p., paper, anth. [Abridged edition].

06599 *The clans of darkness: Scottish stories of fantasy and horror.* London: Victor Gollancz, 1971, 272 p., cloth, anth.

06599A retitled: *Scottish stories of fantasy and horror.* New York: Bonanza Books, 1988, 288 p., cloth, anth.

24917 *Classic horror omnibus, volume I: five classic novels of terror.* London: New English Library, 1979, 653 p., cloth, anth. [Only volume published].

24918 *Dead of night: horror stories from radio, television, and films.* London: William Kimber, 1981, 203 p., cloth, anth.

24919 *Deadly nightshade: strange stories of the dark.* London: Victor Gollancz, 1977, 189 p., cloth, anth.

24920 *Doctor Who: 25 glorious years: XXV.* London: W. H. Allen & Co., 1988, 224 p., cloth, nonf.

24921 *The Doctor Who file.* London: W. H. Allen & Co., 1986, 256 p., cloth, nonf.

24922 *Doctor Who: the key to time: a year-by-year record.* London: W. H. Allen & Co., 1984, 264 p., cloth, nonf.

24923 *Doctor Who: the time-travellers' guide.* London: W. H. Allen & Co., 1987, 272 p., cloth, nonf.

24924 *The Dracula centenary book.* London: Souvenir Press, 1987, 159 p., cloth, nonf.

24925 *The Dracula scrapbook: articles, essays, letters, newspaper cuttings, anecdotes, illustrations, photographs, and memorabilia about the vampire legend.* London: New English Library, 1976, 176 p., cloth, nonf. anth.

24926 *The Edgar Allan Poe scrapbook: articles, essays, letters, anecdotes, illustrations, photographs, and memorabilia about the legendary American genius.* London: New English Library, 1977, 144 p., cloth, nonf. anth.

Everyman's book of classic horror stories—SEE: *The hell of mirrors.*

24927 *The fantastic pulps.* London: Victor Gollancz, 1975, 419 p., cloth, anth.

24928 *The first book of unknown tales of horror.* London: Sidgwick & Jackson, 1976, 184 p., cloth, anth.

24929 *The Frankenstein file.* London: New English Library, 1977, 127 p., paper, anth. [Includes some nonfiction].

24930 *The ghost finders: tales of some famous phantoms.* London: Victor Gollancz, 1978, 192 p., cloth, anth.

24931 *The ghost ship: stories of the phantom Flying Dutchman.* London: William Kimber, 1985, 206 p., cloth, anth.

24932 *Ghost tour: an armchair journey through the supernatural.* London: William Kimber, 1984, 190 p., cloth, anth.

24933 *The ghost's companion: stories of personal encounters with the supernatural.* London: Victor Gollancz, 1975, 191 p., cloth, anth.

24934 *Greasepaint and ghosts: an anthology of strange and supernatural stories from the world of theatre.* London: William Kimber, 1982, 219 p., cloth, anth.

24935 *The H. G. Wells scrapbook: articles, essays, letters, anecdotes, illustrations, photographs, and memorabilia about the prophetic genius of the twentieth century.* London: New English Library, 1978, 144 p., cloth, nonf. anth.

24936 *Hallowe'en hauntings: stories about the most ghostly night of the year.* London: William Kimber, 1984, 223 p., cloth, anth.

06610 *The hell of mirrors.* London: Four Square Books, 1965, 189 p., paper, anth.

06610A retitled: *Everyman's book of classic horror stories.* London: J. M. Dent & Sons, 1976, xiii+239 p., paper, anth.

Irish tales of terror—SEE: *The wild night company.*

24937 *The Jules Verne companion.* London: Pictorial Presentations, 1978, 128 p., cloth, nonf. anth.

More of Christopher Lee's New chamber of horrors—SEE: *Christopher Lee's New chamber of horrors.*

24938 *More tales of unknown horror.* London: New English Library, 1979, 140 p., paper, anth.

24939 *Movie monsters: great horror film stories.* London: Severn House, 1988, 282 p., cloth, anth.

24940 *The mummy: stories of the living corpse.* London: Severn House, 1988, 263 p., cloth, anth.

New chamber of horrors—SEE: *Christopher Lee's New chamber of horrors.*

24941 *Nightcaps and nightmares: ghosts with a touch of humour.* London: William Kimber, 1983, 204 p., cloth, anth.

24942 *The penny dreadful; or, Strange, horrid, & sensational tales!* London: Victor Gollancz, 1975, 382 p., cloth, anth.

A pictorial history of horror stories—SEE: *Terror!*

24943 *Poltergeist: tales of the deadly ghosts.* London: Severn House, 1987, 249 p., cloth, anth.

24944 *The second book of unknown tales of horror.* London: Sidgwick & Jackson, 1978, 207 p., cloth, anth.

24945 *The shilling shockers: stories of terror from the Gothic bluebooks.* London: Victor Gollancz, 1978, 183 p., cloth, anth.

Stories of the walking dead—SEE: *Zombie!*

24946 *Supernatural sleuths: stories of occult investigators.* London: William Kimber, 1986, 224 p., cloth, anth.

24947 *Tales of dungeons and dragons.* London: Century Publishing, 1986, xx+406 p., cloth, anth.

24948 *Tales of unknown horror.* London: New English Library, 1978, 143 p., paper, anth.

24949 *Terror! a history of horror illustrations from the pulp magazines.* London: Souvenir Press, 1976, 176 p., cloth, art.

24949A retitled: *A pictorial history of horror stories: 200 years of spine-chilling illustrations from the pulp magazines.* London: Treasure, 1985, 176 p., cloth, art.

24949B retitled: *The art of horror stories: two hundred years of spine-chilling illustrations.* Secaucus, NJ: Chartwell Books, 1986, 176 p., cloth, art.

24950 *The third book of unknown tales of horror.* London: Sidgwick & Jackson, 1980, 175 p., cloth, anth.

24951 *Vampire: chilling tales of the undead.* London: W. H. Allen, A Target Book, 1985, 240 p., paper, anth.

24952 *Weird tales: a facsimile of the world's most famous fantasy magazine.* St Helier, Jersey: Neville Spearman, 1976, 264 p., cloth, anth.

24953 *Weird tales: a selection, in facsimile, of the best of the world's most famous fantasy magazine, revised edition.* London: Xanadu, 1990, 236 p., cloth, anth.

24954 *Werewolf: horror stories of the man-beast.* London: Severn House, 1987, 250 p., cloth, anth.

06625 *The wild night company: Irish stories of fantasy and horror.* London: Victor Gollancz, 1970, 287 p., cloth, anth.

06625A retitled: *Irish tales of terror.* New York: Bonanza Books, 1988, 317 p., cloth, anth.

24955 *Zombie! stories of the walking dead.* London: Target Books, 1985, 224 p., paper, anth.

24955A retitled: *Stories of the walking dead.* London: Severn House, 1986, 224 p., cloth, anth.

HAJDA, Nina J.—SEE: Mandelik, Nina

HAJJAN, Mohammed el- —SEE: Mrabet, Mohammed

HALAM, Ann—SEE: Jones, Gwyneth

HALBERSTAM, Michael (Joseph), 1932-1980

24956 *The wanting of Levine.* Philadelphia: J. B. Lippincott Co., 1978, 335 p., cloth, novel.

HALBROOK, Duane

24947 *Satan's doll.* Chatsworth, CA: Candid Books, 1975, 223 p., paper, novel.

HALDANE, J(ohn) B(urdon) S(anderson), 1892-1964

24958 *The man with two memories.* London: Merlin Press, 1976, 220 p., cloth, novel.

HALDEMAN, Candace—SEE: Haldeman, Vol

HALDEMAN, Jack C(arroll) II, 1941-

24959 *The fall of winter.* New York: Baen Science Fiction Books, 1985, 284 p., paper, novel.

24960 *Perry's planet.* Toronto, New York: Bantam Books, 1980, 132 p., paper, novel. STAR TREK SERIES.

24961 *Vector analysis.* New York: Berkley Publishing Corp., 1978, 195 p., cloth, novel.

with Jack Dann

21136 *Echoes of thunder.* New York: Tor SF, A Tom Doherty Associates Book, 1991, p. 91-184, paper, story. [Bound with *Run for the stars* / by Harlan Ellison].

with Jack Dann & Gardner Dozois & Susan Casper & Michael Swanwick

19639 *Slow dancing through time.* Kansas City, MO: Ursus Imprints; Shingletown, CA: Mark V. Ziesing, 1990, xvii+253 p., cloth, coll. [All the stories are collaborations by Dozois with other writers, the majority with Jack Dann].

with Joe Haldeman

24962 *There is no darkness.* New York: Ace Books, 1983, 245 p., paper, novel.

with Harry Harrison

24963 *Bill, the galactic hero on the planet of the zombie vampires.* New York: A Bryon Preiss Book, Avon Books, 1991, 213 p., paper, novel. BILL, THE GALACTIC HERO #4.

with Andrew J. Offutt and Vol Haldeman as JOHN CLEVE

24964 *The Iceworld Connection.* New York: Berkley Books, 1983, 209 p., paper, novel. SPACEWAYS #11.

HALDEMAN, Joe (William), 1943-

24965 *All my sins remembered.* New York: St. Martin's Press, 1977, 184 p., cloth, coll.

24966 *Buying time.* Norwalk, CT: Easton Press, 1989, 300 p., cloth, novel.

24966A retitled: *The long habit of living.* London: New English Library, 1989, 300 p., paper, novel.

24968 *Dealing in futures: stories.* New York: Viking Penguin, 1985, 277 p., cloth, coll.

24969 *The forever war.* New York: St. Martin's Press, 1975, 236 p., cloth, novel.

[Winner of the Hugo Award for Best Novel, 1975 (1976); winner of the Nebula Award for Best Novel, 1975 (1976); winner of the *Locus* Award for Best Novel, 1975 (1976)].

24970 *The Hemingway hoax.* New York: William Morrow & Co., 1990, 155 p., cloth, novel.

24971 *Infinite dreams.* New York: St. Martin's Press, 1978, 278 p., cloth, coll.

The long habit of living—SEE: *Buying time.*

24972 *Mindbridge.* New York: St. Martin's Press, 1976, 186 p., cloth, novel.

24973 *More than the sum of his parts.* Eugene, OR: Pulphouse Publishing, 1991, 45 p., cloth, story. SHORT STORY HARDBACKS #9; SHORT STORY PAPERBACKS #14.

24974 *Nebula award stories seventeen.* New York: Holt, Rinehart & Winston, 1983, 291 p., cloth, anth.

24975 *Planet of judgment.* Toronto, New York: Bantam Books, 1977, 151 p., paper, novel. STAR TREK SERIES.

24976 *Study war no more: a selection of alternatives.* New York: St. Martin's Press, 1977, 278 p., cloth, anth.

24977 *Tool of the trade.* New York: William Morrow & Co., 1987, 261 p., cloth, novel.

24978 *World without end: a Star Trek novel.* Toronto, New York: Bantam Books, 1979, 150 p., paper, novel. STAR TREK SERIES.

24979 *Worlds: a novel of the near future.* New York: Viking Press, 1981, 262 p., cloth, novel. WORLDS #1. [Edited by A(nson) Richard Barbour].

24980 *Worlds apart.* New York: Viking Press, 1983, 227 p., cloth, novel. WORLDS #2. [Edited by A(nson) Richard Barbour].

as ROBERT GRAHAM

24981 *Attar's revenge.* New York: Pocket Books, 1975, 144 p., paper, novel. ATTAR THE MERMAN #1.

24982 *War of nerves.* New York: Pocket Books, 1975, 158 p., paper, novel. ATTAR THE MERMAN #2.

with Martin H. Greenberg & Charles G. Waugh

24523 *Body armor: 2000.* New York: Ace Science Fiction Books, 1986, 311 p., paper, anth.

24524 *Spacefighters.* New York: Ace Books, 1988, 296 p., paper, anth.

24525 *Supertanks.* New York: Ace Science Fiction Books, 1987, 262 p., paper, anth.

with Jack C. Haldeman II

24962 *There is no darkness.* New York: Ace Books, 1983, 245 p., paper, novel.

HALDEMAN, Laurie, *with Jean Airey*

16142 *Travel without the Tardis.* London: A Target Book, W. H. Allen & Co., 1986, 160 p., paper, nonf.

HALDEMAN, Linda (Wilson), 1935?-1988

24983 *Esbae: a winter's tale.* New York: Avon, 1981, 224 p., paper, novel.

24984 *The lastborn of Elvinwood.* Garden City, NY: Doubleday & Co., 1978, 237 p., cloth, novel.

24985 *Star of the Sea.* Garden City, NY: Doubleday & Co., 1978, 182 p., cloth, novel.

HALDEMAN, Vol [i.e., Candace Ettlin Haldeman], 1946- , *with Andrew J. Offutt and Jack C. Haldeman II as* JOHN CLEVE

24964 *The Iceworld Connection.* New York: Berkley Books, 1983, 209 p., paper, novel. SPACEWAYS #11.

HALDEMAN-JULIUS, E(manuel), 1889-1951

15813 *Five great ghost stories.* Girard, KS: Haldeman-Julius, 1920?, 127 p., paper, anth.

HALE, Andrew, 1939-

24986 *2020: vision of the future.* Canterbury, England: Ada Press, 1987, 48 p., paper, novel.

HALE, F. J.

24987 *In the sea nymph's lair.* New York: Pageant Books, 1989, 209 p., paper, novel. AFTER THE SPELL WARS #2.

24988 *Ogre castle.* New York: Pageant Books, 1988, 209 p., paper, novel. AFTER THE SPELL WARS #1.

as EDWARD S. HUDSON

24989 *Alien death fleet.* New York: Pageant Books, 1989, 207 p., paper, novel. STAR FRONTIER TRILOGY #1.

HALE, Glenn—SEE: Walker, Robert W.

HALE, James

24990 *The after midnight ghost book.* London: Hutchinson, 1980, 351 p., cloth, anth.
24990A retitled: *The fourth bumper book of ghost stories.* London & Sydney: Pan Books, 1981, 316 p., paper, anth.
The fourth bumper book of ghost stories—SEE: *The after midnight ghost book.*
24991 *The midnight ghost book.* London: Barrie & Jenkins, 1978, 357 p., cloth, anth.
24991A retitled: *The third bumper book of ghost stories.* London & Sydney: Pan Books, 1979, 320 p., paper, anth.
The third bumper book of ghost stories—SEE: *The midnight ghost book.*
24992 *The thirteenth ghost book.* London: Barrie & Jenkins, 1977, 204 p., cloth, anth.
24993 *The twilight book: a new collection of ghost stories.* London: Victor Gollancz, 1981, 183 p., cloth, anth.

with Patricia Parkin

24994 *The 2nd bumper ghost book.* London & Sydney: Pan Books, 1978, 333 p., paper, anth. [Combines *The twelfth ghost book* and *The thirteenth ghost book*].

HALE, Jennifer

24995 *Beyond the dark.* New York: A Berkley Medallion Book, Berkley Publishing Corp., 1978, 220 p., paper, novel.
24996 *Portrait of evil.* New York: Ballantine Books, 1975, 185 p., paper, novel.

*HALE, John (Barry), 1926-

HALE, Michael

24997 *The other child.* New York: Avon, 1986, 297 p., paper, novel.

*HALE, Robert Beverly, 1901-1985

HALES, E(dward) E(lton) Y(oung), 1908-

24998 *Chariot of fire.* London: Hodder & Stoughton, 1977, 191 p., cloth, novel.

HALEY, Claud(e), pseud.—SEE: Fish, Leonard

HALEY, James L(ewis), 1951-

24999 *The lions of Tsavo: a novel.* New York, Toronto: Bantam Books, 1989, 259 p., paper, novel.

*HALEY, Harry F(ranklin), 1883-1965

HALKIN, John, 1927-

25000 *Blood worm.* London: Arrow Books, 1987, 251 p., paper, novel.
25001 *Fangs of the werewolf.* London: Hutchinson Children's Books, 1987, 149 p., cloth, novel.
25002 *Slime.* London: Hamlyn Paperbacks, 1984, 252 p., paper, novel. SLITHER #2.
25003 *Slither.* Feltham: Hamlyn Paperbacks, 1980, 215 p., paper, novel. SLITHER #1.
25004 *Squelch.* London: Hamlyn Paperbacks, 1985, 250 p., paper, novel. SLITHER #3.
25005 *The unholy.* Feltham, England: Hamlyn Paperbacks, 1982, 158 p., paper, novel.

HALL, Adam, pseud.—SEE: Trevor, Elleston

*HALL, Austin (Javen), 1880-1933

HALL, Brian (Patrick), 1935-

25006 *The Wizard of Maldoone.* New York, Paramus, NJ: Paulist Press, 1975, 143 p., cloth, novel.

HALL, Desmond—SEE: Gilmore, Anthony

HALL, Frances (Tebbetts), 1914- , with Piers Anthony

16712 *Pretender: science fiction.* San Bernardino, CA: R. Reginald, The Borgo Press, 1979, 159 p., cloth, novel.

HALL, Hal(bert) W(eldon), 1941-

25007 *Chad Oliver: a preliminary bibliography.* Bryan, TX: Dellwood Press, 1985, 86 p., paper, nonf.
25008 *Science fiction and fantasy book review index, volume 16, 1985.* Bryan, TX: SF-BRI, 1988, 69 p., paper, nonf.
25009 *Science fiction and fantasy book review index, volume 17, 1986.* Bryan, TX: SF-BRI, 1989, vi+71 p., paper, nonf.
25010 *Science fiction and fantasy book review index, volume 18, 1987.* Bryan, TX: SF-BRI, 1990, v+70 p., paper, nonf.
25011 *Science fiction and fantasy reference index, 1878-1985: an international author and subject index to history and criticism.* Detroit: Gale Research Co., 1987, xviii+xx+1460 p. in 2 vols., cloth, nonf.
25012 *Science fiction and fantasy research index, volume 2.* Bryan, TX: SFBRI, 1982, v+72 p., paper, nonf.

25013 *Science fiction and fantasy research index, volume 3.* Bryan, TX: SFBRI, 1983, iv+74 p., paper, nonf.

25014 *Science fiction and fantasy research index, volume 8.* San Bernardino, CA: R. Reginald, The Borgo Press, 1988, iv+68 p., cloth, nonf.

25015 *Science fiction book review index, 1923-1973.* Detroit: Gale Research Co., 1975, xvi+438 p., cloth, nonf.

25016 *Science fiction book review index, 1974-1979.* Detroit: Gale Research Co., 1981, xx+391 p., cloth, nonf.

25017 *Science/fiction collections: fantasy, supernatural, & weird tales.* New York: Haworth Press, 1983, 181 p., cloth, nonf. anth.

25018 *Science fiction research index, volume 1.* Bryan, TX: SFBRI, 1981, iii+27 p., paper, nonf.

25019 *SFBRI: science fiction book review index, v. 5, 1974.* Bryan, TX: H. W. Hall, 1975, 40 p., paper, nonf.

25020 *SFBRI: science fiction book review index, v. 6, 1975.* Bryan, TX: H. W. Hall, 1976, 49 p., paper, nonf.

25021 *SFBRI: science fiction book review index, v. 7, 1976.* Bryan, TX: H. W. Hall, 1977, 58 p., paper, nonf.

25022 *SFBRI: science fiction book review index, v. 8, 1977.* Bryan, TX: SFBRI, 1978, 39 p., paper, nonf.

25023 *SFBRI: science fiction book review index, v. 9, 1978.* Bryan, TX: SFBRI, 1979, 37 p., paper, nonf.

25024 *SFBRI: science fiction book review index, v. 10, 1979.* Bryan, TX: SFBRI, 1980, i+61 p., paper, nonf.

25025 *SFBRI: science fiction book review index, volume 11, 1980.* Bryan, TX: SFBRI, 1981, 40 p., paper, nonf.

25026 *SFBRI: science fiction book review index, volume 12, 1981.* Bryan, TX: SFBRI, 1982, 46 p., paper, nonf.

25027 *SFBRI: science fiction book review index, volume 13, 1982.* Bryan, TX: SFBRI, 1983, 55 p., paper, nonf.

25028 *SFBRI: science fiction book review index, volume 14, 1983.* Bryan, TX: SFBRI, 1984, 61 p., paper, nonf.

25029 *SFBRI: science fiction and fantasy book review index, volume 15, 1984.* Bryan, TX: SFBRI, 1985, 71 p., paper, nonf.

25030 *The work of Chad Oliver: an annotated bibliography & guide.* San Bernardino, CA: R. Reginald, The Borgo Press, 1989, 88 p., cloth, nonf. BIBLIOGRAPHIES OF MODERN AUTHORS #12. [Edited by Boden Clarke].

with Charles N. Brown & William G. Contento

18782 *Science fiction, fantasy, & horror: 1988: a comprehensive bibliography of books and short fiction published in the English language.* Oakland, CA: Locus Press, 1989, viii+463 p., cloth, nonf. [Winner of the J. Lloyd Eaton Award for Best Nonfiction Book of the Year, 1989 (1991)].

18783 *Science fiction, fantasy, & horror: 1989: a comprehensive bibliography of books and short fiction published in the English language.* Oakland, CA: Locus Press, 1990, viii+515 p., cloth, nonf.

18784 *Science fiction, fantasy, & horror: 1990: a comprehensive bibliography of books and short fiction published in the English language.* Oakland, CA: Locus Press, 1991, viii+587 p., cloth, nonf.

with Geraldine L. Hutchins

25031 *Science fiction and fantasy book review index, 1980-1984: an index to more than 13,800 book reviews appearing in over 70 science fiction, fantasy, and general periodicals from 1980 to 1984, and containing "Science fiction and fantasy research index," an index to secondary literature, providing nearly 16,000 subject and author access points to articles, essays, and books featuring the history of, or criticism on, science fiction and fantasy literature, television programs, motion pictures, and graphic arts.* Detroit: Gale Research Co., 1985, xxi+761 p., cloth, nonf.

25032 *Science fiction and fantasy research index, volume 4.* Bryan, TX: SFBRI, 1985, 83 p., paper, nonf.

25033 *Science fiction and fantasy research index, volume 5.* San Bernardino, CA: Borgo, 1985, 115 p., cloth, nonf.

25034 *Science fiction and fantasy research index, volume 6.* San Bernardino, CA: Borgo, 1986, 101 p., cloth, nonf.

with Kenneth R. Johnson & George Michaels

25035 *The science fiction magazines: a bibliographical checklist of titles and issues through 1983.* Bryan, TX: SFBRI, 1983, iv+89 p., paper, nonf.

with Jan Swanbeck

25036 *Science fiction and fantasy research index, volume 7.* San Bernardino, CA: The Borgo Press, 1987, 197 p., cloth, nonf.

HALL, James N., *with Nelson Bond*

18261 *James Branch Cabell: a complete bibliography, with a supplement of current values of Cabell books by Nelson Bond.* New York: Revisionist Press, 1974, xi + 245 p., cloth, nonf.

HALL, John Ryder, pseud.—SEE: Rotsler, William

HALL, Lynn, 1937-

25037 *Dagmar Schultz and the Angel Edna.* New York: Charles Scribner's Sons, 1989, 86 p., cloth, novel. DAGMAR SCHULTZ #2. [The first volume in the series, *The secret life of Dagmar Schultz*, is not SF].
25038 *Dagmar Schultz and the powers of darkness.* New York: Charles Scribner's Sons, 1989, 74 p., cloth, novel. DAGMAR SCHULTZ #3.

HALL, Manly P(almer), 1901-1990

25039 *Shadow forms: a collection of occult stories, rev. ed.* Los Angeles: Philosophical Research Society, 1979, 165 p., cloth, coll.

HALL, Matthew

25040 *Nightmare logic.* New York, Toronto: Bantam Books, 1989, 293 p., paper, novel.

HALL, Norman, 1904-

25041 *Green hailstones.* London: Robert Hale, 1978, 175 p., cloth, novel.

HALL, Robert Lee, 1941-

25042 *Exit Sherlock Holmes: the great detective's final days.* New York: Charles Scribner's Sons, 1977, x + 238 p., cloth, novel. SHERLOCK HOLMES SERIES.

HALL, Rodney, 1935-

25043 *Kisses of the enemy.* Ringwood, Victoria, Australia: Penguin Books, 1987, 622 p., cloth, novel.

HALL, Sandi, 1942-

25044 *The godmothers.* London: The Women's Press, 1982, 183 p., cloth, novel.

25045 *Wingwomen of Hera.* San Francisco, CA: Spinsters/Aunt Lute, 1987, 180 p., paper, novel. COSMIC BOTANISTS TRILOGY #1.

HALL, Willis, 1929-

25046 *The Antelope Company ashore.* London: Bodley Head, 1986, 150 p., cloth, tele. ANTELOPE COMPANY #2.
25047 *The Antelope Company at large.* London: Bodley Head, 1987, 145 p., cloth, tele. ANTELOPE COMPANY #3.
25048 *Dr Jekyll and Mr Hollins.* London: Bodley Head, 1988, 143 p., cloth, novel. HENRY HOLLINS SERIES.
25049 *Dragon days.* London: Bodley Head, 1985, 131 p., cloth, novel.
Henry Hollins and the dinosaur—SEE: *Summer of the dinosaur.*
25050 *The last vampire.* London: Bodley Head, 1982, 157 p., cloth, novel.
25051 *The return of the Antelope Company.* London: Bodley Head, 1985, 174 p., cloth, tele. ANTELOPE COMPANY #1.
25052 *Summer of the dinosaur.* London: Bodley Head, 1977, 189 p., cloth, novel. HENRY HOLLINS SERIES.
25052A retitled: *Henry Hollins and the dinosaur.* London: Bodley Head, 1988, 188 p., cloth, novel. HENRY HOLLINS SERIES.

HALLAHAN, William H(enry)

25053 *Keeper of the children.* New York: William Morrow & Co., 1978, 191 p., cloth, novel.
25054 *The monk: a novel.* New York: William Morrow & Co., 1983, 273 p., cloth, novel.

*HALLAM, (Samuel Benoni) Atlantis, 1915-1987

HALLAMSHIRE, David

25055 *The alien's dictionary.* London: Headline, 1989, 119 p., paper, fiction.

HALLIBURTON, David (Garland), 1933-

25056 *Edgar Allan Poe: a phenomenological view.* Princeton, NJ: Princeton University Press, 1973, 428 p., cloth, nonf.

HALLIWELL, Leslie, 1929-1989

25057 *The dead that walk.* London: Grafton Books, 1986, 261 p., cloth, nonf. coll.
25058 *A demon close behind: a new collection of uneasy tales.* London: Robert Hale, 1987, 240 p., cloth, coll.

25059 *A demon on the stair: stories of the supernatural.* London: Robert Hale, 1988, 240 p., cloth, coll.

25060 *The ghost of Sherlock Holmes: seventeen supernatural stories.* London: Panther, Granada Publishing, 1984, 254 p., paper, coll.

25061 *Return to Shangri-La.* London: Grafton, 1987, 304 p., paper, novel.

HALLOCK, Rusty

37818 *Jewels in the dark.* New York: Ballantine Books, 1986, 72 p., paper, fiction. FIND YOUR FATE—JEM #1.

HALLSTEAD, William Finn III—SEE: Beechcroft, William

HALPERN, Barbara—SEE: Strachey, Barbara

HALPERN, Frank M., 1943-

25062 *International classified directory of dealers in science fiction and fantasy books and related materials.* Haddonfield, NJ: Haddonfield House, 1975, x+90 p., cloth, nonf.

HALPERN, Jay

25063 *The jade unicorn.* New York: Macmillan Publishing Co., 1979, 338 p., cloth, novel.

HALPERN, Marjorie—SEE: Agosin, Marjorie

HAM, Bob

25064 *Alabama bloodbath.* New York, Toronto: Falcon, Bantam Books, 1991, 196 p., paper, novel. OVERLOAD #11.

25065 *Atlanta burn.* New York, Toronto: Bantam Books, 1990, 165 p., paper, novel. OVERLOAD #5.

25066 *Highway warriors.* New York, Toronto: Bantam Books, 1989, 179 p., paper, novel. OVERLOAD #3.

25067 *Huntsville horror.* New York, Toronto: Falcon, Bantam Books, 1991, 216 p., paper, novel. OVERLOAD #9.

25068 *Michigan madness.* New York, Toronto: Falcon, Bantam Books, 1991, 197 p., paper, novel. OVERLOAD #10.

25069 *Nebraska nightmare.* New York, Toronto: Bantam Books, 1990, 168 p., paper, novel. OVERLOAD #6.

25070 *Ozark payback.* New York, Toronto: Bantam Books, 1991, 216 p., paper, novel. OVERLOAD #8.

25071 *Personal war.* New York, Toronto: Bantam Books, 1989, 159 p., paper, novel. OVERLOAD #1.

25072 *Rolling vengeance.* New York, Toronto: Bantam Books, 1990, 238 p., paper, novel. OVERLOAD #7.

25073 *Tennessee terror.* New York, Toronto: Bantam Books, 1989, 260 p., paper, novel. OVERLOAD #4.

25074 *Vegas gamble.* New York, Toronto: Falcon, Bantam Books, 1991, 168 p., paper, novel. OVERLOAD #12.

25075 *The wrath.* New York, Toronto: Bantam Books, 1989, 180 p., paper, novel. OVERLOAD #2.

HAMBLY, Barbara (Joan), 1951-

25076 *The armies of daylight.* New York: A Del Rey Book, Ballantine Books, 1983, 309 p., paper, novel. DARWATH TRILOGY #3.

25077 *Beauty and the beast: a novel.* New York: Avon Books, 1989, 242 p., paper, tele. BEAUTY AND THE BEAST #1.

25078 *Beauty and the beast: Song of Orpheus: a novel.* New York: Avon Books, 1990, 279 p., paper, tele. BEAUTY AND THE BEAST #3.

25079 *The dark hand of magic.* New York: A Del Rey Book, Ballantine Books, 1990, 309 p., paper, novel. SUN WOLF #3.

25080 *Darkmage: The silent tower; The silicon mage.* Garden City, NY: Nelson Doubleday, 1988, 533 p., cloth, coll. WINDROSE #1-2.

25081 *Dragonsbane.* New York: A Del Rey Book, Ballantine Books, 1986, 341 p., paper, novel.

Ghost walker—SEE: Star Trek: Ghost walker.

Immortal blood—SEE: Those who hunt the night.

25082 *Ishmael: a Star Trek novel.* New York: Pocket Books, 1985, 255 p., paper, novel. STAR TREK #23.

25083 *The ladies of Mandrigyn.* New York: A Del Rey Book, Ballantine Books, 1984, 311 p., paper, novel. SUN WOLF #1.

25084 *The rainbow abyss.* London: Grafton, 1991, 256 p., cloth, novel. SUN-CROSS #1.

25085 *The Silent Tower.* New York: A Del Rey Book, Ballantine Books, 1986, 369 p., paper, novel. WINDROSE #1.

25086 *The silicon mage.* London: Unwin Paperbacks, 1988, 340 p., paper, novel. WINDROSE #2.

Song of Orpheus—SEE: Beauty and the beast: Song of Orpheus.

25087 *Star Trek: Ghost walker.* New York, London: Pocket Books, 1991, 273 p., paper, novel. STAR TREK #53.

25088 *Those who hunt the night.* New York: A Del Rey Book, Ballantine Books, 1988, 296 p., cloth, novel. [Winner of the *Locus* Award for Best Horror Novel, 1988 (1989)].

25088A retitled: *Immortal blood.* London: Unwin Paperbacks, 1988, 306 p., paper, novel.

25089 *The time of the Dark.* New York: A Del Rey Book, Ballantine Books, 1982, 263 p., paper, novel. DARWATH TRILOGY #1.

25090 *The unschooled wizard: The ladies of Madrigyn; The witches of Wenshar.* Garden City, NY: Nelson Doubleday, 1987, 600 p., cloth, coll. SUN WOLF #1-2.

25091 *The walls of air.* New York: A Del Rey Book, Ballantine Books, 1983, 297 p., paper, novel. DARWATH TRILOGY #2.

25092 *The witches of Wenshar.* New York: A Del Rey Book, Ballantine Books, 1987, 339 p., paper, novel. SUN WOLF #2.

HAMEL PEIFER, Kathleen—SEE: Dobkin, Kaye

*HAMILTON, Alex (John), <u>1930-</u>

HAMILTON, Andrew

25093 *The host man.* London: Dennis Dobson, 1975, 207 p., cloth, novel.

HAMILTON, Edmond (Moore), 1904-1977

25094 *The best of Edmond Hamilton.* Garden City, NY: Nelson Doubleday, 1977, xvii+334 p., cloth, coll. [Edited by Leigh Brackett].

25095 *Chronicles of the Star Kings.* London: Arrow Books, Venture SF, 1986, 397 p., paper, coll. STAR KINGS #1-2. [Includes *The Star Kings* and *Return to the stars*].

25096 *Starwolf.* New York: Ace Books, 1982, 456 p., paper, coll. STARWOLF #1-3. [Includes *The weapon from beyond*; *The Closed Worlds*; *World of the Starwolves*].

HAMILTON, Elmer Jr.

25097 *Titus from Blakay.* New York, Washington: Vantage Press, 1981, 68 p., cloth, novel.

HAMILTON, Frank(lyn Edward), 1918- , with Link Hullar

25098 *Amazing pulp heroes.* Brooklyn, NY: Griffin Publications, 1988, 59 p., paper, nonf.

HAMILTON, George T.

37819 *Bicentennial tribute to Robert E. Howard.* Yorba Linda, CA: George T. Hamilton, Publisher, 1976 (i.e., 1977?), ix+37 p., paper, nonf. anth. [Limited to 194 copies].

HAMILTON, Jessica, pseud.—SEE: Greenhall, Ken

HAMILTON, Margaret, 1941-

25101 *Spooks and spirits: eight eerie tales by Australian writers.* Sydney, Australia, London: Hodder & Stoughton, 1978, 128 p., cloth, anth.

HAMILTON, Mary M.—SEE: Kaye, M. M.

HAMILTON, Todd Cameron, *with P. J. Beese*

17670 *The guardsman.* New York: Pageant Books, 1988, 313 p., paper, novel.

HAMILTON, Virginia [i.e., Virginia Esther Hamilton Adoff], 1936-

25102 *The dark way: stories from the spirit world.* San Diego, CA: Harcourt Brace Jovanovich, 1990, xiv+154 p., cloth, coll.

25103 *Dustland.* New York: Greenwillow Books, 1980, 180 p., cloth, novel. JUSTICE CYCLE #2.

25104 *The gathering.* New York: Greenwillow Books, 1981, 179 p., cloth, novel. JUSTICE CYCLE #3.

25105 *Justice and her brothers.* New York: Greenwillow Books, 1981, 217 p., cloth, novel. JUSTICE CYCLE #1.

25106 *M. C. Higgins, the great.* New York: Macmillan, 1974, 278 p., cloth, novel.

25107 *The magical adventures of Pretty Pearl.* New York: Harper & Row, A Charlotte Zolotow Book, 1983, 311 p., cloth, novel.

25108 *Sweet whispers, Brother Rush.* New York: Philomel Books, 1982, 215 p., cloth, novel.

HAMLEY, Dennis (C.), 1935-

25109 *The fourth plane at the flypast.* London: André Deutsch, 1985, 119 p., paper, coll.

25110 *Hare's choice.* London: André Deutsch, 1988, 96 p., paper, novel.

25111 *Haunted united.* London: André Deutsch, 1986, 143 p., paper, novel.

15814 *Pageants of despair.* London: André Deutsch, 1974, 175 p., cloth, novel.

25112 *The shirt off a hanged man's back: nine stories of the supernatural.* London: André Deutsch, 1984, 155 p., paper, coll.

HAMM, William, 1929-

25113 *The grey shadows of death.* Winnipeg, Manitoba, Canada: Thirteen Green Publications, 1964, 160 p., paper, novel

HAMMACHER, A(braham) M(arie), 1897-

25114 *Phantoms of the imagination: fantasy in art and literature from Blake to Dali.* New York: Henry N. Abrams, 1981, 364 p., cloth, art.

HAMMIL, Joel, 1909-

25115 *Limbo: a novel.* New York: Arbor House, 1980, 246 p., cloth, novel.

25116 *The trident.* New York: Arbor House, 1981, 251 p., cloth, novel.

HAMMOND, Clement Milton, *with Charles Howard Montague*

25117 *The doctor's mistake; or, What Myrta saw: an experiment with a life: a novel.* Boston: Thomas Downey Jr. & Co., 1888, 146 p., paper, novel.

HAMMOND, J(ohn) R., 1933-

25118 *An Edgar Allan Poe companion: a guide to the short stories, romances, and essays.* Totowa, NJ: Barnes & Noble Books, 1981, xii+205 p., cloth, nonf.

25119 *A George Orwell companion: a guide to the novels, documentaries, and essays.* New York: St. Martin's Press, 1982, xii+278 p., cloth, nonf.

25120 *H. G. Wells and Rebecca West.* New York, London: Harvester Wheatsheaf, 1991, xii+280 p., cloth, nonf.

25121 *H. G. Wells and the modern novel.* New York: St. Martin's Press, 1988, xii+224 p., cloth, nonf.

25122 *An H. G. Wells companion: a guide to the novels, romances, and short stories.* London: Macmillan, 1979, xii+288 p., cloth, nonf.

25123 *H. G. Wells: interviews and recollections.* London: Macmillan, 1980, xii+121 p., cloth, nonf. anth.

25124 *Herbert George Wells: an annotated bibliography of his works.* New York, London: Garland Publishing, 1977, xvi+257 p., cloth, nonf.

25125 *A Robert Louis Stevenson companion: a guide to the novels, essays, and short stories.* London: Macmillan, 1984, x+252 p., cloth, nonf.

with A. H. Watkins & Patrick Parrinder & The H. G. Wells Society

25126 *H. G. Wells: a comprehensive bibliography, 4th ed.* London: H. G. Wells Society, 1986, 58 p., paper, nonf.

HAMMONDS, Michael (Galen), 1942-

25127 *The burning man.* New York: Pinnacle Books, Windsor Publishing Corp., 1991, 432 p., paper, novel.

HAMPSHIRE, Joyce—SEE: Gregorian, Joyce Ballou

HAMPTON, Bill (R.), 1934- , *with Luann Hampton*

25128 *Captive!* New York, Toronto: An Edward Packard Book, Bantam Books, 1989, 116 p., paper, novel. CHOOSE YOUR OWN ADVENTURE #93.

HAMPTON, Jay

25129 *The coven.* Los Angeles: Pinnacle Books, 1978, 278 p., paper, novel.

HAMPTON, Luann, *with Bill Hampton*

25128 *Captive!* New York, Toronto: An Edward Packard Book, Bantam Books, 1989, 116 p., paper, novel. CHOOSE YOUR OWN ADVENTURE #93.

HAN, Suyin, 1917-

25130 *The enchantress.* London: Sidgwick & Jackson, 1985, 345 p., cloth, novel.

HANCOCK, Geoff(rey White), 1946-

25131 *Magic realism: an anthology.* Toronto: Aya Press, 1980, 200 p., cloth, anth.

HANCOCK, Niel (Anderson), 1941-

25132 *Across the far mountain.* New York: Fawcett Popular Library, 1982, 255 p., paper, novel. WILDERNESS OF FOUR #1.

25133 *The bridge of dawn.* New York: Popular Library, 1991, 300 p., paper, novel. WINDAMEIR CIRCLE #4.

25134 *Calix Stay.* New York: Popular Library, 1977, 253 p., paper, novel. CIRCLE OF LIGHT #3.

25135 *Dragon winter.* New York: Popular Library, 1978, 351 p., paper, novel.

25136 *Faragon Fairingay.* New York: Popular Library, 1977, 349 p., paper, novel. CIRCLE OF LIGHT #2.

25137 *The fires of Windameir.* New York: Popular Library, 1985, 407 p., paper, novel. WINDAMEIR CIRCLE #1.

25138 *Greyfax Grimwald.* New York: Popular Library, 1977, 352 p., paper, novel. CIRCLE OF LIGHT #1.

25139 *On the boundaries of darkness.* New York: Popular Library, 1982, 287 p., paper, novel. WILDERNESS OF FOUR #3.

25140 *The plains of the sea.* New York: Popular Library, 1982, 286 p., paper, novel. WILDERNESS OF FOUR #2.

25141 *The road to the Middle Islands.* New York: Warner Books, 1983, 287 p., paper, novel. WILDERNESS OF FOUR #4.

25142 *The sea of silence.* New York: Popular Library, 1987, 374 p., paper, novel. WINDAMEIR CIRCLE #2.

25143 *Squaring the Circle.* New York: Popular Library, 1977, 378 p., paper, novel. CIRCLE OF LIGHT #4.

25144 *A wanderer's return.* New York: Popular Library, 1988, 306 p., paper, novel. WINDAMEIR CIRCLE #3.

HAND, Elizabeth (Francis), 1957-

25145 *Winterlong: a novel.* New York, Toronto: Spectra, Bantam Books, 1990, 442 p., paper, novel.

HAND, Stephen

37820 *Legend of the shadow warriors.* Harmondsworth, Middlesex, England: Puffin Books, 1991, [288] p., paper, fiction. FIGHTING FANTASY GAMEBOOK SERIES.

HANDLEY, Graham (Roderick), 1926-

25146 *Brodie's notes on Aldous Huxley's Brave new world.* London & Sydney: Pan Books, 1977, vi+80 p., paper, nonf.

25147 *Brodie's notes on Aldous Huxley's Brave new world, revised ed.* London & Sydney: Pan Books, 1990, 71 p., paper, nonf.

Brodie's notes on William Golding—SEE: *William Golding: Lord of the flies.*

25148 *John Christopher: The death of grass.* Harmondsworth, Middlesex, England: Penguin Books, 1988, 70 p., paper, nonf.

25149 *William Golding: Lord of the flies.* Bath, Somerset: James Brodie, 1965, 63 p., paper, nonf.

25150 retitled: *Brodie's notes on William Golding, revised ed.* London & Syndey: Pan Books, 1976, vii+63 p., paper, nonf.

25151 *Brodie's notes on William Golding, [second] revised ed.* London & Syndey: Pan Books, 1990, 64 p., paper, nonf.

HANDLEY, Max (Adrian Robert), 1945-

25152 *Meanwhile.* London: Arlington Books, 1977, 286 p., cloth, novel.

HANDLING, Piers

37821 *The shape of rage: the films of David Cronenberg.* Toronto: General Publishing Co.; New York: New York Zoetrope, 1983, vii+216 p., cloth, nonf. anth.

HANEY, Lynn, 1941-

with Arthur Byron Cover

20684 *The Flash Gordon book.* New York: G. P. Putnam's Sons, 1980, [58] p., cloth, movie. FLASH GORDON SERIES. [Adapted by Haney from Cover's novel].

with Alan Dean Foster

23370 *The last starfighter storybook.* New York: G. P. Putnam's Sons, 1984, [47] p., cloth, movie. [Adapted from Foster's novelization].

HANFF, Peter E(dward), 1944- , with Douglas G. Greene

24618 *Bibliographia Oziana: a concise bibliographical checklist of the Oz books by L. Frank Baum and his successors.* Kinderhook, IL: International Wizard of Oz Club, 1976, 103 p., cloth?, nonf.

24619 *Bibliographia Oziana: a concise bibliographical checklist of the Oz books by L. Frank Baum and his successors, rev. and enl. ed.* Kinderhook, IL: International

Wizard of Oz Club, 1988, 146 p., cloth?, nonf.

HANKE, Ken, 1954-

25153 *A critical guide to horror film series.* New York, London: Garland Publishing, 1991, xv+341 p., cloth, nonf.

HANLEY, Elizabeth, pseud.—SEE: DeBreuil, Lorinda

HANLEY, James, 1901-1985

37822 *What Farrar saw, and other stories.* London: André Deutsch, 1984, 295 p., cloth, coll. [Includes the novel *What Farrar saw* (see #06734)].

HANLON, Emily, 1945-

25154 *Circle home: a novel.* New York: Bradbury Press, 1981, 237 p., cloth, novel.

*HANNAN, (Robert) Charles

HANNAY, Margaret P(atterson), 1944-

25156 *C. S. Lewis.* New York: Frederick Ungar Publishing Co., 1981, xiv+299 p., cloth, nonf.

HANRATTY, Peter

25157 *The book of Mordred.* Lake Geneva, WI: New Infinities Productions, 1988, 256 p., paper, novel. ARTHUR #2.
25158 *The last knight of Albion.* New York: Bluejay Books, 1986, 267 p., paper, novel. ARTHUR #1.

HANSEN, Gwen

25159 *Moonspell.* New York: Fawcett Columbine, 1989, 122 p., paper, novel. SECRET OF THE UNICORN QUEEN #6.
25160 *Sun blind.* New York: Fawcett Columbine, 1988, 122 p., paper, novel. SECRET OF THE UNICORN QUEEN #2.

HANSEN, Karl, 1950-

25161 *Dream games.* New York: Ace Science Fiction Books, 1985, 252 p., paper, novel. HYBRID UNIVERSE #2.
25162 *War games.* New York: Playboy Paperbacks, 1981, 288 p., paper, novel. HYBRID UNIVERSE #1.

*HANSEN, Vern [i.e., Victor Joseph Hanson], 1921-

HANSON, Victor—SEE: Hansen, Vern

HARBINSON, Allen—SEE: Harbinson, W. A.

HARBINSON, W(illiam) A(llen), 1941-

25163 *Dream maker.* London: Sphere Books, 1991, 405 p., paper, novel.
 Eden—SEE: *The light of Eden.*
25164 *Genesis.* London: Corgi Books, 1980, 612 p., paper, novel. PROJEKT SAUCER #2.
25165 *Inception.* New York: A Dell Book, 1991, xii+430 p., paper, novel. PROJEKT SAUCER #1.
25166 *The light of Eden.* London: Corgi Books, 1987, 439 p., paper, novel.
25166A retitled: *Eden.* New York: A Dell Book, 1987, 367 p., paper, novel.
25167 *The lodestone* / by Allen Harbinson. London: Sphere Books, 1989, 568 p., paper, novel.
25168 *Otherworld.* London: Corgi Books, 1984, 512 p., paper, novel.
25169 *Revelation.* London: Corgi Books, 1982, 525 p., paper, novel.

HARBOTTLE, Philip (James), 1941-

15815 *E. C. Tubb: an evaluation.* Wallsend-on-Tyne, England: Philip Harbottle, 1964, 20 p., paper, nonf.

*HARBOU, Thea von, 1888-1954

HARCOURT, Glenn, *with Carter Scholz*

25170 *Palimpsests.* New York: Ace Science Fiction Books, 1984, viii+258 p., paper, novel.

HARD, Edward W.—SEE: Hard, T. W.

HARD, T. W. [i.e., Edward Wilhelm Hard Jr.], 1939-

25171 *SUM VII: a novel.* New York: Harper & Row, 1979, 185 p., cloth, novel.

HARDESTY, Steven, 1946-

25172 *Ghost soldiers.* New York: Walker & Co., 1986, 206 p., cloth, novel.

HARDIE, Raymond

25173 *Abyssos.* New York: Tor, A Tom Doherty Associates Book, 1987, 344 p., paper, novel.

HARDING, Lee (John), 1937-

25174 *The altered I: an encounter with science fiction.* Carlton, Victoria, Australia: Norstrilia Press, 1976, 131 p., paper, anth.

25175 *Beyond tomorrow: an anthology of modern science fiction.* South Melbourne, Victoria, Australia: Wren, 1975, 320 p., cloth, anth.

25176 *The children of Atlantis.* Stanmore, New South Wales, Australia: Cassell Australia, 1975, 104 p., paper, novel.

25177 *Displaced person.* Melbourne, Victoria, Australia: Hyland House, 1979, 139 p., cloth, novel.

25177A retitled: *Misplaced persons.* New York: Harper & Row, 1979, 149 p., cloth, novel.

25178 *Fallen spaceman.* Melbourne, Australia: Cassell Australia, 1973, 99 p., cloth, novel.

37823 *Fallen spaceman.* New York: Harper & Row, 1979, 86 p., cloth, novel. [Revised edition].

25179 *The frozen sky.* Stanmore, New South Wales, Australia: Cassell Australia, 1975, 102 p., paper, novel.

25180 *Future Sanctuary.* Toronto, New York: Laser Books, 1976, 190 p., paper, novel.

Misplaced persons—SEE: *Displaced person.*

25181 *Return to tomorrow.* Stanmore, New South Wales, Australia: Cassell Australia, 1976, 112 p., paper, novel.

25182 *Rooms of paradise.* South Yarra, Victoria, Australia: Quartet Books, 1978, viii + 182 p., cloth, anth.

25183 *Waiting for the end of the world.* Melbourne, Victoria, Australia: Hyland House, 1983, 206 p., cloth, novel.

25184 *The web of time.* Stanmore, New South Wales, Australia: Cassell Australia, 1980, 168 p., cloth, novel.

25185 *The weeping sky.* Stanmore, New South Wales, Australia: Cassell Australia, 1977, 197 p., cloth, novel.

25186 *A world of shadows.* London: Robert Hale, 1975, 160 p., cloth, novel.

HARDING, Nancy

25187 *The silver land.* New York, London: Pocket Books, 1989, 611 p., paper, novel.

25188 *Wind child.* New York, London: Pocket Books, 1990, 338 p., paper, novel.

HARDING, Richard, pseud.—SEE: Tine, Robert

HARDY, David A(ndrews), 1936-

25189 *Visions of space: artists journey through the cosmos.* Limpsfield, Surrey, England: Paper Tiger, 1989, 176 p., cloth, art.

with Bob Shaw

25190 *Galactic tours: Thomas Cook out of this world vacations.* New York: Proteus Press, 1981, 95 p., cloth, fiction.

HARDY, Gene B(ennett), 1936-

25191 *Tolkien's The Lord of the Rings and The hobbit: notes, including life of the author, Tolkien's fictional world, The hobbit, The Lord of the Rings, Tolkien's theme of power, history of Middle-Earth, chronology of Middle-Earth, suggested theme topics, a selected bibliography.* Lincoln, NE: Cliffs Notes, 1977, 75 p., paper, nonf. [Edited by James L. Roberts].

HARDY, Hilbert, 1906-

25192 *The cosmos project.* Lewes, East Sussex, England: The Book Guild, 1989, 167 p., cloth, novel.

HARDY, Lyndon (Maurice), 1941-

25193 *Master of the five magics.* New York: A Del Rey Book, Ballantine Books, 1980, viii + 374 p., paper, novel. ARCADIA #1.

25194 *Riddle of the seven realms.* New York: A Del Rey Book, Ballantine Books, 1988, 403 p., paper, novel. ARCADIA #3.

25195 *Secret of the sixth magic.* New York: A Del Rey Book, Ballantine Books, 1984, 366 p., paper, novel. ARCADIA #2.

HARDY, Naomi

25196 *Much of magic and miracles.* New York: Manor Books, 1979, 250 p., paper, novel.

HARDY, Phil(ippe), 1945-

The encyclopedia of horror movies—SEE: *Horror.*

The encyclopedia of science fiction movies—SEE: *Science fiction.*

25197 *Horror.* London: Aurum Press, 1986, 408 p., cloth, nonf. anth.

25197A retitled: *The encyclopedia of horror movies.* London: Octopus Books, 1986, 408 p., cloth, nonf. anth.

25198 *Science fiction.* London: Aurum Press, 1984, 400 p., cloth, nonf. anth.

25199 retitled: *The encyclopedia of science fiction movies.* London: Octopus Books, 1986, 408 p., cloth, nonf. anth. [Revised and updated edition].

25200 *Science fiction, 2nd updated ed.* London: Aurum Press, 1990, [450] p., cloth, nonf. anth. [Expanded edition].

25201 *Science fiction, 3rd updated ed.* London: Aurum Press, 1991, 478 p., cloth, nonf. anth. [Expanded edition].

HARDY, Robin, 1929- , *with Anthony Shaffer*

25202 *The wicker man: a novel.* New York: Crown Publishers, 1978, 216 p., cloth, novel.

HARDY, Thomas, 1840-1928

25203 *The supernatural tales of Thomas Hardy.* London, New York: W. Foulsham & Co., 1988, 288 p., cloth, coll. [Edited by Peter Haining].

*HARDY, W(illiam) G(eorge), 1895-1979

*HARGRAVE, John (Gordon), 1894-1982

HARGREAVES, H(enry) A., 1928-

25204 *North by 2000: a collection of Canadian science fiction.* Toronto: Peter Martin Associates, 1975, 160 p., cloth, coll.

HARGROVE, Marguerite

25205 *The vision and the dream: a novel.* New York: Leisure Books, 1980, 304 p., paper, novel.

HARING, Scott D.

25206 *Duel track.* Lake Geneva, WI: TSR Inc., 1987, 188 p., paper, fiction. CAR WARS ADVENTURE GAMEBOOK #3.

25207 *Green circle blues.* Lake Geneva, WI: TSR Inc., 1987, 190 p., paper, fiction. CAR WARS ADVENTURE GAMEBOOK #5.

HARINGTON, Donald, 1935-

25208 *The cockroaches of Stay More: a novel.* San Diego, CA, New York: A Helen & Kurt Wolff Book, Harcourt Brace Jovanovich, Publishers, 1989, 337 p., cloth, novel.

HARKON, Franz, pseud.

06780 *Spawn of space.* London: Scion Books, 1951, 112 p., paper, novel. SPACE EXPRESS COMPANY #2. [Corrected entry].

as ASTRON DEL MARTIA

04064 *Interstellar espionage.* London: Gaywood Press, 1952, 100 p., paper, novel. SPACE EXPRESS COMPANY #3.

04066 *Space pirates.* London: Gaywood Press, 1951, 112 p., paper, novel. SPACE EXPRESS COMPANY #1.

HARMAN, Nigel

25209 *Look what they've done to my bay!* Sydney, Australia: Nigel Harman, 1987, 194 p., paper, novel.

HARMON, James J.—SEE: Harmon, Jim

HARMON, Jim [i.e., James Judson Harmon], 1933-

25210 *The Godzilla book.* Canoga Park, CA: New Media Books, [1986], 96 p., paper, nonf.

25211 *The man who made maniacs.* Los Angeles: An Epic Original, Art Enterprises, 1961, 155 p., paper, novel.

HARMON, Philip M.

25212 *Study guides for J. R. R. Tolkien's The hobbit and The Lord of the Rings.* Rexburg, ID: Ricks College Press, 1982, 82 leaves, paper, nonf.

HARNESS, Charles L(eonard), 1915-

25213 *The catalyst.* New York: Pocket Books, 1980, 191 p., paper, novel.

25214 *Firebird.* New York: Pocket Books, 1981, 207 p., paper, novel.

06783 *Flight into yesterday.* New York: Bouregy & Curl, 1953, 256 p., cloth, novel.

25215 retitled: *The paradox men.* New York: Crown Publishers, 1984, 205 p., cloth, novel. [Revised edition].

25216 *Krono.* New York: Franklin Watts, 1988, 202 p., cloth, novel.

25217 *Lunar justice.* New York: Avon Books, 1991, 180 p., paper, novel.

25218 *Lurid dreams.* New York: Avon Books, 1990, 187 p., paper, novel.
The paradox men—SEE: *Flight into yesterday.*

25219 *Redworld.* New York: DAW Books, 1986, 229 p., paper, novel.

25220 *The Venetian court.* New York: A Del Rey Book, Ballantine Books, 1982, 202 p., paper, novel.

25221 *Wolfhead.* New York: A Berkley Medallion Book, Berkley Publishing Corp., 1978, 217 p., paper, novel.

HAROLD, Edmund

25222 *Vision tomorrow.* London: Spiritual Venturers Associates, 1981, 210 p., paper, novel.

HARPER, Andrew, *with George McAulay*

25223 *Michael Moorcock: a bibliography.* Baltimore, MD: T-K Graphics, 1976, 29 p., paper, nonf.

HARPER, George W(illiam), 1927-

25224 *Gypsy Earth.* Garden City, NY: Doubleday & Co., 1982, 187 p., cloth, novel.

HARPER, Harry, 1880-1960, *with Claude Grahame-White*

37807 *The air-king's treasure: a story of adventure with airship & aeroplane.* London, New York: Cassell, 1913, vi+312 p., cloth, novel.

HARPER, Rory

25225 *Petrogypsies.* New York: Baen Books, 1989, 275 p., paper, novel.

HARPER, Tara K.

25226 *Shadow leader.* New York: A Del Rey Book, Ballantine Books, 1991, 324 p., paper, novel. WOLFWALKER #2.

25227 *Wolfwalker.* New York: A Del Rey Book, Ballantine Books, 1990, 310 p., paper, novel. WOLFWALKER #1.

HARPUR, Patrick

25228 *Mercurius; or, The marriage of Heaven & Earth.* London: Macmillan London, 1990, xiv+479 p., cloth, novel.

25229 *The serpent's circle.* London: Macmillan, 1985, 231 p., cloth, novel.

HARRELL, Sara (Jeanne) Gordon, 1938-

25230 *Grove of night.* New York: Avon, 1981, 190 p., paper, novel.

HARRINGTON, Alan, 1919-

25231 *Paradise I: a novel.* Boston, Toronto: Little, Brown & Co., 1977, 372 p., cloth, novel.

HARRINGTON, Barbara

25232 *A crock of clear water.* London: Robert Hale, 1987, 207 p., cloth, novel.

HARRINGTON, Barry

25233 *The beyond.* New York: Diamond Books, 1991, 273 p., paper, novel.

HARRIS, Allen Lee

25234 *Deliver us from evil.* Toronto, New York: Bantam Books, 1988, 320 p., paper, novel.

*HARRIS, Barbara S(eger), 1927-

HARRIS, Brian, pseud.—SEE: King, Harold

*HARRIS, Clare Winger, 1891-1968

HARRIS, Deborah Turner, 1951-

25235 *The burning stone.* New York: Tor SF, A Tom Doherty Associates Book, 1987, 307 p., paper, novel. MAGES OF GARILLON #1.

25236 *The gauntlet of malice.* New York: Tor SF, A Tom Doherty Associates Book, 1987, 334 p., paper, novel. MAGES OF GARILLON #2.

25237 *Spiral of fire.* New York: Tor SF, A Tom Doherty Associates Book, 1989, 468 p., paper, novel. MAGES OF GARILLON #3.

with Katherine Kurtz

25238 *The adept.* New York: Ace Books, 1991, 323 p., paper, novel. ADEPT #1.

HARRIS, Geraldine (Rachel), 1951-

25239 *The children of the wind.* New York: Greenwillow Books, 1982, 196 p., cloth, novel. SEVEN CITADELS #2.
25240 *The dead kingdom.* New York: Greenwillow Books, 1983, 182 p., cloth, novel. SEVEN CITADELS #3.
25241 *Prince of the Godborn.* New York: Greenwillow Books, 1982, 186 p., cloth, novel. SEVEN CITADELS #1.
25242 *The seventh gate.* New York: Greenwillow Books, 1983, x+243 p., cloth, novel. SEVEN CITADELS #4.

HARRIS, Gordon (L.)

25243 *Apostle from space.* Plainfield, NJ: Logos International, 1978, v+186 p., paper, novel.

HARRIS, Janet, 1932-1979

25244 *The woman who created Frankenstein: a portrait of Mary Shelley.* New York, Hagerstown, NJ: Harper & Row, Publishers, 1979, 216 p., cloth, nonf.

*HARRIS, John, 1916-1991

HARRIS, John Beynon—SEE: Wyndham, John

HARRIS, Leonard, 1929-

25245 *The Masada Plan: a novel.* New York: Crown Publishers, 1976, 314 p., cloth, novel.

HARRIS, MacDonald [pseud. of Donald William Heiney], 1921-

25246 *The Cathay stories, and other fictions.* Santa Cruz, CA: Story Line Press, 1988, 189 p., cloth, coll.
37824 *The little people.* New York: William Morrow & Co., 1986, 299 p., cloth, novel.
25247 *Screenplay.* New York: Atheneum, 1982, 249 p., cloth, novel.

HARRIS, Marilyn [i.e., Marilyn Harris Springer], 1931-

25248 *Bledding Sorrow.* New York: G. P. Putnam's Sons, 1976, 348 p., cloth, novel.
25249 *The diviner.* New York: G. P. Putnam's Sons, 1982, 287 p., cloth, novel.
25250 *Night games.* Garden City, NY: Doubleday & Co., 1987, 302 p., cloth, novel.

25251 *The portent.* New York: G. P. Putnam's Sons, 1980, 322 p., cloth, novel.

HARRIS, Mark, 1960-

25252 *The Doctor Who technical manual.* London: Severn House, 1983, 62 p., cloth, fiction.

HARRIS, Raymond, 1953-

25253 *The broken worlds.* New York: Ace Science Fiction Books, 1986, 248 p., paper, novel.
25254 *The schizogenic man.* New York: Ace Books, 1990, 229 p., paper, novel.
25255 *Shadows of the white sun.* New York: Ace Books, 1988, 230 p., paper, novel.

with Edgar Allan Poe

25256 *The gold bug.* Providence, RI: A Jamestown Classic, Jamestown Publishers, 1982, 39 p., paper, story. [Adapted from Poe's original edition].
25257 *The masque of the red death.* Providence, RI: A Jamestown Classic, Jamestown Publishers, 1982, 31 p., paper, story. [Adapted from Poe's original edition].
25258 *The tell-tale heart.* Providence, RI: A Jamestown Classic, Jamestown Publishers, 1982, 31 p., paper, story. [Adapted from Poe's original edition].

with Robert Louis Stevenson

25259 *The body snatcher.* Providence, RI: A Jamestown Classic, Jamestown Publishers, 1982, 37 p., paper, story. [Adapted from Stevenson's original edition].
25260 *The bottle imp.* Providence, RI: A Jamestown Classic, Jamestown Publishers, 1982, 40 p., paper, story. [Adapted from Stevenson's original edition].
25261 *Markheim.* Providence, RI: A Jamestown Classic, Jamestown Publishers, 1982, 35 p., paper, story. [Adapted from Stevenson's original edition].
25262 *The strange case of Dr. Jekyll and Mr. Hyde.* Providence, RI: A Jamestown Classic, Jamestown Publishers, 1982, 43 p., paper, story. [Adapted from Stevenson's original edition].

HARRIS, Rosalind Dale- —SEE: Ashe, Rosalind

HARRIS, Rosemary (Jeanne), 1923-

25263 *A quest for Orion.* London, Boston: Faber & Faber, 1978, 233 p., cloth, novel. ORION #1.

25264 *Tower of the stars.* London, Boston: Faber & Faber, 1980, 272 p., cloth, novel. ORION #2.

HARRIS, Steve, 1954-

25265 *Adventureland.* London: Headline, 1990, 376 p., cloth, novel.

25266 *Wulf.* London: Headline, 1991, 440 p., cloth, novel.

HARRIS, Walter, 1925-

25267 *The day I died.* London: A Star Book, W. H. Allen, 1974, 220 p., paper, novel.

HARRISON, Craig, 1942-

25268 *Broken October, New Zealand, 1985: a novel.* Wellington, New Zealand: Reed, 1976, viii+291 p., cloth, novel.

25269 *Days of starlight.* Auckland, New Zealand: Hodder & Stoughton, 1988, 244 p., cloth, novel.

25270 *The quiet Earth.* Auckland, New Zealand: Hodder & Stoughton, 1981, 232 p., cloth, novel.

HARRISON, Harry (Max) [legalized from Henry Maxwell Dempsey], 1925-

25271 *The adventures of the Stainless Steel Rat: The Stainless Steel Rat; The Stainless Steel Rat's revenge; The Stainless Steel Rat saves the world.* Garden City, NY: Nelson Doubleday, 1977, 406 p., cloth, coll. STAINLESS STEEL RAT #1-3. [Includes *The Stainless Steel Rat*; *The Stainless Steel Rat's revenge*; *The Stainless Steel Rat saves the world*].

25272 *The best of Harry Harrison.* New York: Pocket Books, 1976, ix+302 p., paper, coll.

25273 *The best of Harry Harrison.* London: Sidgwick & Jackson, 1976, 315 p., cloth, coll. [Drops one story and the introduction from the American edition, and adds two others].

25274 *The California iceberg.* London: Faber & Faber, 1975, 64 p., cloth, novel.

25275 *Great balls of fire!* London: Pierrot Publishing, 1977, 118 p., cloth, nonf.

25276 *Homeworld.* Toronto, New York: bantam Books, 1980, 199 p., paper, novel. TO THE STARS #1.

25277 *Invasion: Earth.* New York: Ace Books, 1982, ix+211 p., paper, novel.

The Jupiter plague—SEE: *Plague from space.*

25278 *Mechanismo.* London: Pierrot Publishing, 1978, 118 p., paper, nonf.

25279 *The men from PIG and ROBOT.* Harmondsworth, Middlesex: Puffin Books, 1978, 122 p., paper, coll.

06835 *Nova 3.* New York: Walker & Co., 1973, 243 p., cloth, anth.

06835A retitled: *The outdated man.* New York: A Dell Book, 1975, 224 p., paper, anth.

The outdated man—SEE: *Nova 3.*

06838 *Plague from space.* Garden City, NY: Doubleday, 1965, 207 p., cloth, novel.

25280 retitled: *The Jupiter plague.* New York: Tor, A Tom Doherty Associates Book, 1982, 280 p., paper, novel. [Expanded edition].

25281 *Planet of no return.* New York: A Wallaby Book, Simon & Schuster, 1981, 232 p., paper, novel. PLANET OF THE DAMNED #2.

25282 *The planet of robot slaves.* New York: A Byron Preiss Book, Avon Books, 1989, 236 p., paper, novel. BILL, THE GALACTIC HERO #1.

25282A retitled: *Bill, the galactic hero on the planet of robot slaves.* London: Victor Gollancz, 1989, 236 p., cloth, novel. BILL, THE GALACTIC HERO #1.

25283 *A rebel in time.* New York: Tor, A Tom Doherty Associates Book, 1983, 315 p., paper, novel.

25284 *Return to Eden.* Toronto, New York: Bantam Books, 1988, xiii+348 p., cloth, novel. EDEN #3.

25285 *Skyfall.* London: Faber & Faber, 1976, 270 p., cloth, novel.

25286 *The Stainless Steel Rat for president.* New York: Nelson Doubleday, 1982, 185 p., cloth, novel. STAINLESS STEEL RAT #5.

25287 *The Stainless Steel Rat gets drafted.* London: Bantam Press, 1987, 256 p., cloth, novel. STAINLESS STEEL RAT #7.

25288 *A Stainless Steel Rat is born.* London: Titan Books, 1985, 183 p., cloth, novel. STAINLESS STEEL RAT #6.

25289 *The Stainless Steel Rat wants you.* London: Michael Joseph, 1978, 191 p., cloth, novel. SLIPPERY JIM diGRIZ #4.

25290 *Starworld.* Toronto, New York: Bantam Books, 1981, 198 p., paper, novel. TO THE STARS #3.

25291 *To the stars.* Garden City, NY: Nelson Doubleday, 1981, 471 p., cloth, coll. TO THE STARS #1-3. [Includes *Homeworld*; *Wheelworld*; *Starworld*].

25292 *West of Eden.* Toronto, New York: Bantam Books, 1984, xii+483 p., cloth, novel. EDEN #1.

25293 *Wheelworld.* Toronto, New York: Bantam Books, 1981, 181 p., paper, novel. TO THE STARS #2.

25294 *Winter in Eden.* London: Grafton, 1986, 486 p., cloth, novel. EDEN #2.

25295 *You can be The Stainless Steel Rat: an interactive game book.* London: Grafton, 1985, [173] p., paper, fiction. STAINLESS STEEL RAT SERIES.

with Brian W. Aldiss

00164 *Best SF: 1973.* New York: G. P. Putnam's Sons, 1974, 238 p., cloth, anth.

00164A retitled: *The year's best science fiction, no. 7.* London: Sphere Books, 1975, 174 p., paper, anth.

16200 *Best SF: 1974.* Indianapolis, IN, New York: Bobbs-Merrill Co., 1975, 253 p., cloth, anth.

16200A retitled: *The year's best science fiction, no. 8.* London: Sphere Books, 1976, 253 p., paper, anth.

Best SF: 75—SEE: *The ninth annual best SF: 75.*

16201 *Decade, the 1940s.* London: Macmillan, 1975, 213 p., cloth, anth.

16202 *Decade, the 1950s.* London: Macmillan, 1976, 219 p., cloth, anth.

16203 *Decade, the 1960s.* London: Macmillan, 1977, 287 p., cloth, anth.

16204 *Hell's cartographers: some personal histories of science fiction writers.* London: An SF Horizons Production, Weidenfeld & Nicolson, 1975, 246 p., cloth, nonf. anth.

16205 *The ninth annual best SF: 75.* Indianapolis, IN, New York: Bobbs-Merrill Co., 1976, 240 p., cloth, anth.

16205A retitled: *The year's best science fiction, no. 9.* London: Weidenfeld & Nicolson, 1976, 206 p., cloth, anth.

16206 *SF Horizons.* New York: Arno Press, 1975, 64+64 p., cloth, nonf. anth. [The republication in one volume of two magazine issues].

Year's best science fiction, no. 7—SEE: *Best SF: 1973.*

Year's best science fiction, no. 8—SEE: *Best SF: 1974.*

The year's best science fiction, no. 9—SEE: *Best SF: 75.*

with David Bischoff

18013 *Bill, the galactic hero on the planet of tasteless pleasure.* New York: A Byron Preiss Book, Avon Books, 1991, 213 p., paper, novel. BILL, THE GALACTIC HERO #3.

18014 *Bill, the galactic hero on the planet of ten thousand bars.* New York: A Byron Preiss Book, Avon Books, 1991, 214 p., paper, novel. BILL, THE GALACTIC HERO #5.

with Jim Burns

19068 *Planet story.* New York: A&W Visual Library, 1979, 112 p., cloth, novel.

with Gordon R. Dickson

Lifeboat—SEE: *Lifeship.*

21905 *The lifeship.* New York & Hagerstown, NJ: Harper & Row, Publishers, 1976, 181 p., cloth, novel.

21905A retitled: *Lifeboat.* London: Dennis Dobson, 1978, 181 p., cloth, novel.

with Malcolm Edwards

22444 *Spacecraft in fact and fiction.* London: Orbis Books, 1979, 128 p., cloth, nonf.

with Jack C. Haldeman II

24963 *Bill, the galactic hero on the planet of the zombie vampires.* New York: A Bryon Preiss Book, Avon Books, 1991, 213 p., paper, novel. BILL, THE GALACTIC HERO #4.

with Bruce McAllister

25296 *There won't be war.* New York: Tor SF, A Tom Doherty Associates Book, 1991, viii+309 p., paper, anth.

with Willis E. McNelly

25297 *Science fiction novellas.* New York: Charles Scribner's Sons, 1975, x+255 p., paper, anth.

with Robert Sheckley

25298 *Bill, the galactic hero on the planet of bottled brains.* New York: A Byron Preiss Book, Avon Books, 1990, 249 p., paper, novel. BILL, THE GALACTIC HERO #2.

with Leon Stover

25299 *Stonehenge: where Atlantis died.* New York: Tor, A Tom Doherty Associates

Book, 1983, 347 p., paper, novel. [Expanded from #06856].

HARRISON, M(ichael) John, 1945-

The floating gods—SEE: *In Viriconium.*
25300 *The ice monkey, and other stories.* London: Victor Gollancz, 1983, 144 p., cloth, coll.
25301 *In Viriconium.* London: Victor Gollancz, 1982, 126 p., cloth, novel. VIRICONIUM #3.
25301A retitled: *The floating gods.* New York: A Timescape Book, Pocket Books, 1983, 159 p., paper, novel. VIRICONIUM #3.
25302 *The machine in Shaft Ten, and other stories.* St Albans, Hertfordshire, England: Panther, 1975, 174 p., paper, coll.
25303 *A storm of wings: being the second volume of the 'Viriconium' sequence, in which Benedict Paucemanly returns from his long frozen dream in the far side of the Moon, and the Earth submits briefly to the charisma of the Locust.* Garden City, NY: Doubleday & Co., 1980, 177 p., cloth, novel. VIRICONIUM #2.
25304 *Viriconium.* London: Unwin Paperbacks, 1988, 276 p., paper, coll. VIRICONIUM #3-4. [Includes *Viriconium nights* and *In Viriconium*].
25305 *Viriconium nights.* New York: Ace Fantasy Books, 1984, 182 p., paper, coll. VIRICONIUM #4.
25306 *Viriconium nights.* London: Victor Gollancz, 1985, 158 p., cloth, coll. VIRICONIUM #4. [Different contents than the American edition].

HARRISON, Mark (Stephen James), 1951- , *with Lisa Tuttle*

Dreamlands—SEE: *Mark Harrison's Dreamlands.*
25307 *Mark Harrison's Dreamlands.* London: Paper Tiger, 1990, 127 p., cloth, art.

HARRISON, Michael, 1907-1991, *as* MICHAEL EGREMONT

04717 *The bride of Frankenstein.* London: Queensway Press, 1935, 252 p., cloth, movie. FRANKENSTEIN SEQUEL.

HARRISON, Payne

25308 *Storming Intrepid.* New York: Crown Publishers, 1989, 473 p., cloth, novel.
25309 *Thunder of Erebus.* New York: Crown Publishers, 1991, ix+496 p., cloth, novel.

HARRISON, Sue (McHaney), 1950-

25310 *Mother earth, father sky.* New York: Doubleday, 1990, 313 p., cloth, novel. MOTHER EARTH #1.

HARRISON, William (Neal), 1933-

06865 *Roller ball murder.* New York: William Morrow & Co., 1974, 189 p., cloth, coll.
06865A retitled: *Rollerball: 13 selected stories.* London: Futura Publications, An Orbit Book, 1975, 189 p., paper, coll.
Rollerball—SEE: *Roller ball murder.*

HARRY, Bill

25311 *Heroes of the spaceways.* New York, London: Quick Fox, 1981, 127 p., paper, nonf.

HARRYHAUSEN, Ray, 1920-

25312 *Film fantasy scrapbook.* South Brunswick, NJ: A. S. Barnes & Co., 1972, 117 p., paper, nonf.
25313 *Film fantasy scrapbook, 2nd ed., rev.* South Brunswick, NJ: A. S. Barnes & Co., 1974, 142 p., paper, nonf.
25314 *Film fantasy scrapbook, 3rd ed., rev. and enl.* San Diego, New York: A. S. Barnes & Co.; London: The Tantivy Press, 1981, ix+150 p., paper, nonf.

HART, Chris

25315 *The pseudo-nymph: an anthology of NSFA member magazines.* Bolton, England: Chris Hart, 1991, 43 p., paper, anth. [Includes some verse].

HART, Dabney Adams, 1926-

25316 *Through the open door: a new look at C. S. Lewis.* University, AL: University of Alabama Press, 1984, x+164 p., cloth, nonf.

HART, Douglas C., 1950- , *with Robert W. Pohle Jr.*

25317 *The films of Christopher Lee.* Metuchen, NJ: Scarecrow Press, 1983, xxii+227 p., cloth, nonf.

HART, Francis Russell

31546   *The anarchy of light: Neil Gunn: a cele-
         bration.* Dundee, Scotland: Gairfish,
         1991, x+79 p., paper?, nonf. anth.

HARTER, Richard, *with Lisa Raskind*

25318   *The NESFA hymnal.* Cambridge, MA:
         NESFA Press, 1974, 46 p., paper, nonf.
         anth.

HARTLEY, L(eslie) P(oles), 1895-1972

25319   *The complete short stories of L. P. Hartley.*
         London: Hamilton, 1973, x+760 p.,
         cloth, coll.

*HARTLEY, (Harry) Livingston, 1900-<u>1981</u>

HARTMAN, Darlene—SEE: Lang, Simon

**HARTMANN, William K(enneth), 1939- , *with
Pamela Lee & Ron Miller***

25320   *Out of the cradle: exploring the frontiers
         beyond Earth.* New York: Workman
         Publishing, 1984, 190 p., cloth, fiction.
         [Mixes science fiction with nonfiction].

HARTOG, Jan de—SEE: de Hartog, Jan

*HARTRIDGE, Jon, <u>1934-</u>

HARTSHORNE, Henry, 1823-1897

25321   *1931: a glance at the twentieth century.*
         Philadelphia, PA: E. Claxton & Co.,
         1881, 64 p., cloth, story.

HARTWELL, David G(eddes), 1941-

25322   *Age of wonders: exploring the world of sci-
         ence fiction.* New York: Walker & Co.,
         1984, 205 p., cloth, nonf.
         The color of evil—SEE: *The dark descent.*
         The colour of evil—SEE: *The dark de-
         scent.*
25323   *The dark descent.* New York: Tor, A Tom
         Doherty Associates Book, 1987, 1011 p.,
         cloth, anth.
25323A   retitled: *The dark descent 1: The colour of
         evil.* London: Grafton, 1990, 292 p.,
         cloth, anth. [The original book split into
         three volumes].
25323B   retitled: *The dark descent 1: The color of
         evil.* New York: Tor Horror, A Tom
         Doherty Associates Book, 1991, 438 p.,
         paper, anth. [The original book split into
         three volumes].

25323C   retitled: *The dark descent 2: The medusa in
         the shield.* London: Grafton, 1990, 352
         p., cloth, anth. [The original book split
         into three volumes].
25323D   retitled: *The dark descent 3: A fabulous,
         formless darkness.* London: Grafton,
         1991, 352 p., cloth, anth. [The original
         book split into three volumes].
         A fabulous, formless darkness—SEE: *The
         dark descent.*
         The Medusa in the shield—SEE: *The dark
         descent.*
25324   *The world treasury of science fiction.*
         Boston, Toronto: Little, Brown & Co.,
         1989, xix+1083 p., cloth, anth.

with Kathryn Cramer

20772   *Christmas ghosts.* New York: Arbor
         House, 1987, xv+284 p., cloth, anth.
20773   *Masterpieces of fantasy and enchantment.*
         New York: St. Martin's Press, 1988,
         xvi+622 p., cloth, anth.
20774   *Masterpieces of fantasy and wonder.* Gar-
         den City, NY: Doubleday Book and Mu-
         sic Clubs, 1989, xvi+656 p., cloth, anth.
20775   *Spirits of Christmas: twenty other-worldly
         tales.* New York: Wynwood Press,
         1989, 284 p., cloth, anth.

with L. W. Currey

20895   *The battle of the monsters, and other sto-
         ries.* Boston: Gregg Press, 1976, xii+
         238 p., cloth, anth.
20896   *Science fiction and fantasy authors: a bib-
         liography of first printings of their fiction
         and selected nonfiction.* Boston: G. K.
         Hall & Co., 1979, xxix+571 p., cloth,
         nonf.

with L. W. Currey as KILGORE TROUT

20897   *SF-1: a selective bibliography.* Elizabeth-
         town, NY: L. W. Currey, 1971, [32] p.,
         paper, nonf.

HARTZELL, Susan—SEE: Hartzell, Suzy

**HARTZELL, Suzy [i.e., Susan Kathleen
Hartzell], 1959- , *with Dawn Dunn as* PAULINE
DUNN**

22309   *The crawling dark.* New York: Zebra
         Books, Kensington Publishing Corp.,
         1991, 349 p., paper, novel. [Based on
         Dean Koontz's novel, *Phantoms*].
22310   *Demonic color.* New York: Zebra Books,
         Kensington Publishing Corp., 1990, 351

p., paper, novel. [Based on Dean Koontz's novel, *Phantoms*].

22311 *Flesh stealer*. New York: Zebra Books, Kensington Publishing Corp., 1990, 317 p., paper, novel.

HARVEY, David, 1946-

25325 *The song of Middle-Earth: J. R. R. Tolkien's themes, symbols, and myths*. London: George Allen & Unwin, 1985, 143 p., cloth, nonf.

*HARVEY, Frank (Laird), 1913-1982

HARVEY, James—SEE: Fox, Gardner F.

HARVEY, Jean Gilmour, *with Laura Bennett* as LAURA GILMOUR BENNETT

By all that is sacred—SEE: *A wheel of stars*.

17776 *A time and a place*. London: Viking, 1988, 409 p., cloth, novel.

17777 *A wheel of stars*. London: Viking, 1989, 432 p., cloth, novel.

17777a retitled: *By all that is sacred*. New York: Avon Books, 1991, 385 p., paper, novel.

HARVEY, Jon M.

25326 *Cthulhu: tales of the Cthulhu Mythos*. Burton-on-Trent, Staffordshire, England: Spectre Press, 1976, 24 p., paper, anth. CTHULHU MYTHOS.

25327 *Cthulhu 3: tales of the Cthulhu Mythos*. Cardiff, South Wales: Spectre Press, 1978, 24 p., paper, anth.

25328 *Dreams of a dark hue*. Cardiff, South Wales: Spectre Press, 1978, 60 p., paper, anth.

HARVEY, M(ary) Elayn, 1945-

25329 *Warhaven: a novel*. New York: Franklin Watts, 1987, xv+266 p., cloth, novel.

HARVEY, Norman (Bruce), 1931-

25330 *One magpie for sorrow*. London: Robert Hale; Christchurch, New Zealand: Whitcombe & Tombs, 1967, 190 p., cloth, novel.

HARVEY, William Fryer, 1885-1937

37825 *The arm of Mrs. Egan, and other strange stories*. New York: E. P. Dutton, 1952, 256 p., cloth, coll.

HARWELL, Thomas Meade (Jr.), 1913-

25331 *The English gothic novel: a miscellany in four volumes*. Salzburg, Austria: Institut für Anglistik und Amerikanistik, Universität Salzburg, 1986, 4 vols., cloth, nonf. anth.

HARWOOD, John

with Allan Howard

25332 *Tarzan encyclopedia*. ?: Burroughs Bulletin, 1975, 41 p., paper, nonf.

with John F. Roy & Camille Cazedessus Jr.

19680 *ERB-dom: a guide to issues no. 1-25*. Evergreen, CO: Opar Press, 1964, 23 p., paper, nonf.

HASFORD, (Jerry) Gustav, 1947-

25333 *The phantom blooper*. New York, Toronto: Bantam Books, 1990, 243 p., cloth, novel.

*HASSE, Henry L(ouis), 1913-1977

HASSLER, Donald M(ackey II), 1937-

25334 *Comic tones in science fiction: the art of compromise with nature*. Westport, CT, London: Greenwood Press, 1982, xiv+143 p., cloth, nonf. CONTRIBUTIONS TO THE STUDY OF SCIENCE FICTION AND FANTASY #2.

25335 *Hal Clement*. Mercer Island, WA: Starmont House, 1982, 64 p., cloth, nonf. STARMONT READER'S GUIDE #11.

25336 *Isaac Asimov*. Mercer Island, WA: Starmont House, 1991, iii+129 p., cloth, nonf. STARMONT READER'S GUIDE #40.

25337 *Patterns of the fantastic: academic programming at Chicon IV*. Mercer Island, WA: Starmont House, 1983, 105 p., cloth, nonf. anth. STARMONT STUDIES IN LITERARY CRITICISM #2.

25338 *Patterns of the fantastic II*. Mercer Island, WA: Starmont House, 1985, 90 p., cloth, nonf. anth. STARMONT STUDIES IN LITERARY CRITICISM #3.

with Carl B. Yoke

25339 *Death and the serpent: immortality in science fiction and fantasy*. Westport, CT: Greenwood Press, 1985, viii+235 p., cloth, nonf. anth. CONTRIBUTIONS TO

THE STUDY OF SCIENCE FICTION AND FANTASY #13.

HASSON, Moisés (A.)

25340 *Index to Mexican science fiction magazines.* Santiago, Chile: Moisés Hassón, 1991, 52 p., paper, nonf.

HASTINGS, Beverly

25341 *Don't cry, little girl.* New York: Pocket Books, 1987, 256 p., paper, novel.

HASTINGS, William

25342 *A postcript* [sic] *to Homunculus.* England: William Hastings, 1988, p. 245-257, paper, nonf.

HATCH, George

25343 *Guignoir, and other furies.* Long Island City, NY: Horror's Head Press, 1991, 141 p., paper, anth.

*HATCH, Richard W(arren), 1898-1985?

HATCHIGAN, Jessica

25344 *Count Dracula, me, and Norma D.* New York: An Avon Camelot Book, 1987, 116 p., paper, novel.

HATHERLEY, Frank, *with Margaret Aldiss & Malcolm Edwards*

16209 *A is for Brian: a 65th birthday present for Brian W. Aldiss.* London: Avernus, 1988, 128 p., paper, anth. [A festschrift for Brian W. Aldiss which includes some nonf.; limited to 500 copies].

HATHWAY, Alan, 1906-1977

as CLIFFORD GOODRICH

24123 *The football racketeers.* Chicago: Robert Weinberg, 1977, 96 p., paper, novel. PULP CLASSICS #15.

with Harold A. Davis as KENNETH ROBESON

21269 *Doc Savage: Devils of the deep; and, The headless men: two complete adventures in one volume.* Toronto, New York: Bantam Books, 1984, 228 p., paper, coll. DOC SAVAGE #123-124. [*Devils of the deep* by Harold A. Davis; *The headless men* by Alan Hathway].

with Lester Dent as KENNETH ROBESON

21579 *Doc Savage: four complete adventures in one volume: The mindless monsters; The rustling death; King Joe Cay; The thing that pursued.* Toronto, New York: Bantam Books, 1987, 410 p., paper, coll. DOC SAVAGE #131-134. [Cover title: *Doc Savage omnibus, volume 2; The mindless monsters* and *The rustling death* by Alan Hathway; *King Joe Cay* and *The thing that pursued* by Lester Dent].

21590 *Doc Savage: The green eagle; and, The devil's playground: two complete adventures in one volume.* Toronto, New York: Bantam Books, 1983, 217 p., paper, coll. DOC SAVAGE #24-25. [*The devil's playground* by Alan Hathway; *The green eagle* by Lester Dent].

HAUGHNEY, Michael, 1963-

25345 *A dog's chance.* Lewes, East Sussex, England: The Book Guild, 1991, 177 p., cloth, novel.

*HAUN, Blair A., 1891-1968

HAUSHOFER, Marie—SEE: Haushofer, Marlen

HAUSHOFER, Marlen [i.e., Marie Helene Frauendorfer Haushofer], 1920-1970

25346 *The wall.* Pittsburgh, PA: Cleis Press, 1991, 244 p., cloth, novel. [Translation by Shaun Whiteside of *Die wand*].

HAUSMAN, Gerald (Andrews), 1945-

25347 *Stargazer.* Santa Fe, NM: Lotus Press, 1988, 219 p., paper, novel. STARGAZER TRILOGY #1.

HAUTALA, Richard A.—SEE: Hautala, Rick

HAUTALA, Rick [i.e., Richard Andrew Hautala], 1949-

25348 *Cold whisper.* New York: Zebra Books, Kensington Publishing Corp., 1991, 446 p., paper, novel.

25349 *Dead voices.* New York: Warner Books, 1990, 406 p., paper, novel.

25350 *Little brothers.* New York: Zebra Books, Kensington Publishing Corp., 1988, 541 p., paper, novel.

25351 *Moon walker.* New York: Zebra Books, Kensington Publishing Corp., 1989, 544 p., paper, novel.

25352 *Moonbog.* New York: Zebra Books, Kensington Publishing Corp., 1982, 410 p., paper, novel.

25353 *Moondeath.* New York: Zebra Books, Kensington Publishing Corp., 1980, 448 p., paper, novel.

25354 *Night stone.* New York: Zebra Books, Kensington Publishing Corp., 1986, 592 p., paper, novel.

25355 *Winter wake.* New York: Warner Books, 1989, 407 p., paper, novel.

HAVEN, Tom De—SEE: De Haven, Tom

HAWDON, Robin

25356 *A rustle in the grass.* New York: Dodd, Mead & Co., 1984, 244 p., cloth, novel.

HAWES, Louise [i.e., Louise Hawes Jacobson], 1943-

25357 *Nelson Malone meets the man from Mush-Nut.* New York: Lodestar Books, 1986, 116 p., cloth, novel. NELSON MALONE SERIES.

25358 *Nelson Malone saves Flight 942.* New York: Lodestar Books, 1988, 146 p., cloth, novel. NELSON MALONE SERIES.

HAWK, Chester

25359 *Python men of the lost city.* Oak Lawn, IL: Robert Weinberg, 1974, 64 p., paper, novel. PULP CLASSICS #2.

HAWK, Douglas D(aniel), 1948-

25360 *Moonslasher.* New York: A Critic's Choice Paperback from Lorevan Publishing, 1987, 352 p., paper, novel.

25361 *The occult madonna.* New York: A Critic's Choice Paperback from Lorevan Publishing, 1988, 348 p., paper, novel.

HAWKE, Simon [legalized name of Nicholas Valentin Yermakov], 1951-

25362 *The 9 lives of Catseye Gomez.* Arvada, CO: Roadkill Press, 1991, 28 p., paper, story. WIZARD #6.

25363 *The argonaut affair.* New York: Ace Books, 1987, 195 p., paper, novel. TIME WARS #7.

25364 *Batman: To stalk a specter.* New York: Warner Books, 1991, 249 p., paper, movie. BATMAN SERIES.

25365 *The Cleopatra crisis.* New York: Ace Books, 1990, 212 p., paper, novel. TIMEWARS #11.

25366 *The Dracula caper.* New York: Ace Books, 1988, 212 p., paper, novel. TIMEWARS #8.

25367 *Friday the 13th, part I.* New York: A Signet Book, New American Library, 1987, 190 p., paper, movie. FRIDAY THE 13TH #1.

25368 *Friday the 13th, part II: a novel.* New York: A Signet Book, New American Library, 1988, 167 p., paper, movie. FRIDAY THE 13TH #2.

25369 *Friday the 13th, part 3: a novel based on the motion picture Friday the 13th, part 3.* New York: A Signet Book, New American Library, 1988, 172 p., paper, movie. FRIDAY THE 13TH #3.

Friday the 13th, part VI: a novel—SEE: *Jason lives.*

25370 *The hellfire rebellion.* New York: Ace Books, 1990, 192 p., paper, novel. TIMEWARS #10.

The Ivanhoe gambit—SEE: *Timewars: The Ivanhoe gambit.*

25371 *Jason lives: Friday the 13th, part VI: a novel.* New York: A Signet Book, New American Library, 1986, 191 p., paper, movie. FRIDAY THE 13TH #6.

25372 *The Khyber connection.* New York: Ace Science Fiction Books, 1986, 195 p., paper, novel. TIMEWARS #6.

25373 *The Lilliput legion.* New York: Ace Books, 1989, 190 p., paper, novel. TIMEWARS #9.

25374 *The Nautilus sanction.* New York: Ace Science Fiction Books, 1985, xii+196 p., paper, novel. TIMEWARS #5.

25375 *The Pimpernel plot.* New York: Ace Science Fiction Books, 1984, xi+211 p., paper, novel. TIMEWARS #3.

25376 *Predator 2: a novel.* New York: Jove Books, 1990, 231 p., paper, movie. PREDATOR #2.

25377 *Psychodrome.* New York: Ace Books, 1987, 220 p., paper, novel. PSYCHODROME #1.

25378 *The samurai wizard.* New York: Warner Books, 1991, 214 p., paper, novel. WIZARD #5.

25379 *The shapechanger scenario.* New York: Ace Books, 1988, 202 p., paper, novel. PSYCHODROME #2.

25380 *The six-gun solution.* New York: Ace Books, 1991, 225 p., paper, novel. TIMEWARS #12. [Last book in the series].

25381 *The timekeeper conspiracy.* New York: Ace Science Fiction Books, 1984, 215 p., paper, novel. TIMEWARS #2.

25382 *Timewars: The Ivanhoe gambit.* New York: Ace Science Fiction Books, 1984, 209 p., paper, novel. TIMEWARS #1.

To stalk a specter—SEE: *Batman: To stalk a specter.*

25383 *The wizard of 4th Street.* New York: Popular Library, 1987, 247 p., paper, novel. WIZARD #1.

25384 *The wizard of Rue Morgue.* New York: Popular Library, 1990, 201 p., paper, novel. WIZARD #4.

25385 *The wizard of Santa Fe.* New York: Warner Books, 1991, 249 p., paper, novel. WIZARD #6.

25386 *The wizard of Sunset Strip.* New York: Popular Library, 1989, 202 p., paper, novel. WIZARD #3.

25387 *The wizard of Whitechapel.* New York: Popular Library, 1988, 215 p., paper, novel. WIZARD #2.

25388 *The Zenda vendetta.* New York: Ace Science Fiction Books, 1985, xiii+206 p., paper, novel. TIMEWARS #4.

as J. D. MASTERS

25389 *Cold Steele.* New York: Charter Books, 1989, 185 p., paper, novel. STEELE #2.

25390 *Jagged Steele.* New York: Charter Books, 1990, 184 p., paper, novel. STEELE #4.

25391 *Killer Steele.* New York: Charter Books, 1990, 185 p., paper, novel. STEELE #3.

25392 *Renegade Steele.* New York: Berkley Books, 1990, 218 p., paper, novel. STEELE #5.

25393 *Steele.* New York: Charter Books, 1989, 199 p., paper, novel. STEELE #1.

25394 *Target Steele.* New York: Berkley Books, 1990, 198 p., paper, novel. STEELE #6.

as NICHOLAS YERMAKOV

25395 *Clique.* New York: Berkley Books, 1982, 233 p., paper, novel.

25396 *Epiphany.* New York: A Signet Book, New American Library, 1982, 170 p., paper, novel. LAST COMMUNION #2.

25397 *Fall into darkness.* New York: Berkley Books, 1982, 296 p., paper, novel.

25398 *Jehad.* New York: A Signet Book, New American Library, 1984, 224 p., paper, novel. LAST COMMUNION #3.

25399 *Journey from flesh.* New York: Berkley Books, 1981, 195 p., paper, novel.

25400 *Last communion.* New York: A Signet Book, New American Library, 1981, 183 p., paper, novel. LAST COMMUNION #1.

as NICHOLAS YERMAKOV *with Glen A. Larson*

25401 *The living legend.* New York: Berkley Books, 1982, 180 p., paper, tele. BATTLESTAR GALACTICA #6.

25402 *War of the gods.* New York: Berkley Books, 1982, 182 p., paper, tele. BATTLESTAR GALACTICA #7.

HAWKES, (Jessie) Jacquetta (Hopkins), 1910-

37826 *A quest of love.* London: Chatto & Windus, 1980, 219 p., cloth, novel.

HAWKES, Judith, 1949-

25403 *Julian's house.* New York: Ticknor & Fields, 1989, x+354 p., cloth, novel.

HAWKEY, Raymond

End stage—SEE: *It.*

25404 *It.* London: New English Library, 1983, p., cloth, novel. PRESIDENTIAL TRILOGY #3.

25404A retitled: *End stage.* London: Sphere Books, 1988, 317 p., paper, novel. PRESIDENTIAL TRILOGY #3.

25405 *Side-effect.* London: Jonathan Cape, 1979, 255 p., cloth, novel. PRESIDENTIAL TRILOGY #2.

with Roger Bingham

17968 *Wild card.* London: Sphere Books, 1988, 283 p., paper, novel. PRESIDENTIAL TRILOGY #1. [Revised edition of #01309].

HAWKINS, Jim, 1944-

25406 *The Living One.* New York: Fawcett Popular Library, 1980, 188 p., paper, novel.

*HAWKINS, Peter, 1924-

HAWKINS, Ward, 1912-1990

25407 *Blaze of wrath: a novel.* New York: A Del Rey Book, Ballantine Books, 1986, 231 p., paper, novel. HARRY BORG #3.

25408 *Red flame burning: a novel.* New York: A Del Rey Book, Ballantine Books, 1985, 280 p., paper, novel. HARRY BORG #1.

25409 *Sword of fire.* New York: A Del Rey Book, Ballantine Books, 1985, 297 p., paper, novel. HARRY BORG #2.

25410 *Torch of fear: a novel.* New York: A Del Rey Book, Ballantine Books, 1987, 297 p., paper, novel. HARRY BORG #4.

HAWKS, Lee, pseud.—SEE: Pedneau, Dave

HAWTHORNE, Hildegarde

37827 *Faded garden: the collected ghost stories of Hildegarde Hawthorne.* Madison, WI: The Strange Company, 1985, 42 p., paper, coll. [Edited by Jessica Amanda Salmonson; includes some verse].

HAWTHORNE, Violet

25411 *Black moon rising.* New York: Ballantine Books, 1979, 506 p., paper, novel.

HAY, George [i.e., Oswyn Robert Tregonwell Hay], 1922-

25412 *The Edward De Bono science fiction collection.* Leeds, England: Elmfield Press, 1976, 217 p., cloth, anth.

06965 *Flight of the "Hesper".* London: Hamilton & Co. (Stafford), 1952, 112 p., paper, novel. [Corrected entry].

25413 *The necronomicon.* St. Helier, Jersey, Channel Islands: Neville Spearman, 1978, 184 p., cloth, fiction.

25414 *Pulsar 1: an original anthology of science fiction and science futures.* Harmondsworth, Middlesex, England: Penguin Books, 1978, 174 p., paper, anth. [Includes some nonfiction].

25415 *Pulsar 2: an original anthology of science fiction and science futures.* Harmondsworth, Middlesex, England: Penguin Books, 1979, 190 p., paper, anth.

06966 *This planet for sale.* London: Hamilton & Co. (Stafford), 1951, 111 p., paper, novel. [Corrected entry].

as KING LANG

06967 *Terra!* London: Curtis Warren, 1952, 111 p., paper, novel. [Corrected entry].

as ROY SHELDON

06968 *Moment out of time.* London: Hamilton & Co., (Stafford), 1952, 111 p., paper, novel. [Corrected entry].

*HAY, Jacob, 1920-1976

HAY, Oswyn—SEE: Hay, George

HAYASHI, Nancy

25416 *Cosmic Cousin.* New York: E. P. Dutton, 1988, 87 p., cloth, novel.

HAYDEN, Karen

25417 *When the sun shines.* Strathmartine by Dundee, Scotland: ScoTpress, 1983, 47 p., paper, tele. STAR TREK SERIES.

with Vicki Richards

25418 *A human kind of learning.* Strathmartine by Dundee, Scotland: ScoTpress, 1985, 64 p., paper, tele. STAR TREK SERIES.

HAYDOCK, Tim

25419 *The mammoth book of classic chillers.* London: Robinson Publishing, 1986, 693 p., paper, anth.

HAYES, R. Chetwynd- —SEE: Chetwynd-Hayes, R.

HAYES, Ralph (Eugene), 1927-

25420 *Drought!* New York: Zebra Books, Kensington Publishing Corp., 1981, 368 p., paper, novel.

HAYLES, Brian, 1931-1976

25421 *Doctor Who and the ice warriors.* London: A Longbow Book, Allan Wingate, 1976, 144 p., cloth, tele. DOCTOR WHO SERIES.

as GHOST EDITOR with Irene Shubik

25422 *The mind beyond: stories from Irene Shubik's BBC television series.* Harmondsworth, Middlesex, England: Penguin Books, 1976, 239 p., paper, anth.

HAYLES, N(ancy) Katherine (Bruns), 1943-

25423 *The cosmic web: scientific field models and literary strategies in the twentieth century.* Ithaca, NY: Cornell University Press, 1984, 209 p., cloth, nonf.

HAYNES, Betsy (R. Lee), 1937-

25424 *The ghost of the Gravestone Hearth.* Nashville, TN: Thomas Nelson, 1977, 128 p., cloth, novel.

25425 *The power.* New York: Twilight/Dell, 1982, 147 p., paper, novel. TWILIGHT #2.

25426 *The shadows of Jeremy Pimm.* New York: Beaufort Books, 1981, 125 p., cloth, novel.

HAYNES, James (Monroe), 1932-

25427 *Voices in the dark.* New York: Twilight/Dell, 1982, 153 p., paper, novel. TWILIGHT #6.

HAYNES, Mary, 1938-

25428 *Raider's sky: a novel.* New York: Lothrop, Lee & Shepard, 1987, 166 p., cloth, novel.
25429 *Wordchanger.* New York: Lothrop, Lee & Shepard Books, 1983, 252 p., cloth, novel.

HAYNES, Roslynn D.

25430 *H. G. Wells, discoverer of the future: the influence of science on his thought.* New York, London: New York University Press, 1980, xi+238 p., cloth, nonf.

HAYWOOD, Laura W.—SEE: Laurance, Alice

HAZEL, (E.) Paul, 1944-

25431 *The Finnbranch.* London: Sphere Books, 1986, 593 p., paper, coll. FINNBRANCH #1-3.
25432 *Undersea.* Boston: An Atlantic Monthly Press Book, Little, Brown & Co., 1982, ix+224 p., cloth, novel. FINNBRANCH #2.
25433 *Winterking.* Boston: An Atlantic Monthly Press Book, Little, Brown & Co., 1985, 297 p., cloth, novel. FINNBRANCH #3.
25434 *Yearwood.* Boston: An Atlantic Monthly Press Book, Little, Brown & Co., 1980, 276 p., cloth, novel. FINNBRANCH #1.

HAZEN, Barbara Shook, 1930-

25435 *Peter Pan.* London: New English Library, 1976, [128] p., paper, movie.

HEALD, Tim(othy Villiers), 1944-

25436 *The making of Space: 1999: a Gerry Anderson production.* New York: Ballantine Books, 1976, 259 p., paper, nonf.

HEARD, H(enry) F(itzgerald), 1889-1971

07002 *Gabriel and the creatures.* New York: Harper & Brothers, 1952, 244 p., cloth, novel.
07002A retitled: *Wishing well: an outline of the evolution of the mammals, told as a series of stories about how the animals got their*

wishes. London: Faber & Faber, 1953, 198 p., cloth, novel.

HEARN, (Patricio) Lafcadio (Tessima Carlos), 1850-1904

25437 *Selected writings.* New York: Citadel Press, 1949, viii+566 p., cloth, coll. [Includes some nonfiction; edited by Henry Goodman].
25437A retitled: *The selected writings of Lafcadio Hearn.* New York: Citadel Press, Carol Publishing Group, 1991, viii+566 p., paper, coll. [Includes some nonfiction; edited by Henry Goodman].

HEARN, Michael Patrick, 1950-

25438 *The Victorian fairy tale book.* New York: Pantheon Books, 1988, xxvii+385 p., cloth, anth.

with L. Frank Baum

17545 *The wizard of Oz.* New York: Schocken Books, 1983, 305 p., cloth, anth. [Includes text of the novel plus critical essays].

HEARNE, Betsy Gould [i.e., Elizabeth Gould Hearne], 1942-

25439 *Beauty and the beast: visions and revisions of an old tale.* Chicago: University of Chicago Press, 1990, xv+247 p., cloth, nonf.
25440 *Eli's ghost.* New York: Margaret K. McElderry Books, 1987, 104 p., cloth, novel.
25441 *Home.* New York: A Margaret K. McElderry Book, Atheneum, 1979, 126 p., cloth, novel. MEGAN #2.
25442 *South star.* New York: A Margaret K. McElderry Book, Atheneum, 1977, 84 p., cloth, novel. MEGAN #1.

HEARNE, Elizabeth G.—SEE: Hearne, Betsy

HEARTMAN, Charles F(rederick), 1883-1953, with James R. Canny

19314 *A bibliography of first printings of the writings of Edgar Allan Poe: together with a record of first and contemporary later printings of his contributions to annuals, anthologies, periodicals, and newspapers issued during his lifetime: also some spurious Poeana and fakes, revised edition.* Hattiesburg, MS: The

Book Farm, 1943, x+294 p., cloth, nonf.

*HEATH, Peter [pseud. of Peter <u>Heath</u> Fine], 1938-

HEATH-STUBBS, John (Francis Alexander), 1918-

25443 *Charles Williams.* London: Published for the British Council and the National Book League by Longmans, Green & Co., 1955, 44 p., paper, nonf.

HEATHWOOD, Cecilia

25444 *Strange tales of mystery and the paranormal.* England: Excalibur Press, 1991, 180 p., paper, coll. [Includes some nonfiction].

HÉBERT, Anne, 1916-

25445 *Children of the black sabbath.* Don Mills, Ontario, Canada: Musson Book Co., 1977, 198 p., cloth, novel. [Translation by Carol Dunlap-Hébert of *Enfants du Sabbat*].

HEFLEY, Robert M.

25446 *Norman Jacobs & Kerry O'Quinn present Robots.* New York: O'Quinn Studios, 1979, 98 p., paper, nonf.
25447 *Norman Jacobs & Kerry O'Quinn present Robots, second edition.* New York: O'Quinn Studios, 1980, 98 p., paper, nonf.
Robots—SEE: *Norman Jacobs & Kerry O'Quinn present Robots.*

HEIN, Rolland (Neal), 1932-

25448 *The harmony within: the spiritual vision of George MacDonald.* Grand Rapids, MI: Christian University Press, 1982, xix+163 p., cloth, nonf.

HEINE, William C(olbourne), 1919-

Death wind—SEE: *The last Canadian.*
The last American—SEE: *The last Canadian.*
07033 *The last Canadian.* Markham, Ontario, Canada: Simon & Schuster of Canada, 1974, 253 p., paper, novel.
07033A retitled: *Death wind.* New York: Pyramid Books, 1976, 256 p., paper, novel.

07033b retitled: *The last American.* Markham, Ontario: PaperJacks Ltd., 1986, 253 p., paper, novel.

HEINEY, Donald W.—SEE: Harris, MacDonald

HEINLEIN, Robert A(nson), 1907-1988

25449 *The cat who walks through walls: a comedy of manners.* New York: G. P. Putnam's Sons, 1985, 382 p., cloth, novel. LAZARUS LONG SERIES.
25450 *Destination Moon.* Boston: Gregg Press, 1979, xiii+[xiii]+121-176+5-18+24 p., cloth, coll. [Includes some nonfiction; edited by David G. Hartwell].
25451 *Expanded universe: the new worlds of Robert A. Heinlein.* New York: Grosset & Dunlap, 1980, 582 p., cloth, coll.
25452 *Friday.* New York: Holt, Rinehart & Winston, 1982, 368 p., cloth, novel.
25453 *Grumbles from the grave.* New York: A Del Rey Book, Ballantine Books, 1989, xviii+281 p., cloth, nonf. coll. [Edited by Virginia Heinlein; winner of the *Locus* Award for Best Nonfiction, 1989 (1990)].
25454 *A Heinlein trio: The puppet masters; Double star; The door into space.* Garden City, NY: Nelson Doubleday, 1980, 502 p., cloth, coll.
25455 *Job: a comedy of justice.* New York: A Del Rey Book, Ballantine Books, 1984, 376 p., cloth, novel. [Winner of the *Locus* Award for Best Fantasy Novel, 1984 (1985)].
25456 *The notebooks of Lazarus Long.* New York: G. P. Putnam's Sons, 1978, [63] p., paper, fiction.
25457 *The number of the beast.* London: New English Library, 1980, 555 p., cloth, novel.
25458 *The puppet masters.* New York: A Del Rey Book, Ballantine Books, 1990, 340 p., paper, novel. [Expanded edition of #07054].
25459 *Red planet.* New York: A Del Rey Book, Ballantine Books, 1990, 196 p., paper, novel. [Expanded edition of #07055].
25460 *Starship troopers; The moon is a harsh mistress; Time enough for love.* New York: Book-of-the-Month Club, 1991, 309+383+650 p., cloth, coll.
25461 *Stranger in a strange land.* New York: G. P. Putnam's Sons, 1990, 525 p., cloth, novel. [Expanded edition of #07066].
25462 *To sail beyond the sunset: the life and loves of Maureen Johnson: (being the memoirs of a somewhat irregular lady).* New York: An Ace/Putnam Book, 1987, 416 p., cloth, novel. LAZARUS LONG SERIES.

with Rosemary Border

18276 *Space family Stone.* Cambridge, England: Cambridge University Press, 1978, viii+150 p., paper, novel. [Adapted from the original novel by Heinlein].

with David Fickling

23058 *The puppet masters.* Oxford, England: Alpha Books, Oxford University Press, 1979, 96 p., paper, novel. [Adapted from the novel by Heinlein].

HEITLAND, Jon

25463 *The man from U.N.C.L.E. book: the behind-the scenes story of a television classic.* New York: St. Martin's Press, 1987, xv+271 p., paper, nonf.

HELDMAN, Gladys M(edalie), 1922-

25464 *The Harmonetics investigation.* New York: Crown Publishers, 1979, 373 p., cloth, novel.

HELFER, Andrew (J.), 1958-

25465 *Indiana Jones and the cup of the vampire.* New York: Ballantine Books, 1984, 122 p., paper, novel. FIND YOUR FATE ADVENTURE #5; INDIANA JONES SERIES.
25466 *Supergirl, the girl of steel.* New York: An Archway Paperback, Pocket Books, 1984, 118 p., paper, tele. WHICH WAY BOOKS—SUPER POWERS #2.
25467 *Superman, the man of steel.* New York: An Archway Paperback, Pocket Books, 1983, 118 p., paper, tele. WHICH WAY BOOKS—SUPER POWERS #1.

HELFGOTT, Daniel (Andrew), 1952-

25468 *The buried.* New York: Avon, 1981, viii+278 p., paper, novel.

HELLER, Joseph, 1923-

25469 *Picture this.* New York: G. P. Putnam's Sons, 1988, 352 p., cloth, novel.

HELLER, Terry (Lynn), 1947-

25470 *The delights of terror: an aesthetics of the tale of terror.* Urbana & Chicago, IL: University of Illinois Press, 1987, xii+218 p., cloth, nonf.

25471 *The turn of the screw: bewildered vision.* Boston: Twayne Publishers, 1989, xiii+151 p., cloth, nonf.

HELMS, Randel, 1942-

25472 *Tolkien and the Silmarils.* Boston: Houghton Mifflin Co., 1981, xiii+104 p., cloth, nonf.

HELPRIN, Mark, 1947-

25473 *Swan Lake.* Boston: An Ariel Book, Houghton Mifflin Co., 1989, 80 p., cloth, novel.
25474 *Winter's tale.* San Diego, CA, New York: Harcourt Brace Jovanovich, 1983, xii+673 p., cloth, novel.

HELTERMAN, Jeffrey (Alec), 1942-

25475 *The blue frogs.* New York: Manor Books, 1979 (i.e., 1980?), 190 p., paper, novel.

*HELVICK, James [pseud. of Francis Claud Cockburn], 1904-1981

HELYAR, Jane—SEE: Poole, Josephine

HEMINGWAY, Amanda, 1955-

25476 *Pzyche.* London: Faber & Faber, 1982, 235 p., cloth, novel.

HENDERSON, Alexander J(ohn), 1910-

25477 *Aldous Huxley.* London: Chatto & Windus, 1935, xi+258 p., cloth, nonf.

HENDERSON, C(hristopher-John) J(ames), 1951- , *with Byron Preiss*

25478 *Guts.* New York: A Tempo Star Book, Grosset & Dunlap, 1979, viii+178 p., paper, novel.

HENDERSON, (Steven) Dan, 1953?-1991

25479 *Paradise.* New York: Tor, A Tom Doherty Associates Book, 1983, 314 p., paper, novel.

HENDERSON, Philip (Prichard), 1906-1977

25480 *William Morris.* London: Published for the British Council and the National Book League by Longmans, Green & Co., 1952, 43 p., paper, nonf.
25481 *William Morris.* London: Published for the British Council and the National Book

League by Longmans, Green & Co., 1963, 46 p., paper, nonf. [Revised edition].

25482 *William Morris: his life, work, and friends.* London: Thames & Hudson, 1967, 388 p., cloth, nonf.

HENDERSON, Zenna (Chlarson), 1917-1983

25483 *The people collection.* London: Corgi Books, 1991, 594 p., paper, coll. PEOPLE #1-2. [Includes *Pilgrimage*; *The People: no different flesh*; and four other short stories].

HENDRICH, Paula (Marie Griffith), 1928-

25484 *The girl who slipped through time.* New York: Lothrop, Lee & Shepard, 1978, 128 p., cloth, novel.

HENDRICKSON, Walter B(rookfield) Jr., 1936-

25485 *Class G-zero.* Canoga Park, CA: Major Books, 1976, 192 p., paper, novel.

HENDRIX, Howard V(incent), 1959-

25486 *The ecstasy of catastrophe: a study of apocalyptic narrative from Langland to Milton.* New York: Peter Lang, 1990, 394 p., cloth, nonf.
25487 *Testing, testing, 1, 2, 3.* Boise, ID: Eotu Group, 1990, unpaginated, paper, coll.

HENDRY, Frances Mary

25488 *Quest for a babe.* Edinburgh, Scotland: Canongate Publishing, 1990, [250] p., cloth, novel. QUEST #3.
25489 *Quest for a kelpie.* Edinburgh, Scotland: Canongate Publishing, 1986, 156 p., cloth, novel. QUEST #1.
25490 *Quest for a maid.* Edinburgh, Scotland: Canongate Publishing, 1988, 240 p., cloth, novel. QUEST #2.

HENEAGE, Simon, with Henry Ford

23250 *Sidney Sime: master of the mysterious.* London: Thames & Hudson, 1980, 96 p., paper, art.

HENHAM, Ernest G(eorge), 1870-

37828 *The feast of Bacchus: a study in dramatic atmosphere.* London: Brown, Langham & Co., 1907, 320 p., cloth, novel.
37829 *Tenebrae: a novel.* London: Skeffington & Son, 1898, vi+329 p., cloth, novel.

HENIGHAN, Tom

25491 *Strange attractors.* Victoria, British Columbia, Canada: Beach Holme, Tesseracts Books, 1991, [160] p., cloth, novel.
25492 *The well of time.* London: Collins, 1988, 393 p., cloth, novel.

HENNEBERG, Charles [i.e., Charles Henneberg zu Irmelshausen], 1899-1959, with Nathalie Henneberg

25493 *The green gods.* New York: DAW Books, 1980, 173 p., paper, novel. [Translation by C. J. Cherryh of *Les dieux verts*].

HENNEBERG, Nathalie, 1917-1977, with Charles Henneberg

25493 *The green gods.* New York: DAW Books, 1980, 173 p., paper, novel. [Translation by C. J. Cherryh of *Les dieux verts*].

HENRICK, Richard P.

25494 *Cry of the deep.* New York: Zebra Books, Kensington Publishing Corp., 1989, 416 p., paper, novel.
25495 *The phoenix odyssey.* New York: Zebra Books, Kensington Publishing Corp., 1986, 364 p., paper, novel.
25496 *Sea devil.* New York: Zebra Books, Kensington Publishing Corp., 1990, 382 p., paper, novel.
25497 *St. John the pursuer: Vampire in Moscow /* by Richard Henrick. Lake Geneva, WI: TSR Inc., 1988, 382 p., paper, novel. ST. JOHN THE PURSUER #1.
Vampire in Moscow—SEE: *St. John the pursuer: Vampire in Moscow.*
25498 *When duty calls.* New York: Zebra Books, Kensington Publishing Corp., 1988, 415 p., paper, novel.

HENRY, Maeve

25499 *A gift for a gift.* London: Heinemann, 1990, 110 p., cloth, novel.
25500 *The witch king.* London: Orchard Books, 1987, 126 p., cloth, novel.

HENSHALL, David

25501 *Starchild and witchfire.* London: Macmillan, 1990, [176] p., cloth, novel.

HENSLEY, J(oseph) L(ouis), 1926-

25502 *The black roads.* Toronto, New York: Laser Books, 1976, 190 p., paper, novel.

HENSTELL, Diana [pseud. of Diana Silber], 1936-

Deadly friend—SEE: *Friend.*
25503 *Friend.* Toronto, New York: Bantam Books, 1985, 323 p., paper, novel.
25503A retitled: *Deadly friend.* Toronto, New York: Bantam Books, 1986, 323 p., paper, novel.
25504 *New morning dragon.* Toronto, New York: Bantam Books, 1987, 352 p., paper, novel.
25505 *The other side.* Toronto, New York: Bantam Books, 1984, 298 p., paper, novel.

HEPPENSTALL, (John) Rayner, 1911-1981

25506 *Four absentees.* London: Barrie & Rockliff, 1960, 206 p., cloth, nonf.

HERALD, Diana Tixier, with Betty Rosenberg

32656 *Genreflecting: a guide to reading interests in genre fiction, 3rd ed.* Littleton, CO: Libraries Unlimited, 1991, xxv+345 p., cloth, nonf.

HERBERT, A(lan) P(atrick), Sir, 1890-1971

37830 *Made for man.* London: Methuen, 1958, 283 p., cloth, novel.

HERBERT, Brian (Patrick), 1947-

25507 *The garbage chronicles: being an account of the adventures of Tom Javik and Wizzy Malloy in the faraway land of catapulted garbage.* New York: Berkley Books, 1985, 298 p., paper, novel. SIDNEY #2.
25508 *Prisoners of Arionn.* New York: Arbor House, 1987, 356 p., cloth, novel.
25509 *The race for God.* New York: Ace Books, 1990, 295 p., paper, novel.
25510 *Sidney's comet: being an account of the remarkable events which occurred during the approach of the Great Garbage Comet.* New York: Berkley Books, 1983, 266 p., paper, novel. SIDNEY #1.
25511 *Sudanna, Sudanna.* New York: Arbor House, 1985, 251 p., cloth, novel.

with Frank Herbert

25512 *Man of two worlds.* New York: G. P. Putnam's Sons, 1986, 429 p., cloth, novel.

with Marie Landis

25513 *Memorymakers.* New York: A Roc Book, 1991, 206 p., paper, novel.

HERBERT, Frank (Patrick), 1920-1986

25514 *The best of Frank Herbert.* London: Sidgwick & Jackson, 1975, 302 p., cloth, coll. [Edited by Angus Wells].
25514A retitled: *The best of Frank Herbert, 1952-1964.* London: Sphere Books, 1976, 155 p., paper, coll. [The original edition split into two books].
25514B retitled: *The best of Frank Herbert, 1965-1970.* London: Sphere Books, 1976, 170 p., paper, coll. [The original edition split into two books].
25515 *Chapter house: Dune.* London: Victor Gollancz, 1985, 379 p., cloth, novel. DUNE #6.
25515A retitled: *Chapterhouse: Dune.* New York: G. P. Putnam's Sons, 1985, 464 p., cloth, novel. DUNE #6.
Chapterhouse: Dune—SEE: *Chapter house: Dune.*
25516 *Children of Dune.* New York: Berkley Publishing Corp., 1976, 444 p., cloth, novel. DUNE #3.
25517 *Destination: void (revised edition).* New York: A Berkley Book, Berkley Publishing Corp., 1978, ix+276 p., paper, novel. PANDORA #1. [Expanded edition of #07120].
25518 *Direct descent.* New York: Ace Books, 1980, 186 p., paper, novel.
25519 *The Dosadi experiment.* New York: G. P. Putnam's Sons, 1977, 336 p., cloth, novel. JORJ MCKIE #2. [Sequel to *Whipping star*].
07122 *Dune.* Philadelphia: Chilton Book Co., 1965, 412 p., cloth, novel. DUNE #1.
07122A retitled: *The illustrated Dune.* New York: A Berkley Windhover Book, Berkley Publishing Corp., 1977, 531 p., paper, novel.
25520 *Eye.* New York: A Byron Preiss Visual Publications Inc. Book, Berkley Books, 1985, 328 p., paper, coll.
25521 *Four complete novels: The white plague; The Dosadi experiment; The Santaroga barrier; Soul catcher.* New York: Avenel Books, 1984, 579 p., cloth, coll.
25522 *God Emperor of Dune.* New York: G. P. Putnam's Sons, 1981, 411 p., cloth, novel. DUNE #4.

25523 *The great Dune trilogy: Dune; Dune Messiah; Children of Dune.* London: Victor Gollancz, 1979, 911 p., cloth, coll. DUNE #1-3.

37831 *The Heaven makers.* New York: Ballantine Books, 1977, 230 p., paper, novel. [Revised edition of #07127].

25524 *Heretics of Dune.* London: Victor Gollancz, 1984, 384 p., cloth, novel. DUNE #5.

The illustrated Dune—SEE: *Dune.*

25525 *The Maker of Dune: insights of a master of science fiction.* New York: Berkley Books, 1987, 279 p., paper, nonf. coll.

25526 *Nebula winners fifteen.* New York: Harper & Row, 1981, 223 p., cloth, anth.

25527 *The notebooks of Frank Herbert's Dune.* New York: Perigee Books, 1988, [63] p., paper, coll. [Edited by Brian Herbert].

25528 *The priests of psi, and other stories.* London: Victor Gollancz, 1980, 204 p., cloth, coll.

25528A retitled: *The priests of psi.* London & Sydney: Futura, Macdonald & Co., 1981, 204 p., paper, coll.

25529 *The second great Dune trilogy.* London: Victor Gollancz, 1987, 1111 p., cloth, coll. DUNE #4-6. [Includes *God Emperor of Dune; Heretics of Dune; Chapter House: Dune*].

25530 *The white plague.* New York: G. P. Putnam's Sons, 1982, 445 p., cloth, novel.

37832 *Whipping star.* New York: A Berkley Medallion Book, 1977, 188 p., paper, novel. [Revised edition of #07130].

with Rosemary Border

18277 *Dune.* Oxford, England: Oxford University Press, 1980, 144 p., paper, novel. [Adapted from the original novel by Herbert].

with Brian Herbert

25512 *Man of two worlds.* New York: G. P. Putnam's Sons, 1986, 429 p., cloth, novel.

with Bill Ransom

25531 *The ascension factor.* New York: G. P. Putnam's Sons, 1988, 381 p., cloth, novel. PANDORA #4.

25532 *The Jesus incident.* New York: Berkley Publishing Corp., 1979, 405 p., cloth, novel. PANDORA #2.

25533 *The Lazarus effect.* New York: G. P. Putnam's Sons, 1983, 381 p., cloth, novel. PANDORA #3.

HERBERT, James, 1943-

25534 *Creed.* London: Hodder & Stoughton, 1990, 319 p., cloth, novel.

25535 *The dark.* London: New English Library, 1980, 336 p., cloth, novel.

Deadly eyes—SEE: *The rats.*

25536 *Domain.* Sevenoaks, Kent, England: New English Library, 1984, 381 p., cloth, novel. RATS #3.

25537 *The fluke.* London: New English Library, 1977, 191 p., cloth, novel.

25538 *The fog.* London: New English Library, 1975, 301 p., cloth, novel.

25539 *Haunted.* London: Hodder & Stoughton, 1988, 224 p., cloth, novel.

25540 *The Jonah.* London: New English Library, 1981, 253 p., cloth, novel.

25541 *Lair.* London: New English Library, 1979, 244 p., cloth, novel. RATS #2.

25542 *The magic cottage.* London: Hodder & Stoughton, 1986, 309 p., cloth, novel.

25543 *Moon.* Sevenoaks, Kent, England: New English Library, 1985, 313 p., cloth, novel.

25544 *Moon; Shrine; The dark; Fluke.* London: Methuen, 1988, 758 p., cloth, coll.

07133 *The rats.* London: New English Library, 1974, 175 p., cloth, novel. RATS #1.

07133A retitled: *Deadly eyes.* New York: A Signet Book, New American Library, 1983, 205 p., paper, novel. RATS #1.

25545 *Sepulchre.* London: Hodder & Stoughton, 1987, 316 p., cloth, novel.

25546 *Shrine.* Sevenoaks, Kent, England: New English Library, 1983, 432 p., cloth, novel.

25547 *The spear.* London: New English Library, 1978, 279 p., cloth, novel.

25548 *The survivor.* London: New English Library, 1976, 206 p., cloth, novel.

HERBERT, Kathleen

25549 *Bride of the spear.* London: Bodley Head, 1988, 297 p., cloth, novel. DARK AGES #3.

25550 *Ghost in the sunlight.* London: Bodley Head, 1986, 335 p., cloth, novel. DARK AGES #2.

25551 *The lady of the fountain.* Frome, Somerset, England: Bran's Head Books, 1982, 195 p., paper, novel.

25552 *Queen of the lightning.* London: Bodley Head, 1983, 255 p., cloth, novel. DARK AGES #1.

HERBERT, Mary H.

25553 *Dark horse.* Lake Geneva, WI: TSR Inc., 1990, 313 p., paper, novel. DARK HORSE #1.
25554 *Lightning's daughter.* Lake Geneva, WI: TSR Inc., 1991, 308 p., paper, novel. DARK HORSE #2.

HERLEY, Richard, 1950-

25555 *The earth goddess.* London: Heinemann, 1984, 212 p., cloth, novel. PAGANS TRILOGY #3.
25556 *The Flint lord.* London: Heinemann, Peter Davies, 1981, 219 p., cloth, novel. PAGANS TRILOGY #2.
25557 *The pagans.* London: Grafton, 1986, 654 p., paper, coll. PAGANS TRILOGY #1-3.
25558 *The penal colony.* London: Grafton, 1987, [288] p., cloth, novel.
25559 *The stone arrow.* London: Peter Davies, 1978, 220 p., cloth, novel. PAGANS TRILOGY #1.

HERMAN, Alan—SEE: Maxwell, Edward

HERMAN, J(eanne) B.

25560 *Black sabbat.* Canoga Park, CA: Major Books, 1979 (i.e., 1980?), 240 p., paper, novel.

HERMAN, Michaela Rossner- —SEE: Rossner, Michaela

HERNDON, Ursule—SEE: Molinaro, Ursule

*HERR, Dan(iel J.), 1917-1990

HERRIDGE, Charles, *with Stewart Cowley*

20721 *Great space battles.* London: Hamlyn, 1979, 96 p., cloth, coll.

HERRON, Don (Hughes), 1952-

25561 *The dark barbarian: the writings of Robert E. Howard.* Westport, CT & London: Greenwood Press, 1984, xviii+242 p., cloth, nonf. anth. CONTRIBUTIONS TO THE STUDY OF SCIENCE FICTION AND FANTASY #9.
25562 *Feast of fear: conversations with Stephen King.* San Rafael, CA: Underwood-Miller, 1989, x+282 p., cloth, nonf.
25563 *Reign of fear: fiction and film of Stephen King.* Los Angeles, Columbia, PA: Underwood-Miller, 1988, xv+254 p., cloth, nonf. anth. [Limited to 500 copies].

HERSHMAN, Morris, 1926-

The crash of 2086—SEE: *Shareworld.*
07151 *Shareworld.* New York: Walker, 1972, 186 p., cloth, novel.
07151A retitled: *The crash of 2086.* Canoga Park, CA: Major Books, 1976, 175 p., paper, novel.

HERSOM, Kathleen

25564 *The half child.* London: Simon & Schuster, 1990, 152 p., cloth, novel.

HERTER, Loretta M.—SEE: Herter, Lori

HERTER, Lori [i.e., Loretta M. Herter]

25565 *Obsession.* New York: Berkley Books, 1991, 278 p., paper, novel.

HERVEY, Maurice H.

37833 *David Dimsdale, M.D.: a story of past and future.* London: G. Redway, 1897, viii+344 p., cloth, novel.

HERZOG, Arthur (H. III), 1927-

25566 *The craving.* New York: A Dell Book, 1982, 319 p., paper, novel.
25567 *Glad to be here.* New York: Thomas Y. Crowell Publishers, 1979, 251 p., cloth, novel. AMERICA SERIES #2.
25568 *Heat.* New York: Simon & Schuster, 1977, 251 p., cloth, novel.
37834 *Heat.* New York: Tudor Publishing Co., 1989, 277 p., paper, novel. [Revised edition].
25569 *IQ 83.* New York: Simon & Schuster, 1978, 287 p., cloth, novel.
25570 *Make us happy.* New York: Thomas Y. Crowell, Publishers, 1978, vii+247 p., cloth, novel. AMERICA SERIES #1.

HERZOG, Émile—SEE: Maurois, André

*HESKY, Olga L(ynford), 1912-1974

HESS, Joan, 1949-

25571 *Future tense.* New York: Silhouette Books, 1987, 155 p., paper, novel.

HESSE, Hermann, 1877-1962

25572 *Pictor's metamorphoses, and other fantasies.* New York: Farrar, Straus &

Giroux, 1982, xxv+213 p., cloth, coll. [Translation by Rika Lesser].

HETHERINGTON, Keith (James), 1929-

25573 *Patrick.* South Melbourne, Victoria, Australia: Sun Books, 1978, 172 p., cloth, movie.

HEYDRON, Vicki Ann, 1945- , *with Randall Garrett*

25574 *The bronze of Eddarta.* Toronto, New York: Bantam Books, 1983, 165 p., paper, novel. GANDALARA CYCLE #3.
25575 *The Gandalara cycle, volume 1.* Toronto, New York: Bantam Books, 1986, 515 p., paper, coll. GANDALARA CYCLE #1-3.
25576 *The Gandalara cycle, vol. 2.* Toronto, New York: Bantam Books, 1986, 439 p., paper, coll. GANDALARA CYCLE #4-6.
25577 *The glass of Dyskornis.* Toronto, New York: Bantam Books, 1982, 174 p., paper, novel. GANDALARA CYCLE #2.
25578 *Return to Eddarta.* Toronto, New York: Bantam Books, 1985, 149 p., paper, novel. GANDALARA CYCLE #6.
25579 *The river wall.* Toronto, New York: Bantam Books, 1986, 275 p., paper, novel. GANDALARA CYCLE #7.
25580 *The search for Kä.* Toronto, New York: Bantam Books, 1984, 180 p., paper, novel. GANDALARA CYCLE #5.
25581 *The steel of Raithskar.* Toronto, New York: Bantam Books, 1981, 180 p., paper, novel. GANDALARA CYCLE #1.
25582 *The well of Darkness.* Toronto, New York: Bantam Books, 1983, 166 p., paper, novel. GANDALARA CYCLE #4.

HEYM, Stefan [pseud. of Hellmuth Fliegel], 1913-

25583 *The wandering Jew.* New York: A Fred Jordan Book, Holt, Rinehart & Winston, 1984, 298 p., cloth, novel. [Translation of *Ahasver*].

*HEYNE, William P., 1910-1985

HEYWOOD, Victor D.

25584 *Alpha star.* [Woodland Hills, CA]: Decade Press, [1980?], 224 p., paper, novel.

HIBBIN, Sally, *with Michael Klastorin*

25585 *Back to the future: the official book of the complete movie trilogy.* London: Hamlyn, 1990, 79 p., paper, nonf.

HICKMAN, Stephen F., 1949-

25586 *The fantasy art of Stephen Hickman.* Norfolk, VA: Donning Co., 1989, 91 p., cloth, art.
25587 *The Lemurian stone.* New York: Ace Books, 1988, 342 p., paper, novel.

HICKMAN, Tracy (Raye), 1955-

with Margaret Weis

25588 *The Darksword trilogy: Darksword adventures.* Toronto, New York: Bantam Books, 1989, 437 p., paper, nonf. DARKSWORD TRILOGY SERIES.
25589 *Doom of the darksword.* Toronto, New York: Bantam Books, 1988, xi+383 p., paper, novel. DARKSWORD TRILOGY #2.
25590 *Dragon wing.* New York, Toronto: Bantam Books, 1990, 431 p., cloth, novel. DEATH GATE CYCLE #1.
25591 *DragonLance adventures.* Lake Geneva, WI: TSR, 1987, 128 p., cloth, fiction. DRAGONLANCE SERIES; ADVANCED DUNGEONS & DRAGONS REFERENCE BOOKS.
25592 *DragonLance chronicles: Dragons of autumn twilight; Dragons of winter night; Dragons of spring dawning.* Lake Geneva, WI: TRS, 1988, xii+1030 p., paper, coll. DRAGONLANCE CHRONICLES #1-3.
25593 *DragonLance tales: The magic of Krynn; Kender, gully dwarves, and gnomes; Love and war.* Harmondsworth, Middlesex, England: Penguin Books, 1991, 688 p., paper, coll. DRAGONLANCE TALES #1-3.
25594 *Dragons of spring dawning.* Lake Geneva, WI: TSR Inc., 1985, 379 p., paper, novel. DRAGONLANCE CHRONICLES #3.
25595 *Dragons of the autumn twilight.* Lake Geneva, WI: TSR Inc., 1984, 447 p., paper, novel. DRAGONLANCE CHRONICLES #1.
25596 *Dragons of the winter night.* Lake Geneva, WI: TSR Inc., 1985, 399 p., paper, novel. DRAGONLANCE CHRONICLES #2.
25597 *Elven star.* New York, Toronto: Spectra, Bantam Books, 1990, 367 p., cloth, novel. DEATH GATE CYCLE #2.
25598 *Fire sea.* Toronto, New York: Bantam Books, 1991, 364 p., cloth, novel. DEATH GATE CYCLE #3.

25599 *Forging the darksword.* Toronto, New York: Bantam Books, 1988, 391 p., paper, novel. DARKSWORD TRILOGY #1.

25600 *Kender, gully dwarves, and gnomes.* Lake Geneva, WI: TSR Inc., 1987, 367 p., paper, anth. DRAGONLANCE TALES #2.

25601 *Love and war.* Lake Geneva, WI: TSR Inc., 1987, 386 p., paper, anth. DRAGONLANCE TALES #3.

25602 *The magic of Krynn.* Lake Geneva, WI: TSR Inc., 1987, 352 p., paper, anth. DRAGONLANCE TALES #1.

25603 *The paladin of the night.* Toronto, New York: Bantam Books, 1989, 375 p., paper, novel. ROSE OF THE PROPHET #2.

25604 *The prophet of Akhran.* Toronto, New York: Bantam Books, 1989, 390 p., paper, novel. ROSE OF THE PROPHET #3.

25605 *Test of the twins.* Lake Geneva, WI: TSR Inc., 1986, 345 p., paper, novel. DRAGONLANCE LEGENDS #3.

25606 *Time of the twins.* Lake Geneva, WI: TSR Inc., 1986, 398 p., paper, novel. DRAGONLANCE LEGENDS #1.

25607 *Triumph of the darksword.* Toronto, New York: Bantam Books, 1988, 346 p., paper, novel. DARKSWORD TRILOGY #3.

25608 *War of the twins.* Lake Geneva, WI: TSR Inc., 1986, 387 p., paper, novel. DRAGONLANCE LEGENDS #1.

25609 *The will of the wanderer.* Toronto, New York: Bantam Books, 1989, 444 p., paper, novel. ROSE OF THE PROPHET #1.

with Margaret Weis & Mary L. Kirchoff

25610 *Leaves from the inn of the Last Home: the complete Krynn source book.* Lake Geneva, WI: TSR Inc., 1987, 255 p., paper, nonf.

*HICKS, Granville, 1901-<u>1982</u>

HIGGINBOTTOM, David—SEE: Fisk, Nicholas

HIGGINS, D. S(ydney), 1938-

25611 *Rider Haggard: the great storyteller.* London: Cassell, 1981, 266 p., cloth, nonf.

25611A retitled: *Rider Haggard: a biography.* New York: Stein & Day Publishers, 1983, 266 p., cloth, nonf.

with Edgar Allan Poe

25612 *Tales of terror.* London: Cassell, 1980, 46 p., cloth, coll. [Retold by Higgins from Poe's originals].

HIGGINSON, Thomas Wentworth, 1823-1911

37835 *The monarch of dreams.* Boston: Lea & Shepard, 1887, 52 p., cloth, story.

HIGGS, Eric C.

25613 *Doppelganger: a novel.* New York: St. Martin's Press, 1987, 229 p., cloth, novel.

HIGH, Philip E(mpson), 1914-

25614 *Blindfold from the stars.* London: Dennis Dobson, 1979, 192 p., cloth, novel.

25615 *Fugitive from time.* London: Robert Hale, 1978, 188 p., cloth, novel.

HIGHAM, Charles, 1931-

25616 *The midnight tree: a fairy tale of terror.* New York: Pocket Books, 1979, 239 p., paper, novel.

HIGHSMITH, (Mary) Patricia, 1921-

25617 *Tales of natural and unnatural catastrophes.* London: Bloomsbury, 1987, 189 p., cloth, coll.

HIGMAN, Dennis J., 1940-

25618 *Pranks.* New York: Leisure Books, 1987, 431 p., paper, novel.

HILDEBRANDT, Brothers—SEE: Hildebrandt, Greg & Hildebrandt, Tim

HILDEBRANDT, Greg(ory J.), 1939-

with Tim Hildebrandt

25619 *The art of the Brothers Hildebrandt.* New York: Ballantine Books, 1979, 23 p., [40] leaves of plates, paper, art. [Edited by Ian Summers].

with Tim Hildebrandt & Jerry Nichols

25620 *Urshurak.* Toronto, New York: Bantam Books, 1979, 405 p., paper, novel.

with William McGuire

25621 *From Tolkien to Oz.* Parsippany, NJ: Unicorn Publishing House, 1985, [96] p., cloth, art.

HILDEBRANDT, Rita, 1948- , *with Tim Hilde-brandt*

25622 *The fantasy cookbook.* Indianapolis, IN: Bobbs-Merrill Co., 1983, viii+195 p., cloth, nonf.
25623 *Merlin and the dragons of Atlantis.* Indianapolis, IN: Bobbs-Merrill Co., 1983, 197 p., cloth, novel.

HILDEBRANDT, Tim(othy), 1939-

25624 *Rotwang; or, The delirious precision of dreams.* Berkeley, CA: Blue Wind Press, 1976, 139 p., cloth, novel.

with Greg Hildebrandt

25619 *The art of the Brothers Hildebrandt.* New York: Ballantine Books, 1979, 23 p., [40] leaves of plates, paper, art. [Edited by Ian Summers].

with Greg Hildebrandt & Jerry Nichols

25620 *Urshurak.* Toronto, New York: Bantam Books, 1979, 405 p., paper, novel.

with Rita Hildebrandt

25622 *The fantasy cookbook.* Indianapolis, IN: Bobbs-Merrill Co., 1983, viii+195 p., cloth, nonf.
25623 *Merlin and the dragons of Atlantis.* Indianapolis, IN: Bobbs-Merrill Co., 1983, 197 p., cloth, novel.

HILDESHEIMER, Wolfgang, 1916-

25625 *The collected stories of Wolfgang Hildesheimer.* New York: Ecco Press, 1987, vi+197 p., cloth, coll. [Edited and translated by Joachim Neugroschel].

HILDICK, E(dmund) W(allace), 1925-

25626 *The case of the dragon in distress: a McGurk fantasy.* New York: Macmillan Publishing Co.; Toronto: Collier Macmillan Canada; New York: Maxwell Macmillan International Publishing Group, 1991, 153 p., cloth, novel. MCGURK SERIES. [Previous books in this series are mysteries].
25627 *The Ghost Squad and the Ghoul of Grünberg.* New York: E. P. Dutton, 1986, 186 p., cloth, novel. GHOST SQUAD #4.
25628 *The Ghost Squad and the Halloween conspiracy.* New York: E. P. Dutton & Co., 1985, 170 p., cloth, novel. GHOST SQUAD #2.
25629 *Ghost Squad and the menace of the Malevs.* New York: E. P. Dutton, 1988, 200 p., cloth, novel. GHOST SQUAD #6.
25630 *Ghost Squad and the prowling hermits.* New York: E. P. Dutton, 1987, 212 p., cloth, novel. GHOST SQUAD #5.
25631 *The Ghost Squad breaks through.* New York: E. P. Dutton & Co., 1984, 138 p., cloth, novel. GHOST SQUAD #1.
25632 *The Ghost Squad flies Concorde.* New York: E. P. Dutton, 1985, 186 p., cloth, novel. GHOST SQUAD #3.
25633 *Time Explorers*, Inc.. Garden City, NY: Doubleday & Co., 1976, 222 p., cloth, novel.

HILGARTNER, Beth, 1957-

25634 *Colors in the dreamweaver's loom.* Boston: Houghton Mifflin Co., 1989, 241 p., cloth, novel. DREAMWEAVER #1.
25635 *The feast of the trickster.* Boston: Houghton Mifflin Co., 1991, 230 p., cloth, novel. DREAMWEAVER #2.
25636 *A necklace of fallen stars.* Boston: Little, Brown & Co., 1979, 209 p., cloth, novel.

HILL, Albert Fay, 1925- , *with David Campbell Hill*

25637 *The deadly messiah.* New York: Atheneum, 1976, 348 p., cloth, novel.
25638 *Invader.* New York: A Jove Book, 1981, 293 p., paper, novel.

HILL, Carol (De Chellis), 1942-

Amanda & the eleven million mile high dancer—SEE: *The eleven million mile high dancer.*
25639 *The eleven million mile high dancer.* New York: A William Abrahams Book, Holt, Rinehart & Winston, 1985, 447 p., cloth, novel.
25639A retitled: *Amanda & the eleven million mile high dancer.* London: Bloomsbury, 1988, 447 p., paper, novel.

HILL, Cathy, 1944-

25640 *Fantasy art folio.* Los Angeles: Witchcraft & Sorcery, Fantasy Publishing Co. Inc., 1973, [8] p., paper, art.

HILL, David Campbell, *with Albert Fay Hill*

25637 *The deadly messiah.* New York: Atheneum, 1976, 348 p., cloth, novel.
25638 *Invader.* New York: A Jove Book, 1981, 293 p., paper, novel.

HILL, Douglas (Arthur), 1935-

25641 *Alien Citadel.* London: Heinemann, 1984, 122 p., cloth, novel. HUNTSMAN TRILOGY (FINN) #3.
25642 *Alien worlds: stories of adventure on other planets.* London: Heinemann, 1981, 121 p., cloth, anth.
25643 *Blade of the poisoner.* London: Victor Gollancz, 1987, 192 p., cloth, novel. TALENTS #1.
25644 *The caves of Klydor.* London: Victor Gollancz, 1984, 118 p., cloth, novel. COLSEC TRILOGY #2.
25645 *The Colloghi conspiracy.* London: Victor Gollancz, 1990, 237 p., cloth, novel. DEL CURB #2.
25646 *ColSec rebellion.* London: Victor Gollancz, 1985, 121 p., cloth, novel. COLSEC TRILOGY #3.
25647 *Day of the starwind.* London: Victor Gollancz, 1980, 123 p., cloth, novel. LAST LEGIONARY #3.
25648 *Deathwing over Veynaa.* London: Victor Gollancz, 1980, 125 p., cloth, novel. LAST LEGIONARY #2.
25649 *Exiles of ColSec.* London: Victor Gollancz, 1984, 126 p., cloth, novel. COLSEC TRILOGY #1.
25650 *The Fraxilly fracas.* London: Victor Gollancz, 1989, 220 p., cloth, novel. DEL CURB #1.
25651 *Galactic Warlord.* London: Victor Gollancz, 1979, 126 p., cloth, novel. LAST LEGIONARY #1.
25652 *Have your own extra-terrestrial adventure.* London: Sparrow, 1983, 87 p., paper, novel.
25653 *The huntsman.* London: Heinemann, 1982, 135 p., cloth, novel. HUNTSMAN TRILOGY (FINN) #1.
25654 *Master of fiends.* London: Victor Gollancz, 1987, 184 p., cloth, novel. TALENTS #2.
25655 *Penelope's pendant.* London: Macmillan Children's Books, 1990, 103 p., cloth, novel.
25656 *Planet of the Warlord.* London: Victor Gollancz, 1981, 128 p., cloth, novel. LAST LEGIONARY #4.
25657 *Planetfall.* Oxford, England: Oxford University Press, 1986, 96 p., cloth, anth.

25658 *The shape of sex to come.* London & Sydney: Pan Books, 1978, 176 p., paper, anth.
25659 *Warriors of the wasteland.* London: Heinemann, 1983, 124 p., cloth, novel. HUNTSMAN TRILOGY (FINN) #2.
25660 *Young legionary: the earlier adventures of Keill Randor.* London: Victor Gollancz, 1982, 127 p., cloth, novel. LAST LEGIONARY #5.

HILL, Ernest, 1914-

25661 *The Quark invasion.* London: Robert Hale, 1978, 156 p., cloth, novel.

HILL, Helen M(orey), 1915- , *with Pat Pflieger*

25662 *A reference guide to modern fantasy for children.* Westport, CT & London: Greenwood Press, 1984, xvii+690 p., cloth, nonf.

HILL, John, pseud.—SEE: Koontz, Dean R.

HILL, Josiah F.

25665 *The magazine of fantasy & science fiction: index of authors and titles, Volume 1, Number 1 through Volume 54, Number 6, Fall 1949 through June 1978.* Lebanon, NH: 4 Hills Press, 1978, [99] p., paper, nonf.

*HILL, Merton, 1895-1989

HILL, Reginald (Charles), 1936-

37836 *One small step: a Dalziel and Pascoe novella.* London: Crime Club, Collins, 1990, 109 p., cloth, novel. DALZIEL & PASCOE SERIES.
37837 *There are no ghosts in the Soviet Union.* London: Collins, 1987, [208] p., cloth, coll.

HILL, Roger, *with Glen A. Larson*

25666 *The 24-carat assassin: a novel.* London: A Target Book, W. H. Allen & Co., 1984, 154 p., paper, tele. KNIGHT RIDER #4.
25667 *Hearts of stone.* New York: Pinnacle Books, 1984, 233 p., paper, tele. KNIGHT RIDER #3.
25668 *Knight Rider.* New York: Pinnacle Books, 1983, 245 p., paper, tele. KNIGHT RIDER #1.

25669 *Mirror image: a novel.* London: A Target Book, W. H. Allen & Co., 1985, 159 p., paper, tele. KNIGHT RIDER #5.

25670 *Trust doesn't rust.* New York: Pinnacle Books, 1984, 245 p., paper, tele. KNIGHT RIDER #2.

HILL, Russell

25671 *Cold Creek Cash Store.* New York: Ballantine Books, 1986, 151 p., paper, novel.

25672 *Reflections of the future: an elective course in science fiction and fact.* Lexington, MA: Ginn & Co., 1975, viii+261 p., cloth, nonf.

HILL, Susan (Elizabeth), 1942-

25673 *Ghost stories.* London: Hamish Hamilton, 1983, 254 p., cloth, anth.

The Random House book of ghost stories—
SEE: *The Walker book of ghost stories.*

25674 *The Walker book of ghost stories.* London: Walker Books, 1990, 222 p., cloth, anth.

25674A retitled: *The Random House book of ghost stories.* New York: Random House, 1991, 222 p., cloth, anth.

25675 *The woman in black.* London: Hamish Hamilton, 1983, 160 p., cloth, novel.

HILL, William (D.)

25676 *Dawn of the vampire.* New York: Pinnacle Books, Windsor Publishing Corp., 1991, 480 p., paper, novel.

HILLEGAS, Mark R(obert), 1926-

25677 *Shadows of imagination: the fantasies of C. W. Lewis, J. R. R. Tolkien, and Charles Williams, new edition.* Carbondale & Edwardsville, IL: Southern Illinois University Press; London & Amsterdam: Feffer & Simons, 1979, xvii+190 p., cloth, nonf. anth. [A revised edition of #07218].

HILLEGASS, Clifton K(eith), 1918- , *with Frank H. Thompson, Jr.*

25678 *Animal farm: notes.* Lincoln, NE: Cliffs Notes, 1967, 51 p., paper, nonf.

HILLER, B(arbara) B.

37838 *Camp-out on Danger Mountain.* New York, Toronto: Scholastic Inc., 1984, 93 p., paper, fiction. TWISTAPLOT #11.

37839 *The fantastic journey of the space shuttle Astra.* New York, Toronto: Scholastic Inc., 1984, 56 p., paper, fiction. PICK-A-PATH #7.

25679 *Ghostbusters II: a novel.* New York: A Yearling Book, 1989, 87 p., paper, movie. GHOSTBUSTERS #2.

37840 *The secret of 13.* New York, Toronto: Scholastic Inc., 1984, 58 p., paper, fiction. PICK-A-PATH #13.

25680 *Superman IV: a novelization.* New York, Toronto: Scholastic Inc., 1987, 140 p., paper, movie. SUPERMAN #4.

25681 *Teenage mutant ninja turtles: a novelization.* New York: A Yearling Book, 1990, 92 p., paper, movie. TEENAGE MUTANT NINJA TURTLES #1.

with Neil W. Hiller

25682 *Big!* New York: Ballantine Books, 1988, 192 p., paper, movie.

25683 *The far side of the mirror.* New York, Toronto: Scholastic Inc., 1986, 96 p., paper, novel.

25684 *Honey, I shrunk the kids: a novel.* New York, Toronto: Scholastic Inc., 1989, 89 p., paper, movie.

37841 *The Hot Dog Gang caper.* New York, Toronto: Scholastic Inc., 1985, 58 p., paper, fiction. PICK-A-PATH #15.

25685 *Little monsters: a novelization.* New York, Toronto: Scholastic Inc., 1989, 83 p., paper, movie.

25686 *Spacecamp.* New York, Toronto: Scholastic Inc., 1986, 92 p., paper, movie.

HILLER, Neil W., *with B. B. Hiller*

25682 *Big!* New York: Ballantine Books, 1988, 192 p., paper, movie.

25683 *The far side of the mirror.* New York, Toronto: Scholastic Inc., 1986, 96 p., paper, novel.

25684 *Honey, I shrunk the kids: a novel.* New York, Toronto: Scholastic Inc., 1989, 89 p., paper, movie.

37841 *The Hot Dog Gang caper.* New York, Toronto: Scholastic Inc., 1985, 58 p., paper, fiction. PICK-A-PATH #15.

25685 *Little monsters: a novelization.* New York, Toronto: Scholastic Inc., 1989, 83 p., paper, movie.

25686 *Spacecamp.* New York, Toronto: Scholastic Inc., 1986, 92 p., paper, movie.

HILLMAN, S. A.

25687 *Cradle kill.* New York: Berkley Books, 1988, 264 p., paper, novel.

HIMROD, Brenda—SEE: Lane, Megan

HINCHCLIFFE, Philip

25688 *Doctor Who and the keys of Marinus.* London: A Target Book, W. H. Allen, 1980, 127 p., paper, tele. DOCTOR WHO.

25689 *Doctor Who and the masque of Mandragora.* London: Target, W. H. Allen, 1977, 123 p., paper, tele. DOCTOR WHO #42.

25689A retitled: *Doctor Who: The masque of Mandragora.* London: A Target Book, 1991, 123 p., paper, tele. DOCTOR WHO #42.

25690 *Doctor Who and the seeds of doom.* London: A Longbow Book, Allan Wingate, 1977, 128 p., cloth, tele. DOCTOR WHO.

Doctor Who: The masque of Mandragora—SEE: *Doctor Who and the masque of Mandragora.*

The masque of Mandragora—SEE: *Doctor Who and the masque of Mandragora.*

with Terrance Dicks

21852 *The deadly assassin; The seeds of doom.* London: W. H. Allen, 1989, 128+121 p., paper, coll. DOCTOR WHO CLASSICS.

HINDLE, Lee J(ohn), 1965-

25691 *Dragon fall.* New York: An Avon Flare Book, 1984, 139 p., paper, novel.

HINDMAN, Roger

25692 *Far out: some approaches to teaching the speculative literature of science fiction and the supernatural.* Los Angeles: Los Angeles Public Schools, Instructional Planning Division, 1974, iv+120 p., paper, nonf.

HINE, Al(fred Blakelee), 1915-1974

25693 *The Beatles in Help!* New York: A Dell Book, 1965, 156 p., paper, movie.

HINE, Muriel (Coxon)

37842 *The island forbidden to man.* London: Hodder & Stoughton, 1946, 318 p., cloth, novel.

HINES, Anna Grossnickle, 1946-

25694 *Cassie Bowen takes witch lessons.* New York: Dial Books for Young Readers, 1985, 135 p., cloth, novel.

HINES, Bede (Francis), 1918-

25695 *The social world of Aldous Huxley.* Loretto, PA: The Seraphic Press, 1957, 104 p., cloth, nonf.

HINKE, C. J.

25696 *Oz in Canada: a bibliography.* Vancouver, British Columbia, Canada: W. Hoffer, 1982, 85 p., paper, nonf.

HINKEMEYER, Michael T(homas), 1940-

25697 *The creator* / M. Thomas Hinkemeyer. Los Angeles: Pinnacle Books, 1978, 310 p., paper, novel.

25698 *The dark below.* Greenwich, CT: A Fawcett Gold Medal Book, Fawcett Publications, 1975, 207 p., paper, novel.

25698A retitled: *Sea Cliff.* New York: Pocket Books, 1979, 223 p., paper, novel.

25699 *The harbinger.* New York: Pocket Books, 1980, 328 p., paper, novel.

37843 *The Order of the Arrow.* New York: Tor, A Tom Doherty Associates Book, 1990, 313 p., cloth, novel.

Sea Cliff—SEE: *The dark below.*

25700 *Summer Solstice: a novel.* New York: Berkley Publishing Corp., 1976, 256 p., cloth, novel.

as JAN LARA

25701 *Limbo: a novel.* New York: Popular Library, 1988, 250 p., paper, novel.

25702 *Soulcatchers.* New York: Warner Books, 1990, 235 p., paper, novel.

HINTON, Brian

25703 *Michael Moorcock: a bibliography, based on the Moorcock deposit, Bodleian Library, Oxford.* Brighton, England: J. L. Noyce, 1983, 55 p., paper, nonf.

HINTON, C(harles) H(oward), 1853-1907

37844 *Stella; and, An unfinished communication: studies of the unseen.* London: Swan Sonnenschein; New York: Macmillan, 1895, 177 p., cloth, coll.

HINTON, Perry, *with David Fickling*

23059 *Helmquest.* Harmondsworth, Middlesex, England: Puffin Books, 1986, [32] p., paper, novel. FANTASY QUESTBOOK.

23060 *The path of peril.* Harmondsworth, Middlesex, England: Puffin Books, 1984, [32] p., paper, novel. FANTASY QUESTBOOK.

23061 *Starflight zero.* Harmondsworth, Middlesex, England: Puffin Books, 1985, [32] p., paper, novel. FANTASY QUESTBOOK.

23062 *Ten doors of doom.* Harmondsworth, Middlesex, England: Puffin Books, 1987, [32] p., paper, novel. FANTASY QUESTBOOK.

HINTZE, Naomi A., 1909-

25704 *Ghost child.* New York: Fawcett Gold Medal, 1983, 245 p., paper, novel.

HINZ, Christopher (E.), 1951-

25705 *Anachronisms.* New York: St. Martin's Press, 1988, 304 p., cloth, novel.

25706 *Ash Ock.* New York: St. Martin's Press, 1989, 308 p., cloth, novel. PARATWA SAGA #2.

25707 *Liege killer.* New York: St. Martin's Press, 1987, 458 p., cloth, novel. PARATWA SAGA #1.

25708 *The Paratwa.* New York: St. Martin's Press, 1991, 404 p., cloth, novel. PARATWA SAGA #3.

HIPOLITO, Jane (Wilson), 1942- , *with Willis E. McNelly*

The book of Mars—SEE: *Mars, we love you.*

07235 *Mars, we love you: tales of Mars, men, and Martians.* Garden City, NY: Doubleday & Co., 1971, xx+332 p., cloth, anth.

07235A retitled: *The book of Mars: tales of Mars, men, and Martians.* London: Futura Publications, An Orbit Book, 1976, xviii+332 p., paper, anth.

HIPPLE, Theodore W(allace), 1935-

25709 *Tales of mystery and suspense.* Boston: Allyn & Bacon, 1977, ix+260 p., cloth, anth.

with Robert G. Wright

25710 *The worlds of science fiction.* Boston: Allyn & Bacon, 1979, vii+248 p., cloth?, anth.

HIRAI, Kazumasa, 1931-

25711 *Wolfcrest.* Tokyo: Kodansha, 1985, 2 v., paper, novel. [Translation by Edward Lipsett of *Okami no monsho*].

HIRSCH, David

25712 *Moonbase Alpha technical notebook.* New York: Starlog Magazine, 1977, [78] leaves, plaster binder, fiction.

with Barbara Krasnoff

25713 *Science fiction weapons, volume 1.* New York: A Starlog Press Publication, 1979, 35 p., paper, nonf.

with Howard Zimmerman

25714 *Norman Jacobs & Kerry O'Quinn present Spaceships, rev. ed.* New York: A Starlog Press Book, 1980, 98 p., paper, nonf.

Spaceships—SEE: *Norman Jacobs & Kerry O'Quinn present Spaceships, rev. ed.*

HIRSCH, Gordon (Dan), 1943- , *with William Veeder*

25714 *Dr. Jekyll and Mr. Hyde: after one hundred years.* Chicago: University of Chicago Press, 1988, xx+312 p., cloth, nonf. anth.

HIRSCHMAN, Edward, 1950-

25716 *Tarzan at Mars' core.* Annandale, VA: The DeLethein Press, 1977, 151 p., paper, novel. TARZAN SERIES.

HISE, Della Van—SEE: Van Hise, Della

HISE, James V. Van—SEE: Van Hise, James V.

*HITCHCOCK, Alfred (Joseph), Sir, 1899-<u>1980</u>

HITE, Molly (Patricia), 1947-

25717 *Ideas of order in the novels of Thomas Pynchon.* Columbus, OH: Ohio State University Press, 1983, x+183 p., cloth, nonf.

HJORT, James William

25718 *Ebon roses, jewelled skulls.* Buffalo, NY: Weirdbook Press, 1980, 95 p., cloth, coll.

HJORTSBERG, William (Reinhold), 1941-

25719 *Falling angel.* New York: Harcourt Brace Jovanovich, 1978, 242 p., cloth, novel.
25720 *Tales & fables.* Los Angeles: Sylvester & Orphanos, 1985, 80 p., cloth, coll. [Limited to 330 copies in slipcase].

HOARE, Agnes D.—SEE: Hoare, Dorothy

HOARE, Dorothy M. [i.e., Agnes Dorothea Mackenzie Hoare], 1901-

25721 *The works of William Morris and of Yeats in relation to early saga literature.* Cambridge, England: Cambridge University Press, 1937, viii+179 p., cloth, nonf.

HOBAN, Russell (Conwell), 1925-

25722 *The Medusa frequency.* London: Jonathan Cape, 1987, 143 p., cloth, novel.
15816 *The mouse and his child.* New York: Harper & Row, 1967, 181 p., cloth, novel.
25723 *Pilgermann.* London: Jonathan Cape, 1983, 240 p., cloth, novel.
25724 *Riddley Walker.* London: Jonathan Cape, 1980, 220 p., cloth, novel. [Winner of the John W. Campbell Jr. Memorial Award for Best Novel, 1981 (1982)].

HOCH, Edward D(entinger), 1930-

25725 *The Frankenstein factory: a novel of the future.* New York: Warner Paperback Library, 1975, 190 p., paper, novel.
25726 *The quests of Simon Ark.* New York: Mysterious Press, 1984, xii+268 p., cloth, coll. SIMON ARK #3.

HOCHERMAN, Henry W.

25727 *The Gilgul: a novel of possession.* New York: Pinnacle Books, Windsor Publishing Corp., 1990, 350 p., paper, novel.

HOCKE, Martin

25728 *The ancient solitary reign.* London: Grafton, 1989, 358 p., cloth, novel.

HOCKER, Karla, 1946-

25729 *A Christmas charade.* New York: Zebra Books, Kensington Publishing Corp., 1991, 351 p., paper, novel.

HOCKLEY, Chris, 1950-

25730 *Steel ghost.* London: Grafton, 1989, 319 p., paper, novel.

HODDER, William Reginald

37845 *The vampire.* London: William Rider & Son, 1913, viii+306 p., cloth, novel.

HODDER-WILLIAMS, (John) Christopher (Glazebrook), 1926-

25731 *The chromosome game.* London: Mithras, 1984, 216 p., paper, novel.
25732 *The prayer machine.* London: Weidenfeld & Nicolson, 1976, 205 p., cloth, novel.
25733 *The silent voice: a novel.* London: Weidenfeld & Nicolson, 1977, 204 p., cloth, novel.
25734 *The thinktank that leaked.* St. Ives, Cornwall, England: United Writers Publications, 1979, 250 p., cloth, novel.

HODGE, Brian (Keith), 1960-

25735 *Dark advent.* New York: Pinnacle Books, Windsor Publishing Corp., 1988, 448 p., paper, novel.
25736 *Nightlife.* New York: A Dell Book, 1991, 404 p., paper, novel.
25737 *Oasis.* New York: Tor Horror, A Tom Doherty Associates Book, 1989, 312 p., paper, novel.

HODGE, Conrad Vere-—SEE: de Vere, V. C.

HODGELL, P(atricia) C(hristine), 1951-

25738 *Chronicles of the Kencyrath.* London: New English Library, 1988, 608 p., paper, coll. KENCYRATH #1-2. [Includes *God stalk*; *Dark of the moon*].
25739 *Dark of the moon.* New York: An Argo Book, Atheneum, 1985, ix+386 p., cloth, novel. KENCYRATH #2.
25740 *God stalk.* New York: Atheneum, 1982, xi+271 p., cloth, novel. KENCYRATH #1.

HODGES, Doris —SEE: Hunt, Charlotte

HODGMAN, Ann

25741 *Galaxy High School.* Toronto, New York: Bantam Skylark, 1987, 85 p., paper, tele.
25742 *My babysitter is a vampire.* New York, London: A GLC Book, A Minstrel Book, Pocket Books, 1991, 121 p., paper, novel.
25743 *Seaside mystery.* Toronto, New York: An R. A. Montgomery Book, Bantam Books, 1987, 115 p., paper, novel. CHOOSE YOUR OWN ADVENTURE #67.
25744 *There's a batwing in my lunchbox.* New York: A GLC Book, An Avon Camelot Book, 1988, 89 p., paper, novel. FIFTH GRADE MONSTERS #3.

HODGSON, Amanda

25745 *The romances of William Morris.* Cambridge, England: Cambridge University Press, 1987, xii+219 p., cloth, nonf.

HODGSON, William Hope, 1877-1918

25746 *A dream of X.* West Kingston, RI: Donald M. Grant, Publisher, 1977, 141 p., cloth, novel. [An abridged version of *The night land* (see #07287)].
25747 *The haunted "Pampero."* London: Ferret Fantasy, 1980, [8] p., paper, story.
25748 *Masters of terror, volume one.* London: Corgi Books, 1977, 156 p., paper, coll. [Edited by Peter Tremayne].
25749 *Out of the storm: uncollected fantasies.* West Kingston, RI: Donald M. Grant, Publisher, 1975, 304 p., cloth, coll. [Edited by Sam Moskowitz].
25750 *Spectral manifestations.* Oxford, England: Bellknapp Books, 1984, vii+51 p., paper, coll.

HOFFMAN, Alice, 1952-

25751 *Seventh heaven.* Franklin Center, PA: Franklin Library, 1990, 256 p., cloth, novel.

HOFFMAN, Carl

25752 *Monster tayles: two stories.* Rochester, NY: Porkyspine Press, 1983, 114 p., paper, coll.

HOFFMAN, Charles E., 1954- , with Marc A. Cerasini

19683 *Robert E. Howard.* Mercer Island, WA: Starmont House, 1987, 156 p., cloth, nonf. STARMONT READER'S GUIDE #35.

HOFFMAN, Daniel (Gerard), 1923-

25753 *Poe Poe Poe Poe Poe Poe Poe.* Garden City, NY: Doubleday & Co., 1972, xvi+339 p., cloth, nonf.

HOFFMAN, Lee [i.e., Shirley Bell Hoffman], 1932-

25754 *In and out of Quandry.* Cambridge, MA: A Chicon IV Publication, NESFA Press, 1982, iv+63 p., cloth, coll. [Includes some nonfiction; bound with *Up to the sky in ships* / by A. Bertram Chandler].

HOFFMAN, Nina Kiriki, 1955-

25755 *Courting disasters, and other strange affinities: short stories.* Newark, NJ: Wildside Press, 1991, 220 p., cloth, coll. [Limited to 250 copies].
25756 *Legacy of fire.* Eugene, OR: Pulphouse Publishing, 1990, 116 p., cloth, coll. AUTHOR'S CHOICE MONTHLY #14.

HOFFMAN, Paul—SEE: Crypton, Dr.

HOFFMAN, Shirley B.—SEE: Hoffman, Lee

HOFFMAN, Valerie (Jane), 1953- , with Vic Bulluck

18941 *The art of The Empire Strikes Back.* New York: Ballantine Books, 1980, 176 p., cloth, nonf.

HOFFMANN, Curtis H(oward), 1958-

25757 *Project: millennium.* New York: Ace Science Fiction Books, 1987, 199 p., paper, novel.

HOFRICHTER, Paul

25758 *Blood fire.* New York: Leisure Books, 1988, 190 p., paper, novel. ROAD-BLASTER #3.
25759 *Death ride.* New York: Leisure Books, 1988, 192 p., paper, novel. ROAD-BLASTER #2.
25760 *Hell ride.* New York: Leisure Books, 1987, 223 p., paper, novel. ROAD-BLASTER #1.

HOFSTEDE, David

25761 *Hollywood and the comics: film adaptations of comic books & strips.* Las Vegas, NV: Zanne-3 Publishing, 1991, 198 p., paper, nonf. [Cover title].

HOGAN, David (J.), 1953-

25762 *Dark romance: sexuality in the horror film.* Jefferson, NC: McFarland & Co., 1986, xiii+334 p., cloth, nonf.

25763 *Who's who of the horrors and of fantasy films.* San Diego, CA: A. S. Barnes & Co., 1980, 279 p., cloth, nonf.

HOGAN, Ernest

25764 *Ben Bova's discoveries: Cortez on Jupiter.* New York: Tor SF, A Tom Doherty Associates Book, 1990, 244 p., paper, novel.

Cortez on Jupiter—SEE: *Ben Bova's discoveries: Cortez on Jupiter.*

HOGAN, James P(atrick), 1941-

25765 *Code of the lifemaker.* New York: A Del Rey Book, Ballantine Books, 1983, 295 p., cloth, novel.

25766 *Endgame enigma.* Toronto, New York: Bantam Books, 1987, 408 p., cloth, novel.

Entoverse—SEE: *James P. Hogan's Entoverse.*

25767 *The Genesis machine.* New York: A Del Rey Book, Ballantine Books, 1978, 299 p., paper, novel.

25768 *The gentle giants of Ganymede.* New York: A Del Rey Book, Ballantine Books, 1978, 246 p., paper, novel. MINERVAN EXPERIMENT #2.

The giants novels—SEE: *The Minervan experiment.*

25769 *Giants' star.* New York: A Del Rey Book, Ballantine Books, 1981, 315 p., paper, novel. MINERVAN EXPERIMENT #3.

25770 *The infinity gambit.* New York, Toronto: Bantam Books, 1991, 452 p., paper, novel.

25771 *Inherit the stars.* New York: A Del Rey Book, Ballantine Books, 1977, 216 p., paper, novel. MINERVAN EXPERIMENT #1.

25772 *James P. Hogan's Entoverse.* New York: A Del Rey Book, Ballantine Books, 1991, 418 p., cloth, novel. MINERVAN EXPERIMENT #4.

James P. Hogan's The giants novels—SEE: *The Minervan experiment.*

25773 *Minds, machines, and evolution.* Toronto, New York: Bantam Books, 1988, 324 p., paper, coll. [Includes some nonfiction].

25774 *The Minervan experiment: Inherit the stars; The gentle giants of Ganymede; Giants' star.* Garden City, NY: Nelson Doubleday, 1981, 728 p., cloth, coll. MINERVAN EXPERIMENT #1-3.

25774A retitled: *James P. Hogan's The giants novels.* New York: A Del Rey Book, Ballantine Books, 1991, 520 p., cloth, coll. MINERVAN EXPERIMENT #1-3. [Includes *Inherit the stars*; *The gentle giants of Ganymede*; *Giants' star*].

25775 *The mirror maze.* Toronto, New York: Spectra, Bantam Books, 1989, 439 p., paper, novel.

25776 *The Proteus Operation.* Toronto, New York: Bantam Books, 1985, 403 p., cloth, novel.

25777 *Thrice upon a time.* New York: A Del Rey Book, Ballantine Books, 1980, 311 p., paper, novel.

25778 *The two faces of tomorrow.* New York: A Del Rey Book, Ballantine Books, 1979, 392 p., paper, novel.

25779 *Voyage from yesteryear.* Garden City, NY: Nelson Doubleday, 1982, 345 p., cloth, novel.

HOGAN, Robert J(asper), 1897-1963

25780 *The case of the six coffins.* Oak Lawn, IL: Robert Weinberg in Association with Pulp Press, 1975, 95 p., paper, novel. PULP CLASSICS #8.

25781 *G-8 and his battle aces.* Oak Forest, IL: Dimedia Inc., 1985, 192 p., paper, novel. G-8 SERIES.

25782 *The red shadow.* Chicago: Robert Weinberg, 1977, 113 p., paper, novel. PULP CLASSICS #17.

25783 *Scourge of the steel mask: a G-8 air-war thriller.* Oak Forest, IL: Dimedia Inc., 1985, 192 p., paper, novel. G-8 SERIES.

HOGARTH, Peter (J.), 1945- , *with Val Clery*

20189 *Dragons.* New York: A Studio Book, A Jonathan-James Book, Viking Press, 1979, 208 p., cloth, novel.

HOH, Diane, 1937-

25784 *The accident.* New York, Toronto: Point Fiction, Scholastic Inc., 1991, 165 p., paper, novel.

HOHL, Joan

25785 *Window on today.* New York: Berkley Books, 1989, 178 p., paper, novel. WINDOW #2.

25786 *Window on tomorrow.* New York: Berkley Books, 1989, 180 p., paper, novel. WINDOW #3.

25787 *Window on yesterday.* New York: Berkley Books, 1988, 181 p., paper, novel. WINDOW #1.

HOKE, Franklin, *with Helen Hoke*

25788 *Horrifying and hideous hauntings: an anthology.* New York: Lodestar Books, E. P. Dutton, 1986, xi + 116 p., cloth, anth.

HOKE, Helen [i.e., Helen L. Hoke Watts], 1903-1990

25789 *A chilling collection.* New York: Elsevier/Nelson Books, 1979, 140 p., cloth, anth.

Creepies—SEE: *Creepies, creepies, creepies.*

25790 *Creepies, creepies, creepies: a covey of quiver-and-quaver tales.* New York: Franklin Watts, 1978, xii + 178 p., cloth, anth.

25790A retitled: *Creepies: a covey of quiver-and-quaver tales.* London: Franklin Watts, 1978, xiii + 178 p., cloth, anth.

25791 *Demonic, dangerous, & deadly: an anthology.* New York: Lodestar Books, E. P. Dutton, xiii + 143 p., cloth, anth.

25792 *Demons within, & other disturbing tales.* New York: Taplinger Publishing Co., 1977, 189 p., cloth, anth.

25793 *Devils, devils, devils.* New York: Franklin Watts, 1976, 216 p., cloth, anth.

25794 *Eerie, weird, and wicked: an anthology.* Nashville, TN: Thomas Nelson, 1977, 159 p., cloth, anth.

25795 *Fear! fear! fear!* New York: Franklin Watts, 1981, 144 p., cloth, anth.

25796 *Ghastly, ghoulish, gripping tales.* New York: Franklin Watts, 1983, 160 p., cloth, anth.

25797 *Ghostly, grim, and gruesome: an anthology.* Nashville, TN: Thomas Nelson, 1976, 143 p., cloth, anth.

25798 *Ghosts and ghastlies.* New York: Franklin Watts, 1976, 181 p., cloth, anth.

25799 *Giants! giants! giants! from many lands and many times.* New York: Franklin Watts, 1980, 156 p., cloth, anth.

25800 *Haunts, haunts, haunts.* New York: Franklin Watts, 1977, 191 p., cloth, anth.

25801 *Horrors, horrors, horrors.* New York, London: Franklin Watts, 1978, xiii + 177 p., cloth, anth.

25802 *Monsters, monsters, monsters.* New York: Franklin Watts, 1975, 187 p., cloth, anth.

25803 *More ghosts, ghosts, ghosts.* New York, London: Franklin Watts, 1981, x + 130 p., cloth, anth.

25804 *Mysterious, menacing, & macabre: an anthology.* New York: Elsevier/Nelson Books, 1981, 148 p., cloth, anth.

25805 *Sinister, strange, and supernatural: an anthology.* New York: Elsevier/Nelson Books, 1981, 160 p., cloth, anth.

25806 *Spectres, spooks, and shuddery shades.* London, New York: Franklin Watts, 1977, 191 p., cloth, anth.

25807 *Spirits, spooks, and sinister creatures.* New York: Franklin Watts, 1984, 136 p., cloth, anth.

25808 *Tales of fear & frightening phenomena: an anthology.* New York: Lodestar Books, E. P. Dutton, 1982, 132 p., cloth, anth.

25809 *Terrors, terrors, terrors.* New York: Franklin Watts, 1979, 191 p., cloth, anth.

25810 *Terrors, torments, and traumas: an anthology.* Nashville, TN: Thomas Nelson, 1978, 160 p., cloth, anth.

25810A retitled: *Terrors, traumas, and torments: anthology.* London: J. M. Dent & Sons, 1978, 160 p., cloth, anth.

Terrors, traumas, and torments—SEE: *Terrors, torments, and traumas.*

25811 *Thrillers, chillers & killers: an anthology.* New York: Elsevier/Nelson Books, 1979, 192 p., cloth, anth.

25812 *Uncanny tales of unearthly and unexpected horrors: an anthology.* New York: Lodestar Books, E. P. Dutton, 1983, xiii + 126 p., cloth, anth.

25813 *Venomous tales of villainy and vengeance: an anthology.* New York: Lodestar Books, Dutton, 1984, xii + 127 p., cloth, anth.

07326 *Weirdies: a horrifying concatenation of the super-sur-real or almost or not-quite real.* London: Franklin Watts, 1973, 242 p., cloth, anth.

07326A retitled: *Weirdies, weirdies, weirdies: a horrifying concatenation of the super-sur-real or almost or not-quite real.* New York: Franklin Watts, 1975, 242 p., cloth, anth.

Weirdies, weirdies, weirdies—SEE: *Weirdies.*

25815 *Witches, witches, witches, new enl. ed.* New York, London: Franklin Watts, 1977, 230 p., cloth, anth.

with Franklin Hoke

25788 *Horrifying and hideous hauntings: an anthology.* New York: Lodestar Books, E. P. Dutton, 1986, xi+116 p., cloth, anth.

HOKENSON, Jan (Walsh), 1942- , *with Howard Pearce*

25816 *Forms of the fantastic: selected essays from the Third International Conference on the Fantastic in Literature and Film.* Westport, CT & New York: Greenwood Press, 1986, xiv+262 p., cloth, nonf. anth. CONTRIBUTIONS TO THE STUDY OF SCIENCE FICTION AND FANTASY #20.

HOKLIN, Lonn

25817 *The hourglass crisis.* New York: Warner Books, 1987, 374 p., paper, novel.

as JOHN GIDEON

25818 *Greely's Cove.* New York: Jove Books, 1991, 422 p., paper, novel.

HOLDEN, Elizabeth R.—SEE: Lawrence, Louise

HOLDEN, Ursula, 1921-

25819 *Tin toys.* London: Methuen, 1986, 132 p., cloth, novel.

HOLDER, Nancy (Lindsay Jones), 1953-

25820 *Out of this world.* Toronto, New York: Bantam Books, 1985, 182 p., paper, novel.

as LAUREL CHANDLER

27693 *Shades of Moonlight.* New York: A Signet Book, New American Library, 1984, 182 p., paper, novel.

HOLDOM, Lynne

25821 *Capsule reviews.* Lake Jackson, TX: Joanne Burger, 1977, 51 p., paper, nonf.

*HOLDRIDGE, Herbert C(harles), 1892-1974

HOLDSTOCK, Robert (Paul), 1948-

25822 *The bone forest.* London: Grafton, 1991, 229 p., cloth, coll.
25823 *Earthwind.* London: Faber & Faber, 1977, 245 p., cloth, novel.

37846 *Elite: The dark wheel.* Cambridge, England: Acornsoft, 1984, 48 p., paper, story. [Distributed with the *Elite* game].
25824 *Encyclopedia of science fiction.* London: Octopus Books, 1978, 219 p., cloth, nonf.
25825 *Eye among the blind.* London: Faber & Faber, 1976, 219 p., cloth, novel.
25826 *The fetch.* London: Orbit, 1991, 352 p., cloth, novel.
25827 *In the valley of the statues: a collection of short stories.* London: Faber & Faber, 1982, 223 p., cloth, coll.
25828 *Lavondyss: journey to an unknown region.* London: Victor Gollancz, 1988, 367 p., cloth, novel. MYTHAGO #2.
25829 *Mythago Wood.* London: Victor Gollancz, 1984, 252 p., cloth, novel. MYTHAGO #1. [Winner of the World Fantasy Award for Best Fantasy Novel, 1984 (1985)].
25830 *Necromancer.* London: Futura Publications, A Futura Book, 1978, 327 p., paper, novel.
25831 *Where time winds blow.* London, Boston: Faber & Faber, 1981, 286 p., cloth, novel.

as ROBERT BLACK

25832 *Legend of the werewolf.* London: Sphere Books, 1976, 158 p., paper, movie.
25833 *The satanists.* London: Futura, 1978, 176 p., paper, movie.

as CHRIS CARLSEN

25834 *Berserker: Shadow of the wolf.* London: Sphere Books, 1977, 160 p., paper, novel. BERSERKER #1.
25835 *Berserker: The bull chief.* London: Sphere Books, 1977, 175 p., paper, novel. BERSERKER #2.
25836 *Berserker: The horned warrior.* London: Sphere Books, 1979, 172 p., paper, novel. BERSERKER #3.
The bull chief—SEE: *Berserker: The bull chief.*
The horned warrior—SEE: *Berserker: The horned warrior.*
Shadow of the wolf—SEE: *Berserker: Shadow of the wolf.*

as STEVEN EISLER

22498 *The alien world: the complete illustrated guide.* London: Octopus Books, 1980, 96 p., cloth, fiction.
22499 *Space wars: worlds and weapons.* London: Octopus Books, 1978, 96 p., cloth, nonf.

as ROBERT FAULCON

25837 *The ghost dance.* London: Arrow Books, 1983, 192 p., paper, novel. NIGHT-HUNTER #3.

25838 *The ghost dance* / by Robert Holdstock writing as Robert Faulcon. London: Arrow Books, 1987, 411 p., paper, coll. NIGHTHUNTER #3-4.

25839 *The hexing.* London: Arrow Books, 1984, 207 p., paper, novel. NIGHTHUNTER #5.

25840 *The hexing and The labyrinth: Nighthunter collection III.* London: A Legend Book, Century Publishing, 1989, 493 p., paper, coll. NIGHTHUNTER #5-6.

25841 *The labyrinth* / by Robert Holdstock writing as Robert Faulcon. London: Arrow Books, 1987, 283 p., paper, novel. NIGHTHUNTER #6.
Night hunter—SEE: *The Stalking.*

25842 *The shrine.* London: Arrow Books, 1984, 219 p., paper, novel. NIGHTHUNTER #4.

25843 *The stalking.* London: Arrow Books, 1983, 199 p., paper, novel. NIGHT-HUNTER #1.

25844 *The stalking* / by Robert Holdstock writing as Robert Faulcon. London: Arrow Books, 1987, 400 p., paper, coll. NIGHTHUNTER #1-2.

25844A retitled: *Night hunter.* New York: Charter Books, 1987, 184 p., paper, novel. NIGHTHUNTER #1.

25845 *The talisman.* London: Arrow Books, 1983, 200 p., paper, novel. NIGHT-HUNTER #2.

with Malcolm Edwards

22445 *Alien landscapes.* London: Pierrot Publishing, 1979, 116 p., paper, art.

22446 *Lost realms.* Limpsfield, Surrey, England: Paper Tiger, 1984, 114 p., cloth, art.

22447 *Magician: the lost journals of the magus, Geoffrey Carlyle.* Limpsfield, Surrey, England: Paper Tiger, 1982, 127 p., paper, art.

22448 *Realms of fantasy.* Limpsfield, Surrey, England: Paper Tiger, 1983, 120 p., cloth, nonf.

22449 *Tour of the universe: the journey of a lifetime: the recorded diaries of Leio Scott and Caroline Luranski.* London: Pierrot Publishing, 1980, 141 p., cloth, novel.

with Christopher Evans

22819 *Other Edens.* London: Unwin Paperbacks, 1987, ix+237 p., paper, anth.

22820 *Other Edens II.* London: Unwin Paperbacks, 1988, viii+266 p., paper, anth.

22821 *Other Edens III.* London, Sydney: Unwin Paperbacks, 1989, viii+237 p., paper, anth.

with Christopher Priest

25846 *Stars of Albion.* London & Sydney: Pan Books, 1979, 238 p., paper, anth.

with or without Angus Wells as RICHARD KIRK

25847 *Lords of the shadows.* London: Corgi Books, 1979, 204 p., paper, novel. RAVEN #4. [By Robert Holdstock].

25848 *Raven, swordmistress of chaos.* London: Corgi Books, 1978, 174 p., paper, novel. RAVEN #1. [By Robert Holdstock and Angus Wells].

25849 *A time of ghosts.* London: Corgi Books, 1978, 203 p., paper, novel. RAVEN #2. [By Robert Holdstock].

HOLENIA, Alexander Lernet- —SEE: **Lernet-Holenia, Alexander**

HOLKAR, Mo, 1967- , *with Neal Tringham & Ivan Towlson & others as* **M. H. ZOOL**

25850 *Bloomsbury good reading guide to science fiction and fantasy.* London: Bloomsbury, 1989, 160 p., paper, nonf. [A collective pseudonym for the Oxford SF Group].

HOLLAMAN, Keith, *with David Young*

25851 *Magical realist fiction: an anthology.* New York: Longman, 1984, vii+519 p., paper, anth.

HOLLAND, Cecelia (Anastasia), 1943-

25852 *Floating worlds.* New York: Alfred A. Knopf, 1976, 465 p., cloth, novel.

25853 *Pillar of the sky: a novel.* New York: Alfred A. Knopf, 1985, 534 p., cloth, novel.

HOLLAND, Elizabeth (Anne), 1928- , *with Robert Giddings*

23912 *J. R. R. Tolkien: the shores of Middle-Earth.* London: Junction Books, 1981, x+289 p., cloth, nonf.

HOLLAND, Sheila, 1937-

25854 *The masque.* New York: Zebra Books, Kensington Publishing Corp., 1979, 240 p., paper, novel.

HOLLAND, Thomas R(ichard)

25855 *Vonnegut's major works: notes, including life and background, introduction to the works, discussions of Player piano; The sirens of Titan; Mother night; Cat's Cradle; God bless you, Mr. Rosewater; Slaughterhouse-Five; Happy birthday, Wanda June; and Breakfast of champions, special topics, review questions, selected bibliography.* Lincoln, NE: Cliffs Notes, 1973, 58 p., paper, nonf.

HOLLIDAY, Don, pseud.

15817 *Beast of shame.* San Diego, CA: Pillar Books, 1964, 189 p., paper, novel.

HOLLIS, (Maurice) Christopher, 1902-1977

25856 *A study of George Orwell: the man and his works.* London: Hollis & Carter, 1956, viii+212 p., cloth, nonf.

HOLLISTER, Bernard C(lairborne), 1938-

25857 *You and science fiction: a humanistic approach to tomorrow.* Skokie, IL: National Textbook Co., 1976, 349 p., paper, nonf.

HOLLOW, John (Walter), 1939-

25858 *Against the night, the stars: the science fiction of Arthur C. Clarke.* San Diego, CA, New York: Harcourt Brace Jovanovich, 1983, 197 p., cloth, nonf.

25859 *Against the night, the stars: the science fiction of Arthur C. Clarke.* Athens, OH: Ohio University Press, 1987, 217 p., paper, nonf. [Revised and expanded edition].

HOLLOWAY, Brian

as NEIL CHARLES

02888 *Planet Tha.* London: Curtis Warren, 1953, 159 p., cloth, novel.

as VON GRUEN

06436 *The mortals of Reni.* London: Curtis Warren, 1953, 159 p., cloth, novel.

as ARN ROMILUS

12415 *Beyond geo.* London: Curtis Warren, 1953, 159 p., cloth, novel.

as BRIAN SHAW

12962 *Lost world.* London: Curtis Warren, 1953, 159 p., cloth, novel.

HOLLY, Joan (Carol) Hunter, 1932-1982

25860 *Death dolls of Lyra.* New York: Manor Books, 1977, 223 p., paper, novel.

25861 *Keeper.* Toronto, New York: Laser Books, 1976, 191 p., paper, novel.

25862 *Shepherd.* Toronto, New York: Laser Books, 1977, 190 p., paper, novel.

25863 *The wolves and the lambs affair.* Lansing, MI?: Boogums Press, 1977, p., paper, novel. MAN FROM U.N.C.L.E. SERIES.

HOLM, (Else) Anne (Lise), 1922-

15818 *Peter.* New York: Harcourt, Brace & World, 1968, 224 p., cloth, novel.

*HOLM, John Cecil, 1904-1981

HOLMAN, David, *with Larry Pryce*

25864 *Fleshbait.* London: New English Library, 1979, 160 p., paper, novel.

HOLMAN, Russell, *with Arthur Stringer*

37847 *The story without a name.* New York: Grosset & Dunlap, 1924, 316 p., cloth, movie.

HOLME, Constance [i.e., Constance Holme Punchard]

37848 *He-who-came?* London: Chapman & Hall, 1930, 160 p., cloth, novel.

HOLMES, Bruce T(odd), 1946-

25865 *Anvil of the heart.* Evanston, IL: The Haven Corp., 1983, 312 p., cloth, novel.

HOLMES, Charles M(ason), 1923-

25866 *Aldous Huxley and the way to reality.* Bloomington, IN: Indiana University Press, 1970, xiv+238 p., cloth, nonf.

HOLMES, Jeffrey, 1934-

25867 *Farewell to Nova Scotia.* Windsor, Nova Scotia, Canada: Lancelot Press, 1974, 262 p., cloth?, novel.

HOLMES, John Eric, 1930-

25868 *Fantasy role playing games.* New York: Hippocrene Books, 1981, 224 p., cloth, nonf.

25869 *Mahars of Pellucidar.* New York: Ace Books, 1976, 218 p., paper, novel. PELLUCIDAR SERIES.

25870 *The maze of peril.* New York: Space & Time, 1986, 147 p., paper, novel. DUNGEONS & DRAGONS.

with Larry Niven & Jerry Pournelle

25871 *Mordred.* New York: Ace Books, 1980, 216 p., paper, novel. BUCK ROGERS #2. [Sequel to *Armageddon: 2419 AD*].

HOLMES, Robert, 1926-

25872 *Doctor Who: The two doctors.* London: W. H. Allen & Co., 1985, 159 p., cloth, tele. DOCTOR WHO #100.
The two doctors—SEE: Doctor Who: The two doctors.

HOLMES, Ronald

25873 *Macabre military stories.* London: L. Cooper, 1979, viii+175 p., cloth, anth.

25874 *Macabre railway stories.* London: A Star Book, W. H. Allen, 1982, 231 p., paper, anth.

HOLROYD, Sam, pseud.—SEE: Burton, S. H.

HOLSTEAD, Marjorie

25875 *High jinks in the universe.* New York, Washington: Vantage Press, 1990, 69 p., cloth, story.

HOLT, Guy, 1892-1934

25876 *A bibliography of the writings of James Branch Cabell.* Philadelphia: The Centaur Book Shop, 1924, 73 p., cloth, nonf. CENTAUR BIBLIOGRAPHIES #3.

HOLT, John R.

25877 *When we dead awaken.* New York, Toronto: Bantam Books, 1990, 276 p., paper, novel.

HOLT, Michael—SEE: Martin, David

HOLT, Robert Lawrence, 1939-

25878 *Good Friday: a novel.* Blue Ridge Summit, PA: AERO, 1987, 212 p., cloth, novel.

HOLT, Terry, with Sarah Scherling

25879 *The hero and the crown.* Des Moines, IA: Waterwheel Press, 1990, 16 p., paper, nonf.

HOLT, Thomas C. L.—SEE: Holt, Tom

HOLT, Tom [i.e., Thomas Charles Louis Holt], 1961-

25880 *Expecting someone taller.* London: Macmillan, 1987, 218 p., cloth, novel.

25881 *Flying Dutch.* London: Orbit, 1991, 252 p., cloth, novel.

25882 *Who's afraid of Beowulf?* London: Macmillan, 1988, 206 p., cloth, novel.

HOLTON, Scot, 1939?-1991, with Robert Skotak

Fantastic worlds—SEE: Norman Jacobs & Kerry O'Quinn present Fantastic worlds.
25883 *Norman Jacobs & Kerry O'Quinn present Fantastic worlds.* New York: Starlog Press, 1978, 97 p., paper, nonf. anth.

HOLTSMARK, Erling B(ent), 1936-

25884 *Edgar Rice Burroughs.* Boston: Twayne Publishers, 1986, 133 p., cloth, nonf.

25885 *Tarzan and the classics.* Iowa City, IA: University of Iowa, 1979, 13 leaves, paper, nonf.

25886 *Tarzan and tradition: classic myth in popular literature.* Westport, CT & London: Greenwood Press, 1981, xv+196 p., cloth, nonf.

HOLTZMAN, Marcia

25887 *Science fiction: a study guide.* New York: New American Library, 1975, 61 p., paper, nonf.

HOLZER, Hans (W.), 1920-

25888 *The Amityville curse.* New York: Tower Books, 1981, 208 p., paper, novel. AMITYVILLE HORROR SERIES.

25889 *The entry.* New York: Tower Books, 1981, 238 p., paper, novel.

25890 *Psychic detective: The unicorn.* New York: Manor Books, 1976, 192 p., paper, novel. RANDY KNOWLES #3.

25891 *The secret of Amityville.* New York: Leisure Books, 1985, 336 p., paper, novel. AMITYVILLE HORROR SERIES.

The unicorn—SEE: *Psychic detective.*

HOME, William Scott, 1940-

25892 *Hollow faces, merciless moons.* Buffalo, NY: Weirdbook Press, 1977, 95 p., cloth, coll. [Limited to 1250 copies].

*HOME-GALL, Edward R(eginald), <u>1899-</u>

HONAN, William H(olmes), 1930-

37849 *Bywater: the man who invented the Pacific War.* London: Macdonald & Co., 1990, xiv+337 p., cloth, nonf.

HONE, Joseph, 1937-

25893 *Irish ghost stories.* London: Hamilton, 1977, 169 p., cloth, anth.

HONG, Jane (Fay) Cooper, 1954- , *with James M. Ward*

25894 *Forgotten realms fantasy adventure: Pool of radiance.* Lake Geneva, WI: TSR Inc., 1989, 316 p., paper, novel. FORGOTTEN REALMS FANTASY ADVENTURE.
Pool of radiance—SEE: *Forgotten realms fantasy adventure: Pool of radiance.*

HOOBLER, Thomas, 1942/44-

Dr. Chill—SEE: *Dr. Chill's project.*
25895 *Dr. Chill's project.* New York: G. P. Putnam's Sons, 1987, 188 p., cloth, novel.
25895A retitled: *Dr. Chill.* London: Piper, 1989, 188 p., paper, novel.

with Burt Wetanson

25896 *The hunters.* Garden City, NY: Doubleday & Co., 1978, vii+180 p., cloth, novel. HUNTERS #1.
25897 *The treasure hunters.* New York: Playboy Paperbacks, 1983, 248 p., paper, novel. HUNTERS #2.

HOOD, Gwenyth (Elise), 1955-

25898 *The coming of the demons.* New York: William Morrow & Co., 1982, 288 p., cloth, novel.

HOOD, Robert (Maxwell), 1951-

25899 *Day-dreaming on company time: short stories.* Wollongong, New South Wales,

Australia: Five Islands Press, 1988, 96 p., paper, coll.

HOOF, David—SEE: Lorne, David

HOOKER, Ruth, 1920-

25900 *Kennaquhair.* Nashville, TN: Abingdon, 1976, 159 p., cloth, novel.

HOOKS, David

25901 *The spoilers: a novel.* New York: Arbor House, 1985, 396 p., cloth, novel.

HOOPER, Kay, 1957-

25902 *Summer of the unicorn.* Toronto, New York: Bantam Books, 1988, 310 p., paper, novel.

HOOPER, Walter (McGehee), 1931-

25903 *Past watchful dragons: the Narnian Chronicles of C. S. Lewis.* New York: Collier Books, 1979, xi+140 p., paper, nonf.
25904 *Through joy and beyond: a pictorial biography of C. S. Lewis.* New York: Macmillan; London: Collier Macmillan, 1982, xvi+176 p., cloth, nonf.

with Roger Lancelyn Green

24429 *C. S. Lewis: a biography.* London: Collins, 1974, 320 p., cloth, nonf.

HOOVER, Dale

25905 *Shadow twin.* New York: A Dell Book, 1991, 389 p., paper, novel.

HOOVER, H(elen) M(ary), 1935-

25906 *Another Heaven, another Earth.* New York: Viking Press, 1981, 173 p., cloth, novel.
25907 *Away is a strange place to be.* New York: E. P. Dutton, 1990, 167 p., cloth, novel.
25908 *The bell tree.* New York: Viking Press, 1982, 169 p., cloth, novel.
25909 *The dawn palace: the story of Medea.* New York: E. P. Dutton, 1988, 244 p., cloth, novel.
25910 *The Delikon.* New York: Viking Press, 1977, 148 p., cloth, novel.
Journey through the empty—SEE: *Orvis.*
25911 *The lost star.* New York: Viking Press, 1979, 150 p., cloth, novel.

25912 *Orvis*. New York: Viking Kestrel, 1987, 186 p., cloth, novel.

25912A retitled: *Journey through the empty*. London: Lightning, 1990, 185 p., paper, novel.

25913 *The rains of Eridan*. New York: Viking Press, 1977, 183 p., cloth, novel.

25914 *Return to Earth: a novel of the future*. New York: Viking Press, 1980, 172 p., cloth, novel.

25915 *The Shepherd Moon: a novel of the future*. New York: Viking Press, 1984, 149 p., cloth, novel.

25916 *This time of darkness*. New York: Viking Press, 1980, 161 p., cloth, novel.

25917 *Treasures of Morrow*. New York: Four Winds Press, 1976, 171 p., cloth, novel. MORROW #2.

HOOVER, Ralph

25918 *Jabberwocky*. London & Sydney: Pan Books, 1977, 158 p., paper, movie.

HOOVER, Saranne—SEE: Dawson, Saranne

HOOVER, Thomas (Earl), 1941-

25919 *Project Daedalus*. New York, Toronto: Falcon, Bantam Books, 1991, 366 p., paper, novel.

HOPE, Laura Lee, house pseud.—SEE: McQuay, Mike

HOPF, Alice—SEE: Lightner, A. M.

HOPKINS, Harry A(rthur), 1951-

25920 *Fandom directory* [1980]. Langley AFB, VA: Fandom Computer Services, 1980, 304 p., paper, nonf.

25921 *Fandom directory 1981*. Langley Air Force Base, VA: Fandom Computer Services, 1981, 380 p., paper, nonf.

25922 *Fandom directory, number 11, 1989-1990 edition*. Springfield, VA: Fandata, 1989, 495 p., paper, nonf.

25923 *Fandom directory, number 12, 1990-1991 edition*. Springfield, VA: Fandata, 1990, 528 p., paper, nonf.

25924 *Fandom directory, number 13, 1991-1992 edition*. Springfield, VA: Fandata, 1991, 560 p., paper, nonf.

with Mariane S. Hopkins

25925 *Fandom directory, number 5, 1983-1984 edition*. San Bernardino, CA: Fandom Computer Services, 1983, 448 p., paper, nonf.

HOPKINS, Hector K.—SEE: Mannon, Warwick

HOPKINS, James, pseud.—SEE: Nolan, William F.

HOPKINS, Kenneth—SEE: Mannon, Warwick

HOPKINS, Lee Bennett, 1938-

25926 *A-haunting we will go: ghostly stories and poems*. Chicago: A. Whitman, 1977, 128 p., cloth, anth.

25927 *Monsters, ghoulies, and creepy creatures: fantastic stories and poems*. Chicago: A. Whitman, 1977, 128 p., cloth, anth.

25928 *Witching time: mischievous stories and poems*. Chicago: A. Whitman, 1977, 127 p., cloth, anth.

HOPKINS, Mariane (June) S(oroka), 1951-

25929 *Fandom directory 1982*. Newport News, VA: Fandom Computer Services, 1982, 408 p., paper, nonf.

25930 *Fandom directory, number 6: 1984-1985 edition*. San Bernardino, CA: Fandom Computer Services, 1984, 384 p., paper, nonf.

25931 *Fandom directory, number 7, 1985-1986 edition*. San Bernardino, CA: Fandom Computer Services, 1985, 416 p., paper, nonf.

25932 *Fandom directory, number 8, 1986-1987 edition*. San Bernardino, CA: Fandom Computer Services, 1986, 448 p., paper, nonf.

25933 *Fandom directory, number 9, 1987-1988 edition*. Springfield, VA: Fandom Computer Services, 1987, 480 p., paper, nonf.

25934 *Fandom directory, number 10, 1988-1989 edition*. Springfield, VA: Fandata, 1988, 528 p., paper, nonf.

with Harry A. Hopkins

25925 *Fandom directory, number 5, 1983-1984 edition*. San Bernardino, CA: Fandom Computer Services, 1983, 448 p., paper, nonf.

HOPKINSON, Henry Thomas—SEE: Hopkinson, Tom

HOPKINSON, Tom [i.e., Henry Thomas Hopkinson, Sir], 1905-1990

25935 *George Orwell.* London: Published for The British Council and the National Book League by Longmans, Green & Co., 1953, 40 p., paper, nonf.

HOPPE, Stephanie T., 1947-

25936 *The windrider.* New York: DAW Books, 1985, 253 p., paper, novel.

with Theresa Corrigan

20615 *And a deer's ear, eagle's song, & bear's game: animals and women.* Pittsburgh, PA: Cleis Press, 1990, 228 p., cloth, anth.

20616 *With a fly's eye, whale's wit, and woman's heart: animals and women.* San Francisco: Cleis Press, 1989, 234 p., cloth, anth.

HOPPENSTAND, Gary (C.), *with Ray B. Browne*

25937 *The gothic world of Stephen King: landscape of nightmares.* Bowling Green, OH: Bowling Green State University Popular Press, 1988, 143 p., cloth, nonf. anth.

HORAN, Don, *with Norman Stahl as* DONALD N. NORMAN

25938 *Thunder Station: a novel.* New York: Warner Books, 1990, 345 p., paper, novel.

HORBACH, Michael, 1924-1986

25939 *The lioness.* Philadelphia: J. B. Lippincott Co., 1978, 190 p., cloth, novel. [Translation by Ursule Molinaro and Hedwig Rappolt of *Die löwin*].

HORLAK, E. E., pseud.—SEE: Tepper, Sheri S.

HORLER, Sydney, 1888-1954

The charlatan—SEE: *The formula.*
37850 *The evil messenger.* London: Hodder & Stoughton, 1938, 314 p., cloth, novel.
07399 *The formula: a novel of Harley Street.* London: John Long, 1933, 286 p., cloth, novel.
07399A retitled: *The charlatan.* Boston: Little, Brown & Co., 1934, viii+311 p., cloth, novel.

07403 *The mystery of No. 1.* London: Hodder & Stoughton, 1925, 320 p., cloth, novel. PAUL VIVANTI SERIES.
07403A retitled: *The Order of the Octopus.* New York: George H. Doran Co., 1926, 310 p., cloth, novel. PAUL VIVANTI SERIES.
The Order of the Octopus—SEE: *The mystery of No. 1.*
37851 *The worst man in the world: Paul Vivanti again.* London: Hodder & Stoughton, 1929, 314 p., cloth, novel. PAUL VIVANTI SERIES.

*HORN, Edward Newman, 1903-1976

HORN, Phyllis, 1938-

25940 *Lodestar.* Tallahassee, FL: Naiad Press, 1991, 217 p., paper, novel.

*HORNER, Donald William, 1874-

HORNSEY, Pat(ricia E.), *with Penelope Grant*

24358 *Edgar Rice Burroughs.* London: New English Library, 1975, 30 p., paper, nonf. anth.

HOROWITZ, Anthony, 1955-

25941 *The Devil's Door-Bell.* London: Patrick Hardy, 1983, 159 p., cloth, novel. OLD ONES #1.
25942 *Groosham Grange.* London: Methuen, 1988, 110 p., cloth, novel. GROOSHAM GRANGE #1.
25943 *Groosham Grange II: The unholy grail.* London: Methuen's Children's Books, 1991, 128 p., cloth, novel. GROOSHAM GRANGE #2.
The hooded man—SEE: *Robin of Sherwood: The hooded man.*
25944 *The night of the scorpion.* New York: Pacer Books, 1984, 159 p., cloth, novel. OLD ONES #2.
37852 *Robin of Sherwood: The hooded man.* Harmondsworth, Middlesex, England: Puffin Books, 1986, 152 p., paper, tele. ROBIN OF SHERWOOD SERIES.
25945 *The Silver Citadel.* New York: Pacer Books for Young Adults, Berkley Books, 1986, 150 p., paper, novel. OLD ONES #3.
The unholy grail—SEE: *Groosham Grange II.*

HOROWITZ, Lois, 1940-

25946 *She-devil.* New York: Pageant Books, 1989, 334 p., paper, novel.

HORRIGAN, Brian, *with Joseph J. Corn*

20602 *Yesterday's tomorrows: past vision of the American future.* New York: Summit Books; Washington: Smithsonian Institution Traveling Exhibition Service, 1984, xvii+158 p., paper, nonf.

HORSTING, Jessie [i.e., Jessica Horsting Buchanan], 1950-

25947 *Stephen King at the movies.* New York: Starlog Press, 1986, 112 p., paper, nonf.

HORSTMAN, Thomas

25948 *The Kessler alliance.* New York: Belmont Tower Books, 1980, 281 p., paper, novel.

HORTON, Forest W(oody) Jr., 1930-

25949 *The technocrats.* New York: Leisure Books, 1980, 312 p., paper, novel.

HORTON, Gordon T(homas), 1924-

25950 *X-Isle.* London: Robert Hale, 1980, 207 p., cloth, novel.

HORTON, Honey, pseud.

25951 *The sexorcist.* New York: Pleasure Books, 1976, 188 p., paper, novel.

HORVAT, Dilwyn

25952 *Assault on Omega 4.* Oxford, England, Batavia, IL: A Lion Paperback, 1986, 128 p., paper, novel. OPERATION TITAN #2.
25953 *Operation Titan.* Oxford, England, Batavia, IL: A Lion Paperback, 198?, 128 p., paper, novel. OPERATION TITAN #1.

HORVITZ, Leslie (Alan)

25954 *Blood moon.* New York: Pocket Books, 1987, 309 p., paper, novel.
25955 *The dying.* New York: Popular Library, 1987, 440 p., paper, novel.

HORWOOD, William, 1944-

25956 *Callanish.* London: Allen Lane, 1984, 192 p., cloth, novel.
25957 *Duncton found.* London: Century Publishing, 1989, 779 p., cloth, novel. DUNCTON CHRONICLES #3.

25958 *Duncton quest.* London: Century Publishing, 1988, 717 p., cloth, novel. DUNCTON CHRONICLES #2.
25959 *Duncton tales.* London: HarperCollins, 1991, 454 p., cloth, novel. DUNCTON CHRONICLES #4.
25960 *Duncton Wood: a novel.* Richmond upon Thames, England: Country Life, 1980, 543 p., cloth, novel. DUNCTION CHRONICLES #1.
25961 *Skallagrigg.* London: Viking, 1987, 572 p., cloth, novel.
25962 *The stonor eagles.* Richmond upon Thames, England: Country Life, 1982, 555 p., cloth, novel.

HOSHI, Shin'ichi, 1926-

25963 *A bag of surprises.* Tokyo: Kodansha, 1989, 141 p., paper, novel. [Translation by Stanleigh H. Jones of *Enu shi no yuenchi*].
25964 *The capricious robot.* Tokyo: Kodansha, 1986, 155 p., paper, novel. [Translation by Robert Matthew of *Kimagure robotto*].
25965 *The spiteful planet, and other stories.* Tokyo: Tokyo Times, 1978, 207 p., cloth, coll. [Partial translation by Bernard Susser and Tomoyoshi Genkawa of *Hoshi Shin'ichi No sakuhinshu*].
25966 *Tales of Japanese science fiction and fantasy.* Brisbane, Australia: Dept. of Japanese, University of Queensland, 1981?, ii+196 p., paper, coll. [Edited and translated by Robert Matthew].
37853 *There was a knock.* Tokyo: Kodansha International, 1984, 183 p., paper, coll. [Translation by Stanleigh H. Jones of *Nokku no oto ga*].

HOSKEN, John

25967 *Meet Mr Majimpsey.* London: Pavilion, 1987, 176 p., cloth, novel.

HOSKIN, C. H.—SEE: Lobsang Rampa, T.

HOSKINS, Robert (P.), 1933-

25968 *Against tomorrow.* New York: Fawcett Crest, 1979, 287 p., paper, anth.
25969 *The future now: saving tomorrow.* Greenwich, CT: A Fawcett Crest Book, Fawcett Publications, 1977, 286 p., paper, anth.
25970 *Jack-in-the-Box Planet.* Philadelphia, PA: Westminster Press, 1978, 155 p., cloth, novel.

25977A *Legacy of the stars.* London: Robert Hale, 1981, 169 p., cloth, novel. [Originally published under the name John Gregory].

25971 *Master of the stars.* Toronto, New York: Laser Books, 1976, 190 p., paper, novel. MASTER OF THE STARS #1.

25972 *The shattered people.* Garden City, NY: Doubleday & Co., 1975, 182 p, cloth, novel.

25973 *To control the stars.* New York: A Del Rey Book, Ballantine Books, 1977, 188 p., paper, novel. MASTER OF THE STARS #2.

25974 *To escape the stars.* New York: A Del Rey Book, Ballantine Books, 1978, 186 p., paper, novel. MASTER OF THE STARS #3.

25975 *Tomorrow's son.* Garden City, NY: Doubleday & Co., 1977, 183 p., cloth, novel.

as GRACE CORREN

25976 *The attic child.* Los Angeles: Pinnacle Books, 1979, 249 p., paper, novel.

37854 *Evil in the family.* New York: Lancer Books, 1972, 222 p., paper, novel.

as JOHN GREGORY

25977 *Legacy of the stars.* New York: Leisure Books, 1979, 169 p., paper, novel.

as MICHAEL KERR

The gemini run—SEE: *The night runner.*

25978 *The night runner: The gemini run.* New York: Charter, 1979, 214 p., paper, novel.

as MICHAEL KERR, with H. G. Wells

25979 *The island of Dr. Moreau.* New York, Toronto: Scholastic Book Services, 1978, 148 p., paper, novel. [Adapted from Wells's original novel].

HOSSAIN, Rokeya—SEE: Rokeya Begum

*HOTSON, Cornelia Hinkley, 1890-1977

HOUARNER, Gerard Daniel, 1955-

25980 *The bard of sorcery.* New York: A Del Rey Book, Ballantine Books, 1986, 279 p., paper, novel.

HOUGH, Richard—SEE: Carter, Bruce

HOUGHTON, Eric, 1930-

25981 *Gates of glass.* Oxford, England, New York: Oxford University Press, 1987, 136 p., cloth, novel.

25982 *Steps out of time.* London: Methuen Children's Books, 1979, 160 p., cloth, novel.

HOUSE, Brant [pseud. of Paul Chadwick]

25983 *Brand of the metal maiden.* Oak Lawn, IL: Robert Weinberg, 1974, 64 p., paper, novel. PULP CLASSICS #4.

HOUSEHOLD, Geoffrey (Edward West), 1900-1988

25984 *Arrows of desire.* London: Michael Joseph, 1985, 135 p., cloth, novel.

37855 *The cats to come.* London: Michael Joseph, 1975, 62 p., cloth, story.

37856 *Hostage: London: the diary of Julian Despard.* London: Michael Joseph, 1977, 190 p., cloth, novel.

25985 *The sending.* London: Michael Joseph, 1980, 166 p., cloth, novel.

37857 *Summon the bright water.* London: Michael Joseph, 1981, 190 p., cloth, novel.

HOUSH, Barbara, 1937-

25986 *Brakshi: a gypsy fantasy.* Kansas City, MO: Andrews & McMeel, 1980, 151 p., paper, novel.

HOUSTON, David [pseud. of Houston Force Lumpkin III], 1938-

25987 *Alien perspective.* New York: Leisure Books, 1978, 231 p., paper, novel.

25988 *Gods in a vortex.* New York: Leisure Books, 1979, 219 p., paper, novel.

Ice from space—SEE: *Tales of tomorrow: Ice from space.*

25989 *Invaders at ground zero.* New York: Leisure Books, 1981, 208 p., paper, tele. TALES OF TOMORROW #1.

25990 *Norman Jacobs & Kerry O'Quinn present Science fiction heroes.* New York: A Starlog Press Publication, 1980, 34 p., paper, nonf. anth.

25991 *Norman Jacobs & Kerry O'Quinn present Science fiction villains.* New York: A Starlog Press Publication, 1980, 34 p., paper, nonf. anth.

25992 *Red dust.* New York: Leisure Books, 1981, 202 p., paper, tele. TALES OF TOMORROW #2.

Science fiction heroes—SEE: *Norman Jacobs & Kerry O'Quinn present Science fiction heroes.*

Science fiction villains—SEE: *Norman Jacobs & Kerry O'Quinn present Science fiction villains.*

25993 *Substance X.* New York: Leisure Books, 1981, 204 p., paper, tele. TALES OF TOMORROW #3.

25994 *Tales of tomorrow: Ice from space.* New York: Leisure Books, 1982, 201 p., paper, tele. TALES OF TOMORROW #4.

25995 *Wingmaster.* New York: Leisure Books, 1981, 224 p., paper, novel. GODS IN A VORTEX #2.

with Len Wein

25996 *Swamp Thing: a novel.* New York: Tor, A Tom Doherty Associates Book, 1982, 223 p., paper, movie. SWAMP THING #1.

HOUSTON, James (Archibald), 1921-

25997 *Spirit wrestler.* New York: Harcourt Brace Jovanovich, 1980, 306 p., cloth, novel.

HOUTON, Kathleen—SEE: **Kilgore, Kathleen**

HOVORKA, Robert L(eo) Jr., 1955-

25998 *Derelict.* New York: Ace Books, 1988, 199 p., paper, novel.

HOWARD, Allan, with John Harwood

25332 *Tarzan encyclopedia.* ?: Burroughs Bulletin, 1975, 41 p., paper, nonf.

HOWARD, Cary

25999 *Dracula official movie magazine.* Miami, FL: Merit Publications, 1979, [48] p., paper, nonf.

HOWARD, Clark, 1934-

26000 *The last great death stunt.* New York: A Berkley Medallion Book, Berkley Publishing Corp., 1977, 216 p., paper, novel.

HOWARD, Elizabeth [i.e., Elizabeth Howard Mizner], 1907-

26001 *Mystery of the magician.* New York: A Byron Preiss Book, Random House, 1987, 138 p., cloth, novel. MY NAME IS PARIS #2.

26002 *Mystery of the Metro.* New York: A Byron Preiss Book, Random House, 1987, 171 p., cloth, novel. MY NAME IS PARIS #1.

26003 *The scent of mystery.* New York: A Byron Preiss Book, Random House, 1987, 154 p., cloth, novel. MY NAME IS PARIS #3.

HOWARD, Elizabeth Jane, 1923-

37858 *Mr. Wrong.* London: Jonathan Cape, 1975, 223 p., cloth, coll.

HOWARD, Joseph

26004 *Damien: Omen II: a novel.* New York: A Signet Book, New American Library, 1978, 199 p., paper, movie. OMEN #2.

HOWARD, Milford W(riarson), 1862-

15819 *The bishop of the Ozarks.* Los Angeles: Times-Mirror Press, 1923, 232 p., cloth, movie.

HOWARD, Nic

26005 *August Derleth.* Birmingham, England: British Fantasy Society, 1984, 24 p., paper, nonf. MASTERS OF FANTASY #2.

HOWARD, Robert E(rvin), 1906-1936

26006 *The adventures of Lal Singh.* Mount Olive, NC: Cryptic Publications, 1985, 20 p., paper?, coll.

26007 *Black Canaan.* New York: A Berkley Book, Berkley Publishing Corp., 1978, 181 p., paper, coll.

26008 *Black colossus.* West Kingston, RI: Donald M. Grant, Publisher, 1979, 184 p., cloth, coll.

26009 *The book of Robert E. Howard.* New York: Zebra Books, Kensington Publishing Corp., 1976, 345 p., paper, coll. [Edited by Glenn Lord].

07482 *Conan the conqueror; the Hyborean Age.* New York: Gnome Press, 1950, 255 p., cloth, novel. CONAN #9.

07482A retitled: *Conan: The hour of the dragon.* New York: G. P. Putnam's Sons, 1977, viii+296 p., cloth, novel. CONAN SERIES.

Conan: The hour of the dragon—SEE: *Conan the conqueror.*

26010 *Conan: The people of the black circle.* New York: Berkley Publishing Corp., 1977, 293 p, cloth, coll. CONAN SERIES.

26011 *Cthulhu: the mythos and kindred horrors.* New York: Baen Books, 1987, 245 p., paper, coll. [Includes some verse; Edited by David Drake].

07484 *The Dark Man, and others.* Sauk City, WI: Arkham House, 1963, 284 p., cloth, coll.

07484A retitled: *The dead remember: the dark man omnibus, volume 2.* London, Toronto: Panther, Granada Publishing, 1979, 128 p., paper, coll. [The original book split into two volumes].

The dead remember—SEE: The dark man, and others.

26012 *The devil in iron.* West Kingston, RI: Donald M. Grant, Publisher, 1976, 153 p., cloth, coll. CONAN SERIES.

26013 *The gods of Bel-Sagoth.* New York: Ace Books, 1979, 235 p., paper, coll.

26014 *The grey god passes.* Columbia, PA: Charles Miller, 1975, 36 p., paper, story.

26015 *The grim land and others.* Lamoni, IA: Stygian Isle Press, 1976, [32] p., paper, coll. [Includes some verse].

26016 *Hawks of Outremer.* West Kingston, RI: Donald M. Grant, Publisher, 1979, 153 p., cloth, coll. CORMAC MAC ART.

26017 *The hills of the dead.* Toronto, New York: Bantam Books, 1979, xii+141 p., paper, coll. SOLOMON KANE #2.

The hour of the dragon—SEE: Conan the conqueror.

26018 *The illustrated gods of the North.* West Warwick, RI: Necronomicon Press, 1977, [15] p., paper, story.

26019 *The iron man, & other tales of the ring.* West Kingston, RI: Donald M. Grant, Publisher, 1979, 186 p., cloth, coll.

26020 *Jewels of Gwahlur.* West Kingston, RI: Donald M. Grant, Publisher, 1979, 122 p., cloth, coll.

Kull—SEE: Robert E. Howard's Kull.

26021 *The last cat book.* New York: Dodd, Mead & Co., 1984, [61] p., paper, nonf.

26022 *Lord of the dead.* West Kingston, RI: Donald M. Grant, Publisher, 1981, 186 p., cloth, coll.

26023 *The lost valley of Iskander.* West Linn, OR: FAX Collector's Editions, 1974, 194 p, cloth, collection. FRANCIS X. GORDON SERIES.

26024 *Marchers of Valhalla.* West Kingston, RI: Donald M. Grant, Publisher, 1977, 191 p., cloth, coll. [Expanded edition of #07487].

The people of the black circle—SEE: Conan: The people of the black circle.

26025 *Pigeons from Hell.* New York: Zebra Books, Kensington Publishing Corp., 1976, 315 p., paper, coll.

26026 *The pool of the black one.* West Kingston, RI: Donald M. Grant, Publisher, 1986, 134 p., cloth, coll. CONAN SERIES.

26027 *Queen of the black coast.* West Kingston, RI: Donald M. Grant, Publisher, 1978, 118 p., cloth, coll. CONAN SERIES.

26028 *Red nails.* West Kingston, RI: Donald M. Grant, Publisher, 1975, 142 p., cloth, novel. CONAN SERIES.

37859 *Red nails.* New York: Berkley Publishing Corp., 1979, 295 p., cloth, coll. CONAN SERIES. [Includes the short novel, *Red nails*].

26029 *The road of Azrael.* West Kingston, RI: Donald M. Grant, Publisher, 1979, 229 p., cloth, coll.

26030 *The Robert E. Howard omnibus.* London: Futura Publications, An Orbit Book, 1977, 336 p., paper, coll [Different from any other editions].

26031 *Robert E. Howard: selected letters, 1923-1930.* West Warwick, RI: Necronomicon Press, 1990, vi+84 p., paper, nonf. coll. [Edited by Glenn Lord, Rusty Burke, and S. T. Joshi].

26032 *Robert E. Howard: selected letters, 1931-1936.* West Warwick, RI: Necronomicon Press, 1991, 80 p., paper, nonf. coll. [Edited by Glenn Lord].

26033 *Robert E. Howard's Kull.* West Kingston, RI: Donald M. Grant, Publisher, 1985, 247 p., cloth, coll. KULL SERIES.

26034 *Robert E. Howard's World of heroes.* London: Robinson Publishing, 1989, 424 p., paper, coll. [Edited by Mike Ashley].

26035 *Rogues in the house.* West Kingston, RI: Donald M. Grant, Publisher, 1976, 91 p., cloth, coll. CONAN SERIES.

26036 *The second book of Robert Howard.* New York: Zebra Books, Kensington Publishing Corp., 1976, 368 p., paper, coll. [Edited by Glenn Lord].

07490 *Skull-face, and others.* Sauk City, WI: Arkham House, 1946, 475 p., cloth, coll.

07490A *Skull-face, and others.* St Albans, Hertfordshire, England: Panther, 1976, 250 p., paper, coll. [The original book split into two volumes].

07490B retitled: *The valley of the worms, and others.* St Albans, Hertfordshire, England: Panther, 1976, 236 p., paper, coll. [The original book split into two volumes].

26039 *Skulls in the stars.* Toronto, New York: Bantam Books, 1978, xii+173 p., paper, coll. SOLOMON KANE #1.

26040 *The sowers of the thunder.* West Kingston, RI: Donald M. Grant, Publisher, 1979, 285 p., cloth, coll.

26041 *Three-bladed doom.* New York: Zebra Books, Kensington Publishing Corp., 1977, 171 p., paper, novel.

26042 *The tower of the elephant.* West Kingston, RI: Donald M. Grant, Publisher, 1975, 94 p., cloth, coll. CONAN SERIES.

26043 *Valley of the lost.* Columbia, PA: Charles Miller, 1975, [21] p., paper, story.

The valley of the worms, and others—SEE: *Skull-face omnibus.*

26044 *A witch shall be born.* West Kingston, RI: Donald M. Grant, Publisher, 1975, 106 p., cloth, novel. CONAN SERIES.

World of heroes—SEE: *Robert E. Howard's World of heroes.*

with L. Sprague de Camp

Conan: the flame knife—SEE: *Tales of Conan.*

The flame knife—SEE: *Tales of Conan.*

03989 *Tales of Conan.* New York: Gnome Press, 1955, 219 p., cloth, coll. CONAN SERIES.

03989A retitled: *Conan: The flame knife.* New York: Ace Books, 1981, 158 p., paper, coll. CONAN SERIES.

21351 *The treasure of Tranicos.* New York: Ace Books, 1980, 191 p., paper, novel. CONAN SERIES.

with L. Sprague de Camp & Lin Carter

19592 *The Conan chronicles.* London: Orbit, 1989, 569 p., paper, coll. CONAN #1-3.

19593 *The Conan chronicles 2.* London: Orbit, 1990, 531 p., paper, coll. CONAN SERIES. [Includes *Conan the Wanderer; Conan the Adventurer; Conan the Buccaneer.*]

19594 *Conan of Aquilonia.* New York: Prestige Books, 1977, xii+171 p., paper, coll. CONAN #11.

with H. P. Lovecraft, C. L. Moore, A. Merritt & Frank Belknap Long

The challenge from beyond—SEE: *The illustrated challenge from beyond.*

26046 *The illustrated Challenge from beyond.* West Warwick, RI: Necronomicon Press, 1978, [26] p., paper, story.

with Richard A. Lupoff

26047 *The return of Skull-Face.* West Linn, OR: FAX Collector's Editions, 1977, 96 p., cloth, novel. SKULL-FACE #2.

HOWARD, Thomas (Trumbull), 1935-

26049 *The achievement of C. S. Lewis.* Wheaton, IL: Harold Shaw Publishers, 1980, 193 p., cloth, nonf.

26050 *C. S. Lewis: man of letters: a reading of his fiction.* San Francisco: Ignatius Press, 1987, 259 p., cloth, nonf.

26051 *The novels of Charles Williams.* New York, Oxford: Oxford University Press, 1983, xii+220 p., cloth, nonf.

HOWARD, Troy, pseud.—SEE: Paine, Lauran

HOWARTH, William L(ouis), 1940-

26052 *Twentieth century interpretations of Poe's tales: a collection of critical essays.* Englewood Cliffs, NJ: Prentice-Hall, 1971, x+116 p., cloth, nonf. anth.

HOWATCH, Susan, 1940-

26053 *Glamorous powers.* London: Collins, 1988, 514 p., cloth, novel. GLITTERING #2.

26054 *Glittering images.* London: Collins, 1987, [512] p., cloth, novel. GLITTERING #1.

HOWE, Deborah (Jane), 1946-1978, with James Howe

26055 *Bunnicula: a rabbit tale of mystery.* New York: Atheneum, 1979, xii+98 p., cloth, novel. BUNNICULA #1.

HOWE, Imogen

26056 *Fatal attraction.* New York: Twilight/Dell, 1982, 170 p., paper, novel. TWILIGHT #4.

26057 *Vicious circle.* New York: Twilight/Dell, 1983, 148 p., paper, novel. TWILIGHT #13.

HOWE, Irving, 1920-

26058 *1984 revisited: totalitarianism in our century.* New York: Harper & Row, 1983, x+276 p., cloth, nonf. anth.

with George Orwell

26059 *Orwell's Nineteen eighty-four: text, sources, criticism.* New York: Harcourt, Brace & World, 1963, 274 p., cloth, anth. [Includes Orwell's novel plus criticism].

26060 *Orwell's Nineteen eighty-four: text, sources, criticism, second edition.* New York: Harcourt Brace Jovanovich, 1982, x+450 p., cloth, anth. [Includes Orwell's novel plus criticism].

HOWE, James, 1946-

26061 *The celery stalks at midnight.* New York: Atheneum, 1983, xi+111 p., cloth, novel. BUNNICULA #3.
26062 *Howliday Inn.* New York: Atheneum, 1982, vii+195 p., cloth, novel. BUNNICULA #2.
26063 *Nighty-nightmare.* New York: A Jean Karl Book, Atheneum, 1987, 90 p., cloth, novel. BUNNICULA #4.

with Deborah Howe

26055 *Bunnicula: a rabbit tale of mystery.* New York: Atheneum, 1979, xii+98 p., cloth, novel. BUNNICULA #1.

HOWELL, Christopher

Castlevania II: Simon's quest—SEE: *Worlds of power: Castlevania II: Simon's quest.*
Simon's quest—SEE: *Worlds of power: Castlevania II: Simon's quest.*
26064 *Worlds of power: Castlevania II: Simon's quest: a novel based on the best-selling game by Konami.* New York, Toronto: A Seth Godin Production, Scholastic Inc., 1990, 138 p., paper, fiction. WORLDS OF POWER #4.

HOWELL, Scott, pseud.—SEE: King, Albert

HOWELLS, Coral Ann, 1939-

26065 *Love, mystery, and misery: feeling in gothic fiction.* London: University of London, The Athlone Press, 1978, 199 p., paper, nonf.

HOWETT, Dicky, *with Tim Quinn*

26066 *The Doctor Who fun book.* London: A Target Book, W. H. Allen & Co., 1987, 64 p., paper, nonf.

HOWL, Marcia Yvonne (Hurt), 1947- , *with Sharon Jarvis as* JOHANNA HAILEY

26067 *Beloved paradise.* New York: Zebra Books, Kensington Publishing Corp., 1987, 479 p., paper, novel.
26068 *Crystal paradise.* New York: Zebra Books, Kensington Publishing Corp., 1986, 477 p., paper, novel.
26069 *Enchanted paradise.* New York: Zebra Books, Kensington Publishing Corp., 1985, 525 p., paper, novel.

HOWLETT, Winston A., *with Jean Lorrah*

26070 *Flight to the Savage Empire.* New York: A Signet Book, New American Library, 1986, 221 p., paper, novel. SAVAGE EMPIRE #4.
26071 *Wulfston's odyssey.* New York: A Signet Book, New American Library, 1987, 206 p., paper, novel.

HOYLE, Fred, Sir, 1915-

26072 *Comet Halley: a novel in two parts.* London: Michael Joseph, 1985, 410 p., cloth, novel.
26073 *The small world of Fred Hoyle: an autobiography.* London: Michael Joseph, 1986, 187 p., cloth, nonf.

with Geoffrey Hoyle

26074 *The energy pirate.* Loughborough, England: Ladybird, 1982, 51 p., cloth, story.
26075 *The frozen planet of Azuron.* Loughborough, England: Ladybird, 1982, 51 p., cloth, story.
26076 *The giants of Universal Park.* Loughborough, England: Ladybird, 1982, 51 p., cloth, story.
26077 *The incandescent ones.* London: Heinemann, 1977, 183 p., cloth, novel. [Edited by Barbara Hoyle].
26078 *The planet of death.* Loughborough, England: Ladybird, 1982, 51 p., cloth, story.
26079 *The Westminster disaster.* London: Heinemann, 1978, 209 p., cloth, novel. [Edited by Barbara Hoyle].

HOYLE, Geoffrey, 1942- , *with Fred Hoyle*

26074 *The energy pirate.* Loughborough, England: Ladybird, 1982, 51 p., cloth, story.
26075 *The frozen planet of Azuron.* Loughborough, England: Ladybird, 1982, 51 p., cloth, story.
26076 *The giants of Universal Park.* Loughborough, England: Ladybird, 1982, 51 p., cloth, story.
26077 *The incandescent ones.* London: Heinemann, 1977, 183 p., cloth, novel. [Edited by Barbara Hoyle].
26078 *The planet of death.* Loughborough, England: Ladybird, 1982, 51 p., cloth, story.
26079 *The Westminster disaster.* London: Heinemann, 1978, 209 p., cloth, novel. [Edited by Barbara Hoyle].

HOYLE, Trevor, 1940-

Blake's 7—SEE: *Terry Nation's Blake's 7.*

26080 *Earth cult.* London: Panther, 1979, 189 p., paper, novel.

26080A retitled: *This sentient Earth.* New York: Zebra Books, Kensington Publishing Corp., 1979, 236 p., paper, novel.

The gods look down—SEE: *Q: The gods look down.*

26081 *K.I.D.S.* London: Sphere Books, 1987, 308 p., paper, novel.

26082 *The last gasp.* New York: Crown Publishers, 1983, viii+430 p., cloth, novel.

37860 *The last gasp.* London: Grafton Books, 1990, 528 p., paper, novel. [Revised edition].

37861 *The man who travelled on motorways.* London: John Calder; Dallas, TX: River Run Press, 1979, 239 p., cloth, novel.

Project Avalon—SEE: *Terry Nation's Blake's 7: Project Avalon.*

26083 *Q: Seeking the mythical future.* St Albans, Hertfordshire, England: Panther, 1977, 189 p., paper, novel. Q #1.

26084 *Q: The gods look down.* London, Toronto: Panther, Granada Publishing, 1978, 189 p., paper, novel. Q #3.

26085 *Q: Through the eye of time.* St Albans, Hertfordshire, England: Panther, 1977, 173 p., paper, novel. Q #2.

Scorpio attack—SEE: *Terry Nation's Blake's 7: Scorpio attack.*

Seeking the mythical future—SEE: *Q: Seeking the mythical future.*

37862 *The stigma.* London: Sphere Books, 1980, 220 p., paper, novel.

26086 *Terry Nation's Blake's 7: Project Avalon.* London: Arrow Books, 1979, 191 p., paper, tele. BLAKE'S 7 SERIES.

26087 *Terry Nation's Blake's 7: Scorpio attack.* London: British Broadcasting Corporation, 1981, 156 p., cloth, tele. BLAKE'S 7 #3.

26088 *Terry Nation's Blake's Seven: novelisation.* London: Sphere Books, 1977, 204 p., paper, tele. BLAKE'S 7 #1.

26088A retitled: *Terry Nation's Blake's 7: their first adventure.* Secaucus, NJ: Lyle Stuart/Citadel Press, 1988, 204 p., paper, tele. BLAKE'S 7 #1.

This sentient Earth—SEE: *Earth cult.*

Through the eyes of time—SEE: *Q: Through the eyes of time.*

26089 *Vail.* London: John Calder; New York: Riverrun Press, 1984, 188 p., paper, novel.

HOYT, Olga Gruhzit, 1922-

26091 *Lust for blood: the consuming story of vampires.* New York: Stein & Day, 1984, 245 p., cloth, nonf.

HOYT, Richard (Duane), 1941-

26092 *The manna enzyme.* New York: William Morrow & Co., 1982, 263 p., cloth, novel.

HRUSKA, Alan (J.), 1933-

26093 *Borrowed time.* Garden City, NY: The Dial Press, 1984, 254 p., cloth, novel.

HUANZHULOUZHU [pseud. of Li Shanji], 1902-1961

26094 *Blades from the willows.* London: Wellsweep Press, 1991, 256 p., paper, novel. SWORDSMEN'S HAVEN AT WILLOW LAKE #1. [Translation by Robert Chard of *Liu hu xia yin*].

HUBBARD, L(a Fayette) Ron(ald Sr.), 1911-1986

26095 *An alien affair.* Los Angeles: Bridge Publications, 1986, 329 p., cloth, novel. MISSION EARTH #4

26096 *Battlefield Earth: a saga of the year 3000.* New York: St. Martin's Press, 1982, xii+819 p., cloth, novel.

26097 *Black genesis, fortress of evil.* LA: Bridge Publications, 1986, 431 p., cloth, novel. MISSION EARTH #2.

26098 *Death quest.* Los Angeles: Bridge Publications, 1987, 347 p., cloth, novel. MISSION EARTH #6.

26099 *Disaster.* Los Angeles: Bridge Publications, 1987, 337 p., cloth, novel. MISSION EARTH #8.

26100 *The doomed planet.* Los Angeles: Bridge Publications, 1987, 329 p., cloth, novel. MISSION EARTH #10.

26101 *The enemy within.* Los Angeles: Bridge Publications, 1986, 393 p., cloth, novel. MISSION EARTH #3.

Fear; &, Typewriter in the sky—SEE: *Two science fantasy novels.*

26102 *Fortune of fear.* Los Angeles: Bridge Publications, 1986, 365 p., cloth, novel. MISSION EARTH #5.

26103 *The invaders plan.* Los Angeles: Bridge Publications, 1985, xiv+559 p., cloth, novel. MISSION EARTH #1.

07520 *The kingslayer.* Los Angeles: Fantasy Publishing Co., 1949, 208 p., cloth, coll.

07520A retitled: *Seven steps to the Arbiter.* Chatsworth, CA: Major Books, 1975, 192 p., paper, coll.

Seven steps to the Arbiter—SEE: *The kingslayer.*

07525 *Two science fantasy novels by L. Ron Hubbard: Typewriter in the sky; Fear.* New York: Gnome Press, 1951, 256 p., cloth, coll.

07525A retitled: *Fear; &, Typewriter in the sky.* New York: Popular Library, 1977, 286 p., paper, coll.

26104 *Villainy victorious.* Los Angeles: Bridge Publications, 1987, 419 p., cloth, novel. MISSION EARTH #9.

26105 *Voyage of vengeance.* Los Angeles: Bridge Publications, 1987, 381 p., cloth, novel. MISSION EARTH #7.

HUBBARD, L(a Fayette) Ron(ald) Jr., 1934- , with Bent Corydon

20617 *L. Ron Hubbard: messiah or madman?* Secaucus, NJ: Lyle Stuart, 1987, 402 p., cloth, nonf.

HUBERT, Cam [later legalized to Barbara Anne Cameron], 1938-

Dreamspeaker—SEE: *Dreamspeaker and Tem Eyos Ki and the land claims question.*

26106 *Dreamspeaker and Tem Eyos Ki and the land claims question.* Toronto: Clarke, Irwin & Co., 1978, 137 p., cloth, novel.

26106A retitled: *Dreamspeaker.* New York: Avon, 1980, 85 p., paper, novel.

HUBLER, David E(lliot), 1941-

26107 *You gotta believe!* New York: A Signet Book, New American Library, 1983, 222 p., paper, novel.

HUBSCHMAN, Thomas

26108 *Alpha II.* New York: Manor Books, 1979 (i.e., 1980?), 186 p., paper, novel.

26109 *Space Ark.* New York: Tower Books, 1981, 205 p., paper, novel.

HUDDY, Delia, 1934-

26110 *The Humboldt effect.* London: Julia MacRae Books, 1982, 157 p., cloth, novel. TOM HUMBOLDT #2.

26111 *Time piper.* London: Hamilton, 1976, 222 p., cloth, novel. TOM HUMBOLDT #1.

HUDGEONS, Thomas E. III

26112 *The Official 1981 price guide to comic & science fiction books, 4th ed.* Orlando,

FL: House of Collectibles, 1981, 437 p., paper, nonf.

26113 *The Official 1982 price guide to comic & science fiction books, 5th ed.* Orlando, FL: House of Collectibles, 1982, 501 p., paper, nonf.

26114 *The Official 1983 price guide to comic & science fiction books, 6th ed.* Orlando, FL: House of Collectibles, 1983, 526 p., paper, nonf.

26115 *The Official price guide to science fiction and fantasy collectibles, 7th ed.* Orlando, FL: House of Collectibles, 1985, 537 p., paper, nonf.

HUDSON, Edward S., pseud.—SEE: Hale, F. J.

HUDSON, Jan, 1954-

26116 *Water witch.* Toronto, New York: Bantam Books, 1988, 183 p., paper, novel.

HUDSON, Michael, pseud.—SEE: Kube-McDowell, Michael P.

HUDSON, W(illiam) H(enry), 1841-1922

15820 *A little boy lost.* London: Duckworth, 1905, 201 p., cloth, novel.

*HUEMER, Dick [i.e., Richard Martin Huemer], 1898-1979

HUFF, Tanya (Sue), 1957-

26117 *Blood price.* New York: DAW Books, 1991, 272 p., paper, novel.

26118 *Child of the grove.* New York: DAW Books, 1988, 288 p., paper, novel. WIZARD CRYSTAL #1.

26119 *The fire's stone.* New York: DAW Books, 1990, 287 p., paper, novel.

26120 *Gate of darkness, circle of light.* New York: DAW Books, 1989, 272 p., paper, novel.

26121 *The last wizard.* New York: DAW Books, 1989, 288 p., paper, novel. WIZARD CRYSTAL #2.

HUFFMAN, Marlys

26122 *Afternoon of the gosling.* New York: Zebra Books, Kensington Publishing Corp., 1989, 317 p., paper, novel.

HUFFMAN-KLINKOWITZ, Julie, 1956- , with Jerome Klinkowitz & Asa B. Pieratt Jr.

26123 *Kurt Vonnegut: a comprehensive bibliography.* Hamden, CT: Archon Books,

1987, xxiv + 289 p., cloth, nonf. [Expanded edition of #27367].

HUGGINS, Ruth M.—SEE: Arthur, Ruth M.

HUGH, Dafydd ab—SEE: ab Hugh, Dafydd

HUGHART, Barry, 1934-

26124 *The bridge of birds: a novel of an ancient China that never was.* New York: St. Martin's Press, 1984, 248 p., cloth, novel. MASTER LI #1. [Winner of the World Fantasy Award for Best Fantasy Novel, 1984 (1985)].
26125 *Eight skilled gentlemen.* New York: A Foundation Book, Doubleday, 1991, 255 p., cloth, novel. MASTER LI #3.
26126 *The story of the stone.* New York: A Foundation Book, Doubleday, 1988, 236 p., cloth, novel. MASTER LI #2.

*HUGHES, (John) Cledwyn, 1920-1978

HUGHES, Dave W.

26127 *Out on Cloud Nine: a collection of prose and verse.* Cheltenham, Gloucester, England: Zanzibar Productions, 1990, 32 p., paper, coll. [Includes some verse].

HUGHES, David W.—SEE: Hughes, Dave W.

HUGHES, Dennis Talbot

as MARVIN ASHTON

00545 *People of Asa.* London: Curtis Warren, 1953, 159 p., cloth, novel.

as GEORGE SHELDON BROWN

01978 *Destination Mars.* London: Edwin Self, 1951, 128 p., paper, novel.
01979 *The planetoid peril.* London: Edwin Self, 1952, 128 p., paper, novel.

as NEIL CHARLES

02885 *Beyond Zoaster.* London: Curtis Warren, 1953, 159 p., cloth, novel.
02889 *Pre-Gargantua.* London: Curtis Warren, 1953, 159 p., cloth, novel.
02890 *Research opta.* London: Curtis Warren, 1953, 160 p., cloth, novel.
02893 *World of Gol.* London: Curtis Warren, 1953, 159 p., cloth, novel.

as VON KELLAR

08103 *Ionic barrier.* London: Curtis Warren, 1953, 159 p., cloth, novel.

as JOHN LANE

08584 *Mammalia.* London: Curtis Warren, 1953, 159 p., cloth, novel.

as RAND LE PAGE

08916 *Asteroid forma.* London: Curtis Warren, 1953, 159 p., cloth, novel.

as GRANT MALCOM

09585 *Ray Ellis in The Green Mandarin mystery.* London: Curtis Warren, 1950, 127 p., paper, novel.

as RUSSELL REY

12151 *Valley of terror.* London: Curtis Warren, 1953, 159 p., cloth, novel.

as WILLIAM ROGERSOHN

12361 *Amiro.* London: Brown Watson, 1954, 111 p., paper, novel.
12362 *North dimension.* London: Brown Watson, 1954, 111 p., paper, novel.

as ARN ROMILUS

12416 *Brain palaeo.* London: Curtis Warren, 1953, 159 p., cloth, novel.
12417 *Organic destiny.* London: Curtis Warren, 1953, 159 p., cloth, novel.

HUGHES, Edward J.—SEE: Hughes, Ted

HUGHES, Edward P.

26128 *The long mynd.* New York: Baen Science Fiction Books, 1985, 318 p., paper, novel.
26129 *Masters of the fist.* New York: Baen Books, 1989, 281 p., paper, coll.

HUGHES, Monica (Mary Ince), 1925-

26130 *Beckoning lights.* Edmonton, Alberta, Canada: J. M. LeBel Enterprises, 1982, 79 p., cloth, novel.
26131 *Beyond the dark river.* London: Hamish Hamilton, 1979, viii + 152 p., cloth, novel.
26132 *Crisis on Conshelf Ten.* Toronto: Copp Clark Co., 1975, 143 p., cloth. CONSHELF TEN #1.

26133 *Devil on my back.* London: Julia MacRae Books, 1984, 170 p., cloth, novel. ARC ONE #1.

26134 *The dream catcher.* London: Julia MacRae Books, 1986, 171 p., cloth, novel. ARC ONE #2.

26135 *Earthdark.* London: Hamish Hamilton, 1977, 122 p., cloth, novel. CONSHELF TEN #2.

26136 *The guardian of Isis.* London: Hamish Hamilton, 1981, 140 p., cloth, novel. ISIS #2.

26137 *Invitation to the game.* Toronto: Harper-Collins, 1990, 179 p., cloth, novel.

26138 *The Isis pedlar.* Scarborough, Ontario, Canada: Fleet Books, 1982, 121 p., cloth, novel. ISIS #3.

26139 *The keeper of the Isis Light.* London: Hamish Hamilton, 1980, 136 p., cloth, novel. ISIS #1.

26140 *The promise.* Toronto: Stoddart, 1989, 156 p., cloth, novel. SANDWRITER #2.

26141 *Ring-rise, ring-set.* London: Julia MacRae Books; New York: Franklin Watts, 1982, 129 p., cloth, novel.

26142 *Sandwriter.* London: Julia MacRae Books, 1985, 158 p., cloth, novel. SANDWRITER #1.

26143 *The space trap.* Toronto: Greenwood Books, 1983, 153 p., cloth, novel.

26144 *The tomorrow city.* London: Hamish Hamilton, 1978, 137 p., cloth, novel.

HUGHES, Peter Tuesday, pseud.

26145 *The daemon.* Santee, CA: The Blueboy Library, 1977, 184 p., paper, novel.

26146 *The eyes of the basilisk.* Santee, CA: Blueboy Library, 1977, 184 p., paper, novel.

26147 *The phallic worshippers.* Santee, CA: The Blueboy Library, 1977, 184 p., paper, novel.

*HUGHES, Riley, 1914-1981

HUGHES, Robert

26148 *School days.* New York: Charter, 1982, 278 p., paper, novel.

HUGHES, Robert Don, 1949-

26149 *The forging of the dragon.* New York: A Del Rey Book, Ballantine Books, 1989, 291 p., paper, novel. WIZARD & DRAGON #1.

26150 *The power and the prophet.* New York: A Del Rey Books, Ballantine Books, 1985, 339 p., paper, novel. PELMEN #3.

26151 *The prophet of Lamath.* New York: A Del Rey Book, Ballantine Books, 1979, 357 p., paper, novel. PELMEN #1.

26152 *The wizard in waiting.* New York: A Del Rey Book, Ballantine Books, 1982, 357 p., paper, novel. PELMEN #2.

HUGHES, Sara

26153 *Morgan Swift and the kidnapped goddess.* New York: Ballantine Books, 1985, 90 p., paper, novel. FIND YOUR FATE #10.

26154 *Morgan Swift and the treasure of Crocodile Key.* New York: Ballantine Books, 1985, 106 p., paper, novel. FIND YOUR FATE #15.

HUGHES, Ted [i.e., Edward James Hughes], 1930-

26155 *Tales of the early world.* London: Faber & Faber, 1988, 121 p., cloth, coll.

HUGHES, Walter L.—SEE: Walters, Hugh

HUGHES, William

26156 *Deathsport.* London: Sphere Books, 1978, 222 p., paper, movie.

HUGHES, Zach [pseud. of Hugh Zachary], 1928-

26157 *Closed system.* New York: A Signet Book, New American Library, 1986, 222 p., paper, novel.

26158 *The dark side.* New York: A Signet Book, New American Library, 1987, 207 p., paper, novel.

26159 *For Texas and Zed.* New York: Popular Library, 1976, 189 p., paper, novel.

26160 *Gold star.* New York: A Signet Book, New American Library, 1983, 173 p., paper, novel.

26161 *Killbird.* New York: A Signet Book, New American Library, 1980, 171 p., paper, novel.

26162 *Life force.* New York: DAW Books, 1988, 269 p., paper, novel.

26163 *Mother lode.* New York: DAW Books, 1991, 208 p., paper, novel.

26164 *Pressure man.* New York: A Signet Book, New American Library, 1980, 171 p., paper, novel.

26165 *The St. Francis effect.* New York: A Berkley Medallion Book, Berkley Publishing Corp., 1976, 249 p., paper, novel.

26166 *The stork factor.* New York: A Berkley Medallion Book, Berkley Publishing Corp., 1975, 156 p., paper, novel.

26167 *Sundrinker.* New York: DAW Books, 1987, 269 p., paper, novel.

26168 *Thunderworld.* New York: A Signet Book, New American Library, 1982, 151 p., paper, novel. RACK THE HEALER #2.

26169 *Tiger in the stars.* Toronto, New York: Laser Books, 1976, 190 p., paper, novel.

as EVAN INNES

26170 *America 2040.* Toronto, New York: Book Creations Inc., Bantam Books, 1986, 344 p., paper, novel. AMERICA 2040 #1.

26171 *City in the mist.* Toronto, New York: Book Creations Inc., Bantam Books, 1987, 374 p., paper, novel. AMERICA 2040 #3.

26172 *The golden world.* Toronto, New York: Book Creations Inc., Bantam Books, 1986, 373 p., paper, novel. AMERICA 2040 #2.

26173 *The return.* Toronto, New York: Book Creations Inc., Bantam Books, 1988, 374 p., paper, novel. AMERICA 2040 #4.

26174 *The star explorer.* Toronto, New York: Book Creations Inc., Bantam Books, 1988, 322 p., paper, novel. AMERICA 2040 #5.

as HUGH ZACHARY

26175 *The revenant.* New York: An Onyx Book, New American Library, 1988, 239 p., paper, novel.

*HUGI, Maurice Gaspard, 1904-1947

HULKE, Malcolm, 1924-1979

The dinosaur invasion—SEE: *Doctor Who and the dinosaur invasion.*

26176 *Doctor Who and the dinosaur invasion.* London: Longbow Series, Allan Wingate, 1976, 141 p., cloth, tele. DOCTOR WHO.

26177 *Doctor Who and the green death.* London: Target, 1975, 142 p., paper, tele. DOCTOR WHO.

26178 *Doctor Who and the space war.* London: Allan Wingate, 1976, 142 p., cloth, tele. DOCTOR WHO.

26179 *Doctor Who and the war games.* London: A Target Book, W. H. Allen & Co., 1979, 143 p., paper, tele. DOCTOR WHO #70.
The green death—SEE: *Doctor Who and the green death.*
The space war—SEE: *Doctor Who and the space war.*

The war games—SEE: *Doctor Who and the war games.*

with Terrance Dicks

21853 *The making of Doctor Who.* London: Target, 1976, 128 p., paper, nonf. [Revised edition].

HULL, Elizabeth Anne, 1937- , *with Frederik Pohl*

26180 *Tales from the planet Earth.* New York: St. Martin's Press, 1986, xviii+268 p., cloth, anth.

HULLAR, Leonard E.—SEE: Hullar, Link

HULLAR, Link [i.e., Leonard Earl Hullar], 1954- , *with Frank Hamilton*

25098 *Amazing pulp heroes.* Brooklyn, NY: Griffin Publications, 1988, 59 p., paper, nonf.

HUME, Fergus(on Wright), 1859-1932

37863 *The nameless city: a Rommany romance.* London: Osgood, McIlvaine, 1894, iv+274 p., cloth, novel.

HUME, Kathryn, 1945-

26181 *Fantasy and mimesis: responses to reality in western literature.* New York & London: Methuen, 1984, xvi+213 p., cloth, nonf. [Winner of the J. Lloyd Eaton Award for Best Nonfiction Book of the Year, 1984 (1986)].

26182 *Pynchon's mythography: an approach to Gravity's Rainbow.* Carbondale & Edwardsville, IL: Southern Illinois University Press, 1987, xxi+262 p., cloth, nonf.

HUMES, James C(alhoun), 1934- , *with John LeBoutillier*

26183 *Primary.* New York: Manor Books, 1979, 285 p., paper, novel.

HUMPHREYS, J(ohn) R(ichard Adams), 1918-

26184 *Maya red.* New York: Cane Hill Press, 1989, 255 p., paper, novel.

HUMPHRIES, (John) Jefferson, 1955-

26185 *Metamorphoses of the raven: literary overdeterminedness in France and the*

South since Poe. Baton Rouge, LA: Louisiana State University Press, 1985, xix+196 p., cloth, nonf.

HUMPHRYS, Leslie G.—SEE: Condray, Bruno G.

HUNSBURGER, (H.) Ed(ward)

as anonymous co-author with Warren Murphy and Molly Cochran

20219 *Date with death* / by Warren Murphy. New York: Pinnacle Books, 1984, 186 p., paper, novel. DESTROYER #57.

as anonymous co-author with Warren Murphy & Richard Sapir

26186 *The seventh stone.* New York: A Signet Book, New American Library, 1985, 223 p., paper, novel. DESTROYER #62.

*HUNT, Barbara [i.e., Barbara Hunt Watters], 1907-1984

HUNT, Charlotte [pseud. of Doris Marjorie Hodges], 1915-

26187 *The casebook of Dr. Holton: The gilded sarcophagus and The cup of Thanatos.* New York: Ace Books, 1978, 501 p., paper, coll. DR. HOLTON #1-2.

26188 *The casebook of Dr. Holton: The Lotus vellum and The thirteenth treasure.* New York: Ace Books, 1978, 630 p., paper, coll. DR. HOLTON #3-4.

26189 *The cup of Thanatos.* New York: Ace Books, 1978, 221 p., paper, novel. DR. HOLTON #2.

26190 *The gilded sarcophagus.* New York: Ace Books, 1967, 222 p., paper, novel. DR. HOLTON #1.

26191 *The Lotus vellum.* New York: Ace Books, 1970, 222 p., paper, novel. DR. HOLTON #3.

26192 *The thirteenth treasure.* New York: Ace Books, 1972, [222] p., paper, novel. DR. HOLTON #4.

HUNT, Dave [i.e., David Charles Hadden Hunt], 1926-

26193 *The Archon conspiracy.* Eugene, OR: Harvest House Publishers, 1989, 332 p., paper, novel.

HUNT, Lisa, *with Walter Hunt & Richard S. Meyer & Evan Jamieson & Bill Scammell &*

Mark Bloom & Christine Ivey as ARCHITECTS ADVENTURE

18216 *Dzurlord: a Crossroads adventure in the world of Steven Brust's Jhereg* / by Architects Adventure. New York: Tor, A Tom Doherty Associates Book, 1987, 24+[224] p., paper, novel. JHEREG SERIES; CROSSROADS ADVENTURE.

HUNT, Walter, *with Richard S. Meyer & Lisa Hunt & Evan Jamieson & Bill Scammell & Mark Bloom & Christine Ivey as* ARCHITECTS ADVENTURE

18216 *Dzurlord: a Crossroads adventure in the world of Steven Brust's Jhereg* / by Architects Adventure. New York: Tor, A Tom Doherty Associates Book, 1987, 24+[224] p., paper, novel. JHEREG SERIES; CROSSROADS ADVENTURE.

HUNTER, Evan [legalized from Salvatore A. Lombino], 1926-

as ED MCBAIN

37864 *Ghosts: an 87th Precinct novel.* New York: Viking Press, 1980, 212 p., cloth, novel. 87TH PRECINCT SERIES.

07619B *Tomorrow and tomorrow.* London: Sphere Books, 1979, 190 p., paper, novel. [Previously published under the name Hunt Collins].

as HUNT COLLINS

07619 *Tomorrow's world.* New York: Avalon Books, 1956, 223 p., cloth, novel.

07619A retitled: *Tomorrow and tomorrow.* New York: Pyramid Books, 1956, 190 p., paper, novel.

HUNTER, Lynette, 1951-

26194 *Modern allegory and fantasy: rhetorical stances of contemporary writing.* Basingstoke, England: Macmillan, 1989, 215 p., cloth, nonf.

HUNTER, Mollie [i.e., Maureen Mollie Hunter McIlwraith McVeigh], 1922-

07630 *The Bodach.* Glasgow, Scotland: Blackie & Son, 1970, 122 p., cloth, novel. THE WALKING STONES #1.

07630A retitled: *The walking stones: a story of suspense.* New York: Harper & Row, 1970, 143 p., cloth, novel.

26195 *The mermaid summer*. London: Hamish Hamilton, 1988, 127 p., cloth, novel.

26196 *A stranger came ashore*. London: Hamilton, 1975, 118 p., cloth, novel.

26197 *The third eye*. New York: Harper & Row, 1979, 276 p., cloth, novel.
The walking stones—SEE: *The Bodach.*

26198 *The wicked one*. London: Hamilton, 1977, 136 p., cloth, novel.

HUNTER, S. L., pseud.

26199 *Fugitive Steele*. New York: Berkley Books, 1991, 202 p., paper, novel. STEELE #7. [Sequel to the six books written by J. D. Masters].

26200 *Molten Steele*. New York: Berkley Books, 1991, 202 p., paper, novel. STEELE #8.

HUNTER, Thomas O'D.

26201 *Softly walks the beast*. New York: Avon, 1982, 205 p., paper, novel.

HUNTINGTON, John (Willard), 1940-

26202 *Critical essays on H. G. Wells*. Boston: G. K. Hall & Co., 1991, xi+186 p., cloth, nonf. anth.

26203 *The logic of fantasy: H. G. Wells and science fiction*. New York: Columbia University Press, 1982, xv+191 p., cloth, nonf. [Winner of the J. Lloyd Eaton Award for Best Nonfiction Book of the Year, 1982 (1984)].

26204 *Rationalizing genius: ideological strategies in the classic American science fiction short story*. New Brunswick, NJ: Rutgers University Press, 1989, 216 p., cloth, nonf.

HUNTLEY, Noel

26205 *Galactic plan*. Los Angeles: Crescent Publications, 1977, 136 p., paper, novel.

HUNTLEY, Tim(othy Wade), 1939-

26206 *One on me*. New York: DAW Books, 1980, 221 p., paper, novel.

HURD, Florence, 1918-

26207 *The dreamtime*. New York: Ballantine Books, 1989, 403 p., paper, novel.

26208 *Legacy*. New York: Avon, 1977, 377 p., paper, novel.

HURLEY, Graham

26209 *Rules of engagement*. London & Sydney: Pan Books, 1990, 472 p., cloth, novel.

HURLEY, Maxwell, pseud.—SEE: Crawford, Betty Anne

*HURLEY, Richard J(ames), 1906-1976?

HURMENCE, Belinda, 1921-

26210 *A girl called Boy*. New York: A Clarion Book, Ticknor & Fields, 1982, 168 p., cloth, novel.

*HURST, Fannie, 1885-1968

HURWITZ, Johanna (Frank), 1937-

26211 *The adventures of Ali Baba Bernstein*. New York: William Morrow & Co., 1985, 82 p., cloth, novel.

HURWOOD, Bernhardt J(ackson), 1926-1987

26212 *By blood alone*. New York: Charter, 1979, 245 p., paper, novel.

26213 *Kingdom of the spiders: novelization*. New York: Ace Books, 1977, 180 p., paper, movie.

26214 *The Meteor scrapbook*. New York: Ace Books, 1979, 126 p., paper, nonf.

26215 *Strange curses*. New York: Scholastic Book Services, 1975, 112 p., paper, coll.

HUSON, Paul (Anthony), 1942-

26216 *The keepsake*. New York: Warner Books, 1981, 320 p., paper, novel.

26217 *The offering*. London: Inner Circle, 1984, 253 p., cloth, novel.

HUTCHINS, Geraldine L., *with Hal W. Hall*

25031 *Science fiction and fantasy book review index, 1980-1984: an index to more than 13,800 book reviews appearing in over 70 science fiction, fantasy, and general periodicals from 1980 to 1984, and containing "Science fiction and fantasy research index," an index to secondary literature, providing nearly 16,000 subject and author access points to articles, essays, and books featuring the history of, or criticism on, science fiction and fantasy literature, television programs, motion pictures, and graphic arts*. Detroit: Gale Research Co., 1985, xxi+761 p., cloth, nonf.

25032 *Science fiction and fantasy research index, volume 4*. Bryan, TX: SFBRI, 1985, 83 p., paper, nonf.

25033 *Science fiction and fantasy research index, volume 5.* San Bernardino, CA: Borgo, 1985, 115 p., cloth, nonf.

25034 *Science fiction and fantasy research index, volume 6.* San Bernardino, CA: Borgo, 1986, 101 p., cloth, nonf.

HUTCHINSON, David (Christopher), 1960-

26218 *Fools' gold.* London: Abelard, 1979, 160 p., cloth, coll.

26219 *The paradise equation.* London: Abelard, 1981, 95 p., cloth, coll.

26220 *Thumbprints.* London: Abelard, 1978, 159 p., cloth, coll.

26221 *Torn air.* London: Abelard, 1980, 160 p., cloth, coll.

HUTCHINSON, Tom, 1930-

26222 *British science fiction and fantasy.* London: The British Council, 1975, 52 p., paper, nonf.

26223 *Norman Jacobs & Kerry O'Quinn present Special effects, volume 2.* New York: Starlog Press, 1980, 98 p., paper, nonf.

Special effects, volume 2—SEE: *Norman Jacobs & Kerry O'Quinn present Special effects, volume 2.*

with Roy Pickard

26224 *Horrors: a history of horror movies.* London: Optimum Books, 1983, 192 p., cloth, nonf.

HUTCHISON, David (A.), 1946-

Fantastic 3-D—SEE: *Norman Jacobs & Kerry O'Quinn present Fantastic 3-D: a Starlog photo guidebook.*

26225 *Norman Jacobs & Kerry O'Quinn present Fantastic 3-D: a Starlog photo guidebook.* New York: Starlog Press, 1982, 98 p., paper, nonf.

26226 *Norman Jacobs and Kerry O'Quinn present Special effects, vol. 3.* New York: A Starlog Press Publication, 1981, 98 p., paper, nonf.

Special effects, vol. 3—SEE: *Norman Jacobs and Kerry O'Quinn present Special effects, vol. 3.*

26227 *Special effects, volume 4: a Starlog photo book.* New York: Starlog Press, 1984, 98 p., paper, nonf.

HUTCHISON, Don(ald), 1931-

26228 *It's raining corpses in Chinatown.* Mercer Island, WA: Starmont House, 1991,

xxxviii+169 p., cloth, anth. Starmont Popular Culture Studies #9.

HUTSON, Shaun, 1958-

26229 *Assassin.* London: W. H. Allen & Co., 1988, 320 p., cloth, novel.

26230 *Breeding ground.* London: W. H. Allen & Co., 1985, 220 p., cloth, novel. Slugs #2.

26231 *Captives.* London: Macdonald, 1991, 432 p., cloth, novel.

26243A *Deathday.* London: Star Books, W. H. Allen & Co., 1987, 383 p., paper, novel. [Originally published under the name Robert Neville].

26232 *Erebus.* London: A Star Book, W. H. Allen & Co., 1984, 309 p., paper, novel.

26233 *Horror film quiz book.* London: Sphere Books, 1991, 232 p., paper, nonf.

26234 *Nemesis.* London: W. H. Allen & Co., 1989, 347 p., cloth, novel.

26235 *Relics.* London: W. H. Allen & Co., 1986, iv+288 p., cloth, novel.

26236 *Renegades.* London: Macdonald, 1991, 336 p., cloth, novel.

26237 *Shadows.* London: W. H. Allen & Co., 1985, 325 p., cloth, novel.

26238 *The skull.* Feltham, England: Hamlyn Paperbacks, 1982, 188 p., paper, novel.

26239 *Slugs.* London: A Star Book, W. H. Allen & Co., 1982, 208 p., paper, novel. Slugs #1.

26240 *Spawn.* London: A Star Book, W. H. Allen & Co., 1983, 287 p., paper, novel.

26241 *The terminator.* London: A Star Book, W. H. Allen & Co., 1984, 172 p., paper, movie. Terminator #1. [Not the same as the American novelization].

26242 *Victims.* London: W. H. Allen & Co., 1987, 288 p., cloth, novel.

as Robert Neville

26243 *Deathday.* New York: Leisure Books, 1989, 400 p., paper, novel. [Also published under Hutson's real name].

HUTTAR, Charles A(dolph), 1920-

26244 *Imagination and the spirit: essays in literature and the Christian faith, presented to Clyde S. Kilby.* Grand Rapids, MI: William B. Eerdmans Publishing Co., 1971, xvi+496 p., cloth, nonf. anth.

with Peter J. Schakel

26245 *Word and story in C. S. Lewis.* Columbia, MO: University of Missouri Press, 1991, x+316 p., cloth, nonf. anth.

HUXLEY, Aldous (Leonard), 1894-1963

26246 *Letters of Aldous Huxley.* New York & Evanston, IL: Harper & Row, Publishers, 1969, 992 p., cloth, nonf. coll. [Edited by Grover Smith].

HUXLEY, Julian (Sorell, Sir), 1887-1975

26247 *Aldous Huxley, 1894-1963: a memorial volume.* London: Chatto & Windus, 1965, 174 p., cloth, nonf. anth.

HUXLEY, Laura Archera, 1914-

26248 *This timeless moment: a personal view of Aldous Huxley.* London: Chatto & Windus, 1969, 330 p., cloth, nonf.

HUYCK, Willard, 1945- , *with Gloria Katz*

26249 *Indiana Jones and the Temple of Doom: the illustrated screenplay: the complete script.* New York: Ballantine Books, 1984, 121 p., paper, nonf. coll. INDIANA JONES SERIES. [Includes screenplay, designs, & commentary].

HUYGEN, Wil(librord Joseph), 1922-

26250 *Gnomes.* New York: Henry N. Abrams, 1977, [200] p., cloth, fiction. GNOMES #1. [Translation of *Leven en werken van de kabouter*].
26251 *Secrets of the gnomes.* New York: Henry N. Abrams, 1982, [194] p., cloth, fiction. GNOMES #2. [Translation of *De oproep der kabouters*].

HUYGHE, Patrick

26252 *Glowing birds: stories from the edge of science.* Boston, London: Faber & Faber, 1985, ix+241 p., paper, coll.

HYAMS, Edward (Solomon), 1910-1975

37865 *The final agenda.* London: Allen Lane, 1973, 176 p., cloth, novel.
26253 *Morrow's ants.* London: Allen Lane, 1975, 188 p., cloth, novel.

HYAMS, Peter, 1943- , *with Arthur C. Clarke*

20117 *The Odyssey file.* London: Panther, 1985, xxv+132 p., paper, nonf.

HYDE, Christopher, 1949-

26254 *Crestwood Heights.* New York: Avon, 1988, 328 p., paper, novel.
26255 *Egypt Green.* London, New York: Simon & Schuster, 1989, 274 p., cloth, novel.
26256 *Jericho Falls.* New York: Avon, 1986, 312 p., paper, novel.
26257 *Styx.* Chicago: Playboy Press, 1982, 269 p., paper, novel.
26258 *The wave: a novel.* Garden City, NY: Doubleday & Co., 1979, vii+226 p., cloth, novel.
37866 *White lies.* London: Simon & Schuster, 1990, [288] p., cloth, novel.

HYDE, Gregory R.

26259 *C-minor.* Arvada, CO: Roadkill Press, 1991, 12 p., paper, story. [Limited to 200 copies; bound with *Dirtyside down / by Wil McCarthy*].

HYDE, John, 1943-

26260 *The prediction.* London: Futura Books, 1980, [280] p., paper, novel.

*HYDE, Mark Powell, <u>1881-1952</u>

HYDE, Shelley, pseud.—SEE: Reed, Kit

*HYDE-CHAMBERS, Derek <u>(E.), 1913-1980</u>

HYERS, (M.) Conrad, 1933-

15821 *The chickadees: a contemporary fable.* Philadelphia, PA: Westminster Press, 1974, 64 p., cloth, story.

HYLES, Vernon (Ross), 1943- , *with Patrick D. Murphy*

26261 *The poetic fantastic: studies in an evolving genre.* New York: Greenwood Press, 1989, xxv+201 p., cloth, nonf. anth. CONTRIBUTIONS TO THE STUDY OF SCIENCE FICTION AND FANTASY #40.

HYMAN, Jackie (Diamond), 1949-

26262 *Echoes.* New York: William Morrow & Co., 1990, 228 p., cloth, novel.
26263 *Shadowlight.* New York: DAW Books, 1989, 236 p., paper, novel.

as JACQUELINE DIAMOND

26264   *Ghost of a chance.* Toronto, New York: Harlequin Books, 1989, 251 p., paper, novel.

HYNAM, John—SEE: Kippax, John

HYNEMAN, Esther F., 1939-

26265   *Edgar Allan Poe: an annotated bibliography of books and articles in English, 1927-1973.* Boston: G. K. Hall & Co., 1974, xv+335 p., cloth, nonf.

HYNES, Samuel (Lynn), 1924-

26266   *Twentieth century interpretations of 1984: a collection of critical essays.* Englewood Cliffs, NJ: Prentice-Hall, 1971, vi+117 p., cloth, nonf. anth.

26267   *William Golding.* New York: Columbia University Press, 1964, 48 p., paper, nonf.

HYTES, Jason, pseud.

26268   *Erica's magic touch.* New York: Midwood Books, 1976, 189 p., paper, novel.

I

I. S., pseud.—SEE: Schneider, Isador

IBAÑEZ, Félix Marti- —SEE: Marti-Ibañez, Félix

IBBOTSON, Eva, 1925-

26269 *The great ghost rescue.* London: Macmillan, 1975, 128 p., cloth, novel.
26270 *Which witch?* London: Macmillan Publishers, 1979, 197 p., cloth, novel.

IGNAZIO, Fred d'—SEE: d'Ignazio, Fred

IKIN, Van (George), 1951-

26271 *Australian science fiction.* St. Lucia, Queensland, Australia: University of Queensland Press, 1982, xi+320 p., cloth, anth.

INDICK, Ben(jamin) P(hilip), 1923-

26272 *The drama of Ray Bradbury.* Baltimore, MD: T-K Graphics, 1977, [19] p., paper, nonf.
26273 *A gentleman from Providence pens a letter.* Madison, WI: The Strange Company, 1975, [6] leaves, paper, nonf.
26274 *Ray Bradbury: dramatist.* San Bernardino, CA: R. Reginald, The Borgo Press, 1989, 48 p., cloth, nonf. ESSAYS ON FANTASTIC LITERATURE #3. [An expanded and rewritten version of *The drama of Ray Bradbury*].

ING, Dean (Charles), 1931-

26275 *Anasazi.* New York: Ace Books, 1980, 282 p., paper, coll.
26276 *The big lifters.* New York: Tor SF, A Tom Doherty Associates Book, 1988, 243 p., cloth, novel.
26277 *Cathouse.* New York: Baen Books, 1990, 247 p., paper, coll. MAN-KZIN WARS.
26278 *The Chernobyl syndrome.* New York: Baen Books, 1988, 330 p., paper, nonf. coll.
26279 *Firefight 2000.* New York: Baen Books, 1987, 247 p., paper, coll. [Includes some nonfiction].

26280 *High tension.* New York: Ace Books, 1982, 278 p., paper, coll. [Includes some nonfiction].
26281 *The nemesis mission.* New York: Tor, A Tom Doherty Associates Book, 1991, 340 p., cloth, novel.
26282 *Pulling through.* New York: Ace Books, 1983, xix+261 p., paper, coll. [Includes some nonfiction].
26283 *The ransom of Black Stealth One.* New York: St. Martin's Press, 1989, 311 p., cloth, novel.
26284 *Silent thunder.* New York: Tor SF, A Tom Doherty Associates Book, 1991, p. 1-160, paper, novel. [Bound with *Universe 1* by Robert A. Heinlein].
26285 *Single combat.* New York: A Jim Baen Presentation, A Tom Doherty Associates Book, 1983, 375 p., paper, novel. TED QUANTRILL #2.
26286 *Soft targets.* New York: Ace Books, 1979, 217 p., paper, novel.
26287 *Systemic shock.* New York: Ace Books, 1981, 298 p., paper, novel. TED QUANTRILL #1.
26288 *Wild country.* New York: Tor SF, A Tom Doherty Associates Book, 1985, 316 p., paper, novel. TED QUANTRILL #3.

with Larry Niven & Poul Anderson

16454 *The Man-Kzin wars.* New York: Baen Books, 1988, 289 p., paper, coll. MAN-KZIN WARS #1.

with Larry Niven & Jerry Pournelle & S. M. Stirling

26289 *The Man-Kzin wars II.* New York: Baen Books, 1989, ix+306 p., paper, coll. MAN-KZIN WARS #2.

with Mack Reynolds

26290 *Deathwish world.* New York: Baen Science Fiction Books, 1986, 316 p., paper, novel.
26291 *Eternity.* New York: A Baen Book, 1984, 254 p., paper, novel.

26292 *Home sweet home: 2010 A.D..* New York: A Dell/Emerald Book, 1984, 255 p., paper, novel.

26293 *The other time.* New York: A Baen Book, 1984, 308 p., paper, novel.

26294 *Trojan orbit.* New York: A Baen Book, 1985, 374 p., paper, novel. LAGRANGIA #4.

INGALLS, Rachel, 1937-

26295 *The end of tragedy.* London: Faber & Faber, 1987, 184 p., cloth, coll.

INGE, M(ilton) Thomas, 1936- , *with Edgar E. MacDonald*

37867 *James Branch Cabell: centennial essays.* Baton Rouge, LA: Louisiana State University Press, 1983, xii+186 p., cloth, nonf. anth.

INGPEN, Robert (R.), 1936-

with Michael F. Page

26296 *Encyclopaedia of things that never were: creatures, places, and people.* Limpsfield, Surrey, England: Paper Tiger, 1985, 240 p., cloth, nonf.

with Maurice Saxby

26297 *The great deeds of superheroes.* Limpsfield, Surrey, England: Paper Tiger, 1989, 184 p., cloth, coll.

INGRAM, John Henry, 1842-1916

26298 *Edgar Allan Poe: his life, letters, and opinions.* London: W. H. Allen & Co., 1886, vii+488 p., cloth, nonf.

INGRAM, Thomas H.—SEE: Ingram, Tom

INGRAM, Tom [i.e., Thomas Henry Ingram], 1924-

26299 *The night rider: a novel.* New York: Bradbury Press, 1975, 176 p., cloth, novel.

INGRID, Charles, pseud.—SEE: Vilott, Rhondi

INNES, Evan, pseud.—SEE: Hughes, Zach

INNES, J. W. Brodie- —SEE: Brodie-Innes, J. W.

INOUYE, Jon (Masamitsu), 1955-

26300 *A night tide.* Culver City, CA: Randen Publishing Co., 1976, 220 p., paper, coll.

INSINGA, Aron K.

26301 *The Smofcon 3 record.* Cambridge, MA: NESFA Press, 1987, ii+68 p., paper, nonf. anth.

IOANNOU, Greg(ory Phillip), 1953- , *with Lynne Missen*

26302 *Shivers: an anthology of Canadian ghost stories.* Toronto: Seal Books, McClelland-Bantam, 1990, 216 p., paper, anth.

*IONEL [pseud. of Yuval Ronn], <u>1919-1982</u>

IPCAR, Dahlov (Zorach), 1917-

26303 *A dark horn blowing.* New York: Viking Press, 1978, 222 p., cloth, novel.

26304 *The nightmare and her foal, and other stories.* Unity, ME: North Country Press, 1990, 234 p., cloth, coll.

IRELAND, David, 1927-

26305 *A woman of the future: a novel.* New York: George Braziller, 1979, 351 p., cloth, novel.

IRELAND, Kenneth, 1929-

26306 *The werewolf mask.* London: Hodder & Stoughton, 1983, 123 p., cloth, coll.

IRESON, Barbara (Francis), 1927-

The April witch, and other strange tales—SEE: *Fantasy tales.*

26307 *Creepy creatures.* London: Beaver Books, 1978, 189 p., paper, anth.

26308 *Creepy-crawly stories.* London: Hutchinson, 1986, 93 p., cloth, anth.

26309 *Fantasy tales.* London: Faber & Faber, 1977, 218 p., cloth, anth.

26309A retitled: *The April witch and other strange tales.* New York: Charles Scribner's Sons, 1978, x+238 p., cloth, anth.

26310 *Fearfully frightening.* London: Beaver Books, 1984, 175 p., paper, anth.

26311 *Ghostly and ghastly.* London: Beaver Books, 1977, 222 p., paper, anth.

26312 *Ghostly laughter.* London: Beaver Books, 1981, 159 p., paper, anth.

26313 *Spooky stories.* London: Carousel Books, 1975, 126 p., paper, anth.

26313A retitled: *Spooky stories, no. 1.* London: Carousel Books, 1982, 126 p. paper, anth.

26314 *Spooky stories, no. 2.* London: Carousel Books, 1979, 127 p., paper, anth.

26315 *Spooky stories, no. 3.* London: Carousel Books, 1981, 149 p., paper, anth.

26316 *Spooky stories, no. 4.* London: Carousel Books, 1982, 123 p., paper, anth.

26317 *Spooky stories, no. 5.* London: Carousel Books, 1983, 127 p., paper, anth.

26318 *Spooky stories, no. 6.* London: Carousel Books, 1984, 120 p., paper, anth.

26319 *Tales out of time.* London: Faber & Faber, 1979, 212 p., cloth, anth.

IRMELSHAUSEN, Charles Henneberg zu—SEE: Henneberg, Charles

IRONS, John, 1942-

26320 *Watership down in context.* Odense, Denmark: English Institute of Odense University, 1975, 19 p., paper, nonf.

IRONSIDE, Virginia, 1944-

26321 *The human zoo.* London: Walker Books, 1991, 128 p., paper, novel.

26322 *Phantom of Burlap Hall.* London: Walker Books, 1991, 174 p., cloth, novel. BURLAP HALL #3.

26323 *Roseanne and the magic mirror.* London: Walker Books, 1990, [128] p., cloth, novel.

26324 *Spaceboy at Burlap Hall.* London: Walker Books, 1989, 195 p., cloth, novel. BURLAP HALL #2.

26325 *Vampire master.* London: Walker Books, 1987, 175 p., cloth, novel. BURLAP HALL #1.

IRVINE, Mat

26326 *Dr. Who special effects.* London: Hutchinson, 1986, 96 p., cloth, nonf.

IRVINE, Robert

26327 *The devil's breath.* New York: Pinnacle Books, 1982, 280 p., paper, novel.

26328 *Footsteps.* New York: Pinnacle Books, 1982, 311 p., paper, novel.

IRVING, Washington, 1783-1859

26329 *The ghostly tales of Washington Irving.* London: John Calder; Dallas, TX: Riverrun Press, 1979, 152 p., cloth, coll. [Edited by Michael Hayes].

26330 *Washington Irving's tales of the supernatural.* Owings Mills, MD: Stemmer House Publishers, 1982, 307 p., cloth, coll. [Edited by Edward Charles Wagenknecht].

with Mary W. Shelley & John Howard Payne

26331 *The romance of Mary W. Shelley, John Howard Payne, and Washington Irving.* Boston: Bibliophile Society, 1907, 100 p., cloth, nonf. coll.

IRWIN, Joseph James, 1908-

26332 *M. G. "Monk" Lewis.* Boston: Twayne Publishers, 1976, 176 p., cloth, nonf.

*IRWIN, Margaret (Emma Faith), 1889-1967

IRWIN, Robert (Graham), 1946-

26333 *The Arabian nightmare.* London: Dedalus, 1983, 256 p., paper, novel.

26334 *The Arabian nightmare.* Harmondsworth, Middlesex, England: Viking, 1987, 281 p., cloth, novel. [Revised edition].

26335 *The limits of vision.* Harmondsworth, Middlesex, England: Viking in Association with Dedalus, 1986, 119 p., cloth, novel.

IRWIN, Sarita, pseud.—SEE: Zacharia, Irwin

IRWIN, W(illiam) R(obert), 1915-

26336 *The game of the impossible: a rhetoric of fantasy.* Urbana, IL & Chicago: University of Illinois Press, 1976, xii+215 p., cloth, nonf.

IRWIN, Walter (Godfrey), 1950- , with G. B. Love

26337 *The best of the best of Trek: from the magazine for Star Trek fans.* New York: A Roc Book, 1990, xii+369 p., paper, nonf. anth.

26338 *The best of Trek: from the magazine for Star Trek fans.* New York: A Signet Book, New American Library, 1978, xii+239 p., paper, nonf. anth.

26339 *The best of Trek #2: from the magazine for Star Trek fans.* New York: A Signet Book, New American Library, 1980, 196 p., paper, nonf. anth.

26340 *The best of Trek #3: from the magazine for Star Trek fans.* New York: A Signet Book, New American Library, 1981, 196 p., paper, nonf. anth.

26341 *The best of Trek #4: from the magazine for Star Trek fans.* New York: A Signet Book, New American Library, 1981, 215 p., paper, nonf. anth.

26342 *The best of Trek #5: from the magazine for Star Trek fans.* New York: A Signet Book, New American Library, 1982, 202 p., paper, nonf. anth.

26343 *The best of Trek #6: from the magazine for Star Trek fans.* New York: A Signet Book, New American Library, 1983, 191 p., paper, nonf. anth.

26344 *The best of Trek #7: from the magazine for Star Trek fans.* New York: A Signet Book, New American Library, 1984, 205 p., paper, nonf. anth.

26345 *The best of Trek #8: from the magazine for Star Trek fans.* New York: A Signet Book, New American Library, 1985, 221 p., paper, nonf. anth.

26346 *The best of Trek #9: from the magazine for Star Trek fans.* New York: A Signet Book, New American Library, 1985, 207 p., paper, nonf. anth.

26347 *The best of Trek #10: from the magazine for Star Trek fans.* New York: A Signet Book, New American Library, 1986, 204 p., paper, nonf. anth.

26348 *The best of Trek #11: featuring a complete guide to the original episodes: from the magazine for Star Trek fans.* New York: A Signet Book, New American Library, 1986, 204 p., paper, nonf. anth.

26349 *The best of Trek #12: from the magazine for Star Trek fans.* New York: A Signet Book, 1987, 206 p., paper, nonf. anth.

26350 *The best of Trek #13: a brand new collection for Star Trek fans.* New York: A Signet Book, 1988, 204 p., paper, nonf. anth.

26351 *The best of Trek #14: from the magazine for Star Trek fans.* New York: A Signet Book, 1988, 220 p., paper, nonf. anth.

26352 *The best of Trek #15.* New York: A Roc Book, 1990, 207 p., paper, nonf. anth.

26353 *The best of Trek #16.* New York: A Roc Book, 1991, 208 p., paper, nonf. anth.

ISAAC, Rondall

26354 *Stories of the unforeseen.* New York, Washington: Vantage Press, 1979, 118 p., cloth, coll.

ISAACS, Leonard (N.), 1939-1988

26355 *Darwin to double helix: the biological theme in science fiction.* London, Boston: Butterworths, 1977, 64 p., paper, nonf.

ISAACS, Neil D(avid), 1931-1988, *with Rose A. Zimbardo*

26356 *Tolkien: new critical perspectives.* Lexington, KY: University Press of Kentucky, 1981, 175 p., cloth, nonf. anth.

ISBERT, Margot Benary- —SEE: Benary-Isbert, Margot

ISRAEL, Peter, 1933-

26357 *I'll cry when I kill you: a mystery.* New York: Mysterious Press, 1988, 264 p., cloth, novel.

ITH, Lily Van—SEE: Ith, Lily Van

IVANHOE, Mark

37868 *Virgintooth.* San Francisco, CA: III Publishing, 1991, 191 p., paper, novel.

IVERSON, Eric G., pseud.—SEE: Turtledove, Harry

IVEY, Christine, *with Mark Bloom & Bill Scammell & Evan Jamieson & Lisa Hunt & Walter Hunt & Richard S. Meyer as* ARCHITECTS ADVENTURE

18216 *Dzurlord: a Crossroads adventure in the world of Steven Brust's Jhereg* / by Architects Adventure. New York: Tor, A Tom Doherty Associates Book, 1987, 24+[224] p., paper, novel. JHEREG SERIES; CROSSROADS ADVENTURE.

IVORY, James—SEE: Walkham, Walter

J

J., D. N.

26358 *The moon-gazer, and one other: stories.* Hoole, Chester, England: A Haunted Library Publication, Rosemary Pardoe, 1988, 12 p., paper, coll.

JABEZ, Myran—SEE: Livingston, M. Jay

JABLOKOV, Alexander, 1956-

26359 *Carve the sky.* New York: William Morrow & Co., 1991, 298 p., cloth, novel.

JABLONSKI, David, 1953-

26360 *Behold the mighty dinosaur.* New York: Elsevier/Nelson Books, 1981, 256 p., cloth, anth.

JACCOMA, Richard, 1943-

26361 *The werewolf's revenge.* New York: Fawcett Gold Medal, 1991, 296 p., paper, novel. WEREWOLF #2.
26362 *The werewolf's tale.* New York: Fawcett Gold Medal, 1988, 283 p., paper, novel. WEREWOLF #1.
26363 *Yellow peril: the adventures of Sir John Weymouth-Smythe.* New York: Richard Marek Publishers, 1978, 383 p., cloth, novel.

JACKSON, Basil, 1920-

26364 *Epicenter.* New York: W. W. Norton & Co., 1971, 234 p., cloth, novel.
26365 *The night Manhattan burned.* New York: W. W. Norton & Co., 1979, 191 p., cloth, novel.
26366 *Rage under the Arctic.* New York: W. W. Norton & Co., 1974, 220 p., cloth, novel.

JACKSON, David Kelly Jr.

26367 *Poe and the Southern Literary Messenger.* Richmond, VA: Press of the Dietz Printing Co., 1934, xiii+120 p., cloth, nonf.

with Dwight Thomas

26368 *The Poe log: a documentary life of Edgar Allan Poe, 1809-1849.* Boston: G. K. Hall & Co., 1987, xlix+919 p., cloth, nonf.

JACKSON, Jacqueline (Dougan), 1928- , with William Perlmutter

26369 *The endless pavement.* New York: Seabury Press, 1973, 45 p., cloth, novel.

JACKSON, Robert

26370 *Frontier crossings.* Brighton, England: ConSpiracy, 1987, 192 p., cloth, anth. [Includes some nonfiction].

JACKSON, Rosemary (Elizabeth), 1917-

26371 *Fantasy: the literature of subversion.* London & New York: Methuen, 1981, viii+211 p., cloth, nonf.

JACKSON, Shirley (Hardie), 1919-1965

26372 *The lottery, and other stories; The haunting of Hill House; We have always lived in the castle.* New York: Quality Paperback Book Club, 1991, 306+246+214 p., paper, coll.

JACKSON, Steve, 1951-

26373 *Appointment with F.E.A.R.* Harmondsworth, Middlesex, England: Puffin Books, 1985, [276] p., paper, novel. FIGHTING FANTASY GAMEBOOK #17.
26374 *The Citadel of Chaos.* Harmondsworth, Middlesex, England: Puffin Books, 1983, [187] p., paper, novel. FIGHTING FANTASY GAMEBOOK #2.
26375 *Creature of havoc.* Harmondsworth, Middlesex, England: Puffin Books, 1986, 460 p., paper, novel. FIGHTING FANTASY GAMEBOOK #24.
26376 *The crown of kings.* Harmondsworth, Middlesex, England: Puffin Books, 1985, 367 p., paper, novel. SORCERY! #4.

26377 *Fighting fantasy: an introductory role-playing game.* Harmondsworth, Middlesex, England: Puffin Books, 1984, 239 p., paper, novel. FIGHTING FANTASY GAMEBOOK TIE-IN.

House of Hades—SEE: *House of Hell.*

26378 *House of Hell.* Harmondsworth, Middlesex, England: Puffin Books, 1985, [201] p., paper, novel. FIGHTING FANTASY GAMEBOOK #10.

26378A retitled: *House of Hades.* New York: Laurel-Leaf Books, 1985, [224] p., paper, novel. FIGHTING FANTASY GAMEBOOK #10.

37870 *Keep of the Lich-Lord.* Harmondsworth, Middlesex, England: Puffin Books, 1990, [240] p., paper, novel. FIGHTING FANTASY GAMEBOOK #43.

26379 *Kharé—cityport of traps.* Harmondsworth, Middlesex, England: Puffin Books, 1984, [200] p., paper, novel. SORCERY! #2.

26380 *The seven serpents.* Harmondsworth, Middlesex, England: Puffin Books, 1984, 217 p., paper, novel. SORCERY! #3.

26381 *The Shamutanti Hills.* Harmondsworth, Middlesex, England: Puffin Books, 1984, 21+[200] p., paper, novel. SORCERY! #1.

26382 *The sorcery spell book.* Harmondsworth, Middlesex, England: Puffin Books, 1983, 107 p., paper, nonf. SORCERY! SERIES.

26383 *Starship traveler.* Harmondsworth, Middlesex, England: Puffin Books, 1983, [200] p., paper, novel. FIGHTING FANTASY GAMEBOOK #4.

26384 *The Trolltooth wars.* Harmondsworth, Middlesex, England: Puffin Books, 1989, 294 p., paper, fiction.

with Ian Livingstone

37871 *The fighting fantasy poster book.* London: Fantail, 1990, 32 p., paper, art anth.

37872 *Titan: the fighting fantasy world.* Harmondsworth, Middlesex, England: Puffin Books, 1986, 128 p., paper, fiction. FIGHTING FANTASY GAMEBOOK TIE-IN.

26385 *The warlock of Firetop Mountain.* Harmondsworth, Middlesex, England: Puffin Books, 1982, [170] p., paper, novel. FIGHTING FANTASY GAMEBOOK #1.

JACKSON, Steve(n Gary), 1953-

26386 *Battle road.* Lake Geneva, WI: TSR Inc., 1986, [150] p., paper, novel. CAR WARS ADVENTURE GAMEBOOK #1.

with Creede Lambard & Sharleen Lambard

26387 *Fuel's gold.* Lake Geneva, WI: TSR Inc., 1986, 18+[150] p., paper, fiction. CAR WARS ADVENTURE GAMEBOOK #2.

with Ian Livingstone

26388 *Demons of the deep.* Harmondsworth, Middlesex, England: Puffin Books, 1986, 22+[234] p., paper, novel. FIGHTING FANTASY GAMEBOOK #19.

26389 *Robot commando.* Harmondsworth, Middlesex, England: Puffin Books, 1986, [200] p., paper, novel. FIGHTING FANTASY GAMEBOOK #22.

26390 *Scorpion swamp.* Harmondsworth, Middlesex, England: Puffin Books, 1984, 28+[150] p., paper, novel. FIGHTING FANTASY GAMEBOOK #8.

JACKSON, Stuart

26391 *Tracer.* London: Sphere Books, 1990, 301 p., paper, novel.

JACKSON, Tracy, 1962?-

26392 *Too late to see the light.* New York, Washington: Vantage Press, 1978, 202 p., cloth, novel.

JACKSON, William (Godfrey Fothergill, Sir), 1917-

26393 *Alternative Third World War, 1985-2035: a personal history.* London, Washington: Pergamon Press, 1987, xii+247 p., cloth, fiction. THIRD WORLD WAR SERIES.

JACOB, Piers—SEE: Anthony, Piers

JACOBI, Carl (Richard), 1908-

26394 *East of Samarinda.* Bowling Green, OH: Bowling Green State University Popular Press, 1989, 229 p., cloth, coll.

07754 *Revelations in black.* Sauk City, WI: Arkham House, 1947, 272 p., cloth, coll.

07754A retitled: *The tomb from beyond.* St Albans, Hertfordshire, England: Panther, 1977, 144 p., paper, coll. [Abridged edition].

The tomb from beyond—SEE: *Revelations in black.*

JACOBS, James S(wensen), 1945- , with Michael O. Tunnell

26395 *Lloyd Alexander: a bio-bibliography.* Westport, CT, London: Greenwood Press, 1991, x + 145 p., cloth, nonf.

JACOBS, Paul Samuel

26396 *Born into light.* New York, Toronto: Scholastic Inc., 1988, 149 p., cloth, novel.
26397 *Sleepers, wake.* New York, Toronto: Scholastic Inc., 1991, 183 p., cloth, novel.

JACOBS, W(illiam) W(ymark), 1863-1943, with Rod Serling

26398 *Tales of terror: The monkey's paw; The monsters are due on Maple Street.* Boston: Houghton Mifflin Co., 1989, 62 p., paper?, coll.

JACOBSON, Dan, 1929-

37873 *The confessions of Josef Baisz: a novel.* London: Secker & Warburg, 1977, 204 p., cloth, novel.
26399 *Her story: a novel.* London: André Deutsch, 1987, 141 p., cloth, novel.

JACOBSON, Louise H.—SEE: Hawes, Louise

JACOBSON, Mark

26400 *Gojiro.* New York: A Morgan Entrekin Book, Atlantic Monthly Press, 1991, 356 p., cloth, novel.

*JACOMB, C(harles) E(rnest), 1888-

JACQUES, Brian, 1939-

26401 *Mariel of Redwall.* London: Hutchinson's Children's Books, 1991, 336 p., cloth, novel. REDWALL #4.
26402 *Mattimeo.* London: Hutchinson's Children's Books, 1989, 446 p., cloth, novel. REDWALL #3.
26403 *Mossflower.* London: Hutchinson's Children's Books, 1988, 431 p., cloth, novel. REDWALL #1.
26404 *Redwall.* London: Hutchinson's Children's Books, 1986, 351 p., paper, novel. REDWALL #2.
26405 *The Redwall trilogy: Redwall, Mossflower, Mattimeo.* London: Red Fox, 1991, 431 + 351 + 446 p., paper, coll. REDWALL #1-3.

26406 *Seven strange and ghostly tales.* London: Hutchinson, 1991, 151 p., cloth, coll.

JACY, Joanna

26407 *Justin.* New York, Washington: Vantage Press, 1984, 45 p., cloth, story.

JADE, Symon [pseud. of Michael Eckstrom]

26408 *Alter evil.* New York: Pinnacle Books, 1983, 196 p., paper, novel. STARSHIP ORPHEUS #3.
26409 *Cosmic carnage.* New York: Pinnacle Books, 1983, 198 p., paper, novel. STARSHIP ORPHEUS #2.
Return from the dead—SEE: *Starship Orpheus #1.*
26410 *Starship Orpheus #1.* New York: Pinnacle Books, 1982, 181 p., paper, novel. STARSHIP ORPHEUS #1. [Internal half-title: *Return from the dead*].

JADIS, Donna

26411 *The reality barrier.* Baltimore, MD: Marion Catherine McChesney, 1983, 83 p., paper, novel. STAR TREK SERIES.

*JAEGER, C(yril) K(arel Stuart), 1912-

*JAEGER, Muriel, 1893?-

JAFFE, Nora Crow, 1944- , with Patricia L. Skarda

26412 *The evil image: two centuries of gothic short fiction and poetry.* New York: A Meridian Book, New American Library, 1981, xxix + 479 p., paper, anth. [Includes some verse].

*JAFFEE, Irving (Lincoln), 1906-1981

*JAFFEE, Mary (Flora), 1899-1985

JAFFERY, Sheldon (Ronald), 1934-

26413 *The Arkham House companion: fifty years of Arkham House: a bibliographical history and collector's price guide to Arkham House/Mycroft & Moran, including the revised and expanded Horrors and unpleasantries.* Mercer Island, WA: Starmont House, 1989, xv + 184 p., cloth, nonf. STARMONT REFERENCE GUIDE #9. [Incorporates *Horrors and unpleasantries*].
26414 *Future and fantastic worlds: a bibliographical retrospective of DAW Books*

(1972-1987). Mercer Island, WA: Starmont House, 1987, xiii+297 p., cloth, nonf. STARMONT REFERENCE GUIDE #4.

26415 *Horrors and unpleasantries: a bibliographical history & collectors' price guide to Arkham House.* Bowling Green, OH: Bowling Green State University Popular Press, 1982, 142 p., cloth, nonf.

26416 *Selected tales of grim and grue from the horror pulps.* Bowling Green, OH: Bowling Green State University Popular Press, 1987, 195 p., cloth, anth.

26417 *Sensuous science fiction from the weird and spicy pulps* / ed. by Sheldon R. Jaffery. Bowling Green, OH: Bowling Green State University Popular Press, 1984, 164 p., cloth, anth.

26418 *The weirds: a facsimile selection of fiction from the era of the shudder pulps.* Mercer Island, WA: Starmont House, 1987, 173 p., cloth, anth. STARMONT POPULAR CULTURE STUDIES #1.

with Fred Cook

20427 *The collector's guide to Weird tales.* Bowling Green, OH: Bowling Green State University Popular Press, 1985, 162 p., cloth, nonf.

JAGENDORF, M(oritz) A(dolph), 1888-1981

26419 *Tales of mystery.* Morristown, NJ: Silver Burdett Co., 1979, 96 p., cloth, coll.

JAHN, Ernest T(homas), 1936-

26420 *The silent enemy.* New York: Zebra Books, Kensington Publishing Corp., 1980, 220 p., paper, novel.

JAHN, Joseph M.—SEE: Jahn, MIke

JAHN, Michael—SEE: Jahn, Mike

JAHN, Mike [i.e., Joseph Michael Jahn], 1943-

26421 *Armada* / by Michael Jahn. New York: Fawcett Gold Medal, 1981, 221 p., paper, novel.
International incidents—SEE: *The six million dollar man: International incidents.*

26422 *The invisible man* / by Michael Jahn. Greenwich, CT: A Fawcett Gold Medal Book, Fawcett Publications, 1975, 192 p., paper, tele.

26423 *The Olympian strain* / by Michael Jahn. New York: Fawcett Gold Medal, 1980, 221 p., paper, novel.

26424 *The rescue of Athena One: a novel* / by Michael Jahn. New York: Warner Books, 1975, 156 p., paper, tele. SIX MILLION DOLLAR MAN #5.
The secret of Bigfoot Pass—SEE: *The six million dollar man: The secret of Bigfoot Pass.*

26425 *The six million dollar man: International incidents.* New York: A Berkley Medallion Book, Berkley Publishing Corp., 1977, 186 p., paper, tele. SIX MILLION DOLLAR MAN #2.

26426 *The six million dollar man: The secret of Bigfoot Pass.* New York: A Berkley Medallion Book, Berkley Publishing Corp., 1976, 150 p., paper, tele. SIX MILLION DOLLAR MAN SERIES.

26427 *Wine, women, and war: a novel* / by Michael Jahn. New York: Warner Paperback Library, 1975, 158 p., paper, tele. SIX MILLION DOLLAR MAN #1.

as J. D. CAMERON

19235 *City of fear.* New York: Avon Books, 1991, 215 p., paper, novel. OMEGA SUB #3.

19237 *Omega sub.* New York: Avon Books, 1991, 249 p., paper, novel. OMEGA SUB #1.

JAKES, John (William), 1932-

26428 *The best of John Jakes.* New York: DAW Books, 1977, 252 p., paper, coll. [Edited by Martin H. Greenberg and Joseph D. Olander].

26429 *Brak: When the idols walked.* New York: A Kangaroo Book, Pocket Books, 1978, 158 p., paper, novel. BRAK THE BARBARIAN #4.

26430 *The fortunes of Brak.* New York: A Dell Book, 1980, 255 p., paper, coll. BRAK THE BARBARIAN #5.

26431 *Secrets of Stardeep; and, Time gate.* New York: A Signet Book, New American Library, 1982, 153+149 p., paper, coll.
When the idols walked—SEE: *Brak: When the idols walked.*

with Gil Kane

26432 *Excalibur!* New York: A Dell Book, 1980, 509 p., paper, novel.

JAKOBER, Marie, 1941-

26433 *The mind gods: a novel of the future.* Toronto: Macmillan of Canada, 1976, 165 p., cloth, novel.

JAKOBSSON, Ejler, 1911-1986, *as* ANONYMOUS EDITOR

01218   *The best from Galaxy.* New York: Award Books, 1972, 251 p., paper, anth.
01219   *The best from Galaxy, volume II.* New York: Award Books, 1974, 235 p., paper, anth.
01220   *The best from If.* New York: Award Books, 1973, 252 p., paper, anth.
01221   *The best from If, vol. 2.* New York: Award Books, 1974, 235 p., paper, anth.

JAKUBOWSKI, Maxim, 1944-

26434   *Beyond lands of never: a further anthology of modern fantasy.* London: Unwin Paperbacks, 1984, 166 p., paper, anth.
26435   *Lands of never: an anthology of modern fantasy.* London: Unwin Paperbacks, 1983, 167 p., paper, anth.
26436   *Travelling towards epsilon: an anthology of French science fiction.* London: New English Library, 1976, 288 p., cloth, anth. [Translation by Beth Blish and Maxim Jakubowski].
26437   *Twenty houses of the zodiac: an anthology of international science fiction.* London: New English Library, 1979, 237 p., paper, anth.

with Malcolm Edwards

22450   *The complete book of science fiction and fantasy lists.* London, Toronto: Granada, 1983, 350 p., paper, nonf.
22451   retitled: *The SF book of lists.* New York: Berkley Books, 1983, 384 p., paper, nonf. [Expanded edition].
        The SF book of lists—SEE: The complete book of science fiction and fantasy lists.

JALES, Mark

26438   *In his own image.* London: Robert Hale, 1979, 176 p., cloth, novel.
26439   *Normal service will be resumed.* London: Robert Hale, 1980, 224 p., cloth, novel.
26440   *Prelude to exodus.* London: Robert Hale, 1979, 224 p., cloth, novel.

JALESKI, Mary—SEE: Stolz, Mary

JALLIM, Collins

26441   *The Devilgod.* London: Temple House, 1985, 120 p., paper, novel. DEVILGOD #1.
26442   *The Devilgod in the empire of the universal master.* Lewes, East Sussex, England: The Book Guild, 1989, 159 p., cloth, novel. DEVILGOD #2.

JAMERO, Nilo Rodis- —SEE: Rodis-Jamero, Nilo

JAMES, Bernard J.—SEE: James, Dakota

JAMES, Betsy

26443   *Long night dance.* New York: E. P. Dutton, 1989, 170 p., cloth, novel.

JAMES, Dakota [i.e., Bernard Joseph James], 1922-

26444   *Greenhouse: it will happen in 1997.* New York: Donald I. Fine, 1984, 221 p., cloth, novel. GREENHOUSE #1.
26445   *Milwaukee the beautiful.* New York: Donald I. Fine, 1986, 271 p., cloth, novel. GREENHOUSE #2.

JAMES, David, pseud.—SEE: Hagberg, David

JAMES, Donald, 1931-

26447   *The fall of the Russian Empire.* New York: G. P. Putnam's Sons, 1982, 367 p., cloth, novel.

*JAMES, Edward (Frank Willis), 1907-1984

JAMES, Edward (Frederick), 1947-

26448   *Index to Foundation, 1-40.* Dagenham, Essex: Science Fiction Foundation, North East London Polytechnic, 1988, 108 p., paper, nonf.

*JAMES, G(eorge) P(ayne) R(ainsforth), 1799-1860

JAMES, Henry, 1843-1916

26449   *The turn of the screw, and other stories.* London: Everyman Library, J. M. Dent & Sons, 1987, 312 p., paper, coll.

with Diana Stewart

26450   *The turn of the screw.* Milwaukee, WI: Raintree Publishers, 1981, 46 p., cloth, story. [Adapted from James's original story].

with H. G. Wells

26451 *Henry James and H. G. Wells: a record of their friendship, their debate on the art of fiction, and their quarrel.* Urbana, IL: University of Illinois Press, 1958, 272 p., cloth, nonf. coll. [Edited by Leon Edel and Gordon N. Ray].

JAMES, J. Alison

26452 *Sing for a gentle rain.* New York: Atheneum; Toronto: Collier Macmillan Canada; New York: Maxwell Macmillan International Publishing Group, 1990, 211 p., cloth, novel.

JAMES, (David) John

26453 *Men went to Cattraeth.* London: Cassell, 1969, 186 p., cloth, novel. PHOTINUS #3.
26454 *Not for all the gold in Ireland.* London: Cassell, 1968, 281 p., cloth, novel. PHOTINUS #2.

JAMES, L(ana) Dean, 1947-

26455 *Sorcerer's stone.* Lake Geneva, WI: TSR Books, 1991, 312 p., paper, novel.

as LISA DEAN, *with Chris Curry*

20900 *Winter scream.* New York, London: Pocket Books, 1991, 403 p., paper, novel.

JAMES, Laurence, 1942-

Backflash—SEE: *The Rack series: Backflash.*
New life for old—SEE: *Simon Rack: New life for old.*
Planet of the blind—SEE: *The Rack series: Planet of the blind.*
26456 *The Rack series: Backflash.* New York: Pinnacle Books, 1975, 181 p., paper, novel. RACK #3.
26457 *The Rack series: Planet of the blind.* New York: Pinnacle Books, 1975, 150 p., paper, novel. RACK #4.
26458 *Simon Rack: New life for old.* London: Sphere Books, 1975, 142 p., paper, novel. RACK #5.

as JAMES AXLER

Crater Lake—SEE: *Deathlands: Crater Lake.*

26459 *Deathlands: Crater Lake.* Toronto, New York: A Gold Eagle Book from Worldwide, 1987, 250 p., paper, novel. DEATHLANDS #4.
26460 *Deathlands: Dectra chain.* Toronto, New York: A Gold Eagle Book from Worldwide, 1988, 349 p., paper, novel. DEATHLANDS #7.
26461 *Deathlands: Homeward bound.* Toronto, New York: A Gold Eagle Book from Worldwide, 1988, 317 p., paper, novel. DEATHLANDS #5.
26462 *Deathlands: Ice and fire.* Toronto, New York: A Gold Eagle Book from Worldwide, 1988, 349 p., paper, novel. DEATHLANDS #8.
26463 *Deathlands: Latitude zero.* Toronto, New York: A Gold Eagle Book from Worldwide, 1991, 349 p., paper, novel. DEATHLANDS #12.
26464 *Deathlands: Neutron solstice.* Toronto, New York: A Gold Eagle Book from Worldwide, 1987, 252 p., paper, novel. DEATHLANDS #3.
26465 *Deathlands: Northstar rising.* Toronto, New York: A Gold Eagle Book from Worldwide, 1989, 346 p., paper, novel. DEATHLANDS #10.
26466 *Deathlands: Pony soldiers.* Toronto, New York: A Gold Eagle Book from Worldwide, 1988, 348 p., paper, novel. DEATHLANDS #6.
26467 *Deathlands: Red equinox.* Toronto, New York: A Gold Eagle Book from Worldwide, 1989, 299 p., paper, novel. DEATHLANDS #9.
26468 *Deathlands: Red holocaust.* Toronto, New York: A Gold Eagle Book from Worldwide, 1986, 251 p., paper, novel. DEATHLANDS #2.
26469 *Deathlands: Seedling.* Toronto, New York: A Gold Eagle Book from Worldwide, 1991, 349 p., paper, novel. DEATHLANDS #13.
26470 *Deathlands: Time nomads.* Toronto, New York: A Gold Eagle Book from Worldwide, 1990, 348 p., paper, novel. DEATHLANDS #11.
Dectra chain—SEE: *Deathlands: Dectra chain.*
Homeward bound—SEE: *Deathlands: Homeward bound.*
Ice and fire—SEE: *Deathlands: Ice and fire.*
Latitude zero—SEE: *Deathlands: Latitude zero.*
Neutron solstice—SEE: *Deathlands: Neutron solstice.*
Northstar rising—SEE: *Deathlands: Northstar rising.*

Pony soldiers—SEE: *Deathlands: Pony soldiers.*

Red equinox—SEE: *Deathlands: Red equinox.*

Red holocaust—SEE: *Deathlands: Red holocaust.*

Seedling—SEE: *Deathlands: Seedling.*

Time nomads—SEE: *Deathlands: Time nomads.*

as JAMES DARKE

26471 *The escape.* London: Sphere Books, 1984, [160] p., paper, novel. WITCHES #4.

26472 *The feud.* London: Sphere Books, 1986, 160 p., paper, novel. WITCHES #7.

26473 *The plague.* London: Sphere Books, 1986, 160 p., paper, novel. WITCHES #8.

26474 *The prisoner.* London: Sphere Books, 1983, [160] p., paper, novel. WITCHES #1.

26475 *The torture.* London: Sphere Books, 1983, [160] p., paper, novel. WITCHES #3.

26476 *The trial.* London: Sphere Books, 1983, [160] p., paper, novel. WITCHES #2.

26477 *The witches 5*: [title unknown]. London: Sphere Books, 1984?, [160] p., paper, novel. WITCHES #5.

26478 *The witches 6*: [title unknown]. London: Sphere Books, 1985?, [160] p., paper, novel. WITCHES #6.

JAMES, M(ontague) R(hodes), 1862-1936

The book of ghost stories—SEE: *Book of the supernatural.*

26479 *Book of the supernatural.* London, New York: Foulsham, 1979, 128 p., cloth, coll. [Edited by Peter Haining].

26479A retitled: *The book of ghost stories.* New York: Stein & Day, 1982, 128 p., cloth, coll. [Edited by Peter Haining].

26480 *Casting the runes, and other ghost stories.* Oxford, England: Oxford University Press, 1987, xxxviii+352 p., paper, coll. [Edited by Michael Cox].

07815 *The collected ghost stories of M. R. James.* London: Edward Arnold, 1931, 647 p., cloth, coll.

07815B retitled: *The Penguin complete ghost stories of M. R. James.* Harmondsworth, Middlesex, England: Penguin Books, 1984, 361 p., paper, coll.

26481 *The Ghost stories of M. R. James.* Oxford, England, New York: Oxford University Press, 1986, 224 p., cloth, coll. [Edited by Michael Cox].

26482 *M. R. James.* UK: British Fantasy Society, 1987, 24 p., paper, coll. MASTERS OF FANTASY #3. [Edited by Richard Dalby].

The Penguin complete ghost stories of M. R. James—SEE: *The complete ghost stories of M. R. James.*

26483 *Some remarks on ghost stories.* Edinburgh, Scotland: Tragara Press, 1985, 12 p., paper, nonf. [Limited to 115 copies].

37874 *Wailing well.* Stanford Dingley, Berkshire, England: The Mill House Press, 1928, 20 p., cloth, story. [Limited to 157 copies].

26484 *A warning to the curious: the ghost stories of M. R. James.* London: Hutchinson, 1987, xiv+257 p., cloth, coll. [Edited by Ruth Rendell].

JAMES, Martin, pseud.—SEE: Kisner, James

JAMES, Mary (Elliott), 1927-

26485 *Shoebag.* New York, Toronto: Scholastic Inc., 1990, 135 p., cloth, novel.

JAMES, Paul

26486 *Rogan.* London: A Moat Hall Book, Magread Ltd., 1980, 112 p., paper, novel.

JAMES, Peter, 1948-

26487 *Biggles: the untold story.* Harmondsworth, Middlesex, England: Piccolo, 1986, 48 p., paper, nonf.

26488 *Dreamer.* London: Victor Gollancz, 1989, 319 p., cloth, novel.

26489 *Possession.* London: Victor Gollancz, 1988, 282 p., cloth, novel.

26490 *Sweet heart.* London: Victor Gollancz, 1990, 278 p., cloth, novel.

26491 *Twilight.* London: Victor Gollancz, 1991, 316 p., cloth, novel.

JAMES, Philip, pseud.—SEE: Cawthorn, James

JAMES, R. Alan

26492 *No news from Providence.* London: Robert Hale, 1978, 173 p., cloth, novel.

JAMES, Robert

26493 *Blood mist.* New York: Leisure Books, 1987, 365 p., paper, novel.

JAMES, Susan, *with Carol Frisbie*

23548 *Night visions.* Arlington, VA: Pulsar Press, 1979, p., paper, tele. STAR TREK SERIES.

JAMES, Valerie

26494 *Bewitching beloved.* North Hollywood, CA: American Art Enterprises, 1981, 160 p., paper, novel.

*JAMESON, (Margaret) Storm, 1891-1986

JAMIESON, Evan, *with Lisa Hunt & Walter Hunt & Richard S. Meyer & Bill Scammell & Mark Bloom & Christine Ivey as* ARCHITECTS ADVENTURE

18216 *Dzurlord: a Crossroads adventure in the world of Steven Brust's Jhereg* / by Architects Adventure. New York: Tor, A Tom Doherty Associates Book, 1987, 24+[224] p., paper, novel. JHEREG SERIES; CROSSROADS ADVENTURE.

JANESHUTZ, Trish [i.e., Patricia Marie Janeshutz MacGregor], 1947-

26495 *Hidden Lake.* New York: Ballantine Books, 1988, 309 p., paper, novel.

as T. J. MacGregor

26496 *Kin dread.* New York: Ballantine Books, 1990, 309 p., paper, novel.

JANIFER, Laurence M(ark), 1933-

26497 *Knave & the game: a collection of short stories.* Garden City, NY: Doubleday & Co., 1987, xii+173 p., cloth, coll. GERALD KNAVE #3.
26498 *Knave in hand.* New York: Ace Books, 1979, 216 p., paper, novel. GERALD KNAVE #2.
26499 *Reel.* Garden City, NY: Doubleday & Co., 1983, 186 p., cloth, novel.
26500 *Survivor.* New York: Ace Books, 1977, xvi+172 p., paper, novel. GERALD KNAVE #1.

JANOWIAK, Jean Brooks- —SEE: Brooks-Janowiak, Jean

JANSON, Hank, house pseud.—SEE: Frances, Stephen

JANSSON, Tove (Marika), 1914-

26501 *Comet in Moominland.* London: Ernest Benn, 1951, 191 p., cloth, novel. FINN FAMILY MOOMINTROLL #2. [Translation by Elizabeth Portch of *Kometjakten*].
26502 *The exploits of Moominpappa.* London: Ernest Benn, 1952, 156 p., cloth, novel. FINN FAMILY MOOMINTROLL #3. [Translation by Thomas Warburton].
26503 *Finn family Moomintroll.* London: Ernest Benn, 1950, 170 p., cloth, novel. FINN FAMILY MOOMINTROLL #1. [Translation by Elizabeth Portch of *Trollkarlens hatt*].
26503A retitled: *The happy Moomins.* Indianapolis: Bobbs-Merrill Co., 1952, 192 p., cloth, novel. FINN FAMILY MOOMINTROLL #1. [Translation by Elizabeth Portch of *Trollkarlens hatt*].
   The happy Moomins—SEE: *Finn family Moomintroll.*
26504 *Moomin Valley in November.* London: Ernest Benn, 1971, 158 p., cloth, novel. FINN FAMILY MOOMINTROLL #8. [Translation by Kingsley Hart of *Sent: November*].
26505 *Moominland midwinter.* London: Ernest Benn, 1958, 165 p., cloth, novel. FINN FAMILY MOOMINTROLL #5. [Translation by Thomas Warburton of *Trollvinter*].
26506 *Moominpappa at sea.* London: Ernest Benn, 1966, 192 p., cloth, novel. FINN FAMILY MOOMINTROLL #7. [Translation by Kingsley Hart].
26507 *Moominsummer madness.* London: Ernest Benn, 1955, [144] p., cloth, novel. FINN FAMILY MOOMINTROLL #4. [Translation by Thomas Warburton of *Farlig midsommar*].
26508 *Tales from Moominvalley.* New York: Henry Z. Walck; London: Ernest Benn, 1964, 175 p., cloth, coll. FINN FAMILY MOOMINTROLL #6. [Translation by Thomas Warburton].

JANVIER, Thomas A(llibone), 1849-1913

37875 *The women's conquest of New-York: being an account of the rise and progress of the women's rights movement* / by a member of the Committee of Safety of 1908. New York: Harper & Brothers, 1953 (i.e., 1894), 84 p., cloth, story.

JARMAN, Julia

26509 *Ollie and the bogle.* London: Andersen Press, 1987, 135 p., cloth, novel.

*JARRETT, Cora (Hardy), 1877-1969

JARRETT, David

26510 *The gothic form in fiction and its relation to history.* Winchester, England: King Alfred's College, 1980, 35 p., paper, nonf.
26511 *Witherwing.* London: Sphere Books, 1979, 140 p., paper, novel.

JARRY, Alfred, 1873-1907

37876 *The supermale: a modern novel.* London: Jonathan Cape, 1968, 126 p., cloth, novel. [Translation by Barbara Wright of *Le surmâle*].

JARVIE, Clodagh Gibson- —SEE: Gibson-Jarvie, Clodagh

JARVIS, Edward

26512 *Maggots.* London: Arrow Books, 1986, 235 p., paper, novel.

JARVIS, Mike, *with John Spencer*

26513 *Echoes of terror.* London: Hamlyn, 1980, 96 p., cloth, anth.

JARVIS, Robin

26514 *The alchymist's cat.* London: Macdonald & Co., 1991, 330 p., cloth, novel. DEPTFORD HISTORIES #1.
26515 *The crystal prison.* London: Macdonald & Co., 1989, 261 p., cloth, novel. DEPTFORD MICE #2.
26516 *The dark portal.* London: Purnell, 1989, 243 p., cloth, novel. DEPTFORD MICE #1.
26517 *The final reckoning.* London: Simon & Schuster, 1990, xiv+305 p., cloth, novel. DEPTFORD MICE #3.
26518 *The Whitby witches.* London: Sprint, Simon & Schuster, 1991, ix+276 p., cloth, novel.

JARVIS, Sharon (Sylvia), 1943-

26519 *Inside outer space: science fiction professionals look at their craft.* New York: Frederick Ungar Publishing Co., 1985, viii+148 p., cloth, nonf. anth.

with Kathleen Buckley as H. M. MAJOR

18894 *The alien trace.* New York: A Signet Book, New American Library, 1984, 222 p., paper, novel. ALIEN TRACE #1.

18895 *Time twister.* New York: A Signet Book, New American Library, 1984, 255 p., paper, novel. ALIEN TRACE #2.

with Marcia Yvonne Howl as JOHANNA HAILEY

26067 *Beloved paradise.* New York: Zebra Books, Kensington Publishing Corp., 1987, 479 p., paper, novel.
26068 *Crystal paradise.* New York: Zebra Books, Kensington Publishing Corp., 1986, 477 p., paper, novel.
26069 *Enchanted paradise.* New York: Zebra Books, Kensington Publishing Corp., 1985, 525 p., paper, novel.

with Ellen M. Kozak as JARROD COMSTOCK

26520 *The love machine.* New York: Pinnacle Books, 1984, 231 p., paper, novel. THESE LAWLESS WORLDS #1. [Jarvis provided concept and outline].
26521 *Scales of justice.* New York: Pinnacle Books, 1984, 233 p., paper, novel. THESE LAWLESS WORLDS #2. [Jarvis provided concept and outline].

JASON, Jerry, pseud.—SEE: Smith, George H.

JATUES, Ayresome, pseud.—SEE: Locke, George

JAVNA, John

26522 *The best of science fiction TV: the critics' choice from Captain Video to Star Trek, from The Jetsons to Robotech.* New York: Harmony Books, 1987, 144 p., paper, nonf.

JAVOR, Frank A. [pseud. of Francis Anthony Jaworski], 1916-

26523 *The ice beast.* New York: DAW Books, 1990, 224 p., paper, novel. ELI PIKE #3.
26524 *The Rim-world legacy and beyond.* New York: DAW Books, 1991, 253 p., paper, coll. ELI PIKE #1. [Includes *The Rim-World legacy* (see #07860) and two additional stories].
26525 *Scor-sting.* New York: DAW Books, 1990, 223 p., paper, novel. ELI PIKE #2.

JAWORSKI, Francis—SEE: Javor, Frank A.

JAY, Peter, 1937- , *with Michael Stewart*

26526 *Apocalypse 2000: economic breakdown and the suicide of democracy, 1989-2000.* London: Sidgwick & Jackson, 1987, ix +253 p., cloth, fiction. [Includes some nonf.].

JEEVES, (Byron) Terry, 1922-

26527 *Duplicating notes.* Sheffield, England: Terry Jeeves, 1977, [63] p., paper, nonf.

with Mike Ashley

16857 *The complete index to Astounding/Analog: being an index to the 50 years of Astounding stories—Astounding SF & Analog: January 1930-December 1979, together with the Analog annual, the Analog yearbook, & the John W. Campbell memorial anthology.* Oak Forest, IL: Robert Weinberg Publications, 1981, 253 p., cloth, nonf.

JEFFERIES, Mike

26528 *Glitterspike Hall.* London: Fontana, 1989, 41? p., paper, novel. HEIRS TO GNARLS' YRE #1.
26529 *Hall of w. spers.* London: Fontana, 1990, 414 p. paper, novel. HEIRS TO GNARLS MYRE #2.
26530 *Palace of kings.* London: Collins, 1987, 314 p., cloth, novel. LOREMASTERS OF ELUNDIUM #2.
26531 *The road to Underfall.* London: Fontana, 1986, 349 p., paper, novel. LOREMASTERS OF ELUNDIUM #1.
26532 *Shadowlight.* London: Fontana, 1988, 346 p., paper, novel. LOREMASTERS OF ELUNDIUM #3.
26533 *Shadows in the watchgate.* London: Grafton, 1991, 368 p., paper, novel.

JEFFERIES, (John) Richard, 1848-1887

37877 *Bevis: the story of a boy.* London: Sampson Low, Marston, Searle & Rivington, 1882, 3 v., cloth, novel. BEVIS #2.
Sir Bevis: a tale of the fields—SEE: *Wood magic.*
07868 *Wood magic: a fable.* London: Cassell, 1881, 2 v., cloth, novel. BEVIS #1.
07868A retitled: *Sir Bevis: a tale of the fields: ad adaptation of Wood magic.* Boston: Ginn & Co., 1899, xiv +129 p., cloth, novel. BEVIS #1. [Edited by Eliza J. Kelley; abridged edition].

JEFFERS, H(arry) Paul, 1934-

26534 *Secret orders.* New York: Zebra Books, Kensington Publishing Corp., 1989, 352 p., paper, novel.

JEFFERY, G(raham?)

26536 *Erinord.* London: Rex Collings, 1976, 247 p., cloth, novel.

JEFFRIES, Graham—SEE: Graeme, Bruce

JELLOUN, Tahar ben—SEE: ben Jalloun, Tahar

JENKIN, Len

26537 *New Jerusalem.* Los Angeles: Sun & Moon Press, 1986, 214 p., cloth, novel.

JENKINS, Geoffrey, 1920-

26538 *Hold down a shadow.* London: Collins, 1989, 309 p., cloth, novel.

JENKINS, Harry

26539 *An affair of survival: a novel.* New York, Washington: Vantage Press, 1979, 109 p., cloth, novel.

JENKINS, Will F.—SEE: Leinster, Murray

JENNER, Janann V.

26540 *Sandeagozu: a novel.* New York: Harper & Row, 1986, 442 p., cloth, novel.

JENNINGS, Gary—SEE: Quyth, Gabriel

JENNINGS, Jan

26541 *Vampyr.* New York: A Tom Doherty Associates Book, 1981, 304 p., paper, novel.

JENNINGS, Phillip C(harles), 1946-

26542 *The bug life chronicles.* New York: Baen Books, 1989, 304 p., paper, coll.
26543 *Tower to the sky.* New York: Baen Books, 1988, 316 p., paper, novel.

JENNISON, John W(illiam), d. 1969?

as MATTHEW C. BRADFORD

01782 *Invasion from space.* London: Atlantic Book Co., 1954, 128 p., paper, novel.

as GEORGE SHELDON BROWNE

01980 *The yellow planet.* London: Edwin Self, 1954, 100 p., paper, novel.

as EDGAR REES KENNEDY

08163 *Conquerors of Venus*. London: Edwin Self, 1951, 128 p., paper, novel.

08164 *The mystery planet*. London: Edwin Self, 1952, 128 p., paper, novel.

as JOHN THEYDON

14045 *The Angels and the creeping enemy*. London: Armada, 1968, 125 p., paper, tele.

14046 *Calling Thunderbirds*. London: Armada, 1966, 125 p., paper, tele. THUNDERBIRDS #2.

Captain Scarlet—SEE: *Captain Scarlet and the Mysterons.*

14047 *Captain Scarlet and the Mysterons*. London: Armada, 1967, 128 p., paper, tele. CAPTAIN SCARLET #1.

14047A retitled: *Captain Scarlet*. London: Titan, 1989, 119 p., paper, tele. CAPTAIN SCARLET #1.

14048 *Captain Scarlet and the silent saboteur*. London: Armada, 1967, 128 p., paper, tele. CAPTAIN SCARLET #2.

14049 *Lady Penelope: The Albanian affair*. London: Armada, 1967, 128 p., paper, tele. THUNDERBIRDS #5.

14050 *Stingray*. London: Armada, 1965, 157 p., paper, tele. STINGRAY #1.

14051 *Stingray and the monster*. London: Armada, 1966, 125 p., paper, tele. STINGRAY #2.

14052 *Thunderbirds*. London: Armada, 1966, 126 p., paper, tele. THUNDERBIRDS #1.

14053 *Thunderbirds: Ring of fire*. London: Armada, 1966, 125 p., paper, tele. THUNDERBIRDS #3.

JENSEN, Ejner J(acob), 1937-

26544 *The future of Nineteen eighty-four*. Ann Arbor, MI: University of Michigan Press, 1984, viii+209 p., cloth, nonf. anth.

JENSEN, Kris(tine Marie), 1953-

26545 *FreeMaster*. New York: DAW Books, 1990, 285 p., paper, novel. ARDEL #1.

26546 *Mentor*. New York: DAW Books, 1991, 332 p., paper, novel. ARDEL #2.

JENSEN, Paul M(orris), 1944-

26547 *Boris Karloff and his films*. South Brunswick, NJ: A. S. Barnes & Co., 1974, 194 p., cloth?, nonf.

JENSEN, Ruby Jean

26548 *Annabelle*. New York: Zebra Books, Kensington Publishing Corp., 1987, 332 p., paper, novel.

26549 *Baby doll*. New York: Zebra Books, Kensington Publishing Corp., 1991, 477 p., paper, novel.

26550 *Best friends*. New York: Zebra Books, Kensington Publishing Corp., 1985, 318 p., paper, novel.

26551 *Celia*. New York: Zebra Books, Kensington Publishing Corp., 1991, 351 p., paper, novel.

26552 *Chain letter*. New York: Zebra Books, Kensington Publishing Corp., 1987, 382 p., paper, novel.

26553 *Dark angel*. New York: Manor Books, 1978, 302 p., paper, novel.

26554 *Death stone*. New York: Zebra Books, Kensington Publishing Corp., 1989, 315 p., paper, novel.

26555 *The girl who didn't die*. New York: Warner Paperback Library, 1975, 254 p., paper, novel.

26556 *House of illusions*. New York: Zebra Books, Kensington Publishing Corp., 1988, 384 p., paper, novel.

26557 *Jump rope*. New York: Zebra Books, Kensington Publishing Corp., 1988, 383 p., paper, novel.

26558 *The lake* / by R. J. Jensen. New York: Tor, A Tom Doherty Associates Book, 1983, 320 p., paper, novel.

26559 *Lost and found*. New York: Zebra Books, Kensington Publishing Corp., 1990, 320 p., paper, novel.

26560 *MaMa*. New York: Zebra Books, Kensington Publishing Corp., 1983, 303 p., paper, novel.

26561 *Pendulum*. New York: Zebra Books, Kensington Publishing Corp., 1989, 349 p., paper, novel.

26562 *Satan's sister*. Canoga Park, CA: Major Books, 1978 (i.e., 1979?), 160 p., paper, novel.

26563 *Smoke*. New York: Zebra Books, Kensington Publishing Corp., 1988, 366 p., paper, novel.

26564 *Such a good baby: a novel of horror*. New York: Tor, A Tom Doherty Associates Book, 1982, 319 p., paper, novel.

26565 *Vampire child*. New York: Zebra Books, Kensington Publishing Corp., 1990, 285 p., paper, novel.

26566 *Victoria*. New York: Zebra Books, Kensington Publishing Corp., 1990, 352 p., paper, novel.

26567 *Wait and see*. New York: Zebra Books, Kensington Publishing Corp., 1986, 350 p., paper, novel.

JENSON, Martin

26568 *The echo on the stairs.* London: New English Library, 1977, 125 p., paper, novel.
26569 *An odour of decay.* London: New English Library, 1975, 126 p., paper, novel.

JEPPSON, J. O., pseud.—SEE: Asimov, Janet Jeppson

JERGENS, Phillip

26570 *The biota risk.* North Hollywood, CA: American Art Enterprises, 1980, 190 p., paper, novel.

JEROME, Jerome K(lapka), 1859-1927

26571 *After supper ghost stories, and other tales.* Gloucester, England: Alan Sutton, 1985, 175 p., paper, coll.

JERSILD, P(er) C(hristian), 1935-

26572 *After the flood: a novel.* New York: William Morrow & Co., 1986, 251 p., cloth, novel. [Translation by Löne Thygesen Blecher & George Blecher of *Efter floden*].
26573 *A living soul.* Norwich, England: Norvik Press, 1988, 211 p., cloth, novel. [Translation by Rika Lesser of *En levande själ*].

JERVIS, Tabitha, pseud.

26574 *Satan's mistress.* New York: Star Distributors, 1977, 180 p., paper, novel.

JESCHKE, Wolfgang, 1936-

26575 *The last day of creation.* New York: St. Martin's Press, 1982, 222 p., cloth, novel. [Translation by Gertrud Mander of *Der letzte tag der Schopfüng*].
26576 *Midas.* Sevenoaks, Kent, England: New English Library, 1990, 222 p., paper, novel. [Translation by the author of *Midas*].

JETER, K(evin) W., 1950-

26577 *Dark seeker.* New York: Tor Horror, A Tom Doherty Associates Book, 1987, 317 p., paper, novel.
26578 *Death arms.* Bath, Avon, England: Morrigan, 1987, 183 p., cloth, novel. DR. ADDER #3.

26579 *Dr. Adder.* New York: Bluejay Books, 1984, 231 p., cloth, novel. DR. ADDER #1.
26580 *The dreamfields.* Toronto, New York: Laser Books, 1976, 190 p., paper, novel.
26581 *Farewell horizontal.* New York: St. Martin's Press, 1989, 249 p., cloth, novel. CYLINDER TRILOGY #1.
26582 *The glass hammer.* New York: Bluejay Books, 1985, 248 p., paper, novel. DR. ADDER #2.
26583 *In the land of the dead.* Scotforth, Lancashire, England: Morrigan Publications, 1989, 215 p., cloth, novel. [The special edition is limited to 300 copies, and includes added essays by Charles de Lint and Ramsey Campbell; the trade edition contains 204 p.].
26584 *Infernal devices: a mad Victorian fantasy.* New York: A Bluejay Book, St. Martin's Press, 1987, 282 p., cloth, novel.
26585 *Madlands.* New York: St. Martin's Press, 1991, 247 p., cloth, novel.
26586 *Mantis.* New York: Tor Horror, A Tom Doherty Associates Book, 1987, 281 p., paper, novel.
26587 *Morlock night.* New York: DAW Books, 1979, 156 p., paper, novel. TIME MACHINE SEQUEL.
26588 *The night man.* New York: An Onyx Book, New American Library, 1990, 283 p., paper, novel.
26589 *Seeklight.* Don Mills, Ontario, Canada: Laser Books, 1975, 192 p., paper, novel.
26590 *Soul eater.* New York: Tor, A Tom Doherty Associates Book, 1983, 314 p., paper, novel.

as DR ADDER, with Mink Mole (i.e., William Gibson)

23910 *Alligator Alley.* Scotforth, Lancashire, England: Morrigan Publications, 1989, 295 p., cloth, novel.

JEURY, Michel [pseud. of Albert Higon?], 1934-

26591 *Chronolysis.* New York: Macmillan Publishing Co., 1980, x+211 p., cloth, novel. [Translation by Maxim Jakubowski of *Le temps incertain*].

JOELS, Kerry Mark, 1931-

26592 *The Mars One crew manual.* New York: Ballantine Books, 1985, [160] p., cloth, fiction.

JOG, D(attatreya) V(ishnu), 1922-

26593 *Aldous Huxley the novelist.* Bombay: Book Centre, 1963?, xiii+152 p., cloth, nonf.

JOHANSEN, Iris, 1938-

26594 *The forever dream.* Toronto, New York: Bantam Books, 1985, 309 p., paper, novel.

JOHN, Anthony, pseud.—SEE: DeStefano, Anthony & Lettell, John S.

JOHN, Colin, pseud.—SEE: Hagan, Chet

JOHNS, Norma N., pseud.

26595 *Bodoman of Sor.* Dagenham, Essex, England: British Fantasy Society, 1977?, [20] p., paper, story. GOR PARODY.

JOHN, Owen—SEE: Bourne, John

*JOHNS, W(illiam) E(arle), 1893-1968

*JOHNS, Willy [pseud. of Willy John Meeker]

JOHNSEN, Trevor Meldal- —SEE: Meldal-Johnsen, Trevor

JOHNSON, Annabel(l Jones), 1921-

26596 *I am Leaper.* New York, Toronto: Scholastic Book Services, 1990, 105 p., cloth, novel.

with Edgar Johnson

26597 *An alien music.* New York: Four Winds Press, 1982, 184 p., cloth, novel.
26598 *The danger quotient.* New York: Harper & Row, Publishers, 1984, 216 p., cloth, novel.
26599 *A memory of dragons.* New York: Argo, Atheneum, 1986, 170 p., cloth, novel.
26600 *Prisoner of psi.* New York: Argo, Atheneum, 1985, 149 p., cloth, novel.

JOHNSON, Barbara Ferry, 1923-

26601 *Lionors.* New York: Avon, 1975, x+291 p., paper, novel.

JOHNSON, Charles (Richard), 1948-

26602 *Pieces of eight.* Atlanta, GA: Discovery Press, 1988, 110 p., cloth, novel.

26603 *The sorcerer's apprentice.* New York: Atheneum, 1986, 169 p., cloth, coll.

JOHNSON, Denis, 1949-

26604 *Fiskadoro.* New York: Alfred A. Knopf, 1985, 221 p., cloth, novel.

*JOHNSON, Dorothy (Marie), 1905-1984

JOHNSON, E. M.—SEE: Markwick, Edward

JOHNSON, Edgar (Raymond), 1912- , *with Annabel Johnson*

26597 *An alien music.* New York: Four Winds Press, 1982, 184 p., cloth, novel.
26598 *The danger quotient.* New York: Harper & Row, Publishers, 1984, 216 p., cloth, novel.
26599 *A memory of dragons.* New York: Argo, Atheneum, 1986, 170 p., cloth, novel.
26600 *Prisoner of psi.* New York: Argo, Atheneum, 1985, 149 p., cloth, novel.

JOHNSON, Edwin C.—SEE: Johnson, Toby

JOHNSON, Eyvind [pseud. of Eyvind Olof Werner], 1900-1976

26605 *Dreams of roses and fire.* New York: Hippocrene Books, xvi+384 p., cloth, novel. [Translation by Erik J. Friis of *Drömmar om rosor och eld*].

JOHNSON, Forrest B.—SEE: Johnson, Frosty

*JOHNSON, Frosty [i.e., Forrest Bryant Johnson], 1935-

JOHNSON, George Clayton, 1929-

26606 *Scripts and stories written for "The twilight zone".* San Diego, CA: A Shroud Limited Edition, Valcour & Krueger, 1977, viii+185 leaves, paper, coll. [Limited to 100 copies].
26607 *Writing for The Twilight Zone.* Sacramento, CA: Outré House, 1980, ii+130 p., cloth, coll. [Includes four telescripts with commentary].

with William F. Nolan

26608 *Logan: a trilogy.* Baltimore, MD: Maclay & Associates, 1986, 384 p., cloth, coll. LOGAN #1-3.

JOHNSON, James B(lair), 1944-

26609 *Daystar and Shadow.* New York: DAW Books, 1981, 206 p., paper, novel.
26610 *Habu.* New York: DAW Books, 1989, 315 p., paper, novel.
26611 *Mindhopper.* New York: DAW Books, 1988, 269 p., paper, novel.
26612 *Trekmaster.* New York: DAW Books, 1987, 397 p., paper, novel.
26613 *A world lost.* New York: DAW Books, 1991, 316 p., paper, novel.

JOHNSON, Judith A(nne)

26614 *J. R. R. Tolkien: six decades of criticism.* Westport, CT & London: Greenwood Press, 1986, viii+266 p., cloth, nonf.

JOHNSON, Kenneth R(ayner)

26615 *The cheshire cat.* New York: A Dell/Banbury Book, 1983, 327 p., paper, novel.
  Dracula's dog—SEE: *Zoltan, hound of Dracula.*
  Hounds of Dracula—SEE: *Zoltan, hound of Dracula.*
26616 *The succubus* / by Kenneth Rayner Johnson. London: Blond & Briggs, 1979, 249 p., cloth, novel.
26617 *Zoltan, hound of Dracula.* London: Everest Books, 1977, 160 p., paper, movie.
26617A retitled: *Hounds of Dracula: a novel.* New York: A Signet Book, New American Library, 1977, 170 p., paper, movie.
26617B retitled: *Dracula's dog: a novel.* New York: A Signet Book, New American Library, 1978, 170 p., paper, movie.

JOHNSON, Kenneth R(oss), 1948-

with Jerry Boyajian

18374 *Index to the science fiction magazines 1977.* Cambridge, MA: Twaci Press, 1982, 28 p., paper, nonf.
18375 *Index to the science fiction magazines 1978.* Cambridge, MA: Twaci Press, 1982, 28 p., paper, nonf.
18376 *Index to the science fiction magazines 1979.* Cambridge, MA: Twaci Press, 1981, 32 p., paper, nonf.
18377 *Index to the science fiction magazines 1980.* Cambridge, MA: Twaci Press, 1981, 27 p., paper, nonf.
18378 *Index to the science fiction magazines 1981.* Cambridge, MA: Twaci Press, 1982, 32 p., paper, nonf.
18379 *Index to the science fiction magazines 1982.* Cambridge, MA: Twaci Press, 1983, 35 p., paper, nonf.
18380 *Index to the science fiction magazines, 1983.* Cambridge, MA: Twaci Press, 1984, 31 p., paper, nonf.
18381 *Index to the science fiction magazines, 1984.* Cambridge, MA: Twaci Press, 1985, 31 p., paper, nonf.
18382 *Index to the science fiction magazines 1985.* Cambridge, MA: Twaci Press, 1985, 31 p., paper, nonf.
18383 *Index to the semi-professional fantasy magazines, 1982.* Cambridge, MA: Twaci Press, 1983, 27 p., paper, nonf. [First in series.]
18384 *Index to the semi-professional magazines, 1983.* Cambridge, MA: Twaci Press, 1984, 27 p., paper, nonf.

with Hal W. Hall & George Michaels

25035 *The science fiction magazines: a bibliographical checklist of titles and issues through 1983.* Bryan, TX: SFBRI, 1983, iv+89 p., paper, nonf.

JOHNSON, Merle (De Vore), 1874-1935

26618 *A bibliographic check-list of the works of James Branch Cabell, 1904-1921.* New York: F. Shay, 1921, 27 p., paper, nonf.

JOHNSON, Niel M(elvin), 1931-

26619 *George Sylvester Viereck, German-American propagandist.* Urbana, Chicago, IL: University of Illinois Press, 1972, x+282 p., cloth, nonf.

JOHNSON, Norma Tadlock

26620 *Bats on the bedstead.* Boston: Houghton Mifflin Co., 1987, 116 p., cloth, novel.
26621 *The witch house.* New York: An Avon Camelot Book, 1990, 139 p., paper, novel.

JOHNSON, Oliver, 1957-

26622 *Curse of the Pharaoh.* London: Dragon Books, 1985, [172] p., paper, novel. GOLDEN DRAGON FANTASY GAMEBOOK #5.
26623 *The eleven crystals.* London: Corgi Books, 1985, 185 p., paper, novel. DRAGON WARRIORS #3.
26624 *The lord of Shadow Keep.* London: Dragon Books, 1985, [158] p., paper,

novel. GOLDEN DRAGON FANTASY GAMEBOOKS #3.

26625 *The power of darkness.* London: Corgi Books, 1986, 190 p., paper, novel. DRAGON WARRIORS #5.

with Dave Morris

26626 *Blood sword.* Sevenoaks, Kent, England: New English Library, 1987, 299 p., paper, novel. BLOOD SWORD #1.

26627 *The demon's claw.* Sevenoaks, Kent, England: Knight, 1987, 390 p., paper, fiction. BLOOD SWORD #3.

26628 *Doomwalk.* Sevenoaks, Kent, England: Knight, 1988, p., paper, fiction. BLOOD SWORD #4.

26629 *The kingdom of Wyrd.* Sevenoaks, Kent, England: Knight Books, 1987, 330 p., paper, novel. BLOOD SWORD #2.

26630 *The temple of flame.* London: Dragon Books, 1984, [188] p., paper, novel. GOLDEN DRAGON FANTASY GAMEBOOKS #2.

with Dave Morris & Jamie Thomson

26631 *The walls of Spyte.* London: Knight, 1988, 313 p., paper, novel.

JOHNSON, (Walter) Ryerson, 1901- , with Lester Dent as KENNETH ROBESON

04143 *The fantastic island: a Doc Savage adventure.* Toronto, New York: Bantam Books, 1966, 135 p., paper, novel. DOC SAVAGE #14.

04155 *Land of always-night: a Doc Savage adventure.* Toronto, New York: Bantam Books, 1966, 138 p., paper, novel. DOC SAVAGE #13.

04170 *The motion menace: a Doc Savage adventure.* Toronto, New York: Bantam Books, 1971, 123 p., paper, novel. DOC SAVAGE #64.

JOHNSON, Seddon

26632 *Alien, go home!* New York, Toronto: An R. A. Montgomery Book, Bantam Books, 1990, 113 p., paper, novel. CHOOSE YOUR OWN ADVENTURE #101.

26633 *South Pole sabotage.* Toronto, New York: An R. A. Montgomery Book, Bantam Books, 1989, 113 p., paper, novel. CHOOSE YOUR OWN ADVENTURE #89.

JOHNSON, Shane (Thomas), 1959-

Mr. Scott's guide to the Enterprise—SEE: *Star Trek: Mr. Scott's guide to the Enterprise.*

26634 *Star Trek: Mr. Scott's guide to the Enterprise.* New York: Pocket Books, 1987, 125 p., paper, fiction.

26635 *Star Trek: The worlds of the Federation.* New York: Pocket Books, 1989, 155 p., paper, fiction.

The worlds of the Federation—SEE: *Star Trek: The worlds of the Federation.*

JOHNSON, Toby [i.e., Edwin Clark Johnson], 1945-

26636 *Plague: a novel about healing.* Boston: Alyson Publications, 1987, 250 p., paper, novel.

26637 *Secret matter.* South Norwalk, CT: Lavender Press, 1990, 200 p., paper, novel.

JOHNSON, Todd

26638 *Combat command in the world of David Drake's Hammer's Slammers: Slammers down!* New York: Ace Books, 1988, xiv+203 p., paper, novel. COMBAT COMMAND #4.

Slammers down! SEE: *Combat command in the world of David Drake's Hammer's Slammers: Slammers down!*

JOHNSON, Tom, with Will Murray

26639 *Secret Agent X: a history.* Oak Forest, IL: Robert Weinberg, 1980, 96 p., paper, nonf. PULP CLASSICS #22.

26640 *Secret Agent X: a history, revised edition.* Seymour, TX: Fading Shadows Inc., 1991, 96 p., paper, nonf. [Revised edition].

JOHNSON, Wayne L., 1942-

26641 *Ray Bradbury.* New York: Frederick Ungar Publishing Co., 1980, xiii+173 p., cloth, nonf.

JOHNSON, William Oscar

26642 *Hammered gold.* New York: Pocket Books, 1982, 267 p., paper, novel.

26643 *The zero factor.* New York: Pocket Books, 1980, 330 p., paper, novel.

JOHNSTON, J. M.

26644 *Brainchild.* New York: Manor Books, 1979 (i.e., 1980?), 223 p., paper, novel.

JOHNSTON, Joe

26645   *The Star Wars sketchbook.*   New York: Ballantine Books, 1977, 96 p., paper, art.

with Nilo Rodis-Jamero

26646   *The Empire Strikes Back sketchbook.*   New York: Ballantine Books, 1980, 95 p., paper, art.
26647   *The Return of the Jedi sketchbook.*   New York: Ballantine Books, 1983, 96 p., paper, art.

JOHNSTON, Norma

26648   *The watcher in the mist.*   Toronto, New York: A Bantam Starfire Book, 1986, 197 p., paper, novel.
26649   *Whisper of the cat.*   Toronto, New York: Bantam Books, 1988, viii+183 p., paper, novel.

as NICOLE ST. JOHN

26650   *Guinever's gift.*   New York: Random House, 1977, 245 p., cloth, novel.

*JOHNSTON, Thomas, 1945-

JOHNSTON, Velda

26651   *The crystal cat.*   New York: Dodd, Mead & Co., 1985, 184 p., cloth, novel.
26652   *The people from the sea.*   New York: Dodd, Mead & Co., 1979, 234 p., cloth, novel.
26653   *A presence in an empty room.*   New York: Dodd, Mead & Co., 1980, 265 p., cloth, novel.

JOHNSTONE, William W(allace), 1938-

26655   *Alone in the ashes.*   New York: Zebra Books, Kensington Publishing Corp., 1985, 350 p., paper, novel. ASHES #5.
26656   *Anarchy in the ashes.*   New York: Zebra Books, Kensington Publishing Corp., 1984, 432 p., paper, novel. ASHES #3.
26657   *Blood in the ashes.*   New York: Zebra Books, Kensington Publishing Corp., 1985, 396 p., paper, novel. ASHES #4.
26658   *Carnival.*   New York: Zebra Books, Kensington Publishing Corp., 1989, 352 p., paper, novel.
26659   *Cat's cradle.*   New York: Zebra Books, Kensington Publishing Corp., 1986, 412 p., paper, novel.

26660   *Cat's eye.*   New York: Zebra Books, Kensington Publishing Corp., 1989, 397 p., paper, novel.
26661   *Courage in the ashes.*   New York: Zebra Books, Kensington Publishing Corp., 1991, 414 p., paper, novel. ASHES #14.
26662   *A crying shame.*   New York: Zebra Books, Kensington Publishing Corp., 1983, 283 p., paper, novel.
26663   *Danger in the ashes.*   New York: Zebra Books, Kensington Publishing Corp., 1988, 365 p., paper, novel. ASHES #8.
26664   *Darkly the thunder.*   New York: Zebra Books, Kensington Publishing Corp., 1990, 351 p., paper, novel.
26665   *Death in the ashes.*   New York: Zebra Books, Kensington Publishing Corp., 1990, 383 p., paper, novel. ASHES #11.
26666   *Death master.*   New York: Zebra Books, Kensington Publishing Corp., 1987, 269 p., paper, novel.
26667   *The devil's cat.*   New York: Zebra Books, Kensington Publishing Corp., 1987, 380 p., paper, novel. WHITFIELD #4.
26668   *The devil's heart.*   New York: Zebra Books, Kensington Publishing Corp., 1983, 382 p., paper, novel. WHITFIELD #2.
26669   *The devil's kiss.*   New York: Zebra Books, Kensington Publishing Corp., 1980, 449 p., paper, novel. WHITFIELD #1.
26670   *The devil's touch.*   New York: Zebra Books, Kensington Publishing Corp., 1984, 350 p., paper, novel. WHITFIELD #3.
26671   *Eighteen-wheel avenger.*   New York: Zebra Books, Kensington Publishing Corp., 1988, 253 p., paper, novel. RIG WARRIOR #3.
26672   *Fire in the ashes.*   New York: Zebra Books, Kensington Publishing Corp., 1984, 460 p., paper, novel. ASHES #2.
26673   *Fury in the ashes.*   New York: Zebra Books, Kensington Publishing Corp., 1991, 350 p., paper, novel. ASHES #13.
26674   *Jack-in-the-box.*   New York: Zebra Books, Kensington Publishing Corp., 1986, 368 p., paper, novel.
26675   *The nursery.*   New York: Zebra Books, Kensington Publishing Corp., 1983, 351 p., paper, novel.
26676   *Out of the ashes.*   New York: Zebra Books, Kensington Publishing Corp., 1983, 478 p., paper, novel. ASHES #1.
26677   *Rig warrior.*   New York: Zebra Books, Kensington Publishing Corp., 1987, 287 p., paper, novel. RIG WARRIOR #1.
26678   *Rockinghorse.*   New York: Zebra Books, Kensington Publishing Corp., 1986, 428 p., paper, novel.

26679 *Sandman*. New York: Zebra Books, Kensington Publishing Corp., 1988, 432 p., paper, novel.

26680 *Smoke from the ashes*. New York: Zebra Books, Kensington Publishing Corp., 1987, 348 p., paper, novel. ASHES #7.

26681 *Survival in the ashes*. New York: Zebra Books, Kensington Publishing Corp., 1990, 320 p., paper, novel. ASHES #12.

26682 *Sweet dreams*. New York: Zebra Books, Kensington Publishing Corp., 1985, 397 p., paper, novel.

26683 *Toy cemetery*. New York: Zebra Books, Kensington Publishing Corp., 1987, 412 p., paper, novel.

26684 *Trapped in the ashes*. New York: Zebra Books, Kensington Publishing Corp., 1989, 317 p., paper, novel. ASHES #10.

26685 *The uninvited*. New York: Zebra Books, Kensington Publishing Corp., 1982, 301 p., paper, novel.

26686 *Valor in the ashes*. New York: Zebra Books, Kensington Publishing Corp., 1988, 428 p., paper, novel. ASHES #9.

26687 *Watchers in the woods*. New York: Zebra Books, Kensington Publishing Corp., 1991, 352 p., paper, novel.

26688 *Wheels of death*. New York: Zebra Books, Kensington Publishing Corp., 1988, 251 p., paper, novel. RIG WARRIOR #2.

26689 *Wind in the ashes*. New York: Zebra Books, Kensington Publishing Corp., 1986, 363 p., paper, novel. ASHES #6.

26690 *Wolfsbane*. New York: Zebra Books, Kensington Publishing Corp., 1982, 268 p., paper, novel.

with Joseph E. Keene

26691 *Baby grand*. New York: Zebra Books, Kensington Publishing Corp., 1987, 427 p., paper, novel.

JOLLEY, Mark

26692 *Alternative one: the greatest voyage of the Plutonians*. Bognor Regis, West Sussex, England: New Horizons, 1982, 173 p., cloth, novel.

JOLLY, Stratford D.

26693 *The soul of the moor*. London: William Rider, 1911, 226 p., cloth, novel.

JONES, Bruce

26694 *Amberstar: an illustrated cosmic odyssey*. New York: Warner Books, 1980, [94] p., paper, novel.

26695 *Tarotown*. New York: Leisure Books, 1982, 234 p., paper, novel.

26696 *Twisted tales*. San Diego, CA: Blackthorne, 1987, 243 p., paper, coll.

with Armand Eisen

22491 *Sorcerers: a collection of fantasy art*. Kansas City, MO: An Armand Eisen/ Thomas Durwood Production, Ariel Books, 1978, [78] p., paper, art.

JONES, Claude E(dward), 1907- , with Bradford A. Booth

18274 *A concordance of the poetical works of Edgar Allan Poe*. Baltimore, MD: Johns Hopkins Press, 1941, xiv+211 p., cloth, nonf.

JONES, Courtway [i.e., John Alan Jones], 1923-

26697 *In the shadow of the oak king*. New York, London: Pocket Books, 1991, 290 p., paper, novel. KING ARTHUR #1.

JONES, D(ennis) F(eltham), 1918-1981

26698 *Bound in time*. London, Toronto: A Mayflower Book, Granada, 1981, 283 p., paper, novel.

26699 *Colossus and the crab*. New York: A Berkley Medallion Book, Berkley Publishing Corp., 1977, 219 p., paper, novel. COLOSSUS #3.

26700 *Earth has been found: a novel*. New York: A Dell Book, 1979, 267 p., paper, novel.

26700A retitled: *Xeno: science fiction*. London: Sidgwick & Jackson, 1979, 267 p., cloth, novel.

26701 *The floating zombie*. New York: A Berkley Medallion Book, Berkley Publishing Corp., 1975, 216 p., paper, novel.

Xeno—SEE: *Earth has been found*.

JONES, D(avid) J. (Frederick), 1940-

26702 *Souls of the universe*. Braunton, England: Merlin, 1988, 62 p., paper, coll.

JONES, (Robert) Dennis, 1945-

26703 *Winter palace: a novel*. London: Frederick Muller, 1988, 348 p., cloth, novel.

JONES, Diana Wynne, 1934-

26704 *Archer's Goon.* London: Methuen, 1984, 241 p., cloth, novel.

Aunt Maria—SEE: Black Maria.

26705 *Black Maria.* London: Methuen, 1991, 207 p., cloth, novel.

26705A retitled: *Aunt Maria.* New York: Greenwillow Books, 1991, 214 p., cloth, novel.

26706 *Cart & Cwidder.* London: Macmillan, 1975, 193 p., cloth, novel. DALEMARK #1.

26707 *Castle in the air.* London: Methuen Children's Books, 1990, 207 p., cloth, novel. HOWL #2.

26708 *Charmed life.* London: Macmillan, 1977, 209 p., cloth, novel. CHRESTOMANCI #1.

26709 *Dogsbody.* London: Macmillan, 1975, 191 p., cloth, novel.

26710 *Drowned Ammet.* London: Macmillan, 1977, 255 p., cloth, novel. DALEMARK #2.

26711 *Eight days of Luke.* London: Macmillan, 1975, 176 p., cloth, novel.

26712 *Fire and hemlock.* New York: Greenwillow Books, 1984, 341 p., cloth, novel.

26713 *Hidden turnings.* London: Methuen Children's Books, 1989, 183 p., cloth, anth.

26714 *The Homeward Bounders.* London: Macmillan, 1981, 224 p., cloth, novel.

26715 *Howl's moving castle.* London: Methuen's Children's Books, 1986, 212 p., cloth, novel. HOWL #1.

26716 *The lives of Christopher Chant.* New York: Greenwillow Books, 1988, 230 p., cloth, novel. CHRESTOMANCI #4.

26717 *The magicians of Caprona.* London: Macmillan, 1980, 223 p., cloth, novel. CHRESTOMANCI #2.

26718 *The ogre downstairs.* London: Macmillan, 1974, 191 p., cloth, novel.

26719 *Power of three.* London: Macmillan, 1976, 254 p., cloth, novel.

26720 *The spellcoats.* London: Macmillan, 1979, 250 p., cloth, novel. DALEMARK #3.

26721 *A tale of Time City.* New York: Greenwillow Books, 1987, 278 p., cloth, novel.

26722 *The time of the ghost.* London: Macmillan, 1981, 192 p., cloth, novel.

26723 *Warlock at the wheel, and other stories.* London: Macmillan, 1984, 156 p., cloth, coll.

26724 *Witch week.* London: Macmillan, 1982, 210 p., cloth, novel. CHRESTOMANCI #3.

JONES, Douglas C(lyde), 1924-

26725 *The court-martial of George Armstrong Custer.* New York: Charles Scribner's Sons, 1976, 291 p., cloth, novel.

JONES, Frank Earl

15822 *The big-ball: a novel.* Bloomington, IL: Jones Publication, 1958, 156 p., paper, novel.

JONES, Glyn

26727 *Doctor Who: The space museum.* London: W. H. Allen & Co., 1987, 142 p., cloth, tele. DOCTOR WHO #117.

The space museum—SEE: Doctor Who: The space museum.

JONES, Gwyneth (Ann), 1952-

37878 *Dear Hill.* London: Macmillan Children's Books, 1980, 187 p., cloth, novel.

26728 *Divine Endurance.* London: George Allen & Unwin, 1984, xv+233 p., cloth, novel.

26729 *Escape plans.* London: George Allen & Unwin, 1986, 246 p., cloth, novel.

26730 *The hidden ones.* London: Women's Press, 1988, 151 p., paper, novel.

26731 *Kairos.* London: Unwin Hyman, 1988, 260 p., cloth, novel.

37879 *Water in the air.* London, New York: Macmillan, 1977, 179 p., cloth, novel.

26732 *White queen.* London: Victor Gollancz, 1991, 312 p., cloth, novel.

as ANN HALAM

37880 *The alder tree.* London: George Allen & Unwin, 1982, 108 p., cloth, novel.

37881 *Ally, Ally, Aster.* London: George Allen & Unwin, 1981, 118 p., cloth, novel.

26733 *The daymaker.* London, New York: Orchard Books, 1987, 173 p., cloth, novel. INLAND TRILOGY #1.

26734 *King Death's garden.* London, New York: Orchard Books, 1986, 128 p., cloth, novel.

26735 *The skybreaker.* London, New York: Orchard Books, 1990, 208 p., cloth, novel. INLAND TRILOGY #3.

26736 *Transformations.* London, New York: Orchard Books, 1988, 223 p., cloth, novel. INLAND TRILOGY #2.

JONES, J. A.

26737 *Blue lab.* Canoga Park, CA: Major Books, 1978, 189 p., paper, novel.

JONES, J. Jeff, *with Michael Butterworth*

Mind-breaks of space—SEE: *Space 1999: Mind-breaks of space.*

19136 *Space 1999: Mind-breaks of space.* London: A Star Book, W. H. Allen, 1977, 157 p., paper, tele. SPACE 1999 YEAR 2 #2.

JONES, Jeff(rey), 1944-

37882 *Idyl.* Hartford, CT: Blue Star, 1975, [50] p., paper, art.

JONES, Jenny (Huws), 1954-

26738 *The edge of vengeance.* London: Headline, 1991, xi+305 p., cloth, novel. FLIGHT OVER FIRE #2.
26739 *Fly by night.* London: Headline, 1990, 340 p., cloth, novel. FLIGHT OVER FIRE #1.

JONES, John A.—SEE: Jones, Courtway

JONES, John G.

26740 *The Amityville horror II.* New York: Warner Books, 1982, 396 p., paper, novel. AMITYVILLE HORROR #2.
26741 *Amityville horror 3: the final chapter.* Sevenoaks, Kent, England: New English Library, 1984, 271 p., paper, novel. AMITYVILLE HORROR #3.
26741A retitled: *Amityville: the final chapter.* New York: A Jove Book, 1985, xvii+252 p., paper, novel. AMITYVILLE HORROR #3.
26742 *Amityville: the evil escapes.* New York, Los Angeles: Tudor Publishing Co., 1988, 420 p., paper, novel. AMITYVILLE HORROR #5.
26743 *Amityville: The horror returns.* New York, Los Angeles: Tudor Publishing Co., 1989, 280 p., paper, novel. AMITYVILLE HORROR #6.
26744 *Amityville: the untold story.* London: Arrow Books, 1985, 320 p., paper, novel. AMITYVILLE HORROR #4.
The evil escapes—SEE: *Amityville: The evil escapes.*
The final chapter—SEE: *Amityville horror 3.*
The horror returns—SEE: *Amityville: The horror returns.*
26745 *The supernatural.* New York, Los Angeles: Tudor Publishing Co., 1988, 375 p., paper, novel

JONES, John M. III

26746 *U-237 in the Devil's Triangle.* Winter Haven, FL: A Neptune Book, 1975, 106 p., paper, novel.

JONES, John Robert—SEE: Dalmas, John

JONES, Kelvin I.

26747 *The dark entry, and other tales.* Rochester, Kent, England: Sir Hugo Books, 1991, 52 p., paper, coll.
26748 *The obsidian, and other stories.* Rochester, Kent, England: Sir Hugo Boooks, 1990, 51 p., paper, coll.

JONES, (Keith) Lanyon

26749 *The seven deadly sins: stories of the macabre.* London: William Kimber, 1979, 191 p., cloth, coll.

*JONES, L. Q. [pseud. of J. E. McQueen], 1936-

JONES, Lloyd S(cott), 1931-

26750 *Black Rainbow.* Vista, CA: Aeolus Publishing, 1987, 213 p., cloth, novel.

JONES, Marc Edmund, 1888-1980

26751 *Man, magic, and fantasy: the domestication of imagination.* Stanwood, WA: Sabian Publishing Society; Boulder, CO: Shambhala Publications, 1978, vii+215 p., cloth, nonf.

JONES, Marcia Thornton, *with Debbie Dadey*

20961 *Santa Claus doesn't mop floors.* New York, Toronto: A Little Apple Book, Scholastic Inc., 1991, 70 p., paper, novel.
20962 *Vampires don't wear polka dots.* New York, Toronto: A Little Apple Book, Scholastic Inc., 1990, 78 p., paper, novel.
20963 *Werewolves don't go to summer camp.* New York, Toronto: A Little Apple Book, Scholastic Inc., 1991, 92 p., paper, novel.

JONES, Margaret

37883 *Through the Budgerigar.* London: Collins, 1970, 255 p., cloth, novel.

JONES, Mary J., 1938-

26752 *Avalon.* Tallahassee, FL: Naiad Press, 1991, 237 p., paper, novel.

JONES, McClure

26753 *Cast down the stars.* New York: Holt, Rinehart & Winston, 1978, 186 p., cloth, novel.

JONES, Nancy E.—SEE: Luenn, Nancy

JONES, Neal, *with David Pringle*

Deathwing—SEE: *Warhammer 40,000: Deathwing.*
26754 *Warhammer 40,000: Deathwing.* East Sussex, England: GW Books, 1990, 257 p., paper, anth. WARHAMMER SERIES.

*JONES, Neil R(onald), 1909-1988

JONES, Peter A(ndrew), 1951-

26755 *Solar wind.* New York: Perigee Books, 1980, 92 p., paper, art.

JONES, Raymond F., 1915-

26756 *The King of Eolim.* Don Mills, Ontario, Canada: Laser Books, 1975, 190 p., paper, novel.
26757 *Renegades of time.* Don Mills, Ontario, Canada: Laser Books, 1975, 190 p., paper, novel.
26758 *The River and the dream.* Toronto, New York: Laser Books, 1977, 190 p., paper, novel.

with Lester del Rey

21514 *Weeping may tarry.* Los Angeles: Pinnacle Books, 1978, 180 p., paper, novel.

JONES, Robert F(rancis), 1934-

08012 *Blood sport: a journey up the Hassayampa.* New York: Simon & Schuster, 1974, 255 p., cloth, novel.
08012A retitled: *Ratnose: a journey up the Hassayampa.* London: London Magazine Editions, 1975, 255 p., cloth, novel.

JONES, Robert Kenneth, 1926-1986

The lure of Adventure—SEE: *Robert Kenneth Jones' The lure of Adventure.*
26759 *Robert Kenneth Jones' The lure of Adventure.* Mercer Island, WA: Starmont House, 1989, 80 p., cloth, nonf. STARMONT PULP & DIME NOVEL STUDIES #4.
26760 *The shudder pulps: a history of the weird menace magazines of the 1930's.* West

Linn, OR: Fax Collector's Editions, 1975, xv+238 p., cloth, nonf.

JONES, Russ—SEE: Younger, Jack

JONES, Sheila—SEE: MacLeod, Sheila

JONES, Stephen (Gregory), 1953-

26761 *James Herbert: by horror haunted.* London: New English Library, 1991, 288 p., cloth, nonf.
26762 *The mammoth book of terror.* London: Robinson Publishing, 1991, 587 p., paper, anth.

with Clive Barker

17388 *Clive Barker's Shadows in Eden.* Novato, CA, Lancaster, PA: Underwood-Miller, 1991, xv+465 p., cloth, nonf. anth. [Includes material by and about Barker; winner of the Bram Stoker Award for Best Horror Non-Fiction Book, 1991 (1992)].
Shadows in Eden—SEE: *Clive Barker's Shadows in Eden.*

with Ramsey Campbell

19294 *Best new horror.* London: Robinson Publishing, 1990, 390 p., paper, anth. [Winner of the World Fantasy Award for Best Fantasy Anthology, 1990 (1991)].
19295 *Best new horror 2.* London: Robinson Publishing, 1991, 433 p., paper, anth.

with Jo Fletcher

23193 *Gaslight & ghosts.* Wembley, Middlesex, England: 1988 World Fantasy Convention in Association with Robinson Publishing, 1988, 258 p., cloth, anth. [Includes some nonfiction].

with Kim Newman

26763 *Horror: 100 best books.* London: Xanadu, 1988, x+256 p., cloth, nonf. [Winner of the Bram Stoker Award for Best Horror Nonfiction Book, 1989 (1990)].

with Clarence Paget

26764 *Dark voices: the best from the Pan book of horror stories.* London & Sydney: Pan Books, 1990, vii+348 p., cloth, anth.

with David Sutton

26765 *The best horror from Fantasy tales.* London: Robinson Publishing, 1988, xviii+264 p., cloth, anth.

26766 *Dark voices 2: the Pan book of horror.* London & Sydney: Pan Books, 1990, 223 p., paper, anth.

26767 *Dark voices 3: the Pan book of horror.* London & Sydney: Pan Books, 1991, 309 p., paper, anth.

26768 *Fantasy tales 1.* New York: Carroll & Graf, 1990, 104 p., paper, anth.
Fantasy tales 2—SEE: *Fantasy tales 5.*
Fantasy tales 3—SEE: *Fantasy tales 6.*

26769 *Fantasy tales 5.* London: Robinson Publishing, 1990, 201 p., paper, anth.

26769A retitled: *Fantasy tales 2.* New York: Carroll & Graf, 1990, 201 p., paper, anth.

26770 *Fantasy tales 6.* London: Robinson Publishing, 1991, 186 p., paper, anth.

26770A retitled: *Fantasy tales 3.* New York: Carroll & Graf, 1991, 186 p., paper, anth.

26771 *Fantasy tales 7.* London: Robinson Publishing, 1991, 185 p., paper, anth.

JONES, Stephen—SEE: **Gregory, Stephen**

JONES, Terence G.—SEE: **Jones, Terry**

JONES, Terry [i.e., Terence Graham Parry Jones], 1942-

26772 *Fairy tales.* London: Pavilion, 1981, 127 p., cloth, coll.

26773 *Nicobobinus.* London: Pavilion, 1985, 175 p., cloth, novel.

26774 *The saga of Erik the Viking.* London: Pavillion, 1983, 144 p., cloth, novel.

with Brian Froud

23574 *The goblins of Labyrinth.* London: Pavilion, 1986, 137 p., cloth, art.

with Michael Palin

31172 *Ripping yarns.* London: Eyre Methuen, 1978, 186 p., cloth, coll.

JONES, Tim Wynne-—SEE: **Wynne-Jones, Tim**

JONES, Trevor, *with George P. Townsend*

26775 *A book of dreams.* England: Weller Publications, 1991, 80 p., paper, anth.

JONG, Erica (Mann), 1942-

26776 *Serenissima: a novel.* Boston: Houghton Mifflin Co., 1987, 225 p., cloth, novel.

JORDAN, Anne [i.e., Anne Devereaux Jordan Crouse], 1943-

26777 *Fires of the past: thirteen contemporary fantasies about hometowns* / by Anne Devereaux Jordan. New York: St. Martin's Press, 1991, xi+212 p., cloth, anth.

with Edward L. Ferman

23041 *The best horror stories from The magazine of fantasy & science fiction.* New York: St. Martin's Press, 1988, xi+403 p., cloth, anth.

23041A retitled: *The best of modern horror.* London: Viking, 1989, xi+403 p., cloth, anth.

23041B retitled: *The best horror stories from The magazine of fantasy and science fiction, volume 1.* New York: St. Martin's Press, 1989, 260 p., paper, anth. [The original split into two volumes].

23041C retitled: *The best horror stories from The magazine of fantasy and science fiction, volume 2.* New York: St. Martin's Press, 1990, 269 p., paper, anth. [The original split into two volumes].
The best of modern horror—SEE: *The best horror stories from The magazine of fantasy & science fiction.*

JORDAN, Brenda

26778 *The Brentwood witches.* New York: Ace Books, 1987, 186 p., paper, novel.

JORDAN, G(odfrey) P.

26779 *Extraterrestrial cover up.* London: A Target Book, W. H. Allen & Co., 1986, 123 p., paper, novel. STARR FAMILY ADVENTURES #2.

26780 *The Milky Way run.* London: A Target Book, W. H. Allen & Co., 1985, 111 p., paper, novel. STARR FAMILY ADVENTURES #1.

JORDAN, Robert [pseud. of James Oliver Rigney Jr.], 1948-

26781 *Conan the defender.* New York: A Tom Doherty Associates Book, 1982, 287 p., paper, novel. CONAN SERIES.

26782 *Conan the destroyer.* New York: Tor, A Tom Doherty Associates Book, 1984, 271 p., paper, movie. CONAN SERIES.

26783 *Conan the invincible.* New York: Tor, A Tom Doherty Associates Book, 1982, 284 p., paper, novel. CONAN SERIES.

26784 *Conan the magnificent.* New York: Tor, A Tom Doherty Associates Book, 1984, 286 p., paper, novel. CONAN SERIES.

26785 *Conan the triumphant.* New York: Tor, A Tom Doherty Associates Book, 1983, 280 p., paper, novel. CONAN SERIES.

26786 *Conan the unconquered.* New York: Tor, A Tom Doherty Associates Book, 1983, 286 p., paper, novel. CONAN SERIES.

26787 *Conan the victorious.* New York: Tor, A Tom Doherty Associates Book, 1984, 280 p., paper, novel. CONAN SERIES.

26788 *The dragon reborn.* New York: Tor, A Tom Doherty Associates Book, 1991, xxviii+595 p., cloth, novel. WHEEL OF TIME #3.

26789 *The eye of the world.* New York: Tor, A Tom Doherty Associates Book, 1990, xiv+670 p., cloth, novel. WHEEL OF TIME #1.

26790 *The great hunt.* New York: Tor, A Tom Doherty Associates Book, 1990, xxiv+600 p., cloth, novel. WHEEL OF TIME #2.

JORDAN, Sherryl

26791 *The juniper game.* New York, Toronto: Scholastic Inc., 1991, 228 p., cloth, novel.

26792 *A time of darkness.* New York, Toronto: Scholastic Inc., 1990, 246 p., cloth, novel.

JORGENSEN, Ivar, pseud.—SEE: Fairman, Paul W.

JOSEPH, Anne [pseud. of Anna Scot]

26793 *Grandfather.* New York: Zebra Books, Kensington Publishing Corp., 1991, 286 p., paper, novel.

JOSEPH, Franz [pseud. of Franz Joseph Schaubelt], 1914-

26794 *Star Fleet technical manual.* New York: Ballantine Books, 1975, [194] pages in plastic case, fiction.

JOSEPH, Mark (Chester), 1946-

26795 *Mexico 21.* London: Grafton, 1990, 313 p., cloth, novel.

JOSEPH, Michael

26796 *The time of Achamoth.* Auckland, New Zealand & London: Collins, 1977, 181 p., cloth, novel.

*JOSEPH, M(ichael) K(ennedy), 1914-<u>1981</u>

JOSHI, S(unand) T(ryambak), 1958-

26797 *The centennial conference proceedings.* West Warwick, RI: Necronomicon Press, 1991, 80 p., paper, nonf. anth.

26798 *H. P. Lovecraft.* Mercer Island, WA: Starmont House, 1982, 83 p., cloth, nonf.. STARMONT READER'S GUIDE #13.

26799 *H. P. Lovecraft and Lovecraft criticism: an annotated bibliography.* Kent, OH: Kent State University Press, 1981, xxxiv+473 p., cloth, nonf. SERIF SERIES: BIBLIOGRAPHIES AND CHECKLISTS #38.

26800 *H. P. Lovecraft: four decades of criticism.* Athens, OH: Ohio University Press, 1980, xv+246 p., cloth, nonf. anth.

26801 *H. P. Lovecraft: the decline of the west.* Mercer Island, WA: Starmont House, 1990, v+155 p., cloth, nonf. STARMONT STUDIES IN LITERARY CRITICISM #37.

26802 *An index to the selected letters of H. P. Lovecraft.* West Warwick, RI: Necronomicon Press, 1980, 77 p., paper, nonf.

26803 *An index to the selected letters of H. P. Lovecraft, second revised edition.* West Warwick, RI: Necronomicon Press, 1991, 50 p., paper, nonf.

26804 *Selected papers on Lovecraft.* West Warwick, RI: Necronomicon Press, 1989, vi+75 p., paper, nonf. coll.

26805 *The weird tale: Arthur Machen, Lord Dunsany, Algernon Blackwood, Ambrose Bierce, H. P. Lovecraft.* Austin, TX: University of Texas Press, 1990, xii+292 p., cloth, nonf.

with L. D. Blackmore

18093 *H. P. Lovecraft and Lovecraft criticism: an annotated bibliography supplement, 1980-1984.* West Warwick, RI: Necronomicon Press, 1985, iv+72 p., paper, nonf.

with Marc A. Michaud

26807 *Lovecraft's library: a catalogue.* West Warwick, RI: Necronomicon Press, 1980, 90 p., paper, nonf. anth.

with David E. Schultz

26808 *An epicure in the terrible: a centennial anthology of essays in honor of H. P. Love-*

craft. Rutherford, NJ: Fairleigh Dickinson University Press, 1991, 347 p., cloth, nonf. anth.

JOUGUELET, Pierre

26809 *Aldous Huxley*. Paris: Éditions du Temps Présent, 1948, 235 p., paper?, nonf.

JOY, William "Ted", *as anonymous co-author with Warren Murphy*

26810 *Timber line* / by Warren Murphy. Los Angeles: Pinnacle Books, 1980, 181 p., paper, novel. DESTROYER #42.

JOYCE, Graham (William), 1954-

26811 *Dreamside*. London & Sydney: Pan Books, 1991, 246 p., paper, novel.

JOYCE, Jocelyn

26812 *Demon heat*. New York: Masquerade Books, 1991, 162 p., paper, novel.

JOYCE, Tom, *with Christopher P. Stephens*

26813 *A checklist of James P. Blaylock*. Hastings-on-Hudson, NY: Ultramarine, 1991, 17 p., paper, nonf.

26814 *A checklist of Kim Stanley Robinson*. Hastings-on-Hudson, NY: Ultramarine, 1991, 28 p., paper, nonf.

26815 *A checklist of Lucius Shepard*. Hastings-on-Hudson, NY: Ultramarine, 1991, 18 p., paper, nonf.

26816 *A checklist of Tim Powers*. Hastings-on-Hudson, NY: Ultramarine, 1991, 15 p., paper, nonf.

JUDD, A. M.

26817 *The white vampire*. London: John Long, 1914, 319 p., cloth, novel.

JUDD, Cyril, pseud.—SEE: Kornbluth, C. M. & Merril, Judith

JULES-VERNE, Jean, 1892-

26818 *Jules Verne: a biography*. London: Macdonald & Jane's, 1976, x+245 p., cloth, nonf.

JULIUS, E. Haldeman- —SEE: Haldeman-Julius, E.

JUNGMAN, Ann

26819 *Vlad the Drac down under*. London: Young Lions, 1989, 154 p., paper, novel. VLAD THE DRAC #5.

26820 *Vlad the Drac returns*. London: A Dragon Book, Granada, 1984, 110 p., paper, novel. VLAD THE DRAC #2.

26821 *Vlad the Drac superstar*. London: A Dragon Book, Granada, 1985, 110 p., paper, novel. VLAD THE DRAC #3.

26822 *Vlad the Drac: the adventures of a vegetarian vampire*. London: A Dragon Book, Granada, 1982, 112 p., paper, novel. VLAD THE DRAC #1.

26823 *Vlad the Drac vampire*. London: A Dragon Book, Granada, 1988, [110] p., paper, novel. VLAD THE DRAC #4.

JUSTICE, Keith L(eroy), 1949-

26824 *Science fiction, fantasy, and horror reference: an annotated bibliography of works about literature and film*. Jefferson, NC & London: McFarland & Co., Publishers, 1989, xiii+226 p., cloth, nonf.

26825 *Science fiction master index of names*. Jefferson, NC & London: McFarland & Co., Publishers, 1986, vi+394 p., cloth, nonf.

JUTE, André—SEE: McCoy, Andrew

K

KABAKOV, Alexander [i.e., Aleksandr Abramovich Kabakov]

26837 *No return.* New York: William Morrow & Co., 1990, 94 p., cloth, novel. [Translation by Thomas Whitney of *Nevozvrashchenets*].

KADREY, Richard, 1957-

26838 *Metrophage: (a romance of the future).* New York: Ace Books, 1988, 240 p., paper, novel.

KAFKA, Franz, 1883-1924

26839 *Franz Kafka: stories, 1904-1924.* London: Macdonald & Co., 1981, 271 p., cloth, coll. [Translation by J. A. Underwood].

KAGAN, Janet (Megson), 1946-

26840 *Hellspark.* New York: Tor SF, A Tom Doherty Associates Book, 1988, 407 p., paper, novel.
26841 *Mirabile.* New York: Tor, A Tom Doherty Associates Book, 1991, 278 p., cloth, coll.
26842 *Uhura's song: a Star Trek novel.* New York: Pocket Books, 1985, 373 p., paper, novel. STAR TREK #21.

KAGAN, Norman

26843 *The cinema of Stanley Kubrick.* New York: Holt, Rinehart & Winston, 1972, xiii+204 p., cloth, nonf.
26844 *The cinema of Stanley Kubrick, new expanded edition.* New York: A Frederick Ungar Book, Continuum, 1989, xiv+249 p., cloth, nonf.

KAGARLITSKY, Yuli [i.e., Iulii Iosifovich Kagarlitskii], 1926-

26845 *The life and thought of H. G. Wells.* London: Sidgwick & Jackson, 1966, xiv+210 p., cloth, nonf.

KAHLER, Jack

26846 *Rubber dolly.* San Diego, CA: A PEC Giant, Publishers Export Co., 1966, 189 p., paper, novel.

KAHN, Alfred—SEE: Bretnor, Reginald

KAHN, James, 1947-

26847 *The echo vector.* New York: St. Martin's Press, 1988, xi+227 p., cloth, novel.
26848 *Goonies: a novel.* New York: Warner Books, 1985, 193 p., paper, movie. GOONIES #1.
26849 *Indiana Jones and the temple of doom.* New York: Ballantine Books, 1984, 216 p., paper, movie. INDIANA JONES #2.
The other side—SEE: Poltergeist II.
26850 *Poltergeist.* New York: Warner Books, 1982, 301 p., paper, movie. POLTERGEIST #1.
26851 *Poltergeist II: The other side.* New York: Ballantine Books, 1986, 179 p., paper, movie. POLTERGEIST #2.
Return of the Jedi—SEE: Star Wars: Return of the Jedi.
26852 *Star Wars: Return of the Jedi.* New York: A Del Rey Book, Ballantine Books, 1983, 181 p., paper, movie. STAR WARS #3.
26853 *Time's dark laughter.* New York: A Del Rey Book, Ballantine Books, 1982, xiv+318 p., paper, novel. NEW WORLD #2.
26854 *Timefall.* New York: St. Martin's Press, 1987, 295 p., cloth, novel. NEW WORLD #3.
26855 *World enough, and time.* New York: A Del Rey Book, Ballantine Books, 1980, 340 p., paper, novel. NEW WORLD #1.

with George Lucas & Donald F. Glut

24029 *The Star Wars trilogy.* New York: A Del Rey Book, Ballantine Books, 1987, 471 p., paper, anth.

KAHN, Joan, 1914-

26856 *Handle with care: frightening stories.* New York: Greenwillow Books, 1985, xii+209 p., cloth, anth.

26857 *Ready or not, here come fourteen frightening stories!* New York: Greenwillow Books, 1987, 159 p., cloth, anth.

26858 *Some things weird and wicked: twelve stories to chill your bones.* New York: Pantheon Books, 1976, x+243 p., cloth, anth.

KAHN, Obie, pseud.—SEE: Vardeman, Robert & Proctor, Geo. W.

KAINS, Josephine, pseud.—SEE: Goulart, Ron

KALECHOFSKY, Roberta, 1931-

26859 *George Orwell.* New York: Frederick Ungar Publishing Co., 1973, ix+149 p., cloth, nonf.

KAMARCK, Lawrence, 1927-

26860 *The Zinsser implant: a novel.* New York: The Dial Press, 1979, xii+223 p., cloth, novel.

KAMINSKI, Raymond

26861 *The amazons of Somelon.* New York: Leisure Books, 1981, 191 p., paper, novel.

KAMINSKY, Howard, 1940- , with Susan Stanwood Kaminsky as BROOKS STANWOOD

26862 *The glow: a novel.* New York: McGraw-Hill Book Co., 1979, 297 p., cloth, novel.

26863 *The seventh child.* New York: The Linden Press/Simon & Schuster, 1982, 316 p., cloth, novel.

KAMINSKY, Susan Stanwood, with Howard Kaminsky as BROOKS STANWOOD

26862 *The glow: a novel.* New York: McGraw-Hill Book Co., 1979, 297 p., cloth, novel.

26863 *The seventh child.* New York: The Linden Press/Simon & Schuster, 1982, 316 p., cloth, novel.

KAMITSES, Zoë, 1941-

26864 *Moondreamer.* Boston: Little, Brown & Co., 1983, 206 p., cloth, novel.

KANDEL, Michael, 1941-

26865 *Captain Jack Zodiac.* Cambridge, MA: Broken Mirrors Press, 1991, 224 p., cloth, novel.

26866 *In between dragons.* New York, Toronto: Bantam Books, 1990, 181 p., paper, novel.

26867 *Strange invasion.* New York, Toronto: Bantam Books, 1989, 152 p., paper, novel.

KANE, Alex, pseud.—SEE: Lazuta, Gene

KANE, Daniel, 1957-

26868 *Power and magic.* London: GMP Press, 1987, 224 p., paper, novel.

KANE, Gil, 1926- , with John Jakes

26432 *Excalibur!* New York: A Dell Book, 1980, 509 p., paper, novel.

KANER, H(yman), d. 1970?

KANGILASKI, Jaan, 1936-

26869 *Hands of glory.* New York: A Del Rey Book, Ballantine Books, 1981, 295 p., paper, novel. SEEKING SWORD #2.

26870 *The Seeking Sword.* New York: Ballantine Books, 1977, 346 p., paper, novel. SEEKING SWORD #1.

*KANTOR, Hal, 1924-

KAO, Karl S. Y.

26871 *Classical Chinese tales of the supernatural and the fantastic: selections from the third to the tenth century.* Bloomington, IN: Indiana University Press, 1985, x+406 p., cloth, anth.

KAPLAN, Aline Boucher, 1947-

26872 *Khyren.* New York: Baen Books, 1988, 374 p., paper, novel.

26873 *World spirits.* Riverdale, NY: Baen Books, 1991, 403 p., paper, novel.

KAPLAN, Cora, 1940- , with Victor Burgin & James Donald

19047 *Formations of fantasy.* London, New York: Methuen, 1986, 221 p., paper, nonf. anth.

KAPLAN, David Michael, 1946-

26874 *Comfort*. New York: Viking, 1987, 204 p., cloth, coll.

KAPLAN, Robert B(oris), 1928- , with Frank H. Thompson Jr.

26875 *1984: notes*. Lincoln, NE: Cliffs Notes, 1967, 51 p., paper, nonf.

KAPP, Colin, 1928-

26876 *The chaos weapon*. New York: A Del Rey Book, Ballantine Books, 1977, 201 p., paper, novel. CHAOS #2.
26877 *The ion war*. New York: Ace Books, 1978, 252 p., paper, novel.
26878 *The lost worlds of Cronus*. London: New English Library, 1982, 170 p., paper, novel. CAGEWORLD #2.
26879 *Manalone*. St Albans, Hertfordshire, England: Panther, 1977, 197 p., paper, novel.
26880 *Search for the Sun!* London: New English Library, 1982, 172 p., paper, novel. CAGEWORLD #1.
26881 *Star-search*. Sevenoaks, Kent, England: New English Library, 1983, 171 p., paper, novel. CAGEWORLD #4.
26882 *The survival game*. New York: Ballantine Books, 1976, 184 p., paper, novel.
26883 *The tyrant of Hades*. Sevenoaks, Kent, England: New English Library, 1982, 173 p., paper, novel. CAGEWORLD #3.
26884 *The unorthodox engineers*. London: Dennis Dobson, 1979, 216 p., cloth, coll.

KAPRALOV, Yuri

26885 *Castle Dubrava*. New York: E. P. Dutton, 1982, 247 p., cloth, novel.

KARIG, Walter, 1898-1956

26886 *War in the atomic age?* New York: W. H. Wise & Co., 1946, 63 p., paper?, novel.

KARKAINEN, Paul A.

26887 *Narnia explored*. Old Tappan, NJ: Fleming H. Revell Co., 1979, 192 p., cloth, nonf.

KARL, Jean E(dna), 1927-

26888 *Beloved Benjamin is waiting*. New York: E. P. Dutton & Co., 1978, 150 p., cloth, novel.

26889 *But we are not of Earth*. New York: E. P. Dutton & Co., 1981, 170 p., cloth, novel.
26890 *Strange tomorrow*. New York: E. P. Dutton, 1985, 135 p., cloth, novel.
26891 *The turning place: stories of a future past*. New York: E. P. Dutton & Co., 1976, 213 p., cloth, coll.
26891A retitled: *Worlds end and after: stories of a future past*. Glasgow, Scotland: Blackie & Son, 1978, 213 p., cloth, coll.
Worlds end and after—SEE: *The turning place*.

KARLINS, Marvin, 1941- , as ROBERT BROWNE

26892 *The new AToms' bombshell*. New York: A Del Rey Book, Ballantine Books, 1980, 212 p., paper, novel.

KARR, Phyllis Ann, 1944-

26893 *At Amberleaf Fair*. New York: Ace Fantasy Books, 1986, 186 p., paper, novel.
26894 *Frostflower and Thorn*. New York: Berkley Books, 1980, 276 p., paper, novel. FROSTFLOWER #1.
26895 *Frostflower and Windbourne*. New York: Berkley Books, 1982, 234 p., paper, novel. FROSTFLOWER #2.
26896 *The idylls of the queen*. New York: Ace Books, 1982, 341 p., paper, novel.
26897 *Wildraith's last battle*. New York: Ace Books, 1982, 282 p., paper, novel.

KASDAN, Lawrence (Edward), 1949-

26898 *Raiders of the Lost Ark: the illustrated screenplay*. New York: Ballantine Books, 1981, 119 p., paper, movie. [Includes some nonfiction]

KASNER, Michael—SEE: Mackin, Rick

KASSEM, Lou, 1931-

26899 *Dance of death*. New York: Twilight/Dell, 1984, 151 p., paper, novel. TWILIGHT #19.
26900 *A haunting in Williamsburg*. New York: An Avon Camelot Book, 1990, 104 p., paper, novel.

KASSEVGARI, Roman—SEE: Gary, Romain

KAST, Pierre, 1920-1984

26901 *The vampires of Alfama*. London: W. H. Allen & Co., 1976, 181 p., cloth, novel.

[Translation by Peter de Polnay of *Les vampires de l'Alfama*].

KASTLE, Herbert D(avid), 1924-1987

26902 *Edward Berner is alive again!* Englewood Cliffs, NJ: Prentice-Hall, 1975, 263 p., cloth, novel. [Expanded version of *The reassembled man* (see #08078)].

26902A retitled: *The three lives of Edward Berner.* London: W. H. Allen, 1976, 263 p., cloth, novel.

The three lives of Edward Berner—SEE: *Edward Berner is alive again!*

KÄSTNER, Erich, 1899-1974

26903 *The Little Man.* London: Jonathan Cape, 1966, 159 p., cloth, novel. MAXIE #1. [Translation by James Kirkup of *Der kleine mann*].

The Little Man and the big thief—SEE: *The Little Man and the little miss.*

26904 *The Little Man and the little miss.* London: Jonathan Cape, 1969, 184 p., cloth, novel. MAXIE #2. [Translation by James Kirkup of *Der kleine mann und die kleine miss*].

26904A retitled: *The Little Man and the big thief.* New York: Alfred A. Knopf, 1969, 162 p., cloth, novel. MAXIE #2. [Translation by James Kirkup of *Der kleine mann und die kleine miss*].

KATKIN, Pamela E.—SEE: West, Pamela

KATO, Ken, pseud., 1950-

26905 *Yamato: a rage in Heaven: the epic begins...* New York: Warner Books, 1990, xiv+540 p., cloth, novel.

KATZ, Gloria, 1945- , *with Willard Huyck*

26249 *Indiana Jones and the Temple of Doom: the illustrated screenplay: the complete script.* New York: Ballantine Books, 1984, 121 p., paper, nonf. coll. INDIANA JONES SERIES. [Includes screenplay, designs, & commentary].

KATZ, Harvey A., 1927- , *with Martin H. Greenberg & Patricia S. Warrick*

24526 *Introductory psychology through science fiction, 2nd ed.* Chicago: Rand McNally Publishing Co., 1977, vii+550 p., paper, anth.

KATZ, Leslie George, 1918-

26906 *Fairy tales for computers.* Boston: A Nonpareil Book, David R. Godine, 1978, xii+234 p., paper, anth.

KATZ, Shelley

26907 *Alligator.* New York: A Dell Book, 1977, 331 p., paper, novel.

26908 *The Lucifer child.* New York: A Dell Book, 1980, 317 p., paper, novel.

KATZ, Welwyn Wilton, 1948-

26909 *False face.* Vancouver, British Columbia, Canada: Douglas & McIntyre, 1987, 155 p., cloth, novel.

26910 *The prophecy of Tau Ridoo.* Edmonton, Alberta, Canada: Tree Frog Press, 1982, 175 p., paper, novel.

26911 *The third magic.* Vancouver, British Columbia, Canada: A Groundwood Book, Douglas & McIntyre, 1988, 204 p., cloth, novel.

26912 *Whalesinger.* New York: Margaret K. McElderry Books, 1990, 212 p., cloth, novel.

26913 *Witchery hill.* New York: A Margaret K. McElderry Book, Atheneum, 1984, 244 p., cloth, novel.

KATZ, Wendy R(oberta Shapiro), 1945-

26914 *Rider Haggard and the fiction of empire: a critical study of British imperial fiction.* Cambridge, England, New York: Cambridge University Press, 1987, ix+171 p., cloth, nonf.

KATZ, William (Michael), 1940-

26915 *Death dreams.* New York: Ballantine Books, 1979, 297 p., paper, novel.

26916 *Facemaker.* New York: McGraw-Hill Book Co., 1988, 252 p., cloth, novel.

26917 *Ghostflight.* New York: A Dell Book, 1980, 362 p., paper, novel.

26918 *Visions of terror.* New York: Warner Books, 1981, 286 p., paper, novel.

KAUFELT, David A(llan), 1939-

26919 *Spare parts.* New York: Warner Books, 1978, 349 p., paper, novel.

KAUFMAN, Douglas

26920 *The dark realm.* Honesdale, PA: West End Books, 1990, 302 p., paper, novel.

TORG: THE POSSIBILITY WARS #2.
[Novelization of *Possibility Wars* game].

KAUFMANN, Joe

26921 *Spaceman from another planet.* Ilfracombe, England: Arthur H. Stockwell, 1978, 125 p., cloth, novel.

KAVAN, Anna [pseud. of Helen Woods Edmonds], 1904-1968

26922 *My madness: the selected writings of Anna Kavan.* London: Picador, 1990, xiv+318 p., paper, coll. [Edited by Brian W. Aldiss].

KAVENEY, Andrew J.—SEE: Kaveney, Roz

KAVENEY, Roz [legalized from Andrew J. Kaveney], 1949-

26923 *More tales from the Forbidden Planet.* London: Titan Books, 1990, 268 p., cloth, anth.
26924 *Tales from the Forbidden Planet.* London: Titan Books, 1987, 256 p., cloth, anth.

KAY, Charline Bockhold, with Kenneth Kay

26925 *The magic dolls.* St. Petersburg, FL: Valkyrie Press, 1976, 170 p., cloth, novel.

KAY, Guy Gavriel, 1954-

26926 *The darkest road.* Toronto: Collins, 1986, xxv+419 p., cloth, novel. FIONAVAR TAPESTRY #3.
26927 *The summer tree.* Toronto: McClelland & Stewart, 1984, 323 p., cloth, novel. FIONAVAR TAPESTRY #1.
26928 *Tigana.* London, New York: Viking, 1990, 687 p., cloth, novel.
26929 *The wandering fire.* Toronto: Collins, 1986, xvi+298 p., cloth, novel. FIONAVAR TAPESTRY #2.

KAY, Kenneth

with Marshall Goldberg

24057 *Disposable people.* New York: Tower Books, 1980, 316 p., paper, novel.

with Charline Bockhold Kay

26925 *The magic dolls.* St. Petersburg, FL: Valkyrie Press, 1976, 170 p., cloth, novel.

KAY, Susan

26930 *Phantom.* London: Doubleday, 1990, 464 p., cloth, novel.

KAYE, M. M. [i.e., Mary Margaret Kaye Hamilton], 1909-

26931 *The ordinary princess.* Harmondsworth, Middlesex, England: Kestrel Books, 1980, 123 p., cloth, novel.

KAYE, Maggie, pseud.

26932 *Somewhere over the orgy.* New York: A Beeline Classic, 1981, 180 p., paper, novel. OZ PARODY.

KAYE, Marilyn (Janice), 1949-

26933 *Max all over.* Harmondsworth, Middlesex, England: Penguin Books, 1989, 144 p., paper, novel. OUT OF THIS WORLD #6.
26934 *Max flips out.* New York: An Archway Paperback, Pocket Books, 1986, 148 p., paper, novel. OUT OF THIS WORLD #4.
26935 *Max goes bad.* Harmondsworth, Middlesex, England: Penguin Books, 1989, 151 p., paper, novel. OUT OF THIS WORLD #5.
26936 *Max in love.* New York: An Archway Paperback, Pocket Books, 1986, 148 p., paper, novel. OUT OF THIS WORLD #2.
26937 *Max on Earth.* New York: An Archway Paperback, Pocket Books, 1986, 148 p., paper, novel. OUT OF THIS WORLD #1.
26938 *Max on fire.* New York: An Archway Paperback, Pocket Books, 1986, 147 p., paper, novel. OUT OF THIS WORLD #3.
26939 *A witch in Cabin Six.* New York: Avon Camelot, 1990, 119 p., paper, novel. CAMP SUNNYSIDE FRIENDS #7.

KAYE, Marvin (Nathan), 1938-

26940 *The amorous umbrella.* Garden City, NY: Doubleday & Co., 1981, xiii+271 p., cloth, novel. FILLMORE #2.
26941 *Fiends and creatures.* New York: Popular Library, 1975, 190 p., paper, anth.
26942 *Ghosts of night and morning.* New York: Charter Books, 1987, 304 p., cloth, novel. BLUE LIGHT #2.
26943 *The incredible umbrella.* Garden City, NY: Doubleday & Co., 1979, 217 p., cloth, novel. FILLMORE #1.
The Penguin book of witches and warlocks—SEE: *Witches & warlocks: tales of black magic, old & new.*

26944 *The possession of Immanuel Wolf, and other improbable tales.* Garden City, NY: Doubleday & Co., 1981, xv+171 p., cloth, coll.

26945 *Witches & warlocks: tales of black magic, old & new.* Garden City, NY: Guild America Books, 1990, xii+529 p., cloth, anth.

26945A retitled: *The Penguin book of witches and warlocks.* New York: Penguin Books, 1991, xii+529 p., paper, anth.

with Parke Godwin

24048 *A cold blue light.* New York: Charter Books, 1983, 294 p., paper, novel. COLD BLUE LIGHT #1.

24049 *The masters of solitude.* Garden City, NY: Doubleday & Co., 1978, 397 p., cloth, novel. SOLITUDE TRILOGY #1.

24050 *Wintermind.* Garden City, NY: Doubleday & Co., 1982, xiii+291 p., cloth, novel. SOLITUDE TRILOGY #2.

with Saralee Kaye

26946 *Devils & demons: a treasury of fiendish tales old & new.* Garden City, NY: Doubleday & Co., 1987, xv+587 p., cloth, anth.

26947 *Ghosts: a treasury of chilling tales old and new.* Garden City, NY: Doubleday & Co., 1981, xviii+652 p., cloth, anth.

26948 *Haunted America: star-spangled supernatural stories.* New York: Guild America Books, 1991, xii+582 p., cloth, anth.

26949 *Masterpieces of terror and the supernatural: a treasury of spellbinding tales old & new.* Garden City, NY: Doubleday & Co., 1985, xv+623 p., cloth, anth.

26950 *Weird tales: the magazine that never dies.* Garden City, NY: Doubleday Book & Music Clubs, 1988, xxi+582 p., cloth, anth.

with Brother Theodore

26951 *Brother Theodore's chamber of horrors.* New York: Pinnacle Books, 1975, 237 p., paper, anth.

KAYE, Merlin, pseud.

26952 *Penetrators of time.* Encino, CA: World-Wide Publishing Co., 1980, 185 p., paper, novel. [Bound with *The savage princess* / by Raymond E. Banks].

26953 *Rape of the red witch.* Encino, CA: World-Wide Publishing Co., 1980, 184 p., paper, novel.

KAYE, Saralee, *with Marvin Kaye*

26946 *Devils & demons: a treasury of fiendish tales old & new.* Garden City, NY: Doubleday & Co., 1987, xv+587 p., cloth, anth.

26947 *Ghosts: a treasury of chilling tales old and new.* Garden City, NY: Doubleday & Co., 1981, xviii+652 p., cloth, anth.

26948 *Haunted America: star-spangled supernatural stories.* New York: Guild America Books, 1991, xii+582 p., cloth, anth.

26949 *Masterpieces of terror and the supernatural: a treasury of spellbinding tales old & new.* Garden City, NY: Doubleday & Co., 1985, xv+623 p., cloth, anth.

26950 *Weird tales: the magazine that never dies.* Garden City, NY: Doubleday Book & Music Clubs, 1988, xxi+582 p., cloth, anth.

KAYE, Terry

25155 *Mad Max.* Melbourne, Australia: Circus Books, 1979, 200 p., paper, movie. MAD MAX #1.

25155A retitled: *Mad Max 1.* Sydney, Australia: QB Book, 1985, 199 p., paper, movie. MAD MAX #1.

KAZANTZAKIS, Nikos, 1883-1957

26954 *At the palaces of Knossos: a novel.* Athens, OH: Ohio University Press, 1988, 219 p., cloth, novel. [An abridged translation by Themi and Theodora Vasils of *Sta palatia tês Knosou*].

KEA, Neville

26955 *The glass school.* London: Robert Hale, 1980, 159 p., cloth, novel.

26956 *The rats of Megaera.* London: Robert Hale, 1980, 192 p., cloth, novel.

26957 *Scorpion.* London: Robert Hale, 1981, 158 p., cloth, novel.

26958 *The world of Artemis.* London: Robert Hale, 1980, 191 p., cloth, novel.

KEANE, Christopher, *with William D. Black*

18086 *Christmas babies.* New York, London: Pocket Star Books, 1991, 280 p., paper, novel.

KEATING, H(enry) R(eymond) F(itzwalter), 1912-

37884 *A long walk to Wimbledon.* London: Macmillan, 1978, 191 p., cloth, novel.
37885 *The strong man.* London: Heinemann, 1971, 336 p., cloth, novel.

KEEFE, Carolyn, 1928-

26960 *C. S. Lewis: speaker & teacher.* Grand Rapids, MI: Zondervan Publishing House, 1971, 144 p., cloth, nonf.

*KEEFER, Lowell B., 1884-1971

KEEGAN, Mel

26961 *Death's head.* London: Gay Men's Press, 1991, 349 p., paper, novel.

*KEEL, John A. [pseud. of John Alva Kiehle], 1930-

KEELE, Luqman, *with Daniel M. Pinkwater*

26962 *Java Jack.* New York: Thomas Y. Crowell, 1980, 152 p., cloth, novel.

KEEN, Susan Atkinson- —SEE: Atkinson-Keen, Susan

KEENAN, Randall H(ughes), 1932?-1969?

26963 *The major works of H. G. Wells: The time machine, THe invisible man, The war of the worlds, Tono-Bungay.* New York: Monarch Press, 1970, 157 p., paper, nonf.

KEENE, Carolyn, house pseud.

26964 *Nancy Drew: ghost stories.* New York: Simon & Schuster, 1983, 151 p., paper, coll.
26965 *Nancy Drew ghost stories II.* New York: Simon & Schuster, 1985, p., paper, coll. [By Mike McQuay].

*KEENE, Day, 1904-1969

KEENE, Joseph E(ugene), 1938- , *with William W. Johnstone*

26691 *Baby grand.* New York: Zebra Books, Kensington Publishing Corp., 1987, 427 p., paper, novel.

KEENER, Frederick M(ichael), 1937-

26966 *English dialogues of the dead: a critical history, an anthology, and a check list.* New York, London: Columbia University Press, 1973, viii+302 p., cloth, anth. [Includes some nonfiction].

KEEPING, Charles (William James), 1924-1988

Book of classic ghost stories—SEE: *Charles Keeping's Book of classic ghost stories.*
26967 *Charles Keeping's Book of classic ghost stories.* New York: Bedrick; London: Blackie & Son, 1986, 142 p., cloth, anth.
26968 *Charles Keeping's Classic tales of the macabre.* London: Blackie Children's Books, 1987, 172 p., cloth, coll.
Classic tales of the macabre—SEE: *Charles Keeping's Classic tales of the macabre.*

KEGAN, Stephanie

26969 *The baby.* New York: Charter Diamond Books, 1990, 262 p., paper, novel.

KEHRET, Margaret A.—SEE: Kehret, Peg

KEHRET, Peg [i.e., Margaret Ann Kehret], 1936-

26970 *Sisters, long ago.* New York: Cobblehill Books, 1990, 149 p., cloth, novel.

KEITH, (John) Andrew, 1958-

26971 *Combat command in the world of Jack Williamson's The legion of space: The legion of war.* New York: Ace Books, 1988, xvii+234 p., paper, novel. COMBAT COMMAND #5.
The legion of war—SEE: *Combat command in the world of Jack Williamson's The legion of space: The legion of war.*

with Jim Musser

26972 *Technical readout 3050.* Chicago: FASA Corp., 1990, 233 p., paper, fiction. BATTLETECH SERIES.

KEITH, Brandon

26973 *The Man from U.N.C.L.E. and the affair of the gunrunners' gold.* Racine, WI: Whitman Publishing Co., 1967, 212 p., cloth, tele. MAN FROM U.N.C.L.E. SERIES.

KEITH, Darielle

26974 *Dark union.* New York: A Dell/Emerald Book, 1983, 380 p., paper, novel.

KEITH, William H(enry) Jr., 1950-

26975 *BattleTech: Decision at Thunder Rift.* Chicago: FASA Corp., 1986, 374 p., paper, novel. BATTLETECH TRILOGY #1.

26976 *BattleTech: Mercenary's star.* Chicago: FASA Corp., 1987, vii+367 p., paper, novel. BATTLETECH TRILOGY #2.

26977 *BattleTech: The price of glory.* Chicago: FASA Corp., 1987, 321 p., paper, novel. BATTLETECH TRILOGY #3.

Decision at Thunder Rift—SEE: *BattleTech: Decision at Thunder Rift.*

26978 *Doctor Who and the rebel's gamble.* Chicago: FASA Corp., 1986, 371 p., paper, novel. DOCTOR WHO SERIES.

26979 *Doctor Who and the vortex crystal.* Chicago: FASA Corp., 1986, 371 p., paper, novel. DOCTOR WHO SERIES.

Mercenary's star—SEE: *Battletech: Mercenary's star.*

The price of glory—SEE: *BattleTech: The price of glory.*

26980 *Renegades honor.* Chicago: FASA Corp., 1988, 437 p., paper, novel. RENEGADE LEGION #1. [Novelization of game].

as KEITH WILLIAM ANDREWS

16476 *Freedom's rangers.* New York: Berkley Books, 1989, 311 p., paper, novel. FREEDOM'S RANGERS #1.

16477 *Freedom's rangers: Raiders of the Revolution.* New York: Berkley Books, 1989, 202 p., paper, novel. FREEDOM'S RANGERS #2.

16478 *Freedom's rangers: Search and destroy.* New York: Berkley Books, 1990, 203 p., paper, novel. FREEDOM'S RANGERS #3.

16479 *Freedom's rangers: Sink the armada.* New York: Berkley Books, 1990, 217 p., paper, novel. FREEDOM'S RANGERS #5.

16480 *Freedom's rangers: Snow kill.* New York: Berkley Books, 1991, 204 p., paper, novel. FREEDOM'S RANGERS #6.

16481 *Freedom's rangers: Treason in time.* New York: Berkley Books, 1990, 219 p., paper, novel. FREEDOM'S RANGERS #4.

Raiders of the Revolution—SEE: *Freedom's rangers: Raiders of the Revolution.*

Search and destroy—SEE: *Freedom's rangers: Search and destroy.*

Sing the armada—SEE: *Freedom's rangers: Sink the armada.*

Snow kill—SEE: *Freedom's rangers: Snow kill.*

Treason in time—SEE *Freedom's rangers: Treason in time.*

as ROBERT CAIN

19187 *Cybernarc.* New York: HarperPaperbacks, 1991, 245 p., paper, novel. CYBERNARC #1.

19188 *Cybernarc: Gold dragon.* New York: HarperPaperbacks, 1991, 218 p., paper, novel. CYBERNARC #2.

Gold dragon—SEE: *Cybernarc: Gold dragon.*

as KEITH DOUGLASS

22063 *Carrier.* New York: Berkley Books, 1991, 325 p., paper, novel. CARRIER #1.

22064 *Carrier: Viper strike.* New York: Berkley Books, 1991, 329 p., paper, novel. CARRIER #2.

Viper strike—SEE: *Carrier: Viper strike.*

KELLAR, Von, house pseud.—SEE: Hughes, Dennis Talbot

*KELLEAM, Joseph E(veridge), 1913-1975

KELLEHER, Ed, *with Harriette Vidal*

26981 *The breeder.* New York: Leisure Books, 1987, 383 p., paper, novel.

26982 *Madonna.* New York: Leisure Books, 1985, 384 p., paper, novel.

26983 *Prime evil.* New York: Leisure Books, 1988, 293 p., paper, novel.

26984 *The school.* New York: Leisure Books, 1988, 365 p., paper, novel.

26985 *The spell.* New York: Leisure Books, 1990, 312 p., paper, novel.

KELLEHER, Victor (Michael Kitchener), 1939-

26986 *Baily's bones.* Sydney, Australia: Viking Kestrel, 1988, [182] p., cloth, novel.

26987 *The beast of Heaven.* St. Lucia, Queensland, Australia: University of Queensland Press, 1985, 205 p., cloth, novel.

26988 *Brother Night.* London: Julia MacRae Books, 1990, 175 p., cloth, novel.

26989 *Del-Del.* Milsons Point, New South Wales, Australia: Random House Australia, 1991, 224 p., cloth, novel.

26990 *Forbidden paths of Thual.* Ringwood, Victoria, Australia: Kestrel Books, 1979, 154 p., cloth, novel.

26991 *The green piper.* Ringwood, Victoria, Australia & Harmondsworth, Middlesex,

England: Viking/Kestrel, 1984, 178 p., cloth, novel.

26992 *The hunting of Shadroth*. Ringwood, Victoria, Australia & Harmondsworth, Middlesex, England: Kestrel Books, 1981, 191 p., cloth, novel.

37886 *The makers*. Ringwood, Victoria, Australia: Viking Kestrel, 1988, 180 p., cloth, novel.

26993 *Master of the grove*. Ringwood, Victoria, Australia & Harmondsworth, Middlesex, England: Kestrel Books, 1982, 182 p., cloth, novel.

26994 *The Red King*. Ringwood, Victoria, Australia: Viking Kestrel, 1989, [185] p., cloth, novel.

26995 *Taronga*. Ringwood, Victoria, Australia: Viking Kestrel, 1986, 197 p., cloth, novel.

KELLER, Beverly (Lou), 1929?-

26997 *Rosebud, with fangs*. New York: Lothrop, Lee & Shepard Books, 1985, 156 p., cloth, novel.

KELLER, David (M.), 1941-

with Byron Preiss & Megan Miller

26998 *The ultimate Dracula*. New York: A Byron Preiss Book, A Dell Trade Paperback, 1991, viii+358 p., paper, anth.

with Byron Preiss & Megan Miller & John Betancourt

17907 *The ultimate Frankenstein*. New York: A Byron Preiss Book, A Dell Trade Paperback, 1991, viii+327 p., paper, anth.

17908 *The ultimate werewolf*. New York: A Byron Preiss Book, A Dell Trade Paperback, 1991, viii+357 p., paper, anth.

KELLER, David H(enry), 1880-1966

26999 *The human termites: a 1929 science fiction extravaganza*. New Orleans, LA: P.D.A. Enterprises, 1979, 80 p., paper, novel.

27000 *The last magician: nine stories from Weird tales*. New Orleans, LA: P.D.A. Enterprises, 1978, 84 p., paper, coll. [Edited by Patrick H. Adkins].

KELLERHALS-STEWART, Heather, 1937-

27001 *Stuck fast in yesterday*. Vancouver, British Columbia, Canada: A Groundwood Book, Douglas & McIntyre, 1983, 135 p., paper, novel.

KELLEY, Charles

27002 *Nomad VI*. New York, Washington: Vantage Press, 1983, p., cloth, novel.

KELLEY, Leo P(atrick), 1928-

Alien gold—SEE: *Star gold*.

27003 *Backward in time*. Belmont, CA: A Pacemaker Bestsellers Book, Fearon Pitman Publishers, 1979, 57 p., paper, novel. SPACE POLICE #4.

27004 *Dead moon*. Belmont, CA: A Pacemaker Bestsellers Book, Fearon Pitman Publishers, 1979, 59 p., paper, novel. GALAXY 5 #4.

27005 *Death sentence*. Belmont, CA: A Pacemaker Bestsellers Book, Fearon Pitman Publishers, 1979, 58 p., paper, novel. SPACE POLICE #6.

27006 *Earth Two*. Belmont, CA: A Pacemaker Bestsellers Book, Fearon Pitman Publishers, 1979, 59 p., paper, novel. SPACE POLICE #3.

27007 *Galaxy 5: teacher's guide*. Belmont, CA: A Pacemaker Bestsellers Book, Fearon Pitman Publishers, 1979, 55 p., paper, nonf. GALAXY 5 SERIES.

27008 *Good-bye to Earth*. Belmont, CA: A Pacemaker Bestsellers Book, Fearon Pitman Publishers, 1979, 60 p., paper, novel. GALAXY 5 #1.

27009 *King of the stars*. Belmont, CA: A Pacemaker Bestsellers Book, Fearon Pitman Publishers, 1979, 59 p., paper, novel. GALAXY 5 #6.

27010 *Night of fire and blood*. Belmont, CA: Fearon Pitman Publishers, 1979, 59 p., cloth, novel.

27011 *On the red world*. Belmont, CA: A Pacemaker Bestsellers Book, Fearon Pitman Publishers, 1979, 60 p., paper, novel. GALAXY 5 #2.

27012 *Prison satellite*. Belmont, CA: A Pacemaker Bestsellers Book, Fearon Pitman Publishers, 1979, 59 p., paper, novel. SPACE POLICE #1.

27013 *Space police: teacher's guide*. Belmont, CA: A Pacemaker Bestsellers Book, Fearon Pitman Publishers, 1979, 73 p., paper, nonf. SPACE POLICE SERIES.

27014 *Star gold*. Belmont, CA: A Pacemaker Bestsellers Book, Fearon Pitman Publishers, 1979, 60 p., cloth, novel.

27014A retitled: *Alien gold*. Toronto, New York: Bantam Books, 1983, 60 p., paper, novel.

27015 *Sunworld.* Belmont, CA: A Pacemaker Bestsellers Book, Fearon Pitman Publishers, 1979, 59 p., paper, novel. SPACE POLICE #5.

27016 *The time trap.* Belmont, CA: A Pacemaker Bestsellers Book, Fearon-Pitman Publishers, 1977, 59 p., paper, novel.

27017 *Vacation in space.* Belmont, CA: A Pacemaker Bestsellers Book, Fearon Pitman Publishers, 1979, 60 p., paper, novel. GALAXY 5 #3.

27018 *Where no sun shines.* Belmont, CA: A Pacemaker Bestsellers Book, Fearon Pitman Publishers, 1979, 60 p., paper, novel. GALAXY 5 #5.

27019 *Worlds apart.* Belmont, CA: A Pacemaker Bestsellers Book, Fearon Pitman Publishers, 1979, 59 p., paper, novel. SPACE POLICE #2.

*KELLEY, Thomas P., 1905-1982

KELLOGG, M(arjorie) Bradley, 1946-

27020 *Harmony* / by Marjorie Bradley Kellogg. New York: A Roc Book, 1991, 473 p., paper, novel.

27021 *A rumor of angels.* New York: A Signet Book, New American Library, 1983, 277 p., paper, novel.

with William B. Rossow

27022 *Lear's daughters.* Garden City, NY: Nelson Doubleday, 1987, 725 p., cloth, coll. LEAR'S DAUGHTERS #1-2.

27023 *Reign of fire.* New York: A Signet Book, New American Library, 1986, 382 p., paper, novel. LEAR'S DAUGHTERS #2.

27024 *The wave and the flame.* New York: A Signet Book, New American Library, 1986, 358 p., paper, novel. LEAR'S DAUGHTERS #1.

KELLUM, David (Franklin), 1936-

27025 *The falling world of Tristram Pocket.* Edmonton, Alberta, Canada: Tree Frog Press, 1976, 137 p., cloth, novel.

KELLY, David J.

27026 *The Baalbak quest.* North Hollywood, CA: American Art Enterprises, 1980, 159 p., paper, novel. KILLSTAR #1.

27027 *Tower of despair.* North Hollywood, CA: American Art Enterprises, 1980, 158 p., paper, novel. KILLSTAR #2.

KELLY, Frank K., 1914-

27028 *Starship Invincible: science fiction stories of the 30s.* Santa Barbara, CA: A Noel Young Book, Capra Press, 1979, 144 p., cloth, coll.

KELLY, Harold Ernest, 1885?-1970?

as EUGENE ASCHER

00531 *The grim caretaker.* London: Strothers Bookshops, 1944, 50 p., paper, story. LUCIAN CAROLUS SERIES.

00532 *There were no Asper ladies.* London: Mitre Press, 1944, 126 p., paper, novel. LUCIAN CAROLUS SERIES.

00532A retitled: *To kill a corpse.* Manchester, England: World Distributors, 1959, 160 p., paper, novel. LUCIAN CAROLUS SERIES.

To kill a corpse—SEE: *There were no Asper ladies.*

00533 *Uncanny adventures: 5 strange thrillers.* London: Everybody's Books, 1944, 48 p., paper, coll.

as PRESTON YORKE

37887 *Death on priority 1.* London: Mitre Press, 1945, p., paper, novel.

15731 *The gamma ray murders.* London: Everybody's Books, 1943, 128 p., paper, novel.

15732 *Space-time task force.* London: Hector Kelly, 1953, 192 p., paper, novel.

KELLY, James Patrick, 1951-

27029 *Heroines.* Eugene, OR: Pulphouse Publishing, 1990, 118 p., cloth, coll. AUTHOR'S CHOICE MONTHLY #9.

27030 *Look into the sun.* New York: Tor, A Tom Doherty Associates Book, 1989, 281 p., cloth, novel. MESSENGER CHRONICLES #2.

27031 *Planet of whispers.* New York: Bluejay Books, 1984, 234 p., cloth, novel. MESSENGER CHRONICLES #1.

27032 *Writer's workshops.* Eugene, OR: Writer's Notebook Press, Pulphouse Publishing, 1991, 11 p., paper, nonf.

with John Kessel

27033 *Freedom Beach.* New York: A Bluejay International Edition, 1985, 259 p., cloth, novel.

KELLY, Ken, 1946-

27034 *The art of Ken Kelly.* Pittsburgh, PA: Friedlander Publishing Group, 1990, 94 p., paper, art.

KELLY, Maeve, 1930- , with Joni Crone & Mary Dorcy

20823 *Mad and bad fairies: a collection of feminist fairytales.* Dublin: Attic Press, 1987, 60 p., paper, anth.

KELLY, Richard, pseud.—SEE: Laymon, Richard

KELLY, Robert

27035 *The cloud people.* Lake Geneva, WI: TSR Inc., 1991, 311 p., paper, novel.

KELLY, Ronald

27036 *Hindsight.* New York: Zebra Books, Kensington Publishing Corp., 1990, 350 p., paper, novel.
27037 *Moon of the werewolf.* New York: Zebra Books, Kensington Publishing Corp., 1991, 398 p., paper, novel.
27038 *Pitfall.* New York: Zebra Books, Kensington Publishing Corp., 1990, 320 p., paper, novel.
27039 *Something out there.* New York: Zebra Books, Kensington Publishing Corp., 1991, 406 p., paper, novel.

KELLY, Sean, 1940- , with Ted Mann

27040 *The secret.* Toronto, New York: A Byron Preiss Book, Bantam Books, 1982, 224 p., paper, fiction.

KELLY, Shane, 1956?-1986?

27041 *The hidden city.* Encino, CA: World-Wide Publishing Co., 1980, 190 p., paper, novel.

*KELLY, William Patrick, 1848-<u>1916</u>

KELMAN, Judith (Ann), 1945-

27042 *Prime evil.* New York: Berkley Books, 1986, 263 p., paper, novel.
27043 *Where shadows fall.* New York: Berkley Books, 1987, 281 p., paper, novel.
27044 *While angels sleep.* New York: Berkley Books, 1988, 280 p., paper, novel.

KEMP, Earl, 1929- , with Nancy Kemp

08153 *Who killed science fiction? an affectionate autopsy: the second SaFari annual.* Chicago: Earl & Nancy Kemp, 1960, 107 p., paper, nonf. anth. [Corrected entry].
27045 *Why is a fan? the second SaFari annual.* Chicago: Earl & Nancy Kemp, 1961, 64 p., paper, nonf. anth.

KEMP, Ken

27046 *Armageddon revisited.* New York, Washington: Vantage Press, 1979, 211 p., cloth, novel.

KEMP, Nancy, with Earl Kemp

08153 *Who killed science fiction? an affectionate autopsy: the second SaFari annual.* Chicago: Earl & Nancy Kemp, 1960, 107 p., paper, nonf. anth. [Corrected entry].
27045 *Why is a fan? the second SaFari annual.* Chicago: Earl & Nancy Kemp, 1961, 64 p., paper, nonf. anth.

KEMP, Peter, 1942-

27047 *H. G. Wells and the culminating ape.* London: Macmillan, 1982, 225 p., cloth, nonf.

KEMP, Robin

27048 *Equinox.* Lewes, East Sussex, England: Book Guild, 1989, 109 p., cloth, novel.

KENDALL, Carol (Seegar), 1917-

27049 *The Firelings.* London: Bodley Head, 1981, 256 p., cloth, novel.

KENDALL, Gordon, pseud.—SEE: Shwartz, Susan & Lewitt, Shariann N.

KENDALL, John

27050 *Dungeon of darkness.* Lake Geneva, WI: TSR Inc., 1984, 76 p., paper, novel. FANTASY FOREST BOOK #5.
27051 *Under dragon's wing.* Lake Geneva, WI: TSR Inc., 1984, 157 p., paper, novel. ENDLESS QUEST #15.

KENDALL, Mark, 1942-

27052 *Killer flies.* New York: A Signet Book, New American Library, 1983, 159 p., paper, novel.

KENDRICK, Walter (M.), 1947-

27053 *A fire in the sky.* New York: A Tempo Star Book, Grosset & Dunlap, 1978, 171 p., paper, movie.
27054 *The thrill of fear: 250 years of scary entertainment.* New York: Grove Weidenfeld, 1991, xxvi+292 p., cloth, nonf.

KENDYL, Sharice, pseud.—SEE: Michels, Sharry & Carstensen, Bernice

KENEALLY, Thomas (Michael), 1935-

27055 *Ned Kelly and the city of the bees.* London: Jonathan Cape, 1978, 120 p., cloth, novel.
27056 *Passenger.* London, Sydney: Collins, 1979, 189 p., cloth, novel.

KENMORE, Frank J.

27057 *The wire window.* New York: Pinnacle Books, Windsor Publishing Corp., 1988, 348 p., paper, novel.

KENNARD, Jean E., 1936-

27058 *Number and nightmare: forms of fantasy in contemporary fiction.* Hamden, CT: Archon Books, 1975, 244 p., cloth, nonf.

KENNEALY, Patricia [i.e., Patricia Kennealy (originally Kennely) Morrison], 1946-

27059 *The copper crown: (a novel of the Keltiad).* New York: Bluejay Books, 1984, 329 p., cloth, novel. KELTIAD #1.
27060 *The hawk's gray feather: a book of the Keltiad.* New York: A Roc Book, 1990, xiii+400 p., cloth, novel. TALES OF ARTHUR #1.
27061 *The silver branch: a novel of the Keltiad.* New York: NAL Books, 1988, 445 p., cloth, novel. KELTIAD #3.
27062 *The throne of Scone: a book of The Keltiad.* New York: Bluejay Books, 1986, 332 p., cloth, novel. KELTIAD #2.

KENNEDY, Edgar Rees, pseud.—SEE: Jennison, John W.

KENNEDY, J(ohn) Gerald, 1947-

27063 *Poe, death, and the life of writing.* New Haven, CT: Yale University Press, 1987, xi+228 p., cloth, nonf.

KENNEDY, Joseph C.—SEE: Kennedy, X. J.

KENNEDY, Leigh, 1951-

27064 *Faces.* London: Jonathan Cape, 1986, [152] p., cloth, coll.
27065 *The journal of Nicholas the American.* London: Jonathan Cape, 1986, 208 p., cloth, novel.

KENNEDY, Peggy, *with Marty Gear*

23777 *The Kennedy masquerade compendium, revised and expanded edition.* Menands, NY: Firepearl Editions, 1984, v+110 p., paper, nonf.

KENNEDY, (Jerome) Richard, 1932-

27066 *Amy's eyes.* New York: Harper & Row, 1985, 437 p., cloth, novel.
27067 *Inside my feet: the story of a giant.* New York: Harper & Row, 1979, 71 p., cloth, novel.

KENNEDY, William (Joseph Jr.), 1928-

27068 *Quinn's book.* New York: Viking, 1988, 289 p., cloth, novel.

KENNEDY, William P.

27069 *The Masakado lesson.* New York: St. Martin's Press, 1986, 312 p., cloth, novel.

KENNEDY, X. J. [pseud. of Joseph Charles Kennedy], 1929-

27070 *The Owlstone crown.* New York: Atheneum, 1983, 210 p., cloth, novel.

KENNELY, Patricia—SEE: Kennealy, Patricia

KENNETT, Rick

27071 *The reluctant ghost-hunter.* Hoole, Cheshire, England: The Haunted Library, 1991, 35 p., paper, coll. PSYCHIC SLEUTHS #3.

*KENNEY, Douglas C., <u>1947-1980</u>

KENT, Arthur—SEE: Bradwell, James

KENT, Fortune, pseud.—SEE: Toombs, John

KENT, Paul, pseud.—SEE: Toombs, John

KENT, Stephen, *with Drake Douglas*

22055 *Death song.* New York: Leisure Books, 1987, 368 p., paper, novel.

KENTON, L. P., pseud.—SEE: Fanthorpe, R. L.

KENWARD, James (Macara), 1908-

37888 *The story of the poor author, and some of the stories that he told.* Welwyn, Hertfordshire, England: Nisbet, 1959 (i.e., 1960), x+177 p., cloth, novel.

KENYON, Ernest M(onroe), 1920-1980?

27074 *Rogue golem.* New York: Popular Library, 1977, 286 p., paper, novel.

KENYON, Paul [pseud. of Donald Moffatt]

27075 *Black gold.* New York: Pocket Books, 1975, 217 p., paper, novel. BARONESS #8.

KER WILSON, Barbara—SEE: Wilson, Barbara Ker

KERMAN, Judith B(erna), 1945-

27076 *Retrofitting Blade Runner: issues in Ridley Scott's Blade Runner and Philip K. Dick's Do androids dream of electric sheep?* Bowling Green, OH: Bowling Green State University Popular Press, 1991, 291 p., cloth, nonf.

KERN, Gary (Woodward), 1938-

27077 *Orgy & other things.* San Bernardino, CA: A Xenos Book, Distributed by The Borgo Press, 1986, 216 p., cloth, coll.
27078 *Zamyatin's We: a collection of critical essays.* Ann Arbor, MI: Ardis Publishers, 1988, 306 p., cloth, nonf. anth.

KERN, Gregory, pseud.—SEE: Tubb, E. C.

KERNAGHAN, Eileen (Shirley Monk), 1939-

27079 *Journey to Aprilioth.* New York: Ace Books, 1980, 439 p., paper, novel. APRILIOTH #1.
27080 *The Sarsen witch.* New York: Ace Books, 1989, 217 p., paper, novel. APRILIOTH #3.
27081 *Songs from the drowned lands.* New York: Ace Fantasy Books, 1983, 204 p., paper, novel. APRILIOTH #2.

KERR, Howard (Hastings), 1931- , *with John W. Crowley & Charles L. Crow*

20831 *The haunted dusk: American supernatural fiction, 1820-1920.* Athens, GA: University of Georgia Press, 1983, vi+236 p., cloth, nonf. anth.

KERR, Katharine (Nancy Brahtin), 1944-

27082 *The bristling wood.* New York: A Foundation Book, Doubleday, 1989, 357 p., cloth, novel. DEVERRY #3.
27082A retitled: *Dawnspell: The bristling wood.* London: Grafton, 1989, 372 p., paper, novel. DEVERRY #3.
27083 *Daggerspell.* Garden City, NY: Doubleday & Co., 1986, 414 p., cloth, novel. DEVERRY #1.
27084 *Darkspell.* Garden City, NY: Doubleday & Co., 1987, 369 p., cloth, novel. DEVERRY #2.
Dawnspell: The bristling wood—SEE: The bristling wood.
27085 *The dragon revenant.* New York: A Foundation Book, Doubleday, 1990, xi+403 p., cloth, novel. DEVERRY #4.
27085A retitled: *Dragonspell: the southern sea.* London: Grafton, 1990, 378 p., cloth, novel. DEVERRY #4.
Dragonspell: the southern sea—SEE: The dragon revenant.
27086 *Polar City blues: an entertainment.* New York, Toronto: Bantam Books, 1990, 262 p., paper, novel.
27087 *A time of exile: a novel of the Westlands.* New York: A Foundation Book, Doubleday, 1991, 434 p., cloth, novel. DEVERRY #5.

KERR, Michael, pseud.—SEE: Hoskins, Robert

*KERRUISH, Jessie Douglas, d. 1949

KESSEL, John (Joseph Vincent), 1950-

27088 *Another orphan.* New York: Tor SF, A Tom Doherty Associates Book, 1989, 68 p., paper, novel. [Bound with *Enemy mine* / by Barry B. Longyear].
27089 *Good news from outer space.* New York: Tor SF, A Tom Doherty Associates Book, 1989, 402 p., cloth, novel.

with James Patrick Kelly

27033 *Freedom Beach.* New York: A Bluejay International Edition, 1985, 259 p., cloth, novel.

KESSLER, Alan S.

27090 *Night screams: 13 tales of terror.* Salem, MA: Black Pumpkin Press, 1986, 49 p., paper, coll.

KESSLER, Carol Farley, 1936-

27091 *Daring to dream: utopian stories by United States women, 1836-1919.* Boston: Pandora Press, 1984, ix+266 p., paper, nonf.

KESSLER, Peter Lawrence

27092 *Second law.* Lewes, East Sussex, England: The Book Guild, 1990, 377 p., cloth, novel.

KESSLER, Risa, *with Lester del Rey*

21515 *Once upon a time: a treasury of modern fairy tales.* New York: A Del Rey Book, Ballantine Books, 1991, ix+336 p., cloth, anth.

KESTERTON, David, 1948-

27093 *The darkling.* Sauk City, WI: Arkham House, 1982, 259 p., cloth, novel.

KESTEVEN, G. R. [pseud. of Geoffrey Robins Crosher], 1911-

27094 *The awakening water.* London: Chatto & Windus, 1977, 160 p., cloth, novel.
27095 *The pale invaders.* London: Chatto & Windus, 1974, 140 p., cloth, novel.

KETCHUM, Jack [pseud. of Dallas William Mayr], 1946-

37889 *Cover.* New York: Warner Books, 1987, 310 p., paper, novel.
27096 *The girl next door: a novel.* New York: Warner Books, 1989, 232 p., paper, novel.
37890 *Hide and seek.* New York: Ballantine Books, 1984, 194 p., paper, novel.
27097 *Off season.* New York: Ballantine Books, 1980, 184 p., paper, novel. OFF SEASON #1.
27098 *Offspring.* New York: Diamond Books, 1991, 265 p., paper, novel. OFF SEASON #2.
27099 *She wakes.* New York: Berkley Books, 1989, 260 p., paper, novel.

KETTERER, David (Anthony Theodore), 1942-

27100 *Edgar Allan Poe: life, work, and criticism.* Fredericton, New Brunswick, Canada: York Press, 1989, 51 p., paper, nonf.
27101 *Frankenstein's creation: the book, the monster, and human reality.* Victoria, British Columbia, Canada: English Language Studies, University of Victoria, 1979, 124 p., paper, nonf.
27102 *Imprisoned in a tesseract: the life and work of James Blish.* Kent, OH: Kent State University Press, 1987, xv+410 p., cloth, nonf.
27103 *The rationale of deception in Poe.* Baton Rouge, LA: Louisiana State University Press, 1979, xv+285 p., cloth, nonf.

KETTLE, Leroy

with John Brosnan as SIMON IAN CHILDER

18769 *Tendrils.* London: Grafton, 1986, 208 p., paper, novel.

with John Brosnan as HARRY ADAM KNIGHT

Death spore—SEE: *The fungus.*
18770 *The fungus.* London: A Star Book, W. H. Allen & Co., 1985, 220 p., paper, novel.
18770A retitled: *Death spore.* New York: Pinnacle Books, Windsor Publishing Corp., 1990, 256 p., paper, novel.
18771 *Slimer.* London: A Star Book, W. H. Allen & Co., 1983, 156 p., paper, novel.

*KETTLE, (Jocelyn) Pamela, 1934-

KEULEN, Margarete, 1961-

27104 *Radical imagination: feminist conceptions of the future in Ursula Le Guin, Marge Piercy, and Sally Miller Gearhart.* Frankfurt am Main, Germany, New York: Peter Lang, 1991, 122 p., paper, nonf.

KEY, Alexander (Hill), 1904-1979

27105 *The case of the vanishing boy.* New York: An Archway Paperback, Pocket Books, 1979, 213 p., paper, novel.
27106 *Jagger, the dog from elsewhere.* New York: Westminster Press, 1976, 126 p., cloth, novel.
27107 *The magic meadow.* New York: Westminster Press, 1975, 124 p., cloth, novel.
27108 *Return from Witch Mountain.* Philadelphia, PA: Westminster Press, 1978, 144 p., cloth, movie. WITCH MOUNTAIN #2.
27109 *The sword of Aradel.* New York: Westminster Press, 1977, 144 p., cloth, novel.

KEY, L. J.

27110 *The spawn.* New York: A Dell Book, 1983, 383 p., paper, novel.

KEY, Samuel M., pseud.—SEE: de Lint, Charles

KEY, Ted [i.e., Theodore Key], 1912-

27111 *The cat from outer space.* New York: A Kangaroo Book, Pocket Books, 1978, 166 p., paper, movie.

KEY, Theodore—SEE: Key, Ted

KEYE, Don, pseud.

27112 *Plucking Daisy's innocence.* New York: A Beeline Double Novel, 1984, 179 p., paper, novel. [Probably published previously under a different title and byline; Bound with *Lust in bloom* / by Jack N. Rose].

KEYES, Thom, 1943-

37891 *The battle of Disneyland.* London: W. H. Allen & Co., 1974, 190 p., cloth, novel.
37892 *The second coming.* London: W. H. Allen & Co., 1972, 199 p., cloth, novel.

KEYHOE, Donald E(dward), 1897-1988

27113 *The mystery of the dragon's shadow.* Oak Lawn, IL: Robert Weinberg in Association with Pulp Press, 1975, [96] p., paper, anth. PULP CLASSICS #9. [Includes the novel by Keyhoe and several short stories by others].

KEYISHIAN, Harry, 1932-

19063 *Michael Arlen.* Boston: Twayne Publishers, 1975, 150 p., cloth, nonf.

KIDD, A. F., 1953-

27114 *Bells rung backwards.* Ruislip, Middlesex, England: A. F. Kidd, 1991, 50 p., paper, coll.

KIDD, Ronald, 1948-

27115 *The glitch.* New York: A Lodestar Book, E. P. Dutton, 1985, 117 p., cloth, novel.

KIDD, (Mildred) Virginia, 1921-

The eye of the heron, and other stories—SEE: *Millennial women.*
27116 *Millennial women.* New York: Delacorte Press, 1978, 305 p., cloth, anth.
27116A retitled: *The eye of the heron, and other stories.* London, Toronto: Panther, Granada Publishing, 1980, 251 p., paper, anth.

with Ursula K. Le Guin

27117 *Edges: thirteen new tales from the borderlands of the imagination.* New York: Pocket Books, 1980, 239 p., paper, anth.
27118 *Interfaces.* New York: Ace Books, 1980, x+310 p., paper, anth.

KIDDE, Janet, pseud.—SEE: Wolk, George

KIDNER, John, 1923- , *with Jack Anderson*

16359 *Alice in Blunderland.* Washington, DC: Acropolis Books, 1983, 183 p., paper, fiction. ALICE IN WONDERLAND SEQUEL.

KIEHLE, John A.—SEE: Keel, John A.

KIES, Cosette (Nell), 1936-

27119 *Supernatural fiction for teens: 500 good paperbacks to read for wonderment, fear, and fun.* Littleton, CO: Libraries Unlimited, 1987, xii+127 p., paper, nonf.

KILBY, Clyde S(amuel), 1902-1986

27120 *The christian world of C. S. Lewis.* Grand Rapids, MI: William B. Eerdmans Publishing Co., 1964, 198 p., cloth, nonf.
27121 *Images of salvation in the fiction of C. S. Lewis.* Wheaton, IL: Harold Shaw Publishers, 1978, 140 p., paper, nonf.
27122 *Tolkien & the Silmarillion.* Wheaton, IL: Harold Shaw Publishers, 1976, 89 p., cloth, nonf.

with Douglas Gilbert

23926 *C. S. Lewis: images of his world.* Grand Rapids, MI: William B. Eerdmans Publishing Co., 1973, 192 p., cloth, nonf.

KILGORE, Axel

The Siberian alternative—SEE: *They call me the mercenary: The Siberian alternative.*
27123 *They call me the mercenary: The Siberian alternative.* New York: Zebra Books,

Kensington Publishing Corp., 1983, 188 p., paper, novel. THE MERCENARY #14.

KILGORE, Kathleen [i.e., Kathleen Kilgore Houton], 1946-

27124 *The ghost-maker.* Boston: Houghton Mifflin Co., 1984, 206 p., cloth, novel.

KILIAN, Crawford, 1941-

27125 *Brother Jonathan.* New York: Ace Science Fiction Books, 1985, 183 p., paper, novel.

27126 *The empire of time.* New York: A Del Rey Book, Ballantine Books, 1978, 183 p., paper, novel. CHRONOPLANE WARS #1.

27127 *Eyas.* Toronto: McClelland & Stewart, Bantam Seal Books, 1982, 354 p., paper, novel.

27128 *The fall of the republic: a novel of the Chronoplane Wars.* New York: A Del Rey Book, Ballantine Books, 1987, 293 p., paper, novel. CHRONOPLANE WARS #2.

27129 *Gryphon.* New York: A Del Rey Book, Ballantine Books, 1989, 260 p., paper, novel.

27130 *Icequake: a novel.* Vancouver, British Columbia, Canada: Douglas & McIntyre, 1979, 229 p., cloth, novel. ICEQUAKE #1.

27131 *Lifter.* New York: Ace Science Fiction Books, 1986, 201 p., paper, novel.

27132 *Rogue emperor: a novel of the Chronoplane Wars.* New York: A Del Rey Book, Ballantine Books, 1988, 296 p., paper, novel. CHRONOPLANE WARS #3.

27133 *Tsunami.* Vancouver, British Columbia, Canada: Douglas & McIntyre, 1983, 218 p., cloth, novel. ICEQUAKE #2.

KILLOUGH, (Karen) Lee, 1942-

27135 *Aventine.* New York: A Del Rey Book, Ballantine Books, 1982, xiii+171 p., paper, coll.

27136 *Blood hunt.* New York: Tor Horror, A Tom Doherty Associates Book, 1987, 319 p., paper, novel. BLOOD HUNT #1.

27137 *Bloodlinks.* New York: Tor Horror, A Tom Doherty Associates Book, 1988, 345 p., paper, novel. BLOOD HUNT #2.

27138 *Deadly Silents.* New York: A Del Rey Book, Ballantine Books, 1981, 246 p., paper, novel.

27139 *The Doppelgänger gambit.* New York: A Del Rey Book, Ballantine Books, 1979,

261 p., paper, novel. BRILL & MAXWELL #1.

27140 *Dragon's teeth.* New York: Popular Library, 1990, 250 p., paper, novel. BRILL & MAXWELL #3.

27141 *The leopard's daughter.* New York: Popular Library, 1987, 218 p., paper, novel.

27142 *Liberty's world.* New York: DAW Books, 1985, 238 p., paper, novel.

27143 *The Monitor, the miners, and the Shree.* New York: A Del Rey Book, Ballantine Books, 1980, 215 p., paper, novel.

27144 *Spider play.* New York: Popular Library, Warner Books, 1986, 232 p., paper, novel. BRILL & MAXWELL #2.

27145 *A voice out of Ramah.* New York: A Del Rey Book, Ballantine Books, 1979, 211 p., paper, novel.

KILLUS, James (Peter), 1950-

27146 *Book of shadows.* New York: Ace Fantasy Books, 1983, vi+185 p., paper, novel.

27147 *Sunsmoke.* New York: Ace Science Fiction Books, 1985, 182 p., paper, novel.

KILROY-SILK, Robert, 1942-

27148 *The ceremony of innocence: a novel of 1984.* London: Enigma, 1983, 238 p., cloth, novel.

KILWORTH, Garry (Douglas?), 1941-

27149 *Abandonati.* London: Unwin Hyman, 1988, 162 p., cloth, novel.

27150 *Cloudrock.* London, Sydney: Unwin Hyman, 1988, 160 p., cloth, novel.

27151 *Dark hills, hollow clocks: stories from the otherworld.* London: Methuen, 1990, 110 p., cloth, coll.

27152 *The drowners.* London: Methuen Children's Books, 1991, 153 p., cloth, novel.
The foxes of first dark—SEE: *Hunter's moon.*

27153 *Gemini god.* London, Boston: Faber & Faber, 1981, 240 p., cloth, novel.

27154 *Hunter's moon: a story of foxes.* London, Sydney: Unwin Hyman, 1989, 330 p., cloth, novel.

27154A retitled: *The foxes of first dark.* New York: Doubleday, 1990, 371 p., cloth, novel.

27155 *In solitary.* London: Faber & Faber, 1977, 131 p., cloth, novel.

27156 *In the hollow of the deep-sea wave: a novel and seven stories.* London: The Bodley Head, 1989, 232 p., cloth, coll.

27157 *Midnight's sun: a story of wolves.* London: Unwin Hyman, 1990, 317 p., cloth, novel.

27158 *The night of Kadar.* London: Faber & Faber, 1978, 193 p., cloth, novel.

27159 *The rain ghost.* London: Hippo Books, 1989, 147 p., paper, novel.

27160 *The songbirds of pain: stories from the Inscape.* London: Victor Gollancz, 1984, 187 p., cloth, coll.

27161 *Split second.* London, Boston: Faber & Faber, 1979, 191 p., cloth, novel.

A story of foxes—SEE: *Hunter's moon: A story of foxes.*

Theater of timesmiths—SEE: *A theatre of timesmiths.*

27162 *A theatre of timesmiths.* London: Victor Gollancz, 1984, 185 p., cloth, novel.

27162A retitled: *Theater of timesmiths.* New York: Popular Library, Warner Books, 1986, 218 p., paper, novel.

27163 *Trivial tales.* Birmingham, England: Birmingham SF Group, 1988, 16 p., paper, coll.

27164 *The voyage of the Vigilance.* London: Armada, 1988, 142 p., paper, novel. WOODWORLD #2.

27165 *The wizard of Woodworld.* London: Dragon, 1987, 142 p., paper, novel. WOODWORLD #1.

as GARRY DOUGLAS

27166 *Highlander.* London: Grafton, 1986, 252 p., paper, movie.

27167 *The street.* London: Grafton, 1988, 236 p., paper, novel.

KIMBALL, Janus

27168 *Scanners II: the new order.* New York: A Dove Book, Warner Books, 1991, 188 p., paper, movie. SCANNERS #2.

KIMBERLY, Gail [i.e., Gail Kimberly Francis]

27169 *Dracula began.* New York: Pyramid Books, 1976, 160 p., paper, novel. DRACULA SEQUEL.

27170 *Flyer.* New York: Popular Library, 1975, 174 p., paper, novel.

27171 *Star jewel.* New York, Toronto: Scholastic Book Services, 1979, 96 p., paper, novel.

as DAYLE COURTNEY

27172 *The trail of bigfoot.* Cincinnati, OH: Standard Publishing, 1983, 191 p., paper, novel.

KIMBRIEL, Katharine Eliska, 1956-

27173 *Fire sanctuary: a novel.* New York: Popular Library, Warner Books, 1986, 370 p., paper, novel. NUALA #1.

27174 *Fires of Nuala.* New York: Popular Library, 1988, 324 p., paper, novel. NUALA #2.

27175 *Hidden fires.* New York: Warner Books, 1991, 277 p., paper, novel. NUALA #3.

KIMBRO, Jean, pseud.—SEE: Kimbro, John M.

KIMBRO, John M(ilton), 1929-

27176 *Night of tears.* New York: Ballantine Books, 1976, 202 p., paper, novel.

as JEAN KIMBRO

27177 *Twilight return: an astrological gothic novel: Cancer.* New York: Ballantine Books, 1976, 218 p., paper, novel. ASTROLOGICAL GOTHIC NOVEL—CANCER.

as KATHERYN KIMBROUGH

27178 *Alexandria, the ambivalent.* New York: Popular Library, 1981, 256 p., paper, novel. SAGA OF THE PHENWICK WOMEN #36.

27179 *Ann, the gentle.* New York: Popular Library, 1978, 252 p., paper, novel. SAGA OF THE PHENWICK WOMEN #20.

27180 *Augusta, the first.* New York: Popular Library, 1975, 256 p., paper, novel. SAGA OF THE PHENWICK WOMEN #1.

27181 *Augusta, the second.* New York: Popular Library, 1979, 252 p., paper, novel. SAGA OF THE PHENWICK WOMEN #28.

27182 *Barbara, the valiant.* New York: Popular Library, 1977, 255 p., paper, novel. SAGA OF THE PHENWICK WOMEN #16.

27183 *Belinda, the impatient.* New York: Popular Library, 1982, 220 p., paper, novel. SAGA OF THE PHENWICK WOMEN #40. [The last book in the series].

27184 *Carol, the pursued.* New York: Popular Library, 1979, 255 p., paper, novel. SAGA OF THE PHENWICK WOMEN #29.

27185 *Dorothy, the terrified.* New York: Popular Library, 1977, 252 p., paper, novel. SAGA OF THE PHENWICK WOMEN #19.

27186 *Evelyn, the ambitious.* New York: Popular Library, 1978, 254 p., paper, novel. SAGA OF THE PHENWICK WOMEN #23.

27187 *Harriet, the haunted.* New York: Popular Library, 1976, 254 p., paper, novel. SAGA OF THE PHENWICK WOMEN #10.

27188 *Ilene, the superstitious.* New York: Popular Library, 1977, 256 p., paper, novel. SAGA OF THE PHENWICK WOMEN #14.

27189 *Iris, the bewitched.* New York: Popular Library, 1982, 222 p., paper, novel. SAGA OF THE PHENWICK WOMEN #39.

27190 *Isabelle, the frantic.* New York: Popular Library, 1978, 256 p., paper, novel. SAGA OF THE PHENWICK WOMEN #22.

27191 *Jane, the courageous.* New York: Popular Library, 1975, 256 p., paper, novel. SAGA OF THE PHENWICK WOMEN #2.

27192 *Joanne, the unpredictable.* New York: Popular Library, 1976, 256 p., paper, novel. SAGA OF THE PHENWICK WOMEN #8.

27193 *Joyce, the beloved.* New York: Popular Library, 1979, 254 p., paper, novel. SAGA OF THE PHENWICK WOMEN #27.

27194 *Kate, the curious.* New York: Popular Library, 1976, 254 p., paper, novel. SAGA OF THE PHENWICK WOMEN #13.

27195 *Katherine, the returned.* New York: Popular Library, 1980, 256 p., paper, novel. SAGA OF THE PHENWICK WOMEN #30.

27196 *Laura, the imperiled.* New York: Popular Library, 1981, 221 p., paper, novel. SAGA OF THE PHENWICK WOMEN #38.

27197 *Letitia, the dreamer.* New York: Popular Library, 1981, 252 p., paper, novel. SAGA OF THE PHENWICK WOMEN #35.

27198 *Louise, the restless.* New York: Popular Library, 1978, 256 p., paper, novel. SAGA OF THE PHENWICK WOMEN #24.

27199 *Marcia, the innocent.* New York: Popular Library, 1976, 252 p., paper, novel. SAGA OF THE PHENWICK WOMEN #12.

27200 *Margaret, the faithful.* New York: Popular Library, 1975, 254 p., paper, novel. SAGA OF THE PHENWICK WOMEN #3.

27201 *Millijoy, the determined.* New York: Popular Library, 1977, 254 p., paper, novel. SAGA OF THE PHENWICK WOMEN #15.

27202 *Nancy, the daring.* New York: Popular Library, 1976, 255 p., paper, novel. SAGA OF THE PHENWICK WOMEN #11.

27203 *Nellie, the obvious.* New York: Popular Library, 1978, 255 p., paper, novel. SAGA OF THE PHENWICK WOMEN #21.

27204 *Olga, the disillusioned.* New York: Popular Library, 1980, 256 p., paper, novel. SAGA OF THE PHENWICK WOMEN #32.

27205 *Olivia, the tormented.* New York: Popular Library, 1976, 254 p., paper, novel. SAGA OF THE PHENWICK WOMEN #9.

27206 *Ophelia, the anxious.* New York: Popular Library, 1977, 253 p., paper, novel. SAGA OF THE PHENWICK WOMEN #18.

27207 *Patricia, the beautiful.* New York: Popular Library, 1975, 254 p., paper, novel. SAGA OF THE PHENWICK WOMEN #4.

27208 *Peggy, the concerned.* New York: Popular Library, 1980, 256 p., paper, novel. SAGA OF THE PHENWICK WOMEN #31.

27209 *Phyllis, the cautious.* New York: Popular Library, 1980, 256 p., paper, novel. SAGA OF THE PHENWICK WOMEN #33.

27210 *Polly, the worried.* New York: Popular Library, 1979, 256 p., paper, novel. SAGA OF THE PHENWICK WOMEN #25.

27211 *Rachel, the possessed.* New York: Popular Library, 1975, 253 p., paper, novel. SAGA OF THE PHENWICK WOMEN #5.

27212 *Rebecca, the mysterious.* New York: Popular Library, 1975, 255 p., paper, novel. SAGA OF THE PHENWICK WOMEN #7.

27213 *Romula, the dedicated.* New York: Popular Library, 1981, 220 p., paper, novel. SAGA OF THE PHENWICK WOMEN #37.

27214 *Ruth, the unsuspecting.* New York: Popular Library, 1977, 256 p., paper, novel. SAGA OF THE PHENWICK WOMEN #17.

27215 *Susannah, the righteous.* New York: Popular Library, 1975, 253 p., paper, novel. SAGA OF THE PHENWICK WOMEN #6.

27216 *Ursala, the proud.* New York: Popular Library, 1980, 253 p., paper, novel. SAGA OF THE PHENWICK WOMEN #34.

27217 *Yvonne, the confident.* New York: Popular Library, 1979, 253 p., paper, novel. SAGA OF THE PHENWICK WOMEN #26.

KIMBROUGH, Katheryn, pseud.—SEE: Kimbro, John M.

KINCAID, Paul, 1952-

27218 *Keith Roberts.* Folkestone, Kent, England: British Science Fiction Association, 1983, 50 p., paper, nonf. BRITISH SCIENCE FICTION AUTHORS #2.

with Geoff Rippington

27219 *Bob Shaw.* Folkestone, Kent, England: British Science Fiction Association, 1981, 38 p., paper, nonf. BRITISH SCIENCE FICTION WRITERS #1.

KINCAID, Robin, *with Andrew J. Offutt as* JOHN CLEVE

27220 *Assignment: Hellhole.* New York: Berkley Books, 1983, 212 p., paper, novel. SPACEWAYS #14.
27221 *Race across the stars.* New York: Berkley Books, 1984, 225 p., paper, novel. SPACEWAYS #18.

KINDER, Stuart, 1924-

27222 *The cannibal.* London: Grafton, 1988, 171 p., paper, novel.

KING, Albert, 1924-

as MARK BANNON

00850 *The assimilator.* London: Robert Hale, 1974, 191 p., cloth, novel.
27223 *The tomorrow station.* London: Robert Hale, 1975, 175 p., cloth, novel.
00851 *The wayward robot.* London: Robert Hale, 1974, 188 p., cloth, novel.

as PAUL CONRAD

03319 *Ex minus.* London: Robert Hale, 1974, 191 p., cloth, novel.
27224 *Last man on Kluth V.* London: Robert Hale, 1975, 192 p., cloth, novel.
27225 *The slave bug.* London: Robert Hale, 1975, 189 p., cloth, novel.

as FLOYD GIBSON

27226 *The manufactured people.* London: Robert Hale, 1975, 192 p., cloth, novel.
27227 *Shadow of Gastor.* London: Robert Hale, 1975, 182 p., cloth, novel.
05950 *A slip in time.* London: Robert Hale, 1974, 191 p., paper, novel.

as SCOTT HOWELL

07499 *Menace from Magor.* London: Robert Hale, 1974, 190 p., cloth, novel.
27228 *Passage to oblivion.* London: Robert Hale, 1975, 192 p., cloth, novel.

as CHRISTOPHER KING

08241 *Operation Mora.* London: Robert Hale, 1974, 191 p., cloth, novel.
27229 *The world of Jonah Klee.* London: Robert Hale, 1976, 174 p., cloth, novel.

as PAUL MULLER

27230 *Brother Gib.* London: Robert Hale, 1975, 192 p., cloth, novel.
10501 *The man from Ger.* London: Robert Hale, 1974, 191 p., cloth, novel.

KING, Bernard, 1946-

27231 *Blood circle.* London: Sphere Books, 1990, 312 p., paper, novel.
27232 *Death-blinder.* Sevenoaks, Kent, England: New English Library, 1988, 226 p., paper, novel. STARKADDER #3.
27233 *Destroying angel.* London: Sphere Books, 1987, 272 p., paper, novel. CHRONICLES OF THE KEEPER #1.
27234 *Skyfire.* London: Sphere Books, 1988, 238 p., paper, novel. CHRONICLES OF THE KEEPER #3.
27235 *Starkadder.* Sevenoaks, Kent, England: New English Library, 1985, xi+243 p., cloth, novel. STARKADDER #1.
27236 *Time-fighters.* London: Sphere Books, 1987, 253 p., paper, novel. CHRONICLES OF THE KEEPER #2.
27237 *Vargr-moon.* Sevenoaks, Kent, England: New English Library, 1986, xii+243 p., cloth, novel. STARKADDER #2.
27238 *Witch beast.* London: Sphere Books, 1989, [288] p., paper, novel.

KING, Betty, 1948-

27239 *Women of the future: the female main character in science fiction.* Metuchen, NJ & London: Scarecrow Press, 1984, xxi+273 p., cloth, nonf.

KING, Bruce (Alvin), 1933-

27240 *Demon shield.* New York: Lynx Books, 1989, 434 p., paper, novel.

as MARK GRANT

24357 *Christmas slaughter.* New York: Avon Books, 1991, 181 p., paper, novel. MUTANTS AMOK #5.

KING, Christopher, pseud.—SEE: King, Albert

KING, (David) Clive, 1924-

27241 *The seashore people.* Harmondsworth, Middlesex, England: Viking Kestrel, 1987, 95 p., cloth, novel.

KING, Cynthia (Bregman), 1925-

15823 *In the morning of time: the story of the Norse god Balder.* New York: Four Winds Press, 1970, 237 p., cloth, novel.

KING, David, 1960-

27242 *Dreamworks: strange new stories.* Carlton, Victoria, Australia: Norstrilia Press, 1983, viii+198 p., cloth, anth.

with Russell Blackford

18090 *Urban fantasies.* Melbourne, Australia: Ebony Books, 1985, 177 p., paper, anth.

KING, Frank

27243 *Southpaw.* New York: Lynx Books, 1988, 229 p., paper, novel.

KING, Harold, 1945-

27244 *Shelkagari.* New York: Donald I. Fine, 1987, 478 p., cloth, novel.

as BRIAN HARRIS

27245 *World War III: a novelization.* New York: Pocket Books, 1982, 240 p., paper, tele.

KING, John, pseud.—SEE: McKeag, Ernest

KING, John Robert, 1948-

27246 *Bruno Lipshitz and the Disciples of Dogma.* London: Victor Gollancz, 1976, 159 p., cloth, novel.

KING, Keith M.—SEE: Carr, Bentley

KING, Paula—SEE: Downing, Paula

KING, Robert—SEE: Butler, Nathan

*KING, Rufus (Frederick), 1893-1966

KING, Stephen (Edwin), 1947-

27247 *The Bachman books: four early novels: Rage; The long walk; Roadwork; The running man.* New York: New American Library, 1985, x+692 p., cloth, coll.
Black magic and music—SEE: A novelist's perspective of Bangor.

27248 *The breathing method.* Bath, Avon, England: A Lythway Book, Chivers Press, 1984, 106 p., cloth, story.

27249 *Christine: a novel.* West Kingston, RI: Donald M. Grant, Publisher, 1983, 544 p., cloth, novel.

27250 *Cujo.* New York: Viking Press, 1981, 319 p., cloth, novel.

27251 *Cycle of the werewolf.* Westland, MI: The Land of Enchantment, Christopher Zavisa, Publisher, 1983, 114 p., cloth, novel.
Danse macabre—SEE: Stephen King's Danse macabre.

27252 *The dark half.* New York: Viking, 1989, 431 p., cloth, novel.

27253 *The dark tower: The gunslinger.* West Kingston, RI: Donald M. Grant, Publisher, 1982, 224 p., cloth, coll. DARK TOWER #1.
The dark tower II—SEE: The drawing of the three.
The dark tower III—SEE: The waste lands.

27254 *The dead zone.* New York: Viking Press, 1979, 426 p., cloth, novel.

27255 *Different seasons.* New York: Viking Press, 1982, 527 p., cloth, coll.

27256 *Dolan's cadillac.* Northridge, CA: Lord John Press, 1989, 64 p., cloth, story.

27257 *The drawing of the three.* West Kingston, RI: Donald M. Grant, Publisher, 1987, 400 p., cloth, novel. DARK TOWER #2.

27258 *The eyes of the dragon.* Bangor, ME: Philtrum Press, 1984, 314 p., cloth, novel.

27259 *Firestarter.* New York: Viking Press, 1980, p., cloth, novel.

27260 *Four past midnight.* New York: Viking, 1990, xvi+763 p., cloth, coll. [Winner of the Bram Stoker Award for Best Horror Collection, 1990 (1991)].
The gunslinger—SEE: The dark tower: The gunslinger.

27261 *It.* New York: Viking, 1986, x+1138 p., cloth, novel.

27262 *The monkey.* [S.l.: s.n., 1980?], 34 p., paper?, story.

27263 *My pretty pony.* New York: Library Fellows, Whitney Museum of American Art, 1988, unpaginated, cloth, story.

27264 *Needful things.* New York: Viking, 1991, 690 p., cloth, novel.

27265 *Night shift.* Garden City, NY: Doubleday & Co., 1978, xxii+336 p., cloth, coll.

27266 *Nouvelles.* Paris: Presses Pocket, 1990, 223 p., paper, coll. [A bilingual edition in French and English, the French versions translated by Michael Oriano].

27267 *A novelist's perspective of Bangor.* Bangor, ME: [s.n.], 1983, [5] p., paper, nonf. [Cover title: *Black magic and music*].

27268 *Pet sematary.* Garden City, NY: Doubleday & Co., 1983, 373 p., cloth, novel.

27269 *The plant: the opening segment of an ongoing work.* Bangor, ME: Philtrum Press, 1982, 32 p., paper, story. PLANT #1. [Limited to 226 copies].

27270 *The plant, [part 2].* Bangor, ME: Philtrum Press, 1983, 36 p., paper, story. PLANT #2. [Limited to 226 copies].

27271 *The plant, [part 3].* Bangor, ME: Philtrum Press, 1985, 56 p., paper, story. PLANT #3. [Limited to 226 copies].

27272 *'Salem's Lot.* Garden City, NY: Doubleday & Co., 1975, 439 p., cloth, novel.

27273 *The shining.* Garden City, NY: Doubleday & Co., 1977, 447 p., cloth, novel.

27274 *The shining; 'Salem's Lot; Carrie.* London: Octopus Books, Heinemann, 1983, 747 p., cloth, coll.

27275 *The shining; 'Salem's Lot; Night shift; Carrie.* London: Octopus Books, Heinemann, 1981, 991 p., cloth, coll.

27276 *Silver bullet.* New York: A Signet Book, New American Library, 1985, 255 p, paper, coll. [Includes both the story and the screenplay].

27277 *Skeleton crew.* New York: G. P. Putnam's Sons, 1985, 512 p., cloth, coll. [Winner of the *Locus* Award for Best Collection, 1985 (1986)].

27278 retitled: *Stephen King's Skeleton crew.* Santa Cruz, CA: Scream/Press, 1985, xxiv+545 p., cloth, coll. [Expanded edition].

27279 *The stand.* Garden City, NY: Doubleday & Co., 1978, 823 p., cloth, novel.

27280 *The stand: the complete & uncut edition.* New York: Doubleday, 1990, xix+1153 p., cloth, novel. [An expanded edition which restores significant material cut from the original version].

27281 *Stephen King's Danse macabre.* New York: Everest House, 1979, 400 p., cloth, nonf. [Winner of the Hugo Award for Best Nonfiction Book, 1981 (1982); winner of the *Locus* Award for Best Nonfiction, 1981 (1982)].

Stephen King's Skeleton crew—SEE: *Skeleton crew.*

27282 *The tommyknockers.* New York: G. P. Putnam's Sons, 1987, 558 p., cloth, novel.

27283 *The waste lands.* Hampton Falls, NH: Donald M. Grant, Publisher, 1991, 512 p., cloth, novel. DARK TOWER #3.

as RICHARD BACHMAN

27284 *The long walk.* New York: A Signet Book, New American Library, 1979, 244 p., paper, novel.

27285 *The Running Man.* New York: A Signet Book, New American Library, 1982, 219 p., paper, novel.

27286 *Thinner.* New York: New American Library, 1984, 309 p., cloth, novel.

with Peter Straub

27287 *The Talisman.* New York: Viking, G. P. Putnam's Sons, 1984, x+646 p., cloth, novel.

KING, T(homas) Jackson (Jr.), 1948-

27288 *Retread shop.* New York: Popular Library, 1988, 276 p., paper, novel.

KING, Tabitha (Jane), 1949-

27289 *Small world.* New York: Macmillan Publishing Co., 1981, 229 p., cloth, novel.

KING, Tappan (Wright), 1950-

with Beth Meacham

27290 *Nightshade: a novel.* New York: Pyramid Books, 1976, 240 p., paper, novel. WEIRD HEROES #4.

with Viido Polikarpus

27291 *Down Town: a fantasy.* New York: Arbor House, 1985, 293 p., cloth, novel.

KING, Vincent [pseud. of Rex Thomas Vinson], 1935-

27292 *Time snake and superclown.* London: Futura Publications, An Orbit Book, 1976, 191 p., paper, novel.

KING-HALL, Magdalen, 1904-1971

37893 *The life and death of the wicked Lady Skelton.* London: Peter Davies, 1944, 215 p., cloth, novel.

KING-SMITH, Dick, 1922-

27293 *Tumbleweed.* London: Victor Gollancz, 1987, 119 p., cloth, novel.

KINGSBURY, Donald (MacDonald), 1929-

27294 *Courtship rite.* New York: Timescape Books, 1982, 464 p., cloth, novel.

[Winner of the *Locus* Award for Best First Novel, 1982 (1983)].

27294A retitled: *Geta.* London: Panther, 1984, 512 p., paper, novel.
Geta—SEE: *Courtship rite.*

27295 *The moon goddess and the son.* New York: Baen Books, 1987, 409 p., cloth, novel.

KINGSTON, Jeremy, pseud.—SEE: Betancourt, John Gregory

KINNAIRD, John (William), 1924-1980

27296 *Olaf Stapledon.* Mercer Island, WA: Starmont House, 1986, 107 p., cloth, nonf. STARMONT READER'S GUIDE #21.

KINNARD, Roy, 1952-

27297 *Beasts and behemoths: prehistoric creatures in the movies.* Metuchen, NJ & London: Scarecrow Press, 1988, xi+179 p., cloth, nonf.

KINNERLEY, Lynne, *with Ann Grimsley as* LYNDAN DARBY

24747 *Bloodseed.* London: Unwin Paperbacks, 1988, 262 p., paper, novel. EYE OF TIME TRILOGY #2.

24748 *Crystal and steel.* London: Unwin Paperbacks, 1988, 340 p., paper, novel. EYE OF TIME TRILOGY #1.

24749 *Phoenix fire.* London: Unwin Paperbacks, 1989, 202 p., paper, novel. EYE OF TIME TRILOGY #3.

KINSELLA, W(illiam) P(atrick), 1935-

27298 *The alligator report: stories.* Minneapolis, MN: Coffee House Press, 1985, 125 p., paper, coll.

27299 *The further adventures of Slugger McBatt: baseball stories.* Toronto: Collins, 1988, 179 p., cloth, coll.

27300 *The Iowa Baseball Confederacy.* Toronto: Collins, 1986, 310 p., cloth, novel.

27301 *Shoeless Joe.* Boston: Houghton Mifflin Co., 1982, 265 p., cloth, novel.

KIPLING, (Joseph) Rudyard, 1865-1936

27302 *The complete supernatural stories of Rudyard Kipling.* London: W. H. Allen & Co., 1987, 427 p., cloth, coll. [Edited by Peter Haining].

KIPPAX, John [pseud. of John Charles Hynam], 1915-1974

27303 *Where no stars guide.* London & Sydney: Pan Books, 1975, 154 p., paper, novel. VENTURER TWELVE #4.

KIRBAN, Salem

27304 *666.* Huntingdon Valley, PA: Salem Kirban, 1981, 284+185 p., paper, coll. [Includes *666* and *1000*].

KIRBY, T. J.

27305 *Deadly breed.* New York: Zebra Books, Kensington Publishing Corp., 1991, 383 p., paper, novel.

KIRCHHOFF, Frederick (Thomas), 1942-

27306 *William Morris.* London: G. Prior; Boston: Twayne Publishers, 1979, 182 p., cloth, nonf.

27307 *William Morris: the construction of a male self, 1856-1872.* Athens, OH: Ohio University Press, 1990, xv+248 p., cloth, nonf.

KIRCHOFF, Mary L(ynn), 1959-

27308 *Art of the Advanced Dungeons & Dragons fantasy game.* Lake Geneva, WI: TSR Inc., 1989, 126 p., paper, nonf. anth.

27309 *The art of the Dragonlance saga.* Lake Geneva, WI: TSR Inc., 1987, 125 p., paper, art.

27310 *Kendermore.* Lake Geneva, WI: TSR Inc., 1989, 346 p., paper, novel. DRAGONLANCE PRELUDES #2.

27311 *Knight of illusion.* Lake Geneva, WI: TSR Inc., 1986, 159 p., paper, novel. ENDLESS QUEST #33.

27312 *Portrait in blood.* Lake Geneva, WI: TSR Inc., 1985, 222 p., paper, novel. AMAZING STORIES #3.

27313 *Vision of doom.* Lake Geneva, WI: TSR Inc., 1986, 160 p., paper, novel. ENDLESS QUEST #35.

with Douglas Niles

27314 *Flint the king.* Lake Geneva, WI: TSR Inc., 1990, 308 p., paper, novel. DRAGONLANCE PRELUDES II #2.

with James M. Ward

27315 *Light on Quests Mountain.* Lake Geneva, WI: TSR Inc., 1983, 157 p., paper, novel. ENDLESS QUEST #12.

with Margaret Weis & Tracy Hickman

25610   *Leaves from the inn of the Last Home: the complete Krynn source book.*   Lake Geneva, WI: TSR Inc., 1987, 255 p., paper, nonf.

with Steve Winter

27316   *Wanderlust.* Lake Geneva, WI: TSR Inc., 1991, 312 p., paper, novel.   DRAG-ONLANCE SAGA—MEETINGS SEXTET #2.

KIRK, Douglas

27317   *The land of the Nunch.* Canyon Lake, TX: Morton Falls Publishing Co., 1986, 150 p., paper, novel.

KIRK, Philip, pseud.—SEE: Levinson, Leonard

KIRK, Richard, pseud.—SEE: Holdstock, Robert & Wells, Angus

KIRK, Russell (Amos), 1918-

27322   *Lord of the hollow dark.* New York: St. Martin's Press, 1979, 336 p., cloth, novel.

27323   *The princess of all lands.* Sauk City, WI: Arkham House, 1979, viii+238 p., cloth, coll.

27324   *Watchers at the strait gate: mystical tales.* Sauk City, WI: Arkham House, 1984, xiv+256 p., cloth, coll.

KIRK, Tim, 1947- , *with George W. Beahm*

17593   *Kirk's works: an index to the art of Tim Kirk.* Newport News, VA: Heresy Press, 1980, 121 p., cloth, nonf.

KIRSCH, Robert R., 1922-1980, *with Lawrence Clark Powell & Jacob Zeitlin*

27325   *Aldous Huxley, 1894-1963: addresses at a memorial meeting held in the School of Library Service, February 27, 1964.* Los Angeles: University of California, Los Angeles, 1964, 10 p., paper, nonf. coll.

KIRSCH, Steven J., 1951-

27326   *Oath of office.* New York: Fawcett Crest, 1988, 355 p., paper, novel.

*KIRST, Hans Hellmut, 1914-<u>1989</u>

KIRSTEIN, Rosemary

27327   *The steerswoman.* New York: A Del Rey Book, Ballantine Books, 1989, 279 p., paper, novel.

KIRTLEY, Bacil F., 1924- , *with A. Grove Day*

21306   *Horror in paradise: grim and uncanny tales from Hawaii and the South Seas.* Honolulu, HI: Mutual Publishing Co., 1986, 285 p., paper, anth.

KIRWAN-VOGEL, Anna

27328   *The jewel of life.* San Diego, CA: Jane Yolen Books, Harcourt Brace Jovanovich, 1991, ix+118 p., cloth, novel.

KISNER, James (Martin Jr.), 1947-

27329   *Earthblood.* New York: Zebra Books, Kensington Publishing Corp., 1990, 351 p., paper, novel.

27330   *Nero's vice.* New York, Toronto: Beaufort Books, 1981, 160 p., cloth, novel.

27331   *Poison pen.* New York: Zebra Books, Kensington Publishing Corp., 1990, 320 p., paper, novel.

27332   *The quagmire.* New York: Zebra Books, Kensington Publishing Corp., 1991, 351 p., paper, novel.

27333   *Strands* / by James B. Kisner. New York: Leisure Books, 1988, 364 p., paper, novel.

as MARTIN JAMES

27334   *Night glow.* New York: Zebra Books, Kensington Publishing Corp., 1989, 320 p., paper, novel.

27335   *Zombie house.* New York: Pinnacle Books, Windsor Publishing Corp., 1990, 352 p., paper, novel.

KISSLING, Dorothy H.—SEE: Langley, Dorothy

KITSCH, Hieronymous, 1953-

27336   *The heart of R'Lyeh.* London: Unspeakable Tomes, An Aporia Press Imprint, 1989, 72 p., paper, coll. CTHULHU MYTHOS PARODY.

27337   *Tales of the outré: writings celebrating the centenary of H. P. Lovecraft.* England: Unspeakable Tomes, 1990, 43 p., paper, anth.

KITTREDGE, Mary (Elizabeth Talbot), 1949- , with Kevin O'Donnell Jr.

27338   *The shelter.* New York: Tor Horror, A Tom Doherty Associates Book, 1987, 376 p., paper, novel.

KJELGAARD, James A.—SEE: Kjelgaard, Jim

KJELGAARD, Jim [i.e., James Arthur Kjelgaard], 1910-1959, with David Drake

22178   *The hunter returns.* Riverdale, NY: Baen Books, 1991, 275 p., paper, novel. [Expanded and adapted from *Fire-hunter* / by Jim Kjelgaard (see #08301)].

KLAINER, Albert S., 1935-, with Jo-Ann Klainer

08320A   *The 11th plague.* New York: Pinnacle Books, 1976, 178 p., paper, novel. [Originally published in 1973 under the pseud. of L. T. Peters].
27339   *The Judas gene: a novel.* New York: Richard Marek, 1980, 258 p., cloth, novel.

KLAINER, Jo-Ann, with Albert S. Klainer

08320A   *The 11th plague.* New York: Pinnacle Books, 1976, 178 p., paper, novel. [Originally published in 1973 under the pseud. of L. T. Peters].
27339   *The Judas gene: a novel.* New York: Richard Marek, 1980, 258 p., cloth, novel.

KLAPER, Steven

27340   *Agents of insight.* New York: Tor SF, A Tom Doherty Associates Book, 1986, 224 p., paper, novel.

KLASS, Judith A.—SEE: Klass, Judy

KLASS, Judy [i.e., Judith Alexandra Klass], 1967-

  The cry of the Onlies—SEE: *Star Trek: The cry of the Onlies.*
27341   *Star Trek: The cry of the Onlies.* New York, London: Pocket Books, 1989, 255 p., paper, tele.. STAR TREK #46.

KLASTORIN, Michael, with Sally Hibbin

25585   *Back to the future: the official book of the complete movie trilogy.* London: Hamlyn, 1990, 79 p., paper, nonf.

KLAUSE, Annette Curtis

27342   *The silver kiss.* New York: Delacorte Press, 1990, 198 p., cloth, novel.

KLAUSNER, Lawrence David, 1939-

27343   *Hail to the chief.* New York: Carlyle, 1978, 254 p., paper, novel.

KLAVENESS, Jan O'Donnell

27344   *Beyond the cellar door.* New York, Toronto: Scholastic Inc., 1991, 186 p., cloth, novel.
27345   *Ghost island.* New York: Macmillan, 1985, 220 p., cloth, novel.
27346   *The Griffin legacy.* New York: Macmillan, 1983, 184 p., cloth, novel.

KLEIN, Daniel M(artin), 1939-

27347   *Embryo: a novel.* Garden City, NY: Doubleday & Co., 1980, 277 p., cloth, novel.
27348   *Wavelengths.* Garden City, NY: Doubleday & Co., 1982, 276 p., cloth, novel.

*KLEIN, Edward (Joel), 1936-

KLEIN, Gérard, 1937-

27349   *The mote in time's eye.* New York: DAW Books, 1975, 173 p., paper, novel. [Translation by C. J. Richards of *Les tueurs de temps*].

KLEIN, Jeffrey

27350   *The black hole affair.* New York: Zebra Books, Kensington Publishing Corp., 1991, 287 p., paper, novel.

KLEIN, Robin, 1936-

27351   *Games.* Ringwood, Victoria, Australia: Viking Kestrel, 1986, 149 p., cloth, novel.
27352   *Halfway across the galaxy and turn left.* Ringwood, Victoria, Australia: Viking Kestrel, 1986, 144 p., cloth, novel.

KLEIN, T(heodore) E(ibon) D(onald), 1947-

27353   *The ceremonies.* New York: Viking Press, 1984, 502 p., cloth, novel.
27354   *Dark gods: four tales.* New York: Viking, 1985, 259 p., cloth, coll.
27355   *The events at Poroth Farm.* West Warwick, RI: Necronomicon Press, 1990, 40 p., paper, story.

27356 *Great stories from Rod Serling's The Twilight Zone Magazine, 1983 annual.* New York: TZ Publications, 1982, 146 p., paper, anth. [Includes some nonfiction].

27357 *Raising goosebumps for fun and profit.* Round Top, NY: Footsteps Press, 1988, 88 p., paper, nonf. [Limited to 500 copies].

with Robert Bloch & Fritz Leiber

18200 *The first World Fantasy Convention: three authors remember.* West Warwick, RI: Necronomicon Press, 1980, 52 p., paper, nonf.

KLEINBARD, Joan—SEE: Gould, Joan

KLEINBAUM, N. H.

27358 *D.A.R.Y.L.* New York: Pacer Books for Young Adults, 1985, 157 p., paper, movie.

KLEPPLE, Horst, pseud.

27359 *Hard on.* Wilmington, DE: An Eros Goldstripe Publication, 1974, 182 p., paper, novel.

KLEYPAS, Lisa, 1964-

27360 *Give me tonight.* New York: An Onyx Book, New American Library, 1989, 383 p., paper, novel.

KLINE, Otis Adelbert, 1891-1946

The bride of Osiris—SEE: Stories by Otis Adelbert Kline.

27361 *Stories by Otis Adelbert Kline.* Oak Lawn, IL: Robert Weinberg, 1975, 96 p., paper, coll. LOST FANTASIES #1. [Cover title: *The bride of Osiris*].

KLINE, Robert Y(oung)

27362 *Ancestors.* New York: Pageant Books, 1988, 376 p., paper, novel.

27363 *Campfire story.* New York: Charter/ Diamond Books, 1990, 264 p., paper, novel.

KLINKOWITZ, Jerome, 1943-

27364 *Kurt Vonnegut.* London & New York: Methuen, 1982, 96 p., paper, nonf.

27365 *Slaughterhouse-five: reforming the novel and the world.* Boston: Twayne Publishers, 1990, xiii+118 p., cloth, nonf.

with Donald L. Lawler

27366 *Vonnegut in America: an introduction to the life and work of Kurt Vonnegut.* New York: A Seymour Lawrence Book, Delacorte Press, 1977, xv+304 p., cloth, nonf. anth.

with Asa B. Pieratt Jr.

27367 *Kurt Vonnegut, Jr.: a descriptive bibliography and annotated secondary checklist.* Hamden, CT: Archon Books, 1974, xix+138 p., cloth, nonf.

with Asa B. Pieratt Jr. & Julie Huffman-klinkowitz

26123 *Kurt Vonnegut: a comprehensive bibliography.* Hamden, CT: Archon Books, 1987, xxiv+289 p., cloth, nonf. [Expanded edition of #27367].

with John Somer

27368 *The Vonnegut statement.* New York: A Seymour Lawrence Book, Delacorte Press, 1973, xvii+286 p., cloth, nonf. anth.

KLINKOWITZ, Julie Huffman- —SEE: Huffman-klinkowitz, Julie

KLOEPFER, Marguerite (Fonnesbeck), 1916-

27369 *The heart and the scarab.* New York: Avon, 1981, 277 p., paper, novel.

KLYNE, Karl

27370 *Jason and the astronauts.* North Hollywood, CA: American Art Enterprises, 1981, 160 p., paper, novel.

27371 *The last galaxy game.* North Hollywood, CA: American Art Enterprises, 1980, 158 p., paper, novel.

KNAAK, Richard A(llen), 1961-

27372 *Children of the drake: origin of Dragonrealm.* New York: Warner Books, 1991, 284 p., paper, novel. ORIGIN OF DRAGONREALM #2.

27373 *The dragonrealm: Firedrake.* New York: Popular Library, 1989, 268 p., paper, novel. DRAGONREALM #1.

27374 *The dragonrealm: Icedragon.* New York: Popular Library, 1989, 248 p., paper, novel. DRAGONREALM #2.

27375 *The dragonrealm: Shadow steed.* New York: Popular Library, 1990, 263 p., paper, novel. DRAGONREALM #4.

27376 *The dragonrealm: Wolfhelm.* New York: Popular Library, 1990, 251 p., paper, novel. DRAGONREALM #3.

Firedrake—SEE: *The dragonrealm: Firedrake.*

Icedragon—SEE: *The dragonrealm: Icedragon.*

27377 *Kaz, the minotaur.* Lake Geneva, WI: TSR Inc., 1990, 314 p., paper, novel. DRAGONLANCE HEROES II #1.

27378 *The legend of Huma.* Lake Geneva, WI: TSR Inc., 1988, 378 p., paper, novel. DRAGONLANCE SAGA—HEROES #1.

Shadow steed—SEE: *The Dragonrealm: Shadow steed.*

27379 *The shrouded realm: origin of Dragonrealm.* New York: Warner Books, 1991, 297 p., paper, novel. ORIGIN OF DRAGONREALM #1.

Wolfhelm—SEE: *The Dragonrealm: Wolfhelm.*

KNAPP, Bettina L(iebowitz), 1926-

27380 *Edgar Allan Poe.* New York: Frederick Ungar Publishing Co., 1984, 226 p., cloth, nonf.

KNAPP, Lawrence J(oseph)

27381 *The first editions of Philip Jose Farmer* [sic]. Menlo Park, CA: David G. Turner, Bookman, 1976, ii+8 p., paper, nonf. SCIENCE FICTION BIBLIOGRAPHIES #2.

KNEALE, (Thomas) Nigel, 1922-

27382 *Quatermass.* London: Hutchinson, 1979, 271 p., paper, novel.

KNEIFEL, Hans

27383 *Pale country pursuit.* New York: Ace Books, 1977, p. 121-251, paper, novel. ATLAN #3. [Bound with *Robot threat: New York /* by W. W. Shols].

KNERR, M(ichael) E.

27384 *Sasquatch: monster of the northwest woods.* New York: Belmont Tower Books, 1977, 223 p., paper, novel.

KNIGHT, Damon (Francis), 1922-

27385 *Best from Orbit, volumes 1-10.* New York: Berkley Publishing Corp., 1975, 373 p., cloth, anth.

27386 *The best of Damon Knight.* Garden City, NY: Nelson Doubleday, 1976, 307 p., cloth, coll.

27387 *The Clarion awards.* Garden City, NY: Doubleday & Co., 1984, xii+177 p., cloth, anth.

27388 *The Clarion writers' handbook.* [S.l.: s.n.], 1978, 157 p., paper, nonf. [70 copies printed for the Clarion Workshop].

27389 *Creating short fiction.* Cincinnati, OH: Writer's Digest Books, 1981, 215 p., cloth, nonf.

27390 *Creating short fiction.* Cincinnati, OH: Writer's Digest Books, 1985, 212 p., cloth, nonf. [Revised edition].

27391 *CV.* New York: Tor, A Tom Doherty Associates Book, 1985, 285 p., cloth, novel. CV #1.

27392 *Faking out the reader.* Eugene, OR: Writer's Notebook Press, Pulphouse Publishing, 1991, 12 p., paper, nonf.

27393 *The Futurians: the story of the science fiction "family" of the 30's that produced today's top SF writers and editors.* New York: John Day, 1977, viii+276 p., cloth, nonf.

27394 *God's nose.* Eugene, OR: Pulphouse Publishing, 1991, 114 p., cloth, coll. AUTHOR'S CHOICE MONTHLY #21.

27395 *Late Knight edition.* Cambridge, MA: A Boskone Book, NESFA Press, 1985, viii+150 p., cloth, coll.

27396 *The man in the tree.* New York: Berkley Books, 1984, 246 p., paper, novel.

Natural state, and other stories—SEE: *Three novels.*

27397 *The observers.* New York: Tor, A Tom Doherty Associates Book, 1988, 281 p., cloth, novel. CV #2.

27398 *One side laughing: stories unlike other stories.* New York: St. Martin's Press, 1991, 230 p., cloth, coll.

27399 *Orbit 16.* New York: Harper & Row, 1975, 271 p., cloth, anth.

27400 *Orbit 17.* New York: Harper & Row, 1975, 218 p., cloth, anth.

27401 *Orbit 18.* New York: Harper & Row, 1976, 256 p., cloth, anth.

27402 *Orbit 19.* New York, Hagerstown, NJ: Harper & Row, 1977, 262 p., cloth, anth.

27403 *Orbit 20.* New York, Hagerstown, NJ: Harper & Row, 1978, 248 p., cloth, anth.

27404 *Orbit 21.* New York: Harper & Row, 1980, xiii+240 p., cloth, anth.

27405 *A reasonable world.* New York: Tor, A Tom Doherty Associates Book, 1991, 272 p., cloth, novel. CV #3.

27406 *Rule golden; &, Double meaning.* New York: Tor SF, A Tom Doherty Associates Book, 1991, 188 p., paper, coll.

27407 *Rule golden, and other stories.* New York: Avon, 1979, 394 p., paper, coll.

27408 *Science fiction of the thirties.* Indianapolis, IN: Bobbs-Merrill Co., 1975, xii+468 p., cloth, anth.

08378 *Three novels: Rule golden, Natural state, The dying man.* Garden City, NY: Doubleday & Co., 1967, 189 p., cloth, coll.

08378A retitled: *Natural state, and other stories.* London & Sydney: Pan Books, 1975, 189 p., paper, coll.

27409 *Turning points: essays on the art of science fiction.* New York: Harper & Row, 1977, xii+303 p., cloth, nonf. anth.

27410 *The world and Thorinn.* New York: Berkley Publishing Corp., 1980, 214 p., cloth, novel.

with Martin H. Greenberg & Joseph D. Olander

08340 *First flight.* New York: Lancer, 1963, 160 p., paper, anth.

24527 retitled: *First voyages.* New York: Avon, 1981, 373 p., paper, anth. [An expanded and reworked version of Knight's *First flight* (see 08340)].

with Kate Wilhelm

27411 *Better than one.* Boston: Noreascon II, 1980, xiv+76 p., cloth, coll. [Includes some nonfiction].

KNIGHT, Gareth [pseud. of Basil Leslie Wiley], 1930-

27412 *The magical world of the Inklings: J. R. R. Tolkien, C. S. Lewis, Charles Williams, Owen Barfield.* Shaftesbury, England: Element, 1991, 258 p., paper, nonf.

KNIGHT, Harry Adam, pseud.—SEE: Brosnan, John & Kettle, Leroy

KNIGHT, Kathryn L.—SEE: Lasky, Kathryn

KNIGHT, Katie—SEE: Wilhelm, Kate

KNIGHT, Marilyn

27413 *Babydoll.* New York: Zebra Books, Kensington Publishing Corp., 1988, 316 p., paper, novel.

*KNIGHT, Norman L(ouis), 1895-1972

KNIGHT, Robert, pseud.—SEE: Evans, Chris

KNIGHT, Stephen (Thomas), 1940-1985

27414 *Requiem at Rogano.* London: Eyre Methuen, 1979, 319 p., cloth, novel.

27414A retitled: *Rogano: a novel.* Garden City, NY: Doubleday & Co., 1979, 307 p., cloth, novel.
Rogano: a novel—SEE: *Requiem at Rogano.*

KNIGHT, Tony—SEE: Case, Tom

KNOBEL, Philip, 1929?-1982?

27415 *Mr Moon.* New York: A Jove Book, 1979, 318 p., paper, novel.

KNOEPFLMACHER, U(lrich) C(amillus), 1931-, with George Levine

27416 *Endurance of Frankenstein: essays on Mary Shelley's novel.* Berkeley: University of California Press, 1979, xx+341 p., cloth, nonf. anth.

KNOWLES, Anne, 1933-

27417 *Halcyon Island.* London: Blackie & Son, 1980, 96 p., cloth, novel.

KNOWLES, Vernon, 1899-1968

27418 *Sapphires: Here and otherwise; and, Silver nutmegs.* New York: Arno Press, 1978, ix+257+xi+202 p., cloth, coll. [Includes *Here and otherwise* and *Silver nutmegs*].

*KNOWLES, W(illiam) P(lenderleith), 1891-

KNUDSEN, Eric A., 1872-

27419 *Spooky stuffs: Hawaiian ghost stories.* Norfolk Island, Australia: Island Heritage, 1974, 64 p., cloth?, coll.

KOBRYN, A(llen) P(aul), 1949-

27420 *Poseidon's shadow.* New York: Rawson, Wade Associates, 1979, 243 p., cloth, novel.

KOCH, C(hristopher) J(ohn), 1932-

37894 *The doubleman.* London: Chatto & Windus, 1985, [256] p., cloth, novel.

KOCH, Eric, 1919-

27421 *The French kiss: a tongue in cheek political fantasy.* Toronto, Montréal: McClelland & Stewart, 1969, 223 p., cloth, novel.

27422 *The last thing you'd want to know.* Montréal & Plattsburgh, NY: Tundra Books, 1976, 190 p., cloth, novel.

KOCHER, Paul H(arold), 1907-

27423 *A reader's guide to The Silmarillion.* Boston: Houghton Mifflin Co., 1980, 286 p., cloth, nonf.

KOELB, Clayton (Talmadge Jr.), 1942-

27424 *The incredulous reader: literature and the function of disbelief.* Ithaca, NY: Cornell University Press, 1984, 240 p., cloth, nonf.

27425 *The siege of Alesia: a fantasy.* Cambridge, MA: [s.n.], 1964, 49 p., paper?, story.

KOENIG, Walter, 1936-

27426 *Buck Alice and the actor-robot.* New York: A Gap Book, A Critic's Choice Paperback from Lorevan Publishing, 1988, 245 p., paper, novel.

27427 *Chekov's Enterprise: a personal journal of the making of Star Trek—the motion picture.* New York: Pocket Books, 1980, 222 p., paper, nonf.

*KOESTLER, Arthur, 1905-1983

KOFF, Richard M(yram), 1926-

27428 *Christopher.* Millbrae, CA: Celestial Arts, 1981, 109 p., cloth, novel.

KOHILL, Malcolm

Delta and the Bannerman—SEE: *Doctor Who: Delta and the Bannerman.*

27429 *Doctor Who: Delta and the Bannerman.* London: A Target Book, W. H. Allen & Co., 1989, 142 p., paper, tele. DOCTOR WHO #135.

KOHOUT, Pavel, 1928-

37895 *White book: Adam Juracek, professor of drawing and physical education at the Pedagogical Institute in K., vs. Sir Isaac Newton, professor of physics at the University of Cambridge: reconstructed from contemporary records and supplemented by most interesting document.* New

York: George Braziller, 1977, vii+215 p., cloth, novel. [Translation by Alex Page of *Weissbuch*].

KOJA, Kathe, 1960-

27430 *The cipher.* New York: A Dell Book, 1991, 356 p., paper, novel. [Winner of the *Locus* Award for Best First Novel, 1991 (1992); winner of the Bram Stoker Award for Best First Horror Novel, 1991 (1992)].

KOLLER, Jackie French, 1948-

27431 *If I had one wish...* Boston: Little, Brown & Co., 1991, 161 p., cloth, novel.

KOLMAR, Wendy K., 1950- , with Lynette Carpenter

19424 *Haunting the house of fiction: feminist perspectives on ghost stories by American women.* Knoxville, TN: University of Tennessee Press, 1991, x+266 p., cloth, nonf. anth.

KOLTZ, Tony

27432 *Terror island.* Toronto, New York: An Edward Packard Book, Bantam Books, 1986, 121 p., paper, novel. CHOOSE YOUR OWN ADVENTURE #59.

27433 *Vampire express.* Toronto, New York: A Packard/Montgomery Book, Bantam Books, 1984, 118 p., paper, novel. CHOOSE YOUR OWN ADVENTURE #31.

KOLUPAEV, Victor [i.e., Viktor Dmitrievich Kolupaev], 1936-

27434 *Hermit's swing.* New York: Macmillan, 1980, xi+199 p., cloth, coll. [Translation by Helen Saltz Jacobson of *Kacheli Otshel'nika*].

KOMAN, Victor, 1944-

27435 *The Jehovah contract.* New York: Franklin Watts, 1987, 277 p., cloth, novel. [Translation of *Der Jehova-Vertrag* (but originally written in English)].

27436 *Solomon's knife.* New York: Franklin Watts, 1989, 278 p., cloth, novel.

27437 *Starship women.* Encino, CA: World-Wide Publishing Co., 1980, 185 p., paper, novel.

with Andrew J. Offutt as JOHN CLEVE

27438 *The Carnadyne Horde.* New York: Berkley Books, 1984, 212 p., paper, novel. SPACEWAYS #17.
27439 *Jonuta rising!* New York: Berkley Books, 1983, 214 p., paper, novel. SPACEWAYS #13.

KOMATSU, Sakyô, 1931-

The death of the dragon—SEE: *Japan sinks.*
27440 *Japan sinks.* New York: Harper & Row, 1976, 184 p., cloth, novel. [Translation by Michael Gallagher of *Nippon chimbotsu*].
27440A retitled: *The death of the dragon.* London: New English Library, 1978, 192 p., paper, novel. [Translation by Michael Gallagher of *Nippon chimbotsu*].

KONDO, Yoji—SEE: **Kotani, Eric**

KONG, King, pseud.—SEE: **Wager, Walter**

KONVITZ, Jeffrey, 1944-

The apocalypse—SEE: *The guardian*
The beast—SEE: *Monster.*
27441 *The guardian.* Toronto, New York: Bantam Books, 1979, 293 p., paper, novel. SENTINEL #2.
27441A retitled: *Sentinel II.* London: Secker & Warburg, 1979, 256 p., cloth, novel. SENTINEL #2.
27441B retitled: *The apocalypse.* London: New English Library, 1979, 256 p., paper, novel. SENTINEL #2.
27442 *Monster: a tale of Loch Ness.* New York: Ballantine Books, 1982, 374 p., paper, novel.
27442A retitled: *The beast.* Sevenoaks, Kent, England: New English Library, 1983, 441 p., paper, novel.
Sentinel II—SEE: *The guardian.*

KOOIKER, Leonie [pseud. of Hanna Maria Kooyker-Romijn], 1927-

27443 *Legacy of magic.* New York: William Morrow & Co., 1981, 224 p., cloth, novel. CHRIS #2. [Translation by Patricia Crampton of *Het oerlanderboek*].
27444 *The magic stone.* New York: William Morrow & Co., 1978, 224 p., cloth, novel. CHRIS #1. [Translation by Richard and Clara Winston of *Heksensteen*].

KOONTZ, Dean R(ay), 1945-

27446 *The bad place.* New York: G. P. Putnam's Sons, 1990, 382 p., cloth, novel.
27447 *Cold fire.* New York: G. P. Putnam's Sons, 1991, 382 p., cloth, novel.
Darkfall—SEE: *Darkness comes.*
27448 *Darkness comes.* London: W. H. Allen & Co., 1984, 351 p., cloth, novel.
27448A retitled: *Darkfall.* New York: Berkley Books, 1984, 371 p., paper, novel.
27468B *The door to December.* London: Headline, 1991, 312 p., cloth, novel. [Originally published under the name Richard Paige].
27463A *The eyes of darkness.* Arlington Heights, IL: Dark Harvest, 1989, 257 p., cloth, novel. [Originally published under the name Leigh Nichols].
27461B *The face of fear.* London: Headline, 1989, 314 p., paper, novel. [Originally published under the name Brian Coffey].
27464A *The house of thunder.* Arlington Heights, IL: Dark Harvest, 1988, 255 p., cloth, novel. [Originally published under the name Leigh Nichols].
27465A *The key to Midnight.* Arlington Heights, IL: Dark Harvest, 1989, 330 p., cloth, novel. [Originally published under the name Leigh Nichols].
27449 *Lightning.* New York: G. P. Putnam's Sons, 1988, 351 p., cloth, novel.
27469A *The mask.* London: Headline, 1989, 342 p., paper, novel. [Originally published under the name Owen West].
27450 *Midnight.* New York: G. P. Putnam's Sons, 1989, 383 p., cloth, novel.
27451 *Night chills.* New York: Atheneum, 1976, viii+334 p., cloth, novel.
27452 *Nightmare journey.* New York: Berkley Publishing Corp., 1975, 217 p., cloth, novel.
27453 *Oddkins: a fable for all ages.* New York: Warner Books, 1988, 180 p., cloth, novel.
27454 *Phantoms.* New York: G. P. Putnam's Sons, 1983, 352 p., cloth, novel.
27467A *The servants of twilight.* Arlington Heights, IL: Dark Harvest, 1988, 327 p., cloth, novel. [Originally published as *Twilight* under the name Leigh Nichols].
27466A *Shadowfires.* Arlington Heights, IL: Dark Harvest, 1990, 380 p., cloth, novel. [Originally published under the name Leigh Nichols].
27455 *Strangers.* New York: G. P. Putnam's Sons, 1986, 526 p., cloth, novel.
27456 *Three complete novels.* New York: Wings Books, 1991, 739 p., cloth, coll. [In-

cludes *The servants of twilight*; *Darkfall*; *Phantoms*].

27457 *Twilight eyes.* Plymouth, MI: Land of Enchantment, 1985, 263 p., cloth, novel.

27458 *The vision.* New York: G. P. Putnam's Sons, 1977, 287 p., cloth, novel.

27462A *The voice of the night.* London: Headline, 1991, 340 p., cloth, novel. [Originally published under the name Brian Coffey].

27459 *Watchers.* New York: G. P. Putnam's Sons, 1987, 352 p., cloth, novel.

27460 *Whispers.* New York: G. P. Putnam's Sons, 1980, 444 p., cloth, novel.

as BRIAN COFFEY

27461 *The face of fear: a novel of suspense.* Indianapolis, IN: Bobbs-Merrill Co., 1977, 244 p., cloth, novel.

27462 *The voice of the night.* Garden City, NY: Doubleday & Co., 1980, 277 p., cloth, novel.

as K. R. DWYER

27461A *The face of fear.* London: Peter Davies, 1978, 244 p., cloth, novel. [Originally published under the name Brian Coffey].

as JOHN HILL

25663 *Heartbeeps: a novel.* New York: A Jove Book, 1981, 213 p., paper, movie.

25664 *The long sleep.* New York: Popular Library, 1975, 192 p., paper, novel.

as LEIGH NICHOLS

27468A *The door to December.* London: Fontana Books, 1987, 432 p., paper, novel. [Originally published under the name Richard Paige].

27463 *The eyes of darkness.* New York: Pocket Books, 1981, 312 p., paper, novel.

27464 *The house of thunder.* New York: Pocket Books, 1982, 342 p., paper, novel.

27465 *The key to Midnight.* New York: Pocket Books, 1979, 392 p., paper, novel.

27466 *Shadowfires.* New York: Avon, 1987, 436 p., paper, novel.

27467 *Twilight.* New York: Pocket Books, 1984, 440 p., paper, novel.

as RICHARD PAIGE

27468 *The door to December.* New York: A Signet Book, New American Library, 1985, 405 p., paper, novel.

as OWEN WEST

37896 *The funhouse: carnival of terror: a novel.* New York: A Jove Book, 1980, 275 p., paper, movie.

27469 *The mask.* New York: A Jove Book, 1981, 305 p., paper, novel.

as AARON WOLFE

27470 *Invasion.* Don Mills, Ontario: Laser Books, 1975, 190 p., paper, novel.

with Paul Mikol

29844 *Night visions 6: all original stories.* Arlington Heights, IL: Dark Harvest, 1988, 312 p., cloth, anth. [Introduction by Dean R. Koontz].

29844A retitled: *The bone yard.* New York: Berkley Books, 1991, 329 p., paper, anth. [Introduction by Dean R. Koontz].

KOOYKER-ROMIJN, Hanna Maria—SEE: Kooiker, Leonie

KOREL, Charles

27471 *Full alert: a novel.* New York: Zebra Books, Kensington Publishing Corp., 1989, 286 p., paper, novel.

KORNBLATT, Marc

27472 *Flame of the Inquisition.* Toronto, New York: A Byron Preiss Book, Bantam Books, 1986, 124 p., paper, novel. TIME MACHINE #15.

27473 *Paul Revere and the Boston Tea Party.* Toronto, New York: A Byron Preiss Book, A Bantam Skylark Book, 1987, 80 p., paper, novel. TIME TRAVELER #5.

with Susan Nanus

27474 *Mission to World War II.* Toronto, New York: A Byron Preiss Book, Bantam Books, 1986, 125 p., paper, novel. TIME MACHINE #11.

KORNBLUTH, C(yril) M., 1923-1958

27475 *The best of C. M. Kornbluth.* Garden City, NY: Nelson Doubleday, 1976, 312 p., cloth, coll.

with Frederik Pohl

27476 *Before the universe, and other stories: the best of the early work of science fiction's most famous team of collaborators,* in-

cluding four stories never before in book form. Toronto, New York: Bantam Books, 1980, x+203 p., paper, coll.

27477 *Critical mass.* Toronto, New York: Bantam Books, 1977, xi+179 p., paper, coll.

27478 *Gladiator-at-law.* New York: Baen Science Fiction Books, 1986, 251 p., paper, novel. [A revised edition of #08444].

27479 *Not this August.* New York: Tor, A Tom Doherty Associates Book, 1981, 255 p., paper, novel. [An expanded edition by Frederik Pohl of #08438].

27480 *Our best: the best of Frederik Pohl and C. M. Kornbluth.* New York: Baen Books, 1987, 286 p., paper, coll.

27481 *Search the sky.* New York: Baen Science Fiction Books, 1985, 245 p., paper, novel. [A revised edition of #08445].

27482 *The space merchants.* New York: St. Martin's Press, 1985, 169 p., cloth, novel. SPACE MERCHANTS #1. [A revised edition of #08446].

27483 *The Syndic.* New York: Tor, A Tom Doherty Associates Book, 1982, 256 p., paper, novel. [A revision by Frederik Pohl of #08439].

27484 *Venus, Inc.* Garden City, NY: Nelson Doubleday, 1985, 346 p., cloth, coll. SPACE MERCHANTS #1-2.

27485 *Wolfbane.* New York: Baen Science Fiction Books, 1986, 248 p., paper, novel. [A revised version of #08447].

with Judith Merril as CYRIL JUDD

27486 *Gunner Cade, plus Takeoff.* New York: A Jim Baen Presentation, Tor, A Tom Doherty Associates Book, 1983, 320 p., paper, coll. [*Takeoff* is by Kornbluth alone].

KORNWISE, Robert (Ian), 1971?-1987, with Piers Anthony

16713 *Through the ice.* Novato, CA, Lancaster, PA: Underwood-Miller, 1989, 203 p., cloth, novel.

KOSTER, R(ichard) M(orton), 1934-

27487 *The dissertation: a novel.* New York: W. W. Norton & Co., 1975, xix+438 p., cloth, novel. TINIEBLAS TRILOGY #2.

27488 *Mandragon.* New York: W. W. Norton & Co., 1979, 346 p., cloth, novel. TINIEBLAS TRILOGY #3.

27489 *The prince.* New York: W. W. Norton & Co., 1972, 351 p., cloth, novel. TINIEBLAS TRILOGY #1.

KOTANI, Eric [pseud. of Yoji Kondo], 1933-

with Roger Allen MacBride

27490 *Supernova.* New York: Avon Books, 1991, 345 p., paper, novel.

with John Maddox Roberts

27491 *Act of God.* New York: Baen Science Fiction Books, 1985, 282 p., paper, novel. ACT OF GOD #1.

27492 *Between the stars.* New York: Baen Books, 1988, 225 p., paper, novel. ACT OF GOD #3.

27493 *Delta Pavonis.* New York: Baen Books, 1990, 250 p., paper, novel.

27494 *The island worlds.* New York: Baen Books, 1987, 279 p., paper, novel. ACT OF GOD #2.

KOTCH, Thomas

27495 *Possessed!* Encino, CA: World-Wide Publishing Co., 1980, 190 p., paper, novel.

KOTLAN, C(harles) M(ichael), with G. C. Edmondson

22418 *The black magician.* New York: A Del Rey Book, Ballantine Books, 1986, 298 p., paper, novel. CUNNINGHAM #2.

22419 *The Cunningham equations.* New York: A Del Rey Book, Ballantine Books, 1986, 295 p., paper, novel. CUNNINGHAM #1.

22420 *Maximum effort.* New York: A Del Rey Book, Ballantine Books, 1987, 299 p., paper, novel. CUNNINGHAM #3.

22421 *The takeover.* New York: Ace Science Fiction Books, 1984, 284 p., paper, novel.

KOTT, Mike, with Sue Cornwell

20611 *The official price guide to the Star Trek and Star wars collectibles.* New York: House of Collectibles, 1986, 377 p., paper, nonf.

20612 *The official price guide to the Star Trek and Star wars collectibles, 2nd ed.* New York: House of Collectibles, 1987, 415 p., paper, nonf.

20613 *The official price guide to the Star Trek and Star wars collectibles, 3rd ed.* New York: House of Collectibles, 1991, 277 p., paper, nonf.

KOTZWINKLE, William, 1938-

27496 *The ants who took away time.* Garden City, NY: Doubleday & Co., 1978, [64] p., cloth, novel.

The book of the green planet—SEE: *E.T., the book of the green planet.*

27497 *Doctor Rat.* New York: Alfred A. Knopf, 1976, 243 p., cloth, novel. [Winner of the World Fantasy Award for Best Fantasy Novel, 1976 (1977)].

27498 *E.T., the book of the green planet: a new novel.* New York: G. P. Putnam's Sons, 1985, 245 p., cloth, novel. E.T. #2.

27499 *E.T., the extra-terrestrial, in his adventure on Earth: a novel.* New York: G. P. Putnam's Sons, 1982, 246 p., cloth, movie. E.T. #1.

27500 *E.T., the extraterrestrial storybook.* New York: G. P. Putnam's Sons, 1982, [57] p., cloth, movie. E.T. #1.

27501 *E.T.: The storybook of the green planet: a new storybook.* New York: G. P. Putnam's Sons, 1985, 77 p., cloth, novel. E.T. #2.

27502 *The exile.* New York: Seymour Lawrence, E. P. Dutton, 1987, 277 p., cloth, novel.

27503 *Hearts of wood, and other timeless tales.* New York: David R. Godine, 1986, 85 p., cloth, coll.

27504 *Herr Nightingale and the Satin Woman.* New York: Alfred A. Knopf, 1978, 119 p., cloth, novel.

27505 *The hot jazz trio.* Boston: Houghton Mifflin Co., A Seymour Lawrence Book, 1989, 153 p., cloth, coll.

27506 *Jewel of the moon.* New York: G. P. Putnam's Sons, 1985, 160 p., cloth, coll.

27507 *The leopard's tooth.* New York: A Clarion Book, Seabury Press, 1976, 95 p., cloth, novel.

27508 *Superman III: a novel.* New York: Warner Books, 1983, 221 p., paper, movie. SUPERMAN #3.

27509 *Trouble in Bugland: a collection of Inspector Mantis mysteries.* New York: David R. Godine, 1983, 152 p., cloth, coll.

KOUMARAS, Terence J.

27510 *Eye of the devil.* New York: A Critic's Choice Paperback from Lorevan Publishing, 1989, 318 p., paper, novel.

KOVALCHUK, Mikhail—SEE: Gakov, Vladimir

KOZAK, Ellen M., 1944- , with Sharon Jarvis as JARROD COMSTOCK

26520 *The love machine.* New York: Pinnacle Books, 1984, 231 p., paper, novel. THESE LAWLESS WORLDS #1. [Jarvis provided concept and outline].

26521 *Scales of justice.* New York: Pinnacle Books, 1984, 233 p., paper, novel. THESE LAWLESS WORLDS #2. [Jarvis provided concept and outline].

KOZIAKIN, Vladimir

27511 *Flash Gordon mazes.* New York: Grosset & Dunlap, 1980, [63] p., paper, nonf.

27512 *Science fiction mazes.* New York: Tempo Books, Grosset & Dunlap, 1979, [128] p., paper, nonf.

27513 *Star mazes: a celestial collection of out-of-this-world mazes!* New York: Tempo Books, 1978, [63] p., paper, nonf.

27514 *Superman's maze challenge.* New York: Tempo Books, 1978, [63] p., paper, nonf.

KRAFT, David Anthony, 1952-

27515 *The compleat OAK leaves: volume one of the official journal of Otis Adelbert Kline and his works.* Screamer Mountain, GA: A Fictioneer Facsimile Edition, 1980, [196] p., paper, nonf. anth. [Only volume published].

27516 *Ghost knights of Camelot.* New York: A Parachute Press Book, Avon, 1984, 103 p., paper, novel. WIZARDS, WARLOCKS & YOU #4.

37897 *Krull: the storybook based on the film.* New York: Marvel Books, 1983, [64] p., paper, movie.

27517 *Robot race.* New York, Toronto: A Parachute Press Book, Scholastic Inc., 1984, 126 p., paper, novel. MICRO ADVENTURE #6.

with Russ Jones as JACK YOUNGER

27518 *Curse of the pharoahs.* New York: Manor Books, 1976, 215 p, paper, novel.

27519 *Rest in agony.* New York: Carlyle, 1979, 223 p., paper, novel.

KRAILING, Tessa, 1935-

27520 *The nightmare man.* London: Hippo, 1988, 102 p., paper, novel. HAUNTINGS #4.

KRAMER, Dale (Vernon), 1936-

27521 *Charles Robert Maturin.* New York: Twayne Publishers, 1973, 166 p., cloth, nonf.

KRAMER, Dana—SEE: Kramer-Rolls, Dana

KRAMER, Kathryn

27522 *A handbook for visitors from outer space.* New York: Alfred A. Knopf, 1984, 336 p., cloth, novel.

*KRAMER, Nora, 1896?-1984

KRAMER-ROLLS, Dana

27523 *Combat command in the world of Piers Anthony's Bio of a space tyrant: Cut by emerald* / by Dana Kramer. New York: Ace Books, 1987, xix+[175] p., paper, novel. COMBAT COMMAND #1.
Cut by emerald—SEE: *Combat command in the world of Piers Anthony's Bio of a space tyrant: Cut by emerald.*
Home is the hunter—SEE: *Star Trek: Home is the hunter.*
27524 *Star Trek: Home is the hunter* / by Dana Kramer-Rolls. New York, London: Pocket Books, 1990, 278 p., paper, tele. STAR TREK #52.
27525 *Warhorn: a Crossroads adventure in the world of Lynn Abbey's Rifkind, daughter of the bright moon* / by Dana Kramer. New York: Tor, A Tom Doherty Associates Book, 1987, 27+[228] p., paper, novel. CROSSROADS ADVENTURE—RIFKIND.

KRASNOFF, Barbara (Sue), 1954-

27526 *Robots: reel-to-real.* New York: Arco Books, 1982, 154 p., cloth, nonf.
27527 *Star Trek II, the wrath of Khan: the offical movie magazine.* New York: Starlog Press, 1982, 66 p., paper, nonf. anth.

with David Hirsch

27528 *Science fiction weapons, volume 1.* New York: A Starlog Press Publication, 1979, 35 p., paper, nonf.

KRAUS, Bruce R., 1954-

27529 *Encyclopedia Galactica: from the Fleet Library aboard the Battlestar Galactica.* New York: Windmill Books and E. P. Dutton, 1979, [57] p., cloth, fiction.

KRAUZER, Steven M(ark), 1948-

27530 *Brainstorm.* New York, Toronto: Spectra, Bantam Books, 1991, 343 p., paper, novel.

KREEFT, Peter (John), 1937-

27531 *C. S. Lewis: a critical essay.* Grand Rapids, MI: William B. Eerdmans Publishing Co., 1969, 48 p., paper, nonf.

KRENKEL, Roy G(erald), 1918-1983

27532 *Cities & scenes from the ancient world.* Philadelphia, PA: Owlswick Press, 1974, 82 p., cloth, art coll.
27533 *Portfolio from The road of Azrael.* West Kingston, RI: Donald M. Grant, 1979, 4 leaves, paper, art coll.

KRENSKY, Stephen (Alan), 1953-

27534 *A big day for Scepter.* New York: Atheneum, 1977, 112 p., cloth, novel.
27535 *The dragon circle.* New York: Atheneum, 1977, 116 p., cloth, novel. WYND FAMILY #1.
27536 *A ghostly business.* New York: Atheneum, 1984, 144 p., cloth, novel. WYND FAMILY #3.
27537 *A troll in passing.* New York: Atheneum, 1980, 128 p., cloth, novel.
27538 *The witching hour.* New York: Atheneum, 1981, 155 p., cloth, novel. WYND FAMILY #2.

KRENTZ, Jayne Ann

27539 *Crystal flame.* New York: Popular Library, Warner Books, 1986, 375 p., paper, novel.
27540 *Sweet starfire.* New York: Popular Library, Warner Books, 1986, 375 p., paper, novel.
27541 *Witchcraft.* Toronto, New York: Harlequin Books, 1985, 219 p., paper, novel.

as AMANDA GLASS

27542 *Shield's lady.* New York: Popular Library, 1989, 341 p., paper, novel.

KRESS, Nancy (Anne Konigisor), 1948-

27543 *An alien light: a novel.* New York: Arbor House, 1988, 370 p., cloth, novel.

27544 *Beggars in Spain.* Eugene, OR: Axolotl Press, Pulphouse Publishing, 1991, 104 p., cloth, novel. AXOLOTL PRESS #18.
27545 *Brain rose.* New York: William Morrow & Co., 1990, 324 p., cloth, novel.
27545A retitled: *Brainrose.* New York: Avon Books, 1991, 320 p., paper, novel.
27546 *The Golden Grove.* New York: Bluejay Books, 1984, 250 p., cloth, novel.
27547 *The prince of morning bells.* New York: A Timescape Book, Pocket Books, 1981, 224 p., paper, novel.
27548 *Trinity, and other stories.* New York: Bluejay Books, 1985, 279 p., cloth, coll.
27549 *The white pipes.* New York: Bluejay Books, 1985, 218 p., cloth, novel.

*KREUDER, Ernst, 1903-1972

KREUZIGER, Frederick A(lbert)

27550 *Apocalypse and science fiction: a dialectic of religious and secular soteriologies.* Chico, CA: Scholars Press, 1982, vi+247 p., cloth, nonf.
27551 *The religion of science fiction.* Bowling Green, OH: Bowling Green State University Popular Press, 1986, 166 p., cloth, nonf.

KRING, Michael K., 1952-

27552 *Children of the night.* New York: Leisure Books, 1981, 192 p., paper, novel. SPACE MAVERICKS #2.
27553 *The space mavericks.* New York: Leisure Books, 1980, 192 p., paper, novel. SPACE MAVERICKS #1.

KRISHNAMURTI, G.

27554 *The adventures of Rama.* London: Allan Wingate, 1975, 127 p., cloth, novel.

KRISHNAN, Bharathi, 1939-

27555 *Aspects of structure, technique, and quest in Aldous Huxley's major novels.* Uppsala, Sweden: Universitet Uppsala; Stockholm: Almqvist & Wiksell International, 1977, 181 p., paper?, nonf.

KRISNAMOORTHY, P. S.

27556 *Scholar's guide to modern American science fiction.* Hyderabad, India: American Studies Research Centre, 1983, xii+182 p., cloth, nonf.

KROEBER, Karl (Douglas), 1926-

27557 *Romantic fantasy and science fiction.* New Haven, CT: Yale University Press, 1988, vii+188 p., cloth, nonf.

KRONE, Chester (W. Jr.), 1935-

27558 *Blood wrath.* New York: Playboy Paperbacks, 1981, 272 p., paper, novel.

KRONEGGER, Maria Elisabeth, 1932-

27559 *James Joyce and associated image makers.* New Haven, CT: College & University Press, 1968, 206 p., cloth, nonf.

KRUCHTEN, Marcia (Helen), 1932-

27560 *The ghost in the mirror.* Worthington, OH: Willowisp, 1985, 96 p., paper, novel.
27561 *Skyborn.* Worthington, OH: Willowisp Press, 1988, 191 p., paper, novel. OMNI ODYSSEYS #3.
27561A retitled: *Skytorn.* London: Armada Books, 1988, 191 p., paper, novel. OMNI ODYSSEYS #3.

KRUEGER, Ken(neth J.), 1926-

27562 *Unique tales.* Hollywood, CA: Ken Krueger, 1974, [80] p., paper, anth.

KRUEGER, Margery—SEE: Carr, Jayge

KRUEGER, Terry

27563 *Night cries.* New York: A Dell Book, 1985, 272 p., paper, novel.

KRULIK, Nancy E.

27564 *Honey, I shrunk the kids.* New York, Toronto: Scholastic Inc., 1989, 32 p., paper, movie.
27565 *Superman IV.* New York, Toronto: Scholastic Inc., 1987, 30 p., paper, movie. SUPERMAN #4.

KRULIK, Theodore (David), 1948-

27566 *Roger Zelazny.* New York: Ungar, 1986, xiv+178 p., cloth, nonf.

KRÜSS, James, 1926-

27567 *The Happy Islands behind the winds.* New York: Atheneum, 1966, vi+153 p., cloth, novel. CAPTAIN MADIRAN-KOWITCH #1. [Translation by Edelgard von

Heydekampf of *Die glücklichen inseln hinter dem winde, band I*].

27568 *Return to the Happy Islands*. New York: Atheneum, 1967, vi+170 p., cloth, novel. CAPTAIN MADIRANKOWITCH #2. [Translation by Edelgard von Heydekampf of *Die glücklichen inseln hinter dem winde, band II*].

KRUTCH, Joseph Wood, 1893-1970

27569 *Edgar Allan Poe: a study in genius*. New York: Alfred A. Knopf, 1926, x+244 p., cloth, nonf.

KUBAL, David L(awrence), 1936-1982

27570 *Outside the whale: George Orwell's art and politics*. Notre Dame, IN, London: University of Notre Dame Press, 1972, xvii+269 p., cloth, nonf.

KUBASCH, Heike (Andrea)

27571 *Angmar*. Charlottesville, VA: Iron Crown Enterprises, 1982, 48 p., paper, fiction.
The legend of Weathertop—SEE: *Tolkien Quest: The legend of Weathertop*.
27572 *Tolkien quest: The legend of Weathertop*. New York: Berkley Books, 1985, [160] p., paper, novel. TOLKIEN QUEST #2.

KUBASICK, Chris, *with Tom Dowd*

22066 *Virtual realities: a Shadowrun sourcebook*. Chicago: FASA Corp., 1991, 152 p., paper, fiction. SHADOWRUN SERIES.

KUBE-McDOWELL, Michael P(aul) [originally Michael Paul McDowell], 1954-

27573 *Alternities*. New York: Ace Books, 1988, 383 p., paper, novel.
27574 *Empery*. New York: Berkley Books, 1987, 325 p., paper, novel. TRIGON DISUNITY #3.
27575 *Emprise*. New York: Berkley Books, 1985, xiii+304 p., paper, novel. TRIGON DISUNITY #1.
27576 *Enigma*. New York: Berkley Books, 1986, 355 p., paper, novel. TRIGON DISUNITY #2.
27577 *Odyssey*. New York: A Byron Preiss Visual Publications Inc. Book, Ace Books, 1987, xii+211 p., paper, novel. ISAAC ASIMOV'S ROBOT CITY #1.
27578 *The quiet pools*. New York: Ace Books, 1990, 371 p., cloth, novel.

as MICHAEL HUDSON

27579 *Photon: Thieves of light*. New York: Berkley Books, 1987, 215 p., paper, novel. PHOTON SERIES. [An adaptation of the *Photon* game].
Thieves of light—SEE: *Photon: Thieves of light*.

KUBICEK, David, 1944-1990, *with Jeff Mason*

27580 *October dreams: a harvest of horror*. Lincoln, NE: Kubicek & Associates, 1989, xi+162 p., paper, anth.

KUCZKIR, Mary, 1933- , *with Roberta Anderson* *as* FERN MICHAELS

16457 *Without warning*. New York: Pocket Books, 1981, 224 p., paper, novel.

KUEHN, Robert E., 1932-1986?

27581 *Aldous Huxley: a collection of critical essays*. Englewood Cliffs, NJ: Prentice-Hall, 1974, iv+188 p., cloth, nonf. anth.

KUHFELD, Mary Pulvar—SEE: Pulvar, Mary Monica

KUHN, Lan, 1939-

27582 *The outer space connection*. Sydney, Australia: Tomato Press, 1978, 161 p., paper, novel.

KUMAR, Krishan, 1942-

27583 *Utopia and anti-utopia in modern times*. Oxford, England: Basil Blackwell, 1987, x+506 p., cloth, nonf.

KUMMANN, William—SEE: Norman, Elizabeth

KUMMER, Frederic Arnold, 1873-1943

27584 *Shades of Hades: Ladies in Hades; and, Gentlemen in Hades*. New York: Arno Press, 1978, 272+269 p., cloth, coll. HADES #1-2.

KUNETKA, James (W.), 1944- , *with Whitley Strieber*

27585 *Nature's end: the consequences of the twentieth century*. New York: Warner Books, 1986, 418 p., cloth, novel.
27586 *Warday, and the journey onward*. New York: Holt, Rinehart & Winston, 1984, ix+374 p., cloth, novel.

KUNSTLER, James Howard, 1948-

27587 *The hunt.* New York: Tor Horror, A Tom Doherty Associates Book, 1988, 217 p., paper, novel.

KUNTZ, Robert, *with James Ward*

27588 *Advanced Dungeons & Dragons: Deities & Demigods cyclopedia: special reference work.* Lake Geneva, WI: TSR Inc., 1980, 128 p., cloth, nonf. ADVANCED DUNGEONS & DRAGONS REFERENCE BOOKS.
27589 *Advanced Dungeons & Dragons: Deities & Demigods cyclopedia: special reference work.* Lake Geneva, WI: TSR Inc., 1980, 144 p., cloth, nonf. ADVANCED DUNGEONS & DRAGONS REFERENCE BOOKS. [Revised edition].
27590 *Advanced Dungeons & Dragons: Legends & lore.* Lake Geneva, WI: TSR Inc., 1984, 128 p., cloth, nonf. ADVANCED DUNGEONS & DRAGONS REFERENCE BOOKS.

KUPPERBERG, Paul

27591 *Crime campaign.* New York: Pocket Books, 1979, 192 p., paper, novel. SPIDERMAN #2; MARVEL SUPERHEROES #8.
27592 *Murdermoon: a novel.* New York: Pocket Books, 1979, 208 p., paper, novel. INCREDIBLE HULK AND SPIDERMAN #3; MARVEL SUPERHEROES #11.

KUPPIG, C(hristopher) J.

27593 *Nineteen eighty-four to 1984: a companion to the classic novel of our time.* New York: Carroll & Graf Publishers, 1984, 316 p., paper, nonf. anth.

KURLAND, Michael (Joseph), 1938-

27594 *Button bright.* New York: Jove Books, 1990, 268 p., paper, novel.
27595 *Chronicles of elsewhen: Perchance.* New York: A Signet Book, New American Library, 1989, 220 p., paper, novel. CHRONICLES OF ELSEWHEN #1.
27596 *Death by gaslight.* New York: A Signet Book, New American Library, 1982, 279 p., paper, novel.
Perchance—SEE: *Chronicles of elsewhen: Perchance.*
27597 *Pluribus.* Garden City, NY: Doubleday & Co., 1975, 184 p., cloth, novel.

27598 *The princes of Earth.* Nashville, TN: Thomas Nelson, 1978, 190 p., cloth, novel.
27599 *Psi hunt.* New York: Berkley Books, 1980, 184 p., paper, novel.
27600 *Randall Garrett's Lord Darcy in A study in sorcery.* New York: Ace Books, 1989, 184 p., paper, novel. LORD DARCY #5.
27601 *Randall Garrett's Lord Darcy in Ten little wizards.* New York: Ace Books, 1988, 188 p., paper, novel. LORD DARCY #4.
27602 *Star Griffin.* Garden City, NY: Doubleday & Co., 1987, 180 p., cloth, novel.
A study in sorcery—SEE: *Randall Garrett's Lord Darcy in A study in sorcery.*
Ten little wizards—SEE: *Randall Garrett's Lord Darcy in Ten little wizards.*
27603 *Tomorrow knight.* New York: DAW Books, 1976, 156 p., paper, novel.
27604 *The whenabouts of Burr.* New York: DAW Books, 1975, 158 p., paper, novel.

with S. W. Barton

17511 *The last president.* New York: A Bernard Geis Associates Book, William Morrow & Co., 1980, 357 p., cloth, novel.

with H. Beam Piper

27605 *First cycle: a novel.* New York: Ace Books, 1982, 201 p., paper, novel.

KURSKA, Daniel Grotta- —SEE: Grotta-Kurska, Daniel

KURTÉN, Björn (Olof), 1924-1988

27606 *Dance of the tiger: a novel of the ice age.* New York: Pantheon Books, 1980, xxv+255 p., cloth, novel. DANCE #1. [Translation of *Den svarta tigern*].
27607 *Singletusk: a novel of the ice age.* New York: Pantheon, 1986, xi+211 p., cloth, novel. DANCE #2. [Translation of *Mammutens rådare*].

KURTZ, Katherine (Irene), 1944-

27608 *The bishop's heir.* New York: A Del Rey Book, Ballantine Books, 1984, xviii+346 p., cloth, novel. HISTORIES OF KING KELSON #1.
27609 *Camber of Culdi.* New York: A Del Rey Book, Ballantine Books, 1976, xx+314 p., paper, novel. CAMBER #1.
27610 *Camber the heretic.* New York: A Del Rey Book, Ballantine Books, 1981, xi+506 p., paper, novel. CAMBER #3.

27611 *The chronicles of the Deryni: Deryni Rising; Deryni checkmate; High Deryni.* Garden City, NY: Nelson Doubleday, 1985, 752 p., cloth, coll. DERYNI #1-3.

27612 *The Deryni archives.* New York: A Del Rey Book, Ballantine Books, 1986, 325 p., paper, coll. DERYNI SERIES.

27613 *Deryni magic: a grimoire.* New York: A Del Rey Book, Ballantine Books, 1990, 370 p., paper, fiction. DERYNI SERIES.

27614 *The harrowing of Gwynedd.* New York: A Del Rey Book, Ballantine Books, 1989, xii+384 p., cloth, novel. HEIRS OF ST. CAMBER #1.

27615 *The king's justice.* New York: A Del Rey Book, Ballantine Books, 1985, xxv+337 p., cloth, novel. HISTORIES OF KING KELSON #2.

27616 *Lammas night.* New York: Ballantine Books, 1983, 438 p., paper, novel.

27617 *The legacy of Lehr.* New York: Millennium, A Byron Preiss Book, Walker & Co., 1986, 235 p., cloth, novel.

27618 *The quest for Saint Camber.* New York: A Del Rey Book, Ballantine Books, 1986, xxvi+435 p., cloth, novel. HISTORIES OF KING KELSON #3.

27619 *Saint Camber.* New York: A Del Rey Book, Ballantine Books, 1978, x+467 p., cloth, novel. CAMBER #2.

with Deborah Turner Harris

25238 *The adept.* New York: Ace Books, 1991, 323 p., paper, novel. ADEPT #1.

KUSHNER, Donn (Jean), 1927-

27620 *A book dragon.* Toronto: Macmillan of Canada, 1987, 197 p., cloth, novel.

KUSHNER, Ellen (Ruth), 1955-

27621 *Basilisk.* New York: Ace Books, 1980, xi+244 p., paper, anth.

27622 *The enchanted kingdom.* Toronto, New York: An Edward Packard Book, Bantam Books, 1986, 113 p., paper, novel. CHOOSE YOUR OWN ADVENTURE #56.

27623 *Knights of the round table.* Toronto, New York: An Edward Packard Book, Bantam Books, 1988, 114 p., paper, novel. CHOOSE YOUR OWN ADVENTURE #86.

27624 *Mystery of the secret room.* Toronto, New York: An Edward Packard Book, Bantam Books, 1986, 117 p., paper, novel. CHOOSE YOUR OWN ADVENTURE #63.

27625 *Outlaws of Sherwood Forest.* Toronto, New York: A Packard/Montgomery Book, Bantam Books, 1985, 118 p., paper, novel. CHOOSE YOUR OWN ADVENTURE #47.

27626 *Statue of Liberty adventure.* Toronto, New York: A Packard/Montgomery Book, Bantam Books, 1986, 116 p., paper, novel. CHOOSE YOUR OWN ADVENTURE #58.

27627 *Swordspoint: a melodrama of manners.* London: George Allen & Unwin, 1987, 269 p., cloth, novel.

27628 *Thomas, the Rhymer.* New York: William Morrow & Co., 1990, 247 p., cloth, novel. [Winner of the World Fantasy Award for Best Fantasy Novel, 1990 (1991)].

KUTTNER, Catherine—SEE: Moore, C. L.

KUTTNER, Henry, 1915-1958

27629 *The best of Henry Kuttner.* Garden City, NY: Nelson Doubleday, 1975, xii+338 p., cloth, coll.

27630 *Elak of Atlantis.* Brooklyn, NY: Gryphon Books, 1985, 210 p., paper, coll. [Limited to 300 copies].

37898 *Kuttner times three.* Modesto, CA: Virgil Utter, 1988, 29 p., paper, coll. [Limited to 200 copies].

27631 *Prince Raynor.* Brooklyn, NY: Gryphon Publications, 1987, 82 p., paper, coll.

27632 *Secret of the earth star, and others.* Mercer Island, WA: Starmont House, 1991, ix+157 p., cloth, coll. STARMONT FACSIMILE FICTION #6. [Edited by Sheldon Jaffery].

with H. P. Lovecraft

27633 *H. P. Lovecraft letters to Henry Kuttner.* West Warwick, RI: Necronomicon Press, 1990, 32 p., paper, nonf. coll. [Edited by David E. Schultz & S. T. Joshi].

with C. L. Moore

27634 *Chessboard planet, and other stories.* London: Hamlyn Paperbacks, 1983, 187 p., paper, coll.

27635 *Clash by night, and other stories.* London: Hamlyn Paperbacks, 1980, viii+215 p., paper, coll. [Edited by Peter Pinto].

08484A *The mask of Circe.* New York: Ace Books, 1977, 158 p., paper, novel. [Originally published under Kuttner's name only].

The proud robot—SEE: *Robots have no tails.*

08500 *Robots have no tails.* New York: Gnome Press, 1952, 224 p., cloth, coll.

08500B retitled: *The proud robot: the complete Galloway Gallegher stories.* Feltham, England: Hamlyn Paperbacks, 1983, 189 p., paper, coll.

27636 *The startling worlds of Henry Kuttner.* New York: Popular Library, 1987, 357 p., paper, coll. [Includes *Beyond Earth's Gates, Valley of the Flame, The Dark World*; Moore's contribution is uncredited].

KWITZ, Mary DeBall

27637 *The bell tolls at Mousehaven Manor.* New York, Toronto: Scholastic Inc., 1991, 125 p., cloth, novel. MOUSEHAVEN MANOR #2.

27638 *Shadow over Mousehaven Manor.* New York, Toronto: Scholastic Inc., 1989, 160 p., cloth, novel. MOUSEHAVEN MANOR #1.

KYLE, David A(ckerman), 1919-

27639 *The dragon lensman.* Toronto, New York: Bantam Books, 1980, xiv+176 p., paper, novel. LENSMAN SERIES.

27640 *The illustrated book of science fiction ideas & dreams.* London, New York: Hamlyn, 1977, 174 p., cloth, nonf.

27641 *Lensman from Rigel.* Toronto, New York: Bantam Books, 1982, x+212 p., paper, novel. LENSMAN SERIES.

27642 *A pictorial history of science fiction.* London, New York: Hamlyn Publishing Group, 1976, 175 p., cloth, nonf.

27643 *Z-Lensman.* Toronto, New York: Bantam Books, 1983, ix+236 p., paper, novel. LENSMAN SERIES.

KYTLE, Ray(mond), 1941-

27644 *Fire and ice.* New York: David McKay Co., 1975, 246 p., cloth, novel.

L

LA PLANTE, Richard

The killing blow—SEE: *Tegné: The killing blow.*

27645 *Tegné: The killing blow.* London: Sphere Books, 1990, 304 p., paper, novel. TEGNE #2.

27646 *Tegné: Warlord of Zendow.* London: Sphere Books, 1988, 354 p., paper, novel. TEGNE #1.

Warlord of Zendow—SEE: *Tegné: Warlord of Zendow.*

*LA PRADE, Ernest, 1889-1969

LA REE, Gerry de—SEE: De la Ree, Gerry

LA SALLE, Victor, house pseud.

08631 *After the atom.* London: John Spencer & Co., 1953, 108 p., paper, novel. [By Leonard G. Fish].

08632 *Assault from infinity.* London: John Spencer & Co., 1953, 108 p., paper, novel. [By Tom Wade].

08633 *The black sphere.* London: John Spencer & Co., 1952, 108 p., paper, novel. [By Gerald Evans].

06015 *Dawn of the half-gods.* London: John Spencer & Co., 1953, 128 p., paper, novel. [By John Glasby].

05075 *Menace from Mercury.* London: John Spencer & Co., 1954, 128 p., paper, novel. [By R. Lionel Fanthorpe; includes a short story, "More than mortal" / by T. W. (i.e., Tom) Wade].

08634 *The seventh dimension.* London: John Spencer & Co., 1953, 124 p., paper, novel. [By Tom Wade].

08635 *Suns in duo.* London: John Spencer & Co., 1953, 108 p., paper, novel. [By Tom Wade].

08636 *Twilight Zone.* London: John Spencer & Co., 1954, 130 p., paper, novel. [By John Glasby].

08637 *Twilight Zone.* London: Badger Books, 1959, 158 p., paper, coll. [Includes an additional story, "Point of no return," by "Max Chartair" (another pseudonym of Glasby)]. [By John Glasby].

LA SPINA, (Fanny) Greye (Bragg), 1880-1969

27647 *The gargoyle.* Chicago: Robert Weinberg, 1975, [96] p., paper, coll. LOST FANTASIES #3.

LA TOURETTE, Aileen, 1946-

27648 *Cry wolf.* London: Virago, 1986, 192 p., cloth, novel.

LA TOURRETTE, Jacqueline [i.e., Jacqueline La Tourrette Gibeson], 1926-

27649 *An ancient rage.* New York: A Dell Book, 1978, 224 p., paper, novel.

LACEY, Alan

27650 *The love warrior.* London: New English Library, 1975, 128 p., paper, novel.

LACKEY, Mercedes (Ritchie), 1950-

27651 *Arrow's fall.* New York: DAW Books, 1988, 319 p., paper, novel. HERALDS OF VALDEMAR #3.

27652 *Arrow's flight.* New York: DAW Books, 1987, 318 p., paper, novel. HERALDS OF VALDEMAR #2.

27653 *Arrows of the Queen.* New York: DAW Books, 1987, 320 p., paper, novel. HERALDS OF VALDEMAR #1.

27654 *Burning water.* New York: Tor Horror, A Tom Doherty Associates Book, 1989, 314 p., paper, novel. DIANA TREGARDE #1.

27655 *By the sword.* New York: DAW Books, 1991, 492 p., paper, novel.

27656 *Children of the night.* New York: Tor Horror, A Tom Doherty Associates Book, 1990, 313 p., paper, novel. DIANA TREGARDE #2.

27657 *Jinx High.* New York: Tor Horror, A Tom Doherty Associates Book, 1991, 314 p., paper, novel. DIANA TREGARDE #3.

27658 *The last herald-mage.* New York: Guild America Books, 1990, 900 p., cloth, coll. LAST HERALD-MAGE #1-3.

27659 *Magic's pawn.* New York: DAW Books, 1989, 349 p., paper, novel. LAST HERALD-MAGE #1.

27660 *Magic's price.* New York: DAW Books, 1990, 351 p., paper, novel. LAST HERALD-MAGE #3.

27661 *Magic's promise.* New York: DAW Books, 1990, 320 p., paper, novel. LAST HERALD-MAGE #2.

27662 *The oathbound.* New York: DAW Books, 1988, 302 p., paper, novel. VOWS AND HONOR #1.

27663 *Oathbreakers.* New York: DAW Books, 1989, 318 p., paper, novel. VOWS AND HONOR #2.

27664 *Winds of fate.* New York: DAW Books, 1991, 387 p., cloth, novel. MAGE WINDS #1.

with C. J. Cherryh

19899 *Reap the whirlwind.* New York: Baen, 1989, 273 p., paper, novel. SWORD OF KNOWLEDGE #3.

with Ellen Guon

24842 *Knight of ghosts and shadows: an urban fantasy.* New York: Baen Fantasy, 1990, 345 p., paper, novel.

with Andre Norton

27665 *The elvenbane: an epic high fantasy of the Halfblood Chronicles.* New York: Tor, A Tom Doherty Associates Book, 1991, 390 p., cloth, novel.

LACONTE, Ellen, *with Ronald T. LaConte*

27666 *Teaching tomorrow today: a guide to futuristics.* Toronto, New York: Bantam Books, 1975, 139 p., paper, nonf.

LACONTE, Ronald T., *with Ellen LaConte*

27666 *Teaching tomorrow today: a guide to futuristics.* Toronto, New York: Bantam Books, 1975, 139 p., paper, nonf.

LAFFERTY, R(aphael) A(loysius), 1914-

27667 *Annals of Klepsis.* New York: Ace Science Fiction Books, 1983, 212 p., paper, novel.

27668 *Apocalypses.* Los Angeles: Pinnacle Books, 1977, 374 p., paper, coll.

27669 *Archipelago.* Lafayette, LA: Manuscript Press, 1979, 283 p., cloth, novel. ARGOS MYTHOS.

27670 *Aurelia.* Norfolk, Virginia Beach, VA: Starblaze Editions, Donning Co., 1982, 183 p., paper, novel.

27671 *The back door of history.* Weston, Ontario, Canada: United Mythologies Press, 1988, 33 p., paper, coll.

27672 *Cranky old man from Tulsa: interviews with R. A. Lafferty.* Weston, Ontario, Canada: United Mythologies Press, 1990, 25 p., paper, nonf. coll. [Limited to 350 copies].

27673 *Dotty.* Weston, Ontario, Canada: United Mythologies Press, 1990, 96 p., paper, novel. ARGOS MYTHOS.

27674 *The early Lafferty.* Weston, Ontario, Canada: United Mythologies Press, 1988, 37 p., paper, coll. [Limited to 500 copies].

27675 *The early Lafferty II.* Weston, Ontario, Canada: United Mythologies Press, 1990, ii+31 p., paper, coll.

27676 *East of laughter.* Bath, Avon, England: Morrigan Publications, 1988, vii+200 p., cloth, coll. [The trade edition (vii+176 p.) is a novel; the limited edition of 250 copies has an additional story plus an article by Gene Wolfe].

27677 *The elliptical grave.* Weston, Ontario, Canada: United Mythologies Press, 1989, 101+7 p., paper, coll. [The signed edition includes a seven-page short story in addition to the novel].

27678 *Episodes of the Argo.* Weston, Ontario, Canada: United Mythologies Press, 1990, 59 p., paper, coll. ARGOS MYTHOS.

27679 *Four stories.* Polk City, IA: Chris Drumm, 1983, 19 p., paper, coll. DRUMM BOOKLET #7.

27680 *Funnyfingers & Cabrito.* Portland, OR: Pendragon Press, 1976, 45 p., cloth, coll.

27681 *Golden Gate, and other stories.* Minneapolis, MN: Corroboree Press, 1982, 237 p., cloth, coll.

27682 *Half a sky: the Coscuin Chronicles, 1849-1854.* Minneapolis, MN: Corroboree Press, 1984, 235 p., cloth, novel. COSCUIN CHRONICLES, BOOK TWO. [A sequel to *The flame is green*].

27683 *Heart of stone, dear, and other stories.* Polk City, IA: Chris Drumm, 1983, 42 p., paper, coll. DRUMM BOOKLET #12.

27684 *Horns on their heads.* Portland, OR: Pendragon Press, 1976, 33 p., cloth, story.

27685 *How many miles to Babylon.* Weston, Ontario, Canada: United Mythologies Press, 1989, 36 p., paper, story. ARGOS MYTHOS.

27686 *It's down the slippery cellar stairs: nonfiction.* Polk City, IA: Chris Drumm, 1984, 42 p., paper, nonf. coll. DRUMM BOOKLET #14.

27687 *Lafferty in orbit.* Cambridge, MA: Broken Mirrors Press, 1991, 224 p., cloth, coll.

27688 *The man who made models, and other stories.* Polk City, IA: Chris Drumm, 1984, 51 p., paper, coll. DRUMM BOOKLET #18.

27689 *Mischief malicious (and murder most strange).* Weston, Ontario, Canada: United Mythologies Press, 1991, 68 p., paper, coll.

27690 *My heart leaps up (1920-1928), chapters 1 & 2.* Polk City, IA: Chris Drumm, 1986, 54 p., paper, novel. [First part of *In a green tree*]. DRUMM BOOKLET #24.

27691 *My heart leaps up (1920-1928), chapters 3 & 4.* Polk City, IA: Chris Drumm, 1987, 44 p., paper, novel. [First part of *In a green tree*]. DRUMM BOOKLET #26.

27692 *My heart leaps up (1920-1928), chapters 5 & 6.* Polk City, IA: Chris Drumm, 1987, 53 p., paper, novel. [First part of *In a green tree*]. DRUMM BOOKLET #28.

27694 *My heart leaps up (1920-1928), chapters 7 & 8.* Polk City, IA: Chris Drumm, 1988, 49 p., paper, novel. [First part of *In a green tree*]. DRUMM BOOKLET #29.

27695 *My heart leaps up (1920-1928), chapters 9 & 10.* Polk City, IA: Chris Drumm, 1990, 63 p., paper, novel. [First part of *In a green tree*].

27696 *Not to mention camels: a science fiction fantasy.* Indianapolis, IN, New York: Bobbs-Merrill Co., 1976, 215 p., cloth, novel.

27697 *Promontory goats.* Weston, Ontario, Canada: United Mythologies Press, 1988, 22 p., paper, coll. ARGOS MYTHOS.

27698 *Ringing changes.* New York: Ace Science Fiction Books, 1984, xii+275 p., paper, coll.

27699 *Serpent's egg: a fantasy.* Bath, Avon, England: Morrigan Publications, 1987, 177 p., cloth, novel. [Limited to 250 copies; the trade edition (750 copies, 166 p.) lacks the essay added to the end of the special version].

27700 *Sindbad: the thirteenth voyage.* Cambridge, MA: Broken Mirrors Press, 1989, 158 p., paper, novel.

27701 *Slippery, and other stories.* Polk City, IA: Chris Drumm, 1985, 39 p., paper, coll. DRUMM BOOKLET #19.

27702 *Snake in his bosom, and other stories.* Polk City, IA: Chris Drumm, 1983, 43 p., paper, coll. DRUMM BOOKLET #13.

27703 *Through elegant eyes: stories of Austro and the men who knew everything.* Minneapolis, MN: Corroboree Press, 1983, 237 p., cloth, coll.

27704 *True believers.* Weston, Ontario, Canada: United Mythologies Press, 1989, 36 p., paper, nonf. coll.

LAFITTE, Louis—SEE: Curtis, J.-L.

LAFLIN, Jack

27706 *The bees.* New York: Tempo Books, Grosset & Dunlap Publishers, 1977, 153 p., paper, novel.

LAGOWSKI, Barbara (Jean), 1955- , *with Rick Mumma*

27707 *Teen terminators.* New York: Berkley Books, 1989, 219 p., paper, novel.

LAHEY, Michael

27708 *Quest for Apollo.* New York: DAW Books, 1989, 255 p., paper, novel.

*LAHMAN, Damon, <u>1903-1977</u>

LAIDLAW, Marc, 1960-

27709 *Dad's nuke.* New York: Donald I. Fine, 1985, 255 p., cloth, novel.

27710 *Neon lotus.* Toronto, New York: Spectra, Bantam Books, 1988, 294 p., paper, novel.

LAINEZ, Manuel Mujica—SEE: Mujica Lainez, Manuel

*LAING, Alexander (Kinnan), 1903-<u>1976</u>

LAKE, David J(ohn), 1929-

27711 *The changelings of Chaan.* Melbourne, Victoria, Australia: Hyland House, 1985, 170 p., cloth, novel.

27712 *The fourth hemisphere.* St. Kilda, Victoria, Australia: Void Publications, 1980, 208 p., cloth, novel. BREAKOUT #6.

27713 *The gods of Xuma; or, Barsoom revisited.* New York: DAW Books, 1978, 189 p., paper, novel. BREAKOUT #4.

27714 *The man who loved Morlocks: a sequel to The time machine as narrated by The Time Traveller.* Melbourne, Australia: Hyland House, 1981, 128 p., cloth, novel. TIME MACHINE SEQUEL. [A sequel to the novel by H. G. Wells].

27715 *The right hand of Dextra.* New York: DAW Books, 1977, 176 p., paper, novel. BREAKOUT #2.

27716 *Ring of Truth.* St. Kilda, Victoria, Australia: Cory & Collins, 1982, 242 p., paper, novel.

27717 *Walkers on the sky.* New York: DAW Books, 1976, 188 p., paper, novel. BREAKOUT #1.

27718 *Warlords of Xuma.* New York: DAW Books, 1983, 208 p., paper, novel. BREAKOUT #5.

27719 *West of the Moon.* Melbourne, Australia: Hyland House, 1988, 250 p., cloth, novel.

27720 *The Wildings of Westron.* New York: DAW Books, 1977, 189 p., paper, novel. BREAKOUT #3.

LAKIN, Rita

27721 *Demon of the night.* New York: Pyramid Books, 1976, 192 p., paper, novel.

LALLEY, Paul

27722 *The colony.* New York: Carlyle, 1979, 221 p., paper, novel.

LALLY, T(homas) M(ichael)

27723 *Tales, weird and whimsical.* London: Merlin, 1991, 215 p., paper, coll.

LAMB, Hugh (Charles), 1946-

27724 *Cold fear: new tales of terror.* London: W. H. Allen & Co., 1977, 175 p., cloth, anth.

27725 *Forgotten tales of terror.* London: Eyre Methuen, 1978, 170 p., cloth, anth.

27726 *Gaslit nightmares.* London: Futura, 1988, 358 p., paper, anth.

27727 *Gaslit nightmares 2.* London: Futura, 1991, 384 p., paper, anth.

27728 *The man-wolf, and other stories.* London: W. H. Allen & Co., 1978, 202 p., cloth, anth.

27729 *New tales of terror.* London: Magnum, 1980, 192 p., paper, anth.

27730 *Return from the grave.* London: W. H. Allen & Co., 1976, 199 p., cloth, anth.

27731 *The Star Book of horror, no. 1.* London: A Star Book, W. H. Allen & Co., 1975, 156 p., paper, anth.

27732 *The Star Book of horror, no. 2.* London: A Star Book, Wyndham Publications, 1976, 158 p., paper, anth.

27733 *Stories in the dark: tales of terror.* Wellingborough, Northamptonshire, England: William Kimber, 1989, 223 p., cloth, anth.

27734 *Tales from a gas-lit graveyard.* London: W. H. Allen & Co., 1979, 223 p., cloth, anth.

27735 *A taste of fear.* London: W. H. Allen & Co., 1976, 237 p., cloth, anth.

27736 *Terror by gaslight: more Victorian tales of terror.* London: W. H. Allen & Co., 1975, 222 p., cloth, anth.

27737 *The thrill of horror.* London: W. H. Allen & Co., 1975, xiii+207 p., cloth, anth.

27738 *Victorian nightmares.* London: W. H. Allen & Co., 1977, 224 p., cloth, anth.

LAMBARD, Creede

with Sharleen Lambard

27739 *Badlands run.* Lake Geneva, WI: TSR Inc., 1987, 21+[170] p., paper, fiction. CAR WARS ADVENTURE GAMEBOOK #4.

with Sharleen Lambard & Steve Jackson

26387 *Fuel's gold.* Lake Geneva, WI: TSR Inc., 1986, 18+[150] p., paper, fiction. CAR WARS ADVENTURE GAMEBOOK #2.

LAMBARD, Sharleen

with Creede Lambard

27739 *Badlands run.* Lake Geneva, WI: TSR Inc., 1987, 21+[170] p., paper, fiction. CAR WARS ADVENTURE GAMEBOOK #4.

with Creede Lambard & Steve Jackson

26387 *Fuel's gold.* Lake Geneva, WI: TSR Inc., 1986, 18+[150] p., paper, fiction. CAR WARS ADVENTURE GAMEBOOK #2.

LAMBE, Dean R(odney), 1943- , *with Michael Banks*

17338 *The Odysseus solution.* New York: Baen Science Fiction Books, 1986, 279 p., paper, novel.

LAMBERT, Derek (William), 1929-

27740 *The memory man.* London: Arlington Books, 1979, 207 p., cloth, novel.

27741 *The Red Dove.* London: Hamish Hamilton, 1982, 274 p., cloth, novel.

LAMBERT, W(illiam Jay) III, 1948-

27742 *Encores in fade* / by W. Lambert III. North Hollywood, CA: American Art Enterprises, 1981, 160 p., paper, novel.

27743 *Michael: the master* / by W. Lambert III. North Hollywood, CA: American Art Enterprises, 1981, 160 p., paper, novel.

as LAMBERT WILHELM

27744 *Abort Project K!* North Hollywood, CA: American Art Enterprises, 1981, 159 p., paper, novel.

LAMBIRTH, Frank

27745 *Behind the door: a novel.* New York: Popular Library, 1988, 234 p., paper, novel.
27746 *Now I lay me down to sleep...* New York: Popular Library, 1989, 235 p., paper, novel.

LAMBOURNE, David

27747 *The musclemen.* Oxford, England: Oxford University Press, 1991, 141 p., cloth, novel.

LAMBOURNE, Robert, *with Michael Shallis & Michael Shortland*

27748 *Close encounters? science and science fiction.* Bristol & New York: Adam Hilger, 1991, xiii+184 p., paper, nonf.

LAMM, Richard (D.), 1935- , *with Arnold Grossman*

24788 *1988.* New York: St. Martin's Press, 1985, 264 p., cloth, novel.

L'AMOUR, Louis (Dearborn), 1908-1988

27749 *The Californios.* New York: Saturday Review Press, 1974, 188 p., cloth, novel.
27750 *Haunted mesa.* Toronto, New York: Bantam Books, 1987, 357 p., cloth, novel.

LAMPERTI, Claudia (Jane McKay), 1934-

as ANONYMOUS EDITOR

27751 *WomanSpace: future and fantasy stories and art.* Lebanon, NH: New Victoria Publications, 1981, 92 p., paper, anth.

as CLAUDIA MCKAY

27752 *The promise of the rose stone.* Norwich, VT: New Victoria Publishers, 1986, 238 p., paper, novel.

LAMPITT, Dinah, 1937-

27753 *To sleep no more.* London: Michael Joseph, 1987, 451 p., cloth, novel.

LAMPMAN, Evelyn Sibley, 1907-1980

15824 *The shy stegosaurus of Indian Springs.* Garden City, NY: Doubleday & Co., 1962, 232 p., cloth, novel. SHY STEGOSAURUS #2.

LAMPTON, Christopher (F.), 1950-

27754 *Cross of Empire.* Toronto, New York: Laser Books, 1976, 190 p., paper, novel.
27755 *Gateway to Limbo* / by Chris Lampton. Garden City, NY: Doubleday & Co., 1979, 184 p., cloth, novel.

with David Bischoff

18015 *The seeker.* Toronto, New York: Laser Books, 1976, 190 p., paper, novel.

LANCE, Kathryn, 1943-

27756 *Pandora's children.* New York: Popular Library, 1986, 279 p., paper, novel. PANDORA #2.
27757 *Pandora's genes.* New York: Popular Library, 1985, 279 p., paper, novel. PANDORA #1.

as LYNN BEACH

27758 *The attack of the Insecticons.* New York: Ballantine Books, 1985, 74 p., paper, novel. FIND YOUR FATE—JUNIOR TRANSFORMERS #3.
27759 *Conquest of the Time Master.* New York: Avon, 1985, 103 p., paper, novel. WIZARDS, WARRIORS & YOU #8.
The dark—SEE: *Phantom Valley: The dark.*
The evil one—SEE: *Phantom Valley: The evil one.*
27760 *G.I. Joe: Operation: jungle doom.* New York: Ballantine Books, 1986, 88 p., paper, novel. FIND YOUR FATE—G.I. JOE #12.
27761 *G.I. Joe: Operation: time machine.* New York: Ballantine Books, 1987, 89 p., paper, novel. FIND YOUR FATE—G.I. JOE #15.
27762 *The haunted castle of Ravencurse.* New York: A Parachute Press Book, Avon, 1985, 103 p., paper, novel. WIZARDS, WARLOCKS & YOU #5.

H.O.W.L. High—SEE: *Phantom Valley: H.O.W.L. High.*

27763 *Invaders from Darkland.* New York: Avon, 1986, 104 p., paper, novel. WIZARDS, WARRIORS & YOU #15.

27764 *Invisibility island.* New York: Ballantine Books, 1988, 120 p., paper, novel. G.I. JOE #4.

Operation: jungle doom—SEE: *G.I. Joe: Operation: jungle doom.*

Operation: time machine—SEE: *G.I. Joe: Operation: time machine.*

27765 *Phantom Valley: The dark.* New York, London: A Minstrel Book, Pocket Books, 1991, 117 p., paper, novel. PHANTOM VALLEY #2.

27766 *Phantom Valley: The evil one.* New York, London: A Minstrel Book, Pocket Books, 1991, 118 p., paper, novel. PHANTOM VALLEY #1.

27767 *Secrets of the lost island.* New York, Toronto: Scholastic Inc., 1984, 93 p., paper, novel. TWISTAPLOTS #16.

LANCOUR, Gene [pseud. of Gene Louis Fisher], 1947-

27768 *The globes of Llarum.* Garden City, NY: Doubleday & Co., 1980, 186 p., cloth, novel.

27769 *The man-eaters of Cascalon.* Garden City, NY: Doubleday & Co., 1979, 188 p., cloth, novel. DIRSHAN #4.

27770 *Sword for the empire.* Garden City, NY: Doubleday & Co., 1978, 185 p., cloth, novel. DIRSHAN #3.

27771 *The war machines of Kalinth.* Garden City, NY: Doubleday & Co., 1977, 190 p., cloth, novel. DIRSHAN #2.

LAND, Jon

27772 *The alpha deception.* New York: Fawcett Gold Medal, 1988, 357 p., paper, novel. BLAINE MCCRACKEN #2.

27773 *The council of ten.* New York: Fawcett Gold Medal, 1987, 345 p., paper, novel.

27774 *The eighth trumpet.* New York: Fawcett Gold Medal, 1989, 400 p., paper, novel.

27775 *The gamma option.* New York: Fawcett Gold Medal, 1989, 340 p., paper, novel. BLAINE MCCRACKEN #3.

27776 *The Lucifer directive.* New York: Zebra Books, Kensington Publishing Corp., 1984, 462 p., paper, novel.

27777 *The ninth dominion.* New York: Fawcett Gold Medal, 1991, vi+354 p., paper, novel.

27778 *The omega command.* New York: Fawcett Gold Medal, 1986, 371 p., paper, novel. BLAINE MCCRACKEN #1.

27779 *The omicron legion.* New York: Fawcett Gold Medal, 1991, viii+339 p., paper, novel. BLAINE MCCRACKEN #4.

27780 *The Valhalla testament.* New York: Fawcett Gold Medal, 1990, 344 p., paper, novel.

27781 *Vortex.* New York: Zebra Books, Kensington Publishing Corp., 1984, 446 p., paper, novel.

LANDIS, Arthur H(arold), 1917-1986

27782 *Camelot in orbit.* New York: DAW Books, 1978, 175 p., paper, novel. CAMELOT #2.

27783 *Home, to Avalon.* New York: DAW Books, 1982, 223 p., paper, novel. CAMELOT #4

27784 *The magick of Camelot.* New York: DAW Books, 1981, 207 p., paper, novel. CAMELOT #3.

27785 *A world called Camelot.* New York: DAW Books, 1976, 220 p., paper, novel. CAMELOT #1.

LANDIS, Geoffrey A.

27786 *Myths, legends, and true history.* Eugene, OR: Pulphouse Publishing, 1991, 111 p., cloth, coll. AUTHOR'S CHOICE MONTHLY #26.

LANDIS, Marie [i.e., Marie Antoinette Landis Edwards], 1935?- , *with Brian Herbert*

25513 *Memorymakers.* New York: A Roc Book, 1991, 206 p., paper, novel.

*LANDOLFI, Tommaso, 1908-1979

LANDSMAN, Samuel N. B.—SEE: Landsman, Sandy

LANDSMAN, Sandy [i.e., Samuel N. B. Landsman], 1950-

27787 *Castaways on Chimp Island.* New York: Atheneum, 1986, 202 p., cloth, novel.

27788 *The gadget factor.* New York: Atheneum, 1984, 168 p., cloth, novel.

LANE, Ann J(udith), 1931-

27789 *To "Herland" and beyond: the life and work of Charlotte Perkins Gilman.* New York: Pantheon, 1990, xvi+413 p., cloth, nonf.

LANE, Carolyn (Blocker), 1926-

27790 *Echoes in an empty room, and other tales of the supernatural.* New York: Holt, Rinehart & Winston, 1980, 158 p., cloth, coll.

LANE, Daryl, *with William Vernon & David Carson*

19523 *The sound of wonder: interviews from "The science fiction radio show".* Phoenix, AZ: Oryx Press, 1985, 2 v. (I-xi+203 p., II-vi+201 p.), paper, nonf. coll.

*LANE, Jane [pseud. of Elaine Kidner Dakers], 1905-1978

LANE, John, pseud.—SEE: Hughes, Dennis Talbot

LANE, Megan [pseud. of Brenda Himrod]

27791 *The trouble with magic.* New York: A Candlelight Ecstasy Romance, 1985, 192 p., paper, novel.

LANEY, Frances T., *with William H. Evans*

22802 *Howard Phillips Lovecraft (1890-1937): a tentative bibliography* / by Francis T. Laney and William H. Evans. Los Angeles: An "Acolyte" Publication, FAPA, 1943, 12 p., paper, nonf.

*LANG, Gregor [pseud. of Faber Birren], 1900-1988

LANG, King, house pseud.—SEE: Griffiths, David Arthur & Hay, George

LANG, Simon [pseud. of Darlene Hartman], 1934-

27792 *The elluvon gift.* New York: Avon, 1975, 155 p., paper, novel. SKIPJACK #2.

*LANGDON, Norman E(arle), 1888-1967

LANGE, John F.—SEE: Norman, John

LANGE, Oliver, pseud., 1927-

    Defiance—SEE: Vandenberg.
08603 *Vandenberg: a novel.* New York: Stein & Day, 1971, 333 p., cloth, novel.
08603A retitled: *Defiance: an American novel.* New York: Day Books, 1981, 333 p., paper, novel.

LANGFORD, David (Rowland), 1953-

37899 *Critical assembly.* Reading, England: Ansible Information, 1987, 62 p., paper, coll. [Includes some nonfiction].

27793 *The dragonhiker's guide to battlefield covenant at Dune's edge: odyssey two: the collected science fiction and fantasy parodies of David Langford, volume one.* Birmingham, England: Drunken Dragon Press, 1988, 142 p., cloth, coll. [Only volume issued].

37900 *A Novacon garland.* Birmingham, England: Birmingham Science Fiction Group, 1985, 15 p., paper, coll. [Includes some nonfiction; bound with *The interpreter* / by James White].

37901 *Platen stories.* Cambridge, England: Conspiracy 87, 1987, 63 p., paper, nonf. coll.

27794 *The space eater.* London: Arrow Books, 1982, 301 p., paper, novel.

27795 *War in 2080: the future of military technology.* Newton Abbot, England: Westbridge Books, 1979, 229 p., cloth, nonf.

as WILLIAM ROBERT LOOSLEY

27796 *An account of a meeting with denizens of another world, 1871.* Newton Abbot, England: David & Charles, 1979, 96 p., cloth, novel.

with John Grant

24356 *Earthdoom!* London: Grafton, 1987, 303 p., paper, novel.

with Brian Stableford

27797 *The third millennium: a history of the world, A.D. 2000-3000.* London: Sidgwick & Jackson, 1985, 224 p., cloth, fiction.

with Brian M. Stableford & Peter Nicholls

27798 *The science in science fiction.* London: Michael Joseph, 1982, 208 p., cloth, nonf.

LANGFORD, Michèle K.

27799 *Contours of the fantastic: selected essays from the Eighth International Conference on the Fantastic in the Arts.* New York: Greenwood Press, 1990, xiii+232 p., cloth, nonf. anth. CONTRIBUTIONS TO THE STUDY OF SCIENCE FICTION AND FANTASY #41.

LANGHOLM, A. D.—SEE: Davidson, Alan

LANGLEY, Bob [i.e., Robert Langley], 1936-

27800 *Precipice.* New York, Toronto: Falcon, Bantam Books, 1991, 377 p., paper, novel.
27801 *Warlords.* London: Michael Joseph, 1979, 223 p., cloth, novel.

*LANGLEY, Dorothy [pseud. of Dorothy High Kissling], 1904-1969

*LANGLEY, Noel (A.), 1911-1980

LANGLEY, Robert—SEE: Langley, Bob

LANGSAM, Devra M(ichele), 1945-

27802 *Vulcan reflections.* Baltimore, MD: T-K Graphics, 1975, 35 p., paper, nonf. anth.

with Sherna Comerford

20351 *More Vulcan reflections: essays on Spock and his world.* Baltimore, MD: T-K Graphics, 1976, 26 p., paper, nonf. anth. [Cover title].

LANGTON, Jane (Gillson), 1922-

15825 *The astonishing stereoscope.* New York: Harper & Row, 1971, 240 p., cloth, novel. ELEANOR #3.
15826 *The diamond in the window.* New York: Harper & Row, 1962, 242 p., cloth, novel. ELEANOR #1.
27803 *The fledgling.* New York: An Ursula Nordstrom Book, Harper & Row, 1980, ix+182 p., cloth, novel. ELEANOR #4.
15827 *The swing in the summerhouse.* New York: Harper & Row, 1967, 185 p., cloth, novel. ELEANOR #2.

LANIER, Sterling E(dmund), 1927-

27804 *The curious quests of Brigadier Ffellowes.* West Kingston, RI: Donald M. Grant, Publisher, 1986, 254 p., cloth, coll. BRIGADIER FFELLOWES #2.
27805 *Hiero Desteen.* Garden City, NY: Nelson Doubleday, 1984, 532 p., cloth, novel. HIERO DESTEEN #1-2.
27806 *Menace under Marswood.* New York: A Del Rey Book, Ballantine Books, 1983, 214 p., paper, novel.
27807 *Science fiction special (34): Hiero's journey ; The war for the Lot.* London: Sidgwick & Jackson, 1981, 384, 256 p., cloth, coll. HIERO DESTEEN #1.

27808 *The unforsaken Hiero.* New York: A Del Rey Book, Ballantine Books, 1983, 214 p., cloth, novel. HIERO DESTEEN #2.

LANNING, Sereta

27809 *Escape from tomorrow.* Belmont, CA: A Pacemaker Bestsellers Book, Fearon-Pitman Publishers, 1977, 60 p., paper, novel.

LANSDALE, Joe R(ichard Harold), 1951-

27810 *Act of love.* New York: Zebra Books, Kensington Publishing Corp., 1981, 301 p., paper, novel.
27811 *Batman: Captured by the engines.* New York: Warner Books, 1991, vi+241 p., paper, novel. BATMAN SERIES.
27812 *By bizarre hands: stories.* Shingletown, CA: Mark V. Ziesing, 1989, xi+246 p., cloth, coll.
Captured by the engines—SEE: Batman: Captured by the engines.
37902 *Cold in July.* New York, Toronto: Bantam Books, 1989, 195 p., paper, novel.
27813 *Dead in the west.* New York: Space & Time, 1986, 119 p., paper, novel.
27814 *The drive-in: (a "B" movie with blood and popcorn, made in Texas).* Toronto, New York: Bantam, 1988, 158 p., paper, movie. DRIVE-IN #1.
27815 *The drive-in 2: (not just one of them sequels).* New York, Toronto: Bantam Books, 1989, 179 p., paper, novel. DRIVE-IN #2.
27816 *The magic wagon.* Garden City, NY: Doubleday & Co., 1986, x+180 p., cloth, novel.
27817 *The new frontier: the best of today's western fiction.* New York: Doubleday, 1989, 180 p., cloth, anth. [An anthology of westerns, some of them fantastic].
27818 *The nightrunners.* Arlington Heights, IL: Dark Harvest, 1987, 241 p., cloth, novel.
27819 *On the far side of the Cadillac Desert with the dead folks.* Arvada, CO: Roadkill Press, 1991, 45 p., paper, story. [Limited to 500 copies].
37903 *Savage season.* Shingletown, CA: Mark V. Ziesing, 1990, 178 p., cloth, novel.
27820 *The steel valentine.* Eugene, OR: Pulphouse Publishing, 1991, 39 p., cloth, story. SHORT STORY HARDBACKS #7; SHORT STORY PAPERBACKS #11.
27821 *Stories by Mama Lansdale's youngest boy.* Eugene, OR: Pulphouse Publishing, 1991, 130 p., cloth, coll. AUTHOR'S CHOICE MONTHLY #18.

with Pat LoBrutto

27822 *Razored saddles.* Arlington Heights, IL: Dark Harvest, 1989, 268 p., cloth, anth.

LANTZ, Fran(cess Lin), 1952-

27823 *All shook up.* New York: Avon Flare, 1987, 154 p., paper, novel. EILEEN GOUDGE'S SWEPT AWAY #8.
27824 *Star struck.* New York: Avon Flare, 1987, 202 p., paper, novel. EILEEN GOUDGE'S SWEPT AWAY #4.
27825 *Woodstock magic.* New York: Avon Flare, 1986, 166 p., paper, novel. EILEEN GOUDGE'S SWEPT AWAY #2.

LAPKA, Fay S.

27826 *Dark is a color.* Wheaton, IL: Harold Shaw Publisher, 1990, 262 p., cloth, novel. CARO #1.
27826A retitled: *Dark is a colour.* England: Gold Books, 1991, 262 p., paper, novel.
27827 *Hoverlight.* Wheaton, IL: Harold Shaw Publisher, 1991, 285 p., cloth, novel. CARO #2.

LAPLANTE, Jerry (C.)

27828 *In Garde we trust.* New York: Zebra Books, Kensington Publishing Corp., 1979, 240 p., paper, novel. CHAMELEON #2.

LARA, Jan, pseud.—SEE: Hinkemeyer, Michael T.

*LARGE, E(rnest) C(harles), d. 1976

LARGENT, R. Karl

27829 *Ancients.* New York: Leisure Books, 1990, 388 p., paper, novel.
27830 *Black death.* New York: Leisure Books, 1988, 368 p., paper, novel.
27831 *Pagoda.* New York: Leisure Books, 1989, 394 p., paper, novel.
27832 *The prometheus project.* New York: Leisure Books, 1989, 343 p., paper, novel.
27833 *The witch of Sixkill.* New York: Leisure Books, 1990, 367 p., paper, novel.

as SIMON LAWRENCE

27834 *The pond.* New York: Leisure Books, 1990, 389 p., paper, novel.

LARIC, Frank

27835 *Black Cola.* Davenport, FL: A Neptune Book, 1977, 194 p., paper, novel.

LARKIN, David, 1944-

27836 *Fantastic art.* New York: Ballantine Books, 1973, [96] p., paper, art.
27837 *The fantastic kingdom.* New York: Ballantine Books, 1974, [96] p., paper, art.
27838 *Once upon a time: some contemporary illustrators of fantasy.* New York, Toronto: A Peacock Press/Bantam Book, 1976, [99] p., paper, art.

with Alan Lee & Brian Froud

23573 *Faeries.* New York: Henry N. Abrams, 1978, [ca. 200] p., cloth, fiction.

with Sarah Teale

27839 *Giants.* New York: Henry N. Abrams, 1979, 191 p., cloth, fiction.

LARRABEITI, Michael de—SEE: de Larrabeiti, Michael

LARSEN, Jeanne (Louise), 1950-

27840 *Bronze mirror.* New York: Henry Holt & Co., 1991, 337 p., cloth, novel.
27841 *Silk road: a novel of eighth-century China.* New York: Henry Holt & Co., 1989, ix+434 p., cloth, novel.

LARSON, Glen A., 1937-

with Ron Goulart

24255 *Experiment in Terra.* New York: Berkley Books, 1984, 151 p., paper, tele. BATTLESTAR GALACTICA #9.
24256 *Greetings from Earth: a novel.* New York: Berkley Books, 1983, 183 p., paper, tele. BATTLESTAR GALACTICA #8.
24257 *The long patrol: novel.* New York: Berkley Books, 1984, 171 p., paper, tele. BATTLESTAR GALACTICA #10.

with Roger Hill

25666 *The 24-carat assassin: a novel.* London: A Target Book, W. H. Allen & Co., 1984, 154 p., paper, tele. KNIGHT RIDER #4.
25667 *Hearts of stone.* New York: Pinnacle Books, 1984, 233 p., paper, tele. KNIGHT RIDER #3.

25668 *Knight Rider.* New York: Pinnacle Books, 1983, 245 p., paper, tele. KNIGHT RIDER #1.

25669 *Mirror image: a novel.* London: A Target Book, W. H. Allen & Co., 1985, 159 p., paper, tele. KNIGHT RIDER #5.

25670 *Trust doesn't rust.* New York: Pinnacle Books, 1984, 245 p., paper, tele. KNIGHT RIDER #2.

with Michael Resnick

27842 *Galactica discovers Earth.* New York: Berkley Books, 1980, 187 p., paper, tele. BATTLESTAR GALACTICA #5.

with Michael Sloan

27843 *The Hardy Boys and Nancy Drew meet Dracula.* New York: Grosset & Dunlap, 1978, 109 p., paper, novel. HARDY BOYS SERIES.

with Robert Thurston

27844 *Apollo's war: novel.* New York: Berkley Books, 1987, 198 p., paper, tele. BATTLESTAR GALACTICA #13.

27845 *Battlestar Galactica.* New York: A Berkley Book, Berkley Publishing Corp., 1978, 244 p., paper, tele. BATTLESTAR GALACTICA #1.

27846 *The Cylon death machine.* New York: A Berkley Book, Berkley Publishing Corp., 1979, 250 p., paper, tele. BATTLESTAR GALACTICA #2.

27847 *"Die, Chameleon!": novel.* New York: Berkley Books, 1986, 217 p., paper, tele. BATTLESTAR GALACTICA #12.

27848 *The nightmare machine.* New York: Berkley Books, 1985, 216 p., paper, tele. BATTLESTAR GALACTICA #11.

27849 *Surrender the Galactica!* New York: Ace Books, 1988, 203 p., paper, tele. BATTLESTAR GALACTICA #14.

27850 *The tombs of Kobol.* New York: A Berkley Book, Berkley Publishing Corp., 1979, 215 p., paper, tele. BATTLESTAR GALACTICA #3.

27851 *The young warriors.* New York: Berkley Books, 1980, 185 p., paper, tele. BATTLESTAR GALACTICA #4.

with Nicholas Yermakov (i.e., Simon Hawke)

25401 *The living legend.* New York: Berkley Books, 1982, 180 p., paper, tele. BATTLESTAR GALACTICA #6.

25402 *War of the gods.* New York: Berkley Books, 1982, 182 p., paper, tele. BATTLESTAR GALACTICA #7.

LARSON, Majliss

27852 *Pawns and symbols: a Star Trek novel.* New York: Pocket Books, 1985, 277 p., paper, novel. STAR TREK #26.

LARSON, Randall D(ouglas), 1954-

27853 *The complete Robert Bloch: an illustrated, international bibliography.* Sunnyvale, CA: Fandom Unlimited Enterprises, 1986, x+126 p., paper, nonf.

27854 *Musique fantastique: a survey of film music in the fantastic cinema.* Metuchen, NJ: Scarecrow Press, 1985, viii+592 p., cloth, nonf.

27855 *Robert Bloch.* Mercer Island, WA: Starmont House, 1986, 148 p., cloth, nonf. STARMONT READER'S GUIDE #37.

with Robert Bloch

18199 *The Robert Bloch companion: collected interviews, 1969-1986.* Mercer Island, WA: Starmont House, 1989, 156 p., cloth, nonf. anth.

LARSON, Roberta—SEE: Rubenstein, Roberta

LARSON, Ross, 1935-

27856 *Fantasy and imagination in the Mexican narrative.* Tempe, AZ: Center for Latin American Studies, Arizona State University, 1977, xi+154 p., cloth, nonf.

*LASKI, Marghanita, 1915-1988

LASKY, Kathryn [i.e., Kathryn Lasky Knight], 1944-

27857 *Double trouble squared.* San Diego, CA: Harcourt Brace Jovanovich, 1991, 232 p., cloth, novel. STARBUCK FAMILY SERIES.

27858 *Home free.* Phoenix, AZ: Four Winds Press; New York: Macmillan Publishing Co., 1985, 245 p., cloth, novel.

LASSER, Dustin, pseud.

Orgy in orbit—SEE: *Space nymph.*

27859 *Space nymph.* New York: The Cameo Collection, 1978, 180 p., paper, novel. STAR WARS PARODY.

27859A retitled: *Orgy in orbit /* by Traves Tea. New York: A Beeline Double Novel,

1980, 180 p., paper, novel. STAR WARS PARODY. [Bound with: *Janet's sex planet* / by Carrie Onn].

LAST, Martin, 1929-

with Baird Searles

27860 *The science fiction quizbook.* New York, London: Drake Publishers, 1976, 128 p., paper, nonf.

with Baird Searles & Beth Meacham & Michael Franklin

23446 *A reader's guide to fantasy.* New York: Avon, 1982, 217 p., paper, nonf.

LATHAM, David (William), 1950- , with Sheila Latham

27861 *An annotated critical bibliography of William Morris.* London: Harvester Wheatsheaf; New York: St. Martin's Press, 1991, vii+423 p., cloth, nonf.

LATHAM, Robert (Arch), 1959- , with Robert A. Collins

20332 *Science fiction & fantasy book review annual 1988.* Westport, CT, London: Meckler, 1988, ix+486 p., cloth, nonf. anth.

20333 *Science fiction & fantasy book review annual 1989.* Westport, CT, London: Meckler, 1989, ix+624 p., cloth, nonf. anth.

20334 *Science fiction & fantasy book review annual 1990.* New York, Westport, CT: Greenwood Press, 1991, ix+711 p., cloth, nonf. anth.

LATHAM, Sheila (Marie), 1950- , with David Latham

27861 *An annotated critical bibliography of William Morris.* London: Harvester Wheatsheaf; New York: St. Martin's Press, 1991, vii+423 p., cloth, nonf.

LAUDE, Anthony, with H. G. Stenzel

27862 *2001 and beyond: science fiction stories.* London: Longman, 1975, 90 p., paper, anth.

LAUDER, George Dick- —SEE: Dick-Lauder, George

LAUDER, William

27863 *The uncanny.* London: Arrow, 1977, 140 p., paper, movie.

LAUGHLIN, Charlotte (Gay), 1951- , with Daniel J. H. Levack

27864 *De Camp: an L. Sprague de Camp bibliography.* San Francisco, Columbia, PA: Underwood-Miller, 1983, 328 p., cloth, nonf.

LAUMER, (John) Keith, 1925-

27865 *Alien minds.* Riverdale, NY: Baen Books, 1991, 326 p., paper, coll.

27866 *The best of Keith Laumer.* New York: Pocket Books, 1976, 255 p., paper, coll.

27867 *Beyond the Imperium.* New York: Tor, A Tom Doherty Associates Book, 1981, 318 p., paper, coll. IMPERIUM #2-3. [Includes *The other side of time* and *Assignment in nowhere*].

27868 *Bolo: the annals of the Dinochrome Brigade.* New York: Berkley Publishing Corp., 1976, 179 p., cloth, coll. BOLO #1.

27869 *The breaking Earth.* New York: A Tom Doherty Associates Book, TOR Science Fiction, Pinnacle Books, 1981, 287 p., paper, coll. [Includes the novel *Catastrophe Planet* plus stories].

27870 *Chrestomathy.* New York: A Baen Book, 1984, 254 p., paper, coll. [Includes excerpts from his novels].

27871 *The compleat Bolo.* New York: Baen Books, 1990, 314 p., paper, coll. BOLO #1-2. [Includes *Bolo* and *Rogue Bolo*].
Diplomat at arms—SEE: *Retief: Diplomat at arms.*
Emissary to the stars—SEE: *Retief: Emissary to the stars.*

27872 *End as a hero.* New York: Ace Science Fiction Books, 1985, 150 p., paper, novel.

08660 *Envoy to new worlds.* New York: Ace Double, 1963, 134 p., paper, coll. RETIEF #1.

27873 retitled: *Retief: envoy to new worlds.* New York: Baen Books, 1987, 245 p., paper, coll. RETIEF #1. [Expanded edition].

27874 *The galaxy builder.* New York: Ace Science Fiction Books, 1984, 236 p., paper, novel. LAFAYETTE O'LEARY #4.

27875 *The glory game.* New York: A Tom Doherty Associates Book, 1983, 252 p., paper, novel.

27876 *The house in November; special bonus: complete short novel, The other sky.* New

York: Tor, A Tom Doherty Associates Book, 1981, 255 p., paper, coll.

27877 *Judson's Eden.* Riverdale, NY: Baen Books, 1991, 379 p., paper, novel.

27878 *Knight of delusions, plus two bonus stories: Thunderhead and The last command.* New York: Tor, A Tom Doherty Associates Book, 1982, 287 p., paper, coll. [Includes *Night of Delusions* plus stories].

27879 *Once there was a giant.* New York: Tor, A Tom Doherty Associates Book, 1984, 223 p., paper, coll. [Different from the earlier book of the same title].

27880 *Retief and the Pangalactic Pageant of Pulchritude.* New York: Baen Science Fiction Books, 1986, 278 p., paper, coll. RETIEF #6. [Includes *Retief's ransom*].

27881 *Retief at large.* New York: Ace Books, 1978, 440 p., paper, coll. RETIEF SERIES (UNNUMBERED).

27882 *Retief: Diplomat at arms.* New York: A Timescape Book, Pocket Books, 1982, 207 p., paper, coll. RETIEF #9.

27883 *Retief: Emissary to the stars.* New York: A Dell Book, 1975, 171 p., paper, coll. RETIEF #8.

37904 *Retief: Emissary to the stars.* New York: Pocket Books, 1979, 239 p., paper, coll. [Expanded edition].

Retief: Envoy to new worlds—SEE: *Envoy to new worlds.*

27884 *Retief in the ruins.* New York: Baen Books, 1986, 247 p., paper, coll. RETIEF #12.

27885 *Retief to the rescue.* New York: Timescape Books, 1983, 237 p., paper, novel. RETIEF #10.

27886 *Retief unbound.* New York: Ace Books, 1979, 343 p., paper, coll. RETIEF #1 & #6. [Includes *Envoy to new worlds* and *Retief's ransom*].

27887 *The return of Retief.* New York: A Baen Book, 1984, 221 p., paper, novel. RETIEF #11.

27888 *Reward for Retief.* New York: Baen Books, 1989, 340 p., paper, novel. RETIEF #13.

27889 *Rogue Bolo.* New York: Baen Science Fiction Books, 1986, 245 p., paper, novel. BOLO #2.

27890 *Star colony.* New York: St. Martin's Press, 1981, xvii+396 p., cloth, novel.

27891 *The star treasure.* New York: Baen Books, 1986, 271 p., paper, coll. [Adds three stories to the original novel].

27892 *The stars must wait.* New York: Baen Books, 1990, 283 p., paper, novel. BOLO #3.

27893 *Time trap.* New York: Baen Books, 1987, 156 p., paper, novel.

27894 *The ultimax man.* New York: St. Martin's Press, 1978, 217 p., cloth, novel.

27895 *Worlds of the Imperium; special bonus stories: "The war against the Yukks" and "Worldmaster".* New York: Tor, A Tom Doherty Associates Book, 1982, 288 p., paper, coll. IMPERIUM #1.

27896 *Zone yellow: an Imperium novel.* New York: Baen Books, 1990, 247 p., paper, novel. IMPERIUM #4.

with Gordon R. Dickson

21906 *Planet run, plus two bonus stories: "Once there was a giant," by Keith Laumer ; "Call him Lord," by Gordon R. Dickson.* New York: Tor, A Tom Doherty Associates Book, 1982, 287 p., paper, coll. [Includes *Planet run* (see #04377)].

LAUNAY, André (Joseph), 1930-

27897 *The harlequin's son.* London & Sydney: Pan Books, 1986, 239 p., paper, novel.

27898 *Seance.* London & Sydney: Pan Books, 1991, 285 p., paper, novel.

LAURANCE, Alice [pseud. of Laura Alice Weber Haywood], 1938-

27899 *Cassandra rising.* Garden City, NY: Doubleday & Co., 1978, xiii+207 p., cloth, anth.

with Isaac Asimov

17048 *Speculations.* Boston: Houghton Mifflin Co., 1982, xiii+288 p., cloth, anth.

LAURANCE, Andrew

27900 *The black hotel.* London: W. H. Allen & Co., 1983, 191 p., cloth, novel.

The blood of Nostradamus: The link—SEE: *The link.*

Catacomb—SEE: *The hiss.*

27901 *The embryo.* London: A Star Book, W. H. Allen & Co., 1980, 238 p., paper, novel. NOSTRADAMUS #3.

27901A retitled: *The unborn.* New York: Diamond Books, 1991, 236 p. paper, novel. NOSTRADAMUS #1.

27902 *The hiss.* London: A Star Book, W. H. Allen & Co., 1981, 191 p., paper, novel.

27902A retitled: *Catacomb.* New York: Diamond Books, 1991, 219 p., paper, novel.

27903 *The link.* London: A Star Book, W. H. Allen & Co., 1980, 208 p., paper, novel. NOSTRADAMUS #2.

27903A retitled: *The blood of Nostradamus: The link.* New York: Diamond Books, 1991, 206 p., paper, novel. NOSTRADAMUS #2.

27904 *Ouija.* London: A Star Book, W. H. Allen & Co., 1982, 154 p., paper, novel.

The premonition—SEE: *Premonitions of an inherited mind.*

27905 *Premonitions of an inherited mind.* London: A Star Book, W. H. Allen & Co., 1979, 153 p., paper, novel. NOSTRADAMUS #1.

27905A retitled: *The premonition.* New York: Diamond Books, 1991, 197 p., paper, novel. NOSTRADAMUS #1.

The unborn—SEE: *The Embryo.*

LAURENCE, Dan(iel) H(yman), 1920-

27906 *Robert Nathan: a bibliography.* New Haven, CT: Yale University Library, 1960, xi+97 p., cloth, nonf.

LAURIA, Frank (Jonathan), 1935-

27907 *Blue limbo.* New York: Avon Books, 1991, 346 p., paper, novel. DR. ORIENT #7.

27908 *The foundling.* New York: Pocket Books, 1984, 284 p., paper, novel.

27909 *The priestess.* Toronto, New York: Bantam Books, 1978, 246 p., paper, novel. DR. ORIENT #5.

27910 *The Seth papers.* New York: Ballantine Books, 1979, 166 p., paper, novel. DR. ORIENT #6.

LAVALLEY, Al(bert J.), 1935-

27912 *Invasion of the body snatchers.* New Brunswick, NJ & London: Rutgers University Press, 1989, viii+230 p., cloth, nonf. anth. [Includes script of original film and essays].

LAVERS, Norman (Cecil), 1935-

27913 *Jerzy Kosinski.* Boston: Twayne Publishers, 1982, 176 p., cloth, nonf.

27914 *The Northwest Passage: a novel.* New York: Fiction Collective, 1984, 137 p., cloth, novel.

LAW, Richard, 1933- , *with Marleen S. Barr & Ruth Salvaggio*

17446 *Suzy McKee Charnas; Octavia Butler; Joan D. Vinge.* Mercer Island, WA: Starmont House, 1986, 52+44+72 p., cloth, nonf. coll. STARMONT READER'S GUIDE #23.

LAWHEAD, Stephen (R.), 1950-

27915 *Arthur.* Westchester, IL: Crossway Books, 1989, 446 p., paper, novel. PENDRAGON CYCLE #3.

27916 *Dream thief.* Westchester, IL: Crossway Books, 1983, 410 p., paper, novel.

27917 *Emphyrion.* London: Lion, 1990, 900 p., paper, coll. EMPHYRION #1-2.

27918 *Emphyrion: The search for Fierra.* Westchester, IL: Crossway Books, 1985, x+436 p., paper, novel. EMPHYRION #1.

27919 *In the hall of the dragon king.* Westchester, IL: Crossway Books, 1982, 351 p., paper, novel. DRAGON KING TRILOGY #1.

27920 *Merlin.* Westchester, IL: Crossway Books, 1988, 447 p., paper, novel. PENDRAGON CYCLE #2.

27921 *The paradise war.* Oxford, England, Batavia, IL: Lion Publishing, 1991, 416 p., cloth, novel. THE SONG OF ALBION #1.

The search for Fierra—SEE: *Emphyrion: The search for Fierra.*

27922 *The siege of Dome.* Westchester, IL: Crossway Books, 1986, x+458 p., paper, novel. EMPHYRION #2.

27923 *The sword and the flame.* Westchester, IL: Crossway Books, 1984, 313 p., paper, novel. DRAGON KING TRILOGY #3.

27924 *Taliesen.* Westchester, IL: Crossway Books, 1987, 452 p., paper, novel. PENDRAGON CYCLE #1.

27925 *The warlords of Nin.* Westchester, IL: Crossway Books, 1983, 367 p., paper, novel. DRAGON KING TRILOGY #2.

LAWLER, Donald L(ester), 1935-

27926 *Approaches to science fiction.* Boston: Houghton Mifflin Co., 19778, xi+560 p., paper, anth.

27927 *An inquiry into Oscar Wilde's revisions of The picture of Dorian Gray.* New York: Garland Publishing, 1988, 155 p., cloth, nonf.

with Jerome Klinkowitz

27366 *Vonnegut in America: an introduction to the life and work of Kurt Vonnegut.* New York: A Seymour Lawrence Book, Delacorte Press, 1977, xv+304 p., cloth, nonf. anth.

with Oscar Wilde

27928 *The picture of Dorian Gray: authoritative texts, backgrounds, revisions and reac-*

tions, criticism. New York: W. W. Norton & Co., 1988, xiii+462 p., paper, nonf. anth. [Includes the text of Wilde's original novella].

LAWRENCE, Ann (Margaret), 1942-1987

15828 *The half-brothers.* New York: Henry Z. Walck, 1973, 172 p., cloth, novel.

LAWRENCE, J. A. [i.e. Judith Ann Lawrence Blish]

with James Blish

18173 *Mudd's angels.* Toronto, New York: Bantam Books, 1978, xii+177 p., paper, tele. STAR TREK SERIES. [Lawrence's contribution is anonymous].
18174 *Star Trek 12.* Toronto, New York: Bantam Books, 1977, x+177 p., paper, tele. coll. STAR TREK #12.
18175 *Star Trek: the classic episodes 1.* New York, Toronto: Spectra, Bantam Books, 1991, vi+646 p., paper, tele. coll. STAR TREK SERIES.
18176 *Star Trek: the classic episodes 3.* New York, Toronto: Spectra, Bantam Books, 1991, vi+627 p., paper, tele. coll. STAR TREK SERIES.

LAWRENCE, James D.—SEE: Lawrence, Jim

LAWRENCE, Jim [i.e., James Duncan Lawrence], 1918-

27929 *The cutlass clue.* New York: A Signet Vista Book, 1986, 155 p., paper, novel. A.I. GANG #2.
27930 *ESP McGee and the haunted mansion.* New York: An Avon Camelot Book, 1983, 96 p., paper, novel. ESP McGEE #2.

as HUNTER ADAMS

The devil to pay—SEE: *The man from Planet X: The devil to pay.*
27931 *The man from Planet X: The devil to pay.* New York: Pinnacle Books, 1977, 183 p., paper, novel. MAN FROM PLANET X #3.
27932 *The man from Planet X: The she-beast.* New York: Pinnacle Books, 1975, 229 p., paper, novel. MAN FROM PLANET X #1.
27933 *The man from Planet X: Tiger by the tail.* New York: Pinnacle Books, 1975, 210 p., paper, novel. MAN FROM PLANET X #2.

The she-beast—SEE: *The man from Planet X: The she-beast.*
Tiger by the tail—SEE: *The man from Planet X: Tiger by the tail.*

as VICTOR APPLETON II

00435 *Tom Swift and his aquatomic tracker.* New York: Grosset & Dunlap, 1964, 178 p., cloth, novel. TOM SWIFT JR. #A23.
00436 *Tom Swift and his atomic earth blaster.* New York: Grosset & Dunlap, 1954, 210 p., cloth, novel. TOM SWIFT JR. #A5.
00438 *Tom Swift and his deep-sea hydrodome.* New York: Grosset & Dunlap, 1958, 184 p., cloth, novel. TOM SWIFT JR. #A11.
00439 *Tom Swift and his diving seacopter.* New York: Grosset & Dunlap, 1956, 214 p., cloth, novel. TOM SWIFT JR. #A7.
00441 *Tom Swift and his electronic retroscope.* New York: Grosset & Dunlap, 1959, 184 p., cloth, novel. TOM SWIFT JR. #A14.
00441A retitled: *Tom Swift in the jungle of the Mayas.* New York: Grosset & Dunlap, 1972, 184 p., paper, novel. TOM SWIFT JR. #A14.
00443 *Tom Swift and his G-force inverter.* New York: Grosset & Dunlap, 1968, 175 p., cloth, novel. TOM SWIFT JR. #A30.
00446 *Tom Swift and his megascope space prober.* New York: Grosset & Dunlap, 1962, 176 p., cloth, novel. TOM SWIFT JR. #A20.
00447 *Tom Swift and his outpost in space.* NY: Grosset & Dunlap, 1955, 210 p., cloth, novel. TOM SWIFT JR. #A6.
00447A retitled: *Tom Swift and his sky wheel.* New York: Tempo Books, Grosset & Dunlap Publishers, 1977, 210 p., paper, novel. TOM SWIFT JR. #A5 (RENUMBERED).
00448 *Tom Swift and his polar-ray dynasphere.* New York: Grosset & Dunlap, 1965, 177 p., cloth, novel. TOM SWIFT JR. #A25.
00449 *Tom Swift and his repelatron skyway.* New York: Grosset & Dunlap, 1963, 179 p., cloth, novel. TOM SWIFT JR. #A22.
Tom Swift and his sky wheel—SEE: *Tom Swift and his outpost in space.*
00451 *Tom Swift and his sonic boom trap.* New York: Grosset & Dunlap, 1965, 178 p., cloth, novel. TOM SWIFT JR. #A26.
00452 *Tom Swift and his space solartron.* New York: Grosset & Dunlap, 1958, 183 p., cloth, novel. TOM SWIFT JR. #A13.

00453 *Tom Swift and his spectromarine selector.* New York: Grosset & Dunlap, 1960, 184 p., cloth, novel. TOM SWIFT JR. #A15.

00453A retitled: *Tom Swift and the city of gold.* New York: Grosset & Dunlap, 1972, 184 p., paper, novel. TOM SWIFT JR. #A15.

00454 *Tom Swift and his subocean geotron.* New York: Grosset & Dunlap, 1966, 178 p., cloth, novel. TOM SWIFT JR. #A27.

00455 *Tom Swift and his 3-D telejector.* New York: Grosset & Dunlap, 1964, 177 p., cloth, novel. TOM SWIFT JR. #A24.

00456 *Tom Swift and his triphibian atomicar.* New York: Grosset & Dunlap, 1962, 188 p., cloth, novel. TOM SWIFT JR. #A19.

00457 *Tom Swift and his ultrasonic cycloplane.* New York: Grosset & Dunlap, 1957, 182 p., cloth, novel. TOM SWIFT JR. #A10.

00458 *Tom Swift and the asteroid pirates.* New York: Grosset & Dunlap, 1963, 178 p., cloth, novel. TOM SWIFT JR. #A21.

00459 *Tom Swift and the captive planetoid.* New York: Grosset & Dunlap, 1967, 174 p., cloth, novel. TOM SWIFT JR. #A29.

Tom Swift and the city of gold—SEE: *Tom Swift and his spectromarine selector.*

00460 *Tom Swift and the cosmic astronauts.* New York: Grosset & Dunlap, 1960, 178 p., cloth, novel. TOM SWIFT JR. #A16.

00461 *Tom Swift and the electric hydrolung.* New York: Grosset & Dunlap, 1961, 188 p., cloth, novel. TOM SWIFT JR. #A18.

00463 *Tom Swift and the mystery comet.* New York: Grosset & Dunlap, 1966, 178 p., cloth, novel. TOM SWIFT JR. #A28.

00464 *Tom Swift and the visitor from Planet X.* New York: Grosset & Dunlap, 1961, 184 p., cloth, novel. TOM SWIFT JR. #A17.

Tom Swift in the jungle of the Mayas—SEE: *Tom Swift and his electronic retroscope.*

00466 *Tom Swift in the race to the Moon.* New York: Grosset & Dunlap, 1958, 180 p., cloth, novel. TOM SWIFT JR. #A12.

00467 *Tom Swift on the phantom satellite.* New York: Grosset & Dunlap, 1957, 214 p., cloth, novel. TOM SWIFT JR. #A9.

*LAWRENCE, Josephine, 1890?-1978

LAWRENCE, Louise [pseud. of Elizabeth Rhoda Wintle Holden], 1943-

27934 *Calling B for butterfly.* New York: Harper & Row, 1982, 213 p., cloth, novel.

27935 *Cat call.* New York: Harper & Row, Publishers, 1980, 214 p., cloth, novel.

27936 *Children of the dust.* London: Bodley Head, 1985, 168 p., paper, novel.

27937 *The Dram Road.* New York: Harper & Row, 1983, 218 p., cloth, novel.

27938 *The earth witch.* New York: Harper & Row, 1981, 214 p., cloth, novel.

27939 *Extinction is forever, and other stories.* London: Bodley Head, 1990, 189 p., paper, coll.

27940 *Moonwind.* London: Bodley Head, 1986, 153 p., paper, novel.

27941 *Sing and scatter daisies.* New York: Harper & Row, 1977, 236 p., cloth, novel. WYNDCLIFFE #2.

27942 *Star lord.* New York: Harper & Row, 1978, 176 p., cloth, novel.

37905 *Star lord.* London: Bodley Head, 1987, 153 p., paper, novel. [Revised edition].

27943 *The warriors of Taan.* London: Bodley Head, 1986, 196 p., paper, novel.

*LAWRENCE, Margery, 1896?-1969

LAWRENCE, Simon, pseud. SEE: Largent, R. Karl

LAWRENCE, W. H. C.

27944 *The storm of '92: a grandfather's tale told in 1932.* Toronto: Sheppard Publishing Co., 1889, 71 p., cloth, novel.

LAWS, Jay B.

27945 *Steam.* Boston: Alyson Publications, 1991, 389 p., paper, novel.

LAWS, Stephen, 1952-

27946 *The frighteners.* London: Souvenir Press, 1990, 375 p., cloth, novel.

27947 *Ghost train: a novel.* London: Souvenir Press, 1985, [314] p., cloth, novel.

27948 *Spectre.* London: Souvenir Press, 1986, 255 p., cloth, novel.

27949 *The Wyrm.* London: Souvenir Press, 1987, 301 p., cloth, novel.

LAWSON, Jack

27950 *Andro, this is crazy.* New York: An Avon Camelot Book, 1991, 86 p., paper, novel.

LAWSON, Robert N(eale), 1873-1945

15829 *Mr. Twigg's mistake.* Boston: Little, Brown & Co., 1947, 141 p., cloth, novel.

LAWSON, Susan, pseud.—SEE: Weis, Margaret & Moore, Roger E.

LAWSON, Sybil, pseud.

27951 *The possession of Tamara.* New York: Star Distributors, 1977, 180 p., paper, novel.

LAYMON, Carl, pseud.—SEE: Laymon, Richard

LAYMON, Richard (Carl), 1947-

27952 *Allhallow's Eve.* Sevenoaks, Kent, England: New English Library, 1986, 198 p., paper, novel.
27953 *The beast.* Belmont, CA: Fearon-Pitman Publishers, 1986, 61 p., paper, novel. STRANGE OCCURRENCE SQUAD SERIES.
27954 *The Beast House.* London: New English Library, 1986, 304 p., paper, novel.
27955 *Beware!* London: New English Library, 1985, 218 p., paper, novel.
27956 *The cellar.* New York: Warner Books, 1980, 254 p., paper, novel.
27957 *Darkness, tell us.* London: Headline, 1991, 312 p., cloth, novel.
27958 *Flesh.* London: W. H. Allen & Co., 1987, 333 p., cloth, novel.
27959 *Funland.* London: W. H. Allen & Co., 1989, 447 p., cloth, novel.
27960 *Halloween hunt.* Belmont, CA: Fearon, 1987, 60 p., paper, novel.
27961 *The night creature.* Belmont, CA: Fearon-Pitman Publishers, 1986, 61 p., paper, novel. STRANGE OCCURRENCE SQUAD SERIES.
27962 *Night show.* Sevenoaks, Kent, England: New English Library, 1984, 192 p., paper, novel.
27963 *One rainy night.* London: Headline, 1991, 308 p., cloth, novel.
27964 *Resurrection dreams.* London: W. H. Allen & Co., 1988, 352 p., cloth, novel.
27965 *The return.* Belmont, CA: Fearon-Pitman Publishers, 1986, 61 p., paper, novel. STRANGE OCCURRENCE SQUAD SERIES.
27966 *The stake.* London: Headline, 1990, 310 p., cloth, novel.
27967 *Thin air.* Belmont, CA: Fearon-Pitman Publishers, 1986, 61 p., paper, novel. STRANGE OCCURRENCE SQUAD SERIES.

27970A *Tread softly.* New York: Tor Horror, A Tom Doherty Associates Book, 1987, 311 p., paper, novel. [Originally published under the name Richard Kelly].
27968 *The woods are dark.* New York: Warner Books, 1981, 240 p., paper, novel.

as RICHARD KELLY

27969 *Midnight's lair.* London: A Star Book, W. H. Allen & Co., 1988, 253 p., paper, novel.
27970 *Tread softly.* London: Sphere Books, 1986, 285 p., paper, novel.

as CARL LAYMON

27971 *Nightmare lake.* New York: Twilight/Dell, 1983, 146 p., paper, novel. TWILIGHT #11.

LAZENBY, Norman (Austin), 1914- , *as* BENGO MISTRAL

10175 *The Brains of Helle.* London: Gannet Press, 1953, 127 p., paper, novel.

LAZUTA, Eugene M.—SEE: Lazuta, Gene

LAZUTA, Gene [i.e., Eugene Michael Lazuta], 1959-

27972 *Bleeder.* New York: Diamond Books, 1991, 282 p., paper, novel.
27973 *Blood flies.* New York: Charter/Diamond Books, 1990, 265 p., paper, novel.

as ALEX KANE

27974 *The shinglo.* New York: Charter Books, 1989, 281 p., paper, novel.

as DANIEL RAVEN

27975 *Happy cage.* New York: An Onyx Book, New American Library, 1989, 268 p., paper, novel.

LE COMTE, Edward (Semple), 1916-

27976 *I, Eve: a novel.* New York: Atheneum, 1988, 134 p., cloth, novel.

LE FANU, J(oseph Thomas) Sheridan, 1814-1873

27977 *Ghost stories and mysteries.* New York: Dover Publications, 1975, ix+372 p., paper, coll.

27978 *The hours after midnight: tales of terror and the supernatural.* London: Leslie Frewin, 1975, 256 p., cloth, coll.

27979 *The illustrated J. S. Le Fanu: ghost stories and mysteries by a master Victorian storyteller.* Wellingborough, Northamptonshire, England: Crucible, 1988, 319 p., cloth, coll. [Edited by Michael Cox].

27980 *Irish ghost stories of Sheridan Le Fanu.* Dublin, Cork, Ireland: Mercier Press, 1973, iii+133 p., cloth?, coll.

37906 *The Purcell papers.* Sauk City, WI: Arkham House, 1975, ix+241 p., cloth, coll. [Edited by August Derleth; not the same contents as the 1880 edition].

LE GUIN, Ursula K(roeber), 1929-

27981 *The adventure of Cobbler's Rune.* New Castle, VA: Cheap Street, 1982, 32 p., cloth, story. ADVENTURES IN KROY. [Limited to 277 copies].

27982 *Always come home.* New York: Harper & Row, 1985, 523 p., cloth, novel. [Includes an audio tape with songs].

27983 *The beginning place.* New York: Harper & Row, 1980, 183 p., cloth, novel.

27983A retitled: *Threshold.* London: Victor Gollancz, 1980, 183 p., cloth, novel.

27984 *Buffalo gals, and other animal presences.* Santa Barbara, CA: Capra Press, 1987, 196 p., cloth, coll. [Includes some verse].

27985 *Catwings.* New York: Orchard Books, 1988, 39 p., cloth, story. CATWINGS #1.

27986 *Catwings return.* New York: Orchard Books, 1989, 48 p., cloth, story. CATWINGS #2.

27987 *The compass rose: short stories.* Portland, OR: Pendragon Press; San Francisco; Columbia, PA: Underwood-Miller, 1982, 290 p., cloth, coll. [Limited to 550 copies; winner of the *Locus* Award for Best Collection, 1982 (1983)].

27988 *Dancing at the edge of the world: thoughts on words, women, places.* New York: Grove Press, 1989, viii+306 p., cloth, nonf. coll.

27989 *Dreams must explain themselves.* New York: Algol Press, 1975, 36 p., paper, nonf. coll.

27990 *Earthsea: an omnibus comprising A wizard of Earthsea, The tombs of Atuan, The farthest shore.* London: Victor Gollancz, 1977, 191+159+206 p., cloth, coll. EARTHSEA TRILOGY #1-3.

27990A retitled: *The Earthsea trilogy.* Harmondsworth, Middlesex, England: Penguin Books, 1979, 478 p., paper, coll. EARTHSEA TRILOGY #1-3.

27991 *The eye of the heron.* London: Victor Gollancz, 1982, 122 p., cloth, novel.

27992 *The eye of the heron; and, The word for world is forest.* London: Victor Gollancz, 1991, 301 p., paper, coll.

27993 *Five complete novels.* New York: Avenel Books, 1985, 579 p., cloth, coll. [Includes *Rocannon's world, Planet of exile, City of illusions, The left hand of darkness, The word for world is forest*].

27994 *Gwilan's harp.* Northridge, CA: Lord John Press, 1981, [11] p., cloth, story. [Limited to 300 copies].

27995 *In the red zone.* Northridge, CA: Lord John Press, 1983, 29 p., cloth, story?. [Limited to 200 copies].

27996 *The language of the night: essays on fantasy and science fiction.* New York: G. P. Putnam's Sons, 1979, 270 p., cloth, nonf. coll. [Edited by Susan Wood].

27997 *The language of the night: essays on fantasy and science fiction.* London: Women's Press, 1989, 210 p., paper, nonf. coll. [Revised edition].

27998 *The lathe of Heaven; The dispossessed; The wind's twelve quarters.* New York: Book-of-the-Month Club, 1991, 848 p., cloth, coll.

27999 *Leese Webster.* New York: Atheneum, 1979, [31] p., cloth, story.

28001 *Malafrena.* New York: Berkley Publishing Corp., 1979, 369 p., cloth, novel.

28002 *Myth and archetype in science fiction.* Eugene, OR: Writer's Notebook Press, Pulphouse Publishing, 1991, 16 p., paper, nonf.

28003 *Nebula award stories eleven.* London: Victor Gollancz, 1976, 255 p., cloth, anth.

28004 *The new Atlantis.* New York: Tor SF, A Tom Doherty Associates Book, 1989, 42 p., paper, story. [Bound with: *The blind geometer* / by Kim Stanley Robinson].

28005 *Orsinian tales.* New York: Harper & Row, 1976, 179 p., cloth, coll.

28006 *Solomon Leviathan's nine hundred and thirty-first trip around the world.* New Castle, VA: Cheap Street, 1983, 33 p., cloth, story. ADVENTURES IN KROY. [Limited to 277 copies].

28007 *Talk about writing.* Eugene, OR: Writer's Notebook Press, Pulphouse Publishing, 1991, 12 p., paper, nonf.

28008 *Tehanu: the last book of Earthsea.* New York: A Jean Karl Book, Atheneum, 1990, vii+226 p., cloth, novel. EARTHSEA #4. [Winner of the Nebula Award for Best Novel, 1990 (1991); winner of the *Locus* Award for Best Fantasy Novel, 1990 (1991)].

28009   *Three Hainish novels: Rocannon's World; Planet of exile; City of illusions.* Garden City, NY: Nelson Doubleday, 1978, 370 p., cloth, coll.

      The threshold—SEE: *The beginning place.*

28010   *The visionary: the life story of Flicker of the Serpentine of Telina-Na.* Santa Barbara, CA: Capra Press, 1984, 43 p., cloth, story. [An excerpt from *Always coming home;* bound with *Wonders hidden* / by Scott Russell Sanders].

28011   *The water is wide.* Portland, OR: Pendragon Press, 1976, 16 p., cloth, story.

28012   *The wind's twelve quarters: short stories.* New York: Harper & Row, 1975, 303 p., cloth, coll. [Winner of the *Locus* Award for Best Collection, 1975 (1976)].

28013   *The word for world is forest.* New York: A Berkley Medallion Book, Berkley Publishing Corp., 1976, 169 p., paper, novel.

with Virginia Kidd

27117   *Edges: thirteen new tales from the borderlands of the imagination.* New York: Pocket Books, 1980, 239 p., paper, anth.

27118   *Interfaces.* New York: Ace Books, 1980, x+310 p., paper, anth.

with Laura Marshall

28014   *Fire and stone.* New York: Atheneum, 1989, 31 p., cloth, story.

LE PAGE, Rand, house pseud.—SEE: Hughes, Dennis Talbot

LE QUEUX, William (Tufnell), 1864-1927

      The battle of Royston—SEE: *The invasion of 1910.*

37907   *"Cinders" of Harley Street: being some curious leaves from the diary of Villiers Beethom-Saunders, M.D., revealed by his friend and executor, Charles Barrington-Mayne, Esquire, barrister-at-law.* London: Ward, Lock & Co., 1916, 301 p., cloth, novel.

08924   *The invasion of 1910: with a full account of the siege of London.* London: Eveleigh Nash, 1906, 550 p., cloth, novel.

08924B   retitled: *The Battle of Royston, from The invasion of 1910: an important imagination.* Royston: Ellisons' Editions, 1984, 15 p., paper, story. [An excerpt from the original novel].

LEA, Homer, 1876-1912

37908   *The valor of ignorance.* New York, London: Harper & Brothers, 1909, xxii+343 p., cloth, novel.

LEA, Sydney L(ongstreth) W(right) Jr., 1942-

28015   *Gothic to fantastic: readings in supernatural fiction.* New York: Arno Press, 1980, 196 p., cloth, nonf.

LEACH, Christopher, 1925-

28016   *The great book raid.* London: J. M. Dent & Sons, 1979, 144 p., cloth, novel.

28017   *Rosalinda.* London: J. M. Dent & Sons, 1978, 124 p., cloth, novel.

LEADER, Mary (Bartelt)

28018   *Salem's children.* New York: Leisure Books, 1979, 367 p., paper, novel.

*LEAHY, John Martin, 1886-1967

LEAR, Peter [pseud. of Peter Harmer Lovesey], 1936-

28019   *Goldengirl.* London: Cassell, 1977, 377 p., cloth, novel.

LEATHERDALE, Clive, 1949-

28020   *Dracula: the novel & the legend: a study of Bram Stoker's gothic masterpiece.* Wellingborough, Northamptonshire, England: Aquarian Press, 1985, 256 p., cloth, nonf.

28021   *The origins of Dracula: the background to Bram Stoker's gothic masterpiece.* London: William Kimber, 1987, 237 p., cloth, nonf. anth.

LEBLANC, RICHARD

28022   *The fangs of the vampire.* New York, Washington: Vantage Press, 1979, 123 p., cloth, novel.

LEBOUTILLIER, John, with James C. Humes

26183   *Primary.* New York: Manor Books, 1979, 285 p., paper, novel.

LECALE, Errol, pseud.—SEE: McNeilly, Wilfred G.

LEDERER, Paul J.—SEE: Winters, Logan

LEE, A(rthur) Robert, 1941-

28023 *Edgar Allan Poe: the design of order.* London: Vision; Totowa, NJ: Barnes & Noble Books, 1987, 224 p., cloth, nonf. anth.

LEE, Alan, *with Brian Froud & David Larkin*

23573 *Faeries.* New York: Henry N. Abrams, 1978, [ca. 200] p., cloth, fiction.

LEE, Christopher (Frank Carandini), 1922-

28024 *Tall, dark, and gruesome: an autobiography.* London: W. H. Allen & Co., 1977, 284 p., cloth, nonf.

with Michel Parry

28025 *Archives of evil.* London: W. H. Allen & Co., 1977, 172 p., cloth, anth.
28025A retitled: *Christopher Lee's Archives of evil.* London: Mayflower Books, 1979, 160 p., paper, anth.
Christopher Lee's Archives of evil—SEE: *Archives of evil.*
Christopher Lee's omnibus of evil—SEE: *The great villains.*
28026 *Christopher Lee's 'X' certificate, no. 1.* London: W. H. Allen & Co., 1975, 176 p., cloth, anth. [Only volume issued].
28027 *From the archives of evil.* New York: Warner Books, 1976, 205 p., paper, anth.
28028 *From the archives of evil #2.* New York: Warner Books, 1976, 220 p., paper, anth.
28029 *The great villains: an omnibus of evil.* London: W. H. Allen & Co., 1978, 255 p., cloth, anth.
28029A retitled: *Christopher Lee's Omnibus of evil.* London: Mayflower, 1980, 255 p., paper, anth.
28030 *Lurking shadows: an anthology.* London: W. H. Allen & Co., 1979, 157 p., cloth, anth.
Omnibus of evil—SEE: *The great villains.*

LEE, David, pseud.—SEE: Garnett, David S.

LEE, Edward [pseud. of Lee Edward Seymour], 1957-

28031 *Coven.* New York: Diamond Books, 1991, 292 p., paper, novel. COVEN #1.
28032 *Ghouls.* New York: Pinnacle Books, Windsor Publishing Corp., 1988, 444 p., paper, novel.
28033 *Incubi.* New York: Diamond Books, 1991, 280 p., paper, novel. COVEN #2.

***as* PHILIP STRAKER**

37909 *Night date.* New York: Zebra Books, Kensington Publishing Corp., 1982, 381 p., paper, novel. NIGHT #1.
35115 *Night lust.* New York: Zebra Books, Kensington Publishing Corp., 1982, 360 p., paper, novel. NIGHT #2.

*LEE, Elsie [i.e., Elsie Lee Sheridan], 1912-

LEE, (Bert) Gentry, 1942- , *with Arthur C. Clarke*

20119 *Cradle.* London: Victor Gollancz, 1988, 309 p., cloth, novel.
20120 *The garden of Rama.* New York: Bantam Books, 1991, 441 p., cloth, novel. RAMA #3.
20121 *Rama II.* London: Victor Gollancz, 1989, 377 p., cloth, novel. RAMA #2.

LEE, John

28034 *The unicorn dilemma.* New York: Tor SF, A Tom Doherty Associates Book, 1988, 374 p., paper, novel. UNICORN QUEST #2.
28035 *The unicorn quest.* New York: Tor SF, A Tom Doherty Associates Book, 1986, 381 p., paper, novel. UNICORN QUEST #1.
28036 *The unicorn solution.* New York: Tor Fantasy, A Tom Doherty Associates Book, 1991, 372 p., paper, novel. UNICORN QUEST #3.

LEE, Pamela, *with William K. Hartmann & Ron Miller*

25320 *Out of the cradle: exploring the frontiers beyond Earth.* New York: Workman Publishing, 1984, 190 p., cloth, fiction. [Mixes science fiction with nonfiction].

LEE, Robert A(lan), 1934-

Notes on George Orwell's works—SEE: *Orwell's fiction.*
28037 *Orwell's fiction.* Notre Dame, IN: University of Notre Dame Press, 1969, xvii+188 p., cloth, nonf.
28037A retitled: *Notes on George Orwell's works.* Toronto: Coles, 1970, xvii+188 p., cloth, nonf.

LEE, Robert C(orwin Jr.), 1931-

28038 *Once upon another time.* Nashville, TN: Thomas Nelson, 1977, 160 p., cloth, novel.

28039 *Summer of the green star.* Philadelphia, PA: Westminster Press, 1981, 127 p., cloth, novel.
28040 *Timequake.* Philadelphia, PA: Westminster Press, 1982, 151 p., cloth, novel.

LEE, Samantha [pseud. of Maggie Webb]

28041 *Childe Roland.* London: Orbit, 1989, 288 p., paper, novel.

with Robert Louis Stevenson

28042 *Robert Louis Stevenson's Dr. Jekyll and Mr. Hyde.* London: Beaver, 1987, 148 p., paper, novel. [Adapted from Stevenson's original story].

LEE, Sharon, *with Steve Miller*

28043 *Agent of change.* New York: A Del Rey Book, Ballantine Books, 1988, 247 p., paper, novel. AGENT #1.
28044 *Carpe diem.* New York: A Del Rey Book, Ballantine Books, 1989, 292 p., paper, novel. AGENT #2.
28045 *Conflict of honors.* New York: A Del Rey Book, Ballantine Books, 1988, 326 p., paper, novel.

LEE, Stan(ley), 1922-

28046 *The GOD project.* New York: Grove Weidenfeld, 1990, 407 p., cloth, novel.

LEE, Tanith, 1947-

28047 *Anackire.* New York: DAW Books, 1983, 414 p., paper, novel. WARS OF VIS #2.
28048 *The beautiful biting machine.* New Castle, VA: Cheap Street, 1984, 43 p., cloth, story. [Limited to 127 copies].
28049 *The birthgrave.* New York: DAW Books, 1975, 408 p., paper, novel.
28050 *Black unicorn.* New York: A Byron Preiss Book, Dragonflight Books, Atheneum; Toronto: Maxwell Macmillan Canada; New York: Maxwell Macmillan International Publishing Group, 1991, 138 p., cloth, novel.
28051 *The blood of roses.* London: A Legend Book, Century Publishing, 1990, 678 p., cloth, novel.
28052 *The book of the beast.* London: Unwin Paperbacks, 1988, 196 p., paper, novel. SECRET BOOKS OF PARADYS #2.
28053 *The book of the damned.* London: Unwin Paperbacks, 1988, 229 p., paper, coll. SECRET BOOKS OF PARADYS #1.

28054 *The book of the dead.* Woodstock, NY: Overlook Press, 1991, 215 p., cloth, novel. SECRET BOOKS OF PARADYS #3.
28055 *The Castle of Dark.* London: Macmillan, 1978, 180 p., cloth, novel. DARK CASTLE #1.
28056 *Companions on the road.* London: Macmillan, 1975, 122 p., cloth, novel.
28057 *Companions on the road; and, The winter players: two novellas.* New York: St. Martin's Press, 1977, 222 p., cloth, coll. [Originally published separately].
28058 *Cyrion.* New York: DAW Books, 1982, 304 p., paper, novel.
28059 *Dark castle, white horse.* New York: DAW Books, 1986, 302 p., paper, coll. CASTLE OF DARK #1-2. [Includes *The Castle of Dark* and *Prince on a white horse*].
28060 *Day by night.* New York: DAW Books, 1980, 316 p., paper, novel.
28061 *Days of grass.* New York: DAW Books, 1985, 250 p., paper, novel.
28062 *Death's master.* New York: DAW Books, 1979, 348 p., paper, novel. TALES FROM THE FLAT EARTH #2.
28063 *Delirium's Mistress: a novel of the Flat Earth.* New York: DAW Books, 1986, 416 p., paper, novel. TALES FROM THE FLAT EARTH #4.
28064 *Delusion's master.* New York: DAW Books, 1981, 206 p., paper, novel. TALES FROM THE FLAT EARTH #3.
28065 *Don't bite the sun.* New York: DAW Books, 1976, 158 p., paper, novel. DON'T BITE THE SUN #1.
15830 *The dragon hoard.* London: Macmillan, 1971, 169 p., cloth, novel.
28066 *Dreams of dark and light: the great short fiction of Tanith Lee.* Sauk City, WI: Arkham House Publishers, 1986, ix+507 p., cloth, coll.
28067 *Drinking sapphire wine.* New York: DAW Books, 1977, 175 p., paper, novel. DON'T BITE THE SUN #2.
28068 *Drinking sapphire wine [and, Don't bite the Sun].* Feltham, England: Hamlyn Paperbacks, 1979, 300 p., paper, coll. DON'T BITE THE SUN #1-2.
28069 *East of midnight.* London: Macmillan, 1977, 175 p., cloth, novel.
28070 *Electric forest.* Garden City, NY: Nelson Doubleday, 1979, 150 p., paper, novel.
28071 *Forests of the night.* London, Sydney: Unwin Hyman, 1989, 299 p., cloth, coll.
28072 *The gorgon, and other beastly tales.* New York: DAW Books, 1985, 288 p., paper, coll.
28073 *A heroine of the world.* New York: DAW Books, 1989, 448 p., paper, novel.

28074 *Into gold.* Eugene, OR: Pulphouse Publishing, 1991, 47 p., paper, story. SHORT STORY PAPERBACKS #32.

28075 *Kill the dead.* New York: DAW Books, 1980, 172 p., paper, novel.

The lords of darkness—SEE: *Tales from the Flat Earth: The lords of darkness.*

28076 *Lycanthia; or, The children of wolves.* New York: DAW Books, 1981, 220 p., paper, novel.

28077 *Madame Two Swords.* West Kingston, Hampton Falls, RI: Donald M. Grant, Publisher, 1988, 128 p., cloth, novel.

Night's daughter—SEE: *Tales from the Flat Earth: Night's daughter.*

28078 *Night's master.* New York: DAW Books, 1978, 188 p., paper, novel. TALES FROM THE FLAT EARTH #1.

28079 *Night's sorceries: a novel of the Flat Earth.* New York: DAW Books, 1987, 287 p., paper, coll. TALES FROM THE FLAT EARTH #5.

28080 *Prince on a white horse.* London: Macmillan Children's Books, 1982, 157 p., cloth, novel. DARK CASTLE #2.

28081 *Princess Hynchatti & some other surprises.* London: Macmillan, 1972, 150 p., cloth, coll.

28082 *Quest for the white witch.* New York: DAW Books, 1978, 317 p., paper, novel. BIRTHGRAVE #3.

28083 *Red as blood; or, Tales from the Sisters Grimmer.* New York: DAW Books, 1983, 208 p., paper, coll.

28084 *Sabella; or, The blood stone.* New York: DAW Books, 1980, 157 p., paper, novel.

28085 *The secret books of Paradys I & II.* New York: Guild America Books, 1991, 401 p., cloth, coll. SECRET BOOKS OF PARADYS #1-2. [Includes *The book of the damned* and *The book of the beast*].

Shadowfire—SEE: *Vazkor, son of Vazkor.*

28086 *Shon the Taken.* London: Macmillan Children's Books, 1979, 144 p., cloth, novel.

28087 *The silver metal lover.* Garden City, NY: Nelson Doubleday, 1981, 216 p., paper, novel.

28088 *Sometimes, after sunset.* Garden City, NY: Nelson Doubleday, 1981, 311 p., cloth, coll. [Includes *Sabella* and *Kill the dead*].

28089 *The Storm Lord.* New York: DAW Books, 1976, 350 p., paper, novel. WARS OF VIS #1.

28090 *Sung in shadow.* New York: DAW Books, 1983, 349 p., paper, novel.

28091 *Tales from the Flat Earth: Night's daughter.* Garden City, NY: Nelson Double-

day, 1987, 601 p., cloth, coll. TALES FROM THE FLAT EARTH #4-5.

28092 *Tales from the Flat Earth: The lords of darkness.* Garden City, NY: Nelson Doubleday, 1987, 726 p., cloth, coll. TALES FROM THE FLAT EARTH #1-3.

28093 *Tamastara; or, The Indian nights.* New York: DAW Books, 1984, 174 p., paper, coll.

28094 *Unsilent night.* Cambridge, MA: A Boskone Book, NESFA Press, 1981, xii+84 p., cloth, coll. [Includes some verse].

28095 *Vazkor, son of Vazkor.* New York: DAW Books, 1978, 220 p., paper, novel. BIRTHGRAVE #2.

28095A retitled: *Shadowfire.* London: Futura Publications, An Orbit Book, 1978, 220 p., paper, novel. BIRTHGRAVE #2.

28096 *Volkhavaar.* New York: DAW Books, 1977, 192 p., paper, novel.

28097 *The wars of Vis: The storm lord; Anackire.* Garden City, NY: Nelson Doubleday, 1984, 697 p., cloth, coll. WARS OF VIS #1-2. [Includes *The storm lord* and *Anackire*].

28098 *The white serpent: a novel of Vis.* New York: DAW Books, 1988, 396 p., paper, novel. WARS OF VIS #3.

28099 *The winter players.* London: Macmillan, 1976, 104 p., cloth, novel.

28100 *Women as demons: the male perception of women through space and time: stories.* London: The Women's Press, 1989, xii+272 p., paper, coll.

LEE, Vernon [pseud. of Violet Paget], 1856-1935

08783 *The snake lady, and other stories.* New York: Grove Press, 1954, 288 p., cloth, coll.

08783A retitled: *Supernatural tales: excursions into fantasy.* London: Peter Owen, 1987, 222 p., paper, coll.

Supernatural tales: excursions into fantasy—SEE: *The snake lady, and other stories.*

LEE, Walt(er William Jr.), 1931- , with Richard Delap

21542 *Shapes: a romance of horror.* New York: Charter Books, 1987, 324 p., paper, novel.

LEE, Warner, pseud.—SEE: Battin, B. W.

*LEEK, Sybil, 1917-1982

LEESON, Robert (Arthur), 1928-

28101 *At war with tomorrow.* Harlow, England: Longman, 1986, 153 p., cloth, novel. TIME ROPE #3.

28102 *Fire on the cloud.* London: Mammoth, 1991, 158 p., paper, novel. CLOUD VALLEY #2.

28103 *Landing in Cloud Valley.* London: Mammoth, 1991, 143 p., paper, novel. CLOUD VALLEY #1.

28104 *The metro gangs attack.* Harlow, England: Longman, 1986, v+147 p., cloth, novel. TIME ROPE #4.

28105 *Slambash wangs of a compo gormer.* London: Collins, 1987, 288 p., cloth, novel.

37910 *The third class genie.* London: Collins, 1975, 128 p., cloth, novel.

28106 *Three against the world.* Harlow, England: Longman, 1986, v+129 p., cloth, novel. TIME ROPE #2.

28107 *Time rope.* Harlow, England: Longman, 1986, v+135 p., cloth, novel. TIME ROPE #1.

LEFANU, Sarah, 1953-

Feminism and science fiction—SEE: *In the chinks of the worldmachine: feminism and science fiction.*

28108 *In the chinks of the world machine: feminism and science fiction.* London: The Women's Press, 1988, 231 p., cloth, nonf.

28108A retitled: *Feminism and science fiction.* Bloomington, IN: Indiana University Press, 1989, 231 p., cloth, nonf.

with Jen Green

24415 *Despatches from the frontiers of the female mind: an anthology of original stories.* London: Women's Press, 1985, 248 p., paper, anth.

LEGASPI, Pilar F.

28109 *The enchanted pond.* New York, Washington: Vantage Press, 1970, 58 p., cloth, novel.

28110 *The magic ring.* New York: A Geneva Book, Carlton Press, 1971, 79 p., cloth, novel.

LEHMKUHL, Donald

28111 *The flights of Icarus.* New York: A&W Visual Library, A Paper Tiger Book, 1978, 159 p., paper, art. [Edited by Roger & Martyn Dean].

LEIBER, Fritz (Reuter Jr.), 1910-1992

28112 *Bazaar of the bizarre.* West Kingston, RI: Donald M. Grant, Publisher, 1978, 127 p., cloth, coll. FAFHRD & GREY MOUSER SERIES.

28113 *The book of Fritz Leiber.* Boston: Gregg Press, 1980, 2 v. (I-xx+173 p.; II-204 p.), cloth, coll. [Includes *The Book of Fritz Leiber* and *The Second Book of Fritz Leiber*].

28114 *The Change War.* Boston: Gregg Press, 1978, xvi+189 p., cloth, coll. CHANGE-WAR SERIES. [Not the same as the Ace edition].

28115 *Changewar.* New York: Ace Science Fiction Books, 1983, 198 p., paper, coll. CHANGEWAR SERIES.

28116 *Conjure wife; Our lady of darkness.* New York: Tor Fantasy, A Tom Doherty Associates Book, 1991, 347 p., paper, coll.

28117 *Ervool.* Roanoke, VA: Cheap Street, 1980, [8] p., paper, story.

28118 *Fafhrd & me.* Newark, NJ: Wildside Press, 1990, 96 p., cloth, nonf. coll. [Edited by John Gregory Betancourt].

28119 *The ghost light.* New York: Berkley Books, 1984, 368 p., paper, coll. [Winner of the *Locus* Award for Best Collection, 1984 (1985)].

28120 *Heroes and horrors.* Chapel Hill, NC: Whispers Press, 1978, xv+237 p., cloth, coll. [Edited by Stuart David Schiff].

28121 *Ill met in Lankhmar.* New York: Tor Fantasy, A Tom Doherty Associates Book, 1990, 104 p., paper, story. [Bound with *The fair in Emain Macha* / by Charles de Lint].

28122 *In the beginning.* New Castle, VA: Cheap Street, 1983, viii+34 p., cloth, coll. [Limited to 177 copies].

28123 *The knight and knave of swords.* New York: William Morrow & Co., 1988, 303 p., cloth, coll. FAFHRD & GREY MOUSER #7.

28124 *The Leiber chronicles: fifty years of Fritz Leiber.* Arlington Heights, IL: Dark Harvest, 1990, 601 p., cloth, coll. [Edited by Martin H. Greenberg].

28125 *The mystery of the Japanese clock.* Santa Monica, CA: Montgolfier Press, 1982, 42 p., paper, story. [Limited to 300 copies].

28126 *Night's black agents.* New York: A Berkley Medallion Book, Berkley Publishing Corp., 1978, xii+275 p., paper, coll. [Includes the original novel plus two stories].

28127 *Our Lady of Darkness.* New York: Berkley Publishing Corp., 1977, 185 p., cloth, novel. [Winner of the World Fantasy Award for Best Fantasy Novel, 1977 (1978)].

28128 *Quicks around the Zodiac: a farce.* New Castle, VA: Cheap Street, 1983, 25 p., paper, story. [Limited to 125 copies].

28129 *Riches and power: a story for children.* New Castle, VA: Cheap Street, 1982, [17] p., paper, story. [Limited to 62 copies; housed in cloth slipcase].

28130 *Rime Isle.* Chapel Hill, NC: Whispers Press, 1977, iii+185 p., cloth, novel. FAFHRD & GREY MOUSER #6.

28131 retitled: *Swords & ice magic.* New York: Ace Books, 1977, 243 p., paper, coll. FAFHRD & GRAY MOUSER #6. [Expanded edition].

28132 *The second book of Fritz Leiber.* New York: DAW Books, 1975, 204 p., paper, coll.

28133 *Ship of shadows.* London: Victor Gollancz, 1979, 253 p., cloth, coll.

28134 *Ship of shadows.* New York: Tor SF, A Tom Doherty Associates Book, 1989, 77 p., paper, story. [Bound with *No truce with kings* / by Poul Anderson].

Swords & ice magic. SEE: *Rime Isle.*

28135 *Swords' masters.* Garden City, NY: Guild America Books, 1990, 536 p., cloth, coll. FAFHRD & GRAY MOUSER. [Includes *Swords against wizardry, Swords of Lankhmar, Swords and ice magic*].

28136 *The three of swords.* New York: Nelson Doubleday, 1989, 496 p., cloth, coll. FAFHRD & GRAY MOUSER. [Includes *Swords and deviltry, Swords against death, Swords in the mist*].

28137 *The worlds of Fritz Leiber.* New York: Ace Books, 1976, 340 p., paper, coll.

with Robert Bloch & T. E. D. Klein

18200 *The first World Fantasy Convention: three authors remember.* West Warwick, RI: Necronomicon Press, 1980, 52 p., paper, nonf.

with Stuart David Schiff

28138 *World fantasy awards, volume two.* Garden City, NY: Doubleday & Co., 1980, xxxv+248 p., cloth, anth.

LEIBER, Justin (Fritz), 1938-

28139 *Beyond gravity.* New York: Tor SF, A Tom Doherty Associates Book, 1988, 276 p., paper, novel. BEYOND #3.

28140 *Beyond humanity.* New York: Tor SF, A Tom Doherty Associates Book, 1987, 254 p., paper, novel. BEYOND #2.

28141 *Beyond rejection.* New York: A Del Rey Book, Ballantine Books, 1980, vii+179 p., paper, novel. BEYOND #1.

28142 *The sword and the eye.* New York: Tor SF, A Tom Doherty Associates Book, 1985, 252 p., paper, novel. SAGA OF THE HOUSE OF EIGIN #1.

28143 *The sword and the tower.* New York: Tor SF, A Tom Doherty Associates Book, 1986, 216 p., paper, novel. SAGA OF THE HOUSE OF EIGIN #2.

LEIBOLD, Jay, 1957-

28144 *The antimatter formula.* Toronto, New York: An R. A. Montgomery Book, Bantam Books, 1986, 118 p., paper, novel. CHOOSE YOUR OWN ADVENTURE #57.

28145 *Beyond the Great Wall.* Toronto, New York: An R. A. Montgomery Book, Bantam Books, 1987, 116 p., paper, novel. CHOOSE YOUR OWN ADVENTURE #73.

28146 *Fight for freedom.* New York, Toronto: An Edward Packard Book, Bantam Books, 1990, 115 p., paper, novel. CHOOSE YOUR OWN ADVENTURE #107.

28147 *Grand Canyon odyssey.* Toronto, New York: An R. A. Montgomery Book, Bantam Books, 1985, 115 p., paper, novel. CHOOSE YOUR OWN ADVENTURE #43.

28148 *The lost ninja.* New York, Toronto: An R. A. Montgomery Book, Bantam Books, 1991, 116 p., paper, novel. CHOOSE YOUR OWN ADVENTURE #113.

28149 *Return of the ninja.* New York, Toronto: An R. A. Montgomery Book, Bantam Books, 1989, 112 p., paper, novel. CHOOSE YOUR OWN ADVENTURE #92.

28150 *Revenge of the Russian ghost.* New York, Toronto: An R. A. Montgomery Book, Bantam Books, 1990, 117 p., paper, novel. CHOOSE YOUR OWN ADVENTURE #99.

37911 *Sabotage.* Toronto, New York: An R. A. Montgomery Book, Bantam Books, 1984, 132 p., paper, novel. CHOOSE YOUR OWN ADVENTURE #38.

28151 *The search for Aladdin's lamp.* New York, Toronto: An R. A. Montgomery Book, Bantam Books, 1991, 119 p., paper, novel. CHOOSE YOUR OWN ADVENTURE #117.

28152 *Secret of the ninja.* Toronto, New York: An R. A. Montgomery Book, Bantam

Books, 1987, 115 p., paper, novel. CHOOSE YOUR OWN ADVENTURE #66.

37912 *Spy for George Washington.* Toronto, New York: An R. A. Montgomery Book, Bantam Books, 1985, 115 p., paper, novel. CHOOSE YOUR OWN ADVENTURE #48.

28153 *You are a millionaire.* New York, Toronto: An R. A. Montgomery Book, Bantam Books, 1990, 118 p., paper, novel. CHOOSE YOUR OWN ADVENTURE #98.

LEICHTER, Larry R.

28154 *Epidemic!* New York: Zebra Books, Kensington Publishing Corp., 1980, 333 p., paper, novel.

28155 *Mind game.* New York, Washington: Vantage Press, 1989, 293 p., cloth, novel.

LEIGH, Stephen (Walter), 1951-

28156 *The Abraxas marvel circus.* New York: A Roc Book, 1990, 255 p., paper, novel.

28157 *Alien tongue.* New York, Toronto: Spectra, Bantam Books, 1991, xx+327 p., paper, novel. NEXT WAVE #2.

28158 *The bones of God.* New York: Avon, 1986, 289 p., paper, novel.

Changeling—SEE: *Isaac Asimov's Robot city: Robots and aliens: Changeling.*

28159 *The crystal memory.* New York: Avon, 1987, 245 p., paper, novel.

28160 *Dance of the hag.* Toronto, New York: Bantam Books, 1983, 183 p., paper, novel. NEWEDEN #2.

28161 *Isaac Asimov's Robot city: Robots and aliens: Changeling.* New York: A Byron Preiss Visual Publications Book, Ace Books, 1989, xxi+151 p., paper, novel. ISAAC ASIMOV'S ROBOT CITY—ROBOTS & ALIENS #1.

28162 *A quiet of stone.* Toronto, New York: Bantam Books, 1984, 226 p., paper, novel. NEWEDEN #3.

28163 *The secret of the Lona.* New York: A Byron Preiss Visual Publications Book, Ace Books, 1988, 173 p., paper, novel. DR. BONES #1.

28164 *Slow fall to dawn.* Toronto, New York: Bantam Books, 1981, 165 p., paper, novel. NEWEDEN #1.

LEIGHTON, Edward, pseud.—SEE: Barrett, G. J.

LEIMAS, Brooke

28165 *The eighth day.* New York: A Dell Book, 1983, 284 p., paper, novel.

28166 *The intruder.* New York: A Signet Book, New American Library, 1980, 232 p., paper, novel.

28167 *The summer visitors.* New York: A Signet Book, New American Library, 1980, 187 p., paper, novel.

LEININGER, Robert, 1946-

28168 *Black sun.* New York: Avon Books, 1991, 309 p., paper, novel.

LEINSTER, Murray [pseud. of William Fitzgerald Jenkins], 1896-1975

28169 *The best of Murray Leinster.* London: Corgi Books, 1976, 174 p., paper, coll. [Edited by Brian Davis].

28170 *The best of Murray Leinster.* New York: A Del Rey Book, Ballantine Books, 1978, xvi+368 p., paper, coll. [A different selection from the 1976 volume; edited by J. J. Pierce].

28172 *The Med series.* New York: Ace Science Fiction Books, 1983, 380 p., paper, coll. MED SERVICE SERIES #1-3. [Includes *The mutant weapon, S.O.S from three worlds, This world is taboo*].

with Ronald Payne

28173 *Last Murray Leinster interview.* Richmond, VA: Waves Press, 1983, 12 p., paper, nonf.

LEITCH, Patricia, 1933-

15831 *The black loch.* London: Collins, 1963, 192 p., cloth, novel.

LEITHAUSER, Brad, 1953-

28174 *Hence: a novel.* New York: Alfred A. Knopf, 1989, xxiii+319 p., cloth, novel.

LELAND, Lowell P(ond), 1907- , with Thomas L. Wymer & Alice Calderonello & Sara Jayne Steen & R. Michael Evers

19206 *Intersections: the elements of science in science fiction.* Bowling Green, OH: The Popular Press, 1978, viii+130 p., paper, nonf.

LELY, James A.

28175 *Battlestar Galactica.* Mankato, MN: Creative Education, 1979, 32 p., cloth, nonf.

28176 *Star Trek*. Mankato, MN: Creative Education, 1979, 32 p., cloth, nonf.

28177 *Star Wars*. Mankato, MN: Creative Education, 1977, 32 p., cloth, nonf.

LEM, Stanislaw, 1921-

28178 *The chain of chance*. New York & London: A Helen and Kurt Wolff Book, Harcourt Brace Jovanovich, 1978, 179 p., cloth, novel. [Translation by Louis Iribarne of *Katar*].

28179 *The cosmic carnival of Stanislaw Lem: an anthology of entertaining stories by the modern master of science fiction*. New York: Continuum, 1981, xi+271 p., paper, coll. [Edited and translated by Michael Kandel].

28180 *Eden*. San Diego, CA: Harcourt Brace Jovanovich, 1989, 262 p., cloth, novel. [Translation by Marc E. Heine of *Eden*].

28181 *Fiasco*. San Diego, CA: A Helen and Kurt Wolff Book, Harcourt Brace Jovanovich, 1987, viii+322 p., cloth, novel. [Translation by Michael Kandel of *Fiasko*].

28182 *His master's voice*. New York: A Helen & Kurt Wolff Book, Harcourt Brace Jovanovich, 1983, 199 p., cloth, novel. [Translation by Michael Kandel of *Glos Pana*].

28183 *Imaginary magnitude*. San Diego, CA: A Helen & Kurt Wolff Book, Harcourt Brace Jovanovich, 1984, vi+248 p., cloth, coll. [Translation by Marc E. Heine of *Wielkosc urojona*].

28184 *Memoirs of a space traveler: further reminiscences of Ijon Tichy*. New York: Harcourt Brace Jovanovich, 1982, 153 p., cloth, coll. [Translation by Joel Stern and Maria Swiecicka-Ziemianek of *Dzienniki gwiazdowe*].

28185 *Microworlds: writings on science fiction and fantasy*. San Diego, CA: A Helen & Kurt Wolff Book, Harcourt Brace Jovanovich, 1984, xviii+285 p., cloth, nonf. coll. [Edited by Franz Rottensteiner].

28186 *More tales of Pirx the pilot*. San Diego, CA: Harcourt Brace Jovanovich, 1982, 220 p., cloth, coll. [Translation by Louis Iribarne, Michael Kandel, and Magdalena Majcherizyk of part of *Opowiesci o pilocie Pirxie*].

28187 *Mortal engines*. New York: A Continuum Book, Seabury Press, 1977, xxiv+239 p., cloth, coll. [Translation by Michael Kandel].

28188 *One human minute*. San Diego, CA: A Helen and Kurt Wolff Book, Harcourt Brace Jovanovich, 1986, 102 p., cloth, coll. [Translation by Catherine S. Leach].

28189 *A perfect vacuum*. New York, London: A Helen & Kurt Wolff Book, Harcourt Brace Jovanovich, 1978, viii+229 p., cloth, coll. [Translation by Michael Kandel of *Doskonala proznia*].

28190 *Return from the stars*. New York: A Helen & Kurt Wolff Book, Harcourt Brace Jovanovich, 1980, 247 p., cloth, novel. [Translation by Barbara Marszal and Frank Simpson of *Powrót z gwiazd*].

28191 *Solaris; The chain of chance; A perfect vacuum*. Harmondsworth, Middlesex, England: Penguin Books, 1981, 543 p., paper, coll.

28192 *The star diaries*. New York: A Continuum Book, Seabury Press, 1976, x+275 p., cloth, coll. [Translation by Michael Kandel of *Dzienniki gwiazdowe*].

28193 *Tales of Pirx the pilot*. New York: A Helen & Kurt Wolff Book, Harcourt Brace Jovanovich, 1979, 206 p., cloth, coll. [Translation by Louis Iribarne of part of *Opowiesci o pilocie Pirxie*].

28194 *Tales of Pirx the pilot; Return from the stars; The invincible*. Harmondsworth, Middlesex, England: Penguin Books, 1982, 589 p., paper, coll.

LEMURES, Ben

28195 *Spirit of the lagoon*. North Hollywood, CA: American Art Enterprises, 1982, 156 p., paper, novel.

L'ENGLE, Madeleine [i.e., Madeleine L'Engle Camp Franklin], 1918-

28196 *An acceptable time*. New York: Farrar Straus Giroux, 1989, 343 p., cloth, novel. MEG MURRY #5.

28197 *Many waters*. New York: Farrar Straus Giroux, 1986, 310 p., cloth, novel. MEG MURRY #4.

28198 *A swiftly tilting planet*. New York: Farrar, Straus, Giroux, 1978, 278 p., cloth, novel. MEG MURRY #3.

LENTZ, Harris M. III

28199 *Science fiction, horror, and fantasy film and television credits: over 10,000 actors, actresses, directors, producers, screenwriters, cinematographers, art directors, and make-up, special effects, costume, and other people; plus full cross-references from all films and TV shows*. Jefferson, NC & London: McFarland &

Co., 1983, xx+1374 p. in 2 v., cloth, nonf.

28200 *Science fiction, horror, and fantasy film and television credits supplement through 1987.* Jefferson, NC & London: McFarland & Co., 1989, xii+924 p., cloth, nonf.

LENZ, Millicent (Ann)

28201 *Nuclear age literature for youth: the quest for a life-affirming ethic.* Chicago, IL: American Library Association, 1990, xli+316 p., cloth, nonf.

LEOKUM, Leonard, *with Paul Posnick*

28202 *Weather war.* Los Angeles: Pinnacle Books, 1978, 372 p., paper, novel.

LEONARD, Elmore (John Jr.), 1925-

28203 *Touch.* New York: Arbor House, 1987, viii+245 p., cloth, novel.

LEONARD, George H(ugh), 1921-

28204 *Alien.* Chicago: Playboy Press, 1977, 251 p., paper, novel.
28204A retitled: *Alien quest.* London: Sphere Books, 1981, 251 p., paper, novel.
 Alien quest—SEE: *Alien.*
28205 *Beyond control.* New York: Macmillan Publishing Co.; London: Collier Macmillan Publishers, 1975, 165 p., cloth, novel.

as HUGHES COOPER

03387 *Sexmax.* New York: Paperback Library, 1969, 176 p., paper, novel.

LEONARD, Lawrence

28206 *The horn of mortal danger.* London: Julia MacRae Books, 1980, 224 p., cloth, novel.

LEONARD, Raymond, 1941-

28207 *Legacy of the shroud.* London: A Star Book, W. H. Allen & Co., 1988, 233 p., paper, novel.
28208 *The Nostradamus inheritance.* London: Poplar, 1985, 206 p., cloth, novel.
28209 *OMEGA.* London: Poplar, 1986, 196 p., cloth, novel.

*LePIRE, Joe H., <u>1892-1973</u>

LERANGIS, Peter

28210 *The amazing Ben Franklin.* Toronto, New York: A Byron Preiss Book, A Bantam Skylark Book, 1987, 80 p., paper, novel. TIME TRAVELER #4.
28211 *The last of the dinosaurs.* Toronto, New York: A Byron Preiss Book, Bantam Books, 1988, 113 p., paper, novel. TIME MACHINE #22.
28212 *Star Trek IV, the voyage home.* New York: A Wanderer Book, 1986, 91 p., paper, movie. STAR TREK IV.
28213 *The sultan's secret.* New York: Ballantine Books, 1988, 118 p., paper, novel. G.I. JOE #6.
28214 *Time machine, special edition: World War II code breaker.* New York, Toronto: A Byron Preiss Book, Bantam Books, 1989, 159 p., paper, novel. TIME MACHINE (UNNUMBERED).
 World War II code breaker—SEE: *Time machine, special edition: World War II code breaker.*

LERMAN, Rhoda, 1936-

28215 *The book of the night.* New York: Holt, Rinehart & Winston, 1984, 292 p., cloth, novel.

LERNER, Arthur, 1915-

28216 *Psychoanalytically oriented criticism of three American poets: Poe, Whitman, and Aiken.* Rutherford, NJ: Fairleigh Dickinson University Press, 1970, 130 p., cloth, nonf.

LERNER, Edward M.

28217 *Probe.* New York: Warner Books, 1991, 314 p., paper, novel.

LERNER, Frederick Andrew, 1945-

28218 *Modern science fiction and the American literary community.* Metuchen, NJ & London: Scarecrow Press, 1985, xviii+325 p., cloth, nonf.
28219 *A Silverlock companion: the life and works of John Myers Myers* / by Fred Lerner. Center Harbor, NH: Niekas Publications, 1988, 52 p., paper, nonf. anth.

LERNER, Jonathan, 1948-

28220 *Caught in a still place.* London: Serpent's Tail Publishing, 1989, 122 p., paper, novel.

*LERNET-HOLENIA, Alexander (Maria), 1897-1976

LEROE, Ellen (W.), 1949-

28221 *Have a heart, Cupid Delaney.* New York: Lodestar Books, 1986, 148 p., cloth, novel. CUPID DELANEY #1.

28222 *H.O.W.L. High.* New York: A Minstrel Book, Pocket Books, 1991, 132 p., paper, novel.

28223 *Meet your match, Cupid Delaney.* New York: Lodestar Books, 1990, 150 p., cloth, novel. CUPID DELANEY #2.

28224 *The Peanut Butter Poltergeist.* New York: Lodestar Books, 1987, 103 p., cloth, novel.

28225 *Robot raiders.* New York: Harper & Row, 1987, 181 p., cloth, novel. BIXBY WYLER #2.

28226 *Robot romance.* New York: Harper & Row, 1985, 179 p., cloth, novel. BIXBY WYLER #1.

LEROUX, Gaston, 1868-1927

28227 *The Gaston Leroux bedside companion: weird stories by the author of "The phantom of the opera".* London: Victor Gollancz, 1980, 160 p., cloth, coll. [Edited by Peter Haining].

LERT, A. J.

28228 *Manx tales of horror.* Douglas, Isle of Man, United Kingdom: Gordon Publishers, 1974, 112 p., paper, coll.

*LESLIE, Josephine (Aimee Campbell), 1898-1979

LESLIE, Peter, 1922-

28229 *Father Hayes.* New York: Zebra Books, Kensington Publishing Corp., 1976, 205 p., paper, novel. FATHER HAYES #1.

28230 *The Holy spirit.* New York: Zebra Books, Kensington Publishing Corp., 1977, 224 p., paper, novel. FATHER HAYES #3.

28231 *The steeds of Satan.* New York: Zebra Books, Kensington Publishing Corp., 1976, 236 p., paper, novel. FATHER HAYES #2.

LESSER, Milton—SEE: Marlowe, Stephen

LESSING, Doris (May Taylor), 1919-

28232 *Documents relating to the sentimental agents in the Volyen Empire.* London: Jonathan Cape, 1983, 178 p., cloth, novel. CANOPUS IN ARGUS: ARCHIVES #5.

37913 *The fifth child.* London: Jonathan Cape, 1988, 133 p., cloth, novel.

28233 *The making of the representative for Planet 8.* London: Jonathan Cape, 1982, 144 p., cloth, novel. CANOPUS IN ARGUS: ARCHIVES #4.

28234 *The marriages between zones three, four, and five (as narrated by the chroniclers of zone three).* London: Jonathan Cape, 1980, 245 p., cloth, novel. CANOPUS IN ARGUS: ARCHIVES #2.

28235 *Re: colonised planet 5, Shikasta: personal, psychological, historical documents relating to a visit by JOHOR (George Sherban), emissary (grade 9) 87th of the period of the last days.* London: Jonathan Cape, 1979, x+365 p., cloth, novel. CANOPUS IN ARGUS: ARCHIVES #1.

28236 *The Sirian experiments: the report by Ambien II, of the five.* London: Jonathan Cape, 1981, 288 p., cloth, novel. CANOPUS IN ARGUS: ARCHIVES #3.

LESTER, Andrew, pseud.—SEE: Greenhough, Terry

LESTER, Colin (J.)

28237 *The international science fiction yearbook 1979.* London: Pierrot Publishing, 1978, 394 p., paper, nonf. anth.

*LESTER, Edward, 1831-1905

LETTELL, John S., *with Anthony DeStefano as* ANTHONY JOHN

21629 *The predator.* New York: Ballantine Books, 1983, 345 p., paper, novel.

LETTS, Barry, *with Terrance Dicks*

The daemons; The time monster—SEE: *Doctor Who: The Daemons; The time monster.*

21854 *Doctor Who: The Daemons; The time monster.* London: W. H. Allen & Co., 1989, 151 p., paper, tele. coll. DOCTOR WHO CLASSICS #5
The time monster—SEE: *Doctor Who: The Daemons; The time monster.*

LEVACK, Daniel J. H.

28238 *Amber dreams: a Roger Zelazny bibliography.* San Francisco, Columbia, PA: Underwood-Miller, 1983, 151 p., cloth, nonf.

28239 *Dune master: a Frank Herbert bibliography.* Westport, CT: Meckler, 1988, xx+176 p., cloth, nonf. MECKLER'S BIBLIOGRAPHIES ON SCIENCE FICTION, FANTASY, AND HORROR #2.

28240 *PKD: A Philip K. Dick bibliography.* San Francisco, Columbia, PA: Underwood-Miller, 1981, 158 p., cloth, nonf.

28241 *PKD: A Philip K. Dick bibliography, rev. ed.* Westport, CT: Meckler, 1988, 156 p., cloth, nonf. MECKLER'S BIBLIOGRAPHIES ON SCIENCE FICTION, FANTASY, AND HORROR #1.

with Charlotte Laughlin

27864 *De Camp: an L. Sprague de Camp bibliography.* San Francisco, Columbia, PA: Underwood-Miller, 1983, 328 p., cloth, nonf.

with Tim Underwood

28242 *Fantasms: a bibliography of the literature of Jack Vance.* San Francisco, Columbia, PA: Underwood-Miller, 1978, 91 p., cloth, nonf.

with Tim Underwood and Chuck Miller

28243 *Fantasy and science fiction by Jack Vance.* San Francisco, Columbia, PA: Underwood-Miller, 1978, 8 p., paper, nonf.

with Tim Underwood & Kurt Cockrum

20234 *Fantasms II: a bibliography of the works of Jack Vance.* [S.l.: s.n.], 1979, xiii+83, 1, 118, 20 p., paper, nonf.

28244 *Fantasms II: a bibliography of the literature of Jack Vance.* Riverside, CA: Kurt Cockrum, 1979, vi+99 p. on 112 leaves, printout, nonf. [Revised edition].

LEVEN, Jeremy, 1941-

28245 *Creator.* New York: Coward, McCann & Geoghegan, 1980, 490 p., cloth, novel.

28246 *Satan: his psychotherapy and cure by the unfortunate Dr. Kassler, J.S.P.S..* New York: Alfred A. Knopf, 1982, vi+478 p., cloth, novel.

LEVENE, Philip

10432 *City of the hidden eyes.* Manchester, England: World Distributors, 1960, 160 p., paper, radio. [Erroneously credited to J.

L. Morrissey in the first edition of this bibliography].

LEVENTHAL, Lionel—SEE: Russell, Alan K.

LEVI, Primo, 1919-1987

28247 *The mirror maker: stories and essays.* New York: Schocken Books, 1989, xi+176 p., cloth, coll. [Translation by Raymond Rosenthal of *Racconti e saggi*].

28248 *The sixth day, and other tales.* New York: Summit Books, 1990, 222 p., cloth, coll. [Translation by Raymond Rosenthal of *Storie natural* and of *Vizio di forma*].

*LEVIE, Rex Dean, 1937?-

LEVIN, Betty, 1927-

28249 *The binding spell.* New York: Lodestar Books, E. P. Dutton, 1984, 179 p., cloth, novel.

28250 *The forespoken.* New York: Macmillan, 1976, 282 p., cloth, novel. CLAUDIA & EVAN #3.

28251 *A griffon's nest.* New York: Macmillan, 1975, 346 p., cloth, novel. CLAUDIA & EVAN #2. [The first in series is *Sword of Culann* (see #08977)].

28252 *The ice bear.* New York: Greenwillow Books, 1986, 179 p., cloth, novel.

28253 *The keeping-room.* New York: Greenwillow Books, 1981, 247 p., cloth, novel.

LEVIN, Harry (Tuchman), 1912-

28254 *The power of blackness: Hawthorne, Poe, Melville.* New York: Alfred A. Knopf, 1958, 263 p., cloth, nonf.

LEVIN, Ira, 1929-

28255 *The boys from Brazil: a novel.* New York: Random House, 1976, 280 p., cloth, novel.

28256 *Nightmares: three great suspense novels.* London: Michael Joseph, 1981, 460 p., cloth, coll. [Includes *Rosemary's baby*; *The Stepford wives*; *A kiss before dying*].

28257 *Three by Ira Levin.* New York: Random House, 1985, 485 p., cloth, coll. [Includes *Rosemary's baby*; *This perfect day*; *The Stepford wives*].

LEVIN, John, 1944?- , with Frank M. Robinson

28258 *The great divide.* New York: Rawson, Wade Publishers, 1982, 303 p., cloth, novel.

*LEVIN, Meyer, 1905-_1981_

LEVINE, George (Lewis), 1931- , *with U. C. Knoepflmacher*

27416   *Endurance of Frankenstein: essays on Mary Shelley's novel.* Berkeley: University of California Press, 1979, xx+341 p., cloth, nonf. anth.

LEVINE, Sidney, *with Al Dempsey & Joseph Van Winkle*

21549   *Miss Finney kills now and then.* New York: Tor, A Tom Doherty Associates Book, 1982, 256 p., paper, movie.

LEVINSON, Leonard, 1935-

as PHILIP KIRK

27318   *Butler: The Q factor.* New York: Leisure Books, 1984, 239 p., paper, novel. BUTLER #11/12.
27319   *Killer satellites.* New York: Leisure Books, 1980, 235 p., paper, novel. BUTLER #6.
27320   *Killer virus.* New York: Leisure Books, 1983, 238 p., paper, novel. BUTLER #9.
27321   *The laser shuttle.* New York: Leisure Books, 1982, 230 p., paper, novel. BUTLER #7.
        The Q factor—See: *Butler: The Q factor.*

as JONATHAN TRASK

35760   *The camp.* New York: Belmont Tower Books, 1977, 155 p., paper, novel.

LEVY, Edward

28259   *The beast within.* New York: Arbor House, 1981, 269 p., cloth, novel.
28260   *Came a spider.* New York: Arbor House, 1978, 247 p., cloth, novel.

LEVY, Elizabeth (Yelverton), 1942-

28261   *The bride movie storybook.* New York: Random House, 1985, [57] p., cloth, movie.
28262   *Dracula is a pain in the neck.* New York: Harper & Row, 1983, 74 p., cloth, novel.
28263   *Return of the Jedi storybook.* New York: Random House, 1983, 68 p., cloth, movie.
28264   *Running out of magic with Houdini.* New York: Alfred A. Knopf, 1981, 121 p., cloth, novel. RUNNING #2.

28265   *Running out of time.* New York: Alfred A. Knopf, 1980, 121 p., cloth, novel. RUNNING #1.

LÉVY, Maurice

28266   *Lovecraft: a study in the fantastic.* Detroit, MI: Wayne State University Press, 1988, 147 p., cloth, nonf. [Translation by S. T. Joshi of *Lovecraft; ou, Du fantastique*].

LEWINS, Anna, 1956-

28267   *Dream for danger.* London: Blackie, 1987, 140 p., cloth, novel.
28268   *World of strangers.* London: Blackie, 1989, 151 p., cloth, novel.

LEWIS, Anthony R(ichard) "Tony," 1941-

28269   *An annotated bibliography of recursive science fiction.* Cambridge, MA: NESFA Press, 1990, vi+56 p., paper, nonf. [Running title: *Recursion!: science fiction stories about science fiction*; limited to 300 copies].
28270   *The best of Astounding* / by Tony Lewis. New York: Baronet Publishing Co., 1978, 244 p., paper, anth.
28271   *Concordance to Cordwainer Smith.* Boston: New England Science Fiction Association, 1984, iii+90 p., paper, nonf.
28272   *Index to Perry Rhodan, U.S. edition, 25-50.* Boston: New England Science Fiction Association, 1975, 18 p., paper, nonf.

LEWIS, Arthur O(rcutt Jr.), 1920-

28273   *Utopian literature in the Pennsylvania State University Libraries: a selected bibliography.* University Park, PA: Pennsylvania State University Libraries, 1984, xxx+230 p., paper, nonf.

*LEWIS, Benn E., _1908-1979_

LEWIS, C(live) S(taples), 1898-1963

28274   *All my roads before me: the diary of C. S. Lewis, 1922-1927.* London: Collins Fount, 1991, 500 p., cloth, nonf. [Edited by Walter Hooper].
28275   *Boxen: the imaginary world of the young C. S. Lewis.* London: Collins, 1985, 206 p., cloth, coll.

28276 *The cosmic trilogy.* London: The Bodley Head, 1990, 651 p., cloth, coll. PERELANDRA #1-3; RANSOM].

28277 *The dark tower, and other stories.* London: Collins, 1977, 158 p., cloth, coll.

28278 *The essential C. S. Lewis.* New York: Macmillan Publishing Co., 1988, xv + 536 p., cloth, coll. [Edited by Lyle W. Dorsett; includes some nonfiction].

28279 *Letters of C. S. Lewis.* London: Geoffrey Bles, 1966, 308 p., cloth, nonf. coll. [Edited by W. H. Lewis].

28280 *Letters to an American lady.* Grand Rapids, MI: William B. Eerdmans Publishing Co., 1967, 121 p., cloth, nonf. coll. [Edited by Clyde S. Kilby].

28281 *Letters to children.* London: Macmillan, 1985, 120 p., cloth, nonf. coll. [Edited by Lyle W. Dorsett and Marjorie Lampmead].

28282 *Prince Caspian; and, The voyage of the Dawn Treader.* London: Lion, 1989, 381 p., paper, coll. NARNIAN CHRONICLES #4-5.

28283 *The silver chair; and, The last battle.* London: W. H. Smith, 1990, 366 p., cloth, coll. NARNIAN CHRONICLES #6-7.

28284 *They stand together: the letters of C. S. Lewis to Arthur Greeves (1914-1963).* London: Collins, 1979, 592 p., cloth, nonf. coll. [Edited by Walter Hooper].

LEWIS, Canella [pseud. of Jonathan Richards]

28285 *Sensitive encounter.* New York: A Berkley Medallion Book, Berkley Publishing Corp., 1977, 215 p., paper, novel.

LEWIS, Charles [pseud. of Roger Dixon], 1930-

28286 *The Cain factor.* London: Harwood-Smart, 1975, 174 p., cloth, novel.

LEWIS, Gogo, *with Seon Manley*

28287 *Christmas ghosts: an anthology.* Garden City, NY: Doubleday & Co., 1978, xii + 227 p., cloth, anth.

28288 *Fun phantoms: tales of ghostly entertainment.* New York: Lothrop, Lee & Shepard, 1979, 186 p., cloth, anth.

28289 *Ghostly gentlewomen: two centuries of spectral stories by the gentle sex.* New York: Lothrop, Lee & Shepard, 1977, 237 p., cloth, anth.

28290 *The haunted dolls: an anthology.* Garden City, NY: Doubleday & Co., 1980, x + 318 p., cloth, anth.

28291 *Ladies of fantasy: two centuries of sinister stories by the gentle sex.* New York: Lothrop, Lee & Shepard, 1975, 214 p., cloth, anth.

28292 *Ladies of the gothics: tales of romance and terror by the gentle sex.* New York: Lothrop, Lee & Shepard, 1975, 219 p., cloth, anth.

28293 *Masters of shades and shadows: an anthology of great ghost stories.* Garden City, NY: Doubleday & Co., 1978, 214 p., cloth, anth.

28294 *Masters of the macabre: an anthology of mystery, horror, and detection.* Garden City, NY: Doubleday & Co., 1975, 330 p., cloth, anth.

28295 *Nature's revenge: eerie stories of revolt against the human race.* New York: Lothrop, Lee & Shepard, 1978, 154 p., cloth, anth.

28296 *Sisters of sorcery: two centuries of witchcraft stories by the gentle sex.* New York: Lothrop, Lee & Shepard, 1976, 220 p., cloth, anth.

28297 *Women of the weird: eerie stories by the gentle sex.* New York: Lothrop, Lee & Shepard, 1976, 188 p., cloth, anth.

LEWIS, Hilda (Winifred), 1896-1974

15832 *The ship that flew.* London: Oxford University Press, 1939, 320 p., cloth, novel.

LEWIS, Mark

28298 *Kaliban's Christmas: a special tale of magic.* New York: Tor, A Tom Doherty Associates Book, 1988, 55 p., paper, story.

LEWIS, Mary Christianna—SEE: Brand, Christianna

LEWIS, Naomi

28299 *Fantasy books for children.* London: National Book League, 1975, 46 p., paper, nonf.

28300 *Fantasy books for children, rev. ed.* London: National Book League, 1977, 61 p., paper, nonf.

*LEWIS, Oscar, 1893-<u>1992</u>

LEWIS, (Geoffrey) Peter, 1928-

28301 *George Orwell: the road to 1984.* London: Heinemann Quixote Press, 1981, 122 p., cloth, nonf.

LEWIS, Richard, 1945-

The black horde—SEE: *Devil's coach-horse.*

28302 *David Cronenberg's Rabid.* London: Mayflower, 1977, 142 p., paper, movie.

28303 *Devil's coach-horse.* Feltham, England: Hamlyn Paperbacks, 1979, 168 p., paper, novel.

28303A retitled: *The black horde.* New York: A Signet Book, New American Library, 1980, 166 p., paper, novel.

28304 *Night killers.* Feltham, England: Hamlyn Paperbacks, 1983, 208 p., paper, novel.

28305 *Parasite.* Feltham, England: Hamlyn Paperbacks, 1980, 187 p., paper, novel.

28309A *Possessed.* London: Futura, 1983, 313 p., paper, novel. [Originally published under the name Alan Radnor].

Rabid—SEE: *David Cronenberg's Rabid.*

28306 *Spiders.* Feltham, England: Hamlyn Paperbacks, 1978, 153 p., paper, novel.

28307 *The web.* London: Hamlyn Paperbacks, 1981, 204 p., paper, novel.

as ALAN RADNOR

28308 *The force.* Feltham, England: Hamlyn Paperbacks, 1979, 212 p., paper, novel.

28309 *Possessed.* London: Macdonald, 1982, 313 p., cloth, novel.

LEWIS, Roger, 1912-1987

28310 *Numin's curse.* New York: A Berkley Medallion Book, Berkley Publishing Corp., 1976, 215 p., paper, novel.

LEWIS, Sam

with Boyd F. Peterson Jr. & Blaine Pardoe

28311 *Battletech: Wolf Clan sourcebook.* Chicago: FASA Corp., 1991, 128 p., paper, fiction. BATTLETECH SERIES.

with Kevin Stein

28312 *Battletech technical readout 3026: (vehicles and personal equipment).* Chicago: FASA Corp., 1987, 126 p., paper, fiction. BATTLETECH SERIES.

LEWIS, Suford [legalized from Susan McMillan Hereford Lewis], 1943-

28313 *Noreascon II memory book.* Boston, MA: Noreascon II, 1984 (i.e., 1985), 48 p., paper, nonf. anth.

28314 *Proceedings of the Conference of Science Fiction Convention Managers 1972.* Cambridge, MA: NESFA Press, 1987, 14 p., paper, nonf. anth.

LEWIS, Susan M.—SEE: Lewis, Suford

LEWIS, Tim

28315 *Pisspote's progress: the odyssey of a failure.* England: Leomansley Press, 1991, 377 p., paper, novel.

LEWIS, Tony—SEE: Lewis, Anthony R.

LEWITT, S(hariann) N., 1954-

28316 *Angel at apogee.* New York: Berkley Books, 1987, 219 p., paper, novel.

28317 *Blind justice.* New York: Ace Books, 1991, 265 p., paper, novel.

28318 *Cyberstealth.* New York: Ace Books, 1989, 232 p., paper, novel. CYBERSTEALTH #1.

28319 *Dancing vac.* New York: Ace Books, 1990, 236 p., paper, novel. CYBERSTEALTH #2.

28320 *First and final rites* / by Shariann Lewitt. New York: Ace Fantasy Books, 1984, 282 p., paper, novel.

28321 *U.S.S.A., book 2.* New York: A GLC Book, Avon, 1987, 172 p., paper, novel. U.S.S.A. #2.

28322 *U.S.S.A., book 4.* New York: A GLC Book, Avon, 1987, 172 p., paper, novel. U.S.S.A. #4.

as RICK NORTH

30812 *Jack Anderson presents The young astronauts.* New York: Zebra Books, Kensington Publishing Corp., 1990, 159 p., paper, novel. YOUNG ASTRONAUTS #1.

30814 *Space blazers.* New York: Zebra Books, Kensington Publishing Corp., 1990, 157 p., paper, novel. YOUNG ASTRONAUTS #3.

The young astronauts—SEE: *Jack Anderson presents The young astronauts.*

with Susan Shwartz as GORDON KENDALL

28323 *White Wing.* New York: Tor SF, A Tom Doherty Associates Book, 1985, 319 p., paper, novel.

LEWITT, Shariann—SEE: Lewitt, S. N.

LEY, Sandra, 1944-

28324 *Beyond time.* New York: Pocket Books, 1976, xv+268 p., paper, anth.

LEYNER, Mark, 1956-

28325 *My cousin, my gastroenterologist.* New York: Harmony Books, 1990, 154 p., paper, novel.

LEYTON, E. K., pseud.—SEE: Dreadstone, Carl

LHIN, Erik van, pseud.—SEE: Del Rey, Lester

LI, Shanji—SEE: Huanzhulouzhu

LIBMAN, Gary

28326 *Superman (the movie).* Mankato, MN: Creative Education, 1983, 32 p., cloth, nonf.

LICHTENBERG, Jacqueline, 1942-

28327 *City of a million legends.* New York: Berkley Books, 1985, 227 p., paper, novel. MOLT BROTHER #2.
28328 *Dreamspy.* New York: St. Martin's Press, 1989, 337 p., cloth, novel. LUREN #2.
28329 *Dushau.* New York: Popular Library, 1985, 238 p., paper, novel. DUSHAU TRILOGY #1.
28330 *Farfetch.* New York: Popular Library, 1985, 238 p., paper, novel. DUSHAU TRILOGY #2.
28331 *Mahogany trinrose: a Sime/Gen novel.* Garden City, NY: Doubleday & Co., 1981, 214 p., cloth, novel. SIME/GEN #4.
28332 *Molt brother.* New York: Playboy Paperbacks, 1982, 254 p., paper, novel. MOLT BROTHER #1.
28333 *Outreach.* New York: Popular Library, 1986, xv+239 p., paper, novel. DUSHAU TRILOGY #3.
28334 *RenSime.* Garden City, NY: Doubleday & Co., 1984, 178 p., cloth, novel. SIME/GEN #6.
28335 *Those of my blood.* New York: St. Martin's Press, 1988, ix+402 p., cloth, novel. LUREN #1.
28336 *Unto Zeor, forever.* Garden City, NY: Doubleday & Co., 1978, xvi+236 p., cloth, novel. SIME/GEN SERIES #2.

with Jean Lorrah

28337 *Channel's destiny.* Garden City, NY: Doubleday & Co., 1982, 182 p., cloth, novel. SIME/GEN #5.
28338 *First channel.* Garden City, NY: Doubleday & Co., 1980, vi+310 p., cloth, novel. SIME/GEN #3.
28339 *Zelerod's doom: a Sime/Gen novel.* New York: DAW Books, 1986, 277 p., paper, novel. SIME/GEN #8.

with Sondra Marshak & Joan Winston

28340 *Star Trek lives!* Toronto, New York: Bantam Books, 1975, 274 p., paper, nonf.

LIDE, Mary

28341 *Command of the king.* London: Grafton, 1990, 287 p., cloth, novel.

LIEBERMAN, Robert (Howard), 1941-

28342 *Baby: a novel.* New York: Crown Publishers, 1981, 344 p., cloth, novel.
28343 *Perfect people.* New York: A Dell Book, 1986, 294 p., paper, novel.

*LIEBERMAN, Rosalie, 1907?-1979?

LIEBMAN, Arthur, 1926-

28344 *Science fiction: creators and planners.* New York: Richards Rosen Press, 1979, p., cloth, anth.
28345 *Science fiction: masters of today.* New York: Richards Rosen Press, 1981, ix+179 p., cloth, anth.
28346 *Science fiction: the bests of yesterday.* New York: Richards Rosen Press, 1980, 211 p., cloth, anth.

*LIEBSCHER, Walt, 1918-1985

LIEF, Evelyn

28347 *The clone rebellion.* New York: Pocket Books, 1980, 256 p., paper, novel.

LIEF, Ruth Ann

28348 *Homage to Oceania: the prophetic vision of George Orwell.* Athens, OH: Ohio State University Press, 1969, viii+162 p., cloth, nonf.

LIENTZ, Gerald

The lost crowns of Cair Paravel—SEE: *Narnia solo games: The lost crowns of Cair Paravel.*

28349 *Middle-Earth quest: Rescue in Mirkwood.* New York: Berkley Books, 1986, 155 p., paper, novel. MIDDLE-EARTH QUEST #3.

28350 *Narnia solo games: The lost crowns of Cair Paravel.* New York: Berkley Books, 1988, [202] p., paper, novel. NARNIA SOLO GAMES #4.

Rescue in Mirkwood—SEE: *Middle-Earth quest: Rescue in Mirkwood.*

LIFTON-ZOLINE, Pamela—SEE: **Zoline, Pamela**

LIGHT, John, 1943-

28351 *The well of time.* London: Robert Hale, 1981, 222 p., cloth, novel.

LIGHTNER, A. M. [i.e., Alice Martha Lightner Hopf], 1904-1988

28352 *Star circus.* New York: E. P. Dutton, 1977, 169 p., cloth, novel.

LIGOTTI, Thomas, 1953-

28353 *Grimscribe: his lives and works.* London: Robinson Publishing, 1991, 214 p., cloth, coll.

28354 *Songs of a dead dreamer.* Albuquerque, NM: Silver Scarab Press, 1986, 166 p., cloth, coll.

28355 *Songs of a dead dreamer.* London: Robinson Publishing, 1989, x+275 p., paper, coll. [Expanded edition].

LILBURN, Eileen—SEE: **Bigland, Eileen**

LILIUS, Irmelin Sandman—SEE: **Sandman Lilius, Irmelin**

LILLINGTON, Kenneth (James), 1916-

28357 *Full moon.* London: Faber & Faber, 1986, 136 p., cloth, novel.

LINAKER, Michael R.

28358 *Scorpion.* New York: A Signet Book, New American Library, 1981, 159 p., paper, novel. SCORPION #1.

28359 *Scorpion: Second generation.* London: New English Library, 1982, 158 p., paper, novel. SCORPION #2.

Second generation—SEE: *Scorpion: Second generation.*

28360 *The touch of Hell.* London: New English Library, 1981, 158 p., paper, novel.

LINAWEAVER, Brad(ford Swain), 1952-

28361 *Moon of ice.* New York: Arbor House, 1988, 248 p., cloth, novel.

*LINCOLN, Maurice, pseud., 1887-

LINDBERGH, Anne [i.e., Anne Lindberg Feydy Sapieyevski], 1940-

28362 *Bailey's window.* San Diego, CA: Harcourt Brace Jovanovich, 1984, 115 p., cloth, novel.

28363 *The hunky dory dairy.* San Diego, CA: Harcourt Brace Jovanovich, 1986, 147 p., cloth, novel.

28364 *The people in Pineapple Place.* San Diego, CA: Harcourt Brace Jovanovich, 1982, 153 p., cloth, novel. PINEAPPLE PLACE #1.

28365 *The prisoner of Pineapple Place.* San Diego, CA: Harcourt Brace Jovanovich, 1988, ix+178 p., cloth, novel. PINEAPPLE PLACE #2.

28366 *The shadow on the dial.* New York: Harper & Row, 1987, 153 p., cloth, novel.

as ANNE LINDBERGH FEYDY

15805 *Osprey Island.* Boston: Houghton Mifflin Co., 1974, 164 p., cloth, novel.

LINDHOLM, Margaret A.—SEE: **Lindholm, Megan**

LINDHOLM, Megan [i.e., Margaret Astrid Lindholm Ogden], 1952-

28367 *Cloven hooves.* New York, Toronto: Spectra, Bantam Books, 1991, 360 p., paper, novel.

28368 *Harpy's flight.* New York: Ace Books, 1983, 202 p., paper, novel. WINDSINGERS #1.

28369 *The Limbreth Gate.* New York: Ace Fantasy Books, 1984, 232 p., paper, novel. WINDSINGERS #3.

28370 *Luck of the wheels.* New York: Ace Books, 1989, 247 p., paper, novel. WINDSINGERS #4.

28371 *The reindeer people.* New York: Ace Books, 1988, 268 p., paper, novel. REINDEER PEOPLE #1.

28372 *A saga of the reindeer people.* New York: Guild America Books, 1988, 442 p., cloth, coll. REINDEER PEOPLE #1-2.

28373 *The Windsingers.* New York: Ace Fantasy Books, 1984, 268 p., paper, novel. WINDSINGERS #2.

28374 *The Windsingers.* London: Corgi Books, 1986, 637 p., paper, coll. WINDSINGERS #1-3.

28375 *Wizard of the pigeons.* New York: Ace Fantasy Books, 1986, 214 p., paper, novel.

28376 *Wolf's brother.* New York: Ace Books, 1988, 236 p., paper, novel. REINDEER PEOPLE #2.

LINDSAY, David, 1876-1945

28377 *The violet apple.* London: Sidgwick & Jackson, 1978, 252 p., cloth, novel.

28378 *The violet apple; &, The witch.* Chicago: Chicago Review Press, 1976, 395 p., cloth, coll.

LINDSAY, Elizabeth

28379 *The haunting of Sophie Bartholomew.* London: Hippo, 1989, 118 p., paper, novel.

LINDSAY, John V(liet), 1921-

28380 *The edge.* New York: W. W. Norton & Co., 1976, 236 p., cloth, novel.

LINDSAY, Kathleen—SEE: Richmond, Mary

LINDSAY, Richard

28381 *The moon is the key.* London: Robert Hale, 1980, 174 p., cloth, novel.

LINDSEY, (Helen) Johanna (Boston), 1952-

28382 *Warrior's woman.* New York: Avon Books, 1990, 422 p., paper, novel.

LINDSKOOG, Kathryn (Ann), 1934-

28383 *Around the year with C. S. Lewis & his friends.* Norwalk, CT: C. R. Gibson Co., 1986, [400] p., cloth?, nonf. anth.

28384 *The C. S. Lewis hoax.* Portland, OR: Multnomah, 1988, 175 p., cloth, nonf.

28385 *C. S. Lewis: mere Christian.* Glendale, CA: G/L Regal Books, 1973, 242 p., paper, nonf.

28386 *C. S. Lewis: mere Christian, revised and expanded edition.* Downers Grove, IL: InterVarsity Press, 1981, 258 p., paper, nonf.

28387 *C. S. Lewis: mere Christian, third edition, revised and expanded.* Wheaton, IL: Harold Shaw Publishers, 1987, 258 p., paper, nonf.

LINE, David, pseud.—SEE: Davidson, Lionel

LINEBARGER, Paul M. A.—SEE: Smith, Cordwainer

LINEHAN, L.

28388 *BOHACK: symbiotic worlds.* North Hollywood, CA: American Art Enterprises, 1981, 160 p., paper, novel.

LINES, Kathleen (Mary), 1902-1988

28389 *The Faber book of magical tales.* London & Boston: Faber & Faber, 1985, 176 p., paper, anth.

28390 *The haunted and the haunters: stories of ghosts and other apparitions.* London: Bodley Head, 1975, 235 p., cloth, anth.

28390A retitled: *Haunting tales.* London: Beaver Books, 1983, 191 p., paper, anth.
Haunting tales—SEE: *The haunted and the haunters.*

LING, Peter

28391 *Doctor Who: The mind robber.* London: W. H. Allen & Co., 1986, 144 p., cloth, tele. DOCTOR WHO #115.
The mind robber—SEE: *Doctor Who: The mind robber.*

LINKLATER, Eric (Robert Russell), 1899-1974

37914 *A sociable plover, and other stories and conceits.* London: Rupert Hart-Davies, 1957, 222 p., cloth, coll.

37915 *A terrible freedom.* London, Melbourne: Macmillan, 1966, 226 p., cloth, novel.

LINSKILL, William Thomas

28392 *St. Andrews ghost stories.* St. Andrews, Scotland: J. & G. Innes, 1911, 80 p., cloth, coll.

LINSSEN, John

28393 *Tabitha fffoulks: a novel.* New York: Arbor House, 1978, 311 p., cloth, novel.

LINT, Charles de—SEE: De Lint, Charles

LINZNER, Gordon (Bruce), 1949-

28394 *The oni.* New York: Leisure Books, 1986, 399 p., paper, novel.

28395 *The spy who drank blood.* New York: Space & Time, 1984, 127 p., paper, novel.

28396 *The troupe.* New York, London: Pocket Books, 1988, 284 p., paper, novel.

LIPPE, Richard, *with Robin Wood*

37916 *American nightmare: essays on the horror film.* Toronto: Festival of Festivals, 1979, 99 p., paper, nonf. anth.

LIPPINCOTT, David (McCord), 1924-1984

28397 *Black prism.* London: W. H. Allen & Co., 1980, 252 p., cloth, novel.

28397A retitled: *Dark prism.* New York: A Dell Book, 1981, 299 p., paper, novel.

28398 *The blood of October.* New York: A Signet Book, New American Library, 1977, 255 p., paper, novel.
Dark prism—SEE: *Black prism.*

LIPSCOMBE, Robert, 1952-

28399 *The salamander tree.* London: Hamish Hamilton, 1990, 376 p., cloth, novel.

LIPSETT, Suzanne, 1943-

28400 *Remember me: a novel.* San Francisco: Mercury House, 1991, 143 p., cloth, novel.

LIQUORI, Sal, pseud.—SEE: Crawford, Betty Anne

LISLE, Janet Taylor, 1947-

28401 *Afternoon of the elves.* New York: Orchard Books, 1989, 122 p., cloth, novel.

28402 *The lampfish of Twill.* New York: A Richard Jackson Book, Orchard Books, 1991, x+161 p., cloth, novel.

L'ISLE ADAM, Auguste Villiers de—SEE: Villiers de L'Isle Adam, Auguste

LISSON, Deborah

28403 *The devil's own.* Australia: McVitty, 1990, [169] p., cloth, novel.

*LISTON, Edward (J.), 1900-1986

LITTELL, Jonathan, 1969?-

28404 *Bad voltage: a fantasy in 4/4.* New York: A Signet Book, New American Library, 1989, 309 p., paper, novel.

*LITTELL, Robert, 1935?-

LITTKE, Lael (J.), 1929-

28405 *Prom dress.* New York, Toronto: Scholastic Inc., 1989, 167 p., paper, novel.

LITTLE, Bentley

28406 *The mailman.* New York: An Onyx Book, 1991, 320 p., paper, novel.

28407 *The revelation.* New York: St. Martin's Press, 1989, x+289 p., cloth, novel. [Winner of the Bram Stoker Award for Best First Horror Novel, 1990 (1991)].

LITTLE, (T.) Edmund

28408 *The fantasts: studies in J. R. R. Tolkien, Lewis Carroll, Mervyn Peake, Nikolay Gogol, and Kenneth Grahame.* Amersham, England: Avebury, 1984, viii+136 p., paper, nonf.

LITTLE, P. F.—SEE: Wessex, Martyn

LITTLE, Patrick

28409 *A court for owls.* London: Macmillan, 1981, 192 p., cloth, novel.

28410 *The Hawthorne tree.* London: Macmillan, 1980, 191 p., cloth, novel.

28411 *Knight of swords.* London: Macmillan, 1982, 206 p., cloth, novel.

LITTLE, Paul H.—SEE: Minton, Paula

LITTLE, W(illiam) J(ohn) Knox, 1839-1918

37917 *The threshold of the unseen: some romances relating to the other world.* London: Hugh Rees, 1913, 580 p., cloth, coll.

LITTLEFIELD, Hazel [i.e., Hazel G. Littlefield Smith], 1931-

28412 *Lord Dunsay, king of dreams: A personal portrait.* New York: An Exposition-Banner Book, Exposition Press, 1959, 148 p., cloth, nonf.

LIVELY, Adam, 1961-

28413 *Blue fruit.* London: Simon & Schuster, 1988, [144] p., cloth, novel.
28414 *The burnt house.* London: Simon & Schuster, 1989, 264 p., cloth, novel.

LIVELY, Penelope (Margaret), 1933-

28415 *Astercote.* London: Heinemann, 1970, 156 p., cloth, novel.
15833 *The house in Norham Gardens.* London: Heinemann, 1974, 154 p., cloth, novel.
28416 *The revenge of Samuel Stokes.* London: Heinemann, 1981, 122 p., cloth, novel.
28417 *A stitch in time.* London: Heinemann, 1976, 138 p., cloth, novel.
28418 *Treasures of time.* London: Heinemann, 1979, 199 p., cloth, novel.
28419 *Uninvited ghosts, and other stories.* London: Heinemann, 1984, 119 p., cloth, coll.
28420 *The voyage of the QV66.* London: Heinemann, 1978, 172 p., cloth, novel.

LIVESEY, John

28421 *Swallow and the prince of darkness.* London: A Target Book, W. H. Allen & Co., 1986, 152 p., paper, novel.

LIVIA, Anna [pseud. of Anna Livia Julian Brawn], 1955-

28422 *Bulldozer rising.* London: Onlywomen Press, 1988, 188 p., paper, novel.
       Incidents involving mirth—SEE: *Saccharin cyanide.*
28423 *Saccharin cyanide.* London: Onlywomen Press, 1990, 146 p., paper, coll.
28423A retitled: *Incidents involving mirth: short stories.* Portland, OR: Eighth Mountain Press, 1990, 190 p., cloth, coll.

*LIVINGSTON, Berkeley, <u>1909-1975</u>

LIVINGSTON, M. Jay [i.e., Myran Jabez Livingston Jr.], 1934-

28424 *The synapse function.* New York: A Signet Book, New American Library, 1984, 334 p., paper, novel.

LIVINGSTON, Myran J.—SEE: Livingston, M. Jay

LIVINGSTONE, Ian, 1949-

28425 *Casket of souls.* Oxford, England: Oxford University Press, 1987, 32 p., cloth, story.
28426 *Caverns of the snow witch.* Harmondsworth, Middlesex, England: Puffin Books, 1984, 23+[196] p., paper, novel. FIGHTING FANTASY GAMEBOOK #9.
28427 *City of thieves.* Harmondsworth, Middlesex, England: Puffin Books, 1983, 40[200] p., paper, novel. FIGHTING FANTASY GAMEBOOK #5.
28428 *Crypt of the sorcerer.* Harmondsworth, Middlesex, England: Puffin Books, 1987, [235] p., paper, novel. FIGHTING FANTASY GAMEBOOK SERIES.
28429 *Deathtrap dungeon.* Harmondsworth, Middlesex, England: Puffin Books, 1984, [196] p., paper, fiction. FIGHTING FANTASY GAMEBOOK #6.
28430 *Dicing with dragons: an introduction to role-playing games.* London: Routledge & Kegan Paul, 1982, vii+216 p., paper, nonf.
28431 *The forest of doom.* Harmondsworth, Middlesex, England: Puffin Books, 1983, [179] p., paper, fiction. FIGHTING FANTASY GAMEBOOK #3.
28432 *Freeway fighter.* Harmondsworth, Middlesex, England: Penguin Books, 1985, [188] p., paper, novel. FIGHTING FANTASY GAMEBOOK #13.
28433 *Island of the Lizard King.* Harmondsworth, Middlesex, England: Puffin Books, 1984, [179] p., paper, novel. FIGHTING FANTASY GAMEBOOK #7.
28434 *Temple of terror.* Harmondsworth, Middlesex, England: Puffin Books, 1986, [200] p., paper, novel. FIGHTING FANTASY GAMEBOOK #14.
28435 *Trial of champions.* Harmondsworth, Middlesex, England: Puffin Books, 1986, [400] p., paper, novel. FIGHTING FANTASY GAMEBOOK #21.

with Steve Jackson (1951-)

37871 *The fighting fantasy poster book.* London: Fantail, 1990, 32 p., paper, art anth.
37872 *Titan: the fighting fantasy world.* Harmondsworth, Middlesex, England: Puffin Books, 1986, 128 p., paper, fiction. FIGHTING FANTASY GAMEBOOK TIE-IN.
26385 *The warlock of Firetop Mountain.* Harmondsworth, Middlesex, England: Puffin Books, 1982, [170] p., paper, novel. FIGHTING FANTASY GAMEBOOK #1.

with Steve Jackson (1953-)

26388 *Demons of the deep.* Harmondsworth, Middlesex, England: Puffin Books, 1986, 22+[234] p., paper, novel. FIGHTING FANTASY GAMEBOOK #19.
26389 *Robot commando.* Harmondsworth, Middlesex, England: Puffin Books, 1986, [200] p., paper, novel. FIGHTING FANTASY GAMEBOOK #22.
26390 *Scorpion swamp.* Harmondsworth, Middlesex, England: Puffin Books, 1984, [200] p., paper, novel. FIGHTING FANTASY GAMEBOOK #8.

LIVINGSTONE, Mark J., pseud.—SEE: Phillips, Michael R. & Pella, Judith

LIVONI, Cathy (Ann), 1956-

28436 *Element of time.* San Diego, CA: Harcourt Brace Jovanovich, 1983, 182 p., cloth, novel.

LJUNDQUIST, Kent (Paul), 1948-

28437 *The grand and the fair: Poe's landscape aesthetics and pictorial techniques.* Potomac, MD. Scripta Humanistica, 1985, x+216 p., cloth, nonf.

with Frederick S. Frank & Benjamin Franklin Fisher IV & Gary William Crawford

20788 *The 1980 bibliography of gothic studies.* Baton Rouge, LA: Gothic Press, 1983, ii+20 p., paper, nonf. [Limited to 275 copies].

LLEWELLYN, Edward [pseud. of Edward Llewellyn-Thomas], 1917-1984

28438 *The bright companion.* New York: DAW Books, 1980, 176 p., paper, novel. DOUGLAS CONVOLUTION #2.
28439 *The Douglas Convolution.* New York: DAW Books, 1979, 190 p., paper, novel. DOUGLAS CONVOLUTION #1.
28440 *Fugitive in transit.* New York: DAW Books, 1985, 302 p., paper, novel.
28441 *Prelude to chaos.* New York: DAW Books, 1983, 256 p., paper, novel. DOUGLAS CONVOLUTION #3.
28442 *Salvage and destroy.* New York: DAW Books, 1984, 256 p., paper, novel.
28443 *Word-Bringer.* New York: DAW Books, 1986, 222 p., paper, novel.

LLEWELLYN, J. J., *with Rupert Brown & Brian Froud*

18809 *The world of the Dark Crystal.* New York: Alfred A. Knopf, 1983, 128 p., paper, nonf.

LLEWELLYN-THOMAS, Edward—SEE: Llewellyn, Edward

LLOYD, A(lan) R., 1927-

28444 *Dragon pond.* London: Frederick Muller, 1990, 201 p., cloth, novel. KINE SAGA #3.
28445 *Kine.* Feltham, England: Hamlyn Paperbacks, 1982, 255 p., cloth, novel. KINE SAGA #1.
28445A retitled: *Marshworld.* London: Arrow Books, 1990, 255 p., paper, novel. KINE SAGA #1.
Marshworld—SEE: *Kine.*
28446 *Witchwood.* London: Frederick Muller, 1989, xii+223 p., cloth, novel. *Kine Saga #2.*

LLOYD, Caroline

28447 *Animal ghosts.* London: Armada, 1971, 128 p., paper, anth.

LLOYD, Elizabeth

28448 *Witch child.* New York: Zebra Books, Kensington Publishing Corp., 1987, 352 p., paper, novel.
28449 *Witch daughter.* New York: Zebra Books, Kensington Publishing Corp., 1988, 380 p., paper, novel.

LLOYD, J(ohn) A(rthur) T(homas), 1870-1956

28450 *The murder of Edgar Allan Poe.* London: Stanley Paul & Co., 1931, 288 p., cloth, nonf.

LLOYD, (John) Noel, *with Geoffrey Palmer*

28451 *Haunting stories of ghosts and ghouls.* London: Hamlyn, 1982, 256 p., cloth, coll.

LLOYD, Roger B(radshaigh), 1901-

28452 *The undisciplined life: an examination of Aldous Huxley's recent works.* London: Society for Promoting Christian Knowledge, 1932, 32 p., paper, nonf.

LLOYD-SMITH, Allan (Gardner), 1945-

28453 *Uncanny American fiction: Medusa's face.* Basingstoke, England: Macmillan, 1989, xii+186 p., cloth, nonf.

LLOYD WEBBER, Julian, 1951-

28454 *Short sharp shocks: masterclass of the macabre.* London: Weidenfeld & Nicolson, 1990, ix+241 p., cloth, anth.

LLYWELYN, Morgan, 1937-

28455 *Bard: the odyssey of the Irish.* Boston: Houghton Mifflin Co., 1984, 466 p., cloth, novel.
28456 *Druids.* New York: William Morrow & Co., 1991, 456 p., cloth, novel.
28457 *The horse goddess.* Boston: Houghton Mifflin Co., 1982, 417 p., cloth, novel.
28458 *The isles of the blest.* New York: Ace Books, 1989, 170 p., paper, novel.
On raven's wing—SEE: *Red branch.*
28459 *Red branch.* New York: William Morrow, 1989, 558 p., cloth, novel.
28459A retitled: *On raven's wing.* London: Heinemann, 1990, 512 p., cloth, novel.

LOBDELL, Jared (Charles), 1937-

28460 *England and always: Tolkien's world of the rings.* Grand Rapids, MI: William B. Eerdmans Publishing Co., 1981, xiv+94 p., paper, nonf.
28461 *A Tolkien compass: including J. R. R. Tolkien's Guide to the names in The Lord of the Rings.* La Salle, IL: Open Court, 1975, 201 p., cloth, nonf. anth.

LOBEL, Brana, 1942-

28462 *The revenant.* Garden City, NY: Doubleday & Co., 1979, 239 p., cloth, novel.

LoBRUTTO, Patrick

with Joe R. Lansdale

27822 *Razored saddles.* Arlington Heights, IL: Dark Harvest, 1989, 268 p., cloth, anth.

with Shawna McCarthy & Lou Aronica & Amy Stout

16798 *Full spectrum 2.* New York: A Foundation Book, Doubleday, 1989, xi+464 p., cloth, anth.

LOBSANG RAMPA, T. [pseud. of Cyril Henry Hoskin], 1911?-1981

15834 *Living with the lama* / by Mrs. Fifi Greywhiskers, P.S.C., translated from the Siamese cat language [i.e., written by] T. Lobsang Rampa. London: Corgi Books, 1964, 190 p., paper, novel.

LOCHHEAD, Marion (Cleland), 1902-1985

Renaissance of wonder—SEE: *The renaissance of wonder in children's literature.*
28463 *The renaissance of wonder in children's literature.* Edinburgh, Scotland: Canongate, 1977, xiii+169 p., cloth, nonf.
28463A retitled: *Renaissance of wonder: the fantasy worlds of C. S. Lewis, J. R. R. Tolkien, George MacDonald, E. Nesbit, and others.* San Francisco: Harper & Row, 1980, xiii+169 p., cloth, nonf.

LOCKE, Ashley, with Arthur B. Reeve

12111 *Enter Craig Kennedy.* New York: Macaulay Co., 1935, 256 p., cloth, novel. CRAIG KENNEDY #25.

LOCKE, George (Walter), 1936-

28464 *Guardians of the lilac moon; or, The downfall of Darkeevle the Dire.* London: Ferret, 1980, 16 p., paper, story.
28465 *The land of dreams: a review of the work of Sidney H. Sime.* London: Ferret Fantasy, 1975, 64 p., cloth, art.
28466 *The Pearson's weekly: a checklist of fiction, 1890-1939.* London: Ferret, 1990, 140 p., cloth, nonf. [Bound with an additional 36-, 39-, or 75-page signature (at the option of the buyer) containing samples of three different fictions originally published in *Pearson's*].
28467 *Science fiction first editions: a select bibliography and notes for the collector.* London: Ferret, 1978, 96 p., paper, nonf.
28468 *A spectrum of fantasy: the bibliography and biography of a collection of fantastic literature.* London: Ferret, 1980, vi+246 p., cloth, nonf.
28469 *Thirty years of dustwrappers, 1884-1914.* London: Ferret Fantasy, 1988, 33 p., paper, nonf.
28470 *Voyages in space: a bibliography of interplanetary fiction, 1801-1914.* London: Ferret Fantasy, 1975, 80 p., cloth, nonf.

as AYRESOME JATUES

28471 *A spectre-room of fancy.* London: Apocrypha Press, 1989, 48 p., paper, fiction.

LOCKE, Joseph, pseud.—SEE: Garton, Ray

*LOCKRIDGE, Richard (Orson), 1898-1982

LODEN, Erle van—SEE: van Loden, Erle

LOFFICIER, Jean-Marc

28473 *The Doctor Who programme guide.* London: W. H. Allen & Co., 1981, 2 v., cloth, nonf.

28474 *The Doctor Who programme guide, revised and updated edition.* London: A Target Book, W. H. Allen & Co., 1989, 177 p., paper, nonf. [Contains just the first volume of the original work].

28475 *Doctor Who: the terrestrial index.* London: A Target Book, 1991, 247 p., paper, nonf. [Originally published as volume 2 of *The Doctor Who programme guide*].

LOFTING, Hugh (John), 1886-1947

15895 *The twilight of magic.* London: Jonathan Cape, 1930, 285 p., cloth, novel.

LOFTS, Norah (Ethel Robinson), 1904-1983

09136 *Afternoon of an autocrat.* London: Michael Joseph, 1956, 351 p., cloth, novel.

09136A retitled: *The deadly gift.* New York: Pyramid Books, 1976, 317 p., paper, novel.

28476 *The claw.* London: Hodder & Stoughton, 1981, 220 p., cloth, novel.

The deadly gift—SEE: *Afternoon of an autocrat.*

28477 *Gad's Hall.* London: Hodder & Stoughton, 1977, 254 p., cloth, novel. GAD'S HALL #1.

28478 *Gad's Hall; and, The haunting of Gad's Hall.* Garden City, NY: Nelson Doubleday, 1979, 532 p., cloth, coll. GAD'S HALL #1-2.

28479 *Haunted house.* London: Hodder & Stoughton, 1978, 270 p., cloth, novel. GAD'S HALL #2.

28479A retitled: *The haunting of Gad's Hall.* Garden City, NY: Doubleday & Co., 1979, 281 p., cloth, novel. GAD'S HALL #2.

The haunting of Gad's Hall—SEE: *Haunted house.*

Hauntings—SEE: *Is there anybody there?*

09137 *Is there anybody there?* London: Corgi Books, 1974, 174 p., paper, coll.

09137A retitled: *Hauntings: is there anybody there?* Garden City, NY: Doubleday & Co., 1975, 181 p., cloth, coll.

28481A *The little wax doll.* Garden City, NY: Doubleday & Co., 1970, 306 p., cloth, novel. [Originally published as *The devil's own* under the name Peter Curtis].

28480 *The Old Priory.* London: Bodley Head, 1981, 213 p., cloth, novel.

as PETER CURTIS

28481 *The devil's own.* London: Macdonald & Co., 1960, 256 p., cloth, novel.

LOGAN, Carolyn F.

28482 *The power of the Rellard.* Sydney: Angus & Robertson, 1986, 231 p., cloth, novel.

LOGAN, Charles, 1930-

28483 *Shipwreck.* London: Victor Gollancz, 1975, 192 p., cloth, novel.

LOGAN, Les

28484 *The game.* Toronto, New York: Bantam Books, 1983, 149 p., paper, novel. DARK FORCES #1.

28485 *Unnatural talent.* Toronto, New York: Bantam Books, 1983, 166 p., paper, novel. DARK FORCES #7.

LOGAN, Nora

28486 *Dinosaur adventure.* New York, Toronto: Scholastic Inc., 1984, 58 p., paper, story. PICK-A-PATH #11.

28487 *Jungle adventure.* New York, Toronto: Scholastic Inc., 1984, 56 p., paper, story. PICK-A-PATH #9.

28488 *Murf the monster.* New York, Toronto: Scholastic Inc., 1984, 58 p., paper, story. PICK-A-PATH #17.

28489 *RIM, the rebel robot.* New York, Toronto: Scholastic Inc., 1984, 57 p., paper, story. PICK-A-PATH #14.

LOGGEM, Manuel van, 1916-

28490 *New worlds from the Lowlands: fantasy and science fiction of Dutch and Flemish writers.* Merrick, NY: Cross-Cultural Communications, 1982, 223 p., cloth, anth.

LOGSDON, Syd, 1950?-

28491   *A fond farewell to dying.* New York: A Timescape Book, Pocket Books, 1981, 206 p., paper, novel.
28492   *Jandrax.* New York: A Del Rey Book, Ballantine Books, 1979, 153 p., paper, novel.

LOGSTON, Anne

28493   *Shadow.* New York: Ace Books, 1991, 185 p., paper, novel.

LOKKE, Virgil L(lewellyn), 1915- , *with G. R. Thompson*

28494   *Ruined Eden of the present: Hawthorne, Melville, and Poe: critical essays in honor of Darrel Abel.* West Lafayette, IN: Purdue University Press, 1981, xix+383 p., cloth, nonf. anth.

LONDON, Jack [i.e., John Griffith London], 1876-1916

28495   *Curious fragments: Jack London's tales of fantasy fiction.* Port Washington, NY & London: Kennikat Press, 1975, x+223 p., cloth, coll. [Edited by Dale L. Walker].
28496   *The science fiction of Jack London: an anthology.* Boston: Gregg Press, 1975, xxiv+506 p., cloth, coll. [Edited by Richard Gid Powers].
28497   *Selected science fiction & fantasy stories.* Lakemont, GA: Fictioneer Books, 1978, 120 p., cloth, coll.

LONDON, John—SEE: London, Jack

***LONG, Charles R(ussell), 1904-<u>1978</u>**

LONG, Doug, *with Vic Mayhew*

28498   *Fireball.* Toronto, New York: Methuen, 1977, 217 p., cloth, novel.

LONG, Duncan, 1949-

28499   *Anti-Grav unlimited.* New York: Avon Books, 1988, 170 p., paper, novel.

LONG, Frank Belknap, 1903-

28500   *Autobiographical memoir.* West Warwick, RI: Necronomicon Press, 1985, 32 p., paper, nonf.
        The black druid, and other stories—SEE: *The hounds of Tindalos.*

28501   *The early Long.* Garden City, NY: Doubleday & Co., 1975, xxviii+211 p., cloth, coll.
09161   *The hounds of Tindalos.* Sauk City, WI: Arkham House, 1946, 316 p., cloth, coll.
09161B   retitled: *The black druid, and other stories.* St Albans, Hertfordshire, England: Panther, 1975, 174 p., paper, coll. [Abridged edition].
28502   *Howard Phillips Lovecraft: dreamer on the nightside.* Sauk City, WI: Arkham House, 1975, xiv+237 p., cloth, nonf.
28503   *Night fear.* New York: Zebra Books, Kensington Publishing Corp., 1979, 318 p., paper, coll. [Edited by Roy Torgeson].

as LYDA BELKNAP LONG

28504   *The witch tree.* New York: Lancer Books, 1971, 174 p., paper, novel.

with H. P. Lovecraft & A. Merritt & C. L. Moore & Robert E. Howard

        The challenge from beyond—SEE: *The illustrated challenge from beyond.*
26046   *The illustrated Challenge from beyond.* West Warwick, RI: Necronomicon Press, 1978, [26] p., paper, story.

LONG, Gabrielle—SEE: Campbell, Margaret

LONG, John Arthur

28505   *The sign of the guardian.* New York: A Tom Doherty Associates Book, Pinnacle Books, 1981, 253 p., paper, novel.

LONG, Lyda Belknap, pseud.—SEE: Long, Frank Belknap

LONGO, Chris

28506   *The last gene.* Canoga Park, CA: Major Books, 1976, 160 p., paper, novel.

LONGRIGG, Roger—SEE: Taylor, Domini

LONGSTREET, Roxanne

28507   *Stormriders: a Shadow World novel.* Charlottesville, VA: Iron Crown Enterprises, 1990, 287 p., paper, novel.

***LONGSTRETH, T(homas) Morris, 1886-<u>1975</u>**

LONGYEAR, Barry B(rookes), 1942-

28508 *Circus world*. Garden City, NY: Nelson Doubleday, 1980, 181 p., cloth, coll. CIRCUS #2.

28509 *City of Baraboo*. New York: Berkley Publishing Corp., 1980, 240 p., cloth, novel. CIRCUS #1.

28510 *Elephant song*. New York: Berkley Books, 1982, 234 p., paper, novel. CIRCUS #3.

28511 *Enemy mine*. New York: Tor SF, A Tom Doherty Associates Book, 1989, 90 p., paper, story. DRACON #1. [Bound with *Another orphan* / by John Kessel].

28512 *The God box*. New York: A Signet Book, New American Library, 1989, 235 p., paper, novel.

28513 *The homecoming*. New York: Millennium, A Byron Preiss Book, Walker & Co., 1989, 150 p., cloth, novel.

28514 *Infinity hold*. New York: Popular Library, 1989, 281 p., paper, novel.

28515 *It came from Schenectady*. New York: Bluejay Books, 1984, 346 p., cloth, coll.

28516 *Manifest destiny*. New York: Berkley Books, 1980, 245 p., paper, coll.

28517 *Naked came the robot*. New York: Popular Library, 1988, 214 p., paper, novel.

28519 *Science fiction writer's workshop—I: an introduction to fiction mechanics*. Philadelphia, PA: Owlswick Press, 1980, vi + 161 p., cloth, nonf. [Only volume published].

28520 *Sea of glass*. New York: A Bluejay Book, St. Martin's Press, 1987, 375 p., cloth, novel.

28521 *The tomorrow testament*. New York: Berkley Books, 1983, 201 p., paper, novel. DRACON #2.

with David Gerrold

23856 *Enemy mine*. New York: Charter Books, 1985, 218 p., paper, movie. DRACON #1.

LONSDALE, Pamela

28522 *Spooky: stories of the supernatural*. London: Thames Methuen, 1983, 143 p., cloth, anth.

LOOMIS, Gregg

28523 *Voodoo fury*. New York: Diamond Books, 1991, 250 p., paper, novel.

LOONEY, Jack

with Jim Razzi

28524 *The official Ghostbusters II joke, puzzle, and game book*. New York: Newmarket Press, 1989, 93 p., paper, nonf.

with Jim Razzi & Rick Brightfield

18670 *Star games: with a space adventure*. Toronto, New York: Bantam Books, 1978, 128 p., paper, nonf.

LOOSLEY, William Robert, pseud.—SEE: Langford, David

LOPES, Ignácio Brandao—SEE: Lopes, Ignácio

LOPEZ, Barry (Holstun), 1945-

28524 *Crow and Weasel*. San Francisco: North Point Press, 1990, 63 p., cloth, story.

LOPEZ, Enrique Hank, 1920-1985

28525 *The hidden magic of Uxmal*. New York: Fawcett Gold Medal, 1980, 222 p., paper, novel.

LORAINE, Philip [pseud. of Robin Estridge]

09194 *Day of the arrow*. London: Collins, 1964, 192 p., cloth, novel.

09194B retitled: *The eye of the devil*. London: Collins, Fontana Books, 1966, 192 p., paper, novel.
The eye of the devil—SEE: *Day of the arrow*.

*LORD, Beman, 1924-1991

LORD, Gabrielle (Craig), 1946-

37918 *Salt*. Ringwood, Victoria, Australia: McPhee Gribble; New York: Viking Penguin, 1990, 281 p., cloth, novel.

LORD, Glenn (Richard), 1920-

28526 *The Howard collector: by and about Robert E. Howard*. New York: Ace Books, 1979, 267 p., paper, anth. [Includes some nonf.].

28527 *The last Celt: a bio-bibliography of Robert Ervin Howard*. West Kingston, RI: Donald M. Grant, Publisher, 1976, 416 p., cloth, nonf.

with Dennis McHaney

28528 *Fiction of Robert E. Howard: a pocket checklist.* [S.l.]: Dennis McHaney & T. Foster, 1975, [22] p., paper, nonf.

LORD, Graham (John), 1943-

28529 *God and all his angels.* London: Hamilton, 1976, 216 p., cloth, novel.

LORD, J. Edward

28530 *Elixir.* New York: Ballantine Books, 1987, 305 p., paper, novel.

28531 *Incantation.* New York: Ballantine Books, 1987, 281 p., paper, novel.

28532 *Mandrake.* New York: Ballantine Books, 1990, 241 p., paper, novel.

28533 *Upright man.* New York: Ballantine Books, 1989, 258 p., paper, novel.

LORD, Jeffrey, house pseud.

24441 *Blade: Champion of the gods.* New York: Pinnacle Books, 1976, 183 p., paper, novel. RICHARD BLADE #21. [By Roland Green].

24442 *Blade: City of the living dead.* Los Angeles: Pinnacle Books, 1978, 185 p., paper, novel. RICHARD BLADE #26. [By Roland Green].

24443 *Blade: Empire of blood.* New York: Pinnacle Books, 1977, 196 p., paper, novel. RICHARD BLADE #23. [By Roland Green].

24444 *Blade: Guardians of the coral throne.* New York: Pinnacle Books, 1976, 182 p., paper, novel. RICHARD BLADE #20. [By Roland Green].

24445 *Blade: Looters of Tharn.* New York: Pinnacle Books, 1976, 184 p., paper, novel. RICHARD BLADE #19. [By Roland Green].

24446 *Blade: The crystal seas.* New York: Pinnacle Books, 1975, 184 p., paper, novel. RICHARD BLADE #16. [By Roland Green].

24447 *Blade: The forests of Gleor.* New York: Pinnacle Books, 1977, 186 p., paper, novel. RICHARD BLADE #22. [By Roland Green].

24448 *Blade: The mountains of Brega.* New York: Pinnacle Books, 1976, 184 p., paper, novel. RICHARD BLADE #17. [By Roland Green].

24449 *Blade: The Torian pearls.* Los Angeles: Pinnacle Books, 1977, 186 p., paper, novel. RICHARD BLADE #25. [By Roland Green].

24450 *Blade: The towers of Melnon.* New York: Pinnacle Books, 1975, 183 p., paper, novel. RICHARD BLADE #15. [By Roland Green].

24451 *Blade: Warlords of Gaikon.* New York: Pinnacle Books, 1976, 185 p., paper, novel. RICHARD BLADE #18. [By Roland Green].

09198 *The bronze axe.* New York: Macfadden-Bartell, 1969, 191 p., paper, novel. RICHARD BLADE #1. [By Manning Lee Stokes].

Champion of the gods—SEE: *BLADE: CHAMPION OF THE GODS.*

City of the living dead—SEE: *Blade: City of the living dead.*

The crystal seas—SEE: *Blade: The crystal seas.*

06298 *Dimension of dreams.* New York: Pinnacle Books, 1974, 181 p., paper, novel. RICHARD BLADE #11. [By Roland Green].

Dimension of horror—SEE: *Richard Blade: Dimension of horror.*

The dragons of Englor—SEE: *Richard Blade: The dragons of Englor.*

Empire of blood—SEE: *Blade: Empire of blood.*

The forests of Gleor—SEE: *Blade: The forests of Gleor.*

Gladiators of Hapanu—SEE: *Richard Blade: Gladiators of Hapanu.*

The golden steed—SEE: *Richard Blade: The golden steed.*

Guardians of the coral throne—SEE: *Blade: Guardians of the coral throne.*

06299 *Ice dragon: the Richard Blade series.* New York: Pinnacle Books, 1974, 183 p., paper, novel. RICHARD BLADE #10. [By Roland Green].

09199 *The jade warrior.* New York: Macfadden-Bartell, 1969, 192 p., paper, novel. RICHARD BLADE #2. [By Manning Lee Stokes].

09200 *Jewel of Tharn.* New York: Macfadden-Bartell, 1969, 160 p., paper, novel. RICHARD BLADE #3. [By Manning Lee Stokes].

Killer plants of Binaark—SEE: *Richard Blade: Killer plants of Binaark.*

King of Zunga—SEE: *Richard Blade: King of Zunga.*

06300 *Kingdom of Royth: the Richard Blade series.* New York: Pinnacle Books, 1974, 188 p., paper, novel. RICHARD BLADE #9. [By Roland Green].

09201 *Liberator of Jedd.* New York: Macfadden-Bartell, 1971, 224 p., paper, novel. RICHARD BLADE #5. [By Manning Lee Stokes].

Looters of Tharn—SEE: *Blade: Looters of Tharn*.

The Lords of the Crimson River—SEE: *Richard Blade: The Lords of the Crimson River*.

Master of the Hashomi—SEE: *Richard Blade: Master of the Hashomi*.

09202 *Monster of the maze*. New York: Macfadden-Bartell, 1972, 192 p., paper, novel. RICHARD BLADE #6. [By Manning Lee Stokes].

The mountains of Brega—SEE: *Blade: The mountains of Brega*.

09203 *Pearl of Patmos: the Richard Blade series*. New York: Pinnacle Books, 1973, 190 p., paper, novel. RICHARD BLADE #7. [By Manning Lee Stokes].

Pirates of Gohar—SEE: *Richard Blade: Pirates of Gohar*.

Return to Kaldak—SEE: *Richard Blade: Return to Kaldak*.

28534 *Richard Blade: Dimension of horror*. Los Angeles: Pinnacle Books, 1979, 174 p., paper, novel. RICHARD BLADE #30. [By Ray Nelson].

24452 *Richard Blade: Gladiators of Hapanu*. Los Angeles: Pinnacle Books, 1979, 187 p., paper, novel. RICHARD BLADE #31. [By Roland Green].

24453 *Richard Blade: Killer plants of Binaark*. Los Angeles: Pinnacle Books, 1980, 187 p., paper, novel. RICHARD BLADE #33. [By Roland Green].

24454 *Richard Blade: King of Zunga*. New York: Pinnacle Books, 1975, 181 p., paper, novel. RICHARD BLADE #12. [By Roland Green].

24455 *Richard Blade: Master of the Hashomi*. Los Angeles: Pinnacle Books, 1978, 182 p., paper, novel. RICHARD BLADE #27. [By Roland Green].

24456 *Richard Blade: Pirates of Gohar*. Los Angeles: Pinnacle Books, 1979, 181 p., paper, novel. RICHARD BLADE #32. [By Roland Green].

24457 *Richard Blade: Return to Kaldak*. New York: Pinnacle Books, 1983, 216 p., paper, novel. RICHARD BLADE #36. [By Roland Green].

24458 *Richard Blade: The dragons of Englor*. New York: Pinnacle Books, 1977, 182 p., paper, novel. RICHARD BLADE #24. [By Roland Green].

24459 *Richard Blade: The golden steed*. New York: Pinnacle Books, 1975, 182 p., paper, novel. RICHARD BLADE #13. [By Roland Green].

24460 *Richard Blade: The Lords of the Crimson River*. New York: Pinnacle Books, 1981, 182 p., paper, novel. RICHARD BLADE #35. [By Roland Green].

24461 *Richard Blade: The ruins of Kaldac*. New York: Pinnacle Books, 1981, 182 p., paper, novel. RICHARD BLADE #34. [By Roland Green].

24462 *Richard Blade: The temples of Ayocan*. New York: Pinnacle Books, 1975, 182 p., paper, novel. RICHARD BLADE #14. [By Roland Green].

24463 *Richard Blade: Treasure of the stars*. Los Angeles: Pinnacle Books, 1978, 183 p., paper, novel. RICHARD BLADE #29. [By Roland Green].

24464 *Richard Blade: Warriors of Latan*. New York: Pinnacle Books, 1984, 218 p., paper, novel. RICHARD BLADE #37. [By Roland Green].

24465 *Richard Blade: Wizard of Rentoro*. Los Angeles: Pinnacle Books, 1978, 185 p., paper, novel. RICHARD BLADE #28. [By Roland Green].

The ruins of Kaldac—SEE: *Richard Blade: The ruins of Kaldac*.

09204 *Slave of Sarma*. New York: Macfadden-Bartell, 1970, 192 p., paper, novel. RICHARD BLADE #4. [By Manning Lee Stokes].

The temples of Ayocan—SEE: *Richard Blade: The temples of Ayocan*.

The Torian pearls—SEE: *Blade: The Torian pearls*.

The towers of Melnon—SEE: *Blade: The towers of Melnon*.

Treasure of the stars—SEE: *Richard Blade: Treasure of the stars*.

09205 *Undying world*. New York: Pinnacle Books, 1973, 189 p., paper, novel. RICHARD BLADE #8. [By Manning Lee Stokes].

Warlords of Gaikon—SEE: *Blade: Warlords of Gaikon*.

Warriors of Latan—SEE: *Richard Blade: Warriors of Latan*.

Wizard of Rentoro—SEE: *Richard Blade: Wizard of Rentoro*.

LORE, Elana [pseud. of Eleanor Sullivan?]

28535 *Alfred Hitchcock's A choice of evils*. New York: Dial Press, Davis Publications, 1983, 348 p., cloth, anth.

28536 *Alfred Hitchcock's Fatal attractions*. New York: Dial Press, Davis Publications, 1983, 348 p., cloth, anth.

A choice of evils—SEE: *Alfred Hitchcock's A choice of evils*.

Fatal attractions—SEE: *Alfred Hitchcock's Fatal attractions*.

*LORING, Ann, <u>1915-</u>

LORNE, David [pseud. of David Lorne Hoof], 1945-

28537 *The last prisoner.* New York: Avon Books, 1991, 280 p., paper, novel.

LORNQUEST, Olaf [pseud. of Ervine Milton Rips], 1921-

28538 *The moonlovers.* New York: Pinnacle Books, 1975, 162 p., paper, novel.

LORRAH, Jean, 1938?-

28539 *Ambrov Keon: a Sime/Gen novel.* New York: DAW Books, 1986, 256 p., paper, novel. SIME/GEN #7.
28540 *Captives of the Savage Empire.* New York: Berkley Books, 1984, 210 p., paper, novel. SAVAGE EMPIRE #3.
28541 *Dragon Lord of the Savage Empire.* New York: Playboy Paperbacks, 1982, 221 p., paper, novel. SAVAGE EMPIRE #2.
28542 *Empress unborn: a tale of the Savage Empire.* New York: A Signet Book, New American Library, 1988, 206 p., paper, novel. SAVAGE EMPIRE #7.
28543 *Epilogue, part 1.* Murray, KY: Sol Plus Special Edition, Empire Books, 1979, 79 p., paper, novel. STAR TREK SERIES.
28544 *Epilogue, part 2.* Murray, KY: Sol Plus Special Edition, Empire Books, 1979, 131 p., paper, novel. STAR TREK SERIES.
28545 *Full moon rising.* Bronx, NY: Yeoman Press, 1976, 97 p., paper, coll. STAR TREK SERIES.
28546 *The IDIC epidemic: a Star Trek novel.* New York, London: Pocket Books, 1988, 278 p., paper, novel. STAR TREK #38.
28547 *Jean Lorrah's Sarek collection.* Murray, KY: Empire Books, 1980?, p., paper, coll. STAR TREK SERIES.
 Metamorphosis—SEE: *Star Trek, the next generation: Metamorphosis.*
28548 *The night of the twin moons.* Murray, KY: Creative Printers, 1976, iv+158 p., paper, novel. STAR TREK SERIES.
 Sarek collection—SEE: *Jean Lorrah's Sarek collection.*
28549 *Savage Empire.* New York: Playboy Paperbacks, 1981, 224 p., paper, novel. SAVAGE EMPIRE #1.
28550 *Sorcerers of the frozen isles: a tale of the Savage Empire.* New York: A Signet Book, New American Library, 1986, 238 p., paper, novel. SAVAGE EMPIRE #5.

28551 *Star Trek, the next generation: Metamorphosis.* New York, London: Pocket Books, 1990, viii+371 p., paper, novel. STAR TREK: THE NEXT GENERATION (UNNUMBERED).
28552 *Survivors.* New York, London: Pocket Books, 1989, 253 p., paper, novel. STAR TREK: THE NEXT GENERATION #4.
28553 *The Vulcan Academy murders: a Star Trek novel.* New York: Pocket Books, 1984, 280 p., paper, novel. STAR TREK #20.

with Winston A. Howlett

26070 *Flight to the Savage Empire.* New York: A Signet Book, New American Library, 1986, 221 p., paper, novel. SAVAGE EMPIRE #4.
26071 *Wulfston's odyssey.* New York: A Signet Book, New American Library, 1987, 206 p., paper, novel. SAVAGE EMPIRE #6.

with Jacqueline Lichtenberg

28337 *Channel's destiny.* Garden City, NY: Doubleday & Co., 1982, 182 p., cloth, novel. SIME/GEN #5.
28338 *First channel.* Garden City, NY: Doubleday & Co., 1980, vi+310 p., cloth, novel. SIME/GEN #3.
28339 *Zelerod's doom: a Sime/Gen novel.* New York: DAW Books, 1986, 277 p., paper, novel. SIME/GEN #8.

*LORRAINE, Lilith [pseud. of Mary <u>Maude Dunn</u> Wright], 1894-<u>1967</u>

LORTIE, Alain—SEE: Sernine, Daniel

LORTZ, Richard, 1917-1980

28554 *Bereavements.* Sagaponack, NY: The Permanent Press, 1980, 215 p., cloth, novel.
28555 *Children of the night.* New York: A Dell Book, 1974, 160 p., paper, novel.
28555A retitled: *Dracula's children.* Sagaponack, NY: The Permanent Press; London: J. Landesman, 1981, 202 p., cloth, novel.
 Dracula's children—SEE: *Children of the night.*
28556 *Lovers living, lovers dead.* New York: G. P. Putnam's Sons, 1977, 223 p., cloth, novel.

LORY, Robert (Edward), 1936-

28557 *Boris Karloff presents More tales of the frightened.* New York: Pyramid Books, 1975, 126 p., paper, coll.

28558 *Challenge to Dracula.* New York: Pinnacle Books, 1975, 180 p., paper, novel. DRACULA HORROR SERIES #9.

28559 *Dracula's disciple.* New York: Pinnacle Books, 1975, 179 p., paper, novel. DRACULA HORROR SERIES #8.

28560 *Gemini smile, Gemini kill.* New York: Pinnacle Books, 1975, 183 p., paper, novel. HORRORSCOPE #4.

More tales of the frightened—SEE: *Boris Karloff presents: More tales of the frightened.*

*LOTHAR, Ernst, <u>1890-1974</u>

LOTTMAN, Eileen, 1927-

28562 *The bionic woman: Extracurricular activities.* New York: A Berkley Medallion Book, Berkley Publishing Corp., 1977, 186 p., paper, tele. BIONIC WOMAN #2.

28563 *The bionic woman: Welcome home, Jaime: a novel.* New York: A Berkley Medallion Book, Berkley Publishing Corp., 1976, 153 p., paper, tele. BIONIC WOMAN #1.

Extracurricular activities—SEE: *The bionic woman: Extracurricular activities.*

Welcome home, Jaime—SEE: *The bionic woman: Welcome home, Jaime.*

as MOLLY FLUTE

28564 *Through the looking glass.* New York: A Dell Book, 1976, 220 p., paper, movie.

as MAUD WILLIS

28562A *The bionic woman: A question of life.* London: A Star Book, W. H. Allen & Co., 1977, 158 p., paper, tele. BIONIC WOMAN #2. [Previously published under the title *Extracurricular activities* / by Eileen Lottman].

28563A *The bionic woman: Double identity.* London: A Star Book, Wyndham Publications, 1976, 123 p., paper, tele. BIONIC WOMAN #1. [Previously published under the title *Welcome home, Jaime* / by Eileen Lottman].

28565 *The devil's rain.* New York: A Dell Book, 1975, 171 p., paper, movie.

Double identity—SEE: *The bionic woman: Double identity.*

A question of life—SEE: *The bionic woman: A question of life.*

LOUDERBACK, Lew, as NICK CARTER

36631 *Operation Moon Rocket.* New York: Award Books; London: Tandem Books, 1968, 160 p., paper, novel. NICK CARTER SERIES.

LOURIE, Richard, 1940-

28566 *Zero gravity: a novel.* San Diego, CA: Harcourt Brace Jovanovich, 1987, 284 p., cloth, novel.

LOUVISH, Simon, 1947-

28567 *The therapy of Avram Blok: the phantasm of Israel among nations.* London: Heinemann, 1985, 327 p., cloth, novel.

LOVE, E. M.

28568 *Dress up.* New York: Leisure Books, 1988, 366 p., paper, novel.

*LOVE, Edmund G(eorge), 1912-<u>1990</u>

LOVE, G(ordon) B., 1939- , *with Walter Irwin*

26337 *The best of the best of Trek: from the magazine for Star Trek fans.* New York: A Roc Book, 1990, xii + 369 p., paper, nonf. anth.

26338 *The best of Trek: from the magazine for Star Trek fans.* New York: A Signet Book, New American Library, 1978, xii+239 p., paper, nonf. anth.

26339 *The best of Trek #2: from the magazine for Star Trek fans.* New York: A Signet Book, New American Library, 1980, 196 p., paper, nonf. anth.

26340 *The best of Trek #3: from the magazine for Star Trek fans.* New York: A Signet Book, New American Library, 1981, 196 p., paper, nonf. anth.

26341 *The best of Trek #4: from the magazine for Star Trek fans.* New York: A Signet Book, New American Library, 1981, 215 p., paper, nonf. anth.

26342 *The best of Trek #5: from the magazine for Star Trek fans.* New York: A Signet Book, New American Library, 1982, 202 p., paper, nonf. anth.

26343 *The best of Trek #6: from the magazine for Star Trek fans.* New York: A Signet Book, New American Library, 1983, 191 p., paper, nonf. anth.

26344 *The best of Trek #7: from the magazine for Star Trek fans.* New York: A Signet Book, New American Library, 1984, 205 p., paper, nonf. anth.

26345 *The best of Trek #8: from the magazine for Star Trek fans.* New York: A Signet

Book, New American Library, 1985, 221 p., paper, nonf. anth.

26346 *The best of Trek #9: from the magazine for Star Trek fans.* New York: A Signet Book, New American Library, 1985, 207 p., paper, nonf. anth.

26347 *The best of Trek #10: from the magazine for Star Trek fans.* New York: A Signet Book, New American Library, 1986, 204 p., paper, nonf. anth.

26348 *The best of Trek #11: featuring a complete guide to the original episodes: from the magazine for Star Trek fans.* New York: A Signet Book, New American Library, 1986, 204 p., paper, nonf. anth.

26349 *The best of Trek #12: from the magazine for Star Trek fans.* New York: A Signet Book, 1987, 206 p., paper, nonf. anth.

26350 *The best of Trek #13: a brand new collection for Star Trek fans.* New York: A Signet Book, 1988, 204 p., paper, nonf. anth.

26351 *The best of Trek #14: from the magazine for Star Trek fans.* New York: A Signet Book, 1988, 220 p., paper, nonf. anth.

26352 *The best of Trek #15.* New York: A Roc Book, 1990, 207 p., paper, nonf. anth.

26353 *The best of Trek #16.* New York: A Roc Book, 1991, 208 p., paper, nonf. anth.

LOVE, Rosaleen (Lucille), 1940-

28569 *The total devotion machine, and other stories.* London: The Women's Press, 1989, 167 p., paper, coll.

LOVECRAFT, H(oward) P(hillips), 1890-1937

28570 *At the mountains of madness.* West Kingston, RI: Donald M. Grant, Publisher, 1990, 95 p., cloth, story.

The best of H. P. Lovecraft—SEE: *The Dunwich horror, and others.*

28571 *The Californian, 1934-1938.* West Warwick, RI: Necronomicon Press, 1977, 67 leaves, paper, coll.

28572 *The colour out of space.* West Warwick, RI: Necronomicon Press, 1982, [11] p., paper, story.

28573 *The Conservative complete, 1915-1923.* West Warwick, RI: Necronomicon Press, 1977, [124] leaves, paper, anth.

09245 *The Dunwich horror, and others: the best supernatural stories of H. P. Lovecraft.* Sauk City, WI: Arkham House, 1963, 431 p., cloth, coll.

09245B retitled: *The best of H. P. Lovecraft: bloodcurdling tales of horror and the macabre.* New York: A Del Rey Book, Ballantine Books, 1982, 375 p., paper, coll.

28574 *Ex oblivione.* [Glendale, CA]: Miskatonic Edition [i.e., Roy A. Squires], 1969, [9] p., paper, story.

28575 *Four prose poems.* West Warwick, RI: Necronomicon Press, 1990, [14] p., paper, nonf. coll.

28576 *H. P. Lovecraft Christmas book.* West Warwick, RI: Necronomicon Press, 1984, [6] p., paper, story.

28577 *H. P. Lovecraft: commonplace book.* West Warwick, RI: Necronomicon Press, 1987, 81 p. in 2 v., paper, nonf. coll.

28578 *H. P. Lovecraft in "The Eyrie".* West Warwick, RI: Necronomicon Press, 1979, 82 p., paper, nonf. coll. [Edited by S. T. Joshi & Marc A. Michaud].

28579 *H. P. Lovecraft juvenilia, 1895-1905.* West Warwick, RI: Necronomicon Press, 1984, 40 p., paper, coll.

28580 *H. P. Lovecraft writings in the United amateur, 1915-1925.* West Warwick, RI: Necronomicon Press, 1976, 146 p., paper, coll. [Edited by Marc A. Michaud].

28581 *H. P. Lovecraft's Waste paper: a facsimile and transcript of the original draft.* Providence, RI: Brown University, 1979, p. 31-52, paper, story?.

28583 *Herbert West, the reanimator: a short novel.* West Warwick, RI: Necronomicon Press, 1977, 45 p., paper, story.

28583A retitled: *Herbert West, reanimator.* West Warwick, RI: Necronomicon Press, 1985, [31] p., paper, story.

28584 *The history of the Necronomicon.* Oakman, AL: Rebel Press, 1938, 4 p., paper, nonf.

28585 *Looking backward.* West Warwick, RI: Necronomicon Press, 1980, [18] p., paper, nonf.

28586 *The lurking fear.* West Warwick, RI: Necronomicon Press, 1977, [34] p., paper, story.

28587 *Medusa: a portrait.* New York: Oliphant Press, 1975, [5] p., paper, story.

28588 *Memoirs of an inconsequential scribbler.* West Warwick, RI: Necronomicon Press, 1977?, [8] p., paper, nonf.

28589 *Memory.* [Glendale, CA]: Miskatonic Edition [i.e., Roy A. Squires], 1969, [8] p., paper, story.

28590 *The notes & commonplace book employed by the late H. P. Lovecraft, his suggestions for story-writing, analyses of the weird story, and a list of certain basic underlying horrors, & c., & c., designed to stimulate the imagination.* West Warwick, RI: Necronomicon Press, 1978, 45 p., paper, nonf. coll.

28591 *Nyarlathotep.* [Glendale, CA]: Miskatonic Edition [i.e., Roy A. Squires], 1970, [13] p., paper, story.

28592 *The occult Lovecraft.* Saddle River, NJ: Gerry de la Ree, 1975, 40 p., paper, nonf. coll. [Includes commentary by others].

28593 *Re-animator: tales of Herbert West.* Westlake Village, CA: Malibu, 1991, 48 p., paper?, coll. [Edited by Steven Philip Jones].

28594 *Selected letters, volume four, 1932-1934.* Sauk City, WI: Arkham House, 1976, xxxii+424 p., cloth, nonf. coll. [Edited by August Derleth and James Turner].

28595 *Selected letters, volume five, 1934-1937.* Sauk City, WI: Arkham House, 1976, xxxvii+436 p., cloth, nonf. coll. [Edited by Donald Wandrei and James Turner].

28596 *The statement of Randolph Carter: being both the original holograph version and its transcription.* [S.l.]: The Strange Company, 1976, [22] leaves, paper, story.

28597 *To Quebec and the stars.* West Kingston, RI: Donald M. Grant, Publisher, 1976, 318 p., cloth, nonf. coll.

28598 *Uncollected letters.* West Warwick, RI: Necronomicon Press, 1986, iv+47 p., paper, nonf. coll.

28599 *Uncollected prose and poetry.* West Warwick, RI: Necronomicon Press, 1978, vii+80 p., paper, coll. [Includes some nonfiction and verse; edited by S. T. Joshi & Marc A. Michaud].

28600 *Uncollected poetry and prose II.* West Warwick, RI: Necronomicon Press, 1980, vii+51 p., paper, coll. [Includes some verse].
   Waste paper—SEE: H. P. Lovecraft's Waste paper: a facsimile and transcript of the original draft.

28601 *What the Moon brings.* [Glendale, CA]: Miskatonic Edition [i.e., Roy A. Squires], 1970, [12] p., paper, story.

28602 *Writings in the Tryout, including A winter wish, The rutted road, Old Christmas, The wood, The tree.* West Warwick, RI: Necronomicon Press, 1977, 59 p., paper, coll.

with Forrest J Ackerman & Clark Ashton Smith & others

15943 *The boiling point.* West Warwick, RI: Necronomicon Press, 1985, [9] p., paper, nonf.

with R. H. Barlow

17405 *Collapsing cosmoses.* West Warwick, RI: Necronomicon Press, 1977?, [7] p., paper, story.

17406 *The night ocean.* West Warwick, RI: Necronomicon Press, 1982, [23] p., paper, story.

with Willis Conover

20404 *Lovecraft at last.* Arlington, VA: Carrollton Clark, 1975, xxii+272 p., cloth, nonf. coll.

with Nils Helmer Frome

23558 *Howard Phillips Lovecraft and Nils Helmer Frome: a recollection of one of Canada's earliest science fiction fans.* Glenview, IL: Moshassuck Press, 1989, 167 leaves, spiral-bound paper, nonf. coll. [Limited to 110 copies; edited by Sam Moskowitz].

with Henry Kuttner

27633 *H. P. Lovecraft letters to Henry Kuttner.* West Warwick, RI: Necronomicon Press, 1990, 32 p., paper, nonf. coll. [Edited by David E. Schultz & S. T. Joshi].

with A. Merritt & C. L. Moore & Robert E. Howard & Frank Belknap Long

   Challenge from beyond—SEE: The illustrated Challenge from beyond.

26046 *The illustrated Challenge from beyond.* West Warwick, RI: Necronomicon Press, 1978, [26] p., paper, story.

with Clark Ashton Smith

28603 *Letters to H. P. Lovecraft.* West Warwick, RI: Necronomicon Press, 1987, 68 p., paper, nonf. coll. [Edited by Steve Behrends].

with others

09267 *The horror in the museum, and other revisions.* Sauk City, WI: Arkham House, 1970, 383 p., cloth, coll.

09267A retitled: *The horror in the burying ground, and other tales.* St Albans, Hertfordshire, England: Panther, 1975, 211 p., paper, coll. [Abridged edition].

28604 *The horror in the museum, and other revisions, rev. ed.* Sauk City, WI: Arkham House Publishers, 1989, xiii+450 p., cloth, coll. [Stories have been added and removed from the 1970 edition (see #09267); edited by S. T. Joshi].

28605 *The vivisector.* West Warwick, RI: Necronomicon Press, 1990, 13 p., paper, story.

LOVECRAFT, Linda, pseud.—SEE: Parry, Michel

LOVECRAFT, Sonia—SEE: Davis, Sonia H.

LOVEGROVE, James

28606 *The hope.* London: Macmillan, 1990, 232 p., cloth, novel.

LOVEJOY, Jack, 1937-

28607 *The brotherhood of Diablo.* New York: Tor SF, A Tom Doherty Associates Book, 1985, 285 p., paper, novel. VISION OF BEASTS #3.

28608 *Creation descending.* New York: Tor, A Tom Doherty Associates Book, 1984, 222 p., paper, novel. VISION OF BEASTS #1.

28609 *Defenders of Ar.* New York, Toronto: Spectra, Bantam Books, 1990, 311 p., paper, novel. GUARDIANS OF THE THREE #4.

28610 *The hunters.* New York: Tor, A Tom Doherty Associates Book, 1982, 256 p., paper, novel.

28611 *Magus Rex.* New York: A Tom Doherty Associates Book, 1983, 313 p., paper, novel.

28612 *The rebel witch.* New York: Lothrop, Lee & Shepard, 1978, 251 p., cloth, novel.

28613 *The second kingdom.* New York: Tor, A Tom Doherty Associates Book, 1984, 252 p., paper, novel. VISION OF BEASTS #2.

28614 *Star gods.* Canoga Park, CA: Major Books, 1978 (i.e., 1979?), 205 p., paper, novel.

LOVEJOY, William H.

28615 *Black sky.* New York: Zebra Books, Kensington Publishing Corp., 1990, 384 p., paper, novel.

28616 *Seaghost* / by William Lovejoy. New York: Avon Books, 1991, 248 p., paper, novel.

LOVELL, Marc [pseud. of Mark McShane], 1930-

09269 *An enquiry into the existence of vampires.* Garden City, NY: Doubleday & Co., 1974, 181 p., cloth, novel.

09269A retitled: *Vampire in the shadows.* London: Robert Hale, 1976, 181 p., cloth, novel.

28617 *Hand over the mind.* Garden City, NY: Published for the Crime Club by Doubleday & Co., 1979, xii+179 p., cloth, novel.

Vampire in the shadows—SEE: An enquiry into the existence of vampires.

LOVELOCK, James (Ephraim), 1919- , *with Michael Allaby*

16274 *The greening of Mars.* London: André Deutsch, 1984, 165 p., cloth, novel.

LOVEMAN, Samuel, 1885-1976, *with Don Bregenzer*

18570 *A round-table in Poictesme.* Cleveland, OH: Privately Printed by Members of the Colophon Club, 1924, xi+126 p., cloth, nonf. anth.

LOVESEY, Andrew, 1941-

28618 *The half-angels.* London: Sphere Books, 1975, 159 p., paper, novel.

LOVESEY, Peter—SEE: Lear, Peter

LOVIN, Roger (Robert), 1941-

28619 *Apostle.* Norfolk, VA: Starblaze Editions/Donning, 1978, 167 p., paper, novel.

as RODGERS CLEMENS

28620 *The presence.* Greenwich, CT: A Fawcett Gold Medal Book, Fawcett Publications, 1977, 253 p., paper, novel.

LOVISI, Gary (Anthony), 1952-

28621 *The gargoyle.* Brooklyn, NY: Gryphon Publications, 1988, 55 p., paper, coll.

28622 *The saga of Filster Stein.* Brooklyn, NY: Gryphon Publications, 1988, 45 p., paper, story.

28623 *Science fiction detective tales.* Brooklyn, NY: Gryphon Books, 1986, 107 p., paper, nonf.

LOVITT, Chip

28624 *Ghostbusters book of movie madness.* New York, Toronto: Scholastic Inc., 1985, 62 p., paper, nonf.

28625 *The Knight Rider album.* New York, Toronto: Scholastic Inc., 1984, 38 p., paper, nonf.

LOW, Alice, 1926-

28626 *Genie and the witch's spells.* New York: Alfred A. Knopf, 1982, 107 p., cloth, novel.

LOWDER, Chris—SEE: Adrian, Jack

LOWDER, James

Crusade—SEE: *Forgotten realms fantasy adventure: Crusade.*

28627 *Forgotten realms fantasy adventure: Crusade.* Lake Geneva, WI: TSR Inc., 1991, 313 p., paper, novel. EMPIRES TRILOGY #3.

28628 *Knight of the black rose.* Lake Geneva, WI: TSR Inc., 1991, 313 p., paper, novel. RAVENLOFT #2.

with James Ciencin as RICHARD AWLINSON

17145 *Forgotten realms fantasy adventure: Tantras.* Lake Geneva, WI: TSR Inc., 1989, 338 p., paper, novel. AVATAR TRILOGY #2.

Tantras—SEE: *Forgotten realms fantasy adventure: Tantras.*

LOWE, Mary P.—SEE: Adams, Jack

LOWE, Steve(n), 1946?-

28629 *Aurora.* New York: Dodd, Mead & Co., 1985, 260 p., cloth, novel.

LOWENTHAL, Mark M(artin)

28630 *Crispan Magicker.* New York: Avon, 1979, 310 p., paper, novel.

LOWENTROUT, Christine—SEE: Smith, Sherwood

LOWERY, Linda

28631 *Moon dragon summer.* Lake Geneva, WI: TSR Inc., 1984, 157 p., paper, novel. HEARTQUEST #5.

28632 *Secret sorcerers.* Lake Geneva, WI: TSR Inc., 1983, 157 p., paper, novel. HEARTQUEST #3.

28633 *Spell of the winter wizard.* Lake Geneva, WI: TSR Inc., 1983, 156 p., paper, novel. ENDLESS QUEST #11.

LOY, Rosetta, 1931-

28634 *The dust roads of Monferrato.* London: Collins, 1990, 249 p., cloth, novel. [Translation by William Weaver of *Le strade di polvere*].

LUARD, Nicholas (Lambert), 1937-

28635 *Gondar.* London: Century, 1988, 638 p., cloth, novel.

28636 *Kala.* London: Century, 1990, 479 p., cloth, novel.

LUBBOCK, S(amuel) G(urney), *with A. F. Scholfield*

37919 *A memoir of Montague Rhodes James, with a list of his writings.* Cambridge, England: At the University Press, 1939, 86 p., paper, nonf.

LUCANIO, Patrick (Joseph), 1949-

28637 *Them or us: archetypal interpretations of fifties alien invasion films.* Bloomington, IN: Indiana University Press, 1987, x+194 p., cloth, nonf.

LUCAROTTI, John

The Aztecs—SEE: *Doctor Who: The Aztecs.*

28638 *Doctor Who: Marco Polo.* London: W. H. Allen & Co., 1984, 144 p., cloth, tele. DOCTOR WHO #94.

28639 *Doctor Who: The Aztecs.* London: W. H. Allen & Co., 1984, 121 p., cloth, tele. DOCTOR WHO #88.

28640 *Doctor Who: The massacre.* London: W. H. Allen & Co., 1987, 144 p., cloth, tele. DOCTOR WHO #122.

Marco Polo—SEE: *Doctor Who: Marco Polo.*

The massacre—SEE: *Doctor Who: The massacre.*

LUCAS, E(dward) V(errall), 1868-1938, *as* E. D. WARD

14875 *Sir Pulteney: a fantasy.* London: Methuen, 1910, 95 p., cloth, story.

LUCAS, F(rank) L(aurence), 1894-1967

37920 *The woman clothed with the sun, and other stories.* London: Cassell, 1937, 344 p., cloth, coll.

LUCAS, George (Walton Jr.), 1944-

28641 *Star wars: from the adventures of Luke Skywalker.* New York: Ballantine Books, 1976, 220 p., paper, movie. STAR WARS #1. [Attributed to Alan Dean Foster as anonymous co-author].

with James Kahn & Donald F. Glut

24029 *The Star Wars trilogy.* New York: A Del Rey Book, Ballantine Books, 1987, 471 p., paper, anth.

LUCAS, Penelope

28642 *Wilderness moon.* London: Bantam Press, 1991, 396 p., cloth, novel.

LUCAS, Tim

28643 *Your movie guide to horror video tapes and discs.* New York: Signet Books, New American Library, 1985, 128 p., paper, nonf.
28644 *Your movie guide to science fiction/fantasy video tapes and discs.* New York: Signet Books, New American Library, 1985, 128 p., paper, nonf.

LUCENO, James

28645 *A fearful symmetry.* New York: A Del Rey Book, Ballantine Books, 1989, 265 p., paper, novel.
28646 *Illegal alien.* New York: A Del Rey Book, Ballantine Books, 1990, 245 p., paper, novel.

with Brian Daley as JACK MCKINNEY

21001 *Artifact of the system.* New York: A Del Rey Book, Ballantine Books, 1991, 281 p., paper, novel. BLACK HOLE TRAVEL AGENCY #2.
21002 *Battle cry.* New York: A Del Rey Book, Ballantine Books, 1987, 216 p., paper, tele. ROBOTECH #2.
21003 *Battlehymn.* New York: A Del Rey Book, Ballantine Books, 1987, 212 p., paper, tele. ROBOTECH #4.
21004 *Dark powers.* New York: A Del Rey Book, Ballantine Books, 1988, 233 p., paper, tele. SENTINELS #2.
21005 *Death dance.* New York: A Del Rey Book, Ballantine Books, 1988, 185 p., paper, tele. SENTINELS #3.
21006 *The devil's hand.* New York: A Del Rey Book, Ballantine Books, 1988, 214 p., paper, tele. SENTINELS #1.

21007 *Doomsday.* New York: A Del Rey Book, Ballantine Books, 1987, 216 p., paper, tele. ROBOTECH #6.
The end of the circle—SEE: *Robotech: The end of the circle.*
21008 *Event horizon.* New York: A Del Rey Book, Ballantine Books, 1991, 310 p., paper, novel. BLACK HOLE TRAVEL AGENCY #1.
21009 *The final nightmare.* New York: A Del Rey Book, Ballantine Books, 1987, 248 p., paper, tele. ROBOTECH #9.
21010 *Force of arms.* New York: A Del Rey Book, Ballantine Books, 1987, 214 p., paper, tele. ROBOTECH #5.
21011 *Genesis.* New York: A Del Rey Book, Ballantine Books, 1987, 214 p., paper, tele. ROBOTECH #1.
21012 *Homecoming.* New York: A Del Rey Book, Ballantine Books, 1987, 214 p., paper, tele. ROBOTECH #3.
21013 *Invid invasion.* New York: A Del Rey Book, Ballantine Books, 1987, 212 p., paper, tele. ROBOTECH #10.
21014 *Kaduna memories.* New York: A Del Rey Book, Ballantine Books, 1990, 249 p., paper, novel.
21015 *Metal fire.* New York: A Del Rey Book, Ballantine Books, 1987, 216 p., paper, tele. ROBOTECH #8.
21016 *Metamorphosis.* New York: A Del Rey Book, Ballantine Books, 1987, 212 p., paper, tele. ROBOTECH #11.
21017 *Robotech: The end of the circle.* New York: A Del Rey Book, Ballantine Books, 1990, vi+343 p., paper, tele. ROBOTECH #13.
21018 *Rubicon.* New York: A Del Rey Book, Ballantine Books, 1988, 215 p., paper, tele. SENTINELS #5.
21019 *Southern cross.* New York: A Del Rey Book, Ballantine Books, 1987, 215 p., paper, tele. ROBOTECH #7.
21020 *Symphony of light.* New York: A Del Rey Book, Ballantine Books, 1987, 212 p., paper, tele. ROBOTECH #12.
21021 *World killers.* New York: A Del Rey Book, Ballantine Books, 1988, 279 p., paper, tele. SENTINELS #4.

LUCKIE, L(orenzo) F.

28647 *Beware the horse.* New York: Tor, A Tom Doherty Associates Book, 1989, 409 p., paper, novel.

LUDLAM, Harry

37921   *A biography of Dracula: the life story of Bram Stoker*. London, New York: W. Foulsham, 1962, 200 p., cloth, nonf.

*LUDLOW, Edmund, 1898-<u>1979</u>

LUDWIG, Edward W(illiam), 1920-1990

28648   *The 7 shapes of Solomon Bean, and 14 other marvelous stories of science fiction and fantasy*. Los Gatos, CA: Polaris Press, 1983, 225 p., cloth?, coll.

LUENN, Nancy [pseud. of Nancy E. Jones], 1954-

28649   *Arctic unicorn*. New York: Atheneum, 1986, 168 p., cloth, novel.
28650   *Goldclimbers*. New York: Atheneum; Toronto: Maxwell Macmillan Canada; New York: Maxwell Macmillan International Publishing Group, 1991, 184 p., cloth, novel.

LUKE, Mary (M.), 1919-

28651   *The Nonsuch Lure*. New York: Coward, McCann & Geoghegan, 1976, 319 p., cloth, novel.

LUKE, Thomas, pseud.—SEE: Masterton, Graham

LUKEMAN, Tim

28652   *Koren*. Garden City, NY: Doubleday & Co., 1981, 184 p., cloth, novel. RAJAN #2.
28653   *Rajan*. Garden City, NY: Doubleday & Co., 1979, 186 p., cloth, novel. RAJAN #1.
28654   *Witchwood*. New York: Timescape Books, 1983, 190 p., cloth, novel.

*LUKODIANOV, Isai (Borisovich), 1913-<u>1984</u>

LUMLEY, Brian, 1937-

28655   *The clock of dreams*. New York: A Jove/HBJ Book, 1978, 190 p., paper, novel. TITUS CROW #3.
28656   *The compleat Crow*. Buffalo, NY: W. Paul Ganley, 1987, 191 p., cloth, coll. TITUS CROW #6.
37922   *The complete Khash, volume one: Never a backward glance*. Buffalo, NY: W. Paul Ganley, 1991, 181 p., cloth, coll.

28657   *Deadspawn*. London: Grafton, 1991, 586 p., paper, novel. NECROSCOPE #5.
28658   *Deadspeak*. New York: Tor Horror, A Tom Doherty Associates Book, 1990, 487 p., paper, novel. NECROSCOPE #4.
28659   *Demogorgon*. London: Grafton, 1987, 333 p., paper, novel.
28660   *Elysia: the coming of Cthulhu*. Buffalo, NY: W. Paul Ganley, Publisher, 1989, 190 p., cloth, novel. CTHULHU MYTHOS.
28661   *Hero of dreams*. Buffalo, NY: W. Paul Ganley, 1986, ix + 191 p., cloth, novel. DREAMLANDS #1—CTHULHU MYTHOS. [Limited to 200 copies].
28662   *The horror at Oakdeene, and others*. Sauk City, WI: Arkham House, 1977, 229 p., cloth, coll.
28663   *The house of Cthulhu, and other tales of the primal land: fiction*. Buffalo, NY: Weirdbook Press, 1984, 94 p., cloth, coll. TALES OF THE PRIMAL LAND #1.
28664   *House of Cthulhu, and other tales of the primal land: fiction*. London: Headline, 1991, 309 p., paper, coll. TALES OF THE PRIMAL LAND #1. [Adds one story and drops two from the U.S. edition].
28665   *The house of doors*. New York: Tor Horror, A Tom Doherty Associates Book, 1990, 474 p., paper, novel.
28666   *Iced on Aran, and other dreamquests*. London: Headline, 1990, 244 p., paper, coll. DREAMLANDS #4.
28667   *In the moons of Borea*. New York: A Jove/HBJ Book, 1979, 222 p., paper, novel. TITUS CROW #5.
28668   *Khai of ancient Khem*. New York: Berkley Books, 1981, 306 p., paper, novel.
28669   *Mad moon of dreams*. Buffalo, NY: W. Paul Ganley, 1987, vi + 190 p., cloth, novel. DREAMLANDS #3.
28670   *Necroscope*. London: Granada, 1982, p., cloth, novel. NECROSCOPE #1.
   Necroscope II—SEE: Wamphyri!
   Necroscope III—SEE: The source.
   Necroscope IV—SEE: Deadspeak.
   Necroscope V—SEE: Deadspawn.
   Never a backward glance—SEE: The complete Khash, volume one.
28671   *Psychamok*. London: Panther, 1985, 445 p., paper, novel. PSYCH #3.
28672   *Psychomech*. London: Panther, 1984, 351 p., paper, novel. PSYCH #1.
28673   *Psychosphere*. London: Panther, 1984, 272 p., paper, novel. PSYCH #2.
28674   *Ship of dreams*. Buffalo, NY: W. Paul Ganley, Publisher, 1986, vii + 189 p., cloth, novel. DREAMLANDS #2.

28675 *Sorcery in Shad.* London: Headline, 1991, 246 p., paper, novel. TALES OF THE PRIMAL LAND #3.

28676 *The source.* London: Grafton, 1989, 528 p., paper, novel. NECROSCOPE #3.

28677 *Spawn of the winds.* New York: A Jove/HBJ Book, 1978, 191 p., paper, novel. TITUS CROW #4.

28678 *Synchronicity; or, Something.* England: Dagon Press, 1988, 48 p., paper, story. [Limited to 350 copies].

28679 *Tarra Khash: Hrossak!* London: Headline, 1991, 246 p., paper, coll. TALES OF THE PRIMAL LAND #2.

28680 *The transition of Titus Crow.* New York: DAW Books, 1975, 253 p., paper, novel. TITUS CROW #2—CTHULHU MYTHOS. [A direct sequel to *The burrowers beneath*].

28681 *The transition of Titus Crow.* London: Grafton, 1991, 269 p., paper, novel. TITUS CROW #2—CTHULHU MYTHOS. [Revised edition].
Vamphyri!—SEE: *Wamphyri!*

28682 *Wamphyri!* London: Grafton, 1988, 495 p., paper, novel. NECROSCOPE #2.

28682A retitled: *Vamphyri!* New York: Tor Horror, A Tom Doherty Associates Book, 1989, 470 p., paper, novel.

LUMPKIN, Houston—SEE: Houston, David

LUNAN, Duncan (Alasdair), 1945-

28683 *Starfield: the anthology of science fiction by Scottish writers.* Kirkwall, Scotland: Orkney Press, 1989, 211 p., cloth, anth.

*LUND, Ivar, 1882-1975

LUNDQUIST, James (Carl), 1941-

28684 *Kurt Vonnegut.* New York: Frederick Ungar Publishing Co., 1977, ix+124 p., paper, nonf. MODERN LITERATURE MONOGRAPHS SERIES.

LUNDWALL, Sam J(errie), 1941-

28685 *2018 A.D.; or, The King Kong blues.* New York: DAW Books, 1975, 160 p., paper, novel.

28686 *Science fiction: an illustrated history.* New York: Grosset & Dunlap, 1978, 208 p., cloth, nonf.

with Brian W. Aldiss

16207 *The Penguin world omnibus of science fiction.* Harmondsworth, Middlesex, England: Penguin Books, 1986, 320 p., paper, anth.

LUNN, Janet (Louise Swoboda), 1928-

28687 *The root cellar.* Toronto: Lester & Orpen Dennys, 1981, 247 p., cloth, novel.

28688 *Shadow in Hawthorn Bay.* Toronto: Lester & Orpen Dennys, 1986, 216 p., cloth, novel.

LUNN, Richard, 1926-

28689 *Space suits & gum-shoes: an anthology of science fiction and crime stories.* Toronto: Gage, 1980, 275 p., paper?, anth.

LUPOFF, Richard A(llen), 1935-

28690 *Barsoom: Edgar Rice Burroughs and the Martian vision.* Baltimore, MD: Mirage Press, 1976, 161 p., cloth, nonf. [Limited to 1500 copies].

28691 *The black tower.* Toronto, New York: A Byron Preiss Book, Bantam Books, 1988, xii+339 p, paper, novel. PHILIP JOSE FARMER'S THE DUNGEON #1.

28692 *The case of the doctor who had no business; or, The adventure of the second anonymous narrator.* La Grange, NY: Richard A. Lupoff, 1966, 16 p., paper, nonf.

28693 *Circumpolar!* New York: Timescape Books, 1984, 319 p., cloth, novel. TWIN PLANETS #1.

28694 *The comic book killer.* San Francisco: Offspring Press, 1988, 296 p., cloth, novel.

28695 *Countersolar!* New York: Arbor House, 1987, 293 p., cloth, novel. TWIN PLANETS #2.

28696 *The crack in the sky.* New York: A Dell Book, 1976, 207 p., paper, novel.

28696A retitled: *Fool's hill.* London: Sphere Books, 1978, 207 p., paper, novel.

28697 *The digital wristwatch of Philip K. Dick.* San Carlos, CA: Canyon Press, 1985, iii+37 p., cloth, story. [Limited to 350 copies].

28698 *Edgar Rice Burroughs: Master of Adventure.* New York: Ace, 1975, 315 p, paper, critical study. ["Centennial" edition; a reissue of 1965 Canaveral Press edition (see #09328) with "many" revisions].

28699 *The final battle.* New York, Toronto: Spectra, Bantam Books, 1990, 285 p., cloth, novel. PHILIP JOSE FARMER'S THE DUNGEON #6.
Fool's hill—SEE: *A crack in the sky.*

28700 *The Forever City*. New York: Millennium, A Byron Preiss Book, Walker & Co., 1987, 230 p., cloth, novel.

28701 *Galaxy's end*. New York: Ace Books, 1988, 236 p., paper, novel. SUN'S END #2.

28702 *Lisa Kane: a novel of the supernatural*. Indianapolis, IN & New York: Bobbs-Merrill Co., 1976, 128 p., cloth, novel.

28703 *Lovecraft's book*. Sauk City, WI: Arkham House Publishers, 1985, 206 p., cloth, novel.

28704 *Nebogipfel at the end of time*. San Francisco, Columbia, PA: Underwood-Miller, 1979, 18 p., paper, story. [Limited to 300 copies].

37923 *One million centuries*. New York: A Timescape Book, Pocket Books, 1981, 283 p., paper, novel. [Revised edition of #09330].

28705 *The Ova Hamlet papers*. San Francisco: Pennyfarthing Press, 1979, xi+84 p., paper, coll.

28706 *The reader's guide to Barsoom and Amtor*. New York: Richard A. Lupoff, 1963, 84 p., paper, nonf. anth.

28707 *Sandworld*. New York: A Berkley Medallion Book, Berkley Publishing Corp., 1976, 188 p., paper, novel.

28708 *Space war blues*. New York: A Dell Book, 1978, 315 p., paper, novel.

28709 *Stroka Prospekt: a story*. West Branch, IA: Toothpaste Press, 1982, 45 p., cloth, story. [Limited to 950 copies].

28710 *Sun's end*. New York: Berkley Books, 1984, 280 p., paper, novel. SUN'S END #1.

28711 *Sword of the demon: a novel*. New York, Hagerstown, NJ: Harper & Row, Publishers, 1976, 174 p., cloth, novel.

28712 *The triune man*. New York: Berkley Publishing Corp., 1976, 219 p., cloth, novel.

28713 *What if?, volume 1: stories that should have won the Hugo*. New York: Pocket Books, 1980, 266 p., paper, anth.

28714 *What if?, volume 2: stories that should have won the Hugo*. New York: Pocket Books, 1981, 239 p., paper, anth.

as ADDISON E. STEELE

28715 *Buck Rogers in the 25th century*. New York: A Dell Book, 1978, 256 p., paper, tele. BUCK ROGERS #1.

28716 *That man on Beta*. New York: A Dell Book, 1979, 251 p., paper, tele. BUCK ROGERS #2.

with Robert E. Howard

26047 *The return of Skull-Face*. West Linn, OR: FAX Collector's Editions, 1977, 96 p., cloth, novel. SKULL-FACE #2.

LURIE, Alison, 1926-

28717 *Don't tell the grown-ups*. Boston: Little, Brown & Co., 1990, 229 p., cloth, nonf.

LUSTBADER, Eric Van, 1946-

28718 *Angel eyes*. New York: Fawcett Columbine, 1991, 520 p., cloth, novel.

28719 *Beneath an opal moon*. Garden City, NY: Doubleday & Co., 1980, 247 p., cloth, novel. SUNSET WARRIOR #4.

28720 *Dai-San*. Garden City, NY: Doubleday & Co., 1978, 246 p., cloth, novel. SUNSET WARRIOR #3.

28721 *Shallows of night*. Garden City, NY: Doubleday & Co., 1978, 216 p., cloth, novel. Sunset Warrior #2.

28722 *The sunset warrior*. Garden City, NY: Doubleday & Co., 1977, 182 p., cloth, novel. SUNSET WARRIOR #1.

LÜTHI, Max, 1909-

28723 *The European folktale: form and nature*. Philadelphia, PA: Institute for the Study of Human Issues, 1982, xxv+173 p., cloth, nonf.

28724 *The fairy tale as art form and portrait of man*. Bloomington, IN: Indiana University Press, 1984, xi+207 p., cloth, nonf.

28725 *Once upon a time: on the nature of fairy tales*. New York: Frederick Ungar Publishing Co., 1970, 176 p., cloth, nonf.

LUTZ, John (Thomas), 1939-

28726 *Lazarus man*. New York: William Morrow & Co., 1979, 228 p., cloth, novel.

28727 *Ride the lightning*. New York: St. Martin's Press, 1987, 196 p., cloth, novel.

28728 *The shadow man*. New York: William Morrow & Co., 1981, 215 p., cloth, novel.

LYALL, D. K., *with D. M. Foster*

23373 *The empathy experiment*. Sydney: Wild & Woolley, 1977, 201 p., cloth, novel.

LYDAY, David Paul

28729 *Come die for me*. New York: Popular Library, 1977, 192 p., paper, novel.

LYDECKER, John, pseud.—SEE: Gallagher, Stephen

LYDENBERG, Robin (Rector), 1947-

28730 *Word cultures: radical theory and practice in William S. Burroughs's fiction.* Urbana, IL: University of Illinois Press, 1987, xii+205 p., cloth, nonf.

with Jennie Skerl

28731 *William S. Burroughs at the front: critical reception, 1959-1989.* Carbondale & Edwardsville, IL: Southern Illinois University Press, 1991, 274 p., cloth, nonf. anth.

LYLE, Peter

28732 *Rolind of Meru.* New York: Avon, 1977, 173 p., paper, novel.

LYLES, William H(using), 1946-

28733 *Mary Shelley: an annotated bibliography.* New York: Garland Publishing, 1975, xx+297 p., cloth, nonf.

LYMINGTON, John [pseud. of John Newton Chance], 1911-1983

28734 *A caller from overspace.* London: Hodder & Stoughton, 1979, 189 p., cloth, novel.
28735 *The grey ones; A sword above the night.* New York: Manor Books, 1978, 282 p., paper, coll.
28736 *The Laxham haunting.* London: Hodder & Stoughton, 1976, 192 p., cloth, novel.
28737 *The power ball.* London: Robert Hale, 1981, 192 p., cloth, novel.
28738 *A spider in the bath.* London: Hodder & Stoughton, 1975, 190 p., cloth, novel.
28739 *Starseed on Gye Moor.* London: Hodder & Stoughton, 1977, 192 p., cloth, novel.
28740 *The terror version.* London: Robert Hale, 1982, 158 p., cloth, novel.
28741 *The Vale of Sad Banana.* London: Robert Hale, 1984, 192 p., cloth, novel.
28742 *Voyage of the eighth mind.* London: Hodder & Stoughton, 1980, 192 p., cloth, novel.
28743 *The waking of the stone.* London: Hodder & Stoughton, 1978, 190 p., cloth, novel.

LYNCH, Jane—SEE: Gaskell, Jane

LYNCH, Lee, 1945-

28744 *Sue Slate: private eye.* Tallahassee, FL: Naiad Press, 1989, 161 p., paper, novel.

LYNCH, Miriam

28745 *Daughters of Cain.* New York: Manor Books, 1970, 207 p., paper, novel.

LYNDS, Dennis, 1924- , as NICK CARTER

19608 *The samurai kill.* New York: Charter Books, 1986, 200 p., paper, novel. NICK CARTER #215.

LYNGSETH, Joan [pseud. of Joan Davies], 1934-

28746 *Martin's starwars.* Ottawa, Ontario: Borealis Press, 1978, 69 p., cloth, novel.

LYNN, Elizabeth A(nne), 1946-

28747 *The dancers of Arun.* New York: Berkley Publishing Corp., 1979, 263 p., cloth, novel. CHRONICLES OF TORNOR #2.
28748 *A different light.* New York: A Berkley Book, Berkley Publishing Corp., 1978, 183 p., paper, novel.
28749 *The northern girl.* New York: Berkley Publishing Corp., 1980, 382 p., cloth, novel. CHRONICLES OF TORNOR #3.
28750 *The red hawk.* New Castle, VA: Cheap Street, 1983, 67 p., cloth, story. [Limited to 177 copies].
28751 *The Sardonyx net.* New York: Berkley Publishing Corp., 1981, 301 p., cloth, novel.
28752 *The silver horse.* New York: Bluejay Books, 1984, 126 p., cloth, novel.
28753 *Tales from a vanished country.* Eugene, OR: Pulphouse Publishing, 1990, 110 p., cloth, coll. AUTHOR'S CHOICE MONTHLY #10.
28754 *Watchtower.* New York: Berkley Publishing Corp., 1979, 251 p., cloth, novel. CHRONICLES OF TORNOR #1. [Winner of the World Fantasy Award for Best Fantasy Novel, 1979 (1980)].
28755 *The woman who loved the Moon, and other stories.* New York: Berkley Books, 1981, 197 p., paper, coll.

LYNN, Grey

28756 *The return of Karl Marx.* London: Chancery Books Ltd., 1941, 117 p., paper, novel.

LYNN, Ruth Nadelman, 1948-

28757   *Fantasy for children: an annotated checklist.* New York, London: R. R. Bowker Co., 1979, ix+288 p., cloth, nonf.

28758   *Fantasy for children: an annotated checklist and reference guide, 2nd ed.* New York, London: R. R. Bowker Co., 1983, xiv+444 p., cloth, nonf.

28759   *Fantasy literature for children and young adults: an annotated bibliography, 3rd ed.* New York: R. R. Bowker Co., 1989, xlvii+771 p., cloth, nonf.

LYON, Elisabeth (Hart), *with Constance Penley & Lynn Spigel & Janet Bergstrom*

17866   *Close encounters: film, feminism, and science fiction.* Minneapolis, MN, Oxford, England: A Camera Obscura Book, University of Minnesota Press, 1991, xi+298 p., cloth, nonf. anth.

LYON, John, pseud.—SEE: Evans, Chris

LYON, Richard K(enneth), 1933- , *with Andrew J. Offutt*

28760   *Demon in the mirror.* New York: A Kangaroo Book, Pocket Books, 1978, 189 p., paper, novel. WAR OF THE WIZARDS #1.

28761   *The Eyes of Sarsis.* New York: Pocket Books, 1980, 207 p., paper, novel. WAR OF THE WIZARDS #2.

28762   *Web of the spider.* New York: A Timescape Book, Pocket Books, 1981, 292 p., paper, novel. WAR OF THE WIZARDS #3.

LYONS, Lynda, 1949-

28763   *Priorities.* Tallahassee, FL: Naiad Press, 1990, 271 p., paper, novel. CONTROLLERS SERIES.

LYSAGHT, Elizabeth J.

37924   *The veiled picture; or, The wizard's legacy.* London: Simpkin, Marshall & Co., 1890, 160 p., cloth, novel.

M

MACANDREW, Elizabeth, 1924-1983?

28764 *The gothic tradition in fiction.* New York: Columbia University Press, 1979, xi + 289 p., cloth, nonf.

MACAO, Marshall, pseud.—SEE: Tuleja, Thaddeus

MACAPP, C. C. [pseud. of Carroll M(arion?) Capps], 1913-1971

***MACARDLE, Dorothy (Margaret Callan), 1889-1958**

MACARI, Mario D. (Jr.), with Beverly Charette

37655 *Star rangers meet the solar robot.* Lake Geneva, WI: TSR Inc., 1984, 77 p., paper, novel. FANTASY FOREST BOOK #8.

MACARTHUR, D. M.

28765 *Ecology: science and science fiction.* Worcester, MA: Undergraduate Report, Worcester Polytechnic Institute, 1982, 65 p., paper, nonf.

MACAULAY, David (Alexander), 1946-

28766 *Baaa.* Boston: Houghton Mifflin Co., 1985, 61 p., cloth, novel.
28767 *Motel of the Mysteries.* London: Hutchinson, 1979, 96 p., paper, novel.

MACAULAY, (Emilie) Rose, 1881-1958

37925 *And no man's wit.* London: Collins, 1940, 384 p., cloth, novel.
37926 *Mystery at Geneva: an improbable tale of singular happenings.* London: William Collins & Sons, 1922, 259 p., cloth, novel.

MACAULEY, Robie (Mayhew), 1919-

28768 *A secret history of time to come.* New York: Alfred A. Knopf, 1979, 303 p., cloth, novel.

MACAVOY, R(oberta) A(nn), 1949-

28769 *The Book of Kells.* Toronto, New York: Bantam Books, 1985, 340 p., paper, novel.
28770 *Damiano.* Toronto, New York: Bantam Books, 1984, 243 p., paper, novel. DAMIANO #1.
28771 *Damiano's lute.* Toronto, New York: Bantam Books, 1984, 254 p., paper, novel. DAMIANO #2.
28772 *The grey horse.* Toronto, New York: Bantam Books, 1987, 247 p., paper, novel.
28773 *King of the dead.* New York: William Morrow & Co., 1991, 286 p., cloth, novel. LENS OF THE WORLD #2.
28774 *Lens of the world.* New York: William Morrow & Co., 1990, 286 p., cloth, novel. LENS OF THE WORLD #1.
28775 *Raphael.* Toronto, New York: Bantam Books, 1984, 230 p., paper, novel. DAMIANO #3.
28776 *Tea with the black dragon.* Toronto, New York: Bantam Books, 1983, 166 p., paper, novel. BLACK DRAGON #1. [Winner of the *Locus* Award for Best First Novel, 1983 (1984)].
28777 *The Third Eagle: lessons along a minor string.* New York: A Foundation Book, Doubleday, 1989, 301 p., cloth, novel.
28778 *A trio for lute.* Garden City, NY: Nelson Doubleday, 1985, 632 p., cloth, coll. DAMIANO #1-3.
28779 *Twisting the rope: casadh an T'Súgáin.* Toronto, New York: Bantam Books, 1986, 242 p., paper, novel. BLACK DRAGON #2.

MACBETH, George (Mann), 1932-1992

28780 *The transformation.* London: Victor Gollancz, 1975, 96 p., cloth, novel.

MacCLOUD, Malcolm

28781 *A gift of mirrorvax.* New York: An Argo Book, Atheneum, 1981, x + 192 p., cloth, novel.
28782 *The Tera beyond.* New York: Argo, Atheneum, 1981, 190 p., cloth, novel.

MacCONNELL, Colum

28783 *Tark and the Golden Tide.* New York: Leisure Books, 1977, 154 p., paper, novel.

MACDONALD, Andrew [pseud. of William Luther Pierce], 1933-

28784 *Hunter: a novel.* Hillsboro, WV: National Vanguard Books, 1989, 259 p., paper, novel.

28785 *The Turner diaries.* Hillsboro, WV: National Vanguard Books, 1978, iv+211 p., paper, novel.

MACDONALD, Caroline

28786 *The lake at the end of the world.* London: Hodder & Stoughton, 1988, 184 p., cloth, novel.

MACDONALD, D(avid) L(orne), 1955-

28787 *Poor Polidori: a critical biography of the author of "The Vampyre".* Toronto: University of Toronto Press, 1991, xiv+333 p., cloth, nonf.

MacDONALD, Edgar E(dgeworth), 1919- , *with M. Thomas Inge*

37867 *James Branch Cabell: centennial essays.* Baton Rouge, LA: Louisiana State University Press, 1983, xii+186 p., cloth, nonf. anth.

MacDONALD, George, 1824-1905

15836 *At the back of the north wind.* London: Strahan & Co., 1870, 378 p., cloth, novel.

28788 *The day boy and the night girl.* New York: Alfred A. Knopf, 1988, 103 p., cloth, novel.

15837 *The princess and Curdie.* London: Chatto & Windus, 1883, 255 p., cloth, novel. CURDIE #2.

15838 *The princess and the goblin.* London: Strahan & Co., 1871, 313 p., cloth, novel. CURDIE #1.

28789 *The world of George MacDonald: selections from his works of fiction.* Wheaton, IL: Harold Shaw Publishers, 1978, 199 p., cloth, coll.

MACDONALD, James D(ouglas), 1954-

with Debra Doyle

22102 *City by the sea.* Mahwah, NJ: Troll Associates, 1990, 132 p., cloth, novel. CIRCLE OF MAGIC #3.

22103 *The high king's daughter.* Mahwah, NJ: Troll Associates, 1990, 136 p., cloth, novel. CIRCLE OF MAGIC #6.

22104 *The prince's players.* Mahwah, NJ: Troll Associates, 1990, 133 p., cloth, novel. CIRCLE OF MAGIC #4.

22105 *The prisoners of Bell Castle.* Mahwah, NJ: Troll Associates, 1990, 137 p., cloth, novel. CIRCLE OF MAGIC #5.

22106 *Robert Silverberg's Time Tours: Timecrime, Inc.* New York: A Byron Preiss Book, HarperPaperbacks, 1991, 145 p., paper, novel. ROBERT SILVERBERG'S TIME TOURS #3.

22107 *School of wizardry.* Mahwah, NJ: Troll Associates, 1990, 139 p., cloth, novel. CIRCLE OF MAGIC #1.

Timecrime, Inc.—SEE: *Robert Silverberg's Time Tours: Timecrime, Inc..*

22108 *Tournament and tower.* Mahwah, NJ: Troll Associates, 1990, 134 p., cloth, novel. CIRCLE OF MAGIC #2.

with Debra Doyle as NICHOLAS ADAMS

15974 *Horror High: Pep rally.* New York: HarperPaperbacks, 1991, 155 p., paper, novel. HORROR HIGH #7. [By Debra Doyle & James D. Macdonald].

Pep rally—SEE: *Horror High: Pep rally.*

with Debra Doyle as VICTOR APPLETON

16736 *Aquatech warriors.* New York, London: An Archway Paperback, Pocket Books, 1991, 154 p., paper, novel. TOM SWIFT #C6. [By James D. Macdonald and Debra Doyle].

16744 *Monster machine.* New York, London: An Archway Paperback, Pocket Books, 1991, 154 p., paper, novel. TOM SWIFT #C5. [By James D. Macdonald and Debra Doyle].

with Debra Doyle as ROBYN TALLIS

Night of ghosts and lightning—SEE: *Planet builders: night of ghosts and lightning.*

22109 *Planet builders: Night of ghosts and lightning.* New York: Ivy Books, 1989, 185 p., paper, novel. PLANET BUILDERS #2.

22110 *Planet builders: Zero-sum games.* New York: Ivy Books, 1989, 182 p., paper, novel. PLANET BUILDERS #5.

Zero-sum games—SEE: *Planet builders: Zero-sum games.*

MacDONALD, John D(ann), 1916-1986

28790 *Other times, other worlds.* New York: Fawcett Gold Medal, 1978, 287 p., paper, coll.

28791 *Time and tomorrow: Wine of the dreamers; The girl, the gold watch, and everything; Ballroom of the skies.* Garden City, NY: Nelson Doubleday, 1980, 504 p., cloth, coll.

MacDONALD, Michael H., 1945- , *with Andrew A. Tadie*

28792 *G. K. Chesterton and C. S. Lewis: the riddle of joy.* London: Collins, 1989, xx + 304 p., cloth, nonf. anth.

MacDONALD, Philip—SEE: Stuart, W. J.

MacDONALD, Reby Edmund

28793 *The ghosts of Austwick Manor.* New York: A Margaret K. McElderry Book, Atheneum, 1982, 144 p., cloth, novel.

MACDONELL, A(rchibald) G(ordon), 1895-1941

37927 *Lords and masters.* London: Macmillan, 1936, 356 p., cloth, novel.

MacDONNELL, James—SEE: Dark, James

MACE, David (Kendrew), 1951-

28794 *Demon-4.* London: Panther, 1984, 205 p., paper, novel.

28795 *Fire lance.* London: Grafton, 1986, 399 p., paper, novel.

28796 *Frankenstein's children.* London: New English Library, 1990, 252 p., cloth, novel.

28797 *The highest ground.* London: New English Library, 1988, 373 p., cloth, novel.

28798 *Nightrider.* London: Granada, 1985, 304 p., paper, novel.

28799 *Shadow hunters.* London: New English Library, 1991, [272] p., cloth, novel.

MACE, Elisabeth, 1933-

28800 *The ghost diviners.* London: André Deutsch, 1977, 144 p., cloth, novel.
   Out there—SEE: *Ransome revisited.*

28801 *Ransome revisited.* London: André Deutsch, 1975, 139 p., cloth, novel. LEVEN #1.

28801A retitled: *Out there.* New York: Greenwillow Books, 1978, 181 p., cloth, novel. LEVEN #1.

28802 *The Rushton inheritance.* London: André Deutsch, 1978, 160 p., cloth, novel.

28803 *The travelling man.* London: André Deutsch, 1976, 128 p., cloth, novel. LEVEN #2.

28804 *Under siege.* London: André Deutsch, 1988, 167 p., cloth, novel.

MacEOIN, Denis—SEE: Easterman, Daniel

*MacEWEN, Gwendolyn (Margaret), 1941-<u>1987</u>

MACEY, Peter

28805 *Alien culture.* London: Dennis Dobson, 1977, 192 p., cloth, novel.

28806 *Distant relations.* London: Dennis Dobson, 1975, 175 p., cloth, novel.

MacFADDEN, Patrick, *with Rae Murphy & Robert Chodos*

20018 *Your place or mine? an entertainment.* Ottawa, Ontario: Deneau & Greenberg, 1978, 240 p., paper, novel.

MACFARLANE, John

28807 *The door to yesterday.* New York, Washington: Vantage Press, 1982, 183 p., cloth, novel.

MACFARLANE, Elizabeth—SEE: Duke, Madeleine

MACGREGOR, Ellen, 1906-1954, *with Dora Pantell*

28808 *Miss Pickerell and the blue whales.* New York: McGraw-Hill, 1983, 159 p., cloth, novel. MISS PICKERELL #15.

28809 *Miss Pickerell and the supertanker.* New York: McGraw-Hill, 1978, 157 p., cloth, novel. MISS PICKERELL #12.

28810 *Miss Pickerell on the trail.* New York: McGraw-Hill, 1982, 159 p., cloth, novel. MISS PICKERELL #14.

28811 *Miss Pickerell tackles the energy crisis.* New York: McGraw-Hill, 1980, 173 p., cloth, novel. MISS PICKERELL #13.

28812 *Miss Pickerell takes the bull by the horns.* New York: McGraw-Hill, 1976, 160 p., cloth, novel. MISS PICKERELL #10.

28813 *Miss Pickerell to the earthquake rescue.* New York: McGraw-Hill, 1977, 158 p., cloth, novel. MISS PICKERELL #11.

MACGREGOR, James—SEE: McIntosh, J. T.

MacGREGOR, Loren (J.), 1950-

28814　*The net.*　New York: Ace Science Fiction
　　　　Books, 1987, 225 p., paper, novel.

MacGREGOR, Patricia—SEE: Janeshutz, Trish

*MacGREGOR, Richard [pseud. of MacGregor
Urquhardt]

MacGREGOR, Rob

28815　*Crystal skull.*　New York: Ballantine
　　　　Books, 1991, 305 p., paper, novel.
28816　*Indiana Jones and the dance of the giants.*
　　　　New York, Toronto: Falcon, Bantam
　　　　Books, 1991, 230 p., paper, novel. IN-
　　　　DIANA JONES #2.
28817　*Indiana Jones and the last crusade.*　New
　　　　York: Ballantine Books, 1989, 216 p.,
　　　　paper, movie. INDIANA JONES III.
28818　*Indiana Jones and the peril at Delphi.*
　　　　New York, Toronto: Falcon, Bantam
　　　　Books, 1991, 248 p., paper, novel. IN-
　　　　DIANA JONES #1.
28819　*Indiana Jones and the seven veils.*　New
　　　　York, Toronto: Falcon, Bantam Books,
　　　　1991, 275 p., paper, novel. INDIANA
　　　　JONES #3.

MacGREGOR, T. J.—SEE: Janeshutz, Trish

MACHEN, Arthur (Llewellyn Jones), 1863-1947

28820　*Arthur Machen: selected letters: the private
　　　　letters of the master of the macabre.*
　　　　Wellingborough, Northamptonshire, Eng-
　　　　land: Aquarian Press, 1988, 256 p.,
　　　　cloth, nonf. [Edited by Roger Dobson,
　　　　Godfrey Brangham & R. A. Gilbert].
28821　*The collected Arthur Machen.*　London:
　　　　Duckworth, 1988, 380 p., cloth, coll.
　　　　[Edited by Christopher Palmer].
28822　*Guinevere and Lancelot, & others.*　New-
　　　　port News, VA: Purple Mouth, 1986, 47
　　　　p., paper, coll. [Edited by Michael T.
　　　　Shoemaker & Cuyler W. Brooks Jr.; in-
　　　　cludes some nonfiction].

with Morchard Bishop

18051　*Dreams and visions: a brief journey into
　　　　the remarkable imagination of Arthur
　　　　Machen, as recorded by Morchard
　　　　Bishop, with a postscript from the unpub-
　　　　lished portion of The secret glory.*
　　　　Southampton, England: Caermaen Books,
　　　　1987, 7 p., paper, story.

with Robert W. Chambers

19758　*Kings of horror.*　North Hollywood, CA:
　　　　Ken Krueger, 1975, 80 p., paper, coll.

with Vincent Starrett

28823　*Starrett vs. Machen: a record of discovery
　　　　and correspondence.*　St. Louis, MO:
　　　　Autolycus Press, 1977, 119 p., paper?,
　　　　nonf. [Limited to 500 copies].

MACIAS, Carlos Fuentes—SEE: Fuentes, Carlos

MacINTYRE, F(eargus) Gwynplaine, 1949- , *as*
VICTOR APPLETON

16742　*The DNA disaster.*　New York, London:
　　　　An Archway Paperback, Pocket Books,
　　　　1991, 154 p., paper, novel. TOM SWIFT
　　　　#C4.

MACK, Carol K., 1941- , *with David Ehrenfeld*

22486　*Trek or treat.*　New York: Ballantine
　　　　Books, 1977, [95] p., paper, nonf.

MACKAIL, J(ohn) W(illiam), 1859-1945

28824　*The life of William Morris.*　London, New
　　　　York: Longmans, Green & Co., 1899, 2
　　　　v. (I-xv+375 p.; II-viii+364 p.), cloth,
　　　　nonf.
28825　*William Morris: an address delivered the
　　　　XIth November MCCCC at Kelmscott
　　　　House, Hammersmith, before the Ham-
　　　　mersmith Socialist Society.*　Hammer-
　　　　smith, England: Doves Press, 1901, 27
　　　　p., paper?, nonf.
28826　*William Morris and his circle: being an
　　　　address delivered on the occasion of the
　　　　opening of the Morris Exhibition at the
　　　　Municipal School of Art, Oct. 14.*
　　　　Manchester, England: [s.n.], 1909, 22
　　　　p., paper, nonf.

MACKAY, Colin, 1951-

28827　*The song of the forest.*　Edinburgh, Scot-
　　　　land: Canongate Publishing, 1986, 239
　　　　p., cloth, novel.
28828　*The sound of the sea.*　Edinburgh, Scot-
　　　　land: Canongate Publishing, 1989, 217
　　　　p., cloth, novel.

MACKELWORTH, R(onald) W(alter), 1930-

28829　*Shakehole.*　London: Robert Hale, 1981,
　　　　208 p., cloth, novel.
28830　*The year of the painted world.*　London:
　　　　Robert Hale, 1975, 176 p., cloth, novel.

MACKENROTH, Nancy (J.)

28831 *The trees of Zharka.* New York: Popular Library, 1975, 192 p., paper, novel.

MACKENZIE, Jake

28832 *The ghost of the lost mine.* New York, Toronto: Scholastic Inc., 1988, 96 p., paper, novel. SECRET FILES OF DAKOTA KING #4.

28833 *The haunted city of gold.* New York, Toronto: Scholastic Inc., 1987, 95 p., paper, novel. SECRET FILES OF DAKOTA KING #2.

28834 *Operation Black Fang.* New York, Toronto: Scholastic Inc., 1987, 96 p., paper, novel. SECRET FILES OF DAKOTA KING #1.

28835 *Two-wheeled terror.* New York, Toronto: Scholastic Inc., 1988, 96 p., paper, novel. SECRET FILES OF DAKOTA KING #3.

MACKENZIE, (Daisy) Jeanne, 1922-1986, *with Norman MacKenzie*

H. G. Wells—SEE: *The time traveller.*
The life of H. G. Wells—SEE: *The time traveller.*

28836 *The time traveller: the life of H. G. Wells.* London: Weidenfeld & Nicolson, 1973, xii+487 p., cloth, nonf.

28836A retitled: *H. G. Wells: a biography.* New York: Simon & Schuster, 1975, xvi+487 p., cloth, nonf.

28837 retitled: *The life of H. G. Wells, the time traveller, revised edition.* London: Hogarth Press, 1987, xii+500 p., cloth, nonf.

MACKENZIE, Norman (Ian), 1921- , *with Jeanne MacKenzie*

H. G. Wells—SEE: *The time traveller.*
The life of H. G. Wells—SEE: *The time traveller.*

28836 *The time traveller: the life of H. G. Wells.* London: Weidenfeld & Nicolson, 1973, xii+487 p., cloth, nonf.

28836A retitled: *H. G. Wells: a biography.* New York: Simon & Schuster, 1975, xvi+487 p., cloth, nonf.

28837 retitled: *The life of H. G. Wells, the time traveller, revised edition.* London: Hogarth Press, 1987, xii+500 p., cloth, nonf.

MACKENZIE, Steve, pseud.—SEE: Randle, Kevin

MACKENZIE, Trix

28838 *Enchantment.* New York: Warner Books, 1981, 443 p., paper, novel.

MACKEY, Douglas A(lan), 1947-

28839 *Philip K. Dick.* Boston: Twayne Publishers, 1988, 157 p., cloth, nonf.

28840 *The rainbow quest of Thomas Pynchon.* San Bernardino, CA: R. Reginald, The Borgo Press, 1980, 63 p., cloth, nonf. MILFORD SERIES: POPULAR WRITERS OF TODAY #28.

28841 *The work of Ian Watson: an annotated bibliography & guide.* San Bernardino, CA: R. Reginald, The Borgo Press, 1989, 148 p., cloth, nonf. BIBLIOGRAPHIES OF MODERN AUTHORS #18. [Edited by Boden Clarke].

MACKEY, Mary (Lou McGinness), 1945-

28842 *The last warrior queen.* New York: Seaview Press, G. P. Putnam's Sons, 1983, 240 p., cloth, novel.

MACKIE, Mary

28843 *The people of the horse.* London: W. H. Allen & Co., 1987, 415 p., cloth, novel.

MACKIN, Rick [pseud. of William Michael Kasner]

28844 *Chopper cops.* New York: Pinnacle Books, Windsor Publishing Corp., 1990, 222 p., paper, novel. CHOPPER COPS #1.

28845 *Chopper cops: Gulf attack.* New York: Pinnacle Books, Windsor Publishing Corp., 1990, 189 p., paper, novel. CHOPPER COPS #2.

28846 *Chopper cops: Recon strike force.* New York: Pinnacle Books, Windsor Publishing Corp., 1991, 224 p., paper, novel. CHOPPER COPS #3.

28847 *Chopper cops: Sky war.* New York: Pinnacle Books, Windsor Publishing Corp., 1991, 224 p., paper, novel. CHOPPER COPS #4.

Gulf attack—SEE: *Chopper cops: Gulf attack.*
Recon strike force—SEE: *Chopper cops: Recon strike force.*
Sky war—SEE: *Chopper cops: Sky war.*

MACKINNON, Charles—SEE: Stuart, Charles

MACKLEM, Francesca

28852 *Tomorrow and forever.* New York: Leisure Books, 1984, 253 p., paper, novel.

MACKLEY, Jon, 1970-

28853 *Spirit level.* Lewes, East Sussex, England: The Book Guild, 1990, 146 p., cloth, novel.

MACKSEY, Kenneth (John), 1923-

28854 *First clash: combat close-up in World War Three.* London: Arms & Armour Press, 1985, 248 p., cloth, fiction.
28855 *Invasion: the German invasion of England, July 1940.* London: Arms & Armour Press, 1980, 223 p., cloth, fiction. [Includes some nonfiction].

MACLANE, Jack [pseud. of Allen Billy Crider], 1941-

28856 *Blood dreams.* New York: Zebra Books, Kensington Publishing Corp., 1989, 350 p., paper, novel.
28857 *Goodnight Moom.* New York: Zebra Books, Kensington Publishing Corp., 1989, 348 p., paper, novel.
28858 *Just before dark.* New York: Zebra Books, Kensington Publishing Corp., 1990, 288 p., paper, novel.
28859 *Keepers of the beast.* New York: Zebra Books, Kensington Publishing Corp., 1988, 351 p., paper, novel.
28860 *Rest in peace.* New York: Zebra Books, Kensington Publishing Corp., 1990, 319 p., paper, novel.

MACLAY, John (B. Jr.), 1944-

28861 *Mindwarps.* Baltimore, MD: Maclay & Associates, 1991, 144 p., cloth, coll.
19652 *Nukes: four horror writers on the ultimate horror: stories.* Baltimore, MD: Maclay & Associates, 1986, 92 p., paper, anth.
28862 *Other engagements.* Madison, WI: Dream House, 1987, 124 p., cloth, coll. [Includes some verse].

with J. N. Williamson

28863 *Wards of armageddon.* New York: Leisure Books, 1986, 400 p., paper, novel.

MACLEAN, Katherine (Anne), 1925-

28864 *Missing man.* New York: Berkley Publishing Corp., 1975, 252 p., cloth, novel.
28865 *The trouble with you Earth people.* Virginia Beach, VA: Starblaze Editions/ Donning, 1980, 237 p., paper, coll.

with Tom Condit

20374 *Trouble with treaties.* [S.l.]: Lanthorne Press, 1975, 24 p., paper, story.

with Charles V. De Vet

04270 *Cosmic checkmate.* New York: Ace Books, 1962, 96 p., paper, novel. [Bound with *King of the fourth planet* / by Robert Moore Williams].
21444 retitled: *Second game.* New York: DAW Books, 1981, 158 p., paper, novel. [Expanded edition].
Second game—SEE: *Cosmic checkmate.*

with Carl West

28866 *Dark wing.* New York: An Argo Book, Atheneum, 1979, 242 p., cloth, novel.

MACLEISH, Roderick, 1926-

28867 *Prince Ombra.* New York: Congdon & Weed, 1982, 305 p., cloth, novel.

MACLENNAN, (John) Hugh, 1907-1990

28868 *Voices in time.* New York: Toronto: Macmillan of Canada, 1980, 313 p., cloth, novel.

MACLEOD, Charlotte (Matilda Hughes), 1922-

28869 *The curse of the giant hogweed.* Garden City, NY: Doubleday & Co., 1985, 184 p., cloth, novel.

*MACLEOD, Joseph (Todd) Gordon, 1903-1984?

MACLEOD, Sheila [i.e., Sheila MacLeod Jones], 1939-

28870 *Circuit-breaker.* London: Bodley Head, 1978, 163 p., cloth, novel.
28871 *Xanthe and the robots.* London: Bodley Head, 1977, 248 p., cloth, novel.

MACMANUS, Yvonne (Cristina), 1931-

28872 *The presence: a novel of paranormal, psychological horror.* New York: Pinnacle Books, 1982, 275 p., paper, novel.

MacMILLAN, Ian (T.)

28873 *Blakely's ark.* New York: Berkley Books, 1981, 182 p., paper, novel.

MacMINN, Strother, 1918- , *with Syd Mead*

28874 *Sentinel: steel couture—Syd Mead—futurist.* Hendrik-ido-Ambacht, Netherlands: Dragon's Dream, 1979, 157 p., cloth, art.

MACNEE, Patrick, 1922- , *with Marie Cameron*

19245 *Blind in one ear: the Avenger returns.* London: Harrap, 1988, 398 p., cloth, nonf.

MACRAE, G. V.

28875 *G.I. Joe: Operation: robot assassin.* New York: Ballantine Books, 1985, 90 p., paper, novel. FIND YOUR FATE #3—G.I. JOE. [Cover byline gives the authors as H. William Stine and Megan Stine, and the series number as #4; cover byline for *Terror trap*, by H. William Stine and Megan Stine (q.v.), gives the cover author as G. V. Macrae and the series number as #3].
Operation: robot assassin—SEE: G.I. Joe: Operation: robot assassin.

MACVEY, John W(ishart), 1923-

15839 *Journey to Alpha Centauri.* New York: Macmillan Publishing Co., 1965, 256 p., cloth, fiction. [Largely nonfiction speculation, but the book includes a novella-length fictional account of a trip to Alpha Centauri].

*MADARIAGA (y Rojo), Salvador, 1886-1978

MADDEN, Timothy A.

28877 *Outbanker.* Lake Geneva, WI: TSR Inc., 1990, 314 p., paper, novel.

MADDOX, Tom

28878 *Halo.* New York: Tor, A Tom Doherty Associates Book, 1991, viii+216 p., cloth, novel.

MADDUX, Bob

28879 *Fantasy explosion.* Ventura, CA: Regal Books, 1986, 153 p., paper, nonf.

28880 *Gem of the wanderer.* Van Nuys, CA: Bible Voice Inc., 1979, 184 p., paper, novel.

*MADDUX, Rachel, 1912-1983

MADLEE, Dorothy (Haynes), 1917-1980, *with Andre Norton*

28881 *Star Ka'at.* New York: Walker & Co., 1976, 122 p., cloth, novel. STAR KA'ATS #1.
28882 *Star Ka'at world.* New York: Walker & Co., 1978, 130 p., cloth, novel. STAR KA'ATS #2.
28883 *Star Ka'ats and the plant people.* New York: Walker & Co., 1979, 122 p., cloth, novel. STAR KA'ATS #3.
28884 *Star Ka'ats and the winged warriors.* New York: Walker & Co., 1981, 123 p., cloth, novel. STAR KA'ATS #4.

MADSEN, Axel, 1932-

28885 *Unisave.* New York: Ace Books, 1980, 264 p., paper, novel.

MADSEN, David (Lawrence), 1929-

28886 *U.S.S.A..* New York: William Morrow & Co., 1989, 369 p., cloth, novel.

MAFFEI, Fredric

28887 *The life of Humbug.* New York: Manor Books, 1979, 221 p., paper, novel.

MAGEE, Glenn A.

28888 *The U.N.C.L.E. technical manual.* Canoga Park, CA: New Media Books, 1986, 2 v.?, paper, nonf.

with John Peel

28889 *A classic files magazine spotlight on The U.N.C.L.E. files: The mission begins.* Canoga Park, CA: Psi Fi Movie Press, 1986, 2 v. (I-53 p.; II-59 p.), paper, nonf.
28890 *Classic files magazine spotlight on The U.N.C.L.E. files: The show takes off.* Canoga Park, CA: Psi Fi Movie Press, 1986, 2 v. (I-54 p.; II-54 p.), paper, nonf.
The mission begins—SEE: A classic files magazine spotlight on The U.N.C.L.E. files: The mission begins.

The show takes off—SEE: *Classic files magazine spotlight on The U.N.C.L.E. files: The show takes off.*
The U.N.C.L.E. files: The mission begins—SEE: *A classic files magazine spotlight on The U.N.C.L.E. files: The mission begins.*
The U.N.C.L.E. files: The show takes off—SEE: *Classic files magazine spotlight on The U.N.C.L.E. files: The show takes off.*

MAGGIN, Elliot S., 1950-

Last son of Krypton—SEE: *Superman: last son of Krypton.*
Miracle Monday—SEE: *Superman: Miracle Monday.*
28891 *Superman: Last son of Krypton.* New York: Warner Books, 1978, 238 p., paper, novel. SUPERMAN SERIES.
28892 *Superman: Miracle Monday.* New York: Warner Books, 1981, 205 p., paper, novel. SUPERMAN SERIES.

MAGID, Ron, *with Wendy Rathbone & Kay Anderson & Edward Gross & Sheldon Teitelbaum*

16369 *The making of the Trek films.* East Meadow, NY: Image Publishing, 1991, 172 p., paper, nonf.

MAGILL, Frank N(orthen), 1907-

28893 *Science fiction: alien encounter.* Pasadena, CA: Salem Press; Epping, England: R. R. Bowker Co., 1981, xvi+376 p., paper, nonf.

with Keith Neilson

28894 *Survey of modern fantasy literature.* Englewood Cliffs, NJ: Salem Press, 1983, xviii+2538+li p. in 5 v., cloth, nonf. anth.
28895 *Survey of science fiction literature: five hundred 2,000-word essay reviews of world-famous science fiction novels with 2,500 bibliographical references.* Englewood Cliffs, NJ: Salem Press, 1979, xxv+2542+vii p. in 5 v., cloth, nonf. anth.

MAGISTRALE, Anthony (Samuel) "Tony," 1952-

28896 *Landscape of fear: Stephen King's American gothic* / by Tony Magistrale. Bowling Green, OH: Bowling Green State University Popular Press, 1988, 132 p., cloth, nonf.
28897 *The moral voyages of Stephen King.* Mercer Island, WA: Starmont House, 1989, vi+157 p., cloth, nonf. STARMONT STUDIES IN LITERARY CRITICISM #25.
28898 *The Shining reader.* Mercer Island, WA: Starmont House, 1990, xii+220 p, cloth, nonf. anth. STARMONT STUDIES IN LITERARY CRITICISM #30.

MAGISTRALE, Tony—SEE: Magistrale, Anthony

MAGLIO, Mitchell (L.)

28899 *The official Star Trek quiz book.* New York: A Wallaby Book, Pocket Books, 1985, 256 p., paper, nonf.

MAGON, Jymn, *as* ROBYN TALLIS

Horrorvid—SEE: *Planet builders.*
28900 *Planet builders: Horrorvid.* New York: Ivy Books, 1989, 185 p., paper, novel. PLANET BUILDERS #8.

MAGUIRE, Gregory, 1955-

28901 *The daughter of the moon.* New York: Farrar Straus Giroux, 1980, 257 p., cloth, novel.
28902 *The dream stealer.* New York: Harper & Row, 1983, 118 p., cloth, novel.
28903 *I feel like the morning star.* Cambridge, MA: Harper & Row, 1989, viii+275 p., cloth, novel.
28904 *Lightning time.* New York: Farrar Straus Giroux, 1978, 247 p., cloth, novel. DANIEL RIDER #1.
28905 *Lights on the lake.* New York: Farrar Straus Giroux, 1981, 214 p., cloth, novel. DANIEL RIDER #2.

MAHADOO, C. S.

28906 *Twilight escapism.* Vacoas, Mauritius: C. S. Mahadoo, 1974?, 37 p., paper, coll.

MAHN, Klaus—SEE: Mahr, Kurt

MAHONY, Elizabeth—SEE: Winthrop, Elizabeth

MAHR, Kurt [pseud. of Klaus Mahn], 1936-

28907 *Action: Division 3.* New York: Ace Books, 1976, 185 p., paper, novel. PERRY RHODAN #94. [Includes additional fiction and nonfiction].

28908 *The ambassadors from Aurigel.* New York: Ace Books, 1975, 155 p., paper, novel. PERRY RHODAN #64. [Includes additional fiction and nonfiction].

28909 *The atom hell of Grautier.* New York: Ace Books, 1975, 159 p., paper, novel. PERRY RHODAN #71. [Includes additional fiction and nonfiction].

28910 *The beasts below.* Van Nuys, CA: Master Publications, 1979, 64 p., paper, novel. PERRY RHODAN #128. [Translation of *Bestien der unterwelt*].

28911 *Between the galaxies.* Van Nuys, CA: Master Publications, 1978, 56 p., paper, novel. PERRY RHODAN #119. [Translation of *Zwischen den milchstrassen*].

28912 *Caves of the Druufs.* New York: Ace Books, 1975, 157 p., paper, novel. PERRY RHODAN #72. [Includes additional fiction and nonfiction].

28913 *Checkmate: universe.* New York: Ace Books, 1975, 160 p., paper, novel. PERRY RHODAN #74. [Includes additional fiction and nonfiction].

28914 *Death waits in semispace.* New York: Ace Books, 1975, 157 p., paper, novel. PERRY RHODAN #61. [Includes additional fiction and nonfiction].

28915 *Death's demand.* New York: Ace Books, 1977, 121-251 p., paper, novel. PERRY RHODAN #114. [Bound with *Heritage of the lizard people* / by Clark Darlton].

28916 *Desert of death's domain.* New York: Ace Books, 1976, 185 p., paper, novel. PERRY RHODAN #100. [Includes additional fiction and nonfiction].

28917 *Enemy in the dark.* New York: Ace Books, 1975, 203 p., paper, novel. PERRY RHODAN #85. [Includes additional fiction and nonfiction].

28918 *Fortress in time.* Van Nuys, CA: Master Publications, 1978, 55 p., paper, novel. PERRY RHODAN #123. [Translation of *Das Versteck in der zukunft*].

28919 *The idol from Passa.* New York: Ace Books, 1976, 182 p., paper, novel. PERRY RHODAN #98. [Includes additional fiction and nonfiction].

Menace of atomigeddon—SEE: *Perry Rhodan: Menace of atomigeddon.*

28920 *Perry Rhodan: Menace of atomigeddon.* New York: Ace Books, 1977, 110 p., paper, novel. PERRY RHODAN SERIES. [Bound with *Flight from Tarkihl* / by Clark Darlton].

28921 *The plasma monster.* New York: Ace Books, 1976, 186 p., paper, novel. PERRY RHODAN #95. [Includes additional fiction and nonfiction].

28922 *Renegades of the future.* New York: Ace Books, 1975, 155 p., paper, novel. PERRY RHODAN #65. [Includes additional fiction and nonfiction].

28923 *Sgt. Robot.* New York: Ace Books, 1977, 125-252 p., paper, novel. PERRY RHODAN #110. [Includes some nonfiction; Bound with *The stolen spacefleet* / by Clark Darlton].

28924 *Station of the invisibles.* Van Nuys, CA: Master Publications, 1979, 64 p., paper, novel. PERRY RHODAN #133. [Translation of *Station der unsichtbaren*].

28925 *Wonderflower of Utik.* New York: Ace Books, 1976, 181 p., paper, novel. PERRY RHODAN #105. [Includes additional fiction and nonfiction].

MAHY, Margaret (May), 1936-

28926 *Aliens in the family.* New York, Toronto: Scholastic Inc., 1985, 174 p., cloth, novel.

28927 *The blood-and-thunder adventures on Hurricane Peak.* London: Macmillan, 1989, 144 p., cloth, novel.
The boy who bounced, and other magic tales—SEE: *Mahy magic.*

28928 *The changeover: a supernatural romance.* London: J. M. Dent & Sons, 1984, 214 p., cloth, novel.

28929 *Dangerous spaces.* London: Hamish Hamilton, 1991, 131 p., cloth, novel.

28930 *The door in the air, and other stories.* London: J. M. Dent & Sons, 1988, [106] p., cloth, coll.

28931 *The downhill crocodile whizz, and other stories.* London: J. M. Dent & Sons, 1984, 214 p., cloth, coll.

28932 *The haunting.* London: J. M. Dent & Sons, 1982, 135 p., cloth, novel.

28933 *Leaf magic, and five other favourites.* London: J. M. Dent & Sons, 1984, 64 p., cloth, coll.

28934 *Mahy magic: a collection of the most magical stories from the Margaret Mahy story books.* London: J. M. Dent & Sons, 1986, 154 p., cloth, coll.

28934A retitled: *The boy who bounced, and other magic tales.* Harmondsworth, Middlesex, England: Puffin Books, 1988, 154 p., paper, coll.

28935 *The tricksters.* London: J. M. Dent & Sons, 1986, 266 p., cloth, novel.

MAIKOWSKI, Michael F., *with Chris L. Wolf*

28936 *Fire in the sky.* Canoga Park, CA: Major Books, 1978 (i.e., 1979?), 205 p., paper, novel.

MAILE, Ben

28937 *The land of tomorrow.* Lewes, East Sussex, England: The Book Guild, 1990, 161 p., cloth, novel. LAND OF TOMORROW #1.
28938 *Run fox run.* Lewes, East Sussex, England: The Book Guild, 1990, [200] p., cloth, novel. LAND OF TOMORROW #2.

MAILER, Norman (Kingsley), 1923-

28939 *Ancient evenings.* Boston: Little, Brown & Co., 1983, 709 p., cloth, novel.

MAILLET, (Marie) Antonine, 1929-

28940 *The tale of Don l'Orignal.* Toronto: Clarke, Irwin, 1978, 107 p., cloth, novel. [Translation by Barbara Godard of *Don l'Orignal*].

MAIN, Carol

28941 *Betony and the sorcerer.* London: Bodley Head, 1990, 141 p., cloth, novel.
28941A retitled: *Spellbound!* London: Red Fox, 1991, 141 p., paper, novel.
28942 *Planet of adventure.* London: Hodder & Stoughton, 1986, 112 p., cloth, novel. FRASER FAMILY #3.
28943 *Planet of evil.* London: Hodder & Stoughton, 1983, 111 p., cloth, novel. FRASER FAMILY #2.
    Spellbound!—SEE: *Betony and the sorcerer.*
28944 *The white planet.* London: Hodder & Stoughton, 1982, 126 p., cloth, novel. FRASER FAMILY #1.

MAINE, Charles Eric [pseud. of David McIllwain], 1921-1981

    The big death—SEE: *The darkest of nights.*
09562 *The darkest of nights.* London: Hodder & Stoughton, 1962, 254 p., cloth, novel.
28945 retitled: *The big death.* London: Sphere Books, 1978, 223 p., paper, novel. [Revised edition].
    Thirst!—SEE: *The tide went out.*
09572 *The tide went out.* London: Hodder & Stoughton, 1958, 190 p., cloth, novel.
28946 retitled: *Thirst!* London: Sphere Books, 1977, 187 p., paper, novel. [Revised edition].

MAITLAND, Derek, 1943-

37928 *The alpha experience.* London: W. H. Allen & Co., 1974, viii+199 p., cloth, novel.
37929 *The minus tower.* London: MacGibbon & Kee, 1971, 191 p., cloth, novel.

MAITLAND, Margaret, pseud.—SEE: DuBreuil, Linda & Wallmann, Jeffrey M.

MAITLAND, Sara (Louise), 1950-

28947 *The book of spells.* London: Michael Joseph, 1987, 174 p., cloth, coll.

with Lisa Appignanesi

16731 *The Rushdie file.* London: ICA, Fourth Estate, 1989, x+258 p., cloth, nonf. anth.

MAITRE, Doreen

28948 *Literature and possible worlds.* London: Published for Middlesex Polytechnic Press by Pembridge Press, 1983, 128 p., cloth, nonf.

MAITZ, Don(ald), 1953-

28949 *First Maitz: selected works.* Kansas City, MO: Ursus Imprints, 1988, [87] p., cloth, art coll. [Winner of the *Locus* Award for Best Nonfiction, 1988 (1989)].

MAJOR, Austin—SEE: Small, Austin J.

MAJOR, H. M., pseud.—SEE: Jarvis, Sharon & Buckley, Kathleen

MALAMUD, Bernard, 1914-1986

28950 *God's grace.* New York: Farrar Straus Giroux, 1982, 223 p., cloth, novel.

MALCOLM, Andrew I(an), 1927-

28951 *R I P 7: a novel.* Don Mills, Ontario, Canada: Musson Book Co., 1976, 162 p., cloth, novel.

MALCOLM, Donald, 1930-1975

28952 *The Iron Rain.* Toronto, New York: Laser Books, 1976, 190 p., paper, novel.
28953 *The unknown shore.* Toronto, New York: Laser Books, 1976, 191 p., paper, novel.

MALCOM, Grant, pseud.—SEE: Hughes, Dennis Talbot

*MALEC, Alexander, <u>1929-</u>

MALERICH, Edward P.—SEE: Easton, Edward

MALET, Vincent Mills- —SEE: Mills-Malet, Vincent

MALIK, Rex, 1928-

28954 *Future imperfect: science fact and science fiction.* London: Frances Pinter, 1980, ix+219 p., cloth, nonf. anth.

MALINOVSKII, Aleksandr—SEE: Bogdanov, Alexander

MALLETT, Daryl F(urumi), 1969- , *with Robert Reginald*

28955 *Reginald's science fiction and fantasy awards: a comprehensive guide to the awards and their winners, 2nd ed.* San Bernardino, CA: R. Reginald, The Borgo Press, 1991, 248 p., cloth, nonf. BORGO LITERARY GUIDES #1.

MALLINSON, Sue

37930 *The serpent and the butterfly.* London: Robert Hale, 1980, 204 p., cloth, novel.

MALLORY, Lewis

28956 *Gate of fear.* London: Hamlyn Paperbacks, 1981, 156 p., paper, novel.
28957 *The nursery.* London: Hamlyn Paperbacks, 1981, 157 p., paper, novel.

MALMGREN, Carl D(arryl), 1948-

28958 *Worlds apart: narratology of science fiction.* Bloomington, IN: Indiana University Press, 1991, ix+208 p., cloth, nonf.

MALONE, Adrian, *with Sharlene Belanger & Steven Talley*

17673 *The secret.* Boston: Houghton Mifflin Co., 1984, 390 p., cloth, novel.

MALONE, Robert

28959 *The robot book.* New York: Push Pin Press, A Harvest/HBJ Book, 1978, 159 p., paper, nonf.
28960 *Rocketship: an incredible voyage through science fiction and science fact.* NY, Hagerstown: A Push Pin Press Book, Harper & Row, Publishers, 1977, 125 p., paper, nonf.

MALONEY, Mack

28961 *The circle war.* New York: Zebra Books, Kensington Publishing Corp., 1987, 413 p., paper, novel. WINGMAN #2.
The final storm—SEE: *Wingman: The final storm.*
Freedom express—SEE: *Wingman: Freedom express.*
The Lucifer crusade—SEE: *Wingman: The Lucifer crusade.*
Return from the inferno—SEE: *Wingman: Return from the inferno.*
Skyfire—SEE: *Wingman: Skyfire.*
Thunder in the East—SEE: *Wingman: Thunder in the East.*
The twisted cross—SEE: *Wingman: The twisted cross.*
28962 *War heaven.* New York: Zebra Books, Kensington Publishing Corp., 1991, 477 p., paper, novel.
28963 *Wingman.* New York: Zebra Books, Kensington Publishing Corp., 1987, 460 p., paper, novel. WINGMAN #1.
28964 *Wingman: Freedom express.* New York: Zebra Books, Kensington Publishing Corp., 1990, 379 p., paper, novel. WINGMAN #7.
28965 *Wingman: Return from the inferno.* New York: Zebra Books, Kensington Publishing Corp., 1991, 349 p., paper, novel. WINGMAN #9.
28966 *Wingman: Skyfire.* New York: Zebra Books, Kensington Publishing Corp., 1990, 349 p., paper, novel. WINGMAN #8.
28967 *Wingman: The final storm.* New York: Zebra Books, Kensington Publishing Corp., 1989, 350 p., paper, novel. WINGMAN #6.
28968 *Wingman: The Lucifer crusade.* New York: Zebra Books, Kensington Publishing Corp., 1987, 413 p., paper, novel. WINGMAN #3.
28969 *Wingman: The twisted cross.* New York: Zebra Books, Kensington Publishing Corp., 1989, 382 p., paper, novel. WINGMAN #5.
28970 *Wingman: Thunder in the East.* New York: Zebra Books, Kensington Publishing Corp., 1988, 430 p., paper, novel. WINGMAN #4.

MALTA, Demetrio Aguilera—SEE: Aguilera Malta, Demetrio

MALZBERG, Barry N(orman), 1939-

28971 *The best of Barry N. Malzberg.* New York: Pocket Books, 1976, xv+398 p., paper, coll.

28972 *Chorale.* Garden City, NY: Doubleday & Co., 1978, 182 p., cloth, novel.

28973 *Conversations.* Indianapolis, IN, New York: Bobbs-Merrill Co., 1975, 87 p., cloth, novel.

28974 *The cross of fire.* New York: Ace Books, 1982, 168 p., paper, novel.

28975 *Down here in the dream quarter.* Garden City, NY: Doubleday & Co., 1976, xxi+194 p., cloth, coll.

28976 *The engines of the night: science fiction in the eighties.* Garden City, NY: Doubleday & Co., 1982, xii+198 p., cloth, nonf. coll. [Winner of the *Locus* Award for Best Nonfiction, 1982 (1983)].

28977 *Galaxies.* New York: Pyramid Books, 1975, 128 p., paper, novel.

28978 *The Gamesman.* New York: Pocket Books, 1975, 188 p., paper, novel.

28979 *The last transaction.* Los Angeles: Pinnacle Books, 1977, 163 p., paper, novel.

28980 *Malzberg at large.* New York: Ace Books, 1979, 259 p., paper, coll. [Includes *Dwellers of the deep*].

28981 *The man who loved the midnight lady: a collection.* Garden City, NY: Doubleday & Co., 1980, 201 p., cloth, coll.

28982 *The many worlds of Barry Malzberg.* New York: Popular Library, 1975, 159 p., paper, coll.

28983 *The remaking of Sigmund Freud.* New York: A Del Rey Book, Ballantine Books, 1985, xii+275 p., paper, novel.

28984 *Scop.* New York: Pyramid Books, 1976, 128 p., paper, novel.

with Piers Anthony & Martin H. Greenberg & Charles G. Waugh

16714 *Uncollected stars.* New York: Avon, 1986, vii+312 p., paper, anth.

with Edward L. Ferman

23042 *Arena: sports SF.* Garden City, New York: Doubleday & Co., 1976, x+223 p., cloth, anth.

23043 *Final stage: the ultimate SF anthology.* Baltimore: Penguin Books, 1975, 284 p., paper, anth. ["First complete edition of an original anthology published in 1974 with several stories cut" (see #05377)].

23044 *Graven images: three original novellas of science fiction.* Nashville, New York: Thomas Nelson Publishers, 1977, 151 p., cloth, anth.

with Bill Pronzini

28985 *Bug-eyed monsters.* New York, London: A Harvest/HBJ Original, Harcourt Brace Jovanovich, 1980, x+273 p., paper, anth.

28986 *Dark sins, dark dreams: crime in science fiction.* Garden City, NY: Doubleday & Co., 1978, xii+224 p., cloth, anth.

28987 *The end of summer: science fiction of the Fifties.* New York: Ace Books, 1979, 311 p., paper, anth.

28987A retitled: *The fifties: the end of summer.* New York: Baronet Publishing Co., 1979, 311 p., paper, anth.
   The fifties—SEE: *The end of summer.*

28988 *Night screams.* Chicago: Playboy Press, 1979, 262 p., cloth, novel.

37931 *Prose Bowl.* New York: St. Martin's Press, 1980, 180 p., cloth, novel.

28989 *Shared tomorrows: science fiction in collaboration.* New York: St. Martin's Press, 1979, xiv+233 p., cloth, anth.

with Bill Pronzini & Martin H. Greenberg

24574 *The Arbor House treasury of horror and the supernatural.* New York: Arbor House, 1981, 599 p., paper, anth.

24574A retitled: *Great tales of horror & the supernatural.* Secaucus, NJ: Galahad Books, Castle Books, 1985, 597 p., cloth, anth. [Abridged edition].

24574B retitled: *Classic tales of horror and the supernatural.* New York: Quill, 1991, 599 p., paper, anth.

24574C retitled: *The giant book of horror stories.* ?: Magpie, 1991, 597 p., paper, anth. [Abridged edition].
   Classic tales of horror and the supernatural—SEE: *The Arbor House treasury of horror and the supernatural.*
   The giant book of horror stories—SEE: *The Arbor House treasury of horror and the supernatural.*
   Great tales of horror & the supernatural—SEE: *The Arbor House treasury of horror and the supernatural.*

with Martin Harry Greenberg & Joseph D. Olander

24528 *Neglected visions.* Garden City, NY: Doubleday & Co., 1979, ix+211 p., cloth, anth.

MAN, Piter—SEE: Mann, Peter

MANCHEL, Frank, 1935-

28990 *An album of great science fiction films.* New York: Franklin Watts, 1976, 96 p., cloth, nonf.

28991 *An album of great science fiction films, rev. ed.* New York, London: Franklin Watts, 1982, 87 p., cloth, nonf.

28992 *An album of modern horror films.* New York: Franklin Watts, 1983, 90 p., cloth, nonf.

MANCINI, Anthony, 1939-

28993 *Minnie Santangelo & the evil eye.* New York: Coward, McCann & Geoghegan, 1977, 224 p., cloth, novel. MINNIE SANTANGELO #2.

MANCUSO, Ted

28994 *The Granville hypothesis.* New York: Manor Books, 1979, 218 p., paper, novel.

MANDEL, Geoffrey (T.), 1959-

28995 *U.S.S. Enterprise officer's manual.* New York: Interstellar Associates, 1980, [110] p., paper, fiction.

with Eileen Palestine

28996 *Star Fleet medical reference manual.* New York: Ballantine Books, 1977, 160 p., paper, fiction.

MANDELIK, Nina [pseud. of Nina Jana Hajda], 1933-

28997 *Entity.* New York: Diamond Books, 1991, 323 p., paper, novel.

MANDER, Mary R.—SEE: Grylls, Rosalie Glynn

MANDEVILLE, Colin, pseud.

28998 *The last day of New York?* London, New York: Springwood Books; New York: Charterhouse, 1980, 267 p., cloth, novel.

MANDINO, Og, 1923-

28999 *The Christ Commission.* New York: Lippincott & Crowell, 1980, 258 p., cloth, novel.

MANES, Stephen, 1949-

29000 *Chicken trek: the third strange thing that happened to Oscar Noodleman.* New York: E. P. Dutton, 1987, 110 p., cloth, novel. OSCAR NOODLEMAN #3.

37932 *Monstra vs. Irving.* New York: Henry Holt & Co., 1989, 74 p., cloth, novel.

29001 *The Oscar J. Noodleman television network: the second strange thing that happened to Oscar Noodleman.* New York: E. P. Dutton, 1984, 117 p., cloth, novel. OSCAR NOODLEMAN #2.

37933 *Some of the adventures of Rhode Island Red.* New York: J. B. Lippincott, 1990, 117 p., cloth, novel.

29002 *That game from outer space: the first strange thing that happened to Oscar Noodleman.* New York: E. P. Dutton, 1983, 57 p., cloth, novel. OSCAR NOODLEMAN #1.

with Paul Somerson

37934 *Computer monsters.* New York, Toronto: Scholastic Inc., 1984, 171 p., paper, fiction coll.

37935 *Computer space adventures.* New York, Toronto: Scholastic Inc., 1984, 173 p., paper, fiction coll.

MANFRED, Ernest

37936 *Peelah; or, The bewitched maiden of Nepal.* London: Sonnenschein & Co., 1904, 312 p., cloth, novel.

*MANGELS, Arthur C., <u>1892-1966</u>

MANGUEL, Alberto, 1948-

29003 *Black water: the book of fantastic literature.* New York: Clarkson N. Potter, Publishers, 1983, xix+967 p., paper, anth.

29004 *Black water 2: more tales of the fantastic.* Toronto: Lester & Orpen Dennys, 1990, xx+941 p., paper, anth.

29004A retitled: *White fire: further fantastic literature.* London: Picador, 1991, xx+941 p., paper, anth.

29005 *The Oxford book of Canadian ghost stories.* Toronto: Oxford University Press, 1990, xii+276 p., paper, anth.

White fire: further fantastic literature— SEE: *Black water 2: more tales of the fantastic.*

with Gianni Guadalupi

24807　*The dictionary of imaginary places.* New York: Macmillan Publishing Co., 1980, 438 p., cloth, nonf.

24808　*The dictionary of imaginary places.* San Diego, CA: Harcourt Brace Jovanovich, 1987, 454 p., paper, nonf. [Expanded edition].

MANK, Gregory W(illiam), 1950-

29006　*It's alive! the classic cinema saga of Frankenstein.* San Diego: A. S. Barnes & Co., 1981, 196 p., cloth, nonf.

29007　*Karloff and Lugosi: the story of a haunting collaboration, with a complete filmography of their films together.* Jefferson, NC: McFarland & Co., 1990, xii+372 p., cloth, nonf.

MANKOWITZ, (Cyril) Wolf, 1924-

29008　*The devil in Texas.* London: Robert Royce, 1984, 222 p., cloth, novel.

29009　*The exquisite cadaver: being a collage of the lives and times of Lee Llooq, deceased dadaist, surrealist, and petty criminal.* London: André Deutsch, 1990, 248 p., cloth, novel.

29010　*The extraordinary Mr. Poe: a biography of Edgar Allan Poe.* New York: Summit Books, 1978, 248 p., cloth, nonf.

MANLEY, Mark

29011　*Blood sisters.* New York: Charter Books, 1985, 266 p., paper, novel.

29012　*The devil's coin.* New York: Zebra Books, Kensington Publishing Corp., 1990, 318 p., paper, novel.

29013　*Sorcerer: a novel.* New York: Popular Library, 1988, 309 p., paper, novel.

29014　*Throwback.* New York: Popular Library, 1987, 218 p., paper, novel.

MANLEY, Seon, 1921-

29015　*The ghost in the fur garden, and other stories.* New York: Lothrop, Lee & Shepard, 1977, 128 p., cloth, coll.

with Gogo Lewis

28287　*Christmas ghosts: an anthology.* Garden City, NY: Doubleday & Co., 1978, xii+227 p., cloth, anth.

28288　*Fun phantoms: tales of ghostly entertainment.* New York: Lothrop, Lee & Shepard, 1979, 186 p., cloth, anth.

28289　*Ghostly gentlewomen: two centuries of spectral stories by the gentle sex.* New York: Lothrop, Lee & Shepard, 1977, 237 p., cloth, anth.

28290　*The haunted dolls: an anthology.* Garden City, NY: Doubleday & Co., 1980, x+318 p., cloth, anth.

28291　*Ladies of fantasy: two centuries of sinister stories by the gentle sex.* New York: Lothrop, Lee & Shepard, 1975, 214 p., cloth, anth.

28292　*Ladies of the gothics: tales of romance and terror by the gentle sex.* New York: Lothrop, Lee & Shepard, 1975, 219 p., cloth, anth.

28293　*Masters of shades and shadows: an anthology of great ghost stories.* Garden City, NY: Doubleday & Co., 1978, 214 p., cloth, anth.

28294　*Masters of the macabre: an anthology of mystery, horror, and detection.* Garden City, NY: Doubleday & Co., 1975, 330 p., cloth, anth.

28295　*Nature's revenge: eerie stories of revolt against the human race.* New York: Lothrop, Lee & Shepard, 1978, 154 p., cloth, anth.

28296　*Sisters of sorcery: two centuries of witchcraft stories by the gentle sex.* New York: Lothrop, Lee & Shepard, 1976, 220 p., cloth, anth.

28297　*Women of the weird: eerie stories by the gentle sex.* New York: Lothrop, Lee & Shepard, 1976, 188 p., cloth, anth.

MANLOVE, C(olin) N(icholas), 1942-

29016　*C. S. Lewis: his literary achievement.* Basingstoke, Hampshire, England: Macmillan, 1987, x+242 p., cloth, nonf.

29017　*The impulse of fantasy literature.* London: Macmillan, 1983, xiii+174 p., cloth, nonf

29018　*Modern fantasy: five studies.* Cambridge & London: Cambridge University Press, 1975, viii+308 p., cloth, nonf. coll.

29019　*Science fiction: ten explorations.* London: Macmillan, 1986, x+249 p., cloth, nonf. coll.

*MANN, A. Philo [pseud. of Roy Allison Ald]

MANN, Del

29020　*Sands of desire.* Encino, CA: World-Wide Publishing Co., 1980, 181 p., paper, novel.

*MANN, Edward Andrew, 1932-

MANN, James A.—SEE: Mann, Jim

MANN, Jim [i.e., James Anthony Mann], 1955-

29021 *The NESFA index to the science fiction magazines and original anthologies, 1986.* Cambridge, MA: NESFA Press, 1988, vi+82 p., paper, nonf.
29022 *The NESFA index to short SF 1987.* Cambridge, MA: NESFA Press, 1989, vi+140 p., paper, nonf.
29023 *The NESFA index to short SF 1988.* Cambridge, MA: NESFA Press, 1990, viii+135 p., paper, nonf.

*MANN, John (Harvey), 1928-

MANN, Laurie D. T.

29024 *Noreascon 3 memory book.* Cambridge, MA: NESFA Press, 1991, 64 p., paper, nonf. anth.

MANN, Paul

29025 *Prime objective.* New York: Pinnacle Books, Windsor Publishing Corp., 1989, 284 p., paper, novel.

MANN, Peter [i.e., Piter Man], *with Uri Dan*

21052 *Ultimatum: Pu 94.* New York: Leisure Books, 1977, 288 p., paper, novel.

MANN, (Anthony) Phillip, 1942-

29026 *The eye of the queen.* London: Victor Gollancz, 1982, 264 p., cloth, novel
29027 *The fall of the families.* London: Victor Gollancz, 1987, 298 p., cloth, novel. STORY OF THE GARDENER #2.
29028 *Master of Paxwax.* London: Victor Gollancz, 1986, 288 p., cloth, novel. STORY OF THE GARDENER #1.
29029 *Pioneers.* London: Victor Gollancz, 1988, 320 p., cloth, novel.
29030 *Wulfsyarn: a mosaic.* London: Victor Gollancz, 1990, 287 p., cloth, novel.

MANN, Ted, *with Sean Kelly*

27040 *The secret.* Toronto, New York: A Byron Preiss Book, Bantam Books, 1982, 224 p., paper, fiction.

*MANNES, Marya, 1904-1990

*MANNIN, Ethel (Edith), 1900-1984

MANNING, Audrey Smoak

29031 *Bradbury's works, including life and background, Fahrenheit 451, Something wicked this way comes, A medicine for melancholy, The October country, questions for review, selected bibliography.* Lincoln, NE: Cliffs Notes, 1977, 91 p., paper, nonf.

MANNING, Laurence (Edward), 1899-1972

29032 *The man who awoke: a classic novel from the golden age of science fiction.* New York: Ballantine Books, 1975, 170 p., paper, novel.

MANNING-SANDERS, Ruth, 1888-1988

29033 *A cauldron of witches.* London: Pied Piper, 1988, 128 p., cloth, novel.

MANNION, Michael

29034 *Death cloud.* New York: Leisure Books, 1976, 215 p., paper, novel.

MANNIX, Daniel P(ratt IV), 1911-1984

29035 *The secret of the elms.* New York: Reader's Digest Press, 1975, 264 p., cloth, novel.

*MANNON, Warwick [pseud. of Hector Kenneth Hopkins], 1914-1988

MANSON, Cynthia, *with Sheila Williams*

29036 *Tales from Isaac Asimov's science fiction magazine: short stories for young adults.* San Diego, CA: Harcourt Brace Jovanovich, 1986, ix+298 p., cloth, anth.

MANUSHKIN, Fran(ces), 1942-

37937 *The roller coaster ghost.* New York, Toronto: Scholastic Inc., 1983, 60 p., paper, fiction. PICK-A-PATH #2.

*MANVELL, (Arnold) Roger, 1909-1987

MARCELA-FROIDEVAL, François, *with Gary Gygax & David Cook*

20426 *Oriental adventures.* Lake Geneva, WI: TSR Inc., 1985, 144 p., cloth, nonf. ADVANCED DUNGEONS & DRAGONS REFERENCE BOOKS.

MARCH, Gene

29037 *The Shakwa.* New York: Zebra Books, Kensington Publishing Corp., 1979, 203 p., paper, novel.

MARCH, Melisand, 1927-

29038 *The mandrake scream: a novel.* New York: Mason/Charter Publishers, 1975, 353 p., cloth, novel.
29039 *The site.* New York: St. Martin's Press, 1988, x+307 p., cloth, novel.

MARCONI, David (Joseph), 1956- , *with Flint Dille*

Acolytes of darkness—SEE: *Agent 13: Acolytes of darkness.*
21938 *Agent 13: Acolytes of darkness.* Lake Geneva, WI: TSR Inc., 1988, 318 p., paper, novel. AGENT 13, THE MIDNIGHT AVENGER #3. [Bound with *Web of danger* / by Aaron Allston].
21939 *The invisible empire.* Lake Geneva, WI: TSR Inc., 1986, 192 p., paper, novel. AGENT 13, THE MIDNIGHT AVENGER #1.
21940 *The serpentine assassin.* Lake Geneva, WI: TSR Inc., 1986, 192 p., paper, novel. AGENT 13, THE MIDNIGHT AVENGER #2.

MARCUS, Robert B(rown) Jr., 1947-

29040 *Shadow on the stars.* Toronto, New York: Laser Books, 1977, 190 p., paper, novel.

*MARGOLIES, Joseph A(aron), 1889-1982

MARGOLIS, Jack S(elig), 1932-

29041 *Linda Lovelace for president.* Chicago: Playboy Press, 1975, 185 p., paper, novel.

MARGROFF, Robert (Ervien), 1930- , *with Piers Anthony*

16715 *Chimaera's copper.* New York: Tor, A Tom Doherty Associates Book, 1990, 311 p., cloth, novel. DRAGON #3.
16716 *Dragon's gold.* New York: Tor SF, A Tom Doherty Associates Book, 1987, 282 p., paper, novel. DRAGON #1.
16717 *Orc's opal.* New York: Tor, A Tom Doherty Associates Book, 1990, 280 p., cloth, novel. DRAGON #4.
16718 *Serpent's silver.* New York: Tor, A Tom Doherty Associates Book, 1988, 313 p., cloth, novel. DRAGON #2.

MARILL, Alvin H(erbert), 1934- , *with James Robert Parish & Alan G. Barbour*

17359 *Karloff.* Kew Gardens, NY: Cinefax, 1969, [64] p., paper, nonf.

MARINELLI, Jean

29042 *From blight to height.* New York, Washington: Vantage Press, 1979, 75 p., cloth, novel.

MARINI Y COPPEL, Alfredo—SEE: Coppel, Alfred

MARINIS, Rick De—SEE: De Marinis, Rick

MARINO, Lawrence de—SEE: de Marino, Lawrence

MARION, pseud., *as* ANONYMOUS AUTHOR

29043 *Spiderwomon's lesbian fairy tales* [sic]. Stanford, CT: New Moon Communications, 1977, 84 p., paper, coll. ["Marion" is mentioned as author in the text].

MARK, Jan, 1943-

29044 *Aquarius.* Harmondsworth, Middlesex, England: Kestrel Books, 1982, 223 p., cloth, novel.
29045 *Divide and rule.* Harmondsworth, Middlesex, England: Kestrel Books, 1979, 246 p., cloth, novel.
29046 *The Ennead.* Harmondsworth, Middlesex, England: Kestrel Books, 1978, 252 p., cloth, novel.

MARK, Ronald, *with A. Stover*

29047 *Brains for Janes.* New Orleans, LA [i.e., Los Angeles, CA]: Pirate Press, 1948, 47 p., cloth, anth.

MARKOV, Georgii (Ivanov), 1929-1978, *with David Phillips as* DAVID ST. GEORGE

37938 *The Right Honourable Chimpanzee.* London: Secker & Warburg, 1978, 240 p., cloth, novel.

MARKS, Alan, 1957-

29048 *The antenna syndrome.* New York: Belmont Tower Books, 1979, 224 p., paper, novel.

MARKS, Laurie J., 1957-

29049 *Ara's field*. New York: DAW Books, 1991, 270 p., paper, novel. CHILDREN OF TRIAD #3.
29050 *Delan the mislaid*. New York: DAW Books, 1989, 252 p., paper, novel. CHILDREN OF TRIAD #1.
29051 *The moonbane mage*. New York: DAW Books, 1990, 254 p., paper, novel. CHILDREN OF TRIAD #2.

MARKS, Tracy, 1950-

29052 *Science fiction and fantasy trivia*. Arlington, MA: Sagittarius Rising, 1985, 52 p., paper, nonf.

MARKSON, David (Merrill), 1927-

29053 *Wittgenstein's mistress*. Elmwood Park, IL: Dalkey Archive Press, 1988, 240 p., cloth, novel.

*MARKWICK, Edward [pseud. of E. M. Johnson]

MARL, David (J.), *with David Arscott*

16805 *A flight of bright birds*. London: George Allen & Unwin, 1985, 229 p., cloth, novel.
16806 *The frozen city*. London: George Allen & Unwin, 1984, 231 p., cloth, novel.

MARLAND, Michael, 1934-

29054 *Could it be? a collection of stories of the supernatural and horrific*. London: Longman, 1978, 147 p., paper, anth.

MARLEY, Stephen, 1946-

29055 *Mortal mask*. London: Legend, 1991, 404 p., cloth, novel.
29056 *Spirit mirror*. London: Collins, 1988, 334 p., cloth, novel.

MARLIN, Jeffrey, 1940-

29057 *Getting out the ghost*. New York: Pacer Books, 1984, 160 p., cloth, novel.

MARLOW, Max, pseud.—SEE: Nicole, Christopher & Nicole, Diana

MARLOWE, Derek, 1938-

29058 *Nightshade*. London: Weidenfeld & Nicolson, 1975, 192 p., cloth, novel.

MARLOWE, Stephen [pseud. of Milton Lesser], 1928-

29059 *Translation: a novel*. Englewood Cliffs, NJ: Prentice-Hall, 1976, 246 p., cloth, novel.

MARNEY, Dean, 1952-

29060 *The computer that ate my brother*. Boston: Houghton Mifflin Co., 1985, 124 p., cloth, novel.
29061 *The trouble with Jake's double*. New York, Toronto: An Apple Paperback, Scholastic Inc., 1988, 107 p., paper, novel.

MARQUEZ, Gabriel García—SEE: García Márquez, Gabriel

MARR, John S(tuart), 1940- , *with Gwyneth Cravens*

20781 *The black death*. New York: Thomas Congdon Books, E.P. Dutton & Co., 1977, x+302 p., cloth, novel.

MARR, Melissa

29062 *Orphans of the devil*. New York: Star Distributors, 1977, 180 p., paper, novel.

MARRERO, Robert

29063 *Horrors of Hammer*. Key West, FL: RGM Publications, 1984, 131 p., paper, nonf.
Nightmare Theater—SEE: *RGM Productions presents Nightmare Theater.*
29064 *RGM Productions presents Nightmare Theater*. Key West, FL: RGM Publications, 1986, 103 p., paper, nonf.
29065 *Vampires, Hammer style*. Key West, FL: RGM Publications, 1982, 98 p., paper, nonf.

*MARS, Alastair (Campbell Gillespie), 1915-1988

MARSDEN, Simon (Nevile Lewellyn), 1948- , *with Edgar Allan Poe*

29066 *Visions of Poe: a personal selection of Edgar Allan Poe's stories and poems*. Exeter, England: Webb & Bower, 1988, 128 p., cloth, coll. [Edited by Marsden, who also illustrated the book with his photographs].

MARSH, Geoffrey, pseud.—SEE: Grant, Charles L.

MARSH, Ian, *with Peter Darvill-Evans*

21163 *Time lord.* London: Doctor Who Books, 1991, 287 p., paper, nonf.

MARSH, Rosalind J(udith), 1950-

29067 *Soviet science fiction since Stalin: science, politics, and literature.* London: Croom Helm, 1986, 338 p., cloth, nonf.

MARSHAK, Sondra, 1940?-

with Myrna Culbreath

20857 *The fate of the phoenix.* Toronto, New York: Bantam Books, 1979, 262 p., paper, novel. STAR TREK SERIES.
20858 *The price of the phoenix.* Toronto, New York: Bantam Books, 1977, 182 p., paper, novel. STAR TREK SERIES.
20859 *The Prometheus design: a Star Trek novel.* New York: A Timescape Book, Pocket Books, 1982, 190 p., paper, tele. STAR TREK #5.
20860 *Star Trek: the new voyages.* Toronto, New York: Bantam Books, 1976, xvi+237 p., paper, coll. STAR TREK SERIES.
20861 *Star Trek: the new voyages 2.* Toronto, New York: Bantam Books, 1978, xxvii+252 p., paper, anth. STAR TREK SERIES.
20862 *Triangle: a Star Trek novel.* New York: A Timescape Book, Pocket Books, 1983, 188 p., paper, tele. STAR TREK #9.

with Jacqueline Lichtenberg & Joan Winston

28340 *Star Trek lives!* Toronto, New York: Bantam Books, 1975, 274 p., paper, nonf.

with William Shatner & Myrna Culbreath

20863 *Shatner: where no man...: the authorized biography of William Shatner.* New York: A Tempo Star Book, Grosset & Dunlap, 1979, 327 p., paper, nonf.

*MARSHALL, Bruce, 1899-1987

MARSHALL, Deborah A., *with A. C. Crispin*

Death tide—SEE: *V: Death tide.*
20815 *V: Death tide.* New York: Pinnacle Books, 1985, xii+207 p., paper, tele. V #10.

MARSHALL, Gene, *with Carl F. Waedt*

29068 *Incredible adventures #1.* Chicago: Gene Marshall & Carl F. Waedt, 1977, [96] p., paper, anth. INCREDIBLE ADVENTURES #1.
29069 *Incredible adventures #2.* Chicago: Gene Marshall & Carl F. Waedt, 1977, [96] p., paper, anth. INCREDIBLE ADVENTURES #2.

MARSHALL, Laura, 1950- , *with Ursula K. Le Guin*

28014 *Fire and stone.* New York: Atheneum, 1989, 31 p., cloth, story.

MARSHALL, Roderick, 1903-1975

29070 *William Morris and his earthly paradises.* Tisbury, Wiltshire, England: Compton Press, 1979, xvii+315 p., cloth, nonf.

MARSHALL, William (Leonard), 1944-

29071 *Sci fi: a Yellowthread Street mystery.* London: Hamish Hamilton, 1981, 202 p., cloth, novel. [A mystery set at an SF convention].

MARTEN, Jacqueline (Stern)

29072 *Dream walker.* New York: Pocket Books, 1987, 440 p., paper, novel.
Forevermore—SEE: *Visions of the damned.*
29073 *Let the crags comb out her dainty hair.* New York: Popular Library, 1975, 256 p., paper, novel.
29074 *Nightmare in red.* New York: Playboy Paperbacks, 1981, 366 p., paper, novel.
29075 *Visions of the damned.* Chicago: Playboy Press Paperbacks, 1980, 319 p., paper, novel.
29075A retitled: *Forevermore.* New York, London: Pocket Books, 1988, 296 p., paper, novel.

MARTER, Ian

The ark in space—SEE: *Doctor Who and the ark in space.*
29076 *Doctor Who and the ark in space.* London: Allan Wingate, 1977, 140 p., cloth, tele. DOCTOR WHO.
29076A retitled: *Doctor Who: The ark in Space.* London: A Target Book, 1991, 140 p., paper, tele. DOCTOR WHO.

29077 *Doctor Who and the enemy of the world.* London: A Target Book, W. H. Allen, 1981, 127 p., paper, tele. DOCTOR WHO.

29078 *Doctor Who and the Ribos operation.* London: A Target Book, W. H. Allen, 1979, 143 p., paper, tele. DOCTOR WHO.

29079 *Doctor Who and the Sontaran experiment.* London: W. H. Allen, 1978, 127 p., cloth, tele. DOCTOR WHO.

29080 *Doctor Who: Earthshock.* London: W. H. Allen, 1983, 128 p., cloth, tele. DOCTOR WHO #78.

Doctor Who: The ark in space—SEE: *Doctor Who and the ark in space.*

29081 *Doctor Who: The dominators.* London: W. H. Allen & Co., 1984, 126 p., cloth, tele. DOCTOR WHO #86.

29082 *Doctor Who: The dominators; and, The Kryptons.* London: A Star Book, W. H. Allen & Co., 1988, 243 p., cloth, tele. coll. DOCTOR WHO.

29083 *Doctor Who: The invasion.* London: W. H. Allen & Co., 1985, 159 p., cloth, tele. DOCTOR WHO #98.

29084 *Doctor Who: The reign of terror.* London: W. H. Allen & Co., 1987, 160 p., cloth, tele. DOCTOR WHO #119.

29085 *Doctor Who: The rescue.* London: W. H. Allen & Co., 1987, 139 p., cloth, tele. DOCTOR WHO #124.

The Dominators—SEE: *Doctor Who: The dominators.*

The Dominators; and, The Kryptons—SEE: *Doctor Who: The dominators; and, The Kryptons.*

Earthshock—SEE: *Doctor Who: Earthshock.*

29086 *Harry Sullivan's war.* London: A Target Book, W. H. Allen & Co., 1986, 148 p., paper, tele. DOCTOR WHO COMPANIONS #2.

The invasion—SEE: *Doctor Who: The invasion.*

The reign of terror—SEE: *Doctor Who: The reign of terror.*

The rescue—SEE: *Doctor Who: The rescue.*

*MARTI-IBAÑEZ, Félix, 1911-1972

MARTIA, Astron Del—SEE: Del Martia, Astron

MARTIN, Andrew (Jack), 1952-

29087 *The knowledge of ignorance: from Genesis to Jules Verne.* Cambridge, England, New York: Cambridge University Press, 1985, x + 259 p., cloth, nonf.

29088 *The mask of the prophet: the extraordinary fictions of Jules Verne.* Oxford, England: Oxford University Press, 1990, xi + 222 p., cloth, nonf.

MARTIN, Ann M(atthews), 1955-

29089 *Ma and Pa Dracula.* New York: Holiday House, 1989, 122 p., cloth, novel.

MARTIN, Bob, *with Charles Beesley & Michael Weldon & Akira Fitton*

17671 *The psychotronic encyclopedia of film.* New York: Ballantine Books, 1983, xvi + 815 p., paper, nonf.

MARTIN, Carl, 1950- , *with John Dalmas*

21039 *Touch the stars: emergence.* New York: A Tom Doherty Associates Book, 1983, 318 p., paper, novel.

MARTIN, Catherine—SEE: Dexter, Catherine

MARTIN, David, 1935-

Crisis in space—SEE: *Doctor Who: Crisis in space.*

29090 *Doctor Who: Crisis in space.* New York: Ballantine Books, 1986, [96] p., paper, novel. FIND YOUR FATE—DOCTOR WHO #2. [Cover byline and copyright reads Michael Holt].

29091 *Doctor Who: Garden of evil.* New York: Ballantine Books, 1986, [128] p., paper, novel. FIND YOUR FATE—DOCTOR WHO #3.

29092 *Doctor Who: Search for the Doctor.* New York: Ballantine Books, 1986, [127] p., paper, novel. FIND YOUR FATE—DOCTOR WHO #1.

Garden of evil—SEE: *Doctor Who: Garden of evil.*

Search for the Doctor—SEE: *Doctor Who: Search for the Doctor.*

MARTIN, Dick(inson Payne), 1923- , *with David L. Greene*

24617 *The Oz scrapbook.* New York: Random House, 1977, 182 p., cloth, nonf.

MARTIN, Douglas (Ivor), 1939-

29093 *The telling line: essays on fifteen contemporary book illustrators.* New York: Delacorte Press, 1990, 320 p., cloth, nonf. coll.

MARTIN, George R(aymond) R(ichard), 1948-

29094 *Aces abroad: a Wild Cards mosaic novel.* Toronto, New York: Spectra, Bantam Books, 1988, 467 p., paper, anth. WILD CARDS #4.

29095 *Aces high.* Toronto, New York: Bantam Books, 1987, 390 p., paper, anth. WILD CARDS #2.

29096 *The armageddon rag.* New York: Poseidon Press; Kansas City, MO: Nemo Press, 1983, 333 p., cloth, novel. [Limited to 540 copies].

29097 *Down & dirty: a Wild Cards mosaic novel.* Toronto, New York: Spectra, Bantam Books, 1988, 518 p., paper, anth. WILD CARDS #5.

29098 *Dying of the light.* New York: Simon & Schuster, 1977, 365 p., cloth, novel.

29099 *Fevre Dream.* New York: Poseidon Press, 1982, 350 p., cloth, novel.

29100 *Fourth annual volume: new voices 4: the John W. Campbell award nominees.* New York: Berkley Books, 1981, xx+ 262 p., paper, anth.

29101 *The John W. Campbell awards, volume 5.* New York: Bluejay Books, 1984, xviii+ 238 p., paper, anth.

29102 *Jokers wild: a Wild cards mosaic novel.* Toronto, New York: Bantam Books, 1987, 374 p., paper, anth. WILD CARDS #3.

New voices I—SEE: *New voices in science fiction.*

29103 *New voices II.* New York: A Jove/HBJ Book, 1979, 283 p., paper, anth.

29104 *New voices III: the Campbell Award nominees.* New York: Berkley Books, 1980, 259 p., paper, anth.

New voices 4—SEE: *Fourth annual volume: new voices 4.*

29105 *New voices in science fiction: stories by Campbell Award nominees.* New York: Macmillan Publishing Co., 1977, xiv+ 267 p., cloth, anth.

29105A retitled: *New voices I: spellbinding original stories by the next generation of science fiction greats: the Campbell Award nominees.* New York: A Jove/HBJ Book, 1978, 336 p., paper, anth.

29106 *Nightflyers.* New York: Bluejay Books, 1985, 296 p., paper, coll.

29107 *The pear-shaped man.* Eugene, OR: Pulphouse Publishing, 1991, 46 p., cloth, story. SHORT STORY HARDBACKS #24; SHORT STORY PAPERBACKS #37.

29108 *Portraits of his children.* Arlington Heights, IL: Dark Harvest, 1987, 263 p., cloth, coll.

29109 *Sandkings.* New York: A Timescape Book, Pocket Books, 1981, 238 p., paper, coll. [Winner of the *Locus* Award for Best Collection, 1981 (1982)].

29110 *A song for Lya, and other stories.* New York: Avon, 1976, 208 p., paper, coll. [Winner of the *Locus* Award for Best Collection, 1976 (1977)].

29111 *Songs of stars and shadows.* New York: A Kangaroo Book, Pocket Books, 1977, 240 p., paper, coll.

29112 *Songs the dead men sing.* Niles, IL: Dark Harvest, 1983, xvi+290 p., cloth, coll. [Limited to 500 copies].

29113 *Tuf voyaging.* New York: Baen Science Fiction Books, 1986, 374 p., cloth, coll.

29114 *Wild cards: a mosaic novel.* Toronto, New York: Bantam Books, 1986, 410 p., paper, anth.

with Isaac Asimov & Martin H. Greenberg

17049 *The science fiction weight-loss book.* New York: Crown Publishers, 1983, v+249 p., cloth, anth.

with Paul Mikol

The hellbound heart—SEE: *Night visions 3.*

Night visions—SEE: *Night visions 3.*

Night visions: The hellbound heart—SEE: *Night visions 3.*

29115 *Night visions 3.* Niles, IL: Dark Harvest, 1986, 225 p., cloth, anth.

29115A retitled: *Night visions: all original stories.* London: Century Publishing, 1987, 298 p., cloth, anth.

29115B retitled: *Night visions: The hellbound heart.* New York: Berkley Books, 1988, 278 p., paper, anth.

with Melinda M. Snodgrass

29116 *Ace in the hole: a Wild cards mosaic novel.* New York, Toronto: Spectra, Bantam Books, 1990, 385 p., paper, anth. WILD CARDS #6.

29117 *Jokertown shuffle: a Wild Cards mosaic novel.* New York, Toronto: Spectra, Bantam Books, 1991, 390 p., paper, anth. WILD CARDS #9.

29118 *One-eyed jacks: a Wild Card mosaic novel.* New York, Toronto: Spectra, Bantam Books, 1991, 328 p., paper, anth. WILD CARDS #8.

with Melinda M. Snodgrass & John J. Miller

29119   *Dead man's hand: a Wild Card novel.* New York, Toronto: Bantam Books, 1990, 328 p., paper, anth. WILD CARDS #7.

with Lisa Tuttle

29120   *Windhaven.* New York: Timescape Books, 1981, 348 p., cloth, novel.

MARTIN, Graham Dunstan, 1932-

29121   *Catchfire* / by Graham Martin. London: George Allen & Unwin, 1981, 183 p., cloth, novel. GIFTWISH #2.

29122   *The dream wall.* London: Unwin Hyman, 1987, 231 p., cloth, novel.

29123   *Giftwish* / by Graham Martin. London, Boston: George Allen & Unwin, 1980, 200 p., cloth, novel. GIFTWISH #1.

29124   *Half a glass of moonshine.* London: Unwin Hyman, 1988, 179 p., cloth, novel.

29125   *The soul master.* London: George Allen & Unwin, 1984, 292 p., cloth, novel.

29126   *Time-slip.* London: George Allen & Unwin, 1986, 164 p., cloth, novel.

MARTIN, Jack, pseud.—SEE: Etchison, Dennis

MARTIN, John

29127   *Revolt on Jupiter.* New York: Manor Books, 1978, 218 p., paper, novel.

*MARTIN, John S(tuart), 1900-1977

MARTIN, Keith

  Master of chaos—SEE: *Steve Jackson and Ian Livingstone present Master of chaos.*

37939   *Steve Jackson and Ian Livingstone present Master of chaos.* Harmondsworth, Middlesex, England: Puffin Books, 1990, 31+[210] p., paper, fiction. FIGHTING FANTASY GAMEBOOK #41.

37940   *Steve Jackson and Ian Livingstone present Tower of Destruction.* Harmondsworth, Middlesex, England: Puffin Books, 1991, [256] p., paper, fiction. FIGHTING FANTASY GAMEBOOK #46.

  Tower of Destruction—SEE: *Steve Jackson and Ian Livingstone present Tower of Destruction.*

MARTIN, Les [pseud. of Lester Martin Schulman], 1934-

29128   *Blade runner.* New York: Random House, 1982, 91 p., cloth, movie.

29129   *The bride.* New York: Random House, 1985, 93 p., paper, movie. FRANKENSTEIN SERIES.

29130   *Indiana Jones and the last crusade.* New York: Random House, 1989, 107 p., paper, movie. INDIANA JONES SERIES.

29131   *Indiana Jones and the Temple of Doom: a tale of high adventure.* New York: Random House, 1984, 96 p., paper, movie. INDIANA JONES SERIES.

29132   *The invisible castle: a Thundercats thriller.* New York: Random House, 1986, 64 p., paper, tele.

29133   *Raiders of the lost ark: a storybook based on the movie.* New York: Random House, 1981, [57] p., paper, movie. INDIANA JONES SERIES.

29134   *Young Indiana Jones and the gypsy revenge.* New York: Random House, 1991, [123] p., cloth, novel. INDIANA JONES SERIES.

29135   *Young Indiana Jones and the princess of peril.* New York: Random House, 1991, 124 p., cloth, novel. INDIANA JONES SERIES.

29136   *Young Indiana Jones and the secret city.* New York: Random House, 1990, 123 p., cloth, novel. INDIANA JONES SERIES.

29137   *Young Indiana Jones and the tomb of terror.* New York: Random House, 1990, 123 p., cloth, novel. INDIANA JONES SERIES.

with John Polidori

29138   *The vampire.* New York: Random House, 1989, 96 p., cloth, novel. [Adapted from Polidori's original story].

with H. G. Wells

29139   *The time machine.* New York: Random House, 1990, 93 p., cloth, novel. [Adapted from Wells's original novel].

MARTIN, Lori

29140   *The darkling hills.* New York: NAL Books, New American Library, 1986, 327 p., cloth, novel.

MARTIN, Marcia, *with Eric Vinicoff*

29141   *Spacing Dutchman.* Berkeley, CA: Aesir Press, 1978, 55 p., paper, novel.

MARTIN, Philip

29142 *Doctor Who: Invasion of the Ormazoids.* New York: Ballantine Books, 1986, [125] p., paper, novel. FIND YOUR FATE—DOCTOR WHO #5.

29143 *Doctor Who: Mission to Magnus.* London: W. H. Allen & Co., 1990, 122 p., cloth, tele. DOCTOR WHO SERIES.

29144 *Doctor Who: Trial of a time lord: mindwarp.* London: W. H. Allen & Co., 1989, 142 p., cloth, tele. DOCTOR WHO #139.

29145 *Doctor Who: Vengeance on Varus.* London: W. H. Allen & Co., 1988, 137 p., cloth, tele. DOCTOR WHO #106.

Invasion of the Ormazoids—SEE: *Doctor Who: Invasion of the Ormazoids.*

Mindwarp—SEE: *Doctor Who: Trial of a time lord: mindwarp.*

Mission to Magnus—SEE: *Doctor Who: Mission to Magnus.*

Trial of a time lord: Mindwarp—SEE: *Doctor Who: Trial of a time lord: mindwarp.*

Vengeance on Varus—SEE: *Doctor Who: Vengeance on Varus.*

MARTIN, Rod, 1928- , *with John Dalmas*

21040 *The playmasters.* New York: Baen Books, 1987, 317 p., paper, novel.

MARTIN, Russ—SEE: Martin, Russell W.

MARTIN, Russell W(hite), 1933-

29146 *The desecration of Susan Browning.* New York: Playboy Paperbacks, 1981, 254 p., paper, novel.

29147 *The devil and Lisa Black.* New York: Playboy Paperbacks, 1982, 255 p., paper, novel.

29148 *The education of Jennifer Parrish* / by Russ Martin. New York: Tor, A Tom Doherty Associates Book, 1984, 319 p., paper, novel.

29149 *The obsession of Sally Wing* / by Russ Martin. New York: Tor, A Tom Doherty Associates Book, 1983, 286 p., paper, novel.

29150 *The possession of Jessica Young* / by Russ Martin. New York: Tor, A Tom Doherty Associates Book, 1982, 316 p., paper, novel.

29151 *The resurrection of Candy Sterling* / by Russ Martin. Chicago: Playboy Press, 1982, 288 p., paper, novel.

29152 *Rhea.* New York: Ermine Publishers, 1978, 301 p., cloth, novel.

MARTIN, Thomas H.—SEE: Thomas, Martin

MARTIN, Valerie (Metcalf), 1948-

29153 *Mary Reilly.* New York: Doubleday, 1990, 263 p., cloth, novel. DR. JEKYLL & MR. HYDE SEQUEL.

MARTINAC, Paula, 1954-

29154 *Out of time.* Seattle, WA: The Seal Press, 1990, 220 p., paper, novel.

MARTINDALE, T. Chris

29155 *Curse of the werewolf.* Lake Geneva, WI: TSR Inc., 1987, 191 p., paper, fiction. ADVANCED DUNGEONS & DRAGONS ADVENTURE GAMEBOOK #12.

29156 *Demon dance.* New York, London: Pocket Books, 1991, 294 p., paper, novel.

37941 *Duel of the masters.* Lake Geneva, WI: TSR Inc., 1984, 157 p., paper, novel. ENDLESS QUEST #21.

29157 *Nightblood.* New York: Warner Books, 1990, 322 p., paper, novel.

29158 *Prince of thieves.* Lake Geneva, WI: TSR Inc., 1988, 190 p., paper, novel. ADVANCED DUNGEONS & DRAGONS ADVENTURE GAMEBOOK #18.

29159 *Where the chill waits.* New York: Warner Books, 1991, 332 p., paper, novel.

MARTINE [pseud. of Joanna Martine Woolfolk], 1940-

Dance of desire—SEE: *Dance of love.*

29160 *Dance of love.* New York: Pleasure Books, 1979, 188 p., paper, novel. [Probably a reprint of an earlier book published under different title and pseudonym; bound with *Witch bitch* / by Sabrina].

29160A retitled: *Dance of desire.* New York: Pleasure Books, 1980, 188 p., paper, novel. [Bound with *Wild woman* / by Sandy].

MARTINE-BARNES, Adrienne (Zina), 1942-

29161 *The crystal sword.* New York: Avon, 1988, 278 p., paper, novel. CHRONIQUE D'AVEBURY #2.

29162 *The dragon rises.* New York: Ace Science Fiction Books, 1983, 244 p., paper, novel.

29163 *The fire sword.* New York: Avon, 1984, 374 p., paper, novel. CHRONIQUE D'AVEBURY #1.

29164 *The rainbow sword.* New York: Avon Books, 1988, 212 p., paper, novel. CHRONIQUE D'AVEBURY #3.

29165 *The sea sword.* New York: Avon, 1989, 292 p., paper, novel. CHRONIQUE D'AVEBURY #4.

MARTINSEN, Martin, pseud.—SEE: Follett, Ken

MARVIN, Susan [pseud. of Julie Ellis], 1933-

29166 *Chalet Bougy-Villars.* New York: Zebra Books, Kensington Publishing Corp., 1975, 175 p., paper, novel.

29167 *Long dark night of the soul.* New York: A Kangaroo Book, Pocket Books, 1978, 190 p., paper, novel.

MARZOLLO, Jean, 1942-

29168 *39 kids on the block: The green ghost of Appleville.* New York, Toronto: Scholastic Inc., 1989, 92 p., paper, novel. 39 KIDS ON THE BLOCK #1.

The green ghost of Appleville—SEE: 39 kids on the block: The green ghost of Appleville.

29169 *Halfway down Paddy Lane.* New York: Dial Press, 1981, 178 p., cloth, novel.

29170 *Out of time into love.* New York, Toronto: Vagabond Books, Scholastic Book Services, 1981, 165 p., paper, novel.

MASELLO, Robert

29171 *Black horizon.* New York: Jove Books, 1989, 292 p., paper, novel.

29172 *The spirit wood.* New York: Pocket Books, 1987, 345 p., paper, novel.

MASON, Anita (Frances), 1942-

29173 *The illusionist.* London: Macmillan, 1982, 283 p., cloth, novel.

29174 *The war against chaos.* London: Hamish Hamilton, 1988, 252 p., cloth, novel.

MASON, (Laura) Anne, 1941-

29175 *The dancing meteorite.* New York: Harper & Row, Publishers, 1984, 217 p., cloth, novel. DANCING METEORITE #1.

29176 *The stolen law.* New York: Harper & Row, Publishers, 1986, 218 p., cloth, novel. DANCING METEORITE #2.

MASON, Carolyn B.

29177 *Deadly impulse.* New York: Zebra Books, Kensington Publishing Corp., 1989, 300 p., paper, novel.

MASON, Cyn(thia), 1952-

29178 *Wet visions: the rainthology: a collection of soluble stories.* Eugene, OR: Hywetia Press [sic], 1988, 223 p., cloth, anth.

*MASON, David [i.e., Samuel Mason], 1924-1974

MASON, Douglas R(ankine), 1918-

29179 *Euphor unfree.* London: Robert Hale, 1977, 191 p., cloth, novel.

29180 *Mission to Pactolus R.* London: Robert Hale, 1978, 160 p., cloth, novel.

29181 *The omega worm.* London: Robert Hale, 1976, 192 p., cloth, novel. [This is a reprint, possibly of *The resurrection of Roger Diment*].

29182 *Pitman's progress.* Morley, Yorkshire, England: Elmfield Press, 1976, 172 p., cloth, novel.

29183 *The Typhon intervention.* London: Robert Hale, 1981, 206 p., cloth, novel.

as JOHN RANKINE

Android planet—SEE: Space 1999: Android planet.

Astral quest—SEE: Space 1999: Astral quest.

29184 *The bromius phenomenon.* London: Dennis Dobson, 1976, 207 p., cloth, novel.

29185 *Last shuttle to planet Earth.* London: Dennis Dobson, 1980, 182 p., cloth, novel

Lunar attack—SEE: Space 1999: Lunar attack.

29186 *Moon odyssey.* London: Futura Publications, An Orbit Book, 1975, 144 p., paper, tele. SPACE: 1999 #2.

29187 *Phoenix of Megaron.* New York: Pocket Books, 1976, 159 p., paper, tele. SPACE: 1999 SERIES.

29188 *Space 1999: Android planet.* London: Futura Publications, An Orbit Book, 1976, 140 p., paper, tele. SPACE: 1999 #8.

29189 *Space 1999: Astral quest.* London: Futura Publications, An Orbit Book, 1975, 157 p., paper, tele. SPACE: 1999 #6.

29190 *Space 1999: Lunar attack.* London: Futura Publications, An Orbit Book, 1975, 141 p., paper, tele. SPACE: 1999 #5.

29191   *The star of Hesiock.* London: Dennis Dobson, 1980, 217 p., cloth, novel.

29192   *The Thorburn enterprise.* London: Dennis Dobson, 1977, 184 p., cloth, novel.

29193   *The Vort programme.* London: Dennis Dobson, 1979, 191 p., cloth, novel.

MASON, Jeff, *with David Kubicek*

29194   *October dreams: a harvest of horror.* Lincoln, NE: Kubicek & Associates, 1989, xi+162 p., paper, anth.

MASON, Lisa (Susan), 1953-

29195   *Arachne.* New York: William Morrow & Co., 1990, 263 p., cloth, novel.

*MASON, Lowell B(lake), 1893-1983

MASON, Mary, *with Stephen Goldin*

Jade Darcy and the affair of honor—SEE: *The rehumanization of Jade Darcy: Jade Darcy and the affair of honor.*

Jade Darcy and the zen pirates—SEE: *The rehumanization of Jade Darcy: Jade Darcy and the zen pirates.*

24072   *The rehumanization of Jade Darcy: Jade Darcy and the affair of honor.* New York: A Signet Book, New American Library, 1988, 254 p., paper, novel. REHUMANIZATION OF JADE DARCY #1.

24073   *The rehumanization of Jade Darcy: Jade Darcy and the zen pirates.* New York: A Roc Book, 1990, 293 p., paper, novel. REHUMANIZATION OF JADE DARCY #2.

MASON, Paul

29196   *The sword of the templar.* Harmondsworth, Middlesex, England: Puffin Books, 1987, [300] p., paper, fiction. ROBIN OF SHERWOOD SERIES.

with Steve Williams

Black vein prophecy—SEE: *Steve Jackson and Ian Livingstone present Black vein prophecy.*

29197   *The riddling reaver.* Harmondsworth, Middlesex, England: Puffin Books, 1986, 234 p., paper, novel. FIGHTING FANTASY GAMEBOOK.

Slaves of the abyss—SEE: *Steve Jackson and Ian Livingstone present Slaves of the abyss.*

29198   *Steve Jackson and Ian Livingstone present Black vein prophecy.* Harmondsworth, Middlesex, England: Puffin Books, 1990, [200] p., paper, fiction. FIGHTING FANTASY GAMEBOOK #42.

29199   *Steve Jackson and Ian Livingstone present Slaves of the abyss.* Harmondsworth, Middlesex, England: Puffin Books, 1988, 21+[200] p., paper, fiction. FIGHTING FANTASY GAMEBOOK.

MASON, Robert (Caverly), 1942-

29200   *Weapon.* New York: G. P. Putnam's Sons, 1989, 317 p., cloth, novel. WEAPON #1.

MASON, Roger, pseud.—SEE: de Vere, V. C.

MASON, Samuel—SEE: Mason, David

MASON, Simone

29201   *The web of Selagor.* Strathmartine by Dundee, Scotland: ScoTpress, 1977, 39 p., paper, tele. STAR TREK SERIES.

MASON, Tom, 1958-

29202   *Plan 9 from outer space: the original uncensored and uncut screenplay.* Newbury Park, CA: Malibu Graphics, 1990, vi+90 p., paper, nonf. anth. [Includes the screenplay by Edward D. Wood, with additional essays and commentary].

MASSA, Jack [i.e., John Andrew Massa], 1953-

29203   *Mooncrow.* New York: A Berkley Book, Berkley Publishing Corp., 1979, 217 p., paper, novel.

MASSA, John A.—SEE: Massa, Jack

*MASSIE, Chris, pseud., 1880-1964

MASSOGLIA, Martin F.—SEE: Massoglia, Marty

MASSOGLIA, Marty [i.e. Martin Frank Massoglia], 1946-

29204   *Checklist of Ace SF through 1968.* East Lansing, MI: Marty Massoglia, 1969, 11 leaves, paper, nonf.

MASTERS, Anthony, 1940-

29205   *Cries of terror.* London: Arrow Books, 1976, 191 p., paper, anth.

29206   *Klondyker.* London: Sprint, Simon & Schuster, 1991, 110 p., cloth, novel.

29207 *Nobody's child.* London: Hippo, 1989, 133 p., paper, novel.

29208 *Shellshock.* London: Methuen, 1990, 138 p., cloth, novel.

29209 *Traffic.* London: Sprint, Simon & Schuster, 1991, 110 p., cloth, novel.

as RICHARD TATE

29210 *The dead travel fast.* London: Constable, 1971, 191 p., cloth, novel.

with Nicholas Barker

17398 *Red ice.* London: Constable, 1986, 250 p., cloth, novel.

MASTERS, Dexter (Wright), 1908 1989

15840 *The cloud chamber.* Boston: Little, Brown & Co., 1971, 302 p., cloth, novel.

MASTERS, Doug

The Beast—SEE: *TNT: The Beast.*
The Devil's Claw—SEE: *TNT: The Devil's Claw.*
Killer angel—SEE: *TNT: Killer angel.*
Ritual of blood—SEE: *TNT: Ritual of blood.*
Spiral of death—SEE: *TNT: Spiral of death.*

29211 *TNT.* New York: Charter Books, 1985, 216 p., paper, novel. TNT #1.

29212 *TNT: Killer angel.* New York: Charter Books, 1986, 184 p., paper, novel. TNT #5.

29213 *TNT: Ritual of blood.* New York: Charter Books, 1986, 185 p., paper, novel. TNT #6.

29214 *TNT: Spiral of death.* New York: Charter Books, 1985, 197 p., paper, novel. TNT #3.

29215 *TNT: The Beast.* New York: Charter Books, 1985, 201 p., paper, novel. TNT #2.

29216 *TNT: The Devil's Claw.* New York: Charter Books, 1985, 184 p., paper, novel. TNT #4.

MASTERS, J. D., pseud.—SEE: Hawke, Simon

MASTERS, John, 1914-1983

29217 *The Himalayan concerto: a novel of adventure.* London: Michael Joseph, 1976, 293 p., cloth, novel.

MASTERTON, Graham, 1946-

29218 *Black angel.* Wallington, Surrey, England: Severn House, 1991, 312 p., cloth, novel.

29219 *The burning.* New York: Tor, A Tom Doherty Associates Book, 1991, 310 p., cloth, novel.

29219A retitled: *The hymn.* London: Macdonald & Co., 1991, 346 p., cloth, novel.

29220 *Charnel house.* Los Angeles: Pinnacle Books, 1978, 241 p., paper, novel.

29247A *Condor.* New York: A Tom Doherty Associates Book, 1985, 381 p., paper, novel. [Originally published under the name Thomas Luke].

29221 *Death dream.* New York: Tor Horror, A Tom Doherty Associates Book, 1988, 314 p., paper, novel. NIGHT WARRIORS #2.

29222 *Death trance.* New York: Tor Horror, A Tom Doherty Associates Book, 1986, 409 p., paper, novel. [This is a reprint; the original title is unknown].

29223 *The devils of D-Day.* Los Angeles: Pinnacle Books, 1978, 243 p., paper, novel.

29224 *The djinn.* New York: Pinnacle Books, 1977, 210 p., paper, novel.

29225 *Family portrait.* London: Arrow Books, 1985, 427 p., paper, novel.

29225A retitled: *Picture of evil.* New York: Tor, A Tom Doherty Associates Book, 1985, 379 p., paper, novel.

29226 *Famine.* London: Sphere Books, 1981, 376 p., paper, novel.

29227 *Feast.* New York: Pinnacle Books, Windsor Publishing Corp., 1988, 448 p., paper, novel.

29228 *The heirloom.* London: Sphere Books, 1981, 217 p., paper, novel.

29248A *The hell candidate.* London: Severn House, 1985, 384 p., cloth, novel. [Originally published under the name Thomas Luke].

29229 *Hurry monster.* Round Top, NY: Footsteps Press, Bill Munster, Publisher, 1988, 15 p., paper, story. [Limited to 500 copies].

The hymn—SEE: *The burning.*

29230 *Ikon.* London: A Star Book, W. H. Allen, 1983, 376 p., paper, novel.

29231 *Lords of the air.* London: Hamish Hamilton, 1988, 486 p., cloth, novel.

29232 *The manitou.* London: Neville Spearman, 1975, 160 p., cloth, novel. MANITOU #1.

29233 *Mirror.* New York: Tor, A Tom Doherty Associates Book, 1988, 440 p., cloth, novel.

29234 *Night plague.* New York: Tor Horror, A Tom Doherty Associates Book, 1991, 310 p., paper, novel. NIGHT WARRIORS #3.

29235 *Night warriors.* London: Sphere Books, 1986, 409 p., paper, novel. NIGHT WARRIORS #1.

29236 *The pariah.* London: A Star Book, W. H. Allen, 1983, 381 p., paper, novel.

Picture of evil—SEE: *Family portrait.*

29237 *Plague.* London: A Star Book, W. H. Allen, 1977, 318 p., paper, novel.

29238 *Revenge of the manitou.* Los Angeles: Pinnacle Books, 1979, 261 p., paper, novel. MANITOU #2.

29239 *Ritual.* London: Severn House, 1988, 359 p., cloth, novel.

29240 *Sacrifice.* London: W. H. Allen, 1985, 356 p., cloth, novel.

29241 *Scare care.* New York: Tor, A Tom Doherty Associates Book, 1989, xii+403 p., cloth, anth.

29242 *The sphinx.* Los Angeles: Pinnacle Books, 1978, 207 p., paper, novel.

29243 *The Sweetman curve.* New York: Ace Books, 1979, 439 p., paper, novel.

29244 *Tengu.* New York: Tor, A Tom Doherty Associates Book, 1983, 380 p., paper, novel.

29245 *Walkers.* New York: Tor, A Tom Doherty Associates Book, 1989, 345 p., cloth, novel.

29246 *The wells of Hell.* London: Sphere Books, 1981, 219 p., paper, novel.

as THOMAS LUKE

29247 *Condor.* London: A Star Book, W. H. Allen & Co., 1984, 399 p., paper, novel.

29228A *The heirloom.* New York: Pocket Books, 1982, 240 p., paper, novel. [Originally published under the name Masterton].

29248 *The hell candidate.* New York: Pocket Books, 1980, 423 p., paper, novel.

29249 *Phobia.* New York: Pocket Books, 1980, 224 p., paper, movie.

MASTORAKIS, Nico, 1941-

as S. D. NORRIS

29250 *Reckoning.* New York: Charter Books, 1985, 266 p., paper, novel.

with Barnaby Conrad

20406 *Fire below zero.* New York: A Dell Book, 1981, 303 p., paper, novel.

MATHER, Arthur (Richard), 1925-

29251 *The mind breaker.* London: Hodder & Stoughton, 1980, 284 p., cloth, novel.

29252 *The pawn.* Melbourne: Wren, 1975, 182 p., cloth, novel.

MATHER, Melissa [i.e., Melissa Mather Brown], 1917-

29253 *Emelie.* New York: Ballantine Books, 1982, 492 p., paper, novel.

MATHESON, Richard (Burton), 1926-

29254 *Bid time return.* New York: Viking Press, 1975, 278 p., cloth, novel. [Winner of the World Fantasy Award for Best Fantasy Novel, 1975 (1976)].

29254A retitled: *Somewhere in time.* New York: Ballantine Books, 1980, 278 p., paper, novel.

Collected stories—SEE: *Richard Matheson: collected stories.*

29255 *Earthbound.* London: Robinson Publishing, 1989, 186 p., cloth, novel. [Originally published under the name Logan Swanson; restores the author's original text].

The incredible shrinking man—SEE: *The shrinking man.*

29256 *Richard Matheson: collected stories.* Los Angeles: Scream/Press, 1989, 899 p., paper, coll. ["Prevue" edition of 350 copies; winner of the World Fantasy Award for Best Fantasy Collection, 1989 (1990); winner of the Bram Stoker Award for Best Horror Collection, 1989 (1990)].

Shock I—SEE: *Shock!*

09806 *Shock!* New York: Dell, 1961, 191 p., paper, coll.

09806A retitled: *Shock I: thirteen tales to thrill and terrify.* New York: A Berkley Book, Berkley Publishing Corp., 1979, 216 p., paper, coll.

09811 *The shrinking man.* New York: Gold Medal, 1956, 192 p., paper, novel.

09811A retitled: *The incredible shrinking man.* London: Sphere Books, 1988, 217 p., paper, novel.

Somewhere in time—SEE: *Bid time return.*

29257 *Somewhere in time; What dreams may come: two novels of love and fantasy.* Los Angeles: Dream/Press, 1991, iv+505 p., cloth, coll.

29258 *Through channels.* Round Top, NY: Footsteps Press, Bill Munster, 1989, 11 p., paper, story.

29259 *What dreams may come: a novel.* New York: G. P. Putnam's Sons, 1978, 304 p., cloth, novel.

as LOGAN SWANSON

29260 *Earthbound.* New York: Playboy Paperbacks, 1982, 218 p., paper, novel. [Cut without the author's permission].

with Martin H. Greenberg & Charles G. Waugh

24529 *The Twilight Zone: the original stories.* New York: Avon, 1985, 550 p., paper, anth.

MATHESON, Richard Christian, 1953-

29261 *Holiday.* Round Top, NY: Footsteps Press, 1988, 9 p., paper, story. [Limited to 452 copies].
29262 *Scars, and other distinguishing marks.* Los Angeles: Scream/Press, 1987, ix+168 p., cloth, coll.
29263 *Scars, and other distinguishing marks.* New York: Tor Horror, A Tom Doherty Associates Book, 1988, xx+262 p., paper, coll. [Expanded edition].

MATHEWS, Jack, *with Terry Gilliam*

23960 *The battle of Brazil: the authorized story and annotated screenplay of Terry Gilliam's landmark film.* New York: Crown Publishers, 1987, xi+228 p., cloth, nonf. anth.

MATHEWS, Richard (Barrett), 1944-

29264 *Aldiss unbound: the science fiction of Brian W. Aldiss.* San Bernardino, CA: R. Reginald, The Borgo Press, 1977, 64 p., paper, nonf. MILFORD SERIES: POPULAR WRITERS OF TODAY #9.
29265 *The clockwork universe of Anthony Burgess.* San Bernardino, CA: R. Reginald, The Borgo Press, 1978, 63 p., cloth, nonf. MILFORD SERIES: POPULAR WRITERS OF TODAY #19.
29266 *Introductory guide to the utopian and fantasy writing of William Morris.* London: William Morris Centre, 1976, 18 p., paper, nonf.
29267 *Lightning from a clear sky: Tolkien, the Trilogy, and the Silmarillion.* San Bernardino, CA: R. Reginald, The Borgo Press, 1978, 63 p., paper, nonf. MILFORD SERIES: POPULAR WRITERS OF TODAY #15.
29268 *Worlds beyond the world: the fantastic vision of William Morris.* San Bernardino, CA: R. Reginald, The Borgo Press, 1978, 63 p., paper, nonf. MILFORD SERIES: POPULAR WRITERS OF TODAY #13.

with Rick Wilber

29269 *Subtropical speculations: an anthology of Florida science fiction.* Sarasota, FL: Pineapple Press, 1991, 304 p., paper, anth.

*MATSCHAT, Cecile (Hulse), 1895?-1976

*MATTES, Arthur S., 1901-1972

MATTHEW, Robert, 1934-

29270 *Japanese science fiction: a view of a changing society.* London: Routledge & Kegan Paul, 1989, ix+259 p., cloth, nonf.
29271 *The origins of Japanese science fiction.* Brisbane, Australia: University of Queensland Press, 1978, 43 p., paper, nonf.

MATTHEWS, Ann

37942 *Earthquake.* New York: Ballantine Books, 1986, 72 p., paper, novel. FIND YOUR FATE—JUNIOR TRANSFORMERS #4.
29272 *Explorers picture storybook.* New York: Wanderer Books, 1985, [62] p., cloth?, movie.
29273 *Mad Max beyond Thunderdome.* New York: Wanderer Books, 1985, [58] p., cloth?, movie. MAD MAX #3.

MATTHEWS, Becky

29274 *TX fandom 1981.* Dallas, TX: Becky Matthews, 1981, 62 p., paper, nonf.

MATTHEWS, Caitlin, 1952- , *with Rachel Pollack*

29275 *Tarot tales.* London: Legend, Century Hutchinson, 1989, 304 p., paper, anth.

MATTHEWS, Clayton (Hartley), 1918- , *as uncredited co-author with Gary Brandner*

18556 *Energy zero.* New York: Zebra Books, Kensington Publishing Corp., 1976, 203 p., paper, novel. BIG BRAIN #3.

MATTHEWS, Clyde, 1917-

29276 *The Ides of March conspiracy: the year the IRS got what it deserves.* New York: Arbor House, 1979, x+307 p., cloth, novel.

MATTHEWS, Jack [i.e., John Harold Matthews Jr.], 1925-

29277 *Ghostly populations: short stories.* Baltimore, MD, London: Johns Hopkins University Press, 1987, 171 p., cloth, coll.

MATTHEWS, John H. Jr.—SEE: Matthews, Jack

MATTHEWS, Leonard J(ames)

29278 *Super book of ghost stories.* London: Hamlyn, 1977, 507 p., cloth, anth.

MATTHEWS, Patricia (Anne Brisco), 1927-

29279 *Mist of evil.* Wallington, Surrey, England: Severn House, 1990, 192 p., cloth, novel.
29281A *The night visitor.* London: Severn House, 1988, 238 p., cloth, novel. [Originally published under the name Laura Wylie].
29280 *The unquiet.* Wallington, Surrey, England: Severn House, 1991, 279 p., cloth, novel.

as PAT A. BRISCO

01899 *The other people.* Reseda, CA: Powell Publications, 1970, 204 p., paper, novel.

as LAURA WYLIE

29281 *The night visitor.* Los Angeles: Pinnacle Books, 1979, 238 p., paper, novel.

MATTHEWS, Rodney, 1945-

29282 *Last ship home.* Limpsfield, Surrey, England: Paper Tiger, 1989, 134 p., cloth, art.
29283 *The Rodney Matthews portfolio.* Limpsfield, Surrey, England: Paper Tiger, 1990, [64] p., paper, art.

MATUTE, Ana María [i.e., Ana María Matute Ausejo Goicoechea), 1925-

29284 *The heliotrope wall, and other stories.* New York: Columbia University Press, 1989, 103 p., cloth, coll. [Translation by Michael Scott Doyle of *Algunos muchachos*].

MATZKIN, M(yron A.)

29285 *The Outer Fleet.* New York: Manor Books, 1978, 221 p., paper, novel.

MAUGHAM, Robert C.—SEE: Maugham, Robin

*MAUGHAM, Robin [i.e., Robert Cecil Romer Maugham, 2nd Viscount Maugham], 1916-1981

MAUPASSANT, (Henri René Albert) Guy de, 1850-1893

29286 *The dark side of Guy de Maupassant.* London: Xanadu, 1989, xvi+252 p., cloth, coll. [Edited and translated by Arnold Kellett].
29287 *The diary of a madman, and other tales of horror.* London & Sydney: Pan Books, 1976, 170 p., paper, coll. [Edited and translated by Arnold Kellett].

MAURIER, Daphne du—SEE: du Maurier, Daph-ne

MAUROIS, André [pseud. of Émile Salomon Wilhelm Herzog], 1885-1967

15841 *Fatapouis & Thinifers.* New York: Henry Holt, 1940, 92 p., cloth, novel. [Translation by Rosemary Benét of *Patapoufs et Filifers*].
15841A retitled: *Fattypuffs and Thinifers.* London: John Lane, 1941, 92 p., cloth, novel. [Translation by Norman Denny of *Patapoufs et Filifers*].

MAXIM, John R., 1937-

29288 *The Bannerman effect.* New York: Bantam Books, 1990, 390 p., paper, novel. BANNERMAN #2.
29289 *The Bannerman solution.* Toronto, New York: Bantam Books, 1989, 423 p., paper, novel. BANNERMAN #1.
29290 *Bannerman's law.* New York: Bantam Books, 1991, 456 p., paper, novel. BANNERMAN #3.
29291 *Platforms.* New York: G. P. Putnam's Sons, 1980, 308 p., cloth, novel.
29292 *Time out of mind.* Boston: Houghton Mifflin Co., 1986, 502 p., cloth, novel.

MAXON, J. G.

29293 *Progeny.* New York, London: Pocket Books, 1989, 341 p., paper, novel.

MAXWELL, Ann (Elizabeth), 1944-

29294 *Change.* New York: Popular Library, 1975, 224 p., paper, novel.

29295 *Dancer's illusion.* New York: A Signet Book, New American Library, 1983, 190 p., paper, novel. DANCER TRILOGY #3.

29296 *Dancer's luck.* New York: A Signet Book, New American Library, 1983, 171 p., paper, novel. DANCER TRILOGY #2.

29297 *A dead god dancing.* New York: Avon, 1979, 281 p., paper, novel.

29298 *Fire dancer.* New York: A Signet Book, New American Library, 1982, 204 p., paper, novel. DANCER TRILOGY #1.

29299 *The jaws of Menx.* New York: A Signet Book, New American Library, 1981, 248 p., paper, novel.

29300 *Name of a shadow.* New York: Avon, 1980, 280 p., paper, novel.

29301 *The Singer enigma.* New York: Popular Library, 1976, 189 p., paper, novel.

29302 *Timeshadow rider.* New York: Tor SF, A Tom Doherty Associates Book, 1986, 313 p., paper, novel.

*MAXWELL, Edward [pseud. of Ted Allan, originally Alan Herman], 1918-

MAXWELL, John C., pseud.—SEE: Glasby, John

MAXXE, Robert [pseud. of Robert Rosenblum]

29303 *Arcade.* Garden City, NY: Doubleday & Co., 1984, 332 p., cloth, novel.

MAY, John

29304 *Star Wars, the empire strikes back official collectors edition.* Ridgefield, CT: Paradise Press, 1980, 63 p., paper, nonf.

MAY, Julian [i.e., Julian "Judy" May Dikty], 1931-

29305 *The adversary.* London & Sydney: Pan Books, 1984, 477 p., paper, novel. SAGA OF PLIOCENE EXILE #4.

29306 *Brede's tale.* Mercer Island, WA: Starmont House, 1982, 28 p., cloth, story. SAGA OF PLIOCENE EXILE.

29307 *The golden torc.* Boston: Houghton Mifflin Co., 1982, xxv+387 p., cloth, novel. SAGA OF PLIOCENE EXILE #2.

29308 *Intervention: a root tale to the Galactic milieu and a vinculum between it and the Saga of Pliocene exile.* Boston: Houghton Mifflin Co., 1987, 546 p., cloth, novel. GALACTIC MILIEU #1.

29308A retitled: *The surveillance.* New York: A Del Rey Book, Ballantine Books, 1988, 347 p., paper, novel. GALACTIC MILIEU #1A. [The original book split into two volumes].

29308B retitled: *The metaconcert.* New York: A Del Rey Book, Ballantine Books, 1988, 282 p., paper, novel. GALACTIC MILIEU #1B. [The original book split into two volumes].

29309 *The Many-Colored Land.* Boston: Houghton Mifflin Co., 1981, x+419 p., cloth, novel. SAGA OF PLIOCENE EXILE #1. [Winner of the *Locus* Award for Best Science Fiction Novel, 1981 (1982)].

29310 *The Many-colored land; The golden torc.* Garden City, NY: Nelson Doubleday, 1982, viii+755 p., cloth, coll. SAGA OF PLIOCENE EXILE #1-2.

The metaconcert—SEE: *Intervention.*

29311 *The nonborn king.* Boston: Houghton Mifflin Co., 1983, xli+397 p., cloth, novel. SAGA OF PLIOCENE EXILE #3.

29312 *The nonborn king; The adversary.* Garden City, NY: Nelson Doubleday, 1984, 760 p., cloth, coll. SAGA OF PLIOCENE EXILE #3-4.

29313 *A Pliocene companion: being a reader's guide to The many-colored land, The golden torc, The nonborn king, The adversary.* Boston: Houghton Mifflin Co., 1984, xiii+219 p., cloth, nonf.

The surveillance—SEE: *Intervention.*

as LEE N. FALCONER

29314 *Gazeteer of the Hyborian world of Conan, A, including also the world of Kull, and an ethnogeographical dictionary of principal peoples of the era, with reference to the Starmont Map of the Hyborian world.* West Linn, OR: Starmont House, 1977, xiii+119 p., paper, nonf.

as IAN THORNE

29315 *The blob.* Mankato, MN: Crestwood House, 1982, 47 p., cloth, movie.

29316 *Creature from the black lagoon.* Mankato, MN: Crestwood House, 1981, 46 p., cloth, movie.

29317 *The deadly mantis.* Mankato, MN: Crestwood House, 1982, 47 p., cloth, movie.

29318 *Dracula.* Mankato, MN: Crestwood House, 1977, 47 p., cloth, movie.

29319 *Frankenstein.* Mankato, MN: Crestwood House, 1977, 47 p., cloth, movie.

29320 *Frankenstein meets wolfman.* Mankato, MN: Crestwood House, 1981, 47 p., cloth, movie.

29321 *Godzilla.* Mankato, MN: Crestwood House, 1977, 47 p., cloth, nonf.

29322 *It came from outer space.* Mankato, MN: Crestwood House, 1982, 47 p., cloth, movie.

29323 *King Kong.* Mankato, MN: Crestwood House, 1977, 47 p., cloth, nonf. [Includes some fiction].

29324 *Mad scientists.* Mankato, MN: Crestwood House, 1977, 47 p., cloth, nonf. [Includes some fiction].

29325 *The mummy.* Mankato, MN: Crestwood House, 1981, 47 p., cloth, movie.

29326 *The wolf man.* Mankato, MN: Crestwood House, 1977, 48 p., cloth, movie.

with *Marion Zimmer Bradley & Andre Norton*

18493 *Black Trillium.* New York: A Foundation Book, Doubleday, 1990, 409 p., cloth, novel. TRILLIUM #1.

MAY, Karl (Friedrich), 1842-1912

29327 *Ardistan and Djinnistan: a novel.* New York: Seabury Press, 1977, vi+654 p., cloth, novel. [Translation by Michael Shaw of *Ardistan*; and, *Der mir von Dschinnistan*].

MAY, Keith M., 1927-

29328 *Aldous Huxley.* London: Elek, 1972, 252 p., cloth, nonf.

MAY, Robert S.—SEE: May, Robin

MAY, Robin [i.e., Robert Stephen May], 1929-

37943 *Robin of Sherwood and the hounds of Lucifer.* Harmondsworth, Middlesex, England: Puffin Books, 1985, 171 p., paper, tele. ROBIN OF SHERWOOD SERIES.

MAYBURY, Ged

29329 *Time twister.* Auckland, New Zealand: Ashton Scholastic, 1986, 135 p., paper?, novel.

MAYER, Robert, 1939-

29330 *I, JFK.* New York: E. P. Dutton, 1989, 262 p., cloth, novel.

29331 *Superfolks.* New York: The Dial Press, 1977, 231 p., cloth, novel.

MAYHAR, Ardath (Frances Hurst), 1930-

29332 *Exile on Vlahil.* Garden City, NY: Doubleday & Co., 1984, 183 p., cloth, novel.

29333 *Golden dream: a Fuzzy odyssey.* New York: Ace Books, 1982, xiii+303 p., paper, novel. FUZZY SERIES.

29334 *How the gods wove in Kyrannon.* Garden City, NY: Doubleday & Co., 1979, 181 p., cloth, novel. KYRANNON #1.

29335 *Khi to freedom.* New York: Ace Science Fiction Books, 1983, 246 p., paper, novel.

29336 *Lords of the triple moons.* New York: Atheneum, 1983, vii+141 p., cloth, novel. HOUSE OF ENTHALA #1.

29337 *Makra Choria.* New York: An Argo Book, Atheneum, 1987, 193 p., cloth, novel.

29338 *A place of silver silence.* New York: Millennium, A Byron Preiss Book, Walker & Co., 1988, 185 p., cloth, novel.

29339 *The runes of the lyre.* New York: An Argo Book, Atheneum, 1982, x+214 p., cloth, novel. HOUSE OF ENTHALA #2.

29340 *The saga of Grittel Sundotha.* New York: An Argo Book, Atheneum, 1985, viii+196 p., cloth, novel.

29341 *The seekers of Shar-Nuhn.* Garden City, NY: Doubleday & Co., 1980, 188 p., cloth, novel. KYRANNON #2.

29342 *Soul-singer of Tyrnos.* New York: An Argo Book, Atheneum, 1981, viii+195 p., cloth, novel. HOUSE OF ENTHALA #3.

29343 *The sword and the dagger.* Chicago: FASA Corp., 1987, 279 p., paper, novel. BATTLETECH SERIES.

29344 *The wall.* New York: Space & Time, 1987, 121 p., paper, novel.

29345 *Warlock's gift.* Garden City, NY: Doubleday & Co., 1982, 188 p., cloth, novel.

29346 *The world ends in Hickory Hollow.* Garden City, NY: Doubleday & Co., 1985, 182 p., cloth, novel.

with *Ron Fortier*

23299 *Monkey station.* Lake Geneva, WI: TSR Inc., 1989, 311 p., paper, novel.

23300 *Trail of the seahawks.* Lake Geneva, WI: TSR Inc., 1987, 222 p., paper, novel. WINDWALKER SERIES.

MAYHEW, Vic, *with Doug Long*

28498 *Fireball.* Toronto, New York: Methuen, 1977, 217 p., cloth, novel.

MAYLEAS, William—SEE: Saxon, William

MAYNARD, Joe (E.), 1942- , *with Barry Miles*

29347 *William S. Burroughs: a bibliography, 1953-73: unlocking Inspector Lee's word hoard*. Charlottesville, VA: Published for the Bibliographical Society of the University of Virginia by the University Press of Virginia, 1978, xxiii+242 p., cloth, nonf.

MAYNARD, L. H., *with M. P. N. Sims*

29348 *Shadow at midnight: ten ghost stories*. London: William Kimber, 1979, 188 p., cloth, coll.

MAYNARD, Richard (John), 1926-

29349 *The quiet place*. London: Souvenir Press, 1988, 240 p., cloth, novel.
29349A retitled: *The return*. New York: Donald I. Fine, 1988, 240 p., cloth, novel.
The return—SEE: *The quiet place*.

MAYNE, William (James Carter), 1928-

29350 *All the king's men*. London: Jonathan Cape, 1982, 182 p., cloth, coll.
29351 *Antar and the eagles*. London: Walker, 1989, 166 p., cloth, novel.
29352 *IT*. London: Hamish Hamilton, 1977, 189 p., cloth, novel.
29353 *The kelpie*. London: Jonathan Cape, 1987, 80 p., cloth, novel.
29354 *Skiffy and the twin planets*. London: Hamish Hamilton, 1982, 157 p., cloth, novel. SKIFFY #2.

as MARTIN COBALT

Pool of swallows—SEE: *Swallows*.
03112 *Swallows*. London: Heinemann, 1972, 140 p., cloth, novel.
03112A retitled: *Pool of swallows*. Nashville, TN: Thomas Nelson, 1974, 139 p., cloth, novel.

MAYO, (Everett) Clark (III), 1938-

29355 *Kurt Vonnegut: the gospel from outer space: (or, Yes we have no nirvanas)*. San Bernardino, CA: R. Reginald, The Borgo Press, 1977, 64 p., paper, nonf. MILFORD SERIES: POPULAR WRITERS OF TODAY #7.

MAYO, Hope, *with Inge Dupont*

37716 *Morgan Library ghost stories*. New York: Fordham University Press, 1990, 107 p., cloth, anth.

*MAYOR, F(lora) M(acdonald), 1872-1932

MAYR, Dallas—SEE: Ketchum, Jack

MAYS, Phillip T., *with Roy A. Squires*

29356 *The Phil Mays collection of Arkham House ephemerae*. [Glendale, CA: Roy A. Squires], 1985, 10 p., paper, nonf. [Limited to 250 copies].

MAZER, (Diana) Norma Fox, 1931-

29357 *Saturday, the Twelfth of October*. New York: Delacorte Press, 1975, 247 p., cloth, novel.
29358 *Supergirl*. New York: Warner Books, 1984, 230 p., paper, movie.

*MAZZEO, Henry (J. Jr.), 1909?-1980?

MCALEER, Neil, 1942-

29359 *Earthlove: a space fantasy*. San Francisco: Strawberry Hill Press, 1978, 347 p., cloth, novel.

MCALLISTER, Angus

29360 *The Krugg syndrome*. London: Grafton, 1988, 218 p., paper, novel.
37944 *The Canongate strangler*. Glasgow, Scotland: Dog & Bone Press, 1990, 204 p., cloth, novel.

MCALLISTER, Annie Laurie, pseud.—SEE: Cassiday, Bruce

MCALLISTER, Bruce (Hugh), 1946-

29361 *Dream baby*. New York: Tor, A Tom Doherty Associates Book, 1989, xi+434 p., cloth, novel.

as ANONYMOUS EDITOR

29362 *Their immortal hearts: three visions of time*. Reno, NV: West Coast Poetry Review, 1980, 168 p., paper, anth.

with Harry Harrison

25296 *There won't be war*. New York: Tor SF, A Tom Doherty Associates Book, 1991, viii+309 p., paper, anth.

MCALLISTER, Don(ald F.), 1934-

29363 *Cloud world*. Rolling Hills Estates, CA: Quark Publishing Co., 1986, 207 p., paper, novel.

MCARTHUR, Nancy

29364 *The plant that ate dirty socks.* New York: Avon Camelot, 1988, 119 p., paper, novel. PLANT THAT ATE DIRTY SOCKS #1.

29365 *The return of the plant that ate dirty socks.* New York: Avon Camelot, 1990, 136 p., paper, novel. PLANT THAT ATE DIRTY SOCKS #2.

MCAULAY, George, *with Andrew Harper*

25223 *Michael Moorcock: a bibliography.* Baltimore, MD: T-K Graphics, 1976, 29 p., paper, nonf.

MCAULEY, Paul J., 1955-

29366 *Eternal light.* London: Victor Gollancz, 1991, 384 p., cloth, novel. FOUR HUNDRED #3.

29367 *Four hundred billion stars.* New York: A Del Rey Book, Ballantine Books, 1988, 282 p., paper, novel. FOUR HUNDRED BILLION STARS #1.

29368 *The king of the hill.* London: Victor Gollancz, 1991, 216 p., cloth, coll.

29369 *Of the fall.* New York: A Del Rey Book, Ballantine Books, 1989, 343 p., paper, novel. FOUR HUNDRED BILLION STARS #2.

29369A retitled: *Secret harmonies.* London: Victor Gollancz, 1989, 333 p., cloth, novel. FOUR HUNDRED BILLION STARS #2.
Secret harmonies—SEE: *Of the fall.*

MCBAIN, Ed, pseud.—SEE: Hunter, Evan

MCBAIN, Gordon (Duncan III), 1946-1992

29370 *The path of Exoterra.* New York: Avon, 1981, 175 p., paper, novel. EXOTERRA #1.

29371 *Quest of the Dawnstar.* New York: An Avon Flare Book, 1984, 144 p., paper, novel. EXOTERRA #2.

MCBRATNEY, Sam

29372 *The final correction.* London: Abelard, 1978, 126 p., cloth, novel.

29373 *From the Thorenson Dykes.* London: Abelard, 1980, 126 p., cloth, novel.

29374 *The ghosts of Hungryhouse Lane.* London: Hippo, 1988, 108 p., paper, novel.

MCCAFFERY, Larry [i.e., Lawrence Florian McCaffery Jr.], 1946-

29375 *Across the wounded galaxies: interviews with contemporary American science fiction writers.* Urbana & Chicago: University of Illinois Press, 1990, 267 p., cloth, nonf. coll.

29376 *Storming the reality studio: a casebook of cyberpunk and postmodern science fiction.* Durham, NC & London: Duke University Press, 1991, xv+387 p., cloth, nonf. anth.

MCCAFFERY, Lawrence F.—SEE: McCaffery, Larry

MCCAFFREY, Anne (Inez), 1926-

29377 *Alchemy and academe: a collection of original stories concerning themselves with transmutations, mental and elemental, alchemical and academic.* New York: A Del Rey Book, Ballantine Books, 1980, xiii+271 p., paper, anth.

29378 *All the weyrs of Pern.* London: Bantam Press, 1991, 494 p., cloth, novel. PERN #11.

29379 *The coelura.* San Francisco, Columbia, PA: Underwood-Miller, 1983, 77 p., cloth, story.

29380 *The crystal singer.* New York: A Del Rey Book, Ballantine Books, 1982, 311 p., cloth, novel. KILLASHANDRA #1.

29381 *Dinosaur planet.* London: Futura Publications, 1978, [202] p., paper, novel. IRETA #1.

29382 *Dinosaur planet survivors.* New York: A Del Rey Book, Ballantine Books, 1984, 294 p., paper, novel. IRETA #2.

29383 *Dragondrums.* New York: An Argo Book, Atheneum, 1979, 240 p., cloth, novel. PERN #6—HARPER HALL #3.

29384 *The dragonriders of Pern: Dragonflight; Dragonquest; The white dragon.* Garden City, NY: Nelson Doubleday, 1978, 751 p., cloth, coll. PERN #1-3.

29385 *Dragonsdawn.* Norwalk, CT: Easton Press, 1988, 431 p., cloth, novel. PERN #9.

29386 *Dragonsinger.* New York: Atheneum, 1977, 264 p., cloth, novel. PERN #5—HARPER HALL #2.

29387 *Dragonsong.* New York: Atheneum, 1976, 202 p., cloth, novel. PERN #4—HARPER HALL #1.

29388 *Get off the unicorn.* New York: A Del Rey Book, Ballantine Books, 1977, xi+303 p., paper, coll.

29389 *The girl who heard dragons.* New Castle, VA: Cheap Street, 1985, 91 p., cloth, novel. PERN SERIES. [Limited to 199 copies].

29390 *Habit is an old horse.* Seattle, WA: Dryad Press, 1986, 22 p., cloth, coll.

29391 *The Harper Hall of Pern.* Garden City, NY: Nelson Doubleday, 1984, 501 p., cloth, coll. PERN #4-6—HARPER HALL #1-3.

29392 *The Ireta adventure: Dinosaur planet; and, Dinosaur planet survivors.* Garden City, NY: Doubleday & Co., 1985, 376 p., cloth, coll. IRETA #1-2.

29393 *Killashandra.* New York: A Del Rey Book, Ballantine Books, 1985, 303 p., cloth, novel. KILLASHANDRA #2.

29394 *Moreta, dragonlady of Pern.* New York: A Del Rey Book, Ballantine Books, 1983, xiv+286 p., cloth, novel. PERN #7.

29395 *Nerilka's story: a Pern adventure.* New York: A Del Rey Book, Ballantine Books, 1986, xvii+182 p., cloth, novel. PERN #8.

29396 *Nerilka's story; and, The coelura.* London: Bantam Books, 1987, 192 p., cloth, coll. PERN #8.

29397 *Pegasus in flight.* Norwalk, CT: Easton Press, 1990, 290 p., cloth, novel. PEGASUS #2. [Sequel to *To ride Pegasus*].

29398 *The renegades of Pern.* New York: A Del Rey Book, Ballantine Books, 1989, xii+384 p., cloth, novel. PERN #10.

29399 *Rescue run.* Newark, NJ: Wildside Press, 1991, 126 p., cloth, novel. PERN SERIES.

29400 *The Rowan.* New York: An Ace/Putnam Book, 1990, 335 p., cloth, novel. ROWAN #1.

Survivors—SEE: *Dinosaur planet survivors.*

29401 *A time when: being a tale of young Lord Jaxom, his white dragon Ruth, and various fire-lizards.* Cambridge, MA: A Boskone Book, NESFA Press, 1975, 86 p., cloth, story. PERN #3. [An excerpt from the then-forthcoming novel, *The white dragon*].

29402 *The white dragon.* New York: A Del Rey Book, Ballantine Books, 1978, x+497 p., cloth, novel. PERN #3.

29403 *The wings of Pegasus: To ride Pegasus; Pegasus in flight.* New York: Guild America Books, 1991, 446 p., cloth, coll. PEGASUS #1-2.

29404 *The worlds of Anne McCaffrey: Restoree; Decision at Doona; The ship who sang.* London: André Deutsch, 1981, 223+221+205 p., cloth, coll.

with Elizabeth Moon

29405 *Generation warriors.* Riverdale, NY: Baen Books, 1991, 345 p., paper, novel.

PLANET PIRATES #3. [Title page incorrectly lists the author as Jody Lynn Nye].

29406 *Sassinak.* New York: Baen Books, 1990, 333 p., paper, novel. PLANET PIRATES #1.

with Jody Lynn Nye

29407 *The death of sleep.* New York: Baen Books, 1990, 380 p., paper, novel.

29408 *The dragonlover's guide to Pern.* New York: A Del Rey Book, Ballantine Books, 1989, xi+178 p., cloth, nonf. PLANET PIRATES #2.

McCAIG, Donald—SEE: Ashley, Steven

McCAMMON, Robert R(ick), 1952-

29409 *Baal.* New York: Avon, 1978, ix+293 p., paper, novel.

29410 *Bethany's sin: a novel.* New York: Avon, 1980, 342 p., paper, novel.

29411 *Blue world, and other stories.* London, Glasgow: Grafton Books, 1989, viii+306 p., cloth, coll.

29412 *Boy's life.* New York: Pocket Books, 1991, 440 p., paper, novel. [Winner of the Bram Stoker Award for Best Horror Novel, 1991 (1992)].

29413 *The Horror Writers of America present: Under the fang.* New York, London: Pocket Books, 1991, xii+336 p., paper, anth.

29414 *Mine.* New York, London: Pocket Books, 1990, 442 p., cloth, novel. [Winner of the Bram Stoker Award for Best Horror Novel, 1990 (1991)].

29415 *Mystery walk.* New York: Holt, Rinehart & Winston, 1983, 388 p., cloth, novel.

29416 *The Night Boat.* New York: Avon, 1980, 261 p., paper, novel.

29417 *Stinger.* New York, London: Pocket Books, 1988, 538 p., paper, novel.

29418 *Swan song.* New York: Pocket Books, 1987, 956 p., paper, novel. [Winner of the Bram Stoker Award for Best Horror Novel, 1987 (1988)].

29419 *They thirst.* New York: Avon, 1981, 531 p., paper, novel.

Under the fang—SEE: *The Horror Writers of America present: Under the fang.*

29420 *Usher's passing.* New York: Holt, Rinehart & Winston, 1984, 401 p., cloth, novel.

29421 *The wolf's hour.* New York, London: Pocket Books, 1989, 603 p., paper, novel.

with Paul Mikol

29846 *Night visions 8: all original stories.* Arlington Heights, IL: Dark Harvest, 1990 (i.e., 1991?), 255 p., cloth, anth. [Afterword by Robert R. McCammon].

McCARTHY, Patrick A., 1945-

29422 *Olaf Stapledon.* Boston: Twayne Publishers, 1982, 166 p., cloth, nonf.

with Martin Harry Greenberg & Charles Elkins

22546 *The legacy of Olaf Stapledon: critical essays and an unpublished manuscript.* New York: Greenwood Press, 1989, x+132 p., cloth, nonf. anth. CONTRIBUTIONS TO THE STUDY OF SCIENCE FICTION AND FANTASY #34.

McCARTHY, Shawna (Lee), 1954-

Aliens and outworlders—SEE: *Isaac Asimov's Aliens and outworlders.*
Fantasy!—SEE: *Isaac Asimov's Fantasy!*
29423 *Isaac Asimov's Aliens & outworlders.* New York: The Dial Press, Davis Publications, 1983, 288 p., cloth, anth.
29424 *Isaac Asimov's Fantasy!* New York: Dial Press, 1985, 348 p., cloth, anth.
29425 *Isaac Asimov's Space of her own.* New York: The Dial Press, Davis Publications, 1983, 288 p., cloth, anth.
29425A retitled: *Isaac Asimov's Space of your own.* London: Robert Hale, 1984, 286 p., cloth, anth.
Isaac Asimov's Space of your own—SEE: *Isaac Asimov's Space of her own.*
29426 *Isaac Asimov's Wonders of the world.* New York: Dial Press, 1982, 288 p., cloth, anth.
Space of her own—SEE: *Isaac Asimov's Space of her own.*
Space of your own—SEE: *Isaac Asimov's Space of her own.*
Wonders of the world—SEE: *Isaac Asimov's Wonders of the world.*

with Lou Aronica

16797 *Full spectrum.* Toronto, New York: Spectra, Bantam Books, 1988, 483 p., paper, anth. [Winner of the *Locus* Award for Best Anthology, 1988 (1989)].

with Lou Aronica & Amy Stout & Patrick LoBrutto

16798 *Full spectrum 2.* New York: A Foundation Book, Doubleday, 1989, xi+464 p., cloth, anth.

McCARTHY, Wil(liam Terence), 1966-

29427 *Dirtyside down.* Arvada, CO: Roadkill Press, 1991, 13 p., paper, story. [Limited to 200 copies; bound with *C-minor /* by Gregory R. Hyde].

McCARTNEY, P.

29428 *Who sups with the devil?* London: New English Library, 1975, 144 p., paper, novel.

McCARTY, Dennis, 1950-

29429 *Across the Thlassa Mey.* New York: A Del Rey Book, Ballantine Books, 1991, 247 p., paper, novel. THLASSA MEY #4.
29430 *Flight to Thlassa Mey.* New York: A Del Rey Book, Ballantine Books, 1986, 319 p., paper, novel. THLASSA MEY #1.
29431 *Lords of Thlassa Mey.* New York: A Del Rey Book, Ballantine Books, 1989, 294 p., paper, novel. THLASSA MEY #3.
29432 *Warriors of Thlassa Mey.* New York: A Del Rey Book, Ballantine Books, 1987, 337 p., paper, novel. THLASSA MEY #2.

McCARTY, John (Alan), 1944-

29433 *Alfred Hitchcock presents: an illustrated guide to the ten-year television career of the master of suspense.* New York: St. Martin's Press, 1985, xiv+338 p., cloth, nonf.
29434 *Deadly resurrection.* New York: St. Martin's Press, 1990, 264 p., paper, novel.
29435 *The modern horror film: 50 contemporary classics from "The curse of Frankenstein" to "The lair of the white worm".* Secaucus, NJ: Carol Publishing Group, A Citadel Press Book, 1990, 244 p., paper, nonf.
29436 *The official splatter movie guide.* New York: St. Martin's Press, 1989, 145 p., paper, nonf.
29437 *Psychos: eighty years of mad movies, maniacs, and murderous deeds.* New York: St. Martin's Press, 1986, x+211 p., paper, nonf.
29438 *Splatter films: breaking the last taboo: critical survey of the wildly demented subgenre of the horror film that is changing the face of film forever.* Albany, NY: FantaCo Enterprises, 1981, 157 p., paper, nonf.

29439 *Video screams 1983: the official source book to horror, science fiction, fantasy, and related films on videocassette and disc.* Albany, NY: FantaCo Enterprises, 1983, xxxix+253 p., paper, nonf.

with Mark Thomas McGee

29440 *The Little Shop of Horrors book.* New York: St. Martin's Press, 1988, 173 p., paper, nonf.

McCAUGHREAN, Geraldine, 1951-

29441 *Fires' astonishment.* London: Secker & Warburg, 1990, 275 p., cloth, novel.
29442 *A pack of lies: twelve stories in one.* Oxford, England: Oxford University Press, 1988, 168 p., cloth, novel.

McCAUGHREN, Tom

29443 *Run swift, run free.* Dublin, Ireland: Wolfhound Press, 1986, 191 p., cloth, novel. FOXES #3.
29444 *Run to earth.* Dublin, Ireland: Wolfhound Press, 1984, 144 p., cloth, novel. FOXES #2.
29445 *Run to the ark.* Dublin, Ireland: Wolfhound Press, 1991, [144] p., cloth, novel. FOXES #4.
29446 *Run with the wind.* Dublin, Ireland: Wolfhound Press, 1983, 160 p., cloth, novel. FOXES #1.

McCAULEY, Kirby, 1941-

29447 *Beyond midnight.* New York: A Berkley Medallion Book, Berkley Publishing Corp., 1976, x+210 p., paper, anth.
29448 *Dark forces: new stories of suspense and supernatural horror.* New York: Viking Press, 1980, xvi+551 p., cloth, anth. [Winner of the World Fantasy Award for Best Fantasy Single Author Collection/Anthology, 1980 (1981)].
29449 *Frights: new stories of suspense and supernatural terror.* New York: St. Martin's Press, 1976, 293 p., cloth, anth. [Winner of the World Fantasy Award for Best Fantasy Single Author Collection/Anthology, 1976 (1977)].
29449A retitled: *Frights 1: new stories of suspense and the supernatural.* London: Sphere Books, 1979, 157 p., paper, anth. [The original edition split into two volumes].
29449B retitled: *Frights 2: more new stories of suspense and supernatural terror.* London: Sphere, 1979, 159 p., paper, anth.

[The original edition split into two volumes].
Frights 1—SEE: *Frights.*
Frights 2—SEE: *Frights.*

29450 *Night chills: stories of suspense and horror.* New York: Avon, 1975, 260 p., paper, anth.

McCAY, Bill

29451 *Doors to doom.* New York: An Archway Paperback, Pocket Books, 1991, 121 p., paper, novel. NINTENDO ADVENTURE BOOKS #6.
29452 *Koopa capers.* New York: An Archway Paperback, Pocket Books, 1991, 121 p., paper, novel. NINTENDO ADVENTURE BOOKS #4.
29453 *Monster mix-up.* New York: An Archway Paperback, Pocket Books, 1991, 121 p., paper, novel. NINTENDO ADVENTURE BOOKS #3.

as VICTOR APPLETON

16739 *The black dragon.* New York, London: An Archway Paperback, Pocket Books, 1991, 165 p., paper, novel. TOM SWIFT #C1.
16745 *The negative zone.* New York, London: An Archway Paperback, Pocket Books, 1991, 151 p., paper, novel. TOM SWIFT #C2.

McCHESNEY, Marion—SEE: Chesney, Marion

*McCLARY, Thomas Calvert, <u>1909?-1972</u>

McCLOY, Helen—SEE: Clarkson, Helen

McCLUSKY, Thorp

29454 *Loot of the vampire.* Oak Lawn, IL: Robert Weinberg, 1975, 92 p., paper, coll. LOST FANTASIES #2.

McCOLLUM, Michael (Allen), 1946-

29455 *Antares dawn.* New York: A Del Rey Book, Ballantine Books, 1986, 310 p., paper, novel. ANTARES #1.
29456 *Antares passage.* New York: A Del Rey Book, Ballantine Books, 1987, 311 p., paper, novel. ANTARES #2.
29457 *The clouds of Saturn.* New York: A Del Rey Book, Ballantine Books, 1991, 311 p., paper, novel.
29458 *A greater infinity.* New York: A Del Rey Book, Ballantine Books, 1982, 183 p., paper, novel.

29459 *Life PROBE.* New York: A Del Rey Book, Ballantine Books, 1983, 295 p., paper, novel. MAKERS #1.
29460 *Procyon's promise.* New York: A Del Rey Book, Ballantine Books, 1985, 283 p., paper, novel. MAKERS #2.
29461 *Thunder strike!* New York: A Del Rey Book, Ballantine Books, 1989, 403 p., paper, novel.

McCOMAS, Annette Peltz, 1911-

29462 *The eureka years: Boucher and McComas's The magazine of fantasy and science fiction, 1949-54.* Toronto, New York: Bantam Books, 1982, xvii+348 p., paper, anth.

McCONKEY, James (Rodney), 1921-

29463 *Kayo: the authentic and annotated autobiographical novel from outer space.* New York: E. P. Dutton, 1987, x+206 p., cloth, novel.

McCONNELL, Ashley

29464 *Unearthed.* New York: Diamond Books, 1991, 227 p., paper, novel.

McCONNELL, Francis D.—SEE: McConnell, Frank

McCONNELL, Frank [i.e., Francis DeMay McConnell], 1942-

29465 *The science fiction of H. G. Wells.* New York, Oxford: Oxford University Press, 1981, ix+235 p., cloth, nonf.

McCORMACK, Eric (P.), 1938-

37945 *Inspecting the vaults.* Markham, Ontario, Canada: Viking Canada, 1987, xiii+234 p., cloth, coll.
29466 *The Paradise Motel.* Markham, Ontario, Canada: Viking Canada, 1989, 210 p., cloth, novel.

McCORMACK, W(illiam) J(ohn), 1947-

29467 *Sheridan Le Fanu and Victorian Ireland.* Oxford: Clarendon Press, 1980, viii+310 p., cloth, nonf.
29468 *Sheridan Le Fanu and Victorian Ireland, 2nd ed.* Dublin: Lilliput, 1990, [310] p., paper, nonf.

McCORMICK, Lois Elizabeth

29469 *The circle.* New York: Zebra Books, Kensington Publishing Corp., 1978, 256 p., paper, novel.

McCORQUODALE, Barbara—SEE: Cartland, Barbara

McCOY, Andrew [pseud. of André Jute], 1945-

29470 *The Meyeresco helix.* London: Grafton, 1988, 412 p., paper, novel.

McCOY, Glen

29471 *Doctor Who: Timelash.* London: W. H. Allen & Co., 1985, 124 p., cloth, tele. DOCTOR WHO #105.
Timelash—SEE: Doctor Who: Timelash.

McCRUMB, Sharyn, 1948-

29472 *Bimbos of the death sun: murder most fun at the ultimate fantasy con.* Lake Geneva, WI: A Windwalker Book, TSR Inc., 1987, 219 p., paper, novel.

McCULLOUGH, Colleen [i.e., Colleen McCullough-Robinson], 1937-

29473 *A creed for the third millennium.* New York: Harper & Row, 1985, 346 p., cloth, novel.
29474 *The ladies of Missalonghi.* New York: Harper & Row, 1987, 189 p., cloth, novel.

McCUNIFF, Mara, *with Traci Briery*

18628 *The vampire memoirs.* New York: Zebra Books, Kensington Publishing Corp., 1991, 432 p., paper, novel.

McCUTCHAN, Philip (Donald), 1920-

29475 *Flood.* London: Robert Hale, 1991, 190 p., cloth, novel.

McCUTCHEN, Ann—SEE: Broomhead, Ann

McCUTCHEN, R(obert) Terry, 1947?-

29476 *The N.E.S.F.A. index to the science fiction magazines and original anthologies, 1974.* Cambridge, MA: NESFA Press, 1975, ii+44 p., paper, nonf.
29477 *The N.E.S.F.A. index to the science fiction magazines and original anthologies, 1975.* Cambridge, MA: NESFA Press, 1976, iv+36 p., paper, nonf.

29478 *The N.E.S.F.A. index to the science fiction magazines and original anthologies, 1976.* Cambridge, MA: NESFA Press, 1977, iii+38 p., paper, nonf.

McDANIEL, David (Edward), 1939-1977

Number Two—SEE: *The Prisoner #2.*
09894 *The Prisoner #2: Number Two.* New York: Ace, 1969, 158 p., paper, tele. PRIS-ONER #2.
09894A retitled: *The Prisoner: Who is Number Two?* London: New English Library, 1982, 141 p., paper, tele. PRISONER #2.
Who is Number Two?—SEE: *The Pris-oner: Who is Number Two?*

McDEVITT, Jack [i.e., John Charles McDevitt], 1935-

29479 *The Hercules Text.* New York: Ace Sci-ence Fiction Books, 1986, 307 p., paper, novel. [Winner of the *Locus* Award for Best First Novel, 1986 (1987)].
29480 *A talent for war.* New York: Ace Books, 1989, 310 p., paper, novel.

McDEVITT, John C.—SEE: McDevitt, Jack

McDONAGH, Maitland

29481 *Broken mirrors/broken minds: the dark dreams of Dario Argento.* London: Sun Tavern Fields, 1991, 293 p., cloth, nonf.

McDONALD, Collin (A.), 1943-

29482 *Nightwaves: scary tales for after dark.* New York: Cobblehill Books, 1990, 112 p., cloth, coll.

McDONALD, Ian, 1960-

29483 *Desolation road.* Toronto, New York: Spectra, Bantam Books, 1988, 355 p., paper, novel. [Winner of the *Locus* Award for Best First Novel, 1988 (1989)].
29484 *Empire dreams.* Toronto, New York: Spectra, Bantam Books, 1988, 220 p., paper, coll.
29485 *King of morning, queen of day.* New York, Toronto: Spectra, Bantam Books, 1991, 389 p., paper, coll.
29486 *Out on Blue Six.* New York, Toronto: Spectra, Bantam Books, 1989, 335 p., paper, novel.

McDONALD, Kenneth, 1914-

29487 *Red maple: how Canada became the Peo-ple's Republic of Canada in 1981.* Richmond Hill, Ontario, Canada: B.M.G. Publishing, 1975, xiii+117 p., paper, novel.

McDONALD, Steven E(dward), 1956-

29488 *The Janus syndrome.* Toronto, New York: Bantam Books, 1981, 264 p., paper, novel.

McDONELL, (Robert) Terry, 1944-

29489 *California bloodstock.* New York: Mac-millan, 1980, xii+209 p., cloth, novel.

McDONNELL, David

29490 *Star Trek V, the final frontier: the official movie magazine.* New York: Starlog Communications International, 1989, 66 p., paper, nonf. anth.
29491 *Star Trek 25th anniversary celebration.* New York: Starlog Communications In-ternational, 1991, 97 p., paper, nonf. anth.
29492 *Superman IV, the quest for peace: the offi-cial poster magazine.* New York: O'Quinn Studios, 1987, 58 p., paper, nonf.
29493 *Willow: official movie magazine.* New York: O'Quinn Studios, 1988, 66 p., paper, nonf.

with Carr D'Angelo

21082 *Aliens: the official movie magazine.* New York: O'Quinn Studios, 1986, 66 p., paper, nonf. anth.
21083 *Star Trek IV, the voyage home official movie magazine.* New York: O'Quinn Studios, 1986, 65 p., paper, nonf. anth.

with John Sayers & Tim L. Smith

29494 *Starlog science fiction trivia book.* New York: A Signet Book, New American Library, 1986, 208 p., paper, nonf.

McDONOUGH, Alex

29495 *Dragon's blood.* New York: A Byron Preiss Visual Publications Inc. Book, Ace Books, 1991, 155 p., paper, novel. SCORPIO #4.
29496 *Scorpio.* New York: A Byron Preiss Vi-sual Publications Inc. Book, Ace Books, 1990, 164 p., paper, novel. SCORPIO #1.

29497 *Scorpio descending.* New York: A Byron Preiss Visual Publications Inc. Book, Ace Books, 1991, 181 p., paper, novel. SCORPIO #3.

29498 *Scorpio rising.* New York: A Byron Preiss Visual Publications Inc. Book, Ace Books, 1990, 182 p., paper, novel. SCORPIO #2.

McDONOUGH, Craig

29499 *The NESFA hymnal, volume 1: a booke of songs fannish.* Cambridge, MA: NESFA Press, 1976, vi+68 p., paper, nonf. anth.

McDONOUGH, Thomas R(edmond), 1945-

29500 *The architects of hyperspace.* New York: Avon, 1987, 265 p., paper, novel.

McDOWELL, Michael (M.), 1950-

29501 *The amulet.* New York: Avon, 1979, 340 p., paper, novel.

29502 *Cold moon over Babylon.* New York: Avon, 1980, 292 p., paper, novel.

29503 *The elementals.* New York: Avon, 1981, 292 p., paper, novel.

29504 *The flood.* New York: Avon, 1983, 189 p., paper, novel. BLACKWATER #1.

29505 *The fortune.* New York: Avon, 1983, 172 p., paper, novel. BLACKWATER #5.

29506 *The house.* New York: Avon, 1983, 173 p., paper, novel. BLACKWATER #3.

29507 *The levee.* New York: Avon, 1983, 191 p., paper, novel. BLACKWATER #2.

29508 *Rain.* New York: Avon, 1983, 190 p., paper, novel. BLACKWATER #6.

29509 *Toplin: a novel.* Santa Cruz, CA: Scream/Press, 1985, 172 p., cloth, novel.

29510 *The war.* New York: Avon, 1983, 187 p., paper, novel. BLACKWATER #4.

McDOWELL, Michael P. Kube- —SEE: Kube-McDowell, Michael P.

***McELHINEY, Gaile Churchill, 1888-1978**

McELROY, Joseph (Prince), 1930-

29511 *Plus.* New York: Alfred A. Knopf, 1977, 215 p., cloth, novel.

McENROE, Richard S.

29512 *Flight of honor.* Toronto, New York: Bantam Books, 1984, 149 p., paper, novel. FAR STARS AND FUTURE TIMES #2.

29513 *Proteus: voices for the 80's.* New York: Ace Books, 1981, 274 p., paper, anth.

29514 *The shattered stars.* Toronto, New York: Bantam Books, 1984, 182 p., paper, novel. FAR STARS AND FUTURE TIMES #1.

29515 *Skinner.* Toronto, New York: Bantam Books, 1985, 198 p., paper, novel.

with Larry Niven & Jerry Pournelle

29516 *Warrior's blood.* New York: Ace Books, 1981, 311 p., paper, novel. BUCK ROGERS #3.

29517 *Warrior's world.* New York: Ace Books, 1981, 199 p., paper, novel. BUCK ROGERS #4.

McEVOY, Seth

29518 *All geared up.* New York: An Archway Paperback, Pocket Books, 1985, 149 p., paper, novel. NOT QUITE HUMAN #2.

29519 *Batteries not included.* New York: An Archway Paperback, Pocket Books, 1985, 147 p., paper, novel. NOT QUITE HUMAN #1.

29520 *A bug in the system.* New York: An Archway Paperback, Pocket Books, 1985, 148 p., paper, novel. NOT QUITE HUMAN #3.

29521 *Destination: brain.* New York, Toronto: A Byron Preiss Visual Publications Book, Scholastic Inc., 1987, 112 p., paper, novel. EXPLORER #2.

29522 *Escape from Jupiter.* New York, Toronto: A Byron Preiss Visual Publications Book, Scholastic Inc., 1987, 115 p., paper, novel. EXPLORER #4.

29523 *Killer robot.* New York: Pocket Books, 1986, 146 p., paper, novel. NOT QUITE HUMAN #6.

29524 *Reckless robot.* New York: An Archway Paperback, Pocket Books, 1986, 146 p., paper, novel. NOT QUITE HUMAN #4.

29525 *Samuel R. Delany.* New York: Frederick Ungar Publishing Co., 1984, ix+142 p., cloth, nonf.

29526 *Terror at play.* New York: An Archway Paperback, Pocket Books, 1986, 149 p., paper, novel. NOT QUITE HUMAN #5.

with Laure Smith

29527 *Arcade explorers: The electronic hurricane.* New York: Laurel-Leaf Books, 1985, ix+173 p., paper, novel. ARCADE EXPLORERS #3.

29528 *Arcade explorers: Revenge of the Raster gang.* New York: Laurel-Leaf Books,

1985, 175 p., paper, novel. ARCADE EX-PLORERS #2.

29529 *Arcade explorers: Save the Venturians!* New York: Laurel-Leaf Books, 1985, vii+166 p., paper, novel. ARCADE EX-PLORERS #1.

29530 *Arcade explorers: The magnetic ghost of Shadow Island.* New York: Laurel-Leaf Books, 1985, 174 p., paper, novel. AR-CADE EXPLORERS #4.

The electronic hurricane—SEE: *Arcade explorers: The electronic hurricane.*

The magnetic ghost of Shadow Island—SEE: *Arcade explorers: The magnetic ghost of Shadow Island.*

Revenge of the Raster gang—SEE: *Arcade explorers: Revenge of the Raster gang.*

Save the Venturians!—SEE: *Arcade ex-ploreres: Save the Venturians!*

McEWAN, Ian (Russell), 1948-

29531 *The child in time.* London: Jonathan Cape, 1987, 220 p., cloth, novel.

29532 *In between the sheets, and other stories.* London: Jonathan Cape, 1978, 144 p., cloth, coll.

McFERRAN, Douglass SEE: Farren, David

McGANN, Michael, house pseud.

Blood and fire—SEE: *The Marauders: Blood and fire.*

Blood kin—SEE: *The Marauders: Blood kin.*

Convoy strike—SEE: *The Marauders: Convoy strike.*

Fortress of death—SEE: *The Marauders: Fortress of death.*

The ghost warriors—SEE: *The Marauders: The ghost warriors.*

Liar's dice—SEE: *The Marauders: Liar's dice.*

29533 *The Marauders.* New York: Jove Books, 1989, 154 p., paper, novel. MARAUDERS #1. [By Ed Naha].

29534 *The Marauders: Blood and fire.* New York: Jove Books, 1991, 166 p., paper, novel. MARAUDERS #6. [By Ed Naha].

29535 *The Marauders: Blood kin.* New York: Jove Books, 1989, 168 p., paper, novel. MARAUDERS #2. [By Ed Naha].

29536 *The Marauders: Convoy strike.* New York: Jove Books, 1990, 151 p., paper, novel. MARAUDERS #4. [By Ed Naha].

29537 *The Marauders: Fortress of death.* New York: Jove Books, 1991, 184 p., paper, novel. MARAUDERS #7. [By Ed Naha].

29538 *The Marauders: Liar's dice.* New York: Jove Books, 1990, 169 p., paper, novel. MARAUDERS #3. [By Ed Naha].

29539 *The Marauders: The ghost warriors.* New York: Jove Books, 1990, 152 p., paper, novel. MARAUDERS #5. [By Ed Naha].

McGARRITY, Mark, 1943-

29540 *A passing advantage.* New York: Raw-son, Wade, 1980, 235 p., cloth, novel.

McGARRY, Mark J., 1958-

29541 *Blank slate.* New York: A Signet Book, New American Library, 1984, 287 p., paper, novel.

29542 *Sun dogs.* New York: A Signet Book, New American Library, 1981, 181 p., paper, novel.

McGEARY, Duncan

29543 *Icetowers.* New York: Tower Books, 1982, 201 p., paper, novel. GREYLOCK #2.

29544 *Snowcastles.* New York: Tower Books, 1981, 160 p., paper, novel. GREYLOCK #1.

29545 *Star Axe.* New York: Tower Books, 1980, 271 p., paper, novel.

McGECHIE, Alistair, *with Sue Bridgwater*

18625 *Perian's journey.* London: Julia MacRae Books, 1989, 133 p., cloth, novel.

McGEE, Mark Thomas, 1947-

29546 *Roger Corman: the best of the cheap acts.* Jefferson, NC: McFarland & Co., 1988, xiv+247 p., cloth, nonf.

with John McCarty

29440 *The Little Shop of Horrors book.* New York: St. Martin's Press, 1988, 173 p., paper, nonf.

McGHAN, Barry (Robert) 1939-

29547 *Science fiction and fantasy pseudonyms (revised and expanded).* Dearborn, MI: Howard DeVore, 1976, 70 p., paper, nonf.

29548 *Science fiction and fantasy pseudonyms.* Dearborn, MI: Howard DeVore, 1978, v+70 p., paper, nonf.

29549 *Science fiction and fantasy pseudonyms (revised and expanded).* Dearborn, MI:

Howard DeVore, 1979, 77 p., paper, nonf.

McGHAN, H(arlan) P.

29550 *1978 awards for best science fiction; or, The best of 1977, draft ed.* Flint, MI: H. P. McGhan, 1978, 136 p., paper, nonf.

McGHEE, Edward

29551 *The last Caesar.* Los Angeles: Pinnacle Books, 1980, 304 p., paper, novel.

with Robin Moore

29552 *The Chinese ultimatum.* New York: Pinnacle Books, 1976, 338 p., paper, novel.

McGILL, Gordon, 1943-

29553 *The abomination.* New York: A Signet Book, New American Library, 1985, 220 p., paper, novel. OMEN #5.
29554 *Amityville 3-D.* New York: A Signet Book, New American Library, 1984, 159 p., paper, movie. AMITYVILLE HORROR SERIES.
29555 *Armageddon 2000.* New York: A Signet Book, New American Library, 1982, 216 p., paper, novel. OMEN #4.
29556 *The final conflict: a novel.* New York: A Signet Book, New American Library, 1980, 196 p., paper, movie. OMEN #3.
29557 *Stallion.* London: Futura Books, 1989, 176 p., paper, novel.

McGIRT, Dan(iel), 1967-

29558 *Jason Cosmo.* New York: A Signet Book, New American Library, 1989, 235 p., paper, novel. JASON COSMO #1.
29559 *Royal chaos.* New York: A Roc Book, 1990, 239 p., paper, novel. JASON COSMO #2.

McGIVERN, Maureen (Daly), 1921- , *with William P. McGivern*

29560 *The seeing.* New York: Belmont Tower Books, 1980, 284 p., paper, novel.

McGIVERN, Patrick

37946 *American garbage: a collection.* Rotterdam, Netherlands: Futile/Proza Press, 1979, 165 p., paper, coll.

McGIVERN, William P(eter), 1921-1982, *with Maureen McGivern*

29560 *The seeing.* New York: Belmont Tower Books, 1980, 284 p., paper, novel.

McGLAMRY, Beverly—SEE: Cameron, Kate

McGOWEN, Thomas—SEE: McGowen, Tom

McGOWEN, Tom [i.e., Thomas McGowen], 1927-

29561 *King's quest.* Lake Geneva, WI: TSR Inc., 1984, 157 p., paper, novel. ENDLESS QUEST #18.
29562 *The magical fellowship.* New York: Lodestar Books, E. P. Dutton, 1991, 132 p., cloth, novel. AGE OF MAGIC TRILOGY #1.
29563 *The magician's apprentice.* New York: Lodestar Books, 1987, 119 p., cloth, novel. MAGICIAN #1.
29564 *The magicians' challenge.* New York: Lodestar Books, 1989, 138 p., cloth, novel. MAGICIAN #3.
29565 *The magician's company.* New York: Lodestar Books, 1988, 119 p., cloth, novel. MAGICIAN #2.
29566 *The shadow of Fomor.* New York: Lodestar Books, E. P. Dutton, 1991, 119 p., cloth, novel.

McGRATH, Patrick, 1950-

29567 *Blood and water, and other tales.* New York: Poseidon Press, 1988, 192 p., cloth, coll.
29568 *The grotesque: a novel.* New York: Poseidon Press, 1989, 186 p., cloth, novel.

with Bradford Morrow

29569 *The new gothic: a collection of contemporary gothic fiction.* New York: Random House, 1991, xiv+336 p., cloth, anth.

McGRAW, Eloise Jarvis, 1915-

29570 *A really weird summer.* New York: A Margaret K. McElderry Book, Atheneum, 1977, 216 p., cloth, novel.
29571 *The trouble with Jacob.* New York: A Margaret K. McElderry Book, 1988, 280 p., cloth, novel.

McGREGOR, Don

29572 *Dragonflame, & other bedtime nightmares.* Lakemont, GA: Fictioneer Books, 1978, 154 p., paper, coll.
29573 *The variable syndrome.* Clayton, GA: Fictioneer Books, 1981, 140 p., paper, novel.

McGREGOR, Phillip

29574 *Rigger black book.* Chicago: FASA Corp., 1991, 136 p., paper, fiction. SHADOWRUN SERIES.

McGUIRE, Catherine, 1948-

29575 *Raid on Nightmare Castle.* Lake Geneva, WI: TSR Inc., 1983, 157 p., paper, novel. ENDLESS QUEST #14.
29576 *Trouble on Artule.* Lake Geneva, WI: TSR Inc., 1984, 157 p., paper, novel. ENDLESS QUEST #24.

McGUIRE, John J(oseph), 1917-1981, *with H. Beam Piper*

31611 *Four-day planet; Lone star planet.* New York: Ace Books, 1979, 340 p., paper, coll. [*Lone star planet* originally published as *A planet for Texans* (see #09906); John J. McGuire's contribution to the latter is not acknowledged].

McGUIRE, Patrick L(lewellyn), 1949-

29577 *Red stars: political aspects of Soviet science fiction.* Ann Arbor, MI: UMI Research Press, 1985, xvii+152 p., cloth, nonf. STUDIES IN SPECULATIVE FICTION #7.

McGUIRE, William (J.), 1950- , *with Greg Hildebrandt*

25621 *From Tolkien to Oz.* Parsippany, NJ: Unicorn Publishing House, 1985, [96] p., cloth, art.

McHALE, Brian, 1952-

29578 *Postmodernist fiction.* New York: Methuen, 1987, xiii+264 p., cloth, nonf.

McHANEY, Dennis, *with Glenn Lord*

28528 *Fiction of Robert E. Howard: a pocket checklist.* [S.l.]: Dennis McHaney & T. Foster, 1975, [22] p., paper, nonf.

McHARGUE, Georgess, 1941-

15842 *The best of both worlds: an anthology of stories for all ages.* Garden City, NY: Doubleday & Co., 1968, 722 p., cloth, anth.
29579 *The Horseman's Word.* New York: Delacorte Press, 1981, viii+259 p., cloth, novel.
29580 *Stoneflight.* New York: Viking Press, 1975, 223 p., cloth, novel.

*McHUGH, Vincent, 1904-1983

McILWAIN, David—SEE: Maine, Charles Eric

McILWRAITH, Maureen—SEE: Hunter, Mollie

McINERNEY, Judith Whitelock, 1945-

29581 *Judge Benjamin: Superdog.* New York: Holiday House, 1982, 142 p., cloth, novel. JUDGE BENJAMIN #1.
29582 *Judge Benjamin: The superdog gift.* New York: Holiday House, 1986, 128 p., cloth, novel. JUDGE BENJAMIN #5.
29583 *Judge Benjamin: The superdog rescue.* New York: Holiday House, 1984, 138 p., cloth, novel. JUDGE BENJAMIN #3.
29584 *Judge Benjamin: The superdog secret.* New York: Holiday House, 1983, 140 p., cloth, novel. JUDGE BENJAMIN #2.
29585 *Judge Benjamin: The superdog surprise.* New York: Holiday House, 1985, 134 p., cloth, novel. JUDGE BENJAMIN #4.
Superdog—SEE: *Judge Benjamin: Superdog.*
The superdog gift—SEE: *Judge Benjamin: The superdog gift.*
The superdog rescue—SEE: *Judge Benjamin: The superdog rescue.*
The superdog secret—SEE: *Judge Benjamin: The superdog secret.*
The superdog surprise—SEE: *Judge Benjamin: The superdog surprise.*

*McINNES, Graham (Campbell), 1912-1970

McINTOSH, J. T. [pseud. of James Murdoch Macgregor], 1925-

29586 *Norman conquest 2066.* London: Corgi Books, 1977, 156 p., paper, novel.
29587 *A planet called Utopia.* New York: Zebra Books, Kensington Publishing Corp., 1979, 254 p., paper, novel.
29588 *Ruler of the world.* Toronto, New York: Laser Books, 1976, 190 p., paper, novel.
29589 *This is the way the world begins.* London: Corgi Books, 1977, 205 p., paper, novel.

McINTYRE, Clara Frances

29590 *Ann Radcliffe in relation to her time.* New Haven, CT: Yale University Press, 1920, 108 p., cloth, nonf.

McINTYRE, Vonda N(eel), 1948-

29591 *Barbary.* Boston: Houghton Mifflin Co., 1986, 192 p., cloth, novel.

29592 *The bride.* New York: A Dell Book, 1985, 221 p., paper, movie. FRANKENSTEIN SERIES.

29593 *Dreamsnake.* Boston: Houghton Mifflin Co., 1978, 313 p., cloth, novel. [Winner of the Hugo Award for Best Novel, 1978 (1979); winner of the Nebula Award for Best Novel, 1978 (1979); winner of the *Locus* Award for Best Novel, 1978 (1979)].

Enterprise: the first adventure—SEE: *Star Trek: Enterprise: the first adventure.*

29594 *The entropy effect: a Star Trek novel.* New York: A Timescape Book, Pocket Books, 1981, 224 p., paper, tele. STAR TREK #2.

29595 *The exile waiting.* Garden City, NY: Nelson Doubleday, 1975, 215 p., cloth, novel.

29596 *Fireflood, and other stories.* Boston: Houghton Mifflin Co., 1979, 281 p., cloth, coll.

29597 *Screwtop.* New York: Tor SF, A Tom Doherty Associates Book, 1989, 79 p., paper, novel. [Bound with *The girl who was plugged in* / by James Tiptree, Jr.].

The search for Spock—SEE: *Star Trek III: The search for Spock.*

29598 *Star Trek: Enterprise: the first adventure.* New York: Pocket Books, 1986, 371 p., paper, novel. STAR TREK SERIES (UNNUMBERED).

29599 *Star Trek III: The search for Spock: a Star Trek novel.* New York: Pocket Books, 1984, 297 p., paper, movie. STAR TREK #17; STAR TREK III.

29600 *Star Trek IV: The voyage home: a novel.* New York: Pocket Books, 1986, 274 p., paper, movie. STAR TREK IV.

29601 *Star Trek, The wrath of Khan: a novel.* New York: Pocket Books, 1982, 223 p, paper, movie. STAR TREK #7; STAR TREK II.

29602 *Starfarers.* Norwalk, CT: Easton Press, 1989, viii+280 p., cloth, novel. STARFARERS #1.

29603 *Superluminal.* Boston: Houghton Mifflin Co., 1983, 298 p., cloth, novel.

29604 *Transition.* Norwalk, CT: Easton Press, 1990, 290 p., cloth, novel. STARFARERS #2.

The voyage home—SEE: *Star Trek IV: The voyage home: a novel.*

The wrath of Khan—SEE: *Star Trek, The wrath of Khan: a novel.*

with Susan Janice Anderson

16458 *Aurora: beyond equality.* Greenwich, CT: A Fawcett Gold Medal Book, Fawcett Publications, 1976, 222 p., paper, anth.

*McIVER, G(eorge) A.

McKAY, Claudia, pseud.—SEE: Lamperti, Claudia

McKAY, Kenneth

29605 *Indecent relations.* New York: Playboy Paperbacks, 1982, 285 p., paper, novel.

McKEAG, Ernest L(ionel), 1896-1976

as JOHN KING

08243 *Shuna and the lost tribe.* Stoke-on-Trent, England: Harborough Publishing Co., 1951, 128 p., paper, novel. SHUNA #2.

08244 *Shuna, white queen of the jungle.* Stoke-on-Trent, England: Harborough Publishing Co., 1951, 128 p., paper, novel. SHUNA #1.

as JACK MAXWELL

37947 *Invaded by Mars!* London: Champion Library, Amalgamated Press, 1934, 64 p., paper, novel.

37948 *Terror from the stratosphere.* London: Champion Library, Amalgamated Press, 1934, 63 p., paper, novel.

McKEAN, Thomas

29606 *The secret of the seven willows.* New York: Simon & Schuster Books for Young Readers, 1991, 151 p., cloth, novel. DOORS INTO TIME #1.

29607 *Vampire vacation.* New York: An Avon Camelot Book, 1986, 136 p., paper, novel.

McKEE, Erin, *with James Tucker*

29608 *Touchstone: a tribute to Fritz Leiber and Ray Bradbury.* Salt Lake City, UT: The Mysterious Stranger Press, 1978, 88 p., paper, nonf. anth. [Limited to 977 copies].

McKEE, Lynn Armistead

29609 *Woman of the mists.* New York: Diamond Books, 1991, 343 p., paper, novel.

McKENNA, Richard, *as* VICTOR APPLETON II [*not* **the same person as SF writer Richard Milton McKenna, 1913-1964**]

00437 *Tom Swift and his Cosmotron Express.* New York: Grosset & Dunlap, 1970, 180 p., cloth, novel. TOM SWIFT JR. #A32.
00440 *Tom Swift and his Dyna-4 capsule.* New York: Grosset & Dunlap, 1969, 175 p., cloth, novel. TOM SWIFT JR. #A31.
00462 *Tom Swift and the galaxy ghosts.* New York: Grosset & Dunlap, 1971, 180 p., cloth, novel. TOM SWIFT JR. #A33. [Last book in the series].

McKENNEY, Kenneth, 1929-

29610 *The changeling.* New York: Avon, 1985, 292 p., paper, novel. CHANGLING TRILOGY #2.
29611 *The fire cloud.* New York: Simon & Schuster, 1979, 317 p., cloth, novel.
29612 *The moonchild.* New York: Simon & Schuster, 1978, 286 p., cloth, novel. CHANGLING TRILOGY #1.
29613 *The offspring.* New York: Ballantine Books, 1990, 311 p., paper, novel. CHANGLING TRILOGY #3.
29614 *The plants: a novel.* New York: G. P. Putnam's Sons, 1976, 246 p., cloth, novel.

McKENZIE, Ellen Kindt

29615 *Kashka.* New York: Henry Holt & Co., 1987, 258 p., cloth, novel. TAASH #2.

McKENZIE, Melinda—SEE: Snodgrass, Melinda

McKEONE, (Dixie) Lee

29616 *Backblast.* New York: Popular Library, 1989, 218 p., paper, novel. GHOSTER #2.
29617 *Ghoster.* New York: Popular Library, 1988, 218 p., paper, novel. GHOSTER #1.
29618 *Starfire down.* New York: Warner Books, 1991, 216 p., paper, novel. GHOSTER #3.

McKEOWN, Charles, *with Terry Gilliam*

23961 *The adventures of Baron Munchausen.* London: Mandarin, 1989, 212 p., paper, movie.

McKIERNAN, Dennis L., 1932-

29619 *The Brega path.* Garden City, NY: Doubleday & Co., 1986, 221 p., cloth, novel. SILVER CALL DUOLOGY #2.
29620 *The dark tide.* Garden City, NY: Doubleday & Co., 1984, xii+172 p., cloth, novel. IRON TOWER TRILOGY #1.
29621 *The darkest day.* Garden City, NY: Doubleday & Co., 1984, xii+178 p., cloth, novel. IRON TOWER TRILOGY #3.
29622 *Dragondoom.* New York, Toronto: Spectra, Bantam Books, 1990, xvi+485 p., paper, novel.
29623 *Shadows of doom.* Garden City, NY: Doubleday & Co., 1984, xii+174 p., cloth, novel. IRON TOWER TRILOGY #2.
29624 *Trek to Kraggen-Cor.* Garden City, NY: Doubleday & Co., 1986, 188 p., cloth, novel. SILVER CALL DUOLOGY #1. [Sequel to *Iron Tower Trilogy*].

McKILLIP, Patricia A(nne), 1948-

29625 *The changeling sea.* New York: A Jean Karl Book, Atheneum, 1988, 137 p., cloth, novel.
The chronicles of Morgon, Prince of Hed—SEE: *Riddle of stars.*
29626 *Fool's run.* New York: Warner Books, 1987, ix+221 p., cloth, novel.
29627 *Harpist in the wind.* New York: An Argo Book, Atheneum, 1979, 256 p., cloth, novel. HED #3. [Winner of the *Locus* Award for Best Fantasy Novel, 1979 (1980)].
29628 *Heir of sea & fire.* New York: Atheneum, 1978, 204 p., cloth, novel. HED #2.
29629 *The moon and the face.* New York: An Argo Book, Atheneum, 1985, 146 p., cloth, novel. KYREOL #2.
29630 *Moon-Flash.* New York: An Argo Book, Atheneum, 1984, 150 p., cloth, novel. KYREOL #1.
29631 *The night gift.* New York: Atheneum, 1976, 156 p., cloth, novel.
29632 *Riddle of stars: The riddle-master of Hed; Heir of sea and fire; Harpist in the wind.* Garden City, NY: Nelson Doubleday, 1979, 604 p., cloth, coll. HED #1-3.
29632A retitled: *The chronicles of Morgon, Prince of Hed.* London: Sidgwick & Jackson,

1981, 228+204+256 p., cloth, coll. HED #1-3.

29633 *The riddle-master of Hed.* New York: Atheneum, 1978, 228 p., cloth, novel. HED #1.

29634 *The sorceress and the cygnet.* New York: Ace Books, 1991, 231 p., cloth, novel.

29635 *The throme of the Erril of Sherill; with, The harrowing of the dragon of Hoarsbreath.* New York: Tempo Books, 1984, 165 p., paper, coll.

McKINLEY, (Jennifer Carolyn) Robin, 1952-

29636 *Beauty: a retelling of the story of Beauty & the Beast.* New York: Harper & Row, 1978, 247 p., cloth, novel.

29637 *The Blue Sword.* New York: Greenwillow Books, 1982, 272 p., cloth, novel. DAMAR #2.

29638 *The door in the hedge.* New York: Greenwillow Books, 1981, 216 p., cloth, coll.

29639 *The hero and the crown.* New York: Greenwillow Books, 1985, 246 p., cloth, novel. DAMAR #1.

29640 *Imaginary lands.* New York: Ace Books, 1985, 230 p., paper, anth. [Winner of the World Fantasy Award for Best Fantasy Anthology/Collection, 1985 (1986)].

29641 *The outlaws of Sherwood.* New York: Greenwillow Books, 1988, 282 p., cloth, novel.

McKINNEY, Jack, pseud.—SEE: Daley, Brian & Luceno, James

McKINSTRY, Lohr, *with Robert Weinberg*

29642 *The hero pulp index, 2nd ed.* Evergreen, CO: Opar Press, 1971, 48 p., paper, nonf.

McLAREN, Colin (Andrew), 1940-

29643 *Rattus rex.* London: Rex Collings, 1978, 175 p., cloth, novel.

McLAUGHLIN, Dean (Benjamin Jr.), 1931-

29644 *Hawk among the sparrows: three science fiction novellas.* New York: Charles Scribner's Sons, 1976, 198 p., cloth, coll.

McLOUGHLIN, John C., 1949-

29645 *The helix and the sword.* Garden City, NY: Doubleday & Co., 1983, xxiv+234 p., cloth, novel.

29646 *Toolmaker Koan.* New York: Baen Books, 1987, 344 p., cloth, novel.

McMAHAN, Ian (Douglas), 1940-

29647 *ESP McGee and the ghost ship.* New York: Camelot, 1984, 93 p., paper, novel. ESP MCGEE #4.

29648 *The fox's lair.* New York: Macmillan, 1983, 98 p., cloth, novel. MICROKID MYSTERY #2.

29649 *Lake Fear.* New York: Macmillan, 1985, 110 p., cloth, novel. MICROKID MYSTERY.

29650 *The lost forest.* New York: Macmillan, 1985, 113 p., cloth, novel. MICROKID MYSTERY.

McMAHAN, Jeffrey N.

29651 *Somewhere in the night: stories of suspense.* Boston: Alyson Publications, 1989, 182 p., paper, coll. VAMPIRES #1.

29652 *Vampires anonymous: a novel.* Boston: Alyson Publications, 1991, 253 p., paper, novel. VAMPIRES #2.

*McMAHON, Jeremiah, <u>1919-</u>

McMAHON, Neil—SEE: Rhodes, Daniel

McMANUS, Leslie

29653 *Operation backlash.* London: New English Library, 1977, 127 p., paper, novel.

McMULLAN, Kate (Hall), 1947-

37949 *The mystery of the missing mummy.* New York, Toronto: Scholastic Inc., 1984, 57 p., paper, fiction. PICK-A-PATH #10.

with Robert Louis Stevenson

37950 *Dr. Jekyll and Mr. Hyde.* New York: Random House, 1984, 94 p., cloth, story. [Adapted from the Stevenson tale].

McMULLEN, Sean, 1948-

29654 *Australian science fiction and fantasy: (mid-85 to mid-91).* Melbourne, Victoria, Australia: Sean McMullen, 1991, p., paper, nonf.

McMURDIE, Annie Laurie, pseud.—SEE: Cassiday, Bruce

McMURTRY, Stan, 1936-

29655 *The Bunjee venture.* Henley-on-Thames, England: Cressrelles Publishing Co., 1977, 128 p., cloth, novel.

McNALLY, Clare

29656 *Addison House.* New York: Avon Books, 1988, 298 p., paper, novel.
29657 *Come down into darkness.* London: Corgi Books, 1989, 287 p., paper, novel.
29658 *Ghost house.* Toronto, New York: Bantam Books, 1979, 214 p., paper, novel. GHOST HOUSE #1.
29659 *Ghost house; and, Ghost house revenge.* Garden City, NY: Nelson Doubleday, 1981, 434 p., cloth, coll. GHOST HOUSE #1-2.
29660 *Ghost house revenge.* Toronto, New York: Bantam Books, 1981, 232 p., paper, novel. GHOST HOUSE #2.
29661 *Ghost light.* Toronto, New York: Bantam Books, 1982, 226 p., paper, novel.
29662 *Hear the children calling.* New York: An Onyx Book, 1990, 349 p., paper, novel.
29663 *Somebody come and play.* New York: Tor, A Tom Doherty Associates Book, 1987, 311 p., paper, novel.
29664 *What about the baby?* Toronto, New York: Bantam Books, 1983, 245 p., paper, novel.

McNALLY, Raymond T., 1931- , with Radu Florescu

23212 *In search of Frankenstein.* Boston: New York Graphic Society, 1975, xi+244 p., cloth, nonf.

McNAUGHTON, Brian

29665 *Satan's love child.* New York: A Carlyle Special, 1977, 256 p., paper, novel. SATAN #1.
29666 *Satan's mistress.* New York: Carlyle, 1978, 252 p., paper, novel. SATAN #2.
29667 *Satan's seductress.* New York: Carlyle, 1980, 254 p., paper, novel. SATAN #3.
29668 *Satan's surrogate.* New York: Carlyle, 1982, 319 p., paper, novel. SATAN #4.

McNEIL, John, 1939-

29669 *Little brother.* New York: Coward-McCann, 1983, 255 p., cloth, novel.

McNEILE, Herman—SEE: Sapper

McNEILL, Elisabeth [pseud. of Elisabeth D. Taylor]

29670 *Lark returning.* London: Century Hutchinson, 1988, 359 p., cloth, novel.

McNEILL, Janet, 1907-

15843 *Tom's tower.* London: Faber & Faber, 1965, 141 p., cloth, novel.

McNEILL, Warren A., 1903-

29671 *Cabellian harmonics.* New York: Random House, 1928, 103 p., cloth, nonf.

McNEILLY, Wilfred Glassford, 1921-1983

as W. A. BALLINGER

00752 *Drums of the dark gods.* London: Mayflower Books, 1966, 126 p., paper, novel.

as WILFRED GLASSFORD

37951 *Alpha-Omega.* London: New English Library, 1977, 127 p., paper, novel.

as ERROL LECALE

17272 *Blood of my blood.* London: New English Library, 1975, 124 p., paper, novel. SPECIALIST #6.
08760 *Castledoom.* London: New English Library, 1974, 128 p., paper, novel. SPECIALIST #2.
08761 *The death box.* London: New English Library, 1974, 124 p., paper, novel. SPECIALIST #4.
08762 *The severed hand.* London: New English Library, 1974, 127 p., paper, novel. SPECIALIST #3.
08763 *The tigerman of Terrahpur.* London: New English Library, 1973, 128 p., paper, novel. SPECIALIST #1.
17273 *Zombie.* London: New English Library, 1975, 126 p., paper, novel. SPECIALIST #5.

as PETER SAXON

12720 *Corruption.* London: Sphere Books, 1968 (i.e., 1969), 144 p., paper, novel.
00754 *Satan's child.* London: Mayflower Books, 1967, 127 p., paper, novel.

with W. Howard Baker as PETER SAXON

12722 *Dark ways to death.* London: Howard Baker, 1968, 176 p., cloth, novel. GUARDIANS SERIES.

00753 *The darkest night.* London: Mayflower Books, 1966, 157 p., paper, novel.

12725 *The haunting of Alan Mais.* New York: A Berkley Medallion Book, 1969, 143 p., paper, novel. GUARDIANS #3.

00755 *The Torturer.* London: Mayflower Books, 1966, 159 p., paper, novel.

McNELLY, Willis E(verett), 1920-

29672 *The Dune encyclopedia.* New York: G. P. Putnam's Sons, 1984, ix+526 p., cloth, nonf. anth.

with Harry Harrison

25297 *Science fiction novellas.* New York: Charles Scribner's Sons, 1975, x+255 p., paper, anth.

with Jane Hipolito

The book of Mars—SEE: *Mars, we love you.*

07235 *Mars, we love you: tales of Mars, men, and Martians.* Garden City, NY: Doubleday & Co., 1971, xx+332 p., cloth, anth.

07235A retitled: *The book of Mars: tales of Mars, men, and Martians.* London: Futura Publications, An Orbit Book, 1976, xviii+332 p., paper, anth.

McNUTT, Dan J(ames), 1938-

29673 *The eighteenth-century gothic novel: an annotated bibliography of criticism and selected texts.* New York, London: Garland Publishing, 1975, xxii+330 p., cloth, nonf.

McPHEE, James

Blood quest—SEE: *Survival 2000: Blood quest.*

Frozen fire—SEE: *Survival 2000: Frozen fire.*

Renegade war—SEE: *Survival 2000: Renegade war.*

29674 *Survival 2000: Blood quest.* Toronto, New York: A Gold Eagle Book from Worldwide, 1991, 221 p., paper, novel. SURVIVAL 2000 #1.

29675 *Survival 2000: Frozen fire.* Toronto, New York: A Gold Eagle Book from World-

wide, 1991, 216 p., paper, novel. SURVIVAL 2000 #3.

29676 *Survival 2000: Renegade war.* Toronto, New York: A Gold Eagle Book from Worldwide, 1991, 221 p., paper, novel. SURVIVAL 2000 #2.

McQUAY, Michael D.—SEE: McQuay, Mike

McQUAY, Mike [i.e., Michael Dennis McQuay], 1949-

The deadliest show in town—SEE: *Mathew Swain: The deadliest show in town.*

29677 *Escape from New York: a novel.* Toronto, New York: Bantam Books, 1981, 181 p., paper, movie.

Hot time in Old Town—SEE: *Mathew Swain: Hot time in Old Town.*

29678 *Jitterbug.* Toronto, New York: Bantam Books, 1984, 422 p., paper, novel.

29679 *Lifekeeper.* New York: Avon, 1980, 297 p., paper, novel.

29680 *Mathew Swain: Hot time in Old Town.* Toronto, New York: Bantam Books, 1981, 214 p., paper, novel. MATHEW SWAIN #1.

29681 *Mathew Swain: The deadliest show in town.* Toronto, New York: Bantam Books, 1982, 182 p., paper, novel. MATHEW SWAIN #3.

29682 *Mathew Swain: The odds are murder.* Toronto, New York: Bantam Books, 1983, 213 p., paper, novel. MATHEW SWAIN #4.

29683 *Mathew Swain: When trouble beckons.* Toronto, New York: Bantam Books, 1981, 216 p., paper, novel. MATHEW SWAIN #2.

29684 *Memories.* Toronto, New York: Bantam Books, 1987, 400 p., paper, novel.

29685 *Mother Earth.* Toronto, New York: Bantam Books, 1985, xi+370 p., paper, novel. RAMON AND MORGAN #2.

29686 *My science project.* Toronto, New York: Bantam Books, 1985, 169 p., paper, movie.

29687 *The nexus.* New York, Toronto: Spectra, Bantam Books, 1989, 474 p., paper, novel.

The odds are murder—SEE: *Mathew Swain: The odds are murder.*

29688 *Pure blood.* Toronto, New York: Bantam Books, 1985, 280 p., paper, novel. RAMON AND MORGAN #1.

29689 *Suspicion.* New York: A Byron Preiss Visual Productions Inc. Book, Ace Books, 1987, xiii+177 p., paper, novel. ISAAC ASIMOV'S ROBOT CITY #2.

When trouble beckons—SEE: *Mathew Swain: When trouble beckons.*

as VICTOR APPLETON

16748 *Tom Swift: Crater of mystery.* New York: Wanderer Books, Simon & Schuster, 1983, 191 p., cloth, novel. TOM SWIFT #B8.

16746 *Planet of nightmares.* New York: Wanderer Books, Simon & Schuster, 1984, 174 p., paper, novel. TOM SWIFT #B11.

as JACK ARNETT

37952 *Death force.* New York, Toronto: Bantam Books, 1990, 199 p., paper, novel. BOOK OF JUSTICE #3.

37953 *Genocide express.* New York, Toronto: Bantam Books, 1989, 199 p., paper, novel. BOOK OF JUSTICE #1.

37954 *Panama dead.* New York, Toronto: Bantam Books, 1990, 312 p., paper, novel. BOOK OF JUSTICE #4.

37955 *Zaitech sting.* New York, Toronto: Bantam Books, 1990, 200 p., paper, novel. BOOK OF JUSTICE #2.

as LAURA LEE HOPE

37956 *The haunted house mystery.* New York: Wanderer Books, 1985, 123 p., paper, novel. BOBBSEY TWINS #12.

as CAROLYN KEENE

26965 *Nancy Drew ghost stories 2.* New York: Wanderer Books, Simon & Schuster, 1985, 158 p., paper, coll. NANCY DREW SERIES.

McQUEEN, J. E.—SEE: **Jones, L. Q.**

McQUEEN, Ronald A.

29690 *The comic assassin.* London: Robert Hale, 1980, 191 p., cloth, novel.

29691 *The man who knew time.* London: Robert Hale, 1981, 186 p., cloth, novel.

29692 *Mardoc.* London: Robert Hale, 1981, 205 p., cloth, novel.

29693 *The sorcerer of Marakaan.* London: Robert Hale, 1980, 190 p., cloth, novel.

McQUINN, Donald E., 1930-

29694 *Warrior.* New York: A Del Rey Book, Ballantine Books, 1990, 634 p., paper, novel.

McSHANE, Mark—SEE: **Lovell, Marc**

McSHERRY, Frank D(avid) Jr., 1927-

with Martin H. Greenberg & Charles G. Waugh

24530 *Baseball 3000.* New York: Elsevier/Nelson Books, 1981, vi+210 p., cloth, anth.

24531 *Cinemonsters.* Lake Geneva, WI: TSR Inc., 1987, 319 p., paper, anth.

24532 *Civil war ghosts.* Little Rock, AR: August House Publishers, 1991, 204 p., paper, anth.

24533 *Dixie ghosts: haunting, spine-chilling stories from the American South.* Nashville, TN: Rutledge Hill Press, 1988, 208 p., paper, anth.

24534 *Eastern ghosts: haunting, spine-chilling stories from New York, Pennsylvania, New Jersey, Delaware, Maryland, and the District of Columbia.* Nashville, TN: Rutledge Hill Press, 1990, x+208 p., paper, anth.

24535 *Ghosts of the heartland: haunting, spine-chilling stories from the American midwest.* Nashville, TN: Rutledge Hill Press, 1990, 210 p., paper, anth.

24536 *Great American ghost stories.* Nashville, TN: Rutledge Hill Press, 1991, 512 p., cloth, anth.

24537 *Haunted New England: classic tales of the strange and supernatural.* Dublin, NH: Yankee Books, 1988, 287 p., cloth, anth.

24538 *Hollywood ghosts: haunting, spine-chilling stories from America's film capital.* Nashville, TN: Rutledge Hill Press, 1991, 210 p., paper, anth.

24539 *New England ghosts: haunting, spine-chilling stories from the New England states.* Nashville, TN: Rutledge Hill Press, 1990, 213 p., paper, anth.

24540 *Nightmares in Dixie: thirteen horror tales from the American South.* Little Rock, AR: August House, 1987, 260 p., cloth, anth.

24541 *Pirate ghosts of the American coast: stories of hauntings at sea.* Little Rock, AR: August House, 1988, 206 p., paper, anth.

24542 *Red Jack.* New York: DAW Books, 1988, 333 p., paper, anth.

24543 *Strange Maine.* Augusta, ME: Lance Tapley, 1986, 295 p., paper, anth.

24544 *Treasury of American horror stories.* New York: Bonanza Books, 1985, xii+670 p., cloth, anth.

24545 *Western ghosts: haunting, spine-chilling stories from the American West.* Nashville, TN: Rutledge Hill Press, 1990, 215 p., paper, anth.

24546 *Yankee witches.* Augusta, ME: Lance Tapley, Publisher, 1988, 315 p., paper, anth.

with Martin H. Greenberg & Charles G. Waugh & S. M. Stirling

24590 *The fantastic Civil War.* Riverdale, NY: Baen Books, 1991, 307 p., paper, anth.
24591 *Fantastic World War II.* New York: Baen Books, 1990, 281 p., paper, anth.

with Charles G. Waugh

29695 *Spooky sea stories.* Camden, ME: Yankee Books, 1991, 246 p., paper, anth.

McVEIGH, Maureen—SEE: Hunter, Mollie

McWHORTER, George T., 1931-

29696 *Burroughs dictionary: an alphabetical list of proper names, words, phrases, and concepts contained in the published works of Edgar Rice Burroughs.* Lanham, MD & New York: University Press of America, 1987, xiii+446 p., cloth, nonf.
29697 *Edgar Rice Burroughs memorial collection: a catalog.* Louisville, KY: House of Greystoke, 1991, xxv+190 p., paper, nonf. [Limited to 500 copies].

McWILLIAMS, Carey, 1905-1980

29698 *Ambrose Bierce: a biography.* New York: Albert & Charles Boni, 1929, 358 p., cloth, nonf.

MEACHAM, Beth (Ann), 1951-

29699 *Terry's universe.* New York: Tor SF, A Tom Doherty Associates Book, 1988, vi+234 p., cloth, anth. [A festschrift in memory of Terry Carr].

with Wayne Douglas Barlowe & Ian Summers

17408 *Barlowe's Guide to extraterrestrials.* New York: Workman Publishing, 1979, 112+[32] p., cloth, art. [Meacham's contribution is uncredited; winner of the *Locus* Award for Best Art Book, 1979 (1980)].
17409 *Barlowe's Guide to extraterrestrials, 2nd ed.* New York: Workman Publishing, 1987, 112+[32] p., cloth, art.
    Guide to extraterrestrials—SEE: *Barlowe's Guide to extraterrestrials.*

with Vincent DiFate & Ian Summers

Catalog of science fiction hardware—SEE: *DiFate's Catalog of science fiction hardware.*
21918 *DiFate's Catalog of science fiction hardware.* New York: Workman Publishing, 1980, 135 p., cloth, art.

with Tappan King

27290 *Nightshade: a novel.* New York: Pyramid Books, 1976, 240 p., paper, novel. Weird Heroes #4.

with Baird Searles & Michael Franklin

23446 *A reader's guide to fantasy.* New York: Avon, 1982, 217 p., paper, nonf.

with Baird Searles & Michael Franklin & Martin Last

23447 *A reader's guide to science fiction.* New York: Avon, 1979, xv+266 p., paper, nonf.

MEAD, Syd

29700 *Blade Runner sketchbook.* San Diego, CA: Blue Dolphin Enterprises, 1982, 95 p., paper, anth.
29701 *Oblagon.* Tokyo: Oblagon, 1985, 167 p., cloth, art. [In Japanese and English].
29702 *Sentinel II: steel couture.* Tokyo: Kodansha, 1987, 115 p., paper, art.
29703 *Techno fantasy art.* Tokyo, Los Angeles: Oblagon, 1985, [32] p., paper, art.

with Strother MacMinn

28874 *Sentinel: steel couture—Syd Mead—futurist.* Hendrik-ido-Ambacht, Netherlands: Dragon's Dream, 1979, 157 p., cloth, art.

MEADES, Rob(ert), 1964- , with David B. Wake

29704 *Drabble II: double century.* Harold Wood, Essex: Beccon Publications, 1990, 121 p., cloth, anth.
29705 *The Drabble project.* Harold Wood, Essex: Beccon Publciations, 1988, 110 p., cloth, anth.

*MEAGHER, George E(dward), 1895-1967

*MEAGHER, Maude, 1895?-1977?

MEAKIN, Viola

29706 *The ghost ring, and other tales of telepathy.* Ipswich, England: East Anglian Magazine, 1981, 48 p., paper, coll.

MEANEY, (Margaret) Dee Morrison, 1939-

29707 *Death of the raven.* New York: Ace Fantasy Books, 1983, x+245, p., paper, novel. BRANWEN #2.

29708 *Iseult: dreams that are done.* New York: Ace Fantasy Books, 1985, 229 p., paper, novel.

29709 *An unkindness of ravens.* New York: Ace Fantasy Books, 1983, 236 p., paper, novel. BRANWEN #1.

MECKLEM, Todd, 1965- , with Jonathan Falk

22856 *The liquid retreats.* Union, OR: Wordcraft of Oregon, 1991, 43 p., paper, coll.

MECKLER, Jerome, 1941-

29710 *Aldous Huxley: satire and structure.* New York: Barnes & Noble Books, 1969, 223 p., cloth, nonf.

MEEHAN, Thomas C(larke), 1931-

29711 *Essays on Argentine narrators.* Valencia, Spain; Chapel Hill, NC: Albatros Hispanófila, 1982, 196 p., paper, nonf.

MEEKER, Eloise—SEE: Clark, Lydia Benson

MEEKER, W. John—SEE: Johns, Willy

MEIER, Paul

29712 *William Morris, the Marxist dreamer.* Hassocks, Sussex, England: Harvester Press; Atlantic Highlands, NJ. Humanities Press, 1978, xiv+597+lx+lxx p. in 2 v., cloth, nonf. [Translation by Frank Gubb of *La pensée utopique de William Morris*].

MEIER, Shirley (Marie), 1960-

29713 *Shadow's daughter.* Riverdale, NY: Baen Fantasy, 1991, 323 p., paper, novel. FIFTH MILLENNIUM #5.

with S. M. Stirling

29714 *The cage.* New York: Baen, 1989, 402 p., paper, novel. FIFTH MILLENNIUM #3.

29715 *The sharpest edge.* New York: A Signet Book, New American Library, 1986, 255 p., paper, novel. FIFTH MILLENNIUM #2.

with S. M. Stirling & Karen Wehrstein

29716 *Shadow's son.* Riverdale, NY: Baen Books, 1991, 442 p., paper, novel. FIFTH MILLENNIUM #4.

MELADA, Ivan, 1931-

29717 *Sheridan Le Fanu.* Boston: Twayne Publishers, 1987, 142 p., cloth, nonf.

MELAMED, Leo, 1932-

29718 *The tenth planet.* Chicago: Bonus Books, 1987, 318 p., paper, novel.

MELDAL-JOHNSEN, Trevor (Bernard), 1944-

29719 *Always.* New York: Avon, A Bernard Geis Associates Book, 1979, 313 p., paper, novel.

with Dan Sherman as DAN TREVOR

29720 *The night whistlers.* New York: Jove Books, 1991, 234 p., paper, novel. NIGHT WHISTLERS #1.

MELE, Jim, 1950- , with Jean Fiedler

23065 *Isaac Asimov.* New York: Frederick Ungar, 1982, viii+122 p., cloth, nonf.

MELLA, John

37957 *Transformations.* Chicago: Chicago Review Press, 1975, 210 p., cloth, novel.

MELLING, O. R. [pseud. of Geraldine Whelan]

29721 *Falling out of time.* Markham, Ontario: Viking Canada, 1989, 201 p., cloth, novel.

29722 *The singing stone.* Markham, Ontario: Viking Kestrel, 1986, 206 p., cloth, novel.

MELLOR, Anne K(ostelanetz), 1941-

29723 *Mary Shelley: her life, her fiction, her monsters.* London: Methuen, 1988, xx+275 p., cloth, nonf.

MELROSE, Andrea LaSonde [i.e., Andrea La-Sonde Melrose Anastos], 1951-

29724 *Nine visions: a book of fantasies.* New York: Seabury Press, 1983, x+181 p., paper, anth.

MELROSS, Alec Gurney

29725 *Thirteen strange stories.* Dumfries, Scotland: Cairnlea, 1983, 96 p., paper, coll.

MELUCH, R(ebecca) M., 1956-

29726 *Chicago red.* New York: A Roc Book, 1990, 319 p., paper, novel.
29727 *Jerusalem fire.* New York: A Signet Book, New American Library, 1985, 331 p., paper, novel.
29728 *Sovereign.* New York: A Signet Book, New American Library, 1979, 230 p., paper, novel.
29729 *War birds.* New York: A Signet Book, New American Library, 1989, 253 p., paper, novel.
29730 *Wind child.* New York: A Signet Book, New American Library, 1982, 202 p., paper, novel. WIND DANCERS #2.
29731 *Wind dancers.* New York: A Signet Book, New American Library, 1981, 167 p., paper, novel. WIND DANCERS #1.

MELVILLE, Jennie [pseud. of Gwendoline Williams Butler], 1922-

29732 *Tarot's tower.* New York, Toronto: Scholastic Book Services, 1978, 224 p., cloth, novel.

MELVILLE, Pauline

29733 *Shape-shifter: stories.* London: The Women's Press, 1990, 164 p., cloth, coll.

MELVIN, Kenneth B., *with Stanley L. Brodsky & Raymond D. Fowler Jr.*

18715 *Psy-fi one: an anthology of psychology in science fiction.* New York: Random House, 1977, xiii+299 p., paper, anth.

MEMBER of the Committee of Safety of 1908, A, pseud.—SEE: Janvier, Thomas A.

*MENDELSOHN, Felix Jr., 1906-1990

MENDELSON, Drew

29734 *Pilgrimage.* New York: DAW Books, 1981, 220 p., paper, novel.

MENDELSON, Edward, 1946-

29735 *Pynchon: a collection of critical essays.* Englewood Cliffs, NJ: Prentice-Hall, 1978, viii+225 p., cloth, nonf. anth.

MENDONCA, Susan—SEE: Smith, Susan

MENEGAS, Peter

29736 *The nature of the beast.* Toronto, New York: Bantam Books, 1975, 240 p., paper, novel.

*MENEN, (Salvator) Aubrey (Clarence), 1912-1989

MENGER, Lucy, 1928-

29737 *Theodore Sturgeon.* New York: Frederick Ungar Publishing Co., 1981, viii+136 p., cloth, nonf.

MENICK, Jim

29738 *Lingo.* New York: Carroll & Graf, 1991, 334 p., cloth, novel.

MENTZER, Frank, *with Gary Gygax*

24866 *The temple of elemental evil.* Lake Geneva, WI: TSR Inc., 1985, 128 p., paper, novel.

MENVILLE, Douglas (Alver), 1935-

29739 *A historical and critical survey of the science-fiction film /* by Douglas Alver Menville. New York: Arno Press, 1975, xvii+185 p., cloth, nonf. SCIENCE FICTION.
29740 *The work of Ross Rocklynne: an annotated bibliography & guide.* San Bernardino, CA: R. Reginald, The Borgo Press, 1989, 70 p., cloth, nonf. BIBLIOGRAPHIES OF MODERN AUTHORS #17. [Edited by Boden Clarke].

with R. Reginald

29741 *Ancestral voices: an anthology of early science fiction.* New York: Arno Press, 1975, [298] p., cloth, anth. SCIENCE FICTION.
29742 *Ancient hauntings.* New York: Arno Press, 1976, [383] p., cloth, anth. SUPERNATURAL & OCCULT FICTION.

29743 *Dreamers of dreams: an anthology of fantasy.* New York: Arno Press, 1978, [478] p., cloth, anth. LOST RACE & ADULT FANTASY FICTION.

29744 *King Solomon's children: some parodies of H. Rider Haggard.* New York: Arno Press, 1978, [564] p., cloth, anth. LOST RACE & ADULT FANTASY FICTION.

29745 *Phantasmagoria.* New York: Arno Press, 1976, [357] p., cloth, anth. SUPERNATURAL & OCCULT FICTION.

29746 *R.I.P.: five stories of the supernatural.* New York: Arno Press, 1976, [278] p., cloth, anth. SUPERNATURAL & OCCULT FICTION.

29747 *The spectre bridegroom, and other horrors.* New York: Arno Press, 1976, [292] p., cloth, anth. SUPERNATURAL & OCCULT FICTION.

29748 *They: three parodies of H. Rider Haggard's She.* New York: Arno Press, 1978, [592] p., cloth, anth. LOST RACE & ADULT FANTASY FICTION.

29749 *Things to come: an illustrated history of the science fiction film.* New York: Times Books, 1977, xii+212 p., cloth, nonf.

29750 *Worlds of never: three fantastic novels.* New York: Arno Press, 1978, [430] p., cloth, anth. LOST RACE & ADULT FANTASY FICTION.

with R. Reginald & Mary A. Burgess

19041 *Futurevisions: the new golden age of the science fiction film.* North Hollywood, CA: A Greenbriar Book, Newcastle Publishing Co., 1985, 192 p., paper, nonf. [A sequel to *Things to come* (see #29749)].

MERCER, Charles E(dward), 1917-1988

29751 *The Battlestar Galactica storybook.* New York: G. P. Putnam's Sons, 1979, [60] p., cloth, movie. BATTLESTAR GALACTICA.

*MEREDITH, James Creed (Jr.), 1875-1942

MEREDITH, Richard C(arlton), 1937-1979

37958 *At the narrow passage.* Chicago: Playboy Press Paperbacks, 1979, 240 p., paper, novel. TIMELINER #1. [Revised edition of #10024].

37959 *The awakening.* New York: St. Martin's Press, 1979, 296 p., cloth, novel.

29752 *No brother, no friend.* Garden City, NY: Doubleday & Co., 1976, xii+210 p., cloth, novel. TIMELINER #2.

37960 *No brother, no friend.* Chicago: Playboy Press Paperbacks, 1979, 236 p., paper, novel. TIMELINER #2. [Revised edition].

29753 *Run, come see Jerusalem!* New York: Ballantine Books, 1976, 232 p., paper, novel.

29754 *Timeliner trilogy.* London: Arrow Books, 1987, 712 p., paper, coll. TIMELINER #1-3. [Includes *At the narrow passage*; *No brother, no friend*; *Vestiges of time*].

29755 *Vestiges of time.* Garden City, NY: Doubleday & Co., 1978, 186 p., cloth, novel. TIMELINER #3.

37961 *Vestiges of time.* Chicago: Playboy Press Paperbacks, 1979, 236 p., paper, novel. TIMELINER #3. [Revised edition].

MERETZKY, S. Eric

29756 *The cavern of doom.* New York: Tor, A Tom Doherty Associates Book, 1983, 127 p., paper, novel. ZORK #3.

29757 *Conquest at Quendor.* New York: Tor, A Tom Doherty Associates Book, 1984, 127 p., paper, novel. ZORK #4.

29758 *The forces of Krill.* New York: Tor, A Tom Doherty Associates Book, 1983, 126 p., paper, novel. ZORK #1.

29759 *The Malifestro quest.* New York: Tor, A Tom Doherty Associates Book, 1983, 127 p., paper, novel. ZORK #2.

MERLA, Patrick

29760 *The tales of Patrick Merla.* New York: Available Press, Ballantine Books, 1985, 103 p., paper, coll.

MERLE, Robert (Jean Georges), 1908-

29761 *The virility factor: a novel.* New York, St. Louis: McGraw-Hill Book Co., 1977, 344 p., cloth, novel. [Translation by Martin Sokolinsky of *Les hommes protégés*].

MERRIAM, Eve, 1916-1992

29762 *Ab to Zogg: a lexicon for science-fiction and fantasy readers.* New York: Atheneum, 1977, 43 p., cloth, nonf.

*MERRICK, Williston [pseud. of Williston Merrick Ford], 1886-1971

MERRIL, Judith [originally Josephine Juliet Grossman], 1923-

29763 *The best of Judith Merril.* New York: Warner Books, 1976, 254 p., paper, coll.

10033 *Daughters of Earth.* London: Victor Gollancz, 1968, 256 p., cloth, coll.

10033A retitled: *A Judith Merril omnibus: Daughters of Earth, and other stories.* Toronto: McClelland & Stewart, 1985, 383 p., paper, coll.

A Judith Merril omnibus—see: *Daughters of Earth.*

29764 *Tesseracts.* Victoria, British Columbia, Canada: A Tesseract Book, Porcépic Books, 1985, ix+292 p., cloth, anth.

with C. M. Kornbluth as CYRIL JUDD

27486 *Gunner Cade, plus Takeoff.* New York: A Jim Baen Presentation, Tor, A Tom Doherty Associates Book, 1983, 320 p., paper, coll. [*Takeoff* is by Kornbluth alone].

MERRILL, Flora

29765 *Flush of Wimpole Street and Broadway.* New York: Robert M. McBride & Co., 1933, 120 p., cloth, novel.

MERRILL, Robert (Wright), 1944-

29766 *Critical essays on Kurt Vonnegut.* Boston: G. K. Hall & Co., 1990, x+235 p., cloth, nonf. anth.

MERRITT, A(braham P.), 1884-1943

37962 *Woman of the wood.* [Sedalio, CO: M. Doreal, 1948], [50] p., paper, story.

with Hannes Bok

18247 *The fox woman and the blue pagoda; and, The black wheel.* New York: Arno Press, 1976, 109+115 p., cloth, coll.

with H. P. Lovecraft & C. L. Moore & Robert E. Howard & Frank Belknap Long

The challenge from beyond—SEE: *The illustrated challenge from beyond.*

26046 *The illustrated Challenge from beyond.* West Warwick, RI: Necronomicon Press, 1978, [26] p., paper, story.

MERTZ, Barbara—SEE: Michaels, Barbara

MERWIN, Richard

29767 *Agents of fortune: the royal pain.* Lake Geneva, WI: TSR Inc., 1988, 314 p., paper, novel. DOUBLE AGENT BOOK #2.

[Bound with *The hollow earth affair* / by Warren Spector].

MERWIN, Sam(uel Kimball) Jr., 1910-

29768 *Chauvinisto.* Canoga Park, CA: Major Books, 1976, 176 p., paper, novel.

29769 *The house of many worlds.* New York: Ace Books, 1983, 297 p., paper, coll. ELSPETH MARRINER & MACK FRASER #1-2. [Includes *House of many worlds* and *The three faces of time*].

as REBECCA NOYES WINSTEAD

The forbidden mansion—SEE: *Tunnel of darkness.*

29770 *Tunnel of darkness.* Chatsworth, CA: Canyon Books, 1974, 160 p., paper, novel.

29770A retitled: *The forbidden mansion* / by Angela Davidson. Chatsworth, CA: American Art Enterprises, 1981, 160 p., paper, novel.

MESSENT, Peter B.

29771 *Literature of the occult: a collection of critical essays.* Englewood Cliffs, NJ: Prentice-Hall, 1981, xi+188 p., cloth, nonf. anth.

MESSMANN, Jon (J.)

29772 *The deadly deep.* New York: A Signet Book, New American Library, 1976, 222 p., paper, novel.

29773 *Phone call: a novel.* New York: A Signet Book, New American Library, 1979, 214 p., paper, movie.

as NICK CARTER

36402 *The death strain.* New York: Award Books; London: Tandem Books, 1971, 156 p., paper, novel. NICK CARTER SERIES.

19605 *Living death.* New York: Award Books, 1969, 153 p., paper, novel. NICK CARTER SERIES.

19609 *The sea trap.* New York: Award Books; London: Tandem Books, 1969, 156 p., paper, novel. NICK CARTER SERIES.

as CLAUDETTE NICOLE

10681 *The haunting of Drumroe.* Greenwich, CT: Fawcett Gold Medal, 1971, 144 p., paper, novel.

MESSMANN, Richard R., *with James Van Hise*

29774   *Lost in Space technical manual.* Canoga Park, CA: Movie Publishers Services, 1986, 2 v.(?), paper, nonf.

METZGER, Arthur

29775   *A guide to the Gormenghast Trilogy.* Baltimore, MD: T-K Graphics, 1976, 35 p., paper, nonf.
29776   *An index & short history of Unknown.* Baltimore, MD: T-K Graphics, 1976, [27] p., paper, nonf.

METZGER, Robert A(lan), 1956-

29777   *Quad world.* New York: A Roc Book, 1991, 317 p., paper, novel.

METZGER, Thom(as Richard), 1956-

29778   *Shock totem.* New York: An Onyx Book, 1991, 288 p., paper, novel.

with Richard P. Scott

29779   *Big Gurl.* New York: An Onyx Book, New American Library, 1989, 253 p., paper, novel.

MEYER, Bill

15844   *Ultimatum.* New York: A Signet Book, New American Library, 1966, 189 p., paper, novel.

MEYER, Carolyn, 1935-

29780   *Japan: how do hands make peace!* New York: McGraw-Hill Book Co., 1989, [100] p., paper, novel. EARTH INSPECTORS #10.

MEYER, David N. II—SEE: St. Alcorn, Lloyd

MEYER, John (Anthony)

29781   *Nightchild.* New York: Pocket Books, 1978, 224 p., paper, novel.

MEYER, M(athilde) M(arie), 1883-

29782   *H. G. Wells and his family: (as I have known them).* Edinburgh, Scotland: International Publishing Co., 1956, 143 p., cloth, nonf.

MEYER, Miriam Weiss

29783   *Science fiction.* Pleasantville, NY: Reader's Digest Educational Division, 1977, 96 p., paper, anth.

MEYER, Nicholas, 1945-

29784   *The West End horror: a posthumous memoir of John H. Watson, M.D.* New York: E. P. Dutton, 1976, 222 p., cloth, novel.

MEYERS, Jeffrey, 1939-

29785   *George Orwell: the critical heritage.* London: Routledge & Kegan Paul, 1975, xiv+392 p., cloth, nonf. anth.
29786   *A reader's guide to George Orwell.* London: Thames & Hudson, 1975, 192 p., cloth, nonf.

with Valerie Meyers

29787   *George Orwell: an annotated bibliography of criticism.* New York, London: Garland Publishing, 1977, ix+132 p., cloth, nonf.

MEYERS, Ric—SEE: Meyers, Richard S.

MEYERS, Richard S., 1953-

29788   *Cry of the beast.* New York: Pocket Books, 1979, 191 p., paper, novel. INCREDIBLE HULK #2; MARVEL SUPER-HEROES #3.
29789   *Doom star.* New York: Carlyle, 1978, 220 p., paper, novel. DOOMSTAR #1.
29790   retitled: *Doomstar* / by Richard Meyers. New York: Popular Library, Warner Books, 1985, 296 p., paper, novel. DOOMSTAR #1. [Revised edition].
29791   *Doom star, number two.* New York: Carlyle, 1979, 220 p., paper, novel. DOOMSTAR #2.
29791A retitled: *Return to Doomstar* / by Richard Meyers. New York: Popular Library, Warner Books, 1985, 295 p., paper, novel. DOOMSTAR #2.
       Doomstar—SEE: Doom star.
29792   *Fear itself* / by Ric Meyers. New York: A Dell Book, 1991, 264 p., paper, novel. BOOK OF THE UNDEAD #1.
29793   *For one week only: the world of exploitation films.* Piscataway, NJ: New Century Publishers, 1983, xiii+270 p., paper, nonf.
       The great science fiction films—SEE: S-F 2.
29794   *Living hell* / by Ric Meyers. New York: A Dell Book, 1991, 294 p., paper, novel. BOOK OF THE UNDEAD #2.

Return to doomstar—SEE: *Doom star, number two.*

29795 *S-F 2: a pictorial history of science fiction films from "Rollerball" to "Return of the Jedi"* / by Richard Meyers. Secaucus, NJ: Citadel Press, 1984, 255 p., cloth, nonf.

29795A retitled: *The great science fiction films: from "Rollerball" to "Return of the Jedi"* / by Richard Meyers. New York: Carol Publishing Group, A Citadel Press Book, 1990, 255 p., cloth, nonf.

29796 *The world of fantasy films* / by Richard Meyers. South Brunswick & New York: A. S. Barnes & Co.; London: Thomas Yoseloff, 1980, 195 p., cloth, nonf.

as WADE BARKER

37963 *Dragon rising: the year of the Ninja Master: Spring.* New York: Warner Books, 1985, 280 p., paper, novel. YEAR OF THE NINJA MASTER #1.

37964 *The himitsu attack.* New York: Warner Books, 1988, 215 p., paper, novel. WAR OF THE NINJA MASTER #3.

37965 *The kohga ritual.* New York: Warner Books, 1988, 276 p., paper, novel. WAR OF THE NINJA MASTER #1.

37966 *Lion's fire: the year of the Ninja Master: Summer.* New York: Warner Books, 1985, 276 p., paper, novel. YEAR OF THE NINJA MASTER #2.

37967 *Phoenix sword: the year of the Ninja Master: Winter.* New York: Warner Books, 1986, 246 p., paper, novel. YEAR OF THE NINJA MASTER #4.

29797 *Serpent's eye: the year of the Ninja Master: Autumn.* New York: Warner Books, 1985, 243 p., paper, novel. YEAR OF THE NINJA MASTER #3.

29798 *The shibo discipline.* New York: Warner Books, 1988, 208 p., paper, novel. WAR OF THE NINJA MASTER #2.

37968 *The zakka slaughter.* New York: Warner Books, 1988, 246 p., paper, novel. WAR OF THE NINJA MASTER #4.

with Walter Hunt & Lisa Hunt & Evan Jamieson & Bill Scammell & Mark Bloom & Christine Ivey as ARCHITECTS ADVENTURE

18216 *Dzurlord: a Crossroads adventure in the world of Steven Brust's Jhereg* / by Architects Adventure. New York: Tor, A Tom Doherty Associates Book, 1987, 24+[224] p., paper, novel. JHEREG SERIES; CROSSROADS ADVENTURE.

as anonymous co-author with Warren Murphy

29799 *The last temple* / by Warren Murphy. New York: Pinnacle Books, 1977, 180 p., paper, novel. DESTROYER #27.

29800 *Sweet dreams* / by Warren Murphy. New York: Pinnacle Books, 1976, 174 p., paper, novel. DESTROYER #25.

as anonymous co-author with Warren Murphy and Richard Sapir

29801 *The final death.* New York: Pinnacle Books, 1977, 177 p., paper, novel. DESTROYER #29.

MEYERS, Roy L(ethbridge), 1910-1974

37969 *The man they couldn't kill.* Leicester & London, England: Black Friars Press, 1944, 128 p., cloth, novel.

with J. F. Bone

18265 *Gift of the Manti.* Toronto, New York: Laser Books, 1977, 190 p., paper, novel.

MEYERS, Valerie

29802 *George Orwell.* New York: St. Martin's Press, 1991, viii+158 p., cloth, nonf.

with Jeffrey Meyers

29787 *George Orwell: an annotated bibliography of criticism.* New York, London: Garland Publishing, 1977, ix+132 p., cloth, nonf.

MEYERS, Walter E(arl), 1939-

29803 *Aliens and linguists: language study and science fiction.* Athens, GA: University of Georgia Press, 1980, 257 p., cloth, nonf.

MEYNELL, Esther (Hallam Moorhouse), d. 1955

29804 *Portrait of William Morris.* London: Chapman & Hall, 1947, ix+229 p., cloth, nonf.

MEYNELL, Laurence (Walter), 1899-1989

29805 *Strange landing: a tale of adventure.* Toronto: A White Circle Paperback Edition, 1947, 192 p., paper, novel.

MEYRICK, Bette, 1931-

29806 *Time circles.* London: Abelard, 1978, 126 p., cloth, novel.

MEYRINK, Gustav (Meyer-), 1868-1932

29807 *The angel of the west window.* London: Dedalus; Riverside, CA: Ariadne, 1991, 421 p., cloth, novel. [Translation by Mike Mitchell of *Der engel vom westlichen Fenster*].

MEZO, Francine (Marie)

29808 *The fall of worlds.* New York: Avon, 1980, x+310 p., paper, novel. AREIA DARENGA #1.

29809 *No earthly shore.* New York: Avon, 1981, 248 p., paper, novel. AREIA DARENGA #3.

29810 *Unless she burn.* New York: Avon, 1981, 175 p., paper, novel. AREIA DARENGA #2.

*MIAN, Mary (Lawrence Shipman), 1902-

*MICHAEL, Cecil, 1909-1987

MICHAEL, Peter, pseud.—SEE: Michael, Simon & Rosenberg, Peter

MICHAEL, Simon, *with Peter Rosenberg as* PETER MICHAEL

29811 *The usurper.* London: Grafton, 1988, 303 p., paper, novel.

MICHAELS, Barbara [pseud. of Barbara Louise Gross Mertz], 1927-

29812 *Be buried in the rain.* New York: Atheneum, 1985, 241 p., cloth, novel.

29813 *The grey beginning.* New York: Congdon & Weed, 1984, 277 p., cloth, novel.

29814 *Here I stay.* New York: Congdon & Weed, 1983, 288 p., cloth, novel.

29815 *Patriot's dream.* New York: Dodd, Mead & Co., 1976, 344 p., cloth, novel.

29816 *The sea-king's daughter.* New York: Dodd, Mead & Co., 1975, 245 p., cloth, novel.

15845 *Sons of the wolf.* New York: Meredith Press, 1967, 265 p., cloth, novel.

29817 *Wait for what will come.* New York: Dodd, Mead & Co., 1978, 282 p., cloth, novel.

29818 *The wizard's daughter.* New York: Dodd, Mead & Co., 1980, 279 p., cloth, novel.

as ELIZABETH PETERS

29819 *Borrower of the night.* New York: Dodd, Mead & Co., 1973, 247 p., cloth, novel.

29820 *Devil-may-care.* New York: Dodd, Mead & Co., 1977, 275 p., cloth, novel.

29821 *The last camel died at noon.* New York: Warner Books, 1991, 352 p., cloth, novel. AMELIA PEABODY #6.

MICHAELS, Fern, pseud.—SEE: Anderson, Roberta & Kuczkir, Mary

MICHAELS, George, 1923?- , *with Hal W. Hall & Kenneth R. Johnson*

25035 *The science fiction magazines: a bibliographical checklist of titles and issues through 1983.* Bryan, TX: SFBRI, 1983, iv+89 p., paper, nonf.

MICHAELS, Melisa C.

29822 *Far harbor.* New York: Tor SF, A Tom Doherty Associates Book, 1989, 248 p., paper, novel.

29823 *First battle.* New York: Tor SF, A Tom Doherty Associates Book, 1985, 253 p., paper, novel. SKYRIDER #2.

29824 *Floater factor.* New York: Tor SF, A Tom Doherty Associates Book, 1988, 281 p., paper, novel. SKYRIDER #5.

29825 *Last war.* New York: Tor SF, A Tom Doherty Associates Book, 1986, 219 p., paper, novel. SKYRIDER #3.

29826 *Pirate prince.* New York: Tor SF, A Tom Doherty Associates Book, 1987, 254 p., paper, novel. SKYRIDER #4.

29827 *Skirmish.* New York: Tor, A Tom Doherty Associates Book, 1985, 252 p., paper, novel. SKYRIDER #1.

MICHAELS, Philip [possible pseud. of Philippe van Rjndt]

29828 *Come, follow me.* New York: Avon, 1983, 328 p., paper, novel.

29829 *Grail.* New York: Avon, 1982, 330 p., paper, novel.

MICHALSON, Karen

29830 *Victorian fantasy literature: literary battles with church and empire.* Lewiston, NY: Edwin Mellen Press, 1990, 292 p., cloth, nonf.

*MICHAUD, A(lfred) C(harles), 1876-1975

MICHAUD, Marc A., *with S. T. Joshi*

26807 *Lovecraft's library: a catalogue.* West Warwick, RI: Necronomicon Press, 1980, 90 p., paper, nonf. anth.

MICHELINIE, David

29831 *The man who stole tomorrow.* New York: Pocket Books, 1979, 192 p., paper, novel. THE AVENGERS; MARVEL SUPER-HEROES #10.

MICHELS, Sharry, *with Bernice Carstensen as* SHARICE KENDYL

19526 *To share a sunset.* New York: Leisure Books, 1990, 368 p., paper, novel.

MICHELSON, Bennett

29832 *The perfect weapon.* New York: Tower Books, 1980, 239 p., paper, novel.

MIDDLETON, Haydn, 1955-

29833 *The collapsing castle.* London: Hamish Hamilton, 1990, 280 p., cloth, novel. PEOPLE #2.
29834 *The people in the picture.* London, New York: Bantam Press, 1987, 208 p., cloth, novel. PEOPLE #1.
29835 *Son of two worlds: a retelling of the timeless Celtic saga of Pryderi.* London: Century Hutchinson, 1987, 164 p., cloth, novel.

MIEDANER, Terrel

29836 *The soul of Anna Klane.* New York: Coward, McCann & Geogheghan, 1977, 240 p., cloth, novel.

MIESEL, Sandra (Louise), 1941-

29837 *Against time's arrow: the high crusade of Poul Anderson.* San Bernardino, CA: R. Reginald, The Borgo Press, 1978, 64 p., cloth, nonf. MILFORD SERIES: POPULAR WRITERS OF TODAY #18.
29838 *Dreamrider.* New York: Ace Books, 1982, xv+279 p., paper, novel.
29839 retitled: *Shaman.* New York: Baen, 1989, 306 p., paper, novel. [Expanded and rewritten edition].
Shaman—SEE: *Dreamrider.*

with David Drake

22180 *Heads to the storm.* New York: Baen Books, 1989, 273 p., paper, anth.
22181 *A separate star: a science fiction tribute to Rudyard Kipling.* New York: Baen Books, 1989, 278 p., paper, anth.

MIGLIS, John, 1950-

29840 *Killing eyes.* New York: Fawcett Gold Medal, 1984, 185 p., paper, novel.

*MIKES, George [i.e., György Mikes], 1912-1987

MIKLOWITZ, Gloria D(ubov), 1927-

29841 *After the bomb.* New York, Toronto: Scholastic Inc., 1985, 156 p., paper, novel. AFTER THE BOMB #1.
29842 *After the bomb: week one.* New York, Toronto: Scholastic Inc., 1987, 137 p., paper, novel. AFTER THE BOMB #2.

MIKES, György—SEE: Mikes, George

MIKOL, Paul, *as* ANONYMOUS EDITOR

NOTE: The NIGHT VISIONS *anthology series is packaged by Dark Harvest publisher Paul Mikol. The books contain either a guest introduction or afterword by a different writer, with that writer being indicated as "editor" on the jacket copy. The first two volumes were actually compiled by those credited, but beginning with volume three, most of the "editors" have served only as advisers. The books have been listed below in one sequence, the introducers being listed in brackets after each volume.*

The bone yard—SEE: *Night visions 6.*
Dark visions—SEE: *Night visions 5.*
Dead image—SEE: *Night visions 2.*
Hardshell—SEE: *Night visions 4.*
The hellbound heart—SEE: *Night visions 3.*
In the blood—SEE: *Night visions 1.*
Night fears—SEE: *Night visions 4.*
Night terrors—SEE: *Night visions 2.*
Night visions—SEE: *Night visions 3.*

32909 *Night visions 1: all original stories.* Niles, IL: Dark Harvest, 1984, 296 p., cloth, anth. [Introduction (and actually edited) by Alan Ryan].
32909A retitled: *Night visions: In the blood.* New York: Berkley Books, 1988, viii+292 p., paper, anth. [Introduction (and actually edited) by Alan Ryan].
24305 *Night visions 2: all original stories.* Niles, IL: Dark Harvest, 1985, 327 p., cloth, anth. [Introduction (and actually edited) by Charles L. Grant].

24305A retitled: *Night visions: Dead image.* New York: Berkley Books, 1987, 309 p., paper, anth. [Introduction (and actually edited) by Charles L. Grant].

24305B retitled: *Night terrors.* London: Headline, 1989, viii+308 p., paper, anth. [Introduction (and actually edited) by Charles L. Grant].

29115 *Night visions 3.* Niles, IL: Dark Harvest, 1986, 225 p., cloth, anth. [Introduction by George R. R. Martin].

29115A retitled: *Night visions: all original stories.* London: Century Publishing, 1987, 298 p., cloth, anth. [Introduction by George R. R. Martin].

29115B retitled: *Night visions: The hellbound heart.* New York: Berkley Books, 1988, 278 p., paper, anth. [Introduction by George R. R. Martin].

17389 *Night visions 4: all original stories.* Arlington Heights, IL: Dark Harvest, 1987, 275 p., cloth, anth. [Introduction by Clive Barker].

17389A retitled: *Night visions: Hardshell.* New York: Berkley Books, 1988, 279 p., paper, anth. [Introduction by Clive Barker].

17389B retitled: *Night fears.* London: Headline, 1990, 308 p., paper, anth. [Introduction by Clive Barker].

29843 *Night visions 5: all original stories.* Arlington Heights, IL: Dark Harvest, 1988, 274 p., cloth, anth. [Introduction by Douglas E. Winter].

29843A retitled: *Dark visions.* London: Victor Gollancz, 1989, 264 p., cloth, anth. [Introduction by Douglas E. Winter].

29843B retitled: *The skin trade.* NY: Berkley Books, 1990, 329 p., paper, anth. [Introduction by Douglas E. Winter].

29844 *Night visions 6: all original stories.* Arlington Heights, IL: Dark Harvest, 1988, 312 p., cloth, anth. [Introduction by Dean R. Koontz].

29844A retitled: *The bone yard.* New York: Berkley Books, 1991, 329 p., paper, anth. [Introduction by Dean R. Koontz].

29845 *Night visions 7: all original stories.* Arlington Heights, IL: Dark Harvest, 1989, 271 p., cloth, anth. [Introduction (and actually edited) by Stanley Wiater].

29846 *Night visions 8: all original stories.* Arlington Heights, IL: Dark Harvest, 1990 (i.e., 1991?), 255 p., cloth, anth. [Afterword by Robert R. McCammon].

29847 *Night visions 9: all original stories.* Arlington Heights, IL: Dark Harvest, 1991, 260 p., cloth, anth. [Introduction by F. Paul Wilson].

Night visions: Dead image—SEE: *Night visions 2.*
Night visions: Hardshell—SEE: *Night visions 4.*
Night visions: In the blood—SEE: *Night visions 1.*
Night visions: The hellbound heart—SEE: *Night visions 3.*
The skin trade—SEE: *Night visions 5.*

MILAN, Victor (Woodward), 1954-

29848 *The cybernetic samurai.* New York: Arbor House, 1985, 300 p., cloth, novel. CYBERNETIC SHOGUN #1.

29849 *The cybernetic shogun.* New York: William Morrow & Co., 1990, 272 p., cloth, novel. CYBERNETIC SHOGUN #2.

as RICHARD AUSTIN

Armageddon run—SEE: *The Guardians: Armageddon run.*
Brute force—SEE: *The Guardians: Brute force.*
Death charge—SEE: *The guardians: Death charge.*
Death from above—SEE: *The Guardians: Death from above.*
Desolation road—SEE: *The Guardians: Desolation road.*
Devil's deal—SEE: *The Guardians: Devil's deal.*
Freedom fight—SEE: *The Guardians: Freedom fight.*

29850 *The Guardians.* New York: A Jove Book, 1985, 230 p., paper, novel. GUARDIANS #1.

29851 *The Guardians: Armageddon run.* New York: A Jove Book, 1986, 182 p., paper, novel. GUARDIANS #5.

29852 *The Guardians: Brute force.* New York: Jove Books, 1987, 217 p., paper, novel. GUARDIANS #7.

29853 *The Guardians: Death charge.* New York: Jove Books, 1991, 188 p., paper, novel. GUARDIANS #16.

29854 *The Guardians: Death from above.* New York: Jove Books, 1990, 202 p., paper, novel. GUARDIANS #14.

29855 *The Guardians: Desolation road.* New York: Jove Books, 1987, 219 p., paper, novel. GUARDIANS #8.

29856 *The Guardians: Devil's deal.* New York: Jove Books, 1989, 215 p., paper, novel. GUARDIANS #13.

29857 *The Guardians: Freedom fight.* New York: Jove Books, 1988, 201 p., paper, novel. GUARDIANS #10. [Author is credited on cover only].

29858 *The Guardians: Night of the phoenix.* New York: A Jove Book, 1985, 216 p., paper, novel. GUARDIANS #4.

29859 *The Guardians: Plague years.* New York: Jove Books, 1988, 200 p., paper, novel. GUARDIANS #12.

29860 *The Guardians: Snake eyes.* New York: Jove Books, 1990, 198 p., paper, novel. GUARDIANS #15.

29861 *The Guardians: Thunder of Hell.* New York: A Jove Book, 1985, 217 p., paper, novel. GUARDIANS #3.

29862 *The Guardians: Trial by fire.* New York: A Jove Book, 1985, 231 p., paper, novel. GUARDIANS #2.

29863 *The Guardians: Valley of the gods.* New York: Jove Books, 1988, 197 p., paper, novel. GUARDIANS #11.

29864 *The Guardians: Vengeance day.* New York: Jove Books, 1987, 201 p., paper, novel. GUARDIANS #9.

29865 *The Guardians: War zone.* New York: A Jove Book, 1986, 217 p., paper, novel. GUARDIANS #6.

Night of the phoenix—SEE: *The Guardians: Night of the phoenix.*

Plague years—SEE: *The Guardians: Plague years.*

Snake eyes—SEE: *The Guardians: Snake eyes.*

Thunder of Hell—SEE: *The Guardians: Thunder of Hell.*

Trial by fire—SEE: *The Guardians: Trial by fire.*

Valley of the gods—SEE: *The Guardians: Valley of the gods.*

Vengeance day—SEE: *The Guardians: Vengeance day.*

War zone—SEE: *The Guardians: War zone.*

with *Melinda Snodgrass*

29866 *Runespear.* New York: Popular Library, 1987, 278 p., paper, novel.

with *Robert E. Vardeman*

29867 *The city in the glacier.* New York: Playboy Paperbacks, 1980, 224 p., paper, novel. WAR OF POWERS #2.

29868 *Demon of the Dark Ones.* New York: Playboy Paperbacks, 1982, 221 p., paper, novel. WAR OF POWERS #6.

29869 *The Destiny Stone.* New York: Playboy Paperbacks, 1980, 221 p., paper, novel. WAR OF POWERS #3.

29870 *The Fallen Ones.* New York: Playboy Paperbacks, 1982, 222 p., paper, novel. WAR OF POWERS #4.

29871 *In the shadow of Omizantrim.* New York: Playboy Paperbacks, 1982, 222 p., paper, novel. WAR OF POWERS #5.

Istu awakened-SEE: *The war of powers II: Istu awakened.*

29872 *The Sundered Realm.* New York: Playboy Paperbacks, 1980, 222 p., paper, novel. WAR OF POWERS #1.

29873 *The war of powers.* Sevenoaks, Kent, England: New English Library, 1984, 457 p., paper, coll. WAR OF POWERS #1-3. [Includes *The Sundered Realm*; *The city in the glacier*; *The Destiny Stone*].

36113 *The war of powers II: Istu awakened.* Sevenoaks, Kent, England: New English Library, 1985, 511 p., paper, coll. WAR OF POWERS #4-6. [Includes *The Fallen Ones*; *In the shadow of Omizantrim*; *Demon of the Dark Ones*].

MILES, Barry, 1943- , *with Joe Maynard*

29347 *William S. Burroughs: a bibliography, 1953-73: unlocking Inspector Lee's word hoard.* Charlottesville, VA: Published for the Bibliographical Society of the University of Virginia by the University Press of Virginia, 1978, xxiii+242 p., cloth, nonf.

MILES, Ellen (Gross), 1941-

Before Shadowgate—SEE: *Worlds of power: Before Shadowgate: the exciting prequel to the game created by ICOM Simulations, Inc.*

Mega man 2—SEE: *Worlds of power: Mega man 2: a novel based on the best-selling game by CAPCOM.*

Wizards & warriors—SEE: *Worlds of power: Wizards and warriors: a novel based on the best-selling game by Acclaim.*

29874 *Worlds of power: Before Shadowgate: the exciting prequel to the game created by ICOM Simulations, Inc.* New York, Toronto: A Seth Godin Production, Scholastic Inc., 1990, 119 p., paper, fiction. WORLDS OF POWER #8.

29875 *Worlds of power: Mega man 2: a novel based on the best-selling game by CAPCOM.* New York, Toronto: A Seth Godin Production, Scholastic Inc., 1990, 73 p., paper, fiction. WORLDS OF POWER (UNNUMBERED).

29876 *Worlds of power: Wizards & warriors: a novel based on the best-selling game by Acclaim.* New York, Toronto: A Seth Godin Production, Scholastic Inc., 1990,

121 p., paper, fiction. WORLDS OF POWER #5.

MILES, Keith, 1940-

29877 *Arabian adventure.* London: Mirror Books, 1979, 157 p., paper, movie.

MILES, (Mary) Patricia, 1930-

29878 *The gods in winter.* London: Hamilton, 1978, 140 p., cloth, novel.

*MILLARD, Joseph (John), 1908-1989

MILLER, Calvin, 1936-

29879 *Guardians of the Singreale.* San Francisco: Harper & Row, 1982, 216 p., paper, novel. SINGREALE CHRONICLES #1.
29880 *The legend of the brotherstone: the Wise Men's search.* San Francisco: Harper & Row, 1985, xvi+83 p., paper, novel.
29881 *A requiem of love.* Dallas, TX: Word Publishing, 1989, 152 p., paper, novel. SYMPHONY TRILOGY #1.
29882 *Star riders of Ren.* San Francisco: Harper & Row, 1983, 225 p., paper, novel. SINGREALE CHRONICLES #2.
29883 *A symphony in sand.* Dallas, TX: Word Publishing, 1990, 144 p., paper, novel. SYMPHONY TRILOGY #2.
29884 *The valiant papers: a guardian angel's efforts to direct a human's heart to God.* Grand Rapids, MI: Zondervan Publishing House, 1982, 155 p., paper, novel.
29885 *War of the Moonrhymes.* San Francisco & Cambridge: Harper & Row, Publishers, 1984, 214 p., paper, novel. SINGREALE CHRONICLES #3.

MILLER, Carl

29886 *Dragonbound.* New York: Ace Books, 1988, 242 p., paper, novel. DRAGONBOUND #1.
29887 *The goblin plain war.* New York: Ace Books, 1991, 245 p., paper, novel. DRAGONBOUND #3.
29888 *The warrior and the witch.* New York: Ace Books, 1990, 226 p., paper, novel. DRAGONBOUND #2.

MILLER, Charles F.—SEE: Miller, Chuck

MILLER, Chuck [i.e., Charles Franklin Miller Jr.], 1952-

with Tim Underwood

29889 *Bare bones: conversations on terror with Stephen King.* Los Angeles & Columbia, PA: Underwood-Miller, 1988, 259 p., cloth, nonf. anth.
29890 *Fear itself: the horror fiction of Stephen King.* San Francisco, Columbia, PA: Underwood-Miller, 1982, 255 p., cloth, nonf. anth.
29891 *Feast of fear: conversations with Stephen King.* New York: McGraw-Hill Book Co., 1989, 282 p., cloth, nonf. anth.
29892 *Jack Vance.* New York: Taplinger Publishing Co., 1980, 252 p., cloth, nonf. anth.
29893 *Kingdom of fear: the world of Stephen King.* San Francisco & Columbia, PA: Underwood-Miller, 1986, 267 p., cloth, nonf. anth.

with Tim Underwood as ANONYMOUS EDITORS

29894 *The book of the Sixth World Fantasy Convention.* San Francisco, Columbia, PA: Underwood-Miller, 1980, 96 p., cloth, anth. [Includes some nonfiction].

with Tim Underwood and Daniel J. H. Levack

28243 *Fantasy and science fiction by Jack Vance.* San Francisco, Columbia, PA: Underwood-Miller, 1978, 8 p., paper, nonf.

MILLER, David C., *with John H. Way*

29895 *Cardiac arrest.* New York: Charter Books, 1988, 265 p., paper, novel.

MILLER, David Lee, 1951-

29896 *Baby: the storybook.* New York: A Little Simon Book, Simon & Schuster, 1985, [58] p., cloth, movie.

MILLER, David M(erlin), 1934-

29897 *Frank Herbert.* Mercer Island, WA: Starmont House, 1980, 70 p., paper, nonf. STARMONT READER'S GUIDE #5.

MILLER, Faren (Carol), 1950-

29898 *The illusionists.* New York: Warner Books, 1991, 213 p., paper, novel.

MILLER, Frank, 1957-

29899 *Great comic artist file: Frank Miller.* Canoga Park, CA: Heroes Publishing, 1986, 55 p., paper, nonf.

MILLER, Fred D(ycus) Jr., 1944- , *with Nicholas D. Smith*

29900 *Thought probes: philosophy through science fiction.* Englewood Cliffs, NJ: Prentice-Hall, 1981, vi+362 p., cloth, nonf. anth.

29901 *Thought probes: philosophy through science fiction literature, 2nd ed.* Englewood Cliffs, NJ: Prentice-Hall, 1989, 334 p., cloth, nonf. anth.

MILLER, G(eorge) Wayne, 1954-

29902 *Thunder rise.* New York: Arbor House, William Morrow, 1989, 381 p., cloth, novel.

MILLER, George Noyes, 1845-1904, *as* ?

37970 *The strike of a sex: a novel* / by ?. New York: G. W. Dillingham, 1890, 235 p., paper, novel.

MILLER, Hugh—SEE: Watts, John

MILLER, Ian, *with John Blanche*

18120 *Ratspike.* Honesdale, PA: Games Workshop/GW Books, 1990, 140 p., cloth, art.

MILLER, J(ames) P(inckney), 1919-

29903 *The Skook: a novel.* New York: Warner Books, 1984, 307 p., cloth, novel.

MILLER, Jim

29904 *The last chance.* New York, Washington: Vantage Press, 1980, 62 p., cloth, novel.

MILLER, John J(oseph), 1954-

29905 *Buck Rogers: First power play.* Lake Geneva, WI: TSR Inc., 1990, 274 p., paper, novel. BUCK ROGERS—INNER PLANETS TRILOGY #1.
   First power play—SEE: *Buck Rogers: First power play.*

with George R. R. Martin & Melinda M. Snodgrass

29119 *Dead man's hand: a Wild Card novel.* New York, Toronto: Bantam Books, 1990, 328 p., paper, anth. WILD CARDS #7.

MILLER, Larry

29906 *Inseminoid.* London: New English Library, 1981, 158 p., paper, movie.

MILLER, Megan

with David Keller & Byron Preiss

26998 *The ultimate Dracula.* New York: A Byron Preiss Book, A Dell Trade Paperback, 1991, viii+358 p., paper, anth.

with David Keller & Byron Preiss & John Betancourt

17907 *The ultimate Frankenstein.* New York: A Byron Preiss Book, A Dell Trade Paperback, 1991, viii+327 p., paper, anth.

17908 *The ultimate werewolf.* New York: A Byron Preiss Book, A Dell Trade Paperback, 1991, viii+357 p., paper, anth.

MILLER, Miranda (Hyman), 1950-

29907 *Smiles and the millennium.* London: Virago, 1987, 243 p., cloth, novel.

MILLER, Moira

29908 *The doom of Soulis.* London: Pied Piper, Methuen Children's Books, 1987, 126 p., cloth, novel.

MILLER, P(eter) Schuyler, 1912-1974

29909 *Alicia in Blunderland.* Philadelphia, PA: Oswald Train: Publisher, 1983, 117 p., cloth, coll.

MILLER, Patsy Ruth, 1905-

29910 *My Hollywood—when both of us were very young: the memories of Patsy Ruth Miller.* [S.l.]: O'Raghailligh Publishers, 1988, 230+208 p., cloth, nonf.

MILLER, Perry (Gilbert Eddy), 1905-1963

29911 *The raven and the whale: the war of words and wits in the era of Poe and Melville.* New York: Harcourt, Brace & Co., 1956, 370 p., cloth, nonf.

MILLER, Phyllis (Steinfurth), 1920- , *with Andre Norton*

29912 *House of shadows.* New York: A Margaret K. McElderry Book, Atheneum, 1984, 201 p., cloth, novel.

29913 *Seven spells to Sunday.* New York: A Margaret K. McElderry Book, Atheneum, 1979, 136 p., cloth, novel

MILLER, Rex, 1929-

29914 *Frenzy.* New York: An Onyx Book, New American Library, 1988, 302 p., paper, novel. JACK EICHORD #2.

29915 *Iceman.* New York: An Onyx Book, New American Library, 1990, 283 p., paper, novel. JACK EICHORD #5.

29916 *Slice.* New York: An Onyx Book, New American Library, 1990, 317 p., paper, novel. JACK EICHORD #4.

29917 *Slob.* New York: A Signet Book, New American Library, 1987, 301 p., paper, novel. JACK EICHORD #1.

29918 *Stone shadow.* New York: An Onyx Book, New American Library, 1989, 282 p., paper, novel. JACK EICHORD #3.

MILLER, Richard (Connelly), 1925-

29919 *Snail.* New York: Holt, Rinehart & Winston, 1984, 294 p., cloth, novel.

29920 *Sowboy.* London: Bloomsbury, 1991, 230 p., paper, novel. SQUED #2.

29921 *SQUED.* London: Bloomsbury, 1989, 214 p., paper, novel. SQUED #1.

MILLER, Ron, 1947-

29922 *Norman Jacobs & Kerry O'Quinn present Space art.* New York: Starlog Magazine, 1978, 192 p., paper, art.

29923 *Palaces and prisons.* New York: Ace Books, 1991, 246 p., paper, novel. PALACES #1.

29924 *The space art poster book.* Harrisburg, PA: Stackpole Books, 1979, [47] p., paper, art.
Space art—SEE: Norman Jacobs & Kerry O'Quinn present Space art.

with Frederick C. Durant III

22325 *Worlds beyond: the art of Chesley Bonestell.* Norfolk, Virginia Beach, VA: A Starblaze Special, Donning Co., 1983, 133 p., paper, art.

with Pamela Lee & William K. Hartmann

25320 *Out of the cradle: exploring the frontiers beyond Earth.* New York: Workman Publishing, 1984, 190 p., cloth, fiction. [Mixes science fiction with nonfiction].

MILLER, Russell, 1938-

29925 *Bare-faced messiah: the true story of L. Ron Hubbard.* London: Michael Joseph, 1987, 390 p., cloth, nonf.

MILLER, Rusty, 1970?-

29926 *The Jedi master's quizbook: 425 cosmic questions & answers about Star Wars and The Empire Strikes Back.* New York: A Del Rey Book, Ballantine Books, 1982, viii+135 p., paper, nonf.

MILLER, Stephen O.

29927 *Middle Earth: a world in conflict.* Baltimore, MD: T-K Graphics, 1975, 82 p., paper, nonf.

MILLER, Steve(n R.), 1950- , with Sharon Lee

28043 *Agent of change.* New York: A Del Rey Book, Ballantine Books, 1988, 247 p., paper, novel. AGENT #1.

28044 *Carpe diem.* New York: A Del Rey Book, Ballantine Books, 1989, 292 p., paper, novel. AGENT #2.

28045 *Conflict of honors.* New York: A Del Rey Book, Ballantine Books, 1988, 326 p., paper, novel.

MILLER, Thos. Kent [i.e., Thomas Kent Miller], 1945-

29928 *Sherlock Holmes on the roof of the world.* Redlands, CA: Rosemill House, 1987, 75 p., paper, novel. SHE SERIES; SHERLOCK HOLMES SERIES.

MILLER, Walter M(ichael) Jr., 1923-

29929 *The best of Walter M. Miller, Jr.* New York: Pocket Books, 1980, 472 p., paper, coll.

29929A retitled: *Conditionally human, and other stories.* London: Corgi Books,, 1982, 228 p., paper, anth. [Abridged edition].

29929B retitled: *The darfstellar, and other stories.* London: Corgi Books, 1982, 223 p., paper, coll. [Abridged edition].

29930 *The science fiction stories of Walter M. Miller, Jr.* Boston: Gregg Press, 1978, xxv+373 p., cloth, coll.

with Martin H. Greenberg

24547 *Beyond armageddon: twenty-one sermons to the dead.* New York: Donald I. Fine, 1985, 387 p., cloth, anth.

MILLHAUSER, Steven, 1943-

29931 *The Barnum Museum: stories.* New York: Poseidon Press, 1990, 237 p., cloth, coll.

29932 *From the realm of Morpheus.* New York: William Morrow & Co., 1986, 370 p., cloth, novel.

37971 *In the penny arcade: stories.* New York: Alfred A. Knopf, 1986, 164 p., cloth, coll.

MILLHISER, Marlys (Joy), 1938-

29933 *The mirror.* New York: G. P. Putnam's Sons, 1978, 414 p., cloth, novel.

29934 *Nightmare country.* New York: G. P. Putnam's Sons, 1981, 330 p., cloth, novel.

29935 *The threshold.* New York: G. P. Putnam's Sons, 1984, 334 p., cloth, novel.

MILLIES, Suzanne, 1943-

29936 *Science fiction primer for teachers.* Dayton, OH: Pflaum Publishing, 1975, v+ 104 p., paper, nonf.

*MILLIGAN, Alfred L(ee), 1893-1973

MILLS, C(arla) J(ohnson), 1944-

  Egil's book—SEE: *Winter world: Egil's book.*

  Kit's book—SEE: *Winter world: Kit's book.*

29937 *Winter world.* New York: Pageant Books, 1988, 312 p., paper, novel. WINTER WORLD #1.

29938 *Winter world: Egil's book.* New York: Ace Books, 1991, 202 p., paper, novel. WINTER WORLD #2.

29939 *Winter world: Kit's book.* New York: Ace Books, 1991, 181 p., paper, novel. WINTER WORLD #3.

MILLS, Craig (Allan), 1955-

29940 *The bane of Lord Caladon.* New York: A Del Rey Book, Ballantine Books, 1982, 218 p., paper, novel. CALADON #1.

29941 *The dreamer in discord.* New York: A Del Rey Book, Ballantine Books, 1988, 229 p., paper, novel. CALADON #2.

MILLS, D. F. [i.e., Deanie Francis Mills?]

29942 *Deadline.* New York: Diamond Books, 1991, 258 p., paper, novel.

29943 *Spellbound.* New York: Diamond Books, 1991, 309 p., paper, novel.

MILLS, James (Spencer), 1932-

29944 *The power.* New York: Warner Books, 1990, 406 p., cloth, novel.

MILLS, Robert E.

29945 *Star fighters.* New York: Belmont Tower Books, 1978, 220 p., paper, novel. FELLOWSHIP OF LIGHT #2.

29946 *Star force.* New York: Belmont Tower Books, 1978, 238 p., paper, novel. FELLOWSHIP OF LIGHT #3.

29947 *Star quest.* New York: Belmont Tower Books, 1978, 191 p., paper, novel. FELLOWSHIP OF LIGHT #1.

29948 *Under the eye of night.* New York: Leisure Books, 1980, 319 p., paper, novel.

*MILLS, Robert P(ark), 1920-1986

MILLS-MALET, Vincent

37972 *The meteoric Benson: a romance of actuality.* London: Stanley Paul & Co., 1912, 320 p., cloth, novel.

MILLSTEAD, Thomas (Edward)

29949 *Cave of the moving shadows.* New York: The Dial Press, 1979, 217 p., cloth, novel.

MILNE, Janis

29950 *Starship Dunroamin'.* London: J. M. Dent & Sons, 1987, 126 p., cloth, novel.

MILNE, Larry

29951 *Biggles: the movie.* London: Severn House, 1986, 192 p., cloth, movie.

29952 *Ghostbusters.* Sevenoaks, Kent, England: Coronet, 1984, 191 p., paper, movie.

MILNE, Robert Duncan, 1844-1899

29953 *Into the sun, & other stories.* West Kingston, RI: Donald M. Grant, Publisher, 1980, 253 p., cloth, coll. SCIENCE FICTION IN OLD SAN FRANCISCO #2. [Edited by Sam Moskowitz].

MILOSLAVSKII, Nikolai Tolstoi- —SEE: Tolstoi-Miloslavskii, Nikolai

MILSTEAD, John W(illiam), 1924- , *with Martin H. Greenberg & Joseph D. Olander & Patricia Warrick*

24548 *Social problems through science fiction.* New York: St. Martin's Press, 1975, xvi+356 p., cloth, anth.

MILTON, Hilary (Herbert), 1920-

29954 *Craven House terror.* New York: Wanderer Books, Simon & Schuster, 1982, 116 p., paper, novel. PLOT YOUR OWN HORROR STORIES #1.

29954A retitled: *Horror house.* London: Methuen Children's Books, 1984, 116 p., paper, novel

Dining with dinosaurs—SEE: *Museum of the living dead.*

29955 *Dungeon demons.* New York: Wanderer Books, Simon & Schuster, 1985, 119 p., paper, novel. PLOT-IT-YOURSELF HORROR STORIES #8.

29956 *Escape from high doom.* New York: Wanderer Books, Simon & Schuster, 1984, 119 p., paper, novel. PLOT-IT-YOURSELF HORROR STORIES #5.

29957 *Fun house terrors!* New York: Wanderer Books, Simon & Schuster, 1984, 118 p., paper, novel. PLOT-IT-YOURSELF HORROR STORIES #6.

Grand hotel of horror—SEE: *Horror hotel!*

29958 *Horror hotel!* New York: Wanderer Books, Simon & Schuster, 1983, 122 p., paper, novel. PLOT YOUR OWN HORROR STORIES #4.

29958A retitled: *Grand hotel of horror.* London: A Magnet Book, Methuen, 1984, 122 p., paper, novel.

Horror house—SEE: *Craven House terror.*

29959 *Museum of the living dead.* New York: Wanderer Books, Simon & Schuster, 1985, 120 p., paper, novel. PLOT-IT-YOURSELF HORROR STORIES #7.

29959A retitled: *Dining with dinosaurs.* London: A Magnet Book, Methuen, 1985, 120 p., paper, novel.

29960 *Nightmare store.* New York: Wanderer Books, Simon & Schuster, 1982, 121 p., paper, novel. PLOT YOUR OWN HORROR STORIES #2.

Space age terrors!—SEE: *Space-age terrors!*

29961 *Space-age terrors!* New York: Wanderer Books, Simon & Schuster, 1983, 118 p., paper, novel. PLOT YOUR OWN HORROR STORIES #3.

29961A retitled: *Space age terrors!* London: A Magnet Book, Methuen, 1984, 118 p., paper, novel.

29962 *Two from the dead.* Boston: Houghton Mifflin Co., 1983, 184 p., cloth, novel.

MILTON, Joyce, 1946- , *with Jane O'Connor*

37973 *The amazing bubblegum caper.* New York, Toronto: Scholastic Inc., 1983, 60 p., paper, fiction. PICK-A-PATH #4.

37974 *The dandee diamond mystery.* New York, Toronto: Scholastic Book Services, 1982, 56 p., paper, fiction. PICK-A-PATH #1.

MINAHAN, John (English), 1933-

29963 *The great grave robbery.* New York: W. W. Norton & Co., 1990, 251 p., cloth, novel.

MINGHELLA, Anthony, 1954-

29964 *Jim Henson's The storyteller.* London: Boxtree, 1988, 144 p., cloth, tele. coll.

The storyteller—SEE: *Jim Henson's The storyteller.*

MINKOV, Svetoslav, 1902-1966

37975 *The lady with the X-ray eyes.* Sofia, Bulgaria: Foreign Languages Press, 1965, 281 p., cloth, coll. [Translation by Krassimira Noneva].

MINNS, Karen Marie Christa, 1956-

29965 *Virago.* Tallahassee, FL: Naiad Press, 1990, 191 p., paper, novel.

MINSKY, Marvin (Lee), 1927-

29966 *Robotics.* Garden City, NY: Anchor Press, Doubleday & Co., 1985, 317 p., cloth, nonf. anth. [Commentary on robots in fiction and fact].

MINTO, William, 1845-1893

37976 *The crack of doom: a novel.* Edinburgh, Scotland: William Blackwood, 1886, 3 v., cloth, novel.

MINTON, Paula [pseud. of Paul Hugo Little], 1915-1987

29967 *The girl from nowhere.* Chatsworth, CA: Major Books, 1975, 175 p., paper, novel.

MINTON, T. M.—SEE: Bade, Tom

MIRANDA, Vincent, *as* INTRODUCER, d. 1992

29968 *Fantasy voyages: great science fiction from the Saturday evening post, rev. ed.* Indianapolis, IN: Curtis Publishing Co., 1979, 311 p., cloth, anth.

*MIRRLEES, (Helen) Hope, <u>1887</u>-1978

MIRZA, Taqi Ali, *with Adapa Ramakrishna Rao & Satyanarain Singh*

29969 *William Golding: an Indian response: a collection of critical essays on the fiction of William Golding.* New Delhi, India: Arnold-Heinemann, 1987, viii+147 p., cloth, nonf. anth.

MISHA [pseud. of Misha Chocholak]

29970 *Prayers of steel.* Union, OR: Wordcraft, 1988, 43 p., paper, coll.
29971 *Red spider, white web.* Scotforth, Lancaster, England: Morrigan Publications, 1990, 216 p., cloth, novel.

MISSEN, Lynne, *with Greg Ioannou*

26302 *Shivers: an anthology of Canadian ghost stories.* Toronto: Seal Books, McClelland-Bantam, 1990, 216 p., paper, anth.

MISTICHELLI, Judith A(dams), *with Edward J. Gallagher & John A. Van Eerde*

23613 *Jules Verne: a primary and secondary bibliography.* Boston: G. K. Hall & Co., 1980, xxi+387 p., cloth, nonf. MASTERS OF SCIENCE FICTION AND FANTASY.

MISTRAL, Bengo, house pseud.—SEE: Lazenby, Norman & Ward, B.

MITCHELL, Betsy—SEE: Mitchell, Elizabeth

MITCHELL, Elizabeth (L.), 1954-

29972 *After the flames.* New York: Baen Science Fiction Books, 1985, 277 p., paper, anth. ALIEN STARS #2.
29973 *Alien stars.* New York: A Baen Book, 1985, 254 p., paper, anth. ALIEN STARS #1.
29974 *Free lancers.* New York: Baen Books, 1987, 248 p., paper, anth. ALIEN STARS #4.

29975 *Under the wheel.* New York: Baen Books, 1987, 272 p., paper, anth. ALIEN STARS #3.

with Lou Aronica & Amy Stout

16799 *Full spectrum 3.* New York: A Foundation Book, Doubleday, 1991, x+535 p., cloth, anth. [Winner of the *Locus* Award for Best Anthology, 1991 (1992)].

MITCHELL, (Sibyl) Elyne (Keith), 1913-

29976 *Silver brumbies of the south.* London: Hutchinson, 1965, 240 p., cloth, novel. SILVER BRUMBIES #3.
29977 *Silver brumby.* London: Hutchinson, 1958, 191 p., cloth, novel. SILVER BRUMBIES #1.
29978 *Silver brumby kingdom.* London: Hutchinson, 1966, 189 p., cloth, novel. SILVER BRUMBIES #4.
29979 *Silver brumby whirlwind.* London: Hutchinson, 1973, 128 p., cloth, novel. SILVER BRUMBIES #4.
29980 *Silver brumby's daughter.* London: Hutchinson, 1960, 238 p., cloth, novel. SILVER BRUMBIES #2.

MITCHELL, Kirk (John), 1950-

29981 *Cry republic.* New York: Ace Books, 1989, 267 p., paper, novel. PROCURATOR #3.
29982 *Never the Twain.* New York: Ace Books, 1987, 294 p., paper, novel.
29983 *New barbarians.* New York: Ace Science Fiction Books, 1986, 296 p., paper, novel. PROCURATOR #2.
29984 *Procurator.* New York: Ace Science Fiction Books, 1984, 234 p., paper, novel. PROCURATOR #1.

MITCHELL, Peter R.

29985 *The lost sowers of Cathanic.* Bognor Regis, West Sussex, England: New Horizon, 1983, 166 p., cloth, novel.

MITCHELL, Tim, *with David A. Randall & Sigmund Casey Fredericks*

23480 *Science fiction and fantasy: an exhibition, January-April, 1975.* Bloomington, IN: Lilly Library, Indiana University, 1975, 71 p., paper, nonf.

MITCHELL, V. E. [i.e. Victoria Estelle Mitchell Gustafson], 1954-

Enemy unseen—SEE: *Star Trek: Enemy unseen*.

29986 *Star Trek: Enemy unseen.* New York, London: Pocket Books, 1990, 279 p., paper, tele. STAR TREK #51.

MITCHELSON, Austin, *with Nicholas Utechin*

29987 *The earthquake machine.* New York: Belmont Tower Books, 1976, 215 p., paper, novel. SHERLOCK HOLMES SERIES.

MITCHISON, Naomi (Margaret Haldane), 1897-

29988 *Beyond this limit.* London: Jonathan Cape, 1935, 88 p., cloth, novel.

29989 *Beyond this limit: selected shorter fiction of Naomi Mitchison.* Edinburgh, Scotland: Scottish Academy Press in Association with the Association for Scottish Literary Studies, 1986, xix+217 p., paper, coll. [Includes *Beyond this limit*].

29990 *The big house.* London: Faber & Faber, 1950, 169 p., cloth, novel.

29991 *Early in Orcadia.* Glasgow, Scotland: Richard Drew, 1987, 176 p., cloth, novel.

29992 *A girl must live: stories and poems.* Glasgow, Scotland: Richard Drew, 1990, 253 p., cloth, coll. [Includes some verse].

29993 *Not by bread alone: a novel.* London, New York: Marion Boyars, 1983, 167 p., cloth, novel.

29994 *Solution three.* London: Dennis Dobson, 1975, 160 p., cloth, novel.

29995 *Travel light.* London: Faber & Faber, 1952, 147 p., cloth, novel.

29996 *We have been warned: a novel.* London: Constable & Co., 1935, xiv+553 p., cloth, novel.

MITGANG, Herbert, 1920-

29997 *The Montauk fault: a novel.* New York: Arbor House, 1981, 285 p., cloth, novel.

MIXON, Laura J.

Astro pilots—SEE: *Omni: Astropilots*.
Astropilots—SEE: *Omni: Astropilots*.

29998 *Astropilots.* New York, Toronto: Scholastic Inc., 1987, 236 p., paper, novel. OMNI ODYSSEYS #1.

29998A retitled: *Astro pilots.* London: Dragon, 1987, 220 p., paper, novel. OMNI ODYSSEYS #1.

MIZNER, Elizabeth H.—SEE: Howard, Elizabeth

MOBLEY, Jane, 1947-

29999 *Phantasmagoria: tales of fantasy and the supernatural.* Garden City, NY: Anchor Books, Anchor Press/Doubleday, 1977, 439 p., paper, anth.

MODESITT, L(eland) E(xton) Jr., 1943-

30000 *Dawn for a distant Earth.* New York: Tor SF, A Tom Doherty Associates Book, 1987, 340 p., paper, novel. FOREVER HERO #1.

30001 *The ecolitan operation.* New York: Tor SF, A Tom Doherty Associates Book, 1989, 345 p., paper, novel. ECOLITAN TRILOGY #2.

30002 *The ecologic envoy.* New York: Tor SF, A Tom Doherty Associates Book, 1986, 287 p., paper, novel. ECOLITAN TRILOGY #1.

30003 *The ecologic secession.* New York: Tor SF, A Tom Doherty Associates Book, 1990, 344 p., paper, novel. ECOLITAN TRILOGY #3.

30004 *The fires of paratime.* New York: A Timescape Book, Pocket Books, 1982, 239 p., paper, novel.

30005 *The hammer of darkness.* New York: Avon, 1985, 343 p., paper, novel.

30006 *In endless twilight.* New York: Tor SF, A Tom Doherty Associates Book, 1988, 316 p., paper, novel. FOREVER HERO #3.

30007 *The magic of Recluce.* New York: Tor Fantasy, A Tom Doherty Associates Book, 1991, 440 p., cloth, novel. RECLUCE #1.

30008 *The silent warrior.* New York: Tor SF, A Tom Doherty Associates Book, 1987, 280 p., paper, novel. FOREVER HERO #2.

MOERI, Louise, 1924-

30009 *Downwind.* New York: E. P. Dutton, 1984, 121 p., cloth, novel.

*MOFFAT, W. Graham, 1866-

MOFFATT, Derry

30010 *The aristocats.* London: New English Library, 1976, 128 p., paper, movie.

30011 *Dumbo.* London: New English Library, 1975, 125 p., paper, movie.

30012 *Lady and the tramp.* London: New English Library, 1975, 128 p., paper, movie.

30013 *Pete's dragon.* London: New English Library, 1978, 128 p., paper, movie.
30014 *Pinocchio.* London: New English Library, 1975, 144 p., paper, movie.
30015 *Robin Hood.* London: New English Library, 1974, 113 p., paper, movie.
30016 *The sword in the stone.* London: New English Library, 1976, 139 p., paper, movie.

MOFFATT, Donald—SEE: Kenyon, Paul

MOFFATT, James, 1922-

30017 *Queen Kong.* London: Everest Books, 1977, 172 p., paper, movie.

MOFFETT, Judith, 1942-

30018 *Pennterra.* New York: Congdon & Weed, 1987, 382 p., cloth, novel.
30019 *The ragged world: a novel of the Hefn on Earth.* New York: St. Martin's Press, 1991, 341 p., cloth, novel.
30020 *Two that came true.* Eugene, OR: Pulphouse Publishing, 1991, 104 p., cloth, coll. AUTHOR'S CHOICE MONTHLY #19.

MOFFITT, Donald (Anthony), 1936-

30021 *Crescent in the sky.* New York: A Del Rey Book, Ballantine Books, 1990, 280 p., paper, novel. MECHANICAL SKY #1.
30022 *A gathering of stars.* New York: A Del Rey Book, Ballantine Books, 1990, 281 p., paper, novel. MECHANICAL SKY #2.
30023 *The genesis quest.* New York: A Del Rey Book, Ballantine Books, 1986, 341 p., paper, novel. GENESIS QUEST #1.
30024 *The Jupiter theft.* New York: A Del Rey Book, Ballantine Books, 1977, 375 p., paper, novel.
30025 *Second genesis.* New York: A Del Rey Book, Ballantine Books, 1986, 329 p., paper, novel. GENESIS QUEST #2.

MOGEN, David (Lee), 1945-

30026 *Ray Bradbury.* New York: Twayne Publishers, 1986, 186 p., cloth, nonf.
30027 *Wilderness visions: science fiction westerns, volume one.* San Bernardino, CA: R. Reginald, The Borgo Press, 1982, 64 p., cloth, nonf. I.O. EVANS STUDIES IN THE PHILOSOPHY & CRITICISM OF LITERATURE #1.

MOHAN, Kim (Rudolph), 1949- , *with Pamela O'Neill*

30028 *Chase into space.* Delavan, WI: New Infinities Productions, 1988, 318 p., paper, novel. CYBORG COMMANDO #2.
30029 *Planet in peril.* Lake Geneva, WI: New Infinities Productions, 1987, 318 p., paper, novel. CYBORG COMMANDO #1.
30030 *The ultimate prize.* Delavan, WI: New Infinities Productions, 1988, 317 p., paper, novel. CYBORG COMMANDO #3.

MOHAN, Pamela—SEE: O'Neill, Pamela

MOIS, Joseph

37977 *A spot on the Sun.* London: S. Baker, 1954, 62 p., paper, story.

MOLDENHAUER, Joseph J(ohn), 1934-

30031 *A descriptive catalog of Edgar Allan Poe manuscripts in the Humanities Research Center Library, the University of Texas at Austin.* Austin, TX: University of Texas at Austin, 1973, 88 p., paper?, nonf.

MOLE, Mink, pseud.—SEE: Gibson, William

MOLESWORTH, Mary L.—SEE: Molesworth, Mrs.

*MOLESWORTH, Mrs. [i.e., Mary Louisa Molesworth], 1839-1921

MOLINARO, Ursule [i.e., Ursule Molinaro Herndon]

30032 *The autobiography of Cassandra, princess & prophetess of Troy.* Danbury, CT: Archer Editions Press, 1979, 129 p., cloth, novel.

*MOLNAR, E(ugene) F(rank), 1891-1986

MOLSON, Francis J(oseph), 1932-

30033 *Children's fantasy.* Mercer Island, WA: Starmont House, 1989, 97 p., cloth, nonf. STARMONT READER'S GUIDE #33.

MONACO, Richard, 1940-

30034 *Blood and dreams.* New York: Berkley Books, 1985, 230 p., paper, novel. ARTHURIAN CYCLE #4.
30035 *Broken stone.* New York: Ace Fantasy Books, 1985, 230 p., paper, novel. LEITUS #2.
30036 *The final quest.* New York: G. P. Putnam's Sons, 1981, 337 p., cloth, novel. ARTHURIAN CYCLE #3.

30037 *The Grail War.* New York: A Wallaby Book, Pocket Books, 1979, xii+319 p., paper, novel. ARTHURIAN CYCLE #2.

30038 *Journey to the flame.* Toronto, New York: Bantam Books, 1985, 260 p., paper, novel. SHE SEQUEL.

30039 *Parsival; or, A knight's tale.* New York: Macmillan Co., 1977, 343 p., cloth, novel. ARTHURIAN CYCLE #1.

30040 *Runes.* New York: Ace Fantasy Books, 1984, 281 p., paper, novel. LEITUS #1.

30041 *Unto the beast.* Toronto, New York: Bantam Books, 1987, 473 p., paper, novel.

MONAHAN, Brent (Jeffrey), 1948-

30042 *Satan's serenade.* New York, London: Pocket Books, 1989, 208 p., paper, novel.

MONEGAL, Emir Rodriguez—SEE: Rodriguez Monegal, Emir

MONETTE, Paul, 1946?-

30044 *Lightfall.* New York: Avon, 1982, 280 p., paper, novel.

30045 *Nosferatu, the vampyre: a novel.* New York: Avon, 1979, 172 p., paper, movie.

30046 *Predator: a novel.* New York: A Jove Book, 1987, 200 p., paper, movie. PREDATOR #1.

*MONROE, Donald, 1888-1972

MONROE, John B., *with Ken St. Andre & Steve Perrin*

30047 *Stormbringer.* Albany, CA: The Chaosium, 1990, 192 p., paper, art.

*MONROE, Keith, 1917-1973

MONROE, Mary

30048 *The upper room.* New York: St. Martin's Press, 1985, 309 p., cloth, novel.

MONSARRAT, Nicholas (John), 1910-1979

30049 *Darken ship: the unfinished novel.* London: Cassell, 1980, 181 p., cloth, novel. MASTER MARINER #2.

30050 *Running proud.* London: Cassell, 1978, 524 p., cloth, novel. MASTER MARINER #1.

37978 *Smith and Jones.* London: Cassell, 1963, 161 p., cloth, novel.

MONTAGU, Lodovick—SEE: Rees, Richard

MONTAGUE, Charles Howard, *with Clement Milton Hammond*

25117 *The doctor's mistake; or, What Myrta saw: an experiment with a life: a novel.* Boston: Thomas Downey Jr. & Co., 1888, 146 p., paper, novel.

MONTANA, Ron(ald Anthony), 1943-

30051 *The Cathedral Option.* New York: Zebra Books, Kensington Publishing Corp., 1978, 317 p., paper, novel.

Death in the spirit house—SEE: **Strete, Craig**

30052 *The sign of the thunderbird.* New York: Manor Books, 1977, 236 p., paper, novel.

MONTELEONE, Thomas F(rancis), 1946-

30053 *The arts and beyond: visions of man's aesthetic future.* Garden City, NY: Doubleday & Co., 1977, viii+205 p., cloth, anth.

30054 *Borderlands: an anthology of imaginative fiction, volume one.* Baltimore, MD: Maclay & Associates, 1990, 284 p., cloth, anth. [Limited to 750 copies].

30055 *Borderlands 2: an anthology of imaginative fiction.* Baltimore, MD: Borderlands Press, 1991, 275 p., cloth, anth. [Limited to 750 copies].

30056 *Dark stars, and other illuminations.* Garden City, NY: Doubleday & Co., 1981, vii+181 p., cloth, coll.

30057 *Fantasma.* New York: Tor Horror, A Tom Doherty Associates Book, 1989, 277 p., paper, novel.

30058 *Guardian.* Garden City, NY: Doubleday & Co., 1980, 176 p., cloth, novel.

30059 *Lyrica: a novel of horror and desire.* New York: Berkley Books, 1987, 294 p., paper, novel.

30060 *The magnificent gallery.* New York: Tor Horror, A Tom Doherty Associates Book, 1987, 248 p., paper, novel.

Microworlds: tales of the computer age—SEE: *Random access messages of the computer age.*

30061 *Night things.* New York: Fawcett Popular Library, 1980, 316 p., paper, novel.

30062 *Night-train.* New York: Pocket Books, 1984, 337 p., paper, novel.

30063 *Ozymandias.* Garden City, NY: Doubleday & Co., 1981, 179 p., cloth, novel.

30064 *Random access messages of the computer age.* Hasbrouck Heights, NJ: Hayden Book Co., 1984, 193 p., paper, anth.

30064A retitled: *Microworlds: tales of the computer age.* London: Severn House, 1985, 193 p., cloth, anth.

30065 *The secret sea.* New York: Popular Library, 1979, 222 p., paper, novel.

30066 *Seeds of change.* Don Mills, Ontario, Canada: Laser Books, 1975, 190 p., paper, novel.

30067 *The time connection.* New York: Popular Library, 1976, 190 p., paper, novel.

30068 *The time-swept city.* New York: Popular Library, 1977, 287 p., paper, novel.

with David F. Bischoff

18016 *Day of the dragonstar.* New York: Berkley Books, 1983, 291 p., paper, novel. DRAGONSTAR TRILOGY #1.

18017 *Dragonstar destiny* / by David F. Bischoff. New York: Ace Books, 1989, 216 p., paper, novel. DRAGONSTAR TRILOGY #3.

18018 *Night of the Dragonstar* / by David F. Bischoff. New York: Berkley Books, 1985, 264 p., paper, novel. DRAGONSTAR TRILOGY #2.

with John DeChancie

21468 *Crooked house.* New York: Tor Horror, A Tom Doherty Associates Book, 1987, 346 p., paper, novel.

*MONTERROSO, Augusto, 1921-

MONTGOMERIE, Lee, *with John Clute & David Pringle*

20207 *Interzone: the 5th anthology: new science fiction and fantasy writing.* London: New English Library, 1991, 280 p., paper, anth.

MONTGOMERY, L(ucy) M(aud), 1874-1942

30069 *Among the shadows: tales from the darker side.* Toronto: McClelland and Stewart, 1990, 310 p., cloth, coll. [Edited by Rea Wilmshurst].

30070 *Magic for marigold.* Toronto: McClelland & Stewart, 1927, vii+328 p., cloth, novel.

MONTGOMERY, Marion H(oyt) Jr., 1925-

30071 *Why Poe drank liquor.* La Salle, IL: Sherwood Sugden, 1983, 442 p., cloth, nonf.

MONTGOMERY, R(aymond) A. (Jr.), 1936-

30072 *The abominable snowman.* Toronto, New York: Bantam Books, 1982, 116 p., paper, novel. CHOOSE YOUR OWN ADVENTURE #13.

30073 *Almost lost.* New York, Toronto: Bantam Books, 1990, 151 p., paper, novel. TRIO: REBELS IN THE NEW WORLD #3.

30074 *Beyond escape!* Toronto, New York: Bantam Books, 1986, 112 p., paper, novel. CHOOSE YOUR OWN ADVENTURE #61.

30075 *Blood on the handle.* New York, Toronto: Bantam Books, 1989, 112 p., paper, novel. CHOOSE YOUR OWN ADVENTURE #94.

30076 *The brilliant Dr. Wogan.* Toronto, New York: Bantam Books, 1987, 113 p., paper, novel. CHOOSE YOUR OWN ADVENTURE #72.

30077 *Chinese dragons.* New York, Toronto: Bantam Books, 1991, 113 p., paper, novel. CHOOSE YOUR OWN ADVENTURE #109.

30078 *Choose your own adventure super adventure: Danger zones.* Toronto, New York: Bantam Books, 1987, 162 p., paper, novel. CHOOSE YOUR OWN ADVENTURE SUPER ADVENTURE #2.

30079 *Crossing enemy lines.* New York: Bantam Books, 1990, 148 p., paper, novel. TRIO: REBELS IN THE NEW WORLD #2.

Danger zones—SEE: *Choose your own adventure super adventure: Danger zones.*

30080 *Deadly encounter.* New York, Toronto: Bantam Books, 1990, 149 p., paper, novel. TRIO: REBELS IN THE NEW WORLD #6.

30081 *Escape.* Toronto, New York: Bantam Books, 1983, 118 p., paper, novel. CHOOSE YOUR OWN ADVENTURE #20.

30082 *Escape from China.* New York, Toronto: Bantam Books, 1990, 165 p., paper, novel. TRIO: REBELS IN THE NEW WORLD #5.

30083 *Exiled to Earth.* Toronto, New York: Bantam Books, 1989, 113 p., paper, novel. CHOOSE YOUR OWN ADVENTURE #87.

30084 *The hidden evil.* New York, Toronto: Bantam Books, 1990, 152 p., paper, novel. TRIO: REBELS IN THE NEW WORLD #4.

30085 *House of danger.* Toronto, New York: Bantam Books, 1982, 115 p., paper, novel. CHOOSE YOUR OWN ADVENTURE #15.

30086 *The island of time.* New York, Toronto: Bantam Books, 1991, 112 p., paper, novel. CHOOSE YOUR OWN ADVENTURE #115.

30098A *Journey under the sea.* Toronto, New York: Bantam Books, 1979, 117 p., paper, novel. CHOOSE YOUR OWN ADVENTURE #2. [Previously published under the name Robert Mountain].

30087 *The lost jewels of Nabooti.* Toronto, New York: Bantam Books, 1981, 121 p., paper, novel. CHOOSE YOUR OWN ADVENTURE #10.

30088 *Lost on the Amazon.* Toronto, New York: Bantam Books, 1983, 114 p., paper, novel. CHOOSE YOUR OWN ADVENTURE #24.

37979 *Mystery of the Maya.* Toronto, New York: Bantam Books, 1981, 113 p., paper, novel. CHOOSE YOUR OWN ADVENTURE #11.

30089 *Prisoner of the ant people.* Toronto, New York: Bantam Books, 1983, 115 p., paper, novel. CHOOSE YOUR OWN ADVENTURE #25.

37980 *The race forever.* Toronto, New York: Bantam Books, 1983, 116 p., paper, novel. CHOOSE YOUR OWN ADVENTURE #17.

30090 *Return to Atlantis.* Toronto, New York: Bantam Books, 1988, 113 p., paper, novel. CHOOSE YOUR OWN ADVENTURE #78.

30091 *Smoke jumper.* New York, Toronto: Bantam Books, 1991, 112 p., paper, novel. CHOOSE YOUR OWN ADVENTURE #111.

30092 *Space and beyond.* Toronto, New York: Bantam Books, 1980, 117 p., paper, novel. CHOOSE YOUR OWN ADVENTURE #4.

30093 *Stock car champion.* New York, Toronto: Bantam Books, 1989, 113 p., paper, novel. CHOOSE YOUR OWN ADVENTURE #96.

30094 *Track of the bear.* Toronto, New York: Bantam Books, 1988, 112 p., paper, novel. CHOOSE YOUR OWN ADVENTURE #83.

30095 *Traitors from within.* New York: Bantam Books, 1990, 165 p., paper, novel. TRIO: REBELS IN THE NEW WORLD #1.

30096 *Trouble on planet Earth.* Toronto, New York: Bantam Books, 1984, 116 p., paper, novel. CHOOSE YOUR OWN ADVENTURE #29.

30097 *War with the Evil Power Master.* Toronto, New York: Bantam Books, 1984, 118 p., paper, novel. CHOOSE YOUR OWN ADVENTURE #37.

as ROBERT MOUNTAIN

30098 *Journey under the sea.* VT: Vermont Crossroads Press, 1977, 97 p., cloth, novel. CHOOSE YOUR OWN ADVENTURE #2.

with Edward Packard

30099 *Mutiny in space.* New York, Toronto: A Packard/Montgomery Book, Bantam Books, 1989, 116 p., paper, novel. CHOOSE YOUR OWN ADVENTURE #90.

MONTGOMERY, Ramsey

30100 *Grave robbers.* New York, Toronto: An R. A. Montgomery Book, Bantam Books, 1990, 113 p., paper, novel. CHOOSE YOUR OWN ADVENTURE #103.

30101 *The Mona Lisa is missing!* Toronto, New York: An R. A. Montgomery Book, Bantam Books, 1988, 118 p., paper, novel. CHOOSE YOUR OWN ADVENTURE #76.

MONTGOMERY, Rex, pseud.

30102 *Man-made stud.* Santee, CA: Surree, 1977, [160] p., paper, novel.

*MONTGOMERY, Rutherford George, 1894-1985

MONTGOMERY, Wendy

30103 *Tender expressions.* Strathmartine by Dundee, Scotland: ScoTpress, 1985, 59 p., paper, tele. STAR TREK SERIES.

MONTROSE, Catherine—SEE: Cooke, Catherine

MONTROSE, Lester

30104 *Dominique: high priestess of the dark gods.* Sale, Cheshire: Montrose Music & Book Publishers, 1990, 233 p., paper, novel.

MOON, Alan—SEE: Bentley, Peter

MOON, (Susan) Elizabeth (Norris), 1945-

30105 *Divided allegiance.* New York: Baen, 1988, 522 p., paper, novel. DEED OF PAKSENARRION #2

30106 *Lunar activity.* New York: Baen Books, 1990, 278 p., paper, coll.

30107 *Oath of gold.* New York: Baen, 1989, 501 p., paper, novel. DEED OF PAKSENARRION #3.

30108 *Sheepfarmer's daughter.* New York: Baen Books, 1988, 506 p., paper, novel. DEED OF PAKSENARRION #1.

30109 *Surrender none: the legacy of Gird.* New York: Baen Fantasy, 1990, 530 p., paper, novel. DEED OF PAKSENARRIOR PREQUEL.

with Anne McCaffrey

29405 *Generation warriors.* Riverdale, NY: Baen Books, 1991, 345 p., paper, novel. PLANET PIRATES #3. [Title page incorrectly lists the author as Jody Lynn Nye].

29406 *Sassinak.* New York: Baen Books, 1990, 333 p., paper, novel. PLANET PIRATES #1.

MOON, Jay

30110 *Chancellor of Mars: a novel.* Hicksville, NY: Exposition Press, 1978, 191 p., cloth, novel.

MOONCHILD, pseud.—SEE: Fox, Gardner F.

MOONEY, Bel, 1946-

30111 *The stove haunting.* London: Methuen, 1988, 151 p., cloth, novel.

MOONEY, Brian

30112 *Cthulhu 2: tales of the Cthulhu Mythos: The guardians of the gate.* Cardiff, South Wales: Spectre Press, 1977, p. 27-50, paper, story. CTHULHU MYTHOS.

MOONEY, Edward—SEE: Mooney, Ted

MOONEY, Philip F., 1944-

30113 *Science fiction collections in the George Arents Research Library at Syracuse University.* Syracuse, NY: George Arents Research Library, Syracuse University, 1970, 11 p., paper, nonf.

MOONEY, Ted [i.e., Edward Mooney], 1951-

30114 *Easy travel to other planets.* New York: Farrar Straus Giroux, 1981, 278 p., cloth, novel.

30115 *Traffic and laughter.* New York: Alfred A. Knopf, 1990, 401 p., cloth, novel.

MOORCOCK, Michael (John), 1939-

30116 *The adventures of Una Persson and Catherine Cornelius in the twentieth century: a romance.* London: Quartet Books, 1976, 216 p., cloth, novel. JERRY CORNELIUS #7.

The bane of the black sword—SEE: *The stealer of souls.*

30117 *Before armageddon: an anthology of Victorian and Edwardian imaginative fiction published before 1914, volume I.* London: W. H. Allen, 1975, 180 p., cloth, anth.

30118 *The black corridor; The adventures of Una Persson and Catherine Cornelius.* New York: Dial Press, 1979, 346 p., cloth, coll.

30119 *Casablanca.* London: Victor Gollancz, 1989, 267 p., cloth, coll. [Includes some nonfiction].

30120 *The chronicles of Castle Brass: Count Brass; The champion of Garathorm; The quest of Tanelorn.* London & Glasgow: Granada, 1985, 150+138+144 p., cloth, coll. CASTLE BRASS. [Includes *Count Brass, Champion of Garathorm, Quest for Tanelorn*].

30121 *The chronicles of Corum: The bull and the spear; The oak and the ram; The sword and the stallion.* New York: A Berkley Book, Berkley Publishing Corp., 1978, xii+381 p., paper, coll. CORUM #4-6.

30122 *The city in the autumn stars: being a continuation of the story of the von Bek family and its association with Lucifer, Prince of Darkness, and the cure for the world's pain.* London: Grafton Books, 1986, 344 p., cloth, novel. WORLD'S PAIN SERIES.

30123 *The condition of muzak: a Jerry Cornelius novel.* London: Allison & Busby, 1977, 313 p., cloth, novel. JERRY CORNELIUS #4.

30124 *The Cornelius chronicles: The final programme; A cure for cancer; The English assassin; The condition of muzak.* New York: Avon, 1977, xv+974 p., paper, coll. JERRY CORNELIUS #1-4.

30125 *The Cornelius chronicles, vol. II: The lives and times of Jerry Cornelius; The entropy tango.* New York: Avon, 1986, 341 p., paper, coll. JERRY CORNELIUS SERIES.

30126 *The Cornelius chronicles, vol. III: The adventures of Una Persson and Catherine Cornelius in the twentieth century; The alchemist's question.* New York: Avon, 1987, 341 p., paper, coll. JERRY CORNELIUS SERIES.

30127 *The dancers at the end of time.* London: Granada, 1981, viii+603 p., cloth, coll.

DANCERS AT THE END OF TIME #1-3. [Includes *An alien heat*; *The hollow lands*; *The end of all songs*].

30128 *The dragon in the sword: being the third and final story in the history of John Daker, the eternal champion.* New York: Ace Fantasy Books, 1986, 298 p., cloth, novel. ETERNAL CHAMPION #3.

Dying for tomorrow—SEE: *Moorcock's book of martyrs*.

30129 *Elric at the end of time: fantasy stories.* Sevenoaks, Kent, England: New English Library, 1984, 175 p., cloth, coll. [All but two stories are from *Sojan*].

30130 *Elric of Melniboné.* London: Arrow Books, 1975, 191 p., cloth, novel. EL-RIC SERIES. [Parts published previously as *The dreaming city*].

30131 *The Elric Saga, part one: Elric of Melni-boné; The sailor on the seas of fate; The weird of the white wolf.* Garden City, NY: Nelson Doubleday, 1984, 374 p., cloth, coll. ELRIC SERIES.

30132 *The Elric saga, part two: The vanishing tower; The bane of the black sword; Stormbringer.* Garden City, NY: Nelson Doubleday, 1984, 471 p., cloth, coll. ELRIC SERIES.

30133 *The end of all songs.* New York, Hagerstown, NJ: Harper & Row, Publishers, 1976, xi+271 p., cloth, novel. DANCERS AT THE END OF TIME #3. [Author's name appears as "Moorock" on spine].

30134 *England invaded: a collection of fantasy fiction.* London: W. H. Allen, 1977, 245 p., cloth, anth.

30135 *The entropy tango: a comic romance.* London: New English Library, 1981, 153 p., cloth, novel. JERRY CORNELIUS #6.

30136 *Epic pooh.* Dagenham, Essex, England: British Fantasy Society, 1978, [15] p., paper, nonf.

30137 *The eternal champion: a fantastic romance.* New York: Harper & Row, 1978, ix+181 p., cloth, novel. [Expanded edition].

30138 *The fortress of the pearl.* London: Victor Gollancz, 1989, 248 p., cloth, novel. ELRIC SERIES.

30139 *Gloriana; or, The unfulfill'd queen: being a romance.* London: Allison & Busby, 1978, 348 p., cloth, novel. [Winner of the World Fantasy Award for Best Fantasy Novel, 1978 (1979); winner of the John W. Campbell Jr. Memorial Award for Best Novel, 1978 (1979)].

30140 *The golden barge: a fable.* Manchester, England: Savoy Books, 1979, 197 p., paper, novel.

30141 *The history of the Runestaff: The jewel in the skull; The mad god's amulet; The sword of the dawn; The runestaff.* London: Hart-Davis MacGibbon, 1979, 573 p., cloth, coll. HISTORY OF THE RUNE-STAFF #1-4.

30142 *Legends from the end of time.* New York, Evanston, IL: Harper & Row, Publishers, 1976, 182 p., cloth, coll. DANCERS AT THE END OF TIME #4.

30143 *Letters from Hollywood.* London: Harrap, 1986, 232 p., cloth, nonf. coll. [Letters to J. G. Ballard].

30144 *The lives and times of Jerry Cornelius.* London: Allison & Busby, 1976, 176 p., cloth, coll. JERRY CORNELIUS #5.

Messiah at the end of time—SEE: *The transformation of Miss Mavis Ming*.

30145 *Moorcock's book of martyrs.* London: Quartet Books, 1976, 175 p., paper, coll.

30146A retitled: *Dying for tomorrow.* New York: DAW Books, 1978, 192 p., paper, coll.

30147 *My experiences in the Third World War.* Manchester, England: Savoy Books in Association with New English Library, 1980, 156 p., paper, fiction.

30148 *New worlds: an anthology.* London: Flamingo, Fontana Paperbacks, 1983, 512 p., paper, anth.

30149 *The nomad of time.* Garden City, NY: Nelson Doubleday, 1982, 441 p., cloth, coll. OSWALD BASTABLE #1-3. [Includes *The warlord of the air*; *The land leviathan*; *The steel tsar*].

30150 *The opium generals, and other stories.* London: Harrap, 1984, 207 p., cloth, coll.

30151 *The quest for Tanelorn: the chronicles of Castle Brass, being a sequel to the High history of the runestaff, of which this is the third and final volume.* St Albans, England: Mayflower, 1975, 126 p., paper, novel.

30152 *The real life Mr Newman.* Worcester, England: A. J. Callow, 1979, 56 p., paper, story.

30153 *The revenge of the rose.* London: Grafton, 1991, 233 p., cloth, novel. ELRIC SERIES.

30154 *The sailor on the seas of fate.* London: Quartet Books, 1976, 170 p., cloth, novel. ELRIC SERIES.

30155 *SF reprise 5: first-rate science fiction originally published in New worlds magazine.* London: Compact Books, 1967, [256] p., paper, anth.

10298 *The sleeping sorceress: an Elric novel.* London: New English Library, 1971, 140 p., cloth, novel. ELRIC SERIES.

10298A retitled: *The vanishing tower.* New York: DAW Books, 1977, 175 p., paper, novel. ELRIC SERIES.

30156 *Sojan.* Manchester, England: Savoy, 1977, 157 p., paper, coll. [Includes some nonfiction].

10300 *The stealer of souls, and other stories.* London: Neville Spearman, 1963, 215 p., cloth, coll. ELRIC SERIES.

30157 retitled: *The bane of the black sword.* New York: DAW Books, 1977, 157 p., paper, novel. ELRIC SERIES. [Expanded from original edition].

30158 retitled: *The weird of the white wolf.* New York: DAW Books, 1977, 159 p., paper, novel. ELRIC SERIES. [Expanded from original edition].

30159 *The steel tsar: third volume in the Oswald Bastable trilogy.* London, Toronto: A Mayflower Book, Granada, 1981, 153 p., paper, novel. OSWALD BASTABLE #3.

The swords of Corum omnibus—SEE: *The swords trilogy.*

30160 *The swords trilogy.* New York: A Berkley Medallion Book, Berkley Publishing Corp., 1977, x+403 p., paper, coll. CORUM #1-3. [Includes *The king of the swords, The queen of the swords, The knight of the swords*].

30160A retitled: *The swords of Corum omnibus.* London: Grafton, 1986, 512 p., cloth, coll. CORUM #1-3. [Includes *Knight, Queen, King*].

30161 *Tales from the end of time; Legends from the end of time; A messiah at the end of time.* New York: Guild America Books, 1989, 311 p., cloth, coll.

30162 *The transformation of Miss Mavis Ming: a romance of the end of time.* London: W. H. Allen & Co., 1977, 159 p., cloth, novel. DANCERS AT THE END OF TIME.

30162A retitled: *A messiah at the end of time; or, The transformation of Miss Mavis Ming.* New York: DAW Books, 1978, 192 p., paper, novel. DANCERS AT THE END OF TIME.

The vanishing tower—SEE: *The sleeping sorceress.*

30163 *The war hound and the World's Pain: a fable.* New York: Timescape Books, Pocket Books, 1981, 239 p., cloth, novel. WORLD'S PAIN SERIES.

30164 *Warrior of Mars.* London: New English Library, 1981, 384 p., cloth, coll. MARS (MICHAEL KANE) #1-3. [Includes all three Mars books written under the pseudonym of EDWARD P. BRADBURY].

The weird of the white wolf—SEE: *Stealer of souls.*

30165 *Wizardry and wild romance: a study of epic fantasy.* London: Victor Gollancz, 1987, 160 p., cloth, nonf.

with Michael Butterworth

19137 *The time of the Hawklords.* Henley-on-Thames, England: Aidan Ellis, 1976, 255 p., cloth. HAWKLORDS #1. [Mostly written by Butterworth].

with James Cawthorn

19678 *Fantasy: the 100 best books.* London: Xanadu, 1988, 216 p., cloth, nonf. [Mostly written by Cawthorn].

with Philip James [i.e., James Cawthorn]

19679 *The distant suns.* Llanfynydd, Dyfed, Wales: Unicorn Bookshop, 1975, 45 p., paper, novel.

MOORE, Brian, 1921-

30166 *Cold Heaven: a novel.* Toronto: McClelland & Stewart, 1983, 265 p., cloth, novel.

30167 *Fergus.* Toronto: McClelland & Stewart, 1970, 228 p., cloth, novel.

30168 *The great Victorian collection.* Toronto: McClelland & Stewart, 1975, 213 p., cloth, novel.

MOORE, C. L. [i.e., Catherine Lucile Moore Kuttner Reggie], 1911-1987

30170 *The best of C. L. Moore.* Garden City, NY: Nelson Doubleday, 1975, 309 p., cloth, coll. [Edited by Lester del Rey].

Black god's shadow—SEE: *Jirel of Joiry.*

10318 *Jirel of Joiry.* New York: Paperback Library, 1969, 175 p., paper, coll.

10318A retitled: *Black god's shadow.* West Kingston, RI: Donald M. Grant, Publisher, 1977, 252 p., cloth, coll.

Northwest Smith—SEE: *Scarlet dream.*

30171 *Scarlet dream.* West Kingston, RI: Donald M. Grant, Publisher, 1981, 328 p., cloth, coll.

30171A retitled: *Northwest Smith.* New York: Ace Books, 1982, 297 p., paper, coll.

30172 *Vintage season.* New York: Tor SF, A Tom Doherty Associates Book, 1990, p. 1-78, paper, story. [Bound with *In another country* / by Robert Silverberg].

with Henry Kuttner

27634 *Chessboard planet, and other stories.* London: Hamlyn Paperbacks, 1983, 187 p., paper, coll.

27635 *Clash by night, and other stories.* London: Hamlyn Paperbacks, 1980, viii+215 p., paper, coll. [Edited by Peter Pinto].

08484A *The mask of Circe.* New York: Ace Books, 1977, 158 p., paper, novel. [Originally published under Kuttner's name only].

The proud robot—SEE: *Robots have no tails.*

08500 *Robots have no tails.* New York: Gnome Press, 1952, 224 p., cloth, coll.

08500B retitled: *The proud robot: the complete Galloway Gallegher stories.* Feltham, England: Hamlyn Paperbacks, 1983, 189 p., paper, coll.

27636 *The startling worlds of Henry Kuttner.* New York: Popular Library, 1987, 357 p., paper, coll. [Includes *Beyond Earth's Gates, Valley of the Flame, The Dark World*; Moore's contribution is uncredited].

with H. P. Lovecraft & A. Merritt & Robert E. Howard & Frank Belknap Long

The challenge from beyond—SEE: *The illustrated challenge from beyond.*

26046 *The illustrated Challenge from beyond.* West Warwick, RI: Necronomicon Press, 1978, [26] p., paper, story.

MOORE, Darrell (W.)

30173 *The best, worst, and most unusual: horror films.* Skokie, IL: Publications International, 1983, 160 p., paper, nonf.

MOORE, Donald L.

30174 *Memoirs of the apocalypse.* Nashville, TN: Charter House Publishers; London: Springwood Books, 1978, 202 p., cloth, novel.

MOORE, Helen, 1862-1954

30175 *Mary Wollstonecraft Shelley.* Philadelphia, PA: J. B. Lippincott Co., 1886, 346 p., cloth, nonf.

MOORE, P(hyllis) S.

30176 *Williwaw!* St. John's, Newfoundland, Canada: Breakwater Books, 1978, 457 p., cloth, novel.

MOORE, Patrick (Alfred Caldwell), 1923-

30177 *Killer comet: a Scott Saunders space adventure.* London: Armada, 1978, 128 p., paper, novel. SCOTT SAUNDERS #4.

30178 *The moon raiders: a Scott Saunders space adventure.* London: Armada, 1978, 124 p., paper, novel. SCOTT SAUNDERS #3.

30179 *Planet of fear: a Scott Saunders space adventure.* London: Armada, 1977, 128 p., paper, novel. SCOTT SAUNDERS #2.

30180 *The secret of the black hole: a Scott Saunders space adventure.* London: Armada, 1980, 125 p., paper, novel. SCOTT SAUNDERS #6.

30181 *Spy in space: a Scott Saunders space adventure.* London: Armada, 1977, 127 p., paper, novel. SCOTT SAUNDERS #1.

30182 *The terror star: a Scott Saunders space adventure.* London: Armada, 1979, 125 p., paper, novel. SCOTT SAUNDERS #5.

MOORE, Raylyn, 1928-

30183 *What happened to Emily Goode after the Great Exhibition.* Norfolk, VA: Starblaze Editions/Donning, 1978, 188 p., paper, novel.

MOORE, Robert L.—SEE: Moore, Robin

MOORE, Robin [i.e., Robert Lowell Moore Jr.], 1925-

with Bob Foreman

23269 *Two Saturday Yankees; &, Ali in T.V. Land.* New York: Manor Books, 1976, 287 p., paper, coll.

with Gerald G. Griffin

24708 *The death disciple.* Westport, CT: Condor, 1977, 249 p., paper, novel.

24709 *The last coming.* Westport, CT: Condor Books, 1978 (i.e., 1979?), 328 p., paper, novel.

with Edward McGhee

29552 *The Chinese ultimatum.* New York: Pinnacle Books, 1976, 338 p., paper, novel.

with Lewis Perdue

30184 *The trinity implosion.* New York: Manor Books, 1978, 291 p., paper, novel.

MOORE, Roger E(lwood), 1955-

30185   *Conan and the prophecy.* Lake Geneva, WI: TSR Inc., 1984, 157 p., paper, novel. ENDLESS QUEST #20—CONAN SERIES.

30186   *Conan the outlaw.* Lake Geneva, WI: TSR Inc., 1984, 157 p., paper, novel. ENDLESS QUEST #25—CONAN SERIES.

30187   *Jason's first quest.* Lake Geneva, WI: TSR Inc., 1984, 77 p., paper, novel. FANTASY FOREST #9.

30188   *Nightmare realm of Baba Yaga.* Lake Geneva, WI: TSR Inc., 1986, 189 p., paper, novel. ADVANCED DUNGEONS & DRAGONS ADVENTURE GAMEBOOK #8.

30189   *Renegades of Luntar.* Lake Geneva, WI: TSR Inc., 1985, 143 p., paper, novel. ENDLESS QUEST CRIMSON CRYSTAL ADVENTURE #3.

30190   *Search for the pegasus.* Lake Geneva, WI: TSR Inc., 1985, 143 p., paper, novel. ENDLESS QUEST CRIMSON CRYSTAL ADVENTURE #2.

with Margaret Weis as SUSAN LAWSON

30191   *Riddle of the griffon.* Lake Geneva, WI: TSR Inc., 1985, 144 p., paper, novel. ENDLESS QUEST CRIMSON CRYSTAL ADVENTURE #1.

MOORE, Rudin [pseud. of Gary Smith]

30192   *Ultra-vue and selected peripheral visions.* Newport, OR: Gary Smith, 1987, 389 p., paper, coll.

MOORE, Stanley R.

30193   *Nightshade.* New York: An Onyx Book, New American Library, 1989, 331 p., paper, novel.

MOORE, Thomas, 1946-

30194   *The style of connectedness: Gravity's Rainbow and Thomas Pynchon.* Columbia, MO: University of Missouri Press, 1987, 312 p., cloth, nonf.

MOORE, Wallace, pseud.—SEE: Conway, Gerard F.

MOORE, (Joseph) Ward, 1903-1978, *with Robert Bradford*

18446   *Caduceus wild.* Los Angeles: A Futorian Book, Pinnacle Books, 1978, 273 p., paper, novel.

MOORHOUSE, John, *with Paul Newman*

30195   *Colin Wilson: two essays: The English existentialist; and, Spiders and outsiders: (including an interview with the author).* Nottingham, England: Paupers' Press, 1989, 49 p., paper, nonf. coll.

MOORMAN, Charles (Wickliffe), 1925-

30196   *Arthurian triptych: mythic materials in Charles Williams, C. S. Lewis, and T. S. Eliot.* Berkeley & Los Angeles: University of California Press, 1960, ix + 163 p., cloth, nonf.

MOOSER, Stephen, 1941-

30197   *Invasion of the mutants.* New York: An Archway Book, Pocket Books, 1985, 118 p., paper, novel. WHICH WAY BOOKS #17.

30198   *Lights! camera! scream! how to make your own monster movies.* New York: Julian Messner, 1983, 109 p., cloth, nonf.

30199   *Mind bandits.* New York: An Archway Paperback, Pocket Books, 1985, 118 p., paper, novel. WHICH WAY BOOKS #20.

30200   *Monster express.* New York: An Archway Paperback, Pocket Books, 1986, 118 p., paper, novel. WHICH WAY BOOKS #23.

30201   *Monster fun.* New York: Julian Messner, 1979, 96 p., cloth, nonf.

30202   *Nightmare planet.* New York: An Archway Paperback, Pocket Books, 1985, 118 p., paper, novel. WHICH WAY BOOKS #19.

30203   *Space raiders and the planet of doom.* New York: An Archway Paperback, Pocket Books, 1983, 118 p., paper, novel. WHICH WAY BOOKS #11.

30204   *Starship warrior.* New York: An Archway Paperback, Pocket Books, 1984, 118 p., paper, novel. WHICH WAY BOOKS #13.

MORAGA, Gary A. Thompson- —SEE: Thompson, Gary

MORAN, Daniel, pseud.—SEE: Vardeman, Robert E.

MORAN, Daniel Keys, 1962-

30205   *The armageddon blues: a tale of the great wheel of existence.* Toronto, New York: Spectra, Bantam Books, 1988, 205 p., paper, novel. GREAT WHEEL OF EXISTENCE #1.

30206 *Emerald eyes: a tale of the continuing time.* Toronto, New York: Spectra, Bantam Books, 1988, vi+243 p., paper, novel. TALES OF THE CONTINUING TIME #1.

30207 *The long run: a tale of the continuing time.* New York, Toronto: Spectra, Bantam Books, 1989, 372 p., paper, novel. TALES OF THE CONTINUING TIME #2.

30208 *The ring.* Toronto, New York: A Foundation Book, Doubleday, 1988, 467 p., cloth, movie.

MORAN, John C(harles), 1942-

30209 *An F. Marion Crawford companion.* Westport, CT: Greenwood Press, 1981, xxxviii+548 p., cloth, nonf.

30210 *Seeking refuge in Torre San Nicola: an introduction to F. Marion Crawford.* Nashville, TN: The Worthies Library, F. Marion Crawford Memorial Society, 1980, vii+85 p., paper, nonf. [Limited to 150 copies].

MORAN, Richard (Jerome), 1942-

30211 *Cold sea rising.* New York: Arbor House, 1986, 352 p., cloth, novel.

30213 *Dallas down.* New York: Arbor House, William Morrow & Co., 1988, 289 p., cloth, novel.

*MORAVIA, Alberto [pseud. of Alberto Pincherle], 1907-1990

MORDANE, Thomas

30214 *Bloodroot.* New York: A Dell Book, 1982, 285 p., paper, novel.

MORE, Meredith, 1937-

30215 *October obsession.* Tallahassee, FL: Naiad Press, 1988, 182 p., paper, novel.

MORECAMBE, Eric, 1926-1984

30216 *The reluctant vampire.* London: Methuen Children's Books, 1982, 135 p., cloth, novel. RELUCTANT VAMPIRE #1.

30217 *The vampire's revenge.* London: Methuen Children's Books, 1983, 152 p., cloth, novel. RELUCTANT VAMPIRE #2.

MORGAN, Al(bert Edward), 1920-

30218 *The essential man: a novel.* Chicago: Playboy Press, 1977, 280 p., cloth, novel.

MORGAN, Chris, 1946-

30219 *Dark fantasies.* London, Sydney: Legend, Century Hutchinson, 1989, 319 p., cloth, anth.

30220 *Fritz Leiber: a bibliography, 1934-1979.* Birmingham, England: Morganstern, 1979, 36 p., paper, nonf.

30221 *The shape of futures past: the story of prediction.* Exeter, England: Webb & Bower, 1980, 208 p., paper, nonf.

MORGAN, Dan, 1925-

30222 *The concrete horizon.* London: Millington, 1976, 227 p., cloth, novel.

30223 *The country of the mind.* London: Corgi Books, 1975, 189 p., paper, novel. SIXTH PERCEPTION #4.

MORGAN, Dave

30224 *Adverse camber.* London: Robert Hale, 1977, 190 p., cloth, novel.

30225 *Genetic two.* London: Robert Hale, 1976, 175 p., cloth, novel.

30226 *Reiver.* London: Robert Hale, 1975, 192 p., cloth, novel.

MORGAN, Hilda—SEE: Vaughan, Hilda

MORGAN, Hugh

30227 *Rentaghost enterprises.* London: British Broadcasting Corp., 1984, 128 p., cloth, tele. RENTAGHOST #2.

30228 *Rentaghost rules.* London: British Broadcasting Corp., 1985, 144 p., cloth, tele. RENTAGHOST #3.

30229 *Rentaghost unlimited.* London: British Broadcasting Corp., 1982, 126 p., cloth, tele. RENTAGHOST #1.

MORGAN, J(ill) M(eredith), 1946-

30230 *Desert eden.* New York: Pinnacle Books, Windsor Publishing Corp., 1991, 352 p., paper, novel.

as MORGAN FIELDS

30231 *Deadly harvest.* New York: Zebra Books, Kensington Publishing Corp., 1989, 357 p., paper, novel.

30232 *Play time.* New York: Zebra Books, Kensington Publishing Corp., 1988, 319 p., paper, novel.

30233 *Shaman Woods.* New York: Zebra Books, Kensington Publishing Corp., 1990, 304 p., paper, novel.

MORGAN, Kathleen

30234 *Heart's lair.* New York: Leisure Books, 1991, 364 p., paper, novel.
30235 *The knowing crystal.* New York: Leisure Books, 1991, 364 p., paper, novel.

MORGAN, Stanley

30236 *Raven.* New York: Lynx Books, 1989, 339 p., paper, novel.

MORGAN, Ted [legalized from Sanche de Gramont], 1932-

30237 *Literary outlaw: the life and times of William S. Burroughs.* New York: Henry Holt & Co., 1988, viii+659 p., cloth, nonf.

MORGENSTERN, S., pseud.—SEE: Goldman, William

MORHAIM, Joe, *with George Pal*

30238 *Time machine II.* New York: A Dell Book, 1981, 175 p., paper, novel. TIME MACHINE #2.

MORIARTY, Timothy

30239 *Vampire nights.* New York: Pinnacle Books, Windsor Publishing Corp., 1989, 348 p., paper, novel.

MORLAN, A. R.

30240 *The amulet.* New York, Toronto: Spectra, Bantam Books, 1991, 388 p., paper, novel. EWERTON #1.
30241 *The cat with the tulip face.* Eugene, OR: Pulphouse Publishing, 1991, 48 p., paper, story. SHORT STORY PAPERBACKS #29. EWERTON PREQUEL.
30242 *Dark journey.* New York, Toronto: Spectra, Bantam Books, 1991, 596 p., paper, novel. EWERTON #2.

*MORLAND, Nigel, 1905-1986

MORLEY, Adam R.

30243 *Raven.* Lewes, East Sussex, England: The Book Guild, 1989, 205 p., cloth, novel.

*MORLEY, Felix (Muskett), 1894-1982

MORNINGSTAR, Ramón Sender, 1934-

30244 *Zero weather: a future fantasy.* Bodega Bay, CA: Family Publishing Co., 1980, xi+367 p., paper, novel.

MOROZ, Anne (Freeman), 1953-

30245 *No safe place.* New York: Popular Library, Warner Books, 1986, 323 p., paper, novel.

MORPURGO, Michael

30246 *King of the cloud forests.* London: Heinemann, 1987, 145 p., cloth, novel.

MORRELL, David (Bernard), 1943-

30247 *The hundred year Christmas.* West Kingston, RI: Donald M. Grant, Publisher, 1983, 72 p., cloth, story.
30248 *Testament.* New York: M. Evans & Co., 1975, 279 p., cloth, novel.
30249 *The totem: a novel.* New York: M. Evans & Co., 1979, 276 p., cloth, novel.

MORRESSY, John, 1930-

30250 *The drought on Ziax II.* New York: Walker & Co., 1978, 77 p., cloth, novel. ZIAX II #2.
30251 *The drought on Ziax II; and, The humans of Ziax II.* New York, Toronto: Scholastic Book Services, 1978, 55+49 p., paper, coll. ZIAX II #1-2. [Bound back-to-back].
30252 *The extraterritorial.* Toronto, New York: Laser Books, 1977, 190 p., paper, novel.
30253 *Frostworld and dreamfire.* Garden City, NY: Doubleday & Co., 1977, vi+185 p., cloth, novel.
30254 *Graymantle.* New York: Playboy Paperbacks, 1981, 256 p., paper, novel. IRON ANGEL #2.
30255 *Ironbrand.* New York: Playboy Press Paperbacks, 1980, 318 p., paper, novel. IRON ANGEL #1.
30256 *Kedrigern and the charming couple.* New York: Ace Books, 1990, 215 p., paper, novel. KEDRIGERN #4.
30257 *Kedrigern in Wanderland.* New York: Ace Books, 1988, 247 p., paper, novel. KEDRIGERN #3.
30258 *Kingsbane.* New York: Playboy Paperbacks, 1982, 255 p., paper, novel. IRON ANGEL #3.
30259 *A law for the stars.* Toronto, New York: Laser Books, 1976, 192 p., paper, novel.
30260 *The mansions of space.* New York: Ace Science Fiction Books, 1983, 232 p., paper, novel.

10386 *Nail down the stars.* New York: Walker & Co., 1973, 244 p., cloth, novel. DEL WHITBY #2.

10386A retitled: *Stardrift.* New York: Popular Library, 1975, 189 p., paper, novel. DEL WHITBY #2.

30261 *The questing of Kedrigern.* New York: Ace Books, 1987, 202 p., paper, novel. KEDRIGERN #2.

30262 *A remembrance for Kedrigern.* New York: Ace Books, 1990, 233 p., paper, novel. KEDRIGERN #5.

Stardrift—SEE: *Nail down the stars.*

30263 *The time of the Annihilator.* New York: Ace Fantasy Books, 1985, 217 p., paper, novel. IRON ANGEL #4.

30264 *Under a calculating star.* Garden City, NY: Doubleday & Co., 1975, 186 p., cloth, novel. DEL WHITBY #3.

30265 *A voice for Princess.* New York: Ace Fantasy Books, 1986, 213 p., paper, novel. KEDRIGERN #1.

30266 *The windows of forever.* New York: Walker & Co., 1975, 86 p., cloth, novel.

MORRILL, Rowena, 1944-

30267 *The fantastic art of Rowena.* New York: Pocket Books, 1983, p., paper, art.

MORRILL, Sibley S.

30268 *Ambrose Bierce, F. A. Mitchell-Hedges, and the crystal skull.* San Francisco: Cadleon Press, 1972, 83 p., paper, nonf.

*MORRIS, Anthony P(aschal), 1849-1921

MORRIS, Chris(topher Crosby), 1946-

with Janet Morris

30269 *The 40-minute war.* New York: Baen Book, 1984, 281 p., cloth, novel.

30270 *City at the edge of time.* New York: Baen Books, 1988, 312 p., paper, novel. THIEVES' WORLD—TEMPUS #5.

30271 *The little Helliad.* New York: Baen Books, 1988, 302 p., paper, novel. HEROES IN HELL #8.

30272 *M*E*D*U*S*A.* New York: Baen Fiction Books, 1986, 343 p., paper, novel.

30273 *Outpassage.* New York: Pageant Books, 1988, 368 p., paper, novel.

30274 *Storm seed.* New York: Baen Books, 1990, 311 p., paper, novel. THIEVES' WORLD—TEMPUS #7.

30275 *Tempus unbound.* New York: Baen Books, 1989, 277 p., paper, novel. THIEVES' WORLD—TEMPUS #6.

30276 *Threshold.* New York: A Roc Book, 1990, 250 p., cloth, novel. THRESHOLD #1.

with Jane Stump as DANIEL STRYKER

30277 *Cobra.* New York: Jove Books, 1991, 281 p., paper, novel.

30278 *Hawkeye.* New York: Jove Books, 1991, 311 p., paper, novel.

MORRIS, Dave, 1957-

30279 *Buried treasure.* New York: A Dell Book, 1990, 71 p., paper, novel. TEENAGE MUTANT NINJA TURTLES.

30280 *Crypt of the vampire.* London: Dragon Books, 1984, [157] p., paper, novel. GOLDEN DRAGON FANTASY GAMEBOOKS #1.

30281 *Dinobot war.* London: Young Corgi, 1985, 71 p., paper, novel. TRANSFORMERS SERIES.

30282 *Dragon warriors.* London: Corgi Books, 1985, 201 p., paper, novel. DRAGON WARRIORS #1.

30283 *The Eye of the Dragon.* London: Dragon Books, 1985, [190] p., paper, novel. GOLDEN DRAGON FANTASY GAMEBOOKS #4.

30284 *Highway clash.* London: Young Corgi, 1986, 67 p., paper, novel. TRANSFORMERS SERIES.

30285 *Island of fear.* London: Young Corgi, 1986, 67 p., paper, novel. TRANSFORMERS SERIES.

30286 *Knightmare: The labyrinths of fear.* London: Corgi Books, 1989, 94+[62] p., paper, novel. KNIGHTMARE SERIES.

The labyrinths of fear—SEE: *Knightmare: The labyrinths of fear.*

30287 *The lands of legend.* London: Corgi Books, 1986, 271 p., paper, novel. DRAGON WARRIORS #6.

30288 *Out of the shadows.* London: Corgi Books, 1986, 252 p., paper, novel. DRAGON WARRIORS #4.

30289 *Peril from the stars.* London: Young Corgi, 1985, 74 p., paper, novel. TRANSFORMERS SERIES.

30290 *Red herrings.* New York: A Dell Book, 1990, 72 p., paper, novel. TEENAGE MUTANT NINJA TURTLES.

30291 *Six-guns and shurikens.* New York: A Dell Book, 1990, 71 p., paper, novel. TEENAGE MUTANT NINJA TURTLES.

30292 *Sky-high.* New York: A Dell Book, 1990, 74 p., paper, novel. TEENAGE MUTANT NINJA TURTLES.

30293 *Swamp of the scorpion.* London: Young Corgi, 1987, 72 p., paper, novel.
30294 *The way of wizardry.* London: Corgi Books, 1986, 165 p., paper, novel. DRAGON WARRIORS #2.

with Tim Child

20004 *Knightmare.* London: Young Corgi, 1988, 143 p., paper, novel. KNIGHTMARE SERIES.

with Oliver Johnson

26626 *Blood sword.* Sevenoaks, Kent, England: New English Library, 1987, 299 p., paper, novel. BLOOD SWORD #1.
26627 *The demon's claw.* Sevenoaks, Kent, England: Knight, 1987, 390 p., paper, fiction. BLOOD SWORD #3.
26628 *Doomwalk.* Sevenoaks, Kent, England: Knight, 1988, [330] p., paper, fiction. BLOOD SWORD #4.
26629 *The kingdom of Wyrd.* Sevenoaks, Kent, England: Knight Books, 1987, 330 p., paper, novel. BLOOD SWORD #2.
26630 *The temple of flame.* London: Dragon Books, 1984, [188] p., paper, novel. GOLDEN DRAGON FANTASY GAMEBOOKS #2.

with Oliver Johnson & Jamie Thomson

26631 *The walls of Spyte.* London: Knight, 1988, 313 p., paper, novel.

with Yve Newnham

30295 *Castle of Lost Souls.* London: Dragon Books, 1985, [170] p., paper, novel. GOLDEN DRAGON FANTASY GAMEBOOKS #6.

with Jamie Thomson

30296 *The crystal maze: adventure gamebook.* London: Mammoth, 1991, [150] p., paper, novel.

MORRIS, Gregory L(ynn), 1950-

37981 *A world of order and light: the fiction of John Gardner.* Athens, GA: University of Georgia Press, 1984, 259 p., cloth, nonf.

MORRIS, Gwladys Evan

30297 *Tales from Bernard Shaw told in the jungle.* London: George G. Harrap, 1929, 216 p., cloth, coll.

MORRIS, Jan, 1926-

30298 *Last letters from Hav.* New York: Random House, 1985, 203 p., cloth, novel.

MORRIS, Janet (Ellen), 1946-

30299 *Afterwar.* New York: Baen Science Fiction Books, 1985, 284 p., paper, anth.
30300 *Angels in Hell.* New York: Baen Books, 1987, 307 p., paper, anth. HEROES IN HELL #7.
 Beyond Sanctuary—SEE: *Thieves' world: Beyond Sanctuary.*
 Beyond the veil—SEE: *Thieves' world: Beyond the veil.*
 Beyond Wizardwall—SEE: *Thieves' world: Beyond Wizardwall.*
30301 *The carnelian throne* / by Janet E. Morris. Toronto, New York: Bantam Books, 1979, 244 p., paper, novel. SILISTRA #4.
30302 *Cruiser dreams.* New York: G. P. Putnam's Sons, 1981, 274 p., cloth, novel. KERRION EMPIRE #2.
30303 *Crusaders in Hell.* New York: Baen Books, 1987, 287 p., paper, anth. HEROES IN HELL #5.
30304 *Dream dancer.* New York: Berkley Publishing Corp., 1980, 289 p., cloth, novel. KERRION EMPIRE #1.
30305 *Earth dreams.* New York: G. P. Putnam's Sons, 1982, 240 p., cloth, novel. KERRION EMPIRE #3.
30306 *The golden sword* / by Janet E. Morris. Toronto, New York: Bantam Books, 1977, 369 p., paper, novel. SILISTRA #2.
30307 *Heroes in Hell.* New York: Baen Science Fantasy Books, 1986, 274 p., paper, anth. HEROES IN HELL #1.
30308 *High couch of Silistra: (returning creation)* / by Janet E. Morris. Toronto, New York: Bantam Books, 1977, 245 p., paper, novel. SILISTRA #1.
30309 retitled: *Returning creation.* New York: A Baen Book, 1984, 318 p., paper, novel. SILISTRA #1. [Revised and expanded edition].
30310 *Masters in Hell.* New York: Baen Books, 1988, 280 p., paper, anth. HEROES IN HELL #9.
30311 *Prophets in Hell.* New York: Baen Books, 1989, 278 p., paper, anth. HEROES IN HELL #12.
30312 *Rebels in Hell.* New York: Baen Science Fantasy Books, 1986, 308 p., paper, anth. HEROES IN HELL #2.

Returning creation—SEE: *High couch of Silistra.*

30313 *Tempus.* New York: Baen Books, 1987, 277 p., paper, novel. THIEVES' WORLD—TEMPUS #4.

30314 *Thieves' world: Beyond Sanctuary.* New York: Baen Books, 1985, 312 p., cloth, novel. THIEVES' WORLD—TEMPUS #1.

30315 *Thieves' world: Beyond the veil.* New York: Baen Books Fantasy, 1985, 314 p., cloth, novel. THIEVES' WORLD—TEMPUS #2.

30316 *Thieves' world: Beyond Wizardwall.* New York: Baen Fantasy Books, 1986, 278 p., cloth, novel. THIEVES' WORLD—TEMPUS #3.

30317 *War in Hell.* New York: Baen Books, 1988, 277 p., paper, anth. HEROES IN HELL #10.

30318 *Warlord!* New York: Pocket Books, 1987, 376 p., paper, novel.

30319 *Wind from the abyss* / by Janet E. Morris. Toronto, New York: Bantam Books, 1978, 339 p., paper, novel. SILISTRA #3.

with C. J. Cherryh

19900 *The gates of Hell.* New York: Baen Science Fantasy Books, 1986, 250 p., cloth, novel. HEROES IN HELL #3.

19901 *Kings in Hell.* New York: Baen Books, 1987, 375 p., paper, novel. HEROES IN HELL #4.

with David Drake

22182 *Active measures.* New York: Baen Science Fiction Books, 1985, 365 p., paper, novel.

22183 *Explorers in Hell.* New York: Baen Books, 1989, 312 p., paper, novel. HEROES IN HELL #11.

22184 *Kill ratio.* New York: Ace Books, 1987, 268 p., paper, novel.

22185 *Target.* New York: Ace Books, 1989, 312 p., paper, novel.

with Chris Morris

30269 *The 40-minute war.* New York: Baen Book, 1984, 281 p., cloth, novel.

30270 *City at the edge of time.* New York: Baen Books, 1988, 312 p., paper, novel. THIEVES' WORLD—TEMPUS #5.

30271 *The little Helliad.* New York: Baen Books, 1988, 302 p., paper, novel. HEROES IN HELL #8.

30272 *M*E*D*U*S*A.* New York: Baen Fiction Books, 1986, 343 p., paper, novel.

30273 *Outpassage.* New York: Pageant Books, 1988, 368 p., paper, novel.

30274 *Storm seed.* New York: Baen Books, 1990, 311 p., paper, novel. THIEVES' WORLD—TEMPUS #7.

30275 *Tempus unbound.* New York: Baen Books, 1989, 277 p., paper, novel. THIEVES' WORLD—TEMPUS #6.

30276 *Threshold.* New York: A Roc Book, 1990, 250 p., cloth, novel. THRESHOLD #1.

with Jack Vance & C. J. Cherryh

37657 *Rhialto the Marvellous.* New York: Baen Books, 1985, 250 p., paper, anth. DYING EARTH #4; HEROES IN HELL. [Includes Vance's novel, plus the novella "Basileus" by Cherryh and Morris].

MORRIS, (Margaret) Jean, 1924-

30320 *A new magic.* London: The Bodley Head, 1990, 172 p., cloth, novel.

30321 *The Troy game.* London: The Bodley Head, 1987, 112 p., cloth, novel.

MORRIS, Jim, 1940-

30322 *Breeder.* New York: Tor, A Tom Doherty Associates Book, 1988, 306 p., paper, novel.

30323 *The Sheriff of Purgatory.* Garden City, NY: Doubleday & Co., 1979, 218 p., cloth, novel.

30324 retitled: *Spurlock, sheriff of Purgatory.* New York: Tor, A Tom Doherty Associates Book, 1987, 320 p., paper, novel. [Expanded edition].
Spurlock, sheriff of Purgatory—SEE: *The Sheriff of Purgatory.*

*MORRIS, Joe Alex (Sr.), 1904-<u>1990</u>

MORRIS, Kenneth (Vennor), 1879-1937

37982 *Through dragon eyes: a journey to the exotic world of Kenneth Morris.* La Jolla, CA: Ben-Sen Press, 1980, [67] p., paper, coll. [Edited by Helynn Hoffa].

MORRIS, M. E., 1926-

30325 *Alpha Bug.* Novato, CA: Presidio Press, 1986, 236 p., paper, novel.

MORRIS, Mark

The horror club—SEE: *Toady.*

30326 *Stitch.* London: Piatkus, 1991, 423 p., cloth, novel.
30327 *Toady.* London: Piatkus, 1989, v+522 p., cloth, novel.
30327A retitled: *The horror club.* New York, Toronto: Spectra, Bantam Books, 1991, 519 p., paper, novel.

MORRIS, May, 1862-1938

30328 *The introductions to The collected works of William Morris.* New York: Oriole Editions, 1973, viii+761 p. in 2 v., cloth, nonf. coll.
30329 *William Morris: artist, writer, socialist.* Oxford, England: Basil Blackwell, 1936, 2 v., cloth, nonf.

MORRIS SOCIETY—SEE: William Morris Society

MORRIS, William, 1834-1896

30330 *The collected letters of William Morris, Volume I, 1848-1880.* Princeton, NJ: Princeton University Press, 1984, lxiv+626 p., cloth, nonf. coll. [Edited by Norman Kelvin].
30331 *The collected letters of William Morris, Volume II, 1881-1884.* Princeton, NJ: Princeton University Press, 1987, liii+921 p. in 2 v., cloth, nonf. coll. [Edited by Norman Kelvin].
30332 *Golden wings, and other stories.* Van Nuys, CA: Newcastle Publishing Co., 1976, 169 p., paper, coll.
30333 *The juvenilia of William Morris, with a checklist and unpublished early poems.* New York: William Morris Society, 1983, v+90 p., cloth, nonf. coll. [Edited by Florence Boos].
30334 *The letters of William Morris to his family and friends.* London, New York: Longmans, Green & Co., 1950, lxvii+406 p., cloth, nonf. coll. [Edited by Philip Henderson].

MORRIS, Winifred [i.e., Winifred Morris Schecter]

30335 *With magical horses to ride.* New York: Atheneum, 1985, 152 p., cloth, novel.

MORRIS, Wright, 1910-

30336 *The Fork River space project: a novel.* New York, Hagerstown, NJ: Harper & Row, Publishers, 1977, 185 p., cloth, novel.

MORRISON, Chloe—SEE: Morrison, Toni

MORRISON, Dorothy Nafus

30337 *Vanishing act.* New York: Atheneum, 1989, 202 p., cloth, novel.

MORRISON, Greg, *with William R. Forstchen*

23293 *The crystal sorcerers.* New York: Avon Books, 1991, 291 p., paper, novel. CRYSTAL #2.
23294 *The crystal warriors.* New York: Avon Books, 1988, 308 p., paper, novel. CRYSTAL #1.

MORRISON, Louise D(ouglas)

30338 *J. R. R. Tolkien's The fellowship of the Ring: a critical commentary.* New York: Monarch Press, 1976, 98 p., paper, nonf.
30339 *Shirley Jackson's The lottery and other short stories: a critical commentary.* New York: Monarch Press, 1978, 74 p., paper, nonf.

MORRISON, Patricia K.—SEE: Kennealy, Patricia

MORRISON, Toni [i.e., Chloe Anthony Morrison], 1931-

30340 *Beloved.* London: Chatto & Windus, 1987, 285 p., cloth, novel.

MORRISSEY, J. L.—SEE: Levene, Philip

MORROW, Bradford, 1951- , *with Patrick McGrath*

29569 *The new gothic: a collection of contemporary gothic fiction.* New York: Random House, 1991, xiv+336 p., cloth, anth.

MORROW, H. M.

30341 *The black madonna.* New York: A Dell Book, 1991, 288 p., paper, novel.

MORROW, James (Kenneth), 1947-

30342 *The adventures of Smoke Bailey.* Cambridge, MA: Spinnaker, 1983, 76 p., paper?, novel.
30343 *City of truth.* London: Century, 1990, 104 p., cloth, novel.
30344 *The continent of lies.* New York: Holt, Rinehart & Winston, 1984, xi+274 p., cloth, novel.

30345 *Only begotten daughter.* New York: William Morrow & Co., 1990, 312 p., cloth, novel. [Winner of the World Fantasy Award for Best Fantasy Novel, 1990 (1991)].

30346 *Swatting at the cosmos.* Eugene, OR: Pulphouse Publishing, 1990, 107 p., cloth, coll. AUTHOR'S CHOICE MONTHLY #8.

30347 *This is the way the world ends: a novel.* New York: Henry Holt & Co., 1986, 319 p., cloth, novel.

30348 *The wine of violence.* New York: Holt, Rinehart & Winston, 1981, 299 p., cloth, novel.

MORSE, A(lbert) Reynolds, 1914-

30349 *The quest for M. P. Shiel's realm of Redonda.* Cleveland, OH: Reynolds Morse Foundation, 1979, [164] p., paper, nonf.

30350 *Shiel in diverse hands: a collection of essays.* Cleveland, OH: Reynolds Morse Foundation, 1983, 490 p., cloth, nonf. anth.

30351 *The works of M. P. Shiel updated: a study in bibliography, including "About myself," by M. P. Shiel, 1865-1947 (new revised version), with a new appendix on Louis Tracy (1863-1928).* Dayton, OH: Reynolds Morse Foundation in Association with JDS Books, 1980, 858 p. in 2 v., cloth, nonf. WORKS OF M. P. SHIEL #2-3.

MORSE, Brian, 1948-

30352 *Breaking glass.* Cambridge, England: Lutterworth Press, 1986, 107 p., cloth, novel.

30353 *Nick and the genie.* Cambridge, England: Lutterworth Press, 1987, 84 p., cloth, novel.

MORSE, Donald E., 1936-

30354 *The fantastic in world literature and the arts: selected essays from the Fifth International Conference on the Fantastic in the Arts.* New York: Greenwood Press, 1987, xiv+250 p., cloth, nonf. anth. CONTRIBUTIONS TO THE STUDY OF SCIENCE FICTION AND FANTASY #28.

with Csilla Bertha

17890 *More real than reality: the fantastic in Irish literature and the arts.* New York, London: Greenwood Press, 1991, xi+266 p., cloth, nonf. anth. CONTRIBUTIONS TO THE STUDY OF SCIENCE FICTION AND FANTASY #45.

MORSE, Robert E.

30355 *Evocation of Virgil in Tolkien's art: geritol for the classics.* Oak Park, IL: Bolchazy-Carducci Publishers, 1986, ix+66 p., cloth, nonf.

*MORTON, Henry C(anova) V(ollam), 1892-1979

MORTON, J. B. [i.e., John Cameron Andrieu Bingham Michael Morton], 1893-1979

30356 *The death of the dragon: new fairy tales.* London: Eyre & Spottiswoode, 1934, 187 p., cloth, coll.

30357 *Drink up, gentlemen.* London: Chapman & Hall, 1930, 282 p., cloth, novel.

MORTON, John C.—SEE: Morton, J. B.

MORTON, Miriam, 1918?-1985

30358 *Mind over matter.* New York: Silhouette Books, 1987, 156 p., paper, novel.

MORWOOD, Peter [pseud. of Robert Peter Smith], 1956-

30359 *The demon lord.* London: Century Publishing, 1984, 304 p., paper, novel. BOOK OF YEARS #2.

30360 *The dragon lord.* London: Century Publishing, 1986, 318 p., paper, novel. BOOK OF YEARS #3.

30361 *The horse lord.* London: Century, 1983, 254 p., paper, novel. BOOK OF YEARS #1.

30362 *Prince Ivan.* London: Century Publishing, A Legend Book, 1990, 280 p., cloth, novel. PRINCE IVAN #1.

Rules of engagement—SEE: *Star Trek: Rules of engagement.*

30363 *Star Trek: Rules of engagement.* New York, London: Pocket Books, 1990, 245 p., paper, novel. STAR TREK #48.

30364 *The warlord's domain.* London, Sydney: Legend, 1989, 283 p., cloth, novel. BOOK OF YEARS #4.

with Diane Duane

22256 *Keeper of the city.* New York: Bantam Books, 1989, x+309 p., paper, novel. GUARDIANS OF THE THREE #2. [Created by Bill Fawcett].

Mindblast—SEE: *Space cops: Mindblast.*

22257 *The Romulan way: a Star Trek novel.* New York: Pocket Books, 1987, 254 p., paper, novel. STAR TREK #35.

22258 *Space cops: Mindblast.* New York: Avon Books, 1991, 250 p., paper, novel. SPACE COPS #1.

MOSCOVIT, Andrei [pseud. of Igor' Markovich Efimov], 1937-

30365 *The Judgment Day archives: a novel.* San Francisco: Mercury House, 1988, vii + 402 p., cloth, novel. [Translated by Robert Bowie of *Arkhivy strashnogo suda*].

MOSES, Ryan O.

30366 *Evilway.* New York: Zebra Books, Kensington Publishing Corp., 1990, 288 p., paper, novel.

MOSHER, Howard Frank

30367 *Disappearances.* New York: Viking Press, 1977, 255 p., cloth, novel.

MOSHER, Michael, *with David Smith*

30368 *Orwell for beginners.* London: Writers and Readers Publishing Cooperative, 1984, 191 p., paper, nonf.

MOSIG, Dirk Walter, 1943-

30369 *The Miskatonic.* Glenview, IL: Moshassuck Press, 1991, v + 637 p., paper, nonf. anth. [Book reproduction of two volumes of a Lovecraft fanzine].

MOSKOWITZ, Sam (Martin), 1920-

30370 *A. Merritt: reflections in the moon pool: a biography.* Philadelphia, PA: Oswald Train: Publisher, 1985, 399 p., cloth, anth. [Pieces by and about Merritt].

30371 *After all these years...: Sam Moskowitz on his science fiction career.* Center Harbor, NH: Niekas Publications, 1991, 96 p., paper, nonf.

30372 *A canticle for P. Schuyler Miller.* Newark, NJ: Sam Moskowitz, 1975, 11 p., paper, nonf.

30373 *Charles Fort: a radical corpuscle.* Newark, NJ: Sam Moskowitz, 1976, 20 p., paper, nonf.

37983 *Peace and Olaf Stapledon: an editorialized report.* Minneapolis, MN: Gafir Press, 1950, 12 p., paper, nonf.

30374 *Science fiction in old San Francisco, volume I: history of the movement from 1854 to 1890.* West Kingston, RI: Donald M. Grant, Publisher, 1980, 255 p., cloth, nonf. SCIENCE FICTION IN OLD SAN FRANCISCO #1.

30375 *Strange horizons: the spectrum of science fiction.* New York: Charles Scribner's Sons, 1976, v + 298 p., cloth, nonf. coll.

with Gerry de la Ree

21385 *After ten years: a tribute to the late Stanley G. Weinbaum.* Westwood, NJ: Gerry de la Ree, 1945, 28 p., paper, nonf. anth.

MOSS, Peter D.

37984 *Is there life on Earth? a selection of science fiction stories and poems.* Adelaide, Australia: Rigby, 1975, 116 p., paper, anth.

MOSS, Robert (John), 1946-

30376 *Death beam: a novel.* New York: Crown Publishers, 1981, 408 p., cloth, novel.

with Arnaud de Borchgrave

21318 *The spike.* London: Weidenfeld & Nicolson, 1980, 374 p., cloth, novel.

*MOSS, Robert F., 1942-

MOSS, Roger, 1951-

30377 *The game of the pink pagoda.* London: Collins, 1986, 271 p., cloth, novel.

MOSS, Sidney P(hil), 1917-

30378 *Poe's literary battles.* Durham, NC: Duke University Press, 1963, 266 p., cloth, nonf.

30379 *Poe's major crisis: his libel suit and New York's literary world.* Durham, NC: Duke University Press, 1970, xvii + 238 p., cloth, nonf.

MOTSON, Meredith, *with Odd Bjerke*

18061 *The search for Trollhaven.* Boise, ID: Beatty Books, 1977, 172 p., cloth, novel.

MOTTLEY, Charles C., *with Charles M. Mottley*

30380 *The mustard seed.* New York: Popular Library, 1977, 221 p., paper, novel.

MOTTLEY, Charles M., *with Charles C. Mottley*

30380 *The mustard seed.* New York: Popular Library, 1977, 221 p., paper, novel.

MOTTRAM, Eric

30381 *William Burroughs: the algebra of need.* London: Marion Boyars, 1977, 282 p., cloth, nonf.

MOULTON, Deborah

30382 *Children of time.* New York: Dial Books, 1989, 198 p., cloth, novel.
30383 *The first battle of Morn.* New York: Dial Books, 1988, 178 p., cloth, novel.

MOUNDS, Monica, pseud.—SEE: Vardeman, Robert E. & Proctor, Geo. W.

MOUNTAIN, Robert, pseud.—SEE: Montgomery, R. A.

MOWSHOWITZ, Abbe, 1939-

30384 *Inside information: computers in fiction.* Reading, MA: Addison-Wesley Publishing Co., 1977, xxiii+345 p., paper, anth.

MOYLAN, Thomas P.—SEE: Moylan, Tom

MOYLAN, Tom [i.e., Thomas P. Moylan], 1943-

30385 *Demand the impossible: science fiction and the utopian image.* New York & London: Methuen, 1986, viii+242 p., cloth, nonf.

MOZHEIKO, Igor—SEE: Bulychev, Kirill

MRABET, Mohammed [pseud. of Mohammed ben Chaib el-Hajjan], 1940-

30386 *The big mirror.* Santa Barbara, CA: Black Sparrow Press, 1977, 77 p., cloth, story. [Translation by Paul Bowles].

MUDD, Steve

30387 *The planet beyond.* New York: Popular Library, 1990, 234 p., paper, novel. TANGLED WEBS #2.
30388 *Tangled webs.* New York: Popular Library, 1989, 248 p., paper, novel. TANGLED WEBS #1.

MUELLER, Richard

30389 *Ghostbusters: the supernatural spectacular: a novel.* New York: Tor, A Tom Doherty Associates Book, 1985, 250 p., paper, movie. GHOSTBUSTERS #1.
30390 *Jernigan's egg.* New York: Bluejay Books, 1986, 341 p., paper, novel.
30391 *World War I flying ace.* Toronto, New York: A Byron Preiss Book, Bantam Books, 1988, 125 p., paper, novel. TIME MACHINE #24.

*MUGGERIDGE, Malcolm (Thomas), 1903-1990

MUIR, Douglas

30392 *American Reich.* New York: Charter Books, 1985, 419 p., paper, novel.

MUJICA LAINEZ, Manuel, 1910-1984

30393 *The wandering unicorn.* Toronto: Lester & Orpen Dennys, 1982, xi+322 p., cloth, novel. [Translation by Mary Fitton of *El unicornio*].

MULAY, James J.

30394 *The horror film: a guide to more than 700 films on videocassette.* Evanston, IL: CineBooks, 1989, xix+335 p., paper, nonf. anth.

MULLALLY, Frederic, 1920-

30395 *Hitler has won.* London: Macmillan, 1975, ix+293 p., cloth, novel.

MULLEN, R(ichard) D(ale), 1915- , *with Darko Suvin*

30396 *Science-fiction studies: selected articles on science fiction, 1973-1975.* Boston: Gregg Press, 1976, xix+304 p., cloth, nonf. anth.
30397 *Science-fiction studies, second series: selected articles on science fiction, 1976-1977.* Boston: Gregg Press, 1977, xiv+335 p., cloth, nonf. anth.

*MULLEN, Stanley, 1911-1974

MULLEN, Victor

30398 *The toy tree.* Toronto, New York: PaperJacks Ltd., 1988, 265 p., paper, novel.
30399 *Tree house.* New York: Zebra Books, Kensington Publishing Corp., 1989, 304 p., paper, novel.

MULLER, John, house pseud.—SEE: Glasby, John

MULLER, John P(aul), 1940- , *with William J. Richardson*

30400 *The purloined Poe: Lacan, Derrida, and psychoanalytic reading.* Baltimore, MD, London: Johns Hopkins University Press, 1988, xiv+394 p., cloth, nonf.

MULLER, Marcia, 1944- , *with Bill Pronzini*

30401 *Beyond the grave.* New York: Walker & Co., 1986, 236 p., cloth, novel.
30402 *Witches' brew: horror and supernatural stories by women.* New York: Macmillan Publishing Co., 1984, x+323 p., cloth, anth.

MULLER, Paul, pseud.—SEE: King, Albert

MULLER, Robert, 1925-

30403 *Supernatural: seven stories based on the television series on BBC-1.* London: Collins/Fontana, 1977, 192 p., paper, tele. anth.

MULLIN, Chris(topher John), 1947-

30404 *A very British coup.* London: Hodder & Stoughton, 1982, 220 p., cloth, novel.

MULVEY, Thomas, *as* VICTOR APPLETON II

00465 *Tom Swift in the caves of nuclear fire.* New York: Grosset & Dunlap, 1956, 214 p., cloth, novel. TOM SWIFT JR. #A8.

MULVIHILL, Robert

30405 *Reflections on America, 1984: an Orwell symposium.* Athens, GA & London: University of Georgia Press, 1986, x+ 221 p., cloth, nonf. anth.

MUNDIS, Jerrold J., 1941-

30406A *The dogs.* New York: Berkley Books, 1988, 228 p., paper, novel. [Previously published as by Robert Calder].

***as* ROBERT CALDER**

30406 *The dogs.* New York: Delacorte Press, 1976, 228 p., cloth, novel.

MUNDY, Talbot [pseud. of William Lancaster Gribbon], 1879-1940

10524 *Tros of Samothrace.* New York: D. Appleton-Century, 1934, 949 p., cloth, novel. TROS #1.
10524E retitled: *Lud of Lunden.* New York: Zebra Books, Kensington Publishing Corp., 1976, 379 p., paper, novel. TROS #1-A. [The original novel has been broken into three pieces for this reprint edition].
10524F retitled: *Avenging Liafail.* New York: Zebra Books, Kensington Publishing Corp., 1976, 348 p., paper, novel. TROS #1-B.
10524G retitled: *The Praetor's dungeon.* New York: Zebra Books, Kensington Publishing Corp., 1976, 396 p., paper, novel. TROS #1-C.

MUNN, H(arold) Warner, 1903-1981

30407 *In the tomb of the bishop.* West Kingston, RI: Donald M. Grant, Publisher, 1979, 183 p., cloth, coll. TALES OF THE WEREWOLF CLAN #1.
30408 *The master goes home.* West Kingston, RI: Donald M. Grant, Publisher, 1980, 208 p., cloth, coll. TALES OF THE WEREWOLF CLAN #2.
30409 *Merlin's godson.* New York: Ballantine Books, 1976, 311 p., paper, coll. GWALCHMAI #1-2. [Includes *King of the world's edge*; *The ship from Atlantis*].

MUNO, Jean [pseud. of Robert Burniaux], 1924-1988

30410 *Glove of passion, voice of blood.* Seattle, WA: Owl Creek, 1986, 127 p., paper, coll. [Translation by Kim Connell].

*MUNRO, John, <u>1849-1930</u>

MUNRO, Rona, 1959-

30411 *Doctor Who: Survival.* London: A Target Book, W. H. Allen & Co., 1990, 136 p., paper, tele. DOCTOR WHO #150.
Survival—SEE: *Doctor Who: Survival.*

MUNSON, Brad

30412 *The mad throne.* New York: Popular Library, 1979, 316 p., paper, novel.

MUNSTER, Bill, 1947-

30413 *Sudden fear: the horror and dark suspense fiction of Dean R. Koontz.* Mercer Island, WA: Starmont House, 1988, x+182 p., cloth, nonf. anth. STARMONT STUDIES IN LITERARY CRITICISM #24.

MURAKAMI, Haruki, 1949-

30414 *Hard-boiled wonderland and the end of the world: a novel.* Tokyo, New York: Kodansha International, 1991, 400 p., cloth, novel. [Translation by Alfred Birnbaum of *Sekai no owari to hâdo-boirudo wandârando*].

37985 *A wild sheep chase.* Tokyo, New York: Kodansha International, 1989, 299 p., cloth, novel. [Translation by Alfred Birnbaum of *Hitsuji ô meguru boken*].

MURARI, Timeri (Nrupendra), 1941-

30415 *The oblivion tapes.* New York: A Berkley Medallion Book, Berkley Publishing Corp., 1978, 245 p., paper, novel.

MURAV'EV, V(ladimir) S(ergeevich), *as* ANONYMOUS EDITOR

30416 *Science fiction: English and American short stories.* Moscow: Progress Publishers, 1979, 347 p., paper, anth. [Text in English, notes and introduction in Russian].

MURCHISON, Myles, 1942-

30417 *The deathless.* New York: Ballantine Books, 1989, 295 p., paper, novel.

MURDOCK, M(elinda) S(eabrooke), 1947-

Armageddon off Vesta—SEE: *Buck Rogers: Armageddon off Vesta.*
30418 *Buck Rogers: Armageddon off Vesta.* Lake Geneva, WI: TSR Inc., 1989, 279 p., paper, novel. BUCK ROGERS—MARTIAN WARS TRILOGY #3.
30419 *Buck Rogers: Hammer of Mars.* Lake Geneva, WI: TSR Inc., 1989, 279 p., paper, novel. BUCK ROGERS—MARTIAN WARS TRILOGY #2.
30420 *Buck Rogers: Prime squared.* Lake Geneva, WI: TSR Inc., 1990, 276 p., paper, novel. BUCK ROGERS—INNER PLANETS TRILOGY #2.
30421 *Dynteryx.* New York: Popular Library, 1988, 246 p., paper, novel. VENDETTA #2.
Hammer of Mars—SEE: *Buck Rogers: Hammer of Mars.*
Prime squared—SEE: *Buck Rogers: Prime squared.*

30422 *Rebellion 2456.* Lake Geneva, WI: TSR Inc., 1989, 281 p., paper, novel. BUCK ROGERS—MARTIAN WARS TRILOGY #1.
30423 *Vendetta.* New York: Popular Library, 1987, 292 p., paper, novel. VENDETTA #1.
30424 *Web of the Romulans: a Star Trek novel.* New York: A Timescape Book, Pocket Books, 1983, 220 p., paper, novel. STAR TREK #10.

MURNANE, Gerald, 1939-

30425 *Landscape with landscape.* Carlton, Victoria, Australia: Norstrilia Press, 1985, 267 p., cloth, coll.
30426 *The plains.* Carlton, Victoria, Australia: Norstrilia Press, 1982, 126 p., cloth, novel.

MURPHY, Brian, 1939-

30427 *C. S. Lewis.* Mercer Island, WA: Starmont House, 1983, 95 p., cloth, nonf. STARMONT READER'S GUIDE #14.

MURPHY, Gloria

30428 *Nightmare.* New York: Popular Library, 1987, 232 p., paper, novel.

MURPHY, Michael, 1930-

30429 *Golf in the kingdom.* New York: Viking Press, 1972, xiii+205 p., cloth, novel.
30430 *Jacob Atabet: a speculative fiction.* Millbrae, CA: Celestial Arts, 1977, 216 p., paper, novel.

MURPHY, Michael J.

30431 *The celluloid vampires: a history and filmography, 1897-1979.* Ann Arbor, MI: Pierian Press, 1979, xi+351 p., cloth, nonf.

MURPHY, Pat(rice Anne), 1955-

30432 *The city, not long after.* New York, London: A Foundation Book, Doubleday, 1989, 244 p., cloth, novel.
30433 *The falling woman.* New York: Tor, A Tom Doherty Associates Book, 1986, 287 p., cloth, novel. [Winner of the Nebula Award for Best Novel, 1987 (1988)].
30434 *Points of departure.* New York, Toronto: Spectra, Bantam Books, 1990, xiv+316 p., paper, coll.
30435 *The shadow hunter.* New York: Popular Library, 1982, 223 p., paper, novel.

MURPHY, Patrick D(ennis), 1951-

with Vernon Hyles

26261 *The poetic fantastic: studies in an evolving genre.* New York: Greenwood Press, 1989, xxv+201 p., cloth, nonf. anth. CONTRIBUTIONS TO THE STUDY OF SCIENCE FICTION AND FANTASY #40.

with Wu Dingbo

30436 *Science fiction from China.* New York: Praeger Publishers, 1989, 176 p., cloth, anth.

MURPHY, Rae, 1935- , with Patrick MacFadden & Robert Chodos

20018 *Your place or mine? an entertainment.* Ottawa, Ontario: Deneau & Greenberg, 1978, 240 p., paper, novel.

MURPHY, Robert Franklin

30437 *The girl factory.* New York: Zebra Books, Kensington Publishing Corp., 1975, 191 p., paper, novel. GIRL FACTORY #1.
30438 *King's mate.* New York: Zebra Books, Kensington Publishing Corp., 1975, 188 p., paper, novel. GIRL FACTORY #2.
30439 *The man-made woman.* New York: Zebra Books, Kensington Publishing Corp., 1976, 176 p., paper, novel. GIRL FACTORY #3.

MURPHY, Shirley Rousseau, 1928-

30440 *The castle of Hape.* New York: An Argo Book, Atheneum, 1980, viii+172 p., cloth, novel. CHILDREN OF YNELL #3.
30441 *Caves of fire and ice.* New York: An Argo Book, Atheneum, 1980, 174 p., cloth, novel. CHILDREN OF YNELL #4.
30442 *The dragonbards.* New York: Harper & Row, 1988, 249 p., cloth, novel. DRAGONBARDS #3.
30443 *The grass tower.* New York: Atheneum, 1976, 244 p., cloth, novel.
30444 *The ivory lyre.* New York: Harper & Row, 1987, 250 p., cloth, novel. DRAGONBARDS #2.
30445 *The joining of the stone.* New York: An Argo Book, Atheneum, 1981, 169 p., cloth, novel. CHILDREN OF YNELL #5.
30446 *Nightpool.* New York: Harper & Row, 1985, 250 p., cloth, novel. DRAGONBARDS #1.

30447 *The ring of fire.* New York: Atheneum, 1977, 232 p., cloth, novel. CHILDREN OF YNELL #1.
30448 *Silver woven in my hair.* New York: Atheneum, 1977, 121 p., cloth, novel.
30449 *The wolf bell.* New York: An Argo Book, Atheneum, 1979, 182 p., cloth, novel. CHILDREN OF YNELL #2.

with Welch Suggs

30450 *Medallion of the black hound.* New York: Harper & Row, 1989, 182 p., cloth, novel.

MURPHY, Walter F(rancis), 1929-

30451 *The Vicar of Christ.* New York: Macmillan Publishing Co., 1979, 632 p., cloth, novel.

MURPHY, Warren (Burton), 1933-

30452 *Scorpion's dance.* New York: Pinnacle Books, Windsor Publishing Corp., 1990, 477 p., paper, novel.

with Molly Cochran

20216 *Grandmaster.* New York: Pinnacle Books, 1984, 427 p., paper, novel.
20217 *The hand of Lazarus.* New York: Pinnacle Books, Windsor Publishing Corp., 1988, 445 p., paper, novel.
20218 *High priest.* New York: NAL Books, New American Library, 1987, 354 p., cloth, novel.

with Richard Sapir and others

NOTE: Most of the books in this series bear the joint bylines of both writers, even after Richard Sapir's 1987 death; some of the earlier books in the series are bylined by one author only, and many of those bylines changed with subsequent printings. Correct bylines for the first editions appear immediately after individual titles where only one author is recorded on the title page. More than half of the series has been ghostwritten or co-authored with other writers; actual authorship is given at the end of each entry, courtesy of Will Murray. Although individual titles in this series may not be fantastic, the series as a whole has been judged sufficiently fantastic to list every book, including a repetition of the one title listed in the 1700-1974 volume of this bibliography.

30453 *Acid rock.* New York: Pinnacle Books, 1973, 186 p., paper, novel. DESTROYER #13. [By Richard Sapir & Warren Murphy].

30454 *Arabian nightmare.* New York: A Signet Book, 1991, 237 p., paper, novel. DE-STROYER #86. [By Will Murray].

30455 *The arms of Kali.* New York: A Signet Book, New American Library, 1984, 253 p., paper, novel. DESTROYER #59. [By Richard Sapir & Warren Murphy].

30456 *The assassin's handbook.* New York: Pinnacle Books, 1982, xiii+268 p., paper, coll. [By Richard Sapir & Warren Murphy; edited (and written) by Will Murray].

30456A retitled: *Inside Sinanju.* New York: Pinnacle Books, 1985, xiii+268 p., paper, coll. [By Richard Sapir & Warren Murphy; edited (and written) by Will Murray].

30457 *Assassins play-off.* New York: Pinnacle Books, 1975, 178 p., paper, novel. DE-STROYER #20. [By Richard Sapir & Warren Murphy].

20218 *Balance of power.* New York: Pinnacle Books, 1981, viii+183 p., paper, novel. DESTROYER #44. [By Richard Sapir & Warren Murphy & Molly Cochran].

30458 *Bay city blast* / by Warren Murphy. Los Angeles: Pinnacle Books, 1979, 179 p., paper, novel. DESTROYER #38. [By Warren Murphy].

30459 *Blood lust.* New York: A Signet Book, 1991, 256 p., paper, novel. DESTROYER #85. [By Will Murray].

30460 *Blood ties.* New York: A Signet Book, New American Library, 1987, 252 p., paper, novel. DESTROYER #69. [By Warren Murphy & Will Murray].

30461 *Blue smoke and mirrors.* New York: A Signet Book, New American Library, 1989, 224 p., paper, novel. DESTROYER #78. [By Will Murray].

30462 *Bottom line* / by Warren Murphy. Los Angeles: Pinnacle Books, 1979, 178 p., paper, novel. DESTROYER #37. [By Warren Murphy].

30463 *Brain drain.* New York: Pinnacle Books, 1976, 180 p., paper, novel. DESTROYER #22. [By Richard Sapir & Warren Murphy].

30464 *Chained reaction.* Los Angeles: Pinnacle Books, 1978, 178 p., paper, novel. DE-STROYER #34. [By Richard Sapir & Warren Murphy].

30465 *Child's play.* New York: Pinnacle Books, 1976, 183 p., paper, novel. DESTROYER #23. [By Richard Sapir & Warren Murphy].

30466 *Chinese puzzle.* New York: Pinnacle Books, 1972, 187 p., paper, novel. DE-STROYER #3. [By Richard Sapir & Warren Murphy].

30467 *Coin of the realm.* New York: A Signet Book, New American Library, 1989, 256 p., paper, novel. DESTROYER #77. [By Will Murray].

30468 *Created, the Destroyer.* New York: Pinnacle Books, 1971, 187 p., paper, novel. DESTROYER #1. [By Richard Sapir & Warren Murphy].

30469 *Dangerous games* / by Warren Murphy. Los Angeles: Pinnacle Books, 1980, 188 p., paper, novel. DESTROYER #40. [By Warren Murphy & Robert J. Randisi].

20219 *Date with death* / by Warren Murphy. New York: Pinnacle Books, 1984, 186 p., paper, novel. DESTROYER #57. [By Warren Murphy & Molly Cochran & Ed Hunsburger].

30470 *Deadly seeds.* New York: Pinnacle Books, 1975, 180 p., paper, novel. DESTROYER #21. [By Richard Sapir & Warren Murphy].

30471 *Death check.* New York: Pinnacle Books, 1972, 187 p., paper, novel. DESTROYER #2. [By Richard Sapir & Warren Murphy].

30472 *Death sentence.* New York: A Signet Book, 1990, 221 p., paper, novel. DE-STROYER #80. [By Will Murray].

30473 *Death therapy.* New York: Pinnacle Books, 1972, 188 p., paper, novel. DE-STROYER #6. [By Richard Sapir & Warren Murphy].

10535 *Dr. Quake.* New York: Pinnacle Books, 1972, 187 p., paper, novel. DESTROYER #5. [By Richard Sapir & Warren Murphy].

20220 *Dying space* / by Warren Murphy. New York: Pinnacle Books, 1982, 196 p., paper, novel. DESTROYER #47. [By Molly Cochran].

20221 *The eleventh hour.* New York: A Signet Book, New American Library, 1987, 222 p., paper, novel. DESTROYER #70. [By Warren Murphy & Will Murray & Molly Cochran].

30474 *Encounter group* / by Warren Murphy. New York: Pinnacle Books, 1984, 185 p., paper, novel. DESTROYER #56. [By Warren Murphy & Will Murray].

30475 *The end of the game.* New York: A Signet Book, New American Library, 1985, 205 p., paper, novel. DESTROYER #60. [By Richard Sapir & Warren Murphy].

30476 *The final crusade.* New York: A Signet Book, New American Library, 1989, 223 p., paper, novel. DESTROYER #76. [By Will Murray].

29801 *The final death.* New York: Pinnacle Books, 1977, 177 p., paper, novel. DE-

STROYER #29. [By Richard Sapir & Warren Murphy & Ric Meyers].

30477 *Firing line* / by Warren Murphy. Los Angeles: Pinnacle Books, 1980, 180 p., paper, novel. DESTROYER #41. [By Warren Murphy].

30478 *Fool's gold.* New York: Pinnacle Books, 1983, 245 p., paper, novel. DESTROYER #52. [By Richard Sapir & Warren Murphy].

30479 *Funny money.* New York: Pinnacle Books, 1975, 180 p., paper, novel. DESTROYER #18. [By Richard Sapir & Warren Murphy].

30480 *Ground zero.* New York: A Signet Book, 1991, 253 p., paper, novel. DESTROYER #84. [By Will Murray].

30481 *The head men.* Los Angeles: Pinnacle Books, 1977, 197 p., paper, novel. DESTROYER #31. [By Richard Sapir & Warren Murphy].

30482 *Holy terror.* New York: Pinnacle Books, 1975, 182 p., paper, novel. DESTROYER #19. [By Richard Sapir & Warren Murphy].

30483 *Hostile takeover.* New York: A Signet Book, 1990, 252 p., paper, novel. DESTROYER #81. [By Will Murray].

30484 *In enemy hands.* New York: Pinnacle Books, 1977, 178 p., paper, novel. DESTROYER #26. [By Richard Sapir & Warren Murphy].

30485 *Judgment day.* New York: Pinnacle Books, 1974, 184 p., paper, novel. DESTROYER #14. [By Richard Sapir & Warren Murphy].

30486 *Kill or cure.* New York: Pinnacle Books, 1973, 184 p., paper, novel. DESTROYER #11. [By Richard Sapir & Warren Murphy].

30487 *Killer chromosomes.* Los Angeles: Pinnacle Books, 1978, 181 p., paper, novel. DESTROYER #32. [By Richard Sapir & Warren Murphy].

20222 *Killing time* / by Warren Murphy. New York: Pinnacle Books, 1982, 199 p., paper, novel. DESTROYER #50. [By Molly Cochran].

30488 *King's curse.* New York: Pinnacle Books, 1976, 178 p., paper, novel. DESTROYER #24. [By Richard Sapir & Warren Murphy].

30489 *The last alchemist.* New York: A Signet Book, New American Library, 1986, 221 p., paper, novel. DESTROYER #64. [By Richard Sapir & Will Murray].

30490 *Last call* / by Warren Murphy. Los Angeles: Pinnacle Books, 1978, 182 p., paper, novel. DESTROYER #35. [By Warren Murphy].

20223 *Last drop* / by Warren Murphy. New York: Pinnacle Books, 1983, 199 p., paper, novel. DESTROYER #54. [By Molly Cochran].

29799 *The last temple* / by Warren Murphy. New York: Pinnacle Books, 1977, 180 p., paper, novel. DESTROYER #27. [By Warren Murphy & Ric Meyers].

30491 *Last war dance.* New York: Pinnacle Books, 1974, 178 p., paper, novel. DESTROYER #17. [By Richard Sapir & Warren Murphy].

30492 *Line of succession.* New York: A Signet Book, New American Library, 1988, 252 p., paper, novel. DESTROYER #73. [By Warren Murphy & Will Murray].

30493 *Look into my eyes.* New York: A Signet Book, New American Library, 1987, 253 p., paper, novel. DESTROYER #67. [By Richard Sapir].

30494 *Lords of the Earth.* New York: A Signet Book, New American Library, 1985, 254 p., paper, novel. DESTROYER #61. [By Richard Sapir & Warren Murphy].

30495 *Lost yesterday.* New York: A Signet Book, New American Library, 1986, 255 p., paper, novel. DESTROYER #65. [By Richard Sapir & Will Murray].

30496 *Mafia fix.* New York: Pinnacle Books, 1972, 184 p., paper, novel. DESTROYER #4. [By Richard Sapir & Warren Murphy].

20224 *Master's challenge.* New York: Pinnacle Books, 1984, 245 p., paper, novel. DESTROYER #55. [By Richard Sapir & Warren Murphy & Molly Cochran].

30497 *Midnight man* / by Warren Murphy. Los Angeles: Pinnacle Books, 1981, 169 p., paper, novel. DESTROYER #43. [By Warren Murphy & Robert J. Randisi].

30498 *Missing link* / by Warren Murphy. Los Angeles: Pinnacle Books, 1980, 174 p., paper, novel. DESTROYER #39. [By Warren Murphy].

30499 *Mugger blood.* Los Angeles: Pinnacle Books, 1977, 182 p., paper, novel. DESTROYER #30. [By Richard Sapir & Warren Murphy].

30500 *Murder ward.* New York: Pinnacle Books, 1974, 176 p., paper, novel. DESTROYER #15. [By Richard Sapir & Warren Murphy].

30501 *Murder's shield.* New York: Pinnacle Books, 1973, 190 p., paper, novel. DESTROYER #9. [By Richard Sapir & Warren Murphy].

20225 *Next of kin* / by Warren Murphy. New York: Pinnacle Books, 1981, 183 p., paper, novel. DESTROYER #46. [By Molly Cochran].

30502 *Oil slick.* New York: Pinnacle Books, 1974, 179 p., paper, novel. DESTROYER #16. [By Richard Sapir & Warren Murphy].

30503 *An old-fashioned war.* New York: A Signet Book, New American Library, 1987, 221 p., paper, novel. DESTROYER #68. [By Richard Sapir].

30504 *Power play* / by Warren Murphy. Los Angeles: Pinnacle Books, 1979, 180 p., paper, novel. DESTROYER #36. [By Warren Murphy].

30505 *Profit motive.* New York: Pinnacle Books, 1982, 245 p., paper, novel. DESTROYER #48. [By Richard Sapir & Warren Murphy].

30506 *Rain of terror.* New York: A Signet Book, New American Library, 1989, 256 p., paper, novel. DESTROYER #75. [By Will Murray].

30507 *Remo: the adventure begins: a novel.* New York: A Signet Book, New American Library, 1985, 253 p., paper, movie. DESTROYER SERIES (UNNUMBERED). [By Richard Sapir].

30508 *Return engagement.* New York: A Signet Book, New American Library, 1988, 253 p., paper, novel. DESTROYER #71. [By Warren Murphy & Will Murray].

26186 *The seventh stone.* New York: A Signet Book, New American Library, 1985, 223 p., paper, novel. DESTROYER #62. [By Richard Sapir & Warren Murphy & Ed Hunsburger].

30509 *Ship of death.* New York: Pinnacle Books, 1977, 179 p., paper, novel. DESTROYER #28. [By Richard Sapir & Warren Murphy].

20226 *Shock value* / by Warren Murphy. New York: Pinnacle Books, 1983, 199 p., paper, novel. DESTROYER #51. [By Molly Cochran].

30510 *Shooting schedule.* New York: A Signet Book, New American Library, 1990, 255 p., paper, novel. DESTROYER #79. [By Will Murray].

20227 *Skin deep* / by Warren Murphy. New York: Pinnacle Books, 1982, 199 p., paper, novel. DESTROYER #49. [By Molly Cochran].

30511 *Skull duggery.* New York: A Signet Book, 1991, 253 p., paper, novel. DESTROYER #83. [By Will Murray].

30512 *The sky is falling.* New York: A Signet Book, New American Library, 1986, 255 p., paper, novel. DESTROYER #63. [By Richard Sapir & Will Murray].

30513 *Slave safari.* New York: Pinnacle Books, 1973, 186 p., paper, novel. DESTROYER #12. [By Richard Sapir & Warren Murphy].

30514 *Sole survivor.* New York: A Signet Book, New American Library, 1988, 223 p., paper, novel. DESTROYER #72. [By Warren Murphy & Will Murray].

20228 *Spoils of war* / by Warren Murphy. New York: Pinnacle Books, 1981, 182 p., paper, novel. DESTROYER #45. [By Molly Cochran].

30515 *Sue me.* New York: A Signet Book, New American Library, 1986, 221 p., paper, novel. DESTROYER #66. [By Richard Sapir].

30516 *Summit chase* / by Warren Murphy. New York: Pinnacle Books, 1973, 185 p., paper, novel. DESTROYER #8. [By Warren Murphy].

30517 *Survival course.* New York: A Signet Book, 1990, 253 p., paper, novel. DESTROYER #82. [By Will Murray].

29800 *Sweet dreams* / by Warren Murphy. New York: Pinnacle Books, 1976, 174 p., paper, novel. DESTROYER #25. [By Warren Murphy & Ric Meyers].

30518 *Terror squad.* New York: Pinnacle Books, 1973, 188 p., paper, novel. DESTROYER #10. [By Richard Sapir & Warren Murphy].

26810 *Timber line* / by Warren Murphy. Los Angeles: Pinnacle Books, 1980, 181 p., paper, novel. DESTROYER #42. [By Warren Murphy & William "Ted" Joy].

20229 *Time trial* / by Warren Murphy. New York: Pinnacle Books, 1983, 201 p., paper, novel. DESTROYER #53. [By Molly Cochran].

30519 *Total recall* / by Warren Murphy. New York: Pinnacle Books, 1984, 185 p., paper, novel. DESTROYER #58. [By Warren Murphy & Robert J. Randisi].

30520 *Union bust.* New York: Pinnacle Books, 1973, 184 p., paper, novel. DESTROYER #7. [By Richard Sapir & Warren Murphy].

30521 *Voodoo die.* Los Angeles: Pinnacle Books, 1978, 181 p., paper, novel. DESTROYER #33. [By Richard Sapir & Warren Murphy].

30522 *Walking wounded.* New York: A Signet Book, New American Library, 1988, 224 p., paper, novel. DESTROYER #74. [By Will Murray].

MURRAY, Doug(las Louis Jr.), 1947-

30523 *Files magazine spotlight on The Outer Limits files: Nightmare.* Canoga Park, CA: New Media Books, (1986), 53 p., paper, nonf. OUTER LIMITS.

30524 *Files magazine spotlight on The Outer Limits files: The human factor.* Canoga Park, CA: New Media Books, (1986), 51 p., paper, nonf. OUTER LIMITS.

37986 *Files magazine spotlight on The Outer Limits files: The Zanti misfits.* Canoga Park, CA: New Media Books, (1986), 53 p., paper, nonf. OUTER LIMITS.

The human factor—SEE: *Files magazine spotlight on The Outer Limits files: The human factor.*

Nightmare—SEE: *Files magazine spotlight on The Outer Limits files: Nightmare.*

The Zanti misfits—SEE: *Files magazine spotlight on The Outer Limits files: The Zanti misfits.*

with Allan Asherman & Jonathon Green

16837 *Star Wars: the full story.* [S.l.]: Paradise Press, 1977, 62 p., paper, nonf.

MURRAY, E(ugene) B(ernard), 1927-

30525 *Ann Radcliffe.* New York: Twayne Publishers, 1972, 178 p., cloth, nonf.

MURRAY, E(arl) Patrick

30526 *Dream house.* New York: Diamond Books, 1991, 228 p., paper, novel.

30527 *Ten little Indians.* New York: Zebra Books, Kensington Publishing Corp., 1988, 350 p., paper, novel.

MURRAY, Frieda A., *with Roland J. Green*

30528 *The book of Kantela: a novel of high fantasy.* New York: Bluejay Books, 1985, 340 p., paper, novel. THRONE OF SHERRAN TRILOGY #1.

MURRAY, Will [i.e., William Patrick Murray], 1953-

30529 *Doc Savage: reflections in bronze.* Greenwood, MA: Odyssey Publications, 1978, 22 p., paper, nonf.

30530 *The Duende history of the Shadow magazine.* Greenwood, MA: Odyssey Publications, 1980, 128 p., paper, nonf. anth.

30531 *Secrets of Doc Savage.* Greenwood, MA: Odyssey Publications, 1981, 36 p., paper, nonf.

with Lester Dent as KENNETH ROBESON

21585 *Doc Savage: Python Isle.* New York, Toronto: Falcon, Bantam Books, 1991, 207 p., paper, novel. DOC SAVAGE (UNNUMBERED). [With Will Murray].

Python Isle—SEE: *Doc Savage: Python Isle.*

with Tom Johnson

26639 *Secret Agent X: a history.* Oak Forest, IL: Robert Weinberg, 1980, 96 p., paper, nonf. PULP CLASSICS #22.

26640 *Secret Agent X: a history, revised edition.* Seymour, TX: Fading Shadows Inc., 1991, 96 p., paper, nonf. [Revised edition].

as anonymous author or co-author with Warren Murphy and/or Richard Sapir

NOTE: Most of the books in this series bear the joint bylines of Warren Murphy and Richard Sapir, even after the latter's 1987 death; some of the earlier books in the series are bylined by one author only, and many of those bylines changed with subsequent printings. Correct bylines for the first editions appear immediately after individual titles where only one author is recorded on the title page. More than half of the series has been ghostwritten or co-authored with other writers; actual authorship is given at the end of each entry, courtesy of Will Murray.

30454 *Arabian nightmare.* New York: A Signet Book, 1991, 237 p., paper, novel. DESTROYER #86. [By Will Murray].

30456 *The assassin's handbook.* New York: Pinnacle Books, 1982, xiii+268 p., paper, coll. [By Richard Sapir & Warren Murphy; edited (and written) by Will Murray].

30456A retitled: *Inside Sinanju.* New York: Pinnacle Books, 1985, xiii+268 p., paper, coll. [By Richard Sapir & Warren Murphy; edited (and written) by Will Murray].

30459 *Blood lust.* New York: A Signet Book, 1991, 256 p., paper, novel. DESTROYER #85. [By Will Murray].

30460 *Blood ties.* New York: A Signet Book, New American Library, 1987, 252 p., paper, novel. DESTROYER #69. [By Warren Murphy & Will Murray].

30461 *Blue smoke and mirrors.* New York: A Signet Book, New American Library, 1989, 224 p., paper, novel. DESTROYER #78. [By Will Murray].

30467 *Coin of the realm.* New York: A Signet Book, New American Library, 1989, 256 p., paper, novel. DESTROYER #77. [By Will Murray].

30472 *Death sentence.* New York: A Signet Book, 1990, 221 p., paper, novel. DE-STROYER #80. [By Will Murray].

20221 *The eleventh hour.* New York: A Signet Book, New American Library, 1987, 222 p., paper, novel. DESTROYER #70. [By Warren Murphy & Will Murray & Molly Cochran].

30474 *Encounter group* / by Warren Murphy. New York: Pinnacle Books, 1984, 185 p., paper, novel. DESTROYER #56. [By Warren Murphy & Will Murray].

30476 *The final crusade.* New York: A Signet Book, New American Library, 1989, 223 p., paper, novel. DESTROYER #76. [By Will Murray].

30480 *Ground zero.* New York: A Signet Book, 1991, 253 p., paper, novel. DESTROYER #84. [By Will Murray].

30483 *Hostile takeover.* New York: A Signet Book, 1990, 252 p., paper, novel. DE-STROYER #81. [By Will Murray].

Inside Sinanju—SEE: *The assassin's handbook.*

30489 *The last alchemist.* New York: A Signet Book, New American Library, 1986, 221 p., paper, novel. DESTROYER #64. [By Richard Sapir & Will Murray].

30492 *Line of succession.* New York: A Signet Book, New American Library, 1988, 252 p., paper, novel. DESTROYER #73. [By Warren Murphy & Will Murray].

30495 *Lost yesterday.* New York: A Signet Book, New American Library, 1986, 255 p., paper, novel. DESTROYER #65. [By Richard Sapir & Will Murray].

30506 *Rain of terror.* New York: A Signet Book, New American Library, 1989, 256 p., paper, novel. DESTROYER #75. [By Will Murray].

30508 *Return engagement.* New York: A Signet Book, New American Library, 1988, 253 p., paper, novel. DESTROYER #71. [By Warren Murphy & Will Murray].

30510 *Shooting schedule.* New York: A Signet Book, New American Library, 1990, 255 p., paper, novel. DESTROYER #79. [By Will Murray].

30511 *Skull duggery.* New York: A Signet Book, 1991, 253 p., paper, novel. DESTROYER #83. [By Will Murray].

30512 *The sky is falling.* New York: A Signet Book, New American Library, 1986, 255 p., paper, novel. DESTROYER #63. [By Richard Sapir & Will Murray].

30514 *Sole survivor.* New York: A Signet Book, New American Library, 1988, 223 p., paper, novel. DESTROYER #72. [By Warren Murphy & Will Murray].

30517 *Survival course.* New York: A Signet Book, 1990, 253 p., paper, novel. DE-STROYER #82. [By Will Murray].

30522 *Walking wounded.* New York: A Signet Book, New American Library, 1988, 224 p., paper, novel. DESTROYER #74. [By Will Murray].

MURRAY, William, 1926- , *with Chuck Scarborough*

30532 *The Myrmidon Project.* New York: Coward, McCann & Geoghegan, 1981, 311 p., cloth, novel.

MURRAY, William P.—SEE: Murray, Will

MURRY, Colin—SEE: Cowper, Richard

MUSSER, Jim, *with Andrew Keith*

26972 *Technical readout 3050.* Chicago: FASA Corp., 1990, 233 p., paper, fiction. BATTLETECH SERIES.

MYERS, Amy

37987 *After midnight stories.* London: William Kimber, 1985, 222 p., cloth, anth.

30533 *The fifth book of after midnight stories.* London: Robert Hale, 1991, 208 p., cloth, anth.

30534 *The fourth book of after midnight stories.* London: William Kimber, 1988, 192 p., cloth, anth.

30535 *The third book of after midnight stories.* London: William Kimber, 1987, 208 p., cloth, anth.

as ANONYMOUS EDITOR

30536 *The second book of after midnight stories.* London: William Kimber, 1986, 192 p., cloth, anth.

MYERS, Barry

30537 *The Shanee.* New York: Zebra Books, Kensington Publishing Corp., 1975, 302 p., paper, novel.

MYERS, Edward, 1950- , *with Judith Myers*

30538 *A bibliography of the first printings of the writings of Jules Verne in the English language, together with information on numerous reprints, and a key to title interpretation.* New Hartford, CT: Country Lane Books, 1989, 68 p., paper, nonf.

MYERS, Erica

30539 *Akhenaten and Nefertiti: the royal rebels.* New York: Manor Books, 1979, 287 p., paper, novel.

MYERS, Gary

30540 *The house of the worm.* Sauk City, WI: Arkham House, 1975, ix+77 p., cloth, story.

MYERS, Howard L., 1930-1971

30541 *Cloud chamber.* New York: Popular Library, 1977, 255 p., paper, novel.

MYERS, John Myers, 1906-1988

30542 *The harp and the blade.* New York: E. P. Dutton, 1941, 345 p., cloth, novel.
30543 *The moon's fire-eating daughter.* Virginia Beach, VA: Starblaze Editions, Donning Co., 1981, 176 p., cloth, novel. SILVERLOCK #2.

MYERS, Judith, *with Edward Myers*

30538 *A bibliography of the first printings of the writings of Jules Verne in the English language, together with information on numerous reprints, and a key to title interpretation.* New Hartford, CT: Country Lane Books, 1989, 68 p., paper, nonf.

MYERS, Robert E(dward), 1932-

30544 *The intersection of science fiction and philosophy: critical studies.* Westport, CT & London: Greenwood Press, 1983, xvi+262 p., cloth, nonf. anth. CONTRIBUTIONS TO THE STUDY OF SCIENCE FICTION AND FANTASY #4.
30545 *Jack Williamson: a primary and secondary bibliography.* Boston: G. K. Hall & Co., 1980, xiii+93 p., cloth, nonf. MASTERS OF SCIENCE FICTION AND FANTASY.

MYERS, Robert J(ohn), 1924-

30546 *The cross of Frankenstein.* Philadelphia, PA: J. B. Lippincott, 1975, x+208 p., cloth, novel. CROSS OF FRANKENSTEIN SERIES.
30547 *The slave of Frankenstein.* Philadelphia, PA: J. B. Lippincott, 1976, 219 p., cloth, novel. CROSS OF FRANKENSTEIN SERIES.

30548 *The virgin and the vampire: a novel.* New York: Pocket Books, 1977, 207 p., paper, novel.

MYERS, Walter Dean, 1937-

30549 *Ambush in the Amazon.* New York: Puffin Books, 1986, 85 p., paper, novel.
30550 *Brainstorm.* New York: Franklin Watts, 1977, 90 p., cloth, novel.

MYLIUS, Ralph (William), 1945- , *with Warren Norwood*

30551 *The Seren Cenacles.* Toronto, New York: Bantam Books, 1983, 244 p., paper, novel.

MYRA, Harold (Lawrence), 1939-

30552 *Children in the night.* Grand Rapids, MI: Zondervan Publishing House, 1991, 301 p., paper, novel.
30553 *The choice.* Wheaton, IL: Tyndale House Publishers, 1980, 167 p., cloth, novel.
Escape from the twisted planet—SEE: *No man in Eden.*
10553 *No man in Eden.* Waco, TX: Word Inc., 1969, 217 p., cloth, novel.
10553A retitled: *Escape from the twisted planet.* Waco, TX: Word Books, 1981, 217 p., paper, novel.

MYRUS, Don(ald Richard), 1927-

30554 *The best of Omni science fiction, no. 5.* New York: Omni Publications, 1983, [143] p., paper, anth.
30555 *The best of Omni science fiction, no. 6.* New York: Omni Publications, 1983, [143] p., paper, anth.

with Ben Bova

18354 *The best of Omni science fiction.* New York: Omni Society, 1980, 143 p., paper, anth. [Includes some nonfiction].
18355 *The best of Omni science fiction, no. 2.* New York: Omni, 1981, 144 p., paper, anth. [Includes some nonfiction].
18356 *The best of Omni science fiction, no. 3.* New York: Omni Publications, 1982, 143 p., paper, anth. [Includes some nonfiction].
18357 *The best of Omni science fiction, no. 4.* New York: Omni Publications, 1982, 143 p., paper, anth. [Includes some nonfiction].

N

NABOKOV, Vladimir (Vladimirovich), 1899-1977

30556 *The eye*. New York: Phaedra, 1965, 114 p., cloth, novel. [Translation by Dmitri and Vladimir Nabokov of *Sogliadatai*].

30557 *Invitation to a beheading*. New York: G. P. Putnam's Sons, 1959, 223 p., cloth, novel. [Translation by Dmitri and Vladimir Nabokov of *Priglashenie na kazn'*].

NACE, Pierce

30558 *Eat them alive*. New York: Manor Books, 1977, 253 p., paper, novel.

NACHMAN, Elana—SEE: Dykewoman, Elana

NADER, George (Albert), 1940-

30559 *Chrome*. New York: G. P. Putnam's Sons, 1978, 369 p., cloth, novel.

NAHA, Ed, 1950-

30560 *Breakdown*. New York: A Dell Book, 1988, 216 p., paper, novel.

37988 *The films of Roger Corman: brilliance on a budget*. New York: Arco Publications, 1982, xiii+209 p., cloth, nonf.

30561 *Ghostbusters II: a novel*. New York: A Dell Book, 1989, 184 p., paper, movie. GHOSTBUSTERS #2.

30562 *Horrors: from screen to scream: an encyclopedic guide to the greatest horror and fantasy films of all times*. New York: A Flare Book, Avon, 1975, 306 p., paper, nonf.

30563 *The making of Dune*. New York: Berkley Books, 1984, 299 p., paper, nonf.

30564 *Orphans*. New York: A Dell Book, 1989, 184 p., paper, novel.

30565 *The paradise plot*. Toronto, New York: Bantam Books, 1980, 340 p., paper, novel. HARRY PORTER #1.

30566 *Robocop*. New York: A Dell Book, 1987, 189 p., paper, movie. ROBOCOP #1.

30567 *Robocop 2: novel*. New York: Jove Books, 1990, 234 p., paper, movie. ROBOCOP #2.

30568 *Science fiction aliens: a Starlog photo book*. New York: Starlog Magazine, 1977, 97 p., paper, nonf.

30569 *The science fictionary: an A-Z guide to the world of SF authors, films, & TV shows*. New York: Seaview Books, 1980, xii+388 p., cloth, nonf.

30570 *The suicide plague*. Toronto, New York: Bantam Books, 1982, 279 p., paper, novel. HARRY PORTER #2.

as **D. B. DRUMM**

22223 *The children's crusade*. New York: A Dell Book, 1987, 172 p., paper, novel. TRAVELER #11.

22224 *First, you fight*. New York: A Dell Book, 1984, 175 p., paper, novel. TRAVELER #1.

22225 *Ghost dancers*. New York: A Dell Book, 1987, 171 p., paper, novel. TRAVELER #13.

22226 *Hell on Earth*. New York: A Dell Book, 1986, 171 p., paper, novel. TRAVELER #10.

22228 *The prey*. New York: A Dell Book, 1987, 170 p., paper, novel. TRAVELER #12.

22229 *The road ghost*. New York: A Dell Book, 1985, 172 p., paper, novel. TRAVELER #7.

22232 *The stalking time*. New York: A Dell Book, 1986, 174 p., paper, novel. TRAVELER #9.

as **MICHAEL MCGANN**

Blood and fire—SEE: *The Marauders: Blood and fire*.

Blood kin—SEE: *The Marauders: Blood kin*.

Convoy strike—SEE: *The Marauders: Convoy strike*.

Fortress of death—SEE: *The Marauders: Fortress of death*.

The ghost warriors—SEE: *The Marauders: The ghost warriors*.

Liar's dice—SEE: *The Marauders: Liar's dice*.

29533 *The Marauders*. New York: Jove Books, 1989, 154 p., paper, novel. MARAUDERS #1.

705

29534 *The Marauders: Blood and fire.* New York: Jove Books, 1991, 166 p., paper, novel. MARAUDERS #6.

29535 *The Marauders: Blood kin.* New York: Jove Books, 1989, 168 p., paper, novel. MARAUDERS #2.

29536 *The Marauders: Convoy strike.* New York: Jove Books, 1990, 151 p., paper, novel. MARAUDERS #4.

29537 *The Marauders: Fortress of death.* New York: Jove Books, 1991, 184 p., paper, novel. MARAUDERS #7.

29538 *The Marauders: Liar's dice.* New York: Jove Books, 1990, 169 p., paper, novel. MARAUDERS #3.

29539 *The Marauders: The ghost warriors.* New York: Jove Books, 1990, 152 p., paper, novel. MARAUDERS #5.

with Eric Seidman

30571 *Wanted, by the Intergalactic Security Bureau: 20 full-color posters of the most wanted alien criminals.* Toronto, New York: Bantam Books, 1980, [47] p., paper, fiction.

NAHMLOS, John

30572 *Survivors.* New York: Zebra Books, Kensington Publishing Corp., 1982, 336 p., paper, novel.

NANOVIC, John L(eonard), 1906-

30573 *Doc Savage, the supreme adventurer.* Greenwood, MA: Odyssey Publications, 1980, 26 p., paper, story. DOC SAVAGE SERIES. [The original sketch for the *Doc Savage* pulp series].

NANUS, Susan, *with Marc Kornblatt*

27474 *Mission to World War II.* Toronto, New York: A Byron Preiss Book, Bantam Books, 1986, 125 p., paper, novel. TIME MACHINE #11.

NARAYAN, R(asipuram) K(rishnaswami), 1906-

30574 *Gods, demons, and others.* New York: Viking Press, 1964, 241 p., cloth, coll.

NARCEJAC, Thomas [pseud. of Pierre Ayraud], 1908- , *with Pierre Boileau*

26826 *The evil eye.* London: Hutchinson, 1959, 207 p., cloth, coll. [Translation by Geoffrey Sainsbury and James Kirkup of *Le mauvais oeil*].

NARDELLI, Fred

30575 *Frank Frazetta index.* Amsterdam, New York: Fred Nardelli, 1975, 26 p., paper, nonf.

NASSAUER, Bernice—SEE: Rubens, Bernice

NATHAN, David, 1926-

30576 *The story so far.* London: Grafton, 1986, 206 p., paper, novel.

NATHAN, Robert (Gruntal), 1894-1985

30577 *Heaven and Hell and the Megas factor.* New York: Delacorte Press, 1975, 116 p., cloth, novel.

30578 *The rancho of the little loves.* New York: Alfred A. Knopf, 1956, 169 p., cloth, novel.

NATHAN-TURNER, John

30579 *Doctor Who: the companions.* London: Picadilly, 1986, 48 p., cloth, nonf.

30580 *Doctor Who: the Tardis inside out.* London: Picadilly, 1986, 40 p., paper, nonf.

NATHENSON, Joseph

30581 *Deep, very deep space.* New York: Manor Books, 1978, 219 p., paper, novel.

NATION, Terry, 1930-

30582 *Rebecca's world: journey to the forbidden planet.* London: G. Whizzard Publications in Association with André Deutsch, 1975, 114 p., cloth, novel.

30583 *Survivors.* London: Weidenfeld & Nicolson, 1976, 205 p., cloth, novel. SURVIVORS #1.

with John Peel

30584 *The official Doctor Who and the daleks book.* New York: St. Martin's Press, 1988, 212 p., paper, nonf.

***NAVASKY, Victor (S.), 1932-**

NAYLOR, Charles, *with Thomas M. Disch*

21965 *New constellations: an anthology of tomorrow's mythologies.* New York: Harper & Row, 1976, xiii+192 p., cloth, anth.

21966 *Strangeness: a collection of curious tales.*
New York: Charles Scribner's Sons,
1977, viii+309 p., cloth, anth.

NAYLOR, Doug, *with Rob Grant as* GRANT
NAYLOR

24362 *Better than life.* Harmondsworth, Middlesex, England: Viking, 1990, 229 p.,
cloth, movie. RED DWARF #2.
24363 *Red dwarf.* Harmondsworth, Middlesex,
England: Penguin Books, 1989, 298 p.,
paper, movie. RED DWARF #1.

NAYLOR, Grant, pseud.—SEE: Grant, Rob &
Naylor, Doug

NAYLOR, Phyllis Reynolds, 1933-

30585 *Bernie and the Bessledorf ghost.* New
York: Atheneum, A Jean Karl Book,
1990, 132 p., cloth, novel. BESSLEDORF
#2.
30586 *The bodies in the Bessledorf hotel.* New
York: Atheneum, 1986, 132 p., cloth,
novel. BESSLEDORF #1.
30587 *Faces in the water.* New York:
Atheneum, 1981, 167 p., cloth, novel.
YORK TRILOGY #2.
30588 *Footprints at the window.* New York:
Atheneum, 1981, vii+167 p., cloth,
novel. YORK TRILOGY #3.
30589 *Shadows on the wall.* New York:
Atheneum, 1980, 165 p., cloth, novel.
YORK TRILOGY #1.
30590 *The witch herself.* New York: Atheneum,
1978, 164 p., cloth, novel. WITCH'S
SISTER #3.
30591 *Witch water.* New York: Atheneum,
1977, 179 p., cloth, novel. WITCH'S
SISTER #2.
30592 *Witch weed.* New York: Delacorte Press,
1991, 181 p., cloth, novel. WITCH'S
SISTER #5.
30593 *The witch's eye.* New York: Delacorte
Press, 1990, 179 p., cloth, novel.
WITCH'S SISTER #4.
30594 *Witch's sister.* New York: Atheneum,
1975, 150 p., cloth, novel. WITCH'S
SISTER #1.

NAZEL, Joe [i.e., Joseph Nazel]

30595 *The black exorcist.* Los Angeles: Holloway House, 1974, 224 p., paper, novel.
30596 *Satan's master.* Los Angeles, CA: Holloway House, 1974, 224 p., paper, novel.

NAZEL, Joseph—SEE: Nazel, Joe

NEALE, Walter, 1873-1933

30597 *Life of Ambrose Bierce.* New York: Walter Neale, 1929, 489 p., cloth, nonf.

NEBRENSKY, Alex, pseud.—SEE: Cooper,
Parley J.

NEE, David C.—SEE: Nee, Dave

NEE, Dave [i.e., David Chin-Kuo Nee], 1953-

30598 *Michael Bishop: a preliminary bibliography.* Berkeley, CA: The Other Change
of Hobbit, 1983, ii+34 p., paper, nonf.
[Includes 4-page supplement].
30599 *Thomas M. Disch: a preliminary bibliography.* Berkeley, CA: The Other Change
of Hobbit, 1982, ii+30 p., paper, nonf.
[Limited to 125 copies].

NEEDLEMAN, Jacob, 1934-

30600 *The sorcerers: a novel.* San Francisco:
Mercury House, 1986, 235 p., cloth,
novel.

NEEDLEMAN, Rafe

30601 *The official Star Trek trivia book.* New
York: Pocket Books, 1980, 205 p., paper, nonf.

NEEPER, Carolyn A.—SEE: Neeper, Cary

NEEPER, Cary [i.e., Carolyn A. Neeper], 1937-

30602 *A place beyond man.* New York: Charles
Scribner's Sons, 1975, 270 p., cloth,
novel.

NEGLEY, Glenn (Robert), 1907-1988

30603 *Utopia collection of the Duke University
Library.* Durham, NC: Friends of Duke
University Library, 1965, iii+83 p., paper, nonf.
30604 *Utopian literature: a bibliography, with a
supplementary listing of works influential
in utopian thought.* Durham, NC:
Friends of the Library, Duke University,
1975, ca. 250 leaves, paper, nonf.
30605 *Utopian literature: a bibliography, with a
supplementary listing of works influential
in utopian thought.* Lawrence, KS: The
Regents Press of Kansas, 1977,
xxiii+228 p., cloth, nonf. [Expanded
edition].

NEIDERMAN, Andrew, 1940-

30606 *Bloodchild.* New York: Berkley Books, 1990, 268 p., paper, novel.

30607 *Child's play.* New York: Zebra Books, Kensington Publishing Corp., 1985, 302 p., paper, novel.

30608 *The devil's advocate.* New York, London: Pocket Books, 1990, 313 p., paper, novel.

30609 *Illusion.* Toronto, New York: Worldwide, 1987, 285 p., paper, novel.

30610 *The immortals.* New York: Pocket Star Books, 1991, 281 p., paper, novel.

30611 *Imp.* London: Arrow Books, 1986, 314 p., paper, novel.

30612 *Love child.* New York: Tor Horror, A Tom Doherty Associates Book, 1986, 319 p., paper, novel.

30613 *Night howl.* New York: Pocket Books, 1986, 277 p., paper, novel.

30614 *Perfect little angels.* New York: Berkley Books, 1989, 262 p., paper, novel.

30615 *Playmates.* New York: Berkley Books, 1987, 312 p., paper, novel.

30616 *Reflection.* Toronto, New York: Worldwide, 1987, 378 p., paper, novel.

30617 *Sight unseen.* New York: Zebra Books, Kensington Publishing Corp., 1987, 283 p., paper, novel.

30618 *Surrogate child.* New York: Berkley Books, 1988, 294 p., paper, novel.

30619 *Teacher's pet.* New York: Zebra Books, Kensington Publishing Corp., 1986, 319 p., paper, novel.

NEILL, Peter, 1941-

30620 *Acoma: a novel.* New Haven, CT: Leete's Island Books, 1978, 143 p., paper, novel.

NEILSON, Eric

30621 *The golden ax.* Toronto, New York: Bantam Books, 1984, 210 p., paper, novel. HAAKON #1.

37989 *Haakon's iron hand.* Toronto, New York: Bantam Books, 1984, 199 p., paper, novel. HAAKON #3.

30622 *The viking's revenge.* Toronto, New York: Bantam Books, 1984, 213 p., paper, novel. HAAKON #2.

30623 *The war god.* Toronto, New York: Bantam Books, 1984, 231 p., paper, novel. HAAKON #4.

NEILSON, Keith (Townsend Olaf), 1935- , *with Frank N. Magill*

28894 *Survey of modern fantasy literature.* Englewood Cliffs, NJ: Salem Press, 1983, xviii+2538+li p. in 5 v., cloth, nonf. anth.

28895 *Survey of science fiction literature: five hundred 2,000-word essay reviews of world-famous science fiction novels with 2,500 bibliographical references.* Englewood Cliffs, NJ: Salem Press, 1979, xxv+2542+vii p. in 5 v., cloth, nonf. anth.

NEILSON, Marguerite [pseud. of Julia Marguerite Hunter Manchee Tompkins], 1909-

30624 *The bride of Alberburn.* London: Allan Wingate, 1976, 253 p., cloth, novel.

NELSON, Alan, 1911-1966

30625 *Doctor Departure, and others.* Brooklyn, NY: Gryphon Books, 1989, 53 p., paper, coll.

NELSON, Chris, *with Gordon Benson Jr.*

17812 *Bob Shaw: a working bibliography.* Albuquerque, NM: Galactic Central Publications, 1984, 8 p., paper, nonf.

NELSON, John, 1947-

30626 *Starborn: a mystical tale.* Virginia Beach, VA: Donning Co., 1978, 115 p., paper, novel.

NELSON, O. T(erry), 1941-

30627 *The girl who owned a city.* Minneapolis, MN: Lerner Publications Co., 1975, 179 p., cloth, novel.

NELSON, Radell—SEE: Nelson, Ray Faraday

NELSON, Ray Faraday [i.e., Radell Faraday Nelson], 1931-

30628 *Blake's progress* / by R. F. Nelson. Toronto, New York: Laser Books, 1975, 190 p., paper, novel.

30629 retitled: *Timequest.* New York: Tor SF, A Tom Doherty Associates Book, 1985, 286 p., paper, novel. [Revised and rewritten edition].

30630 *The ecolog.* Toronto, New York: Laser Books, 1977, 190 p., paper, novel.

30631 *The Prometheus man: a Nrobook.* Norfolk/Virginia Beach, VA: Starblaze Editions/Donning, 1982, 233 p., paper, novel. TIMEBINDER #1.

30632 *The revolt of the unemployables.* San Francisco: Anthelion Press, 1978, 134 p., paper, novel. TIMEBINDER #2.

30633 *Then beggars could ride* / by R. F. Nelson. Toronto, New York: Laser Books, 1976, 190 p., paper, novel. BEGGARS #1.
Timequest—SEE: *Blake's progress.*

as JEFFREY LORD

Dimension of horror—SEE: *Richard Blade: Dimension of horror.*

28534 *Richard Blade: Dimension of horror.* Los Angeles: Pinnacle Books, 1979, 174 p., paper, novel. RICHARD BLADE #30.

NERI, Penelope

30634 *Forever and beyond.* New York: Zebra Books, Kensington Publishing Corp., 1990, 480 p., paper, novel.

NESBIT, E(dith), 1858-1924

30635 *E. Nesbit's tales of terror.* London: Methuen, 1983, 126 p., cloth, coll. [Edited by Hugh Lamb].

15846 *Harding's luck.* London: Hodder & Stoughton, 1909, 281 p., cloth, novel. ARDEN #2.

15847 *The house of Arden: a story for children.* London: T. Fisher Unwin, 1908, 349 p., cloth, novel. ARDEN #1.

30636 *In the dark: tales of terror by E. Nesbit.* Wellingborough, Northants.: Equation, 1988, 176 p., paper, coll. [Edited by Hugh Lamb].

15848 *Wet magic.* London: T. Werner Laurie, 1913, 274 p., cloth, novel.

NESMITH, Bruce, *with Douglas Niles & Ken Rolston*

30637 *Lankhmar, city of adventure.* Lake Geneva, WI: TSR Inc., 1985, 95 p., paper, novel. FAFHRD & GREY MOUSER.

*NETHERCLIFT, Beryl (Constance), 1911-

NETTER, Susan

30638 *Storm child.* New York: Twilight/Dell, 1983, 150 p., paper, novel. TWILIGHT #17.

NEUFELD, Roger (A.), *with Lloyd Siemans*

30639 *The critical reception of Sir Henry Rider Haggard: an annotated bibliography, 1882-1991.* Greensboro, NC: University of North Carolina at Greensboro, 1991, v+122 p., paper?, nonf.

NEUGROSCHEL, Joachim

Great tales of Jewish occult and fantasy—SEE: *Yenne velt.*
Great works of Jewish fantasy—SEE: *Yenne velt.*
The great works of Jewish fantasy and occult—SEE: *Yenne velt.*

30640 *Yenne velt: the great works of Jewish fantasy and occult.* New York: Stonehill Publishing Co., 1976, 2 v. [I-xi+353 p.; II-357 p.], cloth, anth.

30640A retitled: *Great works of Jewish fantasy.* London: Cassell, 1976, xiii+713 p., cloth, anth.

30640B retitled: *The great works of Jewish fantasy and occult.* Woodstock, NY: Overlook Press, 1986, x+709 p., cloth, anth.

30640C retitled: *The great tales of Jewish occult and fantasy: the dybbuk and 30 other classic stories.* New York: Wings, 1991, x+709 p., cloth, anth.

NEUMANN, Bonnie (Helen) Rayford, 1942-

30641 *The lonely muse: a critical biography of Mary Shelley.* Salzburg, Austria: Institut für Anglistik und Amerikanistik, Universität Salzburg, 1979, 283 p., paper, nonf.

NEVILLE, Katherine, 1945-

30642 *The Eight: a novel.* New York: Ballantine Books, 1989, 550 p., cloth, novel.

NEVILLE, Kris (Ottman), 1925-1980

30643 *The science fiction of Kris Neville.* Carbondale, IL: Southern Illinois University Press, 1984, x+241 p., cloth, coll. [Edited by Barry N. Malzberg & Martin H. Greenberg].

NEVILLE, Robert, pseud.—SEE: Hutson, Shaun

NEVINS, Francis M(ichael) Jr., 1943- , *with Martin H. Greenberg*

24549 *Hitchcock in prime time.* New York: Avon, 1985, 356 p., paper, anth.

NEWARK, T(imothy) P., 1961-

30644 *The land of eternal fire.* London: Frederick Muller, 1990, 232 p., cloth, novel. FALLING EMPIRES #1.

NEWBY, P(ercy) H(oward), 1918-

30645 *Leaning in the wind.* London: Faber & Faber, 1986, 235 p., cloth, novel.

NEWCOMER, Alan Bard, 1946-

30646 *Bardic voices one.* Eugene, OR: Hypatia Press, 1988, 183 p., cloth, anth. [Only 50 copies were produced, although the book itself erroneously states that 825 copies were printed].

30646A retitled: *Spell singers.* New York: DAW Books, 1988, 236 p., paper, anth.
Spell singers—SEE: *Bardic voices one.*

30647 *Strained relations: Eugene writers series one, 1989.* Eugene, OR: Hypatia Press, 1989, 130 p., cloth, anth. [Roughly 155 copies were produced, despite the larger limitation cited in the books].

NEWELL, Neil K., 1953-

30648 *The reluctant wizard.* New York: Manor Books, 1979, 267 p., paper, novel.

*NEWMAN, Howard, 1911-1977

NEWMAN, John, 1942- , *with Michael Unsworth*

30649 *Future war novels: an annotated bibliography of works in English published since 1946.* Phoenix, AZ: Oryx Press, 1984, x+101 p., cloth, nonf.

NEWMAN, Kim (James), 1959-

30650 *Bad dreams.* London, Sydney: Simon & Schuster, 1990, 280 p., cloth, novel.

30651 *Jago.* London, Sydney: Simon & Schuster, 1991, 534 p., cloth, novel.

30652 *The Night Mayor.* London, Sydney: Simon & Schuster, 1989, 186 p., cloth, novel.

30653 *Nightmare movies: wide screen horror since 1968.* New York: Proteus Publishing, 1984, [160] p., paper, nonf.

30654 *Nightmare movies: a critical history of the horror film, 1968-1988, 2nd ed.* London: Bloomsbury, 1988, 256 p., cloth, nonf.

as JACK YEOVIL

Beasts in velvet—SEE: *Warhammer: Beasts in velvet.*
Comeback tour—SEE: *Dark future: Comeback tour: (the sky belongs to the stars).*

30655 *Dark future: Comeback tour: (the sky belongs to the stars).* Brighton, East Sus-

sex, England: GW Books, 1991, 234 p., paper, novel. DARK FUTURE SERIES—DEMON DOWNLOAD #3.

30656 *Dark future: Demon download.* Brighton, East Sussex, England: GW Books, 1990, 253 p., paper, novel. DARK FUTURE SERIES—DEMON DOWNLOAD #1.

30657 *Dark future: Krokodil tears.* Brighton, East Sussex, England: GW Books, 1991, 258 p., paper, novel. DARK FUTURE SERIES—DEMON DOWNLOAD #2.
Demon download—SEE: *Dark future: Demon download.*
Drachenfels—SEE: *Warhammer: Drachenfels.*
Krokodil tears—SEE: *Dark future: Krokodil tears.*

30658 *Warhammer: Beasts in velvet.* Brighton, East Sussex, England: GW Books, 1991, 269 p., paper, novel. WARHAMMER SERIES.

30659 *Warhammer: Drachenfels.* Brighton, East Sussex, England: GW Books, 1989, 247 p., paper, novel. WARHAMMER SERIES.

with Neil Gaiman

23605 *Ghastly beyond belief.* London: Arrow Books, 1985, 343 p., paper, anth.

with Stephen Jones

26763 *Horror: 100 best books.* London: Xanadu, 1988, x+256 p., cloth, nonf. [Winner of the Bram Stoker Award for Best Horror Nonfiction Book, 1989 (1990)].

NEWMAN, Marc

37990 *Longhorn territory.* Toronto, New York: Bantam Books, 1987, 113 p., paper, fiction. CHOOSE YOUR OWN ADVENTURE #74.

NEWMAN, Paul, 1945- , *with John Moorhouse*

30195 *Colin Wilson: two essays: The English existentialist; and, Spiders and outsiders: (including an interview with the author).* Nottingham, England: Paupers' Press, 1989, 49 p., paper, nonf. coll.

NEWMAN, Richard Louis

30660 *On wings of evil.* New York: Leisure Books, 1988, 367 p., paper, novel.

30661 *Siege of Orbitor.* New York: Leisure Books, 1980, 254 p., paper, novel.

NEWMAN, Robert (Howard), 1909-1988

30662 *Night spell.* New York: Atheneum, 1977, 189 p., cloth, novel.
30663 *The shattered stone.* New York: Atheneum, 1975, 231 p., cloth, novel.

NEWMAN, Robert D(ouglas), 1951-

30664 *Understanding Thomas Pynchon.* Columbia, SC: University of South Carolina Press, 1986, viii+155 p., cloth, nonf.

NEWMAN, Sharan (Elizabeth Hill), 1949-

30665 *The chessboard queen.* New York: St. Martin's Press, 1983, 296 p., cloth, novel. GUINEVERE TRILOGY #2.
30666 *The Dagda's harp.* New York: St. Martin's Press, 1976, 187 p., cloth, novel.
30667 *Guinevere.* New York: St. Martin's Press, 1981, 256 p., cloth, novel. GUINEVERE TRILOGY #1.
30668 *Guinevere Evermore.* New York: St. Martin's Press, 1985, 277 p., cloth, novel. GUINEVERE TRILOGY #3.

NEWNHAM, Yve, *with Dave Morris*

30295 *Castle of Lost Souls.* London: Dragon Books, 1985, [170] p., paper, novel. GOLDEN DRAGON FANTASY GAMEBOOKS #6.

NEWTON, Bryan

30669 *Horror stories.* London: Ward Lock Educational, 1978, 127 p., cloth, anth.
30670 *Spook: stories of the unusual.* London: Collins Educational, 1985, 105 p., cloth, anth.

NEWTON, Julius P.

The forgotten planet—SEE: *The forgotten race.*
10668 *The forgotten race.* London: Digit Books, 1963, 158 p., paper, novel.
10668A retitled: *The forgotten planet.* Australia: Bill Ewington Books, 1973, 157 p., paper, novel.

NEWTON, Michael, 1951- , *as* DON PENDLETON

31430 *Mack Bolan: Paradine's gauntlet.* Toronto: A Gold Eagle Book, Worldwide, 1983, 183 p., paper, novel. MACK BOLAN SERIES.

NEYLAND, James (Elwyn), 1939-

30671 *The official Battlestar Galactica scrapbook.* New York: Grosset & Dunlap, 1978, 101 p., paper, nonf.

NICHOLAS, Anna (Katherine), 1917-

30672 *Out of the past: the Indiana ghost stories of Anna Nicholas.* England?: Ghost Story Society, 1991, 30 p., paper, coll.

NICHOLLS, Christopher

30673 *Stolen property.* London: The Bodley Head, 1989, 144 p., cloth, novel.

NICHOLLS, Peter (Douglas), 1939-

Explorations of the marvellous—SEE: *Science fiction at large.*
30674 *Fantastic cinema: an illustrated survey.* London: Ebury, 1984, 224 p., cloth, nonf.
30674A retitled: *The world of fantastic films.* New York: Dodd, Mead & Co., 1984, 224 p., cloth, nonf.
30675 *Science fiction at large: a collection of essays, by various hands, about the interface between science fiction and reality.* London: Victor Gollancz, 1976, 224 p., cloth, nonf. anth.
30675A retitled: *Explorations of the marvellous: the science and the fiction in science fiction.* London: Fontana/Collins, 1978, 224 p., paper, nonf. anth.
The world of fantastic films—SEE: *Fantastic cinema.*

with John Clute

20206 *The encyclopedia of science fiction: an illustrated A to Z.* London, Toronto: Granada, 1979, 672 p., cloth, nonf. anth. [Winner of the Hugo Award for Best Nonfiction Book, 1979 (1980); winner of the *Locus* Award for Best Nonfiction Book, 1979 (1980)].
20206A retitled: *The science fiction encyclopedia.* Garden City, NY: Doubleday & Co., 1979, 672 p., cloth, nonf. anth.
The science fiction encyclopedia—SEE: *The encyclopedia of science fiction.*

with Brian M. Stableford & David Langford

27798 *The science in science fiction.* London: Michael Joseph, 1982, 208 p., cloth, nonf.

NICHOLS, (John) Beverley, 1898-1983

30676 *The mountain of magic: a romance for children.* London: Jonathan Cape, 1950, 302 p., cloth, novel.

30677 *The stream that stood still.* London: Jonathan Cape, 1948, 218 p., cloth, novel.

30678 *The tree that sat down.* London: Jonathan Cape, 1945, 302 p., cloth, novel.

NICHOLS, Jerry, *with The Brothers Hildebrandt*

25620 *Urshurak.* Toronto, New York: Bantam Books, 1979, 405 p., paper, novel.

NICHOLS, Leigh, pseud.—SEE: Koontz, Dean R.

NICHOLS, Robert (Malise Bowyer Jr.), 1919-

30679 *Arrival.* New York: A New Directions Book, 1977, 54 p., paper, fiction. DAILY LIVES IN NGHSI-ALTAI #1.

30680 *Exile.* New York: A New Directions Book, 1979, 108 p., paper, novel. DAILY LIVES IN NGHSI-ALTAI #4.

30681 *Gahr City.* New York: A New Directions Book, 1978, 89 p., paper, fiction. DAILY LIVES IN NGHSI-ALTAI #2.

30682 *The Harditts in Sawna.* New York: A New Directions Book, 1979, 113 p., paper, novel. DAILY LIVES IN NGHSI-ALTAI #3.

with Peter Schumann

30683 *Red shift: an introduction to Ngshi-Altai.* Thetford, VT: Penny Each Press, 1977, p., paper, novel. DAILY LIVES IN NGHSI-ALTAI SERIES.

NICHOLS, (Joanna) Ruth, 1948-

30684 *The burning of the rose.* New York: St. Martin's Press, 1989, 341 p., cloth, novel.

30685 *Song of the pearl.* New York: A Margaret K. McElderry Book, Atheneum, 1976, 158 p., cloth, novel.

NICHOLSON, Malcolm Wheeler- —SEE: Wheeler-Nicholson, Malcolm

NICHOLSON, Norman (Cornthwaite), 1914-1987

30686 *H. G. Wells.* London: Arthur Barker, 1950, 105 p., cloth, nonf.

NICHOLSON, Sam [pseud. of Shirley Nikolaisen]

30687 *Captain Empirical.* New York: Ace Books, 1979, 342 p., paper, novel.

30688 *The Light Bearer.* New York: Berkley Books, 1980, 217 p., paper, novel.

NICKELS, Thom

30689 *Walking water; After all this: two novellas.* Austin, TX: Banned Books, 1989, 170 p., paper, coll.

NICOLE, Christopher (Robin), 1930- , *with Diana Backman as* MAX MARLOW

17161 *Meltdown.* London: New English Library, 1991, 286 p., cloth, novel.

17162 *The red death.* London: New English Library, 1989, 347 p., cloth, novel.

NICOLE, Claudette, pseud.—SEE: Messmann, Jon

*NICOLSON, Marjorie (Hope), 1894-1981

NIEBELSCHUTZ, Wolf (Friedrich Magnus) von, 1913-1960

30690 *The badger of Ghissi.* London: George Allen & Unwin, 1963, 261 p., cloth, novel. [Translation by Barrows Mussey of the first part of *Die kinder der Finsternis*].

NIESEWAND, Peter, 1944-1983

30691 *Fallback.* New York: William Morrow & Co., 1982, 417 p., cloth, novel.

NIGHBERT, David F.

30692 *The clouds of Magellan: a science-fiction novel.* New York: St. Martin's Press, 1991, 308 p., cloth, novel. STRYKER #2.

30693 *Timelapse.* New York: St. Martin's Press, 1988, 294 p., cloth, novel. STRYKER #1.

NIGHTINGALE, Anne Redmon—SEE: Redmon, Anne

NIKOLAISEN, Shirley—SEE: Nicholson, Sam

NIKOLAJEVA, Maria

30694 *Magic code: use of magical patterns in fantasy for children.* Stockholm, Sweden: Almqvist & Wiksell International, 1988, 163 p., paper, nonf.

NILAND, Rosina R.—SEE: Park, Ruth

NILE, Dorothea, pseud.—SEE: Avallone, Michael

NILES, Douglas

Black wizards—SEE: *Forgotten realms fan-tasy adventure: Black wizards.*
Darkwalker on Moonshae—SEE: *Forgotten realms fantasy adventure: Darkwalker on Moonshae.*
Darkwell—SEE: *Forgotten realms fantasy adventure: Darkwell.*
30695 *The DragonLance saga: The kinslayer wars.* Lake Geneva, WI: TSR Inc., 1991, 314 p., paper, novel. DRAGON-LANCE—ELVEN NATIONS TRILOGY #2.
30696 *Dungeoneer's survival guide: a sourcebook for Advanced Dungeons & Dragons game adventures in the unknown depts of Underdark!* Lake Geneva, WI: TSR Inc., 1986, 128 p., paper, nonf.
30697 *Escape from Castle Quarras.* Lake Geneva, WI: TSR Inc., 1985, 189 p., paper, novel. SUPER ENDLESS QUEST ADVENTURE GAMEBOOK #3.
Feathered dragon—SEE: *Forgotten realms fantasy adventure: Feathered dragon.*
30698 *Forgotten realms fantasy adventure: Black wizards.* Lake Geneva, WI: TSR Inc., 1988, 347 p., paper, novel. MOONSHAE TRILOGY #2.
30699 *Forgotten realms fantasy adventure: Dark-walker on Moonshae.* Lake Geneva, WI: TSR Inc., 1987, 380 p., paper, novel. MOONSHAE TRILOGY #1.
30700 *Forgotten realms fantasy adventure: Dark-well.* Lake Geneva, WI: TSR Inc., 1989, 345 p., paper, novel. MOONSHAE TRILOGY #3.
30701 *Forgotten realms fantasy adventure: Feath-ered dragon.* Lake Geneva, WI: TSR Inc., 1991, 316 p., paper, novel. MAZTICA TRILOGY #3.
30702 *Forgotten realms fantasy adventure: Iron-helm.* Lake Geneva, WI: TSR Inc., 1990, 314 p., paper, novel. MAZTICA TRILOGY #1.
30703 *Forgotten realms fantasy adventure: Viper-hand.* Lake Geneva, WI: TSR Inc., 1990, 313 p., paper, novel. MAZTICA TRILOGY #2.
Ironhelm—SEE: *Forgotten realms fantasy adventure: Ironhelm.*
The kinslayer wars—SEE: *Dragonlance saga: The kinslayer wars.*
30704 *Lords of doom: a Dragonlance adventure.* Lake Geneva, WI: TSR Inc., 1986, 160 p., paper, novel. ADVANCED DUNGEONS & DRAGONS ADVENTURE GAMEBOOK #10.
30705 *Tarzan and the well of slaves.* Lake Geneva, WI: TSR Inc., 1985, 157 p., paper, novel. ENDLESS QUEST #26—TARZAN SERIES.
Viperhand—SEE: *Forgotten realms fantasy adventure: Viperhand.*

with Mary Kirchoff

27314 *Flint the king.* Lake Geneva, WI: TSR Inc., 1990, 308 p., paper, novel. DRAG-ONLANCE PRELUDES II #2.

with Bruce Nesmith & Ken Rolston

30706 *Lankhmar, city of adventure.* Lake Geneva, WI: TSR Inc., 1985, 95 p., paper, novel. FAFHRD & GREY MOUSER.

NILES, P. H.

30707 *The science fiction of H. G. Wells: a con-cise guide.* Clifton Park, NY: Auriga, 1980, 58 p., paper, nonf.

NILES, Steve

30708 *Words without pictures.* Forestville, CA: Arcane/Eclipse Books, 1990, iii+180 p., cloth, anth. [Includes some verse].

NIM, P. S.

30709 *Double Mobius sphere: a story of the shape of the universe.* New York: Pocket Books, 1978, 263 p., paper, novel.

NIMMO, Dan (Dean), 1933- , with James Combs & Robert L. Savage

20350 *The Orwellian moment: hindsight and fore-sight in the post-1984 world.* Fayet-teville, AR: University of Arkansas Press, 1989, viii+180 p., cloth, nonf. anth.

NIMMO, Jenny, 1942-

30710 *The chestnut spider.* London: Methuen, 1989, 168 p., cloth, novel. SNOW SPIDER #3.
30711 *Emlyn's moon.* London: Methuen, 1987, 144 p., cloth, novel. SNOW SPIDER #2.
30711A retitled: *Orchard of the crescent moon.* New York: E. P. Dutton, 1989, 170 p., cloth, novel. SNOW SPIDER #2.
Orchard of the crescent moon—SEE: *Em-lyn's moon.*

30712 *Snow spider*. London: Methuen, 1986, 144 p., cloth, novel. SNOW SPIDER #1.

30713 *Ultramarine*. London: Methuen Children's Books, 1990, [176] p., cloth, novel.

NIMOY, Leonard, 1931-

30714 *I am not Spock*. Millbrae, CA: Celestial Arts, 1975, 135 p., cloth, nonf.

NIÑO, Alex

30715 *Satan's tears: the art of Alex Niño*. Detroit, MI: Land of Enchantment, 1977, 301 p., cloth, art. [Edited by Christopher Zavisa and Orvy Jundis].

NISBET, Helen C.

30716 *The raven's beak*. London: Robert Hale, 1979, 159 p., cloth, novel.

NISBET, Hugh A.

30717 *Farewell to Krondahl*. London: Robert Hale, 1980, 192 p., cloth, novel.

NITCHIE, Elizabeth, 1889-

30718 *Mary Shelley, author of "Frankenstein"*. New Brunswick, NJ: Rutgers University Press, 1953, xiv+255 p., cloth, nonf.

NITZSCHE, Jane Chance, 1945-

30719 *Tolkien's art: a 'mythology for England'*. London: Macmillan, 1979, x+164 p., cloth, nonf.

NIVEN, Larry [i.e., Laurence Van Cott Niven], 1938-

30720 *Convergent series*. New York: A Del Rey Book, Ballantine Books, 1979, 227 p., paper, coll. KNOWN SPACE SERIES. [Winner of the *Locus* Award for Best Collection, 1979 (1980)].

30721 *The integral trees*. New York: A Del Rey Book, Ballantine Books, 1984, 240 p., cloth, novel. KNOWN SPACE SERIES—TREES #1. [Winner of the *Locus* Award for Best Science Fiction Novel, 1984 (1985)].

30722 *Limits*. New York: A Del Rey Book, Ballantine Books, 1985, xi+240 p., paper, coll.

30723 *The long ARM of Gil Hamilton*. New York: Ballantine Books, 1976, 182 p., paper, coll. KNOWN SPACE SERIES—GIL HAMILTON #1.

30724 *The magic goes away*. New York: Ace Books, 1978, 213 p., paper, novel. MAGIC #1.

30725 *The magic may return*. New York: Ace Books, 1981, 255 p., paper, anth. MAGIC #2.

30726 *Man-Kzin wars IV*. New York: Baen Books, 1991, 311 p., paper, anth. MAN-KZIN WARS #4.

30727 *More magic*. New York: Berkley Books, 1984, 197 p., paper, anth. MAGIC #3.

30728 *Niven's laws*. Philadelphia, PA: Philadelphia Science Fiction Society, 1984, vii+108 p., cloth, coll. KNOWN SPACE SERIES.

30729 *N-space*. New York: Tor, A Tom Doherty Associates Book, 1990, vi+529 p., cloth, coll. KNOWN SPACE SERIES. [Includes some nonfiction].

30730 *The patchwork girl*. New York: Ace Books, 1980, 206 p., paper, novel. KNOWN SPACE SERIES—GIL HAMILTON #2.

30731 *Playgrounds of the mind*. New York: Tor, A Tom Doherty Associates Book, 1991, 487 p., cloth, coll. KNOWN SPACE SERIES. [Includes some nonfiction].

30732 *The Ringworld engineers*. West Bloomfield, MI: Phantasia Press, 1979, viii+355 p., cloth, novel. KNOWN SPACE SERIES—RINGWORLD #2.

30733 *The smoke ring*. New York: A Del Rey Book, Ballantine Books, 1987, 362 p., cloth, novel. KNOWN SPACE SERIES—TREES #2.

30734 *Tales of known space: the universe of Larry Niven*. New York: Ballantine Books, 1975, xiv+240 p., paper, coll. KNOWN SPACE SERIES.

30735 *The time of the warlock*. Minneapolis, MN: SteelDragon Press, 1984, 183 p., cloth, coll. MAGIC #3. [Includes *The magic goes away*].

30736 *World of Ptavvs; A gift from Earth; Neutron star*. New York: Book-of-the-Month Club, 1991, 160+254+285 p., paper, coll. KNOWN SPACE #1-3.

30737 *A world out of time: a novel*. New York: Holt, Rinehart & Winston, 1976, 243 p., cloth, novel.

with Poul Anderson & Dean Ing

16454 *The Man-Kzin wars*. New York: Baen Books, 1988, 289 p., paper, coll. MAN-KZIN WARS #1.

with Steven Barnes

17428 *Achilles' choice.* New York: Tor, A Tom Doherty Associates Book, 1991, 214 p., cloth, novel.

17429 *The Barsoom project.* New York: Ace Books, 1989, 340 p., paper, novel. DREAM PARK #2.

17430 *The beehive game.* London & Sydney: Pan Books, 1991, 320 p., paper, novel.

17431 *The descent of Anansi.* New York: Tor, A Tom Doherty Associates Book, 1982, 278 p., paper, novel.

17432 *Dream Park.* Huntington Woods, MI: Phantasia Press, 1981, 434 p., cloth, novel. DREAM PARK #1. [Limited to 600 copies].

17433 *Dream Park: The voodoo game.* London & Sydney: Pan Books, 1991, 350 p., paper, novel. DREAM PARK #3.

The voodoo game—SEE: *Dream Park: The voodoo game.*

with Steven Barnes & Jerry Pournelle

17434 *The legacy of Heorot.* London: Victor Gollancz, 1987, 352 p., cloth, novel. HEOROT SERIES.

with Jerry Pournelle

30738 *Footfall.* New York: A Del Rey Book, Ballantine Books, 1985, xxiii+495 p., cloth, novel.

30739 *Inferno.* New York: Pocket Books, 1976, 237 p., paper, novel.

30740 *Lucifer's hammer.* Chicago: Playboy Press Book, 1977, x+494 p., cloth, novel.

30741 *Oath of fealty.* Huntington Woods, MI: Phantasia Press, 1981, 328 p., cloth, novel. [Limited to 750 copies].

with Jerry Pournelle & Michael Flynn

23220 *Fallen angels.* Norwalk, CT: Easton Press, 1991, 394 p., paper, novel.

with Jerry Pournelle & John Eric Holmes

25871 *Mordred.* New York: Ace Books, 1980, 216 p., paper, novel. BUCK ROGERS #2. [Sequel to *Armageddon: 2419 AD*].

with Jerry Pournelle & Richard S. McEnroe

29516 *Warrior's blood.* New York: Ace Books, 1981, 311 p., paper, novel. BUCK ROGERS #3.

29517 *Warrior's world.* New York: Ace Books, 1981, 199 p., paper, novel. BUCK ROGERS #4.

with Jerry Pournelle & John Silbersack

30742 *Rogers' Rangers.* New York: Ace Science Fiction Books, 1983, 235 p., paper, novel. BUCK ROGERS #5.

with Jerry Pournelle & S. M. Stirling & Poul Anderson

16455 *The Man-Kzin wars III.* New York: Baen Books, 1990, 310 p., paper, coll. MAN-KZIN WARS #3.

with Jerry Pournelle & S. M. Stirling & Dean Ing

26289 *The Man-Kzin wars II.* New York: Baen Books, 1989, ix+306 p., paper, coll. MAN-KZIN WARS #2.

NIVEN, Laurence V. C.—SEE: Niven, Larry

NIXON, Joan Lowery, 1927-

30743 *A deadly game of magic.* San Diego, CA: Harcourt Brace Jovanovich, 1983, 148 p., cloth, novel.

30744 *Haunted island.* New York, Toronto: An Apple Paperback, Scholastic Inc., 1987, 123 p., paper, novel.

30745 *The house on Hackman's Hill.* New York, Toronto: An Apple Paperback, Scholastic Inc., 1985, 126 p., paper, novel.

30746 *Whispers from the dead.* New York: Delacorte Press, 1989, 180 p., cloth, novel.

*NIZZI, Guido, 1900-1983

NOAD, Charles E.

30747 *The trees, the jewels, and the rings: a discursive enquiry into things little known on Middle-Earth.* Harrow, England: Tolkien Society, 1977, 44 p., paper, nonf.

NOBES, Patrick, 1933- , with John Wyndham

30748 *Meteor: short stories.* Oxford, England: Oxford University Press, 1991, 106 p., paper, coll. [Adapted by Nobes from several Wyndham tales].

NOBLE, Mark, *with Bob Stickgold*

30750 *Gloryhits.* New York: A Del Rey Book, Ballantine Books, 1978, 296 p., cloth, novel.

NOBLE, Martin, 1947-

30751 *Who framed Roger Rabbit?* London: A Star Book, W. H. Allen & Co., 1988, 147 p., paper, movie. ROGER RABBIT #1.

NOEL, Atanielle Annyn [legalized from Ruth Helen Swycaffer Noel], 1947-

30752 *The Duchess of Kneedeep.* New York: Avon, 1986, 170 p., paper, novel.
30753 *Murder on Usher's Planet.* New York: Avon, 1987, 182 p., paper, novel.
30754 *Speaker to Heaven.* New York: Arbor House, 1987, 279 p., cloth, novel.

as RUTH S. NOEL

30755 *The languages of Tolkien's Middle-Earth.* Baltimore: Houghton Mifflin Co., 1980, 207 p., cloth, nonf.
30756 *The mythology of Middle-Earth.* Boston: Houghton Mifflin Co., 1977, x+198 p., cloth, nonf.

NOEL, Ruth S.—SEE: Noël, Atanielle Annyn

NOESTLINGER, Christine—SEE: Nostlinger, Christine

NOIR, Stephard, pseud.

30757 *Alien plague.* New York: Carlyle, 1979, 224 p., paper, novel.

*NOEL, Sterling, 1903-1984

NOLAN, Madeena Spray, 1943-

30758 *The burning ground.* New York: Pocket Books, 1987, 277 p., paper, novel.
30759 *The gift.* New York: A Dell Book, 1981, 284 p., paper, novel.

NOLAN, William F(rancis), 1928-

30760 *Blood sky.* San Jose, CA: Deadline Publications, 1991, 47 p., paper, nonf. [Limited to 250 copies; an excerpt from the then-forthcoming novel, *Helltracks*].
30761 *Helltracks.* New York: Avon Books, 1991, 248 p., paper, novel.

30762 *How to write horror fiction.* Cincinnati, OH: Writer's Digest Books, 1990, 143 p., cloth, nonf.
30763 *Logan's search.* Toronto, New York: Bantam Books, 1980, 145 p., paper, novel. LOGAN #3.
30764 *Logan's world.* Toronto, New York: Bantam Books, 1977, 149 p., paper, novel. LOGAN #2.
30765 *Look out for Space.* New York: International Polygonics, 1985, 188 p., paper, novel. SAM SPACE #2.
30766 *The Ray Bradbury companion: a life and career history, photolog, and comprehensive checklist of writings, with facsimiles of Ray Bradbury's unpublished and uncollected work in all media.* Detroit, MI: A Bruccoli Clark Book, Gale Research Co., 1975, xiii+339 p, cloth, nonf.
10725 *Ray Bradbury review.* San Diego: William F. Nolan, 1952, 63 p., paper, nonf. anth.
10725A retitled: *William F. Nolan's Ray Bradbury review.* Los Angeles: Graham Press, 1988, [15]+63 p., cloth, anth.
30767 *Things beyond midnight.* Santa Cruz, CA: Scream/Press, 1984, xxiv+217 p., cloth, coll.
William F. Nolan's Ray Bradbury review—SEE: *Ray Bradbury review.*
30768 *Wonderworlds.* London: Victor Gollancz, 1977, 192 p., cloth, coll.
30769 *The work of Charles Beaumont: an annotated bibliography & guide.* San Bernardino, CA: R. Reginald, The Borgo Press, 1986, 48 p., cloth, nonf. BIBLIOGRAPHIES OF MODERN AUTHORS #6. [Edited by Boden Clarke].
30770 *The work of Charles Beaumont: an annotated bibliography & guide, second edition.* San Bernardino, CA: R. Reginald, The Borgo Press, 1990, 92 p., cloth, nonf. BIBLIOGRAPHIES OF MODERN AUTHORS #6. [Expanded edition; edited by Boden Clarke].

as JAMES HOPKINS, *with Boden Clarke*

30771 *The work of William F. Nolan: an annotated bibliography & guide.* San Bernardino, CA: R. Reginald, The Borgo Press, 1988, 224 p., cloth, nonf. BIBLIOGRAPHIES OF MODERN AUTHORS #14.

with Martin H. Greenberg

24550 *The Bradbury chronicles: stories in honor of Ray Bradbury.* New York: A Roc Book, 1991, viii+328 p., cloth, anth. [A festschrift honoring Ray Bradbury].

24551 *Science fiction origins.* New York: Fawcett Popular Library, 1980, 319 p., paper, anth.

24552 *Urban horrors.* Arlington Heights, IL: Dark Harvest, 1990, 246 p., cloth, anth.

with George Clayton Johnson

26608 *Logan: a trilogy.* Baltimore, MD: Maclay & Associates, 1986, 384 p., cloth, coll. LOGAN #1-3.

NOLANE, Richard D.

30772 *Terra SF: the year's best European SF.* New York: DAW Books, 1981, 268 p., paper, anth.

30773 *Terra SF II: the year's best European SF.* New York: DAW Books, 1983, 224 p., paper, anth.

NOLDER, Ann

30774 *Dream of danger.* New York: Tiara Books, 1981, 189 p., paper, novel.

NOLLEN, Scott Allen

30775 *Boris Karloff: a critical account of his screen, stage, radio, television, and recording work.* Jefferson, NC & London: McFarland & Co., 1991, xiii+473 p., cloth, nonf.

NOOTEBOOM, Cees, 1933-

30776 *In the Dutch Mountains: a novel.* Baton Rouge, LA: Louisiana State University Press, 1987, 128 p., cloth, novel. [Translation by Adrienne Dixon of *In Nederland*].

NORDAN, Robert

30777 *Rituals.* New York: Fawcett Gold Medal, 1989, 278 p., paper, novel.

NORDEN, Eric

30778 *Starsongs and unicorns: journeys through time and space.* New York: Manor Books, 1978, 304 p., paper, coll.

NORDSIECK, Graham

30779 *Tales of the unsuspected.* Lewes, East Sussex, England: The Book Guild, 1990, 88 p., cloth, coll.

NORMAN, Barry, 1933-

30780 *End product.* London: Quartet Books, 1975, 248 p., cloth, novel.

NORMAN, Diana

30781 *Fitzempress' law.* London: Hodder & Stoughton, 1980, 284 p., cloth, novel.

NORMAN, Donald N., pseud.—SEE: Stahl, Norman & Horan, Don

NORMAN, Elizabeth [pseud. of William Kummann], 1924-

30782 *Silver, jewels, and jade.* New York: Ballantine Books, 1980, 170 p., paper, novel.

NORMAN, John [pseud. of John Frederick Lange Jr.], 1931-

30783 *Beasts of Gor.* New York: DAW Books, 1978, 444 p., paper, novel. GOR #12.

30784 *Blood brothers of Gor.* New York: DAW Books, 1982, 480 p., paper, novel. GOR #18.

The chieftain—SEE: *The Telnarian histories: The chieftain.*

30785 *Dancer of Gor.* New York: DAW Books, 1985, 479 p., paper, novel. GOR #22.

30786 *Explorers of Gor.* New York: DAW Books, 1979, 464 p., paper, novel. GOR #13.

30787 *Fighting slave of Gor.* New York: DAW Books, 1980, 384 p., paper, novel. GOR #14.

30788 *Guardsman of Gor.* New York: DAW Books, 1981, 304 p., paper, novel. GOR #16.

30789 *Kajira of Gor.* New York: DAW Books, 1983, 446 p., paper, novel. GOR #19.

30790 *Magicians of Gor.* New York: DAW Books, 1988, 492 p., paper, Novel. GOR #25. [Last book in series].

30791 *Marauders of Gor.* New York: DAW Books, 1975, 296 p., paper, Novel. GOR #9.

30792 *Mercenaries of Gor.* New York: DAW Books, 1985, 446 p., paper, novel. GOR #21.

30793 *Players of Gor.* New York: DAW Books, 1984, 396 p., paper, novel. GOR #20.

30794 *Renegades of Gor.* New York: DAW Books, 1986, 444 p., paper, novel. GOR #23.

30795 *Rogue of Gor.* New York: DAW Books, 1981, 318 p., paper, novel. GOR #15.

30796 *Savages of Gor.* New York: DAW Books, 1982, 335 p., paper, novel. GOR #17.

30797 *Slave girl of Gor.* New York: DAW Books, 1977, 446 p., paper, novel. GOR #11.

30798 *The Telnarian histories: The chieftain.* New York: Warner Books, 1991, 294 p., paper, novel. TELNARIAN HISTORIES #1.

30799 *Time slave.* New York: DAW Books, 1975, 380 p., paper, novel.

30800 *Tribesmen of Gor.* New York: DAW Books, 1976, 364 p., paper, novel. GOR #10.

30801 *Vagabonds of Gor.* New York: DAW Books, 1987, 495 p., paper, novel. GOR #24.

NORMAN, Marsha (Williams), 1947-

30802 *The fortune teller.* New York: Random House, 1987, 387 p., cloth, novel.

NORMAN, Roger

30803 *Albion's dream.* London: Faber & Faber, 1990, 184 p., cloth, novel.

NORRIS, Christopher (Charles), 1947-

30804 *Inside the myth: Orwell: views from the left.* London: Lawrence & Wishart, 1984, 287 p., cloth, nonf. anth.

NORRIS, Curtis

Leap of the lion—SEE: *Narnia solo games: Leap of the lion.*

30805 *Narnia solo games: Leap of the lion.* New York: Berkley Books, 1988, [210] p., paper, fiction. NARNIA SOLO GAMES #3.

30806 *Narnia solo games: Return to Deathwater.* New York: Berkley Books, 1988, [188] p., paper, fiction. NARNIA SOLO GAMES #1.

Return to Deathwater—SEE: *Narnia solo games: Return to Deathwater.*

NORRIS, S. D., pseud.—SEE: Mastorakis, Niko

NORTH, David

30807 *Forbidden region: Time warriors.* Toronto, New York: A Gold Eagle Book from Worldwide, 1991, 220 p., paper, novel. TIME WARRIORS #2.

30808 *Fuse point: Time warriors.* Toronto, New York: A Gold Eagle Book from Worldwide, 1991, 221 p., paper, novel. TIME WARRIORS #1.

30809 *The guardian strikes: Time warriors.* Toronto, New York: A Gold Eagle Book from Worldwide, 1991, 218 p., paper, novel. TIME WARRIORS #3.

NORTH, Edmund H(all), 1911-1990, with Franklin Coen

20235 *Meteor.* New York: Warner Books, 1979, 236 p., paper, movie.

NORTH, Eric [pseud. of Bernard Charles Cronin], 1884-1968

37991 *Toad.* London: Hodder & Stoughton, 1929, 320 p., cloth, novel.

NORTH, Rick, house pseud.

30810 *Citizens of Mars.* New York: Zebra Books, Kensington Publishing Corp., 1991, 158 p., paper, novel. YOUNG ASTRONAUTS #6. [By Margaret Wander Bonanno].

30811 *Destination Mars.* New York: Zebra Books, Kensington Publishing Corp., 1991, 172 p., paper, novel. YOUNG ASTRONAUTS #4. [By Margaret Wander Bonanno].

30812 *Jack Anderson presents The young astronauts.* New York: Zebra Books, Kensington Publishing Corp., 1990, 159 p., paper, novel. YOUNG ASTRONAUTS #1. [By S. N. Lewitt].

30813 *Ready for blastoff!* New York: Zebra Books, Kensington Publishing Corp., 1990, 157 p., paper, novel. YOUNG ASTRONAUTS #2. [By John Peel].

30814 *Space blazers.* New York: Zebra Books, Kensington Publishing Corp., 1990, 157 p., paper, novel. YOUNG ASTRONAUTS #3. [By S. N. Lewitt].

30815 *Space pioneers.* New York: Zebra Books, Kensington Publishing Corp., 1991, 174 p., paper, novel. YOUNG ASTRONAUTS #5. [By Mayer Alan Brenner].

The young astronauts—SEE: *Jack Anderson presents The young astronauts.*

NORTHEY, Margot (Elizabeth)

30816 *The haunted wilderness: the gothic and grotesque in Canadian fiction.* Toronto, Buffalo, NY: University of Toronto Press, 1976, 131 p., cloth, nonf.

NORTHROP, Allen C.

30817 *Before the beginning.* New York, Washington: Vantage Press, 1991, 365 p., cloth, novel.

NORTIC, Max, pseud.

30818 *I will return & claim my bed.* New York: Midwood Books, 1982, p. 185-367, paper, novel. [Bound with *Leona's lust /* by Doris Holliday].

NORTON, Alden H(olmes), 1903-1987

NORTON, Alice M.—SEE: Norton, Andre

NORTON, Andre (Alice) [legalized from Alice Mary Norton], 1912-

  The book of Andre Norton—SEE: Many worlds of Andre Norton.
  Crosstime agent—SEE: Quest crosstime.

30819 *Dare to go a-hunting.* New York: Tor, A Tom Doherty Associates Books, 1990, 248 p., cloth, novel. MOON SINGER #2.

30820 *Flight in Yiktor.* New York: Tor, A Tom Doherty Associates Book, 1986, 251 p., cloth, novel. MOON SINGER #3.

30821 *Forerunner.* New York: A Tom Doherty Associates Book, Tor, Pinnacle Books, 1981, 282 p., paper, novel. FORERUNNER #4.

30822 *Forerunner: the second venture.* New York: Tor, A Tom Doherty Associates Book, 1985, 254 p., cloth, novel. FORERUNNER #5.

30823 *Four from the Witch World.* New York: Tor, A Tom Doherty Associates Book, 1989, xi+275 p., cloth, anth. WITCH WORLD #20.

30824 *The gate of the cat.* New York: Ace Books, 1987, 243 p., cloth, novel. WITCH WORLD #19.

30825 *Gryphon in glory.* New York: An Argo Book, A Margaret K. McElderry Book, Atheneum, 1981, 242 p., cloth, novel. WITCH WORLD #13-HIGH HALLACK #5.

30826 *Horn Crown.* New York: DAW Books, 1981, 255 p., paper, novel. WITCH WORLD #14.

30827 *Knave of dreams.* New York: Viking Press, 1975, 252 p., cloth, novel.

30828 *Lore of the Witch World.* New York: DAW Books, 1980, 223 p., paper, coll. WITCH WORLD #12.

30829 *The magic books.* New York: A Signet Book, New American Library, 1988, 383 p., paper, coll. [Includes *Fur magic, Steel magic, Octagon magic*].

10786 *The many worlds of Andre Norton.* Radnor, PA: Chilton Book Co., 1974, 208 p., cloth, coll.

10786A retitled: *The book of Andre Norton.* New York: DAW Books, 1975, 221 p., paper, coll.

30830 *Merlin's mirror.* New York: DAW Books, 1975, 205 p., paper, novel.

30831 *Moon called.* New York: A Wallaby Book, Simon & Schuster, 1982, 301 p., paper, novel.

30832 *Moon mirror.* New York: Tor, A Tom Doherty Associates Book, 1988, 250 p., cloth, coll.

30833 *No night without stars.* New York: A Margaret K. McElderry Book, Atheneum, 1975, 246 p., cloth, novel.

30834 *The opal-eyed fan.* New York: E. P. Dutton, 1977, 212 p., cloth, novel.

30835 *Outside.* New York: Walker & Co., 1975, 126 p., cloth, novel.

30836 *Perilous dreams.* New York: DAW Books, 1976, 199 p., paper, novel.

30837 *Quag Keep.* New York: A Margaret K. McElderry Book, Atheneum, 1978, 224 p., cloth, novel.

10794 *Quest crosstime.* New York: Viking Press, 1965, 253 p., cloth, novel. BLAKE WALKER #2.

10794A retitled: *Crosstime agent.* London: Victor Gollancz, 1975, 253 p., cloth, novel. BLAKE WALKER #2.

30838 *Red Hart magic.* New York: Thomas Y. Crowell, 1976, 179 p., cloth, novel.

10797 *Secret of the lost race.* New York: Ace Books, 1959, 132 p., paper, novel. [Bound with *One against Herculum /* by Jerry Sohl].

10797A retitled: *Wolfshead.* London: Robert Hale, 1977, 157 p., cloth, novel.

30839 *Serpent's tooth.* Winter Park, FL: Andre Norton Ltd., 1987, 52 p., paper, story. WITCH WORLD #18. [Limited to 999 copies].

10809 *Star hunter; &, Voodoo planet.* New York: Ace Books, 1968, 159 p., paper, coll.

10809A retitled: *Voodoo planet; and, Star hunter.* Boston: Gregg Press, 1978, 160 p., paper, coll.

10810 *Star Man's son, 2250 A.D.* New York: Harcourt, Brace & Co., 1952, 248 p., cloth, novel.

10810B retitled: *Star Man's son.* New York: Fawcett Crest, 1978, 224 p., paper, novel.

  Star man's son—SEE: Star man's son, 2250 A.D.

  Tales of the witch world—SEE: Tales of the Witch World 1.

30840 *Tales of the Witch World 1.* New York: Tor, A Tom Doherty Associates Book, 1987, 343 p., cloth, anth.

30840A retitled: *Tales of the witch world.* London & Sydney: Pan Books, 1989, 343 p., paper, anth.

30841 *Tales of the Witch World 2*. New York: Tor, A Tom Doherty Associates Book, 1988, 376 p., cloth, anth.

30842 *Tales of the Witch World 3*. New York: Tor Fantasy, A Tom Doherty Associates Book, 1990, 467 p., cloth, anth.

30843 *Trey of swords*. New York: Grosset & Dunlap, 1977, 180 p., cloth, novel. WITCH WORLD #10.

Voodoo planet; and, Star hunter—SEE: *Star hunter; &, Voodoo planet*.

30844 *Voorloper*. Garden City, New York: Nelson Doubleday, 1980, 214 p., cloth, novel.

30845 *'Ware Hawk*. New York: A Margaret K. McElderry Book, Atheneum, 1983, 214 p., cloth, novel. WITCH WORLD #15.

30846 *Were-Wrath*. New Castle, VA: Cheap Street, 1984, 75 p., cloth, story. WITCH WORLD #16. [Limited to 177 signed and numbered copies].

30847 *Wheel of stars*. New York: A Wallaby Book, Simon & Schuster, 1983, 318 p., paper, novel.

30848 *The white jade fox*. New York: E. P. Dutton, 1975, p., cloth, novel.

30849 *Wizards' worlds*. Norwalk, CT: Easton Press, 1989, 500 p., cloth, coll. [Edited by Ingried Zierhut].

Wolfshead—SEE: *Secret of the lost race*.

30850 *Wraiths of time*. New York: A Margaret K. McElderry Book, Atheneum, 1976, 210 p., cloth, novel.

30851 *Yurth burden*. New York: DAW Books, 1978, 158 p., paper, novel.

30852 *Zarsthor's bane*. New York: Ace Books, 1978, 204 p., paper, novel. WITCH WORLD #11.

with Robert Adams

16024 *Magic in Ithkar*. New York: Tor SF, A Tom Doherty Associates Book, 1985, 317 p., paper, anth.

16024A retitled: *Magic in Ithkar 1*. New York: Tor SF, A Tom Doherty Associates Book, 1988, 317 p., paper, anth.

16025 *Magic in Ithkar 2*. New York: Tor SF, A Tom Doherty Associates Book, 1985, 306 p., paper, anth.

16026 *Magic in Ithkar 3*. New York: Tor SF, A Tom Doherty Associates Book, 1986, 319 p., paper, anth.

16027 *Magic in Ithkar 4*. New York: Tor SF, A Tom Doherty Associates Book, 1987, 278 p., paper, anth.

with Robert Bloch

18197 *The Jekyll legacy*. New York: Tor Horror, A Tom Doherty Associates Book, 1990, 248 p., cloth, novel. DR. JEKYLL & MR. HYDE SEQUEL.

with Marion Zimmer Bradley & Julian May

18493 *Black Trillium*. New York: A Foundation Book, Doubleday, 1990, 409 p., cloth, novel. TRILLIUM #1.

with A. C. Crispin

20816 *Gryphon's eyrie*. New York: Tor, A Tom Doherty Associates Book, 1984, 248 p., cloth, novel. WITCH WORLD #17-HIGH HALLACK #6.

with Michael Gilbert

23928 *The day of the Ness*. New York: Walker & Co., 1975, 119 p., cloth, novel.

with Martin H. Greenberg

24553 *Catfantastic: nine lives and fifteen tales*. New York: DAW Books, 1989, viii+ 320 p., paper, anth.

24554 *Catfantastic II*. New York: DAW Books, 1991, 318 p., paper, anth.

with P. M. Griffin

The turning: storms of victory—SEE: *Witch World: The turning: storms of victory*.

24722 *Witch World: The turning: storms of victory*. New York: Tor Fantasy, A Tom Doherty Associates Book, 1991, 432 p., cloth, novel. WITCH WORLD #21.

with Mercedes Lackey

27665 *The elvenbane: an epic high fantasy of the Halfblood Chronicles*. New York: Tor, A Tom Doherty Associates Book, 1991, 390 p., cloth, novel.

with Dorothy Madlee

28881 *Star Ka'at*. New York: Walker & Co., 1976, 122 p., cloth, novel. STAR KA'ATS #1.

28882 *Star Ka'at world*. New York: Walker & Co., 1978, 130 p., cloth, novel. STAR KA'ATS #2.

28883 *Star Ka'ats and the plant people*. New York: Walker & Co., 1979, 122 p., cloth, novel. STAR KA'ATS #3.

28884 *Star Ka'ats and the winged warriors.* New York: Walker & Co., 1981, 123 p., cloth, novel. Star Ka'ats #4.

with Phyllis Miller

29912 *House of shadows.* New York: A Margaret K. McElderry Book, Atheneum, 1984, 201 p., cloth, novel.
29913 *Seven spells to Sunday.* New York: A Margaret K. McElderry Book, Atheneum, 1979, 136 p., cloth, novel

with Susan Shwartz

30853 *Imperial lady: a fantasy of Han China.* New York: Tor, A Tom Doherty Associates Book, 1989, 293 p., cloth, novel.

with Ingried Zierhut

30854 *Grandmasters' choice.* Cambridge, MA: A Norescon III Book, NESFA Press, 1989, xv+221 p., cloth, anth.

NORTON, Mary, 1903-1992

30855 *Are all the giants dead?* London: J. M. Dent & Sons, 1975, 119 p., cloth, novel.
30856 *The Borrowers avenged.* Harmondsworth, Middlesex, England: Kestrel Books, 1982, 284 p., cloth, novel. Borrowers #6.
30857 *Poor Stainless.* London: J. M. Dent & Sons, 1971, 26 p., cloth, story. Borrowers #5.

NORTON, Michael C(raig), 1947-

30858 *Abomination.* New York: Leisure Books, 1987, 400 p., paper, novel.
30859 *Blizzard.* New York: Leisure Books, 1988, 358 p., paper, novel.

NORVIL, Manning, pseud.—SEE: Bulmer, Kenneth

NORWAY, Nevil—SEE: Shute, Nevil

*NORWOOD, Victor (George Charles), 1920-1983

NORWOOD, Warren (Carl), 1945-

30860 *Final command.* Toronto, New York: Bantam Books, 1986, xiv+252 p., paper, novel. Double Spiral War #3.
Fize of the Gabriel Ratchets—SEE: *The Windhover tapes: Fize of the Gabriel Ratchets.*

Flexing the warp—SEE: *The Windhover tapes: Flexing the warp.*
An image of voices—SEE: *The Windhover tapes: An image of voices.*
30861 *Midway between.* Toronto, New York: Bantam Books, 1984, xiii+235 p., paper, novel. Double-Spiral War #1.
Planet of flowers—SEE: *The Windhover tapes: Planet of flowers.*
30862 *Polar fleet.* Toronto, New York: Bantam Books, 1985, xiii+234 p., paper, novel. Double-Spiral War #2.
30863 *Shudderchild.* Toronto, New York: Bantam Books, 1987, 350 p., paper, novel.
30864 *Trapped!* New York: A Byron Preiss Book, Lynx Omeiga Books, 1989, 304 p., paper, novel. Time Police #2. [With Mel Odom as uncredited co-author].
30865 *True jaguar.* Toronto, New York: Bantam Books, 1988, 324 p., paper, novel.
30866 *Vanished.* New York: A Byron Preiss Book, Lynx Omeiga Books, 1988, 288 p., paper, novel. Time Police #1.
30867 *The Windhover tapes: An image of voices.* Toronto, New York: Bantam Books, 1982, 210 p., paper, novel. Windhover Tapes #1.
30868 *The Windhover tapes: Fize of the Gabriel Ratchets.* Toronto, New York: Bantam Books, 1983, 248 p., paper, novel. Windhover Tapes #3.
30869 *The Windhover tapes: Flexing the warp.* Toronto, New York: Bantam Books, 1983, 231 p., paper, novel. Windhover Tapes #2.
30870 *The Windhover tapes: Planet of flowers.* Toronto, New York: Bantam Books, 1984, 214 p., paper, novel. Windhover Tapes #4.

with Ralph Mylius

30551 *The Seren Cenacles.* Toronto, New York: Bantam Books, 1983, 244 p., paper, novel.

with Mel Odom

30871 *Stranded.* New York: A Byron Preiss Book, Lynx Omeiga Books, 1989, 320 p., paper, novel. Time Police #3.

NÖSTLINGER, Christine, 1936-

30872 *Guardian ghost.* London: Andersen Press, 1986, 142 p., cloth, novel. [Translation by Anthea Bell of *Rosa Riedl, schutzgespenst*].

NOTT, K(athleen) C(ecilia), 1909?-

37992 *The dry deluge.* London: Hogarth Press, 1947, 307 p., cloth, novel.

NOURSE, Alan E(dward), 1928-1992

30873 *The fourth horseman.* New York: Harper & Row, 1983, 362 p., cloth, novel.

NOUX, O'Neil De—SEE: De Noux, O'Neil

NOVAK, Kate

Captain America: Rocket's red glare— SEE: *Rocket's red glare.*

30874 *Lady of the winds.* Lake Geneva, WI: TSR Inc., 1984, 157 p., paper, novel. HEARTQUEST #6.

30875 *Rocket's red glare.* Lake Geneva, WI: TSR Inc., 1986, 190 p., paper, novel. MARVEL SUPERHEROES ADVENTURE GAMEBOOK #2.

30875A retitled: *Captain America: the rocket's red glare.* Harmondsworth, Middlesex, England: Puffin Books, 1987, 190 p., paper, novel.

30876 *The uncanny X-Men: An X-cellent death.* Lake Geneva, WI: TSR Inc., 1987, 192 p., paper, novel. MARVEL SUPERHEROES ADVENTURE GAMEBOOK #6.

An X-cellent death—SEE: The uncanny X-men: An X-cellent death.

with Jeff Grubb

Azure bonds—SEE: Forgotten realms: Azure bonds.

24801 *Forgotten realms: Azure bonds.* Lake Geneva, WI: TSR Inc., 1988, 380 p., paper, novel. FINDER'S STONE TRILOGY #1; FORGOTTEN REALMS FANTASY ADVENTURE.

24802 *Forgotten realms: Song of the saurials.* Lake Geneva, WI: TSR Inc., 1991, 315 p., paper, novel. FINDER'S STONE TRILOGY #3; FORGOTTEN REALMS FANTASY ADVENTURE.

Song of the saurials—SEE: Forgotten realms: Song of the saurials.

24803 *The wyvern's spur.* Lake Geneva, WI: TSR Inc., 1990, 313 p., paper, novel. FINDER'S STONE TRILOGY #2; FORGOTTEN REALMS FANTASY ADVENTURE.

NOVAK, Miroslav, *with Václav Cerny & Zlata Cerná*

19685 *Tales of the uncanny.* London, New York: Hamlyn, 1976, 211 p., cloth, coll. [Translation by Helen Notzl].

*NOWLAN, Philip Francis, 1888-1944

NOYES, Ralph

30877 *A secret property.* London: Quartet, 1985, 186 p., cloth, novel.

NUGENT, James

30878 *The brass halo.* New York: A Critic's Choice Paperback from Lorevan Publishing, 1987, 346 p., paper, novel. TALISMAN #1.

NUGENT, Jean

30879 *Calling outer space.* New York, Toronto: Scholastic Inc., 1985, 93 p., paper, novel. TWISTAPLOT #18.

NUNES, Claude, 1924-

30880 *The sky trapeze.* London: Robert Hale, 1980, 188 p., cloth, novel.

NUTT, Charles L.—SEE: Beaumont, Charles

NYBERG, Björn (Emil Oscar), 1929- , with L. Sprague de Camp & Lin Carter

19595 *Conan the swordsman.* Toronto, New York: Bantam Books, 1978, 274 p., paper, novel. CONAN SERIES.

NYE, Jody Lynn, 1957-

30881 *Dragonfire: a Crossroads adventure in the world of Anne McCaffrey's Pern.* New York: Tor, A Tom Doherty Associates Book, 1988, 19+[256] p., paper, novel. CROSSROADS ADVENTURE; PERN SERIES.

30881 *Dragonharper: a Crossroads adventure in the world of Anne McCaffrey's Pern.* New York: Tor, A Tom Doherty Associates Book, 1987, 23+[289] p., paper, novel. CROSSROADS ADVENTURE; PERN SERIES.

30883 *Encyclopedia of Xanth: a Crossroads adventure in the world of Piers Anthony's Xanth.* New York: Tor, A Tom Doherty Associates Book, 1987, 25+[224] p., paper, novel. CROSSROADS ADVENTURE; XANTH SERIES.

30884 *Ghost of a chance: a Crossroads adventure in the world of Piers Anthony's Xanth.* New York: Tor, A Tom Doherty Associates Book, 1988, 27+[286] p., paper, novel. CROSSROADS ADVENTURE; XANTH SERIES.

30885 *Mythology 101.* New York: Popular Library, 1990, 264 p., paper, novel. MYTHOLOGY #1.

30886 *Mythology abroad.* New York: Warner Books, 1991, 264 p., paper, novel. MYTHOLOGY #2.

with Piers Anthony

16719 *Piers Anthony's Visual guide to Xanth.* New York: Avon, 1989, 236 p., paper, fiction.
Visual guide to Xanth—SEE: *Piers Anthony's Visual guide to Xanth.*

with Anne McCaffrey

29407 *The death of sleep.* New York: Baen Books, 1990, 380 p., paper, novel.

29408 *The dragonlover's guide to Pern.* New York: A Del Rey Book, Ballantine Books, 1989, xi+178 p., cloth, nonf. PLANET PIRATES #2.
Generation warriors—SEE: **McCaffrey, Anne & Moon, Elizabeth**

NYE, Nicholas

30887 *Return to the lost world.* England: Nicholas Nye, 1991, 256 p., cloth, novel. PROFESSOR CHALLENGER SERIES. [Sequel to *The lost world* / by Arthur Conan Doyle].

NYE, Robert, 1939-

30888 *Bee hunter: the adventures of Beowulf.* London: Faber & Faber, 1968, 108 p., cloth, novel.

30888A retitled: *Beowulf: a new telling.* New York: Hill & Wang, 1968, 118 p., cloth, novel.

30888B retitled: *Beowulf, the bee hunter.* London: Faber & Faber, 1972, 108 p., cloth, novel.
Beowulf: a new telling—SEE: *Bee hunter: the adventures of Beowulf.*
Beowulf, the bee hunter—SEE: *Bee hunter: the adventures of Beowulf.*

30889 *Merlin.* London: Hamish Hamilton, 1978, 215 p., cloth, novel.

O

O. R.—SEE: R., O.

OAKDEN, David, 1947-

Ghost stories—SEE: *The Wheaton book of ghost stories*.

30890 *The Wheaton book of ghost stories*. Exeter, England: Wheaton Books, 1979, 114 p., cloth, coll.

30890A retitled: *Ghost stories*. Windermere, FL: Rourke Publications, 1982, 46 p., cloth, coll. [Abridged edition].

30891 *The Wheaton book of witches, wizards, and warlocks*. Exeter, England: Wheaton Books, 1979, 112 p., cloth, coll.

30891A retitled: *Witches and warlocks*. Windermere, FL: Rourke Publications, 1982, 48 p., cloth, coll. [Abridged edition].

30891B retitled: *Wizards and sorcerers*. Windermere, FL: Rourke Publications, 1982, 46 p., cloth, coll. [Abridged edition].

Witches and warlocks; Wizards and sorcerers—SEE: *The Wheaton book of witches, wizards, and warlocks*.

OAKGROVE, Artemis, 1952-

30892 *Dreams of vengeance*. Denver, CO: Lace Publications, 1985, ix+197 p., paper, novel. THRONE TRILOGY #2.

30893 *Nighthawk*. Denver, CO: Lace Publications, 1987, 189 p., paper, novel.

30894 *The raging peace*. Denver, CO: Lace Publications, 1984, 256 p., paper, novel. THRONE TRILOGY #1.

30895 *Throne of council*. Denver, CO: Lace Publications, 1986, xv+151 p., paper, novel. THRONE TRILOGY #3.

OATES, Joyce Carol—SEE: Smith, Rosamond

OBERG, Charlotte H(enley), 1936-

30896 *A pagan prophet: William Morris*. Charlottesville, VA: University Press of Virginia, 1978, 189 p., cloth, nonf.

*OBOLER, Arch, 1907-1987

O'BRANAGAN, Devin

30897 *Spirit warriors*. New York, London: Pocket Books, 1988, 360 p., paper, novel.

30898 *Witch hunt*. New York, London: Pocket Books, 1990, 338 p., paper, novel.

OBRECHT, Fred

30899 *Science fiction and fantasy: 26 classic and contemporary stories*. Woodbury, NY: Barron's Educational Series, 1977, 256 p., paper, anth.

O'BRIEN, Edward W. Jr.

30900 *Insidious garden: a look at horror fiction*. Glenview, IL: Moshassuck Press, 1988, 46 p., paper, nonf. [Limited to 40 copies].

30901 *Young Ronan*. Glenview, IL: Moshassuck Press, 1991, 18 leaves, paper, story. [Limited to 60 copies].

O'BRIEN, (Michael) Fitz-James, 1828-1862

Dream stories and fantasies—SEE: *The supernatural tales of Fitz-James O'Brien, volume two*.

30902 *The fantastic tales of Fitz-James O'Brien*. London: John Calder, 1977, 149 p., cloth, coll. [Edited by Michael Hayes].

Macabre tales—SEE: *The supernatural tales of Fitz-James O'Brien, volume one*.

30903 *The supernatural tales of Fitz-James O'Brien, volume one: Macabre tales*. New York: Doubleday, 1988, xxv+157 p., cloth, coll. [Edited by Jessica Amanda Salmonson].

30904 *The supernatural tales of Fitz-James O'Brien, volume two: Dream stories and fantasies*. New York: Doubleday, 1988, xiv+174 p., cloth, coll. [Edited by Jessica Amanda Salmonson].

37993 *What was it?* New York: Frank Hallman and The Oliphant Press, 1974, [23] p., paper, story. [Limited to 200 copies].

O'BRIEN, Richard

30905 *Evil*. New York: A Dell Book, 1989, 214 p., paper, novel.

O'BRIEN, Robert C. [pseud. of Robert Lesly Carroll Conly], 1918-1973

10899   *Mrs. Frisby and the rats of NIMH.* New York: Atheneum, 1971, 233 p., cloth, novel.

10899A retitled: *The secret of NIMH.* New York, Toronto: An Apple Paperback, Scholastic Book Services, 1982, 249 p., paper, novel. NIMH #1.

    The secret of NIMH—SEE: *Mrs. Frisby and the rats of NIMH.*

30906   *Z for Zachariah.* New York: Atheneum, 1975, 249 p., cloth, novel.

O'BRIEN, Tim, 1946-

30907   *The nuclear age.* New York: Alfred A. Knopf, 1985, 312 p., cloth, novel.

OBSTFELD, Raymond, 1952-

30908   *The reincarnation of Reece Erikson.* New York: Tor, A Tom Doherty Associates Book, 1988, 312 p., paper, novel.

as JASON FROST

23564   *Badland.* New York: Zebra Books, Kensington Publishing Corp., 1984, 254 p., paper, novel. WARLORD #3.

23565   *The cutthroat.* New York: Zebra Books, Kensington Publishing Corp., 1984, 269 p., paper, novel. WARLORD #2.

23566   *Invasion U.S.A.* New York: Pinnacle Books, 1985, 214 p., paper, movie.

23568   *Prisonland.* New York: Zebra Books, Kensington Publishing Corp., 1985, 240 p., paper, novel. WARLORD #4.

23569   *Terminal island.* New York: Zebra Books, Kensington Publishing Corp., 1985, 235 p., paper, novel. WARLORD #5.

23570   *The warlord.* New York: Zebra Books, Kensington Publishing Corp., 1983, 398 p., paper, novel. WARLORD #1.

*OBUKHOVA, Lydia [i.e., Lidiia Alekseevna Obukhova], 1924-

O'CALLAGHAN, Maxine, 1937-

30909   *The bogeyman.* New York: Tor Horror, A Tom Doherty Associates Book, 1986, 320 p., paper, novel.

30910   *Dark visions.* New York: Tor Horror, A Tom Doherty Associates Book, 1988, 346 p., paper, novel.

30911   *Something's calling me home.* New York, London: Pocket Books, 1991, 215 p., paper, novel.

OCAMPO, Silvina, 1906- , with Jorge Luis Borges & Adolfo Bioy Casares

17979   *The book of fantasy.* London: Xanadu, 1988, 384 p., cloth, anth. [Translation of *Antología de la literatura fantástica*].

O'CONNOR, Jane, 1947-

with Joyce Milton

37973   *The amazing bubblegum caper.* New York, Toronto: Scholastic Inc., 1983, 60 p., paper, fiction. PICK-A-PATH #4.

37974   *The dandee diamond mystery.* New York, Toronto: Scholastic Book Services, 1982, 56 p., paper, fiction. PICK-A-PATH #1.

with Jim O'Connor

37994   *The magic top mystery.* New York, Toronto: Scholastic Inc., 1984, 60 p., paper, fiction. PICK-A-PATH #8.

O'CONNOR, Jim, with Jane O'Connor

37994   *The magic top mystery.* New York, Toronto: Scholastic Inc., 1984, 60 p., paper, fiction. PICK-A-PATH #8.

O'CONNOR, Stephen

30912   *Rescue.* New York: Harmony Books, 1989, 180 p., cloth, coll.

OCTOBER, John [pseud. of Christopher John Portway], 1923-

30913   *The anarchy pedlars.* London: Robert Hale, 1976, [160] p., cloth, novel.

O'DAY-FLANNERY, Constance

30914   *Once in a lifetime.* New York: A Zebra Book, Kensington Publishing Corp., 1991, 448 p., paper, novel.

30915   *This time, forever.* New York: A Zebra Book, Kensington Publishing Corp., 1990, 444 p., paper, novel.

30916   *A time for love.* New York: A Zebra Book, Kensington Publishing Corp., 1991, 447 p., paper, novel.

30917   *Time-kept promises.* New York: A Zebra Book, Kensington Publishing Corp., 1988, 511 p., paper, novel.

30918 *Time-kissed destiny*. New York: A Zebra Book, Kensington Publishing Corp., 1987, 509 p., paper, novel.

30919 *Timeless passion*. New York: A Zebra Book, Kensington Publishing Corp., 1986, 493 p., paper, novel.

30920 *Timeswept lovers*. New York: A Zebra Book, Kensington Publishing Corp., 1987, 492 p., paper, novel.

ODIER, Daniel, 1945-

30921 *Cannibal kiss: a novel*. New York: Random House, 1989, 179 p., cloth, novel. [Translation by Lanie Goodman of *Le baiser cannibale*].

with William S. Burroughs

19085 *The job: interviews with William S. Burroughs*. New York: Grove Press, 1974, 224 p., cloth, nonf. coll.

*ODLE, E(dwin) V(incent), 1890-1942

ODOM, Mel(vin Lewis III), 1957-

as DON PENDLETON

30922 *Stoney Man III*. Toronto, New York: Worldwide, 1991, 349 p., paper, novel. STONEY MAN #3.

with Warren Norwood

30871 *Stranded*. New York: A Byron Preiss Book, Lynx Omeiga Books, 1989, 320 p., paper, novel. TIME POLICE #3.

30864 *Trapped!* New York: A Byron Preiss Book, Lynx Omeiga Books, 1989, 304 p., paper, novel. TIME POLICE #2. [Odom's contribution is uncredited].

O'DONNELL, Kevin Jr., 1950-

30923 *Bander Snatch*. Toronto, New York: Bantam Books, 1979, 242 p., paper, novel.

30924 *Caverns*. New York: Berkley Books, 1981, 214 p., paper, novel. JOURNEYS OF MCGILL FEIGHAN #1.

30925 *Cliffs*. New York: Berkley Books, 1986, 246 p., paper, novel. JOURNEYS OF MCGILL FEIGHAN #4.

30926 *Fire on the border*. New York: A Roc Book, 1990, 368 p., paper, novel.

30927 *Lava*. New York: Berkley Books, 1982, 232 p., paper, novel. JOURNEYS OF MCGILL FEIGHAN #3.

30928 *Mayflies*. New York: A Berkley Book, Berkley Publishing Corp., 1979, 295 p., paper, novel.

30929 *ORA:CLE*. New York: Berkley Books, 1984, 343 p., paper, novel.

30930 *Reefs*. New York: Berkley Books, 1981, 220 p., paper, novel. JOURNEYS OF MCGILL FEIGHAN #2.

30931 *War of omission*. Toronto, New York: Bantam Books, 1982, 260 p., paper, novel.

with Mary Kittredge

27338 *The shelter*. New York: Tor Horror, A Tom Doherty Associates Book, 1987, 376 p., paper, novel.

O'DONNELL, Margaret (Jane), 1899-

37995 *The beehive*. London: Eyre Methuen, 1980, 254 p., cloth, novel.

*O'DONNELL, Peter, 1920-

O'DONOHOE, Nicholas B.—SEE: O'Donohoe, Nick

O'DONOHOE, Nick [i.e., Nicholas Benjamin O'Donohoe], 1952-

30932 *Too, too solid flesh*. Lake Geneva, WI: TSR Inc., 1989, 339 p., paper, novel.

OESTRICHER, Joy, *with others*

30933 *Alpha gallery*. Pueblo, CO: SPWAO, 1991, 213 p., paper, coll. [Includes verse and nonfiction].

O'FAOLAIN, Seán, 1900-1991

30934 *And again? a novel*. London: Constable, 1979, 286 p., cloth, novel.

OFFUTT, Andrew J(efferson V), 1934-

30935 *The black sorcerer of the Black Castle*. Aberdeen, MD: Hall Publications, 1976, [18] p., paper, story. CONAN PARODY.

30936 *Chieftain of Andor*. New York: A Dell Book, 1976, 203 p., paper, novel.

30936A retitled: *Clansman of Andor*. London: Robert Hale, 1979, 190 p., cloth, novel.
Clansman of Andor—SEE: *Chieftain of Andor*.

30937 *Conan and the sorcerer*. New York: Sunridge Press, 1978, 186 p., paper, novel. CONAN SERIES.

30938 *Conan the mercenary.* New York: Ace Books, 1980, 184 p., paper, novel. CONAN SERIES.

30939 *Conan: The sword of Skelos.* Toronto, New York: Bantam Books, 1979, 246 p., paper, novel. CONAN SERIES.

30940 *Cormac mac Art: Sword of the Gael.* New York: Zebra Books, Kensington Publishing Corp., 1975, 251 p., paper, novel. CORMAC MAC ART #5.

30941 *Deathknight.* New York: Ace Books, 1990, 225 p., paper, novel.

30942 *The iron lords.* New York: A Jove/HBJ Book, 1979, 224 p., paper, novel. WAR OF THE GODS ON EARTH #1.

30943 *King Dragon.* New York: Ace Books, 1980, 277 p., paper, novel.

30944 *The Lady of the Snowmist.* New York: Ace Fantasy Books, 1983, 215 p., paper, novel. WAR OF THE GODS ON EARTH #3.

30945 *The mists of doom.* New York: Zebra Books, Kensington Publishing Corp., 1977, 255 p., paper, novel. CORMAC MAC ART #1.

30946 *My lord barbarian.* New York: A Del Rey Book, Ballantine Books, 1977, 184 p., paper, novel.

30947 *Shadows out of Hell.* New York: A Berkley Book, Berkley Publishing Corp., 1980, 165 p., paper, novel. WAR OF GODS ON EARTH #2.

30948 *Shadowspawn.* New York: Ace Books, 1987, 278 p., paper, novel. THIEVES' WORLD NOVELS #4.

30949 *The sign of the moonbow.* New York: Zebra Books, Kensington Publishing Corp., 1977, 255 p., paper, novel. CORMAC MAC ART #7.

The sword of Skelos—SEE: *Conan: The sword of Skelos.*

Sword of the Gael—SEE: *Cormac mac Art.*

30950 *Swords against darkness.* New York: Zebra Books, Kensington Publishing Corp., 1977, 288 p., paper, anth.

30950A retitled: *Swords against darkness 1.* New York: Zebra Books, Kensington Publishing Corp., 1990, 288 p., paper, anth.

Swords against darkness 1—SEE: *Swords against darkness.*

30951 *Swords against darkness II.* New York: Zebra Books, Kensington Publishing Corp., 1977, 284 p., paper, anth.

30952 *Swords against darkness III.* New York: Zebra Books, Kensington Publishing Corp., 1978, 288 p., paper, anth.

30953 *Swords against darkness IV.* New York: Zebra Books, Kensington Publishing Corp., 1979, 272 p., paper, anth.

30954 *Swords against darkness V.* New York: Zebra Books, Kensington Publishing Corp., 1979, 288 p., paper, anth.

30955 *The undying wizard.* New York: Zebra Books, Kensington Publishing Corp., 1976, 252 p., paper, novel. CORMAC MAC ART #6.

alone or with various co-authors as JOHN CLEVE

27220 *Assignment: Hellhole.* New York: Berkley Books, 1983, 212 p., paper, novel. SPACEWAYS #14. [With Robin Kincaid].

27438 *The Carnadyne Horde.* New York: Berkley Books, 1984, 212 p., paper, novel. SPACEWAYS #17. [With Victor Koman].

30956 *Corundum's woman.* New York: Playboy Paperbacks, 1982, 224 p., paper, novel. SPACEWAYS #2. [Sole author].

30957 *Escape from Macho.* New York: Playboy Paperbacks, 1982, 223 p., paper, novel. SPACEWAYS #3. [Sole author].

24964 *The Iceworld Connection.* New York: Berkley Books, 1983, 209 p., paper, novel. SPACEWAYS #11. [With Jack C. Haldeman II & Vol Haldeman].

30958 *In quest of Qalara.* New York: Playboy Paperbacks, 1983, 224 p., paper, novel. SPACEWAYS #9. [Sole author].

27439 *Jonuta rising!* New York: Berkley Books, 1983, 214 p., paper, novel. SPACEWAYS #13. [With Victor Koman].

30959 *King of the slavers.* New York: Berkley Books, 1985, 227 p., paper, novel. SPACEWAYS #19. [Sole author].

30960 *The manhuntress.* New York: Playboy Paperbacks, 1982, 224 p., paper, novel. SPACEWAYS #7. [With Geo. W. Proctor].

30961 *Master of Misfit.* New York: Playboy Paperbacks, 1982, 223 p., paper, novel. SPACEWAYS #5. [With Geo. W. Proctor].

30962 *Of alien bondage.* New York: Playboy Paperbacks, 1982, 240 p., paper, novel. SPACEWAYS #1. [Sole author].

30963 *The planet murderer.* New York: Berkley Books, 1984, 224 p., paper, novel. SPACEWAYS #16. [With Dwight V. Swain].

17880 *Pleasure us!* New York: Bee-Line Books, 1971, 187 p., paper, novel. [With D. Bruce Berry].

30964 *Purrfect plunder.* New York: Playboy Paperbacks, 1982, 224 p., paper, novel. SPACEWAYS #6. [Sole author].

27221 *Race across the stars.* New York: Berkley Books, 1984, 225 p., paper, novel. SPACEWAYS #18. [With Robin Kincaid].

30965 *Satana enslaved.* New York: Playboy Paperbacks, 1982, 224 p., paper, novel. SPACEWAYS #4. [Sole author].

10942 *The sexorcist.* New York: Orpheus Series, 1974, 251 p., paper, novel. [Sole author].

10942A retitled: *Unholy revelry.* New York: A Bee Line Banner Book, 1976, 251 p., paper, novel. [Sole author].

22417 *Star slaver.* New York: Berkley Books, 1983, 211 p., paper, novel. SPACEWAYS #12. [With G. C. Edmondson].

24467 *Starship Sapphire.* New York: Berkley Books, 1984, 212 p., paper, novel. SPACEWAYS #15. [With Roland Green].

30966 *Under twin suns.* New York: Playboy Paperbacks, 1982, 220 p., paper, novel. SPACEWAYS #8. [Sole author].
Unholy revelry—SEE: *The sexorcist.*

30967 *The yoke of Shen.* New York: Berkley Books, 1983, 228 p., paper, novel. SPACEWAYS #10. [With Geo. W. Proctor].

with D. Bruce Berry

17879 *Genetic bomb.* New York: Warner Paperback Library, 1975, 207 p., paper, novel.

with Richard K. Lyon

28760 *Demon in the mirror.* New York: A Kangaroo Book, Pocket Books, 1978, 189 p., paper, novel. WAR OF THE WIZARDS #1.

28761 *The Eyes of Sarsis.* New York: Pocket Books, 1980, 207 p., paper, novel. WAR OF THE WIZARDS #2.

28762 *Web of the spider.* New York: A Timescape Book, Pocket Books, 1981, 292 p., paper, novel. WAR OF THE WIZARDS #3.

with Keith Taylor

30968 *The tower of death.* New York: Ace Books, 1982, 246 p., paper, novel. CORMAC MAC ART #2.

30969 *When death birds fly.* New York: Ace Books, 1980, 295 p., paper, novel. CORMAC MAC ART #3.

O'FLAHERTY, Liam, 1896-1984

30970 *The ecstasy of Angus.* London: Joiner & Steele, 1931, 43 p., cloth, story.

OFSHE, Richard, 1941-

30971 *The sociology of the possible.* Englewood Cliffs, NJ: Prentice-Hall, 1970, xvii+391 p., cloth, anth.

37996 *The sociology of the possible, 2nd ed.* Englewood Cliffs, NJ: Prentice-Hall, 1977, xii+381 p., cloth, anth.

OGDEN, Megan—SEE: Lindholm, Megan

O'GREEN, Jennifer—SEE: Roberson, Jennifer

O'GREEN, Mark (Richard), 1953-

30972 *The (w)hole Delvers Catalog.* Amarillo, TX: Task Force Games, 1987, 67 p., paper, fiction.

O'HAR, George M.

30973 *Psychic fair.* New York, London: Pocket Books, 1989, 324 p., paper, novel.

O'HARA, Gerald John

30974 *Malsum.* New York: Avon, 1981, 309 p., paper, novel.

OHLROGGE, Anne—SEE: Stuart, Anne

OKADA, Masaya, 1938-

30975 *Illustrated index to Air Wonder Stories (vol. I, no. 1-vol. I, no. 11, July 1929-May 1930) = Kuchu kyoi monogatari e-i sakuin.* Nagoya, Japan: Masaya Okada, 1973, 79 p., paper, nonf.

O'KEEFE, Claudia (Diane), 1958-

30976 *Black snow days.* New York: Ace Books, 1990, 344 p., paper, novel.

OKRAND, Marc, 1948-

30977 *The Klingon dictionary: English/Klingon, Klingon/English.* New York: Pocket Books, 1985, 172 p., paper, fiction.

OKRI, Ben(jamin), 1959-

30978 *The famished road.* London: Jonathan Cape, 1991, 500 p., cloth, novel.

OKUDA, Michael (Hideo), 1955- , with Rick Sternbach

30979 *The Star Trek, the Next Generation technical manual.* New York, London: Pocket Books, 1991, 183 p., paper, nonf.

OKUN, Lawrence (Eugene), 1929-

30980 *On the 8th day.* Millbrae, CA: Celestial Arts, 1980, 217 p., cloth, novel.
30980A retitled: *On the eighth day.* Chicago: Playboy Paperbacks, 1981, 217 p., paper, novel.
On the eighth day—SEE: *On the 8th day.*

OLAFUR Gunnarsson, 1948-

30981 *Gaga.* Kapuskasing, Ontario, Canada: Penumbra Press, 1988, 68 p., paper, story. [Translation by David McDuff of *Gaga*].

OLAN, Susan Torian

30982 *The earth remembers.* Lake Geneva, WI: TSR Inc., 1990, 317 p., paper, novel.

OLANDER, Joseph D(avid), 1939-

with Isaac Asimov & Martin Harry Greenberg

16966 *100 great science fiction short short stories.* Garden City, NY: Doubleday & Co., 1978, xvi+270 p., cloth, anth.
16967 *The future I.* New York: Fawcett Crest, 1980, 381 p., paper, anth.
16968 *The future in question.* New York: Fawcett Crest, 1980, 381 p., paper, anth.
16969 *Isaac Asimov's Science fiction treasury.* New York: Bonanza Books, 1980, 786 p., cloth, anth. [Includes *The future in question* and *Space mail*].
16970 *Microcosmic tales: 100 wondrous science fiction short-short stories.* New York: Taplinger Publishing Co., 1980, 325 p., cloth, anth.
Science fiction treasury—SEE: *Isaac Asimov's Science fiction treasury.*
16971 *Space mail.* New York: Fawcett Crest, 1980, 416 p., paper, anth.

JOSEPH D. OLANDER, *with Martin H. Greenberg*

24555 *Arthur C. Clarke.* New York: Taplinger Publishing Co., 1977, 254 p., cloth, nonf. anth.
24556 *Criminal justice through science fiction.* New York, London: New Viewpoints, 1977, xvi+239 p., cloth, anth.
24557 *International relations through science fiction.* New York: New Viewpoints, 1978, xviii+236 p., cloth, anth.
24558 *Isaac Asimov.* New York: Taplinger Publishing Co., 1977, 247 p., cloth, nonf. anth.

24559 *Philip K. Dick.* New York: Taplinger Publishing Co., 1983, 256 p., cloth, nonf. anth.
24560 *Ray Bradbury.* New York: Taplinger Publishing Co., 1980, 248 p., cloth, nonf. anth.
24561 *Robert A. Heinlein.* New York: Taplinger Publishing Co., 1978, 268 p., cloth, nonf. anth.
24562 *Science fiction of the fifties.* New York: Avon, 1979, xxiii+438 p., paper, anth.
24563 *Time of passage.* New York: Taplinger Publishing Co., 1978, 292 p., cloth, anth.
24564 *Tomorrow, Inc.: SF stories about business.* New York: Taplinger Publishing Co., 1976, 256 p., cloth, anth.
24565 *Ursula K. Le Guin.* New York: Taplinger Publishing Co., 1979, 258 p., cloth, nonf. anth.

JOSEPH D. OLANDER, *with Martin H. Greenberg & Ralph Clem*

20170 *The city: 2000 A.D.: urban life through science fiction.* Greenwich, CT: A Fawcett Crest Book, Fawcett Publications, 1976, 304 p., paper, anth.
20171 *No room for man: population and the future through science fiction.* Totowa, NJ: Rowman & Littlefield, 1979, 247 p., cloth, anth.

JOSEPH D. OLANDER, *with Martin H. Greenberg & Eric S. Rabkin*

24575 *The end of the world.* Carbondale & Edwardsville, IL: Southern Illinois University Press, 1983, xv+204 p., cloth, nonf. anth.
24576 *No place else: explorations in utopian and dystopian fiction.* Carbondale & Edwardsville, IL: Southern Illinois University Press, 1983, 278 p., cloth, nonf. anth.

JOSEPH D. OLANDER, *with Marting H. Greenberg & Marshall Tymn & L. W. Currey*

20899 *Index to stories in thematic anthologies of science fiction.* Boston: G. K. Hall & Co., 1978, xiii+193 p., cloth, nonf. REFERENCE PUBLICATION IN SCIENCE FICTION.

JOSEPH D. OLANDER, *with Martin H. Greenberg & Patricia S. Warrick*

24566 *Run to starlight: sports through science fiction.* New York: Delacorte Press, 1975, vi+383 p., cloth, anth.
24567 *Science fiction: contemporary mythology: the SFWA-SFRA anthology.* New York: Harper & Row, 1978, xviii+476 p., cloth, anth.. [Includes some nonf.].

JOSEPH D. OLANDER, *with Martin Harry Greenberg & Patricia S. Warrick & Val Clear*

20165 *Marriage and the family through science fiction.* New York: St. Martin's Press, 1976, xiv+358 p., paper, anth.

JOSEPH D. OLANDER, *with Martin H. Greenberg & Patricia Warrick & John W. Milstead*

24548 *Social problems through science fiction.* New York: St. Martin's Press, 1975, xvi+356 p., cloth, anth.

JOSEPH D. OLANDER, *with Martin H. Greenberg & Charles G. Waugh*

24568 *Mysterious visions: great science fiction by masters of the mystery.* New York: St. Martin's Press, 1979, xxvi+516 p., cloth, anth.

JOSEPH D. OLANDER, *with Damon Knight & Martin H. Greenberg*

08340 *First flight.* New York: Lancer, 1963, 160 p., paper, anth.
24527 retitled: *First voyages.* New York: Avon, 1981, 373 p., paper, anth. [An expanded and reworked version of Knight's *First flight* (see 08340)].
First voyages—SEE: *First flight.*

JOSEPH D. OLANDER, *with Barry N. Malzberg & Martin Harry Greenberg*

24528 *Neglected visions.* Garden City, NY: Doubleday & Co., 1979, ix+211 p., cloth, anth.

JOSEPH D. OLANDER, *with Frederik Pohl & Martin H. Greenberg*

24569 *Galaxy: thirty years of innovative science fiction.* Chicago: Playboy Press, 1980, xiii+465 p., cloth, anth.
24570 *The great science fiction series: stories from the best of the series from 1944 to 1980 by twenty all-time favorite writers.*

New York: Harper & Row, 1980, x+419 p., cloth, anth.
24571 *Science fiction of the forties.* New York: Avon, 1978, 377 p., paper, anth.
24572 *Worlds of if.* New York: Bluejay Books, 1986, 438 p., cloth, anth.

JOSEPH D. OLANDER, *with Robert Silverberg & Martin Harry Greenberg*

24584 *Car sinister.* New York: Avon, 1979, 253 p., paper, anth.
24585 *Dawn of time: prehistory through science fiction.* New York: Elsevier/Nelson, 1979, 224 p., cloth, anth.

O'LEARY, Brian (Todd), 1940-

30983 *Mars 1999: exclusive preview of the U.S.-Soviet manned mission.* Harrisburg, PA: Stackpole Books, 1987, 160 p., cloth, fiction. [Includes some nonfiction].

with Richard Duprey

22324 *Spaceship Titanic.* New York: Dodd, Mead & Co., 1983, 230 p., cloth, novel.

O'LEARY, Liam, 1921-

30984 *Welkin's rift.* Masham: Ollavian Press, 1974, 285 p., cloth, novel.

OLDEN, Marc

30985 *Book of Shadows.* New York: Charter Books, 1980, 275 p., paper, novel.
30986 *Poe must die: a novel.* New York: Charter Books, 1978, 466 p., paper, novel.
30987 *Sword of vengeance.* New York: Jove Books, 1990, 341 p., paper, novel.

OLDFIELD, Pamela, 1931-

30988 *The ghosts of Bellering Oast.* London: Blackie, 1987, 79 p., cloth, novel.
30989 *The mill pond ghost, and other stories.* Oxford, England: Lion Publishing, 1991, 149 p., paper, coll.
30990 *Pamela Oldfield's Spine chillers.* London: Blackie, 1987, 92 p., cloth, coll.
Spine chillers—SEE: *Pamela Oldfield's Spine chillers.*

OLDSEY, Bernard S(tanley), 1923-

with Joseph Browne

18814 *Critical essays on George Orwell.* Boston: G. K. Hall & Co., 1986, viii+256 p., cloth, nonf. anth.

with Stanley Weintraub

30991 *The art of William Golding.* New York: Harcourt, Brace & World, 1965, 178 p., cloth, nonf.

*OLECK, Jack, 1914-1981

OLESKER, J(ack?) Bradford, 1949-

30992 *Beyond forever.* New York: A Signet Book, New American Library, 1981, 183 p., paper, novel.
30993 *The siege of Superport.* New York: G. P. Putnam's Sons, 1978, 235 p., cloth, novel.

OLESKER, Jack (same as J. Bradford?)

30994 *Confessional.* New York: Leisure Books, 1990, 361 p., paper, novel.

*OLFSON, Lewy, 1937-

OLIPHANT, Eleana

30995 *The haunting at Lost Lake.* New York: Leisure Books, 1985, 223 p., paper, novel.

OLIPHANT, Margaret—SEE: Oliphant, Mrs.

OLIPHANT, Mrs. [i.e., Margaret Oliphant Wilson Oliphant], 1828-1897

30996 *A beleaguered city, and other stories.* Oxford, England: Oxford University Press, 1988, xxv+338 p., paper, coll. [Edited by Merryn Williams].
30997 *Selected short stories of the supernatural.* Edinburgh, Scotland: Scottish Academic Press, 1985, xiv+256 p., cloth, coll. [Edited by Margaret K. Gray].
30998 *Stories of the seen and unseen.* Edinburgh, Scotland: William Blackwood & Sons, 1896, p., cloth, coll. [Expanded edition of #10969].

OLIVER, (Symmes) Chad(wick), 1928-

30999 *Giants in the dust.* New York: Pyramid Books, 1976, 142 p., paper, novel.

31000 *Unearthly neighbors.* New York: Crown Publishers, 1984, 208 p., cloth, novel. [Revised from the earlier edition (see #10976)].

OLIVER, George—SEE: Onions, Oliver

*OLIVER, Jane [pseud. of Helen Christina Easson Rees], 1903-1970

OLIVER, Laetitia Selwyn

37997 *The expiation of the Lady Anne.* London: Henry J. Drane, 1905, 257 p., cloth, novel.

OLIVER-SMITH, Martha—SEE: Bacon, Martha

OLSEN, Lance

31001 *Live from Earth.* New York: An Available Press Book, Ballantine Books, 1990, 196 p., paper, novel.

OLSEN, Lance (Martin), 1956-

31002 *Eclipse of uncertainty: an introduction to postmodern fantasy.* Westport, CT: Greenwood Press, 1987, xi+134 p., cloth, nonf. CONTRIBUTIONS TO THE STUDY OF SCIENCE FICTION AND FANTASY #26.

OLSHAKER, Mark, 1951-

31003 *Einstein's brain: a novel.* New York: M. Evans & Co., 1981, 323 p., cloth, novel.

OLSON, Eugene E.—SEE: Steiger, Brad

OLSON, Paul F.

31004 *Night prophets: a novel.* New York: An Onyx Book, New American Library, 1989, 350 p., cloth, novel.

with David B. Silva

31005 *Dead end: city limits: an anthology of urban fear.* New York: St. Martin's Press, 1991, xxiii+342 p., cloth, anth.
31006 *Post mortem: new tales of ghostly horror.* New York: St. Martin's Press, 1989, xi+290 p., cloth, anth.

OLTION, Jerry (Brian), 1957-

Alliance—SEE: Isaac Asimov's robot city: robots and aliens: Alliance.

31007 *Frame of reference.* New York: Popular Library, 1987, 262 p., paper, novel.

Humanity—SEE: *Isaac Asimov's robot city: robots and aliens: Humanity.*

31008 *Isaac Asimov's robot city: robots and aliens: Alliance.* New York: A Byron Preiss Visual Publications Inc. Book, Ace Books, 1990, xiii+168 p., paper, novel. ISAAC ASIMOV'S ROBOT CITY: ROBOTS AND ALIENS #4.

31009 *Isaac Asimov's robot city: robots and aliens: Humanity.* New York: A Byron Preiss Visual Publications Inc. Book, Ace Books, 1990, xiii+177 p., paper, novel. ISAAC ASIMOV'S ROBOT CITY: ROBOTS AND ALIENS #6.

31010 *Professionalism.* Eugene, OR: Writer's Notebook Press, Pulphouse Publishing, 1991, 21 p., paper, nonf.

O'MALLEY, Frank—SEE: O'Rourke, Frank

O'MALLEY, Kathleen (Ann), 1955- , *with A. C. Crispin*

20817 *Silent dances.* New York: Ace Books, 1990, vi+275 p., paper, novel. STARBRIDGE #2.

OMDRA 6, pseud.

31011 *Dreamrise.* [Joliet, IL: G. Stempien Publishing Co.], 1976, 270 p., paper, novel.

***O'MEARA, Walter (Andrew), 1897-1989**

O'NEAL, Kathleen M.—SEE: Gear, Kathleen O'Neal

O'NEAL, William B.—SEE: Woods, Jack

***O'NEILL, Joseph (James), 1878-1952**

O'NEILL, Pamela [i.e., Pamela Louise O'Neill Mohan], 1950- , with Kim Mohan

30028 *Chase into space.* Delavan, WI: New Infinities Productions, 1988, 318 p., paper, novel. CYBORG COMMANDO #2.

30029 *Planet in peril.* Lake Geneva, WI: New Infinities Productions, 1987, 318 p., paper, novel. CYBORG COMMANDO #1.

30030 *The ultimate prize.* Delavan, WI: New Infinities Productions, 1988, 317 p., paper, novel. CYBORG COMMANDO #3.

O'NEILL, Timothy R(ue), 1943-

31012 *The individuated hobbit: Jung, Tolkien, and the archetypes of Middle-Earth.*

Boston: Houghton Mifflin Co., 1979, xv+200 p., cloth, nonf.

31013 *Shades of gray.* New York: Viking, 1987, 322 p., cloth, novel.

ONIONS, (George) Oliver [name legally changed to George Oliver], 1873-1961

The first book of ghost stories—SEE: *Widdershins.*

11007 *Widdershins.* London: Martin Secker, 1911, 315 p., cloth, coll.

11007A retitled: *The first book of ghost stories: Widdershins.* New York: Dover Publications, 1978, 206 p., paper, coll.

ONLEY, David C(harles), 1950-

31014 *Shuttle.* New York: Zebra Books, Kensington Publishing Corp., 1981, 414 p., paper, novel.

ONN, Carrie, pseud.—SEE: Vardeman, Robert E. & Proctor, Geo. W.

ONOPA, Robert, 1943-

31015 *The Pleasure Tube.* New York: A Berkley Book, Berkley Publishing Corp., 1979, 212 p., paper, novel.

OPPENHEIM, Shulamith (Levey), 1930-

31016 *The Selchie's seed.* Scarsdale, NY: Bradbury Press, 1975, 82 p., cloth, novel.

31017 *The world invisible.* New York: Ace Fantasy Books, 1984, 198 p., paper, novel.

OPPENHEIMER, Judy, 1942-

31018 *Private demons: the life of Shirley Jackson.* New York: G. P. Putnam's Sons, 1988, 304 p., cloth, nonf.

ORAM, Neil, 1938-

37998 *The balustrade paradox.* London: Sphere Books, 1982, 204 p., paper, novel. THE WARP #3. [This sequence is a novelization of the author's ten-play cycle, *The Warp*].

31019 *Lemmings on the edge.* London: Sphere Books, 1981, 311 p., paper, novel. THE WARP #2.

31020 *The storm's howling through Tiflis.* London: Sphere Books, 1980, 281 p., paper, novel. THE WARP #1.

ORDE, A. J., pseud.—SEE: Tepper, Sheri S.

ORE, Rebecca [pseud. of Rebecca Bard Brown], 1948-

Becoming alien—SEE: *Ben Bova's discoveries: Becoming alien.*
Being alien—SEE: *Ben Bova presents Being alien.*

31021 *Ben Bova presents Being alien.* New York: Tor SF, A Tom Doherty Associates Book, 1989, 277 p., paper, novel. TOM "RED CLAY" #2.

31022 *Ben Bova's discoveries: Becoming alien.* New York: Tor SF, A Tom Doherty Associates Book, 1988, 313 p., paper, novel. TOM "RED CLAY" #1.

31023 *Human to human.* New York: Tor SF, A Tom Doherty Associates Book, 1990, 283 p., paper, novel. TOM "RED CLAY" #3.

31024 *The illegal rebirth of Billy the Kid.* New York: Tor SF, A Tom Doherty Associates Book, 1991, 314 p., paper, novel.

O'REILLY, Timothy, 1954-

31025 *Frank Herbert.* New York: Frederick Ungar Publishing Co., 1981, viii+216 p., cloth, nonf.

ORGILL, Douglas (William), 1922-1984, *with John Gribbin*

24701 *Brother Esau.* London: Bodley Head, 1982, 220 p., cloth, novel.

24702 *The sixth winter.* London: Bodley Head, 1979, 315 p., cloth, novel.

O'RIORDAN, Robert (Garrett), 1943-

31026 *Cadre Lucifer.* New York: Ace Science Fiction Books, 1987, 202 p., paper, novel. CADRE TRILOGY #2.

31027 *Cadre Messiah.* New York: Ace Books, 1988, 204 p., paper, novel. CADRE TRILOGY #3.

31028 *Cadre One.* New York: Ace Science Fiction Books, 1986, 263 p., paper, novel. CADRE TRILOGY #1.

ORKIN, Michael, *with Ed Bogas*

18240 *Survival on Planet X with the Atari home computer.* Reston, VA: A Reston Computer Group Book, 1984, vii+151 p., paper, fiction.

*ORKOW, Ben (Harrison), 1896-1988

ORLANDO, Joe, 1927- , *with Michael Fleisher*

23187 *DC Comics presents: Superman II, the movie magazine.* New York: DC Comics, 1981, 64 p., paper, nonf.
Superman II, the movie magazine—SEE: *DC Comics presents: Superman II, the movie magazine.*

ORLOV, Vladimir (Viktorovich), 1936-

31029 *Danilov the violist.* New York: William Morrow & Co., 1987, 307 p., cloth, novel. [Translation by Antonina W. Bouis of *Al'tist Danilov*].

ORMONDROYD, Edward, 1925-

31030 *All in good time.* Berkeley, CA: Parnassus Press, 1975, 206 p., cloth, novel. SUSAN SHAW #2.

15849 *David and the Phoenix.* Chicago: Follett Publishing Co., 1957, 173 p., cloth, novel.

ORMSBY, Alan

31031 *Movie monsters: monster make-up & monster shows to put on.* New York, Toronto: Scholastic Book Services, 1975, 80 p., paper, nonf.

*O'ROURKE, Frank [pseud. of Frank O'Malley], 1916-1989

ORR, A. [i.e., Alice Ingram Orr Sprague], 1950-

31032 *In the ice king's palace.* New York: Tor, A Tom Doherty Associates Book, 1986, 170 p., cloth, novel. WORLD IN AMBER #2.

31033 *The world in Amber.* New York: Bluejay Books, 1985, 214 p., cloth, novel. WORLD IN AMBER #1.

*ORR, Violet (May), 1904-1989

ORTH, Richard—SEE: Gardner, Richard

ORTON, Joe [i.e., John Kinsley Orton], 1933-1967

31034 *Head to toe.* London: Anthony Blond, 1971, 159 p., cloth, novel.

ORTON, John K.—SEE: Orton, Joe

ORWELL, George [pseud. of Eric Arthur Blair], 1903-1950

31035 *Animal farm; Burmese days; A clergyman's daughter; Coming up for air; Keep the aspidistra flying; Nineteen eighty-four.* London: Secker & Warburg/Octopus Books, 1976, 925 p., cloth, coll.

31036 *The collected essays, journals, and letters of George Orwell, volume I: An age like this, 1920-1940.* New York: Harcourt, Brace & World, 1968, xxiii+574 p., cloth, nonf. coll. [Edited by Sonia Orwell and Ian Angus].

31037 *The collected essays, journals, and letters of George Orwell, volume II: My country right or left, 1940-1943.* New York: Harcourt, Brace & World, 1968, xv+477 p., cloth, nonf. coll. [Edited by Sonia Orwell and Ian Angus].

31038 *The collected essays, journals, and letters of George Orwell, volume III: As I please, 1943-1945.* New York: Harcourt, Brace & World, 1968, xv+435 p., cloth, nonf. coll. [Edited by Sonia Orwell and Ian Angus].

31039 *The collected essays, journals, and letters of George Orwell, volume IV: In front of your nose, 1945-1950.* New York: Harcourt, Brace & World, 1968, xvii+555 p., cloth, nonf. coll. [Edited by Sonia Orwell and Ian Angus].

Orwell: the lost writings—SEE: *Orwell: the war broadcasts.*

31040 *Orwell: the war broadcasts.* London: Duckworth, 1985, 304 p., cloth, nonf. coll. [Edited by W. J. West].

31040A retitled: *Orwell: the lost writings.* New York: Arbor House, 1985, 304 p., cloth, nonf. coll. [Edited by W. J. West].

31041 *Orwell: the war commentaries.* London: Duckworth, 1985, 248 p., cloth, nonf. coll. [Edited by W. J. West].

with Irving Howe

26059 *Orwell's Nineteen eighty-four: text, sources, criticism.* New York: Harcourt, Brace & World, 1963, 274 p., cloth, anth. [Includes Orwell's novel plus criticism].

26060 *Orwell's Nineteen eighty-four: text, sources, criticism, second edition.* New York: Harcourt Brace Jovanovich, 1982, x+450 p., cloth, anth. [Includes Orwell's novel plus criticism].

OSBORN, David (D.), 1923-

31042 *Heads.* Toronto, New York: Bantam Books, 1985, 294 p., paper, novel.

OSBORN, E(dith) M(argot), 1902-

31043 *Short visit to Ergon.* Victoria, British Columbia, Canada: Marlowe House, 1971, 181 p., cloth?, novel.

OSBORNE, Louise

31045 *Rite of the damned.* New York: Popular Library, 1977, 252 p., paper, novel.

OSBORNE, Mary Pope, 1949- , with Will Osborne

31046 *The deadly power of Medusa.* New York, Toronto: Scholastic Inc., 1988, 92 p., paper, novel.

OSBORNE, Victor

31047 *Moondream.* London: Heinemann, 1988, 122 p., cloth, novel.

OSBORNE, Will, 1949- , with Mary Pope Osborne

31046 *The deadly power of Medusa.* New York, Toronto: Scholastic Inc., 1988, 92 p., paper, novel.

OSBORNE, William, 1960- , with Richard Turner

31048 *1998.* London: Sphere Books, 1988, 198 p., paper, novel.

OSCURA, pseud.

37999 *In the shade.* Ealing, England: J. Acworth, 1861, 111 p., cloth, coll. [Includes some verse].

O'SHAUGHNESSY, Michael, 1965-

31049 *The monster book of monsters.* London: Xanadu, 1988, 352 p., cloth, anth.

O'SHEA, (Catherine) Pat(ricia Shiels), 1931-

31050 *Finn MacCool and the small men of deeds.* Oxford, England: Oxford University Press, 1987, 96 p., cloth, novel.

31051 *The hounds of the Morrigan.* Oxford, England: Oxford University Press, 1985, 469 p., cloth, novel.

OSIER, John, 1938-

31052 *Covenant at Coldwater.* Memphis, TN: St. Luke's Press, 1983, 220 p., cloth, novel.

31053 *Rankin: enemy of the state.* Memphis, TN: St. Luke's Press, 1986, 160 p., cloth, novel.

OSMAN, Karen

31054 *Knight of shadows.* Brooklyn, NY: Poison Pen Press, 1982, 115 p., paper, novel. STAR WARS SERIES.

OSTLING, Joan K., *with Joe R. Christopher*

20025 *C. S. Lewis: an annotated checklist of writings about him and his works.* Kent, OH: Kent State University Press, 1974?, xiii+389 p., cloth, nonf. THE SERIF SERIES #30.

O'SULLIVAN, Vincent, 1872-1940

38000 *The next room.* Edinburgh, Scotland: Tragara Press, 1988, 22 p., paper, story. [Limited to 145 copies].

OTFINOSKI, Steven, 1949-

Barracuda run—SEE: *James Bond in Barracuda run.*

31055 *James Bond in Barracuda run.* New York: Ballantine Books, 1985, 121 p., paper, novel. JAMES BOND SERIES.

31056 *Master of the past.* Middletown, CT: Weekly Reader Books, 1987, 118 p., paper, novel.

31057 *Midnight at monster mansion.* New York, Toronto: Scholastic Inc., 1984, 93 p., paper, novel. TWISTAPLOT #13.

31058 *Monsters to know and love: stories of chills and fun.* Middletown, CT: Xerox Education Publications, A Pal Paperback, 1977, 94 p., paper, coll.

31059 *The screaming grave.* Middletown, CT: Weekly Reader Books, 1982, 108 p., paper, coll.?

31060 *The shrieking skull.* Middletown, CT: Weekly Reader Books, 1988, 126 p., paper, coll.?

31061 *Superworld.* New York, Toronto: Scholastic Inc., 1985, 80 p., paper, novel. MAGIC MICRO ADVENTURE #2.

31062 *The third arm, and other strange tales of the supernatural.* Middletown, CT: A Pal Paperback, Xerox Educational Publications, 1977, 96 p., paper, coll.

31063 *Village of the vampires.* Belmont, CA: A Pacemaker Bestsellers Book, Fearon Pitman Publishers, 1978, 59 p., cloth, novel.

31064 *The zombie maker: stories of amazing adventures.* Middletown, CT: A Bluejeans Book, Xerox Educational Publications, 1978, 95 p., paper, coll.

*OTTUM, Bob [i.e., Robert K. Ottum], 1925-1986

OTTUM, Robert—SEE: Ottum, Bob

OULD, Chris, 1959?-

31065 *Road lines.* London: André Deutsch, 1985, 243 p., cloth, novel.

OUNSLEY, Simon, 1953- , *with David Pringle & John Clute*

20208 *Interzone: the 2nd anthology: new science fiction and fantasy writing.* London, Sydney: Simon & Schuster, 1987, x+208 p., cloth, anth.

20209 *Interzone: the 3rd anthology: new science fiction and fantasy writing.* London, Sydney: Simon & Schuster, 1988, viii+184 p., cloth, anth.

20210 *Interzone: the 4th anthology: new science fiction and fantasy writing.* London: Simon & Schuster, 1989, ix+208 p., cloth, anth.

OVALLE, Pilar de—SEE: de Ovalle, Pilar

OVER, Raymond van—SEE: van Over, Raymond

OVERGARD, William (Thomas Jr.), 1926-1990

31066 *The Divide.* New York: A Jove Book, 1980, 244 p., paper, novel.

OVERHOLSER, Stephen, 1944-

31067 *Wild west rider.* Toronto, New York: A Byron Preiss Book, Bantam Books, 1985, 125 p., paper, novel. TIME MACHINE #9.

OVSTEDAL, Barbara—SEE: Paul, Barbara

OWEN, Betty M.

31068 *The ghostmasters: weird stories by famous writers.* New York, Toronto: Scholastic Book Services, 1976, 171 p., paper, anth.

31069 *Starstreak: stories of space.* New York, Toronto: Scholastic Book Services, 1979, 216 p., paper, anth.

OWEN, David, 1939- , *with Jean-Claude Suares & Richard Siegel*

31070 *Fantastic planets*. Danbury, NH: Reed Books, 1979, 160 p., cloth, nonf.

OWEN, J. Bradley

31071 *Dead season*. New York: Leisure Books, 1988, 366 p., paper, novel.

OWEN, Richard, 1942-

31072 *The eye of the gods*. New York: E. P. Dutton, 1978, 204 p., cloth, novel.

OWEN, Thomas, 1910-

31073 *The desolate presence, and other uncanny stories*. London: William Kimber, 1984, 189 p., cloth, coll.

OWEN, William

31074 *Strange Scottish stories*. Norwich, England: Jarrold Colour Publications, 1981, 143 p., cloth, coll.

OWINGS, Mark (Samuel), 1945-

31075 *Murray Leinster (Will F. Jenkins): a bibliography*. Washington, DC: Washington Science Fiction Association, 1970, [9] p., paper, nonf.
31076 *Poul Anderson: bibliography*. Baltimore, MD: Balticon VII, T-K Graphics, 1973, [15] p., paper, nonf.

with Irving Binkin

17978 *A catalog of Lovecraftiana: the Grill/Binkin collection*. Baltimore, MD: Mirage Press, 1975, x+71 p., cloth, nonf.

with Jack L. Chalker

19742 *The science-fantasy publishers: a critical and bibliographic history, 3rd ed., rev. and enlarged*. Westminster, MD: The Mirage Press, 1991, xxviii+744 p., cloth, nonf.

OWSTON, C. E.

31077 *The Scarlet Skull*. New York: Manor Books, 1979, 246 p., paper, novel. [Title reads *The Scarlet Scull* (sic) on title page].

OXFORD SF GROUP—SEE: Zool, M. H.

OXLEY, B. T.

31078 *George Orwell*. London: Evans Brothers, 1967, 144 p., cloth, nonf.

OXLEY, David Anthony

31079 *Three decades to doom: a novel*. New York, Washington: Vantage Press, 1986, 247 p., cloth, novel.

OXLEY, Dorothy (Anne), 1948-

31080 *Quest*. Oxford, England, Batavia, IL: A Lion Paperback, 1990, 188 p., paper, novel.

OZICK, Cynthia, 1928-

31081 *Levitation: five fictions*. New York: Alfred A. Knopf, 1982, 157 p., cloth, coll.

P

PACHTER, Josh, 1951-

31082   *Top fantasy: the authors' choice, selected and introduced by the authors themselves.* London: J. M. Dent & Sons, 1985, viii+311 p., cloth, anth.

31083   *Top science fiction: the authors' choice.* London: J. M. Dent & Sons, 1984, viii+340 p., cloth, anth.

PACKARD, Andrea

31084   *Secret of the sun god.* Toronto, New York: An Edward Packard Book, Bantam Books, 1987, 118 p., paper, novel. CHOOSE YOUR OWN ADVENTURE #68.

PACKARD, Edward, 1931-

31085   *Africa: where do elephants live underground?* New York: McGraw-Hill Book Co., 1989, 104 p., paper, novel. EARTH INSPECTORS #6.

31086   *Alien invaders.* New York, Toronto: A Choose Your Own Adventure Book, Bantam Books, 1991, 110 p., paper, novel. SPACE HAWKS #2.

31087   *America: why is there an eye on the pyramid on the one-dollar bill?* New York: McGraw-Hill Book Co., 1988, 100 p., paper, novel. EARTH INSPECTORS #1.

31088   *The castle of Frome.* Toronto, New York: Bantam Books, 1986, 121 p., paper, novel. ESCAPE FROM THE KINGDOM OF FROME #1.

31089   *The cave of time.* Toronto, New York: Bantam Books, 1979, 115 p., paper, novel. CHOOSE YOUR OWN ADVENTURE #1.

31090   *Choose your own adventure super adventure: Journey to the year 3000.* Toronto, New York: Bantam Books, 1987, 162 p., paper, novel. CHOOSE YOUR OWN ADVENTURE SUPER ADVENTURE #1.

31091   *The comet masters.* New York, Toronto: A Choose Your Own Adventure Book, Bantam Books, 1991, 113 p., paper, novel. SPACE HAWKS #4.

The curse of the haunted mansion—SEE: *The mystery of Chimney Rock.*

31092   *Deadwood City.* Philadelphia, PA: J. B. Lippincott, 1978, 96 p., cloth, novel. CHOOSE YOUR OWN ADVENTURE #8.

31093   *ESP McGee.* New York: An Avon Camelot Book, 1983, 96 p., paper, novel. ESP MCGEE #1.

Exploration infinity—SEE: *The third planet from Altair.*

31094   *Faster than light.* New York, Toronto: A Choose Your Own Adventure Book, Bantam Books, 1991, 119 p., paper, novel. SPACE HAWKS #1.

31095   *The forbidden castle.* Toronto, New York: Bantam Books, 1982, 118 p., paper, novel. CHOOSE YOUR OWN ADVENTURE #14.

31096   *Ghost hunter.* Toronto, New York: Bantam Books, 1986, 117 p., paper, novel. CHOOSE YOUR OWN ADVENTURE #52.

31097   *Hyperspace.* Toronto, New York: Bantam Books, 1983, 116 p., paper, novel. CHOOSE YOUR OWN ADVENTURE #21.

31098   *Inside UFO 54-40.* Toronto, New York: Bantam Books, 1982, 118 p., paper, novel. CHOOSE YOUR OWN ADVENTURE #12.

31099   *Invaders from within.* New York, Toronto: Bantam Books, 1991, 115 p., paper, novel. CHOOSE YOUR OWN ADVENTURE #110.

Journey to the year 3000—SEE: *Choose your own adventure super adventure: Journey to the year 3000.*

31100   *Kidnapped!* New York, Toronto: Bantam Books, 1991, 112 p., paper, novel. CHOOSE YOUR OWN ADVENTURE #116.

Message from space—SEE: *The third planet from Altair.*

38001   *Mountain survival.* Toronto, New York: Bantam Books, 1984, 115 p., paper, novel. CHOOSE YOUR OWN ADVENTURE #28.

31101   *Mutiny in space.* New York: Bantam Books, 1989, 116 p., paper, novel. CHOOSE YOUR OWN ADVENTURE #90.

31102   *The mystery of Chimney Rock.* Toronto, New York: Bantam Books, 1980, 121 p., paper, novel. CHOOSE YOUR OWN ADVENTURE #5.

31102A   retitled: *The curse of the haunted mansion.* Toronto, New York: Bantam Books,

1989, 121 p., paper, novel. CHOOSE YOUR OWN ADVENTURE #5.

31103 *Olympus: what is the secret of the oracle?* New York: McGraw-Hill Book Co., 1988, p., paper, novel. EARTH INSPECTORS #3.

31104 *The perfect planet.* Toronto, New York: Bantam Books, 1988, 116 p., paper, novel. CHOOSE YOUR OWN ADVENTURE #80.

31105 *Return to the Cave of Time.* Toronto, New York: Bantam Books, 1985, 115 p., paper, novel. CHOOSE YOUR OWN ADVENTURE #50.

31106 *Russia: what is the Golden Horde?* New York: McGraw-Hill Book Co., 1989, p., paper, novel. EARTH INSPECTORS #12.

31107 *Skateboard champion.* New York, Toronto: Bantam Books, 1991, 112 p., paper, novel. CHOOSE YOUR OWN ADVENTURE #112.

31108 *Space fortress.* New York, Toronto: A Choose Your Own Adventure Book, Bantam Books, 1991, 113 p., paper, novel. SPACE HAWKS #3.

31109 *Space vampire.* Toronto, New York: Bantam Books, 1987, 118 p., paper, novel. CHOOSE YOUR OWN ADVENTURE #71.

31110 *Sugarcane Island.* Waitsfield, VT: Vermont Crossroads Press, 1976, 105 p., cloth, novel. CHOOSE YOUR OWN ADVENTURE #62; WHICH WAY BOOKS #6.

31111 *Sugarcane Island.* Toronto, New York: Bantam Books, 1986, 117 p., paper, novel. CHOOSE YOUR OWN ADVENTURE #62. [Expanded edition].

31112 *Supercomputer.* Toronto, New York: Bantam Books, 1984, 118 p., paper, novel. CHOOSE YOUR OWN ADVENTURE #39.

31113 *Survival at sea.* Toronto, New York: Bantam Books, 1982, 118 p., paper, novel. CHOOSE YOUR OWN ADVENTURE #16.

31114 *Tenopia Island.* Toronto, New York: Bantam Books, 1986, 133 p., paper, novel. ESCAPE FROM TENOPIA #1.

31115 *The third planet from Altair.* Philadelphia, PA: J. B. Lippincott Co., 1979, 96 p., cloth, novel. CHOOSE YOUR OWN ADVENTURE #7.

31115A retitled: *Exploration infinity.* London: Magnet Books, 1982, 96 p., paper, novel. CHOOSE YOUR OWN ADVENTURE #7.

31115B retitled: *Message from space.* New York: Bantam Books, 1989, 117 p., paper, novel. CHOOSE YOUR OWN ADVENTURE #7.

31116 *Through the black hole.* New York, Toronto: Bantam Books, 1990, 116 p., paper, novel. CHOOSE YOUR OWN ADVENTURE #97.

31117 *Underground kingdom.* Toronto, New York: Bantam Books, 1983, 108 p., paper, novel. CHOOSE YOUR OWN ADVENTURE #18.

31118 *Vampire invaders.* New York, Toronto: Bantam Books, 1991, 111 p., paper, novel. CHOOSE YOUR OWN ADVENTURE #118.

38002 *Who killed Harlowe Thrombey?* Toronto, New York: Bantam Books, 1981, 122 p., paper, novel. CHOOSE YOUR OWN ADVENTURE #9.

31119 *The worst day of your life.* New York, Toronto: Bantam Books, 1990, 116 p., paper, novel. CHOOSE YOUR OWN ADVENTURE #100.

31120 *You are a genius.* New York, Toronto: Bantam Books, 1989, 112 p., paper, novel. CHOOSE YOUR OWN ADVENTURE #95.

31121 *You are a monster.* Toronto, New York: Bantam Books, 1988, 116 p., paper, novel. CHOOSE YOUR OWN ADVENTURE #84.

31122 *You are a shark.* Toronto, New York: Bantam Books, 1985, 114 p., paper, novel. CHOOSE YOUR OWN ADVENTURE #45.

31123 *You are a superstar.* New York, Toronto: Bantam Books, 1989, 115 p., paper, novel. CHOOSE YOUR OWN ADVENTURE #91.

38003 *Your code name is Jonah.* Toronto, New York: Bantam Books, 1979, 114 p., paper, novel. CHOOSE YOUR OWN ADVENTURE #6.

with R. A. Montgomery

30099 *Mutiny in space.* New York, Toronto: A Packard/Montgomery Book, Bantam Books, 1989, 116 p., paper, novel. CHOOSE YOUR OWN ADVENTURE #90.

PAGE, Bill [i.e., William Reese Page], 1953-

31124 *Index to SF cover art, vol. I.* Bryan, TX: Author, 1979, 14 p., paper, nonf.

31125 *Index to SF cover art, vol. II.* Bryan, TX: Dellwood Press, 1980, 16 p., paper, nonf.

31126 *Index to SF cover art, vol. III.* Bryan, TX: Dellwood Press, 1980, 20 p., paper, nonf.

PAGE, Gerald W(ilburn), 1939-

31127 *Nameless places.* Sauk City, WI: Arkham House, 1975, viii+279 p., cloth, anth.
31128 *The year's best horror stories, series IV.* New York: DAW Books, 1976, 208 p., paper, anth.
31129 *The year's best horror stories, series V.* New York: DAW Books, 1977, 237 p., paper, anth.
31130 *The year's best horror stories, series VI.* New York: DAW Books, 1978, 239 p., paper, anth.
31131 *The year's best horror stories, series VII.* New York: DAW Books, 1979, 221 p., paper, anth.

with Hank Reinhardt

31132 *Heroic fantasy.* New York: DAW Books, 1979, 320 p., paper, anth.

with Karl Edward Wagner

38004 *Horrorstory, volume three: The year's best horror stories VII; The year's best horror stories VIII; The year's best horror stories IX.* Novato, CA, Lancaster, PA: Underwood-Miller, 1991 (i.e., 1992), 541 p., cloth, anth.

PAGE, Ian, 1960-

31133 *Beyond the nightmare gate.* London: Beaver Books, 1985, 31+[188] p., paper, novel. WORLD OF LONE WOLF #3. [Edited by Joe Dever].
31134 *The forbidden city.* London: Beaver Books, 1986, 31+[173] p., paper, novel. WORLD OF LONE WOLF #2. [Edited by Joe Dever].
31135 *Grey Star the wizard.* London: Beaver Books, 1985, 33+[200] p., paper, novel. WORLD OF LONE WOLF #1. [Edited by Joe Dever].
31136 *War of the wizards.* London: Beaver Books, 1986, 37+[202] p., paper, novel. WORLD OF LONE WOLF #4. [Edited by Joe Dever].

PAGE, Kathy, 1958-

31137 *As in music: stories.* London: Methuen, 1990, 205 p., cloth, coll.
31138 *Island paradise.* London: Methuen, 1989, 192 p., cloth, novel.

PAGE, Michael F(itzgerald), 1922- , with Robert Ingpen

26296 *Encyclopaedia of things that never were: creatures, places, and people.* Limpsfield, Surrey, England: Paper Tiger, 1985, 240 p., cloth, nonf.

PAGE, Norvell W., 1906-1961

as RANDOLPH CRAIG

20765 *The city condemned to Hell.* Oak Lawn, IL: Robert Weinberg in Association with Pulp Press, 1975, 91 p., paper, novel. PULP CLASSICS #11.
20766 *Satan's incubators.* Oak Lawn, IL: Robert Weinberg in Association with Pulp Press, 1975, 96 p., paper, novel. PULP CLASSICS #12.

as GRANT STOCKBRIDGE

31139 *Builder of the black empire.* New York: Dimedia, 1980, [96] p., paper, novel. SPIDER SERIES.
31140 *The city destroyer.* New York: Pocket Books, 1975, 157 p., paper, novel. SPIDER #3.
31141 *City of flaming shadows.* New York: A Berkley Medallion Book, 1970, 175 p., paper, novel. SPIDER #4.
31142 *Corpse cargo: the Spider thriller.* New York: Dimedia, 1985, 192 p., paper, novel. SPIDER #2.
31143 *Death and the Spider.* New York: Pocket Books, 1975, 143 p., paper, novel. SPIDER #4.
31144 *Death reign of the vampire king.* New York: Pocket Books, 1975, 144 p., paper, novel. SPIDER #1.
31145 *Hordes of the red butcher.* New York: Pocket Books, 1975, 158 p., paper, novel. SPIDER #2.
31146 *Master of the death madness.* New York: Dimedia, 1980, [96] p., paper, novel. SPIDER SERIES.
31147 *Overlord of the damned.* New York: Dimedia, 1980, [96] p., paper, novel. SPIDER SERIES.
31148 *Prince of evil.* New York: Dimedia, 1985, [192] p., paper, novel. SPIDER SERIES.
31149 *Satan's death blast: the Spider thriller.* New York: Dimedia, 1984, 196 p., paper, novel. SPIDER #1.
     Secret city of crime—SEE: *The Spider, master of men!*
     The Spider and the pain master—SEE: *The Spider, master of men!*
31150 *The Spider, master of men!* New York: Carroll & Graf, 1991, 316 p., paper, coll. SPIDER SERIES. [Includes *Secret*

city of crime; and, *The Spider and the pain master*].

31151 *Wings of the black death.* New York: A Berkley Medallion Book, 1969, 144 p., paper, novel. SPIDER #3.

PAGE, P(atricia) K(athleen), 1916-

31152 *The sun and the moon, and other fictions.* Toronto: Anansi, 1973, 204 p., cloth, coll. [Expanded edition; previously published as by Judith Cape].

as JUDITH CAPE

31153 *The sun and the moon.* New York: Creative Age Press, 1944, 200 p., cloth, coll.

PAGE, Thomas (Walker IV), 1942-

31154 *The man who would not die: an unusual ghost story.* New York: Seaview Books, 1981, 263 p., cloth, novel.
31155 *Sigmet active: a novel.* New York: Times Books, 1978, 184 p., cloth, novel.
31156 *The spirit.* New York: Rawson Associates Publishers, 1977, 252 p., cloth, novel.

PAGE, William R.—SEE: Page, Bill

PAGET, Clarence, 1909-1991

31157 *The 26th Pan book of horror stories.* London & Sydney: Pan Books, 1985, 167 p., paper, anth.
31158 *The 27th Pan book of horror stories.* London & Sydney: Pan Books, 1986, 187 p., paper, anth.
31159 *The 28th Pan book of horror stories.* London & Sydney: Pan Books, 1987, 156 p., paper, anth.
31160 *The 29th Pan book of horror stories.* London & Sydney: Pan Books, 1988, 238 p., paper, anth.
31161 *The 30th Pan book of horror stories.* London & Sydney: Pan Books, 1989, 208 p., paper, anth.

with Stephen Jones

26764 *Dark voices: the best from the Pan book of horror stories.* London & Sydney: Pan Books, 1990, vii+348 p., cloth, anth.

PAGET, Violet—SEE: Lee, Vernon

PAHL, Dennis

31162 *Architects of the abyss: the indeterminate fictions of Poe, Hawthorne, and Melville.* Columbia, MO: University of Missouri Press, 1989, xx+121 p., cloth, nonf.

PAIGE, Richard, pseud.—SEE: Koontz, Dean R.

***PAIN, Barry (Eric Odell), 1864-1928**

PAINE, Lauran (Bosworth), 1916-

as ROY AINSWORTHY

00103 *Focolor.* London: Robert Hale, 1973, 184 p., cloth, novel.

as MARK CARREL

38005 *The underground man.* London: Robert Hale, 1975, 182 p., cloth, novel.

as TROY HOWARD

31163 *The harbinger.* London: Robert Hale, 1972, 192 p., cloth, novel.

PAINE, Michael [pseud. of John Curlovich]

31164 *Cities of the dead.* New York: Charter Books, 1988, 246 p., paper, novel.
31165 *The colors of Hell.* New York: Charter Books, 1990, 281 p., paper, novel.
31166 *Owl light.* New York: Charter Books, 1989, 232 p., paper, novel.

PAINTER, Charlotte, 1926-

31167 *Seeing things.* New York: Random House, 1976, 235 p., cloth, novel.

PAIVA, Jean, 1944-1989

31168 *The last gamble.* New York: An Onyx Book, 1990, 294 p., paper, novel.
31169 *The Lilith factor,* The. New York: An Onyx Book, New American Library, 1989, 303 p., paper, novel.

PAL, George, 1908-1980, *with Joe Morhaim*

30238 *Time machine II.* New York: A Dell Book, 1981, 175 p., paper, novel. TIME MACHINE #2.

PALEO, Lyn

with Camilla Decarnin & Eric Garber

21459 *Worlds apart: an anthology of lesbian and gay science fiction and fantasy.* Boston: Alyson Publications, 1986, 293 p., paper, anth.

with Eric Garber

23642 *Uranian worlds: a reader's guide to alternative sexuality in science fiction and fantasy.* Boston: G. K. Hall & Co., 1983, xxvi+177 p., cloth, nonf. REFERENCE PUBLICATION IN SCIENCE FICTION.

23643 *Uranian worlds: a reader's guide to alternative sexuality in science fiction and fantasy, 2nd ed.* Boston: G. K. Hall & Co., 1990, xxvi+286 p., cloth, nonf.

PALESTINE, Eileen, *with Geoffrey Mandel*

28996 *Star Fleet medical reference manual.* New York: Ballantine Books, 1977, 160 p., paper, fiction.

PALEY, Alan L(ouis), 1943-

31170 *George Orwell: writer and critic of modern society.* New York: SamHar Press, 1974, 32 p., paper, nonf.

PALIN, Michael (Edward), 1943-

31171 *The mirrorstone: a ghost story with holograms.* London: Jonathan Cape, 1986, [32] p., cloth, story.

with Terry Jones

31172 *Ripping yarns.* London: Eyre Methuen, 1978, 186 p., cloth, coll.

PALLENBERG, Barbara

31173 *The making of Exorcist II, The: the heretic.* New York: Warner Books, 1977, 208 p., paper, nonf.

*PALM, Gene [pseud. of Luigi Palmisano], 1912-1988

PALMER, Bruce

Of orc-rags, phials, & a far shore—SEE: Visions of paradise in LotR.

31174 *Visions of paradise in LotR.* Baltimore, MD: T-K Graphics, 1976, 29 p., paper, nonf. [Cover title: *Of orc-rags, phials,* & a far shore: visions of paradise in The lord of the rings].

PALMER, David R(eay), 1941-

31175 *Emergence.* Toronto, New York: Bantam Books, 1984, 291 p., paper, novel.

31176 *Threshold.* Toronto, New York: Bantam Books, 1985, 274 p., paper, novel.

PALMER, Geoffrey, 1912- , *with Noel Lloyd*

28451 *Haunting stories of ghosts and ghouls.* London: Hamlyn, 1982, 256 p., cloth, coll.

PALMER, Jane, 1946-

31177 *Moving moosevan.* London: The Women's Press, 1990, 150 p., paper, novel. PLANET DWELLER #2.

31178 *The planet dweller.* London: The Women's Press, 1985, 147 p., paper, novel. PLANET DWELLER #1.

31179 *The watcher.* London: The Women's Press, 1986, 177 p., paper, novel.

PALMER, Jessica

31180 *Dark lullaby.* New York, London: Pocket Books, 1991, 337 p., paper, novel.

PALMER, Michael (Stephen), 1942-

31181 *Extreme measures.* New York, Toronto: Bantam Books, 1991, 390 p., cloth, novel.

31182 *Flashback.* Toronto, New York: Bantam Books, 1988, 385 p., paper, novel.

31183 *The sisterhood.* Toronto, New York: Bantam Books, 1982, 343 p., paper, novel.

PALMER, Thomas—SEE: Palmer, Tom

PALMER, Tom [i.e., Thomas Palmer], 1955-

31184 *Dream science.* New York: Ticknor & Fields, 1990, 308 p., cloth, novel.

*PALMER, William J., 1890-1982

PALMISANO, Luigi—SEE: Palm, Gene

PALTROWITZ, Donna (Milman), 1950- , *with Stuart Paltrowitz*

31185 *The science fiction computer storybook.* New York: Tribeca Communications, 1983, 116 p., paper, coll.

PALTROWITZ, Stuart, 1946- , *with Donna Paltrowitz*

31185 *The science fiction computer storybook.* New York: Tribeca Communications, 1983, 116 p., paper, coll.

PALUMBO, Dennis (James), 1929-

31186 *City wars.* Toronto, New York: Bantam Books, 1979, 152 p., paper, novel.

PALUMBO, Donald (Emanuel), 1949-

31187 *Eros in the mind's eye: sexuality and the fantastic in art and film.* New York, London: Greenwood Press, 1986, xxvi+ 290 p., cloth, nonf. anth. CONTRI-BU-TIONS TO THE STUDY OF SCIENCE FIC-TION AND FANTASY #21.

31188 *Erotic universe: sexuality and fantastic literature.* New York, London: Greenwood Press, 1986, xviii+305 p., cloth, nonf. anth. CONTRIBUTIONS TO THE STUDY OF SCIENCE FICTION AND FAN-TASY #18.

31189 *Spectrum of the fantastic: selected essays from the Sixth International Conference on the Fantastic in the Arts.* New York, London: Greenwood Press, 1988, xx+ 266 p., cloth, nonf. anth. CONTRI-BUTIONS TO THE STUDY OF SCIENCE FIC-TION AND FANTASY #31.

PANATI, Charles, 1943-

31190 *Links.* Boston: Houghton Mifflin Co., 1978, 227 p., cloth, novel.

31191 *Links.* New York: A Berkley Book, Berkley Publishing Corp., 1979, 247 p., paper, novel. [Revised edition with different ending].

31192 *The pleasuring of Rory Malone.* New York: St. Martin's Press, 1982, 297 p., cloth, novel.

PANGBORN, Edgar, 1909-1976

31193 *The company of glory.* New York: Pyramid Books, 1975, 174 p., paper, novel. DAVY #3.

31194 *Still I persist in wondering.* New York: A Dell Book, 1978, 288 p., paper, coll. DAVY #4.

PANSHIN, (Alexis) Alexei, 1940-

31195 *Farewell to yesterday's tomorrow.* New York: Berkley Publishing Corp., 1975, vii+184 p., cloth, coll.

31196 *Transmutations.* Dublin, PA: Elephant Books, 1982, 214 p., cloth, coll. [Includes some nonfiction].

with Cory Panshin

31197 *Earth magic.* New York: Ace Books, 1978, 275 p., paper, novel.

31198 *SF in dimension: a book of explorations.* Chicago: Advent:Publishers, 1976, 342 p., cloth, nonf. coll.

31199 *SF in dimension: a book of explorations, 2nd ed.* Chicago: Advent:Publishers, 1980, xvi+414 p., paper, nonf. coll.

31200 *The world beyond the hill: science fiction and the quest for transcendence.* Los Angeles: J. P. Tarcher, 1989, x+685 p., cloth, nonf. [Winner of the Hugo Award for Best Nonfiction Book, 1989 (1990)].

PANSHIN, Cory (Seidman), 1947- , *with Alexei Panshin*

31197 *Earth magic.* New York: Ace Books, 1978, 275 p., paper, novel.

31198 *SF in dimension: a book of explorations.* Chicago: Advent:Publishers, 1976, 342 p., cloth, nonf. coll.

31199 *SF in dimension: a book of explorations, 2nd ed.* Chicago: Advent:Publishers, 1980, xvi+414 p., paper, nonf. coll.

31200 *The world beyond the hill: science fiction and the quest for transcendence.* Los Angeles: J. P. Tarcher, 1989, x+685 p., cloth, nonf. [Winner of the Hugo Award for Best Nonfiction Book, 1989 (1990)].

PANTELL, Dora (Fuchs)

31201 *Miss Pickerell and the lost world.* New York: Franklin Watts, 1986, 154 p., cloth, novel. MISS PICKERELL #17.

31202 *Miss Pickerell and the war of the computers.* New York: Franklin Watts, 1984, 136 p., cloth, novel. MISS PICKERELL #16.

with Ellen MacGregor

28808 *Miss Pickerell and the blue whales.* New York: McGraw-Hill, 1983, 159 p., cloth, novel. MISS PICKERELL #15.

28809 *Miss Pickerell and the supertanker.* New York: McGraw-Hill, 1978, 157 p., cloth, novel. MISS PICKERELL #12.

28810 *Miss Pickerell on the trail.* New York: McGraw-Hill, 1982, 159 p., cloth, novel. MISS PICKERELL #14.

28811 *Miss Pickerell tackles the energy crisis.* New York: McGraw-Hill, 1980, 173 p., cloth, novel. MISS PICKERELL #13.

28812 *Miss Pickerell takes the bull by the horns.* New York: McGraw-Hill, 1976, 160 p., cloth, novel. MISS PICKERELL #10.

28813 *Miss Pickerell to the earthquake rescue.* New York: McGraw-Hill, 1977, 158 p., cloth, novel. MISS PICKERELL #11.

PAPE, Gordon (Kendrew), 1936- , *with Tony Aspler*

17061 *Chain reaction.* New York: Viking Press, 1978, 284 p., cloth, novel.

PAPE, Sharon B(arbara), 1947-

31203 *Ghost fire.* New York: Pocket Books, 1983, 254 p., paper, novel.

31204 *The godchildren.* New York: Charter Books, 1986, 260 p., paper, novel.

PAPERMAKER, Peter, pseud.—SEE: Thomas, Peter

PAPPAS, Angelos—SEE: Pappazisis, Evangelos

*PAPPAZISIS, Evangelos [pseud. of Angelos Pappas], 1882-1974

PARDOE, Blaine

38006 *Star Trek: the Next Generation first year sourcebook.* Chicago: FASA Corp., 1989, 64 p., paper, nonf.

with Boyd F. Peterson Jr. & Sam Lewis

28311 *Battletech: Wolf Clan sourcebook.* Chicago: FASA Corp., 1991, 128 p., paper, fiction. BATTLETECH SERIES.

PARDOE, Rosemary (Anne), 1951-

31205 *Ghosts & scholars: stories in the tradition of M. R. James.* Liverpool, England: Rosemary Pardoe, 1979, 40 p., paper, anth.

31206 *The James gang.* Hoole, Cheshire, England: Haunted Library, 1991, 16 p., paper, nonf.

as ANONYMOUS EDITOR

16562 *More ghosts & scholars: ghost stories in the tradition of M. R. James.* Runcorn, England: Haunted Library, Rosemary Pardoe, 1980, 46 p., paper, anth.

as MARY ANN ALLEN

31207 *The angry dead.* Liverpool, England: J. Dempsey, Crimson Altar Press, 1986, 37 p., paper, coll.

with Richard Dalby

20988 *Ghosts and scholars: ghost stories in the tradition of M. R. James.* Wellingborough, Northamptonshire, England: Crucible, 1987, 270 p., cloth, anth.

PARENTE, Audrey, 1948-

31208 *Pulp man's odyssey: the Hugh B. Cave story.* Mercer Island, WA: Starmont House, 1988, xiv+146 p., cloth, nonf. STARMONT POPULAR CULTURE STUDIES #6.

PARENTEAU, Shirley (Laurolyn), 1935-

31209 *The talking coffins of Cryo-City.* New York: Elsevier/Nelson Books, 1979, 126 p., cloth, novel.

PARES, Marion—SEE: Grant, Anthony

PARGETER, Edith (Mary), 1913-

15850 *By firelight.* London: William Heinemann, 1948, 324 p., cloth, novel.

15850A retitled: *By this strange fire.* New York: Reynal & Hitchcock, 1948, 310 p., cloth, novel.

PARISE, Frank D., *with Stephen Rich*

31210 *Age of the storyteller.* Burlingame, CA: Advanced Publishing, 1988, xii+263 p., paper, coll.

PARISH, James Robert, 1946-

with Alan G. Barbour & Alvin H. Marill

17359 *Karloff.* Kew Gardens, NY: Cinefax, 1969, [64] p., paper, nonf.

with Michael R. Pitts

31211 *The great science fiction pictures.* Metuchen, NJ: Scarecrow Press, 1977, viii+382 p., cloth, nonf.

31212 *The great science fiction pictures II.* Metuchen, NJ & London: Scarecrow Press, 1991, x+489 p., cloth, nonf.

PARK, Paul (Claiborne), 1954-

31213 *The cult of loving kindness.* New York: William Morrow & Co., 1991, 312 p., cloth, novel. STARBRIDGE CHRONICLES #3.

31214 *Soldiers of paradise: the Starbridge chronicles.* New York: Arbor House, 1987, 280 p., cloth, novel. STARBRIDGE CHRONICLES #1.

The Starbridge Chronicles—SEE: *Soldiers of paradise: the Starbridge chronicles.*

The Starbridge chronicles—SEE: *Sugar rain: the Starbridge chronicles.*

31215 *The sugar festival.* New York: Guild America Books, 1989, 568 p., cloth, coll. STARBRIDGE CHRONICLES #1-2.

31216 *Sugar rain: the Starbridge chronicles.* New York: William Morrow & Co., 1989, 384 p., cloth, novel. STARBRIDGE CHRONICLES #2.

PARK, Ruth [i.e., Rosina Ruth Lucia Park Niland], 1923-

31217 *My sister Sif.* Ringwood, Victoria, Australia: A Robert Sessions Book, Viking Kestrel, 1986, 180 p., cloth, novel.

31218 *Playing Beatie Bow.* Melbourne, Victoria, Australia: Thomas Nelson, 1980, 196 p., cloth, novel.

31219 *Things in corners.* Ringwood, Victoria, Australia: Viking Kestrel, 1989, 196 p., cloth, coll.

PARKER, Benson, *with H. Beam Piper*

31221 *The adventures of Little Fuzzy.* New York: Platt & Munk Publishers, 1983, 43 p., cloth, story. LITTLE FUZZY SERIES. [Adapted from *Little Fuzzy* by Piper].

PARKER, Chris

31222 *Kyoki.* Upton upon Severn, England: Malvern, 1987, 222 p., cloth, novel.

PARKER, Daniel Fitzgeorge- —SEE: Daniel, Mark

PARKER, Helen N(ethercutt), 1947-

31223 *Biological themes in modern science fiction.* Ann Arbor, MI: UMI Research Press, 1984, 109 p., cloth, nonf. STUDIES IN SPECULATIVE FICTION #6.

PARKER, Jennifer

31224 *Daughters of Lucifer.* New York: Star Distributors, 1977, 180 p., paper, novel.

PARKER, Laura [pseud. of Laura Ann Castoro], 1948-

31225 *For love's sake only.* New York: A Dell Book, 1991, 443 p., paper, novel.

PARKER, Marsha (Zurich), 1952-

31226 *Ghosts.* New York: E. P. Dutton & Co., 1982, 264 p., cloth, novel.

PARKER, Patricia L.

31227 *Charles Brockden Brown: a reference guide.* Boston: G. K. Hall & Co., 1980, xxv+132 p., cloth, nonf.

PARKER, Ronn

31228 *Transform node: science fiction mystical adventures.* New York, Washington: Vantage Press, 1990, 115 p., cloth, novel.

PARKIN, Patricia

as ANONYMOUS EDITOR

31229 *The Twelfth ghost book.* London: Barrie & Jenkins, 1976, 192 p., cloth, anth.

with James Hale

24994 *The 2nd bumper ghost book.* London & Sydney: Pan Books, 1978, 333 p., paper, anth. [Combines *The twelfth ghost book* and *The thirteenth ghost book*].

PARKINSON, Dan(iel Edward), 1935-

31230 *The gates of Thorbardin.* Lake Geneva, WI: TSR Inc., 1990, 310 p., paper, novel. DRAGONLANCE HEROES II #2.

31231 *Starsong: a science-fantasy love story.* Lake Geneva, WI: TSR Inc., 1988, 314 p., paper, novel.

PARKINSON, T. L.

31232 *The man upstairs.* New York: E. P. Dutton, 1991, 226 p., cloth, novel.

PARKS, Edd Winfield, 1906-1968

31233 *Edgar Allan Poe as literary critic.* Athens, GA: University of Georgia Press, 1964, 114 p., cloth, nonf.

PARNELL, Frank H(erbert Charles), 1916- , with Mike Ashley

16858 *Monthly terrors: an index to the weird fantasy magazines published in the United States and Great Britain.* Westport, CT, London: Greenwood Press, 1985, xxvii+602 p., cloth, nonf.

PARNOV, Eremei (Iudovich), 1935- , with Mikhail Emtsev

22662 *World soul.* New York: Macmillan Publishing Co.; London: Collier Macmillan Publishers, 1978, viii+178 p., cloth, novel. [Translation by Antonina W. Bouis of *Dusha mira*].

PARRINDER, (John) Patrick, 1944-

31234 *H. G. Wells.* Edinburgh, Scotland: Oliver & Boyd, 1970, 120 p., cloth, nonf.
31235 *H. G. Wells: the critical heritage.* London: Routledge & Kegan Paul, 1972, xv+351 p., cloth, nonf. anth.
31236 *Science fiction: a critical guide.* London & New York: Longman, 1979, 238 p., cloth, nonf. anth.
31237 *Science fiction: its criticism and teaching.* London & New York: Methuen, 1980, xix+166 p., cloth, nonf.
31238 *The war of the worlds: notes.* Harlow, UK: Longman, 1981, 64 p., paper, nonf.

with Christopher Rolfe

31239 *H. G. Wells under revision: proceedings of the International H. G. Wells Symposium, London, July 1986.* Selinsgrove, PA: Susquehanna University Press; London: Associated University Presses, 1990, 263 p., cloth, nonf. anth.

with H. G. Wells Society & A. H. Watkins & J. R. Hammond

24872 *H. G. Wells: a comprehensive bibliography, 4th ed.* London: H. G. Wells Society, 1986, 58 p., paper, nonf.

PARRISH, Barney, pseud.—SEE: Wolk, George

PARRY, Michel (Patrick), 1947-

Christopher Lee's archives of evil—SEE: Archives of evil.
31240 *The fifth Mayflower book of black magic stories.* St Albans, Hertfordshire, England: Mayflower, 1976, 158 p., paper, anth.

31241 *The fourth Mayflower book of black magic stories.* St Albans, Hertfordshire, England: Mayflower, 1976, 192 p., paper, anth.
31242 *Ghostbreakers.* London: Granada, 1985, 128 p., cloth, anth.
31243 *Jack the knife.* St Albans, Hertfordshire, England: Mayflower, 1975, 160 p., paper, anth.
31244 *Reign of terror: great Victorian horror stories.* London: Severn House, 1977, 186 p., cloth, anth.
31245 *Reign of terror: the 1st Corgi book of great Victorian horror stories.* London: Corgi Books, 1976, 187 p., paper, anth.
31246 *Reign of terror: the 2nd Corgi book of great Victorian horror stories.* London: Corgi Books, 1977, 190 p., paper, anth.
31247 *Reign of terror: the 3rd Corgi book of great Victorian horror stories.* London: Corgi Books, 1977, 158 p., paper, anth.
31248 *Reign of terror: the 4th Corgi book of great Victorian horror stories.* London: Corgi Books, 1978, 158 p., paper, anth.
31249 *The rivals of Dracula: a century of vampire fiction.* London: Corgi Books, 1977, 190 p., paper, anth.
31250 *The rivals of Frankenstein: a gallery of monsters.* London: Corgi Books, 1977, 222 p., paper, anth.
31251 *The rivals of King Kong: a rampage of beasts.* London: Corgi Books, 1978, 205 p., paper, anth.
31259A *The roots of evil: weird stories of super plants.* New York: Taplinger Publishing Co., 1976, 190 p., cloth, anth. [Originally published under the name Carlos Cassaba].
31252 *Santa 2000: the science fiction Santa Claus.* London: Granada, 1984, 86 p., cloth, anth.
31262A *Savage horrors: tales of magical fantasy.* New York: Taplinger Publishing Co., 1980, 190 p., cloth, anth. [Originally published under the name Eric Pendragon].
31253 *The sixth Mayflower book of black magic stories.* St Albans, Hertfordshire, England: Mayflower, 1977, 174 p., paper, anth.
31254 *Spaced out.* London, Toronto: Panther, Granada Publishing, 1977, 192 p., paper, anth.
31255 *Superheroes.* London: Sphere Books, 1978, 207 p., paper, anth.
31256 *The supernatural solution: stories of spooks and sleuths.* St Albans, Hertfordshire, England: Panther, 1976, 222 p., paper, anth.

31257 *The third Mayflower book of black magic stories.* St Albans, Hertfordshire, England: Mayflower, 1975, 220 p., paper, anth.

31258 *Waves of terror: weird stories about the sea.* London: Victor Gollancz, 1976, 208 p., cloth, anth.

as CARLOS CASSABA

31259 *Roots of evil: beyond the secret life of plants.* London: Corgi Books, 1976, 191 p., paper, anth.

as LINDA LOVECRAFT

31260 *The devil's kisses.* London: Corgi Books, 1976, 173 p., paper, anth.

31261 *More devil's kisses.* London: Corgi Books, 1977, 188 p., paper, anth.

as ERIC PENDRAGON

31262 *Savage heroes: tales of sorcery and black magic.* London: A Star Book, W. H. Allen, 1977, 190 p., paper, anth.

with Christopher Lee

28025 *Archives of evil.* London: W. H. Allen & Co., 1977, 172 p., cloth, anth.

28025A retitled: *Christopher Lee's Archives of evil.* London: Mayflower Books, 1979, 160 p., paper, anth.

28026 *Christopher Lee's 'X' certificate, no. 1.* London: W. H. Allen & Co., 1975, 176 p., cloth, anth. [Only volume issued].
Christopher Lee's Archives of evil—SEE: *Archives of evil.*
Christopher Lee's omnibus of evil—SEE: *The great villains.*

28027 *From the archives of evil.* New York: Warner Books, 1976, 205 p., paper, anth.

28028 *From the archives of evil #2.* New York: Warner Books, 1976, 220 p., paper, anth.

28029 *The great villains: an omnibus of evil.* London: W. H. Allen & Co., 1978, 255 p., cloth, anth.

28029A retitled: *Christopher Lee's Omnibus of evil.* London: Mayflower, 1980, 255 p., paper, anth.

28030 *Lurking shadows: an anthology.* London: W. H. Allen & Co., 1979, 157 p., cloth, anth.
Omnibus of evil—SEE: *The great villains.*

with Garry Rusoff

31263 *Throne of fire.* London: Orbit, 1975, [207] p., paper, novel. CHARIOTS OF FIRE: GIRADOUX MANUSCRIPT #2.

with Milton Subotsky

31264 *Sex in the 21st century: a collection of SF erotica.* London, Toronto: Panther, Granada Publishing, 1979, 172 p., paper, anth.

PARSONS, James B(unyan), 1921-

31265 *The little book of all colors.* San Francisco: Chinese Materials Center, 1976, 141-269 p., paper, novel.

PARVIN, Brian

31266 *The golden garden.* London: Robert Hale, 1987, 172 p., cloth, novel.

31267 *The moon-keepers.* London: Robert Hale, 1988, 173 p., cloth, novel.

31268 *The singing tree.* London: Robert Hale, 1985, 185 p., cloth, novel.

PASCAL, Francine, 1938-

31269 *Hangin' out with Cici.* New York: Viking Press, 1977, 152 p., cloth, novel.

PASCAL, Jacques, pseud.

31270 *Futuresex.* Chatsworth, CA: World-Wide Publishing Co., 1981, 187 p., paper, novel.

31271 *Virgin's sacrifice.* Encino, CA: World-Wide Publishing Co., 1980, 186 p., paper, novel.

PASCAL, Jamie, *with Laurie Pascal*

38007 *The ballarina mystery.* New York, Toronto: Scholastic Inc., 1984, 58 p., paper, fiction. PICK-A-PATH #12.

38008 *Mystery at Mockingbird Manor.* New York, Toronto: Scholastic Inc., 1983, 57 p., paper, fiction. PICK-A-PATH #6.

PASCAL, Laurie, *with Jamie Pascal*

38007 *The ballarina mystery.* New York, Toronto: Scholastic Inc., 1984, 58 p., paper, fiction. PICK-A-PATH #12.

38008 *Mystery at Mockingbird Manor.* New York, Toronto: Scholastic Inc., 1983, 57 p., paper, fiction. PICK-A-PATH #6.

PASCALL, Jeremy [pseud. of Jeremy James Zupringer], 1946-

31272 *God: the ultimate autobiography.* London: Ebury, 1987, 143 p., cloth, novel.
31273 *The King Kong story.* Secaucus, NJ: Chartwell Books in Association with Phoebus, 1977, 64 p., cloth, novel.
31274 *Satan: the kiss and tell memoirs.* London: Ebury, 1988, 142 p., cloth, novel.

PASNAK, William, 1949-

31275 *In the city of the king.* Vancouver, British Columbia, Canada: Douglas & McIntyre, A Groundwood Book, 1984, 144 p., paper, novel.

PASSAILAIGUE, Tomás—SEE: Bethancourt, T. Ernesto

PASSES, Alan [i.e., Alan Passes-Pazolski], 1943-

31276 *Big step.* London: Allison & Busby, 1977, 166 p., cloth, novel.

PASSEY, Helen K.

31277 *Speak to the rain.* New York: Atheneum, 1989, 167 p., cloth, novel.

PATAI, Daphne, 1943-

31278 *Looking backward, 1988-1888: essays on Edward Bellamy.* Amherst, MA: University of Massachusetts Press, 1988, viii+227 p., cloth, nonf. anth.
31279 *The Orwell mystique: a study in male ideology.* Amherst, MA: University of Massachusetts Press, 1984, x+334 p., cloth, nonf.

PATON WALSH, Jill [i.e., Gillian Paton Walsh], 1937-

31280 *A chance child.* London: Macmillan, 1978, 158 p., cloth, novel.
31281 *The green book.* London: Macmillan Children's, 1981, 112 p., cloth, novel.
31281A retitled: *Shine.* London: Macdonald & Co., 1988, 96 p., paper, novel.
   Shine—SEE: *The green book.*
31282 *Torch.* London: Viking Kestrel, 1987, 176 p., cloth, novel.

PATON, John [pseud. of Frederick John Alford Bateman], 1921-

31283 *Leap to the galactic core.* London: Robert Hale, 1978, 175 p., cloth, novel.

31284 *Proteus.* London: Robert Hale, 1979, 191 p., cloth, novel.
31285 *The sea of rings.* London: Robert Hale, 1979, 192 p., cloth, novel.

PATRICK, DeAnn, pseud.

31286 *Kindred spirits.* New York: A Tapestry Book, Pocket Books, 1982, 310 p., paper, novel.

PATRICK, Lynn, pseud.—SEE: Pinianski, Patricia & Sweeney, Linda

PATTEN, Brian, 1946-

31287 *Mr. Moon's last case.* London: George Allen & Unwin, 1975, 164 p., paper, novel.

PATTERSON, James (Brendan), 1947-

31288 *Black market.* New York: Simon & Schuster, 1986, 365 p., cloth, novel.
31289 *Virgin.* New York: McGraw-Hill Book Co., 1980, xi+252 p., cloth, novel.

PATTERSON, Nancy-Lou, 1929-

31290 *Apple staff and silver crown: a fairy tale.* Erin, Ontario, Canada: Porcupine's Quill, 1985, 223 p., paper, novel.

PATTISON, Barrie, 1940-

31291 *The seal of Dracula.* London: Lorrimer, 1975, 136 p., paper, nonf.

PATTISON, Patrick, *with Donald A. Reed*

31292 *Science fiction film awards: collector's edition.* [Los Angeles]: ESE California, 1981, 107 p., cloth, nonf.

PATTON, Cliff

31293 *The Omni strain.* New York: Zebra Books, Kensington Publishing Corp., 1980, 384 p., paper, novel.

with Leah Patton

31294 *Ghost rig.* New York: Zebra Books, Kensington Publishing Corp., 1981, 576 p., paper, novel.

with Leah Temple

31295 *Fatal analysis.* New York: Zebra Books, Kensington Publishing Corp., 1988, 379 p., paper, novel.

PATTON, Leah, *with Cliff Patton*

31294 *Ghost rig.* New York: Zebra Books, Kensington Publishing Corp., 1981, 576 p., paper, novel.

as LEAH TEMPLE, *with Cliff Patton*

31295 *Fatal analysis.* New York: Zebra Books, Kensington Publishing Corp., 1988, 379 p., paper, novel.

PATTOU, Edith [i.e., Edith Pattou Emery]

31296 *Hero's song.* San Diego, CA: Harcourt Brace Jovanovich, 1991, 290 p., cloth, novel.

PATTRICK, William

Duel, and other horror stories of the road—SEE: *Mysterious motoring stories.*
31297 *Mysterious air stories.* London: W. H. Allen & Co., 1986, 249 p., cloth, anth.
31298 *Mysterious motoring stories.* London: W. H. Allen & Co., 1987, 224 p., cloth, anth.
31298A retitled: *Duel, and other horror stories of the road.* London: A Star Book, W. H. Allen & Co., 1987, 224 p., paper, anth.
31299 *Mysterious railway stories.* London: W. H. Allen & Co., 1984, 255 p., cloth, anth.
31300 *Mysterious sea stories.* London: W. H. Allen & Co., 1985, 247 p., cloth, anth.

PAUL, Barbara [pseud. of Barbara Kathleen Өvstedal], 1925-

31301 *The curse of Halewood.* London: Macdonald & Jane's, 1976, 254 p., cloth, novel.
31301A retitled: *Devil's fire, love's revenge.* New York: St. Martin's Press, 1976, 232 p., cloth, novel.
Devil's fire, love's revenge—SEE: *The curse of Halewood.*

PAUL, Barbara (Jeanne), 1931-

31302 *Bibblings.* New York: A Signet Book, New American Library, 1979, 169 p., paper, novel.

31303 *An exercise for madmen.* New York: A Berkley Book, Berkley Publishing Corp., 1978, 168 p., paper, novel.
31304 *Liars and tyrants and people who turn blue.* Garden City, NY: Doubleday & Co., 1980, 177 p., cloth, novel.
31305 *Pillars of salt.* New York: A Signet Book, New American Library, 1979, 183 p., paper, novel.
31306 *Star Trek: The three-minute universe.* New York, London: Pocket Books, 1988, 265 p., paper, tele. STAR TREK #41.
The three-minute universe—SEE: *Star Trek: The three-minute universe.*
31307 *Under the canopy.* New York: A Signet Book, New American Library, 1980, 245 p., paper, novel.

PAUL, Don de—SEE: **de Paul, Don**

PAUL, Edith de—SEE: **de Paul, Edith**

PAULSEN, Gary (Melvin), 1939-

31308 *Canyons.* New York: Delacorte Press, 1990, 184 p., cloth, novel.
31309 *Meteorite track 291.* New York: A Dell Book in Association with G/M Publishing, 1979, 221 p., paper, novel.
31310 *The night the white dear died.* New York: Delacorte Press, 1990, 104 p., cloth, novel.

with Ray Peekner

31311 *The green recruit.* Independence, MO: Independence Press, 1978, 105 p., cloth, novel.

PAUSACKER, Jennifer—SEE: **Pausacker, Jenny**

PAUSACKER, Jenny [i.e., Jennifer Pausacker], 1948-

31312 *Fast forward.* Sydney, Australia: Angus & Robertson, 1989, [88] p., cloth, novel.

PAUSEWANG, Gudrun, 1928-

The last children—SEE: *The last children of Schevenborn.*
31313 *The last children of Schevenborn.* Saskatoon, Saskatchewan, Canada: Western Producer Prairie Books, 1988, 116 p., cloth, novel. [Translation by Norman Wyatt of *Die letzen kinder von Schewenborn*].
31313A retitled: *The last children.* London: Julia MacRae Books, 1989, 123 p., cloth,

novel. [Translation by Norman Wyatt of *Die letzen kinder von Schewenborn*].

PAUTZ, Peter D(ennis), 1952- , *with Kathryn Cramer*

20776 *Architecture of fear.* New York: Arbor House, 1987, 304 p., cloth, anth.

PAVIC, Milorad, 1929-

31314 *Dictionary of the Khazars: a lexicon novel in 100,000 words.* New York: Alfred A. Knopf, 1988, 338 p., cloth, fiction. [Translation by Christina Pribicevic-Zoric of *Hazarski recnik*].

31315 *Landscape painted with tea.* New York: Alfred A. Knopf, 1990, 337 p., cloth, fiction. [Translation by Christina Pribicevic-Zoric of *Predeo slikan cajem*].

PAVLAT, Robert, 1926-1983, *with Bill Evans*

22803 *Fanzine index: listing most fanzines from the beginning through 1952, including titles, editors' names, and data on each issue.* Flushing, NY: Harold Palmer Piser, Worldfair Publications, 1965, 141 p., paper, nonf.

PAXSON, Diana L(ucile), 1943-

31316 *Brisingamen.* New York: Berkley Books, 1984, 261 p., paper, novel.

31317 *The earthstone.* New York: Tor SF, A Tom Doherty Associates Book, 1987, 278 p., paper, novel. WESTRIA #4.

31318 *Lady of darkness.* New York: A Timescape Book, Pocket Books, 1983, 253 p., paper, novel. WESTRIA #2.

31319 *Lady of light.* New York: A Timescape Book, Pocket Books, 1982, 261 p., paper, novel. WESTRIA #1.

31320 *Lady of light, lady of darkness.* London: New English Library, 1990, 594 p., paper, coll. WESTRIA #1-2. [Includes *Lady of light*; *Lady of darkness*].

31320A retitled: *The mistress of the jewels.* New York: Tor Fantasy, A Tom Doherty Associates Book, 1991, vi+503 p., paper, novel. WESTRIA #1-2. [Includes *Lady of light*; *Lady of darkness*].
The mistress of the jewels—SEE: *Lady of light, lady of darkness*.

31321 *The paradise tree.* New York: Ace Books, 1987, 243 p., paper, novel.

31322 *The sea star.* New York: Tor SF, A Tom Doherty Associates Book, 1988, 374 p., paper, novel. WESTRIA #5.

31323 *The serpent's tooth.* New York: William Morrow & Co., 1991, 402 p., cloth, novel.

31324 *Silverhair the wanderer.* New York: Tor SF, A Tom Doherty Associates Book, 1986, 310 p., paper, novel. WESTRIA #3.

31325 *White mare, red stallion.* New York: Berkley Books, 1986, 242 p., paper, novel.

31326 *The white raven.* New York: William Morrow & Co., 1988, 411 p., cloth, novel.

31327 *The wind crystal.* New York: Tor Fantasy, A Tom Doherty Associates Book, 1990, 308 p., paper, novel. WESTRIA #6.

PAYER, Sue

31328 *Second body.* New York: Belmont Tower Books, 1979, 250 p., paper, novel.

PAYN, James, 1830-1898

38009 *The eavesdropper: an unparalleled experience.* London: Smith, Elder & Co., 1888, 122 p., cloth, novel.

as ANONYMOUS AUTHOR

03667 *The cruise of the anti-torpedo.* London: Tinsley Brothers, 1871, 48 p., paper, story. BATTLE OF DORKING SEQUEL.

PAYNE, Bernal C. Jr., 1941-

31329 *Experiment in terror.* Boston: Houghton Mifflin Co., 1987, 215 p., cloth, novel.

31330 *It's about time.* New York: Macmillan Publishing Co., 1984, 170 p., cloth, novel.

31330A retitled: *Trapped in time.* New York: An Archway Paperback, Pocket Books, 1986, 151 p., paper, novel.

31331 *The late, great Dick Hart.* Boston: Houghton Mifflin Co., 1986, 133 p., cloth, novel.
Trapped in time—SEE: *It's about time*.

*PAYNE, Charles, <u>1909-</u>

PAYNE, Donald Gordon—SEE: Cameron, Ian

PAYNE, John Howard, 1791-1852, *with Mary W. Shelley & Washington Irving*

26331 *The romance of Mary W. Shelley, John Howard Payne, and Washington Irving.* Boston: Bibliophile Society, 1907, 100 p., cloth, nonf. coll.

PAYNE, Phil Stephensen- —SEE: Stephensen-Payne, Phil

*PAYNE, (Pierre Stephen) Robert, 1911-<u>1983</u>

PAYNE, Ronald, *with Murray Leinster*

28173 *Last Murray Leinster interview.* Richmond, VA: Waves Press, 1983, 12 p., paper, nonf.

PAYSON, Patricia

31332 *Science fiction: self-directed study units for grades K-3 and 4-8, gifted, easily adapted for regular classroom use.* Tucson, AZ: Zephyr, 1982, 79 p., paper, nonf.

PAYTON, Crystal, *with Leland Payton*

31333 *Space toys: a collector's guide to science fiction and astronautical toys.* Sedalia, MO: Collectors Compass, 1982, 82 p., paper, nonf.

PAYTON, Leland, *with Crystal Payton*

31333 *Space toys: a collector's guide to science fiction and astronautical toys.* Sedalia, MO: Collectors Compass, 1982, 82 p., paper, nonf.

PAZOLSKI, Alan Passes- —SEE: Passes, Alan

PAZZI, Roberto, 1946-

31334 *Adrift in time.* London: André Deutsch, 1991, 154 p., cloth, novel. [Translation by Vivien Sinott of *La malattia del tempo*].
31335 *The princess and the dragon.* New York: Alfred A. Knopf, 1990, vii+162 p., cloth, novel. [Translation by M. J. Fitzgerald of *La principessa e il drago*].

PEAK, Michael

31336 *Cat house.* New York: A Signet Book, New American Library, 1989, 255 p., paper, novel.

PEAKE, Mervyn (Laurence), 1911-1968

31337 *Boy in darkness.* Exeter, England: Wheaton, 1976, 61 p., paper, story. GORMENGHAST SERIES. [Edited by Kenyon Calthrop].
Gormenghast—SEE: *The Titus books.*

The Gormenghast trilogy—SEE: *The Titus books.*
31338 *Peake's progress: selected writings and drawings of Mervyn Peake.* London: Allen Lane, 1978, 576 p., cloth, coll. [Edited by Maeve Peake].
31339 *The Titus books: Titus Groan, Gormenghast, Titus alone.* Harmondsworth, Middlesex, England: Penguin Books in Association with Eyre & Spottiswoode, 1983, 1023 p., paper, coll. GORMENGHAST TRILOGY #1-3.
31339A retitled: *Gormenghast.* Woodstock, NY: Overlook Press, 1991, 1023 p., paper, coll. GORMENGHAST TRILOGY #1-3.
31339B retitled: *The Gormenghast trilogy.* New York: Viking Overlook, 1988, 1023 p., cloth, coll. GORMENGHAST TRILOGY #1-3.

with Colin Greenland

24661 *Titus unbound.* Oxford, England: Oxford University Press, 1977, 27 p., paper, story. [Adapted from the novel by Peake].

PEARCE, Brenda, 1935-

31340 *Kidnapped into space.* London: Dennis Dobson, 1975, 208 p., cloth, novel.
31341 *Worlds for the grabbing.* London: Dennis Dobson, 1977, 222 p., cloth, novel.

PEARCE, Howard D(ouberley), 1931-

with Robert A. Collins

20330 *The scope of the fantastic: culture, biography, themes, children's literature: selected essays from the First International Conference on the Fantastic in Literature and Film.* Westport, CT & London: Greenwood Press, 1985, xii+284 p., cloth, nonf. anth. CONTRIBUTIONS TO THE STUDY OF SCIENCE FICTION AND FANTASY #11.
20331 *The scope of the fantastic: theory, practice, major authors: selected essays from the First International Conference on the Fantastic in Literature and Film.* Westport, CT & London: Greenwood Press, 1985, xii+295 p., cloth, nonf. anth. CONTRIBUTIONS TO THE STUDY OF SCIENCE FICTION AND FANTASY #10.

with Jan Hokenson

25816 *Forms of the fantastic: selected essays from the Third International Conference on the*

Fantastic in Literature and Film. Westport, CT & New York: Greenwood Press, 1986, xiv+262 p., cloth, nonf. anth. CONTRIBUTIONS TO THE STUDY OF SCIENCE FICTION AND FANTASY #20.

PEARCE, (Ann) Philippa (Christie), 1920-

31342 *The shadow-cage, and other tales of the supernatural.* Harmondsworth, Middlesex, England: Kestrel Books, 1977, 142 p., paper, coll.
31343 *Who's afraid? and other strange stories.* London: Viking Kestrel, 1986, 120 p., cloth, coll.

PEARL, Jacques B.—SEE: Pearl, Jack

PEARL, Jack [i.e., Jacques Bain Pearl], 1923- as STEPHANIE BLAKE

31344 *Secret sins.* New York: Playboy Press Paperbacks, 1980, 398 p., paper, novel.

PEARSON, Kit, 1947-

31345 *A handful of time.* Markham, Ontario, Canada: Viking, 1987, 186 p., cloth, novel.

PEARSON, Michael (Edward Naylor), 1941- , with Amabel Williams-Ellis

31346 *Strange orbits: an anthology of science fiction.* Glasgow, Scotland: Blackie & Son, 1976, 190 p., cloth, anth.
31347 *Strange planets: an anthology of science fiction.* Glasgow, Scotland, London: Blackie & Son, 1977, 176 p., cloth, anth.

PEARSON, Peter

31348 *Postscript for Malpas.* London: Mac-millan, 1975, 158 p., cloth, novel.

PEARY, Dannis—SEE: Peary, Danny

PEARY, Danny [i.e., Dannis Peary], 1949-

31349 *Cult movie stars.* New York: Simon & Schuster, 1991, 608 p., cloth, nonf.
31350 *Cult movies: the classics, the sleepers, the weird, and the wonderful.* New York: Delacorte Press, 1981, xiii+402 p., cloth, nonf.
31351 *Cult movies 2: 50 more of the classics, the sleepers, the weird, and the wonderful.* New York: A Delta Book, 1983, 181 p., paper, nonf.

31352 *Cult movies 3: 50 more of the classics, the sleepers, the weird, and the wonderful.* New York: Simon & Schuster, 1988, 286 p., paper, nonf.
31353 *Omni's screen flights/screen fantasies: the future according to science fiction cinema.* Garden City, NY: Doubleday & Co., A Dolphin Book, 1984, 310 p., cloth, nonf. anth.

PECK, Claudia A(nn)

31354 *Spirit crossings.* New York, Toronto: Spectra, Bantam Books, 1991, 312 p., paper, novel.

*PECK, Ira, <u>1922-</u>

PECK, Louis F., 1904-

31355 *A life of Matthew G. Lewis.* Cambridge, MA: Harvard University Press, 1961, ix+331 p., cloth, nonf.

*PECK, Richard E(arl), <u>1936-</u>

PECK, Richard (Wayne), 1934-

31356 *Anonymously yours.* Englewood Cliffs, NJ: Julian Messner, 1991, 122 p., cloth, nonf.
31357 *Blossom Culp and the sleep of death.* New York: Delacorte Press, 1986, 185 p., cloth, novel. BLOSSOM CULP #4.
31358 *The dreadful future of Blossom Culp.* New York: Delacorte Press, 1983, 183 p., cloth, novel. BLOSSOM CULP #3.
31359 *The ghost belonged to me: a novel.* New York: Viking Press, 1975, 183 p., cloth, novel. BLOSSOM CULP #1.
31360 *Ghosts I have been: a novel.* New York: Viking Press, 1977, 214 p., cloth, novel. BLOSSOM CULP #2.
31361 *Voices after midnight: a novel.* New York: Delacorte Press, 1989, 181 p., cloth, novel.

PECK, Sylvia

31362 *Seal child.* New York: Morrow Junior Books, 1989, 200 p., cloth, novel.

PECKHAM, Virginia, 1925-

38010 *Proud angels: a novel.* New York: Duell, Sloane & Pearce, 1949, 409 p., cloth, novel.

PEDLER, Christopher—SEE: Pedler, Kit

PEDLER, Kit [i.e., Christopher Magnus Howard Pedler], 1927-1981, *with Gerry Davis*

21259 *Doomwatch: The world in danger.* London: Longman, 1975, 90 p., paper, tele.
21260 *The Dynostar menace.* London: Souvenir Press, 1975, 271 p., cloth, novel.
The world in danger—SEE: *Doomwatch: The world in danger.*

PEDNEAU, Dave, 1947-1990

as MARC ELIOT

31363 *How dear the dawn.* New York: Ballantine Books, 1987, 280 p., paper, novel.

as LEE HAWKS

31364 *Night, winter, and death.* New York: Ballantine Books, 1990, 283 p., paper, novel.

PEECHER, John Phillip

31365 *The making of Star Wars: The Return of the Jedi.* New York: A Del Rey Book, Ballantine Books, 1983, 292 p., paper, nonf.

PEEKNER, Ray, *with Gary Paulsen*

31311 *The green recruit.* Independence, MO: Independence Press, 1978, 105 p., cloth, novel.

PEEL, Colin D(udley), 1936-

31366 *Glimpse of forever.* London: Robert Hale, 1980, 191 p., cloth, novel.
31367 *Hell seed.* New York: St. Martin's Press; London: Robert Hale, 1978, 191 p., cloth, novel.

PEEL, John (Ronald), 1954-

15 yrs. later affair—SEE: *Files magazine spotlight on The U.N.C.L.E. files: 15 yrs. later affair.*
All our yesterdays—SEE: *Files magazine spotlight on The Star Trek files: All our yesterdays.*
The animated voyages begin—SEE: *Files magazine spotlight on The Star Trek files: The animated voyages begin.*
The animated voyages end—SEE: *Files magazine spotlight on The Star Trek files: The animated voyages end.*
Assignment: Earth—SEE: *Files magazine spotlight on The Star Trek files: Assignment: Earth.*

The chase—SEE: *Doctor Who: The chase.*
31368 *Classic files magazine spotlight on The Star Trek files: The early voyages.* Canoga Park, CA: Psi Fi Movie Press, 1986, [52] p., paper, nonf.
Daleks' master plan, part 1: Mission to the unknown—SEE: *Doctor Who: The daleks' master plan, part 1: Mission to the unknown.*
Danger awaits—SEE: *The Gerry Anderson's Thunderbirds files: Danger awaits.*
The deadly quest—SEE: *The U.N.C.L.E. files: The deadly quest.*
31369 *Doctor Who.* Los Angeles: Schuster & Schuster, 1987, 289 p., paper, nonf.
Doctor Who: Season four—SEE: *Files magazine spotlight on Doctor Who: Season four.*
Doctor Who: Season one—SEE: *Files magazine spotlight on Doctor Who: Season one.*
Doctor Who: Season three—SEE: *Files magazine spotlight on Doctor Who: Season three.*
Doctor Who: Season two—SEE: *Files magazine spotlight on Doctor Who: Season two.*
31370 *Doctor Who: The chase.* London: A Target Book, W. H. Allen & Co., 1989, 144 p., paper, tele. DOCTOR WHO #140.
31371 *Doctor Who: The daleks' master plan, part 1: Mission to the unknown.* London: W. H. Allen & Co., 1989, 174 p., cloth, tele. DOCTOR WHO #141.
31372 *Doctor Who: The daleks' master plan, part II: The mutation of time.* London: W. H. Allen & Co., 1989, 157 p., cloth, tele. DOCTOR WHO #142.
Doctor Who: The Daleks' master plan, part II: The mutation of time—SEE: *Doctor Who: The daleks' master plan, part II: The mutation of time.*
Doctor Who: The eleventh season—SEE: *Files magazine spotlight on Doctor Who: The eleventh season.*
Doctor Who: The first Baker years—SEE: *Files magazine spotlight on Doctor Who: The first Baker years.*
Doctor Who: The tenth season—SEE: *Files magazine spotlight on Doctor Who: The tenth season.*
The early voyages—SEE: *Classic files magazine spotlight on The Star Trek files: The early voyages.*
The eleventh season—SEE: *Files magazine spotlight on Doctor Who: The eleventh season.*
31373 *The encyclopedia of Star Trek.* Los Angeles: Schuster & Schuster, 1988, 301 p., paper, nonf.

The end of the affair—SEE: *Files magazine spotlight on The U.N.C.L.E. files: The girl from U.N.C.L.E.: The end of the affair.*

The Enterprise incident—SEE: *Files magazine spotlight on The Star Trek files: The Enterprise incident.*

31374 *Files magazine spotlight on Doctor Who: Season four.* Canoga Park, CA: New Media Books, 1986, 2 v. (I-51 p.; II-51 p.), paper, nonf.

31375 *Files magazine spotlight on Doctor Who: Season one.* Canoga Park, CA: New Media Books, 1986, 2 v. (I-49 p.; II-51 p.), paper, nonf.

31376 *Files magazine spotlight on Doctor Who: Season three.* Canoga Park, CA: New Media Books, 1986, 2 v. (I-51 p.; II-[47] p.), paper, nonf.

31377 *Files magazine spotlight on Doctor Who: Season two.* Canoga Park, CA: New Media Books, 1986, 2 v. (I-51 p.; II-51 p.), paper, nonf.

31378 *Files magazine spotlight on Doctor Who: The eleventh season.* Canoga Park, CA: New Media Books, 1986, 51 p., paper, nonf.

31379 *Files magazine spotlight on Doctor Who: The first Baker years.* Canoga Park, CA: New Media Books, 1986, 2 v. (I-53 p., II-55 p.), paper, nonf.

31380 *Files magazine spotlight on Doctor Who: The tenth season.* Canoga Park, CA: New Media Books, 1986, 55 p., paper, nonf.

31381 *Files magazine spotlight on The Fireball XL5 files.* Canoga Park, CA: Psi Fi Movie Press, 1986, 53 p., paper, nonf.

31382 *Files magazine spotlight on The Gerry Anderson's Stingray files.* Canoga Park, CA: Psi Fi Movie Press, 1986, 57 p., paper, nonf.

31383 *Files magazine spotlight on The Star Trek files: All our yesterdays.* Canoga Park, CA: Psi Fi Movie Press, 1985, 51 p., paper, nonf.

31384 *Files magazine spotlight on The Star Trek files: Assignment: Earth.* Canoga Park, CA: Psi Fi Movie Press, 1986, 55 p., paper, nonf.

31385 *Files magazine spotlight on The Star Trek files: Return to tomorrow.* Canoga Park, CA: Psi Fi Movie Press, 1986, 53 p., paper, nonf.

31386 *Files magazine spotlight on The Star Trek files: That which survives.* Canoga Park, CA: Psi Fi Movie Press, 1985, 51 p., paper, nonf.

31387 *Files magazine spotlight on The Star Trek files: The animated voyages begin.*

Canoga Park, CA: Psi Fi Movie Press, 1985, 51 p., paper, nonf.

31388 *Files magazine spotlight on The Star Trek files: The animated voyages end.* Canoga Park, CA: Psi Fi Movie Press, 1985, 51 p., paper, nonf.

31389 *Files magazine spotlight on The Star Trek files: The Enterprise incident.* Canoga Park, CA: Psi Fi Movie Press, 1986, 49 p., paper, nonf.

31390 *Files magazine spotlight on The Star Trek files: The Tholian web.* Canoga Park, CA: Psi Fi Movie Press, 1986, 51 p., paper, nonf.

31391 *Files magazine spotlight on The Star Trek files: Where no man has gone before.* Canoga Park, CA: Psi Fi Movie Press, 1985-86, 2 v. (I-53 p.; II-53 p.), paper, nonf.

31392 *Files magazine spotlight on The Star Trek files: Whom gods destroy.* Canoga Park, CA: Psi Fi Movie Press, 1986, 51 p., paper, nonf.

31393 *Files magazine spotlight on The Twilight Zone files: The new series.* Canoga Park, CA: Psi Fi Movie Press, New Media Books, 1985-86, 2 v. (I-51 p.; II-51 p.), paper, nonf.

31394 *Files magazine spotlight on The U.N.C.L.E. files: 15 yrs. later affair.* Canoga Park, CA: New Media Books, 1985, [51] p., paper, nonf.

31395 *Files magazine spotlight on The U.N.C.L.E. files: The girl from U.N.C.L.E.* Canoga Park, CA: New Media Books, 1985, 2 v. (I-49 p.; II-49 p.), paper, nonf.

31396 *Files magazine spotlight on The U.N.C.L.E. files: The girl from U.N.C.L.E.: The end of the affair.* Canoga Park, CA: New Media Books, 1985, [53] p., paper, nonf.

31397 *Files magazine spotlight on The U.N.C.L.E. files: The man from Thrush.* Canoga Park, CA: New Media Books, 1985, 49 p., paper, nonf.

The Fireball XL5 files—SEE: *Files magazine spotlight on The Fireball XL5 files.*

The first Baker years—SEE: *Files magazine spotlight on Doctor Who: The first Baker years.*

31398 *The Gallifrey chronicles.* London: Doctor Who Books, 1991, 137 p., cloth, fiction. DOCTOR WHO SERIES.

Genesys—SEE: *The new Doctor Who adventures: Timewyrm: genesys.*

The Gerry Anderson's Stingray files—SEE: *Files magazine spotlight on The Gerry Anderson's Stingray files.*

31399 *The Gerry Anderson's Thunderbirds files: International rescue.* Canoga Park, CA: Psi Fi Movie Press, 1986, 65 p., paper, nonf. [Cover title]

31400 *The Gerry Anderson's Thunderbirds files: Danger awaits.* Canoga Park, CA: Psi Fi Movie Press, 1986, 65 p., paper, nonf. [Cover title]

The Girl from U.N.C.L.E.—SEE: *Files magazine spotlight on The U.N.C.L.E. files: The girl from U.N.C.L.E.*

The girl from U.N.C.L.E.: The end of the affair—SEE: *Files magazine spotlight on The U.N.C.L.E. files: The girl from U.N.C.L.E.: The end of the affair.*

International rescue—SEE: *The Gerry Anderson's Thunderbirds files: International rescue.*

Island in the sky—SEE: *The Lost in Space files: Island in the sky.*

31401 *The Lost in Space files.* Granada Hills, CA: Schuster & Schuster, 1987, 241 p., paper, nonf.

31402 *The Lost in Space files: Island in the sky.* Canoga Park, CA: Psi Fi Movie Press, 1986, 57 p., paper, nonf.

31403 *The Lost in Space files: Rocket to Earth.* Canoga Park, CA: Psi Fi Movie Press, 1987, 51 p., paper, nonf.

31404 *The Lost in Space files: War of the robots.* Canoga Park, CA: Psi Fi Movie Press, 1986, 57 p., paper, nonf.

31405 *The Lost in Space files: Wild adventure.* Canoga Park, CA: Psi Fi Movie Press, 1987, 51 p., paper, nonf.

The man from Thrush—SEE: *Files magazine spotlight on The U.N.C.L.E. files: The man from Thrush.*

Mission to the unknown—SEE: *Doctor Who: The daleks' master plan, part 1: Mission to the unknown.*

The mutation of time—SEE: *Doctor Who: The daleks' master plan, part II: The mutation of time.*

31406 *The new Doctor Who adventures: Timewyrm: genesys.* London: Doctor Who Books, 1991, 230 p., paper, tele. DOCTOR WHO: THE NEW ADVENTURES #1.

The new series—SEE: *Files magazine spotlight on The Twilight Zone files: The new series.*

Pieces of fate—SEE: *The U.N.C.L.E. files: Pieces of fate.*

31407 *The Prisoner files.* Canoga Park, CA: New Media Books, 1985-86, 6 v., paper, nonf.

Return to tomorrow—SEE: *Files magazine spotlight on The Star Trek files: Return to tomorrow.*

The rocket to Earth—SEE: *The Lost in Space files: Rocket to Earth.*

Season four—SEE: *Files magazine spotlight on Doctor Who: Season four.*

Season one—SEE: *Files magazine spotlight on Doctor Who: Season one.*

Season three—SEE: *Files magazine spotlight on Doctor Who: Season three.*

Season two—SEE: *Files magazine spotlight on Doctor Who: Season two.*

The Star Trek files: All our yesterdays—SEE: *Files magazine spotlight on The Star Trek files: All our yesterdays.*

The Star Trek files: Assignment: Earth—SEE: *Files magazine spotlight on The Star Trek files: Assignment: Earth.*

The Star Trek files: Return to tomorrow—SEE: *Files magazine spotlight on The Star Trek files: Return to tomorrow.*

The Star Trek files: That which survives—SEE: *Files magazine spotlight on The Star Trek files: That which survives.*

The Star Trek files: The animated voyages begin—SEE: *Files magazine spotlight on The Star Trek files: The animated voyages begin.*

The Star Trek files: The animated voyages end—SEE: *Files magazine spotlight on The Star Trek files: The animated voyages end.*

The Star Trek files: The early voyages—SEE: *Classic files magazine spotlight on The Star Trek files: The early voyages.*

The Star Trek files: The Enterprise incident—SEE: *Files magazine spotlight on The Star Trek files: The Enterprise incident.*

The Star Trek files: The Tholian web—SEE: *Files magazine spotlight on The Star Trek files: The Tholian web.*

The Star Trek files: Where no man has gone before—SEE: *Files magazine spotlight on The Star Trek files: Where no man has gone before.*

The Star Trek files: Whom gods destroy—SEE: *Files magazine spotlight on The Star Trek files: Whom gods destroy.*

The Stingray files—SEE: *Files magazine spotlight on The Gerry Anderson's Stingray files.*

Take me to your leader—SEE: *The U.N.C.L.E. files: Take me to your leader.*

The tenth season—SEE: *Files magazine spotlight on Doctor Who: The tenth season.*

That which survives—SEE: *Files magazine spotlight on The Star Trek files: That which survives.*

The Tholian web—SEE: *Files magazine spotlight on The Star Trek files: The Tholian web.*

Timewyrm: genesys—SEE: *The new Doctor Who adventures: Timewyrm: genesys.*

31408 *The Trek encyclopedia.* Las Vegas, NV: Pioneer Books, 1988, 365 p., paper, nonf.

The Twilight Zone files: The new series—SEE: *Files magazine spotlight on The Twilight Zone files: The new series.*

31409 *The U.N.C.L.E. files: Pieces of fate.* Canoga Park, CA: New Media Books, 1986, 52 p., paper, nonf.

31410 *The U.N.C.L.E. files: Take me to your leader.* Canoga Park, CA: New Media Books, 1986, 58 p., paper, nonf.

31411 *The U.N.C.L.E. files: The deadly quest.* Canoga Park, CA: New Media Books, 1986, 53 p., paper, nonf.

The U.N.C.L.E. files: The man from Thrush—SEE: *Files magazine spotlight on The U.N.C.L.E. files: The man from Thrush.*

War of the robots—SEE: *The Lost in Space files: War of the robots.*

Where no man has gone before—SEE: *Files magazine spotlight on The Star Trek files: Where no man has gone before.*

Whom gods destroy—SEE: *Files magazine spotlight on The Star Trek files: Whom gods destroy.*

Wild adventure—SEE: *The Lost in Space files: Wild adventure.*

as NICHOLAS ADAMS

15977 *I.O.U.* New York: HarperPaperbacks, 1991, 187 p., paper, novel.

15978 *Santa claws.* New York: HarperPaperbacks, 1991, 187 p., paper, novel.

as RICK NORTH

30813 *Ready for blastoff!* New York: Zebra Books, Kensington Publishing Corp., 1990, 157 p., paper, novel. YOUNG ASTRONAUTS #2.

as JOHN VINCENT

31412 *A view to a thrill.* New York: Puffin Books, 1991, 118 p., paper, novel. JAMES BOND JR. #1.

with Glenn A. Magee

28889 *A classic files magazine spotlight on The U.N.C.L.E. files: The mission begins.* Canoga Park, CA: Psi Fi Movie Press, 1986, 2 v. (I-53 p.; II-59 p.), paper, nonf.

28890 *Classic files magazine spotlight on The U.N.C.L.E. files: The show takes off.* Canoga Park, CA: Psi Fi Movie Press, 1986, 2 v. (I-54 p.; II-54 p.), paper, nonf.

The mission begins—SEE: *A classic files magazine spotlight on The U.N.C.L.E. files: The mission begins.*

The show takes off—SEE: *Classic files magazine spotlight on The U.N.C.L.E. files: The show takes off.*

The U.N.C.L.E. files: The mission begins—SEE: *A classic files magazine spotlight on The U.N.C.L.E. files: The mission begins.*

The U.N.C.L.E. files: The show takes off—SEE: *Classic files magazine spotlight on The U.N.C.L.E. files: The show takes off.*

with Terry Nation

30584 *The official Doctor Who and the daleks book.* New York: St. Martin's Press, 1988, 212 p., paper, nonf.

with Dave Rogers

31413 *The Avengers: too many targets.* New York: St. Martin's Press, 1990, 181 p., paper, novel.

Too many targets—SEE: *The Avengers: too many targets.*

PEEPLES, Edwin A(ugustus) Jr., 1915-

15851 *A hole in the hill.* Camden, NJ: Thomas Nelson, 1969, 189 p., cloth, novel.

PEIFER, Kathleen Hamel—SEE: **Dobkin, Kaye**

PEIRCE, Hayford, 1942-

31414 *Ben Bova presents Phylum monsters.* New York: Tor SF, A Tom Doherty Associates Book, 1989, 278 p., paper, novel.

31415 *Ben Bova presents The thirteenth majestral.* New York: Tor SF, A Tom Doherty Associates Book, 1989, 315 p., paper, novel.

31416 *Ben Bova's discoveries: Napoleon disentimed.* New York: Tor SF, A Tom Doherty Associates Book, 1987, 306 p., paper, novel.

Napoleon disentimed—SEE: *Ben Bova's discoveries: Napoleon disentimed.*

Phylum monsters—SEE: *Ben Bova presents Phylum monsters.*

The thirteenth majestral—SEE: *Ben Bova presents The thirteenth majestral.*

PELAN, John C.

31417 *Axolotl special 1.* Eugene, OR: Axolotl Press, Pulphouse Publishing, 1989, 167 p., cloth, anth.

PELLA, Judith, with Michael R. Phillips as MARK J. LIVINGSTONE

31418 *The peacemaker.* Minneapolis, MN: Bethany House Publishers, 1990, 526 p., paper, novel.

PELLOWSKI, Michael (Joseph), 1949-

31419 *Howard the Duck storybook.* London: Armada, 1986, 48 p., paper, movie.

PEMBERTON, Alan

31420 *Journeys of the mind.* Limpsfield, Surrey, England: Paper Tiger, 1983, 143 p., cloth, coll.

PEMBERTON, Clive

38011 *The weird o'it.* London: Henry J. Drane, 1906, p., cloth, coll.

PEMBERTON, Victor

31421 *Doctor Who: Fury from the deep.* London: W. H. Allen & Co., 1986, 189 p., cloth, tele. DOCTOR WHO #110.
31422 *Doctor Who: The Pescatons.* London: A Target Book, 1991, 144 p., paper, novel. DOCTOR WHO #153. [Novelization of an audio record].
Fury from the deep—SEE: *Doctor Who: Fury from the deep.*
The Pescatons—SEE: *Doctor Who: The Pescatons.*

PENDARVES, G. G. [pseud. of Gladys Gordon Trenery], 1885-1938

31423 *The devil's graveyard.* England: British Fantasy Society, 1988, 47 p., paper, coll.

PENDERED, Mary L(ucy), 1858-1940

38012 *Mortmain: a romance.* London & New York: G. P. Putnam's Sons, 1928, 269 p., cloth, novel.

PENDLETON, Don(ald Eugene), 1927-

31424 *Ashes to ashes.* New York: Popular Library, Warner Books, 1986, 210 p., paper, novel. ASHTON FORD #1.
31425 *Eye to eye: an Ashton Ford novel.* New York: Popular Library, Warner Books, 1986, 211 p., paper, novel. ASHTON FORD #2.
31426 *Heart to heart: an Ashton Ford novel.* New York: Popular Library, 1987, 240 p., paper, novel. ASHTON FORD #5.
31427 *Life to life: an Ashton Ford novel.* New York: Popular Library, 1987, 244 p., paper, novel. ASHTON FORD #4.
31428 *Mind to mind: an Ashton Ford novel.* New York: Popular Library, 1987, 244 p., paper, novel. ASHTON FORD #3.
31429 *Time to time: an Ashton Ford novel.* New York: Popular Library, 1988, 215 p., paper, novel. ASHTON FORD #6.

PENDLETON, Don, house pseud.

NOTE: Although Don Pendleton is a real author, his byline also became a house name for Worldwide's Gold Eagle line when he sold them the rights to his Executioner (i.e., Mack Bolan) series.

31430 *Mack Bolan: Paradine's gauntlet.* Toronto: A Gold Eagle Book, Worldwide, 1983, 183 p., paper, novel. MACK BOLAN SERIES. [By Michael Newton].
Paradine's gauntlet—SEE: *Mack Bolan: Paradine's guantlet.*
30922 *Stoney Man III.* Toronto, New York: Worldwide, 1991, 349 p., paper, novel. STONEY MAN #3. [By Mel Odom].

PENDRAGON, Eric, pseud.—SEE: Parry, Michel

PENDRAY, George—SEE: Edwards, Gawain

PENDRY, Eric D(ouglas)

31431 *Way to go home.* London: Secker & Warburg, 1977, 184 p., cloth, novel.

PENLEY, Constance, 1948- , with Elisabeth Lyon & Lynn Spigel & Janet Bergstrom

17866 *Close encounters: film, feminism, and science fiction.* Minneapolis, MN, Oxford, England: A Camera Obscura Book, University of Minnesota Press, 1991, xi+298 p., cloth, nonf. anth.

PENNINGTON, Bruce, 1944-

31432 *The Bruce Pennington portfolio.* Limpsfield, Surrey, England: Paper Tiger, 1990, [64] p., paper, art.

PENNINGTON, David A.—SEE: Daud, David

PENNY, David G(eorge), 1950-

31433 *Out of time.* London: Robert Hale, 1979, 175 p., cloth, novel.
31434 *Starchant.* London: Robert Hale, 1975, 187 p., cloth, novel.
31435 *The sunset people.* London: Robert Hale, 1975, 172 p., cloth, novel.
31436 *Sunshine 43.* London: Robert Hale, 1978, 175 p., cloth, novel.

PEPLOW, Michael W(ebster), 1940- , *with Robert S. Bravard*

18564 *Samuel R. Delany: a primary and secondary bibliography, 1962-1979.* Boston: G. K. Hall & Co., 1980, xiv+178 p., cloth, nonf. MASTERS OF SCIENCE FICTION AND FANTASY.

PEPPER, Frank S(tuart), 1910-1988

31437 *Big deep.* London, Sydney: Mills & Boon, 1977, 93 p., paper, novel.

PEPPIN, Brigid (Mary), 1941-

38013 *Fantasy: the golden age of fantastic illustration.* New York: Watson-Guptill, 1975, 191 p., cloth, art anth.

PERCY, (F.) Walker, 1916-1990

31438 *The Thanatos syndrome.* Franklin Center, PA: Franklin Library, 1987, 372 p., cloth, novel.

PERDUE, (W.) Lewis, 1949-

31439 *The DaVinci legacy.* New York: Pinnacle Books, 1983, 391 p., paper, novel.

with Robin Moore

30184 *The trinity implosion.* New York: Manor Books, 1978, 291 p., paper, novel.

PEREIRA, W(ilfred) D(ennis), 1921-

31440 *Another Eden.* London: Robert Hale, 1976, 189 p., cloth, novel.

31441 *Celeste.* London: Robert Hale, 1979, 159 p., cloth, novel.
31442 *The Charon tapes.* London: Robert Hale, 1975, 184 p., cloth, novel.
31443 *Contact.* London: Robert Hale, 1977, 192 p., cloth, novel.
31444 *The king of hell.* London: Robert Hale, 1978, 188 p., cloth, novel.

PERETTI, Frank E., 1951-

31445 *Piercing the darkness.* Westchester, IL: Crossway Books, 1989, 441 p., paper, novel. DARKNESS #2.
31446 *This present darkness.* Westchester, IL: Crossway Books, 1986, 375 p., paper, novel. DARKNESS #1.
31447 *Tilly.* Westchester, IL: Crossway Books, 1988, 126 p., paper, radio.

PERKINS, Sheldon

31448 *Polaris.* New York: Belmont Tower Books, 1979, 208 p., paper, novel.

PERL, Lila

31449 *Annabelle Starr, E.S.P.* New York: Clarion Books, 1983, 147 p., cloth, novel.

PERLMAN, Dory

31450 *Final test.* New York: Fawcett Columbine, 1988, 122 p., paper, novel. SECRET OF THE UNICORN QUEEN #3.

PERLMUTTER, (Oscar) William, 1920-1975, *with Jacqueline Jackson*

26369 *The endless pavement.* New York: Seabury Press, 1973, 45 p., cloth, novel.

PERRET, Patti, 1955-

31451 *The faces of science fiction: photographs.* New York: Bluejay Books, 1984, [176] p., cloth, nonf.

PERRIN, Pat, *with Wim Coleman*

20296 *The jamais vu papers; or, Misadventures in the worlds of science, myth, and magic.* New York: Harmony Books, 1991, 327 p., cloth, fiction.

PERRIN, Steve

31452 *Spawn of dragonspear.* Lake Geneva, WI: TSR Inc., 1988, 190 p., paper, novel.

ADVANCED DUNGEONS & DRAGONS ADVENTURE GAMEBOOK #17.

with Ken St. Andre & John B. Monroe

30047 *Stormbringer.* Albany, CA: The Chaosium, 1990, 192 p., paper, art.

with Ray Turney

31453 *RuneQuest.* Albany, CA: The Chaosium, 1979, 119 p., paper, fiction.

PERRY, Mark C(hristopher), 1960-

The dead—SEE: *Morigu: The dead.*
The desecration—SEE: *Morigu: The desecration.*
31454 *Morigu: The dead.* New York: Popular Library, Warner Books, 1990, 202 p., paper, novel. MORIGU #2.
31455 *Morigu: The desecration.* New York: Popular Library, Warner Books, 1986, 324 p., paper, novel. MORIGU #1.

with Megahn Perry

31456 *A warlock's blade: a Crossroads adventure in the world of Christopher Stasheff's Warlock of Gramarye.* New York: Tor, A Tom Doherty Associates Book, 1987, 250 p., paper, novel. CROSSROADS ADVENTURE—GRAMARYE SEQUEL.

PERRY, Megahn (Catherine Leahy), 1977- , *with Mark C. Perry*

31456 *A warlock's blade: a Crossroads adventure in the world of Christopher Stasheff's Warlock of Gramarye.* New York: Tor, A Tom Doherty Associates Book, 1987, 250 p., paper, novel. CROSSROADS ADVENTURE—GRAMARYE SEQUEL.

PERRY, Ritchie (John Allen), 1942-

31457 *Fenella Fang.* London: Hutchinson, 1986, 124 p., cloth, novel. FENELLA FANG #1.
31458 *Fenella Fang and the time machine.* London: Hutchinson, 1991, 133 p., cloth, novel. FENELLA FANG #2.

PERRY, Roger [pseud. of Roger William Cowern], 1928-

31459 *Esper's War.* London: Robert Hale, 1981, 188 p., cloth, novel.
31460 *The making of Jason.* London: Robert Hale, 1980, 158 p., cloth, novel.

31461 *Senior citizen.* London: Robert Hale, 1979, 192 p., cloth, novel.

PERRY, Roland, 1946-

Program for a puppet—SEE: *Programme for a puppet.*
31462 *Programme for a puppet.* London: W. H. Allen, 1979, 318 p., cloth, novel.
31462A retitled: *Program for a puppet.* New York: Crown Publishers, 1980, 283 p., cloth, novel.

PERRY, Steve(n Carl), 1947-

31463 *The 97th step.* New York: Ace Books, 1989, 294 p., paper, novel. KHADAJI #5. [Prequel to *The man who never missed*].
31464 *The albino knife.* New York: Ace Books, 1991, 294 p., paper, novel. KHADAJI #6.
31465 *Civil War secret agent.* Toronto, New York: Bantam Books, 1984, 125 p., paper, novel. TIME MACHINE #5.
31466 *Conan the defiant.* New York: Tor, A Tom Doherty Associates Book, 1987, 245 p., paper, novel. CONAN SERIES.
31467 *Conan the fearless.* New York: Tor, A Tom Doherty Associates Book, 1986, 275 p., paper, novel. CONAN SERIES.
31468 *Conan the formidable.* New York: Tor SF, A Tom Doherty Associates Book, 1990, 274 p., paper, novel. CONAN SERIES.
31469 *Conan the free lance.* New York: Tor SF, A Tom Doherty Associates, 1990, 279 p., paper, novel. CONAN SERIES.
31470 *Conan the indomitable.* New York: Tor SF, A Tom Doherty Associates Book, 1989, 273 p., paper, novel. CONAN SERIES.
31471 *The hero curse.* Portland, OR: DimeNovels, 1991, 94 p., paper, novel.
31472 *The Machiavelli interface.* New York: Ace Science Fiction Books, 1986, 197 p., paper, novel. KHADAJI #3.
31473 *The man who never missed.* New York: Ace Science Fiction Books, 1985, 195 p., paper, novel. KHADAJI #1.
31474 *Matadora.* New York: Ace Science Fiction Books, 1986, 211 p., paper, novel. KHADAJI #2.
31475 *The Tularemia gambit.* New York: Fawcett Gold Medal, 1981, 191 p., paper, novel.
31476 *Workshops: the minefields of science fiction.* Eugene, OR: Writer's Notebook Press, Pulphouse Publishing, 1991, 12 p., paper, nonf.

with Michael Reaves

31477 *Dome.* New York: Berkley Books, 1987, 274 p., paper, novel.
31478 *Hellstar.* New York: Berkley Books, 1984, 326 p., paper, novel.
31479 *The omega cage.* New York: Ace Books, 1988, 244 p., paper, novel. KHADAJI #4.
31480 *Sword of the samurai.* Toronto, New York: A Byron Preiss Book, Bantam Books, 1984, 127 p., paper, novel. TIME MACHINE #3.

PERUCHO, Joan, 1920-

31481 *Natural history: a novel.* New York: Alfred A. Knopf, 1988, xii+186 p., cloth, novel. [Translation by David H. Rosenthal of *Les històries naturals*].

PERUTZ, Leo, 1882-1957

31482 *From nine to nine.* New York: Viking Press, 1926, 224 p., cloth, novel. [Translation by Lily Lore of *Zwischen neun und neun*].
 Saint Peter's snow—SEE: *The virgin's brand.*
31483 *The virgin's brand.* London: Butterworth, 1934, 251 p., cloth, novel. [Translation by E. B. G. Stamper & E. M. Hodgson of *St. Petri-schnee*].
31483A retitled: *Saint Peter's snow.* London: Collins-Harvill Press, 1990, 148 p., cloth, novel. [A new translation by Eric Mosbacher of *St. Petri-schnee*].

PESEK, Luděk, 1919-

31484 *Trap for Perseus.* Scarsdale, NY: Bradbury Press, 1980, 168 p., cloth, novel. [Translation by Anthea Bell of *Falle für Perseus*].

*PESIN, Harry, 1919-1984

PETAJA, Emil (Theodore), 1915-

31485 *Photoplay edition.* San Francisco: Sisu Publishers, 1975, 189 p, cloth, nonf.
31486 *Saga of lost earths; and, The star mill.* New York: DAW Books, 1979, 222 p., paper, coll. KALEVALA #1-2.
31487 *The stolen sun; and, Tramontane.* New York: DAW Books, 1979, 223 p., paper, coll. KALEVALA #3-4.

PETERMAN, Michael (Alan), 1942-

31488 *Robertson Davies.* Boston: Twayne Publishers, 1986, 178 p., cloth, nonf.

PETERS, David, pseud.—SEE: David, Peter

PETERS, Elizabeth, pseud.—SEE: Michaels, Barbara

PETERS, Jay

31489 *Pursuit to the future.* Davenport, FL: Laura Books, 1979, 247 p., paper, novel.

*PETERS, Ludovic [pseud. of Peter Ludwig Brent], 1931-1984

PETERS, Maureen—SEE: Darby, Catherine

PETERS, Othello, pseud.

31490 *Satan's daughters.* New York: Zebra Books, Kensington Publishing Corp., 1975, 223 p., paper, novel.
31490A retitled: *Whispers from the dark side of tomorrow.* New York: Zebra Books, Kensington Publishing Corp., 1977, 239 p., paper, novel.
 Whispers from the dark side of tomorrow—SEE: *Satan's daughters.*

PETERS, Ralph, 1952-

31491 *Red Army.* New York: Pocket Books, 1989, 337 p., cloth, novel.
31492 *The war in 2020.* New York, London: Pocket Books, 1991, 434 p., cloth, novel.

PETERS, Saul, *with Kevin Barrett*

17473 *Treason at Helms Deep.* New York: Berkley Books, 1988, [214] p., paper, fiction. MIDDLE-EARTH QUEST.

PETERSEN, Sandy

31493 *Call of Cthulhu: fantasy roleplaying in the worlds of H. P. Lovecraft, 4th ed.* Albany, CA: Chaosium, 1989, 192 p., paper, nonf.
 Field guide to the Cthulhu monsters—SEE: *Petersen's Field guide to the Cthulhu monsters: a field observer's handbook of preternatural entities.*
31494 *Petersen's Field guide to the Cthulhu monsters: a field observer's handbook of preternatural entities.* Albany, CA: Chaosium, 1988, 64 p., paper, art.

with Mark J. Ferrari & Lynn Willis & Tom Sullivan

Field guide to creatures of the dreamlands— SEE: *Petersen's Field guide: creatures of the dreamlands.*

23047 *Petersen's Field guide: creatures of the dreamlands: an album of entities from beyond the wall of sleep.* Albany, CA: Chaosium, 1989, 64 p., paper, art.

PETERSON, Boyd F. Jr., *with Blaine Pardoe & Sam Lewis*

28311 *Battletech: Wolf Clan sourcebook.* Chicago: FASA Corp., 1991, 128 p., paper, fiction. BATTLETECH SERIES.

PETHERICK, Simon, 1960-

31495 *Classic stories of mystery, horror, and suspense.* London: Robert Hale, 1987, 252 p., cloth, anth.

PETREY, Susan C(andace), 1945-1980

31496 *Gifts of blood.* Portland, OR: OSFCI, 1990, 208 p., cloth, coll. [Limited to 500 copies; edited by Debbie Cross and Paul M. Wrigley].

PETROU, David Michael, 1949-

31497 *The making of Superman, the movie.* New York: Warner Books, 1978, 224 p., paper, nonf.

PETSCHEK, Joyce S.

31498 *The silver bird: a tale for those who dream.* Millbrae, CA: Celestial Arts, 1981, xi+173 p., paper, novel.

*PETTERSEN, Rena Oldfield, <u>1887-1972</u>

PETTERSSON, Allan Rune, 1936-

31499 *Frankenstein's aunt.* London: Hodder & Stoughton, 1980, 125 p., cloth, novel. FRANKENSTEIN'S AUNT #1. [Translation by Joan Tate of *Frankensteins faster*].
31500 *Frankenstein's aunt returns.* London: Hodder & Stoughton, 1990, 140 p., cloth, novel. FRANKENSTEIN'S AUNT #2. [Translation of *Frankensteins faster—igen!*]

PETTY, Anne C(otton), 1945-

31501 *One ring to bind them all: Tolkien's mythology.* University, AL: University of Alabama Press, 1979, 122 p., cloth, nonf.

PETYO, Robert

31502 *The Institute.* New York: Manor Books, 1978, 219 p. paper, novel.

PEYTON, Audrey

31503 *Ashes.* London: Robert Hale, 1981, 191 p., cloth, novel.

PEYTON, K. M., pseud.—SEE: Peyton, Kathleen Wendy & Peyton, Michael P.

PEYTON, Kathleen Wendy, 1929- *with Michael P. Peyton as* **K. M. PEYTON**

31504 *A pattern of roses.* London: Oxford University Press, 1972, 132 p., cloth, novel.

PEYTON, Michael, *with Kathleen Wendy Peyton as* **K. M. PEYTON**

31504 *A pattern of roses.* London: Oxford University Press, 1972, 132 p., cloth, novel.

PEYTON, Richard

31505 *The ghost now standing on Platform One: phantoms of the railways in fact and fiction.* London: Souvenir Press, 1990, 322 p., cloth, anth. [Includes some nonfiction].
31505A retitled: *Journey into fear, and other great stories of horror on the railways.* New York: Wings Books, 1991, 322 p., cloth, anth.
Journey into fear, and other great stories of horror on the railways—SEE: *The ghost now standing on Platform One.*

*PEZET, A(lfonso) Washington, 1889-<u>1978</u>

PFAELZER, Jean

31506 *The utopian novel in America, 1886-1896: the politics of form.* Pittsburgh, PA: University of Pittsburgh Press, 1984, xii+211 p., cloth, nonf.

PFAFF, Richard William, 1936-

31507 *Montague Rhodes James.* London: Scholar Press, 1980, xiv+461 p., cloth, nonf.

PFEFFER, Susan (Beth), 1948-

31508 *Future forward.* New York: Delacorte Press, 1989, 123 p., cloth, novel. VCR TIME MACHINE #2.
31509 *Rewind to yesterday.* New York: Delacorte Press, 1988, 138 p., cloth, novel. VCR TIME MACHINE #1.

PFEFFERLE, Seth, 1955-

31510 *Goat's head.* New York: Manor Books, 1977, 369 p., paper, novel.
31511 *Stickman.* New York: Tor Horror, A Tom Doherty Associates Book, 1987, 279 p., paper, novel.

PFEIL, Don—SEE: Pfeil, Donald J.

PFEIL, Donald J.

31512 *Look back to Earth* / by Don Pfeil. New York: Manor Books, 1977, 235 p., paper, novel.
31513 *Through the reality warp.* New York: Ballantine Books, 1976, 164 p., paper, novel.
31514 *Voyage to a forgotten sun.* New York: Ballantine Books, 1975, 181 p., paper, novel.

as WILLIAM ARROW

16802 *Escape from Terror Lagoon.* New York: Ballantine Books, 1976, 138 p., paper, tele. RETURN TO THE PLANET OF THE APES #2.

PFEIL, (John) Fred(erick), 1949-

31515 *Goodman 2020.* Bloomington, IN: Indiana University Press, 1986, 231 p., cloth, novel.

PFLIEGER, Pat(ricia Ann), *with Helen M. Hill*

25662 *A reference guide to modern fantasy for children.* Westport, CT & London: Greenwood Press, 1984, xvii+690 p., cloth, nonf.

PFORDRESHER, John (Charles), 1943- , *with Thomas E. Gage & Edmund J. Farrell & Raymond J. Rodrigues*

22917 *Fantasy: shapes of things unknown.* Glenview, IL & Dallas, TX: Scott, Foresman & Co., 1974, 384 p., paper, anth. [Includes some nonfiction].

PHILBRICK, William R.—SEE: Dantz, William

PHILIP, Neil, 1955-

31516 *Fine anger: a critical introduction to the work of Alan Garner.* London: Collins, 1981, 191 p., cloth, novel.
31517 *The tale of Sir Gawain.* London: Lutterworth Press, 1987, 102 p., cloth, novel.

PHILIPS, F(rancis) C(harles), 1849-1921

38014 *The strange adventures of Lucy Smith.* London: Swan Sonnenschein, Lowrey, 1887, 2 v., cloth, novel.

*PHILIPS, Judson P(entecost), 1903-<u>1989</u>

PHILIPS, Michael (Lawrence), 1942-

31518 *Philosophy and science fiction.* Buffalo, NY: Prometheus Books, 1984, viii+392 p., paper, anth.

*PHILLIPS, Alexander M(oore), 1907-<u>1970</u>

PHILLIPS, Ann, 1930-

31519 *A haunted year.* Oxford, England: Oxford University Press, 1991, 160 p., cloth, novel.
31520 *The multiplying glass.* Oxford, England: Oxford University Press, 1981, 157 p., cloth, novel.
31521 *The oak king and the ash queen.* Oxford, England: Oxford University Press, 1984, 171 p., cloth, novel.

PHILLIPS, David, *with Georgii Markov as* DAVID ST. GEORGE

37938 *The Right Honourable Chimpanzee.* London: Secker & Warburg, 1978, 240 p., cloth, novel.

PHILLIPS, Delbert D(arwal), 1943-

31522 *Spook or spoof? the structure of the supernatural in Russian romantic tales.* Washington, DC: University Press of America, 1982, iv+164 p., cloth, nonf.

PHILLIPS, Dennis—SEE: Daniels, Philip

PHILLIPS, Elizabeth, 1919-

31523 *Edgar Allan Poe, an American imagination: three essays.* Port Washington, NY: Kennikat Press, 1979, 151 p., cloth, nonf. coll.

PHILLIPS, Jill M(eta), 1952-

31524 *Walford's oak: a novel.* New York: A Citadel Press Book, Carol Publishing Group, 1990, 218 p., cloth, novel.

PHILLIPS, Joseph G.

31525 *Mars I: voyage to Earth, year 1489.* Philadelphia & Ardmore, PA: Dorrance & Co., 1977, 107 p., cloth, novel.

PHILLIPS, Lyn [pseud. of James R. Scafidel], 1942-

31526 *The game.* New York: Tor, A Tom Doherty Associates Book, 1982, 288 p., paper, novel.
31527 *Tomb of the shroud.* New York: A Dell/Emerald Book, 1983, 317 p., paper, novel.

PHILLIPS, Michael R(ay), 1946-

31528 *George MacDonald: Scotland's beloved storyteller.* Minneapolis, MN: Bethany House, 1987, 400 p., cloth, nonf.

with Judith Pella as MARK J. LIVINGSTONE

31418 *The peacemaker.* Minneapolis, MN: Bethany House Publishers, 1990, 526 p., paper, novel.

PHILLIPS, Robert (Schaeffer), 1938-

The omnibus of twentieth century ghost stories—SEE: *Triumph of the night: tales of terror and the supernatural by 20th century masters.*
31529 *Triumph of the night: tales of terror and the supernatural by 20th century masters.* New York: Carroll & Graf Publishers, 1989, 374 p., cloth, anth.
31529A retitled: *The omnibus of twentieth century ghost stories.* London: Robinson Publishing, 1990, 373 p., cloth, anth.

PHILLIPS, (C.) Terry

31530 *Gates of death.* Lake Geneva, WI: TSR Inc., 1987, 191 p., paper, fiction. ADVANCED DUNGEONS & DRAGONS ADVENTURE GAMEBOOK #13.
31531 *The soulforge.* Lake Geneva, WI: TSR Inc., 1985, 187 p., paper, nonf. ADVANCED DUNGEONS & DRAGONS ADVENTURE GAMEBOOK #4; DRAGONLANCE SERIES.

PHILLIPS, Tony, house pseud.

City of glass—SEE: *Turbo Cowboys: City of glass.*
Duster trouble—SEE: *Turbo Cowboys: Duster trouble.*
Full throttle—SEE: *Turbo Cowboys: Full throttle.*
Jump start—SEE: *Turbo Cowboys: Jump start.*
Night riders—SEE: *Turbo Cowboys: Night riders.*
Rat trap—SEE: *Turbo Cowboys: Rat trap.*
Spark fire—SEE: *Turbo Cowboys: Spark fire.*
Speed shift—SEE: *Turbo Cowboys: Speed shift.*
Spin out—SEE: *Turbo Cowboys: Spin out.*
Super charge—SEE: *Turbo Cowboys: Super charge.*
17206 *Turbo Cowboys: City of glass.* New York: Ballantine Books, 1989, 140 p., paper, novel. TURBO COWBOYS #10. [By Paul Bagdon].
31532 *Turbo Cowboys: Duster trouble.* New York: Ballantine Books, 1989, 131 p., paper, novel. TURBO COWBOYS #9. [By John Read].
20882 *Turbo Cowboys: Full throttle.* New York: Ballantine Books, 1989, 135 p., paper, novel. TURBO COWBOYS #4. [By Chet Cunningham].
20883 *Turbo Cowboys: Jump start.* New York: Ballantine Books, 1988, 120 p., paper, novel. TURBO COWBOYS #1. [By Chet Cunningham].
17207 *Turbo Cowboys: Night riders.* New York: Ballantine Books, 1989, 134 p., paper, novel. TURBO COWBOYS #7. [By Paul Bagdon].
31533 *Turbo Cowboys: Rat trap.* New York: Ballantine Books, 1989, 135 p., paper, novel. TURBO COWBOYS #6. [By John Read].
20884 *Turbo Cowboys: Spark fire.* New York: Ballantine Books, 1989, 130 p., paper, novel. TURBO COWBOYS #3. [By Chet Cunningham].
17208 *Turbo Cowboys: Speed shift.* New York: Ballantine Books, 1989, 135 p., paper, novel. TURBO COWBOYS #8. [By Paul Bagdon].
20885 *Turbo Cowboys: Spin out.* New York: Ballantine Books, 1989, 136 p., paper, novel. TURBO COWBOYS #2. [By Chet Cunningham].
17209 *Turbo Cowboys: Super charge.* New York: Ballantine Books, 1989, 138 p., paper, novel. TURBO COWBOYS #5. [By Paul Bagdon].

PHILLPOTTS, Eden, 1862-1960

31534 *The girl and the faun.* London: Cecil Palmer & Hayward, 1916, 78 p., cloth, novel.

PHILMUS, Robert M(ichael), 1943- , with Darko Suvin

31535 *H. G. Wells and modern science fiction.* Lewisburg, PA: Bucknell University Press, 1977, 279 p., cloth, nonf. anth.

PHIPSON, Joan [i.e., Joan Margaret Phipson Fitzhardinge], 1912-

31536 *Dinko.* North Ryde, New South Wales, Australia: Methuen, 1985, 190 p., cloth, novel.

31537 *The watcher in the garden.* North Ryde, New South Wales, Australia: Methuen, 1982, 203 p., cloth, novel.

PHY, Allene Stuart, 1937-

31538 *Mary Shelley.* Mercer Island, WA: Starmont House, 1988, 124 p., cloth, nonf. STARMONT READER'S GUIDE #36.

PIACENTINI, Valerie

31539 *The wheel turns.* Strathmartine by Dundee, Scotland: ScoTpress, 1979, 33 p., paper, tele. STAR TREK SERIES.

31540 *Wine of Calvoro.* Strathmartine by Dundee, Scotland: ScoTpress, 1979, 55 p., paper, tele. STAR TREK SERIES.

with Sheila Clark

20093 *The wheel of fate.* Strathmartine by Dundee, Scotland: ScoTpress, 1980, 47 p., paper, tele. STAR TREK SERIES.

PICANO, Felice, 1944-

31541 *Smart as the devil: a novel.* New York: Arbor House, 1975, 308 p., cloth, novel.

31542 *To the seventh power.* New York: William Morrow & Co., 1989, 311 p., cloth, novel.

PICCARD, Mary Ann

31543 *Official Star Trek cooking manual.* Toronto, New York: Bantam Books, 1978, xiv+203 p., paper, nonf.

PICCIRILLI, Thomas E.—SEE: Piccirilli, Tom

PICCIRILLI, Tom [i.e., Thomas Edward Piccirilli], 1965-

31544 *Dark father.* New York, London: Pocket Books, 1990, 280 p., paper, novel.

PICK, J(ohn) B(arclay), 1921-

31545 *Neil M. Gunn: a Highland life.* London: John Murray, 1981, 314 p., cloth, nonf.

with Francis Russell Hart

31546 *The anarchy of light: Neil Gunn: a celebration.* Dundee, Scotland: Gairfish, 1991, x+79 p., paper?, nonf. anth.

PICK, Karl—SEE: Delmont, Joseph

PICKARD, George

31547 *Golden.* New York, Washington: Vantage Press, 1984, 33 p., cloth, story.

PICKARD, Roy, 1937-

31548 *The Hamlyn book of horror and S.F. movie lists.* London: Hamlyn Paperbacks, 1983, 223 p., paper, nonf.

31549 *Science fiction in the movies: an A-Z.* London: Frederick Muller, 1978, 139 p., cloth, nonf.

with Tom Hutchinson

26224 *Horrors: a history of horror movies.* London: Optimum Books, 1983, 192 p., cloth, nonf.

PICKERING, Paul, 1952-

31550 *Charlie Peace: a fable.* New York: Random House, 1991, 309 p., cloth, novel.

PICKNETT, Lynn, as INTRODUCER

31551 *The best horror stories.* London: Hamlyn, 1977, 751 p., cloth, anth.

PIECZENIK, Steve R(ichard)

31552 *Blood heat.* San Diego, CA: Harcourt Brace Jovanovich, 1988, 348 p., cloth, novel.

PIENCIAK, Anne

31553 *J. R. R. Tolkien's Hobbit and Lord of the Rings.* Woodbury, NY: Barron's Educational Series, 1986, 138 p., paper, nonf.

PIENKOWSKI, Jan (Michel), 1936- , *with Joan Aiken*

16137   *A foot in the grave.* London: Jonathan Cape, 1989, 128 p., cloth, coll.

PIERATT, Asa B(radford) Jr., 1938-

with Jerome Klinkowitz

27367   *Kurt Vonnegut, Jr.: a descriptive bibliography and annotated secondary checklist.* Hamden, CT: Archon Books, 1974, xix+138 p., cloth, nonf.

with Jerome Klinkowitz & Julie Huffman-Klinkowitz

26123   *Kurt Vonnegut: a comprehensive bibliography.* Hamden, CT: Archon Books, 1987, xxiv+289 p., cloth, nonf. [Expanded edition of #27367].

PIERCE, Hazel (May) Beasley, 1918-

31554   *A literary symbiosis: science fiction/fantasy mystery.* Westport, CT & London: Greenwood Press, 1983, viii+255 p., cloth, nonf. CONTRIBUTIONS TO THE STUDY OF SCIENCE FICTION AND FANTASY #6.
31555   *Philip K. Dick.* Mercer Island, WA: Starmont House, 1982, 64 p., cloth, nonf. STARMONT READER'S GUIDE #12.

PIERCE, John J(eremy), 1941-

31556   *Foundations of science fiction: a study in imagination and evolution.* Westport, CT: Greenwood Press, 1987, 290 p., cloth, nonf. CONTRIBUTIONS TO THE STUDY OF SCIENCE FICTION AND FANTASY #25.
31557   *Great themes of science fiction.* Westport, CT: Greenwood Press, 1987, 250 p., cloth, nonf. CONTRIBUTIONS TO THE STUDY OF SCIENCE FICTION AND FANTASY #29.
31558   *When world views collide: a study in imagination and evolution.* NY & London: Greenwood Press, 1989, xvii+238 p., cloth, nonf. CONTRIBUTIONS TO THE STUDY OF SCIENCE FICTION AND FANTASY #37.

PIERCE, Meredith Ann, 1958-

31559   *Birth of the Firebringer.* New York: Four Winds Press; London: Collier Macmillan, 1985, 234 p., cloth, novel.
31561   *The darkangel.* Boston & Toronto: An Atlantic Monthly Press Book, Little, Brown & Co., 1982, 223 p., cloth, novel. AERIEL #1.
31560   *The darkangel trilogy: The darkangel; A gathering of gargoyles; The pearl of the soul of the world.* New York: Guild America Books, 1990, 471 p., cloth, novel. AERIEL #1-3.
31562   *A gathering of gargoyles.* Boston & Toronto: An Atlantic Monthly Press Book, Little, Brown & Co., 1984, 263 p., cloth, novel. AERIEL #2.
31563   *The pearl of the soul of the world.* Boston: Joy Street Books, 1990, 243 p., cloth, novel. AERIEL #3.
31564   *The woman who loved reindeer.* Boston: Atlantic Monthly Press, 1985, 242 p., cloth, novel.

PIERCE, Tamora, 1954-

31565   *Alanna: the first adventure.* New York: An Argo Book, Atheneum, 1983, 241 p., cloth, novel. SONG OF THE LIONESS #1.
31566   *In the hand of the goddess.* New York: An Argo Book, Atheneum, 1984, 232 p., cloth, novel. SONG OF THE LIONESS #2.
31567   *Lioness rampant.* New York: A Jean Karl Book, Atheneum, 1988, 320 p., cloth, novel. SONG OF THE LIONESS #4.
31568   *The woman who rides like a man.* New York: An Argo Book, Atheneum, 1986, 253 p., cloth, novel. SONG OF THE LIONESS #3.

PIERCE, William Luther—SEE: MacDonald, Andrew

PIERCY, Marge, 1936-

31569   *He, she, and it.* New York: Alfred A. Knopf, 1991, 446 p., cloth, novel.
31570   *Woman on the edge of time.* New York: Alfred A. Knopf, 1976, 369 p., cloth, novel.

PIKE, Christopher

31571   *Chain letter.* New York: Avon Books, 1986, 185 p., paper, novel.
38015   *Fall into darkness.* New York, London: An Archway Book, Pocket Books, 1990, 213 p., paper, novel.
38016   *Last act.* New York, London: An Archway Book, Pocket Books, 1988, 226 p., paper, novel.

31572 *Remember me.* New York, London: An Archway Book, Pocket Books, 1989, 230 p., paper, novel.

31573 *Sati.* New York: St. Martin's Press, 1990, 217 p., cloth, novel.

31574 *Scavenger hunt.* New York, London: An Archway Book, Pocket Books, 1989, 215 p., paper, novel.

31575 *See you later.* New York, London: Pocket Books, 1990, 226 p., paper, novel.

31576 *Spellbound.* New York: An Archway Paperback, Pocket Books, 1988, 211 p., paper, novel.

31577 *The Tachyon web.* Toronto, New York: Bantam Books, 1986, 197 p., paper, novel.

31578 *Whisper of death.* New York, London: An Archway Paperback, Pocket Books, 1991, 180 p., paper, novel.

31579 *Witch.* New York, London: An Archway Paperback, Pocket Books, 1990, 225 p., paper, novel.

*PILLER, Emanuel (A.), 1907-<u>1985</u>

PINCHERLE, Alberto—SEE: Moravia, Alberto

PINCHIN, Frank J(ames), 1925-1990

31580 *Nexweb.* Sutton Coldfield, England: Newmark Editions, 1990, 222 p., cloth, novel.

31581 *Stargrail.* Chichester, England: Little London Publishers, 1989, 168 p., cloth, novel.

as PETER DAGMAR

03735 *Alien skies.* London: Digit Books, 1962, 160 p., paper, novel.
Mind probe—SEE: *Once in time.*

03736 *Once in time.* London: Digit Books, 1963, 160 p., paper, novel.

03736A retitled: *Mind probe.* Australia: Bill Ewington Books, 1973, 160 p., paper, novel.

03737 *Sands of time.* London: Digit Books, 1963, 155 p., paper, novel.
Spaceways—SEE: *Spykos 4.*

03738 *Spykos 4: strange life-forms on unexplored planets.* London: Digit Books, 1962, 154 p., paper, novel.

03738A retitled: *Spaceways.* Australia: Bill Ewington Books, 1973, 154 p., paper, novel.

31582 *Two equals one.* Lewes, East Sussex, England: Book Guild, 1982, 122 p., cloth, novel.

PIÑERA, Virgilio, 1912-1979

31583 *Cold tales.* Hygiene, CO: Eridanos Press, 1988, 282 p., cloth, coll. [Translation by Mark Schafer and Thomas Christensen of *Cuentos fríos*].

PINES, T(onya)

31584 *Thirteen: 13 tales of horror.* New York, Toronto: Point Fiction, Scholastic Inc., 1991, viii+343 p., paper, anth.

PINI, Richard (Alan), 1950-

31585 *Against the wind.* New York: Tor, A Tom Doherty Associates Book, 1990, 277 p., paper, anth. ELFQUEST: THE BLOOD OF TEN CHIEFS #4.

31586 *Elfquest: Winds of change.* New York: Tor Fantasy, A Tom Doherty Associates Book, 1989, xii+275 p., paper, anth. ELFQUEST: BLOOD OF TEN CHIEFS #3.
Winds of change—SEE: *Elfquest: Winds of change.*

with Robert Asprin & Lynn Abbey

15912 *The blood of ten chiefs.* New York: Tor SF, A Tom Doherty Associates Book, 1986, 314 p., cloth, anth. ELFQUEST #1.

15913 *Elfquest: Wolfsong: The blood of ten chiefs.* New York: Tor SF, A Tom Doherty Associates Book, 1988, 307 p., paper, anth. ELFQUEST #2.
Wolfsong—SEE: *Elfquest: Wolfsong: The blood of ten chiefs.*

with Wendy Pini

31587 *Elfquest: the novel!: Journey to sorrow's end.* San Francisco, Columbia, PA: Underwood-Miller, 1982, 320 p., cloth, novel. ELFQUEST SERIES.

31587A retitled: *Elfquest: the novel.* New York: Playboy Paperbacks, 1982, 320 p., paper, novel. ELFQUEST SERIES.
Journey to sorrow's end—SEE: *Elfquest: the novel.*

PINI, Wendy, 1951- , *with Richard Pini*

31587 *Elfquest: the novel!: Journey to sorrow's end.* San Francisco, Columbia, PA: Underwood-Miller, 1982, 320 p., cloth, novel. ELFQUEST SERIES.

31587A retitled: *Elfquest: the novel.* New York: Playboy Paperbacks, 1982, 320 p., paper, novel. ELFQUEST SERIES.
Journey to sorrow's end—SEE: *Elfquest: the novel.*

PINIANSKI, Patricia, *with Linda Sweeney as* LYNN PATRICK

31588 *Double or nothing.* New York: Candle-light Ecstasy Supreme, Dell, 1985, 287 p., paper, novel.

31589 *More than a dream.* New York: Candle-light Ecstasy Romance, Dell, 1985, [280] p., paper, novel.

PINKWATER, Daniel M(anus), 1941-

31590 *Alan Mendelsohn, the boy from Mars* / by Daniel Pinkwater. New York: E. P. Dutton & Co., 1979, 248 p., cloth, novel.

31591 *Attila the pun: a Magic Moscow story* / by Daniel Pinkwater. New York: Four Winds Press, 1981, 69 p., cloth, novel. MAGIC MOSCOW SERIES.

31592 *Borgel* / by Daniel Pinkwater. New York: Macmillan, 1990, 170 p., cloth, novel.

31593 *Chicago days/Hoboken nights.* Reading, MA: Addison-Wesley, 1991, viii+168 p., cloth, nonf.

31594 *Fat men from space* / by Daniel Manus Pinkwater. New York: Dodd, Mead & Co., 1976, 157 p., cloth, novel.

31595 *Lizard music* / by D. Manus Pinkwater. New York: Dodd, Mead & Co., 1976, 157 p., cloth, novel.

31596 *Slaves of Spiegel: a Magic Moscow story* / by Daniel Pinkwater. New York: Four Winds Press, 1982, 88 p., cloth, novel. MAGIC MOSCOW SERIES.

31597 *The Snarkout boys & the avocado of death* / by Daniel Pinkwater. New York: Loth-rop, Lee & Shepard, 1982, 156 p., cloth, novel. SNARKOUT BOYS #1.

31598 *The Snarkout boys and the Baconburg horror* / by Daniel Pinkwater. New York: Lothrop, Lee & Shepard, 1984, 191 p., cloth, novel. SNARKOUT BOYS #2.

31599 *Wingman* / by Manus Pinkwater. New York: Dodd, Mead & Co., 1975, 63 p., cloth, novel.

31600 *The worms of Kukumlima* / by Daniel Pinkwater. New York: E. P. Dutton & Co., 1981, 152 p., cloth, novel.

31601 *Yobgorgle: mysterious monster of Lake Ontario* / by Daniel M. Pinkwater. Boston: Houghton Mifflin Co., Clarion Books, 1979, 156 p., cloth, novel.

31602 *Young adults.* New York: Tor Books, 1985, 224 p., paper, coll.

with Luqman Keele

26962 *Java Jack.* New York: Thomas Y. Crowell, 1980, 152 p., cloth, novel.

PINTERO, John, 1947-

31603 *The summoning.* New York: Avon, 1979, 220 p., paper, novel.

PIPER, H(orace) Beam, 1904-1964

31604 *Empire.* New York: Ace Books, 1981, 242 p., paper, coll.

31605 *Federation.* New York: Ace Books, 1981, xxx+284 p., paper, coll.

31606 *Fuzzies and other people.* New York: Ace Science Fiction Books, 1984, 216 p., paper, novel. FUZZIES #3.

31607 *The Fuzzy papers: Little Fuzzy; Fuzzy sapiens.* Garden City, NY: Nelson Double-day, 1977, 309 p., cloth, coll. FUZZIES #1-2. [Includes *Little Fuzzy* and *Fuzzy sapiens*].

Fuzzy sapiens—SEE: *The other human race.*

Gunpowder god—SEE: *Lord Kalvan of Otherwhen.*

11522 *Lord Kalvan of Otherwhen.* New York: Ace Books, 1965, 192 p., paper, novel. PARATIME POLICE—LORD KALVAN #1.

11522A retitled: *Gunpowder god.* London: Sphere Books, 1978, 189 p., paper, novel. PARATIME POLICE—LORD KAL-VAN #1.

11523 *The other human race.* New York: Avon Books, 1964, 190 p., paper, novel. FUZZIES #2.

11523A retitled: *Fuzzy sapiens.* New York: Ace Books, 1976, 235 p., paper, novel. FUZZIES #2.

31608 *Paratime.* New York: Ace Books, 1981, 295 p., paper, coll. PARATIME POLICE SERIES.

31609 *Uller uprising.* New York: Ace Science Fiction Books, 1983, xx+201 p., paper, novel.

31610 *The worlds of H. Beam Piper.* New York: Ace Books, 1983, 231 p., paper, coll. [Edited by John F. Carr].

with Michael Kurland

27605 *First cycle: a novel.* New York: Ace Books, 1982, 201 p., paper, novel.

with John J. McGuire

31611 *Four-day planet; Lone star planet.* New York: Ace Books, 1979, 340 p., paper, coll. [*Lone star planet* originally published as *A planet for Texans* (see #09906); John J. McGuire's contribution to the latter is not acknowledged].

with Benson Parker

31221 *The adventures of Little Fuzzy.* New York: Platt & Munk Publishers, 1983, 43 p., cloth, story. LITTLE FUZZY SERIES. [Adapted from *Little Fuzzy* by Piper].

PIRANI, Adam

31612 *The complete Gerry Anderson episode guide.* London: Titan, 1989, 168 p., paper, nonf.

PIRIE, David (Tarbat), 1946-

The complete vampire cinema—SEE: *The vampire cinema.*
31613 *The vampire cinema.* London & New York: Hamlyn, 1977, 176 p., cloth, nonf.
31613A retitled: *The complete vampire cinema.* New York: Crescent, 1977, 176 p., cloth, nonf.

PISERCHIA, Doris (Elaine), 1928-

31614 *A billion days of Earth.* Toronto, New York: Bantam Books, 1976, 210 p., paper, novel.
31615 *The deadly sky.* New York: DAW Books, 1983, 176 p., paper, novel.
31616 *The dimensioneers.* New York: DAW Books, 1982, 176 p., paper, novel.
31617 *Doomtime.* New York: DAW Books, 1981, 173 p., paper, novel.
31618 *Earth in twilight.* New York: DAW Books, 1981, 156 p., paper, novel.
31619 *Earthchild.* New York: DAW Books, 1977, 204 p., paper, novel.
31620 *The Fluger.* New York: DAW Books, 1980, 159 p., paper, novel.
31621 *Spaceling.* Garden City, NY: Nelson Doubleday, 1978, 245 p., cloth, novel.
31622 *The spinner.* Garden City, NY: Nelson Doubleday, 1980, 184 p., cloth, novel.

as CURT SELBY

31623 *Blood County.* New York: DAW Books, 1981, 176 p., paper, novel.
31624 *I, zombie.* New York: DAW Books, 1982, 158 p., paper, novel.

PITKETHLEY, Janice

31625 *When two worlds collide.* Strathmartine by Dundee, Scotland: ScoTpress, 1983, 48 p., paper, tele. STAR TREK SERIES.

PITTS, Michael R., 1947-

31626 *Horror film stars.* Jefferson, NC: McFarland & Co., 1981, vii+324 p., cloth, nonf.
31627 *Horror film stars, 2nd ed.* Jefferson, NC & London: McFarland & Co., 1991, xi+464 p., paper, nonf.

with James Robert Parish

31211 *The great science fiction pictures.* Metuchen, NJ: Scarecrow Press, 1977, viii+382 p., cloth, nonf.
31212 *The great science fiction pictures II.* Metuchen, NJ & London: Scarecrow Press, 1991, x+489 p., cloth, nonf.

*PIZOR, Faith K., 1943-

PJERROU, Mary, 1945-

31628 *Coz: a novel.* San Francisco: Spinsters, Aunt Lute, 1989, xi+224 p., paper, novel.

PLAMONDON, Robert

31629 *Through dungeons deep: fantasy gamers' handbook.* Reston, VA: Reston Publishing Co., 1982, xi+323 p., cloth, nonf.

PLANK, Robert, 1907-1983

31630 *The emotional significance of imaginary beings: a study of the interaction between psychopathology, literature, and reality in the modern world.* Springfield, IL: Thomas, 1968, xi+177 p., cloth, nonf.
31631 *George Orwell's guide through Hell: a psychological study of 1984.* San Bernardino, CA: R. Reginald, The Borgo Press, 1986, 123 p., cloth, nonf. MILFORD SERIES: POPULAR WRITERS OF TODAY #41.

PLANTE, Edmund

31632 *Alone in the house.* New York: An Avon Flare Book, 1991, 166 p., paper, novel.
31633 *Garden of evil.* New York: Leisure Books, 1988, 365 p., paper, novel. SEED #2.
31634 *The new neighbors.* New York: Manor Books, 1979 (i.e., 1980?), 255 p., paper, novel.
31635 *Seed of evil.* New York: Leisure Books, 1988, 367 p., paper, novel. SEED #1.
31636 *Transformation.* New York: Leisure Books, 1987, 351 p., paper, novel.

31637 *Trapped.* New York: Leisure Books, 1989, 355 p., paper, novel.

PLANTE, Richard La—SEE: La Plante, Richard

PLATER, William M(armaduke), 1945-

31638 *The grim phoenix: reconstructing Thomas Pynchon.* Bloomington, IN & London: Indiana University Press, 1978, xvii+268 p., cloth, nonf.

PLATT, Charles (Michael), 1945-

11536 *The city dwellers: science fiction.* London: Sidgwick & Jackson, 1970, 189 p., cloth, novel.

31647 retitled: *Twilight of the city: a novel of the near future.* New York: Macmillan Publishing Co., 1977, 222 p., cloth, novel. [Revised edition].

31639 *Dream makers: the uncommon people who write science fiction: interviews.* New York: Berkley Books, 1980, xvi+284 p., paper, nonf. coll.

31640 retitled: *Who writes science fiction?* Manchester, England: Savoy Books, 1980, 313 p., paper, nonf. coll.

31641 *Dream makers: science fiction and fantasy writers at work: profiles, new revised edition.* London: Xanadu, 1986, 280 p., cloth, nonf. coll. [Selections from the previous two volumes].

31642 *Dream makers, volume II: the uncommon men & women who write science fiction.* New York: Berkley Books, 1983, xv+300 p., paper, nonf. coll. [Winner of the *Locus* Award for Best Nonfiction, 1983 (1984)].

31643 *Free zone: volume one of the epic unilogy*: (*unilogy, a literary work consisting of one volume).* New York: Avon Books, 1989, 233 p., paper, novel.

31649A *Less than human.* London: Grafton, 1987, 238 p., paper, novel. [Originally published under the name Robert Clarke].

31644 *Piers Anthony's Worlds of Chthon: Plasm.* New York: A Signet Book, New American Library, 1987, 284 p., paper, novel. PIERS ANTHONY'S WORLDS OF CHTHON #1.

Plasm—SEE: *Piers Anthony's Worlds of Chthon: Plasm.*

31645 *The silicon man.* New York, Toronto: Spectra, Bantam Books, 1991, 253 p., paper, novel.

31646 *Soma: Piers Anthony's worlds of Chthon.* New York: A Signet Book, New American Library, 1989, 236 p., paper, novel.

PIERS ANTHONY'S WORLDS OF CHTHON #2.

Twilight of the city: a novel of the near future—SEE: *The city dwellers: science fiction.*

Who writes science fiction?—SEE: *Dream makers.*

Worlds of Chthon: Plasm—SEE: *Piers Anthony's Worlds of Chthon: Plasm.*

as ROBERT CLARKE

31648 *Less than human.* New York: Avon, 1986, viii+194 p., paper, novel. [Later reprinted under Platt's own name].

as BLAKELY ST. JAMES

31649 *Christina enchanted.* New York: Playboy Press, 1980, 254 p., paper, novel. CHRISTINA SERIES. [Only one of series which is fantastic].

with Hilary Bailey

New worlds #6—SEE: *New worlds 7.*

00709 *New worlds 7.* London: Sphere, 1974, 213 p., paper, anth.

00709A retitled: *New worlds #6.* New York: Equinox Books, Avon, 1975, 233 p., paper, anth.

PLATT, Kin, 1911-

31650 *Dracula, go home.* New York: A Triumph Book, Franklin Watts, 1979, 87 p., cloth, novel.

31651 *Frank and Stein and me.* New York: A Triumph Book, Franklin Watts, 1982, 124 p., cloth, novel.

31652 *The ghost of Hellsfire Street.* New York: Delacorte Press, 1980, ix+246 p., cloth, novel. SINBAD #3.

as KIRBY CARR

31653 *The impossible spy.* Chatsworth, CA: Major Books, 1976, 176 p., paper, novel.

31654 *They're coming to kill you, Jane!* Chatsworth, CA: Canyon Books, 1975, 192 p., paper, novel. HITMAN #4.

PLATT, Marc, 1914-

Battlefield—SEE: *Doctor Who: Battlefield.*

31655 *Doctor Who: Battlefield.* London: A Target Book, W. H. Allen & Co., 1991, 172 p., paper, tele. DOCTOR WHO #152.

31656 *Doctor Who: Ghost light.* London: A Target Book, W. H. Allen & Co., 1990, 160 p., paper, tele. DOCTOR WHO #149.
Ghost light—SEE: *Doctor Who: Ghost light.*

PLATT, Randall Beth, 1948-

31657 *Out of a forest clearing: an environmental fable.* Santa Barbara, CA: John Daniel & Co., 1991, 220 p., paper, novel.

PLOWRIGHT, Teresa, 1952-

31658 *Dreams of an unseen planet.* New York: Arbor House, 1986, 273 p., cloth, novel.
31659 *Dreams of an unseen planet, rev. ed.* Victoria, British Columbia, Canada: Porcepic Books, Tesseract Books, 1989, 267 p., paper, novel.

PLUM, Claude D. Jr.

31660 *The terratoid guide: a checklist of magazines dealing with fantasy, science-fiction, and horror films.* Hollywood, CA: Claude D. Plum, Jr., 1973, 18 p., paper, nonf.

PLUNKETT, Edward—SEE: Dunsany, Lord

PLUNKETT, Robert L., 1951-

31661 *A California dreamer in King Henry's court.* Simi Valley, CA: Silver Dawn Media, 1990, 213 p., cloth, novel.

PLUNKETT, Susan—SEE: Coon, Susan

POE, Edgar Allan, 1809-1849

31662 *The Edgar Allan Poe bedside companion: morgue and mystery tales.* London: Victor Gollancz, 1980, 188 p., cloth, coll. [Edited by Peter Haining].
31663 *Edgar Allan Poe: letters and documents in the Enoch Pratt Free Library.* New York: Scholars' Facsimiles and Reprints, 1941, 84 p., cloth, nonf. [Edited by Arthur H. Quinn and Richard H. Hart].
31664 *The fall of the House of Usher.* London: A Target Book, W. H. Allen & Co., 1986, 143 p., paper, coll.
The fall of the House of Usher, and other writings—SEE: *Selected writings.*
31665 *Forty-two tales.* London: Octopus, 1979, 638 p., cloth, coll.
31666 *The gold-bug, and other tales.* New York: Dover Publications, 1991, 121 p., paper, coll.

31667 *The illustrated Edgar Allan Poe: a selection of texts together with a poem.* London: Jupiter Books, 1976, xix+236 p., cloth, coll. [Edited by Roy Gasson].
31668 *The science fiction of Edgar Allan Poe.* Harmondsworth, Middlesex, England: Penguin Books, 1976, xxvi+429 p., paper, coll. [Edited by Harold Beaver].
11654 *Selected writings.* Boston: Houghton Mifflin, 1956, 508 p., cloth, coll.
11654A retitled: *The fall of the House of Usher, and other writings.* Harmondsworth, Middlesex, England: Penguin Books, 1986, 539 p., paper, coll.
31669 *The short fiction of Edgar Allan Poe: an annotated edition.* Indianapolis, IN: Bobbs-Merrill Co., 1976, xxvii+633 p., cloth, coll. [Edited by Stuart Levine and Susan Levine].
31670 *Tales of Edgar Allan Poe.* New York: Books of Wonder, 1991, 308 p., cloth, coll.
31671 *Tales of mystery and terror.* Harmondsworth, Middlesex, England: Puffin Books, 1990, 191 p., paper, coll.
31672 *The tell-tale heart, and other writings.* Toronto, New York: Bantam Books, 1982, 432 p., paper, coll.

with Raymond Harris

25256 *The gold bug.* Providence, RI: A Jamestown Classic, Jamestown Publishers, 1982, 39 p., paper, story. [Adapted from Poe's original edition].
25257 *The masque of the red death.* Providence, RI: A Jamestown Classic, Jamestown Publishers, 1982, 31 p., paper, story. [Adapted from Poe's original edition].
25258 *The tell-tale heart.* Providence, RI: A Jamestown Classic, Jamestown Publishers, 1982, 31 p., paper, story. [Adapted from Poe's original edition].

with D. S. Higgins

25612 *Tales of terror.* London: Cassell, 1980, 46 p., cloth, coll. [Retold by Higgins from Poe's originals].

with Simon Marsden

29066 *Visions of Poe: a personal selection of Edgar Allan Poe's stories and poems.* Exeter, England: Webb & Bower, 1988, 128 p., cloth, coll. [Edited by Marsden, who also illustrated the book with his photographs].

with Diana Stewart

31673   *Tales of Edgar Allan Poe.* Milwaukee, WI: Raintree Publishers, 1981, 48 p., cloth, coll. [Adapted from Poe's work].

POHL, Carol (Metcalf Ulf), *with Frederik Pohl*

31674   *Science fiction discoveries.* Toronto, New York: Bantam Books, 1976, x+272 p., paper, anth.

31675   *Science fiction: the great years, volume II.* New York: Ace Books, 1976, 276 p., paper, anth.

POHL, Frederik (George Jr.), 1919-

31676   *Annals of the Heechee.* New York: A Del Rey Book, Ballantine Books, 1987, 338 p., cloth, novel. HEECHEE #4.

31677   *The best of Frederik Pohl.* Garden City, NY: Nelson Doubleday, 1975, 306 p., cloth, coll.

31678   *The best science fiction from Worlds of Tomorrow.* New York: Galaxy Publishing Corp., 1964, 162 p., paper, anth.

31679   *Beyond the blue event horizon.* New York: A Del Rey Book, Ballantine Books, 1980, 327 p., cloth, novel. HEECHEE #2.

31680   *BiPohl: two complete novels.* New York: A Del Rey Book, Ballantine Books, 1982, 313 p., paper, coll. [Includes *The age of the pussyfoot* and *Drunkard's walk*].

31681   *Black star rising.* New York: A Del Rey Book, Ballantine Books, 1985, 282 p., cloth, novel.

31682   *The coming of the quantum cats.* Toronto, New York: Bantam Books, 1986, 296 p., paper, novel.

31683   *The cool war.* New York: A Del Rey Book, Ballantine Books, 1981, 282 p., cloth, novel.

31684   *The day the Martians came.* Norwalk, CT: Easton Press, 1988, 248 p., cloth, coll.

    Demon in the skull—SEE: *A plague of pythons.*

31685   *The early Pohl.* Garden City, NY: Doubleday & Co., 1976, 183 p., cloth, coll.

11766   *The Frederik Pohl omnibus.* London: Victor Gollancz, 1966, 318 p., cloth, coll.

11766A retitled: *Survival kit.* London, Toronto: Panther, Granada Publishing, 1979, 192 p., paper, coll.

31686   *Gateway.* New York: St. Martin's Press, 1977, 313 p., cloth, novel. HEECHEE #1. [Winner of the Hugo Award for Best Novel, 1977 (1978); winner of the Nebula Award for Best Novel, 1977 (1978); winner of the John W. Campbell Jr.

Memorial Award for Best Novel, 1977 (1978); winner of the *Locus* Award for Best Novel, 1977 (1978)].

31687   *The gateway trip: tales and vignettes of the Heechee.* Norwalk, CT: Easton Press, 1990, 241 p., cloth, coll. HEECHEE #5.

31688   *Heechee rendezvous: a novel.* New York: A Del Rey Book, Ballantine Books, 1984, xx+311 p., cloth, novel. HEECHEE #3.

31689   *Homegoing.* Norwalk, CT: Easton Press, 1989, 279 p., cloth, novel.

31690   *In the problem pit.* Toronto, New York: Bantam Books, 1976, 193 p., paper, coll.

31691   *JEM.* New York: St. Martin's Press, 1979, 359 p., cloth, novel.

31692   *Man Plus.* New York: Random House, 1976, 215 p., cloth, novel. [Winner of the Nebula Award for Best Novel, 1976 (1977)].

31693   *The merchants' war.* New York: St. Martin's Press, 1984, x+209 p., cloth, novel. SPACE MERCHANTS #2.

31694   *Midas world: a novel.* New York: St. Martin's Press, 1983, 276 p., cloth, coll.

31695   *Narabedla Ltd.* New York: A Del Rey Book, Ballantine Books, 1988, 375 p., cloth, novel.

31696   *Nebula winners fourteen.* New York: Harper & Row, 1980, xi+259 p., cloth, anth.

31697   *Outnumbering the dead.* London: Legend, 1991, 110 p., cloth, novel.

11772   *A plague of pythons.* New York: Ballantine, 1965, 158 p., paper, novel.

31698   retitled: *Demon in the skull.* New York: DAW Books, 1984, 158 p., paper, novel. [Revised edition].

31699   *Planets three.* New York: Berkley Books, 1982, xi+225 p., paper, coll.

31700   *Pohlstars.* New York: A Del Rey Book, Ballantine Books, 1984, x+257 p., paper, coll.

31701   *The science fiction roll of honor: an anthology of fiction and nonfiction by guests of honor at world science fiction conventions.* New York: Random House, 1975, xvii+264 p., cloth, anth.

31702   *Starburst.* New York: A Del Rey Book, Ballantine Books, 1982, 219 p., cloth, novel.

31703   *Stopping at Slowyear.* Eugene, OR: Axolotl Press, Pulphouse Publishing, 1991, 118 p., cloth, story. AXOLOTL PRESS #21.

    Survival kit—SEE: *The Frederik Pohl omnibus.*

31704   *Syzygy.* Toronto, New York: Bantam Books, 1982, 248 p., paper, novel.

31705   *Terror.* New York: Berkley Books, 1986, 220 p., paper, novel.

31706 *The way the future was: a memoir.* New York: A Del Rey Book, Ballantine Books, 1978, 312 p., cloth, nonf.

31707 *The world at the end of time.* New York: A Del Rey Book, Ballantine Books, 1990, 393 p., cloth, novel.

31708 *The years of the city.* New York: Timescape Books, 1984, 334 p., cloth, novel. [Winner of the John W. Campbell Jr. Memorial Award for Best Novel, 1984 (1985)].

31709 *Yesterday's tomorrows: favorite stories from forty years as a science fiction editor.* New York: Berkley Books, 1982, xiv+431 p., paper, anth.

as INTRODUCER

31710 *The new visions: a collection of modern science fiction art.* Garden City, NY: Doubleday & Co., 1982, vii+87 p., cloth, art.

with Martin H. Greenberg & Joseph D. Olander

24569 *Galaxy: thirty years of innovative science fiction.* Chicago: Playboy Press, 1980, xiii+465 p., cloth, anth.

24570 *The great science fiction series: stories from the best of the series from 1944 to 1980 by twenty all-time favorite writers.* New York: Harper & Row, 1980, x+419 p., cloth, anth.

24571 *Science fiction of the forties.* New York: Avon, 1978, 377 p., paper, anth.

24572 *Worlds of if.* New York: Bluejay Books, 1986, 438 p., cloth, anth.

with Elizabeth Anne Hull

26180 *Tales from the planet Earth.* New York: St. Martin's Press, 1986, xviii+268 p., cloth, anth.

with C. M. Kornbluth

27476 *Before the universe, and other stories: the best of the early work of science fiction's most famous team of collaborators, including four stories never before in book form.* Toronto, New York: Bantam Books, 1980, x+203 p., paper, coll.

27477 *Critical mass.* Toronto, New York: Bantam Books, 1977, xi+179 p., paper, coll.

27478 *Gladiator-at-law.* New York: Baen Science Fiction Books, 1986, 251 p., paper, novel. [A revised edition of #08444].

27479 *Not this August.* New York: Tor, A Tom Doherty Associates Book, 1981, 255 p.,

paper, novel. [An expanded edition by Frederik Pohl of #08438].

27480 *Our best: the best of Frederik Pohl and C. M. Kornbluth.* New York: Baen Books, 1987, 286 p., paper, coll.

27481 *Search the sky.* New York: Baen Science Fiction Books, 1985, 245 p., paper, novel. [A revised edition of #08445].

27482 *The space merchants.* New York: St. Martin's Press, 1985, 169 p., cloth, novel. SPACE MERCHANTS #1. [A revised edition of #08446].

27483 *The Syndic.* New York: Tor, A Tom Doherty Associates Book, 1982, 256 p., paper, novel. [A revision by Frederik Pohl of #08439].

27484 *Venus, Inc.* Garden City, NY: Nelson Doubleday, 1985, 346 p., cloth, coll. SPACE MERCHANTS #1-2.

27485 *Wolfbane.* New York: Baen Science Fiction Books, 1986, 248 p., paper, novel. [A revised version of #08447].

with Carol Pohl

31674 *Science fiction discoveries.* Toronto, New York: Bantam Books, 1976, x+272 p., paper, anth.

31675 *Science fiction: the great years, volume II.* New York: Ace Books, 1976, 276 p., paper, anth.

with Frederik Pohl IV

31711 *Science fiction studies in film.* New York: Ace Books, 1981, 346 p., paper, nonf.

with Jack Williamson

31712 *Farthest star: the saga of Cuckoo.* New York: Ballantine Books, 1975, 246 p., paper, novel. SAGA OF CUCKOO #1.

31713 *Land's end.* New York: Tor, A Tom Doherty Associates Book, 1988, 370 p., cloth, novel.

31714 *The saga of Cuckoo.* Garden City, NY: Nelson Doubleday, 1983, 434 p., cloth, coll. SAGA OF CUCKOO #1-2. [Includes *Farthest star* and *Wall around a star*].

31715 *The singers of time.* New York: A Foundation Book, Doubleday, 1991, 358 p., cloth, novel.

31716 *The starchild trilogy: The reefs of space; Starchild; Rogue star.* Garden City, NY: Nelson Doubleday, 1977, 436 p., cloth, coll. STARCHILD TRILOGY #1-3.

31717 *Wall around a star: the saga of Cuckoo.* New York: A Del Rey Book, Ballantine Books, 1983, 275 p., paper, novel. SAGA OF CUCKOO #2.

POHL, Frederik (George) IV, 1956- , *with Frederik Pohl*

31711　*Science fiction studies in film.*　New York: Ace Books, 1981, 346 p., paper, nonf.

POHLE, Robert W(arren) Jr., 1949-

31718　*Doom of three planets* / by Robert Pohle. New York: Manor Books, 1978, 215 p., paper, novel.

with Douglas C. Hart

25317　*The films of Christopher Lee.*　Metuchen, NJ: Scarecrow Press, 1983, xxii+227 p., cloth, nonf.

POLCOVAR, Jane

31719　*The charming.*　Toronto, New York: Bantam Books, 1984, 151 p., paper, novel. DARK FORCES #15.

POLIDORI, John (William), 1795-1821

with David Campton

19297　*The vampyre.*　London: Hutchinson, 1986, 143 p., cloth, novel.　FLESHCREEPERS. [A retelling of Polidori's "The Vampyre"].

with Les Martin

29138　*The vampire.*　New York: Random House, 1989, 96 p., cloth, novel.　[Adapted from Polidori's original story].

POLIKARPUS, Viido, 1946- , *with Tappan King*

27291　*Down Town: a fantasy.*　New York: Arbor House, 1985, 293 p., cloth, novel.

POLLACK, Rachel (Grace) [legalized from Richard A. Pollack], 1945-

31720　*Alqua dreams.*　New York, Toronto: Franklin Watts, 1987, 246 p., cloth, novel.
31721　*Golden Vanity.*　New York: Berkley Books, 1980, 227 p., paper, novel.
31722　*Unquenchable fire.*　London: Century, 1988, 390 p., cloth, novel.

with Caitlin Matthews

29275　*Tarot tales.*　London: Legend, Century Hutchinson, 1989, 304 p., paper, anth.

POLLACK, Richard A.—SEE: Pollack, Rachel

POLLIN, Burton R(alph), 1916-

31723　*Discoveries in Poe.*　Notre Dame, IN: University of Notre Dame Press, 1970, xii+303 p., cloth, nonf.
31724　*Images of Poe's works: a comprehensive descriptive catalogue of illustrations.*　Westport, CT: Garland Publishing, 1989, xvii+413 p., cloth, nonf.

POLLOCK, Dale (Michael)

31725　*Skywalking: the life and films of George Lucas.*　New York: Harmony Books, 1983, xvi+304 p., cloth, nonf.

POLLOCK, Walter Herries, 1850-1926

38017　*A nine men's morrice: stories collected and re-collected.*　London, New York: Longmans, Green & Co., 1889, 358 p., cloth, coll.

POLLOTTA, Nicholas A.—SEE: Pollotta, Nick

POLLOTTA, Nick [i.e., Nicholas Angelo Pollotta Jr.], 1954-

31726　*Bureau 13.*　New York: Ace Books, 1991, 182 p., paper, novel.　BUREAU 13 #1.

with Phil Foglio

23225　*Illegal aliens.*　Lake Geneva, WI: TSR Inc., 1989, 336 p., paper, novel.

POLNAY, Peter de—SEE: de Polnay, Peter

PONS, Ted

31727　*The devil ground.*　San Diego, CA: Valcour & Krueger, 1977, [36] p., paper, story.　LIBRARY LOVECRAFTIAN #3.

PONT, Denise du—SEE: du Pont, Denise

PONT, Diane du—SEE: du Pont, Diane

POOLE, Josephine [pseud. of Jane Penelope Josephine Helyar], 1933-

31728　*The loving ghosts.*　London: Hutchinson, 1988, 118 p., cloth, novel.
15852　*The visitor: a story of suspense.*　New York: Harper & Row, 1972, 148 p., cloth, novel.

POORTVLIET, Marien—SEE: Poortvliet, Rien

POORTVLIET, Rien [i.e., Marien Poortvliet], 1933?-

31729 *The book of the sandman and the alphabet of sleep.* New York: Harry N. Abrams, 1989, 121 p., cloth, fiction. [Translation of *Het bock van klaas vaak en het ABC van de slaap*].

POPE, Elizabeth Marie, 1917-

31730 *The perilous gard.* Boston: Houghton Mifflin Co., 1974, 280 p., cloth, novel.
15853 *The Sherwood ring.* Boston: Houghton Mifflin Co., 1958, 266 p., cloth, novel.

POPESCU, Petru (Demetru), 1929-

31731 *In hot blood.* New York: Fawcett Gold Medal, 1989, 328 p., paper, novel.
31732 *The last wave.* Sydney: Angus & Robertson, 1977, 227 p., paper, novel.

POPKES, Steven (Earl), 1952-

Caliban landing—SEE: *Isaac Asimov presents Caliban landing.*
31733 *Isaac Asimov presents Caliban landing.* New York: Congdon & Weed in association with Davis Publications, 1987, v+281 p., cloth, novel.
31734 *Slow lightning.* New York: Tor SF, A Tom Doherty Associates Book, 1991, p. 53-241, paper, novel. [Bound with *The longest voyage* / by Poul Anderson].

PORATH, Ellen, *with Mark Anthony*

16641 *Kindred spirits.* Lake Geneva, WI: TSR Inc., 1991, 307 p., paper, novel. DRAGONLANCE SAGA—MEETINGS SEXTET #1.

PORGES, Irwin, 1909-

31735 *Edgar Allan Poe.* Philadelphia, PA: Chilton Book Co., 1963, 191 p., cloth, nonf.
31736 *Edgar Rice Burroughs: the man who created Tarzan.* Provo, UT: Brigham Young University Press, 1975, xix+819 p., cloth, nonf.

PORTER, Andrew (Ian), 1946-

as ANONYMOUS EDITOR

31736 *Experiment perilous: three essays on science fiction.* New York: Algol Press, 1976, 34 p., paper, nonf. anth.

31737 *Exploring Cordwainer Smith.* New York: Algol Press, 1975, 33 p, paper, nonf. anth.

with Harlan Ellison

22607 *The book of Ellison.* New York: Algol Press, 1978, 192 p., cloth, anth. [Includes material by and about Ellison].

PORTER, Barry

31738 *Dark souls.* New York: Zebra Books, Kensington Publishing Corp., 1989, 349 p., paper, novel.
31739 *Junkyard.* New York: Zebra Books, Kensington Publishing Corp., 1989, 284 p., paper, novel.

PORTER, Donald

31740 *Day of the animals.* New York: Ballantine Books, 1977, 168 p., paper, movie.

PORTER, Francis A., 1920-

31741 *SALT twelve.* Santa Barbara, CA: Fithian Press, 1988, 253 p., paper, novel.

PORTNOY, Howard N., 1946-

31742 *Hot rain.* New York: G. P. Putnam's Sons, 1977, 334 p., cloth, novel.

PORTWAY, Christopher—SEE: October, John

PORUSH, David (Hillel), 1952-

31743 *Cybernetic fiction, nerves, and metaphors: postmodern views of artificial intelligence.* Kingston, Ontario, Canada: Studies in Communication and Information Technology, Queen's University, 1988, 33 p., paper, nonf.
31744 *The soft machine: cybernetic fiction.* New York: Methuen, 1985, xii+244 p., cloth, nonf.

POSEY, Carl A(lfred Jr.), 1933-

31745 *Kiev footprint.* New York: Dodd, Mead & Co., 1983, xiii+194 p., cloth, novel.
31746 *Prospero drill.* London: Robert Hale, 1984, 192 p., cloth, novel.

POSNER, Richard, 1944-

31747 *Sparrow's flight.* New York: M. Evans & Co., 1988, 220 p., cloth, novel.

POSNICK, Paul, *with Leonard Leokum*

28202 *Weather war.* Los Angeles: Pinnacle Books, 1978, 372 p., paper, novel.

POSSE, Abel, 1939-

31748 *The dogs of paradise.* New York: Atheneum, 1990, 301 p., cloth, novel. [Translation by Margaret Sayers Peden of *Los perros del paraíso*].

POST, J(eremiah) B(enjamin), 1937-

31749 *An atlas of fantasy, rev. ed.* New York: Ballantine Books, 1979, xiv+210 p., paper, nonf.

POTHAN, Kap, 1929-

31750 *A time to die.* Brisbane, Australia: Jacaranda Press, 1967, 192 p., cloth, novel.

POTOCKI, Jan, *hrabia*, 1761-1815

31751 *Tales from the Saragossa manuscript: (ten days in the life of Alphonse Van Worden).* London: Dedalus, 1990, 159 p., cloth, coll. [Translation by Christine Donougher of *Rekopis znaleziony w Saragossie*].

POTTER, Jeffrey K.

31752 *The art of Skeleton Crew.* Santa Cruz, CA: Scream/Press, 1985, 40 p., paper, art coll.
31753 *The new flesh, volume I.* Los Angeles: Scream/Press, 1986, 15 leaves, paper, art coll.
31754 *The new flesh, volume II.* Los Angeles: Scream/Press, 1986, 15 leaves, paper, art coll.

POTTS, Stephen W(ayne), 1949-

31755 *From here to absurdity: the moral battlefields of Joseph Heller.* San Bernardino, CA: R. Reginald, The Borgo Press, 1982, 64 p., cloth, nonf. MILFORD SERIES: POPULAR WRITERS OF TODAY #36.
31756 *The second Marxian invasion: the fiction of the Strugatsky Brothers.* San Bernardino, CA: R. Reginald, The Borgo Press, 1991, 104 p., cloth, nonf. MILFORD SERIES: POPULAR WRITERS OF TODAY #50.

POUNS, Brauna E.

31757 *Amerika: a novel.* New York: Pocket Books, 1987, 412 p., paper, tele.

POURNELLE, Jerry (Eugene), 1933-

31759 *Birth of fire.* Toronto, New York: Laser Books, 1976, 191 p., paper, novel.
31760 *Black holes, and other marvels.* London: Futura Publications, An Orbit Book, 1978, 334 p., paper, anth.
31761 *Death's head rebellion.* Riverdale, NY: Baen Books, 1990, 403 p., paper, anth. WAR WORLD #2.
31762 *The endless frontier.* New York: Ace Books, 1979, 376 p., paper, anth.
31763 *Exiles to glory.* New York: Ace Books, 1978, 216 p., paper, novel. LAURIE JO HANSEN #2.
31764 *Falkenberg's legion.* New York: Baen Books, 1990, 432 p., paper, novel. FALKENBERG #1-2. [Includes *The mercenary* and *West of honor*].
31764A retitled: *Future history, incorporating The mercenary and West of honor.* London: Futura Publications, 1980, 383 p., paper, coll. FALKENBERG #1-2.
Future history—SEE: *Falkenberg's legion.*
31765 *High justice.* New York: A Kangaroo Book, Pocket Books, 1977, 222 p., paper, coll. LAURIE JO HANSEN #2.
31766 *Janissaries.* New York: Ace Books, 1979, 335 p., paper, novel. JANISSARIES #1.
King David's spaceship—SEE: *A spaceship for the king.*
31767 *Men of war* / by J. E. Pournelle. New York: A Jim Baen Presentation, Tom Doherty Associates, 1984, 368 p., paper, anth. THERE WILL BE WAR #2. [Includes some nonfiction].
31768 *The mercenary.* New York: A Kangaroo Book, Pocket Books, 1977, 223 p., paper, novel. FALKENBERG'S LEGION #2.
31769 *Prince of mercenaries: a novel of Falkenberg's Legion.* New York: Baen Books, 1989, 338 p., paper, novel. FALKENBERG'S LEGION #3.
11839 *A spaceship for the king.* New York: DAW, 1973, 157 p., paper, novel.
31770 retitled: *King David's spaceship.* New York: Simon & Schuster, 1980, 283 p., cloth, novel. [Revised and expanded edition].
31771 *That Buck Rogers stuff.* Los Angeles: Extequer Press, 1977, 111 p., cloth, nonf. coll. [Limited to 500 copies].
31772 *West of honor.* Toronto, New York: Laser Books, 1976, 190 p., paper, novel. FALKENBERG'S LEGION #1.

with Poul Anderson & Larry Niven & S. M. Stirling

16455 *The Man-Kzin wars III.* New York: Baen Books, 1990, 310 p., paper, coll. MAN-KZIN WARS #3.

with Jim Baen

17198 *Far frontiers* / by Jim Baen.... New York: A Baen Book, 1985, 315 p., paper, anth. [Includes some nonfiction].

17199 *Far frontiers, volume II, Spring 1985* / by Jim Baen.... New York: Baen Science Fiction Books, 1985, 319 p., paper, anth. [Includes some nonfiction].

17200 *Far frontiers, Fall edition 1985 [vol. III]* / by Jim Baen.... New York: Baen Science Fiction Books, 1985, 319 p., paper, anth.

17201 *Far frontiers, Winter edition 1985 [vol. IV]* / by Jim Baen. New York: Baen Publishing Enterprises, 1986, 278 p., paper, anth.

17202 *Far frontiers, Summer edition 1986 [vol. V]* / by Jim Baen. New York: Baen Science Fiction Books, 1986, iv+284 p., paper, anth.

17203 *Far frontiers, volume VI, Fall 1986* / by Jim Baen.... New York: Baen Science Fiction Books, 1986, 270 p., paper, anth.

17204 *Far frontiers, Fall edition, 1986 [vol. VII]* / by Jim Baen.... New York: Baen Books, 1986, 279 p., paper, anth. [Last volume in series].

with Jim Baen & John F. Carr

17205 *The science fiction yearbook.* New York: Baen Science Fiction Books, 1985, 344 p., cloth, anth. [includes some nonfiction].

with John F. Carr

19438 *After armageddon.* New York: Tor, A Tom Doherty Associates Book, 1990, 404 p., paper, anth. THERE WILL BE WAR #9.

19439 *Armageddon!* New York: Tor SF, A Tom Doherty Associates Book, 1989, 368 p., paper, anth. THERE WILL BE WAR #8.

19440 *Blood and iron.* New York: Tor, A Tom Doherty Associates Book, 1984, 383 p., paper, anth. THERE WILL BE WAR #3. [Includes some nonfiction].

19441 *Call to battle.* New York: Tor SF, A Tom Doherty Associates Book, 1988, 375 p., paper, anth. THERE WILL BE WAR #7.

19442 *Cities in space.* New York: Ace Books, 1991, 259 p., paper, anth. ENDLESS FRONTIER #3.

19443 *The crash of empire.* New York: Baen Books, 1989, 376 p., paper, anth. IMPERIAL STARS #3.

19444 *Day of the tyrant.* New York: Tor SF, A Tom Doherty Associates Book, 1985, xiv+370 p., paper, anth. THERE WILL BE WAR #4. [Includes some nonfiction].

19445 *The endless frontier, vol. II.* New York: Ace Books, 1982, 429 p., paper, anth.

19446 *Guns of darkness.* New York: Tor SF, A Tom Doherty Associates Book, 1987, 406 p., paper, anth. THERE WILL BE WAR #6.

19447 *Nebula award stories sixteen.* New York: Holt, Rinehart & Winston, 1982, 286 p., cloth, anth.

19448 *Republic and empire.* New York: Baen Books, 1987, 399 p., paper, anth. IMPERIAL STARS #2.

19449 *Sauron dominion.* Riverdale, NY: Baen Books, 1991, 356 p., paper, anth. WAR WORLD #3.

19450 *The stars at war.* New York: Baen Books, 1986, 464 p., paper, anth. IMPERIAL STARS #1.

19451 *The survival of freedom.* New York: Fawcett Crest, 1981, 381 p., paper, anth.

19452 *There will be war.* New York: A Jim Baen Presentation, Tor, A Tom Doherty Associates Book, 1983, 352 p., paper, anth. THERE WILL BE WAR #1. [Includes some nonfiction and verse].

19453 *There will be war, volume V: [Warrior].* New York: Tor SF, A Tom Doherty Associates Book, 1986, 384 p., paper, anth. THERE WILL BE WAR #5.

with John F. Carr and Roland Green

19454 *The burning eye.* New York: Baen Books, 1988, 366 p., paper, anth. WAR WORLD #1.

with Roland Green

Clan and crown—SEE: *Janissaries: Clan and crown.*

24468 *Janissaries: Clan and crown.* New York: Ace Books, 1982, 437 p., paper, novel. JANISSARIES #2.

24469 *Storms of victory.* New York: Ace Science Fiction Books, 1987, xiv+359 p., cloth, novel. JANISSARIES #3.

with Larry Niven

30738 *Footfall.* New York: A Del Rey Book, Ballantine Books, 1985, xxiii+495 p., cloth, novel.

30739 *Inferno.* New York: Pocket Books, 1976, 237 p., paper, novel.

30740 *Lucifer's hammer.* Chicago: Playboy Press Book, 1977, x+494 p., cloth, novel.

30741 *Oath of fealty.* Huntington Woods, MI: Phantasia Press, 1981, 328 p., cloth, novel. [Limited to 750 copies].

with Larry Niven & Steven Barnes

17434 *The legacy of Heorot.* London: Victor Gollancz, 1987, 352 p., cloth, novel. HEOROT SERIES.

with Larry Niven & Michael Flynn

23220 *Fallen angels.* Norwalk, CT: Easton Press, 1991, 394 p., paper, novel.

with Larry Niven & John Eric Holmes

25871 *Mordred.* New York: Ace Books, 1980, 216 p., paper, novel. BUCK ROGERS #2. [Sequel to *Armageddon: 2419 AD*].

with Larry Niven & Richard S. McEnroe

29516 *Warrior's blood.* New York: Ace Books, 1981, 311 p., paper, novel. BUCK ROGERS #3.

29517 *Warrior's world.* New York: Ace Books, 1981, 199 p., paper, novel. BUCK ROGERS #4.

with Larry Niven & John Silbersack

30742 *Rogers' Rangers.* New York: Ace Science Fiction Books, 1983, 235 p., paper, novel. BUCK ROGERS #5.

with Larry Niven & S. M. Stirling & Dean Ing

26289 *The Man-Kzin wars II.* New York: Baen Books, 1989, ix+306 p., paper, coll. MAN-KZIN WARS #2.

with S. M. Stirling

31775 *The children's hour.* Riverdale, NY: Baen Books, 1991, 316 p., paper, novel. MAN-KZIN WARS.

31776 *Go tell the Spartans.* Riverdale, NY: Baen Books, 1991, 345 p., paper, novel. FALKENBERG'S LEGION #4.

POWE, Ronald

31777 *Possessed.* Lewes, East Sussex, England: The Book Guild, 1989, 194 p., cloth, novel. POSSESSED #1.

31778 *Possessed II: the sequel.* Lewes, East Sussex, England: The Book Guild, 1990, 239 p., cloth, novel. POSSESSED #2.

POWELL, Anthony (Dymoke), 1905-

31779 *The fisher king: a novel.* London: Heinemann, 1986, 255 p., cloth, novel.

POWELL, Claire

31780 *Opfer.* Lewes, East Sussex, England: The Book Guild, 1991, 414 p., cloth, coll.

POWELL, Lawrence Clark, 1906-

31781 *The Islandian world of Austin Wright.* Los Angeles: Horace F. Turner, 1957, [16] p., paper, nonf.

with Robert R. Kirsch & Jacob Zeitlin

27325 *Aldous Huxley, 1894-1963: addresses at a memorial meeting held in the School of Library Service, February 27, 1964.* Los Angeles: University of California, Los Angeles, 1964, 10 p., paper, nonf. coll.

POWELL, Mason, pseud.—SEE: DeCles, Jon

POWER, David

31782 *David Lindsay's vision.* Nottingham, England: Paupers' Press, 1991, iv+36 p., paper, nonf.

POWER, M(aurice) S(tephen), 1935-

31783 *Bridle and the silver lady.* London: Heinemann, 1988, iv+192 p., cloth, novel.

POWERS, Louise E.

31784 *Love on the range.* New York: Avon Flare, 1986, 201 p., paper, novel. EILEEN GOUDGE'S SWEPT AWAY #3.

POWERS, Richard (M. Gorman), 1921-

38018 *Spacetimewarp.* Garden City, NY: Nelson Doubleday, 1983, 16 leaves, paper, art.

POWERS, Tim(othy Thomas), 1952-

31785 *The Anubis gates.* New York: Ace Science Fiction Books, 1983, 387 p., paper, novel. [Winner of the *Science Fiction Chronicle* Award for Best Novel, 1983 (1984)].

31786 *Dinner at Deviant's Palace.* New York: Ace Science Fiction Books, 1985, 294 p., paper, novel.

31787 *The drawing of the dark.* New York: A Del Rey Book, Ballantine Books, 1979, 329 p., paper, novel.

31788 *Epitaph in rust* / by Timothy Powers. Toronto, New York: Laser Books, 1976, 190 p., paper, novel. [Abridged edition].

31789 *An epitaph in rust.* Cambridge, MA: A Boskone Book, NESFA Press, 1989, xvi+226 p., cloth, novel. [The original text of this novel has been restored].

Forsake the sky—SEE: *The skies discrowned.*

31790 *Night moves.* Seattle, WA: Axolotl Press, 1986, 40 p., paper, story.

31791 *On stranger tides.* New York: Ace Books, 1987, 325 p., cloth, novel.

31792 *The skies discrowned* / by Timothy Powers. Toronto, New York: Laser Books, 1976, 190 p., paper, novel.

31793 retitled: *Forsake the sky.* New York: Tor SF, A Tom Doherty Associates Book, 1986, 217 p., paper, novel. [Revised edition].

31794 *The stress of her regard.* Lynbrook, NY: Charnel House, 1989, xi+544 p., cloth, novel.

31795 *The way down the hill.* Seattle, WA: Axolotl Press, 1986, 31 p., cloth, story. [Bound with *The pink of fading neon* / by James P. Blaylock].

POWERS, Tom (J.)

31796 *Horror movies.* Minneapolis, MN: Lerner Publications, 1989, 80 p., cloth, nonf.

31797 *Movie monsters.* Minneapolis, MN: Lerner Publications, 1989, 80 p., cloth, nonf.

POWYS, John Cowper, 1872-1963

31798 *Three fantasies.* Manchester: Carcanet Press, 1985, 186 p., cloth, coll.

POYER, David C., 1949-

31799 *The Shiloh project.* New York: Avon, 1981, 244 p., paper, novel.

31800 *Stepfather bank* / by D. C. Poyer. New York: St. Martin's Press, 1987, 277 p., cloth, novel.

as DAVID ANDREISSEN

31801 *Star seed.* Norfolk, Virginia Beach, VA: Starblaze Editions, Donning Co., 1982, 180 p., paper, novel.

POYER, Joe [i.e., Joseph John Poyer Jr.], 1939-

31802 *Tunnel war.* New York: Atheneum, 1979, x+339 p., cloth, novel.

POYER, Joseph—SEE: Poyer, Joe

POZZESSERE, Heather—SEE: Graham, Heather

PRADE, Ernest La—SEE: La Prade, Ernest

PRANTERA, Amanda, 1942-

31803 *The cabalist.* London: Jonathan Cape, 1985, 184 p., cloth, novel.

31804 *Conversations with Lord Byron on perversion, 163 years after his lordship's death.* London: Jonathan Cape, 1987, 174 p., cloth, novel.

31805 *Strange loop.* London: Jonathan Cape, 1984, 175 p., cloth, novel.

PRATCHETT, Terry (David John), 1948-

31806 *The carpet people.* Gerrards Cross, Buckinghamshire, England: Colin Smythe, 1971, 195 p., cloth, novel.

31807 *The colour of magic.* Gerrards Cross, Buckinghamshire, England: Colin Smythe, 1983, 205 p., cloth, coll. DISCWORLD #1.

31808 *The dark side of the Sun.* Gerrards Cross, Buckinghamshire, England: Colin Smythe, 1976, 158 p., cloth, novel.

31809 *Diggers.* London: Doubleday, 1990, 152 p., cloth, novel. BOOK OF THE NOMES #2.

31810 *Equal rites.* London: Victor Gollancz, 1987, 200 p., cloth, novel. DISCWORLD #3.

31811 *Faust Eric.* London: Victor Gollancz, 1990, 126 p., cloth, novel. DISCWORLD #11.

31812 *Guards! guards!* London: Victor Gollancz, 1989, 288 p., cloth, novel. DISCWORLD #8.

31813 *The light fantastic.* Gerrards Cross, Buckinghamshire, England: Colin Smythe,

1986, 189 p., cloth, novel. DISCWORLD #2.

31814   *Mort*. London: Victor Gollancz in Association with Colin Smythe, 1987, 221 p., cloth, novel. DISCWORLD #4.

31815   *Moving pictures*. London: Victor Gollancz, 1990, 279 p., cloth, novel. DISCWORLD #9.

31816   *Pyramids: the book of going forth*. London: Victor Gollancz, 1989, 272 p., cloth, novel. DISCWORLD #7.

31817   *Reaper man*. London: Victor Gollancz, 1991, 253 p., cloth, novel. DISCWORLD #10.

31818   *Sourcery*. London: Victor Gollancz, 1988, 243 p., cloth, novel. DISCWORLD #5.

31819   *Strata*. Gerrards Cross, Buckinghamshire, England: Colin Smythe, 1981, 192 p., cloth, novel.

31820   *Truckers*. London, New York: Doubleday, 1989, 190 p., cloth, novel. BOOK OF THE NOMES #1.

31821   *Wings*. London: Doubleday, 1990, 158 p., cloth, novel. BOOK OF THE NOMES #3.

31822   *Witches abroad*. London: Victor Gollancz, 1991, 252 p., cloth, novel. DISCWORLD #12.

31823   *Wyrd sisters: starring three witches, also kings, daggers, crowns...* London: Victor Gollancz, 1988, 251 p., cloth, novel. DISCWORLD #6.

with Neil Gaiman

23606   *Good omens: the nice and accurate prophecies of Agnes Nutter, witch*. London: Victor Gollancz, 1990, [288] p., cloth, novel.

PRATNEY, William A.—SEE: Pratney, Winkie

PRATNEY, Winkie [i.e., William Alfred Pratney], 1944-

31824   *Star Wars, Star Trek, and the 21st century Christians*. Van Nuys, CA: Bible Voice, 1978, 91 p., paper, nonf.

PRATT, Annis, 1937- , *with L. S. Dembo*

21545   *Doris Lessing: critical studies*. Madison, WI: University of Wisconsin Press, 1974, xi+172 p., cloth, nonf. anth.

PRATT, (Murray) Fletcher, 1897-1956, *with L. Sprague de Camp*

21352   *The compleat enchanter: the magical misadventures of Harold Shea*. Garden City,

NY: Nelson Doubleday, 1975, 341 p., cloth, coll. HAROLD SHEA #1-2. [Includes *The incomplete enchanter* and *The castle of iron*].

  The complete compleat enchanter—SEE: *The intrepid enchanter*.

  The enchanter compleated—SEE: *Wall of serpents*.

  The incompleat enchanter—SEE: *The incomplete enchanter*.

03995   *The incomplete enchanter*. New York: Henry Holt, 1941, 326 p., cloth, novel. HAROLD SHEA #1.

03995A   retitled: *The incompleat enchanter*. London: Sphere Books, 1979, xv+236 p., paper, novel. HAROLD SHEA #1.

21353   *The intrepid enchanter: the complete magical misadventures of Harold Shea*. London: Sphere Books, 1988, xiii+497 p., paper, coll. HAROLD SHEA #1-3.

21353A   retitled: *The complete compleat enchanter*. New York: Baen Books, 1989, 532 p., paper, coll. HAROLD SHEA #1-3.

21354   *Tales from Gavagan's Bar*. Philadelphia, PA: Owlswick Press, 1978, ix+310 p., cloth, coll. [Expanded edition].

03998   *Wall of serpents*. New York: Avalon Books, 1960, 223 p., cloth, novel. HAROLD SHEA #3.

03998A   retitled: *The enchanter compleated*. London: Sphere Books, 1980, 157 p., paper, novel. HAROLD SHEA #3.

PRAWER, S(iegbert) S(aloman), 1925-

31825   *Caligari's children: the film as tale of terror*. Oxford, England, New York: Oxford University Press, 1980, 307 p., cloth, nonf.

PREHODA, Robert W., 1929-

31826   *Your next fifty years*. New York: Ace Books, 1980, 348 p., paper, fiction.

PREISLER, Jerome

31827   *The pact*. New York: Leisure Books, 1989, 363 p., paper, novel.

PREISS, Byron (Cary), 1953-

31828   *The microverse*. New York: Bantam Books, 1989, 352 p., cloth, anth. [Includes some nonfiction].

31829   *The planets*. Toronto, New York: Bantam Books, 1985, 336 p., cloth, anth. [Includes some nonfiction].

31830 *The universe.* Toronto, New York: Bantam Books, 1987, 333 p., cloth, anth. [Includes some nonfiction].

31831 *Weird heroes.* New York: Pyramid Books, 1975, 247 p., paper, anth. WEIRD HEROES #1.

31832 *Weird heroes, volume 2.* New York: Pyramid Books, 1975, 251 p., paper, anth. WEIRD HEROES #2.

31833 *Weird heroes, volume six.* New York: Pyramid Books; Byron Press Visual Publications, 1977, 320 p., paper, anth. WEIRD HEROES #6.

31834 *Weird heroes, volume eight.* New York: A Jove/HBJ Book, Byron Preiss Visual Publications, 1977, 281 p., paper, anth. WEIRD HEROES #8.

with C. J. Henderson

25478 *Guts.* New York: A Tempo Star Book, Grosset & Dunlap, 1979, viii+178 p., paper, novel.

with David Keller & Megan Miller

26998 *The ultimate Dracula.* New York: A Byron Preiss Book, A Dell Trade Paperback, 1991, viii+358 p., paper, anth.

with David Keller & Megan Miller & John Betancourt

17907 *The ultimate Frankenstein.* New York: A Byron Preiss Book, A Dell Trade Paperback, 1991, viii+327 p., paper, anth.

17908 *The ultimate werewolf.* New York: A Byron Preiss Book, A Dell Trade Paperback, 1991, viii+357 p., paper, anth.

with J. Michael Reaves

31835 *Dragonworld.* Garden City, NY: Nelson Doubleday, 1979, 545 p., cloth, novel.

PRESCOT, Dray, pseud.—SEE: Bulmer, Kenneth

*PREST, (Thomas) Peckett, 1810?-1859

PRESTON, Guy

31837 *The bride of Frankenstein.* London: Ferret, 1979, 14 p., cloth, movie. FRANKENSTEIN SERIES.

PRESTON, Harry, 1923-

31838 *Queen of darkness.* New York: Manor Books, 1976, 332 p., paper, novel.

PREUSS, Paul, 1942-

31839 *Breaking strain.* New York: A Byron Preiss Book, Avon, 1987, 265+16 p., paper, novel. ARTHUR C. CLARKE'S VENUS PRIME #1.

31840 *Broken symmetries.* New York: Timescape Books, 1983, 335 p., cloth, novel.

31841 *The diamond moon.* New York: A Byron Preiss Book, Avon Books, 1990, 278 p., paper, novel. ARTHUR C. CLARKE'S VENUS PRIME #5.

31842 *The gates of heaven.* Toronto, New York: Bantam Books, 1980, 210 p., paper, novel.

31843 *Hide and seek.* New York: A Byron Preiss Book, Avon Books, 1989, 281 p., paper, novel. ARTHUR C. CLARKE'S VENUS PRIME #3.

31844 *Human error.* New York: Tor, A Tom Doherty Associates Book, 1985, 350 p., cloth, novel.

31845 *Maelstrom.* New York: A Byron Preiss Book, Avon Books, 1988, 268+16 p., paper, novel. ARTHUR C. CLARKE'S VENUS PRIME #2.

31846 *The Medusa encounter.* New York: A Byron Preiss Book, Avon Books, 1990, 280+16 p., paper, novel. ARTHUR C. CLARKE'S VENUS PRIME #4.

31847 *Re-entry.* Toronto, New York: Bantam Books, 1981, 212 p., paper, novel.

31848 *The shining ones.* New York: A Byron Preiss Book, Avon Books, 1991, 266+[16] p., paper, novel. ARTHUR C. CLARKE'S VENUS PRIME #6. [Last book in the series].

31849 *Starfire.* New York: Tor, A Tom Doherty Associates Book, 1988, 310 p., cloth, novel.

PREUSSLER, Otfried, 1923-

31850 *The tale of the unicorn.* New York: Dial Press, 1989, 25 p., cloth, art. [Translation by Lenny Hort of *Das märchen vom einhorn*].

PRICE, E(dgar) Hoffmann (Trooper), 1898-1988

31851 *The devil wives of Li Fong.* New York: A Del Rey Book, Ballantine Books, 1979, 217 p., paper, novel.

31852 *Far lands, other days.* Chapel Hill, NC: Carcosa House, 1975, xxi+587 p., cloth, coll.

31853 *The Jade enchantress.* New York: A Del Rey Book, Ballantine Books, 1982, 297 p., paper, novel.

31854 *Operation exile.* New York: A Del Rey Book, Ballantine Books, 1986, 281 p., paper, novel. OPERATION #3.

31855 *Operation Isis.* New York: A Del Rey Book, Ballantine Books, 1987, 247 p., paper, novel. OPERATION #4.

31856 *Operation longlife.* New York: A Del Rey Book, Ballantine Books, 1983, 312 p., paper, novel. OPERATION #2.

31857 *Operation misfit.* New York: A Del Rey Book, Ballantine Books, 1980, 284 p., paper, novel. OPERATION #1.

PRICE, John-Allen, 1954-

31858 *Extinction cruise.* New York: Zebra Books, Kensington Publishing Corp., 1987, 496 p., paper, novel.

31859 *The pursuit of the phoenix.* New York: Zebra Books, Kensington Publishing Corp., 1990, 384 p., paper, novel.

PRICE, Michael H., 1947- , *with George Turner*

31860 *Forgotten horrors: early talkie chillers from Poverty Row.* South Brunswick, NJ: A. S. Barnes & Co., 1979, 216 p., cloth, nonf.

PRICE, Patrick L., *with Martin H. Greenberg*

24573 *Fantastic stories: tales of the weird & wondrous.* Lake Geneva, WI: TSR Inc., 1987, 253 p., paper, anth.

PRICE, Robert M(cNair), 1954-

31861 *H. P. Lovecraft and the Cthulhu Mythos.* Mercer Island, WA: Starmont House, 1990, 170 p., cloth, nonf. STARMONT STUDIES IN LITERARY CRITICISM #33.

31862 *The horror of it all: encrusted gems from the "Crypt of Cthulhu".* Mercer Island, WA: Starmont House, 1990, 199 p., cloth, nonf. anth. STARMONT STUDIES IN LITERARY CRITICISM #31.

31863 *Lin Carter: a look behind his imaginary worlds.* Mercer Island, WA: Starmont House, 1991, vi+172 p., cloth, nonf. STARMONT STUDIES IN LITERARY CRITICISM #36.

PRICE, Roger (Damon Mainwaring), 1941-

Four into three—SEE: *The Tomorrow People in Four into three.*
The lost gods—SEE: *The Tomorrow People in The lost gods.*
One law—SEE: *The Tomorrow People in One law.*

31864 *The Tomorrow People in Four into three.* London & Sydney: A Piccolo/TV Times Original, Pan Books, 1975, 140 p., paper, tele. TOMORROW PEOPLE #3.

31865 *The Tomorrow People in One law.* London & Sydney: A Piccolo/TV Times Original, Pan Books, 1976, 125 p., paper, tele. TOMORROW PEOPLE #4.

31866 *The Tomorrow People in The lost gods, with Hitler's last secret and The Thargon menace.* London & Sydney: Piccolo TV Times Original, Pan Books, 1979, 125 p., paper, tele. coll. TOMORROW PEOPLE #5.

PRICE, Susan, 1955-

31867 *The bone dog.* London: Hippo, 1989, 124 p., paper, novel.

31868 *The devil's piper.* London: Faber & Faber, 1973, 166 p., cloth, novel.

31869 *The ghost drum: a cat's tale.* London: Faber & Faber, 1987, 167 p., cloth, novel.

31870 *Ghostly tales.* Loughborough, England: Ladybird, 1987, 50 p., cloth, coll.

31871 *Ghosts at large.* London: Faber & Faber, 1984, 90 p., cloth, coll.

31872 *In a nutshell.* London: Faber & Faber, 1983, 120 p., cloth, novel.

PRICKETT, (Alexander Thomas) Stephen, 1939-

31873 *Victorian fantasy.* Hassocks, Sussex, England: The Harvester Press, 1979, xvi+ 257 p., cloth, nonf.

PRIEST, Christopher (McKenzie), 1943-

31874 *The affirmation.* London, Boston: Faber & Faber, 1981, 213 p., cloth, novel.

31875 *Anticipations.* London, Boston: Faber & Faber, 1978, 214 p., cloth, anth.

31876 *A dream of Wessex.* London: Faber & Faber, 1977, 199 p., cloth, novel.

31876A retitled: *The perfect lover.* New York: Charles Scribner's Sons, 1977, 199 p., cloth, novel.

31877 *The glamour.* London: Jonathan Cape, 1984, 303 p., cloth, novel.

38019 *Indoctrinaire.* London & Sydney: Pan Books, 1979, 192 p., paper, novel. [Revised edition of #11900].

31878 *An infinite summer.* London: Faber & Faber, 1979, 208 p., cloth, coll.

31879 *The last deadloss visions.* Pewsey, Wiltshire, England: Christopher Priest, 1987, 26 p., paper, nonf.

782

31880 *The last deadloss visions*, 2nd ed. Pewsey, Wiltshire, England: Christopher Priest, 1987, 33 p., paper, nonf.

38020 *The making of the lesbian horse*. Birmingham, England: Birmingham Science Fiction Group, 1979, 11 p., paper, story.

The perfect lover—SEE: *A dream of Wessex*.

31881 *The quiet woman*. London: Bloomsbury, 1990, 216 p., cloth, novel.

31882 *The Space Machine: a scientific romance*. London: Faber & Faber, 1976, 363 p., cloth, novel. TIME MACHINE SEQUEL.

31883 *'The truth shall set you free'*. Pewsey, Wiltshire, England: Christopher Priest, 1987, p. 27-34, paper, nonf. [A continuation of *The last deadloss visions*].

with Robert Holdstock

25846 *Stars of Albion*. London & Sydney: Pan Books, 1979, 238 p., paper, anth.

PRIEST, James D.

31884 *Kirins: the spell of No'an*. Shorewood, MN: Yellowstone Press, 1990, 467 p., paper, novel.

*PRIESTLEY, J(ohn) B(oynton), 1894-1984

PRIESTLEY, Margaret, 1919?-

38021 *The ring of fortune*. London: Faber & Faber, 1948, 206 p., cloth, novel. WORLD DIONYSUS #1.

38022 *The three queens*. London: Faber & Faber, 1950, 200 p., cloth, novel. WORLD DIONYSUS #2.

38023 *Tomay is loyal*. London: Faber & Faber, 1951, 183 p., cloth, novel. WORLD DIONYSUS #3.

PRINCE, Alison (Mary), 1931-

31885 *The ghost within*. London: Methuen, 1984, 119 p., cloth, coll.

31886 *The haunted children*. London: Methuen Children's Books, 1988, 125 p., cloth, novel.

31887 *A haunting refrain*. London: Methuen, 1988, 107 p., cloth, coll.

31888 *The others*. London: Methuen, 1986, 207 p., cloth, novel.

31889 *The Type One super robot*. London: Marilyn Marin in Association with André Deutsch, 1986, 127 p., cloth, novel.

PRINCE, Don, 1903-1983

11915 *Tom: a novel*. New York: Julian Messner, 1940, 272 p., cloth, novel.

11915A retitled: *Tom's temptations*. Chicago: Diversey, 1949, 123 p., paper, novel.

PRINGLE, David (William), 1950-

31890 *Dark future: Route 666*. Brighton, East Sussex, England: GW Books, 1990, 254 p., paper, anth. DARK FUTURE SERIES.

31891 *Earth Is the Alien Planet: J. G. Ballard's Four-Dimensional Nightmare*. San Bernardino, CA: R. Reginald, The Borgo Press, 1979, 63 p., cloth, nonf. MILFORD SERIES: POPULAR WRITERS OF TODAY #26.

Ignorant armies—SEE: *Warhammer: Ignorant armies*.

31892 *Imaginary people: a who's who of modern fictional characters*. London, Glasgow: Grafton Books, 1987, x+515 p., cloth, nonf.

31893 *J. G. Ballard: a primary and secondary bibliography*. Boston: G. K. Hall, 1984, xxxvi+156 p., cloth, nonf. MASTERS OF SCIENCE FICTION AND FANTASY.

31894 *Modern fantasy: the hundred best novels: an English-language selection, 1946-1987*. London, Glasgow: Grafton Books, 1988, 278 p., cloth, nonf.

Red thirst—SEE: *Warhammer: Red thirst*.

Route 666—SEE: *Dark future: Route 666*.

31895 *Science fiction: 100 SF authors*. Leeds: Leeds City Libraries, 1978, 24 p., paper, nonf.

31896 *Science fiction: the 100 best novels: an English-language selection, 1949-1984*. London: Xanadu, 1985, 224 p., cloth, nonf.

31897 *Warhammer: Ignorant armies*. Brighton, East Sussex, England: GW Books, 1989, 252 p., paper, anth. WARHAMMER SERIES.

31898 *Warhammer: Red thirst*. Brighton, East Sussex, England: GW Books, 1990, 256 p., paper, anth. WARHAMMER SERIES.

31899 *Warhammer: Wolf riders*. Brighton, East Sussex, England: GW Books, 1989, 236 p., paper, anth. WARHAMMER SERIES.

Wolf riders—SEE: *Warhammer: Wolf riders*.

with Ken Brown as anonymous co-author

31900 *The ultimate guide to science fiction*. London, Glasgow: Grafton Books, 1990, xx+407 p., cloth, nonf.

with John Clute & Colin Greenland

20205 *Interzone: the first anthology: new science fiction and fantasy writing.* London: J. M. Dent & Sons, 1985, 206 p., paper, anth.

with John Clute & Lee Montgomerie

20207 *Interzone: the 5th anthology: new science fiction and fantasy writing.* London: New English Library, 1991, 280 p., paper, anth.

with John Clute & Simon Ounsley

20208 *Interzone: the 2nd anthology: new science fiction and fantasy writing.* London, Sydney: Simon & Schuster, 1987, x + 208 p., cloth, anth.

20209 *Interzone: the 3rd anthology: new science fiction and fantasy writing.* London, Sydney: Simon & Schuster, 1988, viii + 184 p., cloth, anth.

20210 *Interzone: the 4th anthology: new science fiction and fantasy writing.* London: Simon & Schuster, 1989, ix + 208 p., cloth, anth.

with James Goddard

24032 *J. G. Ballard: the first twenty years.* Hayes, Middlesex: Bran's Head Books, 1976, [99] p., cloth, nonf. anth.

with Neal Jones

    Deathwing—SEE: *Warhammer 40,000: Deathwing.*

26754 *Warhammer 40,000: Deathwing.* East Sussex, England: GW Books, 1990, 257 p., paper, anth. WARHAMMER SERIES.

PRINGLE, Eric

    The awakening—SEE: *Doctor Who: The awakening.*

31901 *Doctor Who: The awakening.* London: W. H. Allen & Co., 1985, 144 p., cloth, tele. DOCTOR WHO #95.

PRITCHARD, John W.—SEE: **Wallace, Ian**

PROCHNAU, William (W.), 1937-

31902 *Trinity's child.* New York: A Boston Book, G. P. Putnam's Sons, 1983, 400 p., cloth, novel.

PROCTOR, Geo(rge) W(yatt), 1946-

    The Chicago conversion—SEE: *V: The Chicago conversion.*

31903 *The esper transfer.* Canoga Park, CA: Major Books, 1978, 188 p., paper, novel.

31904 *Fire at the center.* New York: Fawcett Gold Medal, 1981, 220 p., paper, novel.

31905 *Shadowman.* New York: Fawcett Gold Medal, 1980, 254 p., paper, novel.

31906 *Starwings.* New York: Ace Science Fiction Books, 1984, 214 p., paper, novel.

31907 *Stellar fist.* New York: Ace Books, 1989, 229 p., paper, novel.

    The Texas run—SEE: *V: The Texas run.*

31908 *V: The Chicago conversion.* New York: Pinnacle Books, 1985, 184 p., paper, tele. V #4.

31909 *V: The Texas run.* New York: Pinnacle Books, 1985, 183 p., paper, tele. V #11.

as CAER GED

15685 *The coming of Cormac.* New York: Orpheus Series, 1974, 184 p., paper, novel.

as LEE WYATT

15684 *The flesh hunters.* New York: Orpheus Series, 1974, 187 p., paper, novel.

with Arthur C. Clarke

20122 *The science fiction hall of fame, volume III: Nebula winners, 1965-1969.* New York: Avon, 1982, xii + 672 p., paper, anth.

with Andrew J. Offutt as JOHN CLEVE

30960 *The manhuntress.* New York: Playboy Paperbacks, 1982, 224 p., paper, novel. SPACEWAYS #7.

30961 *Master of Misfit.* New York: Playboy Paperbacks, 1982, 223 p., paper, novel. SPACEWAYS #5.

30967 *The yoke of Shen.* New York: Berkley Books, 1983, 228 p., paper, novel. SPACEWAYS #10.

with Steven Utley

31910 *Lone star universe: the first anthology of Texas science fiction authors.* Austin, TX: Heidelberg Publishers, 1976, xviii + 293 p., cloth, anth.

with Robert E. Vardeman

31911 *The beasts of the mist.* New York: Ace Fantasy Books, 1986, 183 p., paper, novel. SWORDS OF RAEMLLYN #5.

31912 *Blood fountain.* New York: Ace Fantasy Books, 1985, 184 p., paper, novel. SWORDS OF RAEMLLYN #3.

31913 *Death's acolyte.* New York: Ace Fantasy Books, 1986, 181 p., paper, novel. SWORDS OF RAEMLLYN #4.

31914 *For crown and kingdom.* New York: Ace Fantasy Books, 1987, 196 p., paper, novel. SWORDS OF RAEMLLYN #6.

31915 *To demons bound.* New York: Ace Fantasy Books, 1985, 215 p., paper, novel. SWORDS OF RAEMLLYN #1.

31916 *A yoke of magic.* New York: Ace Fantasy Books, 1985, 195 p., paper, novel. SWORDS OF RAEMLLYN #2.

with Robert E. Vardeman as EDWARD GEORGE

Intergalactic orgy—SEE: *Pleasure planet.*
Janet's sex planet—SEE: *Pleasure planet.*
Outer space embrace—SEE: *Pleasure planet.*
Playing with desire—SEE: *Pleasure planet.*

05883 *Pleasure planet.* New York: Orpheus Series, 1974, 187 p., paper, novel.

05883A retitled: *Outer space embrace* / by Monica Mounds. New York: A Beeline Classic, 1978, 187 p., paper, novel.

05883B retitled: *Janet's sex planet* / by Carrie Onn. New York: A Beeline Double Novel, 1980, 187 p., paper, novel. [Bound with *Orgy in orbit* / by Traves Tea].

05883C retitled: *Intergalactic orgy* / by Obie Kahn. New York: Late Night Library, 1983, 187 p., paper, novel.

05883D retitled: *Sexual coquette* / by Marv Elous. New York: A Beeline Double Novel, 1985, 187 p., paper, novel. [Bound with *From novice to nymphette* / by Terri Flick].

05883E retitled: *Playing with desire* / by Fred Sparkrock. New York: A Beeline Double Novel, 1986, 187 p., paper, novel.
Sexual coquette—SEE: *Pleasure planet.*

PROFFITT, Josephine—SEE: **Dee, Sylvia**

PRONIN, Barbara

31917 *Syndrome.* New York: Avon, 1986, 292 p., paper, novel.

PRONZINI, Bill [i.e., William John Pronzini], 1943-

31918 *The Arbor House necropolis: Voodoo! a chrestomathy of necromancy; Mummy! a chrestomathy of cryptoology; Ghoul! a chrestomathy of ogrery.* New York: Priam Books, Arbor House, 1981, 727 p., paper, anth.

31918A retitled: *Tales of the dead.* New York: Bonanza Books, 1986, 711 p., cloth, anth. [Slightly abridged].

31919 *Creature! a chrestomathy of "monstery".* New York: Priam Books, Arbor House, 1981, 301 p., cloth, anth.

31920 *Mummy! a chrestomathy of crypto-ology.* New York: Arbor House, 1980, xii+273 p., cloth, anth.

31921 *Specter! a chrestomathy of "spookery".* New York: Arbor House, 1982, 298 p., cloth, anth.
Tales of the dead—SEE: *The Arbor House necropolis.*

31922 *Voodoo! a chrestomathy of necromancy.* New York: Arbor House, 1980, xxii+295 p., cloth, anth.

31923 *Werewolf!* New York: Arbor House, 1979, xx+229 p., cloth, anth.

with Martin H. Greenberg & Barry N. Malzberg

24574 *The Arbor House treasury of horror and the supernatural.* New York: Arbor House, 1981, 599 p., paper, anth.

24574A retitled: *Great tales of horror & the supernatural.* Secaucus, NJ: Galahad Books, Castle Books, 1985, 597 p., cloth, anth. [Abridged edition].

24574B retitled: *Classic tales of horror and the supernatural.* New York: Quill, 1991, 599 p., paper, anth.

24574C retitled: *The giant book of horror stories.* ?: Magpie, 1991, 597 p., paper, anth. [Abridged edition].
Classic tales of horror and the supernatural—SEE: *The Arbor House treasury of horror and the supernatural.*
The giant book of horror stories—SEE: *The Arbor House treasury of horror and the supernatural.*
Great tales of horror & the supernatural—SEE: *The Arbor House treasury of horror and the supernatural.*

with Barry N. Malzberg

28985 *Bug-eyed monsters.* New York, London: A Harvest/HBJ Original, Harcourt Brace Jovanovich, 1980, x+273 p., paper, anth.

28986 *Dark sins, dark dreams: crime in science fiction.* Garden City, NY: Doubleday & Co., 1978, xii+224 p., cloth, anth.

28987 *The end of summer: science fiction of the Fifties.* New York: Ace Books, 1979, 311 p., paper, anth.

28987A retitled: *The fifties: the end of summer.* New York: Baronet Publishing Co., 1979, 311 p., paper, anth.
The fifties—SEE: *The end of summer.*

28988 *Night screams.* Chicago: Playboy Press, 1979, 262 p., cloth, novel.

37931 *Prose Bowl.* New York: St. Martin's Press, 1980, 180 p., cloth, novel.

28989 *Shared tomorrows: science fiction in collaboration.* New York: St. Martin's Press, 1979, xiv+233 p., cloth, anth.

with Marcia Muller

30401 *Beyond the grave.* New York: Walker & Co., 1986, 236 p., cloth, novel.

30402 *Witches' brew: horror and supernatural stories by women.* New York: Macmillan Publishing Co., 1984, x+323 p., cloth, anth.

PRONZINI, William J.—SEE: Pronzini, Bill

PROSE, Francine, 1947-

31924 *Animal magnetism.* New York: G. P. Putnam's Sons, 1978, 190 p., cloth, novel.

31925 *Marie Laveau.* New York: Berkley Publishing Corp., 1977, 342 p., cloth, novel.

*PROSSER, H(arold) L(ee II), 1944-

PROTTER, Eric, 1927-

31926 *A harvest of horrors.* New York: Vanguard Press, 1980, vi+244 p., cloth, anth.

PROUTY, Howard H.

31927 *TZX: the Twilight Zone index.* North Hollywood, CA: [Howard H. Prouty], 1985, 40 p., paper, nonf.

*PRUYN, Leonard, 1898-1973

PRYCE, Larry, with David Holman

25864 *Fleshbait.* London: New English Library, 1979, 160 p., paper, novel.

PTACEK, Kathryn [i.e., Kathryn Anne Ptacek Grant], 1952-

31928 *Blood autumn.* New York: Tor, A Tom Doherty Associates Book, 1985, 349 p., paper, novel.

31929 *Ghost dance.* New York: Tor Horror, A Tom Doherty Associates Book, 1990, 306 p., paper, novel.

31930 *In silence sealed.* New York: Tor Horror, A Tom Doherty Associates Book, 1988, 306 p., paper, novel.

31931 *Kachina.* New York: Tor, A Tom Doherty Associates Book, 1986, 306 p., paper, novel.

31932 *Shadoweyes.* New York: Tor, A Tom Doherty Associates Book, 1984, 314 p., paper, novel.

31933 *Women of darkness.* New York: Tor, A Tom Doherty Associates Book, 1988, x+306 p., cloth, anth.

31934 *Women of darkness II: more original horror and dark fantasy by contemporary women writers.* New York: Tor Horror, A Tom Doherty Associates Book, 1990, vi+280 p., cloth, anth.

as KATHRYN GRANT

31935 *The black jade road.* New York: Ace Books, 1989, 180 p., paper, novel. LAND OF TEN THOUSAND WILLOWS #2.

31936 *The phoenix bells.* New York: Ace Fantasy Books, 1987, 182 p., paper, novel. LAND OF TEN THOUSAND WILLOWS #1.

31937 *The willow garden.* New York: Ace Books, 1989, 196 p., paper, novel. LAND OF TEN THOUSAND WILLOWS #3.

as LES SIMONS

31938 *Gila!* New York: A Signet Book, New American Library, 1981, 166 p., paper, novel.

PULLMAN, Philip (Nicholas), 1946-

31939 *Spring-Heeled Jack.* London: Doubleday, 1989, 112 p., cloth, novel.

PULVER, Mary Monica [i.e., Mary Monica Pulver Kuhfeld], 1943-

31940 *Murder at the war: a modern-day mystery with a medieval setting.* New York: St. Martin's Press, 1987, viii+260 p., cloth, novel.

PUNCHARD, Constance—SEE: Holme, Constance

PUNTER, David (Godfrey), 1949-

31941 *The literature of terror: a history of gothic fictions from 1765 to the present day.*

London & New York: Longman, 1980,
449 p., cloth, nonf.

PURTILL, Richard (Lawrence), 1931-

31942 *Enchantment at Delphi.* San Diego, CA:
Harcourt Brace Jovanovich, 1986, 149 p.,
cloth, novel.
31943 *The golden gryphon feather.* New York:
DAW Books, 1979, 160 p., paper, novel.
31944 *J. R. R. Tolkien: myth, morality, and religion.* San Francisco: Harper & Row,
1984, xi+154 p., cloth, nonf.
31945 *The mirror of Helen.* New York: DAW
Books, 1983, 192 p., paper, novel.
31946 *Murdercon.* Garden City, NY: Doubleday
& Co., 1982, 181 p., cloth, novel.
31947 *The parallel man.* New York: DAW
Books, 1984, 158 p., paper, novel.
31948 *The stolen goddess.* New York: DAW
Books, 1980, 159 p., paper, novel.

PUSTI, Maureen S.

31949 *Neighbors.* New York: Leisure Books,
1991, 395 p., paper, novel.

PUZO, Mario, 1920-

31950 *The fourth K: a novel.* New York: Random House, 1990, 479 p., cloth, novel.

PYE, Lloyd (Anthony, Jr.), 1946-

31951 *Mismatch.* New York: A Dell Book,
1989, 342 p., paper, novel.

PYLE, Hilary, 1936-

31952 *James Stephens: his work and an account
of his life.* London: Routledge & Kegan
Paul, 1965, xi+196 p., cloth, nonf.

PYNCHON, Thomas (Ruggles Jr.), 1937-

31953 *Gravity's rainbow.* New York: Viking
Press, 1973, 760 p., cloth, novel.
38024 *Vineland.* Boston: Little, Brown & Co.,
1990, 385 p., cloth, novel.

Q

QUACKENBUSH, Robert M(ead), 1929-

31954 *Movie monsters and their masters: the birth of the horror film.* Chicago: Albert Whitman & Co., 1980, 47 p., cloth, nonf.

QUEEN, Ellery, house pseud.—SEE: Davidson, Avram

QUEIROS, Eça de [i.e., José Maria de Eça de Queiroz], 1845-1900

15800 *The mandarin, and other stories.* Athens, OH: Ohio University Press, 1965, 176 p., cloth, coll.

QUERRY, Simon

38025 *Adventures on the planets.* London: S. Baker, 1953, 64 p., paper, story.

QUEUX, William Le—SEE: Le Queux, William

QUICK, W. T.

31955 *Dreams of flesh and sand.* New York: A Signet Book, New American Library, 1988, 301 p., paper, novel. DREAMS #1.
31956 *Dreams of gods and men.* New York: A Signet Book, New American Library, 1989, 302 p., paper, novel. DREAMS #2.
31957 *Singularities.* New York: A Roc Book, 1990, 285 p., paper, novel. DREAMS #3.
31958 *Systems: a novel.* New York: A Signet Book, New American Library, 1989, 251 p., paper, novel.
31959 *Yesterday's pawn.* New York: A Signet Book, New American Library, 1989, 254 p., paper, novel.

QUIJANO, Mary L(ouise), 1944-

31960 *Bloodmaster.* New York: Pinnacle Books, Windsor Publishing Corp., 1989, 332 p., paper, novel.

*QUILP, Jocelyn [pseud. of Halliwell Sutcliffe], 1870-1932

*QUILTY, Rafe [pseud. of Rick Trader Whitcombe], 1943-

QUINLIVEN, J. O.

31961 *Bride of the serpents: a story from Terror tales.* North Hollywood, CA: Shroud: Publishers, 1975, 55 p., paper, story. PULP READER #2.

QUINN, Arthur Hobson, 1874-1944

31962 *Edgar Allan Poe: a critical biography.* New York: Appleton-Century, 1941, xvi+804 p., cloth, nonf.

QUINN, Daniel, 1935-

31963 *Dreamer.* New York: Tor Horror, A Tom Doherty Associates Book, 1988, 345 p., paper, novel.

QUINN, Patrick F(rancis), 1918-

31964 *The French face of Edgar Poe.* Carbondale, IL: Southern Illinois University Press, 1957, 310 p., cloth, nonf.

QUINN, Seabury (Grandin), 1889-1969

31965 *The adventures of Jules de Grandin.* New York: Popular Library, 1976, 224 p., paper, coll. JULES DE GRANDIN #1. [Edited by Robert Weinberg].
31966 *Alien flesh.* Philadelphia, PA: Oswald Train: Publisher, 1977, 234 p., cloth, novel.
31967 *The casebook of Jules de Grandin.* New York: Popular Library, 1976, 252 p., paper, coll. JULES DE GRANDIN #2. [Edited by Robert Weinberg].
31968 *The devil's bride.* New York: Popular Library, 1976, 254 p., paper, novel. JULES DE GRANDIN #4. [Edited by Robert Weinberg].
31969 *The hellfire files of Jules de Grandin.* New York: Popular Library, 1976, 222 p., paper, coll. JULES DE GRANDIN #5. [Edited by Robert Weinberg].
31970 *The horror chambers of Jules de Grandin.* New York: Popular Library, 1977, 224

p., paper, coll. JULES DE GRANDIN #6. [Edited by Robert Weinberg].

31971 *The skeleton closet of Jules de Grandin.* New York: Popular Library, 1976, 252 p., paper, coll. JULES DE GRANDIN #3. [Edited by Robert Weinberg].

QUINN, Tim, 1953- , *with Dicky Howett*

26066 *The Doctor Who fun book.* London: A Target Book, W. H. Allen & Co., 1987, 64 p., paper, nonf.

QUIRINO, Joe [i.e, José A. Quirino], 1930-

31972 *Two steps beyond, and other bizarre and nocturnal tales.* Quezon City, Philippines: Interlino Printing Co., 1982, ix + 311 p., cloth?, coll.

QUIRINO, José—SEE: Quirino, Joe

QUYTH, Gabriel [pseud. of Gary Jennings], 1928-

31973 *The lively lives of Crispin Mobey.* New York: Atheneum, 1988, 243 p., cloth, novel.

R

R., O.

31974 *The king who knew not fear: a tale of other days.* London: Philip Lee Warner, Publisher to the Medici Society, 1912, 30 p., cloth, story. [Limited to 500 copies].

RABE, Jean (Marie), 1942-

31975 *Forgotten realms fantasy adventure: Red magic.* Lake Geneva, WI: TSR Inc., 1991, 313 p., paper, novel. THE HARPERS #3.
Red magic—SEE: *Forgotten realms fantasy adventure: Red magic.*

RABIG, Tony

31976 *Keeping up with science fiction.* [S.l.]: Kitchen Table Pamphlets, 1976, 44 p., paper, nonf.

RABIN, Jennifer

31977 *Spellbound.* New York: An Avon Flare Book, 1987, 188 p., paper, novel. EILEEN GOUDGE'S SWEPT AWAY #5.

RABINOWITZ, Ann

31978 *Knight on horseback.* New York: Macmillan Publishing Co.; London: Collier Macmillan Publishing, 1987, 197 p., cloth, novel.

RABKIN, Eric S(tanley), 1946-

31979 *Arthur C. Clarke.* West Linn, OR: Starmont House, 1979, 80 p., paper, nonf. STARMONT READER'S GUIDE #1.
31980 *Arthur C. Clarke.* Mercer Island, WA: Starmont House, 1980, 80 p., paper, nonf. STARMONT READER'S GUIDE #1. [Revised, second edition].
31981 *The fantastic in literature.* Princeton, NJ: Princeton University Press, 1976, xi+234 p., cloth, nonf.
31982 *Fantastic worlds: myths, tales, and stories.* Oxford, England, New York: Oxford University Press, 1979, xvii+478 p., cloth, anth.

31983 *Science fiction: a historical anthology.* Oxford, England, New York: Oxford University Press, 1983, x+529 p., cloth, anth. [Includes some nonfiction].

with Martin H. Greenberg & Joseph D. Olander

24575 *The end of the world.* Carbondale & Edwardsville, IL: Southern Illinois University Press, 1983, xv+204 p., cloth, nonf. anth.
24576 *No place else: explorations in utopian and dystopian fiction.* Carbondale & Edwardsville, IL: Southern Illinois University Press, 1983, 278 p., cloth, nonf. anth.

with Colin Greenland & George E. Slusser

24662 *Storm warnings: science fiction confronts the future.* Carbondale & Edwardsville, IL: Southern Illinois University Press, 1987, xi+278 p., cloth, nonf. anth. PROCEEDINGS OF THE J. LLOYD EATON CONFERENCE ON SCIENCE FICTION AND FANTASY LITERATURE #6.

with Robert Scholes

31984 *Science fiction: history, science, vision.* New York: Oxford University Press, 1977, viii+258 p., cloth, nonf.

with Robert Scholes & George E. Slusser

31985 *Bridges to fantasy.* Carbondale & Edwardsville, IL: Southern Illinois University Press, 1982, xi+231 p., cloth, nonf. anth. PROCEEDINGS OF THE J. LLOYD EATON CONFERENCE ON SCIENCE FICTION AND FANTASY LITERATURE #2.
31986 *Coordinates: placing science fiction and fantasy* / ed. by George E. Slusser... Carbondale & Edwardsville: Southern Illinois University Press, 1983, xii+209 p., cloth, nonf. anth. PROCEEDINGS OF THE J. LLOYD EATON CONFERENCE ON SCIENCE FICTION AND FANTASY LITERATURE #3.

with George E. Slusser

31987 *Aliens: the anthropology of science fiction.* Carbondale & Edwardsville, IL: Southern Illinois University Press, 1987, xx + 243 p., cloth, nonf. anth. PROCEEDINGS OF THE J. LLOYD EATON CONFERENCE ON SCIENCE FICTION AND FANTASY LITERATURE #7.

31988 *Hard science fiction.* Carbondale & Edwardsville, IL: Southern Illinois University Press, 1986, xvi + 284 p., cloth, nonf. anth. PROCEEDINGS OF THE J. LLOYD EATON CONFERENCE ON SCIENCE FICTION AND FANTASY LITERATURE #5.

31989 *Intersections: fantasy and science fiction.* Carbondale & Edwardsville, IL: Southern Illinois University Press, 1987, x + 252 p., cloth, nonf. anth. PROCEEDINGS OF THE J. LLOYD EATON CONFERENCE ON SCIENCE FICTION AND FANTASY LITERATURE #8.

31990 *Mindscapes: the geographies of imagined worlds.* Carbondale & Edwardsville, IL: Southern Illinois University Press, 1989, xiii + 302 p., cloth, nonf. anth. PROCEEDINGS OF THE J. LLOYD EATON CONFERENCE ON SCIENCE FICTION AND FANTASY LITERATURE #9.

31991 *Shadows of the magic lamp: fantasy and science fiction in films.* Carbondale & Edwardsville, IL: Southern Illinois University Press, 1985, xx + 259 p., cloth, nonf. anth. PROCEEDINGS OF THE J. LLOYD EATON CONFERENCE ON SCIENCE FICTION AND FANTASY LITERATURE #4.

RACHLEFF, Owen S(pencer), 1934-

31992 *Enigma.* New York: Leisure Books, 1989, 243 p., paper, novel.

31993 *Eric's image.* New York: Tower Books, 1982, 304 p., paper, novel.

31993A retitled: *The image.* New York: Leisure Books, 1986, 304 p., paper, novel.

The image—SEE: *Eric's image.*

RACINA, Thom [pseud. of Thomas Frank Raucina], 1946-

Blizzard—SEE: *The great Los Angeles blizzard.*

31994 *The great Los Angeles blizzard.* New York: G. P. Putnam's Sons, 1977, 358 p., cloth, novel.

31994A retitled: *Blizzard.* London: New English Library, 1979, 348 p., paper, novel.

RADCLIFFE, Elsa J., 1935-

31995 *Gothic novels of the twentieth century: an annotated bibliography.* Metuchen, NJ, London: Scarecrow Press, 1979, xix + 272 p., cloth, nonf.

RADCLIFFE, (Henry) Garnett, 1899-

38026 *The great Orme terror.* London: Thornton Butterworth, 1935, 254 p., cloth, novel.

RADFORD, Ken

31996 *The cellar.* New York: Holiday House, 1989, 171 p., cloth, novel.

31997 *Haunting at Mill Lane.* Wendover, England: Goodchild, 1983, 153 p., cloth, novel.

31998 *House in the shadows.* Aylesbury, England: Goodchild, 1986, 188 p., cloth, novel.

RADNOR, Alan, pseud.—SEE: Lewis, Richard

RAE, Hugh C(rauford), 1935-

31999 *Harkfast: the making of the king.* London: Constable & Co., 1976, 227 p., cloth, novel.

32000 *The haunting at Waverley Falls.* London: Constable & Co., 1980, 255 p., cloth, novel.

32001 *The traveling soul.* New York: Avon, 1978, 222 p., paper, novel.

as STUART STERN

32002 *The Minotaur factor.* London: Futura Publications, 1977, 318 p., paper, novel.

RAE, Patricia

32003 *The touch.* New York: Tower Books, 1980, 446 p., paper, novel.

RAEPER, William, 1959-

32004 *George MacDonald.* Tring, Hertfordshire, England, Batavia, IL: A Lion Book, 1987, 432 p., cloth, nonf.

32005 *The gold thread: essays on George MacDonald.* Edinburgh, Scotland: Edinburgh University Press, 1990, viii + 198 p., cloth, nonf. anth.

32006 *The troll and the butterfly, and other stories.* London: Malin in Association with André Deutsch, 1987, 126 p., cloth, coll.

RAHMAN, Glenn

32007 *Heir of darkness.* Lake Geneva, WI: New Infinities Productions, 1989, 352 p., paper, novel.

RAIFSNIDER, Barbara, *with James Davis*

21271 *The fire crystal.* San Diego, CA: Infinity Books, 1978, 52 p., paper, novel.

RAILO, Eino

32008 *The haunted castle: a study of the elements of English romanticism.* London: George Routledge & Sons, 1927, xvii+ 388 p., cloth, nonf.

RAINES, Charles A(lanceson), 1927-

32009 *Jules Verne's 20,000 leagues under the sea, and Around the world in 80 days, Journey to the center of the Earth, The mysterious island, Michael Strogoff.* New York: Monarch Press, 1970, 135 p., paper, nonf.

RAINES, Theron, 1925-

32010 *The singing: a fable about what makes us human.* New York: A Morgan Entrekin Book, Atlantic Monthly Press, 1988, 163 p., cloth, novel.

RAINEY, Rich(ard), *as JASON FROST*

23567 *Killer's keep.* New York: Zebra Books, Kensington Publishing Corp., 1987, 236 p., paper, novel. WARLORD #6.

RAISOR, Gary

32011 *Obsessions.* Arlington Heights, IL: Dark Harvest, 1991, 317 p., cloth, anth.

RAKNEM, Ingvald, 1910-

32012 *H. G. Wells and his critics.* Oslo, Norway: Universitets Forlaget, 1962, 475 p., cloth, nonf.

RAMAKRISHNA RAO, Adapa, 1927- , *with Satyanarain Singh & Taqi Ali Mirza*

29969 *William Golding: an Indian response: a collection of critical essays on the fiction of William Golding.* New Delhi, India: Arnold-Heinemann, 1987, viii+147 p., cloth, nonf. anth.

RAMIE, Florence

32013 *Toyland.* New York: Leisure Books, 1986, 395 p., paper, novel.

RAMIREZ, Alice (Louise), *as CANDICE ARKHAM*

32014 *Ancient evil.* New York: Popular Library, 1977, 255 p., paper, novel.

RAMIREZ, Medardo Figueroa—SEE: Figueroa, Medardo

RAMPA, T. Lobsang—SEE: Lobsang Rampa, T.

RAMSAY, Jay, pseud.—SEE: Campbell, Ramsey

RAMSLAND, Katherine (Marie Johnston), 1953-

32015 *Prism of the night: a biography of Anne Rice.* New York: E. P. Dutton, 1991, xiv+385 p., cloth, nonf.

RANADE, Karen—SEE: Blank, Karen

RANALD, Ralph A.

32016 *George Orwell's Animal farm.* New York: Monarch Press, 1965, 106 p., paper, nonf.
32017 *Orwell's 1984, and selected writings.* New York: Monarch Press, 1965, 122 p., paper, nonf.

*RAND, Ayn, 1905-<u>1982</u>

RAND, Peter, 1940-

32018 *The time of the emergency.* Garden City, NY: Doubleday & Co., 1977, 151 p., cloth, novel.

RANDALL, Bob, 1937-

32019 *The calling: a novel.* New York: Simon & Schuster, 1981, 206 p., cloth, novel.
32020 *The next.* New York: Warner Books, 1981, 350 p., paper, novel.

RANDALL, David A(nton), 1905-1975, *with Sigmund Casey Fredericks & Tim Mitchell*

23480 *Science fiction and fantasy: an exhibition, January-April, 1975.* Bloomington, IN: Lilly Library, Indiana University, 1975, 71 p., paper, nonf.

RANDALL, Florence Engel, 1917-

32021 *The watcher in the woods.* New York: Atheneum, 1976, 229 p., cloth, novel.

RANDALL, John D., 1944-

32022 *The Tojo virus.* New York: A Zebra Book, Kensington Publishing Corp., 1991, 511 p., paper, novel.

RANDALL, Marta, 1948-

32023 *A city in the north.* New York: Warner Books, 1976, 222 p., paper, novel.
32024 *Dangerous games.* New York: Pocket Books, 1980, 499 p., paper, novel. NEWHOME #2.
32025 *Islands.* New York: Pyramid Books, 1976, 191 p., paper, novel.
32026 *Islands.* New York: Pocket Books, 1980, 222 p., paper, novel. [Revised edition].
32027 *Journey.* New York: A Kangaroo Book, Pocket Books, 1978, 324 p., paper, novel. NEWHOME #1.
32028 *The Nebula awards #19.* New York: Arbor House, 1984, 255 p., cloth, anth.
32029 *The sword of winter.* New York: Timescape Books, 1983, 269 p., cloth, novel.
32030 *Those who favor fire.* New York: Pocket Books, 1984, 276 p., paper, novel.

with Robert Silverberg

32031 *New dimensions 11.* New York: Pocket Books, 1980, 224 p., paper, anth.
32032 *New dimensions 12.* New York: A Timescape Book, Pocket Books, 1981, 223 p., paper, anth.

RANDALL, Neil

The black road war—SEE: *Combat command in the world of Roger Zelazny's Nine princes in Amber: The black road war.*
32033 *Combat command in the world of Roger Zelazny's Nine princes in Amber: The black road war.* New York: Ace Books, 1988, xvi, [276] p., paper, novel. COMBAT COMMAND #6—AMBER SERIES.
32034 *Seven no-trump: a Crossroads adventure in the world of Roger Zelazny's Amber.* New York: Tor, A Tom Doherty Associates Book, 1988, 249 p., paper, novel. AMBER SEQUEL; CROSSROADS ADVENTURE.
32035 *Storm of dust: a Crossroads adventure in the world of David Drake's Dragon lord.* New York: Tor, A Tom Doherty Associ-

ates Book, 1987, 245 p., paper, novel. DRAGON LORD SEQUEL; CROSSROADS ADVENTURE.

with Bill Fawcett

22992 *Lord of Cragsclaw.* New York, Toronto: Bantam Books, 1989, 392 p., paper, novel. GUARDIANS OF THE THREE #1.

with Roger Zelazny

32036 *Roger Zelazny's Visual guide to Castle Amber.* New York: Avon, 1988, 218 p., paper, fiction.
Visual guide to Castle Amber—SEE: *Roger Zelazny's Visual guide to Castle Amber.*

RANDERS, Nicholas

32037 *Pray serpents prey.* New York: A Critic's Choice Paperback from Lorevan Publishing, 1988, 308 p., paper, novel.

as NICHOLAS GRABOWSKY

32038 *Halloween IV: a novel.* New York: A Critic's Choice Paperback from Lorevan Publishing, 1988, 223 p., paper, movie. HALLOWEEN #4.

RANDISI, Robert J(oseph), 1951-

as J. R. ROBERTS

32039 *Sasquatch hunt.* New York: Charter Books, 1983, 182 p., paper, novel. GUNSMITH #21.

as anonymous co-author with Warren Murphy

30469 *Dangerous games* / by Warren Murphy. Los Angeles: Pinnacle Books, 1980, 188 p., paper, novel. DESTROYER #40. [By Warren Murphy & Robert J. Randisi].
30497 *Midnight man* / by Warren Murphy. Los Angeles: Pinnacle Books, 1981, 169 p., paper, novel. DESTROYER #43. [By Warren Murphy & Robert J. Randisi].
30519 *Total recall* / by Warren Murphy. New York: Pinnacle Books, 1984, 185 p., paper, novel. DESTROYER #58. [By Warren Murphy & Robert J. Randisi].

with Kevin D. Randle

32040 *Once upon a murder.* Lake Geneva, WI: TSR Inc., 1987, 219 p., paper, novel.

RANDLE, Kevin (Douglas), 1949-

32041 *Dawn of conflict.* New York, Toronto: Bantam Books, 1991, 454 p., paper, novel. GLOBAL WAR #1.

Death of a regiment—SEE: *Jefferson's war: Death of a regiment.*

The galactic silver star—SEE: *Jefferson's war: The galactic silver star.*

The January platoon—SEE: *Jefferson's war: The January platoon.*

32042 *Jefferson's war: Death of a regiment.* New York: Ace Books, 1991, 187 p., paper, novel. JEFFERSON'S WAR #5.

32043 *Jefferson's war: The galactic silver star.* New York: Ace Books, 1990, 200 p., paper, novel. JEFFERSON'S WAR #1.

32044 *Jefferson's war: The January platoon.* New York: Ace Books, 1991, 188 p., paper, novel. JEFFERSON'S WAR #4.

32045 *Jefferson's war: The lost colony.* New York: Ace Books, 1991, 185 p., paper, novel. JEFFERSON'S WAR #3.

32046 *Jefferson's war: The price of command.* New York: Ace Books, 1990, 184 p., paper, novel. JEFFERSON'S WAR #2.

The lost colony—SEE: *Jefferson's war: The lost colony.*

The price of command—SEE: *Jefferson's war: The price of command.*

as STEVE MACKENZIE

32047 *Recon.* New York: Avon Books, 1988, 154 p, paper, novel. SEALS #7.

32048 *Sniper.* New York: Avon Books, 1988, 155 p., paper, novel. SEALS #10.

with Robert Cornett

20604 *The Aldebaran campaign.* New York: Ace Books, 1988, 202 p., paper, novel. SEEDS OF WAR #2.

20605 *The Aquarian attack.* New York: Ace Books, 1989, 188 p., paper, novel. SEEDS OF WAR #3.

20606 *Remember Gettysburg!* New York: Charter Books, 1988, 231 p., paper, novel. REMEMBER #2.

20607 *Remember the Alamo!* TA Publications, 1980, [160] p., paper?, novel. REMEMBER #1. [The 1986 Charter Books edition may be revised].

20608 *Remember the Little Bighorn!* New York: Charter Books, 1990, 188 p., paper, novel. REMEMBER #3.

20609 *Seeds of war.* New York: Ace Science Fiction Books, 1986, 265 p., paper, novel. SEEDS OF WAR #1.

with Robert J. Randisi

32040 *Once upon a murder.* Lake Geneva, WI: TSR Inc., 1987, 219 p., paper, novel.

RANDOLPHE, Arabella, pseud.—SEE: Younger, Jack

RANDOM, Alex, pseud.—SEE: Rowland, Donald S.

RANKIN, Ian (James), 1960-

32041 *Westwind.* London: Barrie & Jenkins, 1990, 224 p., cloth, novel.

RANKIN, Robert (Fleming), 1949-

32042 *The antipope.* London & Sydney: Pan Books, 1981, 248 p., paper, novel. BRENTFORD #1.

32043 *Armageddon: the musical.* London: Bloomsbury, 1990, 243 p., cloth, novel. ARMAGEDDON #1.

32044 *The Brentford triangle.* London & Sydney: Pan Books, 1982, 192 p., paper, novel. BRENTFORD #2.

32045 *The Brentford trilogy.* London: Abacus, 1988, 612 p., paper, coll. BRENTFORD #1-3.

32046 *East of Ealing.* London & Sydney: Pan Books, 1984, 192 p., paper, novel. BRENTFORD #3.

32047 *The sprouts of wrath.* London: Abacus, 1988, 247 p., paper, novel. BRENTFORD #4.

32048 *They came and ate us: Armageddon II: the B-movie.* London: Bloomsbury, 1991, 278 p., cloth, novel. ARMAGEDDON #2.

RANKINE, John, pseud.—SEE: Mason, Douglas R.

RANSMAYR, Christoph, 1954-

32049 *The last world: a novel with an Ovidian repertory.* New York: Grove Weidenfeld, 1990, 246 p., cloth, novel. [Translation by John Woods of *Die letzte welt*].

RANSOM, Bill [i.e., William Michael Ransom], 1945-

32050 *Jaguar.* New York: Ace Books, 1990, 294 p., paper, novel.

with Frank Herbert

25531 *The ascension factor.* New York: G. P. Putnam's Sons, 1988, 381 p., cloth, novel. PANDORA #4.

25532 *The Jesus incident.* New York: Berkley Publishing Corp., 1979, 405 p., cloth, novel. PANDORA #2.

25533 *The Lazarus effect.* New York: G. P. Putnam's Sons, 1983, 381 p., cloth, novel. PANDORA #3.

RANSOM, Daniel, pseud.—SEE: Gorman, Ed

RANSOM, William M.—SEE: Ransom, Bill

RAO, Adapa Ramakrishna—SEE: Ramakrishna Rao, Adapa

RASKIND, Lisa

as ANONYMOUS EDITOR

32051 *Boskone XVI filksong book.* Cambridge, MA: NESFA Press, 1979, 34 p., paper, nonf. anth.

with Richard Harter

25318 *The NESFA hymnal.* Cambridge, MA: NESFA Press, 1974, 46 p., paper, nonf. anth.

RASMUSSEN, Alis A., 1958-

32052 *The labyrinth gate.* New York: Baen, 1988, 345 p., paper, novel.

32053 *A passage of stars.* New York, Toronto: Spectra, Bantam Books, 1990, 289 p., paper, novel. HIGHROAD TRILOGY #1.

32054 *The price of ransom.* New York, Toronto: Spectra, Bantam Books, 1990, 289 p., paper, novel. HIGHROAD TRILOGY #3.

32055 *Revolution's shore.* New York, Toronto: Spectra, Bantam Books, 1990, 290 p., paper, novel. HIGHROAD TRILOGY #2.

RASPAIL, Jean, 1925-

32056 *The camp of the saints.* New York: Charles Scribner's Sons, 1975, 311 p., cloth, novel. [Translation by Norman Shapiro of *Le camp des saints*].

RATHBONE, Wendy, *with Kay Anderson & Edward Gross & Ron Magid & Sheldon Teitelbaum*

16369 *The making of the Trek films.* East Meadow, NY: Image Publishing, 1991, 172 p., paper, nonf.

RATHBUN, Mark, *with Graeme Flanagan*

23177 *Richard Matheson: he is legend: an illustrated bio-bibliography.* Chico, CA: Mark Rathbun, 1984, 55 p., paper, nonf.

RATHER, Lois (Marjorie Foster Rodecape), 1905-

32057 *Bittersweet: Ambrose Bierce & women.* Oakland, CA: The Rather Press, 1975, 133 p., cloth, nonf. [Limited to 150 copies].

*RATHJEN, Carl Henry, 1909-1984

RAU, G. Randal

32058 *World tales.* Tempe, AZ: World Fantasy Convention, 1985, 88 p., paper, anth. [Includes some nonfiction].

RAUCH, Earl Mac, 1949-

32059 *Buckaroo Banzai.* New York: Pocket Books, 1984, 222 p., paper, movie.

RAUCHER, Herman, 1928-

32060 *Maynard's house.* New York: G. P. Putnam's Sons, 1980, 240 p., cloth, novel.

RAUCINA, Thomas Frank—SEE: Racina, Thom

RAVEN, Anthony [pseud. of Augustus Rupp]

32061 *The occult Lovecraft.* Saddle River, NJ: Gerry de la Ree, 1975, 40 p., nonf. anth.

RAVEN, Daniel, pseud.—SEE: Lazuta, Gene

RAVENSWOOD, Fritzen [possible pseud. of James Fritzhand?]

32062 *The spawning.* New York: Zebra Books, Kensington Publishing Corp., 1981, 352 p., paper, novel. KEI #2.

32063 *The witching.* New York: Zebra Books, Kensington Publishing Corp., 1980, 426 p., paper, novel. KEI #1.

RAWLINS, Jack (Patrick), 1946-

32064 *Demon prince: the dissonant worlds of Jack Vance.* San Bernardino, CA: R. Reginald, The Borgo Press, 1986, 104 p., cloth, nonf. MILFORD SERIES: POPULAR WRITERS OF TODAY #40.

RAWN, Melanie (Robin), 1953?-

32065 *Dragon prince, book I.* New York: DAW Books, 1988, 574 p., paper, novel. DRAGON PRINCE #1.

32066 *The star scroll.* New York: DAW Books, 1989, 589 p., paper, novel. DRAGON PRINCE #2.

32067 *Stronghold.* New York: DAW Books, 1990, 487 p., cloth, novel. DRAGON STAR #1.

32068 *Sunrunner's fire.* New York: DAW Books, 1990, 479 p., paper, novel. DRAGON PRINCE #3.

RAY, David

32069 *The end of the Fourth Reich: a Rat Catcher adventure.* London: Panther Book, 1966, 142 p., paper, tele.

RAY, Fred Olen, 1954-

32070 *The new poverty row: independent filmmakers as distributors.* Jefferson, NC & London: McFarland & Co., 1991, xiii + 226 p., cloth, nonf.

RAY, Gordon N(orton), 1915-1986

32071 *H. G. Wells & Rebecca West.* New Haven, CT: Yale University Press, 1974, xxvi + 215 p., cloth, nonf.

RAY, Rène [pseud. of Irene Creese], 1912-

32072 *Angel assignment.* Lewes, East Sussex, England: The Book Guild, 1988, 88 p., cloth, novel.

RAY, Robert, 1928-

32073 *Metamorphosis.* London: Robert Hale, 1976, 190 p., cloth, novel.

RAY, Satyajit, 1922-1992

32074 *Stories.* Calcutta, India: Seagull Books in Association with Secker & Warburg, 1987, xii + 190 p., cloth, coll.

32074A retitled: *The unicorn expedition, and other fantastic tales of India.* New York: E. P. Dutton, 1987, xii + 190 p., cloth, coll.
The unicorn expedition, and other fantastic tales of India—SEE: *Stories.*

RAY, Trevor, 1934- , *with Jeremy Burnham*

19061 *Children of the stones.* London: Carousel Books, 1977, 189 p., paper, novel.

19062 *Raven.* London: Corgi Books, 1977, 222 p., paper, tele.

RAYER, Francis G(eorge), 1921-1981, *as Chester Delray*

04071 *Realm of the alien.* Dublin, Ireland: Grafton, 1949, 64 p., paper, story.

RAYMOND, Alice [pseud. of Sharon Anne Salvato], 1938-

32075 *The pact.* New York: Charter Books, 1990, 265 p., paper, novel.

RAYMOND, John, pseud.—SEE: Fish, Leonard G.

RAYMOND, René—SEE: Chase, James Hadley

*RAYNER, William, <u>1929-</u>

RAYNOR, William (J. Jr.), *with Myles Wilder*

32076 *Freeze.* New York: A Critic's Choice Paperback from Lorevan Publishing, 1988, 284 p., paper, novel.

RAZZI, James, 1931-

38027 *Desert flight* / by Jim Razzi. New York: Ballantine Books, 1986, 72 p., paper, novel. FIND YOUR FATE—JUNIOR TRANSFORMERS #5.

32077 *Star Trek intergalactic puzzles: gathered from all over the galaxy: spaced-out puzzles to mystify, amuse, and enlighten Star Trek fans.* Toronto, New York: Bantam Books, 1977, 128 p., paper, nonf.

32078 *Star Trek puzzle manual: puzzles, mazes, and trivia to baffle, enlighten, and amuse Star Trek fans everywhere.* Toronto, New York: Bantam Books, 1976, 128 p., paper, nonf.

32079 *Tales from the weird zone, book 1* / by Jim Razzi. New York: A Minstrel Book, 1986, 69 p., paper, coll.

32080 *Tales from the weird zone, book 2* / by Jim Razzi. New York: A Minstrel Book, 1988, 72 p., paper, coll.

with Jack Looney

28524 *The official Ghostbusters II joke, puzzle, and game book* / by Jim Razzi.... New York: Newmarket Press, 1989, 93 p., paper, nonf.

with Rick Brightfield & Jack Looney

18670 *Star games: with a space adventure.* Toronto, New York: Bantam Books, 1978, 128 p., paper, nonf.

RAZZI, Jim—SEE: Razzi, James

READ, Cameron

32081 *The forsaken.* New York: Pinnacle Books, 1982, 343 p., paper, novel.

READ, John, *as* TONY PHILLIPS

Duster trouble—SEE: *Turbo Cowboys: Duster trouble.*
Rat trap—SEE: *Turbo Cowboys: Rat trap.*
31532 *Turbo Cowboys: Duster trouble.* New York: Ballantine Books, 1989, 131 p., paper, novel. TURBO COWBOYS #9.
31533 *Turbo Cowboys: Rat trap.* New York: Ballantine Books, 1989, 135 p., paper, novel. TURBO COWBOYS #6.

READ, Piers Paul, 1941-

32082 *On the third day: a novel.* London: Secker & Warburg, 1990, 281 p., cloth, novel.

READY, William B(ernard), 1914-1981

32083 *An outline of Lord of the Rings, The hobbit.* Toronto: Forum House, 1971, vi+130 p., paper, nonf.

REAMY, Thomas E.—SEE: Reamy, Tom

REAMY, Tom [i.e., Thomas Earl Reamy], 1935-1977

32084 *Blind voices.* New York: Berkley Publishing Corp., 1978, 254 p., cloth, novel.
32085 *MidAmericon program book.* Kansas City, MO: MidAmericon, 1976, 168 p., cloth, anth. [Includes some nonfiction].
32086 *San Diego Lightfoot Sue, and other stories.* Kansas City, MO: Earth Light Publishers, 1979, xxii+237 p., cloth, coll.

REASONER, Charles F.

32087 *A teacher's guide to the novels of Joan Aiken.* New York: A Dell Book, Laurel-Leaf Library, 1982, 31 p., paper, nonf.
32088 *A teacher's guide to the paperback editions of The Prydain Chronicles by Lloyd Alexander.* New York: A Dell Book, 1982, 30 p., paper, nonf.

REAVES, (James) Michael, 1950-

32089 *The burning realm.* New York: Baen, 1988, 278 p., paper, novel. SHATTERED #2.
32090 *Darkworld detective* / by J. Michael Reaves. Toronto, New York: Bantam Books, 1982, 257 p., paper, novel. DARKWORLD DETECTIVE #1.
32091 *I—alien: a novel* / by J. Michael Reaves. New York: A Tempo Star Book, Grosset & Dunlap, 1978, 185 p., paper, novel.
32092 *The shattered world.* New York: Timescape Books, 1984, 349 p., cloth, novel. SHATTERED WORLD #1.
32093 *Street magic.* New York: Tor, A Tom Doherty Associates Book, 1991, 246 p., cloth, novel.

with Byron Preiss

31835 *Dragonworld* / by J. Michael Reaves... Garden City, NY: Nelson Doubleday, 1979, 545 p., cloth, novel.

with Steve Perry

31477 *Dome.* New York: Berkley Books, 1987, 274 p., paper, novel.
31478 *Hellstar.* New York: Berkley Books, 1984, 326 p., paper, novel.
31479 *The omega cage.* New York: Ace Books, 1988, 244 p., paper, novel. KHADAJI #4.
31480 *Sword of the samurai.* Toronto, New York: A Byron Preiss Book, Bantam Books, 1984, 127 p., paper, novel. TIME MACHINE #3.

REDFINN, Michael

32094 *Being.* New York: Leisure Books, 1988, 367 p., paper, novel.

REDGROVE, Peter W(illiam), 1932-

32095 *The beekeepers: a novel.* London: Routledge & Kegan Paul, 1980, vii+156 p., cloth, novel. BEEKEEPERS #1.
32096 *The facilitators; or, Mister Hole-in-the-Day.* London: Routledge & Kegan Paul, 1982, 173 p., cloth, novel. BEEKEEPERS #2.
32097 *The god of glass: a morality.* London: Routledge & Kegan Paul, 1979, vii+248 p., cloth, novel.
32098 *The one who set out to study fear.* London: Bloomsbury, 1989, 183 p., cloth, radio coll.
32099 *The sleep of the great hypnotist: the life and death and life after death of a mod-*

ern magician. London: Routledge & Kegan Paul, 1979, vii+156 p., cloth, novel.

with Penelope Shuttle

32100 *The glass cottage: a nautical romance.* London: Routledge & Kegan Paul, 1976, 205 p., cloth, novel.
32101 *The terrors of Dr Treviles: a romance.* London: Routledge & Kegan Paul, 1974, 177 p., cloth, novel.

REDMON, Anne [i.e., Anne Redmon Nightingale], 1943-

32102 *Second sight: a novel.* London: Secker & Warburg, 1987, 269 p., cloth, novel.

REE, Gerry de la—SEE: de la Ree, Gerry

REED, Christopher

32103 *The big scratch: a Manx McCatty adventure.* New York: Ballantine Books, 1988, 117 p., paper, novel.

REED, Dana [pseud. of Edwina Berkman]

32104 *Deathbringer.* New York: Leisure Books, 1985, 396 p., paper, novel.
32105 *Demon within.* New York: Leisure Books, 1988, 367 p., paper, novel.
32106 *The gatekeeper.* New York: Leisure Books, 1987, 399 p., paper, novel.
32107 *Hell board.* New York: Leisure Books, 1990, 361 p., paper, novel.
32108 *Margo.* New York: Leisure Books, 1989, 362 p., paper, novel.
32109 *Sister Satan.* New York: Leisure Books, 1984, 400 p., paper, novel.
32110 *The summoning.* New York: Leisure Books, 1988, 368 p., paper, novel.

REED, Donald A(nthony), 1935- , with Patrick Pattison

31292 *Science fiction film awards: collector's edition.* [Los Angeles]: ESE California, 1981, 107 p., cloth, nonf.

REED, Ishmael (Scott), 1938-

32111 *The free-lance pallbearers: an irreverent novel.* Garden City, NY: Doubleday & Co., 1967, 155 p., cloth, novel.
38028 *The terrible threes.* New York: Atheneum, 1989, 180 p., cloth, novel.

32112 *The terrible twos.* New York: St. Martin's Press/Richard Marek, 1982, 178 p., cloth, novel.

*REED, Ivy Kellerman, 1877-<u>1968</u>

REED, John R(obert), 1938-

32113 *The natural history of H. G. Wells.* Athens, OH: Ohio University Press, 1982, x+294 p., cloth, nonf.

REED, Kit [i.e., Lillian Craig Reed], 1932-

32114 *Fort privilege.* Garden City, NY: Doubleday & Co., 1985, 186 p., cloth, novel.
32115 *George Orwell's 1984.* Woodbury, NY: Barron's, 1984, viii+118 p., paper, nonf.
32116 *The killer mice.* London: Victor Gollancz, 1976, 191 p., cloth, coll.
32117 *Magic time.* New York: Berkley Publishing Corp., 1980, 268 p., cloth, novel.
32118 *Other stories and...the attack of the giant baby.* New York: Berkley Books, 1981, 215 p., paper, coll.
32119 *Revenge of the senior citizens, **plus: a short story collection.* Garden City, NY: Doubleday & Co., 1986, 189 p., cloth, coll.

as SHELLEY HYDE

32120 *Blood fever.* New York: Pocket Books, 1982, 188 p., paper, novel.

REED, Lillian—SEE: Reed, Kit

REED, Rick R.

32121 *Obsessed.* New York: A Dell Book, 1991, 392 p., paper, novel.

REED, Robert (David), 1956-

32122 *Black milk: a novel.* New York: Donald I. Fine, 1989, 327 p., cloth, novel.
32123 *Down the bright way.* New York, Toronto: Spectra, Bantam Books, 1991, 312 p., paper, novel.
32124 *The hormone jungle.* New York: Donald I. Fine, 1987, 300 p., cloth, novel.
32125 *The leeshore: a novel.* New York: Donald I. Fine, 1987, 253 p., cloth, novel.

REED, Toni, 1944-

32126 *Demon-lovers and their victims in British fiction.* Lexington, KY: University

Press of Kentucky, 1988, ix + 171 p., cloth, nonf.

REED, Tony, 1962-

32127 *The black book 1: dark fantasies.* London: Creation Press, 1989, 96 p., paper, anth.

REED, Walt, *with Joseph Clement Coll*

20300 *The magic pen of Joseph Clement Coll.* West Kingston, RI: Donald M. Grant, Publisher, 1978, 176 p., cloth, art.

REEMES, Dana M.

32128 *Directed by Jack Arnold.* Jefferson, NC & London: McFarland & Co., 1988, xi + 243 p., cloth, nonf.

REES, Helen—SEE: Oliver, Jane

REES, Richard (Lodowick Edward Montagu, Sir, Bart.), 1900-1970

32129 *George Orwell: fugitive from the camp of victory.* London: Secker & Warburg, 1961, 160 p., cloth, nonf.

REES, Simon, 1958-

32130 *The devil's looking glass.* London: Methuen, 1985, 188 p., paper, novel.

REEVE, Arthur B(enjamin), 1880-1936

15854 *Constance Dunlap, woman detective.* New York: Hearst's International Library, 1916, 342 p., cloth, novel. CRAIG KENNEDY TIE-IN?

15855 *Guy Garrick: an adventure with a scientific gunman.* New York: Hearst's International Library, 1914, 326 p., cloth, novel.

REEVES, L(ynette) P(amela), 1937-

32131 *Harlow's dimension.* London: Robert Hale, 1977, 158 p., cloth, novel.

32132 *If it's blue, it's plague.* London: Robert Hale, 1981, 160 p., cloth, novel.

32133 *Last days of the peacemaker.* London: Robert Hale, 1976, 192 p., cloth, novel.

32134 *The Nairn syndrome.* London: Robert Hale, 1975, 172 p., cloth, novel.

32135 *The stone age venture.* London: Robert Hale, 1977, 155 p., cloth, novel.

32136 *Time search.* London: Robert Hale, 1976, 175 p., cloth, novel.

32137 *A twist in time.* London: Robert Hale, 1978, 175 p., cloth, novel.

REEVES-STEVENS, (Francis) Garfield, 1953-

32138 *Bloodshift.* Toronto: Virgo Press, 1981, 350 p., paper, novel.

32139 *Children of the Shroud.* Toronto: Doubleday Canada, 1987, 319 p., cloth, novel.

32140 *Dark matter.* New York, Toronto: Doubleday, 1990, 375 p., cloth, novel.

32141 *Dreamland.* Toronto: A Seal Book, McClelland-Bantam, 1985, 422 p., paper, novel.

32142 *Nighteyes.* New York: A Foundation Book, Doubleday, 1989, 452 p., cloth, novel.

with Judith Reeves-Stevens

32143 *The chronicles of Galen Sword: Nightfeeder.* New York: A Roc Book, 1991, 285 p., paper, novel. CHRONICLES OF GALEN SWORD #2.
Memory Prime—SEE: *Star Trek: Memory Prime.*
Nightfeeder—SEE: *Chronicles of Galen Sword, The: Nightfeeder.*
Prime directive—SEE: *Star Trek: Prime directive.*

32144 *Shifter.* New York: A Roc Book, 1990, 284 p., paper, novel. CHRONICLES OF GALEN SWORD #1.

32145 *Star Trek: Memory Prime.* New York, London: Pocket Books, 1988, 309 p., paper, tele. STAR TREK #42.

32146 *Star Trek: Prime directive.* New York, London: Pocket Books, 1990, 406 p., cloth, tele. STAR TREK (UNNUMBERED).

REEVES-STEVENS, Judith (Evelyn), 1953?- , *with Garfield Reeves-Stevens*

32143 *The chronicles of Galen Sword: Nightfeeder.* New York: A Roc Book, 1991, 285 p., paper, novel. CHRONICLES OF GALEN SWORD #2.
Memory Prime—SEE: *Star Trek: Memory Prime.*
Nightfeeder—SEE: *Chronicles of Galen Sword, The: Nightfeeder.*
Prime directive—SEE: *Star Trek: Prime directive.*

32144 *Shifter.* New York: A Roc Book, 1990, 284 p., paper, novel. CHRONICLES OF GALEN SWORD #1.

32145 *Star Trek: Memory Prime.* New York, London: Pocket Books, 1988, 309 p., paper, tele. STAR TREK #42.

32146 *Star Trek: Prime directive.* New York, London: Pocket Books, 1990, 406 p., cloth, tele. STAR TREK (UNNUMBERED).

REGALIA, Nanzi, pseud.—SEE: Collins, Nancy A.

REGAN, Dian Curtis

32147 *Jilly's ghost.* New York: An Avon Flare Book, 1990, 137 p., paper, novel.

REGAN, Jackie

32148 *1942: from starship to Lancaster.* Strathmartine by Dundee, Scotland: ScoTpress, 1984, 63 p., paper, tele. STAR TREK SERIES.

REGAN, Robert (Charles), 1930-

32149 *Poe: a collection of critical essays.* Englewood Cliffs, NJ: A Spectrum Book, Prentice-Hall, 1967, 183 p., paper, nonf. anth.

REGGIE, Catherine—SEE: Moore, C. L.

REGINALD, R(obert) [pseud. of Michael Roy Burgess], 1948-

32150 *Science fiction & fantasy awards, including complete checklists of the Hugo Awards, Nebula Awards, Locus Awards, Jupiter Awards, Pilgrim Awards, International Fantasy Awards, Ditmar Awards, August Derleth Awards, World Fantasy Awards, Eaton Awards, Gandalf Awards, British Fantasy Awards, John W. Campbell Memorial Awards, Milford Awards, Prometheus Awards, and selected foreign awards, with a complete index to winners, a list of officers of the Science Fiction Writers of America from the beginning of that organization, a checklist of world science fiction conventions and their guests of honor, and detailed statistical tables.* San Bernardino, CA: R. Reginald, The Borgo Press, 1981, 64 p., cloth, nonf.

32151 *Science fiction and fantasy literature: a checklist, 1700-1974, with Contemporary science fiction authors II.* Detroit: Gale Research Co., 1979, xii+vi+1141+32 p. in 2 v., cloth, nonf. [Incorporates *Stella nova* (see #12119)].

12119 *Stella nova: the contemporary science fiction authors.* Los Angeles: Unicorn & Son, 1970, [358] p., paper, nonf. [Non-bylined; limited to 108 copies].

32152 retitled: *Contemporary science fiction authors, first edition.* New York: Arno Press, 1975, xii+368 p., cloth, nonf. [Revised edition].

as MICHAEL BURGESS

32153 *A guide to science fiction & fantasy in the Library of Congress classification scheme, A.* San Bernardino, CA: R. Reginald, The Borgo Press, 1984, 86 p., cloth, nonf.

32154 *A guide to science fiction and fantasy in the Library of Congress classification scheme, second edition.* San Bernardino, CA: R. Reginald, The Borgo Press, 1988, 168 p., cloth, nonf. [Expanded edition].

32155 *The work of Robert Reginald: an annotated bibliography & guide, second edition.* San Bernardino, CA: R. Reginald, The Borgo Press, 1992, 176 p., cloth, nonf. BIBLIOGRAPHIES OF MODERN AUTHORS #5. [An expanded edition of #22558].

as MICHAEL BURGESS, *with Jeffrey M. Elliot*

22558 *The work of R. Reginald: an annotated bibliography & guide.* San Bernardino, CA: The Borgo Press, 1985, 48 p., cloth, nonf. BIBLIOGRAPHIES OF MODERN AUTHORS #5.

as BODEN CLARKE

32156 *The work of Jeffrey M. Elliot: an annotated bibliography & guide.* San Bernardino, CA: R. Reginald, The Borgo Press, 1984, 50 p., cloth, nonf. BIBLIOGRAPHIES OF MODERN AUTHORS #2.

as BODEN CLARKE, *with James Hopkins*

30771 *The work of William F. Nolan: an annotated bibliography & guide.* San Bernardino, CA: R. Reginald, The Borgo Press, 1988, 224 p., cloth, nonf. BIBLIOGRAPHIES OF MODERN AUTHORS #14.

as C. EVERETT COOPER

32157 *Up your asteroid! a science fiction farce.* San Bernardino, CA: R. Reginald, The Borgo Press, 1977, 47 p., paper, story.

as R. REGINALD AND M. R. BURGESS

32158 *Cumulative paperback index, 1939-1959: A comprehensive bibliographic guide to*

14,000 mass-market paperback books of 33 publishers under 69 imprints. Detroit: Gale Research Co., 1973, xxiv+362 p., cloth, nonf.

as LUCAS WEBB

32159 *The attempted assassination of John F. Kennedy: a political fantasy.* San Bernardino, CA: R. Reginald, The Borgo Press, 1976, 47 p., paper, story.

with Mary A. Burgess & Douglas Menville

19041 *Futurevisions: the new golden age of the science fiction film.* North Hollywood, CA: A Greenbriar Book, Newcastle Publishing Co., 1985, 192 p., paper, nonf. [A sequel to *Things to come* (see #29749)].

with Thaddeus Dikty

21923 *The work of Julian May: an annotated bibliography & guide.* San Bernardino, CA: R. Reginald, The Borgo Press, 1985, 66 p., cloth, nonf. BIBLIOGRAPHIES OF MODERN AUTHORS #3.

with Jeffrey M. Elliot

22560 *If J.F.K. had lived: a political scenario.* San Bernardino, CA: Borgo Press, 1978, 64 p., cloth, novel. BORGO POLITICAL SCENARIOS #1. [Expanded and rewritten version of *The attempted assassination of John F. Kennedy* (see #32159) / by Lucas Webb; Elliot contributed the introduction and minor editing].

22561 *The work of George Zebrowski: an annotated bibliography & guide.* San Bernardino, CA: R. Reginald, The Borgo Press, 1986, 54 p., cloth, nonf. BIBLIOGRAPHIES OF MODERN AUTHORS #4.

22562 *The work of George Zebrowski: an annotated bibliography & guide, second edition.* San Bernardino, CA: R. Reginald, The Borgo Press, 1990, 118 p., cloth, nonf. BIBLIOGRAPHIES OF MODERN AUTHORS #4. [Expanded edition].

with Daryl F. Mallett

28955 *Reginald's science fiction and fantasy awards: a comprehensive guide to the awards and their winners, 2nd ed.* San Bernardino, CA: R. Reginald, The Borgo Press, 1991, 248 p., cloth, nonf.

BORGO LITERARY GUIDES #1. [Expanded edition of #32150].

with Douglas Menville

29741 *Ancestral voices: an anthology of early science fiction.* New York: Arno Press, 1975, [298] p., cloth, anth. SCIENCE FICTION.

29742 *Ancient hauntings.* New York: Arno Press, 1976, [383] p., cloth, anth. SUPERNATURAL & OCCULT FICTION.

29743 *Dreamers of dreams: an anthology of fantasy.* New York: Arno Press, 1978, [478] p., cloth, anth. LOST RACE & ADULT FANTASY FICTION.

29744 *King Solomon's children: some parodies of H. Rider Haggard.* New York: Arno Press, 1978, [564] p., cloth, anth. LOST RACE & ADULT FANTASY FICTION.

29745 *Phantasmagoria.* New York: Arno Press, 1976, [357] p., cloth, anth. SUPERNATURAL & OCCULT FICTION.

29746 *R.I.P.: five stories of the supernatural.* New York: Arno Press, 1976, [278] p., cloth, anth. SUPERNATURAL & OCCULT FICTION.

29747 *The spectre bridegroom, and other horrors.* New York: Arno Press, 1976, [292] p., cloth, anth. SUPERNATURAL & OCCULT FICTION.

29748 *They: three parodies of H. Rider Haggard's She.* New York: Arno Press, 1978, [592] p., cloth, anth. LOST RACE & ADULT FANTASY FICTION.

29749 *Things to come: an illustrated history of the science fiction film.* New York: Times Books, 1977, xii+212 p., cloth, nonf.

29750 *Worlds of never: three fantastic novels.* New York: Arno Press, 1978, [430] p., cloth, anth. LOST RACE & ADULT FANTASY FICTION.

REICHARDT, Jasia, 1933-

32156 *Robots: fact, fiction, and prediction.* London: Thames & Hudson, 1978, 168 p., paper, nonf.

REICHERT, Mickey Zucker [i.e., Miriam Susan Zucker Reichert], 1962-

32157 *By chaos cursed.* New York: DAW Books, 1991, 318 p., paper, novel. BIFROST GUARDIANS #5.

32158 *Dragonrank master.* New York: DAW Books, 1989, 303 p., paper, novel. BIFROST GUARDIANS #3.

32159 *Godslayer.* New York: DAW Books, 1987, 222 p., paper, novel. BIFROST GUARDIANS #1.

32160 *Shadow climber.* New York: DAW Books, 1988, 300 p., paper, novel. BIFROST GUARDIANS #2.

32161 *Shadow's realm.* New York: DAW Books, 1990, 304 p., paper, novel. BIFROST GUARDIANS #4.

REICHERT, Miriam Zucker—SEE: Reichert, Mickey Zucker

REID, Forrest, 1846-1947

32162 *Uncle Stephen.* London: Faber & Faber, 1931, 339 p., cloth, novel.

REID, John Calvin, 1901-

32163 *Bird life in Wington: practical parables for young people.* Grand Rapids, MI: Wm. B. Eerdmans Publishing Co., 1948, 122 p., cloth, coll.

REID BANKS, Lynne [i.e., Lynne Reid Banks Stephenson], 1929-

32164 *The fairy rebel.* London: J. M. Dent & Sons, 1985, 116 p., cloth, novel.

32165 *The farthest-away mountain.* London: Abelard-Schumann, 1976, 140 p., cloth, novel.

32166 *I, Houdini: the autobiography of a self-educated hamster.* London: J. M. Dent & Sons, 1978, 119 p., cloth, novel.

32167 *The Indian in the cupboard.* London: J. M. Dent & Sons, 1980, 160 p., cloth, novel. OMRI #1.

32168 *Maura's angel.* London: J. M. Dent & Sons, 1984, 124 p., cloth, novel.

32169 *Melusine: a mystery.* London: Hamilton Children's Books, 1988, [248] p., cloth, novel.

32170 *Return of the Indian.* London: J. M. Dent & Sons, 1986, 136 p., cloth, novel. OMRI #2.

32171 *The secret of the Indian.* London: Collins, 1989, 144 p., cloth, novel. OMRI #3.

*REIDA, Alvah, 1920-1975

*REIFF, Stephanie (Ann), 1948-

REIFFEL, Leonard, 1927-

32172 *The contaminant.* New York: Harper & Row, 1978, 284 p., cloth, novel.

REILLY, Robert, 1933-

32173 *The transcendant adventure: studies of religion in science fiction/fantasy.* Westport, CT & London: Greenwood Press, 1985, x+266 p., cloth, nonf. anth. CONTRIBUTIONS TO THE STUDY OF SCIENCE FICTION AND FANTASY #12.

REINHARDT, Hank, *with Gerald W. Page*

31132 *Heroic fantasy.* New York: DAW Books, 1979, 320 p., paper, anth.

REINIUS, Trish, 1936-

32174 *The Planet of Tears.* San Rafael, CA: Dawne-Leigh Publications, 1979, 157 p., cloth, novel. WHITE WOLF #1.

32175 *Power of the white wolf.* Reno, NV: Iris I O Publisher, 1985, 160 p., paper, novel. WHITE WOLF #2.

REINO, Joseph

32176 *Stephen King: the first decade, Carrie to Pet Sematary.* Boston: Twayne Publishers, 1988, 162 p., cloth, nonf.

REINSMITH, Richard [pseud. of Richard Rein Smith], 1930-

32177 *The savage stars.* New York: Tower Books, 1981, 192 p., paper, novel.

32178 *Tarzan and the tower of diamonds.* Lake Geneva, WI: TSR Publishers, 1985, 157 p., paper, novel. TARZAN SERIES; ENDLESS QUEST #31.

***as* DAMON CASTLE**

32179 *Starbright.* New York: Leisure Books, 1983, 240 p., paper, novel.

***as* DIANA TOWER**

38029 *Dark diamond.* New York: Ballantine Books, 1975, [155] p., paper, novel. BIRTHSTONE GOTHIC #4.

38030 *A gleam of sapphire.* New York: Ballantine Books, 1975, 153 p., paper, novel. BIRTHSTONE GOTHIC #9.

REIS, Richard H(erbert), 1930-

32180 *George MacDonald.* New York: Twayne Publishers, 1972, 161 p., cloth, nonf.

32181 *George MacDonald's fiction: a twentieth-century view, rev. ed.* Eureka, CA: Sunrise Books Publishers, 1989, 166 p., cloth, nonf.

REISS, Kathryn

32182   *Time windows.* San Diego, CA: Harcourt Brace Jovanovich, 1991, 260 p., cloth, novel.

REISS, Marc, *with Barry William*

32183   *The adversary.* New York: Charter Books, 1979, 298 p., paper, novel.

REIT, Seymour V., 1918-

32184   *Scotland Yard detective.* Toronto, New York: A Byron Preiss Book, Bantam Books, 1987, 125 p., paper, novel. TIME MACHINE #17.
38031   *Voyage with Columbus.* Toronto, New York: A Byron Preiss Book, A Bantam Skylark Book, 1986, 80 p., paper, novel. TIME TRAVELER #1.

REITCI, Rita—SEE: Ritchie, Rita

RELLING, William Jr., 1954-

32185   *Brujo.* New York: Tor Horror, A Tom Doherty Associates Book, 1986, 338 p., paper, novel.
32186   *The infinite man: 21 stories and an afterword.* Los Angeles: Scream/Press, 1989, 215 p., paper, coll.
32187   *New moon.* New York: Tor Horror, A Tom Doherty Associates Book, 1987, 280 p., paper, novel.
32188   *Silent moon.* New York: Tor Horror, A Tom Doherty Associates Book, 1990, 309 p., paper, novel.

REMINGTON, Thomas J(oseph), 1939-

32189   *Selected proceedings of the 1978 Science Fiction Research Association national convention.* Cedar Falls, IA: University of Northern Iowa, 1979, vii+281 p., paper, nonf. anth.

REMS, Jack (Paul), 1955- , *with Jeff Frane*

23422   *A fantasy reader: the seventh World Fantasy Convention book.* Berkeley, CA: Seventh World Fantasy Convention, 1981, x+197 p., cloth, anth.

RENAN, Sheldon (Jackson), 1941- , *with Dr. Crypton*

20852   *Treasure: in search of the golden horse: a puzzle.* New York: An IntraVision

Book, Warner Books, 1984, 81 p., paper, novel.

RENARD, Joseph, 1939-

32190   *The monodyne catastrophe.* Canoga Park, CA: Major Books, 1977, 174 p., paper, novel.

RENAULD, Ron

32191   *Fade to black.* Los Angeles: Pinnacle Books, 1980, 213 p., paper, novel.

as ROSS ANTON COE

32192   *Sorcerer's blood.* New York: Pinnacle Books, 1982, 212 p., paper, novel. WARRIOR OF VENGEANCE #1.
32193   *Trails of peril.* New York: Pinnacle Books, 1982, 190 p., paper, novel. WARRIOR OF VENGEANCE #2.

RENFROE, Martha Kay—SEE: Wren, M. K.

RENNER, Theresa

32194   *Proceedings of Concon (Smofcon I) 1984.* Cambridge, MA: Concon, 1984, 157 p., paper, nonf. anth.

*REPP, Ed(ward) Earl, 1900-<u>1979</u>

RESCH, Kathleen

32195   *The Dark Shadows concordance 1840.* Temple City, CA: Pentagram Publications, 1987, 287 p., paper, nonf. [Cover title].
32196   *The Dark Shadows concordance 1970 parallel time.* Temple City, CA: Pentagram Publications, 1988, 140 p., paper, nonf. [Cover title].
32197   *Paradox* / by Kathy Resch. Santa Clara, CA: Pentagram Publications, 1979, 140 p., paper, novel.

RESNICK, Michael D.—SEE: Resnick, Mike

RESNICK, Mike [i.e., Michael Diamond Resnick], 1942-

32198   *Adventures: being a stirring chronicle of intrigue, romance, danger, hairbreadth escapes, and thrilling triumphs over fierce beasts and fiercer men in the mysterious and exotic dark continent, as recounted by the daring, resourceful, handsome, and modest Christian gentleman who experienced them: a science fiction novel.*

New York: A Signet Book, New American Library, 1985, 239 p., paper, novel.

32199 *The alien heart.* Eugene, OR: Pulphouse Publishing, 1991, 103 p., cloth, coll. AUTHOR'S CHOICE MONTHLY #25.

32200 *The best rootin' tootin' shootin' gunslinger in the whole damned galaxy.* New York: A Signet Book, New American Library, 1983, 204 p., paper, novel. TALES OF THE GALACTIC MIDWAY #4.

32201 *Birthright: the book of man.* New York: A Signet Book, New American Library, 1982, 280 p., paper, novel.

32202 *The branch.* New York: A Signet Book, New American Library, 1984, 191 p., paper, novel.

32203 *Bully!* Eugene, OR: Axolotl Press, Pulphouse Publishing, 1990, 110 p., cloth, novel. AXOLOTL PRESS #15.

32204 *Bwana; &, Bully!* New York: Tor SF, A Tom Doherty Associates Book, 1991, xi+179 p., paper, coll.

32205 *The dark lady: a romance of the far future.* New York: Tor SF, A Tom Doherty Associates Book, 1987, 279 p., paper, novel.

32206 *Eros ascending.* Huntington Woods, MI: Phantasia Press, 1984, 217 p., cloth, novel. TALES OF THE VELVET COMET #1.

32207 *Eros at nadir.* New York: A Signet Book, New American Library, 1986, 252 p., paper, novel. TALES OF THE VELVET COMET #4.

32208 *Eros at zenith.* Huntington Woods, MI: Phantasia Press, 1984, 187 p., cloth, novel. TALES OF THE VELVET COMET #2.

32209 *Eros descending.* New York: A Signet Book, New American Library, 1985, 250 p., paper, novel. TALES OF THE VELVET COMET #3.

32210 *The inn of the Hairy Toad.* New Orleans, LA: Delta Con, 1985, 41 p., paper?, story.

32211 *Ivory: a legend of past and future.* New York: Tor, A Tom Doherty Associates Book, 1988, 374 p., cloth, novel.

32212 *Official guide to comic books and Big Little Books, [2nd ed.].* Florence, AL: House of Collectibles, 1977, ii+264 p., paper, nonf.

32213 *The official guide to fantastic literature: pulps, digests, hardcovers, paperbacks, Star Trek, radio premiums, fanzines, original art, Edgar Rice Burroughs* / by Michael Resnick. Florence, AL: House of Collectibles, 1976, iv+212 p., paper, nonf.

32214 *Official price guide to comic & science fiction books, third edition.* Orlando, FL: House of Collectibles, 1979, 422 p., paper, nonf.

32215 *Paradise: a chronicle of a distant world.* New York: Tor, A Tom Doherty Associates Book, 1989, 323 p., cloth, novel.

32216 *Pink elephants and hairy toads: short stories.* Newark, NJ: Wildside Press, 1991, viii+95 p., cloth, coll. [Limited to 250 copies].

32217 *Santiago: a myth of the far future.* New York: Tor SF, A Tom Doherty Associates Book, 1986, 376 p., paper, novel.

32218 *Second contact.* Norwalk, CT: Easton Press, 1990, 276 p., cloth, novel.

32219 *Shaggy B.E.M. stories.* New Orleans: Nolacon Press, 1988, 262 p., cloth, anth.

32220 *Sideshow.* New York: A Signet Book, New American Library, 1982, 154 p., paper, novel. TALES OF THE GALACTIC MIDWAY #1.

32221 *Soothsayer.* New York: Ace Books, 1991, 279 p., paper, novel. ORACLE TRILOGY #1.

32222 *The Soul Eater.* New York: A Signet Book, New American Library, 1981, 151 p., paper, novel.

32223 *Stalking the unicorn: a fable of tonight.* New York: Tor SF, A Tom Doherty Associates Book, 1987, 314 p., paper, novel.

32224 *Stalking the wild Resnick.* Cambridge, MA: A Boskone Book, NESFA Press, 1991, viii+216 p., cloth, coll. [Includes some nonfiction].

32225 *The three-legged hootch dancer.* New York: A Signet Book, New American Library, 1983, 153 p., paper, novel. TALES OF THE GALACTIC MIDWAY #2.

32226 *Through darkest Resnick with gun and camera.* Washington, DC: Washington Science Fiction Association, 1990, 200 p., cloth, nonf. coll. [Limited to 530 copies].

32227 *Unauthorized autobiographies, and other curiosities.* Detroit: Misfit Press, 1984, [55] p., paper, coll.

32228 *Walpurgis III.* New York: A Signet Book, New American Library, 1982, 166 p., paper, novel.

32229 *The wild alien tamer.* New York: A Signet Book, New American Library, 1983, 191 p., paper, novel. TALES OF THE GALACTIC MIDWAY #3.

with Jack L. Chalker & George Alec Effinger

19743 *The red tape war.* New York: Tor, A Tom Doherty Associates Book, 1991, ix+244 p., cloth, novel.

with Glen A. Larson

27842   *Galactica discovers Earth.* New York: Berkley Books, 1980, 187 p., paper, tele. BATTLESTAR GALACTICA #5.

REUBEN, Paula, 1932- , *with Fitzhugh Dodson*

21991   *The carnival kidnap caper.* La Jolla, CA: Oak Tree Publications, 1979, v+129 p., cloth, novel.

REUBEN, Shelly, 1945-

32230   *Julian Solo.* New York: Dodd, Mead & Co., 1988, 216 p., cloth, novel.

REVERE, John D.

32231   *Death's running mate.* New York: Pinnacle Books, 1985, 183 p., paper, novel. ASSASSIN #4.

REWOLINSKI, Leah

32232   *Star wreck: the generation gap: the spacy spoof that dares to boldly go where nobody wanted to go before.* US: Excellent Words Editorial Services, 1989, [117] p., paper, novel. STAR WRECK #1—STAR TREK, THE NEXT GENERATION PARODY.

REXNER, Romulus, 1920-

32233   *Planetary Legion for Peace: story of their war and our peace, 1940-2000.* [London: s.n.], 1960, 239 p., paper?, fiction.

REY, Judy-Lynn del—SEE: Del Rey, Judy-Lynn

REY, Lester del—SEE: Del Rey, Lester

REY, Russell, pseud.—SEE: Hughes, Dennis Talbot

REYNIAC, Maurice Druon de—SEE: Druon, Maurice

REYNOLDS, Aidan, *with William Charlton*

19820   *Arthur Machen: a short account of his life and work.* London: John Baker for the Richard Press, 1963, xiv+202 p., cloth, nonf.

REYNOLDS, Alfred

Kiteman—SEE: *Kiteman of Karanga.*
32234   *Kiteman of Karanga.* New York: Alfred A. Knopf, 1985, 217 p., cloth, novel.

32234A retitled: *Kiteman.* Toronto, New York: Bantam Books, 1986, 195 p., paper, novel.

REYNOLDS, Baillie, Mrs. [i.e., Gertrude M. Robins Reynolds]

38032   *The relations and what they related: a series of weird stories.* London: Hutchinson & Co., 1902, 314 p., cloth, coll.

REYNOLDS, Bonnie Jones

32235   *The confetti man.* New York: Stein & Day Publishers, 1975, 324 p., cloth, novel.

REYNOLDS, Dallas McC.—SEE: Reynolds, Mack

REYNOLDS, Kathleen N.—SEE: Reynolds, Kay

REYNOLDS, Kay [i.e., Kathleen N. Reynolds], 1951-

32236   *Robotech art 2.* Norfolk, VA: Donning Co., 1987, 131 p., paper, art.

with Ardith Carlton

19406   *Robotech art 1: from the animated series Robotech.* Norfolk, VA: Donning Co., 1986, ix+254 p., paper, art.

REYNOLDS, Mack [i.e., Dallas McCord Reynolds], 1917-1983

32237   *Ability quotient.* New York: Ace Books, 1975, 160 p., paper, novel.
32238   *After utopia.* New York: Ace Books, 1977, 250 p., paper, novel.
32239   *Amazon planet.* New York: Ace Books, 1975, 190 p., paper, novel.
32240   *The best of Mack Reynolds.* New York: Pocket Books, 1976, xiv+365 p., paper, coll.
32241   *The best ye breed.* New York: Ace Books, 1978, 279 p., paper, novel. HOMER CRAWFORD #3.
32242   *Brain world.* New York: Leisure Books, 1978, 204 p., paper, novel.
32243   *Chaos in Lagrangia.* New York: Tor, A Tom Doherty Associates Book, 1984, 256 p., paper, novel. LAGRANGIA #3. [Edited by Dean Ing].
32244   *Compounded interests.* Cambridge, MA: A Boskone Book, NESFA Press, 1983, xii+163 p., cloth, coll.
32245   *Day after tomorrow.* New York: Ace Books, 1976, 181 p., paper, novel.

32246 *Equality: in the year 2000.* New York: Ace Books, 1977, 272 p., paper, novel. JULIAN WEST #2. [A sequel to *Looking Backward from the year 2000* and the Edward Bellamy book, *Looking backward*].

32247 *The five way secret agent; [and, Mercenary from tomorrow].* New York: Ace Books, 1975, 121, 131 p., paper, coll. JOE MAUSER #1.

32248 *The fracas factor.* New York: Leisure Books, 1978, 192 p., paper, novel. JOE MAUSER #4.

32249 *Galactic Medal of Honor.* New York: Ace Books, 1976, 279 p., paper, novel.

32250 *Lagrange Five.* Toronto, New York: Bantam Books, 1979, 227 p., paper, novel. LAGRANGIA #1.

32251 *The Lagrangists.* New York: A Jim Baen Presentation, Tor, A Tom Doherty Associates Book, 1983, 287 p., paper, novel. LAGRANGIA #2. [Edited by Dean Ing].

32252 *Perchance to dream.* New York: Ace Books, 1977, vii+229 p., paper, novel.

32253 *Police patrol: 2000 A.D.* New York: Ace Books, 1977, 181 p., paper, novel.

32254 *Rolltown.* New York: Ace Books, 1976, 165 p., paper, novel.

32255 *Satellite City.* New York: Ace Books, 1975, 238 p., paper, novel.

32256 *Section G: United Planets.* New York: Ace Books, 1976, 186 p., paper, novel. PLANETARY AGENT #5.

32257 *Space search.* New York: Dell/Emerald, 1984, 191 p., paper, novel.

32258 *Space visitor.* New York: Ace Books, 1977, 149 p., paper, novel.

32259 *Tomorrow might be different.* New York: Ace Books, 1975, 190 p., paper, novel.

32260 *The towers of utopia.* Toronto, New York: Bantam Books, 1975, 201 p., paper, novel.

32261 *Trample an empire down.* New York: Leisure Books, 1978, 172 p., paper, novel.

with Michael Banks

17339 *Joe Mauser, mercenary from tomorrow.* New York: Baen Science Fiction Books, 1986, 280 p., paper, novel. JOE MAUSER #1-2. [Previously published in different form as "Mercenary" and "Frigid Fracas" (i.e., *Mercenary from tomorrow* and *The earth war* in book form)].

17340 *Sweet dreams, sweet princes.* New York: Baen Books, 1986, 269 p., paper, novel. JOE MAUSER #3. [Revised edition of *Time gladiator* (see #12183)].

with Dean Ing

26290 *Deathwish world.* New York: Baen Science Fiction Books, 1986, 316 p., paper, novel.

26291 *Eternity.* New York: A Baen Book, 1984, 254 p., paper, novel.

26292 *Home sweet home: 2010 A.D..* New York: A Dell/Emerald Book, 1984, 255 p., paper, novel.

26293 *The other time.* New York: A Baen Book, 1984, 308 p., paper, novel.

26294 *Trojan orbit.* New York: A Baen Book, 1985, 374 p., paper, novel. LAGRANGIA #4.

REYNOLDS, Ted [i.e., Theodore Andrus Reynolds], 1938-

32262 *The tides of God.* New York: Ace Books, 1989, 245 p., paper, novel.

REYNOLDS, Theodore A.—SEE: Reynolds, Ted

*RHEINGOLD, Howard (E.), 1947-

RHINEHART, Luke [pseud. of George Powers Cockcroft], 1932-

32263 *Adventures of Wim.* London: Grafton, 1986, 327 p., cloth, novel.

32264 *Long voyage back.* New York: Delacorte Press, 1983, 395 p., cloth, novel.

RHODES, Daniel [pseud. of Neil McMahon]

32265 *Adversary.* New York: A Thomas Dunne Book, St. Martin's Press, 1988, 354 p., cloth, novel. GUILHEM DE COURDEVAL #2.

32266 *Kiss of death.* New York: A Thomas Dunne Book, St. Martin's Press, 1990, 311 p., cloth, novel.

32267 *Next, after Lucifer.* New York: A Thomas Dunne Book, St. Martin's Press, 1987, 258 p., cloth, novel. GUILHEM DE COURDEVAL #1.

RHODES, Russell L.

32268 *The styx complex.* New York: Dodd, Mead & Co., 1977, 305 p., cloth, novel.

RHYS, Jack

32269 *The eternity merchants.* London: Robert Hale, 1981, 175 p., cloth, novel.

32270 *The five doors.* London: Robert Hale, 1981, 175 p., cloth, novel.

RIBEIRO, Stella Carr—SEE: Carr Ribeiro, Stella

RICCARDO, Martin V.

32271 *Vampires unearthed: the complete multimedia vampire and Dracula bibliography.* New York, London: Garland Publishing, 1983, viii+135 p., cloth, nonf.

RICE, Anne [i.e., Howard Allan Frances O'Brien Rice], 1941-

32272 *Interview with the vampire: a novel.* New York: Alfred A. Knopf, 1976, 371 p., cloth, novel. CHRONICLES OF THE VAMPIRES #1.

32273 *The mummy; or, Ramses the damned: a novel.* New York: Ballantine Books, 1989, 436 p., paper, novel.

32274 *The queen of the damned.* New York: Alfred A. Knopf, 1988, 448 p., cloth, novel. CHRONICLES OF THE VAMPIRE #3.

32275 *The vampire Lestat.* New York: Alfred A. Knopf, 1985, 481 p., cloth, novel. CHRONICLES OF THE VAMPIRES #2.

32276 *The witching hour: a novel.* New York: Alfred A. Knopf, 1990, 965 p., cloth, novel. [Winner of the *Locus* Award for Best Horror/Dark Fantasy Novel, 1990 (1991)].

as A. N. ROQUELAURE

32277 *Beauty's punishment.* New York: E. P. Dutton, 1984, x+233 p., cloth, novel. BEAUTY #2.

32278 *Beauty's release.* New York: E. P. Dutton, 1985, xi+238 p., cloth, novel. BEAUTY #3.

32279 *The claiming of Sleeping Beauty: an erotic novel of tenderness and cruelty for the enjoyment of men and women.* New York: E. P. Dutton, 1983, viii+253 p., cloth, novel. BEAUTY #1.

RICE, Howard A.—SEE: Rice, Anne

RICE, Peter

Damned if we do—SEE: *Renegade legion: Damned if we do.*

32280 *Renegade legion: Damned if we do.* Chicago: FASA Corp., 1990, 270 p., paper, novel. RENEGADE LEGION SERIES.

RICH, Mark (David), 1958-

32281 *Lifting.* Union, OR: Wordcraft of Oregon, 1991, 57 p., paper, coll.

RICH, Stephen (Peter), 1954- , *with Frank D. Parise*

31210 *Age of the storyteller.* Burlingame, CA: Advanced Publishing, 1988, xii+263 p., paper, coll.

RICHARDS, Curtis [pseud. of Richard Curtis?]

32282 *Halloween: a novel.* Toronto, New York: Bantam Books, 1979, 166 p., paper, movie. HALLOWEEN #1.

RICHARDS, Evan

32283 *Solid gold kidnapping: a novel.* New York: Warner Paperback Library, 1975, 158 p., paper, tele. SIX MILLION DOLLAR MAN #2.

RICHARDS, Gregory B.

32284 *Science fiction movies.* New York: A Bison Book, Gallery Books, 1984, 80 p., cloth, nonf.

*RICHARDS, Guy, 1905-<u>1979</u>

RICHARDS, Joel [pseud. of Joel Richard Fruchtman], 1937-

32285 *Pindharee.* New York: Tor SF, A Tom Doherty Associates Book, 1986, 216 p., paper, novel.

RICHARDS, Jonathan—SEE: Lewis, Canella

RICHARDS, Paul

32286 *The unblessed.* New York: Zebra Books, Kensington Publishing Corp., 1982, 398 p., paper, novel.

RICHARDS, Ross, *as* PETER SAXON

12727 *Through the dark curtain.* New York: Lancer Books, 1968, 190 p., paper, novel. GUARDIANS SERIES.

RICHARDS, Sean

32287 *The barbarian swordsmen: great stories of heroic fantasy.* London: Star Books, 1981, 172 p., paper, anth.

RICHARDS, Tony

32288 *The harvest bride.* New York: Tor Horror, A Tom Doherty Associates Book, 1987, 279 p., paper, novel.

RICHARDS, Vicki

32289 *Acceptance.* Strathmartine by Dundee, Scotland: ScoTpress, 1982, 52 p., paper, tele. STAR TREK SERIES.

32290 *Home is where the heart is.* Strathmartine by Dundee, Scotland: ScoTpress, 1982, 53 p., paper, tele. STAR TREK SERIES.

with Karen Hayden

25418 *A human kind of learning.* Strathmartine by Dundee, Scotland: ScoTpress, 1985, 64 p., paper, tele. STAR TREK SERIES.

RICHARDSON, Betty (Joyce), 1935-

32291 *John Collier.* Boston: Twayne Publishers, 1983, 123 p., cloth, nonf.

RICHARDSON, Darrell C(oleman), 1918-

32292 *J. Allen St. John: an illustrated bibliography.* Memphis, TN: Mid-America Publishers, 1991, 111 p., paper, nonf.

RICHARDSON, Jean (Mary)

32293 *Beware! beware!: chiling tales.* London: Hamish Hamilton, 1987, 120 p., cloth, anth.

32294 *Cold feet: an anthology of scary stories.* London: Hodder & Stoughton, 1985, 127 p., cloth, anth.

RICHARDSON, Josephine

32295 *Within the circle: in memoriam F. Lee Baldwin (1913-1987).* Glenview, IL: Moshassuck Press, 1988, 95 p., paper, nonf.

RICHARDSON, Linda, 1944- , *with David Bischoff & Rich Brown*

18012 *A personal demon.* New York: A Signet Book, New American Library, 1985, 253 p., paper, novel.

RICHARDSON, Michael (Allen), 1946-

with John Robert Colombo

20344 *Not to be taken at night: thirteen classic Canadian tales of mystery and the supernatural.* Toronto: Lester & Orpen Dennys, 1981, 189 p., cloth, anth.

with John Robert Colombo & John Bell & Alexandre L. Amprimoz

16353 *CDN SF & F: a bibliography of Canadian science fiction and fantasy.* Toronto: Hounslow Press, 1979, viii+85 p., paper, nonf.

*RICHARDSON, Robert S(hirley), 1902-1981

RICHARDSON, William J., 1920- , *with John P. Muller*

30400 *The purloined Poe: Lacan, Derrida, and psychoanalytic reading.* Baltimore, MD, London: Johns Hopkins University Press, 1988, xiv+394 p., cloth, nonf.

RICHELSON, Geraldine, 1922-

32296 *The Star Wars storybook.* New York: Random House, 1978, [57] p., cloth, movie. STAR WARS SERIES.

with Shep Steneman & Joan D. Vinge

32297 *Star Wars—the first ten years—storybook trilogy: the storybook based on the movies.* New York: Random House, 1987, [175] p., paper, movie coll. STAR WARS #1-3.

RICHEMONT, Enid

32298 *The game.* London: Walker Books Ltd., 1990, 202 p., cloth, novel.

32299 *The time tree.* London: Walker Books Ltd., 1989, 94 p., cloth, novel.

RICHMOND, Fiona

32300 *Galactic girl.* London: A Star Book, W. H. Allen & Co., 1980, 140 p., paper, novel.

RICHMOND, Leigh (Tucker), 1911- , *with Walt Richmond*

32301 *Challenge the hellmaker.* New York: Ace Books, 1976, 202 p., paper, novel.

32302 *Gallagher's glacier.* New York: Ace Books, 1979, 169 p., paper, novel. [Revised and expanded edition of #12227].

12228 *The lost millennium.* New York: Ace Books, 1967, 137 p., paper, novel. [Bound with *The road to the Rim* / by A. Bertram Chandler].

12228A retitled: *Siva!* New York: Ace Books, 1979, xv+172 p., paper, novel.
Phase two—SEE: *The phoenix ship.*

12229 *Phoenix ship.* New York: Ace Books, 1969, 106 p., paper, novel. [Bound with *Earthrim* / by Nick Kamin].

32303 retitled: *Phase two.* New York: Ace Books, 1979, 181 p., paper, novel. [Expanded edition].

32304 *The probability corner.* New York: Ace Books, 1977, 177 p., paper, novel.
Siva!—SEE: *The lost millennium.*

*RICHMOND, Mary [pseud. of Kathleen Lindsay], 1903-1973

RICHMOND, Walt(er F.), 1922-1977, *with Leigh Richmond*

32301 *Challenge the hellmaker.* New York: Ace Books, 1976, 202 p., paper, novel.

32302 *Gallagher's glacier.* New York: Ace Books, 1979, 169 p., paper, novel. [Revised and expanded edition of #12227].

12228 *The lost millennium.* New York: Ace Books, 1967, 137 p., paper, novel. [Bound with *The road to the Rim* / by A. Bertram Chandler].

12228A retitled: *Siva!* New York: Ace Books, 1979, xv+172 p., paper, novel.
Phase two—SEE: *The phoenix ship.*

12229 *Phoenix ship.* New York: Ace Books, 1969, 106 p., paper, novel. [Bound with *Earthrim* / by Nick Kamin].

32303 retitled: *Phase two.* New York: Ace Books, 1979, 181 p., paper, novel. [Expanded edition].

32304 *The probability corner.* New York: Ace Books, 1977, 177 p., paper, novel.
Siva!—SEE: *The lost millennium.*

RICHTER, Peyton E.

32305 *Utopia/dystopia?* Cambridge, MA: Schenkman Publishing Co., 1975, viii+151 p., cloth, nonf. anth.

RICKETT, Arthur Compton- —SEE: Compton-Rickett, Arthur

RICKETT, Joseph Compton- —SEE: Compton-Rickett, Joseph

RICKMAN, Gregg (David)

32306 *To the high castle: Philip K. Dick: a life, 1928-1962.* Long Beach, CA: Fragments West/The Valentine Press, 1989, xxvi+451 p., paper, nonf.

with Philip K. Dick

21740 *Philip K. Dick: in his own words.* Long Beach, CA: Fragments West/The Valentine Press, 1984, xxii+256 p., paper, nonf.

21741 *Philip K. Dick: in his own words, 2nd ed.* Long Beach, CA: Fragments West/ Valentine Press, 1988, xxii+250 p., paper, nonf.

21742 *Philip K. Dick: the last testament.* Long Beach, CA: Fragments West/The Valentine Press, 1985, xxii+241 p., paper, nonf.

*RICO, Don(ato), 1917-1985

RICO, Ul de—SEE: de Rico, Ul

RIDDELL, Charlotte E.—SEE: Riddell, J. H., Mrs.

RIDDELL, J. H., Mrs. [i.e., Charlotte Eliza Lawson Cowan Riddell], 1832-1906

32307 *The collected ghost stories of Mrs. J. H. Riddell.* New York: Dover Publications, 1977, xxvi+345 p., paper, coll.

RIDDELL, Ruth

32308 *Haunted journey.* New York: Atheneum, 1988, 215 p., cloth, novel.

32309 *Shadow witch.* New York: Atheneum, 1989, 202 p., cloth, novel.

RIDDEN, Geoffrey M.

32310 *The Hobbit: notes.* Harlow, England: Longman, 1981, 70 p., paper, nonf.

32311 *J. R. R. Tolkien: Lord of the Rings: notes.* Harlow: Longman, 1984, 80 p., paper, nonf.

RIDGWAY, James M.—SEE: Ridgway, Jim

RIDGWAY, Jim [i.e., James Mervyn Benson Ridgway Jr.], 1930- , *with Michele Benjamin*

17767 *PsiFi: psychological theories and science fictions.* Leicester, England: British Psychological Society, 1987, ix+229 p., paper, nonf.

RIDING, Julia

32312 *Deep space warriors.* London: Robert Hale, 1981, 175 p., cloth, novel.

32313 *Gabion.* London: Robert Hale, 1979, 191 p., cloth, novel.

32314 *Space Traders Unlimited*. London: A Pied Piper Book, Methuen Children's Books, 1987, 156 p., cloth, novel.

32315 *The strange land*. London: Robert Hale, 1980, 157 p., cloth, novel.

RIDLEY, Philip

32316 *Dakota of the White Flats*. London: Collins, 1989, 144 p., cloth, novel.

RIDOUT, Alan (John), 1934- , *with James Gibson*

23874 *Supernatural*. London: John Murray, 1978, 120 p., paper, anth.

RIDSDALE, Angela M(aricia), 1927- , *with Virginia Ferguson*

23031 *Ghost stories*. Melbourne, Australia: Thomas Nelson, 1977, 125 p., paper, anth.

RIEFE, Alan, 1925-

32317 *Scared to death*. New York: Diamond Books, 1991, 276 p., paper, novel.

32318 *Viper*. New York: Charter/Diamond Books, 1990, 271 p., paper, novel.

as BARBARA RIEFE

32319 *This ravaged heart*. Chicago: Playboy Press, 1977, 413 p., paper, novel.

RIEFE, Barbara, pseud.—SEE: Riefe, Alan

RIEMER, James D.

32320 *From satire to subversion: the fantasies of James Branch Cabell*. New York, Westport, CT: Greenwood Press, 1989, xxii+106 p., cloth, nonf. CONTRIBUTIONS TO THE STUDY OF SCIENCE FICTION AND FANTASY #38.

*RIENOW, Leona Train, 1903-1983

*RIENOW, Robert, 1909-1989

RIFBJERG, Klaus (Thorvald), 1931-

32321 *Witness to the future*. Seattle, WA: Fjord Press, 1987, 214 p., paper, novel. [Translation by Steve Murray of *De hellige aber*].

RIFFATERRE, Hermine (B.)

38033 *The occult in language and literature*. New York: New York Literary Forum, 1980, viii+216 p., cloth, nonf. anth.

RIGDON, Charles

32322 *Diosa*. New York: A Kangaroo Book, Pocket Books, 1978, 296 p., paper, novel.

RIGG, Robert B.

32323 *War—1974*. Harrisburg, PA: Military Service Publishing Co., 1958, vii+304 p., cloth, fiction.

RIGNEY, James—SEE: Jordan, Robert

RIKHYE, Ravi, 1946-

32324 *The fourth round, Indo-Pak War, 1984*. New Delhi: ABC Publishing House, 1982, xvi+253 p., cloth, novel.

RILEY, Dick [i.e., Richard Anthony Riley], 1946-

32325 *Critical encounters: writers and themes in science fiction*. New York: Frederick Ungar Publishing Co., 1978, viii+184 p., cloth, nonf. anth.

RILEY, Jame A., *with Scott H. Urban*

32326 *Minor apocalypses, and other small horrors: an anthology of October Society writings*. Atlanta, GA: Unnameable Press, 1985, 40 p., paper, anth. [Includes some verse].

RILEY, Judith (Astria) Merkle, 1942-

32327 *In pursuit of the green lion*. New York: Delacorte Press, 1990, 440 p., cloth, novel. VISION #2.

32328 *A vision of light*. New York: Delacorte Press, 1989, 442 p., cloth, novel. VISION #1.

RILEY, Philip J., 1948-

"The bride of Frankenstein"—SEE: *MagicImage Filmbooks presents "The bride of Frankenstein"*.

"Frankenstein"—SEE: *MagicImage Filmbooks presents "Frankenstein"*.

32329 *MagicImage Filmbooks presents "Abbott and Costello meet Frankenstein"*. Absecon, NJ: MagicImage Filmbooks, 1989, 42+[14]+103 p., paper, nonf.

anth. [Includes screenplay plus commentary].

32330 *MagicImage Filmbooks presents "Dracula": the original 1931 shooting script.* Absecon, NJ: MagicImage Filmbooks, 1990, 88+[199] p., paper, nonf. anth. [Includes screenplay plus commentary].

32331 *MagicImage Filmbooks presents "Frankenstein meets the wolf man": the original 1943 shooting script.* Absecon, NJ: MagicImage Filmbooks, 1990, 127+[20] p., paper, nonf. anth. [Includes screenplay plus commentary].

32332 *MagicImage Filmbooks presents "House of Frankenstein": the original 1944 shooting script.* Absecon, NJ: MagicImage Filmbooks, 1990, 119 p., paper, nonf. anth. [Includes screenplay plus commentary].

32333 *MagicImage Filmbooks presents "Son of Frankenstein": 50th anniversary edition (1939-1989).* Absecon, NJ: MagicImage Filmbooks, 1990, 33+196+[23] p., paper, nonf. anth. [Includes screenplay plus commentary].

32334 *MagicImage Filmbooks presents "The ghost of Frankenstein".* Absecon, NJ: MagicImage Filmbooks, 1990, 45+128+[23] p., paper, nonf. anth. [Includes screenplay plus commentary].

32335 *MagicImage Filmbooks presents "The mummy".* Absecon, NJ: MagicImage Filmbooks, 1989, [192] p., paper, nonf. anth. [Includes screenplay plus commentary].

32336 *MagicImage Filmbooks presents "This island Earth".* Absecon, NJ: MagicImage Filmbooks, 1989, [192] p., paper, nonf. anth. [Includes screenplay plus commentary].

"The Mummy"—SEE: *MagicImage Filmbooks presents "The mummy".*

with Forrest J Ackerman

"The bride of Frankenstein"—SEE: *MagicImage Filmbooks presents "The bride of Frankenstein".*

"Frankenstein"—SEE: *MagicImage Filmbooks presents "Frankenstein".*

15941 *MagicImage Filmbooks presents "The bride of Frankenstein".* Absecon, NJ: MagicImage Filmbooks, 1989, [177] p., paper, nonf. anth. [Includes screenplay plus commentary].

15942 *MagicImage Filmbooks presents "Frankenstein".* Absecon, NJ: MagicImage Filmbooks, 1989, [192] p., paper, nonf. anth. [Includes screenplay plus commentary].

RILEY, Richard A.—SEE: Riley, Dick

RIMEL, Duane W(eldon), 1915-

32337 *The forbidden room: how "The forbidden room" happened.* Glenview, IL: Moshassuck Press, 1988, [19] p., paper, nonf. [Limited to 75 copies].

32338 *To Yith and beyond.* Glenview, IL: Moshassuck Press, 1990, 111 p., paper, nonf. [Limited to 125 copies].

RIMMER, A. J., pseud.

32339 *Space whores.* Encino, CA: World-Wide Publishing Co., 1979, 186 p., paper, novel.

RIMMER, Robert H(enry), 1917-

32340 *Love me tomorrow.* New York: A Signet Book, New American Library, 1978, 455 p., paper, novel.

RIMMER, Steven W(illiam)

32341 *Coven.* New York: Ballantine Books, 1989, 295 p., paper, novel.

RINEHART, Mary Roberts, 1876-1958

32464 *The red lamp.* New York: George H. Doran & Co., 1925, 317 p., cloth, novel.

RING, Thomasina

32342 *Time-spun rapture.* New York: Leisure Books, 1990, 362 p., paper, novel.

RINGBOM, Håkan

32343 *George Orwell as essayist: a stylistic study.* Åbo, Finland: Åbo Akademi, 1973, 78 p., paper?, nonf.

RINGE, Donald A(rthur Jr.), 1923-

32344 *American gothic: imagination and reason in nineteenth-century fiction.* Lexington, KY: University Press of Kentucky, 1982, vii+215 p., cloth, nonf.

32345 *Charles Brockden Brown.* Boston: Twayne Publishers, 1966, 158 p., cloth, nonf.

32346 *Charles Brockden Brown, rev. ed.* Boston: Twayne Publishers, 1991, xii+141 p., cloth, nonf. [Revised edition].

RINGEL, Harry

32347 *The tender seed.* New York: Popular Library, Warner Books, 1986, 278 p., paper, novel.

*RINKOFF, Barbara (Jean Rich), 1923-1975

RIPLEY, Karen

32348 *Prisoner of dreams.* New York: A Del Rey Book, Ballantine Books, 1989, 263 p., paper, novel. PRISONER OF DREAMS #1.

32349 *Tales for the telling; 1: Summer session; Gross purposes: 2.* San Diego: Solo Ventures, 1983, 49 p., paper, coll. INDIANA JONES SERIES.

32350 *The tenth class.* New York: A Del Rey Book, Ballantine Books, 1991, 299 p., paper, novel. PRISONER OF DREAMS #2.

RIPPINGTON, Geoff, with Paul Kincaid

27219 *Bob Shaw.* Folkestone, Kent, England: British Science Fiction Association, 1981, 38 p., paper, nonf. BRITISH SCIENCE FICTION WRITERS #1.

RIPS, Ervine Milton—SEE: Lornquest, Olaf

RITCHIE, Paul, 1923-

38034 *Confessions of a people lover: a novel.* London: Calder & Boyars, 1967 (i.e., 1968), 157 p., cloth, novel.

RITCHIE, Rita [pseud. of Rita Krohne Reitci], 1930-

32351 *Grip of fear.* Chatsworth, CA: Major Books, 1976, 176 p., paper, novel.

RIVERS, Diana, 1931-

32352 *Journey to Zelindar: the personal account of Sair of Semasi: book 986 of the Hadra Archives.* Denver: Lace Publications, 1987, 301 p., paper, novel.

RIVKIN, J. F., pseud. [of two unknown authors]

32353 *The dreamstone.* New York: Ace Books, 1991, 184 p., paper, novel. RUNESWORD #3.

Mistress of ambiguities—SEE: Silverglass: Mistress of ambiguities.

32354 *Silverglass.* New York: Ace Fantasy Books, 1986, 186 p., paper, novel. SILVERGLASS #1.

32355 *Silverglass: Mistress of ambiguities.* New York: Ace Books, 1991, 203 p., paper, novel. SILVERGLASS #4.

32356 *Web of wind.* New York: Ace Books, 1987, 202 p., paper, novel. SILVERGLASS #2.

32357 *Witch of Rhostshyl.* New York: Ace Books, 1989, 172 p., paper, novel. SILVERGLASS #3.

RJNDT, Philippe Van—SEE: Van Rjndt, Philippe

ROACH, Marilynne K(athleen), 1946-

32358 *Encounters with the invisible world: being ten tales of ghosts, witches, & the devil himself in New England.* New York: Thomas Y. Crowell, 1977, 131 p., cloth, coll.

ROAD, Alan

32359 *Doctor Who: the making of a television series.* London: André Deutsch, 1982, 56 p., cloth, nonf.

ROAMAN, Chet, 1939- , with Christopher Swan

32360 *YV88: an eco-fiction of tomorrow.* San Francisco: Sierra Club Books, 1977, viii+248 p., paper, fiction.

ROBBINS, David (Lawrence), 1950-

32361 *Anaheim run.* New York: Leisure Books, 1988, 192 p., paper, novel. ENDWORLD #13.

Anaheim run; Seattle run—SEE: Endworld double: Anaheim run; Seattle run.

Armageddon run—SEE: Endworld: Armageddon run.

32362 *Atlanta run.* New York: Leisure Books, 1989, 188 p., paper, novel. ENDWORLD #17.

32363 *Boston run.* New York: Leisure Books, 1990, 186 p., paper, novel. ENDWORLD #21.

Capital run—SEE: Endworld: Capital run.

Capital run; New York run—SEE: Endworld double: Capital run; New York run.

32363 *Chicago run.* New York: Leisure Books, 1991, 192 p., paper, novel. ENDWORLD #27. [The last book in the series].

32364 *Cincinnati run.* New York: Leisure Books, 1990, 192 p., paper, novel. ENDWORLD #19.

Citadel run—SEE: Endworld: Citadel run.

32365 *Crusher strike.* New York: Leisure Books, 1990, 185 p., paper, novel. BLADE #6.

Dakota run—SEE: *Endworld: Dakota run.*

32366 *Dallas run.* New York: Leisure Books, 1990, 188 p., paper, novel. ENDWORLD #20.

32367 *Dead zone strike.* New York: Leisure Books, ·1990, 190 p., paper, novel. BLADE #10.

32368 *Death master strike.* New York: Leisure Books, 1991, 187 p., paper, novel. BLADE #12.

Denver run—SEE: *Endworld: Denver run.*

32369 *Devil strike.* New York: Leisure Books, 1990, 172 p., paper, novel. BLADE #8.

32370 *Endworld: Armageddon run.* New York: Leisure Books, 1987, 256 p., paper, novel. ENDWORLD #7.

32371 *Endworld: Capital run.* New York: Leisure Books, 1988, 223 p., paper, novel. ENDWORLD #9.

32372 *Endworld: Citadel run.* New York: Leisure Books, 1987, 255 p., paper, novel. ENDWORLD #6.

32373 *Endworld: Dakota run.* New York: Leisure Books, 1987, 256 p., paper, novel. ENDWORLD #5.

32374 *Endworld: Denver run.* New York: Leisure Books, 1987, 223 p., paper, novel. ENDWORLD #8.

32375 *Endworld double: Anaheim run; Seattle run.* New York: Leisure Books, 1991, 192+184 p., paper, coll. ENDWORLD SERIES.

32376 *Endworld double: Capital run; New York run.* New York: Leisure Books, 1991, 223+208 p., paper, coll. ENDWORLD SERIES.

32377 *Endworld double: Liberty run; Houston run.* New York: Leisure Books, 1991, 191+190 p., paper, coll. ENDWORLD SERIES.

32378 *Endworld double: Nevada run; Miami run.* New York: Leisure Books, 1991, 187+188 p., paper, coll. ENDWORLD SERIES. [Author's name does not appear on title page].

32379 *Endworld: New York run.* New York: Leisure Books, 1988, 208 p., paper, novel. ENDWORLD #10.

32380 *Endworld: The Fox run.* New York: Leisure Books, 1986, 255 p., paper, novel. ENDWORLD #1.

32381 *Endworld: The Kalispell run.* New York: Leisure Books, 1987, 255 p., paper, novel. ENDWORLD #4.

32382 *Endworld: Thief River Falls run.* New York: Leisure Books, 1986, 256 p., paper, novel. ENDWORLD #2.

32383 *Endworld: Twin Cities run.* New York: Leisure Books, 1986, 255 p., paper, novel. ENDWORLD #3.

32384 *First strike.* New York: Leisure Books, 1989, 185 p., paper, novel. BLADE #1.

The Fox run—SEE: *Endworld: The Fox run.*

32385 *Green Bay run.* New York: Leisure Books, 1990, 186 p., paper, novel. ENDWORLD #22.

32386 *Houston run.* New York: Leisure Books, 1988, 190 p., paper, novel. ENDWORLD #12.

The Kalispell run—SEE: *Endworld: The Kalispell run.*

32387 *L.A. strike.* New York: Leisure Books, 1990, 184 p., paper, novel. BLADE #9.

32388 *Liberty run.* New York: Leisure Books, 1987, 191 p., paper, novel. ENDWORLD #11.

Liberty run; Houston run—SEE: *Endworld double: Liberty run; Houston run.*

32389 *Madman run.* New York: Leisure Books, 1991, 189 p., paper, novel. ENDWORLD #26.

32390 *Memphis run.* New York: Leisure Books, 1989, 186 p., paper, novel. ENDWORLD #18.

32391 *Miami run.* New York: Leisure Books, 1989, 188 p., paper, novel. ENDWORLD #16.

32392 *Nevada run.* New York: Leisure Books, 1989, 187 p., paper, novel. ENDWORLD #15.

Nevada run; Miami run—SEE: *Endworld double: Nevada run; Miami run.*

32393 *New Orleans run.* New York: Leisure Books, 1991, 190 p., paper, novel. ENDWORLD #24.

New York run—SEE: *Endworld: New York run.*

32394 *Outlands strike.* New York: Leisure Books, 1989, 183 p., paper, novel. BLADE #2.

32395 *Pipeline strike.* New York: Leisure Books, 1989, 184 p., paper, novel. BLADE #4.

32396 *Pirate strike.* New York: Leisure Books, 1989, 170 p., paper, novel. BLADE #5.

32397 *Quest strike.* New York: Leisure Books, 1991, 191 p., paper, novel. BLADE #11.

32398 *Seattle run.* New York: Leisure Books, 1989, 184 p., paper, novel. ENDWORLD #14.

32399 *Spartan run.* New York: Leisure Books, 1991, 189 p., paper, novel. ENDWORLD #25.

32400 *Spectre.* New York: Leisure Books, 1988, 365 p., paper, novel.

32401 *Terror strike.* New York: Leisure Books, 1990, 188 p., paper, novel. BLADE #7.
Thief River Falls run—SEE: *Endworld: Thief River Falls run.*
Twin Cities run—SEE: *Endworld: Twin Cities run.*

32402 *Vampire strike.* New York: Leisure Books, 1989, 188 p., paper, novel. BLADE #3.

32403 *Vengeance strike.* New York: Leisure Books, 1991, 191 p., paper, novel. BLADE #13. [The last book in the series].

32404 *The wereling* / by David L. Robbins. New York: Leisure Books, 1983, 336 p., paper, novel.

32405 *The wrath.* New York: Leisure Books, 1988, 368 p., paper, novel.

32406 *Yellowstone run.* New York: Leisure Books, 1990, 189 p., paper, novel. ENDWORLD #23.

as J. D. CAMERON

19234 *Blood tide.* New York: Avon Books, 1991, 219 p., paper, novel. OMEGA SUB #4.

19236 *Command decision.* New York: Avon Books, 1991, 246 p., paper, novel. OMEGA SUB #2.

ROBBINS, Leonard A(ngus), 1921-

32407 *The pulp magazine index, first series.* Mercer Island, WA: Starmont House, 1989, 3 v. (I-x, 460 p.; II-882 p.; III-810 p.), cloth, nonf.

32408 *The pulp magazine index, second series.* Mercer Island, WA: Starmont House, 1989, viii+583 p., cloth, nonf.

32409 *The pulp magazine index, third series.* Mercer Island, WA: Starmont House, 1990, xii+639 p., cloth, nonf.

32410 *The pulp magazine index, fourth series.* Mercer Island, WA: Starmont House, 1991, xi+567 p., cloth, nonf.

ROBBINS, Thomas E.—SEE: Robbins, Tom

ROBBINS, Tom [i.e., Thomas Eugene Robbins], 1936-

32411 *Jitterbug perfume.* Toronto, New York: Bantam Books, 1984, 342 p., cloth, novel.

32412 *Skinny legs and all.* New York, Toronto: Bantam Books, 1990, 422 p., cloth, novel.

ROBENS, Howard, *with Jack Wassermann*

32413 *Hambo's itch.* Garden City, NY: Doubleday & Co., 1979, 307 p., cloth, novel.

ROBERSON, Jennifer [i.e. Jennifer Mitchell Roberson O'Green], 1953-

32414 *Daughter of the lion.* New York: DAW Books, 1989, 372 p., paper, novel. CHRONICLES OF THE CHEYSULI #6.

32415 *Flight of the raven.* New York: DAW Books, 1990, xi+372 p., paper, novel. CHRONICLES OF THE CHEYSULI #7.

32416 *Legacy of the sword.* New York: DAW Books, 1986, 384 p., paper, novel. CHRONICLES OF THE CHEYSULI #3.

32417 *A pride of princes.* New York: DAW Books, 1988, 453 p., paper, novel. CHRONICLES OF THE CHEYSULI #5.

32418 *Shapechangers.* New York: DAW Books, 1984, 221 p., paper, novel. CHRONICLES OF THE CHEYSULI #1.

32419 *The song of Homana.* New York: DAW Books, 1985, 352 p., paper, novel. CHRONICLES OF THE CHEYSULI #2.

32420 *Sword-breaker.* New York: DAW Books, 1991, 460 p., paper, novel. TIGER & DEL #4.

32421 *Sword-dancer.* New York: DAW Books, 1986, 286 p., paper, novel. TIGER & DEL #1.

32422 *Sword-maker.* New York: DAW Books, 1989, 464 p., paper, novel. TIGER & DEL #3.

32423 *Sword-singer.* New York: DAW Books, 1988, 382 p., paper, novel. TIGER & DEL #2.

32424 *Track of the white wolf.* New York: DAW Books, 1987, 375 p., paper, novel. CHRONICLES OF THE CHEYSULI #4.

ROBERSON, Rick(y James), 1956- , *with Sylvia Louise Engdahl*

22673 *Universe ahead: stories of the future.* New York: Atheneum, 1975, 336 p., cloth, anth.

*ROBERTS, Colin (Henderson), 1909-1990

ROBERTS, J. R., pseud.—SEE: Randisi, Robert J.

ROBERTS, Jane [pseud. of Jane Roberts Butts], 1929-1984

32425 *The further education of Oversoul Seven, The.* Englewood Cliffs, NJ: Prentice-Hall, 1979, 196 p., cloth, novel. OVERSOUL SEVEN #2.

32426 *Oversoul Seven and the Museum of Time.* Englewood Cliffs, NJ: Prentice-Hall, 1984, 134 p., cloth, novel. OVERSOUL SEVEN #3.

ROBERTS, Janet Louise, 1925-1982

32427A *The devil's own.* New York: Pocket Books, 1978, 255 p., paper, novel. [Originally published under the name Louisa Brontë].

12270A *Her demon lover.* New York: A Kangaroo Book, Pocket Books, 1978, 156 p., paper, novel. [Originally published under the name of Louisa Brontë].

12271A *Lord Satan.* New York: Pocket Books, 1979, 159 p., paper, novel. [Originally published under the name of Louisa Brontë].

as LOUISA BRONTE

32427 *The devil's own.* New York: Avon, 1972, [160] p., paper, novel.

12270 *Her demon lover.* New York: Avon, 1973, 156 p., paper, novel.

12271 *Lord Satan.* New York: Avon, 1972, 159 p., paper, novel.

ROBERTS, John Maddox, 1947-

32428 *The black shields.* New York: Tor Fantasy, A Tom Doherty Associates Book, 1991, 377 p., paper, novel. STORMLANDS #2.

32429 *Cestus Dei.* New York: A Jim Baen Presentation, Tor, A Tom Doherty Associates Book, 1983, 283 p., paper, novel.

32430 *The Cingulum.* New York: Tor, A Tom Doherty Associates Book, 1985, 285 p., paper, novel. CINGULUM #1.

32431 *Cloak of illusion.* New York: Tor SF, A Tom Doherty Associates Book, 1985, 287 p., paper, novel. CINGULUM #2.

32432 *Conan the bold.* New York: Tor SF, A Tom Doherty Associates Book, 1989, 282 p., paper, novel. CONAN SERIES.

32433 *Conan the champion.* New York: Tor SF, A Tom Doherty Associates Book, 1987, 280 p., paper, novel. CONAN SERIES.

32434 *Conan the marauder.* New York: Tor SF, A Tom Doherty Associates Book, 1988, 277 p., paper, novel. CONAN SERIES.

32435 *Conan the rogue.* New York: Tor Fantasy, A Tom Doherty Associates Book, 1991, 304 p., paper, novel. CONAN SERIES.

32436 *Conan the valorous.* New York: Tor, A Tom Doherty Associates Book, 1985, 280 p., paper, novel. CONAN SERIES.

32437 *The enigma variations.* New York: Ace Books, 1989, 234 p., paper, novel.

32438 *The islander.* New York: Tor Fantasy, A Tom Doherty Associates Book, 1990, 380 p., paper, novel. STORMLANDS #1.

32439 *King of the wood.* Garden City, NY: Doubleday & Co., 1983, 187 p., cloth, novel.

32440 *Space Angel.* New York: A Del Rey Book, Ballantine Books, 1979, 185 p., paper, novel. SPACE ANGEL #1.

32441 *Spacer: window of the mind.* New York: Ace Books, 1988, 182 p., paper, novel. SPACE ANGEL #2.

32442 *The strayed sheep of Charun.* Garden City, NY: Doubleday & Co., 1977, 183 p., cloth, novel.

32443 *The sword, the jewel, and the mirror.* New York: Tor SF, A Tom Doherty Associates Book, 1988, 277 p., paper, novel. CINGULUM #3.

Window of the mind—SEE: *Spacer: window of the mind.*

with Eric Kotani

27491 *Act of God.* New York: Baen Science Fiction Books, 1985, 282 p., paper, novel. ACT OF GOD #1.

27492 *Between the stars.* New York: Baen Books, 1988, 225 p., paper, novel. ACT OF GOD #3.

27493 *Delta Pavonis.* New York: Baen Books, 1990, 250 p., paper, novel.

27494 *The island worlds.* New York: Baen Books, 1987, 279 p., paper, novel. ACT OF GOD #2.

ROBERTS, Keith (John Kingston), 1935-

32444 *Anita.* Philadelphia, PA: Owlswick Press, 1990, 195 p., cloth, coll. [Includes the contents of the original edition (see #12272), plus one additional story].

32445 *The event.* Scotforth, Lancashire, England: Morrigan Publications, 1989, xii p., paper, story.

32446 *The grain kings: SF stories.* London: Hutchinson of London, 1976, 208 p., cloth, coll.

32447 *Gráinne: a novel.* Salisbury, Wiltshire, England: Kerosina Books, 1987, 175 p., cloth, novel.

32448 *Kaeti & company.* Salisbury, Wiltshire, England: Kerosina Books, 1986, 224 p., cloth, coll.

32449 *Kaeti's apocalypse.* Salisbury, Wiltshire, England: Kerosina Books, 1986, 11 p., paper, story.

32450 *Kiteworld.* London: Victor Gollancz, 1985, 288 p., cloth, novel.

32451 *Ladies from Hell.* London: Victor Gollancz, 1979, 198 p., cloth, coll.

32452 *The Lordly Ones.* London: Victor Gollancz, 1986, 160 p., cloth, coll.

32453 *Molly Zero.* London: Victor Gollancz, 1980, 224 p., cloth, novel.

32454 *The passing of the dragons: the short fiction of Keith Roberts.* New York: A Berkley Medallion Book, Berkley Publishing Corp., 1977, 307 p., paper, coll.

32455 *The road to paradise: a novel.* Worcester Park, Surrey, England: Kerosina Books, 1988 (i.e., 1989), 228 p., cloth, novel.

32456 *Winterwood, and other hauntings.* Scotforth, Lancashire, England: Morrigan Publications, 1989, 182+xii p., cloth, coll. [The special edition (300 copies) includes the story "The event" as an added feature].

ROBERTS, Mark K(elly), 1936-

32457 *Canal Zone conquest.* New York: Popular Library, 1988, 218 p., paper, novel. LIBERTY CORPS #3.

32458 *Costa Rican chaos.* New York: Popular Library, 1988, 164 p., paper, novel. LIBERTY CORPS #6.

32459 *Korean carnage.* New York: Popular Library, 1988, 212 p., paper, novel. LIBERTY CORPS #4.

32460 *The Liberty Corps.* New York: Popular Library, 1987, 313 p., paper, novel. LIBERTY CORPS #1.

32461 *Maracaibo massacre.* New York: Popular Library, 1987, 212 p., paper, novel. LIBERTY CORPS #2.

32462 *Poisoned paradise.* New York: Popular Library, 1988, 194 p., paper, novel. LIBERTY CORPS #5.

us LIONEL DERRICK

21621 *Black massacre.* Los Angeles: Pinnacle Books, 1980, 182 p., paper, novel. PENETRATOR #35.

21622 *Orphan army.* New York: Pinnacle Books, 1982, 196 p., paper, novel. PENETRATOR #47.

21623 *Quaking terror.* New York: Pinnacle Books, 1982, 200 p., paper, novel. PENETRATOR #45.

21624 *Satan's swarm.* New York: Pinnacle Books, 1983, 184 p., paper, novel. PENETRATOR #49.

21625 *Satellite slaughter.* Los Angeles: Pinnacle Books, 1979, 174 p., paper, novel. PENETRATOR #33.

21626 *The supergun mission.* New York: Pinnacle Books, 1977, 147 p., paper, novel. PENETRATOR #21.

ROBERTS, Moss, 1937- , *with C. N. Tay*

32465 *Chinese fairy tales and fantasies.* New York: Pantheon Books, 1979, xx+259 p., cloth, anth.

ROBERTS, Nadine (H.)

32466 *Evil threads.* New York: A Fawcett Juniper Book, 1988, 152 p., paper, novel.

ROBERTS, Nora

32467 *Second nature.* Toronto, New York: Silhouette Books, 1986, 252 p., paper, novel.

32468 *Time was.* Toronto, New York: Silhouette Books, 1989, 250 p., paper, novel. HORNBLOWER SAGA #1.

32469 *Times change.* Toronto, New York: Silhouette Books, 1990, 253 p., paper, novel. HORNBLOWER SAGA #2.

ROBERTS, Peter, 1950-

32470 *British fanzine bibliography.* Dawlish, England: Peter Roberts, 1977, 3 v., paper, nonf.

32471 *The corobite mines.* New York: Manor Books, 1978, 222 p., paper, novel.

32472 *Guide to current fanzines, 5th ed.* Dawlish, England: Peter Roberts, 1978, [13] p., paper, nonf.

Little gem guide to SF fanzines—SEE: *Peter Roberts's Little gem guide to SF fanzines, 4th ed.*

32473 *Peter Roberts's Little gem guide to SF fanzines, 4th ed.* London: Peter Roberts, 1976, [12] p., paper, nonf.

ROBERTS, Richard, 1941-

32474 *Tales for Jung folk: original fairytales for persons of all ages, dramatizing C. G. Jung's archetypes of the collective unconscious.* San Anselmo, CA: Vernal Equinox Press, 1983, 107 p., cloth, coll.

32475 *The wind & the wizard.* San Anselmo, CA: Vernal Equinox Press, 1990, 2 v., cloth, novel.

ROBERTS, Willo Davis, 1928-

32476 *The girl with the silver eyes.* New York: Atheneum, 1980, 181 p., cloth, novel.

32477 *The magic book.* New York: Atheneum, 1986, 150 p., cloth, novel.

ROBERTSON, Alice A.—SEE: St. Luz, Berthe

ROBERTSON, Bruce, 1934-

Fantasy art—SEE: Techniques of fantasy art.

32478 *Techniques of fantasy art.* London: Macdonald & Orbis, 1988, 144 p., cloth, nonf.

32478A retitled: *Fantasy art.* Cincinnati, OH: Northern Lights Books, 1988, 144 p., cloth, nonf.

ROBERTSON, Charles (L.), 1927-

32479 *The children.* Toronto, New York: Bantam Books, 1982, 369 p., paper, novel.

32480 *Red Chameleon.* Toronto, New York: Bantam Books, 1985, 456 p., paper, novel.

ROBERTSON, E(ileen) A(rnot), 1903-1961

38035 *Three came unarmed.* London: Jonathan Cape, 1929, 320 p., cloth, novel.

ROBERTSON, J(anet) R(ussell)

32481 *The crab trees.* London: Robert Hale, 1978, 157 p., cloth, novel.

ROBERTSON, Jennifer—SEE: Robertson, Jenny

ROBERTSON, Jenny [i.e., Jennifer Sinclair Robertson], 1942-

32482 *Fear in the glen.* Oxford, England, Batavia, IL: A Lion Paperback, 1984, 120 p., paper, novel.

ROBERTSON, John [pseud. of John Robert Bensink], 1948- , *with Brett Rutherford*

32483 *Piper.* New York: Zebra Books, Kensington Publishing Corp., 1987, 463 p., paper, novel

ROBERTSON, John W(ooster), 1856-

32484 *Bibliography of the writings of Edgar A. Poe.* San Francisco: Russian Hill Private Press, Edwin & Robert Grabhorn, 1934, 2 v., cloth, nonf. [Limited to 350 copies].

32485 *Edgar A. Poe: a study.* San Francisco: Printed by B. Brough, 1921, 424 p., cloth, nonf.

ROBERTSON, Olivia (Melian), 1917-

15856 *Miranda speaks.* London: Peter Davies, 1950, 220 p., cloth, novel.

ROBERTSON, R. Garcia y—SEE: Garcia y Robertson, R.

ROBESON, Kenneth, house pseud.

NOTE: The Doc Savage and Avenger series have been relisted in their entirety, with new attributions of the real authors behind the house name, Kenneth Robeson; thanks to Will Murray, not only for providing vital identifications gleaned from the original payment records of Street & Smith (publisher of Doc Savage *magazine), but also for continuing the Doc Savage adventures with a new series of original novels.*

18236 *The angry ghost: a Doc Savage adventure.* Toronto, New York: Bantam Books, 1977, 120 p., paper, novel. DOC SAVAGE #86. [By Lester Dent and William G. Bogart].

04132 *The annihilist: a Doc Savage adventure.* Toronto, New York: Bantam Books, 1968, 138 p., paper, novel. DOC SAVAGE #31. [By Lester Dent].

06179 *The Avenger: Black chariots.* New York: Warner Paperback Library, 1974, 142 p., paper, novel. AVENGER #30. [By Ron Goulart].

04915 *The Avenger: Death in slow motion.* New York: Warner Paperback Library, 1973, 158 p., paper, novel. AVENGER #18. [By Paul Ernst].

24244 *The Avenger: Demon Island.* New York: Warner Paperback Library, 1975, 141 p., paper, novel. AVENGER #36. [By Ron Goulart].

24245 *The Avenger: Dr. Time.* New York: Warner Paperback Library, 1974, p., paper, novel. AVENGER #28. [By Ron Goulart].

37729 *The Avenger: House of death.* New York: Warner Paperback Library, 1973, 158 p., paper, novel. AVENGER #15. [By Paul Ernst].

37730 *The Avenger: Justice, Inc.* New York: Paperback Library, 1972, 159 p., paper, novel. AVENGER #1. [By Paul Ernst].

37731 *The Avenger: Midnight murder.* New York: Warner Paperback Library, 1974, 158 p., paper, novel. AVENGER #24. [By Paul Ernst].

37732 *The Avenger: Murder on wheels.* New York: Warner Paperback Library, 1973, 158 p., paper, novel. AVENGER #13. [By Paul Ernst].

04916 *The Avenger: Nevlo.* New York: Warner Paperback Library, 1973, 159 p., paper, novel. AVENGER #17. [By Paul Ernst].

37733 *The Avenger: Pictures of death.* New York: Warner Paperback Library, 1973, 158 p., paper, novel. AVENGER #19. [By Paul Ernst].

06180 *The Avenger: Red moon.* New York: Warner Paperback Library, 1974, 158 p., paper, novel. AVENGER #26. [By Ron Goulart].

04917 *The Avenger: River of ice.* New York: Warner Paperback Library, 1973, 157 p., paper, novel. AVENGER #11. [By Paul Ernst].

37734 *The Avenger: Stockholders in death.* New York: Warner Paperback Library, 1972, 158 p., paper, novel. AVENGER #7. [By Paul Ernst].

04918 *The Avenger: The black death.* New York: Warner Paperback Library, 1974, 158 p., paper, novel. AVENGER #22. [By Paul Ernst].

24246 *The Avenger: The blood countess.* New York: Warner Paperback Library, 1975, p., paper, novel. AVENGER #34. [By Ron Goulart].

37735 *The Avenger: The blood ring.* New York: Warner Paperback Library, 1972, 158 p., paper, novel. AVENGER #6. [By Paul Ernst].

24247 *The Avenger: The cartoon crimes.* New York: Warner Paperback Library, 1974, p., paper, novel. AVENGER #31. [By Ron Goulart].

24248 *The Avenger: The death machine.* New York: Warner Paperback Library, 1975, 142 p., paper, novel. AVENGER #32?. [By Ron Goulart].

37736 *The Avenger: The devil's horns.* New York: Warner Paperback Library, 1972, 160 p., paper, novel. AVENGER #4. [By Paul Ernst].

04919 *The Avenger: The flame breathers.* New York: Warner Paperback Library, 1973, 157 p., paper, novel. AVENGER #12. [By Paul Ernst].

04920 *The Avenger: The frosted death.* New York: Warner Paperback Library, 1972, 157 p., paper, novel. AVENGER #5. [By Paul Ernst].

24249 *The Avenger: The glass man.* New York: Warner Paperback Library, 1975, 142 p., paper, novel. AVENGER #34. [By Ron Goulart].

37737 *The Avenger: The glass mountain.* New York: Warner Paperback Library, 1973, 158 p., paper, novel. AVENGER #8. [By Paul Ernst].

04921 *The Avenger: The green killer.* New York: Warner Paperback Library, 1974, 158 p., paper, novel. AVENGER #20. [By Paul Ernst].

37738 *The Avenger: The happy killers.* New York: Warner Paperback Library, 1974, 158 p., paper, novel. AVENGER #21. [By Paul Ernst].

04922 *The Avenger: The hate master.* New York: Warner Paperback Library, 1973, 158 p., paper, novel. AVENGER #16. [By Paul Ernst].

24250 *The Avenger: The Iron Skull.* New York: Warner Paperback Library, 1975, p., paper, novel. AVENGER #32. [By Ron Goulart].

24251 *The Avenger: The man from Atlantis.* New York: Warner Paperback Library, 1974, p., paper, novel. AVENGER #25. [By Ron Goulart].

24252 *The Avenger: The nightwitch devil.* New York: Warner Paperback Library, 1974, p., paper, novel. AVENGER #29. [By Ron Goulart].

06181 *The Avenger: The purple zombie.* New York: Warner Paperback Library, 1974, 141 p., paper, novel. AVENGER #27. [By Ron Goulart].

04923 *The Avenger: The sky walker.* New York: Warner Paperback Library, 1972, 156 p., paper, novel. AVENGER #3. [By Paul Ernst].

37739 *The Avenger: The smiling dogs.* New York: Warner Paperback Library, 1973, 159 p., paper, novel. AVENGER #10. [By Paul Ernst].

37740 *The Avenger: The Wilder curse.* New York: Warner Paperback Library, 1974, 158 p., paper, novel. AVENGER #23. [By Paul Ernst].

37741 *The Avenger: The yellow hoard.* New York: Warner Paperback Library, 1972, 158 p., paper, novel. AVENGER #2. [By Paul Ernst].

37742 *The Avenger: Three gold crowns.* New York: Warner Paperback Library, 1973, 158 p., paper, novel. AVENGER #14. [By Paul Ernst].

04924 *The Avenger: Tuned for murder.* New York: Warner Paperback Library, 1973, 158 p., paper, novel. AVENGER #9. [By Paul Ernst].

21564 *The awful egg: a Doc Savage adventure.* Toronto, New York: Bantam Books, 1978, 120 p., paper, novel. DOC SAVAGE #92 (or #88?). [By Lester Dent].

The black, black witch—SEE: *Doc Savage: Jiu San; and, The black, black witch.*

The black death—SEE: *The Avenger: The black death.*

03794 *The black spot: a Doc Savage adventure.* Toronto, New York: Bantam Books, 1974, 152 p., paper, novel. DOC SAVAGE #76. [By Laurence Donovan].

The blood ring—SEE: *The Avenger: The blood ring.*

21565 *The boss of terror: a Doc Savage adventure.* Toronto, New York: Bantam Books, 1976, 118 p., paper, novel. DOC SAVAGE #85. [By Lester Dent].

04133 *Brand of the werewolf: a Doc Savage adventure.* Toronto, New York: Bantam Books, 1965, 138 p., paper, novel. DOC SAVAGE #5. [By Lester Dent].

Cargo unknown—SEE: *Doc Savage: Satan black; and, Cargo unknown.*

03795 *Cold death: a Doc Savage adventure.* Toronto, New York: Bantam Books, 1968, 121 p., paper, novel. DOC SAVAGE #21. [By Laurence Donovan].

Cold death—SEE: *Doc Savage: The secret in the sky; and, Cold death.*

04134 *The crimson serpent: a Doc Savage adventure.* Toronto, New York: Bantam Books, 1974, 138 p., paper, novel. DOC SAVAGE #78. [By Lester Dent].

04135 *The czar of fear: a Doc Savage adventure.* Toronto, New York: Bantam Books, 1968, 140 p., paper, novel. DOC SAVAGE #22. [By Lester Dent].

The czar of fear—SEE: *Doc Savage: The czar of fear.*

04136 *The dagger in the sky: a Doc Savage adventure.* Toronto, New York: Bantam Books, 1969, 120 p., paper, novel. DOC SAVAGE #40. [By Lester Dent].

04137 *The deadly dwarf: a Doc Savage adventure.* Toronto, New York: Bantam Books, 1968, 115 p., paper, novel. DOC SAVAGE #28. [By Lester Dent].

Death had yellow eyes—SEE: *Doc Savage: The shape of terror; and, Death had yellow eyes.*

04138 *Death in silver: a Doc Savage adventure.* Toronto, New York: Bantam Books, 1968, 134 p., paper, novel. DOC SAVAGE #26. [By Lester Dent].

Death in silver—SEE: *Doc Savage: Death in silver.*

Death in slow motion—SEE: *The Avenger: Death in slow motion.*

The death machine—SEE: *The Avenger: The death machine.*

Demon Island—SEE: *The Avenger: Demon Island.*

04139 *The derrick devil: a Doc Savage adventure.* Toronto, New York: Bantam Books, 1973, 138 p., paper, novel. DOC SAVAGE #74. [By Lester Dent].

04140 *The devil Genghis.* Toronto, New York: Bantam Books, 1974, 149 p., paper, novel. DOC SAVAGE #79. [By Lester Dent].

04141 *Devil on the Moon: a Doc Savage adventure.* Toronto, New York: Bantam Books, 1970, 120 p., paper, novel. DOC SAVAGE #50. [By Lester Dent].

The devil's horns—SEE: *The Avenger: The devil's horns.*

The devil's playground—SEE: *Doc Savage: The green eagle; and, The devil's playground.*

Devils of the deep—SEE: *Doc Savage: Devils of the deep.*

Doc Savage omnibus—SEE: *Doc Savage: four complete adventures in one volume.*

21566 *Doc Savage: Death in silver; and, Mystery under the sea: two complete adventures in one volume.* Toronto, New York: Bantam Books, 1983, 260 p., paper, coll. DOC SAVAGE #26-27. [By Lester Dent].

21567 *Doc Savage: Devils of the deep; and, The headless men: two complete adventures in one volume.* Toronto, New York: Bantam Books, 1984, 228 p., paper, coll. DOC SAVAGE #123-124. [*Devils of the deep* by Lester Dent and Harold A. Davis; *The headless men* by Alan Hathway].

21568 *Doc Savage: five complete adventures in one volume: Bequest of evil; Death in little houses; Target for death; The death lady; The exploding lake.* New York, Toronto: Bantam Books, 1990, 441 p., paper, coll. DOC SAVAGE #173-177. [Cover title: *Doc Savage omnibus, volume 12; Death in little houses* by Lester Dent and William G. Bogart; *The exploding lake* by Lester Dent; *Target for death* and *The death lady* and *Bequest of evil* by William G. Bogart].

21569 *Doc Savage: five complete adventures in one volume: No light to die by; The monkey suit; Let's kill Ames; Once over lightly; I died yesterday.* Toronto, New York: Bantam Books, 1988, 407 p., paper, coll. DOC SAVAGE #143-147. [Cover title: *Doc Savage omnibus, volume 5*; by Lester Dent].

21570 *Doc Savage: five complete adventures in one volume: Se-Pah-Poo; Colors for murder; Three times a corpse; Death is a round black spot; The devil is Jones.* New York, Toronto: Bantam Books, 1990, 455 p., paper, coll. DOC SAVAGE

#168-172. [Cover title: *Doc Savage omnibus, volume 11*; by Lester Dent].

21571 *Doc Savage: five complete adventures in one volume: The derelict of Skull Shoal; Terror wears no shoes; The green master; Return from Cormoral; Up from Earth's center.* New York, Toronto: Bantam Books, 1990, 441 p., paper, coll. DOC SAVAGE #178-182. [Cover title: *Doc Savage omnibus, volume 13*; by Lester Dent].

21572 *Doc Savage: four complete adventures in one volume: Mystery island; Men of fear; Rock sinister; The pure evil.* Toronto, New York: Bantam Books, 1987, 392 p., paper, coll. DOC SAVAGE #139-142. [Cover title: *Doc Savage omnibus, volume 4*; by Lester Dent].

21573 *Doc Savage: four complete adventures in one volume: The all-white elf; The running skeletons; The angry canary; and The swooning lady.* Toronto, New York: Bantam Books, 1986, 373 p., paper, coll. DOC SAVAGE #127-130. [Cover title: *Doc Savage omnibus, volume I*; by Lester Dent].

21574 *Doc Savage: four complete adventures in one volume: The awful dynasty; The magic forest; Fire and ice; The disappearing lady.* Toronto, New York: Bantam Books, 1988, 378 p., paper, coll. DOC SAVAGE #148-151. [Cover title: *Doc Savage omnibus, volume 6*; The *magic forest*, and *Fire and ice* by Lester Dent and William G. Bogart; *The disappearing lady* and *The awful dynasty* by William G. Bogart].

21575 *Doc Savage: four complete adventures in one volume: The devil's black rock; Waves of death; The too-wise owl; Terror and the lonely widow.* New York, Toronto: Bantam Books, 1989, 425 p., paper, coll. DOC SAVAGE #164-167. [Cover title: *Doc Savage omnibus, volume 10*; by Lester Dent].

21576 *Doc Savage: four complete adventures in one volume: The invisible-box murders; Birds of death; The wee ones; Terror takes 7.* New York: Bantam Books, 1989, 404 p., paper, coll. DOC SAVAGE #160-163. [Cover title: *Doc Savage omnibus, volume 9*; by Lester Dent].

21577 *Doc Savage: four complete adventures in one volume: The men vanished; Five fathoms dead; The terrible stork; Danger lies east.* Toronto, New York: Bantam Books, 1988, 378 p., paper, coll. DOC SAVAGE #152-155. [Cover title: *Doc Savage omnibus, volume 7*; by Lester Dent].

21578 *Doc Savage: four complete adventures in one volume: The mental monster; The pink lady; Weird valley; Trouble on parade.* Toronto, New York: Bantam Books, 1989, 407 p., paper, coll. DOC SAVAGE #156-159. [Cover title: *Doc Savage omnibus, volume 8*; by Lester Dent].

21579 *Doc Savage: four complete adventures in one volume: The mindless monsters; The rustling death; King Joe Cay; The thing that pursued.* Toronto, New York: Bantam Books, 1987, 410 p., paper, coll. DOC SAVAGE #131-134. [Cover title: *Doc Savage omnibus, volume 2*; The *mindless monsters* and *The rustling death* by Alan Hathway; *King Joe Cay* and *The thing that pursued* by Lester Dent].

21580 *Doc Savage: four complete adventures in one volume: The spook of Grandpa Eben; Measures for a coffin; The three devils; Strange fish.* Toronto, New York: Bantam Books, 1987, 378 p., paper, coll. DOC SAVAGE #135-138. [Cover title: *Doc Savage omnibus, volume 3*; by Lester Dent].

21581 *Doc Savage: Hell below; and, The lost giant: two complete adventures in one volume.* Toronto, New York: Bantam Books, 1980, 214 p., paper, coll. DOC SAVAGE #99-100. [By Lester Dent].

21582 *Doc Savage: Jiu San; and, The black, black witch: two complete adventures in one volume.* Toronto, New York: Bantam Books, 1981, 200 p., paper, coll. DOC SAVAGE #107-108. [By Lester Dent].

21583 *Doc Savage: One-eyed mystic; and, The man who fell up: two complete adventures in one volume.* Toronto, New York: Bantam Books, 1982, 213 p., paper, coll. DOC SAVAGE #111-112. [By Lester Dent].

21584 *Doc Savage: Pirate isle; and, The speaking stone: two complete adventures in one volume.* Toronto, New York: Bantam Books, 1983, 200 p., paper, coll. DOC SAVAGE #115-116. [By Lester Dent].

21585 *Doc Savage: Python Isle.* New York, Toronto: Falcon, Bantam Books, 1991, 207 p., paper, novel. DOC SAVAGE (UNNUMBERED). [By Lester Dent and Will Murray].

21586 *Doc Savage: Satan black; and, Cargo unknown: two complete adventures in one volume.* Toronto, New York: Bantam Books, 1980, 213 p., paper, coll. DOC SAVAGE #97-98. [By Lester Dent].

21587 *Doc Savage: The Czar of fear; and, Fortress of Solitude: two complete adventures in one volume.* Toronto, New

York: Bantam Books, 1982, 274 p., paper, coll. DOC SAVAGE #22-23. [By Lester Dent].

21588 *Doc Savage: The goblins; and, The secret of the Su: two complete adventures in one volume.* Toronto, New York: Bantam Books, 1985, 214 p., paper, coll. DOC SAVAGE #125-126. [By Lester Dent].

21589 *Doc Savage: The golden man; and, Peril in the north: two complete adventures in one volume.* Toronto, New York: Bantam Books, 1984, 210 p., paper, coll. DOC SAVAGE #117-118. [By Lester Dent].

21590 *Doc Savage: The green eagle; and, The devil's playground: two complete adventures in one volume.* Toronto, New York: Bantam Books, 1983, 217 p., paper, coll. DOC SAVAGE #24-25. [*The devil's playground* by Alan Hathway; *The green eagle* by Lester Dent].

21591 *Doc Savage: The laugh of death; and, The king of terror: two complete adventures in one volume.* Toronto, New York: Bantam Books, 1984, 216 p., paper, coll. DOC SAVAGE #119-120. [By Lester Dent].

21592 *Doc Savage: The pharaoh's ghost; and, The time terror: two complete adventures in one volume.* Toronto, New York: Bantam Books, 1981, 197 p., paper, coll. DOC SAVAGE #101-102. [By Lester Dent].

21593 *Doc Savage: The secret in the sky; and, Cold death: two complete adventures in one volume.* Toronto, New York: Bantam Books, 1982, 261 p., paper, coll. DOC SAVAGE #20-21. [*The secret in the sky* by Lester Dent; *Cold death* by Laurence Donovan].

21594 *Doc Savage: The shape of terror; and, Death had yellow eyes: two complete adventures in one volume.* Toronto, New York: Bantam Books, 1982, 185 p., paper, coll. DOC SAVAGE #109-110. [By Lester Dent].

21595 *Doc Savage: The talking devil; and, The ten ton snakes: two complete adventures in one volume.* Toronto, New York: Bantam Books, 1982, 183 p., paper, coll. DOC SAVAGE #113-114. [By Lester Dent].

21596 *Doc Savage: The three wild men; and, The fiery menace: two complete adventures in one volume.* Toronto, New York: Bantam Books, 1984, 212 p., paper, coll. DOC SAVAGE #121-122. [By Lester Dent].

21597 *Doc Savage: The whisker of Hercules; and, The man who was scared: two complete adventures in one volume.* Toronto, New York: Bantam Books, 1981, 201 p., paper, coll. DOC SAVAGE #103-104. [By Lester Dent].

21598 *Doc Savage: They died twice; and, The screaming man: two complete adventures in one volume.* Toronto, New York: Bantam Books, 1981, 183 p., paper, coll. DOC SAVAGE #105-106. [By Lester Dent].

04142 *Dust of death: a Doc Savage adventure.* Toronto, New York: Bantam Books, 1969, 139 p., paper, novel. DOC SAVAGE #32. [By Lester Dent and Harold A. Davis].

21599 *The evil gnome: a Doc Savage adventure.* Toronto, New York: Bantam Books, 1976, 120 p., paper, novel. DOC SAVAGE #82. [By Lester Dent].

04143 *The fantastic island: a Doc Savage adventure.* Toronto, New York: Bantam Books, 1966, 135 p., paper, novel. DOC SAVAGE #14. [By Lester Dent and Ryerson Johnson].

The fiery menace—SEE: *Doc Savage: The three wild men; and, The fiery menace.*

04144 *Fear Cay: a Doc Savage adventure.* Toronto, New York: Bantam Books, 1966, 138 p., paper, novel. DOC SAVAGE #11. [By Lester Dent].

04145 *The Feathered Octopus: a Doc Savage adventure.* Toronto, New York: Bantam Books, 1970, 122 p., paper, novel. DOC SAVAGE #48. [By Lester Dent].

The flame breathers—SEE: *The Avenger: The flame breathers.*

04146 *The flaming falcons: a Doc Savage adventure.* Toronto, New York: Bantam Books, 1968, 118 p., paper, novel. DOC SAVAGE #30. [By Lester Dent].

21600 *The flying goblin: a Doc Savage adventure.* Toronto, New York: Bantam Books, 1977, 120 p., paper, novel. DOC SAVAGE #90. [By William G. Bogart].

04147 *Fortress of Solitude: a Doc Savage adventure.* Toronto, New York: Bantam Books, 1968, 118 p., paper, novel. DOC SAVAGE #23. [By Lester Dent].

Fortress of Solitude—SEE: *Doc Savage: The czar of fear; and, Fortress of Solitude.*

04148 *The freckled shark: a Doc Savage adventure.* Toronto, New York: Bantam Books, 1972, 139 p., paper, novel. DOC SAVAGE #67. [By Lester Dent].

The frosted death—SEE: *The Avenger: The frosted death.*

04149 *The giggling ghosts: a Doc Savage adventure.* Toronto, New York: Bantam Books, 1971, 123 p., paper, novel. DOC SAVAGE #56. [By Lester Dent].

The glass man—SEE: *The Avenger: The glass man.*

The glass mountain—SEE: *The Avenger: The glass mountain.*

The goblins—SEE: *Doc Savage: The goblins.*

04150 *The gold ogre: a Doc Savage adventure.* Toronto, New York: Bantam Books, 1969, 122 p., paper, novel. DOC SAVAGE #42. [By Lester Dent].

The golden man—SEE: *Doc Savage: The golden man.*

04151 *The golden peril: a Doc Savage adventure.* Toronto, New York: Bantam Books, 1970, 138 p., paper, novel. DOC SAVAGE #55. [By Lester Dent & Harold A. Davis].

04152 *The green death: a Doc Savage adventure.* Toronto, New York: Bantam Books, 1971, 138 p., paper, novel. DOC SAVAGE #65. [By Harold A. Davis].

04153 *The green eagle: a Doc Savage adventure.* Toronto, New York: Bantam Books, 1968, 114 p., paper, novel. DOC SAVAGE #24. [By Lester Dent].

The green eagle—SEE: *Doc Savage: The green eagle.*

The green killer—SEE: *The Avenger: The green killer.*

The happy killers—SEE: *The Avenger: The happy killers.*

21601 *The hate genius: a Doc Savage adventure.* Toronto, New York: Bantam Books, 1979, 119 p., paper, novel. DOC SAVAGE #94. [By Lester Dent].

The hate master—SEE: *The Avenger: The hate master.*

03796 *Haunted ocean: a Doc Savage adventure.* Toronto, New York: Bantam Books, 1970, 140 p., paper, novel. DOC SAVAGE #51. [By Laurence Donovan].

03797 *He could stop the world: a Doc Savage adventure.* Toronto, New York: Bantam Books, 1970, 140 p., paper, novel. DOC SAVAGE #54. [By Laurence Donovan].

The headless men—SEE: *Doc Savage: Devils of the deep; and, The headless men.*

Hell below—SEE: *Doc Savage: Hell below.*

04154 *Hex: a Doc Savage adventure.* Toronto, New York: Bantam Books, 1969, 120 p., paper, novel. DOC SAVAGE #37. [By Lester Dent and William G. Bogart].

House of death—SEE: *The Avenger: House of death.*

21602 *The incredible radio exploits of Doc Savage, volume 1.* Greenwood, MA: Odyssey Publications, 1982, 128 p., pa-

per, coll. DOC SAVAGE SERIES. [By Lester Dent; only volume published].

The Iron Skull—SEE: *The Avenger: The Iron Skull.*

Jiu San—SEE: *Doc Savage: Jiu San.*

Justice, Inc.—SEE: *The Avenger: Justice, Inc.*

21265 *The king maker.* Toronto, New York: Bantam Books, 1975, 170 p., paper, novel. DOC SAVAGE #80. [By Lester Dent and Harold A. Davis].

The king of terror—SEE: *Doc Savage: The laugh of death; and, The king of terror.*

04155 *Land of always-night: a Doc Savage adventure.* Toronto, New York: Bantam Books, 1966, 138 p., paper, novel. DOC SAVAGE #13. [By Lester Dent and Ryerson Johnson].

04156 *The land of fear: a Doc Savage adventure.* Toronto, New York: Bantam Books, 1973, 136 p., paper, novel. DOC SAVAGE #75. [By Lester Dent and Harold A. Davis].

03798 *Land of long juju: a Doc Savage adventure.* Toronto, New York: Bantam Books, 1970, 140 p., paper, novel. DOC SAVAGE #47. [By Laurence Donovan].

04157 *The land of terror: Doc Savage and his pals in a novel of unusual adventure.* New York: Street & Smith, 1933, 252 p., cloth, novel. DOC SAVAGE #2 (old series); DOC SAVAGE #8 (new series). [By Lester Dent].

The laugh of death—SEE: *Doc Savage: The laugh of death.*

04158 *The living fire menace: a Doc Savage adventure.* Toronto, New York: Bantam Books, 1971, 120 p., paper, novel. DOC SAVAGE #61. [By Harold A. Davis].

The lost giant—SEE: *Doc Savage: Hell below; and, The lost giant.*

04159 *The lost oasis: a Doc Savage adventure.* Toronto, New York: Bantam Books, 1965, 123 p., paper, novel. DOC SAVAGE #6. [By Lester Dent].

03799 *Mad eyes: a Doc Savage adventure.* Toronto, New York: Bantam Books, 1969, 120 p., paper, novel. DOC SAVAGE #34. [By Laurence Donovan].

04160 *Mad Mesa: a Doc Savage adventure.* Toronto, New York: Bantam Books, 1972, 122 p., paper, novel. DOC SAVAGE #66. [By Lester Dent].

21603 *The magic island: a Doc Savage adventure.* Toronto, New York: Bantam Books, 1977, 137 p., paper, novel. DOC SAVAGE #89. [By Lester Dent].

04161 *The Majii: a Doc Savage adventure.* Toronto, New York: Bantam Books,

1971, 140 p., paper, novel. DOC SAVAGE #60. [By Lester Dent].

04162 *The man of bronze: Doc Savage and his pals in a novel of unusual adventure.* New York: Street & Smith, 1933, 252 p., cloth, novel. DOC SAVAGE #1. [By Lester Dent].

04163 *The man who shook the Earth: a Doc Savage adventure.* Toronto, New York: Bantam Books, 1969, 154 p., paper, novel. DOC SAVAGE #43. [By Lester Dent].

The man who fell up—SEE: *Doc Savage: One-eyed mystic; and, The man who fell up.*

The man who was scared—SEE: *Doc Savage: The whisker of Hercules; and, The man who was scared.*

03800 *The men who smiled no more: a Doc Savage adventure.* Toronto, New York: Bantam Books, 1970, 138 p., paper, novel. DOC SAVAGE #45. [By Laurence Donovan].

04164 *The mental wizard: a Doc Savage adventure.* Toronto, New York: Bantam Books, 1970, 135 p., paper, novel. DOC SAVAGE #53. [By Lester Dent].

04165 *Merchants of disaster: a Doc Savage adventure.* Toronto, New York: Bantam Books, 1969, 138 p., paper, novel. DOC SAVAGE #41. [By Lester Dent and Harold A. Davis].

04166 *The Metal Master: a Doc Savage adventure.* Toronto, New York: Bantam Books, 1973, 137 p., paper, novel. DOC SAVAGE #72. [By Lester Dent].

04167 *Meteor menace: a Doc Savage adventure.* Toronto, New York: Bantam Books, 1964, 140 p., paper, novel. DOC SAVAGE #3. [By Lester Dent].

04168 *The Midas man: a Doc Savage adventure.* Toronto, New York: Bantam Books, 1970, 121 p., paper, novel. DOC SAVAGE #46. [By Lester Dent].

Midnight murder—SEE: *The Avenger: Midnight murder.*

04169 *The monsters: a Doc Savage adventure.* Toronto, New York: Bantam Books, 1965, 138 p., paper, novel. DOC SAVAGE #7. [By Lester Dent].

04170 *The motion menace: a Doc Savage adventure.* Toronto, New York: Bantam Books, 1971, 123 p., paper, novel. DOC SAVAGE #64. [By Lester Dent and Ryerson Johnson].

21266 *The mountain monster: a Doc Savage adventure.* Toronto, New York: Bantam Books, 1976, 122 p., paper, novel. DOC SAVAGE #84. [By Harold A. Davis].

04171 *The munitions master: a Doc Savage adventure.* Toronto, New York: Bantam Books, 1971, 135 p., paper, novel. DOC SAVAGE #58. [By Harold A. Davis].

03801 *Murder melody: a Doc Savage adventure.* Toronto, New York: Bantam Books, 1967, 138 p., paper, novel. DOC SAVAGE #15. [By Laurence Donovan].

03802 *Murder mirage: a Doc Savage adventure.* Toronto, New York: Bantam Books, 1973, 153 p., paper, novel. DOC SAVAGE #71. [By Laurence Donovan].

21604 *Mystery on Happy Bones: a Doc Savage adventure.* Toronto, New York: Bantam Books, 1979, 134 p., paper, novel. DOC SAVAGE #96. [By Lester Dent].

04172 *The mystery on the snow: a Doc Savage adventure.* Toronto, New York: Bantam Books, 1972, 149 p., paper, novel. DOC SAVAGE #69. [By Lester Dent].

Murder on wheels—SEE: *The Avenger: Murder on wheels.*

04173 *Mystery under the sea: a Doc Savage adventure.* Toronto, New York: Bantam Books, 1968, 120 p., paper, novel. DOC SAVAGE #27. [By Lester Dent].

Mystery under the sea—SEE: *Doc Savage: Death in silver; and, Mystery under the sea.*

04174 *The Mystic Mullah: a Doc Savage adventure.* Toronto, New York: Bantam Books, 1965, 137 p., paper, novel. DOC SAVAGE #9. [By Lester Dent].

Nevlo—SEE: *The Avenger: Nevlo.*

One-eyed mystic—SEE: *Doc Savage: One-eyed mystic.*

04175 *The other world: a Doc Savage adventure.* Toronto, New York: Bantam Books, 1968, 119 p., paper, novel. DOC SAVAGE #29. [By Lester Dent].

Peril in the north—SEE: *Doc Savage: The golden man; and, Peril in the north.*

04176 *The Phantom City: a Doc Savage adventure.* Toronto, New York: Bantam Books, 1966, 137 p., paper, novel. DOC SAVAGE #10. [By Lester Dent].

The pharaoh's ghost—SEE: *Doc Savage: The pharaoh's ghost.*

Pictures of death—SEE: *The Avenger: Pictures of death.*

Pirate isle—SEE: *Doc Savage: Pirate isle.*

04177 *Pirate of the Pacific: a Doc Savage adventure.* Toronto, New York: Bantam Books, 1967, 136 p., paper, novel. DOC SAVAGE #19. [By Lester Dent].

04178 *The pirate's ghost: a Doc Savage adventure.* Toronto, New York: Bantam Books, 1971, 135 p., paper, novel. DOC SAVAGE #62. [By Lester Dent].

04179 *Poison island: a Doc Savage adventure.* Toronto, New York: Bantam Books, 1971, 118 p., paper, novel. DOC SAVAGE #57. [By Lester Dent].

04180 *The polar treasure: a Doc Savage adventure.* Toronto, New York: Bantam Books, 1965, 122 p., paper, novel. DOC SAVAGE #4. [By Lester Dent].

21267 *The Purple Dragon: a Doc Savage adventure.* Toronto, New York: Bantam Books, 1978, 136 p., paper, novel. DOC SAVAGE #91. [By Lester Dent and Harold A. Davis].

Python Isle—SEE: *Doc Savage: Python Isle.*

04181 *Quest of Qui: a Doc Savage adventure.* Toronto, New York: Bantam Books, 1966, 119 p., paper, novel. DOC SAVAGE #12. [By Lester Dent].

04182 *Quest of the Spider: Doc Savage and his pals in a novel of unusual adventure.* New York: Street & Smith, 1933, 252 p., cloth, novel. DOC SAVAGE #3 (old series; DOC SAVAGE #68 (new series). [By Lester Dent].

04183 *The red skull: a Doc Savage adventure.* Toronto, New York: Bantam Books, 1967, 124 p., paper, novel. DOC SAVAGE #17. [By Lester Dent].

04184 *Red snow: a Doc Savage adventure.* Toronto, New York: Bantam Books, 1969, 139 p., paper, novel. DOC SAVAGE #38. [By Lester Dent].

21605 *The red spider: a Doc Savage adventure.* Toronto, New York: Bantam Books, 1979, 122 p., paper, novel. DOC SAVAGE #95. [By Lester Dent].

21606 *The red terrors: a Doc Savage adventure.* Toronto, New York: Bantam Books, 1976, 136 p., paper, novel. DOC SAVAGE #83. [By Lester Dent].

04185 *Resurrection day: a Doc Savage adventure.* Toronto, New York: Bantam Books, 1969, 119 p., paper, novel. DOC SAVAGE #36. [By Lester Dent].

River of ice—SEE: *The Avenger: River of ice.*

21607 *The Roar Devil: a Doc Savage adventure.* Toronto, New York: Bantam Books, 1977, 153 p., paper, novel. DOC SAVAGE #88. [By Lester Dent].

04186 *The Sargasso ogre: a Doc Savage adventure.* Toronto, New York: Bantam Books, 1967, 140 p., paper, novel. DOC SAVAGE #18. [By Lester Dent].

Satan black—SEE: *Doc Savage: Satan black.*

The screaming man—SEE: *Doc Savage: They died twice; and, The screaming man.*

04187 *The Sea Angel: a Doc Savage adventure.* Toronto, New York: Bantam Books, 1970, 120 p., paper, novel. DOC SAVAGE #49. [By Lester Dent].

04188 *The sea magician: a Doc Savage adventure.* Toronto, New York: Bantam Books, 1970, 137 p., paper, novel. DOC SAVAGE #44. [By Lester Dent].

04189 *The secret in the sky: a Doc Savage adventure.* Toronto, New York: Bantam Books, 1967, 119 p., paper, novel. DOC SAVAGE #20. [By Lester Dent].

The secret in the sky—SEE: *Doc Savage: The secret in the sky.*

The secret of the Su—SEE: *Doc Savage: The goblins; and, The secret of the Su.*

04190 *The seven agate devils: a Doc Savage adventure.* Toronto, New York: Bantam Books, 1973, 134 p., paper, novel. DOC SAVAGE #73. [By Lester Dent].

The shape of terror—SEE: *Doc Savage: The shape of terror.*

The sky walker—SEE: *The Avenger: The sky walker.*

The smiling dogs—SEE: *The Avenger: The smiling dogs.*

04191 *The South Pole terror: a Doc Savage adventure.* Toronto, New York: Bantam Books, 1974, 137 p., paper, novel. DOC SAVAGE #77. [By Lester Dent].

The speaking stone—SEE: *Doc Savage: Pirate isle; and, The speaking stone.*

04192 *Spook Hole: a Doc Savage adventure.* Toronto, New York: Bantam Books, 1972, 138 p., paper, novel. DOC SAVAGE #70. [By Lester Dent].

04193 *The spook legion: a Doc Savage adventure.* Toronto, New York: Bantam Books, 1967, 122 p., paper, novel. DOC SAVAGE #16. [By Lester Dent].

18239 *The spotted men: a Doc Savage adventure.* Toronto, New York: Bantam Books, 1977, 121 p., paper, novel. DOC SAVAGE #87. [By Lester Dent and William G. Bogart].

04194 *The Squeaking Goblin: a Doc Savage adventure.* Toronto, New York: Bantam Books, 1969, 138 p., paper, novel. DOC SAVAGE #35. [By Lester Dent].

Stockholders in death—SEE: *The Avenger: Stockholders in death.*

21608 *The stone man: a Doc Savage adventure.* Toronto, New York: Bantam Books, 1976, 119 p., paper, novel. DOC SAVAGE #81. [By Lester Dent].

04195 *The submarine mystery: a Doc Savage adventure.* Toronto, New York: Bantam Books, 1971, 121 p., paper, novel. DOC SAVAGE #63. [By Lester Dent].

The talking devil—SEE: *Doc Savage: The talking devil.*

The ten ton snakes—SEE: *Doc Savage: The talking devil; and, The ten ton snakes.*

04196 *The terror in the Navy: a Doc Savage adventure.* Toronto, New York: Bantam Books, 1969, 122 p., paper, novel. DOC SAVAGE #33. [By Lester Dent].

They died twice—SEE: *Doc Savage: They died twice.*

04197 *The Thousand-headed Man: a Doc Savage adventure.* Toronto, New York: Bantam Books, 1964, 150 p., paper, novel. DOC SAVAGE #2. [By Lester Dent].

Three gold crowns—SEE: *The Avenger: Three gold crowns.*

The three wild men—SEE: *Doc Savage: The three wild men.*

The time terror—SEE: *Doc Savage: The pharaoh's ghost; and, The time terror.*

Tuned for murder—SEE: *The Avenger: Tuned for murder.*

21609 *Tunnel terror: a Doc Savage adventure.* Toronto, New York: Bantam Books, 1979, 122 p., paper, novel. DOC SAVAGE #93. [By William G. Bogart].

04198 *The vanisher: a Doc Savage adventure.* Toronto, New York: Bantam Books, 1970, 139 p., paper, novel. DOC SAVAGE #52. [By Lester Dent].

The whisker of Hercules—SEE: *Doc Savage: The whisker of Hercules.*

The Wilder curse—SEE: *The Avenger: The Wilder curse.*

04199 *World's Fair goblin: a Doc Savage adventure.* Toronto, New York: Bantam Books, 1969, 122 p., paper, novel. DOC SAVAGE #39. [By Lester Dent and William G. Bogart].

04200 *The yellow cloud: a Doc Savage adventure.* Toronto, New York: Bantam Books, 1971, 121 p., paper, novel. DOC SAVAGE #59. [By Lester Dent].

The yellow hoard—SEE: *The Avenger: The yellow hoard.*

ROBIN, Doris, with *Lee Vibber & Gracia Fay Ellwood*

22608 *In a faraway galaxy: a literary approach to a film saga.* Pasadena, CA: Extequer Press, 1984, 149 p., paper, nonf.

ROBINETT, Stephen (Allen), 1941-

32486 *The man responsible.* New York: Ace Books, 1978, 245 p., paper, novel.

32487 *Projections.* New York: Ace Books, 1979, x+308 p., paper, coll.

32488 *Stargate.* New York: St. Martin's Press, 1976, 218 p., cloth, novel.

as STEVE HAHN

32489 *Mindwipe!* Toronto, New York: Laser Books, 1976, 190 p., paper, novel.

ROBINSON, Colleen McC.—SEE: McCullough, Colleen

ROBINSON, Douglas (Jack), 1954-

32490 *American apocalypse: the image of the end of the world in American literature.* Baltimore: Johns Hopkins University Press, 1985, xviii+283 p., cloth, nonf.

32491 *John Barth's Giles goat-boy: a study.* Jyväskylä, Finland: University of Jyväskylä, 1980, viii+390 p., paper, nonf.

ROBINSON, Eleanor

32492 *Chrysalis of death.* New York: Pocket Books, 1976, 175 p., paper, novel.

The freak—SEE: *The Silverleaf syndrome.*

32493 *The Silverleaf syndrome.* New York: Tower Books, 1980, 224 p., paper, novel.

32493A retitled: *The freak.* New York: Leisure Books, 1985, 224 p., paper, novel.

ROBINSON, Frank M(alcolm), 1926-

32494 *The dark beyond the stars.* New York: Tor, A Tom Doherty Associates Book, 1991, viii+408 p., cloth, novel.

32495 *A life in the day of..., and other stories.* Toronto, New York: Bantam Books, 1981, 261 p., paper, coll.

with John Levin

28258 *The great divide.* New York: Rawson, Wade Publishers, 1982, 303 p., cloth, novel.

with Thomas N. Scortia

32496 *Blowout!* New York: Franklin Watts, 1987, 393 p., cloth, novel.

32497 *The nightmare factor.* Garden City, NY: Doubleday & Co., 1978, 335 p., cloth, novel.

32498 *The prometheus crisis.* Garden City, NY: Doubleday & Co., 1975, xiv+321 p., cloth, novel.

ROBINSON, Frank S(teven), 1947-

32499 *Children of the dragon.* New York: Avon, 1978, viii+438 p., paper, novel.

ROBINSON, Jeanne (Marie Rubbicco), 1948- , with Spider Robinson

32500 *Stardance.* New York: Quantum Science Fiction, Dial Press/James Wade, 1979, x+278 p., cloth, novel. STARDANCE #1.

32501 *Starseed.* New York: Ace Books, 1991, 247 p., cloth, novel. STARDANCE #2.

ROBINSON, Kim Stanley, 1952-

32502 *Black air.* Eugene, OR: Pulphouse Publishing, 1991, 43 p., paper, story. SHORT STORY PAPERBACKS #20.

32503 *The blind geometer.* New Castle, VA: Cheap Street, 1986, 92 p., cloth, story. [Limited to 177 copies].

32504 *The blind geometer; [The return from rainbow bridge].* New York: Tor SF, A Tom Doherty Associates Book, 1989, 87 p., paper, coll. [Bound with *The new Atlantis* / by Ursula K. Le Guin].

32505 *Escape from Kathmandu.* Seattle, WA: Axolotl Press, 1988, 75 p., cloth, coll. AXOLOTL DOUBLE #3; AXOLOTL PRESS #7. [Bound with: *Two views of a cave painting* / by James P. Blaylock].

32506 *Escape from Kathmandu.* Norwalk, CT: Easton Press, 1989, 314 p., cloth, coll. [Expanded edition].

32507 *The gold coast.* New York: St. Martin's Press, 1988, 389 p., cloth, novel. ORANGE COUNTY #2.

32508 *Green Mars.* New York: Tor SF, A Tom Doherty Associates Book, 1988, 113 p., paper, story. [Bound with: *A meeting with Medusa* / by Arthur C. Clarke].

32509 *Icehenge.* New York: Ace Science Fiction Books, 1984, 262 p., paper, novel.

32510 *The memory of whiteness: a scientific romance.* New York: Tom Doherty Associates, 1985, 351 p., cloth, novel.

32511 *The novels of Philip K. Dick.* Ann Arbor, MI: UMI Research Press, 1984, xii+150 p., cloth, nonf. STUDIES IN SPECULATIVE FICTION #9.

32512 *Pacific edge.* London: Unwin Hyman, 1990, 280 p., cloth, novel. ORANGE COUNTY #3. [Winner of the John W. Campbell Jr. Memorial Award for Best Novel, 1990 (1991)].

32513 *The planet on the table.* New York: Tor, A Tom Doherty Associates Book, 1986, xiv+241 p., cloth, coll.

32514 *Remaking history.* New York: Tor, A Tom Doherty Associates Book, 1991, x+274 p., cloth, coll.

32515 *A sensitive dependence on initial conditions.* Eugene, OR: Pulphouse Publishing, 1991, 79 p., cloth, coll. AUTHOR'S CHOICE MONTHLY #20. [Includes some nonfiction].

32516 *A short, sharp shock.* Shingletown, CA: Mark V. Ziesing, 1990, 147 p., cloth, novel.

32517 *The wild shore.* New York: Ace Science Fiction Books, 1984, viii+371 p., paper, novel. ORANGE COUNTY #1. [Winner of the *Locus* Award for Best First Novel, 1984 (1985)].

ROBINSON, Logan (Gilmore), 1949-

32518 *Evil star = Beda.* New York: W. W. Norton & Co., 1986, 238 p., cloth, novel.

ROBINSON, Nigel

Apocalypse—SEE: *Timewyrm: Apocalypse.*

32519 *The Doctor Who crossword book.* London: A Target Book, W. H. Allen & Co., 1982, 125 p., paper, nonf.

32520 *The Doctor Who quiz book.* London: A Target Book, W. H. Allen & Co., 1981, 128 p., paper, nonf.

32521 *Doctor Who: The edge of destruction.* London: W. H. Allen & Co., 1988, 120 p., cloth, tele. DOCTOR WHO #132.

32522 *Doctor Who: The sensorites.* London: W. H. Allen & Co., 1987, 143 p., cloth, tele. DOCTOR WHO #118.

32523 *Doctor Who: The time meddler.* London: W. H. Allen & Co., 1987, 141 p., cloth, tele. DOCTOR WHO #126.

32524 *Doctor Who: The underwater menace.* London: W. H. Allen & Co., 1988, 137 p., cloth, tele. DOCTOR WHO #129.

The edge of destruction—SEE: *Doctor Who: The edge of destruction.*

32525 *The second Doctor Who quiz book.* London: A Target Book, W. H. Allen & Co., 1983, 125 p., paper, nonf.

The sensorites—SEE: *Doctor Who: The sensorites.*

32526 *The third Doctor Who quiz book.* London: A Target Book, W. H. Allen & Co., 1985, 141 p., paper, nonf.

The time meddler—SEE: *Doctor Who: The time meddler.*

32527 *Timewyrm: Apocalypse.* London: Doctor Who Books, 1991, 201 p., paper, tele. DOCTOR WHO: THE NEW ADVENTURES #3.

The underwater menace—SEE: *Doctor Who: The underwater menace*.

with Linda Wilson

32528 *The Tolkien quiz book*. London: Star Books, 1981, 115 p., paper, nonf.

ROBINSON, Paul—SEE: Robinson, Spider

ROBINSON, Roger, 1943-

32529 *Ace science-fiction double books*. Harold Wood, Essex, England: Beccon Publications, 1987, 16 p., paper, nonf.
32530 *DAW science-fiction books*. Harold Wood, Essex, England: Beccon Publications, 1987, 20 p., paper, nonf.
32531 *Hale & Gresham hardback science fiction*. Harold Wood, Essex, England: Beccon Publications, 1988, 16 p., paper, nonf.
32532 *Science fiction and fantasy magazines, 1923-1980*. Harold Wood, Essex, England: Beccon Publications, 1984, 28 p., paper, nonf.
32533 *Who's Hugh? an SF reader's guide to pseudonyms*. Harold Wood, Essex, England: Beccon Publications, 1987, 173 p., cloth, nonf.
32534 *The writings of Henry Kenneth Bulmer*. Harold Wood, Essex, England: Beccon Publications, 1983, 51 p., paper, nonf.
32535 *The writings of Henry Kenneth Bulmer, rev. and updated ed*. Harold Wood, Essex, England: Beccon Publications, 1984, 51 p., paper, nonf.

ROBINSON, Sally, 1959-

32536 *Engendering the subject: gender and self-representation in contemporary women's fiction*. Albany, NY: State University of New York Press, 1991, x+248 p., cloth, nonf.

ROBINSON, Spider [i.e., Paul Robinson], 1948-

32537 *Antinomy*. New York: A Dell Book, 1980, 312 p., paper, coll.
32538 *The best of all possible worlds*. New York: Ace Books, 1980, 373 p., paper, anth.
32539 *Callahan and company: the compleat chronicles of the Crosstime Saloon*. West Bloomfield, MI: Phantasia Press, 1987, xiii+256 p., cloth, coll. CALLAHAN'S CROSSTIME SALOON #1-3.
32539A retitled: *Callahan's crazy crosstime bar*. London: Legend, 1989, 351 p., paper, coll. CALLAHAN'S CROSSTIME SALOON #1-3. [Abridged edition].

Callahan's crazy crosstime bar—SEE: *Callahan and company*.

32540 *Callahan's Crosstime Saloon*. New York: Ace Books, 1977, 170 p., paper, coll. CALLAHAN'S CROSSTIME SALOON #1.
32541 *Callahan's lady*. New York: Ace Books, 1989, 191 p., cloth, coll. CALLAHAN'S CROSSTIME SALOON #4.
32542 *Callahan's secret*. New York: Berkley Books, 1986, xii+172 p., paper, coll. CALLAHAN'S CROSSTIME SALOON #3.
32543 *Copyright violation*. Eugene, OR: Pulphouse Publishing, 1990, 30 p., cloth, story. CONVENTION SERIES #2.
32544 *Kill the editor*. Eugene, OR: Axolotl Press, Pulphouse Publishing, 1991, 153 p., cloth, novel. AXOLOTL SPECIAL EDITION #2. [An excerpt from the forthcoming work, *The lady slings the booze*].
32545 *Melancholy elephants*. Marchmont, Ontario, Canada: Penguin Books Canada, 1984, xiv+239 p., paper, coll.
32546 *Melancholy elephants*. New York: Tor SF, A Tom Doherty Associates Book, 1985, 244 p., paper, coll. [Adds two stories and drops one].
32547 *Mindkiller: a novel of the near future*. New York: Holt, Rinehart & Winston, 1982, viii+278 p., cloth, novel. MINDKILLER #1.
32548 *Night of power*. New York: A Baen Book, 1985, 287 p., cloth, novel.
32549 *Telempath*. New York: Berkley Publishing Corp., 1976, 223 p., cloth, novel.
32550 *Time pressure*. New York: Ace books, 1987, 216 p., cloth, novel. MINDKILLER #2.
32551 *Time travelers strictly cash*. New York: Ace Books, 1981, 200 p., paper, coll. CALLAHAN'S CROSSTIME SALOON #2.
32552 *True minds*. Eugene, OR: Pulphouse Publishing, 1990, 108 p., cloth, coll. AUTHOR'S CHOICE MONTHLY #12. [Includes some verse and nonfiction].

with Jeanne Robinson

32500 *Stardance*. New York: Quantum Science Fiction, Dial Press/James Wade, 1979, x+278 p., cloth, novel. STARDANCE #1.
32501 *Starseed*. New York: Ace Books, 1991, 247 p., cloth, novel. STARDANCE #2.

ROBINSON, Sue

32553 *The amendment: a novel*. New York: Birch Lane Press, 1990, 237 p., cloth, novel.

ROBINSON, Ursula—SEE: Bloom, Robinson

ROBITAILLE, Julie

The beginning—SEE: *Quantum leap: The beginning.*

The ghost and the gumshoe—SEE: *Quantum leap: The ghost and the gumshoe.*

32554 *Quantum leap: The beginning.* London: Corgi Books, 1990, 191 p., paper, tele. QUANTUM LEAP #1.

32555 *Quantum leap: The ghost and the gumshoe.* London: Corgi Books, 1990, 192 p., paper, tele. QUANTUM LEAP #2.

ROBSON, Michael, 1931-

32556 *Holocaust 2000.* London: Sphere Books, 1978, 171 p., paper, movie.

ROCHLIN, Doris, 1932-

32557 *Frobisch's angel.* New York: Taplinger Publishing Co., 1987, 331 p., cloth, novel.

ROCHON, Esther, 1948-

32558 *The shell.* Ottawa, Ontario, Canada: Oberon Press, 1990, 125 p., cloth, novel. [Translation by David Lobdell of *Coquillage*].

ROCK, James A(nthony), 1929-

32559 *Who goes there? a bibliographic dictionary, being a guide to the works of authors who have contributed to the literature of fantasy and science fiction and who have published some or all of their work pseudonymously.* Bloomington, IN: James A. Rock & Co., 1979, viii+201 p., cloth, nonf.

ROCKLIN, Ross—SEE: Rocklynne, Ross

*ROCKLYNNE, Ross [pseud. of Ross Louis Rocklin], 1913-1988

ROCKWOOD, Roy, house pseud.—SEE: Garis, Howard R. & Stratemeyer, Edward L.

RODDA, Emily [pseud. of Jennifer June Rowe], 1948-

32560 *The best-kept secret.* North Ryde, New South Wales, Australia: Angus & Robertson, 1988, 114 p., cloth, novel.

32561 *Finders keepers.* Adelaide, South Australia, Australia: Omnibus Books, 1990, p., cloth, novel.

The pigs are flying!—SEE: *Pigs might fly.*

32562 *Pigs might fly.* North Ryde, New South Wales, Australia: Angus & Robertson, 1986, 118 p., cloth, novel.

32562A retitled: *The pigs are flying!* New York: Greenwillow Books, 1988, 137 p., cloth, novel.

RODDENBERRY, Eugene W.—SEE: Roddenberry, Gene

RODDENBERRY, Gene [i.e., Eugene Wesley Roddenberry], 1921-1991

32563 *Star Trek: the motion picture: a novel.* New York: Simon & Schuster, 1979, 252 p., cloth, movie. STAR TREK #1.

with Susan Sackett

32564 *The making of Star Trek, the motion picture.* New York: A Wallaby Book, Pocket Books, 1980, xvii+221 p., paper, nonf.

RODECAPE, Marjorie—SEE: Rather, Lois

RODGERS, Alan (Paul), 1959-

32565 *Blood of the children.* New York, Toronto: Bantam Books, 1990, 299 p., paper, novel.

32566 *Fire.* New York, Toronto: Bantam Books, 1990, 505 p., paper, novel.

32567 *New life for the dead.* Newark, NJ: Wildside Press, 1991, 134 p., cloth, coll. [Includes some verse].

32568 *Night.* New York, Toronto: Spectra, Bantam Books, 1991, 439 p., paper, novel.

RODGERS, Jesse

38036 *ESP McGee and the dolphin's message.* New York: An Avon Camelot Book, 1984, 92 p., paper, novel. ESP McGEE #6.

RODGERS, Mary, 1931-

32569 *Summer switch.* New York: Harper & Row, 1982, 185 p., cloth, novel. ANNABEL #3.

RODIS-JAMERO, Nilo, *with Joe Johnston*

26646 *The Empire Strikes Back sketchbook.* New York: Ballantine Books, 1980, 95 p., paper, art.

26647 *The Return of the Jedi sketchbook.* New York: Ballantine Books, 1983, 96 p., paper, art.

RODOWSKY, Colby (F.), 1932-

38037 *Keeping time.* New York: Farrar Straus Giroux, 1983, 137 p., cloth, novel.

RODRIGUES, Raymond J., *with John Pfordresher & with Thomas E. Gage & Edmund J. Farrell*

22917 *Fantasy: shapes of things unknown.* Glenview, IL & Dallas, TX: Scott, Foresman & Co., 1974, 384 p., paper, anth. [Includes some nonfiction].

RODRIGUEZ, Christine—SEE: Gentry, Christine

RODRIGUEZ MONEGAL, Emir, 1921-1985

32570 *Jorge Luis Borges: a literary biography.* New York: E. P. Dutton, 1978, ix+502 p., cloth, nonf.

*ROE, Richard L(ionel), 1936-

ROEHM, Bob

32571 *A Thomas Burnett Swann bibliography.* Clarksville, IN: Bob Roehm, 1976, [4] p., paper, nonf.
32572 *A Thomas Burnett Swann bibliography, rev. ed.* Clarksville, IN: Bob Roehm, 1978, [4] p., paper, nonf. [Includes one-page supplement].

ROEMER, Kenneth M(orrison), 1925-

32573 *America as utopia.* New York: Burt Franklin, 1981, vi+410 p., cloth, nonf. anth.
32574 *The obsolete necessity: America in utopian writings, 1888-1900 .* Kent, OH: Kent State University Press, 1976, xiv+239 p., cloth, nonf.

with Gorman Beauchamp & Nicholas D. Smith

17633 *Utopian studies 1.* Lanham, MD: University Press of America, 1987, v+197 p., cloth, nonf. anth.

ROESSNER, Michaela [i.e., Michaela-Marie Roessner-Herman]

32575 *Walkabout woman.* Toronto, New York: Spectra, Bantam Books, 1988, 276 p., paper, novel.

ROESSNER-HERMAN, Michaela—SEE: Roessner, Michaela

*ROGERS, Alva (C.), 1923-1982

ROGERS, Barbara (J.), 1945-

32576 *Project Web.* New York: Dodd, Mead & Co., 1980, 241 p., cloth, novel.

ROGERS, Dave

32577 *The Avengers.* London: ITV Books & Michael Joseph, 1983, 189 p., paper, nonf.
32578 *The Avengers anew: a fantastic story told by an extraordinary fan.* London: Michael Joseph, 1985, 120 p., paper, nonf.
32579 *The complete Avengers: everything you ever wanted to know about The Avengers and The New Avengers.* London: Boxtree Press, 1989, 285 p., paper, nonf. [Includes *The Avengers* and *The Avengers,* with additional material].
32580 *The Prisoner and Danger Man.* London: Boxtree Press, 1989, 254 p., paper, nonf.

with John Peel

31413 *The Avengers: too many targets.* New York: St. Martin's Press, 1990, 181 p., paper, nonf.
*Too many targets—*SEE: *The Avengers; too many targets.*

ROGERS, Deborah Webster, *with Ivor A. Rogers*

32581 *J. R. R. Tolkien.* Boston: Twayne Publishers, 1980, 164 p., cloth, nonf. TWAYNE ENGLISH AUTHOR SERIES #304.
32582 *J. R. R. Tolkien: a critical biography.* New York: Hippocrene Books, 1980, 164 p., cloth, nonf.

ROGERS, Ivor A., *with Deborah Webster Rogers*

32581 *J. R. R. Tolkien.* Boston: Twayne Publishers, 1980, 164 p., cloth, nonf. TWAYNE ENGLISH AUTHOR SERIES #304.
32582 *J. R. R. Tolkien: a critical biography.* New York: Hippocrene Books, 1980, 164 p., cloth, nonf.

ROGERS, Mark

32583 *The dead.* New York: Berkley Books, 1989, 297 p., paper, novel.

ROGERS, Mark E(arl), 1952-

32584 *The adventures of Samurai Cat.* West Kingston, RI: Donald M. Grant, 1984, 124 p., cloth, novel. SAMURAI CAT #1.

32585 *The blood of the lamb: The devouring void.* New York: Ace Books, 1991, ix+213 p., paper, novel. BLOOD OF THE LAMB #2.

32586 *The blood of the lamb: The expected one.* New York: Ace Books, 1991, 230 p., paper, novel. BLOOD OF THE LAMB #1.

32587 *The bridge of Catzad-Dûm, and other stories.* Newark, DE: The Burning Bush Press, 1980, 62 p., paper, coll. [Limited to 500 copies].
The devouring void—SEE: *The blood of the lamb: The devouring void.*
The expected one—SEE: *The blood of the lamb: The expected one.*

32588 *More adventures of Samurai Cat.* New York: Tor Books, 1986, 127 p., paper, novel. SAMURAI CAT #2.

32589 *The nightmare of God.* New York: Ace Books, 1988, 278 p., paper, novel. ZORACHUS #2.

32590 *The runestone.* Newark, DE: The Burning Bush Press, 1979, 71 p., paper, novel. [Limited to 200 copies].

32591 *Samurai Cat in the real world.* New York: Tor Books, 1989, 127 p., paper, novel. SAMURAI CAT #3.

32592 *The sword of Samurai Cat.* New York: Tor Books, 1991, 307 p., paper, novel. SAMURAI CAT #4.

32593 *Zorachus.* New York: Ace Fantasy Books, 1986, 298 p., paper, novel. ZORACHUS #1.

ROGERS, Michael (Alan), 1950-

32594 *Forbidden sequence.* Toronto, New York: Bantam Books, 1988, 329 p., paper, novel.

ROGERS, Patrick F.

32595 *War god.* New York: Pinnacle Books, Windsor Publishing Corp., 1990, 443 p., paper, novel.

ROGERS, Tom, 1948-

32596 *Spaceships.* New York: O'Quinn Studios, 1977, 32 p., paper, nonf.

ROGERS, Wayne

32597 *When the banshee calls: a story from Terror tales.* North Hollywood, CA: Shroud: Publishers, 1975, 54 p., paper, story. PULP READER #1.

ROGERSOHN, William, pseud.—SEE: Hughes, Dennis Talbot

ROGOW, Roberta (Winston), 1942-

32598 *Futurespeak: a fan's guide to the language of science fiction.* New York: Paragon House, 1991, xx+408 p., cloth, nonf.

32599 *Trexindex.* [S.l.: April Publications and Starfleet Productions], 1977, 34 p., paper, nonf.

32600 *Trexindex, volumes II/III.* Brooklyn, NY: Poison Pen Press, 1978, 107 p., paper, nonf.

32601 *Trexindex, volumes IV/V.* Fairlawn, NJ: Roberta Rogow, 1978, 83 p., paper, nonf.

32602 *Trexindex supplement, volume I.* Fairlawn, NJ: Other Worlds Books, 1979, 124 p., paper, nonf.

32603 *Trexindex supplement, volume II.* Fairlawn, NJ: Roberta Rogow, 1980, 72 p., paper, nonf.

32604 *Trexindex second supplement, volume I.* Fairlawn, NJ: Other Worlds Books, 1981, 107 p., paper, nonf.

32605 *Trexindex second supplement, volume II.* Fairlawn, NJ: Other Worlds Books, 1982, 78 p., paper, nonf.

32606 *Trexindex third supplement, volume I.* Fairlawn, NJ: Other Worlds Books, 1984, 94 p., paper, nonf.

32607 *Trexindex third supplement, volume II.* Fairlawn, NJ: Other Worlds Books, (1985?), 64 p., paper, nonf.

32608 *Trexindex fourth supplement, volume one.* Fairlawn, NJ: Other Worlds Books, 1986, 92 p., paper, nonf.

32609 *Trexindex fourth supplement, volume two.* Fairlawn, NJ: Other Worlds Books, 1987, 64 p., paper, nonf.

ROHAN, Michael Scott, 1951-

32610 *The anvil of ice.* London: Macdonald, 1986, 348 p., cloth, novel. WINTER OF THE WORLD #1.

32611 *Chase the morning.* London: Orbit, 1990, 334 p., paper, novel.

32612 *The forge in the forest.* London: Macdonald, 1987, 408 p., cloth, novel. WINTER OF THE WORLD #2.

32613 *The hammer of the sun.* London: Macdonald, 1988, 502 p., cloth, novel. WINTER OF THE WORLD #3.

32614 *Run to the stars* / by Mike Scott Rohan. London: Arrow Books, 1982, 295 p., paper, novel.

with Allan J. Scott as MICHAEL SCOT

Burial rites—SEE: *The Ice King.*
32615 *The Ice King.* London: New English Library, 1986, 252 p., cloth, novel.
32615A retitled: *Burial rites.* New York: Berkley Books, 1987, 248 p., paper, novel.

ROHDE, William L(aurence), *as* NICK CARTER

02747 *The human time bomb: a Killmaster spy chiller.* New York: Award Books; London: Tandem Books, 1969, 154 p., paper, novel. NICK CARTER SERIES.

ROHMER, Richard (H.), 1924-

32616 *Balls!* Don Mills, Ontario, Canada: General Publishing Co., 1980, 346 p., cloth, novel.
32617 *Exodus/UK.* Toronto: McClelland & Stewart, 1975, 256 p., cloth, novel. SEPARATION #1.
32618 *Exxoneration.* London: McClelland & Stewart, 1974, 213 p., cloth, novel. ULTIMATUM #2.
32619 *Periscope red.* Don Mills, Ontario, Canada: General Publishing Co., 1980, 282 p., cloth, novel. TRIAD #1.
32620 *Retaliation.* Don Mills, Ontario, Canada: General Publishing Co., 1982, 293 p., cloth, novel.
32621 *Separation.* Toronto: McClelland & Stewart, 1976, 240 p., cloth, novel. SEPARATION #2.
32622 *Separation two.* Markham, Ontario: PaperJacks Ltd., 1981, 256 p., paper, novel. SEPARATION #3.
32623 *Starmageddon.* Toronto: Irwin, 1986, 241 p., cloth, novel.
32624 *Triad.* Don Mills, Ontario, Canada: General Publishing Co., 1982, 264 p., cloth, novel. TRIAD #2.

ROHMER, Sax [pseud. of Arthur Henry Ward (later Arthur Sarsfield Ward)], 1883-1959

32625 *Fu-Manchu: four classic novels.* Secaucus, NJ: Citadel Press, 1983, 434 p., paper, coll. FU MANCHU SERIES. [Includes *The hand of Fu Manchu, The return of Dr. Fu-Manchu, The yellow claw, Dope*].
12406A *Wulfheim.* London: Bookfinger, 1972, 208 p., cloth, novel. [Originally published under the name Michael Furey].

ROJO, Salvador Madariaga y—SEE: Madariaga, Salvador

ROKEYA, Begum [i.e., Rokeya Sakhawat Hossain, Begum], 1880-1932

32626 *Sultana's dream, and selections from The secluded ones.* New York: Feminist Press, 1988, xii+89 p., paper, coll. [Edited and translated by Roushan Jahan from *Abarodha-basini*].

ROLAND, Howell Jr.

32627 *The living stone.* New York: Manor Books, 1980, 236 p., paper, novel.

ROLAND, Paul

32628 *The curious case of Richard Fielding, and other stories.* England: Lary Press, 1987, 95 p., paper, coll. [Includes some verse].

ROLFE, Christopher, 1938- , *with Patrick Parrinder*

31239 *H. G. Wells under revision: proceedings of the International H. G. Wells Symposium, London, July 1986.* Selinsgrove, PA: Susquehanna University Press; London: Associated University Presses, 1990, 263 p., cloth, nonf. anth.

ROLLO, William

32629 *The big wheel.* London: New English Library, 1984, 283 p., cloth, novel.

ROLLS, Dana Kramer- —SEE: Kramer, Dana

ROLSTON, Ken

32630 *Extreme paranoia: Nobody knows the trouble I've shot.* Honesdale, PA: West End Games, 1991, 346 p., paper, novel.

with Douglas Niles & Bruce Nesmith

30637 *Lankhmar, city of adventure.* Lake Geneva, WI: TSR Inc., 1985, 95 p., paper, novel. FAFHRD & GREY MOUSER.

ROMAINS, Jules [pseud. of Louis Farigoule], 1885-1972

15857 *Tussles with time.* London: Sidgwick & Jackson, 1952, 243 p., cloth, novel.

ROMBERG, Nina [i.e., Nina Romberg Andersson]

32631 *The spirit stalker.* New York: Pinnacle Books, Windsor Publishing Corp., 1989, 315 p., paper, novel.

with C. Dean Andersson as ASA DRAKE

16464 *Crimson kisses.* New York: Avon, 1981, 292 p., paper, novel. DRACULA SEQUEL.
16465 *The lair of ancient dreams.* New York: Avon, 1982, 239 p., paper, novel.

ROMERO, George A(ndrew), 1940- , *with Susanna Sparrow*

32632 *Dawn of the dead.* New York: St. Martin's Press, 1978, 210 p., paper, movie.
32633 *Martin: a novel.* New York: Stein & Day, 1977, 213 p., cloth, novel.

ROMIJN, Hanna Kooyker- —SEE: Kooiker, Leonie

ROMILUS, Arn, house pseud.—SEE: Holloway, Brian & Hughes, Dennis Talbot

ROMINE, Aden F(oster), *with Mary C(ox) Romine*

32634 *The Eternity Stone* / by Aden Foster Romine and Mary Cox Romine. New York: Tower Books, 1981, 335 p., paper, novel.
32635 *The fellowship.* New York: Leisure Books, 1984, 382 p., paper, novel.

ROMINE, Mary C(ox), *with Aden F(oster) Romine*

32634 *The Eternity Stone* / by Aden Foster Romine and Mary Cox Romine. New York: Tower Books, 1981, 335 p., paper, novel.
32635 *The fellowship.* New York: Leisure Books, 1984, 382 p., paper, novel.

ROMKEY, Michael

32636 *Fears point.* New York: Fawcett Gold Medal, 1989, 311 p., paper, novel.
32637 *I, vampire.* New York: Fawcett Gold Medal, 1990, 360 p., paper, novel.

RONALD, Mark, *with A. Stover*

35105 *Brains for Janes.* New Orleans, LA [i.e., Los Angeles, CA]: Pirate Press, 1948, 47 p., cloth, anth.

RONN, Yuval—SEE: Ionel

RONSON, Mark, pseud.—SEE: Alexander, Marc

ROONEY, Charles J. (Jr.), 1935-

32645 *Dreams and visions: a study of American utopias, 1865-1917.* Westport, CT: Greenwood Press, 1985, xi+209 p., cloth, nonf.

*ROOT, Albert (Waldo), 1891-1990

ROQUELAURE, A. N., pseud.—SEE: Rice, Anne

RORVIK, David (Michael), 1946-

32646A *Sabra.* London: Sphere Books, 1983, xiii+287 p., paper, novel. [Originally published as *The sharing* under the name M. M. Faraday].

as M. M. FARADAY

32646 *The sharing.* Toronto, New York: Bantam Books, 1982, xiii+287 p., paper, novel.

ROSCOE, Theodore, 1906-1992

A grave must be deep—SEE: *Theodore Roscoe's A grave must be deep.*
32647 *Theodore Roscoe's A grave must be deep.* Mercer Island, WA: Starmont House, 1989, 120 p., cloth, novel. STARMONT FACSIMILE FICTION #1.
32648 *Theodore Roscoe's Z is for zombie.* Mercer Island, WA: Starmont House, 1989, 140 p., cloth, coll. STARMONT FACSIMILE FICTION #2.
32649 *The wonderful lips of Thibong Linh.* West Kingston, RI: Donald M. Grant, Publisher, 1981, 193 p., cloth, coll.
Z is for zombie—SEE: *Theodore Roscoe's Z is for zombie.*

ROSE, Christine Brooke- —SEE: Brooke-Rose, Christine

ROSE, Mark (Allen), 1939-

32650 *Alien encounters: anatomy of science fiction.* Cambridge, MA & London: Harvard University Press, 1981, 216 p., cloth, nonf. [Winner of the J. Lloyd Eaton Award for Best Nonfiction Book of the Year, 1981 (1983)].

32651 *Science fiction: a collection of critical essays.* Englewood Cliffs, NJ: Prentice-Hall, 1976, x + 174 p., cloth, nonf. anth.

with George E. Slusser & George R. Guffey

24813 *Bridges to science fiction.* Carbondale & Edwardsville, IL: Southern Illinois University Press; London & Amsterdam: Feffer & Simons, 1980, viii + 168 p., cloth, nonf. anth. PROCEEDINGS OF THE J. LLOYD EATON CONFERENCE ON SCIENCE FICTION AND FANTASY LITERATURE #1.

ROSE, Pamela

32652 *Companion: the rest of the story.* Jersey City, NJ: [Pamela Rose?], 1980, p., paper, novel. STAR TREK SERIES.

ROSE, Richard, 1933-

32653 *The Wolf.* New York: Zebra Books, Kensington Publishing Corp., 1980, 286 p., paper, novel.

*ROSE, Stephen (C.), 1936-

ROSENBERG, Betty, 1916-

32654 *Genreflecting: a guide to reading interests in genre fiction.* Littleton, CO: Libraries Unlimited, 1982, 254 p., cloth, nonf.

32655 *Genreflecting: a guide to reading interests in genre fiction, 2nd ed.* Littleton, CO: Libraries Unlimited, 1986, xxviii + 298 p., cloth, nonf.

with Diana Tixier Herald

32656 *Genreflecting: a guide to reading interests in genre fiction, 3rd ed.* Littleton, CO: Libraries Unlimited, 1991, xxv + 345 p., cloth, nonf.

ROSENBERG, Joel, 1954-

32657 *D'Shai.* New York: Ace Books, 1991, 527 p., paper, novel. D'SHAI #1.

32658 *Emile and the Dutchman.* New York: A Signet Book, New American Library, 1986, 254 p., paper, novel. METZADA #2.

32659 *Guardians of the flame: The heroes.* New York: Guild America Books, 1989, 438 p., cloth, coll. GUARDIANS OF THE FLAME #4-5.

32660 *Guardians of the flame: The warriors.* Garden City, NY: Nelson Doubleday, 1985, 722 p., cloth, coll. GUARDIANS OF THE FLAME #1-3.

32661 *The heir apparent.* New York: A Signet Book, New American Library, 1987, 319 p., paper, novel. GUARDIANS OF THE FLAME #4.

32662 *Hero.* New York: A Roc Book, 1990, 259 p., cloth, novel. METADA #4.

The heroes—SEE: *Guardians of the flame: The heroes.*

32663 *Not for glory.* New York: NAL Books, 1988, 232 p., cloth, novel. METZADA #3.

32664 *The road to Ehvenor: a Guardians of the Flame novel.* New York: A Roc Book, 1991, 312 p., cloth, novel. GUARDIANS OF THE FLAME #6.

32665 *The silver crown: a fantastic novel.* New York: A Signet Book, New American Library, 1985, 302 p., paper, novel. GUARDIANS OF THE FLAME #3.

32666 *The sleeping dragon: a fantasy novel.* New York: A Signet Book, New American Library, 1983, 253 p., paper, novel. GUARDIANS OF THE FLAME #1.

32667 *The sword and the chain.* New York: A Signet Book, New American Library, 1984, 251 p., paper, novel. GUARDIANS OF THE FLAME #2.

32668 *Ties of blood and silver.* New York: A Signet Book, New American Library, 1984, 176 p., paper, novel. METZADA #1.

32669 *The warrior lives.* New York: NAL Books, 1989, 260 p., cloth, novel. GUARDIANS OF THE FLAME #5.

The warriors—SEE: *Guardians of the flame: The warriors.*

with Simon Michael as PETER MICHAEL

29811 *The usurper.* London: Grafton, 1988, 303 p., paper, novel.

ROSENBERGER, Joseph (R.)

The Atlantean horror—SEE: *The Death Merchant: The Atlantean horror.*

Blueprint invisibility—SEE: *Death Merchant: Blueprint invisibility.*

32670 *The Budapest action.* New York: Pinnacle Books, 1977, 202 p., paper, novel. DEATH MERCHANT #23.

The burning blue death—SEE: *Death Merchant: The burning blue death.*

32671 *Death Merchant: Blueprint invisibility.* Los Angeles: Pinnacle Books, 1980, 181 p., paper, novel. DEATH MERCHANT #40.

32672 *Death Merchant: Invasion of the clones.* New York: Pinnacle Books, 1976, 181 p., paper, novel. DEATH MERCHANT #16.

32673 *Death Merchant: Island of the damned.* New York: Pinnacle Books, 1981, 185 p., paper, novel. DEATH MERCHANT #44.

32674 *Death Merchant: The Atlantean horror.* New York: Pinnacle Books, 1985, 242 p., paper, novel. DEATH MERCHANT #64.

32675 *Death Merchant: The burning blue death.* Los Angeles: Pinnacle Books, 1980, 183 p., paper, novel. DEATH MERCHANT #38.

32676 *Death Merchant: The Shambhala strike.* Los Angeles: Pinnacle Books, 1978, 208 p., paper, novel. DEATH MERCHANT #30.

32677 *The flight of the Phoenix.* New York: Pinnacle Books, 1982, 198 p., paper, novel. DEATH MERCHANT #52.

32678 *The Greenland mystery.* New York: A Dell Book, 1988, 188 p., paper, novel. DEATH MERCHANT #70.

32679 *Hell in Hindu land.* New York: Pinnacle Books, 1977, 198 p., paper, novel. DEATH MERCHANT #20.

Invasion of the clones—SEE: *Death Merchant: Invasion of the clones.*

Island of the damned—SEE: *Death Merchant: Island of the damned.*

32680 *Operation Skyhook.* New York: Pinnacle Books, 1981, 202 p., paper, novel. DEATH MERCHANT #47 .

32681 *The Pole Star secret.* New York: Pinnacle Books, 1977, 195 p., paper, novel. DEATH MERCHANT #21.

32682 *The psionics war.* New York: Pinnacle Books, 1982, 185 p., paper, novel. DEATH MERCHANT #48.

The Shambhala strike—SEE: *Death Merchant: The Shambhala strike.*

32683 *The Zemlya expedition.* New York: Pinnacle Books, 1976, 177 p., paper, novel. DEATH MERCHANT #17.

ROSENBLUM, Robert—SEE: Maxxe, Robert

ROSENTHAL, Bernard, 1934-

32684 *Critical essays on Charles Brockden Brown.* Boston: G. K. Hall & Co., 1981, vii+246 p., cloth, nonf. anth.

ROSHEIM, David L.

32685 *Galaxy magazine: the dark and the light years.* Chicago, IL: Advent:Publishers, 1986, xvi+343 p., cloth, nonf.

ROSINSKY, Natalie M(yra), 1951-

32686 *Feminist futures: contemporary women's speculative fiction.* Ann Arbor, MI: UMI Research Press, 1984, 146 p., cloth, nonf. STUDIES IN SPECULATIVE FICTION #1.

*ROSKOLENKO, Harry, 1907-1980

*ROSMANITH, Olga (L.), 1893-1978

ROSNY, J.-H., Aîné [pseud. of Joseph-Henri-Honoré Boëx-Borel], 1856-1940

32687 *The Xipehuz; and, The death of the Earth.* New York: Arno Press, 1978, xxii+183 p., cloth, coll. [Translation by George Edgar Slusser of *Le Xipéhuz*; and, *La mort de la terre*].

with Philip José Farmer

22910 *Ironcastle.* New York: DAW Books, 1976, 175 p., paper, novel. [Translation and adaptation by Farmer of *L'Etonnante aventure de Hareton Ironcastle*].

ROSS, A. Joseph

32688 *The Boskone 14 filksong supplement.* Cambridge, MA: NESFA Press, 1977, 27 p., paper, nonf. anth.

32689 *The NESFA hymnal, second edition* / edited by Joe Ross. Cambridge, MA: NESFA Press, 1979, vi+211 p., paper, nonf. anth.

with Kris Benders

17734 *Boskone 10 filksongbook.* Cambridge, MA: New England Science Fiction Association, 1973, 22 p., paper, nonf. anth.

ROSS, Bernard L., pseud.—SEE: Follett, Ken

ROSS, Clarissa, pseud.—SEE: Ross, Dan

ROSS, Dan [i.e., William Edward Daniel Ross], 1912-

as CLARISSA ROSS

32690 *The corridors of fear.* New York: Avon, 1971, 172 p., paper, novel.

32691 *Satan whispers.* New York: Leisure Books, 1981, 297 p., paper, novel.

32692 *Secret of the pale lover.* New York: Lancer Books, 1969, 222 p., paper, novel.

32693 *Summer of the shaman.* New York: Warner Books, 1982, 222 p., paper, novel.

as MARILYN ROSS

38038 *The amethyst of tears.* New York: Beagle Books, 1975, 182 p., paper, novel. BIRTHSTONE GOTHIC #2.

38039 *The ghost and the garnet.* New York: Beagle Books, 1975, 184 p., paper, novel. BIRTHSTONE GOTHIC #1.

38040 *Shadow over Emerald Castle.* New York: Ballantine Books, 1975, 180 p., paper, novel. BIRTHSTONE GOTHIC #5.

ROSS, David D., 1949?-

32694 *The Argus gambit.* New York: St. Martin's Press, 1989, 406 p., cloth, novel. DREAMERS OF THE DAY #1.

32695 *The eighth rank.* New York: St. Martin's Press, 1991, xiii+461 p., cloth, novel. DREAMERS OF THE DAY #2.

ROSS, Ian, pseud.—SEE: Rossmann, John F.

ROSS, Joe—SEE: Ross, A. Joseph

ROSS, Lara, pseud.—SEE: Bennett, Jeff

ROSS, Leona C(urtis), 1953-

32696 *Resurrexit.* New York: Leisure Books, 1986, 384 p., paper, novel.

ROSS, Marilyn, pseud.—SEE: Ross, Dan

ROSS, Raymond J.

32697 *One hundred miles above Earth.* London: Robert Hale, 1981, 192 p., cloth, novel.

ROSS, W. E. D.—SEE: Ross, Dan

ROSSETTI, Lucy Maddox, 1843-1894

32698 *Mrs. Shelley.* London: W. H. Allen & Co., 1890, viii+238 p., cloth, nonf.

ROSSI, Lee D(onald), 1946-

32699 *The politics of fantasy: C. S. Lewis and J. R. R. Tolkien.* Ann Arbor, MI: UMI Research Press, 1984, x+143 p., cloth,

nonf. STUDIES IN SPECULATIVE FICTION #10.

*ROSSITER, Oscar [pseud. of Vernon H. Skeels], 1918-

ROSSMAN, Charles E., *with Douglas A. Rossman*

32700 *Pages from The book of three: a Prydain glossary.* Baltimore, MD: T-K Graphics, 1976?, [30] p., paper, nonf.

ROSSMAN, Douglas A(thon), 1936- , *with Charles E. Rossman*

32700 *Pages from The book of three: a Prydain glossary.* Baltimore, MD: T-K Graphics, 1976?, [30] p., paper, nonf.

ROSSMANN, John F(rancis), 1942-

32701 *The door.* New York: A Signet Book, New American Library, 1975, 168 p., paper, novel. MIND MASTERS #3.

32702 *Shamballah.* New York: A Signet Book, New American Library, 1975, 220 p., paper, novel. MIND MASTERS #2.

as IAN ROSS

32703 *Amazons.* New York: A Signet Book, New American Library, 1976, 172 p., paper, novel. MIND MASTERS #4.

32704 *Recycled souls.* New York: A Signet Book, New American Library, 1976, 170 p., paper, novel. MIND MASTERS #5.

ROSSOW, William B(rigance), 1947- , *with M. Bradley Kellogg*

27022 *Lear's daughters.* Garden City, NY: Nelson Doubleday, 1987, 725 p., cloth, coll. LEAR'S DAUGHTERS #1-2.

27023 *Reign of fire.* New York: A Signet Book, New American Library, 1986, 382 p., paper, novel. LEAR'S DAUGHTERS #2.

27024 *The wave and the flame.* New York: A Signet Book, New American Library, 1986, 358 p., paper, novel. LEAR'S DAUGHTERS #1.

ROSZAK, Theodore, 1933-

32705 *Bugs.* Garden City, NY: Doubleday & Co., 1981, 352 p., cloth, novel.

32706 *Dreamwatcher.* Garden City, NY: Doubleday & Co., 1985, 287 p., cloth, novel.

ROTH, Arthur (Joseph), 1921-

38041 *Crash landing!* New York, Toronto: Scholastic Inc., 1983, 94 p., paper, fiction. TWISTAPLOT #6.

ROTH, Phyllis A(nn), 1945-

32707 *Bram Stoker.* Boston: Twayne Publishers, 1982, 167 p., cloth, nonf.

*ROTHENBERG, Alan B(aer), 1907-1977

ROTHMAN, Charles W.—SEE: Rothman, Chuck

ROTHMAN, Chuck [i.e., Charles Warren Rothman], 1952-

32708 *Staroamer's fate.* New York: Popular Library, Warner Books, 1986, 213 p., paper, novel.

ROTHMAN, Tony, 1953-

32709 *The world is round.* New York: A Del Rey Book, Ballantine Books, 1978, x+447 p., paper, novel.

ROTHSTEIN, Allan, *with Bill Warren*

32710 *Fandom is a way of death.* Los Angeles: L.A.Con II, 1984, 40 p., paper, novel.

ROTSLER, William, 1926-

32711 *And call my killer...Modok!* New York: Pocket Books, 1979, 189 p., paper, novel. IRON MAN; MARVEL SUPERHEROES #6.
32712 *Cavern of horror.* London: Corgi Books, 1985, 120 p., paper, movie. GOONIES #2.
  Distress call—SEE: *Star Trek II: Distress call.*
32713 *The far frontier.* New York: Playboy Press Paperbacks, 1980, 236 p., paper, novel. ZANDRA #2.
32714 *The hidden worlds of Zandra.* Garden City, NY: Doubleday & Co., 1983, 180 p., cloth, novel. ZANDRA #3.
32715 *Mr. Merlin, episode 1: novelization.* New York: Wanderer Books, 1981, 144 p., paper, tele. MR. MERLIN #1.
32716 *Mr. Merlin, episode 2: an original novel.* New York: Wanderer Books, 1981, 160 p., paper, tele. MR. MERLIN #2.
32717 *Nightmare.* New York: Pocket Books, 1979, 188 p., paper, novel. DOCTOR STRANGE; MARVEL SUPERHEROES #7.

32718 *Star Trek II biographies.* New York: Wanderer Books, 1982, 159 p., paper, tele. fiction. STAR TREK SERIES.
32719 *Star Trek II: Distress call.* New York: Wanderer Books, 1982, 126 p., paper, tele. STAR TREK SERIES.
32720 *Star Trek II short stories.* New York: Wanderer Books, Simon & Schuster, 1982, 159 p., paper, coll. STAR TREK SERIES.
32721 *Star Trek III short stories.* New York: Wanderer Books, 1984, 126 p., paper, tele. coll. STAR TREK SERIES.
32722 *Star Trek III: The Vulcan treasure.* New York: Wanderer Books, 1984, 117 p., paper, tele. STAR TREK SERIES.
32722A retitled: *The vulcan treasure.* London: Ravette, 1986, 117 p., paper, tele. STAR TREK SERIES.
32723 *To the land of the electric angel.* New York: Ballantine Books, 1976, 330 p., paper, novel.
  The Vulcan treasure—SEE: *Star Trek III: The Vulcan treasure.*
32724 *Zandra.* Garden City, NY: Doubleday & Co., 1978, 186 p., cloth, novel. ZANDRA #1.

as WILLIAM ARROW

16803 *Man, the hunted animal.* New York: Ballantine Books, 1976, 184 p., paper, tele. RETURN TO THE PLANET OF THE APES #3. [By William Rotsler].
16804 *Visions from nowhere.* New York: Ballantine Books, 1976, 183 p., paper, tele. RETURN TO THE PLANET OF THE APES #1. [By William Rotsler].

as JOHN RYDER HALL

32725 *Futureworld.* New York: Ballantine Books, 1976, 216 p., paper, movie.
32726 *Sinbad and the eye of the tiger: novelization.* New York: A Kangaroo Book, Pocket Books, 1977, 223 p., paper, movie.

with Gregory Benford

17763 *Shiva descending.* New York: Avon, 1980, 394 p., paper, novel.

with Sharman DiVono *as* VICTOR APPLETON

16738 *The astral fortress.* New York: Wanderer Books, Simon & Schuster, 1981, 191 p., paper, novel. TOM SWIFT #B5.

16740 *The city in the stars.* New York: Wanderer Books, Simon & Schuster, 1981, 191 p., paper, novel. TOM SWIFT #B1.

16747 *The rescue mission.* New York: Wanderer Books, Simon & Schuster, 1981, 188 p., paper, novel. TOM SWIFT #B6.

16750 *Tom Swift: Terror on the moons of Jupiter.* New York: Wanderer Books, Simon & Schuster, 1981, 185 p., paper, novel. TOM SWIFT #B2.

16751 *Tom Swift: The alien probe.* New York: Wanderer Books, Simon & Schus-ter, 1981, 186 p., paper, novel. TOM SWIFT #B3.

16752 *Tom Swift: The war in outer space.* New York: Wanderer Books, Simon & Schuster, 1981, 171 p., paper, novel. TOM SWIFT #B4.

ROTTENSTEINER, Franz, 1942-

32727 *The fantasy book: the ghostly, the gothic, the magical, the unreal.* London: Thames & Hudson, 1978, 160 p., paper, nonf.

32728 *The science fiction book: an illustrated history.* London: Thames & Hudson, 1975, 160 p., cloth, nonf.

32729 *The slaying of the dragon: modern tales of the playful imagination.* San Diego, CA: Harcourt Brace Jovanovich, 1984, xv+ 303 p., cloth, anth.

ROTTMAN, Gordon (Leroy), 1947- , *with James B. Adair*

Target Iran—SEE: *WWIII: Behind the lines: Target Iran.*
Target nuke—SEE: *WWIII: Behind the lines: Target nuke.*
Target Texas—SEE: *WWIII: Behind the lines: Target Texas.*

15952 *WWIII: Behind the lines: Target Iran.* New York: Berkley Books, 1991, 282 p., paper, novel. WWIII: BEHIND THE LINES #3.

15953 *WWIII: Behind the lines: Target nuke.* New York: Berkley Books, 1990, 321 p., paper, novel. WWIII: BEHIND THE LINES #2.

15954 *WWIII: Behind the lines: Target Texas.* New York: Berkley Books, 1990, 294 p., paper, novel. WWIII: BEHIND THE LINES #1.

ROUCH, James

32730 *Blind fire.* London: New English Library, 1980, 157 p., paper, novel. ZONE #2.

32731 *Body count.* New York: Zebra Books, Kensington Publishing Corp., 1990, 192 p., paper, novel. ZONE #9.

32732 *Civilian slaughter.* New York: Zebra Books, Kensington Publishing Corp., 1989, 219 p., paper, novel. ZONE #8.

32733 *Hard target.* London: New English Library, 1980, 158 p., paper, novel. ZONE #1.

32734 *Hunter killer.* London: New English Library, 1981, [160] p., paper, novel. ZONE #3.

32735 *Killing ground.* New York: Zebra Books, Kensington Publishing Corp., 1988, 222 p., paper, novel. ZONE #7.

32736 *Overkill.* London: New English Library, 1982, 159 p., paper, novel. ZONE #5.

32737 *Plague bomb.* New York: Zebra Books, Kensington Publishing Corp., 1986, 223 p., paper, novel. ZONE #6.

32738 *Sky strike.* London: New English Library, 1981, [160] p., paper, novel. ZONE #4.

ROUSCH, C(atherine) E.

32739 *Stars or dust.* Laconia, NH: Lori Paige, 1984, 110 p., paper, novel. STAR TREK SERIES.

ROUSSEAU, Victor [pseud. of Victor Rousseau Emanuel], 1879-1960, *with Harl Vincent*

32740 *Red twilight; World's end: two classic novels from Argosy.* Mercer Island, WA: Starmont House, 1991, vi+123 p., cloth, coll. STARMONT FACSIMILE FICTION #13.

ROVIN, Jeff(rey Daniel), 1951-

32741 *Count Dracula's vampire quiz book.* New York: A Signet Book, New American Library, 1979, 154 p., paper, nonf.

32742 *The encyclopedia of monsters.* New York: Facts on File, 1989, ix+390 p., cloth, nonf.

32743 *The encyclopedia of super villains.* New York: Facts on File, 1987, ix+416 p., cloth, nonf.

32744 *The encyclopedia of superheroes.* New York: Facts on File, 1985, xi+443 p., cloth, nonf.

32745 *The fabulous fantasy films.* South Brunswick & New York: A. S. Barnes & Co.; London: Thomas Yoseloff, 1977, 271 p., cloth, nonf.

32746 *The fantasy almanac.* New York: A Dutton Paperback, E. P. Dutton, 1979, 312 p., paper, nonf.

32747 *From Jules Verne to Star Trek.* New York: Drake Publishers, 1977, xi+147 p., paper, nonf.

32748 *From the land beyond beyond: the films of Willis O'Brien and Ray Harryhausen.* New York: A Berkley Windhover Book, Berkley Publishing Corp., 1977, x+277 p., paper, nonf.

32749 *The Madjan.* New York: Charter Books, 1984, 236 p., paper, novel.

32750 *Mars!* Los Angeles: Corwin Books, 1978, xi+244 p., cloth, nonf.

32751 *A pictorial history of science fiction films.* Secaucus, NJ: Citadel Press, 1975, 240 p., cloth, nonf.

32752 *Re-animator: a novel.* New York: Pocket Books, 1987, 223 p., paper, movie. RE-ANIMATOR #1.

32753 *The science fiction collector's catalog.* San Diego: A. S. Barnes & Co.; London: Tantivy Press, 1982, 181 p., paper, nonf.

32754 *The superhero movie & TV quiz book.* New York: A Signet Book, New American Library, 1979, vi+154 p., paper, nonf.

32755 *The supernatural movie quizbook.* New York: Drake Publishers, 1977, 94 p., paper, nonf.

32756 *The transgalactic guide to solar system M-17.* New York: G. P. Putnam's Sons, 1981, 288 p., cloth, fiction.

32757 *The UFO movie quiz book.* New York: A Signet Book, New American Library, 1978, 165 p., paper, nonf.

32758 *The unauthorized Teenage Mutant Ninja Turtles quiz book: an unofficial trivia guide to America's hottest phenomenon.* New York: St. Martin's Paperbacks, 1990, 118 p., paper, nonf.

with Sander Diamond

21705 *Starik.* New York: E. P. Dutton, 1988, 309 p., cloth, novel. [*Starik* is spelled with a backward "r"].

ROWE, Helen—SEE: Cresswell, Helen

ROWE, Jennifer—SEE: Rodda, Emily

ROWE, Nigel (William), 1964-

32759 *The history of science fiction fandom in New Zealand.* Auckland, New Zealand: Nigel Rowe, 1981, 4 v., paper, nonf.

32760 *Timeless sands: a history of science fiction fandom in New Zealand.* Auckland, New Zealand: Martian Way Press, 1983, 106 p., paper, nonf.

ROWE, W(illiam) W(oodin), 1934-

32761 *Nabokov's spectral dimension.* Ann Arbor, MI: Ardis Publishers, 1981, 142 p., cloth, nonf.

ROWLAND, Donald S(ydney), 1928-

32762 *Nightmare planet.* London: Robert Hale, 1976, 190 p., cloth, novel.

32763 *Space venturer.* London: Robert Hale, 1976, 191 p., cloth, novel.

as FENTON BROCKLEY

01903 *Star quest.* London: Robert Hale, 1974, 189 p., paper, novel.

as ROGER CARLTON

32764 *Beyond tomorrow.* London: Robert Hale, 1975, 189 p., cloth, novel.

32765 *Star arrow.* London: Robert Hale, 1975, 192 p., cloth, novel.

as GRAHAM GARNER

32766 *Rifts of time.* London: Robert Hale, 1976, 181 p., cloth, novel.

05788 *Space probe.* London: Robert Hale, 1974, 182 p., cloth, novel.

32767 *Starfall Muta.* London: Robert Hale, 1975, 184 p., cloth, novel.

as ALEX RANDOM

32768 *Cradle of stars.* London: Robert Hale, 1975, 182 p., cloth, novel.

32769 *Dark constellation.* London: Robert Hale, 1975, 189 p., cloth, novel.

12001 *Star Cluster Seven.* London: Robert Hale, 1974, 192 p., cloth, novel.

as ROLAND STARR

32770 *Return from Omina.* London: Robert Hale, 1976, 191 p., cloth, novel. OMINA #4.

32771 *Time factor.* London: Robert Hale, 1975, 189 p., cloth, novel. OMINA #3.

as MARK SUFFLING

32772 *Project Oceanus.* London: Robert Hale, 1975, 189 p., cloth, novel.

32773 *Space crusader.* London: Robert Hale, 1975, 189 p., cloth, novel.

ROWLANDS, D(avid) G., 1941-

32774 *Eye hath not seen—: supernatural anecdotes from the reminiscences of Father D. O'Connor.* Runcorn, Cheshire, England: Rosemary A. Pardoe, 1980, 38 p., paper, coll.

32775 *The living & the dead.* England: Crimson Altar Pres, 1991, 31 p., paper, coll.

with E. G. Swain

Bone to his bone—SEE: *The Stoneground ghost tales*, The.

13908 *The Stoneground ghost tales: compiled from the recollections of the Reverend Roland Batchel, vicar of the parish.* Cambridge, England: W. Heffer & Sons, 1912, 187 p., cloth, coll.

32776 retitled: *Bone to his bone: the Stoneground ghost tales.* Wellingborough, Northamptonshire, England: Equation, 1989, 192 p., paper, coll. [The stories by Rowlands are original to this volume].

ROWLEY, Christopher (B.), 1948-

The battlemaster—SEE: *The Vang: The battlemaster.*

32777 *The Black Ship.* New York: A Del Rey Books, Ballantine Books, 1985, 310 p., paper, novel. FENRILE #2.

32778 *The founder.* New York: A Del Rey Books, Ballantine Books, 1989, 251 p., paper, novel. FENRILE #3.

32779 *Golden sunlands.* New York: A Del Rey Book, Ballantine Books, 1987, 340 p., paper, novel.

The military form—SEE: *The Vang: The military form.*

32780 *Starhammer.* New York: A Del Rey Book, Ballantine Books, 1986, 297 p., paper, novel. VANG #1.

32781 *The Vang: The battlemaster.* New York: A Del Rey Book, Ballantine Books, 1990, 313 p., paper, novel. VANG #3.

32782 *The Vang: The military form.* New York: A Del Rey Book, Ballantine Books, 1988, 369 p., paper, novel. VANG #2.

32783 *The war for eternity.* New York: A Del Rey Book, Ballantine Books, 1983, 337 p., paper, novel. FENRILE #1.

with George Snow

32784 *Star Wars, return of the Jedi* / by Chris Rowley... Newtown, CT: Paradise Press, 1983, 64 p., paper, nonf.

ROY, Archibald—SEE: **Roy, Archie**

ROY, Archie [i.e., Archibald Edmiston Roy], 1924-

32785 *All evil shed away.* London: John Long, 1970, 188 p., cloth, novel.

32786 *Curtained sleep*, The. London: John Long, 1969, 183 p., cloth, novel.

32787 *The dark host.* London: John Long, 1976, 184 p., cloth, novel.

32788 *Deadlight.* London: John Long, 1968, 183 p., cloth, novel.

32789 *Devil in the darkness.* London: John Long, 1978, 184 p., cloth, novel.

32790 *Sable night.* London: John Long, 1973, 184 p., cloth, novel.

ROY, John Flint, 1913-

32791 *A guide to Barsoom: eleven sections of references in one volume dealing with the Martian stories written by Edgar Rice Burroughs.* New York: Ballantine Books, 1976, 200 p., paper, nonf.

with John Harwood & Camille Cazedessus Jr.

19680 *ERB-dom: a guide to issues no. 1-25.* Evergreen, CO: Opar Press, 1964, 23 p., paper, nonf.

ROY, Sue, *with Al Taylor*

32792 *Making a monster: the creation of screen characters by the great makeup artists.* New York: Crown Publishers, 1980, x+278 p, cloth, nonf.

ROYAL, Brian James—SEE: **Fox, Gardner F.**

ROYLE, Nicholas

32793 *Darklands.* London: Edgerton Press, 1991, 116 p., paper, anth.

38042 *Telepathy and literature: essays on the reading mind.* Oxford, England, Cambridge, MA: Basil Blackwell, 1991, 222 p., cloth, nonf. coll.

ROZZI, P. D.

32794 *Waltz with evil.* New York: Zebra Books, Kensington Publishing Corp., 1991, 320 p., paper, novel.

RUBEN, William S.

32795 *Dionysus: the ultimate experiment.* New York: Manor Books, 1977, 208 p., paper, novel. [An expanded edition of

Weightless in Gaza, originally published under the name Fred Shannon].

as FRED SHANNON

12925 *Weightless in Gaza*. New York: Tower Books, 1970, 138 p., paper, novel.

RUBENS, Bernice [i.e., Bernice Ruth Rubens Nassauer], 1928-

32796 *Our father*. London: Hamilton, 1987, 212 p., cloth, novel.
32797 *Spring sonata: a fable*. London: W. H. Allen, 1979, 215 p., cloth, novel.

RUBENSTEIN, Roberta [i.e., Roberta Rubenstein Larson], 1944-

32798 *The novelistic vision of Doris Lessing: breaking the forms of consciousness*. Urbana, Chicago: University of Illinois Press, 1979, 271 p., cloth, nonf.

RUBIE, Peter (Malcolm), 1950-

32799 *Werewolf*. Stamford, CT: Longmeadow Press, 1991, 272 p., cloth, novel.

with James Cohen

20256 *Mindbender*. New York: Lynx Books, 1989, 279 p., paper, novel.

RUBIN, Marty

32800 *The boiled frog syndrome: a novel of love, sex, and politics*. Boston: Alyson Publications, 1987, 231 p., paper, novel.

RUBINSTEIN, Gillian, 1942-

32801 *Beyond the labyrinth*. South Yarra, Victoria, Australia: Hyland House, 1988, 170 p., cloth, novel.
32802 *Skymaze*. Norwood, South Australia, Australia: An Omnibus/Puffin Edition, Omnibus Books, 1989, 193 p., cloth, novel. SPACE DEMONS #2.
32803 *Space demons*. Adelaide, South Australia, Australia: An Omnibus/Puffin Book, 1986, 213 p., cloth, novel. SPACE DEMONS #1.

RUBINYI-ANDERSON, Susan J.—SEE: Anderson, Susan J.

RUCHTI, Ulrich, *with Sybil Taylor*

32804 *Story into film: three tales of the supernatural go from page to screen*. New York: Laurel-Leaf Library, 1978, 256 p., paper, anth.

RUCK, Amy—SEE: Buck, Berta

*RUCK, Berta [i.e., Amy Roberta Ruck], 1878-1978

RUCKER, Rudolf—SEE: Rucker, Rudy

RUCKER, Rudy [i.e., Rudolf von Bitter Rucker], 1946-

32805 *The 57th Frank Kafka*. New York: Ace Books, 1983, 243 p., paper, coll.
32806 *The hollow earth: the narrative of Mason Algiers Reynolds of Virginia*. New York: William Morrow & Co., 1990, 308 p., cloth, novel.
32807 *Master of space and time*. New York: A Bluejay International Edition, 1984, 229 p., cloth, novel.
32808 *Mathenauts: tales of mathematical wonder*. New York: Arbor House, 1987, xvii+300 p., cloth, anth.
32809 *The secret of life*. New York: A Bluejay International Edition, 1985, 246 p., cloth, novel.
32810 *The sex sphere*. New York: Ace Science Fiction Books, 1984, xvi+172 p., paper, novel.
32811 *Software*. New York: Ace Books, 1982, 211 p., paper, novel. SOFTWARE #1.
32812 *Spacetime donuts*. New York: Ace Books, 1981, 196 p., paper, novel.
32813 *Transreal!* Englewood, CO: WCS Books, 1991, xvii+534 p., cloth, coll. [Includes some nonfiction and verse].
32814 *Wetware*. New York: Avon, 1988, 183 p., paper, novel. SOFTWARE #2.
32815 *White light; or, What is Cantor's continuum problem?* New York: Ace Books, 1980, 277 p., paper, novel.

with Robert Anton Wilson & Peter Lamborn Wilson

32816 *Semiotext[e] SF*. Brooklyn. NY: Autonomedia, 1989, 384 p., paper, anth.

RUD, Anthony (Melville), 1893-1942

38043 *The stuffed men*. New York: Macaulay Co., 1935, 250 p., cloth, novel.

RUDDICK, Bob, *with Gery Greer*

24672 *Jason and the aliens down the street.* New York: HarperCollinsPublishers, 1991, 94 p., cloth, novel. JASON #1.

24673 *Let me off this spaceship!* New York: HarperCollinsPublishers, 1991, 54 p., cloth, story.

24674 *Max and me and the time machine.* San Diego, CA: Harcourt Brace Jovanovich, 1983, 114 p., cloth, novel. MAX AND ME #1.

24675 *Max and me and the Wild West.* San Diego, CA: Harcourt Brace Jovanovich, 1988, 138 p., cloth, novel. MAX AND ME #2.

RUDDICK, Nicholas, 1952-

32817 *Christopher Priest.* Mercer Island, WA: Starmont House, 1989, ix+104 p., cloth, nonf. STARMONT READER'S GUIDE #50.

RUDDY, Jon

32818 *The bargain.* New York: Knightsbridge Publishing Co., 1990, 293 p., paper, novel. DRACULA SERIES.

RUDEEN, Louisa—SEE: Ellis, Leigh

*RUDHYAR, Dane [pseud. of Daniel Chenneviere], 1895-1985

RUEMMLER, John David

Night of the Nazgûl—SEE: Tolkien quest: Night of the Nazgûl.

32819 *Northern Mirkwood: realm of the wood-elves.* Charlottesville, VA: Iron Crown Enterprises, 1983, 52 p., paper, fiction.

32820 *Rangers of the North.* Charlottesville, VA: Iron Crown Enterprises, 1984?, 56 p., paper, fiction.

32821 *Tolkien quest: Night of the Nazgûl.* New York: Berkley Books, 1985, [160] p., paper, novel. TOLKIEN QUEST #1.

with Peter C. Fenlon

23024 *The world of Vog Mur.* Charlottesville, VA: Iron Crown Enterprises, 1984, 33 p., paper, fiction.

RUFF, Matt

32822 *Fool on the hill: a novel.* New York: A Morgan Entrekin Book, Atlantic Monthly Press, 1988, 396 p., cloth, novel.

RUFFELL, Ann, 1941-

32823 *Blood brother.* London: Julia MacRae Books, 1980, 171 p., cloth, novel.

32824 *Pyramid power.* London: Julia MacRae Books, 1981, 159 p., cloth, novel.

RÜHEN, Carl, 1937-

32825 *Mad Max 2.* Cammeray, New South Wales, Australia: Horwitz, 1981, 136 p., paper, movie. MAD MAX #2.

RULE, Jane (Vance), 1931-

32826 *Memory board.* London: Pandora, 1987, 256 p., cloth, novel.

RUNDLE, Anne

32827 *Moonbranches.* New York: Macmillan Publishing Co., 1986, 163 p., cloth, novel.

RUNYAN, C(lair) F.

32828 *The flight.* New York, Toronto: Bantam Books, 1991, 453 p., paper, novel.

*RUNYON, Charles W(est), 1928-1987

RUPP, Augustus—SEE: Raven, Anthony

RUPPERT, Peter, 1941-

32829 *Reader in a strange land: the activity of reading literary utopias.* Athens, GA & London: University of Georgia Press, 1986, xiv+193 p., cloth, nonf.

RUSCH, Kristine Kathryn, 1960-

32830 *The best of Pulphouse: the hardback magazine.* New York: St. Martin's Press, 1991, 352 p., cloth, anth.

32831 *Characterization.* Eugene, OR: Pulphouse Publishing, 1990, 22 p., paper, nonf.

32832 *The gallery of his dreams.* Eugene, OR: Axolotl Press, Pulphouse Publishing, 1991, 80 p., cloth, story. AXOLOTL SPECIAL EDITION #1.

32833 *Pulphouse, the hardback magazine: Fall, 1988, issue one.* Eugene, OR: Pulphouse Publishing, 1988, 267 p., cloth, anth.

32834 *Pulphouse, the hardback magazine: Winter, 1988, issue two.* Eugene, OR: Pulphouse Publishing, 1988, 243 p., cloth, anth.

32835 *Pulphouse, the hardback magazine: issue three, Spring, 1989: fantasy.* Eugene, OR: Pulphouse Publishing, 1989, 308 p., cloth, anth.

32836 *Pulphouse, the hardback magazine: issue four, Summer, 1989: science fiction.* Eugene, OR: Pulphouse Publishing, 1989, 247 p., cloth, anth.

32837 *Pulphouse, the hardback magazine: issue five, Fall, 1989: horror.* Eugene, OR: Pulphouse Publishing, 1989, 281 p., cloth, anth.

32838 *Pulphouse, the hardback magazine: issue six, Winter, 1990: fantasy.* Eugene, OR: Pulphouse Publishing, 1990, 306 p., cloth, anth.

32839 *Pulphouse, the hardback magazine: issue seven, Spring, 1990: horror.* Eugene, OR: Pulphouse Publishing, 1990, 311 p., cloth, anth.

32840 *Pulphouse, the hardback magazine: issue eight, Summer, 1990: science fiction.* Eugene, OR: Pulphouse Publishing, 1990, 243 p., cloth, anth.

32841 *Pulphouse, the hardback magazine: issue nine, Fall, 1990: dark fantasy.* Eugene, OR: Pulphouse Publishing, 1990, 259 p., cloth, anth.

32842 *Pulphouse, the hardback magazine: issue ten, Winter, 1991: special issue.* Eugene, OR: Pulphouse Publishing, 1991, 247 p., cloth, anth.

32843 *Pulphouse, the hardback magazine: issue eleven, Spring, 1991: speculative fiction.* Eugene, OR: Pulphouse Publishing, 1991, 311 p., cloth, anth.

32844 *The rules: a short course in the basics.* Eugene, OR: Pulphouse Publishing, 1990, 26 p., paper, nonf.

32845 *Setting.* Eugene, OR: Pulphouse Publishing, 1990, 27 p., paper, nonf.

32846 *The white mists of power.* New York: A Roc Book, 1991, 302 p., paper, novel.

with Dean Wesley Smith

32847 *Science Fiction Writers of America handbook: the professional writer's guide to writing professionally.* Eugene, OR: Writer's Notebook Press, Pulphouse Publishing, 1990, 248 p., paper, nonf. anth. [Winner of the *Locus* Award for Best Nonfiction, 1990 (1991)].

RUSE, Gary Alan, 1946-

32848 *Death hunt on a dying planet: a science fiction novel.* New York: A Signet Book, New American Library, 1988, 396 p., paper, novel.

32849 *The gods of Cerus Major.* Garden City, NY: Doubleday & Co., 1982, 178 p., cloth, novel.

32850 *Morlac: the quest of the green magician.* New York: A Signet Book, New American Library, 1986, 396 p., paper, novel.

RUSH, Alison, 1951-

32851 *The last of Danu's children.* London: George Allen & Unwin, 1981, 238 p., cloth, novel.

RUSHDIE, (Ahmed) Salman, 1947-

32852 *Grimus: a novel.* London: Victor Gollancz, 1975, 319 p., cloth, novel.

32853 *Haroun and the sea of stories.* London: Granta Books in Association with Penguin Books, 1990, 218 p., cloth, novel.

32854 *Midnight's children.* London: Jonathan Cape, 1981, 446 p., cloth, novel.

32855 *The satanic verses.* London: Viking, 1988, 546 p., cloth, novel.

RUSK, James Jr.

32856 *Space slaves.* Woodland Hills, CA: Decade Press, 1980, 220 p., paper, novel.

32857 *Tug of the dwarf star.* Woodland Hills, CA: Decade Press, 1980, 218 p., paper, novel.

RUSKIN, Ronald

32858 *The last panic.* Toronto, New York: Bantam Books, 1979, 279 p., paper, novel.

RUSOFF, Garry

32859 *Spear of fire.* New York: Popular Library, 1977, 223 p., paper, novel. CHARIOTS OF FIRE: GIRADOUX MANUSCRIPT #3.

with Michel Parry

31263 *Throne of fire.* London: Orbit, 1975, [207] p., paper, novel. CHARIOTS OF FIRE: GIRADOUX MANUSCRIPT #2.

RUSS, Joanna (Ruth), 1937-

The adventures of Alyx—SEE: *Alyx.*

32860 *Alyx.* Boston: Gregg Press, 1976, xxiv + 265 p., cloth, coll. [Includes *Picnic on Paradise* (see #12541)].

32860A retitled: *The adventures of Alyx.* New York: A Timescape Book, Pocket Books, 1983, 192 p., paper, coll.

32861 *Extra(ordinary) people.* New York: St. Martin's Press, 1984, 160 p., cloth, coll.

32862 *The female man.* Toronto, New York: Bantam Books, 1975, 214 p., paper, novel.

32863 *The hidden side of the Moon: stories.* New York: St. Martin's Press, 1987, 229 p., paper, coll.

32864 *Kittatinny: a tale of magic.* New York: Daughters Publishing Co., 1978, 92 p., cloth, novel.

32865 *Souls.* New York: Tor SF, A Tom Doherty Associates Book, 1989, 84 p., paper, story. [Bound with: *Houston, Houston, do you read? /* by James Tiptree, Jr.].

32866 *The two of them.* New York: Berkley Publishing Corp., 1978, 226 p., cloth, novel.

32867 *We who are about to....* New York: A Dell Book, 1977, 170 p., paper, novel.

32868 *The Zanzibar cat.* Sauk City, WI: Arkham House Publishers, 1983, xii+244 p., cloth, coll.

RUSSELL, Alan K. [pseud. of Lionel Leventhal]

32869 *The book of the dead: thirteen classic tales of the supernatural.* Poole, New York: New Orchard Editions, 1986, 382 p., cloth, anth.

as ANONYMOUS EDITOR

32870 *Science fiction by the rivals of H. G. Wells: thirty stories and a complete novel.* Secaucus, NJ: Castle Books, 1979, viii+506 p., cloth, anth.

RUSSELL, Eric Frank, 1905-1978

32871 *The best of Eric Frank Russell.* New York: A Del Rey Book, Ballantine Books, 1978, xv+336 p., paper, coll. [Edited by Alan Dean Foster].

32872 *Like nothing on Earth.* London: Dennis Dobson, 1975, 155 p., cloth, coll.

32873 *Sinister barrier.* Reading, PA: Fantasy Press, 1948, 253 p., cloth, novel. [Expanded and heavily revised edition of #12556].

32874 *Wasp.* London: Dennis Dobson, 1958, 202 p., cloth, novel. [Expanded edition of #12561].

RUSSELL, Jean, 1939-1982?

The Magnet book of sinister stories—SEE: *The Methuen book of sinister stories.*
The Magnet book of strange tales—SEE: *The Methuen book of strange tales.*

32875 *The Metheun book of sinister stories.* London: Methuen, 1982, 125 p., cloth, anth.

32875A retitled: *The Magnet book of sinister stories.* London: Methuen Children's Books, 1983, 127 p., paper, anth.

32876 *The Methuen book of strange tales.* London: Methuen, 1980, 142 p., cloth, anth.

32876A retitled: *The Magnet book of strange tales.* London: Methuen Children's, 1980, 144 p., paper, anth.

32877 *Supernatural stories: 13 tales of the unexpected.* London: Orchard Books, 1987, 156 p., cloth, anth. [Selections from *The Magnet book of sinister stories* and *The Magnet book of strange tales*].

RUSSELL, John Robert

32878 *Ta.* New York: Pocket Books, 1975, 207 p., paper, novel.

RUSSELL, Ray (Robert), 1924-

32879 *The book of Hell.* London: Sphere, 1980, 179 p., paper, coll.

32880 *The devil's mirror.* London: Sphere Books, 1980, 189 p., paper, coll.

32881 *Haunted castles: the complete gothic tales of Ray Russell.* Baltimore, MD: Maclay & Associates, 1985, 187 p., cloth, coll.

32882 *Incubus.* New York: William Morrow, 1976, 286 p., cloth, novel.

RUSSELL, Sean

32883 *The initiate brother, book one.* New York: DAW Books, 1991, 480 p., paper, novel.

RUSSELL TAYLOR, Elisabeth, 1930-

32884 *Tales from Barleymill.* London: Abelard-Schuman, 1978, 93 p., cloth, coll.

RUSSO, John (A.), 1939-

32885 *The awakening.* New York: Pocket Books, 1983, 311 p., paper, novel.

32886 *Black cat: a novel of terror.* New York: Pocket Books, 1982, 223 p., paper, novel.

32887 *The complete Night of the living dead filmbook.* Pittsburgh, PA: Imagine, 1985, 120 p., paper, nonf.

32888 *Day care.* New York: Pocket Books, 1985, 255 p., paper, novel.

32889 *Inhuman.* New York: Pocket Books, 1986, 221 p., paper, novel.
32890 *Living things.* New York: Popular Library, 1988, 274 p., paper, novel.
32891 *Return of the living dead.* New York: Dale Books, 1978, 147 p., paper, novel. LIVING DEAD #2.
32892 *Voodoo dawn: a novel.* Pittsburgh, PA: Imagine Inc., 1987, 190 p., paper, novel.

RUSSO, Richard A(nthony), 1946-

32893 *Dreams are wiser than men.* Berkeley, CA: North Atlantic Books, 1987, 374 p., paper, anth. [Includes some verse and nonf].
32894 *Yellow silk: erotic arts and letters.* New York: Harmony, 1990, 296 p., cloth, anth.

RUSSO, Richard Paul, 1954-

32895 *Inner eclipse.* New York: Tor SF, A Tom Doherty Associates Book, 1988, 376 p., paper, novel.
32896 *Subterranean gallery.* New York: Tor SF, A Tom Doherty Associates Book, 1989, 344 p., paper, novel.

RUTHERFORD, Brett, 1947-

32897 *The lost children.* New York: Zebra Books, Kensington Publishing Corp., 1988, 431 p., paper, novel.

with *John Robertson*

32483 *Piper.* New York: Zebra Books, Kensington Publishing Corp., 1987, 463 p., paper, novel

RUTHERFORD, Michael (Andrew), 1946-

32898 *The infinite kingdoms.* Philadelphia, PA: Owlswick Press, 1990, viii+183 p., cloth, coll. [Includes *The tale and its master*].
32899 *The tale and its master.* Delmar, NY: Spring Harbor Press, 1986, 64 p., paper, story.

RUTMAN, Leo, 1935-

32900 *Clash of eagles.* New York: Fawcett Gold Medal, 1990, 530 p., paper, novel.
32901 *Spear of destiny: a novel.* New York: Donald I. Fine, 1988, 280 p., cloth, novel.

RUTTER, Eileen—SEE: Chant, Joy

RUUTH, Marianne, 1933-

32902 *Outbreak.* New York: Manor Books, 1977, 253 p., paper, novel.

RYAN, Alan, 1943-

32903 *The bones wizard.* Garden City, NY: Doubleday & Co., 1988, 178 p., cloth, coll.
32904 *Cast a cold eye.* Niles, IL: Dark Harvest, 1984, 239 p., cloth, novel.
32905 *Dead white.* New York: Tor, A Tom Doherty Associates Book, 1983, 351 p., paper, novel.
32906 *Halloween horrors.* Garden City, NY: Doubleday & Co., 1986, 178 p., cloth, anth.
32907 *Haunting women.* New York: Avon Books, 1988, 210 p., paper, anth.
In the blood—SEE: *Night visions 1.*
32908 *The kill.* New York: Tor, A Tom Doherty Associates Book, 1982, 312 p., paper, novel.
32909 *Night visions 1: all original stories.* Niles, IL: Dark Harvest, 1984, 296 p., cloth, anth.
32909A retitled: *Night visions: In the blood.* New York: Berkley Books, 1988, viii+292 p., paper, anth.
The Penguin book of vampire stories—SEE: *Vampires.*
32910 *Perpetual light.* New York: Warner Books, 1982, 490 p., paper, anth.
32911 *Quadriphobia.* Garden City, NY: Doubleday & Co., 1986, 184 p., cloth, coll.
32912 *Vampires: two centuries of great vampire stories.* Garden City, NY: Doubleday & Co., 1987, xvi+621 p., cloth, anth.
32912A retitled: *The Penguin book of vampire stories.* New York: Penguin Books, 1988, xvi+621 p., paper, anth.

RYAN, Charles, 1937-

32915 *The Capricorn quadrant.* New York: NAL Books, 1990, 325 p., cloth, novel.
32916 *The Panjang incident.* New York: A Signet Book, New American Library, 1989, 399 p., paper, novel.

RYAN, Charles C(arroll), 1946-

32914 *Aboriginal science fiction: tales of the human kind: 1988 annual anthology.* Woburn, MA: Aboriginal SF, 1988, 80 p., paper, anth.

32917 *Starry messenger: the best of Galileo.* New York: St. Martin's Press, 1979, 198 p., cloth, anth.

with John Gregory Betancourt

17909 *Letters of the alien publisher.* Woburn, MA: First Books, 1991, 128 p., paper, nonf. coll.

RYAN, Desmond, 1943- , *with Joel Shurkin*

32918 *Helix.* New York: W. W. Norton, 1979, 240 p., cloth, novel.

RYAN, Thomas J(oseph), 1942-

32919 *The adolescence of P-1.* New York: Macmillan Publishing Co.; London: Collier Macmillan Publishers, 1977, 280 p., cloth, novel.

RYDER, James

32920 *Vicious spiral.* London: Robert Hale, 1976, 189 p., cloth, novel.

RYMAN, Geoff(rey Charles), 1951-

32921 *The child garden; or, A low comedy.* London, Sydney: Unwin Hyman, 1989, viii+388 p., cloth, novel. [Winner of the John W. Campbell Jr. Memorial Award for Best Novel, 1989 (1990)].
32922 *Coming of Enkidu.* Birmingham, England: Birmingham Science Fiction Group, 1989, 16 p., paper, coll. [Includes a play and a piece of a novel in progress].
32923 *The unconquered country: a life history.* London, Boston: George Allen & Unwin, 1986, 134 p., paper, novel.
32924 *The warrior who carried life.* London, Boston: George Allen & Unwin, 1985, 173 p., cloth, novel.

RYMAN, Ras [pseud. of James D. Brown]

32925 *Day of the Ultramind.* London: Robert Hale, 1977, 188 p., cloth, novel.
32926 *The quadrant war.* London: Robert Hale, 1976, 173 p., cloth, novel.
32927 *Weavers of death.* London: Robert Hale, 1981, 192 p., cloth, novel.

*RYMER, James Malcolm, 1814-1884

RYPEL, T(hadeus) C(hester "Ted"), 1949-

Deathwind of Vedun—SEE: *Gonji: Deathwind of Vedun.*

32928 *Fortress of lost worlds.* New York: Zebra Books, Kensington Publishing Corp., 1985, 460 p., paper, novel. GONJI #4.
32929 *Gonji.* New York: Zebra Books, Kensington Publishing Corp., 1986, 448 p., paper, novel. GONJI #5.
32930 *Gonji: Deathwind of Vedun.* New York: Zebra Books, Kensington Publishing Corp., 1982, 427 p., paper, novel. GONJI #1.
32931 *Samurai combat.* New York: Zebra Books, Kensington Publishing Corp., 1983, 464 p., paper, novel. GONJI #3.
32932 *Samurai steel.* New York: Zebra Books, Kensington Publishing Corp., 1982, 464 p., paper, novel. GONJI #2.

S

S., I., pseud.—SEE: Schneider, Isador

SABEN, Lionel

32933   *Replica.* New York: Zebra Books, Kensington Publishing Corp., 1978, 400 p., paper, novel.

SABERHAGEN, Fred(erick Thomas), 1930-

32934   *After the fact.* New York: Baen Books, 1988, 285 p., paper, novel. PILGRIM #2.
         Ardneh's world—SEE: *Changeling Earth.*

12611   *Berserker.* New York: Ballantine Books, 1967, 190 p., paper, coll. BERSERKER #1.

32935   retitled: *The Berserker wars.* New York: Tor, A Tom Doherty Associates Book, 1981, 399 p., paper, coll. BERSERKER #1. [Expanded edition].

32936   *The Berserker attack.* Stamford, CT: Waldenbooks, 1987, 149 p., paper, novel. BERSERKER #9.

32937   *Berserker: Blue death.* New York: Tor SF, A Tom Doherty Associates Book, 1985, 282 p., paper, novel. BERSERKER #8.

32938   *Berserker lies.* New York: Tor SF, A Tom Doherty Associates Book, 1991, xi+208 p., paper, coll. BERSERKER #10.

32939   *Berserker man.* New York: Ace Books, 1979, 220 p., paper, novel. BERSERKER #4.

32940   *The Berserker throne.* New York: Simon & Schuster, 1985, 319 p., cloth, novel. BERSERKER #7.
         The Berserker wars—SEE: *Berserker.*

32941   *Berserker's planet.* New York: DAW Books, 1975, 173 p., paper, novel. BERSERKER #3.
         Berserkers: The ultimate enemy—SEE: *The ultimate enemy.*
         Blue death—SEE: *Berserker: Blue death.*

32942   *The book of Saberhagen.* New York: DAW Books, 1975, 172 p., paper, coll.

32943   *A century of progress.* New York: A Tom Doherty Associates Book, 1983, 315 p., paper, novel.

12615   *Changeling Earth.* New York: DAW, 1973, 176 p., paper, novel. EMPIRE OF THE EAST #3.

12615A   retitled: *Ardneh's world.* New York: Baen Books, 1988, 178 p., paper, novel. EMPIRE OF THE EAST #3.
         Coinspinner's story—SEE: *The fifth book of lost swords: Coinspinner's story.*

32944   *The complete book of swords, comprising the first, second, and third books.* Garden City, NY: Nelson Doubleday, 1985, xi+626 p., cloth, coll. BOOK OF SWORDS #1-3. [Includes *The first book of swords*; *The second book of swords*; *The third book of swords*].

32945   *Dominion.* New York: Tor, A Tom Doherty Associates Book, 1982, 320 p., paper, novel. DRACULA #5.

32946   *The Dracula tape.* New York: Warner Paperback Library, 1975, 206 p., paper, novel. DRACULA #1.

32947   *Earth descended.* New York: Tor, A Tom Doherty Associates Book, 1981, 283 p., paper, coll.

32948   *Empire of the East.* New York: Ace Books, 1979, ix+558 p., paper, coll. EMPIRE OF THE EAST #1-3. [Includes *The broken lands*; *The black mountains*; *Changeling Earth*].
         Farslayer's story—SEE: *The fourth book of lost swords: Farslayer's story.*

32949   *The fifth book of lost swords: Coinspinner's story.* New York: Tor, A Tom Doherty Associates Book, 1989, 244 p., cloth, novel. BOOK OF LOST SWORDS #5.

32950   *The first book of lost swords: Woundhealer's story.* New York: Tor, A Tom Doherty Associates Book, 1986, 281 p., cloth, novel. BOOK OF LOST SWORDS #1.

32951   *The first book of swords.* New York: Tor, A Tom Doherty Associates Book, 1983, 309 p., paper, novel. BOOK OF SWORDS #1.

32952   *The fourth book of lost swords: Farslayer's story.* New York: Tor, A Tom Doherty Associates Book, 1989, 252 p., cloth, novel. BOOK OF LOST SWORDS #4.

32953   *The Frankenstein papers.* New York: Baen Science Fiction Books, 1986, 308 p., paper, novel. FRANKENSTEIN SERIES.

32954   *The golden people.* New York: A Baen Book, 1984, 270 p., paper, novel. [Expanded edition of #12616].

32955 *The Holmes-Dracula file.* New York: Ace Books, 1978, 249 p., paper, novel. DRACULA #2.

32956 *The lost swords: the first triad.* Garden City, NY: Nelson Doubleday, 1988, 602 p., cloth, coll. BOOK OF LOST SWORDS #1-3. [Includes *Woundhealer's story; Sightblinder's story; Stonecutter's story*].

32957 *The lost swords: the second triad.* New York: Guild America Books, 1991, 558 p., cloth, coll. BOOK OF LOST SWORDS #4-6. [Includes *Farslayer's story; Coinspinner's story; Mindsword's story*].

32958 *Love conquers all.* New York: Ace Books, 1979, 284 p., paper, novel.

38044 *Love conquers all.* New York: A Baen Book, 1985, 275 p., paper, novel. [Revised edition].

32959 *The mask of the sun.* New York: Ace Books, 1979, 309 p., paper, novel.

32960 *A matter of taste.* New York: Tor, A Tom Doherty Associates Book, 1990, 284 p., cloth, novel. DRACULA #6.

Mindsword's story—SEE: *The sixth book of lost swords: Mindsword's story.*

32961 *Octagon.* New York: Ace Books, 1981, 272 p., paper, novel.

32962 *An old friend of the family.* New York: Ace Books, 1979, 247 p., paper, novel. DRACULA #3.

32963 *Pyramids.* New York: Baen Books, 1987, 311 p., paper, novel. PILGRIM #1.

32964 *Saberhagen: my best.* New York: Baen Books, 1987, 311 p., paper, coll.

32965 *The second book of lost swords: Sightblinder's story.* New York: Tor, A Tom Doherty Associates Book, 1987, 248 p., cloth, novel. BOOK OF LOST SWORDS #2.

32966 *The second book of swords.* New York: Tor, A Tom Doherty Associates Book, 1983, 313 p., paper, novel. BOOK OF SWORDS #2.

Sightblinder's story—SEE: *The second book of lost swords: Sightblinder's story.*

32967 *The sixth book of lost swords: Mindsword's story.* New York: Tor, A Tom Doherty Associates Book, 1990, 250 p., cloth, novel. BOOK OF LOST SWORDS #6.

32968 *A spadeful of spacetime.* New York: Ace Books, 1981, 214 p., paper, anth.

32969 *Specimens.* New York: Popular Library, 1976, 224 p., paper, novel.

Stonecutter's story—SEE: *The third book of lost swords: Stonecutter's story.*

32970 *The third book of lost swords: Stonecutter's story.* New York: Tor, A Tom Doherty Associates Book, 1988, 249 p., cloth, novel. BOOK OF LOST SWORDS #3.

32971 *The third book of swords.* New York: Tor, A Tom Doherty Associates Book, 1984, 320 p., paper, novel. BOOK OF SWORDS #3.

32972 *Thorn.* New York: Ace Books, 1980, 347 p., paper, novel. DRACULA #4.

32973 *The ultimate enemy.* New York: Ace Books, 1979, 242 p., paper, coll. BERSERKER #5.

32973A retitled: *Berserkers: The ultimate enemy.* New York: Baen Books, 1988, 228 p., paper, coll. BERSERKER #5.

32974 *The veils of Azlaroc.* New York: Ace Books, 1978, 216 p., paper, novel.

32975 *The Water of Thought.* New York: A Tom Doherty Associates Book, TOR Science Fiction, Pinnacle Books, 1981, 251 p., paper, novel. [Expanded edition of #12617].

32976 *The white bull.* New York: Baen, 1988, 323 p., paper, novel.

Woundhealer's story—SEE: *The first book of lost swords: Woundhealer's story.*

with Martin Harry Greenberg

24577 *Machines that kill.* New York: Ace Science Fiction Books, 1984, 326 p., paper, anth.

with Joan Saberhagen

32977 *Pawn to infinity.* New York: Ace Books, 1982, 258 p., paper, anth.

with Roger Zelazny

32978 *The black throne.* New York: Baen Books, 1990, 278 p., paper, novel.

32979 *Coils.* Garden City, New York: Doubleday & Co., 1982, 183 p., cloth, novel.

with others

32980 *Berserker base.* New York: Tor, A Tom Doherty Associates Book, 1985, 316 p., paper, anth. BERSERKER #6. [Collaborative novel].

SABERHAGEN, Joan, *with Fred Saberhagen*

32977 *Pawn to infinity.* New York: Ace Books, 1982, 258 p., paper, anth.

*SABIN, Edwin L(egrand), 1870-1952

SABINE, Ted

32981 *The soulsucker.* New York: Pinnacle Books, 1975, 180 p., paper, novel.

SABRINA, pseud.

32982 *Love witch.* New York: Pleasure Books, 1977, 187 p., paper, novel.
32982A retitled: *Witch bitch.* New York: Pleasure Books, 1979, 187 p., paper, novel. [Bound with *Dance of love*, by Martine]. *Witch bitch*—SEE: *Love witch.*

SACIUK, Olena H(ikawyj), 1940-

32983 *The shape of the fantastic: selected essays from the Seventh International Conference on the Fantastic in the Arts.* New York: Greenwood Press, 1990, 270 p., cloth, nonf. anth. CONTRIBUTIONS TO THE STUDY OF SCIENCE FICTION AND FANTASY #39.

SACKETT, Jeffrey (Allyn), 1949-

32984 *Blood of the impaler.* New York, Toronto: Bantam Books, 1989, viii+340 p., paper, novel.
32985 *Candlemas eve.* Toronto, New York: Bantam Books, 1988, 355 p., paper, novel.
32986 *The demon.* New York, Toronto: Spectra, Bantam Books, 1991, 373 p., paper, novel.
32987 *Mark of the werewolf.* New York, Toronto: Bantam Books, 1990, viii+315 p., paper, novel.
32988 *Stolen souls.* Toronto, New York: Bantam Books, 1987, viii+341 p., paper, novel.

SACKETT, Susan (Deanna), 1943-

32989 *Letters to Star Trek.* New York: Ballantine Books, 1977, 215 p., paper, nonf.

with Fred Goldstein & Stan Goldstein

24098 *Star Trek speaks.* New York: A Wallaby Book, Pocket Books, 1979, 160 p., paper, anth.

with Gene Roddenberry

32564 *The making of Star Trek, the motion picture.* New York: A Wallaby Book, Pocket Books, 1980, xvii+221 p., paper, nonf.

SACKS, Janet

32990 *The best of Science fiction monthly.* London: New English Library, 1975, 189 p., cloth, anth.

32991 *Visions from the future.* London: New English Library, 1976, 128 p., cloth, art.

SACRANIE, Raj

32992 *Stories from outer space.* Secaucus, NJ: Chartwell Books, 1979, 93 p., cloth, coll.

SADLER, Barry, 1940-1989

The African mercenary—SEE: *Casca: The African mercenary.*
The assassin—SEE: *Casca: The assassin.*
The barbarian—SEE: *Casca: The barbarian.*
32993 *Casca: God of death.* New York: Charter, 1979, 218 p., paper, novel. CASCA #2.
32994 *Casca: Panzer soldier.* New York: Charter, 1980, 218 p., paper, novel. CASCA #4.
32995 *Casca: Soldier of fortune.* New York: Charter Books, 1983, vi+181 p., paper, novel. CASCA #8.
32996 *Casca: The African mercenary.* New York: Charter Books, 1984, 217 p., paper, novel. CASCA #12.
32997 *Casca: The assassin.* New York: Charter Books, 1985, 183 p., paper, novel. CASCA #13.
32998 *Casca: The barbarian.* New York: Charter, 1981, 184 p., paper, novel. CASCA #5.
32999 *Casca: The conquistador.* New York: Charter Books, 1984, 172 p., paper, novel. CASCA #10.
33000 *Casca: The damned.* New York: Ace Charter Books, 1982, 204 p., paper, novel. CASCA #7.
33001 *Casca: The eternal mercenary.* New York: Charter, 1979, 246 p., paper, novel. CASCA #1.
33002 *Casca: The legionnaire.* New York: Charter Books, 1984, 169 p., paper, novel. CASCA #11.
33003 *Casca: The Persian.* New York: Charter, 1982, 216 p., paper, novel. CASCA #6.
33004 *Casca: The sentinel.* New York: Charter Books, 1983, 172 p., paper, novel. CASCA #9.
33005 *Casca: The war lord.* New York: Charter, 1980, 182 p., paper, novel. CASCA #3.
The conquistador—SEE: *Casca: The conquistador.*
33006 *The cursed.* New York: Jove Books, 1987, 187 p., paper, novel. CASCA #18.
The damned—SEE: CASCA: THE DAMNED.
33007 *Desert mercenary.* New York: Charter Books, 1986, 188 p., paper, novel. CASCA #16.

The eternal mercenary—SEE: *Casca: The eternal mercenary.*

God of death—SEE: *Casca: God of death.*

The legionnaire—SEE: *Casca: the legionnaire.*

33008 *The mongol.* New York: Jove Books, 1990, 170 p., paper, novel. CASCA #22. [Last book in the series].

Panzer soldier—SEE: *Casca: Panzer soldier.*

The Persian—SEE: *Casca: The Persian.*

33009 *The phoenix.* New York: Charter Books, 1985, 188 p., paper, novel. CASCA #14.

33010 *The pirate.* New York: Charter Books, 1985, 167 p., paper, novel. CASCA #15.

33011 *The samurai.* New York: Jove Books, 1988, 171 p., paper, novel. CASCA #19.

The sentinel—SEE: *Casca: The sentinel.*

Soldier of fortune—SEE: *Casca: soldier of fortune.*

33012 *Soldier of Gideon.* New York: Jove Books, 1988, 168 p., paper, novel. CASCA #20.

33013 *The trench soldier.* New York: Jove Books, 1989, 168 p., paper, novel. CASCA #21.

The war lord—SEE: *Casca: The war lord.*

33014 *The warrior.* New York: Charter Books, 1987, 185 p., paper, novel. CASCA #17.

SADLER, Frank (Orin), 1939-

33015 *The unified ring: narrative art and the science-fiction novel.* Ann Arbor, MI: UMI Research Press, 1984, xv+117 p., cloth, nonf. STUDIES IN SPECULATIVE FICTION #11.

SADOUL, Jacques, 1934-

33016 *2000 A.D.: illustrations from the golden age of science fiction pulps.* Chicago: Henry Regnery, 1975, 175 p., cloth, nonf. [Translation by Eileen B. Hennessy of *Hier, l'an deux mille*].

SAFFRON, Robert, 1918-1985

33017 *The demon device: a novel by Sir Arthur Conan Doyle as communicated to Robert Saffron.* New York: G. P. Putnam's Sons, 1979, 287 p., cloth, novel.

SAGAN, Carl (Edward), 1934-

33018 *Contact: a novel.* New York: Simon & Schuster, 1985, 432 p., cloth, novel. [Winner of the *Locus* Award for Best First Novel, 1985 (1986)].

SAGARA, Michele M.

33019 *Into the dark lands.* New York: A Del Rey Book, Ballantine Books, 1991, 315 p., paper, novel. DARK LANDS #1.

SAGARIN, Edward, 1913-1986

33020 *Flake of Snow: a novel.* New York: Crown, 1975, 217 p, cloth, novel.

SAGE, Alison, *with Dennis Wheatley*

33021 *Dennis Wheatley's The devil rides out.* London: Hutchinson, 1987, 154 p., cloth, novel. [Adapted from the original].

The devil rides out—SEE: *Dennis Wheatley's The devil rides out.*

SAGE, Victor, 1942-

33022 *The gothic novel: a casebook.* Basingstoke, England: Macmillan, 1991, 190 p., cloth, nonf. anth.

33023 *Horror fiction in the Protestant tradition.* London: Macmillan, 1988, xxii+262 p., cloth, nonf.

SAGNIER, Thierry J. (Bright), 1946-

33024 *The IFO report.* New York: Avon, 1983, 295 p., paper, novel.

SAHA, Arthur W(illiam), 1923-

33025 *The year's best fantasy stories: 7.* New York: DAW Books, 1981, 191 p., paper, anth.

33026 *The year's best fantasy stories: 8.* New York: DAW Books, 1982, 191 p., paper, anth.

33027 *The year's best fantasy stories: 9.* New York: DAW Books, 1983, 192 p., paper, anth.

33028 *The year's best fantasy stories: 10.* New York: DAW Books, 1984, 254 p., paper, anth.

33029 *The year's best fantasy stories: 11.* New York: DAW Books, 1985, 238 p., paper, anth.

33030 *The year's best fantasy stories 12.* New York: DAW Books, 1986, xi+226 p., paper, anth.

33031 *The year's best fantasy stories 13.* New York: DAW Books, 1987, 238 p., paper, anth.

33032 *The year's best fantasy stories 14.* New York: DAW Books, 1988, 239 p., paper, anth.

with Donald A. Wollheim

12626 *The 1972 annual world's best SF.* New York: DAW Books, 1972, 302 p., paper, anth.

12626A retitled: *Wollheim's world's best SF, series one.* New York: DAW Books, 1977, 302 p., paper, anth.

12627 *The 1973 annual world's best SF.* New York: DAW Books, 1973, 253 p., paper, anth.

12627A retitled: *Wollheim's world's best SF, series two.* New York: DAW Books, 1978, 253 p., paper, anth.

12628 *The 1974 annual world's best SF.* New York: DAW Books, 1974, 280 p., paper, anth.

12628A retitled: *The world's best SF short stories #1.* Morley, Yorkshire, England: Elmfield Press, 1975, 280 p., cloth, anth.

12628B retitled: *Wollheim's world's best SF, series three.* New York: DAW Books, 1979, 280 p., paper, anth.

33033 *The 1975 annual world's best SF.* New York: DAW Books, 1975, 269 p., paper, anth.

33033A retitled: *The 1975 annual world's best SF: The world's best SF short stories #2.* Morley, Yorkshire, England: Elmfield Press, 1976, 269 p., cloth, anth.

33033B retitled: *Wollheim's world's best SF, series four.* New York: DAW Books, 1980, 269 p., paper, anth.

33034 *The 1976 annual world's best SF.* New York: DAW Books, 1976, 304 p., paper, anth.

33034A retitled: *The world's best SF three.* London: Dennis Dobson, 1979, 304 p., cloth, anth.

33034B retitled: *Wollheim's world's best SF, series five.* New York: DAW Books, 1981, 304 p., paper, anth.

33035 *1977 annual world's best SF.* New York: DAW Books, 1977, 280 p., paper, anth.

33035A retitled: *The world's best SF 4.* London: Dennis Dobson, 1979, 280 p., cloth, anth.

33035B retitled: *Wollheim's world's best SF, series six.* New York: DAW Books, 1982, 280 p., paper, anth.

33036 *The 1978 annual world's best SF.* New York: DAW Books, 1978, 270 p., paper, anth.

33036A retitled: *The world's best SF 5.* London: Dennis Dobson, 1980, 270 p., cloth, anth.

33036B retitled: *Wollheim's world's best SF, series seven.* New York: DAW Books, 1983, 270 p., paper, anth.

33037 *The 1979 annual world's best SF.* New York: DAW Books, 1979, 268 p., paper, anth.

33037A retitled: *Wollheim's world's best SF, series eight.* New York: DAW Books, 1984, 268 p., paper, anth.

33038 *The 1980 annual world's best SF.* New York: DAW Books, 1980, 284 p., paper, anth.

33038A retitled: *Wollheim's world's best SF, series nine.* New York: DAW Books, 1985, 284 p., paper, anth.

33039 *The 1981 annual world's best SF.* New York: DAW Books, 1981, 252 p., paper, anth.

33040 *The 1982 annual world's best SF.* New York: DAW Books, 1982, 304 p., paper, anth.

33041 *The 1983 annual world's best SF.* New York: DAW Books, 1983, 255 p., paper, anth.

33042 *The 1984 annual world's best SF.* New York: DAW Books, 1984, 256 p., paper, anth.

33043 *The 1985 annual world's best SF.* New York: DAW Books, 1985, 302 p., paper, anth.

33044 *The 1986 annual world's best SF.* New York: DAW Books, 1986, 303 p., paper, anth.

33045 *The 1987 annual world's best SF.* New York: DAW Books, 1987, 303 p., paper, anth.

The 1988 annual world's best SF—SEE: *Donald A. Wollheim presents The 1988 annual world's best SF.*

33046 *The 1989 annual world's best SF.* New York: DAW Books, 1989, 315 p., paper, anth.

33047 *The 1990 annual world's best SF.* New York: DAW Books, 1990, vi+341 p., paper, anth. [Last in the series].

33048 *Donald A. Wollheim presents The 1988 annual world's best SF.* New York: DAW Books, 1988, 303 p., paper, anth.

Wollheim's World's best SF, series one—SEE: *1972 annual world's best SF.*

Wollheim's World's best SF, series two—SEE: *1973 annual world's best SF.*

Wollheim's World's best SF, series three—SEE: *1974 annual world's best SF.*

Wollheim's World's best SF, series four—SEE: *1975 annual world's best SF.*

Wollheim's World's best SF, series five—SEE: *1976 annual world's best SF.*

Wollheim's World's best SF, series six—1977 annual world's best SF.

Wollheim's World's best SF, series seven—SEE: *1978 annual world's best SF.*

Wollheim's World's best SF, series eight—SEE: *1979 annual world's best SF.*

Wollheim's World's best SF, series nine—SEE: *1980 annual world's best SF.*

The World's best SF 4—SEE: *The 1977 annual world's best SF.*

The World's best SF 5—SEE: *The 1978 annual world's best SF.*

The World's best SF short stories #1—SEE: *The 1974 annual world's best SF.*

The World's best SF three—SEE: *The 1976 annual world's best SF.*

The World's best SF, series eight—SEE: *1979 annual world's best SF.*

The World's best SF, series five—SEE: *1976 annual world's best SF.*

World's best SF, series four—SEE: *1975 annual world's best SF.*

World's best SF, series nine-SEE: *1980 annual world's best SF.*

World's best SF, series one—SEE: *1972 annual world's best SF.*

World's best SF, series seven—SEE: *1978 annual world's best SF.*

World's best SF, series six—*1977 annual world's best SF.*

World's best SF, series three—SEE: *1974 annual world's best SF.*

World's best SF, series two—SEE: *1973 annual world's best SF.*

*SAHULA-DYCKE, Ignatz, 1900-<u>1982</u>

SAILOR, Charles, 1947-

33049 *The second son.* New York: Avon, 1979, 374 p., paper, novel.

SAINT, H(arry) F., 1941-

33050 *Memoirs of an invisible man.* New York: Atheneum, 1987, 396 p., cloth, novel.

SAINT-AUBIN, Horace de, pseud.—SEE: Balzac, Honoré de

SAINTBURY, Elizabeth, 1913-

33051 *George MacDonald: a short life.* Edinburgh: Canongate, 1987, 152 p., cloth, nonf.

SAINT-JOHN, Kristine

33052 *The minigods.* London: Black Sun, 1984, ix+147 p., paper, novel.

SAKERS, Don, 1958-

33053 *Carmen Miranda's ghost is haunting Space Station Three.* New York: Baen Books, 1990, 305 p., paper, anth.

33054 *The leaves of October.* New York: Baen Books, 1988, 276 p., paper, novel.

SALAY, Tedd

33055 *Dark imaginings.* Czechoslovakia?: Victor Crofansonicus, 1986, 42 p., paper, coll. [Translation by Nadia Nesmerakova; includes some verse].

SALE, Roger (H.), 1932-

33056 *Fairy tales and after: from Snow White to E. B. White.* Cambridge, MA & London: Harvard University Press, 1978, 280 p., cloth, nonf.

33057 *Modern heroism: essays on D. H. Lawrence, William Empson, and J. R. R. Tolkien.* Berkeley, CA & London: University of California Press, 1973, xi+261 p., cloth, nonf. coll.

SALEH, Dennis (Marshall), 1942-

33058 *Science fiction gold: film classics of the 50s.* New York: A Comma Book, McGraw-Hill, 1979, 191 p., paper, nonf.

SALEM, Richard

33059 *New blood.* London: Macdonald Futura, 1981, 221 p., paper, novel.

SALIBA, David R., 1949-

33060 *A psychology of fear: the nightmare formula of Edgar Allan Poe.* Lanham, MD: University Press of America, 1980, ix+267 p., cloth, nonf.

SALIK, pseud.

38045 *A king of dreams and shadows.* London: T. Fisher Unwin, 1894, 211 p., cloth, coll.

SALIKOF, K. S., *with Andrew Fischer*

23113 *Children of darkness.* New York: Manor Books, 1977, 236 p., paper, novel.

SALLE, Victor La, pseud.—SEE: Glasby, John & Evans, Gerald

SALMONSON, Amos—SEE: Salmonson, Jessica Amanda

SALMONSON, Jessica Amanda [legalized from Amos Salmonson], 1950-

33061 *Amazons!* New York: DAW Books, 1979, 206 p., paper, anth. [Winner of the World Fantasy Award for Best Fantasy Single Author Collection/Anthology, 1979 (1980)].

33062 *Amazons II.* New York: DAW Books, 1982, 239 p., paper, anth.

33063 *The Golden Naginata.* New York: Ace Books, 1982, 310 p., paper, novel. TO-MOE GOZEN #2.

33064 *Hag's tapestry.* Runcorn, Cheshire, England: Rosemary Pardoe, 1984, 32 p., paper, story.

33065 *Harmless ghosts.* Hoole, Cheshire, England: Haunted Library, 1990, 25 p., paper, coll.

33066 *The haunted wherry, and other rare ghost stories.* Madison, WI: A Miskatonic University Press Publication, The Strange Company, 1985, vii+97 p., paper, anth.

33067 *Heroic visions.* New York: Ace Fantasy Books, 1983, 214 p., paper, anth.

33068 *Heroic visions II.* New York: Ace Fantasy Books, 1986, xv+206 p., paper, anth.

33069 *John Collier and Fredric Brown went quarrelling through my head: stories.* Buffalo, NY: W. Paul Ganley, Publisher, 1989, 188 p., cloth, coll.

33070 *Ou Lu Khen and the beautiful madwoman.* New York: Ace Fantasy Books, 1985, 243 p., paper, novel.

33071 *A silver thread of madness.* New York: Ace Books, 1989, 179 p., paper, coll.

33072 *The swordswoman.* New York: Tor, A Tom Doherty Associates Book, 1982, 316 p., paper, novel.

33073 *Tales by moonlight.* Chicago: Robert T. Garcia, 1983, xi+218 p., cloth, anth.

33074 *Tales by moonlight II.* New York: Tor Horror, A Tom Doherty Associates Book, 1989, 306 p., paper, anth.

33075 *Thousand shrine warrior.* New York: Ace Fantasy Books, 1984, 275 p., paper, anth. TOMOE GOZEN #3.

33076 *Tomoe Gozen.* New York: Ace Books, 1981, 257 p., paper, novel. TOMOE GOZEN #1.

33077 *What did Miss Darrington see? an anthology of feminist supernatural fiction.* New York: The Feminist Press at the City University of New York, 1989, xxxvii+263 p., cloth, anth.

SALSITZ, R. A. V.—SEE: Vilott, Rhondi

SALSITZ, Rhondi—SEE: Vilott, Rhondi

SALTERBERG, B. J., 1934-

Captivity—SEE: *The outlander: captivity.*

33078 *The outlander: captivity.* Tucson, AZ: Harbinger House, 1989, 293 p., paper, novel. OUTLANDER TRILOGY #1.

SALU, Mary, 1919- , *with Robert T. Farrell*

22919 *J. R. R. Tolkien, scholar and storyteller: essays in memoriam.* Ithaca, NY: Cornell University Press, 1979, 325 p., cloth, nonf. anth.

SALVAGGIO, Ruth, 1951- , *with Marleen S. Barr & Richard Law*

17446 *Suzy McKee Charnas; Octavia Butler; Joan D. Vinge.* Mercer Island, WA: Starmont House, 1986, 52+44+72 p., cloth, nonf. coll. STARMONT READER'S GUIDE #23.

SALVATO, Sharon—SEE: Raymond, Alice

SALVATORE, R(obert) A(nthony), 1959-

Canticle—SEE: *Forgotten realms fantasy adventure: Canticle.*
The crystal shard—SEE: *Forgotten realms fantasy adventure: The crystal shard.*

33079 *Echoes of the fourth magic.* New York: A Roc Book, 1990, 318 p., paper, novel.

Exile—SEE: *Forgotten realms fantasy adventure: Exile.*

33080 *Forgotten realms fantasy adventure: Canticle.* Lake Geneva, WI: TSR Inc., 1991, 313 p., paper, novel. CLERIC QUINTET #1.

33081 *Forgotten realms fantasy adventure: Exile.* Lake Geneva, WI: TSR Inc., 1990, 306 p., paper, novel. DARK ELF TRILOGY #2.

33082 *Forgotten realms fantasy adventure: Homeland.* Lake Geneva, WI: TSR Inc., 1990, 314 p., paper, novel. DARK ELF TRILOGY #1.

33083 *Forgotten realms fantasy adventure: Sojourn.* Lake Geneva, WI: TSR Inc., 1991, 309 p., paper, novel. DARK ELF TRILOGY #3.

33084 *Forgotten realms fantasy adventure: Streams of Silver.* Lake Geneva, WI: TSR Inc., 1989, 342 p., paper, novel. ICEWIND DALE TRILOGY #2.

33085 *Forgotten realms fantasy adventure: The crystal shard.* Lake Geneva, WI: TSR Inc., 1988, 336 p., paper, novel.

33086 *Forgotten realms fantasy adventure: The halfling's gem.* Lake Geneva, WI: TSR Inc., 1990, 314 p., paper, novel. ICE-WIND DALE TRILOGY #3.

The halfling's gem—SEE: *Forgotten realms fantasy adventure: The halfling's gem.*

Homeland—SEE: *Forgotten realms fantasy adventure: Homeland.*

Sojourn—SEE: *Forgotten realms fantasy adventure: Sojourn.*

Streams of silver—SEE: *Forgotten realms fantasy adventure: Streams of Silver.*

33087 *The witch's daughter.* New York: A Roc Book, 1991, 316 p., paper, novel.

SALWAK, Dale (Francis), 1947-

33088 *Interviews with Britain's angry young men.* San Bernardino, CA: R. Reginald, The Borgo Press, 1984, 96 p., cloth, nonf. MILFORD SERIES: POPULAR WRITERS OF TODAY #39.

33089 *Kingsley Amis: in life and letters.* London: Macmillan; New York: St. Martin's Press, 1990, xvii+203 p., cloth, nonf. anth.

SALWAY, Lance

33090 *Beware, this house is haunted!* London: Hippo, 1989, 99 p., paper, coll.

33091 *Black eyes, and other spine chillers.* Leeds: Pepper Press, 1981, 92 p., cloth, anth.

33091A retitled: *The Magnet book of spine chillers.* London: Magnet, 1983, 92 p., paper, anth.

33092 *The darkness under the stairs, and other ghost stories.* London: Lutterworth Press, 1988, 125 p., cloth, coll.

The Magnet book of spine chillers—SEE: *Black eyes.*

33093 *A nasty piece of work, and other ghost stories.* London: Patrick Hardy Books, 1983, 128 p., cloth, coll.

Shivers in the dark—SEE: *They wait, and other spine chillers.*

33094 *They wait, and other spine chillers.* London: Bell & Hyman, 1983, [88] p., cloth, anth.

33094A retitled: *Shivers in the dark.* London: Magnet Books, 1984, 88 p., paper, anth.

*SAMACHSON, Joseph, 1906-_1980_

SAMALMAN, Alexander—SEE: Garth, Will

SAMMON, Paul M(ichael), 1949-

33095 *Splatterpunks: extreme horror.* New York: St. Martin's Press, 1990, 346 p., cloth, anth.

SAMMONS, Martha C(atherine Cragoe), 1949-

33096 *"A better country": the worlds of religious fantasy and science fiction.* New York, London: Greenwood Press, 1988, 168 p., cloth, nonf. CONTRIBUTIONS TO THE STUDY OF SCIENCE FICTION AND FANTASY #32.

33097 *A guide through C. S. Lewis' space trilogy.* Westchester, IL: Cornerstone Books, 1980, 189 p., paper, nonf.

33098 *A guide through Narnia.* Wheaton, IL: Harold Shaw Publishers, 1979, 164 p., paper, nonf.

SAMPSON, Fay (Elizabeth), 1935-

33099 *Black smith's telling.* London: Headline, 1990, 275 p., paper, novel. DAUGHTER OF TINTAGEL #3.

33100 *Finnglas and the stones of choosing.* Tring, Hertfordshire, England: Lion Publishing, 1986, 128 p., paper, novel. PANGUR BAN #4.

33101 *Finnglas of the horses.* Tring, Hertfordshire, England: Lion Publishing, 1985, 112 p., paper, novel. PANGUR BAN #3.

33102 *Pangur Ban, the white cat.* Tring, Hertfordshire, England: Lion Publishing, 1983, 124 p., paper, novel. PANGUR BAN #2.

33103 *The serpent of Senargad.* Littlemore, Oxford, England: Lion Publishing, 1989, 187 p., cloth, novel. PANGUR BAN #5.

33104 *Shape-shifter: the naming of Pangur Ban.* Tring, Hertfordshire, England: Lion Publishing, 1988, 126 p., paper, novel. PANGUR BAN #1.

33105 *Taliesin's telling.* London: Headline, 1991, 277 p., paper, novel. DAUGHTER OF TINTAGEL #4.

33106 *The white horse is running.* Littlemore, Oxford, England: Lion Publishing, 1990, 168 p., paper, novel. PANGUR BAN #6.

33107 *The white nun's telling.* London: Headline, 1989, viii+245 p., paper, novel. DAUGHTER OF TINTAGEL #2.

33108 *The wise woman's telling.* London: Headline, 1989, 229 p., paper, novel. DAUGHTER OF TINTAGEL #1.

SAMPSON, Robert (D.), 1927-

33109 *Deadly excitements: shadows and phantoms.* Bowling Green, OH: Bowling Green State University Popular Press, 1989, 223 p., cloth, nonf.

Glory figures—SEE: *Yesterday's faces: a study of series characters in the early pulp magazines, volume 1: Glory figures.*

33110 *The night master.* Chicago: Pulp Press, 1982, 216 p., cloth, nonf.

33111 *Spider.* Bowling Green, OH: Bowling Green State University Popular Press, 1987, 250 p., cloth, nonf.

Strange days—SEE: *Yesterday's faces: a study of series characters in the early pulp magazines, volume 2: Strange days.*

33112 *Yesterday's faces: a study of series characters in the early pulp magazines, volume 1: Glory figures.* Bowling Green, OH: Bowling Green State University Popular Press, 1983, 270 p., cloth, nonf.

33113 *Yesterday's faces: a study of series characters in the early pulp magazines, volume 2: Strange days.* Bowling Green, OH: Bowling Green State University Popular Press, 1984, 290 p., cloth, nonf.

SAMSON, Joan, 1937-1976

38046 *The auctioneer.* New York: Simon & Schuster, 1975, 239 p., cloth, novel.

SAMUELSON, David N(orman), 1939-

33114 *Arthur C. Clarke: a primary and secondary bibliography.* Boston: G. K. Hall & Co., 1984, xv+256 p., cloth, nonf. MASTERS OF SCIENCE FICTION AND FANTASY.

33115 *Visions of tomorrow: six journeys from outer to inner space.* New York: Arno Press, 1975, 429 p., cloth, nonf.

SAN SOUCI, Robert D(aniel), 1946-

33116 *Blood offerings.* New York: Leisure Books, 1985, 365 p., paper, novel.

33117 *The dreaming.* New York: Berkley Books, 1989, 251 p., paper, novel.

33118 *Emergence.* New York: Avon, 1981, 273 p., paper, novel.

33119 *Short & shivery.* Garden City, NY: Doubleday & Co., 1987, 175 p., cloth, coll.

SANCHEZ, Gali (Riccardo), 1951- , *with Michael Williams*

33120 *Vampires: Chill module.* Cleveland, OH: Pacesetter, 1985, 64 p., paper, novel. [Based on the *Chill* game].

SAND, Margaret, 1932-

33121 *The chanting of children.* New York: Coward, McCann & Gegheghan, 1978, 221 p., cloth, novel.

SANDELIN, Clarence K(enneth), 1915-

33122 *Robert Nathan.* New York: Twayne Publishers, 1968, 171 p., cloth, nonf.

SANDEMAN, Mina

38047 *The rosy cross, and other psychical tales.* Westminster, England: Roxburghe Press, 1896, 264 p., cloth, coll.

38048 *The worship of Lucifer: a novel.* London: Digby & Long, 1897, 218 p., cloth, novel.

SANDERS, J. R.

33123 *The container is ready.* New York, Washington: Vantage Press, date, [200] p., cloth, novel. CONTAINER #1.

33124 *The intergalactic express.* New York, Washington: Vantage Press, 1988, 212 p., cloth, novel. CONTAINER #2.

SANDERS, Joseph L(ee), 1940-

33125 *E. E. "Doc" Smith.* Mercer Island, WA: Starmont House, 1986, 96 p., cloth, nonf. STARMONT READER'S GUIDE #24.

33126 *Roger Zelazny: a primary and secondary bibliography.* Boston: G. K. Hall & Co., 1980, xxx+154 p., cloth, nonf. MASTERS OF SCIENCE FICTION AND FANTASY.

SANDERS, Lawrence, 1920-

33129A *Dark summer.* London: Sphere Books, 1989, 224 p., paper, novel. [Originally published under the name Mark Upton].

33127 *The passion of Molly T.* New York: G. P. Putnam's Sons, 1984, 352 p., cloth, novel.

33128 *The Tomorrow File.* New York: G.P. Putnam's Sons, 1975, 503 p., cloth, novel.

as MARK UPTON

33129 *Dark summer.* New York: Coward, Mc-Cann & Geoghegan, 1979, 255 p., cloth, novel.

SANDERS, Ruth Manning- —SEE: Manning-Sanders, Ruth

SANDERS, Scott Russell, 1945-

33130 *The engineer of beasts.* New York: Orchard Books, 1988, 258 p., cloth, novel.
33131 *The invisible company.* New York: Tor, A Tom Doherty Associates Book, 1989, 313 p., paper, novel.
33132 *Terrarium.* New York: Tor SF, A Tom Doherty Associates Book, 1985, 276 p., paper, novel.

SANDERS, William

33133 *Journey to Fusang.* New York: Popular Library, 1988, 310 p., paper, novel.
33134 *The wild blue and the gray.* New York: Warner Books, 1991, 216 p., paper, novel.

as WILL SUNDOWN

33135 *The hellbound train.* New York: Popular Library, 1990, 214 p., paper, novel. POCKETS #2.
33136 *Pockets of resistance.* New York: Popular Library, 1990, 215 p., paper, novel. POCKETS #1.

SANDISON, Alan, 1932-

33137 *George Orwell: after 1984.* London: Macmillan, 1974, 203 p., cloth, nonf.
33138 *The last man in Europe: an essay on George Orwell.* Basingstoke, Hampshire, England: Macmillan; Dover, NH: Longwood Academic, 1986, 232 p., cloth, nonf.

SANDMAN LILIUS, Irmelin

28356 *Horses of the night.* Oxford, England: Oxford University Press, 1979, 137 p., cloth, novel. [Translation by Joan Tate of *Gångande grå*].

SANFORD, Richard

33139 *The calling.* Sevenoaks, Kent, England: New English Library, 1990, 189 p., cloth, novel.

SANFORD, William R(eynolds), 1927- , *with Carl R. Green*

24399 *The black cat.* Mankato, MN: Crestwood House, 1987, 47 p., cloth, movie.
24400 *Black Friday.* Mankato, MN: Crestwood House, 1985, 48 p., cloth, movie.
24401 *Bride of Frankenstein.* Mankato, MN: Crestwood House, 1985, 48 p., cloth, movie.
24402 *Dracula's daughter.* Mankato, MN: Crestwood House, 1985, 48 p., cloth, movie.
24403 *Ghost of Frankenstein.* Mankato, MN: Crestwood House, 1985, 48 p., cloth, movie.
24404 *House of fear.* Mankato, MN: Crestwood House, 1987, 48 p., cloth, movie.
24405 *The house of the seven gables.* Mankato, MN: Crestwood House, 1987, 48 p., cloth, movie.
24406 *The invisible man.* Mankato, MN: Crestwood House, 1987, 47 p., cloth, movie.
24407 *The mole people.* Mankato, MN: Crestwood House, 1985, 48 p., cloth, movie.
24408 *The murders in the Rue Morgue.* Mankato, MN: Crestwood House, 1987, 47 p., cloth, movie.
24409 *The phantom of the opera.* Mankato, MN: Crestwood House, 1987, 47 p., cloth, movie.
24410 *The raven.* Mankato, MN: Crestwood House, 1985, 48 p., cloth, movie.
24411 *The revenge of the creature.* Mankato, MN: Crestwood House, 1987, 48 p., cloth, movie.
24412 *Tarantula.* Mankato, MN: Crestwood House, 1985, 48 p., cloth, movie.
24413 *Werewolf of London.* Mankato, MN: Crestwood House, 1985, 48 p., cloth, movie.

SANN, Paul, 1914-1986

33140 *Trial in the upper room: a heavenly novel.* New York: A Herbert Michelson Book, Crown Publishers, 1981, 246 p., cloth, novel.

SAPERSTEIN, David (Allan), 1937-

33141 *Cocoon: a novel.* New York: A Jove Book, 1985, 248 p., paper, movie. CO-COON #1.
33142 *Metamorphosis: the Cocoon story continues: a novel.* New York: A Jove Book, 1988, 258 p., paper, movie. COCOON #2.
33143 *Red devil.* New York: Berkley Books, 1989, 312 p., paper, novel.

SAPIEYEVSKI, Anne L.—SEE: Lindbergh, Anne

SAPIR, Richard (Ben), 1936-1987

33144   *The far arena* / by Richard Ben Sapir. New York: Seaview Books, 1978, x + 435 p., cloth, novel.

33145   *Quest* / by Richard Ben Sapir. New York: E. P. Dutton, 1987, vii + 390 p., cloth, novel.

with Warren Murphy and others

NOTE: Most of the books in this series bear the joint bylines of both writers, even after Richard Sapir's 1987 death; some of the earlier books in the series are bylined by one author only, and many of those bylines changed with subsequent printings. Correct bylines for the first editions appear immediately after individual titles where only one author is recorded on the title page. More than half of the series has been ghostwritten or co-authored with other writers; actual authorship is given at the end of each entry, courtesy of Will Murray. Although individual titles in this series may not be fantastic, the series as a whole has been judged sufficiently fantastic to list every book, including a repetition of the one title listed in the 1700-1974 volume of this bibliography.

30453   *Acid rock.* New York: Pinnacle Books, 1973, 186 p., paper, novel. DESTROYER #13. [By Richard Sapir & Warren Murphy].

30454   *Arabian nightmare.* New York: A Signet Book, 1991, 237 p., paper, novel. DESTROYER #86. [By Will Murray].

30455   *The arms of Kali.* New York: A Signet Book, New American Library, 1984, 253 p., paper, novel. DESTROYER #59. [By Richard Sapir & Warren Murphy].

30456   *The assassin's handbook.* New York: Pinnacle Books, 1982, xiii + 268 p., paper, coll. [By Richard Sapir & Warren Murphy; edited (and written) by Will Murray].

30456A retitled: *Inside Sinanju.* New York: Pinnacle Books, 1985, xiii + 268 p., paper, coll. [By Richard Sapir & Warren Murphy; edited (and written) by Will Murray].

30457   *Assassins play-off.* New York: Pinnacle Books, 1975, 178 p., paper, novel. DESTROYER #20. [By Richard Sapir & Warren Murphy].

20218   *Balance of power.* New York: Pinnacle Books, 1981, viii + 183 p., paper, novel. DESTROYER #44. [By Richard Sapir & Warren Murphy & Molly Cochran].

30458   *Bay city blast* / by Warren Murphy. Los Angeles: Pinnacle Books, 1979, 179 p., paper, novel. DESTROYER #38. [By Warren Murphy].

30459   *Blood lust.* New York: A Signet Book, 1991, 256 p., paper, novel. DESTROYER #85. [By Will Murray].

30460   *Blood ties.* New York: A Signet Book, New American Library, 1987, 252 p., paper, novel. DESTROYER #69. [By Warren Murphy & Will Murray].

30461   *Blue smoke and mirrors.* New York: A Signet Book, New American Library, 1989, 224 p., paper, novel. DESTROYER #78. [By Will Murray].

30462   *Bottom line* / by Warren Murphy. Los Angeles: Pinnacle Books, 1979, 178 p., paper, novel. DESTROYER #37. [By Warren Murphy].

30463   *Brain drain.* New York: Pinnacle Books, 1976, 180 p., paper, novel. DESTROYER #22. [By Richard Sapir & Warren Murphy].

30464   *Chained reaction.* Los Angeles: Pinnacle Books, 1978, 178 p., paper, novel. DESTROYER #34. [By Richard Sapir & Warren Murphy].

30465   *Child's play.* New York: Pinnacle Books, 1976, 183 p., paper, novel. DESTROYER #23. [By Richard Sapir & Warren Murphy].

30466   *Chinese puzzle.* New York: Pinnacle Books, 1972, 187 p., paper, novel. DESTROYER #3. [By Richard Sapir & Warren Murphy].

30467   *Coin of the realm.* New York: A Signet Book, New American Library, 1989, 256 p., paper, novel. DESTROYER #77. [By Will Murray].

30468   *Created, the Destroyer.* New York: Pinnacle Books, 1971, 187 p., paper, novel. DESTROYER #1. [By Richard Sapir & Warren Murphy].

30469   *Dangerous games* / by Warren Murphy. Los Angeles: Pinnacle Books, 1980, 188 p., paper, novel. DESTROYER #40. [By Warren Murphy & Robert J. Randisi].

20219   *Date with death* / by Warren Murphy. New York: Pinnacle Books, 1984, 186 p., paper, novel. DESTROYER #57. [By Warren Murphy & Molly Cochran & Ed Hunsburger].

30470   *Deadly seeds.* New York: Pinnacle Books, 1975, 180 p., paper, novel. DESTROYER #21. [By Richard Sapir & Warren Murphy].

30471   *Death check.* New York: Pinnacle Books, 1972, 187 p., paper, novel. DESTROYER #2. [By Richard Sapir & Warren Murphy].

30472 *Death sentence.* New York: A Signet Book, 1990, 221 p., paper, novel. DE-STROYER #80. [By Will Murray].

30473 *Death therapy.* New York: Pinnacle Books, 1972, 188 p., paper, novel. DE-STROYER #6. [By Richard Sapir & Warren Murphy].

10535 *Dr. Quake.* New York: Pinnacle Books, 1972, 187 p., paper, novel. DESTROYER #5. [By Richard Sapir & Warren Murphy].

20220 *Dying space* / by Warren Murphy. New York: Pinnacle Books, 1982, 196 p., paper, novel. DESTROYER #47. [By Molly Cochran].

20221 *The eleventh hour.* New York: A Signet Book, New American Library, 1987, 222 p., paper, novel. DESTROYER #70. [By Warren Murphy & Will Murray & Molly Cochran].

30474 *Encounter group* / by Warren Murphy. New York: Pinnacle Books, 1984, 185 p., paper, novel. DESTROYER #56. [By Warren Murphy & Will Murray].

30475 *The end of the game.* New York: A Signet Book, New American Library, 1985, 205 p., paper, novel. DESTROYER #60. [By Richard Sapir & Warren Murphy].

30476 *The final crusade.* New York: A Signet Book, New American Library, 1989, 223 p., paper, novel. DESTROYER #76. [By Will Murray].

29801 *The final death.* New York: Pinnacle Books, 1977, 177 p., paper, novel. DE-STROYER #29. [By Richard Sapir & Warren Murphy & Ric Meyers].

30477 *Firing line* / by Warren Murphy. Los Angeles: Pinnacle Books, 1980, 180 p., paper, novel. DESTROYER #41. [By Warren Murphy].

30478 *Fool's gold.* New York: Pinnacle Books, 1983, 245 p., paper, novel. DESTROYER #52. [By Richard Sapir & Warren Murphy].

30479 *Funny money.* New York: Pinnacle Books, 1975, 180 p., paper, novel. DE-STROYER #18. [By Richard Sapir & Warren Murphy].

30480 *Ground zero.* New York: A Signet Book, 1991, 253 p., paper, novel. DESTROYER #84. [By Will Murray].

30481 *The head men.* Los Angeles: Pinnacle Books, 1977, 197 p., paper, novel. DE-STROYER #31. [By Richard Sapir & Warren Murphy].

30482 *Holy terror.* New York: Pinnacle Books, 1975, 182 p., paper, novel. DESTROYER #19. [By Richard Sapir & Warren Murphy].

30483 *Hostile takeover.* New York: A Signet Book, 1990, 252 p., paper, novel. DE-STROYER #81. [By Will Murray].

30484 *In enemy hands.* New York: Pinnacle Books, 1977, 178 p., paper, novel. DE-STROYER #26. [By Richard Sapir & Warren Murphy].

30485 *Judgment day.* New York: Pinnacle Books, 1974, 184 p., paper, novel. DE-STROYER #14. [By Richard Sapir & Warren Murphy].

30486 *Kill or cure.* New York: Pinnacle Books, 1973, 184 p., paper, novel. DESTROYER #11. [By Richard Sapir & Warren Murphy].

30487 *Killer chromosomes.* Los Angeles: Pinnacle Books, 1978, 181 p., paper, novel. DESTROYER #32. [By Richard Sapir & Warren Murphy].

20222 *Killing time* / by Warren Murphy. New York: Pinnacle Books, 1982, 199 p., paper, novel. DESTROYER #50. [By Molly Cochran].

30488 *King's curse.* New York: Pinnacle Books, 1976, 178 p., paper, novel. DESTROYER #24. [By Richard Sapir & Warren Murphy].

30489 *The last alchemist.* New York: A Signet Book, New American Library, 1986, 221 p., paper, novel. DESTROYER #64. [By Richard Sapir & Will Murray].

30490 *Last call* / by Warren Murphy. Los Angeles: Pinnacle Books, 1978, 182 p., paper, novel. DESTROYER #35. [By Warren Murphy].

20223 *Last drop* / by Warren Murphy. New York: Pinnacle Books, 1983, 199 p., paper, novel. DESTROYER #54. [By Molly Cochran].

29799 *The last temple* / by Warren Murphy. New York: Pinnacle Books, 1977, 180 p., paper, novel. DESTROYER #27. [By Warren Murphy & Ric Meyers].

30491 *Last war dance.* New York: Pinnacle Books, 1974, 178 p., paper, novel. DE-STROYER #17. [By Richard Sapir & Warren Murphy].

30492 *Line of succession.* New York: A Signet Book, New American Library, 1988, 252 p., paper, novel. DESTROYER #73. [By Warren Murphy & Will Murray].

30493 *Look into my eyes.* New York: A Signet Book, New American Library, 1987, 253 p., paper, novel. DESTROYER #67. [By Richard Sapir].

30494 *Lords of the Earth.* New York: A Signet Book, New American Library, 1985, 254 p., paper, novel. DESTROYER #61. [By Richard Sapir & Warren Murphy].

30495 *Lost yesterday.* New York: A Signet Book, New American Library, 1986, 255 p., paper, novel. DESTROYER #65. [By Richard Sapir & Will Murray].

30496 *Mafia fix.* New York: Pinnacle Books, 1972, 184 p., paper, novel. DESTROYER #4. [By Richard Sapir & Warren Murphy].

20224 *Master's challenge.* New York: Pinnacle Books, 1984, 245 p., paper, novel. DESTROYER #55. [By Richard Sapir & Warren Murphy & Molly Cochran].

30497 *Midnight man* / by Warren Murphy. Los Angeles: Pinnacle Books, 1981, 169 p., paper, novel. DESTROYER #43. [By Warren Murphy & Robert J. Randisi].

30498 *Missing link* / by Warren Murphy. Los Angeles: Pinnacle Books, 1980, 174 p., paper, novel. DESTROYER #39. [By Warren Murphy].

30499 *Mugger blood.* Los Angeles: Pinnacle Books, 1977, 182 p., paper, novel. DESTROYER #30. [By Richard Sapir & Warren Murphy].

30500 *Murder ward.* New York: Pinnacle Books, 1974, 176 p., paper, novel. DESTROYER #15. [By Richard Sapir & Warren Murphy].

30501 *Murder's shield.* New York: Pinnacle Books, 1973, 190 p., paper, novel. DESTROYER #9. [By Richard Sapir & Warren Murphy].

20225 *Next of kin* / by Warren Murphy. New York: Pinnacle Books, 1981, 183 p., paper, novel. DESTROYER #46. [By Molly Cochran].

30502 *Oil slick.* New York: Pinnacle Books, 1974, 179 p., paper, novel. DESTROYER #16. [By Richard Sapir & Warren Murphy].

30503 *An old-fashioned war.* New York: A Signet Book, New American Library, 1987, 221 p., paper, novel. DESTROYER #68. [By Richard Sapir].

30504 *Power play* / by Warren Murphy. Los Angeles: Pinnacle Books, 1979, 180 p., paper, novel. DESTROYER #36. [By Warren Murphy].

30505 *Profit motive.* New York: Pinnacle Books, 1982, 245 p., paper, novel. DESTROYER #48. [By Richard Sapir & Warren Murphy].

30506 *Rain of terror.* New York: A Signet Book, New American Library, 1989, 256 p., paper, novel. DESTROYER #75. [By Will Murray].

30507 *Remo: the adventure begins: a novel.* New York: A Signet Book, New American Library, 1985, 253 p., paper, movie.

DESTROYER SERIES (UNNUMBERED). [By Richard Sapir].

30508 *Return engagement.* New York: A Signet Book, New American Library, 1988, 253 p., paper, novel. DESTROYER #71. [By Warren Murphy & Will Murray].

26186 *The seventh stone.* New York: A Signet Book, New American Library, 1985, 223 p., paper, novel. DESTROYER #62. [By Richard Sapir & Warren Murphy & Ed Hunsburger].

30509 *Ship of death.* New York: Pinnacle Books, 1977, 179 p., paper, novel. DESTROYER #28. [By Richard Sapir & Warren Murphy].

20226 *Shock value* / by Warren Murphy. New York: Pinnacle Books, 1983, 199 p., paper, novel. DESTROYER #51. [By Molly Cochran].

30510 *Shooting schedule.* New York: A Signet Book, New American Library, 1990, 255 p., paper, novel. DESTROYER #79. [By Will Murray].

20227 *Skin deep* / by Warren Murphy. New York: Pinnacle Books, 1982, 199 p., paper, novel. DESTROYER #49. [By Molly Cochran].

30511 *Skull duggery.* New York: A Signet Book, 1991, 253 p., paper, novel. DESTROYER #83. [By Will Murray].

30512 *The sky is falling.* New York: A Signet Book, New American Library, 1986, 255 p., paper, novel. DESTROYER #63. [By Richard Sapir & Will Murray].

30513 *Slave safari.* New York: Pinnacle Books, 1973, 186 p., paper, novel. DESTROYER #12. [By Richard Sapir & Warren Murphy].

30514 *Sole survivor.* New York: A Signet Book, New American Library, 1988, 223 p., paper, novel. DESTROYER #72. [By Warren Murphy & Will Murray].

20228 *Spoils of war* / by Warren Murphy. New York: Pinnacle Books, 1981, 182 p., paper, novel. DESTROYER #45. [By Molly Cochran].

30515 *Sue me.* New York: A Signet Book, New American Library, 1986, 221 p., paper, novel. DESTROYER #66. [By Richard Sapir].

30516 *Summit chase* / by Warren Murphy. New York: Pinnacle Books, 1973, 185 p., paper, novel. DESTROYER #8. [By Warren Murphy].

30517 *Survival course.* New York: A Signet Book, 1990, 253 p., paper, novel. DESTROYER #82. [By Will Murray].

29800 *Sweet dreams* / by Warren Murphy. New York: Pinnacle Books, 1976, 174 p., paper, novel. DESTROYER #25. [By Warren Murphy & Ric Meyers].

30518 *Terror squad.* New York: Pinnacle Books, 1973, 188 p., paper, novel. DESTROYER #10. [By Richard Sapir & Warren Murphy].

26810 *Timber line* / by Warren Murphy. Los Angeles: Pinnacle Books, 1980, 181 p., paper, novel. DESTROYER #42. [By Warren Murphy & William "Ted" Joy].

20229 *Time trial* / by Warren Murphy. New York: Pinnacle Books, 1983, 201 p., paper, novel. DESTROYER #53. [By Molly Cochran].

30519 *Total recall* / by Warren Murphy. New York: Pinnacle Books, 1984, 185 p., paper, novel. DESTROYER #58. [By Warren Murphy & Robert J. Randisi].

30520 *Union bust.* New York: Pinnacle Books, 1973, 184 p., paper, novel. DESTROYER #7. [By Richard Sapir & Warren Murphy].

30521 *Voodoo die.* Los Angeles: Pinnacle Books, 1978, 181 p., paper, novel. DESTROYER #33. [By Richard Sapir & Warren Murphy].

30522 *Walking wounded.* New York: A Signet Book, New American Library, 1988, 224 p., paper, novel. DESTROYER #74. [By Will Murray].

SAPPER [pseud. of Herman Cyril McNeile], 1888-1937

38049 *The final count.* London: Hodder & Stoughton, 1926, 319 p., cloth, novel.

SARABANDE, William

Beyond the sea of ice—SEE: *The first Americans: Beyond the sea of ice.*
Corridor of storms—SEE: *The first Americans: Corridor of storms.*

33146 *The first Americans: Beyond the sea of ice.* Toronto, New York: Book Creations Inc., Bantam Books, 1987, 373 p., paper, novel. FIRST AMERICANS #1.

33147 *The first Americans: Corridor of storms.* Toronto, New York: Book Creations Inc., Bantam Books, 1988, 423 p., paper, novel. FIRST AMERICANS #2.

33148 *The first Americans: Forbidden land.* New York, Toronto: Book Creations Inc., Bantam Books, 1989, 434 p., paper, novel. FIRST AMERICANS #3.

33149 *The first Americans: The sacred stones.* New York, Toronto: Domain, Book Creations Inc., Bantam Books, 1991, 580 p., paper, novel. FIRST AMERICANS #5.

33150 *The first Americans: Walkers of the wind.* New York: Book Creations Inc., Bantam Books, 1990, 420 p., paper, novel. FIRST AMERICANS #4.

Forbidden land—SEE: *The first Americans: Forbidden land.*
The sacred stones—SEE: *The first Americans: The sacred stones.*
Walkers of the wind—SEE: *The first Americans: Walkers of the wind.*

33151 *Wolves of the dawn.* Toronto, New York: Bantam Books, 1987, 453 p., paper, novel.

SARALEGUI, Jorge

33152 *Last rites.* New York: Charter Books, 1985, 279 p., paper, novel.

33153 *Looker.* New York: Charter Books, 1990, 217 p., paper, novel.

33154 *Shadow stalker.* New York: Charter Books, 1987, 322 p., paper, novel.

SARAMAGO, José, 1922-

33155 *Baltasar and Blimunda.* San Diego, CA: Harcourt Brace Jovanovich, 1987, 336 p., cloth, novel. [Translation by Giovanni Pontiero of *Memorial do convento*].

SARAZEN, Nicholas, pseud.—SEE: Cooper, Rick & Davis, Mark

*SARBAN [pseud. of John William Wall], 1910-1989

SARGENT, Craig, pseud.—SEE: Stacy, Jan

SARGENT, H(enry) B.

33156 *Carthaginian for a day: an historical romance.* New York: Sargent Collett, 1981, xxv+130 p., paper, novel.

SARGENT, Lyman Tower, 1940-

33157 *British and American utopian literature, 1516-1975: an annotated bibliography.* Boston: G. K. Hall & Co., 1979, xxvi+324 p., cloth, nonf. REFERENCE PUBLICATION IN SCIENCE FICTION.

33158 *British and American utopian literature, 1516-1986: an annotated, chronological bibliography.* New York, London: Garland Publishing Co., 1988, xix+559 p., cloth, nonf.

SARGENT, Pamela, 1948-

33159 *Alien child.* New York: Harper & Row, 1988, 246 p., cloth, novel.

33160 *The alien upstairs.* Garden City, NY: Doubleday & Co., 1983, 181 p., cloth, novel.

33161 *The best of Pamela Sargent.* Chicago: Academy Chicago, 1987, xxxii+322 p., cloth, anth. [Edited by Martin H. Greenberg].

33162 *Bio-futures: science fiction stories about biological metamorphosis.* New York: Vintage Books, Random House, 1976, xxxv+344 p., paper, anth.

33163 *Cloned lives.* Greenwich, CT: A Fawcett Gold Medal Book, Fawcett Publications, 1976, 336 p., paper, novel.

33164 *Earthseed: a novel.* New York, Hagerstown, NJ: Harper & Row, Publishers, 1983, 289 p., cloth, novel.

33165 *Elvira's zoo.* Tulsa, OK: Educational Development Corp., 1979, 16 p., paper, story.

33166 *Eye of the comet.* New York, Hagerstown, NJ: Harper & Row, 1984, 275 p., cloth, novel. EARTHMINDS TRILOGY #2.

33167 *The golden space.* New York: Timescape Books, 1982, 272 p., cloth, novel.

33168 *Homesmind.* New York, Hagerstown, NJ: Harper & Row, 1984, 278 p., cloth, novel. EARTHMINDS TRILOGY #3.

33169 *More women of wonder: science fiction novelettes by women about women.* New York: Vintage Books, Random House, 1976, liii+305 p., paper, anth.

33170 *The mountain cage.* New Castle, VA: Cheap Street, 1983, 31 p., paper, story. [Limited to 125 copies].

33171 *The new women of wonder: recent science fiction stories by women about women.* New York: Vintage Books, Random House, 1978, xxxiv+363 p., paper, anth.

33172 *Pamela Sargent: a checklist.* New Castle, VA: Cheap Street, 1983, 8 p., paper, story. [Limited to 125 copies].

33173 *The shore of women.* New York: Crown Publishers, 1986, 469 p., cloth, novel.

33174 *Starshadows: ten stories.* New York: Ace Books, 1977, 205 p., paper, coll.

33175 *The sudden star.* New York: Fawcett Gold Medal, 1979, 285 p., paper, novel.

33175A retitled: *The white death.* London: Fontana Books, 1980, 254 p., paper, novel.

33176 *Venus of dreams.* Toronto, New York: Bantam Books, 1986, 536 p., paper, novel. VENUS TRILOGY #1.

33177 *Venus of shadows.* Toronto, New York: A Foundation Book, Doubleday, 1988, 544 p., cloth, novel. VENUS TRILOGY #2.

33178 *Watchstar.* New York: Pocket Books, 1980, 238 p., paper, novel. EARTHMINDS TRILOGY #1.

The white death—SEE: *The sudden star.*

33179 *Women of wonder: science fiction stories by women about women.* New York: Vintage Books, 1975, lxiv+285 p., paper, anth.

with Ian Watson

33180 *Afterlives: an anthology of stories about life after death.* New York: Vintage Books, 1986, xviii+494 p., paper, anth.

SARGENT, Sarah, 1937-

33181 *Jonas McFee, A.T.P.* New York: Bradbury Press, 1989, 119 p., cloth, novel.

33182 *Watermusic.* Boston: Ticknor & Fields, 1986, 120 p., cloth, novel.

SARRANTONIO, Al, 1952-

33183 *The boy with penny eyes.* New York: Tor Horror, A Tom Doherty Associates Book, 1987, 278 p., paper, novel.

33184 *Campbell Wood.* Garden City, NY: Doubleday & Co., 1986, 180 p., cloth, novel.

33185 *Cold night.* New York: Tor, A Tom Doherty Associates Book, 1989, 181 p., cloth, novel.

33186 *House haunted.* New York, Toronto: Spectra, Bantam Books, 1991, 277 p., paper, novel.

33187 *Moonbane.* New York, Toronto: Bantam Books, 1989, 196 p., paper, novel.

33188 *October.* New York, Toronto: Bantam Books, 1990, 224 p., paper, novel.

33189 *Totentanz.* New York: Tor, A Tom Doherty Associates Book, 1985, 285 p., paper, novel.

33190 *The worms.* Garden City, New York: Doubleday & Co., 1985, 179 p., cloth, novel.

*SARTRE, Jean-Paul (Charles Aymard), 1905-1980

SATTY, Harvey J(erome), 1936- , with Curtis C. Smith

33191 *Olaf Stapledon: a bibliography.* Westport, CT: Greenwood Press, 1984, xxxviii+167 p., cloth, nonf.

*SAUER, Julia L(ina), 1891-1983

*SAUL, George Brandon, 1901-1986

SAUL, John (Woodruff III), 1942-

All fall down—SEE: *The God project.*
33192 *Brainchild.* Toronto, New York: Bantam Books, 1985, 342 p., paper, novel.
33193 *Comes the blind fury.* New York: A Dell Book, 1980, 383 p., paper, novel.
33194 *Creature.* New York, Toronto: Bantam Books, 1989, 329 p., cloth, novel.
33195 *Cry for the strangers.* New York: A Dell Book, 1979, 415 p., paper, novel.
33196 *Darkness.* New York, Toronto: Bantam Books, 1991, 341 p., cloth, novel.
33197 *The God project.* Toronto, New York: Bantam Books, 1982, 311 p., cloth, novel.
33197A retitled: *All fall down.* London: Corgi Books, 1983, 311 p., cloth, novel.
33198 *Hellfire.* Toronto, New York: Bantam Books, 1986, 344 p., paper, novel.
33199 *Nathaniel.* Toronto, New York: Bantam Books, 1984, 343 p., paper, novel.
33200 *Second child.* New York, Toronto: Bantam Books, 1990, 341 p., cloth, novel.
33201 *Sleepwalk.* New York, Toronto: Bantam Books, 1991, 499 p., paper, novel.
33202 *Suffer the children.* New York: A Dell Book, 1977, 378 p., paper, novel.
33203 *The unloved.* Toronto, New York: Bantam Books, 1988, 358 p., paper, novel.
33204 *The unwanted.* Toronto, New York: Bantam Books, 1987, 339 p., paper, novel.
33205 *When the wind blows.* New York: A Dell Book, 1981, 348 p., paper, novel.

SAUNDERS, Charles R(obert), 1946-

33206 *Imaro.* New York: DAW Books, 1981, 208 p., paper, novel. IMARO #1.
33207 *The quest for Cush.* New York: DAW Books, 1984, 205 p., paper, novel. IMARO #2.
33208 *Robert E. Howard: adventure unlimited.* Gananoque, Ontario, Canada: Shadow Press, 1976, p., paper?, nonf.
33209 *The trail of Bohu.* New York: DAW Books, 1985, 222 p., paper, novel. IMARO #3.

SAUNDERS, David, 1948-

33210 *Encyclopaedia of the worlds of Doctor Who, A-D.* London: Picadilly Press, 1987, 128 p., cloth, nonf.
33211 *Encyclopaedia of the worlds of Doctor Who, E-K.* London: Picadilly Press, 1989, 127 p., cloth, nonf.
33212 *Encyclopaedia of the worlds of Doctor Who, L-R.* London: Picadilly Press, 1990, 140 p., cloth, nonf.

SAUNDERS, Elizabeth A., 1948-

33213 *When the black lotus blooms.* Atlanta, GA: Unnameable Press, 1990, 322 p., cloth, anth. [Includes some verse].

SAUNDERS, G. K.

33214 *The stranger.* Sydney & London: Whitcombe & Tombs, 1978, 217 p., cloth, tele.

SAUNDERS, Hilary—SEE: Browne, Barum

*SAUNDERS, Jake, 1947-

SAUNDERS, Richard, 1947-

33215 *Ambrose Bierce: the making of a misanthrope.* San Francisco: Chronicle Books, 1985, 111 p., paper, nonf.

SAUTER, Eric, 1948-

33216 *Predators.* New York: Pocket Books, 1988, 360 p., paper, novel.

SAVAGE, Adrian [pseud. of Joe Serrano]

33217 *Blake House.* New York, London: Pocket Books, 1990, 254 p., paper, novel.
33218 *Unholy communion.* New York, London: Pocket Books, 1988, 255 p., paper, novel.

SAVAGE, D(ouglas) J(oseph), 1950-

33219 *The glass lady: the space shuttle novel.* Canton, OH: Daring Books, 1985, 388 p., cloth, novel.

SAVAGE, David S., 1910-

33220 *Mysticism and Aldous Huxley: an examination of Heard-Huxley theories.* Yonkers, NY: O. Baradinsky, 1947, [28] p., paper, nonf.

SAVAGE, Robert L(ynn), 1939- , with James Combs & Dan Nimmo

20350 *The Orwellian moment: hindsight and foresight in the post-1984 world.* Fayetteville, AR: University of Arkansas Press, 1989, viii+180 p., cloth, nonf. anth.

SAVARIN, Julian Jay

33221 *The archives of Haven.* London: Corgi Books, 1977, 206 p., paper, novel. LEMMUS #3.

33222 *Arena.* London: Robert Hale, 1979, 224 p., cloth, novel.

33223 *Beyond the Outer Mirr.* London: Corgi Books, 1976, 253 p., paper, novel. LEMMUS #2.

SAVCHENKO, Vladimir (Ivanovich), 1933-

33224 *Self-discovery.* New York: Macmillan Publishing Co.; London: Collier Macmillan Publishers, 1979, xiv+305 p., cloth, novel. [Translation by Antonina W. Bouis of *Otkrytie sebia*].

*SAVILLE, (Leonard) Malcolm, 1901-1982

SAVINI, Tom, 1950-

Bizarro—SEE: *Grande illusions.*

33225 *Grande illusions: learn-by-example guide to the art and technique of special make-up effects from the films of Tom Savini.* Pittsburgh, PA: Imagine, 1983, 135 p., paper, nonf.

33225A retitled: *Bizarro.* New York: Harmony Books, 1983, 135 p., paper, nonf.

SAVORY, Gerald

33226 *Count Dracula.* London: Corgi Books, 1977, 142 p., paper, tele. DRACULA SERIES.

SAVORY, Teo, 1909-1989

33227 *A clutch of fables.* Greensboro, NC: Unicorn Press, 1977, 87 p., cloth, coll. [Limited to 326 copies].

SAWARD, Eric

Attack of the cybermen—SEE: *Doctor Who: Attack of the cybermen.*

33228 *Doctor Who and the visitation.* London: W. H. Allen, 1982, 121 p., cloth, tele. DOCTOR WHO.

33229 *Doctor Who: Attack of the cybermen.* London: W. H. Allen & Co., 1989, 138 p., cloth, tele. DOCTOR WHO #138.

33230 *Doctor Who: Slipback.* London: W. H. Allen & Co., 1986, 144 p., cloth, radio. DOCTOR WHO (UNNUMBERED).

33231 *Doctor Who: The twin dilemma.* London: W. H. Allen & Co., 1985, 138 p., cloth, tele. DOCTOR WHO #103.

Slipback—SEE: *Doctor Who: Slipback.*

The twin dilemma—SEE: *Doctor Who: The twin dilemma.*

SAWDE, Derek

33232 *The sceptre mortal.* London: Oriflamme Publishing, 1985, ix+294 p., paper, novel.

SAWYER, Robert J(ames), 1960-

33233 *Golden fleece.* New York: Popular Library, 1990, 197 p., paper, novel.

SAXBY, William, *with Robert Ingpen*

26297 *The great deeds of superheroes.* Limpsfield, Surrey, England: Paper Tiger, 1989, 184 p., cloth, coll.

SAXON, Peter, house pseud.

12719 *Black Honey.* London: Mayflower Books, 1968, 157 p., paper, novel. [By W. Howard Baker].

12720 *Corruption.* London: Sphere Books, 1968 (i.e., 1969), 144 p., paper, novel. [By Wilfred G. McNeilly].

12721 *The curse of Rathlaw.* New York: Lancer Books, 1968, 190 p., paper, novel. GUARDIANS SERIES. [By W. Howard Baker & Martin Thomas].

12722 *Dark ways to death.* London: Howard Baker, 1968, 176 p., cloth, novel. GUARDIANS #2. [By W. Howard Baker & Wilfred G. McNeilly].

00753 *The darkest night.* London: Mayflower Books, 1966, 157 p., paper, novel. [By W. Howard Baker & Wilfred G. McNeilly].

12723 *The disorientated man.* London: Mayflower Books, 1966, 126 p., paper, novel. [By W. Howard Baker & Stephen D. Frances].

12723A retitled: *Scream and scream again.* New York: Paperback Library, 1967, 158 p., paper, novel. [By W. Howard Baker & Stephen D. Frances].

12725 *The haunting of Alan Mais.* New York: Berkley Books, 1969, 143 p., paper, novel. GUARDIANS #3. [By W. Howard Baker & Wilfred G. McNeilly].

12724 *The killing bone.* New York: Berkley Books, 1969, 159 p., paper, novel. GUARDIANS #1. [By W. Howard Baker].

00754 *Satan's child.* London: Mayflower Books, 1967, 127 p., paper, novel. [By Wilfred G. McNeilly].

Scream and scream again—SEE: *The disorientated man.*

00755 *The Torturer.* London: Mayflower Books, 1966, 159 p., paper, novel. [By W. Howard Baker & Wilfred G. McNeilly].

12727 *Through the dark curtain.* New York: Lancer Books, 1968, 190 p., paper, novel. GUARDIANS SERIES. [By Ross Richards].

12728 *Vampire's moon.* New York: Belmont Books, 1970, 176 p., paper, novel. [By W. Howard Baker].

12726 *The vampires of Finistère.* New York: A Berkley Medallion Book, 1970, 190 p., paper, novel. GUARDIANS #4. [By Rex Dolphin].

SAXON, William [pseud. of William Mayleas], 1927-

33234 *Mind bender.* New York: Avon Books, 1989, 250 p., paper, novel.

SAXTON, Josephine (Mary Howard), 1935-

33235 *The consciousness machine; Jane Saint and the backlash: the further adventures of Jane Saint.* London: The Women's Press, 1989, 167 p., paper, coll. JANE SAINT #2.

33236 *Little tours of Hell.* London: Routledge & Kegan Paul, 1986, 146 p., cloth, coll.

33237 *The power of time.* London: Chatto & Windus, 1985, 222 p., cloth, coll.

33238 *Queen of the states.* London: The Women's Press, 1986, 175 p., paper, novel.

33239 *The travails of Jane Saint.* London: Virgin Books, 1980, 128 p., paper, novel. JANE SAINT #1.

33240 retitled: *The travails of Jane Saint, and other stories.* London: The Women's Press, 1986, 194 p., paper, coll. JANE SAINT #1. [Expanded edition].

SAXTON, Mark, 1914-1988

33241 *Havoc in Islandia.* Boston: Houghton Mifflin Co., 1982, 241 p., cloth, novel. ISLANDIA #4.

33242 *The two kingdoms: a novel of Islandia.* Boston: Houghton Mifflin Co., 1979, vii+242 p., cloth, novel. ISLANDIA #3.

SAXTON, Peter, house pseud.—SEE: Frances, Stephen & Baker, W. Howard

SAYER, George

33243 *Jack: C. S. Lewis and his times.* San Francisco: Harper & Row, 1988, xvii+278 p., cloth, nonf.

SAYERS, John, *with David McDonnell & Tim L. Smith*

29494 *Starlog science fiction trivia book.* New York: A Signet Book, New American Library, 1986, 208 p., paper, nonf.

SAYRE, Cheryl—SEE: Curry, Chris

SAYRE, Rose, *with Jim Villani*

33244 *Science fiction.* Youngstown, OH: Pig Iron Press, 1982, 95 p., paper?, anth.

SCAFIDEL, James R.—SEE: Phillips, Lyn

SCALES, Derek P(ercival), 1921-

33245 *Aldous Huxley and French literature.* Sydney, Australia: Sydney University Press for the Australia Humanities Research Council, 1969, 94 p., cloth, nonf.

SCAMMELL, Bill, *with Evan Jamieson & Lisa Hunt & Walter Hunt & Richard S. Meyer & Mark Bloom & Christine Ivey as* ARCHITECTS ADVENTURE

18216 *Dzurlord: a Crossroads adventure in the world of Steven Brust's Jhereg /* by Architects Adventure. New York: Tor, A Tom Doherty Associates Book, 1987, 24+[224] p., paper, novel. JHEREG SERIES; CROSSROADS ADVENTURE.

SCANLON, Noel

33246 *Apparitions.* London: Robert Hale, 1984, 208 p., cloth, novel.

33247 *Black ashes.* New York: St. Martin's Press, 1985, 222 p., cloth, novel.

SCANLON, Paul, *with Michael Gross*

24784 *The book of Alien.* New York: Heavy Metal Communications, 1979, [12] p., paper, nonf.

SCANZIANI, Piero, 1908-dead

33248 *The white book.* Windsor, England: Eureka Publishers, 1991, 307 p., cloth, novel. [Translation by Linda Lappin of *Libro blanco*].

SCAPARRO, Jack

33249 *The attic.* New York: A Zebra Book, Kensington Publishing Corp., 1991, 350 p., paper, novel.

33250 *Deathsong.* New York: A Zebra Book, Kensington Publishing Corp., 1989, 346 p., paper, novel.

33251 *The dollkeeper.* New York: A Zebra Book, Kensington Publishing Corp., 1987, 380 p., paper, novel.

33252 *Hocus-pocus.* New York: A Zebra Book, Kensington Publishing Corp., 1988, 405 p., paper, novel.

33253 *Worst enemies.* New York: A Dell Book, 1983, 351 p., paper, novel.

SCARBOROUGH, Charles—SEE: Scarborough, Chuck

SCARBOROUGH, Chuck [i.e., Charles Bishop Scarborough III], 1943- , *with William Murray*

30532 *The Myrmidon Project.* New York: Coward, McCann & Geoghegan, 1981, 311 p., cloth, novel.

SCARBOROUGH, Elizabeth (Ann), 1947-

33254 *Bronwyn's bane.* Toronto, New York: Bantam Books, 1983, 286 p., paper, novel. ARGONIA #3.

33255 *The christening quest* / by Elizabeth Ann Scarborough. Toronto, New York: Bantam Books, 1985, 231 p., paper, novel. ARGONIA #4.

33256 *The drastic dragon of Draco*, Texas. Toronto, New York: Bantam Books, 1986, 247 p., paper, novel.

33257 *The goldcamp vampire; or, The sanguinary sourdough.* Toronto, New York: Bantam Books, 1987, 247 p., paper, novel.

33258 *The harem of Aman Akbar; or, The djinn decanted.* Toronto, New York: Bantam Books, 1984, 265 p., paper, novel.

33259 *The healer's war* / by Elizabeth Ann Scarborough. New York: A Foundation Book, Doubleday, 1988, 303 p., cloth, novel. [Winner of the Nebula Award for Best Novel, 1989 (1990)].

33260 *Nothing sacred.* New York: A Foundation Book, Doubleday, 1991, 342 p., cloth, novel.

33261 *Phantom banjo.* New York, Toronto: Spectra, Bantam Books, 1991, 263 p., paper, novel. SONGKILLER SAGA #1.

33262 *Picking the ballad's bones.* New York, Toronto: Spectra, Bantam Books, 1991, 242 p., paper, novel. SONGKILLER SAGA #2.

33263 *Song of sorcery* / by Elizabeth Ann Scarborough. Toronto, New York: Bantam Books, 1982, 216 p., paper, novel. ARGONIA #1.

33264 *Songs from the seashell archives, volume I: Song of sorcery; The unicorn creed.* Toronto, New York: Bantam Books, 1987, 552 p., paper, coll. ARGONIA #1-2. [Includes *Song of Sorcery*; *Unicorn creed*].

33265 *Songs from the seashell archives, vol. 2: Bronwyn's bane; The christening quest* / by Elizabeth Ann Scarborough. Toronto, New York: Spectra, Bantam Books, 1988, 390 p., paper, coll. ARGONIA #3-4.

33266 *The unicorn creed.* Toronto, New York: Bantam Books, 1983, v+340 p., paper, novel. ARGONIA #2.

SCARFONE, Jay, *with John Fricke & William Stillman*

23512 *The Wizard of Oz: the official 50th anniversary pictorial history.* New York: Warner Books, 1989, 245 p., cloth, nonf.

SCARMAN, George

33267 *The victim.* London: Corgi Books, 1982, 234 p., paper, novel.

SCHAEFER, Jack (Warner), 1907-1991

33268 *Conversations with a pocket gopher.* Santa Barbara, CA: A Noel Young Book, Capra Press, 1978, 126 p., paper, coll.

SCHAEFFER, Susan Fromberg, 1941-

33269 *The dragons of North Chittendon.* New York: A Little Simon Book, Simon & Schuster, 1986, 208 p., cloth, novel.

33270 *The Four Hoods and Great Dog.* New York: St. Martin's Press, 1988, 131 p., cloth, novel.

SCHAFFER, Gene, 1941-

33271 *Countdown to doomsday.* North Hollywood, CA: American Art Enterprises, 1982, 154 p., paper, novel.

SCHAKEL, Peter J(ames), 1941-

33272 *The longing for a form: essays on the fiction of C. S. Lewis.* Kent, OH: Kent State University Press, 1977, xvii+234 p., cloth, nonf. anth.

33273 *Reading with the heart: the way into Narnia.* Grand Rapids, MI: William B. Eerdmans Publishing Co., 1979, xiv + 154 p., cloth, nonf.

33274 *Reason and imagination in C. S. Lewis: a study of "Till we have faces".* Grand Rapids, MI: William B. Eerdmans Publishing Co., 1984, xii + 208 p., paper, nonf.

with Charles A. Huttar

26245 *Word and story in C. S. Lewis.* Columbia, MO: University of Missouri Press, 1991, x + 316 p., cloth, nonf. anth.

*SCHAPER, Edzard (Hellmuth), 1908-1984

SCHATT, Stanley, 1943-

33275 *Kurt Vonnegut, Jr.* Boston: Twayne Publishers, 1976, 174 p., cloth, nonf.

SCHAUBELT, F. J.—SEE: Joseph, Franz

SCHECTER, Winifred—SEE: Morris, Winifred

SCHEER, K(arl) H(erbert), 1928-1991

33276 *The blue system.* New York: Ace Books, 1976, 182 p., paper, novel. PERRY RHODAN #99. [Includes additional fiction and nonfiction].

33277 *The Columbus affair.* New York: Ace Books, 1975, 157 p., paper, novel. PERRY RHODAN #80. [Includes additional fiction and nonfiction].

33278 *Crimson universe.* New York: Ace Books, 1975, 175 p., paper, novel. PERRY RHODAN #67. [Includes additional fiction and nonfiction].

33279 *The Crystal Prince.* New York: Ace Books, 1977, 131 p., paper, novel. ATLAN #4. [Bound with *War of the ghosts* / by Clark Darlton].

33280 *Duel under the double sun.* New York: Ace Books, 1977, 189 p., paper, novel. PERRY RHODAN #108. [Includes additional fiction and nonfiction].

33281 *The guns of Everblack.* Van Nuys, CA: Master Publications, 1979, 62 p., paper, novel. PERRY RHODAN #126. [Translation of *Die kanonen von Everblack*].

33282 *The last days of Atlantis.* New York: Ace Books, 1975, 155 p., paper, novel. PERRY RHODAN #62. [Includes additional fiction and nonfiction].

33283 *The mystery of the Anti.* New York: Ace Books, 1976, 187 p., paper, novel.

PERRY RHODAN #88. [Includes additional fiction and nonfiction].

33284 *Planet Mechanica.* New York: Ace Books, 1977, 115-252 p., paper, novel. PERRY RHODAN #112. [Bound with *Seeds of ruin* / by William Voltz].

33285 *Power key.* New York: Ace Books, 1975, 157 p., paper, novel. PERRY RHODAN #78. [Includes additional fiction and nonfiction].

33286 *The robot invitation.* Van Nuys, CA: Master Publications, 1979, 64 p., paper, novel. PERRY RHODAN #136. [Translation of *Roboter lassen bitten...*].

33287 *Savior of the empire.* New York: Ace Books, 1977, 126 p., paper, novel. PERRY RHODAN #117. [Bound with *The shadows attack* / by Clark Darlton].

33288 *The target star.* New York: Ace Books, 1976, 184 p., paper, novel. PERRY RHODAN #92. [Includes additional fiction and nonfiction].

SCHEICK, William J(oseph), 1941- , *with J. Randolph Cox*

33289 *H. G. Wells: a reference guide.* Boston: G. K. Hall & Co., 1988, xxxiii + 430 p., cloth, nonf. anth.

SCHELLINGER, Paul E(dward), 1962- , *with Noelle Watson*

33290 *Twentieth-century science-fiction writers, 3rd ed.* Chicago & London: St James Press, 1991, xxvi + 1016 p., cloth, nonf. anth.

SCHENCK, Hilbert (van Nydeck Jr.), 1926-

33291 *At the eye of the ocean.* New York: A Timescape Book, Pocket Books, 1981, 224 p., paper, novel.

33292 *Chronosequence.* New York: Tor, A Tom Doherty Associates Book, 1988, 314 p., cloth, novel.

33293 *A rose for armageddon.* New York: A Timescape Book, Pocket Books, 1982, 175 p., paper, novel.

33294 *Steam bird.* New York: Tor SF, A Tom Doherty Associates Book, 1988, 213 p., paper, coll.

33295 *Wave rider.* New York: Pocket Books, 1980, 237 p., paper, coll.

SCHERLING, Sarah, *with Terry Holt*

25879 *The hero and the crown.* Des Moines, IA: Waterwheel Press, 1990, 16 p., paper, nonf.

SCHICK, Lawrence, 1953-

33296 *Heroic worlds: a history and guide to role-playing games.* Buffalo, NY: Prometheus Books, 1991, 448 p., cloth, nonf.

SCHIFF, Gert (K. A.), 1926-1990

33297 *Images of horror and fantasy.* New York: Henry N. Abrams Publishers, 1978, 159 p., cloth, art.

33298 *Images of horror and fantasy: the Bronx Museum of the Arts, November 15 through December 31, 1977.* Bronx, NY: Bronx Museum of the Arts, 1977, [22] p., paper, art.

SCIIIFF, Stuart David, 1946-

33299 *Death.* New York: Playboy Paperbacks, 1982, 237 p., paper, anth.

33300 *Mad scientists: an anthology of fantasy and horror.* Garden City, NY: Doubleday & Co., 1980, 300 p., cloth, anth.

33300 *Whispers: an anthology of fantasy and horror.* Garden City, NY: Doubleday & Co., 1977, xii+226 p., cloth, anth.

33302 *Whispers II.* Garden City, NY: Doubleday & Co., 1979, xii+237 p., cloth, anth.

33303 *Whispers III.* Garden City, NY: Doubleday & Co., 1981, viii+182 p., cloth, anth.

33304 *Whispers IV.* Garden City, NY: Doubleday & Co., 1983, 182 p., cloth, anth.

33305 *Whispers V.* Garden City, NY: Doubleday & Co., 1985, 208 p., cloth, anth.

33306 *Whispers VI.* Garden City, NY: Doubleday & Co., 1987, viii+181 p., cloth, anth.

with Fritz Leiber

28138 *World fantasy awards, volume two.* Garden City, NY: Doubleday & Co., 1980, xxxv+248 p., cloth, anth.

SCHLEE, Ann, 1934-

33307 *The vandal.* London: Macmillan Children's Books, 1979, 173 p., cloth, novel.

SCHLOBIN, Roger C(lark), 1944-

33308 *Aesthetics of fantasy art and literature.* Notre Dame, IN: University of Notre Dame Press; Brighton, Sussex, England: Harvester Press, 1982, xvi+288 p., cloth, nonf. coll.

33309 *Andre Norton: a primary and secondary bibliography.* Boston: G. K. Hall &

Co., 1980, xxxii+68 p., cloth, nonf. MASTERS OF SCIENCE FICTION AND FANTASY.

33310 *The literature of fantasy: a comprehensive, annotated bibliography of modern fantasy fiction.* New York, London: Garland Publishing, 1979, xxxv+425 p., cloth, nonf.

33311 *Urania's daughters: a checklist of women science-fiction writers, 1692-1982.* Mercer Island, WA: Starmont House, 1983, xiii+79 p., cloth, nonf. STARMONT REFERENCE GUIDE #1.

with Glen Cook

20461 *A Glen Cook bibliography.* [S.l.: s.n.], 1983, [1] p., paper, nonf.

with Marshall Tymn

33312 *The year's scholarship in science fiction and fantasy: 1976-1979.* Kent, OH: Kent State University Press, 1982, ix+251 p., cloth, nonf.

33313 *The year's scholarship in science fiction and fantasy, The: 1972-1975.* Kent, OH: Kent State University Press, 1979, xvi+222 p., cloth, nonf.

with Marshall Tymn & L. W. Currey

20898 *A research guide to science fiction studies: an annotated checklist of primary and secondary sources for fantasy and science fiction.* New York, London: Garland Publishing, 1977, ix+165 p., cloth, nonf.

SCHLUETER, Paul (George Jr.), 1933-

33314 *The novels of Doris Lessing.* Carbondale & Edwardsville, IL: Southern Illinois University Press; London & Amsterdam: Feffer & Simon, 1973, x+144 p., cloth, nonf.

SCHMIDT, Arno (Otto), 1914-1979

33315 *The egghead republic: a short novel from the Horse Latitudes.* London & Boston: Marion Boyars, 1979, 164 p., cloth, novel. [Translation by Michael Horovitz of *Die Gelehrtenrepublik*].

SCHMIDT, Dan

33316 *Armageddon, USA.* New York, Toronto: Falcon, Bantam Books, 1991, 192 p., paper, novel. EAGLE FORCE #9.

SCHMIDT, Dennis (A.)

33317 *City of crystal shadow.* New York: Ace Books, 1990, 180 p., paper, novel. QUESTIONER TRILOGY #2.

33318 *Dark paradise.* New York: Ace Books, 1990, 186 p., paper, novel. QUESTIONER TRILOGY #3.

The first name—SEE: *Twilight of the gods: The first name.*

33319 *Groa's other eye.* New York: Ace Fantasy Books, 1986, 295 p., paper, novel. TWILIGHT OF THE GODS #2.

33320 *Kensho.* New York: Ace Books, 1979, 314 p., paper, novel. KENSHO #2.

33321 *Labyrinth.* New York: Ace Books, 1989, 179 p., paper, novel. QUESTIONER TRILOGY #1.

33322 *Satori.* New York: Ace Books, 1981, 293 p., paper, novel. KENSHO #3.

33323 *Three trumps sounding.* New York: Ace Books, 1988, 342 p., paper, novel. TWILIGHT OF THE GODS #3.

33324 *Twilight of the gods: The first name.* New York: Ace Fantasy Books, 1985, 307 p., paper, novel. TWILIGHT OF THE GODS #1.

33325 *Wanderer.* New York: Ace Science Fiction Books, 1985, 202 p., paper, novel. KENSHO #4.

33326 *Way-farer.* New York: Ace Books, 1978, 277 p., paper, novel. KENSHO #1.

SCHMIDT, Stanley (Albert), 1944-

33327 *6 decades: the best of Analog.* New York: Davis Publications, 1986, 128 p., paper, anth.

33328 *Aliens from Analog.* New York: The Dial Press, Davis Publications, 1983, 286 p., cloth, anth. ANALOG ANTHOLOGY #7.

33329 *The Analog anthology #1.* New York: Davis Publications, 1980, 380 p., paper, anth. ANALOG ANTHOLOGY #1. [Cover title reads: *Fifty years of the best from Astounding science fiction and Analog science fiction/science fact*].

33329A retitled: *Analog's Golden anniversary anthology.* New York: Longmeadow Press, Davis Publications, 1980, 380 p., cloth, anth. ANALOG ANTHOLOGY #1.

33330 *The Analog anthology #2.* New York: Davis Publications, 1981, 288 p., paper, anth. ANALOG ANTHOLOGY #2. [Cover title reads: *Readers' choice*].

33330A retitled: *Analog: Readers' choice.* New York: Dial Press, Davis Publications, 1981, 284 p., cloth, anth. ANALOG ANTHOLOGY #2.

Analog: Readers' choice—SEE: *The Analog anthology #2.*

33331 *Analog: Writers' choice.* New York: The Dial Press, Davis Publications, 1983, 288 p., cloth, anth. ANALOG ANTHOLOGY #5.

Analog: Writers' choice, volume II—SEE: *Writers' choice, volume II.*

33332 *Analog yearbook II.* New York: Ace Books, 1981, 294 p., paper, anth.

33333 *Analog's Children of the future.* New York: The Dial Press, Davis Publications, 1982, 288 p., cloth, anth. ANALOG ANTHOLOGY #3.

33334 *Analog's Expanding universe.* New York: Longmeadow Press, Davis Publications, 1986, 285 p., cloth, anth. ANALOG ANTHOLOGY #10.

Analog's Golden anniversary anthology—SEE: *The Analog anthology #1.*

33335 *Analog's Lighter side.* New York: The Dial Press, Davis Publications, 1982, 287 p., cloth, anth. ANALOG ANTHOLOGY #4.

Analog's War and peace—SEE: *War and peace.*

Children of the future—SEE: *Analog's Children of the future.*

Expanding universe—SEE: *Analog's Expanding universe.*

33336 *From mind to mind: tales of communication from Analog.* New York: Dial Press, Davis Publications, 1984, 288 p., cloth, anth. ANALOG ANTHOLOGY #9.

Golden anniversary anthology—SEE: *Analog's Golden anniversary anthology.*

33337 *Lifeboat Earth.* New York: A Berkley Book, Berkley Publishing Corp., 1978, 244 p., paper, novel. KYYRA #2.

33338 *Newton and the quasi-apple.* Garden City, NY: Doubleday & Co., 1975, 180 p, paper, novel.

33339 *The sins of the fathers.* New York: A Berkley Medallion Book, Berkley Publishing Corp., 1976, 184 p., paper, novel. KYYRA #1.

33340 *Tweedlioop.* New York: Tor, A Tom Doherty Associates Book, 1986, 233 p., cloth, novel.

33341 *Unknown.* New York: Baen Books, 1988, 304 p., paper, anth.

33342 *War and peace: possible futures from Analog.* New York: The Dial Press, Davis Publications, 1983, 288 p., cloth, anth. ANALOG ANTHOLOGY #6. [Cover title reads: *Analog's War and peace*].

33343 *Writers' choice, volume II.* New York: The Dial Press, Davis Publications, 1984, 285 p., cloth, anth. ANALOG ANTHOL-

OGY #8. [Cover reads: *Analog: writers' choice, volume II*].

with Martin H. Greenberg

24578 *Unknown worlds: tales from beyond.* New York: Galahad Books, 1988, 517 p., cloth, anth.

SCHMITZ, James H(enry), 1911-1981

33345 *The best of James H. Schmitz.* Cambridge, MA: NESFA Press, 1991, xi+244 p., cloth, coll. [Edited by Mark L. Olson]. *Legacy*—SEE: *A tale of two clocks.*

12768 *A tale of two clocks.* New York: Torquil, 1962, 206 p., cloth, novel. HUB SERIES.

12768A retitled: *Legacy.* New York: Ace Books, 1979, 346 p., paper, novel. HUB SERIES.

12769 *The Telzey toy.* New York: DAW Books, 1973, 175 p., paper, coll. TELZEY #3; HUB SERIES.

12769A retitled: *The Telzey toy, and other stories.* New York: Ace Books, 1982, 211 p., paper, coll. TELZEY SERIES.

SCHNECK, Paul D., 1952-

33346 *Mork & Mindy.* Mankato, MN: Creative Education, 1980, 32 p., cloth, nonf.

SCHNEIDER, Isidor, 1896-1977, as I. S.

33347 *Doctor Transit.* New York: Boni & Liveright, 1925, 285 p., cloth, novel.

SCHNEIDER, Joyce Anne, 1942-

33348 *Darkness falls.* New York, London: Pocket Books, 1989, 310 p., cloth, novel.

33349 *Stryker's children: a novel.* New York: Arbor House, 1984, 240 p., cloth, novel.

SCHNEIDER, Meg (F.)

33350 *The ghost in the picture.* New York, Toronto: Scholastic Inc., 1988, 151 p., paper, novel.

SCHNURNBERGER, Lynn Edelman, 1949-

33351 *Star Trek: the motion picture make-your-own costume book.* New York: A Wallaby Book, Pocket Books, 1979, x+118 p., cloth, nonf. STAR TREK SERIES.

SCHOCH, Tim

33352 *Creeps.* New York: An Avon Camelot Book, 1985, 156 p., paper, novel.

33353 *Flash Fry, private eye.* New York: Avon Camelot, 1986, 90 p., paper, novel.

SCHOCHET, Victoria

with John Silbersack

33354 *The Berkley showcase, vol. 1: new writings in science fiction and fantasy.* New York: Berkley Books, 1980, 280 p., paper, anth.

33355 *The Berkley showcase, vol. 2: new writings in science fiction and fantasy.* New York: Berkley Books, 1980, 200 p., paper, anth.

33356 *The Berkley showcase, vol. 3.* New York: Berkley Books, 1981, 248 p., paper, anth.

33357 *The Berkley showcase, vol. 4: New writings in science fiction and fantasy.* New York: Berkley Books, 1981, 199 p., paper, anth.

with Melissa Singer

33358 *The Berkley showcase, vol. 5: new writings in science fiction and fantasy.* New York: Berkley Books, 1982, 266 p., paper, anth.

SCHODER, Judith

33359 *The blood suckers.* New York: A Jem Book, Julian Messner, 1981, 63 p., cloth, nonf.

SCHOELL, William, 1951-

33360 *Bride of Satan.* New York: Leisure Books, 1986, 396 p., paper, novel.

33361 *Comic book heroes of the screen.* Secaucus, NJ: A Citadel Press Book, Carol Publishing Group, 1991, 239 p., cloth, nonf.

33362 *The dragon.* New York: Leisure Books, 1989, 361 p., paper, novel.

33363 *Fatal beauty.* New York: St. Martin's Paperbacks, 1990, 277 p., paper, novel.

33364 *Late at night.* New York: Leisure Books, 1986, 382 p., paper, novel.

33365 *The pact.* New York: St. Martin's Press, 1988, 206 p., paper, novel.

33366 *Saurian.* New York: Leisure Books, 1988, 365 p., paper, novel.

33367 *Shivers.* New York: Leisure Books, 1985, 398 p., paper, novel.

33368 *Spawn of Hell.* New York: Leisure Books, 1984, 399 p., paper, novel.

33369 *Stay out of the shower: 25 years of shocker films, beginning with "Psycho".* New

York: Dembner Books, 1985, vii+184 p., paper, nonf.

SCHOEMAN, Karel, 1939-

33370 *Promised land: a novel.* New York: Summit Books, 1978, 205 p., cloth, novel. [Translation by Marion V. Friedman of *Na die Geliefde Land*].

SCHOEPFLIN, Harold—SEE: Vincent, Harl

SCHOFIELD, Alfred Taylor, 1846-1929

38050 *Another world; or, The fourth dimension.* London: Swan Sonnenschein, 1888, 92 p., cloth, story.

as LUKE THEOPHILUS COURTENAY

03480 *Travels in the interior; or, The wonderful adventures of Luke and Belinda.* London: Ward & Downey, 1887, 316 p., cloth, novel.

SCHOFIELD, Stephen

33371 *In search of C. S. Lewis: interviews with Kenneth Tynan, A. J. P. Taylor, Malcolm Muggeridge, and others who knew Lewis: contains previously unpublished letters and photographs.* South Plainfield, NJ: Bridge Publishing, 1983, xiii+220 p., paper, nonf. anth.

SCHOLES, Katherine (Anne), 1959-

33372 *The landing: a night of birds.* Melbourne, Australia: Hill of Content, 1987, 62 p., cloth, novel.

SCHOLES, Robert (Edward), 1929-

33373 *Fabulation and metafiction.* Urbana, IL: University of Illinois Press, 1979, 222 p., cloth, nonf.
33374 *The left hand of difference: Le Guin & Derrida.* New Orleans, LA: Graduate School of Tulane University, 1983, 18 p., paper, nonf.
33375 *Structural fabulation: an essay on fiction of the future.* Notre Dame & London: University of Notre Dame Press, 1975, xi+111 p., cloth, nonf.

with Eric S. Rabkin

31984 *Science fiction: history, science, vision.* New York: Oxford University Press, 1977, viii+258 p., cloth, nonf.

with George E. Slusser & Eric S. Rabkin

31985 *Bridges to fantasy.* Carbondale & Edwardsville, IL: Southern Illinois University Press, 1982, xi+231 p., cloth, nonf. anth.
31986 *Coordinates: placing science fiction and fantasy.* Carbondale & Edwardsville: Southern Illinois University Press, 1983, xii+209 p., cloth, nonf. anth.

SCHOLFIELD, A(lwyn) F(aber), 1884- , *with S. G. Lubbock*

37919 *A memoir of Montague Rhodes James, with a list of his writings.* Cambridge, England: At the University Press, 1939, 86 p., paper, nonf.

SCHOLTEN, Willem, 1927-

33376 *Charles Robert Maturin, the terror-novelist.* New York: Garland Publishing, 1980, 197 p., cloth, nonf.

SCHOLZ, Carter, 1953-

33377 *Cuts.* Polk City, IA: Chris Drumm, 1985, 56 p., paper, coll. DRUMM BOOKLET #20.

with Glenn Harcourt

25170 *Palimpsests.* New York: Ace Science Fiction Books, 1984, viii+258 p., paper, novel.

SCHOMBURG, Alex, 1905- , *with Jon Gustafson*

24845 *Chroma: the art of Alex Schomburg.* Poughkeepsie, NY: Father Tree Press, 1986, 108 p., cloth, art.

*SCHOONOVER, Lawrence (Lovell), 1906-1980

SCHOW, David J., 1955-

33378 *The kill riff.* New York: Tor, A Tom Doherty Associates Book, 1988, 406 p., cloth, novel.
33379 *Lost angels.* New York: An Onyx Book, New American Library, 1990, 252 p., paper, coll.
33380 *Sedalia.* Eugene, OR: Pulphouse Publishing, 1991, 47 p., cloth, story. SHORT STORY HARDBACKS #16; SHORT STORY PAPERBACKS #25.

33381 *Seeing red.* New York: Tor Horror, A Tom Doherty Associates Book, 1990, xiii+268 p., paper, coll.

33382 *The shaft.* London: Macdonald, 1990, 361 p., cloth, novel.

33383 *Silver scream: stories.* Arlington Heights, IL: Dark Harvest, 1988, 369 p., cloth, anth.

with Jeffrey Frentzen

23504 *The Outer Limits: the official companion.* New York: Ace Science Fiction Books, 1986, 406 p., paper, nonf.

SCHRAFF, Anne E(laine), 1939-

38051 *The sorceress and the book of spells.* New York: Berkley Books, 1988, 150 p., paper, fiction. NARNIA SOLO GAMES #2.

*SCHRAMM, Wilbur (Lang), 1907-1987

SCHREIBER, Harvey K(eith)

33384 *The eagle and the sword.* New York: Popular Library, 1979, 256 p., paper, novel.

SCHULMAN, J(oseph) Neil, 1953-

33385 *Alongside night: a novel.* New York: Crown Publishers, 1979, 181 p., cloth, novel.

33386 *The rainbow cadenza: a novel in logosata form.* New York: Simon & Schuster, 1983, 303 p., cloth, novel.

SCHULMAN, Lester Martin—SEE: Martin, Les

SCHULMAN, Paul H., with Gary Gerani

23838 *Fantastic television.* New York: Harmony Books, 1977, 192 p., cloth, nonf.

SCHULTZ, David E., 1952- , with S. T. Joshi

26808 *An epicure in the terrible: a centennial anthology of essays in honor of H. P. Lovecraft.* Rutherford, NJ: Fairleigh Dickinson University Press, 1991, 347 p., cloth, nonf. anth.

SCHULZE, Dallas

33387 *Of dreams and magic.* Toronto, New York: Harlequin Books, 1989, 253 p., paper, novel.

SCHULZE, Doris

33388 *Friendship and duty.* Strathmartine by Dundee, Scotland: ScoTpress, 1985, 59 p., paper, tele. STAR TREK SERIES.

with Irene Wohlfahrt

33389 *Crystal clear.* Strathmartine by Dundee, Scotland: ScoTpress, 1988?, 78 p., paper, novel. STAR TREK SERIES.

SCHUMANN, Peter, with Robert Nichols

30683 *Red shift: an introduction to Ngshi-Altai.* Thetford, VT: Penny Each Press, 1977, p., paper, novel. DAILY LIVES IN NGHSI-ALTAI SERIES.

SCHUMER, Arlen

33390 *Visions from the Twilight Zone.* San Francisco: Chronicle Books, 1991, 169 p., cloth, nonf.

SCHUSTER, Hal, 1955-

The Avengers files—SEE: *Comics file magazine spotlight on The Avengers files, Earth's mightiest super-heroes.*

Batman—SEE: *Comics file magazine spotlight on Batman.*

33391 *Comics file magazine spotlight on The Avengers files, Earth's mightiest super-heroes.* Canoga Park, CA: Psi Fi Movie Press, 1986, 51 p., paper, nonf. anth.

33392 *Comics file magazine spotlight on The Spider-Man files.* Canoga Park, CA: Heroes Publishing, 1986, [49] p., paper, nonf. anth.

33393 *Comics file magazine spotlight on The X-Men file: Sons of X-Men.* Canoga Park, CA: Psi Fi Movie Press, 1986, 53 p., paper, nonf. anth.

33394 *Comics file magazine spotlight on Batman.* Canoga Park, CA: Heroes Publishing, 1986, 63 p., paper, nonf. anth.

33395 *Critic's choice file looks at the X-Men.* Canoga Park, CA: Heroes Publishing, 1987, 49 p., paper, nonf. anth.

33396 *File magazine spotlight on Robotech.* Canoga Park, CA: Psi Fi Movie Press, 1986, 51 p., paper, nonf. anth.

Robotech—SEE: *File magazine spotlight on Robotech.*

Sons of X-Men—SEE: *Comics file magazine spotlight on The X-Men file: Sons of X-Men.*

The Spider-Man files—SEE: *Comics file magazine spotlight on The Spider-Man files.*

33397 *Star Trek 20th anniversary tribute: the voyage continues.* Canoga Park, CA: New Media Books, 1986, 81 p., paper, nonf. anth.
The X-Men file: Sons of X-Men—SEE: *Comics file magazine spotlight on The X-Men file: Sons of X-Men.*

SCHUTZ, J(oseph) W(illard), 1912-1984

33398 *The moon microbe.* London: Robert Hale, 1976, 175 p., cloth, novel.
33399 *People of the rings.* London: Robert Hale, 1975, 192 p., cloth, novel.

SCHUYLER, George S(amuel), 1895-1977

33400 *Black empire.* Boston: Northeastern University Press, 1991, 368 p., cloth, novel.

SCHWADER, Ann (Marie) K(ennedy), 1960-

33401 *Blood rights.* Arvada, CO: Roadkill Press, 1991, 30 p., paper, story. [Bound with *Flame thrower* / by Lucy Taylor].

SCHWARTZ, Betty Ann, 1927-

33402 *Great ghost stories.* New York: A Little Simon Book, Simon & Schuster, 1985, xiii + 177 p., cloth, anth.

SCHWARTZ, Sheila (Ruth), 1929-

33403 *Earth in transit: science fiction and contemporary problems.* New York: Laurel-Leaf Library, 1976, 271 p., paper, anth.

SCHWARZ-BART, Simone, 1938-

33404 *Between two worlds: a novel.* New York: A Cornelia & Michael Bessie Book, Harper & Row, 1981, 270 p., cloth, novel. [Translation by Barbara Bray of *Ti Jean l'horizon*].

SCHWEITZER, Darrell (Charles), 1952-

33405 *Conan's world and Robert E. Howard.* San Bernardino, CA: R. Reginald, The Borgo Press, 1978, 64 p., paper, nonf. MILFORD SERIES: POPULAR WRITERS OF TODAY #17.
33406 *Discovering H. P. Lovecraft.* Mercer Island, WA: Starmont House, 1987, xii + 153 p., cloth, nonf. anth. STARMONT STUDIES IN LITERARY CRITICISM #6.
33407 *Discovering modern horror fiction.* Mercer Island, WA: Starmont House, 1985, 156

p., cloth, nonf. anth. STARMONT STUDIES IN LITERARY CRITICISM #4.
33408 *Discovering modern horror fiction II.* Mercer Island, WA: Starmont House, 1988, 169 p., cloth, nonf. anth. STARMONT STUDIES IN LITERARY CRITICISM #16.
33409 *Discovering Stephen King.* Mercer Island, WA: Starmont House, 1985, 219 p., cloth, nonf. anth. STARMONT STUDIES IN LITERARY CRITICISM #8.
33410 *The dream quest of H. P. Lovecraft.* San Bernardino, CA: R. Reginald, The Borgo Press, 1978, 63 p., paper, nonf. MILFORD SERIES: POPULAR WRITERS OF TODAY #12.
33411 *Essays Lovecraftian.* Baltimore, MD: T-K Graphics, 1976, iv + 114 p., paper, nonf. anth.
33412 *Exploring fantasy worlds: essays on fantastic literature.* San Bernardino, CA: R. Reginald, The Borgo Press, 1985, 112 p., cloth, nonf. anth. I. O. EVANS STUDIES IN THE PHILOSOPHY & CRITICISM OF LITERATURE #3.
33413 *Lovecraft in the cinema.* Baltimore, MD: T-K Graphics, 1975, [22] p., paper, nonf.
33414 *The meaning of life.* Polk City, IA: Chris Drumm, 1988, 50 p., paper, coll. DRUMM BOOKLET #30.
33415 *Pathways to Elfland: the writings of Lord Dunsany.* Philadelphia, PA: Owlswick Press, 1989, xvi + 180 p., cloth, nonf.
33416 *Science fiction voices #1: interviews with science fiction writers.* San Bernardino, CA: R. Reginald, The Borgo Press, 1979, 63 p., cloth, nonf. coll. MILFORD SERIES: POPULAR WRITERS OF TODAY #23.
33417 *Science fiction voices #5: interviews with American science fiction writers of the golden age.* San Bernardino, CA: R. Reginald, The Borgo Press, 1981, 64 p., cloth, nonf. coll. MILFORD SERIES: POPULAR WRITERS OF TODAY #35.
33418 *SF voices.* Baltimore, MD: T-K Graphics, 1976, 122 p., paper, nonf. coll.
33419 *The Shattered Goddess.* Virginia Beach, Norfolk, VA: Starblaze Editions/Donning, 1982, 183 p., paper, novel.
33420 *Tom O'Bedlam's night out, and other strange excursions.* Buffalo, NY: W. Paul Ganley, 1985, vii + 191 p., cloth, coll.
33421 *We are all legends.* Virginia Beach, VA: Starblaze Editions/Donning, 1981, 193 p., paper, novel.

33422 *The white isle.* Philadelphia, PA: Owlswick Press, 1989 (i.e., 1990), viii+139 p., cloth, novel.

with George H. Scithers

33423 *Another round at the spaceport bar.* New York: Avon Books, 1989, viii+248 p., paper, anth.
33424 *Tales from the spaceport bar.* New York: Avon, 1987, xv+235 p., paper, anth.

with George Scithers & John Ashmead

16862 *Constructing scientifiction & fantasy.* Lake Geneva, WI: TSR Inc., 1982, 31 p., paper, nonf.

with George H. Scithers & John M. Ford

23260 *On writing science fiction: (the editors strike back!).* Philadelphia, PA: Owlswick Press, 1981, vii+227 p., cloth, nonf. anth.

SCHWERIN, Doris (Halpern), 1922-

The missing years—SEE: *Rainbow walkers.*
33425 *Rainbow walkers.* New York: Villard Books, 1985, 406 p., cloth, novel.
33425A retitled: *The missing years.* London: Piatkus, 1986, 416 p., cloth, novel.

SCITHERS, George H(arry), 1929-

Adventures of science fiction—SEE: *Isaac Asimov's Adventures of science fiction.*
33426 *Asimov's choice: Black holes & bug-eyedmonsters.* New York: Davis Publications, 1977, 223 p., paper, anth.
33427 *Asimov's choice: Comets & computers.* New York: Dale Books, 1978, 221 p., paper, anth.
33428 *Asimov's choice: Dark stars & dragons.* New York: Dale Books, 1978, 223 p., paper, anth.
33429 *Asimov's choice: Extraterrestrials & eclipses.* New York: Dale Books, 1978, 206 p., paper, anth.
Astronauts & androids—SEE: *Asimov's choice: Astronauts & androids.*
Black holes & bug-eyed monsters—SEE: *Asimov's choice: Black holes & bug-eyed monsters.*
Comets & computers—SEE: *Asimov's choice: Comets & computers.*
Dark stars & dragons—SEE: *Asimov's choice: Dark stars & dragons.*

Extraterrestrials & eclipses—SEE: *Asimov's choice: Extraterrestrials & eclipses.*
Isaac Asimov's Adventures of science fiction—SEE: *Isaac Asimov's Science fiction anthology, volume 3.*
33430 *Isaac Asimov's Marvels of science fiction.* New York: The Dial Press, Davis Publications, 1979, 287 p., cloth, anth. ISAAC ASIMOV'S SCIENCE FICTION ANTHOLOGY #2.
33431 *Isaac Asimov's Science fiction anthology, volume 3.* New York: Davis Publications, 1980, 284 p., paper, anth. ISAAC ASIMOV'S SCIENCE FICTION ANTHOLOGY #3.
33431A retitled: *Isaac Asimov's Adventures of science fiction.* New York: The Dial Press, Davis Publications, 1980, 284 p., cloth, anth. ISAAC ASIMOV'S SCIENCE FICTION ANTHOLOGY #3.
33432 *Isaac Asimov's Science fiction anthology, volume 4.* New York: Davis Publications, 1980, 288 p., paper, anth. ISAAC ASIMOV'S SCIENCE FICTION ANTHOLOGY #4.
33432A retitled: *Isaac Asimov's Worlds of science fiction.* New York: The Dial Press, Davis Publications, 1980, 284 p., cloth, anth. ISAAC ASIMOV'S SCIENCE FICTION ANTHOLOGY #4.
33433 *Isaac Asimov's Science fiction anthology, volume 5.* New York: Davis Publications, 1981, 285 p., paper, anth. ISAAC ASIMOV'S SCIENCE FICTION ANTHOLOGY #5.
33433A retitled: *Isaac Asimov's Near futures and far.* New York: The Dial Press, Davis Publications, 1981, 285 p., cloth, anth. ISAAC ASIMOV'S SCIENCE FICTION ANTHOLOGY #5.
Isaac Asimov's Worlds of science fiction—SEE: *Isaac Asimov's Science fiction anthology, volume 4.*
Marvels of science fiction—SEE: *Isaac Asimov's Marvels of science fiction.*
Near futures and far—SEE: *Isaac Asimov's Science fiction anthology, volume 5.*
Worlds of science fiction—SEE: *Isaac Asimov's Science fiction anthology, volume 4.*

as ANONYMOUS EDITOR

33434 *Asimov's choice: Astronauts & androids.* New York: Davis Publications, 1977, 220 p., paper, anth.
Astronauts & androids—SEE: *Asimov's choice: Astronauts & androids.*

33435 *Isaac Asimov's Science fiction anthology, volume 1.* New York: Davis Publications, 1978, 288 p., paper, anth. ISAAC ASIMOV'S SCIENCE FICTION ANTHOLOGY #1.

33435A retitled: *Isaac Asimov's Masters of science fiction.* New York: Davis Publications, 1978, 288 p., cloth, anth. ISAAC ASIMOV'S SCIENCE FICTION ANTHOLOGY #1. *Masters of science fiction*—SEE: *Isaac Asimov's Science fiction anthology, volume 1.*

with Darrell Schweitzer

33423 *Another round at the spaceport bar.* New York: Avon Books, 1989, viii+248 p., paper, anth.

33424 *Tales from the spaceport bar.* New York: Avon, 1987, xv+235 p., paper, anth.

with Darrell Schweitzer & John Ashmead

16862 *Constructing scientifiction & fantasy.* Lake Geneva, WI: TSR Inc., 1982, 31 p., paper, nonf.

with Darrell Schweitzer & John M. Ford

23260 *On writing science fiction: (the editors strike back!).* Philadelphia, PA: Owlswick Press, 1981, vii+227 p., cloth, nonf. anth.

SCLIAR, Moacyr (Jaime), 1937-

33437 *The carnival of the animals.* New York: Available Press, 1986, 86 p., paper, coll. [Translation by Eloah F. Giacomelli of *O carnival dos animals*].

33438 *The centaur in the garden.* New York: Available Press, Ballantine Books, 1985, 216 p., paper, novel. [Translation by Margaret A. Neves of *O centauro no jardin*].

33439 *The enigmatic eye.* New York: Ballantine Books, 1989, 100 p., paper, coll. [Translation by Eloah F. Giacomelli of *O olho enigmatico*].

33440 *The gods of Raquel.* New York: Available Press, 1986, 107 p., paper, coll. [Translation by Eloah F. Giacomelli of *Os Deuses de Raquel*].

33441 *Max and the cats.* New York: Available Press, 1990, 99 p., paper, coll. [Translation by Eloah F. Giacomelli of *Max os felinos*].

33442 *The strange nation of Rafael Mendes.* New York: Harmony Books, 1987, 309 p., cloth, novel. [Translation by Eloah F. Giacomelli of *A estranha naçao de Rafael Mendes*].

SCORTIA, Thomas N(icholas), 1926-1986

33443 *The best of Thomas N. Scortia.* Garden City, NY: Doubleday & Co., 1981, xii+244 p., cloth, coll. [Edited by George Zebrowski].

33444 *Caution! Inflammable!* Garden City, NY: Doubleday & Co., 1975, xi+28 p., cloth, coll.

with Frank M. Robinson

32496 *Blowout!* New York: Franklin Watts, 1987, 393 p., cloth, novel.

32497 *The nightmare factor.* Garden City, NY: Doubleday & Co., 1978, 335 p., cloth, novel.

32498 *The prometheus crisis.* Garden City, NY: Doubleday & Co., 1975, xiv+321 p., cloth, novel.

with George Zebrowski

33445 *Human-machines: an anthology of stories about cyborgs.* New York: Vintage Books, Random House, 1975, xxv+252 p., paper, anth.

SCOT, Anna—SEE: **Joseph, Anne**

SCOT, Michael, pseud.—SEE: **Rohan, Mike Scott & Scott, Allan J.**

SCOTT, A. G., pseud.--SEE: **Sharman, Nick**

SCOTT, Alan, 1947-

The Anthrax mutation—SEE: *Project Drac-ula.*

12819 *Project Dracula.* London: Sphere Books, 1971, 319 p., paper, novel.

12819A retitled: *The anthrax mutation.* New York: Pyramid Books, 1976, 319 p., paper, novel.

SCOTT, Allan (J.), 1952-

33446 *The dragon in the stone.* London: Orbit, 1991, ix+301 p., paper, novel.

with Michael Scott Rohan as MICHAEL SCOT

Burial rites—SEE: *The Ice King.*

32615 *The Ice King.* London: New English Library, 1986, 252 p., cloth, novel.

32615A retitled: *Burial rites.* New York: Berkley Books, 1987, 248 p., paper, novel.

SCOTT, Anna—SEE: Joseph, Anne

SCOTT, Bill [i.e., William Neville Scott], 1923-

33447 *Boori*. Melbourne, Australia, New York: Oxford University Press, 1978, 148 p., cloth, novel. BOORI #1.

33448 *The darkness under the hills*. Melbourne, Australia, New York: Oxford University Press, 1980, 176 p., cloth, novel. BOORI #2.

SCOTT, Eleanor

38052 *Randalls round*. London: Ernest Benn, 1929, 255 p., cloth, novel.

SCOTT, Hugh

33449 *A box of tricks*. London: Walker Books, 1991, 125 p., cloth, novel.

33450 *The camera obscura*. London: Walker Books, 1990, 112 p., cloth, novel.

33451 *The gargoyle*. London: Walker Books, 1991, 171 p., cloth, novel.

33452 *The haunted sand*. London: Walker Books, 1990, 149 p., cloth, novel.

33453 *The shaman's stone*. London: Andersen Press, 1988, 144 p., cloth, novel.

33454 *Something watching*. London: Walker Books, 1990, 168 p., cloth, novel.

33455 *Why weeps the brogan?* London: Walker Books, 1989, 103 p., cloth, novel.

SCOTT, J(ames) E(dward), 1911-

33456 *A bibliography of the works of Sir Henry Rider Haggard, 1856-1925*. Takeley, Hertfordshire, England: Elkin Matthews, 1947, 258 p., cloth, nonf. [Limited to 500 copies].

SCOTT, Jeremy, pseud.—SEE: Dick, Kay

SCOTT, Jody (Huguelet Wood), 1923-

33457 *I, vampire*. New York: Ace Fantasy Books, 1984, 206 p., paper, novel. STERLING O'BLIVION #2.

33458 *Passing for human*. New York: DAW Books, 1977, 191 p., paper, novel. STERLING O'BLIVION #1.

SCOTT, Kathryn Leigh, 1943-

33459 *The Dark Shadows companion: 25th anniversary collection*. Los Angeles, London: Pomegranate Press, 1990, 208 p., cloth, nonf. anth.

33460 *My scrapbook memories of Dark Shadows*. Los Angeles, London: Pomegranate Press, 1986, 152 p., cloth, nonf.

SCOTT, Mary

33461 *Nudists may be encountered*. London: Serpent's Tail, 1991, 160 p., paper, coll.

SCOTT, Melissa

33462 *A choice of destinies*. New York: Baen Science Fiction Books, 1986, 314 p., paper, novel.

33463 *The empress of Earth*. New York: Baen Books, 1987, 346 p., paper, novel. SILENCE LEIGH #3.

33464 *Five-twelfths of Heaven*. New York: Baen Science Fiction Books, 1985, 339 p., paper, novel. SILENCE LEIGH #1.

33465 *The game beyond*. New York: A Baen Book, 1984, 350 p., paper, novel.

33466 *The kindly ones*. New York: Baen Books, 1987, 371 p., paper, novel.

33467 *Mighty good road*. New York: A Baen Book, 1990, 306 p., paper, novel.

33468 *The roads of Heaven*. Garden City, NY: Nelson Doubleday, 1988, 760 p., cloth, coll. SILENCE LEIGH #1-3.

33469 *Silence in solitude*. New York: Baen Books, 1986, 313 p., paper, novel. SILENCE LEIGH #2.

with Lisa A. Barnett

17435 *The armor of light*. New York: Baen Fantasy, 1988, 504 p., paper, novel.

SCOTT, Michael, 1959-

33470 *Banshee*. London: Mandarin, 1990, 248 p., paper, novel.

33471 *A bright enchantment*. London: Sphere Books, 1985, 115 p., paper, novel. TALES FROM THE LAND OF ERIN #1.

33472 *The children of Lir: an Irish legend*. London: Methuen Children's Books, Magnet Books, 1986, 88 p., paper, novel.

33473 *Death's law*. London: Sphere Books, 1989, 276 p., paper, novel. TALES OF THE BARD #3.

33474 *Demon's law*. London: Sphere Books, 1988, 293 p., paper, novel. TALES OF THE BARD #2.

33475 *A golden dream*. London: Sphere Books, 1985, 114 p., paper, novel. TALES FROM THE LAND OF ERIN #2.

33476 *Image*. London: Sphere Books, 1991, 356 p., paper, novel.

33477 *The last of the Fianna.* London: A Pied Piper Book, Methuen Children's Books, 1987, 112 p., cloth, novel.

33478 *Magician's law.* London: Sphere Books, 1987, 305 p., paper, novel. TALES OF THE BARD #1.

33479 *The quest of the sons.* London: Methuen Children's Books, A Pied Piper Book, 1988, 158 p., cloth, novel.

33480 *A silver wish.* London: Sphere Books, 1985, 115 p., paper, novel. TALES FROM THE LAND OF ERIN #3.

33481 *The song of the children of Lir.* Dublin: De Vogel Ltd., 1983, 96 p., cloth?, novel.

33482 *Wind lord.* Dublin: Wolfhound, 1991, [160] p., paper, novel.

with Gloria Gaghan

23599 *Navigator: the voyage of Saint Brendan.* London: Methuen, 1988, 205 p., paper, novel.

SCOTT, Michael, pseud.

33483 *Gay exorcist.* New York: Gay Library Editions, Midwood Books, 1976, 219 p., paper, novel.

SCOTT, R. C.

33484 *Blood sport.* Toronto, New York: Bantam Books, 1984, 134 p., paper, novel. DARK FORCES #14.

SCOTT, R(eginald) T(homas) M(aitland), 1882-

33485 *The Spider strikes!* New York: A Berkley Medallion Book, 1969, 159 p., paper, novel. SPIDER #1.

33486 *The wheel of death.* New York: A Berkley Medallion Book, 1969, 144 p., paper, novel. SPIDER #2.

SCOTT, Richard P., *with Thom Metzger*

29779 *Big Gurl.* New York: An Onyx Book, New American Library, 1989, 253 p., paper, novel.

SCOTT, Sandra

33487 *Demon legacy.* Encino, CA: World-Wide Publishing Co., 1980, 184 p., paper, novel.

33488 *From dust to lust.* Chatsworth, CA: World-Wide Publishing Co., 1981, 183 p., paper, novel.

33489 *Mystic passions.* Chatsworth, CA: World-Wide Publishing Co., 1981, 191 p., paper, novel.

SCOTT, Tanya Gardiner- —SEE: Gardiner-Scott, Tanya

SCOTT, Walter, Sir, 1771-1832

33490 *The supernatural short stories of Sir Walter Scott.* London: John Calder, 1977, 217 p., cloth, coll. [Edited by Michael Hayes].

SCOTT, William N.—SEE: Scott, Bill

*SCOTT MONCRIEFF, D(avid William Hardy), 1907-1987

SCOTTEN, (William) Cordell, 1921-

33491 *Isaac Asimov's robot city: robots and aliens: Renegade.* New York: A Byron Preiss Visual Publications Inc. Book, Ace Books, 1989, 178 p., paper, novel. ISAAC ASIMOV'S ROBOT CITY: ROBOTS AND ALIENS #2.
Renegade—SEE: *Isaac Asimov's robot city: robots and aliens: Renegade.*

*SCRIRE. O.T.O. 4=7 [pseud. of Gerald Brosseau Gardner], 1884-1964

*SCRYMSOUR, Ella (M.), 1888-

SCUPHAM, A. G.

33492 *Duty to the devil, and other ghost stories.* London: William Kimber, 1981, 207 p., cloth, coll.

SCYOC, Sydney J. Van—SEE: Van Scyoc, Sydney J.

*'SEA-LION' [pseud. of Geoffrey Martin Bennett], 1909-1983

SEARLES, (William) Baird, 1934-

33493 *Films of science fiction and fantasy.* New York: AFI Press, Henry N. Abrams, 1988, 239 p., cloth, nonf.

33494 *Stranger in a strange land & other works: notes, including life of the author, science fiction in the '30s, discussions of the novels and short stories, Heinlein's "Future History" framework, Heinlein's major themes, a selected bibliography.* Lincoln, NE: Cliffs Notes, 1975, 59 p., paper, nonf.

with Martin Last

27860   *The science fiction quizbook.* New York, London: Drake Publishers, 1976, 128 p., paper, nonf.

with Martin Last & Beth Meacham & Michael Franklin

23447   *A reader's guide to science fiction.* New York: Avon, 1979, xv+266 p., paper, nonf.

with Beth Meacham & Michael Franklin

23446   *A reader's guide to fantasy.* New York: Avon, 1982, 217 p., paper, nonf.

with Brian Thomsen

33495   *Halflings, hobbits, warrows, & weefolk: a collection of tales of heroes short in stature.* New York: Warner Books, 1991, vi+275 p., paper, anth.

SEARLS, Hank [i.e., Henry Hunt Searls Jr.], 1922-

33496   *Sounding.* New York: Ballantine Books, 1982, 214 p., cloth, novel.

SEARLS, Henry—SEE: Searls, Henry

SEBASTIAN, Tim(othy), 1952-

33497   *Saviour's gate.* London: Simon & Schuster, 1991, 266 p., cloth, novel.
33498   *Spy shadow.* London: Simon & Schuster, 1989, 281 p., cloth, novel.

SEBEOK, Thomas A(lbert), 1920- , *with Umberto Eco*

22387   *The sign of three: Dupin, Holmes, Peirce.* Bloomington, IN: Indiana University Press, 1983, xi+236 p., cloth, nonf. anth.

*SECHRIST, (Anne) Elizabeth Hough, <u>1902-1991</u>

SEE, Carolyn (Penelope), 1934-

33499   *Golden days.* New York: McGraw-Hill Book Co., 1986, 196 p., cloth, novel.

SEED, David (A.), 1946-

33501   *The fictional labyrinths of Thomas Pynchon.* Iowa City, IA: University of Iowa Press, 1988, x+268 p., cloth, nonf.

SEFTON, Catherine [pseud. of Martin Waddell], 1941-

33502   *The blue misty monsters.* London, Boston: Faber & Faber, 1985, 106 p., cloth, novel.
33503   *Emer's ghost.* London: Hamish Hamilton, 1981, 137 p., cloth, novel.
33504   *The ghost girl.* London: Hamish Hamilton, 1985, 124 p., cloth, novel.

SEGAL, Judith Z(elda), 1948-

33505   *Protocols: a guide to the world of fanzines: helpful hints for editors, authors, artists, & readers.* Patterson, NJ: Allen Mc-Clearnen, 1980, 55 p., paper, nonf.
33506   *Understanding Kraith: a compilation of words, phrases, ideas, and interpretations, as set forth in the Kraith Universe series.* Pawling, NY: J. Z. Segal, n.d., 40 p., paper, nonf.

SEGER, Maura

33507   *Perchance to dream.* New York: Avon Books, 1989, 311 p., paper, novel.

SEGRAVES, Kelly L(ee), 1942-

33508   *Dinosaur dilemma.* San Diego, CA: Beta Books, 1977, 196 p., paper, novel.
33509   *The only game in town.* San Diego, CA: Beta Books, 1976, 79 p., paper, novel.
33510   *When you're dead, you're dead.* San Diego, CA: Beta Books, 1975, 95 p., paper, novel.

SEIDMAN, Eric, *with Ed Naha*

30571   *Wanted, by the Intergalactic Security Bureau: 20 full-color posters of the most wanted alien criminals.* Toronto, New York: Bantam Books, 1980, [47] p., paper, fiction.

SEIGNOLLE, Claude, 1917-

33511   *The nightcharmer, and other tales of Claude Seignolle.* College Station, TX: Texas A&M University Press, 1983, 115 p., cloth, coll. [Translated by Eric Hollingsworth Deudon].

SEINGALT, Giacomo Casanova de—SEE: Casanova de Seingalt, Jacques

SELBY, Curt, pseud.—SEE: Piserchia, Doris

SELDEN, George [pseud. of George Selden Thompson], 1929-1989

15859 *Harry Cat's pet puppy.* New York: Farrar, Straus & Giroux, 1974, 167 p., cloth, novel. TUCKER & HARRY #3.
15860 *Tucker's countryside.* New York: Farrar, Straus & Giroux, 1969, 166 p., cloth, novel. TUCKER & HARRY #2.

SELDEN, Neil R(oy), 1931-

33512 *Drawing the dead.* New York: Twilight/Dell, 1983, 156 p., paper, novel. TWILIGHT #16.

SELDON, Keith, *with Jocelyn Almond*

16320 *The faceless tarot.* London: Dunscaith Publishing, 1989, 155 p., paper, novel.

SELIG, Elaine Booth, 1935-

33513 *Demon summer.* New York: Pocket Books, 1979, 224 p., paper, novel.

SELINGER, Bernard (George), 1949-

33514 *Le Guin and identity in contemporary fiction.* Ann Arbor, MI: UMI Research Press, 1988, 183 p., cloth, nonf. STUDIES IN SPECULATIVE FICTION #16.

SELLERS, Con(nie Leslie Jr.), 1922-1992

12872 *F.S.C.* Chicago: Novel Books, 1963, 182 p., paper, novel. [Corrected entry].
12872A retitled: *The pleasure mongers.* Chicago: Novel Books, 1964, 128 p., paper, novel.
12872B retitled: *Mr. Tomorrow.* San Diego, CA: Papillon Books, 1974, 160 p., paper, novel.

as RIC ARANA

33515 *The silent seducers.* Canoga Park, CA: Challenge Books, 1967, 222 p., paper, novel.

SELLERS, Mary (Frances Raineri), 1925-

33516 *The cry of the cat.* New York: Warner Books, 1975, 237 p., paper, novel.
33517 *The house on Black Bayou.* New York: Warner Paperback Library, 1975, 255 p., paper, novel.
33518 *Night shadows.* New York: A Berkley Medallion Book, Berkley Publishing Corp., 1977, 311 p., paper, novel.

33519 *Race of the dark gambler.* New York: Warner Books, 1977, 315 p., paper, novel.

SELLIER, Charles E. Jr., 1925?-1983?, *with Robert Weverka*

33520 *The Boogens.* Toronto, New York: Bantam Books, 1981, 182 p., paper, movie.
33521 *Hangar 18.* Toronto, New York: Bantam Books, 1980, 166 p., paper, movie.

SELLIN, Bernard

33522 *The life and works of David Lindsay.* Cambridge, New York: Cambridge University Press, 1981, xxiii+257 p., cloth, nonf.

SELTZER, David, 1920?-

33523 *The omen.* New York: A Signet Book, New American Library, 1976, 202 p., paper, movie. OMEN #1.
33524 *Prophecy.* New York: Ballantine Books, 1979, 247 p., paper, movie.

SELVES, David, 1949-

33525 *Life goes on forever...* Haywards Heath, West Sussex, England: Ansty Publishers, 1987, 430 p., cloth, novel.

SENF, Carol A(nn)

33526 *The vampire in 19th century English literature.* Bowling Green, OH: Bowling Green State University Popular Press, 1988, 204 p., cloth, nonf.

SENN, (Oscar) Steve(n), 1950-

33527 *Born of flame: a Spacebread story.* New York: An Argo Book, Atheneum, 1982, vii+200 p., cloth, novel. SPACEBREAD SERIES.
33528 *A circle in the sea.* New York: An Argo Book, Atheneum, 1981, 256 p., cloth, novel.
33529 *The double disappearance of Walter Fozbek.* New York: Hastings House, 1980, 120 p., cloth, novel. FOZBEK #1.
33530 *Loonie Louie meets the space fungus.* New York: An Avon Camelot Book, 1991, 106 p., paper, novel.
33531 *Ralph Fozbek and the amazing black hole patrol.* New York: An Avon Camelot Book, 1986, 102 p., paper, novel. FOZBEK #2.

33532 *The sand witch.* New York: An Avon Camelot Book, 1987, 88 p., paper, novel.

33533 *Spacebread.* New York: An Argo Book, Atheneum, 1981, 216 p., cloth, novel. SPACEBREAD #1.

SERLING, Carol, with Martin H. Greenberg & Charles G. Waugh

Night gallery reader—SEE: *Rod Serling's Night gallery reader.*

24579 *Rod Serling's Night gallery reader.* New York: Dembner Books, 1987, x+326 p., cloth, anth.

SERLING, Robert (Jerome), 1918-

33534 *Air Force One is haunted.* New York: St. Martin's Press, 1985, xiii+241 p., cloth, novel. JEREMY HAINES #2. [Sequel to *The president's plane is missing*].

33535 *Something's alive on the Titanic.* New York: St. Martin's Press, 1990, 399 p., cloth, novel.

SERLING, Rod(man Edward), 1924-1975 (SEE ALSO: Dickson, Gordon R.)

33536 *Into The Twilight Zone: A new collection of startling explorations into the realm of the supernatural.* Mattituck, NY: Rivercity Press, 1976, 168 p., cloth, coll. [This may be a reprint from an earlier Serling or Walter Gibson title, or a selection of stories from previous collections].

Other worlds—SEE: *Rod Serling's Other worlds.*

33537 *Rod Serling's Other worlds.* Toronto, New York: Bantam Books, 1978, x+244 p., paper, anth.

33538 *Stories from The Twilight Zone.* Toronto, New York: Bantam Books, 1986, xiii+418 p., paper, tele. coll. TWILIGHT ZONE #1-3.

with W. W. Jacobs

26398 *Tales of terror: The monkey's paw; The monsters are due on Maple Street.* Boston: Houghton Mifflin Co., 1989, 62 p., paper?, coll.

SERNINE, Daniel [pseud. of Alain Lortie], 1955-

33539 *Argus steps in.* Windsor, Ontario, Canada: Black Moss Press, 1990, 170 p., paper, novel. ARGUS SERIES. [Translation by David Homel of *Argus intervient*].

38053 *The Scorpion's treasure.* Windsor, Ontario, Canada: Black Moss Press, 1990, 143 p., paper, novel. GRANDVERGER SERIES. [Translation by Frances Morgan of *Le trésor du Scorpion*].

38054 *The sword of Arhapal.* Windsor, Ontario, Canada: Black Moss Press, 1990, 181 p., paper, novel. GRANDVERGER SERIES. [Translation by Frances Morgan of *L'Epée Arhapal*].

33540 *Those who watch over Earth.* Windsor, Ontario, Canada: Black Moss Press, 1990, 109 p., paper, novel. ARGUS SERIES. [Translation by David Homel of *Organisation Argus*].

SERRANO, Joe—SEE: Savage, Adrian

SERVICE, Pamela F., 1945-

33541 *Being of two minds.* New York: A Jean Karl Book, Atheneum; Toronto: Maxwell Macmillan Canada; New York: Maxwell Macmillan International, 1991, 169 p., cloth, novel.

33542 *A question of destiny.* New York: An Argo Book, Atheneum, 1986, 160 p., cloth, novel.

33543 *The reluctant god.* New York: A Jean Karl Book, Atheneum, 1988, 211 p., cloth, novel.

33544 *Stinker from space.* New York: Charles Scribner's Sons, 1988, 83 p., cloth, novel.

33545 *Tomorrow's magic.* New York: A Jean Karl Book, Atheneum, 1987, 191 p., cloth, novel. WINTER #2.

33546 *Under alien stars.* New York: A Jean Karl Book, Atheneum, 1990, 214 p., cloth, novel.

33547 *Vision quest.* New York: A Jean Karl Book, Atheneum, 1989, 136 p., cloth, novel.

33548 *When the night wind howls.* New York: Atheneum, 1987, 153 p., cloth, novel.

33549 *Winter of magic's return.* New York: Atheneum, 1985, 192 p., cloth, novel. WINTER #1.

SERVISS, Garrett P(utnam), 1851-1929

33550 *The moon maiden.* [Los Angeles: Fantasy Publishing Co., Inc., 1978], 97 p., paper, novel.

SESSA, Aldo, 1939- , with Ray Bradbury

18443 *The bridge of forever.* New York: Rizzoli, 1981, 130 p., cloth, fiction.

SETH, Marie

33551 *Dream of the dead.* Belmont, CA: A Pacemaker Bestsellers Book, Fearon-Pitman Publishers, 1977, 59 p., paper, novel.

SETLOWE, Richard

33552 *The experiment: a novel.* New York: Holt, Rinehart & Winston, 1980, 299 p., cloth, novel.
33553 *The haunting of Suzanna Blackwell: a novel.* New York: Holt, Rinehart & Winston, 1984, 355 p., cloth, novel.

*SETON, Anya, 1904?-1990

SEVERANCE, Carol (Ann Wilcox), 1944-

33554 *Reefsong.* New York: A Del Rey Book, Ballantine Books, 1991, 311 p., paper, novel.

*SÉVERIN, Jean, 1911-1987

SEWELL, (Michael) Brocard, 1912-

33555 *Arthur Machen: essays.* Llandeilo, Carmarathenshire, South Wales: St Albert's Press, 1960, 43 p., paper, nonf. anth. [Limited to 350 copies].
33556 *Montague Summers: a memoir.* London: Cecil & Amelia Woolf, 1965, xviii+185 p., cloth, nonf.
33557 *Three essays: Father Vincent McNabb; A modern hand-printer: Edward Walters; "Voyage to a beginning": the introduction to Colin Wilson's autobiography.* Nottingham, England: Paupers' Press, 1988, 22 p., paper, nonf. coll.

with Cecil Woolf

33558 *Corvo, 1860-1960: a collection of essays by various hands to commemorate the birth of Fr. Rolfe, Baron Corvo.* Aylesford, England: Saint Albert's Press, 1961, xiv+155 p., cloth, nonf. anth.
33558A retitled: *New quests for Corvo: a collection of essays by various hands.* Mayfair, England: Icon Books, 1965, 128 p., cloth, nonf. anth.
New quests for Corvo—SEE: *Corvo, 1860-1960: a collection of essays by various hands to commemorate the birth of Fr. Rolfe, Baron Corvo.*

SEYMOUR, Lee—SEE: Lee, Edward

SEYMOUR, Miranda [pseud. of Miranda Jane Sinclair], 1948-

33559 *Count Manfred.* London: Hutchinson, 1976, 283 p., cloth, novel.
33560 *The reluctant devil: a cautionary tale.* London: Heinemann, 1990, 214 p., cloth, novel.
33561 *The vampire of Verdonia.* London: André Deutsch, 1986, 100 p., cloth, novel.

SHAARA, Michael (Joseph Jr.), 1929-1988

33562 *The herald.* New York: McGraw-Hill Book Co., 1981, 229 p., cloth, novel.
33563 *Soldier boy.* New York: A Timescape Book, Pocket Books, 1982, 255 p., paper, coll.

SHACKLEFORD, Jack D., 1938-

33564 *The eve of midsummer.* London: Corgi Books, 1977, 189 p., paper, novel.
33565 *The house of the magus.* London: New English Library, 1979, 237 p., paper, novel.
33566 *The source.* Sevenoaks, Kent, England: New English Library, 1985, 346 p., paper, novel.
33567 *The Strickland demon.* London: Corgi Books, 1977, 142 p., paper, novel.
33568 *Tanith.* London: Corgi Books, 1977, 188 p., paper, novel.

SHACKLETON-HILL, Angela

33569 *Greensight.* London: George Allen & Unwin, 1984, 371 p., cloth, novel.

SHACOCHIS, Bob [i.e., Robert G. Shacochis], 1951-

33570 *The next new world: stories.* New York: Crown Publishers, 1989, 209 p., cloth, coll.

SHACOCHIS, Robert G.—SEE: Shacochis, Bob

*SHADEGG, Stephen C., 1909-1990

SHADWELL, Thomas, pseud.—SEE: Cover, Arthur Byron & Sullivan, Tim & Bethancourt, John Gregory

*SHAFER, Robert (Jones), 1920-

SHAFFER, Anthony (Joshua), 1926- , *with Robin Hardy*

25202 *The wicker man: a novel.* New York: Crown Publishers, 1978, 216 p., cloth, novel.

SHAFFER, Eugene Carl

33571 *The clones.* Woodland Hills, CA: Decade Press, 1980, 217 p., paper, novel.
33572 *Panic 7.* Woodland Hills, CA: Decade Press, 1980, 223 p., paper, novel.

SHAGAN, Steve, 1927-

33573 *The discovery.* New York: A Perigord Press Book, William Morrow & Co., 1984, 355 p., cloth, novel.
33574 *Pillars of fire.* New York, London: Pocket Books, 1990, 371 p., cloth, movie.

SHAHAR, Eluki bes—SEE: bes Shahar, Eluki

SHAHEEN, Jack G(eorge), 1935-

33575 *Nuclear war films.* Carbondale & Edwardsville, IL: University of Illinois Press; London & Amsterdam: Feffer & Simons Inc., 1978, xx + 193 p., cloth, nonf. anth.

SHALLIS, Michael, *with Robert Lambourne & Michael Shortland*

27748 *Close encounters? science and science fiction.* Bristol, England, New York: Adam Hil-ger, 1991, xiii + 184 p., paper, nonf.

SHANJI, Li—SEE: Huanzhulouzhu

SHANKS, Edward, 1892-1953

33576 *Edgar Allan Poe.* London: Macmillan & Co., 1937, x + 176 p., cloth, nonf.

SHANNON, Doris, 1924-

33577 *The seekers.* Greenwich, CT: A Fawcett Gold Medal Book, Fawcett Publications, 1975, 176 p., paper, novel.

SHANNON, Fred, pseud.—SEE: Ruben, William S.

SHAPIRO, Neil (L.)

33578 *Mind call.* Canoga Park, CA: Major Books, 1978 (i.e., 1979?), 160 p., paper, novel.
33579 *Planet without a name.* Canoga Park, CA: Major Books, 1976, 160 p., paper, novel.

SHAPIRO, Stanley, 1925-1990

33580 *Simon's soul.* New York: G. P. Putnam's Sons, 1977, 227 p., cloth, novel.
33581 *A time to remember.* New York: Random House, 1986, 191 p., cloth, novel.

SHAREE, Keith

33582 *Gulliver's fugitives.* New York, London: Pocket Books, 1990, 282 p., paper, tele. STAR TREK: THE NEXT GENERATION #11.

SHARMAN, Nick [pseud. of Scott Grønmark], 1952-

33583 *The cats.* London: New English Library, 1977, 160 p., paper, novel.
33584 *Childmare.* London: Hamlyn Paperbacks, 1980, 205 p., paper, novel. [Also published as by A. G. Scott].
33585 *Judgment day.* New York: A Signet Book, New American Library, 1982, 316 p., paper, novel.
Next!—SEE: You're next!
33586 *The scourge.* New York: A Signet Book, New American Library, 1980, 199 p., paper, novel.
33587 *The surrogate.* New York: A Signet Book, New American Library, 1980, 249 p., paper, novel.
33588 *The switch.* Sevenoaks, Kent, England: New English Library, 1984, 299 p., paper, novel.
33589 *You're next!* Sevenoaks, Kent, England: New English Library, 1986, 352 p., paper, novel.
33589A retitled: *Next!* New York: A Signet Book, New American Library, 1986, 287 p., paper, novel.

as SCOTT GRONMARK

33590 *Steel gods.* New York: Corgi Books, 1990, 286 p., paper, novel.

as A. G. SCOTT

33584A *Childmare.* New York: A Signet Book, New American Library, 1981, 199 p., paper, novel. [Originally published under the name Nick Sharman].

SHARMAT, Mitchell, 1927-

33591 *A girl of many parts.* New York: Laurel-Leaf Books, 1988, 151 p., paper, novel.

SHARP, Allen (W.)

33592 *Book of science fiction.* Cambridge, England: Cambridge University Press, 1987, 352 p., cloth, coll.

33593 *The dark awakening: can you destroy an ancient sorcery?* Cambridge, England: Cambridge University Press, 1986, [96] p., paper, novel. STORYTRAILS.

33594 *The deadly trap: caught up in the web of a strange prophecy, can you avoid the trap?* Cambridge, England: Cambridge University Press, 1983, [74] p., paper, novel. STORYTRAILS.

33595 *The evil of Mr. Happiness: can you defeat the schemes of a criminal mastermind?* Cambridge, England: Cambridge University Press, 1983, [44] p., paper, novel. STORYTRAILS.

33596 *The eye of Heaven: can you save the victim of a web of mystery?* Cambridge, England: Cambridge University Press, 1985, [96] p., paper, novel. STORYTRAILS.

33597 *The hands of Pablo Santos.* Cambridge, England: Cambridge University Press, 1985, [96] p., paper, novel. STORYTRAILS.

33598 *The haunters of Marsh Hall: can you find the secret of the ghostly guardian?* Cambridge, England: Cambridge University Press, 1982, [37] p., paper, novel. STORYTRAILS.

33599 *The island of the walking dead: can you save the victim of a terrifying revenge?* Cambridge, England: Cambridge University Press, 1986, [96] p., paper, novel. STORYTRAILS.

33600 *Night of the comet: can you destroy the giants from the sea?* Cambridge, England: Cambridge University Press, 1983, [44] p., paper, novel. STORYTRAILS.

33601 *Return of the undead: can you destroy the vampire of Valdah?* Cambridge, England: Cambridge University Press, 1984, [90] p., paper, novel. STORYTRAILS.

33602 *The second conquest: can you change the world's future?* Cambridge, England: Cambridge University Press, 1985, [96] p., paper, novel. STORYTRAILS.

33603 *The stone of Badda: can you face the deadly guardians of Otherworld?* Cambridge, England: Cambridge University Press, 1982, [37] p., paper, novel. STORYTRAILS.

33604 *Terror in the fourth dimension: can you return from a 2000 year journey through time?* Cambridge, England: Cambridge University Press, 1982, [44] p., paper, novel. STORYTRAILS.

33605 *The tomb of Amenosis: can you stop a war, solve a riddle as old as Genesis?* Cambridge, England: Cambridge University Press, 1983, [90] p., paper, novel. STORYTRAILS.

33606 *The wolf with no tail: can you discover Kutzka's ancient secret?* Cambridge, England: Cambridge University Press, 1987, [90] p., paper, novel. STORYTRAILS.

SHARP, Luke

Chasms of malice—SEE: *Steve Jackson and Ian Livingstone present Chasms of malice.*
Fangs of fury—SEE: *Steve Jackson and Ian Livingstone present Fangs of fury.*

33607 *Steve Jackson and Ian Livingstone present Chasms of malice.* Harmondsworth, Middlesex, England: Puffin Books, 1988, 29+[200] p., paper, fiction. FIGHTING FANTASY GAMEBOOK SERIES.

33608 *Steve Jackson and Ian Livingstone present Fangs of fury.* Harmondsworth, Middlesex, England: Puffin Books, 1989, 399 p., paper, fiction. FIGHTING FANTASY GAMEBOOK #39.

SHARP, Margery, 1905-1991

33609 *Bernard the brave: a Miss Bianca story.* Boston: Little, Brown & Co., 1977, 128 p., cloth, novel. MISS BIANCA #8.

33610 *Bernard into battle: a Miss Bianca story.* Boston: Little, Brown & Co., 1978, 87 p., cloth, novel. MISS BIANCA #9.

SHARPE, John Rufus III

33611 *Hogar, Lord of the Asyr.* New York: A Signet Book, New American Library, 1987, 239 p., paper, novel.

SHARPE, Vera, pseud.

33612 *Queen of evil.* New York: Bizarre Library, 1975, 190 p., paper, novel.

SHATNER, Lisabeth, *with William Shatner*

33613 *The captain's log: William Shatner's Personal account of the making of Star Trek V, The final frontier.* New York: Pocket Books, 1989, 224 p., paper, nonf.

SHATNER, William, 1931-

33614 *TekLab*. New York: An Ace/Putnam Book, 1991, 223 p., cloth, novel. TEK-WAR #3. [Attributed to Ron Goulart as anonymous co-author].

33615 *TekLords*. New York: An Ace/Putnam Book, 1991, 223 p., cloth, novel. TEK-WAR #2. [Attributed to Ron Goulart as anonymous co-author].

33616 *TekWar*. West Bloomfield, MI: Phantasia Press, 1989, 216 p., cloth, novel. TEK-WAR #1. [Attributed to Ron Goulart as anonymous co-author].

with Sondra Marshak & Myrna Culbreath

20863 *Shatner: where no man...: the authorized biography of William Shatner*. New York: A Tempo Star Book, Grosset & Dunlap, 1979, 327 p., paper, nonf.

with Lisabeth Shatner

33613 *The captain's log: William Shatner's Personal account of the making of Star Trek V, The final frontier*. New York: Pocket Books, 1989, 224 p., paper, nonf.

*SHAW, Arnold, 1909-1989

SHAW, Bob [i.e., Robert Shaw], 1931-

33617 *The best of the bushel*. Epsom, Surrey, England: Paranoid/Inca Press, 1979, 60 p., paper, nonf. coll.

33618 *A better mantrap: nine science fiction and fantasy stories*. London: Victor Gollancz, 1982, 192 p., cloth, coll.

33619 *The Ceres solution*. London: Victor Gollancz, 1981, 191 p., cloth, novel.

33620 *Cosmic kaleidoscope*. London: Victor Gollancz, 1976, 188 p., cloth, coll.

33621 *Dagger of the mind*. London: Victor Gollancz, 1979, 173 p., cloth, novel.

33622 *Dark night in Toyland*. London: Victor Gollancz, 1989, 192 p., cloth, coll.

33623 *The Eastercon speeches*. Epsom, Surrey, England: Paranoid/Inca Press, 1979, 50 p., paper, nonf. coll.

33624 *Fire pattern*. London: Victor Gollancz, 1984, 190 p., cloth, novel.

33625 *The fugitive worlds*. London: Victor Gollancz, 1989, 254 p., cloth, novel. LAND AND OVERLAND #3.

12953 *Ground zero man*. New York: Avon, 1971, 160 p., paper, novel.

12953A retitled: *The peace machine*. London: Victor Gollancz, 1985, 160 p., cloth, novel. [Revised and updated edition].

33626 *Killer planet*. London: Victor Gollancz, 1989, 105 p., cloth, novel.

33627 *Medusa's children*. London: Victor Gollancz, 1977, 184 p., cloth, novel.

33628 *Messages found in an oxygen bottle*. Cambridge, MA: NESFA Press, 1986, iv + 103 p., cloth, coll. [Includes some nonfiction; bound with *Between two worlds* / by Terry Carr].

33629 *Orbitsville*. London: Victor Gollancz, 1975, 224 p., cloth, novel. ORBITSVILLE #1.

33630 *Orbitsville departure*. London: Victor Gollancz, 1983, 166 p., cloth, novel. ORBITSVILLE #2.

33631 *Orbitsville judgement*. London: Victor Gollancz, 1990, 281 p., cloth, novel. ORBITSVILLE #3.

The peace machine—SEE: *Ground zero man*.

33632 *The ragged astronauts*. London: Victor Gollancz, 1986, 310 p., cloth, novel. LAND AND OVERLAND #1.

33633 *The shadow of heaven, rev. ed.* London: Victor Gollancz, 1991, 174 p., cloth, novel. [Expanded edition of #12958].

33634 *Ship of strangers*. London: Victor Gollancz, 1978, 160 p., cloth, novel.

Terminal velocity—SEE: *Vertigo*.

33635 *Vertigo*. London: Victor Gollancz, 1978, 160 p., cloth, novel.

38055 retitled: *Terminal velocity*. London: Victor Gollancz, 1991, 192 p., cloth, novel. [Expanded edition].

33636 *Who goes here?* London: Victor Gollancz, 1977, 160 p., cloth, coll.

33637 *Who goes here? and, The Giaconda caper*. London: Victor Gollancz, 1988, 253 p., paper, coll. [Expanded edition].

33638 *The wooden spaceships*. London: Victor Gollancz, 1988, 294 p., cloth, novel. LAND AND OVERLAND #2.

33639 *A wreath of stars*. London: Victor Gollancz, 1976, 189 p., cloth, novel.

with David Hardy

25190 *Galactic tours: Thomas Cook out of this world vacations*. New York: Proteus Press, 1981, 95 p., cloth, fiction.

SHAW, Brian, house pseud.—SEE: Holloway, Brian

*SHAW, Larry T. [i.e., Lawrence Taylor Shaw], 1924-1985

SHAW, Lawrence T.—SEE: Shaw, Larry T.

SHAW, Robert—SEE: Shaw, Bob

SHAY, Don

33640 *Making Ghostbusters: the screenplay by Dan Ackroyd and Harold Ramis, with notes, quotes, and anecdotes.* New York: Zoetrope, 1985, 223 p., paper, nonf. anth.

with Jody Duncan

22294 *The making of T2, Terminator 2: Judgment day.* New York, Toronto: Bantam Books, 1991, 127 p., paper, nonf.

SHEA, George, 1940-

38056 *ESP McGee to the rescue.* New York: An Avon Camelot Book, 1984, 96 p., paper, novel. ESP MCGEE #5.
33641 *I died here.* Belmont, CA: Fearon Pitman Publishers, 1977, 60 p., cloth, novel.
33642 *Nightmare Nina.* Mankato, MN: Creative Education, 1978, 56 p., cloth, novel.

SHEA, J. Vernon, 1912-1981

33643 *H. P. Lovecraft: the house and the shadows.* West Warwick, RI: Necronomicon Press, 1982, 20 p., paper, nonf.
33644 *In search of Lovecraft.* West Warwick, RI: Necronomicon Press, 1991, 42 p., paper, nonf. coll. [Includes some verse and two stories].

SHEA, Michael (Sinclair MacAuslan), 1938-

33645 *Tomorrow's men: a novel.* London: Weidenfeld & Nicolson, 1982, 204 p., cloth, novel.

SHEA, Michael, 1946-

33646 *Color out of time.* New York: DAW Books, 1984, 191 p., paper, novel. CTHULHU MYTHOS. [A sequel to H. P. Lovecraft's *The color out of space*].
33646A retitled: *The colour out of time.* London: Grafton, 1986, 160 p., paper, novel.
The colour out of time—SEE: *Color out of time.*
33647 *Fat face.* Seattle, WA: Axolotl Press, 1987, 36 p., cloth, story. CTHULHU MYTHOS; AXOLOTL PRESS #5.
33648 *In Yana, the touch of undying.* New York: DAW Books, 1985, 318 p., paper, novel.
33649 *Nifft the Lean.* New York: DAW Books, 1982, 304 p., paper, coll. DYING EARTH SEQUEL. [Winner of the World Fantasy Award for Best Fantasy Novel, 1982 (1983)].

33650 *Polyphemus: stories.* Sauk City, WI: Arkham House Publishers, 1987, x+245 p., cloth, coll.

SHEA, Robert (Joseph), 1933-

33651 *Shaman.* New York: Ballantine Books, 1991, 519 p., paper, novel.

with Robert Anton Wilson

33652 *The eye in the pyramid.* New York: A Dell Book, 1975, 304 p., paper, novel. ILLUMINATUS! #1.
33653 *The golden apple.* New York: A Dell Book, 1975, 272 p., paper, novel. ILLUMINATUS! #2.
33654 *The Illuminatus! trilogy: The eye in the pyramid, The golden apple, and Leviathan.* New York: A Dell Trade Paperback, 1984, 805 p., paper, coll. ILLUMINATUS! #1-3.
33655 *Leviathan.* New York: A Dell Book, 1975, 253 p., paper, novel. ILLUMINATUS! #3.

SHEARING, Joseph, pseud.—SEE: Campbell, Margaret

SHECKLEY, Robert, 1928-

33656 *After the fall.* New York: Ace Books, 1980, x+212 p., paper, anth.
The alchemical marriage of Alistair Crompton—SEE: *Crompton divided.*
33657 *Alien starswarm.* Portland, OR: Dime-Novels, 1990, 93 p., paper, novel.
33658 *The collected short stories of Robert Sheckley, book one.* Eugene, OR: Pulphouse Publishing, 1991, 331 p., cloth, coll. [Limited to 300 copies].
33659 *The collected short stories of Robert Sheckley, book two.* Eugene, OR: Pulphouse Publishing, 1991, 380 p., cloth, coll. [Limited to 300 copies].
33660 *The collected short stories of Robert Sheckley, book three.* Eugene, OR: Pulphouse Publishing, 1991, 360 p., cloth, coll. [Limited to 300 copies].
33661 *The collected short stories of Robert Sheckley, book four.* Eugene, OR: Pulphouse Publishing, 1991, 275 p., cloth, coll. [Limited to 300 copies].
33662 *The collected short stories of Robert Sheckley, book five.* Eugene, OR: Pulphouse Publishing, 1991, 344 p., cloth, coll. [Limited to 300 copies].
33663 *Crompton divided.* New York: Holt, Rinehart & Winston, 1978, 234 p., cloth, novel.

33663A retitled: *The alchemical marriage of Alistair Crompton.* London: Michael Joseph, 1978, 191 p., cloth, novel.

33664 *Dramoles: an intergalactic soap opera.* New York: Holt, Rinehart & Winston, 1983, 204 p., cloth, novel.

33665 *Futuropolis.* New York: A & W Visual Library, 1978, [118] p., cloth, nonf.

33666 *Hunter/victim.* New York: A Signet Books, New American Library, 1988, 269 p., paper, novel. VICTIM #3.

33667 *Is that what people do?: short stories.* New York: Holt, Rinehart & Winston, 1984, 402 p., cloth, coll.

12978 *Journey beyond tomorrow.* New York: Signet, 1962, 144 p., paper, novel.

12978A retitled: *Journey of Joenes.* London: Sphere Books, 1978, 191 p., paper, novel.

Journey of Joenes—SEE: *Journey beyond tomorrow.*

33668 *Minotaur maze.* Eugene, OR: Axolotl Press, Pulphouse Publishing, 1990, 110 p., cloth, novel. AXOLOTL PRESS #17.

33669 *Options.* New York: Pyramid Books, 1975, 158 p., paper, novel.

33670 *The people trap; plus, Mindswap.* New York: Ace Books, 1981, 469 p., paper, coll.

33671 *The robot who looked like me.* London: Sphere Books, 1978, 189 p., paper, coll.

33672 *The status civilization; and, Notions: unlimited.* New York: Ace Books, 1979, 469 p., paper, coll.

33673 *Victim prime.* London: Methuen, 1987, 202 p., cloth, novel. VICTIM #2.

33674 *Watchbird.* Eugene, OR: Pulphouse Publishing, 1990, 35 p., cloth, story.

33675 *The wonderful world of Robert Sheckley.* Toronto, New York: Bantam Books, 1979, xii + 195 p., paper, coll.

33676 *Xolotl.* Eugene, OR: Pulphouse Publishing, 1991, 41 p., cloth, story. SHORT STORY HARDBACKS #3; SHORT STORY PAPERBACKS #3.

with Harry Harrison

25298 *Bill, the galactic hero on the planet of bottled brains.* New York: A Byron Preiss Book, Avon Books, 1990, 249 p., paper, novel. BILL, THE GALACTIC HERO #2.

with Roger Zelazny

33677 *Bring me the head of Prince Charming.* New York, Toronto: Bantam Books, 1991, 279 p., cloth, novel.

*SHECTER, Ben, 1935-

SHEDLEY, Ethan I. [pseud. of Boris Beizer], 1934-

33678 *Earth ship and star song: a novel.* New York: The Viking Press, 1979, 215 p., cloth, novel.

SHEFFIELD, Charles (A.), 1935-

33679 *Between the strokes of night.* New York: Baen Science Fiction Books, 1985, 346 p., paper, novel.

33680 *Divergence.* Norwalk, CT: Easton Press, 1991, 281 p., cloth, novel. HERITAGE UNIVERSE #2.

33681 *Erasmus magister.* New York: Ace Books, 1982, 217 p., paper, novel.

33682 *Hidden variables.* New York: Ace Books, 1981, 359 p., paper, coll.

33683 *The McAndrew chronicles.* New York: A Jim Baen Presentation, Tor, A Tom Doherty Associates Books, 1983, 243 p., paper, novel.

33684 *My brother's keeper.* New York: Ace Books, 1982, 216 p., paper, novel.

33685 *The Nimrod hunt.* New York: Baen Science Fiction Books, 1986, 401 p., paper, novel.

33686 *Proteus manifest.* New York: Guild America Books, 1989, 406 p., cloth, coll. PROTEUS #1-2.

33687 *Proteus unbound.* London: New English Library, 1989, 267 p., paper, novel. PROTEUS #2.

33688 *Sight of Proteus.* New York: Ace Books, 1978, 282 p., paper, novel. PROTEUS #1.

33689 *Summertide.* New York: A Del Rey Book, Ballantine Books, 1990, 257 p., cloth, novel. HERITAGE UNIVERSE #1.

33690 *Trader's world.* New York: A Del Rey Book, Ballantine Books, 1988, 279 p., paper, novel.

33691 *Vectors.* New York: Ace Books, 1979, 432 p., paper, coll.

33692 *The web between the worlds.* New York: Ace Books, 1979, 274 p., paper, novel.

with David Bischoff

18019 *The Selkie.* New York: Macmillan Publishing Co., 1982, 375 p., cloth, novel.

SHEFNER, Evelyn, 1919-

33693 *Common body, royal bones: three stories.* Minneapolis, MN: Coffee House Press, 1987, 119 p., paper, coll.

SHEFNER, Vadim (Sergeevich), 1915-

33694 *The unman; Kovrigin's chronicles.* New York: Macmillan Publishing Co.; London: Collier Macmillan Publishers, 1980, vi+233 p., cloth, coll. [Translation by Alice Stone Nakhimovky and Alexander Nakhimovsky of *Chelovek s piatiu "ne"*, and by Antonina W. Bouis of *Devushka u obryva*].

SHELDEN, Michael

33695 *Orwell: a biography.* New York: HarperCollinsPublishers, 1991, 497 p., cloth, nonf.

SHELDON, Alice—SEE: Tiptree, James Jr.

SHELDON, Charlie

33696 *Fat chance.* New York, London: Pocket Books, 1991, 259 p., paper, novel.

SHELDON, Lita (Koko)

33697 *An author list of Star Wars fan fiction.* Tsaile, AZ: Lita Sheldon, 1984, 33+4 leaves, paper, nonf.
33698 *A Star Wars bibliography.* Tsaile, AZ: Lita Sheldon, 1980, 160 p., paper, nonf.
33699 *A Star Wars bibliography, 1973-1987.* Everett, WA: Lita Sheldon, 1987, 78 p., paper, nonf.
33700 *A Star Wars fanzine index, volume 1.* Tsaile, TZ: Lita Sheldon, 1981, 125 p., paper, nonf.

SHELDON, Roy, house pseud.—SEE: Hay, George

SHELDON, Sidney, 1917-

33701 *The doomsday conspiracy.* New York: William Morrow & Co., 1991, 412 p., cloth, novel.

SHELDON, Walter J., 1917-1979?

33702 *The beast.* New York: Fawcett Gold Medal, 1980, 288 p., paper, novel.

*SHELDON, William D(enley), 1915-

SHELLEY, Mary Wollstonecraft, 1797-1851

33703 *The journals of Mary Shelley, 1814-1844.* Oxford: Clarendon Press, 1987, lxii+x+735 p. in 2 v., cloth, nonf. coll. [Edited by Paula R. Feldman and Diana Scott-Kilvert].

33704 *The letters of Mary Wollstonecraft Shelley.* Norman, OK: University of Oklahoma Press, 1944, 2 v. (I-xxxii+379 p.; II-xx+390 p.), cloth, nonf. coll. [Edited by Frederick L. Jones].
33705 *The letters of Mary Wollstonecraft Shelley, volume I: "A part of the elect".* Baltimore, MD & London: Johns Hopkins University Press, 1980, xlv+591 p., cloth, nonf. coll. [Edited by Betty T. Bennett].
33706 *The letters of Mary Wollstonecraft Shelley, volume II: "Treading in unknown paths".* Baltimore, MD & London: Johns Hopkins University Press, 1983, lii+360 p., cloth, nonf. coll. [Edited by Betty T. Bennett].
33707 *The letters of Mary Wollstonecraft Shelley, volume III: "What years I have spent!"* Baltimore, MD & London: Johns Hopkins University Press, 1988, li+473 p., cloth, nonf. coll. [Edited by Betty T. Bennett].
33708 *The Mary Shelley reader.* Oxford, England, New York: Oxford University Press, 1990, 420 p., cloth, coll. [Includes some nonfiction].
"A part of the elect"—SEE: *The letters of Mary Wollstonecraft Shelley, volume I.*
"Treading in unknown paths"—SEE: *The letters of Mary Wollstonecraft Shelley, volume II.*
"What years I have spent!"—SEE: *The letters of Mary Wollstonecraft Shelley, volume III.*

with Tom Barling

17400 *Frankenstein.* London: Corgi Books, 1976, 96 p., paper, novel. [Adapted from the original novel by Shelley].

with T. Ernesto Bethancourt

17917 *Frankenstein.* Belmont, CA: David S. Lake, A Fearon Classic, 1986, v+74 p., paper, novel. [Adapted from Shelley's novel].

with David Campton

19298 *Frankenstein.* London: Hutchinson, 1987, 143 p., cloth, novel. [A retelling of Mary Shelley's novel].

with John Howard Payne & Washington Irving

26331 *The romance of Mary W. Shelley, John Howard Payne, and Washington Irving.* Boston: Bibliophile Society, 1907, 100 p., cloth, nonf. coll.

with Diana Stewart

33709 *Frankenstein.* Milwaukee, WI: Raintree Publishers, 1981, 48 p., cloth, story. [Adapted from Shelley's original work].

with John Stoker

35062 *The illustrated Frankenstein.* Newton Abbot, England: Westridge Books, 1980, 128 p., paper, nonf.

SHELLEY, Richard M.—SEE: Shelley, Rick

SHELLEY, Rick [i.e., Richard Michael Shelley], 1947-

33710 *The hero of Varay.* New York: A Roc Book, 1991, 256 p., paper, novel. VARAYAN MEMOIR #2.

33711 *Son of the hero.* New York: A Roc Book, 1990, 256 p., paper, novel. VARAYAN MEMOIR #1.

SHELVANKAR, Krishnaro S(hivarao)

33712 *Ends are means: a critique of social values.* London: Drummond, 1938, 146 p., cloth, nonf.

SHENNAN, Margaret, 1933-

33713 *The devil's diagonal.* London: Swallow, 1989, 124 p., paper, novel.

SHEPARD, Leslie (Alan), 1917-

33714 *The book of Dracula.* New York: Wings Books, 1991, 269, 288 p., cloth, anth. [Includes *The Dracula book of great horror stories*; *The Dracula book of great vampire stories*].

33715 *The Dracula book of great horror stories.* Secaucus, NJ: Citadel Press, 1981, 288 p., cloth, anth.

33716 *The Dracula book of great vampire stories.* Secaucus, NJ: Citadel Press, 1977, 269 p., cloth, anth.

SHEPARD, Lucius (Taylor), 1947-

33717 *The ends of the earth: 14 stories.* Sauk City, WI: Arkham House Publishers, 1991, x+484 p., cloth, coll.

33718 *The father of stones.* Baltimore, MD, Washington, DC: Washington Science Fiction Association, 1989, 133 p., cloth, novel. [Limited to 578 copies].

33719 *Green eyes.* New York: Ace Science Fiction Books, 1984, xii+275 p., paper, novel.

33720 *The jaguar hunter.* Sauk City, WI: Arkham House Publishers, 1987, xii+404 p., cloth, coll. [Winner of the World Fantasy Award for Best Fantasy Anthology/Collection, 1987 (1988); winner of the *Locus* Award for Best Collection, 1987 (1988)].

33721 *The jaguar hunter.* London: Paladin, 1988, 429 p., paper, coll. [Drops 1 story, adds 3].

33722 *Kalimantan.* London: Legend, 1990, 160 p., cloth, novel.

33723 *Life during wartime.* Toronto, New York: Bantam Books, 1987, 438 p., paper, novel.

33724 *The scalehunter's beautiful daughter.* Willimantic, CT: Mark V. Ziesing, 1988, 153 p., cloth, novel.

with Robert Frazier

23475 *Nantucket slayrides: three short novels.* Nantucket, MA: Eel Grass Press, 1989, 219 p., cloth, coll.

SHERIDAN, Elsie L.—SEE: Lee, Elsie

SHERIDAN, Thomas, *with E. E. Smith*

33725 *E. E. "Doc" Smith, father of star wars.* West Warwick, RI: Necronomicon Press, 1977, [8] p., paper, nonf.

SHERMAN, Cordelia C.—SEE: Sherman, Delia

SHERMAN, Dan(iel Michael), 1950- , *with Trevor Meldal-Johnsen as* DAN TREVOR

29720 *The night whistlers.* New York: Jove Books, 1991, 234 p., paper, novel. NIGHT WHISTLERS #1.

SHERMAN, Delia [i.e., Cordelia Caroline Sherman], 1951-

33726 *Through a brazen mirror.* New York: Ace Books, 1989, 233 p., paper, novel.

SHERMAN, Harold M(orrow), 1898-1987

33727 *The green man and his return: an amazing UFO pre-vision of the coming of the space people! written in 1946-47! complete reprint of the original text of The green man and The green man returns.* Amherst, WI: Published for Nor-man Creamer, Suttons Bay, MI, and Harold M. Sherman, Mountain View, AR, by Amherst Press, 1979, 214 p., paper, coll.

SHERMAN, Joel Henry, 1957-

33728 *Corpseman.* New York: A Del Rey Book, Ballantine Books, 1988, 277 p., paper, novel.

33729 *Random factor.* New York: A Del Rey Book, Ballantine Books, 1991, 329 p., paper, novel.

SHERMAN, Jory (Tecumseh), 1932-

33730 *The bamboo demons.* Los Angeles: Pinnacle Books, 1979, 182 p., paper, novel. CHILL #3.

33731 *Chill.* Los Angeles: Pinnacle Books, 1978, 244 p., paper, novel. CHILL #2.

33732 *House of scorpions.* Los Angeles: Pinnacle Books, 1980, 176 p., paper, novel. CHILL #6.

33733 *The phoenix man.* Los Angeles: Pinnacle Books, 1980, 175 p., paper, novel. CHILL #5.

33734 *The reincarnation of Jenny James.* New York: Carlyle, 1979, 222 p., paper, novel.

33735 *Satan's seed.* Los Angeles: Pinnacle Books, 1978, 213 p., paper, novel. CHILL #1.

33736 *Shadows.* Los Angeles: Pinnacle Books, 1980, 181 p., paper, novel. CHILL #7.
Vampire—SEE: *Vegas vampire.*

33737 *Vegas vampire.* Los Angeles: Pinnacle Books, 1980, 176 p., paper, novel. CHILL #4.

33737A retitled: *Vampire.* London: New English Library, 1981, 176 p., paper, novel.

as FRANK ANVIE

33738 *Diana's devilish seduction.* New York: Orpheus Books, 1976, 251 p., paper, novel. [Cover byline says Frank Anvic].

SHERMAN, Josepha

33739 *The dark gods.* New York: Fawcett Columbine, 1989, 117 p., paper, novel. SECRET OF THE UNICORN QUEEN #5.

38057 *Golden Girl and the crystal of doom.* New York: Ballantine Books, 1986, 72 p., paper, novel. FIND YOUR FATE—GOLDEN GIRL #3.

33740 *The horse of flame.* New York: Avon Books, 1990, 345 p., paper, novel.

38058 *The invisibility factor.* New York: Ballantine Books, 1986, 72 p., paper, novel. FIND YOUR FATE—JUNIOR TRANSFORMERS #9.

33741 *The shining falcon.* New York: Avon Books, 1989, 341 p., paper, novel.

33742 *Song of the dark druid: a Dungeons & Dragons adventure book.* Lake Geneva, WI: TSR Inc., 1987, 157 p., paper, novel. ENDLESS QUEST #36.

33743 *Swept away.* New York: Fawcett Columbine, 1988, 121 p., paper, novel. SECRET OF THE UNICORN QUEEN #1.

SHERRED, T(homas) L., 1915-1985, *with Lloyd Biggle, Jr.*

17951 *Alien main.* Garden City, NY: Doubleday & Co., 1985, 182 p., cloth, novel. ALIEN ISLAND #2.

SHERRELL, Carl, 1929-1990

33744 *Arcane.* New York: A Jove/HBJ Book, 1978, 320 p., paper, novel.

33745 *The curse.* New York: Pageant Books, 1989, 469 p., paper, novel.

33746 *Raum.* New York: Avon, 1977, 189 p., paper, novel. RAUM #1.

33747 *Skraelings.* Lake Geneva, WI: New Infinities Productions, 1987, 224 p., paper, novel. RAUM #2.

33748 *The space prodigal.* New York: A Dell Book, 1981, 512 p., paper, novel.

SHERWOOD, Deborah

33749 *Blood sisters.* New York: Zebra Books, Kensington Publishing Corp., 1988, 352 p., paper, novel.

SHERWOOD, Martin (Anthony), 1942-

33750 *Maxwell's demon.* London: New English Library, 1976, 172 p., cloth, novel.

33751 *Survival.* London: New English Library, 1975, 128 p., cloth, novel.

SHETTERLY, Emma—SEE: Bull, Emma

SHETTERLY, Will(iam Howard), 1955-

33752 *Cats have no lord.* New York: Ace Fantasy Books, 1985, 225 p., paper, novel. KEVIN FIKKAN #1.

33753 *Elsewhere.* San Diego, CA: Harcourt Brace Jovanovich, 1991, xii+248 p., cloth, novel.

33754 *The tangled lands.* New York: Ace Books, 1989, 247 p., paper, novel. KEVIN FIKKAN #2.

33755 *Witch blood.* New York: Ace Fantasy Books, 1986, 197 p., paper, novel.

with Emma Bull

Festival week—SEE: *Liavek: Festival week.*

18935 *Liavek.* New York: Ace Fantasy Books, 1985, 274 p., paper, anth.

18936 *Liavek: Festival week.* New York: Ace Books, 1990, 275 p., paper, anth. LIAVEK #5.

18938 *Liavek: Spells of binding.* New York: Ace Books, 1988, 245 p., paper, anth. LIAVEK #4.

18937 *Liavek: The players of luck.* New York: Ace Fantasy Books, 1986, 290 p., paper, anth. LIAVEK #2.

18939 *Liavek: Wizard's row.* New York: Ace Fantasy Books, 1987, 212 p., paper, anth. LIAVEK #3.

The players of luck—SEE: *Liavek: The players of luck.*

Spells of binding—SEE: *Liavek: Spells of binding.*

Wizard's row—SEE: *Liavek: Wizard's row.*

SHETTLE, Andrea

33756 *Flute song music.* New York: An Avon Flare Book, 1990, 217 p., paper, novel.

SHI-KUO, Chang—SEE: Chang, Shi-Kuo

SHIEL, M(atthew) P(hipps), 1865-1947

33757 *The Empress of the Earth, 1898; The purple cloud, 1901; "Some short stories": offprints of the original editions.* Cleveland, OH: Reynolds Morse Foundation, 1979, xxxii+148+vi+60+iv+157 p., cloth, coll. WORKS OF M. P. SHIEL, VOL. 1.

33758 *The new king, plus an unpublished dialog with Cummings King Monk omitted from The pale ape of 1911.* Cleveland, OH: Reynolds Morse Foundation, 1980, 170 p., cloth, coll.

33759 *Prince Zaleski; and, Cummings King Monk.* Sauk City, WI: Mycroft & Moran, 1977, v+219 p., cloth, coll.

33760 *Xélucha, and others.* Sauk City, WI: Arkham House, 1975, viii+243 p., cloth, coll.

SHINE, Deborah, 1932-

33761 *Ghost stories.* London: Octopus Books, 1980, 349 p., cloth, anth.

SHINER, Lewis (Gordon), 1950-

33762 *Deserted cities of the heart.* New York: A Foundation Book, Doubleday & Co., 1988, 273 p., cloth, novel.

33763 *The edges of things.* Washington, DC: Washington Science Fiction Association, 1991, xi+216 p., cloth, coll. [Limited to 600 copies].

33764 *Frontera.* New York: A Baen Book, 1984, 286 p., paper, novel.

33765 *Nine hard questions about the nature of the universe.* Eugene, OR: Pulphouse Publishing, 1990, 120 p., cloth, coll. AUTHOR'S CHOICE MONTHLY #4.

33766 *Twilight time.* Eugene, OR: Pulphouse Publishing, 1991, 46 p., cloth, story. SHORT STORY HARDBACKS #17; SHORT STORY PAPERBACKS #30.

33767 *When the music's over: a benefit anthology.* New York, Toronto: Spectra, Bantam Books, 1991, ix+322 p., paper, anth.

SHINN, Thelma J. (Wardrop), 1942-

33768 *Worlds within women: mythology and mythmaking in fantastic literature by women.* New York, London: Greenwood Press, 1986, xiv+214 p., cloth, nonf. CONTRIBUTIONS TO THE STUDY OF SCIENCE FICTION AND FANTASY #22.

SHIPMAN, David, 1932-

33769 *A pictorial history of science fiction films.* London: Hamlyn, 1985, 172 p., cloth, nonf.

SHIPPEY, T(homas) A(lan), 1943-

33770 *Fictional space: essays on contemporary science fiction* / ed. by Tom Shippey. Oxford, England: Basil Blackwell; Atlantic Highlands, NJ: Humanities Press, 1991, vii+227 p., cloth, nonf. anth.

33771 *The road to Middle-Earth.* London, Boston: George Allen & Unwin, 1982, xii+252 p., cloth, nonf.

SHIPTON, Alyn

33772 *Fantasy.* London: John Murray, 1982, 119 p., paper, anth.

*SHIRAS, Wilmar H(ouse), 1908-1990

SHIRLEY, John (Patrick), 1953-

The black hole of Carcosa—SEE: *Kamus of Kadizhar: The black hole of Carcosa.*

38059 *The brigade.* New York: Avon, 1981, 254 p., paper, novel.

33773 *Cellars.* New York: Avon, 1982, 295 p., paper, novel.

33774 *City come a-walkin'.* New York: A Dell Book, 1980, 204 p., paper, novel.

33775 *Dracula in love.* New York: Zebra Books, Kensington Publishing Corp., 1983, 283 p., paper, novel.

33776 *Eclipse.* New York: Bluejay Books, 1985, 341 p., paper, novel. SONG CALLED YOUTH #1.

33777 *Eclipse corona.* New York: Popular Library, Warner Books, 1990, 293 p., paper, novel. SONG CALLED YOUTH #3.

33778 *Eclipse penumbra.* New York: Popular Library, Warner Books, 1988, 322 p., paper, novel. SONG CALLED YOUTH #2.

33779 *Heatseeker.* Los Angeles: Scream/Press, 1989, v+246 p., cloth, coll.

33780 *In darkness waiting.* New York: An Onyx Book, New American Library, 1988, 269 p., paper, novel.

33781 *Kamus of Kadizhar: The black hole of Carcosa: a tale of the Darkworld detective.* New York: St. Martin's Press, 1988, 184 p., paper, novel. KAMUS OF KADHIZHAR #2. [Sequel to Michael Reaves' *Darkworld detective*].

33782 *A splendid chaos: an interplanetary fantasy.* New York: Franklin Watts, 1988, 357 p., cloth, novel.

33783 *Three-ring psychus.* New York: Zebra Books, Kensington Publishing Corp., 1980, 240 p., paper, novel.

33784 *Transmaniacon.* New York: Zebra Books, Kensington Publishing Corp., 1979, 271 p., paper, novel.

38060 *Wetbones: a novel.* Shingletown, CA: Mark V. Ziesing, 1991, 273 p., cloth, novel.

as **D. B. DRUMM**

22222 *Border war.* New York: A Dell Book, 1985, 172 p., paper, novel. TRAVELER #6.

22227 *Kingdom come.* New York: A Dell Book, 1984, 176 p., paper, novel. TRAVELER #2.

22230 *Road war.* New York: A Dell Book, 1985, 158 p., paper, novel. TRAVELER #5.

22231 *The stalkers.* New York: A Dell Book, 1984, 176 p., paper, novel. TRAVELER #3.

22233 *Terminal road.* New York: A Dell Book, 1986, 173 p., paper, novel. TRAVELER #8.

22234 *To kill a shadow.* New York: A Dell Book, 1984, 173 p., paper, novel. TRAVELER #4.

SHOBER, Joyce Lee, 1932- , *with Claire John Eschelbach*

22733 *Aldous Huxley: a bibliography, 1916-1959.* Berkeley & Los Angeles: University of California Press, 1961, x+150 p., cloth, nonf.

SHOBIN, David, 1945-

33785 *The seeding.* New York: The Linden Press/Simon & Schuster, 1982, 223 p., cloth, novel.

33786 *The unborn.* New York: Linden Press/Simon & Schuster, 1981, 311 p., cloth, novel.

SHOCK, Julian, pseud.—SEE: Williamson, J. N.

SHOLS, W. W.

33787 *Perry Rhodan: Robot threat: New York.* New York: Ace Books, 1977, 117 p., paper, novel. PERRY RHODAN SERIES. [Bound with *Pale country pursuit* / by Hans Kneifel].

33788 *Perry Rhodan: The wasp men attack.* New York: Ace Books, 1977, 123 p., paper, novel. PERRY RHODAN SERIES. [Bound with *Spider desert* / by Ernst Vlcek].

Robot threat: New York—SEE: *Perry Rhodan: Robot threat: New York.*

The wasp men attack—SEE: *Perry Rhodan: The wasp men attack.*

*SHORES, Louis, 1904-1981

SHORT, Robert L(ester), 1932-

33789 *The gospel from outer space.* San Francisco: Harper & Row, 1983, ix+96 p., paper, nonf.

SHORTER, Philip

33790 *A handful of silver.* New York: Manor Books, 1978, 274 p., paper, novel.

SHORTLAND, Michael, *with Robert Lambourne & Michael Shallis*

27748 *Close encounters? science and science fiction.* Bristol & New York: Adam Hilger, 1991, xiii + 184 p., paper, nonf.

SHRADER, Alan Ross

33791 *Satan's chance.* New York: Ace Books, 1982, 388 p., paper, novel.

SHREFFLER, Philip A.

33792 *The H. P. Lovecraft companion.* Westport, CT & London: Greenwood Press, 1977, xvi + 198 p., cloth, nonf.

SHREVE, Susan Richards, 1939-

33793 *Queen of hearts: a novel.* New York: Simon & Schuster, 1986, 354 p., cloth, novel.

SHRYACK, Dennis, *with Michael Butler*

19116 *The car: a novel.* New York: A Dell Book, 1977, 235 p., paper, movie.

SHUBIK, Irene, *with Brian Hayles (as uncredited co-editor)*

25422 *The mind beyond: stories from Irene Shubik's BBC television series.* Harmondsworth, Middlesex, England: Penguin Books, 1976, 239 p., paper, anth.

SHULER, Linda Lay

33794 *She who remembers.* New York: Arbor House, 1988, 400 p., cloth, novel. TIME CIRCLE #1.

*SHUMWAY, Harry Irving, 1883-<u>1974</u>

SHUPP, Mike, 1946-

33795 *Death's gray land.* New York: A Del Rey Book, Ballantine Books, 1991, 322 p., paper, novel. DESTINY MAKERS #4.
33795A retitled: *Death's grey land.* London: Headline, 1991, 322 p., paper, novel.
33796 *The last reckoning.* New York: A Del Rey Book, Ballantine Books, 1991, 371 p., paper, novel. DESTINY MAKERS #5.

33797 *Morning of creation.* New York: A Del Rey Book, Ballantine Books, 1986, 304 p., paper, novel. DESTINY MAKERS #2.
33798 *Soldier of another fortune.* New York: A Del Rey Book, Ballantine Books, 1988, 396 p., paper, novel. DESTINY MAKERS #3.
33799 *With fate conspire.* New York: A Del Rey Book, Ballantine Books, 1985, 306 p., paper, novel. DESTINY MAKERS #1.

SHURKIN, Joel N., 1938- , *with Desmond Ryan*

32918 *Helix.* New York: W. W. Norton, 1979, 240 p., cloth, novel.

SHUTE, Nevil [pseud. of Nevil Shute Norway], 1899-1960

33800 *No highway.* London: William Heinemann, 1948, 314 p., cloth, novel.

SHUTTLE, Penelope (Diane), 1947-

38061 *The mirror of the giant.* London, Boston: Marion Boyars, 1980, 164 p., cloth, novel.

with Peter W. Redgrove

32100 *The glass cottage: a nautical romance.* London: Routledge & Kegan Paul, 1976, 205 p., cloth, novel.
32101 *The terrors of Dr Treviles: a romance.* London: Routledge & Kegan Paul, 1974, 177 p., cloth, novel.

SHWARTZ, Susan (Martha), 1949-

33801 *Arabesques: more tales of the Arabian nights.* New York: Avon Books, 1988, xi, 258 p., paper, anth.
33802 *Arabesques 2.* New York: Avon Books, 1989, viii + 373 p., paper, anth.
33803 *Byzantium's crown / by Susan M. Shwartz.* New York: Popular Library, 1987, 272 p., paper, novel. HEIRS TO BYZANTIUM #1.
33804 *Habitats.* New York: DAW Books, 1984, 220 p., paper, anth.
33805 *Hecate's cauldron / by Susan M. Shwartz.* New York: DAW Books, 1982, 256 p., paper, anth.
33806 *Heritage of flight.* New York: Tor SF, A Tom Doherty Associates Book, 1989, 338 p., paper, novel.
33807 *Moonsinger's friends: an anthology in honor of Andre Norton.* New York: Bluejay Books, 1985, 342 p., cloth, anth.

33808 *Queensblade* / by Susan M. Shwartz. New York: Popular Library, 1988, 280 p., paper, novel. HEIRS TO BYZANTIUM #3.

33809 *Silk roads and shadows.* New York: Tor SF, A Tom Doherty Associates Book, 1988, 337 p., paper, novel.

33810 *The woman of flowers* / by Susan M. Shwartz. New York: Popular Library, 1987, 308 p., paper, novel. HEIRS TO BYZANTIUM #2.

with Shariann N. Lewitt as GORDON KENDALL

28323 *White Wing.* New York: Tor SF, A Tom Doherty Associates Book, 1985, 319 p., paper, novel.

with Andre Norton

30853 *Imperial lady: a fantasy of Han China.* New York: Tor, A Tom Doherty Associates Book, 1989, 293 p., cloth, novel.

SIBLEY, Agnes (Marie), 1914-1979

33811 *Charles Williams.* Boston: Twayne Publishers, 1982, 160 p., cloth, nonf.

SIBLEY, Brian, 1949-

C. S. Lewis: Through the shadowlands— SEE: *Shadowlands: The story of C. S. Lewis and Joy Davidman.*

33812 *The land of Narnia: Brian Sibley explores the world of C. S. Lewis.* London: Collins Lions, 1989, 96 p., paper, nonf.

33813 *Shadowlands: The story of C. S. Lewis and Joy Davidman.* London: Hodder & Stoughton, 1985, 192 p., paper, nonf.

33813A retitled: *C. S. Lewis: through the shadowlands.* Old Tappan, NJ: Fleming H. Revell Co., 1985, 192 p., paper, nonf.

33814 *Snow White and the seven dwarfs & the making of the classic film.* New York: Simon & Schuster, 1987, 88 p., cloth, nonf.

*SIBSON, Francis H(enry), 1899-

SICILIANO, Sam (Joseph), 1947-

33815 *Blood farm: an Iowa gothic.* New York: Pageant Books, 1988, 336 p., paper, novel.

SICLARI, Joseph D.

33816 *MagiCon original bookmark anthology.* Orlando, FL: MagiCon, 1989, 8 p., paper, anth.

SIDDONS, (Sybil) Anne Rivers, 1936-

33817 *The house next door.* New York: Simon & Schuster, 1978, 346 p., cloth, novel.

SIDNEY, Kathleen M(arion), 1944-

33818 *Michael and the magic man.* New York: A Berkley Book, Berkley Publishing Corp., 1980, 213 p., cloth, novel.

SIDNEY-FRYER, Donald, 1934-

33819 *Emperor of dreams: a Clark Ashton Smith bibliography.* West Kingston, RI: Donald M. Grant, 1978, 303 p., cloth, nonf.

33820 *The last of the great romantic poets.* Albuquerque, NM: Silver Scarab Press, 1973, 27 p., paper, nonf.

SIEBERS, Tobin, 1953-

33821 *The romantic fantastic.* Ithaca, NY & London: Cornell University Press, 1984, 194 p., cloth, nonf.

SIEGEL, Barbara (B.), 1952?-, with Scott Siegel

38062 *Battle drive.* New York: Ballantine Books, 1985, 72 p., paper, novel. FIND YOUR FATE—JUNIOR TRANSFORMERS #2.

Beyond terror—SEE: *Ghostworld: Beyond terror.*

33822 *The burning land.* New York: An Archway Paperback, Pocket Books, 1987, 152 p., paper, novel. FIREBRATS #1.

38063 *The champ of TV wrestling.* New York: An Archway Paperback, Pocket Books, 1986, 118 p., paper, novel. WHICH WAY BOOKS #22.

33823 *G.I. Joe: Operation: death stone.* New York: Ballantine Books, 1986, 88 p., paper, novel. FIND YOUR FATE—G.I. JOE #6.

33824 *G.I. Joe: Operation: sink or swim.* New York: Ballantine Books, 1987, 89 p., paper, novel. FIND YOUR FATE—G.I. JOE #17.

33825 *G.I. Joe: Operation: snow job.* New York: Ballantine Books, 1987, 89 p., paper, novel. FIND YOUR FATE—G.I. JOE #13.

33826 *Ghost riders of Goldspur.* New York, Toronto: Scholastic Inc., 1985, 93 p., paper, novel. TWISTAPLOTS #17.

33827 *Ghostworld: Beyond terror.* New York, London: An Archway Paperback, Pocket Books, 1991, 148 p., paper, novel. GHOSTWORLD #1.

33828 *Ghostworld: Midnight chill.* New York, London: An Archway Paperback, Pocket Books, 1991, 148 p., paper, novel. GHOSTWORLD #2.

Midnight chill—SEE: *Ghostworld: Midnight chill.*

Operation: death stone—SEE: *G.I. Joe: Operation: death stone.*

Operation: sink or swim—SEE: *G.I. Joe: Operation: sink or swim.*

Operation: snow job—SEE: *G.I. Joe: Operation: snow job.*

Phaser fight—SEE: *Star Trek: Phaser fight.*

38064 *Project brain drain.* New York: Ballantine Books, 1986, 72 p., paper, novel. FIND YOUR FATE—JUNIOR TRANSFORMERS #8.

33829 *The scarlet shield of Shalimar.* New York: Avon, 1986, 103 p., paper, novel. WIZARDS, WARRIORS & YOU #12.

33830 *Shockwave.* New York: An Archway Paperback, Pocket Books, 1988, 150 p., paper, novel. FIREBRATS #4.

33831 *Star Trek: Phaser fight.* New York: An Archway Paperback, Pocket Books, 1986, 118 p., paper, novel. WHICH WAY BOOKS #24; STAR TREK SERIES.

33832 *Survivors.* New York: An Archway Paperback, Pocket Books, 1987, 150 p., paper, novel. FIREBRATS #2.

33833 *Tanis, the shadow years.* Lake Geneva, WI: TSR Inc., 1990, 320 p., paper, novel. DRAGONLANCE PRELUDES II #3.

33834 *Thunder Mountain.* New York: An Archway Paperback, Pocket Books, 1987, 146 p., paper, novel. FIREBRATS #3.

33835 *The warrior women of Weymouth.* New York: Avon, 1986, 104 p., paper, novel. WIZARDS, WARRIORS & YOU #18.

SIEGEL, Mark (Richard), 1949-

33836 *Hugo Gernsback, father of modern science fiction, with essays on Frank Herbert and Bram Stoker.* San Bernardino, CA: The Borgo Press, 1988, 96 p., cloth, nonf. coll. MILFORD SERIES: POPULAR WRITERS OF TODAY #45.

33837 *James Tiptree, Jr.* Mercer Island, WA: Starmont House, 1986, 89 p., cloth, nonf. STARMONT READER'S GUIDE #22.

33838 *Pynchon: creative paranoia in Gravity's rainbow.* Port Washington, NY, London: National University Press Publications, Kennikat Press, 1978, viii+136 p., cloth, nonf.

33839 *Tom Robbins.* Boise, ID: Boise State University, 1980, 52 p., paper, nonf.

*SIEGEL, Martin, 1938-1972

SIEGEL, Richard

with John H. Butterfield

19128 *The extraterrestrial report.* New York: A&W Visual Library, 1978, 128 p., paper, fiction.

with Jean-Claude Suarès

33840 *Alien creatures.* Los Angeles: Reed Books, 1978, 160 p., cloth, nonf.

with Jean-Claude Suarès & David Owen

31070 *Fantastic planets.* Danbury, NH: Reed Books, 1979, 160 p., cloth, nonf.

SIEGEL, Robert (Harold), 1939-

33841 *Alpha Centauri.* Westchester, IL: Cornerstone Books, 1980, 255 p., cloth, novel.

33842 *Whalesong.* Westchester, IL: Crossway Books, 1981, 143 p., paper, novel.

33843 *White whale: a novel.* San Francisco: HarperSanFrancisco, 1991, 228 p., cloth, novel.

SIEGEL, Scott (Warren), 1951-

33844 *Beat the devil.* Toronto, New York: Bantam Books, 1983, 118 p., paper, novel. DARK FORCES #10.

33845 *The companion.* Toronto, New York: Bantam Books, 1983, 134 p., paper, novel. DARK FORCES #8.

33846 *Revenge of the falcon knight.* New York: A Parachute Press Book, Avon, 1985, 103 p., paper, novel. WIZARDS, WARRIORS & YOU #6.

with Barbara Siegel

38062 *Battle drive.* New York: Ballantine Books, 1985, 72 p., paper, novel. FIND YOUR FATE—JUNIOR TRANSFORMERS #2.

Beyond terror—SEE: *Ghostworld: Beyond terror.*

33822 *The burning land.* New York: An Archway Paperback, Pocket Books, 1987, 152 p., paper, novel. FIREBRATS #1.

38063 *The champ of TV wrestling.* New York: An Archway Paperback, Pocket Books, 1986, 118 p., paper, novel. WHICH WAY BOOKS #22.

33823 *G.I. Joe: Operation: death stone.* New York: Ballantine Books, 1986, 88 p., paper, novel. FIND YOUR FATE—G.I. JOE #6.

33824 *G.I. Joe: Operation: sink or swim.* New York: Ballantine Books, 1987, 89 p., paper, novel. FIND YOUR FATE—G.I. JOE #17.

33825 *G.I. Joe: Operation: snow job.* New York: Ballantine Books, 1987, 89 p., paper, novel. FIND YOUR FATE—G.I. JOE #13.

33826 *Ghost riders of Goldspur.* New York, Toronto: Scholastic Inc., 1985, 93 p., paper, novel. TWISTAPLOTS #17.

33827 *Ghostworld: Beyond terror.* New York, London: An Archway Paperback, Pocket Books, 1991, 148 p., paper, novel. GHOSTWORLD #1.

33828 *Ghostworld: Midnight chill.* New York, London: An Archway Paperback, Pocket Books, 1991, 148 p., paper, novel. GHOSTWORLD #2.

Midnight chill—SEE: Ghostworld: Midnight chill.

Operation: death stone—SEE: G.I. Joe: Operation: death stone.

Operation: sink or swim—SEE: G.I. Joe: Operation: sink or swim.

Operation: snow job—SEE: G.I. Joe: Operation: snow job.

Phaser fight—SEE: Star Trek: Phaser fight.

38064 *Project brain drain.* New York: Ballantine Books, 1986, 72 p., paper, novel. FIND YOUR FATE—JUNIOR TRANSFORMERS #8.

33829 *The scarlet shield of Shalimar.* New York: Avon, 1986, 103 p., paper, novel. WIZARDS, WARRIORS & YOU #12.

33830 *Shockwave.* New York: An Archway Paperback, Pocket Books, 1988, 150 p., paper, novel. FIREBRATS #4.

33831 *Star Trek: Phaser fight.* New York: An Archway Paperback, Pocket Books, 1986, 118 p., paper, novel. WHICH WAY BOOKS #24; STAR TREK SERIES.

33832 *Survivors.* New York: An Archway Paperback, Pocket Books, 1987, 150 p., paper, novel. FIREBRATS #2.

33833 *Tanis, the shadow years.* Lake Geneva, WI: TSR Inc., 1990, 320 p., paper, novel. DRAGONLANCE PRELUDES II #3.

33834 *Thunder Mountain.* New York: An Archway Paperback, Pocket Books, 1987, 146 p., paper, novel. FIREBRATS #3.

33835 *The warrior women of Weymouth.* New York: Avon, 1986, 104 p., paper, novel. WIZARDS, WARRIORS & YOU #18.

*SIEGELE, H(erman) H(ugo), 1883-<u>1983</u>

SIEGMAN, Meryl

33847 *Volcano!* Toronto, New York: An R. A. Montgomery Book, Bantam Books, 1987, 111 p., paper, novel. CHOOSE YOUR OWN ADVENTURE #64.

SIEGRIST, Robert R.

33848 *Rotunda.* Westport, CT: Condor Books, 1977, 610 p., paper, novel.

SIEMANS, Lloyd, *with Roger Neufeld*

30639 *The critical reception of Sir Henry Rider Haggard: an annotated bibliography, 1882-1991.* Greensboro, NC: University of North Carolina at Greensboro, 1991, v+122 p., paper?, nonf.

SIEVERT, John, house pseud.

33849 *C.A.D.S.* New York: Zebra Books, Kensington Publishing Corp., 1985, 398 p., paper, novel. C.A.D.S. #1. [By Ryder Syvertsen & Jan Stacy].

33850 *Cybertech killing zone.* New York: Zebra Books, Kensington Publishing Corp., 1989, 222 p., paper, novel. C.A.D.S. #8. [By Ryder Syvertsen].

16221 *Death zone attack.* New York: Zebra Books, Kensington Publishing Corp., 1991, 176 p., paper, novel. C.A.D.S. #11. [By David Alexander].

33851 *Doom commander.* New York: Zebra Books, Kensington Publishing Corp., 1989, 220 p., paper, novel. C.A.D.S. #7. [By Ryder Syvertsen].

16222 *Recon by fire.* New York: Zebra Books, Kensington Publishing Corp., 1990, 222 p., paper, novel. C.A.D.S. #10. [By David Alexander].

16223 *Suicide attack.* New York: Zebra Books, Kensington Publishing Corp., 1990, 224 p., paper, novel. C.A.D.S. #9. [By David Alexander].

16224 *Tech assassins.* New York: Zebra Books, Kensington Publishing Corp., 1991, 192 p., paper, novel. C.A.D.S. #12. [By David Alexander].

33852 *Tech battleground.* New York: Zebra Books, Kensington Publishing Corp., 1986, 285 p., paper, novel. C.A.D.S. #2. [By Ryder Syvertsen].

33853 *Tech commando.* New York: Zebra Books, Kensington Publishing Corp., 1986, 252 p., paper, novel. C.A.D.S. #3. [By Ryder Syvertsen].

33854 *Tech inferno.* New York: Zebra Books, Kensington Publishing Corp., 1988, 255 p., paper, novel. C.A.D.S. #6. [By Ryder Syvertsen].

33855 *Tech Satan.* New York: Zebra Books, Kensington Publishing Corp., 1988, 286 p., paper, novel. C.A.D.S. #5. [By Ryder Syvertsen].

33856 *Tech strike force.* New York: Zebra Books, Kensington Publishing Corp., 1987, 270 p., paper, novel. C.A.D.S. #4. [By Ryder Syvertsen].

SILAS, A. E.

33857 *The panorama egg.* New York: DAW Books, 1978, 224 p., paper, novel.

SILBER, Diana—SEE: Henstell, Diana

SILBERSACK, John (Walter), 1954-

as ANONYMOUS AUTHOR

33858 *Science fiction.* New York: A Jove Book, 1981, 58 p., paper, novel. [Attributed to Silbersack; cover gives title as *No frills science fiction*].

with Jerry Pournelle & Larry Niven

30742 *Rogers' Rangers.* New York: Ace Science Fiction Books, 1983, 235 p., paper, novel. BUCK ROGERS #5.

with Victoria Schochet

33354 *The Berkley showcase, vol. 1: new writings in science fiction and fantasy.* New York: Berkley Books, 1980, 280 p., paper, anth.

33355 *The Berkley showcase, vol. 2: new writings in science fiction and fantasy.* New York: Berkley Books, 1980, 200 p., paper, anth.

33356 *The Berkley showcase, vol. 3.* New York: Berkley Books, 1981, 248 p., paper, anth.

33357 *The Berkley showcase, vol. 4: New writings in science fiction and fantasy.* New York: Berkley Books, 1981, 199 p., paper, anth.

SILK, Robert Kilroy- —SEE: Kilroy-Silk, Robert

SILKE, James R.

33859 *Frank Frazetta's Death Dealer: Prisoner of the horned helmet.* New York: Tor SF, A Tom Doherty Associates Book, 1988, 314 p., paper, novel. FRANK FRAZETTA'S DEATH DEALER #1.

33860 *Lords of destruction.* New York: Tor SF, A Tom Doherty Associates Book, 1989, 342 p., paper, novel. FRANK FRAZETTA'S DEATH DEALER #2.

33861 *Plague of knives.* New York: Tor Fantasy, A Tom Doherty Associates Book, 1990, 311 p., paper, novel. FRANK FRAZETTA'S DEATH DEALER #4.

Prisoner of the horned helmut—SEE: *Frank Frazetta's Death Dealer: Prisoner of the horned helmet.*

33862 *Tooth and claw.* New York: Tor Fantasy, A Tom Doherty Associates Book, 1989, 342 p., paper, novel. FRANK FRAZETTA'S DEATH DEALER #3.

SILVA, David B., 1950-

33863 *The best of the Horror Show, an adventure in terror.* Chicago: 2AM Publications, 1987, vii + 125 p., paper, anth.

33864 *Child of darkness.* New York: Leisure Books, 1986, 399 p., paper, novel.

33865 *Come thirteen / by David Silva.* New York: Leisure Books, 1988, 348 p., paper, novel.

with Paul F. Olson

31005 *Dead end: city limits: an anthology of urban fear.* New York: St. Martin's Press, 1991, xxiii + 342 p., cloth, anth.

31006 *Post mortem: new tales of ghostly horror.* New York: St. Martin's Press, 1989, xi + 290 p., cloth, anth.

SILVA, Joseph, pseud.—SEE: Goulart, Ron

SILVER, Alain (Joel), 1947- , with James Ursini

33866 *The vampire film.* South Brunswick, NJ: A. S. Barnes & Co., 1975, 238 p., cloth, nonf.

SILVER, Carole (Gretta), 1937-

33867 *The golden chain: essays on William Morris and pre-Raphaelitism.* New York: William Morris Society, 1982, vii + 148 p., cloth, nonf. anth.

33868 *The romance of William Morris.* Athens, OH: Ohio University Press, 1982, xviii + 233 p., cloth, nonf.

with Florence S. Boos

18273 *Socialism and the literary artistry of William Morris.* Columbia, MO: University of Missouri Press, 1990, vii+177 p., cloth, nonf. anth.

with Joseph Dunlap

22301 *Studies in the late romances of William Morris: papers presented at the annual meeting of the Modern Language Association, December 1975.* New York: William Morris Society, 1976, 139 p., paper, nonf. anth.

SILVERBERG, Karen—SEE: Haber, Karen

SILVERBERG, Robert, 1935-

33869 *The aliens: seven stories of science fiction.* Nashville, TN & New York: Thomas Nelson, 1976, 189 p., cloth, anth.
33870 *Alpha 6.* New York: A Berkley Medallion Book, Berkley Publishing Corp., 1976, x+211 p., paper, anth.
33871 *Alpha 7.* New York: A Berkley Medallion Book, Berkley Publishing Corp., 1977, x+240 p., paper, anth.
33872 *Alpha 8.* New York: A Berkley Medallion Book, Berkley Publishing Corp., 1977, x+242 p., paper, anth.
33873 *Alpha 9.* New York: A Berkley Book, Berkley Publishing Corp., 1978, ix+180 p., paper, anth.
33874 *The androids are coming: seven stories of science fiction.* New York: Elsevier/Nelson Books, 1979, 183 p., cloth, anth.
33875 *At winter's end.* New York: Warner Books, 1988, 404 p., cloth, novel. NEW SPRINGTIME #1.
33875A retitled: *Winter's end.* London: Legend, 1990, 491 p., paper, novel. NEW SPRINGTIME #1.
33876 *The best of New Dimensions.* New York: Pocket Books, 1979, xiv+333 p., paper, anth.
33877 *The best of Robert Silverberg.* New York: Pocket Books, 1976, xiv+258 p., paper, coll.
33877A retitled: *The best of Robert Silverberg, volume one.* Boston: Gregg Press, 1978, 258 p., cloth, coll.
The best of Robert Silverberg, volume one—SEE: *The best of Robert Silverberg.*
33878 *The best of Robert Silverberg, volume two.* Boston: Gregg Press, 1978, xxi+323 p., cloth, coll.
33879 *Beyond the gate of worlds.* New York: Tor SF, A Tom Doherty Associates Book, 1991, 280 p., paper, anth.

33880 *Beyond the safe zone: collected stories of Robert Silverberg.* New York: Donald I. Fine, 1986, 472 p., cloth, coll.
33881 *The book of skulls; Nightwings; Dying inside.* New York: Book-of-the-Month Club, 1991, 222+190+245 p., paper, coll.
33882 *Born with the dead.* New York: Tor SF, A Tom Doherty Associates Book, 1988, 96 p., paper, story. [Not the same as the collection of the same title; bound with *The saliva tree* / by Brian W. Aldiss].
33883 *Capricorn games.* New York: Random House, 1976, 180 p., cloth, coll.
33884 *The conglomeroid cocktail party.* New York: Arbor House, 1984, 284 p., cloth, coll.
33885 *Conquerors from the darkness; and, Master of life and death.* New York: Ace Books, 1979, xiv+386 p., paper, coll. [Includes two books previously published as separate volumes].
33886 *The crystal ship: three original novellas of science fiction.* Nashville, TN, New York: Thomas Nelson, 1976, 208 p., cloth, anth.
33887 *Dangerous interfaces.* New York: Baen Books, 1990, 296 p., paper, anth. TIME GATE #2.
33888 *The desert of stolen dreams.* San Francisco, Columbia, PA: Underwood-Miller, 1981, 96 p., cloth, story. MAJIPOOR #1-A.
33889 *Drug themes in science fiction.* Rockville, MD: National Institute on Drug Abuse, 1974, vii+55 p., paper, nonf.
33890 *Earth is the strangest planet: ten stories of science fiction.* Nashville, TN, New York: Thomas Nelson, 1977, 189 p., cloth, anth.
33891 *The edge of space: three original novellas of science fiction.* New York: Elsevier/Nelson Books, 1979, 224 p., cloth, anth.
33892 *Explorers of space: eight stories of science fiction.* Nashville, TN, New York: Thomas Nelson, 1975, 253 p., cloth, anth.
33893 *The face of the waters.* London: Grafton, 1991, 348 p., cloth, novel.
33894 *The feast of St. Dionysus: five science fiction stories.* New York: Charles Scribner's Sons, 1975, 255 p., cloth, coll.
33895 *Galactic dreamers: science fiction as visionary literature.* New York: Random House, 1977, xii+275 p., cloth, anth.
33896 *Gilgamesh the king.* New York: Arbor House, 1984, 320 p., cloth, novel.
33897 *Hawksbill Station.* New York: Tor SF, A Tom Doherty Associates Book, 1990, 86

p., paper, story. [The original version of the novel of the same title; bound with *Press enter ■ /* by John Varley].

33898 *Homefaring.* Huntington Woods, MI: Phantasia Press, 1983, 102 p., cloth, novel. [Limited to 450 copies].

33899 *In another country.* New York: Tor SF, A Tom Doherty Associates Book, 1990, p. 79-200, paper, novel. [Bound with *Vintage season /* by C. L. Moore].

33900 *The infinite web: eight stories of science fiction.* New York: Dial Locus, 1977, xiii+239 p., cloth, anth.

33901 *Invaders from Earth; and, To worlds beyond.* New York: Ace Books, 1980, 408 p., paper, coll. [Includes two books previously published as separate volumes].

33902 *Letters from Atlantis.* New York: Dragonflight Books, A Byron Preiss Book, Atheneum; Toronto: Collier Macmillan Canada; New York: Maxwell Macmillan International Publishing Group, 1990, 136 p., cloth, novel.

33903 *Lion time in Timbuctoo.* Eugene, OR: Axolotl Press, Pulphouse Publishing, 1990, 112 p., cloth, novel. AXOLOTL PRESS #13.

33904 *Lord Valentine's castle.* New York: Harper & Row, 1980, vii+444 p., cloth, novel. MAJIPOOR #1. [Winner of the *Locus* Award for Best Fantasy Novel, 1980 (1981)].

33905 *Lost worlds, unknown horizons: nine stories of science fiction.* Nashville, TN, New York: Thomas Nelson, 1978, 172 p., cloth, anth.

33906 *Majipoor chronicles: a novel.* New York: Arbor House, 1982, 314 p., cloth, novel. MAJIPOOR #2.

33907 *The masks of time; Born with the dead; Dying inside.* Toronto, New York: Bantam Books, 1988, 561 p., paper, coll.

33908 *The Nebula awards #18.* New York: Arbor House, 1983, 302 p., cloth, anth.

33909 *Needle in a timestack.* London: Sphere, 1979, 149 p., paper, coll. [Contents are different from the previous collection of this title (see #13116)].

33910 *The new Atlantis, and other novellas of science fiction.* New York: Hawthorn Books, 1975, 180 p., cloth, anth.

33911 *New dimensions science fiction, number 5.* New York: Harper & Row, 1975, 234 p., cloth, anth.

33912 *New dimensions science fiction, number 6.* New York: Harper & Row, 1976, 247 p., cloth, anth.

33913 *New dimensions science fiction, number 7.* New York: Harper & Row, 1977, vi+229 p., cloth, anth.

33914 *New dimensions science fiction, number 8.* New York: Harper & Row, 1978, 215 p., cloth, anth.

33915 *New dimensions science fiction, number 9.* New York: Harper & Row, 1979, vi+212 p., cloth, anth.

33916 *New dimensions science fiction, number 10.* New York: Harper & Row, 1980, 188 p., cloth, anth.
The new springtime—SEE: *The queen of springtime.*

33917 *Nightwings.* New York: Tor SF, A Tom Doherty Associates Book, 1989, 81 p., paper, story. [The original version of the novel of the same title; bound with *The last castle /* by Jack Vance].

33918 *Project Pendulum.* New York: Millennium, A Byron Preiss Book, Walker & Co., 1987, 200 p., cloth, novel.

33919 *The queen of springtime.* London: Victor Gollancz, 1989, 415 p., cloth, novel. NEW SPRINGTIME #2.

33919A retitled: *The new springtime.* New York: Warner Books, 1990, 358 p., cloth, novel. NEW SPRINGTIME #2.

33920 *A Robert Silverberg omnibus: The man in the maze; Nightwings; Downward to the Earth.* New York: Harper & Row, 1981, x+544 p., cloth, coll.

33921 *Robert Silverberg's Worlds of wonder.* New York: Warner Books, 1987, xiv+352 p., cloth, anth.

33922 *Sailing to Byzantium.* San Francisco, Columbia, PA: Underwood-Miller, 1985, 114 p., cloth, novel.

33923 *Science fiction special (30): Invaders from Earth ; The best of Robert Silverberg.* London: Sidgwick & Jackson, 1978, 142, xiv+258 p., cloth, coll.

33924 *The secret sharer.* Los Angeles, Columbia, PA: Underwood-Miller, 1988, 107 p., cloth, novel.

33925 *Shadrach in the furnace.* Indianapolis, IN, New York: Bobbs-Merrill Co., 1976, 245 p., cloth, novel.

33926 *The shores of tomorrow: eight stories of science fiction.* Nashville, TN & New York: Thomas Nelson, 1976, 191 p., cloth, coll.

33927 *The silent invaders.* New York: Tor SF, A Tom Doherty Associates Book, 1985, 216 p., paper, coll. [Adds the story, "Valley Beyond Time" to the novel (see #13138)].

33928 *The songs of summer, and other stories.* London: Victor Gollancz, 1979, 173 p., cloth, coll.

33929 *Star of Gypsies.* New York: Donald I. Fine, 1986, 397 p., cloth, novel.

33930 *The stochastic man.* New York: Harper & Row, 1975, 229 p., cloth, novel.

33931 *Strange gifts: eight stories of science fiction.* Nashville, TN: Thomas Nelson, 1975, 206 p., cloth, anth.

33932 *Sunrise on Mercury, and other science fiction stories.* Nashville, TN & New York: Thomas Nelson, 1975, 175 p., cloth, coll.

33933 *Thebes of the hundred gates.* Eugene, OR: Axolotl Press, Pulphouse Publishing, 1991, 110 p., cloth, story. AXOLOTL PRESS #22.

33934 *Three novels: Thorns; Downward to the Earth; The world inside.* Toronto, New York: Spectra, Bantam Books, 1988, viii+487 p., paper, coll.

33935 *To the land of the living.* London: Victor Gollancz, 1989, 301 p., cloth, novel. GILGAMESH #2.

33936 *Tom O'Bedlam.* New York: Donald I. Fine, 1985, 320 p., cloth, novel.

33937 *Triax: three original novellas.* Los Angeles: Pinnacle Books, 1977, 214 p., paper, anth.

33938 *Trips in time: nine stories of science fiction.* Nashville, TN, New York: Thomas Nelson, 1977, 174 p., cloth, anth.

33939 *Valentine Pontifex.* New York: Arbor House, 1983, 347 p., cloth, novel. MAJIPOOR #3.

Winter's end—SEE: *At winter's end.*

33940 *World of a thousand colors.* New York: Arbor House, 1982, 329 p., cloth, coll.

Worlds of wonder—SEE: *Robert Silverberg's Worlds of wonder.*

with Isaac Asimov

17050 *Child of time.* London: Victor Gollancz, 1991, 302 p., cloth, novel.

17051 *Nightfall.* London: Victor Gollancz, 1990, 352 p., cloth, novel.

with Roger Elwood

22637 *Epoch.* New York: Berkley Publishing Corp., 1975, viii+623 p., cloth, anth. [Winner of the *Locus* Award for Best Anthology, 1975 (1976)].

with Bill Fawcett

22993 *Time gate.* New York: Baen Books, 1989, 277 p., paper, anth. TIME GATE #1.

with Martin H. Greenberg

24581 *The Arbor House treasury of great science fiction short novels.* New York: Arbor House, 1980, x+768 p., paper, anth.

24581A retitled: *Worlds imagined: 14 short science fiction novels.* New York: Avenel Books, 1989, x+704 p., cloth, anth.

24582 *The Arbor House treasury of modern science fiction.* New York: Priam Books, Arbor House, 1980, xii+754 p., paper, anth.

24582A retitled: *Great science fiction of the 20th century.* New York: Avenel Books, 1987, x+726 p., cloth, anth.

24583 *The Arbor House treasury of science fiction masterpieces.* New York: Arbor House, 1983, 538 p., cloth, anth.

24583A retitled: *Great tales of science fiction.* Secaucus, NJ: Galahad Books, Castle Books, 1985, 529 p., cloth, anth. [Abridged edition].

24586 *The fantasy hall of fame.* New York: Arbor House, 1983, 431 p., cloth, anth.

24586A retitled: *The mammoth book of fantasy all-time greats.* London: Robinson, 1988, 431 p., paper, anth.

Great science fiction of the 20th century—SEE: *The Arbor House treasury of modern science fiction.*

Great tales of science fiction—SEE: *The Arbor House treasury of science fiction masterpieces.*

The mammoth book of fantasy all-time greats—SEE: *The fantasy hall of fame.*

24587 *The time travelers: a science fiction quartet.* New York: Donald I. Fine, 1985, 284 p., cloth, anth.

Worlds imagined—SEE: *The Arbor House treasury of great science fiction short novels.*

with Martin H. Greenberg & Joseph D. Olander

24584 *Car sinister.* New York: Avon, 1979, 253 p., paper, anth.

24585 *Dawn of time: prehistory through science fiction.* New York: Elsevier/Nelson, 1979, 224 p., cloth, anth.

with Martin H. Greenberg & Charles G. Waugh

24588 *Neanderthals.* New York: A Signet Book, New American Library, 1987, 351 p., paper, anth. ISAAC ASIMOV'S WONDERFUL WORLDS OF SCIENCE FICTION #6.

24589 *The science fictional dinosaur.* New York: An Avon Flare Book, 1982, 224 p., paper, anth.

with Karen Haber

24877 *The mutant season.* New York: A Foundation Book, Doubleday, 1989, xi+ 289 p., cloth, novel. MUTANT #1.

24878 *Universe 1.* New York: A Foundation Book, Doubleday, 1990, xiii+449 p., cloth, anth.

with Marta Randall

32031 *New dimensions 11.* New York: Pocket Books, 1980, 224 p., paper, anth.

32032 *New dimensions 12.* New York: A Timescape Book, Pocket Books, 1981, 223 p., paper, anth.

SILVERMAN, Kenneth (Eugene), 1936-

33941 *Edgar Allan Poe: mournful and never-ending remembrance.* New York: Harper-CollinsPublishers, 1991, ix+564 p., cloth, nonf.

SILVERSTEIN, Herma, 1937-

33942 *Mad, mad Monday.* New York: Lodestar Books, 1988, 120 p., cloth, novel.

SILVERTHORN, Richard Jay

33943 *Satan's spawn.* New York: Avon Books, 1988, 247 p., paper, novel.

SILVETTE, Herbert—SEE: Dogbolt, Barnaby

SIMAK, Clifford D(onald), 1904-1988

33944 *The autumn land, and other stories.* London: Mandarin, 1990, 172 p., paper, coll. [Edited by Francis Lyall].

33945 *The best of Clifford D. Simak.* London: Sidgwick & Jackson, 1975, 253 p., cloth, coll. [Edited by Angus Wells].

33946 *Brother, and other stories.* London: Severn House, 1986, 165 p., cloth, coll. [Edited by Francis Lyall].
Catface—SEE: Mastodonia.

33947 *City.* New York: Ace Books, 1981, 267 p., paper, coll. [Expanded from #13175 to include the final story in the series].

33948 *Enchanted pilgrimage.* New York: Berkley Publishing Corp., 1975, 218 p., cloth, novel.

33949 *The fellowship of the talisman.* New York: A Del Rey Book, Ballantine Books, 1978, 346 p., cloth, novel.

33950 *A heritage of stars.* New York: Berkley Publishing Corp., 1977, 219 p., cloth, novel.

33951 *Highway of eternity.* New York: A Del Rey Book, Ballantine Books, 1986, 289 p., cloth, novel.

33951A retitled: *Highway to eternity.* London: Severn House, 1987, 289 p., cloth, novel.
Highway to eternity—SEE: Highway of eternity.

33952 *The immigrant, and other stories.* London: Mandarin, 1991, 189 p., paper, coll. [Edited by Francis Lyall].

33953 *The marathon photograph, and other stories.* London: Severn House, 1986, 171 p., cloth, coll.

33954 *Mastodonia.* New York: A Del Rey Book, Ballantine Books, 1978, 251 p., cloth, novel.

33954A retitled: *Catface: science fiction.* London: Sidgwick & Jackson, 1978, 252 p., cloth, novel.

33955 *Off-planet.* London: Methuen, 1988, 223 p., cloth, coll. [Edited by Francis Lyall].

33956 *Project Pope.* New York: A Del Rey Book, Ballantine Books, 1981, 313 p., cloth, novel.

33957 *Shakespeare's planet.* New York: Berkley Publishing Corp., 1976, 188 p., cloth, novel.

33958 *Skirmish: the great short fiction of Clifford D. Simak.* New York: G. P. Putnam's Sons, 1977, 320 p., cloth, coll.

33959 *Special deliverance.* New York: A Del Rey Book, Ballantine Books, 1982, 217 p., cloth, novel.

33960 *The visitors.* New York: A Del Rey Book, Ballantine Books, 1980, 282 p., cloth, novel.

33961 *Where the evil dwells.* New York: A Del Rey Book, Ballantine Books, 1982, 249 p., cloth, novel.

SIME, S(idney) H(erbert), 1867-1941

33962 *Beasts that might have been.* London: Ferret Fantasy, 1974, [23] p., paper, art.

SIMMONS, Dan, 1948-

33963 *Banished dreams.* Arvada, CO: Roadkill Press, 1990, 27 p., paper, story. [Limited to 300 copies].

33964 *Carrion comfort: a new novel.* Arlington Heights, IL: Dark Harvest, 1989, 636 p., cloth, novel. [Winner of the *Locus* Award for Best Horror Novel, 1989 (1990); winner of the Bram Stoker Award for Best Horror Novel, 1989 (1990)].

33966 *Entropy's bed at midnight.* Northridge, CA: Lord John Press, 1990, 35 p., cloth, story. [Limited to 300 copies].

33967 *The fall of Hyperion.* New York: A Foundation Book, Doubleday, 1990, 517 p., cloth, novel. HYPERION #2. [Winner of the *Locus* Award for Best Science Fiction Novel, 1990 (1991); winner of the *Science Fiction Chronicle* Award for Best Novel, 1990 (1991)].

33968 *Going after the rubber chicken.* Arvada, CO: Roadkill Press, 1991, 72 p., paper, nonf. coll.

33969 *Hyperion.* New York: A Foundation Book, Doubleday, 1989, 481 p., cloth, novel. HYPERION #1. [Winner of the Hugo Award for Best Novel, 1989 (1990); winner of the *Locus* Award for Best Science Fiction Novel, 1989 (1990)].

33970 *Hyperion cantos.* New York: Guild America Books, 1990, 929 p., cloth, coll. HYPERION #1-2.

33971 *Phases of gravity.* New York, Toronto: Spectra, Bantam Books, 1989, 278 p., paper, novel.

33972 *Prayers to broken stones: a collection.* Arlington Heights, IL: Dark Harvest, 1991, viii+322 p., cloth, coll. [Winner of the Bram Stoker Award for Best Horror Collection, 1991 (1992)].

33973 *The Song of Kali.* New York: Bluejay Books, 1985, 311 p., cloth, novel. [Winner of the World Fantasy Award for Best Fantasy Novel, 1985 (1986)].

33974 *Summer of night.* New York: G. P. Putnam's Sons, 1991, 555 p., cloth, novel. [Winner of the *Locus* Award for Best Horror/Dark Fantasy Novel, 1991 (1992)].

SIMMONS, Geoffrey (S.), 1943?-

33975 *The Adam experiment: a novel.* New York: Arbor House, 1978, viii+199 p., cloth, novel.

33976 *Pandemic: a novel.* New York: Arbor House, 1980, 218 p., cloth, novel.

SIMMONS, John

33977 *The sharing.* New York: Fawcett Gold Medal, 1983, 310 p., paper, novel.

SIMMONS, Ted (Conrad), 1916-

33978 *Middlearth: a modern pilgrimage by foot and greyhound to Middle-Earth (after J. R. R. Tolkien), with Nikon and notepad.* San Rafael, CA: Fur Line Press, 1976, 70 p., paper, novel.

SIMMONS, Wm. Mark [i.e., William Mark Simmons]

33979 *In the net of dreams.* New York: Popular Library, 1990, 308 p., paper, novel.

SIMON, Heather

33980 *The fox and the hound.* New York: An Archway Paperback, 1981, 167 p., paper, movie.

SIMON, Jean

33981 *Darksong.* New York: Zebra Books, Kensington Publishing Corp., 1990, 347 p., paper, novel.

33982 *Descendants.* New York: Pageant Books, 1989, 368 p., paper, novel.

33983 *Sweet revenge.* New York: Zebra Books, Kensington Publishing Corp., 1991, 319 p., paper, novel.

33984 *Wild card.* New York: Zebra Books, Kensington Publishing Corp., 1991, 288 p., paper, novel.

SIMON, Jo Ann [pseud. of Joanna Haessig Campbell Bruce], 1946-

33985 *Beloved captain.* New York: Avon, 1988, 314 p., paper, novel.

SIMON, Leonard (J.), 1937-

33986 *Reborn.* New York: Arbor House, 1979, 274 p., cloth, novel.

SIMON, Madeleine [pseud. of Morris Simon?]

33987 *Isle of illusion.* Lake Geneva, WI: TSR Inc., 1983, 157 p., paper, novel. HEARTQUEST #4.

33988 *Talisman of Valdegarde.* Lake Geneva, WI: TSR Inc., 1983, 157 p., paper, novel. HEARTQUEST #2.

SIMON, Morris

33989 *Blade of the young samurai.* Lake Geneva, WI: TSR Inc., 1984, 157 p., paper, novel. ENDLESS QUEST #23.

33990 *Captive planet.* Lake Geneva, WI: TSR Inc., 1984, 157 p., paper, novel. ENDLESS QUEST #17.

33991 *Castle in the clouds.* Lake Geneva, WI: TSR Inc., 1984, 77 p., paper, novel. FANTASY FOREST BOOK #7.

33992 *Clash of the sorcerers.* Lake Geneva, WI: TSR Inc., 1986, 189 p., paper, novel.

KINGDOM OF SORCERY #3; ADVANCED DUNGEONS & DRAGONS GAMEBOOK #11.

33993 *The fireseed*. Lake Geneva, WI: TSR Inc., 1985, 157 p., paper, novel. ENDLESS QUEST #30.

33994 *Jaguar!* Lake Geneva, WI: TSR Inc., 1985, 222 p., paper, novel. AMAZING STORIES #2.

33995 *Mystery of the ancients*. Lake Geneva, WI: TSR Inc., 1985, 157 p., paper, novel. ENDLESS QUEST #28.

33996 *Prisoners of Pax Tharkas*. Lake Geneva, WI: TSR Inc., 1985, 189 p., paper, novel. SUPER ENDLESS QUEST ADVENTURE GAMEBOOK #1.

33997 *Sceptre of power*. Lake Geneva, WI: TSR Inc., 1986, 190 p., paper, novel. KINGDOM OF SORCERY #1; ADVANCED DUNGEONS & DRAGONS GAMEBOOK #7.

33998 *The sorcerer's crown*. Lake Geneva, WI: TSR Inc., 1986, 190 p., paper, novel. KINGDOM OF SORCERY #2; ADVANCED DUNGEONS & DRAGONS GAMEBOOK #9.

SIMON, Seymour, 1931-

33999 *Creatures from lost worlds*. Philadelphia, PA, New York: J. B. Lippincott Co., 1979, 80 p., cloth, nonf.

34000 *Mad scientists, weird doctors, and time travelers in movies, TV, and books*. Philadelphia, PA, New York: J. B. Lippincott Co., 1981, 57 p., cloth, nonf.

34001 *Space monsters from movies, TV, and books*. Philadelphia, PA, New York: J. B. Lippincott Co., 1977, 80 p., cloth, nonf.

SIMONS, Les, pseud.—SEE: Ptacek, Kathryn

SIMPSON, Carla

34002 *Always, my love*. New York: Zebra Books, Kensington Publishing Corp., 1990, 512 p., paper, novel.

with Pamela Wallace as PAMELA SIMPSON

34003 *Partners in time*. New York, Toronto: Bantam Books, 1990, 297 p., paper, novel.

SIMPSON, George E(dward), 1944- , *with Neal R. Burger*

19031 *Ghostboat*. New York: A Dell Book, 1976, 412 p., paper, novel.

19032 *Thin air*. New York: A Dell Book, 1978, 318 p., paper, novel.

SIMPSON, Leo (James Pascal), 1934-

34004 *The peacock papers*. Toronto: Macmillan of Canada, 1973, 226 p., cloth, novel.

SIMPSON, Mark S(herman)

34005 *The Russian gothic novel and its British antecedents*. Columbus, OH: Slavica Publishers, 1986, 110 p., paper, nonf.

SIMPSON, Pamela, pseud.—SEE: Wallace, Pamela & Simpson, Carla

SIMPSON, Patricia

34006 *Whisper of midnight*. New York: Harper-Paperbacks, 1991, 297 p., paper, novel.

SIMS, D(enise) N(atalie), 1940-

34007 *The pastime of eternity*. London: Robert Hale, 1975, 190 p., cloth, novel.

SIMS, M(ichael) P. N., 1952- , *with L. H. Maynard*

29348 *Shadow at midnight: ten ghost stories*. London: William Kimber, 1979, 188 p., cloth, coll.

SINCLAIR, Andrew (Annandale), 1935-

34008 *Gog: a novel*. London: Weidenfeld & Nicolson, 1967, 486 p., cloth, novel. ALBION TRIPTYCH #1.

34009 *King Ludd*. London: Hodder & Stoughton, 1988, 352 p., cloth, novel. ALBION TRIPTYCH #3.

38065 *Magog: a novel*. London: Weidenfeld & Nicolson, 1972, 328 p., cloth, novel. ALBION TRIPTYCH #2.

SINCLAIR, Clive (John), 1948-

34010 *Blood libels*. London: Allison & Busby, 1985, 190 p., cloth, novel.

SINCLAIR, Iain (MacGregor), 1943-

34011 *Downriver: (or, The vessels of wrath): a narrative in twelve tales*. London: Paladin, 1991, 407 p., cloth, novel.

SINCLAIR, Miranda—SEE: Seymour, Miranda

SINCLAIR, Quinn

34012   *The boy who could draw tomorrow.* New York: A Dell/Emerald Book, 1984, 221 p., paper, novel.

SINGER, A. L.

  Bases loaded II, second season—SEE: *Worlds of power: Bases loaded II, second season: a novel based on the best-selling game by Jaleco.*

  Blaster master—SEE: *Worlds of power: Blaster master.*

  Infiltrator—SEE: *Worlds of power: Infiltrator: a novel based on the best-selling game by MINDSCAPE.*

34013   *Little monsters: a novelization.* New York, Toronto: Point, Scholastic Inc., 1989, 152 p., paper, movie.

  Ninja gaiden—SEE: *Worlds of power: Ninja gaiden.*

34014   *The Rescuers Downunder.* New York, Toronto: Scholastic Inc., 1990, 73 p., paper, movie. RESCUERS SERIES.

34015   *Worlds of power: Bases loaded II, second season: a novel based on the best-selling game by Jaleco.* New York, Toronto: A Seth Godin Production, Scholastic Inc., 1991, 72 p., paper, fiction. WORLDS OF POWER (UNNUMBERED).

34016   *Worlds of power: Blaster master: a novel based on the best-selling game by Sunsoft.* New York, Toronto: A Seth Godin Production, Scholastic Inc., 1990, 119 p., paper, fiction. WORLDS OF POWER #1.

34017   *Worlds of power: Infiltrator: a novel based on the best-selling game by MINDSCAPE.* New York, Toronto: A Seth Godin Production, Scholastic Inc., 1991, 122 p., paper, fiction. WORLDS OF POWER #7.

34018   *Worlds of power: Ninja gaiden: a novel based on the best-selling game by Tecmo.* New York, Toronto: A Seth Godin Production, Scholastic Inc., 1990, 120 p., paper, fiction. WORLDS OF POWER #3.

SINGER, Isaac Bashevis, 1904-1991

34019   *The king of the fields.* New York: Farrar Straus Giroux, 1988, 244 p., cloth, novel. [Translation by the author of *Der kenig fun di felder*].

SINGER, Judith, 1926-

34020   *Threshold.* Toronto, New York: Bantam Books, 1975, 248 p., paper, novel.

SINGER, Kurt (Deutsch), 1911-

34021   *The first Target book of horror.* London: Target, 1984, 143 p., paper, anth. [The stories in this volume and its successors were reassembled from three previous anthologies, including *They are possessed*].

34022   *The fourth Target book of horror.* London: Target, 1985, 142 p., paper, anth.

34023   *The second Target book of horror.* London: Target, 1984, 144 p., paper, anth.

34024   *The Star bumper horror book 1.* London: A Star Book, W. H. Allen & Co., 1986, 144 p., paper, anth. [Reprinted from Target series].

34025   *The Star bumper horror book 2.* London: A Star Book, W. H. Allen & Co., 1986, 142 p., paper, anth. [Reprinted from Target series].

34026   *They are possessed.* London: W. H. Allen & Co., 1976, 246 p., cloth, anth. [Includes some nonfiction].

34027   *The third Target book of horror.* London: Target, 1985, 142 p., paper, anth.

SINGER, Marilyn, 1948-

34028   *Charmed.* New York: Atheneum; Toronto: Collier Macmillan Canada; New York: Maxwell Macmillan International Publishing Group, 1990, 219 p., cloth, novel.

34029   *Ghost hunt.* New York: Harper & Row, 1987, 182 p., cloth, novel.

34030   *Horsemaster.* New York: An Argo Book, Atheneum, 1985, 179 p., cloth, novel.

34031   *Mitzi Meyer, fearless warrior queen.* New York, Toronto: An Apple Paperback, Scholastic Inc., 1987, 140 p., paper, novel.

34032   *Storm rising.* New York, Toronto: Scholastic Inc., 1989, 215 p., cloth, novel.

SINGER, Melissa, *with Victoria Schochet*

33358   *The Berkley showcase, vol. 5: new writings in science fiction and fantasy.* New York: Berkley Books, 1982, 266 p., paper, anth.

SINGER, Rochelle [i.e., Shelley Singer], 1939-

34033   *The Demeter flower.* New York: St. Martin's Press, 1980, 224 p., cloth, novel.

SINGER, Shelley—SEE: Singer, Rochelle

SINGH, Kirpal

with R. S. Bhathal & Dudley de Souza

17923 *Singapore science fiction.* Singapore: Rotary Club of Jurongtown, Singapore Science Centre, 1980, ix+116 p., cloth, anth.

with Michael J. Tolley

34034 *The stellar gauge: essays of science fiction writers.* Carlton, Victoria, Australia: Norstrilia Press, 1980, 288 p., cloth, nonf. anth.

SINGH, Satyanarain, with Adapa Ramakrishna Rao & Taqi Ali Mirza

29969 *William Golding: an Indian response: a collection of critical essays on the fiction of William Golding.* New Delhi, India: Arnold-Heinemann, 1987, viii+147 p., cloth, nonf. anth.

SINOR, John, 1930-

34035 *Finsterhall of San Pasqual.* San Diego, CA: Joyce Press, 1976, 80 p., paper, novel.

34036 *Ghosts of Cabrillo Lighthouse.* San Diego, CA: Joyce Press, 1977, 79 p., paper, novel.

SIROTA, Michael B.—SEE: Sirota, Mike

SIROTA, Mike [i.e., Michael Barry Sirota], 1946-

34037 *Berbora.* New York: Manor Books, 1978, 282 p., paper, novel. BERBORA #1.

34038 *Bicycling through space and time.* New York: Ace Books, 1991, 202 p., paper, novel.

34039 *The caves of Reglathium.* New York: Manor Books, 1978, 272 p., paper, novel. DANNUS #3.

34040 *The conquerors of Reglathium.* New York: Manor Books, 1978, 237 p., paper, novel. DANNUS #2.

34041 *Dark straits of Reglathium .* New York: Manor Books, 1978, 236 p., paper, novel. DANNUS #4.

34042 *Demon shadows* / by Michael B. Sirota. New York, Toronto: Bantam Books, 1990, 233 p., paper, novel.

34043 *The demons of Zammar.* New York: Zebra Books, Kensington Publishing Corp., 1981, 271 p., paper, novel. RO-LAN #4.

34044 *Flight from Berbora.* New York: Manor Books, 1978, 237 p., paper, novel. BERBORA #2.

34045 *The Golden Hawk of Zandraya.* New York: Zebra Books, Kensington Publishing Corp., 1981, 288 p., paper, novel.

34046 *Journey to Mesharra.* New York: Zebra Books, Kensington Publishing Corp., 1980, 299 p., paper, novel. RO-LAN #3.

34047 *Master of Boranga.* New York: Zebra Books, Kensington Publishing Corp., 1980, 317 p., paper, novel. RO-LAN #1.

34048 *The prisoner of Reglathium.* New York: Manor Books, 1978, 240 p., paper, novel. DANNUS #1.

34049 *The shrouded walls of Boranga.* New York: Zebra Books, Kensington Publishing Corp., 1980, 288 p., paper, novel. RO-LAN #2.

34050 *Slaves of Reglathium.* New York: Manor Books, 1978, 255 p., paper, novel. DANNUS #5.

34051 *The twentieth son of Ornon.* New York: Zebra Books, Kensington Publishing Corp., 1980, 251 p., paper, novel.

34052 *The well* / by Michael B. Sirota. New York: Bantam Books, 1991, 242 p., paper, novel.

SITWELL, (Francis) Osbert (Sacheverell), Sir, Bart., 1892-1969

34053 *Triple fugue.* London: Grant Richards, 1924, 327 p., cloth, coll.

SKAF, Robert

34054 *The story of the planet Candy.* New York, Washington: Vantage Press, 1990, 201 p., cloth, novel.

SKAL, David J.

34055 *Antibodies.* Boston: Congdon & Weed, 1988, vi+169 p., cloth, novel.

34056 *Hollywood gothic: the tangled web of Dracula from novel to stage to screen.* New York: W. W. Norton & Co., 1990, 242 p., cloth, nonf.

34057 *Scavengers.* New York: Pocket Books, 1980, 204 p., paper, novel.

34058 *When we were good.* New York: Pocket Books, 1981, 188 p., paper, novel.

SKALDASPILLIR, Sigfriour, pseud.—SEE: Broxon, Mildred Downey

SKARDA, Patricia L(yn), 1946- , with Nora Crow Jaffe

26412 *The evil image: two centuries of gothic short fiction and poetry.* New York: A Meridian Book, New American Library, 1981, xxix+479 p., paper, anth. [Includes some verse].

SKEELS, Vernon—SEE: Rossiter, Oscar

SKEETERS, Paul W., 1905-1983

34059 *Sidney H. Sime, master of fantasy.* Pasadena, CA: Ward Ritchie Press, 1978, 127 p., paper, art.

SKELTON, Robin, 1925-

34060 *Fires of the kindred.* Victoria, British Columbia, Canada: A Tesseract Book, Porcépic Books, 1987, 158 p., paper, novel.

SKERL, Jennie

34061 *William S. Burroughs.* Boston: Twayne Publishers, 1985, 127 p., cloth, nonf.

with Robin Lydenberg

28731 *William S. Burroughs at the front: critical reception, 1959-1989.* Carbondale & Edwardsville, IL: Southern Illinois University Press, 1991, 274 p., cloth, nonf. anth.

SKIDMORE, Ian, 1929-

34062 *Island fling.* London: W. H. Allen & Co., 1982, 172 p., cloth, novel.

SKIMIN, Robert (Elwayne), 1929-1990

34063 *Gray victory.* New York: St. Martin's Press, 1988, xii+378 p., cloth, novel.

*SKINKLE, Dorothy E., <u>1906?-1983?</u>

SKINNER, Ainslie [pseud. of Paula Gosling], 1939-

34064 *Mind's eye: a novel.* London: Secker & Warburg, 1980, 276 p., cloth, novel.
34064A retitled: *The harrowing.* New York: Rawson, Wade Publishers, 1981, 335 p., cloth, novel.

SKINNER, Michael, 1953-

34065 *First air: a novel of air combat in the Persian Gulf.* Novato, CA: Presidio Press, 1991, 403 p., cloth, novel.

SKIPP, John (M.), 1957- , with Craig Spector

34066 *The book of the dead.* Willimantic, CT: Mark V. Ziesing, 1989, xiv+334 p., cloth, anth.
34067 *The bridge: a horror story.* New York, Toronto: Spectra, Bantam Books, 1991, 419 p., paper, novel.
34068 *The cleanup.* Toronto, New York: Bantam Books, 1987, 379 p., paper, novel.
34069 *Dead lines: a novel of horror.* Toronto, New York: Bantam Books, 1989, 309 p., paper, novel.
34070 *Fright night.* New York: Tor, A Tom Doherty Associates Book, 1985, 250 p., paper, movie.
34071 *The light at the end.* Toronto, New York: Bantam Books, 1986, 385 p., paper, novel.
34072 *The scream.* Toronto, New York: Spectra, Bantam Books, 1988, 420 p., paper, novel.

SKLAR, Richard (Lawrence), 1930- , as VICTOR APPLETON II

00444 *Tom Swift and his giant robot.* New York: Grosset & Dunlap, 1954, 211 p., cloth, novel. TOM SWIFT JR. #A4.

SKOLSKY, Syd (Cohen), 1917-

34073 *The affectionism society: a novel.* South Miami, FL: Earth Publishing Enterprises, 1977, 442 p., paper, novel.

SKOTAK, Robert, with Scott Holton

Fantastic worlds—SEE: *Norman Jacobs & Kerry O'Quinn present Fantastic worlds.*
25883 *Norman Jacobs & Kerry O'Quinn present Fantastic worlds.* New York: Starlog Press, 1978, 97 p., paper, nonf. anth.

SKY, Kathleen (McKinney Goldin), 1943-

34074 *Birthright.* Toronto, New York: Laser Books, 1975, 190 p., paper, novel.
34075 *Death's angel: a Star Trek novel.* Toronto, New York: Bantam Books, 1981, 213 p., paper, novel. STAR TREK SERIES.
34076 *Ice prison.* Toronto, New York: Laser Books, 1976, 190 p., paper, novel.
34077 *Vulcan!* Toronto, New York: Bantam Books, 1978, xiv+175 p., paper, novel. STAR TREK SERIES.

34078 *Witchdame*. New York: Berkley Books, 1985, 323 p., paper, novel.

SLADE, Derek

34079 *Invasion*. London: Oriflamme Publishing, 1990, 497 p., paper, novel.

SLADE, Joseph W(arren), 1941-

34080 *Thomas Pynchon*. New York: Warner Paperback Library, 1974, 256 p., paper, nonf.

SLADE, Michael, pseud.—SEE: Clarke, Jay & Banks, John & Clarke, Lee & Covell, Richard

SLADEK, John (Thomas), 1937-

34081 *Alien accounts*. London: Panther, 1982, 202 p., paper, coll.

38066 *The best of John Sladek*. New York: Pocket Books, 1981, 220 p., paper, coll.

34082 *Blood and gingerbread*. New Castle, VA: Cheap Street, 1990, 68 p., cloth, story. [Limited to 111 copies].

34083 *Bugs*. London: Macmillan, 1989, 213 p., cloth, novel.

34084 *Flatland*. New Castle, VA: Cheap Street, 1982, 21 p., paper, story.

34085 *Keep the giraffe burning*. London, Toronto: Panther, Granada Publishing, 1977 (i.e., 1978), 205 p., paper, coll.

34086 *Love among the Xoids*. Polk City, IA: Chris Drumm, 1984, 15 p., paper, fiction. DRUMM BOOKLET #15.

34087 *The lunatics of Terra*. London: Victor Gollancz, 1984, 192 p., cloth, coll.

34088 *Red noise*. New Castle, VA: Cheap Street, 1982, 28 p., paper, story.

34089 *Roderick at random; or, Further education of a young machine*. London: Granada, 1983, 317 p., paper, novel. RODERICK #2.

34090 *Roderick; or, The education of a young machine*. London: Granada Publishers, 1980, 347 p., cloth, novel. RODERICK #1.

34091 *Tik-Tok*. London: Victor Gollancz, 1983, 184 p., cloth, novel.

SLATEN, Jeff, *with Albert C. Ellis*

22574 *Death jag*. New York: Manor Books, 1979, 235 p., paper, novel.

SLATER, Ian, 1941-

34092 *Orwell: the road to Airstrip One*. New York: W. W. Norton & Co., 1985, 302 p., cloth, nonf.

34093 *Rage of battle*. New York: Fawcett Crest, 1991, 342 p., paper, novel.

World in flames—SEE: *WW III: World in flames*.

34094 *WW III*. New York: Fawcett Gold Medal, 1990, 441 p., paper, novel. WW III #1.

34095 *WW III: World in flames*. New York: Fawcett Gold Medal, 1991, 434 p., paper, novel. WW III #2.

SLATER, Jim, 1929-

34096 *The boy who saved Earth*. Garden City, NY: Doubleday & Co., 1979, 121 p., cloth, novel.

SLATER, Ken(neth Frederick), 1917-

34097 *British science fiction book index 1955*. Wisbech, Cambridgeshire, England: Fantast (Medway) Ltd., 1956, 14 p., paper, nonf.

34098 *A checklist of science fiction, fantasy, and supernatural stories available in paperback in Britain, January 1966*. Wisbech, Cambridgeshire, England: Fantast (Medway) Ltd., 1966, 30 p., paper, nonf.

SLAUGHTER, Frank G(ill), 1908-

34099 *Devil's gamble: a novel of demonology*. Garden City, NY: Doubleday & Co., 1977, 304 p., cloth, novel.

SLAUGHTER, Pamela

34100 *Ravished*. Toronto, New York: Bantam Books, 1983, 200 p., paper, novel.

SLAVICSEK, Bill

with Curtis Smith

34101 *The Star Wars sourcebook*. Honesdale, PA: West End Games, 1987, 142 p., paper, nonf.

with C. J. Tramontana

34102 *Storm knights*. Honesdale, PA: West End Books, 1990, 317 p., paper, novel. TORG: THE PROBABILITY WARS #1. [Based on the *Probability Wars* game].

SLAVITT, David R.—SEE: Sutton, Henry

SLEATOR, William (Warner III), 1945-

34103 *Among the dolls.* New York: E. P. Dutton, 1975, 70 p., cloth, novel.

34104 *The boy who reversed himself.* New York: E. P. Dutton, 1986, 167 p., cloth, novel.

34105 *The duplicate.* New York: E. P. Dutton, 1988, 154 p., cloth, novel.

34106 *Fingers.* New York: Atheneum, 1983, 197 p., cloth, novel.

34107 *The green futures of Tycho.* New York: E. P. Dutton & Co., 1981, 133 p., cloth, novel.

34108 *Interstellar pig.* New York: E. P. Dutton, 1984, 197 p., cloth, novel.

34109 *Into the dream.* New York: E. P. Dutton, 1979, 137 p., cloth, novel.

34110 *Singularity.* New York: E. P. Dutton, 1985, 170 p., cloth, novel.

34111 *The spirit house.* New York: E. P. Dutton Children's Books, 1991, 134 p., cloth, novel.

Strange attractions—SEE: *Strange attractors.*

34112 *Strange attractors.* New York: E. P. Dutton, 1990, 169 p., cloth, novel.

34112A retitled: *Strange attractions.* London: Heinemann, 1991, 186 p., cloth, novel.

SLEIGH, Barbara, 1906-1982

34113 *Broomstocks and beasticles: stories and verse about witches and strange creatures.* London: Hodder & Stoughton, 1981, 153 p., cloth, anth.

34114 *Carbonel and Calidor: being the further adventures of a royal cat.* Harmondsworth, Middlesex, England: Kestrel Books, 1978, 214 p., cloth, novel. CARBONEL #3.

SLOAN, Carolyn, 1937-

34115 *Don't go near the water.* London: Hippo, 1988, 101 p., paper, novel.

34116 *The sea child.* London: The Bodley Head, 1987, 127 p., cloth, novel.

SLOAN, Michael (Fred), 1946- , with Glen A. Larson

34117 *The Hardy Boys and Nancy Drew meet Dracula.* New York: Grosset & Dunlap, 1978, 109 p., paper, tele. HARDY BOYS SERIES; NANCY DREW SERIES.

SLOANE, Ben

Blown dead—SEE: *Horn: Blown dead.*

34118 *Horn: Blown dead.* Toronto, New York: A Gold Eagle Book from Worldwide, 1990, 301 p., paper, novel. HORN #2.

34119 *Horn: Hot zone.* Toronto, New York: A Gold Eagle Book from Worldwide, 1990, 300 p., paper, novel. HORN #1.

34120 *Horn: Outland strip.* Toronto, New York: A Gold Eagle Book from Worldwide, 1991, 299 p., paper, novel. HORN #3.

34121 *Horn: Ultimate weapon.* Toronto, New York: A Gold Eagle Book from Worldwide, 1991, 300 p., paper, novel. HORN #4.

Hot zone—SEE: *Horn: Hot zone.*
Outland strip—SEE: *Horn: Outland strip.*
Ultimate weapon—SEE: *Horn: Ultimate weapon.*

SLOANE, Robert C.

34122 *A nice place to live: a novel.* New York: Crown Publishers, 1981, 278 p., cloth, novel. MARINO FAMILY #1.

34123 *The vengeance: a novel.* New York: Crown Publishers, 1983, 247 p., cloth, novel. MARINO FAMILY #2.

SLONAKER, Larry

34124 *Voice of the visitor.* New York: Avon, 1986, 227 p., paper, novel.

SLONCZEWSKI, Joan (Lyn), 1956-

34125 *A door into Ocean.* New York: Arbor House, 1985, 403 p., cloth, novel. [Winner of the John W. Campbell Jr. Memorial Award for Best Novel, 1986 (1987)].

34126 *Still forms on Foxfield.* New York: A Del Rey Book, Ballantine Books, 1980, 214 p., paper, novel.

34127 *The wall around Eden.* New York: William Morrow & Co., 1989, 288 p., cloth, novel.

SLOTE, Alfred, 1926-

34128 *Clone catcher.* New York: J. B. Lippincott, 1982, 154 p., cloth, novel.

34129 *C.O.L.A.R.: a tale of outer space.* New York: J. B. Lippincott, 1981, 145 p., cloth, novel. DANNY ONE #3.

34130 *The devil rides with me, and other fantastic stories.* New York: Methuen, 1980, 83 p., cloth, coll.

34131 *My robot buddy.* Philadelphia, PA: J. B. Lippincott Co., 1975, 92 p., cloth, novel. DANNY ONE #1.

34132 *My trip to Alpha I.* Philadelphia, PA: J. B. Lippincott Co., 1978, 94 p., cloth, novel. DANNY ONE #2.

34133 *Omega Station.* New York: J. B. Lippincott, 1983, 147 p., cloth, novel. DANNY ONE #4.

34134 *The trouble on Janus.* New York: J. B. Lippincott, 1985, xii+175 p., cloth, novel. DANNY ONE #5.

SLUNG, Michele (Beth), 1947-

34135 *I shudder at your touch.* New York: A Roc Book, 1991, 379 p., cloth, anth.

SLUSSER, George Edgar, 1939-

34136 *The Bradbury chronicles.* San Bernardino, CA: R. Reginald, The Borgo Press, 1977, 63 p., paper, nonf. MILFORD SERIES: POPULAR WRITERS OF TODAY #4.

34137 *The classic years of Robert A. Heinlein.* San Bernardino, CA: R. Reginald, The Borgo Press, 1977, 63 p., paper, nonf. MILFORD SERIES: POPULAR WRITERS OF TODAY #11.

34138 *The Delany intersection: Samuel R. Delany considered as a writer of semi-precious words.* San Bernardino, CA: R. Reginald, The Borgo Press, 1977, 64 p., paper, nonf. MILFORD SERIES: POPULAR WRITERS OF TODAY #10.

34139 *The farthest shores of Ursula K. Le Guin.* San Bernardino, CA: R. Reginald, The Borgo Press, 1976, 60 p., paper, nonf. MILFORD SERIES: POPULAR WRITERS OF TODAY #3.

34140 *Harlan Ellison: unrepentant harlequin.* San Bernardino, CA: R. Reginald, The Borgo Press, 1977, 63 p., paper, nonf. MILFORD SERIES: POPULAR WRITERS OF TODAY #6.

34141 *Robert A. Heinlein: stranger in his own land.* San Bernardino, CA: R. Reginald, The Borgo Press, 1976, 60 p., paper, nonf. MILFORD SERIES: POPULAR WRITERS OF TODAY #1.

34142 *Robert A. Heinlein: stranger in his own land, second edition.* San Bernardino, CA: R. Reginald, The Borgo Press, 1977, 64 p., paper, nonf. MILFORD SERIES: POPULAR WRITERS OF TODAY #1. [Completely rewritten from the original].

34143 *The space odysseys of Arthur C. Clarke.* San Bernardino, CA: R. Reginald, The Borgo Press, 1978, 64 p., paper, nonf. MILFORD SERIES: POPULAR WRITERS OF TODAY #8.

as INTRODUCER

34144 *Dictionary catalog of the J. Lloyd Eaton Collection of Science Fiction and Fantasy Literature.* Boston: G. K. Hall & Co., 1982, 3 v., cloth, nonf. [vol. 1-v+558 p., vol. 2-575 p., vol. 3-568 p.].

with George R. Guffey & Mark Rose

24813 *Bridges to science fiction.* Carbondale & Edwardsville, IL: Southern Illinois University Press; London & Amsterdam: Feffer & Simons, 1980, viii+168 p., cloth, nonf. anth. PROCEEDINGS OF THE J. LLOYD EATON CONFERENCE ON SCIENCE FICTION AND FANTASY LITERATURE #1.

with Eric S. Rabkin

31987 *Aliens: the anthropology of science fiction.* Carbondale & Edwardsville, IL: Southern Illinois University Press, 1987, xx+243 p., cloth, nonf. anth. PROCEEDINGS OF THE J. LLOYD EATON CONFERENCE ON SCIENCE FICTION AND FANTASY LITERATURE #7.

31988 *Hard science fiction.* Carbondale & Edwardsville, IL: Southern Illinois University Press, 1986, xvi+284 p., cloth, nonf. anth. PROCEEDINGS OF THE J. LLOYD EATON CONFERENCE ON SCIENCE FICTION AND FANTASY LITERATURE #5.

31989 *Intersections: fantasy and science fiction.* Carbondale & Edwardsville, IL: Southern Illinois University Press, 1987, x+252 p., cloth, nonf. anth. PROCEEDINGS OF THE J. LLOYD EATON CONFERENCE ON SCIENCE FICTION AND FANTASY LITERATURE #8.

31990 *Mindscapes: the geographies of imagined worlds.* Carbondale & Edwardsville, IL: Southern Illinois University Press, 1989, xiii+302 p., cloth, nonf. anth. PROCEEDINGS OF THE J. LLOYD EATON CONFERENCE ON SCIENCE FICTION AND FANTASY LITERATURE #9.

31991 *Shadows of the magic lamp: fantasy and science fiction in films.* Carbondale & Edwardsville, IL: Southern Illinois University Press, 1985, xx+259 p., cloth, nonf. anth. PROCEEDINGS OF THE J. LLOYD EATON CONFERENCE ON SCIENCE FICTION AND FANTASY LITERATURE #4.

with Eric S. Rabkin & Colin Greenland

24662 *Storm warnings: science fiction confronts the future.* Carbondale & Edwardsville, IL: Southern Illinois University Press,

1987, xi+278 p., cloth, nonf. anth. PROCEEDINGS OF THE J. LLOYD EATON CONFERENCE ON SCIENCE FICTION AND FANTASY LITERATURE #6.

with Eric S. Rabkin & Robert Scholes

31985 *Bridges to fantasy.* Carbondale & Edwardsville, IL: Southern Illinois University Press, 1982, xi+231 p., cloth, nonf. anth. PROCEEDINGS OF THE J. LLOYD EATON CONFERENCE ON SCIENCE FICTION AND FANTASY LITERATURE #2.

31986 *Coordinates: placing science fiction and fantasy* / ed. by George E. Slusser... Carbondale & Edwardsville: Southern Illinois University Press, 1983, xii+209 p., cloth, nonf. anth. PROCEEDINGS OF THE J. LLOYD EATON CONFERENCE ON SCIENCE FICTION AND FANTASY LITERATURE #3.

*SMALL, Austin J. [originally Austin Small Major], <u>1894-1929</u>

SMALL, Beatrice, 1937-

34145 *A moment in time.* New York: Ballantine Books, 1991, 496 p., paper, novel.

SMALL, Christopher, 1919-

34146 *Ariel like a harpy: Shelley, Mary, and Frankenstein.* London: Victor Gollancz, 1972, 352 p., cloth, nonf.
34146A retitled: *Mary Shelly's Frankenstein: tracing the myth.* Pittsburgh, PA: University of Pittsburgh Press, 1973, 352 p., cloth, nonf.
   Mary Shelley's Frankenstein—SEE: *Ariel like a harp: Shelley, Mary, and Frankenstein.*
34147 *The road to Miniluv: George Orwell, the state, and God.* London: Victor Gollancz, 1975, 220 p., cloth, nonf.

SMALL, David, 1945- , *with Randy Small*

34148 *A guidebook for winner adventurers.* New York: A Pournelle Users Guide, Baen Computer Books, 1985, 339 p., paper, nonf.

SMALL, Randy, *with David Small*

34148 *A guidebook for winner adventurers.* New York: A Pournelle Users Guide, Baen Computer Books, 1985, 339 p., paper, nonf.

SMALLDON, Jeffrey (Lewis), 1953-

34149 *Human nature stained: Colin Wilson and the existential study of modern murder.* Nottingham, England: Paupers' Press, 1991, 38 p., paper, nonf.

SMART, Brian

38067 *Best of the Midwest's science fiction, fantasy, and horror.* [U.S.]: ESA Books, 1991, 286 p., paper, anth.

SMEDS, Dave, 1955-

34150 *Hennesy's test.* Belmont, CA: Fearon Educational, 1987, 30 p., paper, story.
34151 *The schemes of dragons.* New York: Ace Books, 1989, 246 p., paper, novel. WAR OF THE DRAGONS #2.
34152 *Sinking ship.* Belmont, CA: Fearon Educational, 1987, 29 p., paper, story.
34153 *The sorcery within.* New York: Ace Fantasy Books, 1985, 295 p., paper, novel. WAR OF THE DRAGONS #1.

SMITH, A(nthony) C(harles) H(ockley), 1935-

34154 *The dark crystal: a novel.* London: Futura, 1982, 176 p., paper, movie.
34155 *Labyrinth: a novel.* London: Virgin Books, 1986, 183 p., paper, movie.

SMITH, A(nthony) C(orby), 1925-

34156 *A glimpse of judgement.* London: Robert Hale, 1978, 175 p., cloth, novel.

SMITH, Albert Brewster, 1930-

34157 *Théophile Gautier and the fantastic.* University, MS: Romance Monographs, 1977, 149 p., cloth, nonf.

SMITH, Allan Lloyd- —SEE: Lloyd-Smith, Allan

SMITH, Andrew

34158 *Doctor Who: Full circle.* London: A Star Book, W. H. Allen, 1982, 123 p., paper, tele. DOCTOR WHO.
   Full circle—SEE: *Doctor Who: Full circle.*

SMITH, Basil A(lec), 1908-1969

34159 *The scallion stone.* Chapel Hill, NC: Whispers Press, 1980, xv+148 p., cloth, coll.

SMITH, C(harles) Alphonso, 1864-1924

34160 *Edgar Allan Poe: how to know him.* New York: Garden City Publishing Co., 1921, 350 p., cloth, nonf.

SMITH, Cara Lockhart

34161 *Parchment House.* London: Methuen, 1989, [144] p., cloth, novel.

SMITH, Cheryl A.

34162 *The falcon and the serpent.* Westchester, IL: Crossway Books, 1990, 318 p., paper, novel.

SMITH, Clark Ashton, 1893-1961

19641 *As it is written* / by Clark Ashton Smith. West Kingston, RI: Donald M. Grant, Publisher, 1982, 125 p., cloth, novel. [Originally thought to have been written by Smith, and published under his name, but later determined from payment records of the original pulp magazine publisher to have been penned by De-Lysle Ferree Cass].

34163 *The black book of Clark Ashton Smith.* Sauk City, WI: Arkham House, 1979, xi+141 p., cloth, nonf. coll. [Edited by R. A. Hoffman and Donald Sydney-Fryer; includes some verse].

34164 *The city of the Singing Flame.* New York: A Timescape Book, Pocket Books, 1981, 240 p., paper, coll.

34165 *The devil's notebook: collected epigrams and pensés of Clark Ashton Smith.* Mercer Island, WA: Starmont House, 1990, xv+82 p., cloth, coll. STARMONT POPULAR CULTURE STUDIES #16. [Compiled by Donald Sidney-Fryer; edited by Don Herron].

34166 *The last incantation.* New York: A Timescape Book, Pocket Books, 1982, 262 p., paper, coll.

34167 *The monster of the prophecy.* New York: A Timescape Book, Pocket Books, 1983, 238 p., paper, coll.

38068 *The mortuary.* [Glendale, CA: Roy A. Squires], 1971, 4 leaves, paper, story. [Limited to 180 copies].

38069 *Mother of toads.* West Warwick, RI: Necronomicon Press, 1987, 15 p., paper, coll. [Edited by Steve Behrends].

34168 *Nostalgia of the unknown: the complete prose poetry.* West Warwick, RI: Necronomicon Press, 1988, viii+32 p., paper, coll.

38070 *Prince Alcouz and the magician.* [Glendale, CA: Roy A. Squires], 1971, 8 p., paper, story. [Limited to 180 copies].

34169 *A rendezvous in Averoigne: best fantastic tales of Clark Ashton Smith.* Sauk City, WI: Arkham House Publishers, 1988, x+472 p., cloth, coll.

34170 *Strange shadows: the uncollected fiction and essays of Clark Ashton Smith.* New York, London: Greenwood Press, 1989, xxiv+281 p., cloth, coll. CONTRIBUTIONS TO THE STUDY OF SCIENCE FICTION AND FANTASY #36. [Includes some nonfiction; edited by Steve Behrends, Donald Sidney-Fryer, and Rah Hoffman].

38071 *Untold tales.* Bloomfield, NY: Cryptic Publications, 1984, p., paper, coll.

38072 *The vaults of Yoh-Vombis.* West Warwick, RI: Necronomicon Press, 1988, vi+9 p., paper, coll. [Edited by Steve Behrends].

with H. P. Lovecraft

28603 *Letters to H. P. Lovecraft.* West Warwick, RI: Necronomicon Press, 1987, 68 p., paper, nonf. coll. [Edited by Steve Behrends].

with H. P. Lovecraft & Forrest J Ackerman, et al.

15943 *The boiling point.* West Warwick, RI: Necronomicon Press, 1985, [9] p., paper, nonf.

SMITH, Cordwainer [pseud. of Paul Myron Anthony Linebarger], 1913-1966

34171 *The best of Cordwainer Smith.* Garden City, New York: Nelson Doubleday, 1975, 342 p., cloth, coll. [Edited by J. J. Pierce].

34171A retitled: *The rediscovery of man.* London: Victor Gollancz, 1988, 377 p., paper, coll. [Edited by J. J. Pierce].

34172 *The Instrumentality of mankind.* New York: A Del Rey Book, Ballantine Books, 1979, xvii+238 p., paper, coll. INSTRUMENTALITY SERIES.

34173 *Norstrilia.* New York: Ballantine Books, 1975, 277 p., paper, novel. INSTRUMENTALITY SERIES. [Incorporates *The planet buyer* and *The underpeople*].

The rediscovery of man—SEE: *The best of Cordwainer Smith.*

SMITH, Curtis

34174 *Test of the ninja.* Lake Geneva, WI: TSR Inc., 1985, 189 p., paper, novel. AD-

VANCED DUNGEONS & DRAGONS GAME-BOOK #5.

with Bill Slavicsek

34101　*The Star Wars sourcebook.* Honesdale, PA: West End Games, 1987, 142 p., paper, nonf.

SMITH, Curtis C(ooper), 1939-

34175　*Twentieth-century science-fiction writers.* London: Macmillan, 1981, xviii+642 p., cloth, nonf. anth.

34176　*Twentieth-century science-fiction writers, second edition.* Chicago & London: St. James Press, 1986, xviii+933 p., cloth, nonf. anth.

with Harvey J. Satty

33191　*Olaf Stapledon: a bibliography.* Westport, CT: Greenwood Press, 1984, xxxviii+167 p., cloth, nonf.

SMITH, D(avid) Alexander, 1953-

34177　*Homecoming.* New York: Ace Books, 1990, 296 p., paper, novel. MARATHON #3.

34178　*Marathon.* New York: Ace Books, 1982, 250 p., paper, novel. MARATHON #1.

34179　*Rendezvous.* New York: Ace Books, 1988, 280 p., paper, novel. MARATHON #2.

SMITH, David C(layton), 1929-

34180　*H. G. Wells: desperately mortal: a biography.* New Haven, CT, London: Yale University Press, 1986, xviii+634 p., cloth, nonf.

SMITH, David C(laude), 1952-

34181　*The eyes of night.* New York: Avon Books, 1991, 254 p., paper, novel. FAIR RULES #2.

34182　*The fair rules of evil.* New York: Avon Books, 1989, 180 p., paper, novel. FAIR RULES #1.

34183　*The fall of the First World: The master of evil.* New York: Pinnacle Books, 1983, 334 p., paper, novel. FALL OF THE FIRST WORLD #1.

34184　*The fall of the First World: The passing of the gods.* New York: Pinnacle Books, 1983, 344 p., paper, novel. FALL OF THE FIRST WORLD #3.

34185　*The fall of the First World: Sorrowing vengeance.* New York: Pinnacle Books, 1983, 341 p., paper, novel. FALL OF THE FIRST WORLD #2.

34186　*The ghost army.* New York: Zebra Books, Kensington Publishing Corp., 1983, 256 p., paper, novel. ORON #5.

The master of evil—SEE: *The fall of the First World: The master of evil.*

34187　*Mosutha's magic: Oron.* New York: Zebra Books, Kensington Publishing Corp., 1982, 272 p., paper, novel. ORON #3.

34188　*Oron.* New York: Zebra Books, Kensington Publishing Corp., 1978, 395 p., paper, novel. ORON #1.

The passing of the gods—SEE: *The fall of the First World: The passing of the gods.*

34189　*The sorcerer's shadow.* New York: Zebra Books, Kensington Publishing Corp., 1978, 368 p., paper, novel. ORON #2.

Sorrowing vengeance—SEE: *The fall of the First World: Sorrowing vengeance.*

34190　*The valley of Ogrum.* New York: Zebra Books, Kensington Publishing Corp., 1982, 251 p., paper, novel. ORON #4.

34191　*The witch of the Indies.* New York: Zebra Books, Kensington Publishing Corp., 1977, 254 p., paper, novel. BLACK VULMEA SERIES.

with Richard L. Tierney

34192　*Against the prince of Hell.* New York: Ace Books, 1983, 200 p., paper, novel. RED SONJA #5.

34193　*Demon night.* New York: Ace Books, 1982, 209 p., paper, novel. RED SONJA #2.

34194　*Endithor's daughter.* New York: Ace Books, 1982, 217 p., paper, novel. RED SONJA #4.

34195　*For the witch of the mists.* New York: Zebra Books, Kensington Publishing Corp., 1978, 234 p., paper, novel. BRAN MAK MORN #3.

34196　*The ring of Ikribu.* New York: Ace Books, 1981, 246 p., paper, novel. RED SONJA #1.

34197　*Star of doom.* New York: Ace Fantasy Books, 1983, 199 p., paper, novel. RED SONJA #6.

34198　*When Hell laughs.* New York: Ace Books, 1982, 183 p., paper, novel. RED SONJA #3.

SMITH, David N(orman), 1952- , *with Michael Mosher*

30368 *Orwell for beginners.* London: Writers and Readers Publishing Cooperative, 1984, 191 p., paper, nonf.

SMITH, David VanMeter

34199 *Trinity grove.* New York: Avon Books, 1990, 277 p., paper, novel.

SMITH, Dean Wesley, 1950-

34200 *Laying the music to rest.* New York: Popular Library, 1989, 194 p., paper, novel.

***with Jon Gustafson as* SMITH GUSTAFSON**

24846 *The Moscow Moffia presents Rat tales.* Eugene, OR: Hyratia Press [sic], 1987, v+114 p., cloth, anth. [Limited to 144 copies].
Rat tales—SEE: *The Moscow Mafia presents Rat tales.*

with Kristine Kathryn Rusch

32847 *Science Fiction Writers of America handbook: the professional writer's guide to writing professionally.* Eugene, OR: Writer's Notebook Press, Pulphouse Publishing, 1990, 248 p., paper, nonf. anth. [Winner of the *Locus* Award for Best Nonfiction, 1990 (1991)].

SMITH, Dick King- —SEE: King-Smith, Dick

*SMITH, Dodie [i.e., Dorothy Gladys Smith], 1896-1990

SMITH, Doris Buchanan, 1934-

34201 *Voyages.* New York: Viking, 1989, 169 p., cloth, novel.

SMITH, Dorothy G.—SEE: Smith, Dodie

SMITH, E(dward) E(lmer) "Doc", 1890-1965

34202 *The best of E. E. "Doc" Smith.* London: Futura Publications, An Orbit Book, 1975, 285 p., paper, coll.
34203 *Masters of space.* New York: Jove Books, 1979, 158 p., paper, coll.

with Gordon Eklund

Alien realms—SEE: *Lord Tedric: Alien realms.*

22509 *Black knight of the Iron Sphere.* New York: Baronet Publishing Co., 1979, 216 p., paper, novel. LORD TEDRIC #3.
22509A retitled: *Lord Tedric: The black knight of the Iron Sphere.* London: A Star Book, W. H. Allen, 1979, 140 p., paper, novel. LORD TEDRIC #3. [The British editions do not mention Eklund as author].
22510 *Lord Tedric.* New York: Baronet Publishing Co., 1978, 221 p., paper, novel. LORD TEDRIC #1.
22511 *Lord Tedric: Alien realms.* London: Star Books, 1980, 143 p., paper, novel. LORD TEDRIC #4.
22512 *Lord Tedric; Alien realms.* London: A Star Book, W. H. Allen, 1980, 159+143 p., paper, coll. LORD TEDRIC #1 & 4.
Lord Tedric: The black knight of the Iron Sphere—SEE: *The black knight of the Iron Sphere.*
22513 *Space pirates.* New York: Baronet Publishing Co., 1979, 223 p., paper, novel. LORD TEDRIC #2.

with Lloyd Arthur Eshbach

24074 *Subspace encounter.* New York: Berkley Books, 1983, 198 p., paper, novel. SUBSPACE EXPLORERS #2. ["Edited" (but actually completed) by Eshbach].

with Stephen Goldin

24075 *Appointment at Bloodstar.* New York: A Jove/HBJ Book, 1978, 189 p., paper, novel. FAMILY D'ALEMBERT #5.
24075A retitled: *The Bloodstar conspiracy.* London: Panther, 1978, 158 p., paper, novel. FAMILY D'ALEMBERT SERIES.
The Bloodstar conspiracy—SEE: *Appointment at Bloodstar.*
24076 *The clockwork traitor.* New York: Pyramid Books, 1977, 158 p., paper, novel. FAMILY D'ALEMBERT #3.
24077 *Eclipsing binaries.* New York: Berkley Books, 1983, 184 p., paper, novel. FAMILY D'ALEMBERT #8.
24078 *Getaway world.* New York: Pyramid Books, 1977, 191 p., paper, novel. FAMILY D'ALEMBERT #4.
24079 *Imperial stars.* New York: Pyramid Books, 1976, 143 p., paper, novel. FAMILY D'ALEMBERT #1.
24080 *The Omicron invasion.* New York: Berkley Books, 1984, 184 p., paper, novel. FAMILY D'ALEMBERT #9.
24081 *Planet of treachery.* New York: Berkley Books, 1982, 199 p., paper, novel. FAMILY D'ALEMBERT #7.

24082 *The Purity plot.* New York: Berkley Books, 1980, 184 p., paper, novel. FAMILY D'ALEMBERT #6.
24083 *Revolt of the galaxy.* New York: Berkley Books, 1985, 186 p., paper, novel. FAMILY D'ALEMBERT SERIES #10.
24084 *Strangler's moon.* New York: Pyramid Books, 1976, 159 p., paper, novel. FAMILY D'ALEMBERT #2.

with Thomas Sheridan

33725 *E. E. "Doc" Smith, father of star wars.* West Warwick, RI: Necronomicon Press, 1977, [8] p., paper, nonf.

SMITH, Ella, 1933-

34204 *The transference.* New York: Playboy Paperbacks, 1982, 319 p., paper, novel.

SMITH, Evelyn E., 1927-

34205 *The copy shop.* Garden City, NY: Doubleday & Co., 1985, x+178 p., cloth, novel.
34206 *Unpopular planet.* New York: A Dell Book, 1975, 335 p., paper, novel.

SMITH, Evieline Lates

34207 *Tomorrow's reality.* New York, Washington: Vantage Press, 1980, 78 p., cloth, novel.

SMITH, Frederik N., 1940-

34208 *The genres of Gulliver's travels.* Newark, DE: University of Delaware Press; London: Associated University Presses, 1990, 265 p., cloth, nonf. anth.

SMITH, Gary—SEE: Moore, Rudin

SMITH, George H(enry), 1922-

34209 *The island snatchers.* New York: DAW Books, 1978, 189 p., paper, novel. ANNWN SERIES.
34210 *The second war of the worlds.* New York: DAW Books, 1976, 174 p., paper, novel. ANNWN SERIES.

as JERRY JASON

15861 *Sexodus.* Hollywood, CA: Boudoir Limited Editions, 1963, 160 p., paper, novel.

as HAL STRYKER

34211 *NYPD 2025.* New York: Pinnacle Books, 1985, 185 p., paper, novel.

SMITH, George O(liver), 1911-1981

34212 *The complete Venus Equilateral.* New York: Ballantine Books, 1976, xi+468 p., paper, coll. [Expanded edition of #13370].
34213 *The worlds of George O.* Toronto, New York: Bantam Books, 1982, x+338 p., paper, coll.

SMITH, Gordon (Winslow), 1907-

34214 *Mervyn Peake: a personal memoir.* London: Victor Gollancz, 1984, 128 p., cloth, nonf.

SMITH, Gregory Blake, 1951-

34215 *The devil in the dooryard.* New York: William Morrow & Co., 1986, 336 p., cloth, novel.

SMITH, Gregory J(on)

34216 *Captive planet.* Minneapolis, MN: Bethany House Publishers, 1986, 176 p., paper, novel. STARQUEST #1.
34217 *Operation master planet.* Minneapolis, MN: Bethany House Publishers, 1986, 189 p., paper, novel. STARQUEST #2.

SMITH, Guy N(ewman), 1939-

34218 *Abomination.* London: Arrow Books, 1986, 208 p., paper, novel.
34219 *Accursed.* Sevenoaks, Kent, England: New English Library, 1983, 239 p., paper, novel.
34220 *Alligators.* London: Arrow Books, 1987, 176 p., paper, novel.
34221 *Bats out of hell.* London: New English Library, 1978, 157 p., paper, novel.
34222 *The black fedora.* London: Sphere Books, 1991, 236 p., paper, novel.
34223 *Blood circuit.* Sevenoaks, Kent, England: New English Library, 1983, 216 p., paper, novel.
34224 *The blood merchants.* London: New English Library, 1982, 160 p., paper, novel. SABAT #2.
34225 *Bloodshow.* London: Arrow Books, 1987, 207 p., paper, novel.
34226 *The camp.* London: Sphere Books, 1989, 288 p., paper, novel.
34227 *Cannibal cult.* London: New English Library, 1982, 154 p., paper, novel. SABAT #3.

34228 *Cannibals*. London: Arrow Books, 1986, 208 p., paper, novel.

34229 *Caracal*. London: New English Library, 1980, 172 p., paper, novel.

34230 *Carnivore*. London: Arrow Books, 1990, 202 p., paper, novel.

34231 *Crabs moon*. Sevenoaks, Kent, England: New English Library, 1984, [160] p., paper, novel. CRABS #5.

34232 *Crabs on the rampage*. London: New English Library, 1981, 157 p., paper, novel. CRABS #4.

34233 *Crabs: The human sacrifice*. London: New English Library, 1988, 171 p., paper, novel. CRABS SERIES.

34234 *Deathbell*. Feltham, England: Hamlyn Paperbacks, 1980, 200 p., paper, novel. DEATHBELL #1.

34235 *Demons*. London: Arrow Books, 1987, 200 p., paper, novel. DEATHBELL #2.

34236 *Doomflight*. London: Hamlyn Paperbacks, 1981, 221 p., paper, novel.

34237 *The druid connection*. London: New English Library, 1983, 148 p., paper, novel. SABAT #4.

34238 *Entombed*. Feltham, England: Hamlyn Paperbacks, 1982, 191 p., paper, novel.

34239 *The festering*. London: Arrow Books, 1989, 191 p., paper, novel.

34240 *Fiend*. London: Sphere Books, 1988, 311 p., paper, novel.

34241 *The ghoul*. London: Sphere Books, 1976, 128 p., paper, movie.

34242 *The graveyard vultures*. London: New English Library, 1982, 160 p., paper, novel. SABAT #1.

The human sacrifice—SEE: *Crabs: The human sacrifice*.

34243 *The island*. London: Arrow Books, 1988, 191 p., paper, novel.

34244 *Killer crabs*. London: New English Library, 1978, 158 p., paper, novel. CRABS #2.

34245 *The legend of Sleepy Hollow*. London: New English Library, 1976, 129 p., paper, movie.

34246 *Locusts*. Feltham, England: Hamlyn Paperbacks, 1979, 230 p., paper, novel.

34247 *The lurkers*. Feltham, England: Hamlyn Paperbacks, 1982, 158 p., paper, novel.

34248 *Mania*. London: Sphere Books, 1989, 234 p., paper, novel.

34249 *Manitou doll*. London: Hamlyn Paperbacks, 1981, 236 p., paper, novel.

34250 *The master*. London: Arrow Books, 1988, 208 p., paper, novel.

34251 *The neophyte*. London: New English Library, 1986, 312 p., paper, novel.

34252 *Night of the crabs*. London: New English Library, 1976, 144 p. paper, novel. CRABS #1.

34253 *The origin of the crabs*. London: New English Library, 1979, 157 p., paper, novel. CRABS #3.

34254 *Phobia*. London: Grafton, 1990, 252 p., paper, novel.

34255 *The plague*. London: New English Library, 1987, 160 p., paper, novel. THIRST #2.

34256 *The Pluto pact*. Feltham, England: Hamlyn Paperbacks, 1982, 187 p., paper, novel.

34257 *The resurrected*. London: Grafton, 1991, 223 p., paper, novel.

34258 *Return of the werewolf*. London: New English Library, 1977, 112 p., paper, novel. WEREWOLF #2.

34259 *Satan's snowdrop*. Feltham, England: Hamlyn Paperbacks, 1980, 219 p., paper, novel.

34260 *Sleeping beauty*. London: New English Library, 1975, 121 p., paper, movie.

34261 *The slime beast*. London: New English Library, 1976, 110 p., paper, novel.

34262 *Snakes*. Sevenoaks, Kent, England: New English Library, 1986, 170 p., paper, novel.

34263 *Snow White and the snow dwarfs*. London: New English Library, 1975, 123 p., paper, movie.

34264 *The son of the werewolf*. London: New English Library, 1978, 124 p., paper, novel. WEREWOLF #3.

34265 *The Sucking Pit*. London: New English Library, 1975, 111 p., paper, novel.

34266 *Thirst*. London: New English Library, 1980, 219 p., paper, novel. THIRST #1.

34267 *Throwback*. London: New English Library, 1985, 256 p., paper, novel.

34268 *The undead*. Sevenoaks, Kent, England: New English Library, 1983, 176 p., paper, novel.

34269 *The unseen*. London: Sphere Books, 1990, 268 p., paper, novel.

34270 *The walking dead*. Sevenoaks, Kent, England: New English Library, 1984, 160 p., paper, novel.

34271 *Warhead*. London: New English Library, 1981, 256 p., paper, novel.

34272 *Wolfcurse*. London: New English Library, 1981, 176 p., paper, novel.

34273 *The wood*. Sevenoaks, Kent, England: New English Library, 1985, 171 p., paper, novel.

SMITH, Hazel L.—SEE: Littlefield, Hazel

SMITH, James V. Jr.

34274 *Almost human.* New York: A Dell Book, 1990, 338 p., paper, novel.
34275 *Beastmaker.* New York: A Dell Book, 1988, 382 p., paper, novel. BEAST #1.
34276 *Beaststalker.* New York: A Dell Book, 1988, 373 p., paper, novel. BEAST #2.
34277 *The lurker.* New York: A Dell Book, 1989, 295 p., paper, novel.

SMITH, Janet Patton

34278 *The ghost in the swing.* Austin, TX: Steck-Vaughn Co., 1973, 216 p., cloth, novel.
34279 *The twisted room.* New York: Twilight/Dell, 1983, 154 p., paper, novel. TWILIGHT #12.

SMITH, Jasper

34280 *The specialist.* London: Hamlyn Paperbacks, 1979, 207 p., paper, novel.

SMITH, Jeffrey D.

34281 *Women in science fiction: a symposium.* Baltimore, MD: Jeffrey D. Smith, 1975, 156 p., paper, nonf.

SMITH, John

34282 *Rolling thunder.* New York: Zebra Books, Kensington Publishing Corp., 1987, 333 p., paper, novel.

SMITH, John Selby

34283 *Power point.* New York: Warner Books, 1982, 317 p., paper, novel.

SMITH, Julia (Mary Wylie), *with Mark Smith as* JONATHAN WYLIE

34284 *The age of chaos.* London: Corgi Books, 1989, 351 p., paper, novel. UNBALANCED EARTH TRILOGY #3.
The center of the circle—SEE: *The centre of the circle.*
34285 *The centre of the circle.* London: Corgi Books, 1987, 350 p., paper, novel. SERVANTS OF ARK #2.
34285A retitled: *The center of the circle.* Toronto, New York: Spectra, Bantam Books, 1988, 276 p., paper, novel. SERVANTS OF ARK #2.
34286 *Dream-weaver.* London: Corgi Books, 1991, 655 p., paper, novel.

34287 *Dreams of stone.* London: Corgi Books, 1989, 362 p., paper, novel. UNBALANCED EARTH TRILOGY #1.
34288 *The first named.* London: Corgi Books, 1987, 348 p., paper, novel. SERVANTS OF ARK #1.
34289 *The lightless kingdom.* London: Corgi Books, 1989, 350 p., paper, novel. UNBALANCED EARTH TRILOGY #2.
34290 *The mage-born child.* London: Corgi Books, 1988, 349 p., paper, novel. SERVANTS OF ARK #3.

SMITH, Julie Dean, 1960-

34291 *Call of madness.* New York: A Del Rey Book, Ballantine Books, 1990, 311 p., paper, novel. CAITHAN CRUSADE #1.
34292 *Mission of magic.* York: A Del Rey Book, Ballantine Books, 1991, 324 p., paper, novel. CAITHAN CRUSADE #2.

SMITH, Kay Nolte, 1932-

34293 *Mindspell.* London: Hodder & Stoughton, 1984, 311 p., cloth, novel.

SMITH, Keith

15862 *OGF: being the private papers of George Cockburn, bus conductor, a resident of Hurstfield, a suburb of Sydney, Australia.* Sydney, Australia: Ure Smith, 1965, 259 p., cloth, novel.

SMITH, Kent

34294 *Future X: a novel.* Los Angeles: Holloway House, 1990, 384 p., paper, novel.

SMITH, L(isa) J.

34295 *The awakening.* New York: HarperPaperbacks, 1991, 311 p., paper, novel. VAMPIRE DIARIES #1.
34296 *The fury.* New York: HarperPaperbacks, 1991, 309 p., paper, novel. VAMPIRE DIARIES #3.
34297 *Heart of valor.* New York: Macmillan; Toronto: Collier Macmillan Canada; New York: Maxwell Macmillan International Publishing Group, 1990, 227 p., cloth, novel. SOLSTICE #2.
34298 *The night of the solstice.* New York: Macmillan Publishing Co., 1987, 231 p., cloth, novel. SOLSTICE #1.
34299 *The struggle.* New York: HarperPaperbacks, 1991, 313 p., paper, novel. VAMPIRE DIARIES #2.

SMITH, L. K., pseud.

34300 *Serpent lady.* New York: Bizarre Library, 1977, 190 p., paper, novel.

SMITH, L. Neil, 1946-

34301 *Brightsuit MacBear.* New York: Avon, 1988, 212 p., paper, novel. NORTH AMERICAN CONFEDERACY #3.

34302 *Contact and commune.* New York: Questar, Popular Library, 1990, 199 p., paper, novel. CONTACT AND COMMUNE #1.

34303 *Converse and conflict.* New York: Popular Library, 1990, 199 p., paper, novel. CONTACT AND COMMUNE #2.

34304 *The crystal empire.* New York: A Bluejay International Edition, Tor Books, 1986, ix + 449 p., cloth, novel.

34305 *The Gallatin divergence.* New York: A Del Rey Book, Ballantine Books, 1985, 223 p., paper, novel. NORTH AMERICAN CONFEDERACY #2.

34306 *Henry Martyn.* New York: Tor, A Tom Doherty Associates Book, 1989, 437 p., cloth, novel.

34307 *Lando Calrissian and the Flamewind of Oseon: a novel.* New York: A Del Rey Book, Ballantine Books, 1983, 181 p., paper, novel. LANDO CALRISSIAN #2; STAR WARS.

34308 *Lando Calrissian and the Mindharp of Sharu: a novel.* New York: A Del Rey Book, Ballantine Books, 1983, 182 p., paper, novel. LANDO CALRISSIAN #1; STAR WARS.

34309 *Lando Calrissian and the Starcave of ThonBoka: a novel.* New York: A Del Rey Book, Ballantine Books, 1983, 181 p., paper, novel. LANDO CALRISSIAN #3; STAR WARS.

34310 *The Nagasaki vector.* New York: A Del Rey Book, Ballantine Books, 1983, 242 p., paper, novel. WIN BEAR #3.

34311 *The Probability Broach.* New York: A Del Rey Book, Ballantine Books, 1980, 275 p., paper, novel. WIN BEAR #1.

34312 *Taflak Lysandra.* New York: Avon Books, 1988, 230 p., paper, novel.

34313 *Their Majesties' Bucketeers.* New York: A Del Rey Book, Ballantine Books, 1981, 182 p., paper, nove.

34314 *Tom Paine Maru.* New York: A Del Rey Book, Ballantine Books, 1984, xiii + 273 p., paper, novel. NORTH AMERICAN CONFEDERACY #1.

34315 *The Venus belt.* New York: A Del Rey Book, Ballantine Books, 1981, 211 p., paper, novel. WIN BEAR #2.

34316 *The wardove.* New York: Berkley Books, 1986, 223 p., paper, novel.

SMITH, Laure, *with Seth McEvoy*

29527 *Arcade explorers: The electronic hurricane.* New York: Laurel-Leaf Books, 1985, ix + 173 p., paper, novel. ARCADE EXPLORERS #3.

29528 *Arcade explorers: Save the Venturians!* New York: Laurel-Leaf Books, 1985, vii + 166 p., paper, novel. ARCADE EXPLORERS #1.

29529 *Arcade explorers: Revenge of the Raster gang.* New York: Laurel-Leaf Books, 1985, 175 p., paper, novel. ARCADE EXPLORERS #2.

29530 *Arcade explorers: The magnetic ghost of Shadow Island.* New York: Laurel-Leaf Books, 1985, 174 p., paper, novel. ARCADE EXPLORERS #4.

The electronic hurricane—SEE: *Arcade explorers: The electronic hurricane.*

The magnetic ghost of Shadow Island—SEE: *Arcade explorers: The magnetic ghost of Shadow Island.*

Revenge of the Raster gang—SEE: *Arcade explorers: Revenge of the Raster gang.*

Save the Venturians!—SEE: *Arcade exploreres: Save the Venturians!*

SMITH, Lindsay, *with Diana Attias*

17102 *The Empire Strikes Back notebook.* New York: Ballantine Books, 1980, 127 p., paper, nonf.

SMITH, Lynn S.

34317 *Space voyages, 1591-1920: a bibliography of works held in the Library of the University of California, Riverside.* Riverside, CA: University of California, Riverside, 1979, [47] p., paper, nonf.

SMITH, Mark (Jonathan Andrew)

with Julia Smith as JONATHAN WYLIE

34284 *The age of chaos.* London: Corgi Books, 1989, 351 p., paper, novel. UNBALANCED EARTH TRILOGY #3.

The center of the circle—SEE: *The centre of the circle.*

34285 *The centre of the circle.* London: Corgi Books, 1987, 350 p., paper, novel. SERVANTS OF ARK #2.

34285A retitled: *The center of the circle.* Toronto, New York: Spectra, Bantam Books,

1988, 276 p., paper, novel. SERVANTS OF ARK #2.

34286 *Dream-weaver.* London: Corgi Books, 1991, 655 p., paper, novel.

34287 *Dreams of stone.* London: Corgi Books, 1989, 362 p., paper, novel. UNBALANCED EARTH TRILOGY #1.

34288 *The first named.* London: Corgi Books, 1987, 348 p., paper, novel. SERVANTS OF ARK #1.

34289 *The lightless kingdom.* London: Corgi Books, 1989, 350 p., paper, novel. UNBALANCED EARTH TRILOGY #2.

34290 *The mage-born child.* London: Corgi Books, 1988, 349 p., paper, novel. SERVANTS OF ARK #3.

with Jamie Thomson

34318 *Arena of death.* London: Armada, 1987, 2 v., paper, fiction. DUELMASTER #4.

34319 *Assassin!* Sevenoaks, Kent, England: Knight Books, 1985, 254 p., paper, fiction. WAY OF THE TIGER #2.

34320 *At the end of time.* London: Sphere Books, 1986, [171] p., paper, novel. FALCON #6.

34321 *Avenger!* Sevenoaks, Kent, England: Knight Books, 1985, 256 p., paper, fiction. WAY OF THE TIGER #1.

34322 *Blood valley.* London: Armada, 1986, 2 v., paper, fiction. DUELMASTER #2.

34323 *Challenge of the Magi.* London: Armada Books, 1986, 2 v., paper, novel. DUELMASTER #1.

34324 *Duelmaster.* London: Armada Books, 1986, 2 v., paper, novel. DUELMASTER #2.

34325 *The dying sun.* London: Sphere Books, 1986, [190] p., paper, novel. FALCON #5.

34326 *Inferno!* Sevenoaks, Kent, England: Knight Books, 1987, [224] p., paper, fiction. WAY OF THE TIGER #6.

34327 *Lost in time.* London: Sphere Books, 1985, [190] p., paper, novel. FALCON #4.

34328 *Mechanon.* London: Sphere Books, 1985, [190] p., paper, novel. FALCON #2.

34329 *Overlord!* Sevenoaks, Kent, England: Knight Books, 1986, 253 p., paper, novel. WAY OF THE TIGER #4.

34330 *The rack of Baal.* London: Sphere Books, 1985, [190] p., paper, novel. FALCON #3.

34331 *The renegade lord.* London: Sphere Books, 1985, [190] p., paper, novel. FALCON #1.

34332 *The shattered realm.* London: Armada, 1987, 2 v., paper, fiction. DUELMASTER #3.

34333 *Sword of the samurai.* Harmondsworth, Middlesex, England: Puffin Books, 1986, [236] p., paper, novel. FIGHTING FANTASY GAMEBOOK #20.

34334 *Talisman of death.* Harmondsworth, Middlesex, England: Puffin Books, 1985, [250] p., paper, novel. FIGHTING FANTASY GAMEBOOK #11.

34335 *Usurper!* London: Knight Books, 1985, 269 p., paper, novel. WAY OF THE TIGER #3.

34336 *Warbringer!* Sevenoaks, Kent, England: Knight Books, 1986, 255 p., paper, novel. WAY OF THE TIGER #5.

SMITH, Martha Oliver- —SEE: Bacon, Martha

SMITH, Martin (William) Cruz, 1942-

38073 *Canto for a gypsy.* New York: G. P. Putnam's Sons, 1972, 191 p., cloth, novel. GYPSY #2.

38074 *Gypsy in amber.* New York: G. P. Putnam's Sons, 1971, 192 p., cloth, novel. GYPSY #1.

38075 *Gypsy in amber; and, Canto for a gypsy.* Garden City, NY: Nelson Doubleday, 1984, 283 p., cloth, novel. GYPSY #1-2.

34337 *Nightwing.* New York: W. W. Norton & Co., 1977, 255 p., cloth, novel.

as NICK CARTER

35806 *Code name: werewolf.* New York: Award Books, 1973, 167 p., paper, novel. NICK CARTER SERIES.

31758 *The devil's dozen.* New York: Award Books, 1973, 184 p., paper, novel. NICK CARTER SERIES.

34389 *The Inca death squad.* New York: Award Books, 1972, 169 p., paper, novel. NICK CARTER SERIES.

SMITH, Nicholas D(abney), 1949-

34338 *Philosophers look at science fiction.* Chicago: Nelson-Hall, 1982, xi+204 p., cloth, nonf. anth.

with Marleen Barr

17447 *Women and utopia: critical interpretations.* Lanham, MD, New York: University Press of America, 1983, 171 p., cloth, nonf. anth.

with Michael S. Cummings

20875 *Utopian studies II.* Lanham, MD: University Press of America, 1989, 154 p., cloth, nonf. anth.

with Fred D. Miller Jr.

29900 *Thought probes: philosophy through science fiction.* Englewood Cliffs, NJ: Prentice-Hall, 1981, vi+362 p., cloth, nonf. anth.

29901 *Thought probes: philosophy through science fiction literature, 2nd ed.* Englewood Cliffs, NJ: Prentice-Hall, 1989, 334 p., cloth, nonf. anth.

with Kenneth Roemer & Gorman Beauchamp

17633 *Utopian studies 1.* Lanham, MD: University Press of America, 1987, v+197 p., cloth, nonf. anth.

SMITH, Peter C(harles Horstead), 1940-

34339 *The haunted sea: supernatural stories.* London: William Kimber, 1975, 240 p., cloth, anth.

34340 *Haunted shores: thirteen stories of the supernatural.* London: William Kimber, 1980, 207 p., cloth, anth.

34341 *The phantom coach: thirteen journeys into the unknown.* London: William Kimber, 1979, 189 p., cloth, anth.

34342 *Undesirable properties: thirteen haunted houses.* London: William Kimber, 1977, 216 p., cloth, anth.

34343 *Uninvited guests: thirteen unwelcome visitors.* London: William Kimber, 1984, 191 p., cloth, anth.

SMITH, Phil

34344 *The incredible melting man.* London: New English Library, 1978, 159 p., paper, movie.

34345 *The resurrection machine.* London: New English Library, 1978, 205 p., paper, novel.

SMITH, R(alph) A(ndrews), 1905-1959

34346 *High road to the Moon: from imagination to reality: the collected pictures of R. A. Smith.* [England]: Space Educational Aids for the British Interplanetary Society, 1979, 120 p., paper, art.

SMITH, R. Dixon, 1944-

34347 *Lost in the Rentharpian Hills: spanning the decades with Carl Jacobi.* Bowling Green, OH: Bowling Green State University Popular Press, 1985, 146 p., cloth, nonf.

SMITH, Richard R.—SEE: Reinsmith, Richard

SMITH, Robert Arthur, 1944-

34348 *Deadly admirer.* New York: Fawcett Gold Medal, 1987, 294 p., paper, novel.

34349 *Kramer project.* Toronto: Doubleday Canada; Garden City, NY: Doubleday & Co., 1975, 203 p., cloth, novel.

34350 *The prey.* Greenwich, CT: A Fawcett Gold Medal Book, Fawcett Publications, 1977, 448 p., paper, novel.

34351 *Silent witness.* New York: Fawcett Crest, 1991, 246 p., paper, novel.

34352 *The toymaker.* New York: Fawcett Gold Medal, 1984, 281 p., paper, novel.

34353 *Vampire notes.* New York: Fawcett Gold Medal, 1990, 241 p., paper, novel.

SMITH, Robert Charles—SEE: Charles, Robert

SMITH, Robert Houston, 1931-

34354 *Patches of godlight: the pattern of thought of C. S. Lewis.* Athens, GA: University of Georgia Press, 1981, xi+275 p., cloth, nonf.

SMITH, Robert Peter—SEE: Morwood, Peter

SMITH, Ronald L(ande), 1952-

34355 *Poe in the media: screen, songs, and spoken word recordings.* New York: Garland Publishing, 1990, x+226 p., cloth, nonf.

SMITH, Rosamond [pseud. of Joyce Carol Oates], 1938-

34356 *Lives of the twins.* New York: Simon & Schuster, 1987, 236 p., cloth, novel.

SMITH, Sherwood [pseud. of Christine I. Smith Lowentrout], 1951-

34357 *Wren to the rescue.* San Diego, CA: Jane Yolen Books, Harcourt Brace Jovanovich, 1990, 216 p., cloth, novel.

as NICHOLAS ADAMS

Final curtain—SEE: *Horror High: Final curtain.*

15969 *Horror High: Final curtain.* New York: HarperPaperbacks, 1991, 156 p., paper, novel. HORROR HIGH #8. [By Sherwood Smith].

as ROBYN TALLIS

34358 *Planet builders: Fire in the sky.* New York: Ivy Books, 1989, 186 p., paper, novel. PLANET BUILDERS #10.

34359 *Planet builders: Giants of Elenna.* New York: Ivy Books, 1989, 184 p., paper, novel. PLANET BUILDERS #9.

34360 *Planet builders: Rebel from Alphorion.* New York: Ivy Books, 1989, 183 p., paper, novel. PLANET BUILDERS #3.

34361 *Planet builders: Visions from the sea.* New York: Ivy Books, 1989, 186 p., paper, novel. PLANET BUILDERS #4.

SMITH, Stephanie A(nn)

34362 *The boy who was thrown away.* New York: An Argo Book, Atheneum, 1987, 249 p., cloth, novel. SNOW-EYES #2.

34363 *Snow-Eyes.* New York: An Argo Book, Atheneum, 1985, 184 p., cloth, novel. SNOW-EYES #1.

SMITH, Susan [i.e., Susan Vernon Smith Mendonca], 1950-

34364 *Changing places.* New York, Toronto: Scholastic Inc., 1986, 155 p., paper, novel.

34365 *Confessions of a teenage frog.* New York: An Archway Paperback, Pocket Books, 1987, 133 p., paper, novel. SAMANTHA SLADE #2.

Monster-sitter—SEE: *Samantha Slade, monster-sitter.*

34366 *Our friend, public nuisance #1.* New York: An Archway Paperback, Pocket Books, 1987, 135 p., paper, novel. SAMANTHA SLADE #3.

34367 *Samantha Slade, monster-sitter.* New York: An Archway Paperback, Pocket Books, 1987, 129 p., paper, novel. SAMANTHA SLADE #1.

34367A retitled: *Monster-sitter.* London: Hippo, 1989, 109 p., paper, novel. SAMANTHA SLADE #1.

34368 *The terrors of rock and roll.* New York: An Archway Paperback, Pocket Books, 1988, 147 p., paper, novel. SAMANTHA SLADE #4.

SMITH, Terrence Lore, 1942-1988, *with David Alan Doman*

21995 *Yours truly, from Hell.* New York: St. Martin's Press, 1987, 336 p., cloth, novel.

SMITH, Tevis Clyde, 1908-1984

34369 *Report on a writing man & other reminiscences of Robert E. Howard.* West Warwick, RI: Necronomicon Press, 1991, 48 p., paper, nonf. coll. [Edited by Rusty Burke].

SMITH, Thomas G(raham), 1938-

34370 *Industrial Light & Magic: the art of special effects.* New York: A Del Rey Book, Ballantine Books, 1986, xi+279 p., cloth, nonf.

SMITH, Tim(othy) L(awrence), 1924-1990?, *with David McDonnell & John Sayers*

34371 *Starlog science fiction trivia book.* New York: A Signet Book, New American Library, 1986, 208 p., paper, nonf.

SMITH, Trevor Dudley- —SEE: Trevor, Elleston

SMITH, Walter J(ames), 1917-

34372 *Fourth gear.* London: Robert Hale, 1981, 174 p., cloth, novel.

*SMITH, Wayland [pseud. of Victor Bayley], 1880-1972

SMOKE, Stephen L., 1949-

34373 *The Atlantean document: a novel.* Palm Springs, CA: ETC Publications, 1982, 199 p., cloth, novel.

34374 *Deliver us from evil* / by Stephen Smoke. New York: Berkley Books, 1989, 282 p., paper, novel.

*SNELL, Edmund, 1889-

SNELL, Gordon

34375 *Tom's amazing machine.* London: Hutchinson, 1988, 157 p., cloth, novel. TOM'S AMAZING MACHINE #1.

34376 *Tom's amazing machine takes a trip.* London: Radius, 1990, 144 p., cloth, novel. TOM'S AMAZING MACHINE #3.

34377 *Tom's amazing machine zaps back.* London: Hutchinson Children's Books, 1989, 182 p., cloth, novel. TOM'S AMAZING MACHINE #2.

SNELLINGS, John (H.)

34378 *Carvings.* New York: Leisure Books, 1987, 397 p., paper, novel.

SNO, William

34379 *Carnival of demons.* New York: Avon, 1986, 104 p., paper, novel. WIZARDS, WARRIORS & YOU #14.

38076 *G.I. Joe: Operation: dragon fire.* New York: Ballantine Books, 1985, 90 p., paper, novel. FIND YOUR FATE—G.I. JOE #2.

34380 *G.I. Joe: Operation: night flight.* New York: Ballantine Books, 1986, 88 p., paper, novel. FIND YOUR FATE—G.I. JOE #10.

34381 *G.I. Joe: Operation: tiger strike.* New York: Ballantine Books, 1987, 89 p., paper, novel. FIND YOUR FATE—G.I. JOE #19.

Operation: night flight—SEE: *G.I. Joe: Operation: night flight.*

Operation: tiger strike—SEE: *G.I. Joe: Operation: tiger strike.*

SNODGRASS, Melinda M(arilyn), 1951-

34382 *Circuit.* New York: Berkley Books, 1986, 232 p., paper, novel. CIRCUIT #1.

34383 *Circuit breaker.* New York: Berkley Books, 1987, 263 p., paper, novel. CIRCUIT #2.

34384 *Final circuit / by Melinda Snodgrass.* New York: Ace Books, 1988, 244 p., paper, novel. CIRCUIT #3.

34385 *Queen's gambit declined.* New York: Popular Library, 1989, 244 p., paper, novel.

34386 *The tears of the Singers: a Star Trek novel.* New York: Pocket Books, 1984, 252 p., paper, novel. STAR TREK #19.

34387 *A very large array: New Mexico science fiction and fantasy.* Albuquerque, NM: University of New Mexico Press, 1987, v+264 p., cloth, anth.

as MELINDA MCKENZIE

34388 *Magic to do: Paul's story.* New York: A Signet Book, New American Library, 1985, 182 p., paper, novel.

with George R. R. Martin

29116 *Ace in the hole: a Wild cards mosaic novel.* New York, Toronto: Spectra, Bantam Books, 1990, 385 p., paper, anth. WILD CARDS #6.

29117 *Jokertown shuffle: a Wild Cards mosaic novel.* New York, Toronto: Spectra, Bantam Books, 1991, 390 p., paper, anth. WILD CARDS #9.

29118 *One-eyed jacks: a Wild Card mosaic novel.* New York, Toronto: Spectra, Bantam Books, 1991, 328 p., paper, anth. WILD CARDS #8.

with George R. R. Martin & John J. Miller

29119 *Dead man's hand: a Wild Card novel.* New York, Toronto: Bantam Books, 1990, 328 p., paper, anth. WILD CARDS #7.

with Victor Milán

29866 *Runespear.* New York: Popular Library, 1987, 278 p., paper, novel.

SNODGRASS, Richard, 1940-

34390 *There's something in the back yard.* New York: Viking, 1989, 322 p., cloth, novel.

SNOW, Bradley, 1953-

34391 *Andy.* Bramalea, Ontario, Canada: Downhome Publishing, 1990, 203 p., paper, novel.

*SNOW, C(harles) P(ercy), Baron Snow, 1905-1980

SNOW, George, with Chris Rowley

32784 *Star Wars, return of the Jedi.* Newtown, CT: Paradise Press, 1983, 64 p., paper, nonf.

SNOW, Jack, 1907-1956

34392 *Who's who in Oz.* Chicago: Reilly & Lee Co., 1954, 277 p., cloth, nonf.

SNYDER, Colleen K., 1954-

34393 *Journey to Amanah: the beginning.* Nashville, TN: Broadman Press, 1991, 206 p., paper, novel.

SNYDER, Eugene V.—SEE: Snyder, Gene

SNYDER, Gene [i.e., Eugene Vincent Snyder], 1943-

34394 *Dark dreaming.* New York: Playboy Press, 1981, 302 p., paper, novel.

34395 *Mind war.* New York: Playboy Press Paperbacks, 1980, 366 p., paper, novel.
34396 *The Ogden enigma.* New York: Playboy Press Paperbacks, 1980, 318 p., paper, novel.
34397 *The Sigma project.* New York: Jove Books, 1988, 311 p., paper, novel.
34398 *Tomb Seven.* New York: Charter Books, 1985, 279 p., paper, novel.

with William Jon Watkins

34399 *The litany of Sh'reev.* Garden City, NY: Doubleday & Co., 1976, 179 p., cloth, novel.

SNYDER, Midori

34400 *New moon.* New York: Ace Books, 1989, 280 p., paper, novel. QUEEN'S QUARTER #1.
34401 *Sadar's keep.* London: Unwin Paperbacks, 1990, 362 p., paper, novel. QUEEN'S QUARTER #2.
34402 *Soulstring.* New York: Ace Books, 1987, 182 p., paper, novel.

SNYDER, Zilpha K(eatley), 1927-

34403 *And all between.* New York: Atheneum, 1976, 216 p., cloth, novel. GREEN-SKY #2.
34404 *Below the root.* New York: Atheneum, 1975, 231 p., cloth, novel. GREEN-SKY #1.
34405 *The changeling.* New York: Atheneum, 1970, 220 p., cloth, novel.
34406 *The Egypt game.* New York: Atheneum, 1967, 215 p., cloth, novel.
34407 *A fabulous creature.* New York: Atheneum, 1981, p., cloth, novel.
      The ghosts of Stone Hollow—SEE: *The truth about Stone Hollow.*
15863 *Season of ponies.* New York: Atheneum, 1964, 133 p., cloth, novel.
34408 *Song of the gargoyle.* New York: Delacorte Press, 1991, 232 p., cloth, novel.
34409 *Squeak saves the day, and other Tooley tales.* New York: Delacorte Press, 1988, 116 p., cloth, coll.
13430 *The truth about Stone Hollow.* New York: Atheneum, 1974, 211 p., cloth, novel.
13430A retitled: *The ghosts of Stone Hollow.* Guildford, England: Lutterworth Press, 1978, 207 p., cloth, novel.
34410 *Until the celebration.* New York: Atheneum, 1977, 214 p., cloth, novel. GREEN-SKY #3.
34411 *The witches of worm.* New York: Atheneum, 1972, 183 p., cloth, novel.

SOBCHACK, Vivian Carol, 1940-

34412 *The limits of infinity: the American science fiction film, 1950-75.* South Brunswick, NJ & New York: A. S. Barnes & Co.; London: Thomas Yoseloff, 1980, 246 p., cloth, nonf.
34413 retitled: *Screening space: the American science fiction film, 2nd enlarged ed.* New York: Frederick Ungar Publishing Co., 1987, 345 p., cloth, nonf. [Expanded edition].
      Screening space—SEE: *The limits of infinity.*

SOBEL, Irwin Philip, 1901-1991

34414 *The virus killer.* Garden City, NY: Doubleday & Co., 1975, 260 p. cloth, novel.

SOBOL, Donald J., 1924-

34415 *The amazing power of Ashur Fine.* New York: Macmillan, 1986, 114 p., cloth, novel.
34416 *The best animal stories of science fiction and fantasy.* New York: Frederick Warne, 1979, 195 p., cloth, anth.

SOESBE, Douglas

34417 *Scream play.* New York: Charter/Diamond Books, 1990, 268 p., paper, novel.

SOHL, Gerald A.—SEE: Sohl, Jerry

SOHL, Jerry [i.e., Gerald Allen Sohl Sr.], 1913-

34418 *Death sleep.* New York: Fawcett Gold Medal, 1983, 248 p., paper, novel.
34419 *I, Aleppo.* Toronto, New York: Laser Books, 1976, 190 p., paper, novel.

as NATHAN BUTLER

34420 *Kaheesh.* New York: Fawcett Gold Medal, A Joan Hitzig McDonnell Book, 1983, 217 p., paper, novel.

SOHMER, Steve

34421 *Favorite son.* Toronto, New York: Bantam Books, 1987, 484 p., cloth, novel.
34421A retitled: *Favourite son.* London: Bantam Press, 1988, 484 p., cloth, novel.

SOLDATI, Mario, 1906-

34422 *The emerald: a novel.* New York: A Helen & Kurt Wolff Book, Harcourt Brace Jovanovich, 1977, 347 p., cloth, novel. [Translation by William Weaver of *Lo smeraldo*].

SOLIS, Catherine Duque

34423 *The returning.* New York: Popular Library, 1982, 220 p., paper, novel.

SOLOGUB, Fëdor [pseud. of Fëdor Kuzmich Teternikov], 1863-1927

38077 *The created legend.* London: Martin Secker, 1916, 318 p., cloth, novel. [A translation by John Cournos of Part One of *Tvorimaia legenda*].

38078 *The created legend.* Ann Arbor, MI: Ardis, 1979, 3 v., cloth, novel. [Translation by Samuel D. Cloran of *Tvorimaia legenda*; the volumes also have individual titles: Part One-*Drops of blood*; Part Two-*Queen Ortruda*; Part Three-*Smoke and ashes*].

Drops of blood—SEE: *The created legend.*
Queen Ortruda—SEE: *The created legend.*
Smoke and ashes—SEE: *The created legend.*

38079 *The sweet-scented name, and other fairy tales, fables, and stories.* London: Constable & Co., 1915, xi+239 p., cloth, coll. [Translation by Stephen Graham].

SOMER, John (Laddie), 1936- , with Jerome Klinkowitz

27368 *The Vonnegut statement.* New York: A Seymour Lawrence Book, Delacorte Press, 1973, xvii+286 p., cloth, nonf. anth.

SOMERSON, Paul, with Stephen Manes

37934 *Computer monsters.* New York, Toronto: Scholastic Inc., 1984, 171 p., paper, fiction coll.

37935 *Computer space adventures.* New York, Toronto: Scholastic Inc., 1984, 173 p., paper, fiction coll.

SOMERLOTT, Robert, 1928-

15864 *The inquisitor's house.* New York: Viking Press, 1968, 377 p., cloth, novel.

SOMMER-BODENBURG, Angela, 1948-

34424 *The little vampire.* London: Andersen Press, 1982, 143 p., cloth, novel. LITTLE VAMPIRE #1. [Translation of *Der kleine vampir*].

34424A retitled: *My friend, the vampire.* New York: Dial Books for Young Readers, 1984, 155 p., cloth, novel. LITTLE VAMPIRE #1. [Translation of *Der kleine vampir*].

34425 *The little vampire goes on holiday.* London: Andersen Press, 1985, 139 p., cloth, novel. LITTLE VAMPIRE #4. [Translation by Sarah Gibson of *Der kleine vampir auf dem bauernhof*].

34425A retitled: *The little vampire on the farm.* London: Hippo, 1986, 139 p., paper, novel. LITTLE VAMPIRE #4. [Translation by Sarah Gibson of *Der kleine vampir auf dem bauernhof*].

34425B retitled: *The vampire on the farm.* New York: Dial Books for Young Readers, 1989, 135 p., cloth, novel. LITTLE VAMPIRE #4. [Tranlation by Sarah Gibson of *Der kleine vampir auf dem bauernhof*].

34426 *The little vampire in danger.* London: Simon & Schuster Young Books, 1991, [112] p., cloth, novel. LITTLE VAMPIRE SERIES.

34427 *The little vampire in love.* London: Andersen Press, 1986, 125 p., cloth, novel. LITTLE VAMPIRE #5. [Translation by Sarah Gibson of *Der kleine vampir und die grosse liebe*].

34427A retitled: *The vampire in love.* New York: Dial Books for Young Readers, 1991, 131 p., cloth, novel. LITTLE VAMPIRE #5. [Translation by Sarah Gibson of *Der kleine vampir und die grosse liebe*].

34428 *The little vampire in the vale of doom.* London: Simon & Schuster Young Books, 1991, [112] p., cloth, novel. LITTLE VAMPIRE SERIES.

34429 *The little vampire moves in.* London: Andersen Press, 1982, 155 p., cloth, novel. LITTLE VAMPIRE #2. [Translation by Sara Gibson of *Der kleine vampir zieht um*].

34429A retitled: *The vampire moves in.* New York: Dial Books for Young Readers, 1985, 154 p., cloth, novel. LITTLE VAMPIRE #2. [Translation by Sara Gibson of *Der kleine vampir zieht um*].

The little vampire on the farm—SEE: *The little vampire goes on holiday.*

34430 *The little vampire takes a trip.* London: Andersen Press, 1984, 135 p., cloth, novel. LITTLE VAMPIRE #3. [Translation by Sarah Gibson of *Der kleine vampir verreist*].

34430A retitled: *The vampire takes a trip.* New York: Dial Books for Young Readers, 1985, 155 p., cloth, novel. LITTLE VAMPIRE #3. [Translation by Sarah Gibson of *Der kleine vampir verreist*].

My friend, the vampire—SEE: *The little vampire.*

The vampire in love—SEE: *The little vampire in love.*

The vampire moves in—SEE: *The little vampire moves in.*

The vampire on the farm—SEE: *The little vampire goes on holiday.*

SOMMERS, Beverly

34431 *Time and again.* Toronto, New York: Worldwide Library, 1987, 253 p., paper, novel.

SOMTOW, S. P., pseud.—SEE: Sucharitkul, Somtow

SONDERS, Mark, pseud.—SEE: Berlyn, Michael

SONNTAG, Linda, 1950-

34432 *The ghost story treasury.* London: Kingfisher, 1987, 87 p., cloth, anth.

SOREN, David

38080 *The rise and fall of the horror film: an art historical approach to fantasy cinema.* Columbia, MO: Lucas Bros. Publishers, 1977, ii+108 p., cloth, nonf.

SORENSEN, Ian

34433 *The best of Con-runner: a selection of articles from the Con running fanzine.* Harold Wood, Essex, England: Produced for Beccon Publications by Roger Robinson, 1987, 36 p., paper, nonf. anth.

SORENSON, Villy, 1929-

34434 *The downfall of the gods.* Lincoln, NE: University of Nebraska Press, 1990, 123 p., cloth, novel. [Translation by Paula Hostrup-Jessen of *En Gudefortaelling*].

SORRELS, Roy (W.)

34435 *The eyes of Torie Webster.* New York: Pinnacle Books, Windsor Publishing Corp., 1990, 288 p., paper, novel.

SOSNA, Sharon (Madelyn), 1950-

34536 *In this age of stone.* New York: Manor Books, 1978, 197 p., paper, novel.

SOUCI, Robert D. San—SEE: San Souci, Robert D.

SOUZA, Dudley de, *with R. S. Bhathal & Kirpal Singh*

17923 *Singapore science fiction.* Singapore: Rotary Club of Jurongtown, Singapore Science Centre, 1980, ix+116 p., cloth, anth.

SOUZA, Márcio, 1946-

34537 *The order of the day: an unidentified flying opus.* New York: A Bard Book, Avon Books, 1986, xvi+223 p., paper, novel. [Translation by Thomas Colchie of *Ordem do dia*].

SPANO, Charles A. Jr., 1948- , *with Theodore R. Cogswell*

20242 *Spock, messiah!* Toronto, New York: Bantam Books, 1976, 182 p., paper, novel. STAR TREK SERIES.

SPARER, Laurie A.—SEE: Taylor, L. A.

SPARGER, Rex

34538 *The bargain.* Toronto, New York: Bantam Books, 1983, 152 p., paper, novel. DARK FORCES #5.

34539 *The doll.* Toronto, New York: Bantam Books, 1983, 135 p., paper, novel. DARK FORCES #3.

SPARK, Muriel [i.e., Muriel Sarah Camberg Spark Stanford], 1918-

34540 *Child of light: a reassessment of Mary Wollstonecraft Shelley.* Hadleigh, Essex, England: Tower Bridge Publications, 1951, xii+235 p., cloth, nonf.

34540A retitled: *Mary Shelley: a biography.* New York: E. P. Dutton, 1987, 248 p., cloth, nonf. [Winner of the Bram Stoker Award for Best Horror Nonfiction Book, 1987 (1988)].

Mary Shelley: a biography—SEE: *Child of light.*

SPARKROCK, Fred, pseud.—SEE: Vardeman, Robert E. & Proctor, Geo. W.

SPARKS, Beatrice (Mathews), 1918-

34541 *Jay's journal* / edited [i.e., written] by Beatrice Sparks. New York: Times Books, 1979, ix+179 p., cloth, novel.

SPARROW, Susanna, *with George A. Romero*

32632 *Dawn of the dead.* New York: St. Martin's Press, 1978, 210 p., paper, movie.
32633 *Martin: a novel.* New York: Stein & Day, 1977, 213 p., cloth, novel.

SPEARING, Judith (Mary Harlow), 1922-

34542 *Ghosts who went to school.* New York: Atheneum, 1966, 183 p., cloth, novel. TEMPLE STREET #1.
34543 *The museum house ghosts.* New York: Atheneum, 1969, 181 p., cloth, novel. TEMPLE STREET #2.

SPEARS, Heather, 1934-

34544 *Moonfall.* Victoria, British Columbia, Canada: A Tesseract Book, Beach Holme Publishers, 1991, 239 p., paper, novel.

SPEARS, Kermit

34545 *The touch of love.* New York, Washington: Vantage Press, 1990, 158 p., cloth, novel.

SPECTOR, Craig, 1958- , *with John Skipp*

34066 *The book of the dead.* Willimantic, CT: Mark V. Ziesing, 1989, xiv+334 p., cloth, anth.
34067 *The bridge: a horror story.* New York, Toronto: Spectra, Bantam Books, 1991, 419 p., paper, novel.
34068 *The cleanup.* Toronto, New York: Bantam Books, 1987, 379 p., paper, novel.
34069 *Dead lines: a novel of horror.* Toronto, New York: Bantam Books, 1989, 309 p., paper, novel.
34070 *Fright night.* New York: Tor, A Tom Doherty Associates Book, 1985, 250 p., paper, movie.
34071 *The light at the end.* Toronto, New York: Bantam Books, 1986, 385 p., paper, novel.
34072 *The scream.* Toronto, New York: Spectra, Bantam Books, 1988, 420 p., paper, novel.

SPECTOR, Robert Donald, 1922-

34546 *The English gothic: a bibliographic guide to writers from Horace Walpole to Mary Shelley.* Westport, CT & London: Greenwood Press, 1984, xiii+269 p., cloth, nonf.

SPECTOR, Warren

34547 *The Hollow Earth affair.* Lake Geneva, WI: TSR Inc., 1988, 314 p., paper, anth. DOUBLE AGENT BOOK #2. [Bound with *Agents of fortune: the royal pain* / by Richard Merwin].
34548 *The Thing: One thing after another.* Lake Geneva, WI: TSR Inc., 1987, 191 p., paper, fiction. MARVEL SUPERHEROES ADVENTURE GAMEBOOK #5.

SPEDDING, [Alison]

34549 *A cloud over water.* London: Unwin Hyman, 1988, 348 p., paper, novel. WALK IN THE DARK #2.
34550 *The road and the hills.* London: George Allen & Unwin, 1986, 431 p., cloth, novel. WALK IN THE DARK #1.
34551 *Streets of the city.* London: Unwin Hyman, 1988, 338 p., paper, novel. WALK IN THE DARK #3.

SPEER, Flora (M.)

34552 *Destiny's lovers.* New York: Leisure Books, 1990, 361 p., paper, novel.

SPEER, Jack Bristol, 1915-1989

34553 *Fancyclopedia.* Los Angeles: Los Angeles Science Fiction Society, 1944, 97 p., paper, nonf.

SPELMAN, Dick, 1931-

34554 *A preliminary checklist of science fiction and fantasy published by Ballantine Books (1953-1974).* North Hollywood, CA: Institute for Specialized Literature, 1976, 42 leaves, paper, nonf.
34555 *A preliminary checklist of science fiction and fantasy published by Ballantine Books (1953-1977).* North Hollywood, CA: Institute for Specialized Literature, 1977, 76 leaves, paper, nonf.
34556 *Science fiction and fantasy published by Ace Books (1953-1968).* North Hollywood, CA: Institute for Specialized Literature, 1976, 62 p., paper, nonf.
34557 *Science fiction and fantasy published by Arkham House and Mycroft & Moran (1939-1976).* North Hollywood, CA:

Institute for Specialized Literature, 1977, 10 leaves, paper, nonf.

34558 *Science fiction and fantasy published by Arkham House and Mycroft & Moran (1939-1976), rev. ed.* North Hollywood, CA: Institute for Specialized Literature, 1978, 10 leaves, paper, nonf.

34559 *Science fiction and fantasy published by Avalon Books and Bouregy & Curl.* North Hollywood, CA: Institute for Specialized Literature, 1977, 10 leaves, paper, nonf.

SPELMAN, Mary—SEE: Towne, Mary

SPENCE, Catherine Helen, 1825-1910

34560 *Handfasted.* Harmondsworth, Middlesex, England: Published for the Literature Board of the Australian Council by Penguin Books, 1984, ix+378 p., paper, novel.
34561 *A week in the future.* Sydney, Australia: Hale & Iremonger, 1987, 136 p., cloth, novel.

SPENCE, Michele

34562 *Rebekka Moon.* New York: A Dell Book, 1983, 383 p., paper, novel.

SPENCER, John (Barry), 1944-

34563 *A case for Charley.* London: Fontana Books, 1984, 192 p., paper, novel. CHARLEY #1.
34564 *Charley gets the picture.* London: Fontana Books, 1985, 160 p., paper, novel. CHARLEY #2.
34565 *The electronic lullaby meat market.* London: Quartet Books, 1975, 117 p., paper, novel.

with Mike Jarvis

26513 *Echoes of terror.* London: Hamlyn, 1980, 96 p., cloth, anth.

SPENCER, Kathleen (Louise), 1947-

34566 *Charles Williams.* Mercer Island, WA: Starmont House, 1986, 104 p., cloth, nonf. STARMONT READER'S GUIDE #25.

*SPENCER, Scott, 1945-

SPERRY, Ralph A(ddison), 1944-

34567 *Status quotient: the carrier.* New York: Avon, 1981, 253 p., paper, novel.

SPICER, Dorothy [i.e., Dorothy Gladys Spicer Fraser]

34568 *The crystal ball.* New York: Ballantine Books, 1975, 151 p., paper, novel.

SPICER, (William) Michael (Hardy), 1943-

34569 *Final act.* London: Severn House, 1981, 160 p., cloth, novel.

SPIELBERG, Steven (Alan), 1947-

34570 *Close encounters of the third kind.* New York: Delacorte Press, 1977, 256 p., cloth, movie. [Attributed to Leslie Waller as anonymous co-author].
34571 *Close encounters of the third kind.* New York: A Dell Book, 1980, 272 p., paper, movie. [Attributed to Leslie Waller as anonymous co-author; revised and expanded edition].

SPELMAN, Brenda Gates

34572 *Stalker Lord.* New York: Manor Books, 1979, 185 p., paper, novel.
34573 *Umbar.* Charlottesville, VA: Iron Crown Enterprises, 1982, 52 p., paper, fiction.

SPIERING, Frank, 1946-

34574 *Berserker.* New York: A Jove Book, 1981, 248 p., paper, novel.

SPIGEL, Lynn, *with Elisabeth Lyon & Constance Penley & Janet Bergstrom*

17866 *Close encounters: film, feminism, and science fiction.* Minneapolis, MN, Oxford, England: A Camera Obscura Book, University of Minnesota Press, 1991, xi+298 p., cloth, nonf. anth.

SPIGNESI, Stephen (John), 1953-

34575 *The shape under the sheet: the complete Stephen King encyclopedia.* Ann Arbor, MI: Popular Culture Ink, 1991, xx+780 p., cloth, nonf.
34576 *The Stephen King quiz book.* New York: A Signet Book, 1990, 203 p., paper, nonf.

SPILLSBURY, Julian—SEE: Tempest, John

SPINA, Greye La—SEE: La Spina, Greye

SPINNER, Stephanie, 1943-

34577 *Daily planet: a world of news every day!* New York: Random House, 1981, 24 + 16 p., paper, fiction. SUPERMAN II TIE-IN.

with Jonathan Etra

22791 *Aliens for breakfast.* New York: A Stepping Stone Book, Random House, 1988, 62 p., paper, story.
22792 *Aliens for lunch.* New York: A Stepping Stone Book, Random House, 1991, 62 p., paper, story.

with Bram Stoker

34578 *Dracula.* New York: Random House, 1982, 94 p., cloth, novel. [Adapted from Stoker's novel].

SPINRAD, Norman (Richard), 1940-

34579 *Child of fortune.* New York: Bantam Books, 1985, xii + 483 p., cloth, novel.
34580 *Little heroes.* Toronto, New York: Bantam Books, 1987, 486 p., cloth, novel.
34581 *The mind game.* New York: A Jove Book, 1980, 342 p., paper, novel.
34581A retitled: *The process.* London: Arrow Books, 1983, 342 p., paper, novel.
34582 *No direction home: an anthology of science-fiction stories.* New York: Pocket Books, 1975, 238 p., paper, anth.
34583 *Other Americas.* Toronto, New York: Spectra, Bantam Books, 1988, xiv + 273 p., paper, coll.
 The process—SEE: *The mind game.*
34584 *The reasons behind the SFWA model paperback contract.* [S.l.]: Science Fiction Writers of America, 1978, 10 p., paper, nonf.
34585 *Riding the torch.* New York: Bluejay Books, 1984, 166 p., paper, novel.
34586 *Russian spring.* New York: Bantam Books, 1991, 567 p., cloth, novel.
34587 *Science fiction in the real world.* Carbondale & Edwardsville, IL: Southern Illinois University Press, 1990, xvi + 233 p., cloth, nonf.
34588 *Songs from the stars.* New York: Simon & Schuster, 1980, 286 p., cloth, novel.
34589 *The star-spangled future.* New York: Ace Books, 1979, 401 p., paper, coll.
34590 *Staying alive: a writer's guide.* Norfolk, Virginia Beach, VA: Donning Company/Publishers, 1983, 162 p., paper, nonf.

34591 *The Void Captain's tale.* New York: Timescape Books, 1983, 250 p., cloth, novel.
34592 *A world between.* New York: Pocket Books, 1979, 343 p., paper, novel.

SPIVACK, Charlotte (Ruth Kesler Roscoe), 1926-

34593 *Merlin's daughters: contemporary women writers of fantasy.* Westport, CT: Greenwood Press, 1987, xi + 185 p., cloth, nonf. CONTRIBUTIONS TO THE STUDY OF SCIENCE FICTION AND FANTASY #23.
34594 *Ursula K. Le Guin.* Boston: Twayne Publishers, 1984, 182 p., cloth, nonf.

SPOFFORD, Harriet (Elizabeth) Prescott, 1835-1921

34595 *The amber gods, and other stories.* New Brunswick, NJ: Rutgers University Press, 1989, xxxix + 222 p., cloth, coll. [Edited by Alfred Bendixen].

SPRAGUE, Alice—SEE: Orr, A.

SPRAGUE, Claire (Sacks), 1926-

34596 *In pursuit of Doris Lessing: nine nations reading.* New York: St. Martin's Press, 1990, ix + 163 p., cloth, nonf.
34597 *Rereading Doris Lessing: narrative patterns of doubling and repetition.* Chapel Hill, NC: University of North Carolina Press, 1987, 210 p., cloth, nonf.

with Virginia Tiger

34598 *Critical essays on Doris Lessing.* Boston: G. K. Hall & Co., 1986, ix + 237 p., cloth, nonf. anth.

SPRECHMAN, J(ulius) R.

34599 *Caribe: a novel.* New York: E. P. Dutton, 1986, 280 p., cloth, novel.

SPRINGER, Marilyn—SEE: Harris, Marilyn

SPRINGER, Nancy (Connor), 1948-

34600 *Apocalypse.* New York: Baen Fantasy, 1989, 341 p., paper, novel.
34601 *The black beast.* New York: A Timescape Book, Pocket Books, 1982, 192 p., paper, novel. BOOK OF ISLE #4.
34602 *The Book of Suns.* New York: A Kangaroo Book, Pocket Books, 1977, 291 p., paper, novel. BOOK OF ISLE #1.

34603 retitled: *The silver sun.* New York: Pocket Books, 1980, 292 p., paper, novel. BOOK OF ISLE #1. [Expanded edition].

34604 *The Book of Vale.* Garden City, NY: Nelson Doubleday, 1984, 340 p., cloth, coll. BOOK OF ISLE #4-5. [Includes *The black beast* and *The golden swan*].

34605 *Chains of gold.* New York: Arbor House, 1986, 230 p., cloth, novel.

34606 *Chance, & other gestures of the hand of fate.* New York: Baen Books, 1987, 240 p., paper, coll.

34607 *Godbond.* New York: Tor SF, A Tom Doherty Associates Book, 1988, 278 p., paper, novel. SEA KING #3.

34608 *The golden swan.* New York: A Timescape Book, Pocket Books, 1983, 176 p., paper, novel. BOOK OF ISLE #5.

34609 *The hex witch of Seldom.* New York: Baen, 1989, 276 p., cloth, novel.

34610 *Madbond.* New York: Tor SF, A Tom Doherty Associates Book, 1987, 214 p., paper, novel. SEA KING #1.

34611 *Mindbond.* New York: Tor SF, A Tom Doherty Associates Book, 1987, 243 p., paper, novel. SEA KING #2.

34612 *Mythic realism in fantasy.* Eugene, OR: Writer's Notebook Press, Pulphouse Publishing, 1991, 10 p., paper, nonf.

34613 *Red wizard.* New York: Atheneum, 1990, 138 p., cloth, novel.

34614 *The sable moon.* New York: Pocket Books, 1981, 263 p., paper, novel. BOOK OF ISLE #3.

The silver sun—SEE: *The Book of Suns.*

34615 *The white hart.* New York: Pocket Books, 1979, 222 p., paper, novel. BOOK OF ISLE #2.

34616 *Wings of flame.* New York: Tor, A Tom Doherty Associates Book, 1985, 252 p., cloth, novel.

SPRUILL, Steven G(regory), 1946-

34617 *The genesis shield* / by Steven Spruill. New York: Tor, A Tom Doherty Associates Book, 1985, 374 p., paper, novel.

34618 *Hellstone.* New York: Playboy Paperbacks, 1981, 320 p., paper, novel.

34619 *The Imperator plot* / by Steven Spruill. Garden City, NY: Doubleday & Co., 1983, 187 p., cloth, novel. KANE & PENDRAKE #2.

34620 *Keepers of the gate.* Garden City, NY: Doubleday & Co., 1977, 181 p., cloth, novel.

34621 *Painkiller* / by Steven Spruill. New York: St. Martin's Press, 1990, 278 p., cloth, novel.

34622 *Paradox planet: a Kane and Pendrake novel.* New York: A Foundation Book, Doubleday, 1988, 182 p., cloth, novel. KANE & PENDRAKE #3.

34623 *The psychopath plague.* Garden City, NY: Doubleday & Co., 1978, 180 p., cloth, novel. KANE & PENDRAKE #1.

SQUIRE, J(ohn) C(ollings), Sir, 1884-1958

34624 *If it had happened otherwise.* London: Sidgwick & Jackson, 1972, p., cloth, anth. [Adds two additional fictions to the original edition (see #13507)].

SQUIRES, Roy A. (Jr.), 1920-1988

34625 *The private press of Roy A. Squires: a checklist of imprints.* Glendale, CA: [Roy A. Squires], 1970, 4 p., paper, nonf.

34626 *The private press of Roy A. Squires: a descriptive listing of publications, 1962-1979.* Glendale, CA: Roy A. Squires, 1987, 16 p., paper, nonf. [Expanded edition; limited to 80 copies].

with Joseph Bell

17702 *The books of Clark Ashton Smith.* Toronto: Soft Books, 1987, [10]+27 p., paper, nonf. [Limited to 300 copies].

with Phillip T. Mays

29356 *The Phil Mays collection of Arkham House ephemerae.* [Glendale, CA: Roy A. Squires], 1985, 10 p., paper, nonf. [Limited to 250 copies].

SQUIRREL, Alan

34627 *Miracle man.* Lewes, East Sussex, England: The Book Guild, 1989, 177 p., cloth, novel.

ST. ALCORN, Lloyd [pseud. of David N. Meyer II]

34628 *Halberd: dream warrior.* New York: A Signet Book, New American Library, 1987, 253 p., paper, novel. DREAM QUEST #1.

34629 *On the shoulders of giants.* New York: A Signet Book, New American Library, 1988, 252 p., paper, novel. DREAM QUEST #2.

34630 *The serpent mound.* New York: A Signet Book, New American Library, 1989, 253 p., paper, novel. DREAM QUEST #3.

ST. ANDRE, Ken(neth Eugene), 1947- , *with Steve Perrin & John B. Monroe*

30047 *Stormbringer*. Albany, CA: The Chaosium, 1990, 192 p., paper, art.

ST. ARMAND, Barton Levi, 1943-

34631 *H. P. Lovecraft, New England decadent.* Albuquerque, NM: Silver Scarab Press, 1979, 56 p., cloth, nonf.
34632 *The roots of horror in the fiction of H. P. Lovecraft.* Elizabethtown, NY: Dragon Press, 1977, viii + 102 p., cloth, nonf.

ST. CLAIR, David, 1932-

34633 *Bloodline.* London: Corgi Books, 1989, 351 p., paper, novel.
   Child possessed—SEE: *Watseka.*
34634 *The devil rocked her cradle.* London: Corgi Books, 1987, 362 p., paper, novel.
34635 *Mine to kill.* London: Corgi Books, 1985, ix + 351 p., paper, novel.
34636 *Watseka: America's most extraordinary case of possession and exorcism.* Chicago: Playboy Press, 1977, vi + 310 p., cloth, novel.
34636A retitled: *Child possessed.* London: Corgi Books, 1979, 300 p., cloth, novel.

ST. CLAIR, Elizabeth [pseud. of Susan Handler Cohen], 1938-

34637 *Trek or treat.* New York: Zebra Books, Kensington Publishing Corp., 1980, 221 p., paper, novel.

ST. CLAIR, Henry

   Evening tales for the winter—SEE: *Tales of terror.*
15858 *Tales of terror; or, The mysteries of magic: a selection of wonderful and supernatural stories.* Boston: C. Gaylord, 1835, 277 p., cloth, anth.
15858A retitled: *Evening tales for the winter: being a selection of wonderful & supernatural stories.* New York: R. Marsh, 1856, 370 p., cloth, anth.

ST. CLAIR, Margaret (Neeley), 1911-

34638 *The best of Margaret St. Clair.* Chicago: Academy Chicago Publishers, 1985, 271 p., cloth, coll. [Edited by Martin H. Greenberg].

ST. CLAIR, William (Linn)

34639 *The Godwins and the Shelleys.* New York: W. W. Norton & Co., 1989, xvi + 572 p., cloth, nonf.

ST. GEORGE, David, pseud.—SEE: Phillips, David & Markov, Georgii

ST. GEORGE, E(lizabeth) A(nn), 1937-

34640 *Beyond the reach of night.* London: Spook Enterprises, 1983, 185 leaves, paper, novel.
34641 *Joyflame of Algol.* London: Spook Enterprises, 1983, 193 leaves, paper, novel.
34642 *The prophetess.* London: Spook Enterprises, 1983, 186 leaves, paper, novel.
34643 *South of eternity.* London: Spook Enterprises, 1983, 191 leaves, paper, novel.
34644 *A sword for Alosando.* London: Spook Enterprises, 1982, 189 leaves, paper, novel.
34645 *The thirteenth eternity.* London: Spook Enterprises, 1982, 182 leaves, paper, novel.
34646 *Voyage to the cat star.* London: Spook Enterprises, 1985, 240 leaves, paper, novel.
34647 *The winds of Salpurtaim.* London: Spook Enterprises, 1983, 183 leaves, paper, novel.
34648 *Witch might.* London: Spook Enterprises, 1987, 178 leaves, paper, novel.

ST. GEORGE, Judith, 1931-

34649 *Haunted.* New York: G. P. Putnam's Sons, 1980, 158 p., cloth, novel.
34650 *In the shadow of the bear.* New York: G. P. Putnam's Sons, 1983, 144 p., cloth, novel.
34651 *The mysterious girl in the garden.* New York: G. P. Putnam's Sons, 1981, 64 p., cloth, novel.
34652 *Who's scared?, not me!* New York: G. P. Putnam's Sons, 1987, 174 p., cloth, novel.

ST. JAMES, Blakely, house pseud.—SEE: Platt, Charles

ST. JOHN, Nicole, pseud.—SEE: Johnston, Norma

*ST. LUZ, Berthe [pseud. of Alice Alberthe Robertson], 1871-1968

ST. PIERRE, Dennis

34653 *The Marshal.* New York: Warner Books, 1981, 268 p., paper, novel.

STABENOW, Dana (Helen), 1952-

34654 *A handful of stars.* New York: Ace Books, 1991, 215 p., paper, novel. SECOND STAR #2.

34655 *Second star.* New York: Ace Books, 1991, 202 p., paper, novel. SECOND STAR #1.

STABLEFORD, Brian M(ichael), 1948-

34656 *The angel of pain.* London: Simon & Schuster, 1991, 400 p., cloth, novel. WEREWOLVES #2.

34657 *Balance of power.* New York: DAW Books, 1979, 173 p., paper, novel. DAEDALUS MISSION #5.

34658 *The castaways of Tanagar.* New York: DAW Books, 1981, 319 p., paper, novel.

34659 *The centre cannot hold.* London: New English Library, 1990, 304 p., paper, novel. ASGARD #3.

34660 *The City of the Sun.* New York: DAW Books, 1978, 189 p., paper, novel. DAEDALUS MISSION #4.

34661 *A clash of symbols: the triumph of James Blish.* San Bernardino, CA: R. Reginald, The Borgo Press, 1979, 62 p., cloth, nonf. MILFORD SERIES: POPULAR WRITERS OF TODAY #24.

34662 *The cosmic perspective.* Polk City, IA: Chris Drumm, 1985, 19 p., paper, coll. [Bound with *Custer's last stand*]. DRUMM BOOKLET #21.

34663 *Critical threshold.* New York: DAW Books, 1977, 160 p., paper, novel. DAEDALUS MISSION #2.

34664 *Custer's last stand.* Polk City, IA: Chris Drumm, 1985, 25 p., paper, coll. [Bound with *The cosmic perspective*]. DRUMM BOOKLET #21.

34665 *The Dedalus book of British fantasy: the 19th century.* Sawtry, Cambridgeshire, England: Dedalus, 1991, 416 p., cloth, anth.

34666 *The Dedalus book of decadence: (moral ruins).* Sawtry, Cambridgeshire, England: Dedalus with the Support of the Eastern Arts Association, 1990, 283 p., cloth, anth.

34667 *The empire of fear.* London: Simon & Schuster, 1988, 390 p., cloth, novel.

34668 *The face of Heaven.* London: Quartet Books, 1976, 151 p., paper, novel.

34669 retitled: *The realms of Tartarus.* New York: DAW Books, 1977, 448 p., paper, novel. [Expanded edition].

34670 *The Florians.* New York: DAW Books, 1976, 158 p., paper, novel. DAEDALUS MISSION #1.

34671 *The gates of Eden.* New York: DAW Books, 1983, 176 p., paper, novel.

34672 *Invaders from the centre.* London: New English Library, 1990, 256 p., paper, novel. ASGARD #2.

34673 *Journey to the center.* Garden City, New York: Doubleday & Co., 1982, 153 p., cloth, novel. ASGARD #1.

34674 retitled: *Journey to the centre.* London: New English Library, 1989, 201 p., paper, novel. ASGARD #1. [Revised and expanded edition].

Journey to the centre—SEE: Journey to the center.

34675 *The last days of the edge of the world.* London: Hutchinson, 1978, 173 p., cloth, novel.

34676 *Man in a cage.* New York: John Day Co., 1975, ix+294 p., cloth, novel.

34677 *Masters of science fiction: essays on six science fiction authors.* San Bernardino, CA: R. Reginald, The Borgo Press, 1981, 64 p., cloth, nonf. coll. MILFORD SERIES: POPULAR WRITERS OF TODAY #32.

34678 *The mind-riders.* New York: DAW Books, 1976, 143 p., paper, novel.

34679 *Optiman.* New York: DAW Books, 1980, 190 p., paper, novel.

34679A retitled: *War games.* London & Sydney: Pan Books, 1981, 205 p., paper, novel.

34680 *The paradox of the Sets.* New York: DAW Books, 1979, 176 p., paper, novel. DAEDALUS MISSION #6.

The realms of Tartarus—SEE: The face of Heaven.

34681 *Scientific romance in Britain, 1890-1950.* London: Fourth Estate, 1985, 372 p., cloth, nonf. [Winner of the J. Lloyd Eaton Award for Best Nonfiction Book of the Year, 1985 (1987)].

34682 *Sexual chemistry: sardonic tales of the genetic revolution.* London: Simon & Schuster, 1991, 229 p., cloth, coll.

34683 *Slumming in voodooland.* Eugene, OR: Pulphouse Publishing, 1991, 40 p., paper, story. SHORT STORY PAPERBACKS #26.

34684 *The sociology of science fiction.* San Bernardino, CA: R. Reginald, The Borgo Press, 1987, 189 p., cloth, nonf. I.O. EVANS STUDIES IN THE PHILOSOPHY & CRITICISM OF LITERATURE #4.

34685 *Swan song.* New York: DAW Books, 1975, 158 p., paper, novel. STAR-PILOT GRAINGER #6.

34686 *Tales of the wandering Jew.* Sawtry, Cambridgeshire, England: Dedalus, 1991, 368 p., paper, anth. [Includes some verse].

34687 *The walking shadow.* London: Fontana/ Collins, 1979, 224 p., paper, novel.
War games—SEE: *Optiman.*

34688 *The way to write science fiction.* London: Elm Tree Books, 1989, xiii+97 p., cloth, nonf.

34689 *The werewolves of London.* London: Simon & Schuster, 1989, 390 p., cloth, novel. WEREWOLVES #1.

34690 *Wildeblood's empire.* New York: DAW Books, 1977, 192 p., paper, novel. DAEDALUS MISSION #3.

as BRIAN CRAIG

28848 *Dark future: Ghost dancers.* Brighton, East Sussex, England: GW Books, 1991, 240 p., paper, novel. DARK FUTURE SERIES.
Ghost dancers—SEE: *Dark future: Ghost dancers.*
Plague demon—SEE: *Warhammer: Plague demon.*
Storm warriors—SEE: *Warhammer: Storm warriors.*

28849 *Warhammer: Plague demon.* Brighton, East Sussex, England: GW Books, 1990, 235 p., paper, novel. WARHAMMER SERIES—MINSTREL ORFEO #2.

28850 *Warhammer: Storm warriors.* Brighton, East Sussex, England: GW Books, 1991, 271 p., paper, novel. WARHAMMER SERIES—MINSTREL ORFEO #3.

28851 *Warhammer: Zaragoz.* Brighton, East Sussex, England: GW Books, 1989, 245 p., paper, novel. WARHAMMER SERIES—MINSTREL ORFEO #1.
Zaragoz—SEE: *Warhammer: Zaragoz.*

with David Langford

27797 *The third millennium: a history of the world, A.D. 2000-3000.* London: Sidgwick & Jackson, 1985, 224 p., cloth, fiction.

with David Langford & Peter Nicholls

27798 *The science in science fiction.* London: Michael Joseph, 1982, 208 p., cloth, nonf.

STACKPOLE, Michael (Austin), 1957-

34691 *Battletech: Blood legacy* / by Michael A. Stackpole. Chicago: FASA Corp., 1990, 319 p., paper, novel. BATTLETECH: BLOOD OF KERENSKY #2. [Novelization of game].

34692 *Battletech: Lethal heritage* / by Michael A. Stackpole. Chicago: FASA Corp., 1989, 332 p., paper, novel. BATTLETECH: BLOOD OF KERENSKY #1. [Novelization of game].

34693 *Battletech: Lost destiny* / by Michael A. Stackpole. Chicago: FASA Corp., 1991, 332 p., paper, novel. BATTLETECH: BLOOD OF KERENSKY #3. [Novelization of game].

34694 *Battletech: Warrior: Coupe.* Chicago: FASA Corp., 1989, xi+324 p., paper, novel. BATTLETECH: WARRIOR #3. [Novelization of game].

34695 *Battletech: Warrior: En garde.* Chicago: FASA Corp., 1988, 337 p., paper, novel. BATTLETECH: WARRIOR #2. [Novelization of game].

34696 *Battletech: Warrior: Riposte.* Chicago: FASA Corp., 1988, 299 p., paper, novel. BATTLETECH: WARRIOR #1. [Novelization of game].
Blood legacy—SEE: *Battletech: Blood legacy.*
Coupe—SEE: *Battletech: Warrior: Coupe.*

34697 *A dark conspiracy: A gathering evil.* Bloomington, IL: GDW Books, 1991, 327 p., paper, novel. DARK CONSPIRACY #1. [Novelization of game].

34698 *A dark conspiracy: Evil ascending.* Bloomington, IL: GDW Books, 1991, 319 p., paper, novel. DARK CONSPIRACY #2. [Novelization of game].
En garde—SEE: *Battletech: Warrior: En garde.*
Evil ascending—SEE: *A dark conspiracy: Evil ascending.*
A gathering evil—SEE: *Dark conspiracy: A gathering evil.*
Lethal heritage—SEE: *Battletech: Lethal heritage.*
Lost destiny—SEE: *Battletech: Lost destiny.*
Riposte—SEE: *Battletech: Warrior: Riposte.*
Warrior: Coupe—SEE: *Battletech: Warrior: Coupe.*
Warrior: En garde—SEE: *Battletech: Warrior: En garde.*
Warrior: Riposte—SEE: *Battletech: Warrior: Riposte.*

STACY, Jan, 1948-1989

as CRAIG SARGENT

34699 *The cutthroat cannibals.* New York: Popular Library, 1988, 170 p., paper, novel. LAST RANGER #8.

34700 *The damned disciples.* New York: Popular Library, 1988, 167 p., paper, novel. LAST RANGER #9.

34701 *Is this the end?* New York: Popular Library, 1989, 168 p., paper, novel. LAST RANGER #10. [Last of the series].

34702 *The last ranger.* New York: Popular Library, Warner Books, 1986, 215 p., paper, novel. LAST RANGER #1.

34703 *The madman's mansion.* New York: Popular Library, Warner Books, 1986, 216 p., paper, novel. LAST RANGER #3.

34704 *The rabid brigadier.* New York: Popular Library, 1987, 216 p., paper, novel. LAST RANGER #4.

34705 *The savage stronghold.* New York: Popular Library, Warner Books, 1986, 217 p., paper, novel. LAST RANGER #2.

34706 *The vile village.* New York: Popular Library, 1988, 169 p., paper, novel. LAST RANGER #7.

34707 *The war weapons.* New York: Popular Library, 1987, 171 p., paper, novel. LAST RANGER #5.

34708 *The warlord's revenge.* New York: Popular Library, 1988, 184 p., paper, novel. LAST RANGER #6.

with Ryder Syvertsen

34709 *The great book of movie monsters.* Chicago: Contemporary Books, 1983, 352 p., paper, nonf.

with Ryder Syvertsen as JOHN SIEVERT

33849 *C.A.D.S.* New York: Zebra Books, Kensington Publishing Corp., 1985, 398 p., paper, novel. C.A.D.S. #1.

with Ryder Syvertsen as RYDER STACY

34710 *Bloody America.* New York: Zebra Books, Kensington Publishing Corp., 1985, 271 p., paper, novel. DOOMSDAY WARRIOR #4.

34711 *Doomsday warrior.* New York: Zebra Books, Kensington Publishing Corp., 1984, 347 p., paper, novel. DOOMSDAY WARRIOR #1.

34712 *The last American.* New York: Zebra Books, Kensington Publishing Corp., 1984, 267 p., paper, novel. DOOMSDAY WARRIOR #3.

34713 *Red America.* New York: Zebra Books, Kensington Publishing Corp., 1984, 267 p., paper, novel. DOOMSDAY WARRIOR #2.

STACY, Ryder, pseud.—SEE: Stacy, Jan & Syvertsen, Ryder

*STAHL, Ben(jamin), 1910-1987

STAHL, Norman, 1931- , with Don Horan as DONALD N. NORMAN

25938 *Thunder Station: a novel.* New York: Warner Books, 1990, 345 p., paper, novel.

STAICAR, Thomas E.—SEE: Staicar, Tom

STAICAR, Tom [i.e., Thomas Edward Staicar], 1946-

34714 *Critical encounters II: writers and themes in science fiction.* New York: Frederick Ungar Publishing Co., 1982, viii+165 p., cloth, nonf. anth.

34715 *The feminine eye: science fiction and the women who write it.* New York: Frederick Ungar, 1982, viii+148 p., cloth, nonf. anth.

34716 *Fritz Leiber.* New York: Frederick Ungar Publishing Co., 1983, ix+134 p., cloth, nonf.

STAIG, Laurence

34717 *Dark toys and consumer goods.* London: Macmillan Children's Books, 1989, 150 p., cloth, coll.

34718 *Digital vampires.* London: Collins, 1989, 144 p., cloth, novel.

34719 *The glimpses.* London: Macmillan Children's Books, 1989, 177 p., cloth, novel.

34720 *The network.* London: Collins, 1989, ix+177 p., cloth, novel.

34721 *Smoke-stack lightning.* London: Walker Books, 1991, [96] p., cloth, novel.

STALLMAN, Robert, 1930-1980

34722 *The beast.* New York: A Timescape Book, Pocket Books, 1982, 192 p., paper, novel. BOOK OF THE BEAST #3.

34722A retitled: *The book of the beast: the final book in the trilogy.* London: Mayflower, 1982, 224 p., paper, novel. BOOK OF THE BEAST #3.
The book of the beast—SEE: The beast.

34723 *The captive.* New York: A Timescape Book, Pocket Books, 1981, 207 p., paper, novel. BOOK OF THE BEAST #2.

34724 *The orphan.* New York: Pocket Books, 1980, 240 p., paper, novel. BOOK OF THE BEAST #1.

STAMBAUGH, E. B.

34725 *Mantis*. London: Futura, 1989, 288 p., paper, novel.

STAMEY, Sara (Lucinda), 1953-

34726 *Double blind*. New York: Ace Books, 1990, 275 p., paper, novel. WILD CARD RUN #3.

34727 *Wild card run*. New York: Berkley Books, 1987, 232 p., paper, novel. WILD CARD RUN #1.

34728 *Win, lose, draw*. New York: Ace Books, 1988, 263 p., paper, novel. WILD CARD RUN #2.

STAMPER, J(udith) B(auer), 1947-

34729 *13 Shadow Lane* / by Judith Bauer Stamper. Middletown, CT: Weekly Reader Books, 1987, 62 p., paper, novel..

34730 *Autobot alert!* / by Judith Bauer Stamper. New York: Ballantine Books, 1986, 72 p., paper, fiction. FIND YOUR FATE— JUNIOR TRANSFORMERS #7.
Bionic commando—SEE: Worlds of power: Bionic commando: a novel based on the best-selling game by CAPCOM.

34731 *Decepticon poison* / by Judith Bauer Stamper. New York: Ballantine Books, 1986, 72 p., paper, fiction. FIND YOUR FATE— JUNIOR TRANSFORMERS #6.

34732 *More tales for the midnight hour: 13 stories of horror*. New York, Toronto: An Apple Paperback, Scholastic Inc., 1987, 117 p., paper, coll.

34733 *The secret of Rainbow Island* / by Judith Bauer Stamper. New York: Ballantine Books, 1986, 73 p., paper, fiction. FIND YOUR FATE—JEM #3.

34734 *Still more tales for the midnight hour*. New York, Toronto: An Apple Paperback, Scholastic Inc., 1989, 117 p., paper, coll.

34735 *Tales for the midnight hour*. New York, Toronto: Apple, Scholastic Book Services, 1977, 124 p., paper, coll.

34736 *Worlds of power: Bionic commando: a novel based on the best-selling game by CAPCOM*. New York, Toronto: A Seth Godin Production, Scholastic Inc., 1991, 117 p., paper, fiction. WORLDS OF POWER #6.

STANARD, Mary (Mann Page) Newton, 1865-1929

34737 *The dreamer: a romantic rendering of the life-story of Edgar Allan Poe*. Philadelphia, PA, London: J. B. Lippincott Co., 1925, 381 p., cloth, nonf.

STANDIFORD, Les(ter Alan), 1945-

34738 *Spill*. New York: Atlantic Monthly Press, 1991, 326 p., cloth, novel.

STANDRING, Lesley

34739 *The Doctor Who illustrated A-Z*. London: W. H. Allen, 1985, 121 p., cloth, nonf.

STANFORD, Muriel—SEE: Spark, Muriel

STANG, Ivan, 1949-

34740 *Three-fisted tales of "Bob"*. New York: Fireside Books, Simon & Schuster, 1990, 351 p., paper, anth.

STANGERUP, Henrik, 1937-

34741 *The man who wanted to be guilty*. London, Boston: Marion Boyars, 1982, 124 p., cloth, novel. [Translation by David Gress-Wright of *Manden der ville være skyldig*].

STANLEY, Colin (Frederick), 1952-

34742 *Colin Wilson, a celebration: essays and recollections*. London: Cecil Woolf, 1988, 240 p., cloth, nonf. anth.

34743 *The nature of freedom, and other essays*. Nottingham, England: Paupers' Press, 1990, 33 p., paper, nonf. coll.

34744 *The work of Colin Wilson: an annotated bibliography & guide*. San Bernardino, CA: R. Reginald, The Borgo Press, 1989, 312 p., cloth, nonf. BIBLIOGRAPHIES OF MODERN AUTHORS #1. [Edited by Boden Clarke].

STANLEY, John (W.), 1940-

34745 *The creature features movie guide; or, An A to Z encyclopedia to the cinema of the fantastic; or, Is there a mad doctor in the house?* Pacifica, CA: Creatures at Large, 1981, 208 p., paper, nonf.

34746 *The creature features movie guide; or, An A to Z encyclopedia to the cinema of the fantastic; or, Is there a mad doctor in the house?* New York: Warner Books, 1984, xv + 304 p., paper, nonf. [Revised edition].

34747 *Revenge of the Creature features movie guide; or, An A to Z encyclopedia to the cinema of the fantastic; or, Is there a mad doctor in the house?, rev. ed.* Pacifica, CA: Creatures at Large, 1988, xxiv+420 p., paper, nonf. [Second revised edition].

34748 *World War III.* New York: Avon, 1976, 361 p., paper, novel.

STANNARD, Russell

34749 *Black holes and Uncle Albert.* London: Faber & Faber, 1991, 160 p., cloth, novel. UNCLE ALBERT #2.

34750 *The time and space of Uncle Albert.* London: Faber & Faber, 1989, 120 p., cloth, novel. UNCLE ALBERT #1.

STANSKY, Peter (David Lyman), 1932-

34751 *On Nineteen Eighty-Four.* New York, San Francisco: W. H. Freeman & Co., 1983, xi+226 p., cloth, nonf. anth.

34752 *Redesigning the world: William Morris, the 1880s, and the arts and crafts.* Princeton, NJ: Princeton University Press, 1985, xvi+293 p., cloth, nonf.

34753 *William Morris.* Oxford, New York: Oxford University Press, 1983, x+96 p., cloth, nonf.

34754 *William Morris, C. R. Ashbee, and the arts and crafts.* London: Nine Elms Press, 1984, 15 p., paper, nonf.

with William Abrahams

15920 *Orwell: the transformation.* London: Constable, 1979, xi+240 p., cloth, nonf.

15921 *The unknown Orwell.* London: Constable, 1972, xvi+271 p., cloth, nonf.

STANTON, Ken, pseud.—SEE: Stokes, Manning Lee

STANTON, Mary, 1947-

34755 *The heavenly horse from the outermost west.* New York: Baen Books, 1988, 344 p., paper, novel. HORSE #1.

34756 *Piper at the gate.* New York: Baen Fantasy, 1989, 306 p., paper, novel. HORSE #2.

34756A retitled: *Piper at the gates of dawn.* London: New English Library, 1989, 308 p., cloth, novel. HORSE #2.
Piper at the gates of dawn—SEE: *Piper at the gate.*

STANWOOD, Brooks—SEE: Kaminsky, Howard & Kaminsky, Susan Stanwood

STAPLEDON, Agnes (Zena Miller), 1894?-1983?, with Olaf Stapledon

34757 *Letters across the world: the love letters of Olaf Stapledon and Agnes Miller, 1913-1919.* Kensington, NSW: New South Wales University Press, 1987, xli+382 p., cloth, nonf. coll. [Edited by Robert Crossley].

34757A retitled: *Talking across the world: the love letters of Olaf Stapledon and Agnes Miller.* Hanover, NH: University Press of New England, 1987, xli+382 p., cloth, nonf. coll. [Edited by Robert Crossley].
Talking across the world—SEE: *Letters across the world: the love letters of Olaf Stapledon and Agnes Miller, 1913-1919.*

STAPLEDON, Michael, as INTRODUCER

34761 *The best science fiction stories.* London: Hamlyn Publishing Group, 1977, 750 p., cloth, anth.

STAPLEDON, (William) Olaf, 1886-1950

34758 *Far future calling: uncollected science fiction and fantasies of Olaf Stapledon.* Philadelphia, PA: Oswald Train: Publisher, 1979, 275 p., cloth, coll. [Edited by Sam Moskowitz].

34759 *Nebula maker.* Hayes, Middlesex, England: Bran's Head Books, 1976, x+126 p., cloth, novel. [An early version of *Star maker*].

34760 *Nebula maker; and, Four encounters.* New York: Dodd, Mead & Co., 1983, x+260 p., cloth, coll.

with Agnes Stapledon

34757 *Letters across the world: the love letters of Olaf Stapledon and Agnes Miller, 1913-1919.* Kensington, NSW: New South Wales University Press, 1987, xli+382 p., cloth, nonf. coll. [Edited by Robert Crossley].

34757A retitled: *Talking across the world: the love letters of Olaf Stapledon and Agnes Miller.* Hanover, NH: University Press of New England, 1987, xli+382 p., cloth, nonf. coll. [Edited by Robert Crossley].
Talking across the world—SEE: *Letters across the world: the love letters of Olaf Stapledon and Agnes Miller, 1913-1919.*

STARKEY, David, 1952-

34762 *Wishes and fears.* Rockford, IL: 2AM Publications, 1988, 48 p., paper, story.

STARKEY, Naomi

34763   *The lost and the dreamer.* London: Minstrel, 1990, 288 p., paper, novel.

STARKS, Christopher

34764   *Possession.* New York: Fawcett Gold Medal, 1983, 182 p., paper, novel.

STARKS, Richard, 1947-

34765   *The brood: novelization.* London: Mayflower, 1979, 184 p., paper, movie.

STARLIN, Jim, 1950- , *with Daina Graziunas*

24390   *Among madmen.* New York: A Roc Book, 1990, 268 p., paper, novel.

STARR, Bill

34766   *The treasure of Wonderwhat.* New York: Ballantine Books, 1976, 232 p., paper, novel. FARSTAR & SON #2.

34767   *The way to Dawnworld.* New York: Ballantine Books, 1975, 249 p., paper, novel. FARSTAR & SON #1.

STARR, Roland, pseud.—SEE: Rowland, Donald S.

STARRETT, (Charles) Vincent (Emerson), 1886-1974, *with Arthur Machen*

28823   *Starrett vs. Machen: a record of discovery and correspondence.* St. Louis, MO: Autolycus Press, 1977, 119 p., paper?, nonf. [Limited to 500 copies].

STASHEFF, Christopher, 1944-

34768   *A company of stars.* New York: A Del Rey Book, Ballantine Books, 1991, 309 p., cloth, novel. STARSHIP TROUPERS #1.

34769   *Escape velocity.* New York: Ace Science Fiction Books, 1983, 249 p., paper, novel. GRAMARYE #1.

34770   *Her Majesty's wizard.* New York: A Del Rey Book, Ballantine Books, 1986, 342 p., paper, novel.

    King Kobold revived—SEE: *King Kobold.*

13572   *King Kobold.* New York: Ace, 1971, 254 p., paper, novel. GRAMARYE #3.

34771   retitled: *King Kobold revived.* New York: Ace Science Fiction Books, 1984, 216 p., paper, novel. GRAMARYE #3. [Revised edition].

34772   *Odd warlock out.* New York: Guild America Books, 1989, 632 p., cloth, coll.

GRAMARYE #8-10. [Includes *The warlock heretical*; *The warlock's companion*; *The warlock insane*].

34773   *To the magic born.* Garden City, NY: Nelson Doubleday, 1986, 501 p., cloth, coll. GRAMARYE #1-2. [Includes *Escape velocity*; *Warlock in spite of himself*].

34774   *Warlock and son.* New York: Ace Books, 1991, 234 p., paper, novel. GRAMARYE #12.

34775   *The warlock enlarged.* Garden City, NY: Nelson Doubleday, 1986, 664 p., cloth, coll. GRAMARYE #3-5. [Includes *King Kobold revived*; *Warlock unlocked*; *Warlock enraged*].

34776   *The warlock enlarged.* London & Sydney: Pan Books, 1991, 442 p., paper, coll. GRAMARYE #4-5. [Includes *The warlock unlocked*; *The warlock enraged*].

34777   *The warlock enraged.* New York: Ace Science Fiction Books, 1985, 251 p., paper, novel. GRAMARYE #5.

34778   *The warlock heretical.* New York: Ace Books, 1987, 233 p., paper, novel. GRAMARYE #8.

34779   *The warlock insane.* New York: Ace Books, 1989, 247 p., paper, novel. GRAMARYE #10.

34780   *The warlock is missing.* New York: Ace Science Fiction Books, 1986, 201 p., paper, novel. GRAMARYE #7.

34781   *The warlock rock.* New York: Ace Books, 1990, 275 p., paper, novel. GRAMARYE #11.

34782   *Warlock to the magic born.* London: Pan Books, 1990, 696 p., paper, coll. GRAMARYE #1-3. [Includes *Escape velocity*; *Warlock in spite of himself*; *King Kobold revived*].

34783   *The warlock unlocked.* New York: Ace Books, 1982, 282 p., paper, novel. GRAMARYE #4.

34784   *The warlock wandering.* New York: Ace Science Fiction Books, 1986, 297 p., paper, novel. GRAMARYE #6.

34785   *The warlock's companion.* New York: Ace Books, 1988, 235 p., paper, novel. GRAMARYE #9.

34786   *The warlock's night out.* New York: Guild America Books, 1988, 437 p., cloth, coll. GRAMARYE #6-7. [Not the same as the Pan Books edition; includes *The warlock wandering*; *The warlock is missing*].

34787   *The warlock's night out.* London & Sydney: Pan Books, 1991, 576 p., cloth, coll. GRAMARYE #6-8. [Not the same as the Guild America edition; includes *The warlock wandering*; *The warlock is missing*; *The warlock heretical*].

34788   *A wizard in bedlam.* Garden City, NY: Doubleday & Co., 1979, 187 p., cloth, novel.

with Bill Fawcett

22994   *The crafters.* New York: Ace Books, 1991, viii+246 p., paper, anth.

STASHOWER, Daniel (Meyer), 1960-

34789   *The adventures of the ectoplasmic man.* New York: William Morrow & Co., 1985, 203 p., cloth, novel. SHERLOCK HOLMES.

STASZAK, Lucille

34790   *A twist of mind.* North Riverside, IL: Pandora Publications, 1981, 56 p., paper, novel.

STATEHAM, B. R.

34791   *Banners of the Sa'yen.* New York: DAW Books, 1981, 207 p., paper, novel.

STATON, Mary

34792   *From the legend of Biel.* New York: Ace Books, 1975, 333 p., paper, novel.

STAUDINGER, Michael C.

34793   *The falcon rises.* Lake Geneva, WI: TSR Inc., 1991, 314 p., paper, novel.

STCHUR, John (W.)

34794   *Down on the farm.* New York: St. Martin's Press, 1987, 216 p., cloth, novel.
34795   *Paddywhack.* New York: St. Martin's Press, 1989, 297 p., cloth, novel.

STEAD, C(hristian) K(arlson), 1932-

38081   *Smith's dream.* Auckland, New Zealand: Longman Paul, 1971, 142 p., cloth, novel.

*STEAD, Christina (Ellen), 1902-1983

STEAKLEY, John, 1951-

34796   *Armor.* New York: DAW Books, 1984, 426 p., paper, novel.
34797   *Vampire$.* New York: A Roc Book, 1990, 357 p., paper, novel.

STEARN, Jess, *with Taylor Caldwell*

19213   *The romance of Atlantis.* New York: William Morrow & Co., 1975, 285 p., cloth, novel.

STEARNS, Albert—SEE: Thorpe, Fred

STEARNS, Pamela (Fujimoto), 1935-

34798   *Into the painted bear lair.* Boston: Houghton Mifflin Co., 1976, 153 p., cloth, novel.
34799   *The pool and the dancing bear.* Boston: An Atlantic Monthly Book, Little, Brown & Co., 1979, 167 p., cloth, novel.

STEBEL, S(idney) L(ee), 1924-

34800   *Spring thaw.* New York: Walker & Co., 1989, 236 p., cloth, novel.

STEED, Neville

34801   *Hallowes' hell.* London: Headline, 1990, 276 p., cloth, novel.

STEELBAUGH, Larry

34802   *Fireball.* New York: Berkley Books, 1990, 186 p, paper, novel. TANKWAR #2.
34803   *Firebrand.* New York: Berkley Books, 1991, 201 p, paper, novel. TANKWAR #4.
34804   *Firestorm.* New York: Berkley Books, 1991, 202 p, paper, novel. TANKWAR #3.
34805   *Tankwar.* New York: Berkley Books, 1990, 229 p, paper, novel. TANKWAR #1.

STEELE, Addison E., pseud.—SEE: Lupoff, Richard A.

STEELE, Allen (Mulherrin Jr.), 1958-

34806   *Clarke County, space.* New York: Ace Books, 1990, 231 p., paper, novel.
34807   *Lunar descent.* New York: Ace Books, 1991, 325 p., paper, novel. ORBITAL DECAY #2.
34808   *Orbital decay.* New York: Ace Books, 1989, 324 p., paper, novel. ORBITAL DECAY #1. [Winner of the *Locus* Award for Best First Novel, 1989 (1990)].

STEELE, Curtis, house pseud.

21233   *Cavern of the damned.* Oak Forest, IL: Dimedia/Pulp Press, 1980, [96] p., paper, novel. OPERATOR 5 SERIES. [By Frederick C. Davis].

21234 *Legions of starvation.* Oak Forest, IL: Dimedia/Pulp Press, 1980, [96] p., paper, novel. OPERATOR 5 SERIES. [By Frederick C. Davis].

34809 *Revolt of the devil men.* Readers Press, 1975, p., paper, novel. OPERATOR 5 SERIES. [By Emile C. Tepperman]

21235 *Scourge of the invisible death.* Oak Forest, IL: Dimedia/Pulp Press, 1980, [96] p., paper, novel. OPERATOR 5 SERIES. [By Frederick C. Davis].

STEELE, Linda

34810 *Ibts.* New York: DAW Books, 1985, 221 p., paper, novel.

STEELE, Mary Q(uintard Goven), 1922-1992

34811 *Because of the sand witches there.* New York: Greenwillow Books, 1975, 183 p., cloth, novel.

34812 *The owl's kiss: three stories.* New York: Greenwillow Books, 1978, 113 p., cloth, coll.

34813 *The True Men.* New York: Greenwillow Books, 1976, 144 p., cloth, novel.

34814 *Wish, come true.* New York: Greenwillow Books, 1979, 115 p., cloth, novel.

STEEN, Sara Jayne, 1949- , *with Thomas L. Wymer & Alice Calderonello & Lowell P. Leland & R. Michael Evers*

19206 *Intersections: the elements of science in science fiction.* Bowling Green, OH: The Popular Press, 1978, viii+130 p., paper, nonf.

*STEEVES, Harrison R(oss), 1881-1981

STEFANO, Anthony De—SEE: De Stefano, Anthony

STEIGER, Brad [pseud. of Eugene E. Olson], 1936-

34815 *The Chindi.* New York: A Dell Book, 1980, 288 p., paper, novel.

34816 *The hypnotist.* New York: A Dell Book, 1979, 346 p., paper, novel.

STEIN, Baker

34817 *Unholy goddess.* New York: Zebra Books, Kensington Publishing Corp., 1981, 397 p., paper, novel.

STEIN, Benjamin (J.), 1944-

34818 *The Croesus conspiracy.* New York: Simon & Schuster, 1978, 320 p., cloth, novel.

with Herbert Stein

34819 *On the brink: a novel.* New York: Simon & Schuster, 1977, 315 p., cloth, novel.

STEIN, Duffy [pseud. of Melvin H. Berger], 1927-

34820 *The ghost child.* New York: A Dell Book, 1982, 396 p., paper, novel.

34821 *The Owlsfane horror.* New York: A Dell Book, 1981, 474 p., paper, novel.

STEIN, Herbert, 1915?-1989?, *with Benjamin Stein*

34819 *On the brink: a novel.* New York: Simon & Schuster, 1977, 315 p., cloth, novel.

STEIN, Kevin (Todd), 1965-

34822 *Brothers Majere.* Lake Geneva, WI: TSR Inc., 1989, 349 p., paper, novel. DRAGONLANCE SAGA—PRELUDES #3.

with Sam Lewis

28312 *Battletech technical readout 3026: (vehicles and personal equipment).* Chicago: FASA Corp., 1987, 126 p., paper, fiction. BATTLETECH SERIES.

STEIN, Murray, 1943- , *with Lionel Corbett*

20578 *Psyche's stories: modern Jungian interpretations of fairy tales, volume 1.* Wilmette, IL: Chiron Publications, 1991, viii+166 p., cloth, nonf. anth.

STEINBECK, John (Ernst), 1902-1968

34823 *The acts of King Arthur and his noble knights from the Winchester manuscripts of Thomas Malory and other sources.* New York: Farrar, Straus & Giroux, 1976, xiii+363 p., cloth, coll.

STEINER, Barbara (Annette), 1934-

34824 *Ghost cave.* San Diego, CA: Harcourt Brace Jovanovich, 1990, vi+135 p., cloth, novel.

34825 *The photographer.* New York: An Avon Flare Book, 1989, 138 p., paper, novel.

STEINER, Merrilee

34826 *Pirate moon.* New York: Avon Flare, 1987, 168 p., paper, novel. EILEEN GOUDGE'S SWEPT AWAY #7.

STEINHOFF, William R(ichard), 1914-

34827 *George Orwell and the origins of 1984.* Ann Arbor, MI: University of Michigan Press, 1975, 288 p., cloth, nonf.
34827A retitled: *The road to 1984.* London: Weidenfeld & Nicolson, 1975, 288 p., cloth, nonf.
The road to 1984—SEE: *George Orwell and the origins of 1984.*

STEMPLE, Jane—SEE: Yolen, Jane

STENEMAN, Shep, 1945-

34828 *The Black Hole storybook.* New York: Random House, 1979, 61 p., cloth, movie.
34829 *Star Wars, The Empire Strikes Back storybook.* New York: Random House, 1980, [58] p., cloth, movie. STAR WARS.

with Joan D. Vinge & Geraldine Richelson

32297 *Star Wars—the first ten years—storybook trilogy: the storybook based on the movies.* New York: Random House, 1987, [175] p., paper, movie coll. STAR WARS #1-3.

STENZEL, H(elmut) G(eorg), *with Anthony Laude*

27862 *2001 and beyond: science fiction stories.* London: Longman, 1975, 90 p., paper, anth.

STEPHEN, David, 1910-

34830 *Bodach the badger.* London: Century Publishing, 1983, 191 p., cloth, novel.
34831 *String Lug the fox.* Boston: Little, Brown & Co., 1952, 174 p., cloth, novel.

STEPHEN, Martin, 1949-

34832 *The invisible man: notes.* London: Longman, 1980, 79 p., paper, nonf.

STEPHENS, Brynne, 1958-

34833 *The Dream Palace.* New York: Baen Fantasy Books, 1986, 259 p., paper, novel.

STEPHENS, Christopher P(eyton), 1943-

34834 *A checklist of Anne Rice.* Hastings-on-Hudson, NY: Ultramarine, 1991, 11 p., paper, nonf.
34835 *A checklist of Dean R. Koontz.* Hastings-on-Hudson, NY: Ultramarine, 1987, 14 p., paper, nonf.
34836 *A checklist of Dean R. Koontz, 2nd ed.* Hastings-on-Hudson, NY: Ultramarine, 1989, p., paper, nonf.
34837 *A checklist of Dean R. Koontz, 3rd ed.* Hastings-on-Hudson, NY: Ultramarine, 1990, 20 p., paper, nonf.
34838 *A checklist of Dean R. Koontz, 4th ed.* Hastings-on-Hudson, NY: Ultramarine, 1991, 22 p., paper, nonf.
34839 *A checklist of Gene Wolfe.* Hastings-on-Hudson, NY: Ultramarine, 1989, p., paper, nonf.
34840 *A checklist of Gene Wolfe, 2nd ed.* Hastings-on-Hudson, NY: Ultramarine, 1990, 37 p., paper, nonf.
34841 *A checklist of Gene Wolfe, 3rd ed.* Hastings-on-Hudson, NY: Ultramarine, 1991, 40 p., paper, nonf.
34842 *A checklist of K. W. Jeter.* Hastings-on-Hudson, NY: Ultramarine, 1991, 13 p., paper, nonf.
34843 *A checklist of Morrigan Press and Kerosina Press.* Hastings-on-Hudson, NY: Ultramarine, 1989, 18 p., paper, nonf.
34844 *A checklist of Phantasia Press.* Hastings-on-Hudson, NY: Ultramarine, 1991, 19 p., paper, nonf.
34845 *A checklist of Philip K. Dick.* Hastings-on-Hudson, NY: Ultramarine, 1989, p., paper, nonf.
34846 *A checklist of Philip K. Dick, 2nd ed.* Hastings-on-Hudson, NY: Ultramarine, 1990, 46 p., paper, nonf.
34847 *A checklist of Philip K. Dick, 3rd ed.* Hastings-on-Hudson, NY: Ultramarine, 1991, 47 p., paper, nonf.
34848 *A checklist of Robertson Davies.* Hastings-on-Hudson, NY: Ultramarine, 1990, p., paper, nonf.
34849 *A checklist of Robertson Davies, 2nd ed.* Hastings-on-Hudson, NY: Ultramarine, 1991, 16 p., paper, nonf.
34850 *A checklist of Roger Zelazny.* Hastings-on-Hudson, NY: Ultramarine, 1989, p., paper, nonf.
34851 *A checklist of Roger Zelazny, 2nd ed.* Hastings-on-Hudson, NY: Ultramarine, 1990, 20 p., paper, nonf.
34852 *A checklist of Roger Zelazny, 3rd ed.* Hastings-on-Hudson, NY: Ultramarine, 1991, 47 p., paper, nonf.

34853 *A checklist of Samuel R. Delany.* Hastings-on-Hudson, NY: Ultramarine, 1990, p., paper, nonf.

34854 *A checklist of Samuel R. Delany, 2nd ed.* Hastings-on-Hudson, NY: Ultramarine, 1991, 18 p., paper, nonf.

34855 *A checklist of the publications of Dennis McMillan.* Hastings-on-Hudson, NY: Ultramarine, 1991, 19 p., paper, nonf.

34856 *A checklist of the Tor Doubles.* Hastings-on-Hudson, NY: Ultramarine, 1990, p., paper, nonf.

34857 *A checklist of the Tor Doubles, 2nd ed.* Hastings-on-Hudson, NY: Ultramarine, 1991, 18 p., paper, nonf.

34858 *A checklist of Thomas M. Disch.* Hastings-on-Hudson, NY: Ultramarine, 1987, p., paper, nonf.

34859 *A checklist of Thomas M. Disch, 2nd ed.* Hastings-on-Hudson, NY: Ultramarine, 1989, 22 p., paper, nonf.

34860 *A checklist of Thomas M. Disch, 3rd ed.* Hastings-on-Hudson, NY: Ultramarine, 1991, 22 p., paper, nonf.

34861 *A checklist of Ultramarine Press.* Hastings-on-Hudson, NY: Ultramarine, 1989, p., paper, nonf.

34862 *A checklist of Ultramarine Press, 2nd ed..* Hastings-on-Hudson, NY: Ultramarine, 1991, 18 p., paper, nonf.

34863 *A checklist of Wilson Tucker.* Hastings-on-Hudson, NY: Ultramarine, 1990, p., paper, nonf.

34864 *A checklist of Wilson Tucker, 2nd ed.* Hastings-on-Hudson, NY: Ultramarine, 1991, 18 p., paper, nonf.

with Tom Joyce

26813 *A checklist of James P. Blaylock.* Hastings-on-Hudson, NY: Ultramarine, 1991, 17 p., paper, nonf,

26814 *A checklist of Kim Stanley Robinson.* Hastings-on-Hudson, NY: Ultramarine, 1991, 28 p., paper, nonf.

26815 *A checklist of Lucius Shepard.* Hastings-on-Hudson, NY: Ultramarine, 1991, 18 p., paper, nonf.

26816 *A checklist of Tim Powers.* Hastings-on-Hudson, NY: Ultramarine, 1991, 15 p., paper, nonf.

STEPHENS, Henrietta—SEE: Buckmaster, Henrietta

STEPHENS, J(ohn) Hall, 1925-

34865 *Lift off.* Seaford, East Sussex, England: Rodmell Press, 1989, 148 p., paper, novel.

STEPHENS, James, 1882-1950

34866 *Letters of James Stephens.* London: Macmillan, 1974, xxiv+481 p., cloth, nonf. coll. [Edited by Richard J. Finneran].

STEPHENSEN-PAYNE, Phil(ip Andrew), 1952-

34867 *Andre Norton: a working bibliography.* Leeds, West Yorkshire, England & Albuquerque, NM: Galactic Central Publications, 1991, 74 p., paper, nonf.

34868 *Brian Wilson Aldiss: a working bibliography.* Leeds, West Yorkshire, England & Albuquerque, NM: Galactic Central Publications, 1987, 80 p., paper, nonf. GALACTIC CENTRAL BIBLIOGRAPHIES FOR THE AVID READER #26.

34869 *Brian Wilson Aldiss, a man for all seasons: a working bibliography, 2nd ed.* Leeds, West Yorkshire, England & Albuquerque, NM: Galactic Central Publications, 1990, 9+138 p., paper, nonf. GALACTIC CENTRAL BIBLIOGRAPHIES FOR THE AVID READER #26.

34870 *Christopher Samuel Youd: a working bibliography.* Leeds, West Yorkshire, England & Albuquerque, NM: Galactic Central Publications, 1987, 19 p., paper, nonf. GALACTIC CENTRAL BIBLIOGRAPHIES FOR THE AVID READER #25.

34871 *Christopher Samuel Youd, master of all genres: a working bibliography, 2nd ed.* Leeds, West Yorkshire, England & Albuquerque, NM: Galactic Central Publications, 1990, 9+33 p., paper, nonf. GALACTIC CENTRAL BIBLIOGRAPHIES FOR THE AVID READER #25.

34872 *Clifford D. Simak: a working bibliography.* Leeds, West Yorkshire, England & Albuquerque, NM: Galactic Central Publications, 1991, 64 p., paper, nonf.

34873 *Eric Frank Russell, our sentinel in space: a working bibliography, 2nd rev. ed.* Leeds, West Yorkshire, England & Albuquerque, NM: Galactic Central Publications, 1988, 9+35 p., paper, nonf. GALACTIC CENTRAL BIBLIOGRAPHIES FOR THE AVID READER #24.

34874 *Frank Herbert, a voice from the desert: a working bibliography.* Leeds, West Yorkshire, England & Albuquerque, NM: Galactic Central Publications, 1990, 9+48 p., paper, nonf. GALACTIC CENTRAL BIBLIOGRAPHIES FOR THE AVID READER #36.

34875 *Fred Saberhagen, Berserker man: a working bibliography.* Leeds, West Yorkshire, England & Albuquerque, NM: Galactic Central Publications, 1991, 9 + 28 p., paper, nonf. GALACTIC CENTRAL BIBLIOGRAPHIES FOR THE AVID READER #37.

34876 *Gene Wolfe: a working bibliography.* Leeds, West Yorkshire, England & Albuquerque, NM: Galactic Central Publications, 1991, 53 p., paper, nonf.

34877 *George R. R. Martin: a working bibliography.* Leeds, West Yorkshire, England & Albuquerque, NM: Galactic Central Publications, 1987, 16 p., paper, nonf. GALACTIC CENTRAL BIBLIOGRAPHIES FOR THE AVID READER #27.

34878 *George R. R. Martin, the ace from New Jersey: a working bibliography, 2nd rev. ed.* Leeds, West Yorkshire, England & Albuquerque, NM: Galactic Central Publications, 1989, 9 + 23 p., paper, nonf. GALACTIC CENTRAL BIBLIOGRAPHIES FOR THE AVID READER #27.

34879 *John Wyndham, creator of the cosy catastrophe: a working bibliography, 2nd rev. ed.* Leeds, West Yorkshire, England & Albuquerque, NM: Galactic Central Publications, 1989, 9 + 39 p., paper, nonf. GALACTIC CENTRAL BIBLIOGRAPHIES FOR THE AVID READER #16.

34880 *Piers Anthony: biblio of an ogre: a working bibliography.* Leeds, West Yorkshire, England & Albuquerque, NM: Galactic Central Publications, 1990, 9 + 45 p., paper, nonf. GALACTIC CENTRAL BIBLIOGRAPHIES FOR THE AVID READER #35.

34881 *Roger Zelazny: a working bibliography.* Leeds, West Yorkshire, England & Albuquerque, NM: Galactic Central Publications, 1991, 65 p., paper, nonf.

with Gordon Benson Jr.

17813 *Anne McCaffrey, dragonlady and more: a working bibliography.* Albuquerque, NM: Galactic Central Publications, 1984, 9 p., paper, nonf. GALACTIC CENTRAL BIBLIOGRAPHIES FOR THE AVID READER #13.

17814 *Anne McCaffrey, dragonlady and more: a working bibliography, 3rd rev. ed.* Leeds, West Yorkshire, England & Albuquerque, NM: Galactic Central Publications, 1989, 9 + 30 p., paper, nonf. GALACTIC CENTRAL BIBLIOGRAPHIES FOR THE AVID READER #13.

17815 *Bob Shaw, artist at ground zero, 4th rev. ed.* Leeds, West Yorkshire, England & Albuquerque, NM: Galactic Central Publications, 1989, 9 + 32 p., paper,

nonf. GALACTIC CENTRAL BIBLIOGRAPHIES FOR THE AVID READER #14.

17816 *Cyril M. Kornbluth: a working bibliography.* Leeds, West Yorkshire, England & Albuquerque, NM: Galactic Central Publications, 1988, 28 p., paper, nonf. GALACTIC CENTRAL BIBLIOGRAPHIES FOR THE AVID READER #29.

17817 *Cyril M. Kornbluth, the cynical scrutineer: a working bibliography, 2nd rev. ed.* Leeds, West Yorkshire, England & Albuquerque, NM: Galactic Central Publications, 1990, 9 + 39 p., paper, nonf. GALACTIC CENTRAL BIBLIOGRAPHIES FOR THE AVID READER #29.

17818 *Eric Frank Russell: a working bibliography.* Leeds, West Yorkshire, England & Albuquerque, NM: Galactic Central Publications, 1986, 19 p., paper, nonf.

17819 *Frederik Pohl, merchant of excellence: a working bibliography.* Leeds, West Yorkshire, England & Albuquerque, NM: Galactic Central Publications, 1989, 9 + 109 p., paper, nonf. GALACTIC CENTRAL BIBLIOGRAPHIES FOR THE AVID READER #34.

17820 *Fritz Leiber, sardonic swordsman: a working bibliography, 2nd rev. ed.* Leeds, West Yorkshire, England & Albuquerque, NM: Galactic Central Publications, 1990, 9 + 90 p., paper, nonf. GALACTIC CENTRAL BIBLIOGRAPHIES FOR THE AVID READER #22.

17821 *Gordon Rupert Dickson, first Dorsai: a working bibliography, 4th rev. ed.* Leeds, West Yorkshire, England & Albuquerque, NM: Galactic Central Publications, 1990, 9 + 62 p., paper, nonf. GALACTIC CENTRAL BIBLIOGRAPHIES FOR THE AVID READER #2.

17822 *Harry Maxwell Harrison, stainless steel talent: a working bibliography, 4th rev. ed.* Leeds, West Yorkshire, England & Albuquerque, NM: Galactic Central Publications, 1989, 9 + 71 p., paper, nonf. GALACTIC CENTRAL BIBLIOGRAPHIES FOR THE AVID READER #9.

17823 *Jack Vance: a working bibliography.* Leeds, West Yorkshire, England & Albuquerque, NM: Galactic Central Publications, 1988, 46 p., paper, nonf. GALACTIC CENTRAL BIBLIOGRAPHIES FOR THE AVID READER #28.

17824 *Jack Vance, a fantasmic imagination: a working bibliography, 2nd rev. ed.* Leeds, West Yorkshire, England & Albuquerque, NM: Galactic Central Publications, 1990, 9 + 61 p., paper, nonf. GALACTIC CENTRAL BIBLIOGRAPHIES FOR THE AVID READER #28.

17825 *James Tiptree Jr., a lady of letters: a working bibliography.* Leeds, West Yorkshire, England & Albuquerque, NM: Galactic Central Publications, 1989, 9+ 26 p., paper, nonf. GALACTIC CENTRAL BIBLIOGRAPHIES FOR THE AVID READER #31.

17826 *John Brunner, shockwave writer: a working bibliography, 3rd ed.* Leeds, West Yorkshire, England & Albuquerque, NM: Galactic Central Publications, 1989, 9+ 79 p., paper, nonf. GALACTIC CENTRAL BIBLIOGRAPHIES FOR THE AVID READER #11.

17827 *John Wyndham Parkes Lucas Beynon Harris: a bibliography.* Leeds, West Yorkshire, England & Albuquerque, NM: Galactic Central Publications, 1985, 18 p., paper, nonf. GALACTIC CENTRAL BIBLIOGRAPHIES FOR THE AVID READER #16.

17828 *Keith Laumer, ambassador to space: a working bibliography, 2nd rev. ed.* Leeds, West Yorkshire, England & Albuquerque, NM: Galactic Central Publications, 1990, 9+41 p., paper, nonf. GALACTIC CENTRAL BIBLIOGRAPHIES FOR THE AVID READER #30.

17829 *Marion Zimmer Bradley, mistress of magic: a working bibliography.* Leeds, West Yorkshire, England & Albuquerque, NM: Galactic Central Publications, 1991, 9+ 51 p., paper, nonf. GALACTIC CENTRAL BIBLIOGRAPHIES FOR THE AVID READER #40.

17830 *Philip José Farmer, good-natured groundbreaker: a working bibliography, 2nd rev. ed.* Leeds, West Yorkshire, England & Albuquerque, NM: Galactic Central Publications, 1990, 9+63 p., paper, nonf. GALACTIC CENTRAL BIBLIOGRAPHIES FOR THE AVID READER #23.

17831 *Philip Kindred Dick, metaphysical conjurer: a working bibliography, 3rd rev. ed.* Leeds, West Yorkshire, England & Albuquerque, NM: Galactic Central Publications, 1990, 9+102 p., paper, nonf. GALACTIC CENTRAL BIBLIOGRAPHIES FOR THE AVID READER #18.

17832 *Poul Anderson, myth-master and wondermaker: a working bibliography, 5th ed.* Leeds, West Yorkshire, England & Albuquerque, NM: Galactic Central Publications, 1989, 9+123 p., paper, nonf. GALACTIC CENTRAL BIBLIOGRAPHIES FOR THE AVID READER #1.

17833 *Theodore Sturgeon, sculptor of love and hate: a working bibliography.* Leeds, West Yorkshire, England & Albuquerque, NM: Galactic Central Publica-

tions, 1989, 9+75 p., paper, nonf. GALACTIC CENTRAL BIBLIOGRAPHIES FOR THE AVID READER #32.

STEPHENSON, Andrew M(ichael), 1946-

34882 *Nightwatch.* London: Futura Publications, An Orbit Book, 1977, 238 p., paper, novel.

34883 *The wall of years.* London: Futura Publications, An Orbit Book, 1979, 384 p., paper, novel.

38082 *The wall of years.* New York: A Dell Book, 1980, 431 p., paper, novel. [Expanded edition].

STEPHENSON, Gregory (K.), 1947-

34884 *Out of the night and into the dream: a thematic study of the fiction of J. G. Ballard.* New York: Greenwood Press, 1991, 182 p., cloth, nonf. CONTRIBUTIONS TO THE STUDY OF SCIENCE FICTION AND FANTASY #47.

STEPHENSON, Lynne—SEE: Reid Banks, Lynne

STEPHENSON, Neal, 1959-

34885 *Zodiac: the eco-thriller.* New York: Atlantic Monthly Press, 1988, 283 p., cloth, novel.

STERLING, (Michael) Bruce, 1954-

34886 *The artificial kid.* New York: Harper & Row, 1980, 245 p., cloth, novel.

34887 *Crystal express.* Sauk City, WI: Arkham House Publishers, 1989, viii+264 p., cloth, coll.

34888 *Involution ocean.* New York: A Jove/HBJ Book, 1977 (i.e., 1978), 191 p., paper, novel.

34889 *Islands in the net.* New York: Arbor House, 1988, 348 p., cloth, novel. [Winner of the John W. Campbell Jr. Memorial Award for Best Novel, 1988 (1989)].

34890 *Mirrorshades: the cyberpunk anthology.* New York: Arbor House, 1986, xiv+ 239 p., cloth, anth.

34891 *Schismatrix.* New York: Arbor House, 1985, 288 p., cloth, novel.

with William Gibson

23910 *The difference engine.* London: Victor Gollancz, 1990, 383 p., cloth, novel.

STERMAN, Betsy, 1927- , *with Samuel Sterman*

34892 *Too much magic.* New York: J. B. Lippincott, 1987, 154 p., cloth, novel.

STERMAN, Samuel, 1918- , *with Betsy Sterman*

34892 *Too much magic.* New York: J. B. Lippincott, 1987, 154 p., cloth, novel.

STERN, David, 1958-

34893 *Nightmare world.* New York: A Byron Preiss Visual Publications Inc. Book, Ace Books, 1989, 171 p., paper, novel. DR. BONES #5.

*STERN, Philip Van Doren, 1900-1984

STERN, Steve, 1947-

34894 *Lazar Malkin enters Heaven: stories.* New York: Viking, 1986, 249 p., cloth, coll.

STERN, Steven L.

34895 *Hex.* New York, London: Pocket Books, 1989, 362 p., paper, novel.

STERN, Stuart, pseud.—SEE: Rae, Hugh C.

STERNBACH, Richard M.—SEE: Sternback, Rick

STERNBACH, Rick [i.e., Richard Michael Sternbach], 1951- , *with Michael Okuda*

30979 *The Star Trek, the Next Generation technical manual.* New York, London: Pocket Books, 1991, 183 p., paper, nonf.

STETTEN, George

34896 *Weissenbaum's eye.* Syracuse, NY: Zwitter Press, 1989, 208 p., paper, novel.

STEUSSY, Martha J.—SEE: Steussy, Marti

STEUSSY, Marti [i.e., Martha Jane Steussy], 1955-

34897 *Dreams of dawn.* New York: A Del Rey Book, Ballantine Books, 1988, 313 p., paper, novel. FOREST #2.
34898 *Forest of the night.* New York: A Del Rey Book, Ballantine Books, 1987, 265 p., paper, novel. FOREST #1.

STEVENS, Garfield Reeves- —SEE: Reeves-Stevens, Garfield

STEVENS, Gordon, 1945-

34899 *And all the King's men.* London: Chapmans, 1990, 495 p., cloth, novel.

STEVENS, Judith Reeves- —SEE: Reeves-Stevens, Judith

STEVENSON, Bruce, *with Robin Stevenson*

34900 *Sword of Caesar.* Toronto, New York: A Byron Preiss Book, Bantam Books, 1987, 126 p., paper, novel. TIME MACHINE #18.

STEVENSON, Drew, 1947-

34901 *The case of the visiting vampire.* New York: Dodd, Mead & Co., 1986, 124 p., cloth, novel.

STEVENSON, E(dward P.), 1943-

34902 *The avenging spirit.* New York: Twilight/Dell, 1983, 148 p., paper, novel. TWILIGHT #10.

STEVENSON, Florence

34903 *Dark encounter.* New York: A Signet Book, New American Library, 1977, 168 p., paper, novel.
34904 *Household.* New York: Leisure Books, 1989, 392 p., paper, novel.
34905 *Moonlight variations.* New York: A Jove Book, 1981, 213 p., paper, novel.
34906 *The silent watcher.* New York: Award Books, 1975, 169 p., paper, novel. KITTY TELFAIR #6.
34907 *The sisterhood.* New York: Leisure Books, 1989, 342 p., paper, novel.

STEVENSON, John, *as* NICK CARTER

19606 *The Q-Man.* New York: Charter, 1981, 217 p., paper, novel. NICK CARTER SERIES.

STEVENSON, Laura C(aroline), 1946-

34908 *The island and the ring.* Boston: Houghton Mifflin Co., 1991, 275 p., cloth, novel.

STEVENSON, Robert Louis (Balfour), 1850-1894

15865 *The body-snatcher.* New York: Merriam Co., 1895, 61 p., cloth, story.

34909 *The body snatcher, and other stories.* New York: A Signet Book, New American Library, 1988, 350 p., paper, coll. [Edited by Jeffrey Meyers].

34910 *The complete shorter fiction.* London: Robinson Publishing, 1991, 664 p., cloth, coll. [Edited by Peter Stoneley].

34911 *The strange case of Dr Jekyll and Mr Hyde, and other stories.* Harmondsworth, Middlesex, England: Penguin Books, 1979, 304 p., paper, coll.

34912 *The supernatural short stories of Robert Louis Stevenson.* London: John Calder, 1976, 182 p., cloth, coll. [Edited by Michael Hayes].

with T. Ernesto Bethancourt

17918 *Dr. Jekyll and Mr. Hyde.* Belmont, CA: Fearon Education, A Fearon Classic, 1985, 90 p., paper, novel. [Adapted from Stevenson's novella].

with Rosemary Border

18278 *Dr Jekyll and Mr Hyde.* Oxford, England: Oxford University Press, 1991, 75 p., paper, novel. [Adapted from the original novel by Stevenson].

with Joan Cameron

19239 *The strange case of Dr. Jekyll and Mr. Hyde.* Loughborough, England: Ladybird, 1986, 51 p., paper, novel. [Adapted from Stevenson's novel].

with Raymond Harris

25259 *The body snatcher.* Providence, RI: A Jamestown Classic, Jamestown Publishers, 1982, 37 p., paper, story. [Adapted from Stevenson's original edition].

25260 *The bottle imp.* Providence, RI: A Jamestown Classic, Jamestown Publishers, 1982, 40 p., paper, story. [Adapted from Stevenson's original edition].

25261 *Markheim.* Providence, RI: A Jamestown Classic, Jamestown Publishers, 1982, 35 p., paper, story. [Adapted from Stevenson's original edition].

25262 *The strange case of Dr. Jekyll and Mr. Hyde.* Providence, RI: A Jamestown Classic, Jamestown Publishers, 1982, 43 p., paper, story. [Adapted from Stevenson's original edition].

with Samantha Lee

Dr. Jekyll and Mr. Hyde—SEE: *Robert Louis Stevenson's Dr. Jekyll and Mr. Hyde.*

28042 *Robert Louis Stevenson's Dr. Jekyll and Mr. Hyde.* London: Beaver, 1987, 148 p., paper, novel. [Adapted from Stevenson's original story].

with Kate McMullan

37950 *Dr. Jekyll and Mr. Hyde.* New York: Random House, 1984, 94 p., cloth, story. [Adapted from the Stevenson tale].

STEVENSON, Robin

with Tom Bade

17171 *Switchback.* New York: Pinnacle Books, Windsor Publishing Corp., 1988, 447 p., paper, novel.

with Ellen Frankel

23435 *George Washington and the Constitution.* Toronto, New York: A Byron Preiss Book, A Bantam Skylark Book, 1987, 80 p., paper, novel. Time Traveler #6.

with Bruce Stevenson

34900 *Sword of Caesar.* Toronto, New York: A Byron Preiss Book, Bantam Books, 1987, 126 p., paper, novel. Time Machine #18.

STEVER, David, *with Jerry Boyajian*

18385 *A John Schoenherr SF checklist.* Somerville, MA: Paratime Press, 1977, [36] p., paper, nonf.

STEVERMER, Caroline (J.)

34913 *The alchemist: Death of a Borgia.* New York: Charter Books, 1981, 200 p., paper, novel.

34914 *The serpent's egg.* New York: Ace Books, 1988, 200 p., cloth, novel.

with Patricia C. Wrede

34915 *Sorcery and Cecelia: an epistolary fantasy.* New York: Ace Books, 1988, 197 p., cloth, novel.

STEWART, Alan, *with Elke Stewart*

34916 *SF yearbook 1976.* London: BSFA Ltd., 1976, 57 p., paper, nonf.

STEWART, Alex

34917   *Arrows of Eros*. London: New English Library, 1989, 262 p., paper, anth.

with Neil Gaiman

23607   *Temps, volume 1*. London: A Roc Book, 1991, 353 p., paper, anth.

STEWART, Desmond (Stirling), 1924-1981

34918   *The vampire of Mons*. London: Hamilton, 1976, 169 p., cloth, novel.

STEWART, Diana

with Henry James

26450   *The turn of the screw*. Milwaukee, WI: Raintree Publishers, 1981, 46 p., cloth, story. [Adapted from James's original story].

with Edgar Allan Poe

31673   *Tales of Edgar Allan Poe*. Milwaukee, WI: Raintree Publishers, 1981, 48 p., cloth, coll. [Adapted from Poe's work].

with Mary Shelley

33709   *Frankenstein*. Milwaukee, WI: Raintree Publishers, 1981, 48 p., cloth, story. [Adapted from Shelley's original work].

STEWART, Elke, *with Alan Stewart*

34916   *SF yearbook 1976*. London: BSFA Ltd., 1976, 57 p., paper, nonf.

*STEWART, George R(ippey), 1895-1980

STEWART, Heather Kellerhals- —SEE: Kellerhals-Stewart, Heather

STEWART, Janet, 1939-

34919   *Time is, time was, time yet to be: (inscription on an old sundial)*. Strathmartine by Dundee, Scotland: ScoTpress, 1982, 61 p., paper, tele. STAR TREK SERIES.

STEWART, Kerry [i.e., Linda Stewart]

34920   *Ruby*. New York: A Berkley Medallion Book, Berkley Publishing Corp., 1978, 201 p., paper, movie.

STEWART, Linda—SEE: Stewart, Kerry

STEWART, Mary (Florence Elinor), 1916-

13686   *The crystal cave*. London: Hodder & Stoughton, 1970, 464 p., cloth, novel. MERLIN #1.

13686A   retitled: *Merlin of the crystal cave*. London: Coronet, 1991, 464 p., paper, novel. MERLIN #1.

34921   *The crystal cave; The hollow hills; Wildfire at midnight; Airs above the ground*. London: Heinemann; Secker & Warburg; Octopus, 1978, 862 p., cloth, coll. MERLIN #1-2.

34922   *Four complete novels*. New York: Avenel Books, 1983, 694 p., cloth, coll. [Includes *Touch not the cat; The Gabriel hounds; This rough magic; My brother Michael*].

34923   *The last enchantment*. London: Hodder & Stoughton, 1979, 448 p., cloth, novel. MERLIN #3.

34924   *Mary Stewart's Merlin trilogy*. New York: William Morrow & Co., 1980, 919 p., cloth, coll. MERLIN #1-3. [Includes *The crystal cave; The hollow hills; The last enchantment*].

     Merlin of the crystal cave—SEE: *The crystal cave*.

     Merlin trilogy—SEE: *Mary Stewart's Merlin trilogy*.

34925   *Thornyhold*. London: Hodder & Stoughton, 1988, 224 p., cloth, novel.

34926   *Touch not the cat*. London: Hodder & Stoughton, 1976, 301 p., cloth, novel.

34927   *A walk in Wolf Wood*. London: Hodder & Stoughton, 1980, 128 p., cloth, novel.

34928   *The wicked day*. London: Hodder & Stoughton, 1983, 350 p., cloth, novel. MERLIN #4.

STEWART, Michael (James), 1933- , *with Peter Jay*

26526   *Apocalypse 2000: economic breakdown and the suicide of democracy, 1989-2000*. London: Sidgwick & Jackson, 1987, ix + 253 p., cloth, fiction. [Includes some nonfiction].

STEWART, Michael, 1945-

34929   *Birthright*. London: Collins, 1990, 320 p., cloth, novel.

34930   *Blindsight*. London: Macmillan, 1987, 263 p., cloth, novel.

34931   *Far cry*. London: Macmillan, 1984, 206 p., cloth, novel.

34932 *Grace.* London: Collins, 1989, 351 p., cloth, novel.

34933 *Monkey-shines.* London: Macmillan, 1983, 249 p., cloth, novel.

34933A retitled: *Monkey shines.* New York: Random House, 1983, 256 p., cloth, novel.

34934 *Prodigy.* London: Macmillan, 1988, 292 p., cloth, novel.

STEWART, (Gordon) Neil, 1912-

34935 *Australian stories of horror and suspense from the early days.* Sydney, Australia: Australasian Book Society, 1978, 272 p., cloth, anth.

STEWART, R(obert) J., 1948-

34936 *Merlin and woman: second Merlin Conference.* London: Blandford, 1988, 190 p., cloth, anth. [Mostly nonfiction; includes three fantasy stories].

STEWART, Ramona, 1922-

34937 *The nightmare candidate.* New York: Delacorte Press, 1980, 213 p., cloth, novel.

34938 *Sixth sense.* New York: Delacorte Press, 1979, 211 p., cloth, novel.

STICKGOLD, Bob, 1945-

34939 *The California coven project.* New York: A Del Rey Book, Ballantine Books, 1981, 280 p., paper, novel.

with Mark Noble

30750 *Gloryhits.* New York: A Del Rey Book, Ballantine Books, 1978, 296 p., cloth, novel.

STIEGLER, Marc

34940 *David's sling.* New York: Baen Books, 1988, 346 p., paper, novel.

34941 *The gentle seduction.* New York: Baen Books, 1990, 277 p., paper, coll.

with Joseph H. Delaney

21519 *Valentina: soul in sapphire.* New York: A Baen Book, 1984, 318 p., paper, novel.

STIGWOOD, Robert (Colin), 1934- , *with Dee Anthony*

16640 *The official "Sgt. Pepper's Lonely Hearts Club Band" scrapbook: the making of a* hit movie musical. New York: A Wallaby Book, Pocket Books, 1978, 80 p., paper, nonf.

STILLMAN, Ron

Black phantom—SEE: *Tracker: Black phantom.*

34942 *Blood money.* New York: Diamond Books, 1991, 185 p., paper, novel. TRACKER #3.

Death hunt—SEE: *Tracker: Death hunt.*
Firekill—SEE: *Tracker: Firekill.*
Green lightning—SEE: *Tracker: Green lightning.*

34943 *Tracker.* New York: Charter/Diamond Books, 1990, 187 p., paper, novel. TRACKER #1.

34944 *Tracker: Black phantom.* New York: Diamond Books, 1991, 184 p., paper, novel. TRACKER #4.

34945 *Tracker: Death hunt.* New York: Diamond Books, 1991, 166 p., paper, novel. TRACKER #6.

34946 *Tracker: Firekill.* New York: Diamond Books, 1991, 166 p., paper, novel. TRACKER #5.

34947 *Tracker: Green lightning.* New York: Charter/Diamond Books, 1990, 172 p., paper, novel. TRACKER #2.

STILLMAN, William, *with John Fricke & Jay Scarfone*

23512 *The Wizard of Oz: the official 50th anniversary pictorial history.* New York: Warner Books, 1989, 245 p., cloth, nonf.

***STILSON, Charles B(illings), 1880-1932**

STINE, G(eorge) Harry, 1928-

34948 *The bastaard rebellion* [sic]. New York: Pinnacle Books, Windsor Publishing Corp., 1988, 432 p., paper, novel. WARBOTS #3.

34949 *Blood siege.* New York: Pinnacle Books, Windsor Publishing Corp., 1990, 352 p., paper, novel. WARBOTS #9.

34950 *Force of arms.* New York: Pinnacle Books, Windsor Publishing Corp., 1990, 368 p., paper, novel. WARBOTS #8.

34951 *Guts and glory.* New York: Pinnacle Books, Windsor Publishing Corp., 1991, 382 p., paper, novel. WARBOTS #10.

34952 *The lost battalion.* New York: Pinnacle Books, Windsor Publishing Corp., 1989, 352 p., paper, novel. WARBOTS #6.

34953 *Operation High Dragon.* New York: Pinnacle Books, Windsor Publishing Corp.,

1989, 414 p., paper, novel. WARBOTS #5.

34954 *Operation iron fist.* New York: Pinnacle Books, Windsor Publishing Corp., 1989, 368 p., paper, novel. WARBOTS #7.

34955 *Operation Steel Band.* New York: Pinnacle Books, Windsor Publishing Corp., 1988, 428 p., paper, novel. WARBOTS #2.

34956 *Sierra Madre.* New York: Pinnacle Books, Windsor Publishing Corp., 1988, 398 p., paper, novel. WARBOTS #4.

34957 *Warbots.* New York: Pinnacle Books, Windsor Publishing Corp., 1988, 476 p., paper, novel. WARBOTS #1.

as LEE CORREY

34958 *The abode of life: a Star Trek novel.* New York: A Timescape Book, Pocket Books, 1982, 207 p., paper, tele. STAR TREK #6.

34959 *Manna.* New York: DAW Books, 1984, 239 p., paper, novel.

34960 *A matter of Metalaw.* New York: DAW Books, 1986, 256 p., paper, novel.

34961 *Shuttle down.* New York: A Del Rey Book, Ballantine Books, 1981, 216 p., paper, novel.

34962 *Space doctor.* New York: A Del Rey Book, Ballantine Books, 1981, 245 p., paper, novel.

34963 *Star driver: a novel.* New York: A Del Rey Book, Ballantine Books, 1980, 245 p., paper, novel.

STINE, H(arlan) William, 1946- , *with Megan Stine*

34964 *Baseball card fever.* New York: Fawcett Columbine, 1989, 74 p., paper, novel. JEFFREY AND THE FOURTH GRADE GHOST #2.

34965 *Big brother blues.* New York: Fawcett Columbine, 1990, 75 p., paper, novel. JEFFREY AND THE FOURTH GRADE GHOST #6.

34966 *Camp Duck Down.* New York: Fawcett Columbine, 1990, 74 p., paper, novel. JEFFREY AND THE FOURTH GRADE GHOST #5.

34967 *Christmas visitors.* New York: Fawcett Columbine, 1988, 70 p., paper, novel. JEFFREY AND THE THIRD GRADE GHOST #3.

34968 *Conquest of the barbarians.* New York: Avon, 1986, 104 p., paper, novel. WIZARDS, WARRIORS & YOU #17.

38083 *The formula for trouble.* New York, Toronto: Scholastic Book Services,

1983, 110 p., paper, fiction. TWISTAPLOT #3.

34969 *Frozen danger.* New York, Toronto: Scholastic Book Services, 1981, 32 p., paper, story.

34970 *G.I. Joe: Operation: Death-ray.* New York: Ballantine Books, 1986, 88 p., paper, novel. FIND YOUR FATE—G.I. JOE #8.

34971 *G.I. Joe: Operation: poison dart.* New York: Ballantine Books, 1987, 89 p., paper, novel. FIND YOUR FATE—G.I. JOE #16.

38084 *G.I. Joe: Operation: terror trap.* New York: Ballantine Books, 1985, 89 p., paper, novel. FIND YOUR FATE—G.I. JOE #3.

34972 *Haunted halloween.* New York: Fawcett Columbine, 1988, 70 p., paper, novel. JEFFREY AND THE THIRD GRADE GHOST #2.

34973 *The imposter king.* New York: Avon, 1986, 103 p., paper, novel. WIZARDS, WARRIORS & YOU #11.

34974 *Indiana Jones and the dragon of vengeance.* New York: Ballantine Books, 1985, 118 p., paper, novel. FIND YOUR FATE ADVENTURE #8; INDIANA JONES SERIES.

34975 *Indiana Jones and the mask of the elephant.* New York: Ballantine Books, 1987, 120 p., paper, novel. FIND YOUR FATE ADVENTURE #17; INDIANA JONES SERIES.

34976 *Journey to Vernico 5.* New York, Toronto: Scholastic Inc., 1984, 93 p., paper, novel. TWISTAPLOT #12.

34977 *Jungle quest.* New York, Toronto: A Parachute Press Book, Scholastic Inc., 1984, 126 p., paper, novel. MICRO ADVENTURE #2.

34978 *The mad doctor.* New York, Toronto: Scholastic Book Services, 1978, 31 p., paper, story.

34979 *Mad science.* New York: Fawcett Columbine, 1990, 74 p., paper, novel. JEFFREY AND THE FOURTH GRADE GHOST #4.

34980 *Max is back.* New York: Fawcett Columbine, 1989, 74 p., paper, novel. JEFFREY AND THE FOURTH GRADE GHOST #1.

34981 *Max onstage.* New York: Fawcett Columbine, 1989, 74 p., paper, novel. JEFFREY AND THE THIRD GRADE GHOST #5.

34982 *Max saves the day.* New York: Fawcett Columbine, 1989, 74 p., paper, novel. JEFFREY AND THE THIRD GRADE GHOST #6.

34983　*Max's secret formula*. New York: Fawcett Columbine, 1989, 74 p., paper, novel. JEFFREY AND THE FOURTH GRADE GHOST #3.

34984　*Monster madness*. New York, Toronto: Scholastic Book Services, 1978, [64] p., paper, story.

34985　*Mysterious Max*. New York: Fawcett Columbine, 1988, 68 p., paper, novel. JEFFREY AND THE THIRD GRADE GHOST #1.

　　　Operation: death-ray—SEE: *G.I. Joe: Operation: death-ray.*

　　　Operation: poison dart—SEE: *G.I. Joe: Operation: Poison dart.*

　　　Operation Robot Assassin—SEE: *G.I. Joe: Operation Robot Assassin.*

34986　*Pet day surprise*. New York: Fawcett Columbine, 1989, 72 p., paper, novel. JEFFREY AND THE THIRD GRADE GHOST #4.

34987　*Race into the past*. New York, Toronto: Scholastic Inc., 1983, 93 p., paper, novel. TWISTAPLOT #8.

34988　*The shortest sheriff in the west*. New York, Toronto: Sprint, Scholastic Book Services, 1980, 32 p., paper, fiction.

34989　*The spear of Azzura: a Thundercats thriller*. New York: Random House, 1986, 64 p., paper, novel. THUNDERCATS SERIES.

34990　*Spellbound*. New York, Toronto: Scholastic Inc., 1985, 126 p., paper, novel. MICRO ADVENTURE #10.

34991　*Super Susan*. New York, Toronto: Sprint, Scholastic Book Services, 1979, 96 p., paper, novel.

34992　*The thundercats and the ghost warrior*. New York: Random House, 1985, 80 p., paper, novel. THUNDERCATS SERIES.

34993　*The thundercats and the snowmen of Hook Mountain*. New York: Random House, 1985, 80 p., paper, novel. THUNDERCATS SERIES.

34994　*Tournament for terror*. New York: Avon, 1986, 103 p., paper, novel. WIZARDS, WARRIORS & YOU #10.

34995　*Who kidnapped Princess Saralinda?* New York: A Parachute Press Book, Avon, 1984, 103 p., paper, novel. WIZARDS, WARLOCKS & YOU #3.

34996　*Wizards of wonder*. New York, Toronto: A Parachute Press Book, Scholastic Inc., 1985, 80 p., paper, novel. MAGIC MICRO ADVENTURE #3.

STINE, Jovial Bob—SEE: Stine, R. L.

STINE, Megan (Gray), 1950- , *with H. William Stine*

34964　*Baseball card fever*. New York: Fawcett Columbine, 1989, 74 p., paper, novel. JEFFREY AND THE FOURTH GRADE GHOST #2.

34965　*Big brother blues*. New York: Fawcett Columbine, 1990, 75 p., paper, novel. JEFFREY AND THE FOURTH GRADE GHOST #6.

34966　*Camp Duck Down*. New York: Fawcett Columbine, 1990, 74 p., paper, novel. JEFFREY AND THE FOURTH GRADE GHOST #5.

34967　*Christmas visitors*. New York: Fawcett Columbine, 1988, 70 p., paper, novel. JEFFREY AND THE THIRD GRADE GHOST #3.

34968　*Conquest of the barbarians*. New York: Avon, 1986, 104 p., paper, novel. WIZARDS, WARRIORS & YOU #17.

38083　*The formula for trouble*. New York, Toronto: Scholastic Book Services, 1983, 110 p., paper, fiction. TWISTAPLOT #3.

34969　*Frozen danger*. New York, Toronto: Scholastic Book Services, 1981, 32 p., paper, story.

34970　*G.I. Joe: Operation: Death-ray*. New York: Ballantine Books, 1986, 88 p., paper, novel. FIND YOUR FATE—G.I. JOE #8.

34971　*G.I. Joe: Operation: poison dart*. New York: Ballantine Books, 1987, 89 p., paper, novel. FIND YOUR FATE—G.I. JOE #16.

38084　*G.I. Joe: Operation: terror trap*. New York: Ballantine Books, 1985, 89 p., paper, novel. FIND YOUR FATE—G.I. JOE #3.

34972　*Haunted halloween*. New York: Fawcett Columbine, 1988, 70 p., paper, novel. JEFFREY AND THE THIRD GRADE GHOST #2.

34973　*The imposter king*. New York: Avon, 1986, 103 p., paper, novel. WIZARDS, WARRIORS & YOU #11.

34974　*Indiana Jones and the dragon of vengeance*. New York: Ballantine Books, 1985, 118 p., paper, novel. FIND YOUR FATE ADVENTURE #8; INDIANA JONES SERIES.

34975　*Indiana Jones and the mask of the elephant*. New York: Ballantine Books, 1987, 120 p., paper, novel. FIND YOUR FATE ADVENTURE #17; INDIANA JONES SERIES.

34976　*Journey to Vernico 5*. New York, Toronto: Scholastic Inc., 1984, 93 p., paper, novel. TWISTAPLOT #12.

34977　*Jungle quest*. New York, Toronto: A Parachute Press Book, Scholastic Inc.,

1984, 126 p., paper, novel. MICRO ADVENTURE #2.

34978 *The mad doctor.* New York, Toronto: Scholastic Book Services, 1978, 31 p., paper, story.

34979 *Mad science.* New York: Fawcett Columbine, 1990, 74 p., paper, novel. JEFFREY AND THE FOURTH GRADE GHOST #4.

34980 *Max is back.* New York: Fawcett Columbine, 1989, 74 p., paper, novel. JEFFREY AND THE FOURTH GRADE GHOST #1.

34981 *Max onstage.* New York: Fawcett Columbine, 1989, 74 p., paper, novel. JEFFREY AND THE THIRD GRADE GHOST #5.

34982 *Max saves the day.* New York: Fawcett Columbine, 1989, 74 p., paper, novel. JEFFREY AND THE THIRD GRADE GHOST #6.

34983 *Max's secret formula.* New York: Fawcett Columbine, 1989, 74 p., paper, novel. JEFFREY AND THE FOURTH GRADE GHOST #3.

34984 *Monster madness.* New York, Toronto: Scholastic Book Services, 1978, [64] p., paper, story.

34985 *Mysterious Max.* New York: Fawcett Columbine, 1988, 68 p., paper, novel. JEFFREY AND THE THIRD GRADE GHOST #1.

Operation: death-ray—SEE: *G.I. Joe: Operation: death-ray.*

Operation: poison dart—SEE: *G.I. Joe: Operation: Poison dart.*

Operation Robot Assassin—SEE: *G.I. Joe: Operation Robot Assassin.*

34986 *Pet day surprise.* New York: Fawcett Columbine, 1989, 72 p., paper, novel. JEFFREY AND THE THIRD GRADE GHOST #4.

34987 *Race into the past.* New York, Toronto: Scholastic Inc., 1983, 93 p., paper, novel. TWISTAPLOT #8.

34988 *The shortest sheriff in the west.* New York, Toronto: Sprint, Scholastic Book Services, 1980, 32 p., paper, fiction.

34989 *The spear of Azzura: a Thundercats thriller.* New York: Random House, 1986, 64 p., paper, novel. THUNDERCATS SERIES.

34990 *Spellbound.* New York, Toronto: Scholastic Inc., 1985, 126 p., paper, novel. MICRO ADVENTURE #10.

34991 *Super Susan.* New York, Toronto: Sprint, Scholastic Book Services, 1979, 96 p., paper, novel.

34992 *The thundercats and the ghost warrior.* New York: Random House, 1985, 80 p., paper, novel. THUNDERCATS SERIES.

34993 *The thundercats and the snowmen of Hook Mountain.* New York: Random House, 1985, 80 p., paper, novel. THUNDERCATS SERIES.

34994 *Tournament for terror.* New York: Avon, 1986, 103 p., paper, novel. WIZARDS, WARRIORS & YOU #10.

34995 *Who kidnapped Princess Saralinda?* New York: A Parachute Press Book, Avon, 1984, 103 p., paper, novel. WIZARDS, WARLOCKS & YOU #3.

34996 *Wizards of wonder.* New York, Toronto: A Parachute Press Book, Scholastic Inc., 1985, 80 p., paper, novel. MAGIC MICRO ADVENTURE #3.

STINE, R(obert) L(awrence), 1943-

34997 *Amazing adventures of me, myself, and I /* by Jovial Bob Stine. New York, Toronto: Bantam Books, 1991, 66 p., paper, novel.

34998 *The baby-sitter.* New York, Toronto: Point Fiction, Scholastic Inc., 1989, 167 p., paper, novel. BABY-SITTER #1.

34999 *The baby-sitter II.* New York, Toronto: Point Fiction, Scholastic Inc., 1991, 166 p., paper, novel. BABY-SITTER #2.

35000 *The badlands of Hark.* New York, Toronto: Scholastic Inc., 1985, [109] p., paper, novel. HARK #1.

35001 *The boyfriend.* New York, Toronto: Point Fiction, Scholastic Inc., 1990, 165 p., paper, novel.

35003 *Cavern of the Phantoms.* New York: Avon, 1986, 104 p., paper, novel. WIZARDS, WARRIORS & YOU #13.

35004 *Challenge of the Wolf Knight.* New York: Avon, 1985, 103 p., paper, novel. WIZARDS, WARRIORS & YOU #7.

35005 *Fear Street: Halloween party.* New York, London: An Archway Paperback, Pocket Books, 1990, 147 p., paper, novel. FEAR STREET SERIES.

35006 *Fear Street: Haunted.* New York, London: An Archway Paperback, Pocket Books, 1990, 164 p., paper, novel. FEAR STREET SERIES.

35007 *Fear Street: Lights out.* New York, London: An Archway Paperback, Pocket Books, 1991, 163 p., paper, novel. FEAR STREET SERIES.

35008 *Fear Street: Missing.* New York, London: An Archway Paperback, Pocket Books, 1990, 168 p., paper, novel. FEAR STREET SERIES.

35009 *Fear Street: Party summer.* New York, London: An Archway Paperback, Pocket Books, 1991, 215 p., paper, novel. FEAR STREET SERIES.

35010   *Fear Street: Silent night.* New York, London: An Archway Paperback, Pocket Books, 1991, 216 p., paper, novel. FEAR STREET SERIES.

35011   *Fear Street: Ski weekend.* New York, London: An Archway Paperback, Pocket Books, 1991, 165 p., paper, novel. FEAR STREET SERIES.

35012   *Fear Street: The fire game.* New York, London: An Archway Paperback, Pocket Books, 1991, 145 p., paper, novel. FEAR STREET SERIES.

35013   *Fear Street: The new girl.* New York, London: An Archway Paperback, Pocket Books, 1989, 168 p., paper, novel. FEAR STREET SERIES.

35014   *Fear Street: The overnight.* New York, London: An Archway Paperback, Pocket Books, 1989, 148 p., paper, novel. FEAR STREET SERIES.

35015   *Fear Street: The secret bedroom.* New York, London: An Archway Paperback, Pockct Books, 1991, 167 p., paper, novel. FEAR STREET SERIES.

35016   *Fear Street: The sleepwalker.* New York, London: An Archway Paperback, Pocket Books, 1990, 164 p., paper, novel. FEAR STREET SERIES.

35017   *Fear Street: The stepsister.* New York, London: An Archway Paperback, Pocket Books, 1990, 165 p., paper, novel. FEAR STREET SERIES.

35018   *Fear Street: The surprise party.* New York, London: An Archway Paperback, Pocket Books, 1989, 167 p., apper, novel. FEAR STREET SERIES.

35019   *Fear Street: The wrong number.* New York, London: An Archway Paperback, Pocket Books, 1990, 165 p., paper, novel. FEAR STREET SERIES.

The fire game—SEE: *Fear Street: The fire game.*

35020   *The forest of twisted dreams.* New York: A Parachute Press Book, Avon, 1984, 103 p., paper, novel. WIZARDS, WARRIORS & YOU #1.

38085   *G.I. Joe: Operation: deadly decoy.* New York: Ballantine Books, 1986, 88 p., paper, novel. FIND YOUR FATE—G.I. JOE #7.

35021   *G.I. Joe: Operation: mindbender.* New York: Ballantine Books, 1986, 88 p., paper, novel. FIND YOUR FATE—G.I. JOE #9.

35022   *G.I. Joe: Serpentor and the mummy warrior.* New York: Ballantine Books, 1987, 88 p., paper, novel. FIND YOUR FATE—G.I. JOE #20.

35023   *Ghostbusters II: a novel* / by Jovial Bob Stine. New York, Toronto: Scholastic Inc., 1989, [46] p., paper, movie. GHOSTBUSTERS #2.

38086   *Golden Girl and the vanishing unicorn.* New York: Ballantine Books, 1986, 72 p., paper, novel. FIND YOUR FATE—GOLDEN GIRL #1.

35024   *Golden sword of Dragonwalk.* New York, Toronto: Scholastic Book Services, 1983, 94 p., paper, novel. TWISTAPLOT #4.

Halloween party—SEE: *Fear Street: Halloween party.*

Haunted—SEE: *Fear Street: Haunted.*

35025   *Horrors of the haunted museum.* New York, Toronto: Scholastic Inc., 1983, 93 p., paper, novel. TWISTAPLOT #9.

35026   *Indiana Jones and the ape slaves of Howling Island.* New York: Ballantine Books, 1987, 116 p., paper, novel. FIND YOUR FATE ADVENTURE #16; INDIANA JONES SERIES.

35027   *Indiana Jones and the cult of the mummy's crypt.* New York: Ballantine Books, 1985, 117 p., paper, novel. FIND YOUR FATE ADVENTURE #7; INDIANA JONES SERIES.

35028   *Indiana Jones and the curse of Horror Island.* New York: Ballantine Books, 1984, 118 p., paper, novel. FIND YOUR FATE ADVENTURE #1; INDIANA JONES SERIES.

35029   *Indiana Jones and the giants of the Silver Tower.* New York: Ballantine Books, 1984, 122 p., paper, novel. FIND YOUR FATE ADVENTURE #3; INDIANA JONES SERIES.

38087   *Instant millionaire.* New York, Toronto: Scholastic Inc., 1984, 93 p., paper, fiction. TWISTAPLOT #14.

35030   *The invaders of Hark.* New York, Toronto: Scholastic Inc., 1985, [111] p., paper, novel. HARK #2.

38088   *James Bond in Win, place or die.* New York: Ballantine Books, 1985, 118 p., paper, novel. FIND YOUR FATE ADVENTURE #11; JAMES BOND SERIES.

35031   *Jerks-in-training.* New York, Toronto: An Apple Paperback, Scholastic Inc., 1991, 130 p., paper, novel. SPACE CADETS #1.

35032   *Jungle raid.* New York: Ballantine Books, 1988, 121 p., paper, novel. G.I. JOE #5.

Lights out—SEE: *Fear Street: Lights out.*

35033   *Losers in space.* New York, Toronto: An Apple Paperback, Scholastic Inc., 1991, 130 p., paper, novel. SPACE CADETS #2.

Missing—SEE: *Fear Street: Missing.*

35034   *My secret indentity: a novelization* / by Jovial Bob Stine. New York, Toronto:

An Apple Paperback, Scholastic Inc., 1989, 103 p., paper, tele.

The new girl—SEE: *Fear Street: The new girl.*

Operation: mindbender—SEE: *G.I. Joe: Operation: mindbender.*

The overnight—SEE: *Fear Street: The overnight.*

Party summer—SEE: *Fear Street: Party summer.*

The secret bedroom—SEE: *Fear Street: The secret bedroom.*

Serpentor and the mummy warrior—SEE: *G.I. Joe: Serpentor and the mummy warrior.*

35035 *Siege of Serpentor.* New York: Ballantine Books, 1988, 120 p., paper, novel. G.I. JOE #1.

Silent night—SEE: *Fear Street: Silent night.*

Ski weekend—SEE: *Fear Street: Ski weekend.*

The sleepwalker—SEE: *Fear Street: The sleepwalker.*

35036 *The snowman.* New York, Toronto: Point Fiction, Scholastic Inc., 1991, 181 p., paper, novel.

35037 *Spaceballs: the book* / by Jovial Bob Stine. New York, Toronto: Scholastic Inc., 1987, 122 p., paper, movie.

The stepsister—SEE: *Fear Street: The stepsister.*

The surprise party—SEE: *Fear Street: The surprise party.*

35038 *The time raider.* New York, Toronto: Scholastic Book Services, 1982, 94 p., paper, novel. TWISTAPLOT #1.

35039 *Twisted.* New York, Toronto: A Point Book, Scholastic Inc., 1987, 168 p., paper, novel.

The wrong number—SEE: *Fear Street: The wrong number.*

as ERIC AFFABEE

35040 *Attack on the King.* New York: Avon, 1986, 104 p., paper, novel. WIZARDS, WARRIORS & YOU #16.

35041 *The Dragon Queen's revenge.* New York: Avon, 1986, 103 p., paper, novel. WIZARDS, WARRIORS & YOU #9.

38089 *G.I. Joe: The Everglades Swamp terror.* New York: Ballantine Books, 1986, 88 p., paper, novel. FIND YOUR FATE—G.I. JOE #5.

35042 *G.I. Joe: Operation: Star Raider.* New York: Ballantine Books, 1985, 88 p., paper, novel. FIND YOUR FATE—G.I. JOE #1.

Operation: Star Raider—SEE: *G.I. Joe: Operation: Star Raider.*

35043 *The siege of the dragonriders.* New York: A Parachute Press Book, Avon, 1984, 103 p., paper, novel. WIZARDS, WARLOCKS & YOU #2.

STIRLING, S(tephen) M(ichael), 1953-

35044 *Marching through Georgia.* New York: Baen Books, 1988, 410 p., paper, novel. DRAKA #1.

35045 *Power.* Riverdale, NY: Baen Books, 1991, 323 p., paper, anth.

35046 *Snowbrother.* New York: A Signet Book, New American Library, 1985, 251 p., paper, novel. FIFTH MILLENNIUM #1.

35047 *The stone dogs.* New York: Baen Books, 1990, 522 p., paper, novel. DRAKA #3.

35048 *Under the yoke.* New York: Baen Books, 1989, 501 p., paper, novel. DRAKA #2.

with David Drake

22186 *The forge.* Riverdale, NY: Baen Books, 1991, 323 p., paper, novel. GENERALS #1.

with Frank D. McSherry Jr. & Charles G. Waugh & Martin Harry Greenberg

24590 *The fantastic Civil War.* Riverdale, NY: Baen Books, 1991, 307 p., paper, anth.

24591 *Fantastic World War II.* New York: Baen Books, 1990, 281 p., paper, anth.

with Shirley Meier

29714 *The cage.* New York: Baen, 1989, 402 p., paper, novel. FIFTH MILLENNIUM #3.

29715 *The sharpest edge.* New York: A Signet Book, New American Library, 1986, 255 p., paper, novel. FIFTH MILLENNIUM #2.

with Shirley Meier & Karen Wehrstein

29716 *Shadow's son.* Riverdale, NY: Baen Books, 1991, 442 p., paper, novel. FIFTH MILLENNIUM #4.

with Larry Niven & Dean Ing & Jerry Pournelle

26289 *The Man-Kzin wars II.* New York: Baen Books, 1989, ix+306 p., paper, coll. MAN-KZIN WARS #2.

with Larry Niven & Jerry Pournelle & Poul Anderson

16455 *The Man-Kzin wars III.* New York: Baen Books, 1990, 310 p., paper, coll. MAN-KZIN WARS #3.

with Jerry Pournelle

31775 *The children's hour.* Riverdale, NY: Baen Books, 1991, 316 p., paper, novel. MAN-KZIN WARS.

31776 *Go tell the Spartans.* Riverdale, NY: Baen Books, 1991, 345 p., paper, novel. FALKENBERG'S LEGION #4.

STITH, John E(dward), 1947-

35049 *Death tolls.* New York: Ace Books, 1987, 230 p., paper, novel.

35050 *Deep quarry.* New York: Ace Books, 1989, 186 p., paper, novel.

35051 *Memory blank.* New York: Ace Science Fiction Books, 1986, 230 p., paper, novel.

35052 *Redshift rendezvous.* New York: Ace Books, 1990, 256 p., paper, novel.

35053 *Scapescope.* New York: Ace Science Fiction Books, 1984, 218 p., paper, novel.

STIVENS, Dal(las George), 1911-

35054 *The unicorn, and other tales.* Sydney, Australia: Wild & Woolley, 1976, 127 p., cloth, coll.

STOCK, Stuart H., *with Kenneth Von Gunden*

35055 *Twenty all-time great science fiction films.* Westport, CT: Arlington House, 1982, v+250 p., cloth, nonf.

STOCKBRIDGE, Grant, house pseud.

31139 *Builder of the black empire.* New York: Dimedia, 1980, [96] p., paper, novel. SPIDER SERIES. [By Norvell W. Page].

31140 *The city destroyer.* New York: Pocket Books, 1975, 157 p., paper, novel. SPIDER #3. [By Norvell W. Page].

31141 *City of flaming shadows.* New York: A Berkley Medallion Book, 1970, 175 p., paper, novel. SPIDER #4. [By Norvell W. Page].

31142 *Corpse cargo: the Spider thriller.* New York: Dimedia, 1985, 192 p., paper, novel. SPIDER #2. [By Norvell W. Page].

31143 *Death and the Spider.* New York: Pocket Books, 1975, 143 p., paper, novel. SPIDER #4. [By Norvell W. Page].

31144 *Death reign of the vampire king.* New York: Pocket Books, 1975, 144 p., paper, novel. SPIDER #1. [By Norvell W. Page].

31145 *Hordes of the red butcher.* New York: Pocket Books, 1975, 158 p., paper, novel. SPIDER #2. [By Norvell W. Page].

31146 *Master of the death madness.* New York: Dimedia, 1980, [96] p., paper, novel. SPIDER SERIES. [By Norvell W. Page].

31147 *Overlord of the damned.* New York: Dimedia, 1980, [96] p., paper, novel. SPIDER SERIES. [By Norvell W. Page].

31148 *Prince of evil.* New York: Dimedia, 1985, [192] p., paper, novel. SPIDER SERIES. [By Norvell W. Page].

31149 *Satan's death blast: the Spider thriller.* New York: Dimedia, 1984, 196 p., paper, novel. SPIDER #1. [By Norvell W. Page].

Secret city of crime—SEE: *The Spider, master of men!*

The Spider and the pain master—SEE: *The Spider, master of men!*

31150 *The Spider, master of men!* New York: Carroll & Graf, 1991, 316 p., paper, coll. SPIDER SERIES. [By Norvell W. Page; includes *Secret city of crime*; and, *The Spider and the pain master*].

35056 *The Spider, master of men!* New York: Carroll & Graf, 1991, 316 p., paper, coll. SPIDER #2. [Includes *Dictator of the damned*; and, *The mill-town massacres*]. [By Emile C. Tepperman].

31151 *Wings of the black death.* New York: A Berkley Medallion Book, 1969, 144 p., paper, novel. SPIDER #3. [By Norvell W. Page].

STOCKTON, Francis R.—SEE: Stockton, Frank R.

STOCKTON, Frank R. [i.e., Francis Richard Stockton], 1834-1902

35057 *The fairy tales of Frank Stockton.* New York: A Signet Classic, 1990, 432 p., paper, coll. [Edited by Jack Zipes].

STOKER, Abraham—SEE: Stoker, Bram

STOKER, Bram [i.e., Abraham Stoker], 1847-1912

35058 *The annotated Dracula.* New York: Clarkson N. Potter, 1975, xviii+362 p., cloth, novel. [Edited by Leonard Wolf].

35059 *The essential Dracula: the completely illustrated & annotated edition of Bram Stoker's classic novel.* New York: Mayflower Books, 1979, 320 p., cloth, novel. [Edited by Raymond McNally & Radu Florescu].

13726 *Dracula.* Westminster, England: Archibald Constable, 1897, 390 p., cloth, novel.

13726A retitled: *The illustrated Dracula: original text.* Secaucus, NJ: Chartwell Books, 1975, 184 p., cloth, novel. [Includes stills from the Dracula movies].

35060 *Midnight tales.* London: Peter Owen, 1990, 182 p., cloth, coll. [Edited by Peter Haining].

35061 *Shades of Dracula: Bram Stoker's uncollected stories.* London: William Kimber, 1982, 204 p., cloth, coll. [Edited by Peter Haining].

with Tom Barling

17401 *Dracula.* London: Corgi Books, 1976, 96 p., paper, novel. [Adapted from the original novel by Stoker].

with Joan Cameron

19240 *Dracula.* Loughborough, England: Ladybird, 1984, 51 p., paper, novel. [Adapted from Stoker's novel].

with John Davey

21186 *Tales of horror.* London: Heinemann Educational, 1983, v+56 p., paper, coll. [Adapted by Davey from Stoker's original tales].

with Derek Farmer

22864 *Blood from the mummy's tomb.* London: Fleshcreepers, Century Hutchinson, 1986, 144 p., cloth, novel. [An adaptation of Bram Stoker's *Jewel of seven stars*].

with Derek Farmer writing as DEREK ALLEN

22864A *Blood from the mummy's tomb.* New York: Barron's Educational Series, 1988, 138 p., cloth?, novel. [An adaptation of Stoker's *Jewel of seven stars*; previously published under the name Derek Farmer].

with Stephanie Spinner

34578 *Dracula.* New York: Random House, 1982, 94 p., cloth, novel. [Adapted from Stoker's novel].

STOKER, John, *with Mary Wollstonecraft Shelley*

35062 *The illustrated Frankenstein.* Newton Abbot, England: Westridge Books, 1980, 128 p., paper, nonf.

STOKES, Coleman—SEE: Coleman, Clay

STOKES, Manning Lee, 1911-1976

as NICK CARTER

19607 *The red rays.* New York: Award Books; London: Tandem Books, 1969, 153 p., paper, novel. NICK CARTER SERIES.

as JEFFREY LORD

09198 *The bronze axe.* New York: Macfadden-Bartell, 1969, 191 p., paper, novel. RICHARD BLADE #1.

09199 *The jade warrior.* New York: Macfadden-Bartell, 1969, 192 p., paper, novel. RICHARD BLADE #2.

09200 *Jewel of Tharn.* New York: Macfadden-Bartell, 1969, 160 p., paper, novel. RICHARD BLADE #3.

09201 *Liberator of Jedd.* New York: Macfadden-Bartell, 1971, 224 p., paper, novel. RICHARD BLADE #5.

09202 *Monster of the maze.* New York: Macfadden-Bartell, 1972, 192 p., paper, novel. RICHARD BLADE #6.

09203 *Pearl of Patmos: the Richard Blade series.* New York: Pinnacle Books, 1973, 190 p., paper, novel. RICHARD BLADE #7.

09204 *Slave of Sarma.* New York: Macfadden-Bartell, 1970, 192 p., paper, novel. RICHARD BLADE #4.

09205 *Undying world.* New York: Pinnacle Books, 1973, 189 p., paper, novel. RICHARD BLADE #8.

as KEN STANTON

13549 *Operation mermaid.* New York: Manor Books, 1974, 192 p., paper, novel. AQUANAUTS #11.

13548 *Operation sea monster.* New York: Manor Books, 1974, 190 p., paper, novel. AQUANAUTS #10.

AUTHOR INDEX

STOLBOV, Bruce

35063 *Last fall.* Garden City, NY: Doubleday & Co., 1987, 175 p., cloth, novel.

STOLZ, Mary [i.e., Mary Slattery Stolz Jaleski], 1920-

35064 *Cat in the mirror.* New York: Harper & Row, 1975, 199 p., cloth, novel.
35065 *Quentin Corn.* Boston: David R. Godine, 1985, 121 p., cloth, novel.

*STONE, Alma, 1908-

STONE, Andrew—SEE: Stone, Andy

STONE, Andy [i.e., Andrew Stone]

35066 *Song of the Kingdom.* Garden City, NY: Doubleday & Co., 1979, 229 p., cloth, novel.

STONE, Charlotte

35067 *Cheon of Weltanland: The four wishes.* New York: DAW Books, 1983, 205 p., paper, novel.
The four wishes—SEE: Cheon of Weltanland: The four wishes.

STONE, Elna

35068 *The secret of the willows.* New York: Belmont Books, 1970, 171 p., paper, novel.
35069 *The visions of Esmaree.* New York: St. Martin's Press, 1976, 264 p., cloth, novel.
35070 *The visitation.* New York: St. Martin's Press, 1980, 314 p., cloth, novel.

STONE, George

35071 *Blizzard: a novel.* New York: Grosset & Dunlap, 1977, x+214 p., cloth, novel.
35071A retitled: *Freeze.* London: Corgi Books, 1979, 220 p., paper, novel.

STONE, Graham (Brice), 1926-

35072 *Australian science fiction index: supplement, 1968/1975.* Sydney, Australia: Australian Science Fiction Association, 1976, vii+48 p., paper, nonf.
07700 *Index to British science fiction magazines, 1934-1953.* Canberra City, Australia: Australian Science Fiction Association, 1968-71, 176 in 5 v., paper, nonf.

[Corrected entry; published anonymously].
35073 *Index to British science fiction magazines, 1934-1953.* Canberra & Sydney, Australia: Australian Science Fiction Association, 1977-80, 3 v. (vol. 1-viii+213 p., vol. 2-vii+174, vol. 3-vii+221 p.), paper, nonf. [Expanded edition].

STONE, Harry, 1926-

35074 *Dickens and the invisible world: fairy tales, fantasy, and novel-making.* Bloomington, IN: Indiana University Press, 1979, xii+370 p., cloth, nonf.

*STONE, Idella Purnell, 1901-1982

*STONE, Isobel, 1891?-1969?

STONE, Josephine Rector [pseud. of Jeanne Dixon], 1936-

35075 *Green is for Galanx.* New York: An Argo Book, Atheneum, 1980, 170 p., cloth, novel.
35076 *The mudhead.* New York: An Argo Book, Atheneum, 1980, 140 p., cloth, novel.
35077 *Praise all the moons of morning.* New York: An Argo Book, Atheneum, 1979, 172 p., cloth, novel.
35078 *Those who fall from the Sun.* New York: Atheneum, 1978, 153 p., cloth, novel.

*STONE, Leslie F(rances), 1905-1991

STONE, Mike

35079 *Allison's baby.* New York: A Dell Book, 1988, 272 p., paper, novel.

STONE, Paul, pseud.

35080 *Devil meat.* Wilmington, DE: An Eros Goldstripe Publication, 1975, 180 p., paper, novel.

STONE, Richard, 1940-

35081 *The devil's engineering.* Sevenoaks, Kent, England: Ashgrove, 1980, 256 p., cloth, novel.

STONE-BLACKBURN, Susan (Beth Cole), 1941-

35082 *Robertson Davies, playwright: a search for the self on the Canadian stage.* Vancouver, British Columbia, Canada: University of British Columbia Press, 1985, 249 p., cloth, nonf.

STONER, Samuel G.

35083 *Science fiction and fantasy: a price guide to hardback first trade printings.* Portland, OR: Samuel G. Stoner, 1988, v+86 p., paper, nonf.

STONOR, Oliver—SEE: Bishop, Morchard

STOREY, Alice

38090 *Golden Girl in the land of dreams.* New York: Ballantine Books, 1986, 72 p., paper, novel. FIND YOUR FATE—GOLDEN GIRL #2.

STOREY, Anthony, 1928-

35084 *The centre holds: a novel.* London: Calder & Boyars, 1973, 167 p., cloth, novel. MESSIAH #2.
35085 *The rector: a novel.* London: Calder & Boyars, 1970, 167 p., cloth, novel. MESSIAH #1.
35086 *The saviour: a novel.* London: Marion Boyars, 1978, 186 p., cloth, novel. MESSIAH #3.

STOREY, (Elizabeth) Margaret (Carlton), 1926-

35087 *The double wizard.* London, Boston: Faber & Faber, 1979, 113 p., cloth, novel. TIMOTHY, ELLEN & MELINDA #5.
35088 *A quarrel of witches.* London: Faber & Faber, 1970, 135 p., cloth, novel. TIMOTHY, ELLEN & MELINDA #2.
35089 *The sleeping witch.* London, Boston: Faber & Faber, 1971, 141 p., cloth, novel. TIMOTHY, ELLEN & MELINDA #3.
35090 *The stone sorcerer.* London, Boston: Faber & Faber, 1967, 84 p., cloth, novel.
35090A retitled: *The stone wizard.* London, Boston: Faber & Faber, 1979, 84 p., cloth, novel.
       The stone wizard—SEE: *The stone sorcerer.*
35091 *Timothy and the two witches.* London, Boston: Faber & Faber, 1967, 76 p., cloth, novel. TIMOTHY, ELLEN & MELINDA #1.
35092 *A war of wizards.* London, Boston: Faber & Faber, 1976, 133 p., cloth, novel. TIMOTHY, ELLEN & MELINDA #4.

STORM, Hyemeyohsts, 1935-

35093 *Song of Heyoehkah.* San Francisco: Harper & Row, 1981, 302 p., cloth, novel.

STOROSCHUK, Stephen, *with Gerry Goldberg & Fred Corbett*

20576 *Nighttouch.* Don Mills, Ontario, Canada: General Publishing, 1977, 156 p., cloth, anth. [Includes some nonfiction and verse].

STORR, Catherine (Cole), 1913-

35094 *The castle boy.* London: Faber & Faber, 1983, 160 p., cloth, novel.
       The magic drawing pencil—SEE: *Marianne dreams.*
35095 *Marianne dreams.* London: Faber & Faber, 1958, 191 p., cloth, novel.
35095A retitled: *The magic drawing pencil.* New York: A. S. Barnes & Co., 1960, 191 p., cloth, novel.
35096 *Unnatural fathers.* London: Quartet Books, 1976, 153 p., cloth, novel.

STORY, Jack Trevor, 1917-1991

35097 *Up river.* London: Duckworth, 1979, 154 p., cloth, novel.
35097A retitled: *The screwrape lettuce.* Manchester, England: Savoy Books, 1982, 154 p., paper, novel.

STOUGHTON, Richard P.

35098 *ULTIMA One.* North Hollywood, CA: American Art Enterprises, 1980, 191 p., paper, novel.

STOUT, Amy (Leah), 1960-

with Lou Aronica & Patrick LoBrutto & Shawna McCarthy

16798 *Full spectrum 2.* New York: A Foundation Book, Doubleday, 1989, xi+464 p., cloth, anth.

with Lou Aronica & Betsy Mitchell

16799 *Full spectrum 3.* New York: A Foundation Book, Doubleday, 1991, x+535 p., cloth, anth. [Winner of the *Locus* Award for Best Anthology, 1991 (1992)].

STOUT, Mike

35099 *W.H.A.M.* London: Sphere Books, 1971, 157 p., paper, novel.

STOUT, Rex (Todhunter), 1886-1975

35100 *Under the Andes.* New York: Penzler Books, Mysterious Press, 1985, xix+286 p., cloth, novel.

STOUT, Tim, 1946-

35101 *The Doomsdeath chronicles.* London: Abelard, 1980, 126 p., cloth, coll.
35102 *Hollow laughter.* London: Abelard, 1978, 126 p., cloth, coll.
35103 *The raging.* London: Grafton, 1987, 256 p., paper, novel.

*STOUTENBURG, Adrien (Pearl), 1916-1982

STOVALL, Floyd, 1896-

35104 *Edgar Allan Poe the poet: essays new and old on the man and his work.* Charlottesville, VA: University Press of Virginia, 1969, vii+273 p., cloth, nonf. coll.

STOVER, A., with Mark Ronald

35105 *Brains for Janes.* New Orleans, LA [i.e., Los Angeles, CA]: Pirate Press, 1948, 47 p., cloth, anth.

STOVER, Leon (Eugene), 1929-

35106 *Harry Harrison.* Boston: Twayne Publishers, 1990, xviii+141 p., cloth, nonf.
35107 *Robert A. Heinlein.* Boston: Twayne Publishers, 1987, 147 p., cloth, nonf.
35108 *The shaving of Karl Marx: an instant novel of ideas, after that manner of Thomas Love Peacock, in which Lenin and H. G. Wells talk about the political meaning of the scientific romances.* Lake Forest, IL: Chiron Press, 1982, iii+118 p., paper, novel.

with Harry Harrison

25299 *Stonehenge: where Atlantis died.* New York: Tor, A Tom Doherty Associates Book, 1983, 347 p., paper, novel. [Expanded from #06856].

with H. G. Wells

35109 *The prophetic soul: a reading of H. G. Wells' Things to come, together with his film treatment, Whither mankind?, and postproduction script (both never before published).* Jefferson, NC: McFarland & Co., 1987, xix+301 p., cloth, nonf.

STOW, (Julian) Randolph, 1935-

35110 *Visitants.* London: Secker & Warburg, 1979, 188 p., cloth, novel.

STRACHAN, Ian

35111 *Picking up the threads.* London: Hippo, 1989, 110 p., paper, novel.

STRACHEY, Barbara [i.e., Barbara Strachey Halpern], 1912-

35112 *Journeys of Frodo: an atlas of J. R. R. Tolkien's The Lord of the Rings.* London, Boston: George Allen & Unwin, 1981, [110] p., cloth, nonf.

STRACZYNSKI, J(oseph) Michael, 1954-

35113 *Demon night.* New York: E. P. Dutton, 1988, 340 p., cloth, novel.
35113 *OtherSyde.* New York: E. P. Dutton, 1990, 294 p., cloth, novel.
35114 *Tales from The New Twilight Zone.* New York, Toronto: Spectra, Bantam Books, 1989, xiii+255 p., paper, tele. coll.

STRAKER, Philip, pseud.—SEE: Lee, Edward

STRASBERG, Daoma—SEE: Winston, Daoma

STRASSER, Todd, 1950-

35116 *The mall from outer space.* New York, Toronto: Scholastic Inc., 1987, 116 p., paper, novel.

STRASSL, Hubert—SEE: Walker, Hugh

STRATEMEYER, Edward L., 1862-1930

as VICTOR APPLETON

15786 *Don Sturdy in the port of lost ships; or, Adrift in the Sargasso Sea.* New York: Grosset & Dunlap, 1926, 214 p., cloth, novel. DON STURDY #6.

with Howard R. Garis as ROY ROCKWOOD

NOTE: Stratemeyer outlined these books, which were then completed by Garis.

12339 *Five thousand miles underground; or, The mystery of the center of the Earth.* New York: Cupples & Leon, 1908, 242 p., cloth, novel. GREAT MARVEL SERIES #3.

12340 *Lost on the Moon; or, In quest of the field of diamonds.* New York: Cupples & Leon, 1911, 248 p., cloth, novel. GREAT MARVEL SERIES #5.

12341 *On a torn-away world; or, The captives of the great earthquake.* New York: Cupples & Leon, 1913, 246 p., cloth, novel. GREAT MARVEL SERIES #6.

12342 *Through space to Mars; or, The longest journey on record.* New York: Cupples & Leon, 1910, 248 p., cloth, novel. GREAT MARVEL SERIES #4.

12343 *Through the air to the North Pole; or, The wonderful cruise of the Electric Monarch.* New York: Cupples & Leon, 1906, 240 p., cloth, novel. GREAT MARVEL SERIES #1.

12344 *Under the ocean to the South Pole; or, The strange cruise of the submarine wonder.* New York: Cupples & Leon, 1907, 248 p., cloth, novel. GREAT MARVEL SERIES #2.

STRATTON, Monica—SEE: Dickens, Monica

STRAUB, Peter (Francis), 1943-

35117 *20 under 35.* London: Sceptre, 1988, p., cloth, anth.

35118 *Blue rose.* San Francisco, Columbia, PA: Underwood-Miller, 1985, 92 p., cloth, novel.

35119 *Floating dragon.* San Francisco, Columbia, PA: Underwood-Miller, 1982, 560 p., cloth, novel.
Full circle—SEE: *Julia.*

35120 *The general's wife.* West Kingston, RI: Donald M. Grant, Publisher, 1982, 128 p., cloth, story. [A previously unpublished portion of the original manuscript of *Floating dragon*].

35121 *Ghost story.* New York: Coward, McCann & Geoghegan, 1979, 483 p., cloth, novel.

35122 *Houses without doors.* London: Grafton Books, 1990, [288] p., cloth, coll.

35123 *If you could see me now.* New York: Coward, McCann & Geoghegan, 1977, 287 p., cloth, novel.

35124 *Julia.* New York: Coward, McCann & Geoghegan, 1975, 287 p., cloth, novel.

35124A retitled: *Full circle.* London: Corgi Books, 1977, 254 p., paper, novel.

35125 *Koko.* New York: E. P. Dutton, 1988, xi+562 p., paper, novel. [Winner of the World Fantasy Award for Best Fantasy Novel, 1988 (1989)].

35126 *Mrs. God.* Hampton Falls, NH: Donald M. Grant, 1990, 195 p., cloth, novel.
Shadow land—SEE: *Shadowland.*

35127 *Shadowland.* New York: Coward, McCann & Geoghegan, 1980, 417 p., cloth, novel.

35127A retitled: *Shadow land.* London: Collins, 1981, 417 p., cloth, novel.

35128 *Wild animals: three novels: Julia; If you could see me now; Under Venus.* New York: Viking, G. P. Putnam's Sons, 1984, 591 p., cloth, coll.

with Stephen King

27287 *The Talisman.* New York: Viking, G. P. Putnam's Sons, 1984, x+646 p., cloth, novel.

STRAUCH, Katina—SEE: Alexis, Katina

STRAUS, Dennis (David), 1940?- , with Sheila Ascher as ASCHER/STRAUS

16815 *The other planet: a novel.* Kingston, NY: McPherson, 1988, 244 p., cloth, novel.

26090 *Red moon/red lake.* New York: Top Stories, 1984, 28 p., paper, story.

16816 *Red moon, red lake: stories.* Kingston, NY: McPherson, 1988, 128 p., cloth, coll.

STRAUSS, Erwin S(heehan), 1943-

35129 *The blackdex and the bluedex.* Cambridge, MA: MIT Science Fiction Society, 1965, 232 p., paper, nonf.

35130 *The complete guide to science fiction conventions.* Port Townsend, WA: Loompanics Unlimited, 1983, 56 p., paper, nonf.

35131 *The index to the S-F magazines 1966.* Cambridge, MA: MIT Science Fiction Society, 1967, 56 p., paper, nonf.

STRAUSS, Victoria

35132 *Worldstone.* New York: The Four Winds Press, 1985, 245 p., cloth, novel.

STREIB, Dan(iel Thomas), 1928-

38091 *The bloody rose.* New York: Fawcett Gold Medal, 1985, 215 p., paper, novel. COUNTER FORCE #8.

35133 *Counter Force.* New York: Fawcett Gold Medal, 1983, 183 p., paper, novel. COUNTER FORCE #1.

38092 *Death shuttle.* New York: Fawcett Gold Medal, 1983, 186 p., paper, novel. COUNTER FORCE #3.

38093 *The karate killers.* New York: Fawcett Gold Medal, 1983, 199 p., paper, novel. COUNTER FORCE #4.

35134 *The mind breakers: a Counter Force novel.* New York: Fawcett Gold Medal, 1984, 197 p., paper, novel. COUNTER FORCE #7.

38094 *Terror for sale.* New York: Fawcett Gold Medal, 1984, 170 p., paper, novel. COUNTER FORCE #5.

38095 *Titans duel.* New York: Fawcett Gold Medal, 1984, 200 p., paper, novel. COUNTER FORCE #6.

38096 *The Trident hijacking.* New York: Fawcett Gold Medal, 1983, 200 p., paper, novel. COUNTER FORCE #2.

STRETE, Craig (Kee), 1950-

35135 *The bleeding man, and other science fiction stories.* New York: Greenwillow Books, 1977, ix+118 p., cloth, coll.

35136 *Death chants: short stories* / by Craig Kee Strete. New York: Doubleday & Co., 1988, xii+188 p., cloth, coll.

35137 *Death in the spirit house* / by Craig Kee Strete. New York: Doubleday & Co., A Foundation Book, 1988, 179 p., cloth, novel. [Based on the then-unpublished novel, *Face in the snow* / by Ron Montana].

38097 *Dreams that burn in the night.* Garden City, NY: Doubleday & Co., 1982, 183 p., cloth, novel.

35138 *If all else fails...* Garden City, NY: Doubleday & Co., 1980, viii+182 p., cloth, coll. [Originally published in 1976 in the Netherlands as *Als al andere faalt*].

as SOVEREIGN FALCONER

35139 *To make death love us.* Garden City, NY: Doubleday & Co., 1987, 181 p., cloth, novel.

STRICK, Philip, 1939-

35140 *Antigrav.* London: Hutchinson, 1975, 184 p., cloth, anth.

35141 *Science fiction movies.* London: Octopus, 1976, 160 p., cloth, nonf.

STRICKLAND, A(lbert) W(esley), 1940-

35142 *A collection of great science fiction films.* Bloomington, IN: T.I.S. Publications, 1979, 179 p., cloth, nonf.

with Forrest J Ackerman

15944 *A reference guide to American science fiction films, volume 1.* Bloomington, IN: T.I.S. Publications, 1981, xvii+397 p., cloth, nonf. [Only volume published].

STRICKLAND, (William) Brad(ley), 1947-

35143 *Children of the knife.* New York: An Onyx Book, 1990, 317 p., paper, novel.

35144 *Moon dreams.* New York: A Signet Book, New American Library, 1988, 288 p., paper, novel. JEREMY MOON #1.

35145 *Nul's quest.* New York: A Signet Book, New American Library, 1989, 274 p., paper, novel. JEREMY MOON #2.

35146 *ShadowShow.* New York: An Onyx Book, New American Library, 1988, 372 p., paper, novel.

35147 *To stand beneath the sun.* New York: A Signet Book, New American Library, 1986, 256 p., paper, novel.

35148 *Wizard's mole: a fantasy novel.* New York: A Roc Book, 1991, 284 p., paper, novel. JEREMY MOON #3.

STRIEBER, (Louis) Whitley, 1945-

35150 *Billy.* New York: G. P. Putnam's Sons, 1990, 317 p., cloth, novel.

35151 *Black Magic.* New York: William Morrow & Co., 1982, 298 p., cloth, novel.

35158A *Catmagic.* New York: Tor, A Tom Doherty Associates Book, 1986, 441 p., cloth, novel. [Previously published under the joint byline "Jonathan Barry" and Whitley Strieber].

35152 *The hunger.* New York: William Morrow & Co., 1981, 320 p., cloth, novel.

35153 *Majestic.* New York: G. P. Putnam's Sons, 1989, 317 p., cloth, novel. [Partially based on *An account of a meeting with denizens of another world, 1871* / by William Robert Loosley (i.e., David Langford)].

38098 *Majestic.* London: Macdonald & Co., 1990, [320] p., cloth, novel. [Partially based on *An account of a meeting with denizens of another world, 1871* / by William Robert Loosley (i.e., David Langford); revised edition].

35154 *The Night Church* New York: Simon & Schuster, 1983, 317 p., cloth, novel.

35155 *The wild.* New York: Tor, A Tom Doherty Associates Book, 1991, 378 p., paper, novel.

35156 *Wolf of Shadows.* New York, San Francisco: Alfred A. Knopf/Sierra Club Books, 1985, 105 p., cloth, novel.

35157 *The Wolfen.* New York: William Morrow & Co., 1978, 252 p., cloth, novel.

as JONATHAN BARRY *and* WHITLEY STRIEBER

35158 *Catmagic.* New York: Tor, A Tom Doherty Associates Book, 1986, 441 p., cloth, novel.

with James W. Kunetka

27585 *Nature's end: the consequences of the twentieth century.* New York: Warner Books, 1986, 418 p., cloth, novel.
27586 *Warday, and the journey onward.* New York: Holt, Rinehart & Winston, 1984, ix+374 p., cloth, novel.

STRINGER, Arthur (John Arbuthnott), 1874-1950, *with Russell Holman*

37847 *The story without a name.* New York: Grosset & Dunlap, 1924, 316 p., cloth, movie.

STROTHER, Pat—SEE: Wallace, Pat

STRUGATSKY, Arkady (Natanovich), 1925-1991, *with Boris Strugatsky*

35159 *Beetle in the anthill.* New York: Macmillan, 1980, ix+217 p., cloth, novel. MAXIM TRILOGY #1. [Translation by Antonina W. Bouis of *Zhuk v muraveinike*].
35160 *Definitely maybe: a manuscript discovered under unusual circumstances.* New York: Macmillan Publishing Co.; London: Collier Macmillan Publishers, 1978, xi+143 p., cloth, novel. [Translation by Antonina W. Bouis of *Za milliard let do kontsa sveta*].
35161 *Far rainbow; The second invasion from Mars.* New York: Macmillan; London: Collier Macmillan, 1979, ix+240 p., cloth, coll. [Translation by Antonina W. Bouis of *Dalekaia raduga*; and by Gary Kern of *Vtoroe nashestvie Marsian*].
35162 *The final circle of paradise.* New York: DAW Books, 1976, 172 p., paper, novel. [Translation by Leonid Renen of *Khishchne veshchi veka*].
35163 *Monday begins on Saturday.* New York: DAW Books, 1977, 222 p., paper, novel. [Translation by Leonid Renen of *Ponedel'nik nachinaetsia v subbotu*].
35164 *Noon: 22nd century.* New York: Macmillan; London: Collier Macmillan, 1978, xv+319 p., cloth, novel. [Translation of Patrick L. McGuire of *Vozrashchenie: polden' 22i vek*].
35165 *Prisoners of power.* New York: Macmillan Publishing Co.; London: Collier Macmillan Publishers, 1977, ix+286 p.,

cloth, novel. MAXIM TRILOGY #1. [Translation by Helen Saltz Jacobson of *Obitaemyi ostrov*].
35166 *Roadside picnic.* London: Victor Gollancz, 1978, ix+145 p., cloth, novel. [Translation by Antonina W. Bouis of *Piknik na obochine*].
35167 *Roadside picnic/Tale of the Troika.* New York: Macmillan Co., 1977, x+245 p., cloth, coll. [Translation by Antonina W. Bouis of *Piknik na obochine* and *Skazka o troike*].
35168 *The snail on the slope.* Toronto, New York: Bantam Books, 1980, 243 p., paper, novel. [Translation by Alan Meyers of *Ulitka na sklone*].
35169 *Space apprentice.* New York: Macmillan; London: Collier Macmillan, 1981, xiii+231 p., cloth, novel. [Translation by Antonina W. Bouis of *Stazhery*].
35170 *The time wanderers.* New York: Richardson & Steirman, 1986, 213 p., cloth, novel. MAXIM TRILOGY #3. [Translation by Antonina W. Bouis of *Volny gasiat veter*].
35171 *The ugly swans.* New York: Macmillan Publishing Co.; London: Collier Macmillan Publishers, 1979, 234 p., cloth, novel. [Translation by Alice Stone and Alexander Nakhimovsky of *Gadkie lebedi*].

with Boris Strugatsky as ANONYMOUS EDITORS

10223 *The molecular cafe: science-fiction stories.* Moscow: Mir Publishers, 1968, 279 p., paper, anth.

STRUGATSKY, Boris (Natanovich), 1933- , *with Arkady Strugatsky*

35159 *Beetle in the anthill.* New York: Macmillan, 1980, ix+217 p., cloth, novel. MAXIM TRILOGY #1. [Translation by Antonina W. Bouis of *Zhuk v muraveinike*].
35160 *Definitely maybe: a manuscript discovered under unusual circumstances.* New York: Macmillan Publishing Co.; London: Collier Macmillan Publishers, 1978, xi+143 p., cloth, novel. [Translation by Antonina W. Bouis of *Za milliard let do kontsa sveta*].
35161 *Far rainbow; The second invasion from Mars.* New York: Macmillan; London: Collier Macmillan, 1979, ix+240 p., cloth, coll. [Translation by Antonina W. Bouis of *Dalekaia raduga*; and by Gary Kern of *Vtoroe nashestvie Marsian*].
35162 *The final circle of paradise.* New York: DAW Books, 1976, 172 p., paper, novel.

[Translation by Leonid Renen of *Khishchne veshchi veka*].

35163 *Monday begins on Saturday.* New York: DAW Books, 1977, 222 p., paper, novel. [Translation by Leonid Renen of *Ponedel'nik nachinaetsia v subbotu*].

35164 *Noon: 22nd century.* New York: Macmillan; London: Collier Macmillan, 1978, xv+319 p., cloth, novel. [Translation of Patrick L. McGuire of *Vozrashchenie: polden' 22i vek*].

35165 *Prisoners of power.* New York: Macmillan Publishing Co.; London: Collier Macmillan Publishers, 1977, ix+286 p., cloth, novel. MAXIM TRILOGY #1. [Translation by Helen Saltz Jacobson of *Obitaemyi ostrov*].

35166 *Roadside picnic.* London: Victor Gollancz, 1978, ix+145 p., cloth, novel. [Translation by Antonina W. Bouis of *Piknik na obochine*].

35167 *Roadside picnic/Tale of the Troika.* New York: Macmillan Co., 1977, x+245 p., cloth, coll. [Translation by Antonina W. Bouis of *Piknik na obochine* and *Skazka o troike*].

35168 *The snail on the slope.* Toronto, New York: Bantam Books, 1980, 243 p., paper, novel. [Translation by Alan Meyers of *Ulitka na sklone*].

35169 *Space apprentice.* New York: Macmillan; London: Collier Macmillan, 1981, xiii+231 p., cloth, novel. [Translation by Antonina W. Bouis of *Stazhery*].

35170 *The time wanderers.* New York: Richardson & Steirman, 1986, 213 p., cloth, novel. MAXIM TRILOGY #3. [Translation by Antonina W. Bouis of *Volny gasiat veter*].

35171 *The ugly swans.* New York: Macmillan Publishing Co.; London: Collier Macmillan Publishers, 1979, 234 p., cloth, novel. [Translation by Alice Stone and Alexander Nakhimovsky of *Gadkie lebedi*].

with Arkady Strugatsky as ANONYMOUS EDITORS

10223 *The molecular cafe: science-fiction stories.* Moscow: Mir Publishers, 1968, 279 p., paper, anth.

STRUTTON, Bill [i.e., William Harold Strutton], 1918-

13797 *Doctor Who and the Zarbi.* London: Frederick Muller, 1965, 174 p., cloth, tele. DOCTOR WHO #2.
13797A retitled: *Doctor Who: The web planet.* London: A Target Book, 1991, 174 p,

paper, tele. DOCTOR WHO #73 (RENUMBERED).
Doctor Who: The web planet—SEE: *Doctor Who and the Zarbi.*
The web planet—SEE: *Doctor Who and the Zarbi.*

STRUTTON, William H.—SEE: Strutton, Bill

STRYKER, Daniel, pseud.—SEE: Stump, Jane & Morris, Christopher

STRYKER, Hal, pseud.—SEE: Smith, George H.

STUART, Alex R., pseud.—SEE: Gordon, Stuart

STUART, Anne [i.e., Anne Kristine Stuart Ohlrogge]

35172 *Bewitching hour.* Toronto, New York: Harlequin Books, 1986, 252 p., paper, novel.

STUART, Charles [pseud. of Charles Roy MacKinnon], 1924-

35173 *England: what is the secret of the stones?* New York: McGraw-Hill Book Co., 1990, 105 p., paper, novel. EARTH INSPECTORS #11.

STUART, Donald—SEE: Verner, Gerald

STUART, (Henry) Francis M(ontgomery), 1902-

35174 *Faillandia.* Dublin, Ireland: Raven Arts Press, 1985, 352 p., paper, novel.
35175 *A hole in the head.* London: M. Brian & O'Keeffe, 1977, 215 p., cloth, novel.
35176 *Pigeon Irish.* London: Victor Gollancz, 1932, 288 p., cloth, novel.
35177 *Try the sky.* London: Victor Gollancz, 1933, 287 p., cloth, novel.
35178 *Women and God: a novel.* London: Jonathan Cape, 1931, 251 p., cloth, novel.

STUART, L. T.

35179 *The House of the Lions.* Toronto, New York: Bantam Books, 1983, 184 p., paper, novel.

STUART, Rick, with John Terra

35180 *Star Trek the next generation officer's manual.* Chicago: FASA Corp., 1988, 144 p., paper, fiction. STAR TREK TIE-IN.

*STUART, W. J. [pseud. of Philip MacDonald], 1899-1980

STUBBS, Harry Clement—SEE: Clement, Hal

STUBBS, John Heath- —SEE: Heath-Stubbs, John

STUDEBAKER, Donald—SEE: DeCles, Jon

STUMP, Jane (Barr), 1936- , *with Christopher Morris as* DANIEL STRYKER

30277 *Cobra.* New York: Jove Books, 1991, 281 p., paper, novel.
30278 *Hawkeye.* New York: Jove Books, 1991, 311 p., paper, novel.

STURGEON, Theodore (Hamilton) [legalized from Edward Hamilton Waldo], 1918-1985

35181 *Alien cargo.* New York: Bluejay Books, 1984, 284 p., cloth, coll.
35182 *The cosmic rape; and, "To marry Medusa".* Boston: Gregg Press, 1977, xxxiv+231 p., cloth, coll.
35183 *The dreaming jewels; The cosmic rape; Venus plus X.* New York: Book-of-the-Month Club, 1990, 217+160+160 p., cloth, coll.
35184 *Godbody.* New York: Donald I. Fine, 1986, 159 p., cloth, novel.
35185 *The golden helix.* Garden City, NY: Nelson Doubleday, 1979, viii+247 p., cloth, coll.
35186 *Maturity: three stories.* Minneapolis, MN: Minneapolis Science Fiction Society, 1979, 144 p., cloth, coll. [Edited by Scott Imes and Stuart W. Wells III; limited to 750 copies].
35187 *Pruzy's pot.* Eugene, OR: Hypatia Press, 1986, vii+15+xi p., cloth, story. [Limited to 477 copies].
35188 *The stars are the Styx.* New York: A Dell Book, 1979, 382 p., paper, coll.
35189 *To marry Medusa.* New York: Baen Books, 1987, 251 p., paper, coll.
35190 *A touch of Sturgeon: stories.* London: Simon & Schuster, 1987, xiv+234 p., cloth, coll. [Edited by David Pringle].
35191 *Visions and venturers.* New York: A Dell Book, 1978, 300 p., paper, coll.
35192 *[Widget], the [wadget], and The boff.* New York: Tor SF, A Tom Doherty Associates Book, 1989, 123 p., paper, story. [Bound with: *The ugly little boy* / by Isaac Asimov].

STURGIS, Susanna J.

35193 *Memories and visions: women's fantasy & science fiction.* Freedom, CA: The Crossing Press, 1989, 207 p., cloth, anth.
35194 *Tales of magic realism by women: dreams in a minor key.* Freedom, CA: Crossing Press, 1991, 235 p., paper, anth.
35195 *The women who walk through fire: women's fantasy & science fiction, vol. 2.* Freedom, CA: Crossing Press, 1990, 275 p., cloth, anth.

STUTZMAN, Esther Friesner- —SEE: Friesner, Esther

SUARES, Jean-Claude, 1942- *with David Owen & Richard Siegel*

31070 *Fantastic planets.* Danbury, NH: Reed Books, 1979, 160 p., cloth, nonf.

with Richard Siegel

33840 *Alien creatures.* Los Angeles: Reed Books, 1978, 160 p., cloth, nonf.

SUBOTSKY, Milton, 1921-1991, *with Michel Parry*

31264 *Sex in the 21st century: a collection of SF erotica.* London, Toronto: Panther, Granada Publishing, 1979, 172 p., paper, anth.

SUCHARITKUL, Somtow (Papinian), 1952-

The alien swordmaster—SEE: *V: The alien swordmaster.*
35196 *The Aquiliad.* New York: A Timescape Book, Pocket Books, 1983, 224 p., paper, novel. AQUILIAD #1.
35197 *The darkling wind: chronicles of the High Inquest.* Toronto, New York: Bantam Books, 1985, 384 p., paper, novel. CHRONICLES OF THE HIGH INQUEST SERIES #4.
35198 *The Fallen Country.* Toronto, New York: Bantam Books, 1986, 198 p., paper, novel.
35199 *Fire from the wine dark sea.* Norfolk, Virginia Beach, VA: Starblaze Editions, Donning Co., 1983, 301 p., paper, coll.
35200 *Light on the sound.* New York: A Timescape Book, Pocket Books, 1982, 255 p., paper, novel. CHRONICLES OF THE HIGH INQUEST #1.
35201 *The light on the sound.* Toronto, New York: Bantam Books, 1986, 275 p., paper, novel. CHRONICLES OF THE HIGH INQUEST #1. [Expanded edition].

35202 *Mallworld.* Norfolk, Virginia Beach, VA: The Donning Co., 1981, 195 p., paper, novel.

35203 *Starship & Haiku.* New York: A Timescape Book, Pocket Books, 1981, 207 p., paper, novel. [Winner of the *Locus* Award for Best First Novel, 1981 (1982)].

Symphony of terror—SEE: *V: Symphony of terror.*

35204 *The throne of madness.* New York: A Timescape Book, Pocket Books, 1983, 254 p., paper, novel. CHRONICLES OF THE HIGH INQUEST #2.

35205 *Utopia hunters: chronicles of the High Inquest.* Toronto, New York: Bantam Books, 1984, 255 p., paper, novel. CHRONICLES OF THE HIGH INQUEST #3.

35206 *V: Symphony of terror.* New York: Tor SF, A Tom Doherty Associates Book, 1988, 244 p., paper, tele. V SERIES.

35207 *V: The alien swordmaster.* New York: Pinnacle Books, 1985, 185 p., paper, tele. V #7.

as S. P. SOMTOW

35208 *Aquila and the iron horse.* New York: A Del Rey Book, Ballantine Books, 1988, 261 p., paper, novel. AQUILIAD #2.

35209 *Aquila and the sphinx.* New York: A Del Rey Book, Ballantine Books, 1988, 242 p., paper, novel. AQUILIAD #3.

Aquila in the new world—SEE: *The Aquiliad.*

35196A *The Aquiliad: Aquila in the new world.* New York: A Del Rey Book, Ballantine Books, 1988, 247 p., paper, novel. AQUILIAD #1. [Originally published under the name Somtow Sucharitkul].

35210 *Moon dance: a novel.* New York: Tor, A Tom Doherty Associates Book, 1990, 564 p., cloth, novel.

35211 *Riverrun.* New York: Avon Books, 1991, x+259 p., paper, novel. RIVERRUN #1.

35212 *The shattered horse.* New York: Tor, A Tom Doherty Associates Book, 1986, 464 p., cloth, novel.

35203A *Starship & Haiku.* New York: A Del Rey Book, Ballantine Books, 1988, 210 p., paper, novel. [Originally published under the name Somtow Sucharitkul].

35213 *Vampire junction.* Norfolk, VA: Donning Company, Publishers, 1984, 280 p., cloth, novel. VALENTINE #1.

SUCKLING, Nigel

35214 *The clothmerchant's apprentice: the first volume in the tale of Rufus, the clothmerchant's apprentice, showing his early days and the beginning of his acquaintance with the Golden Wheel.* London: Big O Publishing, 1979, 143 p., paper, fiction.

with Ciruelo Cabral

19162 *Ciruelo.* Limpsfield, Surrey, England: Paper Tiger, 1990, 128 p., cloth, art.

SUDBERY, Rodie, 1943-

35215 *The silk and the skin.* London: André Deutsch, 1976, 144 p., cloth, novel.

35216 *Somewhere else.* London: André Deutsch, 1978 144 p., cloth, novel.

SUFFLING, Mark, pseud.—SEE: Rowland, Donald S.

SUGAR, Andrew

Bio blitz—SEE: *The Enforcer: Bio blitz.*

35217 *The Enforcer: Bio blitz.* New York: Manor Books, 1975, 188 p., paper, novel. ENFORCER #5.

35218 *The Enforcer: Kill deadline.* New York: Manor Books, 1979, 221 p., paper, novel. ENFORCER #7. [Series number is given as #6 on book].

35219 *The Enforcer: Steel trap.* New York: Manor Books, 1975, 188 p., paper, novel. ENFORCER #6.

Kill deadline—SEE: *The Enforcer: Kill deadline.*

Steel trap—SEE: *The Enforcer: Steel trap.*

SUGGS, Welch, *with Shirley Rousseau Murphy*

30450 *Medallion of the black hound.* New York: Harper & Row, 1989, 182 p., cloth, novel.

SULLIVAN, C(harles) W(illiam) III, 1944-

35220 *Welsh Celtic myth in modern fantasy.* NY & Westport, CT: Greenwood Press, 1989, xiii+181 p., cloth, nonf. CONTRIBUTIONS TO THE STUDY OF SCIENCE FICTION AND FANTASY #35.

SULLIVAN, E(dward) D. S., 1918-

35221 *The utopian vision: seven essays on the quincentennial of Sir Thomas More.* San Diego, CA: San Diego State University Press, 1983, 265 p., cloth, nonf. anth.

SULLIVAN, Eleanor (Regis), 1928-1991

35222 *Alfred Hitchcock's book of horror stories 1.* London: Coronet Books, 1983, [208] p., paper, anth. [This series includes stories from a variety of Hitchcock anthologies published in the United States].

35223 *Alfred Hitchcock's book of horror stories, book 2.* Sevenoaks, Kent, England: Coronet Books, 1984, [208] p., paper, anth. [Partially adapted from *Alfred Hitchcock's tales to take your breath away*].

35224 *Alfred Hitchcock's book of horror stories, book 3.* Sevenoaks, Kent, England: Coronet Books, 1984, 206 p., paper, anth. [Partially adapted from *Alfred Hitchcock's tales to take your breath away*].

35225 *Alfred Hitchcock's book of horror stories, no. 4.* Sevenoaks, Kent, England: Coronet Books, 1985, 188 p., paper, anth. [Partially adapted from *Alfred Hitchcock's tales to make your blood run cold*].

35226 *Alfred Hitchcock's book of horror stories 5.* London: Coronet Books, 1986, 204 p., paper, anth. [Partially adapted from *Alfred Hitchcock's tales to make your blood run cold*].

35227 *Alfred Hitchcock's book of horror stories, book 6.* London: Coronet Books, 1987, 190 p., paper, anth. [Partially adapted from *Alfred Hitchcock's Tales to make your hair stand on end*].

35228 *Alfred Hitchcock's book of horror stories, book 7.* London: Coronet Books, 1988, 157 p., paper, anth. [Partially adapted from *Alfred Hitchcock's Tales to make your hair stand on end*].

35229 *Alfred Hitchcock's book of horror stories, book 8.* London: Coronet Books, 1988, 223 p., paper, anth. *[Partially adapted from Alfred Hitchcock's Tales to keep you spellbound]*.

35230 *Alfred Hitchcock's book of horror stories, book 9.* London: Coronet Books, 1989, 208 p., paper, anth. *[Partially adapted from Alfred Hitchcock's Tales to keep you spellbound]*.

35231 *Alfred Hitchcock's Tales to make your blood run cold.* New York: Dial Press, 1978, 349 p., cloth, anth.

35232 *Alfred Hitchcock's tales to make your teeth chatter.* New York: Dial Press, 1980, 350 p., cloth, anth.

35233 *Alfred Hitchcock's Tales to send chills down your spine.* New York: Dial Press, 1979, 348 p., cloth, anth.

35234 *Tales of terror.* New York: Galahad Books, 1986, 631 p., cloth, anth.

SULLIVAN, Faith, 1933-

35235 *Mrs. Demming and the mythical beast.* New York: Macmillan Publishing Co., 1985, 341 p., cloth, novel.

35236 *Watchdog.* New York: McGraw-Hill, 1982, 248 p., cloth, novel.

SULLIVAN, Jack, 1946-

35237 *Elegant nightmares: the English ghost story from Le Fanu to Blackwood.* Athens, OH: Ohio University Press, 1978, 155 p., cloth, nonf.

35238 *Lost souls: a collection of English ghost stories.* Athens, OH: Ohio University Press, 1983, x+430 p., cloth, anth.

35239 *The Penguin encyclopedia of horror and the supernatural.* New York: A Promised Land Production, Viking, 1986, xxviii+482 p., cloth, nonf. anth.

SULLIVAN, Mary W(ilson), 1907-

35240 *Earthquake 2099.* New York: Lodestar Books, E. P. Dutton, 1982, 119 p., cloth, novel.

SULLIVAN, Mike

35241 *Station Zero-Zero.* Canoga Park, CA: Major Books, 1978 (i.e., 1979?), 238 p., paper, novel.

SULLIVAN, Sheila (P.), 1927-

The calling of Bara—SEE: *Summer rising.*

35242 *Summer rising.* London: Weidenfeld & Nicolson, 1975, 260 p., cloth, novel.

35242A retitled: *The calling of Bara.* New York: E. P. Dutton, 1976, 260 p., cloth, novel.

SULLIVAN, Thomas (William), 1940-

35243 *Born burning.* London & Sydney: Pan Books, 1991, 262 p., paper, novel.

35244 *Diapason.* New York: Condor, 1978, 166 p., paper, novel.

SULLIVAN, Tim(othy Robert), 1948-

35245 *Cold shocks.* New York: Avon Books, 1991, viii+309 p., paper, anth.

35246 *Destiny's end.* New York: Avon Books, 1988, 305 p., paper, novel.

The Florida project—SEE: *V: The Florida project.*

35247 *The Martian viking.* New York: Avon Books, 1991, 242 p., paper, novel.

The New England resistance—SEE: *V: The New England resistance.*

35248 *The parasite war.* New York: Avon Books, 1989, 246 p., paper, novel.

To conquer the throne—SEE: *V: To conquer the throne.*

35249 *Tropical chills.* New York: Avon Books, 1988, xii+258 p., paper, anth.

35250 *V: The Florida project.* New York: Pinnacle Books, 1985, 178 p., paper, tele. V #5.

35251 *V: The New England resistance.* New York: Pinnacle Books, 1985, 180 p., paper, tele. V #9.

35252 *V: To conquer the throne.* New York: Tor SF, A Tom Doherty Associates Book, 1987, 216 p., paper, tele. V SERIES.

with David Bischoff as MARK GRANT

18010 *Mutants amok.* New York: Avon Books, 1991, 216 p., paper, novel. MUTANTS AMOK #1.

with Arthur Byron Cover and John Gregory Betancourt as THOMAS SHADWELL

The dinosaur trackers—SEE: *Robert Silverberg's Time tours: The dinosaur trackers.*

20683 *Robert Silverberg's Time tours: The dinosaur trackers.* New York: A Byron Preiss Book, HarperPaperbacks, 1991, 138 p., paper, novel. ROBERT SILVERBERG'S TIME TOURS #4.

SULLIVAN, Tom, *with Mark J. Ferrari & Sandy Petersen & Lynn Willis*

Field guide to creatures of the dreamlands—SEE: *Petersen's Field guide: creatures of the dreamlands.*

23047 *Petersen's Field guide: creatures of the dreamlands: an album of entities from beyond the wall of sleep.* Albany, CA: Chaosium, 1989, 64 p., paper, art.

SUMMERFIELD, Geoffrey, 1931-

35253 *Fantasy and reason: children's literature in the eighteenth century.* London: Methuen, 1984, 315 p., cloth, nonf.

SUMMERS, Dennis, pseud.—SEE: Barrett, G. J.

SUMMERS, Ian, 1939-

35254 *Tomorrow and beyond: masterpieces of science fiction art.* Leicester, England: Windward, 1978, 158 p., paper, art.

with Vincent DiFate & Beth Meacham

Catalog of science fiction hardware—SEE: *DiFate's Catalog of science fiction hardware.*

21918 *DiFate's Catalog of science fiction hardware.* New York: Workman Publishing, 1980, 135 p., cloth, art.

with Wayne Douglas Barlowe & Beth Meacham

17408 *Barlowe's Guide to extraterrestrials.* New York: Workman Publishing, 1979, 112+[32] p., cloth, art. [Meacham's contribution is uncredited; winner of the *Locus* Award for Best Art Book, 1979 (1980)].

17409 *Barlowe's Guide to extraterrestrials, 2nd ed.* New York: Workman Publishing, 1987, 112+[32] p., cloth, art.

Guide to extraterrestrials—SEE: *Barlowe's Guide to extraterrestrials.*

SUMMERS, (Alphonsus Joseph-Mary Augustus) Montague, 1880-1948

The Penguin supernatural omnibus—SEE: *The supernatural omnibus.*

13866 *The supernatural omnibus: being a collection of stories of apparitions, witchcraft, werewolves, diabolism, necromancy, Satanism, divination, sorcery, goetry, voodoo, possession, occult doom, and destiny.* London: Victor Gollancz, 1931, 622 p., cloth, anth.

13866B retitled: *The Penguin supernatural omnibus: being a collection of stories of apparitions, witchcraft, werewolves, diabolism, necromancy, satanism, divination, sorcery, goety, voodoo, possession, occult, doom, and destiny.* Harmondsworth, Middlesex, England: Penguin Books, 1984, 573 p., paper, anth.

SUNDOWN, Will, pseud.—SEE: Sanders, William

SUNLIGHT, pseud.

35255 *Womonseed: a vision.* Little River, CA: Tough Dove Books, 1986, 231 p., paper, novel.

SUNSTEIN, Emily W(eisberg), 1924-

35256 *Mary Wollstonecraft Shelley: romance and reality.* Boston, Toronto: Little, Brown & Co., 1989, xi+478 p., cloth, nonf.

SUSANN, Jacqueline, 1918-1974

35257 *Yargo.* Toronto, New York: Bantam Books, 1979, 347 p., paper, novel.

SÜSKIND, Patrick, 1949-

35258 *Perfume: the story of a murderer.* New York: Alfred A. Knopf, 1986, 255 p., cloth, novel. [Translation by John E. Woods of *Das parfum*; winner of the World Fantasy Award for Best Fantasy Novel, 1986 (1987)].

SUSSEX, Lucy (Jane), 1957-

35259 *My lady tongue, & other tales.* Australia: Heinemann, 1990, 280 p., paper, coll.

with Jenny Blackford & Russell Blackford & Norman Talbot

18088 *Contrary modes: proceedings of the World Science Fiction Conference, Melbourne, Australia, 1985.* Melbourne, Australia: Ebony Books in Association with Department of English, University of Newcastle, 1985, 154 p., paper, nonf. anth.

SUSSMAN, Herbert L., 1937-

38099 *Victorians and the machine: the literary response to technology.* Cambridge, MA: Harvard University Press, 1968, viii+261 p., cloth, nonf.

SUSTER, Gerald, 1951-

35260 *The devil's maze.* New York: A Dell Book, 1983, 254 p., paper, novel.
35261 *The elect.* London: Sphere Books, 1980, 244 p., paper, novel.

SUTCLIFF, Rosemary, 1920-1992

35262 *The light beyond the forest: the quest for the Holy Grail.* London: Bodley Head, 1979, 148 p., cloth, novel. KING ARTHUR #1.
35263 *The road to Camlann.* London: Bodley Head, 1981, 143 p., cloth, novel. KING ARTHUR #3.
35264 *The sword and the circle: King Arthur and the knights of the Round Table.* London:

Bodley Head, 1981, 260 p., cloth, novel. KING ARTHUR #2.
35265 *Sword at sunset.* London: Hodder & Stoughton, 1963, 480 p., cloth, novel.
35266 *Tristan and Iseult.* London: Bodley Head, 1971, 134 p., cloth, novel.

SUTCLIFFE, Halliwell—SEE: Quilp, Jocelyn

SUTER, Jon Michael, 1941-

35267 *The adventure of the bald bibliophile.* Ada, OK: Hasserl Bindery, 1977, 152 leaves, paper?, novel. [Sequel to *Perpidious*].
35268 *The adventures of the mustard jar.* Ada, OK: Hasserl Bindery, 1976, 45 leaves, paper?, novel.
35269 *The autocrats of Oz.* Ada, OK: Hasserl Bindery, 1976, 2 v., paper?, novel. OZ SERIES. [Sequel to *Blueankle*].
35270 *Blueankle.* Ada, OK: Hasserl Bindery, 1976, 60 leaves, paper?, novel. [Sequel to *The passing of Fu Manchu*].
35271 *The case of the limping librarian.* Ada, OK: Hasserl Bindery, 1978, 271 leaves, paper?, novel. [Sequel to *The orange knight of Oz*].
35272 *The case of the perpidious president.* Ada, OK: Hasserl Bindery, 1978, 2 v., paper?, novel. [Sequel to *The autocrats of Oz*].
35273 *The orange knight of Oz.* Ada, OK: Hasserl Bindery, 1976, 138 leaves, paper?, novel. OZ SERIES. [Sequel to *The adventures of the mustard jar*].
35274 *The passing of Fu Manchu.* Ada, OK: Hasserl Bindery, 1976, 160 leaves, paper?, novel. FU MANCHU SERIES. [Sequel to *The case of the limping librarian*].

SUTHERLAND, Jon, *with Simon Farrell*

22920 *Bardik the thief.* London: Magnet, 1987, [192] p., paper, fiction. CITY OF SHADOWS #2.
22921 *Coreus the prince.* London: Magnet, 1987, [192] p., paper, fiction. CITY OF SHADOWS #1.
22922 *Darian: master magician.* London: Magnet Books, 1987, [200] p., paper, fiction. GLADE OF DREAMS #1.
22923 *Issel: warrior king.* London: Magnet Books, 1987, [200] p., paper, fiction. GLADE OF DREAMS #2.

SUTHERLAND, Judith L.

35275 *The problematic fictions of Poe, James, and Hawthorne.* Columbia, MO: University of Missouri Press, 1984, ix+133 p., cloth, nonf.

SUTIN, Lawrence, 1951-

35276 *Divine invasions: a life of Philip K. Dick.* New York: Harmony Books, 1989, xiv+352 p., cloth, nonf.

SUTPHEN, Richard (Charles), 1937-

35277 *Sexpunks & savage sagas.* Agoura Hills, CA: Spine-Tingling Press, 1991, 255 p., cloth, coll.

SUTTON, David (Ambrose), 1947-

35278 *The satyr's head.* London: Corgi Books, 1975, 159 p., paper, anth.

with Stephen Jones

26765 *The best horror from Fantasy tales.* London: Robinson Publishing, 1988, xviii+264 p., cloth, anth.
26766 *Dark voices 2: the Pan book of horror.* London & Sydney: Pan Books, 1990, 223 p., paper, anth.
26767 *Dark voices 3: the Pan book of horror.* London & Sydney: Pan Books, 1991, 309 p., paper, anth.
26768 *Fantasy tales 1.* New York: Carroll & Graf, 1990, 104 p., paper, anth.
Fantasy tales 2—SEE: *Fantasy tales 5.*
Fantasy tales 3—SEE: *Fantasy tales 6.*
26769 *Fantasy tales 5.* London: Robinson Publishing, 1990, 201 p., paper, anth.
26769A retitled: *Fantasy tales 2.* New York: Carroll & Graf, 1990, 201 p., paper, anth.
26770 *Fantasy tales 6.* London: Robinson Publishing, 1991, 186 p., paper, anth.
26770A retitled: *Fantasy tales 3.* New York: Carroll & Graf, 1991, 186 p., paper, anth.
26771 *Fantasy tales 7.* London: Robinson Publishing, 1991, 185 p., paper, anth.

SUTTON, Henry [pseud. of David Rytman Slavitt], 1935-

35279 *The sacrifice: a novel of the occult.* New York: Grosset & Dunlap, 1978, 245 p., cloth, novel.

SUTTON, Jeff(erson Howard), 1913-1979

35280 *Cassady.* New York: St. Martin's Press, 1979, 205 p., cloth, novel.

*SUTTON, (Homer) Lee, 1916-1978

SUVIN, Darko (Ronald), 1930-

35281 *Metamorphosis of science fiction: on the poetics and history of a literary genre.* New Haven, CT & London: Yale University Press, 1979, xviii+317 p., cloth, nonf.
35282 *Positions and presuppositions in science fiction.* Kent, OH: Kent State University Press, 1988, xviii+227 p., cloth, nonf.
35283 *Russian science fiction, 1956-1974: a bibliography: original books, translated books, and an annotated checklist of criticism, with an appendix on criticism of Russian SF before 1956.* Elizabethtown, NY: Dragon Press, 1976, vi+73 p., cloth, nonf.
35284 *Victorian science fiction in the UK: the discourses of knowledge and of power.* Boston: G. K. Hall, 1983, xvii+461 p., cloth, nonf.

with R. D. Mullen

30396 *Science-fiction studies: selected articles on science fiction, 1973-1975.* Boston: Gregg Press, 1976, xix+304 p., cloth, nonf. anth.
30397 *Science-fiction studies, second series: selected articles on science fiction, 1976-1977.* Boston: Gregg Press, 1977, xiv+335 p., cloth, nonf. anth.

with Robert Philmus

31535 *H. G. Wells and modern science fiction.* Lewisburg, PA: Bucknell University Press, 1977, 279 p., cloth, nonf. anth.

SVENDSEN, Hanne Marie, 1933-

35285 *The gold ball.* New York: Alfred A. Knopf, 1989, 245 p., cloth, novel. [Translation by Jorgen Schiott of *Guldkuglen*].

SWAHN, Sven (Christer), 1933-

35286 *The island through the gate.* London: Methuen, 1973, 160 p., cloth, novel. [Translation of *Hausporten*].

SWAIN, Dwight V(reeland), 1915-1992

35287 *Monster.* New York: Pinnacle Books, Windsor Publishing Corp., 1991, 256 p., paper, novel.

with Andrew J. Offutt as JOHN CLEVE

30963 *The planet murderer.* New York: Berkley Books, 1984, 224 p., paper, novel. SPACEWAYS #16.

SWAIN, E(dmund) G(ill), 1861-1938

Bone to his bone—SEE: *The Stoneground ghost tales.*

13908 *The Stoneground ghost tales: compiled from the recollections of the Reverend Roland Batchel, vicar of the parish.* Cambridge, England: W. Heffer & Sons, 1912, 187 p., cloth, coll.

with David Rowlands

35288 retitled: *Bone to his bone: the Stoneground ghost tales.* Wellingborough, Northamptonshire, England: Equation, 1989, 192 p., paper, coll. [Expanded edition; the stories by Rowlands are original to this volume].

*SWAIN, Virginia, 1899-1984?

SWAN, Christopher (Cushing), 1946- , *with Chet Roaman*

32360 *YV88: an eco-fiction of tomorrow.* San Francisco: Sierra Club Books, 1977, viii+248 p., paper, fiction.

SWAN, Mark E(lbert), 1871-

15866 *Top o' the world: a once upon a time tale.* New York: E. P. Dutton, 1908, 194 p., cloth, novel. [Adapted from the musical of the same name].

*SWAN, Thor, 1903-1978

SWANBECK, Jan (B.), 1948- , *with Hal W. Hall*

25036 *Science fiction and fantasy research index, volume 7.* San Bernardino, CA: The Borgo Press, 1987, 197 p., cloth, nonf.

SWANN, Ingo, 1933-

35289 *Star fire.* Also: London: Souvenir Press, 1978, 314 p., cloth, novel.

SWANN, Thomas Burnett (Jr.), 1928-1976

35290 *A. A. Milne.* New York: Twayne Publishers, 1971, 153 p., cloth, novel.

35291 *Cry Silver Bells.* New York: DAW Books, 1977, 192 p., paper, novel. ANCIENT HISTORY #2—MINOTAUR #1.

35292 *The gods abide.* New York: DAW Books, 1976, 160 p., paper, novel. ANCIENT HISTORY #10.

35293 *Lady of the bees.* New York: Ace Books, 1976, 199 p., paper, novel. ANCIENT HISTORY #7—MELLONIA #3.

35294 *The Minikins of Yam.* New York: DAW Books, 1976, 156 p., paper, novel. ANCIENT HISTORY #1.

35295 *The Not-world.* New York: DAW Books, 1975, 160 p., paper, novel. ANCIENT HISTORY #13.

35296 *Queens walk in the dusk.* Forest Park, GA: Heritage Press, 1977, 139 p., cloth, novel. ANCIENT HISTORY #5—MELLONIA #1.

35297 *The tournament of thorns.* New York: Ace Books, 1976, 167 p., paper, novel. ANCIENT HISTORY #11.

35298 *Will-o-the-wisp.* London: Corgi Books, 1976, 160 p., paper, novel. ANCIENT HISTORY #12.

38100 *Wonder and whimsy: the fantastic world of Christina Rossetti.* Francestown, NH: M. Joes, 1960, 111 p., cloth, nonf.

SWANSON, Logan, pseud.—SEE: Matheson, Richard

SWANWICK, Michael (Josephus), 1950-

35299 *Gravity's angels: 13 stories.* Sauk City, WI: Arkham House Publishers, 1991, x+302 p., cloth, coll.

35300 *Griffin's egg.* London: Legend, 1990, 101 p., cloth, novel.

35301 *In the Drift.* New York: Ace Science Fiction Books, 1985, ix+195 p., paper, novel.

35302 *Stations of the tide.* Norwalk, CT: Easton Press, 1991, 252 p., cloth, novel. [Winner of the Nebula Award for Best Novel, 1991 (1992); winner of the *Science Fiction Chronicle* Award for Best Novel, 1991 (1992)].

35303 *Vacuum flowers.* New York: Arbor House, 1987, 248 p., cloth, novel.

with Gardner Dozois & Susan Casper & Jack C. Haldeman II & Jack Dann

19639 *Slow dancing through time.* Kansas City, MO: Ursus Imprints; Shingletown, CA:

Mark V. Ziesing, 1990, xvii+253 p., cloth, coll. [All the stories are collaborations by Dozois with other writers, the majority with Jack Dann].

SWAZEE, Ruth

35304 *A time of night.* New York: Manor Books, 1978, 208 p., paper, novel.

SWEEN, R(oger) D(avid), 1940-

35305 *Reference sources for the study of speculative literature.* Redway, MN: The Karrmann Library, University of Wisconsin-Platteville, 1973?, [48] p., paper, nonf. SPECULATIVE LITERATURE BIBLIOGRAPHY #2.
35306 *Speculative literature used in U.S. academic courses.* Redway, MN: The Karrmann Library, University of Wisconsin-Platteville, 1972?, [40] p., paper, nonf.

SWEENEY, Joyce (Kay), 1955-

35307 *The dream collector.* New York: Delacorte Press, 1989, 196 p., cloth, novel.

SWEENEY, Linda, *with Patricia Pinianski as* LYNN PATRICK

31588 *Double or nothing.* New York: Candlelight Ecstasy Supreme, Dell, 1985, 287 p., paper, novel.
31589 *More than a dream.* New York: Candlelight Ecstasy Romance, Dell, 1985, [280] p., paper, novel.

SWEETSER, Wesley (Duaine), 1919-

35308 *Arthur Machen.* New York: Twayne Publishers, 1964, 175 p., cloth, nonf.
35309 *Arthur Machen: a miscellany.* Llandeilo, Wales: St. Alberts Press, 1960, 43 p., paper, nonf.

with Adrian Goldstone

24105 *A bibliography of Arthur Machen.* Austin, TX: University of Texas, 1965, 180 p., cloth, nonf.
35310 *Machen* / by Wesley Sweetser; *Men about Machen* / by Adrian H. Goldstone. Llandeilo, Wales: St. Alberts Press, 1960, 24 p., paper, nonf. coll.

SWIFT, Rebecca

35311 *Project Norouz.* New York: Tower Books, 1982, 512 p., paper, novel.

SWIGART, Rob, 1941-

35312 *A.K.A.: a cosmic fable.* Boston: Houghton Mifflin Co., 1978, 226 p., cloth, novel.
38101 *The book of abbreviations: a novel.* New York: E. P. Dutton, 1981, 278 p., cloth, novel.
35313 *Portal: a dataspace retrieval.* New York: St. Martin's Press, 1988, 346 p., cloth, novel.
35314 *The time trip.* Boston: Houghton Mifflin Co., 1979, 329 p., cloth, novel.
35315 *Toxin.* New York: St. Martin's Press, 1989, 385 p., paper, novel. VECTOR #2.
35316 *Vector.* New York: Bluejay Books, 1986, 288 p., cloth, novel. VECTOR #1.
35317 *Venom.* New York: St. Martin's Press, 1991, 248 p., cloth, novel.

SWINDELLS, Robert E(dward), 1939-

35318 *Brother in the land.* Oxford, England: Oxford University Press, 1984, 153 p., cloth, novel.
35319 *Follow a shadow.* New York: Holiday House, 1990, 148 p., cloth, novel.
35320 *The ghost messengers.* London: Hodder & Stoughton, 1985, 95 p., cloth, novel.
35321 *Ghost ship to Ganymede.* Exeter, England: Wheaton, 1980, 76 p., cloth, novel.
35322 *Hydra.* London: Doubleday, 1991, 208 p., cloth, novel.
35323 *The moonpath, and other tales of the bizarre.* Exeter, England: Wheaton, 1979, 54 p., cloth, coll.
35324 *Room 13.* London, New York: Doubleday, 1989, 157 p., cloth, novel.
35325 *A serpent's tooth.* London: Hamish Hamilton Children's Books, 1988, 136 p., cloth, novel.
35326 *The Wheaton book of science fiction stories.* Exeter, England: Wheaton Books, 1982, 67 p., cloth, coll.
35327 *When darkness comes.* Leicester, England: Brockhampton Press, 1973, 152 p., cloth, novel.
35328 *World-eater.* London: Hodder & Stoughton, 1981, 103 p., cloth, novel.

SWINFEN, Ann

35329 *In defence of fantasy: a study of the genre in English and American literature.* London: Routledge & Kegan Paul, 1984, x+253 p., cloth, nonf.

SWITHIN, Antony

35330 *The lords of the Stoney Mountains.* London: Fontana, 1991, 374 p., paper, novel. PERILOUS QUEST FOR LYONESSE #2.

38102 *Princes of Sandastre.* London: Fontana, 1990, xiii+220 p., paper, novel. PERILOUS QUEST FOR LYONESSE #1.

SWYCAFFER, Jefferson P(utnam), 1956-

35331 *Become the hunted.* New York: Avon, 1985, 160 p., paper, novel. CONDORDAT #1.

35332 *The empire's legacy* / by Jefferson Swycaffer. Delavan, WI: New Infinities Productions, 1988, 331 p., paper, novel. TALES OF THE CONCORDAT #1.

35333 *Not in our stars.* New York: Avon, 1984, 222 p., paper, novel. CONCORDAT #2.

35334 *The Praesidium of Archive.* New York: Avon, 1986, 197 p., paper, coll. CONCORDAT #4.

35335 *Revolt and rebirth* / by Jefferson Swycaffer. Delavan, WI: New Infinities Productions, 1988, 329 p., paper, novel. Tales of the CONCORDAT #3.

35336 *The universal prey.* New York: Avon, 1985, 191 p., paper, novel. CONCORDAT #3.

35337 *Voyage of the planetslayer* / by Jefferson Swycaffer. Delavan, WI: New Infinities Productions, 1988, 302 p., paper, novel. TALES OF THE CONCORDAT #2.

35338 *Warsprite.* Lake Geneva, WI: TSR Inc., 1990, 313 p., paper, novel.

35339 *Web of futures.* Lake Geneva, WI: TSR Inc., 1991, 312 p., paper, novel.

SWYCAFFER, Ruth Helen—SEE: Noel, Atanielle Annyn

SYKALA, U(rsula)

35340 *Mystical encounters.* Irchester, England: Castle Books, 1982, 102 p., paper, coll.

SYKES, S(ondra) C(atharine), 1943-

35341 *Red genesis.* New York, Toronto: Spectra, Bantam Books, 1991, xx+360 p., paper, novel. NEXT WAVE #1.

35342 *U.S.S.A., book 3.* New York: A GLC Book, Avon, 1987, 170 p., paper, novel. U.S.S.A. #3.

SYMES, Mike

35343 *Boskone XVI portfolio.* Cambridge, MA: NESFA Press, 1979, 5 leaves, paper, art coll.

SYMONS, Allene (K.), 1944-

35344 *Vagabond prophet: a novel of Nostradamus & his time.* New York: Avon, 1983, 185 p., paper, novel.

SYMONS, (Dorothy) Geraldine, 1909-

Crocuses were over, Hitler was dead—SEE: *Now and then.*

35345 *Now and then.* London: Faber & Faber, 1977, 147 p., cloth, novel.

35345A retitled: *Crocuses were over, Hitler was dead.* Philadelphia, PA: J. B. Lippincott, 1977, 158 p., cloth, novel.

SYMONS, Julian (Gustave), 1912-

35346 *The tell-tale heart: the life and works of Edgar Allan Poe.* New York: A Joan Kahn Book, Harper & Row, 1978, x+259 p., cloth, nonf.

SYNGE, (Phyllis) Ursula, 1930-1981?

35347 *Swan's wing.* London: Bodley Head, 1984, 155 p., cloth, novel.

SYVERTSEN, Ryder (Otto), 1941-

35348 *Cave of the master.* New York: Pinnacle Books, Windsor Publishing Corp., 1990, 255 p., paper, novel. MYSTIC REBEL #5. [Cover title].

35349 *The dancing dead.* New York: Pinnacle Books, Windsor Publishing Corp., 1988, 320 p., paper, novel. MYSTIC REBEL #2.

35350 *Darkness descends.* New York: Pinnacle Books, Windsor Publishing Corp., 1988, 320 p., paper, novel. MYSTIC REBEL #3.

35351 *Fortress of forbidden destiny.* New York: Pinnacle Books, Windsor Publishing Corp., 1991, 288 p., paper, novel. MYSTIC REBEL #6.

35352 *Mystic rebel.* New York: Pinnacle Books, Windsor Publishing Corp., 1988, 384 p., paper, novel. MYSTIC REBEL #1.

35353 *Temple of dark destiny.* New York: Pinnacle Books, Windsor Publishing Corp., 1989, 320 p., paper, novel. MYSTIC REBEL #4.

alone or with Jan Stacy as JOHN SIEVERT

33849 *C.A.D.S.* New York: Zebra Books, Kensington Publishing Corp., 1985, 398 p., paper, novel. C.A.D.S. #1. [With Jan Stacy].

33850 *Cybertech killing zone.* New York: Zebra Books, Kensington Publishing Corp., 1989, 222 p., paper, novel. C.A.D.S. #8.

33851 *Doom commander.* New York: Zebra Books, Kensington Publishing Corp., 1989, 220 p., paper, novel. C.A.D.S. #7.

33852 *Tech battleground.* New York: Zebra Books, Kensington Publishing Corp., 1986, 285 p., paper, novel. C.A.D.S. #2.

33853 *Tech commando.* New York: Zebra Books, Kensington Publishing Corp., 1986, 252 p., paper, novel. C.A.D.S. #3.

33854 *Tech inferno.* New York: Zebra Books, Kensington Publishing Corp., 1988, 255 p., paper, novel. C.A.D.S. #6.

33855 *Tech Satan.* New York: Zebra Books, Kensington Publishing Corp., 1988, 286 p., paper, novel. C.A.D.S. #5.

33856 *Tech strike force.* New York: Zebra Books, Kensington Publishing Corp., 1987, 270 p., paper, novel. C.A.D.S. #4.

alone or with Jan Stacy as RYDER STACY

35354 *American death orbit.* New York: Zebra Books, Kensington Publishing Corp., 1988, 251 p., paper, novel. DOOMSDAY WARRIOR #14.

35355 *American defiance.* New York: Zebra Books, Kensington Publishing Corp., 1986, 269 p., paper, novel. DOOMSDAY WARRIOR #7.

35356 *American dream machine.* New York: Zebra Books, Kensington Publishing Corp., 1990, 190 p., paper, novel. DOOMSDAY WARRIOR #18.

35357 *American Eden.* New York: Zebra Books, Kensington Publishing Corp., 1987, 268 p., paper, novel. DOOMSDAY WARRIOR #11.

35358 *American glory.* New York: Zebra Books, Kensington Publishing Corp., 1986, 255 p., paper, novel. DOOMSDAY WARRIOR #8.

35359 *American nightmare.* New York: Zebra Books, Kensington Publishing Corp., 1987, 256 p., paper, novel. DOOMSDAY WARRIOR #10.

35360 *American overthrow.* New York: Zebra Books, Kensington Publishing Corp., 1989, 223 p., paper, novel. DOOMSDAY WARRIOR #16.

35361 *American paradise.* New York: Zebra Books, Kensington Publishing Corp., 1988, 251 p., paper, novel. DOOMSDAY WARRIOR #13.

35362 *American rebellion.* New York: Zebra Books, Kensington Publishing Corp., 1985, 255 p., paper, novel. DOOMSDAY WARRIOR #6. [Cover title].

35363 *American ultimatum.* New York: Zebra Books, Kensington Publishing Corp., 1989, 224 p., paper, novel. DOOMSDAY WARRIOR #15.

35364 *America's final defense.* New York: Zebra Books, Kensington Publishing Corp., 1991, 224 p., paper, novel. DOOMSDAY WARRIOR #19. [Last book in the series].

35365 *America's last declaration.* New York: Zebra Books, Kensington Publishing Corp., 1985, 256 p., paper, novel. DOOMSDAY WARRIOR #5. [Cover title].

35366 *America's sword.* New York: Zebra Books, Kensington Publishing Corp., 1990, 221 p., paper, novel. DOOMSDAY WARRIOR #17.

35367 *America's zero hour.* New York: Zebra Books, Kensington Publishing Corp., 1986, 255 p., paper, novel. DOOMSDAY WARRIOR #9.

34710 *Bloody America.* New York: Zebra Books, Kensington Publishing Corp., 1985, 271 p., paper, novel. DOOMSDAY WARRIOR #4. [With Jan Stacy].

34711 *Doomsday warrior.* New York: Zebra Books, Kensington Publishing Corp., 1984, 347 p., paper, novel. DOOMSDAY WARRIOR #1. [With Jan Stacy].

34712 *The last American.* New York: Zebra Books, Kensington Publishing Corp., 1984, 267 p., paper, novel. DOOMSDAY WARRIOR #3. [With Jan Stacy].

34713 *Red America.* New York: Zebra Books, Kensington Publishing Corp., 1984, 267 p., paper, novel. DOOMSDAY WARRIOR #2. [With Jan Stacy].

with Adrian Fletcher

23191 *Psychic spawn: a novel.* New York: Popular Library, 1987, 376 p., paper, novel.

with Jan Stacy

34709 *The great book of movie monsters.* Chicago: Contemporary Books, 1983, 352 p., paper, nonf.

SZOLLOSI, Thomas

35368   *The proving*. Garden City, NY: Doubleday & Co., 1988, 256 p., cloth, novel.

SZYDLOW, Jarl, pseud.—SEE: Vigliante, Mary

SZYDLOWSKI, Mary—SEE: Vigliante, Mary

T

TABLER, Joseph

35369 *Capitol Hill clones*. North Hollywood, CA: American Art Enterprises, 1981, 206 p., paper, novel.
35370 *The meteoric affair*. North Hollywood, CA: American Art Enterprises, 1982, 156 p., paper, novel.
35371 *The microwave caper*. North Hollywood, CA: American Art Enterprises, 1981, 222 p., paper, novel.

TABOR, Margaret

Nightmare street—SEE: *Unity Penfold*.
38103 *The understudy*. London: Severn House, 1983, 254 p., cloth, novel.
35372 *Unity Penfold*. London: Heinemann, 1980, 202 p., cloth, novel.
35372A retitled: *Nightmare street*. New York: Pocket Books, 1982, 224 p., paper, novel.

TABORI, Paul [legalized from Pál Tábori], 1908-1974

38104 *The frontier*. London: Sampson Low, Marston, 1950, vii+264 p., cloth, novel.
15867 *The talking tree*. London: Sampson Low, Marston, 1950, 246 p., cloth, novel.

TADIE, Andrew A., *with Michael H. MacDonald*

28792 *G. K. Chesterton and C. S. Lewis: the riddle of joy*. London: Collins, 1989, xx+304 p., cloth, nonf. anth.

TAHOURDIN, Barbara Ker—SEE: Wilson, Barbara Ker

TAIT, George B.—SEE: Barclay, Alan

TAKEI, George, 1939- , *with Robert Asprin*

17083 *Mirror friend, mirror foe*. Chicago: Playboy Press Paperbacks, 1979, 223 p., paper, novel.

TALBOT, Michael (Coleman), 1953-1992

35373 *The bog*. New York: William Morrow & Co., 1986, 310 p., cloth, novel.
35374 *The delicate dependency: a novel of the vampire life*. New York: Avon, 1982, 406 p., paper, novel.
35375 *Night things*. New York: William Morrow & Co., 1988, 274 p., cloth, novel.

TALBOT, Norman (Clare), 1936- , *with Jenny Blackford & Russell Blackford & Lucy Sussex*

18088 *Contrary modes: proceedings of the World Science Fiction Conference, Melbourne, Australia, 1985*. Melbourne, Australia: Ebony Books in Association with Department of English, University of Newcastle, 1985, 154 p., paper, nonf. anth.

TALL, Stephen [pseud. of Compton Newby Crook], 1908-1981

35377 *The people beyond the wall*. New York: DAW Books, 1980, 204 p., paper, novel.
35378 *The ramsgate paradox*. New York: A Berkley Medallion Book, Berkley Publishing Corp., 1976, 186 p., paper, novel. STARDUST #2.
35379 *The Stardust voyages*. New York: A Berkley Medallion Book, Berkley Publishing Corp., 1975, 230 p., paper, coll. STARDUST #1.

TALLARICO, Anthony—SEE: Tallarico, Tony

TALLARICO, Tony [i.e., Anthony Tallarico], *with D. J. Arneson [i.e., "Dr. Drew"]*

16778 *The aliens are here!* Mahwah, NJ: Watermill Press, 1980, 64 p., paper, coll.
16779 *Beware of the supernatural*. Mahwah, NJ: Watermill Press, 1980, 63 p., paper, coll.
16780 *Black Star chronicles*. Mahwah, NJ: Watermill Press, 1981, 96 p., paper, coll.
16781 *Ghost horse mystery*. Mahwah, NJ: Watermill Press, 1981, 96 p., paper, novel.
16782 *The haunted planet*. Mahwah, NJ: Watermill Press, 1980, 96 p., paper, coll.
16783 *Monster madness*. Mahwah, NJ: Watermill Press, 1980, 64 p., paper, coll.
16784 *The secret drawing guide to creating space creatures / by "Dr. Drew"*. Mahwah,

NJ: Watermill Press, 1981, 48 p., paper, nonf.

TALLEY, Steven, *with Sharlene Belanger & Adrian Malone*

17673 *The secret.* Boston: Houghton Mifflin Co., 1984, 390 p., cloth, novel.

TALLIS, Robyn, house pseud.

Children of the storm—SEE: *Planet builders: Children of the storm.*
Fire in the sky—SEE: *Planet builders: Fire in the sky.*
Giants of Elenna—SEE: *Planet builders: Giants of Elenna.*
Horrorvid—SEE: *Planet builders: Horrorvid.*
Mountain of stolen dreams—SEE: *Planet builders: Mountain of stolen Dreams.*
Night of ghosts and lightning—SEE: *Planet builders: Night of ghosts and lightning.*
Night of two new moons—SEE: *Planet builders: Night of two new moons.*

35380 *Planet builders: Children of the storm.* New York: Ivy Books, 1989, 179 p., paper, novel. PLANET BUILDERS #7. [By Mary Frances Zambreno].

34358 *Planet builders: Fire in the sky.* New York: Ivy Books, 1989, 186 p., paper, novel. PLANET BUILDERS #10. [By Sherwood Smith].

34359 *Planet builders: Giants of Elenna.* New York: Ivy Books, 1989, 184 p., paper, novel. PLANET BUILDERS #9. [By Sherwood Smith].

28900 *Planet builders: Horrorvid.* New York: Ivy Books, 1989, 185 p., paper, novel. PLANET BUILDERS #8. [By Jymn Magon].

20711 *Planet builders: Mountain of stolen dreams.* New York: Ivy Books, 1988, 185 p., paper, novel. PLANET BUILDERS #1. [By Bruce Coville].

22109 *Planet builders: Night of ghosts and lightning.* New York: Ivy Books, 1989, 185 p., paper, novel. PLANET BUILDERS #2. [By Debra Doyle and James D. Macdonald].

20712 *Planet builders: Night of two new moons.* New York: Ivy Books, 1989, 183 p., paper, novel. PLANET BUILDERS #6. [By Bruce Coville].

34360 *Planet builders: Rebel from Alphorion.* New York: Ivy Books, 1989, 186 p., paper, novel. PLANET BUILDERS #3. [By Sherwood Smith].

34361 *Planet builders: Visions from the sea.* New York: Ivy Books, 1989, 186 p., paper, novel. PLANET BUILDERS #4. [By Sherwood Smith].

22110 *Planet builders: Zero-sum games.* New York: Ivy Books, 1989, 182 p., paper, novel. PLANET BUILDERS #5. [By Debra Doyle and James D. Macdonald].

Rebel from Alphorion—SEE: *Planet builders: Rebel from Alphorion.*
Visions from the sea—SEE: *Planet builders: Visions from the sea.*
Zero-sum games—SEE: *Planet builders: Zero-sum games.*

TALMADGE-BICKMORE, Deborah

35381 *The apprentice.* New York: A Del Rey Book, Ballantine Books, 1990, 263 p., paper, novel.

TAMLYN, Pete

35382 *Green and pleasant land: the British 1920s-1930s Cthulhu sourcepack.* Eastwood, England: Games Workshop, 1987, 88 p., paper, nonf. anth.

with Marc Gascoigne

Blacksand!—SEE: *Steve Jackson and Ian Livingstone present Blacksand!*
Dungeoneer—SEE: *Steve Jackson and Ian Livingstone present Dungeoneer.*

23745 *Steve Jackson and Ian Livingstone present Blacksand!* Harmondsworth, Middlesex, England: Puffin Books, 1990, vi+362 p., paper, fiction. FIGHTING FANTASY GAMEBOOK.

23746 *Steve Jackson and Ian Livingstone present Dungeoneer.* Harmondsworth, Middlesex, England: Puffin Books, 1989, 394 p., paper, fiction. FIGHTING FANTASY GAMEBOOK.

TAMMINGA, Frederick W(illiam), 1935-

35383 *Prescription Z.* Richmond Hill, Ontario, Canada: Scholastic-Tab Publications, 1975, 96 p., paper, novel.

TANNEHILL, Jayne

The Oregon invasion—SEE: *V: The Oregon invasion.*

35384 *V: The Oregon invasion.* New York: Tor SF, A Tom Doherty Associates Book, 1988, 215 p., paper, tele. V SERIES.

TANNEN, Mary, 1943-

35385 *Huntley Nutley and the missing link.* New York: Alfred A. Knopf, 1983, 121 p., cloth, novel.

35386 *The lost legend of Finn.* New York: Alfred A. Knopf, 1982, 144 p., cloth, novel. FINN #2.

35387 *Second sight.* New York: Alfred A. Knopf, 1988, 259 p., cloth, novel.

35388 *The wizard children of Finn.* New York: Alfred A. Knopf, 1981, 214 p., cloth, novel. FINN #1.

TANNER, Mack

35389 *Target: intruder.* New York: Pinnacle Books, Windsor Publishing Corp., 1990, 320 p., paper, novel.

TANNER, Tony, 1935-

35390 *Thomas Pynchon.* London, New York: Methuen, 1982, 95 p., paper, nonf.

TAPP, Kathy Kennedy, 1949-

35391 *Flight of the moth-kin.* New York: Margaret K. McElderry Books, 1987, 118 p., cloth, novel. MOTH-KIN #2.
The ghostmobile—SEE: The scorpio ghosts and the black hole gang.

35392 *Moth-kin magic.* New York: A Margaret K. McElderry Book, Atheneum, 1983, 122 p., cloth, novel. MOTH-KIN #1.

35393 *The scorpio ghosts and the black hole gang.* New York: Harper & Row, 1987, 151 p., cloth, novel. MOTH-KIN #3.

35393a retitled: *The ghostmobile.* New York, Toronto: An Apple Paperback, Scholastic Inc., 1988, 151 p., paper, novel. MOTH-KIN #2.

TARABILDA, James (Thomas), 1948-

35394 *Black sun.* New York: Leisure Books, 1980, 348 p., paper, novel.

TARDIVEL, Jules-Paul, 1851-1905

35395 *For my country: an 1895 religious and separatist vision of Quebec in the mid-twentieth century.* Toronto, Buffalo, NY: University of Toronto Press, 1975, xl+210 p., cloth, novel. [Translation by Sheila Fischman of *Pour la patrie: roman du XXe siècle*].

TARR, Judith, 1955-

35396 *Alamut.* New York: A Foundation Book, Doubleday, 1989, 478 p., cloth, novel. ALAMUT #1.

35397 *Ars magica.* New York, Toronto: Spectra, Bantam Books, 1989, 276 p., paper, novel.

35398 *Avaryan rising.* Garden City, NY: Nelson Doubleday, 1988, 851 p., cloth, coll. AVARYAN RISING #1-3.

35399 *The dagger and the cross: a novel of the Crusades.* New York: A Foundation Book, Doubleday, 1991, 474 p., cloth, novel. ALAMUT #2.

35400 *A fall of princes.* New York: Tor, A Tom Doherty Associates Book, 1988, 401 p., cloth, novel. AVARYAN RISING #3.

35401 *The Golden Horn.* New York: Bluejay International Edition, 1985, 262 p., cloth, novel. HOUND AND THE FALCON #2.

35402 *The hall of the mountain king.* New York: Tor, A Tom Doherty Associates Book, 1986, 278 p., cloth, novel. AVARYAN RISING #1.

35403 *The hound and the falcon.* Garden City, NY: Nelson Doubleday, 1986, 728 p., cloth, coll. HOUND AND THE FALCON #1-3.

35404 *The hounds of God.* New York: A Bluejay International Edition, 1986, 344 p., cloth, novel. HOUND AND THE FALCON #3.

35405 *The isle of glass.* New York: A Bluejay International Edition, 1985, 276 p., cloth, novel. HOUND AND THE FALCON #1.

35406 *The lady of Han-Gilden.* New York: Tor, A Tom Doherty Associates Book, 1987, 310 p., cloth, novel. AVARYAN RISING #2.

35407 *A wind in Cairo.* Toronto, New York: Spectra, Bantam Books, 1989, 261 p., paper, novel.

TARRANT, Desmond, 1924-

35408 *James Branch Cabell: the dream and the reality.* Norman, OK: University of Oklahoma Press, 1967, xii+292 p., cloth, nonf.

TARZAN, Deloris Lehman, *with D. D. Chapman*

19803 *Red tide.* New York: Ace Books, 1975, 239 p., paper, novel.

TASSELI, D. Van—SEE: Van Tasseli, D.

TATE, Peter

35409 *Faces in the flames: fourth in a series of small wars.* Garden City, NY: Doubleday & Co., 1976, 207 p., cloth, novel. SIMEON #3.

35410 *Greencomber.* Garden City, NY: Doubleday & Co., 1979, 182 p., cloth, novel.

35411 *Seagulls under glass, and other stories.* Garden City, NY: Doubleday & Co., 1975, 230 p., cloth, coll.

TATE, Richard, pseud.—SEE: Masters, Anthony

TATTERSALL, (Honor) Jill, 1931-

35412 *Chanters Chase: a novel.* London: Hodder & Stoughton, 1978, 203 p., cloth, novel.

TAY, C. N., *with Moss Roberts*

32465 *Chinese fairy tales and fantasies.* New York: Pantheon Books, 1979, xx+259 p., cloth, anth.

TAYLOR, Al(an James), 1949- , *with Sue Roy*

32792 *Making a monster: the creation of screen characters by the great makeup artists.* New York: Crown Publishers, 1980, x+278 p, cloth, nonf.

TAYLOR, Angus (MacDonald), 1945-

35413 *Philip K. Dick & the umbrella of light.* Baltimore, MD: T-K Graphics, 1975, [52] p., paper, nonf.

TAYLOR, Bernard (Irvin), 1936-

35414 *Charmed life.* London: Grafton, 1991, 366 p., paper, novel.

35415 *The godsend.* London: Souvenir Press, 1976, 208 p., cloth, novel.

35416 *The moorstone sickness.* Loughton, England: Piatkus, 1982, 161 p., cloth, novel.

35416A retitled: *Moorstone.* New York: St. Martin's Press, 1988, 161 p., paper, novel. *Moorstone*—SEE: *Moorstone sickness.*

35417 *The reaping: a novel.* London: Souvenir Press, 1980, 237 p., cloth, novel.

35418 *Sweetheart, sweetheart.* London: Souvenir Press, 1977, 335 p., cloth, novel.

TAYLOR, Charles D(oonan), 1938-

35419 *Boomer.* New York, London: Pocket Books, 1990, 335 p., paper, novel.

35420 *Choke point.* New York: Charter Books, 1986, 326 p., paper, novel. BERNIE RYNG SERIES.

35421 *Counterstrike.* New York: Jove Books, 1988, 273 p., paper, novel. BERNIE RYNG SERIES.

35422 *Deep sting.* New York: Pocket Star Books, 1991, x+371 p., paper, novel. BERNIE RYNG SERIES.

35423 *First salvo.* New York: Charter Books, 1985, 311 p., paper, novel. BERNIE RYNG SERIES.

35424 *Show of force.* New York: St. Martin's Press, 1980, 281 p., cloth, novel.

35425 *Silent hunter.* New York: Charter Books, 1987, 339 p., paper, novel.

35426 *The sunset patriots.* New York: Charter, 1982, 450 p., paper, novel.

35427 *War ship.* New York: Jove Books, 1989, ix+307 p., paper, novel.

TAYLOR, Cora (Lorraine), 1936-

35428 *Julie.* Saskatoon, Saskatchewan, Canada: Western Producer Prairie Books, 1985, 101 p., cloth, novel. JULIE #1.

35429 *Julie's secret.* Saskatoon, Saskatchewan, Canada: Western Producer Prairie Books, 1991, 117 p., cloth, novel. JULIE #2.

TAYLOR, Derek

35430 *The mirrorwell express.* England: Droylata Books, 1991, 63 p., paper, story.

TAYLOR, Domini [pseud. of Roger Erskine Longrigg], 1929-

35431 *Gemini.* London: Hamish Hamilton, 1984, 225 p., cloth, novel.

TAYLOR, Elisabeth D.—SEE: McNeill, Elisabeth

TAYLOR, Elisabeth Russell—SEE: Russell Taylor, Elisabeth

TAYLOR, G(eorge) J(effrey), 1944- , *with R. V. Fodor*

23221 *Impact!* New York: Leisure Books, 1979, 302 p., paper, novel.

TAYLOR, Geoff

35432 *The fantasy art of Geoff Taylor.* London: Corgi Books, 1991, 32 p., paper, art coll.

TAYLOR, Janelle (Diane Williams), 1944-

35433 *Moondust and madness.* Toronto, New
York: Bantam Books, 1986, xvi+415 p.,
paper, novel.

TAYLOR, Jenny (Bourne), 1949-

35434 *Notebooks/memoirs/archives: reading and
rereading Doris Lessing.* Boston, London: Routledge & Kegan Paul, 1982,
xi+251 p., cloth, nonf. anth.

TAYLOR, Jeri, 1946?-

35435 *Star Trek, the next generation: Unification:
a novel.* New York, London: Pocket
Books, 1991, x | 245 p., paper, tele.
STAR TREK: THE NEXT GENERATION
(UNNUMBERED).
Unification—SEE: *Star Trek, the next generation: Unification.*

TAYLOR, Keith (John), 1946-

35436 *Bard.* New York: Ace Books, 1981, 293
p., paper, novel. BARD #1.
35437 *Bard II.* New York: Ace Fantasy Books,
1984, 260 p., paper, novel. BARD #2.
35437A retitled: *The first longship.* London:
Headline, 1989, 260 p., paper, novel.
BARD #2.
35438 *The cauldron of plenty.* New York: Ace
Books, 1989, 214 p., paper, novel.
DANANS #2.
35439 *Felimid's homecoming.* London: Headline, 1991, 280 p., paper, novel. BARD
#5.
The first longship—SEE: *Bard II.*
35440 *Lances of Nengesdul.* St. Kilda, Victoria,
Australia: Cory & Collins, 1982, 196 p.,
paper, novel.
35441 *Ravens' gathering.* New York: Ace
Books, 1987, 235 p., paper, novel.
BARD #4.
35442 *Search for the starblade.* New York: Ace
Books, 1990, 248 p., paper, novel.
DANANS #3.
35443 *The sorcerers' sacred isle.* New York:
Ace Books, 1989, 218 p., paper, novel.
DANANS #1.
35444 *The wild sea.* New York: Ace Fantasy
Books, 1986, 202 p., paper, novel.
BARD #3.

with Andrew J. Offutt

30968 *The tower of death.* New York: Ace
Books, 1982, 246 p., paper, novel.
CORMAC MAC ART #2.

30969 *When death birds fly.* New York: Ace
Books, 1980, 295 p., paper, novel.
CORMAC MAC ART #3.

**TAYLOR, L. A. [i.e., Laurie Aylma Taylor
Sparer], 1939-**

35445 *The blossom of Erda.* New York: St.
Martin's Press, 1986, 247 p., cloth,
novel.

TAYLOR, Lisa, 1959-

35446 *All on a winter's day.* London: Hippo,
1989, 138 p., paper, novel.

TAYLOR, Lucy (Campbell), 1950?-

35447 *Flame thrower.* Arvada, CO: Roadkill
Press, 1991, 30 p., paper, story. [Bound
with *Blood rights* / by Ann K. Schwader].

TAYLOR, R. G.

35448 *Futura man, an orphan in time.* New
York, Washington: Vantage Press, 1979,
198 p., cloth, novel.

TAYLOR, Roger

35449 *The call of the sword.* London: Headline,
1988, 280 p., paper, novel. HAWKLAN
#1.
35450 *Dream finder.* London: Headline, 1991,
436 p., cloth, novel.
35451 *The fall of Fyorlund.* London: Headline,
1989, 467 p., paper, novel. HAWKLAN
#2.
35452 *Into Narsindal.* London: Headline, 1990,
533 p., paper, novel. HAWKLAN #4.
35453 *The waking of Orthlund.* London: Headline, 1989, 472 p., paper, novel. HAWKLAN #3.

TAYLOR, Sheila Ortiz, 1939-

35454 *Spring forward/fall back: a novel.* Tallahassee, FL: Naiad Press, 1985, 257 p.,
paper, novel.

**TAYLOR, Sybil (Renee), 1933- , with Ulrich
Ruchti**

32804 *Story into film: three tales of the supernatural go from page to screen.* New York:
Laurel-Leaf Library, 1978, 256 p., paper,
anth.

TEA, Traves, pseud.—SEE: Lasser, Dustin

TEACHER, Rebecca, 1948-

35455 *Rainbow magic.* Lewes, East Sussex, England: The Book Guild, 1990, 141 p., cloth, novel.

TEACHERS COLLEGE LIBRARY

35456 *Science fiction.* Auckland, New Zealand: Teachers College Library, 1984, 25 p., paper, nonf.

TEAGUE, Robert, 1929- , with Michael Goodwin

24127 *A guide to the Commonwealth: the official guide to Alan Dean Foster's Humanx Commonwealth universe.* Roy, UT: Galagraphics Press, 1985, 70 p., paper, nonf.

TEALE, Sarah, with David Larkin

27839 *Giants.* New York: Henry N. Abrams, 1979, 191 p., cloth, fiction.

TEDFORD, William G.

35457 *Hydrabyss red.* New York: Leisure Books, 1981, 232 p., paper, novel. TIMEQUEST #2.

35458 *Nemydia Deep.* New York: Leisure Books, 1981, 287 p., paper, novel. TIMEQUEST #3.

35459 *Rashanyn dark.* New York: Leisure Books, 1981, 281 p., paper, novel. TIMEQUEST #1.

35460 *Silent galaxy.* New York: Leisure Books, 1981, 283 p., paper, novel.

TEED, Jack Hamilton, pseud.—SEE: Adrian, Jack

TEITELBAUM, Sheldon, with Ron Magid & Wendy Rathbone & Kay Anderson & Edward Gross

16369 *The making of the Trek films.* East Meadow, NY: Image Publishing, 1991, 172 p., paper, nonf.

TELFORD, Robert

35462 *Storm haven.* London: Headline, 1990, 373 p., cloth, novel.

TELLA, Alfred

35463 *Sundered soul: a mythic tale.* Washington, DC: Three Continents Press, 1990, 226 p., cloth, novel.

TELLES, Lygia Fagundes, 1923-

35464 *Tigrela, and other stories.* New York: Avon Bard, 1986, 152 p., paper, coll. [Translation by Margaret A. Neves of *Seminário dos ratos*].

TELOTTE, J(ay) P(aul), 1949-

35465 *Dreams of darkness: fantasy and the films of Val Lewton.* Urbana, IL & Chicago: University of Illinois Press, 1985, 223 p., cloth, nonf.

TEM, Melanie

35466 *Daddy's side.* Arvada, CO: Roadkill Press, 1991, 19 p., paper, story. [Limited to 300 copies].

35467 *Prodigal.* New York: A Dell Book, 1991, 377 p., paper, novel. [Winner of the Bram Stoker Award for Best First Horror Novel, 1991 (1992)].

TEM, Steve Rasnic, 1950-

35468 *Absences.* Hoole, Chester, Cheshire, England: The Haunted Library, 1991, 32 p., paper, coll.

35469 *Celestial inventory.* Polk City, IA: Chris Drumm, 1991, 54 p., paper, story. DRUMM BOOKLET #36.

35470 *Excavation.* New York: Avon, 1987, 280 p., paper, novel.

35471 *Fairytales.* Arvada, CO: Roadkill Press, 1990, 27 p., paper, story. [Limited to 400 copies].

35472 *One view: creating characters in fantasy and horror fiction.* Eugene, OR: Writer's Notebook Press, Pulphouse Publishing, 1991, 14 p., paper, nonf.

TEMPEST, John [pseud. of Julian Spillsbury]

35473 *Vision of the hunter.* New York: Harper & Row, 1989, 266 p., cloth, novel.

TEMPLE, Leah—SEE: Patton, Leah

TEMPLE, Robin, pseud.—SEE: Wood, S. Andrew

*TEMPLE, William F(rederick), 1914-1989

TEMPLETON, Charles (Bradley), 1915-

35474 *Act of God.* Toronto: McClelland & Stewart, 1977, 319 p., cloth, novel.

TENNANT, Emma (Christina), 1937-

35475   *The bad sister: a novel.* London: Victor Gollancz, 1978, 223 p., cloth, novel.
  The crack—SEE: *Time of the crack.*

35476   *Hotel de Dream.* London: Victor Gollancz, 1976, 190 p., cloth, novel.

35477   *The last of the country house murders.* London: Jonathan Cape, 1974, 160 p., cloth, novel.

35478   *Queen of stones.* London: Jonathan Cape, 1982, 160 p., cloth, novel.

35478   *Sisters and strangers: a moral tale.* London: Grafton, 1990, 184 p., cloth, novel.

14028   *The time of the crack.* London: Jonathan Cape, 1973, 142 p., cloth, novel.

14028A retitled: *The crack.* Harmondsworth, Middlesex, England: Penguin Books, 1978, 112 p., paper, novel.

35479   *Two women of London: the strange case of Ms Jekyll and Mrs Hyde.* London: Faber & Faber, 1989, 121 p., cloth, novel.

35480   *Wild nights.* London: Jonathan Cape, 1979, 134 p., cloth, novel.

TEPPER, Sheri S., 1929-

35481   *After long silence.* Toronto, New York: Bantam Books, 1987, 343 p., paper, novel.

35481A retitled: *The enigma score.* London: Corgi Books, 1989, 384 p., paper, novel.

35482   *The awakeners.* Garden City, NY: Nelson Doubleday, 1987, 437 p., cloth, coll. AWAKENERS #1-2.

35483   *Beauty: a novel.* New York: A Foundation Book, Doubleday, 1991, 412 p., cloth, novel. [Winner of the *Locus* Award for Best Fantasy Novel, 1991 (1992)].

35484   *Blood heritage.* New York: Tor, A Tom Doherty Associates Book, 1986, 287 p., paper, novel. BLOOD HERITAGE #1.

35485   *The bones.* New York: Tor Horror, A Tom Doherty Associates Book, 1987, 315 p., paper, novel. BLOOD HERITAGE #2.

35486   *The chronicles of Mavin Manyshaped.* London: Corgi Books, 1986, 436 p., paper, coll. TRUE GAME SERIES—MAVIN #1-3.

35487   *Dervish daughter.* New York: Tor SF, A Tom Doherty Associates Book, 1986, 218 p., paper, novel. TRUE GAME SERIES; JINIAN #2.

35488   *The end of the game.* Garden City, NY: Nelson Doubleday, 1987, 528 p., cloth, coll. JINIAN #1-3.
  The enigma score—SEE: *After long silence.*

35489   *The flight of Mavin Manyshaped.* New York: Ace Fantasy Books, 1985, 186 p., paper, novel. TRUE GAME SERIES—MAVIN #2.

35490   *The gate to Women's Country.* New York: A Foundation Book, Doubleday, 1988, 278 p., cloth, novel.

35491   *Grass.* New York: A Foundation Book, Doubleday, 1989, 426 p., cloth, novel.

35492   *Jinian Footseer.* New York: Tor SF, A Tom Doherty Associates Book, 1985, 284 p., paper, novel. TRUE GAME SERIES; JINIAN #1.

35493   *Jinian Star-eye.* New York: Tor SF, A Tom Doherty Associates Book, 1986, 252 p., paper, novel. TRUE GAME SERIES; JINIAN #3.

35494   *King's Blood Four.* New York: Ace Fantasy Books, 1983, 202 p., paper, novel. TRUE GAME #1.

35495   *Marianne, the madame, and the momentary gods.* New York: Ace Books, 1988, 178 p., paper, novel. MARIANNE #2.

35496   *Marianne, the magus, and the manticore.* New York: Ace Fantasy Books, 1985, 185 p., paper, novel. MARIANNE #1.

35497   *Marianne, the matchbox, and the malachite mouse.* New York: Ace Books, 1989, 167 p., paper, novel. MARIANNE #3.

35498   *The Marianne trilogy.* London: Corgi Books, 1990, 524 p., paper, coll. MARIANNE #1-3.

35499   *Necromancer Nine.* New York: Ace Fantasy Books, 1983, 175 p., paper, novel. TRUE GAME #21.

35500   *Northshore.* New York: Tor, A Tom Doherty Associates Book, 1987, 248 p., cloth, novel. AWAKENERS #1.

35501   *Raising the stones.* New York: A Foundation Book, Doubleday, 1990, 453 p., cloth, novel.

35502   *The revenants.* New York: Ace Fantasy Books, 1984, 342 p., paper, novel.

35503   *The search of Mavin Manyshaped.* New York: Ace Fantasy Books, 1985, 168 p., paper, novel. TRUE GAME SERIES—MAVIN #3.

35504   *The song of Mavin Manyshaped.* New York: Ace Fantasy Books, 1985, 183 p., paper, novel. TRUE GAME SERIES—MAVIN #1

35505   *Southshore.* New York: Tor, A Tom Doherty Associates Book, 1987, 250 p., cloth, novel. AWAKENERS #2.

35508A *Still life.* London: Corgi Books, 1989, 246 p., paper, novel. [Originally published under the name E. E. Horlak].

35506   *The true game.* London: Corgi Books, 1985, 543 p., paper, coll. TRUE GAME #1-3.

35507 *Wizard's Eleven.* New York: Ace Fantasy Books, 1984, xiv+187 p., paper, novel. TRUE GAME #3.

as E. E. HORLAK

35508 *Still Life.* Toronto, New York: Spectra, Bantam Books, 1989, 200 p., paper, novel.

TEPPERMAN, Emile C.

as CURTIS STEELE

34809 *Revolt of the devil men.* Chicago?: Readers Press, 1975, [96] p., paper, novel. OPERATOR 5 SERIES.

as GRANT STOCKBRIDGE

35056 *The Spider, master of men!* New York: Carroll & Graf, 1991, 316 p., paper, coll. SPIDER #2. [Includes *Dictator of the damned*; and, *The mill-town massacres*].

TERLOUW, Jan (Cornelis), 1931-

35510 *How to become king—1976.* Glasgow, Scotland: Blackie & Son, 1976, 128 p., cloth, novel. [Translation of *Koning van katoren*].

TERMAN, Douglas (J.), 1933-

35511 *By balloon to the Sahara* / by D. Terman. Toronto, New York: Bantam Books, 1979, 117 p., paper, novel.
35511a retitled: *Danger in the desert.* New York: Bantam Books, 1989, 117 p., paper, novel. CHOOSE YOUR OWN ADVENTURE #3.
Danger in the desert—SEE: *By balloon to the Sahara.*
35512 *First strike.* New York: Charles Scribner's Sons, 1979, 368 p., cloth, novel.
35513 *Free flight.* New York: Charles Scribner's Sons, 1980, 349 p., cloth, novel.

TERRA, John, *with Rick Stuart*

35180 *Star Trek the next generation officer's manual.* Chicago: FASA Corp., 1988, 144 p., paper, fiction. STAR TREK TIE-IN.

TERRIFIC, Ted, pseud.

35514 *Star whores.* New York: Pleasure Books, 1979, 188 p., paper, novel.

TERRY, Bridget

35515 *The Popeye story.* New York: A Tom Doherty Associates Book, 1980, 285 p., paper, nonf.

TESSIER, Thomas, 1947-

35516 *The Fates.* London: Futura, 1978, 203 p., paper, novel.
35517 *Finishing touches.* New York: Atheneum, 1986, 243 p., cloth, novel.
35518 *The nightwalker.* London: Macmillan, 1979, 158 p., cloth, novel.
35519 *Phantom.* New York: Atheneum, 1982, ix+274 p., cloth, novel.
35520 *Rapture.* New York: Atheneum, 1987, 310 p., cloth, novel.
35521 *Shockwaves.* London: Fontana, 1983, 222 p., paper, novel.

TESSLER, Stephanie (Gordon), 1940- , *with Judith Enderle*, as JEFFIE ROSS GORDON

22668 *A touch of genius.* New York: Silhouette Books, 1986, 157 p., paper, novel.
22669 *A touch of magic.* New York: Silhouette Books, 1987, 155 p., paper, novel.

TEUNISSEN, John J(ames), 1933-

35522 *Other worlds: fantasy and science fiction since 1939.* Winnipeg, Manitoba, Canada: University of Manitoba, 1980, xiv+225 p., cloth, nonf. coll.

TEVIS, Walter (Stone Jr.), 1928-1984

35523 *Far from home.* Garden City, NY: Doubleday & Co., 1981, 181 p., cloth, coll.
35524 *Mockingbird.* Garden City, NY: Doubleday & Co., 1980, 247 p., cloth, novel.
35525 *The steps of the sun.* Garden City, NY: Doubleday & Co., 1983, 251 p., cloth, novel.

with David Fickling

23063 *The man who fell to Earth.* Oxford, England: Alpha Books, Oxford University Press, 1979, 94 p., paper, novel. [Adapted from the novel by Tevis].

TEWELES, Claude

35526 *The stalker.* New York: Zebra Books, Kensington Publishing Corp., 1984, 334 p., paper, novel.
35527 *The wilds.* New York: A Dell Book, 1989, 213 p., paper, novel.

THACKERAY, William Makepeace, 1811-1863, *as* M. A. TITMARSH

15869 *The rose and the ring; or, The history of Prince Giglio and Prince Bulbo: a fireside pantomime for great and small children* / by M. A. Titmarsh. London: Smith, Elder & Co., 1855, 128 p., cloth, novel.

15869A *The rose and the ring; or, The history of Prince Giglio and Prince Bulbo* / by W. M. Thackeray. Boston: Estes & Lauriat, 1883, 148 p., cloth, novel.

THACKERY, Anne

35528 *Ragnarok.* London: Bantam Press, 1989, 192 p., paper, novel.

THAL, Herbert Van—SEE: Van Thal, Herbert

*THANE, Elswyth (Beebe), 1900-1984

THAYER, Nancy, 1943-

35529 *Spirit lost.* New York: Charles Scribner's Sons, 1988, 199 p., cloth, novel.

THAYER, Tiffany (Ellsworth), 1902-1959

35530 *33 sardonics I can't forget.* New York: Philosophical Library, 1946, 389 p., cloth, anth.

THEMERSON, Stefan, 1910-1988

38105 *Hobson's Island.* London: Faber & Faber, 1988, [250] p., cloth, novel.

38106 *The mystery of the sardine.* London: Faber & Faber, 1986, 194 p., cloth, novel.

*THEODAMUS [pseud. of Theodore Glass], 1896-1970

THEODORE, Brother [pseud. of Theodore Gottlieb], *with Marvin Kaye*

26951 *Brother Theodore's chamber of horrors.* New York: Pinnacle Books, 1975, 237 p., paper, anth.

THEROUX, Paul (Edward), 1941-

38107 *The black house.* Boston: Houghton Mifflin Co., 1974, 245 p., cloth, novel.

35531 *O-Zone.* New York: G. P. Putnam's Sons, 1986, 527 p., cloth, novel.

THESMAN, Jean

35532 *Appointment with a stranger.* Boston: Houghton Mifflin Co., 1989, 166 p., cloth, novel.

THEYDON, John, pseud.—SEE: Jennison, John

THIESSEN, J(ames) Grant, 1947-

35533 *The science fiction collector, volume one.* Altona, Manitoba, Canada: Pandora's Books, 1981, [222] p., cloth, nonf. anth.

35534 *The science fiction collector, volume two.* Altona, Manitoba, Canada: Pandora's Books, 1981, [196] p., cloth, nonf. anth.

35535 *The science fiction collector, volume three.* Altona, Manitoba, Canada: Pandora's Books, 1981, [196] p., cloth, nonf. anth.

THODY, Philip (Malcolm Waller), 1928-

35536 *Aldous Huxley: a biographical introduction.* London: Studio Vista, 1973, 144 p., cloth, nonf.

35536A retitled: *Huxley: a biographical introduction.* New York: Charles Scribner's Sons, 1973, 144 p., cloth, nonf.

THOET, Felicity

35537 *The book of the dun cow teacher's guide.* New York: Pocket Books Education Dept., 1979?, 31 p., paper, nonf.

THOKAR, Greg(ory Allen), 1955-

35538 *Noreascon Three souvenir book.* Cambridge, MA: NESFA Press, 1989, 192 p., paper, anth. [Includes some nonfiction].

*THOM, Robert, 1929-1979

THOMAS, Bill, *with Bill Warren*

35539 *Keep watching the skies!: American science fiction movies of the fifties, volume 1, 1950-1957.* Jefferson, NC & London: McFarland & Co., 1982, xvi+467 p., cloth, nonf.

35540 *Keep watching the skies!: American science fiction movies of the fifties, volume II, 1958-1962.* Jefferson, NC & London: McFarland & Co., 1987, xx+839 p., cloth, nonf.

THOMAS, Craig (David), 1942-

35541 *Firefox.* London: Michael Joseph, 1977, 288 p., cloth, novel. FIREFOX #1.

35542 *Firefox down!* London: Michael Joseph, 1983, 340 p., cloth, novel. FIREFOX #2.

35543 *Sea Leopard.* London: Michael Joseph, 1981, 315 p., cloth, novel.

as DAVID GRANT

35544 *Moscow 5000.* London: Michael Joseph, 1979, 445 p., cloth, novel.

with David Fickling

23064 *Firefox.* Oxford, England: Alpha Books, Oxford University Press, 1980, 96 p., paper, novel. [Adapted from the novel by Thomas].

THOMAS, D(onald) M(ichael), 1935-

38108 *Ararat.* London: Victor Gollancz, 1983, 191 p., cloth, novel. RUSSIAN QUARTET #1.

38109 *Birthstone: a novel.* London: Victor Gollancz, 1980, 160 p., cloth, novel.

38110 *Birthstone: a novel.* Harmondsworth, Middlesex, England: Penguin Books, 1982, 157 p., paper, novel. [Revised edition].

38111 *The devil and the floral papers.* London: Robson Books, 1978, 64 p., cloth, story.

35545 *Sphinx.* Toronto: Lester & Orpen Dennys, 1986, 248 p., cloth, novel. RUSSIAN QUARTET #3.

38112 *Summit.* London: Victor Gollancz, 1987, 160 p., cloth, novel. RUSSIAN QUARTET #4.

38113 *Swallow.* London: Victor Gollancz, 1984, 312 p., cloth, novel. RUSSIAN QUARTET #2.

38114 *The white hotel: a novel.* London: Victor Gollancz, 1981, 240 p., cloth, novel.

THOMAS, Donna, *with Peter Thomas*

35546 *Yotan's vision.* Santa Cruz, CA: [The Good Book Press], 1980, [25] p., cloth, story. [Limited to 150 copies].

THOMAS, Dwight (Rembert), 1944- , *with David K. Jackson*

26368 *The Poe log: a documentary life of Edgar Allan Poe, 1809-1849.* Boston: G. K. Hall & Co., 1987, xlix+919 p., cloth, nonf.

THOMAS, Edward Llewellyn- —SEE: Llewellyn, Edward

THOMAS, Edward M(orley)

35547 *Orwell.* London: Oliver & Boyd, 1965, 114 p., cloth, nonf.

THOMAS, Elizabeth Marshall, 1931-

35548 *The animal wife.* Boston: Houghton Mifflin Book, 1990, 289 p., cloth, novel. REINDEER MOON #2.

35549 *Reindeer moon.* Boston: A Peter Davison Book, Houghton Mifflin Book, 1987, 338 p., cloth, novel. REINDEER MOON #1.

THOMAS, Francis, 1912-1977

35550 *Cityscape.* London: Heinemann, 1988, 144 p., cloth, novel.

35551 *Gull against the wind: a thriller of the future.* Monmouth, Gwent, Wales: M. Thomas, 1980, 167 p., paper, novel.

THOMAS, Jane Resh, 1936-

35552 *The princess in the pigpen.* Boston: Clarion Books, 1989, 130 p., cloth, novel.

THOMAS, Joyce Carol (Haynes), 1938-

35553 *Journey.* New York, Toronto: Scholastic Inc., 1988, 153 p., cloth, novel.

THOMAS, Martin [pseud. of Thomas Hector Martin], 1913-1985, *with W. Howard Baker as* PETER SAXON

12721 *The curse of Rathlaw.* New York: Lancer Books, 1968, 190 p., paper, novel. GUARDIANS SERIES.

THOMAS, Michele Y.

35554 *Crystal shadows.* New York: Zebra Books, Kensington Publishing Corp., 1989, 397 p., paper, novel.

THOMAS, Peter, *with Donna Thomas*

35546 *Yotan's vision.* Santa Cruz, CA: [The Good Book Press], 1980, [25] p., cloth, story. [Limited to 150 copies].

as PETER PAPERMAKER

35555 *The tale of Cara-sou and his magic word.* Santa Cruz, CA: The Good Book Press, 1979, [12] p., cloth, coll. [Limited to 30 copies].

35556 *The three cedars: a collection of short stories.* Santa Cruz, CA: The Good Book

Press, 1978, 19 p., cloth, coll. [Limited to 150 copies].

*THOMAS, Theodore L(ockard), 1920-

THOMAS, Thomas T(hurston), 1948-

35557 *First citizen.* New York: Baen Books, 1987, 373 p., paper, novel.
35558 *Me: a novel of self-discovery.* Riverdale, NY: Baen Books, 1991, 341 p., paper, novel.

as THOMAS WREN

35559 *The doomsday effect.* New York: Baen Science Fiction Books, 1986, 290 p., paper, novel.

with David Drake

22187 *An honorable defense.* New York: Baen Books, 1988, 310 p., paper, novel. CRISIS OF EMPIRE #1.

with Roger Zelazny

35560 *The mask of Loki.* Riverdale, NY: Baen Fantasy, 1990, 340 p., paper, novel.

THOMEY, Tedd, 1920-

35561 *The prodigy plot.* New York: Warner Books, 1987, 330 p., paper, novel.

THOMPSON, Allyn

35562 *The Azriel uprising.* Toronto, New York: Bantam Books, 1982, 181 p., paper, novel.

THOMPSON, Diane, *with Les Daniels*

21100 *Thirteen tales of terror.* New York: Charles Scribner's Sons, 1977, xviii+260 p., paper, anth.

THOMPSON, Don(ald Arthur), 1935- , *with Maggie Thompson*

35563 *The official price guide to science fiction and fantasy collectibles, 3rd ed.* New York: House of Collectibles, 1989, viii+482 p., paper, nonf.

THOMPSON, Donald

35564 *The ancient enemy.* New York: Fawcett Gold Medal, 1979, 220 p., paper, novel.

35565 *The next encounter.* New York: Fawcett Gold Medal, 1982, 224 p., paper, novel.

THOMPSON, E(dward) P(almer), 1924-

35566 *The communism of William Morris: a lecture given on 4th May 1959 in the Hall of Art Workers' Guild, London.* London: William Morris Society, 1965, 19 p., paper, nonf.
35567 *The Sykaos papers: being an account of the voyages of the poet Oi Paz to the system of Strim in the seventeenth century, selected and edited by Q* / by Edward Palmer Thompson. London: Bloomsbury, 1988, viii+482 p., cloth, novel.
35568 *William Morris: romantic to revolutionary.* London: Lawrence & Wishart, 1955, 908 p., cloth, nonf.

THOMPSON, Eugene A.—SEE: Thompson, Gene

THOMPSON, Frank H. Jr., 1926-

with Clifton K. Hillegass

25678 *Animal farm: notes.* Lincoln, NE: Cliffs Notes, 1967, 51 p., paper, nonf.

with Robert K. Kaplan

26875 *1984: notes.* Lincoln, NE: Cliffs Notes, 1967, 51 p., paper, nonf.

THOMPSON, G(ary) R(ichard), 1937-

35569 *Romantic gothic tales, 1790-1840.* New York: Perennial Library, Harper & Row, 1979, x+337 p., paper, anth.

with Virgil L. Lokke

28494 *Ruined Eden of the present: Hawthorne, Melville, and Poe: critical essays in honor of Darrel Abel.* West Lafayette, IN: Purdue University Press, 1981, xix+383 p., cloth, nonf. anth.

THOMPSON, Gary [i.e., Gary Allen Thompson-Moraga], 1951-

35570 *Chumash.* New York: Leisure Books, 1986, 400 p., paper, novel.

THOMPSON, Gene [i.e., Eugene Allen Thompson], 1924-

35571 *Lupe.* New York: Random House, 1977, 285 p., cloth, novel.

THOMPSON, George S.—SEE: Selden, George

*THOMPSON, Harlan (Howard), 1894-<u>1987</u>

THOMPSON, Harrison R.

35572 *Seventh sense.* New York: Manor Books, 1979 (i.e., 1980?), 335 p., paper, novel.

THOMPSON, Howard

35573 *The glitterball.* London: Methuen, 1979, 127 p., cloth, movie.

THOMPSON, Joyce (Marie), 1948-

Bigfoot and the Hendersons—SEE: *Harry and the Hendersons.*
35574 *The blue chair: a novel.* New York: Avon, 1977, 246 p., paper, novel.
35575 *Conscience Place: a novel.* Garden City, NY: Doubleday & Co., 1984, 225 p., cloth, novel.
35576 *Harry and the Hendersons: a novel.* New York: Berkley Books, 1987, 233 p., paper, movie.
35576A retitled: *Bigfoot and the Hendersons.* Harmondsworth, Middlesex, England: Puffin Books, 1987, 189 p., paper, movie.

THOMPSON, Julian F(rancis), 1927-

35577 *Goofbang value daze.* New York, Toronto: Scholastic Inc., 1989, 261 p., cloth, coll.
35578 *The grounding of group 6.* New York: Avon Flare Books, 1983, 282 p., paper, novel.
35579 *Herb Seasoning.* New York, Toronto: Point Fiction, Scholastic Inc., 1990, 280 p., cloth, novel.
35580 *A question of survival.* New York: Avon Flare, 1984, 293 p., paper, novel.

THOMPSON, Maggie [i.e., Margaret Curtis Thompson], *with Don Thompson*

35563 *The official price guide to science fiction and fantasy collectibles, 3rd ed.* New York: House of Collectibles, 1989, viii+482 p., paper, nonf.

THOMPSON, Paul (Richard), 1935-

35581 *The work of William Morris.* London: Heinemann, 1967, xvi+300 p., cloth, nonf.

35582 *The work of William Morris, 2nd ed.* London: Quartet Books, 1977, ix+325 p., cloth, nonf.
35583 *The work of William Morris, 3rd ed.* Oxford, England: Oxford University Press, 1991, xvi+318 p., cloth, nonf.

THOMPSON, Paul B., 1951-

35584 *Sundipper.* New York: St. Martin's Press, 1987, 215 p., paper, novel.

with Tonya R. Carter

19614 *Darkness & light.* Lake Geneva, WI: TSR Inc., 1989, 377 p., paper, novel. DRAG-ONLANCE PRELUDES #1.
19615 *DragonLance saga: Firstborn.* Lake Geneva, WI: TSR Inc., 1991, 305 p., paper, novel. ELVEN NATIONS TRILOGY #1.
19615 *DragonLance saga: The Qualinesti.* Lake Geneva, WI: TSR Inc., 1991, 310 p., paper, novel. ELVEN NATIONS TRILOGY #3.
Firstborn—SEE: *DragonLance saga: Firstborn.*
The Qualinesti—SEE: *DragonLance saga: The Qualinesti.*
19616 *Red sands: an Arabian adventure.* Lake Geneva, WI: TSR Inc., 1988, 338 p., paper, novel.
19617 *Riverwind the plainsman.* Lake Geneva, WI: TSR Inc., 1990, 313 p., paper, novel. DRAGONLANCE PRELUDES II #1.

THOMPSON, Raymond H(enry), 1941-

35585 *Bibliography of Arthurian literature, from the nineteenth to twentieth centuries, in the Newberry Library, Chicago.* Wolfville, Nova Scotia, Canada: Raymond H. Thompson, 1982, 29 leaves, paper, nonf.
35586 *Gordon R. Dickson: a primary and secondary bibliography.* Boston: G. K. Hall, 1983, xix+108 p., cloth, nonf. MASTERS OF SCIENCE FICTION AND FANTASY.
35587 *The return from Avalon: a study of the Arthurian legend in modern fiction.* Westport, CT: Greenwood Press, 1985, 206 p., cloth, nonf. CONTRIBUTIONS TO THE STUDY OF SCIENCE FICTION AND FANTASY #14.

THOMPSON, Robert E(lliott), 1921-

35588 *The trial of Lee Harvey Oswald.* New York: Ace Books, 1977, 181 p., paper, movie.

THOMPSON, V. M.

35589 *Deadly nature.* New York: Zebra Books, Kensington Publishing Corp., 1988, 429 p., paper, novel.

35590 *Project God.* New York: Zebra Books, Kensington Publishing Corp., 1989, 352 p., paper, novel.

THOMPSON, W(illiam) R(och), 1955-

35591 *Sideshow.* New York: Baen Books, 1988, 346 p., paper, novel.

THOMPSON, William Irwin, 1938-

35592 *Islands out of time: a memoir of the last days of Atlantis: a metafiction.* Garden City, NY: The Dial Press, Doubleday & Co., 1985, xv+222 p., cloth, novel.

THOMPSON-MORAGA, Gary A.—SEE: Thompson, Gary

THOMSEN, Brian, *with Baird Searles*

33495 *Halflings, hobbits, warrows, & weefolk: a collection of tales of heroes short in stature.* New York: Warner Books, 1991, vi+275 p., paper, anth.

*THOMSON, Christine Campbell, 1897-1985

THOMSON, David, 1941-

38115 *Suspects.* London: Secker & Warburg, 1985, [288] p, cloth, novel.

38116 *Warren Beatty: a life and a story.* London: Secker & Warburg, 1987, [346] p, cloth, fiction.

38116A retitled: *Warren Beatty and Desert Eyes: a life and a story.* Garden City, NY: Doubleday & Co., 1987, xii+399 p., cloth, fiction.

THOMSON, Jamie

with Dave Morris

30296 *The crystal maze: adventure gamebook.* London: Mammoth, 1991, [150] p., paper, novel.

with Dave Morris & Oliver Johnson

26631 *The walls of Spyte.* London: Knight, 1988, 313 p., paper, novel.

with Mark Smith

34318 *Arena of death.* London: Armada, 1987, 2 v., paper, fiction. DUELMASTER #4.

34319 *Assassin!* Sevenoaks, Kent, England: Knight Books, 1985, 254 p., paper, fiction. WAY OF THE TIGER #2.

34320 *At the end of time.* London: Sphere Books, 1986, [171] p., paper, novel. FALCON #6.

34321 *Avenger!* Sevenoaks, Kent, England: Knight Books, 1985, 256 p., paper, fiction. WAY OF THE TIGER #1.

34322 *Blood valley.* London: Armada, 1986, 2 v., paper, fiction. DUELMASTER #2.

34323 *Challenge of the Magi.* London: Armada Books, 1986, 2 v., paper, novel. DUELMASTER #1.

34324 *Duelmaster.* London: Armada Books, 1986, 2 v., paper, novel. DUELMASTER #2.

34325 *The dying sun.* London: Sphere Books, 1986, [190] p., paper, novel. FALCON #5.

34326 *Inferno!* Sevenoaks, Kent, England: Knight Books, 1987, [224] p., paper, fiction. WAY OF THE TIGER #6.

34327 *Lost in time.* London: Sphere Books, 1985, p., paper, novel. FALCON #4.

34328 *Mechanon.* London: Sphere Books, 1985, p., paper, novel. FALCON #2.

34329 *Overlord!* Sevenoaks, Kent, England: Knight Books, 1986, 253 p., paper, novel. WAY OF THE TIGER #4.

34330 *The rack of Baal.* London: Sphere Books, 1985, p., paper, novel. FALCON #3.

34331 *The renegade lord.* London: Sphere Books, 1985, p., paper, novel. FALCON #1.

34332 *The shattered realm.* London: Armada, 1987, 2 v., paper, fiction. DUELMASTER #3.

34333 *Sword of the samurai.* Harmondsworth, Middlesex, England: Puffin Books, 1986, [236] p., paper, novel. FIGHTING FANTASY GAMEBOOK #20.

34334 *Talisman of death.* Harmondsworth, Middlesex, England: Puffin Books, 1985, [250] p., paper, novel. FIGHTING FANTASY GAMEBOOK #11.

34335 *Usurper!* London: Knight Books, 1985, 269 p., paper, novel. WAY OF THE TIGER #3.

34336 *Warbringer!* Sevenoaks, Kent, England: Knight Books, 1986, 255 p., paper, novel. WAY OF THE TIGER #5.

THOMSON, Rupert, 1955-

35593 *Dreams of leaving.* London: Bloomsbury, 1987, 435 p., cloth, novel.

THORNBURG, Mary K(atherine) Patterson, 1940-

35594 *The monster in the mirror: gender and the sentimental/gothic myth in Frankenstein.* Ann Arbor, MI: UMI Research Press, 1987, 154 p., cloth, nonf. STUDIES IN SPECULATIVE FICTION #14.

THORNBURG, Newton (Kendall), 1930-

35595 *Valhalla.* Boston: Little, Brown & Co., 1980, 337 p., cloth, novel.

THORNE, Ian, pseud.—SEE: May, Julian

THORNER, J(onathan) Lincoln, 1949-

35596 *A guide through the worlds of Robert A. Heinlein.* Brooklyn, NY: Gryphon Books, 1989, 48 p., paper, nonf.

THORNLEY, Diann, 1957-

35597 *Ganwold's child.* Xenia, OH: Synapse, 1991, 437 p., paper, novel.

THORNTON, Lawrence, 1937-

35598 *Imagining Argentina.* London: Bloomsbury, 1987, 214 p., cloth, novel.

THORPE, Fred [pseud. of Albert Stearns], d. 1899

35599 *Through the Earth; or, Jack Nelson's invention.* New York: Street & Smith, 1909, 31 p., paper, novel.

THORPE, Michael, 1932-

35600 *Doris Lessing.* London: Published for the British Council by Longman Group Ltd., 1973, 37 p., paper, nonf.
35601 *Doris Lessing's Africa.* London: Evans Brothers, 1978, x+117 p., cloth, nonf.

THORSON, James L(lewellyn), 1934- , with Marilyn P. Fletcher

23195 *Reader's guide to twentieth-century science fiction.* Chicago & London: American Library Association, 1989, xiv+673 p., cloth, nonf.

THRALL, Debra

35602 *Demon stalking.* New York: Manor Books, 1979, 248 p., paper, novel.

THURLO, Aimée

35603 *Strangers who linger.* Toronto, New York: Harlequin Books, 1991, 253 p., paper, novel.

THURLOW, David (Michael), 1932-

35604 *The sleepers.* London: Robert Hale, 1980, 175 p., cloth, novel.

THURSTON, Robert (Donald), 1936-

35605 *Alicia II.* New York: Berkley Publishing Corp., 1978, 419 p., cloth, novel.
35606 *Bloodname.* New York: A Roc Book, 1991, 287 p., paper, novel. BATTLETECH: LEGEND OF THE JADE PHOENIX #2.
35607 *Falcon guard.* New York: A Roc Book, 1991, 253 p., paper, novel. BATTLETECH: LEGEND OF THE JADE PHOENIX #3.
 Intruder—SEE: Isaac Asimov's robot city: robots and aliens: Intruder.
35608 *Isaac Asimov's Robot city: Robots and aliens: Intruder.* New York: A Byron Preiss Visual Publications Inc. Book, Ace Books, 1990, xv+195 p., paper, novel. ISAAC ASIMOV'S ROBOT CITY; ROBOTS AND ALIENS #3.
35609 *Q Colony.* New York: Ace Science Fiction Books, 1985, 218 p., paper, novel.
35610 *Robot jox: the novel.* New York: Avon Books, 1989, 230 p., paper, movie. RUGGER #1.
35611 *A set of wheels.* New York: Berkley Books, 1983, 281 p., paper, novel.
35612 *Way of the clans.* New York: A Roc Book, 1991, 268 p., paper, novel. BATTLETECH: LEGEND OF THE JADE PHOENIX #1.

with Glen A. Larson

27844 *Apollo's war: novel.* New York: Berkley Books, 1987, 198 p., paper, tele. BATTLESTAR GALACTICA #13.
27845 *Battlestar Galactica.* New York: A Berkley Book, Berkley Publishing Corp., 1978, 244 p., paper, tele. BATTLESTAR GALACTICA #1.
27846 *The Cylon death machine.* New York: A Berkley Book, Berkley Publishing Corp., 1979, 250 p., paper, tele. BATTLESTAR GALACTICA #2.
27847 *"Die, Chameleon!": novel.* New York: Berkley Books, 1986, 217 p., paper, tele. BATTLESTAR GALACTICA #12.
27848 *The nightmare machine.* New York: Berkley Books, 1985, 216 p., paper, tele. BATTLESTAR GALACTICA #11.

27849 *Surrender the Galactica!* New York: Ace Books, 1988, 203 p., paper, tele. BATTLESTAR GALACTICA #14.

27850 *The tombs of Kobol.* New York: A Berkley Book, Berkley Publishing Corp., 1979, 215 p., paper, tele. BATTLESTAR GALACTICA #3.

27851 *The young warriors.* New York: Berkley Books, 1980, 185 p., paper, tele. BATTLESTAR GALACTICA #4.

THYNN, Alexander (George, Viscount Weymouth], 1932-

35613 *The king is dead.* England: Longleat House, 1977, p., cloth?, novel.

TIDYMAN, Ernest, 1928-1984

38117 *Absolute zero.* New York: Dial Press, 1971, 182 p., cloth, novel.

TIEDMAN, Richard

35614 *Jack Vance: science fiction stylist.* Wabash, IN: Robert & Juanita Coulson, 1965, 30 p., paper, nonf. [Cover title].

TIERNEY, Richard (Louis), 1936-

35615 *The winds of Zarr /* by Richard L. Tierney. Albuquerque, NM: Silver Scarab Press, 1975, 77 p., paper, story.

with David C. Smith

34192 *Against the prince of Hell.* New York: Ace Books, 1983, 200 p., paper, novel. RED SONJA #5.

34193 *Demon night.* New York: Ace Books, 1982, 209 p., paper, novel. RED SONJA #2.

34194 *Endithor's daughter.* New York: Ace Books, 1982, 217 p., paper, novel. RED SONJA #4.

34195 *For the witch of the mists.* New York: Zebra Books, Kensington Publishing Corp., 1978, 234 p., paper, novel. BRAN MAK MORN #3.

34196 *The ring of Ikribu.* New York: Ace Books, 1981, 246 p., paper, novel. RED SONJA #1.

34197 *Star of doom.* New York: Ace Fantasy Books, 1983, 199 p., paper, novel. RED SONJA #6.

34198 *When Hell laughs.* New York: Ace Books, 1982, 183 p., paper, novel. RED SONJA #3.

TIGER, Virginia (Marie), 1940-

35616 *William Golding: the dark fields of discovery.* London: Calder & Boyars, 1974, 244 p., cloth, nonf.

with Claire Sprague

34598 *Critical essays on Doris Lessing.* Boston: G. K. Hall & Co., 1986, ix+237 p., cloth, nonf. anth.

TIGGES, John (Thomas), 1932-

35617 *As evil does.* New York: Leisure Books, 1987, 384 p., paper, novel.

35618 *Book of the dead.* New York: Leisure Books, 1989, 358 p., paper, novel.

35619 *Comes the wraith.* New York: Leisure Books, 1990, 362 p., paper, novel.

35620 *Evil dreams.* New York: Leisure Books, 1986, 397 p., paper, novel.

35621 *Garden of the incubus.* New York: Leisure Books, 1982, 319 p., paper, novel. INCUBUS #1.

35622 *Hands of Lucifer.* New York: Leisure Books, 1987, 384 p., paper, novel.

35623 *The immortal.* New York: Leisure Books, 1986, 397 p., paper, novel.

35624 *Kevin Browne's Nightales: stories.* New York: Upper West Side Publishing, 1990, 293 p., paper, movie coll.

35625 *Kiss not the child.* New York: Leisure Books, 1985, 380 p., paper, novel. INCUBUS #3.

Nightales—SEE: *Kevin Browne's Nightales: stories.*

35626 *Unto the altar.* New York: Leisure Books, 1985, 400 p., paper, novel. INCUBUS #2.

35627 *Venom.* New York: Leisure Books, 1988, 363 p., paper, novel.

35628 *Vessel.* New York: Leisure Books, 1988, 362 p., paper, novel.

as WILLIAM ESSEX

35629 *From below.* New York: Leisure Books, 1989, 359 p., paper, novel.

35630 *The pack.* New York: Leisure Books, 1987, 384 p., paper, novel.

35631 *Slime.* New York: Leisure Books, 1988, 365 p., paper, novel.

TIGNOR, Beth

35632 *Tryst of Dark shadows.* North Riverside, IL: Pandora, 1981, p., paper, novel.

TILLEY, Patrick, 1928-

35634 *Blood river.* London: Sphere Books, 1988, 361 p., paper, novel. AMTRAK WARS #4.

35635 *Cloud warrier.* London: Sphere, 1983, 311 p., paper, novel. AMTRAK WARS #1.

35636 *Death bringer.* London: Sphere Books, 1989, 373 p., paper, novel. AMTRAK WARS #5.

35637 *Earth-thunder.* London: Sphere Books, 1990, 484 p., paper, novel. AMTRAK WARS #6.

35638 *Fade-out.* London: Hodder & Stoughton, 1975, 369 p., cloth, novel.

35639 *Fade-out.* London: Grafton, 1987, 541 p., paper, novel. [Expanded edition].

35640 *The first family.* London: Sphere Books, 1985, 344 p., paper, novel. AMTRAK WARS #2.

35641 *Iron master.* London: Sphere Books, 1987, 405 p., paper, novel. AMTRAK WARS #3.

35642 *Mission: a novel.* Boston: Little, Brown & Co., 1981, 472 p., cloth, novel.

35643 *Xan.* London: Grafton, 1985, 332 p., paper, novel.

with Fernando Fernandez

23045 *Dark visions: an illustrated guide to the Amtrak wars.* London: Sphere, 1988, 64 p., paper, fiction. AMTRAK WARS SERIES.

TILLEY, Robert J.

35644 *The big losers.* Delavan, WI: New Infinities Productions, 1988, 270 p., paper, novel.

*TILLYARD, Aelfrida (Catherine Wetenhall), 1883-

TILTON, Lois (Ann), 1946-

35645 *Vampire winter.* New York: Pinnacle Books, Windsor Publishing Corp., 1990, 320 p., paper, novel.

TIMLETT, Peter Valentine, 1933-

35646 *The power of the serpent.* London: Corgi Books, 1976, 246 p., paper, novel. ATLANTIS #2.

35647 *The twilight of the serpent.* London: Corgi Books, 1977, ix+210 p., paper, novel. ATLANTIS #3.

*TIMLIN, William M(itcheson), 1892-1943

TIMMERMAN, John H(ager), 1945-

35648 *Other worlds: the fantasy genre.* Bowling Green, OH: Bowling Green State University Popular Press, 1983, 124 p., cloth, nonf.

TIMMES, G. D.—SEE: de Timms, Graeme

TIMMES, Graeme de—SEE: de Timms, Graeme

TIMMS, G. D.—SEE: de Timms, Graeme

TIMMS, Graeme de—SEE: de Timms, Graeme

TIMPERLEY, Rosemary (Kenyon), 1920-1988

35649 *The haunted garden.* London: Robert Hale, 1966, 191 p., cloth, novel.

35650 *Juliet.* London: Robert Hale, 1974, 190 p., cloth, novel.

35651 *The man with the beard.* London: Robert Hale, 1977, 192 p., cloth, novel.

35652 *The nameless one.* London: Robert Hale, 1978, 192 p., cloth, novel.

35653 *The phantom husband.* London: Robert Hale, 1977, 188 p., cloth, novel.

35654 *The stranger.* London: Robert Hale, 1976, 176 p., cloth, novel.

35655 *Walk to San Michele.* London: Robert Hale, 1971, 192 p., cloth, novel.

TIMSON, Keith, 1945-

35656 *A far magic shore.* London: Orbit Books, Futura, 1989, 299 p., paper, novel. FALL OF THE DISENCHANTED #1.

TINE, Robert

35657 *Bill & Ted's bogus journey: a novel.* New York: Berkley Books, 1991, 201 p., paper, movie.

35658 *Broken Eagle.* New York: Pinnacle Books, 1985, 230 p., paper, novel.

35659 *Midnight city.* New York: A Signet Book, New American Library, 1987, 284 p., paper, novel.

as RICHARD HARDING

35660 *Bay City burnout.* New York: Pinnacle Books, 1985, 184 p., paper, novel. OUTRIDER #4.

35661 *Blood highway.* New York: Pinnacle Books, 1984, 214 p., paper, novel. OUTRIDER #3.

35662 *Built to kill.* New York: Pinnacle Books, 1985, 181 p., paper, novel. OUTRIDER #5.

35663 *Fire and ice.* New York: Pinnacle Books, 1984, 217 p., paper, novel. OUTRIDER #2.

35664 *The outrider.* New York: Pinnacle Books, 1984, 213 p., paper, novel. OUTRIDER #1.

TINTNER, Adeline R., 1912-

35665 *The pop world of Henry James: from fairy tales to science fiction.* Ann Arbor, MI: UMI Research Press, 1989, xxv+317 p., cloth, nonf.

TIPTREE, James Jr. [pseud. of Alice Hastings Bradley Davey Sheldon], 1915-1987

35666 *Brightness falls from the air.* New York: Tor, Tom Doherty Associates, 1985, 382 p., cloth, novel. GREAT CENTRAL LIBRARY #1.

35667 *Byte beautiful: eight science fiction stories.* Garden City, NY: Doubleday & Co., 1985, xiv+177 p., cloth, coll.

35668 *The color of Neanderthal eyes.* New York: Tor SF, A Tom Doherty Associates Book, 1990, 76 p., paper, story. [Bound with *And strange at Ecbatan the trees* / by Michael Bishop].

35669 *Crown of stars.* New York: Tor, A Tom Doherty Associates Book, 1988, 340 p., cloth, coll.

35670 *The girl who was plugged in.* New York: Tor SF, A Tom Doherty Associates Book, 1989, 57 p., paper, story. [Bound with *Screwtop* / by Vonda N. McIntyre].

35671 *Her smoke rose up forever: the great years of James Tiptree, Jr..* Sauk City, WI: Arkham House Publishers, 1990, xv+520 p., cloth, coll. [Edited by James Turner].

35672 *Houston, Houston, do you read?* New York: Tor SF, A Tom Doherty Associates Book, 1989, 92 p., paper, story. [Bound with *Souls* / by Joanna Russ].

35673 *Out of the everywhere, and other extraordinary visions.* New York: A Del Rey Book, Ballantine Books, 1981, 276 p., paper, coll.

35674 *Star songs of an old primate.* New York: A Del Rey Book, Ballantine Books, 1978, xii+270 p., paper, coll.

35675 *The starry rift.* New York: Tor, A Tom Doherty Associates Book, 1986, 250 p., cloth, coll. GREAT CENTRAL LIBRARY #2.

35676 *Tales of the Quintana Roo: stories.* Salk City: Arkham House Publishers, 1986, [111] p., cloth, coll. [Winner of the World Fantasy Award for Best Fantasy Anthology/Collection, 1986 (1987)].

35677 *Up the walls of the world.* New York: Berkley Publishing Corp., 1978, 319 p., cloth, novel.

35678 *Warm worlds and otherwise.* New York: Ballantine Books, 1975, xviii+222 p., paper, coll.

TITELMAN, Carol (Wikarska)

35679 *The art of Star Wars.* New York: Ballantine Books, 1979, 175 p., cloth, nonf.

TITLE, Elise

35680 *Shadow of the moon.* Toronto, New York: Harlequin Books, 1991, 253 p., paper, novel.

TITMARSH, M. A., pseud.—SEE: Thackeray, W. M.

T'LAN, K. S., *with D. Dubois*

22261 *T'Zad'U, part 2.* Brackley, Northamptonshire, England: [s.n.], 1982, p., paper, novel. STAR TREK SERIES.

TOBIAS, Michael (Charles), 1947?-

38118 *After Eden.* San Diego, CA: Avant Books, 1985, 390 p., paper, fiction. [Includes some nonfiction].

35681 *Fatal exposure.* New York, London: Pocket Books, 1991, 281 p., paper, tele.

35682 *Voice of the planet.* New York, Toronto: Spectra, Bantam Books, 1990, 388 p., paper, tele.

TOBIAS, Sara, pseud.

35683 *Starship stud.* New York: Pleasure Books, 1979, 192 p., paper, novel.

TODD, Casey

38119 *Dinobots strike back.* New York: Ballantine Books, 1985, 72 p., paper, fiction. FIND YOUR FATE—JUNIOR TRANSFORMERS #1.

*TODD, Ruthven, 1914-_1978_

*TODOROV, Tzvetan, _1939-_

TOFTE, Arthur (R.), 1902-1980

35684 *Crash landing on Iduna.* Don Mills, Ontario, Canada: Laser Books, 1975, 190 p., paper, novel.

35685 *The day the Earth stood still.* New York: Scholastic Book Services, 1976, 156 p., paper, movie.

35686 *The ghost hunters.* Canoga Park, CA: Major Books, 1978 (i.e., 1979?), 176 p., paper, novel.

35687 *Survival planet: a novel of the future.* Indianapolis, IN, New York: Bobbs-Merrill Co., 1977, 187 p., cloth, novel.

35688 *Walls within walls.* Don Mills, Ontario, Canada: Laser Books, 1975, 190 p., paper, novel.

TOLKIEN, Christopher (John Reuel), 1924-

35689 *The Silmarillion: J. R. R. Tolkien: A brief account of the book and its making.* Boston: Houghton Mifflin Co., 1977, [5] p., paper, nonf.

TOLKIEN, J(ohn) R(onald) R(euel), 1892-1973

35690 *The annotated Hobbit.* Boston: Houghton Mifflin Co., 1988, 336 p., cloth, novel. [Edited by Douglas A. Anderson].

35691 *The book of lost tales, part 1.* London: George Allen & Unwin, 1983, 297 p., cloth, coll. HISTORY OF MIDDLE-EARTH #1. [Edited by Christopher Tolkien].

35692 *The book of lost tales, part II.* London: George Allen & Unwin, 1984, vi+385 p., cloth, coll. HISTORY OF MIDDLE-EARTH #2. [Edited by Christopher Tolkien].

35693 *Catalogue of an exhibition of drawings by J. R. R. Tolkien at the Ashmolean Museum, Oxford, 14th December-27th February, 1976-1977, and at the National Book League, 7 Albermarle Street, London W1, 2nd March-7th April, 1977.* Oxford, England: Ashmolean Museum; London: National Book League, 1976, [37] p., paper, art.

35694 *Farmer Giles of Ham; The adventures of Tom Bombadil.* London: Unwin Books, 1975, 144 p., paper, coll.

35695 *The Father Christmas letters.* London: George Allen & Unwin, 1976, [46] p., cloth, coll.

35696 *The filmbook of J. R. R. Tolkien's The Lord of the Rings.* Toronto: Methuen, 1978, 76 p., paper, movie.

35697 *The Grey Havens: An excerpt from The return of the king.* Brookline, MA: At the Sing of the Pilcrow, 1990, [10] p., paper?, story. LORD OF THE RINGS #3. [An excerpt from *The Return of the King*].

35698 *Lays of Beleriand.* London: George Allen & Unwin, 1985, 393 p., cloth, coll. HISTORY OF MIDDLE-EARTH #3. [Edited by Christopher Tolkien].

35699 *Letters of J. R. R. Tolkien: A selection.* London, Boston: George Allen & Unwin, 1981, 463 p., cloth, nonf. coll. [Edited by Humphrey Carpenter & Christopher Tolkien].

35700 *The Lord of the Rings.* London: Unwin Paperbacks, 1978, 1077 p., paper, coll. LORD OF THE RINGS #1-3.

35701 *The lost road, and other writings.* London: Unwin Hyman, 1987, 455 p., cloth, coll. HISTORY OF MIDDLE-EARTH #5. [Edited by Christopher Tolkien].

35702 *The monsters and the critics, and other essays.* London: George Allen & Unwin, 1983, 240 p., cloth, nonf. coll. [Edited by Christopher Tolkien].

35703 *Pictures by J. R. R. Tolkien.* London, Boston: George Allen & Unwin, 1979, [103] p., cloth, art.

35704 *The return of the shadow.* London, Boston: Unwin Hyman, 1988, xii+497 p., cloth, coll. HISTORY OF MIDDLE-EARTH #6; HISTORY OF THE LORD OF THE RINGS #1. [Edited by Christopher Tolkien].

35705 *The shaping of Middle-Earth: The Quenta, the Ambarkanta, and the Annals, together with the earliest 'Silmarillion' and the first map.* London, Boston: George Allen & Unwin, 1986, 380 p., cloth, coll. HISTORY OF MIDDLE-EARTH #4. [Edited by Christopher Tolkien].

35706 *The Silmarillion.* London: George Allen & Unwin, 1977, 365 p., cloth, coll. [Edited by Christopher Tolkien].

35707 *Smith of Wootton Major; and, Leaf by Niggle.* London: Unwin Paperbacks, 1983, 78 p., paper, coll.

35708 *The treason of Isengard.* London, Boston: Unwin Hyman, 1989, vi+504 p., cloth, coll. HISTORY OF MIDDLE-EARTH #7; HISTORY OF THE LORD OF THE RINGS #2. [Edited by Christopher Tolkien].

35709 *Tree and leaf; Smith of Wootton Major; The homecoming of Beorhtnoth, Beorhthelm's son.* London: Unwin Books, 1975, 175 p., paper, coll.

35710 *Unfinished tales of Númenor and Middle-Earth.* London: George Allen & Unwin, 1980, 472 p., cloth, coll. [Edited by Christopher Tolkien].

35711 *The war of the ring.* London, Boston: Unwin Hyman, 1990, xi+476 p., cloth, coll. HISTORY OF MIDDLE-EARTH #8;

HISTORY OF THE LORD OF THE RINGS #3. [Edited by Christopher Tolkien].

TOLLEY, Michael J., *with Kirpal Singh*

34034 *The stellar gauge: essays of science fiction writers.* Carlton, Victoria, Australia: Norstrilia Press, 1980, 288 p., cloth, nonf. anth.

TOLNAY, Thomas—SEE: Tolnay, Tom

TOLNAY, Tom [i.e., Thomas Tolnay]

35712 *Celluloid gangs.* New York: Walker & Co., 1990, 190 p., cloth, novel.

TOLSTOI, Aleksei (Nikolaevich), Graf, 1882-1945

14174 *Aelita.* Moscow: Foreign Languages Publishing House, 1957, 275 p., cloth, novel. [Translation of *Aëlita*].
14174A *Aelita.* New York: Macmillan Publishing Co., 1981, x+167 p., cloth, novel. [New translation by Antonina W. Bouis of *Aëlita*].
14174B *Aelita; or, The decline of Mars.* Ann Arbor, MI: Ardis, 1985, 176 p., cloth, novel. [New translation by Leland Fetzer of *Aëlita*].
14175 *The death box.* London: Methuen, 1936, 375 p., cloth, novel. [Translation by Bernard Guilbert Guerney of *Giperboloid inzhernera Garina*].
14175A *The Garin death ray.* Moscow: Foreign Languages Publishing House, 1955, 342 p., cloth, novel. [Translation of *Giperboloid inzhernera Garina*].
14175B *Engineer Garin and his death ray.* Moscow: Raduga Publishers, 1987, 204 p., cloth, novel. [Abridge translation by George Hanna of *Giperboloid Inzhernera Garina*].

TOLSTOI-Miloslavskii, Nikolai—SEE: Tolstoy, Nikolai

TOLSTOY, Alexey—SEE: Tolstoi, Aleksei

TOLSTOY, Nikolai [i.e., Nikolai Dimitrievich Tolstoi-Miloslavskii], 1935-

35713 *The coming of the king: the first book of Merlin.* London: Bantam Books, 1988, 606 p., cloth, novel.
35714 *The quest for Merlin.* London: Hamish Hamilton, 1985, xix+322 p., cloth, nonf.

TOMALIN, Ruth

35715 *Gone away.* London, Boston: Faber & Faber, 1979, 158 p., cloth, novel.
35716 *A summer ghost.* London, Boston: Faber & Faber, 1986, 108 p., cloth, novel.
35717 *W. H. Hudson: a biography.* London, Boston: Faber & Faber, 1982, 314 p., cloth, nonf.

TOMAN, M(ichael) D(avid), 1949-

35718 *Science fiction bibliography.* Lansing, MI: Lansing Community College, Dept. of Library Services, 1975, 13 leaves, paper, nonf.

TOMINO, Yoshiyuki

35719 *Awakening.* New York: A Del Rey Book, Ballantine Books, 1990, x+212 p., paper, tele. GUNDAM MOBILE SUIT #1. [Translation by Frederik L. Schodt].
35720 *Confrontation.* New York: A Del Rey Book, Ballantine Books, 1991, x+213 p., paper, tele. GUNDAM MOBILE SUIT #3 (title page says #2). [Translation by Frederik L. Schodt].
35721 *Escalation.* New York: A Del Rey Book, Ballantine Books, 1990, xi+209 p., paper, tele. GUNDAM MOBILE SUIT #2. [Translation by Frederik L. Schodt].

TOMKINS, Julia M. Hunter Manchee—SEE: Neilson, Marguerite

TOMPKINS, Julia M.—SEE: Neilson, Marguerite

TOMPKINS, Robert, 1944-

35722 *Futurescapes: explorations in fact and science fiction.* Toronto: Methuen, 1977, 176 p., paper, anth. [Includes some nonfiction and verse].

*TOMPKINS, Walker A(llison), 1909-1988

TONKIN, Peter (Francis), 1950-

35723 *The journal of Edwin Underhill.* London: Hodder & Stoughton, 1981, 192 p., cloth, novel.

*TOOKER, Richard, 1902-1988

TOOMBS, Jane (Ellen Jamison) Jenke, 1926-

35724 *The fog maiden.* New York: Ballantine Books, 1976, 186 p., paper, novel.

35725 *Point of lost souls.* New York: Avon, 1975, 160 p., paper, novel.

38120 *A topaz for my lady fair.* New York: Ballantine Books, 1975, 153 p., paper, novel. BIRTHSTONE GOTHIC #11.

TOOMBS, John, 1927-

as FORTUNE KENT

27072 *The opal legacy.* New York: Ballantine Books, 1975, 156 p., paper, novel. BIRTHSTONE GOTHIC #10.

as PAUL KENT

27073 *The crib.* Toronto, New York: Bantam Books, 1987, 218 p., paper, novel.

TOPOL, Allan, 1941-

35726 *The fourth of July war: a novel.* New York: William Morrow & Co., 1978, 311 p., cloth, novel.

TOPOL, B. H.

35727 *A fistful of ego: a novel.* Great Neck, NY: Todd & Honeywell, 1985, 260 p., cloth, novel.

TORDAY, Ursula—SEE: Blackstock, Charity

TORGESON, Roy

35728 *Chrysalis.* New York: Zebra Books, Kensington Publishing Corp., 1977, 270 p., paper, anth.

35729 *Chrysalis, volume 2.* New York: Zebra Books, Kensington Publishing Corp., 1978, 284 p., paper, anth.

35730 *Chrysalis 3.* New York: Zebra Books, Kensington Publishing Corp., 1978, 284 p., paper, anth.

35731 *Chrysalis 4.* New York: Zebra Books, Kensington Publishing Corp., 1979, 301 p., paper, anth.

35732 *Chrysalis 5.* New York: Zebra Books, Kensington Publishing Corp., 1979, 288 p., paper, anth.

35733 *Chrysalis 6.* New York: Zebra Books, Kensington Publishing Corp., 1979, 285 p., paper, anth.

35734 *Chrysalis 7.* New York: Zebra Books, Kensington Publishing Corp., 1979, 287 p., paper, anth.

35735 *Chrysalis 8.* Garden City, NY: Doubleday & Co., 1980, xii+211 p., cloth, anth.

35736 *Chrysalis 9.* Garden City, NY: Doubleday & Co., 1981, 186 p., cloth, anth.

35737 *Chrysalis 10.* Garden City, NY: Doubleday & Co., 1983, 182 p., cloth, anth.

35738 *Other worlds 1.* New York: Zebra Books, Kensington Publishing Corp., 1979, 282 p., paper, anth.

35739 *Other worlds 2.* New York: Zebra Books, Kensington Publishing Corp., 1980, 281 p., paper, anth.

with Howard Frank

23434 *The 1977 science fiction & fantasy magazine checklist & price guide, 1923-1976.* Port Washington, NY: Science Fiction Resources, 1977, 50 p., paper, nonf.

TOUPONCE, William F(erdinand), 1948-

35740 *Frank Herbert.* Boston: Twayne Publishers, 1990, 136 p., cloth, nonf.

35741 *Isaac Asimov.* Boston: Twayne Publishers, 1991, xv+122 p., cloth, nonf.

35742 *Ray Bradbury.* Mercer Island, WA: Starmont House, 1989, iv+110 p., cloth, nonf. STARMONT READER'S GUIDE #31.

35743 *Ray Bradbury and the poetics of reverie: fantasy, science fiction, and the reader.* Ann Arbor, MI: UMI Press, 1984, xxiii+131 p., cloth, nonf. STUDIES IN SPECULATIVE FICTION #2.

TOURETTE, Aileen La—SEE: La Tourette, Aileen

TOURNEY, Leonard D(on), 1942-

35744 *Familiar spirits.* New York: A Joan Kahn Book, St. Martin's Press, 1984, 230 p., cloth, novel.

TOURRETTE, Jacqueline La—SEE: La Tourrette, Jacqueline

TOWER, Diana, pseud.—SEE: Reinsmith, Richard

TOWER, Harker, pseud.

15870 *Two weird tales.* [S.l.]: Neptune Readers, 1971, 160 p., paper, coll.

TOWLSON, Ivan, 1967- , with Neal Tringham & Mo Holkar & others as M. H. ZOOL

25850 *Bloomsbury good reading guide to science fiction and fantasy.* London: Bloomsbury, 1989, 160 p., paper, nonf. [A collective pseudonym for the Oxford SF Group].

*TOWNE, Anthony, 1928-1980

TOWNE, Mary [pseud. of Mary Spelman], 1934-

35745 *Goldenrod.* New York: Atheneum, 1977, 180 p., cloth, novel.
35746 *Paul's game: a novel.* New York: Delacorte Press, 1983, 186 p., cloth, novel.

TOWNSEND, George P., *with Trevor Jones*

26775 *A book of dreams.* England: Weller Publications, 1991, 80 p., paper, anth.

TOWNSEND, John (Howard)

38121 *The rocket-ship saboteurs.* London: Chatto & Windus, 1959, 167 p., cloth, novel.

TOWNSEND, John Rowe, 1922-

The creatures—SEE: *King creature, come.*
35747 *The fortunate isles: a novel.* New York: J. B. Lippincott, 1989, 248 p., cloth, novel.
35748 *The islanders.* Oxford, England, New York: Oxford University Press, 1981, 192 p., cloth, novel.
35749 *King creature, come.* Oxford, England, New York: Oxford University Press, 1980, 187 p., cloth, novel.
35749A retitled: *The creatures.* New York: J. B. Lippincott, 1980, 248 p., cloth, novel.
35750 *Noah's castle.* London, New York: Oxford University Press, 1975, 180 p., cloth, novel.
35751 *The persuading stick.* Harmondsworth, Middlesex, England: Viking Kestrel, 1986, 91 p., cloth, novel.
Visitors—SEE: *The Xanadu manuscript.*
35752 *The Xanadu manuscript.* Oxford, England, New York: Oxford University Press, 1977, 170 p., cloth, novel.
35752A retitled: *The visitors.* Philadelphia, PA: J. B. Lippincott, 1977, 221 p., cloth, novel.

TOWNSEND, Tom

35753 *Panzer spirit.* New York: Pageant Books, 1988, 274 p., paper, novel.

TOWNSLEY, John

35754 *Who's who in Star Trek.* London: A Star Book, W. H. Allen & Co., 1988, 109 p., paper, nonf. STAR TREK SERIES.

TRACY, Ann B(laisdell), 1941-

35755 *The gothic novel, 1790-1830: plot summaries and index to motifs.* Lexington, KY: University Press of Kentucky, 1981, vii+216 p., cloth, nonf.
35756 *Patterns of fear in the gothic novel, 1790-1830.* New York: Arno Press, 1980, 350 p., cloth, nonf.

*TRACY, Don(ald Fiske), 1905-1976

TRACY, Louis, 1863-1928

38122 *The turning point.* New York: E. J. Clode, 1923, 362 p., cloth, novel.

TRAINOR, Joseph

35757 *Family crypt.* New York: Twilight, 1984, 168 p., paper, novel. TWILIGHT #20.
35758 *Watery grave.* New York: Twilight/Dell, 1983, 168 p., paper, novel. TWILIGHT #18.

TRAINOR, Sandy [possible pseud. of Robert Tralins]

35758 *Future sex.* New York: Pleasure Books, 1979, 176 p., paper, novel.

TRAINOR, Starr [possible pseud. of Robert Tralins]

35759 *Pleasure planet.* New York: Pleasure Books, 1979, 178 p., paper, novel.

TRALINS, (Sandor) Robert, 1926-

35759 *Signal intruder.* New York: Pinnacle Books, Windsor Publishing Corp., 1991, 318 p., paper, novel.

TRAMONTANA, C. J., *with Bill Slavicsek*

34102 *Storm knights.* Honesdale, PA: West End Books, 1990, 317 p., paper, novel. TORG: THE PROBABILITY WARS #1. [Based on the *Probability Wars* game].

TRASK, Jonathan, pseud.—SEE: Levinson, Leonard

TRAVEN, B. [pseud. of (Hermann Albert) Otto (Maximilian) Feige], 1882-1969

35761 *The creation of the sun and the moon.* Westport, CT & Berkeley, CA: Lawrence Hill & Co., Creative Arts Book Co., 1977, 65 p., paper, fiction.

TRAVERS, P(amela) L(yndon), 1906-

35762 *Mary Poppins in Cherry Tree Lane.* London: Collins, 1982, 91 p., cloth, novel. MARY POPPINS #5.

TREBOR, Robert, pseud.

35763 *An XT called Stanley.* New York: DAW Books, 1983, 221 p., paper, novel.

TREDELL, Nicolas

35764 *The novels of Colin Wilson.* London: Vision Press; Totowa, NJ: Barnes & Noble Books, 1982, 157 p., cloth, nonf.

TREMAYNE, Peter [pseud. of Peter Berresford Ellis], 1943-

35765 *Angelus!* London: Panther, 1985, 239 p., paper, novel.

35766 *The ants.* London: Sphere Books, 1979, 182 p., paper, novel.

35767 *Bloodmist.* New York: Baen Books, 1988, 310 p., paper, novel.
Bloodright—SEE: *Dracula unborn.*

35768 *The buccaneers of Lan-Kern.* London: Methuen, 1983, 201 p., cloth, novel. LAN-KERN SERIES.

35769 *The curse of Loch Ness.* London: Sphere Books, 1979, 230 p., paper, novel.

35770 *The destroyers of Lan-Kern.* London: Methuen, 1982, 183 p., cloth, novel. LAN-KERN SERIES.

35771 *Dracula unborn.* Folkestone, England: Bailey Brothers & Swinfen, 1977, 222 p., cloth, novel. DRACULA #1.

35771A retitled: *Bloodright.* New York: Walker & Co., 1979, 222 p., cloth, novel. DRACULA #1.

35772 *Dracula, my love.* Folkestone, England: Bailey Brothers & Swinfen, 1980, iv+154 p., cloth, novel. DRACULA #3.

35773 *The fires of Lan-Kern.* Folkestone, England: Bailey Bros. & Swinfen, 1980, ii+272 p., cloth, novel. LAN-KERN #1.

35774 *Hound of Frankenstein.* London, Sydney: Mills & Boon, 1977, 96 p., paper, novel. FRANKENSTEIN SERIES.

35775 *Irish masters of fantasy: an anthology with introduction and biographical essays.* Portmarnock, Ireland: Wolfhound Press, 1979, 220 p., cloth, anth.

35775A retitled: *The wondersmith, and other macabre tales.* Dublin: Wolfhound Press, 1988, 220 p., paper, coll.

35776 *Island of shadows.* London: Mandarin, 1991, 316 p., paper, novel.

35777 *Kiss of the cobra.* London: Sphere Books, 1984, 182 p., paper, novel.

35778 *The Morgow rises!* London: Sphere Books, 1982, 183 p., paper, novel.

35779 *My lady of hyBrasil, and other stories.* West Kingston, RI: Donald M. Grant, Publisher, 1987, 160 p., cloth, coll.

35780 *Nicor!* London: Sphere Books, 1987, 211 p., paper, novel.

35781 *Raven of destiny.* London: Methuen, 1984, 286 p., cloth, novel.

35782 *Ravenmoon.* London: Methuen, 1988, 256 p., cloth, novel.

35783 *The revenge of Dracula.* Folkestone, England: Bailey Brothers & Swinfen, 1978, 203 p., cloth, novel. DRACULA #2.

35784 *Snowbeast!* London: Sphere Books, 1983, 216 p., paper, novel.

35785 *Swamp!* London: Sphere, 1985, 185 p., paper, novel.

35786 *Trollnight.* London: Sphere Books, 1987, 247 p., paper, novel.

35787 *The vengeance of She.* London: Sphere Books, 1978, 187 p., paper, novel. SHE SEQUEL.
The wondersmith, and other macabre tales—SEE: *Irish masters of fantasy.*

35788 *Zombie!* London: Sphere Books, 1981, 183 p., paper, novel.

as PETER BERRESFORD ELLIS

35790 *H. Rider Haggard: a voice from the infinite.* London & Henley: Routledge & Kegan Paul, 1978, xiv+291 p., cloth, nonf.

35791 *The last adventurer: the life of Talbot Mundy, 1879-1940.* West Kingston, RI: Donald M. Grant, Publisher, 1984, 279 p., cloth, nonf.

with Jeanne Youngson

35792 *Freak show vampire; and, The hungry grass.* Chicago: Adams Press, 1981, 110 p., paper, coll.

TRENERY, Gladys Gordon—SEE: Pendarves, G. G.

TREVELYAN, Julia

35793 *The tower room.* New York: A Signet Book, New American Library, 1979, 168 p., paper, novel.

TREVOR, Dan, pseud.—SEE: Meldal-Johnsen, Trevor & Sherman, Dan

TREVOR, Elleston [legalized from Trevor Dudley-Smith], 1920-

35794 *Deathwatch: a novel.* New York: Beaufort Books, 1984, 277 p., cloth, novel.
38123 *Forbidden kingdom.* London: Lutterworth Press, 1955, 126 p., cloth, novel.
35796A *The sibling.* New York: Jove Books, 1989, 301 p., paper, novel. [Originally published under the name Adam Hall].
35795 *The theta syndrome.* London: New English Library, 1977, 205 p., cloth, novel.

as ADAM HALL

35796 *The sibling.* Chicago: Playboy Press Paperbacks, 1979, 301 p., paper, novel.

TREVOR, (Lucy) Meriol, 1919-

38124 *The fires and the stars.* London: Faber & Faber, 1950, 228 p., cloth, novel. WORLD DIONYSUS #3.
38125 *The forest and the kingdom.* London: Faber & Faber, 1949, 222 p., cloth, novel. WORLD DIONYSUS #1.
38126 *Merlin's ring.* London: Collins, 1957, 192 p., cloth, novel.

TREVOR, William [i.e., William Trevor Cox], 1928-

35797 *The children of Dynmouth.* London: Bodley Head, 1976, 222 p., cloth, novel.

TRIMBLE, Betty—SEE: Trimble, Bjo

TRIMBLE, Bjo [i.e., Betty Joann Conway Trimble], 1933-

35798 *The official Starlog communications handbook, volume 1.* New York: Starlog Press, 1979, 92 p., paper, nonf.
35799 *On the good ship Enterprise: my 15 years with Star Trek.* Norfolk, Virginia Beach, VA: A Starblaze Special, The Donning Company, Publishers, 1982, 286 p., paper, nonf. STAR TREK SERIES.
35800 *The Star Trek concordance.* New York: Ballantine Books, 1976, 256 p., paper, nonf. STAR TREK SERIES.

*TRIMBLE, Louis (Preston), 1917-1988

TRINGHAM, Neal, 1966- , *with Mo Holkar & Ivan Towlson & others as M. H. ZOOL*

25850 *Bloomsbury good reading guide to science fiction and fantasy.* London: Bloomsbury, 1989, 160 p., paper, nonf. [A

collective pseudonym for the Oxford SF Group].

TRONCHE, Philippe—SEE: Curval, Philippe

TROPP, Martin, 1945-

35801 *Images of fear: how horror stories helped shape modern culture, 1818-1918.* Jefferson, NC & London: McFarland & Co., 1990, xiii+235 p., cloth, nonf.
35802 *Mary Shelley's monster: the story of Frankenstein.* Boston: Houghton Mifflin Co., 1976, xii+192 p., cloth, nonf.

TROPPENBERG, Ulderico di—SEE: De Rico, Ul

TROUT, Kilgore, pseud.—SEE: Farmer, Philip José; SEE ALSO: Currey, L. W. & Hartwell, David G.

TROWELL, Michael

35803 *Colin Wilson, the positive approach: a response to a critic.* Nottingham, England: Paupers' Press, 1990, 35 p., paper, nonf.

TRUESDALE, Dave, *with David Gerrold*

23857 *Norman Jacobs & Kerry O'Quinn present Starlog's science fiction yearbook, vol. 1.* New York: A Starlog Press Book, 1979, 111 p., paper, nonf. anth.
Starlog's science fiction yearbook, vol. 1—SEE: *Norman Jacobs & Kerry O'Quinn present Starlog's science fiction yearbook, vol. 1.*

TRUSCOTT, Gerry, 1955- , *with Candas Jane Dorsey*

22039 *Tesseracts³.* Victoria, British Columbia, Canada: A Tesseract Book, Porcépic Books, 1991, x+437 p., paper, coll. [Includes some verse].

TRUZZI, Marcello, 1935-

35804 *Chess in literature.* New York: Equinox Books, Avon, 1975, 421 p., paper, anth.

*TRYON, Thomas, 1926-1991

TSANG, Eric

35805 *The solar wind.* Lewes, East Sussex, England: The Book Guild, 1991, 134 p., cloth, novel.

TSIOLKOVSKII, Konstantin (Eduardovich), 1857-1935

14257 *The call of the cosmos.* Moscow: Foreign Languages Publishing House, 1961, 472 p., cloth, coll. [Includes some nonfiction].

14257A retitled: *The science fiction of Konstantin Tsiolkovsky.* Seattle, WA: University Press of the Pacific, 1979, 454 p., cloth, coll. [Abridged edition; supposedly (but not actually) edited by "Adam Starchild"].

TSUTSUI, Yasutaka, 1934-

35807 *What the maid saw.* Tokyo: Kodansha International, 1990, 189 p., cloth, coll. [Translation by Adam Kabat of *Kazoku hakkei*].

TUBB, E(dwin) C(harles), 1919-

Alien seed—SEE: *Space 1999: Alien seed.*
35808 *Angado.* New York: DAW Books, 1984, 159 p., paper, novel. DUMAREST #29.
Breakaway—SEE: *Space 1999: Breakaway.*
Collision course—SEE: *Space 1999: Collision course.*
35809 *The coming event.* New York: DAW Books, 1982, 160 p., paper, novel. DUMAREST #26.
35810 *Death wears a white face.* London: Robert Hale, 1979, 175 p., cloth, novel.
35811 *Earth is heaven.* New York: DAW Books, 1982, 160 p., paper, novel. DUMAREST #27.
Earthfall—SEE: *Space 1999: Earthfall.*
35812 *Eloise.* New York: DAW Books, 1975, 156 p., paper, novel. DUMAREST #12.
35813 *Eye of the zodiac.* New York: DAW Books, 1975, 176 p., paper, novel. DUMAREST #13.
35814 *Haven of darkness.* New York: DAW Books, 1977, 173 p., paper, novel. DUMAREST #16.
35815 *Iduna's universe.* New York: DAW Books, 1979, 156 p., paper, novel. DUMAREST #21.
35816 *Incident on Ath.* New York: DAW Books, 1978, 188 p., paper, novel. DUMAREST #18.
35817 *Jack of Swords.* New York: DAW Books, 1976, 152 p., paper, novel. DUMAREST #14.
35818 *The luck machine.* London: Dennis Dobson, 1980, 188 p., cloth, novel.

35819 *Mayenne; and, Jondelle.* New York: DAW Books, 1981, 159, 159 p., paper, coll. DUMAREST #9-10.
35820 *Melome.* New York: DAW Books, 1983, 160 p., paper, novel. DUMAREST #28.
35821 *Melome; and, Angado.* London: Legend, 1988, 317 p., paper, coll. DUMAREST #28-29.
35822 *Nectar of heaven.* New York: DAW Books, 1981, 160 p., paper, novel. DUMAREST #24.
35823 *Pawn of the Omphalos.* New York: Fawcett Gold Medal, 1980, 156 p., paper, novel.
35824 *The primitive.* London: Futura Publications, An Orbit Book, 1977, 142 p., paper, novel.
35825 *Prison of night.* New York: DAW Books, 1977, 160 p., paper, novel. DUMAREST #17.
35826 *The Quillian Sector.* New York: DAW Books, 1978, 158 p., paper, novel. DUMAREST #19.
Rogue planet—SEE: *Space 1999: Rogue planet.*
35827 *Space 1999: Alien seed.* London: Futura Publications, An Orbit Book, 1976, 138 p., paper, tele. SPACE: 1999 #7.
35828 *Space 1999: Breakaway.* London: Futura Publications, An Orbit Book, 1975, 143 p., paper, tele. SPACE: 1999 #1.
35829 *Space 1999: Collision course.* London: Futura Publications, An Orbit Book, 1975, 143 p., paper, tele. SPACE: 1999 #4.
35830 *Space 1999: Earthfall.* London: Futura Publications, An Orbit Book, 1977, 284 p., paper, tele. SPACE: 1999 #10.
35831 *Space 1999: Rogue planet.* London: Futura Publications, An Orbit Book, 1976, 143 p., paper, tele. SPACE: 1999 #9.
35832 *Spectrum of a forgotten sun.* New York: DAW Books, 1976, 157 p., paper, novel. DUMAREST #15.
35833 *Stardeath.* New York: A Del Rey Book, Ballantine Books, 1983, 182 p., paper, novel.
35834 *Stellar assignment.* London: Robert Hale, 1979, 175 p., cloth, novel.
35835 *Symbol of Terra.* New York: DAW Books, 1984, 237 p., paper, novel. DUMAREST #30.
35836 *Symbol of Terra; and, The temple of truth.* London: Legend, 1989, 460 p., paper, coll. DUMAREST #30-31.
35837 *The Temple of truth.* New York: DAW Books, 1985, 222 p., paper, novel. DUMAREST #31. [Last of the series].

35838 *The terra data.* New York: DAW Books, 1980, 172 p., paper, novel. DUMAREST #22.

35839 *The Terridae.* New York: DAW Books, 1981, 160 p., paper, novel. DUMAREST #25.

35840 *Web of sand.* New York: DAW Books, 1979, 156 p., paper, novel. DUMAREST #20.

35841 *World of promise.* New York: DAW Books, 1980, 160 p., paper, novel. DUMAREST #23.

as GREGORY KERN

35842 *Beyond the galactic lens.* New York: DAW Books, 1975, 156 p., paper, novel. CAP KENNEDY #16.

35843 *The Galactiad.* New York: DAW Books, 1983, 128 p., paper, novel. CAP KENNEDY #17. [First published in Germany as *Das kosmiche duelle*].

35844 *The ghosts of Epidoris.* New York: DAW Books, 1975, 124 p., paper, novel. CAP KENNEDY #14.

35845 *Mimics of Dephene.* New York: DAW Books, 1975, 126 p., paper, novel. CAP KENNEDY #15.

TUCK, Donald H(enry), 1922-

35846 *Authors' book listing.* Lindisfarne, Tasmania: The Compiler, 1975, 32 p., paper, nonf.

35847 *The encyclopedia of science fiction and fantasy through 1968: a bibliographic survey of the fields of science fiction, fantasy, and weird fiction through 1968, volume 2: who's who, M-Z.* Chicago: Advent:Publishers, 1978, xvii-xx + 287-530 p., cloth, nonf.

35848 *The encyclopedia of science fiction and fantasy through 1968: a bibliographic survey of the fields of science fiction, fantasy, and weird fiction through 1968, volume 3: miscellaneous.* Chicago: Advent:Publishers, 1982, xxv-xxviii + 531-920 p., cloth, nonf. [Winner of the Hugo Award for Best Nonfiction Book, 1983 (1984)].

TUCKER, Bob—SEE: Tucker, Wilson

TUCKER, George, 1775-1861

38127 *A century hence; or, A romance of 1941.* Charlottesville, VA: University Press of Virginia, 1977, xx + 135 p., cloth, novel. [Edited by Donald R. Noble].

TUCKER, James, 1929- , *with Erin McKee*

29608 *Touchstone: a tribute to Fritz Leiber and Ray Bradbury.* Salt Lake City, UT: The Mysterious Stranger Press, 1978, 88 p., paper, nonf. anth. [Limited to 977 copies].

TUCKER, (Arthur) Wilson ("Bob"), 1914-

35849 *The best of Wilson Tucker.* New York: A Timescape Book, Pocket Books, 1982, 191 p., paper, coll.

35850 *Neo-fan's guide to science fiction fandom / by Bob Tucker.* Hartford City, IN: Robert & Juanita Coulson, 1966, 16 p., paper, nonf.

35851 *Resurrection days.* New York: A Timescape Book, Pocket Books, 1981, 191 p., paper, novel.

TUCKEY, John S(utton), 1921-1987

35852 *The devil's race-track: Mark Twain's great dark writings.* Berkeley, CA & Los Angeles: University of California Press, 1980, xx + 385 p., paper, nonf. anth.

TUDOR, Andrew (Frank), 1942-

35853 *Monsters and mad scientists: a cultural history of the horror movie.* Oxford, England: Basil Blackwell, 1989, 239 p., cloth, nonf.

TULEJA, Thaddeus V. (Francis), 1944-

35854 *Land of precious snow.* New York: Python, 1977, 188 p., paper, novel.

as MARSHALL MACAO

09397 *The Kuk-Abdullah conspiracy.* New York: Freeway Press, 1973, 197 p., paper, novel. K'ING KUNG FU #4.

09400 *Mark of the vulture.* New York: Freeway Press, 1974, 186 p., paper, novel. K'ING KUNG FU #7.

09399 *New York necromancy.* New York: Freeway Press, 1974, 180 p., paper, novel. K'ING KUNG FU #6.

09396 *The rape of Sun Lee Fong.* New York: Freeway Press, 1973, 187 p., paper, novel. K'ING KUNG FU #3.

09398 *Red plague in Bolivia.* New York: Freeway Press, 1974, 178 p., paper, novel. K'ING KUNG FU #5.

09395 *Return of the opium wars.* New York: Freeway Press, 1973, 189 p., paper, novel. K'ING KUNG FU #2.

09394 *Son of the flying tiger.* New York: Freeway Press, 1973, 188 p., paper, novel. KʼING KUNG FU #1.

TULLOCH, John, 1942- , with Manuel Alvarado

16329 *Doctor Who: the unfolding text.* London: Macmillan Press, 1983, xi+342 p., cloth, nonf.

TULLOCK, Joyce

35855 *When heroes die: a starchild's quest.* Baton Rouge, LA: Odyssey Press, 1983, 142 p., paper, novel. STAR TREK SERIES.

TULLY, John (Kimberley), 1923-

35856 *Natfact 7.* London: Methuen, 1984, 207 p., cloth, novel.

TUNING, William, 1935-1982

35857 *Fuzzy bones.* New York: Ace Books, 1981, 375 p., paper, novel. FUZZIES SEQUEL.
35858 *Tornado alley.* New York: Ace Books, 1978, 240 p., paper, novel.

TUNNELL, Michael O('Grady)

35859 *The Prydain companion: a reference guide to Lloyd Alexander's Prydain Chronicles.* NY & Westport, CT: Greenwood Press, 1989, xvii+257 p., cloth, nonf.

with James S. Jacobs

26395 *Lloyd Alexander: a bio-bibliography.* Westport, CT, London: Greenwood Press, 1991, x+145 p., cloth, nonf.

TUREK, Leslie (Jean)

35860 *If I ran the zoo con: the Smofcon 3 game.* Cambridge, MA: MCFI, 1986, iv+109 p., paper, nonf. anth.
35861 *If I ran the zoo con: the Smofcon 3 game, second edition.* Cambridge, MA: NESFA Press, 1987, iv+109 p., paper, nonf. anth.
35862 *The Noreascon proceedings: the Twenty-Ninth World Science Fiction Convention, Boston, Massachusetts, September 3-6, 1971.* Cambridge, MA: NESFA Press, 1976, 191 p., cloth, nonf. anth.

TURGENEV, Ivan (Sergeevich), 1818-1883

35863 *The mysterious tales of Ivan Turgenev.* Canberra, Australia: Australian National University, Faculty of Arts, 1979, xxxiv+192 p., cloth, coll. [Edited and translated by Robert Dessaix].

TURK, H(arold) C., 1958-

35864 *Ben Bova's discoveries: Ether ore.* New York: Tor SF, A Tom Doherty Associates Book, 1987, 282 p., paper, novel.
35865 *Black body: a novel.* New York: Villard Books, 1989, 517 p., cloth, novel.
Ether ore—SEE: Ben Bova's discoveries: Ether ore.

TURMAN, John (Ray)

35866 *Saxon and the sorceress.* Austin, TX: Morganland Press, 1978, p., paper, novel.

TURNBULL, Ann (Christine), 1943-

35867 *The frightened forest.* Harmondsworth, Middlesex, England: Kestrel Books, 1974, 124 p., cloth, novel.
35868 *Maroo of the winter caves.* New York: Clarion Books, 1984, 136 p., cloth, novel.
35869 *The Wolf King.* Harmondsworth, Middlesex, England: Kestrel Books, 1975, 159 p., cloth, novel.

TURNBULL, Gerry

35870 *A Star Trek catalog.* New York: Grosset & Dunlap, 1979, 160 p., cloth, nonf. STAR TREK SERIES.

TURNER, Ann W(arren), 1945-

35871 *Rosemary's witch.* New York: A Charlotte Zolotow Book, HarperCollins-Publishers, 1991, 164 p., cloth, novel.

TURNER, Frederick (Hodson Jr.), 1943-

35872 *A double shadow: fiction.* New York: Berkley Publishing Corp., 1978, 252 p., cloth, novel.

TURNER, George (Reginald), 1916-

35873 *Beloved son.* London: Faber & Faber, 1978, 375 p., cloth, novel. ETHICAL CULTURE #1.
35874 *Brain child.* New York: William Morrow & Co., 1991, 407 p., cloth, novel.

Drowning towers—SEE: *The sea and the summer.*

35875 *In the heart or in the head: an essay in time travel.* Carlton, Victoria, Australia: Norstrilia Press, 1984, 239 p., cloth, nonf.

35876 *A pursuit of miracles.* North Adelaide, South Australia, Australia: Aphelion Publications, 1990, xii+209 p., paper, coll.

35877 *The sea and the summer.* London: Faber & Faber, 1987, 352 p., cloth, novel.

35877A retitled: *Drowning towers.* New York: Arbor House, 1988, 318 p., cloth, novel.

35878 *Vaneglory: a science fiction novel.* London: Faber & Faber, 1981, 320 p., cloth, novel. ETHICAL CULTURE #2.

35879 *The view from the edge: a workshop of science fiction stories.* Carlton, Victoria, Australia: Norstrilia Press, 1977, 124 p., paper, anth. [Includes some nonfiction].

35880 *Yesterday's men.* London: Faber & Faber, 1983, 223 p., cloth, novel. ETHICAL CULTURE #3.

TURNER, George E(ugene), 1925-

35881 *Cinema of adventure, romance & terror: from the archives of American cinematographer.* Hollywood, CA: ASC Press, 1989, 298 p., cloth, nonf. anth.

with Orville Goldner

24090 *The making of King Kong: the story behind a film classic.* South Brunswick, NJ: A. S. Barnes & Co., 1975, 271 p., cloth, nonf.

with Michael H. Price

31860 *Forgotten horrors: early talkie chillers from Poverty Row.* South Brunswick, NJ: A. S. Barnes & Co., 1979, 216 p., cloth, nonf.

TURNER, James (Allen), 1945- , with August Derleth as ANONYMOUS EDITORS

21619 *Tales of the Cthulhu Mythos* / by H. P. Lovecraft and divers hands. Sauk City, WI: Arkham House, 1989, xiv+529 p., cloth, anth. [Drops 4 stories from 1969 version (see #04228), and adds 7].

TURNER, James (Ernest), 1909-1975

35861 *Staircase to the sea: fourteen ghost stories.* London: William Kimber, 1974, 212 p., cloth, coll.

35862 *The way shadows fall: fourteen ghost stories.* London: William Kimber, 1975, 221 p., cloth, coll.

TURNER, Richard, *with William Osborne*

31048 *1998.* London: Sphere Books, 1988, 198 p., paper, novel.

TURNER, Sandra (Stephens), 1945-

35863 *The house of time travel.* New York, Washington: Vantage Press, 1981, 127 p., cloth, novel.

TURNER, Vickery

35864 *The testimony of Daniel Pagels.* London: Macdonald, 1991, 354 p., cloth, novel.

TURNEY, Ray, *with Steve Perrin*

31453 *RuneQuest.* Albany, CA: The Chaosium, 1979, 119 p., paper, fiction.

TURTLEDOVE, Harry (Norman), 1949-

Agent of Byzantium—SEE: *Isaac Asimov presents Agent of Byzantium.*
A different flesh—SEE: *Isaac Asimov presents A different flesh.*

35865 *Earthgrip.* New York: A Del Rey Book, Ballantine Books, 1991, 264 p., paper, coll. TALES FROM THE TRADERS' WORLD #1.

35866 *An emperor for the legion.* New York: A Del Rey Book, Ballantine Books, 1987, 322 p., paper, novel. VIDESSOS CYCLE #2.

35867 *Isaac Asimov presents A different flesh.* New York: Congdon & Weed, 1988, xi+292 p., cloth, novel.

35868 *Isaac Asimov presents Agent of Byzantium.* New York: Congdon & Weed, 1987, x+246 p., cloth, coll.

35869 *Kaleidoscope.* New York: A Del Rey Book, Ballantine Books, 1990, 249 p., paper, coll.

35870 *Krispos of Videssos.* New York: A Del Rey Book, Ballantine Books, 1991, 355 p., paper, novel. VIDESSOS CYCLE #6; TALE OF KRISPOS #2.

35871 *Krispos rising.* New York: A Del Rey Book, Ballantine Books, 1991, 353 p., paper, novel. VIDESSOS CYCLE #5; TALE OF KRISPOS #1.

35872 *The legion of Videssos.* New York: A Del Rey Book, Ballantine Books, 1987, 413 p., paper, novel. VIDESSOS CYCLE #3.

35873 *The misplaced legion.* New York: A Del Rey Book, Ballantine Books, 1987, 323 p., paper, novel. VIDESSOS CYCLE #1.

35874 *Noninterference.* New York: A Del Rey Book, Ballantine Books, 1988, 213 p., paper, novel.

35875 *The pugnacious peacemaker.* New York: Tor SF, A Tom Doherty Associates Book, 1990, p. 89-185, paper, story. [Bound with *The wheels of if /* by L. Sprague de Camp].

35876 *Swords of the legion.* New York: A Del Rey Book, Ballantine Books, 1987, 394 p., paper, novel. VIDESSOS CYCLE #4.

35877 *A world of difference.* New York: A Del Rey Book, Ballantine Books, 1990, 308 p., paper, novel.

as ERIC IVERSON

35878 *Wereblood /* by Erik Iverson. New York: Belmont Tower Books, 1979, 144 p., paper, novel. GERIN #1. [Cover byline reads Eric Iverson].

35879 *Werenight.* New York: Belmont Tower Books, 1979, 140 p., paper, novel. GERIN #2.

TUTTLE, Lisa, 1952-

35880 *Catwitch.* Garden City, NY: Doubleday & Co., 1983, 79 p., cloth, novel.

35881 *Familiar spirit.* New York: Berkley Books, 1983, 218 p., paper, novel.

35882 *Gabriel.* London: Severn House, 1987, 216 p., cloth, novel.

35883 *A nest of nightmares.* London: Sphere Books, 1986, 208 p., paper, coll.

35884 *Skin of the soul: new horror stories by women.* London: Women's Press, 1990, 231 p., cloth, anth.

35885 *A spaceship built of stone, and other stories.* London: The Women's Press, 1987, 192 p., paper, coll.

with Mark Harrison

Dreamlands—SEE: *Mark Harrison's Dream-lands.*

25307 *Mark Harrison's Dreamlands.* London: Paper Tiger, 1990, 127 p., cloth, art.

with George R. R. Martin

29120 *Windhaven.* New York: Timescape Books, 1981, 348 p., cloth, novel.

TUYL, Rosealtha Van—SEE: Van Tuyl, Zaara

TUYL, Zaara Van—SEE: Van Tuyl, Zaara

TWAIN, Mark [pseud. of Samuel Langhorne Clemens], 1835-1910

35886 *The science fiction of Mark Twain.* Hamden, CT: Archon Books, 1984, xxxiii+ 385 p., cloth, coll. [Edited by David Ketterer].

TWEED, Thomas F(rederic), 1890-1940

14365 *Blind mouths: a novel.* London: Arthur Barker, 1934, 386 p., cloth, novel.

14365A retitled: *Destiny's man.* New York: Farrar & Rinehart, 1935, 386 p., cloth, novel.

TWEEDSMUIR, Baron—SEE: Buchan, John

TWITCHELL, James B(uell), 1943-

35887 *Dreadful pleasures: an anatomy of modern horror.* New York, Oxford: Oxford University Press, 1985, viii+353 p., cloth, nonf.

35888 *The living dead: a study of the vampire in romantic literature.* Durham, NC: Duke University Press, 1981, 219 p., cloth, nonf.

TWITCHELL, Paul, 1908-1971

35889 *East of danger.* Menlo Park, CA: Illuminated Way Press, 1978, 180 p., paper, novel.

15871 *Talons of time.* San Diego, CA: Illuminated Way Press, 1974, 188 p., paper, novel.

35890 *The three masks of Gaba.* Menlo Park, CA: Illuminated Way Press, 1983, 199 p., paper, novel.

TYERS, Kathleen—SEE: Tyers, Kathy

TYERS, Kathy [i.e., Kathleen Luanne Moore Tyers], 1952-

35891 *Crystal witness.* Toronto, New York: Spectra, Bantam Books, 1989, 276 p., paper, novel.

35892 *Firebird.* Toronto, New York: Bantam Books, 1987, 265 p., paper, novel. FIREBIRD #1.

35893 *Fusion fire.* Toronto, New York: Spectra, Bantam Books, 1988, 231 p., paper, novel. FIREBIRD #2.

35894 *Shivering world.* New York, Toronto: Spectra, Bantam Books, 1991, 421 p., paper, novel.

TYLER, J. E. A(nthony)

35895   *The new Tolkien companion.* London: Macmillan, 1979, xiii+649 p., cloth, nonf.

35896   *The Tolkien companion.* London: Macmillan, 1976, 531 p., cloth, nonf.

TYLER, Tony—SEE: Tyler, J. E. A.

TYMN, Marshall B(enton), 1937-

35897   *American fantasy and science fiction: toward a bibliography of works published in the United States, 1948-1973.* West Linn, OR: FAX Collector's Editions, 1979, ix+228 p., paper, nonf.

35898   *A basic reference shelf for science fiction teachers.* Monticello, IL: Council of Planning Librarians, 1978, 13 p., paper, nonf.

35899   *Horror literature: a core collection and reference guide.* New York, London: R. R. Bowker Co., 1981, xviii+559 p., cloth, nonf. anth.

35900   *Recent critical studies on fantastic literature: an annotated checklist.* Monticello, IL: Council of Planning Librarians, 1978, 21 p., paper, nonf.

35901   *The science fiction reference book: a comprehensive handbook and guide to the history, literature, scholarship, and related activities of the science fiction and fantasy fields.* Mercer Island, WA: Starmont House, 1981, ix+536 p., cloth, nonf.

35902   *Science fiction: a teacher's guide and resource book.* Mercer Island, WA: Starmont House, 1988, x+140 p., cloth, nonf. STARMONT REFERENCE GUIDE #5.

35903   *Survey of science fiction literature: bibliographical supplement.* Englewood Cliffs, NJ: Salem Press, 1982, xiv+183 p., paper, nonf.

35904   *Teacher's guide to science fiction.* [S.l.: s.n.], 1981, 54 p., paper, nonf.

35905   *The year's scholarship in science fiction, fantasy, and horror literature: 1980.* Kent, OH: Kent State University Press, 1983, viii+110 p., paper, nonf.

35906   *The year's scholarship in science fiction, fantasy, and horror literature, 1981.* Kent, OH: Kent State University Press, 1984, viii+103 p., paper, nonf.

35907   *The year's scholarship in science fiction, fantasy, and horror literature, 1982.* Kent, OH: Kent State University Press, 1985, x+107 p., paper, nonf.

with Mike Ashley

16859   *Science fiction, fantasy, and weird fiction magazines.* Westport, CT, London: Greenwood Press, 1985, xxx+970 p., cloth, nonf. anth.

with Robert H. Boyer & Kenneth J. Zahorski

18399   *Fantasy literature: a core collection and reference guide.* New York, London: R. R. Bowker Co., 1979, xiii+273 p., cloth, nonf.

with L. W. Currey & Martin H. Greenberg & Joseph D. Olander

20899   *Index to stories in thematic anthologies of science fiction.* Boston: G. K. Hall & Co., 1978, xiii+193 p., cloth, nonf. REFERENCE PUBLICATION IN SCIENCE FICTION.

with L. W. Currey & Roger C. Schlobin

20898   *A research guide to science fiction studies: an annotated checklist of primary and secondary sources for fantasy and science fiction.* New York, London: Garland Publishing, 1977, ix+165 p., cloth, nonf.

with Roger C. Schlobin

33312   *The year's scholarship in science fiction and fantasy: 1976-1979.* Kent, OH: Kent State University Press, 1982, ix+251 p., cloth, nonf.

33313   *The year's scholarship in science fiction and fantasy, The: 1972-1975.* Kent, OH: Kent State University Press, 1979, xvi+222 p., cloth, nonf.

TYRRELL, Margot (Lesley), 1948- , *with Toss Gascoigne & Jo Goodman*

23747   *Dream time: new stories by sixteen award-winning authors.* Ringwood, Victoria, Australia: Penguin Books, 1989, 184 p., paper, anth.

*TYSON, J(ohn) Aubrey, 1870-<u>1930</u>

U

UEDA, Tsutomu

35908 *A study of Huxley*. Tokyo: Elihosha, 1955, 256 p., cloth, nonf.

UGRINSKY, Alexej, *with Courtney T. Wemyss*

35909 *George Orwell*. New York, Westport, CT: Greenwood Press, 1987, viii+204 p., cloth, nonf. anth.

UHRMAN, Esther, 1921-

35910 *Mithras the Second*. Philadelphia, PA: Dorrance & Co., 1988, 91 p., cloth, novel.

UNDERWOOD, Peter, 1923-

35911 *Horror man: the life of Boris Karloff*. London: Leslie Frewin, 1972, 238 p., cloth, nonf.

35911A retitled: *Karloff: the life of Boris Karloff*. New York: Drake Publishers, 1972, 238 p., cloth, nonf.
Karloff: the life of Boris Karloff—SEE: *Horror man*.

35912 *Thirteen famous ghost stories*. London, Melbourne: J. M. Dent & Sons; New York: E. P. Dutton, 1977, 203 p., cloth, anth.

35913 *The vampire's bedside companion: the amazing world of vampires in fact and fiction*. London: Leslie Frewin, 1975, 248 p., cloth, anth. [Includes some non-fiction].

UNDERWOOD, Tim (Edward), 1948-

with Daniel J. H. Levack

28242 *Fantasms: a bibliography of the literature of Jack Vance*. San Francisco, Columbia, PA: Underwood-Miller, 1978, 91 p., cloth, nonf.

with Daniel J. H. Levack & Kurt Cockrum

20234 *Fantasms II: a bibliography of the works of Jack Vance*. [S.l.: s.n.], 1979, xiii+83, 1, 118, 20 p., paper, nonf.

28244 *Fantasms II: a bibliography of the literature of Jack Vance*. Riverside, CA: Kurt Cockrum, 1979, vi+99 p. on 112 leaves, printout, nonf. [Revised edition; this book consists of unbound computer printout sheets gathered together into a binder].

with Daniel J. H. Levack & Chuck Miller

28243 *Fantasy and science fiction by Jack Vance*. San Francisco, Columbia, PA: Underwood-Miller, 1978, 8 p., paper, nonf.

with Chuck Miller

29889 *Bare bones: conversations on terror with Stephen King*. Los Angeles & Columbia, PA: Underwood-Miller, 1988, 259 p., cloth, nonf. anth.

29890 *Fear itself: the horror fiction of Stephen King*. San Francisco, Columbia, PA: Underwood-Miller, 1982, 255 p., cloth, nonf. anth.

29891 *Feast of fear: conversations with Stephen King*. New York: McGraw-Hill Book Co., 1989, 282 p., cloth, nonf. anth.

29892 *Jack Vance*. New York: Taplinger Publishing Co., 1980, 252 p., cloth, nonf. anth.

29893 *Kingdom of fear: the world of Stephen King*. San Francisco & Columbia, PA: Underwood-Miller, 1986, 267 p., cloth, nonf. anth.

with Chuck Miller as ANONYMOUS EDITORS

29894 *The book of the Sixth World Fantasy Convention*. San Francisco, Columbia, PA: Underwood-Miller, 1980, 96 p., cloth, anth. [Includes some nonfiction].

UNKEFER, Duane, 1937-

35914 *Gray eagles*. New York: Beech Tree Books, 1986, 467 p., cloth, novel.

UNSWORTH, Michael (E.), *with John Newman*

30649 *Future war novels: an annotated bibliography of works in English published since*

1946. Phoenix, AZ: Oryx Press, 1984, x + 101 p., cloth, nonf.

UPCHURCH, Boyd—SEE: Boyd, John

UPDIKE, John (Hoyer), 1932-

35915 *The chaste planet.* Worcester, MA: Metacom Press, 1980, 16 p., paper, story. [Limited to 300 copies].
35916 *The witches of Eastwick.* Franklin Center, PA: Franklin Library, 1984, 307 p., cloth, novel.

UPTON, Mark, pseud.—SEE: Sanders, Lawrence

UPWARD, Allen, 1863-1926

38128 *High treason.* London: Primrose Press, 1903, 60 p., cloth, story. HIGH TREASON #1.
14391 *Romance of politics: The fourth conquest of England: a sequel to "Treason".* London: Tyndale Press, 1904, 72 p., cloth, story. HIGH TREASON #2.

URBAN, Scott H., *with Jame A. Riley*

32326 *Minor apocalypses, and other small horrors: an anthology of October Society writings.* Atlanta, GA: Unnameable Press, 1985, 40 p., paper, anth. [Includes some verse].

URE, Jean (Neville), 1924-

35917 *Plague 99.* London: Methuen Teens Collection, 1989, 149 p., cloth, novel.
35917A retitled: *Plague.* San Diego, CA: Harcourt Brace Jovanovich, 1991, 218 p., cloth, novel.
Plague—SEE: *Plague 99.*

URICK, Kevin, 1952-

35918 *Snow World: a novel.* Adelphi, MD: White Ewe Press, 1983, 477 p., cloth, novel.

URQUHARDT, MacGregor—SEE: MacGregor, Richard

URQUHART, Fred(erick Burrows), 1912-

35919 *Seven ghosts in search.* London: William Kimber, 1983, 220 p., cloth, coll.

URQUHART, Jane, 1949-

35920 *Changing heaven.* Toronto: McClelland & Stewart, 1990, 258 p., cloth, novel.

URSINI, James, 1947- , *with Alain Silver*

33866 *The vampire film.* South Brunswick, NJ: A. S. Barnes & Co., 1975, 238 p., cloth, nonf.

USHER, Gray, 1903- , *with Shaun Usher*

35921 *Festival of fiends.* Folkestone, England: Bailey Brothers & Swinfen, 1976, 164 p., cloth, coll.
35922 *The graveyard companion: tales of hauntings and horrors.* Folkestone, England: Bailey Brothers & Swinfen, 1975, 102 p., cloth, coll.

USHER, Shaun, 1937- , *with Gray Usher*

35921 *Festival of fiends.* Folkestone, England: Bailey Brothers & Swinfen, 1976, 164 p., cloth, coll.
35922 *The graveyard companion: tales of hauntings and horrors.* Folkestone, England: Bailey Brothers & Swinfen, 1975, 102 p., cloth, coll.

USTINOV, Peter (Alexander), 1921-

35923 *The old man and Mr. Smith: a fable.* Boston: Little, Brown & Co., 1991, 261 p., cloth, novel.

UTECHIN, Nicholas, *with Austin Mitchelson*

29987 *The earthquake machine.* New York: Belmont Tower Books, 1976, 215 p., paper, novel. SHERLOCK HOLMES SERIES.

UTLEY, Steven, 1948- , *with Geo. W. Proctor*

31910 *Lone star universe: the first anthology of Texas science fiction authors.* Austin, TX: Heidelberg Publishers, 1976, xviii + 293 p., cloth, anth.

UTTER, Virgil S(tarbuck) Jr., 1925- , *with Gordon Benson Jr.*

17834 *Catherine Lucille Moore & Henry Kuttner, a marriage of souls and talent: a working bibliography.* Modesto, CA & Albuquerque, NM: Galactic Central Publications, 1986, 45 p., paper, nonf. GALACTIC CENTRAL BIBLIOGRAPHIES FOR THE AVID READER #21.
17835 *Catherine Lucille Moore & Henry Kuttner, a marriage of souls and talent: a working*

bibliography, 3rd rev. ed. Leeds, West Yorkshire, England & Albuquerque, NM: Galactic Central Publications, 1989, v+ 92 p., paper, nonf. GALACTIC CENTRAL BIBLIOGRAPHIES FOR THE AVID READER #21.

V

VACCARO, María Angélica

35924 *Animal?* New York, Washington: Vantage Press, 1982, 95 p., cloth, coll. [Translation by Bobbi Ciriza Whiteside].

VAL BAKER, Denys—SEE: Baker, Denys Val

VALDEMI, Maria (L.), 1947-

35925 *The demon lover: a novel of supernatural passion.* New York: Tor, A Tom Doherty Associates Book, 1981, 320 p., paper, novel.

VALE, Brenda, 1949-

35926 *Albion.* Barnstaple, England: Spindlewood, 1982, 181 p., cloth, novel.

***VALE, Rena (Marie), 1898-1983**

VALENTINE, Mark

35927 *14 Bellchamber Tower.* England: Crimson Altar Press, 1987, 35 p., paper, coll.

with Roger Dobson

21985 *Arthur Machen: apostle of wonder.* Oxford, England: Caermaen Books, 1985, ix+61 p., paper, nonf. anth.
21986 *Arthur Machen: artist and mystic.* Oxford, England: Caermaen Books, 1986, xii+54 p., paper, nonf. anth. [Limited to 300 copies].

VALENZA, Anji

35928 *Snow on the moon: an anthology of the Klysadel universe.* Brooklyn, NY: T'Kuhtian Press, 1978, 188 p., paper, coll.

VALLEJO, Boris, 1941-

35929 *The fantastic art of Boris.* New York: Ballantine Books, 1978, 12 p., [40] plates, cloth, art.
35930 *Fantasy art techniques.* New York: Arco Publishing, 1985, 127 p., cloth, nonf.

with Doris Vallejo

35931 *Mirage.* New York: Ballantine Books, 1982, [50] p., cloth, fiction.

VALLEJO, Doris

35932 *Enchantment: stories.* New York: Ballantine Books, 1984, 107 p., cloth, coll.
35933 *Windsound.* New York: Berkley Books, 1981, 186 p., paper, novel.

with Boris Vallejo

35931 *Mirage.* New York: Ballantine Books, 1982, [50] p., cloth, fiction.

VALMONT, Alejo Carpentier y—SEE: Carpentier y Valmont, Alejo

VALTOS, William M.

35934 *Resurrection: a novel of horror and suspense.* New York: Richardson, Steirman & Black, 1988, 251 p., cloth, novel.

VAN ALLSBURG, Chris, 1949-

35935 *The wretched stone.* Boston: Houghton Mifflin Co., 1991, unpaginated, cloth, novel.

VAN ASH, Cay, 1918-

35936 *The fires of Fu Manchu.* New York: Harper & Row, 1987, 277 p., cloth, novel. FU MANCHU SERIES.
35937 *Ten years beyond Baker Street: Sherlock Holmes matches wits with the diabolical Dr. Fu Manchu.* New York: Harper & Row, 1984, xi+339 p., cloth, novel. FU MANCHU SERIES.

VAN ASTEN, Gail

35938 *The blind knight.* New York: Ace Books, 1988, 218 p., paper, novel.
35939 *Charlemagne's champion.* New York: Ace Books, 1990, 295 p., paper, novel. CHARLEMAGNE'S CHAMPION #1.

35940 *The dark sword's lover.* New York: Ace Books, 1990, 282 p., paper, novel. CHARLEMAGNE'S CHAMPION #2.

VAN DOREN, Carl (Clinton), 1885-1950

35941 *James Branch Cabell.* New York: Robert M. McBride & Co., 1932, 89 p., cloth, nonf.

VAN EERDE, John A(ndrews), 1916- , *with Edward J. Gallagher & Judith A. Mistichelli*

23613 *Jules Verne: a primary and secondary bibliography.* Boston: G. K. Hall & Co., 1980, xxi+387 p., cloth, nonf. MASTERS OF SCIENCE FICTION AND FANTASY.

VAN GORES, Alida

35942 *Mermaid's song.* New York: A Signet Book, New American Library, 1989, 396 p., paper, novel.
35943 *Mermaid's song.* New York: A Signet Book, New American Library, 1989, 396 p., paper, novel.

VAN GREENAWAY, Peter, 1929-1988

35944 *The evening fool.* London: Hutchinson, 1964, 312 p., cloth, novel.
35945 *graffiti: a novel.* London: Victor Gollancz, 1983, 184 p., cloth, novel.
35946 *Manrissa man.* London: Victor Gollancz, 1982, 208 p., cloth, novel.
35947 *Mutants: a novel.* London: Victor Gollancz, 1986, 237 p., cloth, novel.

VAN HISE, Della, 1955-

35948 *Killing time.* New York: Pocket Books, 1985, 311 p., paper, novel. STAR TREK #24.

VAN HISE, James V., 1949-

35949 *Addams family revealed: an unauthorized look at America's spookiest family.* Las Vegas, NV: Pioneer Books, 1991, 157 p., paper, nonf. ADDAMS FAMILY SERIES.
        The arrival—SEE: *The V files, book one: The arrival.*
35950 *Batmania.* Las Vegas, NV: Pioneer Books, 1989, 145 p., paper, nonf. BATMAN SERIES.
35951 *Batmania: plus the story of the incredible Batman television revival.* Las Vegas, NV: Pioneer Books, 1989, 145 p., paper, nonf. BATMAN SERIES.

35952 *The best of Enterprise Incidents: the magazine for Star Trek fans.* Las Vegas, NV: Pioneer Books, 1990, 99 p., paper, nonf. anth. STAR TREK SERIES.
35953 *Cartoon files magazine spotlight on The Jonny Quest files.* Canoga Park, CA: Psi Fi Movie Press, 1986, 51 p., paper, nonf. JONNY QUEST SERIES.
35954 *Comics file magazine spotlight on The Fantastic Four files.* Canoga Park, CA: Psi Fi Movie Press, 1986, 66 p., paper, nonf. FANTASTIC FOUR SERIES.
35955 *Comics file magazine spotlight on The Superman files.* Canoga Park, CA: Heroes Publishing, 1986, 58 p., paper, nonf. SUPERMAN SERIES.
35956 *Comics file magazine spotlight on X-Men files.* Canoga Park, CA: Psi Fi Movie Press, 1986, 65 p., paper, nonf. X-MEN SERIES.
35957 *Critic's choice file focuses on Warmen: issues 1 through 4.* Canoga Park, CA: Psi Fi Movie Press, 1987, 51 p., paper, nonf.
        Dark Shadows handbook—SEE: *Files magazine focus on Dark Shadows.*
35958 *The EC Comics story.* Canoga Park, CA: Psi Fi Movie Press, 1987, 54 p., paper, nonf.
35959 *Enterprise incidents presents Stephen King.* Tampa, FL: New Media Publishers, 1984, 58 p., paper, nonf. anth.
        The Fantastic Four files—SEE: *Comics file magazine spotlight on The Fantastic Four files.*
35960 *Files magazine focus on Dark Shadows.* Granada Hills, CA: Pop Cult Inc., 1988, 57 p., paper, nonf. DARK SHADOWS SERIES. [Cover title: *Dark Shadows handbook*].
35961 *How to draw art for comic books: lessons from the masters: Corben, Elder, Foster, Kane, Kubert, Kurtzman, Raymond, Spiegleman, Sprang, Williamson.* Las Vegas, NV: Pioneer Books, 1989, 146 p., paper, nonf.
35962 *The illustrated guide to Clive Barker.* Las Vegas, NV: Pioneer Books, 1989, 110 p., paper, nonf.
35963 *The illustrated Stephen King.* Las Vegas, NV: Pioneer Books, 1989, 90 p., paper, nonf.
35964 *It's a bird—it's a plane—no, it's the television adventures of Superman.* Las Vegas, NV: Schuster & Schuster, 1989, 111 p., paper, nonf. SUPERMAN SERIES.
        The Jonny Quest files—SEE: *Cartoon files magazine spotlight on The Jonny Quest files.*

35965 *Lost in Space 25th anniversary tribute book.* Las Vegas, NV: Pioneer Books, 1990, 170 p., paper, nonf. LOST IN SPACE SERIES.

35966 *Serial adventures.* Las Vegas, NV: Pioneer Books, 1990, 154 p., paper, nonf.

The serial adventures of Batman—SEE: *Serial adventures presents The serial adventures of Batman.*

35967 *Serial adventures presents The serial adventures of Batman.* Las Vegas, NV: Pioneer Books, 1989, 98 p., paper, nonf. BATMAN SERIES.

35968 *Silver Surfer: an analysis of issues #1-9.* Canoga Park, CA: Psi Fi Movie Press, 1987, 49 p., paper, nonf. SILVER SURFER SERIES.

35969 *Star Trek 25th anniversary celebration.* Las Vegas, NV: Pioneer Books, 1991, 152 p., paper, nonf. STAR TREK SERIES.

35970 *Stephen King & Clive Barker: the illustrated guide to the masters of the macabre.* Las Vegas, NV: Pioneer Books, 1990, 146 p., paper, nonf. [Includes *The illustrated guide to Clive Barker*].

Stephen King—SEE: *Enterprise incidents presents Stephen King.*

The Superman files—SEE: *Comics file magazine spotlight on The Superman files.*

35971 *Swamp Thing finale.* Canoga Park, CA: Psi Fi Movie Press, 1987, 57 p., paper, nonf. SWAMP THING SERIES.

35972 *The Trek crew book.* Las Vegas, NV: Pioneer Books, 1989, 95 p., paper, nonf. STAR TREK SERIES.

35973 *The Trek fan's handbook.* Las Vegas, NV: Pioneer Books, 1990, 109 p., paper, nonf. STAR TREK SERIES.

35974 *Trek: the lost years.* Las Vegas, NV: Pioneer Books, 1989, 121 p., paper, nonf. STAR TREK SERIES. [Cover and spine credit says Edward Gross].

35975 *Trek: the next generation.* Las Vegas, NV: Pioneer Books, 1991, 153 p., paper, nonf. STAR TREK SERIES.

35976 *The V files, book one: The arrival.* Canoga Park, CA: Psi Fi Movie Press, 1985, 2 v. (I-49 p.; II-54 p.), paper, nonf. anth. V SERIES.

35977 *Video superheroes.* Las Vegas, NV: Pioneer Books, 1991, 141 p., paper, nonf.

X-Men files—SEE: *Comics file magazine spotlight on X-Men files.*

with Edward Gross

24782 *The Dark Shadows tribute book.* Las Vegas, NV: Pioneer Books, 1990, 144 p., paper, nonf.

*VAN ITH, Lily [pseud. of Emilie Ida Friedli], 1889-1974

VAN LHIN, Erik, pseud.—SEE: Del Rey, Lester

*VAN LODEN, Erle [pseud. of Lisle Willis], 1919-

VAN LOGGEM, Manuel—see: Loggem, Manuel van

VAN LUSTBADER, Eric—SEE: Lustbader, Eric Van

VAN OVER, Raymond, 1934-

35978 *Monsters you never heard of.* New York: Tempo Books, 1983, xii+148 p., paper, coll.

35979 *The twelfth child.* New York: Pinnacle Books, Windsor Publishing Corp., 1990, 320 p., paper, novel.

35980 *Whisper.* New York: Pinnacle Books, Windsor Publishing Corp., 1991, 287 p., paper, novel.

VAN RJNDT, Philippe, 1950-

35981 *Samaritan.* Toronto: Lester & Orpen Dennys, 1983, 406 p., cloth, novel.

35982 *The trial of Adolf Hitler: a novel.* Toronto: Lester & Orpen Dennys, 1978, 334 p., cloth, novel.

VAN SCYOC, Sydney J(oyce), 1939-

35983 *Bluesong.* New York: Berkley Books, 1983, 261 p., paper, novel. SUNSTONE SCROLLS #2.

35984 *Cloudcry.* New York: Berkley Publishing Corp., 1977, 216 p., cloth, novel.

35985 *Darkchild.* New York: Berkley Books, 1982, 249 p., paper, novel. SUNSTONE SCROLLS #1.

35986 *Daughters of the sunstone.* Garden City, NY: Nelson Doubleday, 1985, 697 p., cloth, coll. SUNSTONE SCROLLS #1-3.

35987 *Deepwater dreams.* New York: Avon Books, 1991, 249 p., paper, novel.

35988 *Drowntide.* New York: Berkley Books, 1987, 220 p., paper, novel.

35989 *Feather stroke.* New York: Avon Books, 1989, 264 p., paper, novel.

35990 *StarMother.* New York: Berkley Publishing Corp., 1976, 186 p., cloth, novel.

35991 *Starsilk*. New York: Berkley Books, 1984, 245 p., paper, novel. SUNSTONE SCROLLS #3.

35992 *Sunwaifs*. New York: Berkley Books, 1981, 214 p., paper, novel.

VAN SICKLE, V. A. [pseud. of Arthur Hawthorne Carhart], 1892-

38129 *The wrong body*. New York: Alfred A. Knopf, 1937, 273 p., cloth, novel.

VAN TASSEL, D(ennie L.), 1939-

35993 *Computers, computers, computers: in fiction and in verse*. Nashville, TN: Thomas Nelson Books, 1977, 192 p., cloth, nonf. anth.

VAN THAL, Herbert (Maurice), 1904-1983

35994 *The 16th Pan book of horror stories*. London & Sydney: Pan Books, 1975, 205 p., paper, anth.

35995 *The 17th Pan book of horror stories*. London & Sydney: Pan Books, 1976, 205 p., paper, anth.

35996 *The 18th Pan book of horror stories*. London & Sydney: Pan Books, 1977, 190 p., paper, anth.

35997 *The 19th Pan book of horror stories*. London & Sydney: Pan Books, 1978, 192 p., paper, anth.

35998 *The 20th Pan book of horror stories*. London & Sydney: Pan Books, 1979, 191 p., paper, anth.

35999 *The 21st Pan book of horror stories*. London & Sydney: Pan Books, 1980, 174 p., paper, anth.

36000 *The 22nd Pan book of horror stories*. London & Sydney: Pan Books, 1981, 189 p., paper, anth.

36001 *The 23rd Pan book of horror stories*. London & Sydney: Pan Books, 1982, 158 p., paper, anth.

36002 *The 24th Pan book of horror stories*. London & Sydney: Pan Books, 1983, 158 p., paper, anth.

36003 *The 25th Pan book of horror stories*. London & Sydney: Pan Books, 1984, 157 p., paper, anth.

36004 *The second bedside book of strange stories*. London: Arthur Barker, 1976, 168 p., cloth, anth.

36005 *Tales to make the flesh creep: an anthology of classic stories*. London: Constable, 1977, xix+282 p., cloth, anth.

VAN TUYL, Rosealtha—SEE: Van Tuyl, Zaara

*VAN TUYL, Zaara [i.e., Rosealtha Van Tuyl], 1901-1989

VAN VOGT, A(lfred) E(lton), 1912-

36006 *The anarchistic colossus*. New York: Ace Books, 1977, 248 p., paper, novel.

36007 *The best of A. E. Van Vogt*. New York: Pocket Books, 1976, 256 p., paper, coll.

The Blal—SEE: *Monsters*.

14539 *The book of Ptath*. Reading, PA: Fantasy Press, 1947, 227 p., cloth, novel.

14539A retitled: *Two hundred million A.D.* New York: Paperback Library, 1964, 159 p., paper, novel.

14539B retitled: *Ptath*. New York: Zebra Books, Kensington Publishing Corp., 1976, 204 p., paper, novel.

14540 *The book of van Vogt*. New York: DAW Books, 1972, 191 p., paper, coll.

14540A retitled: *Lost: fifty suns*. New York: DAW Books, 1979, 191 p., paper, coll.

Computer eye—SEE: Computerworld.

36008 *Computerworld*. New York: DAW Books, 1983, 203 p., paper, novel.

36008A retitled: *Computer eye*. New York: DAW Books, 1985, 203 p., paper, novel.

36009 *Cosmic encounter*. Garden City, NY: Doubleday & Co., 1980, 207 p., cloth, novel.

Earth factor X—SEE: *Secret galactics*.

36010 *The enchanted village*. Dearborn Heights, MI: Misfit Press for Conclave and Loscon, 1979, 24 p., paper, story. [Limited to 550 copies].

14548 *Future glitter*. New York: Ace, 1973, 216 p., paper, novel.

14548A retitled: *Tyranopolis*. London: Sphere Books, 1977, 170 p., paper, novel.

36011 *The Gryb*. New York: Zebra Books, Kensington Publishing Corp., 1976, 217 p., paper, coll.

14549 *The house that stood still*. New York: A Corwin Book, Greenberg: Publisher, 1950, 210 p., cloth, novel.

14549A retitled: *The mating cry: a prize science fiction novel selected by Galaxy magazine for Beacon Books*. New York: Beacom Books, 1960, 160 p., paper, novel.

14549B retitled: *The undercover aliens*. St Albans, England: Panther, 1976, 173 p., paper, novel.

Lost: fifty suns—SEE: *The book of van Vogt*.

14555 *Monsters*. New York: Paperback Library, 1965, 154 p., paper, coll.

14555A retitled: *The Blal*. New York: Zebra Books, Kensington Publishing Corp., 1976, 224 p., paper, coll.

36012 *Null A3.* Beverly Hills, CA: Morrison, Raven-Hill Co., 1984, 213 p., cloth, novel. NULL-A #3. [Limited to 750 copies].

36013 *Pendulum.* New York: DAW Books, 1978, 158 p., paper, coll.

Ptath—SEE: *The book of Ptath.*

36014 *Reflections of A. E. van Vogt: the autobiography of a science fiction giant, with a complete bibliography.* Lakemont, GA: Fictioneer Books, 1975, 136 p., paper, nonf. [Edited by David Anthony Kraft].

36015 *Renaissance.* New York: Pocket Books, 1979, 190 p., paper, novel.

14561 *The secret galactics.* Englewood Cliffs, NJ: Reward, 1974, 215 p., paper, novel.

14561A retitled: *Earth factor X.* New York: DAW Books, 1976, 174 p., paper, novel.

36016 *Supermind.* New York: DAW Books, 1977, 176 p., paper, novel.

14565 *The three eyes of evil; and, Earth's last fortress: two science fiction novels.* London: Sidgwick & Jackson, 1973, 218 p., cloth, coll. [*The three eyes of evil* was originally published as *Siege of the unseen*].

14565A retitled: *Earth's last fortress; The three eyes of evil.* London: Sphere, 1977, 173 p., paper, coll.

38130 *Tomorrow on the march: the text of a speech delivered July 4, 1946 at the Pacificon by the Guest of Honor, A. E. van Vogt.* Los Angeles: Time-Binder Press, 1946, [14] p., paper, nonf. [Cover title].

Tyranopolis—SEE: *Future glitter.*

The undercover aliens—SEE: *The house that stood still.*

36017 *The universe maker; and, The proxy intelligence: science fiction.* London: Sidgwick & Jackson, 1976, 196 p., cloth, coll.

36018 *The weapon shops of Isher; and, The weapon makers.* London: New English Library, 1988, 265 p., paper, coll. ISHER #1-2.

VAN WINKLE, Joseph, *with Al Dempsey & Sidney Levine*

21549 *Miss Finney kills now and then.* New York: Tor, A Tom Doherty Associates Book, 1982, 256 p., paper, movie.

*VAN WINKLE, Monica F., <u>1892-1985</u>

VAN **ZELLER, Claude**—SEE: **Vennings, Hugh**

VANCE, J. Emily, *with Beverly Volker*

36019 *The rack; &, All the king's horses, all the king's men.* [S.l.]: J. Emily Vance, 1977?, 114-170, 106-194 p., paper, coll. STAR TREK SERIES.

VANCE, Jack [i.e., John Holbrook Vance], 1916-

Alastor 933—SEE: *Marune: Alastor 933.*
Alastor 1716—SEE: *Wyst: Alastor 1716*

14438 *The Anome; Durdane, Book I.* New York: Dell, 1973, 224 p., paper, novel. DURDANE #1.

14438A retitled: *The faceless man.* New York: Ace Books, 1978, 224 p., paper, novel. DURDANE #1.

36020 *Araminta Station.* Los Angeles, Columbia, PA: Underwood-Miller, 1987, xviii+ 458 p., cloth, novel. CADWAL CHRONICLES #1. [Limited to 500 copies].

36021 *The augmented agent, and other stories.* San Francisco, Columbia, PA: Underwood-Miller, 1986, 237 p., cloth, coll.

36022 *The bagful of dreams.* San Francisco, Columbia, PA: Underwood-Miller, 1979, 37 p., cloth, story. DYING EARTH SERIES. [Limited to 600 copies].

36023 *The best of Jack Vance.* New York: Pocket Books, 1976, x+274 p., paper, coll.

36024 *Big planet.* San Francisco, Columbia, PA: Underwood-Miller, 1978, 236 p., cloth, novel. BIG PLANET #1. [An expanded edition of #14440; restores the uncut original text].

36025 *The Book of Dreams.* San Francisco, Columbia, PA: Underwood-Miller, 235 p., cloth, novel. DEMON PRINCES #5.

Chasch—SEE: *Planet of adventure #1: City of the Chasch.*

36026 *Chateau D'If, and other stories.* Novato, CA, Lancaster, PA: Underwood-Miller, 1990, 284 p., cloth, coll.

The complete Magnus Ridolph—SEE: *The many worlds of Magnus Ridolph.*

36027 *Cugel's saga.* San Francisco, Columbia, PA: Underwood-Miller, 1983, 334 p., cloth, novel. DYING EARTH SERIES. [Limited to 550 copies].

36028 *The dark side of the Moon: stories of the future.* San Francisco, Columbia, PA: Underwood-Miller, 1986, 275 p., cloth, coll.

36029 *Durdane.* London: Victor Gollancz, 1989, 613 p., paper, coll. DURDANE #1-3. [Includes *Faceless, Brave, Asutra*].

Durdane, Book I—SEE: *The Anome: Durdane, Book I.*

Dust of far suns—SEE: *Future tense.*

36030 *Ecce and old Earth.* Novato, CA, Lancaster, PA: Underwood-Miller, 1991,

313 p., cloth, novel. CADWAL CHRONICLES #2. [Limited to 587 copies].

14447 *Eight fantasms and magics: a science fiction adventure.* New York: Macmillan, 1969, 288 p., cloth, novel.

14447A retitled: *Fantasms and magics: a science fantasy adventure.* London, Toronto: Mayflower, Granada Publishing, 1978, 192 p., paper, coll.

36031 *The face.* New York: DAW Books, 1979, 224 p., paper, novel. DEMON PRINCES #4.

The faceless man—SEE: *The Anome.*

Fantasms and magics—SEE: *Eight fantasms and magics: a science fiction adventure.*

14450 *Future tense.* New York: Ballantine Books, 1964, 160 p., paper, coll.

14450A retitled: *Dust of far suns.* New York: DAW Books, 1981, 160 p., paper, coll.

36032 *Galactic effectuator.* San Francisco, Columbia, PA: Underwood-Miller, 1980, 171 p., cloth, coll. GAEAN REACH #6.

Gold and iron (Slaves of the Klau)—SEE: *Slaves of the Klau.*

36033 *Green magic.* San Francisco, Columbia, PA: Underwood-Miller, 1979, 16 p., paper, story. [Limited to 300 copies].

36034 *Green magic: the fantasy realms of Jack Vance.* San Francisco, Columbia, PA: Underwood-Miller, 1979, 273 p., cloth, coll. [Limited to 600 copies].

The green pearl—SEE: *Lyonesse: The green pearl.*

36035 *Light from a lone star.* Cambridge, MA: A Lone Star Con Book, NESFA Press, 1985, xiii+125 p., cloth, coll. [Includes some nonfiction].

36036 *Lost moons.* San Francisco, Columbia, MO: Underwood-Miller, 1982, 250 p., cloth, coll.

36037 *Lyonesse: Madouc.* Novato, CA, Lancaster, PA: Underwood-Miller, 1989, 358 p., cloth, novel. LYONESSE #3. [Limited to 600 copies]. [Winner of the World Fantasy Award for Best Fantasy Novel, 1989 (1990)].

36037A retitled: *Madouc.* New York: Ace Books, 1990, 426 p., paper, novel. LYONESSE #3.

36038 *Lyonesse: The green pearl.* San Francisco, Columbia, PA: Underwood-Miller, 1985, 360 p., cloth, novel. LYONESSE #2. [Limited to 600 copies].

36038A retitled: *The green pearl.* New York: Berkley Books, 1986, 408 p., paper, novel. LYONESSE #2.

Madouc—SEE: *Lyonesse: Madouc.*

The magnificent showboats of the Lower Vissel River, Lune XXIII South, Big Planet: (Showboat world)—SEE: *Showboat world.*

36039 *The many worlds of Magnus Ridolph.* New York: DAW Books, 1980, 174 p., paper, coll. [Adds two additional stories to the original edition (see #14456)].

36040 retitled: *The complete Magnus Ridolph.* San Francisco, Columbia, PA: Underwood-Miller, 1984, 204 p., cloth, coll. [Expanded edition; adds two more stories to the 1980 DAW edition].

36041 *Marune: Alastor 933.* New York: Ballantine Books, 1975, 169 p., paper, novel. GAEAN REACH #3.

36042 *Maske: Thaery.* New York: Berkley Publishing Corp., 1976, 215 p., cloth, novel. GAEAN REACH #4.

The moon moth, and other stories—SEE: *The world between, and other stories.*

36043 *Morreion.* San Francisco, Columbia, PA: Underwood-Miller, 1979, 106 p., cloth, novel. DYING EARTH SERIES.

36044 *The Narrow Land.* New York: DAW Books, 1982, 176 p., paper, coll.

36045 *Nopalgarth: three complete novels: Nopalgarth, The houses of Iszm, Son of the tree.* New York: DAW Books, 1980, 272 p., paper, coll. [Includes *Nopalgarth, The houses of Iszm, Son of the tree*; *Nopalgarth* is retitling of *The brains of Earth*].

14459 *Planet of adventure #1: City of the Chasch.* New York: Ace, 1968, 157 p., paper, novel. TSCHAI #1.

14459A retitled: *Chasch.* New York: Bluejay Books, 1986, 200 p., paper, novel. TSCHAI #1.

Planet of adventure #2—SEE: *Servants of the Wankh: Planet of adventure #2.*

36046 *The planet of adventure omnibus.* London: Grafton, 1985, 536 p., paper, coll. PLANET OF ADVENTURE #1-4.

36047 *Rhialto the Marvellous.* San Francisco, Columbia, PA: Brandywyne Books, 1984, 198 p., cloth, novel. DYING EARTH #4. [Limited to 1000 boxed copies].

14461 *Servants of the Wankh: Planet of adventure #2.* New York: Ace, 1969, 158 p., paper, novel. TSCHAI #2.

14461A retitled: *Wankh.* New York: Bluejay Books, 1986, 193 p., paper, novel. TSCHAI #2.

36048 *The seventeen virgins.* San Francisco, Columbia, PA: Underwood-Miller, 1979, 33 p., paper, story. DYING EARTH SERIES. [Limited to 600 copies].

36049 *The seventeen virgins; The bagful of dreams: the adventures of Cugel the Clever.* San Francisco, Columbia, PA:

Underwood-Miller, 1979, 33+37 p., cloth, coll. DYING EARTH SERIES. [Limited to 111 copies].

36050 *Showboat world.* New York: Pyramid Books, 1975, 188 p., paper, novel. BIG PLANET #2.

36050A retitled: *The magnificent showboats of the Lower Vissel River, Lune XXIII South, Big Planet: (Showboat world).* San Francisco, Columbia, PA: Underwood-Miller, 1983, 171 p., cloth, novel. BIG PLANET #2.

14462 *Slaves of the Klau.* New York: Ace Books, 1958, 129 p., paper, novel. [Bound with *Big planet /* by Jack Vance].

36051 retitled: *Gold and iron: (Slaves of the Klau).* San Francisco, Columbia, PA: Underwood-Miller, 1982, 126 p., cloth, novel. [An expanded edition which restores the original text].

36052 *Suldrun's garden.* San Francisco, Columbia, PA: Underwood-Miller, 1983, 406 p., cloth, novel. LYONESSE #1. [Limited to 550 copies].

Thaery—SEE: *Maske: Thaery.*

Wankh—SEE: *Servants of the Wankh: Planet of adventure #2.*

14470 *The world between, and other stories.* New York: Ace Double, 1965, 134 p., paper, coll.

14470A retitled: *The moon moth, and other stories.* London: Dennis Dobson, 1975, 125 p., cloth, coll.

36053 *Wyst: Alastor 1716.* New York: DAW Books, 1978, 222 p., paper, novel. GAEAN REACH #5.

with C. J. Cherryh & Janet Morris

37657 *Rhialto the Marvellous.* New York: Baen Books, 1985, 250 p., paper, anth. DYING EARTH #4; HEROES IN HELL. [Includes Vance's novel, plus the novella "Basileus" by Cherryh and Morris].

VANCE, John Holbrook—SEE: Vance, Jack

VANCE, Steve, 1952-

36054 *The abyss.* New York: Leisure Books, 1989, 361 p., paper, novel.

36055 *All the shattered worlds.* New York: Manor Books, 1979, 292 p., paper, novel.

36056 *The Asgard run.* New York: Leisure Books, 1990, 309 p., paper, novel.

36057 *The hybrid.* New York: Tower Books, 1981, 224 p., paper, novel.

36058 *The Hyde effect.* New York: Leisure Books, 1986, 399 p., paper, novel.

36059 *Planet of the Gawfs.* New York: Leisure Books, 1978, 173 p., paper, novel.

36060 *Shapes.* New York: Leisure Books, 1991, 442 p., paper, novel.

36061 *Spook.* New York: Soho Press, 1990, 234 p., cloth, novel.

VANDE VELDE, Vivian, 1951-

36062 *A hidden magic.* New York: Crown Publishers, 1985, 117 p., cloth, novel.

36063 *User unfriendly.* San Diego, CA: Jane Yolen Books, Harcourt Brace Jovanovich, 1991, viii+244 p., cloth, novel.

36064 *A well-timed enchantment.* New York: Crown Publishers, 1990, vi+184 p., cloth, novel.

VANDERMEER, Jeff

36065 *The book of frog.* Gainesville, FL: Ministry of Whimsy Press, 1989, 45 p., paper, coll.

*VANE, (Vane Hunt) Sutton, 1888-1963

VANHEE, Gregory G., 1935?-

36066 *Night strike.* New York: Avon Books, 1990, 375 p., paper, novel.

VANN, Gerald, 1906-

36067 *On being human: St. Thomas and Mr. Aldous Huxley.* London: Sheed & Ward, 1934, 110 p., cloth, nonf.

VANSITTART, Peter, 1920-

36068 *The dark tower: tales from the past.* London: Macdonald & Co., 1965, 135 p., cloth, coll.

36069 *The death of Robin Hood: a novel.* London: Peter Owen, 1981, 224 p., cloth, novel.

36070 *The game and the ground.* London: Max Reinhardt, 1956, 187 p., cloth, novel.

36071 *I am the world: a romance.* London: Chatto & Windus, 1942, 320 p., cloth, novel.

36072 *Lancelot: a novel.* London: Peter Owen, 1978, 192 p., cloth, novel.

36073 *Parsifal: a novel.* London: Peter Owen, 1988, 256 p., cloth, novel.

36074 *The shadow land: more stories from the past.* London: Macdonald & Co., 1967, 128 p., cloth, coll.

36075 *The story teller: a novel.* London: Peter Owen, 1968, 285 p., cloth, novel.

VARDEMAN, Robert E(dward), 1947-

36076 *The alien web.* New York: Avon, 1987, 166 p., paper, novel. MASTERS OF SPACE #2.

36077 *Ancient heavens.* New York: Avon Books, 1989, 246 p., paper, novel.

36078 *Cenotaph Road.* New York: Ace Science Fiction Books, 1983, 224 p., paper, novel. CENOTAPH ROAD #1.

36079 *Colors of chaos.* New York: Ace Books, 1988, 202 p., paper, novel. WEAPONS OF CHAOS #3.

36080 *Crisis at Starlight.* New York: Ace Books, 1990, 199 p., paper, novel. BIOWARRIORS #2.

36081 *The crystal clouds.* New York: Avon, 1985, 222 p., paper, novel. JADE DEMONS #3.

36082 *Deathfall.* New York: An Onyx Book, 1991, 384 p., paper, novel.

36083 *The Demon Crown trilogy: The glass warrior; Phantoms on the wind; A symphony of storms.* London: New English Library, 1990, 277+281+280 p., paper, coll. DEMON CROWN TRILOGY #1-3.

36084 *Echoes of chaos.* New York: Berkley Books, 1986, 183 p., paper, novel. WEAPONS OF CHAOS #1.

36085 *Equations of chaos.* New York: Ace Books, 1987, 201 p., paper, novel. WEAPONS OF CHAOS #2.

36086 *Fire and fog.* New York: Ace Science Fiction Books, 1984, 215 p., paper, novel. CENOTAPH ROAD #5.

36087 *The frozen waves.* New York: Avon, 1985, 204 p., paper, novel. JADE DEMONS #2.

36088 *The glass warrior.* New York: Tor SF, A Tom Doherty Associates Book, 1989, 277 p., paper, novel. DEMON CROWN TRILOGY #1.

36089 *The infinity plague.* New York: Ace Books, 1989, 202 p., paper, novel. BIOWARRIORS #1.

36090 *Iron Tongue.* New York: Ace Science Fiction Books, 1984, 217 p., paper, novel. CENOTAPH ROAD #4.

36091 *The Jade Demons quartet: The quaking lands; The frozen waves; The crystal clouds; The white fire.* London: New English Library, 1987, 206+204+222+199 p., paper, coll. JADE DEMONS #1-4.

The keys to paradise—SEE: entry under pseudonym Robert Moran (below).

36092 *The Klingon gambit: a Star Trek novel.* New York: A Timescape Book, Pocket Books, 1981, 158 p., paper, novel. STAR TREK #3.

36093 *Masters of space.* London: New English Library, 1990, 214+166+169 p., paper, coll. MASTERS OF SPACE #1-3. [Includes *The stellar death plan; The alien web; A plague in paradise*].

36094 *Masters of space: The stellar death plan.* New York: Avon, 1987, 214 p., paper, novel. MASTERS OF SPACE #1.

36095 *Mutiny on the Enterprise: a Star Trek novel.* New York: A Timescape Book, Pocket Books, 1983, 189 p., paper, novel. STAR TREK #12.

36096 *Phantoms on the wind.* New York: Tor Fantasy, A Tom Doherty Associates Book, 1989, 281 p., paper, novel. DEMON CROWN TRILOGY #2.

36097 *Pillar of night.* New York: Ace Science Fiction Books, 1984, 200 p., paper, novel. CENOTAPH ROAD #6.

36098 *A plague in paradise.* New York: Avon, 1987, 169 p., paper, novel. MASTERS OF SPACE #3.

36099 *The quaking lands.* New York: Avon, 1985, 206 p., paper, novel. JADE DEMONS #1.

36100 *Road to the stars.* New York: Harper & Row, 1988, 213 p., cloth, novel.

36101 *The sandcats of Rhyl.* Canoga Park, CA: Major Books, 1978, 192 p., paper, novel.

36102 *The screaming knife.* New York: Avon Books, 1990, 217 p., paper, novel. PETER THORNE #1.

36103 *The sorcerer's skull.* New York: Ace Science Fiction Books, 1983, 223 p., paper, novel. CENOTAPH ROAD #2.

36104 *Space vectors.* New York: Ace Books, 1990, 198 p., paper, novel. BIOWARRIORS #3.

The stellar death plan—SEE: *Masters of space: The stellar death plan.*

36105 *A symphony of storms.* New York: Tor Fantasy, A Tom Doherty Associates Book, 1990, 280 p., paper, novel. DEMON CROWN TRILOGY #3.

36106 *Weapons of chaos: Echoes of chaos; Equations of chaos; Colors of chaos.* London: New English Library, 1989, 596 p., paper, coll. WEAPONS OF CHAOS #1-3.

36107 *The white fire.* New York: Avon, 1986, 199 p., paper, novel. JADE DEMONS #4.

36108 *World of mazes.* New York: Ace Science Fiction Books, 1983, 219 p., paper, novel. CENOTAPH ROAD #3.

as VICTOR APPLETON

Gateway to doom—SEE: *Tom Swift: Gateway to doom.*

16749 *Tom Swift: Gateway to doom.* New York: Wanderer Books, Simon & Schuster,

1983, 175 p., paper, novel. Tom Swift
#B9.

as NICK CARTER

19603 *Doctor DNA.* New York: Ace Charter
Books, 1982, 196 p., paper, novel. NICK
CARTER SERIES.

19610 *The solar menace.* New York: Charter,
1981, 215 p., paper, novel. NICK CAR-
TER SERIES.

as DANIEL MORAN

36109 *The flame key.* New York: Tor SF, A
Tom Doherty Associates Book, 1987, 222
p., paper, novel. KEYS TO PARADISE #1.

36110 *Key of ice and steel* / by Robert E. Vardeman writing as Daniel Moran. New
York: Tor SF, A Tom Doherty Associates Book, 1988, 216 p., paper, novel.
KEYS TO PARADISE #3.

36111 *The keys to paradise* / by Robert E.
Vardeman. London: New English Library, 1986, 540 p., paper, coll. KEYS
TO PARADISE #1-3. [Includes *The flame
key*; *The skeleton lord's key*; *Key of ice
and steel*].

36112 *The skeleton lord's key* / by Robert E.
Vardeman writing as Daniel Moran. New
York: Tor SF, A Tom Doherty Associ-
ates Book, 1987, 186 p., paper, novel.
KEYS TO PARADISE #2.

with Victor Milán

29867 *The city in the glacier.* New York: Playboy Paperbacks, 1980, 224 p., paper,
novel. WAR OF POWERS #2.

29868 *Demon of the Dark Ones.* New York:
Playboy Paperbacks, 1982, 221 p., paper,
novel. WAR OF POWERS #6.

29869 *The Destiny Stone.* New York: Playboy
Paperbacks, 1980, 221 p., paper, novel.
WAR OF POWERS #3.

29870 *The Fallen Ones.* New York: Playboy Paperbacks, 1982, 222 p., paper, novel.
WAR OF POWERS #4.

29871 *In the shadow of Omizantrim.* New York:
Playboy Paperbacks, 1982, 222 p., paper,
novel. WAR OF POWERS #5.
Istu awakened-SEE: *The war of powers II:
Istu awakened*.

29872 *The Sundered Realm.* New York: Playboy
Paperbacks, 1980, 222 p., paper, novel.
WAR OF POWERS #1.

29873 *The war of powers.* Sevenoaks, Kent,
England: New English Library, 1984,
457 p., paper, coll. WAR OF POWERS #1-

3. [Includes *The Sundered Realm*; *The
city in the glacier*; *The Destiny Stone*].

36113 *The war of powers II: Istu awakened.*
Sevenoaks, Kent, England: New English
Library, 1985, 511 p., paper, coll. WAR
OF POWERS #4-6. [Includes *The Fallen
Ones*; *In the shadow of Omizantrim*; *De-
mon of the Dark Ones*].

with Geo. W. Proctor

31911 *The beasts of the mist.* New York: Ace
Fantasy Books, 1986, 183 p., paper,
novel. SWORDS OF RAEMLLYN #5.

31912 *Blood fountain.* New York: Ace Fantasy
Books, 1985, 184 p., paper, novel.
SWORDS OF RAEMLLYN #3.

31913 *Death's acolyte.* New York: Ace Fantasy
Books, 1986, 181 p., paper, novel.
SWORDS OF RAEMLLYN #4.

31914 *For crown and kingdom.* New York: Ace
Fantasy Books, 1987, 196 p., paper,
novel. SWORDS OF RAEMLLYN #6.

31915 *To demons bound.* New York: Ace Fantasy Books, 1985, 215 p., paper, novel.
SWORDS OF RAEMLLYN #1.

31916 *A yoke of magic.* New York: Ace Fantasy
Books, 1985, 195 p., paper, novel.
SWORDS OF RAEMLLYN #2.

with Geo. W. Proctor as EDWARD GEORGE

Intergalactic orgy—SEE: *Pleasure planet*.
Janet's sex planet—SEE: *Pleasure planet*.
Outer space embrace—SEE: *Pleasure
planet*.
Playing with desire—SEE: *Pleasure
planet*.

05883 *Pleasure planet.* New York: Orpheus Series, 1974, 187 p., paper, novel.

05883A retitled: *Outer space embrace* / by Monica
Mounds. New York: A Beeline Classic,
1978, 187 p., paper, novel.

05883B retitled: *Janet's sex planet* / by Carrie
Onn. New York: A Beeline Double
Novel, 1980, 187 p., paper, novel.
[Bound with *Orgy in orbit* / by Traves
Tea].

05883C retitled: *Intergalactic orgy* / by Obie Kahn.
New York: Late Night Library, 1983,
187 p., paper, novel.

05883D retitled: *Sexual coquette* / by Marv Elous.
New York: A Beeline Double Novel,
1985, 187 p., paper, novel. [Bound with
From novice to nymphette / by Terri
Flick].

05883E retitled: *Playing with desire* / by Fred
Sparkrock. New York: A Beeline Dou-
ble Novel, 1986, 187 p., paper, novel.
Sexual coquette—SEE: *Pleasure planet*.

VARLEY, John (Herbert), 1947-

36114 *The Barbie murders.* New York: Berkley Books, 1980, 260 p., paper, coll. [Winner of the *Locus* Award for Best Collection, 1980 (1981)].

36114A retitled: *Picnic on Nearside.* New York: Berkley Books, 1984, 260 p., paper, coll.

36115 *Blue champagne.* Niles, IL: Dark Harvest, 1986, 400 p., cloth, coll. [Limited to 300 copies; winner of the *Locus* Award for Best Collection, 1986 (1987)].

36116 *Demon.* New York: G. C. Putnam's Sons, 1984, 464 p., cloth, novel. GAEA #3.

36117 *Millennium.* New York: Berkley Books, 1983, 249 p., paper, novel.

36118 *The Ophiuchi hotline.* New York: Quantum Science Fiction, Dial Press/James Wade, 1977, 237 p., cloth, novel.

36119 *The persistence of vision.* New York: Quantum Science Fiction, Dial Press/James Wade, 1978, xv+316 p., cloth, coll.

36119A retitled: *In the hall of the Martian kings: science fiction.* London: Sidgwick & Jackson, 1978, xvii+316 p., cloth, coll.

36120 *The persistence of vision.* New York: Tor SF, A Tom Doherty Associates Book, 1991, p. 113-188, paper, story. [Bound with *Nanoware time* / by Ian Watson].

Picnic on Nearside—SEE: *The Barbie murders.*

36121 *Press enter* ■. New York: Tor SF, A Tom Doherty Associates Book, 1990, 98 p., paper, story. [Bound with *Hawksbill Station* / by Robert Silverberg].

36122 *Tango Charlie and Foxtrot Romeo.* New York: Tor SF, A Tom Doherty Associates Book, 1989, 101 p., paper, story. [Bound with *The star pit* / by Samuel R. Delany].

36123 *Titan.* New York: Berkley Publishing Corp., 1979, 302 p., cloth, novel. GAEA #1. [Winner of the *Locus* Award for Best Science Fiction Novel, 1979 (1980)].

36124 *Wizard.* New York: Berkley Publishing Corp., 1980, 354 p., cloth, novel. GAEA #2.

VARMA, Devendra P., Sir, 1923-

15872 *Gothic flame: being a history of the gothic novel in England, its origins, efflorescence, and residuary influences.* London: Arthur Barker, 1957, 246 p., cloth, nonf.

VARNADO, S(eaborn) L(owrey), 1929-

36125 *Haunted presence: the numinous in gothic fiction.* Tuscaloosa, AL & London: University of Alabama Press, 1987, 160 p., cloth, nonf.

VARNEY, Allen

36126 *Doctor Strange: Through six dimensions.* Lake Geneva, WI: TSR Inc., 1987, 188 p., paper, fiction. MARVEL SUPER-HEROES ADVENTURE GAMEBOOK #4.

Through six dimensions—SEE: *Doctor Strange: Through six dimensions.*

with Greg Costikyan

20638 *The Willow sourcebook.* New York: Tor, An Eric Goldberg Associates Sourcebook, 1988, 90 p., paper, nonf.

VASBINDER, Samuel Holmes

36127 *Scientific attitudes in Mary Shelley's Frankenstein.* Ann Arbor, MI: UMI Research Press, 1984, 111 p., cloth, nonf. STUDIES IN SPECULATIVE FICTION #8.

VAUGHAN, Hilda [pseud. of Hilda Campbell Morgan], 1892-1985

15873 *Iron and gold.* London: Macmillan, 1948, 233 p., cloth, novel.

VAUGHAN, Ralph E.

The adventure of the ancient gods—SEE: *Sherlock Holmes in The adventure of the ancient gods.*

36128 *Sherlock Holmes in The adventure of the ancient gods.* Brooklyn, NY: Gryphon Books, 1990, 37 p., paper, story. SHERLOCK HOLMES SERIES.

VAZ, Mark Cotta

36129 *Tales of the dark knight: Batman's first fifty years, 1939-1989.* New York: Ballantine Books, 1989, xiv+210 p., paper, nonf. BATMAN SERIES.

VEEDER, William (R.), 1940-

36130 *Mary Shelley & Frankenstein: the fate of androgyny.* Chicago: University of Chicago Press, 1986, ix+277 p., cloth, nonf.

with Gordon Hirsch

25714 *Dr. Jekyll and Mr. Hyde: after one hundred years.* Chicago: University of Chicago

Press, 1988, xx+312 p., cloth, nonf. anth.

VEGETTI, Ernesto

36131 *Repertory of the Italian professionals in science fiction and fantasy 1981.* Milano, Italy: World SF Italy, 1981, 44 p., paper, nonf.

36132 *Repertory of the Italian professionals in science fiction and fantasy 1982-1983.* Milano, Italy: World SF Italy, 1984, [114] p., paper, nonf.

VELASCO, Raymond L.

36133 *A guide to the Star Wars universe, illustrated throughout.* New York: A Del Rey Book, Ballantine Books, 1984, xlvii+215 p., paper, nonf.

VELDE, Vivian Vande—SEE: Vande Velde, Vivian

VELER, Richard P(aul), 1936-

36134 *Papers on Poe: essays in honor of John Ward Ostrom.* Springfield, OH: Chantry Music Press, 1972, vii+236 p., cloth, nonf. anth.

VELEY, Charles (Ronald), 1943-

36135 *Children of the dark.* Garden City, NY: Doubleday & Co., 1979, 331 p., cloth, novel.

36136 *Night whispers.* Garden City, NY: Doubleday & Co., 1980, 330 p., cloth, novel.

36137 *Play to live.* New York: Twilight/Dell, 1982, 151 p., paper, novel. TWILIGHT #7.

VENABLES, Hubert, d. 1980

36138 *The Frankenstein diaries.* New York: Viking Press, 1980, 120 p., cloth, novel. FRANKENSTEIN SERIES.

*VENNINGS, Hugh [pseud. of Claude van Zeller], 1905-1984

VENTERS, Archie

36139 *Highland vengeance.* London: Robert Hale, 1978, 174 p., cloth, novel.

VENTURO, Betty Lou—SEE: Baker, Betty

*VERCORS [pseud. of Jean Marcel Bruller], 1902-1991

VERDE, Campo, pseud.—SEE: Greenfield, Irving A.

VERE, V. C. de—SEE: de Vere, V. C.

VERE-HODGE, Conrad—SEE: de Vere, V. C.

VERNAM, Glenn R., 1896-1980

36140 *The power of the gods.* New York: Manor Books, 1979, 293 p., paper, novel.

VERNE, Jean Jules- —SEE: Jules-Verne, Jean

VERNE, Jules (Gabriel), 1828-1905

36141 *The annotated Jules Verne: From the Earth to the Moon direct in ninety-seven hours and twenty minutes.* New York: Thomas Y. Crowell Publishers, 1978, xix+171 p., cloth, novel. [Edited by Walter James Miller; translation of *De la Terre à la Lune*].

36142 *The annotated Jules Verne: Twenty thousand leagues under the sea.* New York: Thomas Y. Crowell Publishers, 1976, xxii+362 p., cloth, novel. [Edited by Walter James Miller; translation of *Vingt mille lieues sous les mers*].

36143 *The best of Jules Verne: three complete, illustrated novels.* Secaucus, NJ: Castle Books, 1978, viii+470 p., cloth, coll. [Includes *Around the world in eighty days*; *The clipper of the clouds*; *Journey to the centre of the Earth*].

36144 *Collected novels.* Secaucus, NJ: Castle Books, 1984, 837 p., cloth, coll. [Includes *Around the world in eighty days*; *The clipper in the clouds*; *A journey to the centre of the Earth*; *From the Earth to the Moon*; *20,000 leagues under the sea*].

36145 *The complete Twenty thousand leagues under the sea.* Bloomington, IN: Indiana University Press, 1991, ix+499 p., cloth, novel. [Edited by Emanuel J. Mickel; a new translation of *Vingt mille lieues sous les mers*].

From the Earth to the Moon direct in ninety-seven hours and twenty minutes—SEE: *The annotated Jules Verne: From the Earth to the Moon direct in ninety-seven hours and twenty minutes.*

Twenty thousand leagues under the sea—SEE: *The annotated Jules Verne: Twenty thousand leagues under the sea*; and, *The complete Twenty thousand leagues under the sea.*

with Tom Barling

17402 *20,000 leagues under the sea*. London: Piccolo Adventure Library, 1977, 125 p., paper, novel. [Adapted from the original novel by Verne; translation of *Vingt mille lieues sous les mers*].

VERNER, Gerald [pseud. of Donald Stuart], 1896-1980

36146 *The vampire men*. London: Wright & Brown, 1941, 252 p., cloth, novel.

VERNON, John, 1943-

38131 *Peter Doyle: a novel*. New York: Random House, 1991, 417 p., cloth, novel.

VERNON, William, *with Daryl Lane & David Carson*

19523 *The sound of wonder: interviews from "The science fiction radio show"*. Phoenix, AZ: Oryx Press, 1985, 2 v. (I-xi+203 p., II-vi+201 p.), paper, nonf. coll.

VERRETTE, Joyce, 1939-

36147 *To love and to conquer*. New York: A Dell Trade Paperback, 1984, 445 p., paper, novel.

VERRILL, A(lpheus) Hyatt, 1871-1954

38132 *The boy adventurers in the unknown land*. New York: G. P. Putnam's Sons, 1924, v+257 p., cloth, novel. BOY ADVENTURERS SERIES.
38133 *The radio detectives under the sea*. New York, London: D. Appleton & Co., 1922, 283 p., cloth, novel. RADIO DETECTIVES SERIES.

*VERRON, Robert (J.), 1935?-1984

VERSEAU, Dominique

The girl from erosphere—SEE: *Yolanda, The girl from erosphere*.
Slaves of space—SEE: *Yolanda: Slaves of space*.
36148 *Yolanda, The girl from erosphere*. New York: Grove Press, 1975, 190 p., paper, novel. YOLANDA #1. [Translation by Sam Flores].
36149 *Yolanda: Slaves of space*. New York: Grove Press, 1976, 205 p., paper, novel. YOLANDA #2.

VERSLUIS, Arthur, 1959-

36150 *Telos*. New York: Arkana, 1987, 156 p., paper, novel.

VESSER, Carolyn (Hansen), 1934-

36151 *Hellwalker*. New York: Tor SF, A Tom Doherty Associates Book, 1988, 283 p., paper, novel.

VET, Charles V. De—SEE: De Vet, Charles V.

VIAN, Boris, 1920-1959

38134 *Heartsnatcher*. London: Rapp & Whiting, 1968, 245 p., cloth, novel. [Translation by Stanley Chapman of *L'Arrache-coeur*].

VIBBER, Lee, *with Doris Robin & Gracia Fay Ellwood*

22608 *In a faraway galaxy: a literary approach to a film saga*. Pasadena, CA: Extequer Press, 1984, 149 p., paper, nonf.

VICTOR, Cindy

36152 *Covenant with death*. New York: Charter Books, 1989, 249 p., paper, novel.

VICTOR, Steve

36153 *Sin & sorcery*. Chatsworth, CA: World-Wide Publishing Co., 1981, 186 p., paper, novel.
36154 *When the aliens come*. Encino, CA: World-Wide Publishing Co., 1981, 182 p., paper, novel.

VICTOROFF, Jeffrey Ivan

36155 *The wild type*. New York: Crown Publishers, 1989, 233 p., cloth, novel.

VIDAL, Eugene—SEE: Vidal, Gore

VIDAL, Gore [i.e., Eugene Luther "Gore" Vidal Jr.], 1925-

36156 *Kalki: a novel*. Franklin Center, PA: Franklin Library, 1978, 315 p., cloth, novel.

VIDAL, Harriette, *with Ed Kelleher*

26981 *The breeder*. New York: Leisure Books, 1987, 383 p., paper, novel.
26982 *Madonna*. New York: Leisure Books, 1985, 384 p., paper, novel.

26983   *Prime evil.* New York: Leisure Books, 1988, 293 p., paper, novel.
26984   *The school.* New York: Leisure Books, 1988, 365 p., paper, novel.
26985   *The spell.* New York: Leisure Books, 1990, 312 p., paper, novel.

VIERECK, George Sylvester, 1884-1962

36157   *Gloria: a novel.* London: Duckworth, 1952, 158 p., cloth, novel.
14674   retitled: *The nude in the mirror.* New York: Woodford Press, 1953, 253 p., cloth, novel. [Revised edition].

VIGLIANTE, Mary [i.e., Mary Vigliante Szydlowski], 1946-

36158   *The colony.* New York: Manor Books, 1979, 190 p., paper, novel. AFTERMATH #2.
36159   *The land.* New York: Manor Books, 1979, 218 p., paper, novel. AFTERMATH #1.
36160   *Source of evil.* New York: Manor Books, 1979, 192 p., paper, novel.
36161   *Worship the night.* New York: Tower Books, 1982, 280 p., paper, novel.

as JARL SZYDLOW

36162   *The Ark.* New York: Manor Books, 1978, 224 p., paper, novel.

VIJAYAN, O(ttupulakkal) V(elukutty)

36163   *The saga of Dharmapuri.* New York: Penguin Books, 1989, 160 p., paper, novel. [Translation by the author of *Dharmapuraanam*].

VILLANI, Jim, 1948- , *with Rose Sayre*

33244   *Science fiction.* Youngstown, OH: Pig Iron Press, 1982, 95 p., paper?, anth.

VILLASEÑOR, Gervasio Gallardo—SEE: Gallardo, Gervasio

VILLIERS DE L'ISLE ADAM, Auguste, Comte de, 1838-1889

36164   *The Eve of the future Eden: L'Eve future.* Lawrence, KS: Coronado Press, 1981, xiii+260 p., cloth, novel. [Translation by Marilyn Gaddis Rose of *L'Eve future*].
36164A retitled: *Tomorrow's Eve.* Urbana, IL: University of Illinois Press, 1982, xxv+222 p., cloth, novel. [A different translation by Robert M. Adams of *L'Eve future*].
        Tomorrow's Eve—SEE: *Eve of the future.*

VILLIERS, Margot

36165   *The serpent of Lilith.* New York: Pocket Books, 1976, 254 p., paper, novel.

VILOTT, Rhondi [i.e., Rhondi A. Vilott-Salsitz]

36166   *Aphrodite's Mirror.* New York: A Signet Book, New American Library, 1985, 186 p., paper, novel.
36167   *Black dragon's curse.* New York: A Signet Book, New America Library, 1984, 188 p., paper, novel.
36168   *Challenge of the Pegasus Grail.* New York: A Signet Book, New American Library, 1984, 189 p., paper, novel.
36169   *The dungeons of Dregnor.* New York: A Signet Book, New American Library, 1984, 189 p., paper, novel.
36170   *Hall of the Gargoyle King.* New York: A Signet Book, New American Library, 1985, 188 p., paper, novel.
36171   *Maiden of Greenwold.* New York: A Signet Book, New American Library, 1985, 189 p., paper, novel.
36172   *Pledge of peril.* New York: A Signet Book, New American Library, 1985, 188 p., paper, novel.
36173   *Runesword!* New York: A Signet Book, New American Library, 1984, 203 p., paper, novel.
36174   *Secret of the sphinx.* New York: A Signet Book, New American Library, 1985, 185 p., paper, novel.
36175   *Spellbound.* New York: A Signet Book, New American Library, 1984, 189 p., paper, novel.
36176   *Storm rider.* New York: A Signet Book, New American Library, 1985, 188 p., paper, novel.
36177   *Sword Daughter's quest.* New York: A Signet Book, New American Library, 1984, 205 p., paper, novel.
36178   *The towers of Rexor.* New York: A Signet Book, New American Library, 1984, 189 p., paper, novel.
36179   *The unicorn crown.* New York: A Signet Book, New American Library, 1984, 189 p., paper, novel.

as CHARLES INGRID

36180   *Alien salute.* New York: DAW Books, 1989, 252 p., paper, novel. SAND WARS #4.

36181 *Celestial hit list.* New York: DAW Books, 1988, 285 p., paper, novel. SAND WARS #3.

36182 *Challenge met.* New York: DAW Books, 1990, 270 p., paper, novel. SAND WARS #6.

36183 *Lasertown blues.* New York: DAW Books, 1988, 286 p., paper, novel. SAND WARS #2.

36184 *The last recall.* New York: DAW Books, 1991, 336 p., paper, novel. MARKED MAN #2.

36185 *The marked man.* New York: DAW Books, 1989, 253 p., paper, novel. MARKED MAN #1.

36186 *Radius of doubt.* New York: DAW Books, 1991, 348 p., paper, novel. PATTERNS OF CHAOS #1.

36187 *Return fire.* New York: DAW Books, 1989, 252 p., paper, novel. SAND WARS #5.

36188 *Solar kill.* New York: DAW Books, 1987, 301 p., paper, novel. SAND WARS #1.

as R. A. V. SALSITZ

36189 *Daughter of destiny.* New York: A Signet Book, New American Library, 1988, 271 p., paper, novel.

36190 *Night of dragons.* New York: A Roc Book, 1990, 254 p., paper, novel. DRAGONS #3.

36191 *The unicorn dancer.* New York: A Signet Book, New American Library, 1986, 252 p., paper, novel.

36192 *Where dragons lie.* New York: A Signet Book, New American Library, 1985, 255 p., paper, novel. DRAGONS #1.

36193 *Where dragons rule.* New York: A Signet Book, New American Library, 1986, 253 p., paper, novel. DRAGONS #2.

VILOTT-SALSITZ, Rhondi—SEE: Vilott, Rhondi

VINCENT, Harl [i.e., Harold Vincent "Harl" Schoepflin], 1893-1968, *with Victor Rousseau*

32740 *Red twilight; World's end: two classic novels from Argosy.* Mercer Island, WA: Starmont House, 1991, vi+123 p., cloth, coll. STARMONT FACSIMILE FICTION #13.

VINCENT, John, pseud.—SEE: Peel, John

VINGE, Joan D. [i.e., Joan Carol Dennison Vinge Frenkel], 1948-

36194 *Alien blood: Psion; Catspaw.* Garden City, New York: Nelson Doubleday, 1988, 633 p., cloth, coll. PSION #1-2.

Cats paw—SEE: *Catspaw.*

36195 *Catspaw.* New York: Warner Books, 1988, 392 p., cloth, novel. PSION #2.

36195A retitled: *Cats paw.* London: Victor Gollancz, 1989, [400] p., cloth, novel. PSION #2.

36196 *The Dune storybook.* New York: G. C. Putnam's Sons, 1984, [62] p., cloth, movie. DUNE SERIES.

36197 *Eyes of amber, and other stories.* New York: A Signet Book, New American Library, 1979, 248 p., paper, coll.

36198 *Fireship.* New York: A Dell Book, 1978, 191 p., paper, coll.

36198A retitled: *Fireship; and, Mother and child: science fiction.* London: Sidgwick & Jackson, 1980, 191 p., cloth, coll.

Fireship; and, Mother and child—SEE: *Fireship.*

36199 *Heaven chronicles.* New York: Warner Books, 1991, 275 p., paper, coll. HEAVEN CHRONICLES #1-2. [Includes *The outcasts of Heaven Belt* and *Legacy*].

36200 *Joan D. Vinge omnibus.* London: Sidgwick & Jackson, 1983, 191+198 p., cloth, coll. [Includes *Fireship* and *The outcasts of Heaven Belt*].

36201 *Ladyhawke.* New York: A Signet Book, New American Library, 1985, 252 p., paper, movie.

36202 *Mad Max beyond Thunderdome: a novelization.* New York: Warner Books, 1985, 219 p., paper, movie. MAD MAX #3.

36203 *The outcasts of Heaven Belt.* New York: A Signet Book, New American Library, 1978, 198 p., paper, novel. HEAVEN CHRONICLES #1.

36204 *Phoenix in the ashes.* New York: A Bluejay International Edition, 1985, 230 p., cloth, coll.

36205 *Psion.* New York: Delacorte Press, 1982, 346 p., cloth, novel. PSION #1.

Return of the Jedi—SEE: *Star Wars: Return of the Jedi: the storybook based on the movie.*

36206 *Return to Oz: a novel.* New York: A Del Rey Book, Ballantine Books, 1985, 214 p., paper, movie. OZ SERIES.

36207 *Santa Claus, the movie: a novel.* New York: Berkley Books, 1985, 244 p., paper, movie.

36208 *Santa Claus, the movie storybook.* New York: Grosset & Dunlap, 1985, [58] p., cloth, movie.

36209 *The snow queen.* New York: A Quantum Book, The Dial Press, 1980, 536 p., cloth, novel. SNOW QUEEN CYCLE #1. [Winner of the Hugo Award for Best Novel, 1980 (1981); winner of the *Locus* Award for Best Science Fiction Novel, 1980 (1981)].

36210 *Star Wars: Return of the Jedi: the storybook based on the movie.* New York: Random House, 1983, [60] p., cloth, movie. STAR WARS SERIES.

36211 *The summer queen.* New York: Warner Books, 1991, 670 p., cloth, novel. SNOW QUEEN CYCLE #3.

36212 *Tin soldier.* New York: Tor SF, A Tom Doherty Associates Book, 1990, 68 p., paper, story. [Bound with *Riding the torch* / by Norman Spinrad].

36213 *Willow: based on the motion picture.* New York: Random House, 1988, 125 p., paper, movie. WILLOW SERIES.

36214 *World's end.* New York: Bluejay Books, 1984, 230 p., cloth, novel. SNOW QUEEN CYCLE #2.

with Edgar Rice Burroughs

19075 *Tarzan, king of the apes.* New York: Random House, 1983, 104 p., cloth, novel. [Adapted from the original novel by Burroughs].

with Shep Steneman & Geraldine Richelson

32297 *Star Wars—the first ten years—storybook trilogy: the storybook based on the movies.* New York: Random House, 1987, [175] p., paper, movie coll. STAR WARS #1-3.

VINGE, Vernor (Steffen), 1944-

36215 *Across realtime.* Garden City, NY: Nelson Doubleday, 1986, 532 p., cloth, coll. REALTIME #1-2. [Includes *The peace war; Marooned in realtime*].

36216 *Across realtime.* Riverdale, NY: Baen Books, 1991, 545 p., paper, coll. [An expanded edition which includes *The peace war; Marooned in realtime; The ungoverned*].

14685 *Grimm's world.* New York: Berkley Medallion, 1969, 176 p., paper, novel.

38135 retitled: *Tatja Grimm's world.* New York: Baen Books, 1987, 277 p., paper, coll. [Expanded edition].

36217 *Marooned in realtime.* New York: A Bluejay International Edition, 1986, 270 p., cloth, novel. REALTIME #2.

36218 *The peace war.* New York: A Bluejay International Edition, 1984, 286 p., cloth, novel. REALTIME #1.

Tatja Grimm's world—SEE: *Grimm's world.*

36219 *Threats...and other promises.* New York: Baen Books, 1988, 320 p., paper, coll.

36220 *True names.* New York: Bluejay Books, 1984, 153 p., paper, novel.

36221 *True names...and other dangers.* New York: Baen Books, 1987, 275 p., paper, coll.

36222 *The witling.* New York: DAW Books, 1976, 173 p., paper, novel.

VINICOFF, Eric

36223 *Maiden flight.* New York: Baen Books, 1988, 405 p., paper, novel.

with Marcia Martin

29141 *Spacing Dutchman.* Berkeley, CA: Aesir Press, 1978, 55 p., paper, novel.

VINSON, Rex—SEE: King, Vincent

VINTER, Michael, 1927-

36224 *Along came a spider.* London: Robert Hale, 1980, 188 p., cloth, novel.

as T. S. J. GIBBARD

36225 *The starseed mission.* London: Robert Hale, 1980, 191 p., cloth, novel.

36226 *The Torold core.* London: Robert Hale, 1980, 189 p., cloth, novel.

05935 *Vandals of eternity.* London: Robert Hale, 1974, 191 p., cloth, novel.

VIRG, Leo, pseud.

15874 *Twenty trillion light-years through space.* New York: Vantage Press, 1958, 126 p., cloth, novel.

VIVELO, Jackie [i.e., Jacqueline J. Vivelo], 1943-

36227 *A trick of the light: stories to read at dusk.* New York: G. P. Putnam's Sons, 1987, 124 p., cloth, coll.

VIVELO, Jacqueline—SEE: Vivelo, Jackie

VIVIAN, E(velyn) Charles (Henry) [legalized from Charles Henry Cannell], 1882-1947

36228 *Aia: Fields of sleep; and, People of the darkness.* New York: Arno Press, 1978, 288+288 p., cloth, coll. AIA #1-2.

VIVIAN, Herbert, 1865- , *as* A WELL-KNOWN AUTHOR

38136 *The master sinner: a romance.* London: John Long, 1901, 181 p., cloth, novel.

VIVIERS, Lyn

36229 *Blood of others.* Strathmartine by Dundee, Scotland: ScoTpress, 1988, 69 p., paper, novel. STAR TREK SERIES.
36230 *Fallen angel.* Strathmartine by Dundee, Scotland: ScoTpress, 1990, 78 p., paper, novel. STAR TREK SERIES.
36231 *Know thine enemy.* Strathmartine by Dundee, Scotland: ScoTpress, 1984, 47 p., paper, novel. STAR TREK SERIES.

VIXEN, Richard M., pseud.

36232 *Deep foot.* Eugene, OR: Avant-Garde Creations, 1977, vii+125 p., paper, novel. DEEP FOOT #1.
36233 *Deeper foot: sequel to Deep foot.* Eugene, OR: Avant-Garde Creations, 1977, vi+ 135 p., paper, novel. DEEP FOOT #2.

VLCEK, Ernst

36234 *Spider desert.* New York: Ace Books, 1977, 125-252 p., paper, novel. ATLAN #1. [Bound with *The wasp men attack* / by W. W. Shols].

VOGEL, Anna Kirwan- —SEE: Kirwan-Vogel, Anna

VOGT, A. E. van—SEE: van Vogt, A. E.

VOIGT, Cynthia, 1942-

36235 *Building blocks.* New York: Atheneum, 1984, 128 p., cloth, novel.
36236 *Jackaroo.* New York: An Argo Book, Atheneum, 1985, 291 p., cloth, novel.
36237 *On fortune's wheel.* New York: Atheneum, 1990, 276 p., cloth, novel.

VOINOVICH, Vladimir (Nikolaevich), 1932-

36238 *Moscow 2042.* San Diego, CA, New York: Harcourt Brace Jovanovich, 1987, viii+424 p., cloth, novel. [Translation by Richard Lourie of *Moskorep*].

VOLKER, Beverly, *with J. Emily Vance*

36019 *The rack; &, All the king's horses, all the king's men.* [S.l.]: J. Emily Vance,

1977?, 114-170, 106-194 p., paper, coll. STAR TREK SERIES.

VOLLMAN, William T., 1959-

36239 *The ice-shirt.* London: André Deutsch, 1990, 404 p., cloth, novel. SEVEN DREAMS #1.
36240 *The rainbow stories.* New York: Atheneum, 1989, 541 p., cloth, coll.
36241 *You bright and risen angels: a cartoon.* London: André Deutsch, 1990, xvi+635 p., cloth, novel.

VOLSKY, Paula

36242 *The curse of the witch-queen.* New York: A Del Rey Book, Ballantine Books, 1982, 345 p., paper, novel.
36243 *Illusion.* London: Victor Gollancz, 1991, 656 p., cloth, novel.
36244 *The luck of Relian Kru.* New York: Ace Fantasy Books, 1987, 294 p., paper, novel.
36245 *The sorcerer's curse.* New York: Ace Books, 1989, 299 p., paper, novel. SORCERER #3.
36246 *The sorcerer's heir.* New York: Ace Books, 1988, 279 p., paper, novel. SORCERER #2.
36247 *The sorcerer's lady.* New York: Ace Fantasy Books, 1986, 264 p., paper, novel. SORCERER #1.

VOLTAIRE [pseud. of François-Marie Arouet], 1694-1778

36248 *Micromegas, (and other stories).* London: Dedalus, 1989, 171 p., paper, coll.

VOLTZ, William (Willi), 1938-1984

36249 *The emperor and the monster.* New York: Ace Books, 1977, 188 p., paper, novel. PERRY RHODAN #107. [Includes additional fiction and nonfiction].
36250 *Friend to mankind.* New York: Ace Books, 1976, 197 p., paper, novel. PERRY RHODAN #91. [Includes additional fiction and nonfiction].
Green—SEE: *Horn: Green.*
36251 *Horn: Green.* New York: Ace Books, 1976, 187 p., paper, novel. PERRY RHODAN #96. [Includes additional fiction and nonfiction].
36252 *The horror.* New York: Ace Books, 1975, 160 p., paper, novel. PERRY RHODAN #66. [Iincludes additional fiction and nonfiction].

36253 *Humans keep out!* Van Nuys, CA: Master Publications, 1979, 64 p., paper, novel. PERRY RHODAN #135. [Translation of *Für menschen verboten!*].

36254 *Killers from hyperspace.* Van Nuys, CA: Master Publications, 1978, 59 p., paper, novel. PERRY RHODAN #120. [Translation of *Mörder aus dem hyperraum*].

Moluk—SEE: *Secret mission: Moluk.*

36255 *The psycho duel.* New York: Ace Books, 1977, 119-250 p., paper, novel. PERRY RHODAN #116. [Bound with *Saboteurs in A-1* / by Kurt Brand].

36256 *Robots, bombs, and mutants.* Van Nuys, CA: Master Publications, 1979, 63 p., paper, novel. PERRY RHODAN #125. [Translation of *Roboter, bomben, und mutanten*].

36257 *Secret mission: Moluk.* New York: Ace Books, 1975, 168 p., paper, novel. PERRY RHODAN #84. [Includes additional fiction and nonfiction].

36258 *Seeds of ruin.* New York: Ace Books, 1977, 113 p., paper, novel. PERRY RHODAN #111. [Bound with *Planet Mechanica* / by K. H. Scheer].

36259 *The sleepers.* New York: Ace Books, 1975, 159 p., paper, novel. PERRY RHODAN #79. [Includes additional fiction and nonfiction].

36260 *Spoor of the Antis.* New York: Ace Books, 1976, 188 p., paper, novel. PERRY RHODAN #102. [Includes additional fiction and nonfiction].

36261 *World without mercy.* Van Nuys, CA: Master Publications, 1979, 64 p., paper, novel. PERRY RHODAN #131. [Translation of *Die laurins kommen!*].

VON ALMEDINGEN, Martha—SEE: Almedingen, E. M.

VON FRANZ, Marie Luise SEE: Franz, Marie Luise von

VON GUNDEN, Kenneth (Ray), 1946-

36262 *Flights of fancy: the great fantasy films.* Jefferson, NC & London: McFarland & Co., 1989, viii+295 p., cloth, nonf.

36263 *K-9 Corps.* New York: Ace Books, 1991, 229 p., paper, novel. K-9 CORPS #1.

36264 *K-9 Corps: Under fire.* New York: Ace Books, 1991, 250 p., paper, novel. K-9 CORPS #2.

36265 *StarSpawn.* New York: Ace Books, 1990, 250 p., paper, novel.

Under fire—SEE: *K-9 Corps: Under fire.*

with Stuart H. Stock

35055 *Twenty all-time great science fiction films.* Westport, CT: Arlington House, 1982, v+250 p., cloth, nonf.

VON HARBOU, Thea—SEE: Harbou, Thea von

VON NIEBELSCHUTZ, Wolf—SEE: Niebelschutz, Wolf von

VONARBURG, Élisabeth (Ferron-Wehrlin Morché), 1947-

36266 *The silent city.* Vancouver, British Columbia, Canada: A Tesseract Book, Porcépic Books, 1988, 209 p., paper, novel. [Translation by Jane Brierley of *Le silence de la cité*].

VONNEGUT, Kurt (Jr.), 1922-

36267 *Cat's cradle; God bless you, Mr. Rosewater; Slaughterhouse-Five.* New York: Book-of-the-Month Club, 1990, 231+271+186 p., cloth, coll.

36268 *Dead-Eye Dick.* New York: A Seymour Lawrence Book, Delacorte Press, 1982, xiii+240 p., cloth, novel.

36269 *Galápagos: a novel.* Franklin Center, PA: Franklin Library, 1985, 295 p., cloth, novel.

36270 *Hocus pocus.* Franklin Center, PA: Franklin Library, 1990, 302 p., cloth, novel.

VOORHEES, Richard (Joseph), 1916-

36271 *The paradox of George Orwell.* Lafayette, IN: Purdue University, 1961, 127 p., cloth, nonf.

VORNHOLT, John (Blair), 1951-

36272 *Contamination.* New York, London: Pocket Books, 1991, xi+273 p., paper, novel. STAR TREK: THE NEXT GENERATION #16.

36273 *Masks.* New York, London: Pocket Books, 1989, 277 p., paper, novel. STAR TREK: THE NEXT GENERATION #7.

VOS, Luk de, 1949-

36274 *Just the other day: essays on the future of the future.* Antwerpent, Belgium: EXA, 1985, xxx+556 p., paper?, nonf. coll. [Text in Dutch, English, French, and German].

36275 *Science fiction: status or status quo?* Antwerpen/Gent, Belgium: Restant Uit-gaven, 1977, 214 p., cloth, nonf.

VOSS BARK, Conrad, 1913-

36276 *The big wave.* London: New English Lib-rary, 1979, 174 p., paper, novel.

VYSE, Michael

36277 *The outer reaches.* London: Faber & Faber, 1980, 158 p., cloth, coll.
36278 *Overworld.* London: Faber & Faber, 1980, 154 p., cloth, novel.

W

W. W. [pseud. of William Bloom], 1948-

The prophets of evil—SEE: *Qhe!: The prophets of evil.*

36279 *Qhe!: The prophets of evil.* London: A Star Book, W. H. Allen, 1976, 174 p., paper, novel. QHE #4.

36280 *The riches.* St Albans, England: Mayflower, 1975, 157 p., paper, novel. QHE #3.

WADDELL, Martin—SEE: Sefton, Catherine

WADE, Elizabeth

36281 *Anatola: the autobiography of an Abyssinian cat.* New York: Manor Books, 1976, 140 p., paper, novel.

36282 *The ashes of Tamar.* New York: Zebra Books, Kensington Publishing Corp., 1978, 416 p., paper, novel.

WADE, Thomas W.—SEE: Wade, Tom

WADE, Tom [i.e., Thomas W. Wade]

14750 *The world of Theda.* London: Digit Books, 1962, 154 p., paper, novel.

14750A retitled: *The unknown world.* Australia: Bill Ewington Books, 1973, 155 p., paper, novel.

as VICTOR LA SALLE

08632 *Assault from infinity.* London: John Spencer & Co., 1953, 108 p., paper, novel.

08634 *The seventh dimension.* London: John Spencer & Co., 1953, 124 p., paper, novel.

08635 *Suns in duo.* London: John Spencer & Co., 1953, 108 p., paper, novel.

as VICTOR WADEY

14752 *A planet named Terra.* London: Digit Books, 1962, 160 p., paper, novel.

14753 *The united planets.* London: Digit Books, 1962, 160 p., paper, novel.

as KARL ZEIGFRIED

15758 *Beyond the galaxy.* London: John Spencer & Co., 1953, 124 p., paper, novel.

15759 *Chaos in Arcturus.* London: John Spencer & Co., 1953, 124 p., paper, novel.

15760 *Chariot into time.* London: John Spencer & Co., 1953, 128 p., paper, novel.

*WADELTON, Maggie-Owen [i.e., Maggie Jeanne Wadelton], 1890-1972

WAEDT, Carl F., *with Gene Marshall*

29068 *Incredible adventures #1.* Chicago: Gene Marshall & Carl F. Waedt, 1977, [96] p., paper, anth. INCREDIBLE ADVENTURES #1.

29069 *Incredible adventures #2.* Chicago: Gene Marshall & Carl F. Waedt, 1977, [96] p., paper, anth. INCREDIBLE ADVENTURES #2.

WAELTI-WALTERS, Jennifer (R.), 1942-

36283 *Fairy tales and the female imagination.* Montréal, Canada: Eden Press, 1982, 161 p., cloth, nonf.

WAGAR, W(alter) Warren, 1932-

36284 *H. G. Wells and the world state.* New Haven, CT: Yale University Press, 1961, x+301 p., cloth, nonf.

36285 *A short history of the future.* Chicago: University of Chicago Press, 1989, 323 p., cloth, fiction.

36286 *Terminal visions: the literature of last things.* Bloomington, IN: Indiana University Press, 1982, xiii+241 p., cloth, nonf.

WAGENKNECHT, Edward (Charles), 1900-

36287 *Edgar Allan Poe: the man behind the legend.* New York: Oxford University Press, 1963, 276 p., cloth, nonf.

36288 *Seven masters of supernatural fiction.* New York, London: Greenwood Press, 1991, viii+210 p., cloth, nonf. CONTRIBUTIONS TO THE STUDY OF SCIENCE FICTION AND FANTASY #46.

WAGER, Walter (Herman), 1924- , as KING KONG

36289 *My side.* New York: Macmillan Publishing Co.; London: Collier Macmillan Publishers, 1976, vi+119 p., cloth, novel. KING KONG SERIES.

WAGGONER, Diana

36290 *The hills of faraway: a guide to fantasy.* New York: Atheneum, 1978, x+326 p., cloth, nonf.

WAGNER, Jack

36291 *The great change.* Trinidad, CA: Trinidad Press, 1979, 269 p., cloth, novel.

WAGNER, Jane

36292 *The NESFA hymnal, volume 2.* Cambridge, MA: NESFA Press, 1987, 123 p., paper, nonf. anth.

WAGNER, Karl Edward, 1945-

36293 *Bloodstone.* New York: Warner Paperback Library, 1975, 303 p., paper, novel. KANE SERIES.
36294 *The book of Kane.* West Kingston, RI: Donald M. Grant, Publisher, 1985, 224 p., cloth, coll. KANE SERIES.
36295 *Bran Mak Morn: Legion from the shadows.* New York: Zebra Books, Kensington Publishing Corp., 1976, 249 p., paper, novel. BRAN MAK MORN #2.
36295A retitled: *Legion from the shadows.* New York: Baen Books, 1988, 247 p., paper, novel. BRAN MAK MORN #2.
36296 *Conan: The road of kings.* Toronto, New York: Bantam Books, 1979, 209 p., paper, novel. CONAN SERIES.
36297 *Dark crusade.* New York: Warner Books, 1976, 222 p., paper, novel. KANE SERIES.
14759 *Darkness weaves with many shades.* Reseda, CA: Powell Publications, 1970, 205 p., paper, novel. KANE #1.
38137 retitled: *Darkness weaves.* New York: Warner Books, 1978, 288 p., paper, novel. KANE #1. [Expanded edition].
Darkness weaves—SEE: *Darkness weaves with many shades.*
36298 *Echoes of valor.* New York: Tor SF, A Tom Doherty Associates Book, 1987, 286 p., paper, anth.
36299 *Echoes of valor II.* New York: Tor, A Tom Doherty Associates Book, 1989, 274 p., cloth, anth.

36300 *Echoes of valor III.* New York: Tor Fantasy, A Tom Doherty Associates Book, 1991, 374 p., paper, anth.
36301 *Horrorstory, volume four: The year's best horror stories X; The year's best horror stories XI; The year's best horror stories XII.* Novato, CA, Lancaster, PA: Underwood-Miller, 1990, 641 p., cloth, anth.
36302 *Horrorstory, volume five: The year's best horror stories XIII; The year's best horror stories XIV; The year's best horror stories XV.* Novato, CA, Lancaster, PA: Underwood-Miller, 1989, 709 p., cloth, anth.
36303 *In a lonely place.* New York: Warner Books, 1983, 265 p., paper, coll.
36304 *Intensive scare.* New York: DAW Books, 1990, 303 p., paper, anth.
36305 *Karl Edward Wagner presents The year's best horror stories XV.* New York: DAW Books, 1987, 300 p., paper, anth.
36306 *Karl Edward Wagner presents The year's best horror stories XVI.* New York: DAW Books, 1988, 303 p., paper, anth.
36307 *Karl Edward Wagner presents The year's best horror stories XVII.* New York: DAW Books, 1989, x+351 p., paper, anth.
Legion from the shadows—SEE: *Bran Mak Morn.*
36308 *Night winds.* New York: Warner Books, 1978, 286 p., paper, coll. KANE SERIES.
The road of kings—SEE: *Conan: The road of kings.*
36309 *The sign of the salamander.* Columbus, OH: Gary Hoppenstand, 1975, 57 p., paper, novel.
36310 *Unthreatened by the morning light.* Eugene, OR: Pulphouse Publishing, 1989, 101 p., cloth, coll. AUTHOR'S CHOICE MONTHLY #2.
36311 *Where the summer ends.* Eugene, OR: Pulphouse Publishing, 1991, 43 p., cloth, story. SHORT STORY HARDBACKS #19; SHORT STORY PAPERBACKS #31.
36312 *Why not you and I?* New York: Tor Horror, A Tom Doherty Associates Book, 1987, 306 p., paper, coll.
36313 *Why not you and I?* Arlington Heights, IL: Dark Harvest, 1987, 240 p., cloth, coll. [Expanded edition].
36314 *The year's best horror stories XIV.* New York: DAW Books, 1986, 291 p., paper, anth.
The year's best horror stories XV—SEE: *Karl Edward Wagner presents The year's best horror stories XV.*

The year's best horror stories XVI—SEE: *Karl Edward Wagner presents The year's best horror stories XVI.*

The year's best horror stories XVII—SEE: *Karl Edward Wagner presents The year's best horror stories XVII.*

36315 *The year's best horror stories XVIII.* New York: DAW Books, 1990, 367 p., paper, anth.

36316 *The year's best horror stories: XIX.* New York: DAW Books, 1991, xiii+366 p., paper, anth.

36317 *The year's best horror stories, series VIII.* New York: DAW Books, 1980, 221 p., paper, anth.

36318 *The year's best horror stories, series IX.* New York: DAW Books, 1981, 223 p., paper, anth.

36319 *The year's best horror stories, series X.* New York: DAW Books, 1982, 240 p., paper, anth.

36320 *The year's best horror stories, series XI.* New York: DAW Books, 1983, 237 p., paper, anth.

36321 *The year's best horror stories, series XII.* New York: DAW Books, 1984, 239 p., paper, anth.

36322 *The year's best horror stories, series XIII.* New York: DAW Books, 1985, 251 p., paper, anth.

with David Drake

22188 *Killer.* New York: A Baen Book, 1985, 270 p., paper, novel.

with Gerald W. Page

38004 *Horrorstory, volume three: The year's best horror stories VII; The year's best horror stories VIII; The year's best horror stories IX.* Novato, CA, Lancaster, PA: Underwood-Miller, 1991 (i.e., 1992), 541 p., cloth, anth.

WAGNER, Robin S.

36323 *The incredible shrinking Mork.* New York: Pocket Books, 1980, 160 p., paper, tele. MORK & MINDY #2.

WAGNER, Sharon (Blythe), 1936-

36324 *Bride of the Dullahan.* Garden City, NY: Doubleday & Co., 1976, 185 p., cloth, novel.

36325 *Circle of evil.* New York: Lancer Books, 1971, 254 p., paper, novel.

36326 *Country of the wolf.* New York: Lancer Books, 1970, 189 p., paper, novel.

36327 *Dark sun at midnight.* New York: Ace Books, 1976, 217 p., paper, novel.

36328 *Echoes of an ancient love.* New York: Ballantine Books, 1976, 236 p., paper, novel.

36329 *House of doom, house of desire.* New York: Zebra Books, Kensington Publishing Corp., 1980, 253 p., paper, novel.

36330 *The turquoise talisman.* New York: Ballantine Books, 1975, 185 p., paper, novel. BIRTHSTONE GOTHIC #12.

36331 *Winter evil.* New York: Lancer Books, 1972, 319 p., paper, novel.

WAHLÖÖ, Per, 1926-1975

38138 *The generals.* London: Michael Joseph, 1974, 278 p., cloth, novel. [Translation by Joan Tate of *Generalerna*].

38139 *Murder on the 31st floor.* London: Michael Joseph, 1966, 189 p., cloth, novel. [Translation by Joan Tate of *Mord på 31:a våningen*].

38139A retitled: *The thirty-first floor.* New York: Alfred A. Knopf, 1967, 207 p., cloth, novel. [Translation by Joan Tate of *Mord på 31:a våningen*].

38140 *The steel spring.* London: Michael Joseph, 1970, 188 p., cloth, novel. [Translation by Joan Tate of *Stålsprånget*].

The thirty-first floor—SEE: *Murder on the 31st floor.*

WAJENBERG, Earl, 1953- , with Clayton Emery

22650 *4-D funhouse.* Lake Geneva, WI: TSR Inc., 1985, 219 p., paper, novel. AMAZING STORIES #1.

WAKE, David B., 1964- , with Rob Meades

29704 *Drabble II: double century.* Harold Wood, Essex: Beccon Publications, 1990, 121 p., cloth, anth.

29705 *The Drabble project.* Harold Wood, Essex: Beccon Publciations, 1988, 110 p., cloth, anth.

WAKEFIELD, H(erbert) Russell, 1888-1964

36332 *The best ghost stories of H. Russell Wakefield.* London: John Murray, 1978, 232 p., cloth, coll. [Edited by Richard Dalby].

WAKEFIELD, Tom, 1935-

36333 *The love siege.* London: Routledge & Kegan Paul, 1979, vi+176 p., cloth, novel.

WALDEN, Mark

36334 *Beyond the 13th sun.* North Hollywood, CA: American Art Enterprises, 1981, 160 p., paper, novel.

WALDMAN, Frank, 1919-1990

36335 *The Pink Panther strikes again.* New York: Ballantine Books, 1976, 123 p., paper, movie.

WALDO, Edward H.—SEE: Sturgeon, Theodore

WALDROP, Howard, 1946-

36336 *All about strange monsters of the recent past: neat stories.* Kansas City, MO: Ursus Imprints, 1987, 125 p., cloth, coll. [Limited to 600 copies].

36337 *A dozen tough jobs.* Willimantic, CT: Mark V. Ziesing, 1989, 135 p., cloth, novel.

36338 *Howard who?: twelve outstanding stories of speculative fiction.* Garden City, NY: Doubleday & Co., 1986, 181 p., cloth, coll.

36339 *Night of the cooters: more neat stories.* Kansas City, MO: Ursus Imprints; Shingletown, CA: Mark V. Ziesing, 1990 (i.e., 1991), xiii+231 p., cloth, coll. [Winner of the *Locus* Award for Best Collection, 1991 (1992)].

36340 *Night of the cooters: more neat stuff.* London: Legend, 1991, 326 p., paper, coll. [Includes the contents of the Ursus/Ziesing collection, plus the novel, *A dozen tough jobs*].

36341 *Strange monsters of the recent past.* New York: Ace Books, 1991, xii+208 p., paper, coll. [Includes *All about strange monsters of the recent past* and *A dozen tough jobs*].

36342 *Strange things in close-up: the nearly complete Howard Waldrop.* London: Legend, 1989, vii+363 p., paper, coll. [Includes *Howard Who?* and *All about strange monsters of the recent past*].

36343 *Them bones.* New York: Ace Science Fiction Books, 1984, xi+225 p., paper, novel.

WALKER, Alice (Malsenior), 1944-

38141 *The temple of my familiar.* San Diego, CA: Harcourt Brace Jovanovich, 1989, 416 p., cloth, novel.

*WALKER, David (Harry), 1911-1992

WALKER, Hugh [pseud. of Hubert Strassl], 1941-

36344 *Army of darkness.* New York: Daw Books, 1979, 155 p., paper, novel. MAGIRA #2. [Translation by Christine Priest of *Das heer der Finsternis*].

36345 *Messengers of darkness.* New York: DAW Books, 1979, 156 p., paper, novel. MAGIRA #3. [Translation by Christine Priest of *Boten der Finsternis*].

36346 *War-gamers' world.* New York: DAW Books, 1978, 160 p., paper, novel. MAGIRA #1. [Translation by Christine Priest of *Reiter der Finsternis*].

WALKER, I(an) M(alcolm)

36347 *Edgar Allan Poe: the critical heritage.* London, Boston: Routledge & Kegan Paul, 1986, xvii+419 p., cloth, nonf. anth.

WALKER, Irma (Ruth Roden), 1921-

36348 *Inherit the Earth.* New York: An Argo Book, Atheneum, 1981, 262 p., cloth, novel.

WALKER, Leola H.

36349 *Horror, supernatural, occult 1985.* Baton Rouge, LA: Louisiana State Library, Section for the Blind and Physically Handicapped, 1985, [31] p., paper, nonf.

WALKER, Mary Alexander, 1927-

36350 *The Scathach and Maeve's daughter.* New York: Atheneum, 1990, 119 p., cloth, novel.

WALKER, Nancy A(nne Cheney), 1942-

36351 *Feminist alternatives: irony and fantasy in the contemporary novel by women.* Jackson, MS: University Press of Mississippi, 1991, 220 p., cloth, nonf.

WALKER, Paul

36352 *The altar.* New York: Pocket Books, 1983, 224 p., paper, novel.

WALKER, Paul, 1921-

36353 *Speaking of science fiction: the Paul Walker interviews.* Oradell, NJ: Luna Publications, 1978, x+425 p., cloth, nonf. coll.

WALKER, Robert W(ayne), 1948-

36354 *Aftershock.* New York: St. Martin's Press, 1987, 248 p., paper, novel.

36355 *Brain watch.* New York: Leisure Books, 1985, 349 p., paper, novel.

36356 *Burning obsession.* New York: Pinnacle Books, Windsor Publishing Corp., 1989, 304 p., paper, novel.

36357 *Dead man's float.* New York: Pinnacle Books, Windsor Publishing Corp., 1988, 347 p., paper, novel.

36358 *Disembodied.* New York: St. Martin's Press, 1988, 263 p., paper, novel.

36359 *Dr. O.* New York: Zebra Books, Kensington Publishing Corp., 1991, 320 p., paper, novel. [Author's name is given as "Glenn Hale" on spine and cover].

36360 *Dying breath.* New York: Pinnacle Books, Windsor Publishing Corp., 1989, 320 p., paper, novel.

36361 *Razor's edge.* New York: Pinnacle Books, Windsor Publishing Corp., 1989, 318 p., paper, novel.

36362 *Salem's child.* New York: Leisure Books, 1987, 399 p., paper, novel.

36363 *Search for the Nile.* Toronto, New York: A Byron Preiss Book, Bantam Books, 1986, 127 p., paper, novel. TIME MACHINE #12.

36364 *Sub-zero!* New York: Belmont Tower Books, 1979, 189 p., paper, novel.

as GEOFFREY CAINE

36365 *Curse of the vampire.* New York: Diamond Books, 1991, 247 p., paper, novel. ABRAHAM STROUD #1.

36366 *Wake of the werewolf.* New York: Diamond Books, 1991, 233 p., paper, novel. ABRAHAM STROUD #2.

WALKHAM, Walter [pseud. of James Harvey Trevithick Ivory], 1921-

36367 *When Earth trembled.* London: Robert Hale, 1980, 192 p., cloth, novel.

WALL, John W.—SEE: Sarban

WALL, Mervyn (Eugene Welply), 1908-

36368 *The complete Fursey.* Dublin, Ireland: Wolfhound Press, 1985, [432] p., cloth, coll. FURSEY #1-2. [Includes *The unfortunate Fursey* and *The return of Fursey*].

36369 *The garden of echoes: a fable for children and grown-ups.* Finglas, Dublin, Ireland: Fingal Books, 1988, 109 p., cloth, novel.

WALL, William

36370 *Devils in candy houses.* San Diego, CA: Papillon Books, 1974, 216 p., paper, novel.

36370A retitled: *Murder with grace.* Woodland Hills, CA: Decade Press, 1980, 216 p., paper, novel.

WALLACE, Carol McD., 1955-

36371 *Waking dream.* New York: St. Martin's Press, 1987, 210 p., cloth, novel.

WALLACE, David Foster, 1962-

36372 *The broom of the system.* New York: Viking, 1987, 467 p., cloth, novel.

WALLACE, David Rains, 1945-

36373 *The vermilion parrot: a novel.* New York: Random House, Sierra Club, 1991, 217 p., cloth, novel. TURQUOISE DRAGON #2.

36374 *The turquoise dragon: a mystery.* San Francisco: A Yolla Bolly Press Book, Sierra Club, 1985, 230 p., cloth, novel. TURQUOISE DRAGON #1.

WALLACE, (Richard Horatio) Edgar, 1875-1932

36375 *The death room: strange and startling stories.* London: William Kimber, 1986, 222 p., cloth, coll. [Edited by Jack Adrian].

WALLACE, Ian [pseud. of John Wallace Pritchard], 1912-

36376 *Heller's leap.* New York: DAW Books, 1979, 317 p., paper, novel. CLAUDINE ST. CYR #5; CROYD #6.

36377 *The Lucifer comet.* New York: DAW Books, 1980, 302 p., paper, novel. CROYD #7.

36378 *Megalomania.* New York: DAW Books, 1989, x+179 p., paper, novel. CROYD #8.

36379 *The rape of the Sun.* New York: DAW Books, 1982, 287 p., paper, novel.

36380 *The sign of the mute Medusa.* New York: Popular Library, 1977, 255 p., paper, novel. CLAUDINE ST. CYR #4.

36381 *The world asunder.* New York: DAW Books, 1976, 252 p., paper, novel. PAN SAGITTARIUS #4.

36382 *Z-sting.* New York: DAW Books, 1978, 222 p., paper, novel. CROYD #5.

WALLACE, Irving, 1916-1990

36383 *The pigeon project.* New York: Simon & Schuster, 1979, 383 p., cloth, novel.

WALLACE, James, pseud.—SEE: Barrett, G. J.

WALLACE, Jim

36384 *Rock and roll mystery.* Toronto, New York: An R. A. Montgomery Book, Bantam Books, 1987, 118 p., paper, novel. CHOOSE YOUR OWN ADVENTURE #69.

36385 *Search for the mountain gorillas.* Toronto, New York: An R. A. Montgomery Book, Bantam Books, 1985, 118 p., paper, novel. CHOOSE YOUR OWN ADVENTURE #41.

WALLACE, Pamela, 1949-

36386 *The fires of Beltane.* Los Angeles: Pinnacle Books, 1978, 307 p., paper, novel.

with Carla Simpson as PAMELA SIMPSON

34003 *Partners in time.* New York, Toronto: Bantam Books, 1990, 297 p., paper, novel.

WALLACE, Pat [i.e., Patricia Wallace Strother], 1929-

36387 *House of Scorpio* / by Pat Wallace. New York: Avon, 1975, 612 p., paper, novel.

36388 *The wand and the star* / by Pat Wallace. New York: A Kangaroo Book, Pocket Books, 1978, 339 p., paper, novel.

WALLACE, Patricia [i.e., Patricia Wallace Estrada]

36389 *Blood lies.* New York: Zebra Books, Kensington Publishing Corp., 1991, 319 p., paper, novel.

36390 *The children's ward.* New York: Zebra Books, Kensington Publishing Corp., 1985, 364 p., paper, novel.

36391 *Deadly grounds.* New York: Zebra Books, Kensington Publishing Corp., 1989, 319 p., paper, novel.

36392 *Lullabye.* New York: Zebra Books, Kensington Publishing Corp., 1990, 287 p., paper, novel.

36393 *Monday's child.* New York: Zebra Books, Kensington Publishing Corp., 1989, 288 p., paper, novel.

36394 *Night whisper.* New York: Zebra Books, Kensington Publishing Corp., 1987, 364 p., paper, novel.

36395 *Only child.* New York: Zebra Books, Kensington Publishing Corp., 1985, 332 p., paper, novel.

36396 *See no evil.* New York: Zebra Books, Kensington Publishing Corp., 1988, 286 p., paper, novel.

36397 *The taint.* New York: Zebra Books, Kensington Publishing Corp., 1983, 351 p., paper, novel.

36398 *Thrill.* New York: Zebra Books, Kensington Publishing Corp., 1990, 383 p., paper, novel.

36399 *Traces.* New York: Zebra Books, Kensington Publishing Corp., 1982, 333 p., paper, novel.

36400 *Twice blessed.* New York: Zebra Books, Kensington Publishing Corp., 1986, 333 p., paper, novel.

36401 *Water baby.* New York: Zebra Books, Kensington Publishing Corp., 1987, 301 p., paper, novel.

WALLER, Gregory A(lbert), 1950-

36403 *American horrors: essays on the modern American horror film.* Urbana & Chicago, IL: University of Illinois Press, 1988, 228 p., cloth, nonf. anth.

36404 *The living and the undead: from Stoker's Dracula to Romero's Dawn of the dead.* Urbana & Chicago: University of Illinois Press, 1986, 376 p., cloth, nonf.

WALLER, Leslie, 1923- , with Louise Waller

15875 *Take me to your leader.* New York: G. P. Putnam's Sons, 1961, unpaginated, paper, fiction.

WALLER, Louise, with Leslie Waller

15875 *Take me to your leader.* New York: G. P. Putnam's Sons, 1961, unpaginated, paper, fiction.

*WALLERSTEIN, James S., 1910-<u>1990</u>

WALLING, William (Herbert), 1926-

36405   *The world I left behind me.* New York: St. Martin's Press, 1979, 224 p., cloth, novel.

WALLING, William A.

36406   *Mary Shelley.* New York: Twayne Publishers, 1972, 173 p., cloth, nonf.

WALLIS, G. McDonald—SEE: Campbell, Hope

*WALLIS, George C., 1871-1956

WALLIS, Redmond (Frankton), 1933-

36407   *The mills of space.* London: Purnell Books, 1989, 181 p., cloth, novel. TRIANGULUM TRILOGY #2.
36408   *Starbloom.* London: Purnell Books, 1989, 158 p., cloth, novel. TRIANGULUM TRILOGY #1.

WALLMANN, Jeffrey M(iner), 1941-

36409   *Deathtrek.* New York: Tower Books, 1980, 172 p., paper, novel.

with Linda DuBreuil as MARGARET MAITLAND

22268   Love's golden circle. New York: Leisure Books, 1978, 304 p., paper, novel.

*WALLOP, (John) Douglass (III), 1920-1985

WALLRAPP, Lynn (Rogers)

36410   *Murmuring ever.* New York: Manor Books, 1975, 224 p., paper, novel.

WALSDORF, John J.

36411   *William Morris in private press and limited editions: a descriptive bibliography of books about William Morris, 1891-1981.* Phoenix, AZ: Oryx Press, 1983, xxvi+ 602 p., cloth, nonf.

WALSH, Chad, 1914-1991

36412   *C. S. Lewis: apostle to the skeptics.* New York: Macmillan Publishing Co., 1949, xiii+176 p., cloth, nonf.
36413   *The literary legacy of C. S. Lewis.* NY & London: Harcourt Brace Jovanovich, 1979, xi+269 p., cloth, nonf.

WALSH, Jill Paton—SEE: Paton Walsh, Jill

WALSH, John Evangelist (Jr.), 1927-

36414   *Plumes in the dust: the love affair of Edgar Allan Poe and Fanny Osgood.* Chicago: Nelson Hall, 1980, 163 p., cloth, nonf.
36415   *Poe the detective: the curious circumstances behind The mystery of Marie Roget.* New Brunswick, NJ: Rutgers University Press, 1968, 154 p., cloth, nonf.

WALSH, Robb

36416   *Kingdom of the dwarfs.* New York: Centaur Books, 1980, 140 p., cloth, novel.

*WALTARI, Mika (Toimi), 1908-1979

WALTER, Dorothy C.

36417   *Lovecraft and Benefit Street.* North Montpelier: Driftwood Press, 1943?, 14 p., paper, nonf. [Limited to 150 copies].

WALTER, Elizabeth (Margaret)

36418   *Dead woman, and other haunting experiences.* London: Collins & Harvill Press, 1975, 192 p., cloth, coll.
36419   *In the mist, and other uncanny encounters.* Sauk City, WI: Arkham House, 1979, xi+202 p., cloth, coll.

WALTERS, Hugh [pseud. of Walter Llewellyn Hughes], 1910-

36420   *The blue aura.* London: Faber & Faber, 1979, 127 p., cloth, novel. CHRIS GODFREY #20.
36421   *Boy astronaut.* London: Abelard-Schuman, 1977, 61 p., cloth, novel. CHRIS GODFREY #17.
36422   *The caves of Drach.* London: Faber & Faber, 1977, 136 p., cloth, novel. CHRIS GODFREY #18.
36423   *The dark triangle.* London: Faber & Faber, 1981, 125 p., cloth, novel. CHRIS GODFREY #22.
36424   *First family on the Moon.* London: Abelard, 1979, 79 p., cloth, novel. CHRIS GODFREY #21.
36425   *The last disaster.* London: Faber & Faber, 1978, 136 p., cloth, novel. CHRIS GODFREY #19.
36426   *Murder on Mars.* London: Faber & Faber, 1975, 131 p., cloth, novel. CHRIS GODFREY #16.
36427   *P-K.* London: Severn House, 1986, 139 p., cloth, novel. CHRIS GODFREY #24.

36428 *School on the Moon.* London: A Grasshopper Book, Abelard, 1981, 74 p., cloth, novel. CHRIS GODFREY #23.

WALTERS, Jennifer Waelti- —SEE: Waelti-Walters, Jennifer

WALTERS, R. R.

36429 *Ladies in waiting.* New York: Tor Horror, A Tom Doherty Associates Book, 1986, 411 p., paper, novel.
36430 *Lily.* New York: Tor Horror, A Tom Doherty Associates Book, 1988, 408 p., paper, novel.
36431 *Ludlow's Mill.* New York: Tor, A Tom Doherty Associates Book, Pinnacle Books, 1981, 300 p., paper, novel.
36432 *The ritual.* New York: Charter, 1980, 218 p., paper, novel.
36433 *Wind chimes.* New York: Zebra Books, Kensington Publishing Corp., 1991, 352 p., paper, novel.

WALTHER, Daniel, 1940-

36434 *The book of Shai.* New York: DAW Books, 1984, 157 p, paper, novel. SHAI #1. [Translation by C. J. Cherryh of *Le livre de Swa*].
36435 *Shai's destiny.* New York: DAW Books, 1985, 223 p., paper, novel. SHAI #2. [Translation by C. J. Cherryh of *Le destin de Swa*].

*WALTON, Bryce, 1918-<u>1988</u>

WALTON, Evangeline [i.e., Evangeline Walton Ensley], 1907-

36436 *The sword is forged.* New York: Timescape Books, 1982, 347 p., cloth, novel.

WANDREI, Donald (A.), 1908-1987

36437 *Colossus: the collected science fiction of Donald Wandrei.* Minneapolis, MN: Fedogan & Bremer, 1989, xxix+421 p., cloth, coll. [Edited by Philip J. Rahman & Dennis E. Weiler].

WANGERIN, Walter Jr., 1944-

36438 *The book of sorrows.* New York: Harper & Row, 1985, x+339 p., cloth, novel. COOP #2.
36439 *The book of the dun cow.* NY, Hagerstown: Harper & Row, 1978, ix+241 p., cloth, novel. COOP #1.

WANNAN, Bill [i.e., William Fielding Wannan], 1915-

36440 *Australian horror stories.* South Yarra, Victoria, Australia: Currey O'Neil, 1983, 280 p., cloth, anth.

WANNAN, William F.—SEE: Wannan, Bill

WARD, Arthur Henry—SEE: Rohmer, Sax

WARD, Arthur Sarsfield—SEE: Rohmer, Sax

WARD, B. [i.e., Edward Ward?], *as* BENGO MISTRAL

10176 *Pirates of Cerebus.* London: Gannet Press, 1953, 128 p., paper, novel.

WARD, E. D., pseud.—SEE: Lucas, E. V.

WARD, Edward—SEE: Ward, B.

WARD, Harold—SEE: Zorro, pseud.

WARD, James M(ichael), 1951-

36441 *Battle for the ancient robot.* Lake Geneva, WI: TSR Inc., 1985, 2 v., paper, novel. [*Vol. 1: You are Michael Renshaw, Earth star pilot; vol. 2: You are E-Ben, a powerful robot*].
36442 *Castle Arcania.* Lake Geneva, WI: TSR Inc., 1985, 2 v., paper, novel. [*Vol. 1: You are Eric Sunsword, legendary knight of the northern marches; vol. 2: You are Neves, an ancient and powerful wizard*].
36443 *Challenge of Druid's Grove.* Lake Geneva, WI: TSR Inc., 1985, 2 v., paper, novel. [*Vol. 1: You are Arkane, a great Wizard; vol. 2: You are Renwood, a powerful druid*].
36444 *Conan the undaunted.* Lake Geneva, WI: TSR Inc., 1984, 157 p., paper, novel. ENDLESS QUEST #19; CONAN SERIES.
Daredevil vs. Kingpin—SEE: The king takes a dare; Daredevil vs. Kingpin.
36445 *Dragonsword of Lankhmar.* Lake Geneva, WI: TSR Inc., 1986, 2 v., paper, novel. FAFHRD & GRAY MOUSER SERIES. [*Vol. 1: You are Fafhrd and the Gray Mouser; vol. 2: You are Thieves' Guild assassins*].
36446 *G.I. Joe: Operation: Weapons disaster.* New York: Ballantine Books, 1986, 88 p., paper, novel. FIND YOUR FATE—G.I. JOE #11.
36447 *Greyhawk adventures: a compendium of Greyhawk campaign ideas for the AD&D playing system.* Lake Geneva, WI: TSR,

1988, 128 p., paper, nonf. ADVANCED DUNGEONS & DRAGONS SERIES; GREYHAWK SERIES.

36448 *The king takes a dare; Daredevil vs. Kingpin.* Lake Geneva, WI: TSR, 1987, 2 v., paper, fiction.

Operation: Weapons disaster—SEE: *G.I. Joe: Operation weapons disaster.*

36449 *Revenge of the red dragon.* Lake Geneva, WI: TSR Inc., 1985, 2 v., paper, novel. [*Vol. 1: You are Flametongue, an ancient red dragon; vol. 2: You are Raven Quickblade, the black knight*].

36450 *The ring, the sword, and the unicorn.* Lake Geneva, WI: TSR Inc., 1983, 75 p., paper, novel. FANTASY FOREST BOOK #1.

Weapons disaster—SEE: *G.I. Joe: Operation: Weapons disaster.*

with Jean Blashfield

18130 *Faerie mound of dragonkind.* Lake Geneva, WI: TSR Inc., 1987, 157 p., paper, novel. CATACOMBS BOOKS #1.

18131 *Gnomes-100, dragons-0.* Lake Geneva, WI: TSR, 1987, [156] p., paper, fiction. CATACOMBS BOOKS #2.

with Jerry Epperson

22691 *Night of the wolverine.* Lake Geneva, WI: TSR Inc., 1986, 190 p., paper, novel. MARVEL SUPERHEROES ADVENTURE GAMEBOOK #3.

with Jane Cooper Hong

25894 *Forgotten realms fantasy adventure: Pool of radiance.* Lake Geneva, WI: TSR Inc., 1989, 316 p., paper, novel. FORGOTTEN REALMS FANTASY ADVENTURE.

Pool of radiance—SEE: *Forgotten realms fantasy adventure: Pool of radiance.*

with Mary L. Kirchoff

27315 *Light on Quests Mountain.* Lake Geneva, WI: TSR Inc., 1983, 157 p., paper, novel. ENDLESS QUEST #12.

with Robert Kuntz

27588 *Advanced Dungeons & Dragons: Deities & Demigods cyclopedia: special reference work.* Lake Geneva, WI: TSR Inc., 1980, 128 p., cloth, nonf. ADVANCED DUNGEONS & DRAGONS REFERENCE BOOKS.

27589 *Advanced Dungeons & Dragons: Deities & Demigods cyclopedia: special reference*

work. Lake Geneva, WI: TSR Inc., 1980, 144 p., cloth, nonf. ADVANCED DUNGEONS & DRAGONS REFERENCE BOOKS. [Revised edition].

27590 *Advanced Dungeons & Dragons: Legends & lore.* Lake Geneva, WI: TSR Inc., 1984, 128 p., cloth, nonf. ADVANCED DUNGEONS & DRAGONS REFERENCE BOOKS.

*WARD, Lynd (Kendall), 1905-1985

*WARD, Richard Heron, 1910-1969

WARDE, Beatrice—SEE: Beaujon, Paul

WARDMAN, Gordon

36451 *Reparations.* London: Secker & Warburg, 1987, 196 p., cloth, novel.

WARE, Malcolm

36452 *Sublimity in the novels of Ann Radcliffe: a study of the influence upon her craft of Edmund Burke's Enquiry into the origin of our ideas of the sublime and beautiful.* Upsala, Sweden: Lundequistka, 1963, 62 p., paper, nonf.

WARFIELD, Wayne

38142 *The ultimate guide to Howardia, 1925-1975.* [Aberdeen, MD]: Hall Publications, 1976, p., paper, nonf. anth.

WARICHA, Jean

38143 *The video caper.* New York: Ballantine Books, 1986, 72 p., paper, fiction. FIND YOUR FATE—JEM #2.

WARNER, Michael, with R. D. Warner

36453 *Galactic Rift.* New York: Manor Books, 1979, 239 p., paper, novel.

WARNER, Mignon

36454 *The tarot murders.* London: Robert Hale, 1978, 192 p., cloth, novel.

WARNER, R. D., with Michael Warner

36453 *Galactic Rift.* New York: Manor Books, 1979, 239 p., paper, novel.

WARNER, Reginald E.—SEE: Warner, Rex

*WARNER, Rex [i.e., Reginald Ernest Warner], 1905-1986

WARNER, Sylvia Townsend, 1893-1978

36455 *Kingdoms of elfin.* London: Chatto & Windus, 1977, 222 p., cloth, coll.
36456 *Selected stories of Sylvia Townsend Warner.* New York: Viking Press, 1988, 440 p., cloth, coll.
36457 *T. H. White: a biography.* New York: Viking Press, 1967, 352 p., cloth, nonf.

WARREN, Alan [pseud. of Alan John Ziegenfuss], 1952-

36458 *Roald Dahl.* Mercer Island, WA: Starmont House, 1988, vi+105 p., cloth, nonf.

WARREN, Bill [i.e., William Bond Warren], 1943-

with Allan Rothstein

32710 *Fandom is a way of death.* Los Angeles: L.A.Con II, 1984, 40 p., paper, novel.

with Bill Thomas

35539 *Keep watching the skies!: American science fiction movies of the fifties, volume 1, 1950-1957.* Jefferson, NC & London: McFarland & Co., 1982, xvi+467 p., cloth, nonf.
35540 *Keep watching the skies!: American science fiction movies of the fifties, volume II, 1958-1962.* Jefferson, NC & London: McFarland & Co., 1987, xx+839 p., cloth, nonf.

WARREN, Chad

36459 *Alien heaven.* London: Robert Hale, 1976, 175 p., cloth, novel.

WARREN, George, 1934-

36460 *Dominant species.* Virginia Beach, VA: The Donning Company/Publishers, 1979, 153 p., paper, novel.

as NICK CARTER

19604 *The doomsday spore.* New York: Charter, 1979, 242 p., paper, novel. NICK CARTER SERIES.

WARREN, Patricia Nell, 1936-

36461 *One is the sun.* New York: Ballantine Books, 1991, 535 p., paper, novel.

WARREN, Val

36462 *Lost lands, mythical kingdoms, and unknown worlds.* New York: HM Communications, 1979, 128 p., cloth?, nonf.

WARREN, William B.—SEE: Warren, Bill

WARRICK, Patricia S(cott), 1925-

36463 *The cybernetic imagination in science fiction.* Cambridge, MA & London: MIT Press, 1980, xvii+282 p., cloth, nonf.
36464 *Mind in motion: the fiction of Philip K. Dick.* Carbondale & Edwardsville, IL: Southern Illinois University Press, 1987, xxiii+222 p., cloth, nonf.

with Isaac Asimov & Martin H. Greenberg

16972 *Machines that think: the best science fiction stories about robots and computers.* New York: Holt, Rinehart & Winston, 1984, 627 p., cloth, anth.

with Martin H. Greenberg

24592 *The new awareness: religion through science fiction.* New York: Delacorte Press, 1975, xii+485 p., cloth, anth.

with Martin H. Greenberg & Harvey A. Katz

24526 *Introductory psychology through science fiction, 2nd ed.* Chicago: Rand McNally Publishing Co., 1977, vii+550 p., paper, anth.

with Martin H. Greenberg & Joseph D. Olander

24566 *Run to starlight: sports through science fiction.* New York: Delacorte Press, 1975, vi+383 p., cloth, anth.
24567 *Science fiction: contemporary mythology: the SFWA-SFRA anthology.* New York: Harper & Row, 1978, xviii+476 p., cloth, anth. [Includes some nonfiction].

with Martin Harry Greenberg & Joseph D. Olander & Val Clear

20165 *Marriage and the family through science fiction.* New York: St. Martin's Press, 1976, xiv+358 p., paper, anth.

with Martin H. Greenberg & Joseph D. Olander & John W. Milstead

24548 *Social problems through science fiction.* New York: St. Martin's Press, 1975, xvi+356 p., cloth, anth.

with Martin H. Greenberg & Charles G. Waugh

24593 *Science fiction: the Science Fiction Research Association anthology.* New York: Harper & Row, 1988, xi+522 p., cloth, anth.

WARRINGTON, Freda

36465 *A blackbird in amber.* New York: New English Library, 1988, 437 p., paper, novel. BLACKBIRD #3.
36466 *A blackbird in darkness.* London: New English Library, 1986, 473 p., paper, novel. BLACKBIRD #2.
36467 *A blackbird in silver.* London: New English Library, 1986, 302 p., paper, novel. BLACKBIRD #1.
36468 *A blackbird in twilight.* New York: New English Library, 1988, 387 p., paper, novel. BLACKBIRD #4.
36469 *The rainbow gate.* New York: New English Library, 1990, 381 p., cloth, novel.

WARTOFSKY, (William) Victor, 1931-

36470 *The passage.* New York: Tower Books, 1980, 188 p., paper, novel.

WASHBURN, Mark—SEE: Frey, James N.

*WASON, Sandys, 1870?-

WASSER, Margaret

36471 *The priory.* New York, London: Pocket Books, 1989, 281 p., paper, novel.

WASSERMANN, Jack, 1929- , *with Howard Robens*

32413 *Hambo's itch.* Garden City, NY: Doubleday & Co., 1979, 307 p., cloth, novel.

WAT, Aleksander [pseud. of Aleksander Chwat], 1900-1967

36472 *Lucifer unemployed.* Evanston, IL: Northwestern University Press, 1991, xii+123 p., cloth, coll. [Translation by Lillian Vallee of *Bezrobotny Lucyfer*].

WATERFIELD, Robin (Anthony Herschel), 1952-

38144 *Masks of mayhem.* Harmondsworth, Middlesex, England: Puffin Books, 1986, [200] p., paper, fiction. FIGHTING FANTASY GAMEBOOK SERIES.
Phantoms of fear—SEE: *Steve Jackson and Ian Livingstone present Phantoms of fear.*
36473 *Rebel planet.* Harmondsworth, Middlesex, England: Puffin Books, 1985, [205] p., paper, fiction. FIGHTING FANTASY GAMEBOOK #18.
36474 *Steve Jackson and Ian Livingstone present Phantoms of fear.* Harmondsworth, Middlesex, England: Puffin Books, 1987, [400] p., paper, fiction. FIGHTING FANTASY GAMEBOOK SERIES.

with Wilfred Davies

21252 *The money spider.* Harmondsworth, Middlesex, England: Puffin Books, 1988, 280 p., paper, fiction. FIGHTING FANTASY GAMEBOOK SERIES.
21253 *The water spider.* Harmondsworth, Middlesex, England: Puffin Books, 1988, 300 p., paper, fiction. FIGHTING FANTASY GAMEBOOK SERIES.

WATERLOO, Stanley, 1846-1913

14904 *The story of Ab: a tale of the time of the cave man.* Chicago: Way & Williams, 1897, 351 p., cloth, novel.
14904A retitled: *A tale of the time of the cave men: being the story of Ab.* London: Adam & Charles Black, 1904, xi+363 p., cloth, novel.

*WATERS, T(homas) A(llen), 1938-

*WATKIN, Lawrence Edward, 1901-1981

WATKINS, A. H.

36475 *Catalogue of the H. G. Wells Collection in the Bromley Public Libraries.* Bromley, England: London Borough of Bromley Public Libraries, 1974, xi+196 p., cloth, nonf.

with Patrick Parrinder & H. G. Wells Society & J. R. Hammond

24872 *H. G. Wells: a comprehensive bibliography, 4th ed.* London: H. G. Wells Society, 1986, 58 p., paper, nonf.

WATKINS, Diana—SEE: Gabaldon, Diana

WATKINS, Graham (Karl)

36476 *Dark winds.* New York: Berkley Books, 1989, 328 p., paper, novel.
36477 *The fire within.* New York: Berkley Books, 1991, 556 p., paper, novel.

WATKINS, Ivor

36478 *Blood snarl.* London: Macdonald Futura, 1980, 347 p., cloth, novel.
38145 *Demon.* London: Macdonald, 1983, 219 p., cloth, novel.

WATKINS, Leslie

36479 *The killing of Idi Amin.* London: Everest Books, 1976, 208 p., cloth, novel.

WATKINS, William John, 1942-

36480 *The centrifugal rickshaw dancer.* New York: Popular Library, Warner Books, 1985, 233 p., paper, novel. LEGRANGE LEAGUE #1.
36481 *Going to See the End of the Sky.* New York: Popular Library, Warner Books, 1986, 230 p., paper, novel. LEGRANGE LEAGUE #2.
36482 *The last deathship off Antares.* New York: Popular Library, 1989, 204 p., paper, novel.

with Gene Snyder

34399 *The litany of Sh'reev* / by William Jon Watkins... Garden City, NY: Doubleday & Co., 1976, 179 p., cloth, novel.

WATKINS, William Jon—SEE: Watkins, William John

WATNEY, John (Basil), 1915-

36483 *Mervyn Peake.* London: Michael Joseph, 1976, 255 p., cloth, nonf.

WATSON, Andy, *with Mark V. Ziesing*

36484 *Journal wired.* Willimantic, CT: Mark V. Ziesing, 1989, 118 p., paper, anth. [This publication later became a magazine].

WATSON, Elena M., 1958-

36485 *Television horror movie hosts: 68 vampires, mad scientists and other denizens of the late-night airwaves examined and inter-viewed.* Jefferson, NC & London: McFarland & Co., Publishers, 1991, xiv+242 p., cloth, nonf.

*WATSON, Henry Crocker Marriott, 1835-

WATSON, Ian, 1943-

36486 *Alien embassy.* London: Victor Gollancz, 1977, 208 p., cloth, novel.
36487 *The book of Being.* London: Victor Gollancz, 1985, 184 p., cloth, novel. BLACK CURRENT TRILOGY #3.
36488 *The book of Ian Watson.* Willimantic, CT: Mark V. Ziesing, 1985, 380 p., cloth, coll. [Includes some nonfiction].
36489 *The Book of the River.* London: Victor Gollancz, 1984, 208 p., cloth, novel. BLACK CURRENT TRILOGY #1.
36490 *The Book of the Stars.* London: Victor Gollancz, 1984, 192 p., cloth, novel. BLACK CURRENT TRILOGY #2.
36491 *The Books of the Black Current.* Garden City, NY: Nelson Doubleday, 1986, 536 p., cloth, coll. BLACK CURRENT TRILOGY #1-3.
36492 *Chekhov's journey.* London: Victor Gollancz, 1983, 183 p., cloth, novel.
36493 *Converts.* London: Panther, Granada Publishing, 1984, 191 p., paper, novel.
36494 *Deathhunter.* London: Victor Gollancz, 1981, 173 p., cloth, novel.
36495 *Evil water, and other stories.* London: Victor Gollancz, 1987, 200 p., cloth, coll.
36496 *The fire worm.* London: Victor Gollancz, 1988, 207 p., cloth, novel.
36497 *The flies of memory.* London: Victor Gollancz, 1990, 220 p., cloth, novel.
36498 *The Gardens of Delight.* London: Victor Gollancz, 1980, 176 p., cloth, novel.
36499 *God's world.* London: Victor Gollancz, 1979, 254 p., cloth, novel.
        Inquisitor—SEE: *Warhammer 40,000: Inquisitor.*
36500 *Japan tomorrow.* Osaka, Japan: Bunken Shuppan, 1977, 112 p., paper, coll. [Introduction and notes in Japanese].
36501 *The Jonah kit.* London: Victor Gollancz, 1975, 221 p., cloth, novel.
36502 *The Martian Inca.* London: Victor Gollancz, 1977, 207 p., cloth, novel.
36503 *Meat.* London: Headline, 1988, 246 p., paper, novel.
36504 *Miracle visitors.* London: Victor Gollancz, 1978, 239 p., cloth, novel.
36505 *Nanoware time.* New York: Tor SF, A Tom Doherty Associates Book, 1991, p. 1-111, paper, story. [Bound with *The persistence of vision* / by John Varley].

36506 *Pictures at an exhibition.* Cardiff, Wales: Greystoke Mobray, 1981, 168 p., paper, anth.

36507 *The power.* London: Headline, 1987, 232 p., paper, novel.

36508 *Queenmagic, Kingmagic.* London: Victor Gollancz, 1986, 205 p., cloth, novel.

36509 *Salvage rites, and other stories.* London: Victor Gollancz, 1989, 223 p., cloth, coll.

36510 *Slow birds, and other stories.* London: Victor Gollancz, 1985, 190 p., cloth, coll.

36511 *Stalin's teardrops, and other stories.* London: Victor Gollancz, 1991, 270 p., cloth, coll.

36512 *Sunstroke, and other stories.* London: Victor Gollancz, 1982, 190 p., cloth, coll.

36513 *The very slow time machine: science fiction stories.* London: Victor Gollancz, 1979, 189 p., cloth, coll. [Cover title: *The very slow time machine, and other stories*].

36514 *Warhammer 40,000: Inquisitor.* Brighton, East Sussex, England: GW Books, 1990, 246 p., paper, novel. WARHAMMER SERIES—INQUISITION WAR #1.

36515 *Whores of Babylon.* London: Grafton Books, 1988, 302 p., paper, novel.

with Michael Bishop

18050 *Changes: stories of metamorphosis: an anthology of speculative fiction about startling metamorphoses, both psychological and physical.* New York: Ace Science Fiction Books, 1983, 259 p., paper, anth.

18051 *Under heaven's bridge.* London: Victor Gollancz, 1980 (i.e., 1981), 159 p., cloth, novel. URBAN NUCLEUS SERIES.

with Pamela Sargent

33180 *Afterlives: an anthology of stories about life after death.* New York: Vintage Books, 1986, xviii+494 p., paper, anth.

WATSON, Jane Werner, 1915-

36516 *The case of the vanishing spaceship.* New York: Coward, McCann & Geoghegan, 1982, 109 p., cloth, novel.

WATSON, John H., pseud.—SEE: Estleman, Loren D. or Collins, Randall

WATSON, Julia—SEE: Fitzgerald, Julia

WATSON, Noelle (Anne), 1958- , with Paul E. Schellinger

33290 *Twentieth-century science-fiction writers, 3rd ed.* Chicago & London: St James Press, 1991, xxvi+1016 p., cloth, nonf. anth.

WATSON, Patrick, 1929-

36517 *Alter ego: a novel.* Toronto: Lester & Orpen Dennys, 1978, 255 p., cloth, novel.

WATSON, Robert, 1947-

36518 *Whilom.* New York: Atlantic Monthly Press, 1990, 216 p., cloth, novel.

WATSON, Simon

36519 *No man's land.* London: Victor Gollancz, 1975, 190 p., cloth, novel.

WATT, Donald, 1938-

36520 *Aldous Huxley: the critical heritage.* London & Boston: Routledge & Kegan Paul, 1975, xxiv+493 p., cloth, nonf. anth.

WATT-EVANS, Lawrence [pseud. of Lawrence Watt Evans], 1954-

36521 *The blood of a dragon.* New York: A Del Rey Book, Ballantine Books, 1991, 231 p., paper, novel.

36522 *The Book of Silence.* New York: A Del Rey Book, Ballantine Books, 1984, 326 p., paper, novel. LORDS OF DUS #4.

36523 *The chromosomal code.* New York: Avon, 1984, 204 p., paper, novel.

36524 *The Cyborg and the Sorcerers.* New York: A Del Rey Book, Ballantine Books, 1982, 248 p., paper, novel. WAR SURPLUS #1.

36525 *Denner's wreck.* New York: Avon, 1988, 199 p., paper, novel.

36526 *The lure of the basilisk.* New York: A Del Rey Book, Ballantine Books, 1980, 195 p., paper, novel. LORDS OF DUS #1.

36527 *The misenchanted sword.* New York: A Del Rey Book, Ballantine Books, 1985, 292 p., paper, novel. LEGEND OF ETHSHAR #1.

36528 *Newer York: stories of science fiction and fantasy about the world's greatest city.* New York: A Roc Book, 1991, xi+370 p., paper, anth.

36529 *The nightmare people.* New York: An Onyx Book, 1990, 254 p., paper, novel.

36530 *Nightside city.* New York: A Del Rey Book, Ballantine Books, 1989, 227 p., paper, novel.

36531 *The Seven Altars of Dûsarra.* New York: A Del Rey Book, Ballantine Books, 1981, 227 p., paper, novel. LORDS OF DUS #2.

36532 *Shining steel.* New York: Avon, 1986, 216 p., paper, novel.

36533 *The sword of Bheleu.* New York: A Del Rey Book, Ballantine Books, 1983, 272 p., paper, novel. LORDS OF DUS #3.

36534 *The unwilling warlord.* New York: A Del Rey Book, Ballantine Books, 1989, 309 p., paper, novel. LEGEND OF ETHSHAR #3.

36535 *With a single spell.* New York: A Del Rey Book, Ballantine Books, 1987, 263 p., paper, novel. LEGEND OF ETHSHAR #2.

36536 *The wizard and the war machine.* New York: A Del Rey Book, Ballantine Books, 1987, 291 p., paper, novel. WAR SURPLUS #2.

WATTERS, Barbara—SEE: Hunt, Barbara

WATTS, Harold H(olliday), 1906-

36537 New York: Twayne Publishers, 1969, 182 p., cloth, nonf.

WATTS, Helen—SEE: Hoke, Helen

WATTS, John [pseud. of Hugh Miller], 1937-

36538 *Head of state.* London: New English Library, 1979, 171 p., cloth, novel.

WAUGH, Carol-Lynn Rössel, 1947- , *with Isaac Asimov & Martin H. Greenberg*

16973 *13 horrors of Halloween.* New York: Avon, 1983, 175 p., paper, anth.

WAUGH, Charles G(ordon), 1943-

CHARLES G. WAUGH, *with Robert Adams & Martin H. Greenberg*

16023 *Barbarians.* New York: A Signet Book, New American Library, 1986, 368 p., paper, anth.

CHARLES G. WAUGH, *with Robert Adams & Pamela Crippen Adams & Martin H. Greenberg*

15982 *Barbarians II.* New York: A Signet Book, New American Library, 1988, xi+364 p., paper, anth. [Charles Waugh was an uncredited co-editor for this book].

CHARLES G. WAUGH, *with Poul Anderson & Martin H. Greenberg*

16450 *Mercenaries of tomorrow.* New York: A Critic's Choice Paperback from Lorevan Publishing, 1985, xi+372 p., paper, anth.

16451 *Space wars.* New York: Tor SF, A Tom Doherty Associates Book, 1988, 372 p., paper, anth.

16452 *Terrorists of tomorrow.* New York: A Critic's Choice Paperback from Lorevan Publishing, 1986, 376 p., paper, anth.

16453 *Time wars.* New York: Tor SF, A Tom Doherty Associates Book, 1986, 374 p., paper, anth.

CHARLES G. WAUGH, *with Piers Anthony & Barry Malzberg & Martin H. Greenberg*

16714 *Uncollected stars.* New York: Avon, 1986, vii+312 p., paper, anth.

CHARLES G. WAUGH, *with Isaac Asimov & Martin H. Greenberg*

16974 *The 13 crimes of science fiction.* Garden City, NY: Doubleday & Co., 1979, 455 p., cloth, anth.

16975 *After the end.* Milwaukee, WI: Raintree Publishers, 1981, 48 p., cloth, anth.

Asimov's extraterrestrials—SEE: *Young extraterrestrials.*

16976 *Asimov's ghosts & monsters.* London: Armada, 1988, 413 p., paper, anth. [Includes *Young ghosts* and *Young monsters*].

Asimov's ghosts—SEE: *Young ghosts.*

Asimov's monsters—SEE: *Young monsters.*

Asimov's mutants—SEE: *Young mutants.*

16977 *Baker's dozen: thirteen short fantasy novels.* New York: Greenwich House, 1984, ix+612 p., cloth, anth.

16977A retitled: *The mammoth book of short fantasy novels.* London: Robinson Publishing, 1986, 612 p., paper, anth.

16978 *Baker's dozen: thirteen short science fiction novels.* New York: Bonanza Books, 1985, ix+574 p., cloth, anth.

16978A retitled: *The mammoth book of short science fiction novels.* London: Robinson Publishing, 1986, 612 p., paper, anth.

The best fantasy of the 19th century—SEE: *Isaac Asimov presents the best fantasy of the 19th century.*

The best horror and supernatural of the 19th century—SEE: *Isaac Asimov presents The best horror and supernatural of the 19th century.*

The best science fiction firsts—SEE: *Isaac Asimov presents The best science fiction firsts.*

The best science fiction of the 19th century—SEE: *Isaac Asimov presents The best science fiction of the 19th century.*

16979 *Bug awful.* Milwaukee, WI: Raintree Publishers, 1984, 48 p., cloth, anth. Martin Harry.

16980 *Catastrophes!* New York: Fawcett Crest, 1981, 413 p., paper, anth.

16981 *Caught in the organ draft: biology in science fiction.* New York: Farrar Straus Giroux, 1983, xi+276 p., cloth, anth.

16982 *Children of the future.* Milwaukee, WI: Raintree Publishers, 1984, 48 p., cloth, anth.

16983 *Comets.* New York: A Signet Book, New American Library, 1986, xii+339 p., paper, anth. ISAAC ASIMOV'S WONDERFUL WORLDS OF SCIENCE FICTION #4.

16984 *Computer crimes and capers.* Chicago: Academy Chicago Publishers, 1983, 235 p., cloth, anth.

16985 *Cosmic knights.* New York: A Signet Book, New American Library, 1985, 339 p., paper, anth. ISAAC ASIMOV'S MAGICAL WORLDS OF FANTASY #3.

16986 *Curses.* New York: A Signet Book, New American Library, 1989, 350 p., paper, anth. ISAAC ASIMOV'S MAGICAL WORLDS OF FANTASY #11.

16987 *The deadly sins and cardinal virtues of science fiction.* New York: Bonanza Books, 1982, 317, 350 p., cloth, anth. [Includes both books].

16988 *Dragon tales.* New York: Fawcett Crest, 1982, 318 p., paper, anth.

16989 *Earth invaded.* Milwaukee, WI: Raintree Publishers, 1982, 46 p., cloth, anth.

16990 *Encounters.* London: Headline, 1988, 399 p., paper, anth.

Extraterrestrials—SEE: *Young extraterrestrials.*

16991 *Faeries: Isaac Asimov's magical worlds of fantasy.* New York: A Roc Book, 1991, 374 p., paper, coll. ISAAC ASIMOV'S MAGICAL WORLDS OF FANTASY (UNNUMBERED).

16992 *Fantastic creatures: an anthology of fantasy and science fiction.* New York: Franklin Watts, 1981, 155 p., cloth, anth.

16993 *Flying saucers.* New York: Fawcett Crest, 1982, 349 p., paper, anth.

16994 *Ghosts.* New York: A Signet Book, New American Library, 1988, 347 p., paper, anth. ISAAC ASIMOV'S MAGICAL WORLDS OF FANTASY #10.

Ghosts & monsters—SEE: *Asimov's Ghosts & monsters.*

16995 *Giants.* New York: A Signet Books, New American Library, 1985, 351 p., paper, anth. ISAAC ASIMOV'S MAGICAL WORLDS OF FANTASY #5.

16996 *Great science fiction stories by the world's great scientists.* New York: Donald I. Fine, 1985, 400 p., cloth, anth.

Great tales of classic science fiction—SEE: *The mammoth book of classic science fiction: short novels of the 1930s.*

16997 *Hallucination orbit: psychology in science fiction.* New York: Farrar Straus Giroux, 1983, 279 p., cloth, anth.

16998 *The immortals.* Milwaukee, WI: Raintree Publishers, 1984, 48 p., cloth, anth.

16999 *Intergalactic empires.* New York: A Signet Book, New American Library, 1983, 303 p., paper, anth. ISAAC ASIMOV'S WONDERFUL WORLDS OF SCIENCE FICTION #1.

17000 *Invasions.* New York: A Roc Book, 1990, 382 p., paper, anth. ISAAC ASIMOV'S WONDERFUL WORLDS OF SCIENCE FICTION #10.

17001 *Isaac Asimov presents Tales of the occult: stories.* Buffalo, NY: Prometheus Books, 1989, 354 p., cloth, anth.

17002 *Isaac Asimov presents The best fantasy of the 19th century.* New York: Beaufort Books, 1982, 368 p., cloth, anth.

17003 *Isaac Asimov presents The best horror and supernatural of the 19th century.* New York: Beaufort Books, 1983, 368 p., cloth, anth.

17004 *Isaac Asimov presents The best science fiction firsts.* New York: Beaufort Books, 1984, 249 p., cloth, anth.

17005 *Isaac Asimov presents The best science fiction of the 19th century.* New York: Beaufort Books, 1981, 316 p., cloth, anth.

17006 *Isaac Asimov's Magical worlds of fantasy: Witches & wizards.* New York: Bonanza Books, 1985, 649 p., cloth, anth. [Includes *Witches* and *Wizards*].

17007 *The last man on Earth.* New York: Fawcett Crest, 1982, 352 p., paper, anth.

17008 *Mad scientists.* Milwaukee, WI: Raintree Publishers, 1982, 48 p., cloth, anth.

17009 *Magical wishes.* New York: A Signet Book, New American Library, 1986, 350 p., paper, anth. ISAAC ASIMOV'S MAGICAL WORLDS OF FANTASY #7.

Magical worlds of fantasy—SEE: *Isaac Asimov's Magical worlds of fantasy.*

17010 *The Mammoth book of classic science fiction: short novels of the 1930s.* London:

Robinson, 1988, xiii+572 p., paper, anth.

17010A retitled: *Great tales of classic science fiction.* New York: Galahad, 1990, 498 p., cloth, anth.

17011 *The mammoth book of golden age science fiction: short novels of the 1940s.* New York: Carroll & Graf, 1989, 504 p., paper, anth.

17012 *The mammoth book of new world science fiction: short novels of the 1960s.* New York: Carroll & Graf, 1991, 506 p., paper, anth.

The mammoth book of short fantasy novels—SEE: *Baker's dozen: thirteen short fantasy novels.*

The mammoth book of short science fiction novels—SEE: *Baker's dozen: thirteen short science fiction novels.*

17013 *The mammoth book of vintage science fiction: short novels of the 1950s.* London: Robinson, 1990, 503 p., paper, anth.

17014 *Monsters.* New York: A Signet Book, New American Library, 1988, 349 p., paper, anth. ISAAC ASIMOV'S WONDERFUL WORLDS OF SCIENCE FICTION #8.

17015 *Mutants.* Milwaukee, WI: Raintree Publishers, 1982, 46 p., cloth, anth.

Mutants—SEE: *Young mutants.*

Mythic beasts—SEE: *Mythical beasties.*

17016 *Mythical beasties.* New York: A Signet Book, New American Library, 1986, 343 p., paper, anth. ISAAC ASIMOV'S MAGICAL WORLDS OF FANTASY #6.

17016A retitled: *Mythic beasts.* London: Robinson, 1988, 343 p., paper, anth.

17017 *Robots.* New York: A Signet Book, New American Library, 1989, 351 p., paper, anth. ISAAC ASIMOV'S WONDERFUL WORLDS OF SCIENCE FICTION #9.

17018 *Science fiction A to Z: a dictionary of great S.F. themes.* Boston: Houghton Mifflin Co., 1982, xvii+651 p., cloth, anth.

17019 *The science fictional Olympics.* New York: A Signet Book, New American Library, 1984, 356 p., paper, anth. ISAAC ASIMOV'S WONDERFUL WORLDS OF SCIENCE FICTION #2.

17020 *The science fictional solar system.* New York: Harper & Row, 1979, ix+317 p., cloth, anth.

17021 *The seven cardinal virtues of science fiction.* New York: Fawcett Crest, 1981, 350 p., paper, anth.

17022 *The seven deadly sins of science fiction.* New York: Fawcett Crest, 1980, 317 p., paper, anth.

17023 *Sherlock Holmes through time and space.* New York: Bluejay Book, 1984, 355 p., cloth, anth.

17024 *Space mail, volume II.* New York: Fawcett Crest, 1982, 380 p., paper, anth.

17025 *Space shuttles.* New York: A Signet Book, New American Library, 1987, 384 p., paper, anth. ISAAC ASIMOV'S WONDERFUL WORLDS OF SCIENCE FICTION #7.

17026 *Spells.* New York: A Signet Book, New American Library, 1985, 350 p., paper, anth. ISAAC ASIMOV'S MAGICAL WORLDS OF FANTASY #4.

17027 *Starships.* New York: Fawcett Crest, 1983, 342 p., paper, anth.

17028 *Supermen.* New York: A Signet Book, New American Library, 1984, 350 p., paper, anth. ISAAC ASIMOV'S WONDERFUL WORLDS OF SCIENCE FICTION #3.

Tales of the occult—SEE: *Isaac Asimov presents Tales of the occult.*

17029 *Thinking machines.* Milwaukee, WI: Raintree Publishers, 1981, 48 p., cloth, anth.

17030 *Those amazing electronic thinking machines: an anthology of robot and computer stories* / by Isaac Asimov, Martin S. Greenberg & Charles H. Waugh [sic]. New York: Franklin Watts, 1983, 147 p., cloth, anth.

17031 *Time warps.* Milwaukee, WI: Raintree Publishers, 1984, 48 p., cloth, anth.

17032 *Tin stars.* New York: A Signet Book, New American Library, 1986, 351 p., paper, anth. ISAAC ASIMOV'S WONDERFUL WORLDS OF SCIENCE FICTION #5.

17033 *Tomorrow's TV.* Milwaukee, WI: Raintree Publishers, 1982, 48 p., cloth, anth.

17034 *Travels through time.* Milwaukee, WI: Raintree Publishers, 1981, 47 p., cloth, anth.

17035 *TV: 2000.* New York: Fawcett Crest, 1982, 352 p., paper, anth.

17036 *The twelve frights of Christmas.* New York: Avon, 1986, 263 p., paper, anth.

17037 *Wild inventions.* Milwaukee, WI: Raintree Publishers, 1981, 46 p., cloth, anth.

17038 *Witches.* New York: A Signet Book, New American Library, 1984, 350 p., paper, anth. ISAAC ASIMOV'S MAGICAL WORLDS OF FANTASY #2.

17039 *Wizards.* New York: A Signet Book, New American Library, 1983, 303 p., paper, anth. ISAAC ASIMOV'S MAGICAL WORLDS OF FANTASY #1.

17040 *Young extraterrestrials.* New York: Harper & Row, 1984, xiv+240 p., cloth, anth.

17040A retitled: *Asimov's extraterrestrials.* London: Dragon Books, 1986, 204 p., paper, anth.

17040A retitled: *Asimov's extraterrestrials*. London: Dragon Books, 1986, 204 p., paper, anth.

17040B retitled: *Extraterrestrials*. New York: Harper & Row, 1988, xiv+240 p., paper, anth.

17041 *Young ghosts*. New York: Harper & Row, 1985, xiv+210 p., cloth, anth.

17041A retitled: *Asimov's ghosts*. London: Dragon Books, 1986, 202 p., paper, anth.

17042 *Young immortals*. New York: Harper & Row, 1985, vii+213 p., cloth, anth.

17043 *Young monsters*. New York: Harper & Row, 1985, 213 p., cloth, anth.

17043A retitled: *Asimov's monsters*. London: Dragon Books, 1986, 203 p., paper, anth.

17044 *Young mutants*. New York: Harper & Row, 1984, 256 p., cloth, anth.

17044A retitled: *Asimov's mutants*. London: Dragon Books, 1986, 201 p., paper, anth.

17044B retitled: *Mutants*. New York: Harper & Row, 1988, 256 p., paper, anth.

17045 *Young star travelers*. New York: Harper & Row, 1986, xiii+209 p., cloth, anth.

17046 *Young witches & warlocks*. New York: Harper & Row, 1987, xvi+207 p., cloth, anth.

CHARLES G. WAUGH, *with Gordon R. Dickson & Martin H. Greenberg*

21904 *Robot warriors*. New York: Ace Books, 1991, x+240 p., paper, anth.

CHARLES G. WAUGH, *with David Drake & Martin H. Greenberg*

22174 *The eternal city*. New York: Baen Books, 1990, 280 p., paper, anth.

22175 *Space dreadnoughts*. New York: Ace Books, 1990, xiii+220 p., paper, anth.

22176 *Space gladiators*. New York: Ace Books, 1989, 310 p., paper, anth.

22177 *Space infantry*. New York: Ace Books, 1989, xii+244 p., paper, anth.

CHARLES G. WAUGH, *with Martin H. Greenberg*

24594 *Alternative histories: eleven stories of the world as it might have been*. New York & London: Garland Publishing, 1986, 363 p., cloth, anth.

24595 *The Arbor House celebrity book of horror stories*. New York: Arbor House, 1982, 448 p., cloth, anth.

24596 *Back from the dead*. New York: DAW Books, 1991, 364 p., paper, anth.

24597 *Baker's dozen: 13 short horror novels*. New York: Bonanza Books, 1987, ix+758 p., cloth, anth.

24598 *Battlefields beyond tomorrow: science fiction war stories*. New York: Bonanza Books, 1987, xiii+650 p., cloth, anth.

24506 *Christmas on Ganymede, and other stories*. New York: Avon Books, 1990, viii+243 p., paper, anth. [Charles Waugh was an uncredited co-editor for this book].

24599 *Cults! an anthology of secret societies, sects, and the supernatural*. New York: Beaufort Books, 1983, 358 p., cloth, anth.

24600 *Cults of horror*. New York: DAW Books, 1990, 350 p., paper, anth.

24601 *Devil worshippers*. New York: DAW Books, 1990, 348 p., paper, anth.

24602 *East Coast ghosts*. Wilmington, DE: Middle Atlantic Press, 1989, 310 p., paper, anth.

24603 *Hollywood unreel: fantasies about Hollywood and the movies*. New York: Taplinger Publishing Co., 1982, 308 p., cloth, anth.

24604 *House shudders: an anthology of haunted house stories*. New York: DAW Books, 1987, 332 p., paper, anth.

24605 *Love, 3000*. New York: Elsevier/Nelson Books, 1980, 240 p., cloth, anth.

24606 *Vamps: an anthology of female vampire stories*. New York: DAW Books, 1987, 365 p., paper, anth.

CHARLES G. WAUGH, *with Martin H. Greenberg & Tim Cottrill*

20644 *Science fiction and fantasy series and sequels: a bibliography, volume 1: books*. New York, London: Garland Publishing, 1986, xix+398 p., cloth, nonf. [Only volume published].

CHARLES G. WAUGH, *with Martin H. Greenberg & Rosalind M. Greenberg*

24522 *14 vicious valentines*. New York: Avon Books, 1988, vii+196 p., paper, anth.

CHARLES G. WAUGH, *with Martin H. Greenberg & Frank D. McSherry Jr.*

24530 *Baseball 3000*. New York: Elsevier/Nelson Books, 1981, vi+210 p., cloth, anth.

24531 *Cinemonsters*. Lake Geneva, WI: TSR Inc., 1987, 319 p., paper, anth.

24532 *Civil war ghosts*. Little Rock, AR: August House Publishers, 1991, 204 p., paper, anth.

TN: Rutledge Hill Press, 1988, 208 p., paper, anth.

24534 *Eastern ghosts: haunting, spine-chilling stories from New York, Pennsylvania, New Jersey, Delaware, Maryland, and the District of Columbia.* Nashville, TN: Rutledge Hill Press, 1990, x+208 p., paper, anth.

24535 *Ghosts of the heartland: haunting, spine-chilling stories from the American midwest.* Nashville, TN: Rutledge Hill Press, 1990, 210 p., paper, anth.

24536 *Great American ghost stories.* Nashville, TN: Rutledge Hill Press, 1991, 512 p., cloth, anth.

24537 *Haunted New England: classic tales of the strange and supernatural.* Dublin, NH: Yankee Books, 1988, 287 p., cloth, anth.

24538 *Hollywood ghosts: haunting, spine-chilling stories from America's film capital.* Nashville, TN: Rutledge Hill Press, 1991, 210 p., paper, anth.

24539 *New England ghosts: haunting, spine-chilling stories from the New England states.* Nashville, TN: Rutledge Hill Press, 1990, 213 p., paper, anth.

24540 *Nightmares in Dixie: thirteen horror tales from the American South.* Little Rock, AR: August House, 1987, 260 p., cloth, anth.

24541 *Pirate ghosts of the American coast: stories of hauntings at sea.* Little Rock, AR: August House, 1988, 206 p., paper, anth.

24542 *Red Jack.* New York: DAW Books, 1988, 333 p., paper, anth.

24543 *Strange Maine.* Augusta, ME: Lance Tapley, 1986, 295 p., paper, anth.

24544 *Treasury of American horror stories.* New York: Bonanza Books, 1985, xii+670 p., cloth, anth.

24545 *Western ghosts: haunting, spine-chilling stories from the American West.* Nashville, TN: Rutledge Hill Press, 1990, 215 p., paper, anth.

24546 *Yankee witches.* Augusta, ME: Lance Tapley, Publisher, 1988, 315 p., paper, anth.

CHARLES G. WAUGH, *with Martin H. Greenberg & Joseph D. Olander*

24568 *Mysterious visions: great science fiction by masters of the mystery.* New York: St. Martin's Press, 1979, xxvi+516 p., cloth, anth.

CHARLES G. WAUGH, *with Martin H. Greenberg & Carol Serling*

Night gallery reader—SEE: *Rod Serling's Night gallery reader.*

24579 *Rod Serling's Night gallery reader.* New York: Dembner Books, 1987, x+326 p., cloth, anth.

CHARLES G. WAUGH, *with Martin H. Greenberg & Patricia Warrick*

24593 *Science fiction: the Science Fiction Research Association anthology.* New York: Harper & Row, 1988, xi+522 p., cloth, anth.

CHARLES G. WAUGH, *with Martin H. Greenberg & Jenny-Lynn Waugh*

24607 *101 science fiction stories.* New York: Avenel Books, 1986, xvii+651 p., cloth, anth.

CHARLES G. WAUGH, *with Joe Haldeman & Martin H. Greenberg*

24523 *Body armor: 2000.* New York: Ace Science Fiction Books, 1986, 311 p., paper, anth.

24524 *Spacefighters.* New York: Ace Books, 1988, 296 p., paper, anth.

24525 *Supertanks.* New York: Ace Science Fiction Books, 1987, 262 p., paper, anth.

CHARLES G. WAUGH, *with Richard Matheson & Martin H. Greenberg*

24529 *The Twilight Zone: the original stories.* New York: Avon, 1985, 550 p., paper, anth.

CHARLES G. WAUGH, *with Frank D. McSherry Jr.*

29695 *Spooky sea stories.* Camden, ME: Yankee Books, 1991, 246 p., paper, anth.

CHARLES G. WAUGH, *with Robert Silverberg & Martin H. Greenberg*

24588 *Neanderthals.* New York: A Signet Book, New American Library, 1987, 351 p., paper, anth. ISAAC ASIMOV'S WONDERFUL WORLDS OF SCIENCE FICTION #6.

24589 *The science fictional dinosaur.* New York: An Avon Flare Book, 1982, 224 p., paper, anth.

CHARLES G. WAUGH, *with S. M. Stirling & Frank D. McSherry Jr. & Martin H. Greenberg*

24590   *The fantastic Civil War.* Riverdale, NY: Baen Books, 1991, 307 p., paper, anth.

24591   *Fantastic World War II.* New York: Baen Books, 1990, 281 p., paper, anth.

CHARLES G. WAUGH, *with Jane Yolen & Martin H. Greenberg*

24612   *Dragons & dreams: a collection of new fantasy and science fiction stories.* New York: Harper & Row, 1986, x+180 p., cloth, anth.

24613   *Spaceships & spells: a collection of new fantasy and science-fiction stories.* New York: Harper & Row, 1987, 182 p., cloth, anth.

WAUGH, Frederick J(udd), 1861-

38146   *The clan of Munes.* New York: Charles Scribner's Sons, 1916, 56 p., cloth, art.

WAUGH, Harriet, 1944-

36539   *Kate's house: a novel.* London: Weidenfeld & Nicolson, 1983, 217 p., cloth, novel.

WAUGH, Jenny-Lynn, 1968- , *with Charles G. Waugh & Martin H. Greenberg*

24607   *101 science fiction stories.* New York: Avenel Books, 1986, xvii+651 p., cloth, anth.

WAY, John H., *with David C. Miller*

29895   *Cardiac arrest.* New York: Charter Books, 1988, 265 p., paper, novel.

*WAY, Peter (Howard), 1936-

WAYNE, Charles M., pseud.

15876   *The duke of sin.* New York: Vantage Press, 1954, 74 p., cloth, story.

WAYNE, Matt

36540   *Brain drain.* New York: An Archway Paperback, Pocket Books, 1991, 121 p., paper, novel. NINTENDO ADVENTURE BOOKS #12.

36541   *The crystal trap.* New York: An Archway Paperback, Pocket Books, 1991, 121 p., paper, novel. NINTENDO ADVENTURE BOOKS #9.

36542   *Flown the Koopa.* New York: An Archway Paperback, Pocket Books, 1991, 121 p., paper, novel. NINTENDO ADVENTURE BOOKS #8.

36543   *The shadow prince.* New York: An Archway Paperback, Pocket Books, 1991, 121 p., paper, novel. NINTENDO ADVENTURE BOOKS #10.

36544   *Unjust desserts.* New York: An Archway Paperback, Pocket Books, 1991, 121 p., paper, novel. NINTENDO ADVENTURE BOOKS #11.

WEATHERBY, W(illiam) J(ohn)

36545   *Goliath.* Toronto, New York: A Quicksilver Book, Bantam Books, 1981, ix+273 p., paper, novel.

36546   *Salman Rushdie: sentenced to death.* New York: Carroll & Graf, 1990, 258 p., cloth, nonf.

WEATHERS, Brenda, 1936-

36547   *The house at Pelham Falls.* Tallahassee, FL: Naiad Press, 1986, 226 p., paper, novel.

WEAVER, Gertrude—SEE: Dunn, Gertrude

WEAVER, Lydia

36548   *Splashman.* New York: A Signet Vista Book, New American Library, 1985, 190 p., paper, novel.

WEAVER, Michael D., 1961-

36549   *Bloodfang.* New York: Avon Books, 1989, 215 p., paper, novel. THYRI #3.

36550   *Mercedes nights.* New York: St. Martin's Press, 1987, 240 p., cloth, novel.

36551   *My father immortal.* New York: St. Martin's Press, 1989, 228 p., cloth, novel.

36552   *Nightreaver.* New York: Avon Books, 1988, 187 p., paper, novel. THYRI #2.

36553   *Wolf-dreams.* New York: Avon, 1987, 186 p., paper, novel. THYRI #1.

36554   *Wolf-dreams.* London: New English Library, 1989, 686 p., paper, coll. THYRI #1-3.

WEAVER, Tom, 1958- , *with Michael Brunas & John Brunas*

18827   *Interviews with B science fiction and horror movie makers: writers, producers, directors, actors, moguls, and makeup.* Jefferson, NC & London: McFarland & Co., 1988, xi+413 p., cloth, nonf.

[Michael and John Brunas are listed as research associates].

18828 *Science fiction stars and horror heroes: interviews with actors, producers, and writers of the 1940s through 1960s.* Jefferson, NC & London: McFarland & Co., 1991, xiii+448 p., cloth, nonf. [Michael and John Brunas are listed as research associates].

18829 *Universal horrors: the studio's classic films, 1931-1946.* Jefferson, NC & London: McFadden & Co., 1990, viii+616 p., cloth, nonf.

*WEBB, A(ugustus) C(aesar), 1894-<u>1985</u>

WEBB, Don, 1960-

36555 *Uncle Ovid's exercise book: fictions.* Normal, IL: Illinois State University; NY, Boulder: Fiction Collective, 1988, 154 p., cloth, coll.

WEBB, Jackie

36556 *Wilkes the wizard.* London: Granada, 1985, 144 p., cloth, novel. WILKES THE WIZARD #1.
36557 *Wilkes the wizard and the S.P.A.M.* London: Grafton, 1986, 144 p., cloth, novel. WILKES THE WIZARD #2.

WEBB, Lucas, pseud.—SEE: Reginald, Robert

WEBB, Maggie—SEE: Lee, Samantha

WEBB, Sharon (Lynn), 1936-

36558 *The adventures of Terra Tarkington.* Toronto, New York: Bantam Books, 1985, 204 p., paper, novel.
36559 *Earth song.* New York: An Argo Book, Atheneum, 1983, 190 p., cloth, novel. EARTH SONG TRIAD #2.
36560 *Earthchild.* New York: Atheneum, 1982, 192 p., cloth, novel. EARTH SONG TRIAD #1.
36561 *The halflife.* New York: Tor Books, 1989, 406 p., cloth, novel.
36562 *Pestis 18.* New York: Tor, A Tom Doherty Associates Book, 1987, viii+400 p., cloth, novel.
36563 *Ram song.* New York: Argo, Atheneum, 1984, 218 p., cloth, novel. EARTH SONG TRIAD #3.

WEBB, William Thomas, 1918-

36564 *After the inferno.* London: Robert Hale, 1977, 190 p., cloth, novel.

36565 *Cheyney's robot.* London: Robert Hale, 1978, 192 p., cloth, novel.
36566 *The Dimension Lords.* London: Robert Hale, 1979, 192 p., cloth, novel.
36567 *The eye of Hollerl-Ra.* London: Robert Hale, 1977, 190 p., cloth, novel.
36568 *The fate of the Phral.* London: Robert Hale, 1980, 191 p., cloth, novel.
36569 *The froth eater.* London: Robert Hale, 1980, 190 p., cloth, novel.
36570 *Poisoned planet.* London: Robert Hale, 1978, 192 p., cloth, novel.
36571 *The Time Druids.* London: Robert Hale, 1978, 188 p., cloth, novel.

WEBBER, Julian Lloyd—SEE: Lloyd Webber, Julian

WEBBERT, Doreen (Lee Erlenwein), 1934- , *with Jean Goddin*

24033 *Fantasy cookbook.* Tucson, AZ: World Fantasy Convention, 1991, 86 p., paper, nonf.

WEBER, David

36572 *Mutineers' moon.* Riverdale, NY: Baen Books, 1991, 315 p., paper, novel.

with Steve White

36573 *Insurrection.* Riverdale, NY: Baen Books, 1990, 408 p., paper, novel.

WEBER, Nancy, 1942-

36574 *The playgroup.* New York: St. Martin's Press/Richard Marek, 1982, 263 p., cloth, novel.

as LINDSAY WEST

36575 *Empire of the ants: novelization.* New York: Ace Books, 1977, 180 p., paper, movie.

WEBER, Ronald, 1934-

36576 *Seeing Earth: literary responses to space exploration.* Athens, OH: Ohio University Press, 1985, xiv+138 p., cloth, nonf.

WEBSTER, Ernest, 1923-

36577 *The Friulan plot.* London: Robert Hale, 1980, 192 p., cloth, novel.

WEBSTER, Joanne

36578 *The love genie.* London: Hodder & Stoughton, 1978, 118 p., cloth, novel.

WEBSTER, Josh (Lew), 1949-

36579 *The beckoning.* New York: A Dell Book, 1980, 272 p., paper, novel.
36580 *Ceremonies.* New York: Berkley Books, 1982, 296 p., paper, novel.
36581 *The doll.* New York: Zebra Books, Kensington Publishing Corp., 1986, 348 p., paper, novel.
36582 *Quarantine.* Toronto, New York: Worldwide, 1988, 384 p., paper, novel.

WEBSTER, Lyn, 1950-

36583 *The illumination of Alice J. Cunningham.* London: Dedalus, 1987, 306 p., cloth, novel.

*WECHTER, Nell Wise, 1913-<u>1989</u>

WEDGELOCK, Colin

36584 *Short circuit: a novel.* London: Sphere Books, 1986, 185 p., paper, movie.

WEEDMAN, Jane Branham

36585 *Samuel R. Delany.* Mercer Island, WA: Starmont House, 1982, 79 p., cloth, nonf. STARMONT READER'S GUIDE #10.
36586 *Women worldwalkers: new dimensions of science fiction and fantasy* / by Jane B. Weedman. Lubbock, TX: Texas Tech Press, 1985, 250 p., cloth, nonf. anth.

WEEKS, John (Howard), 1949-

36587 *The dream weavers: short stories by the nineteenth-century pre-Raphaelite poet-painters.* Santa Barbara, CA: A Banquo Book, Woodbridge Press Publishing Co., 1980, 191 p., paper, anth.

WEEKS, Stephen, *with Henry Whittington*

36588 *Sword of the valiant: the legend of Sir Gawain and the Green Knight.* London: Robert Hale, 1984, 151 p., cloth, movie.

WEHMEYER, Lillian (Mabel) Biermann, 1933-

36589 *Images in a crystal ball: world futures in novels for young people.* Littleton, CO: Libraries Unlimited, 1981, 211 p., cloth, nonf.

WEHRSTEIN, Karen (Miriam), 1961-

36589 *Lion's heart.* Riverdale, NY: Baen Fantasy, 1991, 410 p., paper, novel. FIFTH MILLENNIUM #6.
36590 *Lion's soul.* Riverdale, NY: Baen Fantasy, 1991, 324 p., paper, novel. FIFTH MILLENNIUM #7.

with S. M. Stirling & Shirley Meier

29716 *Shadow's son.* Riverdale, NY: Baen Books, 1991, 442 p., paper, novel. FIFTH MILLENNIUM #4.

WEIGEL, John A(rthur), 1912-

36591 *Colin Wilson.* Boston: Twayne Publishers, 1975, 157 p., cloth, nonf.

WEIN, Len [i.e., Leonard Norman Wein], 1948-

with David Houston

25996 *Swamp Thing: a novel.* New York: Tor, A Tom Doherty Associates Book, 1982, 223 p., paper, movie. SWAMP THING #1.

with Marv Wolfman

36592 *The Marvel superheroes.* New York: Pocket Books, 1979, 208 p., paper, anth. MARVEL SUPERHEROES #9.
36593 *Mayhem in Manhattan.* New York: A Kangaroo Book, Pocket Books, 1978, 176 p., paper, novel. SPIDERMAN #1; MARVEL SUPERHEROES #1.

with Marv Wolfman & Joseph Silva [i.e., Ron Goulart]

24258 *Stalker from the stars.* New York: Pocket Books, 1978, 174 p., paper, novel. INCREDIBLE HULK #1; MARVEL SUPERHEROES #2.

WEIN, Leonard N.—SEE: Wein, Len

WEINBAUM, Stanley G(rauman), 1902-1935

14959 *The best of Stanley G. Weinbaum.* Reading, PA: Fantasy Press, 1949, 289 p., cloth, coll.
14959A *A Martian odyssey, and others.* London: Sphere, 1977, 316 p., paper, coll.
A Martian odyssey, and others—SEE: *The best of Stanley G. Weinbaum.*

WEINBERG, George (H.)

36594 *Numberland: a fable.* New York: St. Martin's Press, 1987, 119 p., cloth, novel.

WEINBERG, Larry [i.e., Lawrence E. Weinberg]

36595 *The curse.* Toronto, New York: Bantam Books, 1984, 133 p., paper, novel. DARK FORCES #13.

36596 *Dragonslayer: the storybook based on the movie.* New York: Random House, 1981, [57] p., cloth, movie.

36597 *The empire strikes back.* New York: Random House, 1985, 68 p., cloth, movie. STAR WARS SERIES.

36598 *Frankenstein.* New York: Random House, 1982, 94 p., cloth, movie. [Adapted from the novel by Shelley].

36599 *Island of the walking dead.* New York: Wanderer Books, 1986, 56 p., paper, novel. CHUCK NORRIS & THE KARATE KOMMANDOS #2.

36600 *Menace in space.* New York: Wanderer Books, 1986, 54 p., cloth, novel. CHUCK NORRIS & THE KARATE KOMMANDOS #1.

36601 *Star Trek III, the search for Spock storybook* / by Lawrence Weinberg. New York: Little Simon, Simon & Schuster, 1984, [57] p., paper, movie. STAR TREK SERIES.

36602 *Star Wars: adaptation.* New York: Random House, 1985, 68 p., cloth, movie. STAR WARS SERIES.

36603 *Star Wars: the making of the movie.* New York: Random House, 1980, 69 p., cloth, nonf. STAR WARS SERIES.

36604 *Tron: the storybook.* New York: Little Simon, 1982, [57] p., cloth, movie.

36605 *Wicket and the dandelion warriors: an Ewok adventure.* New York: Random House, 1985, 29 p., cloth, story. STAR WARS SERIES.

WEINBERG, Lawrence E.—SEE: Weinberg, Larry

WEINBERG, Robert (Edward), 1946-

36607 *Annotated guide to Robert E. Howard's sword & sorcery.* West Linn, OR: Starmont House, 1976, vii+152 p., paper, nonf.

36608 *The armageddon box.* Newark, NJ: Wildside Press, 1991, 222 p., cloth, novel. ALEX WERNER #2.

36609 *A biographical dictionary of science fiction and fantasy artists.* New York, Westport, CT: Greenwood Press, 1988, xvi+346 p., cloth, nonf. anth.

36610 *The black lodge.* New York, London: Pocket Books, 1991, 275 p., paper, novel.

36611 *The devil's auction.* Philadelphia, PA: Owlswick Press, Weird Tales Library, 1988, 155 p., cloth, novel. ALEX WERNER #1.

36612 *Devils in the dark.* Chicago: Robert Weinberg, 1979, 96 p., paper, anth. WEIRD MENACE CLASSICS #4.

36613 *The eighth green man (and other strange folk).* Mercer Island, WA: Starmont House, 1989, vi+171 p., cloth, anth. STARMONT POPULAR FICTION #2.

36614 *Lester Dent: the man behind Doc Savage.* Oak Lawn, IL: Robert Weinberg, 1974, 127 p., paper, nonf. anth.

36615 *A reader's guide to the Cthulhu Mythos.* Hillside, NJ: Robert Weinberg, 1969, p., paper, nonf.

36616 *The Weird tales story.* West Linn, OR: FAX Collector's Editions, 1977, ix+134 p., cloth, nonf.

as ANONYMOUS EDITOR

36617 *The angel.* Oak Lawn, IL: Robert Weinberg, 1975, [96] p., paper, anth. PULP CLASSICS #10.

36618 *The chair where terror sat.* Chicago: Robert Weinberg, 1977, 96 p., paper, anth. WEIRD MENACE CLASSICS #3.

36619 *The corpse factory.* Chicago: Robert Weinberg, 1977, 96 p., paper, anth. WEIRD MENACE CLASSICS #1.

36620 *The dance of the skeletons.* Chicago: Robert Weinberg, 1980, 96 p., paper, anth. WEIRD MENACE CLASSICS #6.

36621 *The death dealers: fantastic sleuths battling diabolical villains.* Chicago: Robert Weinberg, 1980, 96 p., paper, anth. PULP CLASSICS #21.

36622 *Death orchids, & other bizarre tales.* Chicago: Robert Weinberg, 1976, 96 p., paper, anth. PULP CLASSICS #13.

26726 *The emperor of death.* Chicago: Robert Weinberg, 1979, [96] p., paper, anth. PULP CLASSICS #20.

04387 *Famous fantastic classics #1.* West Linn, OR: FAX Collector's Editions, 1974, 128 p., paper, anth. [Previously attributed to T. E. Dikty].

36623 *Famous fantastic classics #2.* West Linn, OR: FAX Collector's Editions, 1975, 128 p., paper, anth.

36624 *Famous pulp classics #1*. West Linn, OR: FAX Collector's Editions, 1975, 128 p., paper, anth. [Only volume issued].

36625 *The lake of life*. Chicago: Robert Weinberg, 1978, 80 p., paper, anth. LOST FANTASIES #8.

36626 *Lost fantasies #4*. Chicago: Robert Weinberg, 1976, 80 p., paper, anth. LOST FANTASIES #4.

36627 *Lost fantasies #5*. Chicago: Robert Weinberg, 1977, 96 p., paper, anth. LOST FANTASIES #5.

36628 *Lost fantasies #6*. Chicago: Robert Weinberg, 1977, 96 p., paper, anth. LOST FANTASIES #6.

36629 *Satan's roadhouse*. Chicago: Robert Weinberg, 1977, 96 p., paper, anth. WEIRD MENACE CLASSICS #2.

36626 *The sin eaters*. Chicago: Robert Weinberg, 1979, 96 p., paper, anth. LOST FANTASIES #9.

36630 *Slaves of the blood wolves*. Chicago: Robert Weinberg, 1979, 96 p., paper, anth. WEIRD MENACE CLASSICS #5.

with Joel Frieman

23529 *A tribute to Unknown worlds*. Newark, NJ: Joel Frieman, 1969, 22 p., paper, nonf.

with Martin H. Greenberg

24608 *Lovecraft's legacy*. New York: Tor, A Tom Doherty Associates Book, 1990, 334 p., cloth, anth.

with Martin H. Greenberg & Stefan R. Dziemianowicz

22354 *Famous fantastic mysteries: 30 great tales of fantasy and horror from the classic pulp magazines Famous fantastic mysteries & Fantastic novels*. New York: Gramercy Books, 1991, xiii+449 p., cloth, anth.

22355 *Rivals of Weird tales: 30 great fantasy & horror stories from the weird fiction pulps*. New York: Bonanza Books, 1990, xx+486 p., cloth, anth.

22356 *Weird tales: 32 unearthed terrors*. New York: Bonanza Books, 1988, xv+665 p., cloth, anth.

with Lohr McKinstry

29642 *The hero pulp index, 2nd ed.* Evergreen, CO: Opar Press, 1971, 48 p., paper, nonf.

WEINER, Andrew (Simon), 1949-

36632 *Distant signals, and other stories*. Vancouver, British Columbia, Canada: A Tesseract Book, Porcépic Press, 1990, 236 p., paper, coll.

36633 *Isaac Asimov presents Station Gehenna*. New York: Congdon & Weed, 1987, 216 p., cloth, novel.

Station Gehenna—SEE: *Isaac Asimov presents Station Gehenna*.

WEINER, Ellis, 1951-

Doon—SEE: *National Lampoon's Doon*.

36634 *The great Muppet caper*. Toronto, New York: Bantam Books, 1981, 96 p., paper, movie.

36635 *Howard the Duck*. New York: Berkley Books, 1986, 232 p., paper, movie.

36636 *National Lampoon's Doon*. New York: Pocket Books, 1984, 221 p., paper, novel. DUNE PARODY. [Parody of Frank Herbert's *Dune* series].

WEINER, Homer

36637 *Spacewater blues*. Los Angeles: Sonica Press, 1980, 253 p., cloth, novel.

WEINSTEIN, Elliot

36638 *The fillostrated fan dictionary*. North Hollywood, CA: "O" Press, 1975, 171 p. in 2 v., paper, nonf.

WEINSTEIN, Howard, 1954-

36639 *The covenant of the crown: a Star Trek novel*. New York: A Timescape Book, Pocket Books, 1981, 191 p., paper, novel. STAR TREK #4.

36640 *Deep domain: a Star Trek novel*. New York: Pocket Books, 1987, 275 p., paper, novel. STAR TREK #33.

36641 *Exiles*. New York, London: Pocket Books, 1990, 271 p., paper, novel. STAR TREK: THE NEXT GENERATION #14.

Path to conquest—SEE: *V: Path to conquest*.

36642 *Perchance to dream*. New York, London: Pocket Books, 1991, xi+242 p., paper, novel. STAR TREK: THE NEXT GENERATION #19.

36643 *Power hungry*. New York, London: Pocket Books, 1989, x+276 p., paper, novel. STAR TREK: THE NEXT GENERATION #6.

Prisoners and pawns—SEE: *V: Prisoners and pawns*.

36644 *V: Path to conquest.* New York: Tor, A Tom Doherty Associates Book, 1987, 209 p., paper, tele. V SERIES.

36645 *V: Prisoners and pawns.* New York: Pinnacle Books, 1985, vi+181 p., paper, tele. V #6.

with A. C. Crispin

East Coast crisis—SEE: *V: East Coast crisis.*

20818 *V: East Coast crisis.* New York: Pinnacle Books, 1984, xi+305 p., paper, tele. V #2.

WEINTRAUB, William, 1926-

36646 *The underdogs.* Toronto: McClelland & Stewart, 1979, 225 p., cloth, novel.

WEIS, Margaret (Edith Baldwin), 1948-

36647 *The art of Dungeons & Dragons fantasy game* / by Margaret Baldwin Weis. Lake Geneva, WI: TSR Inc., 1985, 127 p., paper, art.

36648 *The endless catacombs* / by Margaret Baldwin Weis. Lake Geneva, WI: TSR Inc., 1984, 157 p., paper, novel. ENDLESS QUEST #22.

36649 *King's sacrifice.* New York, Toronto: Spectra, Bantam Books, 1991, 519 p., paper, novel. STAR OF THE GUARDIANS #3.

36650 *King's test.* New York, Toronto: Spectra, Bantam Books, 1990, 450 p., paper, novel. STAR OF THE GUARDIANS #2.

36651 *The lost king.* New York, Toronto: Spectra, Bantam Books, 1990, 457 p., paper, novel. STAR OF THE GUARDIANS #1.

with Tracy Hickman

25588 *The Darksword trilogy: Darksword adventures.* Toronto, New York: Bantam Books, 1989, 437 p., paper, nonf. DARKSWORD TRILOGY SERIES.

25589 *Doom of the darksword.* Toronto, New York: Bantam Books, 1988, xi+383 p., paper, novel. DARKSWORD TRILOGY #2.

25590 *Dragon wing.* New York, Toronto: Bantam Books, 1990, 431 p., cloth, novel. DEATH GATE CYCLE #1.

25591 *DragonLance adventures.* Lake Geneva, WI: TSR, 1987, 128 p., cloth, fiction. DRAGONLANCE SERIES; ADVANCED DUNGEONS & DRAGONS REFERENCE BOOKS.

25592 *DragonLance chronicles: Dragons of autumn twilight; Dragons of winter night;*

Dragons of spring dawning. Lake Geneva, WI: TRS, 1988, xii+1030 p., paper, coll. DRAGONLANCE CHRONICLES #1-3.

25593 *DragonLance tales: The magic of Krynn; Kender, gully dwarves, and gnomes; Love and war.* Harmondsworth, Middlesex, England: Penguin Books, 1991, 688 p., paper, coll. DRAGONLANCE TALES #1-3.

25594 *Dragons of spring dawning.* Lake Geneva, WI: TSR Inc., 1985, 379 p., paper, novel. DRAGONLANCE CHRONICLES #3.

25595 *Dragons of the autumn twilight.* Lake Geneva, WI: TSR Inc., 1984, 447 p., paper, novel. DRAGONLANCE CHRONICLES #1.

25596 *Dragons of the winter night.* Lake Geneva, WI: TSR Inc., 1985, 399 p., paper, novel. DRAGONLANCE CHRONICLES #2.

25597 *Elven star.* New York, Toronto: Spectra, Bantam Books, 1990, 367 p., cloth, novel. DEATH GATE CYCLE #2.

25598 *Fire sea.* Toronto, New York: Bantam Books, 1991, 364 p., cloth, novel. DEATH GATE CYCLE #3.

25599 *Forging the darksword.* Toronto, New York: Bantam Books, 1988, 391 p., paper, novel. DARKSWORD TRILOGY #1.

25600 *Kender, gully dwarves, and gnomes.* Lake Geneva, WI: TSR Inc., 1987, 367 p., paper, anth. DRAGONLANCE TALES #2.

25601 *Love and war.* Lake Geneva, WI: TSR Inc., 1987, 386 p., paper, anth. DRAGONLANCE TALES #3.

25602 *The magic of Krynn.* Lake Geneva, WI: TSR Inc., 1987, 352 p., paper, anth. DRAGONLANCE TALES #1.

25603 *The paladin of the night.* Toronto, New York: Bantam Books, 1989, 375 p., paper, novel. ROSE OF THE PROPHET #2.

25604 *The prophet of Akhran.* Toronto, New York: Bantam Books, 1989, 390 p., paper, novel. ROSE OF THE PROPHET #3.

25605 *Test of the twins.* Lake Geneva, WI: TSR Inc., 1986, 345 p., paper, novel. DRAGONLANCE LEGENDS #3.

25606 *Time of the twins.* Lake Geneva, WI: TSR Inc., 1986, 398 p., paper, novel. DRAGONLANCE LEGENDS #1.

25607 *Triumph of the darksword.* Toronto, New York: Bantam Books, 1988, 346 p., paper, novel. DARKSWORD TRILOGY #3.

25608 *War of the twins.* Lake Geneva, WI: TSR Inc., 1986, 387 p., paper, novel. DRAGONLANCE LEGENDS #1.

25609 *The will of the wanderer.* Toronto, New York: Bantam Books, 1989, 444 p., paper, novel. ROSE OF THE PROPHET #1.

with Tracy Hickman & Mary L. Kirchoff

25610 *Leaves from the inn of the Last Home: the complete Krynn source book.* Lake Geneva, WI: TSR Inc., 1987, 255 p., paper, nonf.

with Roger E. Moore as SUSAN LAWSON

30191 *Riddle of the griffon.* Lake Geneva, WI: TSR Inc., 1985, 144 p., paper, novel. ENDLESS QUEST CRIMSON CRYSTAL ADVENTURE #1.

WEISBECKER, A(lan) C.

36652 *Cosmic banditos: a contrabandista's quest for the meaning of life.* New York: Vintage Books, Random House, 1986, 193 p., paper, novel.

WEISENBURGER, Steven (C.)

38147 *A Gravity rainbow's companion: sources and contexts for Pynchon's novel.* Athens, GA & London: University of Georgia Press, 1988, 345 p., cloth, nonf.

WEISER, Melvin

36653 *The trespasser.* New York: Avon, 1981, 281 p., paper, novel.
36654 *Within the web.* New York: A Dell Book, 1984, 272 p., paper, novel.

WEISMAN, Jordan K.

Into the shadows—SEE: *Shadowrun: Into the shadows.*
36655 *Shadowrun: Into the shadows: anthology.* Chicago: FASA Corp., 1990, 286 p., paper, anth. [Stories based around the game *Shadowrun*].

WEISS, Ellen, 1953-

36656 *Indiana Jones and the gold of Genghis Khan.* New York: Ballantine Books, 1985, 117 p., paper, novel. FIND YOUR FATE ADVENTURE #9; INDIANA JONES SERIES.

WELBY, Philip

36657 *The pleasure domes of Sigma 93.* London: Robert Hale, 1978, 191 p., cloth, novel.

WELDON, Fay, 1931-

36658 *The cloning of Joanna May.* London: Collins, 1989, 265 p., cloth, novel.
36659 *Female friends.* London: Heinemann, 1975, 311 p., cloth, novel.
38148 *Puffball.* London: Hodder & Stoughton, 1980, 255 p., cloth, novel.
36660 *The rules of life.* London: Hutchinson, 1987, 79 p., cloth, novel.
36661 *Wolf: the mechanical dog.* London: Collins, 1988, 48 p., cloth, story.

WELDON, John, *with James Bjornstad*

18062 *Playing with fire.* Chicago: Moody Press, 1984, 91 p., paper, nonf.

WELDON, Michael (James), 1952- , *with Charles Beesley & Bob Martin & Akiru Fitton*

17671 *The psychotronic encyclopedia of film.* New York: Ballantine Books, 1983, xvi+815 p., paper, nonf.

WELDRICK, Valerie (Eileen)

36662 *The Blakeley ghost.* Ringwood, Victoria, Australia: Hutchinson of Australia, 1980, 112 p., cloth, novel.
36663 *Time sweep.* London: Hutchinson, 1976, 131 p., cloth, novel.

WELFARE, Mary

36664 *Yeti of the glen.* London: A Pied Piper Book, Methuen Children's Books, 1987, 96 p., cloth, novel.

*WELLARD, James (Howard), 1909-1987

WELLBROCK, Gladys Bale, *with Patricia Bale Cox as* G. F. BALE

20744 *If thoughts could kill.* New York: Charter/Diamond Books, 1990, 291 p., paper, novel.

WELLER, M(ike) J.

36665 *Kobald, the first Showdwortian.* London: ITMA, 1990, 14 p., paper, story.

*WELLES, (George) Orson, 1915-1985

WELLES, Patricia

36666 *The ghost of S.W.1.* New York: Donald I. Fine, 1986, 286 p., cloth, novel.
36666A retitled: *Sara's ghost.* Toronto, New York: PaperJacks Ltd., 1987, 286 p., paper, novel.

Sara's ghost—SEE: *The ghost of S.W.1.*

WELLES, Paul O'M., 1926-

36667 *Project Lambda.* Port Washington, NY: Ashley Books, 1979, iii+316 p., cloth, novel.

WELLING, Lois

36668 *Continuum.* Champaign, IL: Lois Welling, 1983, 29 p., paper, story. STAR TREK SERIES.

36669 *The displaced.* Champaign, IL: Lois Welling, 1982?, 126 p., paper, novel. STAR TREK SERIES.

36670 *Transition.* Champaign, IL: Lois Welling, 1982, xviii+156 p., paper, novel. STAR TREK SERIES.

WELL-KNOWN AUTHOR, A—SEE: Vivian, Herbert

WELLMAN, Manly Wade (Sr.), 1903-1986

36671 *After dark.* Garden City, NY: Doubleday & Co., 1980, 184 p., cloth, novel. SILVER JOHN #3.

36672 *The Beyonders.* New York: Warner Books, 1977, 189 p., paper, novel.

36673 *Cahena: a dream of the past.* Garden City, NY: Doubleday & Co., 1986, 182 p., cloth, novel.

36674 *The hanging stones.* Garden City, NY: Doubleday & Co., 1982, 172 p., cloth, novel. SILVER JOHN #5.

John the balladeer—SEE: *Who fears the devil?*

36675 *Lonely vigils.* Chapel Hill, NC: Carcosa, 1981, xii+376 p., cloth, coll. JOHN THUNSTONE #1.

36676 *The lost and the lurking.* Garden City, NY: Doubleday & Co., 1981, 179 p., cloth, novel. SILVER JOHN #4.

36677 *The old gods waken.* Garden City, NY: Doubleday & Co., 1979, 186 p., cloth, novel. SILVER JOHN #2.

36678 *The school of darkness.* Garden City, NY: Doubleday & Co., 1985, 182 p., cloth, novel. JOHN THUNSTONE #3.

36679 *Twice in time.* New York: Baen Books, 1988, 214 p., paper, coll. [Includes the original text of 1957 novel (see #14998) plus an additional novelette].

36680 *The valley so low: Southern mountain stories.* Garden City, NY: Doubleday & Co., 1987, 212 p., cloth, coll. [Edited by Karl Edward Wagner].

36681 *The voice of the mountain.* Garden City, NY: Doubleday & Co., 1984, 178 p., cloth, novel. SILVER JOHN #6.

36682 *What dreams may come.* Garden City, NY: Doubleday & Co., 1983, 175 p., cloth, novel. JOHN THUNSTONE #2.

14999 *Who fears the devil?* Sauk City, WI: Arkham House, 1963, 213 p., cloth, coll. SILVER JOHN #1.

36683 retitled: *John the balladeer.* New York: Baen Books, 1988, 306 p., paper, coll. SILVER JOHN #1. [Expanded edition; edited by Karl Edward Wagner].

with Wade Wellman

36684 *Sherlock Holmes's War of the worlds.* New York: Warner Books, 1975, 208 p., paper, novel. WAR OF THE WORLDS SEQUEL.

WELLMAN, (Manly) Wade (Jr.), 1937- , *with Manly Wade Wellman*

36684 *Sherlock Holmes's War of the worlds.* New York: Warner Books, 1975, 208 p., paper, novel. WAR OF THE WORLDS SEQUEL.

WELLS, Angus, 1943-

36685 *Forbidden magic.* London: Orbit, 1991, 586 p., paper, novel. GODWARS #1.

36686 *The usurper.* London: Sphere Books, 1989, 346 p., paper, novel. THE KINGDOMS #2.

36687 *The way beneath.* London: Orbit, 1990, 345 p., paper, novel. THE KINGDOMS #3.

36688 *The wrath of Ashar.* London: Michael Joseph, 1988, 360 p., cloth, novel. THE KINGDOMS #1.

as IAN EVANS

22823 *Star maidens: a novel.* London: Corgi Books, 1977, 175 p., paper, tele.

with or without Robert Holdstock as RICHARD KIRK

36689 *The frozen god.* London: Corgi Books, 1978, 174 p., paper, novel. RAVEN #3. [By Angus Wells].

25848 *Raven, swordmistress of chaos.* London: Corgi Books, 1978, 174 p., paper, novel. RAVEN #1. [By Robert Holdstock and Angus Wells].

36690 *A time of dying.* London: Corgi Books, 1979, 190 p., paper, novel. RAVEN #5. [By Angus Wells].

WELLS, Arvin R(obert), 1927-

36691 *Jesting Moses: a study in Cabellian comedy.* Gainesville, FL: University of Florida Press, 1962, ix+146 p., cloth, nonf.

WELLS, Basil (Eugene), 1912- , with Paul Ernst

14962 *Dr. Satan.* Oak Lawn, IL: Robert Weinberg, 1974, 95 p, paper, coll. [Corrected entry; includes five Dr. Satan stories by Ernst, and one by Wells].

WELLS, Catherine [i.e., Catherine Jean Wells Dimenstein], 1952-

36692 *The earth is all that lasts.* New York: A Del Rey Book, Ballantine Books, 1991, viii+339 p., paper, novel.

WELLS, Geoffrey H(arry), 1900-

36693 *The works of H. G. Wells, 1887-1925: a bibliography, dictionary, and subject-index.* London: George Routledge & Sons, 1926, xxv+274 p., cloth, nonf.

as GEOFFREY WEST

36694 *H. G. Wells: a sketch for a portrait.* London: G. Howe, 1930, 316 p., cloth, nonf.

WELLS, H(erbert) G(eorge), 1886-1946

36695 *The collector's book of science fiction by H. G. Wells.* Secaucus, NJ: Castle Books, 1978, vii+514 p., cloth, coll. [Edited by Alan K. Russell].
The complete science fiction treasury of H. G. Wells—SEE: *Seven famous novels.*

36696 *The definitive time machine: a critical edition of H. G. Wells's scientific romance.* Bloomington, IN: Indiana University Press, 1987, xi+218 p., cloth, novel. [Edited by Harry M. Geduld].

36697 *Early writings in science and science fiction.* Berkeley & Los Angeles, CA: University of California Press, 1975, xiv+249 p., cloth, coll. [Edited by Robert M. Philmus & David Y. Hughes].

36698 *The empire of the ants, and 8 science fiction stories.* New York: Grosset & Dunlap, 1977, p., cloth, coll.

36699 *The empire of the ants, and other short stories.* Paris: Le Livre de Poche, 1991, 311 p., paper, coll. [A bilingual edition in French and English; translations by Joseph Dobrinsky].

36700 *The empire of the ants (and other stories).* New York, Toronto: Scholastic Book Services, 1977, 152 p., paper, coll.

36701 *Experiment in autobiography: discoveries and conclusions of a very ordinary brain (since 1866).* New York: Macmillan Publishing Co., 1934, xi+718 p., cloth, nonf.

36702 *The H. G. Wells science fiction treasury.* New York: Chatham River Perss, 1984, x+688 p., cloth, coll.

36703 *H. G. Wells short stories.* London: Folio Society, 1990, xvii+262 p., cloth, coll. [Edited by Tim Heald].

36704 *H. G. Wells's literary criticism.* Brighton, Sussex, England: Harvester Press; Totowa, NJ: Barnes & Noble Books, 1980, xiii+261 p., cloth, nonf. coll. [Edited by Patrick Parrinder & Robert Philmus].

36705 *A man with a nose, and the other uncollected short stories of H. G. Wells.* London, Dover, NH: Athlone Presss, 1984, ix+212 p., cloth, coll. [Edited by J. R. Hammond].

15061 *Seven famous novels.* New York: Alfred A. Knopf, 1934, 860 p., cloth, coll. [Includes *The time machine, The island of Doctor Moreau, The invisible man, The war of the worlds, The first men in the moon, The food of the gods,* and *In the days of the comet*].

15061A retitled: *The complete science fiction treasury of H. G. Wells.* New York: Avenel Books, 1978, 860 p., cloth, coll.

36706 *Three more novels of the future.* Garden City, NY: Nelson Doubleday, 1981, xiii+395 p., cloth, coll. [Includes *The Island of Dr. Moreau, Story of the days to come, The first men in the moon*].

36707 *Three novels of the future.* Garden City, NY: Nelson Doubleday, 1979, xii+368 p., cloth, coll. [Includes *The time machine, The invisible man, The war of the worlds*].

36708 *The time machine; The invisible man.* New York: A Signet Classic, New American Library, 1984, xxiii+278 p., paper, coll.

36709 *The time machine; The invisible man; The war of the worlds.* Franklin Center, PA: Franklin Library, 1982, 418 p., cloth, coll.

36710 *The time machine; The island of Dr Moreau; The first men in the Moon; The food of the gods; In the days of the comet; The war of the worlds.* London: Heinemann/Octopus Books, 1977, 828 p., cloth, coll.

36711 *The time machine, The; The island of Dr. Moreau; The invisible man; The first men on the Moon; The food of the gods; The war of the worlds.* New York: Octopus, 1982, 666 p., cloth, coll.

36712 *The war of the worlds; The invisible man; The time machine.* [S.l.]: Longmeadow Press, 1983, 283 p., cloth, coll.

36713 *Works of H. G. Wells: The wonderful visit; Kipps; The wife of Sir Isaac Harman; Love and Mr. Lewisham; plus 14 short stories, including The crystal egg, The star, In the abyss, and A dream of armageddon.* New York: Avenel Books, 1982, ix+726 p., cloth, coll.

with T. Ernesto Bethancourt

17919 *The time machine.* Belmont, CA: David S. Lake, A Fearon Classic, 1986, vi+74 p., paper, novel. [Adapted from Wells's novel].

with Simon Freeman

23491 *The country of the blind.* Cambridge, England: Cambridge University Press, 1977, 24 p., paper, story. [Adapted from Wells's novel].

with Henry James

26451 *Henry James and H. G. Wells: a record of their friendship, their debate on the art of fiction, and their quarrel.* Urbana, IL: University of Illinois Press, 1958, 272 p., cloth, nonf. coll. [Edited by Leon Edel and Gordon N. Ray].

with Michael Kerr [i.e., Robert Hoskins]

25979 *The island of Dr. Moreau.* New York, Toronto: Scholastic Book Services, 1978, 148 p., paper, novel. [Adapted from Wells's original novel].

with Les Martin

29139 *The time machine.* New York: Random House, 1990, 93 p., cloth, novel. [Adapted from Wells's original novel].

with Leon Stover

35109 *The prophetic soul: a reading of H. G. Wells' Things to come, together with his film treatment, Whither mankind?, and postproduction script (both never before*

published). Jefferson, NC: McFarland & Co., 1987, xix+301 p., cloth, nonf.

with Betty Ren Wright

36714 *The time machine.* Milwaukee, WI: Raintree Publishers, 1981, 47 p., cloth, novel. [Adapted from the novel by Wells].

WELLS, (Frank Charles) Robert, 1929-

36715 *The spacejacks.* New York: A Berkley Medallion Book, Berkley Publishing Corp., 1975, 186 p., paper, novel.

WELLS, Rosemary, 1943-

38149 *Through the hidden door.* New York: Dial Books for Young Readers, 1987, 264 p., cloth, novel.

WELLS, Stuart W. III

36716 *The science fiction and heroic fantasy author index.* Duluth, MN: Purple Unicorn Books, 1978, xxi+186 p., cloth, nonf.

WELLS SOCIETY—SEE: H. G. Wells Society

WELLS, William K.

36717 *Chaos.* New York: Tor, A Tom Doherty Associates Book, 1987, 373 p., paper, novel.

36718 *Effigies.* New York: A Dell Book, 1980, 442 p., paper, novel.

WELSH, Frank, 1931-

36719 *First blood: tales of horror from the border country.* London: Constable, 1985, 184 p., cloth, coll.

WELSH, Paul, 1953-

36720 *The spine chillers.* Ilfracombe, England: Arthur H. Stockwell, 1975, 68 p., cloth, nonf.

WELTY, Wayne V.

36721 *The evil place.* New York: Manor Books, 1979, 185 p., paper, novel.

WEMYSS, Courtney T(itus Jr.), 1922- , with Alexej Ugrinsky

35909   *George Orwell.*   New York, Westport, CT: Greenwood Press, 1987, viii+204 p., cloth, nonf. anth.

WENDELL, Carolyn (Joan), 1942-

36722   *Alfred Bester.*   Mercer Island, WA: Starmont House, 1982, 72 p., paper, nonf. STARMONT READER'S GUIDE #6.

WENDLAND, Albert (William), 1948-

36723   *Science, myth, and the fictional creation of alien worlds.*   Ann Arbor, MI: UMI Research Press, 1985, 200 p., cloth, nonf. STUDIES IN SPECULATIVE FICTION #12.

WENDORF, Patricia, 1928-

36724   *Blanche.*   London: Hamish Hamilton, 1986, 376 p., cloth, novel. PATTERAN TRILOGY #2.
36725   *Bye bye blackbird.*   London: Hamish Hamilton, 1987, 388 p., cloth, novel. PATTERAN TRILOGY #3.
36726   *Larksleve.*   London: Hamish Hamilton, 1985, 278 p., cloth, novel. PATTERAN TRILOGY #1.

WENK, Richard

36727   *Batman: The doomsday prophecy.*   New York: Pocket Books, 1986, 119 p., paper, novel. WHICH WAY BOOKS—SUPER POWERS #4; BATMAN SERIES.
       The doomsday prophecy—SEE: *Batman: The doomsday prophecy.*
36728   *The great baseball championship.*   New York, Toronto: Scholastic Inc., 1983, 59 p., paper, fiction. PICK-A-PATH #3.
36729   *Indiana Jones and the Eye of the Fates.*   New York: Ballantine Books, 1984, 122 p., paper, novel. FIND YOUR FATE ADVENTURE #4; INDIANA JONES SERIES.
36730   *Indiana Jones and the Legion of Death.*   New York: Ballantine Books, 1984, 120 p., paper, novel. FIND YOUR FATE ADVENTURE #6; INDIANA JONES SERIES.
38150   *The super trail bike race.*   New York, Toronto: Scholastic Inc., 1983, 58 p., paper, fiction. PICK-A-PATH #5.
36731   *Tales from the crypt, volume 3.*   New York: Random House, 1991, 96 p., paper, coll. [Adapted from the comic book of the same name].

*WENTZ, W(alter) J(ames), 1902?-1990?

WENZEL, David, 1950- , with Lin Carter

19596   *Middle Earth: the world of Tolkien illustrated.*   New York: Centaur Books, 1977, 64 p., paper, nonf.

WERLIN, Mark, with Marvin Werlin

36732   *The savior.*   New York: Simon & Schuster, 1978, 384 p., cloth, novel.
36732A   retitled: *The saviour.*   London: Severn House, 1979, 384 p., cloth, novel. *The saviour*—SEE: *The savior.*

WERLIN, Marvin, with Mark Werlin

36732   *The savior.*   New York: Simon & Schuster, 1978, 384 p., cloth, novel.
36732A   retitled: *The saviour.*   London: Severn House, 1979, 384 p., cloth, novel. *The saviour*—SEE: *The savior.*

WERNER, Eyvind—SEE: Johnson, Eyvind

WERNICK, Saul, 1921-1982

36733   *Blood tide.*   New York: A Dell Book, 1979, 443 p., paper, novel.
36734   *Cain's touch.*   New York: A Dell Book, 1978, 319 p., paper, novel.
36735   *The fire ants.*   New York: Award Books, 1976, 220 p., paper, novel.

*WERTHAM, Fredric, 1895-1981

WESCOTT, Earle, 1947-

36736   *Winter wolves.*   Dublin, NH: Yankee Publishing, 1988, 192 p., cloth, novel.

WESSEX, Martyn [pseud. of P. F. Little]

36737   *The chain reaction.*   London: Robert Hale, 1976, 189 p., cloth, novel.

WEST, Anthony (Panther), 1914-1987

36738   *H. G. Wells: aspects of a life.*   London: Hutchinson, 1984, 405 p., cloth, nonf.

WEST, Carl, with Katherine MacLean

28866   *Dark wing.*   New York: An Argo Book, Atheneum, 1979, 242 p., cloth, novel.

WEST, Chassie L.

36739   *Dead ringer.*   New York, Toronto: A Parachute Press Book, Scholastic Inc.,

1985, 126 p., paper, novel. MICRO ADVENTURE #9.

36740 *Million dollar gamble.* New York, Toronto: A Parachute Press Book, Scholastic Inc., 1984, 126 p., paper, novel. MICRO ADVENTURE #3.

WEST, Geoffrey—SEE: Wells, Geoffrey

WEST, Lindsay, pseud.—SEE: Weber, Nancy

*WEST, (Mary) Jessamyn, <u>1902-1984</u>

WEST, Owen, pseud.—SEE: Koontz, Dean R.

WEST, Pamela [i.e., Pamela Elizabeth West Katkin], 1945-

36741 *20/20 vision.* New York: A Del Rey Book, Ballantine Books, 1990, 228 p., paper, novel.

36742 *Yours truly, Jack the Ripper.* New York: A Joan Kahn Book, St. Martin's Press, 1987, 323 p., cloth, novel.

WEST, Paul (Noden), 1930-

36743 *The universe, and other fictions.* New York: Overlook Press, 1988, 187 p., cloth, coll.

*WEST, Rebecca [pseud. of Cecily Isobel Andrews], 1892-<u>1983</u>

WEST, Richard C(arroll), 1944-

36744 *Tolkien criticism: an annotated checklist, revised edition.* Kent, OH: Kent State University Press, 1981, xiv+177 p., cloth, nonf. SERIF SERIES: BIBLIOGRAPHIES AND CHECKLISTS #39.

WEST, Uta—SEE: Auden, Renée

*WEST, (George) Wallace, 1900-<u>1980</u>

WEST, Morris L(anglo), 1916-

38151 *The clowns of God: a novel.* New York: William Morrow & Co., 1981, 370 p., cloth, novel.

38152 *The navigator.* New York: William Morrow & Co., 1976, 407 p., cloth, novel.

WESTALL, Robert (Atkinson), 1929-

36745 *Antique dust: ghost stories.* London: Viking, 1989, 213 p., cloth, coll.

36746 *Blitzcat.* London: Macmillan Children's Books, 1989, 231 p., cloth, novel.

36747 *Break of dark.* London: Chatto & Windus, 1982, 182 p., cloth, coll.

36748 *The call, and other stories.* London, New York: Viking, 1989, 118 p., cloth, coll.

36749 *The cats of Seroster.* London: Macmillan Children's Books, 1984, 278 p., cloth, novel.

36750 *The creature in the dark.* London: Blackie Children's Books, 1988, [144] p., cloth, novel.

36751 *The devil on the road.* London: Macmillan, 1978, 247 p., cloth, novel.

36752 *Futuretrack 5.* Harmondsworth, Middlesex, England: Kestrel Books, 1983, 252 p., cloth, novel.

36753 *Ghost abbey.* London: Macmillan Children's Books, 1988, 172 p., cloth, novel.

36754 *Ghost stories.* London: Kingfisher, 1988, 253 p., cloth, anth.

36755 *Ghosts and journeys: short stories.* London: Macmillan Children's Books, 1988, 168 p., cloth, coll.

36756 *The haunting of Chas McGill, and other stories.* London: Macmillan, 1983, 155 p., cloth, coll.

36757 *Old man on a horse.* London: Hippo, 1989, 83 p., paper, story.

36758 *The promise.* London: Macmillan Children's Books, 1990, 169 p., cloth, novel.

36759 *Rachel and the angel, and other stories.* London: Macmillan, 1986, 192 p., cloth, coll.

36760 *The scarecrows.* London: Chatto & Windus, 1981, 159 p., cloth, novel.

36761 *The stones of Muncaster Cathedral: two stories of the supernatural.* London: Viking Children's Books, 1991, 156 p., cloth, coll.

36762 *Urn burial.* Harmondsworth, Middlesex, England: Viking Kestrel, 1987, 157 p., cloth, novel.

36763 *A walk on the wild side.* London: Methuen, 1989, 143 p., cloth, coll.

36764 *The watch house.* London: Macmillan, 1977, 228 p., cloth, novel.

36765 *The wind eye.* London: Macmillan, 1976, 212 p., cloth, novel.

36766 *Yaxley's cat.* London: Macmillan Children's Books, 1991, 137 p., cloth, novel.

WESTCOTT, C. T.

36767 *Blood and bone.* New York: A Dell Book, 1989, 249 p., paper, novel. EAGLEHEART #3.

36768 *Broadsides and brass: the autobiography of Colonel William T. Bucko, USFAC (ret.).* New York: A Dell Book, 1989, 240 p., paper, novel. EAGLEHEART #2.

36769 *Silver wings and leather jackets: the autobiography of Colonel William T. Bucko, USFAC (ret.)*. New York: A Dell Book, 1989, 227 p., paper, novel. EAGLE-HEART #1.

WESTERLY, Daniel [pseud. of Bairj Donabedian]

36770 *Devotion*. New York: Pocket Books, 1987, 279 p., paper, novel.

WESTERMAN, Percy F(rancis), 1876-1959

15877 *The rival submarines*. London: S. W. Partridge, 1913, 432 p., cloth, novel.

WESTLAKE, Abby, *with Donald E. Westlake*

36771 *Transylvania Station: a Mohonk mystery*. Miami Beach, FL: Dennis McMillen Publications, 1987, 125 p., cloth, novel.

WESTLAKE, Donald E(dwin Edmund), 1933-

36772 *Tomorrow's crimes*. New York: The Mysterious Press, 1989, 263 p., cloth, coll. [Includes *Anarchaos* (see #15169)].

with Abby Westlake

36771 *Transylvania Station: a Mohonk mystery*. Miami Beach, FL: Dennis McMillen Publications, 1987, 125 p., cloth, novel.

WESTLAKE, Michael, 1942-

38153 *One zero and the night controller*. London: Routledge & Kegan Paul, 1980, 222 p., cloth, novel.
36773 *The utopian*. London: Carcanet, 1989, 158 p., cloth, novel.

WESTON, Peter, 1944-

36774 *Andromeda 1: an original SF anthology*. London: Futura Publications, An Orbit Book, 1976, 206 p., paper, anth.
36775 *Andromeda 2: an original SF anthology*. London: Futura Publications, An Orbit Book, 1977, 202 p., paper, anth.
36776 *Andromeda 3: an original SF anthology*. London: Futura Publications, An Orbit Book, 1978, 240 p., paper, anth.

WESTON, Susan B(rown), 1943-

36777 *Children of the light*. New York: St. Martin's Press, 1985, 262 p., cloth, novel.

WESTWOOD, Chris

36778 *Calling all monsters*. London: Viking Kestrel, 1990, 192 p., cloth, novel.
36779 *Dark brigade*. London: Headline, 1991, 340 p., paper, novel.
He came from the shadows—SEE: *A light in the black*.
36780 *A light in the black*. London: Viking Kestrel, 1989, 207 p., paper, novel.
36780A retitled: *He came from the shadows*. New York: HarperCollinsPublishers, 1991, 215 p., cloth, novel.

WETANSON, Burt, *with Thomas Hoobler*

25896 *The hunters*. Garden City, NY: Doubleday & Co., 1978, vii+180 p., cloth, novel. HUNTERS #1.
25897 *The treasure hunters*. New York: Playboy Paperbacks, 1983, 248 p., paper, novel. HUNTERS #2.

*WETMORE, Claude H(azeltine), 1862-<u>1944</u>

WETZEL, George T., 1921-1983

38154 *Fragments imagae*. Dundalk, MD: George T. Wetzel, 1955, 22 p., paper, coll.
36781 *The gothic horror, and other weird tales*. Buffalo, NY: Weirdbook Press, 1978, 63 p., cloth, coll.

with R. Alain Everts

37746 *Winifred Virginia Jackson, Lovecraft's lost romance*. Madison, WI: The Strange Company, 1975?, 13 p., paper, nonf.

WEVERKA, Robert, 1926-

36782 *Circle of iron: a novel*. New York: Warner Books, 1979, 221 p., paper, movie.
36783 *Spectre*. Toronto, New York: Bantam Books, 1979, 154 p., paper, movie.

with Charles E. Sellier Jr.

33520 *The Boogens*. Toronto, New York: Bantam Books, 1981, 182 p., paper, movie.
33521 *Hangar 18*. Toronto, New York: Bantam Books, 1980, 166 p., paper, movie.

WEYMOUTH, Viscount—SEE: Thynn, Alexander

WEYN, Suzanne, 1955-

36784 *Into the dream.* New York: Fawcett Columbine, 1989, 123 p., paper, novel. SECRET OF THE UNICORN QUEEN #4.

WEYRICH, Becky Lee

36785 *Contents for sale.* New York: Manor Books, 1978, 223 p., paper, novel.
36786 *Through caverns infinite.* New York: Manor Books, 1978, 254 p., paper, novel.

WHALEN, (William) Patrick, 1944-

36787 *Monastery.* New York, London: Pocket Books, 1988, 346 p., paper, novel.
36788 *Night thirst.* New York, London: Pocket Books, 1991, 356 p., paper, novel.
36789 *Out of the night.* New York, London: Pocket Books, 1990, 310 p., paper, novel.

WHALEY, Barton—SEE: Barton, S. W.

WHAM, Tom

36790 *Prospero's island: a Crossroads adventure in the world of L. Sprague de Camp and Fletcher Pratt's The incomplete enchanter.* New York: Tor, A Tom Doherty Associates Book, 1987, 33+[214] p., paper, novel. HAROLD SHEA SERIES; CROSSROADS ADVENTURE.

with Rose Estes

22765 *Skryling's blade.* New York: Ace Books, 1990, 220 p., paper, novel. RUNESWORD #2.

WHARTON, William [pseud. of Albert Du Aimé], 1926-

36791 *Franky Furbo: a novel.* New York: An Owl Book, Henry Holt & Co., 1989, ix+228 p., cloth, novel.

WHATMORE, D(enys) E(dwin)

36792 *H. Rider Haggard: a bibliography.* London: Mansell Publishing Ltd., 1987, xix+187 p., cloth, nonf.

WHEATLEY, Dennis (Yeats), 1897-1977

36793 *The devil rides out; The haunting of Toby Jugg; Gateway to Hell; To the devil—a daughter.* London: Heinemann/Octopus, 1977, 864 p., cloth, coll.
38155 *The fabulous valley: a novel.* London: Hutchinson, 1934, 288 p., cloth, novel.

with Alison Sage

33021 *Dennis Wheatley's The devil rides out.* London: Hutchinson, 1987, 154 p., cloth, novel. [Adapted from the original].
The devil rides out—SEE: *Dennis Wheatley's The devil rides out.*

WHEELER, David

36794 *No, but I saw the movie.* Harmondsworth, Middlesex, England: Penguin Books, 1989, 411 p., paper, anth.

WHEELER, J(ohn) Craig, 1943-

36795 *The Krone experiment.* Dallas, TX: Pressworks, 1986, 412 p., cloth, novel.

WHEELER, Scott

36796 *Matters of form.* New York: DAW Books, 1987, 240 p., paper, novel.

*WHEELER-NICHOLSON, Malcolm, 1890-1968

WHELAN, Geraldine—SEE: Melling, O. R.

WHELAN, Michael (Raymond), 1950-

36797 *Michael Whelan's Works of wonder.* New York: A Del Rey Book, Ballantine Books, 1987, xiv+109 p., cloth, art. [Winner of the Hugo Award for Best Nonfiction Book, 1987 (1988)].
36798 *Wonderworks: science fiction and fantasy art.* Norfolk, VA: Donning Co., 1979, 119 p., cloth, art. [Edited by Kelly & Polly Freas].
Works of wonder—SEE: *Michael Whelan's Works of wonder.*

WHITAKER, Alexandra

36799 *Dream sister.* Boston: Houghton Mifflin Co., 1986, 156 p., cloth, novel.

*WHITAKER, David, 1930-1980

WHITBOURN, John

36800 *Binscombe tales.* Hoole, Chester, England: Haunted Library, Rosemary Pardoe 1989, 44 p., paper, coll.

36801 *Rollover night*. Hoole, Chester, England: Haunted Library, 1990, 36 p., paper, coll.

WHITBY, Sharon, pseud.—SEE: Darby, Catherine

WHITCOMB, Mary Burg

36802 *Tee-Bo the incredible talking dog leads the way in the great hort hunt*. Racine, WI: Golden Books, 1978 (or 1975?), 210 p., cloth, novel. TEE-BO SERIES.
36803 *Tee-Bo the incredible talking dog on the trail of the persnickety prowler*. Racine, WI: Golden Press, 1975, 138 p., cloth, novel.

WHITCOMBE, Rick T.—SEE: Quilty, Rafe

WHITE, Alan, 1924-

36804 *Black alert*. London: Grafton, 1985, 328 p., cloth, novel.

WHITE, Alicen

36805 *The watching eye*. New York: A Dell Book, 1977, 223 p., paper, novel.

WHITE, Anthony G(ene), 1946-

36806 *Science fiction and architecture: a selected bibliography*. Monticello, IL: Vance Bibliographies, 1979, 12 p., paper, nonf.

WHITE, (George) Ared, 1881-1941

38156 *Seven tickets to Singapore*. Boston: Houghton Mifflin Co., 1939, 255 p., cloth, novel.

WHITE, Edmund (Valentine III), 1940-

36807 *Caracole*. New York: E. P. Dutton, 1985, 342 p., cloth, novel.

WHITE, Ellen Emerson

36808 *The president's daughter*. New York: An Avon Flare Book, 1984, 247 p., paper, novel. PRESIDENT'S DAUGHTER #1.
38157 *White House autumn*. New York: An Avon Flare Book, 1985, 209 p., paper, novel. PRESIDENT'S DAUGHTER #2.

*WHITE, F(rederick) M(errick), 1859-

WHITE, Gill(ian Mary), 1936-

36809 *The plague stone*. London: Century, 1990, 222 p., cloth, novel.

WHITE, James, 1928-

36810 *Ambulance ship*. New York: A Del Rey Book, Ballantine Books, 1979, xvii+184 p., paper, novel. SECTOR GENERAL #4.
36811 *Code blue—emergency: (a Sector General novel)*. New York: A Del Rey Book, Ballantine Books, 1987, 280 p., paper, novel. SECTOR GENERAL #7.
36812 *Federation world*. New York: A Del Rey Book, Ballantine Books, 1988, 283 p., paper, novel.
36813 *Futures past*. New York: A Del Rey Book, Ballantine Books, 1982, 228 p., paper, coll.
36814 *Futures past*. London: Orbit, 1988, 228 p., paper, coll. [Drops one story from the original edition and adds another].
38158 *The interpreter*. Birmingham, England: Birmingham Science Fiction Group, 1985, 14 p., paper, story. [Bound with *A Novacon garland* / by David Langford].
36815 *Monsters and medics*. New York: A Del Rey Book, Ballantine Books, 1977, 266 p., paper, coll. [Includes *Second ending* (see #15239)].
36816 *Sector General*. New York: A Del Rey Book, Ballantine Books, 1983, 196 p., paper, coll. SECTOR GENERAL #5.
36817 *The silent stars go by*. New York: A Del Rey Book, Ballantine Books, 1991, 441 p., paper, novel.
36818 *Star healer*. New York: A Del Rey Book, Ballantine Books, 1985, 217 p., paper, novel. SECTOR GENERAL #6.
36819 *Underkill: a science fiction novel*. London: Corgi Books, 1979, 176 p., paper, novel.

WHITE, Jane [pseud. of Jane Brady], 1934-1985

36820 *Comet: a novel*. London: Hamilton, 1975, 222 p., cloth, novel.

WHITE, John, 1924-

36821 *Gaal the conqueror*. Downers Grove, IL: InterVarsity Press, 1989, 312 p., paper, novel. ARCHIVES OF ANTHROPOS #4.
36822 *The iron sceptre*. Downers Grove, IL: InterVarsity Press, 1981, 408 p., paper, novel. ARCHIVES OF ANTHROPOS #2.
36823 *The sword bearer*. Downers Grove, IL: InterVarsity Press, 1986, 294 p., paper, novel. ARCHIVES OF ANTHROPOS #3.
36824 *The tower of Geburah: a children's fantasy*. Downers Grove, IL: InterVarsity Press,

1978, 402 p., paper, novel. ARCHIVES OF ANTHROPOS #1.

WHITE, Jon (Ewbank) Manchip, 1924-

36825 *Death by dreaming.* Newton & Cambridge, MA: Apple-Wood Books, 1981, 134 p., cloth, novel.

36826 *Fevers and chills/three extravagant tales: Nightclimber; The game of Troy; The garden game.* Woodstock, New York: A Foul Play Press Book, The Countryman Press, 1983, 212 p., cloth, coll.

WHITE, Jude—SEE: Deveraux, Jude

WHITE, Mary Alice, 1920-

36827 *The land of the possible: a report of the first visit to Prire.* New York: Warner Books, 1979, 285 p., paper, novel.

WHITE, Matthew (Hagy), 1956- , with Jaffer Ali

16272 *The official Prisoner companion.* New York: Warner Books, 1988, ix+244 p., paper, nonf.

WHITE, Steve, with David Weber

36573 *Insurrection.* Riverdale, NY: Baen Books, 1990, 408 p., paper, novel.

WHITE, T(erence) H(anbury), 1906-1964

36828 *The book of Merlyn: the unpublished conclusion to The once and future king.* Austin, TX & London: University of Texas Press, 1977, xx+137 p., cloth, novel. ONCE & FUTURE KING #5.

15249 *Gone to ground: a novel.* London: Collins, 1935, 267 p., cloth, novel. [A set of linked tales].

15249A retitled: *The Maharajah, and other stories.* London: Macdonald & Co., 1981, 192 p., cloth, coll.

WHITE, Ted [i.e., Theodore Edward White], 1938-

with Dave Bischoff

18020 *Forbidden world: a science fiction novel.* New York: Popular Library, 1978, 224 p., paper, novel.

with Marv Wolfman

36829 *Phoenix: a novel.* New York: Pyramid Books, 1977, 216 p., paper, novel. WEIRD HEROES #5.

WHITE, Theodore E.—SEE: White, Ted

WHITE, Tim(othy Thomas Anthony), 1952-

36830 *Chiaroscuro.* Limpsfield, Surrey, England: Dragon's World, 1989, 144 p., paper, art.

36831 *The science fiction and fantasy world of Tim White.* London: New English Library, 1981, 143 p. cloth, art.

WHITE, William Luther, 1931-

36832 *The image of man in C. S. Lewis.* Nashville, TN: Abingdon Press, 1969, 239 p., cloth, nonf.

WHITEFORD, Wynne (Noel), 1915-

36833 *Breathing space only.* St. Kilda, Victoria, Australia: Void Publications, 1980, 150 p., cloth, novel.

36834 *The Hyades contact.* New York: Ace Books, 1987, 249 p., paper, novel.

36835 *Lake of the sun.* New York: Ace Books, 1989, 249 p., paper, novel.

36836 *Sapphire road.* St. Kilda, Victoria, Australia: Cory & Collins, 1982, 267 p., paper, novel.

36837 *The specialist.* New York: Ace Books, 1990, 246 p., paper, novel.

36838 *Thor's hammer.* St. Kilda, Victoria, Australia: Cory & Collins, 1983, 150 p., paper, novel.

WHITEHEAD, Elizabeth (Mathews), 1930-

38159 *Shadows end.* London: William Kimber, 1984, 191 p., cloth, novel.

WHITEHEAD, Henry S(t. Clair), 1882-1932

The black beast, and other uncanny tales—SEE: *Jumbee, and other uncanny tales.*

15271 *Jumbee, and other uncanny tales.* Sauk City, WI: Arkham House, 1944, 394 p., cloth, coll.

15271A retitled: *Jumbee, and other voodoo tales.* St Albans, England: Mayflower, 1976, 190 p., paper, coll. [The original book split into two volumes].

15271B retitled: *The black beast, and other uncanny tales.* St Albans, England: Mayflower, 1976, 189 p., paper, coll.

[The original book split into two volumes].

WHITEHEAD, Victoria, 1944-

36839 *Chimney witch chase.* London: Orchard Books, 1987, 126 p., cloth, novel. CHIMNEY WITCH #2.

38160 *Chimney witch Christmas.* London: Orchard Books, 1988, 128 p., cloth, novel. CHIMNEY WITCH #3.

36840 *The chimney witches.* London: Orchard Books, 1986, 143 p., cloth, novel. CHIMNEY WITCH #1.

38161 *The witches of Creaky-Cranky Castle.* London: Orchard Books, 1991, 160 p., cloth, novel. CHIMNEY WITCH #4.

WHITELAW, Stella, 1941- , *with Judy Gardiner & Mark Ronson*

23659 *Grimalkin's tales: strange and wonderful cat stories.* London: Hamlyn Paperbacks, 1983, 160 p., paper, anth.

WHITESON, Leon, 1930-

David Cronenberg's Scanners—SEE: *Scanners.*

36841 *Scanners.* New York: Tower Books, 1981, 204 p., paper, movie. SCANNERS #1.

36841A retitled: *David Cronenberg's Scanners: a novel.* London: Mayflower, 1981, 158 p., paper, movie. SCANNERS #1.

WHITMAN, Sarah Helen Power, 1803-1878

36842 *Poe's Helen remembers.* Charlottesville, VA: University Press of Virginia, 1979, 528 p., cloth, nonf. coll. [Edited by John Carl Miller].

WHITMORE, Andrew

36843 *The fortress of eternity.* New York: Avon Books, 1990, 251 p., paper, novel.

WHITMORE, Charles (Stanleigh), 1949-

36844 *Winter's daughter: the saying of Signe Ragnhilds-datter.* New York: Timescape Books, 1984, 220 p., cloth, novel.

WHITNEY, Phyllis A(yame), 1903-

36845 *Rainbow in the mist.* New York: Doubleday & Co., 1989, 310 p., cloth, novel.

WHITTEN, Les(lie Hunter Jr.), 1928-

36846 *The alchemist.* New York: Charter House, 1973, 368 p., cloth, novel.

*WHITTINGTON, Harry (Benjamin), 1915-1989

WHITTINGTON, Henry, *with Stephen Weeks*

36588 *Sword of the valiant: the legend of Sir Gawain and the Green Knight.* London: Robert Hale, 1984, 151 p., cloth, movie.

WHYTE, H. Walter

36847 *Deep freeze.* New York: Manor Books, 1977, 220 p., paper, novel.

WIATER, Stanley (Steven), 1953-

36848 *Dark dreamers: conversations with the masters of horror.* Novato, CA, Lancaster, PA: Underwood-Miller, 1990, 206 p., cloth, nonf. anth. [Limited to 350 copies; winner of the Bram Stoker Award for Best Horror Nonfiction Book, 1990 (1991)].

36849 *The official teenage mutant ninja turtles treasury.* New York: Villard Books, 1991, xx + 122 p., paper, nonf.

with Paul Mikol

29845 *Night visions 7: all original stories.* Arlington Heights, IL: Dark Harvest, 1989, 271 p., cloth, anth. [Introduction by Stanley Wiater].

WIBBERLEY, Leonard (Patrick O'Connor), 1915-1983

36850 *The crime of Martin Coverly.* New York: Farrar Straus Giroux, 1980, 167 p., cloth, novel.

36851 *Homeward to Ithaka.* New York: William Morrow, 1978, 192 p., cloth, novel.

The mouse that saved the West—SEE: *The true and secret history of how the world oil crisis was solved by the Duchy of Grand Fenwick; or, The Mouse that saved the West.*

36852 *One in four.* New York: William Morrow & Co., 1976, 250 p., cloth, novel.

36853 *The true and secret history of how the world oil crisis was solved by the Duchy of Grand Fenwick; or, The Mouse that saved the West.* New York: William Morrow, 1981, 187 p., cloth, novel. GRAND FENWICK #5.

WICKIZER, Mary A.—SEE: Burgess, Mary A.

WIDMER, Kingsley, 1925-

36854 *Counterings: utopian dialectics in contemporary contexts.* Ann Arbor, MI: UMI Research Press, 1988, viii+196 p., cloth, nonf. STUDIES IN SPECULATIVE FICTION #17.

WIETEN, Alida (Alberdina Ibbellina)

36855 *Mrs. Radcliffe: her relation towards romanticism: with an appendix on the novels falsely ascribed to her.* Amsterdam: H. J. Paris, 1926, 146 p., cloth, nonf.

WIGGINS, Marianne, 1947-

36856 *John Dollar.* New York: Harper & Row, 1989, 214 p., cloth, novel.

WIGGINS, Robert A(lonzo), 1921-

36857 *Ambrose Bierce.* Minneapolis, MN: University of Minnesota Press, 1964, 48 p., paper, nonf.

*WIGNALL, T(revor) C., 1883-1958

WIGNELL, Edel [i.e., Edna Wignell], 1936-

36858 *Escape by deluge.* Australia: Walter McVitty Books, 1989, [156] p., cloth, novel.

WIGNELL, Edna—SEE: Wignell, Edel

WILBER, Alix

36859 *The wives' tale.* New York: W. W. Norton & Co., 1991, 351 p., cloth, novel.

WILBER, Rick [i.e., Richard Arnold Wilber], 1948- , *with Richard Mathews*

29269 *Subtropical speculations: an anthology of Florida science fiction.* Sarasota, FL: Pineapple Press, 1991, 304 p., paper, anth.

WILBER, Richard A.—SEE: Wilber, Rick

*WILCOX, Don, 1908-

WILCOX, Robert K(alleen), 1943-

36860 *Fatal glimpse.* New York: Leisure Books, 1981, 239 p., paper, novel.
36861 *The centre of the wheel.* London: Robert Hale, 1980, 224 p., cloth, novel.

WILDE, Kelley

36862 *Makoto.* New York: Tor, A Tom Doherty Associates Book, 1990, x+406 p., cloth, novel.
36863 *Mastery.* New York: A Dell Book, 1991, 450 p., paper, novel.
36864 *The suiting.* New York: Tor, A Tom Doherty Associates Book, 1988, 245 p., cloth, novel. [Winner of the Bram Stoker Award for Best First Horror Novel, 1988 (1989)].

WILDE, Nicholas

36865 *Into the dark.* London: Collins, 1987, 172 p., cloth, novel.

WILDE, Oscar (Fingal O'Flahertie Wills), 1854-1900

36866 *Fairy tales and stories, including The happy prince, The selfish giant, and Lord Arthur Savile's crime.* London: Octopus, 1980, 335p, cloth, coll.
36867 *The picture of Dorian Gray, and other writings.* Toronto, New York: Bantam Books, 1982, xix+487 p., paper, coll.

with Donald L. Lawler

27928 *The picture of Dorian Gray: authoritative texts, backgrounds, revisions and reactions, criticism.* New York: W. W. Norton & Co., 1988, xiii+462 p., paper, nonf. anth. [Includes the text of Wilde's original novella].

WILDER, Cherry [pseud. of Cherry Barbara Lockett Anderson Grimm], 1930-

36868 *Cruel designs.* London: Piatkus, 1988, 304 p., cloth, novel.
36869 *The luck of Brin's Five.* New York: Atheneum, 1977, vii+230 p., cloth, novel. TORIN #1.
36870 *The nearest fire.* New York: An Argo Book, Atheneum, 1980, xi+226 p., cloth, novel. TORIN #2.
36871 *A princess of the Chameln.* New York: Atheneum, 1984, 275 p., cloth, novel. RULERS OF HYLOR #1.
36872 *Second nature.* New York: A Timescape Book, Pocket Books, 1982, 254 p., paper, novel.
36873 *The summer's king.* New York: Atheneum, 1986, 244 p., cloth, novel. RULERS OF HYLOR #3.

36874 *The tapestry warriors.* New York: An Argo Book, Atheneum, 1983, 264 p., cloth, novel. TORIN #3.

36875 *Yorath the wolf.* New York: An Argo Book, Atheneum, 1984, 178 p., cloth, novel. RULERS OF HYLOR #2.

WILDER, Myles, *with William Raynor*

32076 *Freeze.* New York: A Critic's Choice Paperback from Lorevan Publishing, 1988, 284 p., paper, novel.

WILDING, Michael, 1942-

36876 *Scenic drive.* Sydney, Australia: Wild & Woolley, 1976, 99 p., cloth, novel.

WILE, Edith B.

36877 *One way weekend.* Port Washington, NY: Ashley Books, 1989, 294 p., cloth, novel.

WILEY, Basil Leslie—SEE: Knight, Gareth

WILEY, Elizabeth

36878 *Concordance to the poetry of Edgar Allan Poe.* Selinsgrove, PA: Susquehanna University Press; London: Associated University Presses, 1989, 745 p., cloth, nonf.

WILHELM, Kate [i.e., Katie Gertrude Meredeth Wilhelm Knight], 1928-

36879 *Cambio Bay.* New York: St. Martin's Press, 1990, 294 p., cloth, novel.

36880 *Children of the wind: five novellas.* New York: St. Martin's Press, 1989, 263 p., cloth, coll.

36881 *Clarion SF.* New York: A Berkley Medallion Book, Berkley Publishing Corp., 1977, xi+176 p., paper, anth.

36882 *The Clewiston test.* New York: Farrar, Straus, Giroux, 1976, 244 p., cloth, novel.

36883 *Crazy time.* New York: St. Martin's Press, 1988, 248 p., cloth, novel.

36884 *The dark door.* New York: St. Martin's Press, 1988, 248 p., cloth, novel. MIKLEJOHN & LEIDL #2.

36885 *Death qualified: a mystery of chaos.* New York: St. Martin's Press, 1991, 438 p., cloth, novel

36886 *Fault lines: a novel.* New York, Hagerstown, NJ: Harper & Row, Publishers, 1977, 195 p., cloth, novel.

36887 *The girl who fell into the sky.* Eugene, OR: Pulphouse Publishing, 1991, 50 p., cloth, story. SHORT STORY HARDBACKS #5; SHORT STORY PAPERBACKS #9.

38162 *The Hamlet trap.* New York: St. Martin's Press, 1987, 234 p., cloth, novel. MIKLEJOHN & LEIDL #1.

36888 *Huysman's pets.* New York: Bluejay Books, 1986, 247 p., cloth, novel.

36889 *The infinity box.* New York: Tor SF, A Tom Doherty Associates Book, 1989, 76 p., paper, story. [Bound with *He who shapes* / by Roger Zelazny].

36890 *Infinity box: a collection of speculative fiction.* New York: Harper & Row, 1975, 318 p., cloth, coll.

36891 *Juniper time: a novel.* New York: Harper & Row, 1979, 280 p., cloth, novel.

36892 *Listen, listen.* Boston: Houghton Mifflin Co., 1981, 301 p., cloth, coll.

36893 *A sense of shadow.* Boston: Houghton Mifflin Co., 1981, 215 p., cloth, novel.

38163 *Smart house.* New York: St. Martin's Press, 1989, 266 p., cloth, novel. MIKLEJOHN & LEIDL #3.

36894 *Somerset dreams, and other fictions.* New York, Hagerstown, NJ: Harper & Row, Publishers, 1978, xiv+174 p., cloth, coll.

36895 *State of grace.* Eugene, OR: Pulphouse Publishing, 1991, 98 p., cloth, coll. AUTHOR'S CHOICE MONTHLY #16.

38164 *Sweet, sweet poison.* New York: St. Martin's Press, 1990, 262 p., cloth, novel. MIKLEJOHN & LEIDL #4.

36896 *Welcome, chaos.* Boston: Houghton Mifflin Co., 1983, 285 p., cloth, novel.

36897 *Where late the sweet birds sang.* New York: Harper & Row, 1976, 251 p., cloth, novel. [Winner of the Hugo Award for Best Novel, 1976 (1977); winner of the *Locus* Award for Best Novel, 1976 (1977)].

with Damon Knight

27411 *Better than one.* Boston: Noreascon II, 1980, xiv+76 p., cloth, coll. [Includes some nonfiction].

with Richard Wilhelm

36898 *The hills are dancing.* Minneapolis, MN: Corroboree Press, 1985, 97 p., cloth, nonf. [Some fiction fragments included].

WILHELM, Lambert, pseud.—SEE: Lambert, W. III

WILHELM, Richard, 1953- , *with Kate Wilhelm*

36898 *The hills are dancing.* Minneapolis, MN: Corroboree Press, 1985, 97 p., cloth, nonf. [Some fiction fragments included].

WILKES, Marilyn Z.

36899 *C.L.U.T.Z.* New York: Dial Press, 1982, 120 p., cloth, novel. C.L.U.T.Z. #1.
36900 *C.L.U.T.Z. and the fizzion formula.* New York: Dial Books for Young Readers, 1985, 136 p., cloth, novel. C.L.U.T.Z. #2.

WILKIE, Christine

36901 *Through the narrow gate: the mythological consciousness of Russell Hoban.* Rutherford, NJ: Fairleigh Dickinson University Press, 1989, 135 p., cloth, nonf.

WILKINS, Cary, 1954-

The Mammoth book of classic fantasy—SEE: *A treasury of fantasy.*
36902 *A treasury of fantasy: heroic adventures in imaginary lands.* New York: Avenel Books, 1981, viii+504 p., cloth, anth.
36902A retitled: *The mammoth book of classic fantasy: heroic adventures in imaginary lands.* London: Robinson Publishing, 1987, viii+472 p., paper, anth.

WILKINSON, Sandra

36903 *Brain death.* New York: Pinnacle Books, Windsor Publishing Corp., 1988, 396 p., paper, novel.

WILKINSON, Vernon (Francis), 1916-

36904 *After the bomb: flight to utopia.* Auckland, New Zealand: Interface Press, 1984, vi+145 p., paper, novel.

*WILLARD, Mildred Wilds, 1911-<u>1978</u>

WILLARD, Nancy, 1936-

36905 *Firebrat.* New York: A Lucas/Evans Book, Alfred A. Knopf, 1988, 120 p., cloth, novel.
36906 *The island of the grass king: the further adventures of Anatole.* New York: Harcourt Brace Jovanovich, 1979, 120 p., cloth, novel. ANATOLE #2.
36907 *Sailing to Cythera, and other Anatole stories.* New York: Harcourt Brace Jovano-

vich, 1974, 74 p., cloth, coll. ANATOLE #1.
36908 *Things invisible to see.* New York: Alfred A. Knopf, 1984, 263 p., cloth, novel.
36909 *Uncle Terrible: more adventures of Anatole.* New York: Harcourt Brace Jovanovich, 1982, 120 p., cloth, novel. ANATOLE #3.

WILLARD, Tom

Blood river—SEE: *Strike fighters: Blood river.*
Bold forager—SEE: *Strike fighters: Bold forager.*
Desert star—SEE: *Strike fighters: Desert star.*
Red dancer—SEE: *Strike fighters: Red dancer.*
36910 *Strike fighters.* New York: HarperPaperbacks, 1990, 262 p., paper, novel. STRIKE FIGHTERS #1.
36911 *Strike fighters: Blood river.* New York: HarperPaperbacks, 1991, 261 p., paper, novel. STRIKE FIGHTERS #7.
36912 *Strike fighters: Bold forager.* New York: HarperPaperbacks, 1990, 259 p., paper, novel. STRIKE FIGHTERS #2.
36913 *Strike fighters: Desert star.* New York: HarperPaperbacks, 1991, 265 p., paper, novel. STRIKE FIGHTERS #6.
36914 *Strike fighters: Red dancer.* New York: HarperPaperbacks, 1991, 257 p., paper, novel. STRIKE FIGHTERS #5.
36915 *Strike fighters: Sudden fury.* New York: HarperPaperbacks, 1991, 262 p., paper, novel. STRIKE FIGHTERS #4.
36916 *Strike fighters: War chariot.* New York: HarperPaperbacks, 1990, 259 p., paper, novel. STRIKE FIGHTERS #3.
Sudden fury—SEE: *Strike fighters: Sudden fury.*
War chariot—SEE: *Strike fighters: War chariot.*

as BILL DOLAN

36917 *Akrikorps.* New York: HarperPaperbacks, 1991, 249 p., paper, novel. AFRIKORPS #1.
36918 *Akrikorps: Iron horse.* New York: HarperPaperbacks, 1991, 245 p., paper, novel. AFRIKORPS #2.
Iron horse—SEE: *Akrikorps: Iron horse.*

*WILLEFORD, Charles (Ray III), 1919-<u>1988</u>

WILLETT, John (William Mills), 1932-

36919 *Aubade for Gamelon.* New York: A Baen Book, 1984, 343 p., paper, novel.
36920 *The singer in the stone.* Boston: Houghton Mifflin Co., 1981, 86 p., cloth, novel.

WILLIAM MORRIS SOCIETY

36913 *The work of William Morris: an exhibition arranged by the William Morris Society.* London: William Morris Society, 1975, 62 p., paper, nonf.

WILLIAM, Barry, *with Marc Reiss*

32183 *The adversary.* New York: Charter Books, 1979, 298 p., paper, novel.

WILLIAMS, Arthur J.

36914 *A fast ride to hell.* New York, Washington: Vantage Press, 1990, 51 p., cloth, story.

WILLIAMS, Bronwyn, pseud.—SEE: Browning, Dixie & Williams, Mary

WILLIAMS, Charles M.

36915 *New avenues in science fiction.* New York: A Geneva Book, Carlton Press, 1984, 31 p., cloth, nonf.?

WILLIAMS, Christopher Hodder- —SEE: Hodder-Williams, Christopher

WILLIAMS, David (L.), 1939-

36916 *Second sight: a novel.* New York: Simon & Schuster, 1977, 221 p., cloth, novel.

WILLIAMS, Di, *with Norma Brown & Jane Broughton*

18772 *Herzone: fantasy short stories by women.* Manchester, England: Crocus, 1991, 103 p., paper, anth.

WILLIAMS, Eric C(yril), 1918-

36917 *The drop in.* Morley, Yorkshire, England: Elmfield Press, 1977, 166 p., cloth, novel.
36918 *Homo telekins.* London: Robert Hale, 1981, 208 p., cloth, novel.
36919 *Largesse from Triangulum.* London: Robert Hale, 1979, 190 p., cloth, novel.
36920 *Time for mercy.* London: Robert Hale, 1979, 159 p., cloth, novel.

WILLIAMS, Gordon (Maclean), 1939-

36921 *The microcolony.* Toronto, New York: Bantam Books, 1979, 248 p., paper, novel. MICRONAUTS #2.
36921A retitled: *Micronaut world.* London: New English Library, 1981, 221 p., paper, novel. MICRONAUTS #2.
  Micronaut world—SEE: *The microcolony.*
36922 *The micronauts.* Toronto, New York: Bantam Books, 1977, 282 p., paper, novel. MICRONAUTS #1.
36923 *Revolt of the micronauts.* Toronto, New York: Bantam Books, 1981, x+170 p., paper, novel. MICRONAUTS #3.

WILLIAMS, Graham

36924 *Doctor Who: The nightmare fair.* London: A Target Book, W. H. Allen & Co., 1989, 143 p., paper, tele. DOCTOR WHO SERIES.
  The nightmare fair—SEE: *Doctor Who: The nightmare fair.*

WILLIAMS, Ian

36925 *The lies that bind.* London: Purnell, Macdonald & Co., 1989, 254 p., cloth?, novel.

WILLIAMS, Jay, 1914-1978

36925 *The magic grandfather.* New York: Four Winds Press, 1979, 149 p., cloth, novel.
36926 *The time of the Kraken.* New York: Four Winds Press, 1977, 168 p., cloth, novel.
36927 *Unearthly beasts, and other strange people.* London: Macmillan, 1979, 110 p., cloth, coll.

with Raymond Abrashkin

15924 *Danny Dunn and the universal glue.* New York: McGraw-Hill Book Co., 1977, 160 p., cloth, novel. DANNY DUNN #15. [The final book in the series].
15925 *Danny Dunn, scientific detective.* New York: McGraw-Hill Book Co., 1975, 172 p., cloth, novel. DANNY DUNN #14.
  Scientific detective—SEE: *Danny Dunn: Scientific detective.*

WILLIAMS, (Dorothy) Jeanne, 1930-

36928 *The cave dreamers.* New York: Avon, 1983, 576 p., paper, novel.
36929 *The Heaven Sword.* New York: Avon, 1985, 448 p., paper, novel.

WILLIAMS, John A(lfred), 1925-

36930 *Captain Blackman: a novel.* Garden City, NY: Doubleday & Co., 1972, 336 p., cloth, novel.

WILLIAMS, Kit, 1946?-

36931 *Kit Williams.* New York: Alfred A. Knopf, 1984, [32] p., cloth, fiction.
36932 *Masquerade.* London: Jonathan Cape, 1979, [31] p., cloth, fiction.
36933 *Masquerade: the complete book with the answer explained.* London: Jonathan Cape, 1982, [46] p., cloth, fiction. [Expanded edition].
36934 *Out of one eye.* London: Jonathan Cape, 1986, 112 p., cloth, art.

WILLIAMS, Mary, 1925?-

36935 *Chill company: ghost stories from Cornwall.* London: William Kimber, 1976, 192 p., cloth, coll.
36936 *The dark god: a novel of the occult, and other supernatural stories.* London: William Kimber, 1979, 192 p., cloth, coll.
36937 *The dark land: a book of Cornish ghost stories.* London: William Kimber, 1975, 223 p., cloth, coll.
36938 *Ghostly carnival: Cornish ghost stories.* London: William Kimber, 1980, 175 p., cloth, coll.
36939 *The haunted garden: ghost stories.* London: William Kimber, 1986, 174 p., cloth, coll.
36940 *The haunted valley, and other ghost stories.* London: William Kimber, 1978, 192 p., cloth, coll.
36941 *Haunted waters.* London: William Kimber, 1987, 190 p., cloth, coll.
36942 *Ravenscarne, and other ghost stories.* London: Piatkus, 1991, 195 p., cloth, coll.
36943 *They walk at twilight: stories of ghosts and the occult.* London: William Kimber, 1977, 192 p., cloth, coll.
36944 *Unseen footsteps: ghost stories.* London: William Kimber, 1977, 190 p., cloth, coll.
36945 *Where no birds sing: stories of the macabre.* London: William Kimber, 1978, 191 p., cloth, coll.
36946 *Where phantoms stir: ghost stories.* London: William Kimber, 1976, 192 p., cloth, coll.
36947 *Whisper in the night: ghost stories.* London: William Kimber, 1979, 189 p., cloth, coll.

with Dixie Browning as BRONWYN WILIAMS

18817 *White witch.* Toronto, New York: Harlequin Books, 1988, 301 p., paper, novel.

WILLIAMS, Michael (Leon), 1952-

36948 *A forest lord.* New York: Warner Books, 1991, 291 p., paper, novel. FROM THIEF TO KING #2.
36949 *Galen beknighted.* Lake Geneva, WI: TSR Inc., 1990, 317 p., paper, novel. DRAGONLANCE HEROES II #3.
36950 *A sorcerer's apprentice.* New York: Popular Library, 1990, 280 p., paper, novel. FROM THIEF TO KING #1.
36951 *Weasel's luck.* Lake Geneva, WI: TSR Inc., 1988, 347 p., paper, novel. DRAGONLANCE HEROES #3.

with Gali Sanchez

33120 *Vampires: Chill module.* Cleveland, OH: Pacesetter, 1985, 64 p., paper, fiction. [Based on the *Chill* game].

WILLIAMS, Michael Lindsay, 1940-

36952 *FTL: further than life.* New York: Avon, 1987, 327 p., paper, novel. MARTIAN #2.
36953 *Martian spring.* New York: Avon, 1986, 277 p., paper, novel. MARTIAN #1.

WILLIAMS, Mona (Goodwyn), 1916-

36954 *The messenger.* New York: Rawson Associates Publishers, 1977, 301 p., cloth, novel.
36955 *This house is burning.* New York: Rawson Associates Publishers, 1978, 262 p., cloth, novel.

*WILLIAMS, Nick (Van) Boddie (Sr.), 1906-1992

WILLIAMS, Nigel, 1948-

36956 *Black magic.* London: Hutchinson, 1988, 117 p., cloth, novel.

WILLIAMS, Paul (Steven), 1948- , with Philip K. Dick

21743 *Only apparently real.* New York: Arbor House, 1986, viii+184 p., paper, nonf.

WILLIAMS, Paul O(sborne), 1935-

36957 *An ambush of shadows.* New York: A Del Rey Book, Ballantine Books, 1983, 248 p., paper, novel. PELBAR CYCLE #5.

36958 *The breaking of Northwall.* New York: A Del Rey Book, Ballantine Books, 1981, 280 p., paper, novel. PELBAR CYCLE #1.

36959 *The dome in the forest.* New York: A Del Rey Book, Ballantine Books, 1981, 214 p., paper, novel. PELBAR CYCLE #3.

36960 *The ends of the circle.* New York: A Del Rey Book, Ballantine Books, 1981, 203 p., paper, novel. PELBAR CYCLE #2.

36961 *The fall of the shell.* New York: A Del Rey Book, Ballantine Books, 1982, 214 p., paper, novel. PELBAR CYCLE #4.

36962 *Gifts of the Gordobuc vandal.* New York: A Del Rey Book, Ballantine Books, 1989, 210 p., paper, novel.

36963 *The song of the axe.* New York: A Del Rey Book, Ballantine Books, 1984, 248 p., paper, novel. PELBAR CYCLE #6.

36964 *The sword of forbearance.* New York: A Del Rey Book, Ballantine Books, 1985, 245 p., paper, novel. PELBAR CYCLE #7.

WILLIAMS, Raymond (Henry), 1921-1988

38165 *The fight for Manod.* London: Chatto & Windus, 1979, 207 p., cloth, novel.

36965 *George Orwell.* New York: Viking Press, 1971, 102 p., cloth, nonf.

36966 *George Orwell: a collection of critical essays.* Englewood Cliffs, NJ: Prentice-Hall, 1974, viii+182 p., cloth, nonf. anth.

36967 *The volunteers.* London: Eyre Methuen, 1978, 208 p., cloth, novel.

WILLIAMS, Robert P.—SEE: Williams, Tad

WILLIAMS, Roger, 1947-

36969 *Aftermath.* London: A Star Book, W. H. Allen, 1982, 185 p., paper, novel.

WILLIAMS, Russ

36970 *The night hunter.* Far Hills, NJ: New Horizon Press, 1990, 448 p., paper, novel.

WILLIAMS, Sheila

with Charles Ardai

16763 *Why I left Harry's All-Night Hamburgers, and other stories from Isaac Asimov's Science Fiction Magazine.* New York: Delacorte Press, 1990, ix+285 p., cloth, anth.

with Gardner Dozois

22135 *Isaac Asimov's Robots.* New York: Ace Books, 1991, xiv+209 p., paper, anth.
Robots—SEE: *Isaac Asimov's Robots.*

with Cynthia Manson

29036 *Tales from Isaac Asimov's science fiction magazine: short stories for young adults.* San Diego, CA: Harcourt Brace Jovanovich, 1986, ix+298 p., cloth, anth.

WILLIAMS, Sidney

36971 *Azarius.* New York: Pinnacle Books, Windsor Publishing Corp., 1989, 446 p., paper, novel.

36972 *Blood hunter.* New York: Pinnacle Books, Windsor Publishing Corp., 1990, 317 p., paper, novel.

36973 *Gnelfs.* New York: Pinnacle Books, Windsor Publishing Corp., 1991, 352 p., paper, novel.

36974 *Night brothers.* New York: Pinnacle Books, Windsor Publishing Corp., 1989, 448 p., paper, novel.

WILLIAMS, Steve, with Paul Mason

Black vein prophecy—SEE: *Steve Jackson and Ian Livingstone present Black vein prophecy.*

29197 *The riddling reaver.* Harmondsworth, Middlesex, England: Puffin Books, 1986, 234 p., paper, novel. FIGHTING FANTASY GAMEBOOK.

Slaves of the abyss—SEE: *Steve Jackson and Ian Livingstone present Slaves of the abyss.*

29198 *Steve Jackson and Ian Livingstone present Black vein prophecy.* Harmondsworth, Middlesex, England: Puffin Books, 1990, [200] p., paper, fiction. FIGHTING FANTASY GAMEBOOK #42.

29199 *Steve Jackson and Ian Livingstone present Slaves of the abyss.* Harmondsworth, Middlesex, England: Puffin Books, 1988, 21+[200] p., paper, fiction. FIGHTING FANTASY GAMEBOOK.

WILLIAMS, Tad [i.e., Robert Paul Williams], 1957-

36975 *The dragonbone chair.* New York: DAW Books, 1988, 654 p., cloth, novel. MEMORY, SORROW & THORN #1.

36976 *Stone of farewell.* New York: DAW Books, 1990, xvii+589 p., cloth, novel. MEMORY, SORROW & THORN #2.

36977 *Tailchaser's song.* New York: DAW Books, 1985, xv+333 p., cloth, novel.

*WILLIAMS, Tennessee [i.e., Thomas Lanier Williams], <u>1911-1983</u>

WILLIAMS, Thomas (Alonzo), 1926-1990

36978 *Tsuga's children.* New York: Random House, 1977, 239 p., cloth, novel.

WILLIAMS, Thomas L.—SEE: Williams, Tennessee

WILLIAMS, Ursula Moray, 1911-

15878 *The Line.* Harmondsworth, Middlesex, England: Puffin Books, 1974, 127 p., paper, coll.

15879 *Malkin's mountain.* London: George G. Harrap, 1948, 140 p., cloth, novel. RUDI #2.

15880 *The three toymakers.* London: George G. Harrap, 1945, 142 p., cloth, novel. RUDI #1.

WILLIAMS, Victoria (Ann Vilchez), 1955-

36979 *Future love: a science fiction anthology.* Basingstoke, England: Topliners, Macmillan, 1977, 125 p., paper, anth.

WILLIAMS, Walter Jon, 1953-

36980 *Ambassador of progress.* New York: Tor, A Tom Doherty Associates Book, 1984, 432 p., paper, novel.

36981 *Angel Station.* New York: Tor, A Tom Doherty Associates Book, 1989, 393 p., cloth, novel.

36982 *The crown jewels.* New York: Tor SF, A Tom Doherty Associates Book, 1987, 247 p., paper, novel. CROWN JEWELS #1.

36983 *Days of atonement.* New York: Tor, A Tom Doherty Associates Book, 1991, 437 p., cloth, novel.

36984 *Dinosaurs.* Eugene, OR: Pulphouse Publishing, 1991, 44 p., cloth, story. SHORT STORY HARDBACKS #12; SHORT STORY PAPERBACKS #18.

36985 *Elegy for angels and dogs.* New York: Tor SF, A Tom Doherty Associates Book, 1990, p. 63-187, paper, story. [Bound with *Graveyard heart* / by Roger Zelazny].

36986 *Facets.* New York: Tor, A Tom Doherty Associates Book, 1990, xi+321 p., cloth, coll.

36987 *Hardwired.* New York: Tor, A Tom Doherty Associates Book, 1986, 343 p., cloth, novel. HARDWIRED #1.

36988 *Hardwired: the sourcebook.* Berkeley, CA: R. Talsorian Games, 1989, 94 p., paper?, fiction.

36989 *House of shards.* New York: Tor SF, A Tom Doherty Associates Book, 1988, 309 p., paper, novel. CROWN JEWELS #2.

36990 *Knight moves.* New York: Tor, A Tom Doherty Associates Book, 1985, 317 p., paper, novel.

36991 *Solip:system.* Eugene, OR: Axolotl Press, Pulphouse Publishing, 1989, 71 p., cloth, story. HARDWIRED #3; AXOLOTL PRESS #11.

36992 *Voice of the whirlwind.* New York: Tor, A Tom Doherty Associates Book, 1987, 278 p., cloth, novel. HARDWIRED #2.

WILLIAMS-ELLIS, (Mary) Amabel (Nassau Strachey, Lady), 1894-1984, *with Michael Pearson*

31346 *Strange orbits: an anthology of science fiction.* Glasgow, Scotland: Blackie & Son, 1976, 190 p., cloth, anth.

31347 *Strange planets: an anthology of science fiction.* Glasgow, Scotland, London: Blackie & Son, 1977, 176 p., cloth, anth.

WILLIAMSON, Chester C.—SEE: Williamson, Chet

WILLIAMSON, Chet [i.e., Chester Carlton Williamson], 1948-

36993 *Ash Wednesday.* New York: Tor Horror, A Tom Doherty Associates Book, 1987, 372 p., cloth, novel.

36994 *Dreamthorp: a new novel.* Arlington Heights, IL: Dark Harvest, 1989, 325 p., cloth, novel.

36995 *The house of fear: a study in comparative religions.* Round Top, NY: Footsteps Press, 1989, 23 p., paper, story. [Limited to 500 copies].

36996 *Lowland rider.* New York: Tor Horror, A Tom Doherty Associates Book, 1988, 342 p., paper, novel.

36997 *Reign.* Arlington Heights, IL: Dark Harvest, 1990, 348 p., cloth, novel.

36998 *Soulstorm.* New York: Tor Horror, A Tom Doherty Associates Book, 1986, 311 p., paper, novel.

WILLIAMSON, Duncan, 1928-

36999   *The broonie, silkies, & fairies: travellers' tales.* Edinburgh, Scotland: Canongate, 1985, 157 p., cloth, coll.

WILLIAMSON, Gerald N.—SEE: Williamson, J. N.

WILLIAMSON, J. N. [i.e., Gerald Neal "Jerry" Williamson], 1932-

37000   *Babel's children.* New York: A Dell/ Emerald Book, 1984, 284 p., paper, novel.

37001   *The banished.* New York: Playboy Paperbacks, 1981, 255 p., paper, novel.

37002   *The best of masques.* New York: Berkley Books, 1988, xi+288 p., paper, anth.

37003   *The black school.* New York: A Dell Book, 1989, 273 p., paper, novel.

37004   *Brotherkind.* New York: Leisure Books, 1982, 286 p., paper, novel.

37005   *Dead to the world.* New York: Leisure Books, 1988, 366 p., paper, novel.

37006   *Death-angel.* New York: Zebra Books, Kensington Publishing Corp., 1981, 303 p., paper, novel. LAMIA ZACHARIUS #2.

37007   *Death-coach.* New York: Zebra Books, Kensington Publishing Corp., 1981, 318 p., paper, novel. LAMIA ZACHARIUS #1.

37008   *Death-doctor.* New York: Zebra Books, Kensington Publishing Corp., 1982, 272 p., paper, novel. LAMIA ZACHARIUS #4.

37009   *Death-school.* New York: Zebra Books, Kensington Publishing Corp., 1982, 302 p., paper, novel. LAMIA ZACHARIUS #3.

37010   *The dentist.* New York: A Dell/Emerald Book, 1983, 254 p., paper, novel.

37011   *Evil offspring.* New York: Leisure Books, 1987, 394 p., paper, novel.

37012   *The evil one.* New York: Zebra Books, Kensington Publishing Corp., 1982, 333 p., paper, novel.

    Flesh creepers—SEE: *Masques III.*

37013   *Ghost.* New York: Leisure Books, 1984, 283 p., paper, novel.

37014   *Ghost mansion.* New York: Zebra Books, Kensington Publishing Corp., 1981, 350 p., paper, novel. MINNIFIELD #1.

37015   *Hell storm.* New York: A Dell Book, 1991, 269 p., paper, novel.

37016   *Horror house.* New York: Playboy Paperbacks, 1981, 299 p., paper, novel.

37017   *Horror mansion.* New York: Zebra Books, Kensington Publishing Corp., 1982, 300 p., paper, novel. MIN-NIFIELD #2.

37018   *The Houngan.* New York: Leisure Books, 1980, 304 p., paper, novel.

37018A retitled: *Profits.* New York: Leisure Books, 1984, 304 p., paper, novel.

37019   *How to write tales of horror, fantasy & science fiction.* Cincinnati, OH: Writer's Digest Books, 1987, 242 p., cloth, nonf. anth.

37020   *The longest night.* New York: Leisure Books, 1985, 367 p., paper, novel.

37021   *Masques: all new works of horror and the supernatural.* Baltimore, MD: Maclay & Associates, 1984, 306 p., cloth, anth.

37022   *Masques II: all-new stories of horror and the supernatural.* Baltimore, MD: Maclay & Associates, 1987, 221 p., cloth, anth.

37023   *Masques two.* London: Severn House, 1989, 221 p., cloth, anth.

37024   *Masques III: all-new works of horror and the supernatural.* New York: St. Martin's Press, 1989, xv+317 p., cloth, anth.

37024A retitled: *Flesh creepers.* London: Robson, 1990, 317 p., cloth, anth.

37025   *Masques IV: all-new works of horror & the supernatural.* Baltimore, MD: Maclay and Associates, 1991, 246 p., cloth, anth.

    Masques two—SEE: *Masques II.*

37026   *The naked flesh of feeling.* Eugene, OR: Pulphouse Publishing, 1991, 107 p., cloth, coll. AUTHOR'S CHOICE MONTHLY #24.

37027   *The new devil's dictionary: creepy clichés and sinister synonyms.* Buffalo, NY: W. Paul Ganley, 1985, 57 p., cloth, nonf. coll.

37028   *The night seasons.* New York: Zebra Books, Kensington Publishing Corp., 1991, 398 p., paper, novel.

37029   *Noonspell.* New York: Leisure Books, 1987, 368 p., paper, novel.

37030   *The offspring.* New York: Leisure Books, 1984, 304 p., paper, novel.

37031   *Playmates.* New York: Leisure Books, 1982, 303 p., paper, novel.

37032   *Premonition.* New York: Leisure Books, 1981, 287 p., paper, novel.

    Profits—SEE: *The Houngan.*

37033   *Queen of Hell.* New York: Leisure Books, 1981, 285 p., paper, novel.

37034   *The ritual.* New York: Leisure Books, 1979, 318 p., paper, novel.

37035   *Shadows of death.* New York: A Dell Book, 1989, 278 p., paper, novel.

37036   *The Tulpa.* New York: Leisure Books, 1981, 238 p., paper, novel.

as JULIAN SHOCK

37037 *Extraterrestrial.* New York: Zebra Books, Kensington Publishing Corp., 1982, 302 p., paper, novel.

with John Maclay

28863 *Wards of armageddon.* New York: Leisure Books, 1986, 400 p., paper, novel.

WILLIAMSON, Jack [i.e., John Stewart Williamson], 1908-

37038 *The alien intelligence.* New Orleans, LA: P.D.A. Enterprises, 1980, 79 p., paper, coll.

37039 *The best of Jack Williamson.* New York: A Del Rey Book, Ballantine Books, 1978, xiv+386 p., paper, coll.

37040 *Brother to demons, brother to gods.* Indianapolis & New York: Bobbs-Merrill Co., 1979, 228 p., cloth, novel.

37041 *But not warriors: a novel.* New York: Lynx Books, 1989, 229 p., cloth, novel.

37042 *Dreadful sleep.* Chicago: Robert Weinberg, 1977, 80 p., paper, novel. LOST FANTASIES #7.

37043 *The early Williamson.* Garden City, NY: Doubleday & Co., 1975, xvi+199 p., cloth, coll.

37044 *Firechild.* New York: Bluejay Books, 1986, 377 p., cloth, novel.

37045 *The humanoid touch.* Huntington Woods, MI: Phantasia Press, 1980, 210 p., cloth, novel. HUMANOIDS #2. [Limited to 500 copies].

37046 *The humanoids.* Garden City, NY: Nelson Doubleday, 1980, 245 p., cloth, coll. HUMANOIDS #1. [Expanded edition; includes original story].

37047 *Into the eighth decade.* Eugene, OR: Pulphouse Publishing, 1990, 118 p., cloth, coll. AUTHOR'S CHOICE MONTHLY #5.

37048 *Lifeburst.* New York: A Del Rey Book, Ballantine Books, 1984, xvi+271 p., cloth, novel.

37049 *Manseed.* New York: A Del Rey Book, Ballantine Books, 1982, 217 p., cloth, novel.

37050 *Mazeway.* Norwalk, CT: Easton Press, 1990, 290 p., cloth, novel.

37051 *The power of blackness.* New York: Berkley Publishing Corp., 1976, 183 p., cloth, novel.

37052 *The queen of the Legion.* New York: A Timescape Book, Pocket Books, 1983, 260 p., paper, novel. LEGION OF SPACE #4.

15449 *Seetee ship/Seetee shock.* New York: Lancer, 1972, 445 p., paper, coll. SEETEE #1-2.

15449A retitled: *Seetee.* New York: A Jove Book, 1979, 448 p., paper, coll. SEETEE #1-2.
Seetee—SEE: *Seetee ship/Seetee shock.*

37053 *Teaching science fiction: education for tomorrow.* Philadelphia: Owlswick Press, 1980, vii+261 p., cloth, nonf.

37054 *Teaching SF, 3rd ed.* Portales, NM: Jack Williamson, 1975, 69 p., paper, nonf.

37055 *Three from the Legion.* Garden City, NY: Nelson Doubleday, 1979, 536 p., cloth, coll. LEGION OF SPACE #1-3.

37056 *Wonder's child: my life in science fiction.* New York: Bluejay Books, 1984, x+276 p., cloth, nonf. [Winner of the Hugo Award for Best Nonfiction Book, 1984 (1985)].

with M. J. Breuer

18619 *The birth of a new republic.* New Orleans, LA: P.D.A. Enterprises, 1981, 80 p., paper, story.

with Frederik Pohl

31712 *Farthest star: the saga of Cuckoo.* New York: Ballantine Books, 1975, 246 p., paper, novel. SAGA OF CUCKOO #1.

31713 *Land's end.* New York: Tor, A Tom Doherty Associates Book, 1988, 370 p., cloth, novel.

31714 *The saga of Cuckoo.* Garden City, NY: Nelson Doubleday, 1983, 434 p., cloth, coll. SAGA OF CUCKOO #1-2. [Includes *Farthest star* and *Wall around a star*].

31715 *The singers of time.* New York: A Foundation Book, Doubleday, 1991, 358 p., cloth, novel.

31716 *The starchild trilogy: The reefs of space; Starchild; Rogue star.* Garden City, NY: Nelson Doubleday, 1977, 436 p., cloth, coll. STARCHILD TRILOGY #1-3.

31717 *Wall around a star: the saga of Cuckoo.* New York: A Del Rey Book, Ballantine Books, 1983, 275 p., paper, novel. SAGA OF CUCKOO #2.

WILLIAMSON, John S.—SEE: Williamson, Jack

WILLIAMSON, Philip G.

37057 *Dinbig of Khimmur.* London: Grafton, 1991, 375 p., cloth, novel. FIRSTWORLD CHRONICLES #1.

WILLIAMSON, Roger

37058   *The sun at night: a novel.*   Minneapolis, MN: Vann Press, 1989, v+124 p., paper, novel.

WILLINGHAM, Calder (Baynard) Jr., 1922-

38166   *The building of Venus Four.*   New York: Manor Books, 1977, 317 p., paper, novel.

WILLIS, Connie [i.e., Constance Elaine Trimmer Willis], 1945-

37059   *Daisy, in the sun.*   Eugene, OR: Pulphouse Publishing, 1991, 45 p., cloth, story. SHORT STORY HARDBACKS #20; SHORT STORY PAPERBACKS #33.
37060   *Fire watch.*   New York: A Bluejay International Edition, 1985, 274 p., cloth, coll.
37061   *Lincoln's dreams.*   Toronto, New York: Bantam Books, 1987, 212 p., cloth, novel. [Winner of the John W. Campbell Jr. Memorial Award for Best Novel, 1987 (1988)].

with Cynthia Felice

23022   *Light raid.*   New York: Ace Books, 1989, 229 p., cloth, novel.
23023   *Water witch: a novel.*   New York: Ace Books, 1982, 216 p., paper, novel.

WILLIS, Constance E.—SEE: Willis, Connie

WILLIS, Donald C(halmers), 1947-

37062   *Horror and science fiction films II.*   Metuchen, NJ & London: Scarecrow Press, 1982, xiv+474 p., cloth, nonf.
37063   *Horror and science fiction films III.*   Metuchen, NJ & London: Scarecrow Press, 1984, xiii+335 p., cloth, nonf.
37064   *Variety's complete science fiction reviews.*   New York, London: Garland Publishing, 1985, xiv+479 p., cloth, nonf. anth.

WILLIS, George—SEE: Armstrong, Anthony

WILLIS, John Randolph

37065   *Pleasures forevermore: the theology of C. S. Lewis.*   Chicago: A Campion Book, Loyola University Press, 1983, xx+157 p., cloth, nonf.

WILLIS, Lisle—SEE: Van Loden, Erle

WILLIS, Lynn, *with Mark J. Ferrari & Sandy Petersen & Tom Sullivan*

Field guide to creatures of the dreamlands—SEE: Petersen's Field guide: creatures of the dreamlands.
23047   *Petersen's Field guide: creatures of the dreamlands: an album of entities from beyond the wall of sleep.*   Albany, CA: Chaosium, 1989, 64 p., paper, art.

WILLIS, Maud, pseud.—SEE: Lottman, Eileen

WILLIS, Paul J., 1955-

37066   *No clock in the forest: an alpine tale.*   Wheaton, IL: Crossway Books, 1991, 209 p., paper, novel.

WILLSON, Harry

37067   *A world for the meek: a fantasy novel.*   Albuquerque, NM: Amador Publishers, 1987, 184 p., paper, novel.

WILSON, A(ndrew) N(orman), 1950-

37068   *C. S. Lewis: a biography.*   London: Collins, 1990, xviii+334 p., cloth, novel.

WILSON, Alison M(orley), 1932-

37069   *August Derleth: a bibliography.*   Metuchen, NJ & London: Scarecrow Press, 1983, xxvi+229 p., cloth, nonf. SCARECROW AUTHOR BIBLIOGRAPHIES #59.

WILSON, Angus (Frank Johnstone), Sir, 1913-1991

38167   *The strange ride of Rudyard Kipling: his life and works.*   London: Secker & Warburg, 1977, xiv+370 p., cloth, nonf.

WILSON, Anna

37070   *Hatching stones.*   London: Onlywomen Press, 1991, 131 p., paper, novel.

WILSON, Anne Deirdre, 1934-

37071   *Magical quest: the use of magic in Arthurian romance.*   Manchester, England: Manchester University Press, 1988, 242 p., cloth, nonf.

WILSON, Barbara Ker [i.e., Barbara Ker Wilson Tahourdin], 1929-

37072 *A handful of ghosts: thirteen eerie tales of Australian writers.* Sydney, Australia: Hodder & Stoughton, 1976, 180 p., cloth, anth.

WILSON, Colin (Henry), 1931-

The delta—SEE: *Spider world: The delta.*
The desert—SEE: *Spider world: The desert.*
37073 *Existentially speaking: essays on the philosophy of literature.* San Bernardino, CA: R. Reginald, The Borgo Press, 1989, 143 p., cloth, nonf. coll. I.O. EVANS STUDIES IN THE PHILOSOPHY & CRITICISM OF LITERATURE #7.
The fortress—SEE: *Spider world: The tower.*
37074 *The haunted man: the strange genius of David Lindsay.* San Bernardino, CA: R. Reginald, The Borgo Press, 1979, 63 p., cloth, nonf. MILFORD SERIES: POPULAR WRITERS OF TODAY #20.
Lifeforce—SEE: *The space vampires.*
37075 *The personality surgeon.* Sevenoaks, Kent, England: New English Library, 1985, 339 p., cloth, novel.
37076 *Science fiction as existentialism.* Hayes, Middlesex, England: Bran's Head Books, 1978, 16 p., paper, nonf.
37077 *The space vampires.* London: Hart-Davis, MacGibbon, 1976, 214 p., cloth, novel.
37077A retitled: *Lifeforce.* New York: Warner Books, 1985, 220 p., paper, novel.
37078 *Spider world: The delta.* London: Grafton, 1987, 304 p., cloth, novel. SPIDER WORLD #2.
37079 *Spider world: The tower.* London: Grafton, 1987, 398 p., cloth, novel. SPIDER WORLD #1.
37079A retitled: *Spider world: The desert.* New York: Ace Books, 1988, 163 p., paper, novel. SPIDER WORLD #1-A. [The original novel split into three pieces].
37079B retitled: *The tower.* New York: Ace Books, 1989, 181 p., paper, novel. SPIDER WORLD #1-B. [The original novel split into three pieces].
37079C retitled: *The fortress.* New York: Ace Books, 1989, 149 p., paper, novel. SPIDER WORLD #1-C. [The original novel split into three pieces].
The tower—SEE: *Spider world: The tower.*

WILSON, David Henry, 1937-

37080 *The coachman rat.* Taunton, Somerset, England: Hope Corner, 1987, 132 p., paper, novel. [Translation of *Ashmadi*].

WILSON, Eric (Hamilton), 1940-

37081 *The vampires of Ottawa.* Don Mills, Ontario, Canada: Collins, 1984, 97 p., cloth, novel.

WILSON, F(rancis) Paul, 1946-

37082 *Ad statum perspicuum.* Eugene, OR: Pulphouse Publishing, 1990, 115 p., cloth, coll. AUTHOR'S CHOICE MONTHLY #13.
37083 *Black wind.* New York: Tor, A Tom Doherty Associates Book, 1988, 465 p., cloth, novel.
37084 *Buckets.* Eugene, OR: Pulphouse Publishing, 1991, 47 p., paper, story. SHORT STORY PAPERBACKS #36.
37085 *Dydeetown world.* Norwalk, CT: Easton Press, 1989, 303 p., cloth, coll.
37086 *An enemy of the state.* Garden City, NY: Doubleday & Co., 1980, xiv+269 p., cloth, novel. LANAGUE FEDERATION #3.
37087 *Healer.* Garden City, NY: Doubleday & Co., 1976, 183 p., cloth, novel. LANAGUE FEDERATION #1.
37088 *The keep.* New York: William Morrow & Co., 1981, 347 p., cloth, novel. ADVERSARY #1.
37089 *Midnight mass.* Eugene, OR: Axolotl Press, Pulphouse Publishing, 1990, 85 p., cloth, novel. AXOLOTL PRESS #16.
37090 *Pelts.* Round Top, NY: Footsteps Press, 1990, 30 p., paper, story.
37091 *Reborn: a novel.* Arlington Heights, IL: Dark Harvest, 1990, 315 p., cloth, novel. ADVERSARY #2.
37092 *Reprisal: a novel.* Arlington Heights, IL: Dark Harvest, 1991, 332 p., cloth, novel. ADVERSARY #3.
37092A retitled: *Reprisals.* London: New English Library, 1991, 336 p., paper, coll. ADVERSARY #3.
Reprisals—SEE: *Reprisal.*
37093 *Sibs.* Arlington Heights, IL: Dark Harvest, 1991, 280 p., cloth, novel.
37094 *Soft and others: 16 stories of wonder and dread.* New York: Tor, A Tom Doherty Associates Book, 1989, xi+306 p., cloth, coll.
37095 *The Tery.* New York: Baen Books, 1990, 246 p., paper, coll.
37096 *The tomb.* New York: Whispers Press, 1984, 365 p., cloth, novel.
37097 *The touch.* New York: G. P. Putnam's Sons, 1986, 367 p., cloth, novel.

37098 *Wheels within wheels: a novel of the LaNague Federation.* Garden City, NY: Doubleday & Co., 1978, x + 176 p., cloth, novel. LANAGUE FEDERATION #2.

with Paul Mikol

29847 *Night visions 9: all original stories.* Arlington Heights, IL: Dark Harvest, 1991, 260 p., cloth, anth. [Introduction by F. Paul Wilson].

WILSON, G. L.

38168 *Murder goes underground.* London: Fiction House, 1949, 96 p., paper, novel.

WILSON, Gahan, 1930-

37099 *Eddy Deco's last caper: an illustrated mystery.* New York: Times Books, 1987, 213 p., cloth, novel.
37100 *Everybody's favorite duck.* New York: Mysterious Press, 1988, 202 p., cloth, novel.
Favorite tales of horror—SEE: *Gahan Wilson's Favorite tales of horror.*
37101 *First World Fantasy Awards.* Garden City, NY: Doubleday & Co., 1977, 311 p., cloth, anth.
37102 *Gahan Wilson's Favorite tales of horror.* New York: Tempo Books, Grosset & Dunlap Publishers, 1976, 186 p., paper, anth.

WILSON, (Leslie) Granville, 1912-

37103 *The terror cubes.* London, Toronto: A Dragon Book, Granada, 1982, 111 p., paper, novel.
37104 *War of the computers.* London, Toronto: A Dragon Book, Granada, 1981, 92 p., paper, novel.

WILSON, John Anthony Burgess—SEE: Burgess, Anthony

WILSON, Linda, *with Nigel Robinson*

32528 *The Tolkien quiz book.* London: Star Books, 1981, 115 p., paper, nonf.

WILSON, Mary

37105 *The changeling.* New York: A Dell Book, 1975, 176 p., paper, novel.

WILSON, Merzie

37106 *Nealites: Doc Genius and Henry the Stud.* New York, Washington: Vantage Press, 1980, 256 p., cloth, novel.

WILSON, Peter Lamborn, 1945- , *with Robert Anton Wilson & Rudy Rucker*

32816 *Semiotext[e] SF.* Brooklyn. NY: Autonomedia, 1989, 384 p., paper, anth.

WILSON, Richard, 1920-1987

37107 *Adventures in the space trade.* Polk City, IA: Drumm Books, 1986, 20 p., paper, nonf. DRUMM BOOKLET #23. [Bound with *A Richard Wilson checklist* / by Chris Drumm].
37108 *Aunt Fritzi.* Polk City, IA: Chris Drumm, 1987, [5] p., paper, story. DRUMM BOOKLET.
37109 *The kid from Ozone Park & other stories.* Polk City, IA: Chris Drumm, 1987, 63 p., paper, coll. DRUMM BOOKLET #27.

WILSON, Robert

37110 *Tentacles of dawn.* Canoga Park, CA: Major Books, 1978 (i.e., 1979?), 191 p., paper, novel.

WILSON, Robert Anton, 1932-

37111 *The earth will shake: a novel.* Los Angeles: Jeremy Tarcher, 1982, 369 p., cloth, novel. HISTORICAL ILLUMINATUS CHRONICLES #1.
37112 *The homing pigeons.* New York: Pocket Books, 1981, 206 p., paper, novel. SCHRÖDINGER'S CAT #3.
37113 *Masks of the Illuminati.* New York: A Timescape Book, Pocket Books, 1981, 294 p., paper, novel.
37114 *Nature's god.* New York: A Roc Book, 1991, 225 p., paper, novel. HISTORICAL ILLUMINATUS CHRONICLES #3.
37115 *Right where you are sitting now: further tales of the Illuminati.* Berkeley, CA: And/Or Press, 1982, ix + 207 p., paper, coll. ILLUMINATI SERIES.
37116 *Schrödinger's cat trilogy.* New York: A Dell Book, 1988, 545 p., paper, coll. SCHRÖDINGER'S CAT #1-3.
37117 *Schrödinger's cat: The universe next door.* New York: Pocket Books, 1979, 256 p., paper, novel. SCHRÖDINGER'S CAT #1.
37118 *The trick top hat.* New York: Pocket Books, 1981, 254 p., paper, novel. SCHRÖDINGER'S CAT #2.
The universe next door—SEE: *Schrödinger's cat.*

37119 *The widow's son.* New York: Bluejay Books, 1985, 343 p., paper, Novel. HISTORICAL ILLUMINATUS CHRONICLES #2.

with Rudy Rucker & Peter Lamborn Wilson

32816 *Semiotext[e] SF.* Brooklyn. NY: Autonomedia, 1989, 384 p., paper, anth.

with Robert Shea

33652 *The eye in the pyramid.* New York: A Dell Book, 1975, 304 p., paper, novel. ILLUMINATUS! #1.

33653 *The golden apple.* New York: A Dell Book, 1975, 272 p., paper, novel. ILLUMINATUS! #2.

33654 *The Illuminatus! trilogy: The eye in the pyramid, The golden apple, and Leviathan.* New York: A Dell Trade Paperback, 1984, 805 p., paper, coll. ILLUMINATUS! #1-3.

33655 *Leviathan.* New York: A Dell Book, 1975, 253 p., paper, novel. ILLUMINATUS! #3.

WILSON, Robert C(harles), 1951-

37120 *The Crooked Tree.* New York: G. P. Putnam's Sons, 1980, 350 p., cloth, novel.

37121 *Icefire.* New York: G. P. Putnam's Sons, 1984, 379 p., cloth, novel.

WILSON, Robert C(harles), 1953-

37122 *A bridge of years.* New York: A Foundation Book, Doubleday, 1991, 237 p., paper, novel. [The cloth edition of this book was never actually published, although an ISBN for a cloth version appears on the copyright page].

37123 *The divide.* New York: A Foundation Book, Doubleday, 1990, 249 p., cloth, novel.

37124 *Gypsies.* New York: A Foundation Book, Doubleday, 1989, 237 p., cloth, novel.

37125 *A hidden place.* Toronto, New York: Bantam Books, 1986, 212 p., paper, novel.

37126 *Memory wire.* Toronto, New York: Spectra, Bantam Books, 1987, 219 p., paper, novel.

WILSON, Robert Hendrie

37127 *A blank card.* London: Robert Hale, 1977, 189 p., cloth, novel.

37128 *The Frisk donation.* London: Robert Hale, 1979, 160 p., cloth, novel.

37129 *The gods alone.* London: Robert Hale, 1975, 190 p., cloth, novel.

37130 *Ring of rings.* London: Robert Hale, 1976, 189 p., cloth, novel.

WILSON, Rudy

37131 *The red truck.* New York: Alfred A. Knopf, 1987, 178 p., cloth, novel.

WILSON, Snoo, 1948-

37132 *Inside Babel.* London: Chatto & Windus, 1985, 208 p., cloth, novel. SPACEACHE #2.

37133 *Spaceache.* London: Chatto & Windus, 1984, [160] p., cloth, novel. SPACEACHE #1.

WILSON, Steve, 1943-

37134 *The lost traveller: a motorcycle grail quest and science fiction western.* London: Macmillan, 1976, 245 p., cloth, novel.

WILTSHIRE, David, 1935-

37135 *Child of Vodyanoi.* London: Robert Hale, 1978, 208 p., cloth, novel.

37135A retitled: *The nightmare man.* London: Hamlyn Paperbacks, 1981, 192 p., paper, novel.

37136 *Genesis II.* London: Robert Hale, 1981, 189 p., cloth, novel.

37137 *The homosaur.* London: Robert Hale, 1978, 206 p., cloth, novel.

The nightmare man—SEE: *Child of Vodyanoi.*

as JOHN BEDFORD

38169 *The Titron madness.* London: Robert Hale, 1984, 187 p., cloth, novel.

WIMBLE, Edward

37138 *Death in Dunwich.* Kirkwood, NJ: Theatre of the Mind, 1983, 34 p., paper, story. CTHULHU MYTHOS.

WIND, David, *as* MONICA BARRIE

37139 *Queen of knights* / by David Wind writing as Monica Barrie. New York: Pocket Books, 1985, 372 p., paper, novel.

WINDLING, Terri, 1958-

37140 *Faery!* New York: Ace Fantasy Books, 1985, 308 p., paper, anth.

37141 *Life on the border.* New York: Tor Fantasy, A Tom Doherty Associates Book, 1991, 372 p., paper, anth. BORDERTOWN SERIES.

with Mark Alan Arnold

16789 *Borderland.* New York: A Signet Book, New American Library, 1986, 252 p., paper, anth. BORDERLANDS #1.

16790 *Bordertown: a chronicle of the Borderlands.* New York: A Signet Book, New American Library, 1986, 253 p., paper, anth. BORDERLANDS #2.

16791 *Elsewhere.* New York: Ace Books, 1981, 366 p., paper, anth. [Winner of the World Fantasy Award for Best Fantasy Anthology/Collection, 1981 (1982)].

16792 *Elsewhere: tales of fantasy, vol. II.* New York: Ace Books, 1982, 388 p., paper, anth.

16793 *Elsewhere: tales of fantasy, vol. III.* New York: Ace Fantasy Books, 1984, 404 p., paper, anth.

with Ellen Datlow

Demons and dreams—SEE: *The year's best fantasy: first annual collection.*

Demons and dreams 2—SEE: *The year's best fantasy: second annual collection.*

21178 *The year's best fantasy: first annual collection.* New York: St. Martin's Press, 1988, xxxv+491 p., cloth, anth. [Winner of the World Fantasy Award for Best Fantasy Anthology, 1988 (1989)].

21178A retitled: *Demons and dreams: the best fantasy and horror 1.* London: Legend, 1989, xxxiv+482 p., cloth, anth.

21179 *The year's best fantasy: second annual collection.* New York: St. Martin's Press, 1989, lvii+579 p., cloth, anth. [Winner of the World Fantasy Award for Best Fantasy Anthology, 1989 (1990)].

21179A retitled: *Demons and dreams: the best fantasy and horror 2.* London: Legend, 1989, lvii+579 p., paper, anth.

21180 *The year's best fantasy and horror: third annual collection.* New York: St. Martin's Press, 1990, liii+563 p., cloth, anth.

21181 *The year's best fantasy and horror: fourth annual collection.* New York: St. Martin's Press, 1991, liv+552 p., cloth, anth.

WINDSOR, Patricia (Frances), 1938-

37142 *The Christmas killer.* New York, Toronto: Scholastic Inc., 1991, 263 p., cloth, novel.

37143 *The hero.* New York: Delacorte Press, 1988, 224 p., cloth, novel.

37144 *Killing time.* New York: Harper & Row, 1980, 188 p., cloth, novel.

37145 *Two weirdos and a ghost.* New York: A Yearling Book, 1991, 122 p., paper, novel.

37146 *A very weird and moogly Christmas.* New York: A Yearling Book, 1991, 101 p., paper, novel.

as COLIN DANIEL

37147 *Demon tree.* New York: Twilight/Dell, 1983, 153 p., paper, novel. TWILIGHT #9.

WINGROVE, David (John), 1954-

37148 *The broken wheel.* London: New English Library, 1990, xiv+433 p., cloth, novel. CHUNG KUO #2.

37149 *The immortals of science fiction.* London: Pierrot Publishing, 1980, 113 p., paper, nonf.

37150 *The middle kingdom.* London: New English Library, 1989, 501 p., cloth, novel. CHUNG KUO #1.

37151 *The science fiction film source book.* Harlow, Essex, England: Longman, 1985, vi+312 p., cloth, nonf.

37152 *The science fiction source book.* Harlow, Essex, England: Longman, 1984, 320 p., cloth, nonf.

37153 *The white mountain.* London: New English Library, 1991, 432 p., cloth, novel. CHUNG KUO #3.

with Brian W. Aldiss

16208 *Trillion year spree: the history of science fiction.* London: Victor Gollancz, 1986, 511 p., cloth, nonf. [An expansion of *Billion year spree* (see #00123); winner of the Hugo Award for Best Nonfiction Book, 1986 (1987); winner of the *Locus* Award for Best Nonfiction, 1986 (1987); winner of the J. Lloyd Eaton Award for Best Nonfiction Book of the Year, 1986 (1988)].

with Brian Griffin

24707 *Apertures: a study of the writings of Brian W. Aldiss.* Westport, CT & London: Greenwood Press, 1984, xvi+261 p., cloth, nonf. CONTRIBUTIONS TO THE

STUDY OF SCIENCE FICTION AND FAN-
TASY #8.

WINKLE, Joseph Van—SEE: Van Winkle, Joseph

WINKLE, Monica F. Van—SEE: Van Winkle, Monica

WINN, Rowland (Denis Guy, 4th Baron St. Oswald), 1916-1984

15881 *My dear, it's Heaven.* London: Cassell, 1950, 224 p., cloth, novel.

*WINSHIP, Glen B(rion), 1887-1966

WINSKI, Norman

37154 *The sword and the sorcerer.* New York: Pinnacle Books, 1982, 217 p., paper, movie.

WINSLOW, Pauline Glen, 1934?-

37155 *I, Martha Adams.* London: Arlington, 1982, 340 p., cloth, novel.
37156 *Judgement day.* London: Arlington, 1984, 299 p., cloth, novel.
37156A retitled: *Judgment day.* New York: St. Martin's Press, 1986, 250 p., cloth, novel.
Judgment day—SEE: Judgement day.

WINSTEAD, Rebecca Noyes, pseud.—SEE: Merwin, Sam Jr.

WINSTON, Daoma [i.e., Daoma Winston Strasberg], 1922-

37157 *Seminar in evil.* New York: Lancer Books, 1972, 205 p., paper, novel.
15500A *The sorcerers.* London: Severn House, 1988, 160 p., cloth, novel. [Originally published in 1973 under the name Dorian Winslow].
37158 *Sweet familiarity: a novel.* New York: Arbor House, 1981, 254 p., cloth, novel.
37159 *The vampire curse.* New York: Paperback Library, 1971, 142 p., paper, novel.
37160 *The vampire curse.* New York: Paperback Library, 1971, 142 p., paper, novel.

WINSTON, Joan

37161 *The making of the Trek conventions; or, How to throw a party for 12,000 of your most intimate friends.* Garden City, NY: Doubleday & Co., 1977, xii+252 p., cloth, nonf.

with Jacqueline Lichtenberg & Sondra Marshak

28340 *Star Trek lives!* Toronto, New York: Bantam Books, 1975, 274 p., paper, nonf.

WINSTONE, C. A.

38170 *Possessed.* New York: St. Martin's Press; London: Robert Hale, 1979, 221 p., cloth, novel.

WINTER, Douglas E., 1950-

The art of darkness—SEE: Stephen King: the art of darkness.
37162 *Black wine.* Arlington Heights, IL: Dark Harvest, 1986, 167 p., cloth, anth.
37163 *Faces of fear: encounters with the creators of modern horror.* New York: Berkley Books, 1985, 277 p., paper, nonf. coll.
37164 *Prime evil.* New York: NAL Books, New American Library, 1988, 322 p., cloth, anth.
37165 *Shadowings: the reader's guide to horror fiction, 1981-82.* Mercer Island, WA: Starmont House, 1983, xi+148 p., cloth, nonf. anth. STARMONT STUDIES IN LITERARY CRITICISM #1.
37166 *Splatter: a cautionary tale: a story.* Round Top, NY: Footsteps Press, 1987, iv+47 p., paper, story. [Limited to 526 copies].
37167 *Stephen King.* Mercer Island, WA: Starmont House, 1982, 128 p., cloth, nonf. STARMONT READER'S GUIDE #16.
37168 *Stephen King: the art of darkness.* New York: NAL Books, New American Library, 1984, xix+252 p., cloth, nonf.
37169 *Stephen King: the art of darkness, updated ed.* New York: Plume Books, New American Library, 1986, xix+297 p., paper, nonf.
37169A retitled: *The art of darkness: the life and fiction of the master of the macabre, Stephen King.* Sevenoaks, Kent, England: New English Library, 1989, p., paper, nonf.

with Paul Mikol

Dark visions—SEE: Night visions 5.
29843 *Night visions 5: all original stories.* Arlington Heights, IL: Dark Harvest, 1988, 274 p., cloth, anth. [Introduction by Douglas E. Winter].
29843A retitled: *Dark visions.* London: Victor Gollancz, 1989, 264 p., cloth, anth. [Introduction by Douglas E. Winter].

29843B retitled: *The skin trade.* NY: Berkley Books, 1990, 329 p., paper, anth. [Introduction by Douglas E. Winter].
The skin trade—SEE: *Night visions 5.*

WINTER, Pat (DeGraw)

37170 *Driver.* New York: Pinnacle Books, 1982, 309 p., paper, novel.

WINTER, Steve, 1955- , *with Mary Kirchoff*

27316 *Wanderlust.* Lake Geneva, WI: TSR Inc., 1991, 312 p., paper, novel. DRAG-ONLANCE SAGA—MEETINGS SEXTET #2.

***WINTERFELD, Henry, 1901-1990**

WINTERS, Logan [pseud. of Paul Joseph Lederer]

37171 *Hunt the beast down.* New York: Tower Books, 1981, 159 p., paper, novel. SPECTROS #2.
37172 *Natchez.* New York: Tower Books, 1981, 176 p., paper, novel. SPECTROS #3.
37173 *The silver canyon.* New York: Tower Books, 1981, 174 p., paper, novel. SPECTROS #4.
37174 *Silverado.* New York: Tower Books, 1981, 159 p., paper, novel. SPECTROS #1.

WINTERS, Mick, pseud.—SEE: Wooley, John & Wolfe, Ron

WINTERSON, Jeanette, 1959-

37175 *Sexing the cherry.* London: Bloomsbury, 1989, 167 p., cloth, novel.

WINTHROP, Elizabeth [i.e., Elizabeth Winthrop Mahony], 1948-

37176 *The castle in the attic.* New York: Holiday House, 1985, 179 p., cloth, novel.

WINTLE, Elizabeth—SEE: Lawrence, Louise

WIPPERSBERG, W(alter) J. M., 1945-

37177 *Bad times for ghosts.* San Diego, CA: Harcourt Brace Jovanovich, 1986, 156 p., cloth, novel. [Translation of *Schlechte zeiten für gespenster* / by Edna McCown].

WISDOM, Linda Randall

37178 *Free spirits.* Toronto, New York: Harlequin Books, 1991, 253 p., paper, novel.

WISE, Barbara Ann Gordon- —SEE: Gordon-Wise, Barbara Ann

WISE, David, 1930-

37179 *The Samarkand dimension.* New York: Avon Books, 1988, 262 p., paper, novel.

WISE, S.

37180 *The Darkover dilemma.* Baltimore, MD: T-K Graphics, 1976, 28 p., paper, nonf.

WISEMAN, David, 1916-

37181 *Adam's Common.* Boston: Houghton Mifflin Co., 1984, 175 p., cloth, novel.
37182 *Blodwen and the Guardians.* Boston: Houghton Mifflin Co., 1983, 163 p., cloth, novel.
37183 *The Devil's Cauldron.* London: Hippo, 1989, 104 p., paper, novel.
The fate of Jeremy Visick—SEE: *Jeremy Visick.*
37184 *Jeremy Visick.* Boston: Houghton Mifflin Co., 1981, 170 p., cloth, novel.
37184A retitled: *The fate of Jeremy Visick.* Harmondsworth, England: Kestrel Books, 1982, 159 p., cloth, novel.
37185 *Thimbles: a novel.* Boston: Houghton Mifflin Co., 1982, 134 p., cloth, novel.

WISEMAN, Rex

37186 *The Okora mask.* New York: Belmont Tower Books, 1979, 251 p., paper, novel.

WISHER, W(illiam) H.

with James Cameron

19238 *Terminator 2: Judgment day: the book of the film: an illustrated screenplay.* New York: Applause Books, 1991, 318 p., paper, anth.

with Randall Frakes

23415 *The Terminator: a novel.* Toronto, New York: Bantam Books, 1985, 240 p., paper, movie. TERMINATOR #1. [Completely different from the British novelization of the same title].

WISLER, G(ary) Clifton, 1950-

37187 *The Antrian messenger.* New York: E. P. Dutton, 1986, 117 p., cloth, novel. Antrian #1.

37188 *The mind trap.* New York: Lodestar Books, 1990, 118 p., cloth, novel. ANTRIAN #3.

37189 *The seer.* New York: Lodestar Books, 1988, 134 p., cloth, novel. ANTRIAN #2.

WISMER, Don(ald Richard), 1946-

37190 *Planet of the dead.* New York: Baen Books, 1988, 275 p., paper, novel.

37191 *A roil of stars.* Riverdale, NY: Baen Books, 1991, 281 p., paper, novel.

37192 *Starluck* / by Donald Wismer. Garden City, NY: Doubleday & Co., 1982, 186 p., cloth, novel.

37193 *Warrior planet.* New York: Baen Books, 1987, 275 p., paper, novel.

WITKIEWICZ, Stanislaw Ignacy, 1885-1939

37194 *Insatiability: a novel in two parts.* Urbana & Chicago: University of Illinois Press, 1977, xlv+447 p., cloth, novel. [Translation by Louis Iribarne of *Nienasycenie*].

*WITT, Currie B., <u>1908-1990</u>

WITTIG, Monique, 1935-

37195 *Across the Acheron.* London: Peter Owen, 1987, 119 p., cloth, novel. [Translation by David Le Vay of *Virgile*].

with Sande Zeig

37196 *Lesbian peoples: material for a dictionary.* New York: Avon, 1979, 170 p., paper, fiction.

WLUDYKA, Peter

37197 *The past is another country.* New York: Simon & Schuster, 1988, 396 p., cloth, novel.

*WOBIG, Ellen, 1911-<u>1989</u>

WODHAMS, (Herbert) Jack, 1931-

37198 *Future war.* St. Kilda, Victoria, Australia: Cory & Collins, 1982, 184 p., paper, coll.

37199 *Looking for Blücher.* St. Kilda, Victoria, Australia: Void Publications, 1980, 207 p., cloth, novel.

37200 *Ryn.* St. Kilda, Victoria, Australia: Cory & Collins, 1982, 196 p., paper, novel.

WOHLFAHRT, Irene, *with Doris Schulze*

33389 *Crystal clear.* Strathmartine by Dundee, Scotland: ScoTpress, 1988?, 78 p., paper, novel. STAR TREK SERIES.

WOLD, Allen (Lester), 1943-

Below the threshold—SEE: *V: Below the threshold.*

The Crivit experiment—SEE: *V: The crivit experiment.*

37201 *Crown of the serpent* / by Allen L. Wold. New York: Popular Library, 1989, 250 p., paper, novel.

37202 *The eye in the stone* / by Allen L. Wold. New York: Pageant Books, 1988, 344 p., paper, novel.

37203 *Jewels of the dragon* / by Allen L. Wold. New York: Popular Library, Warner Books, 1986, 263 p., paper, novel.

37204 *The planet masters.* New York: St. Martin's [sic], 1979, 230 p., cloth, novel.

The pursuit of Diana—SEE: *V: The pursuit of Diana.*

37205 *Star god* / by Allen L. Wold. New York: St. Martin's Press, 1980, xiv+191 p., cloth, novel.

37206 *V: Below the threshold.* New York: Tor SF, A Tom Doherty Associates Book, 1988, 246 p., paper, tele. V SERIES.

37207 *V: The Crivit experiment.* New York: Pinnacle Books, 1985, 181 p., paper, tele. V #8.

37208 *V: The pursuit of Diana.* New York: Pinnacle Books, 1984, 186 p., paper, tele. V #3.

WOLF, Barbara H(errman), 1932- , *with Jack C. Wolf*

37209 *Tales of the occult.* Greenwich, CT: A Fawcett Crest Book, Fawcett Publications, 1975, 416 p., paper, anth.

WOLF, Chris L., *with Michael F. Maikowski*

28936 *Fire in the sky.* Canoga Park, CA: Major Books, 1978 (i.e., 1979?), 205 p., paper, novel.

WOLF, Gary K(enneth), 1941-

37210 *A generation removed.* Garden City, NY: Doubleday & Co., 1977, 188 p., cloth, novel.

37211 *Killerbowl.* Garden City, NY: Doubleday & Co., 1975, 161 p., cloth, novel.

37212 *The resurrectionist.* Garden City, NY: Doubleday & Co., 1979, 181 p., cloth, novel.

37213 *Who censored Roger Rabbit?* New York: St. Martin's Press, 1981, 214 p., cloth, novel. ROGER RABBIT #1.

37214 *Who p-p-plugged Roger Rabbit?* New York: Villard Books, 1991, 255 p., cloth, novel. ROGER RABBIT #2.

WOLF, Jack C(lifford), 1922- , *with Barbara H. Wolf*

37209 *Tales of the occult.* Greenwich, CT: A Fawcett Crest Book, Fawcett Publications, 1975, 416 p., paper, anth.

WOLF, Joan

37215 *Daughter of the red deer.* New York: E. P. Dutton, 1991, 420 p., cloth, novel.

37216 *The road to Avalon.* New York: NAL Books, 1988, 358 p., cloth, novel.

WOLF, Joyce, 1949-

37217 *The white spider.* New York: Leisure Books, 1987, 400 p., paper, novel.

WOLF, Leonard, 1923-

Complete book of terror—SEE: *Wolf's Complete book of terror.*

37218 *A dream of Dracula: in search of the living dead.* Boston: Little, Brown & Co., 1972, xlii+327 p., cloth, nonf.

37219 *Horror: a connoisseur's guide to literature and film.* New York, Oxford: Facts on File, 1989, 262 p., cloth, nonf.

37220 *Wolf's Complete book of terror.* New York: Clarkson N. Potter, 1979, xvi+473 p., cloth, anth.

WOLFE, Aaron, pseud.—SEE: Koontz, Dean R.

*WOLFE, Bernard, 1915-1985

WOLFE, Chris Anne

37221 *Shadows of Aggar.* Norwich, VT: New Victoria Publishers, 1991, 308 p., paper, novel.

WOLFE, Gary K(ent), 1946-

37222 *Critical terms for science fiction and fantasy: a glossary and guide to scholarship.* New York, Westport, CT: Green-

wood Press, 1986, xxxvi+162 p., cloth, nonf.

37223 *David Lindsay.* Mercer Island, WA: Starmont House, 1982, 64 p., cloth, nonf. STARMONT READER'S GUIDE #9.

37224 *The known and the unknown: iconography of science fiction.* Kent, OH: Kent State University Press, 1979, xvii+250 p., cloth, nonf. [Winner of the J. Lloyd Eaton Award for Best Nonfiction Book of the Year, 1979 (1981)].

37225 *Science fiction dialogues.* Chicago: Academy Chicago, 1982, viii+227 p., paper, nonf. anth.

WOLFE, Gene (Rodman), 1931-

37226 *The Arimaspian legacy.* New Castle, VA: Cheap Street, 1987, 14 p., paper, story. [Limited to about 100 copies].

37227 *Bibliomen: twenty characters waiting for a book.* New Castle, VA: Cheap Street, 1984, 68 p., cloth, coll. [Limited to 191 copies].

Book of days—SEE: *Gene Wolfe's Book of days.*

37228 *The book of the new sun, vols. I and II.* London: Sidgwick & Jackson, 1983, 604 p., cloth, coll. BOOK OF THE NEW SUN #1-2.

38171 *The book of the new sun, vols. III and IV.* London: Sidgwick & Jackson, 1985, 302+317 p., cloth, coll. BOOK OF THE NEW SUN #3-4.

37229 *The boy who hooked the sun: a tale from the Book of the wonders of Urth and sky.* New Castle, VA: Cheap Street, 1985, 11 p., paper, story. BOOK OF THE NEW SUN SERIES.

37230 *The castle of the otter.* Willimantic, CT: Ziesing Brothers, 1982, 113 p., cloth, nonf. coll. BOOK OF THE NEW SUN TIE-IN. [Includes some fiction; limited to 520 copies].

37231 *Castleview.* New York: Tor, A Tom Doherty Associates Book, 1990, 279 p., cloth, novel.

37232 *The citadel of the Autarch.* New York: Timescape Books, 1983, 317 p., cloth, novel. BOOK OF THE NEW SUN #4. [Winner of the John W. Campbell Jr. Memorial Award for Best Novel, 1983 (1984)].

37233 *The claw of the conciliator.* New York: Timescape Books, 1981, 303 p., cloth, novel. BOOK OF THE NEW SUN #2. [Winner of the Nebula Award for Best Novel, 1981 (1982); winner of the *Science Fiction Chronicle* Award for Best Novel, 1981 (1982); winner of the *Locus*

Award for Best Fantasy Novel, 1981 (1982)].

37234 *The death of Doctor Island.* New York: Tor SF, A Tom Doherty Associates Book, 1990, 62 p., paper, story. [Bound with *Fugue state* / by John M. Ford].

37235 *The devil in a forest.* Chicago: Follett Publishing Co., 1976, 224 p., cloth, novel.

37236 *Empires of foliage and flower: a tale from The book of the wonders of Urth and sky.* New Castle, VA: Cheap Street, 1987, 80 p., cloth, story. BOOK OF THE NEW SUN SEQUEL. [Limited to 199 copies].

37237 *Endangered species.* Norwalk, CT: Easton Press, 1989, vi+506 p., cloth, coll.

37238 *Free live free.* Willimantic, CT: Mark V. Ziesing, 1984, 496 p., cloth, novel. [Limited to 750 copies].

37239 *Gene Wolfe's Book of days.* Garden City, NY: Doubleday & Co., 1981, 182 p., cloth, coll.

37240 *The hero as werwolf.* Eugene, OR: Pulphouse Publishing, 1991, 44 p., cloth, story. SHORT STORY HARDBACKS #22; SHORT STORY PAPERBACKS #40.

37241 *The island of Doctor Death and other stories, and other stories.* New York: Pocket Books, 1980, 410 p., paper, coll.

37242 *Letters home.* Weston, Ontario, Canada: United Mythologies Press, 1991, 185 p., cloth, nonf. coll.

37243 *The old woman whose rolling pin is the sun.* New Castle, VA: Cheap Street, 1991, 15 p., paper, story.

37244 *Plan[e]t engineering.* Cambridge, MA: A Boskone Book, The NESFA Press, 1984, xvii+155 p., cloth, coll.

37245 *Seven American nights.* New York: Tor SF, A Tom Doherty Associates Book, 1989, 84 p., paper, story. [Bound with *Sailing to Byzantium* / by Robert Silverberg].

37246 *The shadow of the torturer.* New York: Simon & Schuster, 1980, 303 p., cloth, novel. BOOK OF THE NEW SUN #1. [Winner of the World Fantasy Award for Best Fantasy Novel, 1980 (1981)].

37247 *Slow children at play.* New Castle, VA: Cheap Street, 1989, 17 p., paper, story.

37248 *Soldier of Arete.* New York: Tor, A Tom Doherty Associates Book, 1989, x+354 p., cloth, novel. LATRO #2.

37249 *Soldier of the mist.* New York: Tor, A Tom Doherty Associates Book, 1986, xiv+335 p., cloth, novel. LATRO #1. [Winner of the *Locus* Award for Best Fantasy Novel, 1986 (1987)].

37250 *Storeys from the old hotel.* Worcester Park, Surrey, England: Kerosina, 1988, 299 p., cloth, coll. [Winner of the World Fantasy Award for Best Fantasy Collection, 1988 (1989)].

37251 *The sword of the Lictor.* New York: Timescape Books, 1981, 302 p., cloth, novel. BOOK OF THE NEW SUN #3. [Winner of the *Science Fiction Chronicle* Award for Best Novel, 1982 (1983); winner of the *Locus* Award for Best Fantasy Novel, 1982 (1983)].

37252 *The sword of the Lictor: science fiction; The citadel of the Autarch: science fiction.* London: Sidgwick & Jackson, 1985, 301+317 p., cloth, coll. BOOK OF THE NEW SUN #3-4.

37253 *There are doors.* New York: Tor, A Tom Doherty Associates Book, 1988, 313 p., cloth, novel.

37254 *The Urth of the new sun.* London: Victor Gollancz, 1987, 371 p., cloth, novel. BOOK OF THE NEW SUN #5. [Winner of the *Science Fiction Chronicle* Award for Best Novel, 1987 (1988)].

37255 *The Wolfe Archipelago.* Willimantic, CT: Ziesing Brothers, 1983, xiii+119 p., cloth, coll.

WOLFE, L. Stephen, *with Roy L. Wysack*

37256 *Handbook for space pioneers: a manual of the Galactic Association (Earth Branch).* New York: Grosset & Dunlap, 1978, 197 p., paper, fiction.

*WOLFE, Louis, 1905-1985

WOLFE, Ron(ald Lee), 1945-

with John Wooley

37257 *Old fears.* New York: Franklin Watts, 1982, 280 p., cloth, novel.

with John Wooley as MICK WINTERS

37258 *Full moon.* New York: Berkley Books, 1989, 327 p., paper, novel.

WOLFF, Robert Lee, 1915-1980

37259 *The golden key: a study of the fiction of George MacDonald.* New Haven, CT: Yale University Press, 1961, ix+425 p., cloth, nonf.

37260 *Strange stories, and other explorations in Victorian fiction.* Boston: Gambit, 1971, xiv+378 p., cloth, nonf.

WOLFF, Robert Sherman

37261 *Caves of Mars*. Hamden, CT: Linnet Books, 1988, x+160 p., cloth, novel. FALCON GOLD SPACE ADVENTURES #1.

WOLFMAN, Marv, 1946-

37262 *Doomsday*. New York: Pocket Books, 1979, 191 p., paper, novel. FANTASTIC FOUR SERIES; MARVEL SUPERHEROES #5.

with Len Wein

36592 *The Marvel superheroes*. New York: Pocket Books, 1979, 208 p., paper, anth. MARVEL SUPERHEROES #9.

36593 *Mayhem in Manhattan*. New York: A Kangaroo Book, Pocket Books, 1978, 176 p., paper, novel. SPIDERMAN #1; MARVEL SUPERHEROES #1.

with Lein Wein and Joseph Silva [i.e., Ron Goulart]

24258 *Stalker from the stars*. New York: Pocket Books, 1978, 174 p., paper, novel. INCREDIBLE HULK #1; MARVEL SUPER HEROES #2.

with Ted White

36829 *Phoenix: a novel*. New York: Pyramid Books, 1977, 216 p., paper, novel. WEIRD HEROES #5.

WOLITZER, Meg, 1959-

37263 *The dream book*. New York: Greenwillow Books, 1986, 148 p., cloth, novel.

WOLK, George

as JANET KIDDE

37264 *The prophetess*. New York: A Jove/HBJ Book, 1978, 254 p., paper, novel.

as BARNEY PARRISH

37265 *The closed circle: a novel*. Chicago: Playboy Press, 1976, 190 p., paper, novel.

WOLLHEIM, Donald A(llen), 1914-1990

37266 *The best from the rest of the world: European science fiction*. Garden City, NY: Doubleday & Co., 1976, xix+267 p., cloth, anth.

37267 *The DAW science fiction reader*. New York: DAW Books, 1976, 207 p., paper, anth.

37268 *Fanciful tales of time and space, Fall, 1936*. West Warwick, RI: Marc A. Michaud, 1977, 45 p., paper, anth. [Reproduction of a magazine issue].

37269 *The men from Ariel*. Cambridge, MA: A Boskone Book, NESFA Press, 1982, 116 p., cloth, coll.

37270 *Up there, and other strange directions*. Cambridge, MA: A Nolacon II Book, NESFA Press, 1988, v+148 p., cloth, coll.

with Arthur W. Saha

12626 *The 1972 annual world's best SF*. New York: DAW Books, 1972, 302 p., paper, anth.

12626A retitled: *Wollheim's world's best SF, series one*. New York: DAW Books, 1977, 302 p., paper, anth.

12627 *The 1973 annual world's best SF*. New York: DAW Books, 1973, 253 p., paper, anth.

12627A retitled: *Wollheim's world's best SF, series two*. New York: DAW Books, 1978, 253 p., paper, anth.

12628 *The 1974 annual world's best SF*. New York: DAW Books, 1974, 280 p., paper, anth.

12628A retitled: *The world's best SF short stories #1*. Morley, Yorkshire, England: Elmfield Press, 1975, 280 p., cloth, anth.

12628B retitled: *Wollheim's world's best SF, series three*. New York: DAW Books, 1979, 280 p., paper, anth.

33033 *The 1975 annual world's best SF*. New York: DAW Books, 1975, 269 p., paper, anth.

33033A retitled: *The 1975 annual world's best SF: The world's best SF short stories #2*. Morley, Yorkshire, England: Elmfield Press, 1976, 269 p., cloth, anth.

33033B retitled: *Wollheim's world's best SF, series four*. New York: DAW Books, 1980, 269 p., paper, anth.

33034 *The 1976 annual world's best SF*. New York: DAW Books, 1976, 304 p., paper, anth.

33034A retitled: *The world's best SF three*. London: Dennis Dobson, 1979, 304 p., cloth, anth.

33034B retitled: *Wollheim's world's best SF, series five*. New York: DAW Books, 1981, 304 p., paper, anth.

33035 *1977 annual world's best SF*. New York: DAW Books, 1977, 280 p., paper, anth.

33035A retitled: *The world's best SF 4*. London: Dennis Dobson, 1979, 280 p., cloth, anth.

33035B retitled: *Wollheim's world's best SF, series six*. New York: DAW Books, 1982, 280 p., paper, anth.

33036 *The 1978 annual world's best SF*. New York: DAW Books, 1978, 270 p., paper, anth.

33036A retitled: *The world's best SF 5*. London: Dennis Dobson, 1980, 270 p., cloth, anth.

33036B retitled: *Wollheim's world's best SF, series seven*. New York: DAW Books, 1983, 270 p., paper, anth.

33037 *The 1979 annual world's best SF*. New York: DAW Books, 1979, 268 p., paper, anth.

33037A retitled: *Wollheim's world's best SF, series eight*. New York: DAW Books, 1984, 268 p., paper, anth.

33038 *The 1980 annual world's best SF*. New York: DAW Books, 1980, 284 p., paper, anth.

33038A retitled: *Wollheim's world's best SF, series nine*. New York: DAW Books, 1985, 284 p., paper, anth.

33039 *The 1981 annual world's best SF*. New York: DAW Books, 1981, 252 p., paper, anth.

33040 *The 1982 annual world's best SF*. New York: DAW Books, 1982, 304 p., paper, anth.

33041 *The 1983 annual world's best SF*. New York: DAW Books, 1983, 255 p., paper, anth.

33042 *The 1984 annual world's best SF*. New York: DAW Books, 1984, 256 p., paper, anth.

33043 *The 1985 annual world's best SF*. New York: DAW Books, 1985, 302 p., paper, anth.

33044 *The 1986 annual world's best SF*. New York: DAW Books, 1986, 303 p., paper, anth.

33045 *The 1987 annual world's best SF*. New York: DAW Books, 1987, 303 p., paper, anth.

The 1988 annual world's best SF—SEE: *Donald A. Wollheim presents The 1988 annual world's best SF*.

33046 *The 1989 annual world's best SF*. New York: DAW Books, 1989, 315 p., paper, anth.

33047 *The 1990 annual world's best SF*. New York: DAW Books, 1990, vi+341 p., paper, anth.

33048 *Donald A. Wollheim presents The 1988 annual world's best SF*. New York: DAW Books, 1988, 303 p., paper, anth.

Wollheim's World's best SF, series one—SEE: *1972 annual world's best SF*.
Wollheim's World's best SF, series two—SEE: *1973 annual world's best SF*.
Wollheim's World's best SF, series three—SEE: *1974 annual world's best SF*.
Wollheim's World's best SF, series four—SEE: *1975 annual world's best SF*.
Wollheim's World's best SF, series five—SEE: *1976 annual world's best SF*.
Wollheim's World's best SF, series six—*1977 annual world's best SF*.
Wollheim's World's best SF, series seven—SEE: *1978 annual world's best SF*.
Wollheim's World's best SF, series eight—SEE: *1979 annual world's best SF*.
Wollheim's World's best SF, series nine—SEE: *1980 annual world's best SF*.
The World's best SF 4—SEE: *The 1977 annual world's best SF*.
The World's best SF 5—SEE: *The 1978 annual world's best SF*.
The World's best SF short stories #1—SEE: *The 1974 annual world's best SF*.
The World's best SF three—SEE: *The 1976 annual world's best SF*.
The World's best SF, series eight—SEE: *1979 annual world's best SF*.
The World's best SF, series five—SEE: *1976 annual world's best SF*.
World's best SF, series four—SEE: *1975 annual world's best SF*.
World's best SF, series nine-SEE: *1980 annual world's best SF*.
World's best SF, series one—SEE: *1972 annual world's best SF*.
World's best SF, series seven—SEE: *1978 annual world's best SF*.
World's best SF, series six—*1977 annual world's best SF*.
World's best SF, series three—SEE: *1974 annual world's best SF*.
World's best SF, series two—SEE: *1973 annual world's best SF*.

WOLSON, Morton

37271 *The nightmare blonde*. New York, London: Pocket Books, 1988, 255 p., paper, novel.

WOLVERTON, Dave [i.e., John David Wolverton], 1957-

37272 *On my way to paradise.* New York, Toronto: Spectra, Bantam Books, 1989, 521 p., paper, novel.

37273 *Serpent catch.* New York, Toronto: Spectra, Bantam Books, 1991, 418 p., paper, novel.

WOLVERTON, John D.—SEE: Wolverton, Dave

WOMACK, Jack, 1956-

37274 *Ambient.* New York: Weidenfeld & Nicolson, 1987, 259 p., cloth, novel. TERRAPLANE #1.

37275 *Heathern.* London: Unwin Hyman, 1990, 255 p., cloth, novel. TERRAPLANE #3.

37276 *Terraplane: a novel.* London: Weidenfeld & Nicolson, 1988, 227 p., cloth, novel. TERRAPLANE #2.

WONGAR, B. [pseud. of Streten Bozic], 1938?-

37277 *Gabo Djara.* New York: Dodd, Mead & Co., 1987, xiii+242 p., cloth, novel. NUCLEAR TRILOGY #3.

37278 *Karan.* New York: Dodd, Mead & Co., 1985, xix+248 p., cloth, novel. NUCLEAR TRILOGY #2.

37279 *Walg: a novel of Australia.* New York: Dodd, Mead & Co., 1983, xviii+213 p., cloth, novel. NUCLEAR TRILOGY #1.

WOOD, Barbara (Lewandowski), 1947-

37280 *Childsong.* Garden City, NY: Doubleday & Co., 1981, 254 p., cloth, novel.

37281 *The Magdalene scrolls.* Garden City, NY: Doubleday & Co., 1978, 253 p., cloth, novel.

37282 *The watch gods.* London: New English Library, 1981, 347 p., cloth, novel.

37283 *Yesterday's child.* Garden City, NY: Doubleday & Co., 1979, 259 p., cloth, novel.

WOOD, Bari, 1936-

37284 *Amy girl.* New York: NAL Books, New American Library, 1987, 346 p., cloth, novel.

37285 *The killing gift: a novel.* New York: G. P. Putnam's Sons, 1975, 254 p., cloth, novel.

37286 *The tribe.* New York: New American Library, 1981, 339 p., cloth, novel.

with Jack Geasland

    Dead ringers—SEE: *Twins: Dead ringers.*

23780 *Twins: a novel.* New York: G. P. Putnam's Sons, 1977, 316 p., cloth, novel.

23781A retitled: *Dead ringers.* London: Sphere Books, 1988, 346 p., paper, novel.

WOOD, Bridget

37287 *The minstrel's lute.* London: Robert Hale, 1987, 208 p., cloth, novel. LUTE #1.

37288 *Satanic lute.* London: Robert Hale, 1987, 208 p., cloth, novel. LUTE #2.

37289 *Wolfking.* London: Headline, 1991, 376 p., cloth, novel.

WOOD, Christopher (Hovelle), 1935-

37288 *James Bond and Moonraker.* New York: A Jove Book, 1979, 222 p., paper, movie.

*WOOD, Edward D(avis) Jr., 1924-1978

WOOD, J. A.

37289 *We alien seed.* London: Robert Hale, 1979, 191 p., cloth, novel.

WOOD, John, 1942-

37290 *In a secret place.* Dublin, Ireland: Wolfhound, 1986, 128 p., cloth, novel.

WOOD, Robert, 1953-

37291 *The avatar.* London: Poplar, 1987, 290 p., cloth, novel.

WOOD, Robert P.—SEE: Wood, Robin

WOOD, Robin [i.e., Robert Paul Wood], 1931-

37292 *The people of Pern.* Norfolk, VA: Donning Co., 1988, 151 p., cloth, art.

with Richard Lippe

37916 *American nightmare: essays on the horror film.* Toronto: Festival of Festivals, 1979, 99 p., paper, nonf. anth.

WOOD, S(amuel) Andrew, 1890- , as ROBIN TEMPLE

38172 *The Aztec temple.* London: Blackie, 1955, vii+48 p., cloth, story.

WOOD, Susan (Joan), 1948-1980

06038　*The poison maiden and the great bitch: female stereotypes in Marvel superhero comics* / by Susan Wood Glicksohn. Baltimore, MD: T-K Graphics, 1974, 36 p., paper, nonf.

37293　*The poison maiden & the great bitch: female stereotypes in Marvel superhero comics.* San Bernardino, CA: R. Reginald, The Borgo Press, 1989, 28 p., cloth, nonf. [Revised edition; edited by Robert Reginald].

WOOD, Susan T.

37294　*The colonists and the Chronicles of Novae.* New York, Washington: Vantage Press, 1986, 215 p., cloth, novel.

*WOOD, Wallace, 1927-1981

WOODARD, Edwin (Udell), *with Heather Woodard Bischoff*

18021　*Storehouses of the snow.* New York: Leisure Books, 1980, 284 p, paper, novel.

WOODARD, Wayne—SEE: Bok, Hannes

WOODBERRY, George E(dward), 1855-1930

37295　*Edgar Allan Poe.* Boston: Houghton Mifflin Co., 1885, xxxi+354 p., cloth, nonf.

WOODBRIDGE, Benjamin M(ather), 1884-1969

37296　*The supernatural in Hawthorne and Poe.* Colorado Springs, CO: Colorado College, 1911, p. 135-154, paper, nonf.

*WOODBURY, David O(akes), 1896-1981

WOODCOCK, George, 1912-

37297　*The crystal spirit: a study of George Orwell.* New York: Minerva Press, 1966, vii+366 p., cloth, nonf.

37298　*Dawn and the darkest hour: a study of Aldous Huxley.* New York: Viking, 1971, 299 p., cloth, nonf.

37299　*Orwell's message: 1984 and the present.* Madeira Park, British Columbia, Canada: Harbour Publishing, 1984, 193 p., paper, nonf.

*WOODHOUSE, Martin (Charlton), 1932-

WOODLEY, Richard

37300　*Ark of doom.* New York: A Dell Book, 1978, 171 p., paper, tele. MAN FROM ATLANTIS #4.

37301　*Death scouts.* New York: A Dell Book, 1977, 190 p., paper, tele. MAN FROM ATLANTIS #2.

37302　*It's alive!* New York: Ballantine Books, 1977, 156 p., paper, movie.

37303　*Killer spores.* New York: A Dell Book, 1978, 176 p., paper, tele. MAN FROM ATLANTIS #3.

37304　*Man from Atlantis #1.* New York: A Dell Book, 1977, 204 p., paper, tele. MAN FROM ATLANTIS #1.

WOODROFFE, Patrick, 1940-

37305　*A closer look.* Limpsfield, Surrey, England: Paper Tiger, 1986, 127 p., paper, art.

37306　*The Dorbott of Vacuo; or, How to live with the Fluxus Quo.* Limpsfield, Surrey, England: Dragon's World, 1987, 79 p., cloth, story.

37307　*Mythopoeikon: fantasies, monsters, nightmares, daydreams.* London: Dragon's World, 1976, 155 p., paper, art.

37308　*The Second Earth: the Pentateuch retold.* Limpsfield, Surrey, England: Paper Tiger, 1987, 143 p., cloth, art.

WOODROW, Terry—SEE: Bluejay

WOODRUFF, Elvira

37309　*George Washington's socks.* New York, Toronto: Scholastic Inc., 1991, 166 p., cloth, novel.

WOODRUFF, Stuart C.

37310　*The short stories of Ambrose Bierce: a study in polarity.* Pittsburgh, PA: University of Pittsburgh Press, 1964, 193 p., cloth, nonf.

WOODS, Jack [pseud. of William B. O'Neal]

37311　*Wolffile.* New York: Pageant Books, 1988, 337 p., paper, novel.

WOODS, Stuart (Chevalier), 1938-

37312　*Under the lake.* New York: Simon & Schuster, 1987, 301 p., cloth, novel.

WOODSON, Thomas (Miller), 1931-

37313 *Twentieth century interpretations of The fall of the house of Usher: a collection of critical essays.* Englewood Cliffs, NJ: Prentice-Hall, 1969, iii+122 p., cloth, nonf. anth.

WOOLEY, John (Steven), 1949-

with Ron Wolfe

37257 *Old fears.* New York: Franklin Watts, 1982, 280 p., cloth, novel.

with Ron Wolfe as MICK WINTERS

37258 *Full moon.* New York: Berkley Books, 1989, 327 p., paper, novel.

WOOLF, Cecil, *with Brocard Sewell*

33558 *Corvo, 1860-1960: a collection of essays by various hands to commemorate the birth of Fr. Rolfe, Baron Corvo.* Aylesford, England: Saint Albert's Press, 1961, xiv+155 p., cloth, nonf. anth.
33558A retitled: *New quests for Corvo: a collection of essays by various hands.* Mayfair, England: Icon Books, 1965, 128 p., cloth, nonf. anth.
   New quests for Corvo—SEE: *Corvo, 1860-1960: a collection of essays by various hands to commemorate the birth of Fr. Rolfe, Baron Corvo.*

WOOLFOLK, Joanne—SEE: Martine

WOOLFOLK, William, 1917-

37314 *The Adam project.* New York: Fawcett Gold Medal, 1984, 280 p., paper, novel.
37315 *The president's doctor.* Chicago: Playboy Press, 1975, 309 p., cloth, novel.
37316 *The Sendai: a novel.* New York: Fawcett Popular Library, 1981, 288 p., paper, novel.

WOOLLEY, Persia, 1935-

37317 *Child of the northern spring.* New York: Poseidon Press, 1987, 428 p., cloth, novel. GUINEVERE #1.
   Guinevere, queen of the summer stars—SEE: *Queen of the summer stars.*
37318 *Guinevere: The legend in autumn.* New York: Poseidon Press, 1991, 432 p., cloth, novel. GUINEVERE #3.

37319 *Queen of the summer stars.* New York: Poseidon Press, 1990, 415 p., cloth, novel. GUINEVERE #2.
37319A retitled: *Guinevere, queen of the summer stars.* London: Grafton, 1991, 495 p., paper, novel. GUINEVERE #2.

WOOLRICH, Cornell (George Hopley-), 1903-1968

37320 *The fantastic stories of Cornell Woolrich.* Carbondale & Edwardsville, IL: Southern Illinois University Press, 1981, xxvi+334 p., cloth, coll. [Edited by Charles G. Waugh and Martin H. Greenberg].
15882 *Savage bride.* New York: Gold Medal Books, 1950, 178 p., paper, novel.
37321 *Vampire's honeymoon.* New York: Carroll & Graf, 1985, 223 p., paper, coll.

*WOOLSEY, Janette, 1904-_1989_

WOOLVERTON, Linda

37322 *Star wind.* Boston: Houghton Mifflin Co., 1986, viii+181 p., cloth, novel.

*WOOTTON, Barbara (Frances Adam), Baroness Wootton of Abinger, 1897-_1988_

*WORMSER, Richard (Edward), 1908-_1977_

WORTH, Valerie [i.e., Valerie Worth Bahlke], 1933-

37323 *Fox Hill.* New York: Farrar, Straus & Giroux, 1986, 148 p., cloth, novel.

WORTIS, Edward—SEE: Avi

WORTS, George F(rank), 1892-1967

37324 *The monster of the lagoon.* Mercer Island, WA: Starmont House, 1991, viii+145 p., cloth, coll. STARMONT FACSIMILE FICTION #14.

WRATISLAW, A(lbert) C(harles), 1862-

38173 *King Charles & Mr. Perkins.* Edinburgh, Scotland: William Blackwood & Sons, 1931, 320 p., cloth, novel.

WREDDEN, Margaret, *with Peter Cave*

19676 *Pisces rising.* London: Sidgwick & Jackson, 1978, 189 p., cloth, novel.

WREDE, Patricia C(ollins), 1953-

37325 *Caught in crystal.* New York: Ace Fantasy Books, 1987, 293 p., paper, novel. LYRA #3.

37326 *Daughter of witches.* New York: Ace Fantasy Books, 1983, 215 p., paper, novel. LYRA #2.

37327 *Dealing with dragons.* San Diego, CA: Harcourt Brace Jovanovich, 1990, x+212 p., cloth, novel. ENCHANTED FOREST CHRONICLES #1.

37328 *The harp of Imach Thyssel.* New York: Ace Fantasy Books, 1985, 234 p., paper, novel.

37329 *Mairelon the magician.* New York: Tor Books, 1991, 280 p., cloth, novel.

37330 *Searching for dragons.* San Diego, CA: Harcourt Brace Jovanovich, 1991, x+242 p., cloth, novel. ENCHANTED FOREST CHRONICLES #2.

37331 *The seven towers.* New York: Ace Fantasy Books, 1984, 264 p., paper, novel.

37332 *Shadow magic.* New York: Ace Books, 1982, 279 p., paper, novel. LYRA #1.

37333 *Snow White and Rose Red.* New York: Tor, A Tom Doherty Associates Book, 1989, xiii+273 p., cloth, novel.

37334 *Talking to dragons.* New York: Tempo Books, 1985, 232 p., paper, novel.

with Caroline Stevermer

34915 *Sorcery and Cecelia: an epistolary fantasy.* New York: Ace Books, 1988, 197 p., cloth, novel.

WREN, M. K. [pseud. of Martha Kay Renfroe], 1938-

37335 *A gift upon the shore.* New York: Ballantine Books, 1990, 375 p., cloth, novel.

37336 *House of the wolf.* New York: Berkley Books, 1981, 310 p., paper, novel. PHOENIX LEGACY #3.

37337 *Shadow of the swan.* New York: Berkley Books, 1981, xiv+338 p., paper, novel. PHOENIX LEGACY #2.

37338 *The Sword of the Lamb.* New York: Berkley Books, 1981, 436 p., paper, novel. PHOENIX LEGACY #1.

WREN, Thomas, pseud.—SEE: Thomas, Thomas T.

WRIGHT, Betty Ren, 1927-

37339 *Christina's ghost.* New York: Holiday House, 1985, 105 p., cloth, novel.

37340 *The dollhouse murders.* New York: Holiday House, 1983, vii+149 p., cloth, novel.

37341 *A ghost in the house.* New York, Toronto: Scholastic Inc., 1991, 164 p., cloth, novel.

37342 *A ghost in the window.* New York: Holiday House, 1987, 152 p., cloth, novel. SECRET WINDOW #2.

37343 *The ghost of Ernie P.* New York: Holiday House, 1990, 130 p., cloth, novel.

37344 *Ghosts beneath our feet.* New York: Holiday House, 1984, 137 p., cloth, novel.

37345 *The Pike River phantom.* New York: Holiday House, 1988, 153 p., cloth, novel.

37346 *The secret window.* New York: Holiday House, 1982, 149 p., cloth, novel. SECRET WINDOW #1.

with H. G. Wells

36714 *The time machine.* Milwaukee, WI: Raintree Publishers, 1981, 47 p., cloth, novel. [Adapted from the novel by Wells].

WRIGHT, Eugene A.—SEE: Wright, Gene

WRIGHT, Evan—SEE: Graham, David

WRIGHT, Gary (Staples), 1930-

37347 *The road west.* Lake Geneva, WI: TSR Inc., 1990, 314 p., paper, novel.

WRIGHT, Gene [i.e., Eugene Alden Wright], 1939-

37348 *Horrorshows: the A-to-Z of horror in film, TV, radio, & theater.* New York: Facts on File, 1986, viii+286 p., cloth, nonf.

37349 *The science fiction image: the illustrated encyclopedia of science fiction in film, television, radio, and in the theater.* New York: Facts on File Publications, 1983, 336 p., cloth, nonf.

37349A retitled: *Who's who & what's what in science fiction film, television, radio, and theater.* New York: Bonanza Books, 1985, ix+336 p., cloth, nonf.

Who's who & what's what in science fiction film, television, radio, and theater—SEE: *The science fiction image.*

WRIGHT, Glover [i.e., Geoffrey Glover-Wright], 1940-

37350 *The hound of heaven.* London: Hutchinson, 1984, 314 p., cloth, novel.

*WRIGHT, Grahame, 1947-<u>1977</u>

WRIGHT, Gregory Scott Jr., *with Guier S. Wright III as* GUY GREGORY

37351 *Heroes of Zara Keep.* Toronto, New York: Bantam Books, 1982, 197 p., paper, novel.

WRIGHT, Guier S. III, *with Gregory Scott Wright Jr. as* GUY GREGORY

37351 *Heroes of Zara Keep.* Toronto, New York: Bantam Books, 1982, 197 p., paper, novel.

WRIGHT, Helen (S.)

37352 *A matter of oaths.* London: Methuen, 1988, 283 p., paper, novel.

*WRIGHT, Lee, <u>1904?-1986</u>

WRIGHT, Mabel Osgood, 1859-1934

15883 *Wabeno, the magician: the sequel to "Tommy-Anne and the three hearts".* New York: Macmillan, 1899, 346 p., cloth, novel.

WRIGHT, Mary M.—SEE: Lorraine, Lilith

WRIGHT, Meg

37353 *As new wine.* Strathmartine by Dundee, Scotland: ScoTpress, 1979, 77 p., paper, tele. STAR TREK SERIES.
37354 *Closer than a brother.* Strathmartine by Dundee, Scotland: ScoTpress, 1983, 129 p., paper, tele. STAR TREK SERIES.
37355 *The female of the species is more deadly than the male.* Strathmartine by Dundee, Scotland: ScoTpress, 1982, 70 p., paper, tele. STAR TREK SERIES.
37356 *The tribe of Jen-Wae.* Strathmartine by Dundee, Scotland: ScoTpress, 1981, 92 p., paper, tele. STAR TREK SERIES.

WRIGHT, Robert G(ranger), 1937- , *with Theodore W. Hipple*

25710 *The worlds of science fiction.* Boston: Allyn & Bacon, 1979, vii+248 p., cloth?, anth.

WRIGHT, S(ydney) Fowler, 1874-1967

37357 *Deluge: a romance; and, Dawn.* New York: Arno Press, 1975, 395+349 p., cloth, coll. DELUGE SERIES #1-2.

WRIGHT, Stephen, 1946-

37358 *M31: a family romance.* New York: Crown Publishers, 1988, 214 p., cloth, novel.

WRIGHT, T(errance) M(ichael), 1947-

37359 *Boundaries.* New York: Tor Horror, A Tom Doherty Associates Book, 1990, 277 p., paper, novel.
37360 *The children of the island.* New York: A Jove Book, 1983, 243 p., paper, novel.
37361 *The island.* New York: Tor Horror, A Tom Doherty Associates Book, 1988, 278 p., cloth, novel.
37362 *The last vampire.* London: Victor Gollancz, 1991, 221 p., cloth, novel.
37363 *A Manhattan ghost story.* New York: Tor, A Tom Doherty Associates Book, 1984, 381 p., paper, novel. MANHATTAN #1.
37364 *Nursery tale.* New York: Playboy Paperbacks, 1982, 288 p., paper, novel.
37365 *The people of the dark.* New York: Tor, A Tom Doherty Associates Book, 1985, 288 p., paper, novel.
37366 *The place.* New York: Tor Horror, A Tom Doherty Associates Book, 1989, 278 p., cloth, novel.
37367 *The playground.* New York: Tor, A Tom Doherty Associates Book, 1982, 315 p., paper, novel.
37368 *The school.* New York: Tor Horror, A Tom Doherty Associates Book, 1990, 245 p., cloth, novel.
37369 *Strange seed: a novel.* New York: Everest House Publishers, 1978, 236 p., cloth, novel.
37370 *The waiting room.* New York: Tor Horror, A Tom Doherty Associates Book, 1986, 342 p., paper, novel. MANHATTAN #2.
37371 *The woman next door.* New York: Playboy Paperbacks, 1981, 255 p., paper, novel.

as F. W. ARMSTRONG

37372 *The changing.* New York: Tor, A Tom Doherty Associates Book, 1985, 244 p., paper, novel. CHANGING #1.
37373 *The devouring.* New York: Tor Horror, A Tom Doherty Associates Book, 1987, 284 p., paper, novel. CHANGING #2.

WRIGHT, T(imothy) Lucien, 1947-

37374 *The hunt.* New York: Pinnacle Books, Windsor Publishing Corp., 1991, 320 p., paper, novel.

WRIGHTSON, Berni, 1948- , with Christopher Zavisa

37375 *Berni Wrightson: a look back.* Detroit, MI: Land of Enchantment, 1979, 358 p., cloth, art.

WRIGHTSON, (Alice) Patricia, 1921-

37376 *Balyet.* London: Hutchinson, 1989, 102 p., cloth, novel.
37377 *Behind the wind.* Richmond, Victoria, Australia: Hutchinson of Australia, 1981, 156 p., cloth, novel. BOOK OF WIRRUN #3.
37377A retitled: *Journey behind the wind.* New York: A Margaret K. McElderry Book, Atheneum, 1981, 156 p., cloth, novel. BOOK OF WIRRUN #3.
37378 *The dark bright water.* Richmond, Victoria, Australia: Hutchinson of Australia, 1978, 223 p., cloth, novel. BOOK OF WIRRUN #2.
37379 *The ice is coming.* Richmond South, Victoria, Australia: Hutchinson of Australia, 1977, 222 p., cloth, novel. BOOK OF WIRRUN #1.
Journey behind the wind—SEE: *Behind the wind.*
37380 *A little fear.* London: Hutchinson, 1983, 110 p., cloth, novel.
37381 *Moon-dark.* London: Hutchinson, 1987, 146 p., cloth, novel.
37382 *Night outside.* New York: Atheneum, 1985, 67 p., cloth, story.
37383 *The song of Wirrun.* London: Century, 1987, [592] p., cloth, coll. BOOK OF WIRRUN #1-3. [Includes *The ice is coming; The dark bright water; Journey behind the wind*].

WU, Dingbo, with Patrick G. Murphy

30436 *Science fiction from China.* New York: Praeger Publishers, 1989, 176 p., cloth, anth.

WU, William F(ranking), 1951-

37384 *The cosmic bomber.* New York: A Byron Preiss Visual Publications Inc. Book, Ace Books, 1989, 151 p., paper, novel. DR. BONES #2.

37385 *Cyborg.* New York: A Byron Preiss Visual Publications Inc. Book, Ace Books, 1987, 170 p., paper, novel. ISAAC ASIMOV'S ROBOT CITY #3.
37386 *Hong on the range.* New York: Millennium, A Byron Preiss Book, Walker & Co., 1989, 286 p., cloth, novel.
37387 *Masterplay.* New York: Popular Library, 1987, 215 p., paper, novel.
37388 *Perihelion.* New York: A Byron Preiss Visual Publications Inc. Book, Ace Books, 1988, 162 p., paper, novel. ISAAC ASIMOV'S ROBOT CITY #6.
37389 *Robert Silverberg's Time tours: The Robin Hood ambush.* New York: A Byron Preiss Book, Harper & Row, 1990, 140 p., paper, novel. ROBERT SILVERBERG'S TIME TOURS #1.
The Robin Hood ambush—SEE: *Robert Silverberg's Time tours: The Robin Hood ambush.*
37390 *The shade of Lo Man Gong.* Eugene, OR: Pulphouse Publishing, 1991, 37 p., paper, story. SHORT STORY PAPERBACKS #35.
37391 *Yellow peril: Chinese Americans in American fiction, 1850-1940.* Hamden, CT: Shoe String Press, 1982, ix+241 p., cloth, nonf.

WUCKEL, Dieter, with Bruce Cassiday

19645 *The illustrated history of science fiction.* New York: Ungar, 1989, viii+251 p., cloth, nonf. [Translation by Jenny Vowles of *Science fiction: eine illustrierte literaturgeschichte*].

WULETICH-BRINBERG, Sybil, 1921-

37392 *Poe: the rational of the uncanny.* New York: Peter Lang, 1988, xi+223 p., cloth, nonf.

WÜLFING, Sulamith, 1901-

37393 *The fantastic art of Sulamith Wulfing.* Toronto, New York: Peacock Press/Bantam Books, 1978, [94] p., paper, art.

WUORIO, Eva-Lis, 1918-

37394 *Escape if you can: 13 tales of the preternatural.* New York: Viking Press, 1977, 116 p., cloth, coll.

WURFEL, Clifford (Randall), 1927-

37395 *An introduction to the J. Lloyd Eaton Collection of Science Fiction and Fantasy.*

Riverside, CA: Special Collections Department, University Library, University of California, Riverside, 1979, 13 p., paper, nonf.

*WURLITZER, Rudolph, 1937-

WURTS, Janny [i.e., Janice Wurts?], 1953-

37396 *Keeper of the keys.* New York: Ace Books, 1988, 269 p., paper, novel. CYCLE OF FIRE #2.

37397 *Shadowfane.* New York: Ace Books, 1988, 259 p., paper, novel. CYCLE OF FIRE #3.

37398 *Sorcerer's legacy.* New York: Ace Books, 1982, 246 p., paper, novel.

37399 *Stormwarden.* New York: Ace Fantasy Books, 1984, 325 p., paper, novel. CYCLE OF FIRE #1.

with Raymond E. Feist

23013 *Daughter of the empire.* Garden City, NY: Doubleday & Co., 1987, 394 p., cloth, novel. EMPIRE #1.

23014 *Servant of the empire.* New York: A Foundation Book, Doubleday, 1990, 580 p., cloth, novel. EMPIRE #2.

WYATT, Joan (Portis), 1934?-

37400 *A Middle Earth album: paintings inspired by J. R. R. Tolkien's The lord of the rings.* New York: Simon & Schuster, 1979, 63 p., cloth, art.

WYATT, Lee, pseud.—SEE: Proctor, Geo. W.

WYATT, Patrick, pseud.

37401 *Irish rose.* London: Michael Joseph, 1975, 213 p., cloth, novel.

WYATT, Stephen (John), 1948-

37402 *Doctor Who: Paradise Towers.* London: W. H. Allen & Co., 1988, 143 p., cloth, tele. DOCTOR WHO #134.

37403 *Doctor Who: The greatest show in the galaxy.* London: W. H. Allen & Co., 1989, 141 p., cloth, tele. DOCTOR WHO #144.
The greatest show in the galaxy—SEE: Doctor Who: The greatest show in the galaxy.
Paradise Towers—SEE: Doctor Who: Paradise Towers.

WYKES, (Douglas) Alan, 1914-

37404 *H. G. Wells in the cinema.* London: Jupiter Books, 1977, 176 p., cloth, nonf.

38174 *Happyland: a story.* London: Duckworth, 1952, 222 p., cloth, novel.

WYLDE, Thomas (Clarke), 1946-

37405 *Garukan blood.* New York: A Byron Preiss Visual Publications Inc. Book, Ace Books, 1989, 173 p., paper, novel. DR. BONES #3.

37406 *Journey to Rilla.* New York: A Byron Preiss Visual Publications Inc. Book, Ace Books, 1990, 189 p., paper, novel. DR. BONES #6.

37407 *Pitfall.* Toronto, New York: A Byron Preiss Book, Bantam Books, 1988, xii + 198 p., paper, novel. ROGER ZELAZNY'S ALIEN SPEEDWAY #2.

37408 *Roger Zelazny's alien speedway: The web.* Toronto, New York: Bantam Books, 1988, 245 p., paper, novel. ROGER ZELAZNY'S ALIEN SPEEDWAY #3.
The web—SEE: Roger Zelazny's alien speedway: The web.

WYLIE, Jonathan, pseud.—SEE: Smith, Mark & Smith, Julia

WYLIE, Laura, pseud.—SEE: Matthews, Patricia

WYMER, Thomas L(ee), 1938-

with Alice Calderonello & Lowell P. Leland & Sara Jayne Steen & R. Michael Evers

19206 *Intersections: the elements of science in science fiction.* Bowling Green, OH: The Popular Press, 1978, viii + 130 p., paper, nonf.

with Thomas D. Clareson

20070 *Voices for the future, volume three.* Bowling Green, OH: Bowling Green University Popular Press, 1984, 220 p., cloth, nonf. anth.

with David Cowart

20714 *Twentieth-century American science-fiction writers.* Detroit, MI: A Bruccoli Clark Book, Gale Research Co., 1981, 2 v. [I—xv + 306 p.; II—ix + 346 p.], cloth, nonf.

WYNDHAM, John [pseud. of John Wyndham Parkes Lucas Beynon Harris], 1903-1969

15699 *The best of John Wyndham.* London: Sphere, 1973, 318 p., paper, coll.

15699A retitled: *The best of John Wyndham, 1932-1949.* London: Sphere Books, 1977, 170 p., paper, coll. [The original book split into two volumes].

15699B retitled: *The best of John Wyndham, 1951-1960.* London: Sphere Books, 1977, 159 p., paper, coll. [The original book split into two volumes].

37409 *The day of the triffids; The kraken wakes; The chrysalids; The seeds of time; Trouble with lichen; The Midwich cuckoos.* London: Heinemann/Octopus, 1980, 860 p., cloth, coll.

37412A *Exiles on Asperus.* London: Severn House, 1979, 156 p., cloth, coll. [Originally published under the name John Beynon].

37410 *The man from beyond, and other stories.* London: Michael Joseph, 1975, 283 p., cloth, coll.

15716B *The secret people.* London: Coronet Books, 1972, 192 p., paper, novel. [Corrected entry; originally published under the names John Beynon and John Beynon Harris].

15715B *Stowaway to Mars.* London: Michael Joseph, 1974, 190 p., cloth, novel. [Originally published under the name John Beynon].

37411 *Web.* London: Michael Joseph, 1979, 187 p., cloth, novel.

as JOHN BEYNON

37412 *Exiles on Asperus.* London: Coronet Books, Hodder & Stoughton, 1979, 156 p., paper, coll.

with Patrick Nobes

30748 *Meteor: short stories.* Oxford, England: Oxford University Press, 1991, 106 p., paper, coll. [Adapted by Nobes from several Wyndham tales].

WYNNE, John

37413 *The sighting.* New York: Tree Line, 1978, 26 p., paper?, story.

WYNNE-JONES, Tim(othy), 1948-

37414 *Fastyngange: a novel.* Toronto: Lester & Orpen Dennys, 1988, 312 p., cloth, novel.

37414A retitled: *Voices.* London: Hodder & Stoughton, 1990, 312 p., cloth, novel.
Voices—SEE: *Fastyngange.*

WYNORSKI, Jim, 1950-

37415 *They came from outer space: 12 classic science fiction tales that became major motion pictures.* Garden City, NY: Doubleday & Co., 1980, xix+363 p., cloth, anth.

WYSACK, Roy L., *with L. Stephen Wolfe*

37256 *Handbook for space pioneers: a manual of the Galactic Association (Earth Branch).* New York: Grosset & Dunlap, 1978, 197 p., paper, fiction.

WYSOCKI, R(aymond) J.

37416 *The science fiction, fantasy, weird, hero magazine checklist.* Westlake, OH: R. J. Wysocki with Cooperation from the Cleveland Science Fiction Connection, 1985, iv+90 p., paper, nonf.

X

X, Madeleine

37417 *I am a vampire.* Hoboken, NJ: Essex, 1974, p., paper, novel.

Y

YAMASHITA, Karen Tei, 1951-

37418 *Through the arc of the rain forest: a novel.* Minneapolis, MN: Coffee House Press, 1990, 212 p., paper, novel.

YANEZ, José Donoso—SEE: Donoso, José

*YANIKIAN, Gourgen (Migirdik), 1895-1984

YARBRO, Chelsea Quinn, 1942-

Ariosto Furioso—SEE: Ariosto.
37419 *Ariosto: Ariosto Furioso, a romance for an alternate renaissance.* New York: Pocket Books, 1980, 361 p., paper, novel.
Bad medicine—SEE: Ogilvie, Tallant, and Moon.
37420 *A baroque fable.* New York: Berkley Books, 1986, 243 p., paper, novel.
37421 *Beastnights.* New York: Warner Books, 1989, 330 p., paper, novel.
37422 *Blood games: a novel of historical horror.* New York: St. Martin's Press, 1979, 458 p., cloth, novel. SAINT GERMAIN #3.
37423 *A candle for D'Artagnan: an historical horror novel.* New York: Tor Horror, A Tom Doherty Associates Book, 1989, ix+485 p., cloth, novel. ATTA OLIVIA CLEMENS #3.
37424 *Cautionary tales.* Garden City, NY: Doubleday & Co., 1978, x+204 p., cloth, coll.
37425 *CQY.* New Castle, VA: Cheap Street, 1982, [10] p., paper, nonf.
37426 *Crusader's torch.* New York: Tor, A Tom Doherty Associates Book, 1988, xiii+459 p., cloth, novel. ATTA OLIVIA CLEMENS #2.
37428 *Dead & buried: novelization.* New York: Warner Books, 1980, 304 p., paper, movie.
37429 *False dawn.* Garden City, NY: Doubleday & Co., 1978, 208 p., cloth, novel.
False notes—SEE Music when sweet voices die.
37430 *Firecode.* New York: Popular Library, 1987, 453 p., paper, novel.
37431 *A flame in Byzantium.* New York: Tor, A Tom Doherty Associates Book, 1987,

ix+470 p., cloth, novel. ATTA OLIVIA CLEMENS #1.
37432 *The godforsaken.* New York: Warner Books, 1983, 393 p., paper, novel.
37433 *Hôtel Transylvania: a novel of forbidden love.* New York: St. Martin's Press, 1978, 279 p., cloth, novel. SAINT-GERMAIN #1.
37434 *Hyacinths.* Garden City, NY: Doubleday & Co., 1983, 210 p., cloth, novel.
37435 *A mortal glamour.* Toronto, New York: Bantam Books, 1985, 308 p., paper, novel.
37436 *Music when sweet voices die.* New York: G. P. Putnam's Sons, 1979, 264 p., cloth, novel. CHARLIE MOON #2.
37436A retitled: *False notes / by C. Q. Yarbro.* New York: Jove Books, 1991, 245 p., paper, novel. CHARLIE MOON #2.
37437 *Nomads: novelization.* Toronto, New York: Bantam Books, 1984, 232 p., paper, novel.
37438 *Ogilvie, Tallant, and Moon.* New York: G. P. Putnam's Sons, 1976, 214 p., cloth, novel. CHARLIE MOON #1.
37438A retitled: *Bad medicine / by C. Q. Yarbro.* New York: Jove Books, 1990, 243 p., paper, novel. CHARLIE MOON #1.
37439 *On Saint Hubert's thing.* New Castle, VA: Cheap Street, 1982, [32] p., paper, story. [Limited to 333 copies].
37440 *Out of the house of life.* New York: Warner Books, 1990, xi+446 p., cloth, novel. SAINT-GERMAIN #7.
37441 *The palace: an historical horror novel.* New York: St. Martin's Press, 1978, 408 p., cloth, novel. SAINT GERMAIN #2.
37442 *Path of the eclipse: an historical horror novel.* New York: St. Martin's Press, 1981, xi+447 p., cloth, novel. SAINT GERMAIN #4.
37443 *Poison fruit / by C. Q. Yarbro.* New York: Jove Books, 1991, 245 p., paper, novel. CHARLIE MOON #3.
37444 *The Saint-Germain chronicles.* New York: A Timescape Book, Pocket Books, 1983, 206 p., paper, coll. SAINT-GERMAIN #6.
37445 *Signs & portents.* Santa Cruz, CA: Dream/Press, 1984, 162 p., cloth, coll.

37446 *Sins of omission.* New York: A Signet Book, New American Library, 1980, ix+245 p., paper, novel.

37447 *The spider glass.* Eugene, OR: Pulphouse, 1991, 51 p., cloth, story. SAINT-GERMAIN #8; SHORT STORY HARDBACKS #10; SHORT STORY PAPERBACKS #16.

37448 *Taji's syndrome.* New York: Popular Library, 1988, 439 p., paper, novel.

37449 *Tempting fate.* New York: St. Martin's Press, 1982, 662 p., cloth, novel. SAINT GERMAIN #5.

37450 *Time of the fourth horseman.* Garden City, NY: Nelson Doubleday, 1976, 183 p., cloth, novel.

37451 *To the high redoubt.* New York: Popular Library, Warner Books, 1985, 370 p., paper, novel.

YARIV, Fran Pokras

37452 *The hallowing.* New York: A Jove Book, 1980, 255 p., paper, movie.

YATES, Alan (Geoffrey), 1923-1985

37453 *Coriolanus, the Chariot!* New York: Ace Books, 1978, 245 p., paper, novel.

as CARTER BROWN

37454 *So what killed the vampire?* New York: A Signet Book, New American Library, 1966, 127 p., paper, novel.

YATES, Jessica

37455 *Dragons and warrior daughters.* London: Lions, 1989, 223 p., paper, anth.

YATES, W(illarm) R(olla), 1950-

37456 *Diasporah.* New York: Baen Science Fiction Books, 1985, 307 p., paper, novel.

YEAGER, David Clark, *with Isaac Asimov & Martin H. Greenberg*

17047 *Fantastic reading: stories and activities for grades 5-8.* Glenview, IL: A Goodyear Book, Scott, Foresman & Co., 1984, xiii+169 p., paper?, anth.

YEFIMOV, Igor—SEE: Moscovit, Andrei

YEHUDA, Nachman Ben- —SEE: Ben-Yehuda, Nachman

YEOVIL, Jack, pseud.—SEE: Newman, Kim

YEP, Laurence (Michael), 1948-

37457 *Dragon cauldron.* New York: HarperCollinsPublishers, 1991, 312 p., cloth, novel. SHIMMER AND THORN #3.

37458 *Dragon of the lost sea.* New York: Harper & Row, 1982, 213 p., cloth, novel. SHIMMER AND THORN #1.

37459 *Dragon steel.* New York: Harper & Row, Publishers, 1985, 276 p., cloth, novel. SHIMMER AND THORN #2.

37460 *Monster Makers, Inc.* New York: Arbor House, 1986, 219 p., cloth, novel.

37461 *Seademons: a novel.* New York: Harper & Row, 1977, 185 p., cloth, novel.

37462 *Shadow lord: a Star Trek novel.* New York: Pocket Books, 1985, 280 p., paper, novel. STAR TREK #22.

37463 *Tongues of jade.* New York: HarperCollinsPublishers, 1991, 194 p., cloth, coll.

YERBY, Frank (Garvin), 1916-1991

37464 *Tobias and the angel.* New York: The Dial Press, 1975, 315 p., cloth, novel.

YERMAKOV, Nicholas—SEE: Hawke, Simon

*YERSHOV, Peter, 1895-<u>1965</u>

YIN, Leslie—SEE: Charteris, Leslie

YNTEMA, Sharon

37465 *More than 100: women science fiction writers.* Freedom, CA: The Crossing Press, 1988, 193 p., cloth, nonf. [Cover title reads: *More than 100 woman science fiction writers: an annotated bibliography*].

YOKE, Carl B(ernard), 1937-

37466 *Phoenix from the ashes: the literature of the remade world.* New York: Greenwood Press, 1987, ix+247 p., cloth, nonf. anth. CONTRIBUTIONS TO THE STUDY OF SCIENCE FICTION AND FANTASY #30.

37467 *Roger Zelazny.* West Linn, OR: Starmont House, 1979, 111 p., paper, nonf. STARMONT READER'S GUIDE #2.

37468 *Roger Zelazny and Andre Norton: proponents of individualism.* Columbus, OH: State Library of Ohio, 1979, 26 p., paper, nonf.

with Donald M. Hassler

25339 *Death and the serpent: immortality in science fiction and fantasy.* Westport, CT: Greenwood Press, 1985, viii+235 p., cloth, nonf. anth. CONTRIBUTIONS TO THE STUDY OF SCIENCE FICTION AND FANTASY #13.

YOLEN, Jane [i.e., Jane Hyatt Yolen Stemple], 1939-

37469 *2041 A.D.: twelve stories about the future by top science fiction writers.* New York: Delacorte Press, 1991, xi+222 p., cloth, anth.

37470 *The books of Great Alta.* New York: Guild America Books, 1990, 426 p., cloth, coll. GREAT ALTA #1-2. [Includes *Sister Light, Sister Dark*; *White Jenna*].

37471 *The boy who spoke chimp.* New York: Alfred A. Knopf, 1981, 120 p., cloth, novel.

37472 *Cards of grief.* New York: Ace Fantasy Books, 1984, x+193 p., paper, novel.

37473 *The devil's arithmetic.* New York: Viking Kestrel, 1988, 170 p., cloth, novel.

37474 *Dragonfield, and other stories.* New York: Ace Fantasy Books, 1985, xiii+241 p., paper, coll.

37475 *Dragon's blood: a fantasy.* New York: Delacorte Press, 1982, xii+243 p., cloth, novel. PIT DRAGONS #1.

37476 *The dragon's boy.* New York: Harper & Row, 1990, 120 p., cloth, novel.

37477 *Dream weaver.* Cleveland, OH, New York: Collins, 1979, 80 p., cloth, coll.

37478 *The faery flag.* New York: Orchard Books, 1989, 120 p., cloth, coll. [Includes some verse].

37479 *Heart's blood.* New York: Delacorte Press, 1984, xiii+238 p., cloth, novel. PIT DRAGONS #2.

37480 *The lady and the merman: a tale.* Easthampton, MA: Pennyroyal Press, 1979, [21] p, cloth, story. [Limited to 100 copies].

37481 *Merlin's booke: thirteen stories and poems about the arch-mage.* New York: Ace Books, 1986, xiii+176 p., paper, coll. [Includes some verse].

37482 *The mermaid's three wisdoms.* New York: Collins & World, 1978, 112 p., cloth, novel.

37483 *Neptune rising: songs and tales of the undersea folk.* New York: Philomel Books, 1982, 149 p., cloth, coll. [Includes some verse].

37484 *The robot and Rebecca: the mystery of the code-carrying kids.* New York: Alfred A. Knopf, 1980, 89 p., cloth, novel.

37485 *A sending of dragons.* London: Julia MacRae Books, 1987, 184 p., cloth, novel. PIT DRAGONS #3.

37486 *Shape shifters: fantasy and science fiction tales about humans who can change their shapes.* New York: Seabury Press, 1978, viii+182 p., cloth, anth.

37487 *Sister Light, sister Dark.* New York: Tor, A Tom Doherty Associates Book, 1988, 244 p., cloth, novel. GREAT ALTA #1.

37488 *The sword and the stone.* Eugene, OR: Pulphouse Publishing, 1991, 45 p., cloth, story. SHORT STORY HARDBACKS #14; SHORT STORY PAPERBACKS #27.

37489 *Tales of wonder.* New York: Schocken Books, 1983, xii+275 p., cloth, coll.

37490 *Touch magic: fantasy, faerie, and folklore in the literature of childhood.* New York: Philomel Books, 1981, 96 p., cloth, nonf.

37491 *White Jenna.* New York: Tor, A Tom Doherty Associates Book, 1989, 265 p., cloth, novel. GREAT ALTA #2.

37492 *The whitethorn wood, and other magicks.* Ottawa, Ontario, Canada: Triskell Press, 1984, 30 p., cloth, coll. [Includes some verse].

37493 *The wizard of Washington Square.* New York: World Publishing Co., 1969, 126 p., cloth, novel.

37494 *Wizard's hall.* San Diego, CA: Harcourt Brace Jovanovich, 1991, x+133 p., cloth, novel.

with Martin H. Greenberg

24609 *Things that go bump in the night: a collection of original stories.* New York: Harper & Row, 1989, 280 p., cloth, anth.

24610 *Vampires: a collection of original stories.* New York: HarperCollinsPublishers, 1991, xi+228 p., cloth, anth.

24611 *Werewolves: a collection of original stories.* New York: Harper & Row, 1988, xi+271 p., cloth, anth.

with Martin H. Greenberg & Charles G. Waugh

24612 *Dragons & dreams: a collection of new fantasy and science fiction stories.* New York: Harper & Row, 1986, x+180 p., cloth, anth.

24613 *Spaceships & spells: a collection of new fantasy and science-fiction stories.* New York: Harper & Row, 1987, 182 p., cloth, anth.

YORK, Carol Beach, 1928-

37495 *Beware of this shop.* Nashville, TN: Thomas Nelson, 1977, 127 p., cloth, novel.

37496 *The ghost of the Isherwoods.* New York: Franklin Watts, 1966, 118 p., cloth, novel.

37497 *I will make you disappear.* Nashville, TN: Thomas Nelson, 1974, 111 p., cloth, novel.

37498 *Miss Know It All and the magic house: a Butterfield Square story.* Toronto, New York: Bantam Skylark, 1989, 90 p., paper, novel. BUTTERFIELD SQUARE #2.

37499 *Miss Know It All and the wishing lamp: a Butterfield Square story.* Toronto, New York: Bantam Skylark, 1987, 88 p., paper, novel. BUTTERFIELD SQUARE #1.

37500 *Nights in ghostland.* New York: An Archway Paperback, Pocket Books, 1987, 121 p., paper, novel.

37501 *On that dark night.* Toronto, New York: Bantam Books, 1985, 128 p., paper, novel.

37502 *Rabbit magic.* New York, Toronto: Scholastic Inc., 1991, 81 p., paper, novel.

37503 *When midnight comes.* New York: Elsevier/Nelson Books, 1979, 121 p., cloth, novel.

37504 *Where evil is.* New York: An Archway Paperback, Pocket Books, 1987, 117 p., paper, novel.

YORK, (Margaret) Elizabeth, 1927-

37505 *The Medea legend.* New York: Pocket Books, 1975, 262 p., paper, novel.

YORK, Rebecca, pseud.—SEE: Buckholtz, Eileen & Glick, Ruth

YORKE, Erin

37506 *Yesterday and tomorrow.* Toronto, New York: Worldwide, 1987, 379 p., paper, novel.

YORKE, Henry—SEE: Green, Henry

YORKE, Preston, pseud.—SEE: Kelly, Harold Ernest

YOUD, Christopher—SEE: Christopher, John

YOUNG ADULT REVIEWERS OF CALIFORNIA

37507 *Fantasy for young adults* / prepared by Young Adult Reviewers of Southern California. Temple City, CA: Temple City Public Library, 1974?, 40 p., paper, nonf.

YOUNG, B(ertram) A(lfred), 1912-

37508 *The colonists from space.* London: William Kimber, 1979, 208 p., cloth, coll.

YOUNG, Charles

37509 *The last man on Earth.* Lewes, East Sussex, England: The Book Guild, 1991, 319 p., cloth, novel.

YOUNG, David (Pollock), 1936- , with Keith Hollaman

25851 *Magical realist fiction: an anthology.* New York: Longman, 1984, vii+519 p., paper, anth.

YOUNG, Donna J.

37510 *Retreat, as it was!: a fantasy.* Weatherby Lake, MO: Naiad Press, 1979, 106 p., cloth, novel.

YOUNG, Ella, 1867-1956

15884 *The unicorn with silver shoes.* New York: Longmans, Green & Co., 1932, 215 p., cloth, novel.

YOUNG, James M.—SEE: Young, Jim

YOUNG, Jim [i.e., James Maxwell Young], 1951-

37511 *The face of the deep.* New York: Pocket Books, 1979, 223 p., paper, novel.

YOUNG, Meredith Lady

37512 *Agartha: a journey to the stars.* Walpole, NH: Stillpoint Publishing, 1984, 340 p., paper, novel.

YOUNG, Robert F(ranklin), 1915-1986

37513 *Eridahn.* New York: A Del Rey Book, Ballantine Books, 1983, 146 p., paper, novel.

37514 *The last Yggdrasill.* New York: A Del Rey Book, Ballantine Books, 1982, 135 p., paper, novel.

37515 *Starfinder.* New York: Pocket Books, 1980, 205 p., paper, novel.

37516 *The vizier's second daughter.* New York: DAW Books, 1985, 203 p., paper, novel.

YOUNGER, Jack [pseud. of Russ Jones], 1927?-

37517 *Claw*. New York: Manor Books, 1976, 219 p., paper, novel.

27518 *Curse of the pharoahs*. New York: Manor Books, 1976, 215 p., paper, novel. [With David Anthony Kraft].

37518 *Demon*. New York: Carlyle, 1979, 256 p., paper, novel.

37519 *Devlin*. New York: Manor Books, 1976, 222 p., paper, novel.

27519 *Rest in agony*. New York: Carlyle, 1979, 223 p., paper, novel. [With David Anthony Kraft].

37520 *Satan sublets*. New York: Carlyle, 1979, 190 p., paper, novel.

as ARABELLA RANDOLPHE

37521 *The vampire tapes*. New York: A Berkley Medallion Book, Berkley Publishing Corp., 1977, 247 p., paper, novel.

YOUNGSON, Jeanne (Keyes), 1924-

37522 *A child's garden of vampires*. Chicago: Adams Press, 1980, 61 p., paper, anth.

37523 *The Count Dracula book of classic vampire stories*. Chicago: Adams Press, 1981, 175 p., cloth, anth.

37524 *The Count Dracula cookbook*. Chicago: Adams Press, 1979, 60 p., paper?, coll.

37525 *The Count Dracula fan club book of vampire stories*. Chicago: Adams Press, 1980, 91 p., paper?, anth.

37526 *Count Dracula's favorite Christmas cookie recipes*. New York: Dracula Press, 1988, 12 p., paper?, nonf.

37527 *The further perils of Dracula*. Chicago: Adams Press, 1979, 50 p., paper, story. DRACULA SERIES.

with Peter Tremayne

35792 *Freak show vampire; and, The hungry grass*. Chicago: Adams Press, 1981, 110 p., paper, coll.

YOURCENAR, Marguerite [originally Marguerite de Crayencour], 1903-1987

37528 *Oriental tales*. New York: Farrar, Straus & Giroux, 1985, 147 p., cloth, coll. [Translation by Alberto Manguel of *Nouvelles Orientales*].

YOURELL, Agnes Bond

38175 *A manless world*. New York: G. W. Dillingham, 1891, 169 p., cloth, novel.

YOURGRAU, Barry

37529 *Wearing dad's head*. Salt Lake City, UT: Gibbs M. Smith, Peregrine Smith Books, 1987, 128 p., paper, coll.

YOUSSEF, Michael

37530 *Earth king*. Westchester, IL: Crossway Books, 1988, 384 p., paper, novel.

YULE, Andrew, 1936-

37531 *Losing the light: Terry Gilliam and the Munchausen saga*. New York: Applause Books, 1991, 247 p., cloth, nonf.

YULSMAN, Jerry

37532 *Elleander Morning: a novel*. New York: St. Martin's Press, 1984, 294 p., cloth, novel.

Z

ZACHARIA, Irwin

37533   *Brotherhood of evil.* North Hollywood, CA: American Art Enterprises, 1982, 156 p., paper, novel. PROTECTOR #1.

37534   *Landshark.* North Hollywood, CA: American Art Enterprises, 1982, 156 p., paper, novel.

37535   *Princess of darkness.* North Hollywood, CA: American Art Enterprises, 1982, 156 p., paper, novel. PROTECTOR #2.

37536   *Reddy or not.* North Hollywood, CA: American Art Enterprises, 1982, 156 p., paper, novel. PROTECTOR #3.

37537   *Three to get Reddy.* North Hollywood, CA: American Art Enterprises, 1982, 220 p., paper, novel. PROTECTOR #4.

as SARITA IRWIN

37538   *To love a vampire.* North Hollywood, CA: American Art Enterprises, 1982, 219 p., paper, novel.

ZACHARY, Fay Nedra, 1931-

37539   *Cradle and all...* New York: Pageant Books, 1989, 301 p., paper, novel.

37540   *Fertility rights* / by Fay N. Zachary. New York: Zebra Books, Kensington Publishing Corp., 1987, 507 p., paper, novel.

ZACHARY, Hugh—SEE: Hughes, Zach

ZACHARY, Judy

37541   *No other love.* Santa Clara, CA: Pentagram Publications, 1978, 87 p., paper, novel.

ZAHAVA, Irene, 1951-

37542   *Hear the silence: stories by women of myth, magic, & renewal.* Trumansburg, NY: The Crossing Press, 1986, 194 p., cloth, anth.

ZAHN, Timothy, 1951-

The Backlash mission—SEE: *Blackcollar: The Backlash mission.*

37543   *The Blackcollar.* New York: DAW Books, 1983, 272 p., paper, novel. BLACKCOLLAR #1.

37544   *Blackcollar: The Backlash mission.* New York: DAW Books, 1986, 288 p., paper, novel. BLACKCOLLAR #2.

37545   *Cascade point.* New York: Tor SF, A Tom Doherty Associates Book, 1988, 82 p., paper, story. [Bound with *Hard-fought* / by Greg Bear].

37546   *Cascade point, and other stories.* New York: A Bluejay International Edition, 1986, 405 p., cloth, coll.

37546A   retitled: *Cascade point.* New York: Baen Books, 1987, 405 p., paper, coll.

Cascade point—SEE: *Cascade point, and other stories.*

37547   *Cobra.* New York: Baen Science Fiction Books, 1985, 346 p., paper, novel. COBRA #1.

37548   *Cobra bargain.* New York: Baen Books, 1988, 409 p., paper, novel. COBRA #3.

37549   *Cobra strike.* New York: Baen Science Fiction Books, 1986, 344 p., paper, novel. COBRA #2.

37550   *A coming of age.* New York: A Bluejay International Edition, 1985, 292 p., cloth, novel.

37551   *Deadman switch.* New York: Baen Books, 1988, 373 p., paper, novel.

37552   *Heir to the empire.* New York: Bantam Books, 1991, 361 p., cloth, movie. STAR WARS #1.

37553   *Spinneret.* New York: Bluejay Books, 1985, 339 p., cloth, novel.

37554   *Time bomb, and Zahndry others.* New York: Baen Books, 1988, 312 p., paper, coll.

37555   *Triplet.* New York: Baen Books, 1987, 369 p., paper, novel.

37556   *Warhorse.* New York: Baen Books, 1990, 347 p., paper, novel.

ZÄHNER, Lilly

38176   *Demon and saint in the novels of Aldous Huxley.* Bern, Switzerland: Francke, 1975, 201 p., cloth, nonf.

ZAHORSKI, Kenneth J(ames), 1939-

37557 *Peter Beagle.* Mercer Island, WA: Starmont House, 1988, 124 p., cloth, nonf. STARMONT READER'S GUIDE #44.

with Robert H. Boyer

18400 *Dark imaginings: a collection of gothic fantasy.* New York: A Delta Book, 1978, 398 p., paper, anth.

18401 *Fantasists on fantasy: a collection of critical reflections.* New York: A Discus Book, Avon Books, 1984, 287 p., paper, nonf. anth.

18402 *The fantastic imagination: an anthology of high fantasy.* New York: Avon, 1977, ix+325 p., paper, anth.

18403 *The fantastic imagination II: an anthology of high fantasy.* New York: Avon, 1978, xi+307 p., paper, anth.

18404 *Lloyd Alexander, Evangeline Walton Ensley, Kenneth Morris: a primary and secondary bibliography.* Boston: G. K. Hall & Co., 1981, xvi+291 p., cloth, nonf. MASTERS OF SCIENCE FICTION AND FANTASY.

18405 *The phoenix tree: an anthology of myth fantasy.* New York: Avon, 1980, xxii+279 p., paper, anth.

18406 *Visions of wonder: an anthology of Christian fantasy.* New York: Avon, 1981, 240 p., paper, anth.

with Robert H. Boyer & Marshall Tymn

18399 *Fantasy literature: a core collection and reference guide.* New York, London: R. R. Bowker Co., 1979, xiii+273 p., cloth, nonf.

ZAKI, Hoda M(oukhtar), 1950-

37558 *Phoenix renewed: the survival and mutation of utopian thought in North American science fiction, 1965-1982.* Mercer Island, WA: Starmont House, 1988, 151 p., cloth, nonf. STARMONT STUDIES IN LITERARY CRITICISM #22.

ZAMBRENO, Mary Frances, 1954-

37559 *A plague of sorcerers.* San Diego, CA: Harcourt Brace Jovanovich, 1991, 257 p., cloth, novel.

as ROBYN TALLIS

35380 *Planet builders: Children of the storm.* New York: Ivy Books, 1989, 179 p., paper, novel. PLANET BUILDERS #7.

ZAMEENZAD, Adam

37560 *Cyrus Cyrus.* London: Viking, 1990, 578 p., cloth, novel.

ZAROULIS, N(ancy) L.

37561 *The Poe papers: a tale of passion.* New York: G. P. Putnam's Sons, 1977, 252 p., cloth, novel.

ZAVISA, Christopher, *with Berni Wrightson*

37375 *Berni Wrightson: a look back.* Detroit, MI: Land of Enchantment, 1979, 358 p., cloth, art.

ZAWIDOSKI, Gregory—SEE: Burgess, Mason

ZAYED, Georges (H.), 1916-

37562 *The genius of Edgar Allan Poe.* Cambridge, MA: Schenkman Publishing Co., 1985, ix+223 p., cloth, nonf.

ZEBROWSKI, George (Thaddeus) [anglicized from Jerzy Tadeuz Zebrowski], 1945-

37563 *Adrift in space.* Tulsa, OK: Educational Development Corp., 1979, 10 p., paper, story.

37564 *Ashes and stars.* New York: Ace Books, 1977, vii+197 p., paper, novel. OMEGA POINT TRILOGY #1.

37565 *The firebird* / by George Zebrowsky [sic]. Tulsa, OK: Educational Development Corp., 1979, 7 p., paper, story.

37566 *Macrolife.* New York, Hagerstown, NJ: Harper & Row, Publishers, 1979, 285 p., cloth, novel.

38177 *Macrolife.* Norwalk, CT: Easton Press, 1990, 284 p., cloth, novel. [Revised edition].

37567 *The monadic universe.* New York: Ace Books, 1977, xviii+170 p., paper, coll.

37568 *The monadic universe.* New York: Ace Science Fiction Books, 1985, xx+167 p., paper, coll. [Revised and expanded edition].

37569 *Nebula awards #20: SFWA's choices for the best science fiction and fantasy, 1984.* San Diego, CA, New York: Harcourt Brace Jovanovich, 1985, xi+372 p., cloth, anth.

37570 *Nebula awards #21: SFWA's choices for the best science fiction and fantasy, 1985.*

San Diego, CA, New York: Harcourt Brace Jovanovich, 1987, xiii+334 p., cloth, anth.

37571 *Nebula awards #22: SFWA's choices for the best science fiction and fantasy, 1986.* San Diego, CA, New York: Harcourt Brace Jovanovich, 1988, xii+365 p., cloth, anth.

37572 *The omega point trilogy.* New York: Ace Science Fiction Books, 1983, viii+295 p., paper, coll. OMEGA POINT #1-3. [Includes *The omega point, Ashes and stars, Mirror of minds*].

37573 *A silent shout.* Tulsa, OK: Educational Development Corp., 1979, 13 p., paper, story.

37574 *The star web.* Toronto, New York: Laser Books, 1975, 173 p., paper, novel.

37575 *The stars will speak.* New York: Harper & Row, 1985, 216 p., cloth, novel. BERNAL ONE #2.

37576 *Stranger suns.* Norwalk, CT: Easton Press, 1991, 310 p., cloth, novel.

37577 *Sunspacer: a novel.* New York: Harper & Row, Publishers, 1984, 309 p., cloth, novel. BERNAL ONE #1.

37578 *Synergy: new science fiction, number one.* San Diego, CA, New York: An Original Harvest/HBJ Book, Harcourt Brace Jovanovich, Publishers, 1987, xvii+243 p., paper, anth.

37579 *Synergy: new science fiction, number two.* San Diego, CA, New York: An Original Harvest/HBJ Book, Harcourt Brace Jovanovich, Publishers, 1988, xii+225 p., paper, anth.

37580 *Synergy: new science fiction, number three.* San Diego, CA, New York: An Original Harvest/HBJ Book, Harcourt Brace Jovanovich, Publishers, 1988 (i.e., 1989), x+223 p., paper, anth.

37581 *Synergy: new science fiction, number four.* San Diego, CA, New York: An Original Harvest/HBJ Book, Harcourt Brace Jovanovich, Publishers, 1989, xi+262 p., paper, anth.

37582 *Tomorrow today.* Santa Cruz, CA: Unity Press, 1975, 188 p., cloth, anth.

with Isaac Asimov & Martin H. Greenberg

17052 *Creations: the quest for origins in story and science.* New York: Crown Publishers, 1983, xii+351 p., cloth, anth.

with Jack Dann

21137 *Faster than light: an original anthology about interstellar travel.* New York,

Hagerstown, NJ: Harper & Row, Publishers, 1976, xviii+321 p., cloth, anth.

with Thomas N. Scortia

33445 *Human-machines: an anthology of stories about cyborgs.* New York: Vintage Books, Random House, 1975, xxv+252 p., paper, anth.

ZEBROWSKI, Jerzy—SEE: Zebrowski, George

ZEDDIES, Ann Tonsor, 1951-

37583 *Deathgift.* New York: A Del Rey Book, Ballantine Books, 1989, 329 p., paper, novel.

ZEIG, Sande, with Monique Wittig

37196 *Lesbian peoples: material for a dictionary.* New York: Avon, 1979, 170 p., paper, fiction.

ZEIGFRIED, Karl, house pseud.

15758 *Beyond the galaxy.* London: John Spencer & Co., 1953, 124 p., paper, novel. [By Tom Wade].

15759 *Chaos in Arcturus.* London: John Spencer & Co., 1953, 124 p., paper, novel. [By Tom Wade].

15760 *Chariot into time.* London: John Spencer & Co., 1953, 128 p., paper, novel. [By Tom Wade].

15761 *"Dark Centauri".* London: John Spencer & Co., 1954, 130 p., paper, novel. [By John Glasby].

15762 *The uranium seekers.* London: John Spencer & Co., 1953, 128 p., paper, novel. [By John Glasby].

*ZEITLIN, Ida, <u>1885?-1984?</u>

ZEITLIN, Jacob (Israel), 1902-1987, with Lawrence Clark Powell & Robert R. Kirsch

27325 *Aldous Huxley, 1894-1963: addresses at a memorial meeting held in the School of Library Service, February 27, 1964.* Los Angeles: University of California, Los Angeles, 1964, 10 p., paper, nonf. coll.

ZELAZNY, Roger (Joseph), 1937-

37584 *The authorized illustrated book of Roger Zelazny.* New York: Baronet Books, 1978, [96] p., cloth, coll. [Edited and adapted by Byron Preiss].

37584A retitled: *The illustrated Zelazny.* New York: Ace Books, 1979, 192 p., paper, coll. [Edited and adapted by Byron Preiss].

37585 *The bells of Shoredan.* San Francisco, Columbia, PA: Underwood-Miller, 1979, 12 p., paper, story. DILVISH #1. [Limited to 275 copies].

37586 *Blood of Amber.* New York: Arbor House, 1986, 215 p., cloth, novel. AMBER #7.

37587 *Bridge of ashes.* New York: A Signet Book, New American Library, 1976, 154 p., paper, novel.

37588 *Changeling.* New York: An Ace Book, 1980, 272 p., paper, novel.

37589 *The changing land: a novel of Dilvish the Damned.* New York: Ace Books, 1981, p., paper, novel. DILVISH #2.

37590 *The chronicles of Amber.* Garden City, NY: Nelson Doubleday, 1979, 2 v. (I-338 p., II-434 p.), cloth, coll. AMBER #1-5. [Volume one includes *Nine Princes* and *The guns of Avalon*; volume two includes *Sign of the unicorn, The hand of Oberon, The Courts of Chaos*].

37591 *The Courts of Chaos.* Garden City, NY: Doubleday & Co., 1978, 183 p., cloth, novel. AMBER #5.

37592 *A dark traveling.* New York: Millennium, A Byron Preiss Book, Walker & Co., 1987, 143 p., cloth, novel.

37592A retitled: *A dark travelling.* London: Hutchinson, 1989, 109 p., cloth, novel.

A dark travelling—SEE: *A dark traveling.*

37593 *Dilvish, the Damned.* New York: A Del Rey Book, Ballantine Books, 1982, 215 p., paper, coll. DILVISH #3.

37594 *The doors of his face, the lamps of his mouth.* Eugene, OR: Pulphouse Publishing, 1991, 46 p., cloth, story. SHORT STORY HARDBACKS #8; SHORT STORY PAPERBACKS #13.

37595 *Doorways in the sand.* New York: Harper & Row, 1976, 185 p., cloth, novel.

37596 *Eye of cat.* San Francisco, Columbia, PA: Underwood-Miller, 1982, 216 p., cloth, novel. [Limited to 350 copies].

37597 *For a breath I tarry.* San Francisco, Columbia, PA: Underwood-Miller, 1980, 66 p., cloth, novel. [Limited to 600 copies].

37598 *Frost and fire.* New York: William Morrow, 1989, 288 p., cloth, coll.

37599 *The graveyard heart.* New York: Tor SF, A Tom Doherty Associates Book, 1990, p. 1-62, paper, story. [Bound with *Elegy for angels and dogs* / by Walter Jon Williams].

37600 *The hand of Oberon.* Garden City, NY: Doubleday & Co., 1976, 181 p., cloth, novel. AMBER #4.

37601 *He who shapes.* New York: Tor SF, A Tom Doherty Associates Book, 1989, 107 p., paper, novel. [Bound with *The infinity box* / by Kate Wilhelm].

37602 *Home is the hangman.* New York: Tor SF, A Tom Doherty Associates Book, 1990, 96 p., paper, story. [Bound with *We, in some strange power's employ, move on a rigorous line* / by Samuel R. Delany].

The illustrated Zelazny—SEE: *The authorized illustrated book of Roger Zelazny.*

37603 *Knight of shadows.* New York: William Morrow, 1989, 251 p., cloth, novel. AMBER #9.

37604 *The last defender of Camelot.* San Francisco, Columbia, PA: Underwood-Miller, 1980, 32 p., cloth, story. [Limited to 300 copies].

37605 *The last defender of Camelot.* New York: Pocket Books, 1980, vii+308 p., paper, coll.

37606 *Madwand.* Huntington Woods, MI: Phantasia Press, 1981, 254 p., cloth, novel. CHANGELING SAGA #2. [Limited to 750 copies].

37607 *My name is Legion.* New York: Ballantine Books, 1976, 213 p., paper, novel.

37608 *Prince of chaos.* New York: William Morrow, 1991, 225 p., cloth, novel. AMBER #10.

37609 *A rhapsody in Amber.* New Castle, VA: Cheap Street, 1981, 32 p., paper, coll. AMBER tie-in. [Includes some verse].

37610 *Roadmarks.* New York: A Del Rey Book, Ballantine Books, 1979, 185 p., cloth, novel.

37611 *Sign of chaos.* New York: Arbor House, 1987, 214 p., cloth, novel. AMBER #8.

37612 *Sign of the unicorn.* Garden City, NY: Doubleday & Co., 1975, 186 p., cloth, novel. AMBER #3.

37613 *Today we choose faces; and, Bridge of ashes.* New York: A Signet Book, New American Library, 1981, 174+154 p., paper, coll.

37614 *Trumps of doom.* New York: Arbor House, 1985, 183 p., cloth, novel. AMBER #6. [Winner of the *Locus* Award for Best Fantasy Novel, 1985 (1986)].

37615 *Unicorn variations.* New York: Timescape Books, 1983, 252 p., cloth, coll. [Winner of the *Locus* Award for Best Collection, 1983 (1984)].

37616 *Wizard world.* New York: Baen Books, 1989, 411 p., paper, coll. [Includes *Changeling; Madwand*].

with Philip K. Dick

21744 *Deus irae.* Garden City, NY: Doubleday & Co., 1976, 182 p., cloth, novel.

with Neil Randall

32036 *Roger Zelazny's Visual guide to Castle Amber.* New York: Avon, 1988, 218 p., paper, fiction.
Visual guide to Castle Amber—SEE: *Roger Zelazny's Visual guide to Castle Amber.*

with Fred Saberhagen

32978 *The black throne.* New York: Baen Books, 1990, 278 p., paper, novel.
32979 *Coils.* Garden City, New York: Doubleday & Co., 1982, 183 p., cloth, novel.

with Robert Sheckley

33677 *Bring me the head of Prince Charming.* New York, Toronto: Bantam Books, 1991, 279 p., cloth, novel.

with Thomas T. Thomas

35560 *The mask of Loki.* Riverdale, NY: Baen Fantasy, 1990, 340 p., paper, novel.

ZELDIN, Theodore, 1933-

38178 *Happiness.* London: Collins-Harvill, 1988, 320 p., cloth, novel.

ZELLER, Claude van—SEE: Vennings, Hugh

ZENTZ, Gregory L.

37617 *Jupiter's ghost: next generation science fiction.* New York: Praeger Publishing, 1991, xxx+158 p., cloth, nonf.

ZETFORD, Tully, pseud.—SEE: Bulmer, Kenneth

ZETTERHOLM, Tore (Ulf Axel), 1915-

37618 *Six Six Six.* New York: A Dell Book, 1974, 267 p., paper, novel. [Translation by Thomas Teal of *666*].

ZETTNER, Pat

37619 *The shadow warrior.* New York: Atheneum, 1990, 220 p., cloth, novel.

ZEZZA, Carlo, 1936-

37620 *The love potion.* New York: M. Evans & Co., 1975, 402 p., cloth, novel.
37621 *Paris 2005.* New York: M. Evans & Co., 1990, ix+372 p., cloth, novel.

ZHEMAITIS, Sergei (Georgievich), 1908-

37622 *Eternal wind.* Moscow: Mir Publishers, 1975, 392 p., cloth, novel. [Translation by Gladys Evans of *Vechnyi veter*].

ZHURAVLEVA, Valentina (Nikolaevna), *with Genrikh Al'tov*

16328 *Ballad of the stars.* New York: Macmillan, 1982, 280 p., cloth, coll.

ZICREE, Marc Scott, 1955-

37623 *The Twilight Zone companion.* Toronto, New York: Bantam Books, 1982, 447 p., paper, nonf.
37624 *The Twilight Zone companion, rev. and exp. 30th anniversary edition.* New York, Toronto: Bantam Books, 1989, 466 p., paper, nonf.

ZIDE, Donna Comeaux

37625 *Lost splendor.* New York: Warner Books, 1980, 463 p., paper, novel.

ZIEGENFUSS, Alan—SEE: Warren, Alan

ZIEGFELD, Richard E(van), 1948-

37626 *Stanislaw Lem.* New York: Frederick Ungar Publishing Co., 1985, x+188 p., cloth, nonf.

ZIELINSKI, David, 1953-

37627 *A genuine monster.* New York: Atlantic Monthly Press, 1990, 236 p., cloth, novel.

ZIERHUT, Ingried, *with Andre Norton*

30854 *Grandmasters' choice.* Cambridge, MA: A Norescon III Book, NESFA Press, 1989, xv+221 p., cloth, anth.

ZIESING, Mark V(incent), 1953- , *with Andy Watson*

36484 *Journal wired.* Willimantic, CT: Mark V. Ziesing, 1989, 118 p., paper, anth. [This book was continued as a magazine].

ZIFF, Gil

37628 *Tibet: being the recollections and adventures of the hermit called Small Ears: a novel.* New York: Crown Publishers, 1981, xx+360 p., cloth, novel.

ZIMBARDO, Rose A(bdelnour), 1932- , with Neil D. Isaacs

26356 *Tolkien: new critical perspectives.* Lexington, KY: University Press of Kentucky, 1981, 175 p., cloth, nonf. anth.

ZIMBERT, Jonathan A.

37629 *The official art of 2010.* New York: A Wallaby Book, Pocket Books, 1984, 93 p., paper, nonf.

ZIMMER, Paul Edwin, 1943-

37630 *A gathering of heroes.* New York: Ace Books, 1987, 368 p., paper, novel. DARK BORDER #3.
37631 *Ingulf the mad.* New York: Ace, 1989, 247 p., paper, novel.
37632 *King Chondos' ride.* New York: Playboy Paperbacks, 1982, 412 p., paper, novel. DARK BORDER #2.
37633 *The lost prince.* New York: Playboy Paperbacks, 1982, 349 p., paper, novel. DARK BORDER #1.
37634 *Woman of the elfmounds.* Ottawa: Triskell Press, 1979, 63 p., paper, novel.

with Marion Zimmer Bradley

18494 *The survivors.* New York: DAW Books, 1979, 238 p., paper, novel. RED MOON #2.

with Jon DeCles

21477 *Blood of the Colyn Muir.* New York: Avon Books, 1988, 245 p., paper, novel.

ZIMMERMAN, Howard

37635 *The best of Starlog, the magazine of the future, vol. I.* New York: O'Quinn Studios, 1980, 98 p., paper, nonf. anth.

with David Hirsch

25714 *Norman Jacobs & Kerry O'Quinn present Spaceships, rev. ed.* New York: A Starlog Press Book, 1980, 98 p., paper, nonf.

Spaceships—SEE: Norman Jacobs & Kerry O'Quinn present Spaceships, rev. ed.

ZIMMERMAN, R(obert) D(ingwall), 1952-

37636 *Mindscream.* New York: Donald I. Fine, 1989, xii+260 p., cloth, novel.

ZIMMERMAN, Werner—SEE: Douglas, Drake

ZINDELL, David, 1952-

37637 *Neverness.* New York: Donald I. Fine, 1988, 458 p., cloth, novel.

ZINOVIEV, Alexander [i.e., Aleksandr Aleksandrovich Zinoviev], 1922-

38179 *The yawning heights.* London: Bodley Head, 1979, 828 p., cloth, novel. [Translation by Gordon Clough of *Ziiaiushchie vysoty*].

ZIPES, Jack (David), 1937-

37638 *Beauties, beasts, and enchantments: classic French fairy tales.* New York: NAL Books, New American Library, 1989, p., cloth, anth.
37639 *Breaking the magic spell: radical theories of folk and fairy tales.* London: Heinemann, 1979, xix+201 p., cloth, nonf.
37640 *Don't bet on the prince: contemporary feminist fairy tales in North American and England.* New York: Methuen, 1986, xiv+270 p., cloth, anth.
37641 *Fairy tales and fables from the Weimar days.* Hanover, NH: University Press of New England, 1989, ix+211 p., cloth, anth.
37641A retitled: *Utopian tales from Weimar.* Edinburgh, Scotland: Polygon, 1990, ix+211 p., paper, anth.
37642 *Fairy tales and the art of subversion: the classical genre for children and the process of civilization.* New York: Wildman Press, 1983, 214 p., cloth, nonf.
37643 *Spells of enchantment: the wondrous fairy tales of western culture.* New York: Viking, 1991, 814 p., cloth, anth.
Utopian tales from Weimar—SEE: Fairy tales and fables from the Weimar days.
37644 *Victorian fairy tales: the revolt of the fairies and elves.* London: Methuen, 1987, 381 p., cloth, anth.

ZODROW, John (Rester), 1944-

37645   *In the name of the father.* New York: A Dell Book, 1980, 317 p., paper, novel.

ZOLA, Émile (Édouard Charles Antoine), 1840-1902

38180   *Truth.* London: Blackwood, Scott & Co., 1903, x+587 p., cloth, novel. [Translation by Ernest Alfred Vizatelly of *Vérité*].

ZOLINE, Pamela [i.e., Pamela Lifton-Zoline], 1941-

38181   *Annika and the wolves.* Minneapolis, MN: Coffee House Press, 1985, [27] p., cloth, story.

37646   *Busy about the tree of life, and other stories.* London: The Women's Press, 1988, 187 p., paper, coll.

37646A retitled: *The heat death of the universe, and other stories.* Kingston, NY: McPherson, 1988, 204 p., cloth, coll.
The heat death of the universe, and other stories—SEE: *Busy about the tree of life.*

ZOOL, M. H., pseud.—SEE: Holkar, Mo & Towlson, Ivan & Tringham, Neal

ZORRO [pseud. of Harold Ward]

37647   *12 must die: a horror mystery straight from the devil's notebook.* Chicago: Robert Weinberg, 1979, 96 p., paper, novel. PULP CLASSICS #19.

ZOSS, Joel, 1944-

37648   *Chronicle.* New York: Pocket Books, 1980, 127 p., paper, novel.

ZU IRMELSHAUSEN, Charles Henneberg—SEE: Henneberg, Charles

ZUBER, Bernie, *with Bart Andrews*

16472   *The Tolkien quiz book: 1001 questions about Tolkien's tales of Middle-Earth and other fantasies.* New York: A Signet Book, New American Library, 1979, 154 p., paper, nonf.

ZUCKER, Miriam S.—SEE: Reichert, Mickey Zucker

ZUK, Beverly C.

37649   *The honorable sacrifice.* Lombard, IL: Beverly C. Zuk, 1981, ii+92 p., paper, novel.

37650   *The third verdict.* Lombard, IL: Beverly C. Zuk, 1982, iv+132 p., paper, novel. STAR TREK SERIES.

ZUPRINGER, Jeremy—SEE: Pascall, Jeremy

ZWERDLING, Alex, 1932-

37651   *Orwell and the left.* New Haven, CT, London: Yale University Press, 1974, xii+215 p., cloth, nonf.

TITLE INDEX

A

2nd bumper ghost book, The * Hale, James & Patricia Parkin

3 by Asimov: three science fiction tales * Asimov, Isaac

3 by Finney * Finney, Jack

4-D funhouse * Emery, Clayton & Earl Wajenberg

6 decades: the best of Analog * Schmidt, Stanley

6:02: a novel of horror * Clements, Mark A.

7 shapes of Solomon Bean, and 14 other marvelous stories of science fiction and fantasy, The * Ludwig, Edward W.

9 lives of Catseye Gomez, The * Hawke, Simon

10 ghosts * Grimshaw, Nigel & Paul Groves

10 strange tales * Grimshaw, Nigel & Paul Groves

11th plague, The * Klainer, Albert S. & Jo-Ann Klainer

12 must die: a horror mystery straight from the devil's notebook * Zorro

13 crimes of science fiction, The * Asimov, Isaac & Martin H. Greenberg & Charles G. Waugh

13 ghosts: a collection of original ghost stories with suggestions for varied work in English * Grimshaw, Nigel & Paul Groves

13 horror stories * Grimshaw, Nigel & Paul Groves

13 horrors of Halloween * Asimov, Isaac & Carol-Lynn Rössel Waugh & Martin H. Greenberg

13 sci-fi stories * Grimshaw, Nigel & Paul Groves

13 Shadow Lane * Stamper, J. B.

13 sinister stories * Griffin, John & Nigel Grimshaw & Paul Groves

13 weird tales: a collection of original strange stories with suggestions for varied work in English * Grimshaw, Nigel & Paul Groves

14 Bellchamber Tower * Valentine, Mark

14 vicious valentines * Greenberg, Martin H. & Rosalind M. Greenberg & Charles G. Waugh

15 yrs. later affair * Peel, John

16th Pan book of horror stories, The * Van Thal, Herbert

17th Pan book of horror stories, The * Van Thal, Herbert

18th Pan book of horror stories, The * Van Thal, Herbert

19th Pan book of horror stories, The * Van Thal, Herbert

20 under 35 * Straub, Peter

20th Pan book of horror stories, The * Van Thal, Herbert

21st century Foss * Foss, Chris

21st Pan book of horror stories, The * Van Thal, Herbert

22nd Pan book of horror stories, The * Van Thal, Herbert

23rd Pan book of horror stories, The * Van Thal, Herbert

24-carat assassin, The: a novel * Hill, Roger & Glen A. Larson

24th Pan book of horror stories, The * Van Thal, Herbert

25th Pan book of horror stories, The * Van Thal, Herbert

26th Pan book of horror stories, The * Paget, Clarence

27th Pan book of horror stories, The * Paget, Clarence

28th Pan book of horror stories, The * Paget, Clarence

29th Pan book of horror stories, The * Paget, Clarence

30th Pan book of horror stories, The * Paget, Clarence

33 sardonics I can't forget * Thayer, Tiffany

39 kids on the block: The green ghost of Appleville * Marzollo, Jean

40-minute war, The * Morris, Chris & Janet Morris

50-meter monsters, and other horrors, The: six tales of terror * Elwood, Roger

57th Frank Kafka, The * Rucker, Rudy

65 great spine chillers * Danby, Mary

65 great tales of horror * Danby, Mary

65 great tales of the supernatural * Danby, Mary

97th step, The * Perry, Steve

100 great fantasy short short stories * Asimov, Isaac & Terry Carr & Martin H. Greenberg

100 great science fiction short short stories * Asimov, Isaac & Martin H. Greenberg & Joseph D. Olander

100 magical stories * anon.

101 science fiction stories * Greenberg, Martin H. & Charles G. Waugh & Jenny-Lynn Waugh

666 * Anson, Jay

666 * Kirban, Salem

1876 * Barney

1931: a glance at the twentieth century * Hartshorne, Henry

1942: from starship to Lancaster * Regan, Jackie

1972 annual world's best SF * Saha, Arthur W. & Donald A. Wollheim

1973 annual world's best SF * Saha, Arthur W. & Donald A. Wollheim

1974 annual world's best SF, The * Saha, Arthur W. & Donald A. Wollheim

1975 annual world's best SF, The * Saha, Arthur W. & Donald A. Wollheim

1976 annual world's best SF, The * Saha, Arthur W. & Donald A. Wollheim

1977 annual world's best SF * Saha, Arthur W. & Donald A. Wollheim

1977 science fiction & fantasy magazine checklist & price guide, 1923-1976, The * Frank, Howard & Roy Torgeson

1978 annual world's best SF, The * Saha, Arthur W. & Donald A. Wollheim

1978 awards for best science fiction, or, The best of 1977, draft ed. * McGhan, H. P.

1979 annual world's best SF, The * Saha, Arthur W. & Donald A. Wollheim

1980 annual world's best SF, The * Saha, Arthur W. & Donald A. Wollheim

1980 bibliography of gothic studies, The * Crawford, Gary William & Frederick S. Frank & Benjamin Franklin Fisher IV & Kent Ljungquist

1981 annual world's best SF, The * Saha, Arthur W. & Donald A. Wollheim

1982 annual world's best SF, The * Saha, Arthur W. & Donald A. Wollheim

1982, Janine * Gray, Alasdair

1983 annual world's best SF, The * Saha, Arthur W. & Donald A. Wollheim

1984 annual world's best SF, The * Saha, Arthur W. & Donald A. Wollheim

1984: notes * Thompson, Frank. H. Jr. & Clifton K. Hillegass

1984 revisited: totalitarianism in our century * Howe, Irving
1984: Spring: a choice of futures * Clarke, Arthur C.
1985 * Burgess, Anthony
1985: a historical report (Hongkong 2036), from the Hungarian of *** * Dalos, György
1985 annual world's best SF, The * Saha, Arthur W. & Donald A. Wollheim
1986 annual world's best SF, The * Saha, Arthur W. & Donald A. Wollheim
1987 annual world's best SF, The * Saha, Arthur W. & Donald A. Wollheim
1988 * Grossman, Arnold & Richard Lamm
1988 annual world's best SF, The * Saha, Arthur W. & Donald A. Wollheim
1989 annual world's best SF, The * Saha, Arthur W. & Donald A. Wollheim
1990 * Gregson, Maureen
1990 annual world's best SF, The * Saha, Arthur W. & Donald A. Wollheim
1998 * Osborne, William & Richard Turner
2000 A.D.: illustrations from the golden age of science fiction pulps * Sadoul, Jacques
2001 A.D. * Foster, George C.
2001: a space odyssey; The city and the stars; The deep range; A fall of moondust; Rendezvous with Rama * Clarke, Arthur C.
2001 and beyond: science fiction stories * Laude, Anthony & H. G. Stenzel
2010: odyssey two * Clarke, Arthur C.
2018 A.D.; or, The King Kong blues * Lundwall, Sam J.
20/20 vision * West, Pamela
2020: vision of the future * Hale, Andrew
2041 A.D.: twelve stories about the future by top science fiction writers * Yolen, Jane
2061: odyssey three * Clarke, Arthur C.
2076: the American Tricentennial * Bryant, Edward
2084 * Gaida, Davida
2150 * Alexander, Thea
2150 A.D. * Alexander, Thea
20,000 leagues under the sea * Barling, Tom & Jules Verne
AI war, The * Berry, Stephen Ames
A. A. Milne * Swann, Thomas Burnett
A Is for Brian * Aldiss, Margaret & Frank Hatherley & Malcolm Edwards Bennett
A. Merritt * Foust, Ronald
A. Merritt: reflections in the moon pool: a biography * Moskowitz, Sam
Aardvark affair, The * Brandner, Gary
Ab to Zogg: a lexicon for science-fiction and fantasy readers * Merriam, Eve
Abandonati * Kilworth, Garry
Abduction: the UFO conspiracy * Bischoff, David
Ability quotient * Reynolds, Mack
Abode of life, The: a Star Trek novel * Stine, G. Harry, *as* LEE CORREY
Abominable snowman, The * Montgomery, R. A.
Abomination, The * McGill, Gordon
Abomination * Norton, Michael C.
Abomination * Smith, Guy N.
Aboriginal science fiction: tales of the human kind: 1988 annual anthology * Ryan, Charles C.
Abort Project K! * Lambert, William J. III *as* LAMBERT WILHELM
About the body * Burns, Christopher
About time: twelve stories * Finney, Jack
Above & below: a guide to Beauty and the Beast * Gross, Edward
Abracadabra * Gresham, Stephen

Abraxas marvel circus, The * Leigh, Stephen
Absences * Tem, Steve Rasnic
Absolute zero * Tidyman, Ernest
Abyss, The * Vance, Steve
Abyss, The: a novel * Card, Orson Scott
Abyss, The: a novel * Cunningham, Jere
Abyss of light, An * Gear, Kathleen O'Neal, *as* KATHLEEN M. O'NEAL
Abyssos * Hardie, Raymond
Academy of terror * Grant, Charles L., *as* STEVEN CHARLES
Acceptable time, An * L'Engle, Madeleine
Acceptance * Richards, Vicki
Accident, The * Hoh, Diane
An account of a meeting with denizens of another world, 1871 * Langford, David as WILLIAM ROBERT LOOSLEY
Accursed, The * Burdick, G. S.
Accursed * Smith, Guy N.
Ace alpha-numeric annotated science fiction checklist, An * Dillon, Peter C.
Ace in the hole: a Wild cards mosaic novel * Martin, George R. R. & Melinda M. Snodgrass
Ace science-fiction double books * Robinson, Roger
Aces abroad: a Wild Cards mosaic novel * Martin, George R. R.
Aces high * Martin, George R. R.
Achievement of C. S. Lewis, The * Howard, Thomas
Achilles' choice * Barnes, Steven & Larry Niven
Achon! the first book of the watchers * Gordon, Stuart
Acolytes of darkness * Marconi, David & Flint Dille
Acoma: a novel * Neill, Peter
Across a wine-dark sea * Bryan, Jessica
Across realtime * Vinge, Vernor
Across the Acheron * Wittig, Monique
Across the dark metropolis * De Larrabeiti, Michael
Across the far mountain * Hancock, Niel
Across the misty sea * Barrett, Neal Jr.
Across the sea of suns * Benford, Gregory
Across the Thlassa Mey * McCarty, Dennis
Across the wounded galaxies: interviews with contemporary American science fiction writers * McCaffery, Larry
Act of God * Kotani, Eric & John Maddox Roberts
Act of God * Templeton, Charles
Act of love * Lansdale, Joe R.
Act of Providence * Brennan, Joseph Payne & Donald Grant
Action: Division 3 * Mahr, Kurt
Active measures * Drake, David & Janet Morris
Acts of King Arthur and his noble knights from the Winchester manuscripts of Thomas Malory and other sources, The * Steinbeck, John
Acts of the apostates, The * Farrington, Geoffrey
Ad statum perspicuum * Wilson, F. Paul
Adam! * Baker, Mike
Adam experiment, The: a novel * Simmons, Geoffrey
Adam project, The * Woolfolk, William
Adam's Common * Wiseman, David
Addams chronicles, The: everything you ever wanted to know about the Addams Family * Cox, Stephen
Addams Family, The: a novelization * Calmenson, Stephanie
Addams Family, The: a novelization * Faucher, Elizabeth
Addams Family revealed: an unauthorized look at America's spookiest family * Van Hise, James
Adding machine, The: collected essays * Burroughs, William S.
Addison House * McNally, Clare
Adept, The * Harris, Deborah Turner & Katherine Kurtz

After all these years...: Sam Moskowitz on his science fiction career * Moskowitz, Sam

After armageddon * Carr, John F. & Jerry Pournelle

After dark * Wellman, Manly Wade

After Eden * Tobias, Michael

After long silence * Tepper, Sheri S.

After magic * Boston, Bruce

After man: a zoology of the future * Dixon, Dougal

After midnight * anon.

After midnight * Grant, Charles L.

After midnight ghost book, The * Hale, James

After midnight stories * Myers, Amy

After such knowledge * Blish, James

After sundown * Boyll, Randall

After supper ghost stories, and other tales * Jerome, Jerome K.

After ten years: a tribute to Stanley G. Weinbaum, 1902-1935 * De la Ree, Gerry & Sam Moskowitz

After the apocalypse * Fox, W. Randolph

After the atom * Fish, Leonard G. as VICTOR LA SALLE

After the bomb * Miklowitz, Gloria D.

After the bomb: flight to utopia * Wilkinson, Vernon

After the bomb: week one * Miklowitz, Gloria D.

After the end * Asimov, Isaac & Martin H. Greenberg & Charles Waugh

After the fact * Saberhagen, Fred

After the fall * Sheckley, Robert

After the flames * Mitchell, Elizabeth

After the flood: a novel * Jersild, P. C.

After the inferno * Webb, William Thomas

After the Omen * Allnutt, Frank

After the zap * Armstrong, Michael

After utopia * Reynolds, Mack

Afterdark princess, The * Dalton, Annie

Afterlife * Attwood, Tony

Afterlives: an anthology of stories about life after death * Sargent, Pamela & Ian Watson

Aftermath * Abbey, Lynn & Robert Lynn Asprin

Aftermath * Barton, James

Aftermath * Williams, Roger

Afternoon foreplay * Feddup, I. M.

Afternoon of an autocrat * Lofts, Norah

Afternoon of the elves * Lisle, Janet Taylor

Afternoon of the gosling * Huffman, Marlys

Aftershock * Walker, Robert W.

Afterwar * Morris, Janet

Against infinity * Benford, Gregory

Against the age: an introduction to William Morris * Faulkner, Peter

Against the fall of night; and, Beyond the fall of night * Clarke, Arthur C. & Greg Benford

Against the horde * Gemmell, David A.

Against the night, the stars: the science fiction of Arthur C. Clarke * Hollow, John

Against the prince of Hell * Smith, David C. & Richard L. Tierney

Against the wind * Pini, Richard

Against time's arrow: the high crusade of Poul Anderson * Miesel, Sandra

Against tomorrow * Hoskins, Robert

Agartha: a journey to the stars * Young, Meredith Lady

Age like this, 1920-1940, An * Orwell, George

Age of chaos, The * Smith, Julia & Mark Smith, *as* JONATHAN WYLIE

Age of the storyteller * Parise, Frank D. & Stephen Rich

Age of wonders: exploring the world of science fiction * Hartwell, David G.

Agent 13: Acolytes of darkness * Dille, Flint & David Marconi

Agent of Byzantium * Turtledove, Harry

Agent of change * Lee, Sharon & Steve Miller

Agents of destruction * Brand, Kurt

Agents of insight * Klaper, Steven

Agnes Cecilia * Gripe, Maria

Agnes day * Grant, Charles L., *as* LIONEL FENN

Agnostic island, The * Gould, F. J.

Agonies of time * Christchild, Ravan

Agviq: the whale * Armstrong, Michael

A-haunting we will go: ghostly stories and poems * Hopkins, Lee

Aia: Fields of sleep; and, People of the darkness * Vivian, E. Charles

Aiki: a novel * Gilbert, John

Air Force One is haunted * Serling, Robert

Air of Mars, and other stories of time and space, The * Ginsburg, Mirra

Air-king's treasure, The: a story of adventure with airship & aeroplane * Grahame-White, Claude & Harry Harper

Airship Nine * Block, Thomas H.

A.K.A.: a cosmic fable * Swigart, Rob

Akhenaten and Nefertiti: the royal rebels * Myers, Erica

Akrikorps * Williard, Tom, *as* BILL DOLAN

Akrikorps: Iron horse * Williard, Tom, *as* BILL DOLAN

Alabama bloodbath * Ham, Bob

Alamut * Tarr, Judith

Alan Mendelsohn, the boy from Mars * Pinkwater, Daniel M.

Alanna: the first adventure * Pierce, Tamora

Alasdair Gray * Gray, Alasdair

Albanian affair, The * Jennison, John as JOHN THEYDON

Albatross * Duncan, Kirk & Rico Gusman

Albino knife, The * Perry, Steve

Albion * Grant, John

Albion * Vale, Brenda

Albion's dream * Norman, Roger

Album of great science fiction films, An * Manchel, Frank

Album of great science fiction films, An, rev. ed. * Manchel, Frank

Album of modern horror films, An * Manchel, Frank

Alchemical marriage of Alistair Crompton, The * Sheckley, Robert

Alchemist, The * Whitten, Les

Alchemist, The: Death of a Borgia * Stevermer, Caroline

Alchemists, The * Gravel, Geary

Alchemy and academe: a collection of original stories concerning themselves with transmutations, mental and elemental, alchemical and academic * McCaffrey, Anne

Alchemy unlimited * Clark, Douglas W.

Alchymist's cat, The * Jarvis, Robin

Aldair, across the misty sea * Barrett, Neal Jr.

Aldair in Albion * Barrett, Neal Jr.

Aldair, master of ships * Barrett, Neal Jr.

Aldair: the legion of beasts * Barrett, Neal Jr.

Aldebaran campaign, The * Cornett, Robert & Kevin Randle

Alder tree, The * Jones, Gwyneth A. as ANN HALAM

Aldiss unbound: the science fiction of Brian W. Aldiss * Mathews, Richard

Aldous Huxley * Brooke, Jocelyn

Aldous Huxley * Henderson, Alexander J.

Aldous Huxley * Jouguelet, Pierre

Aldous Huxley * May, Keith M.

Aldous Huxley * Watts, Harold H.

Aldous Huxley, 1894-1963: a memorial volume * Huxley, Julian

Aldous Huxley, 1894-1963: addresses at a memorial meeting held in the School of Library Service, Febru-

Alien to femininity: speculative fiction and feminist theory * Barr, Marleen S.

Alien tongue * Leigh, Stephen

Alien trace, The * Buckley, Kathleen & Sharon Jarvis, *as* H. M. MAJOR

Alien upstairs, The * Sargent, Pamela

Alien wargames * Godfrey, Martyn N.

Alien web, The * Vardeman, Robert E.

Alien within, The * Bolton, Johanna M.

Alien within, The * Bova, Ben

Alien within, The * DeBolt, Adriana

Alien world, The: the complete illustrated guide * Holdstock, Robert as STEVEN EISLER

Alien worlds * Collins, Paul

Alien worlds: stories of adventure on other planets * Hill, Douglas

Alien worlds: three novellas of science fiction by award winning authors * Brown, Charles N.

Aliens! * Dann, Jack & Gardner Dozois

Aliens * Dozois, Gardner

Aliens: 3 novellas * Bova, Ben

Aliens: a novelization * Foster, Alan Dean

Aliens and linguists: language study and science fiction * Meyers, Walter E.

Aliens and outworlders * McCarthy, Shawna

Aliens are here, The! * Arneson, D. J. & Tony Tallarico

Alien's dictionary, The * Hallamshire, David

Aliens for breakfast * Spinner, Stephanie & Jonathan Etra

Aliens for lunch * Spinner, Stephanie & Jonathan Etra

Aliens from Analog * Schmidt, Stanley

Aliens in space: an illustrated guide to the inhabited galaxy * Caldwell, Steven

Aliens in the family * Mahy, Margaret

Aliens in the home: the child in horror fiction * Bussing, Sabine

Aliens: official movie magazine * D'Angelo, Carr & David McDonnell

Aliens, The: seven stories of science fiction * Silverberg, Robert

Aliens: the anthropology of science fiction * Slusser, George E. & Eric S. Rabkin

Aliens, travelers, and other strangers * DeGaris, Roger *as* ANONYMOUS

Alight in the void * Anderson, Poul

All about strange monsters of the recent past: neat stories, 2nd ed. * Waldrop, Howard

All & more * Aiken, Joan

All darkness met * Cook, Glen

All evil shed away * Roy, Archie

All fall down * Saul, John

All geared up * McEvoy, Seth

All heads turn when the hunt goes by * Farris, John

All in good time * Ormondroyd, Edward

All my roads before me: the diary of C. S. Lewis, 1922-1927 * Lewis, C. S.

All my sins remembered * Haldeman, Joe

All on a winter's day * Taylor, Lisa

All our tomorrows * Allbeury, Ted

All our yesterdays * Peel, John

All shook up * Lantz, Fran

All the clocks are melting * Boston, Bruce

All the devils are here * Deyo, David D. Jr.

All the gods are dead * Baker, Howard

All the king's men * Mayne, William

All the lies that are my life * Ellison, Harlan

All the money in the world * Brittain, Bill

All the shattered worlds * Vance, Steve

All the weyrs of Pern * McCaffrey, Anne

All these Earths * Busby, F. M.

All you've ever wanted, and other stories * Aiken, Joan

Allan Quatermain * Haggard, H. Rider

Allan Quatermain and the lost city of gold * Haggard, H. Rider

Allhallow's Eve * Laymon, Richard

Alliance * Oltion, Jerry

Allies of Antares * Bulmer, Kenneth, *as* DRAY PRESCOT & ALAN BURT AKERS

Alligator * Cerf, Christopher & Michael K. Frith as I*N FL*M*NG

Alligator Alley * Adder, Dr & Mink Mole

Alligator report, The: stories * Kinsella, W. P.

Alligators * Smith, Guy N.

Allison's baby * Stone, Mike

Allistar: journey through a mind * Aigner, Kurt W.

All-white elf, The * Dent, Lester as KENNETH ROBESON

Ally, Ally, Aster * Jones, Gwyneth A. as ANN HALAM

Almighty me * Bausch, Robert

Almost human * Smith, James V. Jr.

Almost lost * Montgomery, R. A.

Alone in the ashes * Johnstone, William W.

Alone in the house * Plante, Edmund

Along came a spider * Alexis, Athena

Along came a spider * Vinter, Michael

Alongside night: a novel * Schulman, J. Neil

Alpha II * Hubschman, Thomas

Alpha 6 * Silverberg, Robert

Alpha 7 * Silverberg, Robert

Alpha 8 * Silverberg, Robert

Alpha 9 * Silverberg, Robert

Alpha box, The * Dalton, Annie

Alpha Bug * Morris, M. E.

Alpha Centauri * Siegel, Robert

Alpha death * Conway, Norman

Alpha deception, The * Land, Jon

Alpha experience, The * Maitland, Derek

Alpha gallery * Oestricher, Joy et al.

Alpha star * Heywood, Victor D.

Alpha trap, The * Byrne, Stuart J.

Alpha-omega * McNeilly, Wilfred G. as WILFRED GLASSFORD

Alqua dreams * Pollack, Rachel

Altar, The * Walker, Paul

Alter ego: a novel * Watson, Patrick

Alter evil * Jade, Symon

Alteration, The * Amis, Kingsley

Altered egos * Girard, Kenneth

Altered I, The: an encounter with science fiction * Harding, Lee

Altered states: a novel * Chayefsky, Paddy

Alternate Asimovs, The * Asimov, Isaac

Alternate empires * Benford, Gregory & Martin H. Greenberg

Alternate heroes * Benford, Gregory & Martin H. Greenberg

Alternate wars * Benford, Gregory & Martin H. Greenberg

Alternate worlds: the illustrated history of science fiction * Gunn, James

Alternative histories: eleven stories of the world as it might have been * Greenberg, Martin H. & Charles G. Waugh

Alternative one: the greatest voyage of the Plutonians * Jolley, Mark

Alternative persons: the entities of science fiction and myth * Gooch, Stan

Alternative: the epilog to Orion * Downs, Gerry

Alternative Third World War, 1985-2035: a personal history * Jackson, William

Alternatives * Adams, Pamela Crippen & Robert Adams

Alternities * Kube-McDowell, Michael P.

Anaheim run * Robbins, David
Anaheim run; Seattle run * Robbins, David
Analog annual * Bova, Ben
Analog anthology #1, The * Schmidt, Stanley
Analog anthology #2, The * Schmidt, Stanley
Analog: readers' choice * Schmidt, Stanley
Analog: The best of science fiction * anon.
Analog: writers' choice * Schmidt, Stanley
Analog yearbook, The * Bova, Ben
Analog yearbook II * Schmidt, Stanley
Analog's Children of the future * Schmidt, Stanley
Analog's Expanding universe * Schmidt, Stanley
Analog's Golden anniversary anthology * Schmidt, Stanley
Analog's lighter side * Schmidt, Stanley
Anarch lords, The * Chandler, A. Bertram
Anarchistic colossus, The * van Vogt, A. E.
Anarchy in the ashes * Johnstone, William W.
Anarchy of light, The: Neil Gunn: a celebration * Pick, J. B.
Anarchy pedlars, The * October, John
Anasazi * Ing, Dean
Anatola: the autobiography of an Abyssinian cat * Wade, Elizabeth
Anatomies of egotism: a reading of the last novels of H. G. Wells * Bloom, Robert
Anatomy of horror: the masters of occult fiction * Barclay, Glen St. John
Anatomy of wonder: a critical guide to science fiction, 2nd ed. * Barron, Neil
Anatomy of wonder: a critical guide to science fiction, 3rd ed. * Barron, Neil
Anatomy of wonder: science fiction * Barron, Neil
Ancestors * Kline, Robert Y.
Ancestral voices: an anthology of early science fiction * Menville, Douglas & R. Reginald
Ancient curse of the Baskervilles, The * Cook, Michael L. as MICHAEL COOKE
Ancient dreams * Alexander, Marc
Ancient enemy, The * Thompson, Donald
Ancient evenings * Mailer, Norman
Ancient evil * Brennan, J. H.
Ancient evil * Ramirez, Alice as CANDICE ARKHAM
Ancient hauntings * Menville, Douglas & R. Reginald
Ancient heavens * Vardeman, Robert E.
Ancient images * Campbell, Ramsey
Ancient light * Gentle, Mary
Ancient lights * Grubb, Davis
Ancient mysteries reader, The * Haining, Peter
Ancient of days * Bishop, Michael
Ancient rage, An * La Tourrette, Jacqueline
Ancient solitary reign, The * Hocke, Martin
Ancients * Largent, R. Karl
And a deer's ear, eagle's song, and bear's game: animals and women * Corrigan, Theresa & Stephanie T. Hoppe
And afterward, the dark: seven tales * Copper, Basil
And again? a novel * O'Faoláin, Seán
And all between * Snyder, Zilpha K.
And all the King's men * Stevens, Gordon
And call my killer...Modok! * Rotsler, William
And don't forget the one red rose * Davidson, Avram
And eternity * Anthony, Piers
And gold was ours * Brandewyne, Rebecca
And having writ...: a science fiction novel * Bensen, D. R.
And love survived * Chetwynd-Hayes, R.
And no man's wit * Macaulay, Rose
And not make dreams your master * Goldin, Stephen

And on the eighth day * Davidson, Avram as ELLERY QUEEN
And still the Earth: an archival narration * Brandao, Ignacio de Loyola
And strange at Ecbatan the trees: a novel * Bishop, Michael
And the devil will drag you under: a novel * Chalker, Jack L.
And the gods laughed: a collection of science fiction and fantasy * Brown, Fredric
...And the lurid glare of the comet * Aldiss, Brian W.
And the rafters were singing: a tale of Cerin Songweaver * de Lint, Charles
And then there'll be fireworks * Elgin, Suzette Haden
And this is Laura * Conford, Ellen
Andre Norton: a primary and secondary bibliography * Schlobin, Roger C.
Andre Norton: fables & futures * Braude, Anne Janet
Andrew Lang: a critical bibliography of the works of Andrew Lang * Green, Roger Lancelyn
Andro, this is crazy * Lawson, Jack
Android planet * Mason, Douglas R. as JOHN RANKINE
Androids are coming, The: seven stories of science fiction * Silverberg, Robert
Andromeda 1: an original SF anthology * Weston, Peter
Andromeda 2: an original SF anthology * Weston, Peter
Andromeda 3: an original SF anthology * Weston, Peter
Andromeda vein, The * Dickenson, Sylvia
Andy * Snow, Bradley
Angado * Tubb, E. C.
Angel, The * Weinberg, Robert
Angel assignment * Ray, Rène
Angel at apogee * Lewitt, S. N.
Angel eyes * Lustbader, Eric Van
Angel fire * Greeley, Andrew M.
Angel of darkness * de Lint, Charles as SAMUEL M. KEY
Angel of pain, The * Stableford, Brian M.
Angel of passion * Arrow, Jay as GORDON BRADFORD
Angel of the west window, The * Meyrink, Gustav
Angel Station * Williams, Walter Jon
Angel with the sword * Cherryh, C. J.
Angels * Barton, James
Angels and awakenings: stories of the miraculous by great modern writers * Grey, M. Cameron
Angels and the creeping enemy, The * Jennison, John as JOHN THEYDON
Angels in Hell * Morris, Janet
Angelus! * Tremayne, Peter
Angelwalk: a modern fable * Elwood, Roger
Angmar * Kubasch, Heike
Angriff technique, The * Gardner, Tonita S.
Angry canary, The * Dent, Lester as KENNETH ROBESON
Angry candy * Ellison, Harlan
Angry dead, The * Pardoe, Rosemary as MARY ANN ALLEN
Angry ghost, The: a Doc Savage adventure * Dent, Lester & William G. Bogart as KENNETH ROBESON
Animal? * Vaccaro, Maria Angelica
Animal Farm and Nineteen Eighty-Four * Calder, Jenni
Animal farm; Burmese days; A clergyman's daughter; Coming up for air; Keep the aspidistra flying; Nineteen eighty-four * Orwell, George
Animal farm, George Orwell * Griffin, John
Animal farm: notes * Fink, Howard
Animal farm: notes * Thompson, Frank H. Jr. & Robert B. Kaplan
Animal ghosts * Lloyd, Caroline
Animal ghosts: a new collection * Davis, Richard
Animal magnetism * Prose, Francine
Animal wife, The * Thomas, Elizabeth Marshall

April fools * Cusick, Richie Tankersley
April witch, The * Bradbury, Ray
April witch, and other strange tales, The * Ireson, Barbara
Aquarian attack, The * Cornett, Robert & Kevin Randle
Aquarius * Mark, Jan
Aquarius mission: a novel * Caidin, Martin
Aquatech warriors * Macdonald, James D. and Debra Doyle as VICTOR APPLETON
Aqueduct, The: (a Martian chronicle) * Bradbury, Ray
Aquila and the iron horse * Sucharitkul, Somtow as S. P. SOMTOW
Aquila and the sphinx * Sucharitkul, Somtow as S. P. SOMTOW
Aquila in the new world * Sucharitkul, Somtow as S. P. SOMTOW
Aquiliad, The * Sucharitkul, Somtow
Ara's field * Marks, Laurie J.
Arabesques 2 * Shwartz, Susan
Arabesques: more tales of the Arabian nights * Shwartz, Susan
Arabian adventure * Miles, Keith
Arabian nightmare, The * Irwin, Robert
Arabian nightmare * Murphy, Warren & Richard Sapir
Arabian nights entertainments * anon.
Arachnaphobia: a novel * Edwards, Nicholas
Arachne * Mason, Lisa
Arafel's saga * Cherryh, C. J.
Araminta Station * Vance, Jack
Ararat * Thomas, D. M.
Arbor House celebrity book of horror stories, The * Greenberg, Martin H. & Charles G. Waugh
Arbor House necropolis, The: Voodoo! a chrestomathy of necromancy; Mummy! a chrestomathy of cryptoology; Ghoul! a chrestomathy of ogrery * Pronzini, Bill
Arbor House treasury of great science fiction short novels, The * Greenberg, Martin H. & Robert Silverberg
Arbor House treasury of horror and the supernatural, The * Greenberg, Martin H. & Bill Pronzini & Barry N. Malzberg
Arbor House treasury of modern science fiction, The * Greenberg, Martin H. & Robert Silverberg
Arbor House treasury of science fiction masterpieces, The * Greenberg, Martin H. & Robert Silverberg
Arc of infinity * Dicks, Terrance
Arc of the dream * Attanasio, A. A.
Arcade * Maxxe, Robert
Arcade explorers: Revenge of the Raster gang * McEvoy, Seth & Laure Smith
Arcade explorers: Save the Venturians! * Smith, Laure & Seth McEvoy
Arcade explorers: The electronic hurricane * McEvoy, Seth & Laure Smith
Arcade explorers: The magnetic ghost of Shadow Island * McEvoy, Seth & Laure Smith
Arcane * Sherrell, Carl
Archer's Goon * Jones, Diana Wynne
Archipelago * Lafferty, R. A.
Architect of sleep, The * Boyett, Steven R.
Architects of hyperspace, The * McDonough, Thomas R.
Architects of the abyss: the indeterminate fictions of Poe, Hawthorne, and Melville * Pahl, Dennis
Architecture of desire, The * Gentle, Mary
Architecture of fear * Cramer, Kathryn & Peter D. Pautz
Archives of evil * Lee, Christopher & Michel Parry
Archives of Haven, The * Savarin, Julian Jay
Archivist, The: a black romance * Alderman, Gil
Archon conspiracy, The * Hunt, Dave
Arctic unicorn * Luenn, Nancy
Arcturus landing * Dickson, Gordon R.

Ardennes tapes, The * Benford, Timothy B.
Ardistan and Djinnistan: a novel * May, Karl
Ardneh's world * Saberhagen, Fred
Are all the giants dead? * Norton, Mary
Arena * Savarin, Julian Jay
Arena of death * Smith, Mark & Jamie Thomson
Arena: sports SF * Ferman, Edward L. & Barry N. Malzberg
Argh: the tale of a tiger * Buckingham, M. E.
Argonaut affair, The * Hawke, Simon
Argus gambit, The * Ross, David D.
Argus steps in * Sernine, Daniel
ARIEL * Bickham, Jack M.
Ariel * Durwood, Thomas
Ariel: a book of the Change * Boyett, Steven R.
Ariel like a harpy: Shelley, Mary, and Frankenstein * Small, Christopher
Ariel, the book of fantasy, volume four * Durwood, Thomas
Ariel, the book of fantasy, volume three * Durwood, Thomas
Ariel, the book of fantasy, volume two * Durwood, Thomas
Aries I * Grant, John
Arimaspian legacy, The * Wolfe, Gene
Ariosto: Ariosto Furioso, a romance for an alternate renaissance * Yarbro, Chelsea Quinn
Ariosto Furioso * Yarbro, Chelsea Quinn
Aristocats, The * Moffatt, Derry
Ark, The * Erickson, Paul
Ark, The * Vigliante, Mary as JARL SZYDLOW
Ark in space, The * Marter, Ian
Ark of doom * Woodley, Richard
Ark Sakura, The * Abe, Kobo
Ark Two * Appleton, Victor
Arkham evil, The * Diaper, John
Arkham House companion, The: fifty years of Arkham House: a bibliographical history and collector's price guide to Arkham House/Mycroft & Moran, including the revised and expanded Horrors and unpleasantries * Jaffery, Sheldon
Arm of Mrs. Egan, and other strange stories, The * Harvey, William Fryer
Armada * Jahn, Michael
Armada of Antares * Bulmer, Kenneth as ALAN BURT AKERS
Armada sci-fi 1 * Davis, Richard
Armada sci-fi 2 * Davis, Richard
Armada sci-fi 3 * Davis, Richard
Armageddon! * Carr, John F. & Jerry Pournelle
Armageddon 2000 * McGill, Gordon
Armageddon blues, The: a tale of the great wheel of existence * Moran, Daniel Keys
Armageddon box, The * Weinberg, Robert
Armageddon crazy, The * Farren, Mick
Armageddon off Vesta * Murdock, M. S.
Armageddon rag, The * Martin, George R. R.
Armageddon revisited * Kemp, Ken
Armageddon run * Milán, Victor as RICHARD AUSTIN
Armageddon run * Robbins, David
Armageddon: the musical * Rankin, Robert
Armageddon, USA * Schmidt, Dan
Armies of daylight, The * Hambly, Barbara
Armlet of the gods, The * Eshbach, Lloyd Arthur
Armor * Steakley, John
Armor of light, The * Barnett, Lisa A. & Melissa Scott
Arms of Kali, The * Murphy, Warren & Richard Sapir
Army of darkness * Walker, Hugh
Around the year with C. S. Lewis & his friends * Lindskoog, Kathryn

B

Baaa * Macaulay, David
Baal * McCammon, Robert R.
Baalbak quest, The * Kelly, David J.
Babel's children * Williamson, J. N.
Baby, The * Kegan, Stephanie
Baby: a novel * Don, Ian
Baby: a novel * Lieberman, Robert
Baby doll * Jensen, Ruby Jean
Baby grand * Johnstone, William W. & Joseph E. Keene
Baby: the storybook * Miller, David Lee
Babydoll * Knight, Marilyn
Babylon * Esler, Anthony
Babylon Gate, The * Byers, Edward A.
Babysitter, The * Gorman, Ed as DANIEL RANSOM
Baby-sitter, The * Stine, R. L.
Baby-sitter II, The * Stine, R. L.
Bachman books, The: four early novels: Rage; The long
    walk; Roadwork; The running man * King, Stephen
Back door of history, The * Lafferty, R. A.
Back from the dead * Greenberg, Martin H. & Charles
    G. Waugh
Back to nature * Alexander, Robert
Back to the future: a novel * Gipe, George
Back to the future: a story * Fleming, Robert Loren
Back to the future, part II: a novel * Gardner, Craig
    Shaw
Back to the future, part III: a novel * Gardner, Craig
    Shaw
Back to the future: the official book of the complete movie
    trilogy * Hibbin, Sally & Michael Klastorin
Backblast * McKeone, Lee
Backflash * James, Laurence
Backlash * Farrar, Stewart
Backlash * Fisk, Nicholas
Backlash mission, The * Zahn, Timothy
Backward in time * Kelley, Leo P.
Backwater man, The * Clements, David
Back-yard war, The * Fisk, Nicholas
Bad blood * Farris, John
Bad dreams * Newman, Kim
Bad medicine * Yarbro, Chelsea Quinn
Bad night for Ali Baba, A * Gardner, Craig Shaw
Bad place, The * Koontz, Dean R.
Bad sister, The: a novel * Tennant, Emma
Bad spell in Yurt, A * Brittain, C. Dale
Bad times for ghosts * Wippersberg, W. J. M.
Bad voltage: a fantasy in 4/4 * Littell, Jonathan
Badger in the bag, The: a tale of Cerin Songweaver * de
    Lint, Charles
Badger of Ghissi, The * Niebelschutz, Wolf von
Badland * Obstfeld, Raymond as JASON FROST
Badlands of Hark, The * Stine, R. L.
Badlands run * Lambard, Creede & Sharleen Lambard
Bag of surprises, A * Hoshi, Shin'ichi
Bagdad * Dennis, Ian
Bagful of dreams, The * Vance, Jack
Bailey's window * Lindbergh, Anne
Baily's bones * Kelleher, Victor
Bait of dreams, A: a five-summer quest * Clayton, Jo

Baker's dozen: 13 short horror novels * Greenberg,
    Martin H. & Charles G. Waugh
Baker's dozen: thirteen short fantasy novels * Asimov,
    Isaac & Martin H. Greenberg & Charles G. Waugh
Baker's dozen: thirteen short science fiction novels *
    Asimov, Isaac & Martin H. Greenberg & Charles G.
    Waugh
Balance of power * Stableford, Brian M.
Ballad of Beta-2, The * Delany, Samuel R.
Ballad of Beta-2, The; and, Empire star * Delany,
    Samuel R.
Ballad of Favour * Dickens, Monica
Ballad of the stars * Al'tov, Genrikh & Valentina Zhu-
    ravleva
Ballantine Books: the first decade: a bibliographical his-
    tory & guide of the publisher's early years *
    Aronovitz, David
Ballantine teachers' guide to science fiction, The * Allen,
    L. David
Ballarina mystery, The * Pascal, Jamie & Laurie Pascal
Balls! * Rohmer, Richard
Balook * Anthony, Piers
Baltasar and Blimunda * Saramago, Jose
Balthazar * Durrell, Lawrence
Balustrade paradox, The * Oram, Neil
Balyet * Wrightson, Patricia
Bamboo demons, The * Sherman, Jory
Bander Snatch * O'Donnell, Kevin Jr.
Bane * Donnelly, Joe
Bane of Lord Caladon, The * Mills, Craig
Bane of nightmares * Cole, Adrian
Bane of the black sword, The * Moorcock, Michael
Banished, The * Williamson, J. N.
Banished dreams * Simmons, Dan
Bannerman effect, The * Maxim, John R.
Bannerman solution, The * Maxim, John R.
Bannerman's law * Maxim, John R.
Banners of the Sa'yen * Stateham, B. R.
Banshee * Barton, Dan
Banshee * Scott, Michael
Bantam Spectra sampler, The * Aronica, Lou
Barbara, the valiant * Kimbro, John M. as KATHERYN
    KIMBROUGH
Barbarian, The * Sadler, Barry
Barbarian of world's end, The * Carter, Lin
Barbarian swordsmen, The: great stories of heroic fan-
    tasy * Richards, Sean
Barbarian victim * Bedford, Clive
Barbarians * Adams, Robert & Martin H. Greenberg &
    Charles G. Waugh
Barbarians II * Adams, Pamela Crippen & Robert Adams
    & Martin H. Greenberg [& Charles G. Waugh]
Barbarians and black magicians * Carter, Lin
Barbary * McIntyre, Vonda N.
Barbie murders, The * Varley, John
Bard * Taylor, Keith
Bard II * Taylor, Keith
Bard of sorcery, The * Houarner, Gerard Daniel
Bard: the odyssey of the Irish * Llywelyn, Morgan

Bardic voices one * Newcomer, Alan Bard
Bardik the thief * Farrell, Simon & Jon Sutherland
Bare bones: conversations on terror with Stephen King *
  Miller, Chuck & Tim Underwood
Bare-faced messiah: the true story of L. Ron Hubbard *
  Miller, Russell
Bargain, The * Ruddy, Jon
Bargain, The * Sparger, Rex
Barking dogs * Green, Terence M.
Barlowe's Guide to extraterrestrials * Barlowe, Wayne
  Douglas & Ian Summers & Beth Meacham
Barlowe's Guide to extraterrestrials, 2nd ed. * Barlowe,
  Wayne Douglas & Ian Summers & Beth Meacham
Barmy Jeffers and the Quasimodo walk * Brennan, J. H.
Barmy Jeffers and the shrinking potion * Brennan, J. H.
Barnard's Planet * Boyd, John
Barnstormer in Oz, A; or, A rationalization and extrap-
  olation of the split-level continuum * Farmer, Philip
  José
Barnum Museum, The: stories * Millhauser, Steven
Baroque fable, A * Yarbro, Chelsea Quinn
Barracuda * Greenfield, Irving A.
Barracuda run * Otfinoski, Steven
Barrayar * Bujold, Lois McMaster
Barrow * Deakins, John
Barsoom: Edgar Rice Burroughs and the Martian vision *
  Lupoff, Richard A.
Barsoom project, The * Barnes, Steven & Larry Niven
Bart science fiction triplet #1 * Greenberg, Martin H. as
  ANONYMOUS EDITOR
Baseball 3000 * Greenberg, Martin H. & Frank D. Mc-
  Sherry Jr. & Charles G. Waugh
Baseball card fever * Stine, H. William & Megan Stine
Bases loaded II, second season * Singer, A. L.
Basic reference shelf for science fiction teachers, A *
  Tymn, Marshall B.
Basilisk * Kushner, Ellen
Bassumtyte treasure, The * Curry, Jane Louise
Bastaard rebellion, The * Stine, G. Harry
Batman * Gardner, Craig Shaw
Batman * Schuster, Hal
Batman: Captured by the engines * Lansdale, Joe R.
Batman murders, The * Gardner, Craig Shaw
Batman official souvenir magazine * Gerani, Gary
Batman: The doomsday prophecy * Wenk, Richard
Batman: To stalk a specter * Hawke, Simon
Batmania * Van Hise, James
Batmania: plus the story of the incredible Batman televi-
  sion revival * Van Hise, James
Bats on the bedstead * Johnson, Norma Tadlock
Bats out of hell * Smith, Guy N.
Batteries not included * McEvoy, Seth
*batteries not included: a novel * Drew, Wayland
Battle begins, The * Ahern, Jerry
Battle circle: a trilogy: Sos the Rope; Var the Stick; Neq
  the Sword * Anthony, Piers
Battle cry * Daley, Brian & James Luceno as JACK
  MCKINNEY
Battle drive * Siegel, Barbara & Scott Siegel
Battle for Terra Two, The * Berry, Stephen Ames
Battle for the ancient robot * Ward, James M.
Battle of Astar, The * Brightfield, Richard
Battle of Brazil, The: the authorized story and annotated
  screenplay of Terry Gilliam's landmark film *
  Gilliam, Terry & Jack Mathews
Battle of Disneyland, The * Keyes, Thom
Battle of Royston, The * Le Queux, William
Battle of the dragons * Brightfield, Richard
Battle of the monsters, and other stories, The * Currey,
  L. W. & David G. Hartwell

Battle of the ring * Gunnarsson, Thorarinn
Battle road * Jackson, Steve
Battle station * Bova, Ben
Battle stations * Greenfield, Irving A.
Battleblade Warnor * Gascoigne, Marc
Battlefield * Platt, Marc
Battlefield Earth: a saga of the year 3000 * Hubbard, L.
  Ron
Battlefields beyond tomorrow: science fiction war stories
  * Greenberg, Martin H. & Charles G. Waugh
Battlehymn * Daley, Brian & James Luceno as JACK
  MCKINNEY
Battlemaster, The * Rowley, Christopher
Battlestar Galactica * Larson, Glen A. & Robert
  Thurston
Battlestar Galactica * Lely, James A.
Battlestar Galactica storybook, The * Mercer, Charles E.
Battlestations!: a Star Trek novel * Carey, Diane
BattleTech: Blood legacy * Stackpole, Michael
BattleTech: Decision at Thunder Rift * Keith, William H.
  Jr.
BattleTech: Heir to the dragon * Charrette, Robert N.
BattleTech: Lethal heritage * Stackpole, Michael
BattleTech: Lost legacy * Stackpole, Michael
BattleTech: Mercenary's star * Keith, William H. Jr.
BattleTech technical readout 3026 * Stein, Kevin & Sam
  Lewis
BattleTech technical readout 3050 * Keith, Andrew &
  Jim Musser
BattleTech: The price of glory * Keith, William H. Jr.
BattleTech: Warrior: Coupe * Stackpole, Michael
BattleTech: Warrior: En garde * Stackpole, Michael
BattleTech: Warrior: Riposte * Stackpole, Michael
BattleTech: Wolf Clan sourcebook * Peterson, Boyd F.
  Jr. & Blaine Pardoe & Sam Lewis
BattleTech: Wolves on the border * Charrette, Robert N.
Baudelaire on Poe; critical papers * Baudelaire, Charles
Baxter: a novel of inhuman evil * Greenhall, Ken as JES-
  SICA HAMILTON
Bay City burnout * Tine, Robert as RICHARD HARDING
Bazaar of the bizarre * Leiber, Fritz
Be buried in the rain * Michaels, Barbara
Be careful what you wish for * Barnes, Megan
Beach dogs, The * Dann, Colin
Beadbonny ash * Finlay, Winifred
Beamriders! * Caidin, Martin
Beard's Roman women: a novel * Burgess, Anthony
Bearing an hourglass * Anthony, Piers
Beast, The * Fast, Jonathan
Beast, The * Konvitz, Jeffrey
Beast, The * Laymon, Richard
Beast, The * Masters, Doug
Beast, The * Sheldon, Walter J.
Beast, The * Stallman, Robert
Beast House, The * Laymon, Richard
Beast of Heaven, The * Kelleher, Victor
Beast of shame * Holliday, Don
Beast rising * Almquist, Gregg
Beast within, The * Levy, Edward
Beastmaker * Smith, James V. Jr.
Beastmarks * Attanasio, A. A.
Beastnights * Yarbro, Chelsea Quinn
Beasts * Crowley, John
Beasts * George, Stephen R.
Beasts and behemoths: prehistoric creatures in the movies
  * Kinnard, Roy
Beasts below, The * Mahr, Kurt
Beasts; Engine summer; Little, big * Crowley, John
Beasts in velvet * Newman, Kim as JACK YEOVIL

Bernard into battle * Sharp, Margery
Bernard the brave * Sharp, Margery
Bernard Wolfe * Geduld, Carolyn
Berni Wrightson: a look back * Wrightson, Berni & Christopher Zavisa
Bernie and the Bessledorf ghost * Naylor, Phyllis Reynolds
Berryhill * Bennett, Barbara Curry
Berserker * Saberhagen, Fred
Berserker * Spiering, Frank
Berserker attack, The * Saberhagen, Fred
Berserker base * Saberhagen, Fred
Berserker: Blue death * Saberhagen, Fred
Berserker lies * Saberhagen, Fred
Berserker man * Saberhagen, Fred
Berserker: Shadow of the wolf * Holdstock, Robert as CHRIS CARLSEN
Berserker: The bull chief * Holdstock, Robert as CHRIS CARLSEN
Berserker: The horned warrior * Holdstock, Robert as CHRIS CARLSEN
Berserker throne, The * Saberhagen, Fred
Berserker wars, The * Saberhagen, Fred
Berserker's planet * Saberhagen, Fred
Berserkers: The ultimate enemy * Saberhagen, Fred
Best animal stories of science fiction and fantasy, The * Sobol, Donald J.
Best fantasy of the 19th century, The * Asimov, Isaac & Martin H. Greenberg & Charles G. Waugh
Best fantasy stories from The magazine of fantasy & science fiction, The * Ferman, Edward L.
Best friend insurance * Gormley, Beatrice
Best friends * Jensen, Ruby Jean
Best from Fantasy and science fiction, 22nd series, The * Ferman, Edward L.
Best from Fantasy & science fiction, 23rd series, The * Ferman, Edward L.
Best from Fantasy & science fiction, 24th series, The * Ferman, Edward L.
Best from Fantasy & science fiction: a 40th anniversary anthology * Ferman, Edward L.
Best from Galaxy, The * Jakobsson, Ejler as ANONYMOUS EDITOR
Best from Galaxy, volume II, The * Jakobsson, Ejler as ANONYMOUS EDITOR
Best from Galaxy, volume III, The * Baen, James Patrick
Best from Galaxy, volume IV, The * Baen, James Patrick
Best from If, The * Jakobsson, Ejler as ANONYMOUS EDITOR
Best from If, vol. 2, The * Jakobsson, Ejler as ANONYMOUS EDITOR
Best from If, volume III, The * Baen, James Patrick
Best from Orbit, volumes 1-10 * Knight, Damon
Best from the rest of the world, The: European science fiction * Wollheim, Donald A.
Best from Universe, The * Carr, Terry
Best ghost stories, The * anon.
Best ghost stories, The * Fowkes, Charles as INTRODUCER
Best ghost stories of H. Russell Wakefield, The * Wakefield, H. Russell
Best horror and supernatural of the 19th century, The * Asimov, Isaac & Martin H. Greenberg & Charles G. Waugh
Best horror from Fantasy tales, The * Jones, Stephen & David Sutton
Best horror stories, The * anon.
Best horror stories, The * Picknett, Lynn as INTRODUCER
Best horror stories from The magazine of fantasy & science fiction, The * Ferman, Edward L. & Anne Jordan

Best horror stories of Arthur Conan Doyle, The * Doyle, Arthur Conan
Best Japanese science fiction stories, The * Apostolou, John L. & Martin H. Greenberg
Best new horror * Campbell, Ramsey & Stephen Jones
Best new horror 2 * Campbell, Ramsey & Stephen Jones
Best new SF 2 * Dozois, Gardner
Best new SF 3 * Dozois, Gardner
Best new SF 4 * Dozois, Gardner
Best new SF 5 * Dozois, Gardner
Best of A. E. van Vogt, The * van Vogt, A. E.
Best of all possible worlds, The * Robinson, Spider
Best of Ambrose Bierce, The * Bierce, Ambrose
Best of Analog, The * Bova, Ben
Best of Astounding, The * Lewis, Anthony R.
Best of Avram Davidson, The * Davidson, Avram
Best of Barry N. Malzberg, The * Malzberg, Barry N.
Best of Beaumont * Beaumont, Charles
Best of both worlds, The: an anthology of stories for all ages * McHargue, Georgess
Best of British SF 1, The * Ashley, Mike
Best of British SF 2, The * Ashley, Mike
Best of C. L. Moore, The * Moore, C. L.
Best of C. M. Kornbluth, The * Kornbluth, C. M.
Best of Clifford D. Simak, The * Simak, Clifford D.
Best of Con-runner, The: a selection of articles from the Con running fanzine * Sorensen, Ian
Best of Cordwainer Smith, The * Smith, Cordwainer
Best of Damon Knight, The * Knight, Damon
Best of Destinies, The * Baen, James Patrick
Best of E. E. 'Doc' Smith, The * Smith, E. E.
Best of Edmond Hamilton, The * Hamilton, Edmond
Best of Enterprise incidents, The * Van Hise, James
Best of Enterprise Incidents, The: the magazine for Star Trek fans * Van Hise, James
Best of Eric Frank Russell, The * Russell, Eric Frank
Best of Frank Herbert, The * Herbert, Frank
Best of Frederik Pohl, The * Pohl, Frederik
Best of Fredric Brown, The * Brown, Fredric
Best of H. P. Lovecraft, The * Lovecraft, H. P.
Best of Hal Clement, The * Clement, Hal
Best of Harry Harrison, The * Harrison, Harry
Best of Henry Kuttner, The * Kuttner, Henry
Best of Isaac Asimov's science fiction magazine, The * Dozois, Gardner
Best of J. G. Ballard, The * Ballard, J. G.
Best of Jack Vance, The * Vance, Jack
Best of Jack Williamson, The * Williamson, Jack
Best of James Blish, The * Blish, James
Best of James H. Schmitz, The * Schmitz, James H.
Best of John Brunner, The * Brunner, John
Best of John Collier, The * Collier, John
Best of John Jakes, The * Jakes, John
Best of John Sladek, The * Sladek, John
Best of John W. Campbell, The * Campbell, John W.
Best of John Wyndham, The, 1932-1949 * Wyndham, John
Best of John Wyndham, The, 1951-1960 * Wyndham, John
Best of Judith Merril, The * Merril, Judith
Best of Jules Verne, The: three complete, illustrated novels * Verne, Jules
Best of Keith Laumer, The * Laumer, Keith
Best of L. Sprague de Camp, The * de Camp, L. Sprague
Best of Leigh Brackett, The * Brackett, Leigh
Best of Lester del Rey, The * del Rey, Lester
Best of Mack Reynolds, The * Reynolds, Mack
Best of Margaret St. Clair, The * St. Clair, Margaret
Best of Marion Zimmer Bradley, The * Bradley, Marion Zimmer

Best SF of the year 16 * Carr, Terry
Best SF stories of Brian W. Aldiss, 2nd rev. ed. * Aldiss, Brian W.
Best short stories of Fredric Brown, The * Brown, Fredric
Best short stories of J. G. Ballard, The * Ballard, J. G.
Best short stories of Rider Haggard, The * Haggard, H. Rider
Best supernatural stories of John Buchan, The * Buchan, John
Best supernatural stories of Wilkie Collins, The * Collins, Wilkie
Best supernatural tales of Arthur Conan Doyle, The * Doyle, Arthur Conan
Best ye breed, The * Reynolds, Mack
Best, worst, and most unusual: horror films, The * Moore, Darrell
Bestiary! * Dann, Jack & Gardner Dozois
Bestiary Mountain * Forrester, John
Best-kept secret, The * Rodda, Emily
Beta Colony * Enstrom, Robert
Bethany's Sin: a novel * McCammon, Robert R.
Betony and the sorcerer * Main, Carol
Betrayal, The * Cherryh, C. J.
Better country, A: the worlds of religious fantasy and science fiction * Sammons, Martha C.
Better mantrap, A: nine science fiction and fantasy stories * Shaw, Bob
Better than life * Grant, Rob & Doug Naylor as GRANT NAYLOR
Better than one * Knight, Damon & Kate Wilhelm
Between friends: letters of James Branch Cabell and others * Cabell, James Branch
Between the galaxies * Mahr, Kurt
Between the stars * Kotani, Eric & John Maddox Roberts
Between the strokes of night * Sheffield, Charles
Between two worlds * Carr, Terry
Between two worlds: a novel * Schwarz-Bart, Simone
Betz cell, The * Barnard, Keith
Bevis: the story of a boy * Jefferies, Richard
Beware! * Laymon, Richard
Beware! beware!: chiling tales * Richardson, Jean
Beware more beasts * Elwood, Roger & Vic Ghidalia
Beware of the Brain Sharpeners * Curtis, Philip
Beware of the supernatural * Arneson, D. J. & Tony Tallarico
Beware of this shop * York, Carol Beach
Beware the child * Foster, Ruth
Beware the horse * Luckie, L. F.
Beware the Tektrons * Cameron, Ian & George Erskine
Beware, this house is haunted! * Salway, Lance
Bewitched and bewildered: a spooky love story * Borisoff, Norman
Bewitched by the Brain Sharpeners * Curtis, Philip
Bewitching beloved * James, Valerie
Bewitching hour * Stuart, Anne
Bewitching of Alison Allbright, The * Davidson, Alan
Bewitching of Alison Allbright, The * Davidson, Alan as A. D. LANGHOLM
Bewitchments of love and hate, The * Constantine, Storm
Beyond, The * Harrington, Barry
Beyond 1984: a remembrance of things future * Bradbury, Ray
Beyond armageddon: twenty-one sermons to the dead * Greenberg, Martin H. & Walter M. Miller Jr.
Beyond control * Leonard, George H.
Beyond escape! * Montgomery, R. A.
Beyond forever * Olesker, J. Bradford
Beyond geo * Holloway, Brian as ARN ROMILUS
Beyond gravity * Leiber, Justin

Beyond heaven's river * Bear, Greg
Beyond humanity * Leiber, Justin
Beyond lands of never: a further anthology of modern fantasy * Jakubowski, Maxim
Beyond lies the wub: the collected stories of Philip K. Dick, volume one * Dick, Philip K.
Beyond midnight * McCauley, Kirby
Beyond reality: 8 stories of science fiction * Carr, Terry
Beyond rejection * Leiber, Justin
Beyond Sanctuary * Morris, Janet
Beyond shattered illusions * Dexter, Carmen
Beyond silence * Cameron, Eleanor
Beyond terror * Siegel, Barbara & Scott Siegel
Beyond that river * Christopher, Paul
Beyond the 13th sun * Walden, Mark
Beyond the blue event horizon * Pohl, Frederik
Beyond the cellar door * Klaveness, Jan O'Donnell
Beyond the curve: (and other stories) * Abe, Kobo
Beyond the Dar al-Harb * Dickson, Gordon R.
Beyond the dark * Hale, Jennifer
Beyond the dark river * Hughes, Monica
Beyond the door * Blackwood, Gary L.
Beyond the Draak's Teeth * Bennett, Marcia J.
Beyond the fall of night * Clarke, Arthur C. & Gregory Benford
Beyond the galactic lens * Tubb, E. C. as GREGORY KERN
Beyond the galaxy * Wade, Tom as KARL ZEIGFRIED
Beyond the gaslight: science in popular fiction, 1895-1905 * Evans, Dik & Hilary Evans
Beyond the gate of worlds * Silverberg, Robert
Beyond the grave * Muller, Marcia & Bill Pronzini
Beyond the Great Wall * Leibold, Jay
Beyond the horizon: an anthology of science fact and science fiction * anon.
Beyond the Imperium * Laumer, Keith
Beyond the labyrinth * Rubinstein, Gillian
Beyond the moons * Cook, David "Zeb"
Beyond the nightmare gate * Page, Ian
Beyond the Outer Mirr * Savarin, Julian Jay
Beyond the reach of night * St. George, E. A.
Beyond the safe zone: collected stories of Robert Silverberg * Silverberg, Robert
Beyond the sea of ice * Sarabande, William
Beyond the solar system * Fish, Leonard G. as CLAUDE HALEY
Beyond the starlit frost * Brandewyne, Rebecca
Beyond the stars * Asimov, Isaac
Beyond the stars * Conn, Phoebe
Beyond the veil * Morris, Janet
Beyond the void * Blakeney, Jay D. as SEAN DALTON
Beyond this limit * Mitchison, Naomi
Beyond this limit: selected shorter fiction of Naomi Mitchison * Mitchison, Naomi
Beyond time * Ley, Sandra
Beyond tomorrow * Rowland, Donald S. as ROGER CARLTON
Beyond tomorrow: an anthology of modern science fiction * Harding, Lee
Beyond Wizardwall * Morris, Janet
Beyond world's end * Beachcroft, Nina
Beyond Zoaster * Hughes, Dennis Talbot as NEIL CHARLES
Beyonders, The * Wellman, Manly Wade
Bibblings * Paul, Barbara
Bibliographia Oziana: a concise bibliographical checklist of the Oz books by L. Frank Baum and his successors * Greene, Douglas G. & Peter E. Hanff
*Bibliographia Oziana: a concise bibliographical checklist of the Oz books by L. Frank Baum and his succes-

Blood is not enough: 17 stories of vampirism * Datlow, Ellen
Blood island * Farber, James
Blood kin * Naha, Ed as MICHAEL MCGANN
Blood kiss, The * Etchison, Dennis
Blood knot * Algozin, Bruce
Blood legacy * Foster, Prudence
Blood legacy * Stackpole, Michael
Blood libels * Sinclair, Clive
Blood lies * Wallace, Patricia
Blood lust * Dee, Ron
Blood lust * Murphy, Warren & Richard Sapir
Blood merchants, The * Smith, Guy N.
Blood mist * James, Robert
Blood money * Stillman, Ron
Blood moon * Alexander, Jan
Blood moon * Burgess, Mason
Blood moon * Horvitz, Leslie
Blood music * Bear, Greg
Blood of a dragon, The * Watt-Evans, Lawrence
Blood of Amber * Zelazny, Roger
Blood of Dracula, The * Adrian, Jack as JACK HAMILTON TEED
Blood of innocents * Arbucci, John
Blood of my blood * McNeilly, Wilfred G. as ERROL LECALE
Blood of Nostradamus, The: The link * Laurance, Andrew
Blood of October, The * Lippincott, David
Blood of others * Viviers, Lyn
Blood of roses, The * Lee, Tanith
Blood of ten chiefs, The * Abbey, Lynn & Robert Lynn Asprin & Richard Pini
Blood of the children * Rodgers, Alan
Blood of the Colyn Muir * DeCles, Jon & Paul Edwin Zimmer
Blood of the impaler * Sackett, Jeffrey
Blood of the lamb, The: The devouring void * Rogers, Mark E.
Blood of the lamb, The: The expected one * Rogers, Mark E.
Blood of the tiger * Estes, Rose
Blood of the wolf * Goddin, Jeffrey
Blood offerings * San Souci, Robert D.
Blood on the bayou * Donaldson, D. J.
Blood on the handle * Montgomery, R. A.
Blood on the Moon * Cohen, Barney
Blood price * Huff, Tanya
Blood quest * McPhee, James
Blood red! * Dennis, K. C.
Blood red roses * Armstrong, Sarah
Blood red sky * Emmerton, Anton
Blood rights * Schwader, Ann K.
Blood ring, The * Ernst, Paul as KENNETH ROBESON
Blood rite * Anderson, Michael Falconer
Blood rites * Bergstrom, Elaine
Blood river * Tilley, Patrick
Blood river * Willard, Tom
Blood river down * Grant, Charles L. as LIONEL FENN
Blood ruby * Alexander, Jan
Blood sabbath * Clark, Leigh
Blood siege * Stine, G. Harry
Blood sisters * Manley, Mark
Blood sisters * Sherwood, Deborah
Blood sky * Nolan, William F.
Blood snarl * Watkins, Ivor
Blood sport * Scott, R. C.
Blood sport: a journey up the Hassayampa * Jones, Robert F.

Blood stones, The * Conway, Gerard F. as WALLACE MOORE
Blood storm * Gladney, Heather
Blood stripe * Blankenship, William D.
Blood suckers, The * Schoder, Judith
Blood summer * Cooper, Louise
Blood sword * Johnson, Oliver & Dave Morris
Blood thirst * Freed, L. A.
Blood tide * Robbins, David as J. D. CAMERON
Blood tide * Wernick, Saul
Blood ties * Abbey, Lynn & Robert Lynn Asprin
Blood ties * Murphy, Warren & Richard Sapir
Blood valley * Smith, Mark & Jamie Thomson
Blood wedding * Goulart, Ron
Blood will have blood * Barnes, Linda
Blood wings * Gresham, Stephen
Blood worm * Halkin, John
Blood wrath * Krone, Chester
Blood-and-thunder adventures on Hurricane Peak, The * Mahy, Margaret
Bloodchild * Neiderman, Andrew
Bloodcircle * Elrod, P. N.
Blooded on Arachne * Bishop, Michael
Bloodfang * Weaver, Michael D.
Bloodline * St. Clair, David
Bloodlinks * Killough, Lee
Bloodlist * Elrod, P. N.
Bloodmaster * Quijano, Mary L.
Bloodmist * Tremayne, Peter
Bloodname * Thurston, Robert
Bloodright * Tremayne, Peter
Bloodrock * Ferrie, Richard
Bloodroot * Mordane, Thomas
Bloodseed * Grimsley, Ann & Lynne Kinnerley as LYNDAN DARBY
Bloodshift * Reeves-Stevens, Garfield
Bloodshow * Smith, Guy N.
Bloodsongs * Bailey, Robin W.
Bloodstalk * Goulart, Ron
Bloodstar conspiracy, The * Goldin, Stephen & E. E. Smith
Bloodstone * Wagner, Karl Edward
Bloodstone, The * Eulo, Ken
Bloodthirst * Alexander, Marc as MARK RONSON
Bloodthirst: a Star Trek novel * Dillard, J. M.
Bloodwind, The * Grant, Charles L.
Bloody America * Stacy, Jan & Ryder Syvertsen as RYDER STACY
Bloody chamber, and other stories, The * Carter, Angela
Bloody rose, The * Streib, Dan
Bloody seas * Greenfield, Irving A.
Bloody sun, The * Bradley, Marion Zimmer
Bloody sun, The; and, "To keep the oath" * Bradley, Marion Zimmer
Bloomsbury good reading guide to science fiction and fantasy * Zool, M. H.
Blossom Culp and the sleep of death * Peck, Richard
Blossom of Erda, The * Taylor, L. A.
Blossoms * Antieau, Kim
Blow my mind * Fox, Gardner F. as ROD GRAY
Blown dead * Sloane, Ben
Blowout! * Robinson, Frank M. & Thomas N. Scortia
Blue Adept * Anthony, Piers
Blue aura, The * Walters, Hugh
Blue chair, The: a novel * Thompson, Joyce
Blue champagne * Varley, John
Blue death * Saberhagen, Fred
Blue frogs, The * Helterman, Jeffrey
Blue fruit * Lively, Adam
Blue Hawk, The * Dickinson, Peter

Book of Suns, The * Springer, Nancy
Book of the beast, The * Lee, Tanith
Book of the beast, The * Stallman, Robert
Book of the damned, The * Lee, Tanith
Book of the dead, The * Lee, Tanith
Book of the dead, The * Skipp, John & Craig Spector
Book of the dead * Tigges, John
Book of the dead, The: thirteen classic tales of the super-natural * Russell, Alan K.
Book of the dragon, The * Allen, Judy & Jeanne Griffiths
Book of the dun cow, The * Wangerin, Walter Jr.
Book of the dun cow teacher's guide, The * Thoet, Felicity
Book of the green planet, The * Kotzwinkle, William & Steven Spielberg
Book of the new sun, The, vols. I and II * Wolfe, Gene
Book of the night, The * Lerman, Rhoda
Book of the River, The * Watson, Ian
Book of the sandman and the alphabet of sleep, The * Poortvliet, Rien
Book of the Sixth World Fantasy Convention, The * Underwood, Tim & Chuck Miller
Book of the Stars, The * Watson, Ian
Book of the supernatural * James, M. R.
Book of Vale, The * Springer, Nancy
Book of van Vogt * van Vogt, A. E.
Book of Virgil Finlay, The: being the drawings of Virgil Finlay (1914-1971), from the collection of Gerry de la Ree * Finlay, Virgil
Books of blood, The * Barker, Clive
Books of blood, volumes IV, V & VI * Barker, Clive
Books of Clark Ashton Smith, The * Bell, Joseph & Roy A. Squires
Books of Clive Barker, The * Bell, Joseph
Books of Great Alta, The * Yolen, Jane
Books of the Black Current, The * Watson, Ian
Books of William Morris described, The, with some account of his doings in literature and in the allied crafts * Forman, H. Buxton
Boomer * Taylor, Charles D.
Boori * Scott, Bill
Bordeaux narrative, The * Courlander, Harold
Border to terrorism * Burchett, Jay & M. Ann Evans
Border war * Shirley, John as D. B. DRUMM
Borderland * Arnold, Mark Alan & Terri Windling
Borderlands: an anthology of imaginative fiction, volume one * Monteleone, Thomas F.
Borderlands 2: an anthology of imaginative fiction * Monteleone, Thomas F.
Borders just beyond, The * Brennan, Joseph Payne
Borders of infinity * Bujold, Lois McMaster
Bordertown: a chronicle of the Borderlands * Arnold, Mark Alan & Terri Windling
Borgel * Pinkwater, Daniel M.
Boris Karloff: a critical account of his screen, stage, radio, television, and recording work * Nollen, Scott Allen
Boris Karloff and his films * Jensen, Paul M.
Boris Karloff presents More tales of the frightened * Lory, Robert
Born burning * Sullivan, Thomas
Born into light * Jacobs, Paul Samuel
Born of flame: a Spacebread story * Senn, Steve
Born of the sun * Cross, Gillian
Born to exile * Eisenstein, Phyllis
Born to howl * Gilden, Mel
Born with the dead * Silverberg, Robert
Borribles, The * De Larrabeiti, Michael
Borribles, The: Across the dark metropolis * De Larrabeiti, Michael

Borribles go for broke, The * De Larrabeiti, Michael
Borrowed time * Hruska, Alan
Borrower of the night * Michaels, Barbara as ELIZABETH PETERS
Borrowers avenged, The * Norton, Mary
Boskone 9 filk-song book, The * Blank, Karen
Boskone 10 filksongbook * Benders, Kris & A. Joseph Ross
Boskone 14 filksong supplement, The * Ross, A. Joseph
Boskone XVI filksong book * Raskind, Lisa
Boskone XVI portfolio * Symes, Mike
Boss of terror, The: a Doc Savage adventure * Dent, Lester as KENNETH ROBESON
Boston run * Robbins, David
Bottle imp, The * Harris, Raymond & Robert Louis Stevenson
Boucher bibliography, A * Briney, R. E. & D. W. Dickensheet & J. R. Christopher
Bound for Australia * Bailey, Nancy
Bound in time * Jones, D. F.
Boundaries * Dee, Ron
Boundaries * Wright, T. M.
Bowl of Baal, The * Bennet, Robert Ames
Bowman Test, The * Elias, Albert J.
Box of nothing, A * Dickinson, Peter
Box of tricks, A * Scott, Hugh
Boxen: the imaginary world of the young C. S. Lewis * Lewis, C. S.
Boy adventurers in the unknown land, The * Verrill, A. Hyatt
Boy astronaut * Walters, Hugh
Boy from the burren, The * Gilluly, Sheila
Boy in darkness * Peake, Mervyn
Boy of the painted cave * Denzel, Justin
Boy who bounced, and other magic tales, The * Mahy, Margaret
Boy who could draw tomorrow, The * Sinclair, Quinn
Boy who hooked the sun, The: a tales from the Book of the wonders of Urth and sky * Wolfe, Gene
Boy who reversed himself, The * Sleator, William
Boy who saved Earth, The * Slater, Jim
Boy who spoke chimp, The * Yolen, Jane
Boy who was thrown away, The * Smith, Stephanie A.
Boy with penny eyes, The * Sarrantonio, Al
Boyfriend, The * Stine, R. L.
Boys from Brazil, The: a novel * Levin, Ira
Boy's life * McCammon, Robert R.
Bradbury chronicles, The * Slusser, George Edgar
Bradbury chronicles, The: stories in honor of Ray Bradbury * Greenberg, Martin H. & William F. Nolan
Bradbury's works, including life and background, Fahrenheit 451, Something wicked this way comes, A medicine for melancholy, The October country, questions for review, selected bibliography * Manning, Audrey Smoak
Brain * Cook, Robin
Brain 2000 * Gann, Ernest K.
Brain child * Dibble, Birney
Brain child * George, Stephen R.
Brain child * Turner, George
Brain dead * Brieno, Linda
Brain death * Wilkinson, Sandra
Brain drain * Murphy, Warren & Richard Sapir
Brain drain * Wayne, Matt
Brain eaters, The * Brandner, Gary
Brain fever * Dee, Ron
Brain of Morbius, The * Dicks, Terrance
Brain on Quartz Mountain, The * Anderson, Margaret
Brain palaeo * Hughes, Dennis Talbot as Arn Romilus
Brain rose * Kress, Nancy

British and American utopian literature, 1516-1986: an annotated, chronological bibliography * Sargent, Lyman Tower

British fanzine bibliography * Roberts, Peter

British science fiction and fantasy * Hutchinson, Tom

British science fiction book index 1955 * Slater, Ken

Broadsides and brass: the autobiography of Colonel William T. Bucko, USFAC (ret.) * Westcott, C. T.

Brockden Brown and the rights of women * Clark, David Lee

Brodie's notes on Aldous Huxley's Brave new world * Handley, Graham

Brodie's notes on Aldous Huxley's Brave new world, revised edition * Handley, Graham

Brodie's notes on H. G. Wells's The war of the worlds * Dowling, Kevin

Brodie's notes on John Wyndham's 'The Chrysalids' * Gooden, Philip

Brodie's notes on William Golding * Handley, Graham

Brokedown palace * Brust, Steven

Broken citadel, The * Gregorian, Joyce Ballou

Broken cycle, The * Chandler, A. Bertram

Broken Eagle * Tine, Robert

Broken mirrors/broken minds: the dark dreams of Dario Argento * McDonagh, Maitland

Broken October, New Zealand, 1985: a novel * Harrison, Craig

Broken stone * Monaco, Richard

Broken symmetries * Preuss, Paul

Broken wheel, The * Wingrove, David

Broken worlds, The * Harris, Raymond

Bromius phenomenon, The * Mason, Douglas R. as JOHN RANKINE

Brontomek! * Coney, Michael

Bronwyn's bane * Scarborough, Elizabeth

Bronze axe, The * Stokes, Manning Lee as JEFFREY LORD

Bronze king, The * Charnas, Suzy McKee

Bronze mirror * Larsen, Jeanne

Bronze of Eddarta, The * Garrett, Randall & Vicki Ann Heydron

Brooch of azure midnight, The * Gay, Anne

Brood, The: novelization * Starks, Richard

Broom of the system, The * Wallace, David Foster

Broomstocks and beasticles: stories and verse about witches and strange creatures * Sleigh, Barbara

Broonie, silkies, & fairies, The: travellers' tales * Williamson, Duncan

Brother, and other stories * Simak, Clifford D.

Brother Esau * Gribbin, John & Douglas Orgill

Brother Gib * King, Albert as PAUL MULLER

Brother in the land * Swindells, Robert E.

Brother Jonathan * Kilian, Crawford

Brother monster * Brown, Fredric

Brother Night * Kelleher, Victor

Brother Theodore's chamber of horrors * Kaye, Marvin & Brother Theodore

Brother to demons, brother to gods * Williamson, Jack

Brother to the lion * Estes, Rose

Brotherhood of Diablo, The * Lovejoy, Jack

Brotherhood of evil * Zacharia, Irwin

Brotherkind * Williamson, J. N.

Brothers * Goldman, William

Brothers in arms * Bujold, Lois McMaster

Brothers in arms: a Miles Vorkosigan adventure * Bujold, Lois McMaster

Brothers Majere * Stein, Kevin

Brothers of Earth * Cherryh, C. J.

Brothers of the head * Aldiss, Brian W.

Brothers of the head; and, Where the lines converge * Aldiss, Brian W.

Brownstone, The * Eulo, Ken

Bruce Pennington portfolio, The * Pennington, Bruce

Brujo * Relling, William Jr.

Bruno Lipshitz and the Disciples of Dogma * King, John Robert

Brutal conquest * Ahern, Jerry

Brute force * Milán, Victor as RICHARD AUSTIN

Buccaneers of Lan-Kern, The * Tremayne, Peter

Buck Alice and the actor-robot * Koenig, Walter

Buck Rogers: Armageddon off Vesta * Murdock, M. S.

Buck Rogers: Arrival * anon.

Buck Rogers: First power play * Miller, John J.

Buck Rogers: Hammer of Mars * Murdock, M. S.

Buck Rogers in the 25th century * Lupoff, Richard A. as ADDISON E. STEELE

Buck Rogers: Matrix cubed * Bloom, Britton

Buck Rogers: Prime squared * Murdock, M. S.

Buckaroo Banzai * Rauch, Earl Mac

Buckets * Wilson, F. Paul

Budapest action, The * Rosenberger, Joseph

Buddy Holly is alive and well on Ganymede * Denton, Bradley

Budspy * Dvorkin, David

Buffalo gals, and other animal presences * Le Guin, Ursula K.

Bug awful * Asimov, Isaac & Martin H. Greenberg & Charles G. Waugh

Bug in the system, A * McEvoy, Seth

Bug life chronicles, The * Jennings, Phillip C.

Bug wars, The Asprin, Robert Lynn

Bug-eyed monsters * Malzberg, Barry N. & Bill Pronzini

Bugs * Roszak, Theodore

Bugs * Sladek, John

Builder of the black empire * Page, Norvell W. as GRANT STOCKBRIDGE

Building blocks * Voigt, Cynthia

Building of Venus Four, The * Willingham, Calder

Built to kill * Tine, Robert as RICHARD HARDING

Bull chief, The * Holdstock, Robert as CHRIS CARLSEN

Bulldozer rising * Livia, Anna

Bulldozers, and fables and fantasies for adults * Das, Manoj

Bully! * Resnick, Mike

Bumper book of ghost stories, The * Chambers, Aidan

Bundle of nerves, A: stories of horror, suspense, and fantasy * Aiken, Joan

Bunduki * Edson, J. T.

Bunduki and Dawn * Edson, J. T.

Bunjee venture, The * McMurtry, Stan

Bunnicula: a rabbit tale of mystery * Howe, James and Deborah Howe

Bureau 13 * Pollotta, Nick

Bureau of lost souls, The * Fowler, Christopher

Burial rites * Rohan, Michael Scott & Allan J. Scott as MICHAEL SCOT

Buried, The * Helfgott, Daniel

Buried treasure * Morris, Dave

Burning * Chambers, Jane

Burning, The * Fair, Jeff

Burning, The * Masterton, Graham

Burning blue death, The * Rosenberger, Joseph

Burning book, The * Gee, Maggie

Burning chrome * Gibson, William

Burning eye, The * Carr, John F. & Jerry Pournelle & Roland Green

Burning ground, The * Nolan, Madeena Spray

Burning land, The * Siegel, Barbara & Scott Siegel

Burning man, The * Hammonds, Michael

Burning mountain, The: a novel of the invasion of Japan * Coppel, Alfred

C

C. S. Lewis * Christopher, Joe R.
C. S. Lewis * Hannay, Margaret P.
C. S. Lewis * Murphy, Brian
C. S. Lewis: a biography * Green, Roger Lancelyn & Walter Hooper
C. S. Lewis: a biography * Wilson, A. N.
C. S. Lewis: a critical essay * Kreeft, Peter
C. S. Lewis: an annotated checklist of writings about him and his works * Christopher, Joe R. & Joan K. Ostling
C. S. Lewis and his world * Barratt, David
C. S. Lewis and the truth of myth * Freshwater, Mark Edwards
C. S. Lewis: apostle to the skeptics * Walsh, Chad
C. S. Lewis at the breakfast table, and other reminiscences * Como, James T.
C. S. Lewis, defender of the faith * Cunningham, Richard B.
C. S. Lewis: his literary achievement * Manlove, C. N.
C. S. Lewis hoax, The * Lindskoog, Kathryn
C. S. Lewis: images of his world * Gilbert, Douglas & Clyde S. Kilby
C. S. Lewis, man of letters: a reading of his fiction * Howard, Thomas
C. S. Lewis: mere Christian * Lindskoog, Kathryn
C. S. Lewis: mere Christian, rev. and expanded edition * Lindskoog, Kathryn
C. S. Lewis: mere Christian, 3rd rev. and expanded edition * Lindskoog, Kathryn
C. S. Lewis: speaker and teacher * Keefe, Carolyn
C. S. Lewis, spinner of tales: a guide to his fiction * Gibson, Evan K.
C. S. Lewis: the art of enchantment * Glover, Donald E.
C. S. Lewis: through the shadowlands * Sibley, Brian
Cabal * Barker, Clive
Cabal, The * Dunn, Saul
Cabal, The * Dunn, Saul as PHILIP DUNN
Cabal: the nightbreed * Barker, Clive
Cabalist, The * Prantera, Amanda
Cabellian harmonics * McNeill, Warren A.
Cabinet of Dr. Caligari, The: texts, contexts, histories * Budd, Mike
Cachalot: a novel * Foster, Alan Dean
Cache, The; includes two bonus stories: They twinkled like jewels and Rastignac the devil * Farmer, Philip José
Cactus garden, A * Bannister, Jo
Cadavers: stories of speculative fiction * De Noux, O'Neil
Cadre Lucifer * O'Riordan, Robert
Cadre Messiah * O'Riordan, Robert
Cadre One * O'Riordan, Robert
C.A.D.S. * Syvertsen, Ryder & Jan Stacy as JOHN SIEVERT
Caduceus wild * Bradford, Robert & Ward Moore
Caesar's time legions * Betancourt, John Gregory as JEREMY KINGSTON
Cafe Purgatorium: three original novels of horror and the supernatural * anon.

Cage, The * Meier, Shirley & S. M. Stirling
Cahena: a dream of the past * Wellman, Manly Wade
Cain factor, The * Lewis, Charles
Cain's touch * Wernick, Saul
Cajun nights * Donaldson, D. J.
Cal * Asimov, Isaac
Calabrinia falling: a fantasy * De Ovalle, Pilar
Caliban landing * Popkes, Steven
California bloodstock * McDonnell, Terry
California countdown * Dever, Joe
California coven project, The * Stickgold, Bob
California dreamer in King Henry's court, A * Plunkett, Robert L.
California dreaming * Garlick, Nicholas
California iceberg, The * Harrison, Harry
Californian, 1934-1938, The * Lovecraft, H. P.
Californios, The * L'Amour, Louis
Caligari's children: the film as tale of terror * Prawer, S. S.
Calix Stay * Hancock, Niel
Call, and other stories, The * Westall, Robert
Call back yesterday * Forman, James D.
Call of Cthulhu: fantasy roleplaying in the worlds of H. P. Lovecraft, 4th ed. * Petersen, Sandy
Call of madness * Smith, Julie Dean
Call of the cosmos, The * Tsiolkovskii, Konstantin
Call of the sword, The * Taylor, Roger
Call to arms, A * Foster, Alan Dean
Call to arms * Griffin, P. M.
Call to battle * Carr, John F. & Jerry Pournelle
Call to darkness, A * Friedman, Michael Jan
Callahan and company: the compleat chronicles of the Crosstime Saloon * Robinson, Spider
Callahan's crazy crosstime bar * Robinson, Spider
Callahan's Crosstime Saloon * Robinson, Spider
Callahan's lady * Robinson, Spider
Callahan's secret * Robinson, Spider
Callanish * Horwood, William
Caller from eternity * Brand, Kurt
Caller from overspace, A * Lymington, John
Calling, The * Sanford, Richard
Calling, The: a novel * Randall, Bob
Calling all monsters * Westwood, Chris
Calling B for butterfly * Lawrence, Louise
Calling Dr. Patchwork * Goulart, Ron
Calling of Bara, The * Sullivan, Sheila
Calling of the three, The * Emerson, Ru
Calling outer space * Nugent, Jean
Calling Thunderbirds * Jennison, John as JOHN THEYDON
Callipygia: further adventures in Terra Magica * Carter, Lin
Calvin nullifier, The * DeWeese, Gene
Caly * Combes, Sharon
Camber of Culdi * Kurtz, Katherine
Camber the heretic * Kurtz, Katherine
Cambio Bay * Wilhelm, Kate
Came a spider * Levy, Edward
Camelot in orbit * Landis, Arthur H.
Camera obscura, The * Scott, Hugh

Cameron's closet * Brandner, Gary
Cameron's terror * Brandner, Gary
Camp, The * Smith, Guy N.
Camp, The * Trask, Jonathan
Camp Duck Down * Stine, H. William & Megan Stine
Camp of the saints, The * Raspail, Jean
Campbell Wood * Sarrantonio, Al
Campfire chillers * Freeman, E. M.
Campfire stories: things that go bump in the night *
　　Forgey, William W.
Campfire story * Kline, Robert Y.
*Campfire tales: ghoulies, ghosties, and long-leggety
　　beasties* * Forgey, William W.
Camp-out on Danger Mountain * Hiller, B. B.
Can I get there by candlelight? * Doty, Jean Slaughter
Canal dreams * Banks, Iain M.
Canal Zone conquest * Roberts, Mark K.
Candle for D'Artagnan, A: an historical horror novel *
　　Yarbro, Chelsea Quinn
Candle in the wind * Bernau, George
Candlemas eve * Sackett, Jeffrey
Canfield decision, The * Agnew, Spiro T.
Canned meat: a science fiction novel * Geis, Richard E.
Cannibal, The * Kinder, Stuart
Cannibal cult * Smith, Guy N.
Cannibal kiss: a novel * Odier, Daniel
Cannibals * Smith, Guy N.
Canongate strangler, The * McAllister, Angus
Canticle * Salvatore, R. A.
Canticle for P. Schuyler Miller, A * Moskowitz, Sam
Canto for a gypsy * Smith, Martin Cruz
Canyons * Paulsen, Gary
Capella's Golden Eyes * Evans, Chris D.
Capital run * Robbins, David
Capital run; New York run * Robbins, David
Capitol Hill clones * Tabler, Joseph
Capitol: the Worthing Chronicle * Card, Orson Scott
Capricious robot, The * Hoshi, Shin'ichi
Capricorn games * Silverberg, Robert
Capricorn One * Follett, Ken as BERNARD L. ROSS
Capricorn One * Goulart, Ron
Capricorn quadrant, The * Ryan, Charles
Capsule, The * Hagberg, David
Capsule reviews * Holdom, Lynne
Captain America: Rocket's red glare * Novak, Kate
Captain Blackman: a novel * Williams, John A.
Captain Butcher's body * Corbett, Scott
Captain Empirical * Nikolaisen, Shirley as SAM
　　NICHOLSON
Captain Jack Zodiac * Kandel, Michael
Captain Quad * Costello, Sean
Captain Scarlet * Jennison, John as JOHN THEYDON
Captain Scarlet and the Mysterons * Jennison, John as
　　JOHN THEYDON
Captain Scarlet and the silent saboteur * Jennison, John
　　as JOHN THEYDON
Captain Sinbad * Diamond, Graham
Captain's honor, The * Dvorkin, Daniel & David
　　Dvorkin
*Captain's log, The: William Shatner's personal account of
　　the making of Star Trek V, the final frontier* * Shatner,
　　Lisabeth & William Shatner
Captive! * Hampton, Bill & Luann Hampton
Captive, The * Stallman, Robert
Captive in time, A: a Stoner McTavish mystery * Dreher,
　　Sarah
Captive planet * Simon, Morris
Captive planet * Smith, Gregory J.
Captive Scorpio * Bulmer, Kenneth as ALLAN BURT AK-
　　ERS

Captives * Hutson, Shaun
Captives of the Savage Empire * Lorrah, Jean
Captured by the engines * Lansdale, Joe R.
Car, The: a novel * Butler, Michael & Dennis Shryack
Car sinister * Greenberg, Martin H. & Robert Silverberg
　　& Joseph D. Olander
Caracal * Smith, Guy N.
Caracole * White, Edmund
Caravan * Goldin, Stephen
Caravan to China * Gaskin, Carol
*Carbonel and Calidor: being the further adventures of a
　　royal cat* * Sleigh, Barbara
*Card catalogue: the science fiction and fantasy of Orson
　　Scott Card* * Collings, Michael R.
Cardiac arrest * Miller, David C. & John H. Way
Cardography * Card, Orson Scott
Cards of grief * Yolen, Jane
Cargo unknown * Dent, Lester as KENNETH ROBESON
Caribe: a novel * Sprechman, J. R.
Carmen dog * Emshwiller, Carol
Carmen Miranda's ghost is haunting Space Station Three
　　* Sakers, Don
Carnadyne Horde, The * Offutt, Andrew J. & Victor
　　Koman as JOHN CLEVE
Carnelian cat, The * DeWeese, Gene as JEAN DeWEESE
Carnelian throne, The * Morris, Janet E.
Carnifex Mardi Gras * Carr, John F.
Carnival * Johnstone, William W.
Carnival kidnap caper, The * Dodson, Fitzhugh & Paula
　　Reuben
Carnival of demons * Sno, William
Carnival of the animals, The * Scliar, Moacyr
Carnivore * Smith, Guy N.
Carnosaur * Brosnan, John as HARRY ADAM KNIGHT
Carol, the pursued * Kimbro, John M. as KATHERYN
　　KIMBROUGH
Carpathians, The * Frame, Janet
Carpe diem * Lee, Sharon & Steve Miller
Carrier * Keith, William H. Jr. as KEITH DOUGLASS
Carrier: Viper strike * Keith, William H. Jr. as KEITH
　　DOUGLASS
Carrion * Brandner, Gary
Carrion comfort: a new novel * Simmons, Dan
Cart & Cwidder * Jones, Diana Wynne
Carthaginian for a day: an historical romance * Sargent,
　　H. B.
Cartoon crimes, The * Goulart, Ron as KENNETH ROBE-
　　SON
Cartoon files magazine spotlight on The Jonny Quest files
　　* Van Hise, James
Cartoonist, The * Costello, Sean
Carve the sky * Jablokov, Alexander
Carvings * Snellings, John
Casablanca * Moorcock, Michael
*Casanova's "Icosameron"; or, The story of Edward and
　　Elizabeth, who spent eighty-one years in the land of
　　the Megamicres, original inhabitants of Protocosmos
　　in the interior of our globe* * Casanova de Seingalt,
　　Jacques
Casca: God of death * Sadler, Barry
Casca: Panzer soldier * Sadler, Barry
Casca: Soldier of fortune * Sadler, Barry
Casca: The African mercenary * Sadler, Barry
Casca: The assassin * Sadler, Barry
Casca: The barbarian * Sadler, Barry
Casca: The conquistador * Sadler, Barry
Casca: The damned * Sadler, Barry
Casca: The eternal mercenary * Sadler, Barry
Casca: The legionnaire * Sadler, Barry
Casca: The Persian * Sadler, Barry

Cats to come, The * Household, Geoffrey
Catspaw * Vinge, Joan D.
Cattle mutilators, The * Dalton, John J.
Catweazle and the magic zodiac * Carpenter, Richard
Catwings * Le Guin, Ursula K.
Catwings return * Le Guin, Ursula K.
Catwitch * Tuttle, Lisa
Caught in a still place * Lerner, Jonathan
Caught in crystal * Wrede, Patricia C.
Caught in the organ draft: biology in science fiction *
   Asimov, Isaac & Martin H. Greenberg & Charles G.
   Waugh
Cauldron of fear, The * Dever, Joe
Cauldron of plenty, The * Taylor, Keith
Cauldron of witches, A * Manning-Sanders, Ruth
Caution! Inflammable! * Scortia, Thomas N.
Cautionary tales * Yarbro, Chelsea Quinn
Cave beyond time * Bosse, Malcolm J.
Cave dreamers, The * Williams, Jeanne
Cave of the master * Syvertsen, Ryder
Cave of the moving shadows * Millstead, Thomas
Cave of time, The * Packard, Edward
Cavemen of Venus, The * Glasser, Allen
Cavern of doom, The * Meretzky, S. Eric
Cavern of horror * Rotsler, William
Cavern of the damned * Davis, Frederick C. as CURTIS
   STEELE
Cavern of the Phantoms * Stine, R. L.
Caverns * O'Donnell, Kevin Jr.
Caverns of Kalte, The * Chalk, Gary & Joe Dever
Caverns of Mornas, The * Brightfield, Richard
Caverns of the snow witch * Livingstone, Ian
Caves of Androzani, The * Dicks, Terrance
Caves of Drach, The * Walters, Hugh
Caves of fire and ice * Murphy, Shirley Rousseau
Caves of Klydor, The * Hill, Douglas
Caves of madness, The * Conway, Gerard F. as WAL-
   LACE MOORE
Caves of Mars * Wolff, Robert Sherman
Caves of Reglathium, The * Sirota, Mike
Caves of steel, The * Asimov, Isaac & Rosemary Border
Caves of the Druufs * Mahr, Kurt
*CDN SF & F: a bibliography of Canadian science fiction
   and fantasy* * Amprimoz, Alexandre L. & John
   Robert Colombo & John Bell & Michael Richardson
Celery stalks at midnight, The * Howe, James
Celeste * Pereira, W. D.
Celestial chess * Bontly, Thomas
Celestial hit list * Vilott, Rhondi as CHARLES INGRID
Celestial inventory * Tem, Steve Rasnic
Celestial steam locomotive, The * Coney, Michael
Celestial Toymaker, The * Bingeman, Alison & Gerry
   Davis
Celia * Jensen, Ruby Jean
Cellar, The * Laymon, Richard
Cellar, The * Radford, Ken
Cellars * Shirley, John
Celluloid gangs * Tolnay, Tom
*Celluloid vampires, The: a history and filmography,
   1897-1979* * Murphy, Michael J.
*Celtia: a collection of posters and drawings in the celtic
   style* * Fitzpatrick, Jim
Cenotaph Road * Vardeman, Robert E.
Centaur Aisle * Anthony, Piers
Centaur in the garden, The * Scliar, Moacyr
Centaurian quest * Elder, Michael
Centenarian, The; or, The two Beringhelds * Balzac,
   Honoré de as HORACE DE SAINT-AUBIN
Centennial conference proceedings, The * Joshi, S. T.

Center of the circle, The * Smith, Julia & Mark Smith as
   JONATHAN WYLIE
Centigrade 233 * Benford, Gregory
Central heat * Dvorkin, David
Centre cannot hold, The * Stableford, Brian M.
Centre holds, The: a novel * Storey, Anthony
Centre of the circle, The * Smith, Julia & Mark Smith as
   JONATHAN WYLIE
Centre of the wheel, The * Wilcox, Ronald
Centrifugal rickshaw dancer, The * Watkins, William
   John
Centrifuge * Green, Hilary
Centurion, The * De Hartog, Jan
Century hence, A; or, A romance of 1941 * Tucker,
   George
Century of progress, A * Saberhagen, Fred
Century's end * Griffin, Russell M.
Cerberus * Budrys, Algis
Cerberus: a wolf in the fold * Chalker, Jack L.
Cereal box adventures, The * Bartholomew, Barbara
Ceremonies, The * Klein, T. E. D.
Ceremonies * Webster, Josh
Ceremony * Cook, Glen
Ceremony of innocence, The: a novel of 1984 * Kilroy-
   Silk, Robert
Ceres solution, The * Shaw, Bob
Cestus Dei * Roberts, John Maddox
Chad Oliver: a preliminary bibliography * Hall, Hal W.
Chain letter * Jensen, Ruby Jean
Chain letter * Pike, Christopher
Chain of attack: a Star Trek novel * DeWeese, Gene
Chain of chance, The * Lem, Stanislaw
Chain reaction * Aspler, Tony & Gordon Pape
Chain reaction, The * Wessex, Martyn
Chaining the lady * Anthony, Piers
Chains of gold * Springer, Nancy
Chair where terror sat, The * Weinberg, Robert E.
Chalet Bougy-Villars * Marvin, Susan
Chalet Diabolique * Coffman, Virginia
Chalet of the devil * Coffman, Virginia
Challenge, The * Ahern, Jerry
Challenge * Collins, Warwick
Challenge from beyond, The * Howard, Robert E. & C.
   L. Moore & H. P. Lovecraft & A. Merritt & Frank
   Belknap Long
Challenge met * Vilott, Rhondi as CHARLES INGRID
Challenge of Druid's Grove * Ward, James M.
Challenge of the clans * Flint, Kenneth C.
Challenge of the Magi * Smith, Mark & Jamie Thomson
Challenge of the Pegasus Grail * Vilott, Rhondi
Challenge of the Wolf Knight * Stine, R. L.
Challenge the hellmaker * Richmond, Leigh & Walt
   Richmond
Challenge to Dracula * Lory, Robert
Challengers of the unknown * Goulart, Ron
Chamber of horrors * anon.
Chameleon variant, The * Ehrenfeld, David & Carol K.
   Mack
Champ of TV wrestling, The * Siegel, Barbara & Scott
   Siegel
Champion of the gods * Green, Roland as JEFFREY LORD
Champion of the last battle: a Horseclans novel * Adams,
   Robert
Champions of the Sidhe * Flint, Kenneth C.
Chance, & other gestures of the hand of fate * Springer,
   Nancy
Chance child, A * Paton Walsh, Jill
Chancellor of Mars: a novel * Moon, Jay
Change, The * Foster, George C.
Change * Maxwell, Ann

Change War, The * Leiber, Fritz
Changeling * Leigh, Stephen
Changeling, The * McKenney, Kenneth
Changeling, The * Snyder, Zilpha K.
Changeling, The * Wilson, Mary
Changeling * Zelazny, Roger
Changeling Earth * Saberhagen, Fred
Changeling sea, The * McKillip, Patricia A.
Changelings of Chaan, The * Lake, David J.
Changeover, The: a supernatural romance * Mahy, Margaret
Changer's moon * Clayton, Jo
Changes, The: a trilogy, comprising The devil's children, Heartsease, The weathermonger * Dickinson, Peter
Changes: stories of metamorphosis: an anthology of speculative fiction about startling metamorphoses, both psychological and physical * Bishop, Michael & Ian Watson
Changes trilogy, The * Dickinson, Peter
Changewar * Leiber, Fritz
Changing, The * Wright, T. M. as F. W. ARMSTRONG
Changing heaven * Urquhart, Jane
Changing land, The: a novel of Dilvish the Damned * Zelazny, Roger
Changing places * Smith, Susan
Changing the past * Berger, Thomas
Channel's destiny * Lichtenberg, Jacqueline & Jean Lorrah
Chant * Chesbro, George C. as DAVID CROSS
Chant: Code of blood * Chesbro, George C. as DAVID CROSS
Chant: Silent killer * Chesbro, George C. as DAVID CROSS
Chanters Chase: a novel * Tattersall, Jill
Chanting, The * Haaf, Beverly T.
Chanting of children, The * Sand, Margaret
Chantry guild, The * Dickson, Gordon R.
Chanur's homecoming * Cherryh, C. J.
Chanur's venture * Cherryh, C. J.
Chaos * Wells, William K.
Chaos comes to Chivvy Chase * Curtis, Philip
Chaos in Arcturus * Wade, Tom as KARL ZEIGFRIED
Chaos in Lagrangia * Reynolds, Mack
Chaos kid, The * Peters, David
Chaos weapon, The * Kapp, Colin
Chapter house: Dune * Herbert, Frank
Chapterhouse: Dune * Herbert, Frank
Characterization * Rusch, Kristine Kathryn
Charg, monster: from the Shadow's private annals * Gibson, Walter B. as MAXWELL GRANT
Chariot into time * Wade, Tom as KARL ZEIGFRIED
Chariot of fire * Hales, E. E. Y.
Charisma * Coney, Michael
Charlatan, The * Horler, Sydney
Charlcie Arrow & the magic red cape * Beamer, Charles
Charlemagne's champion * Van Asten, Gail
Charles and Elizabeth: a novel * Burley, W. J.
Charles Beaumont: selected stories * Beaumont, Charles
Charles Brockden Brown * Ringe, Donald A.
Charles Brockden Brown, rev. ed. * Ringe, Donald A.
Charles Brockden Brown: a reference guide * Parker, Patricia L.
Charles Brockden Brown: an American tale * Axelrod, Alan
Charles Brockden Brown: pioneer voice of America * Clark, David Lee
Charles Fort: a radical corpuscle * Moskowitz, Sam
Charles Fort never mentioned wombats * Coulson, Robert & Gene DeWeese

Charles Keeping's Book of classic ghost stories * Keeping, Charles
Charles Keeping's Classic tales of the macabre * Keeping, Charles
Charles Robert Maturin * Kramer, Dale
Charles Robert Maturin, the terror-novelist * Scholten, Willem
Charles W. S. Williams: a checklist * Glenn, Lois
Charles Williams * Heath-Stubbs, John
Charles Williams * Sibley, Agnes
Charles Williams * Spencer, Kathleen
Charles Williams: an exploration of his life and work * Hadfield, A. M.
Charles Williams: poet of theology * Cavaliero, Glen
Charley gets the picture * Spencer, John
Charlie Peace: a fable * Pickering, Paul
Charlotte Perkins Gilman reader, The: The yellow wallpaper, and other fiction * Gilman, Charlotte Perkins
Charmed * Singer, Marilyn
Charmed life * Jones, Diana Wynne
Charmed life * Taylor, Bernard
Charming, The * Polcovar, Jane
Charnel house * Masterton, Graham
Charon: a dragon at the gate * Chalker, Jack L.
Charon tapes, The * Pereira, W. D.
Charon's ark * Gauger, Rick
Chartered libertine, The * Allen, Ralph
Chasch * Vance, Jack
Chase, The * Peel, John
Chase into space * Mohan, Kim & Pamela O'Neill
Chase the morning * Rohan, Michael Scott
Chasm of doom, The * Chalk, Gary & Joe Dever
Chasms of malice * Sharp, Luke
Chaste planet, The * Updike, John
Chateau D'If, and other stories * Vance, Jack
Chauvinisto * Merwin, Sam Jr.
Checklist of Ace SF through 1968 * Massoglia, Marty
Checklist of Anne Rice, A * Stephens, Christopher P.
Checklist of British science-fiction and fantasy, part 1: magazines, original & reprint * Bentcliffe, Eric
Checklist of Dean R. Koontz, A * Stephens, Christopher P.
Checklist of Dean R. Koontz, A, 2nd ed. * Stephens, Christopher P.
Checklist of Dean R. Koontz, A, 3rd ed. * Stephens, Christopher P.
Checklist of Dean R. Koontz, A, 4th ed. * Stephens, Christopher P.
Checklist of fantastic literature, The * Bleiler, E. F.
Checklist of Gene Wolfe, A * Stephens, Christopher P.
Checklist of Gene Wolfe, A, 2nd ed. * Stephens, Christopher P.
Checklist of Gene Wolfe, A, 3rd ed. * Stephens, Christopher P.
Checklist of James P. Blaylock, A * Joyce, Tom & Christopher P. Stephens
Checklist of K. W. Jeter, A * Stephens, Christopher P.
Checklist of Kim Stanley Robinson, A * Joyce, Tom & Christopher P. Stephens
Checklist of Lucius Shepard, A * Joyce, Tom & Christopher P. Stephens
Checklist of Morrigan Press and Kerosina Press, A * Stephens, Christopher P.
Checklist of Phantasia Press, A * Stephens, Christopher P.
Checklist of Philip K. Dick, A * Stephens, Christopher P.
Checklist of Philip K. Dick, A, 2nd ed. * Stephens, Christopher P.
Checklist of Philip K. Dick, A, 3rd ed. * Stephens, Christopher P.

Checklist of Robertson Davies, A * Stephens, Christopher P.

Checklist of Robertson Davies, A, 2nd ed. * Stephens, Christopher P.

Checklist of Roger Zelazny, A * Stephens, Christopher P.

Checklist of Roger Zelazny, A, 2nd ed. * Stephens, Christopher P.

Checklist of Roger Zelazny, A, 3rd ed. * Stephens, Christopher P.

Checklist of Samuel R. Delany, A * Stephens, Christopher P.

Checklist of Samuel R. Delany, A, 2nd ed. * Stephens, Christopher P.

Checklist of science fiction, fantasy, and supernatural stories available in paperback in Britain, January 1966, A * Slater, Ken

Checklist of science-fiction and supernatural literature, The * Bleiler, E. F.

Checklist of the publications of Dennis McMillan, A * Stephens, Christopher P.

Checklist of the Tor Doubles, A * Stephens, Christopher P.

Checklist of the Tor Doubles, A, 2nd ed. * Stephens, Christopher P.

Checklist of Thomas M. Disch, A * Stephens, Christopher P.

Checklist of Thomas M. Disch, A, 2nd ed. * Stephens, Christopher P.

Checklist of Thomas M. Disch, A, 3rd ed. * Stephens, Christopher P.

Checklist of Tim Powers, A * Joyce, Tom & Christopher P. Stephens

Checklist of Ultramarine Press, A * Stephens, Christopher P.

Checklist of Ultramarine Press, A, 2nd ed. * Stephens, Christopher P.

Checklist of Wilson Tucker, A * Stephens, Christopher P.

Checklist of Wilson Tucker, A, 2nd ed. * Stephens, Christopher P.

Checkmate: universe * Mahr, Kurt

Cheerleader, The * Cooney, Caroline B.

Chekhov's journey * Watson, Ian

Chekov's Enterprise: a personal journal of the making of Star Trek—the motion picture * Koenig, Walter

Cheon of Weltanland: The four wishes * Stone, Charlotte

Chernevog * Cherryh, C. J.

Chernobyl syndrome, The * Ing, Dean

Cherron * Combes, Sharon

Cheshire cat, The * Johnson, Ken

Chess in literature * Truzzi, Marcello

Chess king: a novel * Chang, Shi-Kuo

Chess with a dragon * Gerrold, David

Chessboard planet, and other stories * Kuttner, Henry & C. L. Moore

Chessboard queen, The * Newman, Sharan

Chessmen of doom, The * Bellairs, John

Chestnut spider, The * Nimmo, Jenny

Cheyney's robot * Webb, William Thomas

Chiaroscuro * White, Tim

Chicago conversion, The * Proctor, Geo. W.

Chicago days/Hoboken nights * Pinkwater, Daniel M.

Chicago red * Meluch, R. M.

Chicago run * Robbins, David

Chickadees, The: a contemporary fable * Hyers, Conrad

Chicken trek: the third strange thing that happened to Noodleman * Manes, Stephen

Chieftain, The * Norman, John

Chieftain of Andor * Offutt, Andrew J.

Child across the sky, A * Carroll, Jonathan

Child garden, The; or, A low comedy * Ryman, Geoff

Child in time, The * McEwan, Ian

Child of darkness * Silva, David B.

Child of demons * Burgess, Mason

Child of fortune * Spinrad, Norman

Child of good fortune, The * De Haan, Tom

Child of light: a reassessment of Mary Wollstonecraft Shelley * Spark, Muriel

Child of night * Edwards, Anne

Child of Saturn * Edgerton, Teresa

Child of shadows * Coyne, John

Child of the air * Chetwin, Grace

Child of the grove * Huff, Tanya

Child of the northern spring * Woolley, Persia

Child of time * Asimov, Isaac & Robert Silverberg

Child of tomorrow * Bartholomew, Barbara

Child of Vodyanoi * Wiltshire, David

Child possessed * St. Clair, David

Child's garden of vampires, A * Youngson, Jeanne

Child's play * Conte, Sal

Child's play * Neiderman, Andrew

Child's play 2: a novel * Costello, Matthew J.

Child's play 3: a novel * Costello, Matthew J.

Childe Roland * Lee, Samantha

Childgrave * Greenhall, Ken

Childmare * Sharman, Nick

Childmare * Sharman, Nick as A. G. SCOTT

Children, The * Robertson, Charles

Children in the night * Myra, Harold

Children of Anthi, The * Blakeney, Jay D.

Children of Arable * Belden, David

Children of Ashgaroth, The * Ford, Richard

Children of Atlantis, The * Harding, Lee

Children of darkness * Fischer, Andrew & K. S. Salikof

Children of Dune * Herbert, Frank

Children of Dynmouth, The * Trevor, William

Children of Flux & Anchor * Chalker, Jack L.

Children of Hamlin, The * Carter, Carmen

Children of Hastur: The heritage of Hastur; Sharra's exile * Bradley, Marion Zimmer

Children of Lir, The: an Irish legend * Scott, Michael

Children of Shiny Mountain, The * Dvorkin, David

Children of the dark * Veley, Charles

Children of the dragon, The * Estes, Rose

Children of the dragon * Robinson, Frank S.

Children of the drake: origin of Dragonrealm * Knaak, Richard A.

Children of the dust * Lawrence, Louise

Children of the future * Asimov, Isaac & Martin H. Greenberg & Charles G. Waugh

Children of the future * Schmidt, Stanley

Children of the island, The * Wright, T. M.

Children of the knife * Strickland, Brad

Children of the light * Weston, Susan B.

Children of the Maker * Babbitt, Lucy Cullyford

Children of the night * Bingley, Margaret

Children of the night * Kring, Michael K.

Children of the night * Lackey, Mercedes

Children of the night * Lortz, Richard

Children of the rainbow * Darby, Catherine as SHARON WHITBY

Children of the shadows * Freeman, Don L.

Children of the Shroud * Reeves-Stevens, Garfield

Children of the stones * Burnham, Jeremy & Trevor Ray

Children of the storm * Tallis, Robyn

Children of the thunder * Brunner, John

Children of the wind, The * Harris, Geraldine

Children of the wind: five novellas * Wilhelm, Kate

Children of time * Moulton, Deborah

Children's crusade, The * Naha, Ed as D. B. DRUMM

Children's fantasy * Molson, Francis J.

Cinder * De Marinis, Rick

"Cinders" of Harley Street: being some curious leaves from the diary of Villiers Beethom-Saunders, M.D., revealed by his friend and executor, Charles Barrington-Mayne, Esquire, barrister-at-law * Le Queux, William

Cinefantastique * Annan, David

Cinema of adventure, romance & terror: from the archives of American cinematographer * Turner, George E.

Cinema of mystery and fantasy * Annan, David

Cinema of Stanley Kubrick, The * Kagan, Norman

Cinemonsters * Greenberg, Martin H. & Charles G. Waugh & Frank D. McSherry Jr.

Cineverse cycle, The * Gardner, Craig Shaw

Cingulum, The * Roberts, John Maddox

Cinnabar * Bryant, Edward

Cinnabar * Diamond, Graham

Cipher, The * Koja, Kathe

Circle, The * McCormick, Lois Elizabeth

Circle, crescent, star * Dibell, Ansen

Circle home: a novel * Hanlon, Emily

Circle in the sea, A * Senn, Steve

Circle of death * Frey, James N.

Circle of evil * Wagner, Sharon

Circle of iron: a novel * Weverka, Robert

Circle of Rowan, A * Darby, Catherine

Circle of the gods, The * Canning, Victor

Circle war, The * Maloney, Mack

Circuit * Snodgrass, Melinda M.

Circuit breaker * Snodgrass, Melinda M.

Circuit-breaker * MacLeod, Sheila

Circumpolar! * Lupoff, Richard A.

Circus of fear * Estes, Rose

Circus world * Longyear, Barry B.

Cirque: a novel of the far future * Carr, Terry

Ciruelo * Cabral, Ciruelo & Nigel Suckling

Citadel of Chaos, The * Jackson, Steve

Citadel of the Autarch, The * Wolfe, Gene

Citadel run * Robbins, David

Citadels on Earth * Hagberg, David as ANONYMOUS AUTHOR

Citadels under attack * Hagberg, David as ANONYMOUS AUTHOR

Cities & scenes from the ancient world * Krenkel, Roy G.

Cities in flight, volume 1 * Blish, James

Cities in flight, volume 2 * Blish, James

Cities in space * Carr, John F. & Jerry Pournelle

Cities of the dead * Paine, Michael

Cities of the red night * Burroughs, William S.

Citizen Phaid * Farren, Mick

Citizen vampire * Daniels, Les

Citizens of Mars * Bonanno, Margaret Wander as RICK NORTH

City, The * Haigh, Richard

City * Simak, Clifford D.

City, The: 2000 A.D.: urban life through science fiction * Clem, Ralph & Martin H. Greenberg & Joseph D. Olander

City and the desert, The * George B. Tait as ALAN BARCLAY

City at the edge of time * Morris, Chris & Janet Morris

City by the sea * Doyle, Debra & James D. Macdonald

City come a-walkin' * Shirley, John

City condemned to Hell, The * Page, Norvell W. as RANDOLPH CRAIG

City destroyer, The * Page, Norvell W. as GRANT STOCKBRIDGE

City dwellers, The: science fiction * Platt, Charles

City in darkness * Grubb, Jeff

City in the autumn stars, The: being a continuation of the story of the von Bek family and its association with Lucifer, Prince of Darkness, and the cure for the world's pain * Moorcock, Michael

City in the glacier, The * Milán, Victor & Robert E. Vardeman

City in the mist * Hughes, Zach as EVAN INNES

City in the north, A * Randall, Marta

City in the stars, The * DiVono, Sharman & William Rotsler as VICTOR APPLETON

City jitters * Fowler, Christopher

City, not long after, The * Murphy, Pat

City of a million legends * Lichtenberg, Jacqueline

City of Baraboo * Longyear, Barry B.

City of crystal shadow * Schmidt, Dennis

City of darkness: a novel * Bova, Ben

City of fear * Jahn, Michael as J. D. CAMERON

City of flaming shadows * Page, Norvell W. as GRANT STOCKBRIDGE

City of glass * Bagdon, Paul as TONY PHILLIPS

City of hawks * Gygax, Gary

City of masques * Brennert, Alan

City of sorcery * Bradley, Marion Zimmer

City of the Chasch * Vance, Jack

City of the first time * Barrett, G. J.

City of the hidden eyes * Levene, Philip

City of the living dead * Green, Roland as JEFFREY LORD

City of the Singing Flame, The * Smith, Clark Ashton

City of the Sun, The * Stableford, Brian M.

City of thieves * Livingstone, Ian

City of truth * Morrow, James

City of whispering stone, The * Chesbro, George C.

City outside the world, The * Carter, Lin

City vagabonds, The * Dann, Colin

City war * Chapman, John

City wars * Palumbo, Dennis

Cityscape * Thomas, Francis

Civil war ghosts * Greenberg, Martin H. & Frank D. McSherry Jr. & Charles G. Waugh

Civil War secret agent * Perry, Steve

Civilian slaughter * Rouch, James

Claiming of Sleeping Beauty, The: an erotic novel of tenderness and cruelty for the enjoyment of men and women * Rice, Anne as A. N. ROQUELAURE

Clairvoyant, The * Clement, Henry

Clairvoyant countess, The * Gilman, Dorothy

Clan and crown * Green, Roland & Jerry Pournelle

Clan ground * Bell, Clare

Clan of Golgotha Scalp, The * Anderson, Michael Falconer

Clan of Munes, The * Waugh, Frederick J.

Clan of the cats, The * Adams, Robert

Clan of the Cave Bear, The: a novel * Auel, Jean M.

Clans of darkness * Haining, Peter

Clansman of Andor * Offutt, Andrew J.

Clarion * Greenleaf, William

Clarion awards, The * Knight, Damon

Clarion SF * Wilhelm, Kate

Clarion writers' handbook, The * Knight, Damon

Clark Ashton Smith * Behrends, Steve

Clarke County, space * Steele, Allen

Clash by night, and other stories * Kuttner, Henry & C. L. Moore

Clash of eagles * Rutman, Leo

Clash of symbols, A: the triumph of James Blish * Stableford, Brian M.

Clash of the sorcerers * Simon, Morris

Clash of the titans: novelization * Foster, Alan Dean

Class G-zero * Hendrickson, Walter B. Jr.

Class Six climb * Cochrane, William E.

Clypsis * Carver, Jeffrey A.
C-minor * Hyde, Gregory R.
Coachman rat, The * Wilson, David Henry
Cobra * Morris, Christopher & Jane Stump as DANIEL STRYKER
Cobra * Zahn, Timothy
Cobra bargain * Zahn, Timothy
Cobra connection, The * Foley, Louise Munro
Cobra strike * Zahn, Timothy
Cobweb across the moon * Darby, Catherine
Cobwebwalking * Banerji, Sara
Cockroaches of Stay More, The: a novel * Harington, Donald
Cocoon: a novel * Saperstein, David
Code blue—emergency: (a Sector General novel) * White, James
Code name: Clone * Cooper, Margaret
Code name Peregrine * Blakeney, Jay D. as SEAN DALTON
Code name: werewolf * Smith, Martin Cruz as NICK CARTER
Code of blood * Chesbro, George C. as DAVID CROSS
Code of the lifemaker * Hogan, James P.
Coelura, The * McCaffrey, Anne
Coils * Saberhagen, Fred & Roger Zelazny
Coin of the realm * Murphy, Warren & Richard Sapir
Coincidental art of Charles Brockden Brown, The * Grabo, Norman S.
Coinspinner's story * Saberhagen, Fred
C.O.L.A.R.: a tale of outer space * Slote, Alfred
Cold blood * Chizmar, Richard T.
Cold blue light, A * Godwin, Parke & Marvin Kaye
Cold cash war, The * Asprin, Robert Lynn
Cold cash warrior * Asprin, Robert Lynn & Bill Fawcett
Cold chills * Bloch, Robert
Cold Christmas * Beachcroft, Nina
Cold copper tears * Cook, Glen
Cold Creek Cash Store * Hill, Russell
Cold death * Donovan, Laurence as KENNETH ROBESON
Cold death: a Doc Savage adventure * Donovan, Laurence as KENNETH ROBESON
Cold eye * Blunt, Giles
Cold fear: new tales of terror * Lamb, Hugh
Cold feet: an anthology of scary stories * Richardson, Jean
Cold fire * Koontz, Dean R.
Cold hand in mine: strange stories * Aickman, Robert
Cold Heaven: a novel * Moore, Brian
Cold in July * Lansdale, Joe R.
Cold moon over Babylon * McDowell, Michael
Cold moons, The * Clement, Aeron
Cold night * Sarrantonio, Al
Cold print * Campbell, Ramsey
Cold room, The * Caine, Jeffrey
Cold sea rising * Moran, Richard
Cold shocks * Sullivan, Tim
Cold smell of sacred stone, The * Chesbro, George C.
Cold Steele * Hawke, Simon as J. D. MASTERS
Cold tales * Piñera, Virgilio
Cold victory * Anderson, Poul
Cold whisper * Hautala, Rick
Cold wind from Orion, A: a novel * Asnin, Scott
Cold-Eyes * Dwyer, James Francis
Colin Wilson * Weigel, John A.
Colin Wilson, a celebration: essays and recollections * Stanley, Colin
Colin Wilson collection of Howard F. Dossor, The * Dossor, Howard F.
Colin Wilson: the man and his mind * Dossor, Howard F.

Colin Wilson: the outsider and beyond * Bendau, Clifford P.
Colin Wilson, the positive approach: a response to a critic * Trowell, Michael
Colin Wilson: two essays: The English existentialist; and, Spiders and outsiders: (including an interview with the author) * Moorhouse, John & Paul Newman
Collapsing castle, The * Middleton, Haydn
Collapsing cosmoses * Barlow, R. H. & H. P. Lovecraft
Collected Arthur Machen, The * Machen, Arthur
Collected essays, journalism, and letters of George Orwell, The, volume I: An age like this, 1920-1940 * Orwell, George
Collected essays, journalism, and letters of George Orwell, The, volume II: My country right or left, 1940-1943 * Orwell, George
Collected essays, journalism, and letters of George Orwell, The, volume III: As I please, 1943-1945 * Orwell, George
Collected essays, journalism, and letters of George Orwell, The, volume IV: In front of your nose, 1945-1950 * Orwell, George
Collected fantasies * Davidson, Avram
Collected ghost stories of M. R. James, The * James, M. R.
Collected ghost stories of Mrs. J. H. Riddell, The * Riddell, J. H., Mrs.
Collected letters of William Morris, The, Volume I, 1848-1880 * Morris, William
Collected letters of William Morris, The, Volume II, 1881-1884 * Morris, William
Collected novels * Verne, Jules
Collected novels: King Solomon's mines, Maiwa's revenge, Cleopatra, She * Haggard, H. Rider
Collected short stories of Roald Dahl, The * Dahl, Roald
Collected short stories of Robert Sheckley, book five, The * Sheckley, Robert
Collected short stories of Robert Sheckley, book four, The * Sheckley, Robert
Collected short stories of Robert Sheckley, book one, The * Sheckley, Robert
Collected short stories of Robert Sheckley, book three, The * Sheckley, Robert
Collected short stories of Robert Sheckley, book two, The * Sheckley, Robert
Collected stories * Matheson, Richard
Collected stories of Wolfgang Hildesheimer, The * Hildesheimer, Wolfgang
Collection of great science fiction films, A * Strickland, A. W.
Collector's book of science fiction by H. G. Wells, The * Wells, H. G.
Collector's guide to Weird tales, The * Cook, Fred & Sheldon R. Jaffery
Collidescope * Chetwin, Grace
Collision course * Bayley, Barrington J.
Collision course * Tubb, E. C.
Collision with chronos * Bayley, Barrington J.
Collisions: a novel * Clarke, A. F. N.
Colloghi conspiracy, The * Hill, Douglas
Colonists and the Chronicles of Novae, The * Wood, Susan T.
Colonists from space, The * Young, B. A.
Colony * Bova, Ben
Colony, The * Lalley, Paul
Colony, The * Vigliante, Mary
Colony in peril * Griffin, P. M.
Color of evil, The * Hartwell, David G.
Color of Neanderthal eyes, The * Tiptree, James Jr.
Color out of time * Shea, Michael

Cosmic critiques: how & why ten science fiction stories work * Asimov, Isaac & Martin H. Greenberg

Cosmic crusaders: Two complete novels: Baphomet's meteor; Cosmic crusade * Barbet, Pierre

Cosmic dancers, The: exploring the physics of science fiction * Goswami, Amit & Maggie Goswami

Cosmic encounter * van Vogt, A. E.

Cosmic encounters * Austin, R. G.

Cosmic kaleidoscope * Shaw, Bob

Cosmic knights * Asimov, Isaac & Martin H. Greenberg & Charles G. Waugh

Cosmic perspective, The * Stableford, Brian M.

Cosmic rape * Bennett, Jeff

Cosmic rape, The; and, "To marry Medusa" * Sturgeon, Theodore

Cosmic trilogy, The * Lewis, C. S.

Cosmic web, The: scientific field models and literary strategies in the twentieth century * Hayles, N. Katherine

Cosmos project, The * Hardy, Hilbert

Costa Rican chaos * Roberts, Mark K.

Costumes, creatures, and characters * Chancellor, Ann Layman

Could it be? a collection of stories of the supernatural and horrific * Marland, Michael

Council of Ten, The * Land, Jon

Count Dracula * Savory, Gerald

Count Dracula book of classic vampire stories, The * Youngson, Jeanne

Count Dracula cookbook, The * Youngson, Jeanne

Count Dracula fan club book of vampire stories, The * Youngson, Jeanne

Count Dracula, me, and Norma D. * Hatchigan, Jessica

Count Dracula's favorite Christmas cookie recipes * Youngson, Jeanne

Count Dracula's vampire quiz book * Rovin, Jeff

Count Manfred * Seymour, Miranda

Count of eleven, The * Campbell, Ramsey

Count Zero * Gibson, William

Countdown to doomsday * Schaffer, Gene

Countdown to midnight: twelve great stories about nuclear war * Franklin, H. Bruce

Countdown World War III: Operation Black Sea * Davies, W. X.

Countdown WWIII: Operation choke point: a novel * Davies, W. X.

Countdown WWIII: Operation North Africa: a novel * Davies, W. X.

Countdown WWIII: Operation Persian Gulf: a novel * Davies, W. X.

Counter Force * Streib, Dan

Counter Force: Beware the Tektrons * Cameron, Ian & George Erskine

Counter Force: Find the Tektrons * Cameron, Ian & Erskine, George

Counterattack * Drake, David & Bill Fawcett

Counterings: utopian dialectics in contemporary contexts * Widmer, Kingsley

Counterprobe * Douglas, Carole Nelson

Countersolar! * Lupoff, Richard A.

Counterstrike * Taylor, Charles D.

Counting the cost * Drake, David

Country of the blind, The * Freeman, Simon & H. G. Wells

Country of the mind, The * Morgan, Dan

Country of the wolf * Wagner, Sharon

Coupe * Stackpole, Michael

Courage in the ashes * Johnstone, William W.

Court for owls, A * Little, Patrick

Court of a thousand suns, The * Bunch, Chris & Allan Cole

Courting disasters, and other strange affinities: short stories * Hoffman, Nina Kiriki

Court-martial of George Armstrong Custer, The * Jones, Douglas C.

Courts of Chaos, The * Zelazny, Roger

Courtship rite * Kingsbury, Donald

Coven * Lee, Edward

Coven, The * Hampton, Jay

Coven * Rimmer, Steven W.

Covenant, The * Anderson, Michael Falconer

Covenant at Coldwater * Osier, John

Covenant of the crown, The: a Star Trek novel * Weinstein, Howard

Covenant with death * Victor, Cindy

Cover * Ketchum, Jack

Cowboy Feng's space bar and grille * Brust, Steven

Cowboy heaven * Goulart, Ron

Coyote: a novel * Gadol, Peter

Coz: a novel * Pjerrou, Mary

CQY * Yarbro, Chelsea Quinn

Crab trees, The * Robertson, J. R.

Crabs: The human sacrifice * Smith, Guy N.

Crabs moon * Smith, Guy N.

Crabs on the rampage * Smith, Guy N.

Crack, The * Tennant, Emma

Crack in the sky, The * Lupoff, Richard A.

Crack of doom, The * Minto, William

Cracken at critical * Aldiss, Brian W.

Crackpot * Goulart, Ron

Cradle * Clarke, Arthur C. & Gentry Lee

Cradle and all... * Zachary, Fay Nedra

Cradle demon, and other stories of fantasy and terror, The * Chetwynd-Hayes, R.

Cradle kill * Hillman, S. A.

Cradle of stars * Rowland, Donald S. as ALEX RANDOM

Craft of science fiction, The: a symposium on writing science fiction and science fantasy * Bretnor, Reginald

Crafters, The * Fawcett, Bill & Christopher Stasheff

Cranky old man from Tulsa: interviews with R. A. Lafferty * Lafferty, R. A.

Crash landing! * Roth, Arthur

Crash landing on Iduna * Tofte, Arthur

Crash of '79, The * Erdman, Paul

Crash of 2086, The * Hershman, Morris

Crash of empire, The * Carr, John F. & Jerry Pournelle

Crater Lake * James, Laurence as JAMES AXLER

Crater of mystery * McQuay, Mike as VICTOR APPLETON

Craven house terror * Milton, Hilary

Craving, The * Herzog, Arthur

Crawling dark, The * Dunn, Dawn & Susan Hartzell as PAULINE DUNN

Crazy Indian, The * Bogart, William G.

Crazy time * Wilhelm, Kate

Created legend, The * Sologub, Fëdor

Creating short fiction * Knight, Damon

Creating short fiction, rev. ed. * Knight, Damon

Creation descending * Lovejoy, Jack

Creation of Dino De Laurentiis' King Kong, The * Bahrenburg, Bruce

Creation of the sun and the moon, The * Traven, B.

Creation of tomorrow, The: fifty years of magazine science fiction * Carter, Paul A.

Creation story verbatim * Gold, E. J.

Creations: the quest for origins in story and science * Asimov, Isaac & George Zebrowski & Martin H. Greenberg

Creator, The * Hinkemeyer, Michael T.

Creator * Leven, Jeremy

Crusader's torch * Yarbro, Chelsea Quinn
Crusher strike * Robbins, David
Cry for the demon * Grice, Julia
Cry for the strangers * Saul, John
Cry havoc * Forman, James D.
Cry in the night, A * Ellis, Carol
Cry in the woods, A * Ball, Donna
Cry of a seagull * Dickens, Monica
Cry of the beast * Meyers, Richard S.
Cry of the cat, The * Sellers, Mary
Cry of the deep * Henrick, Richard P.
Cry of the Onlies, The * Klass, Judy
Cry republic * Mitchell, Kirk
Cry Silver Bells * Swann, Thomas Burnett
Cry vampire! * Dicks, Terrance
Cry wolf * Black, Ian Stuart
Cry wolf * Chronister, Alan B.
Cry wolf * La Tourette, Aileen
Crying shame, A * Johnstone, William W.
Crypt of the sorcerer * Livingstone, Ian
Crypt of the vampire * Morris, Dave
Crypts of terror, The * Brennan, J. H.
Crystal and steel * Grimsley, Ann & Lynne Kinnerley as LYNDAN DARBY
Crystal ball, The * Spicer, Dorothy
Crystal cage, The * Bayer, Sandy
Crystal cat, The * Johnston, Velda
Crystal cave, The * Stewart, Mary
Crystal cave, The; The hollow hills; Wildfire at midnight; Airs above the ground * Stewart, Mary
Crystal city, The * Etchemendy, Nancy
Crystal clear * Schulze, Doris & Irene Wohlfahrt
Crystal clouds, The * Vardeman, Robert E.
Crystal Crown, The * Clough, B. W.
Crystal curtain, The * Bayer, Sandy
Crystal empire, The * Smith, L. Neil
Crystal express * Sterling, Bruce
Crystal flame * Krentz, Jayne Ann
Crystal keep, The * Gilluly, Sheila
Crystal maze, The: adventure gamebook * Morris, Dave & Jamie Thomson
Crystal memory, The * Leigh, Stephen
Crystal of a hundred dreams: a portfolio * Fabian, Stephen E.
Crystal of power, The * DeBolt, Adriana
Crystal palace, The * Eisenstein, Phyllis
Crystal paradise * Howl, Marcia Yvonne & Sharon Jarvis as JOHANNA HAILEY
Crystal phoenix * Berlyn, Michael
Crystal Prince, The * Scheer, K. H.
Crystal prison, The * Jarvis, Robin
Crystal seas, The * Green, Roland as JEFFREY LORD
Crystal shadows * Thomas, Michele Y.
Crystal shard, The * Salvatore, R. A.
Crystal ship, The: three original novellas of science fiction * Silverberg, Robert
Crystal singer, The * McCaffrey, Anne
Crystal skull * MacGregor, Rob
Crystal sorcerers, The * Forstchen, William R. & Greg Morrison
Crystal spirit, The: a study of George Orwell * Woodcock, George
Crystal stair, The * Chetwin, Grace
Crystal sword, The * Martine-Barnes, Adrienne
Crystal trap, The * Wayne, Matt
Crystal warriors, The * Forstchen, William R. & Greg Morrison
Crystal witness * Tyers, Kathy
Crystal world, The; Crash; Concrete island * Ballard, J. G.

Crystals of air and water * Goldin, Stephen
Crystals of Mida, The * Green, Sharon
Cthulhu: tales of the Cthulhu Mythos * Harvey, Jon M.
Cthulhu 2: tales of the Cthulhu Mythos: The guardians of the gate * Mooney, Brian
Cthulhu 3: tales of the Cthulhu Mythos * Harvey, Jon M.
Cthulhu: the mythos and kindred horrors * Howard, Robert E.
CTZ paradigm, The * Francois, Yves Régis
Cuckoo plant, The * Ford, Adam
Cuckoo tree, The * Aiken, Joan
Cuckoo's egg * Cherryh, C. J.
Cugel's saga * Vance, Jack
Cujo * King, Stephen
Cult * Frail, Edward J.
Cult movie stars * Peary, Danny
Cult movies 2: 50 more of the classics, the sleepers, the weird, and the wonderful * Peary, Danny
Cult movies 3: 50 more of the classics, the sleepers, the weird, and the wonderful * Peary, Danny
Cult movies: the classics, the sleepers, the weird, and the wonderful * Peary, Danny
Cult of loving kindness, The * Park, Paul
Cults!: an anthology of secret societies, sects, and the supernatural * Greenberg, Martin H. & Charles G. Waugh
Cults of horror * Greenberg, Martin H. & Charles G. Waugh
Cumulative paperback index, 1939-1959 * Reginald, R. & M. R. Burgess
Cunningham equations, The * Edmondson, G. C. & C. M. Kotlan
Cup of clay * Douglas, Carole Nelson
Cup of Thanatos, The * Hunt, Charlotte
Curious case of Richard Fielding, and other stories, The * Roland, Paul
Curious fragments: Jack London's tales of fantasy fiction * London, Jack
Curious quests of Brigadier Ffellowes, The * Lanier, Sterling E.
Curse * Farson, Daniel
Curse, The * Grant, Charles L.
Curse, The * Sherrell, Carl
Curse, The * Weinberg, Larry
Curse of Batterslea Hall, The * Brightfield, Richard
Curse of Fenric, The * Briggs, Ian
Curse of Frankenstein, The * Brennan, J. H.
Curse of Halewood, The * Paul, Barbara
Curse of Halewood, The * Paul, Barbara
Curse of Loch Ness, The * Tremayne, Peter
Curse of Sagamore, The * Dalkey, Kara
Curse of Slagfid, The * Boyer, Elizabeth H.
Curse of the blue figurine, The * Bellairs, John
Curse of the Fleers, The * Copper, Basil
Curse of the giant hogweed, The * MacLeod, Charlotte
Curse of the haunted mansion, The * Packard, Edward
Curse of the obelisk, The * Goulart, Ron
Curse of the Pharaoh * Johnson, Oliver
Curse of the pharoahs * Younger, Jack
Curse of the ring, The: an archetypal translation of Richard Wagner's The rhinegold * Gorham, Melvin
Curse of the snake god, The * Chetwynd-Hayes, R.
Curse of the sunken treasure * Austin, R. G.
Curse of the vampire, The * Alexander, Karl
Curse of the vampire * Walker, Robert W. as GEOFFREY CAINE
Curse of the werewolf, The * Biegel, Paul
Curse of the werewolf * Martindale, T. Chris
Curse of the witch-queen, The * Volsky, Paula
Curse of Valkyrie House * Cunningham, Cathy

D

Daddy's home * Anderson, Paul Dale
Daddy's little girl * Gorman, Ed as DANIEL RANSOM
Daddy's side * Tem, Melanie
Dad's nuke * Laidlaw, Marc
Daemon, The * Hughes, Peter Tuesday
Daemon in Lithuania * Guigonnat, Henri
Daemons, The; The time monster * Dicks, Terrance &
   Barry Letts
Dagda's harp, The * Newman, Sharan
Dagger * Drake, David
Dagger and the bird, The: a story of suspense * Greaves,
   Margaret
Dagger and the cross, The: a novel of the Crusades *
   Tarr, Judith
Dagger in the sky, The: a Doc Savage adventure * Dent,
   Lester as KENNETH ROBESON
Dagger of the mind * Shaw, Bob
Daggerspell * Kerr, Katharine
Dagmar Schultz and the Angel Edna * Hall, Lynn
Dagmar Schultz and the powers of darkness * Hall, Lynn
Dagon * Chappell, Fred
Dahut * Anderson, Karen & Poul Anderson
Daily planet: a world of news every day! * Spinner,
   Stephanie
Daily voices * Goldstein, Lisa
Dai-San * Lustbader, Eric Van
Daisy, in the sun * Willis, Connie
Dakota run * Robbins, David
Dalek invasion of Earth, The * Dicks, Terrance
Dalek invasion of Earth, The; and, The crusaders *
   Dicks, Terrance
Daleks' master plan, part 1: Mission to the unknown *
   Peel, John
Dallas down * Moran, Richard
Dallas run * Robbins, David
Damiano * MacAvoy, R. A.
Damiano's lute * MacAvoy, R. A.
Damien: Omen II: a novel * Howard, Joseph
Damnation game, The * Barker, Clive
Damned, The * Sadler, Barry
Damned disciples, The * Stacy, Jan as CRAIG SARGENT
Damned if we do * Rice, Peter
Dance band on the Titanic * Chalker, Jack L.
Dance of blood, The * Farrar, Stewart
Dance of death * Kassem, Lou
Dance of demons * Gygax, Gary
Dance of desire * Martine
Dance of love * Martine
Dance of the apocalypse * Eklund, Gordon
Dance of the hag * Leigh, Stephen
Dance of the skeletons, The * Weinberg, Robert
Dance of the tiger: a novel of the ice age * Kurten, Bjorn
Dance of the warriors * Esser, Kevin
Dancer of Gor * Norman, John
Dancers at the end of time, The * Moorcock, Michael
Dancer's illusion * Maxwell, Ann
Dancers in the afterglow * Chalker, Jack L.
Dancer's luck * Maxwell, Ann
Dancers of Arun, The * Lynn, Elizabeth A.

Dancing at the edge of the world: thoughts on words,
   women, places * Le Guin, Ursula K.
Dancing dead, The * Syvertsen, Ryder
Dancing meteorite, The * Mason, Anne
Dancing vac * Lewitt, S. N.
Dancing with mermaids * Gibson, Miles
Dandee diamond mystery, The * O'Connor, Jane &
   Joyce Milton
Dandelion caper, The * DeWeese, Gene
Danger!: space pirates * Freeman, Maggie
Danger at Anchor Mine * Foley, Louise Munro
Danger awaits * Peel, John
Danger in the ashes * Johnstone, William W.
Danger in the desert * Terman, Douglas
Danger lies east * Dent, Lester as KENNETH ROBESON
Danger quotient, The * Johnson, Annabel & Edgar John-
   son
Danger zones * Montgomery, R. A.
Dangerous games * Randall, Marta
Dangerous interfaces * Silverberg, Robert
Dangerous quest * Creasey, John
Dangerous spaces * Mahy, Margaret
Danielle, book two * Clayton, Sheena
Danilov the violist * Orlov, Vladimir
Danni's desperate journey * Grocott, Ann
Danny Dunn and the universal glue * Abrashkin, Ray-
   mond & Jay Williams
Danny Dunn, scientific detective * Abrashkin, Raymond
   & Jay Williams
Danse macabre * King, Stephen
Daphne du Maurier's Classics of the macabre * Du Mau-
   rier, Daphne
Dare to go a-hunting * Norton, Andre
Daredevil park * Compton, Sara & Spencer Compton
Daredevils, Ltd. * Goulart, Ron
Darfstellar, and other stories, The * Miller, Walter M.
   Jr.
Dargason * Cooper, Colin
Darian: master magician * Farrell, Simon & Jon Suther-
   land
Daring to dream: utopian stories by United States women,
   1836-1919 * Kessler, Carol Farley
Dark, The * Franklin, Max
Dark, The * Herbert, James
Dark, The * Lance, Kathryn as LYNN BEACH
Dark abyss, The * Coville, Bruce
Dark advent * Hodge, Brian
Dark angel * Forestal, Sean
Dark angel * Graham, Jean
Dark angel * Jensen, Ruby Jean
Dark ashram * Giroux, Leo Jr.
Dark awakening, The: can you destroy an ancient sor-
   cery? * Sharp, Allen
Dark backward, The * Buchanan, Marie
Dark banquet: a feast of twelve great ghost stories *
   Child, Lincoln
Dark barbarian, The: the writings of Robert E. Howard *
   Herron, Don
Dark behind the curtain, The * Cross, Gillian

DAW science-fiction books * Robinson, Roger
Dawn and the darkest hour: a study of Aldous Huxley * Woodcock, George
Dawn chorus * Garden, Donald J.
Dawn for a distant Earth * Modesitt, L. E. Jr.
Dawn of conflict * Randle, Kevin
Dawn of the dead * Romero, George A. & Susanna Sparrow
Dawn of the half-gods * Glasby, John as VICTOR LA SALLE
Dawn of the vampire * Hill, William
Dawn of time * Del Martia, Astron
Dawn of time: prehistory through science fiction * Greenberg, Martin H. & Joseph D. Olander & Robert Silverberg
Dawn palace, The: the story of Medea * Hoover, H. M.
Dawn song * Green, Sharon
Dawn: xenogenesis * Butler, Octavia E.
Dawn's uncertain light * Barrett, Neal Jr.
Dawnspell: The bristling wood * Kerr, Katharine
Day after tomorrow * Reynolds, Mack
Day boy and the night girl, The * MacDonald, George
Day by night * Lee, Tanith
Day care * Russo, John
Day eight * Ayrton, Elisabeth Walshe
Day for damnation, A * Gerrold, David
Day for damnation, A, rev. ed. * Gerrold, David
Day gone by, The: an autobiography * Adams, Richard
Day I died, The * Harris, Walter
Day in the life of Jay Peter Sweetly, A * Golis, Paul
Day lasts more than a hundred years, The * Aitmatov, Chingiz
Day of the animals * Porter, Donald
Day of the arrow * Loraine, Philip
Day of the beasts * Glasby, John as JOHN MULLER
Day of the cheetah * Brown, Dale
Day of the Daleks, The * Dicks, Terrance
Day of the dinosaurs, The * Bunting, Eve
Day of the dissonance, The * Foster, Alan Dean
Day of the dove * Blish, James
Day of the dragonstar * Bischoff, David & Thomas F. Monteleone
Day of the earthlings * Bunting, Eve
Day of the Klesh, The * Foster, M. A.
Day of the mad dogs * Anne, David
Day of the Ness, The * Gilbert, Michael & Andre Norton
Day of the starwind * Hill, Douglas
Day of the stranger: further memoires of Robert E. Howard * Ellis, Novalyne Price
Day of the triffids, The; The kraken wakes; The chrysalids; The seeds of time; Trouble with lichen; The Midwich cuckoos * Wyndham, John
Day of the tyrant * Carr, John F. & Jerry Pournelle
Day of the Ultramind * Ryman, Ras
Day of their return, The * Anderson, Poul
Day of wrath, The * Gansovsky, Sever
Day seven * Bickham, Jack M.
Day the Earth stood still, The * Tofte, Arthur
Day the gods died, The * Ernsting, Walter
Day the Martians came, The * Pohl, Frederik
Day the Sun came through, The * Campbell, Clive S.
Day the world went sane, The * Barba, Harry
Daybreak on a different mountain: a fantasy novel * Greenland, Colin
Day-dreaming on company time: short stories * Hood, Robert
Daylight and nightmare: uncollected stories and fables * Chesterton, G. K.
Daymaker, The * Jones, Gwyneth as ANN HALAM
Days after, The * Dorman, Thomas

Days between stations: a novel * Erickson, Steve
Days of atonement * Williams, Walter Jon
Days of grass * Lee, Tanith
Days of Perky Pat, The: the collected stories of Philip K. Dick, volume four * Dick, Philip K.
Days of starlight * Harrison, Craig
Daystar and Shadow * Johnson, James B.
Dayworld * Farmer, Philip José
Dayworld breakup * Farmer, Philip José
Dayworld rebel * Farmer, Philip José
DC Comics presents: Superman II, the movie magazine * Fleisher, Michael & Joe Orlando
de Camp: an L. Sprague de Camp bibliography * Laughlin, Charlotte & Daniel J. H. Levack
De historia et veritate unicornis = On the history and truth of the unicorn * Green, Michael
De mojo blues: de quest of HighJohn de Conqueror * Flowers, A. R.
Dead, The * Perry, Mark C.
Dead, The * Rogers, Mark
Dead & buried: novelization * Yarbro, Chelsea Quinn
Dead babies * Amis, Martin
Dead end: city limits: an anthology of urban fear * Olson, Paul F. & David B. Silva
Dead god dancing, A * Maxwell, Ann
Dead image * Grant, Charles L. & Paul Mikol
Dead in the west * Lansdale, Joe R.
Dead kingdom, The * Harris, Geraldine
Dead lines: a novel of horror * Skipp, John & Craig Spector
Dead man's float * Walker, Robert W.
Dead man's hand: a Wild Card novel * Martin, George R. R. & John J. Miller & Melinda M. Snodgrass
Dead moon * Kelley, Leo P.
Dead morn * Anthony, Piers & Roberto Fuentes
Dead of night: horror stories from radio, television, and films * Haining, Peter
Dead of winter, The * Abbey, Lynn & Robert Lynn Asprin
Dead remember, The * Howard, Robert E.
Dead ringer * West, Chassie L.
Dead ringers * Wood, Bari & Jack Geasland
Dead season * Owen, J. Bradley
Dead smile, The * Crawford, F. Marion
Dead that walk, The * Halliwell, Leslie
Dead to the world * Williamson, J. N.
Dead travel fast, The * Masters, Anthony as RICHARD TATE
Dead valley, The * Cram, Ralph Adams
Dead voices * Hautala, Rick
Dead white * Ryan, Alan
Dead woman, and other haunting experiences * Walter, Elizabeth
Dead zone, The * King, Stephen
Dead zone strike * Robbins, David
Dead-Eye Dick * Vonnegut, Kurt
Deadfall * Laumer, Keith
Deadliest show in town, The * McQuay, Mike
Deadlight * Roy, Archie
Deadline * Mills, D. F.
Deadly admirer * Smith, Robert Arthur
Deadly assassin, The ; The seeds of doom * Dicks, Terrance as PHILIP HINCHCLIFFE
Deadly breed * Kirby, T. J.
Deadly communion * Brookes, Owen
Deadly cyborgs, The * Edwards, Paul
Deadly deep, The * Messmann, Jon
Deadly dwarf, The: a Doc Savage adventure * Dent, Lester as KENNETH ROBESON
Deadly election, The * Castle, Mort

Death orchids, & other bizarre tales * Weinberg, Robert
Death planet * Griffin, P. M.
Death qualified: a mystery of chaos * Wilhelm, Kate
Death quest * Alexander, David
Death quest * Hubbard, L. Ron
Death reign of the vampire king * Page, Norvell W. as
GRANT STOCKBRIDGE
Death ride * Hofrichter, Paul
Death Riders of Hel * Andersson, C. Dean *as* ASA DRAKE
Death room, The: strange and startling stories * Wallace,
Edgar
Death scouts * Woodley, Richard
Death screen * Beaird, Richard F.
Death sentence * Kelley, Leo P.
Death sentence * Murphy, Warren & Richard Sapir
Death shuttle * Streib, Dan
Death sleep * Sohl, Jerry
Death song * Douglas, Drake & Stephen Kent
Death spore * Brosnan, John & Leroy Kettle *as* HARRY
ADAM KNIGHT
Death stone * Jensen, Ruby Jean
Death strain, The * Messmann, Jon *as* NICK CARTER
Death tide * Crispin, A. C. & Deborah A. Marshall
Death to the Daleks * Dicks, Terrance
Death tolls * Stith, John E.
Death trance * Masterton, Graham
Death waits in semispace * Mahr, Kurt
Death watch * Compton, D. G.
Death wears a white face * Tubb, E. C.
Death wind * Heine, William C.
Death worms of Kratos, The * Cooper, Edmund *as*
RICHARD AVERY
Death zone attack * Alexander, David *as* JOHN SIEVERT
Death-angel * Williamson, J. N.
Deathbeast * Gerrold, David
Deathbell * Smith, Guy N.
Deathbird stories: a pantheon of modern gods * Ellison,
Harlan
Death-blinder * King, Bernard
Deathbringer * Reed, Dana
Deathchain * Greenhall, Ken
Death-coach * Williamson, J. N.
Deathday * Hutson, Shaun
Deathday * Hutson, Shaun *as* ROBERT NEVILLE
Death-doctor * Williamson, J. N.
Deathfall * Vardeman, Robert E.
Deathgame * Goulart, Ron
Deathgift * Zeddies, Ann Tonsor
Deathhunter * Watson, Ian
Deathknight * Offutt, Andrew J.
Deathlands: Crater Lake * James, Laurence *as* JAMES
AXLER
Deathlands: Dectra chain * James, Laurence *as* JAMES
AXLER
Deathlands: Homeward bound * James, Laurence *as*
JAMES AXLER
Deathlands: Ice and fire * James, Laurence *as* JAMES
AXLER
Deathlands: Latitude zero * James, Laurence *as* JAMES
AXLER
Deathlands: Neutron solstice * James, Laurence *as* JAMES
AXLER
Deathlands: Northstar rising * James, Laurence *as* JAMES
AXLER
Deathlands: Pilgrimage to Hell * Adrian, Jack
Deathlands: Pony soldiers * James, Laurence *as* JAMES
AXLER
Deathlands: Red equinox * James, Laurence *as* JAMES
AXLER

Deathlands: Red holocaust * James, Laurence *as* JAMES
AXLER
Deathlands: Seedling * James, Laurence *as* JAMES AXLER
Deathlands: Time nomads * James, Laurence *as* JAMES
AXLER
Deathless, The * Murchison, Myles
Deathlight * Ahern, Jerry *as* NICK CARTER
Death's angel: a Star Trek novel * Sky, Kathleen
Death's acolyte * Proctor, Geo. W. & Robert E. Varde-
man
Death's demand * Mahr, Kurt
Death's gray land * Shupp, Mike
Death's grey land * Shupp, Mike
Death's head * Keegan, Mel
Death's head rebellion * Pournelle, Jerry
Death's law * Scott, Michael
Death's little sister * Decker, Jake
Death's master * Lee, Tanith
Death's running mate * Revere, John D.
Deathscape * Peters, David
Death-school * Williamson, J. N.
Deathsong * Borton, Douglas
Deathsong * Scaparro, Jack
Deathsport * Hughes, William
Deathstone, The * Eulo, Ken
Deathtrap dungeon * Livingstone, Ian
Deathtrek * Wallmann, Jeffrey M.
Deathwalkers * Brandner, Gary
Deathward * Byers, Richard Lee
Deathwatch: a novel * Trevor, Elleston
Deathwind of Vedun * Rypel, T. C.
Deathwing * Jones, Neal & David Pringle
Deathwing over Veynaa * Hill, Douglas
Deathwish world * Ing, Dean & Mack Reynolds
Deathworms of Kratos, The * Cooper, Edmund
Decade, the 1940s * Aldiss, Brian W. & Harry Harrison
Decade, the 1950s * Aldiss, Brian W. & Harry Harrison
Decade, the 1960s * Aldiss, Brian W. & Harry Harrison
Deceiver, The * Cooper, Louise
Deceivers, The * Bester, Alfred
Decepticon poison * Stamper, J. B.
Deception: the UFO conspiracy * Bischoff, David
Decision at Thunder Rift * Keith, William H. Jr.
Decision time * Ahern, Jerry
Dectra chain * James, Laurence, *as* JAMES AXLER
Dedalus book of British fantasy, The: the 19th century *
Stableford, Brian M.
*Deeds of the ever-glorious: histories of the Tsolyani le-
gions* * Barker, M. A. R.
Deep, The * Crowley, John
Deep domain: a Star Trek novel * Weinstein, Howard
Deep foot * Vixen, Richard M.
Deep freeze * Whyte, H. Walter
Deep kill * Greenfield, Irving A.
Deep quarry * Stith, John E.
Deep rescue * Greenfield, Irving A.
Deep six: a novel * Cussler, Clive
Deep space processional * Beaumont, Roger & R. Snow-
den Ficks
Deep space warriors * Riding, Julia
Deep sting * Taylor, Charles D.
Deep, very deep space * Nathenson, Joseph
Deep wizardry * Duane, Diane
DeepCore * Adair, James B.
Deeper foot: sequel to Deep foot * Vixen, Richard M.
Deeper than the darkness * Benford, Gregory
Deepwater dreams * Van Scyoc, Sydney J.
Defenders of Ar * Lovejoy, Jack
Defiance * Lange, Oliver

Deryni magic: a grimoire * Kurtz, Katherine
Descendants * Simon, Jean
Descent * Dee, Ron
Descent of Anansi, The * Barnes, Steven & Larry Niven
Descriptive catalog of Edgar Allan Poe manuscripts in the Humanities Research Center Library, the University of Texas at Austin, A * Moldenhauer, Joseph J.
Desecration, The * Perry, Mark C.
Desecration of Susan Browning, The * Martin, Russell W.
Desert, The * Wilson, Colin
Desert eden * Morgan, J. M.
Desert flight * Razzi, Jim
Desert mercenary * Sadler, Barry
Desert of death's domain * Mahr, Kurt
Desert of stolen dreams, The * Silverberg, Robert
Desert star * Willard, Tom
Deserted cities of the heart * Shiner, Lewis
Design of William Morris' The earthly paradise * Boos, Florence Saunders
Desolate presence, and other uncanny stories, The * Owen, Thomas
Desolation road * McDonald, Ian
Desolation road * Milán, Victor as RICHARD AUSTIN
Despatches from the frontiers of the female mind: an anthology of original stories * Green, Jen & Sarah Lefanu
Desperate measures * Faust, Joe Clifford
Destination brain Asimov, Isaac
Destination: brain * McEvoy, Seth
Destination Mars * Bonanno, Margaret Wander as RICK NORTH
Destination Mars * Hughes, Dennis Talbot as GEORGE SHELDON BROWN
Destination Moon * Fanthorpe, R. Lionel as L. P. KENTON
Destination Moon * Heinlein, Robert A.
Destination: mutiny * Blakeney, Jay D. as SEAN DALTON
Destination: void * Herbert, Frank
Destined to survive * Bentley, Peter
Destinies: the paperback magazine of science fiction and speculative fact, November-December, 1978 * Baen, James Patrick
Destinies: the paperback magazine of science fiction and speculative fact, February-March, 1979 * Baen, James Patrick
Destinies: the paperback magazine of science fiction and speculative fact, April-June, 1979 * Baen, James Patrick
Destinies: the paperback magazine of science fiction and speculative fact, August-September, 1979 * Baen, James Patrick
Destinies: the paperback magazine of science fiction and speculative fact, October-December, 1979 * Baen, James Patrick
Destinies: the paperback magazine of science fiction and speculative fact: February-March, 1980 * Baen, James Patrick
Destinies: the paperback magazine of science fiction and speculative fact: Spring edition, 1980 * Baen, James Patrick
Destinies: the paperback magazine of science fiction and speculative fact: Summer edition, 1980 * Baen, James Patrick
Destinies: the paperback magazine of science fiction and speculative fact: Fall edition, 1980 * Baen, James Patrick
Destinies: the paperback magazine of science fiction and speculative fact, Spring edition, 1981 * Baen, James Patrick

Destinies: the paperback magazine of science fiction and speculative fact: vol. 3, no. 2 * Baen, James Patrick
Destiny Dice, The * Bischoff, David
Destiny of the sword, The * Duncan, Dave
Destiny Stone, The * Milán, Victor & Robert E. Vardeman
Destiny's end * Sullivan, Tim
Destiny's lovers * Speer, Flora
Destiny's man * Tweed, Thomas F.
Destroyer, The: Funny money * Sapir, Richard & Warren Murphy
Destroyers of Lan-Kern, The * Tremayne, Peter
Destroying angel * King, Bernard
Deus ex machina * Brummels, J. V.
Deus irae * Dick, Philip K. & Roger Zelazny
Devices of darkness, The * English, Jean
Devil and Lisa Black, The * Martin, Russell W.
Devil and Max Devlin, The: a novel * Grossbach, Robert
Devil and the floral dance, The * Thomas, D. M.
Devil and W. Kaspar, The * Appel, Benjamin
Devil by the sea * Bawden, Nina
Devil country * Cameron, Ian
Devil Genghis * Dent, Lester as KENNETH ROBESON
Devil ground, The * Pons, Ted
Devil in a forest, The * Wolfe, Gene
Devil in iron, The * Howard, Robert E.
Devil in Texas, The * Mankowitz, Wolf
Devil in the Atlas, The: a study of modern satanism * Gurney, David
Devil in the darkness * Roy, Archie
Devil in the dooryard, The * Smith, Gregory Blake
Devil is Jones, The * Dent, Lester as KENNETH ROBESON
Devil made me do it, The! twenty tales of subtle horror * Anderson, Paul Dale
Devil meat * Stone, Paul
Devil on my back * Hughes, Monica
Devil on the Moon: a Doc Savage adventure * Dent, Lester as KENNETH ROBESON
Devil on the road, The * Westall, Robert
Devil pony * Christopher, Matt
Devil, poor devil, The! a novel * Burdekin, Kay as MURRAY CONSTANTINE
Devil rides out, The * Sage, Alison & Dennis Wheatley
Devil rides out, The; The haunting of Toby Jugg; Gateway to Hell; To the devil—a daughter * Wheatley, Dennis
Devil rides with me, and other fantastic stories, The * Slote, Alfred
Devil rocked her cradle, The * St. Clair, David
Devil strike * Robbins, David
Devil take the hindmost * Green, Simon
Devil to pay, The * Lawrence, Jim as HUNTER ADAMS
Devil wind * Alexander, Paul & Laurie Bridges
Devil wives of Li Fong, The * Price, E. Hoffmann
Devil world * Eklund, Gordon
Devil worshippers * Greenberg, Martin H. & Charles G. Waugh
Devilgod, The * Jallim, Collins
Devilgod in the empire of the universal master, The * Jallim, Collins
Devil-may-care * Michaels, Barbara as ELIZABETH PETERS
Devils * Asimov, Isaac & Martin H. Greenberg
Devil's advocate, The * Neiderman, Andrew
Devil's advocate, The: an Ambrose Bierce reader * Bierce, Ambrose
Devil's alternative, The * Forsyth, Frederick
Devils and demons: a collection * Dickson, Gordon R. as ROD SERLING

Dinobot war * Morris, Dave
Dinobots strike back * Todd, Casey
Dinosaur adventure * Logan, Nora
Dinosaur dilemma * Bosco, Clyde
Dinosaur dilemma * Segraves, Kelly L.
Dinosaur planet * McCaffrey, Anne
Dinosaur planet survivors * McCaffrey, Anne
Dinosaur tales * Bradbury, Ray
Dinosaur that followed me home, The * Coville, Bruce
Dinosaur trackers, The * Cover, Arthur Byron & Tim
  Sullivan & John Gregory Betancourt as THOMAS
  SHADWELL
Dinosaur trap, The * Bunting, Eve
Dinosaurs! * Dann, Jack & Gardner Dozois
Dinosaurs * Williams, Walter Jon
Dionysus * Ruben, William S.
Diosa * Rigdon, Charles
Diplomacy Guild, The * Greenberg, Martin H.
Diplomat at arms * Laumer, Keith
Direct descent * Herbert, Frank
Directed by Jack Arnold * Reemes, Dana M.
Dirge for Sabis, A * Cherryh, C. J. & Leslie Fish
Dirk Gently's holistic detective agency * Adams, Douglas
Dirty tricks * Effinger, George Alec
Dirtyside down * McCarthy, Wil
Disagreement with death, A * Gardner, Craig Shaw
Disappearances * Mosher, Howard Frank
Disappearing dwarf, The * Blaylock, James P.
Disappearing lady, The * Dent, Lester & William G.
  Bogart as KENNETH ROBESON
Disaster * Hubbard, L. Ron
Disciples of Cthulhu, The * Berglund, Edward P.
Disciples of dread * Cave, Hugh B.
Discontented ghost, The * Corbett, Scott & Oscar Wilde
Discovered! * Coleman, Clay
Discoveries in Poe * Pollin, Burton R.
Discovering H. P. Lovecraft * Schweitzer, Darrell
Discovering modern horror fiction * Schweitzer, Darrell
Discovering modern horror fiction II * Schweitzer, Dar-
  rell
Discovering Stephen King * Schweitzer, Darrell
Discovery, The * Shagan, Steve
*Discovery of the future, The: the ways science fiction de-
  veloped* * Gunn, James
Disembodied * Walker, Robert W.
Displaced, The * Welling, Lois
Displaced person * Harding, Lee
Disorientated man, The * Frances, Stephen & W.
  Howard Baker as PETER SAXON
Disposable people * Goldberg, Marshall & Kenneth Kay
Dissertation, The: a novel * Koster, R. M.
Distant country, A: a novel * Ferris, Paul
Distant relations * Macey, Peter
Distant signals, and other stories * Weiner, Andrew
Distant stars * Delany, Samuel R.
Distant suns, The * Cawthorn, James as PHILIP JAMES &
  Michael Moorcock
Distant worlds * Collins, Paul
Distress call * Rotsler, William
Divergence * Sheffield, Charles
Divide, The * Overgard, William
Divide, The * Wilson, Robert Charles
Divide and conquer * Becker, Margot
Divide and rule * de Camp, L. Sprague
Divide and rule * Mark, Jan
Divided allegiance * Moon, Elizabeth
Divine Endurance * Jones, Gwyneth
Divine invasion, The * Dick, Philip K.
Divine invasions: a life of Philip K. Dick * Sutin,
  Lawrence

Divine queen, The * Corby, Adam
Divine right * Cherryh, C. J.
Diviner, The * Harris, Marilyn
Division of the spoils * Green, Roland
*Dixie ghosts: haunting, spine-chilling stories from the
  American south* * Greenberg, Martin H. & Charles
  G. Waugh & Frank D. McSherry Jr.
Djinn, The * Masterton, Graham
Dmitri * Cohen, Jamey
DNA disaster, The * MacIntyre, F. Gwynplaine as VIC-
  TOR APPLETON
Do androids dream of electric sheep? * Dick, Philip K.
Doc and Fluff: the distopian tale of a girl and her biker *
  Califia, Pat
*Doc Savage: Death in silver; and, Mystery under the sea:
  two complete adventures in one volume* * Dent, Lester
  as KENNETH ROBESON
*Doc Savage: Devils of the deep; and, The headless men:
  two complete adventures in one volume* * Davis,
  Harold A. & Alan Hathway as KENNETH ROBESON
*Doc Savage: Escape from Loki: Doc Savage's first ad-
  venture* * Farmer, Philip José
*Doc Savage: five complete adventures in one volume: Be-
  quest of evil; Death in little houses; Target for death;
  The death lady; The exploding lake* * Dent, Lester &
  Harold A. Davis & William G. Bogart as KENNETH
  ROBESON
*Doc Savage: five complete adventures in one volume: No
  light to die by; The monkey suit; Let's kill Ames; Once
  over lightly; I died yesterday* * Dent, Lester as KEN-
  NETH ROBESON
*Doc Savage: five complete adventures in one volume: Se-
  Pah-Poo; Colors for murder; Three times a corpse;
  Death is a round black spot; The devil is Jones* *
  Dent, Lester as KENNETH ROBESON
*Doc Savage: five complete adventures in one volume: The
  derelict of Skull Shoal; Terror wears no shoes; The
  green master; Return from Cormoral; Up from
  Earth's center* * Robeson, Kenneth
*Doc Savage: four complete adventures in one volume:
  Mystery island; Men of fear; Rock sinister; The pure
  evil* * Dent, Lester as KENNETH ROBESON
*Doc Savage: four complete adventures in one volume:
  The all-white elf; The running skeletons; The angry
  canary; and The swooning lady* * Dent, Lester as
  KENNETH ROBESON
*Doc Savage: four complete adventures in one volume:
  The awful dynasty; The magic forest; Fire and ice;
  The disappearing lady* * Dent, Lester & William G.
  Bogart as KENNETH ROBESON
*Doc Savage: four complete adventures in one volume:
  The devil's black rock; Waves of death; The too-wise
  owl; Terror and the lonely widow* * Dent, Lester as
  KENNETH ROBESON
*Doc Savage: four complete adventures in one volume:
  The invisible-box murders; Birds of death; The wee
  ones; Terror takes 7* * Dent, Lester as KENNETH
  ROBESON
*Doc Savage: four complete adventures in one volume:
  The men vanished; Five fathoms dead; The terrible
  stork; Danger lies east* * Dent, Lester as KENNETH
  ROBESON
*Doc Savage: four complete adventures in one volume:
  The mental monster; The pink lady; Weird valley;
  Trouble on parade* * Dent, Lester as KENNETH
  ROBESON
*Doc Savage: four complete adventures in one volume:
  The mindless monsters; The rustling death; King Joe
  Cay; The thing that pursued* * Dent, Lester & Alan
  Hathway as KENNETH ROBESON

Doctor Who and the monster of Peladon * Dicks, Terrance
Doctor Who and the mutants * Dicks, Terrance
Doctor Who and the nightmare of Eden * Dicks, Terrance
Doctor Who and the planet of evil * Dicks, Terrance
Doctor Who and the planet of the Daleks * Dicks, Terrance
Doctor Who and the planet of the spiders * Dicks, Terrance
Doctor Who and the power of Kroll * Dicks, Terrance
Doctor Who and the Pyramids of Mars * Dicks, Terrance
Doctor Who and the rebel's gamble * Keith, William H. Jr.
Doctor Who and the revenge of the Cybermen * Dicks, Terrance
Doctor Who and the Ribos operation * Marter, Ian
Doctor Who and the robots of death * Dicks, Terrance
Doctor Who and the seeds of doom * Hinchcliffe, Philip
Doctor Who and the Sontaran experiment * Marter, Ian
Doctor Who and the space war * Hulke, Malcolm
Doctor Who and the state of decay * Dicks, Terrance
Doctor Who and the stones of blood * Dicks, Terrance
Doctor Who and the sunmakers * Dicks, Terrance
Doctor Who and the talons of Weng-Chiang * Dicks, Terrance
Doctor Who and the tenth planet * Davis, Gerry
Doctor Who and the terror of the Autons * Dicks, Terrance
Doctor Who and the time warrior * Dicks, Terrance
Doctor Who and the tomb of the cybermen * Davis, Gerry
Doctor Who and the underworld * Dicks, Terrance
Doctor Who and the visitation * Saward, Eric
Doctor Who and the vortex crystal * Keith, William H. Jr.
Doctor Who and the war games * Hulke, Malcolm
Doctor Who and the warriors' gate * Gallagher, Stephen as JOHN LYDECKER
Doctor Who and the web of fear * Dicks, Terrance
Doctor Who and the Zarbi * Strutton, Bill
Doctor Who: Arc of infinity * Dicks, Terrance
Doctor Who: Attack of the cybermen * Saward, Eric
Doctor Who: Battlefield * Platt, Marc
Doctor Who: Black orchid * Dudley, Terence
Doctor Who: Castrovalva * Bidmead, Christopher H.
Doctor Who cookbook, The * Downie, Gary
Doctor Who: Crisis in space * Martin, David
Doctor Who crossword book, The * Robinson, Nigel
Doctor Who: Cybermen * Banks, David
Doctor Who: Death to the Daleks * Dicks, Terrance
Doctor Who: Delta and the Bannerman * Kohill, Malcolm
Doctor Who dinosaur book, The * Dicks, Terrance
Doctor Who: Dragonfire * Briggs, Ian
Doctor Who: Earthshock * Marter, Ian
Doctor Who: Enlightenment * Clegg, Barbara
Doctor Who file, The * Haining, Peter
Doctor Who: Four to doomsday * Dicks, Terrance
Doctor Who: Frontios * Bidmead, Christopher H.
Doctor Who: Full circle * Smith, Andrew
Doctor Who fun book, The * Howell, Dicky & Tim Quinn
Doctor Who: Fury from the deep * Pemberton, Victor
Doctor Who: Galaxy Four * Emms, William
Doctor Who: Garden of evil * Martin, David
Doctor Who: Ghost light * Platt, Marc
Doctor Who illustrated A-Z, The * Standring, Lesley
Doctor Who: Inferno * Dicks, Terrance
Doctor Who: Invasion of the Ormazoids * Martin, Philip
Doctor Who: Kinda * Dicks, Terrance
Doctor Who: Logopolis * Bidmead, Christopher H.
Doctor Who: Marco Polo * Lucarotti, John
Doctor Who: Mawdryn undead * Grimwade, Peter

Doctor Who: Meglos * Dicks, Terrance
Doctor Who: Mission to Magnus * Martin, Philip
Doctor Who: Mission to Venus * Emms, William
Doctor Who monster book, The * Dicks, Terrance
Doctor Who: Mysterious planet * Dicks, Terrance
Doctor Who omnibus, The * Dicks, Terrance
Doctor Who: Paradise Towers * Wyatt, Stephen
Doctor Who pattern book, The * Gammon, Joy
Doctor Who: Planet of fire * Grimwade, Peter
Doctor Who: Planet of giants * Dicks, Terrance
Doctor Who programme guide, The * Lofficier, Jean-Marc
Doctor Who quiz book, The * Robinson, Nigel
Doctor Who: Race against time * Baker, Jane & Pip Baker
Doctor Who: Remembrance of the Daleks * Aaronovitz, Ben
Doctor Who: Search for the Doctor * Martin, David
Doctor Who: Season four * Peel, John
Doctor Who: Season one * Peel, John
Doctor Who: Season three * Peel, John
Doctor Who: Season two * Peel, John
Doctor Who: Silver nemesis * Clarke, Kevin
Doctor Who: Slipback * Saward, Eric
Doctor Who: Snakedance * Dicks, Terrance
Doctor Who: Survival * Munro, Rona
Doctor Who technical manual, The * Harris, Mark
Doctor Who: Terminus * Gallagher, Stephen as JOHN LYDECKER
Doctor Who: Terror of the Vervoids * Baker, Jane & Pip Baker
Doctor Who: The ambassadors of death * Dicks, Terrance
Doctor Who: The Ark * Erickson, Paul
Doctor Who: The ark in space * Marter, Ian
Doctor Who: The auton invasion * Dicks, Terrance
Doctor Who: The awakening * Pringle, Eric
Doctor Who: The Aztecs * Lucarotti, John
Doctor Who: The brain of Morbius * Dicks, Terrance
Doctor Who: The caves of Androzani * Dicks, Terrance
Doctor Who: The Celestial Toymaker * Bingeman, Alison & Gerry Davis
Doctor Who: The chase * Peel, John
Doctor Who: the companions * Nathan-Turner, John
Doctor Who: The curse of Fenric * Briggs, Ian
Doctor Who: The Daemons; The time monster * Dicks, Terrance & Barry Letts
Doctor Who: The Dalek invasion of Earth * Dicks, Terrance
Doctor Who: The Dalek invasion of Earth; and, The crusaders * Dicks, Terrance
Doctor Who: The Daleks' master plan, part 1: Mission to the unknown * Peel, John
Doctor Who: The Daleks' master plan, part II: The mutation of time * Peel, John
Doctor Who: The day of the Daleks * Dicks, Terrance
Doctor Who: The dominators * Marter, Ian
Doctor Who: The dominators; and, The Kryptons * Marter, Ian
Doctor Who: the early years * Bentham, Jeremy
Doctor Who: The edge of destruction * Robinson, Nigel
Doctor Who: The eleventh season * Peel, John
Doctor Who: The face of evil; and, The sunmakers * Dicks, Terrance
Doctor Who: The faceless ones * Dicks, Terrance
Doctor Who: The first Baker years * Peel, John
Doctor Who: The five doctors * Dicks, Terrance
Doctor Who: The genesis of the Daleks * Dicks, Terrance
Doctor Who: The greatest show in the galaxy * Wyatt, Stephen

Doomsday * Daley, Brian & James Luceno as JACK
  McKINNEY
Doomsday * Wolfman, Marv
Doomsday clock * Benoist, Elizabeth S.
Doomsday conspiracy, The * Sheldon, Sidney
Doomsday effect, The * Thomas, Thomas T. as THOMAS
  WREN
Doomsday plus twelve * Forman, James D.
Doomsday prophecy, The * Wenk, Richard
Doomsday spore, The * Warren, George as NICK CARTER
Doomsday ultimatum, The * Follett, James
Doomsday warrior * Stacy, Jan & Ryder Syvertsen as
  RYDER STACY
Doomsday world * Carter, Carmen & Michael Jan
  Friedman & Peter David & Robert Greenberger
Doomsdeath chronicles, The * Stout, Tim
Doomstalker * Brandner, Gary
Doomstalker * Cook, Glen
Doomstar * Downey, Jack
Doomstar * Meyers, Richard S.
Doomtime * Piserchia, Doris
Doomwalk * Johnson, Oliver & Dave Morris
Doomwatch: The world in danger * Davis, Gerry & Kit
  Pedler
Doon * Weiner, Ellis
Door, The * Rossmann, John F.
Door between, The * Garden, Nancy
Door in the air, and other stories, The * Mahy, Margaret
Door in the hedge, The * McKinley, Robin
Door in the tree, The * Corlett, William
Door into fire, The * Duane, Diane
Door into Ocean, A * Slonczewski, Joan
Door into shadow, The * Duane, Diane
Door into terror * Coulson, Juanita
Door to December, The * Koontz, Dean R.
Door to December, The * Koontz, Dean R. as LEIGH
  NICHOLS
Door to December, The * Koontz, Dean R. as RICHARD
  PAIGE
Door to yesterday, The * MacFarlane, John
Doorkeepers, The * Curley, Chris
Doors of his face, the lamps of his mouth, The * Zelazny,
  Roger
Doors of the universe, The * Engdahl, Sylvia Louise
Doors to doom * McCay, Bill
Doorways in the sand * Zelazny, Roger
Doppelganger: a novel * Higgs, Eric C.
Doppelgänger gambit, The * Killough, Lee
*Dorbott of Vacuo, The; or, How to live with the Fluxus
  Quo* * Woodroffe, Patrick
Doris Lessing * Bloom, Harold
Doris Lessing * Brewster, Dorothy
Doris Lessing * Thorpe, Michael
*Doris Lessing and women's appropriation of science fic-
  tion* * Clare, Mariette
Doris Lessing: critical studies * Pratt, Annis & L. S.
  Dembo
Doris Lessing: life, work, and criticism * Fishburn,
  Katherine
Doris Lessing's Africa * Thorpe, Michael
Dorothea dreams * Charnas, Suzy McKee
Dorothy of Oz * Baum, Roger S.
Dorothy, the terrified * Kimbro, John M. as KATHERYN
  KIMBROUGH
Dorsai! * Dickson, Gordon R.
Dorsai companion, The * Dickson, Gordon R.
Dorsai's command * Denning, Troy & Gordon R. Dick-
  son & Cory Glaberson
Dosadi experiment, The * Herbert, Frank
Dotty * Lafferty, R. A.

Double blind * Stamey, Sara
Double disappearance of Walter Fozbek, The * Senn,
  Steve
Double, double * Friedman, Michael Jan
Double exposure * Anthony, Piers
Double helix fall * Ferguson, Neil
Double identity * Lottman, Eileen as MAUD WILLIS
*Double Mobius sphere: a story of the shape of the uni-
  verse* * Nim, P. S.
Double Nocturne * Felice, Cynthia
Double or nothing * Pinianski, Patricia & Linda Sweeney
  as LYNN PATRICK
Double planet * Chown, Marcus & John Gribbin
Double shadow, A: fiction * Turner, Frederick
Double time * Elder, Michael
Double trouble * Bosco, Clyde
Double trouble * DeClements, Barthe & Christopher
  Greimes
Double trouble squared * Lasky, Kathryn
Double wizard, The * Storey, Margaret
Double your pleasure: the Ace SF double * Corrick,
  James A.
Double Z: from the Shadow's private annals * Gibson,
  Walter B. as MAXWELL GRANT
Doubleman, The * Koch, C. J.
Douglas Convolution, The * Llewellyn, Edward
Dover Beach * Bowker, Richard
Down & dirty: a Wild Cards mosaic novel * Martin,
  George R. R.
Down here in the dream quarter * Malzberg, Barry N.
Down on the farm * Stchur, John
Down river * Gallagher, Steve
Down the bright way * Reed, Robert
Down the long wind * Bradshaw, Gillian
Down the stream of stars * Carver, Jeffrey A.
Down to a sunless sea * Carter, Lin
Down to a sunless sea * Graham, David
Down Town: a fantasy * King, Tappan & Viido Polikar-
  pus
Downbelow station * Cherryh, C. J.
Down-bound train * Garnett, Bill
Downfall of the gods, The * Sorenson, Villy
Downhill crocodile whizz, and other stories, The * Mahy,
  Margaret
*Downriver: (or, The vessels of wrath): a narrative in
  twelve tales* * Sinclair, Iain
Downtime * Felice, Cynthia
Downtime * Fox, Peter
Downtiming the night side * Chalker, Jack L.
Downwind * Moeri, Louise
Dozen tough jobs, A * Waldrop, Howard
Dr. Adder * Jeter, K. W.
Dr. Chill * Hoobler, Thomas
Dr. Chill's project * Hoobler, Thomas
Dr. Cyclops * Garth, Will
Dr. Dredd's wagon of wonders * Brittain, Bill
Dr Jekyll and Mr Hollins * Hall, Willis
Dr. Jekyll and Mr. Holmes * Estleman, Loren D. as DR.
  JOHN H. WATSON, AS EDITED BY LOREN D. ESTLEMAN
Dr. Jekyll and Mr. Hyde * Bethancourt, T. Ernesto &
  Robert Louis Stevenson
Dr Jekyll and Mr Hyde * Border, Rosemary & Robert
  Louis Stevenson
Dr. Jekyll and Mr. Hyde * McMullan, Kate & Robert
  Louis Stevenson
Dr. Jekyll and Mr. Hyde: after one hundred years *
  Hirsch, Gordon & William Veeder
Dr. Nikola returns * Boothby, Guy
Dr. O * Walker, Robert W.
Dr. Pak's preschool * Brin, David

Dungeon master's guide, revised and updated * Cook, David "Zeb"

Dungeon of darkness * Kendall, John

Dungeon of dread * Estes, Rose

Dungeoneer! * Gascoigne, Marc & Pete Tamlyn

Dungeoneer's survival guide: a sourcebook for Advanced Dungeons & Dragons game adventures in the unknown depts of Underdark! * Niles, Douglas

Dungeons of Dregnor, The * Vilott, Rhondi

Dungeons of Kuba * Diamond, Graham

Dungeons of Torgar, The * Dever, Joe

Dunwich horror and others, The * Lovecraft, H. P.

Duplicate, The * Sleator, William

Duplicate lovers * Burch, Ralph

Duplicating notes * Jeeves, Terry

Durdane * Vance, Jack

Dushau * Lichtenberg, Jacqueline

Dusk * Dee, Ron

Dust of death: a Doc Savage adventure * Dent, Lester and Harold A. Davis as KENNETH ROBESON

Dust of far suns * Vance, Jack

Dust roads of Monferrato, The * Loy, Rosetta

Dust to dust * Carl, Lillian Stewart

Duster trouble * Read, John as TONY PHILLIPS

Dustland * Hamilton, Virginia

Duty to the devil, and other ghost stories * Scupham, A. G.

Dwellers in darkness * Derleth, August

Dwellers in the crucible: a Star Trek novel * Bonanno, Margaret Wander

Dwelling, The * Elliott, Tom

Dydeetown world * Wilson, F. Paul

Dying, The * Horvitz, Leslie

Dying breath * Walker, Robert W.

Dying for tomorrow * Moorcock, Michael

Dying light * Chandler, Evan

Dying of fright: masterpieces of the macabre * Daniels, Les

Dying of paradise * Gallagher, Stephen as STEPHEN COUPER

Dying of the light * Martin, George R. R.

Dying space * Murphy, Warren

Dying sun, The * Blackwood, Gary L.

Dying sun, The * Smith, Mark & Jamie Thomson

Dynamo & the tree, The: my twins and I journeying in a technate in the year 1981 * Brown, William Glenn

Dynostar menace, The * Davis, Gerry & Kit Pedler

Dynteryx * Murdock, M. S.

Dystopian visions * Elwood, Roger

Dzurlord: a Crossroads adventure in the world of Steven Brust's Jhereg * Bloom, Mark & Bill Scammell & Evan Jamieson & Lisa Hunt & Walter Hunt & Richard S. Meyer & Christine Ivey as ARCHITECTS ADVENTURE

E

E. C. Tubb: an evaluation * Harbottle, Philip
E. E. "Doc" Smith * Sanders, Joseph L.
E. E. "Doc" Smith, father of Star wars * Sheridan, Thomas & E. E. Smith
E. Nesbit's tales of terror * Nesbit, E.
Eagle and the sword, The * Schreiber, Harvey K.
Eagle's Nest, The * Carter, John
Ealdwood * Cherryh, C. J.
Early del Rey * del Rey, Lester
Early H. G. Wells, The: a study of the scientific romances * Bergonzi, Bernard
Early harvest * Bear, Greg
Early in Orcadia * Mitchison, Naomi
Early Lafferty, The * Lafferty, R. A.
Early Lafferty II, The * Lafferty, R. A.
Early Long, The * Long, Frank Belknap
Early Pohl, The * Pohl, Frederik
Early science fiction stories of Thomas M. Disch, The * Disch, Thomas M.
Early voyages, The * Peel, John
Early Williamson, The * Williamson, Jack
Early writings in science and science fiction * Wells, H. G.
Earth * Brin, David
Earth again redeemed, The: May 26 to July 1, 1984, on this Earth of ours and its alter ego: a science fiction novel * Green, Martin
Earth and elsewhere * DeGaris, Roger
Earth book of stormgate, The * Anderson, Poul
Earth cult * Hoyle, Trevor
Earth descended * Saberhagen, Fred
Earth dreams * Morris, Janet
Earth factor X * van Vogt, A. E.
Earth fire * Ahern, Jerry
Earth goddess, The * Herley, Richard
Earth has been found: a novel * Jones, D. F.
Earth in transit: science fiction and contemporary problems * Schwartz, Sheila
Earth in twilight * Piserchia, Doris
Earth invaded * Asimov, Isaac & Martin H. Greenberg & Charles G. Waugh
Earth invaded * Evans, Chris as NATHAN ELLIOTT
Earth is all that lasts, The * Wells, Catherine
Earth is heaven * Tubb, E. C.
Earth Is the Alien Planet: J. G. Ballard's Four-Dimensional Nightmare * Pringle, David
Earth is the strangest planet: ten stories of science fiction * Silverberg, Robert
Earth king * Youssef, Michael
Earth lords, The * Dickson, Gordon R.
Earth magic * Panshin, Alexei & Cory Panshin
Earth remembers, The * Olan, Susan Torian
Earth search * Follett, James
Earth ship and star song: a novel * Shedley, Ethan I.
Earth song * Webb, Sharon
Earth Two * Kelley, Leo P.
Earth watch * Barrett, G. J.
Earth watch * Borsheim, Roger M.
Earth will shake, The: a novel * Wilson, Robert Anton

Earth witch, The * Lawrence, Louise
Earthblood * Kisner, James
Earthbound * Ball, Donna as REBECCA FLANDERS
Earthbound * Matheson, Richard
Earthbound * Matheson, Richard as LOGAN SWANSON
Earthchange * Cooper, Clare
Earthchild * Piserchia, Doris
Earthchild * Webb, Sharon
Earthclan: Startide rising, The uplift war * Brin, David
Earthdance: a romance of reincarnation * Connolly, Eileen
Earthdark * Hughes, Monica
Earthdoom! * Grant, John & David Langford
Earthfall * Brown, Jerry Earl
Earthfall * Tubb, E. C.
Earthgrip * Turtledove, Harry
Earthlove: a space fantasy * McAleer, Neil
Earthquake * Matthews, Ann
Earthquake 2099 * Sullivan, Mary W.
Earthquake machine, The * Mitchelson, Austin & Nicholas Utechin
Earth's children * Auel, Jean M.
Earthsea: an omnibus comprising A wizard of Earthsea, The tombs of Atuan, The farthest shore * Le Guin, Ursula K.
Earthsea trilogy, The * Le Guin, Ursula K.
Earthseed: a novel * Sargent, Pamela
Earth-shaker, The * Carter, Lin
Earthshock * Marter, Ian
Earthstar magic * Chew, Ruth
Earthstone, The * Paxson, Diana L.
Earth-thunder * Tilley, Patrick
Earthwind * Holdstock, Robert
East Coast crisis * Crispin, A. C. & Howard Weinstein
East Coast ghosts * Greenberg, Martin H. & Charles G. Waugh
East of danger * Twitchell, Paul
East of Faling * Rankin, Robert
East of laughter * Lafferty, R. A.
East of midnight * Lee, Tanith
East of Samarinda * Jacobi, Carl
East wind coming, An * Cover, Arthur Byron
Eastercon speeches, The * Shaw, Bob
Eastern ghosts: haunting, spine-chilling stories from New York, Pennsylvania, New Jersey, Delaware, Maryland, and the District of Columbia * Greenberg, Martin H. & Frank D. McSherry Jr. & Charles G. Waugh
Easy travel to other planets * Mooney, Ted
Eat them alive * Nace, Pierce
Eaters of the dead: the manuscript of ibn Fadlan, relating his experiences with the Northmen in A.D. 922 * Crichton, Michael
Eavesdropper, The: an unparalleled experience * Payn, James
Ebon roses, jewelled skulls * Hjort, James William
EC Comics story, The * Van Hise, James
Ecce and old Earth * Vance, Jack
Ecce hominid * Friesner, Esther M.
Echo on the stairs, The * Jenson, Martin

Echo vector, The * Kahn, James
Echoes* Brandner, Gary
Echoes * Hyman, Jackie
Echoes answer, The * Chapman, Clodagh
Echoes from the macabre: selected stories * Du Maurier, Daphne
Echoes in an empty room, and other tales of the supernatural * Lane, Carolyn
Echoes of an ancient love * Wagner, Sharon
Echoes of chaos * Vardeman, Robert E.
Echoes of evil * Comfort, Iris
Echoes of terror * Jarvis, Mike & John Spencer
Echoes of the fourth magic * Salvatore, R. A.
Echoes of thunder * Dann, Jack & Jack C. Haldeman II
Echoes of valor * Wagner, Karl Edward
Echoes of valor II * Wagner, Karl Edward
Echoes of valor III * Wagner, Karl Edward
Echoing silence, The * Beckett, Jenifer
Eclipse * Frister, Robert Allen
Eclipse * Shirley, John
Eclipse corona * Shirley, John
Eclipse of the Kai * Dever, Joe & John Grant
Eclipse of uncertainty: an introduction to postmodern fantasy * Olsen, Lance
Eclipse penumbra * Shirley, John
Eclipses * Felice, Cynthia
Eclipsing binaries * Goldin, Stephen & E. E. Smith
Ecolitan operation, The * Modesitt, L. E. Jr.
Ecolog, The * Nelson, Ray Faraday
Ecologic envoy, The * Modesitt, L. E. Jr.
Ecologic secession, The * Modesitt, L. E. Jr.
Ecology: science and science fiction * MacArthur, D. M.
Ecotopia emerging * Callenbach, Ernest
Ecotopia: the notebooks and reports of William Weston * Callenbach, Ernest
Ecotopian sketchbook, The: a book for drawing, coloring, writing, collaging, designing, thinking about & creating a new world * Clancy, Judith S.
Ecstasy of Angus, The * O'Flaherty, Liam
Ecstasy of catastrophe, The: a study of apocalyptic narrative from Langlund to Milton * Hendrix, Howard V.
Ed Dean is queer: a novel * Diaman, N. A.
Edd Cartier: the known and the unknown * Cartier, Edd
Eddie's blue winged dragon * Adler, C. S.
Eddy Deco's last caper: an illustrated mystery * Wilson, Gahan
Eden * Harbinson, W. A.
Eden * Lem, Stanislaw
Eden's eyes * Costello, Sean
Eden's lost * Elliott, Sumner Locke
Edgar A. Poe; a study * Robertson, John W.
Edgar Allan Poe * Asselineau, Roger
Edgar Allan Poe * Bloom, Harold
Edgar Allan Poe * Buranelli, Vincent
Edgar Allan Poe, 2nd ed. * Buranelli, Vincent
Edgar Allan Poe * Knapp, Bettina L.
Edgar Allan Poe * Porges, Irwin
Edgar Allan Poe * Shanks, Edward
Edgar Allan Poe * Woodberry, George E.
Edgar Allan Poe: a bibliography of criticism, 1827-1967 * Dameron, J. Lasley & Irby B. Cauthen
Edgar Allan Poe: a critical biography * Quinn, Arthur Hobson
Edgar Allan Poe: a phenomenological view * Halliburton, David
Edgar Allan Poe: a study in genius * Krutch, Joseph Wood
Edgar Allan Poe, an American imagination: three essays * Phillips, Elizabeth

Edgar Allan Poe: an annotated bibliography of books and articles in English, 1827-1973 * Hyneman, Esther F.
Edgar Allan Poe and Ambrose Bierce * Adams, Anthony
Edgar Allan Poe as literary critic * Parks, Edd Winfield
Edgar Allan Poe bedside companion, The: morgue and mystery tales * Poe, Edgar Allan
Edgar Allan Poe companion, An: a guide to the short stories, romances, and essays * Hammond, J. R.
Edgar Allan Poe: his life, letters, and opinions * Ingram, John H.
Edgar Allan Poe: how to know him * Smith, C. Alphonso
Edgar Allan Poe: letters and documents in the Enoch Pratt Free Library * Poe, Edgar Allan
Edgar Allan Poe: life, work, and criticism * Ketterer, David
Edgar Allan Poe: mournful and never-ending remembrance * Silverman, Kenneth
Edgar Allan Poe scrapbook, The: articles, essays, letters, anecdotes, illustrations, photographs, and memorabilia about the legendary American genius * Haining, Peter
Edgar Allan Poe: the critical heritage * Walker, I. M.
Edgar Allan Poe: the design of order * Lee, A. Robert
Edgar Allan Poe: the man behind the legend * Wagenknecht, Edward
Edgar Allan Poe: the unknown Poe * Foye, Raymond
Edgar Pangborn: a bibliography * Benson, Gordon Jr.
Edgar Poe the poet: essays new and old on the man and his work * Stovall, Floyd
Edgar Rice Burroughs * Grant, Penelope & Pat Hornsey
Edgar Rice Burroughs * Holtsmark, Erling B.
Edgar Rice Burroughs checklist, An * Cummings, David George
Edgar Rice Burroughs: Master of Adventure * Lupoff, Richard A.
Edgar Rice Burroughs memorial collection: a catalog * McWhorter, George T.
Edgar Rice Burroughs: the man who created Tarzan * Porges, Irwin
Edge, The * Lindsay, John V.
Edge in my voice, An * Ellison, Harlan
Edge of destruction, The * Robinson, Nigel
Edge of evening, The * Gray, Nicholas Stuart
Edge of immortality, The * Ajemian, Diran
Edge of space, The: three original novellas of science fiction * Silverberg, Robert
Edge of the infinite, The * Butterworth, Michael
Edge of the universe, The: what is our destiny? is there life after death? what incredible secret lies in the depths of space? * Allen, Harold W. G.
Edge of the world, The * Gordon, John
Edge of tomorrow, The * Asimov, Isaac
Edge of tomorrow, The * Finlay, D. G.
Edge of vengeance, The * Jones, Jenny
Edges of reality: confrontations with the uncanny, the macabre, and the mad * anon.
Edges of things, The * Shiner, Lewis
Edges: thirteen new tales from the borderlands of the imagination * Kidd, Virginia & Ursula K. Le Guin
Edinburgh stories, The * Doyle, Arthur Conan
Edith and the mermaids * Crowder, Fay
Edmond Dantès: a sequel to the Count of Monte-Cristo * Flagg, Edmund
Education of Jennifer Parrish, The * Martin, Russell W.
Edward Berner is alive again! * Kastle, Herbert D.
Edward De Bono science fiction collection, The * Hay, George
Eerie, weird, and wicked: an anthology * Hoke, Helen
Effigies * Wells, William K.

Empire dreams * McDonald, Ian
Empire of blood * Green, Roland as JEFFREY LORD
Empire of fear, The * Stableford, Brian M.
Empire of the ants, and 8 science fiction stories, The *
  Wells, H. G.
Empire of the ants, The, and other short stories * Wells,
  H. G.
Empire of the ants (and other stories), The * Wells, H. G.
Empire of the ants: novelization * Weber, Nancy as
  LINDSAY WEST
Empire of the East * Saberhagen, Fred
Empire of the nine, The * Farmer, Philip José
Empire of the senseless * Acker, Kathy
Empire of time, The * Kilian, Crawford
Empire strikes back, The * Glut, Donald F.
Empire strikes back, The * Weinberg, Larry
Empire strikes back notebook, The * Attias, Diana &
  Lindsay Smith
Empire strikes back sketchbook, The * Johnston, Joe &
  Nilo Rodis-Jamero
*Empire strikes out, The: Kurd Lasswitz, Hans Dominik,
  and the development of German science fiction* * Fis-
  cher, William B.
Empire's horizon * Brizzolara, John
Empire's legacy, The * Swycaffer, Jefferson P.
Empires of Flux & Anchor * Chalker, Jack L.
*Empires of foliage and flower: a tale from The book of the
  wonders of Urth and sky* * Wolfe, Gene
Empress of Earth, The * Scott, Melissa
*Empress of the Earth, 1898, The; The purple cloud, 1901;
  "Some short stories": offprints of the original editions*
  * Shiel, M. P.
Empress unborn: a tale of the Savage Empire * Lorrah,
  Jean
Emprise * Kube-McDowell, Michael P.
Empty palace * Barclay, Ben
Empty sleeve * Garfield, Leon
Empty throne, The * Elliott, Janice
Empty world * Christopher, John
En garde * Stackpole, Michael
Enchanted isles, The * Flint, Kenneth C. as CASEY
  FLYNN
Enchanted kingdom, The * Kushner, Ellen
Enchanted land, The * Dawson, Saranne
Enchanted paradise * Howl, Marcia Yvonne & Sharon
  Jarvis as JOHANNA HAILEY
Enchanted pilgrimage * Simak, Clifford D.
Enchanted planet, The * Barbet, Pierre
Enchanted pond, The * Legaspi, Pilar F.
Enchanted village, The * van Vogt, A. E.
Enchanter * Bailey, Robin W.
Enchanter compleated, The * de Camp, L. Sprague &
  Fletcher Pratt
Enchanters' end game * Eddings, David
Enchantment * MacKenzie, Trix
Enchantment at Delphi * Purtill, Richard
Enchantment: stories * Vallejo, Doris
Enchantments of flesh and spirit, The * Constantine,
  Storm
Enchantress, The * Han, Suyin
Enchantress of world's end, The * Carter, Lin
Encores in fade * Lambert, William J. III
Encounter at Farpoint * Gerrold, David
Encounter program * Enstrom, Robert
Encounter three * Caidin, Martin
Encounters * Asimov, Isaac & Martin H. Greenberg &
  Charles G. Waugh
Encounters * Erskine, Barbara

*Encounters with the invisible world: being ten tales of
  ghosts, witches, & the devil himself in New England* *
  Roach, Marilynne K.
Encyclopaedia of the worlds of Doctor Who, A-D * Saun-
  ders, David
Encyclopaedia of the worlds of Doctor Who, E-K * Saun-
  ders, David
Encyclopaedia of the worlds of Doctor Who, L-R * Saun-
  ders, David
*Encyclopaedia of things that never were: creatures,
  places, and people* * Ingpen, Robert & Michael F.
  Page
*Encyclopedia Galactica: from the Fleet Library aboard
  the Battlestar Galactica* * Kraus, Bruce
Encyclopedia of American comics, The * Goulart, Ron
Encyclopedia of horror, The * Davis, Richard
Encyclopedia of horror movies, The * Hardy, Phil
Encyclopedia of monsters, The * Rovin, Jeff
Encyclopedia of science fiction * Holdstock, Robert
Encyclopedia of science fiction, The: an illustrated A to Z
  * Nicholls, Peter & John Clute
*Encyclopedia of science fiction and fantasy through 1968,
  The: a bibliographic survey of the fields of science
  fiction, fantasy, and weird fiction through 1968, vol-
  ume 2: who's who, M-Z* * Tuck, Donald H.
*Encyclopedia of science fiction and fantasy through 1968,
  The: a bibliographic survey of the fields of science
  fiction, fantasy, and weird fiction through 1968, vol-
  ume 3: miscellaneous* * Tuck, Donald H.
Encyclopedia of science fiction movies, The * Hardy, Phil
Encyclopedia of Star Trek, The * Peel, John
Encyclopedia of super villains, The * Rovin, Jeff
Encyclopedia of superheroes, The * Rovin, Jeff
*Encyclopedia of Trekkie memorabilia: identification and
  value guide* * Gentry, Christine & Sally Gibson-
  Downs
Encyclopedia of TV science fiction, The * Fulton, Roger
*Encyclopedia of Xanth: a Crossroads adventure in the
  world of Piers Anthony's Xanth* * Nye, Jody Lynn
End as a hero * Laumer, Keith
End is coming, The * Ahern, Jerry
End of all songs, The * Moorcock, Michael
End of exile * Bova, Ben
End of summer, The: science fiction of the Fifties *
  Malzberg, Barry N. & Bill Pronzini
End of the affair, The * Peel, John
End of the circle, The * Daley, Brian & James Luceno as
  JACK McKINNEY
End of the circle * Gomery, Percy
*End of the dreams, The: three short novels about space,
  happiness, and immortality* * Gunn, James
End of the Empire * Gilliland, Alexis A.
End of the Fourth Reich, The: a Rat Catcher adventure *
  Ray, David
End of the game, The * Tepper, Sheri S.
End of the matter, The * Foster, Alan Dean
End of the world, The * Greenberg, Martin H. & Eric S.
  Rabkin & Joseph D. Olander
End of the world news, The: an entertainment * Burgess,
  Anthony
End of this day's business, The * Burdekin, Katharine
End of tragedy, The * Ingalls, Rachel
*End of utopia: a study of Aldous Huxley's Brave new
  world* * Firchow, Peter E.
End product * Norman, Barry
End stage * Hawkey, Raymond
Endangered species * Wolfe, Gene
Ende: a diary of the Third World War * Guha, Anton-
  Andreas
Ender's game * Card, Orson Scott

Erasmus magister * Sheffield, Charles
ERB-dom: a guide to issues no. 1-25 * Cazedessus, Camille Jr. & John Harwood & John F. Roy
Erebus * Hutson, Shaun
Eric * Pratchett, Terry
Eric and us: a remembrance of George Orwell * Buddicom, Jacintha
Eric Frank Russell: a working bibliography * Stephensen-Payne, Phil & Gordon Benson Jr.
Eric Frank Russell, our sentinel in space: a working bibliography, 2nd rev. ed. * Stephensen-Payne, Phil
Eric of Zanthodon * Carter, Lin
Erica's magic touch * Hytes, Jason
Eric's image * Rachleff, Owen S.
Eridahn * Young, Robert F.
Erinord * Jeffery, G.
Érinsaga: the mythological paintings of Jim Fitzpatrick * Fitzpatrick, Jim
Ernestine takes over: a novel * Brooks, Walter R.
Ernst Ellert returns! * Ernsting, Walter as CLARK DARLTON
Eros ascending * Resnick, Mike
Eros at nadir * Resnick, Mike
Eros at zenith * Resnick, Mike
Eros descending * Resnick, Mike
Eros in the mind's eye: sexuality and the fantastic in art and film * Palumbo, Donald
Erotic universe: sexuality and fantastic literature * Palumbo, Donald
Erotic world of faery, The * Duffy, Maureen
Eroticism in the fantasy cinema * George, Bill
Erthring Cycle, The * Drew, Wayland
Ervool * Leiber, Fritz
Esbae: a winter's tale * Haldeman, Linda
Escalation * Tomino, Yoshiyuki
Escalator down * Balfour, B. Gabriel
Escape * Ahern, Jerry
Escape! * Coleman, Clay
Escape, The * James, Laurence as JAMES DARKE
Escape * Montgomery, R. A.
Escape across the cosmos * Fox, Gardner F.
Escape by deluge * Wignell, Edel
Escape Carthus * Browne, C. J.
Escape from Castle Quarras * Niles, Douglas
Escape from China * Montgomery, R. A.
Escape from high doom * Milton, Hilary
Escape from Jupiter * McEvoy, Seth
Escape from Kathmandu * Robinson, Kim Stanley
Escape from Loki * Farmer, Philip José
Escape from Lost Island * Coleman, Clay
Escape from Lost Island: Attack! * Coleman, Clay
Escape from Lost Island: Discovered! * Coleman, Clay
Escape from Lost Island: Escape! * Coleman, Clay
Escape from Lost Island: Mutiny! * Coleman, Clay
Escape from Lost Island: Revenge! * Coleman, Clay
Escape from Macho * Offutt, Andrew J. as JOHN CLEVE
Escape from New York: a novel * McQuay, Mike
Escape from Robotropolis * D'Ignazio, Fred
Escape from Splatterbang * Fisk, Nicholas
Escape from Terror Lagoon * Pfeil, Donald J. as WILLIAM ARROW
Escape from the city of gold * Faircloth, Cyril E.
Escape from tomorrow * Lanning, Sereta
Escape from tyrannosaurus * Bunting, Eve
Escape if you can: 13 tales of the preternatural * Wuorio, Eva-Lis
Escape plans * Jones, Gwyneth
Escape plus * Bova, Ben
Escape to tomorrow * Effinger, George Alec
Escape velocity * Stasheff, Christopher

ESP McGee * Packard, Edward
ESP McGee and the dolphin's message * Rodgers, Jesse
ESP McGee and the ghost ship * McMahan, Ian
ESP McGee and the haunted mansion * Lawrence, Jim
ESP McGee and the mysterious magician * Ernst, Kathryn F.
ESP McGee to the rescue * Shea, George
Esper! * Bucar, Cary A.
Esper transfer, The * Proctor, Geo. W.
Esper's War * Perry, Roger
ESPionage * Doxey, William
Essays Lovecraftian * Schweitzer, Darrell
Essays on Argentine narrators * Meehan, Thomas C.
Essence of evil, The * Faust, Joe Clifford
Essential C. S. Lewis, The * Lewis, C. S.
Essential Dracula, The: the completely illustrated & annotated edition of Bram Stoker's classic novel * Stoker, Bram
Essential Ellison, The: a 35-year retrospective * Ellison, Harlan
Essential man, The: a novel * Morgan, Al
E.T., the book of the green planet: a new novel * Kotzwinkle, William
E.T., the extraterrestrial * Gelfland, M. Howard
E.T., the extra-terrestrial, in his adventure on Earth: a novel * Kotzwinkle, William
E.T., the extraterrestrial storybook * Kotzwinkle, William
E.T.: The storybook of the green planet: a new storybook * Kotzwinkle, William
Eternal bliss * Fahy, Christopher
Eternal champion, The: a fantastic romance * Moorcock, Michael
Eternal city, The * Drake, David & Martin H. Greenberg & Charles G. Waugh
Eternal enemy, The * Berlyn, Michael
Eternal fountain, The * Dorer, Frances & Nancy Dorer
Eternal light * McAuley, Paul J.
Eternal mercenary, The * Sadler, Barry
Eternal wind * Zhemaitis, Sergei
Eternity * Bear, Greg
Eternity * Ing, Dean & Mack Reynolds
Eternity brigade, The * Goldin, Stephen
Eternity merchants, The * Rhys, Jack
Eternity Stone, The * Romine, Aden F. & Mary C. Romine
Ethan of Athos * Bujold, Lois McMaster
Etheldreda, Princess of East Anglia, Queen of Northumbria, saint of Ely, born A.D. 630, died A.D. 679 * Caldecott, Moyra
Ether ore * Turk, H. C.
Euphor unfree * Mason, Douglas R.
Eureka years, The: Boucher and McComas's The magazine of fantasy and science fiction, 1949-54 * McComas, Annette Peltz
Europe: why was a city built to capture a castle? * Compton, Sara
European folktale, The: form and nature * Luthi, Max
Euryale * Dalkey, Kara
Eva * Dickinson, Peter
Evangelist, The * Dunn, Saul
Evangelist, The * Dunn, Saul as PHILIP DUNN
Eve: her story * Farmer, Penelope
Eve of midsummer, The * Shackleford, Jack D.
Eve of the future Eden, The: L'Eve future * Villiers de L'Isle Adam, Auguste, comte de
Evelyn, the ambitious * Kimbro, John M. as KATHERYN KIMBROUGH
(Even more) compleat Feghoot, The: the many lives and greatest exploits of history's punniest space-time traveler * Bretnor, Reginald as GRENDEL BRIARTON

F

Fall of the First World, The: Sorrowing vengeance * Smith, David C.

Fall of the First World, The: The master of evil * Smith, David C.

Fall of the First World, The: The passing of the gods * Smith, David C.

Fall of the House of Usher, The * Poe, Edgar Allan

Fall of the House of Usher, and other writings, The * Poe, Edgar Allan

Fall of the republic, The: a novel of the Chronoplane Wars * Kilian, Crawford

Fall of the Russian Empire, The * James, Donald

Fall of the shell, The * Williams, Paul O.

Fall of the sky lords, The * Brosnan, John

Fall of the white ship Avatar * Daley, Brian

Fall of winter, The * Haldeman, Jack C. II

Fall of worlds, The * Mezo, Francine

Fallback * Niesewand, Peter

Fallen angel * Viviers, Lyn

Fallen angel: a novel * Elwood, Roger

Fallen angels * Flynn, Michael & Larry Niven & Jerry Pournelle

Fallen Country, The * Sucharitkul, Somtow

Fallen Ones, The * Vardeman, Robert E. &.Victor Milán

Fallen spaceman * Harding, Lee

Falling angel * Hjortsberg, William

Falling free * Bujold, Lois McMaster

Falling out of time * Melling, O. R.

Falling torch * Budrys, Algis

Falling toward forever * Eklund, Gordon

Falling woman, The * Murphy, Pat

Falling world of Tristram Pocket, The * Kellum, David

False dawn * Yarbro, Chelsea Quinn

False face * Katz, Welwyn Wilton

False front * Ernsting, Walter as CLARK DARLTON

False notes * Yarbro, Chelsea Quinn

Familiar spirit * Tuttle, Lisa

Familiar spirits * Tourney, Leonard D.

Family: a novel * Donovan, John

Family crypt * Trainor, Joseph

Family portrait * Masterton, Graham

Family reunion * Cooper, Rick & Mark Davis as NICHOLAS SARAZEN

Famine * Masterton, Graham

Famished road, The * Okri, Ben

Famous and rich * Austin, R. G.

Famous fantastic classics #1 * Weinberg, Robert as ANONYMOUS EDITOR

Famous fantastic classics #2 * Weinberg, Robert as ANONYMOUS EDITOR

Famous fantastic mysteries: 30 great tales of fantasy and horror from the classic pulp magazines Famous fantastic mysteries & Fantastic novels * Dziemianowicz, Stefan R. & Robert Weinberg & Martin H. Greenberg

Famous pulp classics #1 * Weinberg, Robert as ANONYMOUS EDITOR

Fanciful tales of time and space, Fall, 1936 * Wollheim, Donald A.

Fancyclopedia * Speer, Jack Bristol

Fandom directory [1980] * Hopkins, Harry A.

Fandom directory 1981 * Hopkins, Harry A.

Fandom directory 1982 * Hopkins, Mariane S.

Fandom directory, number 5, 1983-1984 edition * Hopkins, Harry A. & Mariane S. Hopkins

Fandom directory, number 6: 1984-1985 edition * Hopkins, Mariane S.

Fandom directory, number 7, 1985-1986 edition * Hopkins, Mariane S.

Fandom directory, number 8, 1986-1987 edition * Hopkins, Mariane S.

Fandom directory, number 9, 1987-1988 edition * Hopkins, Mariane S.

Fandom directory, number 10, 1988-1989 edition * Hopkins, Mariane S.

Fandom directory, number 11, 1989-1990 edition * Hopkins, Harry A.

Fandom directory, number 12, 1990-1991 edition * Hopkins, Harry A.

Fandom directory, number 13, 1991-1992 edition * Hopkins, Marianne S.

Fandom harvest * Carr, Terry

Fandom is a way of death * Rothstein, Allan & Bill Warren

Fandom is for the young; or, One convention too many * Flanery, Karen "K-nut" & Nana Grasmick

Fane * Alexander, David M.

Fang, the gnome * Coney, Michael

Fanglith * Dalmas, John

Fangs * Forsythe, Richard

Fangs of fury * Sharp, Luke

Fangs of the hooded demon, The: a Lincoln Blackthorne adventure * Grant, Charles L. as GEOFFREY MARSH

Fangs of the vampire, The * LeBlanc, Richard

Fangs of the werewolf * Halkin, John

Fantasies of Harlan Ellison, The * Ellison, Harlan

Fantasies two * Griffith, William

Fantasists on fantasy: a collection of critical reflections * Boyer, Robert H. & Kenneth J. Zahorski

Fantasma * Monteleone, Thomas F.

Fantasms: a bibliography of the literature of Jack Vance * Levack, Daniel J. H. & Tim Underwood

Fantasms II: a bibliography of the works of Jack Vance * Cockrum, Kurt & Daniel J. H. Levack & Tim Underwood

Fantasms and magics * Vance, Jack

Fantastic 3-D * Hutchison, David

Fantastic: a new collection of scenes from all-time favorite films featuring Boris Karloff * Barbour, Alan G.

Fantastic adventures of Robin Hood, The * Greenberg, Martin H.

Fantastic art * Larkin, David

Fantastic art of Boris, The * Vallejo, Boris

Fantastic art of Frank Frazetta, The * Frazetta, Frank

Fantastic art of Rowena, The * Morrill, Rowena

Fantastic art of Sulamith Wulfing, The * Wulfing, Sulamith

Fantastic Chicago * Greenberg, Martin H.

Fantastic cinema: an illustrated survey * Nicholls, Peter

Fantastic Civil War, The * Greenberg, Martin H. & S. M. Stirling & Frank D. McSherry Jr. & Charles G. Waugh

Fantastic creatures: an anthology of fantasy and science fiction * Asimov, Isaac & Martin H. Greenberg & Charles G. Waugh

Fantastic Four files, The * Van Hise, James

Fantastic freshman, The: a novel * Brittain, Bill

Fantastic imagination, The: an anthology of high fantasy * Boyer, Robert H. & Kenneth J. Zahorski

Fantastic imagination II, The: an anthology of high fantasy * Boyer, Robert H. & Kenneth J. Zahorski

Fantastic in literature, The * Rabkin, Eric S.

Fantastic in world literature and the arts, The: selected essays from the Fifth International Conference on the Fantastic in the Arts * Morse, Donald E.

Fantastic island, The: a Doc Savage adventure * Dent, Lester and Ryerson Johnson as KENNETH ROBESON

Fantastic journey of the space shuttle Astra, The * Hiller, B. B.

Fantastic kingdom, The * Larkin, David

Far frontier, The * Rotsler, William
Far frontiers * Pournelle, Jerry & Jim Baen
Far frontiers, Fall edition 1985 [vol. III] * Baen, James Patrick & Jerry Pournelle
Far frontiers, Fall edition, 1986 [vol. VII] * Baen, James Patrick & Jerry Pournelle
Far frontiers, Summer edition 1986 [vol. V] * Baen, James Patrick & Jerry Pournelle
Far frontiers, volume II, Spring 1985 * Baen, James Patrick & Jerry Pournelle
Far frontiers, volume VI, Fall 1986 * Baen, James Patrick & Jerry Pournelle
Far frontiers, Winter edition 1985 [vol. IV] * Baen, James Patrick & Jerry Pournelle
Far future calling: uncollected science fiction and fantasies of Olaf Stapledon * Stapledon, Olaf
Far harbor * Michaels, Melisa C.
Far islands, and other tales of fantasy, The * Buchan, John
Far lands, other days * Price, E. Hoffmann
Far magic shore, A * Timson, Keith
Far out: some approaches to teaching the speculative literature of science fiction and the supernatural * Hindman, Roger
Far rainbow; The second invasion from Mars * Strugatsky, Arkady & Boris Strugatsky
Far reaches of fear, The * Campbell, Ramsey
Far side of forever, The * Green, Sharon
Far side of the mirror, The * Hiller, B. B. & Neil W. Hiller
Far stars war, The * Fawcett, Bill
Far Traveler, The * Chandler, A. Bertram
Far Traveller * Chandler, A. Bertram
Far travellers: three science fiction novellas * Brown, Charles N.
Faragon Fairingay * Hancock, Niel
Farewell horizontal * Jeter, K. W.
Farewell, Miss Julie Logan: a wintry tale * Barrie, J. M.
Farewell party, The * Bandy, Franklin
Farewell to Krondahl * Nisbet, Hugh A.
Farewell to Nova Scotia * Holmes, Jeffrey
Farewell to yesterday's tomorrow * Panshin, Alexei
Farfetch * Lichtenberg, Jacqueline
Farm, The * Haigh, Richard
Farmer Giles of Ham; The adventures of Tom Bombadil * Tolkien, J. R. R.
Farseekers, The * Carmody, Isobelle
Farside cannon * Allen, Roger MacBride
Farslayer's story * Saberhagen, Fred
Farthest shores of Ursula K. Le Guin, The * Slusser, George Edgar
Farthest star: the saga of Cuckoo * Pohl, Frederik & Jack Williamson
Farthest-away mountain, The * Reid Banks, Lynne
Fast forward * Pausacker, Jenny
Fast gun, The * Edson, J. T.
Fast ride to Hell, A * Williams, Arthur J.
Faster than light * Packard, Edward
Faster than light: an original anthology about interstellar travel * Dann, Jack & George Zebrowski
Fastyngange: a novel * Wynne-Jones, Tim
Fat chance * Sheldon, Charles
Fat face * Shea, Michael
Fat man in history, The * Carey, Peter
Fat man in history, and other stories, The * Carey, Peter
Fat men from space * Pinkwater, Daniel M.
Fatal analysis * Patton, Cliff & Leah Patton as LEAH TEMPLE
Fatal attraction * Howe, Imogen
Fatal attractions * Lore, Elana

Fatal beauty * Schoell, William
Fatal destinies: the Edgar Poe essays * Baudelaire, Charles
Fatal exposure * Tobias, Michael
Fatal glimpse * Wilcox, Robert K.
Fatal shadows * George, Sara
Fatal woman, The: three tales * Glassco, John
Fatapouis & Thinifers * Maurois, André
Fate of an eagle, The * Greenfield, Irving A.
Fate of Jeremy Visick, The * Wiseman, David
Fate of the phoenix, The * Culbreath, Myrna & Sondra Marshak
Fate of the Phral, The * Webb, William Thomas
Fates, The * Tessier, Thomas
Father Christmas letters, The * Tolkien, J. R. R.
Father Hayes * Leslie, Peter
Father of stones, The * Shepard, Lucius
Father to the man * Gribbin, John
Father to the stars * Farmer, Philip José
Father-thing, The: the collected stories of Philip K. Dick, volume three * Dick, Philip K.
Fattypuffs and Thinifers * Maurois, André
Fault lines: a novel * Wilhelm, Kate
Faust Eric * Pratchett, Terry
Favor for a ghost * Christopher, Matt
Favored child, The * Gregory, Philippa
Favorite son * Sohmer, Steve
Favorite tales of horror * Wilson, Gahan
Favourite son * Sohmer, Steve
F-cubed * Da Cruz, Daniel
Fear * Daniels, Les
Fear * Gates, R. Patrick
Fear and trembling * Bloch, Robert
Fear; &, Typewriter in the sky * Hubbard, L. Ron
Fear book * Byrne, John L.
Fear Cay: a Doc Savage adventure * Dent, Lester as KENNETH ROBESON
Fear! fear! fear! * Hoke, Helen
Fear in the glen * Robertson, Jenny
Fear in yesterday's rings, The * Chesbro, George C.
Fear itself * Meyers, Richard S.
Fear itself: the horror fiction of Stephen King * Miller, Chuck & Tim Underwood
Fear of Samuel Walton, The * Green, Roger J.
Fear stalks the bayou * Coulson, Juanita
Fear Street: Halloween party * Stine, R. L.
Fear Street: Haunted * Stine, R. L.
Fear Street: Lights out * Stine, R. L.
Fear Street: Missing * Stine, R. L.
Fear Street: Party summer * Stine, R. L.
Fear Street: Silent night * Stine, R. L.
Fear Street: Ski weekend * Stine, R. L.
Fear Street: The fire game * Stine, R. L.
Fear Street: The new girl * Stine, R. L.
Fear Street: The overnight * Stine, R. L.
Fear Street: The secret bedroom * Stine, R. L.
Fear Street: The sleepwalker * Stine, R. L.
Fear Street: The stepsister * Stine, R. L.
Fear Street: The surprise party * Stine, R. L.
Fear Street: The wrong number * Stine, R. L.
Fearful symmetry, A * Luceno, James
Fearfully frightening * Ireson, Barbara
Fearless master of the jungle * Edson, J. T.
Fears * Grant, Charles L.
Fears point * Romkey, Michael
Feast * Masterton, Graham
Feast of Bacchus, The: a study in dramatic atmosphere * Henham, Ernest G.
Feast of fear * Ghidalia, Vic

Files magazine spotlight on The Star Trek files: The animated voyages begin * Peel, John

Files magazine spotlight on The Star Trek files: The animated voyages end * Peel, John

Files magazine spotlight on The Star Trek files: The Enterprise incident * Peel, John

Files magazine spotlight on The Star Trek files: The Tholian web * Peel, John

Files magazine spotlight on The Star Trek files: Where no man has gone before * Peel, John

Files magazine spotlight on The Star Trek files: Whom gods destroy * Peel, John

Files magazine spotlight on The Star Trek III files, The search for Spock * Gross, Edward

Files magazine spotlight on The Twilight Zone files: The new series * Peel, John

Files magazine spotlight on The U.N.C.L.E. files: 15 yrs. later * Peel, John

Files magazine spotlight on The U.N.C.L.E. files: The girl from U.N.C.L.E. * Peel, John

Files magazine spotlight on The U.N.C.L.E. files: The girl from U.N.C.L.E.: The end of the affair * Peel, John

Files magazine spotlight on The U.N.C.L.E. files: The man from T.H.R.U.S.H. affair * Peel, John

Files magazine spotlight on The V files, book five: Conclusion * Gross, Edward

Files magazine spotlight on The V files, book four: They're back * Gross, Edward

Fillostrated fan dictionary, The * Weinstein, Elliot

Film fantasy scrapbook * Harryhausen, Ray

Filmbook of J. R. R. Tolkien's The Lord of the Rings, The * Tolkien, J. R. R.

Films of Christopher Lee, The * Hart, Douglas C. & Robert W. Pohle Jr.

Films of Roger Corman, The: brilliance on a budget * Naha, Ed

Films of science fiction and fantasy * Searles, Baird

Films of Stephen King, The * Collings, Michael R.

Final act * Spicer, Michael

Final addiction, The * Condon, Richard

Final agenda, The * Hyams, Edward

Final assault * Berry, Stephen Ames

Final battle, The * Lupoff, Richard A.

Final circle of paradise, The * Strugatsky, Arkady & Boris Strugatsky

Final circuit * Snodgrass, Melinda M.

Final command * Norwood, Warren

Final conflict, The: a novel * McGill, Gordon

Final correction, The * McBratney, Sam

Final count, The * Sapper

Final countdown, The: a novel * Caidin, Martin

Final crusade, The * Murphy, Warren & Richard Sapir

Final curtain * Smith, Sherwood as NICHOLAS ADAMS

Final death, The * Murphy, Warren & Richard Sapir

Final encyclopedia, The * Dickson, Gordon R.

Final frontier, The * Dillard, J. M.

Final nexus, The * DeWeese, Gene

Final nightmare, The * Daley, Brian & James Luceno as JACK MCKINNEY

Final planet, The * Greeley, Andrew M.

Final quest, The * Monaco, Richard

Final rain * Ahern, Jerry

Final reckoning, The * Jarvis, Robin

Final reckonings: the selected stories of Robert Bloch, volume 1 * Bloch, Robert

Final reflection, The: a Star Trek novel * Ford, John M.

Final Shadows * Grant, Charles L.

Final stage: the ultimate SF anthology * Ferman, Edward L. & Barry N. Malzberg

Final storm, The * Maloney, Mack

Final test * Perlman, Dory

Find the changeling * Benford, Gregory & Gordon Eklund

Find the Tektrons * Cameron, Ian & George Erskine

Find your own truth * Charrette, Robert N.

Finders keepers * Rodda, Emily

Fine anger: a critical introduction to the work of Alan Garner * Philip, Neil

Fine frights: stories that scared me * Campbell, Ramsey

Fingers * Sleator, William

Fingers of death: from the Shadow's private annals * Gibson, Walter B. as MAXWELL GRANT

Finish line * Goldin, Stephen

Finishing touches * Tessier, Thomas

Finlay's femmes: a portfolio * Finlay, Virgil

Finlay's lost drawings * Finlay, Virgil

Finn Family Moomintroll * Jansson, Tove

Finn MacCool and the small men of deeds * O'Shea, Pat

Finnbranch, The * Hazel, Paul

Finnglas and the stones of choosing * Sampson, Fay

Finnglas of the horses * Sampson, Fay

Finnsburg encounter, The * Dickerson, Matthew T.

Finsterhall of San Pasqual * Sinor, John

Fintan's tower * Fisher, Catherine

Fire, The * Cooney, Caroline B.

Fire * Rodgers, Alan

Fire and fog * Vardeman, Robert E.

Fire and hemlock * Jones, Diana Wynne

Fire and ice * Dent, Lester as KENNETH ROBESON

Fire and ice * Kytle, Ray

Fire and ice * Tine, Robert as RICHARD HARDING

Fire and stone * Le Guin, Ursula K. & Laura Marshall

Fire ants, The * Wernick, Saul

Fire at the center * Proctor, Geo. W.

Fire below zero * Conrad, Barnaby & Nico Mastorakis

Fire cloud, The * McKenney, Kenneth

Fire crossing * Franklin, Cheryl J.

Fire crystal, The * Davis, James & Barbara Raifsnider

Fire dancer * Maxwell, Ann

Fire demon, The * Dille, Flint & Gary Gygax

Fire from the wine dark sea * Sucharitkul, Somtow

Fire game, The * Stine, R. L.

Fire get * Franklin, Cheryl J.

Fire in his hands, The * Cook, Glen

Fire in the abyss * Gordon, Stuart

Fire in the ashes * Johnstone, William W.

Fire in the blood * Elrod, P. N.

Fire in the sky, A * Kendrick, Walter

Fire in the sky * Maikowski, Michael F. & Chris L. Wolf

Fire in the sky * Tallis, Robyn

Fire in the sun, A * Effinger, George Alec

Fire lance * Mace, David

Fire lily * Camp, Deborah

Fire lord * Franklin, Cheryl J.

Fire mask * Grant, Charles L.

Fire on the border * O'Donnell, Kevin Jr.

Fire on the cloud * Leeson, Robert

Fire on the mountain * Bisson, Terry

Fire on the water * Chalk, Gary & Joe Dever

Fire pattern * Shaw, Bob

Fire planet * Griffin, P. M.

Fire queen * Grabien, Deborah

Fire sanctuary: a novel * Kimbriel, Katharine Eliska

Fire sea * Hickman, Tracy & Margaret Weis

Fire sword, The * Martine-Barnes, Adrienne

Fire throne mountain * Bixby, E. Rew

Fire watch * Willis, Connie

Fire when it comes, The * Godwin, Parke

Fire within, The * Watkins, Graham

Fire wolf * Brennan, J. H.

Five doors, The * Rhys, Jack
Five fathoms dead * Dent, Lester as KENNETH ROBESON
Five for infinity * Barker, Thomas W.
Five great ghost stories * Haldeman-Julius, E.
Five thousand miles underground; or, The mystery of the center of the Earth * Garis, Howard R. & Edward L. Stratemeyer as ROY ROCKWOOD
Five way secret agent, The; [and, Mercenary from tomorrow] * Reynolds, Mack
Five-twelfths of Heaven * Scott, Melissa
Fize of the Gabriel Ratchets * Norwood, Warren
Flag full of stars, A * Ferguson, Brad
Flake of Snow: a novel * Sagarin, Edward
Flame breathers, The * Ernst, Paul as KENNETH ROBESON
Flame in Byzantium, A * Yarbro, Chelsea Quinn
Flame key, The * Vardeman, Robert E. as DANIEL MORAN
Flame knife, The * de Camp, L. Sprague & Robert E. Howard
Flame of the Inquisition * Kornblatt, Marc
Flame thrower * Taylor, Lucy
Flame upon the ice, The * Forstchen, William R.
Flamers * Fisk, Nicholas
Flaming falcons, The: a Doc Savage adventure * Dent, Lester as KENNETH ROBESON
Flamesong * Barker, M. A. R.
Flameweaver * Ball, Margaret
Flash Fry, private eye * Schoch, Tim
Flash Gordon: a novel * Cover, Arthur Byron
Flash Gordon book, The * Cover, Arthur Byron & Lynn Haney
Flash Gordon: Massacre in the 22nd century * Hagberg, David as ANONYMOUS AUTHOR
Flash Gordon mazes * Koziakin, Vladimir
Flash Gordon: The war of the Cybernauts * Cassiday, Bruce as CARSON BINGHAM
Flashback * Palmer, Michael
Flashing swords! #3: Warriors and wizards * Carter, Lin
Flashing swords! #4: Barbarians and black magicians * Carter, Lin
Flashing swords! no. 5: Demons and daggers * Carter, Lin
Flashpoint * Duke, Madeleine
Flatland * Sladek, John
Flatliners: a novel * Fleischer, Leonore
Flaunting moon, The * Darby, Catherine
Fledger * Barrett, Nicholas
Fledgling, The * Langton, Jane
Fleet, The * Drake, David & Bill Fawcett
Fleet of the damned * Bunch, Chris & Allan Cole
Fleetwood correspondence, The: a devilish tale of temptation * Griffin, William
Flesh * Laymon, Richard
Flesh; and, Lord Tyger * Farmer, Philip José
Flesh creepers * Williamson, J. N.
Flesh hunters, The * Proctor, Geo. W. as LEE WYATT
Flesh stealer * Dunn, Dawn & Susan Hartzell as PAULINE DUNN
Fleshbait * Holman, David & Larry Pryce
Flexing the warp * Norwood, Warren
Fliers of Antares * Bulmer, Kenneth as ALAN BURT AKERS
Flies of memory, The * Watson, Ian
Flight, The * Runyan, C. F.
Flight from Berbora * Sirota, Mike
Flight from Nevèrÿon * Delany, Samuel R.
Flight from Tarkihl * Ernsting, Walter as CLARK DARLTON
Flight from the dark * Chalk, Gary & Joe Dever
Flight in Yiktor * Norton, Andre

Flight into the unknown * Bartholomew, Barbara
Flight into yesterday * Harness, Charles L.
Flight of bright birds, A * Arscott, David & David Marl
Flight of dragons, The * Dickinson, Peter
Flight of honor * McEnroe, Richard S.
Flight of Mavin Manyshaped, The * Tepper, Sheri S.
Flight of the Dragonfly, The * Forward, Robert L.
Flight of the Endeavor, The * Farrell, Jackson T.
Flight of the "Hesper" * Hay, George
Flight of the moth-kin * Tapp, Kathy Kennedy
Flight of the old dog: a novel * Brown, Dale
Flight of the Phoenix, The * Rosenberger, Joseph
Flight of the raven * Buckholtz, Eileen & Ruth Glick as REBECCA YORK
Flight of the raven * Roberson, Jennifer
Flight of the Sandpiper * Benjamin, Jacob
Flight to Lucifer, The: a gnostic fantasy * Bloom, Harold
Flight to Opar * Farmer, Philip José
Flight to the Savage Empire * Howlett, Winston A. & Jean Lorrah
Flight to Thlassa Mey * McCarty, Dennis
Flights of fancy: the great fantasy films * Von Gunden, Kenneth
Flights of Icarus, The * Lehmkuhl, Donald
Flint knife, The * Benson, E. F.
Flint lord, The * Herley, Richard
Flint the king * Kirchoff, Mary L. & Douglas Niles
Flinx in flux * Foster, Alan Dean
Floater * Brandner, Gary
Floater factor * Michaels, Melisa C.
Floating dragon * Straub, Peter
Floating gods, The * Harrison, M. John
Floating worlds * Holland, Cecelia
Floating Zombie, The * Jones, D. F.
Flood * McCutchan, Philip
Flood, The * McDowell, Michael
Flood tide * Cherryh, C. J.
Florians, The * Stableford, Brian M.
Florida project, The * Sullivan, Tim
Flounder, The * Grass, Günther
Flowers of evil * Charles, Robert
Flown the Koopa * Wayne, Matt
Fluger, The * Piserchia, Doris
Fluke, The * Herbert, James
Flush of Wimpole Street and Broadway * Merrill, Flora
Flute song music * Shettle, Andrea
Flux; The tin angel: two novels * Goulart, Ron
Fly by night * Jones, Jenny
Flyer * Kimberly, Gail
Flying Dutch * Holt, Tom
Flying goblin, The: a Doc Savage adventure * Bogart, William G. as KENNETH ROBESON
Flying saucers * Asimov, Isaac & Martin H. Greenberg & Charles G. Waugh
Flying spy, The: a history of G-8 * Carr, Nick
Flying to nowhere * Fuller, John
Flying warlord, The * Frankowski, Leo
Focolor * Paine, Lauren as ROY AINSWORTHY
Focus on Jack Cole * Goulart, Ron
Focus pocus * Gormley, Beatrice
Fog, The * Cooney, Caroline B.
Fog, The * Herbert, James
Fog, The: a novel * Etchison, Dennis
Fog horn, The * Bradbury, Ray
Fog horn, and other stories, The * Bradbury, Ray
Fog hounds, wind cat, sea mice * Aiken, Joan
Fog maiden, The * Toombs, Jane Jenke
Folk of the air, The * Beagle, Peter S.
Folk of the fringe, The * Card, Orson Scott
Follow a shadow * Swindells, Robert E.

Forgotten realms fantasy adventure: Ironhelm * Niles, Douglas

Forgotten realms fantasy adventure: Pool of radiance * Ward, James M. & Jane Cooper Hong

Forgotten realms fantasy adventure: Red magic * Rabe, Jean

Forgotten realms fantasy adventure: Shadowdale * Ciencin, Scott as RICHARD AWLINSON

Forgotten realms fantasy adventure: Sojourn * Salvatore, R. A.

Forgotten realms fantasy adventure: Spellfire * Greenwood, Ed

Forgotten realms fantasy adventure: Streams of Silver * Salvatore, R. A.

Forgotten realms fantasy adventure: Tantras * Ciencin, Scott & James Lowder as RICHARD AWLINSON

Forgotten realms fantasy adventure: The crystal shard * Salvatore, R. A.

Forgotten realms fantasy adventure: The halfling's gem * Salvatore, R. A.

Forgotten realms fantasy adventure: The parched sea * Denning, Troy as RICHARD AWLINSON

Forgotten realms fantasy adventure: Viperhand * Niles, Douglas

Forgotten realms fantasy adventure: Waterdeep * Denning, Troy as RICHARD AWLINSON

Forgotten realms: Song of the saurials * Grubb, Jeff & Kate Novak

Forgotten realms: The wyvern's spur * Novak, Kate & Jeff Grubb

Forgotten tales of terror * Lamb, Hugh

Fork River space project, The: a novel * Morris, Wright

Forlorn hope, The * Drake, David

Formations of fantasy * Burgin, Victor & James Donald & Cora Kaplan

Former king, The * Corby, Adam

Forms of the fantastic: selected essays from the Third International Conference on the Fantastic in Literature and Film * Hokenson, Jan & Howard Pearce

Formula, The: a novel of Harley Street * Horler, Sydney

Formula fiction? an anatomy of American science fiction, 1930-1940 * Cioffi, Frank

Formula for trouble, The * Stine, H. William & Megan Stine

Forrest J Ackerman presents Mr. Monster's movie gold * Ackerman, Forrest J

Forrest J Ackerman, famous monster of filmland * Ackerman, Forrest J

Forrest J Ackerman's Fantastic movie memories * Ackerman, Forrest J

Forsake the sky * Powers, Tim

Forsaken, The * Fulgham, Steven Ray

Forsaken, The * Gorman, Ed as DANIEL RANSOM

Forsaken, The * Read, Cameron

Fort privilege * Reed, Kit

Fortress * Drake, David

Fortress, The * Wilson, Colin

Fortress and the fire, The * Friedman, Michael Jan

Fortress in time * Mahr, Kurt

Fortress island * Estey, Dale

Fortress of death * Naha, Ed as MICHAEL MCGANN

Fortress of eternity, The * Whitmore, Andrew

Fortress of forbidden destiny * Syvertsen, Ryder

Fortress of lost worlds * Rypel, T. C.

Fortress of Solitude: a Doc Savage adventure * Dent, Lester as KENNETH ROBESON

Fortress of the pearl, The * Moorcock, Michael

Fortunate isles, The: a novel * Townsend, John Rowe

Fortune, The * McDowell, Michael

Fortune for Kregen, A * Bulmer, Kenneth as DRAY PRESCOT & ALAN BURT AKERS

Fortune of fear * Hubbard, L. Ron

Fortune teller, The * Norman, Marsha

Fortune's light * Friedman, Michael Jan

Fortunes of Brak, The * Jakes, John

Forty thousand in Gehenna * Cherryh, C. J.

Forty-two tales * Poe, Edgar Allan

Forward! * Dickson, Gordon R.

Foucault's pendulum * Eco, Umberto

Found wanting * Carter, Lin

Foundation and Earth * Asimov, Isaac

Foundation; I, robot * Asimov, Isaac

Foundation trilogy, The: Foundation, Foundation and Empire, Second Foundation; The stars, like dust; The naked sun; I, robot * Asimov, Isaac

Foundation's edge * Asimov, Isaac

Foundation's friends: stories in honor of Isaac Asimov * Greenberg, Martin H.

Foundations of science fiction: a study in imagination and evolution * Pierce, John J.

Founder, The * Rowley, Christopher

Founder member * Gardner, John E.

Foundling, The * Lauria, Frank

Fountains of Paradise, The * Clarke, Arthur C.

Four absentees * Heppenstall, Rayner

Four complete novels * Stewart, Mary

Four complete novels: The white plague; The Dosadi experiment; The Santaroga barrier; Soul catcher * Herbert, Frank

Four from the Witch World * Norton, Andre

Four great SF novels * Clarke, Arthur C.

Four Hoods and Great Dog, The * Schaeffer, Susan Fromberg

Four hundred billion stars * McAuley, Paul J.

Four into three * Price, Roger

Four lords of the diamond * Chalker, Jack L.

Four moons of Darkover * Bradley, Marion Zimmer & the Friends of Darkover

Four past midnight * King, Stephen

Four prose poems * Lovecraft, H. P.

Four stories * Lafferty, R. A.

Four thaumastic tales * Griffith, Clem

Four to doomsday * Dicks, Terrance

Four wishes, The * Stone, Charlotte

Four-day planet; Lone star planet * Piper, H. Beam & John J. McGuire

Four-dimensional nightmare, The * Ballard, J. G.

Fours Crossing * Garden, Nancy

Fourteenth Armada ghost book, The * Danby, Mary

Fourteenth Fontana book of great ghost stories, The * Chetwynd-Hayes, R.

Fourteenth Fontana book of great horror stories, The * Danby, Mary

Fourth annual volume: new voices 4: the John W. Campbell award nominees * Martin, George R. R.

Fourth Armada ghost book, The * Chetwynd-Hayes, R.

Fourth book of after midnight stories, The * Myers, Amy

Fourth book of lost swords, The * Saberhagen, Fred

Fourth book of Virgil Finlay, The: the fantasy art of Virgil Finlay * Finlay, Virgil

Fourth bumper book of ghost stories, The * Hale, James

Fourth connection * Bagnall, R. D.

Fourth conquest of England, The: a sequel to "Treason" * Upward, Allen

Fourth gear * Smith, Walter J.

Fourth hemisphere, The * Lake, David J.

Fourth horseman, The * Nourse, Alan E.

Fourth K, The: a novel * Puzo, Mario

Friends of the Horseclans II * Adams, Pamela Crippen & Robert Adams
Friendship and duty * Schulze, Doris
Fright * Collins, Charles M.
Fright line * Byers, Richard Lee
Fright night * Skipp, John & Craig Spector
Frightened forest, The * Turnbull, Ann
Frighteners, The * Laws, Stephen
Frighteners 2 * Danby, Mary
Frights * McCauley, Kirby
Frights 1: new stories of suspense and the supernatural * McCauley, Kirby
Frights 2: more new stories of suspense and supernatural terror * McCauley, Kirby
Fringe, The * de Timms, Graeme as G. D. TIMMS
Frisk donation, The * Wilson, Robert Hendrie
Fritz Leiber * Frane, Jeff
Fritz Leiber * Staicar, Tom
Fritz Leiber: a bibliography, 1934-1979 * Morgan, Chris
Fritz Leiber: a working bibliography * Benson, Gordon Jr.
Fritz Leiber, sardonic swordsman: a working bibliography, 2nd rev. ed. * Benson, Gordon Jr. & Phil Stephensen-Payne
Friulan plot, The * Webster, Ernest
Frobisch's angel * Rochlin, Doris
Frog people, The * Carlson, Dale
From a changeling star * Carver, Jeffrey A.
From afar * Fearn, John Russell
From below * Tigges, John as WILLIAM ESSEX
From blight to height * Marinelli, Jean
From dust to lust * Scott, Sandra
From fiction to film: Ambrose Bierce's "An occurrence at Owl Creek Bridge" * Barrett, Gerald R. & Thomas L. Erskine
From here to absurdity: the moral battlefields of Joseph Heller * Potts, Stephen W.
From Jules Verne to Star Trek * Rovin, Jeff
From mind to mind: tales of communication from Analog * Schmidt, Stanley
From my guy to sci-fi: genre and women's writing in the postmodern world * Carr, Helen
From nine to nine * Perutz, Leo
From satire to subversion: the fantasies of James Branch Cabell * Riemer, James D.
From sea to shining star * Chandler, A. Bertram
From the archives of evil * Lee, Christopher & Michel Parry
From the archives of evil #2 * Lee, Christopher & Michel Parry
From the ashes * Hagan, Chet
From The blob to Star wars: the science fiction movie quiz book: 1001 trivia teasers for sci-fi fans * Andrews, Bart & Howard Davenport
From the Earth to the Moon direct in ninety-seven hours and twenty minutes * Verne, Jules
From the heart of darkness * Drake, David
From the land beyond beyond: the films of Willis O'Brien and Ray Harryhausen * Rovin, Jeff
From the legend of Biel * Staton, Mary
From the mist * Dawson, Saranne
From the realm of Morpheus * Millhauser, Steven
From the Thoreson Dykes * McBratney, Sam
From Tolkien to Oz * Hildebrandt, Greg & William McGuire
Frontera * Shiner, Lewis
Frontier * Tabori, Paul
Frontier crossings * Jackson, Robert
Frontier of the dark * Chandler, A. Bertram
Frontier worlds * Collins, Paul

Frontiersville High * Bowkett, Stephen
Frontios * Bidmead, Christopher H.
Frost * Bailey, Robin W.
Frost and fire * Zelazny, Roger
Frost on the moon * Darby, Catherine
Frosted death, The * Ernst, Paul as KENNETH ROBESON
Frostflower and Thorn * Karr, Phyllis Ann
Frostflower and Windbourne * Karr, Phyllis Ann
Frostworld and dreamfire * Morressy, John
Froth eater, The * Webb, William Thomas
Frozen city, The * Marl, David & David Arscott
Frozen danger * Stine, H. William & Megan Stine
Frozen fire * McPhee, James
Frozen god, The * Holdstock, Robert & Angus Wells as RICHARD KIRK
Frozen planet of Azuron, The * Hoyle, Fred & Geoffrey Hoyle
Frozen sky, The * Harding, Lee
Frozen waves, The * Vardeman, Robert E.
F.S.C. * Sellers, Con
FTL: further than life * Williams, Michael Lindsay
Fuel's gold * Jackson, Steve & Creede Lambard & Sharleen Lambard
Fugitive from time * High, Philip E.
Fugitive in transit * Llewellyn, Edward
Fugitive Steele * Hunter, S. L.
Fugitive worlds, The * Shaw, Bob
Fugue state * Ford, John M.
Fulfilments of fate and desire, The * Constantine, Storm
Full alert: a novel * Korel, Charles
Full circle * Smith, Andrew
Full circle * Straub, Peter
Full house * Alexander, Robert as JOAN BUTLER
Full moon * Lillington, Kenneth
Full moon * Wolfe, Ron & John Wooley as MICK WINTERS
Full moon rising * Lorrah, Jean
Full spectrum * Aronica, Lou & Shawna McCarthy
Full spectrum 2 * Aronica, Lou & Shawna McCarthy & Amy Stout & Patrick LoBrutto
Full spectrum 3 * Aronica, Lou & Amy Stout & Betsy Mitchell
Full throttle * Cunningham, Chet as TONY PHILLIPS
Fu-Manchu: four classic novels * Rohmer, Sax
Fun house * Girard, Kenneth
Fun house terrors! * Milton, Hilary
Fun phantoms: tales of ghostly entertainment * Lewis, Gogo & Seon Manley
Fundamental Disch, The * Disch, Thomas M.
Funeral for the eyes of fire, A * Bishop, Michael
Fungus, The * Brosnan, John & Leroy Kettle as HARRY ADAM KNIGHT
Fungus garden, The * Brett, Brian
Funhouse, The: carnival of terror: a novel * Koontz, Dean R. as OWEN WEST
Funland * Laymon, Richard
Funny money * Murphy, Warren & Richard Sapir
Funnyfingers & Cabrito * Lafferty, R. A.
Further adventures of Batman, The * Greenberg, Martin H.
Further adventures of Doctor Who, The: Doctor Who and the deadly assassin; Doctor Who and the face of evil; Doctor Who and the robots of death * Dicks, Terrance
Further adventures of Halley's Comet, The * Batchelor, John Calvin
Further adventures of Lucky Starr, The * Asimov, Isaac
Further adventures of Slugger McBatt, The: baseball stories * Kinsella, W. P.

G

G. K. Chesterton and C. S. Lewis: the riddle of joy *
MacDonald, Michael H. & Andrew A. Tadie
G-8 and his battle aces * Hogan, Robert J.
Gaal the conqueror * White, John
Gabion * Riding, Julia
Gabo Djara * Wongar, B.
Gabriel * Tuttle, Lisa
Gabriel and the creatures * Heard, H. F.
Gabriel inheritance, The * Dyer, Alfred
Gad: a novel * Geller, Stephen
Gadget factor, The * Landsman, Sandy
Gad's Hall * Lofts, Norah
Gad's Hall; and, The haunting of Gad's Hall * Lofts, Norah
Gaga * Olafur Gunnarsson
Gahan Wilson's Favorite tales of horror * Wilson, Gahan
Gahr City * Nichols, Robert
Gaian expedient, The * Drew, Wayland
Galactiad, The * Tubb, E. C. as GREGORY KERN
Galactic adventures * anonymous
Galactic aliens * Frank, Alan
Galactic arena, The * DeBolt, Adriana as CHRISTOPHER DANE
Galactic chronicles * Christopher, Paul
Galactic convoy * Baldwin, Bill
Galactic dreamers: science fiction as visionary literature * Silverberg, Robert
Galactic effectuator * Vance, Jack
Galactic empires: an anthology of way-back-when futures * Aldiss, Brian W.
Galactic girl * Richmond, Fiona
Galactic invaders, The * Berry, James R.
Galactic Medal of Honor * Reynolds, Mack
Galactic plan * Huntley, Noel
Galactic Rift * Warner, Michael & R. D. Warner
Galactic silver star, The * Randle, Kevin
Galactic tours: Thomas Cook out of this world vacations * Hardy, David A. & Bob Shaw
Galactic Warlord * Hill, Douglas
Galactic warriors * Bischoff, David
Galactic whirlpool, The: a Star Trek novel * Gerrold, David
Galactica discovers Earth * Larson, Glen A. & Michael Resnick
Galápagos: a novel * Vonnegut, Kurt
Galaxies * Malzberg, Barry N.
Galaxy 5: teacher's guide * Kelley, Leo P.
Galaxy builder, The * Laumer, Keith
Galaxy checklist, The: covering the period October 1950 to December 1958 * Dollner, Karl
Galaxy Four * Emms, William
Galaxy High School * Hodgman, Ann
Galaxy Jane * Goulart, Ron
Galaxy magazine: the dark and the light years * Rosheim, David L.
Galaxy of strangers, A * Biggle, Lloyd Jr.
Galaxy: the best of my years * Baen, James Patrick

Galaxy: thirty years of innovative science fiction * Greenberg, Martin H. & Frederik Pohl & Joseph D. Olander
Galaxy's end * Lupoff, Richard A.
Galen beknighted * Williams, Michael
Gallagher's glacier * Richmond, Leigh & Walt Richmond
Gallatin divergence, The * Smith, L. Neil
Gallery of his dreams, The * Rusch, Kristine Kathryn
Gallery of horror * Grant, Charles L.
Gallicenae * Anderson, Karen & Poul Anderson
Gallifrey chronicles, The * Peel, John
Galloping galaxies * Block, Bob
Game, The * Logan, Les
Game, The * Phillips, Lyn
Game, The * Richemont, Enid
Game and the ground, The * Vansittart, Peter
Game beyond, The * Scott, Melissa
Game master's guide for Sanctuary * Abbey, Lynn et al.
Game of empire, The * Anderson, Poul
Game of fox and lion, The * Chase, Robert R.
Game of the impossible, The: a rhetoric of fantasy * Irwin, W. R.
Game of the pink pagoda, The * Moss, Roger
Gamearth * Anderson, Kevin J.
Gameplay * Anderson, Kevin J.
Gameplayers * Bowkett, Stephen
Gameplayers of Zan, The * Foster, M. A.
Games * Klein, Robin
Game's end * Anderson, Kevin J.
Games of the strong * Adams, Glenda
Gamesman, The * Malzberg, Barry N.
Gamma option, The * Land, Jon
Gamma ray murders, The * Kelly, Harold Ernest as PRESTON YORKE
Gandalara cycle, volume 1, The * Garrett, Randall & Vicki Ann Heydron
Gandalara cycle, vol. 2, The * Garrett, Randall & Vicki Ann Heydron
Gants * Abshire, Richard K. & William R. Clair
Ganwold's child * Thornley, Diann
Gap into conflict, The: The real story * Donaldson, Stephen R.
Gap into vision, The: Forbidden knowledge * Donaldson, Stephen R.
Garbage chronicles, The: being an account of the adventures of Tom Javik and Wizzy Malloy in the faraway land of catapulted garbage * Herbert, Brian
Garden, The * Berger, Yves
Garden of echoes, The: a fable for children and grownups * Wall, Mervyn
Garden of evil * Martin, David
Garden of evil * Plante, Edmund
Garden of Rama, The * Clarke, Arthur C. & Gentry Lee
Garden of the incubus * Tigges, John
Garden of the shaped, The * Finch, Sheila
Garden of winter, The * Eklund, Gordon
Gardens of Delight, The * Watson, Ian
Gardens of Dorr, The * Biegel, Paul

Ghost ring, and other tales of telepathy, The * Meakin, Viola

Ghost ship * Carey, Diane

Ghost ship, The: stories of the phantom Flying Dutchman * Haining, Peter

Ghost ship to Ganymede * Swindells, Robert E.

Ghost soldiers * Hardesty, Steven

Ghost Squad and the Ghoul of Grünberg, The * Hildick, E. W.

Ghost Squad and the Halloween conspiracy, The * Hildick, E. W.

Ghost Squad and the menace of the Malevs * Hildick, E. W.

Ghost Squad and the prowling hermits * Hildick, E. W.

Ghost Squad breaks through, The * Hildick, E. W.

Ghost Squad flies Concorde, The * Hildick, E. W.

Ghost stories * Border, Rosemary

Ghost stories * Ferguson, Virginia & Angela M. Ridsdale

Ghost stories * Hill, Susan

Ghost stories * Oakden, David

Ghost stories * Shine, Deborah

Ghost stories * Westall, Robert

Ghost stories and mysteries * Le Fanu, J. Sheridan

Ghost stories and phantom fancies * Friswell, Hain

Ghost stories of Canada * Clery, Val

Ghost stories of Charles Dickens, The * Dickens, Charles

Ghost stories of M. R. James, The * James, M. R.

Ghost story * Straub, Peter

Ghost story treasury, The * Sonntag, Linda

Ghost that came alive, The * Crume, Vic

Ghost tour: an armchair journey through the supernatural * Haining, Peter

Ghost tower, The * Blashfield, Jean

Ghost train: a novel * Laws, Stephen

Ghost walker * Hambly, Barbara

Ghost warriors, The * Naha, Ed as MICHAEL MCGANN

Ghost who fell in love, The * Cartland, Barbara

Ghost within, The * Prince, Alison

Ghost wore gray, The * Coville, Bruce

Ghostboat * Burger, Neal R. & George E. Simpson

Ghostbreakers * Parry, Michel

Ghostbusters * Milne, Larry

Ghostbusters II: a novel * Hiller, B. B.

Ghostbusters II: a novel * Naha, Ed

Ghostbusters II: a novel * Stine, R. L.

Ghostbusters: a storybook * Digby, Anne

Ghostbusters book of movie madness * Lovitt, Chip

Ghostbusters: the supernatural spectacular: a novel * Mueller, Richard

Ghoster * McKeone, Lee

Ghostflight * Katz, William

Ghosthunt * Clayton, Jo

Ghostly and ghastly * Ireson, Barbara

Ghostly business, A * Krensky, Stephen

Ghostly carnival: Cornish ghost stories * Williams, Mary

Ghostly companions * Alcock, Vivien

Ghostly encounters * Griffiths, Vivien

Ghostly gentlewomen: two centuries of spectral stories by the gentle sex * Lewis, Gogo & Seon Manley

Ghostly, grim, and gruesome: an anthology * Hoke, Helen

Ghostly laughter * Ireson, Barbara

Ghostly populations: short stories * Matthews, Jack

Ghostly tales * Price, Susan

Ghostly tales of Washington Irving, The * Irving, Washington

Ghost-maker, The * Kilgore, Kathleen

Ghostmasters, The: weird stories by famous writers * Owen, Betty M.

Ghostmobile, The * Tapp, Kathy Kennedy

Ghosts * Asimov, Isaac & Martin H. Greenberg & Charles G. Waugh

Ghosts * Chambers, Aidan & Nancy Chambers

Ghosts * Parker, Marsha

Ghosts: a treasury of chilling tales old and new * Kaye, Marvin & Saralee Kaye

Ghosts: an 87th Precinct novel * Hunter, Evan as ED MCBAIN

Ghosts and ghastlies * Hoke, Helen

Ghosts and journeys: short stories * Westall, Robert

Ghosts & monsters * Asimov, Isaac & Martin H. Greenberg & Charles G. Waugh

Ghosts and scholars: ghost stories in the tradition of M. R. James * Dalby, Richard & Rosemary Pardoe

Ghosts & scholars: stories in the tradition of M. R. James * Pardoe, Rosemary

Ghosts and shadows * Edwards, Dorothy

Ghosts at large * Price, Susan

Ghosts beneath our feet * Wright, Betty Ren

Ghost's companion, The: stories of personal encounters with the supernatural * Haining, Peter

Ghosts for Christmas * Dalby, Richard

Ghosts four * Chambers, Aidan as MALCOLM BLACKLIN

Ghosts from the mist of time * Chetwynd-Hayes, R.

Ghosts I have been: a novel * Peck, Richard

Ghosts in country houses * Baker, Denys Val

Ghosts in country villages: stories of mystery and the supernatural * Baker, Denys Val

Ghosts of Austwick Manor, The * MacDonald, Reby Edmund

Ghosts of Bellering Oast, The * Oldfield, Pamela

Ghosts of Cabrillo Lighthouse * Sinor, John

Ghosts of Departure Point, The * Bunting, Eve

Ghosts of Epidoris, The * Tubb, E. C. as GREGORY KERN

Ghosts of Gallows Cross, The * Dicks, Terrance

Ghosts of Hungryhouse Lane, The * McBratney, Sam

Ghosts of night and morning * Kaye, Marvin

Ghosts of Stone Hollow, The * Snyder, Zilpha Keatley

Ghosts of Stony Clove, The * Charbonneau, Eileen

Ghosts of the heartland: haunting, spine-chilling stories from the American midwest * Greenberg, Martin H. & Frank D. McSherry Jr. & Charles G. Waugh

Ghosts of the heaviside layers, and other fantasms * Dunsany, Lord

Ghosts of wind and shadow * de Lint, Charles

Ghosts that haunt you * Chambers, Aidan

Ghosts who went to school * Spearing, Judith

Ghost-sitter, The * Elfman, Blossom

Ghostwood * de Lint, Charles

Ghostworld: Beyond terror * Siegel, Barbara & Scott Siegel

Ghostworld: Midnight chill * Siegel, Barbara & Scott Siegel

Ghoul * Alexander, Marc as MARK RONSON

Ghoul * Banks, John & Richard Covell & Lee Clarke & Jay Clarke as MICHAEL SLADE

Ghoul, The * Smith, Guy N.

Ghouls * Lee, Edward

G.I. Joe: Operation: deadly decoy * Stine, R. L.

G.I. Joe: Operation: death stone * Siegel, Scott & Barbara Siegel

G.I. Joe: Operation: death-ray * Stine, H. William & Megan Stine

G.I. Joe: Operation: dragon fire * Sno, William

G.I. Joe: Operation: jungle doom * Lance, Kathryn as LYNN BEACH

G.I. Joe: Operation: killer comet * Ballard, S. M.

G.I. Joe: Operation: mindbender * Stine, R. L.

G.I. Joe: Operation: night flight * Sno, William

Glow of candles, and other stories, A * Grant, Charles L.
Glowing birds: stories from the edge of science *
    Huyghe, Patrick
Gnelfs * Williams, Sidney
Gnole, The * Aldridge, Alan
Gnome man's land * Friesner, Esther M.
Gnomes * Huygen, Wil
Gnome's engine, The * Edgerton, Teresa
Gnomes-100, dragons-0 * Blashfield, Jean & James M.
    Ward
Go tell the Spartans * Pournelle, Jerry & S. M. Stirling
Goat dance * Clegg, Douglas
Goat's head * Pfefferle, Seth
Goblin market * Bowes, Richard
Goblin moon * Edgerton, Teresa
Goblin plain war, The * Miller, Carl
Goblins * Froud, Brian
Goblins, The * Robeson, Kenneth
Goblins of Labyrinth, The * Froud, Brian & Terry Jones
God and all his angels * Lord, Graham
God box, The * Longyear, Barry B.
God Emperor of Dune * Herbert, Frank
God game * Greeley, Andrew M.
God help the Queen * Cush, Geoffrey
God in science fiction, The * Bradbury, Ray
God killer, The * Green, Simon
God of a thousand faces * Anderson, Michael Falconer
God of death * Sadler, Barry
God of glass, The: a morality * Redgrove, Peter W.
God of Tarot * Anthony, Piers
GOD project, The * Lee, Stan
God project, The * Saul, John
God stalk * Hodgell, P. C.
God: the ultimate autobiography * Pascall, Jeremy
Goda war, The * Blakeney, Jay D.
Godbody * Sturgeon, Theodore
Godbond * Springer, Nancy
Godchildren, The * Pape, Sharon B.
Godforsaken, The * Yarbro, Chelsea Quinn
Godmothers, The * Hall, Sandi
Gods abide, The * Swann, Thomas Burnett
Gods alone, The * Wilson, Robert Hendrie
Gods, demons, and others * Narayan, R. K.
God's grace * Malamud, Bernard
Gods in a vortex * Houston, David
Gods in anger, The * Cole, Adrian
Gods in winter, The * Miles, Patricia
Gods laughed, The * Anderson, Poul
Gods look down, The * Hoyle, Trevor
God's nose * Knight, Damon
Gods of Bel-Sagoth, The * Howard, Robert E.
Gods of Cerus Major, The * Ruse, Gary Alan
Gods of Raquel, The * Scliar, Moacyr
Gods of Riverworld * Farmer, Philip José
Gods of the Greataway * Coney, Michael
Gods of Xuma, The; or, Barsoom revisited * Lake, David
    J.
Gods' temptress, The * Greenfield, Irving A.
God's world * Watson, Ian
Godsend, The * Taylor, Bernard
Godsfire * Felice, Cynthia
Godslayer * Reichert, Mickey Zucker
Godwins and the Shelleys, The * St. Clair, William
Godzilla * May, Julian as IAN THORNE
Godzilla book, The * Harmon, Jim
Gog: a novel * Sinclair, Andrew
Going * Elliott, Sumner Locke
Going after the rubber chicken * Simmons, Dan
Going to See the End of the Sky * Watkins, William John
Gojiro * Jacobson, Mark

Gold and iron * Vance, Jack
Gold ball, The * Svendsen, Hanne Marie
Gold bug, The * Harris, Raymond & Edgar Allan Poe
Gold coast, The * Robinson, Kim Stanley
Gold dragon * Cain, Robert
Gold ogre, The: a Doc Savage adventure * Dent, Lester
    as KENNETH ROBESON
Gold star * Hughes, Zach
Gold thread, The: essays on George MacDonald *
    Raeper, William
Gold-bug, and other tales, The * Poe, Edgar Allan
Goldcamp vampire, The; or, The sanguinary sourdough *
    Scarborough, Elizabeth
Goldchester: more adventures in high fantasy * Dillow,
    Jeffrey C.
Goldclimbers * Luenn, Nancy
Golden * Pickard, George
Golden age, The: a novel * FitzGibbon, Constantine
Golden age of science fiction, The * Amis, Kingsley
Golden anniversary anthology * Schmidt, Stanley
Golden apple, The * Shea, Robert & Robert Anton Wil-
    son
Golden astronauts, The * Haigh, Richard
Golden ax, The * Neilson, Eric
Golden barge, The: a fable * Moorcock, Michael
*Golden chain, The: essays on William Morris and pre-
    Raphaelitism* * Silver, Carole
Golden child, The * Chesbro, George C.
Golden days * See, Carolyn
Golden dream, A * Scott, Michael
Golden dream: a Fuzzy odyssey * Mayhar, Ardath
Golden fleece * Sawyer, Robert J.
Golden garden, The * Parvin, Brian
Golden Gate, and other stories * Lafferty, R. A.
Golden Girl and the crystal of doom * Sherman, Josepha
Golden Girl and the vanishing unicorn * Stine, R. L.
Golden Girl in the land of dreams * Storey, Alice
Golden Grove, The * Kress, Nancy
Golden gryphon feather, The * Purtill, Richard
Golden Hawk of Zandraya, The * Sirota, Mike
Golden helix, The * Sturgeon, Theodore
Golden Horn, The * Tarr, Judith
*Golden key, The: a study of the fiction of George Mac-
    Donald* * Wolff, Robert Lee
Golden man, The * Dick, Philip K.
Golden man, The * Robeson, Kenneth
Golden Naginata, The * Salmonson, Jessica Amanda
Golden people, The * Saberhagen, Fred
Golden peril, The: a Doc Savage adventure * Dent,
    Lester & Harold A. Davis as KENNETH ROBESON
Golden Scorpio * Bulmer, Kenneth as ALAN BURT AKERS
Golden space, The * Sargent, Pamela
Golden steed, The * Green, Roland as JEFFREY LORD
Golden sunlands * Rowley, Christopher
Golden swan, The * Springer, Nancy
Golden sword, The * Morris, Janet
Golden sword of Dragonwalk * Stine, R. L.
Golden thread, The * Charnas, Suzy McKee
Golden torc, The * May, Julian
Golden Troubadour, The * Bell, Gordon B.
Golden Vanity * Pollack, Rachel
Golden wings, and other stories * Morris, William
Golden witchbreed * Gentle, Mary
Golden world, The * Hughes, Zach as EVAN INNES
Golden years of science fiction, The * Asimov, Isaac &
    Martin H. Greenberg
Goldengirl * Lear, Peter
Goldenrod * Towne, Mary
Golem * Anson, Barbara
Golem^{100} * Bester, Alfred

Gravity's rainbow companion, A: sources and contexts for Pynchon's novel * Weisenburger, Steven
Gray eagles * Unkefer, Duane
Gray Fist: from the Shadow's private annals * Gibson, Walter B. as MAXWELL GRANT
Gray magic: a Stoner McTavish mystery * Dreher, Sarah
Gray shadows of death, The * Hamm, William
Gray victory * Skimin, Robert
Graymantle * Morressy, John
Grayspace beast, The * Eklund, Gordon
Greasepaint and ghosts: an anthology of strange and supernatural stories from the world of theatre * Haining, Peter
Greasy Lake, and other stories * Boyle, T. Coraghessan
Great American ghost stories * Greenberg, Martin H. & Frank D. McSherry Jr. & Charles G. Waugh
Great and secret show, The: the first book of The art * Barker, Clive
Great balls of fire! * Harrison, Harry
Great baseball championship, The * Wenk, Richard
Great book of movie monsters, The * Stacy, Jan & Ryder Syvertsen
Great book raid, The * Leach, Christopher
Great change, The * Wagner, Jack
Great comic artist file: Frank Miller * Miller, Frank
Great comic book artists, The * Goulart, Ron
Great deeds of superheroes, The * Ingpen, Robert & Maurice Saxby
Great divide, The * Levin, John & Frank M. Robinson
Great drake, The * Cappelli, Mario
Great Dune trilogy, The: Dune; Dune Messiah; Children of Dune * Herbert, Frank
Great escape, A * Dann, Colin
Great fetish, The * de Camp, L. Sprague
Great ghost rescue, The * Ibbotson, Eva
Great ghost stories * Schwartz, Betty Ann
Great ghost stories in large print * Allen, Mary C.
Great ghost story book, The * anon.
Great gradepoint mystery, The * Bartholomew, Barbara
Great grave robbery, The * Minahan, John
Great hunt, The * Jordan, Robert
Great Kings' War * Carr, John F. & Roland Green
Great Los Angeles blizzard, The * Racina, Thom
Great monsters of the movies * Davidson, Robert K.
Great Muppet caper, The * Weiner, Ellis
Great Orme terror, The * Radcliffe, Garnett
Great science fiction films, The * Meyers, Richard S.
Great science fiction from the movies * Edelson, Edward
Great science fiction of the 20th century * Greenberg, Martin H. & Robert Silverberg
Great science fiction pictures, The * Parish, James Robert & Michael R. Pitts
Great science fiction pictures II, The * Parish, James Robert & Michael R. Pitts
Great science fiction series, The: stories from the best of the series from 1944 to 1980 by twenty all-time favorite writers * Greenberg, Martin H. & Frederik Pohl & Joseph D. Olander
Great science fiction stories, The * Asimov, Isaac & Martin H. Greenberg
Great science fiction stories: 2001: a space odyssey / Arthur C. Clarke ; The demolished man / Alfred Bester; The day of the triffids / John Wyndham; I, robot / Isaac Asimov * anon.
Great science fiction stories by the world's great scientists * Asimov, Isaac & Martin H. Greenberg & Charles G. Waugh
Great short tales of mystery and terror * anon.
Great Sky River * Benford, Gregory

Great space battles * Cowley, Stewart & Charles Herridge
Great stories from Rod Serling's The Twilight Zone Magazine, 1983 annual * Klein, T. E. D.
Great stories from The Twilight Zone magazine * anon.
Great tales of classic science fiction * Asimov, Isaac & Martin H. Greenberg & Charles G. Waugh
Great tales of horror & the supernatural * Greenberg, Martin H. & Bill Pronzini & Barry N. Malzberg
Great tales of Jewish occult and fantasy * Neugroschel, Joachim
Great tales of madness & the macabre * Ardai, Charles
Great tales of science fiction * Greenberg, Martin H. & Robert Silverberg
Great tales of the supernatural * Dowrick, Stephanie
Great themes of science fiction * Pierce, John J.
Great Victorian collection, The * Moore, Brian
Great villains, The: an omnibus of evil * Lee, Christopher & Michel Parry
Great wheel, The * Gregorian, Joyce Ballou
Great work of time * Crowley, John
Great works of Jewish fantasy * Neugroschel, Joachim
Great works of Jewish fantasy and occult, The * Neugroschel, Joachim
Greater infinity, A * McCollum, Michael
Greatest show in the galaxy, The * Wyatt, Stephen
Greatheart Silver * Farmer, Philip José
Greely's Cove * Hoklin, Lonn as JOHN GIDEON
Green and pleasant land: the British 1920s-1930s Cthulhu sourcepack * Tamlyn, Pete
Green Bay run * Robbins, David
Green book, The * Paton Walsh, Jill
Green circle blues * Haring, Scott
Green death, The: a Doc Savage adventure * Davis, Harold A. as KENNETH ROBESON
Green eagle, The: a Doc Savage adventure * Dent, Lester as KENNETH ROBESON
Green eyes * Shepard, Lucius
Green Eyes: from the Shadow's private annals * Gibson, Walter B. as MAXWELL GRANT
Green futures of Tycho, The * Sleator, William
Green ghost, and other stories, The * Danby, Mary
Green ghost of Appleville, The * Marzollo, Jean
Green god, The * Dvorkin, David
Green goddess, The * Edwards, Paul
Green gods, The * Henneberg, Charles & Nathalie Henneberg
Green hailstones * Hall, Norman
Green Hydra, The * Dille, Flint & Gary Gygax
Green is for Galanx * Stone, Josephine Rector
Green killer, The * Ernst, Paul as KENNETH ROBESON
Green knight, The * Chapman, Vera
Green lama, The: an amazing exploit taken right out of the case-book of the Green Lama, in which his unusual powers are put to the test * Crossen, Kendell Foster & Frederick C. Davis
Green lightning * Stillman, Ron
Green magic * Vance, Jack
Green magic: the fantasy realms of Jack Vance * Vance, Jack
Green man, The * Abbey, Lynn
Green man and his return, The: an amazing UFO pre-vision of the coming of the space people! written in 1946-47! complete reprint of the original text of The green man and The green man returns * Sherman, Harold M.
Green Mandarin mystery, The * Hughes, Dennis Talbot as Grant Malcom
Green mansions * Cannon, Martin
Green Mars * Robinson, Kim Stanley

Guardians, The: Valley of the gods * Milán, Victor as RICHARD AUSTIN

Guardians, The: Vengeance day * Milán, Victor as RICHARD AUSTIN

Guardians, The: War zone * Milán, Victor as RICHARD AUSTIN

Guards! guards! * Pratchett, Terry

Guardsman, The * Beese, P. J. & Todd Cameron Hamilton

Guardsman of Gor * Norman, John

Guess what's coming to dinner?: the extraterrestrial etiquette guide * Fivelson, Scott

Guide through C. S. Lewis' space trilogy, A * Sammons, Martha C.

Guide through Narnia, A * Sammons, Martha C.

Guide through the worlds of Robert A. Heinlein, A * Thorner, J. Lincoln

Guide to Barsoom, A: eleven sections of references in one volume dealing with the Martian stories written by Edgar Rice Burroughs * Roy, John Flint

Guide to current fanzines, 5th ed. * Roberts, Peter

Guide to fantasy art techniques, The * Dean, Martyn & Chris Evans

Guide to reference sources of science fiction materials in the collections of San Diego State University Library * Barclay, Bernice

Guide to science fiction & fantasy in the Library of Congress classification scheme, A * Reginald, R. as MICHAEL BURGESS

Guide to science fiction and fantasy in the Library of Congress classification scheme, second edition, A * Reginald, Robert as MICHAEL BURGESS

Guide to supernatural fiction, The: a full description of 1,775 books from 1750 to 1960, including ghost stories, weird fiction, stories of supernatural horror, fantasy, gothic novels, occult fiction, and similar literature, with author, title, and motif indexes * Bleiler, E. F.

Guide to the Commonwealth, A: the official guide to Alan Dean Foster's Humanx Commonwealth universe * Goodwin, Michael & Robert Teague

Guide to the extraterrestrials * Barlowe, Wayne Douglas & Ian Summers & Beth Meacham

Guide to the extraterrestrials, 2nd ed. * Barlowe, Wayne Douglas & Ian Summers & Beth Meacham

Guide to the Gormenghast trilogy, A * Metzger, Arthur

Guide to the gothic: an annotated bibliography of criticism * Frank, Frederick S.

Guide to the Star Wars universe, illustrated throughout, A * Velasco, Raymond L.

Guidebook for winner adventurers, The * Small, David & Randy Small

Guided tour * Dickson, Gordon R.

Guignoir, and other furies * Hatch, George

Guinever's gift * Norma Johnston as NICOLE ST. JOHN

Guinevere * Newman, Sharan

Guinevere and Lancelot & others * Machen, Arthur

Guinevere Evermore * Newman, Sharan

Guinevere, queen of the summer stars * Woolley, Persia

Guinevere: The legend in autumn * Woolley, Persia

Gulf attack * Mackin, Rick

Gull against the wind: a thriller of the future * Thomas, Francis

Gulliver's fugitives * Sharee, Keith

Gunfighters, The * Cotton, Donald

Gunner Cade, plus Takeoff * Merril, Judith & C. M. Kornbluth as CYRIL JUDD

Gunpowder god * Piper, H. Beam

Guns of darkness * Carr, John F. & Jerry Pournelle

Guns of Everblack, The * Scheer, K. H.

Gunslinger, The * King, Stephen

Gush * Abbott, Keith

Gusliar wonders * Bulychev, Kirill

Guts * Henderson, C. J. & Byron Preiss

Guts and glory * Stine, G. Harry

Gutter of creation, The * Dwinnell, R. M.

Guy Garrick: an adventure with a scientific gunman * Reeve, Arthur B.

Gwilan's harp * Le Guin, Ursula K.

Gypsies * Wilson, Robert Charles

Gypsy Earth * Harper, George W.

Gypsy in amber * Smith, Martin Cruz

Gypsy in amber; and, Canto for a gypsy * Smith, Martin Cruz

H

H. G. Wells * Batchelor, John
H. G. Wells * Belgion, Montgomery
H. G. Wells, rev. ed. * Belgion, Montgomery
H. G. Wells * Beresford, J. D.
H. G. Wells * Brome, Vincent
H. G. Wells * Costa, Richard Hauer
H. G. Wells, rev. ed. * Costa, Richard Hauer
H. G. Wells * Crossley, Robert
H. G. Wells * Nicholson, Norman
H. G. Wells * Parrinder, Patrick
H. G. Wells: a biography * MacKenzie, Jeanne & Norman MacKenzie
H. G. Wells: a collection of critical essays * Bergonzi, Bernard
H. G. Wells: a comprehensive bibliography * H. G. Wells Society
H. G. Wells: a comprehensive bibliography, 2nd ed. * H. G. Wells Society
H. G. Wells: a comprehensive bibliography, 3rd ed. * H. G. Wells Society
H. G. Wells: a comprehensive bibliography, 4th ed. * H. G. Wells Society & Patrick Parrinder & A. H. Watkins & J. R. Hammond
H. G. Wells: a reference guide * Cox, J. Randolph & William J. Scheick
H. G. Wells: a sketch for a portrait * Wells, Geoffrey, as GEOFFREY WEST
H. G. Wells and his critics * Raknem, Ingvald
H. G. Wells and his family: (as I have known them) * Meyer, M. M.
H. G. Wells and modern science fiction * Philmus, Robert M. & Darko Suvin
H. G. Wells and Rebecca West * Hammond, John R.
H. G. Wells & Rebecca West * Ray, Gordon N.
H. G. Wells and the culminating ape * Kemp, Peter
H. G. Wells and the modern novel * Hammond, J. R.
H. G. Wells and the world state * Wagar, W. Warren
H. G. Wells: aspects of a life * West, Anthony
H. G. Wells: author in agony * Borrello, Alfred
H. G. Wells companion, An: a guide to the novels, romances, and short stories * Hammond, J. R.
H. G. Wells: desperately mortal: a biography * Smith, David C.
H. G. Wells, discoverer of the future: the influence of science on his thought * Haynes, Roslynn D.
H. G. Wells: first citizen of the future * Ferrell, Keith
H. G. Wells: his turbulent life and times * Dickson, Lovat
H. G. Wells in the cinema * Wykes, Alan
H. G. Wells: interviews and recollections * Hammond, J. R.
H. G. Wells science fiction treasury, The * Wells, H. G.
H. G. Wells scrapbook, The: articles, essays, letters, anecdotes, illustrations, photographs, and memorabilia about the prophetic genius of the twentieth century * Haining, Peter
H. G. Wells short stories * Wells, H. G.
H. G. Wells: the critical heritage * Parrinder, Patrick

H. G. Wells under revision: proceedings of the International H. G. Wells Symposium, London, July 1986 * Parrinder, Patrick & Christopher Rolfe
H. G. Wells's literary criticism * Parrinder, Patrick & Robert M. Philmus
H. G. Wells's literary criticism * Wells, H. G.
H. P. Lovecraft * Cannon, Peter
H. P. Lovecraft * Joshi, S. T.
H. P. Lovecraft: a bibliography, rev. ed. * Brennan, Joseph Payne
H. P. Lovecraft: a critical study * Burleson, Donald R.
H. P. Lovecraft: a symposium * anon.
H. P. Lovecraft and Lovecraft criticism: an annotated bibliographical supplement, 1980-1984 * Blackmore, Leigh & S. T. Joshi
H. P. Lovecraft and Lovecraft criticism: an annotated bibliography * Joshi, S. T.
H. P. Lovecraft and the Cthulhu Mythos * Price, Robert M.
H. P. Lovecraft Christmas book * Lovecraft, H. P.
H. P. Lovecraft: commonplace book * Lovecraft, H. P.
H. P. Lovecraft companion, The * Shreffler, Philip A.
H. P. Lovecraft: four decades of criticism * Joshi, S. T.
H. P. Lovecraft: his life, his work * Faig, Kenneth W. Jr.
H. P. Lovecraft in "The Eyrie" * Lovecraft, H. P.
H. P. Lovecraft juvenilia, 1895-1905 * Lovecraft, H. P.
H. P. Lovecraft letters to Henry Kuttner * Kuttner, Henry & H. P. Lovecraft
H. P. Lovecraft memorial plaque, The * anon.
H. P. Lovecraft, New England decadent * St. Armand, Barton Levi
H. P. Lovecraft: the decline of the west * Joshi, S. T.
H. P. Lovecraft: the house and the shadows * Shea, J. Vernon
H. P. Lovecraft writings in the United amateur, 1915-1925 * Lovecraft, H. P.
H. P. Lovecraft's Waste paper: a facsimile and transcript of the original draft * Lovecraft, H. P.
H. R. Giger * Giger, H. R.
H. R. Giger ARh+ * Giger, H. R.
H. R. Giger's biomechanics * Giger, H. R.
H. R. Giger's Necronomicon * Giger, H. R.
H. R. Giger's Necronomicon 2 * Giger, H. R.
H. Rider Haggard: a bibliography * Whatmore, D. E.
H. Rider Haggard: a voice from the infinite * Tremayne, Peter as PETER BERRESFORD ELLIS
Haakon's iron hand * Neilson, Eric
HAB Theory, The: a novel * Eckert, Allan W.
Habit is an old horse * McCaffrey, Anne
Habitats * Shwartz, Susan
Habu * Johnson, James B.
Hacker, The * Day, Chet
Hag's tapestry * Salmonson, Jessica Amanda
Hail Hibbler * Goulart, Ron
Hail to the chief * Klausner, Lawrence David
Hal Clement * Hassler, Donald M.
Hal Clement checklist, A * Drumm, Chris
Hal Clement (Harry Clement Stubbs) * Benson, Gordon Jr.

Hal Clement, scientist with a mission: a working bibliography * Benson, Gordon Jr.

Halberd: dream warrior * St. Alcorn, Lloyd

Halcyon Island * Knowles, Anne

Hale & Gresham hardback science fiction * Robinson, Roger

Half a glass of moonshine * Martin, Graham Dunstan

Half a life, and other stories * Bulychev, Kirill

Half a sky: the Coscuin Chronicles, 1849-1854 * Lafferty, R. A.

Half child, The * Hersom, Kathleen

Half in shadow * Counselman, Mary Elizabeth

Half Moon down * Gresham, Stephen

Half-angels, The * Lovesey, Andrew

Half-brothers, The * Lawrence, Ann

Halflife, The * Webb, Sharon

Halfling's gem, The * Salvatore, R. A.

Halflings, hobbits, warrows, & weefolk: a collection of tales of heroes short in stature * Searles, Baird & Brian Thomsen

Halfmen of O, The * Gee, Maurice

Halfway across the galaxy and turn left * Klein, Robin

Halfway down Paddy Lane * Marzollo, Jean

Halfway man * Drew, Wayland

Hall of the Gargoyle King * Vilott, Rhondi

Hall of the mountain king, The * Tarr, Judith

Hall of whispers * Jefferies, Mike

Halloween II * Etchison, Dennis as JACK MARTIN

Halloween III: Season of the witch * Etchison, Dennis as JACK MARTIN

Halloween IV: a novel * Randers, Nicholas as NICHOLAS GRABOWSKY

Halloween: a novel * Richards, Curtis

Hallowe'en hauntings: stories about the most ghostly night of the year * Haining, Peter

Halloween horrors * Ryan, Alan

Halloween hunt * Laymon, Richard

Halloween party * Stine, R. L.

Hallowes' hell * Steed, Neville

Hallowing, The * Yariv, Fran Pokras

Halls of the Evolvulus, The * Barrett, G. J.

Hallucination orbit: psychology in science fiction * Asimov, Isaac & Martin H. Greenberg & Charles G. Waugh

Halo * Cook, Paul

Halo * Day, Chet

Halo * Maddox, Tom

Hambo's itch * Robens, Howard & Jack Wassermann

Hamish Hamilton book of magicians, The * Green, Roger Lancelyn

Hamish Hamilton book of other worlds, The * Green, Roger Lancelyn

Hamlet trap, The * Wilhelm, Kate

Hamlyn book of horror, The * Farson, Daniel

Hamlyn book of horror and S.F. movie lists, The * Pickard, Roy

Hammer and the horn, The * Friedman, Michael Jan

Hammer of darkness, The * Modesitt, L. E. Jr.

Hammer of Mars * Murdock, M. S.

Hammer of the sun, The * Rohan, Michael Scott

Hammered gold * Johnson, William Oscar

Hammer's Slammers * Drake, David

Hammer's Slammers: At any price * Drake, David

Hammer's Slammers: Counting the cost * Drake, David

Hammer's Slammers: Rolling hot * Drake, David

Hammer's Slammers: The warrior * Drake, David

Hammock beneath the mangoes, A: stories from Latin America * Colchie, Thomas

Hampton sisters, The: a novel * Conners, Bernard F.

Han Solo and the lost legacy: from the adventures of Luke Skywalker * Daley, Brian

Han Solo at Star's End, from the adventures of Luke Skywalker * Daley, Brian

Han Solo's revenge, from the adventures of Luke Skywalker * Daley, Brian

Hand, The * Brandel, Marc

Hand of Ganz, The: a science fiction novel * Haiblum, Isidore

Hand of Lazarus, The * Cochran, Molly & Warren Murphy

Hand of Oberon, The * Zelazny, Roger

Hand of Zei, The * de Camp, L. Sprague

Hand over the mind * Lovell, Marc

Handbook for space pioneers: a manual of the Galactic Association (Earth Branch) * Wolfe, L. Stephen & Roy L. Wysack

Handbook for visitors from outer space, A * Kramer, Kathryn

Handfasted * Spence, Catherine Helen

Handful of ghosts, A: thirteen eerie tales of Australian writers * Wilson, Barbara Ker

Handful of silver, A * Shorter, Philip

Handful of stars, A * Stabenow, Dana

Handful of time, A * Pearson, Kit

Handle with care: frightening stories * Kahn, Joan

Handmaid's tale, The * Atwood, Margaret

Hands in the dark: from the Shadow's private annals * Gibson, Walter B. as MAXWELL GRANT

Hands of glory * Kangilaski, Jaan

Hands of Lucifer * Tigges, John

Hands of Pablo Santos, The * Sharp, Allen

Hangar 18 * Sellier, Charles E. Jr. & Robert Weverka

Hangin' out with Cici * Pascal, Francine

Hanging stones, The * Wellman, Manly Wade

Hannes Bok memorial showcase of fantasy art, The * Bok, Hannes

Hannes Bok sketchbook, A * Bok, Hannes

Happening worlds of John Brunner, The: critical explorations in science fiction * De Bolt, Joe

Happiness * Zeldin, Theodore

Happiness patrol, The * Curry, Graeme

Happy cage * Lazuta, Gene as DANIEL RAVEN

Happy ending * Brown, Fredric

Happy Islands behind the winds, The * Krüss, James

Happy killers, The * Ernst, Paul as KENNETH ROBESON

Happy Moomins, The * Jansson, Tove

Happyland: a story * Wykes, Alan

Harbinger, The * Hinkemeyer, Michael T.

Harbinger, The * Paine, Lauran as TROY HOWARD

Harbor of doom * Greenfield, Irving A.

Hard on * Klepple, Horst

Hard rock * Coleman, Clay as NICHOLAS ADAMS

Hard science fiction * Slusser, George Edgar & Eric S. Rabkin

Hard sell * Anthony, Piers

Hard target * Rouch, James

Hard-boiled wonderland and the end of the world: a novel * Murakami, Haruki

Hardfought * Bear, Greg

Harding's luck * Nesbit, E.

Harditts in Sawna, The * Nichols, Robert

Hardshell * Mikol, Paul & Barker, Clive

Hardwired * Williams, Walter Jon

Hardwired angel * Dorsey, Candas & Nora Abercrombie

Hardwired: the sourcebook * Williams, Walter Jon

Hardy Boys and Nancy Drew meet Dracula, The * Larson, Glen A. & Michael Sloan

Hardy Boys ghost stories, The * Dixon, Franklin W.

Haunting of SafeKeep, The * Bunting, Eve
Haunting of Sophie Bartholomew, The * Lindsay, Elizabeth
Haunting of Suzanna Blackwell, The: a novel * Setlowe, Richard
Haunting refrain, A * Prince, Alison
Haunting stories of ghosts and ghouls * Lloyd, Noel & Geoffrey Palmer
Haunting tales * Lines, Kathleen
Haunting with Louisa: the ghost ferry * Cates, Emily
Haunting women * Ryan, Alan
Hauntings * Lofts, Norah
Hauntings: The wooden gun * Beresford, Elizabeth
Haunts, haunts, haunts * Hoke, Helen
Have a heart, Cupid Delaney * Leroe, Ellen W.
Have your own extra-terrestrial adventure * Hill, Douglas
Haven, The * Diamond, Graham
Haven of darkness * Tubb, E. C.
Havoc in Islandia * Saxton, Mark
Hawaiian U.F.O. aliens * Gilden, Mel
Hawk among the sparrows: three science fiction novellas * McLaughlin, Dean
Hawk & Fisher * Green, Simon
Hawk & Fisher: Guard against dishonor * Green, Simon
Hawk & Fisher: The god killer * Green, Simon
Hawk & Fisher: Winner takes all * Green, Simon
Hawk & Fisher: Wolf in the fold * Green, Simon
Hawk in silver, A * Gentle, Mary
Hawk of May * Bradshaw, Gillian
Hawkeye * Morris, Christopher & Jane Stump as DANIEL STRYKER
Hawkmistress! * Bradley, Marion Zimmer
Hawk's flight * Chase, Carol
Hawk's gray feather, The: a book of the Keltiad * Kennealy, Patricia
Hawks of Fellheath, The * Fisher, Paul R.
Hawks of Outremer * Howard, Robert E.
Hawksbill Station * Silverberg, Robert
Hawksmoor * Ackroyd, Peter
Hawthorne tree, The * Little, Patrick
He came from the shadows * Westwood, Chris
He could stop the world: a Doc Savage adventure * Donovan, Laurence as KENNETH ROBESON
He, she, and it * Piercy, Marge
He who shapes * Zelazny, Roger
Head of state * Watts, John
Head to toe * Orton, Joe
Headless men, The * Hathway, Alan as KENNETH ROBESON
Heads * Bear, Greg
Heads * Osborn, David
Heads to the storm * Drake, David & Sandra Miesel
Healer * Dickinson, Peter
Healer * Wilson, F. Paul
Healer's war, The * Scarborough, Elizabeth
Hear the children calling * McNally, Clare
Hear the silence: stories by women of myth, magic, & renewal * Zahava, Irene
Hearing trumpet, The * Carrington, Leonora
Hearse, The * Clement, Henry
Heart and the scarab, The * Kloepfer, Marguerite
Heart beat * Dong, Eugene & Spyros Andreopoulos
Heart of red iron * Gotlieb, Phyllis
Heart of R'Lyeh, The * Kitsch, Hieronymous
Heart of stone, and other stories * Lafferty, R. A.
Heart of the comet * Benford, Gregory & David Brin
Heart of the fire, The: a novel * Fallingstar, Cerridwen
Heart of valor * Smith, L. J.
Heart to heart: an Ashton Ford novel * Pendleton, Don

Heartbeeps: a novel * Koontz, Dean R. as JOHN HILL
Heartbreaker * Coleman, Clay as NICHOLAS ADAMS
Hearth of Ruvaig, The * Douglas, Iain
Heartland * Hagberg, David
Heartlight * Barron, T. A.
Heart's blood * Yolen, Jane
Heart's lair * Morgan, Kathleen
Hearts of stone * Hill, Roger & Glen A. Larson
Hearts of wood, and other timeless tales * Kotzwinkle, William
Heartsnatcher * Vian, Boris
Heat * Herzog, Arthur
Heat death of the universe, and other stories, The * Zoline, Pamela
Heathern * Womack, Jack
Heatseeker * Shirley, John
Heatshield * Anderson, Don
Heaven and Hell * Berbrich, Joan D.
Heaven and Hell and the Megas factor * Nathan, Robert
Heaven can wait: a novel * Fleischer, Leonore
Heaven cent * Anthony, Piers
Heaven chronicles * Vinge, Joan D.
Heaven makers, The * Herbert, Frank
Heaven Sword, The * Williams, Jeanne
Heavenly breakfast: an essay on the winter of love * Delany, Samuel R.
Heavenly horse from the outermost west, The * Stanton, Mary
Heavenly host, The * Asimov, Isaac
Heavy time * Cherryh, C. J.
Hecate's cauldron * Shwartz, Susan
Hedgework and guessery * de Lint, Charles
Heechee rendezvous: a novel * Pohl, Frederik
Hegira * Bear, Greg
Height of the scream, The * Campbell, Ramsey
Heinlein trio, A: The puppet masters; Double star; The door into space * Heinlein, Robert A.
Heir apparent, The * Rosenberg, Joel
Heir of darkness * Rahman, Glenn
Heir of Reingarth * Douglas, Carole Nelson
Heir of sea & fire * McKillip, Patricia A.
Heir to the dragon * Charrette, Robert N.
Heir to the empire * Zahn, Timothy
Heirloom, The * Masterton, Graham
Heirloom, The * Masterton, Graham as THOMAS LUKE
Heirs of Hammerfell, The * Bradley, Marion Zimmer
Heliotrope wall, and other stories, The * Matute, Ana Maria
Helix * Ryan, Desmond & Joel Shurkin
Helix and the sword, The * McLoughlin, John C.
Hell below * Robeson, Kenneth
Hell board * Reed, Dana
Hell candidate, The * Masterton, Graham
Hell candidate, The * Masterton, Graham as THOMAS LUKE
Hell hound * Greenhall, Ken
Hell in Hindu land * Rosenberger, Joseph
Hell no we won't go!: resisting the draft during the Vietnam War * Gottlieb, Sherry Gershon
Hell of mirrors, The * Haining, Peter
Hell on Earth * Naha, Ed as D. B. DRUMM
Hell ride * Hofrichter, Paul
Hell seed * Peel, Colin D.
Hell storm * Williamson, J. N.
Hellbane * Esler, Anthony
Hellborn * Brandner, Gary
Hell-bound heart, The * Barker, Clive
Hellbound heart, The * Mikol, Paul as ANONYMOUS EDITOR & George R. R. Martin
Hellbound magic * Green, Sharon

Horrors: a history of horror movies * Hutchinson, Tom & Roy Pickard

Horrors and unpleasantries: a bibliographical history & collectors' price guide to Arkham House * Jaffery, Sheldon

Horrors: from screen to scream: an encyclopedic guide to the greatest horror and fantasy films of all times * Naha, Ed

Horrors, horrors, horrors * Hoke, Helen

Horrors of Hammer * Marrero, Robert

Horrors of the haunted museum * Stine, R. L.

Horrorshows: the A-to-Z of horror in film, TV, radio, & theater * Wright, Gene

Horrorstory, volume five: The year's best horror stories XIII; The year's best horror stories XIV; The year's best horror stories XV * Wagner, Karl Edward

Horrorstory, volume four: The year's best horror stories X; The year's best horror stories XI; The Year's best horror stories XII * Wagner, Karl Edward

Horrorstory, volume three: The year's best horror stories VII; The year's best horror stories VIII; The year's best horror stories IX * Wagner, Karl Edward & Gerald W. Page

Horrorvid * Tallis, Robyn

Horse fantastic * Greenberg, Martin H. & Rosalind M. Greenberg

Horse goddess, The * Llywelyn, Morgan

Horse lord, The * Morwood, Peter

Horse of flame, The * Sherman, Josepha

Horseclans: Friends of the Horseclans II * Adams, Pamela Crippen & Robert Adams

Horseclans odyssey: a Horseclans novel * Adams, Robert

Horsegirl, The * Ash, Constance

Horselords * Cook, David

Horseman's Word, The * McHargue, Georgess

Horsemaster * Singer, Marilyn

Horses of heaven * Bradshaw, Gillian

Horses of the night * Sandman Lilius, Irmelin

Horses of the north * Adams, Robert

Horsewoman in Godsland, A * Edwards, Claudia J.

Hosea Globe and the fantastical peg-legged Chu * Beeks, Graydon

Hospital ship, The * Bax, Martin

Host, The * Emshwiller, Peter R.

Host man, The * Hamilton, Andrew

Hostage for Hinterland, A * Darnay, Arsen

Hostage: London: the diary of Julian Despard * Household, Geoffrey

Hostage of the sea * Baldry, Cherith

Hostage of Zir, The * de Camp, L. Sprague

Hostage one * Albertazzie, Ralph & David E. Fisher

Hostile takeover * Murphy, Warren & Richard Sapir

Hot blood: tales of provocative horror * Friend, Lonn & Jeff Gelb

Hot Dog Gang caper, The * Hiller, B. B. & Neil W. Hiller

Hot jazz trio, The * Kotzwinkle, William

Hot rain * Portnoy, Howard N.

Hot sleep: the Worthing chronicle * Card, Orson Scott

Hot time in Old Town * McQuay, Mike

Hot zone * Sloane, Ben

Hotel de Dream * Tennant, Emma

Hôtel Transylvania: a novel of forbidden love * Yarbro, Chelsea Quinn

Hotter blood: more tales of erotic horror * Garrett, Michael & Jeff Gelb

Houdini detective, The * Conner, Michael

Hound and the falcon, The * Tarr, Judith

Hound dog Moses and the promised land * Edmonds, Walter D.

Hound of Culain, The * Flint, Kenneth C.

Hound of Frankenstein * Tremayne, Peter

Hound of Heaven * Addington, Sarah

Hound of heaven, The * Wright, Glover

Hounds of Dracula * Johnson, Ken

Hounds of God, The * Tarr, Judith

Hounds of heaven, The * Burgess, Eric & Arthur Friggens

Hounds of the Morrigan, The * O'Shea, Pat

Hounds of Tindalos * Long, Frank Belknap

Houngan, The * Williamson, J. N.

Hour of blue, The * Froese, Robert

Hour of last things, and other stories, An * Elliott, George P.

Hour of the dragon, The * Howard, Robert E.

Hour of the gate, The * Foster, Alan Dean

Hour of the Oxrun dead, The * Grant, Charles L.

Hour of the scorpion * Costello, Matthew J.

Hour of the thin ox, The * Greenland, Colin

Hourglass crisis, The * Hoklin, Lonn

Hours after midnight, The: tales of terror and the supernatural * Le Fanu, J. Sheridan

House, The * Fritts, William

House, The * McDowell, Michael

House at Pelham Falls, The * Weathers, Brenda

House between the worlds, The * Bradley, Marion Zimmer

House haunted * Sarrantonio, Al

House in Norham Gardens, The * Lively, Penelope

House in November, The; special bonus: complete short novel, The other sky * Laumer, Keith

House in the shadows * Radford, Ken

House in the snow, The * Engh, M. J.

House next door, The * Siddons, Anne Rivers

House of another kind * Fritts, William

House of Arden, The: a story for children * Nesbit, E.

House of Caine, The * Eulo, Ken

House of cards * Cave, Peter

House of cards * Dobbs, Michael

House of Cthulhu, and other tales of the primal land: fiction, The * Lumley, Brian

House of danger * Montgomery, R. A.

House of death * Ernst, Paul as KENNETH ROBESON

House of doom, house of desire * Wagner, Sharon

House of doors, The * Lumley, Brian

House of Dracula, The * Chetwynd-Hayes, R.

House of fear * Green, Carl R. & William R. Sanford

House of fear, The: a study in comparative religions * Williamson, Chet

House of fear, The: notes from down below * Carrington, Leonora

House of Hades * Jackson, Steve

House of Hell * Jackson, Steve

House of horror, The: the complete story of Hammer Films, 2nd ed. * Adkinson, Robert V. & Allen Eyles & Nicholas Fry

House of illusions * Jensen, Ruby Jean

House of many worlds, The * Merwin, Sam Jr.

House of rats, The * Elboz, Stephen

House of Scorpio * Wallace, Patricia

House of scorpions * Sherman, Jory

House of shadows * Miller, Phyllis & Andre Norton

House of shards * Williams, Walter Jon

House of silence * Daniels, Dorothy

House of the hatchet * Bloch, Robert

House of the Lions, The * Stuart, L. T.

House of the magus, The * Shackleford, Jack D.

House of the seven gables, The * Green, Carl R. & William R. Sanford

House of the spirits, The * Allende, Isabel

I

Introductory psychology through science fiction, 2nd. ed. * Greenberg, Martin H. & Harvey A. Katz & Patricia S. Warrick

Intruder, The * Leimas, Brooke

Intruder * Thurston, Robert

Intrusion, The * Combs, David

Intrusions: strange tales * Aickman, Robert

Intuit * Clement, Hal

Inuit * Bell, M. Shayne

Invaded by Mars! * McKeag, Ernest as JACK MAXWELL

Invader * Hill, Albert Fay & David Campbell Hill

Invaders! * Dickson, Gordon R.

Invaders at ground zero * Houston, David

Invaders from Darkland * Lance, Kathryn as LYNN BEACH

Invaders from Earth; and, To worlds beyond * Silverberg, Robert

Invaders from Mars: a novel * Garton, Ray

Invaders from the centre * Stableford, Brian M.

Invaders from within * Packard, Edward

Invaders of Hark, The * Stine, R. L.

Invaders of the planet Earth * Brightfield, Richard

Invaders plan, The * Hubbard, L. Ron

Invasion * Gerrold, David

Invasion * Koontz, Dean R. as AARON WOLFE

Invasion, The * Marter, Ian

Invasion * Slade, Derek

Invasion: 2200 A.D. * Goldsmith, Howard

Invasion: Earth * Harrison, Harry

Invasion from below the Earth * Curtis, Philip

Invasion from space * Jennison, John W. as MATTHEW C. BRADFORD

Invasion of 1910, The * Le Queux, William

Invasion of the black slime, and other tales of horror * Austin, R. G.

Invasion of the blue lights * Glick, Ruth

Invasion of the body snatchers * LaValley, Al

Invasion of the Brain Sharpeners * Curtis, Philip

Invasion of the clones * Rosenberger, Joseph

Invasion of the comet people * Curtis, Philip

Invasion of the mutants * Mooser, Stephen

Invasion of the Ormazoids * Martin, Philip

Invasion of Willow Springs * Ellis, Terry

Invasion: the German invasion of England, July 1940 * Macksey, Kenneth

Invasion U.S.A. * Obstfeld, Raymond as JASON FROST

Invasions * Asimov, Isaac & Martin H. Greenberg & Charles G. Waugh

Invid invasion * Daley, Brian & James Luceno as JACK McKINNEY

Invincible Doc Savage, The * Gruskin, Ed

Invisibility factor, The * Sherman, Josepha

Invisibility island * Lance, Kathryn as LYNN BEACH

Invisible castle, The: a Thundercats thriller * Martin, Les

Invisible company, The * Sanders, Scott Russell

Invisible death * Carter, Lin

Invisible empire, The * Côté, Denis

Invisible empire, The * Dille, Flint & David Marconi

Invisible fire * Graversen, Pat

Invisible force, The * Appleton, Victor

Invisible man, The * Green, Carl R. & William R. Sanford

Invisible man, The * Jahn, Mike

Invisible man, The: notes * Stephen, Martin

Invisible rival * Algozin, Bruce

Invisible-box murders, The * Dent, Lester as KENNETH ROBESON

Invisibles, The * Dark, James

Invitation to a beheading * Nabokov, Vladimir

Invitation to Camelot: an Arthurian anthology of short stories * Godwin, Parke

Invitation to the game * Hughes, Monica

Involution ocean * Sterling, Bruce

Ion war, The * Kapp, Colin

Ionic barrier * Hughes, Dennis Talbot as VON KELLAR

I.O.U. * Peel, John as NICHOLAS ADAMS

Iowa Baseball Confederacy, The * Kinsella, W. P.

IQ 83 * Herzog, Arthur

Ira Levin * Fowler, Douglas

Ireta adventure, The: Dinosaur planet; and, Dinosaur planet survivors * McCaffrey, Anne

Iris * Barton, William & Michael Capobianco

Iris, the bewitched * Kimbro, John M. as KATHERYN KIMBROUGH

Irish ghost stories * Hone, Joseph

Irish ghost stories of Sheridan Le Fanu * Le Fanu, J. Sheridan

Irish masters of fantasy: an anthology with introduction and biographical essays * Tremayne, Peter

Irish rose * Wyatt, Patrick

Irish tales of terror * Haining, Peter

Iron and gold * Vaughan, Hilda

Iron horse * Willard, Tom as BILL DOLAN

Iron lords, The * Offutt, Andrew J.

Iron man, & other tales of the ring, The * Howard, Robert E.

Iron master * Tilley, Patrick

Iron Rain, The * Malcolm, Donald

Iron sceptre, The * White, John

Iron Skull, The * Goulart, Ron as KENNETH ROBESON

Iron Tongue * Vardeman, Robert E.

Iron wolf, and other stories, The * Adams, Richard

Ironbrand * Morressy, John

Ironcastle * Farmer, Philip José & J. H. Rosny Ainé

Ironhelm * Niles, Douglas

Irrational numbers * Effinger, George Alec

Irsud * Clayton, Jo

Is anybody there? * Lofts, Norah

Is that what people do?: short stories * Sheckley, Robert

Is there life on a plastic planet? * Ames, Mildred

Is there life on Earth? a selection of science fiction stories and poems * Moss, Peter D.

Is this the end? * Stacy, Jan as CRAIG SARGENT

Isaac Asimov * Fiedler, Jean & Jim Mele

Isaac Asimov * Greenberg, Martin H. & Joseph D. Olander

Isaac Asimov * Hassler, Donald M.

Isaac Asimov * Touponce, William F.

Isaac Asimov presents A different flesh * Turtledove, Harry

Isaac Asimov presents Agent of Byzantium * Turtledove, Harry

Isaac Asimov presents Caliban landing * Popkes, Steven

Isaac Asimov presents Sin of origin * Barnes, John

Isaac Asimov presents Station Gehenna * Weiner, Andrew

Isaac Asimov presents Tales of the occult: stories * Asimov, Isaac & Martin H. Greenberg & Charles G. Waugh

Isaac Asimov presents The best fantasy of the 19th century * Asimov, Isaac & Martin H. Greenberg & Charles G. Waugh

Isaac Asimov presents The best horror and supernatural of the 19th century * Asimov, Isaac & Martin H. Greenberg & Charles G. Waugh

Isaac Asimov presents The best science fiction firsts * Asimov, Isaac & Martin H. Greenberg & Charles G. Waugh

Ishmael: A Star Trek novel * Hambly, Barbara
Isis pedlar, The * Hughes, Monica
Iskiir * Easton, M. Coleman
Iskra incident, The * Butler, Jimmie H.
Island, The * Benchley, Peter
Island, The * Smith, Guy N.
Island, The * Wright, T. M.
Island and the ring, The * Stevenson, Laura C.
Island called Moreau, An: a novel * Aldiss, Brian W.
Island fling * Skidmore, Ian
Island forbidden to man, The * Hine, Muriel
Island in the sky * Peel, John
Island of Crimea, The: a novel * Aksyonov, Vassily
Island of Doctor Death and other stories, and other stories, The * Wolfe, Gene
Island of Dr. Moreau, The * Hoskins, Robert as MICHAEL KERR & H. G. Wells
Island of Dr. Moreau, The: novelization * Goulart, Ron as JOSEPH SILVA
Island of fear * Brightfield, Richard
Island of fear * Morris, Dave
Island of one, The * Bunting, Eve
Island of peril, The * Creasey, John
Island of shadows * Tremayne, Peter
Island of the damned * Rosenberger, Joseph
Island of the dead, The * Elder, Michael
Island of the grass king, The: the further adventures of Anatole * Willard, Nancy
Island of the Lizard King * Livingstone, Ian
Island of the walking dead * Weinberg, Larry
Island of the walking dead, The: Can you save the victim of a terrifying revenge? * Sharp, Allen
Island of the weird * Gilden, Mel
Island of time, The * Montgomery, R. A.
Island paradise * Page, Kathy
Island snatchers, The * Smith, George H.
Island through the gate, The * Swahn, Sven
Island worlds, The * Kotani, Eric & John Maddox Roberts
Islander, The * Roberts, John Maddox
Islanders, The * Townsend, John Rowe
Islandia revisited * Farmer, Richard N.
Islandian world of Austin Wright, The * Powell, Lawrence Clark
Islands * Randall, Marta
Islands in the net * Sterling, Bruce

Islands in the sky * Clarke, Arthur C. & Suzan Davies
Islands of terror * Austin, R. G.
Islands out of time: a memoir of the last days of Atlantis: a metafiction * Thompson, William Irwin
Isle of destiny: a novel of ancient Ireland * Flint, Kenneth C.
Isle of glass, The * Tarr, Judith
Isle of illusion * Anderson, Betty
Isle of illusion * Simon, Madeleine
Isle of the shapeshifters * Coontz, Otto
Isle of view * Anthony, Piers
Isles of the blest, The * Llywelyn, Morgan
Israfel: the life and times of Edgar Allen Poe * Allen, Hervey
Issel: warrior king * Farrell, Simon & Jon Sutherland
Istu awakened * Milán, Victor & Robert Vardeman
IT * Aulich, Chris
It * Hawkey, Raymond
It * King, Stephen
IT * Mayne, William
It came from outer space * May, Julian as IAN THORNE
It came from Schenectady * Longyear, Barry B.
It lives again * Dixon, James
It looks alive to me! * Baum, Thomas
It's a bird—it's a plane—no, it's the television adventures of Superman * Van Hise, James
It's about time * Payne, Bernal C. Jr.
It's about time: a witches' brew of comedy, tragedy, and ghosts * Cooper, Margaret C.
It's alive! * Woodley, Richard
It's alive! the classic cinema saga of Frankenstein * Mank, Gregory W.
It's been fun * Friesner, Esther M.
It's down the slippery cellar stairs: non-fiction * Lafferty, R. A.
It's loose * Battin, B. W. as WARNER LEE
It's raining corpses in Chinatown * Hutchison, Don
It's time: a nuclear novel * Bluejay
Italo Calvino: metamorphoses of fantasy * Carter, Albert Howard III
Ivan Efremov's theory of Soviet science fiction * Grebens, G. V.
Ivanhoe gambit, The * Hawke, Simon
Ivory: a legend of past and future * Resnick, Mike
Ivory lyre, The * Murphy, Shirley Rousseau

J

J. G. Ballard * Brigg, Peter
J. G. Ballard: a primary and secondary bibliography * Pringle, David
J. G. Ballard: the first twenty years * Goddard, James & David Pringle
J. R. R. Tolkien * Crabbe, Katharyn W.
J. R. R. Tolkien * Rogers, Deborah Webster & Ivor A. Rogers
J. R. R. Tolkien: a biography * Carpenter, Humphrey
J. R. R. Tolkien: a critical biography * Rogers, Ivor A. & Deborah Webster Rogers
J. R. R. Tolkien: architect of Middle Earth: a biography * Grotta-Kurska, Daniel
J. R. R. Tolkien: Lord of the Rings: notes * Ridden, Geoffrey M.
J. R. R. Tolkien: myth, morality, and religion * Purtill, Richard
J. R. R. Tolkien, scholar and storyteller: essays in memoriam * Farrell, Robert T. & Mary Salvaggio
J. R. R. Tolkien: six decades of criticism * Johnson, Judith A.
J. R. R. Tolkien: the shores of Middle-Earth * Giddings, Robert & Elizabeth Holland
J. R. R. Tolkien: this far land * Giddings, Robert
J. R. R. Tolkien's Hobbit and Lord of the Rings * Pienciak, Anne
J. R. R. Tolkien's The fellowship of the Ring * Morrison, Louise D.
J. R. R. Tolkien's The lord of the rings: a fantasy film * Ackerman, Forrest J
J. T. McIntosh: memoir & bibliography * Covell, Ian
Jabberwocky * Hoover, Ralph
Jack Anderson presents The young astronauts * Lewitt, S. N. as RICK NORTH
Jack: C. S. Lewis and his times * Sayer, George
Jack (John Stewart) Williamson, child and father of wonder * Benson, Gordon Jr.
Jack London * Beauchamp, Gorman
Jack of Swords * Tubb, E. C.
Jack, the giant-killer * de Lint, Charles
Jack the knife * Parry, Michel
Jack the Ripper * Casper, Susan & Gardner Dozois
Jack Vance * Miller, Chuck & Tim Underwood
Jack Vance, a fantasmic imagination: a working bibliography, 2nd rev. ed. * Benson, Gordon Jr. & Phil Stephensen-Payne
Jack Vance: science fiction stylist * Tiedman, Richard
Jack Williamson: a primary and secondary bibliography * Myers, Robert E.
Jackaroo * Voigt, Cynthia
Jackbird: tales of illusion & identity * Boston, Bruce
Jack-in-the-box * Johnstone, William W.
Jack-in-the-Box Planet * Hoskins, Robert
Jacob Atabet: a speculative fiction * Murphy, Michael
Jade Darcy and the affair of honor * Goldin, Stephen & Mary Mason
Jade Darcy and the zen pirates * Goldin, Stephen & Mary Mason
Jade Demons quartet, The * Vardeman, Robert E.

Jade dragon; &, House of ghosts * Gibson, Walter B.
Jade enchantress, The * Price, E. Hoffmann
Jade unicorn, The * Halpern, Jay
Jade warrior, The * Stokes, Manning Lee as JEFFREY LORD
Jagged Steele * Hawke, Simon as J. D. MASTERS
Jagger, the dog from elsewhere * Key, Alexander
Jago * Newman, Kim
Jaguar * Ransom, Bill
Jaguar! * Simon, Morris
Jaguar hunter, The * Shepard, Lucius
Jaiyavara: a novel * Glaze, Eleanor
Jamais vu papers, The; or, Misadventures in the worlds of science, myth, and magic * Coleman, Wim & Pat Perrin
James Bond and Moonraker * Wood, Christopher
James Bond in Barracuda run * Otfinoski, Steven
James Bond in Programmed for danger * Favors, Jean M.
James Bond in Strike it dead * Siegel, Barbara & Scott Siegel
James Bond in Win, place or die * Stine, R. L.
James Branch Cabell * Davis, Joe Lee
James Branch Cabell * Van Doren, Carl
James Branch Cabell: a bibliography of his writings, biography, and criticism * Brewer, Frances Joan
James Branch Cabell: a complete bibliography * Hall, James N.
James Branch Cabell: a complete bibliography, with a supplement of current values of Cabell books by Nelson Bond * Bond, Nelson & James N. Hall
James Branch Cabell: centennial essays * Inge, M. Thomas & Edgar E. MacDonald
James Branch Cabell: the dream and the reality * Tarrant, Desmond
James Gunn checklist, A * Drumm, Chris
James Herbert: by horror haunted * Jones, Stephen
James Joyce and associated image makers * Kronegger, Maria Elisabeth
James P. Hogan's Entoverse * Hogan, James P.
James P. Hogan's The giants novels * Hogan, James P.
James Stephens: his work and an account of his life * Pyle, Hilary
James Tiptree, Jr. * Siegel, Mark
James Tiptree Jr., a lady of letters: a working bibliography * Benson, Gordon Jr. & Phil Stephensen-Payne
James White, doctor to aliens: a working bibliography * Benson, Gordon Jr.
Jamie the Red * Dickson, Gordon R. & Roland Green
Jandrax * Logsdon, Syd
Jane, the courageous * Kimbro, John M. as KATHERYN KIMBROUGH
Janet's sex planet * Vardeman, Robert E. & Geo. W. Proctor as CARRIE ONN
Janine * Gray, Alasdair
Janissaries * Pournelle, Jerry
Janissaries: Clan and crown * Green, Roland & Jerry Pournelle
January platoon, The * Randle, Kevin

Janus syndrome, The * McDonald, Steven E.
Japan: how do hands make peace! * Meyer, Carolyn
Japan sinks * Komatsu, Sakyô
Japan tomorrow * Watson, Ian
Japanese science fiction: a view of a changing society *
   Matthew, Robert
Jason and the aliens down the street * Ruddick, Bob &
   Gery Greer
Jason and the Argonauts * Evslin, Bernard
Jason and the astronauts * Klyne, Karl
Jason Cosmo * McGirt, Dan
Jason lives: Friday the 13th, part VI: a novel * Hawke,
   Simon
Jason's first quest * Moore, Roger E.
Java Jack * Keele, Luqman & Daniel M. Pinkwater
Jaws of Menx, The * Maxwell, Ann
Jaws that bite, the claws that catch, The * Coney,
   Michael
Jay-Jay and the Peking monster * Evarts, Hal G. Jr.
Jay's journal * Sparks, Beatrice
Jean Lorrah's Sarek collection * Lorrah, Jean
*Jeannie Jemima Jones: the adventures of a runaway girl
   on a desert island* * Blunderland Cartoonist, The
Jedera adventure, The * Alexander, Lloyd
*Jedi master's quizbook, The: 425 cosmic questions & an-
   swers about Star Wars and The Empire strikes back* *
   Miller, Rusty
Jefferson's war: Death of a regiment * Randle, Kevin
Jefferson's war: The galactic silver star * Randle, Kevin
Jefferson's war: The January platoon * Randle, Kevin
Jefferson's war: The lost colony * Randle, Kevin
Jefferson's war: The price of command * Randle, Kevin
Jehad * Hawke, Simon as NICHOLAS YERMAKOV
Jehovah contract, The * Koman, Victor
Jekyll legacy, The * Bloch, Robert & Andre Norton
JEM * Pohl, Frederik
Jenny * Blumenfeld, Yorick
Jenny Ewing: my diary * Blumenfeld, Yorick as ANONY-
   MOUS AUTHOR
Jeremy Case * DeWeese, Gene
Jeremy Thatcher, dragon hatcher: a magic shop book *
   Coville, Bruce
Jeremy Visick * Wiseman, David
Jericho 52 * Caidin, Martin
Jericho Falls * Hyde, Christopher
Jerks-in-training * Stine, R. L.
Jernigan's egg * Mueller, Richard
Jerusalem fire * Meluch, R. M.
Jerusalem man, The * Gemmell, David A.
Jerzy Kosinski * Lavers, Norman
Jerzy Kosinski: the literature of violation * Everman,
   Welch D.
Jesting Moses: a study in Cabellian comedy * Wells,
   Arvin R.
Jesus incident, The * Herbert, Frank & Bill Ransom
Jesus on Mars * Farmer, Philip José
Jet Smoke and the dragon fire * Ashton, Charles
Jewel of Bas, The * Brackett, Leigh
Jewel of life, The * Kirwan-Vogel, Anna
Jewel of Tharn * Stokes, Manning Lee as JEFFREY LORD
Jewel of the moon * Kotzwinkle, William
*Jewel-hinged jaw, The: notes on the language of science
   fiction* * Delany, Samuel R.
Jewels in the dark * Hallock, Rusty
Jewels of Elvish, The * Berberick, Nancy Varian
Jewels of Gwahlur * Howard, Robert E.
Jewels of the dragon * Wold, Allen
Jewels of wonder: an anthology of heroic fantasies *
   Ashley, Mike
Jhereg * Brust, Steven

Jilly's ghost * Regan, Dian Curtis
Jim Burns portfolio, The * Burns, Jim
Jim Button and Luke the engine driver * Ende, Michael
Jim Henson's The storyteller * Minghella, Anthony
Jinian Footseer * Tepper, Sheri S.
Jinian Star-eye * Tepper, Sheri S.
Jinx High * Lackey, Mercedes
Jinx on a Terran inheritance * Daley, Brian
Jirel of Joiry * Moore, C. L.
Jitterbug * McQuay, Mike
Jitterbug perfume * Robbins, Tom
Jiu San * Dent, Lester as KENNETH ROBESON
Joan D. Vinge omnibus * Vinge, Joan D.
Joanne, the unpredictable * Kimbro, John M. as KATH-
   ERYN KIMBROUGH
Joan-of-Arc replay, The * Barbet, Pierre
Job: a comedy of justice * Heinlein, Robert A.
Job, The: interviews with William S. Burroughs * Bur-
   roughs, William S. & Daniel Odier
Joe Bob goes back to the drive-in * Briggs, Joe Bob
Joe Bob goes to the drive-in * Briggs, Joe Bob
Joe Gosh * De Haven, Tom
Joe Haldeman * Gordon, Joan
Joe Mauser, mercenary from tomorrow * Banks, Michael
   A. & Mack Reynolds
John Barth's Giles goat-boy: a study * Robinson, Dou-
   glas
John Brunner: a working bibliography * Benson, Gordon
   Jr.
*John Brunner, shockwave writer: a working bibliography,
   3rd ed.* * Benson, Gordon Jr. & Phil Stephensen-
   Payne
John Christopher: The death of grass * Handley, Graham
John Collier * Richardson, Betty
*John Collier and Fredric Brown went quarrelling through
   my head: stories* * Salmonson, Jessica Amanda
John Collier reader, The * Collier, John
John Dollar * Wiggins, Marianne
John L. Byrne's Fear book * Byrne, John L.
John Midas in the dreamtimes * Catling, Patrick Skene
John Schoenherr SF checklist, A * Boyajian, Jerry &
   David Stever
John Sladek checklist, A: Pre-publication version *
   Drumm, Chris
John the balladeer * Wellman, Manly Wade
John W. Campbell awards, volume 5, The * Martin,
   George R. R.
John W. Campbell letters, volume 1, The * Campbell,
   John W.
*John Wyndham, creator of the cosy catastrophe: a work-
   ing bibliography, 2nd rev. ed.* * Stephensen-Payne,
   Phil
*John Wyndham Parkes Lucas Beynon Harris: a bibliog-
   raphy* * Stephensen-Payne, Phil & Gordon Benson Jr.
Johnny Transplant: a novel * Ault, O. E.
Johnny Zed * Betancourt, John Gregory
Joining of the stone, The * Murphy, Shirley Rousseau
Jokers wild: a Wild cards mosaic novel * Martin, George
   R. R.
Jokertown shuffle: a Wild Cards mosaic novel * Martin,
   George R. R. & Melinda M. Snodgrass
Jon Pertwee book of monsters, The * Davis, Richard
Jonah, The * Herbert, James
Jonah kit, The * Watson, Ian
*Jonah watch, The: a true-life ghost story in the form of a
   novel* * Cady, Jack
Jonas McFee, A.T.P. * Sargent, Sarah
Jonny Quest files, The * Van Hise, James
Jonuta rising! * Offutt, Andrew J. & Victor Koman as
   JOHN CLEVE

K

K9 and company * Dudley, Terence
K-9 Corps * Von Gunden, Kenneth
K-9 Corps: Under fire * Von Gunden, Kenneth
Kachina * Ptacek, Kathryn
Kaduna memories * Daley, Brian & James Luceno as
     JACK MCKINNEY
Kaeti & company * Roberts, Keith
Kaeti's apocalypse * Roberts, Keith
Kaheesh * Sohl, Jerry as NATHAN BUTLER
Kairos * Jones, Gwyneth
Kajira of Gor * Norman, John
Kak-Abdullah conspiracy, The * Tuleja, Thaddeus as
     MARSHALL MACAO
Kala * Luard, Nicholas
Kaleidoscope * Turtledove, Harry
Kalevide, The * Goble, Lou
Kaliban's Christmas: a special tale of magic * Lewis,
     Mark
Kalif's war, The * Dalmas, John
Kalimantan * Shepard, Lucius
Kalispell run, The * Robbins, David
Kalki: a novel * Vidal, Gore
Kamikaze legacy, The * Ahern, Jerry & Sharon Ahern
Kampus: a novel * Gunn, James
Kamus of Kadizhar: The black hole of Carcosa: a tale of
     the Darkworld detective * Shirley, John
Kane * Borton, Douglas
Kane's odyssey * Bickham, Jack M. as JEFF CLINTON
Karan * Wongar, B.
Karate killers, The * Streib, Dan
Kar-Chee reign, The; Rogue dragon * Davidson, Avram
Karl Edward Wagner presents The year's best horror sto-
     ries XV * Wagner, Karl Edward
Karl Edward Wagner presents The year's best horror sto-
     ries XVI * Wagner, Karl Edward
Karl Edward Wagner presents The year's best horror sto-
     ries XVII * Wagner, Karl Edward
Karloff * Barbour, Alan G. & James Robert Parish &
     Alvin H. Marill
Karloff and Lugosi: the story of a haunting collaboration,
     with a complete filmography of their films together *
     Mank, Gregory
Karloff: the life of Boris Karloff * Underwood, Peter
Karma: a novel of retribution and transcendence * Dar-
     nay, Arsen
Karma affair, The * Darnay, Arsen
Karma Corps, The * Barrett, Neal Jr.
Karma machine, The * Davidson, Michael
Kashka * McKenzie, Ellen Kindt
Kate Crackernuts * Briggs, K. M.
Kate, the curious * Kimbro, John M. as KATHERYN KIM-
     BROUGH
Kate's house: a novel * Waugh, Harriet
Katherine, the returned * Kimbro, John M. as KATHERYN
     KIMBROUGH
Kayo: the authentic and annotated autobiographical novel
     from outer space * McConkey, James
Kaz, the minotaur * Knaak, Richard A.

Kecksies, and other twilight tales * Campbell, Margaret
     as MARJORIE BOWEN
Kedrigern and the charming couple * Morressy, John
Kedrigern in Wanderland * Morressy, John
Keep, The * Wilson, F. Paul
Keep of the ancient king * Carr, Mike
Keep of the Lich-Lord * Jackson, Steve
Keep the giraffe burning * Sladek, John
Keep watching the skies!: American science fiction movies
     of the fifties, volume 1, 1950-1957 * Thomas, Bill &
     Bill Warren
Keep watching the skies!: American science fiction movies
     of the fifties, volume II, 1958-1962 * Thomas, Bill &
     Bill Warren
Keeper * Holly, Joan Hunter
Keeper of the children * Hallahan, William H.
Keeper of the city * Duane, Diane & Peter Morwood
Keeper of the Isis Light, The * Hughes, Monica
Keeper of the keys * Wurts, Janny
Keepers of Edanvant * Douglas, Carole Nelson
Keepers of the beast * MacLane, Jack
Keepers of the gate * Spruill, Steven G.
Keepers of the peace * Brooke, Keith
Keepers of the secrets * Farmer, Philip Jose
Keeper's price, and other stories, The * Bradley, Marion
     Zimmer & the Friends of Darkover
Keeping time * Bear, David
Keeping time * Rodowsky, Colby
Keeping up with science fiction * Rabig, Tony
Keeping-room, The * Levin, Betty
Keepsake, The * Huson, Paul
Keith Laumer, ambassador to space: a working bibliog-
     raphy, 2nd rev. ed. * Benson, Gordon Jr. & Phil
     Stephensen-Payne
Keith Roberts * Kincaid, Paul
Kellory the warlock * Carter, Lin
Kelly country * Chandler, A. Bertram
Kelpie, The * Mayne, William
Kender, gully dwarves, and gnomes * Hickman, Tracy &
     Margaret Weis
Kendermore * Kirchoff, Mary L.
Kennaquhair * Hooker, Ruth
Kennedy masquerade compendium, rev. and expanded
     ed., The * Kennedy, Peggy & Marty Gear
Kensho * Schmidt, Dennis
Kent Montana and the once and future thing * Grant,
     Charles L. as LIONEL FENN
Kent Montana and the really ugly thing from Mars *
     Grant, Charles L. as LIONEL FENN
Kent Montana and the reasonably invisible man * Grant,
     Charles L. as LIONEL FENN
Kesrick * Carter, Lin
Kesrith * Cherryh, C. J.
Kessler alliance, The * Horstman, Thomas
Kestrel, The * Alexander, Lloyd
Kevin Browne's Nightales: stories * Tigges, John
Key for the nonesuch, A * Gravel, Geary
Key of ice and steel * Vardeman, Robert E. as DANIEL
     MORAN

Key to Fredric Brown's wonderland, A: a study and an annotated bibliographical checklist * Baird, Newton D.

Key to Midnight, The * Koontz, Dean R.

Key to Midnight, The * Koontz, Dean R. as LEIGH NICHOLS

Key West, 2720 A.D. * Eakins, William

Keys to paradise, The * Vardeman, Robert E. as DANIEL MORAN

Khai of ancient Khem * Lumley, Brian

Khalindaine * Burns, Richard

Khan's persuasion, The * Felice, Cynthia

Kharé—cityport of traps * Jackson, Steve

Khi to freedom * Mayhar, Ardath

Khyber connection, The * Hawke, Simon

Khyren * Kaplan, Aline Boucher

Kid from Ozone Park, & other stories, The * Wilson, Richard

Kidnap in space * Evans, Chris as NATHAN ELLIOTT

Kidnapped! * Packard, Edward

Kidnapped into space * Pearce, Brenda

Kidnapper, The * Bloch, Robert

K.I.D.S. * Hoyle, Trevor

Kiev footprint * Posey, Carl A.

Kif strike back, The * Cherryh, C. J.

Kill, The * Ryan, Alan

Kill deadline * Sugar, Andrew

Kill ratio * Drake, David & Janet Morris

Kill riff, The * Schow, David J.

Kill the dead * Lee, Tanith

Kill the editor * Robinson, Spider

Killashandra * McCaffrey, Anne

Killbird * Hughes, Zach

Killer * Drake, David & Karl Edward Wagner

Killer angel * Masters, Doug

Killer chromosomes * Murphy, Warren & Richard Sapir

Killer comet: a Scott Saunders space adventure * Moore, Patrick

Killer crabs * Smith, Guy N.

Killer flies * Kendall, Mark

Killer mice, The * Reed, Kit

Killer planet * Shaw, Bob

Killer plants of Binaark * Green, Roland as JEFFREY LORD

Killer robot * McEvoy, Seth

Killer satellites * Kirk, Philip

Killer spores * Woodley, Richard

Killer station * Caidin, Martin

Killer Steele * Hawke, Simon as J. D. MASTERS

Killer virus * Kirk, Philip

Killerbowl * Wolf, Gary K.

Killers from hyperspace * Voltz, William

Killer's keep * Rainey, Rich as JASON FROST

Killing blow, The * La Plante, Richard

Killing bone, The * Baker, W. Howard as PETER SAXON

Killing eyes * Miglis, John

Killing gift, The: a novel * Wood, Bari

Killing glance, The * Finlay, D. G.

Killing ground * Rouch, James

Killing of Idi Amin, The * Watkins, Leslie

Killing of the saints, The * Abella, Alex

Killing time * Murphy, Warren

Killing time * Van Hise, Della

Killing time * Windsor, Patricia

Killing touch, The * Braun, Matthew as WARREN BURKE

Killing wedge, The * Ahern, Jerry

Kilroy and the gull * Benchley, Nathaniel

Kin dread * Janeshutz, Trish as T. J. MACGREGOR

Kin of Ata are waiting for you, The * Bryant, Dorothy

Kinda * Dicks, Terrance

Kindly ones, The * Scott, Melissa

Kindred * Butler, Octavia E.

Kindred spirits * Anthony, Mark & Ellen Porath

Kindred spirits * Brennert, Alan

Kindred spirits * Patrick, DeAnn

Kindred spirits: an anthology of gay and lesbian science fiction stories * Elliot, Jeffrey M.

Kine * Lloyd, A. R.

King, The * Barthelme, Donald

King and joker * Dickinson, Peter

King Arthur's daughter * Chapman, Vera

King awakes, The * Elliott, Janice

King beyond the gate, The * Gemmell, David A.

King Charles & Mr. Perkins * Wratislaw, A. C.

King Chondos' ride * Zimmer, Paul Edwin

King creature, come * Townsend, John Rowe

King David's spaceship * Pournelle, Jerry

King Death * Cohn, Nik

King Death's garden * Jones, Gwyneth as ANN HALAM

King Dragon * Offutt, Andrew J.

King is dead, The * Thynn, Alexander

King Joe Cay * Dent, Lester as KENNETH ROBESON

King Kobold * Stasheff, Christopher

King Kobold revived * Stasheff, Christopher

King Kong * May, Julian as IAN THORNE

King Kong story, The * Pascall, Jeremy

King Ludd * Sinclair, Andrew

King maker, The * Dent, Lester & Harold A. Davis as KENNETH ROBESON

King of dreams and shadows, A * Salik

King of Eolim, The * Jones, Raymond F.

King of hell, The * Pereira, W. D.

King of light and shadows, The * Cole, Adrian

King of morning, queen of day * McDonald, Ian

King of Satan's eyes, The * Grant, Charles L. as GEOFFREY MARSH

King of shadows, The * Caldecott, Moyra

King of terror, The * Robeson, Kenneth

King of terrors, The: tales of madness and death * Bloch, Robert

King of the cloud forests * Morpurgo, Michael

King of the Copper Mountains, The * Biegel, Paul

King of the dead * MacAvoy, R. A.

King of the fields, The * Singer, Isaac Bashevis

King of the hill, The * McAuley, Paul J.

King of the Murgos * Eddings, David

King of the scepter'd isle * Coney, Michael

King of the sea * Bickerton, Derek

King of the slavers * Offutt, Andrew J. as JOHN CLEVE

King of the stars * Kelley, Leo P.

King of the vagabonds * Dann, Colin

King of the wood * Roberts, John Maddox

King of Ys, The * Anderson, Karen & Poul Anderson

King of Ys, The: Roma mater * Anderson, Karen & Poul Anderson

King of Ys, The, volume 2 * Anderson, Karen & Poul Anderson

King of Zunga * Green, Roland as JEFFREY LORD

King Solomon's children: some parodies of H. Rider Haggard * Menville, Douglas & R. Reginald

King Solomon's mines; She; Allan Quatermain * Haggard, H. Rider

King takes a dare, The; Daredevil vs. kingpin * Ward, James M.

King who knew not fear, The: a tale of other days * R., O.

King Windom * Farris, John

Kingdom come * Shirley, John as D. B. DRUMM

Kingdom of fear: the world of Stephen King * Miller, Chuck & Tim Underwood

L

L. P. Hartley * Bloomfield, Paul
L. P. Hartley, rev. ed. * Bloomfield, Paul
L. Ron Hubbard: messiah or madman? * Corydon, Bent
   & L. Ron Hubbard Jr.
L. Ron Hubbard presents Writers of the future * Budrys,
   Algis
L. Ron Hubbard presents Writers of the future, volume II
   * Budrys, Algis
L. Ron Hubbard presents Writers of the future, volume
   III: (14 great new tales from the Writers of the Future
   International Talent Search) * Budrys, Algis
L. Ron Hubbard presents Writers of the future, volume
   IV: (16 new top-rated tales from his Writers of the
   Future International Talent Search) * Budrys, Algis
L. Ron Hubbard presents Writers of the future, volume V:
   the year's 14 best tales from his Writers of the Future
   International Writing-Talent Program * Budrys, Algis
L. Ron Hubbard presents Writers of the future, volume
   VI: (the year's 18 best tales from his Writers of the
   Future International Writing Program * Budrys, Algis
L. Ron Hubbard presents Writers of the future, volume
   VII: the year's 18 best tales from his Writers of the
   Future International Writing Program * Budrys, Algis
L.A. strike * Robbins, David
Labyrinth, The * Holdstock, Robert as ROBERT FAULCON
Labyrinth * Schmidt, Dennis
Labyrinth: a novel * Smith, A. C. H.
Labyrinth: a storybook * Gikow, Louise
Labyrinth gate, The * Rasmussen, Alis A.
Labyrinth of dreams, The * Chalker, Jack L.
Labyrinth of lies * Berry, Adrian
Labyrinth of worlds * Cole, Adrian
Labyrinth: the photo album * Grand, Rebecca
Labyrinths of fear, The * Morris, Dave
Lacey and his friends * Drake, David
Ladies from Hell * Roberts, Keith
Ladies in waiting * Walters, R. R.
Ladies of fantasy: two centuries of sinister stories by the
   gentle sex * Lewis, Gogo & Seon Manley
Ladies of Mandrigyn, The * Hambly, Barbara
Ladies of Missalonghi, The * McCullough, Colleen
Ladies of the gothics: tales of romance and terror by the
   gentle sex * Lewis, Gogo & Seon Manley
Lady and the merman, The: a tale * Yolen, Jane
Lady and the tramp * Moffatt, Derry
Lady blade, lord fighter * Green, Sharon
Lady Ermyntrude and the plumber: a love story of
   MCMXX * Fendall, Percy
Lady of darkness * Paxson, Diana L.
Lady of Han-Gilden, The * Tarr, Judith
Lady of Hay * Erskine, Barbara
Lady of light * Paxson, Diana L.
Lady of light, lady of darkness * Paxson, Diana L.
Lady of the bees * Swann, Thomas Burnett
Lady of the fountain, The * Herbert, Kathleen
Lady of the Haven: adventures of the Empire princess *
   Diamond, Graham
Lady of the Snowmist, The * Offutt, Andrew J.
Lady of the winds * Novak, Kate

Lady Penelope: The Albanian affair * Jennison, John as
   JOHN THEYDON
Lady with the X-ray eyes, The * Minkov, Svetoslav
Ladygrove: the third adventure of Dr Caspian and Bron-
   wen * Burke, John
Ladyhawke * Vinge, Joan D.
Lafferty in orbit * Lafferty, R. A.
Lagoon * Drake, Alison
Lagrange Five * Reynolds, Mack
Lagrangists, The * Reynolds, Mack
Laid in the future * Fox, Gardner F. as ROD GRAY
Lair * Herbert, James
Lair of ancient dreams, The * Andersson, C. Dean &
   Nina Romberg as ASA DRAKE
Lair of the Lich * Algozin, Bruce
Lake, The * Cooke, John Peyton
Lake, The * Jensen, Ruby Jean
Lake at the end of the world, The * MacDonald, Caroline
Lake Fear * McMahan, Ian
Lake of fire, The * Bailey, Robin W.
Lake of life, The * Weinberg, Robert
Lake of the sun * Whiteford, Wynne
Lamarchos * Clayton, Jo
Lamia * Gardine, Michael
Lammas night * Kurtz, Katherine
Lamp from the warlock's tomb, The * Bellairs, John
Lampfish of Twill, The * Lisle, Janet Taylor
Lanark: a life in four books * Gray, Alasdair
Lancelot: a novel * Vansittart, Peter
Lances of Nengesdul * Taylor, Keith
Land, The * Vigliante, Mary
Land beyond, The * Alderman, Gil
Land beyond, The * Corlett, William
Land beyond the gate, The * Eshbach, Lloyd Arthur
Land beyond the north, The * Green, Roger Lancelyn
Land of always-night: a Doc Savage adventure * Dent,
   Lester and Ryerson Johnson as KENNETH ROBESON
Land of dreams * Blaylock, James P.
Land of dreams, The: a review of the work of Sidney H.
   Sime * Locke, George
Land of eternal fire, The * Newark, T. P.
Land of fear: a Doc Savage adventure * Dent, Lester &
   Harold A. Davis as KENNETH ROBESON
Land of Froud, The * Froud, Brian
Land of Laughs, The * Carroll, Jonathan
Land of long juju: a Doc Savage adventure * Donovan,
   Laurence as KENNETH ROBESON
Land of Narnia, The: Brian Sibley explores the world of
   C. S. Lewis * Sibley, Brian
Land of precious snow * Tuleja, Thaddeus V.
Land of terror, The: Doc Savage and his pals in a novel
   of unusual adventure * Dent, Lester as KENNETH
   ROBESON
Land of the Nunch, The * Kirk, Douglas
Land of the possible, The: a report of the first visit to
   Prire * White, Mary Alice
Land of tomorrow, The * Maile, Ben
Land where the serpents rule * Lee, S.
Landing, The: a night of birds * Scholes, Katherine

Little professor, intuitionist, The: a transactional analysis of Isaac Asimov's The gods themselves * Hull, Elizabeth Anne

Little shop of horrors * Egan, Robert & Louise Egan

Little shop of horrors book, The * McCarty, John & Mark Thomas McGee

Little tours of Hell * Saxton, Josephine

Little vampire, The * Sommer-Bodenburg, Angela

Little vampire goes on holiday, The * Sommer-Bodenburg, Angela

Little vampire in danger, The * Sommer-Bodenburg, Angela

Little vampire in love, The * Sommer-Bodenburg, Angela

Little vampire in the vale of doom, The * Sommer-Bodenburg, Angela

Little vampire moves in, The * Sommer-Bodenburg, Angela

Little vampire on the farm, The * Sommer-Bodenburg, Angela

Little vampire takes a trip, The * Sommer-Bodenburg, Angela

Little wax doll, The * Lofts, Norah

Little Wilson and big God * Burgess, Anthony

Live from Earth * Olsen, Lance

Live girls * Garton, Ray

Lively lives of Crispin Mobey, The * Quyth, Gabriel

Lives and times of Jerry Cornelius, The * Moorcock, Michael

Lives of Christopher Chant, The * Jones, Diana Wynne

Lives of the twins * Smith, Rosamund

Living & the dead, The * Rowlands, D. G.

Living and the undead, The: from Stoker's Dracula to Romero's Dawn of the dead * Waller, Gregory A.

Living dark, The * Gresham, Stephen

Living dead, The * Goddin, Jeffrey

Living dead, The: a study of the vampire in romantic literature * Twitchell, James B.

Living death * Messmann, Jon as NICK CARTER

Living end, The * Elkin, Stanley

Living fire, and other S.F. stories * Fisk, Nicholas

Living fire menace: a Doc Savage adventure * Davis, Harold A. as KENNETH ROBESON

Living hell * Meyers, Richard S.

Living in ether: a novel * Geary, Patricia

Living in fear: a history of horror in the mass media * Daniels, Les

Living legend, The * Larson, Glen A. & Simon Hawke as NICHOLAS YERMAKOV

Living One, The * Hawkins, Jim

Living soul, A * Jersild, P. C.

Living stone, The * Roland, Howell Jr.

Living things * Russo, John

Living with the lama * Lobsang Rampa, T.

Living with the reptiles * DiSilvestro, Roger L.

Lizard music * Pinkwater, Daniel M.

Lizard war, The * Dalmas, John

Lizards of Trianada, The * Casciani, Patricia Nada

Lizard's tail, The * Brandel, Marc

Lizzie Borden * Engstrom, Elizabeth

Lloyd Alexander, Evangeline Walton Ensley, Kenneth Morris: a primary and secondary bibliography * Boyer, Robert H. & Kenneth J. Zahorski

Loch, The * Caird, Janet

Loch Ness conspiracy * Bateman, John

Locked in time * Duncan, Lois

Locos: a comedy of gestures * Alfau, Felipe

Locus, the newspaper of the science fiction field, numbers 1-103, 1968-1971 * Brown, Charles N.

Locus, the newspaper of the science fiction field, numbers 104-207, 1972-1977 * Brown, Charles N.

Locusts * Smith, Guy N.

Lodestar * Horn, Phyllis

Lodestar project, The * Bradley, David

Lodestone, The * Harbinson, W. A.

Logan: a trilogy * Johnson, George Clayton & William F. Nolan

Logan's search * Nolan, William F.

Logan's world * Nolan, William F.

Logic of fantasy, The: H. G. Wells and science fiction * Huntington, John

Logopolis * Bidmead, Christopher H.

Lon of 1000 faces * Ackerman, Forrest J

London fields * Amis, Martin

Lone sentinel, The * Dereske, Jo

Lone star universe: the first anthology of Texas science fiction authors * Proctor, Geo. W. & Steven Utley

Lone Wolf adventures, The * Chalk, Gary & Joe Dever

Lonely muse, The: a critical biography of Mary Wollstonecraft Shelley * Neumann, Bonnie Rayford

Lonely vigils * Wellman, Manly Wade

Long after midnight * Bradbury, Ray

Long ARM of Gil Hamilton, The * Niven, Larry

Long dark night of the soul * Marvin, Susan

Long dark tea-time of the soul, The * Adams, Douglas

Long forgetting, The * Byers, Edward A.

Long habit of living, The * Haldeman, Joe

Long mynd, The * Hughes, Edward P.

Long night, The * Anderson, Poul

Long night dance * James, Betsy

Long night of the grave, The * Grant, Charles L.

Long orbit, The * Farren, Mick

Long patrol, The: novel * Goulart, Ron & Glen A. Larson

Long run, The: a tale of the continuing time * Moran, Daniel Keys

Long shot for Rosinante * Gilliland, Alexis A.

Long sleep, The * Koontz, Dean R. as JOHN HILL

Long trip to teatime, A * Burgess, Anthony

Long view, The * Busby, F. M.

Long voyage back * Rhinehart, Luke

Long walk, The * King, Stephen as RICHARD BACHMAN

Long walk to Wimbledon, A * Keating, H. R. F.

Long way home, The * Anderson, Poul

Longborn the inexhaustible * Cole, Adrian

Longest night, The * Williamson, J. N.

Longest voyage, The * Anderson, Poul

Longhorn territory * Newman, Marc

Longing for a form, The: essays on the fiction of C. S. Lewis * Schakel, Peter J.

Look away * Effinger, George Alec

Look back to Earth * Pfeil, Donald J.

Look into my eyes * Murphy, Warren & Richard Sapir

Look into the sun * Kelly, James Patrick

Look out for Space * Nolan, William F.

Look what they've done to my bay! * Harman, Nigel

Looker * Saralegui, Jorge

Looking ahead: the vision of science fiction * Allen, Dick & Lori Allen

Looking backward * Lovecraft, H. P.

Looking backward, 1988-1888: essays on Edward Bellamy * Patai, Daphne

Looking for Blücher * Wodhams, Jack

Looking for Hamlet: a haunting at Deeping Lake * Campbell, Hope

Looking for Ilyriand * Ashton, Jay

Loonie Louis meets the space fungus * Senn, Steve

Loose connections * Claiborne, Sybil

Loot of the vampire * McClusky, Thorp

Looters of Tharn * Green, Roland as JEFFREY LORD

Lord Conrad's lady * Frankowski, Leo

M

M. C. Higgins, the great * Hamilton, Virginia
M. G. "Monk" Lewis * Irwin, Joseph James
M is for monster * Gilden, Mel
M. R. James * James, M. R.
M. R. James: an informal portrait * Cox, Michael
M31: a family romance * Wright, Stephen
Ma and Pa Dracula * Martin, Ann M.
Ma Qui, and other phantoms * Brennert, Alan
Macabre military stories * Holmes, Ronald
Macabre railway stories * Holmes, Ronald
Macabre tales * O'Brien, Fitz-James
Mace of souls, The: a novel of the Six Kingdoms * Fergusson, Bruce
Machen; Men about Machen * Sweetser, Wesley & Adrian Goldstone
Machiavelli interface, The * Perry, Steve
Machine in Shaft Ten, and other stories, The * Harrison, M. John
Machine sex, and other stories * Dorsey, Candas Jane
Machines that kill * Greenberg, Martin H. & Fred Saberhagen
Machines that think: the best science fiction stories about robots and computers * Asimov, Isaac & Martin H. Greenberg & Patricia S. Warrick
Mack Bolan: Paradine's gauntlet * Newton, Michael as DON PENDLETON
Mack Reynolds checklist, A: notes toward a bibliography * Drumm, Chris & George Flynn
Macra terror, The * Black, Ian Stuart
Macrocosmic conflict, The * Bischoff, David
Macrolife * Zebrowski, George
Macunaíma * Andrade, Mario de
Mad and bad fairies: a collection of feminist fairytales * Crone, Joni & Maeve Kelly & Mary Dorcey
Mad doctor, The * Stine, H. William & Megan Stine
Mad doctors, monsters, and mummies: lobby card posters from Hollywood horrors! * Gifford, Denis
Mad empress of Callisto * Carter, Lin
Mad eyes: a Doc Savage adventure * Donovan, Laurence as KENNETH ROBESON
Mad goblin, The * Farmer, Philip José
Mad, mad Monday * Silverstein, Herma
Mad Max * Kaye, Terry
Mad Max 1 * Kaye, Terry
Mad Max 2 * Rühen, Carl
Mad Max: Beyond Thunderdome * Matthews, Ann
Mad Max: Beyond Thunderdome: a novelization * Vinge, Joan D.
Mad Mesa: a Doc Savage adventure * Dent, Lester as KENNETH ROBESON
Mad moon of dreams * Lumley, Brian
Mad Roy's light * King, Paula
Mad science * Stine, H. William & Megan Stine
Mad scientists * Asimov, Isaac & Martin H. Greenberg & Charles G. Waugh
Mad scientists * May, Julian as IAN THORNE
Mad scientists: an anthology of fantasy and horror * Schiff, Stuart David

Mad scientists, weird doctors, and time travelers in movies, TV, and books * Simon, Seymour
Mad throne, The * Munson, Brad
Madame Two Swords * Lee, Tanith
Madbond * Springer, Nancy
Made for man * Herbert, A. P.
Madjan, The * Rovin, Jeff
Madlands * Jeter, K. W.
Madman run * Robbins, David
Madman's army * Adams, Robert
Madman's mansion, The * Stacy, Jan as CRAIG SARGENT
Madness emerging * Cole, Adrian
Madness from Mars, A * Barrett, G. J. as DENNIS SUMMERS
Madness season, The * Friedman, C. S.
Madonna * Kellcher, Ed & Harriette Vidal
Madouc * Vance, Jack
Madwand * Zelazny, Roger
Maelstrom * Preuss, Paul
Maeve * Clayton, Jo
Magazine of fantasy and science fiction, The: a 30-year retrospective * Ferman, Edward L.
Magazine of fantasy and science fiction, April 1965, The * Ferman, Edward L. & Martin H. Greenberg
Magazine of fantasy & science fiction, The: index of authors and titles, Volume 1, Number 1 through Volume 54, Number 6, Fall 1949 through June 1978 * Hill, Josiah F.
Magdalene scrolls, The * Wood, Barbara
Mage-born child, The * Smith, Julia & Mark Smith as JONATHAN WYLIE
Magefire, The * Baliol, Alexander
Maggot, A * Fowles, John
Maggots * Jarvis, Edward
Magic * Goldman, William
Magic book, The * Roberts, Willo Davis
Magic books, The * Norton, Andre
Magic casement * Duncan, Dave
Magic casements * Alexander, Marc
Magic cave, The * Chew, Ruth
Magic code: use of magical patterns in fantasy for children * Nikolajeva, Maria
Magic coin, The * Chew, Ruth
Magic cottage, The * Herbert, James
Magic cup, The: an Irish legend * Greeley, Andrew M.
Magic deer, The * Beasley, Conger Jr.
Magic dolls, The * Kay, Charline Bockhold & Kenneth Kay
Magic door, The * Fast, Howard
Magic drawing pencil, The * Storr, Catherine
Magic for marigold * Montgomery, L. M.
Magic for sale * Davidson, Avram
Magic forest, The * Dent, Lester & William G. Bogart as KENNETH ROBESON
Magic goes away, The * Niven, Larry
Magic grandfather, The * Williams, Jay
Magic in Ithkar * Adams, Robert & Andre Norton
Magic in Ithkar 1 * Adams, Robert & Andre Norton
Magic in Ithkar 2 * Adams, Robert & Andre Norton

Magic in Ithkar 3 * Adams, Robert & Andre Norton
Magic in Ithkar 4 * Adams, Robert & Andre Norton
Magic in the park * Chew, Ruth
Magic island, The: a Doc Savage adventure * Dent, Lester as KENNETH ROBESON
Magic kingdom for sale—sold! * Brooks, Terry
Magic kiss, and other tales of princes and princesses, The * Bradman, Tony
Magic labyrinth, The * Farmer, Philip José
Magic labyrinth of Philip José Farmer, The * Chapman, Edgar L.
Magic may return, The * Niven, Larry
Magic meadow, The * Key, Alexander
Magic mean machine, The * Gormley, Beatrice
Magic mirror, The: lost supernatural and mystery stories * Blackwood, Algernon
Magic mix-up, The * Becker, Eve
Magic of Krynn, The * Hickman, Tracy & Margaret Weis
Magic of Recluce, The * Modesitt, L. E. Jr.
Magic of the black mirror * Chew, Ruth
Magic of the past, The * Aldiss, Brian W.
Magic of the unicorn, The * Goodman, Deborah Lerme
Magic of Xanth, The * Anthony, Piers
Magic pen of Joseph Clement Coll, The * Coll, Joseph Clement & Walt Reed
Magic realism * Hancock, Geoffrey
Magic ring, The * Legaspi, Pilar F.
Magic show * Alexander, Paul & Laurie Bridges
Magic shuttle, The * Goodman, Deborah Lerme
Magic spectacles, The * Blaylock, James P.
Magic spectacles, and other tales, The * Cowper, Richard
Magic stone, The * Kooiker, Leonie
Magic talisman, The * Blaine, John
Magic time * Reed, Kit
Magic to burn * Fritz, Jean
Magic to do: Paul's story * Snodgrass, Melinda M. as MELINDA MCKENZIE
Magic touch, The * Bacon, Peggy
Magic wagon, The * Lansdale, Joe R.
Magical adventures of Pretty Pearl, The * Hamilton, Virginia
Magical coach, The * Adler, C. S.
Magical cupboard, The * Curry, Jane Louise
Magical fellowship, The * McGowen, Tom
Magical quest: the use of magic in Arthurian romance * Wilson, Anne Deirdre
Magical realism and the fantastic: resolved versus unresolved antinomy * Chanady, Amaryll Beatrice
Magical realist fiction: an anthology * Hollaman, Keith & David Young
Magical wishes * Asimov, Isaac & Martin H. Greenberg & Charles G. Waugh
Magical world of the Inklings, The: J. R. R. Tolkien, C. S. Lewis, Charles Williams, Owen Barfield * Knight, Gareth
Magical worlds of fantasy * Asimov, Isaac & Martin H. Greenberg & Charles G. Waugh
Magicats! * Dann, Jack & Gardner Dozois
Magicats II * Dann, Jack & Gardner Dozois
Magician * Feist, Raymond E.
Magician: Apprentice * Feist, Raymond E.
Magician: Master * Feist, Raymond E.
Magician: the lost journals of the magus, Geoffrey Carlyle * Edwards, Malcolm & Robert Holdstock
Magician out of Manchuria, The * Finney, Charles
Magicians, The * Gunn, James
Magician's apprentice, The * McGowen, Tom
Magician's bane * Beamer, Charles
Magician's challenge, The * McGowen, Tom

Magician's company, The * McGowen, Tom
Magician's gambit * Eddings, David
Magician's law * Scott, Michael
Magicians of Caprona, The * Jones, Diana Wynne
Magicians of Erianne * Berry, James R.
Magicians of Gor * Norman, John
Magician's ring, The * Gaskin, Carol
Magician's sleeve, The * Conaway, J. C.
MagicImage Filmbooks presents "Frankenstein" * Ackerman, Forrest J & Philip J. Riley
MagicImage Filmbooks presents "The bride of Frankenstein" * Ackerman, Forrest J & Philip J. Riley
Magicimage Filmbooks presents "The mummy" * Riley, Philip J.
Magick of Camelot, The * Landis, Arthur H.
MagiCon original bookmark anthology * Siclari, Joseph D.
Magic's pawn * Lackey, Mercedes
Magic's price * Lackey, Mercedes
Magic's promise * Lackey, Mercedes
Magination, The * Etkin, Anne
Magnamund companion, The * Chalk, Gary & Joe Dever
Magnet book of sinister stories, The * Russell, Jean
Magnet book of spine chillers, The * Salway, Lance
Magnet book of strange tales, The * Russell, Jean
Magnetic ghost of Shadow Island, The * McEvoy, Seth & Laure Smith
Magnetic storm * Dean, Martyn & Colin Greenland & Roger Dean
Magnificent gallery, The * Monteleone, Thomas F.
Magnificent showboats of the Lower Vissel River, Lune XXIII South, Big Planet, The: (Showboat world) * Vance, Jack
Magog: a novel * Sinclair, Andrew
Magus Rex * Lovejoy, Jack
Maharajah, and other stories, The * White, T. H.
Mahars of Pellucidar * Holmes, John Eric
Mahogany trinrose: a Sime/Gen novel * Lichtenberg, Jacqueline
Mahy magic: a collection of the most magical stories from the Margaret Mahy story books * Mahy, Margaret
Maia * Adams, Richard
Maiden, The * Deveraux, Jude
Maiden flight * Vinicoff, Eric
Maiden of Greenwold * Vilott, Rhondi
Maiden's end * Boyle, Josephine
Mailman, The * Little, Bentley
Mail-order wings * Gormley, Beatrice
Main event, The * Beebee, Chris
Main Street D.O.A. * Peters, David
Mairelon the magician * Wrede, Patricia C.
Majestic * Strieber, Whitley
Majii, The: a Doc Savage adventure * Dent, Lester as KENNETH ROBESON
Majipoor chronicles: a novel * Silverberg, Robert
Major Corby and the unidentified flying object * DeWeese, Gene
Major works of H. G. Wells, The: The time machine, THe invisible man, The war of the worlds, Tono-Bungay * Keenan, Randall H.
Major works of H. P. Lovecraft, The: a critical commentary * Gatto, John Taylor
Make us happy * Herzog, Arthur
Make way for dragons! * Gunnarsson, Thorarinn
Maker of Dune, The: insights of a master of science fiction * Herbert, Frank
Makers, The * Kelleher, Victor
Makeshift god, The * Griffin, Russell M.
Making a monster: the creation of screen characters by the great makeup artists * Roy, Sue & Al Taylor

Man who had no idea, The: a collection of stories * Disch, Thomas M.

Man who knew time, The * McQueen, Ronald A.

Man who lifted the mountain, and other fantasies, The * Das, Manoj

Man who loved Morlocks, The: a sequel to The time machine as narrated by The Time Traveller * Lake, David J.

Man who loved the midnight lady, The: a collection * Malzberg, Barry N.

Man who made maniacs, The * Harmon, Jim

Man who made models, and other stories, The * Lafferty, R. A.

Man who melted, The * Dann, Jack

Man who never missed, The * Perry, Steve

Man who pulled down the sky, The * Barnes, John

Man who shook the Earth, The: a Doc Savage adventure * Dent, Lester as KENNETH ROBESON

Man who stole tomorrow, The * Michelinie, David

Man who travelled on motorways, The * Hoyle, Trevor

Man who used the universe, The * Foster, Alan Dean

Man who wanted to save Canada, The: a prophetic novel * Childerhose, R. J.

Man who was God, The * Chase, Glen

Man who was Poe, The: a novel * Avi

Man who was scared, The * Dent, Lester as KENNETH ROBESON

Man who would not die, The: an unusual ghost story * Page, Thomas

Man who wrote Dracula: a biography of Bram Stoker, The * Farson, Daniel

Man with a nose, A, and the other uncollected short stories of H. G. Wells * Wells, H. G.

Man with the beard, The * Timperley, Rosemary

Man with two faces, The * Brand, Kurt

Man with two memories, The * Haldane, J. B. S.

Man worth loving, A * Browning, Pamela

Manalone * Kapp, Colin

Mandala * Bischoff, David

Mandarin, and other stories, The * Eça de Queiroz

Mandragon * Koster, R. M.

Mandrake * Lord, J. Edward

Mandrake scream, The: a novel * March, Melisand

Mandrake the magician * Ashman, Howard

Mandricardo: new adventures in Terra Magica * Carter, Lin

Mandrill * Gardner, Richard

Man-eaters of Cascalon, The * Lancour, Gene

ManFac * Caidin, Martin

Manhattan ghost story, A * Wright, T. M.

Manhattan project, The * Bischoff, David

Manhounds of Antares; and, Arena of Antares * Bulmer, Kenneth as DRAY PRESCOT & ALAN BURT AKERS

Manhuntress, The * Offutt, Andrew J. & Geo. W. Proctor as JOHN CLEVE

Mania * Smith, Guy N.

Maniac * Friedman, Stuart

Manifest destiny * Longyear, Barry B.

Manipulator, The * Brookins, Dana

Manitou, The * Masterton, Graham

Manitou doll * Smith, Guy N.

Mankind on the run * Dickson, Gordon R.

Mankind under the leash * Disch, Thomas M.

Man-Kzin wars, The * Anderson, Poul & Larry Niven & Dean Ing

Man-Kzin wars II, The * Ing, Dean & Larry Niven & Jerry Pournelle & S. M. Stirling

Man-Kzin wars III, The * Anderson, Poul & Jerry Pournelle & S. M. Stirling & Larry Niven

Man-Kzin wars IV * Niven, Larry

Manless world, A * Yourell, Agnes Bond

Manly Wade Wellman, the gentleman from Chapel Hill: a memorial working bibliography * Benson, Gordon Jr.

Man-made stud * Montgomery, Rex

Man-made woman, The * Murphy, Robert Franklin

Manna * Stine, G. Harry as LEE CORREY

Manna enzyme, The * Hoyt, Richard

Mannequin * Byrne, Robert

Manrissa man * Van Greenaway, Peter

Manse, The * Cantrell, Lisa W.

Manseed * Williamson, Jack

Manshape * Brunner, John

Mansions of space, The * Morressy, John

Manstopper * Borton, Douglas

Mantis * Jeter, K. W.

Mantis * Stambaugh, E. B.

Mants of Myrmedon, The * Burgess, Eric & Arthur Friggens

Manufactured people, The * King, Albert as FLOYD GIBSON

Man-wolf, and other stories, The * Lamb, Hugh

Manx tales of horror * Lert, A. J.

Manxmouse * Gallico, Paul

Many facets of Stephen King, The * Collings, Michael R.

Many futures, many worlds: theme and form in science fiction * Clareson, Thomas D.

Many waters * L'Engle, Madeleine

Many worlds of Andre Norton * Norton, Andre

Many worlds of Barry Malzberg, The * Malzberg, Barry N.

Many worlds of Larry Niven, The, 2nd ed. * Drumm, Chris & Paul Guptill

Many worlds of Magnus Ridolph, The * Vance, Jack

Many worlds of Poul Anderson * Anderson, Poul

Many-Colored Land, The * May, Julian

Many-colored land, The; The golden torc * May, Julian

Maori * Foster, Alan Dean

Maps in a mirror: the short fiction of Orson Scott Card * Card, Orson Scott

Maracaibo massacre * Roberts, Mark K.

Marathon * Smith, D. Alexander

Marathon photograph, and other stories, The * Simak, Clifford D.

Marauders, The * Naha, Ed as MICHAEL MCGANN

Marauders, The: Blood and fire * Naha, Ed as MICHAEL MCGANN

Marauders, The: Blood kin * Naha, Ed as MICHAEL MCGANN

Marauders, The: Convoy strike * Naha, Ed as MICHAEL MCGANN

Marauders, The: Fortress of death * Naha, Ed as MICHAEL MCGANN

Marauders, The: Liar's dice * Naha, Ed as MICHAEL MCGANN

Marauders of Gor * Norman, John

Marauders, The: The ghost warriors * Naha, Ed as MICHAEL MCGANN

Marchers of Valhalla * Howard, Robert E.

Marching through Georgia * Stirling, S. M.

Marcia, the innocent * Kimbro, John M. as KATHERYN KIMBROUGH

Marco Polo * Lucarotti, John

Marco Polo and the sleeping beauty * Davidson, Avram & Grania Davis

Mardi Gras mystery, The * Foley, Louise Munro

Mardoc * McQueen, Ronald A.

Margaret St. Clair * Benson, Gordon Jr.

Margaret, the faithful * Kimbro, John M. as KATHERYN KIMBROUGH

Margo * Reed, Dana

Massacre, The * Lucarotti, John
Massacre in the 22nd century * Hagberg, David as ANONYMOUS AUTHOR
Master, The * Cooper, Louise
Master * Feist, Raymond E.
Master, The * Smith, Guy N.
Master cat, The: the true and unexpurgated story of Puss in Boots * Garnett, David
Master cure, The * Buck, Charles H.
Master file, The * Elliott, Elton T. & Richard E. Geis as RICHARD ELLIOTT
Master goes home, The * Munn, H. Warner
Master of Boranga * Sirota, Mike
Master of chaos, The * Adams, Terry A.
Master of chaos * Martin, Keith
Master of evil, The * Smith, David C.
Master of fiends * Hill, Douglas
Master of ghosts * Barrett, G. J. as DENNIS SUMMERS
Master of hawks * Bushyager, Linda E.
Master of karate * Brightfield, Richard
Master of kung fu * Brightfield, Richard
Master of mazes, The * Gaskin, Carol
Master of Misfit * Offutt, Andrew J. & Geo. W. Proctor as JOHN CLEVE
Master of Norriya, The * Drew, Wayland
Master of Paxwax * Mann, Phillip
Master of Ravenloft * Blashfield, Jean
Master of ships * Barrett, Neal Jr.
Master of space and time * Rucker, Rudy
Master of tae kwon do * Brightfield, Richard
Master of the fearful depths * Adkins, Patrick H.
Master of the five magics * Hardy, Lyndon
Master of the game * Gygax, Gary
Master of the grove * Kelleher, Victor
Master of the Hashomi * Green, Roland as JEFFREY LORD
Master of the past * Otfinoski, Steven
Master of the red butcher * Page, Norvell W. as GRANT STOCKBRIDGE
Master of the Sidhe * Flint, Kenneth C.
Master of the stars * Hoskins, Robert
Master of the temple * Ericson, Eric
Master Wolf: a novel of quest and romance, sorcery and death * Estes, Rose
Masterpieces of fantasy and enchantment * Cramer, Kathryn & David G. Hartwell
Masterpieces of fantasy and wonder * Cramer, Kathryn & David G. Hartwell
Masterpieces of science fiction * Durwood, Thomas & Armand Eisen
Masterpieces of terror and the supernatural: a treasury of spellbinding tales old & new * Kaye, Marvin & Sar-alee Kaye
Masterplay * Wu, William F.
Master's challenge * Murphy, Warren & Richard Sapir
Masters in Hell * Morris, Janet
Masters of darkness, The * Dever, Joe
Masters of darkness * Etchison, Dennis
Masters of darkness II * Etchison, Dennis
Masters of darkness III * Etchison, Dennis
Masters of Everon * Dickson, Gordon R.
Masters of Flux & Anchor * Chalker, Jack L.
Masters of glass * Easton, M. Coleman
Masters of horror * Cohen, Daniel
Masters of horror & suspense: The interlopers, The specter, The tell-tale heart, The cask of Amontillado * anon.
Masters of science fiction * Scithers, George H.
Masters of science fiction: essays on six science fiction authors * Stableford, Brian M.

Masters of shades and shadows: an anthology of great ghost stories * Lewis, Gogo & Seon Manley
Masters of solitude, The * Godwin, Parke & Marvin Kaye
Masters of space * Smith, E. E.
Masters of space * Vardeman, Robert E.
Masters of space: The stellar death plan * Vardeman, Robert E.
Masters of terror, volume one * Hodgson, William Hope
Masters of the fist * Hughes, Edward P.
Masters of the macabre: an anthology of mystery, horror, and detection * Lewis, Gogo & Seon Manley
Mastery * Wilde, Kelley
Mastodonia * Simak, Clifford D.
Matadora * Perry, Steve
Mathenauts: tales of mathematical wonder * Rucker, Rudy
Mathew Swain: Hot time in Old Town * McQuay, Mike
Mathew Swain: The deadliest show in town * McQuay, Mike
Mathew Swain: The odds are murder * McQuay, Mike
Mathew Swain: When trouble beckons * McQuay, Mike
Matilda at the speed of light * Broderick, Damien
Matilda's stepchildren * Chandler, A. Bertram
Matrix, The * Bannister, Jo
Matrix cubed * Bloom, Britton
Matrix man * Dietz, William C.
Matrix witch * Douglis, Marjie
Matter for men, A * Gerrold, David
Matter of evolution, A * Barker, D. A.
Matter of Metalaw, A * Stine, G. Harry as LEE CORREY
Matter of oaths, A * Wright, Helen
Matter of taste, A * Saberhagen, Fred
Matter of time, A * Byrne, Beverly
Matter of time, A * Cook, Glen
Matter's end * Benford, Gregory
Matters of form * Wheeler, Scott
Matthew G. Lewis, Charles Robert Maturin, and the Germans: an interpretative study of the influence of German literature on two Gothic novels * Conger, Syndy M.
Mattimeo * Jacques, Brian
Maturity: three stories * Sturgeon, Theodore
Maui: the demigod * Goldsberry, Steven
Maurai & Kith * Anderson, Poul
Maura's angel * Reid Banks, Lynne
Maverick * Bethke, Bruce
Mawdryn undead * Grimwade, Peter
Max all over * Kaye, Marilyn
Max and me and the time machine * Greer, Gery & Bob Ruddick
Max and me and the Wild West * Greer, Gery & Bob Ruddick
Max and the cats * Scliar, Moacyr
Max flips out * Kaye, Marilyn
Max goes bad * Kaye, Marilyn
Max in love * Kaye, Marilyn
Max is back * Stine, H. William & Megan Stine
Max Lakeman and the beautiful stranger: a novel * Cohen, Jon
Max on Earth * Kaye, Marilyn
Max on fire * Kaye, Marilyn
Max onstage * Stine, H. William & Megan Stine
Max saves the day * Stine, H. William & Megan Stine
Maximum effort * Edmondson, G. C. & C. M. Kotlan
Max's book * Crawford, Betty Anne as MAXWELL HURLEY
Max's secret formula * Stine, H. William & Megan Stine
Maxwell's demon * Sherwood, Martin
Maxwell's demons * Bova, Ben
Maya red * Humphreys, J. R.

Meridian 144 * Files, Meg
Merlin * Lawhead, Stephen
Merlin * Nye, Robert
Merlin and the dragons of Atlantis * Hildebrandt, Rita & Tim Hildebrandt
Merlin and woman: second Merlin Conference * Stewart, R. J.
Merlin dreams * Dickinson, Peter
Merlin of the crystal cave * Stewart, Mary
Merlin trilogy * Stewart, Mary
Merlin's booke: thirteen stories and poems about the arch-mage * Yolen, Jane
Merlin's daughters: contemporary women writers of fantasy * Spivack, Charlotte
Merlin's godson * Munn, H. Warner
Merlin's mirror * Norton, Andre
Merlin's ring * Trevor, Meriol
Mermaid summer, The * Hunter, Mollie
Mermaids! * Dann, Jack & Gardner Dozois
Mermaid's song * Van Gores, Alida
Mermaid's three wisdoms, The * Yolen, Jane
Merman's children, The * Anderson, Poul
Merovingen nights: Angel with the sword * Cherryh, C. J.
Merovingen nights: Divine right * Cherryh, C. J.
Merovingen nights: Endgame * Cherryh, C. J.
Merovingen nights: Festival moon * Cherryh, C. J.
Merovingen nights: Fever season * Cherryh, C. J.
Merovingen nights: Flood tide * Cherryh, C. J.
Merovingen nights: Smuggler's gold * Cherryh, C. J.
Merovingen nights: Troubled waters * Cherryh, C. J.
Merry Christmas, Ms Minerva * Cooper, Edmund
Mervyn Peake * Watney, John
Mervyn Peake, 1911-1968: exhibition of manuscripts, drawings, illustrations * Gilmour, Maeve
Mervyn Peake: a biographical and critical exploration * Batchelor, John
Mervyn Peake: a personal memoir * Smith, Gordon
Message from space * Packard, Edward
Messages: a collection of shivery tales * Darke, Marjorie
Messages found in an oxygen bottle * Shaw, Bob
Messenger, The * Dickens, Monica
Messenger, The * Williams, Mona
Messengers of darkness * Walker, Hugh
Messiah at the end of time * Moorcock, Michael
Messiah choice, The * Chalker, Jack L.
Messiah Stone, The * Caidin, Martin
Metaconcert, The * May, Julian
Metal fire * Daley, Brian & James Luceno as JACK McKINNEY
Metal gear * Frost, Alexander
Metal Master, The: a Doc Savage adventure * Dent, Lester as KENNETH ROBESON
Metalstorm * Alexander, David
Metamorphoses of the Raven: literary overdeterminedness in France and the South since Poe * Humphries, Jefferson
Metamorphosis * Daley, Brian & James Luceno as JACK McKINNEY
Metamorphosis * Lorrah, Jean
Metamorphosis * Ray, Robert
Metamorphosis of science fiction: on the poetics and history of a literary genre * Suvin, Darko
Metamorphosis: the Cocoon story continues: a novel * Saperstein, David
Meteor * Coen, Franklin & Edmund H. North
Meteor menace: a Doc Savage adventure * Dent, Lester as KENNETH ROBESON
Meteor scrapbook, The * Hurwood, Bernhardt J.
Meteor: short stories * Nobes, Patrick & John Wyndham

Meteoric affair, The * Tabler, Joseph
Meteoric Benson, The: a romance of actuality * Mills-Malet, Vincent
Meteorite track 291 * Paulsen, Gary
Methods of madness: a collection * Garton, Ray
Methuen book of sinister stories, The * Russell, Jean
Methuen book of strange tales, The * Russell, Jean
Metro gangs attack, The * Leeson, Robert
Metrognome, and other stories, The * Foster, Alan Dean
Metrophage: (a romance of the future) * Kadrey, Richard
Mexico 21 * Joseph, Mark
Meyeresco helix, The * McCoy, Andrew
Miami run * Robbins, David
Miamigrad * Ahern, Jerry & Sharon Ahern
Michael and the magic man * Sidney, Kathleen M.
Michael and the secret war * Golds, Cassandra
Michael Arlen * Keyishian, Harry
Michael Bishop: a preliminary bibliography * Nee, Dave
Michael Moorcock: a bibliography * Harper, Andrew & George McAulay
Michael Moorcock: a bibliography, based on the Moorcock deposit, Bodleian Library, Oxford * Hinton, Brian
Michael Moorcock: a reader's guide * Davey, John
Michael: the master * Lambert, William J. III
Michael Whelan's Works of wonder * Whelan, Michael
Michaelmas * Budrys, Algis
Michigan madness * Ham, Bob
Mickelsson's ghosts: a novel * Gardner, John
Microcolony, The * Williams, Gordon
Microcosmic tales: 100 wondrous science fiction short-short stories * Asimov, Isaac & Martin H. Greenberg & Joseph D. Olander
Micromegas, (and other stories) * Voltaire
Micronaut world * Williams, Gordon
Micronauts, The * Williams, Gordon
Microverse, The * Preiss, Byron
Microwave caper, The * Tabler, Joseph
Microworlds: tales of the computer age * Monteleone, Thomas F.
Microworlds: writings on science fiction and fantasy * Lem, Stanislaw
MidAmerican program book * Reamy, Tom
Midas * Jeschke, Wolfgang
Midas man, The: a Doc Savage adventure * Dent, Lester as KENNETH ROBESON
Midas world: a novel * Pohl, Frederik
Middle Earth: a world in conflict * Miller, Stephen O.
Middle Earth album, A: paintings inspired by J. R. R. Tolkien's The lord of the rings * Wyatt, Joan
Middle Earth: the world of Tolkien illustrated * Carter, Lin & David Wenzel
Middle kingdom, The * Wingrove, David
Middlearth: a modern pilgrimage by foot and greyhound to Middle-Earth (after J. R. R. Tolkien), with Nikon and notepad * Simmons, Ted
Middle-Earth quest: A spy in Isengard * Amthor, Terry K.
Middle-Earth quest: Rescue in Mirkwood * Lientz, Gerald
Middle-Earth quiz book, The * Buchholz, Suzanne
Midget planet, The * Faircloth, Cyril E.
Midnight * Grant, Charles L.
Midnight * Koontz, Dean R.
Midnight at monster mansion * Otfinoski, Steven
Midnight at the Well of Souls * Chalker, Jack L.
Midnight blue * Fisk, Pauline
Midnight boy * Gresham, Stephen
Midnight chill * Siegel, Barbara & Scott Siegel
Midnight city * Tine, Robert
Midnight ghost book, The * Hale, James

Mirror of Helen, The * Purtill, Richard
Mirror of her dreams, The * Donaldson, Stephen R.
Mirror of shadows, A * Daniels, Dorothy
Mirror of the giant, The * Shuttle, Penelope
Mirror planet, The * Bunting, Eve
Mirrorshades: the cyberpunk anthology * Sterling, Bruce
Mirrorstone, The: a ghost story with holograms * Palin, Michael
Mirrorwell express, The * Taylor, Derek
Miscast barbarian, The: a biography of Robert E. Howard (1906-1936) * de Camp, L. Sprague
Miscast gentleman, The * Easton, Edward
Mischief malicious (and murder most strange) * Lafferty, R. A.
Misenchanted sword, The * Watt-Evans, Lawrence
Miskatonic, The * Mosig, Dirk Walter
Mismatch * Pye, Lloyd
Misplaced legion, The * Turtledove, Harry
Misplaced persons * Harding, Lee
Miss Finney kills now and then * Dempsey, Al & Joseph Van Winkle & Sidney Levine
Miss Ghost * Arthur, Ruth M.
Miss Know It All and the magic house: a Butterfield Square story * York, Carol Beach
Miss Know It All and the wishing lamp: a Butterfield Square story * York, Carol Beach
Miss Pickerell and the blue whales * MacGregor, Ellen & Dora Pantell
Miss Pickerell and the lost world * Pantell, Dora
Miss Pickerell and the supertanker * MacGregor, Ellen & Dora Pantell
Miss Pickerell and the war of the computers * Pantell, Dora
Miss Pickerell on the trail * MacGregor, Ellen & Dora Pantell
Miss Pickerell tackles the energy crisis * MacGregor, Ellen & Dora Pantell
Miss Pickerell takes the bull by the horns * MacGregor, Ellen & Dora Pantell
Miss Pickerell to the earthquake rescue * MacGregor, Ellen & Dora Pantell
Missing * Stine, R. L.
Missing heart, The * Cowper, Richard
Missing man * MacLean, Katherine
Missing persons league, The * Bonham, Frank
Missing years, The * Schwerin, Doris
Mission: a novel * Tilley, Patrick
Mission begins, The * Magee, Glenn A. & John Peel
Mission of magic * Smith, Julie Dean
Mission of the secret spy squad * Buckholtz, Eileen & Ruth Glick
Mission to Magnus * Martin, Philip
Mission to Mars * Fleming, Robert Loren
Mission to Moulokin * Foster, Alan Dean
Mission to Pactolus R. * Mason, Douglas R.
Mission to the unknown * Peel, John
Mission to universe * Dickson, Gordon R.
Mission to Venus * Emms, William
Mission to World War II * Kornblatt, Marc & Susan Nanus
Mission: Tori * Bolton, Johanna M.
Mission underground * Griffin, P. M.
Mist of evil * Matthews, Patricia
Mister Touch * Bosse, Malcolm J.
Mistress of ambiguities * Rivkin, J. F.
Mistress of the jewels, The * Paxson, Diana L.
Mistress of torment * Bedford, Clive
Mists and magic * Edwards, Dorothy
Mists of Avalon, The * Bradley, Marion Zimmer
Mists of doom, The * Offutt, Andrew J.

Mists of the ages * Green, Sharon
Mists of time, The * Anderson, Margaret J.
Mithras the Second * Uhrman, Esther
Mitzi Meyer, fearless warrior queen * Singer, Marilyn
Mixed doubles * Da Cruz, Daniel
Mockingbird * Tevis, Walter
Model, The * Aickman, Robert
Modern allegory and fantasy: rhetorical stances of contemporary writing * Hunter, Lynette
Modern fantasy: five studies * Manlove, C. N.
Modern fantasy: the hundred best novels: an English-language selection, 1946-1987 * Pringle, David
Modern heroism: essays on D. H. Lawrence, William Empson, and J. R. R. Tolkien * Sale, Roger
Modern horror film, The: 50 contemporary classics from "The curse of Frankenstein" to "The lair of the white worm" * McCarty, John
Modern masters of horror * Coffey, Frank
Modern science fiction and the American literary community * Lerner, Frederick Andrew
Modern science fiction: its meaning and its future, [second edition] * Bretnor, Reginald
Mojo and the pickle jar * Bell, Douglas
Mole men want your eyes, The * Davis, Frederick C.
Mole people, The * Green, Carl R. & William R. Sanford
Molecular cafe, The: science-fiction stories * Strugatsky, Arkady & Boris Strugatsky as ANONYMOUS EDITORS
Molecular ramjet, and other bedtime stories * Carlson, Larry G.
Molly Dear: the autobiography of an android; or, How I came to my senses, was repaired, escaped my master, and was educated in the ways of the world * Fine, Stephen
Molly Zero * Roberts, Keith
Molt brother * Lichtenberg, Jacqueline
Molten Steele * Hunter, S. L.
Moment in time, A * Small, Beatrice
Moment of the magician, The * Foster, Alan Dean
Moment out of time * Hay, George as ROY SHELDON
Momo * Ende, Michael
Mona Lisa is missing, The! * Montgomery, Ramsey
Mona Lisa overdrive * Gibson, William
Monadic universe, The * Zebrowski, George
Monarch of dreams, The * Higginson, Thomas Wentworth
Monastery * Whalen, Patrick
Monday begins on Saturday * Strugatsky, Arkady & Boris Strugatsky
Monday's child * Wallace, Patricia
Money spider, The * Davies, Wilfred & Robin Waterfield
Mongol, The * Sadler, Barry
Mongster * Boyll, Randall
Monitor, the miners, and the Shree, The * Killough, Lee
Monk, The: a novel * Hallahan, William H.
Monkey, The * King, Stephen
Monkey brain sushi: new tastes in Japanese fiction * Birnbaum, Alfred
Monkey shines * Stewart, Michael
Monkey suit, The * Dent, Lester as KENNETH ROBESON
Monkey station * Fortier, Ron & Ardath Mayhar
Monkey-shines * Stewart, Michael
Monochrome: the Readercon anthology * Cholfin, Bryan
Monodyne catastrophe, The * Renard, Joseph
Monster * Crowcroft, Peter
Monster * Swain, Dwight V.
Monster: a tale of Loch Ness * Konvitz, Jeffrey
Monster and horror movies * Aylesworth, Thomas G.
Monster at Christmas, A * Canty, Thomas
Monster book of monsters, The * O'Shaughnessy, Michael

Moral voyages of Stephen King, The * Magistrale, Anthony

Mordred * Holmes, John Eric & Larry Niven & Jerry Pournelle

More adventures of Samurai Cat * Rogers, Mark E.

More city jitters * Fowler, Christopher

More classics of the horror film * Everson, William K.

More devil's kisses * Parry, Michel as LINDA LOVECRAFT

More fantasy by Fabian: the art of Stephen E. Fabian * Fabian, Stephen E.

More fifth grade magic * Gormley, Beatrice

More ghosts & scholars: ghost stories in the tradition of M. R. James * Pardoe, Rosemary as ANONYMOUS EDITOR

More ghosts, ghosts, ghosts * Hoke, Helen

More haunted stories * Furman, A. L.

More magic * Niven, Larry

More of Christopher Lee's new chamber of horrors * Haining, Peter

More real than reality: the fantastic in Irish literature and the arts * Bertha, Csilla & Donald E. Morse

More Roald Dahl tales of the unexpected * Dahl, Roald

More shapes than one * Chappell, Fred

More tales for the midnight hour: 13 stories of horror * Stamper, J. B.

More tales from the Forbidden Planet * Kaveney, Roz

More tales of Pirx the pilot * Lem, Stanislaw

More tales of the frightened * Lory, Robert

More tales of the unexpected * Dahl, Roald

More tales of unknown horror * Haining, Peter

More teen-age haunted stories * Furman, A. L.

More than 100: women science fiction writers * Yntema, Sharon

More than a dream * Pinianski, Patricia & Linda Sweeney as LYNN PATRICK

More than complete Hitchhiker's guide, The: five stories * Adams, Douglas

More than one universe: the collected stories of Arthur C. Clarke * Clarke, Arthur C.

More than the sum of his parts * Haldeman, Joe

More than weird * Godfrey, Martyn N.

More than you bargained for, and other stories * Aiken, Joan

More Vulcan reflections: essays on Spock and his world * Comerford, Sherna & Devra M. Langsam

More wandering stars: outstanding stories of Jewish fantasy and science fiction * Dann, Jack

More women of wonder: science fiction novelettes by women about women * Sargent, Pamela

Moreau's other island: a novel * Aldiss, Brian W.

Moreta, Dragonlady of Pern * McCaffrey, Anne

Morgan Library ghost stories * Dupont, Inge & Hope Mayo

Morgan Swift and the kidnapped goddess * Hughes, Sara

Morgan Swift and the treasure of Crocodile Key * Hughes, Sara

Morgana: a novel * Buchanan, Marie

Morgow rises!, The * Tremayne, Peter

Morigu: The dead * Perry, Mark C.

Morigu: The desecration * Perry, Mark C.

Mork & Mindy * Church, Ralph

Mork & Mindy * Schneck, Paul D.

Morlac: the quest of the green magician * Ruse, Gary Alan

Morlock night * Jeter, K. W.

Morning of creation * Shupp, Mike

Morphodite, The * Foster, M. A.

Morreion * Vance, Jack

Morrow's ants * Hyams, E.

Mort * Pratchett, Terry

Mortal engines * Lem, Stanislaw

Mortal fear * Cook, Robin

Mortal glamour, A * Yarbro, Chelsea Quinn

Mortal gods: a novel * Fast, Jonathan

Mortal instruments, The * Bethancourt, T. Ernesto

Mortal mask * Marley, Stephen

Mortals of Reni, The * Holloway, Brian as VON GRUEN

Mortmain: a romance * Pendered, Mary L.

Mortorio two * Burgess, Eric & Arthur Friggens

Mortuary, The * Smith, Clark Ashton

Moscow 2042 * Voinovich, Vladimir

Moscow 5000 * Thomas, Craig as DAVID GRANT

Moscow Moffia presents Rat tales, The * Gustafson, Jon & Dean Wesley Smith as SMITH GUSTAFSON

Moscow option, The: an alternative Second World War * Downing, David

Mossflower * Jacques, Brian

Most ancient song * Flint, Kenneth C. as CASEY FLYNN

Mostly magic * Chew, Ruth

Mosutha's magic: Oron * Smith, David C.

Mote in time's eye, The * Klein, Gérard K.

Motel of the Mysteries * Macaulay, David

Moth Manor: a gothic tale * Bacon, Martha

Moth to the flame * Dougherty, Kathleen

Mother Earth * McQuay, Mike

Mother earth, father sky * Harrison, Sue

Mother lode * Hughes, Zach

Mother of storms * Cole, Adrian

Mother of toads * Smith, Clark Ashton

Motherland * DiCarlantonio, Martin

Motherlines * Charnas, Suzy McKee

Motherstone * Gee, Maurice

Moth-kin magic * Tapp, Kathy Kennedy

Moths * Ashe, Rosalind

Motion menace, The: a Doc Savage adventure * Dent, Lester and Ryerson Johnson as KENNETH ROBESON

Motion of light in water, The: sex and science fiction writing in the East Village, 1957-1965 * Delany, Samuel R.

Motion of light in water, The: sex and science fiction writing in the East Village, 1957-1965; with, The column at the market's edge * Delany, Samuel R.

Motion picture, The * Gross, Edward

Motto excelsior, The * De Vere, V. C.

Motto excelsior, books II-IV, The * De Vere, V. C.

Motto excelsior, books V-VIII, The * De Vere, V. C.

Mound, and other SF stories from the Low Lands, The * anon.

Mountain cage, The * Sargent, Pamela

Mountain monster, The: a Doc Savage adventure * Davis, Harold A. as KENNETH ROBESON

Mountain of magic, The: a romance for children * Nichols, Beverley

Mountain of mirrors * Estes, Rose

Mountain of stolen dreams * Tallis, Robyn

Mountain run * Dever, Joe

Mountain survival * Packard, Edward

Mountain walks, The: a Peace Company novel * Green, Roland

Mountain witch * Grant, Charles L. as FELICIA ANDREWS

Mountains at the bottom of the world, The * Cameron, Ian

Mountains of Brega, The * Green, Roland as JEFFREY LORD

Mountains of Channadran, The * Dexter, Susan

Mouse and his child, The * Hoban, Russell

Mouse that saved the West, The * Wibberley, Leonard

Movement of mountains, The * Blumlein, Michael

Movie fantastic: beyond the dream machine * Annan, David

My enemy, my ally: a Star Trek novel * Duane, Diane
My experiences in the Third World War * Moorcock, Michael
My fantoms * Gautier, Théophile
My father immortal * Weaver, Michael D.
My friend, the vampire * Sommer-Bodenburg, Angela
My heart leaps up (1920-1928), chapters 1 & 2 * Lafferty, R. A.
My heart leaps up (1920-1928), chapters 3 & 4 * Lafferty, R. A.
My heart leaps up (1920-1928), chapters 5 & 6 * Lafferty, R. A.
My heart leaps up (1920-1928), chapters 7 & 8 * Lafferty, R. A.
My heart leaps up (1920-1928), chapters 9 & 10 * Lafferty, R. A.
My lady of hyBrasil, and other stories * Tremayne, Peter
My lady tongue, & other tales * Sussex, Lucy
My lord barbarian * Offutt, Andrew J.
My madness: the selected writings of Anna Kavan * Kavan, Anna
My name is legion * Zelazny, Roger
My pretty pony * King, Stephen
My robot buddy * Slote, Alfred
My science project * McQuay, Mike
My science project: a novel * Don, Ian
My scrapbook memories of Dark shadows * Scott, Kathryn Leigh
My secret admirer * Ellis, Carol
My secret indentity: a novelization * Stine, R. L.
My side * Wager, Walter as KING KONG
My sister Sif * Park, Ruth
My teacher fried my brains * Coville, Bruce
My teacher glows in the dark * Coville, Bruce
My teacher is an alien * Coville, Bruce
My time or yours * Blake, William Dorsey
My trip to Alpha I * Slote, Alfred
My way * Barton, James
Myrmidon Project, The * Murray, William & Chuck Scarborough
Myself and Marco Polo * Griffiths, Paul
Mysteries of the worm: all the Cthulhu Mythos stories of Robert Bloch * Bloch, Robert
Mysterious air stories * Pattrick, William
Mysterious cure, The, and other stories of Pshrinks Anonymous * Asimov, Janet Jeppson as J. O. JEPPSON
Mysterious girl in the garden, The * St. George, Judith
Mysterious house, The * Blackwood, Algernon
Mysterious Max * Stine, H. William & Megan Stine
Mysterious, menacing, & macabre: an anthology * Hoke, Helen
Mysterious motoring stories * Pattrick, William
Mysterious planet, The * del Rey, Lester
Mysterious planet * Dicks, Terrance
Mysterious railway stories * Pattrick, William
Mysterious sea stories * Pattrick, William
Mysterious tales of Ivan Turgenev, The * Turgenev, Ivan
Mysterious visions: great science fiction by masters of the mystery * Greenberg, Martin H. & Charles G. Waugh & Joseph D. Olander
Mystery at Geneva: an improbable tale of singular happenings * Macaulay, Rose
Mystery at Mockingbird Manor * Pascal, Jamie & Laurie Pascal
Mystery fanfare: a composite annual index to mystery and related fanzines, 1963-1981 * Cook, Michael L.
Mystery for Christmas * Dalby, Richard
Mystery in Dracula's castle, The * Crume, Vic
Mystery island * Dent, Lester as KENNETH ROBESON

Mystery of Atlantis, The * Gasperini, Jim
Mystery of Chimney Rock, The * Packard, Edward
Mystery of Echo Lodge * Foley, Louise Munro
Mystery of Misty Island Inn, The * Cates, Emily
Mystery of No. 1, The * Horler, Sydney
Mystery of the ancients * Simon, Morris
Mystery of the Anti, The * Scheer, K. H.
Mystery of the dragon's shadow, The * Keyhoe, Donald E.
Mystery of the hidden trap, The * Carlson, Dale
Mystery of the Highland crest, The * Foley, Louise Munro
Mystery of the Japanese clock, The * Leiber, Fritz
Mystery of the Maya * Montgomery, R. A.
Mystery of the midnight menace * Garden, Nancy
Mystery of the missing mummy, The * McMullan, Kate
Mystery of the night raiders * Garden, Nancy
Mystery of the sacred stones * Foley, Louise Munro
Mystery of the sardine, The * Themerson, Stefan
Mystery of the secret marks * Garden, Nancy
Mystery of the secret room * Kushner, Ellen
Mystery of the shining children, The * Carlson, Dale
Mystery of the witches' bridge * Carleton, Barbee Oliver
Mystery of Ura Senke, The * Gilligan, Shannon
Mystery on Happy Bones: a Doc Savage adventure * Dent, Lester as KENNETH ROBESON
Mystery on the snow: a Doc Savage adventure * Dent, Lester as KENNETH ROBESON
Mystery planet, The * Jennison, John W. as EDGAR REES KENNEDY
Mystery under the sea: a Doc Savage adventure * Dent, Lester as KENNETH ROBESON
Mystery walk * McCammon, Robert R.
Mystic Mullah, The: a Doc Savage adventure * Dent, Lester as KENNETH ROBESON
Mystic passions * Scott, Sandra
Mystic rebel * Syvertsen, Ryder
Mystical encounters * Sykala, Ursula
Mysticism and Aldous Huxley: an examination of Heard-Huxley theories * Savage, David S.
Mystique: tales of wonder * Chinn, Mike
Myth adventures * Asprin, Robert Lynn
Myth alliances * Asprin, Robert Lynn
Myth and archetype in science fiction * Le Guin, Ursula K.
Myth conceptions * Asprin, Robert Lynn
Myth directions * Asprin, Robert Lynn
M.Y.T.H. Inc. in action * Asprin, Robert Lynn
M.Y.T.H. Inc. link * Asprin, Robert Lynn
Myth makers, The * Cotton, Donald
Myth makers, The; and, The gunfighters * Cotton, Donald
Mythago Wood * Holdstock, Robert
Mythic beasts * Asimov, Isaac & Martin H. Greenberg & Charles G. Waugh
Mythic realism in fantasy * Springer, Nancy
Mythical beasties * Asimov, Isaac & Martin H. Greenberg & Charles G. Waugh
Myth-ing persons * Asprin, Robert Lynn
Myth-nomers and im-pervections * Asprin, Robert Lynn
Mythology 101 * Nye, Jody Lynn
Mythology abroad * Nye, Jody Lynn
Mythology of Middle-Earth, The * Noel, Ruth S.
"Mythopoeikon": fantasies, monsters, nightmares, daydreams * Woodroffe, Patrick
Myths and realities: the mysterious Mr. Poe * Fisher, Benjamin Franklin IV
Myths, legends, and true history * Landis, Geoffrey A.
Myths of the near future * Ballard, J. G.

N

Night howl * Neiderman, Andrew
Night hunter * Holdstock, Robert *as* ROBERT FAULCON
Night hunter, The * Williams, Russ
Night in the Netherhells, A * Gardner, Craig Shaw
Night killers * Lewis, Richard
Night launch * Cohen, Stephen Paul & Jake Garn
Night lust * Lee, Edward *as* PHILIP STRAKER
Night man, The * Jeter, K. W.
Night Manhattan burned, The * Jackson, Basil
Night mare * Anthony, Piers
Night master, The * Sampson, Robert
Night Mayor, The * Newman, Kim
Night maze * Dalton, Annie
Night moves * Powers, Tim
Night nemesis, The * Davis, Frederick C.
Night ocean, The * Barlow, Robert H. & H. P. Lovecraft
Night of dragons * Vilott, Rhondi *as* R. A. V. SALSITZ
Night of fire and blood * Kelley, Leo P.
Night of ghosts and lightning * Tallis, Robyn
Night of Kadar, The * Kilworth, Garry
Night of power * Robinson, Spider
Night of tears * Kimbro, John M.
Night of the claw * Campbell, Ramsey
Night of the claw * Campbell, Ramsey *as* JAY RAMSAY
Night of the comet: can you destroy the giants from the sea? * Sharp, Allen
Night of the cooters: more neat stories * Waldrop, Howard
Night of the crabs * Smith, Guy N.
Night of the deathship, The * Barrett, G. J.
Night of the Dragonstar * Bischoff, David & Thomas F. Monteleone
Night of the living shark! * Bischoff, David
Night of the Nazgûl * Ruemmler, John David
Night of the phoenix * Milán, Victor *as* RICHARD AUSTIN
Night of the Sasquatch * Ashlee, Ted
Night of the scorpion, The * Horowitz, Anthony
Night of the seventh darkness * Easterman, Daniel
Night of the solstice, The * Smith, L. J.
Night of the toy dragons, The * Cohen, Barney
Night of the twin moons, The * Lorrah, Jean
Night of the wolf * Callahan, Jay
Night of the wolf * Forest, Salambo
Night of the wolverine * Epperson, Jerry & James M. Ward
Night of two new moons * Tallis, Robyn
Night outside * Wrightson, Patricia
Night plague * Masterton, Graham
Night prayers * Coffey, Frank
Night probe! * Cussler, Clive
Night prophets: a novel * Olson, Paul F.
Night rider, The: a novel * Ingram, Tom
Night riders * Bagdon, Paul *as* TONY PHILLIPS
Night runner, The: The gemini run * Hoskins, Robert *as* MICHAEL KERR
Night screams * Malzberg, Barry N. & Bill Pronzini
Night screams: 13 tales of terror * Kessler, Alan S.
Night seasons, The * Williamson, J. N.
Night shadows * Sellers, Mary
Night shift * King, Stephen
Night show * Laymon, Richard
Night songs * Grant, Charles L.
Night spell * Newman, Robert
Night stalking: a 20th anniversary Kolchak companion * Dawidziak, Mark
Night stands at the door: a novel * Blake, Katherine
Night stone * Hautala, Rick
Night strike * Vanhee, Gregory G.
Night terrors * Grant, Charles L. & Paul Mikol
Night the white dear died, The * Paulsen, Gary

Night things * Monteleone, Thomas F.
Night things * Talbot, Michael
Night thirst * Whalen, Patrick
Night tide, A * Inouye, Jon
Night touch * Gresham, Stephen
Night visions * Frisbie, Carol & Susan James
Night visions 1: all original stories * Ryan, Alan
Night visions 2: all original stories * Grant, Charles L.
Night visions 3: all original stories * Martin, George R. R. & Paul Mikol
Night visions 4: all original stories * Barker, Clive & Paul Mikol
Night visions 5: all original stories * Mikol, Paul & Douglas E. Winter
Night visions 6: all original stories * Koontz, Dean R. & Paul Mikol
Night visions 7: all original stories * Mikol, Paul & Stanley Wiater
Night visions 8: all original stories * McCammon, Robert R. & Paul Mikol
Night visions 9: all original stories * Wilson, F. Paul & Paul Mikol
Night visions: The hellbound heart * Martin, George R. R.
Night visitor, The * Matthews, Patricia
Night visitor, The * Matthews, Patricia *as* LAURA WYLIE
Night visitors: the rise and fall of the English ghost story * Briggs, Julia
Night voices: strange stories * Aickman, Robert
Night walkers, The * Coontz, Otto
Night warriors * Masterton, Graham
Night whisper * Wallace, Patricia
Night whispers * Veley, Charles
Night whistlers, The * Meldal-Johnsen, Trevor & Dan Sherman *as* DAN TREVOR
Night winds * Wagner, Karl Edward
Night, winter, and death * Pedneau, Dave *as* LEE HAWKS
Nightales: stories * Tigges, John
Nightbirds on Nantucket * Aiken, Joan
Nightblood * Martindale, T. Chris
Nightbreed chronicles, The * Barker, Clive
Nightcaps and nightmares: ghosts with a touch of humour * Haining, Peter
Nightcharmer, and other tales of Claude Seignolle, The * Seignolle, Claude
Nightchild * Baker, Scott
Nightchild * Meyer, John
Nighteyes * Reeves-Stevens, Garfield
Nightfall * Asimov, Isaac & Robert Silverberg
Nightfall * Farris, John
Nightfeeder * Reeves-Stevens, Garfield & Judith Reeves-Stevens
Nightfire * Aultman, Mark
Nightflight: a novel * Cadnum, Michael
Nightflyer * Fahy, Christopher
Nightflyers * Martin, George R. R.
Nighthawk * OakGrove, Artemis
Nightingale, The * Dalkey, Kara
Nightlife * Hodge, Brian
Nightmare * Murphy, Gloria
Nightmare * Murray, Doug
Nightmare * Rotsler, William
Nightmare and her foal, and other stories, The * Ipcar, Dahlov
Nightmare begins, The * Ahern, Jerry
Nightmare blonde, The * Wolson, Morton
Nightmare blue * Dozois, Gardner & George Alec Effinger
Nightmare candidate, The * Stewart, Ramona
Nightmare child * Gorman, Ed *as* DANIEL RANSOM

No more magic * Avi
No news from Providence * James, R. Alan
No night without stars * Norton, Andre
No ordinary man * Browning, Robert
No other love * Zachary, Judy
No place else: explorations in utopian and dystopian fiction * Greenberg, Martin H. & Eric S. Rabkin & Joseph D. Olander
No place for me * DeClements, Barthe
No return * Kabakov, Alexander
No room for man: population and the future through science fiction * Clem, Ralph & Martin H. Greenberg & Joseph D. Olander
No safe place * Moroz, Anne
No such thing as a witch * Chew, Ruth
No survivors * Ahern, Jerry
No swimming in Dark Pond, and other chilling tales * Gorog, Judith
No truce with kings * Anderson, Poul
No way street * Clemence, Bruce
No world of their own * Anderson, Poul
Noah's castle * Townsend, John Rowe
Nobody's child * Masters, Anthony
Nocturnal * Eulo, Ken
Nocturne * Cooper, Louise
Nomad VI * Kelley, Charles
Nomad of time, The * Moorcock, Michael
Nomads: novelization * Yarbro, Chelsea Quinn
Nonborn king, The * May, Julian
Nonborn king, The; The adversary * May, Julian
Noninterference * Turtledove, Harry
Non-literary influences on science fiction: (an essay) * Budrys, Algis
Nonsuch Lure, The * Luke, Mary
Noon: 22nd century * Strugatsky, Arkady & Boris Strugatsky
Noonan: a novel about baseball, ESP, & time warps * Fisher, Leonard Everett
Noonspell * Williamson, J. N.
Noose of light, A * Cullen, Seamus
Nopalgarth: three complete novels: Nopalgarth, The houses of Iszm, Son of the Tree * Vance, Jack
Nor crystal tears * Foster, Alan Dean
Nora Maeve and Sebi * Greeley, Andrew M.
Norby and the court jester * Asimov, Isaac & Janet Asimov
Norby and the invaders * Asimov, Isaac & Janet Asimov
Norby and the lost princess * Asimov, Isaac & Janet Asimov
Norby and the oldest dragon * Asimov, Isaac & Janet Asimov
Norby and the queen's necklace * Asimov, Isaac & Janet Asimov
Norby and Yobo's great adventure * Asimov, Isaac & Janet Asimov
Norby chronicles, The * Asimov, Isaac & Janet Asimov
Norby down to Earth * Asimov, Isaac & Janet Asimov
Norby finds a villain * Asimov, Isaac & Janet Asimov
Norby: robot for hire * Asimov, Isaac & Janet Asimov
Norby, the mixed-up robot * Asimov, Isaac & Janet Asimov
Norby through space and time * Asimov, Isaac & Janet Asimov
Norby's other secret * Asimov, Isaac & Janet Asimov
Noreascon proceedings, The: the Twenty-Ninth World Science Fiction Convention, Boston, Massachusetts, September 3-6, 1971 * Turek, Leslie
Noreascon 3 memory book * Mann, Laurie D. T.
Noreascon Three souvenir book * Thokar, Greg
Noreascon II memory book * Lewis, Suford

Norgil: more tales of prestidigitection * Gibson, Walter B.
Norgil the magician * Gibson, Walter B.
Normal service will be resumed * Jales, Mark
Norman conquest 2066 * McIntosh, J. T.
Norman Jacobs & Kerry O'Quinn present Fantastic 3-D: a Starlog photo guidebook * Hutchison, David
Norman Jacobs & Kerry O'Quinn present Fantastic worlds * Holton, Scot & Robert Skotak
Norman Jacobs & Kerry O'Quinn present Robots * Hefley, Robert M.
Norman Jacobs & Kerry O'Quinn present Science fiction heroes * Houston, David
Norman Jacobs & Kerry O'Quinn present Science fiction villains * Houston, David
Norman Jacobs & Kerry O'Quinn present Space art * Miller, Ron
Norman Jacobs & Kerry O'Quinn present Spaceships, rev. ed. * Hirsch, David & Howard Zimmerman
Norman Jacobs & Kerry O'Quinn present Special effects, volume 2 * Hutchinson, Tom
Norman Jacobs and Kerry O'Quinn present Special effects, vol. 3 * Hutchison, David
Norman Jacobs & Kerry O'Quinn present Starlog's science fiction yearbook, vol. 1 * Gerrold, David & Dave Truesdale
Norman Jacobs and Kerry O'Quinn present TV episode guides: science fiction, adventure, and superheroes * Gerani, Gary
Norstrilia * Smith, Cordwainer
North by 2000: a collection of Canadian science fiction * Hargreaves, H. A.
North dimension * Hughes, Dennis Talbot as WILLIAM ROGERSOHN
North Pole, and Charlie Wilson's adventures in search of it, The * Frost, Thomas
Northern girl, The * Lynn, Elizabeth A.
Northern Mirkwood: realm of the wood-elves * Ruemmler, John David
Northshore * Tepper, Sheri S.
Northstar rising * James, Laurence as JAMES AXLER
Northwest Passage, The: a novel * Lavers, Norman
Northwest Smith * Moore, C. L.
Northworld * Drake, David
Nosferatu, the vampyre: a novel * Monette, Paul
No-sided professor, and other tales of fantasy, humor, mystery, and philosophy, The * Gardner, Martin
Nostalgia of the unknown: the complete prose poetry * Smith, Clark Ashton
Nostradamus: a novel * Greene, Liz
Nostradamus inheritance, The * Leonard, Raymond
Not after midnight: thirteen stories to haunt your dreams * Alexander, Marc
Not by bread alone: a novel * Mitchison, Naomi
Not for all the gold in Ireland * James, John
Not for glory * Rosenberg, Joel
Not in our stars * Swycaffer, Jefferson P.
Not now, but now * Fisher, M. F. K.
Not this August * Kornbluth, C. M. & Frederik Pohl
Not to be taken at night: thirteen classic Canadian tales of mystery and the supernatural * Colombo, John Robert & Michael Richardson
Not to mention camels: a science fiction fantasy * Lafferty, R. A.
Not wanted on the voyage * Findley, Timothy
Not your average Joe * Delaney, Michael
Notebooks, memoirs, archives: reading and rereading Doris Lessing * Taylor, Jenny
Notebooks/memoirs/archives: reading and rereading Doris Lessing * Taylor, Jenny

O

O master Caliban! a novel * Gotlieb, Phyllis
Oak king and the ash queen, The * Phillips, Ann
Oak king's daughter, The: a tale of Cerin Songweaver *
de Lint, Charles
Oasis * Hodge, Brian
Oasis Project, The * Arthur, David Stuart
Oath of fealty * Niven, Larry & Jerry Pournelle
Oath of gold * Moon, Elizabeth
Oath of office * Kirsch, Steven J.
Oath of the renunciates * Bradley, Marion Zimmer
Oath to Mida, An * Green, Sharon
Oathbound, The * Lackey, Mercedes
Oathbreakers * Lackey, Mercedes
Obelisk * Ehly, Ehren M.
Obernewtyn * Carmody, Isobelle
Oblagon * Mead, Syd
Oblivion tapes, The * Murari, Timeri
Obscene bird of night, The * Donoso, Jose
Observers, The * Knight, Damon
Obsessed * Reed, Rick R.
Obsession * Campbell, Ramsey
Obsession * Horler, Len
Obsession of Sally Wing, The * Martin, Russell W.
Obsessions * Raisor, Gary
Obsidian, and other stories, The * Jones, Kelvin I.
Obsolete necessity, The: America in utopian writings,
1888-1900 * Roemer, Kenneth M.
Occult coxsman, The * Arrow, Jay
Occult in language and literature, The * Riffaterre, Her-
mine
Occult Lovecraft, The * Lovecraft, H. P.
Occult Lovecraft, The * Raven, Anthony
Occult madonna, The * Hawk, Douglas D.
Octagon * Saberhagen, Fred
October * Sarrantonio, Al
October dreams: a harvest of horror * Kubicek, David &
Jeff Mason
October obsession * More, Meredith
October's baby * Cook, Glen
Odd warlock out * Stasheff, Christopher
Oddkins: a fable for all ages * Koontz, Dean R.
Odds are murder, The * McQuay, Mike
Odour of decay, An * Jenson, Martin
Odysseus solution, The * Banks, Michael A. & Dean R.
Lambe
Odyssey * Kube-McDowell, Michael P.
Odyssey file, The * Clarke, Arthur C. & Peter Hyams
Odyssey of a barbarian: the biography of George
Sylvester Viereck * Gertz, Elmer
Odyssey project, The * De Marino, Lawrence
Odyssey to freedom, An: four themes in Colin Wilson's
novels * Bergström, K. Gunnar
Of alien bondage * Offutt, Andrew J. as JOHN CLEVE
Of beginnings and endings * Adams, Robert
Of chiefs and champions * Adams, Robert
Of dreams and magic * Schulze, Dallas
Of man and mantra: a trilogy: Omnivore, Orn, Ox * An-
thony, Piers

Of muppets & men: the making of The muppet show *
Finch, Christopher
Of myths and monsters * Adams, Robert
Of orc-rags, phials, & a far shore * Palmer, Bruce
Of quests and kings * Adams, Robert
Of space/time and the river * Benford, Gregory
Of the fall * McAuley, Paul J.
Off season * Ketchum, Jack
Offering, The * Huson, Paul
Offerings * Bade, Tom as T. M. MINTON
Officers of the bridge, The * Carnes, Ralph L. & Valerie
Carnes
Official 1981 price guide to comic & science fiction
books, The, 4th ed. * Hudgeons, Thomas E. III
Official 1982 price guide to comic & science fiction
books, The, 5th ed. * Hudgeons, Thomas E. III
Official 1983 price guide to comic & science fiction
books, The, 6th ed. * Hudgeons, Thomas E. III
Official Advanced Dungeons & Dragons Unearthed ar-
cana: a compendium of new ideas and new discover-
ies for AD&D campaigns, of benefit to players and
dungeon masters alike * Gygax, Gary
Official art of 2010, The * Zimbert, Jonathan A.
Official Batman batbook, The * Eisner, Joel
Official Battlestar Galactica scrapbook, The * Neyland,
James
Official correspondence between the Honorable the First
Minister of Duffy and His Exalted Majesty Night
Blooming Ceres, Monarch of the Moon, Emperor of
the Starry Isles, etc., etc., relative to the construction
of the Imperial, Lunar, Grand, Mid-Air, Lunatic Gov-
ernmental Railway, also the reports of the Chief En-
gineer, and the draft treaty in relation to same, with
the speech from the throne * anonymous
Official Counter Force reference book, The: the back-
ground on the Counter Force characters and the
world they live in * Erskine, George & Ian Cameron
Official Doctor Who and the daleks book, The * Nation,
Terry & John Peel
Official Ghostbusters II joke, puzzle, and game book, The
* Looney, Jack & Jim Razzi
Official guide to comic books and Big Little Books, [2nd
ed.] * Resnick, Mike
Official guide to fantastic literature, The: pulps, digests,
hardcovers, paperbacks, Star Trek, radio premiums,
fanzines, original art, Edgar Rice Burroughs *
Resnick, Mike
Official price guide to comic & science fiction books,
third edition * Resnick, Mike
Official price guide to science fiction and fantasy col-
lectibles, The, 3rd ed. * Thompson, Don & Maggie
Thompson
Official price guide to science fiction and fantasy collectibles, The, 7th ed. * Hudgeons, Thomas E. III
Official price guide to Star Trek and Star Wars collectibles * anonymous
Official price guide to Star Trek and Star Wars col-
lectibles, 2nd ed. * anonymous

Official price guide to Star Trek and Star Wars collectibles, 3rd ed. * anonymous

Official price guide to the Star Trek and Star wars collectibles, The * Cornwell, Sue & Mike Kott

Official price guide to the Star Trek and Star wars collectibles, The, 2nd ed. * Cornwell, Sue & Mike Kott

Official price guide to the Star Trek and Star wars collectibles, The, 3rd ed. * Cornwell, Sue & Mike Kott

Official Prisoner companion, The * Ali, Jaffer & Matthew White

Official "Sgt. Pepper's Lonely Hearts Club Band" scrapbook, The: the making of a hit movie musical * Anthony, Dee & Robert Stigwood

Official splatter movie guide, The * McCarty, John

Official Star Trek cooking manual * Piccard, Mary Ann

Official Star Trek quiz book, The * Maglio, Mitchell

Official Star Trek trivia book, The * Needleman, Rafe

Official Starlog communications handbook, volume 1, The * Trimble, Bjo

Official teenage mutant ninja turtles treasury, The * Wiater, Stanley

Off-planet * Simak, Clifford D.

Offspring * Ketchum, Jack

Offspring, The * McKenney, Kenneth

Offspring, The * Williamson, J. N.

Offworld * Daniels, Max

Ogden enigma, The * Snyder, Gene

OGF: being the private papers of George Cockburn, bus conductor, a resident of Hurstfield, a suburb of Sydney, Australia * Smith, Keith

Ogilvie, Tallant, and Moon * Yarbro, Chelsea Quinn

Ogre * Alexander, Marc as MARK RONSON

Ogre castle * Hale, F. J.

Ogre downstairs, The * Jones, Diana Wynne

Ogre, ogre * Anthony, Piers

Oh heavenly dog * Camp, Joe

Oil-planet * Elder, Michael

Oil-seeker * Elder, Michael

Okora mask, The * Wiseman, Rex

Oktober * Gallagher, Stephen

Olaf Stapledon * Kinnaird, John

Olaf Stapledon * McCarthy, Patrick A.

Olaf Stapledon: a bibliography * Satty, Harvey J. & Curtis C. Smith

Olaf Stapledon: a man divided * Fiedler, Leslie A.

Old fears * Wolfe, Ron & John Wooley

Old firm, The * Alexander, Robert as JOAN BUTLER

Old friend of the family, An * Saberhagen, Fred

Old funny stuff, The * Effinger, George Alec

Old gent, The * Conover, Willis

Old gods waken, The * Wellman, Manly Wade

Old magic, An * Arthur, Ruth M.

Old man and Mr. Smith, The * Ustinov, Peter

Old man on a horse * Westall, Robert

Old Nathan * Drake, David

Old Priory, The * Lofts, Norah

Old tin sorrows: from the files of Garrett, P.I. * Cook, Glen

Old wives' fairy tale book, The * Carter, Angela

Old Woman whose rolling pin is the sun, The * Wolfe, Gene

Old-fashioned war, An * Murphy, Warren & Richard Sapir

Olga, the disillusioned * Kimbro, John M. as KATHERYN KIMBROUGH

Olivia, the tormented * Kimbro, John M. as KATHERYN KIMBROUGH

Ollie and the bogle * Jarman, Julia

Olympiad * Frith, Nigel

Olympian strain, The * Jahn, Mike

Olympus: what is the secret of the oracle? * Packard, Edward

Omcri matrix, The * Blakeney, Jay D.

OMEGA * Leonard, Raymond

Omega: a novel * Farrar, Stewart

Omega cage, The * Perry, Steve & Michael Reaves

Omega command, The * Land, Jon

Omega operation, The * Conway, Norman

Omega point trilogy, The * Zebrowski, George

OMEGA Project, The * Griffin, Brian

Omega rebellion, The * Denning, Troy

Omega Station * Slote, Alfred

Omega sub * Jahn, Mike as J. D. CAMERON

Omega worm, The * Mason, Douglas R.

Omega Zone, The * Dever, Joe

OMEGA-MINUS * Allbeury, Ted

Omen, The * Seltzer, David

Omens of Kregen * Bulmer, Kenneth as DRAY PRESCOT & ALAN BURT AKERS

Omicron invasion, The * Goldin, Stephen & E. E. Smith

Omicron legion, The * Land, Jon

Omni: Astropilots * Mixon, Laura J.

Omni strain, The * Patton, Cliff

Omnibus of evil * Lee, Christopher & Michel Parry

Omnibus of twentieth century ghost stories, The * Phillips, Robert

Omni's screen flights/screen fantasies: the future according to science fiction cinema * Peary, Danny

On a pale horse * Anthony, Piers

On a torn-away world; or, The captives of the great earthquake * Garis, Howard R. & Edward L. Stratemeyer as ROY ROCKWOOD

On alien wings * Goulart, Ron

On All Hollows' Eve * Chetwin, Grace

On being human: St. Thomas and Mr. Aldoux Huxley * Vann, Gerald

On fortune's wheel * Voigt, Cynthia

On meeting witches at wells * Gorog, Judith

On my honor * Black, Malachi

On my way to paradise * Wolverton, Dave

On Nineteen Eighty-Four * Stansky, Peter

On raven's wing * Llywelyn, Morgan

On Saint Hubert's thing * Yarbro, Chelsea Quinn

On stranger tides * Powers, Tim

On that dark night * York, Carol Beach

On the 8th day * Okun, Lawrence

On the boundaries of darkness * Hancock, Niel

On the brink: a novel * Stein, Benjamin & Herbert Stein

On the devil's court * Deuker, Carl

On the eighth day * Okun, Lawrence

On the far side of the Cadillac Desert with the dead folks * Lansdale, Joe R.

On the flip side * Fisk, Nicholas

On the good ship Enterprise: my 15 years with Star Trek * Trimble, Bjo

On the history and truth of the unicorn * Green, Michael

On the red world * Kelley, Leo P.

On the rim of the mandala * Cook, Paul

On the road to Baghdad: a picaresque novel of magical adventures, begged, borrowed, and stolen from the Thousand and one nights * GüOn, Güneli

On the run * Dickson, Gordon R.

On the seas of destiny * Emerson, Ru

On the shoulders of giants * St. Alcorn, Lloyd

On the third day * Delahaye, Michael

On the third day: a novel * Read, Piers Paul

On the wasteland * Arthur, Ruth M.

On wings of evil * Newman, Richard Louis

On wings of song * Disch, Thomas M.

On writing * Chalker, Jack L.

P

P. L. Travers * Demers, Patricia
Pacemaker * Brieno, Linda
Pacific book of Australian SF, The * Baxter, John
Pacific book of science fiction, The * Baxter, John
Pacific edge * Robinson, Kim Stanley
Pacific vortex! * Cussler, Clive
Pack, The * Fuller, John G.
Pack, The * Tigges, John as WILLIAM ESSEX
Pack of lies, A: twelve stories in one * McCaughrean, Geraldine
Package in hyperspace, A * Asimov, Janet Jeppson
Pact, The * Preisler, Jerome
Pact, The * Raymond, Alice
Pact, The * Schoell, William
Paddywhack * Stchur, John
Pagan prophet, A: William Morris * Oberg, Charlotte H.
Pagans, The * Herley, Richard
Pageants of despair * Hamley, Dennis
Pages from The book of three: a Prydain glossary * Rossman, Charles E. & Douglas A. Rossman
Pagoda * Largent, R. Karl
Pain * Carson, Michael
Pain gain * Carr, John F.
Paingod, and other delusions * Ellison, Harlan
Painkiller * Spruill, Steven G.
Painted devils: strange stories * Aickman, Robert
Palace, The: an historical horror novel * Yarbro, Chelsea Quinn
Palace of kings * Jefferies, Mike
Palace without chairs * Brophy, Brigid
Palaces and prisons * Miller, Ron
Paladin, The * Cherryh, C. J.
Paladin of the night, The * Hickman, Tracy & Margaret Weis
Pale blue nightgown: a book of tales * Golding, Louis
Pale country pursuit * Kneifel, Hans
Pale invaders, The * Kesteven, G. R.
Pale rider: a novelization * Foster, Alan Dean
Pale shadow of science, The * Aldiss, Brian W.
Palimpsests * Harcourt, Glenn & Carter Scholz
Pallahaxi tide * Coney, Michael
Palm dome, The * Fulton, Liz
Palomino blonde * Allbeury, Ted
Pamela Oldfield's Spine chillers * Oldfield, Pamela
Pamela Sargent: a checklist * Sargent, Pamela
Pan * Dibble, Birney
Panama dead * McQuay, Mike as JACK ARNETT
Panchronicon plot, The * Goulart, Ron
Pandemic: a novel * Simmons, Geoffrey
Pandemonium * Barker, Clive
Pandemonium * Brown, Michael
Pandora principle, The * Clowes, Carolyn
Pandora stone, The * Greenleaf, William
Pandora's children * Lance, Kathryn
Pandora's genes * Lance, Kathryn
Panglor * Carver, Jeffrey A.
Pangur Ban the white cat * Sampson, Fay
Panic 7 * Shaffer, Eugene Carl
Panic of '89, The * Erdman, Paul

Panjang incident, The * Ryan, Charles
Panorama egg, The * Silas, A. E.
Panzer soldier * Sadler, Barry
Panzer spirit * Townsend, Tom
Paper dragons * Blaylock, James P.
Paper grail, The * Blaylock, James P.
Papers on Poe: essays in honor of John Ward Ostrom * Veler, Richard P.
Papio * Kelleher, Victor
Para * Abrams, R. Vaughan
Paradine's gauntlet * Newton, Michael as DON PENDLETON
Paradise * Henderson, Dan
Paradise I: a novel * Harrington, Alan
Paradise: a chronicle of a distant world * Resnick, Mike
Paradise equation, The * Hutchinson, David
Paradise found; or, Where the sex problem has been solved: a story from South America * Armstrong, Charles W.
Paradise Motel, The * McCormack, Eric
Paradise plot, The * Naha, Ed
Paradise Towers * Wyatt, Stephen
Paradise tree, The * Paxson, Diana L.
Paradise war, The * Lawhead, Stephen
Paradise zone, The * Barrett, G. J.
Paradox * Resch, Kathleen
Paradox alley * DeChancie, John
Paradox men, The * Harness, Charles L.
Paradox of George Orwell, The * Voorhees, Richard
Paradox of the Sets, The * Stableford, Brian M.
Paradox planet: a Kane and Pendrake novel * Spruill, Steven G.
Parallel man, The * Purtill, Richard
Paranoia and science fiction * anon.
Parasite, The * Campbell, Ramsey
Parasite * Lewis, Richard
Parasite war, The * Sullivan, Tim
Paratime * Piper, H. Beam
Paratwa, The * Hinz, Christopher
Parched sea, The * Denning, Troy as RICHARD AWLINSON
Parchment House * Smith, Cara Lockhart
Parents of Howard Phillips Lovecraft, The * Faig, Kenneth W. Jr.
Pariah, The * Masterton, Graham
Paris 2005 * Zezza, Carlo
Parsifal: a novel * Vansittart, Peter
Parsival; or, A knight's tale * Monaco, Richard
Parsley Sage, Rosemary, & time * Curry, Jane Louise
Part of the elect, A * Shelley, Mary Wollstonecraft
Partaker, The: a novel of fantasy * Chetwynd-Hayes, R.
Particle theory * Bryant, Edward
Particolored unicorn, The: an entertainment * DeCles, Jon
Partners in time * Simpson, Carla & Pamela Wallace as PAMELA SIMPSON
Party summer * Stine, R. L.
Passage, The * Wartofsky, Victor
Passage at arms * Cook, Glen

1263

Passage of stars, A * Rasmussen, Alis A.
Passage to oblivion * King, Albert as SCOTT HOWELL
Passenger * Keneally, Thomas
Passing advantage, A * McGarrity, Mark
Passing for human * Scott, Jody
Passing of Fu Manchu, The * Suter, Jon Michael
Passing of the dragons, The: the short fiction of Keith Roberts * Roberts, Keith
Passing of the gods, The * Smith, David C.
Passion moon rising * Brandewyne, Rebecca
Passion of Ayn Rand, The * Branden, Barbara
Passion of Molly T., The * Sanders, Lawrence
Passion of new Eve, The * Carter, Angela
Passionate ghost, The * Allen, Sheila Rosalynd
Passionate invaders, the * Clare, John
Passionate warriors * Gronau, Mary Ellen
Past eight o'clock: goodnight stories * Aiken, Joan
Past forgetting: memoirs of the Hammer years * Cushing, Peter
Past is another country, The * Wludyka, Peter
Past of forever, The * Coulson, Juanita
Past times * Anderson, Poul
Past watchful dragons: the Narnian Chronicles of C. S. Lewis * Hooper, Walter
Pastime of eternity, The * Sims, D. N.
Pastoral vision of William Morris, The: the earthly paradise * Calhoun, Blue
Patch of the Odin soldier, The * Grant, Charles L. as GEOFFREY MARSH
Patches of godlight: the pattern of thought of C. S. Lewis * Smith, Robert Houston
Patchwork girl, The * Niven, Larry
Path of Exoterra, The * McBain, Gordon
Path of peril, The * Fickling, David & Perry Hinton
Path of the eclipse: an historical horror novel * Yarbro, Chelsea Quinn
Path through the circle of time * Lee, S.
Path to conquest * Weinstein, Howard
Pathfinders, The * Gravel, Geary
Paths in darkness * Cole, Adrian
Paths of the perambulator, The * Foster, Alan Dean
Pathways to Elfland: the writings of Lord Dunsany * Schweitzer, Darrell
Patricia, the beautiful * Kimbro, John M. as KATHERYN KIMBROUGH
Patrick * Hetherington, Keith
Patrimony, The: a Horseclans novel * Adams, Robert
Patriot's dream * Michaels, Barbara
Pattern of expectation, 1644-2001, The * Clarke, I. F.
Pattern of roses, A * Peyton, Kathleen Wendy & Michael P. Peyton as K. M. PEYTON
Pattern of silver strings, A: a tale of Cerin Songweaver * de Lint, Charles
Patternmaster * Butler, Octavia E.
Patterns of fear in the gothic novel, 1790-1830 * Tracy, Ann B.
Patterns of the fantastic: academic programming at Chicon IV * Hassler, Donald M.
Patterns of the fantastic II * Hassler, Donald M.
Patterns: stories * Cadigan, Pat
Paul Revere and the Boston Tea Party * Kornblatt, Marc
Paul's game: a novel * Towne, Mary
Paul's volcano * Gormley, Beatrice
Pawn, The * Mather, Arthur
Pawn of prophecy * Eddings, David
Pawn of the Omphalos * Tubb, E. C.
Pawn to infinity * Saberhagen, Fred & Joan Saberhagen
Pawns and symbols: a Star Trek novel * Larson, Majliss
Paz * Grae, Camarin

Peace and Olaf Stapledon: an editorialized report * Moskowitz, Sam
Peace Company * Green, Roland
Peace machine, The * Shaw, Bob
Peace under earth: dialogues from the year 1946 * Beaujon, Paul
Peace war, The * Vinge, Vernor
Peacekeepers * Bova, Ben
Peacekeepers, The * DeWeese, Gene
Peacemaker, The * Dozois, Gardner
Peacemaker, The * Pella, Judith & Michael R. Phillips as MARK J. LIVINGSTONE
Peacock papers, The * Simpson, Leo
Peake's progress: selected writings and drawings of Mervyn Peake * Peake, Mervyn
Peanut Butter Express, The * Gagher, John E.
Peanut Butter Poltergeist, The * Leroe, Ellen W.
Pearl of Patmos * Stokes, Manning Lee as JEFFREY LORD
Pearl of the soul of the world, The * Pierce, Meredith Ann
Pear-shaped man, The * Martin, George R. R.
Pearson's weekly, The: a checklist of fiction, 1890-1939 * Locke, George
Pedant and the shuffly, The * Bellairs, John
Peelah; or, The bewitched maiden of Nepal * Manfred, Ernest
Pegasus in flight * McCaffrey, Anne
Peggy, the concerned * Kimbro, John M. as KATHERYN KIMBROUGH
Pellafino * Cardew, Christopher
Pelts * Wilson, F. Paul
Pen friend from another planet * Curtis, Philip
Pen—the brush—the well, The: a work of imagination * Fraser, Ronald
Penal colony, The * Herley, Richard
PENDEX, The: an index of pen names and house names in fantastic, thriller, and series literature * Bates, Susannah
Pendragon chronicles, The: heroic fantasy from the time of King Arthur * Ashley, Mike
Pendulum * Jensen, Ruby Jean
Pendulum * van Vogt, A. E.
Penelope's pendant * Hill, Douglas
Penetrators of time * Kaye, Merlin
Penfriend, The * Ballantyne, David
Penguin book of ghost stories, The * Cuddon, J. A.
Penguin book of horror stories, The * Cuddon, J. A.
Penguin book of vampire stories, The * Ryan, Alan
Penguin book of witches and warlocks, The * Kaye, Marvin
Penguin complete ghost stories of M. R. James, The * James, M. R.
Penguin encyclopedia of horror and the supernatural, The * Sullivan, Jack
Penguin science fiction omnibus, The: an anthology * Aldiss, Brian W.
Penguin supernatural omnibus, The * Summers, Montague
Penguin world omnibus of science fiction, The * Aldiss, Brian W. & Sam J. Lundwall
Pennterra * Moffett, Judith
Penny dreadful, The; or, Strange, horrid, & sensational tales! * Haining, Peter
Penny dreadfuls and other Victorian horrors * Anglo, Michael
Pentecost and the chosen one * Corbett, W. J.
Pentecost of Lickey Top * Corbett, W. J.
People beyond the wall, The * Tall, Stephen
People collection, The * Henderson, Zenna
People exchange, The * Baylus, Robert F.

Phases of gravity * Simmons, Dan
Phaze doubt * Anthony, Piers
Philadelphia adventure, The * Alexander, Lloyd
Philip José Farmer * Brizzi, Mary T.
Philip José Farmer: a working bibliography * Benson, Gordon Jr.
Philip José Farmer, good-natured groundbreaker: a working bibliography, 2nd rev. ed. * Benson, Gordon Jr. & Phil Stephensen-Payne
Philip K. Dick * Greenberg, Martin H. & Joseph D. Olander
Philip K. Dick * Mackey, Douglas A.
Philip K. Dick * Pierce, Hazel Beasley
Philip K. Dick & the umbrella of light * Taylor, Angus
Philip K. Dick: electric shepherd * Gillespie, Bruce
Philip K. Dick: in his own words * Dick, Philip K. & Gregg Rickman
Philip K. Dick: in his own words, 2nd ed. * Dick, Philip K. & Gregg Rickman
Philip K. Dick is dead, alas * Bishop, Michael
Philip K. Dick: the dream connection * Apel, D. Scott
Philip K. Dick: the last testament * Dick, Philip K. & Gregg Rickman
Philip Kindred Dick: a preliminary working bibliography * Benson, Gordon Jr.
Philip Kindred Dick, metaphysical conjurer: a working bibliography, 3rd rev. ed. * Benson, Gordon Jr. & Phil Stephensen-Payne
Philip Wylie: the man and his work * Barshay, Robert Howard
Philosophers, The * Comfort, Alex
Philosophers look at science fiction * Smith, Nicholas D.
Philosophy and science fiction * Philips, Michael
Philosophy of horror, The; or, Paradoxes of the heart * Carroll, Noel
Phobia * Masterton, Graham as THOMAS LUKE
Phobia * Smith, Guy N.
Phoenix * Brust, Steven
Phoenix, The * Sadler, Barry
Phoenix: a novel * White, Ted & Marv Wolfman
Phoenix bells, The * Ptacek, Kathryn as KATHRYN GRANT
Phoenix: Dark messiah * Alexander, David
Phoenix: Death quest * Alexander, David
Phoenix fire * Grimsley, Ann & Lynne Kinnerley as LYNDAN DARBY
Phoenix from the ashes: the literature of the remade world * Yoke, Carl B.
Phoenix: Ground zero * Alexander, David
Phoenix guards, The * Brust, Steven
Phoenix in the ashes * Vinge, Joan D.
Phoenix man, The * Sherman, Jory
Phoenix: Metalstorm * Alexander, David
Phoenix odyssey, The * Henrick, Richard P.
Phoenix of Megaron * Mason, Douglas R. as JOHN RANKINE
Phoenix renewed: the survival and mutation of utopian thought in North American science fiction, 1965-1982 * Zaki, Hoda M.
Phoenix ship * Richmond, Leigh & Walt Richmond
Phoenix sword: the year of the Ninja Master: Winter * Meyers, Richard S. as WADE BARKER
Phoenix tree, The: an anthology of myth fantasy * Boyer, Robert H. & Kenneth J. Zahorski
Phoenix without ashes: a novel of the starlost * Bryant, Edward & Harlan Ellison
Phone call: a novel * Messmann, Jon
Photographer, The * Steiner, Barbara
Photon: Thieves of light * Kube-McDowell, Michael P. as MICHAEL HUDSON
Photoplay edition * Petaja, Emil

Phthor * Anthony, Piers
Phule's company * Asprin, Robert Lynn
Phyllis, the cautious * Kimbro, John M. as KATHERYN KIMBROUGH
Phylum monsters * Peirce, Hayford
Picking the ballad's bones * Scarborough, Elizabeth
Picking up the threads * Strachan, Ian
Picnic on Nearside * Varley, John
Pictorial history of horror movies, A, rev. ed. * Gifford, Denis
Pictorial history of horror stories, A * Haining, Peter
Pictorial history of science fiction, A * Kyle, David A.
Pictorial history of science fiction films, A * Rovin, Jeff
Pictorial history of science fiction films, A * Shipman, David
Pictor's metamorphoses, and other fantasies * Hesse, Hermann
Picture of Dorian Gray, and other writings, The * Wilde, Oscar
Picture of Dorian Gray, The: authoritative texts, backgrounds, revisions and reactions, criticism * Wilde, Oscar & Donald Lawler
Picture of evil * Masterton, Graham
Picture this * Heller, Joseph
Pictures at an exhibition * Watson, Ian
Pictures by J. R. R. Tolkien * Tolkien, J. R. R.
Pictures from an exhibition * Gordon, Giles
Pictures of death * Ernst, Paul as KENNETH ROBESON
Pieces of eight * Johnson, Charles
Pieces of fate * Peel, John
Piecework * Brin, David
Piercing, The * Coyne, John
Piercing the darkness * Peretti, Frank E.
Piers Anthony * Collings, Michael R.
Piers Anthony: biblio of an ogre: a working bibliography * Stephensen-Payne, Phil
Piers Anthony's Hasan * Anthony, Piers
Piers Anthony's Visual guide to Xanth * Anthony, Piers & Jody Lynn Nye
Piers Anthony's Worlds of Chthon: Plasm * Platt, Charles
Pig ignorant * Fisk, Nicholas
Pig Plantagenet, The * Andrews, Allen
Pig, the prince, & the unicorn, The * Brush, Karen A.
Pigeon Irish * Stuart, Francis M.
Pigeon project, The * Wallace, Irving
Pigeons from Hell * Howard, Robert E.
Pigs are flying, The! * Rodda, Emily
Pigs might fly * Rodda, Emily
Pike River phantom, The * Wright, Betty Ren
Pilgermann * Hoban, Russell
Pilgrimage * Mendelson, Drew
Pilgrimage to Hell * Adrian, Jack
Pillar of night * Vardeman, Robert E.
Pillar of the sky: a novel * Holland, Cecelia
Pillars of eternity, The * Bayley, Barrington J.
Pillars of eternity, The; and, The garments of Caean * Bayley, Barrington J.
Pillars of fire * Shagan, Steve
Pillars of Pentegarn * Estes, Rose
Pillars of salt * Paul, Barbara
Pilot error: a novel * Barbree, Jay
Pimpernel plot, The * Hawke, Simon
Pindharee * Richards, Joel
Pines, The * Dunbar, Robert
Pink elephants and hairy toads * Resnick, Mike
Pink lady, The * Dent, Lester as KENNETH ROBESON
Pink of fading neon, The * Blaylock, James P.
Pink Panther strikes again, The * Waldman, Frank
Pinocchio * Moffatt, Derry
Pinocchio in Venice * Coover, Robert

Planetary Legion for Peace: story of their war and our peace, 1940-2000 * Rexner, Romulus

Planetfall * Cover, Arthur Byron

Planetfall * Hill, Douglas

Planetoid of amazement, The * Gilden, Mel

Planetoid peril, The * Hughes, Dennis Talbot as GEORGE SHELDON BROWN

Planets, The * Boylan, James Finney

Planets, The * Preiss, Byron

Planets of peril * Butterworth, Michael

Planets of wonder: a treasury of space opera * Carr, Terry

Planets three * Pohl, Frederik

Planiverse, The: computer contact with a two-dimensional world * Dewdney, A. K.

Planks of reason: essays on the horror film * Grant, Barry Keith

Plant, [part 2], The * King, Stephen

Plant, [part 3], The * King, Stephen

Plant, The: the opening segment of an ongoing work * King, Stephen

Plant people, The * Carlson, Dale

Plant that ate dirty socks, The * McArthur, Nancy

Plants, The: a novel * McKenney, Kenneth

Plasm * Platt, Charles

Plasma monster, The * Mahr, Kurt

Platen stories * Langford, David

Platforms * Maxim, John R.

Platypus of Doom, and other nihilists, The * Cover, Arthur Byron

Play time * Morgan, J. M. as MORGAN FIELDS

Play to live * Veley, Charles

Player of games, The * Banks, Iain M.

Players at the game of people * Brunner, John

Players handbook * Gygax, Gary

Players of Gor * Norman, John

Players of luck, The * Bull, Emma & Will Shetterly

Playground, The * Wright, T. M.

Playgrounds of the mind * Niven, Larry

Playgroup, The * Weber, Nancy

Playing Beatie Bow * Park, Ruth

Playing with desire * Vardeman, Robert E. & Geo. W. Proctor as FRED SPARKROCK

Playing with fire * Bjornstad, James & John Weldon

Playmasters, The * Dalmas, John & Rod Martin

Playmates * Neiderman, Andrew

Playmates * Williamson, J. N.

Pleasure domes of Sigma 93, The * Welby, Philip

Pleasure mongers, The * Sellers, Con

Pleasure planet * Trainor, Starr

Pleasure planet * Vardeman, Robert E. & Geo. W. Proctor as EDWARD GEORGE

Pleasure Tube, The * Onopa, Robert

Pleasure us! * Offutt, Andrew J. & D. Bruce Berry as JOHN CLEVE

Pleasurehouse 13 * Anders, Agnetha

Pleasures forevermore: the theology of C. S. Lewis * Willis, John Randolph

Pleasuring of Rory Malone, The * Panati, Charles

Pledge of peril * Vilott, Rhondi

Pliocene companion, A: being a reader's guide to The many-colored land, The golden torc, The nonborn king, The adversary * May, Julian

Plucking Daisy's innocence * Keye, Don

Plumes in the dust: the love affair of Edgar Allan Poe and Fanny Osgood * Walsh, John Evangelist

Pluribus * Kurland, Michael

Plus * McElroy, Joseph

Pluto pact, The * Smith, Guy N.

Pocket of silence, A * Freeman, Barbara C.

Pockets of resistance * Sanders, William as WILL SUNDOWN

Poe: a biography * Bittner, William Robert

Poe: a collection of critical essays * Regan, Robert

Poe: a critical study * Davidson, Edward H.

Poe and his poetry * Chase, Lewis

Poe and his times: the artist and his milieu * Fisher, Benjamin Franklin IV

Poe and the British magazine tradition * Allen, Michael L.

Poe and the Southern literary messenger * Jackson, David Kelly

Poe, death, and the life of writing * Kennedy, J. Gerald

Poe in the media: screen, songs, and spoken word recordings * Smith, Ronald L.

Poe log, The: a documentary life of Edgar Allan Poe, 1809-1849 * Thomas, Dwight & David K. Jackson

Poe must die: a novel * Olden, Marc

Poe papers, The: a tale of passion * Zaroulis, N. L.

Poe Poe Poe Poe Poe Poe Poe * Hoffman, Daniel

Poe the detective: the curious circumstances behind The mystery of Marie Roget * Walsh, John Evangelist

Poe's Helen remembers * Whitman, Sarah

Poe's literary battles * Moss, Sidney P.

Poe's major crisis: his libel suit and New York's literary world * Moss, Sidney P.

Poetic fantastic, The: studies in an evolving genre * Hyles, Vernon & Patrick D. Murphy

Poetics of imperialism, The: translation and colonization from The tempest to Tarzan * Cheyfitz, Eric

Pohlstars * Pohl, Frederik

Point man, The * Englehart, Stephen

Point of impact * Douglas, Iain

Point of lost souls * Toombs, Jane Jenke

Points of departure * Murphy, Pat

Poison fruit * Yarbro, Chelsea Quinn

Poison island: a Doc Savage adventure * Dent, Lester as KENNETH ROBESON

The poison maiden and the great bitch: female stereotypes in Marvel superhero comics * Wood, Susan

Poison pen * Kisner, James

Poisoned paradise * Roberts, Mark K.

Poisoned planet * Webb, William Thomas

Poisoned pussy, The * Fox, Gardner F. as ROD GRAY

Polar City blues: an entertainment * Kerr, Katharine

Polar fleet * Norwood, Warren

Polar treasure, The: a Doc Savage adventure * Dent, Lester as KENNETH ROBESON

Polaris * Perkins, Sheldon

Pole Star secret, The * Rosenberger, Joseph

Police patrol: 2000 A.D. * Reynolds, Mack

Police your planet * del Rey, Lester as LESTER DEL REY & ERIK VAN LHIN

Politician * Anthony, Piers

Politics of fantasy, The: C. S. Lewis and J. R. R. Tolkien * Rossi, Lee D.

Polly charms the sleeping woman * Davidson, Avram

Polly, the worried * Kimbro, John M. as KATHERYN KIMBROUGH

Poltergeist * Kahn, James

Poltergeist: tales of the deadly ghosts * Haining, Peter

Poltergeist II: The other side * Kahn, James

Poltergeists, ghosts, and psychic encounters * Austin, R. G.

Poly: new speculative writing * Ballentine, Lee

Polyphemus: stories * Shea, Michael

Pond, The * Largent, R. Karl as SIMON LAWRENCE

Pony soldiers * James, Laurence as JAMES AXLER

Pool and the dancing bear, The * Stearns, Pamela

Pool of radiance * Hong, Jane Cooper & James M. Ward

Pool of swallows * Mayne, William as MARTIN COBALT
Pool of the black one, The * Howard, Robert E.
Poor Stainless * Norton, Mary
Poor Tom's ghost * Curry, Jane Louise
Pop world of Henry James, The: from fairy tales to science fiction * Tintner, Adeline R.
Popeye story, The * Terry, Bridget
Pornucopia * Anthony, Piers
Port Eternity * Cherryh, C. J.
Port of saints * Burroughs, William S.
Portal: a dataspace retrieval * Swigart, Rob
Portal of evil * Darvill-Evans, Peter
Portent, The * Harris, Marilyn
Portfolio * Fabian, Stephen E.
Portfolio from The road of Azrael * Krenkel, Roy G.
Portfolio of drawings by William Dixon based on the novels of Edgar Rice Burroughs, A * Dixon, William
Portrait in blood * Kirchoff, Mary L.
Portrait of Ambrose Bierce * de Castro, Adolphe
Portrait of evil * Hale, Jennifer
Portrait of William Morris * Meynell, Esther
Portraits of his children * Martin, George R. R.
Portraits of the past * DuBreuil, Linda as KATE CAMERON
Poseidon target, The * Canon, Jack as NICK CARTER
Poseidon's shadow * Kobryn, A. P.
Positions and presuppositions in science fiction * Suvin, Darko
Possess & conquer * Brown, Wenzell
Possessed! * Kotch, Thomas
Possessed * Lewis, Richard
Possessed * Lewis, Richard as ALAN RADNOR
Possessed * Powe, Ronald
Possessed * Winstone, C. A.
Possessed II: the sequel * Powe, Ronald
Possession * Davies, L. P.
Possession * James, Peter
Possession * Starks, Christopher
Possession of Immanuel Wolf, and other improbable tales, The * Kaye, Marvin
Possession of Jessica Young, The * Martin, Russell W.
Possession of Tamara, The * Lawson, Sybil
Post mortem: new tales of ghostly horror * Olson, Paul F. & David B. Silva
Postcript to Homunculus, A [sic] * Hastings, William
Postman, The * Brin, David
Postmodernist fiction * McHale, Brian
Postscript for Malpas * Pearson, Peter
Poul Anderson: bibliography * Owings, Mark
Poul Anderson, myth-master and wonder-maker: an interim bibliography * Benson, Gordon Jr.
Poul Anderson, myth-master and wonder-maker: an interim bibliography (1947-1986), 4th rev. ed. * Benson, Gordon Jr.
Poul Anderson, myth-master and wonder-maker: a working bibliography, 5th ed. * Benson, Gordon Jr. & Phil Stephensen-Payne, Phil
Power, The * Conte, Sal
Power, The * Haynes, Betsy
Power, The * Mills, James
Power * Stirling, S. M.
Power, The * Watson, Ian
Power and magic * Kane, Daniel
Power and the prophet, The * Hughes, Robert Don
Power ball, The * Lymington, John
Power exchange, The: a novel * Erwin, Alan R.
Power hungry * Weinstein, Howard
Power key * Scheer, K. H.
Power of blackness, The * Williamson, Jack
Power of blackness, The: Hawthorne, Poe, Melville * Levin, Harry

Power of darkness, The * Johnson, Oliver
Power of the gods, The * Vernam, Glenn R.
Power of the Rellard, The * Logan, Carolyn F.
Power of the serpent, The * Timlett, Peter Valentine
Power of the white wolf * Reinius, Trish
Power of three * Jones, Diana Wynne
Power of time, The * Saxton, Josephine
Power play * Cameron, Kenneth M.
Power point * Smith, John Selby
Power that preserves, The * Donaldson, Stephen R.
Power twins, The * Follett, Ken
Power twins and the worm puzzle, The: a science fantasy for young people * Follett, Ken as MARTIN MARTINSON
Power's price * Brand, Kurt
Practice effect, The * Brin, David
Praesidium of Archive, The * Swycaffer, Jefferson P.
Praetor's dungeon, The * Mundy, Talbot
Praise all the moons of morning * Stone, Josephine Rector
Pranks * Higman, Dennis J.
Pray serpents prey * Randers, Nicholas
Prayer machine, The * Hodder-Williams, Christopher
Prayers of steel * Misha
Prayers to broken stones: a collection * Simmons, Dan
Precious cargo * Faust, Joe Clifford
Precipice * Langley, Bob
Precog * Duigon, Lee
Predator, The * DeStefano, Anthony & John S. Lettell as ANTHONY JOHN
Predator: a novel * Monette, Paul
Predator 2: a novel * Hawke, Simon
Predators * Sadler, Mark
Prediction, The * Hyde, John
Pre-Gargantua * Hughes, Dennis Talbot as NEIL CHARLES
Prehistoric epic! * Cirilius, Marcus
Preliminary checklist of science fiction and fantasy published by Ballantine Books (1953-1974), A * Spelman, Dick
Preliminary checklist of science fiction and fantasy published by Ballantine Books (1953-1977), A * Spelman, Dick
Prelude to chaos * Llewellyn, Edward
Prelude to exodus * Jales, Mark
Prelude to Foundation * Asimov, Isaac
Premonition, The * Laurance, Andrew
Premonition * Williamson, J. N.
Premonitions * Bonham, Frank
Premonitions of an inherited mind * Laurance, Andrew
Prentice Alvin * Card, Orson Scott
Pre-revolutionary Russian science fiction: (seven utopias and a dream) * Fetzer, Leland
Prescription Z * Tamminga, Frederick W.
Presence, The * Bunn, T. Davis
Presence, The * Lovin, Roger as RODGERS CLEMENS
Presence, The: a novel of paranormal, psychological horror * MacManus, Yvonne
Presence in an empty room, A * Johnston, Velda
Presenting William Sleator * Davis, James E. & Davis, Hazel K.
Preserver * Foster, M. A.
President's daughter, The * White, Ellen Emerson
President's doctor, The * Woolfolk, William
Press enter ■ * Varley, John
Pressure man * Hughes, Zach
Pretender, The * Cooper, Louise
Pretender: science fiction * Anthony, Piers & Frances Hall

Prevailing spirits: a book of Scottish ghost stories * Gordon, Giles

Prey, The * Naha, Ed as D. B. DRUMM

Prey, The * Smith, Robert Arthur

Price and reference guide to books written by Edgar Rice Burroughs, 2nd ed. * Bergen, James A. Jr.

Price of command, The * Randle, Kevin

Price of fear, The * Davis, Richard

Price of glory, The * Keith, William H. Jr.

Price of power, The: a journey into an incredible world of magic and peril * Estes, Rose

Price of ransom, The * Rasmussen, Alis A.

Price of the phoenix, The * Culbreath, Myrna & Sondra Marshak

Price of victory, The * Asprin, Robert Lynn & Lynn Abbey

Pride of Chanur, The * Cherryh, C. J.

Pride of princes, A * Roberson, Jennifer

Priestess, The * Lauria, Frank

Priests of Ferris, The * Gee, Maurice

Priests of psi, and other stories, The * Herbert, Frank

Primal screen, The: a history of science fiction film * Brosnan, John

Primary * Humes, James C. & John LeBoutillier

Primavera * David, Marjorie

Prime directive * Reeves-Stevens, Garfield & Judith Reeves-Stevens

Prime evil * Kelleher, Ed & Harriette Vidal

Prime evil * Kelman, Judith

Prime evil * Winter, Douglas E.

Prime objective * Mann, Paul

Prime squared * Murdock, M. S.

Primitive, The * Tubb, E. C.

Prince, The * Koster, R. M.

Prince Alcouz and the magician * Smith, Clark Ashton

Prince Caspian; and, The voyage of the Dawn Treader * Lewis, C. S.

Prince in waiting trilogy, The * Christopher, John

Prince Ivan * Morwood, Peter

Prince of chaos * Zelazny, Roger

Prince of dreams * Bishop, Carly

Prince of evil * Page, Norvell W. as GRANT STOCKBRIDGE

Prince of mercenaries: a novel of Falkenberg's Legion * Pournelle, Jerry

Prince of morning bells, The * Kress, Nancy

Prince of stars, The * Dennis, Ian

Prince of stars in the cavern of time, The * Dennis, Ian

Prince of the blood * Feist, Raymond E.

Prince of the Godborn * Harris, Geraldine

Prince of thieves * Martindale, T. Chris

Prince of whales, The: a fantasy adventure * Fisher, R. L.

Prince Ombra * MacLeish, Roderick

Prince on a white horse * Lee, Tanith

Prince Raynor * Kuttner, Henry

Prince who hiccupped, and other tales, The: being some fairy tales for grown-ups * Armstrong, Anthony

Prince Zaleski; and, Cummings King Monk * Shiel, M. P.

Princes of Earth, The * Kurland, Michael

Princes of Sandastre * Swithin, Antony

Princes of the air, The * Ford, John M.

Prince's players, The * Doyle, Debra & James D. Macdonald

Princess and Curdie, The * MacDonald, George

Princess and the dragon, The * Pazzi, Roberto

Princess and the goblin, The * MacDonald, George

Princess and the pauper, The: an erotic fairy tale * Davis, Gwen

Princess and the thorn, The * Fisher, Paul R.

Princess Daphne, The: a novel * Delaro, Selina & Edward Heron-Allen

Princess Hynchatti & some other surprises * Lee, Tanith

Princess in the pigpen, The * Thomas, Jane Resh

Princess of all lands, The * Kirk, Russell

Princess of darkness * anon.

Princess of darkness * Zacharia, Irwin

Princess of Flames, The * Emerson, Ru

Princess of the Chameln, A * Wilder, Cherry

Priorities * Lyons, Lynda

Priory, The * Wasser, Margaret

Prism of the night: a biography of Anne Rice * Ramsland, Katherine

Prison of night * Tubb, E. C.

Prison planet * Dietz, William C.

Prison satellite * Kelley, Leo P.

Prison ship * Caidin, Martin

Prisoner, The * Laurence, James as JAMES DARKE

Prisoner and Danger Man, The * Rogers, Dave

Prisoner files, The * Peel, John

Prisoner, The: Number Two * McDaniel, David

Prisoner of Blackwood Castle, The * Goulart, Ron

Prisoner of dreams * Ripley, Karen

Prisoner of Elderwood * Algozin, Bruce

Prisoner of Malville Hall, The * Daniels, Dorothy

Prisoner of Pineapple Place, The * Lindbergh, Anne

Prisoner of psi * Johnson, Annabel & Edgar Johnson

Prisoner of Reglathium, The * Sirota, Mike

Prisoner of the ant people * Montgomery, R. A.

Prisoner of the horned helmet * Silke, James R.

Prisoner of the planets * Fast, Jonathan

Prisoner of vampires * Garden, Nancy

Prisoner of Zhamanak, The * de Camp, L. Sprague

Prisoners and pawns * Weinstein, Howard

Prisoners of Arionn * Herbert, Brian

Prisoners of Bell Castle, The * Doyle, Debra & James D. Macdonald

Prisoners of paradise * Cross, Ronald Anthony

Prisoners of Pax Tharkas * Simon, Morris

Prisoners of power * Strugatsky, Arkady & Boris Strugatsky

Prisoners of the stars * Asimov, Isaac

Prisoners of time, The * Dever, Joe

Prisonland * Obstfeld, Raymond as JASON FROST

Private demons: the life of Shirley Jackson * Oppenheimer, Judy

Private diaries of Sir H. Rider Haggard, 1914-1925, The * Haggard, H. Rider

Private life of H. P. Lovecraft, The * Davis, Sonia H.

Private press of Roy A. Squires, The: a checklist of imprints * Squires, Roy A.

Private press of Roy A. Squires, The: a descriptive listing of publications, 1962-1979, [2nd ed.] * Squires, Roy A.

Privateers * Bova, Ben

Pro * Dickson, Gordon R.

Probability Broach, The * Smith, L. Neil

Probability corner, The * Richmond, Leigh & Walt Richmond

Probe * Douglas, Carole Nelson

Probe * Lerner, Edward M.

Problematic fictions of Poe, James, and Hawthorne, The * Sutherland, Judith L.

Proceedings of Concon (Smofcon I) 1984 * Renner, Theresa

Proceedings of the Conference of Science Fiction Convention Managers 1972 * Lewis, Suford

Process, The * Spinrad, Norman

Procurator * Mitchell, Kirk

Procyon's promise * McCollum, Michael

Q

Q Colony * Thurston, Robert
Q factor, The * Kirk, Philip
Q: Seeking the mythical future * Hoyle, Trevor
Q: The gods look down * Hoyle, Trevor
Q: Through the eye of time * Hoyle, Trevor
Qhe!: The prophets of evil * W. W.
Q-in-law * Peters, David as PETER DAVID
Q-Man, The * Stevenson, John as NICK CARTER
Quad world * Metzger, Robert A.
Quadrant war, The * Ryman, Ras
Quadriphobia * Ryan, Alan
Quag Keep * Norton, Andre
Quagmire, The * Kisner, James
Quaking lands, The * Vardeman, Robert E.
Quaking terror * Roberts, Mark as LIONEL DERRICK
Qualinesti, The * Carter, Tonya R. & Paul B. Thompson
Quantum leap: The beginning * Robitaille, Julie
Quantum leap: The ghost and the gumshoe * Robitaille, Julie
Quantum science fiction special (1): In the ocean of night / Gregory Benford ; The Ophiuchi hotline / John Varley * anon.
Quantum special (2): The far call / Gordon R. Dickson ; In the hall of the Martian kings / John Varley * anon.
Quarantine * Webster, Josh
Quark invasion, The * Hill, Ernest
Quarrel of witches, A * Storey, Margaret
Quarrel with the Moon * Conaway, J. C.
Quarreling, they met the dragon * Baker, Sharon
Quarter of eight, A; &, The freak show murders * Gibson, Walter B.
Quas Starbrite * Berry, James R.
Quatermass * Kneale, Nigel
Queen Kong * Moffatt, James
Queen of angels * Bear, Greg
Queen of darkness * Preston, Harry
Queen of evil * Sharpe, Vera
Queen of hearts, The * Dobkin, Kaye
Queen of hearts: a novel * Shreve, Susan Richards
Queen of Hell * Williamson, J. N.
Queen of knights * Wind, David as MONICA BARRIE
Queen of sorcery * Eddings, David
Queen of springtime, The * Silverberg, Robert
Queen of stones * Tennant, Emma
Queen of the black coast * Howard, Robert E.
Queen of the damned, The * Rice, Anne
Queen of the Legion, The * Williamson, Jack
Queen of the lightning * Herbert, Kathleen
Queen of the looking glass * Cassiday, Bruce as ANNIE LAURIE MCALLISTER
Queen of the states * Saxton, Josephine
Queen of the summer stars * Woolley, Persia
Queen of Zamba, The * de Camp, L. Sprague
Queen Ortruda * Sologub, Fëdor
Queenmagic, Kingmagic * Watson, Ian
Queen's cadet, and other tales, The * Grant, James
Queen's gambit declined * Snodgrass, Melinda M.
Queens of Deliria * Butterworth, Michael
Queens walk in the dusk * Swann, Thomas Burnett

Queensblade * Shwartz, Susan
Quelling eye, The * Gordon, John
Quentin Corn * Stolz, Mary
Quest, The * Ahern, Jerry
Quest * Bischoff, David
Quest, The * DeMille, Nelson
Quest * Oxley, Dorothy
Quest * Sapir, Richard
Quest crosstime * Norton, Andre
Quest for a babe * Hendry, Frances
Quest for a kelpie * Hendry, Frances
Quest for a maid * Hendry, Frances
Quest for Apollo * Lahey, Michael
Quest for Cush, The * Saunders, Charles R.
Quest for King Arthur * Ashby, Ruth
Quest for lost heroes * Gemmell, David A.
Quest for M. P. Shiel's realm of Redonda, The * Morse, A. Reynolds
Quest for Merlin, The * Tolstoy, Nikolai
Quest for Orion, A * Harris, Rosemary
Quest for Queenie, The * Ball, Brian
Quest for Saint Camber, The * Kurtz, Katherine
Quest for Tanelorn, The: the chronicles of Castle Bruss, being a sequel to the High history of the runestaff, of which this is the third and final volume * Moorcock, Michael
Quest for the 36, The * Billias, Stephen
Quest for the cities of gold * Glatzer, Richard
Quest for the Demon Gate * Fawcett, Bill
Quest for the dragon's eye * Fawcett, Bill
Quest for the elf king * Fawcett, Bill
Quest for the Faradawn * Ford, Richard
Quest for the unicorn's horn * Fawcett, Bill
Quest for the Well of Souls * Chalker, Jack L.
Quest for the white witch * Lee, Tanith
Quest of love, A * Hawkes, Jacquetta
Quest of Qui: a Doc Savage adventure * Dent, Lester as KENNETH ROBESON
Quest of the absolute, The: Séraphita * Balzac, Honoré de
Quest of the Dawnstar * McBain, Gordon
Quest of the DNA cowboys, The * Farren, Mick
Quest of the Gypsy: a novel * Goulart, Ron
Quest of the Quidnuncs, The * Curtis, Philip
Quest of the seventh carrier * Albano, Peter
Quest of the sons, The * Scott, Michael
Quest of the Spider: Doc Savage and his pals in a novel of unusual adventure * Dent, Lester as KENNETH ROBESON
Quest strike * Robbins, David
Quester's endgame: a novel of the Diadem * Clayton, Jo
Questing hero, The * Cook, Hugh
Questing of Kedrigern, The * Morressy, John
Question and answer * Anderson, Poul
Question of destiny, A * Service, Pamela F.
Question of life, A * Lottman, Eileen as MAUD WILLIS
Question of reality, A * Barker, D. A.
Question of survival, A * Thompson, Julian F.
Question quest * Anthony, Piers

R

R. A. Lafferty checklist, A: a bibliographical chronology
    with notes and index * Drumm, Chris
Rabbit magic * York, Carol Beach
Rabelaisian reprise * Carr, Jayge
Rabid * Anne, David
Rabid * Lewis, Richard
Rabid brigadier, The * Stacy, Jan as CRAIG SARGENT
Race across the stars * Offutt, Andrew J. & Robin Kin-
    caid as JOHN CLEVE
Race against time * Baker, Jane & Pip Baker
Race for God, The * Herbert, Brian
Race forever, The * Montgomery, R. A.
Race into the past * Stine, H. William & Megan Stine
Race of the dark gambler * Sellers, Mary
Rachel and the angel, and other stories * Westall, Robert
Rachel, the possessed * Kimbro, John M. as KATHERYN
    KIMBROUGH
Rack, The; &, All the king's horses, all the king's men *
    Vance, J. Emily
Rack of Baal, The * Smith, Mark & Jamie Thomson
Rack series, The: Backlash * James, Laurence
Rack series, The: Planet of the blind * James, Laurence
Radiant Warrior, The * Frankowski, Leo
Radical imagination: feminist conceptions of the future in
    Ursula Le Guin, Marge Piercy, and Sally Miller
    Gearhart * Keulen, Margarete
Radical utopias * anon.
Radio detectives under the sea, The * Verrill, A. Hyatt
Radio Free Albemuth * Dick, Philip K.
Radio plays * Compton, D. G.
Radius of doubt * Vilott, Rhondi as CHARLES INGRID
Radix * Attanasio, A. A.
Raft * Baxter, Stephen
Rafters were singing, The: a tale of Cerin Songweaver *
    de Lint, Charles
Rag, a bone, and a hank of hair, A * Fisk, Nicholas
Rage for revenge, A * Gerrold, David
Rage of battle * Slater, Ian
Rage under the Arctic * Jackson, Basil
Ragged astronauts, The * Shaw, Bob
Ragged world, The: a novel of the Hefn on Earth * Mof-
    fett, Judith
Raging, The * Stout, Tim
Raging peace, The * OakGrove, Artemis
Ragnarok * Compton, D. G. & John Gribbin
Ragnarok * Thackery, Anne
Rahne * Coon, Susan
Raid on Nightmare Castle * McGuire, Catherine
Raiders of the lost ark: a storybook based on the movie *
    Martin, Les
Raiders of the lost Ark: novel * Black, Campbell
Raiders of the lost ark: the illustrated screenplay * Kas-
    dan, Lawrence
Raiders of the Revolution * Andrews, Keith William
Raider's sky: a novel * Haynes, Mary
Rain * Gallagher, Stephen
Rain * McDowell, Michael
Rain ghost, The * Kilworth, Garry
Rain of terror * Murphy, Warren & Richard Sapir

Rainbow abyss, The * Hambly, Barbara
Rainbow annals, The * Davis, Grania
Rainbow cadenza, The: a novel in logosata form *
    Schulman, J. Neil
Rainbow gate, The * Warrington, Freda
Rainbow goblins, The * de Rico, Ul
Rainbow in the mist * Whitney, Phyllis A.
Rainbow magic * Teacher, Rebecca
Rainbow quest of Thomas Pynchon, The * Mackey, Dou-
    glas A.
Rainbow stories, The * Vollman, William T.
Rainbow sword, The * Martine-Barnes, Adrienne
Rainbow walkers * Schwerin, Doris
Rains of Eridan, The * Hoover, H. M.
Raise the Titanic! * Cussler, Clive
Raising goosebumps for fun and profit * Klein, T. E. D.
Raising the stones * Tepper, Sheri S.
Rajan * Lukeman, Tim
Rally cry * Forstchen, William R.
Ralph Fozbek and the amazing black hole patrol * Senn,
    Steve
Ram of Sweetriver, The * Dann, Colin
Ram song * Webb, Sharon
Rama II * Clarke, Arthur C. & Gentry Lee
Ramsey Campbell * Crawford, Gary William
Ramsgate paradox, The * Tall, Stephen
Rancho of the little loves, The * Nathan, Robert
Randall Garrett's Lord Darcy in A study in sorcery *
    Kurland, Michael
Randall Garrett's Lord Darcy in Ten little wizards *
    Kurland, Michael
Randalls round * Scott, Eleanor
Random access messages of the computer age * Mon-
    teleone, Thomas F.
Random factor * Sherman, Joel Henry
Random House book of ghost stories, The * Hill, Susan
Rangers of the North * Ruemmler, John David
Rankin: enemy of the state * Osier, John
Ranks of bronze * Drake, David
Ransom of Black Stealth One, The * Ing, Dean
Ransome revisited * Mace, Elisabeth
Rape of Shavi, The * Emecheta, Buchi
Rape of Sun Lee Fong, The * Tuleja, Thaddeus as MAR-
    SHALL MACAO
Rape of the red witch * Kaye, Merlin
Rape of the Sun, The * Wallace, Ian
Raped by the devil * anon.
Raphael * MacAvoy, R. A.
Rapture * Tessier, Thomas
Rapture effect, The * Carver, Jeffrey A.
Rare Frazetta, The * Frazetta, Frank
Rasco and the rats of NIMH * Conly, Jane Leslie
Rashanyn dark * Tedford, William G.
Rat, The * Grass, Gunter
Rat report, The * FitzGibbon, Constantine
Rat trap * Read, John as TONY PHILLIPS
Ratha and Thistle-Chaser * Bell, Clare
Ratha's creature * Bell, Clare
Rationale of deception in Poe, The * Ketterer, David

Rationalizing genius: ideological strategies in the classic American science fiction short story * Huntington, John

Ratner's Star * DeLillo, Don

Ratnose: a journey up the Hassayampa * Jones, Robert F.

Rats, The * Herbert, James

Rats and gargoyles * Gentle, Mary

Rats of Megaera, The * Kea, Neville

Ratspike * Blanche, John & Ian Miller

Raum * Sherrell, Carl

Raven * Burnham, Jeremy & Trevor Ray

Raven, The * Green, Carl R. & William R. Sanford

Raven * Morgan, Stanley

Raven * Morley, Adam R.

Raven, and the whale, The: the war of words and wits in the era of Poe and Melville * Miller, Perry

Raven in the glass, The * Downie, Jill

Raven of destiny * Tremayne, Peter

Raven, swordmistress of chaos * Holdstock, Robert & Angus Wells as RICHARD KIRK

Ravenloft: Vampire of the mists * Golden, Christie

Ravenmoon * Tremayne, Peter

Raven's beak, The * Nisbet, Helen C.

Ravens' gathering * Taylor, Keith

Ravens of the moon, The * Grant, Charles L.

Ravenscarne, and other ghost stories * Williams, Mary

Ravished * Slaughter, Pamela

Raw pain Max * Andersson, C. Dean

Rax * Coney, Michael

Ray Bradbury * Bradbury, Ray

Ray Bradbury * Greenberg, Martin H. & Joseph D. Olander

Ray Bradbury * Johnson, Wayne L.

Ray Bradbury * Mogen, David

Ray Bradbury * Touponce, William F.

Ray Bradbury and the poetics of reverie: fantasy, science fiction, and the reader * Touponce, William F.

Ray Bradbury companion, The: a life and career history, photolog, and comprehensive checklist of writings, with facsimiles of Ray Bradbury's unpublished and uncollected work in all media * Nolan, William F.

Ray Bradbury: dramatist * Indick, Ben P.

Ray Bradbury review * Nolan, William F.

Ray Ellis in The Green Mandarin mystery * Hughes, Dennis Talbot as GRANT MALCOM

Razored saddles * Lansdale, Joe R. & Pat LoBrutto

Razor's edge * Walker, Robert W.

Re: colonised planet 5, Shikasta: personal, psychological, historical documents relating to a visit by Johor (George Sherban), emissary (grade 9) 87th of the period of the last days * Lessing, Doris

Reach: a novel * Gibson, Edward

Reader in a strange land: the activity of reading literary utopias * Ruppert, Peter

Reader's guide to Barsoom and Amtor, The * Lupoff, Richard A.

Reader's guide to fantasy, A * Franklin, Michael & Baird Searles & Beth Meacham

Reader's guide to George Orwell, A * Meyers, Jeffrey

Reader's guide to science fiction, A * Franklin, Michael & Baird Searles & Martin Last & Beth Meacham

Reader's guide to the Cthulhu Mythos, A * Weinberg, Robert

Reader's guide to The Silmarillion, A * Kocher, Paul H.

Reader's guide to twentieth-century science fiction * Fletcher, Marilyn P. & James L. Thorson

Reading Poe, reading Freud: the romantic imagination in crisis * Bloom, Clive

Reading with the heart: the way into Narnia * Schakel, Peter J.

Ready for blastoff! * Peel, John as RICK NORTH

Ready or not, here come fourteen frightening stories! * Kahn, Joan

Real life Mr Newman, The * Moorcock, Michael

Real story, the * Donaldson, Stephen R.

Reality barrier, The * Jadis, Donna

Reality matrix, The * Dalmas, John

Really weird summer, A * McGraw, Eloise Jarvis

Realm beneath, The * Clough, B. W.

Realm of chaos * Brennan, J. H.

Realm of the alien * Rayer, Francis G. as CHESTER DELRAY

Realm of the gods * Cooke, Catherine

Realm seven * Chiu, Tony

Realms of darkness * Danby, Mary

Realms of fantasy * Edwards, Malcolm & Robert Holdstock

Realms of Tartarus, The * Stableford, Brian M.

Realms of wizardry * Carter, Lin

Re-animator: a novel * Rovin, Jeff

Re-animator: tales of Herbert West * Lovecraft, H. P.

Reap: the Baycon guest-of-honor speech * Farmer, Philip José

Reap the east wind * Cook, Glen

Reap the whirlwind * Cherryh, C. J. & Mercedes Lackey

Reaper man * Pratchett, Terry

Reaping, The: a novel * Taylor, Bernard

Reason and imagination in C. S. Lewis: a study of Till we have faces * Schakel, Peter J.

Reasonable world, A * Knight, Damon

Reasons behind the SFWA model paperback contract, The * Spinrad, Norman

Reavers of Skaith, The * Brackett, Leigh

Rebecca, the mysterious * Kimbro, John M. as KATHERYN KIMBROUGH

Rebecca's world: journey to the forbidden planet * Nation, Terry

Rebekka Moon * Spence, Michele

Rebel angels, The * Davies, Robertson

Rebel attack * Bischoff, David as MARK GRANT

Rebel dynasty, The, volume 1: Star rebel; Rebel's quest * Busby, F. M.

Rebel dynasty, The, volume 2: The alien debt; Rebel's seed * Busby, F. M.

Rebel from Alphorion * Tallis, Robyn

Rebel in time, A * Harrison, Harry

Rebel of Antares * Bulmer, Kenneth as DRAY PRESCOT & ALAN BURT AKERS

Rebel planet * Waterfield, Robin

Rebel prince, The * Green, Sharon

Rebel witch, The * Lovejoy, Jack

Rebellion 2456 * Murdock, M. S.

Rebellion, The * Ahern, Jerry

Rebels in Hell * Morris, Janet

Rebels of Merka * Funnell, Augustine

Rebel's quest * Busby, F. M.

Rebels' seed * Busby, F. M.

Rebirth, The * Cherryh, C. J.

Reborn * Simon, Leonard

Reborn: a novel * Wilson, F. Paul

Recent critical studies on fantastic literature: an annotated checklist * Tymn, Marshall B.

Reckless robot * McEvoy, Seth

Reckoning * Norris, S. D.

Reclamation of a queen, The: Guinevere in modern fantasy * Gordon-Wise, Barbara Ann

Recluse 1927, The * Cook, W. Paul

Rehumanization of Jade Darcy, The: Jade Darcy and the affair of honor * Goldin, Stephen & Mary Mason

Rehumanizaion of Jade Darcy, The: Jade Darcy and the zen pirates * Mason, Mary & Stephen Goldin

Reign * Williamson, Chet

Reign of fear: fiction and film of Stephen King * Herron, Don

Reign of fire * Kellogg, M. Bradley & William B. Rossow

Reign of terror, The * Marter, Ian

Reign of terror: great Victorian horror stories * Parry, Michel

Reign of terror: the 1st Corgi book of great Victorian horror stories * Parry, Michel

Reign of terror: the 2nd Corgi book of great Victorian horror stories * Parry, Michel

Reign of terror: the 3rd Corgi book of great Victorian horror stories * Parry, Michel

Reign of terror: the 4th Corgi book of great Victorian horror stories * Parry, Michel

Reimann curse, The * DeWeese, Gene as JEAN DeWEESE

Reincarnation in Venice * Ehrlich, Max

Reincarnation of Jenny James, The * Sherman, Jory

Reincarnation of Reece Erikson, The * Obstfeld, Raymond

Reindeer moon * Thomas, Elizabeth Marshall

Reindeer people, The * Lindholm, Megan

Reiver * Morgan, Dave

Relations and what they related, The: a series of weird stories * Reynolds, Mrs. Baillie

Relics * Hutson, Shaun

Relife * Barton, Dan

Religion, The * Condé, Nicholas

Religion of science fiction, The * Kreuziger, Frederick A.

Reluctant devil, The: a cautionary tale * Seymour, Miranda

Reluctant ghost, The * Allen, Sheila Rosalynd

Reluctant ghost-hunter, The * Kennett, Rick

Reluctant god, The * Service, Pamela F.

Reluctant king, The * de Camp, L. Sprague

Reluctant swordsman, The * Duncan, Dave

Reluctant vampire, The * Morecambe, Eric

Reluctant wizard, The * Newell, Neil K.

Remaking history * Robinson, Kim Stanley

Remaking of Sigmund Freud, The * Malzberg, Barry N.

Remarkable aerial voyage, A * Bilderdijk, Willem

Remarkable journey of Prince Jen, The * Alexander, Lloyd

Remember Gettysburg! * Cornett, Robert & Kevin Randle

Remember me * Pike, Christopher

Remember me: a novel * Lipsett, Suzanne

Remember the Alamo! * Cornett, Robert & Kevin Randle

Remember the Little Bighorn! * Cornett, Robert & Kevin Randle

Remembrance for Kedrigern, A * Morressy, John

Remembrance of the Daleks * Aaronovitz, Ben

Rememory * Betancourt, John Gregory

Remo: the adventure begins: a novel * Murphy, Warren & Richard Sapir

Remscéla * Frost, Gregory

Renaissance * van Vogt, A. E.

Renaissance of wonder * Lochhead, Marion

Renaissance of wonder in children's literature, The * Lochhead, Marion

Renaissance of wonder: the fantasy worlds of C. S. Lewis, J. R. R. Tolkien, George MacDonald, E. Nesbit, and others * Lochhead, Marion

Rendezvous * Smith, D. Alexander

Rendezvous in Averoigne, A: best fantastic tales of Clark Ashton Smith * Smith, Clark Ashton

Rendezvous on a lost world * Chandler, A. Bertram

Rendezvous with Rama * Clarke, Arthur C. & David Fickling

Renegade * DeWeese, Gene

Renegade * Scotten, Cordell

Renegade legion: Damned if we do * Rice, Peter

Renegade lord, The * Smith, Mark & Jamie Thomson

Renegade of Callisto * Carter, Lin

Renegade of Kregen * Bulmer, Kenneth as ALAN BURT AKERS

Renegade Steele * Hawke, Simon as J. D. MASTERS

Renegade war * McPhee, James

Renegades * Hutson, Shaun

Renegades honor * Keith, William H. Jr.

Renegades of Gor * Norman, John

Renegades of Luntar * Moore, Roger E.

Renegades of Pern, The * McCaffrey, Anne

Renegades of the future * Mahr, Kurt

Renegades of time * Jones, Raymond F.

RenSime * Lichtenberg, Jacqueline

Rentaghost enterprises * Morgan, Hugh

Rentaghost rules * Morgan, Hugh

Rentaghost unlimited * Morgan, Hugh

Rent-a-nymph * Bennett, Jeff as HANNAH BRONTO

Renunciates of Darkover * Bradley, Marion Zimmer & the Friends of Darkover

Reparations * Wardman, Gordon

Repertory of the Italian professionals in science fiction and fantasy 1981 * Vegetti, Ernesto

Repertory of the Italian professionals in science fiction and fantasy 1982-1983 * Vegetti, Ernesto

Replay * Grimwood, Ken

Replica * Bowker, Richard

Replica * Saben, Lionel

Report on a writing man & other reminiscences of Robert E. Howard * Smith, Tevis Clyde

Reprisal, The * Ahern, Jerry

Reprisal: a novel * Wilson, F. Paul

Reprisals * Wilson, F. Paul

Republic and empire * Carr, John F. & Jerry Pournelle

Requiem at Rogano * Knight, Stephen

Requiem for a princess * Arthur, Ruth M.

Requiem for a ruler of worlds * Daley, Brian

Requiem for Anthi * Blakeney, Jay D.

Requiem for the conqueror * Gear, W. Michael

Requiem of love, A * Miller, Calvin

Rereading Doris Lessing: narrative patterns of doubling and repetition * Sprague, Claire

Rerun: a novel * Crichton, Neil

Rescue, The * Marter, Ian

Rescue * O'Connor, Stephen

Rescue in Mirkwood * Lientz, Gerald

Rescue mission, The * DiVono, Sharman & William Rotsler as VICTOR APPLETON

Rescue of Athena One, The: a novel * Jahn, Mike

Rescue of Ranor, The * Belden, Wilanne Schneider

Rescue run * McCaffrey, Anne

Rescuers Downunder, The * Singer, A. L.

Research guide to science fiction studies, A: an annotated checklist of primary and secondary sources for fantasy and science fiction * Currey, L. W. & Marshall Tymn & Roger C. Schlobin

Research opta * Hughes, Dennis Talbot as Neil Charles

Resolutions in time * Clark, Dale

Resolved, you're dead * Coleman, Clay as NICHOLAS ADAMS

Resonating bodies * Alexander, Lynne

Rest in agony * Younger, Jack

Rest in peace * MacLane, Jack

Revenge of the rose, The * Moorcock, Michael
Revenge of the Russian ghost * Leibold, Jay
Revenge of the senior citizens, **plus: a short story collection * Reed, Kit
Revenge of the Valkyrie * Gunnarsson, Thorarinn
Revenge of the wizard's ghost, The * Bellairs, John
Reverend Mama * Cooper, Parley J.
Revolt and rebirth * Swycaffer, Jefferson P.
Revolt of Aphrodite, The * Durrell, Lawrence
Revolt of the devil men * Tepperman, Emile C. as CURTIS STEELE
Revolt of the dwarves * Estes, Rose
Revolt of the galaxy * Goldin, Stephen & E. E. "Doc" Smith
Revolt of the micronauts * Williams, Gordon
Revolt of the unemployables, The * Nelson, Ray Faraday
Revolt on Jupiter * Martin, John
Revolt on Majipoor: a Crossroads adventure in the world of Robert Silverberg's Majipoor * Costello, Matthew J.
Revolution from Rosinante, The * Gilliland, Alexis A.
Revolution island * Fane, Julian
Revolution's shore * Rasmussen, Alis A.
Reward for Retief * Laumer, Keith
Rewind to yesterday * Pfeffer, Susan
Rewolf of Oz, The * Baum, Roger S.
RGM Productions presents Nightmare Theater * Marrero, Robert
Rhanna at war * Fraser, Christine Marion
Rhapsody in Amber, A * Zelazny, Roger
Rhea * Martin, Russell W.
Rhetoric of the unreal, The: studies in narrative and structure, especially of the fantastic * Brooke-Rose, Christine
Rhialto the Marvellous * Vance, Jack
Rhialto the Marvellous * Vance, Jack & C. J. Cherryh & Janet Morris
Rhinegold * Gorham, Melvin
Rhino Ritz: an American mystery * Abbott, Keith
Richard and the Vratch * Gormley, Beatrice
Richard Blade: Dimension of horror * Nelson, Ray Faraday as JEFFREY LORD
Richard Blade: Gladiators of Hapanu * Green, Roland as JEFFREY LORD
Richard Blade: Killer plants of Binaark * Green, Roland as JEFFREY LORD
Richard Blade: King of Zunga * Green, Roland as JEFFREY LORD
Richard Blade: Master of the Hashomi * Green, Roland as JEFFREY LORD
Richard Blade: Pirates of Gohar * Green, Roland as JEFFREY LORD
Richard Blade: Return to Kaldak * Green, Roland as JEFFREY LORD
Richard Blade: The dragons of Englor * Green, Roland as JEFFREY LORD
Richard Blade: The golden steed * Green, Roland as JEFFREY LORD
Richard Blade: The Lords of the Crimson River * Green, Roland as JEFFREY LORD
Richard Blade: The ruins of Kaldac * Green, Roland as JEFFREY LORD
Richard Blade: The temples of Ayocan * Green, Roland as JEFFREY LORD
Richard Blade: Treasure of the stars * Green, Roland as JEFFREY LORD
Richard Blade: Warriors of Latan * Green, Roland as JEFFREY LORD
Richard Blade: Wizard of Rentoro * Green, Roland as JEFFREY LORD

Richard Matheson: collected stories * Matheson, Richard
Richard Matheson: he is legend: an illustrated bio-bibliography * Flanagan, Graeme & Mark Rathbun
Richard Wilson checklist, A * Drumm, Chris
Riches, The * W. W.
Riches and power: a story for children * Leiber, Fritz
Riddle and the rune, The * Chetwin, Grace
Riddle of stars: The riddle-master of Hed; Heir of sea and fire; Harpist in the wind * McKillip, Patricia A.
Riddle of the griffon * Moore, Roger E. & Margaret Weis as SUSAN LAWSON
Riddle of the seven realms * Hardy, Lyndon
Riddle of the Wren, The * de Lint, Charles
Riddle-master of Hed, The * McKillip, Patricia A.
Riddley Walker * Hoban, Russell
Riddling reaver, The * Mason, Paul & Steve Williams
Ride the lightning * Lutz, John
Ride the wind * Gordon, John
Rider Haggard * Etherington, Norman
Rider Haggard: a biography * Higgins, D. S.
Rider Haggard and the fiction of empire: a critical study of British imperial fiction * Katz, Wendy R.
Rider Haggard: his life and works * Cohen, Morton N.
Rider Haggard: his life and work, 2nd ed. * Cohen, Morton N.
Rider Haggard: the great storyteller * Higgins, D. S.
Riders of the Dragon * DeBolt, Adriana as CHRISTOPHER DANE
Riders of the Sidhe, The * Flint, Kenneth C.
Riders of the winds * Chalker, Jack L.
Ridge, The * Cantrell, Lisa W.
Riding the torch * Spinrad, Norman
Rift, The * Peters, David as PETER DAVID
Rifts of time * Rowland, Donald S. as GRAHAM GARNER
Rig warrior * Johnstone, William W.
Rigger black book * McGregor, Phillip
Right hand of Dextra, The * Lake, David J.
Right Honourable Chimpanzee, The * Phillips, David & Georgii Markov as DAVID ST. GEORGE
Right where you are sitting now: further tales of the Illuminati * Wilson, Robert Anton
Rim of eternity, The * Geddes, Adrienne
Rim of space, The; The ship from outside * Chandler, A. Bertram
RIM, the rebel robot * Logan, Nora
Rime Isle * Leiber, Fritz
Rimrunners * Cherryh, C. J.
Rim-world legacy and beyond, The * Javor, Frank A.
Ring, The * Moran, Daniel Keys
Ring cycle, The * Gorham, Melvin
Ring of Allaire, The * Dexter, Susan
Ring of Charon, The * Allen, Roger MacBride
Ring of fire * Jennison, John as JOHN THEYDON
Ring of fire, The * Murphy, Shirley Rousseau
Ring of fortune, The * Priestley, Margaret
Ring of Ikribu, The * Smith, David C. & Richard L. Tierney
Ring of rings * Wilson, Robert Hendrie
Ring of the ruby dragon * Black, Jeannie
Ring of truth * Lake, David J.
Ring, the sword, and the unicorn, The * Ward, James M.
Ring, the witch, and the crystal, The: an Ewok adventure, based on the television movie Ewoks * Dubowksi, Cathy East
Ringing changes * Lafferty, R. A.
Ring-rise, ring-set * Hughes, Monica
Rings of Kether, The * Chapman, Andrew
Rings of Saturn, The * Cover, Arthur Byron
Rings of Tantalus, The * Cooper, Edmund

Robert Silverberg: a primary and secondary bibliography * Clareson, Thomas D.

Robert Silverberg omnibus, A: The man in the maze; Nightwings; Downward to the Earth * Silverberg, Robert

Robert Silverberg's Time tours: Caesar's time legions * Betancourt, John Gregory as JEREMY KINGSTON

Robert Silverberg's Time Tours: Glory's end * Ciencin, Scott as NICK BARON

Robert Silverberg's Time tours: The Dinosaur trackers * Cover, Arthur Byron & Tim Sullivan & John Gregory Betancourt as THOMAS SHADWELL

Robert Silverberg's Time Tours: The Pirate paradox * Ciencin, Scott as NICK BARON & Greg Cox

Robert Silverberg's Time tours: The Robin Hood ambush * Wu, William F.

Robert Silverberg's Time Tours: Timecrime, Inc. * Doyle, Debra & James D. Macdonald

Robert Silverberg's Worlds of wonder * Silverberg, Robert

Robertson Davies * Peterman, Michael

Robertson Davies, playwright: a search for the self on the Canadian stage * Stone-Blackburn, Susan

Robin Hood * Moffatt, Derry

Robin Hood ambush, The * Wu, William F.

Robin Hood, prince of thieves * Green, Simon

Robin of Sherwood and the hounds of Lucifer * May, Robin

Robin of Sherwood: The hooded man * Horowitz, Anthony

Robin of Sherwood: The time of the wolf * Carpenter, Richard

Robinsheugh * Dunlop, Eileen

Robocop * Naha, Ed

Robocop 2: novel * Naha, Ed

Robot * Grimwade, Peter

Robot adept * Anthony, Piers

Robot and Rebecca, The: the mystery of the code-carrying kids * Yolen, Jane

Robot birthday, The * Bunting, Eve

Robot book, The * Malone, Robert

Robot collection, The: the robot novels * Asimov, Isaac

Robot commando * Jackson, Steve & Ian Livingstone

Robot dreams * Asimov, Isaac

Robot in the closet, The * Goulart, Ron

Robot in the glass * Barrett, G. J. as DENNIS SUMMERS

Robot invitation, The * Scheer, K. H.

Robot jox: the novel * Thurston, Robert

Robot novels, The * Asimov, Isaac

Robot people, The * Bunting, Eve

Robot race * Kraft, David Anthony

Robot raiders * Leroe, Ellen W.

Robot revolt * Fisk, Nicholas

Robot romance * Leroe, Ellen W.

Robot: the mechanical monster * Annan, David

Robot threat: New York * Shols, W. W.

Robot trouble * Coville, Bruce

Robot visions * Asimov, Isaac

Robot warriors * Greenberg, Martin H. & Charles G. Waugh & Gordon R. Dickson

Robot who looked like me, The * Sheckley, Robert

Robotech * Schuster, Hal

Robotech art 1: from the animated series Robotech * Carlton, Ardith & Kay Reynolds

Robotech art 2 * Reynolds, Kay

Robotech: The end of the circle * Daley, Brian & James Luceno as JACK MCKINNEY

Robotics * Minsky, Marvin

Robotria * Barrett, G. J.

Robots * Asimov, Isaac & Martin H. Greenberg & Charles G. Waugh

Robots * Dozois, Gardner & Sheila Williams

Robots * Hefley, Robert M.

Robots and empire * Asimov, Isaac

Robots, androids, and mechanical oddities: the science fiction of Philip K. Dick * Dick, Philip K.

Robots, bombs, and mutants * Voltz, William

Robots: fact, fiction, and prediction * Reichardt, Jasia

Robots have no tails—Proud robot, The: the complete Galloway Gallegher stories * Kuttner, Henry & C. L. Moore

Robots of Dawn, The * Asimov, Isaac

Robots: reel-to-real * Krasnoff, Barbara

Robots, robots, robots * Geduld, Harry M. & Ronald Gottesman

Roboworld * Dicks, Terrance

Rocheworld * Forward, Robert L.

Rock and a hard place, A * Peters, David as PETER DAVID

Rock and roll mystery * Wallace, Jim

Rock sinister * Dent, Lester as KENNETH ROBESON

Rocket jockey * del Rey, Lester

Rocket to Earth * Peel, John

Rocketeer: a novel * Fontes, Ron

Rocketeer, The: a novel * Peters, David as PETER DAVID

Rocket's red glare * Novak, Kate

Rocketship: an incredible voyage through science fiction and science fact * Malone, Robert

Rocket-ship saboteurs, The * Townsend, John

Rockinghorse * Johnstone, William W.

Rod of light, The * Bayley, Barrington J.

Rod Serling: the dreams and nightmares of life in the Twilight Zone: a biography * Engel, Joel

Rod Serling's Devils and demons: a collection * Dickson, Gordon R. as ROD SERLING

Rod Serling's Night gallery reader * Greenberg, Martin H. & Carol Serling & Charles G. Waugh

Rod Serling's Other worlds * Serling, Rod

Rod Serling's Triple W: witches, warlocks, and werewolves: a collection * Dickson, Gordon R. as ROD SERLING

Rod Serling's Twilight zone * Gibson, Walter B.

Roderick at random; or, Further education of a young machine * Sladek, John

Roderick; or, The education of a young machine * Sladek, John

Rodney Matthews portfolio, The * Matthews, Rodney

Rogan * James, Paul

Rogano: a novel * Knight, Stephen

Roger Corman: the best of the cheap acts * McGee, Mark Thomas

Roger Zelazny * Krulik, Theodore

Roger Zelazny * Yoke, Carl B.

Roger Zelazny: a primary and secondary bibliography * Sanders, Joseph L.

Roger Zelazny and Andre Norton: proponents of individualism * Yoke, Carl B.

Roger Zelazny's alien speedway: The web * Wylde, Thomas

Roger Zelazny's Visual guide to Castle Amber * Randall, Neil & Roger Zelazny

Rogers' Rangers * Niven, Larry & John Silbersack & Jerry Pournelle

Rogue Bolo * Laumer, Keith

Rogue emperor: a novel of the Chronoplane Wars * Kilian, Crawford

Rogue golem * Kenyon, Ernest M.

Rogue of Gor * Norman, John

Rogue pirate * Betancourt, John Gregory

Running proud * Monsarrat, Nicholas
Running skeletons, The * Dent, Lester as KENNETH ROBESON
Running wild * Ballard, J. G.
Rusalka * Cherryh, C. J.
Rush of golden wings, A * Baldry, Cherith
Rushdie file, The * Appignanesi, Lisa & Sara Maitland
Rushton inheritance, The * Mace, Elisabeth
Russia: what is the Golden Horde? * Packard, Edward
The Russian gothic novel and its British antecedents * Simpson, Mark S.
Russian hide-and-seek: a melodrama * Amis, Kingsley
Russian revolution 1985: a contemporary fable * Downing, David

Russian science fiction, 1956-1974: a bibliography: original books, translated books, and an annotated checklist of criticism, with an appendix on criticism of Russian SF before 1956 * Suvin, Darko
Russian spring * Spinrad, Norman
Rust * Calif, R. C.
Rustle in the grass, A * Hawdon, Robin
Rustling death, The * Dent, Lester & Alan Hathway as KENNETH ROBESON
Ruth, the unsuspecting * Kimbro, John M. as KATHERYN KIMBROUGH
Ryn * Wodhams, Jack
Rynosseros * Dowling, Terry

S

Sabazel * Carl, Lillian Stewart
Sabella; or, The blood stone * Lee, Tanith
Saberhagen: my best * Saberhagen, Fred
Sable moon, The * Springer, Nancy
Sable night * Roy, Archie
Sabotage * Leibold, Jay
Saboteurs in A-1 * Brand, Kurt
Sabra * Rorvik, David
Saccharin cyanide * Livia, Anna
Sacred families: three novellas * Donoso, José
Sacred night, The * ben Jelloun, Tahar
Sacred stones, The * Sarabande, William
Sacred visions * Cassutt, Michael & Andrew M. Greeley
Sacrifice * Drake, Morgan
Sacrifice * Masterton, Graham
Sacrifice, The: a novel of the occult * Slavitt, David R. as
    HENRY SUTTON
Sacrifice for the Quagga God * Edson, J. T.
Sacrifice of Ruanon, The * Dever, Joe & John Grant
Sadar's keep * Snyder, Midori
Sadness of witches, The * Elliott, Janice
Saga of Cuckoo, The * Pohl, Frederik & Jack Williamson
Saga of Dharmapuri, The * Vijayan, O. V.
Saga of Erik the Viking, The * Jones, Terry
Saga of Filster Stein, The * Lovisi, Gary
Saga of Grittel Sundotha, The * Mayhar, Ardath
Saga of lost earths; and, The star mill * Petaja, Emil
Saga of old city: a novel of swordplay, thievery, and
    magic * Gygax, Gary
Saga of the reindeer people, A * Lindholm, Megan
Sail with pirates * Gasperini, Jim
Sailing to Byzantium * Silverberg, Robert
Sailing to Cythera, and other Anatole stories * Willard,
    Nancy
Sailor on the seas of fate, The * Moorcock, Michael
Saint Camber * Kurtz, Katherine
Saint Peter's snow * Perutz, Leo
Saint Peter's wolf * Cadnum, Michael
Saint-Germain chronicles, The * Yarbro, Chelsea Quinn
Saints and strangers * Carter, Angela
Salamander tree, The * Lipscombe, Robert
Salem's child * Walker, Robert W.
Salem's children * Leader, Mary
'Salem's Lot * King, Stephen
Saliva tree, The * Aldiss, Brian W.
Salman Rushdie: sentenced to death * Weatherby, W. J.
Salome's slave * Bedford, Clive
Sal's book * Crawford, Betty Anne as SAL LIQUORI
Salt * Lord, Gabrielle
SALT twelve * Porter, Francis A.
Salvage and destroy * Llewellyn, Edward
Salvage rites, and other stories * Watson, Ian
Samain * Atkins, Meg Elizabeth
Samantha Slade, monster-sitter * Smith, Susan
Samaritan * Van Rjndt, Philippe
Samarkand * Diamond, Graham
Samarkand dawn * Diamond, Graham
Samarkand dimension, The * Wise, David
Sambaqui: a novel of pre-history * Ribeiro, Stella Carr

Same blood * Blakeslee, Mermer
Samraj * Aron, Elaine
Samuel R. Delany * McEvoy, Seth
Samuel R. Delany * Weedman, Jane Branham
Samuel R. Delany: a primary and secondary bibliogra-
    phy, 1962-1979 * Bravard, Robert S. & Michael W.
    Peplow
Samurai, The * Sadler, Barry
Samurai Cat in the real world * Rogers, Mark E.
Samurai combat * Rypel, T. C.
Samurai kill, The * Lynds, Dennis as NICK CARTER
Samurai steel * Rypel, T. C.
Samurai wizard, The * Hawke, Simon
San Diego Lightfoot Sue, and other stories * Reamy, Tom
Sanctuary * Asprin, Robert Lynn
Sanctuary, The * Chandler, Glenn
Sand child, The * ben Jelloun, Tahar
Sand witch, The * Senn, Steve
Sandcats of Rhyl, The * Vardeman, Robert E.
Sandeagozu: a novel * Jenner, Janann V.
Sandkings * Martin, George R. R.
Sandman * Gray, Linda Crockett as LINDA CROCKETT
Sandman * Johnstone, William W.
Sandman's dust * Bukiet, Melvin Jules
Sandoval transmissions, The * Dagnol, Jules N.
Sands of desire * Mann, Del
Sands of time * Pinchin, Frank as PETER DAGMAR
Sandworld * Lupoff, Richard A.
Sandwriter * Hughes, Monica
Sanity plea: schizophrenia in the novels of Kurt Vonnegut
    * Broer, Lawrence R.
Santa 2000: the science fiction Santa Claus * Parry,
    Michel
Santa Claus doesn't mop floors * Dadey, Debbie & Mar-
    cia Thornton Jones
Santa Claus, the movie: a novel * Vinge, Joan D.
Santa Claus, the movie storybook * Vinge, Joan D.
Santa claws * Peel, John as NICHOLAS ADAMS
Santiago: a myth of the far future * Resnick, Mike
Sapphire road * Whiteford, Wynne
Sapphire rose, The * Eddings, David
Sapphires: Here and otherwise; and, Silver nutmegs *
    Knowles, Vernon
Saraband of lost time * Grant, Richard
Sarah Canary * Fowler, Karen Joy
Sara's ghost * Welles, Patricia
Sardia: a story of love * Daniels, Cora Lynn
Sardonyx net, The * Lynn, Elizabeth A.
Sargasso * Corley, Edwin
Sargasso ogre, The: a Doc Savage adventure * Dent,
    Lester as KENNETH ROBESON
Sarsen witch, The * Kernaghan, Eileen
Sasquatch hunt * Randisi, Robert J. as J. R. ROBERTS
Sasquatch: monster of the northwest woods * Knerr, M.
    E.
Sassinak * McCaffrey, Anne & Elizabeth Moon
Satan black * Dent, Lester as KENNETH ROBESON
Satan help me * Battin, B. W.

Satan: his psychotherapy and cure by the unfortunate Dr. Kassler, J.S.P.S. * Leven, Jeremy
Satan sublets * Younger, Jack
Satan: the kiss and tell memoirs * Pascall, Jeremy
Satan whispers * Ross, Dan as CLARISSA ROSS
Satana enslaved * Offutt, Andrew J. as JOHN CLEVE
Satanic lute * Wood, Bridget
Satanic orgy * Blackmoor, Edmund
Satanic verses, The * Rushdie, Salman
Satanic virgin * anon.
Satanists, The * Holdstock, Robert as ROBERT BLACK
Satan's chance * Shrader, Alan Ross
Satan's child * McNeilly, Wilfred G. as PETER SAXON
Satan's daughters * Peters, Othello
Satan's death blast: the Spider thriller * Page, Norvell W. as GRANT STOCKBRIDGE
Satan's doll * Halbrook, Duane
Satan's incubators * Page, Norvell W. as RANDOLPH CRAIG
Satan's love child * McNaughton, Brian
Satan's manor * Andrews, Mark
Satan's master * Nazel, Joe
Satan's mistress * Jervis, Tabitha
Satan's mistress * McNaughton, Brian
Satan's roadhouse * Weinberg, Robert
Satan's seductress * McNaughton, Brian
Satan's seed * Sherman, Jory
Satan's serenade * Monahan, Brent
Satan's servant * Battin, B. W.
Satan's sister * Jensen, Ruby Jean
Satan's snowdrop * Smith, Guy N.
Satan's spawn * Silverthorn, Richard Jay
Satan's surrogate * McNaughton, Brian
Satan's swarm * Roberts, Mark as LIONEL DERRICK
Satan's tears: the art of Alex Niño * Niño, Alex
Satan's victor * Dark, Jon
Satellite City * Reynolds, Mack
Satellite slaughter * Roberts, Mark as LIONEL DERRICK
Sati * Pike, Christopher
Satori * Schmidt, Dennis
Saturday, the Twelfth of October * Mazer, Norma Fox
Saturn game, The * Anderson, Poul
Saturn Three: a novelisation * Gallagher, Stephen
Saturnalia * Callin, Grant
Saturn's missing rings * Douglas, Iain
Satyr * Gray, Linda Crockett
Satyrday: a fable * Bauer, Steven
Satyr's head, The * Sutton, David
Saucer Hill * Adler, Paul
Saurian * Schoell, William
Sauron dominion * Pournelle, Jerry & John F. Carr
Savage bride * Woolrich, Cornell
Savage empire * Lorrah, Jean
Savage heroes: tales of sorcery and black magic * Parry, Michel as ERIC PENDRAGON
Savage horde, The * Ahern, Jerry
Savage horrors: tales of magical fantasy * Parry, Michel
Savage mountains, The: a Horseclans novel * Adams, Robert
Savage princess, The * Banks, Raymond E.
Savage Scorpio * Bulmer, Kenneth as ALAN BURT AKERS
Savage season * Lansdale, Joe R.
Savage stars, The * Reinsmith, Richard
Savage stronghold, The * Stacy, Jan as CRAIG SARGENT
Savage tomorrow * Donohue, Trevor
Savage web, The * Darby, Catherine as SHARON WHITBY
Savages, The * Black, Ian Stuart
Savages of Gor * Norman, John
Save Sirrushany! also Agotha, Princess Gwyn, and all the fearsome beasts * Baker, Betty

Save the Venturians! * McEvoy, Seth & Laure Smith
Savior, The * Werlin, Mark & Marvin Werlin
Savior of the empire * Scheer, K. H.
Saviour, The * Werlin, Mark & Marvin Werlin
Saviour, The: a novel * Storey, Anthony
Saviour's gate * Sebastian, Tim
Savoy book, The * Britton, David & Michael Butterworth
Savoy dreams * Britton, David & Michael Butterworth
Saxon and the sorceress * Turman, John
Sa'-Zada tales, The * Fraser, W. A.
Scalehunter's beautiful daughter, The * Shepard, Lucius
Scales of justice * Jarvis, Sharon & Ellen M. Kozak as JARROD COMSTOCK
Scallion stone, The * Smith, Basil A.
Scanner darkly, A * Dick, Philip K.
Scanners * Whiteson, Leon
Scanners II: the new order * Kimball, Janus
Scapescope * Stith, John E.
Scarborough Hall * Boyd, John as BOYD UPCHURCH
Scare care * Masterton, Graham
Scare tactics * Farris, John
Scarecrow * Cusick, Richie Tankersley
Scarecrows, The * Westall, Robert
Scared stiff: tales of sex and death * Campbell, Ramsey
Scared to death * Riefe, Alan
Scarlet dream * Moore, C. L.
Scarlet Scull, The * Owston, C. E.
Scarlet serenade * Forward, Robert
Scarlet Shield of Shalimar, The * Siegel, Barbara & Scott Siegel
Scarlet Skull, The * Owston, C. E.
Scarlet sorcerer * Dever, Joe
Scars, and other distinguishing marks * Matheson, Richard Christian
Scary book, The * Calmenson, Stephanie & Joanna Cole
Scathach and Maeve's daughter, The * Walker, Mary Alexander
Scatterlings * Carmody, Isobelle
Scavenger hunt * Goldin, Stephen
Scavenger hunt * Pike, Christopher
Scavengers * Skal, David J.
Scavenger's hunt * Bicknell, Arthur
Scenic drive * Wilding, Michael
Scent of magic, The * Chittenden, Margaret
Sceptre mortal, The * Sawde, Derek
Sceptre of power * Simon, Morris
Schemes of dragons, The * Smeds, Dave
Schimmelhorn file, The: memoirs of a dirty old genius * Bretnor, Reginald
Schimmelhorn's gold * Bretnor, Reginald
Schismatrix * Sterling, Bruce
Schizogenic man, The * Harris, Raymond
Scholars and soldiers: a story collection * Gentle, Mary
Scholar's guide to modern American science fiction * Krisnamoorthy, P. S.
School, The * Kelleher, Ed & Harriette Vidal
School, The * Wright, T. M.
School days * Hughes, Robert
School of darkness, The * Wellman, Manly Wade
School of wizardry * Doyle, Debra & James D. Macdonald
School on the Moon * Walters, Hugh
Schooled by the devil * anon.
Schoolhouse * Duigon, Lee
Schrödinger's cat: The universe next door * Wilson, Robert Anton
Schrödinger's cat trilogy * Wilson, Robert Anton
Sci fi: a Yellowthread Street mystery * Marshall, William
Science fiction * Gibson, James
Science fiction * Hardy, Phil

Secret gardens: a study of the golden age of children's literature * Carpenter, Humphrey
Secret harmonies * McAuley, Paul J.
Secret history of time to come, A * Macauley, Robie
Secret in the Argentine jungle, The * Gronowski, Paul
Secret in the sky, The: a Doc Savage adventure * Dent, Lester as KENNETH ROBESON
Secret life of Algernon Pendleton, The * Greenan, Russell
Secret life of Dilly McBean, The * Haas, Dorothy
Secret life of houses, The * Bradfield, Scott
Secret matter * Johnson, Toby
Secret mission: Moluk * Voltz, William
Secret of 13, The * Hiller, B. B.
Secret of Amityville, The * Holzer, Hans
Secret of Barnabas, The * Gross, Edward
Secret of Bigfoot Pass, The * Jahn, Mike
Secret of Dinosaur Bog, The * Gilden, Mel
Secret of life, The * Rucker, Rudy
Secret of NIMH, The * O'Brien, Robert C.
Secret of Rainbow Island, The * Stamper, J. B.
Secret of Seven Oaks, The * Coulson, Juanita
Secret of Stonehenge, The * Cantwell, Lois as MILO DENNISON
Secret of the black hole, The: a Scott Saunders space adventure * Moore, Patrick
Secret of the earth star, and others * Kuttner, Henry
Secret of the elms, The * Mannix, Daniel P.
Secret of the Indian, The * Reid Banks, Lynne
Secret of the invisible city, The * Carlson, Dale
Secret of the knights * Gasperini, Jim
Secret of the Lona, The * Leigh, Stephen
Secret of the lost race * Norton, Andre
Secret of the ninja * Leibold, Jay
Secret of the pale lover * Ross, Dan as CLARISSA ROSS
Secret of the pyramids * Brightfield, Richard
Secret of the round beast, The * Forrester, John
Secret of the royal treasure * Gaskin, Carol
Secret of the seven willows, The * McKean, Thomas
Secret of the sixth magic * Hardy, Lyndon
Secret of the sphinx * Vilott, Rhondi
Secret of the Su, The * Dent, Lester as KENNETH ROBESON
Secret of the sun god * Packard, Andrea
Secret of the third eye, The * Carlson, Dale
Secret of the underground room, The * Bellairs, John
Secret of the willows, The * Stone, Elna
Secret Operation Brain, The * Carlson, Dale
Secret orders * Jeffers, H. Paul
Secret people, The * Wyndham, John
Secret property, A * Noyes, Ralph
Secret Scorpio * Bulmer, Kenneth as ALAN BURT AKERS
Secret sea, The * Monteleone, Thomas F.
Secret sharer, The * Silverberg, Robert
Secret sins * Pearl, Jack as STEPHANIE BLAKE
Secret sorcerers * Lowery, Linda
Secret treasure of Tibet, The * Brightfield, Richard
Secret weavers, The: stories of the fantastic by women of Argentina and Chile * Agosin, Marjorie
Secret window, The * Wright, Betty Ren
Secret world of Polly Flint, The * Cresswell, Helen
Secrets of Doc Savage * Murray, Will
Secrets of Stardeep; and, Time gate * Jakes, John
Secrets of synchronicity, The * Fast, Jonathan
Secrets of the deep * Dickson, Gordon R.
Secrets of the gnomes * Huygen, Wil
Secrets of the lost island * Lance, Kathryn as LYNN BEACH
Secrets of the samurai * Gaskin, Carol
Section G: United Planets * Reynolds, Mack
Sector General * White, James

Sedalia * Schow, David J.
Seductions * Garton, Ray
See no evil * Wallace, Patricia
See you later * Pike, Christopher
Seed of evil, The * Bayley, Barrington J.
Seed of evil * Plante, Edmund
Seeding, The * Shobin, David
Seeding stars, The; and, Galactic cluster * Blish, James
Seedling * James, Laurence as JAMES AXLER
Seeds of change * Monteleone, Thomas F.
Seeds of death, The * Dicks, Terrance
Seeds of doom, The; The deadly assassin / Terrance Dicks * Hinchcliffe, Philip
Seeds of evil * Bingley, Margaret
Seeds of ruin * Voltz, William
Seeds of war * Cornett, Robert & Kevin Randle
Seedseekers, The * Garrett, Dave
Seeing, The * McGivern, Maureen & William P. McGivern
Seeing Earth: literary responses to space exploration * Weber, Ronald
Seeing knife, The * Crawley, Fenton
Seeing red * Schow, David J.
Seeing things * Painter, Charlotte
Seeker, The * Bischoff, David & Christopher Lampton
Seekers, The * Dvorkin, David
Seekers, The * Shannon, Doris
Seekers and the sword, The * Friedman, Michael Jan
Seekers of Shar-Nuhn, The * Mayhar, Ardath
Seeking refuge in Torre San Nicola: an introduction to F. Marion Crawford * Moran, John C.
Seeking Sword, The * Kangilaski, Jaan
Seeking the dream brother * Bennett, Marcia J.
Seeking the mythical future * Hoyle, Trevor
Seeklight * Jeter, K. W.
Seer, The * Wisler, G. Clifton
Seeress of Kell, The * Eddings, David
Seetee * Williamson, Jack
Seetee ship/Seetee shock * Williamson, Jack
Seg the bowman * Bulmer, Kenneth as DRAY PRESCOT & ALAN BURT AKERS
Segra and Stargull * Downing, Peggy
Segra and the magician * Downing, Peggy
Segra in diamond castle * Downing, Peggy
Selchie's seed, The * Oppenheim, Shulamith
Selected critical studies of Baudelaire * Baudelaire, Charles
Selected fragments * De la Ree, Gerry
Selected letters, 1923-1930 * Howard, Robert E.
Selected letters of Philip K. Dick: 1974 * Dick, Philip K.
Selected letters, volume five, 1934-1937 * Lovecraft, H. P.
Selected letters, volume four, 1932-1934 * Lovecraft, H. P.
Selected papers on Lovecraft * Joshi, S. T.
Selected proceedings of the 1978 Science Fiction Research Association national convention * Remington, Thomas J.
Selected science fiction & fantasy stories * London, Jack
Selected short stories of the supernatural * Oliphant, Mrs.
Selected stories * Beaumont, Charles
Selected stories of Sylvia Townsend Warner * Warner, Sylvia Townsend
Selected tales of grim and grue from the horror pulps * Jaffery, Sheldon
Selected writings * Hearn, Lafcadio
Selected writings * Poe, Edgar Allan
Selected writings of Lafcadio Hearn, The * Hearn, Lafcadio

Sex in the 21st century: a collection of SF erotica * Parry, Michel & Milton Subotsky

Sex life on the planet Mars * Brown, Fredric

Sex slaves * Crane, Martin

Sex sphere, The * Rucker, Rudy

Sexing the cherry * Winterson, Jeanette

Sexmax * Leonard, George H. as HUGHES COOPER

Sexodus * Smith, George H. as JERRY JASON

Sexorcist, The * Horton, Honey

Sexorcist, The * Offutt, Andrew J. as JOHN CLEVE

Sexpunks & savage sagas * Sutphen, Richard

Sexual chemistry: sardonic tales of the genetic revolution * Stableford, Brian M.

Sexual coquette * Vardeman, Robert E. & Geo. W. Proctor as MARV ELOUS

SF 1 * Davis, Richard

SF 2 * Davis, Richard

S-F 2: a pictorial history of science fiction films from "Rollerball" to "Return of the Jedi" * Meyers, Richard S.

SF 4: science fiction stories * Davis, Richard

SF book of lists, The * Edwards, Malcolm & Maxim Jakubowski

SF choice 77 * Ashley, Mike

SF Horizons * Aldiss, Brian W. & Harry Harrison

SF in dimension: a book of explorations * Panshin, Alexei & Cory Panshin

SF in dimension: a book of explorations, 2nd ed. * Panshin, Alexei & Cory Panshin

SF: inventing the future * Appleford, R. Duncan

SF published in 1973 * Burger, Joanne

SF published in 1974 * Burger, Joanne

SF published in 1975 * Burger, Joanne

SF published in 1976 * Burger, Joanne

SF published in 1977 * Burger, Joanne

SF reprise 3 * anon.

SF reprise 4 * anon.

SF reprise 5: first-rate science fiction originally published in New worlds magazine * Moorcock, Michael

SF reprise 6 * anon.

SF sampler * Elwood, Roger

SF voices * Schweitzer, Darrell

SF yearbook 1976 * Stewart, Alan & Elke Stewart

SF-1: a selective bibliography * Currey, L. W. & David G. Hartwell as KILGORE TROUT

SFBRI: science fiction and fantasy book review index, volume 15, 1984 * Hall, Hal W.

SFBRI: science fiction book review index, v. 5, 1974 * Hall, Hal W.

SFBRI: science fiction book review index, v. 6, 1975 * Hall, Hal W.

SFBRI: science fiction book review index, v. 7, 1976 * Hall, Hal W.

SFBRI: science fiction book review index, v. 8, 1977 * Hall, Hal W.

SFBRI: science fiction book review index, v. 9, 1978 * Hall, Hal W.

SFBRI: science fiction book review index, v. 10, 1979 * Hall, Hal W.

SFBRI: science fiction book review index, volume 11, 1980 * Hall, Hal W.

SFBRI: science fiction book review index, volume 12, 1981 * Hall, Hal W.

SFBRI: science fiction book review index, volume 13, 1982 * Hall, Hal W.

SFBRI: science fiction book review index, volume 14, 1983 * Hall, Hal W.

SFWA handbook, The * Broxon, Mildred Downey

Sgt. Pepper's Lonely Hearts Club Band: a novel * Edwards, Henry

Sgt. Robot * Mahr, Kurt

Shade * Devenport, Emily

Shade of Lo Man Gong, The * Wu, William F.

Shade of the tree * Anthony, Piers

Shades of dark: ghost stories * Chambers, Aidan

Shades of darkness: a novel * Cowper, Richard

Shades of Dracula: Bram Stoker's uncollected stories * Stoker, Bram

Shades of evil * Cave, Hugh B.

Shades of gray * O'Neill, Timothy R.

Shades of Hades: Ladies in Hades; and, Gentlemen in Hades * Kummer, Frederic Arnold

Shades of moonlight * Holder, Nancy as LAUREL CHANDLER

Shadow * Duncan, Dave

Shadow, The * Garnett, Bill

Shadow * Logston, Anne

Shadow, The: A quarter of eight & The freak show murders * Gibson, Walter B.

Shadow and evil in fairy tales * Franz, Marie-Luise von

Shadow, and other strange tales, The * Goldsmith, Howard

Shadow and the Golden Master, The * Gibson, Walter B.

Shadow at midnight: ten ghost stories * Maynard, L. H. & M. P. N. Sims

Shadow child * Citro, Joseph

Shadow climber * Reichert, Mickey Zucker

Shadow, The: Crime over Casco & The Mother Goose murders * Gibson, Walter B.

Shadow dance * Borton, Douglas

Shadow dancers * Carl, Lillian Stewart

Shadow dancers * Curry, Jane Louise

Shadow dancers, The * Chalker, Jack L.

Shadow forms: a collection of occult stories, rev. ed. * Hall, Manly P.

Shadow games: first book of the South * Cook, Glen

Shadow gate, The * Ball, Margaraet

Shadow guests, The * Aiken, Joan

Shadow hunter, The * Murphy, Pat

Shadow hunters * Mace, David

Shadow in Hawthorn Bay * Lunn, Janet

Shadow, The: Jade dragon & House of ghosts * Gibson, Walter B.

Shadow land * Straub, Peter

Shadow land, The: more stories from the past * Vansittart, Peter

Shadow leader * Harper, Tara K.

Shadow lord: a Star Trek novel * Yep, Laurence

Shadow magic * Wrede, Patricia C.

Shadow Man, The * Gresham, Stephen

Shadow man, The * Lutz, John

Shadow masque * Comfort, Iris

Shadow of a broken man * Chesbro, George C.

Shadow of a shade: a survey of vampirism in literature * Carter, Margaret L.

Shadow of all night falling, A * Cook, Glen

Shadow of alpha, The * Grant, Charles L.

Shadow of death, A * Creasey, John as GORDON ASHE

Shadow of Earth * Eisenstein, Phyllis

Shadow of Fomor, The * McGowen, Tom

Shadow of Gastor * King, Albert as FLOYD GIBSON

Shadow of Heaven, The, rev. ed. * Shaw, Bob

Shadow of his wings, The * Fergusson, Bruce

Shadow of the beast * DiPego, Gerald

Shadow of the Gloom-World, The * Eldridge, Roger

Shadow of the moon * Title, Elise

Shadow of the seventh moon * Berberick, Nancy Varian

Shadow of the ship, The * Franson, Robert Wilfred

Shadow of the swan * Wren, M. K.

Shadow of the torturer, The * Wolfe, Gene

Shape under the sheet, The: the complete Stephen King encyclopedia * Spignesi, Stephen J.
Shapechanger, The * Ergas, Elizabeth
Shapechanger scenario, The * Hawke, Simon
Shapechangers * Roberson, Jennifer
Shapers * Chase, Robert R.
Shaper's legacy * Finch, Sheila
Shapes * Vance, Steve
Shapes: a romance of horror * Delap, Richard & Walt Lee
Shapes of midnight, The: horror * Brennan, Joseph Payne
Shape-shifter: stories * Melville, Pauline
Shape-shifter: the naming of Pangur Ban * Sampson, Fay
Shapeshifters, The * Coontz, Otto
Shaping of Middle-Earth, The: the Quenta, the Ambarkanta, and the Annals, together with the earliest 'Silmarillion' and the first map * Tolkien, J. R. R.
Shaping the dawn * Finch, Sheila
Shards of honor * Bujold, Lois McMaster
Shards of honour * Bujold, Lois McMaster
Shared fantasies: role-playing games as social worlds * Fine, Gary Alan
Shared tomorrows: science fiction in collaboration * Malzberg, Barry N. & Bill Pronzini
Shareworld * Hershman, Morris
Sharing, The * Rorvik, David as M. M. FARADAY
Sharing, The * Simmons, John
Sharp practice: a novel * Farris, John
Sharpest edge, The * Meier, Shirley & S. M. Stirling
Sharra's exile * Bradley, Marion Zimmer
Shatner: where no man...: the authorized biography of William Shatner * Culbreath, Myrna & William Shatner & Sondra Marshak
Shatter * Farris, John
Shatterday * Ellison, Harlan
Shattered chain, The: a Darkover novel * Bradley, Marion Zimmer
Shattered glass * Bergstrom, Elaine
Shattered Goddess, The * Schweitzer, Darrell
Shattered horse, The * Sucharitkul, Somtow as S. P. SOMTOW
Shattered moon * Green, Kate
Shattered people, The * Hoskins, Robert
Shattered realm, The * Smith, Mark & Jamie Thomson
Shattered sphere, The * Abbey, Lynn & Robert Lynn Asprin
Shattered stars, The * McEnroe, Richard S.
Shattered stone, The * Newman, Robert
Shattered world, The * Reaves, Michael
Shaving of Karl Marx, The: an instant novel of ideas, after that manner of Thomas Love Peacock, in which Lenin and H. G. Wells talk about the political meaning of the scientific romances * Stover, Leon
Shawn * Geller, Uri
She comes when you're leaving & other stories * Boston, Bruce
She waits * Clement, Henry
She wakes * Ketchum, Jack
She who remembers * Shuler, Linda Lay
She-beast, The * Lawrence, Jim as HUNTER ADAMS
She-devil * Horowitz, Lois
Shee, The * Donnelly, Joe
Sheepfarmer's daughter * Moon, Elizabeth
Sheet lightning * Alexander, Robert as JOAN BUTLER
Shelkagari * King, Harold
Shell, The * Rochon, Esther
Shellshock * Masters, Anthony
Shelter * Asher, Marty
Shelter, The * Kittredge, Mary & Kevin O'Donnell Jr.
Shelter in bedlam, The * Beaujon, Paul

Shepherd, The * Forsyth, Frederick
Shepherd * Holly, Joan Hunter
Shepherd Moon, The: a novel of the future * Hoover, H. M.
Sheridan Le Fanu * Browne, Nelson
Sheridan Le Fanu * Melada, Ivan
Sheridan Le Fanu and Victorian Ireland * McCormack, W. J.
Sheridan Le Fanu and Victorian Ireland, 2nd ed. * McCormack, W. J.
Sheriff of Purgatory, The * Morris, Jim
Sherlock Holmes in The adventure of the ancient gods * Vaughan, Ralph E.
Sherlock Holmes on the roof of the world * Miller, Thos. Kent
Sherlock Holmes through time and space * Asimov, Isaac & Martin H. Greenberg & Charles G. Waugh
Sherlock Holmes vs. Dracula; or, The adventure of the sanguinary count * Estleman, Loren D. as JOHN H. WATSON, AS EDITED BY LOREN D. ESTLEMAN
Sherlock Holmes's war of the worlds * Wellman, Manly Wade & Wade Wellman
Sherwood * Godwin, Parke
Sherwood ring, The * Pope, Elizabeth Marie
Shibo discipline, The * Meyers, Richard S. as WADE BARKER
Shiel in diverse hands: a collection of essays * Morse, A. Reynolds
Shield of time, The * Anderson, Poul
Shield's lady * Krentz, Jayne Ann as AMANDA GLASS
Shift, The * Cook, Hugh
Shift key, The * Brunner, John
Shifter * Reeves-Stevens, Garfield & Judith Reeves-Stevens
Shilling shockers, The: stories of terror from the Gothic bluebooks * Haining, Peter
Shiloh project, The * Poyer, David C.
Shine * Paton Walsh, Jill
Shines the name * Acres, Mark
Shinglo, The * Lazuta, Gene as ALEX KANE
Shining, The * King, Stephen
Shining falcon, The * Sherman, Josepha
Shining ones, The * Preuss, Paul
Shining pool, The * Carlson, Dale & Carlson, Danny
Shining reader, The * Magistrale, Anthony
Shining, The; 'Salem's Lot; Carrie * King, Stephen
Shining, The; 'Salem's Lot; Night shift; Carrie * King, Stephen
Shining steel * Watt-Evans, Lawrence
Shiny Mountain * Dvorkin, David
Ship of death * Murphy, Warren & Richard Sapir
Ship of dreams * Lumley, Brian
Ship of shadows * Leiber, Fritz
Ship of strangers * Shaw, Bob
Ship that flew, The * Lewis, Hilda
Ship that sailed the time stream, The * Edmondson, G. C.
Ship to the stars, A * Arai, Motoko
Shipwreck * Logan, Charles
Shirley Jackson * Friedman, Lenemaja
Shirley Jackson's The lottery and other short stories: a critical commentary * Morrison, Louise D.
Shirt off a hanged man's back, The: nine stories of the supernatural * Hamley, Dennis
Shiva: an adventure of the ice age * Brennan, J. H.
Shiva accused * Brennan, J. H.
Shiva descending * Benford, Gregory & William Rotsler
Shivering world * Tyers, Kathy
Shivers * Schoell, William
Shivers: an anthology of Canadian ghost stories * Ioannou, Greg & Lynne Missen

Silent slaughter * Beere, Peter
Silent stars go by, The * White, James
Silent thunder * Ing, Dean
Silent Tower, The * Hambly, Barbara
Silent voice, The: a novel * Hodder-Williams, Christopher
Silent warrior, The * Modesitt, L. E. Jr.
Silent watcher, The * Stevenson, Florence
Silent witness * Smith, Robert Arthur
Silicon mage, The * Hambly, Barbara
Silicon man, The * Platt, Charles
Silk and the skin, The * Sudbery, Rodie
Silk road: a novel of eighth-century China * Larsen, Jeanne
Silk roads and shadows * Shwartz, Susan
SillyOZbuls of Oz, The * Baum, Roger S.
Silmarillion, The * Tolkien, J. R. R.
Silmarillion, The: J. R. R. Tolkien: a brief account of the book and its making * Tolkien, Christopher
Silvabamba * D'Amelio, Dan
Silver arm, The * Fitzpatrick, Jim
Silver bird, the: a tale for those who dream * Petschek, Joyce S.
Silver branch, The: a novel of the Keltiad * Kennealy, Patricia
Silver brumbies of the south * Mitchell, Elyne
Silver brumby * Mitchell, Elyne
Silver brumby kingdom * Mitchell, Elyne
Silver brumby whirlwind * Mitchell, Elyne
Silver brumby's daughter * Mitchell, Elyne
Silver bullet * King, Stephen
Silver canyon, The * Winters, Logan
Silver chair, The; and, The last battle * Lewis, C. S.
Silver Citadel, The * Horowitz, Anthony
Silver coach, The * Adler, C. S.
Silver crown, The: a fantastic novel * Rosenberg, Joel
Silver curlew, The * Farjeon, Eleanor
Silver glove, The * Charnas, Suzy McKee
Silver horse, The * Lynn, Elizabeth A.
Silver, jewels, and jade * Norman, Elizabeth
Silver kiss, The * Klause, Annette Curtis
Silver land, The * Harding, Nancy
Silver link, the silken tie, The * Ames, Mildred
Silver man, The * Clark, Catherine Anthony
Silver metal lover, The * Lee, Tanith
Silver Mountain, The * Friesner, Esther M.
Silver nemesis * Clarke, Kevin
Silver on the tree * Cooper, Susan
Silver pillow, The: a tale of witchcraft * Disch, Thomas M.
Silver scream: stories * Schow, David J.
Silver skull, The: a novel of sorcery * Daniels, Les
Silver spike, The * Cook, Glen
Silver sun, The * Springer, Nancy
Silver Surfer: an analysis of issues #1-9 * Van Hise, James
Silver thread of madness, A * Salmonson, Jessica Amanda
Silver tower * Brown, Dale
Silver vortex, The * Caldecott, Moyra
Silver wings and leather jackets: the autobiography of Colonel William T. Bucko, USFAC (ret.) * Westcott, C. T.
Silver wish, A * Scott, Michael
Silver woven in my hair * Murphy, Shirley Rousseau
Silverado * Winters, Logan
Silvered cage, The * Fearn, John Russell as HUGO BLAYN
Silverglass * Rivkin, J. F.
Silverglass: Mistress of ambiguities * Rivkin, J. F.
Silverhair the wanderer * Paxson, Diana L.

Silverleaf syndrome, The * Robinson, Eleanor
Silverlock companion, A: the life and works of John Myers Myers * Lerner, Frederick Andrew
Silverthorn * Feist, Raymond E.
Simon Rack: New life for old * James, Laurence
Simon's quest * Howell, Christopher
Simon's soul * Shapiro, Stanley
Sin & sorcery * Victor, Steve
Sin eater, The * Weinberg, Robert
Sin of origin * Barnes, John
Sinbad and the eye of the tiger: novelization * Rotsler, William as JOHN RYDER HALL
Sindbad: the thirteenth voyage * Lafferty, R. A.
Sing and scatter daisies * Lawrence, Louise
Sing for a gentle rain * James, J. Alison
Sing me a moon * Darby, Catherine
Singapore science fiction * Bhathal, R. S. & Dudley de Souza & Kirpal Singh
Singer enigma, The * Maxwell, Ann
Singer in the stone, The * Willett, John
Singers of time, The * Pohl, Frederik & Jack Williamson
Singing, The: a fable about what makes us human * Raines, Theron
Singing stone, The * Melling, O. R.
Singing stones * Finlay, Winifred
Singing tree, The * Parvin, Brian
Single combat * Ing, Dean
Singletusk: a novel of the ice age * Kurten, Bjorn
Singularities * Quick, W. T.
Singularity * Sleator, William
Sinister and supernatural stories * Adams, Richard
Sinister barrier * Russell, Eric Frank
Sinister power, The * Brand, Kurt
Sinister ray, The * Dent, Lester
Sinister, strange, and supernatural: an anthology * Hoke, Helen
Sinister studios of KESP-TV, The * Foley, Louise Munro
Sink the armada * Andrews, Keith William
Sinking ship * Smeds, Dave
Sins of omission * Yarbro, Chelsea Quinn
Sins of Rachel Ellis, The * Caveney, Philip
Sins of the fathers, The * Schmidt, Stanley
Sins of the flesh * Davis, Don & Jay Davis
Sir Bevis: a tale of the fields * Jefferies, Richard
Sir Harold and the gnome king * de Camp, L. Sprague
Sir Pulteney: a fantasy * Lucas, E. V. as E. D. WARD
Siren * Gray, Linda Crockett
Sirens: the second book of illustrations * Achilleos, Chris
Sirian experiments, The: the report by Ambien II, of the five * Lessing, Doris
Sister Light, Sister Dark * Yolen, Jane
Sister Satan * Reed, Dana
Sisterhood, The * Palmer, Michael
Sisterhood, The * Stevenson, Florence
Sisters and strangers: a moral tale * Tennant, Emma
Sisters, long ago * Kehret, Peg
Sisters of sorcery: two centuries of witchcraft stories by the gentle sex * Lewis, Gogo & Seon Manley
Site, The * March, Melisand
Siva! * Richmond, Leigh & Walt Richmond
Six million dollar man, The: International incidents * Jahn, Mike
Six million dollar man, The: The secret of Bigfoot Pass * Jahn, Mike
Six of Swords * Douglas, Carole Nelson
Six Six Six * Zetterholm, Tore
Six-gun solution, The * Hawke, Simon
Six-guns and shurikens * Morris, Dave
Sixteenth Fontana book of great ghost stories, The * Chetwynd-Hayes, R.

Slow freight * Busby, F. M.
Slow lightning * Popkes, Steven
Slugs * Hutson, Shaun
Slumming in voodooland * Stableford, Brian M.
Small colonial war, A * Frezza, Robert
Small pinch of weather, A, and other stories * Aiken, Joan
Small world * King, Tabitha
Small world of Fred Hoyle, The: an autobiography * Hoyle, Fred
Smart as the devil: a novel * Picano, Felice
Smart dragons, foolish elves * Foster, Alan Dean & Martin H. Greenberg
Smart house * Wilhelm, Kate
Smart rats: a novel * Baird, Thomas
Smile on the void: the mythhistory of Ralph M'Botu Kitaj * Gordon, Stuart
Smiles and the millennium * Miller, Miranda
Smiling dogs, The * Ernst, Paul as KENNETH ROBESON
Smiling trip, The * Courtier, S. H.
Smith and Jones * Monsarrat, Nicholas
Smith of Wootton Major; and, Leaf by Niggle * Tolkien, J. R. R.
Smithereens * Battin, B. W.
Smith's dream * Stead, C. K.
Smofcon 3 record, The * Insinga, Aron K.
Smoke * Jensen, Ruby Jean
Smoke and ashes * Sologub, Fëdor
Smoke from the ashes * Johnstone, William W.
Smoke jumper * Montgomery, R. A.
Smoke ring, The * Niven, Larry
Smoke-stack lightning * Staig, Laurence
Smoking land, The: a Max Brand popular classic * Brand, Max
Smoky-House * Goudge, Elizabeth
Smugglers, The * Dicks, Terrance
Smuggler's gold * Cherryh, C. J.
Snail * Miller, Richard
Snail on the slope, The * Strugatsky, Arkady & Boris Strugatsky
Snake eyes * Milán, Victor as RICHARD AUSTIN
Snake in his bosom, and other stories * Lafferty, R. A.
Snake lady, and other stories, The * Lee, Vernon
Snake oil wars, The; or, Scheherazade Ginsberg strikes again * Godwin, Parke
Snakedance * Dicks, Terrance
Snakegod * Goulart, Ron
Snakes * Smith, Guy N.
Snares of Ibex, The * Clayton, Jo
Snarkout boys & the avocado of death, The * Pinkwater, Daniel M.
Snarkout boys and the Baconburg horror, The * Pinkwater, Daniel M.
Sneezing spell, The * Becker, Eve
Sniper * Randle, Kevin as STEVE MACKENZIE
Snow, The * Cooney, Caroline B.
Snow kill * Andrews, Keith William
Snow on the moon: an anthology of the Klysadel universe * Valenza, Anji
Snow queen, The * Vinge, Joan D.
Snow spider * Nimmo, Jenny
Snow White and Rose Red * Wrede, Patricia C.
Snow White and the seven dwarfs & the making of the classic film * Sibley, Brian
Snow White and the snow dwarfs * Smith, Guy N.
Snow World: a novel * Urick, Kevin
Snowbeast! * Tremayne, Peter
Snowbrother * Stirling, S. M.
Snowcastles * McGeary, Duncan
Snow-Eyes * Smith, Stephanie A.

Snowman * Bogner, Norman
Snowman, The * Stine, R. L.
Snows of Jaspre, The * Caraker, Mary
So long, and thanks for all the fish * Adams, Douglas
So what killed the vampire? * Yates, Alan as CARTER BROWN
So you want to be a wizard? * Duane, Diane
Sociable plover, and other stories and conceits, A * Linklater, Eric
Social problems through science fiction * Greenberg, Martin H. & John W. Milstead & Joseph D. Olander & Patricia Warrick
Social world of Aldous Huxley, The * Hines, Bede
Socialism and the literary artistry of William Morris * Boos, Florence Saunders & Carole Silver
Sociology of science fiction, The * Stableford, Brian M.
Sociology of the possible, The * Ofshe, Richard
Sociology of the possible, 2nd ed., The * Ofshe, Richard
Soft and others: 16 stories of wonder and dread * Wilson, F. Paul
Soft Book publications: first five years, 1981-1986 * Bell, Joseph
Soft machine, The: cybernetic fiction * Porush, David
Soft machine, The; Nova express; The wild boys: three novels * Burroughs, William S.
Soft targets * Ing, Dean
Soft wars * Bringsjord, Selmer
Soft whisper of the dead, The * Grant, Charles L.
Softly walks the beast * Hunter, Thomas O'D.
Software * Rucker, Rudy
Sojan * Moorcock, Michael
Sojourn * Salvatore, R. A.
Solar kill * Vilott, Rhondi as CHARLES INGRID
Solar menace, The * Vardeman, Robert E. as NICK CARTER
Solar wind * Jones, Peter A.
Solar wind, The * Tsang, Eric
Solaris; The chain of chance; A perfect vacuum * Lem, Stanislaw
Soldier boy * Shaara, Michael
Soldier of another fortune * Shupp, Mike
Soldier of arete * Wolfe, Gene
Soldier of fortune * Sadler, Barry
Soldier of Gideon * Sadler, Barry
Soldier of the mist * Wolfe, Gene
Soldiers of paradise: the Starbridge chronicles * Park, Paul
Sole survivor * Murphy, Warren & Richard Sapir
Solid gold kidnapping: a novel * Richards, Evan
Solip:system * Williams, Walter Jon
Solitary voice, A: Vardis Fisher: a collection of essays * Grover, Dorys C.
Solo kill * Cochrane, William E. as S. KYE BOULT
Solomon Leviathan's nine hundred and thirty-first trip around the world * Le Guin, Ursula K.
Solomon's knife * Koman, Victor
Solution: escape * Cooper, Margaret
Solution three * Mitchison, Naomi
Soma: Piers Anthony's world of Chthon * Platt, Charles
Some facts in the case of William Hope Hodgson, master of phantasy * Everts, R. Alain
Some kind of paradise: the emergence of American science fiction * Clareson, Thomas D.
Some kind of wonderer * Bischoff, David
Some of my best friends are monsters * Coville, Bruce
Some of the adventures of Rhode Island Red * Manes, Stephen
Some remarks on ghost stories * James, M. R.
Some summer lands * Gaskell, Jane

Sound of winter, The * Cover, Arthur Byron
Sound of wonder, The: interviews from "The science fiction radio show" * Carson, David & William Vernon & Daryl Lane
Sounding * Searls, Hank
Source, The * Lumley, Brian
Source, The * Shackleford, Jack D.
Source of evil * Vigliante, Mary
Source of magic, The * Anthony, Piers
Sourcery * Pratchett, Terry
South of eternity * St. George, E. A.
South Pole sabotage * Johnson, Seddon
South Pole terror, The: a Doc Savage adventure * Dent, Lester as KENNETH ROBESON
South star * Hearne, Betsy Gould
Southern cross * Daley, Brian & James Luceno as JACK MCKINNEY
Southpaw * King, Frank
Southshore * Tepper, Sheri S.
Souvenir book of Mr. Science Fiction's fantasy museum * Ackerman, Forrest J
Sovereign * Meluch, R. M.
Soviet science fiction since Stalin: science, politics, and literature * Marsh, Rosalind J.
Sowboy * Miller, Richard
Sowers of the thunder, The * Howard, Robert E.
Space 3: a collection of science fiction stories * Davis, Richard
Space 4: a collection of science-fiction stories * Davis, Richard
Space 5: a collection of science fiction stories * Davis, Richard
Space 6: a collection of science fiction stories * Davis, Richard
Space 7: a collection of science fiction stories * Davis, Richard
Space 8: a collection of science fiction stories * Davis, Richard
Space 9: a collection of science fiction stories * Davis, Richard
Space 1999: Alien seed * Tubb, E. C.
Space 1999: Android planet * Mason, Douglas R. as JOHN RANKINE
Space 1999: Astral quest * Mason, Douglas R. as JOHN RANKINE
Space 1999: Breakaway * Tubb, E. C.
Space 1999: Collision course * Tubb, E. C.
Space 1999: Earthfall * Tubb, E. C.
Space 1999: Lunar attack * Mason, Douglas R. as JOHN RANKINE
Space 1999: Mind-breaks of space * Butterworth, Michael & J. Jeff Jones
Space 1999: Planets of peril * Butterworth, Michael
Space 1999: Rogue planet * Tubb, E. C.
Space 1999: The psychomorph * Butterworth, Michael
Space 1999: The space-jackers * Butterworth, Michael
Space 1999: The time fighters * Butterworth, Michael
Space: 2000 to 2100 A.D. * Cowley, Stewart
Space age terrors! * Milton, Hilary
Space and beyond * Montgomery, R. A.
Space Angel * Roberts, John Maddox
Space apprentice * Strugatsky, Arkady & Boris Strugatsky
Space Ark * Hubschman, Thomas
Space art * Miller, Ron
Space art poster book, The * Miller, Ron
Space assassin * Chapman, Andrew
Space attack * Buckholtz, Eileen & Ruth Glick
Space beyond, The * Campbell, John W.
Space blazers * Lewitt, S. N. as RICK NORTH

Space cops: Mindblast * Duane, Diane & Peter Morwood
Space crusader * Rowland, Donald S. as MARK SUFFLING
Space demons * Rubinstein, Gillian
Space doctor * Stine, G. Harry as LEE CORREY
Space dreadnoughts * Drake, David & Martin H. Greenberg & Charles G. Waugh
Space eater, The * Langford, David
Space family Stone * Border, Rosemary & Robert A. Heinlein
Space folk * Anderson, Poul
Space fortress * Packard, Edward
Space gladiators * Drake, David & Martin H. Greenberg & Charles G. Waugh
Space Guardian, The * Daniels, Max
Space guardians, The * Ball, Brian
Space hawks * Blakeney, Jay D. as SEAN DALTON
Space infantry * Drake, David & Martin H. Greenberg & Charles G. Waugh
Space lust * Bellmore, Cynthia
Space Machine, The: a scientific romance * Priest, Christopher
Space mail * Asimov, Isaac & Martin H. Greenberg & Joseph D. Olander
Space mail, volume II * Asimov, Isaac & Martin H. Greenberg & Charles G. Waugh
Space mavericks, The * Kring, Michael K.
Space merchants, The * Kornbluth, C. M. & Frederik Pohl
Space monsters from movies, TV, and books * Simon, Seymour
Space museum, The * Jones, Glyn
Space nymph * Lasser, Dustin
Space odyssey * anon.
Space odysseys: an anthology of way-back-when futures * Aldiss, Brian W.
Space odysseys of Arthur C. Clarke, The * Slusser, George Edgar
Space of her own * McCarthy, Shawna
Space of your own * McCarthy, Shawna
Space patrol * Goodman, Julius
Space Patrol: the official guide to the Galactic Security Force * Caldwell, Steven
Space people, The * Bunting, Eve
Space pioneers * Brenner, Mayer Alan as RICK NORTH
Space pirates, The * Dicks, Terrance
Space pirates * Eklund, Gordon & E. E. Smith
Space pirates * Harkon, Franz as ASTRON DEL MARTIA
Space police: teacher's guide * Kelley, Leo P.
Space probe * Rowland, Donald S. as GRAHAM GARNER
Space prodigal, The * Sherrell, Carl
Space raiders and the planet of doom * Mooser, Stephen
Space scavengers, The * Cartmill, Cleve
Space search * Reynolds, Mack
Space shuttles * Asimov, Isaac & Martin H. Greenberg & Charles G. Waugh
Space slaves * Rusk, James Jr.
Space Station ICE-3 * Coville, Bruce
Space suits & gum-shoes: an anthology of science fiction and crime stories * Lunn, Richard
Space to let * Alexander, Robert as JOAN BUTLER
Space toys: a collector's guide to science fiction and astronautical toys * Payton, Crystal & Leland Payton
Space Traders Unlimited * Riding, Julia
Space train * Haile, Terence
Space trap * Coulson, Juanita
Space trap, The * Hughes, Monica
Space vampire * Packard, Edward
Space vampires, The * Wilson, Colin
Space vectors * Vardeman, Robert E.
Space venturer * Rowland, Donald S.

Starlog's science fiction yearbook, vol. 1 * Gerrold, David & Dave Truesdale
Starluck * Wismer, Don
Starmageddon * Rohmer, Richard
Starman: a novel * Foster, Alan Dean
Starmen, The * Brackett, Leigh
Starmen of Llyrdis, The * Brackett, Leigh
StarMother * Van Scyoc, Sydney J.
Staroamer's fate * Rothman, Chuck
Starpirate's brain * Goulart, Ron
Starquake * Forward, Robert L.
Starrett vs. Machen: a record of discovery and correspondence * Machen, Arthur & Vincent Starrett
Starrigger * DeChancie, John
Starry messenger: the best of Galileo * Ryan, Charles C.
Starry rift, The * Tiptree, James Jr.
Stars are the Styx, The * Sturgeon, Theodore
Stars at war, The * Carr, John F. & Jerry Pournelle
Stars' End * Cook, Glen
Stars in my pocket like grains of sand * Delany, Samuel R.
Stars in our hands * Cooper, Susan
Stars in shroud, The * Benford, Gregory
Stars must wait, The * Laumer, Keith
Stars of Albion * Holdstock, Robert & Christopher Priest
Stars or dust * Roush, C. E.
Stars will judge, The * Greenfield, Irving A.
Stars will speak, The * Zebrowski, George
Star-search * Kapp, Colin
Starseed * Robinson, Jeanne & Spider Robinson
Starseed mission, The * Vinter, Michael as T. S. J. GIB-BARD
Starseed on Gye Moor * Lymington, John
Starshadows: ten stories * Sargent, Pamela
Starship * Anderson, Poul
Starship & Haiku * Sucharitkul, Somtow
Starship & Haiku * Sucharitkul, Somtow as S. P. SOMTOW
Starship Death * Garrett, Randall
Starship Dunroamin * Milne, Janis
Starship Invincible: science fiction stories of the 30s * Kelly, Frank K.
Starship Orpheus #1 * Jade, Symon, pseud.
Starship Sapphire * Offutt, Andrew J. & Roland Green as JOHN CLEVE
Starship stud * Tobias, Sara
Starship traveler * Jackson, Steve
Starship troopers; The moon is a harsh mistress; Time enough for love * Heinlein, Robert A.
Starship warrior * Mooser, Stephen
Starship women * Koman, Victor
Starships * Asimov, Isaac & Martin H. Greenberg & Charles G. Waugh
Starsilk * Van Scyoc, Sydney J.
Starsong: a science-fantasy love story * Parkinson, Dan
Starsongs and unicorns; journeys through time and space * Norden, Eric
Star-spangled crunch, The * Condon, Richard
Star-spangled future, The * Spinrad, Norman
StarSpawn * Von Gunden, Kenneth
Starspinner * Aycock, Dale
Starstone, The * Chetwin, Grace
Starstormers * Fisk, Nicholas
Starstreak: stories of space * Owen, Betty M.
Starstrike * Gear, W. Michael
Start of the end of it all, The * Emshwiller, Carol
Start of the end of it all, and other stories, The * Emshwiller, Carol
Startide rising * Brin, David

Startling worlds of Henry Kuttner, The * Kuttner, Henry & C. L. Moore [uncredited]
Starwings * Proctor, Geo. W.
Starwolf * Hamilton, Edmond
Starwolves, The * Gunnarsson, Thorarinn
Starwolves: Battle of the ring * Gunnarsson, Thorarinn
Starwolves: Tactical error * Gunnarsson, Thorarinn
Starworld * Harrison, Harry
State of grace * Wilhelm, Kate
State of play * Buckley, Doug
State of the art, The * Banks, Iain M.
State visit * Egleton, Clive
Statement of Randolph Carter, The: being both the original holograph version and its transcription * Lovecraft, H. P.
Statesman * Anthony, Piers
Station Gehenna * Weiner, Andrew
Station of the invisibles * Mahr, Kurt
Station Zero-Zero * Sullivan, Mike
Stationfall * Cover, Arthur Byron
Stations of the nightmare * Farmer, Philip José
Stations of the tide * Swanwick, Michael
Statue of Liberty adventure * Kushner, Ellen
Status civilization, The; and, Notions: unlimited * Sheckley, Robert
Status quotient: the carrier * Sperry, Ralph A.
Staveworld * Evans, Chris as NATHAN ELLIOTT
Stay out of the shower: 25 years of shocker films, beginning with "Psycho" * Schoell, William
Staying alive: a writer's guide * Spinrad, Norman
Stealer of souls * Moorcock, Michael
Stealers' sky * Abbey, Lynn & Robert Lynn Asprin
Stealing time * Edwards, Nicky
Stealth * Durham, Guy
Steam * Laws, Jay B.
Steam bird * Schenck, Hilbert
Steeds of Satan, The * Leslie, Peter
Steel albatross, The * Carpenter, Scott
Steel brother * Dickson, Gordon R.
Steel eye, The * Gottfried, Chet
Steel ghost * Hockley, Chris
Steel gods * Sharman, Nick as SCOTT GRONMARK
Steel of Raithskar, The * Garrett, Randall & Vicki Ann Heydron
Steel spring, The * Wahlöö, Per
Steel, the mist, and the blazing sun, The * Anvil, Christopher
Steel trap * Sugar, Andrew
Steel tsar, The: third volume in the Oswald Bastable trilogy * Moorcock, Michael
Steel valentine, The * Lansdale, Joe R.
Steele * Hawke, Simon as J. D. MASTERS
Steeleye: The Wideways * Dunn, Saul
Steeleye: Waterspace * Dunn, Saul
Steerswoman, The * Kirstein, Rosemary
Stella; and, An unfinished communication: studies of the unseen * Hinton, C. H.
Stella nova: the contemporary science fiction authors * Reginald, R.
Stellar assignment * Tubb, E. C.
Stellar death plan, The * Vardeman, Robert E.
Stellar fist * Proctor, Geo. W.
Stellar gauge, The: essays of science fiction writers * Singh, Kirpal & Michael J. Tolley
Stellar science-fiction stories #2 * del Rey, Judy-Lynn
Stellar science-fiction stories #3 * del Rey, Judy-Lynn
Stellar science-fiction stories #4 * del Rey, Judy-Lynn
Stellar science-fiction stories #5 * del Rey, Judy-Lynn
Stellar science-fiction stories #6 * del Rey, Judy-Lynn
Stellar science-fiction stories #7 * del Rey, Judy-Lynn

Stories * Ray, Satyajit
Stories about not being afraid of ghosts * anonymous
Stories about not being afraid of ghosts, 2nd ed. * anonymous
Stories by Mama Lansdale's youngest boy * Lansdale, Joe R.
Stories by Otis Adelbert Kline * Kline, Otis Adelbert
Stories from outer space * Sacranie, Raj
Stories from the Twilight zone * Serling, Rod
Stories in the dark: tales of terror * Lamb, Hugh
Stories of fear * Baker, Denys Val
Stories of haunted inns * Baker, Denys Val
Stories of horror and suspense: an anthology * Baker, Denys Val
Stories of Ray Bradbury, The * Bradbury, Ray
Stories of Ronald Blythe, The * Blythe, Ronald
Stories of terror * Foster, John L.
Stories of the macabre * Baker, Denys Val
Stories of the night: an anthology * Baker, Denys Val
Stories of the occult, and other tales of mystery * Baker, Denys Val
Stories of the strange & sinister * Baker, Frank
Stories of the supernatural * Baker, Denys Val
Stories of the unforeseen * Isaac, Rondall
Stories of the walking dead * Haining, Peter
Stork factor, The * Hughes, Zach
Storm child * Netter, Susan
Storm haven * Telford, Robert
Storm knights * Slavicsek, Bill & C. J. Tramontana
Storm Lord, The * Lee, Tanith
Storm of '92, The: a grandfather's tale told in 1932 * Lawrence, W. H. C.
Storm of dust: a Crossroads adventure in the world of David Drake's Dragon lord * Randall, Neil
Storm of wings, A: being the second volume of the 'Viriconium' sequence, in which Benedict Paucemanly returns from his long frozen dream in the far side of the Moon, and the Earth submits briefly to the charisma of the Locust * Harrison, M. John
Storm over Valla * Bulmer, Kenneth, as DRAY PRESCOT & ALAN BURT AKERS
Storm rider * Vilott, Rhondi
Storm rising * Singer, Marilyn
Storm season * Asprin, Robert Lynn
Storm seed * Morris, Chris & Janet Morris
Storm shield * Flint, Kenneth C.
Storm upon Ulster, A * Flint, Kenneth C.
Storm warnings: science fiction confronts the future * Greenland, Colin & George Slusser & Eric S. Rabkin
Storm warriors * Stableford, Brian, as BRIAN CRAIG
Stormblade * Berberick, Nancy Varian
Stormbringer * Monroe, John B. & Ken St. Andre & Steve Perrin
Storming Intrepid * Harrison, Payne
Storming the reality studio: a casebook of cyberpunk and postmodern science fiction * McCaffery, Larry
Stormqueen! A Darkover novel * Bradley, Marion Zimmer
Stormriders: a Shadow World novel * Longstreet, Roxanne
Storm's howling through Tiflis, The * Oram, Neil
Storms of victory * Green, Roland & Jerry E. Pournelle
Stormwarden * Wurts, Janny
Story into film: three tales of the supernatural go from page to screen * Ruchti, Ulrich & Sybil Taylor
Story of Ab, The: a tale of the time of the cave man * Waterloo, Stanley
Story of Freginald, The * Brooks, Walter R.
Story of Pepita and Corindo, The * Cowper, Richard
Story of the planet Candy, The * Skaf, Robert

Story of the poor author, and some of the stories that he told, The * Kenward, James
Story of the stone, The * Hughart, Barry
Story so far, The * Nathan, David
Story teller, The: a novel * Vansittart, Peter
Storyteller, The * Minghella, Anthony
Storyteller and the Jann, The * Goldin, Stephen
Stout-hearted cat, The: a fable for cat lovers * Frey, Alexander M.
Stove haunting, The * Mooney, Bel
Stowaway to Mars * Wyndham, John
Strained relations: Eugene writers series one, 1989 * Newcomer, Alan Bard
Straits of Messina, The * Delany, Samuel R.
Stranded * Grae, Camarin
Stranded * Norwood, Warren & Mel Odom
Strands * Kisner, James
Strands of starlight * Baudino, Gael
Strange adventures of Lucy Smith, The * Philips, F. C.
Strange and amazing facts about Star Trek * Cohen, Daniel
Strange attractions * Sleator, William
Strange attractors * Henighan, Tom
Strange attractors * Sleator, William
Strange attractors: original Australian speculative fiction * Broderick, Damien
Strange bedfellows * Burkholz, Herbert
Strange case of Dr. Jekyll and Mr. Hyde, The * Cameron, Joan & Robert Louis Stevenson
Strange case of Dr. Jekyll and Mr. Hyde, The * Harris, Raymond & Robert Louis Stevenson
Strange case of Dr Jekyll and Mr Hyde, and other stories, The * Stevenson, Robert Louis
Strange curses * Hurwood, Bernhardt J.
Strange days * Sampson, Robert
Strange encounters * Bischoff, David
Strange eons * Bloch, Robert
Strange fish * Dent, Lester as KENNETH ROBESON
Strange ghost stories * Arneson, D. J.
Strange gifts: eight stories of science fiction * Silverberg, Robert
Strange glory * Goldberg, Gerry
Strange horizons: the spectrum of science fiction * Moskowitz, Sam
Strange invasion * Kandel, Michael
Strange land, The * Riding, Julia
Strange landing: a tale of adventure * Meynell, Laurence
Strange loop * Prantera, Amanda
Strange Maine * Greenberg, Martin H. & Charles G. Waugh & Frank D. McSherry Jr.
Strange monster stories * Arneson, D. J.
Strange monsters of the recent past * Waldrop, Howard
Strange nation of Rafael Mendes, The * Scliar, Moacyr
Strange night writing of Jessamine Colter, The * DeFelice, Cynthia C.
Strange orbits: an anthology of science fiction * Pearson, Michael & Amabel Williams-Ellis
Strange planets: an anthology of science fiction * Pearson, Michael & Amabel Williams-Ellis
Strange ride of Rudyard Kipling, The: his life and works * Wilson, Angus
Strange Scottish stories * Owen, William
Strange seed: a novel * Wright, T. M.
Strange shadows: the uncollected fiction and essays of Clark Ashton Smith * Smith, Clark Ashton
Strange stories, and other explorations in Victorian fiction * Wolff, Robert Lee
Strange tales from CBS Radio Mystery Theater * Brown, Himan
Strange tales from the Strand * Adrian, Jack

Strange tales of mystery and the paranormal * Heathwood, Cecilia

Strange things happen in the woods * Bunting, Eve

Strange things in close-up: the nearly complete Howard Waldrop * Waldrop, Howard

Strange tomorrow * Karl, Jean E.

Strange toys * Geary, Patricia

Strange visitor * Conway, Laura

Strange wine: fifteen new stories from the nightside of the world * Ellison, Harlan

Strange world of science fiction * anonymous

Strangeness: a collection of curious tales * Disch, Thomas M. & Charles Naylor

Stranger * Dickson, Gordon R.

Stranger, The * Saunders, G. K.

Stranger, The * Timperley, Rosemary

Stranger came ashore, A * Hunter, Mollie

Stranger from the stars * Etchemendy, Nancy

Stranger in a strange land * Heinlein, Robert A.

Stranger in a strange land & other works: notes * Searles, Baird

Stranger suns * Zebrowski, George

Stranger than tomorrow: three stories of the future * Carew, Jan R.

Stranger to herself, A * Bailey, Hilary

Stranger with my face * Duncan, Lois

Strangers, The * Castle, Mort

Strangers * Dozois, Gardner

Strangers * Koontz, Dean R.

Strangers from the sky * Bonanno, Margaret Wander

Strangers who linger * Thurla, Aimée

Strangler's moon * Goldin, Stephen & E. E. Smith

Strata * Pratchett, Terry

Strategem, and other stories, The * Crowley, Aleister

Strayed sheep of Charun, The * Roberts, John Maddox

Stream that stood still, The * Nichols, Beverley

Streams of silver * Salvatore, R. A.

Street, The * Kilworth, Garry, as GARRY DOUGLAS

Street magic * Reaves, Michael

Streetlethal * Barnes, Steven

Streets of the city * Spedding, [Alison]

Strength of stones * Bear, Greg

Strength of stones, new rev. ed. * Bear, Greg

Stress of her regard, The * Powers, Tim

Strickland demon, The * Shackleford, Jack D.

Strike Eagle * Beason, Doug

Strike fighters * Willard, Tom

Strike fighters: Blood river * Willard, Tom

Strike fighters: Bold forager * Willard, Tom

Strike fighters: Desert star * Willard, Tom

Strike fighters: Red dancer * Willard, Tom

Strike fighters: Sudden fury * Willard, Tom

Strike fighters: War chariot * Willard, Tom

Strike it dead * Siegel, Barbara & Scott Siegel

Strike of a sex, The * Miller, George Noyes as ?

Strike zone * Peters, David, as PETER DAVID

String in the harp, A * Bond, Nancy

String Lug the fox * Stephen, David

Strings * Duncan, Dave

Striped holes * Broderick, Damien

Stroka Prospekt: a story * Lupoff, Richard A.

Strokes: essays and reviews, 1966-1986 * Clute, John

Strong man, The * Keating, H. R. F.

Strongest man in the world, The * Cebulash, Mel

Stronghold * Rawn, Melanie

Structural fabulation: an essay on fiction of the future * Scholes, Robert

Struggle, The * Ahern, Jerry

Struggle, The * Smith, L. J.

Stryker's children: a novel * Schneider, Joyce Anne

Stuck fast in yesterday * Kellerhals-Stewart, Heather

Studies in the late romances of William Morris: papers presented at the annual meeting of the Modern Language Association, December 1975 * Dunlap, Joseph & Carole Silver

Study guides for J. R. R. Tolkien's The hobbit and The Lord of the Rings * Harmon, Philip M.

Study in sorcery, A * Kurland, Michael

Study of George Orwell, A: the man and his works * Hollis, Christopher

Study of Huxley, A * Ueda, Tsutomu

Study war no more: a selection of alternatives * Haldeman, Joe

Stuffed dog, The * De Polnay, Peter

Stuffed men, The * Rud, Anthony

Stunts * Grant, Charles L.

Style of connectedness, The: Gravity's Rainbow and Thomas Pynchon * Moore, Thomas

Styx * Hyde, Christopher

Styx complex, The * Rhodes, Russell L.

Suaine and the crow-god * Gordon, Stuart

Sublimity in the novels of Ann Radcliffe: a study of the influence upon her craft of Edmund Burke's Enquiry into the origin of our ideas of the sublime and beautiful * Ware, Malcolm

Submarine mystery, The: a Doc Savage adventure * Dent, Lester as KENNETH ROBESON

Submarine tour, A * Balch, Frank

Subsidy, The * Galen, James

Subspace encounter * Smith, E. E. & Lloyd Arthur Eshbach

Substance under pressure: artistic coherence and evolving form in the novels of Doris Lessing * Draine, Betsy

Substance X * Houston, David

Subterranean * Buxton, James

Subterranean gallery * Russo, Richard Paul

Subtropical speculations: an anthology of Florida science fiction * Mathews, Richard & Rick Wilber

Sub-zero! * Walker, Robert W.

Succubus * Greenfield, Irving A., as CAMPO VERDE

Succubus, The * Johnson, Ken

Such a good baby: a novel of horror * Jensen, Ruby Jean

Such stuff as screams are made of * Bloch, Robert

Sucking Pit, The * Smith, Guy N.

Suculent witch, The * Bourns, Marsha

Sudanna, Sudanna * Herbert, Brian

Sudden death * Fretts, Bruce, as NICHOLAS ADAMS

Sudden fear: the horror and dark suspense fiction of Dean R. Koontz * Munster, Bill

Sudden fury * Willard, Tom

Sudden star, The * Sargent, Pamela

Sue me * Murphy, Warren & Richard Sapir

Sue Slate: private eye * Lynch, Lee

Suffer the children * Saul, John

Sugar festival, The * Park, Paul

Sugar rain: the Starbridge Chronicles * Park, Paul

Sugarcane Island * Packard, Edward

Suicide attack * Alexander, David, as JOHN SIEVERT

Suicide, Inc. * Goulart, Ron

Suicide plague, The * Naha, Ed

Suicide run * Greenfield, Irving A.

Suiting, The * Wilde, Kelley

Suldrun's garden * Vance, Jack

Sultana's dream, and selections from The secluded ones * Hossein, Rokeya Sakhawat

Sultan's secret, The * Lerangis, Peter

Sultan's turret, The * Cullen, Seamus

SUM VII: a novel * Hard, T. W.

Sum of all fears, The * Clancy, Tom

Sum of things, The * Green, Roland
Summer birds, The * Farmer, Penelope
Summer ghost, A * Tomalin, Ruth
Summer magic * Chew, Ruth
Summer of fear * Duncan, Lois
Summer of night * Simmons, Dan
Summer of the dinosaur * Hall, Willis
Summer of the green star * Lee, Robert C.
Summer of the shaman * Ross, Dan, *as* CLARISSA ROSS
Summer of the unicorn * Hooper, Kay
Summer people * Elliott, Janice
Summer queen, The * Vinge, Joan D.
Summer rising * Sullivan, Sheila
Summer Solstice: a novel * Hinkemeyer, Michael T.
Summer switch * Rodgers, Mary
Summer tree, The * Kay, Guy Gavriel
Summer visitors, The * Leimas, Brooke
Summerfair * Dibell, Ansen
Summer's king, The * Wilder, Cherry
Summertide * Sheffield, Charles
Summit * Bowker, Richard
Summit * Thomas, D. M.
Summon the bright water * Household, Geoffrey
Summoned, The * Fulgham, Steven Ray
Summoning, The * Pintoro, John
Summoning, The * Reed, Dana
Sun and the moon, The * Page, P. K., *as* JUDITH CAPE
Sun and the moon, and other fictions, The * Page, P. K.
Sun at night, The: a novel * Williamson, Roger
Sun blind * Hansen, Gwen
Sun bubble: a novel * Gaskell, Jane
Sun chemist, The * Davidson, Lionel
Sun dogs * McGarry, Mark J.
Sun horse, The * Clark, Catherine Anthony
Sun rises into the sky, and other stories, The * Dawson, Fielding
Sun, the moon, and the stars, The * Brust, Steven
Sunbound, The * Felice, Cynthia
Sunburn Lake * De Haven, Tom
Sunburst * Fisk, Nicholas
Sunder, Eclipse & Seed * Guttenberg, Elyse
Sundered Realm, The * Vardeman, Robert E. & Victor Milán
Sundered soul: a mythic tale * Tella, Alfred
Sundipper * Thompson, Paul B.
Sundiver * Brin, David
Sundrinker * Corley, James
Sundrinker * Hughes, Zach
Sunfall * Cherryh, C. J.
Sung in blood * Cook, Glen
Sung in shadow * Lee, Tanith
Sunglasses after dark * Collins, Nancy A.
Sunrise on Mercury, and other science fiction stories * Silverberg, Robert
Sunrise west * Carlson, William K.
Sunrunner's fire * Rawn, Melanie
Sun's end * Lupoff, Richard A.
Suns in duo * Wade, Tom as VICTOR LA SALLE
Sunset gun, The * Cameron, Kenneth M., *as* GEORGE BARTRAM
Sunset patriots, The * Taylor, Charles D.
Sunset people, The * Penny, David G.
"Sunset Terrace imagery in Lovecraft," and other essays * Cannon, Peter
Sunset warrior, The * Lustbader, Eric Van
Sunshaker's war: a tale of David Sullivan * Deitz, Tom
Sunshine 43 * Penny, David G.
Sunsmoke * Killus, James
Sunspacer: a novel * Zebrowski, George
SunStop 8 * Fisher, Lou

Sunstrike * Carpozi, George Jr.
Sunstroke, and other stories * Watson, Ian
Sunwaifs * Van Scyoc, Sydney J.
Sunwatch * Dorer, Frances & Nancy Dorer, *as* FRANK DORN
Sunworld * Kelley, Leo P.
Super book of ghost stories * Matthews, Leonard J.
Super charge * Bagdon, Paul as TONY PHILLIPS
Super Susan * Stine, H. William & Megan Stine
Super trail bike mystery * Wenk, Richard
Supercomputer * Packard, Edward
Superdog * McInerney, Judith Whitelock
Superdog gift, The * McInerney, Judith Whitelock
Superdog rescue, The * McInerney, Judith Whitelock
Superdog secret, The * McInerney, Judith Whitelock
Superdog surprise, The * McInerney, Judith Whitelock
Superfolks * Mayer, Robert
Supergirl * Mazer, Norma Fox
Supergirl, the girl of steel * Helfer, Andrew
Supergun mission, The * Roberts, Mark as LIONEL DERRICK
Superhero movie & TV quiz book, The * Rovin, Jeff
Superheroes * Parry, Michel
Superheroes on screen * Gross, Edward
Superheroes on screen files, The: Superman and Spider-Man * Gross, Edward
Superhorror * Campbell, Ramsey
Superluminal * McIntyre, Vonda N.
Supermale, The: a modern novel * Jarry, Alfred
Superman II, the movie magazine * Fleisher, Michael & Joe Orlando
Superman III: a novel * Kotzwinkle, William
Superman IV * Hiller, B. B.
Superman IV * Krulik, Nancy E.
Superman IV, the quest for peace: the official poster magazine * McDonnell, David
Superman and Spider-Man * Gross, Edward
Superman at fifty: the persistence of a legend * Dooley, Dennis & Gary Engle
Superman files, The * Van Hise, James
Superman: Last son of Krypton * Maggin, Elliot S.
Superman: Miracle Monday * Maggin, Elliot S.
Superman, serial to cereal * Grossman, Gary H.
Superman, the man of steel * Helfer, Andrew
Superman (the movie) * Libman, Gary
Superman's maze challenge * Koziakin, Vladimir
Supermen * Asimov, Isaac & Martin H. Greenberg & Charles G. Waugh
Supermind * van Vogt, A. E.
Supernatural * Gibson, James & Alan Ridout
Supernatural, The * Jones, John G.
Supernatural fiction for teens: 500 good paperbacks to read for wonderment, fear, and fun * Kies, Cosette
Supernatural fiction writers: fantasy and horror * Bleiler, E. F.
Supernatural in Hawthorne and Poe, The * Woodbridge, Benjamin M.
Supernatural movie quizbook, The * Rovin, Jeff
Supernatural omnibus, The * Summers, Montague
Supernatural romance of Suzanne, The conquest of demon Cabeto, and Allen Mountain ghosts * Barrow, Louis
Supernatural: seven stories based on the television series on BBC-1 * Muller, Robert
Supernatural short stories of Charles Dickens, The * Dickens, Charles
Supernatural short stories of Robert Louis Stevenson, The * Stevenson, Robert Louis
Supernatural short stories of Sir Walter Scott, The * Scott, Walter, Sir

Sword & sorcery annual, special—1975 * anon.
Sword and the chain, The * Rosenberg, Joel
Sword and the circle, The: King Arthur and the knights of the Round Table * Sutcliff, Rosemary
Sword and the dagger, The * Mayhar, Ardath
Sword and the Eye, The * Leiber, Justin
Sword and the flame, The * Lawhead, Stephen
Sword and the satchel, The * Boyer, Elizabeth
Sword and the sorcerer, The * Winski, Norman
Sword and the stone, The * Yolen, Jane
Sword and the tower, The * Leiber, Justin
Sword at sunset * Sutcliff, Rosemary
Sword bearer, The * White, John
Sword Daughter's quest * Vilott, Rhondi
Sword for Alosando, A * St. George, E. A.
Sword for Kregen, A * Bulmer, Kenneth as DRAY PRESCOT & ALAN BURT AKERS
Sword for the empire * Lancour, Gene
Sword in the stone, The * Moffatt, Derry
Sword is forged, The * Walton, Evangeline
Sword of Allah, The * Elliott, Elton T. & Richard E. Geis as RICHARD ELLIOTT
Sword of Aradel, The * Key, Alexander
Sword of Arhapal, The * Sernine, Daniel
Sword of Bheleu, The * Watt-Evans, Lawrence
Sword of Caesar * Stevenson, Bruce & Robin Stevenson
Sword of Calandra, The * Dexter, Susan
Sword of chaos, and other stories * Bradley, Marion Zimmer & the Friends of Darkover
Sword of fire * Hawkins, Ward
Sword of forbearance, The * Williams, Paul O.
Sword of Hachiman, The: a novel of early Japan * Guest, Lynn
Sword of Orley, The * Farrar, Stewart
Sword of Poyana, The * Bailey, Gerald Earl
Sword of Sagamore, The * Dalkey, Kara
Sword of Samurai Cat, The * Rogers, Mark E.
Sword of Shandar, The * Besaw, Victor
Sword of Shannara, The * Brooks, Terry
Sword of Skelos, The * Offutt, Andrew J.
Sword of the demon: a novel * Lupoff, Richard A.
Sword of the Gael * Offutt, Andrew J.
Sword of the Lamb, The * Wren, M. K.
Sword of the Lictor, The * Wolfe, Gene
Sword of the Lictor, The: science fiction; The citadel of the Autarch: science fiction * Wolfe, Gene
Sword of the Nurlingas * Bailey, Gerald Earl
Sword of the samurai * Perry, Steve & Michael Reaves
Sword of the samurai * Smith, Mark & Jamie Thomson
Sword of the sun, The * Dever, Joe
Sword of the sun, The * Dever, Joe & John Grant
Sword of the templar, The * Mason, Paul
Sword of the valiant: the legend of Sir Gawain and the Green Knight * Weeks, Stephen & Henry Whittington
Sword of vengeance * Olden, Marc
Sword of winter, The * Randall, Marta
Sword Point * Coyle, Harold W.
Sword smith, The * Arnason, Eleanor
Sword, the jewel, and the mirror, The * Roberts, John Maddox
Swordbearer, The * Cook, Glen

Sword-breaker * Roberson, Jennifer
Sword-dancer * Roberson, Jennifer
Sword-maker * Roberson, Jennifer
SwordQuest: Quest for the Demon Gate * Fawcett, Bill
SwordQuest: Quest for the dragon's eye * Fawcett, Bill
SwordQuest: Quest for the elf king * Fawcett, Bill
SwordQuest: Quest for the unicorn's horn * Fawcett, Bill
Swords against darkness * Offutt, Andrew J.
Swords against darkness 1 * Offutt, Andrew J.
Swords against darkness II * Offutt, Andrew J.
Swords against darkness III * Offutt, Andrew J.
Swords against darkness IV * Offutt, Andrew J.
Swords against darkness V * Offutt, Andrew J.
Swords & ice magic * Leiber, Fritz
Swords' masters * Leiber, Fritz
Swords of Corum omnibus, The * Moorcock, Michael
Swords of Mars; and, Synthetic men of Mars * Burroughs, Edgar Rice
Swords of Raemllyn: To demons bound * Vardeman, Robert E. & Geo. W. Proctor
Swords of the horseclans * Adams, Robert
Swords of the legion * Turtledove, Harry
Swords of Zinjaban, The * de Camp, Catherine Crook & L. Sprague de Camp
Swords trilogy, The * Moorcock, Michael
Sword-singer * Roberson, Jennifer
Swordspoint: a melodrama of manners * Kushner, Ellen
Swordswoman, The * Salmonson, Jessica Amanda
Sworn allies * Drake, David & Bill Fawcett
Sykaos papers, The: being an account of the voyages of the poet Oi Paz to the system of Strim in the seventeenth century, selected and edited by Q * Thompson, E. P.
Sylvia game, The * Alcock, Vivien
Symbiote's crown * Baker, Scott
Symbiotic mind, The * Dyer, Alfred
Symbol of Terra * Tubb, E. C.
Symbol of Terra; and, The temple of truth * Tubb, E. C.
Symphony in sand, A * Miller, Calvin
Symphony of light * Daley, Brian & James Luceno as JACK MCKINNEY
Symphony of storms, A * Vardeman, Robert E.
Symphony of terror * Sucharitkul, Somtow
Synapse function, The * Livingston, M. Jay
Synaptic manhunt * Farren, Mick
Synchronicity; or, Something * Lumley, Brian
Syndic, The * Kornbluth, C. M.
Syndrome * Pronin, Barbara
Synergy: new science fiction, number four * Zebrowski, George
Synergy: new science fiction, number one * Zebrowski, George
Synergy: new science fiction, number three * Zebrowski, George
Synergy: new science fiction, number two * Zebrowski, George
Synners * Cadigan, Pat
Synthetics, The * Clark, Karen
Systemic shock * Ing, Dean
Systems: a novel * Quick, W. T.
Syzygy * Pohl, Frederik

T

Tales of fantasy and fear * Finlay, Winifred
Tales of fear and fantasy * Chetwynd-Hayes, R.
Tales of fear & frightening phenomena: an anthology * Hoke, Helen
Tales of horror * Davey, John & Bram Stoker
Tales of Japanese science fiction and fantasy * Hoshi, Shin'ichi
Tales of known space: the universe of Larry Niven * Niven, Larry
Tales of love and death * Aickman, Robert
Tales of magic realism by women: dreams in a minor key * Sturgis, Susanna J.
Tales of mystery * Jagendorf, M. A.
Tales of mystery and horror * anon.
Tales of mystery and suspense * Hipple, Theodore W.
Tales of mystery and terror * Poe, Edgar Allan
Tales of myth and fantasy * Falconar, A. E. I.
Tales of natural and unnatural catastrophes * Highsmith, Patricia
Tales of Nevèrÿon * Delany, Samuel R.
Tales of Patrick Merla, The * Merla, Patrick
Tales of Pirx the pilot * Lem, Stanislaw
Tales of Pirx the pilot; Return from the stars; The invincible * Lem, Stanislaw
Tales of Robin Hood * Emery, Clayton
Tales of science fiction and the supernatural * Groves, Ann
Tales of sorcery and witchcraft * Finlay, Winifred
Tales of terror * Higgins, D. S. & Edgar Allan Poe
Tales of terror * Sullivan, Eleanor
Tales of terror and darkness * Blackwood, Algernon
Tales of terror and mystery * Doyle, Arthur Conan
Tales of terror from outer space * Chetwynd-Hayes, R.
Tales of terror; or, The mysteries of magic: a selection of wonderful and supernatural stories * St. Clair, Henry
Tales of terror: The monkey's paw; The monsters are due on Maple Street * Jacobs, W. W. & Rod Serling
Tales of the Cthulhu Mythos * Derleth, August & James Turner as ANONYMOUS EDITORS
Tales of the dark * Child, Lincoln
Tales of the dark #2 * Child, Lincoln
Tales of the dark #3 * Child, Lincoln
Tales of the dark knight: Batman's first fifty years, 1939-1989 * Vaz, Mark Cotta
Tales of the dead * Pronzini, Bill
Tales of the early world * Hughes, Ted
Tales of the falcon * Buckholtz, Eileen & Ruth Glick as REBECCA YORK
Tales of the hidden world * Chetwynd-Hayes, R.
Tales of the Horseclans: collectors' edition, books 1, 2, 3 * Adams, Robert
Tales of the Lovecraft collectors * Faig, Kenneth W. Jr.
Tales of the occult * Asimov, Isaac & Martin H. Greenberg & Charles G. Waugh
Tales of the occult * Wolf, Barbara H. & Jack C. Wolf
Tales of the outré: writings celebrating the centenary of H. P. Lovecraft * Kitsch, Hieronymous
Tales of the Quintana Roo: stories * Tiptree, James Jr.
Tales of the sacred and the supernatural * Eliade, Mircea
Tales of the Scientific Crime Club * Cummings, Ray
Tales of the supernatural * Blackwood, Algernon
Tales of the uncanny * anon.
Tales of the uncanny * Cerna, Zlata & Vaclav Cerny & Miroslav Novak
Tales of the unexpected * Dahl, Roald
Tales of the unsuspected * Nordsieck, Graham
Tales of the wandering Jew * Stableford, Brian M.
Tales of the witch world * Norton, Andre
Tales of the Witch World 1 * Norton, Andre
Tales of the Witch World 2 * Norton, Andre

Tales of the Witch World 3 * Norton, Andre
Tales of tomorrow: Ice from space * Houston, David
Tales of unknown horror * Haining, Peter
Tales of witchcraft * Dalby, Richard
Tales of Wonder * Fearn, John Russell
Tales of wonder * Yolen, Jane
Tales out of time * Ireson, Barbara
Tales to make the flesh creep: an anthology of classic stories * Van Thal, Herbert
Tales, weird and whimsical * Lally, T. M.
Taliesen * Lawhead, Stephen
Taliesin's telling * Sampson, Fay
Talisman, The * Holdstock, Robert as ROBERT FAULCON
Talisman, The * Straub, Peter & Stephen King
Talisman of death * Smith, Mark & Jamie Thomson
Talisman of Valdegarde * Simon, Madeleine
Talk about writing * Le Guin, Ursula K.
Talk: conversations with William Golding * Biles, Jack I. & William Golding
Talking across the world * Stapledon, Agnes & Olaf Stapledon
Talking car, The * Fisk, Nicholas
Talking coffins of Cryo-City, The * Parenteau, Shirley
Talking devil, The * Dent, Lester as KENNETH ROBESON
Talking man * Bisson, Terry
Talking to dragons * Wrede, Patricia C.
Talking tree, The * Tabori, Paul
Tall, dark, and gruesome: an autobiography * Lee, Christopher
Tall stones, The * Caldecott, Moyra
Talons of Scorpio * Bulmer, Kenneth as DRAY PRESCOT & ALAN BURT AKERS
Talons of Time * Twitchell, Paul
Taltos * Brust, Steven
Taltos and the paths of the dead * Brust, Steven
Taltos the assassin * Brust, Steven
Tam Lin * Dean, Pamela
Tamastara; or, The Indian nights * Lee, Tanith
Tambu * Asprin, Robert Lynn
Taming the Forest King * Edwards, Claudia J.
Tanelorn archives, The: a primary and secondary bibliography of the works of Michael Moorcock, 1949-1979 * Bilyeu, Richard
Tangents * Bear, Greg
Tangerine * Gray, Linda Crockett
Tangled lands, The * Shetterly, Will
Tangled webs * Mudd, Steve
Tango Charlie and Foxtrot Romeo * Varley, John
Tanis, the shadow years * Siegel, Barbara & Scott Siegel
Tanith * Shackleford, Jack D.
Tankwar * Steelbaugh, Larry
Tantras * Ciencin, Scott & James Lowder as RICHARD AWLINSON
Tapestry of magics, A * Daley, Brian
Tapestry of time, A * Cowper, Richard
Tapestry warriors, The * Wilder, Cherry
Tara of the twilight * Carter, Lin
Tarantula * Green, Carl R. & William R. Sanford
Target * Drake, David & Janet Morris
Target for death * Dent, Lester & William G. Bogart as KENNETH ROBESON
Target: intruder * Tanner, Mack
Target Iran * Adair, James B. & Gordon Rottman
Target nuke * Adair, James B. & Gordon Rottman
Target star, The * Scheer, K. H.
Target Steele * Hawke, Simon as J. D. MASTERS
Target Texas * Adair, James B. & Gordon Rottman
Tark and the Golden Tide * MacConnell, Colum
Taronga * Kelleher, Victor
Tarot * Anthony, Piers

Ten-ton monster * Austin, R. G.
Teot's war * Gladney, Heather
Tera beyond, The * MacCloud, Malcolm
Terminal island * Obstfeld, Raymond as JASON FROST
Terminal road * Shirley, John as D. B. DRUMM
Terminal velocity * Shaw, Bob
Terminal visions: the literature of last things * Wagar, W. Warren
Terminator, The * Hutson, Shaun
Terminator 2 * Frakes, Randall
Terminator 2: Judgment day: the book of the film: an illustrated screenplay * Cameron, James & William Wisher
Terminator, The: a novel * Frakes, Randall & W. H. Wisher
Terminus * Edwards, Peter
Terminus * Gallagher, Stephen as JOHN LYDECKER
Terra! * Benni, Stefano
Terra! * Hay, George as KING LANG
Terra data, The * Tubb, E. C.
Terra nostra * Fuentes, Carlos
Terra SF: the year's best European SF * Nolane, Richard D.
Terra SF II: the year's best European SF * Nolane, Richard D.
Terraplane: a novel * Womack, Jack
Terrarium * Sanders, Scott Russell
Terratoid guide, The: a checklist of magazines dealing with fantasy, science-fiction, and horror films * Plum, Claude D. Jr.
Terrible freedom, A * Linklater, Eric
Terrible stork, The * Dent, Lester as KENNETH ROBESON
Terrible threes, The * Reed, Ishmael
Terrible twos, The * Reed, Ishmael
Terridae, The * Tubb, E. C.
Terror, The * Ahern, Jerry
Terror * Pohl, Frederik
Terror!: a history of horror illustrations from the pulp magazines * Haining, Peter
Terror and the lonely widow * Dent, Lester as KENNETH ROBESON
Terror at Octagon House * Coffman, Ardis
Terror at play * McEvoy, Seth
Terror begins, The * Gross, Edward
Terror by gaslight: more Victorian tales of terror * Lamb, Hugh
Terror by night, and other strange tales * Goldsmith, Howard
Terror cubes, The * Wilson, Granville
Terror for sale * Streib, Dan
Terror from the stratosphere * McKeag, Ernest as JACK MAXWELL
Terror in Australia * Gilligan, Shannon
Terror in the fourth dimension: can you return from a 2000 year journey through time? * Sharp, Allen
Terror in the navy, The: a Doc Savage adventure * Dent, Lester as KENNETH ROBESON
Terror island * Koltz, Tony
Terror of Dr Treviles, The: a romance * Redgrove, Peter W. & Penelope Shuttle
Terror of Frankenstein * Glut, Donald F.
Terror of the Vervoids * Baker, Jane & Pip Baker
Terror on Kabran * Brightfield, Richard
Terror on the moons of Jupiter * DiVono, Sharman & William Rotsler as VICTOR APPLETON
Terror star, The: a Scott Saunders space adventure * Moore, Patrick
Terror strike * Robbins, David
Terror takes 7 * Dent, Lester as KENNETH ROBESON
Terror under the Earth * Brightfield, Richard

Terror under the tent * Anderson, Mary
Terror version, The * Lymington, John
Terror wears no shoes * Dent, Lester as KENNETH ROBESON
Terrorist trap, The * Gilligan, Shannon
Terrorists of tomorrow * Anderson, Poul & Martin H. Greenberg & Charles G. Waugh
Terrors * Grant, Charles L.
Terrors of rock and roll, The * Smith, Susan
Terrors of uncertainty: the cultural contexts of horror fiction * Grixti, Joseph
Terrors, terrors, terrors * Hoke, Helen
Terrors, traumas, and torments * Hoke, Helen
Terrors, torments, and traumas: an anthology * Hoke, Helen
Terrorsaur! * Dicks, Terrance
Terry Carr's best science fiction and fantasy of the year #16 * Carr, Terry
Terry Carr's best science fiction of the year [#14] * Carr, Terry
Terry Carr's best science fiction of the year #15 * Carr, Terry
Terry Nation's Avon: a terrible aspect * Darrow, Paul
Terry Nation's Blake's 7: Afterlife * Attwood, Tony
Terry Nation's Blake's 7: Project Avalon * Hoyle, Trevor
Terry Nation's Blake's 7: Scorpio attack * Hoyle, Trevor
Terry Nation's Blake's 7: the programme guide * Attwood, Tony
Terry Nation's Blake's 7: Their first adventure * Hoyle, Trevor
Terry Nation's Blake's Seven: novelisation * Hoyle, Trevor
Terry Nation's Dalek special * Dicks, Terrance
Terry's universe * Meacham, Beth
Tery, The * Wilson, F. Paul
Tesseract * Addison, Joseph
Tesseracts * Merril, Judith
Tesseracts^2 * Gotlieb, Phyllis & Douglas Barbour
Tesseracts^3 * Dorsey, Candas Jane & Gerry Truscott
Test of fire * Bova, Ben
Test of honor * Bujold, Lois McMaster
Test of the ninja * Smith, Curtis
Test of the twins * Hickman, Tracy & Margaret Weis
Testament * Morrell, David
Testament of Andros, The * Blish, James
Testimony of Daniel Pagels, The * Turner, Vickery
Testing, testing, 1, 2, 3 * Hendrix, Howard V.
Tetrarch * Comfort, Alex
Texas on the rocks * Da Cruz, Daniel
Texas run, The * Proctor, Geo. W.
Texas triumphant * Da Cruz, Daniel
Thanatos syndrome, The * Percy, Walker
That Buck Rogers stuff * Pournelle, Jerry
That game from outer space: the first strange thing that happened to Oscar Noodleman * Manes, Stephen
That man on Beta * Lupoff, Richard A. as ADDISON E. STEELE
That which survives * Peel, John
Theater of timesmiths * Kilworth, Garry
Theatre of timesmiths, A * Kilworth, Garry
Thebes of the hundred gates * Silverberg, Robert
Their immortal hearts: three visions of time * McAllister, Bruce as ANONYMOUS EDITOR
Their Majesties' Bucketeers * Smith, L. Neil
Their master's war * Farren, Mick
The-Land-Where-the-Sun-Goes-Down * Brady, Richard
Them * French, Robert
Them bones * Waldrop, Howard
Them or us: archetypal interpretations of fifties' alien invasion films * Lucanio, Patrick

Thirteenth ghost book, The * Hale, James
Thirteenth majestral, The * Peirce, Hayford
Thirteenth treasure, The * Hunt, Charlotte
Thirty years of dustwrappers, 1884-1914 * Locke, George
Thirty-first floor, The * Wahlöö, Per
This darkening universe * Biggle, Lloyd Jr.
This house is burning * Williams, Mona
This is the way the world begins * McIntosh, J. T.
This is the way the world ends: a novel * Morrow, James
This is your life, Bhodi Li * Peters, David
This place has no atmosphere * Danziger, Paula
This planet for sale * Hay, George
This present darkness * Peretti, Frank E.
This ravaged heart * Riefe, Alan as BARBARA RIEFE
This second Earth * Glasby, John as B. L. BOWERS
This sentient Earth * Hoyle, Trevor
This time forever * Chittenden, Margaret
This time, forever * O'Day-Flannery, Constance
This time of darkness * Hoover, H. M.
This timeless moment: a personal view of Aldous Huxley * Huxley, Laura Archera
This world and nearer ones: essays exploring the familiar * Aldiss, Brian W.
Tholian web, The * Peel, John
Thomas Burnett Swann: a brief critical biography and annotated bibliography * Collins, Robert A.
Thomas Burnett Swann bibliography, A * Roehm, Bob
Thomas Burnett Swann bibliography, A, rev. ed. * Roehm, Bob
Thomas M. Disch: a preliminary bibliography * Nee, Dave
Thomas Pynchon * Slade, Joseph W.
Thomas Pynchon * Tanner, Tony
Thomas the Rhymer * Kushner, Ellen
Thor's hammer * Whiteford, Wynne
Thor's hammer: on or near Earth * Bretnor, Reginald
Thora's sacrifice * Brand, Kurt
Thorburn enterprise, The * Mason, Douglas R. as JOHN RANKINE
Thorn * Saberhagen, Fred
Thorn key, The * Cooper, Louise
Thornyhold * Stewart, Mary
Those amazing electronic thinking machines: an anthology of robot and computer stories * Asimov, Isaac & Martin H. Greenberg & Charles G. Waugh
Those gentle voices: a Promethean romance of the spaceways * Effinger, George Alec
Those of my blood * Lichtenberg, Jacqueline
Those who fall from the Sun * Stone, Josephine Rector
Those who favor fire * Randall, Marta
Those who hunt the night * Hambly, Barbara
Those who watch over Earth * Sernine, Daniel
Thought probes: philosophy through science fiction * Miller, Fred D. Jr. & Nicholas D. Smith
Thought probes: philosophy through science fiction literature, 2nd ed. * Smith, Nicholas D. & Fred D. Miller Jr.
Thoughtworld * Greenhough, Terry
Thousand ages, A * Ellis, D. E.
Thousand coffins affair, The * Avallone, Michael & Terry Carr
Thousand shrine warrior * Salmonson, Jessica Amanda
Thousand-headed man, The: a Doc Savage adventure * Dent, Lester as KENNETH ROBESON
Thousandstar * Anthony, Piers
Thrall and the dragon's heart, The * Boyer, Elizabeth
Threats...and other promises * Vinge, Vernor
Three against the world * Leeson, Robert
Three by Ira Levin * Levin, Ira

Three came unarmed * Robertson, E. A.
Three cedars, The: a collection of short stories * Thomas, Peter as PETER PAPERMAKER
Three complete novels * Koontz, Dean R.
Three complete novels and five short stories * du Maurier, Daphne
Three corners to nowhere * Caidin, Martin
Three damosels, The * Chapman, Vera
Three decades to doom: a novel * Oxley, David Anthony
Three devils, The * Dent, Lester as KENNETH ROBESON
Three doctors, The * Dicks, Terrance
Three dreams and a nightmare, and other tales of the dark * Gorog, Judith
Three essays: Father Vincent McNabb; A modern handprinter: Edward Walters; "Voyage to a beginning": the introduction to Colin Wilson's autobiography * Sewell, Brocard
Three eyes of evil, The; and, Earth's last fortress * van Vogt, A. E.
Three famous du Maurier novels * du Maurier, Daphne
Three fantasies * Powys, John Cowper
Three from the Legion * Williamson, Jack
Three gold crowns * Ernst, Paul as KENNETH ROBESON
Three Hainish novels: Rocannon's World; Planet of exile; City of illusions * Le Guin, Ursula K.
Three lives of Edward Berner, The * Kastle, Herbert D.
Three masks of Gaba, The * Twitchell, Paul
Three midnight stories * Drake, Alexander W.
Three modern satirists: Waugh, Orwell, and Huxley * Greenblatt, Stephen
Three more novels of the future * Wells, H. G.
Three novels * Knight, Damon
Three novels: Hordubal, Meteor, An ordinary life * Capek, Karel
Three novels of the future * Wells, H. G.
Three novels: Thorn; Downward to the Earth; The world inside * Silverberg, Robert
Three of swords, The * Leiber, Fritz
Three plusketeers and the garden slugs, The * de Lint, Charles
Three queens, The * Priestley, Margaret
Three spirits of Vandermeer Manor, The * Anderson, Mary
Three supernatural novels of the Victorian period * Bleiler, E. F.
Three times a corpse * Dent, Lester as KENNETH ROBESON
Three to Dorsai!: three novels from the Childe Cycle: Necromancer; Tactics of mistake; Dorsai! * Dickson, Gordon R.
Three to get Reddy * Zacharia, Irwin
Three tomorrows: American, British, and Soviet science fiction * Griffiths, John
Three toymakers, The * Williams, Ursula Moray
Three trumps sounding * Schmidt, Dennis
Three wild men, The * Dent, Lester as KENNETH ROBESON
Three-bladed doom * Howard, Robert E.
Three-Eyes * Gordon, Stuart
Three-fisted tales of "Bob" * Stang, Ivan
Three-legged hootch dancer, The * Resnick, Mike
Three-minute universe, The * Paul, Barbara
Three-quarters * de Timms, Graeme
Three-ring psychus * Shirley, John
Threshold * Le Guin, Ursula K.
Threshold, The * Millhiser, Marlys
Threshold * Morris, Chris & Janet Morris
Threshold * Palmer, David R.
Threshold * Singer, Judith

Tom Swift and his aquatomic tracker * Lawrence, Jim as VICTOR APPLETON II

Tom Swift and his atomic earth blaster * Lawrence, Jim as VICTOR APPLETON II

Tom Swift and his Cosmotron Express * McKenna, Richard as VICTOR APPLETON II

Tom Swift and his deep-sea hydrodome * Lawrence, Jim as VICTOR APPLETON II

Tom Swift and his diving seacopter * Lawrence, Jim as VICTOR APPLETON II

Tom Swift and his Dyna-4 capsule * McKenna, Richard as VICTOR APPLETON II

Tom Swift and his electronic retroscope * Lawrence, Jim as VICTOR APPLETON II

Tom Swift and his flying lab * Dougherty, William as VICTOR APPLETON II

Tom Swift and his G-force inverter * Lawrence, Jim as VICTOR APPLETON II

Tom Swift and his giant robot * Sklar, Richard as VICTOR APPLETON II

Tom Swift and his jetmarine * Almquist, John as VICTOR APPLETON II

Tom Swift and his megascope space prober * Lawrence, Jim as VICTOR APPLETON II

Tom Swift and his outpost in space * Lawrence, Jim as VICTOR APPLETON II

Tom Swift and his polar-ray dynasphere * Lawrence, Jim as VICTOR APPLETON II

Tom Swift and his repelatron skyway * Lawrence, Jim as VICTOR APPLETON II

Tom Swift and his rocket ship * Almquist, John as VICTOR APPLETON II

Tom Swift and his sky wheel * Lawrence, Jim as VICTOR APPLETON II

Tom Swift and his sonic boom trap * Lawrence, Jim as VICTOR APPLETON II

Tom Swift and his space solartron * Lawrence, Jim as VICTOR APPLETON II

Tom Swift and his spectromarine selector * Lawrence, Jim as VICTOR APPLETON II

Tom Swift and his subocean geotron * Lawrence, Jim as VICTOR APPLETON II

Tom Swift and his triphibian atomicar * Lawrence, Jim as VICTOR APPLETON II

Tom Swift and his ultrasonic cycloplane * Lawrence, Jim as VICTOR APPLETON II

Tom Swift and the asteroid pirates * Lawrence, Jim as VICTOR APPLETON II

Tom Swift and the captive planetoid * Lawrence, Jim as VICTOR APPLETON II

Tom Swift and the city of gold * Lawrence, Jim as VICTOR APPLETON II

Tom Swift and the cosmic astronauts * Lawrence, Jim as VICTOR APPLETON II

Tom Swift and the electric hydrolung * Lawrence, Jim as VICTOR APPLETON II

Tom Swift and the galaxy ghosts * McKenna, Richard as VICTOR APPLETON II

Tom Swift and the mystery comet * Lawrence, Jim as VICTOR APPLETON II

Tom Swift and the planet stone; or, Discovering the secret of another world * Adams, Harriet as VICTOR APPLETON

Tom Swift and the visitor from Planet X * Lawrence, Jim as VICTOR APPLETON II

Tom Swift: Crater of mystery * McQuay, Mike as VICTOR APPLETON

Tom Swift: Gateway to doom * Vardeman, Robert E. as VICTOR APPLETON

Tom Swift in the caves of nuclear fire * Mulvey, Thomas as VICTOR APPLETON II

Tom Swift in the jungle of the Mayas * Lawrence, Jim as VICTOR APPLETON II

Tom Swift in the race to the Moon * Lawrence, Jim as VICTOR APPLETON II

Tom Swift on the phantom satellite * Lawrence, Jim as VICTOR APPLETON II

Tom Swift: Terror on the moons of Jupiter * DiVono, Sharman & William Rotsler as VICTOR APPLETON

Tom Swift: The alien probe * DiVono, Sharman & William Rotsler as VICTOR APPLETON

Tom Swift: The war in outer space * DiVono, Sharman & William Rotsler as VICTOR APPLETON

Tomay is loyal * Priestley, Margaret

Tomb, The * Wilson, F. Paul

Tomb from beyond, The * Jacobi, Carl

Tomb of Amenosis, The: can you stop a war, solve a riddle as old as Genesis? * Sharp, Allen

Tomb of the shroud * Phillips, Lyn

Tomb Seven * Snyder, Gene

Tombley's walk * Brown, Crosland

Tombs of Kobol, The * Larson, Glen A. & Robert Thurston

Tommyknockers, The * King, Stephen

Tomoe Gozen * Salmonson, Jessica Amanda

Tomorrow and a day * Frances, Stephen as HANK JANSON

Tomorrow and beyond: masterpieces of science fiction art * Summers, Ian

Tomorrow and forever * Macklem, Francesca

Tomorrow and tomorrow * Eldershaw, M. Barnard

Tomorrow and tomorrow * Hunter, Evan as ED MCBAIN

Tomorrow and tomorrow * Hunter, Evan as HUNT COLLINS

Tomorrow and tomorrow and tomorrow * Eldershaw, M. Barnard

Tomorrow city, The * Hughes, Monica

Tomorrow connection, The * Bethancourt, T. Ernesto

Tomorrow File, The * Sanders, Lawrence

Tomorrow, Inc.: SF stories about business * Greenberg, Martin H. & Joseph D. Olander

Tomorrow is another day * Coles, Lesley

Tomorrow knight * Kurland, Michael

Tomorrow may be even worse: an alphabet of science fiction clichés * Brunner, John

Tomorrow might be different * Reynolds, Mack

Tomorrow: new worlds of science fiction * Elwood, Roger

Tomorrow on the march: the text of a speech delivered July 4, 1946 at the Pacificon by the Guest of Honor, A. E. van Vogt * van Vogt, A. E.

Tomorrow People in Four into three, The * Price, Roger

Tomorrow People in One law, The * Price, Roger

Tomorrow People in The lost gods, with Hitler's last secret and The Thargon menace, The * Price, Roger

Tomorrow station, The * King, Albert as MARK BANNON

Tomorrow testament, The * Longyear, Barry B.

Tomorrow today * Zebrowski, George

Tomorrow's crimes * Westlake, Donald E.

Tomorrow's eve * Villiers de L'Isle Adam, Auguste, comte de

Tomorrow's heritage * Coulson, Juanita

Tomorrow's magic * Service, Pamela F.

Tomorrow's men: a novel * Shea, Michael

Tomorrow's reality * Smith, Evieline Lates

Tomorrow's son * Hoskins, Robert

Tomorrow's sphinx * Bell, Clare

Tomorrow's TV * Asimov, Isaac & Martin H. Greenberg & Charles G. Waugh

Transcendant adventure, The: studies of religion in science fiction/fantasy * Reilly, Robert

Transcendental tales from Isaac Asimov's science fiction magazine * Dozois, Gardner

Transference, The * Smith, Ella

Transfigurations * Bishop, Michael

Transform node: science fiction mystical adventures * Parker, Ronn

Transformation, The * MacBeth, George

Transformation * Plante, Edmund

Transformation of Miss Mavis Ming, The: a romance of the end of time * Moorcock, Michael

Transformations * Jones, Gwyneth as ANN HALAM

Transformations * Mella, John

Transformer * Foster, M. A.

Transgalactic guide to solar system M-17, The * Rovin, Jeff

Transition * McIntyre, Vonda N.

Transition * Welling, Lois

Transition of Titus Crow, The * Lumley, Brian

Translation: a novel * Marlowe, Stephen

Transmaniacon * Shirley, John

Transmigration of Timothy Archer, The * Dick, Philip K.

Transmitters: an imaginary documentary, 1969-1984 * Broderick, Damien

Transmutations * Gerrand, Rob

Transmutations * Panshin, Alexei

Transreal! * Rucker, Rudy

Transylvania Station: a Mohonk mystery * Westlake, Abby & Donald E. Westlake

Trap for Perseus * Pesek, Ludek

Trapped! * Norwood, Warren

Trapped * Plante, Edmund

Trapped in the ashes * Johnstone, William W.

Trapped in the black box * Austin, R. G.

Trapped in the sea kingdom * Brightfield, Richard

Trapped in time * Chew, Ruth

Trapped in time * Payne, Bernal C. Jr.

TRAUMA * Craig, Robert

Travails of Jane Saint, and other stories, The * Saxton, Josephine

Travel light * Mitchison, Naomi

Travel without the Tardis * Airey, Jean & Laurie Haldeman

Traveling soul, The * Rae, Hugh C.

Traveller * Adams, Richard

Travelling man, The * Mace, Elisabeth

Travelling towards epsilon: an anthology of French science fiction * Jakubowski, Maxim

Travels * Crichton, Michael

Travels in the interior; or, The wonderful adventures of Luke and Belinda * Schofield, Alfred Taylor as LUKE THEOPHILUS COURTENAY

Travels through time * Asimov, Isaac & Martin H. Greenberg & Charles G. Waugh

Tread softly * Laymon, Richard

Tread softly * Laymon, Richard as RICHARD KELLY

Treading in unknown paths * Shelley, Mary Wollstonecraft

Treason * Card, Orson Scott

Treason at Helms Deep * Barrett, Kevin & Saul Peters

Treason in time * Andrews, Keith William

Treason of Isengard, The * Tolkien, J. R. R.

Treasure: a novel * Cussler, Clive

Treasure diver * Goodman, Julius

Treasure Hunters, The * Hoobler, Thomas & Burt Wetanson

Treasure: in search of the golden horse: a puzzle * Crypton, Dr. & Sheldon Renan

Treasure in the heart of the maze, The * Carr, Jayge

Treasure of Alpheus Winterborn, The * Bellairs, John

Treasure of light * Gear, Kathleen O'Neal as KATHLEEN M. O'NEAL

Treasure of the Onyx Dragon, The * Gilligan, Alison

Treasure of the stars * Green, Roland as JEFFREY LORD

Treasure of Tranicos, The * de Camp, L. Sprague & Robert E. Howard

Treasure of Wonderwhat, The * Starr, Bill

Treasure planet * Evans, Chris as NATHAN ELLIOTT

Treasures of Morrow * Hoover, H. M.

Treasures of time * Lively, Penelope

Treasury of American horror stories * Greenberg, Martin H. & Charles G. Waugh & Frank D. McSherry Jr.

Treasury of fantasy, A: heroic adventures in imaginary lands * Wilkins, Cary

Treasury of gothic and supernatural, A * anon.

Treasury of modern fantasy, A * Carr, Terry & Martin Harry Greenberg

Treasury of Victorian ghost stories, A * Bleiler, E. F.

Tree and leaf; Smith of Wootton Major; The homecoming of Beorhtnoth, Beorhthelm's son * Tolkien, J. R. R.

Tree house * Mullen, Victor

Tree of swords and jewels, The * Cherryh, C. J.

Tree that sat down, The * Nichols, Beverley

Trees of Zharka, The * Mackenroth, Nancy

Trees, the jewels, and the rings, The: a discursive enquiry into things little known on Middle-Earth * Noad, Charles E.

Trek crew book, The * Van Hise, James

Trek encyclopedia, The * Peel, John

Trek fan's handbook, The * Van Hise, James

Trek or treat * Ehrhardt, Eleanor & Terry Flanagan

Trek or treat * St. Clair, Elizabeth

Trek: the lost years * Gross, Edward

Trek: the lost years * Van Hise, James

Trek: The next generation * Van Hise, James

Trek to Kraggen-Cor * McKiernan, Dennis L.

Trek to madworld: a Star Trek novel * Goldin, Stephen

Trekker cookbook, The * Cantor, Johanna T.

Trekkie quiz book, The * Andrews, Bart & Brad Dunning

Trekmaster * Johnson, James B.

Trellisane confrontation, The: a Star Trek novel * Dvorkin, David

Trembling of Borealis, The * D'Argenteuil, Paul

Trembling world, The * Fearn, John Russell as Franz Harkon

Trench soldier, The * Sadler, Barry

Trespasser, The * Weiser, Melvin

Trexindex * Rogow, Roberta

Trexindex supplement * Rogow, Roberta

Trey of swords * Norton, Andre

Triad * Finch, Sheila

Triad * Rohmer, Richard

Trial, The * Laurence, James as JAMES DARKE

Trial by fire * Milán, Victor as RICHARD AUSTIN

Trial in the upper room: a heavenly novel * Sann, Paul

Trial of a time lord: Mindwarp * Martin, Philip

Trial of Adolf Hitler, The: a novel * Van Rjndt, Philippe

Trial of champions * Livingstone, Ian

Trial of Lee Harvey Oswald, The * Thompson, Robert E.

Trial of the seventh carrier * Albano, Peter

Triangle: a Star Trek novel * Culbreath, Myrna & Sondra Marshak

Triax: three original novellas * Silverberg, Robert

Tribe, The * Chandler, Glenn

Tribe, The * Wood, Bari

Tribe of Gum, The * Coburn, Anthony

Tribe of Jen-Wae, The * Wright, Meg

Tribe of the dead * Brandner, Gary

Tribesmen of Gor * Norman, John

Turbo Cowboys: Jump start * Cunningham, Chet as TONY PHILLIPS
Turbo Cowboys: Night riders * Bagdon, Paul as TONY PHILLIPS
Turbo Cowboys: Rat trap * Read, John as TONY PHILLIPS
Turbo Cowboys: Spark fire * Cunningham, Chet as TONY PHILLIPS
Turbo Cowboys: Speed shift * Bagdon, Paul as TONY PHILLIPS
Turbo Cowboys: Spin out * Cunningham, Chet as TONY PHILLIPS
Turbo Cowboys: Super charge * Bagdon, Paul as TONY PHILLIPS
Turlough and the Earthlink dilemma * Attwood, Tony
Turn of the screw, The * James, Henry & Diana Stewart
Turn of the screw, The, and other stories * James, Henry
Turn of the screw, The: bewildered vision * Heller, Terry
Turner diaries, The * Macdonald, Andrew
Turning place, The: stories of a future past * Karl, Jean E.
Turning point, The * Tracy, Louis
Turning points: essays on the art of science fiction * Knight, Damon
Turning, The: storms of victory * Griffin, P. M. & Andre Norton
Turning wheel, and other stories, The * Dick, Philip K.
Turquoise dragon, The: a mystery * Wallace, David Rains
Turquoise talisman, The * Wagner, Sharon
Tussles with time * Romains, Jules
TV: 2000 * Asimov, Isaac & Martin H. Greenberg & Charles G. Waugh
TV episode guides * Gerani, Gary
Tweedlioop * Schmidt, Stanley
Twelfth Armada ghost book, The * Danby, Mary
Twelfth child, The * Van Over, Raymond
Twelfth Fontana book of great ghost stories, The * Chetwynd-Hayes, R.
Twelfth Fontana book of great horror stories, The * Danby, Mary
Twelfth ghost book, The * Parkin, Patricia as ANONYMOUS EDITOR
Twelve fair kingdoms * Elgin, Suzette Haden
Twelve frights of Christmas, The * Asimov, Isaac & Martin H. Greenberg & Charles G. Waugh
Twelve robbers, The * Biegel, Paul
Twentieth century interpretations of 1984: a collection of critical essays * Hynes, Samuel
Twentieth century interpretations of Poe's tales: a collection of critical essays * Howarth, William L.
Twentieth century interpretations of The fall of the house of Usher: a collection of critical essays * Woodson, Thomas
Twentieth Fontana book of great ghost stories, The * Chetwynd-Hayes, R.
Twentieth son of Ornon, The * Sirota, Mike
Twentieth-century American science-fiction writers * Cowart, David & Thomas L. Wymer
Twentieth-century science-fiction writers * Smith, Curtis C.
Twentieth-century science-fiction writers, second edition * Smith, Curtis C.
Twentieth-century science-fiction writers, third edition * Schellinger, Paul E. & Noelle Watson
Twenty all-time great science fiction films * Stock, Stuart H. & Kenneth Von Gunden
Twenty houses of the zodiac: an anthology of international science fiction * Jakubowski, Maxim
Twenty thousand leagues under the sea * Verne, Jules
Twenty trillion light-years through space * Virg, Leo

Twenty-one letters of Ambrose Bierce * Bierce, Ambrose
Twenty-seven stairs: a novel * Finn, Ralph L.
Twice blessed * Wallace, Patricia
Twice in time * Wellman, Manly Wade
Twice upon a time: a novel * Appel, Allen
Twilight * James, Peter
Twilight * Koontz, Dean R. as LEIGH NICHOLS
Twilight at the Well of Souls: the legacy of Nathan Brazil * Chalker, Jack L.
Twilight book, The: a new collection of ghost stories * Hale, James
Twilight escapism * Mahadoo, C. S.
Twilight eyes * Koontz, Dean R.
Twilight of magic, The * Lofting, Hugh
Twilight of the city: a novel of the near future * Platt, Charles
Twilight of the gods: The first name * Schmidt, Dennis
Twilight of the serpent, The * Timlett, Peter Valentine
Twilight realm, The * Evans, Chris as CHRISTOPHER CARPENTER
Twilight return: an astrological gothic novel: Cancer * Kimbro, John M. as JEAN KIMBRO
Twilight time * Shiner, Lewis
Twilight Zone * Glasby, John as VICTOR LA SALLE
Twilight zone companion, The * Zicree, Marc Scott
Twilight zone companion, The, rev. and exp. 30th anniversary edition * Zicree, Marc Scott
Twilight Zone files, The: The new series * Peel, John
Twilight zone: the movie: a novel * Bloch, Robert
Twilight zone, The: the original stories * Greenberg, Martin H. & Charles G. Waugh & Richard Matheson
Twilight's kingdoms * Asire, Nancy
Twin Cities run * Robbins, David
Twin dilemma, The * Saward, Eric
Twin Peaks behind-the-scenes: an unofficial visitors guide to Twin Peaks * Altman, Mark A.
Twin souls: a romance of duality * anon.
Twins: a novel * Geasland, Jack & Bari Wood
Twist in time, A * Reeves, L. P
Twist of mind, A * Staszak, Lucille
Twisted * Stine, R. L.
Twisted circuits * Gowar, Mick
Twisted cross, The * Maloney, Mack
Twisted room, The * Smith, Janet Patton
Twisted tales * Jones, Bruce
Twisters: stories of the sinister and macabre * Bowles, Steve
Twisting the rope: casadh an t'súgáin * MacAvoy, R. A.
Twistor * Cramer, John
Two came calling * Dorer, Frances & Nancy Dorer
Two deaths of Quincas Wateryell, The * Amado, Jorge
Two doctors, The * Holmes, Robert
Two equals one * Pinchin, Frank J. as PETER DAGMAR
Two fables * Dahl, Roald
Two faces of Silenus, The * Clarke, Pauline
Two faces of tomorrow, The * Hogan, James P.
Two from the dead * Milton, Hilary
Two Hawks from Earth * Farmer, Philip José
Two in hiding, The * Emerson, Ru
Two kingdoms, The: a novel of Islandia * Saxton, Mark
Two of them, The * Russ, Joanna
Two queens of Lochrin * Crawford, Betty Anne as LEE CREIGHTON
Two Saturday Yankees; &, Ali in T.V. Land * Foreman, Bob & Robin Moore
Two science fantasy novels * Hubbard, L. Ron
Two songs this archangel sings * Chesbro, George C.
Two steps beyond, and other bizarre and nocturnal tales * Quirino, Joe
Two strange tales * Eliade, Mircea

U

Underground kingdom * Packard, Edward
Underground man, The * Paine, Lauren as MARK CARREL
Underkill: a science fiction novel * White, James
Undersea * Hazel, Paul
Undersea people, The * Bunting, Eve
Understanding contemporary American science fiction: the formative period, 1926-1970 * Clareson, Thomas D.
Understanding Kraith: a compilation of words, phrases, ideas, and interpretations, as set forth in the Kraith Universe series * Segal, Judith Z.
Understanding Kurt Vonnegut * Allen, William Rodney
Understanding science fiction * Banks, Michael A.
Understanding Thomas Pynchon * Newman, Robert D.
Understanding Ursula K. Le Guin * Cummins, Elizabeth
Understudy, The * Tabor, Margaret
Understudy magic * Gormley, Beatrice
Undertow * Douglas, Drake
Underwater menace, The * Robinson, Nigel
Undesirable properties: thirteen haunted houses * Smith, Peter C.
Undesired princess, The; &, The enchanted bunny * de Camp, L. Sprague & David Drake
Undisciplined life, The: an examination of Aldous Huxley's recent works * Lloyd, Roger B.
Undying land, The * Gilmour, William
Undying wizard, The * Offutt, Andrew J.
Undying world * Stokes, Manning Lee as JEFFREY LORD
Unearthed * McConnell, Ashley
Unearthed arcana * Gygax, Gary
Unearthly beasts, and other strange people * Williams, Jay
Unearthly child, An * Dicks, Terrance
Unearthly neighbors * Oliver, Chad
Uneasy alliances * Abbey, Lynn & Robert Lynn Asprin
Unexpected universe of Doris Lessing, The * Fishburn, Katherine
Unfinished tales of Númenor and Middle-Earth * Tolkien, J. R. R.
Unforsaken Hiero, The * Lanier, Sterling E.
Unhappy princess, The * Cowper, Richard
Unholy, The * Anderson, Michael Falconer
Unholy, The * Cooper, Parley J. as ALEX NEBRENSKY
Unholy, The * Halkin, John
Unholy communion * Savage, Adrian
Unholy goddess * Stein, Baker
Unholy grail, The * Horowitz, Anthony
Unholy revelry * Offutt, Andrew J. as JOHN CLEVE
Unholy smile, The * Douglas, Gregory A.
Unicorn, The * Holzer, Hans
Unicorn affair, The * Fritzhand, James & Frank Glicksman
Unicorn & dragon * Abbey, Lynn
Unicorn, and other tales, The * Stivens, Dal
Unicorn creed, The * Scarborough, Elizabeth
Unicorn crown, The * Vilott, Rhondi
Unicorn dancer, The * Vilott, Rhondi as R. A. V. SALSITZ
Unicorn dilemma, The * Lee, John
Unicorn expedition, and other fantastic tales of India, The * Ray, Satyajit
Unicorn gambit, The * Bischoff, David
Unicorn mountain * Bishop, Michael
Unicorn point * Anthony, Piers
Unicorn quest, The * Lee, John
Unicorn solution, The * Lee, John
Unicorn trade, The * Anderson, Karen & Poul Anderson
Unicorn treasury, The: stories, poems, and unicorn lore * Coville, Bruce
Unicorn variations * Zelazny, Roger

Unicorn with silver shoes, The * Young, Ella
Unicorns! * Dann, Jack & Gardner Dozois
Unicorns in the rain * Cohen, Barbara
Unidentified flying oddball * Crume, Vic
Unification * Taylor, Jeri
Unified ring, The: narrative art and the science-fiction novel * Sadler, Frank
Uninvited, The * Farris, John
Uninvited, The * Johnstone, William W.
Uninvited ghosts, and other stories * Lively, Penelope
Uninvited guests: thirteen unwelcome visitors * Smith, Peter C.
Union forever * Forstchen, William R.
Unique tales * Krueger, Kenneth
Unisave * Madsen, Axel
United planets, The * Wade, Tom as VICTOR WADEY
Unity Penfold * Tabor, Margaret
Universal horrors: the studio's classic films, 1931-1946 * Brunas, Michael & Tom Weaver & John Brunas
Universal prey, The * Swycaffer, Jefferson P.
Universe, The * Preiss, Byron
Universe 1 * Haber, Karen & Robert Silverberg
Universe 6 * Carr, Terry
Universe 7 * Carr, Terry
Universe 8 * Carr, Terry
Universe 9 * Carr, Terry
Universe 10 * Carr, Terry
Universe 11 * Carr, Terry
Universe 12 * Carr, Terry
Universe 13 * Carr, Terry
Universe 14 * Carr, Terry
Universe 15 * Carr, Terry
Universe 16 * Carr, Terry
Universe 17 * Carr, Terry
Universe ahead: stories of the future * Engdahl, Sylvia Louise & Rick Roberson
Universe, and other fictions, The * West, Paul
Universe maker, The; and, The proxy intelligence: science fiction * van Vogt, A. E.
Universe next door, The * Wilson, Robert Anton
University of California, Riverside dictionary catalogue of the J.Lloyd Eaton Collection of Science Fiction and Fantasy Literature * Slusser, George Edgar AS INTRODUCER
Unjust desserts * Wayne, Matt
Unkindness of ravens, An * Meaney, Dee Morrison
Unknown * Schmidt, Stanley
Unknown Orwell, The * Abrahams, William & Peter Stansky
Unknown shore, The * Malcolm, Donald
Unknown world, The * Wade, Tom
Unknown worlds: tales from beyond * Greenberg, Martin H. & Stanley Schmidt
Unleashed powers * Brand, Kurt
Unless she burn * Mezo, Francine
Unlikely ones, The * Brown, Mary
Unlikely stories, mostly * Gray, Alasdair
Unlimited dream company, The * Ballard, J. G.
Unloved, The * Saul, John
Unman, The; Kovrigin's chronicles * Shefner, Vadim
Unnatural causes: based on the Central television series * anon.
Unnatural fathers * Storr, Catherine
Unnatural talent * Logan, Les
Unofficial tale of Beauty and the Beast, The * Gross, Edward
Unofficial tale of Beauty and the Beast, The, 2nd ed. * Gross, Edward
Unorthodox engineers, The * Kapp, Colin
Unpopular planet * Smith, Evelyn E.

V

Voice of the visitor * Slonaker, Larry
Voice of the whirlwind * Williams, Walter Jon
Voice out of Ramah, A * Killough, Lee
Voices * Aiken, Joan
Voices * Wynne-Jones, Tim
Voices after midnight: a novel * Peck, Richard
Voices at the late hour: a novel * Carpelan, Bo
Voices for the future: essays on major science fiction writers, volume I * Clareson, Thomas D.
Voices for the future: essays on major science fiction writers, volume two * Clareson, Thomas D.
Voices for the future, volume three * Clareson, Thomas D. & Thomas L. Wymer
Voices in an empty house: a novel * Aiken, Joan
Voices in the dark * Haynes, James
Voices in the fog * DuBreuil, Linda as KATE CAMERON
Voices in time * MacLennan, Hugh
Voices of doom: tales of terror and the uncanny * Copper, Basil
Voices of time, The * Ballard, J. G.
Void Captain's tale, The * Spinrad, Norman
Volcano * Fisk, Nicholas
Volcano! * Siegman, Meryl
Volcano ogre, The * Carter, Lin
Volkhavaar * Lee, Tanith
Volume II of Steven Spielberg's Amazing stories * Bauer, Steven
Volunteers, The * Williams, Raymond
Volunteers for Frago * Brand, Kurt
Vφlve: Scandinavian views on science fiction: selected papers from the Scandinavian Science-Fiction Festival, 1977 * Dollerup, Cay
Vonnegut: a preface to his novels * Giannone, Richard
Vonnegut in America: an introduction to the life and work of Kurt Vonnegut * Klinkowitz, Jerome & Donald L. Lawler
Vonnegut statement, The * Klinkowitz, Jerome & John Somer
Vonnegut's major works: notes, including life and background, introduction to the works, discussions of Player piano; The sirens of Titan; Mother night; Cat's Cradle; God bless you, Mr. Rosewater; Slaughterhouse-Five; Happy birthday, Wanda June; and Breakfast of champions, special topics, review questions, selected bibliography * Holland, Thomas R.
Voodoo * Deaver, Jeffrey Wilds
Voodoo!: a chrestomathy of necromancy * Pronzini, Bill
Voodoo dawn: a novel * Russo, John

Voodoo die * Murphy, Warren & Richard Sapir
Voodoo fury * Loomis, Gregg
Voodoo game, The * Barnes, Steven & Larry Niven
Voodoo planet; and, Star hunter * Norton, Andre
Voorloper * Norton, Andre
Vor game, The * Bujold, Lois McMaster
Vorkosigan's game * Bujold, Lois McMaster
Vort programme, The * Mason, Douglas R. as JOHN RANKINE
Vortex * Bond, Larry
Vortex * Land, Jon
Votan treasure, The * Collins, Jackson
Vow, The * Foster, Prudence
Voyage begun, The * Bond, Nancy
Voyage from yesteryear * Hogan, James P.
Voyage home, The * McIntyre, Vonda N.
Voyage of Mael Duin's curragh, The * Aakhus, Patricia
Voyage of terror * Brennan, J. H.
Voyage of the eighth mind * Lymington, John
Voyage of the planetslayer * Swycaffer, Jefferson P.
Voyage of the QV66, The * Lively, Penelope
Voyage of the Star Wolf * Gerrold, David
Voyage of the Trigon * DeBolt, Adriana
Voyage of the Vigilance, The * Kilworth, Garry
Voyage of vengeance * Hubbard, L. Ron
Voyage to a forgotten sun * Pfeil, Donald J.
Voyage to adventure * Ford, John M. as MICHAEL J. DODGE
Voyage to Inshneefa, A: the first-hand account of the fifth voyage of Lemuel Gulliver * Brady, John Paul
Voyage to the cat star * St. George, E. A.
Voyage to the city of the dead * Foster, Alan Dean
Voyage to the red planet * Bisson, Terry
Voyage with Columbus * Reit, Seymour V.
Voyager in night * Cherryh, C. J.
Voyagers * Bova, Ben
Voyagers! * Claro, Joe
Voyages * Smith, Doris Buchanan
Voyages in space: a bibliography of interplanetary fiction, 1801-1914 * Locke, George
Vulcan! * Sky, Kathleen
Vulcan Academy murders, The: a Star Trek novel * Lorrah, Jean
Vulcan language guide * anon.
Vulcan reflections * Langsam, Devra M.
Vulcan treasure, The * Rotsler, William
Vulcan's glory * Fontana, D. C.

W

W. H. Hudson: a biography * Tomalin, Ruth
Wabeno feast, The * Drew, Wayland
Wabeno, the magician: the sequel to "Tommy-Anne and
    the three hearts" * Wright, Mabel Osgood
Wailing well * James, M. R.
Wait and see * Jensen, Ruby Jean
Wait for what will come * Michaels, Barbara
Wait till Helen comes: a ghost story * Hahn, Mary
    Downing
Waiting darkness, The * Bingley, Alice
Waiting for the end of the world * Harding, Lee
Waiting for the galactic bus * Godwin, Parke
Waiting room, The * Wright, T. M.
Waiting spirits * Coville, Bruce
Wake of the werewolf * Walker, Robert W. as GEOFFREY
    CAINE
Waking dream * Wallace, Carol McD.
Waking nightmares * Campbell, Ramsey
Waking of Orthlund, The * Taylor, Roger
Waking of the stone, The * Lymington, John
Walden Three * Catran, Jack
Walford's oak: a novel * Phillips, Jill M.
Walg: a novel of Australia * Wongar, B.
Walk in Wolf Wood, A * Stewart, Mary
Walk on the wild side, A * Westall, Robert
Walk the dark valley * Benjamin, Jacob
Walk the Moons Road * Aikin, Jim
Walk to San Michele * Timperley, Rosemary
Walk to the end of the world; and, Motherlines * Char-
    nas, Suzy McKee
Walk with the dead * Finster, E. Burke
Walkabout woman * Roessner, Michaela
Walkaway clause, The * Dalmas, John
Walker book of ghost stories, The * Hill, Susan
Walker of worlds * De Haven, Tom
Walker Percy, a Southern wayfarer * Allen, William
    Rodney
Walkers * Brandner, Gary
Walkers * Masterton, Graham
Walkers of the wind * Sarabande, William
Walkers on the sky * Lake, David J.
Walking dead, The * Smith, Guy N.
Walking on glass * Banks, Iain M.
Walking shadow, The * Stableford, Brian M.
Walking stone, The * Hunter, Mollie
Walking water; After all this: two novellas * Nickels,
    Thom
Walking wounded * Murphy, Warren & Richard Sapir
Wall, The * Haushofer, Marlen
Wall, The * Mayhar, Ardath
Wall around a star: a saga of Cuckoo * Williamson, Jack
    & Frederik Pohl
Wall around Eden, The * Slonczewski, Joan
Wall of serpents * de Camp, L. Sprague & Fletcher Pratt
Wall of years, The * Stephenson, Andrew M.
Walls of air, The * Hambly, Barbara
Walls of fear * Cramer, Kathryn
Walls of Spyte, The * Johnson, Oliver & Dave Morris &
    Jamie Thomson

Walls within walls * Tofte, Arthur
Walpurgis III * Resnick, Mike
Walrus and the warwolf, The * Cook, Hugh
Walter de la Mare: an exploration * Atkins, John Alfred
Waltz with evil * Rozzi, P. D.
Waltzing wizard, The: cartoons * Gilliland, Alexis A.
Wamphyri! * Lumley, Brian
Wand and the star, The * Wallace, Patricia
Wand, The: the return to Mesmeria * Eckert, Allan W.
Wanderer * Schmidt, Dennis
Wanderer's return, A * Hancock, Niel
Wanderground, The: stories of the hill women * Gearhart,
    Sally Miller
Wandering fire, The * Kay, Guy Gavriel
Wandering ghost: the odyssey of Lafcadio Hearn * Cott,
    Jonathan
Wandering Jew, The * Heym, Stefan
Wandering Jew, The: an account of his last adventures,
    with an appendix of selected memoirs * Clough, S. D.
    P.
Wandering unicorn, The * Mujica Láinez, Manuel
Wandering worlds, The * Greenhough, Terry
Wanderings of Wuntvor, The * Gardner, Craig Shaw
Wanderlust * Kirchoff, Mary L. & Steve Winter
Wandor's flight * Green, Roland
Wandor's journey * Green, Roland
Wandor's voyage * Green, Roland
Wankh, The * Vance, Jack
Wanted, by the Intergalactic Security Bureau: 20 full-
    color posters of the most wanted alien criminals *
    Naha, Ed & Eric Seidman
Wanted: UFO * Gormley, Beatrice
Wanting, The * Black, Campbell
Wanting factor, The * DeWeese, Gene
Wanting of Levine, The * Halberstam, Michael
War, The * McDowell, Michael
War against chaos, The * Mason, Anita
War against the Chtorr, The: Invasion * Gerrold, David
War and peace: possible futures from Analog * Schmidt,
    Stanley
War birds * Meluch, R. M.
War chariot * Willard, Tom
War crimes: short stories * Carey, Peter
War fever * Ballard, J. G.
War for eternity, The * Rowley, Christopher
War for the oaks * Bull, Emma
War games * Hansen, Karl
War games * Stableford, Brian M.
War Games of Zelos, The * Cooper, Edmund
War Games of Zelos, The * Cooper, Edmund as RICHARD
    AVERY
War god, The * Neilson, Eric
War god * Rogers, Patrick F.
War heaven * Maloney, Mack
War hound and the World's Pain, The: a fable * Moor-
    cock, Michael
War in 2020, The * Peters, Ralph
War in 2080: the future of military technology * Lang-
    ford, David

War in Hell * Morris, Janet
War in outer space, The * DiVono, Sharman & William Rotsler as VICTOR APPLETON
War in the atomic age? * Karig, Walter
War lord, The * Sadler, Barry
War machine, The * Allen, Roger MacBride & David Drake
War machines, The * Black, Ian Stuart
War machines of Kalinth, The * Lancour, Gene
War of 1974, The * Fisette, James J.
War of nerves * Haldeman, Joe as ROBERT GRAHAM
War of omission * O'Donnell, Kevin Jr.
War of powers, The * Milán, Victor & Robert Vardeman
War of powers II, The: Istu awakened * Milán, Victor & Robert Vardeman
War of shadows, A * Chalker, Jack L.
War of the Citadels * Hagberg, David as ANONYMOUS AUTHOR
War of the computers * Wilson, Granville
War of the Cybernauts, The * Cassiday, Bruce as CARSON BINGHAM
War of the ghosts * Ernsting, Walter as CLARK DARLTON
War of the gods * Larson, Glen A. & Simon Hawke as NICHOLAS YERMAKOV
War of the maelstrom * Chalker, Jack L.
War of the Moonrhymes * Miller, Calvin
War of the ring, The * Tolkien, J. R. R.
War of the robots * Peel, John
War of the roses, The * Fowler, Karen Joy
War of the sky lords * Brosnan, John
War of the twins * Hickman, Tracy & Margaret Weis
War of the wing-men * Anderson, Poul
War of the witches * Dicks, Terrance
War of the wizards, The * Gaskin, Carol
War of the wizards * Page, Ian
War of the worlds, The * Evans, Mary Ann & H. G. Wells
War of the worlds, The: notes * Parrinder, Patrick
War of the worlds, The; The invisible man; The time machine * Wells, H. G.
War of the worlds: The resurrection: a novel * Dillard, J. M.
War of wizards, A * Storey, Margaret
War ship * Taylor, Charles D.
War stars: the superweapon and the American imagination * Franklin, H. Bruce
War weapons, The * Stacy, Jan as CRAIG SARGENT
War with the Evil Power Master * Montgomery, R. A.
War world * Dietz, William C.
War zone * Milán, Victor as RICHARD AUSTIN
War—1974 * Rigg, Robert B.
Warbots * Stine, G. Harry
Warbringer! * Smith, Mark & Jamie Thomson
Warchild * Bowes, Richard
Warday, and the journey onward * Kunetka, James & Whitley Strieber
Wardens of the weir, The * Gray, Nicholas Stuart
Wardove, The * Smith, L. Neil
Wards of armageddon * Maclay, John & J. N. Williamson
'Ware Hawk * Norton, Andre
War-gamers' world * Walker, Hugh
WarGames: a novel * Bischoff, David
Wargods of Ludorbis * Cole, Adrian
Warhammer 40,000: Deathwing * Jones, Neal & David Pringle
Warhammer 40,000: Inquisitor * Watson, Ian
Warhammer: Beasts in velvet * Newman, Kim as JACK YEOVIL

Warhammer: Drachenfels * Newman, Kim as JACK YEOVIL
Warhammer: Ignorant armies * Pringle, David
Warhammer: Konrad * Garnett, David S. as DAVID FERRING
Warhammer: Plague demon * Stableford, Brian as BRIAN CRAIG
Warhammer: Red thirst * Pringle, David
Warhammer: Shadowbreed * Garnett, David S. as DAVID FERRING
Warhammer: Storm warriors * Stableford, Brian as BRIAN CRAIG
Warhammer: Wolf riders * Pringle, David
Warhammer: Zaragoz * Stableford, Brian as BRIAN CRAIG
Warhaven: a novel * Harvey, M. Elayn
Warhead * Smith, Guy N.
Warhorn: a Crossroads adventure in the world of Lynn Abbey's Rifkind, daughter of the bright moon * Kramer, Dana
Warhorse * Zahn, Timothy
Warlock * Cook, Glen
Warlock * Flynn, J. M.
Warlock: a novel * Garton, Ray
Warlock and son * Stasheff, Christopher
Warlock at the wheel, and other stories * Jones, Diana Wynne
Warlock enlarged, The * Stasheff, Christopher
Warlock enraged, The * Stasheff, Christopher
Warlock heretical, The * Stasheff, Christopher
Warlock insane, The * Stasheff, Christopher
Warlock is missing, The * Stasheff, Christopher
Warlock of Firetop Mountain, The * Jackson, Steve & Ian Livingstone
Warlock of Rhada, The * Coppel, Alfred as ROBERT CHAM GILMAN
Warlock rock, The * Stasheff, Christopher
Warlock to the magic born * Stasheff, Christopher
Warlock unlocked, The * Stasheff, Christopher
Warlock wandering, The * Stasheff, Christopher
Warlock's blade, A: a Crossroads adventure in the world of Christopher Stasheff's Warlock of Gramarye * Perry, Mark C. & Megahn Perry
Warlock's companion, The * Stasheff, Christopher
Warlock's gift * Mayhar, Ardath
Warlock's night out, The * Stasheff, Christopher
Warlord! * Morris, Janet
Warlord, The * Obstfeld, Raymond as JASON FROST
Warlord of Antares * Bulmer, Kenneth as DRAY PRESCOT & ALAN BURT AKERS
Warlord of Ghandor * DowDell, Del
Warlord of Heaven * Cole, Adrian
Warlord of Zendow * La Plante, Richard
Warlords * Langley, Bob
Warlord's domain, The * Morwood, Peter
Warlords of Gaikon * Green, Roland as JEFFREY LORD
Warlords of Nin, The * Lawhead, Stephen
Warlords of Xuma * Lake, David J.
Warlord's revenge, The * Stacy, Jan as CRAIG SARGENT
Warlord's world * Anvil, Christopher
Warm worlds and otherwise * Tiptree, James Jr.
Warmonger * Greenfield, Irving A.
*War*Moon* * Cooper, Tom
Warning, The * Byron, Amanda
Warning to the curious, A: the ghost stories of M. R. James * James, M. R.
Warning whispers: new weird tales * Burrage, A. M.
Warnings, The * Buffie, Margaret
Warren Beatty: a life and a story * Thomson, David
Warren Beatty and Desert Eyes: a life and a story * Thomson, David

Wearing dad's head * Yourgrau, Barry
Weasel's luck * Williams, Michael
Weather war * Leokum, Leonard & Paul Posnick
Weatherhawk * Crowder, Herbert
Weaver of dreams * Baddeley, Pam
Weavers of death * Ryman, Ras
Weaveworld * Barker, Clive
Web, The * Ahern, Jerry
Web, The * Lewis, Richard
Web, The * Wylde, Thomas
Web * Wyndham, John
Web between the worlds, The * Sheffield, Charles
Web of angels * Ford, John M.
Web of danger / by Aaron Allston ; Agent 13: acolytes of darkness / by Flint Dille and David Marconi * Allston, Aaron & Flint Dille & David Marconi
Web of darkness * Bradley, Marion Zimmer
Web of defeat * Grant, Charles L. as LIONEL FENN
Web of futures * Swycaffer, Jefferson P.
Web of light * Bradley, Marion Zimmer
Web of sand * Tubb, E. C.
Web of Selagor, The * Mason, Simone
Web of spider, The * Gear, W. Michael
Web of the Chozen, The * Chalker, Jack L.
Web of the Magi, The, and other stories * Cowper, Richard
Web of the Romulans: a Star Trek novel * Murdock, M. S.
Web of the spider * Lyon, Richard K. & Andrew Offutt
Web of time, The * Harding, Lee
Web of wind * Rivkin, J. F.
Web of wizardry, The * Coulson, Juanita
Web planet, The * Strutton, Bill
Webs * Baker, Scott
Wednesday witch, The * Chew, Ruth
Wee ones, The * Dent, Lester as KENNETH ROBESON
Week in the future, A * Spence, Catherine Helen
Weekend book of science fiction * Gendall, Stuart
Weekend in the Jurassic * Atkinson-Keen, Susan
Weekend vacation * Girard, Kenneth
Weeping may tarry * del Rey, Lester & Raymond F. Jones
Weeping sky, The * Harding, Lee
Weetzie Bat * Block, Francesca Lia
Weightless in Gaza * Ruben, William S. as FRED SHANNON
Weird disappearance of Jordan Hall, The * Angell, Judie
Weird gathering, and other tales, The: "supernatural" women in American popular fiction, 1800-1850 * Curran, Ronald
Weird heroes * Preiss, Byron
Weird heroes, volume 2 * Preiss, Byron
Weird heroes, volume eight * Preiss, Byron
Weird heroes, volume six * Preiss, Byron
Weird legacies * Ashley, Mike
Weird o'it, The * Pemberton, Clive
Weird of the white wolf, The * Moorcock, Michael
Weird tale, The: Arthur Machen, Lord Dunsany, Algernon Blackwood, Ambrose Bierce, H. P. Lovecraft * Joshi, S. T.
Weird tales * Durie, Alistair
Weird tales #1 * Carter, Lin
Weird tales #2 * Carter, Lin
Weird tales #3 * Carter, Lin
Weird tales #4 * Carter, Lin
Weird tales: 32 unearthed terrors * Dziemianowicz, Stefan R. & Robert Weinberg & Martin H. Greenberg
Weird tales: a facsimile of the world's most famous fantasy magazine * Haining, Peter

Weird tales: a selection, in facsimile, of the best from the world's most famous fantasy magazine, revised edition * Haining, Peter
Weird tales story, The * Weinberg, Robert
Weird tales: the magazine that never dies * Kaye, Marvin & Saralee Kaye
Weird valley * Dent, Lester as KENNETH ROBESON
Weird zone, The * Black, Christopher
Weirdbook sampler, The * Ganley, W. Paul
Weirdies: a horrifying concatenation of the super-sur-real or almost or not-quite real * Hoke, Helen
Weirdies, weirdies, weirdies: a horrifying concatenation of the super-sur-real or almost or not-quite real * Hoke, Helen
Weirds, The: a facsimile selection of fiction from the era of the shudder pulps * Jaffery, Sheldon
Weissenbaum's eye * Stetten, George
Welcome, chaos * Wilhelm, Kate
Welcome home, Jaime * Lottman, Eileen
Welcome to reality: the nightmares of Philip K. Dick * Anton, Uwe
Welcome to the giants * Curtis, Philip
Welkin's rift * O'Leary, Liam
Well, The * Cady, Jack
Well, The * Sirota, Mike
Well of Darkness, The * Garrett, Randall & Vicki Ann Heydron
Well of Shiuan * Cherryh, C. J.
Well of time, The * Henighan, Tom
Well of time, The * Light, John
Wells of Hell, The * Masterton, Graham
Well-timed enchantment, A * Vande Velde, Vivian
Welsh Celtic myth in modern fantasy * Sullivan, C. W. III
Werebeasts of Hel * Andersson, C. Dean as ASA DRAKE
Wereblood * Turtledove, Harry as ERIC IVERSON
Wereboy! * Dicks, Terrance
Wereling, The * Robbins, David
Werenight * Turtledove, Harry as ERIC IVERSON
Werewolf! * Pronzini, Bill
Werewolf * Rubie, Peter
Werewolf and the wormlord, The * Cook, Hugh
Werewolf, come home * Gilden, Mel
Werewolf: horror stories of the man-beast * Haining, Peter
Werewolf in legend, fact, & art, The * Copper, Basil
Werewolf mask, The * Ireland, Kenneth
Werewolf of London, The * Dreadstone, Carl
Werewolf of London * Green, Carl R. & William R. Sanford
Werewolf's revenge, The * Jaccoma, Richard
Werewolf's tale, The * Jaccoma, Richard
Werewolves: a collection of original stories * Greenberg, Martin H. & Jane Yolen
Werewolves don't go to summer camp * Dadey, Debbie & Marcia Thornton Jones
Werewolves of Kregen * Bulmer, Kenneth as DRAY PRESCOT & ALAN BURT AKERS
Werewolves of London, The * Stableford, Brian M.
WerewolveSS [Nazi insignia] * Ahern, Jerry & Sharon Ahern
Were-Wrath * Norton, Andre
West End horror, The: a posthumous memoir of John H. Watson, M.D. * Meyer, Nicholas
West of Eden * Harrison, Harry
West of honor * Pournelle, Jerry
West of January * Duncan, Dave
West of the Moon * Lake, David J.
Western ghosts: haunting, spine-chilling stories from the American west * Greenberg, Martin H. & Frank D. McSherry Jr. & Charles G. Waugh

Whilom * Watson, Robert
Whim of the dragon, The * Dean, Pamela
Whipping star * Herbert, Frank
Whirligig of time, The * Biggle, Lloyd Jr.
Whirlwind * Alexander, David
Whirlwind, The: the 34th Dr Palfrey adventure *
    Creasey, John
Whisker of Hercules, The * Dent, Lester as KENNETH
    ROBESON
Whisper * Van Over, Raymond
Whisper down the moon * Darby, Catherine
Whisper in the night: ghost stories * Williams, Mary
*Whisper in the night, A: stories of horror, suspense, and
    fantasy* * Aiken, Joan
Whisper in the night, A: tales of terror and suspense *
    Aiken, Joan
Whisper of blood, A * Datlow, Ellen
Whisper of death * Pike, Christopher
Whisper of midnight * Simpson, Patricia
Whisper of the axe, The: a novel * Condon, Richard
Whisper of the cat * Johnston, Norma
Whispering corner * Alexander, Marc as MARK RONSON
Whispering sea, The * Goldsmith, Howard
Whispers II * Schiff, Stuart David
Whispers III * Schiff, Stuart David
Whispers IV * Schiff, Stuart David
Whispers V * Schiff, Stuart David
Whispers VI * Schiff, Stuart David
Whispers: an anthology of fantasy and horror * Schiff,
    Stuart David
Whispers from the dark side of tomorrow * Peters, Oth-
    ello
Whispers from the dead * Nixon, Joan Lowery
Whispers of heavenly death * Coins, Wally
Whistler's Lane * Fraser, Anthea
Whitby witches, The * Jarvis, Robin
*White book: Adam Juracek, professor of drawing and
    physical education at the Pedagogical Institute in K.,
    vs. Sir Isaac Newton, professor of physics at the Uni-
    versity of Cambridge: reconstructed from contempo-
    rary records and supplemented by most interesting
    document* * Kohout, Pavel
White bull, The * Saberhagen, Fred
White death, The * Sargent, Pamela
White dragon, The * McCaffrey, Anne
White fire, The * Vardeman, Robert E.
White fire: further fantastic literature * Manguel, Alberto
White gold wielder * Donaldson, Stephen R.
White hart, The * Springer, Nancy
White horse is running, The * Sampson, Fay
White hotel, The: a novel * Thomas, D. M.
White House autumn * White, Ellen Emerson
White House mess, The * Buckley, Christopher
White isle, The * Schweitzer, Darrell
White jade fox, The * Norton, Andre
White Jenna * Yolen, Jane
White lies * Hyde, Christopher
White light; or, What is Cantor's continuum problem? *
    Rucker, Rudy
White mambo * Allen, Marilyn
White mare, red stallion * Paxson, Diana L.
White mists of power, The * Rusch, Kristine Kathryn
White mountain, The * Wingrove, David
White nun's telling, The * Sampson, Fay
White pipes, The * Kress, Nancy
White plague, The * Herbert, Frank
White planet, The * Main, Carol
White queen * Jones, Gwyneth
White rabbit, The * Dobkin, Kaye
White raven, The * Paxson, Diana L.

White regiment, The * Dalmas, John
White Rose, The * Cook, Glen
White serpent, The: a novel of Vis * Lee, Tanith
White ship, The: a novel of adventure * Cameron, Ian
White spider, The * Wolfe, Joyce
White vampire, The * Judd, A. M.
White whale: a novel * Siegel, Robert
White Wing * Lewitt, S. N. & Susan Shwartz as GORDON
    KENDALL
White witch * Browning, Dixie & Mary Williams as
    BRONWYN WILLIAMS
Whitethorn wood, and other magicks, The * Yolen, Jane
Whiz kid and the carnival caper, The * Crume, Vic
Who censored Roger Rabbit? * Wolf, Gary K.
Who framed Roger Rabbit * Noble, Martin
Who goes here? * Shaw, Bob
Who goes here? and, The Giaconda caper * Shaw, Bob
Who goes there? * Campbell, John W.
*Who goes there?: a bibliographic dictionary, being a
    guide to the works of authors who have contributed to
    the literature of fantasy and science fiction and who
    have published some or all of their work pseudony-
    mously* * Rock, James A.
*Who is Ayn Rand?: an analysis of the novels of Ayn Rand
    * * Branden, Nathaniel & Barbara Branden
Who is Frances Rain? * Buffie, Margaret
Who is Number Two? * McDaniel, David
Who kidnapped Princess Saralinda? * Stine, H. William
    & Megan Stine
Who killed Harlowe Thrombey? * Packard, Edward
*Who killed science fiction?: an affectionate autopsy: the
    second SaFari annual* * Kemp, Earl & Nancy Kemp
Who knew there'd be ghosts? * Brittain, Bill
Who made Stevie Crye?: a novel of the American South *
    Bishop, Michael
Who needs enemies?... * Foster, Alan Dean
Who p-p-plugged Roger Rabbit? * Wolf, Gary K.
Who sups with the devil? * McCartney, P.
Who writes science fiction? * Platt, Charles
(W)hole Delvers Catalog, The * O'Green, Mark
Whom gods destroy * Peel, John
Whom the gods destroy * Bosshardt, Robert\
Whores of Babylon * Watson, Ian
Who's afraid? and other strange stories * Pearce,
    Philippa
Who's afraid of Beowulf? * Holt, Tom
Who's Hugh?: an SF reader's guide to pseudonyms *
    Robinson, Roger
Who's scared? not me! * St. George, Judith
*Who's who & what's what in science fiction film, televi-
    sion, radio, and theater* * Wright, Gene
Who's who in H. G. Wells * Ash, Brian
Who's who in horror and fantasy fiction * Ashley, Mike
Who's who in Oz * Snow, Jack
Who's who in science fiction * Ash, Brian
Who's who in Star Trek * Asherman, Allan
Who's who in Star Trek * Townsley, John
Who's who of the horrors and of fantasy films * Hogan,
    David
*Why I left Harry's All-Night Hamburgers, and other sto-
    ries from Isaac Asimov's science fiction magazine* *
    Ardai, Charles & Sheila Williams
Why is a fan?: the second SaFari annual * Kemp, Earl &
    Nancy Kemp
Why not you and I? * Wagner, Karl Edward
Why Poe drank liquor * Montgomery, Marion
Why weeps the brogan? * Scott, Hugh
Wicked * Arven, Andrea
Wicked and the witless, The * Cook, Hugh
Wicked cyborg, The * Goulart, Ron

Willow: official movie magazine * McDonnell, David

Willow sourcebook, The * Costikyan, Greg & Allen Varney

Willow: the storybook based on the movie * Dubowski, Cathy East

Win, lose, draw * Stamey, Sara

Win, place or die * Stine, R. L.

Wind & the wizard, The * Roberts, Richard

Wind Boy, The * Eliot, Ethel Cook

Wind child * Harding, Nancy

Wind child * Meluch, R. M.

Wind chimes * Walters, R. R.

Wind crystal, The * Paxson, Diana L.

Wind dancers * Meluch, R. M.

Wind eye, The * Westall, Robert

Wind from a burning woman, The * Bear, Greg

Wind from Bukhara, A * Engh, M. J.

Wind from nowhere, A * Gray, Nicholas Stuart

Wind from the abyss * Morris, Janet

Wind in Cairo, A * Tarr, Judith

Wind in the ashes * Johnstone, William W.

Wind in the willows, The * Grahame, Kenneth

Wind lord * Scott, Michael

Wind over Stonehenge * Dorre, Pamela

Windhaven * Martin, George R. R. & Lisa Tuttle

Windhover tapes, The: An image of voices * Norwood, Warren

Windhover tapes, The: Fize of the Gabriel Ratchets * Norwood, Warren

Windhover tapes, The: Flexing the warp * Norwood, Warren

Windhover tapes, The: Planet of flowers * Norwood, Warren

Windigo: an anthology of fact and fantastic fiction * Colombo, John Robert

Windmaster's bane * Deitz, Tom

Window of the mind * Roberts, John Maddox

Window on today * Hohl, Joan

Window on tomorrow * Hohl, Joan

Window on yesterday * Hohl, Joan

Windows * Compton, D. G.

Windows of forever, The * Morressy, John

Windrider, The * Hoppe, Stephanie T.

Winds of Altair, The * Bova, Ben

Winds of change * Pini, Richard

Winds of change, and other stories, The * Asimov, Isaac

Winds of fate * Lackey, Mercedes

Winds of Salpurtaim, The * St. George, E. A.

Winds of Zarr, The * Tierney, Richard

Wind's twelve quarters, The: short stories * Le Guin, Ursula K.

Windsingers, The * Lindholm, Megan

Windsound * Vallejo, Doris

Wine of Calvoro * Piacentini, Valerie

Wine of violence, The * Morrow, James

Wine, women, and war: a novel * Jahn, Mike

Wine-dark sea, The * Aickman, Robert

Winged assassin, The * Cooke, Catherine

Winged colt of Casa Mia, The * Byars, Betsy

Wingman * Maloney, Mack

Wingman * Pinkwater, Daniel M.

Wingman: Freedom express * Maloney, Mack

Wingman: Return from the inferno * Maloney, Mack

Wingman: Skyfire * Maloney, Mack

Wingman: The final storm * Maloney, Mack

Wingman: The Lucifer crusade * Maloney, Mack

Wingman: The twisted cross * Maloney, Mack

Wingman: Thunder in the East * Maloney, Mack

Wingmaster * Houston, David

Wings * Pratchett, Terry

Wings: a novel * Brittain, Bill

Wings of flame * Springer, Nancy

Wings of omen * Abbey, Lynn & Robert Lynn Asprin

Wings of Pegasus, The: To ride Pegasus; Pegasus in flight * McCaffrey, Anne

Wings of power * Carl, Lillian Stewart

Wings of the black death * Page, Norvell W. as GRANT STOCKBRIDGE

Wings of the Eagle, The * Dorer, Frances & Nancy Dorer

Wingwomen of Hera * Hall, Sandi

Winifred Virginia Jackson, Lovecraft's lost romance * Everts, R. Alain & George Wetzel

Winner takes all * Green, Simon

Winners * Anderson, Poul

Winning Scheherezade * Gorog, Judith

Winston three three three * Barker, Dennis

Winter evil * Wagner, Sharon

Winter in Aphelion: the adventures of Skarry the Dreamer * Dixon, Chris

Winter in Eden * Harrison, Harry

Winter king, The * Carl, Lillian Stewart

Winter lord * Brooks-Janowiak, Jean

Winter of magic's return * Service, Pamela F.

Winter of the birds, The * Cresswell, Helen

Winter of the world, The * Anderson, Poul

Winter of the world, The; and, The Queen of Air and Darkness, and other stories * Anderson, Poul

Winter palace * Jones, Dennis

Winter plain, The * Bannister, Jo

Winter players, The * Lee, Tanith

Winter reckoning * Brennan, Noel-Anne

Winter scream * James, L. Dean as LISA DEAN & Chris Curry

Winter swan, The * Christopher, John as CHRISTOPHER YOUD

Winter wake * Hautala, Rick

Winter wolves * Wescott, Earle

Winter world * Mills, C. J.

Winter world: Egil's book * Mills, C. J.

Winter world: Kit's book * Mills, C. J.

Winterflight: a novel * Bayly, Joseph

Winterking * Hazel, Paul

Winterlong: a novel * Hand, Elizabeth

Wintermind * Godwin, Parke & Marvin Kaye

Winter's daughter: the saying of Signe Ragnhilds-datter * Whitmore, Charles

Winter's end * Silverberg, Robert

Winter's tale * Helprin, Mark

Winterwood, and other hauntings * Roberts, Keith

Wire window, The * Kenmore, Frank J.

Wise child * Furlong, Monica

Wise man's story, The: a Christmas tale for dreamers * Bailey, Albert Edward

Wise one * Elwood, Roger

Wise woman's telling, The * Sampson, Fay

Wise-woman * Forde, R. A.

Wish at the baby's grave, A * Bull, Angela

Wish come true * Gabhart, Ann

Wish, come true * Steele, Mary Q.

Wish giver, The: three tales of Coven Tree * Brittain, Bill

Wish you were here * Brown, Rita Mae & Sneaky Pie Brown

Wishbringer * Gardner, Craig Shaw

Wishes + fears * Starkey, David

Wishing people, The * Beachcroft, Nina

Wishing tree, The * Chew, Ruth

Wishing well: an outline of the evolution of the mammals, told as a series of stories about how the animals got their wishes * Heard, H. F.

Wizardry and wild romance: a study of epic fantasy * Moorcock, Michael

Wizardry compiled, The * Cook, Rick

Wizardry cursed, The * Cook, Rick

Wizards * Asimov, Isaac & Martin H. Greenberg * Charles G. Waugh

Wizards and sorcerers * Oakden, David

Wizards and the warriors, The * Cook, Hugh

Wizards & warriors * Miles, Ellen

Wizards and warriors: two complete play-as-you-read fantasy games * Dillow, Jeffrey C.

Wizard's bane * Cook, Rick

Wizard's daughter, The * Michaels, Barbara

Wizard's Eleven * Tepper, Sheri S.

Wizard's hall * Yolen, Jane

Wizard's mole: a fantasy novel * Strickland, Brad

Wizards of wonder * Stine, H. William & Megan Stine

Wizard's row * Bull, Emma & Will Shetterly

Wizards' worlds * Norton, Andre

Wizenbeak * Gilliland, Alexis A.

Wolf, The * Rose, Richard

Wolf and iron * Dickson, Gordon R.

Wolf bell, The * Murphy, Shirley Rousseau

Wolf Clan sourcebook * Peterson, Boyd F. Jr. & Blaine Pardoe & Sam Lewis

Wolf in shadow * Gemmell, David A.

Wolf in the fold * Green, Simon

Wolf kill * Almquist, Gregg

Wolf King, The * Turnbull, Ann

Wolf man, The * May, Julian as IAN THORNE

Wolf moon * de Lint, Charles

Wolf of Shadows * Strieber, Whitley

Wolf riders * Pringle, David

Wolf: the mechanical dog * Weldon, Fay

Wolf tracks * Case, David

Wolf with no tail, The: can you discover Kutzka's ancient secret? * Sharp, Allen

Wolf worlds, The * Bunch, Chris & Allan Cole

Wolfbane * Kornbluth, C. M. & Frederik Pohl

Wolfcrest * Hirai, Kazumasa

Wolfcurse * Smith, Guy N.

Wolf-dreams * Weaver, Michael D.

Wolfe Archipelago, The * Wolfe, Gene

Wolfen, The * Strieber, Whitley

Wolffile * Woods, Jack

Wolfhead * Harness, Charles L.

Wolfhelm * Knaak, Richard A.

Wolfking * Wood, Bridget

Wolfman, The * Ramsey Campbell as CARL DREADSTONE

Wolf's brother * Lindholm, Megan

Wolf's Complete book of terror * Wolf, Leonard

Wolf's hour, The * McCammon, Robert R.

Wolfsbane * Johnstone, William W.

Wolfshead * Norton, Andre

Wolfsong * Abbey, Lynn & Robert Lynn Asprin & Richard Pini

Wolfsong: the blood of ten chiefs * Pini, Richard & Robert Asprin & Lynn Abbey

Wolfwalker * Harper, Tara K.

Wollheim's World's best SF, series eight * Saha, Arthur W. & Donald A. Wollheim

Wollheim's World's best SF, series five * Saha, Arthur W. & Donald A. Wollheim

Wollheim's World's best SF, series four * Saha, Arthur W. & Donald A. Wollheim

Wollheim's World's best SF, series nine * Saha, Arthur W. & Donald A. Wollheim

Wollheim's World's best SF, series one * Saha, Arthur W. & Donald A. Wollheim

Wollheim's World's best SF, series seven * Saha, Arthur W. & Donald A. Wollheim

Wollheim's World's best SF, series six * Saha, Arthur W. & Donald A. Wollheim

Wollheim's World's best SF, series three * Saha, Arthur W. & Donald A. Wollheim

Wollheim's World's best SF, series two * Saha, Arthur W. & Donald A. Wollheim

Wolves and the lambs affair, The * Holly, Joan Hunter

Wolves of Aam, The * Curry, Jane Louise

Wolves of memory, The * Effinger, George Alec

Wolves of the dawn * Sarabande, William

Wolves of Willoughby Chase, The * Aiken, Joan

Wolves on the border * Charrette, Robert N.

Woman clothed with the sun, and other stories, The * Lucas, F. L.

Woman in black, The * Hill, Susan

Woman in space, A * Cavanaugh, Sara

Woman next door, The * Wright, T. M.

Woman of fire * Grabien, Deborah

Woman of flowers, The * Shwartz, Susan

Woman of passion, A: the life of E. Nesbit, 1858-1924 * Briggs, Julia

Woman of the elfmounds * Zimmer, Paul Edwin

Woman of the future, A: a novel * Ireland, David

Woman of the Horseclans, A: a Horseclans novel * Adams, Robert

Woman of the iron people, A * Arnason, Eleanor

Woman of the mists * McKee, Lynn Armistead

Woman of the wood * Merritt, A.

Woman on the edge of time * Piercy, Marge

Woman who created Frankenstein, The: a portrait of Mary Shelley * Harris, Janet

Woman who is the midnight wind, The * Green, Terence M.

Woman who loved reindeer, The * Pierce, Meredith Ann

Woman who loved the Moon, and other stories, The * Lynn, Elizabeth A.

Woman who rides like a man, The * Pierce, Tamora

Woman who slept with demons, The * Ericson, Eric

WomanSpace: future and fantasy stories and art * Lamperti, Claudia as ANONYMOUS EDITOR

Women and God: a novel * Stuart, Francis M.

Women and the warlords, The * Cook, Hugh

Women and utopia: critical interpretations * Barr, Marleen S. & Nicholas D. Smith

Women as demons: the male perception of women through space and time: stories * Lee, Tanith

Women in science fiction: a symposium * Smith, Jeffrey D.

Women of darkness * Ptacek, Kathryn

Women of darkness II: more original horror and dark fantasy by contemporary women writers * Ptacek, Kathryn

Women of the future: the female main character in science fiction * King, Betty

Women of the weird: eerie stories by the gentle sex * Lewis, Gogo & Seon Manley

Women of vision * Du Pont, Denise

Women of wonder: science fiction stories by women about women * Sargent, Pamela

Women who walk through fire, The: women's fantasy & science fiction, vol. 2 * Sturgis, Susanna J.

Women worldwalkers: new dimensions of science fiction and fantasy * Weedman, Jane Branham

Women's conquest of New-York, The: being an account of the rise and progress of the women's rights movement * Janvier, Thomas A.

Women's utopias in nineteenth and twentieth century fiction * Albinski, Nan Bowman

World of difference, The * Coles, Lesley
World of difference, A * Cooper, Edmund
World of difference, A * Turtledove, Harry
World of fantastic films, The * Nicholls, Peter
World of fantasy films, The * Meyers, Richard S.
World of George MacDonald, The: selections from his works of fiction * MacDonald, George
World of George Orwell, The * Gross, Miriam
World of Gol * Hughes, Dennis Talbot as NEIL CHARLES
World of H. G. Wells, The * Brooks, Van Wyck
World of heroes * Howard, Robert E.
World of Jonah Klee, The * King, Albert as CHRISTOPHER KING
World of mazes * Vardeman, Robert E.
World of order and light, A: the fiction of John Gardner * Morris, Gregory L.
World of Oz, The * Eyles, Allen
World of promise * Tubb, E. C.
World of Ptavvs; A gift from Earth; Neutron star * Niven, Larry
World of science fiction, The: 1926-1976: the history of a subculture * del Rey, Lester
World of shadows, A * Harding, Lee
World of Star Trek, revised edition * Gerrold, David
World of Star Wars, The: a compendium of fact and fantasy from Star Wars and The Empire strikes back * Frederickson, Anthony
World of strangers * Lewins, Anna
World of the Dark Crystal, The * Brown, Rupert & J. J. Llewellyn & Brian Froud
World of The Neverending story * anon.
World of the sower, The * Douglas, Iain
World of Theda, The * Wade, Tom
World of tiers, The * Farmer, Philip José
World of tiers 1 * Farmer, Philip José
World of tiers 2 * Farmer, Philip José
World of Vog Mur, The * Fenlon, Peter C. & John David Ruemmler
World out of time, A: a novel * Niven, Larry
World soul * Emtsev, Mikhail & Eremei Parnov
World spirits * Kaplan, Aline Boucher
World tales * Rau, G. Randal
World treasury of science fiction, The * Hartwell, David G.
World unknown, A * Clagett, John
World War I flying ace * Mueller, Richard
World War II code breaker * Lerangis, Peter
World War III * Stanley, John
World War III: a novelization * King, Harold as BRIAN HARRIS
World without end: a Star Trek novel * Haldeman, Joe
World without mercy * Voltz, William
World-birth * Desmond, Shaw
World-eater * Swindells, Robert E.
Worldmaker * Ellis, Albert C.
Worlds: a novel of the near future * Haldeman, Joe
Worlds apart * Haldeman, Joe
Worlds apart * Kelley, Leo P.
Worlds apart: a study of Earth and Vulcan in fiction and article * Elson, Jenny
Worlds apart: an anthology of lesbian and gay science fiction and fantasy * DeCarnin, Camilla & Eric Garber & Lyn Paleo
Worlds apart: narratology of science fiction * Malmgren, Carl D.
Worlds at war: an illustrated study of interplanetary conflict * Caldwell, Steven
World's best SF 4, The * Saha, Arthur W. & Donald A. Wollheim

World's best SF 5, The * Saha, Arthur W. & Donald A. Wollheim
World's best SF, series eight * Saha, Arthur W. & Donald A. Wollheim
World's best SF, series five * Saha, Arthur W. & Donald A. Wollheim
World's best SF, series four * Saha, Arthur W. & Donald A. Wollheim
World's best SF, series nine * Saha, Arthur W. & Donald A. Wollheim
World's best SF, series one * Saha, Arthur W. & Donald A. Wollheim
World's best SF, series seven * Saha, Arthur W. & Donald A. Wollheim
World's best SF, series six * Saha, Arthur W. & Donald A. Wollheim
World's best SF, series three * Saha, Arthur W. & Donald A. Wollheim
World's best SF, series two * Saha, Arthur W. & Donald A. Wollheim
World's best SF short stories #1, The * Saha, Arthur W. & Donald A. Wollheim
World's best SF three, The * Saha, Arthur W. & Donald A. Wollheim
Worlds beyond: the art of Chesley Bonestell * Durant, Frederick C. III & Ron Miller & Chesley Bonestell
Worlds beyond the world: the fantastic vision of William Morris * Mathews, Richard
World's end * Vinge, Joan D.
Worlds end and after * Karl, Jean E.
World's Fair goblin: a Doc Savage adventure * Dent, Lester & William G. Bogart as KENNETH ROBESON
Worlds for the grabbing * Pearce, Brenda
World's greatest monster quiz, The * Carlinsky, Dan & Edwin Goodgold
Worlds imagined * Greenberg, Martin H. & Robert Silverberg
Worlds of Anne McCaffrey, The: Restoree; Decision at Doona; The ship who sang * McCaffrey, Anne
Worlds of Chthon: Plasm * Platt, Charles
Worlds of Fritz Leiber, The * Leiber, Fritz
Worlds of George O., The * Smith, George O.
Worlds of H. Beam Piper, The * Piper, H. Beam
Worlds of If * Greenberg, Martin H. & Frederik Pohl & Joseph D. Olander
Worlds of never: three fantastic novels * Menville, Douglas & R. Reginald
Worlds of power: Bases loaded II, second season: a novel based on the best-selling game by Jaleco * Singer, A. L.
Worlds of power: Before Shadowgate: the exciting prequel to the game created by ICOM Simulations, Inc. * Miles, Ellen
Worlds of power: Bionic commando: a novel based on the best-selling game by CAPCOM * Stamper, J. B.
Worlds of power: Blaster master: a novel based on the best-selling game by Sunsoft * Singer, A. L.
Worlds of power: Castlevania II: Simon's quest: a novel based on the best-selling game by Konami * Howell, Christopher
Worlds of power: Infiltrator: a novel based on the best-selling game by MINDSCAPE * Singer, A. L.
Worlds of power: Mega man 2: a novel based on the best-selling game by CAPCOM * Miles, Ellen
Worlds of power: Metal gear: a novel based on the best-selling game by Ultragames * Frost, Alexander
Worlds of power: Ninja garden: a novel based on the best-selling game by Tecmo * Singer, A. L.
Worlds of power: Wizards & warriors: a novel based on the best-selling game by Acclaim * Miles, Ellen

X

Xan * Tilley, Patrick
Xanadu manuscript, The * Townsend, John Rowe
Xanthe and the robots * MacLeod, Sheila
Xartella * Dieudonné, Florence Carpenter
X-cellent death, An * Novak, Kate
Xélucha, and others * Shiel, M. P.
Xeno: science fiction * Jones, D. F.
Xenocide * Card, Orson Scott
Xenogenesis * Butler, Octavia E.

Xipehuz, The; and, The death of the Earth * Rosny, J.-H., Aîné
X-Isle * Horton, Gordon T.
X-Men file, The: Sons of X-Men * Schuster, Hal
X-Men files * Van Hise, James
Xolotl * Sheckley, Robert
Xorandor * Brooke-Rose, Christine
XT called Stanley, An * Trebor, Robert

Y

Y chromosome, The * Gom, Leona
Yage letters, The * Burroughs, William S. & Allen Ginsberg
Yamato: a rage in Heaven: the epic begins... * Kato, Ken
Yankee witches * Greenberg, Martin H. & Charles G. Waugh & Frank D. McSherry Jr.
Yargo * Susann, Jacqueline
Yaril's children * Bennett, Marcia J.
Yarrow: an autumn tale * de Lint, Charles
Yawning heights, The * Zinoviev, Alexander
Yaxley's cat * Westall, Robert
Year and a day, A * Furlong, Monica
Year before yesterday, The * Aldiss, Brian W.
Year king * Farmer, Penelope
Year of the bat: the history of DC Comics: fifty years of fantastic imagination * Goulart, Ron
Year of the painted world, The * Mackelworth, R. W.
Year of the ransom, The * Anderson, Poul
Year of the Spiatnik, The: a novel * Betchov, Robert
Year's best fantasy and horror, The: fourth annual collection * Datlow, Ellen & Terri Windling
Year's best fantasy and horror, The: third annual collection * Datlow, Ellen & Terri Windling
Year's best fantasy, The: first annual collection * Datlow, Ellen & Terri Windling
Year's best fantasy, The: second annual collection * Datlow, Ellen & Terri Windling
Year's best fantasy stories, The * Carter, Lin
Year's best fantasy stories: 2, The * Carter, Lin
Year's best fantasy stories: 3, The * Carter, Lin
Year's best fantasy stories: 4, The * Carter, Lin
Year's best fantasy stories: 5, The * Carter, Lin
Year's best fantasy stories: 6, The * Carter, Lin
Year's best fantasy stories: 7, The * Saha, Arthur W.
Year's best fantasy stories: 8, The * Saha, Arthur W.
Year's best fantasy stories: 9, The * Saha, Arthur W.
Year's best fantasy stories: 10, The * Saha, Arthur W.
Year's best fantasy stories: 11, The * Saha, Arthur W.
Year's best fantasy stories 12, The * Saha, Arthur W.
Year's best fantasy stories 13, The * Saha, Arthur W.
Year's best fantasy stories 14, The * Saha, Arthur W.
Year's best horror stories XIV, The * Wagner, Karl Edward
Year's best horror stories XV, The * Wagner, Karl Edward
Year's best horror stories XVI, The * Wagner, Karl Edward
Year's best horror stories XVII, The * Wagner, Karl Edward
Year's best horror stories XVIII, The * Wagner, Karl Edward
Year's best horror stories: XIX, The * Wagner, Karl Edward
Year's best horror stories, series III, The * Davis, Richard
Year's best horror stories, series IV, The * Page, Gerald W.
Year's best horror stories, series V, The * Page, Gerald W.

Year's best horror stories, series VI, The * Page, Gerald W.
Year's best horror stories, series VII, The * Page, Gerald W.
Year's best horror stories, series VIII, The * Wagner, Karl Edward
Year's best horror stories, series IX, The * Wagner, Karl Edward
Year's best horror stories, series X, The * Wagner, Karl Edward
Year's best horror stories, series XI, The * Wagner, Karl Edward
Year's best horror stories, series XII, The * Wagner, Karl Edward
Year's best horror stories, series XIII, The * Wagner, Karl Edward
Year's best science fiction, The: eighth annual collection * Dozois, Gardner
Year's best science fiction, The: fifth annual collection * Dozois, Gardner
Year's best science fiction, The, first annual collection * Dozois, Gardner
Year's best science fiction, The: fourth annual collection * Dozois, Gardner
Year's best science fiction, no. 7 * Aldiss, Brian W. & Harry Harrison
Year's best science fiction, no. 8 * Aldiss, Brian W. & Harry Harrison
Year's best science fiction, no. 9, The * Aldiss, Brian W. & Harry Harrison
Year's best science fiction, second annual collection, The * Dozois, Gardner
Year's best science fiction, The: seventh annual collection * Dozois, Gardner
Year's best science fiction, The: sixth annual collection * Dozois, Gardner
Year's best science fiction, third annual collection, The * Dozois, Gardner
Year's finest fantasy * Carr, Terry
Year's finest fantasy, volume 2, The * Carr, Terry
Years of light: a celebration of Leslie A. Crouch: a compilation and a commentary * Colombo, John Robert & Leslie A. Crouch
Years of the city, The * Pohl, Frederik
Year's scholarship in science fiction and fantasy, The: 1972-1975 * Schlobin, Roger C. & Marshall Tymn
Year's scholarship in science fiction and fantasy, The: 1976-1979 * Schlobin, Roger C. & Marshall Tymn
Year's scholarship in science fiction, fantasy, and horror literature, The: 1980 * Tymn, Marshall B.
Year's scholarship in science fiction, fantasy, and horror literature, 1981, The * Tymn, Marshall B.
Year's scholarship in science fiction, fantasy, and horror literature, 1982, The * Tymn, Marshall B.
Yearwood * Hazel, Paul
Yellow cloud, The * Dent, Lester as KENNETH ROBESON
Yellow fog * Daniels, Les
Yellow hoard, The * Ernst, Paul as KENNETH ROBESON

Yellow peril: Chinese Americans in American fiction, 1850-1940 * Wu, William F.

Yellow peril: The adventures of Sir John Weymouth-Smythe * Jaccoma, Richard

Yellow planet, The * Jennison, John W. as GEORGE SHELDON BROWNE

Yellow silk: erotic arts and letters * Russo, Richard A.

Yellow wallpaper, The * Gilman, Charlotte Perkins

Yellow wallpaper, and other writings, The * Gilman, Charlotte Perkins

Yellowstone run * Robbins, David

Yendi * Brust, Steven

Yenne velt: the great works of Jewish fantasy and occult * Neugroschel, Joachim

Yesterday and tomorrow * Yorke, Erin

Yesterday's child * Wood, Barbara

Yesterday's children * Gerrold, David

Yesterday's faces: a study of series characters in the early pulp magazines, volume 1: Glory figures * Sampson, Robert

Yesterday's faces: a study of series characters in the early pulp magazines, volume 2: Strange days * Sampson, Robert

Yesterday's men * Turner, George

Yesterday's passion * Biggs, Cheryl

Yesterday's pawn * Quick, W. T.

Yesterday's son: a Star Trek novel * Crispin, A. C.

Yesterday's tomorrows: a historical survey of future societies * Armytage, Walter

Yesterday's tomorrows: favorite stories from forty years as a science fiction editor * Pohl, Frederik

Yesterday's tomorrows: past vision of the American future * Corn, Joseph J. & Brian Horrigan

Yeti of the glen * Welfare, Mary

Ylana of Callisto * Carter, Lin

Yngling, The * Dalmas, John

Yobgorgle: mysterious monster of Lake Ontario * Pinkwater, Daniel M.

Yoke of magic, A * Proctor, Geo. W. & Robert E. Vardeman

Yoke of Shen, The * Offutt, Andrew J. & Geo. W. Procter as JOHN CLEVE

Yolanda: Slaves of space * Verseau, Dominique

Yolanda, The girl from erosphere * Verseau, Dominique

Yonder comes the other end of time * Elgin, Suzette Haden

Yorath the wolf * Wilder, Cherry

Yotan's vision * Thomas, Donna & Peter Thomas

You and science fiction: a humanistic approach to tomorrow * Hollister, Bernard C.

You are a genius * Packard, Edward

You are a millionaire * Leibold, Jay

You are a monster * Packard, Edward

You are a shark * Packard, Edward

You are a superstar * Packard, Edward

You bright and risen angels * Vollman, William T.

You can be The Stainless Steel Rat: an interactive game book * Harrison, Harry

You gotta believe! * Hubler, David E.

You must remember us—? * Daventry, Leonard

You never believe me, and other stories * Grubb, Davis

You remember me! * Fisk, Nicholas

You see the future * Goodman, Deborah Lerme

Young adults * Pinkwater, Daniel M.

Young astronauts, The * Lewitt, S. N. as RICK NORTH

Young Bleys * Dickson, Gordon R.

Young blood * Alexis, Katina

Young extraterrestrials * Asimov, Isaac & Martin H. Greenberg & Charles G. Waugh

Young ghosts * Asimov, Isaac & Martin H. Greenberg & Charles G. Waugh

Young immortals * Asimov, Isaac & Martin H. Greenberg & Charles G. Waugh

Young Indiana Jones and the Gypsy revenge * Martin, Les

Young Indiana Jones and the princess of peril * Martin, Les

Young Indiana Jones and the secret city * Martin, Les

Young Indiana Jones and the tomb of terror * Martin, Les

Young legionary: the earlier adventures of Keill Randor * Hill, Douglas

Young monsters * Asimov, Isaac & Martin H. Greenberg & Charles G. Waugh

Young mutants * Asimov, Isaac & Martin H. Greenberg & Charles G. Waugh

Young Rissa * Busby, F. M.

Young Ronan * O'Brien, Edward W. Jr.

Young star travelers * Asimov, Isaac & Martin H. Greenberg & Charles G. Waugh

Young student, The * Cowper, Richard

Young warriors, The * Larson, Glen A. & Robert Thurston

Young witches & warlocks * Asimov, Isaac & Martin H. Greenberg & Charles G. Waugh

Your code name is Jonah * Packard, Edward

Your movie guide to horror video tapes and discs * Lucas, Tim

Your movie guide to science fiction/fantasy video tapes and discs * Lucas, Tim

Your next fifty years * Prehoda, Robert W.

Your place or mine?: an entertainment * Chodos, Robert & Patrick MacFadden & Rae Murphy

You're next! * Sharman, Nick

Yours till forever * Gifaldi, David

Yours truly, from Hell * Doman, David Alan & Terrence Lore Smith

Yours truly, Jack the Ripper * Bloch, Robert

Yours truly, Jack the Ripper * West, Pamela

Youth without youth, and other novellas * Eliade, Mircea

You've had your time: being the second part of the confessions of Anthony Burgess * Burgess, Anthony

Yuckers! * Gilden, Mel

Yurth burden * Norton, Andre

YV88: an eco-fiction of tomorrow * Roaman, Chet & Christopher Swan

Yvgenie * Cherryh, C. J.

Yvonne, the confident * Kimbro, John M. as KATHERYN KIMBROUGH

Z

Z for Zachariah * O'Brien, Robert C.
Z is for zombie * Gilden, Mel
Zaitech sting * McQuay, Mike as JACK ARNETT
Zakka slaughter, The * Meyers, Richard S. as WADE
  BARKER
Zalma * Ellis, T. Mullett
Zamba of the jungle * Fish, Leonard G. as JOHN RAY-
  MOND
Zamyatin's We: a collection of critical essays * Kern,
  Gary
Zandra * Rotsler, William
Zanthodon * Carter, Lin
Zanti misfits, The * Murray, Doug
Zanzibar cat, The * Russ, Joanna
Zaragoz * Stableford, Brian as BRIAN CRAIG
Zarkon, Lord of the Unknown and his Omega Crew: In-
  visible death * Carter, Lin
Zarkon, Lord of the Unknown and his Omega Crew: The
  volcano ogre * Carter, Lin
Zarkon, Lord of the Unknown, in Invisible death, a case
  from the files of Omega * Carter, Lin
Zarkon, Lord of the Unknown, in The Earth-shaker, a
  case from the files of Omega * Carter, Lin
Zarkon, Lord of the Unknown, in The nemesis of evil, a
  case from the files of Omega * Carter, Lin
Zarkon, Lord of the Unknown, in The volcano ogre, a
  case from the files of Omega * Carter, Lin
Zarsthor's bane * Norton, Andre
Zeitgeist machine, The: a new anthology of science fiction
  * Broderick, Damien
Zelde M'Tana * Busby, F. M.
Zelerod's doom: a Sime/Gen novel * Lichtenberg,
  Jacqueline & Jean Lorrah
Zemba: from the Shadow's private annals * Gibson,
  Walter B. as MAXWELL GRANT

Zemlya expedition, The * Rosenberger, Joseph
Zen and the art of writing; and, The joy of writing: two
  essays * Bradbury, Ray
Zen gun, The * Bayley, Barrington J.
Zen in the art of writing * Bradbury, Ray
Zenda vendetta, The * Hawke, Simon
Zenith: the best in new British science fiction * Garnett,
  David S.
Zenith 2: the best in new British science fiction * Garnett,
  David S.
Zero factor, The * Johnson, William Oscar
Zero gravity: a novel * Lourie, Richard
Zero plus ten * Ball, Florence E.
Zero weather: a future fantasy * Morningstar, Ramon
  Sender
Zero-sum games * Tallis, Robyn
Zeta base * Alguire, Judith
Zinsser implant, The: a novel * Kamarck, Lawrence
Z-Lensman * Kyle, David A.
Zoboa * Caidin, Martin
Zodiac: the eco-thriller * Stephenson, Neal
Zoltan, hound of Dracula * Johnson, Ken
Zombie * McNeilly, Wilfred G. as ERROL LECALE
Zombie! * Tremayne, Peter
Zombie house * Kisner, James as MARTIN JAMES
Zombie maker, The: stories of amazing adventures * Otfi
  noski, Steven
Zombie!: stories of the walking dead * Haining, Peter
Zombies that ate Pittsburgh, The: the films of George A.
  Romero * Gagne, Paul R.
Zone yellow: an Imperium novel * Laumer, Keith
Zorachus * Rogers, Mark E.
Zork chronicles, The * Effinger, George Alec
Z-sting * Wallace, Ian
Zulus * Everett, Percival

SERIES INDEX

SERIES INDEX

SCOPE NOTE: Included in this section are books associated with personal, jointly authored, or publisher-sponsored series in the fields of science fiction, fantasy, or horror (including nonfiction books about the genres). Excluded are those series in which only one book has been issued through the end of 1991, or those fiction series in which less than half the published books are fantastic. Some of the series included in the 1979 version of this bibliography are repeated here verbatim where new entries have been added to the series in question; in a few instances where the number of entries in the 1979 set far outweigh the number of new titles added, a "see" reference back to the original listing has been made at the appropriate point in the text. Where no specific series name has been associated with a series, a series title has been invented, based either on the leading character(s) or background setting, or on the first book title in the series.

1984 SEQUELS (various authors)

1. *1984.* [George Orwell]. (1948)
2. *1985.* [Anthony Burgess]. (1978)
3. *1985: a historical report (Hongkong 2036)* [György Dalos]. (1983)

2001 SERIES (Arthur C. Clarke)

1. *2001: a space odyssey.* (1968)
2. *2010: odyssey two.* (1982)
3. *2061: odyssey three.* (1988)

THE A.I. GANG (various authors)

1. *Operation Sherlock.* [Bruce Coville]. (1986)
2. *The cutlass clue.* [Jim Lawrence]. (1986)
3. *Robot trouble.* [Bruce Coville]. (1986)
4. *Forever begins tomorrow.* [Bruce Coville]. (1986)

ABRACADABRA (Eve Becker)

1. *Thirteen means magic.* (1989)
2. *The love potion.* (1989)
3. *The magic mix-up.* (1989)
4. *The sneezing spell.* (1990)
5. *Instant popularity.* (1990)
6. *Too much magic.* (1990)

ABRAHAM STROUD (Robert Walker as GEOFFREY CAINE)

1. *Curse of the vampire.* (1991)
2. *Wake of the werewolf.* (1991)

ACT OF GOD (Eric Kotani & John Maddox Roberts)

1. *Act of God.* (1985)
2. *The island worlds.* (1987)
3. *Between the stars.* (1988)

ADDAMS FAMILY (various authors)

1. *The Addams family.* [Jack Sharkey]. (1965)
2. *The Addams family strikes back.* [William Miksch]. (1965)

Associated Titles

The Addams chronicles: everything you ever wanted to know about the Addams family [Stephen Cox] (1991)

The Addams family: a novelization. [Stephanie Calmenson]. (1991)

The Addams Family: a novelization. [Elizabeth Faucher]. (1991)

Addams family revealed: an unauthorized look at America's spookiest family [James Van Hise] (1991)

ADVANCED DUNGEONS & DRAGONS ADVENTURE GAMEBOOK (various authors)

SUPER ENDLESS QUEST ADVENTURE GAMEBOOKS

1. *Prisoners of Pax Tharkas.* [Morris Simon]. (1985)
2. *The ghost tower.* [Jean Blashfield]. (1985)
3. *Escape from Castle Quarras.* [Douglas Niles]. (1985)

ADVANCED DUNGEONS & DRAGONS ADVENTURE GAMEBOOK

4. *The Soulforge.* [Terry Phillips]. (1985)
5. *Test of the ninja.* [Curtis Smith]. (1985)
6. *Master of Ravenloft.* [Jean Blashfield]. (1986)
7. *Sceptre of power.* KINGDOM OF SORCERY #1. [Morris Simon]. (1986)
8. *Nightmare realm of Baba Yaga.* [Roger E. Moore]. (1986)
9. *The sorcerer's crown.* KINGDOM OF SORCERY #2. [Morris Simon]. (1986)
10. *Lords of doom: a DragonLance adventure.* [Douglas Niles]. (1986)
11. *Clash of the sorcerers.* KINGDOM OF SORCERY #3. [Morris Simon]. (1986)
12. *Curse of the werewolf.* [Chris T. Martindale]. (1987)
13. *Gates of death.* [Terry Phillips]. (1987)
14. *Trail sinister.* [James Brumbaugh]. (1987)
15. *The vanishing city.* [Allen Varney]. (1987)
16. *Shadow over Nordmaar.* [Dezra Despain]. (1988)
17. *Spawn of dragonspear.* [Steve Perrin]. (1988)
18. *Prince of thieves.* [Chris T. Martindale]. (1988)

ADVANCED FIGHTING FANTASY GAMEBOOK—SEE: FIGHTING FANTASY GAMEBOOK

ADVENTURES IN KROY (Ursula K. Le Guin)

1. *The adventure of Cobbler's Rune.* (1982)
2. *Solomon Leviathan's nine hundred and thirty-first trip around the world.* (1983)

ADVENTURES OF CONRAD STARGARD (Leo Frankowski)

1. *The cross-time engineer.* (1986)
2. *The high-tech knight.* (1989)
3. *The radiant Warrior.* (1989)
4. *The flying warlord.* (1989)
5. *Lord Conrad's lady.* (1990)

ADVENTURES OF THE EMPIRE PRINCESS—SEE: THE HAVEN

THE ADVERSARY (F. Paul Wilson)

1. *The keep.* (1981)
2. *Reborn: a novel.* (1990)
3. *Reprisal: a novel.* (1991)
3A. *Reprisals.* (1991)

ADVISE & CONSENT (Allen Drury)

1. *Advise and consent.* (1959)
2. *A shade of difference.* (1962)
3. *Capable of honor.* (1966)
4. *Preserve and protect.* (1968)
5. *Come Nineveh, come Tyre.* (1973)
6. *The promise of joy.* (1975)

AERIEL (Meredith Ann Pierce)

1. *The Darkangel.* (1982)
2. *A gathering of gargoyles.* (1984)
3. *The pearl of the soul of the world.* (1990)
1-3. *The Darkangel trilogy: The Darkangel; A gathering of gargoyles; The pearl of the soul of the world.* (1990)

AFRIKORPS (Tom Williard as BILL DOLAN)

1. *Akrikorps.* (1991)
2. *Akrikorps: Iron horse.* (1991)

AFTER SUCH KNOWLEDGE (James Blish)

1. *Doctor Mirabilis.* (1964) [not SF]
2. *Black Easter.* (1968)
3. *The day after judgment.* (1971)
4. *A case of conscience.* (1958)
1-4. *After such knowledge.* (1991)

AFTER THE BOMB (Gloria D. Miklowitz)

1. *After the bomb.* (1985)
2. *After the bomb: week one.* (1987)

AFTER THE SPELL WARS (F. J. Hale)

1. *Ogre castle.* (1988)
2. *In the sea nymph's lair.* (1989)

AFTERMATH (Mary Vigliante)

1. *The land.* (1979)
2. *The colony.* (1979)

AGENT 13, THE MIDNIGHT AVENGER (Flint Dille & David Marconi)

1. *The invisible empire.* (1986)
2. *The serpentine assassin.* (1986)
3. *Acolytes of darkness.* (1988)

AGENT OF CHANGE (Steve Miller & Sharon Lee)

1. *Agent of change.* (1988)
2. *Carpe diem.* (1989)

AIA (E. Charles Vivian)

1. *Fields of sleep.* (1923)
2. *People of the darkness.* (1924)
1-2. *Aia: Fields of sleep; and, People of the darkness.* (1978)

ALACRITY FITZHUGH (Brian Daley)

1. *Requiem for a ruler of worlds.* (1985)
2. *Jinx on a Terran inheritance.* (1985)
3. *Fall of the white ship Avatar.* (1987)

ALAMUT (Judith Tarr)

1. *Alamut.* (1989)
2. *The dagger and the cross: a novel of the Crusades.* (1991)

ALARIC THE MINSTREL (Phyllis Eisenstein)

1. *Born to exile.* (1978)
2. *In the red lord's reach.* (1989)

ALASTOR CLUSTER—SEE: GAEAN REACH

ALBION TRIPTYCH (Andrew Sinclair)

1. *Gog.* (1967)
2. *Magog.* (1972)
3. *King Ludd.* (1988)

ALDAIR (Neal Barrett Jr.)

1. *Aldair in Albion.* (1976)
2. *Aldair, master of ships.* (1977)
3. *Aldair, across the misty sea.* (1980)
4. *Aldair: the legion of beasts.* (1982)

ALEX BALFOUR (Allen Appel)

1. *Time after time.* (1985)
2. *Twice upon a time: a novel.* (1988)
3. *Till the end of time.* (1990)

ALEX WERNER (Robert Weinberg)

1. *The devil's auction.* (1988)
2. *The armageddon box.* (1991)

ALICE IN WONDERLAND SERIES (Lewis Carroll)

1. *Alice's adventures in wonderland* (1865)
2. *Through the looking-glass, and what Alice found there* (1872)

SEQUELS AND PARODIES

Alice in Blunderland. [Jack Anderson & John Kidner]. (1983)
Alicia in Blunderland. [P. Schuyler Miller]. (1983)
Alice through the needle's eye. [Gilbert Adair]. (1984)

ALIEN (Alan Dean Foster)

1. *Alien.* (1979)
2. *Aliens: a novelization.* (1986)

ALIEN ISLAND (T. L. Sherred)

1. *Alien Island.* (1970)
2. *Alien main.* [with Lloyd Biggle Jr.]. (1985)

ALIEN SPEEDWAY—SEE: ROGER ZELAZNY'S ALIEN SPEEDWAY

ALIEN STARS (Elizabeth Mitchell)

1. *Alien stars.* (1985)
2. *After the flames.* (1985)
3. *Under the wheel.* (1987)
4. *Free lancers.* (1987)

ALIEN TRACE (Kathleen Buckley & Sharon Jarvis as H. M. MAJOR)

1. *The alien trace.* (1984)
2. *Time twister.* (1984)

ALIENS (Jonathan Etra & Stephanie Spinner)

1. *Aliens for breakfast.* (1988)
2. *Aliens for lunch.* (1991)

ALVIN MAKER (Orson Scott Card)

1. *Seventh son.* (1987)
2. *Red prophet.* (1988)
3. *Prentice Alvin.* (1989)
1-3. *Hatrack River: the Tales of Alvin Maker, part one.* (1989)

AMAZING SPIDERMAN—SEE: MARVEL SUPERHEROES

AMAZING STORIES (various authors)

1. *4-D funhouse.* [Clayton Emery & Earl Wajenberg]. (1985)
2. *Jaguar!* [Morris Simon]. (1985)
3. *Portrait in blood.* [Mary L. Kirchoff]. (1985)

AMBER (Roger Zelazny)

1. *Nine princes in Amber.* (1970)
2. *The guns of Avalon.* (1972)
3. *Sign of the unicorn.* (1975)
4. *The hand of Oberon.* (1976)
5. *The Courts of Chaos.* (1978)
6. *Trumps of doom.* (1985)
7. *Blood of Amber.* (1986)
8. *Sign of chaos.* (1987)
9. *Knight of shadows.* (1989)
10. *Prince of chaos.* (1991)
1-5. *The chronicles of Amber.* (1979)

Associated Titles

Combat command in the world of Roger Zelazny's Nine princes in Amber: The black road war. [Neil Randall]. (1988)
A rhapsody in Amber [tie-in]. (1981)
Roger Zelazny's Visual guide to Castle Amber [Neil Randall & Roger Zelazny] (1988)
Seven no-trump: a Crossroads adventure in the world of Roger Zelazny's Amber. [Neil Randall]. (1988)

AMERICA 2040 (Zach Hughes as EVAN INNES)

1. *America 2040.* (1986)
2. *The golden world.* (1986)
3. *City in the mist.* (1987)
4. *The return.* (1988)
5. *The star explorer.* (1988)

AMERICA SERIES (Arthur Herzog)

1. *Make us happy.* (1978)
2. *Glad to be here.* (1979)

AMITYVILLE HORROR (various authors)

1. *The Amityville horror.* [Jay Anson]. (1977). [Published as nonfiction]
2. *The Amityville horror II.* [John G. Jones]. (1982)
3. *Amityville horror 3: the final chapter.* [John G. Jones]. (1984)
3A. *Amityville: the final chapter.* [John G. Jones]. (1985)
4. *Amityville 3-D.* [Gordon McGill]. (1984)
5. *Amityville: the untold story.* [John G. Jones]. (1985)
6. *The secret of Amityville.* [Hans Holzer]. (1985)
7. *Amityville: the evil escapes.* [John G. Jones]. (1988)
8. *Amityville: The horror returns.* [John G. Jones]. (1989)

AMTRAK WARS (Patrick Tilley)

1. *Cloud warrior.* (1983)
2. *The first family.* (1985)
3. *Iron master.* (1987)
4. *Blood river.* (1988)
5. *Death bringer.* (1989)
6. *Earth-thunder.* (1990)

Associated Titles

Dark visions: an illustrated guide to the Amtrak wars. [with Fernando Fernandez]. (1988)

AMUN (Moyra Caldecott)

1. [unknown title]
2. *The son of the sun.* (1986)
3. *Daughter of Ra.* (1990)

ANALOG ANTHOLOGY (Stanley Schmidt)

1. *The Analog anthology #1.* (1980)
1A. *Analog's Golden anniversary anthology.* (1980)
2. *The Analog anthology #2.* (1981)
2A. *Analog: Readers' choice.* (1981)
3. *Analog's Children of the future.* (1982)
4. *Analog's lighter side.* (1982)
5. *Analog: writers' choice.* (1983)

6. *War and peace: possible futures from Analog.* (1983)
7. *Aliens from Analog.* (1983)
8. *Writers' choice, volume II.* (1984)
9. *From mind to mind: tales of communication from Analog.* (1984)
10. *Analog's Expanding universe.* (1986)

ANATOLE (Nancy Willard)

1. *Sailing to Cythera, and other Anatole stories.* (1974)
2. *The island of the grass king: the further adventures of Anatole.* (1979)
3. *Uncle Terrible: more adventures of Anatole.* (1982)

ANCIENT HISTORY (Thomas Burnett Swann)

1. *The Minikins of Yam.* (1976)
2. *Cry Silver Bells.* MINOTAUR #1. (1977)
3. *The forest of forever.* MINOTAUR #2. (1971)
4. *Day of the minotaur.* MINOTAUR #3. (1966)
5. *Queens walk in the dusk.* MELLONIA #1. (1977)
6. *Green Phoenix.* MELLONIA #2. (1972)
7. *Lady of the bees.* MELLONIA #3. (1976)
8. *Wolfwinter.* (1972)
9. *The Weirwoods.* (1967)
10. *The gods abide.* (1976)
11. *The tournament of thorns.* (1976)
12. *Will-of-the-wisp.* (1976)
13. *The Not-world.* (1975)
14. *The goat without horns.* (1971)

ANGEL'S LUCK (Joe Clifford Faust)

1. *Desperate measures.* (1989)
2. *Precious cargo.* (1990)
3. *The essence of evil.* (1990)

ANGELWALK (Roger Elwood)

1. *Angelwalk: a modern fable.* (1988)
2. *Fallen angel: a novel.* (1990)

ANNABEL ANDREWS (Mary Rodgers)

1. *Freaky Friday.* (1972)
2. *A billion for Boris.* (1974)
3. *Summer switch.* (1982)

ANNWN SERIES (George H. Smith)

1. *Scourge of the blood cult.* (1961)
2. *Kar Kaballa.* (1969)
3. *Witch Queen of Lochlann.* (1969)
4. *The second war of the worlds.* (1976)
5. *The island snatchers.* (1978)

ANTARES (Michael McCollum)

1. *Antares dawn.* (1986)
2. *Antares passage.* (1987)

ANTELOPE COMPANY (Willis Hall)

1. *The return of the Antelope Company.* (1985)
2. *The Antelope Company ashore.* (1986)
3. *The Antelope Company at large.* (1987)

ANTHI (Jay D. Blakeney)

1. *The children of Anthi.* (1985)
2. *Requiem for Anthi.* (1990)

ANTHONY MONDAY (John Bellairs)

1. *The treasure of Alpheus Winterborn.* (1978)
2. *The dark secret of Weatherend.* (1984)
3. *The lamp from the warlock's tomb.* (1988)

ANTRIAN (G. Clifton Wisler)

1. *The Antrian messenger.* (1986)
2. *The seer.* (1988)
3. *The mind trap.* (1990)

APPRENTICE ADEPT (Piers Anthony)

1. *Split infinity.* (1980)
2. *Blue adept.* (1981)
3. *Juxtaposition.* (1982)
4. *Out of Phaze.* (1987)
5. *Robot adept.* (1988)
6. *Unicorn point.* (1989)
7. *Phaze doubt.* (1990)
1-3. *Double exposure.* (1982)

APRILIOTH (Eileen Kernaghan)

1. *Journey to Aprilioth.* (1980)
2. *Songs from the drowned lands.* (1983)
3. *The Sarsen witch.* (1989)

AQUILIAD (Somtow Sucharitkul as S. P. SOMTOW)

1. *The Aquiliad.* [As Somtow Sucharitkul]. (1983)
1A. *Aquila in the new world.* (1988)
2. *Aquila and the iron horse.* (1988)
3. *Aquila and the sphinx.* (1988)

ARABIAN NIGHTS TRILOGY (Craig Shaw Gardner)

1. *The other Sinbad.* (1991)
2. *A bad night for Ali Baba.* (1991)

ARC ONE (Monica Hughes)

1. *Devil on my back.* (1984)
2. *The dream catcher.* (1986)

ARCADE EXPLORERS (Seth McEvoy & Laure Smith)

1. *Save the Venturians!* (1985)
2. *Revenge of the Raster gang.* (1985)
3. *The electronic hurricane.* (1985)
4. *The magnetic ghost of Shadow Island.* (1985)

ARCADIA (Lyndon Hardy)

1. *Master of the five magics.* (1980)
2. *Secret of the sixth magic.* (1984)
3. *Riddle of the seven realms.* (1988)

ARCHIVES OF ANTHROPOS (John White)

1. *The tower of Geburah.* (1978)
2. *The iron sceptre.* (1981)
3. *The sword bearer.* (1986)
4. *Gaal the conqueror.* (1989)

ATLANTEAN CHRONICLES (Marion Zimmer Bradley)

1. *Web of light.* (1983)
2. *Web of darkness.* (1983)
1-2. *Web of darkness.* (1985)
1-2. *The fall of Atlantis.* (1987)

ATLANTEAN EARTH—SEE: CIRCLE OF LIGHT

ATLANTIS (Peter Valentine Timlett)

1. *The seedbearers.* (1974)
2. *The power of the serpent.* (1976)
3. *The twilight of the serpent.* (1977)

ATTA OLIVIA CLEMENS (Chelsea Quinn Yarbro)

1. *A flame in Byzantium.* (1987)
2. *Crusader's torch.* (1988)
3. *A candle for D'Artagnan.* (1989)

ATTAR THE MERMAN (Joe Haldeman as ROBERT GRAHAM)

1. *Attar's revenge.* (1975)
2. *War of nerves.* (1975)

AUDREY ROSE (Frank De Felitta)

1. *Audrey Rose: a novel.* (1975)
2. *For love of Audrey Rose.* (1982)

AUSTRAS FAMILY (Elaine Bergstrom)

1. *Shattered glass.* (1989)
2. *Blood alone.* (1990)
3. *Blood rites.* (1991)

AUTHOR'S CHOICE MONTHLY (various authors)

1. *The old funny stuff.* [George Alec Effinger]. (1989)
2. *Unthreatened by the morning light.* [Karl Edward Wagner]. (1989)
3. *Daily voices.* [Lisa Goldstein]. (1989)
4. *Nine hard questions about the nature of the universe.* [Lewis Shiner]. (1990)
5. *Into the eighth decade.* [Jack Williamson]. (1990)
6. *Peripheral vision.* [Karen Joy Fowler]. (1990)
7. *Neon twilight.* [Edward Bryant]. (1990)
8. *Swatting at the cosmos.* [James Morrow]. (1990)
9. *Heroines.* [James Patrick Kelly]. 1990)
10. *Tales from a vanished country.* [Elizabeth A. Lynn]. (1990)
11. *Skyrocket Steele conquers the universe, and other media tales.* [Ron Goulart]. (1990)
12. *True minds.* [Spider Robinson]. (1990)
13. *Ad statum perspicuum.* [F. Paul Wilson]. (1990)
14. *Legacy of fire.* [Nina Kiriki Hoffman]. (1990)
15. *Emphatically not SF, almost.* [Michael Bishop]. (1990)
16. *State of grace.* [Kate Wilhelm]. (1991)
17. *Ma Qui, and other phantoms.* [Alan Brennert]. (1991)
18. *Stories by Mama Lansdale's youngest boy.* [Joe R. Lansdale]. (1991)
19. *Two that came true.* [Judith Moffett]. (1991)
20. *A sensitive dependence on initial conditions.* [Kim Stanley Robinson]. (1991)
21. *God's nose.* [Damon Knight]. (1991)
22. *Hedgework and guessery.* [Charles de Lint]. (1991)

23. *It's been fun.* [Esther M. Friesner]. (1991)
24. *The naked flesh of feeling.* [J. N. Williamson]. (1991)
25. *The alien heart.* [Mike Resnick]. (1991)
26. *Myths, legends, and true history.* [Geoffrey A. Landis]. (1991)

AUTUMN ANGELS (Arthur Byron Cover)

1. *Autumn angels.* (1975)
2. *The Platypus of Doom, and other nihilists.* (1976)
3. *An east wind rising.* (1979)

AUTUMN WORLD (Geary Gravel)

1. *The alchemists.* (1984)
2. *The Pathfinders.* (1986)

AVARYAN RISING (Judith Tarr)

1. *The hall of the mountain king.* (1986)
2. *The lady of Han-Gilden.* (1987)
3. *A fall of princes.* (1988)
1-3. *Avaryan rising.* (1988)

AVATAR TRILOGY—SEE: FORGOTTEN REALMS FANTASY ADVENTURE

THE AVENGER (Paul Ernst and Ron Goulart as KENNETH ROBESON)

1. *Justice, Inc.* [Paul Ernst]. (1972)
2. *The yellow hoard.* [Paul Ernst]. (1972)
3. *The sky walker.* [Paul Ernst]. (1972)
4. *The devil's horns.* [Paul Ernst]. (1972)
5. *The frosted death.* [Paul Ernst]. (1972)
6. *The blood ring.* [Paul Ernst]. (1972)
7. *Stockholders in death.* [Paul Ernst]. (1972)
8. *The glass mountain.* [Paul Ernst]. (1973)
9. *Tuned for murder.* [Paul Ernst]. (1973)
10. *The smiling dogs.* [Paul Ernst]. (1973)
11. *River of ice.* [Paul Ernst]. (1973)
12. *The flame breathers.* [Paul Ernst]. (1973)
13. *Murder on wheels.* [Paul Ernst]. (1973)
14. *Three gold crowns.* [Paul Ernst]. (1973)
15. *House of death.* [Paul Ernst]. (1973)
16. *The hate master.* [Paul Ernst]. (1973)
17. *Nevlo.* [Paul Ernst]. (1973)
18. *Death in slow motion.* [Paul Ernst]. (1973)
19. *Pictures of death.* [Paul Ernst]. (1973)
20. *The green killer.* [Paul Ernst]. (1974)
21. *The happy killers.* [Paul Ernst]. (1974)
22. *The black death.* [Paul Ernst]. (1974)
23. *The Wilder curse.* [Paul Ernst]. (1974)
24. *Midnight murder.* [Paul Ernst]. (1974)
25. *The man from Atlantis.* [Ron Goulart]. (1974)
26. *Red moon.* [Ron Goulart]. (1974)
27. *The purple zombie.* [Ron Goulart]. (1974)
28. *Dr. Time.* [Ron Goulart]. (1974)
29. *The nightwitch devil.* [Ron Goulart]. (1974)
30. *Black chariots.* [Ron Goulart]. (1974)
31. *The cartoon crimes.* [Ron Goulart]. (1974)
32. *The death machine.* [Ron Goulart]. (1975)
33. *The blood countess.* [Ron Goulart]. (1975)
34. *The glass man.* [Ron Goulart]. (1975)
35. *The Iron Skull.* [Ron Goulart]. (1975)
36. *Demon Island.* [Ron Goulart]. (1975)

THE AVENGERS—SEE: MARVEL SUPERHEROES

AVERIDAN (B. W. Clough)

1. *The Crystal Crown.* (1984)
2. *The dragon of Mishbil.* (1985)
3. *The realm beneath.* (1986)
4. *The name of the sun.* (1988)

AWAKENERS (Sheri S. Tepper)

1. *Northshore.* (1987)
2. *Southshore.* (1987)
1-2. *The Awakeners.* (1987)

AYLA—SEE: EARTH'S CHILDREN

BABY-SITTER (R. L. Stine)

1. *The baby-sitter.* (1989)
2. *The baby-sitter II.* (1991)

BACK TO THE FUTURE (various authors)

1. *Back to the future: a novel.* [George Gipe]. (1985)
2. *Back to the future, part II: a novel.* [Craig Shaw Gardner]. (1989)
3. *Back to the future, part III: a novel.* [Craig Shaw Gardner]. (1990)

Associated Titles

Back to the future: a story. (adapted from Gipe's novelization). [Robert Loren Fleming] (1985)
Back to the future: the official book of the complete movie trilogy. [Sally Hibbin & Michael Klastorin]. {1990}

BALLAD OF WUNTVOR (Craig Shaw Gardner)

1. *A difficulty with dwarves.* (1987)
2. *An excess of enchantments.* (1988)
3. *A disagreement with death.* (1989)
1-3. *The wanderings of Wuntvor.* (1989)

BALZAN OF THE CAT PEOPLE (Gerard F. Conway as WALLACE MOORE)

1. *The blood stones.* (1975)
2. *The caves of madness.* (1975)
3. *The lights of Zetar.* (1975)

BANNERMAN (John R. Maxim)

1. *The Bannerman solution.* (1989)
2. *The Bannerman effect.* (1990)
3. *Bannerman's law.* (1991)

BAPHOMET (Pierre Barbet)

1. *Baphomet's meteor.* (1972)
2. *Cosmic crusade.* (1980)
1-2. *Cosmic crusaders: Two complete novels.* (1980)

BARCLAY (Michael Elder)

1. *Nowhere on Earth.* (1972)
2. *The perfumed planet.* (1973)
2A. *Flight to terror.* (1973)
3. *Down to Earth.* (1973)
4. *The seeds of frenzy.* (1974)
5. *The island of the dead.* (1975)

BARD: FELIMID MAC FAL (Keith Taylor)

1. *Bard.* (1981)
2. *Bard II.* (1984)
2A. *The first longship.* (1989)
3. *The wild sea.* (1986)
4. *Ravens' gathering.* (1987)
5. *Felimid's homecoming.* (1991)

BARMY JEFFERS (J. H. Brennan)

1. *Barmy Jeffers and the Quasimodo walk.* (1988)
2. *Return of Barmy Jeffers and the Quasimodo walk.* (1988)
3. *Barmy Jeffers and the shrinking potion.* (1989)

BARNUM SYSTEM (Ron Goulart)

1. *The fire-eater.* (1970)
2. *Death cell.* (1971)
3. *Plunder.* (1972)
4. *Shaggy planet.* (1972)
5. *A whiff of madness.* (1976)
6. *The wicked cyborg.* (1978)
7. *Empire 99.* (1980)
8. *The cyborg king.* (1981)
9. *Daredevils, Ltd.* (1987)

BARONESS (Paul Kenyon)

1. *The ecstasy connection.* (1974)
2. *Diamonds are for dying.* (1974)
3. *Death is a ruby light.* (1974)
4. *Hard-core murder.* (1974)
5. *Operation Doomsday.* (1974)
6. *Sonic slave.* (1974)
7. *Flicker of doom.* (1974)
8. *Black gold.* (1975)

BATMAN SERIES (various authors)

Batman: The doomsday prophecy. [Richard Wenk]. (1986)
Batman. [Craig Shaw Gardner]. (1989)
The Batman murders. [Craig Shaw Gardner]. (1990)
The further adventures of Batman. [Martin H. Greenberg]. (1989)
The further adventures of the Joker. [Martin H. Greenberg]. (1990)
Batman: Captured by the engines. [Joe R. Lansdale]. (1991)
Batman: To stalk a specter. [Nicholas Yermakov as SIMON HAWKE]. (1991)

Associated Titles

Batman. [Hal Schuster]. (1986)
Batman official souvenir magazine. [Gary Gerani]. (1989)
Batmania: plus the story of the incredible Batman television revival. [James Van Hise]. (1989)

BATTLE CIRCLE (Piers Anthony)

1. *Sos the Rope.* (1968)
2. *Var the Stick.* (1972)
3. *Neq the Sword.* (1975)
1-3. *Battle circle: a trilogy.* (1978)

BATTLESTAR GALACTICA (Glen A. Larson with various co-authors)

1. *Battlestar Galactica.* [with Robert Thurston]. (1978)
2. *The Cylon death machine.* [with Robert Thurston]. (1979)
3. *The tombs of Kobol.* [with Robert Thurston]. (1979)
4. *The young warriors.* [with Robert Thurston]. (1980)
5. *Galactica discovers Earth.* [with Michael Resnick]. (1980)
6. *The living legend.* [with Nicholas Yermakov]. (1982)
7. *War of the gods.* [with Nicholas Yermakov]. (1982)
8. *Greetings from Earth.* [with Ron Goulart]. (1983)
9. *Experiment in Terra.* [with Ron Goulart]. (1984)
10. *The long patrol.* [with Ron Goulart]. (1984)
11. *The nightmare machine.* [with Robert Thurston]. (1985)
12. *Die, Chameleon!* [with Robert Thurston]. (1986)
13. *Apollo's war.* [with Robert Thurston]. (1987)
14. *Surrender the Galactica!* [with Robert Thurston]. (1988)

Associated Titles

Battlestar Galactica. [James Lely]. (1979)
The Battlestar Galactica storybook. [Charles E. Mercer]. (1979)
Encyclopedia Galactica. [Bruce R. Kraus]. (1979)

BATTLETECH SERIES (various authors)

Miscellaneous Titles

Heir to the dragon. [Robert N. Charrette]. (1989)
Wolves on the border. [Robert N. Charrette]. (1989)
The sword and the dagger. [Ardath Mayhar]. (1987)

BATTLETECH TRILOGY (William H. Keith Jr.)

1. *Decision at Thunder Rift.* (1986)
2. *Mercenary's star.* (1987)
3. *The price of glory.* (1987)

BLOOD OF KERENSKY (Michael Stackpole)

1. *Lethal heritage.* (1990)
2. *Blood legacy.* (1990)
3. *Lost legacy.* (1991)

LEGEND OF THE JADE PHOENIX (Robert Thurston)

1. *Way of the clans.* (1991)
2. *Bloodname.* (1991)
3. *Falcon guard.* (1991)

WARRIOR (Michael Stackpole)

1. *Riposte.* (1988)
2. *En garde.* (1988)
3. *Coupe.* (1989)

BEAST (James V. Smith Jr.)

1. *Beastmaker.* (1988)
2. *Beaststalker.* (1988)

BEAUTY (Anne Rice as A. N. ROQUELAURE)

1. *The claiming of Sleeping Beauty.* (1983)

2. *Beauty's punishment.* (1984)
3. *Beauty's release.* (1985)

BEAUTY AND THE BEAST (various authors)

1. *Beauty and the beast.* [Barbara Hambly]. (1989)
2. *Masques.* [Ru Emerson], (1990)
3. *Song of Orpheus.* [Barbara Hambly]. (1990)

BEKLAN EMPIRE (Richard Adams)

1. *Shardik.* (1974)
2. *Maia.* (1984)

THE BELGARIAD (David Eddings)

1. *Pawn of prophecy.* (1982)
2. *Queen of sorcery.* (1982)
3. *Magician's gambit.* (1983)
4. *Castle of wizardry.* (1984)
5. *Enchanters' end game.* (1984)
1-5. *The Belgariad.* (1985)

THE MALLOREON

1. *Guardians of the west.* (1987)
2. *King of the Murgos.* (1988)
3. *Demon lord of Karanda.* (1988)
4. *Sorceress of Darshiva.* (1989)
5. *The seeress of Kell.* (1991)

BERBORA (Mike Sirota)

1. *Berbora.* (1978)
2. *Flight from Berbora.* (1978)

BERNAL ONE (George Zebrowski)

1. *Sunspacer: a novel.* (1984)
2. *The stars will speak.* (1985)

BERNIE RYNG (Charles D. Taylor)

First salvo. (1985)
Choke point. (1986)
Counterstrike. (1988)
Deep sting. (1991)

BERSERKER (Robert Holdstock as CHRIS CARLSEN)

1. *Shadow of the wolf.* (1977)
2. *The bull chief.* (1977)
3. *The horned warrior.* (1979)

BERSERKER (Fred Saberhagen)

1. *Berserker.* (1967)
1A. *The Berserker wars.* (1981)
2. *Brother assassin.* (1969)
2A *Brother Berserker.* (1969)
3. *Berserker's planet.* (1975)
4. *Berserker man.* (1979)
5. *The ultimate enemy.* (1979)
5A. *Berserkers: The ultimate enemy.* (1988)
6. *Berserker base.* (1985)
7. *The Berserker throne.* (1985)
8. *Berserker: Blue death.* (1985)
9. *The Berserker attack.* (1987)
10. *Berserker lies.* (1991)

BESSLEDORF (Phyllis Reynolds Naylor)

1. *The bodies in the Bessledorf hotel.* (1986)
2. *Bernie and the Bessledorf ghost.* (1990)

BESTIARY TRILOGY (John Forrester)

1. *Bestiary Mountain.* (1985)
2. *The secret of the round beast.* (1986)
3. *The forbidden beast.* (1988)

BEYOND (Justin Leiber)

1. *Beyond rejection.* (1980)
2. *Beyond humanity.* (1987)
3. *Beyond gravity.* (1988)

BIBLIOGRAPHIES OF MODERN AUTHORS (various authors)

1. *The work of Colin Wilson: an annotated bibliography & guide.* [Colin Stanley]. (1989)
2. *The work of Jeffrey M. Elliot, The: an annotated bibliography & guide.* [R. Reginald as BODEN CLARKE]. (1984)
3. *The work of Julian May: an annotated bibliography & guide.* [Thaddeus Dikty & R. Reginald]. (1985)
4. *The work of George Zebrowski: an annotated bibliography & guide.* [Jeffrey M. Elliot & R. Reginald]. (1986)
4A. *The work of George Zebrowski: an annotated bibliography & guide, second edition.* [Jeffrey M. Elliot & R. Reginald]. (1990)
5. *The work of R. Reginald, The: an annotated bibliography & guide.* [Michael Burgess & Jeffrey M. Elliot]. (1985)
5A. *The work of Robert Reginald: an annotated bibliography & guide, second edition.* [Michael Burgess]. (1992)
6. *The work of Charles Beaumont: an annotated bibliography & guide.* [William F. Nolan]. (1986)
6A. *The work of Charles Beaumont, The: an annotated bibliography & guide, second edition.* [William F. Nolan]. (1990)
7. *The work of Katherine Kurtz: an annotated bibliography & guide.* [Boden Clarke]. (1992)
8. *The work of Reginald Bretnor: an annotated bibliography & guide.* [Scott Alan Burgess]. (1989)
9. *The work of Brian W. Aldiss: an annotated bibliography & guide.* [Margaret Aldiss]. (1992)
10. *The work of Bruce McAllister: an annotated bibliography & guide.* [David Ray Bourquin]. (1985)
10A. *The work of Bruce McAllister, The: an annotated bibliography & guide, rev. ed.* [David Ray Bourquin]. (1986)
11. *The work of Dean Ing: an annotated bibliography & guide.* [Scott Alan Burgess]. (1990)
12. *The work of Chad Oliver: an annotated bibliography & guide.* [Hal W. Hall]. (1989)
13. *The work of Pamela Sargent: an annotated bibliography & guide.* [Jeffrey M. Elliot]. (1990)
14. *The work of William F. Nolan, The: an annotated bibliography & guide.* [William F. Nolan as JAMES HOPKINS & R. Reginald as BODEN CLARKE]. (1988)
15. *The work of Louis L'Amour: an annotated bibliography & guide.* [Hal W. Hall]. (1991). Not SF.
16. *The work of Jack Dann: an annotated bibliography & guide.* [Jeffrey M. Elliot]. (1990)
17. *The work of Ross Rocklynne: an annotated bibliography & guide.* [Douglas Menville]. (1989)
18. *The work of Ian Watson: an annotated bibliography & guide.* [Douglas A. Mackey]. (1989)

BIFROST GUARDIANS (Mickey Zucker Reichert)

1. *Godslayer.* (1987)
2. *Shadow climber.* (1988)
3. *Dragonrank master.* (1989)
4. *Shadow's realm.* (1990)
5. *By chaos cursed.* (1991)

BIG BRAIN (Gary Brandner)

1. *The aardvark affair.* (1975)
1A. *The big brain.* (1991)
2. *The Beelzebub business.* (1975)
3. *Energy zero.* (1976)

BIG PLANET (Jack Vance)

1. *Big planet.* (1957/1978).
2. *Showboat world.* (1975)

BILL, THE GALACTIC HERO (Harry Harrison with others)

1. *The planet of robot slaves.* (1989)
1A. *Bill, the galactic hero on the planet of robot slaves.* (1989)
2. *Bill, the galactic hero on the planet of bottled brains.* [with Robert Sheckley]. (1990)
3. *Bill, the galactic hero on the planet of tasteless pleasure.* [with David Bischoff]. (1991)
4. *Bill, the galactic hero on the planet of the zombie vampires.* [with Jack C. Haldeman II]. (1991)
5. *Bill, the galactic hero on the planet of ten thousand bars.* [with David Bischoff]. (1991)

BIO OF A SPACE TYRANT (Piers Anthony)

1. *Refugee.* (1983)
2. *Mercenary.* (1984)
3. *Politician.* (1985)
4. *Executive.* (1985)
5. *Statesman.* (1986)

Associated title

Combat command in the world of Piers Anthony's Bio of a space tyrant: Cut by emerald. [Dana Kramer]. (1987)

BIONIC WOMAN (Eileen Lottman)

1. *Welcome home, Jaime: a novel.* (1976)
1A. *Double identity.* [as MAUD WILLIS]. (1976)
2. *Extracurricular activities.* (1977)
2A. *A question of life.* [as MAUD WILLIS]. (1977)

BIOWARRIORS (Robert E. Vardeman)

1. *The infinity plague.* (1989)
2. *Crisis at Starlight.* (1990)
3. *Space vectors.* (1990)

BIRD OF KINSHIP (Richard Cowper)

1. *The road to Corlay.* (1978)
2. *A dream of kinship.* (1981)
3. *A tapestry of time.* (1982)

BIRTHGRAVE (Tanith Lee)

1. *The birthgrave.* (1975)
2. *Vazkor, son of Vazkor.* (1978)
2A. *Shadowfire.* (1978)
3. *Quest for the white witch.* (1978)

BIRTHSTONE GOTHIC (various authors)

1. *The ghost and the garnet.* [Marilyn Ross]. (1975)
2. *The amethyst tears.* [Marilyn Ross]. (1975)
3. *Stone of blood.* [Juanita Coulson]. (1975)
4. *Dark diamond.* [Diana Tower]. (1975)
5. *Shadow over Emerald Castle.* [Marilyn Ross]. (1975)
6. *The moonstone spirit.* [Gene DeWeese as JEAN DE-WEESE]. (1975)
7. *Blood ruby.* [Jan Alexander]. (1975)
8. *The carnelian cat.* [Gene DeWeese as JEAN DE-WEESE]. (1975)
9. *A gleam of sapphire.* [Diana Tower]. (1975)
10. *The opal legacy.* [Fortune Kent]. (1975)
11. *A topaz for my lady fair.* [Jane Toombs]. (1975)
12. *The turquoise talisman.* [Sharon Wagner]. (1975)

BIXBY WYLER (Ellen W. Leroe)

1. *Robot romance.* (1985)
2. *Robot raiders.* (1987)

BLACK COMPANY—SEE: **CHRONICLES OF THE BLACK COMPANY**

BLACK CURRENT TRILOGY (Ian Watson)

1. *The Book of the River.* (1984)
2. *The Book of the Stars.* (1984)
3. *The Book of Being.* (1985)
1-3. *The Books of the Black Current.* (1986)

BLACK DRAGON (R. A. MacAvoy)

1. *Tea with the black dragon.* (1983)
2. *Twisting the rope: casadh an t'súgáin.* (1986)

BLACK HARVEST (Ann Cheetham)

1. *Black harvest.* (1983)
2. *The beggar's curse.* (1984)
3. *The witch of Lagg.* (1985)
4. *The pit.* (1987)

BLACK HOLE TRAVEL AGENCY (Brian Daley & James Luceno as JACK MCKINNEY)

1. *Event horizon.* (1991)
2. *Artifact of the system.* (1991)

BLACKBIRD (Freda Warrington)

1. *A blackbird in silver.* (1986)
2. *A blackbird in darkness.* (1986)
3. *A blackbird in amber.* (1988)
4. *A blackbird in twilight.* (1988)

BLACKCOLLAR (Timothy Zahn)

1. *The Blackcollar.* (1983)
2. *The Backlash mission.* (1986)

BLACKWATER (Michael McDowell)

1. *The flood.* (1983)
2. *The levee.* (1983)
3. *The house.* (1983)
4. *The war.* (1983)
5. *The fortune.* (1983)
6. *Rain.* (1983)

BLADE—SEE: ENDWORLD

BLAINE MCCRACKEN (Jon Land)

1. *The Omega command.* (1986)
2. *The Alpha deception.* (1988)
3. *The Gamma option.* (1989)
4. *The Omicron legion.* (1991)

BLAKE WALKER (Andre Norton)

1. *The crossroads of time.* (1956)
2. *Quest crosstime* (1965)
2A. *Crosstime agent.* (1975)

BLAKE'S 7 (various authors)

1. *Terry Nation's Blake's seven: novelisation.* [Trevor Hoyle]. (1977)
1A. *Terry Nation's Blake's 7: their first adventure.* [Trevor Hoyle]. (1988)
2. *Project Avalon.* [Trevor Hoyle]. (1979)
3. *Scorpio attack.* [Trevor Hoyle]. (1981)
4. *Afterlife.* [Tony Attwood]. (1984)
5. *Terry Nation's Avon: a terrible aspect.* [Paul Darrow]. (1989)

BLESSING TRILOGY (William Barnwell)

1. *The Blessing Papers.* (1980)
2. *Imram.* (1981)
3. *The Sigma curve.* (1981)

BLOOD HERITAGE (Sheri S. Tepper)

1. *Blood heritage.* (1986)
2. *The bones.* (1987)

BLOOD HUNT (Lee Killough)

1. *Blood hunt.* (1987)
2. *Bloodlinks.* (1988)

BLOOD OF NOSTRADAMUS—SEE: NOSTRADAMUS

BLOOD OF THE LAMB (Mark E. Rogers)

1. *The expected one.* (1991)
2. *The devouring void.* (1991)

BLOOD SWORD (Oliver Johnson & Dave Morris)

1. *Blood sword.* (1987)
2. *The kingdom of Wyrd.* (1987)
3. *The demon's claw.* (1987)
4. *Doomwalk.* (1988)

BLOSSOM CULP (Richard Peck)

1. *The ghost belonged to me: a novel.* (1975)
2. *Ghosts I have been: a novel.* (1977)

3.   *The dreadful future of Blossom Culp.* (1983)
4.   *Blossom Culp and the sleep of death.* (1986)

BLUE LIGHT (Marvin Kaye)

1.   *A cold blue light.* [With Parke Godwin]. (1983)
2.   *Ghosts of night and morning.* (1987)

BOB FULTON (Jerome Beatty Jr.)

1.   *Bob Fulton's amazing soda-pop stretcher.* (1963)
2.   *Bob Fulton's terrific time machine.* (1964)

BOBBIE TOPPIN (Dana Brookins)

1.   *Soul-eater.* (1985)
2.   *The manipulator.* (1989)

BOLO (Keith Laumer)

1.   *Bolo: the annals of the Dinochrome Brigade.* (1976)
2.   *Rogue Bolo.* (1986)
3.   *The stars must wait.* (1990)
1-2.   *The compleat Bolo.* (1990)

BONES (Jonathan Carroll)

1.   *Bones of the moon.* (1987)
2.   *Sleeping in flame.* (1988)
3.   *A child across the sky.* (1989)

BOOK OF ISLE (BOOK OF SUNS) (Nancy Springer)

1.   *The Book of Suns.* (1977)
1A.   *The silver sun.* (1980)
2.   *The white hart.* (1979)
3.   *The sable moon.* (1981)
4.   *The black beast.* (1982)
5.   *The golden swan.* (1983)
4-5.   *The Book of Vale.* (1984)

BOOK OF LOST SWORDS—SEE: BOOK OF SWORDS

BOOK OF SUNS—SEE: BOOK OF ISLE

BOOK OF SWORDS (Fred Saberhagen)

1.   *The first book of swords.* (1983)
2.   *The second book of swords.* (1983)
3.   *The third book of swords.* (1984)
1-3.   *The complete book of swords.* (1985)

BOOK OF LOST SWORDS

1.   *Woundhealer's story.* (1986)
2.   *Sightblinder's story.* (1987)
3.   *Stonecutter's story.* (1988)
4.   *Farslayer's story.* (1989)
5.   *Coinspinner's story.* (1989)
6.   *Mindsword's story.* (1990)
1-3.   *The lost swords: the first triad.* (1988)
4-6.   *The lost swords: the second triad.* (1991)

BOOK OF THE BEAST (Robert Stallman)

1.   *The orphan.* (1980)
2.   *The captive.* (1981)
3.   *The beast.* (1982)
3A.   *The book of the beast.* (1982)

BOOK OF THE NEW SUN (Gene Wolfe)

1.   *The shadow of the torturer.* (1980)
2.   *The claw of the conciliator.* (1981)
3.   *The sword of the Lictor.* (1981)
4.   *The citadel of the Autarch.* (1983)
5.   *The Urth of the new sun.* (1987)
1-2.   *The book of the new sun, vols. I and II.* (1983)
3-4.   *The sword of the Lictor.* (1985)

Associated Titles

The boy who hooked the sun: a tale from the Book of the wonders of Urth and sky. (1985)
Empires of foliage and flower: a tale from The book of the wonders of Urth and sky. (1987)

BOOK OF THE NOMES (Terry Pratchett)

1.   *Truckers.* (1989)
2.   *Diggers.* (1990)
3.   *Wings.* (1990)

BOOK OF THE UNDEAD (Ric Meyers)

1.   *Fear itself.* (1991)
2.   *Living hell.* (1991)

BOOK OF WIRRUN (Patricia Wrightson

1.   *The ice is coming.* (1977)
2.   *The dark bright water.* (1978)
3.   *Journey behind the wind.* (1981)
1-3.   *The song of Wirrun.* (1987)

BOOK OF WRAETHTHU (Storm Constantine)

1.   *The enchantments of flesh and spirit.* (1987)
2.   *The bewitchments of love and hate.* (1988)
3.   *The fulfilments of fate and desire.* (1989)

BOOK OF YEARS (Peter Morwood)

1.   *The horse lord.* (1983)
2.   *The demon lord.* (1984)
3.   *The dragon lord.* (1986)
4.   *The warlord's domain.* (1989)

BOOKS OF BLOOD (Clive Barker)

1.   *Clive Barker's Books of blood, volume I.* (1984)
2.   *Clive Barker's Books of blood, volume II.* London: Sphere Books, (1984)
3.   *Clive Barker's Books of blood, volume III.* (1984)
4.   *Clive Barker's Books of blood, volume IV.* (1985)
4A.   *The inhuman condition: tales of terror.* (1986) [Abridged edition]
5.   *Clive Barker's Books of blood, volume V.* (1985)
5A.   *In the flesh.* (1986)
5B.   *The books of blood V.* (1988)
6.   *Clive Barker's Books of blood, volume VI.* (1985)
6A.   *Books of blood VI.* (1991)
1-3.   *The books of blood.* (1985)

BOORI (Bill Scott)

1.   *Boori.* (1978)
2.   *Darkness under the hills.* (1980)

BORDERLANDS (Mark Alan Arnold & Terri Windling)

1. *Borderland.* (1986)
2. *Bordertown.* (1986)

BORGO BIOVIEWS (various authors)

1. *Starclimber: the literary adventures and autobiography of Raymond Z. Gallun.* [Raymond Z. Gallun with Jeffrey M. Elliot]. (1991)
2. *Adventures of a freelancer: the literary exploits and autobiography of Stanton A. Coblentz.* [Stanton A. Coblentz with Jeffrey M. Elliot]. (1992)
3. *Deathman pass me by: two years on Death Row.* [Philip Brasfield with Jeffrey M. Elliot]. (1983)
4. *Legends and lovers: fourteen profiles.* [William F. Nolan]. (1993)
5. *Ah Julian! a memoir of Julian Brodetsky.* [Leonard Wibberley]. (1987)
6. *Perfecting visions, slaying cynics: The life and works of George Zebrowski.* [George Zebrowski]. (1993)
7. *Orchids for Doc: The literary adventures and autobiography of Robert A. W. "Doc" Lowndes.* {Robert A. Lowndes with Jeffrrey M. Elliot]. (1993)
8. *Bibi Mkuba: My experiences during wartime in German East Afrika.* [Ada Schnee]. (1993)
9. *Whip and spur: The memoirs of a Civil War officer.* [Col. George E. Waring, Jr.; introduction by Reginald Bretnor]. (1993)
10. *Parting shots: Tales from the last days of horse-drawn field artillery in the U.S. Army (1938-1942).* [Tom Tompkins]. (1993)

BORGO LITERARY GUIDES (various authors)

1. *Reginald's science fiction and fantasy awards: a comprehensive guide to the awards and their winners, 2nd ed.* [Daryl F. Mallett & Robert Reginald]. (1991). [3rd ed., 1992].
2. *A catalogue of Little Blue Books.* [Boden Clarke]. (1993)
3. *The Milford Series: Popular Writers of Today: An index to Volumes 1-37.* [R. Reginald & Mary A. Burgess]. (1993)
4. *The Locus Index: A guide to the people, places, and things in the newspaper of the science fiction field.* [Boden Clarke & Mary A. Burgess]. (1993)
5. *A Robert A. Heinlein cyclopedia: A guide to the persons, places, and things in the fiction of America's most popular science fiction author.* [Nancy Bailey Downing]. (1993)
6. *Victorian criticism of American writers: a guide to British criticism of American writers in the leading British periodicals of the Victorian period, 1824-1900.* [Arnella K. Turner]. (1991)
7. *British science fiction paperbacks, 1949-1956; An annotated bibliography.* [Philip Harbottle & Stephen Holland]. (1992)
8. *The Transylvanian library: A consumer's guide to vampire fiction.* [Greg Cox]. (1992)
9. *The other side of the sky: An annotated bibliography of space stations in science fiction, 1869-1990.* [Gary Westfahl]. (1993)
10. *Hall's Science fiction and fantasy magazines: A bibliographical checklist of titles and issues, 2nd ed.* [Hal W. Hall & Daryl F. Mallett]. (1993)

THE BORRIBLES (Michael De Larrabeiti)

1. *The Borribles.* (1976)
2. *The Borribles go for broke.* (1981)
3. *The Borribles: Across the dark metropolis.* (1986)

THE BORROWERS (Mary Norton)

1. *The Borrowers.* (1952)
2. *The Borrowers afield.* (1955)
3. *The Borrowers afloat.* (1959)
4. *The Borrowers aloft.* (1961)
5. *Poor Stainless.* (1971)
6. *The Borrowers avenged.* (1982)
1-4 *The Borrowers omnibus.* (1966)
1-4 *The complete adventures of the Borrowers.* (1967)

THE BRAIN SHARPENERS/MR BROWSER (Philip Curtis)

1. *Mr Browser and the Brain Sharpeners.* (1979)
1A. *Invasion of the Brain Sharpeners.* (1981)
2. *Mr Browser meets the Burrowers.* (1980)
2A. *Invasion from below the Earth.* (1981)
3. *Mr Browser and the comet crisis.* (1981)
3A. *Invasion of the comet people.* (1983)
4. *The revenge of the Brain Sharpeners.* (1982)
5. *Beware of the Brain Sharpeners.* (1983)
6. *Mr Browser and the mini-meteorites.* (1983)
7. *Mr Browser in the space museum.* (1985)
8. *Bewitched by the Brain Sharpeners.* (1986)
9. *The Brain Sharpeners abroad.* (1987)
10. *Chaos comes to Chivvy Chase.* (1988)
11. *Mr Browser and the space maggots.* (1989)
12. *Mr Browser meets the mind shrinkers.* (1989)

BRAK THE BARBARIAN (John Jakes)

1. *Brak the barbarian.* (1968)
2. *Brak the barbarian versus the sorceress.* (1969)
2A. *The sorceress.* (1970)
3. *Brak the barbarian versus the mark of the demons.* (1969)
3A. *The mark of the demons.* (1970)
4. *When the idols walked.* (1978)
5. *The fortunes of Brak.* (1980)

BRAN MAK MORN (various authors)

1. *Bran Mak Morn.* [Robert E. Howard]. (1969)
2. *Legion from the shadows.* [Karl Edward Wagner]. (1976/1988)
3. *For the witch of the mists.* [David C. Smith & Richard Tierney]. (1978)

BRAN TREGARE—SEE: RISSA KERGUELEN

BRANDYJACK (Augustine Funnell)

1. *Brandyjack.* (1976)
2. *Rebels of Merka.* (1976)

BRANWEN (Dee Morrison Meaney)

1. *An unkindness of ravens.* (1983)
2. *Death of the raven.* (1983)

BRAVE LITTLE TOASTER (Thomas M. Disch)

1. *The brave little toaster.* (1986)
2. *The brave little toaster goes to Mars.* (1988)

BREAKOUT (David J. Lake)

1. *Walkers on the sky.* (1976)
2. *The right hand of Dextra.* DEXTRA #1. (1977)
3. *The Wildings of Westron.* DEXTRA #2. (1977)
4. *The gods of Xuma; or, Barsoom revisited.* XUMA #1. (1978)
5. *Warlords of Xuma.* XUMA #2. (1983)
6. *The fourth hemisphere.* (1980)

BRENTFORD (Robert Rankin)

1. *The antipope.* (1981)
2. *The Brentford triangle.* (1982)
3. *East of Ealing.* (1984)
4. *The sprouts of wrath.* (1988)
1-3. *The Brentford trilogy.* (1988)

BRIGADIER FFELLOWES (Sterling F. Lanier)

1. *The peculiar exploits of Brigadier Ffellowes.* (1972)
2. *The curious quests of Brigadier Ffellowes.* (1986)

BRILL & MAXWELL (Lee Killough)

1. *The doppelgänger gambit.* (1979)
2. *Spider play.* (1986)
3. *Dragon's teeth.* (1990)

BRITISH SCIENCE FICTION AUTHORS (various authors)

1. *Bob Shaw.* [Paul Kincaid & Geoff Rippington]. (1981)
2. *Keith Roberts.* [Paul Kincaid]. (1983)

BROWNSTONE (Ken Eulo)

1. *The brownstone.* (1980)
2. *The bloodstone.* (1981)
3. *The deathstone.* (1982)

BRYNCHMACHRYE (Tom De Haan)

1. *A mirror for princes.* (1987)
2. *The child of good fortune.* (1989)

BUCK ROGERS (various authors)

ACE BOOKS SERIES

1. *Armageddon: 2419 A.D.* [Philip Francis Nowlan]. (1962)
2. *Mordred.* [Larry Niven & John Eric Holmes & Jerry Pournelle]. (1980)
3. *Warrior's blood.* [Richard S. McEnroe & Larry Niven & Jerry Pournelle]. (1981)
4. *Warrior's world.* [Richard S. McEnroe & Larry Niven & Jerry Pournelle]. (1981)
5. *Rogers' Rangers.* [Larry Niven & John Silbersack & Jerry Pournelle]. (1983)

DELL BOOKS SERIES

1. *Buck Rogers in the 25th century.* [Richard A. Lupoff as ADDISON E. STEELE]. (1978)
2. *That man on Beta.* [Richard A. Lupoff as ADDISON E. STEELE]. (1979)

INNER PLANETS TRILOGY

1. *First power play.* [John J. Miller]. (1990)
2. *Prime squared.* [M. S. Murdock]. (1990)
3. *Matrix cubed.* [Britton Bloom]. (1991)

MARTIAN WARS TRILOGY (M. S. Murdock)

1. *Rebellion 2456.* (1989)
2. *Hammer of Mars.* (1989)
3. *Armageddon off Vesta.* (1989)

BUNDUKI (J. T. Edson)

1. *Bunduki.* (1975)
2. *Bunduki and Dawn.* (1976)
3. *Sacrifice for the Quagga God.* (1976)
4. *Fearless master of the jungle.* (1980)

BUNNICULA (James Howe)

1. *Bunnicula.* [with Deborah Howe]. (1979)
2. *Howliday Inn.* (1982)
3. *The celery stalks at midnight.* (1983)
4. *Nighty-nightmare.* (1987)

BURLAP HALL (Virginia Ironside)

1. *Vampire master.* (1987)
2. *Spaceboy at Burlap Hall.* (1989)
3. *Phantom of Burlap Hall.* (1991)

BUTTERFIELD SQUARE SERIES (Carol Beach York)

1. *Miss Know It All and the wishing lamp.* (1987)
2. *Miss Know It All and the magic house.* (1989)

CABAL (Saul (Philip) Dunn)

1. *The Cabal.* (1978)
2. *The black moon.* (1978)
3. *The evangelist.* (1979)

CADRE TRILOGY (Robert O'Riordan)

1. *Cadre One.* (1986)
2. *Cadre Lucifer.* (1987)
3. *Cadre Messiah.* (1988)

C.A.D.S. (various authors as JOHN SIEVERT)

1. *C.A.D.S.* [Ryder Syvertsen & Jan Stacy]. (1985)
2. *Tech battleground.* [Ryder Syvertsen]. (1986)
3. *Tech commando.* [Ryder Syvertsen]. (1986)
4. *Tech strike force.* [Ryder Syvertsen]. (1987)
5. *Tech Satan.* [Ryder Syvertsen]. (1988)
6. *Tech inferno.* [Ryder Syvertsen]. (1988)
7. *Doom commander.* [Ryder Syvertsen]. (1989)
8. *Cybertech killing zone.* [Ryder Syvertsen]. (1989)
9. *Suicide attack.* [David Alexander]. (1990)
10. *Recon by fire.* [David Alexander]. (1990)
11. *Death zone attack.* [David Alexander]. (1991)
12. *Tech assassins.* [David Alexander]. (1991)

CADWAL CHRONICLES (Jack Vance)

1. *Araminta Station.* (1987)
2. *Ecce and old Earth.* (1991)

CAGEWORLD (Colin Kapp)

1. *Search for the Sun!* (1982)

2. *The lost worlds of Cronus.* (1982)
3. *The tyrant of Hades.* (1982)
4. *Star-search.* (1983)

CAITHAN CRUSADE (Julie Dean Smith)

1. *Call of madness.* (1990)
2. *Mission of magic.* (1991)

CAITLIN (Ann Downer)

1. *The spellkey.* (1987)
2. *The glass salamander.* (1989)

CALADON (Craig Mills)

1. *The bane of Lord Caladon.* (1982)
2. *The dreamer in discord.* (1988)

CALLAHAN'S CROSSTIME SALOON (Spider Robinson

1. *Callahan's Crosstime Saloon.* (1977)
2. *Time travelers strictly cash.* (1981)
3. *Callahan's secret.* (1986)
4. *Callahan's lady.* (1989)
1-3. *Callahan and company.* (1987)
1-3. *Callahan's crazy crosstime bar.* (1989)

CALLIE (Jane Louise Curry)

1. *Beneath the hill.* (1967)
2. *The daybreakers.* (1970)
3. *The birdstones.* (1977)

CALVIN WILLEFORD (Gene DeWeese)

1. *Black suits from outer space.* (1985)
1A. *Beepers from outer space.* (1985)
2. *The dandelion caper.* (1986)
3. *The Calvin nullifier.* (1987)

CAMBER OF CULDI—SEE: DERYNI CHRONICLES

CAMELOT (Arthur H. Landis)

1. *A world called Camelot.* (1976)
2. *Camelot in orbit.* (1978)
3. *The magick of Camelot.* (1981)
4. *Home, to Avalon.* (1982)

CAMP HAUNTED HILLS (Bruce Coville)

1. *How I survived my summer vacation.* (1988)
2. *Some of my best friends are monsters.* (1988)
3. *The dinosaur that followed me home.* (1990)

CANOPUS IN ARGUS: ARCHIVES (Doris Lessing)

1. *Re: colonised planet 5, Shikasta: personal, psychological, historical documents relating to a visit by Johor (George Sherban), emissary (grade 9) 87th of the period of the last days.* (1979)
2. *The marriages between zones three, four, and five (as narrated by the chroniclers of zone three).* (1980)
3. *The Sirian experiments: the report by Ambien II, of the five.* (1981)
4. *The making of the representative for Planet 8.* (1982)

5. *Documents relating to the sentimental agents in the Volyen Empire.* (1983)

CAP KENNEDY (E. C. Tubb *as* GREGORY KERN)

1. *Galaxy of the lost.* (1973)
2. *Slave ship from Sergan.* (1973)
3. *Monster of Metelaze.* (1973)
4. *Enemy within the skull.* (1974)
5. *Jewel of Jarhen.* (1974)
6. *Seetee alert!* (1974)
7. *The Gholan Gate.* (1974)
8. *The eater of worlds.* (1974)
9. *Earth enslaved.* (1974)
10. *Planet of dread.* (1974)
11. *Spawn of Laban.* (1974)
12. *The genetic buccaneer.* (1974)
13. *A world aflame.* (1974)
14. *The ghosts of Epidoris.* (1975)
15. *Mimics of Dephene.* (1975)
16. *Beyond the galactic lens.* (1975)
17. *The Galactiad.* (1983)

CAPTAIN AMERICA—SEE: MARVEL SUPERHEROES & MARVEL SUPERHEROES ADVENTURE GAMEBOOKS

CAPTAIN MADIRANKOWITCH (James Krüss)

1. *Happy Islands behind the winds.* (1966)
2. *Return to the Happy Islands.* (1967)

CAPTAIN PYANFAR—SEE: CHANUR

CAR WARS ADVENTURE GAMEBOOK (various authors)

1. *Battle road.* [Steve Jackson]. (1986)
2. *Fuel's gold.* [Steve Jackson & Creede Lambard & Sharleen Lambard]. (1987)
3. *Dueltrack.* [Scott D. Haring]. (1987)
4. *Badlands run.* [Creede Lambard & Sharleen Lambard]. (1987)
5. *Green circle blues.* [Scott D. Haring]. (1987)

CARBONEL (Barbara Sleigh)

1. *Carbonel.* (1955)
1A. *Carbonel, the king of the cats.* (1957)
2. *The kingdom of Carbonel.* (1959)
3. *Carbonel and Calidor.* (1978)

CARO (Fay S. Lapka)

1. *Dark is a color.* (1990)
2. *Hoverlight.* (1991)

CARRIER (various authors as KEITH DOUGLASS)

1. *Carrier.* [William K. Keith Jr.]. (1991)
2. *Viper strike.* [William K. Keith Jr.]. (1991)

CASCA, THE ETERNAL MERCENARY (Barry Sadler)

1. *The eternal mercenary.* (1979)
2. *God of death.* (1979)
3. *The war lord.* (1980)
4. *Panzer soldier.* (1980)
5. *The barbarian.* (1981)
6. *The Persian.* (1982)
7. *The damned.* (1982)
8. *Soldier of fortune.* (1983)

CHARLEMAGNE'S CHAMPION (Gail Van Asten)

1. *Charlemagne's champion.* (1990)
2. *The dark sword's lover.* (1990)

CHARLEY (John Spencer)

1. *A case for Charley.* (1984)
2. *Charley gets the picture.* (1985)

CHARLIE MOON (Chelsea Quinn Yarbro)

1. *Ogilvie, Tallant, and Moon.* (1976)
1A. *Bad medicine.* (1990)
2. *Music when sweet voices die.* (1979)
2A. *False notes.* (1991)
3. *Poison fruit.* (1991)

CHILD'S PLAY (Matthew J. Costello)

1. [never novelized]
2. *Child's play 2: a novel.* (1990)
3. *Child's play 3: a novel.* (1991)

CHILDE CYCLE (Gordon R. Dickson)

1. *Necromancer.* (1962)
1A. *No room for man.* (1963)
2. *Tactics of mistake.* (1971)
3. *Soldier, ask not.* (1967)
4. *The genetic general.* (1960)
4A. *Dorsai!* (1976)
5. *The spirit of Dorsai.* (1979)
6. *Lost Dorsai.* (1980)
7. *Young Bleys.* (1991)
8. *The final encyclopedia.* (1984)
9. *The Chantry guild.* (1988)
   Three to Dorsai!: three novels from the Childe Cycle: Necromancer; Tactics of mistake; Dorsai! (1975)

Associated Title

Dorsai's command. [Troy Denning & Gordon R. Dickson & Cory Glaberson]. (1989)
The Dorsai companion. [Gordon R. Dickson]. (1986)

CHILDREN OF THE STARS (Juanita Coulson)

1. *Tomorrow's heritage.* (1981)
2. *Outward bound.* (1982)
3. *Legacy of Earth.* (1989)
4. *The past of forever.* (1989)

CHILDREN OF TRIAD (Laurie J. Marks)

1. *Delan the mislaid.* (1989)
2. *The moonbane mage.* (1990)
3. *Ara's field.* (1991)

CHILDREN OF YNELL (Shirley Rousseau Murphy)

1. *The ring of fire.* (1977)
2. *The wolf bell.* (1979)
3. *The castle of Hape.* (1980)
4. *Caves of fire and ice.* (1980)
5. *The joining of the stone.* (1981)

CHILL (Jory Sherman)

1. *Satan's seed.* (1978)
2. *Chill.* (1978)
3. *The bamboo demons.* (1979)
4. *Vegas vampire.* (1980)
5. *The phoenix man.* (1980)
6. *House of scorpions.* (1980)
7. *Shadows.* (1980)

CHIMNEY WITCH (Victoria Whitehead)

1. *The chimney witches.* (1986)
2. *Chimney witch chase.* (1987)
3. *Chimney witch Christmas.* (1988)
4. *The witches of Creaky-Cranky Castle.* (1991)

CHIP SERIES (NOT QUITE HUMAN) (Seth McEvoy)

1. *Batteries not included.* (1985)
2. *All geared up.* (1985)
3. *A bug in the system.* (1985)
4. *Reckless robot.* (1986)
5. *Terror at play.* (1986)
6. *Killer robot.* (1986)

CHOCKY (John Wyndham and others)

1. *Chocky.* [John Wyndham]. (1968)
2. *Chocky's challenge.* [Mark Daniel]. (1986)

CHOOSE YOUR OWN ADVENTURE (various authors)

1. *The cave of time.* [Edward Packard]. (1979)
2. *Journey under the sea.* [R. A. Montgomery as ROBERT MOUNTAIN]. (1977)
3. *By balloon to the Sahara.* [Douglas Terman]. (1979).
3A. *Danger in the desert.* [Douglas Terman]. (1989)
4. *Space and beyond.* [R. A. Montgomery]. (1980)
5. *The mystery of Chimney Rock.* [Edward Packard]. (1980)
5A. *The curse of the haunted mansion.* [Edward Packard]. (1989)
6. *Your code name is Jonah.* [Edward Packard]. (1979)
7. *The third planet from Altair.* [Edward Packard]. (1979)
7A. *Exploration infinity.* [Edward Packard]. (1982)
7B. *Message from space.* [Edward Packard]. (1989)
8. *Deadwood City.* [Edward Packard]. (1978)
9. *Who killed Harlowe Thrombey?* [Edward Packard]. (1981)
10. *The lost Jewels of Nabooti.* [R. A. Montgomery]. (1981)
11. *Mystery of the Maya.* [R. A. Montgomery]. (1981)
12. *Inside UFO 54-40.* [Edward Packard]. (1982)
13. *The abominable snowman.* [R. A. Montgomery]. (1982)
14. *The forbidden castle.* [Edward Packard]. (1982)
15. *House of danger.* [R. A. Montgomery]. (1982)
16. *Survival at sea.* [Edward Packard]. (1982)
17. *The race forever.* [R. A. Montgomery]. (1983)
18. *Underground kingdom.* [Edward Packard]. (1983)
19. *Secret of the pyramids.* [Richard Brightfield]. (1983)
20. *Escape.* [R. A. Montgomery]. (1983)
21. *Hyperspace.* [Edward Packard]. (1983)
22. *Space patrol.* [Julius Goodman]. (1983)
23. *The lost tribe.* [Louis Munro Foley]. (1983)
24. *Lost on the Amazon.* [R. A. Montgomery]. (1983)
25. *Prisoner of the ant people.* [R. A. Montgomery]. (1983)

CHRIS (Leonie Kooiker)

1. *The magic stone.* (1978)
2. *Legacy of magic.* (1981)

CHRIS GODFREY (Hugh Walters)

1. *Blast off at Woomera.* (1957)
2. *The domes of Pico.* (1958)
3. *Operation Columbus.* (1960)
4. *Moon Base One.* (1961)
5. *Expedition Venus.* (1962)
6. *Destination Mars.* (1963)
7. *Terror by satellite.* (1964)
8. *Journey to Jupiter.* (1965)
9. *Mission to Mercury.* (1965)
10. *Spaceship to Saturn.* (1967)
11. *The Mohole mystery.* (1968)
12. *Nearly Neptune.* (1969)
13. *First contact?* (1971)
14. *Passage to Pluto.* (1973)
15. *Tony Hale, space detective.* (1973)
16. *Murder on Mars.* (1975)
17. *Boy astronaut.* (1977)
18. *Caves of Drach.* (1977)
19. *The last disaster.* (1978)
20. *The blue aura.* (1979)
21. *First family on the Moon.* (1979)
22. *The dark triangle.* (1981)
23. *School on the Moon.* (1981)
24. *P-K.* (1986)

CHRONICLE OF GREYSTONE BAY

1. *The first chronicles of Greystone Bay.* (1985)
2. *Doom city.* (1987)
3. *The SeaHarp Hotel.* (1990)

CHRONICLES OF AN AGE OF DARKNESS (Hugh Cook)

1. *The wizards and the warriors.* (1986)
2. *The wordsmiths and the warguild.* (1987)
3. *The women and the warlords.* (1987)
4. *The walrus and the warwolf.* (1988)
5. *The wicked and the witless.* (1989)
6. *Wishstone and the wonderworkers.* (1990)
7. *The wazir and the witch.* (1990)
8. *The werewolf and the wormlord.* (1991)

WIZARD WAR CHRONICLES (U.S. edition)

1. *Wizard war.* [A retitling of *The wizards and the warriors*]. (1988)
2. *The questing hero.* [The first half of *The wordsmiths and the warguild*]. (1987)
3. *The hero's return.* [The second half of *The wordsmiths and the warguild*]. (1988)
4. *The oracle.* [A retitling of *The women and the warlords*]. (1989)
5. *Lords of the sword.* [A retitling of *The walrus and the warwolf*]. (1991)

THE CHRONICLES OF CORUM (Michael Moorcock)

THE SWORDS TRILOGY

1. *The Knight of the Swords.* (1971)
2. *The Queen of the Swords.* (1971)
3. *The King of the Swords.* (1971)
1-3. *The swords trilogy.* (1977)

1-3. *The swords of Corum omnibus.* (1986)

THE CHRONICLES OF CORUM

4. *The bull and the spear.* (1973)
5. *The oak and the ram.* (1973)
6. *The sword and the stallion.* (1974)
4-6. *The chronicles of Corum.* (1978)

CHRONICLES OF GALEN SWORD (Garfield Reeves-Stevens & Judith Reeves-Stevens)

1. *Shifter.* (1990)
2. *Nightfeeder.* (1991)

CHRONICLES OF KYLIX (Lin Carter)

1. *Quest of Kadji.* (1971)
2. *The wizard of Zao.* (1978)

CHRONICLES OF MORGAINE (C. J. Cherryh)

1. *Gate of Ivrel.* (1976)
2. *Well of Shiuan.* (1978)
3. *Fires of Azeroth.* (1979)
4. *Exile's gate.* (1988)
1-3. *The book of Morgaine.* (1979)
1-3. *The chronicles of Morgaine.* (1985)

Associated Title

The witchfires of Leth: a Crossroads adventure in the world of C. J. Cherryh's Morgaine. [Dan Greenburg]. (1987)

CHRONICLES OF NARNIA (C. S. Lewis)

1. *The lion, the witch, and the wardrobe.* (1950)
2. *Prince Caspian.* (1951)
3. *The voyage of the Dawn Treader.* (1952)
4. *The silver chair.* (1953)
5. *The horse and his boy.* (1954)
6. *The magician's nephew.* (1955)
7. *The last battle.* (1956)
1-7. *The Chronicles of Narnia; with, The Lion of Judah in never-Never Land.* (1973)
4-5. *Prince Caspian; and, The voyage of the Dawn Treader.* (1989)
6-7. *The silver chair; and, The last battle.* (1990)

CHRONICLES OF THE BLACK COMPANY (Glen Cook)

1. *The Black Company.* (1984)
2. *Shadows linger.* (1984)
3. *The White Rose.* (1985)
4. *Shadow games: first book of the South.* (1989)
5. *Dreams of steel: second book of the South.* (1990)
6. *The silver spike.* (1989)
1-3. *Annals of the Black Company.* (1986)

CHRONICLES OF THE CHEYSULI (Jennifer Roberson)

1. *Shapechangers.* (1984)
2. *The song of Homana.* (1985)
3. *Legacy of the sword.* (1986)
4. *Track of the white wolf.* (1987)
5. *A pride of princes.* (1988)
6. *Daughter of the lion.* (1989)
7. *Flight of the raven.* (1990)

CHRONICLES OF THE HIGH INQUEST (Somtow Sucharitkul)

1. *Light on the sound.* (1982/1986)
2. *The throne of madness.* (1983)
3. *Utopia hunters.* (1984)
4. *The darkling wind.* (1985)

CHRONICLES OF THE KEEPER (Bernard King)

1. *Destroying angel.* (1987)
2. *Time-fighters.* (1987)
3. *Skyfire.* (1988)

CHRONICLES OF THE KING'S TRAMP (Tom De Haven)

1. *Walker of worlds.* (1990)
2. *The end-of-everything man.* (1991)

CHRONICLES OF THE TWELVE KINGDOMS (Esther M. Friesner)

1. *Mustapha and his wise dog.* (1985)
2. *Spells of mortal weaving.* (1986)
3. *The witchwood cradle.* (1987)
4. *The water king's laughter.* (1989)

CHRONICLES OF THE VAMPIRES (Anne Rice)

1. *Interview with the vampire: a novel.* (1976)
2. *The vampire Lestat.* (1985)
3. *The queen of the damned.* (1988)

CHRONICLES OF TINTAGEL (Rebecca Brandewyne)

1. *Passion moon rising.* (1988)
2. *Beyond the starlit frost.* (1991)

CHRONICLES OF TORNOR (Elizabeth A. Lynne)

1. *Watchtower.* (1979)
2. *The dancers of Arun.* (1979)
3. *The northern girl.* (1980)

CHRONIQUE D'AVEBURY (Adrienne Martine-Barnes)

1. *The fire sword.* (1984)
2. *The crystal sword.* (1988)
3. *The rainbow sword.* (1988)
4. *The sea sword.* (1989)

CHRONOPLANE WARS (Crawford Kilian)

1. *The empire of time.* (1978)
2. *The fall of the republic.* (1987)
3. *Rogue emperor.* (1988)

CHTHON (Piers Anthony)

1. *Chthon.* (1967)
2. *Phthor.* (1975)

PIERS ANTHONY'S WORLD OF CHTHON

1. *Plasm.* [Charles Platt]. (1987)
2. *Soma.* [Charles Platt]. (1989)

CHUCK NORRIS & THE KARATE KOMMANDOS (Larry Weinberg)

1. *Menace in space.* (1986)
2. *Island of the walking dead.* (1986)

CHUNG KUO (David Wingrove)

1. *The middle kingdom.* (1989)
2. *The broken wheel.* (1990)
3. *The white mountain.* (1991)

CINEVERSE CYCLE (Craid Shaw Gardner)

1. *Slaves of the volcano god.* (1989)
2. *Bride of the slime monster.* (1990)
3. *Revenge of the fluffy bunnies.* (1990)
1-3. *The Cineverse cycle.* (1991)

CINGULUM (John Maddox Roberts)

1. *The Cingulum.* (1985)
2. *Cloak of illusion.* (1985)
3. *The sword, the jewel, and the mirror.* (1988)

CIPOLA SEQUENCE (Chris Beebee)

1. *The hub.* (1987)
2. *The main event.* (1989)

CIRCLE OF LIGHT [ATLANTEAN EARTH] (Niel Hancock)

1. *Greyfax Grimwald.* (1977)
2. *Faragon Fairingay.* (1977)
3. *Calix Stay.* (1977)
4. *Squaring the Circle.* (1977)

WILDERNESS OF FOUR

1. *Across the far mountain.* (1982)
2. *The plains of the sea.* (1982)
3. *On the boundaries of bleakness.* (1982)
4. *The road to the Middle Islands.* (1983)

WINDAMEIR CIRCLE

1. *The fires of Windameir.* (1985)
2. *The sea of silence.* (1987)
3. *A wanderer's return.* (1988)
4. *The bridge of dawn.* (1991)

Associated Titles

Dragon winter. (1978)

CIRCLE OF MAGIC (Debra Doyle & James D. Macdonald)

1. *School of wizardry.* (1990)
2. *Tournament and tower.* (1990)
3. *City by the sea.* (1990)
4. *The prince's players.* (1990)
5. *The prisoners of Bell Castle.* (1990)
6. *The high king's daughter.* (1990)

CIRCUIT (Melinda M. Snodgrass)

1. *Circuit.* (1986)
2. *Circuit breaker.* (1987)
3. *Final circuit.* (1988)

CIRCUS (Barry B. Longyear)

1. *City of Baraboo.* (1980)

2. *Circus world.* (1980)
3. *Elephant song.* (1982)

CITIES IN FLIGHT (James Blish)

1. *They shall have stars.* (1956)
2. *A life for the stars.* (1962)
3. *Earthman, come home.* (1955)
4. *The triumph of time.* (1958)
1-2. *Cities in flight, volume 1.* (1991)
1-4. *Cities in flight.* (1970)
3-4. *Cities in flight, volume 2.* (1991)

CITY JITTERS (Christopher Fowler)

1. *City jitters.* (1986)
2. *More city jitters.* (1988)

CITY OF SHADOWS (Simon Farrell & Jon Sutherland)

1. *Coreus the prince.* (1987)
2. *Bardik the thief.* (1987)

CLAUDIA & EVAN (Betty Levin)

1. *The sword of Culann.* (1973)
2. *A griffon's nest.* (1975)
3. *The forespoken.* (1976)

CLAUDINE ST. CYR AND CROYD (Ian Wallace)

CLAUDINE ST. CYR SERIES

1. *Dr. Orpheus.* (1968)
2. *Deathstar voyage.* (1969)
3. *The purloined prince.* (1971)
4. *The sign of the mute Medusa.* (1977)
5. *Heller's leap.* (1979)

CROYD

1. *Croyd.* (1967)
2. *Dr. Orpheus.* (1968)
3. *Deathstar voyage.* (1969)
4. *A voyage to Dari.* (1974)
5. *Z-sting.* (1978)
6. *Heller's leap.* (1979)
7. *The Lucifer comet.* (1980)
8. *Megalomania.* (1989)

PAN SAGITTARIUS

1. *Deathstar voyage.* (1969)
2. *Pan Sagittarius.* (1973)
3. *A voyage to Dari.* (1974)
4. *The world asunder.* (1976)

CLERIC QUINTET—SEE: FORGOTTEN REALMS FANTASY ADVENTURE

CLOAKMASTER CYCLE (various authors)

1. *Spelljammer: Beyond the moons.* [David Cook]. (1991)
2. *Spelljammer: Into the void.* [Nigel Findley]. (1991)

CLOUD VALLEY (Robert Leeson)

1. *Landing in Cloud Valley.* (1991)
2. *Fire on the cloud.* (1991)

CLUSTER (Piers Anthony)

1. *Cluster.* (1977)
1A. *Vicinity cluster.* (1979)
2. *Chaining the lady.* (1978)
3. *Kirlian quest.* (1978)
4. *Thousandstar.* (1980)
5. *Viscous circle.* (1982)

C.L.U.T.Z. (Marilyn Z. Wilkes)

1. *C.L.U.T.Z.* (1982)
2. *C.L.U.T.Z. and the fizzion formula.* (1985)

COBRA (Timothy Zahn)

1. *Cobra.* (1985)
2. *Cobra strike.* (1986)
3. *Cobra bargain.* (1988)

COCOON (David Saperstein)

1. *Cocoon: a novel.* (1985)
2. *Metamorphosis.* (1988)

COLD CASH WAR (Robert Lynn Asprin and others)

1. *Cold cash war.* (1977)

Associated Title

2. *Combat command in the world of Robert Asprin's Cold cash war: Cold cash warrior.* [Robert Lynn Asprin and Bill Fawcett]. (1989)

COLOSSUS (D. F. Jones)

1. *Colossus.* (1966)
2. *The fall of Colossus.* (1974)
3. *Colossus and the crab.* (1977)

COLSEC TRILOGY (Douglas Hill)

1. *Exiles of ColSec.* (1984)
2. *The caves of Klydor.* (1984)
3. *ColSec rebellion.* (1985)

COMBAT COMMAND (various authors)

1. *Combat command in the world of Piers Anthony's Bio of a space tyrant: Cut by emerald.* [Dana Kramer]. (1987)
2. *Combat command in the world of Robert A. Heinlein's Starship troopers: Shines the name.* [Mark Acres]. (1987)
3. *Combat command in the world of Keith Laumer's Star colony: The Omega rebellion.* [Troy Denning]. (1987)
4. *Combat command in the world of David Drake's Hammer's Slammers: Slammers down!* [Todd Johnson]. (1988)
5. *Combat command in the world of Jack Williamson's The legion of space: The legion of war.* [Andrew Keith]. (1988)
6. *Combat command in the world of Roger Zelazny's Nine princes in Amber: The black road war.* [Neil Randll]. (1988)

7. *Combat command in the world of Jerry E. Pournelle's Janissaries: Lord of lances.* [Mark Acres]. (1988)
8. *Dorsai's command.* [Troy Denning & Gordon R. Dickson & Cory Glaberson]. (1989)
9. *Combat command in the world of Robert Asprin's Cold cash war: Cold cash warrior.* [Robert Lynn Asprin & Bill Fawcett]. (1989)

COMBAT HEROES (Joe Dever)

1. *White warlord.* WHITE WARLORD #1. (1986)
2. *Black baron.* WHITE WARLORD #2. (1986)
3. *Emerald enchanter.* EMERALD ENCHANTER #1. (1986)
4. *Scarlet sorcerer.* EMERALD ENCHANTER #2. (1986)

COMMONWEALTH SERIES—SEE: THRANX SERIES

COMPANIONS OF DOCTOR WHO—SEE: DOCTOR WHO

CONAN SERIES (various authors; by publication date)

Red nails. [Robert E. Howard]. (1975)
The tower of the elephant. [Robert E. Howard]. (1975)
A witch shall be born. [Robert E. Howard]. (1975)
The devil in iron. [Robert E. Howard]. (1976)
Rogues in the house. [Robert E. Howard]. (1976)
Conan of Aquilonia. [Lin Carter & Robert E. Howard & L. Sprague de Camp]. (1977)
Conan: the hour of the dragon. [Robert E. Howard]. (1977)
Conan: the people of the black circle. [Robert E. Howard]. (1977)
Conan and the sorcerer. [Andrew J. Offutt]. (1978)
Conan the swordsman. [Lin Carter & L. Sprague de Camp & Bjorn Nyberg]. (1978)
Queen of the black coast. [Robert E. Howard]. (1978)
Conan the liberator. [Lin Carter & L. Sprague de Camp]. (1979)
Conan: The road of kings. [Karl Edward Wagner]. (1979)
Conan: The sword of Skelos. [Andrew J. Offutt]. (1979)
Conan and the spider god. [L. Sprague de Camp] (1980)
Conan the rebel. [Poul Anderson]. (1980)
The treasure of Tranicos. [L. Sprague de Camp & Robert E. Howard]. (1980)
Conan: The flame knife. [L. Sprague de Camp & Robert E. Howard]. (1981)
Conan the barbarian. [Lin Carter & L. Sprague de Camp]. (1982)
Conan the defender. [Robert Jordan]. (1982)
Conan the invincible. [Robert Jordan]. (1982)
Conan the triumphant. [Robert Jordan]. (1983)
Conan the unconquered. [Robert Jordan]. (1983)
Conan the destroyer. [Robert Jordan]. (1984)
Conan the magnificent. [Robert Jordan]. (1984)
Conan the victorious. [Robert Jordan]. (1984)
Conan the undaunted. [James M. Ward]. (1984)
Conan and the prophecy. [Roger E. Moore]. (1984)
Conan the outlaw. [Roger E. Moore]. (1984)
Conan the valorous. [John Maddox Roberts]. (1985)
Conan the fearless. [Steve Perry]. (1986)
Conan the raider. [Leonard Carpenter]. (1986)
Conan the renegade. [Leonard Carpenter]. (1986)

The pool of the black one. [Robert E. Howard]. (1986)
Conan the champion. [John Maddox Roberts]. (1987)
Conan the marauder. [John Maddox Roberts]. (1988)
Conan the valiant. [Roland Green]. (1988)
Conan the warlord. [Leonard Carpenter]. (1988)
The Conan chronicles. [Lin Carter & Robert E. Howard & L. Sprague de Camp]. (1989)
Conan the bold. [John Maddox Roberts]. (1989)
Conan the hero. [Leonard Carpenter]. (1989)
Conan the indomitable. [Steve Perry]. (1989)
The Conan chronicles 2. [Lin Carter & Robert E. Howard & L. Sprague de Camp]. (1990)
Conan the great. [Leonard Carpenter]. (1989) (i.e., (1990))
Conan the formidable. [Steve Perry]. (1990)
Conan the free lance. [Steve Perry]. (1990)
Conan the guardian. [Roland Green]. (1991)
Conan the outcast. [Leonard Carpenter]. (1991)
Conan the rogue. [John Maddox Roberts]. (1991)

Parodies and Pastiches

The black sorcerer of the Black Castle. [Andrew J. Offutt]. (1976)
The leopard of Poitain. [Raul Garcia Capella]. (1985)

CONCORDAT (Jefferson P. Swycaffer)

1. *Become the hunted.* (1985)
2. *Not in our stars.* (1984)
3. *The universal prey.* (1985)
4. *The Praesidium of Archive.* (1986)

CONJURERS (David Gurney)

1. *The conjurers.* (1972)
2. *The devil in the Atlas: a study of modern satanism.* (1976)

CONSHELF TEN (Monica Hughes)

1. *Crisis on Conshelf Ten.* (1975)
2. *Earthdark.* (1977)

CONTACT AND COMMUNE (L. Neil Smith)

1. *Contact and commune.* (1990)
2. *Converse and conflict.* (1990)

CONTAINER (J. R. Sanders)

1. *The container is ready.* (1988?)
2. *The intergalactic express.* (1988)

CONTRIBUTIONS TO THE STUDY OF SCIENCE FICTION AND FANTASY (various authors)

1. *The mechanical god: machines in science fiction.* [Thomas P. Dunn and Richard D. Erlich]. (1982)
2. *Comic tones in science fiction: the art of compromise with nature.* [Donald M. Hassler]. (1982)
3. *Formula fiction? an anatomy of American science fiction, 1930-1940.* [Frank Cioffi]. (1982)
4. *The intersection of science fiction and philosophy: critical studies.* [Robert E. Myers]. (1983)

5. *H. P. Lovecraft: a critical study.* [Donald R. Burleson]. (1983)
6. *A literary symbiosis: science fiction/fantasy mystery.* [Hazel Beasley Pierce]. (1983)
7. *Clockwork worlds: mechanized environments in SF.* [Thomas P. Dunn and Richard D. Erlich]. (1983)
8. *Apertures: a study of the writings of Brian W. Aldiss.* [Brian Griffin and David Wingrove]. (1984)
9. *The dark barbarian: the writings of Robert E. Howard.* [Don Herron]. (1984)
10. *The scope of the fantastic: theory, practice, major authors: selected essays from the First International Conference on the Fantastic in Literature and Film.* [Robert A. Collins and Howard D. Pearce]. (1985)
11. *The scope of the fantastic: culture, biography, themes, children's literature: selected essays from the First International Conference on the Fantastic in Literature and Film.* [Robert A. Collins and Howard D. Pearce]. (1985)
12. *The transcendant adventure: studies of religion in science fiction/fantasy.* [Robert Reilly]. (1985)
13. *Death and the serpent: immortality in science fiction and fantasy.* [Donald M. Hassler and Carl B. Yoke]. (1985)
14. *The return from Avalon: a study of the Arthurian legend in modern fiction.* [Raymond H. Thompson]. (1985)
15. *The comedy of the fantastic: ecological perspectives on the fantasy novel.* [Don D. Elgin]. (1985)
16. *Some kind of paradise: the emergence of American science fiction.* [Thomas D. Clareson]. (1985)
17. *The unexpected universe of Doris Lessing.* [Katherine Fishburn]. (1985)
18. *Erotic universe: sexuality and fantastic literature.* [Donald Palumbo]. (1986)
19. *Aspects of fantasy: selected essays from the Second International Conference on the Fantastic in Literature and Film.* [William Coyle]. (1986)
20. *Forms of the fantastic: selected essays from the Third International Conference on the Fantastic in Literature and Film.* [Jan Hokenson and Howard D. Pearce]. (1986)
21. *Eros in the mind's eye: sexuality and the fantastic in art and film.* [Donald Palumbo]. (1986)
22. *Worlds within women: mythology and mythmaking in fantastic literature by women.* [Thelma J. Shinn]. (1986)
23. *Merlin's daughters: contemporary women writers of fantasy.* [Charlotte Spivack]. (1987)
24. *Reflections on the fantastic: selected essays from the Fourth International Conference on the Fantastic in the Arts.* [Michael R. Collings]. (1986)
25. *Foundations of science fiction: a study in imagination and evolution.* [John J. Pierce]. (1987)
26. *Eclipse of uncertainty: an introduction to postmodern fantasy.* [Lance Olsen]. (1987)
27. *Alien to femininity: speculative fiction and feminist theory.* [Marleen S. Barr]. (1987)
28. *The fantastic in world literature and the arts.* [Donald E. Morse]. (1987)
29. *Great themes of science fiction.* [John J. Pierce]. (1987)
30. *Phoenix from the ashes: the literature of the remade world.* [Carl B. Yoke]. (1987)
31. *Spectrum of the fantastic: selected essays from the Sixth International Conference on the Fantastic in the Arts.* [Donald Palumbo]. (1988)
32. *"A better country": the worlds of religious fantasy and science fiction.* [Martha C. Sammons]. (1988)
33. *The way to ground zero: the atomic bomb in American science fiction.* [Martha Bartter]. (1988)
34. *The legacy of Olaf Stapledon: critical essays and an unpublished manuscript.* [Olaf Stapledon; edited by Charles Elkins, Patrick A. McCarthy, and Martin Harry Greenberg]. (1989)
35. *Welsh Celtic myth in modern fantasy.* [C. W. Sullivan, III]. (1989)
36. *Strange shadows: the uncollected fiction and essays of Clark Ashton Smith.* [Clark Ashton Smith]. (1989)
37. *When world views collide: a study in imagination and evolution.* [John J. Pierce]. (1989)
38. *From satire to subversion: the fantasies of James Branch Cabell.* [James D. Riemer]. (1989)
39. *The shape of the fantastic: selected essays from the Seventh International Conference on the Fantastic in the Arts.* [Olena H. Saciuk]. (1990)
40. *The poetic fantastic: studies in an evolving genre.* [Vernon Hyles and Patrick D. Murphy]. (1989)
41. *Contours of the fantastic: selected essays from the Eighth International Conference on the Fantastic in the Arts.* [Michele K. Langford]. (1990)
42. *In the image of God: theme, characterization, and landscape in the fiction of Orson Scott Card.* [Michael R. Collings]. (1990)
43. *The Connecticut Yankee in the twentieth century: travel to the past in science fiction.* [Bud Foote]. (1991)
44. *The reclamation of a queen: Guinevere in modern fantasy.* [Barbara Ann Gordon-Wise]. (1991)
45. *More real than reality: the fantastic in Irish literature and the arts.* [Csilla Bertha and Donald E. Morse]. (1991)
46. *Seven masters of supernatural fiction.* [Edward Wagenknecht]. (1991)
47. *Out of the night and into the dream: a thematic study of the fiction of J. G. Ballard.* [Gregory Stephenson]. (1991)

THE COOP (Walter Wangerin, Jr.)

1. *The book of the dun cow.* (1978)
2. *The book of sorrows.* (1985)

CORAMONDE (Brian Daley)

1. *The doomfarers of Coramonde.* (1977)
2. *The starfollowers of Coramonde.* (1979)

CORD—SEE: THE ALIEN TRACE

CORMAC MAC ART (Robert E. Howard and others)

1. *The mists of doom.* [Andrew Offutt]. (1977)
2. *The tower of death.* [[Andrew Offutt & Keith Taylor]. (1982)
3. *When death birds fly.* [Andrew Offutt & Keith Taylor]. (1980)
4. *Tigers of the sea.* [Robert E. Howard]. (1974)
5. *Cormac mac Art: Sword of the Gael.* [Andrew Offutt]. (1975)
6. *The undying wizard.* [Andrew Offutt]. (1976)
7. *The sign of the moonbow.* [Andrew Offutt]. (1977)

Unnumbered Title

Hawks of Outremer. [Robert E. Howard]. (1979)

COUNTDOWN WORLD WAR III (W. X. Davies)

1. *Operation North Africa.* (1984)
2. *Operation Black Sea.* (1984)
3. *Operation choke point.* (1984)
4. *Operation Persian Gulf.* (1984)

COUNTER FORCE (Dan Streib)

1. *Counter Force.* (1983)
2. *The Trident hijacking.* (1983)
3. *Death shuttle.* (1983)
4. *The karate killers.* (1983)
5. *Terror for sale.* (1984)
6. *Titans duel.* (1984)
7. *The mind breakers.* (1984)
8. *The bloody rose.* (1985)

COUNTER FORCE (Ian Cameron & George Erskine)

Beware the Tektrons. (1988)
Find the Tektrons. (1988)
The official Counter Force reference book. (1986)

COVEN (Edward Lee)

1. *Coven.* (1991)
2. *Incubi.* (1991)

COVEN TREE (Bill Brittain)

1. *Devil's donkey.* (1981)
2. *The wish giver: three tales of Coven Tree.* (1983)
3. *Dr. Dredd's wagon of wonders.* (1987)
4. *Professor Popkin's prodigious Polish.* (1990)

COYOTE JONES (Suzette Haden Elgin)

1. *The Communipaths.* (1970)
2. *Furthest.* (1971)
3. *At the Seventh Level.* (1972)
4. *Star anchored, star angered.* (1979)
5. *Yonder comes the other end of time.* (1986)
1-3. *Communipath worlds.* (1980)

CRABS (Guy N. Smith)

1. *Night of the crabs.* (1976)
2. *Killer crabs.* (1978)
3. *The origin of the crabs.* (1979)
4. *Crabs on the rampage.* (1981)
5. *Crabs moon.* (1984)
6. *Crabs: The human sacrifice.* (1988)

CRIMSON CHALICE (Vincent Canning)

1. *The crimson chalice.* (1976)
2. *The circle of the gods.* (1977)
3. *The immortal wound.* (1978)
1-3. *The crimson chalice trilogy.* (1980)

CRIMSON CRYSTAL ADVENTURE—SEE: ENDLESS QUEST CRIMSON CRYSTAL ADVENTURE

CRISIS OF EMPIRE (various authors)

1. *An honorable defense.* [David Drake & Thomas T. Thomas]. (1988)
2. *Cluster command.* [William C. Dietz & David Drake]. (1989)

3. *The war machine.* [Roger MacBride Allen & David Drake]. (1989)

CROSS OF FRANKENSTEIN—SEE: FRANKENSTEIN

CROSSROADS ADVENTURES

Deryni challenge: a Crossroads adventure in the world of Katherine Kurtz's Deryni. [Stephen Billias]. (1988)
Dragonfire: a Crossroads adventure in the world of Anne McCaffrey's Pern. [Jody Lynn Nye]. (1988)
Dragonharper: a Crossroads adventure in the world of Anne McCaffrey's Pern. [Jody Lynn Nye]. (1987)
Dzurlord: a Crossroads adventure in the world of Steven Brust's Jhereg. [Mark Bloom & Bill Scammell & Evan Jamieson & Lisa Hunt & Walter Hunt & Richard S. Meyer & Christine Ivey as ARCHITECTS ADVENTURE]. (1987)
Encyclopedia of Xanth: a Crossroads adventure in the world of Piers Anthony's Xanth. [Jody Lynn Nye]. (1987)
Ghost of a chance: a Crossroads adventure in the world of Piers Anthony's Xanth. [Jody Lynn Nye]. (1988)
Prospero's island: a Crossroads adventure in the world of L. Sprague de Camp and Fletcher Pratt's The incomplete enchanter. (Harold Shea series). [Tom Wham]. (1987)
Revolt on Majipoor: a Crossroads adventure in the world of Robert Silverberg's Majipoor. [Matthew J. Costello as MATT COSTELLO]. (1987)
Seven no-trump: a Crossroads adventure in the world of Roger Zelazny's Amber. [Neil Randall]. (1988)
Storm of dust: a Crossroads adventure in the world of David Drake's Dragon lord. [Neil Randall]. (1987)
Warhorn: a Crossroads adventure in the world of Lynn Abbey's Rifkind, daughter of the bright moon. [Dana Kramer]. (1987)
A warlock's blade: a Crossroads adventure in the world of Christopher Stasheff's Warlock of Gramarye. [Mark C. Perry & Megahn Perry]. (1987)
The witchfires of Leth: a Crossroads adventure in the world of C. J. Cherryh's Morgaine. [Dan Greenburg]. (1987)

CROWN JEWELS (Walter Jon Williams)

1. *The crown jewels.* (1987)
2. *House of shards.* (1988)

CROYD SERIES—SEE: CLAUDINE ST. CYR

THE COLOUR OUT OF SPACE (H. P. Lovecraft and others)

The Dunwich horror, and others; the best supernatural stories of H. P. Lovecraft. (1963)
retitled: *The colour out of space, and others.* (1964)
Color out of time. [Michael Shea]. (1984)

CRYSTAL CURTAIN (Sandy Bayer)

1. *The crystal curtain.* (1988)
2. *The crystal cage.* (1991)

CRYSTAL WARRIORS (William R. Forstchen & Greg Morrison)

1. *The crystal warriors.* (1988)
2. *The crystal sorcerers.* (1991)

CTHULHU MYTHOS (various authors)
[SEE ALSO: TITUS CROW SERIES (Brian Lumley)]

   Dagon. [Fred Chappell]. (1968)
   Cthulhu: tales of the Cthulhu Mythos. [Jon M. Harvey]. (1976)
   The disciples of Cthulhu. [Edward P. Berglund]. (1976)
   The horror on the beach: a tale in the Cthulhu Mythos. [Alan Dean Foster]. (1978)
   Strange eons. [Robert Bloch]. (1978)
   Mysteries of the worm: all the Cthulhu Mythos stories of Robert Bloch. [Robert Bloch]. (1981)
   The Arkham evil. [John Diaper]. (1983)
   Death in Dunwich. [Edward Wimble]. (1983)
   Pursuit to Kadath. [John Diaper & Bob Gallagher]. (1983)
   Tide of desire. [Sheena Clayton]. (1983)
   Hero of dreams. [Brian Lumley; Dreamlands #1.]. (1986)
   Fat face. [Michael Shea]. (1987)
   The Fred Chappell reader. [Fred Chappell]. (1987)
   Elysia: the coming of Cthulhu. [Brian Lumley]. (1989)
   The heart of R'Lyeh. [Hieronymous Kitsch]. (1989)

THE CULTURE (Iain M. Banks)

1. *Consider Phlebas.* (1987)
2. *The player of games.* (1988)
3. *The state of the art.* (1989)
4. *Use of weapons.* (1990)

CUNNINGHAM & BLACK (G. C. Edmondson & C. M. Kotlan)

1. *The Cunningham equations.* (1986)
2. *The black magician.* (1986)
3. *Maximum effort.* (1987)

CUPID DELANEY (Ellen Leroe)

1. *Have a heart, Cupid Delaney.* (1986)
2. *Meet your match, Cupid Delaney.* (1990)

CV (Damon Knight)

1. *CV.* (1985)
2. *The observers.* (1988)
3. *A reasonable world.* (1991)

CYBERNARC (various authors as ROBERT CAIN)

1. *Cybernarc.* [William H. Keith Jr.]. (1991)
2. *Gold dragon.* [William H. Keith Jr.]. (1991)

CYBERNETIC (Victor Milán)

1. *The cybernetic samurai.* (1985)
2. *The cybernetic shôgun.* (1990)

CYBERSTEALTH (S. N. Lewitt)

1. *Cyberstealth.* (1989)

2. *Dancing vac.* (1990)

CYBORG—SEE: SIX MILLION DOLLAR MAN

CYBORG COMMANDO (Kim Mohan & Pamela O'Neill)

1. *Planet in peril.* (1987)
2. *Chase into space.* (1988)
3. *The ultimate prize.* (1988)

CYCLE OF FIRE (Janny Wurts)

1. *Stormwarden.* (1984)
2. *Keeper of the keys.* (1988)
3. *Shadowfane.* (1988)

CYTEEN (C. J. Cherryh)

1. *Cyteen.* (1988)
1A. *Cyteen: The betrayal.* (1989)
1B. *Cyteen: The rebirth.* (1989)
1C. *Cyteen: The vindication.* (1989)

D'ALEMBERT FAMILY—SEE: FAMILY D'ALEMBERT

DAEDALUS (Brian M. Stableford)

1. *The florians.* (1976)
2. *Critical threshold.* (1977)
3. *Wildeblood's empire.* (1977)
4. *The city of the Sun.* (1978)
5. *Balance of power.* (1979)
6. *The paradox of the Sets.* (1979)

DAGMAR SCHULTZ (Lynn Hall)

1. *The secret life of Dagmar Schultz.* [not SF].
2. *Dagmar Schultz and the Angel Edna.* (1989)
3. *Dagmar Schultz and the powers of darkness.* (1989)

DAHLGREN (Phyllis Gotlieb)

1. *O master Caliban!: a novel.* (1976)
2. *Heart of red iron.* (1989)

DAILY LIVES IN NGHSI-ALTAI (various authors)

1. *Arrival.* [Robert Nichols]. (1977)
2. *Gahr City.* [Robert Nichols]. (1978)
3. *The Harditts in Sawna.* [Robert Nichols]. (1979)
4. *Exile.* [Robert Nichols]. (1979)

Associated Title

   Red shift: an introduction to Ngshi-Altai. [Robert Nichols & Peter Schumann]. (1977)

DALEMARK (Diana Wynne Jones)

1. *Cart & Cwidder.* (1975)
2. *Drowned Ammet.* (1977)
3. *The spellcoats.* (1979)

DAMAR (Robin McKinley)

1. *The hero and the crown.* (1985)
2. *The Blue Sword.* (1982)

DAMIANO DELSTREGO (R. A. MacAvoy)

1. *Damiano.* (1984)
2. *Damiano's lute.* (1984)
3. *Raphael.* (1984)
1-3. *A trio for lute.* (1985)

DANANS (Keith Taylor)

1. *The sorcerers' sacred isle.* (1989)
2. *The cauldron of plenty.* (1989)
3. *Search for the starblade.* (1990)

DANCE (Björn Kurtén)

1. *Dance of the tiger.* (1980)
2. *Singletusk.* (1986)

DANCE OF THE GODS (Mayer Alan Brenner)

1. *Catastrophe's spell.* (1989)
2. *Spell of intrigue.* (1990)

DANCER TRILOGY (Ann Maxwell)

1. *Fire dancer.* (1982)
2. *Dancer's luck.* (1983)
3. *Dancer's illusion.* (1983)

DANCERS AT THE END OF TIME (Michael Moorcock)

1. *An alien heat.* (1972)
2. *The hollow lands.* (1974)
3. *The end of all songs.* (1976)
4. *Legends from the end of time.* (1976)
5. *The transformation of Miss Mavis Ming.* (1977)
5A. *A messiah at the end of time.* (1978)
1-3. *The dancers at the end of time.* (1981)

DANCING GODS (Jack L. Chalker)

1. *The River of Dancing Gods.* (1984)
2. *Demons of the Dancing Gods.* (1984)
3. *Vengeance of the Dancing Gods.* (1985)
4. *Songs of the Dancing Gods.* (1990)

DANIEL RIDER (Gregory Maguire)

1. *Lightning time.* (1978)
2. *Lights on the lake.* (1981)

DANNUS (Mike Sirota)

1. *The prisoner of Reglathium.* (1978)
2. *The conquerors of Reglathium.* (1978)
3. *The caves of Reglathium.* (1978)
4. *Dark straits of Reglathium.* (1978)
5. *Slaves of Reglathium.* (1978)

DANNY DUNN (Raymond Abrashkin & Jay Williams)

1. *Danny Dunn and the anti-gravity paint.* (1956)
2. *Danny Dunn on a desert island.* (1957)
3. *Danny Dunn and the homework machine.* (1958)
4. *Danny Dunn and the weather machine.* (1959)
5. *Danny Dunn on the ocean floor.* (1960)
6. *Danny Dunn and the fossil cave.* (1961)
7. *Danny Dunn and the heat ray.* (1962)
8. *Danny Dunn, time traveller.* (1963)
9. *Danny Dunn and the automatic house.* (1965)
10. *Danny Dunn and the voice from space.* (1967)
11. *Danny Dunn and the smallifying machine.* (1969)
12. *Danny Dunn and the swamp monster.* (1971)
13. *Danny Dunn, invisible boy.* (1974)
14. *Danny Dunn, scientific detective.* (1975)
15. *Danny Dunn and the universal glue.* (1977)

DANNY ONE (Alfred Slote)

1. *My robot buddy.* (1975)
2. *My trip to Alpha I.* (1978)
3. *C.O.L.A.R.: a tale of outer space.* (1981)
4. *Omega Station.* (1983)
5. *The trouble on Janus.* (1985)

DARK AGES (Kathleen Herbert)

1. *Queen of the lightning.* (1983)
2. *Ghost in the sunlight.* (1986)
3. *Bride of the spear.* (1988)

DARK ANGEL (Jean Graham)

1. *Dark angel.* (1977)
2. *Dark lord.* (1980)

DARK BORDER (Paul Edwin Zimmer)

1. *The lost prince.* (1982)
2. *King Chondos' ride.* (1982)
3. *A gathering of heroes.* (1987)

DARK CASTLE (Tanith Lee)

1. *The Castle of Dark.* (1978)
2. *Prince on a white horse.* (1982)

DARK CONSPIRACY (Michael Stackpole)

1. *A gathering evil.* (1991)
2. *Evil ascending.* (1991)

DARK ELF TRILOGY—SEE: FORGOTTEN REALMS FANTASY ADVENTURE

DARK FORCES (various authors)

1. *The game.* [Les Logan]. (1983)
2. *Magic show.* [Laurie Bridges and Paul Alexander]. (1983)
3. *The doll.* [Rex Sparger]. (1983)
4. *Devil wind.* [Laurie Bridges and Paul Alexander]. (1983)
5. *The bargain.* [Rex Sparger]. (1983)
6. *Swamp witch.* [Laurie Bridges and Paul Alexander]. (1983)
7. *Unnatural talent.* [Les Logan]. (1983)
8. *The companion.* [Scott Siegel]. (1983)
9. *Eyes of the tarot.* [Bruce Coville]. (1983)
10. *Beat the devil.* [Scott Siegel]. (1983)
11. *Waiting spirits.* [Bruce Coville]. (1984)
12. *The Ashton horror.* [Laurie Bridges]. (1984)
13. *The curse.* [Larry Weinberg]. (1984)
14. *Blood sport.* [R. C. Scott]. (1984)
15. *The charming.* [Jane Polcovar]. (1984)

DARK FUTURE SERIES (various authors)

Dark future: Route 666. [David Pringle]. (1990)

Dark future: Ghost dancers. [Brian Stableford as BRIAN CRAIG]. (1991)

DEMON DOWNLOAD (Kim Newman as JACK YEOVIL)

1. *Demon download.* (1990)
2. *Krokodil tears.* (1991)
3. *Comeback tour: (the sky belongs to the stars).* (1991)

DARK HORSE (Mary H. Herbert)

1. *Dark horse.* (1990)
2. *Lightning's daughter.* (1991)

DARK IS RISING (Susan Cooper)

1. *Over sea, under stone.* (1965)
2. *The dark is rising.* (1973)
3. *Greenwitch.* (1974)
4. *The grey king.* (1975)
5. *Silver on the tree.* (1977)
1-5. *The dark is rising sequence.* (1984)

DARK TOWER (Stephen King)

1. *The gunslinger.* (1982)
2. *The drawing of the three.* (1987)
3. *The waste lands.* (1991)

DARKEST AMERICA (Neal Barrett Jr.)

1. *Through darkest America.* (1986)
2. *Dawn's uncertain light.* (1989)

DARKNESS (Frank E. Peretti)

1. *This present darkness.* (1986)
2. *Piercing the darkness.* (1989)

DARKOVER SERIES. (Marion Zimmer Bradley)

Reading Order

1. *Darkover landfall.* (1972)
2. *The spell sword.* (1974)
3. *Star of danger.* (1965)
4. *The winds of Darkover.* (1970)
5. *The bloody sun.* (1964)
6. *The heritage of Hastur.* (1975)
7. *The Sword of Aldones.* (1962)
8. *The planet savers.* (1962)
9. *The world wreckers.* (1971)

Publication Order

The shattered chain: a Darkover novel. (1976)
The forbidden tower: a Darkover novel. (1977)
Stormqueen! A Darkover novel. (1978)
The bloody sun. (1979)
The bloody sun; and, "To keep the oath". (1979)
The planet savers; The sword of Aldones. (1980)
Two to conquer. (1980)
Sharra's exile. (1981)
Children of Hastur: The heritage of Hastur; Sharra's exile. (1982)
Hawkmistress!. (1982)
Thendara House. (1983)
City of sorcery. (1984)
Oath of the renunciates. (1984)

The heirs of Hammerfell. (1989)

DARKOVER ANTHOLOGIES (with the Friends of Darkover)

The Keeper's price, and other stories. (1980)
Sword of chaos, and other stories. (1982)
The other side of the mirror, and other Darkover stories. (1987)
Red sun of Darkover. (1987)
Four moons of Darkover. (1988)
Leroni of Darkover. (1991)
Renunciates of Darkover. (1991)

DARKSWORD TRILOGY (Tracy Hickman & Margaret Weis)

1. *Forging the darksword.* (1988)
2. *Doom of the darksword.* (1988)
3. *Triumph of the darksword.* (1988)
1-3. *The Darksword trilogy.* (1989)

DARKWAR TRILOGY (Glen Cook)

1. *Doomstalker.* (1985)
2. *Warlock.* (1985)
3. *Ceremony.* (1986)

DARKWORLD DETECTIVE: KAMUS OF KADHIZHAR (Michael Reaves & others)

1. *Darkworld detective.* (1982)
2. *Kamus of Kadizhar: The black hole of Carcosa: a tale of the Darkworld detective.* [By John Shirley]. (1988)

DARWATH TRILOGY (Barbara Hambly)

1. *The time of the Dark.* (1982)
2. *The walls of air.* (1983)
3. *The armies of daylight.* (1983)

DAUGHTER OF TINTAGEL (Fay Sampson)

1. *The wise woman's telling.* (1989)
2. *The white nun's telling.* (1989)
3. *Black smith's telling.* (1990)
4. *Taliesin's telling.* (1991)

DAVID SULLIVAN (Tom Deitz)

1. *Windmaster's bane.* (1986)
2. *Fireshaper's doom: a tale of vengeance.* (1987)
3. *Darkthunder's way.* (1989)
4. *Sunshaker's war: a tale of David Sullivan.* (1990)
5. *Stoneskin's revenge: a tale of Calvin McIntosh.* (1991)

DAVY (Edgar Pangborn)

1. *Davy.* (1964)
2. *The judgment of Eve.* (1966)
3. *The company of glory.* (1975)
4. *Still I persist in wondering.* (1978)

DAYBREAK (Colin Greenland)

1. *Daybreak on a different mountain: a fantasy novel.* (1984)
2. *The hour of the thin ox.* (1987)
3. *Other voices.* (1988)

3.   *High Deryni.* (1973)
1-3.   *The chronicles of the Deryni: Deryni Rising; Deryni checkmate; High Deryni.* (1985)

CAMBER OF CULDI

1.   *Camber of Culdi.* (1976)
2.   *Saint Camber.* (1978)
3.   *Camber the heretic.* (1981)

THE HISTORIES OF KING KELSON

1.   *The bishop's heir.* (1984)
2.   *The king's justice.* (1985)
3.   *The quest for Saint Camber.* (1986)

THE HEIRS OF SAINT CAMBER

1.   *The harrowing of Gwynedd.* (1989)

ASSOCIATED TITLES

The Deryni archives. [Katherine Kurtz]. (1986)
Deryni challenge: a Crossroads adventure in the world of Katherine Kurtz's Deryni. [Stephen Billias]. (1988)

DESTINY MAKERS (Mike Shupp)

1.   *With fate conspire.* (1985)
2.   *Morning of creation.* (1986)
3.   *Soldier of another fortune.* (1988)
4.   *Death's gray land.* (1991)
5.   *The last reckoning.* (1991)

DESTROYER (various writers as Warren Murphy & Richard Sapir)

1.   *Created, the Destroyer.* (1971)
2.   *Death check.* (1972)
3.   *Chinese puzzle.* (1972)
4.   *Mafia fix.* (1972)
5.   *Dr. Quake.* (1972)
6.   *Death therapy.* (1972)
7.   *Union bust.* (1973)
8.   *Summit chase.* (1973)
9.   *Murder's shield.* (1973)
10.   *Terror squad.* (1973)
11.   *Kill or cure.* (1973)
12.   *Slave safari.* (1973)
13.   *Acid rock.* (1973)
14.   *Judgment day.* (1974)
15.   *Murder ward.* (1974)
16.   *Oil slick.* (1974)
17.   *Last war dance.* (1974)
18.   *Funny money.* (1975)
19.   *Holy terror.* (1975)
20.   *Assassins play-off.* (1975)
21.   *Deadly seeds.* (1975)
22.   *Brain drain.* (1976)
23.   *Child's play.* (1976)
24.   *King's curse.* (1976)
25.   *Sweet dreams.* (1976)
26.   *In enemy hands.* (1977)
27.   *The last temple.* (1977)
28.   *Ship of death.* (1977)
29.   *The final death.* (1977)
30.   *Mugger blood.* (1977)
31.   *The head men.* (1977)
32.   *Killer chromosomes.* (1978)

33.   *Voodoo die.* (1978)
34.   *Chained reaction.* (1978)
35.   *Last call.* (1978)
36.   *Power play.* (1979)
37.   *Bottom line.* (1979)
38.   *Bay city blast.* (1979)
39.   *Missing link.* (1980)
40.   *Dangerous games.* (1980)
41.   *Firing line.* 1980)
42.   *Timber line.* (1980)
43.   *Midnight man.* (1981)
44.   *Balance of power.* (1981)
45.   *Spoils of war.* (1981)
46.   *Next of kin.* (1981)
47.   *Dying space.* (1982)
48.   *Profit motive.* (1982)
49.   *Skin deep.* (1982)
50.   *Killing time.* (1982)
51.   *Shock value.* (1983)
52.   *Fool's gold.* (1983)
53.   *Time trial.* (1983)
54.   *Last drop.* (1983)
55.   *Master's challenge.* (1984)
56.   *Encounter group.* (1984)
57.   *Date with death.* (1984)
58.   *Total recall.* (1984)
59.   *The arms of Kali.* (1984)
60.   *The end of the game.* (1985)
61.   *Lords of the Earth.* (1985)
62.   *The seventh stone.* (1985)
63.   *The sky is falling.* (1986)
64.   *The last alchemist.* (1986)
65.   *Lost yesterday.* (1986)
66.   *Sue me.* (1986)
67.   *Look into my eyes.* (1987)
68.   *An old-fashioned war.* (1987)
69.   *Blood ties.* (1987)
70.   *The eleventh hour.* (1987)
71.   *Return engagement.* (1988)
72.   *Sole survivor.* (1988)
73.   *Line of succession.* (1988)
74.   *Walking wounded.* (1988)
75.   *Rain of terror.* (1989)
76.   *The final crusade.* (1989)
77.   *Coin of the realm.* (1989)
78.   *Blue smoke and mirrors.* (1989)
79.   *Shooting schedule.* (1990)
80.   *Death sentence.* (1990)
81.   *Hostile takeover.* (1990)
82.   *Survival course.* (1990)
83.   *Skull duggery.* (1991)
84.   *Ground zero.* (1991)
85.   *Blood lust.* (1991)
86.   *Arabian nightmare.* (1991)

Associated Titles

The assassin's handbook. [edited (and written) by Will Murray]. (1982)
retitled: *Inside Sinanju.* [edited (and written) by Will Murray]. (1985)
Remo: the adventure begins: a novel. (1985)

DEVERRY (Katharine Kerr)

1.   *Daggerspell.* (1986)
2.   *Darkspell.* (1987)
3.   *The bristling wood.* (1989)
3A.   *Dawnspell: The bristling wood.* (1989)
4.   *The dragon revenant.* (1990)

4A. *Dragonspell: the southern sea.* (1990)
5. *A time of exile: a novel of the Westlands.* (1991)

DEVILGOD (Collins Jallim)

1. *The devilgod.* (1985)
2. *The devilgod in the empire of the universal master.* (1989)

DEWEY ANNALS (Chet Hagan)

1. *Bon marché.* (1988)
2. *From the ashes.* (1989)

DEXTRA—SEE: BREAKOUT

DIADEM (Jo Clayton)

1. *Diadem from the stars.* (1977)
2. *Lamarchos.* (1978)
3. *Irsud.* (1978)
4. *Maeve.* (1979)
5. *Star hunters.* (1980)
6. *The Nowhere Hunt.* (1981)
7. *Ghosthunt.* (1983)
8. *The snares of Ibex.* (1984)
9. *Quester's endgame.* (1986)
10. *Shadowplay.* SHADITH'S QUEST #1. (1990)
11. *Shadowspeer.* SHADITH'S QUEST #2. (1990)
12. *Shadowkill.* SHADITH'S QUEST #3. (1991)

DIANA SANTEE (Sharon Green)

1. *Mind guest.* (1984)
2. *Gateway to Xanadu.* (1985)

DIANA TREGARDE (Mercedes Lackey)

1. *Burning water.* (1989)
2. *Children of the night.* (1990)
3. *Jinx High.* (1991)

DIDO TWITE (Joan Aiken)

1. *The wolves of Willoughby Chase.* (1962)
2. *Black hearts in Battersea.* (1964)
3. *Nightbirds on Nantucket.* (1966)
4. *The stolen lake.* (1981)
5. *The cuckoo tree.* (1971)
6. *Dido and Pa.* (1986)
7. *The whispering mountain.* (1968)

DILVISH THE DAMNED (Roger Zelazny)

1. *The bells of Shoredan.* (1979)
2. *The changing land.* (1981)
3. *Dilvish, the Damned.* (1982)

DINOSAUR MACHINES SERIES (Eve Bunting)

The creature of Cranberry Cove. (1976)
The day of the dinosaurs. (1975)
Death of a dinosaur. (1975)
The demon. (1976)
The dinosaur trap. (1975)
Escape from tyrannosaurus. (1975)
The ghost. (1976)
The tongue of the ocean. (1976)

DIRK GENTLY (Douglas Adams)

1. *Dirk Gently's holistic detective agency.* (1987)
2. *The long dark tea-time of the soul.* (1988)

DIRK PITT (Clive Cussler)

1. *Pacific vortex!* (1983)
2. *The Mediterranean caper.* (1973)
2A. *Mayday!* (1978)
3. *Iceberg.* (1975)
4. *Raise the Titanic!* (1976)
5. *Vixen 03.* (1978)
6. *Night probe!* (1981)
7. *Deep six: a novel.* (1984)
8. *Cyclops: a novel.* (1986)
9. *Treasure: a novel.* (1988)
10. *Dragon: a novel.* (1990)

DIRSHAN (Gene Lancour)

1. *The Lerios mecca.* (1973)
2. *The war machines of Kalinth.* (1977)
3. *Sword for the empire.* (1978)
4. *The man-eaters of Cascalon.* (1979)

DISCWORLD (Terry Pratchett)

1. *The colour of magic.* (1983)
2. *The light fantastic.* (1986)
3. *Equal rites.* (1987)
4. *Mort.* (1987)
5. *Sourcery.* (1988)
6. *Wyrd sisters.* (1988)
7. *Pyramids: the book of going forth.* (1989)
8. *Guards! guards!* (1989)
9. *Moving pictures.* (1990)
10. *Reaper man.* (1991)
11. *Faust Eric.* [with Josh Kirby]. (1991)
12. *Witches abroad.* (1991)

DOC SAVAGE (various authors as KENNETH ROBESON)

1. *The man of bronze.* (1964)
2. *The Thousand-Headed Man.* (1964)
3. *Meteor menace.* (1964)
4. *The polar treasure.* (1965)
5. *Brand of the werewolf.* (1965)
6. *The lost oasis.* (1965)
7. *The monsters.* (1965)
8. *The land of terror.* (1965)
9. *The Mystic Mullah.* (1965)
10. *The Phantom City.* (1966)
11. *Fear Cay.* (1966)
12. *Quest of Qui.* (1966)
13. *Land of always-night.* (1966)
14. *The fantastic island.* (1966)
15. *Murder melody.* (1967)
16. *The spook legion.* (1967)
17. *The red skull.* (1967)
18. *The Sargasso Ogre.* (1967)
19. *Pirate of the Pacific.* (1967)
20. *The secret in the sky.* (1967)
21. *Cold death.* (1968)
20-21. *The secret in the sky; and, Cold death: two complete adventures in one volume.* (1982)
22. *The czar of fear.* (1968)
23. *Fortress of Solitude.* (1968)
22-23. *The Czar of fear; and, Fortress of Solitude: two complete adventures in one volume.* (1982)
24. *The green eagle.* (1968)

25. *The devil's playground.* (1968)
24-25.   *Doc Savage: The green eagle; and, The devil's playground: two complete adventures in one volume.* (1983)
26. *Death in silver.* (1968)
27. *Mystery under the sea.* (1968)
26-27.   *Doc Savage: Death in silver; and, Mystery under the sea: two complete adventures in one volume.* (1983)
28. *The deadly dwarf.* (1968)
29. *The other world.* (1968)
30. *The flaming falcons.* (1968)
31. *The Annihilist.* (1968)
32. *Dust of death.* (1969)
33. *The terror in the Navy.* (1969)
34. *Mad eyes.* (1969)
35. *The Squeaking Goblin.* (1969)
36. *Resurrection day.* (1969)
37. *Hex.* (1969)
38. *Red snow.* (1969)
39. *World's Fair goblin.* (1969)
40. *The dagger in the sky.* (1969)
41. *Merchants of disaster.* (1969)
42. *The gold ogre.* (1969)
43. *The man who shook the Earth.* (1969)
44. *The sea magician.* (1970)
45. *The men who smiled no more.* (1970)
46. *The Midas man.* (1970)
47. *Land of long juju.* (1970)
48. *The Feathered Octopus.* (1970)
49. *The Sea Angel.* (1970)
50. *Devil on the Moon.* (1970)
51. *Haunted ocean.* (1970)
52. *The vanisher.* (1970)
53. *The mental wizard.* (1970)
54. *He could stop the world.* (1970)
55. *The golden peril.* (1970)
56. *The giggling ghosts.* (1971)
57. *Poison island.* (1971)
58. *The munitions master.* (1971)
59. *The yellow cloud.* (1971)
60. *The Majii.* (1971)
61. *The living-fire menace.* (1971)
62. *The pirate's ghost.* (1971)
63. *The submarine mystery.* (1971)
64. *The motion menace.* (1971)
65. *The green death.* (1971)
66. *Mad Mesa.* (1972)
67. *The freckled shark.* (1972)
68. *Quest of the Spider.* (1972)
69. *The mystery on the snow.* (1972)
70. *Spook Hole.* (19772)
71. *Murder mirage.* (1972)
72. *The Metal Master.* (1973)
73. *The seven agate devils.* (1973)
74. *The derrick devil.* (1973)
75. *The land of fear.* (1973)
76. *The black spot.* (1974)
77. *The South Pole terror.* (1974)
78. *The crimson serpent.* (1974)
79. *The devil Genghis.* (1974)
80. *The king maker.* (1975)
81. *The stone man.* (1976)
82. *The evil gnome.* (1976)
83. *The red terrors.* (1976)
84. *The mountain monster.* (1976)
85. *The boss of terror.* (1976)
86. *The angry ghost.* (1977)
87. *The spotted men.* (1977)
88. *The Roar Devil.* (1977)

89. *The magic island.* (1977)
90. *The flying goblin.* (1977)
91. *The Purple Dragon.* (1978)
92. *The awful egg.* (1978)
93. *Tunnel terror.* (1979)
94. *The hate genius.* (1979)
95. *The red spider.* (1979)
96. *Mystery on Happy Bones.* (1979)
97-98.   *Satan black; and, Cargo unknown.* (1980)
99-100.   *Hell below; and, The lost giant.* (1980)
101-102. *The pharaoh's ghost; and, The time terror.* (1981)
103-104. *The whisker of Hercules; and, The man who was scared.* (1981)
105-106. *They died twice; and, The screaming man.* (1981)
107-108. *Jiu San; and, The black, black witch.* (1981)
109-110. *The shape of terror; and, Death had yellow eyes.* (1982)
111-112. *One-eyed mystic; and, The man who fell up.* (1982)
113-114. *The talking devil; and, The ten ton snakes.* (1982)
115-116. *Pirate isle; and, The speaking stone.* (1983)
117-118. *The golden man; and, Peril in the north.* (1984)
119-120. *The laugh of death; and, The king of terror.* (1984)
121-122. *The three wild men; and, The fiery menace.* (1984)
123-124. *Devils of the deep; and, The headless men.* (1984)
125-126. *The goblins; and, The secret of the Su.* (1985)
127-130. *The all-white elf; The running skeletons; The angry canary; and The swooning lady.* (1986)
131-134. *The mindless monsters; The rustling death; King Joe Cay; The thing that pursued.* (1987)
135-138. *The spook of Grandpa Eben; Measures for a coffin; The three devils; Strange fish.* (1987)
139-142. *Mystery island; Men of fear; Rock sinister; The pure evil.* (1987)
143-147. *No light to die by; The monkey suit; Let's kill Ames; Once over lightly; I died yesterday.* (1988)
148-151. *The awful dynasty; The magic forest; Fire and ice; The disappearing lady.* (1988)
152-155. *The men vanished; Five fathoms dead; The terrible stork; Danger lies east.* (1988)
156-159. *The mental monster; The pink lady; Weird valley; Trouble on parade.* (1989)
160-163. *The invisible-B murders; Birds of death; The wee ones; Terror takes 7.* (1989)
164-167. *The devil's black rock; Waves of death; The too-wise owl; Terror and the lonely widow.* (1989)
168-172. *Se-Pah-Poo; Colors for murder; Three times a corpse; Death is a round black spot; The devil is Jones.* (1990)
173-177. *Bequest of evil; Death in little houses; Target for death; The death lady; The exploding lake.* (1990)
178-182. *The derelict of Skull Shoal; Terror wears no shoes; The green master; Return from Cormoral; Up from Earth's center.* (1990)
183. *Escape from Loki: Doc Savage's first adventure.* [Philip José Farmer]. (1991)
184. *Python Isle.* [Will Murray *as* Kenneth Robeson]. (1991)

Pastiches and Associated Titles

Doc Savage, the supreme adventurer. [John L. Nanovic]. (1980)

The incredible radio exploits of Doc Savage, volume 1. [Lester Dent; only volume published]. (1982)
The invincible Doc Savage. [Ed Gruskin]. (1983)
The crazy Indian. [William G. Bogart]. (1987)

DOCTOR STRANGE—SEE: MARVEL SUPERHEROES

DOCTOR WHO (various authors)

Note: The Doctor Who books were originally issued as unnumbered volumes until #81 (1983). The first eighty volumes in the series have been assigned numbers below that correspond to publication order. In the last few years a number of these books have been reissued with reinserted numbers that appear to have no correspondence either with the original publication order or the order in which the original TV episodes were aired. These have been indicated in the body of the entry as alternative series numbers.

1. *Doctor Who in an exciting adventure with the Daleks.* [David Whitaker]. (1964)
2. *Doctor Who and the Zarbi.* [Bill Strutton]. (1965)
2A. *Doctor Who: The web planet.* [Bill Strutton]. (1991). [reissued as #73]
3. *Doctor Who and the crusaders.* [David Whitaker]. (1965)
4. *Doctor Who and the cave monsters.* [Malcolm Hulke]. (1974)
5. *Doctor Who and the Auton invasion.* [Terrance Dicks]. (1974)
5A. *Doctor Who: The auton invasion.* [Terrance Dicks]. (1991)
6. *Doctor Who and the doomsday weapon.* [Malcolm Hulke]. (1974)
7. *Doctor Who and the day of the Daleks.* [Terrance Dicks]. (1974)
7A. *Doctor Who: The day of the Daleks.* [Terrance Dicks]. (1991). [reissued as #18]
8. *Doctor Who and the Daemons.* [Barry Letts]. (1974)
9. *Doctor Who and the Sea-Devils.* [Malcolm Hulke]. (1974)
10. *Doctor Who and the abominable snowmen.* [Terrance Dicks]. (1974)
11. *Doctor Who and the curse of Peladon.* [Brian Hayles]. (1974)
12. *Doctor Who and the Cybermen.* [Gerry Davis]. (1974)
13. *Doctor Who and the giant robot.* [Terrance Dicks]. (1975)
14. *Doctor Who and the terror of the Autons.* [Terrance Dicks]. (1975)
15. *Doctor Who and the green death.* [Malcolm Hulke]. (1975)
16. *Doctor Who and the planet of the spiders* [Terrance Dicks]. (1975)
16A. *Doctor Who: The planet of the spiders.* [Terrance Dicks]. (1991). [reissued as #48]
17. *Doctor Who and the three doctors.* [Terrance Dicks]. (1975). [reissued as #64]
18. *Doctor Who and the Loch Ness monster.* [Terrance Dicks]. (1976)
19. *Doctor Who and the tenth planet.* [Gerry Davis]. (1976)
20. *Doctor Who and the dinosaur invasion.* [Malcolm Hulke]. (1976)
21. *Doctor Who and the ice warriors.* [Brian Hayles]. (1976)
22. *Doctor Who and the revenge of the Cybermen.* [Terrance Dicks]. (1976)

22A. *Doctor Who: The revenge of the Cybermen.* [Terrance Dicks]. (1991). [reissued as #51]
23. *Doctor Who and the genesis of the Daleks.* [Terrance Dicks]. (1976)
24A. *Doctor Who: The genesis of the Daleks.* [Terrance Dicks]. (1991)
24. *Doctor Who and the web of fear.* [Terrance Dicks]. (1976)
25. *Doctor Who and the space war.* [Malcolm Hulke]. (1976)
26. *Doctor Who and the planet of the Daleks.* [Terrance Dicks]. (1976)
27. *Doctor Who and the Pyramids of Mars.* [Terrance Dicks]. (1976)
28. *Doctor Who and the carnival of monsters.* [Terrance Dicks]. (1977)
29. *Doctor Who and the seeds of doom.* [Philip Hinchcliffe]. (1977)
30. *Doctor Who and the Dalek invasion of Earth.* [Terrance Dicks]. (1977)
30A. *Doctor Who: The Dalek invasion of Earth.* [Terrance Dicks]. (1990)
31. *Doctor Who and the claws of Axos.* [Terrance Dicks]. (1977)
32. *Doctor Who and the brain of Morbius.* [Terrance Dicks]. (1977)
32A. *Doctor Who: The brain of Morbius.* [Terrance Dicks]. (1991)
33. *Doctor Who and the planet of evil.* [Terrance Dicks]. (1977)
34. *Doctor Who and the mutants.* [Terrance Dicks]. (1977)
35. *Doctor Who and the deadly assassin.* [Terrance Dicks]. (1977)
36. *Doctor Who and the talons of Weng-Chiang.* [Terrance Dicks]. (1977)
37. Doctor Who and the masque of Mandragora. [Philip Hinchcliffe]. (1977)
37A. *Doctor Who: The masque of Mandragora.* [Philip Hinchcliffe]. (1991). [reissued as #42]
38. *Doctor Who and the face of evil.* [Terrance Dicks]. (1978)
39. *Doctor Who and the horror of Fang Rock.* [Terrance Dicks]. (1978)
40. *Doctor Who and the tomb of the cybermen.* [Gerry Davis]. (1978)
43. *Doctor Who and the android invasion.* [Terrance Dicks]. (1978)
44. *Doctor Who and the Sontaran experiment.* [Ian Marter]. (1978)
41. *Doctor Who and the time warrior.* [Terrance Dicks]. (1978)
42. Doctor Who and death to the Daleks. [Terrance Dicks]. (1978). [reissued as #20]
43. *Doctor Who and the android invasion.* [Terrance Dicks]. (1978)
44. *Doctor Who and the Sontaran experiment.* [Ian Marter]. (1978)
45. *Doctor Who and the hand of fear.* [Terrance Dicks]. (1979)
46. *Doctor Who and the invisible enemy.* [Terrance Dicks]. (1979)
47. *Doctor Who and the robots of death.* [Terrance Dicks]. (1979)
48. *Doctor Who and the image of the Fendahl.* (1979)
49. *Doctor Who and the war games.* [Malcolm Hulke]. (1979). [reissued as #70]
50. *Doctor Who and the destiny of the Daleks.* [Terrance Dicks]. (1979)

51. *Doctor Who and the Ribos operation.* [Ian Marter]. (1979)
52. *Doctor Who and the ark in space.* [Ian Marter]. (1977)
52A. *Doctor Who: The ark in Space.* [Ian Marter]. (1991)
53. *Doctor Who and the underworld.* [Terrance Dicks]. (1980)
54. *Doctor Who and the invasion of time.* [Terrance Dicks]. (1980)
55. *Doctor Who and the stones of blood.* [Terrance Dicks]. (1980)
56. *Doctor Who and the androids of Tara.* [Terrance Dicks]. (1980)
57. *Doctor Who and the power of Kroll.* [Terrance Dicks]. (1980)
58. *Doctor Who and the armageddon factor.* [Terrance Dicks]. (1980)
59. *Doctor Who and the keys of Marinus.* [Philip Hinchcliffe]. (1980)
60. *Doctor Who and the nightmare of Eden.* [Terrance Dicks]. (1980). [reissued as #45]
61. *Doctor Who and the horns of Nimon.* [Terrance Dicks]. (1980)
62. *Doctor Who and the monster of Peladon.* [Terrance Dicks]. (1980)
63. *Doctor Who and the creature from the pit.* [David Fisher]. (1981)
64. *Doctor Who and the enemy of the world.* [Ian Marter]. (1981)
65. *Doctor Who and an unearthly child.* [Terrance Dicks]. (1981)
65A. *Doctor Who: An unearthly child.* [Terrance Dicks]. (1990). [reissued as #68]
66. *Doctor Who and the state of decay.* [Terrance Dicks]. (1982)
67. *Doctor Who and the warriors' gate.* [Stephen Gallagher as JOHN LYDECKER]. (1982)
68. *Doctor Who and the Keeper of Traken.* [Terrance Dicks]. (1982)
69. *Doctor Who and the Leisure Hive.* [David Fisher]. (1982)
70. *Doctor Who and the visitation.* [Eric Saward]. (1982)
71. *Doctor Who: Full circle.* [Andrew Smith]. (1982)
72. *Doctor Who and the sunmakers.* [Terrance Dicks]. (1982)
73. *Doctor Who: Logopolis.* [Christopher H. Bidmead]. (1982)
74. *Doctor Who: Time flight.* [Peter Grimwade]. (1983)
75. *Doctor Who: Meglos.* [Terrance Dicks]. (1983)
76. *Doctor Who: Castrovalva.* [Christopher H. Bidmead]. (1983)
77. *Doctor Who: four to doomsday.* [Terrance Dicks]. (1983)
78. *Doctor Who: Earthshock.* [Ian Marter]. (1983)
79. *Doctor Who: Terminus.* [Stephen Gallagher as JOHN LYDECKER]. (1983)
80. *Doctor Who: Arc of infinity.* [Terrance Dicks]. (1983)
81. *Doctor Who: The five doctors.* [Terrance Dicks]. (1983)
82. *Doctor Who: Mawdryn undead.* [Peter Grimwade]. (1983)
83. *Doctor Who: Snakedance.* [Terrance Dicks]. (1984)
84. *Doctor Who: Kinda.* [Terrance Dicks]. (1983)
85. *Doctor Who: Enlightenment.* [Barbara Clegg]. (1984)
86. *Doctor Who: The dominators.* [Ian Marter]. (1984)
87. *Doctor Who: Warriors of the deep.* [Terrance Dicks]. (1984)

88. *Doctor Who: The Aztecs.* [John Lucarotti]. (1984)
89. *Doctor Who: Inferno.* [Terrance Dicks]. (1984)
90. *Doctor Who: The Highlanders.* [Gerry Davis]. (1984)
91. *Doctor Who: Frontios.* [Christopher H. Bidmead]. (1984)
92. *Doctor Who: The caves of Androzani.* [Terrance Dicks]. (1984)
93. *Doctor Who: Planet of fire.* [Peter Grimwade]. (1984)
94. *Doctor Who: Marco Polo.* [John Lucarotti]. (1984)
95. *Doctor Who: The awakening.* [Eric Pringle]. (1985)
96. *Doctor Who: The mind of evil.* [Terrance Dicks]. (1985)
97. *Doctor Who: The myth makers.* [Donald Cotton]. (1985)
98. *Doctor Who: The invasion.* [Ian Marter]. (1985)
99. *Doctor Who: The Krotons.* [Terrance Dicks]. (1985)
100. *Doctor Who: The two doctors.* [Robert Holmes]. (1985)
101. *Doctor Who: The gunfighters.* [Donald Cotton]. (1985)
102. *Doctor Who: The time monster.* [Terrance Dicks]. (1985)
103. *Doctor Who: The twin dilemma.* [Eric Saward]. (1985)
104. *Doctor Who: Galaxy Four.* [William Emms]. (1985)
105. *Doctor Who: Timelash.* [Glen McCoy]. (1985)
106. *Doctor Who: Vengeance on Varus.* [Philip Martin]. (1988)
107. *Doctor Who: The mark of the Rani.* [Jane Baker & Pip Baker]. (1986)
108. *Doctor Who: The king's demons.* [Terence Dudley]. (1986)
109. *Doctor Who: The savages.* [Ian Stuart Black]. (1986)
110. *Doctor Who: Fury from the deep.* [Victor Pemberton]. (1986)
111. *Doctor Who: The Celestial Toymaker.* [Alison Bingeman & Gerry Davis]. (1986)
112. *Doctor Who: The seeds of death.* [Terrance Dicks]. (1986)
113. *Doctor Who: Black orchid.* [Terence Dudley]. (1986)
114. *Doctor Who: The Ark.* [Paul Erickson]. (1986)
115. *Doctor Who: The mind robber.* [Peter Ling]. (1986)
116. *Doctor Who: The faceless ones.* [Terrance Dicks]. (1986)
117. *Doctor Who: Slipback.* [Eric Saward]. (1986)
118. *Doctor Who: The sensorites.* [Nigel Robinson]. (1987)
119. *Doctor Who: The reign of terror.* [Ian Marter]. (1987)
120. *Doctor Who: The Romans.* [Donald Cotton]. (1987)
121. *Doctor Who: The ambassadors of death.* [Terrance Dicks]. (1987)
122. *Doctor Who: The massacre.* [John Lucarotti]. (1987)
123. *Doctor Who: The Macra terror.* [Ian Stuart Black]. (1987)
124. *Doctor Who: The rescue.* [Ian Marter]. (1987)
125. *Doctor Who: Terror of the Vervoids.* [Jane Baker & Pip Baker]. (1987)
126. *Doctor Who: The time meddler.* [Nigel Robinson]. (1987)
127. *Doctor Who: Time and the Rani.* [Jane Baker & Pip Baker]. (1987)
128. *Doctor Who: Mysterious planet.* [Terrance Dicks]. (1987)
129. *Doctor Who: The underwater menace.* [Nigel Robinson]. (1988)

130. *Doctor Who: The wheel in space.* [Terrance Dicks]. (1988)
131. *Doctor Who: The ultimate foe.* [Jane Baker & Pip Baker]. (1988)
132. *Doctor Who: The edge of destruction.* [Nigel Robinson]. (1988)
133. *Doctor Who: The smugglers.* [Terrance Dicks]. (1988)
134. *Doctor Who: Paradise Towers.* [Stephen Wyatt]. (1988)
135. *Doctor Who: Delta and the Bannerman.* [Malcolm Kohill]. (1989)
136. *Doctor Who: The war machines.* [Ian Stuart Black]. (1988)
137. *Doctor Who: Dragonfire.* [Ian Briggs]. (1989)
138. *Doctor Who: Attack of the cybermen.* [Eric Saward]. (1989)
139. *Doctor Who: Trial of a time lord: mindwarp.* [Philip Martin]. (1989)
140. *Doctor Who: The chase.* [John Peel]. (1989)
141. *Doctor Who: The Daleks' master plan, part 1: Mission to the unknown.* [John Peel]. (1989)
142. *Doctor Who: The Daleks' master plan, part II: The mutation of time.* [John Peel]. (1989)
143. *Doctor Who: Silver nemesis.* [Kevin Clarke]. (1989)
144. *Doctor Who: The greatest show in the galaxy.* [Stephen Wyatt]. (1989)
145. *Doctor Who: Planet of giants.* [Terrance Dicks]. (1990)
146. *Doctor Who: The happiness patrol.* [Graeme Curry]. (1989)
147. *Doctor Who: The space pirates.* [Terrance Dicks]. (1990)
148. *Doctor Who: Remembrance of the Daleks.* [Ben Aaronovitz]. (1990)
149. *Doctor Who: Ghost light.* [Marc Platt]. (1990)
150. *Doctor Who: Survival.* [Rona Munro]. (1990)
151. *Doctor Who: The curse of Fenric.* [Ian Briggs]. (1990)
152. *Doctor Who: Battlefield.* [Marc Platt]. (1991)
153. *Doctor Who: The Pescatons.* [Victor Pemberton]. (1991)

Associated Titles

The adventures of Doctor Who: Doctor Who and the genesis of the Daleks; Doctor Who and the revenge of the cybermen; Doctor Who and the Loch Ness monster. [Terrance Dicks]. (1979)
The adventures of K9, and other mechanical creatures. [Terrance Dicks]. (1979)
The Doctor Who omnibus. [Terrance Dicks]. (1983)
Doctor Who and the rebel's gamble. [William H. Keith Jr.]. (1986)
Doctor Who and the vortex crystal. [William H. Keith Jr.]. (1986)
The further adventures of Doctor Who: Doctor Who and the deadly assassin; Doctor Who and the face of evil; Doctor Who and the robots of death. [Terrance Dicks]. (1986)
The tribe of Gum. [Anthony Coburn]. (1987)
Doctor Who: The nightmare fair. [Graham Williams]. (1989)
Doctor Who: Ultimate evil. [Wally K. Daly]. (1989)
Doctor Who: Cybermen. [David Banks]. (1990)
Doctor Who: Mission to Magnus. [Philip Martin]. (1990)
The Gallifrey chronicles. [John Peel]. (1991)

PINNACLE BOOKS SERIES

1. *Doctor Who and the day of the Daleks.* [Terrance Dicks]. (1979)
2. *Doctor Who and the doomsday weapon.* [Malcolm Hulke]. (1979)
3. *Doctor Who and the dinosaur invasion.* [Malcolm Hulke]. (1979)
4. *Doctor Who and the genesis of the Daleks.* [Terrance Dicks]. (1979)
5. *Doctor Who and the revenge of the Cybermen.* [Terrance Dicks]. (1979)
6. *Doctor Who and the Loch Ness monster.* [Terrance Dicks]. (1979)
7. *Doctor Who and the talons of Wang-Chiang.* [Terrance Dicks]. (1979)
8. *Doctor Who and the masque of Mandragora.* [Philip Hinchcliffe]. (1979)
9. *Doctor Who and the Android invasion.* [Terrance Dicks]. (1980)
10. *Doctor Who and the seeds of doom.* [Philip Hinchcliffe]. (1980)

DOCTOR WHO CLASSICS

1. *Doctor Who: The dalek invasion of Earth; and, The crusaders.* [Terrance Dicks]. (1988)
2. *Doctor Who: The dominators; and, The Kryptons.* [Ian Marter]. (1988)
3. *Doctor Who: The myth makers; and, The gunfighters.* [Donald Cotton]. (1988)
4. *Doctor Who: The mind of evil; and, The claws of Axos.* [Terrance Dicks]. (1989)
5. *Doctor Who: The Daemons; The time monster.* [Terrance Dicks & Barry Letts]. (1989)
6. *Doctor Who and the seeds of doom; The deadly assassin.* [Philip Hinchcliffe & Terrance Dicks]. (1989)
7. *Doctor Who: The face of evil; and, The sunmakers.* [Terrance Dicks]. (1989)

DOCTOR WHO COMPANIONS

1. *The companions of Doctor Who: Turlough and the Earthlink dilemma.* [Tony Attwood]. (1985)
2. *Harry Sullivan's war.* [Ian Marter]. (1986)
3. *K9 and company.* (1987)

DOCTOR WHO: THE NEW ADVENTURES

1. *Timewyrm: Genesys.* [John Peel]. (1991)
2. *Timewyrm: Exodus.* [Terrance Dicks]. (1991)
3. *Timewyrm: Apocalypse.* [Nigel Robinson]. (1991)
4. *Timewyrm: Revelation.* [Paul Cornell]. (1991)

DOCTOR WHO FIND YOUR FATE—SEE: FIND YOUR FATE—DOCTOR WHO

DOMINIC FLANDRY—SEE: FUTURE HISTORY

DON SEBASTIEN (Les Daniels)

1. *The black castle: a novel of the macabre.* (1978)
2. *The silver skull: a novel of sorcery.* (1979)
3. *Citizen vampire.* (1981)
4. *Yellow fog.* (1986)
5. *No blood spilled.* (1991)

DON'T BITE THE SUN (Tanith Lee)

1. *Don't bite the sun.* (1976)
2. *Drinking sapphire wine.* (1977)
1-2. *Drinking sapphire wine [and, Don't bite the Sun].* (1979)

DOOM-QUEST OF ARA-KARN (Adam Corby)

1. *The former king.* (1981)
2. *The divine queen.* (1982)

DOOMSDAY (James D. Forman)

1. *Call back yesterday.* (1981)
2. *Doomsday plus twelve.* (1984)

DOOMSDAY WARRIOR (Jan Stacy & Ryder Syvertsen as RYDER STACY)

1. *Doomsday warrior.* (1984)
2. *Red America.* (1984)
3. *The last American.* (1984)
4. *Bloody America.* (1985)
5. *America's last declaration.* (1985)
6. *American rebellion.* (1985)
7. *American defiance.* (1986)
8. *American glory.* (1986)
9. *America's zero hour.* (1986)
10. *American nightmare.* (1987)
11. *American Eden.* (1987)
12. *Death, American style.* (1987)
13. *American paradise.* (1988)
14. *American death orbit.* (1988)
15. *American ultimatum.* (1989)
16. *American overthrow.* (1989)
17. *America's sword.* (1990)
18. *American dream machine.* (1990)
19. *America's final defense.* (1991)

DOOMSTAR (Richard S. Meyers)

1. *Doom star.* (1978)
1A. *Doomstar.* (1985)
2. *Doom star, number two.* (1979)
2A. *Return to Doomstar.* (1985)

DORSAI—SEE: CHILDE CYCLE

DOUBLE AGENT BOOK (Richard Merwin & Warren Spector)

1. *Web of danger* / by Aaron Allston ; *Agent 13: Acolytes of darkness* / by Flint Dille & David Marconi. (1988)
2. *The Hollow Earth affair* / by Warren Spector ; *Agents of fortune: the royal pain* / by Richard Merwin. (1988)

DOUBLE-SPIRAL WAR (Warren Norwood)

1. *Midway between.* (1984)
2. *Polar fleet.* (1985)
3. *Final command.* (1986)

DOUGLAS CONVOLUTION (Edward Llewellyn)

1. *The Douglas Convolution.* (1979)
2. *The bright companion.* (1980)
3. *Prelude to chaos.* (1983)

DOWNBELOW STATION (C. J. Cherryh)

1. *Downbelow station.* (1981)
2. *Merchanter's luck.* (1982)
3. *Forty thousand in Gehenna.* (1983)

DR. ADDER (K. W. Jeter)

1. *Dr. Adder.* (1984)
2. *The glass hammer.* (1985)
3. *Death arms.* (1987)

DR. BONES (various authors)

1. *The secret of the Lona.* [Stephen Leigh]. (1988)
2. *The cosmic bomber.* [William F. Wu]. (1989)
3. *Garukan blood.* [Thomas Wylde]. (1989)
4. *The dragons of Komako.* [John Gregory Betancourt]. (1989)
5. *Nightmare world.* [David Stern]. (1989)
6. *Journey to Rilla.* [Thomas Wylde]. (1990)

DR. CASPIAN & BRONWEN (John Burke)

1. *The devil's footsteps.* (1976)
2. *The black charade: a Dr. Caspian story.* (1977)
3. *Ladygrove: the third adventure of Dr Caspian and Bronwen.* (1978)

DR. HOLTON (Charlotte Hunt)

1. *The gilded sarcophagus.* (1967)
2. *The cup of Thanatos.* (1978)
3. *The Lotus vellum.* (1970)
4. *The thirteenth treasure.* (1972)
1-2. *The casebook of Dr. Holton: The gilded sarcophagus and The cup of Thanatos.* (1978)
3-4. *The casebook of Dr. Holton: The Lotus vellum and The thirteenth treasure.* (1978)

DR. JEKYLL & MR. HYDE SEQUELS (various authors)

Frankenstein; Dracula; Dr. Jekyll and Mr. Hyde. [anonymous]. (1978)
The strange case of Dr Jekyll and Mr Hyde, and other stories. [Robert Louis Stevenson]. (1979)
Dr. Jekyll and Mr. Holmes. [Loren D. Estleman as DR. JOHN H. WATSON]. (1979) [See also: SHERLOCK HOLMES]
The strange case of Dr. Jekyll and Mr. Hyde. [Raymond Harris & Robert Louis Stevenson]. (1982)
Dr. Jekyll and Mr. Hyde. [Kate McMullan & Robert Louis Stevenson]. (1984)
Dr. Jekyll and Mr. Hyde. [T. Ernesto Bethancourt & Robert Louis Stevenson]. (1985)
The strange case of Dr. Jekyll and Mr. Hyde. [Joan Cameron & Robert Louis Stevenson]. (1986)
Robert Louis Stevenson's Dr. Jekyll and Mr. Hyde. [Samantha Lee & Robert Louis Stevenson]. (1987)
Dr Jekyll and Mr Hollins. [Willis Hall]. HENRY HOLLINS SERIES. (1988)
Two women of London: the strange case of Ms Jekyll and Mrs Hyde. [Emma Tennant]. (1989)
The Jekyll legacy. [Robert Bloch & Andre Norton]. (1990)
Mary Reilly. [Valerie Martin]. (1990)
Dr Jekyll and Mr Hyde. [Rosemary Border & Robert Louis Stevenson]. (1991)

Associated titles

The definitive Dr. Jekyll and Mr. Hyde companion. [Harry M. Geduld]. (1983)
Dr. Jekyll and Mr. Hyde: after one hundred years. [Gordon Hirsch & William Veeder]. (1988)

DR. NIKOLA (Guy Boothby)

1. *A bid for fortune.* (1895)
1A. *Enter Dr. Nikola!* (1975)
2. *Doctor Nikola.* (1896)
2A. *Dr. Nikola returns.* (1976)
3. *The lust of hate.* (1898)
4. *Dr. Nikola's experiment.* (1899)
5. *'Farewell, Nikola!'* (1899)

DR. ORIENT (Frank Lauria)

1. *Doctor Orient.* (1970)
2. *Raga Six.* (1972)
3. *Lady Sativa.* (1973)
4. *Baron Orgaz.* (1974)
5. *The priestess.* (1978)
6. *The Seth papers.* (1979)
7. *Blue limbo.* (1991)

DRACON (Barry B. Longyear)

1. *Enemy mine.* (1985/1989)
2. *The tomorrow testament.* (1983)

DRACULA CHQVELO (various authors)

Dracula began. [Gail Kimberly]. (1976)
Count Dracula. [Gerald Savory]. (1977)
The blood of Dracula. [Jack Hamilton Tccd]. (1977)
Dracula's daughter. [CARL DREADSTONE]. (1977)
Sherlock Holmes vs. Dracula; or, The adventure of the sanguinary count. [Loren D. Estleman as DR. JOHN H. WATSON]. (1978)
The further perils of Dracula. [Jeanne Youngson]. (1979)
Crimson kisses. [C. Dean Andersson & Nina Romberg *as* ASA DRAKE]. (1981)
Dhampire. [Scott Baker]. (1982)
Prisoner of vampires. [Nancy Garden]. (1984)
The bargain. [Jon Ruddy]. (1990)

DRACULA SERIES (Fred Saberhagen)

1. *The Dracula tape.* (1975)
2. *The Holmes-Dracula file.* (1978)
3. *An old friend of the family.* (1979)
4. *Thorn.* (1980)
5. *Dominion.* (1982)
6. *A matter of taste.* (1990)

DRACULA SERIES (Peter Tremayne)

1. *Dracula unborn.* (1977)
1A. *Bloodright.* (1979)
2. *The revenge of Dracula.* (1978)
3. *Dracula, my love.* (1980)

DRACULA HORROR SERIES (Robert Lory)

1. *Dracula returns.* (1973)
2. *The hand of Dracula.* (1973)
3. *Dracula's brother.* (1973)

4. *Dracula's gold.* (1973)
5. *Drums of Dracula.* (1974)
6. *The witching of Dracula.* (1974)
7. *Dracula's lost world.* (1974)
8. *Dracula's disciple.* (1975)
9. *Challenge to Dracula.* (1975)

DRACULA'S CHILDREN (R. Chetwynd-Hayes)

1. *Dracula's children.* (1987)
2. *The house of Dracula.* (1987)

DRAGON (Piers Anthony & Robert Margroff)

1. *Dragon's gold.* (1987)
2. *Serpent's silver.* (1988)
3. *Chimaera's copper.* (1990)
4. *Orc's opal.* (1990)

DRAGON AND THE GEORGE (Gordon R. Dickson)

1. *The dragon and the George.* (1976)
2. *The dragon knight.* (1990)

DRAGON KING TRILOGY (Stephen Lawhead)

1. *In the hall of the dragon king.* (1982)
2. *The warlords of Nin.* (1983)
3. *The sword and the flame.* (1984)

DRAGON LORD (David Drake and others)

The dragon lord. (1979)

Associated Title

Storm of dust: a Crossroads adventure in the world of David Drake's Dragon lord. [Neil Randall]. (1987)

DRAGON PRINCE (Melanie Rawn)

1. *Dragon prince, book I.* (1988)
2. *The star scroll.* (1989)
3. *Sunrunner's fire.* (1990)

DRAGON WARRIORS (various authors)

1. *Dragon warriors.* [Dave Morris]. (1985)
2. *The way of wizardry.* [Dave Morris]. (1986)
3. *The eleven crystals.* [Oliver Johnson]. (1985)
4. *Out of the shadows.* [Dave Morris]. (1986)
5. *The power of darkness.* [Oliver Johnson]. (1986)
6. *The lands of legend.* [Dave Morris]. (1986)

DRAGONBARDS (Shirley Rousseau Murphy)

1. *Nightpool.* (1985)
2. *The ivory lyre.* (1987)
3. *The dragonbards.* (1988)

DRAGONBOUND (Carl Miller)

1. *Dragonbound.* (1988)
2. *The warrior and the witch.* (1990)
3. *The goblin plain war.* (1991)

DRAGONFALL 5 (Brian Earnshaw)

1. *Dragonfall 5 and the space cowboys.* (1972)

2. *Dragonfall 5 and the Royal Beast.* (1972)
3. *Dragonfall 5 and the empty planet.* (1973)
4. *Dragonfall 5 and the hijackers.* (1974)
5. *Dragonfall 5 and the master mind.* (1975)
6. *Dragonfall 5 and the super horse.* (1977)
7. *Dragonfall 5 and the haunted world.* (1979)

DRAGONLANCE SERIES

Unaffiliated Titles

The Soulforge. [Terry Phillips]. (1985)
Lords of doom: a DragonLance adventure. [Douglas Niles]. (1986)
DragonLance adventures. [Tracy Hickman & Margaret Weis]. (1987)
Brothers Majere. [Kevin Stein]. (1989)

DRAGONLANCE CHRONICLES (Tracy Hickman & Margaret Weis)

1. *Dragons of the autumn twilight.* (1984)
2. *Dragons of the winter night.* (1985)
3. *Dragons of spring dawning.* (1985)
1-3. *DragonLance chronicles.* (1988)

DRAGONLANCE HEROES (various authors)

1. *The legend of Huma.* [Richard A. Knaak]. (1988)
2. *Stormblade.* [Nancy Varian Berberick]. (1988)
3. *Weasel's luck.* (1988)

DRAGONLANCE HEROES II (various authors)

1. *Kaz, the minotaur.* [Richard A. Knaak]. (1990)
2. *The gates of Thorbardin.* [Dan Parkinson]. (1990)
3. *Galen beknighted.* [Michael Williams]. (1990)

DRAGONLANCE LEGENDS (Tracy Hickman & Margaret Weis)

1. *Time of the twins.* (1986)
2. *War of the twins.* (1986)
3. *Test of the twins.* (1986)
1-3. *The DragonLance legends.* (1988)

DRAGONLANCE PRELUDES (various authors)

1. *Darkness & light.* [Tonya R. Carter & Paul B. Thompson]. (1989)
2. *Kendermore.* [Mary L. Kirchoff]. (1989)

DRAGONLANCE PRELUDES II (various authors)

1. *Riverwind the plainsman.* [Tonya R. Carter & Paul B. Thompson]. (1990)
2. *Flint the king.* [Mary L. Kirchoff & Douglas Niles]. (1990)
3. *Tanis, the shadow years.* [Barbara Siegel & Scott Siegel]. (1990)

DRAGONLANCE TALES (Tracy Hickman & Margaret Weis)

1. *The magic of Krynn.* (1987)
2. *Kender, gully dwarves, and gnomes.* (1987)
3. *Love and war.* (1987)
1-3. *DragonLance tales.* (1991)

ELVEN NATIONS TRILOGY (various authors)

1. *Firstborn.* [Tonya R. Carter & Paul B. Thompson]. (1991)
2. *The kinslayer wars.* [Douglas Niles]. (1991)
3. *The Qualinesti.* [Tonya R. Carter & Paul B. Thompson]. (1991)

MEETINGS SEXTET (various authors)

1. *Kindred spirits.* [Mark Anthony & Ellen Porath]. (1991)
2. *Wanderlust.* [Mary L. Kirchoff & Steve Winter]. (1991)

DRAGONREALM (Richard A. Knaak)

1. *Firedrake.* (1989)
2. *Icedragon.* (1989)
3. *Wolfhelm.* (1990)
4. *Shadow steed.* (1990)

DRAGONRIDERS OF PERN—SEE: PERN

DRAGONS (Gary Gentile)

1. *A time for dragons.* (1989)
2. *Dragons past.* (1990)
3. *No future for dragons.* (1990)

DRAGONS (Thorarinn Gunnarsson)

1. *Make way for dragons!* (1990)
2. *Human, beware!* (1990)

DRAGONS (Rhondi Vilott *as* R. A. V. SALSITZ)

1. *Where dragons lie.* (1985)
2. *Where dragons rule.* (1986)
3. *Night of dragons.* (1990)

DRAGON'S EGG (Robert L. Forward)

1. *Dragon's Egg.* (1980)
2. *Starquake.* (1985)

DRAGON'S PAWN (Carol L. Dennis)

1. *Dragon's pawn.* (1987)
2. *Dragon's knight.* (1989)
3. *Dragon's queen.* (1991)

DRAGONSTAR TRILOGY (David F. Bischoff & Thomas F. Monteleone)

1. *Day of the dragonstar.* (1983)
2. *Night of the dragonstar.* (1985)
3. *Dragonstar destiny* (1989)

DRAGONSWORD (Gael Baudino)

1. *Dragon sword, volume I.* (1988)
1A. *Dragonsword.* (1991)
2. *Duel of dragons.* (1991)

DRAKA (S. M. Stirling)

1. *Marching through Georgia.* (1988)
2. *Under the yoke.* (1989)
3. *The stone dogs.* (1990)

DRAY PRESCOT (Kenneth Bulmer as DRAY PRESCOT & ALAN BURT AKERS)

1. *Transit to Scorpio.* (1972)
2. *The suns of Scorpio.* (1973)
3. *Warrior of Scorpio.* (1973)
4. *Swordships of Scorpio.* (1973)
5. *Prince of Scorpio.* (1974)
6. *Manhounds of Antares.* (1974)
7. *Arena of Antares.* (1974)
8. *Fliers of Antares.* (1975)
9. *Bladesman of Antares.* (1975)
10. *Avenger of Antares.* (1975)
11. *Armada of Antares.* (1976)
12. *The tides of Kregen.* (1976)
13. *Renegade of Kregen.* (1976)
14. *Krozair of Kregen.* (1977)
15. *Secret Scorpio.* (1977)
16. *Savage Scorpio.* (1978)
17. *Captive Scorpio.* (1978)
18. *Golden Scorpio.* (1978)
19. *A life for Kregen.* (1979)
20. *A sword for Kregen.* (1979)
21. *A fortune for Kregen.* (1979)
22. *A victory for Kregen.* (1980)
23. *Beasts of Antares.* (1980)
24. *Rebel of Antares.* (1980)
25. *Legions of Antares.* (1981)
26. *Allies of Antares.* (1981)
27. *Mazes of Antares.* (1982)
28. *Delia of Vallia.* (1982)
29. *Fires of Scorpio.* (1983)
30. *Talons of Scorpio.* (1983)
31. *Masks of Scorpio.* (1984)
32. *Seg the bowman.* (1984)
33. *Werewolves of Kregen.* (1985)
34. *Witches of Kregen.* (1985)
35. *Storm over Valla.* (1985)
36. *Omens of Kregen.* (1985)
37. *Warlord of Antares.* (1988)
6-7. *Manhounds of Antares; and, Arena of Antares.* (1981)

DREAD EMPIRE (Glen Cook)

1. *A shadow of all night falling.* (1979)
2. *October's baby.* (1980)
3. *All darkness met.* (1980)
4. *The fire in his hands.* (1984)
5. *With mercy twoard none.* (1985)
6. *Reap the east wind.* (1987)
7. *An ill fate marshalling.* (1988)

DREAM LORDS (Adrian Cole)

1. *A plague of nightmares.* (1975)
2. *Lord of nightmares.* (1975)
3. *Bane of nightmares.* (1976)

DREAM PARK (Steven Barnes & Larry Niven)

1. *Dream Park.* (1981)
2. *The Barsoom project.* (1989)

DREAM QUEST (Lloyd St. Alcorn)

1. *Halberd: dream warrior.* (1987)
2. *On the shoulders of giants.* (1988)
3. *The serpent mound.* (1989)

DREAMERS OF THE DAY (David D. Ross)

1. *The Argus gambit.* (1989)
2. *The eighth rank.* (1991)

DREAMLANDS (Brian Lumley)

1. *Hero of dreams.* (1986)
2. *Ship of dreams.* (1986)
3. *Mad moon of dreams.* (1987)
4. *Iced on Aran, and other dreamquests.* (1990)

DREAMS (W. T. Quick)

1. *Dreams of flesh and sand.* (1988)
2. *Dreams of men and gods.* (1989)
3. *Singularities.* (1990)

DREAMWEAVER (Beth Hilgartner)

1. *Colors in the dreamweaver's loom.* (1989)
2. *The feast of the trickster.* (1991)

DRENAI SAGA—LEGEND TRILOGY (David A. Gemmell)

1. *Legend.* (1986)
1A. *Against the horde.* (1988)
2. *The king beyond the gate.* (1985)
3. *Waylander.* (1986)
4. *Quest for lost heroes.* (1990)
1-3. *Drenai tales.* (1991)

DRINKER OF SOULS (Jo Clayton)

1. *Drinker of souls.* (1986)
2. *Blue magic.* (1988)
3. *A gathering of stones.* (1989)
1-3. *The soul drinker.* (1989)

DRIVE-IN (Joe R. Lansdale)

1. *The drive-in: (a "B" movie with blood and popcorn, made in Texas).* (1988)
2. *The drive-in 2: (not just one of them sequels).* (1989)

DRUMM BOOKLETS (various authors)

1. *[Catalog One].* A dealer's catalog.
2. *A Hal Clement checklist.* [Chris Drumm]. (1983)
3. *A Mack Reynolds checklist: notes toward a bibliography.* [Chris Drumm & George Flynn]. (1983)
4. *A Tom Disch checklist.* [Chris Drumm]. (1983)
5. *An Algis Budrys checklist.* [Chris Drumm]. (1983)
6. *An R. A. Lafferty checklist: a bibliographical chronology with notes and index.* [Chris Drumm]. (1983)
7. *Four stories.* [R. A. Lafferty]. (1983)
8. *A Larry Niven checklist.* [Chris Drumm]. (1983)
9. *Non-literary influences on science fiction.* [Algis Budrys]. (1983)
10. *A John Sladek checklist: pre-publication version.* [Chris Drumm]. (1984)
11. *Laughing Kelly, and other verses.* [R. A. Lafferty]. (1983)
12. *Heart of stone, dear, and other stories.* [R. A. Lafferty]. (1983)
13. *Snake in his bosom, and other stories.* [R. A. Lafferty]. (1983)
14. *It's down the slippery cellar stairs: non-fiction.* [R. A. Lafferty]. (1984)

15. *Love among the Xoids.* [John Sladek]. (1984)
16. *A James Gunn checklist.* [Chris Drumm]. (1984)
17. *Tiger! Tiger!* [James Gunn]. (1984)
18. *The man who made models, and other stories.* [R. A. Lafferty]. (1984)
19. *Slippery, and other stories.* [R. A. Lafferty]. (1985)
20. *Cuts.* [Carter Scholz]. (1985)
21. *The cosmic perspective; and Custer's last stand.* [Brian Stableford]. ()
22. *Leigh Brackett: American writer.* [John L. Carr]. ()
23. *Adventures in the space trade; and A Richard Wilson checklist.* [Richard Wilson; Chris Drumm]. (1986)
24. *My heart leaps up (1920-1928), chapters 1 & 2.* [R. A. Lafferty]. (1986)
25. *J. T. McIntosh: Memoir & bibliography.* [Ian Covell]. (1987)
26. *My heart leaps up (1920-1928), chapters 3 & 4.* [R. A. Lafferty]. (1987)
27. *The kid from Ozone Park & other stories.* [Richard Wilson]. (1987)
28. *My heart leaps up (1920-1928), chapters 5 & 6.* [R. A. Lafferty]. (1987)
29. *My heart leaps up (1920-1928), chapters 7 & 8.* [R. A. Lafferty]. (1988)
30. *The meaning of life and other awesome cosmic revelations: three curious tales.* [Darrell Schweitzer]. (1988)
31. *Skin trades.* [Bruce Boston]. (1988)
32. *The Null-A worlds of A. E. van Vogt.* [H. L. Drake]. (1989)
33. *The many worlds of Larry Niven, 2nd ed.* [Chris Drumm & Paul Guptill]. (1989)
34. *Hypertales and metafictions.* [Bruce Boston]. (1990)
35. *My heart leaps up (1920-1928), chapters 9 & 10.* [R. A. Lafferty]. (1990)
36. *Celestial inventory.* [Steve Rasnic Tem]. (1991)
37. *A Cordwainer Smith checklist.* [Mike Bennett]. (1991)

DUEL OF SORCERY (Jo Clayton)

1. *Moongather.* (1982)
2. *Moonscatter.* (1983)
3. *Changer's moon.* (1985)

DUELMASTER (Mark Smith & Jamie Thomson)

1. *Challenge of the Magi.* (1986)
2. *Blood valley.* (1986). [Both books are listed as #2]
2. *Duelmaster.* (1986). [Both books are listed as #2]
3. *The shattered realm.* (1987)
4. *Arena of death.* (1987)

DUMAREST (E. C. Tubb)

1. *The winds of Gath.* (1967)
1A. *Gath.* (1968)
2. *Derai.* (1968)
3. *Toyman.* (1969)
4. *Kalin.* (1969)
5. *The jester at Scar.* (1970)
6. *Lallia.* (1971)
7. *Technos.* (1972)
8. *Mayenne.* (1973)
9. *Veruchia.* (1973)
10. *Jondelle.* (1973)
11. *Zenya.* (1974)
12. *Eloise.* (1975)
13. *Eye of the zodiac.* (1975)

14. *Jack of Swords.* (1976)
15. *Spectrum of a forgotten sun.* (1976)
16. *Haven of darkness.* (1977)
17. *Prison of night.* (1977)
18. *Incident on Ath.* (1978)
19. *The Quillian Sector.* (1978)
20. *Web of sand.* (1979)
21. *Iduna's universe.* (1979)
22. *The Terra data.* (1980)
23. *World of promise.* (1980)
24. *Nectar of heaven.* (1981)
25. *The Terridae.* (1981)
26. *The Coming Event.* (1982)
27. *Earth is heaven.* (1982)
28. *Melome.* (1983)
29. *Angado.* (1984)
30. *Symbol of Terra.* (1984)
31. *The Temple of truth.* (1985)
9-10. *Mayenne; and, Jondelle.* (1981)
28-29. *Melome; and, Angado.* (1988)
30-31. *Symbol of Terra; and, The temple of truth.* (1989)

DUNCTON CHRONICLES (William Horwood)

1. *Duncton Wood: a novel.* (1980)
2. *Duncton quest.* (1988)
3. *Duncton found.* (1989)
4. *Duncton tales.* (1991)

DUNE (Frank Herbert)

1. *Dune.* (1965)
2. *Dune messiah.* (1969)
3. *Children of Dune.* (1976)
4. *God Emperor of Dune.* (1981)
5. *Heretics of Dune.* (1984)
6. *Chapter house: Dune.* (1985)
6A. *Chapterhouse: Dune.* (1985)
1-3. *The great Dune trilogy.* (1979)
4-6. *The second great Dune trilogy.* (1987)

DUNGEON SERIES—SEE: PHILIP JOSE FARMER'S DUNGEON SERIES

DURDANE (Jack Vance)

1. *The Anome.* (1973)
1A. *The faceless man.* (1978)
2. *The brave free men.* (1973)
3. *The Asutra.* (1974)
1-3. *Durdane.* (1989)

DUSHAU TRILOGY (Jacqueline Lichtenberg)

1. *Dushau.* (1985)
2. *Farfetch.* (1985)
3. *Outreach.* (1986)

DYING EARTH (Jack Vance)

1. *The dying earth.* (1950)
2. *The eyes of the overworld.* (1966)
3. *Morreion.* (1979)
4. *Cugel's saga.* (1983)
5. *Rhialto the Marvellous.* (1984)

Pastiches and Sequels

Nifft the Lean. [Michael Shea]. (1982)

EAGLE (Frances Dorer & Nancy Dorer)

1. *By daybreak the Eagle.* (1980)
2. *Return of the Eagle.* (1980)
3. *The wings of the Eagle.* (1980)

EAGLEHEART (C. T. Westcott)

1. *Silver wings and leather jackets.* (1989)
2. *Broadsides and brass.* (1989)
3. *Blood and bone.* (1989)

EALDWOOD (C. J. Cherryh)

1. *The dreamstone.* (1983)
2. *The tree of swords and jewels.* (1983)
1-2. *Arafel's saga.* (1983)
1-2. *Ealdwood.* (1991)

EARTH INSPECTORS (various authors)

1. *America: why is there an eye on the pyramid on the one-dollar bill?* [Edward Packard]. (1988)
2. *Amazon: where do fish swim through the treetops?* [Sara Compton]. (1988)
3. *Olympus: what is the secret of the oracle?* [Edward Packard]. (1988)
4. *Australia: find the flying foxes!* [Louise Munro Foley]. (1988)
5. *Venice: who are the three?* [Sara Compton]. (1989)
6. *Africa: where do elephants live underground?* [Edward Packard]. (1989)
7. *China: why was an army made of clay?* [Richard Brightfield]. (1989)
8. *U.S.A.: what is the great American invention?* [Richard Brightfield]. (1989)
9. *Europe: why was a city built to capture a castle?* [Sara Compton]. (1989)
10. *Japan: how do hands make peace!* [Carolyn Meyer]. (1989)
11. *England: what is the secret of the stones?* [Charles Stuart]. (1990)
12. *Russia: what is the Golden Horde?* [Edward Packard]. (1989)

EARTH SEARCH (James Follett)

1. *Earth search.* (1981)
2. *Torus.* (1990)

EARTH SONG TRIAD (Sharon Webb)

1. *Earthchild.* (1982)
2. *Earth song.* (1983)
3. *Ram song.* (1984)

EARTHCLAN (David Brin)

1. *Startide rising.* (1983)
2. *The uplift war.* (1987)
1-2. *Earthclan.* (1987)

EARTHMINDS TRILOGY (Pamela Sargent)

1. *Watchstar.* (1980)
2. *Eye of the comet.* (1984)
3. *Homesmind.* (1984)

EARTH'S CHILDREN (AYLA) (Jean M. Auel)

1. *The clan of the Cave Bear: a novel.* (1980)
2. *The valley of horses: a novel.* (1982)
3. *The mammoth hunters.* (1985)
4. *The plains of passage.* (1990)
1-3. *Earth's children.* (1987)

EARTH'S END—SEE: EMPIRE OF THE EAST

EARTHSEA (Ursula K. Le Guin)

1. *A wizard of Earthsea.* (1968)
2. *The tombs of Atuan.* (1971)
3. *The farthest shore.* (1972)
4. *Tehanu: the last book of Earthsea.* (1990)
1-3. *The Earthsea trilogy.* (1979)
1-3. *Earthsea.* (1977)

EBENEZUM (Craig Shaw Gardner)

1. *A malady of magicks.* (1986)
2. *A multitude of monsters.* (1986)
3. *A night in the Netherhells.* (1987)
4. *A difficulty with dwarves.* (1987)
1-3. *The exploits of Ebenezum.* (1987)

ECOLITAN TRILOGY (L. E. Modesitt, Jr.)

1. *The ecologic envoy.* (1986)
2. *The ecolitan operation.* (1989)
3. *The ecologic secession.* (1990)

ECOTOPIA (Ernest Callenbach)

1. *Ecotopia emerging.* (1981)
2. *Ecotopia: the notebooks and reports of William Weston.* (1975)

Associated Titles

The Ecotopian sketchbook: a book for drawing, coloring, writing, collaging, designing, thinking about & creating a new world. [Judith S. Clancy]. (1981)

EDEN (Harry Harrison)

1. *West of Eden.* (1984)
2. *Winter in Eden.* (1986)
3. *Return to Eden.* (1988)

EILEEN GOUDGE'S SWEPT AWAY (various authors)

1. *Gone with the wish.* [Eileen Goudge]. (1986)
2. *Woodstock magic.* [Fran Lantz]. (1986)
3. *Love on the range.* [Louise E. Powers]. (1986)
4. *Star struck.* [Fran Lantz]. (1987)
5. *Spellbound.* [Jennifer Rabin]. (1987)
6. *Once upon a kiss.* [Mar Garrido]. (1987)
7. *Pirate moon.* [Merrilee Steiner]. (1987)
8. *All shook up.* [Fran Lantz]. (1987)

ELEANOR (Jane Langton)

1. *The diamond in the window.* (1962)
2. *The swing in the summerhouse.* (1967)
3. *The astonishing stereoscope.* (1971)
4. *The fledgling.* (1980)

ELENIUM (David Eddings)

1. *The diamond throne.* (1989)

2.   *The ruby knight.* (1990)
3.   *The sapphire rose.* (1991)

ELFQUEST SERIES (Richard Pini & Wendy Pini)

Elfquest: the novel. (1982)

BLOOD OF TEN CHIEFS (various authors)

1.   *The blood of ten chiefs.* [Lynn Abbey & Robert Lynn Asprin & Richard Pini]. (1986)
2.   *Wolfsong.* [Lynn Abbey & Robert Lynn Asprin & Richard Pini]. (1988)
3.   *Winds of change.* [Richard Pini]. (1989)
4.   *Against the wind.* [Richard Pini]. (1990)

ELI PIKE (Frank A. Javor)

1.   *The rim-world legacy and beyond.* (1991)
2.   *Scor-sting.* (1990)
3.   *The ice beast.* (1990)

ELRIC (Michael Moorcock)

1.   *Elric of Melniboné.* (1972)
1A. *The dreaming city.* (1972)
1B. *Elric of Melniboné.* (1975). [Parts published previously as *The dreaming city*].
2.   *The sailor on the seas of fate.* (1976)
3.   *The weird of the white wolf.* (1977)
4.   *The sleeping sorceress.* (1971)
4A. *The vanishing tower.* (1977)
5.   *The stealer of souls, and other stories.* (1963)
5A. *The bane of the black sword* (1977)
6.   *Stormbringer.* (1965)
1-3. *The Elric Saga, part one: Elric of Melniboné; The sailor on the seas of fate; The weird of the white wolf.* (1984)
4-6. *The Elric saga, part two: The vanishing tower; The bane of the black sword; Stormbringer.* (1984)

Associated Titles

The singing citadel; four tales of heroic fantasy. (1970)
The Jade Man's eyes. (1973)
Elric at the end of time: fantasy stories. (1984)
The fortress of the pearl. (1989)
The revenge of the rose. (1991)

ELSPETH MARRINER & MACK FRASER (Sam Merwin, Jr.)

1.   *The house of many worlds.* (1951)
2.   *Three faces of time.* (1955)
1-2. *The house of many worlds.* (1983)

ELVEN NATIONS TRILOGY—SEE: DRAGONLANCE SAGA

EMPHYRION (Stephen Lawhead)

1.   *Emphyrion: The search for Fierra.* (1985)
2.   *The siege of Dome.* (1986)
1-2. *Emphyrion.* (1990)

EMPIRE (Raymond E. Feist & Janny Wurts)

1.   *Daughter of the empire.* (1987)
2.   *Servant of the empire.* (1990)

EMPIRE OF THE EAST: EARTH'S END (Fred Saberhagen)

1.   *The Broken Lands.* (1968)
2.   *The Black Mountains.* (1971)
3.   *Changeling Earth.* (1973)
3A. *Ardneh's world.* (1988)
1-3. *Empire of the East.* (1979)

EMPIRES TRILOGY—SEE: FORGOTTEN REALMS FANTASY ADVENTURE

ENCHANTED FOREST CHRONICLES (Patricia C. Wrede)

1.   *Dealing with dragons.* (1990)
2.   *Searching for dragons.* (1991)

ENDER WIGGINS (Orson Scott Card)

1.   *Ender's game.* (1985/1991)
2.   *Speaker for the dead.* (1986/1991)
3.   *Xenocide.* (1991)
1-2. *Ender's war.* (1986)

ENDLESS FRONTIER (Jerry Pournelle)

1.   *The endless frontier.* (1979)
2.   *The endless frontier, vol. II.* [with John F. Carr]. (1982)
3.   *Cities in space.* [with John F. Carr]. (1991)

ENDLESS QUEST (various authors)

1.   *Dungeon of dread.* [Rose Estes]. (1982)
2.   *Mountain of mirrors.* [Rose Estes]. (1982)
3.   *Pillars of Pentegarn.* [Rose Estes]. (1982)
4.   *Return to Brookmere.* [Rose Estes]. (1982)
5.   *Revolt of the dwarves.* [Rose Estes]. (1983)
6.   *Revenge of the rainbow dragons.* [Rose Estes]. (1983)
7.   *Hero of Washington Square.* [Rose Estes]. (1983)
8.   *Villains of Volturnus.* [Jean Blashfield]. (1983)
9.   *Robbers and robots.* [Mike Carr]. (1983)
10. *Circus of fear.* [Rose Estes]. (1983)
11. *Spell of the winter wizard.* [Linda Lowery]. (1983)
12. *Light on Quests Mountain.* [Mary L. Kirchoff & James M. Ward]. (1983)
13. *Dragon of doom.* [Rose Estes]. (1983)
14. *Raid on Nightmare Castle.* [Catherine McGuire]. (1983)
15. *Under dragon's wing.* [John Kendall]. (1984)
16. *The dragon's ransom.* [Laura French]. (1984)
17. *Captive planet.* [Morris Simon]. (1984)
18. *King's quest.* [Tom McGowen]. (1984)
19. *Conan the undaunted.* [James M. Ward]. (1984)
20. *Conan and the prophecy.* [Roger E. Moore]. (1984)
21. *Duel of the masters.* [Chris Martindale]. (1984)
22. *The endless catacombs.* [Margaret Weis]. (1984)
23. *Blade of the young samurai.* [Morris Simon]. (1984)
24. *Trouble on Artule.* [Catherine McGuire]. (1984)
25. *Conan the outlaw.* [Roger E. Moore]. (1984)
26. *Tarzan and the well of slaves.* [Douglas Niles]. (1985)
27. *Lair of the Lich.* [Bruce Algozin]. (1985)
28. *Mystery of the ancients.* [Morris Simon]. (1985)
29. *Tower of darkness.* [Regina Oehler Fultz]. (1985)
30. *The fireseed.* [Morris Simon]. (1985)
31. *Tarzan and the tower of diamonds.* [Richard Reinsmith]. (1985)
32. *Prisoner of Elderwood.* [Bruce Algozin]. (1986)
33. *Knight of illusion.* [Mary L. Kirchoff]. (1986)
34. *Claw of the dragon.* [Bruce Algozin]. (1986)

35. *Vision of doom.* [Mary L. Kirchoff]. (1986)
36. *Song of the dark druid.* [Josepha Sherman] (1987)

ENDLESS QUEST CRIMSON CRYSTAL ADVENTURE

1. *Riddle of the griffon.* [Susan Lawson]. (1985)
2. *Search for the pegasus.* [Roger E. Moore]. (1985)
3. *Renegades of Luntar.* [Roger E. Moore]. (1985)
4. *Stop that witch!* [Mary Clark]. (1985)

ENDWORLD (David Robbins)

1. *The Fox run.* (1986)
2. *Thief River Falls run.* (1986)
3. *Twin Cities run.* (1986)
4. *The Kalispell run.* (1987)
5. *Dakota run.* (1987)
6. *Citadel run.* (1987)
7. *Armageddon run.* (1987)
8. *Denver run.* (1987)
9. *Capital run.* (1988)
10. *New York run.* (1988)
11. *Liberty run.* (1987)
12. *Houston run.* (1988)
13. *Anaheim run.* (1988)
14. *Seattle run.* (1988)
15. *Nevada run.* (1989)
16. *Miami run.* (1989)
17. *Atlanta run.* (1989)
18. *Memphis run.* (1989)
19. *Cincinnati run.* (1990)
20. *Dallas run.* (1990)
21. *Boston run.* (1990)
22. *Green Bay run.* (1990)
23. *Yellowstone run.* (1990)
24. *New Orleans run.* (1991)
25. *Spartan run.* (1991)
26. *Madman run.* (1991)
27. *Chicago run.* (1991)
9-10. *Capital run; New York run.* (1991)
11-12. *Liberty run; Houston run.* (1991)
13-14. *Anaheim run; Seattle run.* (1991)
15-16. *Nevada run; Miami run.* (1991)

BLADE SERIES

1. *First strike.* (1989)
2. *Outlands strike.* (1989)
3. *Vampire strike.* (1989)
4. *Pipeline strike.* (1989)
5. *Pirate strike.* (1989)
6. *Crusher strike.* (1990)
7. *Terror strike.* (1990)
8. *Devil strike.* (1990)
9. *L.A. strike.* (1990)
10. *Dead zone strike.* (1990)
11. *Quest strike.* (1991)
12. *Death master strike.* (1991)
13. *Vengeance strike.* (1991)

ENFORCER (Andrew Sugar)

1. *The Enforcer.* (1973)
2. *Calling Doctor Kill!* (1973)
3. *Kill city.* (1973)
4. *Kill deadline.* (1973)
5. *Bio blitz.* (1975)
6. *Steel trap.* (1975)
7. *Kill deadline.* (1979)

EON (Greg Bear)

1. *Eon.* (1985)
2. *Eternity.* (1988)

EPIC TALES OF THE FIVE (Diane Duane)

1. *The door into fire.* (1979)
2. *The door into shadow.* (1984)

ERIC BRIGHTEYES (H. Rider Haggard and others)

1. *Eric Brighteyes.* (1891)
2. *A witch's welcome.* [Mildred Downey Broxon as SIGFRIOUR SKALDASPILLIR]. (1979)

ERIC CARSTAIRS (Lin Carter)

1. *Journey to the underground world.* (1979)
2. *Zanthodon.* (1980)
3. *Hurok of the stone age.* (1981)
4. *Darya of the bronze age.* (1981)
5. *Eric of Zanthodon.* (1982)

ERIC JOHN STARK (Leigh Brackett)

1. *People of the Talisman.* (1964)
2. *The secret of Sinharat.* (1964)
3. *The reavers of Skaith.* (1976)
1-3. *The Book of Skaith.* (1976)

ERTHRING CYCLE (Wayland Drew)

1. *The memoirs of Alcheringia.* (1984)
2. *The Gaian expedient.* (1985)
3. *The master of Norriya.* (1986)
1-3. *The Erthring Cycle.* (1986)

ESCAPE FROM LOST ISLAND (Clay Coleman)

1. *Escape from Lost Island.* (1990)
2. *Attack!* (1990)
3. *Mutiny!* (1991)
4. *Discovered!* (1991)
5. *Revenge!* (1991)
6. *Escape!* (1991)

ESCAPE FROM TENOPIA (various authors)

1. *Tenopia Island.* [Edward Packard]. (1986)
2. *Trapped in the sea kingdom.* [Richard Brightfield]. (1986)
3. *Terror on Kabran.* [Richard Brightfield]. (1986)
4. *Star system Tenopia.* [Richard Brightfield]. (1986)

ESCAPE FROM THE KINGDOM OF FROME (various authors)

1. *The castle of Frome.* [Edward Packard]. (1986)
2. *The forest of the king.* [Richard Brightfield]. (1987)
3. *The caverns of Mornas.* [Richard Brightfield]. (1987)
4. *The battle of Astar.* [Richard Brightfield]. (1987)

ESP McGEE (various authors)

1. *ESP McGee.* [Edward Packard]. (1983)
2. *ESP McGee and the haunted mansion.* [Jim Lawrence]. (1983)
3. *ESP McGee and the mysterious magician.* [Kathryn F. Ernst]. (1983)

4.   *ESP McGee and the ghost ship.* [Ian McMahan]. (1984)
5.   *ESP McGee to the rescue.* [George Shea]. (1984)
6.   *ESP McGee and the dolphin's message.* [Jesse Rodgers]. (1984)

ESSAYS ON FANTASTIC LITERATURE (various authors)

1.   *It's down the slippery cellar stairs.* [R. A. Lafferty]. (1986)
2.   *Blond barbarians & noble savages.* [L. Sprague de Camp]. (1986)
3.   *Ray Bradbury: dramatist.* [Ben P. Indick]. (1989)
3A. *Ray Bradbury: dramtist, 2nd ed.* [Ben P. Indick]. (1989)
4.   *Non-literary influences on science fiction.* [Algis Budrys]. (1987)
5.   *The poison maiden & the great bitch: female stereotypes in Marvel Superhero Comics.* [Susan Wood]. (1989)

E.T., THE EXTRA-TERRESTRIAL (William Kotzwinkle)

1.   *E.T., the extra-terrestrial, in his adventure on Earth: a novel.* (1982)
1A. *E.T., the extraterrestrial storybook.* (1982)
2.   *E.T., the book of the green planet: a new novel.* (1985)
2A. *E.T.: The storybook of the green planet: a new storybook.* (1985),
2B. *E.T.: The book of the green planet: a new novel.* [with Steven Spielberg]. (1985)

ETERNAL CHAMPION (Michael Moorcock)

1.   *The Eternal Champion.* (1970)
2.   *Phoenix in obsidian.* (1970)
2A. *The Silver Warriors.* (1973)
3.   *The dragon in the sword: being the third and final story in the history of John Daker, the eternal champion.* (1986)

ETHICAL CULTURE (George Turner)

1.   *Beloved son.* (1978)
2.   *Vaneglory: a science fiction novel.* (1981)
3.   *Yesterday's men.* (1983)

EUNOSTOS—SEE: ANCIENT HISTORY

EWERTON (A. R. Morlan)

1.   *The amulet.* (1991)
2.   *Dark journey.* (1991)
3.   *The cat with the tulip face.* (1991)

EXCHAMELEON (Ron Goulart)

1.   *Daredevils, Ltd.* (1987)
2.   *Starpirate's brain.* (1987)
3.   *Everybody comes to Cosmo's.* (1988)

EXILES (Ben Bova)

1.   *Exiled from Earth.* (1971)
2.   *Flight of exiles.* (1972)
3.   *End of exile.* (1975)
1-3. *The exiles trilogy: three novels.* (1980)

EXITORN ADVENTURES (Peggy Downing)

1.   *Brill and the Dragators.* (1987)
2.   *Segra and Stargull.* (1987)
3.   *Segra in diamond castle.* (1988)
4.   *Brill and the Zinders.* (1988)
5.   *Segra and the magician.* (1989)
6.   *Brill and the puffire volcano.* (1989)

THE EXORCIST—SEE: LT. KINDERMAN

EXOTERRA (Gordon McBain)

1.   *The path of Exoterra.* (1981)
2.   *Quest of the Dawnstar.* (1984)

EXPENDABLES (Edmund Cooper as RICHARD AVERY)

1.   *The death worms of Kratos.* (1975)
1A. *The deathworms of Kratos.* [Edmund Cooper]. (1977)
2.   *The rings of Tantalus.* (1975)
2A. *The rings of Tantalus.* [Edmund Cooper]. (1977)
3.   *The War Games of Zelos.* (1975)
3A. *The War Games of Zelos.* [Edmund Cooper]. (1980)
4.   *The venom of Argus.* (1976)

EXPLORER (various authors)

1.   *Journey to the center of the atom!* [Carol Gaskin]. (1987)
2.   *Destination: brain.* [Seth McEvoy]. (1987)
3.   [unknown title]
4.   *Escape from Jupiter.* [Seth McEvoy]. (1987)

EYE OF TIME TRILOGY (Ann Grimsley & Lynne Kinnerley as LYNDAN DARBY)

1.   *Crystal and steel.* (1988)
2.   *Bloodseed.* (1988)
3.   *Phoenix fire.* (1989)

EYES (Stuart Gordon)

1.   *One-Eye.* (1973)
2.   *Two-Eyes.* (1974)
3.   *Three-Eyes.* (1975)
1-3. *The Eyes trilogy.* (1978)

FADED SUN (C. J. Cherryh)

1.   *Kesrith.* (1978)
2.   *Shon'jir.* (1978)
3.   *Kutath.* (1979)
1-3. *The faded sun trilogy.* (1987)

FADING WORLDS (Geary Gravel)

1.   *A key for the nonesuch.* (1990)
2.   *The return of the Breakneck Boys.* (1991)

FAFHRD & GRAY MOUSER (Fritz Leiber)

1.   *Swords and deviltry.* (1970)
2.   *Swords against death.* (1970)
3.   *Swords in the mist.* (1968)
4.   *Swords against wizardry* ((1968)
5.   *The swords of Lankhmar.* (1968)
6.   *Rime Isle.* (1977)
6A. *Swords & ice magic.* (1977)
7.   *Bazaar of the bizarre.* (1978)

8. *The knight and knave of swords.* (1988)
9. *The three of swords.* (1989)
10. *Swords' masters.* (1990)

Pastiches and Sequels

Lankhmar, city of adventure. [Bruce Nesmith & Douglas Niles & Ken Rolston]. (1985)
Dragonsword of Lankhmar. [James M. Ward]. (1986)

FAIR RULES (David C. Smith)

1. *The fair rules of evil.* (1989)
2. *The eyes of night.* (1991)

FALCON (Mark Smith & Jamie Thomson)

1. *The renegade lord.* (1985)
2. *Mechanon.* (1985)
3. *The rack of Baal.* (1985)
4. *Lost in time.* (1985)
5. *The dying sun.* (1986)
6. *At the end of time.* (1986)

FALKENBERG'S LEGION—SEE: FUTURE HISTORY

FALL OF THE FIRST WORLD (David C. Smith)

1. *The master of evil.* (1983)
2. *Sorrowing vengeance.* (1983)
3. *The passing of the gods.* (1983)

FAMILY D'ALEMBERT (Stephen Goldin & E. E. "Doc" Smith)

1. *Imperial stars.* (1976)
2. *Strangler's moon.* (1976)
3. *The clockwork traitor.* (1977)
4. *Getaway world.* (1977)
5. *Appointment at Bloodstar.* (1978)
6. *The Purity plot.* (1980)
7. *Planet of treachery.* (1982)
8. *Eclipsing binaries.* (1983)
9. *The Omicron invasion.* (1984)
10. *Revolt of the galaxy.* (1985)

FANGLITH (John Dalmas)

1. *Fanglith.* (1985)
2. *Return to Fanglith.* (1987)

FANTASTIC FOUR—SEE: MARVEL SUPERHEROES

FANTASTIC VOYAGE (Isaac Asimov)

1. *Fantastic voyage; a novel.* (1966)
2. *Fantastic voyage II: Destination brain.* (1987)

FANTASY FOREST (various authors)

1. *The ring, the sword, and the unicorn.* [James M. Ward]. (1983)
2. *Ruins of Rangar.* [Mike Carr]. (1983)
3. *Shadowcastle.* [Michael Gray]. (1983)fw'
4. *Keep of the ancient king.* [Mike Carr]. (1983)
5. *Dungeon of darkness.* [David Kendall]. (1984)
6. *Star rangers and the spy.* [Jean Blashfield & Beverly Charette]. (1984)
7. *Castle in the clouds.* [Morris Simon]. (1984)

8. *Star rangers meet the solar robot.* [Beverly Charette & Mario D. Macari]. (1984)
9. *Jason's first quest.* [Roger E. Moore]. (1984)
10. *The lost wizard.* [Michael Gray]. (1984)

FANTASY QUEST BOOK (David Fickling & Perry Hinton)

The path of peril. (1984)
Starflight zero. (1985)
Helmquest. (1986)
Ten doors of doom. (1987)

FANTASY READERS GUIDE (Mike Ashley)

1. *Fantasy readers guide to Ramsey Campbell.* (1980)
2. *A complete index and annotated commentary to the John Spencer fantasy publications (1950-66).* (1979)

FAR FRONTIERS (Jerry Pournell & Jim Baen

1. *Far frontiers.* (1985)
2. *Far frontiers, volume II, Spring 1985.* (1985)
3. *Far frontiers, Fall edition 1985 [vol. III].* (1985)
4. *Far frontiers, Winter edition 1985 [vol. IV].* (1986)
5. *Far frontiers, Summer edition 1986 [vol. V].* (1986)
6. *Far frontiers, volume VI, Fall 1986.* (1986)
7. *Far frontiers, Fall edition, 1986 [vol. VII].* (1986)

FAR SIDE OF FOREVER (Sharon Green)

1. *The far side of forever.* (1987)
2. *Hellhound magic.* (1989)

FAR STARS AND FUTURE TIMES (Richard S. McEnroe)

1. *The shattered stars.* (1984)
2. *Flight of honor.* (1984)

FARADAWN TRILOGY (Richard Ford)

1. *Quest for the Faradawn.* (1982)
2. *Melvaig's vision.* (1984)
3. *The children of Ashgaroth.* (1986)

THE FARM (Richard Haigh)

1. *The farm.* (1984)
2. *The city.* (1986)

FARSTAR & SON (Bill Starr)

1. *The way to Dawnworld.* (1975)
2. *The treasure of Wonderwhat.* (1976)

FARTHING WOOD (Colin Dann)

1. *The animals of Farthing Wood.* (1979)
2. *In the grip of winter.* (1981)
3. *In the path of the storm.* (1989)

FATHER HAYES (Peter Leslie)

1. *Father Hayes.* (1976)
2. *The steeds of Satan.* (1976)
3. *The Holy spirit.* (1977)

FEAR STREET (R. L. Stine)

The fire game. (1991)

Haunted. (1990)
Halloween party. (1990)
Lights out. (1991)
Missing. (1990)
The new girl. (1989)
The overnight. (1989)
Party summer. (1991)
The secret bedroom. (1991)
Silent night. (1991)
Ski weekend. (1991)
The sleepwalker. (1990)
The stepsister. (1990)
The surprise party. (1989)
The wrong number. (1990)

FEGHOOT (Reginald Bretnor as GRENDEL BRIARTON)

Through time and space with Ferdinand Feghoot; the first forty-five Feghoot adventures, with five more never previously heard of. (1962)
The compleat Feghoot: the many lives and greatest exploits of history's punniest space-time traveller. (1975)
The (even more) compleat Feghoot: the many lives and greatest exploits of history's punniest space-time traveler. (1980)

FELIMID MAC FAL—SEE: BARD

FELLOWSHIP OF LIGHT (Robert E. Mills)

1. *Star quest.* (1978)
2. *Star fighters.* (1978)
3. *Star force.* (1978)

FENELLA FANG (Ritchie Perry)

1. *Fenella Fang.* (1986)
2. *Fenella Fang and the time machine.* (1991)

FENRILE (Christopher Rowley)

1. *The war for eternity.* (1983)
2. *The Black Ship.* (1985)
3. *The founder.* (1989)

FIFTH GRADE MAGIC (Beatrice Gormley)

1. *Fifth grade magic.* (1982)
2. *More fifth grade magic.* (1989)

FIFTH GRADE MONSTERS (Mel Gilden)

1. *M is for monster.* (1987)
2. *Born to howl.* (1987)
3. *There's a batwing in my lunchbox.* [By Ann Hodgman]. (1988)
4. *The pet of Frankenstein.* (1988)
5. *Z is for zombie.* (1988)
6. *Monster mashers.* (1989)
7. *Things that go bark in the park.* (1989)
8. *Yuckers!* (1989)
9. *The monster in Creeps Head Bay.* (1990)
10. *How to be a vampire in one easy lesson.* (1990)
11. *Island of the weird.* (1990)
12. *Werewolf, come home.* (1990)
13. *Monster boy.* (1991)
14. *Troll patrol.* (1991)
15. *The secret of Dinosaur Bog.* (1991)

FIFTH MILLENNIUM (S. M. Stirling and others)

1. *Snowbrother.* (1985)
2. *The sharpest edge.* [With Shirley Meier]. (1986)
3. *The cage.* [With Shirley Meier]. (1989)
4. *Shadow's son.* [With Shirley Meier & Karen Wehrstein]. (1991)
5. *Shadow's daughter.* [By Shirley Meier]. (1991)
6. *Lion's heart.* [By Karen Wehrstein]. (1991)
7. *Lion's soul.* [By Karen Wehrstein]. (1991)

FIGHTING FANTASY GAMEBOOK (various authors)

1. *The warlock of Firetop Mountain.* [Steve Jackson & Ian Livingstone]. (1982)
2. *The citadel of Chaos.* [Steve Jackson]. (1983)
3. *The forest of doom.* [Ian Livingstone]. (1983)
4. *Starship traveler.* [Steve Jackson]. (1983)
5. *City of thieves.* [Ian Livingstone]. (1983)
6. *Deathtrap dungeon.* [Ian Livingstone]. (1984)
7. *Island of the Lizard King.* [Ian Livingstone]. (1984)
8. *Scorpion swamp.* [Steve Jackson (1953-) & Ian Livingstone]. (1984)
9. *Caverns of the snow witch.* [Ian Livingstone]. (1984)
10. *House of Hell.* [Steve Jackson]. (1985)
10A. *House of Hades.* [Steve Jackson]. (1985)
11. *Talisman of death.* [Mark Smith & Jamie Thomson]. (1985)
12. *Space assassin.* [Andrew Chapman]. (1985)
13. *Freeway fighter.* [Ian Livingstone]. (1985)
14. *Temple of terror.* [Ian Livingstone]. (1986)
15. *The rings of Kether.* [Andrew Chapman]. (1986)
16. *Seas of blood.* [Andrew Chapman]. (1985)
17. *Appointment with F.E.A.R.* [Steve Jackson]. (1985)
18. *Rebel planet.* [Robin Waterfield]. (1985)
19. *Demons of the deep.* [Steve Jackson (1953-) & Ian Livingstone]. (1986)
20. *Sword of the samurai.* [Mark Smith & Jamie Thomson]. (1986)
21. *Trial of champions.* [Ian Livingstone]. (1986)
22. *Robot commando.* [Steve Jackson (1953-) & Ian Livingstone]. (1986)
23. *Masks of mayhem.* [Robin Waterfield]. (1986)
24. *Creature of havoc.* [Steve Jackson]. (1986)
25. *Beneath Nightmare Castle.* [Peter Darvill-Evans]. (1987)
29. *Midnight rogue.* [Graeme Davis]. (1987)
39. *Fangs of fury.* [Luke Sharp]. (1989)
42. *Black vein prophecy.* [Paul Mason & Steve Jackson]. (1990)
43. *Keep of the Lich-Lord.* [Steve Jackson]. (1990)
46. *Tower of destruction.* [Keith Martin]. (1991)

Series Numbers Unknown

Crypt of the sorcerer. [Ian Livingstone]. (1987)
The riddling reaver. [Paul Mason & Steve Williams]. (1986)
Phantoms of fear. [Robin Waterfield]. (1987)
Battleblade Warrior. [Marc Gascoigne]. (1988)
Money spider. [Robin Waterfield & Peter Davies]. (1988)
Water spider. [Robin Waterfield & Peter Davies]. (1988)
Chasms of malice. [Luke Sharp]. (1988)
Slaves of the abyss. [Paul Mason & Steve Williams]. (1988)
Sky lord. [Martin Allen]. (1988)
Portal of evil. [Peter Darvill-Evans]. (1989)

Dungeoneer. [Marc Gascoigne & Pete Tamlyn].
ADVANCED FIGHTING FANTASY GAMEBOOK. (1989)

Blacksand! [Marc Gascoigne & Pete Tamlyn]. AD-
VANCED FIGHTING FANTASY GAMEBOOK. (1990)

Legend of the shadow warriors. [Stephen Hand].
(1991)

Demonstealer. [Marc Gascoigne]. (1991)

Spectral stalker. [Peter Darvill-Evans]. (1991)

Associated Titles

Fighting fantasy: an introductory role-playing game.
[Steve Jackson]. (1984)

Titan: the fighting fantasy world. [Steve Jackson &
Ian Livingstone]. (1986)

Fighting fantasy poster book. [Steve Jackson & Ian
Livingstone]. (1990)

FILLMORE (Marvin Kaye)

1. *The incredible umbrella.* (1979)
2. *The amorous umbrella.* (1981)

FIND YOUR FATE ADVENTURE (various authors)

1. *Indiana Jones and the curse of Horror Island.* [R.
   L. Stine]. (1984)
2. *Indiana Jones and the lost treasure of Sheba.* [Rose
   Estes]. (1984)
3. *Indiana Jones and the giants of the Silver Tower.*
   [R. L. Stine]. (1984)
4. *Indiana Jones and the Eye of the Fates.* [Richard
   Wenk]. (1984)
5. *Indiana Jones and the cup of the vampire.* [Andrew
   Helfer]. (1984)
6. *Indiana Jones and the Legion of Death.* [Richard
   Wenk]. (1984)
7. *Indiana Jones and the cult of the mummy's crypt.*
   [R. L. Stine]. (1985)
8. *Indiana Jones and the dragon of vengeance.* [H.
   William Stine & Megan Stine]. (1985)
9. *Indiana Jones and the gold of Genghis Khan.* [Ellen
   Weiss]. (1985)
10. *Morgan Swift and the kidnapped goddess.* [Sara
    Hughes]. (1985)
11. *James Bond in Win, place, or die.* [R. L. Stine].
    (1985)
12. *James Bond in Strike it deadly.* [Barbara & Scott
    Siegel]. (1985)
13. *James Bond in Programmed for danger.* [Jean M.
    Favors]. (1985)
14. *James Bond in Barracuda run.* [Steven Otfinoski].
    (1985)
15. *Morgan Swift and the treasure of Crocodile Key.*
    [Sara Hughes]. (1985)
16. *Indiana Jones and the ape slaves of Howling Island.*
    [R. L. Stine]. (1987)
17. *Indiana Jones and the mask of the elephant.* [H.
    William Stine & Megan Stine]. (1987)

FIND YOUR FATE—DOCTOR WHO (various authors)

1. *Search for the Doctor.* [David Martin]. (1986)
2. *Crisis in space.* [David Martin]. (1986)
3. *Garden of evil.* [David Martin]. (1986)
4. *Mission to Venus.* [William Emms]. (1986)
5. *Invasion of the Ormazoids.* [Philip Martin]. (1986)
6. *Race against time.* [Jane Baker & Pip Baker]. (1986)

FIND YOUR FATE—G.I. JOE (various authors)

1. *Operation: Star Raider.* [R. L. Stine *as* ERIC AF-
   FABEE]. (1985)
2. *Operation: Dragon fire.* [William Sno]. (1985)
3. Operation: *Terror trap.* [H. William & Megan
   Stine]. (1985)
4. *Operation: robot assassin.* [G. V. Macrae]. (1985)
5. *The Everglades swamp terror.* [R. L. Stine as ERIC
   AFFABEE]. (1986)
6. *Operation: Death stone.* [Barbara Siegel & Scott
   Siegel]. (1986)
7. *Operation: Deadly decoy.* [R. L. Stine]. (1986)
8. *Operation: Death-ray.* [H. William Stine & Megan
   Stine]. (1986)
9. *Operation: Mindbender.* [R. L. Stine]. (1986)
10. *Operation: night flight.* [William Sno]. (1986)
11. *Operation: weapons disaster.* [James M. Ward].
    (1986)
12. *Operation: Jungle doom.* [Kathryn Lance as LYNN
    BEACH]. (1986)
13. *Operation: Snow job.* [Barbara Siegel & Scott
    Siegel]. (1987)
14. *Operation: Thunderbolt.* [K. C. Edwards]. (1987)
15. *Operation: Time machine.* [Kathryn Lance as LYNN
    BEACH]. (1987)
16. *Operation: Poison dart.* [H. William Stine & Megan
    Stine]. (1987)
17. *Operation: Sink or swim.* [Barbara Siegel & Scott
    Siegel]. (1987)
18. *Operation: Killer comet.* [S. M. Ballard]. (1987)
19. *Operation: Tiger strike.* [William Sno]. (1987)
20. *Serpentor and the mummy warrior.* [R. L. Stine].
    (1987)

FIND YOUR FATE—JEM (various authors)

1. *Jewels in the dark.* [Rusty Hallock]. (1986)
2. *The video caper.* [Jean Waricha]. (1986)
3. *The secret of Rainbow Island.* [Judith Bauer Stam-
   per]. (1986)

FIND YOUR FATE—JUNIOR GOLDEN GIRL
[GOLDEN GIRL AND THE GUARDIANS OF THE GEMSTONES]
(various authors)

1. *Golden Girl and the vanishing unicorn.* [R. L.
   Stine]. (1986)
2. *Golden Girl in the land of dreams.* [Alice Storey].
   (1986)
3. *Golden Girl and the crystal of doom.* [Josepha
   Sherman]. (1986)

FIND YOUR FATE—JUNIOR TRANSFORMERS
(various authors)

1. *Dinobots strike back.* [Casey Todd]. (1985)
2. *Battle drive.* [Barbara Siegel & Scott Siegel]. (1985)
3. *The attack of the Insecticons.* [Kathryn Lance as
   LYNN BEACH]. (1985)
4. *Earthquake.* [Ann Matthews]. (1986)
5. *Desert flight.* [Jim Razzi]. (1986)
6. *Decepticon poison.* [Judith Bauer Stamper]. (1986)
7. *Autobot alert!* [Judith Bauer Stamper]. (1986)
8. *Project brain drain.* [Barbara Siegel & Scott Siegel].
   (1986)
9. *The invisibility factor.* [Josepha Sherman]. (1986)

FINDER'S STONE TRILOGY—SEE: FORGOTTEN REALMS FANTASY ADVENTURE

FINN (Mary Tannen)

1. *The wizard children of Finn.* (1981)
2. *The lost legend of Finn.* (1982)

FINN FAMILY MOOMINTROLL (Tove Jansson)

1. *Finn Family Moomintroll.* (1950)
1A. *The happy Moomins.* (1952)
2. *Comet in Moominland.* (1951)
3. *The exploits of Moominpappa.* (1952)
4. *Moominsummer madness.* (1955)
5. *Moominland midwinter.* (1958)
6. *Tales from Moominvalley.* (1964)
7. *Moominpappa at sea.* (1966)
8. *Moomin Valley in November.* (1971)

FINN MACCUMHAL (Kenneth C. Flint)

1. *Challenge of the clans.* (1986)
2. *Storm shield.* (1986)
3. *The dark druid.* (1987)

FINNBRANCH (Paul Hazel)

1. *Yearwood.* (1980)
2. *Undersea.* (1982)
3. *Winterking.* (1985)
1-3. *The Finnbranch.* (1986)

FIONAVAR TAPESTRY (Guy Gavriel Kay)

1. *The summer tree.* (1984)
2. *The wandering fire.* (1986)
3. *The darkest road.* (1986)

FIREBALL (John Christopher)

1. *Fireball.* (1981)
2. *New found land.* (1983)
3. *Dragondance.* (1986)
3A. *Dragon dance.* (1986)

FIREBIRD (Kathy Tyers)

1. *Firebird.* (1987)
2. *Fusion fire.* (1988)

FIREBRATS (Barbara Siegel & Scott Siegel)

1. *The burning land.* (1987)
2. *Survivors.* (1987)
3. *Thunder Mountain.* (1987)
4. *Shockwave.* (1988)

FIREFOX: MATTHEW GANT (Craig Thomas)

1. *Firefox.* (1977)
2. *Firefox down!* (1983)

FIRST AMERICANS (William Sarabande)

1. *Beyond the sea of ice.* (1987)
2. *Corridor of storms.* (1988)
3. *Forbidden land.* (1989)
4. *Walkers of the wind.* (1990)
5. *The sacred stones.* (1991)

FIRSTFLIGHT (Chris Claremont)

1. *FirstFlight.* (1987)
2. *Grounded!* (1991)

FLASH GORDON (various authors)

ACE BOOKS SERIES
(David Hagberg as ANONYMOUS AUTHOR)

1. *Massacre in the 22nd century.* (1980)
2. *War of the Citadels.* (1980)
3. *Crisis on Citadel II.* (1980)
4. *Forces from the Federation.* (1981)
5. *Citadels under attack.* (1981)
6. *Citadels on Earth.* (1981)

AVON BOOKS SERIES

1. *The lion men of Mongo.* [Ron Goulart as CON STEFFANSON]. (1974)
2. *The plague of sound.* [Ron Goulart as CON STEFFANSON]. (1974)
3. *The space circus.* [Ron Goulart as CON STEFFANSON]. (1974)
4. *The time trap of Ming XIII.* [Bruce Cassidy as CON STEFFANSON]. (1974)
5. *The witch queen of Mongo.* [Bruce Cassiday as CARSON BINGHAM]. (1974)
6. *The war of the Cybernauts.* [Bruce Cassiday as CARSON BINGHAM]. (1975)

MOVIE TIE-INS

Flash Gordon: a novel. [Arthur Byron Cover]. (1980)
The Flash Gordon book. [Arthur Byron Cover & Lynn Haney]. (1980)

Associated Title

Flash Gordon in the caverns of Mongo. [Alex Raymond]. (1937)

THE FLEET (David Drake & Bill Fawcett)

1. *The fleet.* (1988)
2. *Counterattack.* (1988)
3. *Breakthrough.* (1989)
4. *Sworn allies.* (1990)
5. *Total war.* (1990)
6. *Crisis.* (1991)

FLIGHT IN YIKTOR: LYDIS (Andre Norton)

1. *Flight in Yiktor.* [LYDIS #3]. (1986)
2. *Dare to go a-hunting.* (1990)

LYDIS SERIES

1. *Moon of three rings.* (1966)
2. *Exiles of the stars.* (1971)
3. *Flight in Yiktor.* (1986)

FLIGHT OVER FIRE (Jenny Jones)

1. *Fly by night.* (1990)
2. *The edge of vengeance.* (1991)

FLINX (Alan Dean Foster)

1. *For love of Mother-not.* (1983)

2A. *Secret harmonies.* (1989)
3.   *Eternal light.* (1991)

FOUR LORDS OF THE DIAMOND (Jack L. Chalker)

1.   *Lilith: a snake in the grass.* (1981)
2.   *Cerberus: a wolf in the fold.* (1982)
3.   *Charon: a dragon at the gate.* (1982)
4.   *Medusa: a tiger by the tail.* (1983)
1-4. *Four lords of the diamond.* (1983)

FOURS CROSSING (Nancy Garden)

1.   *Fours Crossing.* (1981)
2.   *Watersmeet.* (1983)
3.   *The door between.* (1987)

FOXES (Tom McCaughren)

1.   *Run with the wind.* (1983)
2.   *Run to earth.* (1984)
3.   *Run swift, run free.* (1986)
4.   *Run to the ark.* (1991)

FOZBEK (Steve Senn)

1.   *The double disappearance of Walter Fozbek.* (1980)
2.   *Ralph Fozbek and the amazing black hole patrol.* (1986)

FRANK FRAZETTA'S DEATH DEALER (James R. Silke)

1.   *Prisoner of the horned helmet.* (1988)
2.   *Lords of destruction.* (1989)
3.   *Tooth and claw.* (1989)
4.   *Plague of knives.* (1990)

FRANKENSTEIN SEQUELS (various authors)

The bride of Frankenstein. [Ramsey Campbell *as* CARL DREADSTONE]. (1977)
Hound of Frankenstein. [Peter Tremayne]. (1977)
The Frankenstein diaries. [Hubert Venables]. (1980)
The bride. [Les Martin]. (1985)
The bride. [Vonda N. McIntyre]. (1985)
The curse of Frankenstein. [J. H. Brennan]. (1986)
The Frankenstein papers. [Fred Saberhagen]. (1986)

THE CROSS OF FRANKENSTEIN (Robert J. Myers)

1.   *The cross of Frankenstein.* (1975)
2.   *The slave of Frankenstein.* (1976)

FRANKENSTEIN'S AUNT (Allan Rune Pettersson)

1.   *Frankenstein's aunt.* (1980)
2.   *Frankenstein's aunt returns.* (1990)

THE NEW ADVENTURES OF FRANKENSTEIN (Donald F. Glut)

1.   *Frankenstein lives again.* (1977)
1A. *Frankenstein lives again!* (1981)
2.   *Terror of Frankenstein.* (1977)
3.   *Bones of Frankenstein.* (1977)
4.   *Frankenstein meets Dracula.* (1977)

FRASER FAMILY (Carol Main)

1.   *The white planet.* (1982)

2.   *Planet of evil.* (1983)
3.   *Planet of adventure.* (1986)

FREEDOM'S RANGERS (various authors as KEITH WILLIAM ANDREWS)

1.   *Freedom's rangers.* [William K. Keith Jr.]. (1989)
2.   *Raiders of the Revolution.* [William K. Keith Jr.]. (1989)
3.   *Search and destroy.* [William K. Keith Jr.]. (1990)
4.   *Treason in time.* [William K. Keith Jr.]. (1990)
5.   *Sink the armada.* [William K. Keith Jr.]. (1990)
6.   *Snow kill.* [William K. Keith Jr.]. (1991)

FREEWAY WARRIOR (Joe Dever)

1.   *Highway holocaust.* (1988)
2.   *Slaughter Mountain run.* (1988)
2A. *Mountain run.* (1990)
3.   *The Omega Zone.* (1989)
4.   *California countdown.* (1989)

FRIDAY THE 13TH (Simon Hawke)

1.   *Friday the 13th, part I.* (1987)
2.   *Friday the 13th, part II: a novel.* (1988)
3A. *Friday the 13th, part 3, 3-D.* [Michael Avallone]. (1982.
3B. *Friday the 13th, part 3: a novel based on the motion picture Friday the 13th, part 3.* (1988)
4.   [Never novelized]
5.   [Never novelized]
6.   *Jason lives: Friday the 13th, part VI: a novel.* (1986)

FROM THIEF TO KING (Michael Williams)

1.   *A sorcerer's apprentice.* (1990)
2.   *A forest lord.* (1991)

FROST (Robin W. Bailey)

1.   *Frost.* (1983)
2.   *Skull Gate.* (1985)
3.   *Bloodsongs.* (1986)

FROSTFLOWER (Phyllis Ann Karr)

1.   *Frostflower and Thorn.* (1980)
2.   *Frostflower and Windbourne.* (1982)

FU MANCHU SERIES (Sax Rohmer and others)

Fu-Manchu: four classic novels. (1983)
The passing of Fu Manchu. [Jon Michael Suter]. (1976)
1.   *Ten years beyond Baker Street: Sherlock Holmes matches wits with the diabolical Dr. Fu Manchu.* [Cay Van Ash]. (1984)
2.   *The fires of Fu Manchu.* [Cay Van Ash]. (1987)

FURSEY (Mervyn Wall)

1.   *The unfortunate Fursey.* (1946)
2.   *The return of Fursey.* (1948)
1-2. *The complete Fursey.* (1985)

FUTURE AT WAR (Reginald Bretnor)

1.   *Thor's hammer.* (1979)

2. *The spear of Mars.* (1980)
3. *Orion's sword.* (1980)

FUTURE HISTORY: POLESOTECHNIC LEAGUE (Poul Anderson)

FUTURE HISTORY

1. *Let the spacemen beware!* POLESOTECHNIC LEAGUE #1. (1963)
1A. retitled: *The night face.* (1978)
2. *The day of their return.* (1973)
3. The people of the wind. POLESOTECHNIC LEAGUE #2. (1973)
2-3. *The people of the wind; and, The day of their return.* (1982)

DAVID FALKAYN

The trouble twisters. (1966)

DOMINIC FLANDRY

We claim these stars! (1959)
Earthman, go home! (1960)
Mayday orbit. (1961)
Agent of the Terran Empire. (1965)
Ensign Flandry. (1966)
Flandry of Terra. (1965)
The rebel worlds. (1969)
A circus of hells. (1970)
A knight of ghosts and shadows. (1974)
retitled: *Knight Flandry.* (1980)
A stone in heaven. (1979)
The game of empire. (1985)

NICHOLAS VAN RIJN

1. *Satan's world.* POLESOTECHNIC LEAGUE #3. (1969)
2. Trader to the stars. POLESOTECHNIC LEAGUE #4. (1964)
3. War of the wing-men. POLESOTECHNIC LEAGUE #5. (1958)
3A. retitled: *The man who counts.* (1978)
4. *Mirkheim.* POLESOTECHNIC LEAGUE #6. (1977)
5. *The earth book of stormgate.* (1978)
6. *The long night.* (1983)

POLESOTECHNIC LEAGUE

1. *Let the spacemen beware!* (1963)
2. *The people of the wind.* (1973)
3. *Satan's world.* (1969)
4. *Trader to the stars.* (1964)
5. *War of the wing-men.* (1958)
6. *Mirkheim.* (1977)

FUTURE HISTORY SERIES (Jerry Pournelle)

The mote in God's eye. [*with* Larry Niven]. (1974)
The mercenary. FALKENBERG #1. (1977)
West of honor. FALKENBERG #2. (1976)
Future history, incorporating The mercenary and West of honor. (1980)
Prince of mercenaries: a novel of Falkenberg's Legion. FALKENBERG #3. (1989)
Falkenberg's legion. (1990)
Go tell the Spartans. FALKENBERG #4. [*with* S. M. Stirling]. (1991)

FUTURE HISTORY: LAZARUS LONG (Robert A. Heinlein)

FUTURE HISTORY

The green hills of Earth. (1951)
The man who sold the Moon. (1950)
Universe. (1951)
Orphans of the sky [includes *Universe*]. (1963)
The past through tomorrow [an omnibus volume]. (1973)

LAZARUS LONG

1. *Methuselah's children.* (1958)
2. *Time enough for love; the lives of Lazarus Long; a novel.* (1973)
3. *The cat who walks through walls: a comedy of manners.* (1985)
4. *To sail beyond the sunset: the life and loves of Maureen Johnson: (being the memoirs of a somewhat irregular lady).* (1987)
The notebooks of Lazarus Long. (1978)

FUZZIES (H. Beam Piper and others)

1. *Little Fuzzy.* (1962)
2. *The other human race.* (1964)
2A. *Fuzzy sapiens.* (1976)
3. *Fuzzies and other people.* (1984)
1-2. *The Fuzzy papers.* (1977)

Associated Titles

Fuzzy bones. [William Tuning]. (1981)
Golden dream: a Fuzzy odyssey. [Ardath Mayhar]. (1982)
The adventures of Little Fuzzy. [with Benson Parker]. (1983)

G-8 SERIES (Robert J. Hogan)

G-8 and his battle aces. (1985)
Scourge of the steel mask: a G-8 air-war thriller. (1985)

GAD'S HALL (Norah Lofts)

1. *Gad's Hall.* (1977)
2. *Haunted house.* (1978)
2A. *The haunting of Gad's Hall.* (1979)
1-2. *Gad's Hall; and, The haunting of Gad's Hall.* (1979)?

GAEA (John Varley)

1. *Titan.* (1979)
2. *Wizard.* (1980)
3. *Demon.* (1984)

THE GAEAN REACH (Jack Vance)

1. *Trullion: Alastor 2262.* (1973)
2. *The Gray Prince.* (1975)
3. *Marune: Alastor 933.* (1975)
4. *Maske: Thaery.* (1976)
5. *Wyst: Alastor 1716.* (1978)
6. *Galactic Effectuator.* (1980)

GALACTIC CENTRAL BIBLIOGRAPHIES FOR THE AVID READER (Gordon Benson Jr. & Phil Stephensen-Payne & Virgil S. Utter Jr.)

1. *Phil. Poul Anderson, myth-master and wonder-maker: a working bibliography, 5th ed.* [Gordon Benson Jr. & Phil Stephensen-Payne]. (1989)
2. *Gordon Rupert Dickson, first Dorsai: a working bibliography, 4th rev. ed.* [Gordon Benson Jr. & Phil Stephensen-Payne]. (1990)
3. *Arthur Bertram Chandler, master navigator of space: a working bibliography, 2nd ed.* [Gordon Benson Jr.]. (1989)
4. *Hal Clement, scientist with a mission: a working bibliography.* [Gordon Benson Jr.]. (1989)
5. *Edgar Pangborn: a bibliography.* [Gordon Benson Jr.]. (1985)
6. *Henry Beam Piper.* [Gordon Benson Jr.]. (1985)
7. *William Tenn (Philip Klass).* [Gordon Benson Jr.]. (1987)
8. *Arthur Wilson "Bob" Tucker.* [Gordon Benson Jr.]. (1985)
9. *Harry Maxwell Harrison, stainless steel talent: a working bibliography, 4th rev. ed.* [Gordon Benson Jr. & Phil Stephensen-Payne]. (1989)
10. *Jack (John Stewart) Williamson, child and father of wonder.* [Gordon Benson Jr.]. (1985)
11. *John Brunner, shockwave writer: a working bibliography, 3rd ed.* [Gordon Benson Jr. & Phil Stephensen-Payne]. (1989)
12. *James White, doctor to aliens: a working bibliography.* [Gordon Benson Jr.]. (1986)
13. *Anne McCaffrey, dragonlady and more: a working bibliography, 3rd rev. ed.* [Gordon Benson Jr. & Phil Stephensen-Payne]. (1989)
14. *Bob Shaw, artist at ground zero, 4th rev. ed.* [Gordon Benson Jr. & Phil Stephensen-Payne]. (1989)
15. *Margaret St. Clair.* [Gordon Benson Jr.]. (1986)
16. *John Wyndham Parkes Lucas Beynon Harris: a bibliography.* [Phil Stephensen-Payne]. (1988?)
16A. *John Wyndham, creator of the cosy catastrophe: a working bibliography, 2nd rev. ed.* [Phil Stephensen-Payne]. (1989)
17. *Manly Wade Wellman, the gentleman from Chapel Hill: a memorial working bibliography.* [Gordon Benson Jr.]. (1986)
18. *Philip Kindred Dick, metaphysical conjurer: a working bibliography, 3rd rev. ed.* [Gordon Benson Jr. & Phil Stephensen-Payne]. (1990)
20. *Leigh Douglass Brackett and Edmond Hamilton: a working bibliography.* [Gordon Benson Jr.]. (1988)
21. *Catherine Lucille Moore & Henry Kuttner, a marriage of souls and talent: a working bibliography, 3rd rev. ed.* [Gordon Benson Jr. & Virgil S. Utter Jr.]. (1989)
22. *Fritz Leiber, sardonic swordsman: a working bibliography, 2nd rev. ed.* [Gordon Benson Jr. & Phil Stephensen-Payne]. (1990)
23. *Philip José Farmer, good-natured groundbreaker: a working bibliography, 2nd rev. ed.* [Gordon Benson Jr. & Phil Stephensen-Payne]. (1990)
24. *Eric Frank Russell, our sentinel in space: a working bibliography, 2nd rev. ed.* [Phil Stephensen-Payne]. (1988)
25. *Christopher Samuel Youd, master of all genres: a working bibliography, 2nd ed.* [Phil Stephensen-Payne]. (1990)
26. *Brian Wilson Aldiss, a man for all seasons: a working bibliography, 2nd ed.* [Phil Stephensen-Payne]. (1990)
27. *George R. R. Martin, the ace from New Jersey: a working bibliography, 2nd rev. ed.* [Phil Stephensen-Payne]. (1989)
28. *Jack Vance, a fantasmic imagination: a working bibliography, 2nd rev. ed.* [Gordon Benson Jr. & Phil Stephensen-Payne]. (1990)
29. *Cyril M. Kornbluth, the cynical scrutineer: a working bibliography, 2nd rev. ed.* [Gordon Benson Jr. & Phil Stephensen-Payne]. (1990)
30. *Keith Laumer, ambassador to space: a working bibliography, 2nd rev. ed.* [Gordon Benson Jr. & Phil Stephensen-Payne]. (1990)
31. *James Tiptree Jr., a lady of letters: a working bibliography.* [Gordon Benson Jr. & Phil Stephensen-Payne]. (1989)
32. *Theodore Sturgeon, sculptor of love and hate: a working bibliography.* [Gordon Benson Jr. & Phil Stephensen-Payne]. (1989)
34. *Frederik Pohl, merchant of excellence: a working bibliography.* [Gordon Benson Jr. & Phil Stephensen-Payne]. (1989)
35. *Piers Anthony: biblio of an ogre: a working bibliography.* [Phil Stephensen-Payne]. (1990)
36. *Frank Herbert, a voice from the desert: a working bibliography.* [Phil Stephensen-Payne]. (1990)
37. *Fred Saberhagen, Berserker man: a working bibliography.* [Phil Stephensen-Payne]. (1991)
40. *Marion Zimmer Bradley, mistress of magic: a working bibliography.* [Gordon Benson Jr. & Phil Stephensen-Payne]. (1991)

GALACTIC CONNECTIVITY SEQUENCE (David Belden)

1. *Children of Arable.* (1987)
2. *To warm the Earth.* (1988)

GALACTIC MILIEU—SEE: SAGA OF PLIOCENE EXILE

GALAXY 5 (Leo P. Kelley)

1. *Good-bye to Earth.* (1979)
2. *On the red world.* (1979)
3. *Vacation in space.* (1979)
4. *Dead moon.* (1979)
5. *Where no sun shines.* (1979)
6. *King of the stars.* (1979)

Associated Title

Galaxy 5: teacher's guide. (1979)

GAME (Robert R. Chase)

1. *The game of fox and lion.* (1986)
2. *Crucible.* (1991)

GAMEARTH TRILOGY (Kevin J. Anderson)

1. *Gamearth.* (1989)
2. *Gameplay.* (1989)
3. *Game's end.* (1990)

GAMESTER WARS (William R. Forstchen)

1. *The Alexandrian ring.* (1987)
2. *The assassin gambit.* (1988)

GAMING MAGI (David Bischoff)

1. *The Destiny Dice*. (1985)
2. *Wraith Board*. (1985)
3. *The unicorn gambit*. (1986)

GANDALARA CYCLE (Randall Garrett & Vicki Ann Heydron)

1. *The steel of Raithskar*. (1981)
2. *The glass of Dyskornis*. (1982)
3. *The bronze of Eddarta*. (1983)
4. *The well of darkness*. (1983)
5. *The search for Kä*. (1984)
6. *Return to Eddarta*. (1985)
7. *The river wall*. (1986)
1-3. *The Gandalara cycle, volume 1*. (1986)
4-6. *The Gandalara cycle, vol. 2*. (1986)

GANTS (Richard K. Abshire & William R. Clair)

1. *Gants*. (1985)
2. *The shaman tree*. (1989)

GAP INTO CONFLICT (Stephen R. Donaldson)

1. *The real story*. (1990)
2. *Forbidden knowledge*. (1991)

GARRETT (Glen Cook)

1. *Sweet silver blues*. (1987)
2. *Bitter gold hearts*. (1988)
3. *Cold copper tears*. (1988)
4. *Old tin sorrows*. (1989)
5. *Dread brass shadows*. (1990)
6. *Red iron nights*. (1991)
1-3. *The Garrett files*. (1989)

GATE TRILOGY (William Corlett)

1. *The gate of Eden*. (1974)
2. *The land beyond*. (1975)
3. *Return to the gate*. (1975)

GATES OF LUCIFER (Lloyd Arthur Eshbach)

1. *The land beyond the gate*. (1984)
2. *The armlet of the gods*. (1986)
3. *The sorceress of Scath*. (1988)
4. *The scroll of Lucifer*. (1990)

GENESIS (Donald Moffitt)

1. *The genesis quest*. (1986)
2. *Second genesis*. (1986)

GERALD KNAVE (Laurence M. Janifer)

1. *Survivor*. (1977)
2. *Knave in hand*. (1979)
3. *Knave & the game*. (1987)

GERIN (Harry Turtledove as ERIC IVERSON)

1. *Wereblood*. (1979)
2. *Werenight*. (1979)

GHOST (Duncan Ball)

1. *The ghost and the gogglebox*. (1984)
2. *The ghost and the gory story*. (1987)

GHOST HOUSE (Clare McNelly)

1. *Ghost house*. (1979)
2. *Ghost house revenge*. (1981)
1-2. *Ghost house; and, Ghost house revenge*. (1981)

GHOST SQUAD (E. W. Hildick)

1. *The Ghost Squad breaks through*. (1984)
2. *The Ghost Squad and the Halloween conspiracy*. (1985)
3. *The Ghost Squad flies Concorde*. (1985)
4. *The Ghost Squad and the Ghoul of Grünberg*. (1986)
5. *The Ghost Squad and the prowling hermits*. (1987)
6. *The Ghost Squad and the menace of the Malevs*. (1988)

GHOSTBUSTERS (various authors)

1. *Ghostbusters: a storybook*. [Anne Digby]. (1984)
2A. *Ghostbusters II: a novel*. [B. B. Hiller]. (1989)
2B. *Ghostbusters II*. [Ed Naha]. (1989)
2C. *Ghostbusters II: a novel*. [R. L. Stine]. (1989)

GHOSTER (Lee McKeone)

1. *Ghoster*. (1988)
2. *Backblast*. (1989)
3. *Starfire down*. (1991)

GHOSTWORLD (Barbara Siegel & Scott Siegel)

1. *Beyond terror*. (1991)
2. *Midnight chill*. (1991)

G.I. JOE (various authors)

1. *Siege of Serpentor*. [R. L. Stine]. (1988)
2. *Divide and conquer*. [Margot Becker]. (1988)
3. *Fool's gold*. [S. M. Ballard]. (1988)
4. *Invisibility island*. [Kathryn Lance as LYNN BEACH]. (1988)
5. *Jungle raid*. [R. L. Stine]. (1988)
6. *The sultan's secret*. [Peter Lerangis]. (1988)

G.I. JOE: FIND YOUR FATE—SEE: FIND YOUR FATE: G.I. JOE

GIANT UNDER THE SNOW (John Gordon)

1. *The giant under the snow*. (1968)
2. *Ride the wind*. (1989)

GIFTWISH (Graham Martin)

1. *Giftwish*. (1980)
2. *Catchfire*. (1981)

GILGAMESH (Robert Silverberg)

1. *Gilgamesh the king*. (1984)
2. *To the land of the living*. (1989)

GIRADOUX MANUSCRIPT—SEE: CHARIOTS OF FIRE

GIRL FACTORY (Robert Franklin Murphy)

1. *The girl factory.* (1975)
2. *King's mate.* (1975)
3. *The man-made woman.* (1976)

GLADE OF DREAMS (Simon Farrell & Jon Sutherland)

1. *Darian: master magician.* (1987)
2. *Issel: warrior king.* (1987)

GLITTERING (Susan Howatch)

1. *Glittering images.* (1987)
2. *Glamorous powers.* (1988)

GLORY ROAD (Robert A. Heinlein and others)

1. *Glory road.* (1963)
2. *Fate's trick.* [Matthew J. Costello]. (1988)

GNOME (Esther M. Friesner)

1. *Gnome man's land.* (1991)
2. *Harpy High.* (1991)

GNOMES (Wil Huygen)

1. *Gnomes.* (1977)
2. *Secrets of the gnomes.* (1982)

GOBLIN (Teresa Edgerton)

1. *Goblin moon.* (1991)
2. *The gnome's engine.* (1991)

G.O.D. INC. (Jack L. Chalker)

1. *The labyrinth of dreams.* (1987)
2. *The shadow dancers.* (1987)
3. *The maze in the mirror.* (1989)

GODS IN A VORTEX (David Houston)

1. *Gods in a vortex.* (1979)
2. *Wingmaster.* (1981)

GODS OF IRELAND (Kenneth C. Flint as CASEY FLYNN)

1. *Most ancient song.* (1991)
2. *The enchanted isles.* (1991)

GOLDEN DRAGON FANTASY GAMEBOOKS (various authors)

1. *Crypt of the vampire.* [Dave Morris]. (1984)
2. *The temple of flame.* [Oliver Johnson & Dave Morris]. (1984)
3. *The lord of Shadow Keep.* [Oliver Johnson]. (1985)
4. *The eye of the Dragon.* [Dave Morris]. (1985)
5. *Curse of the Pharaoh.* [Oliver Johnson]. (1985)
6. *Castle of Lost Souls.* [Dave Morris & Yve Newnham]. (1985)

GOLDEN GIRL AND THE GUARDIANS OF THE GEMSTONES—SEE: FIND YOUR FATE—JUNIOR GOLDEN GIRL

GONDWANE EPIC (Lin Carter)

1. *The warrior of world's end.* (1974)
2. *The enchantress of world's end.* (1975)
3. *The immortal of world's end.* (1976)
4. *The barbarian of world's end.* (1977)
5. *The pirate of world's end.* (1978)

GONJI: KNIGHTS OF WONDER (T. C. Rypel)

1. *Deathwind of Vedun.* (1982)
2. *Samurai steel.* (1982)
3. *Samurai combat.* (1983)
4. *Fortress of lost worlds.* (1985)
5. *Gonji.* (1986)

GOONIES (various authors)

1. *Goonies.* [James Kahn]. (1985)
2. *Cavern of horror.* [William Rotsler]. (1985)

GOR (John Norman)

1. *Tarnsman of Gor.* (1966)
2. *Outlaw of Gor.* (1967)
3. *Priest-Kings of Gor.* (1968)
4. *Nomads of Gor.* (1969)
5. *Assassin of Gor.* (1970)
6. *Raiders of Gor.* (1971)
7. *Capitve of Gor.* (1972)
8. *Hunters of Gor.* (1974)
9. *Marauders of Gor.* (1975)
10. *Tribesmen of Gor.* (1976)
11. *Slave girl of Gor.* (1977)
12. *Beasts of Gor.* (1978)
13. *Explorers of Gor.* (1979)
14. *Fighting slave of Gor.* (1980)
15. *Rogue of Gor.* (1981)
16. *Guardsman of Gor.* (1981)
17. *Savages of Gor.* (1982)
18. *Blood brothers of Gor.* (1982)
19. *Kajira of Gor.* (1983)
20. *Players of Gor.* (1984)
21. *Mercenaries of Gor.* (1985)
22. *Dancer of Gor.* (1985)
23. *Renegades of Gor.* (1986)
24. *Vagabonds of Gor.* (1987)
25. *Magicians of Gor.* (1988)
1-3. *Gor omnibus.* (1972)

Parodies

Bodoman of Sor. [Norma N. Johns]. (1977?)

GORD THE ROGUE (Gary Gygax)

1. *Sea of death.* (1987)
2. *Night arrant: a collection of short stories featuring Gord, his friends, and his foes.* (1987)
3. *City of hawks.* (1987)
4. *Come endless darkness.* (1988)
5. *Dance of demons.* (1988)

GORMENGHAST (Mervyn Peake)

1. *Titus Groan.* (1946)
2. *Gormenghast.* (1950)
3. *Titus alone.* (1959/1970)
1-3. *The Titus books.* (1983)
1-3. *The Gormenghast trilogy.* (1988)
1-3. *Gormenghast.* (1991)

Associated Title

Boy in darkness. (1976)

GRAILQUEST (J. H. Brennan)

1. *The castle of darkness.* (1984)
2. *The den of dragons.* (1984)
3. *The gateway of doom.* (1984)
4. *Voyage of terror.* (1985)
5. *Kingdom of horror.* (1985)
6. *Realm of chaos.* (1986)

GRAMARYE (Christopher Stasheff)

1. *Escape velocity.* (1983)
2. *The warlock in spite of himself.* (1969)
3. *King Kobold.* (1971)
3A. *King Kobold revived.* (1984)
4. *The Warlock unlocked.* (1982)
5. *The Warlock enraged.* (1985)
6. *The Warlock wandering.* (1986)
7. *The Warlock is missing.* (1986)
8. *The Warlock heretical.* (1987)
9. *The Warlock's companion.* (1988)
10. *The Warlock insane.* (1989)
11. *The Warlock rock.* (1990)
12. *Warlock and son.* (1991)
1-2. *To the magic born.* (1986)
1-3. *Warlock to the magic born.* (1990)
3-5. *The Warlock enlarged.* (1986)
4-5. *The Warlock enlarged.* (1991)
6-7. *The Warlock's night out.* (1990)
6-8. *The Warlock's night out.* (1991)
8-10. *Odd warlock out.* (1989)

Associated titles

A warlock's blade: a Crossroads adventure in the world of Christopher Stasheff's Warlock of Gramarye. [Megahn Perry & Mark C. Perry]. (1987)

GRAND FENWICK (Leonard Wibberley)

1. *Beware of the mouse.* (1958)
2. *The mouse that roared.* (1955)
2A. *The wrath of grapes.* (1955)
3. *The mouse on the Moon.* (1962)
4. *The mouse on Wall Street.* (1969)
5. *The true and secret history of how the world oil crisis was solved by the Duchy of Grand Fenwick; or, The Mouse that saved the West.* (1981)

GRANDVERGER SERIES (Daniel Sernine)

The Scorpion's treasure. (1990)
The sword of Arhapal. (1990)

GREAT ALTA (Jane Yolen)

1. *Sister Light, Sister Dark.* (1988)
2. *White Jenna.* (1989)
1-2. *The Books of Great Alta.* (1990)

GREAT CENTRAL LIBRARY (James Tiptree Jr.)

1. *Brightness falls from the air.* (1985)
2. *The starry rift.* (1986)

GREAT ISSUES OF THE DAY (various authors)

1. *The future of the space program; Large corporations & society: discussions with 22 science-fiction writers.* [Jeffrey M. Elliot]. (1981)
2. *The trilemma of world oil politics.* [Sheikh R. Ali & Jeffrey M. Elliot]. (1991)
3. *Fidel by Fidel: a new interview with Dr. Fidel Castro Ruz, President of the Republic of Cuba.* [Rep. Mervyn M. Dymally & Jeffrey M. Elliot]. (1993)
4. *To kill or not to kill: thoughts on capital punishment.* [Rep. William L. Clay Sr.]. (1990)

GREAT SKY RIVER (Gregory Benford)

1. *Great Sky River.* (1987)
2. *Tides of light.* (1989)

GREATAWAY: SONG OF EARTH (Michael Coney)

1. *The celestial steam locomotive.* (1983)
2. *Gods of the Greataway.* (1984)
3. *Fang, the gnome.* (1988)
4. *King of the scepter'd isle.* (1989)

GREEN KNOWE (L. M. Boston)

1. *The children of Green Knowe.* (1954)
2. *The chimneys of Green Knowe.* (1958)
2A. *Treasure of Green Knowe.* (1958)
3. *The river at Green Knowe.* (1959)
4. *A stranger at Green Knowe.* (1961)
5. *An enemy at Green Knowe.* (1964)
6. *Guardians of the house.* (1974)
7. *The stones of Green Knowe.* (1976)

GREEN LION TRILOGY (Teresa Edgerton)

1. *Child of Saturn.* (1989)
2. *The moon in hiding.* (1989)
3. *The work of the sun.* (1990)

GREEN STAR (Lin Carter)

1. *Under the green star.* (1972)
2. *When the green star calls.* (1973)
3. *By the light of the green star.* (1974)
4. *As the Green Star rises.* (1975)
5. *In the Green Star's glow.* (1976)

GREENBRIAR QUEEN (Sheila Gilluly)

1. *Greenbriar queen.* (1988)
2. *The crystal keep.* (1988)
3. *Ritnym's daughter.* (1989)

GREENHOUSE (Dakota James)

1. *Greenhouse: it will happen in 1997.* (1984)
2. *Milwaukee the beautiful.* (1986)

GREEN-SKY (Zilpha K. Snyder)

1. *Below the root.* (1975)
2. *And all between.* (1976)
3. *Until the celebration.* (1977)

GREMLINS (various authors)

1. *Gremlins.* [George Gipe]. (1984)
2. *Gremlins 2: the new batch.* [David Bischoff]. (1990)

Associated Title

The Gremlins story book. [Mary Carey]. 1984

GREYHAWK ADVENTURES (various authors)

1. Saga of old city: a novel of swordplay, thievery, and magic. [Gary Gygax]. (1985)
2. Artifact of evil: a novel of fantastic action in a world where magic is law. [Gary Gygax]. (1986)
3. Master Wolf: a novel of quest and romance, sorcery and death. [Rose Estes]. (1987)
4. The price of power: a journey into an incredible world of magic and peril. [Rose Estes]. (1987)
5. The demon hand: a journey to a land of wizards, demons, and magical gems. [Rose Estes]. (1988)
6. The name of the game: a journey to a land of wizards, kings, and magical gems. [Rose Estes]. (1988)
7. The eyes have it: an adventure in a land of wizards, demons, and fire-breathing dragons. [Rose Estes]. (1989)

GREYLOCK (Duncan McGeary)

1. Snowcastles. (1981)
2. Icetowers. (1982)

GRIMES SAGA (A. Bertram Chandler)

The big black mark. (1975)
The broken cycle. (1975)
The way back. (1976)
Far Traveller. (1977)
retitled: The Far Traveler. (1979)
Star courier. (1977)
To keep the ship. (1978)
Matilda's stepchildren. (1979)
Star loot. (1980)
The Anarch lords. (1981)
The wild ones. (1984)
The last Amazon. (1984)

Grimes Doubles

1. The road to the Rim; [and, The hard way up]. (1978)
2. The inheritors; [and, Gateway to never]. (1978)
3. The dark dimensions; [and, The Rim gods]. (1978)
4. Into the alternate universe; [and, Contraband from otherspace]. (1979)
5. The Commodore at sea; [and, Spartan planet]. (1979)

RIM SERIES

Spartan planet. [retitling of False fatherland]. (1969)
The last Amazon. (1984)

GUARDIANS (Victor Milán as RICHARD AUSTIN)

1. The Guardians. (1985)
2. Trial by fire. (1985)
3. Thunder of Hell. (1985)
4. Night of the phoenix. (1985)
5. Armageddon run. (1986)
6. War zone. (1986), 217
7. Brute force. (1987)
8. Desolation road. (1987)
9. Vengeance day. (1987)

10. Freedom fight. (1988)
11. Valley of the gods. (1988)
12. Plague years. (1988)
13. Devil's deal. (1989)
14. Death from above. (1990)
15. Snake eyes. (1990)
16. Death charge. (1991)

GUARDIANS (various authors as PETER SAXON)

1. The killing bone. [W. Howard Baker]. (1969)
2. Dark ways to death. [W. Howard Baker & Wilfred G. McNeilly]. (1968)
3. The haunting of Alan Mais. [W. Howard Baker & Wilfred G. McNeilly]. (1969)
4. The vampires of Finistère. [author unknown]. (1970)

Unnumbered books

The Guardians / by W. Howard Baker. (1967)
The curse of Rathlaw. [Martin Thomas & W. Howard Baker]. (1968)
Through the dark curtain. [author unknown]. (1968)

GUARDIANS OF THE FLAME (Joel Rosenberg)

1. The sleeping dragon: a fantasy novel. (1983)
2. The sword and the chain. (1984)
3. The silver crown: a fantastic novel. (1985)
4. The heir apparent. (1987)
5. The warrior lives. (1989)
6. The road to Ehvenor. (1991)
1-3. Guardians of the flame: The warriors. (1985)
4-5. Guardians of the flame: The heroes. (1989)

GUARDIANS OF THE TALL STONES—SEE: SACRED STONES

GUARDIANS OF THE THREE (various authors)

1. Lord of Cragsclaw. [Bill Fawcett & Neil Randall]. (1989)
2. Keeper of the city. [Diane Duane & Peter Morwood]. (1989)
3. The wizard of Tizare. [Matthew J. Costello]. (1990)
4. Defenders of Ar. [Jack Lovejoy]. (1990)

GUILHEM DE COURDEVAL (Daniel Rhodes)

1. Next, after Lucifer. (1987)
2. Adversary. (1988)

GUINEVERE (Sharan Newman)

1. Guinevere. (1981)
2. The chessboard queen. (1983)
3. Guinevere Evermore. (1985)

GUINEVERE (Persia Woolley)

1. Child of the northern spring. (1987)
2. Queen of the summer stars. (1990)
2A. Guinevere, queen of the summer stars. (1991)
3. Guinevere: The legend in autumn. (1991)

GULLIVER'S TRAVELS (Jonathan Swift and others)

Travels into several remote nations of the world [*Gulliver's Travels*]. (1726)
The new Gulliver; or, The adventures of Lemuel Gulliver Jr. in Capovolta: a novel. [Esmé Dodderidge]. (1979)
A voyage to Inshneefa: the first-hand account of the fifth voyage of Lemuel Gulliver. [John Paul Brady]. (1987)

GUNA SEQUENCE (Gill Alderman)

1. *The archivist: a black romance.* (1989)
2. *The land beyond.* (1990)

GUNDAM MOBILE SUIT (Yoshiyuki Tomino)

1. *Awakening.* (1990)
2. *Escalation.* (1990)
3. *Confrontation.* (1991)

GUNJER (Isidore Haiblum)

1. *Interworld.* (1977)
2. *Specterworld.* (1991)

GWALCHMAI (H. Warner Munn)

1. *King of the world's edge.* (1966)
2. *The ship from Atlantis.* (1967
3. *Merlin's ring.* (1974)
1-2. *Merlin's godson.* (1976)

GYPSY (Ron Goulart)

1. *Quest of the Gypsy.* (1976)
2. *Eye of the Vulture: a novel.* (1977)

HAAKON (Eric Neilson)

1. *The golden ax.* (1984)
2. *The Viking's revenge.* (1984)
3. *Haakon's iron hand.* (1984)
4. *The war god.* (1984)

HADES (Frederic Arnold Kummer)

1. *Ladies in Hades.* (1928)
2. *Gentlemen in Hades.* (1930)
1-2. *Shades of Hades.* (1978)

HADON OF ANCIENT OPAR (Edgar Rice Burroughs & Philip José Farmer)

Tarzan and the jewels of Opar. [Edgar Rice Burroughs]. (1918)

Hadon of Ancient Opar

1. *Hadon of ancient Opar.* [Prequel to *Tarzan and the jewels of Opar*]. (1974)
2. *Flight to Opar.* (1976)

HALLOWEEN (various authors)

1. *Halloween: a novel.* [Curtis Richards]. (1979)
2. *Halloween II.* [Dennis Etchison *as* JACK MARTIN]. (1981)

3. *Halloween III: Season of the witch.* [Dennis Etchison *as* JACK MARTIN]. (1982)
4. *Halloween IV: a novel.* [Nicholas Randers *as* NICHOLAS GRABOWSKY]. (1988)

HAMMER'S SLAMMERS (David Drake)

1. *Hammer's Slammers.* (1979/1987)
2. *Cross the stars.* (1984)
3. *At any price.* (1985)
4. *Counting the cost.* (1987)
5. *Rolling hot.* (1989)
6. *The warrior.* (1991)

Associated Title

Combat command in the world of David Drake's Hammer's Slammers: Slammers down! [Todd Johnson]. (1988)

HARDWIRED (Walter Jon Williams)

1. *Hardwired.* (1986)
2. *Voice of the whirlwind.* (1987)
3. *Solip:system.* (1989)

HARK (R. L. Stine)

1. *The badlands of Hark.* (1985)
2. *The invaders of Hark.* (1985)

HAROLD SHEA (L. Sprague de Camp & Fletcher Pratt)

1 *The incomplete enchanter.* (1941)
1A. *The incompleat enchanter.* (1979)
2. *The castle of iron.* (1950)
3. *Wall of serpents.* (1960)
3A. *The enchanter compleated.* (1980)
1-2. *The compleat enchanter: the magical misadventures of Harold Shea.* (1975)
1-3. *Intrepid enchanter: the complete magical misadventures of Harold Shea.* (1988)
1-3. *The complete compleat enchanter.* (1989)

Associated Titles

Crossroads adventure. Prospero's island: a Crossroads adventure in the world of L. Sprague de Camp and Fletcher Pratt's The incomplete enchanter. [Tom Wham]. (1987)
Sir Harold and the gnome king. [L. Sprague de Camp]. (1991)

HARPER HALL—SEE: PERN

HARPERS TRILOGY—SEE: FORGOTTEN REALMS FANTASY ADVENTURE

HARRY BORG (Ward Hawkins)

1. *Red flame burning: a novel.* (1985)
2. *Sword of fire.* (1985)
3. *Blaze of wrath: a novel.* (1986)
4. *Torch of fear: a novel.* (1987)

HARRY PORTER (Ed Naha)

1. *The paradise plot.* (1980)
2. *The suicide plague.* (1982)

HAUNTING WITH LOUISA (Emily Cates)

1. *The ghost in the attic.* (1990)
2. *The mystery of Misty Island Inn.* (1990)
3. *Haunting with Louisa: the ghost ferry.* (1991)

HAUNTINGS (various authors)

1. [unknown title]
2. [unknown title]
3. [unknown title]
4. *The nightmare man.* [Tessa Krailing]. (1988)
5. *A wish at the baby's grave.* [Angela Bull]. (1988)

THE HAVEN: STACY-ADVENTURES OF THE EMPIRE PRINCESS (Graham Diamond)

1. *The Haven.* (1977)
2. *Lady of the Haven.* STACY #1. (1978)
3. *Dungeons of Kuba.* STACY #2. (1979)
4. *The Falcon of Eden.* STACY #3. (1980)
5. *The beasts of Hades.* STACY #4. (1981)

HAWK & FISHER (Simon Green)

1. *Hawk & Fisher.* (1990)
1A. *No haven for the guilty.* (1990)
2. *Winner takes all.* (1991)
2A. *Devil take the hindmost.* (1991)
3. *The god killer.* (1991)
4. *Wolf in the fold.* (1991)
5. *Guard against dishonor.* (1991)

HAWKLAN (Roger Taylor)

1. *The call of the sword.* (1988)
2. *The fall of Fyorlund.* (1989)
3. *The waking of Orthlund.* (1989)
4. *Into Narsindal.* (1990)

HAWKLORDS (various authors)

1. *The time of the Hawklords.* [Michael Butterworth & Michael Moorcock]. (1976)
2. *Queens of Deliria.* [Michael Butterworth]. (1977)

HEARTQUEST (various authors)

1. *Ring of the ruby dragon.* [Jeannie Black]. (1983)
2. *Talisman of Valdegarde.* [Madeleine Simon]. (1983)
3. *Secret sorcerers.* [Linda Lowery]. (1983)
4. *Isle of illusion.* [Madeleine Simon]. (1983)
5. *Moon dragon summer.* [Linda Lowery]. (1984)
6. *Lady of the winds.* [Kate Novak]. (1984)

HEAVEN CHRONICLES (Joan D. Vinge)

1. *The outcasts of Heaven Belt.* (1978)
2. *Legacy.* (1991)
1-2. *Heaven chronicles.* (1991)

HED (Patricia A. McKillip)

1. *The riddle-master of Hed.* (1978)
2. *Heir of sea & fire.* (1978)
3. *Harpist in the wind.* (1979)
1-3. *Riddle of stars.* (1979)
1-3. *The chronicles of Morgon, Prince of Hed.* (1981)

HEECHEE (Frederik Pohl)

1. *Gateway.* (1977)
2. *Beyond the blue event horizon.* (1980)
3. *Heechee rendezvous: a novel.* (1984)
4. *Annals of the Heechee.* (1987)
5. *The gateway trip: tales and vignettes of the Heechee.* (1990)

HEIRS OF ST. CAMBER—SEE: DERYNI CHRONICLES

HEIRS TO BYZANTIUM (Susan M. Shwartz)

1. *Byzantium's crown.* (1987)
2. *The woman of flowers.* (1987)
3. *Queensblade.* (1988)

HEIRS TO GNARLSMYRE (Mike Jefferies)

1. *Glitterspike Hall.* (1989)
2. *Hall of whispers.* (1990)

HEL (C. Dean Andersson as ASA DRAKE)

1. *Warrior Witch of Hel.* (1985)
2. *Death Riders of Hel.* (1986)
3. *Werebeasts of Hel.* (1986)

HELLICONIA (Brian W. Aldiss)

1. *Helliconia spring.* (1982)
2. *Helliconia summer.* (1983)
3. *Helliconia winter.* (1985)

HELMSMAN (Bill Baldwin)

1. *The helmsman.* (1985)
2. *Galactic convoy.* (1987)
3. *The trophy.* (1990)
4. *The mercenaries.* (1991)

HENRY HOLLINS (Willis Hall)

1. *The summer of the dinosaur.* (1977)
1A. *Henry Hollins and the dinosaur.* (1988)
2. *Dr Jekyll and Mr Hollins.* (1988)

HERALD CHILDE (Philip José Farmer)

1. *The image of the beast.* (1968)
2. *Blown.* (1969)
3. *Traitor to the living.* (1973)
1-2. *Image of the beast.* (1979)

HERALDS OF VALDEMAR (Mercedes Lackey)

1. *Arrows of the Queen.* (1987)
2. *Arrow's flight.* (1987)
3. *Arrow's fall.* (1988)

HERBIE SERIES (various authors)

1. *The love bug.* [Mel Cebulash]. (1969)
2. *Herbie rides again.* [Mel Cebulash]. (1974)
3. *Herbie goes to Monte Carlo.* [Vic Crume]. (1977)
4. *Herbie goes bananas.* [Joe Claro]. (1980)
5. *Herbie the matchmaker.* [Joe Claro]. (1982)

HERITAGE UNIVERSE (Charles Sheffield)

1. *Summertide.* (1990)

2. *Divergence.* (1991)

HEROES IN HELL (Janet Morris with various co-authors)

1. *Heroes in Hell.* (1986)
2. *Rebels in Hell.* (1986)
3. *The gates of Hell.* [With C. J. Cherryh]. (1986)
4. *Masters in Hell.* (1988)
5. *Kings in Hell.* [With C. J. Cherryh]. (1987)
6. *Angels in Hell.* (1987)
7. *Crusaders in Hell.* (1987)
8. *Legions of Hell.* [By C. J. Cherryh]. (1987)
9. *War in Hell.* (1988)
10. *The Little Helliad.* [With Chris Morris]. (1988)
11. *Explorers in Hell.* [With David Drake]. (1989)
12. *Prophets in Hell.* (1989)

HEROES INC. (Kyle Crocco)

1. *Heroes, Inc.* (1991)
2. *Heroes wanted.* (1991)

HIERO DESTEEN (Sterling E. Lanier)

1. *Hiero's journey.* (1973)
2. *The unforsaken Hiero.* (1983)
1-2. *Hiero Desteen.* (1984)

HIGH TREASON (Allen Upward)

1. *High treason.* (1903)
2. *Romance of politics: The fourth conquest of England* (1904)

HIGHROAD TRILOGY (Alis A. Rasmussen)

1. *A passage of stars.* (1990)
2. *Revolution's shore.* (1990)
3. *The price of ransom.* (1990)

HILL OF SUMMER (Allen Drury)

1. *The hill of summer: a novel of the Soviet conquest.* (1981)
2. *The roads of Earth: a novel.* (1984)

HISTORICAL ILLUMINATUS CHRONICLES (Robert Anton Wilson)

1. *The earth will shake: a novel.* (1982)
2. *The widow's son.* (1985)
3. *Nature's god.* (1991)

HISTORIES OF KING KELSON—SEE: DERYNI CHRONICLES

HISTORY OF MIDDLE-EARTH (J. R. R. Tolkien; edited by Christopher Tolkien)

1. *The book of lost tales, part I.* (1983)
2. *The book of lost tales, part II.* (1984)
3. *Lays of Beleriand.* (1985)
4. *The shaping of Middle-Earth: the Quenta, the Ambarkanta, and the Annals, together with the earliest 'Silmarillion' and the first map.* (1986)
5. *The lost road, and other writings.* (1987)
6. *The return of the shadow.* HISTORY OF THE LORD OF THE RINGS #1. (1988)
7. *The treason of Isengard.* HISTORY OF THE LORD OF THE RINGS #2. (1989)

8. *The war of the ring.* HISTORY OF THE LORD OF THE RINGS #3. (1990)

HISTORY OF THE LORD OF THE RINGS—SEE: HISTORY OF MIDDLE-EARTH

HISTORY OF THE RUNESTAFF (Michael Moorcock)

1. *The jewel in the skull.* (1967)
2. *Sorcerer's amulet.* (1968)
2A. *The Mad God's amulet.* (1969)
3. *Sword of the dawn.* (1968)
4. *The secret of the Runestaff.* (1969)
4A. retitled: *The Runestaff.*
1-4. *The history of the Runestaff.* (1979)

HITCHHIKER (Douglas Adams)

1. *The hitch hiker's guide to the galaxy.* (1979)
1A. *The hitchhiker's guide to the galaxy.* (1980)
2. *The Restaurant at the End of the Universe.* (1980)
3. *Life, the universe and everything.* (1982)
4. *So long, and thanks for all the fish.* (1984)
1-3. *The hitchhiker's trilogy.* (1983)
1-4. *The hitchhiker's guide to the galaxy.* (1986)
1-4. *The Hitchhiker's quartet.* (1986)
1-4. *The more than complete Hitchhiker's guide.* (1987)

HOKA (Poul Anderson & Gordon R. Dickson)

1. *Earthman's burden.* (1957)
2. *Star Prince Charlie.* (1975)
3. *Hoka!* (1983)

HOLDERLY HALL (Linda DuBreuil as KATE CAMERON)

1. *The legend of Holderly Hall.* (1974)
2. *Shadows of the past.* (1974)
3. *Voices in the fog.* (1975)
4. *Deadly nightshade.* (1975)
5. *Music from the past.* (1975)
6. *Portraits of the past.* (1975)

HOMER CRAWFORD (Mack Reynolds)

1. *Blackman's burden.* (1972)
2. *Border, breed, nor birth.* (1972)
3. *The best ye breed.* (1978)

HONEY B (Stephen Goldin)

1. *Scavenger hunt.* (1976)
2. *Finish line.* (1976)

HOOD'S ARMY TRILOGY (Chris Evans as NATHAN ELLIOTT)

1. *Earth invaded.* (1986)
2. *Staveworld.* (1986)
3. *The liberators.* (1986)

HOOK (Kenneth Bulmer as TULLY ZETFORD)

1. *Whirlpool of stars.* (1974)
2. *The boosted man.* (1974)
3. *Secret under the Caribbean.* (1964)
4. *Hook: Virility gene.* (1975)

HORN (Ben Sloane)

1. *Hot zone*. (1990)
2. *Blown dead*. (1990)
3. *Outland strip*. (1991)
4. *Ultimate weapon*. (1991)

HORROR HIGH (various authors as NICHOLAS ADAMS)

1. *Mr. Popularity*. [Clay Coleman]. (1990)
2. *Resolved, you're dead*. [Clay Coleman]. (1990)
3. *Heartbreaker*. [Clay Coleman]. (1991)
4. *New kid on the block*. [Clay Coleman]. (1991)
5. *Hard rock*. [Clay Coleman]. (1991)
6. *Sudden death*. [Bruce Fretts]. (1991)
7. *Pep rally*. [Debra Doyle & James D. Macdonald]. (1991)
8. *Final curtain*. [Sherwood Smith]. (1991)

HORRORSCOPE (Robert Lory)

1. *The green flames of Aries*. (1974)
2. *The revenge of Taurus*. (1974)
3. *The curse of Leo*. (1974)
4. *Gemini smile, Gemini kill*. (1975)

HORSE (Mary Stanton)

1. *The heavenly horse from the outermost west*. (1988)
2. *Piper at the gate*. (1989)
2A. *Piper at the gates of dawn*. (1989)

HORSECLANS (Robert Adams)

1. *The coming of the Horseclans*. (1975/1982)
2. *Swords of the Horseclans*. (1977)
3. *Revenge of the Horseclans*. (1977)
4. *A cat of silvery hue*. (1979)
5. *The savage mountains*. (1980)
6. *The patrimony*. (1980)
7. *Horseclans odyssey*. (1981)
8. *The death of a legend*. (1981)
9. *The witch goddess*. (1982)
10. *Bili the Axe*. (1983)
11. *Champion of the last battle*. (1983)
12. *A woman of the Horseclans*. (1983)
13. *Horses of the north*. (1985)
14. *A man called Milo Morai*. (1986)
15. *The memories of Milo Morai*. (1986)
16. *Trumpets of war*. (1987)
17. *Madman's army*. (1987)
18. *The clan of the cats*. (1988)
1-3. *Tales of the Horseclans*. (1985)

Associated titles

Friends of the Horseclans. [with Pamela Crippen Adams]. (1987)
Horseclans: Friends of the Horseclans II. [with Pamela Crippen Adams]. (1989)

HORSEGIRL (Constance Ash)

1. *The horsegirl*. (1988)
2. *The stalking horse*. (1990)

HOUND AND THE FALCON (Judith Tarr)

1. *The isle of glass*. (1985)
2. *The Golden Horn*. (1985)

3. *The hounds of God*. (1986)
1-3. *The hound and the falcon*. (1986)

HOUSE OF ENTHALA (Ardath Mayhar)

1. *Lords of the triple moons*. (1983)
2. *Runes of the lyre*. (1982)
3. *Soul singer of Tyrnos*. (1981)

HOUSE OF ZEOR—SEE: SIME/GEN

HOWL (Diana Wynne Jones)

1. *Howl's moving castle*. (1986)
2. *Castle in the air*. (1990)

HOWLING (Gary Brandner)

1. *The howling*. (1977)
2. *The howling II*. (1978)
3. *The howling III*. (1985)
3A. *Echoes*. (1985)

THE HUB: TELZEY SERIES (James H. Schmitz)

THE HUB SERIES

1. *A tale of two clocks*. (1962)
2. *A nice day for screaming, and other tales of The Hub*. (1965)
3. *The demon breed*. (1968)
4. *A pride of monsters*. (1970)

THE TELZEY SERIES

1. *The universe against her*. (1964)
2. *The Lion Game*. (1973)
3. *The Telzey Toy*. (1973)
3A. *The Telzey toy, and other stories*. (1982)

HUMANOIDS (Jack Williamson)

1. *The humanoids*. (1980)
2. *The humanoid touch*. (1980)

HUMANX SERIES—SEE: THRANX SERIES

HUNTER (Norman Conway)

1. *The omega operation*. (1974)
2. *Alpha death*. (1975)

HUNTER (Rose Estes)

1. *The hunter*. (1990)
2. *The hunter on Arena*. (1991)

HUNTERS (Thomas Hoobler & Burt Wetanson)

1. *The hunters*. (1978)
2. *The treasure hunters*. (1983)

HUNTSMAN TRILOGY (Douglas Hill)

1. *The huntsman*. (1982)
2. *Warriors of the wasteland*. (1983)
3. *Alien Citadel*. (1984)

HYBRID UNIVERSE (Karl Hansen)

1. *War games.* (1981)
2. *Dream games.* (1985)

HYDRONAUTS (Carl L. Biemiller)

1. *The hydronauts.* (1970)
2. *Follow the whales.* (1973)
3. *Escape from the Crater.* (1974)
1-2. *The hydronaut adventures.* (1981)

HYPERION (Dan Simmons)

1. *Hyperion.* (1989)
2. *The fall of Hyperion.* (1990)
1-2. *Hyperion cantos.* (1990)

I.O. EVANS STUDIES IN THE PHILOSOPHY & CRITICISM OF LITERATURE (various authors)

1. *Wilderness visions: science fiction westerns, volume one.* [David Mogen]. (1982)
2. *The pulp western: a popular history of the western fiction magazine in America.* [John A. Dinan]. (1983)
3. *Exploring fantasy worlds: essays on fantastic literature.* [Darrell Schweitzer]. (1985)
4. *The sociology of science fiction.* [Brian M. Stableford]. (1987)
5. *Sleepless nights in the procrustean bed: essays.* [Harlan Ellison]. (1984)
6. *Voices of the River Plate: interviews with writers of Argentina and Uruguay.* [Clark M. Zlotchew]. (1993)
7. *Existentially speaking: essays on the philosophy of literature.* [Colin Wilson]. (1989)
8. *Shamrocks and sea silver, and other illuminations.* [Leonard Wibberley]. (1992)
9. *Literary masters: an exercise in autobiography.* [Jeffrey M. Elliot]. (1993)
10. *Still the frame holds: essays on women, poets, and writers.* [Sheila Roberts]. (1993)
11. *Inside science fiction: essays on fantastic literature.* [James Gunn]. (1992)

ICE PROPHET (William R. Forstchen)

1. *Ice prophet.* (1983)
2. *The flame upon the ice.* (1984)
3. *A darkness upon the ice.* (1985)

ICEQUAKE (Crawford Kilian)

1. *Icequake.* (1979)
2. *Tsunami.* (1983)

ICERIGGER (Alan Dean Foster)

1. *Icerigger.* (1974)
2. *Mission to Moulokin.* (1979)
3. *The deluge drivers.* (1987)

ICEWIND DALE TRILOGY—SEE: FORGOTTEN REALMS FANTASY ADVENTURE

ILLUMINATI (Robert Anton Wilson & Robert Shea)

1. *The eye in the pyramid.* (1975)
2. *The golden apple.* (1975)

3. *Leviathan.* (1975)
4. *Right where you are sitting now.* [Robert Anton Wilson]. (1982)
1-3. *The Illuminatus! trilogy.* (1984)

IMPERIUM (Keith Laumer)

1. *Worlds of the Imperium.* (1962)
2. *The other side of time.* (1965)
3. *Assignment in nowhere.* (1968)
4. *Zone yellow.* (1990)

INCARNATIONS OF IMMORTALITY (Piers Anthony)

1. *On a pale horse.* (1983)
2. *Bearing an hourglass.* (1984)
3. *With a tangled skein.* (1985)
4. *Wielding a red sword.* (1986)
5. *Being a green mother.* (1987)
6. *For love of evil.* (1988)
7. *And eternity.* (1990)

INCOMER (Margaret Elphinstone)

1. *The incomer.* (1987)
2. *A sparrow's flight.* (1989)

INCREDIBLE HULK—SEE: MARVEL SUPERHEROES

INDIANA JONES

BANTAM BOOKS SERIES (Rob MacGregor)

1. *Indiana Jones and the peril at Delphi.* (1991)
2. *Indiana Jones and the dance of the giants.* (1991)
3. *Indiana Jones and the seven veils.* (1991)

MOVIE ADAPTATIONS

1. *Raiders of the lost Ark: novel.* [Campbell Black]. (1981)
2A. *Indiana Jones and the temple of doom.* [James Kahn]. (1984)
2B. *Indiana Jones and the temple of doom: a storybook based on the movie.* [Michael French]. (1984)
3A. *Indiana Jones and the last crusade.* [Rob MacGregor]. (1989)
3B. *Indiana Jones and the last crusade.* [Les Martin]. (1989)
3C. *Indiana Jones and the last crusade: storybook.* [Anne Digby]. (1989)

YOUNG INDIANA JONES (Les Martin)

Young Indiana Jones and the secret city. (1990)
Young Indiana Jones and the tomb of terror. (1990)
Young Indiana Jones and the gypsy revenge. (1991)
Young Indiana Jones and the princess of peril. (1991)

Associated Title

Indiana Jones and the Temple of Doom: the illustrated screenplay: the complete script. [Willard Huyck & Gloria Katz]. (1984)

INDIANA JONES—SEE ALSO: FIND YOUR FATE

INDIGO (Louise Cooper)

1. *Nemesis.* (1988)
2. *Inferno.* (1988)
3. *Infanta.* (1989)
4. *Nocturne.* (1989)
5. *Troika.* (1991)
6. *Avatar.* (1991)

INHERITOR (Marion Zimmer Bradley)

1. *The inheritor.* (1984)
2. *Witch hill.* (1990)

INLAND TRILOGY (Gwyneth Jones as ANN HALAM)

1. *The daymaker.* (1987)
2. *Transformations.* (1988)
3. *The skybreaker.* (1990)

INNER PLANETS TRILOGY—SEE: BUCK ROGERS

INQUESTOR—SEE: CHRONICLES OF THE HIGH INQUEST

INSTRUMENTALITY (Cordwainer Smith)

You will never be the same. (1963)
The planet buyer. (1964)
Space lords. (1965)
Quest of the three worlds. (1966)
The underpeople. (1968)
Under old Earth, and other explorations. (1970)
Stardreamer. (1971)
Norstrilia. [Incorporates *The planet buyer* and *The underpeople*]. (1975)
The Instrumentality of mankind. (1979)

INTERPLANETARIAS—SEE: KRISHNA

IRETA (Anne McCaffrey)

1. *Dinosaur planet.* (1978)
2. *Dinosaur planet survivors.* (1984)
1-2. *The Ireta adventure: Dinosaur planet; and, Dinosaur planet survivors.* (1985)

IRON ANGEL (John Morressy)

1. *Ironbrand.* (1980)
2. *Graymantle.* (1981)
3. *Kingsbane.* (1982)
4. *The time of the Annihilator.* (1985)

IRON MAN—SEE: MARVEL SUPERHEROES

IRON TOWER TRILOGY—SEE: MITHGARIAN SERIES

ISAAC ASIMOV'S MAGICAL WORLDS OF FANTASY (Isaac Asimov & Martin H. Greenberg & Charles G. Waugh)

1. *Wizards.* (1983)
2. *Witches.* (1984)
3. *Cosmic knights.* (1985)
4. *Spells.* (1985)
5. *Giants.* (1985)
6. *Mythical beasties.* (1986)
7. *Magical wishes.* (1986)
8. *Devils.* (1987)
9. *Atlantis.* (1988)

10. *Ghosts.* (1988)
11. *Curses.* (1989)
(12) *Faeries.* (1991)

ISAAC ASIMOV'S ROBOT CITY (various authors)

1. *Odyssey.* [Michael P. Kube-McDowell]. (1987)
2. *Suspicion.* [Mike McQuay]. (1987)
3. *Cyborg.* [William F. Wu]. (1987)
4. *Prodigy.* [Arthur Byron Cover]. (1988)
5. *Refuge.* [Rob Chilson]. (1988)
6. *Perihelion.* [William F. Wu]. (1988)

ROBOTS & ALIENS

1. *Changeling.* [Stephen Leigh]. (1989)
2. *Renegade.* [Cordell Scotten]. (1989)
3. *Intruder.* [Robert Thurston]. (1990)
4. *Alliance.* [Jerry Oltion]. (1990)
5. *Maverick.* [Bruce Bethke]. (1990)
6. *Humanity.* [Jerry Oltion]. (1990)

ISAAC ASIMOV'S SCIENCE FICTION ANTHOLOGY (George H. Scithers)

1. *Isaac Asimov's Science fiction anthology, volume 1.* [ANONYMOUSLY EDITED]. (1978)
1A. *Isaac Asimov's Masters of science fiction.* [ANONYMOUSLY EDITED]. (1978)
2. *Isaac Asimov's Marvels of science fiction.* (1979)
3. *Isaac Asimov's Science fiction anthology, volume 3.* (1980)
3A. *Isaac Asimov's Adventures of science fiction.* (1980)
4. *Isaac Asimov's Science fiction anthology, volume 4.* (1980)
4A. *Isaac Asimov's Worlds of science fiction.* (1980)
5. *Isaac Asimov's Science fiction anthology, volume 5.* (1981)
5A. *Isaac Asimov's Near futures and far.* (1981)

ISAAC ASIMOV'S WONDERFUL WORLDS OF SCIENCE FICTION (Isaac Asimov & Martin H. Greenberg & Charles G. Waugh)

1. *Intergalactic empires.* (1983)
2. *The science fictional Olympics.* (1984)
3. *Supermen.* (1984)
4. *Comets.* (1986)
5. *Tin stars.* (1986)
6. *Neanderthals.* [Edited by Robert Silverberg & Martin H. Greenberg & Charles G. Waugh]. (1987)
7. *Space shuttles.* (1987)
8. *Monsters.* (1988)
9. *Robots.* (1989)
10. *Invasions.* (1990)

ISAAC'S UNIVERSE (Martin H. Greenberg)

1. *The Diplomacy Guild.* (1990)
2. *Phases in chaos.* (1991)

ISIS (Monica Hughes)

1. *The keeper of the Isis Light.* (1980)
2. *The guardian of Isis.* (1981)
3. *The Isis pedlar.* (1982)

ISLANDIA (Austin Tappan Wright and Mark Saxton)

1. *Islandia.* [Austin Tappan Wright]. (1942)
2. *The Islar.* [Mark Saxton]. (1969)
3. *The two kingdoms.* [Mark Saxton]. (1979)
4. *Havoc in Islandia.* [Mark Saxton]. (1982)

Associated Titles

The Islandian world of Austin Wright. [Lawrence Clark Powell]. (1957)
Islandia revisited. [Richard N. Farmer]. (1983)

IT'S ALIVE! (various authors)

1. *It's alive!* [Richard Woodley]. 1977
2. *It lives again.* [James Dixon]. (1978)

JACK EICHORD (Rex Miller)

1. *Slob.* (1987)
2. *Frenzy.* (1988)
3. *Stone shadow.* (1989)
4. *Slice.* (1990)

JACK SUMNER (Ron Goulart)

1. *Death cell.* (1971)
2. *Plunder.* (1972)
3. *A whiff of madness.* (1976)

JACK, THE GIANT-KILLER (Charles de Lint)

1. *Jack, the giant-killer.* (1987)
2. *Drink down the moon.* (1990)

JADE DEMONS (Robert E. Vardeman)

1. *The quaking lands.* (1985)
2. *The frozen waves.* (1985)
3. *The crystal clouds.* (1985)
4. *The white fire.* (1986)
1-4. *The Jade Demons quartet.* (1987)

JALAV (Sharon Green)

1. *The Crystals of Mida.* (1982)
2. *An Oath to Mida.* (1983)
3. *Chosen of Mida.* (1984)
4. *The will of the gods.* (1985)
5. *To battle the gods.* (1986)

JAMES BOND SERIES—SEE: FIND YOUR FATE ADVENTURE

JAN DARZEK (Lloyd Biggle, Jr.)

1. *All the colors of darkness.* (1963)
2. *Watchers of the dark.* (1966)
3. *This darkening universe.* (1976)
4. *The whirligig of time.* (1979)

JANDAR (Lin Carter)

1. *Jandar of Callisto.* (1972)
2. *Black Legion of Callisto.* (1972)
3. *Sky pirates of Callisto.* (1973)
4. *Mad empress of Callisto.* (1975)
5. *Mind wizards of Callisto.* (1975)
6. *Lankar of Callisto.* (1975)

7. *Ylana of Callisto.* (1977)
8. *Renegade of Callisto.* (1978)

JANE SAINT (Josephine Saxton)

1. *The travails of Jane Saint, and other stories.* (1986)
2. *The consciousness machine; Jane Saint and the backlash: the further adventures of Jane Saint.* (1989)

JANISSARIES (Jerry Pournelle & Roland Green)

1. *Janissaries.* [Jerry Pournelle only]. (1979)
2. *Clan and crown.* (1982)
3. *Storms of victory.* (1987)

Associated Title

Combat command in the world of Jerry E. Pournelle's Janissaries: Lord of lances. [Mark Acres]. (1988)

JASON COSMO (Dan McGirt)

1. *Jason Cosmo.* (1989)
2. *Royal chaos.* (1990)

JASON STRIKER (Piers Anthony & Roberto Fuentes)

1. *Kiai!* (1974)
2. *Mistress of death.* (1974)
3. *The bamboo bloodbath.* (1974)
4. *Ninja's revenge.* (1975)
5. *Amazon slaughter.* (1976)

JEB STUART HO (Mick Farren)

1. *The quest of the DNA cowboys.* (1976)
2. *Synaptic manhunt.* (1976)
3. *The neural atrocity.* (1977)
4. *The last stand of the DNA cowboys.* (1989)

JEFFERSON'S WAR (Kevin Randle)

1. *The galactic silver star.* (1990)
2. *The price of command.* (1990)
3. *The lost colony.* (1991)
4. *The January platoon.* (1991)
5. *Death of a regiment.* (1991)

JEFFREY AND THE ... GHOST (H. William Stine & Megan Stine)

...And the Third Grade Ghost

1. *Mysterious Max.* (1988)
2. *Haunted halloween.* (1988)
3. *Christmas visitors.* (1988)
4. *Pet day surprise.* (1989)
5. *Max onstage.* (1989)
6. *Max saves the day.* (1989)

...And the Fourth Grade Ghost

1. *Max is back.* (1989)
2. *Baseball card fever.* (1989)
3. *Max's secret formula.* (1989)
4. *Mad science.* (1990)
5. *Camp Duck Down.* (1990)
6. *Big brother blues.* (1990)

JEM—SEE: FIND YOUR FATE—JEM

JENNY DEAN (Dale Carlson)

1. *The mystery of the shining children.* (1983)
2. *The mystery of the hidden trap.* (1983)
3. *The secret of the third eye.* (1983)
4. *The secret of the invisible city.* (1984)

JEREMY HAINES (Robert Serling)

1. *The President's plane is missing.* (1967)
2. *Air Force One is haunted.* (1985)

JEREMY MOON (Brad Strickland)

1. *Moon dreams.* (1988)
2. *Nul's quest.* (1989)
3. *Wizard's mole: a fantasy novel.* (1991)

JERRY CORNELIUS (Michael Moorcock)

1. *The final programme.* (1968)
2. *A cure for cancer.* (1971)
3. *The English assassin.* (1972)
4. *The condition of muzak.* (1977)
5. *The lives and times of Jerry Cornelius.* (1976)
6. *The entropy tango.* (1981)
7. *The adventures of Una Persson and Catherine Cornelius in the twentieth century: a romance.* (1976)
1-4. *The Cornelius chronicles: The final programme; A cure for cancer; The English assassin; The condition of muzak.* (1977)
5-6. *The Cornelius chronicles, vol. II: The lives and times of Jerry Cornelius; The entropy tango.* (1986)
7. *The Cornelius chronicles, vol. III: The adventures of Una Persson and Catherine Cornelius in the twentieth century; The alchemist's question.* (1987)

Associated Titles

The nature of the catastrophe. [with Langdon Jones]. (1971)
The opium general. (1984)

JHEREG (Steven Brust)

1. *Jhereg.* (1983)
2. *Yendi.* (1984)
3. *Teckla.* (1987)
4. *Taltos.* (1988)
4A. *Taltos and the paths of the dead.* (1991)
5. *Phoenix.* (1990)
1-3. *Taltos the assassin.* (1991)

Associated Title

Dzurlord: a Crossroads adventure in the world of Steven Brust's Jhereg. [Mark Bloom & Bill Scammell & Evan Jamieson & Lisa Hunt & Walter Hunt & Richard S. Meyer & Christine Ivey as ARCHITECTS ADVENTURE]. (1987)

JINIAN—SEE: TRUE GAME SERIES

JOE KARNS (Robert Coulson & Gene DeWeese)

1. *Now you see it/him/them...* (1975)
2. *Charles Fort never mentioned wombats.* (1977)

JOE MAUSER (Mack Reynolds)

1. *Mercenary from tomorrow.* (1968)
2. *The Earth war.* (1963)
3. *Time gladiator.* (1966)
3A. *Sweet dreams, sweet princes.* [with Michael A. Banks]. (1986) [Revised edition].
4. *The fracas factor.* (1978)
1-2. *Joe Mauser, mercenary from tomorrow.* [with Michael A. Banks]. (1986). [Previously published in different form as "Mercenary" and "Frigid Fracas" (i.e., *Mercenary from tomorrow* and *The Earth war* in book form)].

JOHN DAKER—SEE: ETERNAL CHAMPION

JOHN HARRISON (Stephen Ames Berry)

1. *The biofab war.* (1984)
2. *The battle for Terra Two.* (1986)
3. *The AI war.* (1987)
4. *Final assault.* (1988)

JOHN NORRIS (Elton T. Elliott & Richard E. Geis *as* RICHARD ELLIOTT)

1. *The Sword of Allah.* (1984)
2. *The burnt lands.* (1985)

JOHN THUNSTONE SERIES (Manly Wade Wellman)

1. *Lonely vigils.* (1981)
2. *What dreams may come.* (1983)
3. *The school of darkness.* (1985)

JOHNNY DIXON (John Bellairs)

1. *The curse of the blue figurine.* (1983)
2. *The mummy, the will, and the crypt.* (1983)
3. *The spell of the sorcerer's skull.* (1984)
4. *The revenge of the wizard's ghost.* (1985)
5. *The eyes of the killer robot.* (1986)
6. *The trolly to yesterday.* (1989)
7. *The chessmen of doom.* (1989)
8. *The secret of the underground room.* (1990)

JONATHAN BING (James P. Blaylock)

1. *The elfin ship.* (1982)
2. *The disappearing dwarf.* (1983)
3. *The stone giant.* (1989)

JORIAN (L. Sprague de Camp)

1. *The Goblin Tower.* (1968)
2. *The clocks of Iraz.* (1971)
3. *The fallible fiend.* (1973)
4. *The unbeheaded king.* (1983)
1,2,4. *The reluctant king.* (1985)

JORJ McKIE (Frank Herbert)

1. *Whipping star.* (1970)
2. *The Dosadi experiment.* (1977)

JOSHUA (Joseph F. Girzone)

1. *Joshua.* (1983)
2. *Joshua and the children.* (1989)

JOURNEYS OF MCGILL FEIGHAN (Kevin O'Donnell, Jr.)

1. *Caverns.* (1981)
2. *Reefs.* (1981)
3. *Lava.* (1982)
4. *Cliffs.* (1986)

JUDGE BENJAMIN (Judith Whitelock McInerney)

1. *Judge Benjamin: Superdog.* (1982)
2. *The superdog secret.* (1983)
3. *The superdog rescue.* (1984)
4. *The superdog surprise.* (1985)
5. *The superdog gift.* (1986)

JULES DE GRANDIN (Seabury Quinn)

1. *The adventures of Jules de Grandin.* (1976)
2. *The casebook of Jules de Grandin.* (1976)
3. *The skeleton closet of Jules de Grandin.* (1976)
4. *The devil's bride.* (1976)
5. *The hellfire files of Jules de Grandin.* (1976)
6. *The horror chambers of Jules de Grandin.* (1977)

JULIAN WEST SERIES (Edward Bellamy & others)

1. *Looking backward, 2000-1887.* (1888)
2. *Equality.* (1897)

THE YEAR 2000 (Mack Reynolds)

1. *Looking back from the year 2000.* (1973)
2. *Equality: in the year 2000.* (1977)

JULIE (Cora Taylor)

1. *Julie.* (1985)
2. *Julie's secret.* (1991)

JUNIOR GOLDEN GIRL—SEE: FIND YOUR FATE JUNIOR GOLDEN GIRL

JUNIOR TRANSFORMERS—SEE: FIND YOUR FATE JUNIOR TRANSFORMERS

JUSTICE CYCLE (Virginia Hamilton)

1. *Justice and her brothers.* (1981)
2. *Dustland.* (1980)
3. *The gathering.* (1981)

K-9 CORPS (Kenneth Von Gunden)

1. *K-9 Corps.* (1991)
2. *Under fire.* (1991)

KALEVALA (Emil Petaja)

1. *Saga of lost Earths.* (1966)
2. *The star mill.* (1966)
3. *The stolen sun.* (1967)
4. *Tramontane.* (1967)
1-2. *Saga of lost earths; and, The star mill.* (1979)
3-4. *The stolen sun; and, Tramontane.* (1979)

KAMUS OF KADHIZHAR—SEE: DARKWORLD DETECTIVE

KANE (Karl Edward Wagner)

1. *Darkness weaves with many shades.* (1971)

1A. *Darkness weaves.* (1978)
2. *Death Angel's shadow.* (1973)
3. *Bloodstone.* (1975)
4. *Dark crusade.* (1976)
5. *Night winds.* (1978)
6. *The book of Kane.* (1985)

KANE & PENDRAKE (Steven G. Spruill)

1. *The psychopath plague.* (1978)
2. *The Imperator plot.* (1983)
3. *Paradox planet.* (1988)

KANTMORIE (Ansen Dibell)

1. *Pursuit of the Screamer.* (1978)
2. *Circle, crescent, star.* (1981)
3. *Summerfair.* (1982)

KAR-CHEE (Avram Davidson)

1. *Rogue dragon.* (1965)
2. *The Kar-Chee reign.* (1966)
1-2. *The Kar-Chee reign; Rogue dragon.* (1979)

KATHERINE MORTENHOE (D. G. Compton)

1. *The unsleeping eye.* (1974)
1A. *The continuous Katherine Mortenhoe.* (1974)
2. *Windows.* (1979)

KEDRIGERN (John Morressy)

1. *A voice for Princess.* (1986)
2. *The questing of Kedrigern.* (1987)
3. *Kedrigern in Wanderland.* (1988)
4. *Kedrigern and the charming couple.* (1990)
5. *A remembrance for Kedrigern.* (1990)

KEI (Fritzen Ravenswood)

1. *The witching.* (1980)
2. *The spawning.* (1981)

KELTIAD (Patricia Kennealy)

1. *The copper crown.* (1984)
2. *The throne of Scone.* (1986)
3. *The silver branch.* (1988)

KENCYRATH (PC Hodgell)

1. *God stalk.* (1982)
2. *Dark of the moon.* (1985)
1-2. *Chronicles of the Kencyrath.* (1988)

KENDRIC & IRISSA—SEE: SWORD & CIRCLET

KENSHO (Dennis Schmidt)

1. *Wayfarer.* (1978)
2. *Kensho.* (1979)
3. *Satori.* (1981)
4. *Wanderer.* (1985)

KENT MONTANA (Charles L. Grant *as* LIONEL FENN)

1. *Kent Montana and the really ugly thing from Mars.* (1990)

2.   *Kent Montana and the reasonably invisible man.* (1991)
3.   *Kent Montana and the once and future thing.* (1991)

KERRION EMPIRE (Janet Morris)

1.   *Dream dancer.* (1980)
2.   *Cruiser dreams.* (1981)
3.   *Earth dreams.* (1982)

KEVIN FIKKAN (Will Shetterly)

1.   *Cats have no lord.* (1985)
2.   *The tangled lands.* (1989)

KEYS TO PARADISE (Robert E. Vardeman *as* DANIEL MORAN)

1.   *The flame key.* (1987)
2.   *The skeleton lord's key.* (1987)
3.   *Key of ice and steel.* (1988)
1-3. *The keys to paradise.* (1986)

KEYS TO THE DIMENSIONS (Kenneth Bulmer)

1.   *The key to Irunium.* (1967)
2.   *The key to Venudine.* (1968)
3.   *The Wizards of Senchuria.* (1969)
4.   *The ships of Durostorum.* (1970)
5.   *The Hunters of Jundagai.* (1971)
6.   *The Chariots of Ra.* (1972)
7.   *The Diamond Contessa.* (1983)

KHADAJI (Steve Perry and others)

1.   *The man who never missed.* (1985)
2.   *Matadora.* (1986)
3.   *The Machiavelli interface.* (1986)
4.   *The omega cage.* [With Michael Reaves]. (1988)
5.   *The 97th step.* (1989)
6.   *The albino knife.* (1991)

KHALINDAINE (Richard Burns)

1.   *Khalindaine.* (1985)
2.   *Troubadour.* (1988)

KILLASHANDRA (Anne McCaffrey)

1.   *The crystal singer.* (1982)
2.   *Killashandra.* (1985)

KILLSTAR (David J. Kelly)

1.   *The Baalbak quest.* (1980)
2.   *Tower of despair.* (1980)

KINE SAGA (A. R. Lloyd)

1.   *Kine.* (1982)
1A. *Marshworld.* (1990)
2.   *Witchwood.* (1989)
3.   *Dragon pond.* (1990)

KING ARTHUR (Rosemary Sutcliff)

1.   *The light beyond the forest: the quest for the Holy Grail.* (1979)
2.   *The sword and the circle: King Arthur and the knights of the Round Table.* (1981)

3.   *The road to Camlann.* (1981)

Related titles

In the shadow of the oak king. [Courtway Jones]. (1991)

KING KONG (various authors)

King Kong. [Delos Lovelace]. (1932)
My side. [Walter Wager *as* KING KONG]. (1976)

Associated Titles

The girl in the hairy paw: King Kong as myth, movie, and monster. [Harry M. Geduld & Ronald Gottesman]. (1976)
King Kong. [Julian May *as* IAN THORNE]. (1977)
The King Kong story. [Jeremy Pascall]. (1977)

KING OF YS (Poul Anderson & Karen Anderson)

1.   *The king of Ys: Roma mater.* (1986)
2.   *Gallicenae.* (1987)
3.   *Dahut.* (1988)
4.   *The dog and the wolf.* (1988)
1-2. *The king of Ys.* (1987)
3-4. *The king of Ys, volume 2.* (1988)

KING VICTOR (Peter Dickinson)

1.   *King and joker.* (1976)
2.   *Skeleton-in-waiting.* (1989)

KINGDOM OF SORCERY—SEE: ADVANCED DUNGEONS & DRAGONS GAMEBOOK

THE KINGDOMS (Angus Wells)

1.   *The wrath of Ashar.* (1988)
2.   *The usurper.* (1989)
3.   *The way beneath.* (1990)

KINSMAN (Ben Bova)

1.   *Millennium.* (1976)
2.   *Kinsman.* (1979)
1-2. *The Kinsman saga.* (1987)

KIOGA (William L. Chester)

1.   *Hawk of the wilderness.* (1936)
2.   *Kioga of the wilderness.* (1976)
3.   *One against a wilderness.* (1977)
4.   *Kioga of the unknown land.* (1978)

KITTY TELFAIR (Florence Stevenson)

1.   *The witching hour.* (1971)
2.   *Where Satan dwells.* (1971)
3.   *Altar of evil.* (1973)
4.   *Mistress of Devil's Manor.* (1973)
5.   *The sorcerer of the castle.* (1974)
6.   *The silent watcher.* (1975)

KNIGHT RIDER (Roger Hill & Glen A. Larson)

1.   *Knight Rider.* (1983)
2.   *Trust doesn't rust.* (1984)
3.   *Hearts of stone.* (1984)

2. *Lyonesse: The green pearl.* (1985)
2A. *The green pearl.* (1986)
3. *Lyonesse: Madouc.* (1989)
3A. *Madouc.* (1990)

LYRA (Patricia C. Wrede)

1. *Shadow magic.* (1982)
2. *Daughter of witches.* (1983)
3. *Caught in crystal.* (1987)

MAD MAX (various authors)

1. *Mad Max.* [Terry Kaye]. (1979)
1A. *Mad Max 1.* [Terry Kaye]. (1985)
2. *Mad Max 2.* [Carl Ruhan]. (1981)
3 *Mad Max beyond Thunderdome.* [Ann Matthews]. (1985)
3A. *Mad Max beyond Thunderdome: a novelization.* [Joan D. Vinge]. (1985)

MAGES OF GARILLON (Deborah Turner Harris)

1. *The burning stone.* (1987)
2. *The gauntlet of malice.* (1987)
3. *Spiral of fire.* (1989)

MAGIC (Larry Niven)

1. *The magic goes away.* (1978)
2. *The magic may return.* (1981)
3. *More magic.* (1984)

MAGIC KINGDOM OF LANDOVER (Terry Brooks)

1. *Magic kingdom for sale—sold!* (1986)
2. *The black unicorn.* (1987)
3. *Wizard at large.* (1988)

MAGIC MICRO ADVENTURE (various authors)

1. *Captain Kid and the pirates.* [Eileen Buckholtz & Ruth Glick]. (1985)
2. *Superworld.* [Steven Otfinoski]. (1985)
3. *Wizards of wonder.* [H. William Stine & Megan Stine]. (1985)
4. *The cats of Castle Mountain.* [Eileen Buckholtz & Ruth Glick] (1985)

MAGIC MOSCOW (Daniel M. Pinkwater)

1. *Attila the pun.* (1981)
2. *Slaves of Spiegel.* (1982)

MAGICAL TALES OF THE TAORMIN (Cheryl J. Franklin)

1. *Fire get.* (1987)
2. *Fire lord.* (1989)
3. *Fire crossing.* (1991)

MAGICAL WORLDS OF FANTASY—SEE: ISAAC ASIMOV'S MAGICAL WORLDS OF FANTASY

MAGICIAN (Tom McGowen)

1. *The magician's apprentice.* (1987)
2. *The magician's company.* (1988)
3. *The magicians' challenge.* (1989)

MAGICIAN'S HOUSE (William Corlett)

1. *The steps up the chimney.* (1990)
2. *The door in the tree.* (1991)
3. *The tunnel behind the waterfall.* (1991)

MAGIRA (Hugh Walker)

1. *War-gamers' world.* (1978)
2. *Army of darkness.* (1979)
3. *Messengers of darkness.* (1979)

MAJIPOOR (Robert Silverberg)

1. *Lord Valentine's castle.* (1980)
1A. *The desert of stolen dreams.* (1981)
2. *Majipoor chronicles: a novel.* (1982)
3. *Valentine Pontifex.* (1983)

Associated Title

Revolt on Majipoor: a Crossroads adventure in the world of Robert Silverberg's Majipoor. [Matthew J. Costello as MATT COSTELLO]. (1987)

MAKERS (Michael McCollum

1. *Life PROBE.* (1983)
2. *Procyon's promise.* (1985)

THE MALLOREON—SEE: THE BELGARIAD

MAN FROM ATLANTIS (Richard Woodley)

1. *Man from Atlantis #1.* (1977)
2. *Death scouts.* (1977)
3. *Killer spores.* (1978)
4. *Ark of doom.* (1978)

MAN FROM PLANET X (Jim Lawrence as HUNTER ADAMS)

1. *The she-beast.* (1975)
2. *Tiger by the tail.* (1975)
3. *The devil to pay.* (1977)

THE MAN FROM U.N.C.L.E. (various authors)

The Man from U.N.C.L.E. [Michael Avallone & Terry Carr]. (1965)
The Man from U.N.C.L.E. and the affair of the gun-runners' gold. [Brandon Keith]. (1967)
The wolves and the lambs affair. [Joan Hunter Holly]. (1977)

A MAN OF HIS WORD (Dave Duncan)

1. *Magic casement.* (1990)
2. *Faery lands forlorn.* (1991)
3. *Perilous seas.* (1991)

MAN-KZIN WARS (various authors; SEE ALSO: KNOWN SPACE)

1. *The Man-Kzin wars.* [Poul Anderson & Larry Niven & Dean Ing]. (1988)
2. *The Man-Kzin wars II.* [Dean Ing & Larry Niven & Jerry Pournelle & S. M. Stirling]. (1989)
3. *The Man-Kzin wars III.* [Poul Anderson & Jerry Pournelle & S. M. Stirling & Larry Niven]. (1990)
4. *Man-Kzin wars IV.* [Larry Niven]. (1991)

ASSOCIATED TITLES

Cathouse. [Dean Ing]. (1990)
The children's hour. [Jerry Pournelle & S. M. Stirling]. (1991)
Inconstant star. [Poul Anderson]. (1991)

MANHATTAN GHOST (T. M. Wright)

1. *A Manhattan ghost story*. (1984)
2. *The waiting room*. (1986)

MANITOU (Graham Masterton)

1. *The manitou*. (1975)
2. *Revenge of the manitou*. (1979)

THE MANSE (Lisa W. Cantrell)

1. *The manse*. (1987)
2. *Torments*. (1990)

MARATHON (D. Alexander Smith)

1. *Marathon*. (1982)
2. *Rendezvous*. (1988)
3. *Homecoming*. (1990)

MARATHON MAN (William Goldman)

1. *Marathon man*. (1974)
2. *Brothers*. (1987)

THE MARAUDERS (various authors as MICHAEL MCGANN)

1. *The marauders*. [Ed Naha]. (1989)
2. *Blood kin*. [Ed Naha]. (1989)
3. *Liar's dice*. [Ed Naha]. (1990)
4. *Convoy strike*. [Ed Naha]. (1990)
5. *The ghost warriors*. [Ed Naha]. (1990)
6. *Blood and fire*. [Ed Naha]. (1991)
7. *Fortress of death*. [Ed Naha]. (1991)

MARIA LOONEY (Jerome Beatty, Jr.)

1. *Maria Looney on the red planet*. (1977)
2. *Maria Looney and the cosmic circus*. (1978)
3. *Maria Looney and the remarkable robot*. (1979)

MARIANNE (Sheri S. Tepper)

1. *Marianne, the magus, and the manticore*. (1985)
2. *Marianne, the madame, and the momentary gods*. (1988)
3. *Marianne, the matchbox, and the malachite mouse*. (1989)
1-3. *The Marianne trilogy*. (1990)

MARID AUDRAN (George Alec Effinger)

1. *When gravity fails*. (1987)
2. *A fire in the sun*. (1989)
3. *The exile kiss*. (1991)

MARINO FAMILY (Robert C. Sloane)

1. *A nice place to live: a novel*. (1981)
2. *The vengeance: a novel*. (1983)

MARKED MAN (Rhondi Vilott as CHARLES INGRID)

1. *The marked man*. (1989)
2. *The last recall*. (1991)

MARRAKESH (Graham Diamond)

1. *Marrakesh*. (1981)
2. *Marrakesh nights*. (1984)

MARS (Lin Carter)

1. *The man who loved Mars*. (1973)
2. *The valley where time stood still*. (1974)
3. *The city outside the world*. (1977)
4. *Down to a sunless sea*. (1984)

MARS—SEE: MICHAEL KANE

MARTIAN (Michael Lindsay Williams)

1. *Martian spring*. (1986)
2. *FTL: further than life*. (1987)

MARTIAN WARS TRILOGY—SEE: BUCK ROGERS

MARTIN WEBSTER—SEE: DELUGE SERIES

MARVEL SUPERHEROES (various authors)

OLD SERIES

1. *The Avengers battle the Earth-wrecker*. [Otto Binder]. (1967)
2. *Captain America: the great gold steal*. [Ted White]. (1968)

NEW SERIES

1. *Amazing Spiderman: Mayhem in Manhattan*. [Len Wein & Marv Wolfman]. (1978)
2. *Incredible Hulk: Stalker from the stars*. [Len Wein & Marv Wolfman & Ron Goulart as JOSEPH SILVA]. (1978)
3. *Incredible Hulk: Cry of the beast*. [Richard S. Myers]. (1979)
4. *Captain America: Holocaust for hire*. [Ron Goulart as JOSEPH SILVA]. (1979)
5. *Fantastic Four: Doomsday*. [Marv Wolfman]. (1979)
6. *Iron Man: And call my killer...Modok!* [William Rotsler]. (1979)
7. *Doctor Strange: Nightmare*. [William Rotsler]. (1979)
8. *Amazing Spiderman: Crime campaign*. [Paul Kupperberg]. (1979)
9. *The Marvel superheroes*. [Len Wein & Marv Wolfman]. (1979)
10. *Avengers: The man who stole tomorrow*. [David Michelinie]. (1979)
11. *Incredible Hulk & Spiderman: Murdermoon: a novel*. [Paul Kupperberg]. (1979)

Associated Titles

Comics file magazine spotlight on The Fantastic Four files. [James V. Van Hise]. (1986)

MARVEL SUPERHEROES ADVENTURE GAMEBOOKS (various authors)

1. *City in darkness*. [Jeff Grubb]. (1986)

2. *Rocket's red glare.* [Kate Novak]. (1986)
3. *Night of the wolverine.* [Jerry Epperson & James M. Ward]. (1986)
4. *Doctor Strange: through six dimensions.* [Allen Varney]. (1987)
5. *The Thing: one thing after another.* [Warren Spector]. (1987)
6. *The uncanny X-Men: An X-cellent death.* [Kate Novak]. (1987)
7. *The amazing Spider-Man: As the world burns.* [Peter David]. (1987)

MARY POPPINS (P. L. Travers)

1. *Mary Poppins.* (1934)
2. *Mary Poppins comes back.* (1935)
3. *Mary Poppins opens the door.* (1943)
4. *Mary Poppins in the park.* (1952)
5. *Mary Poppins in Cherry Tree Lane.* (1982)

MASK (Catherine Cooke)

1. *Mask of the wizard.* (1985)
2. *Veil of shadow.* (1987)
3. *The hidden temple.* (1988)

MASTER LI (Barry Hughart)

1. *The bridge of birds: a novel of an ancient China that never was.* (1984)
2. *The story of the stone.* (1988)
3. *Eight skilled gentlemen.* (1991)

MASTER MARINER (Nicholas Monsarrat)

1. *Running proud.* (1978)
2. *Darken ship: the unfinished novel.* (1980)

MASTER OF THE STARS (Robert Hoskins)

1. *Master of the stars.* (1976)
2. *To control the stars.* (1977)
3. *To escape the stars.* (1978)

MASTERS OF FANTASY (various authors)

1. *Peter Tremayne.* [Jo Fletcher]. (1984)
2. *August Derleth.* [Nic Howard]. (1984)
3. *M. R. James.* [M. R. James]. (1987)

MASTERS OF SCIENCE FICTION AND FANTASY (various authors)

1. *Theodore Sturgeon: a primary and secondary bibliography.* [Lahna F. Diskin]. (1980),
2. *Clifford D. Simak: a primary and secondary bibliography.* [Muriel R. Becker]. (1980)
3. *Jack Williamson: a primary and secondary bibliography.* [Robert E. Myers]. (1980)
4. *Andre Norton: a primary and secondary bibliography.* [Roger C. Schlobin]. (1980)
5. *Samuel R. Delany: a primary and secondary bibliography, 1962-(1979).* [Robert S. Bravard & Michael W. Peplow]. (1980)
6. *Jules Verne: a primary and secondary bibliography.* [Edward J. Gallagher & Judith A. Mistichelli & John A. Van Eerde]. (1980)
7. *Roger Zelazny: a primary and secondary bibliography.* [Joseph L. Sanders]. (1980)

8. *Leigh Brackett, Marion Zimmer Bradley, Anne McCaffrey: a primary and secondary bibliography.* [Rosemarie Arbur]. (1982),
9. *Lloyd Alexander, Evangeline Walton Ensley, Kenneth Morris: a primary and secondary bibliography.* [Robert H. Boyer & Kenneth J. Zahorski]. (1981)
10. *Ursula K. Le Guin: a primary and secondary bibliography.* [Elizabeth Cummins Cogell]. (1983)
11. *Gordon R. Dickson: a primary and secondary bibliography.* [Raymond H. Thompson]. (1983)
12. *Robert Silverberg: a primary and secondary bibliography.* [Thomas D. Clareson]. (1983)
13. *J. G. Ballard: a primary and secondary bibliography.* [David Pringle]. (1984)
14. *Arthur C. Clarke: a primary and secondary bibliography.* [David Samuelson]. (1984)

MASTERS OF SPACE (Robert E. Vardeman)

1. *Masters of space: The stellar death plan.* (1987)
2. *The alien web.* (1987)
3. *A plague in paradise.* (1987)
1-3. *Masters of space.* (1990)

MATHEW SWAIN (Mike McQuay)

1. *Hot time in Old Town.* (1981)
2. *When trouble beckons.* (1981)
3. *The deadliest show in town.* (1982)
4. *The odds are murder.* (1983)

MATTHEW DILKE (Lindsay Gutteridge)

1. *Cold war in a country garden.* (1971)
2. *Killer pine.* (1973)
3. *Fratricide is a gas.* (1975)

MATTHEW GANT—SEE: FIREFOX

MAVIN—SEE: TRUE GAME SERIES

MAX AND ME (Gery Greer & Bob Ruddick)

1. *Max and me and the time machine.* (1983)
2. *Max and me and the Wild West.* (1988)

MAX: OUT OF THIS WORLD (Marilyn Kaye)

1. *Max on Earth.* (1986)
2. *Max in love.* (1986)
3. *Max on fire.* (1986)
4. *Max flips out.* (1986)
5. *Max goes bad.* (1989)
6. *Max all over.* (1989)

MAXIE: THE LITTLE MAN (Erich Kästner)

1. *The Little Man* (1966)
2. *The Little Man and the little miss.* (1969)
2A. *The Little Man and the big thief* (1969)

MAZTICA TRILOGY—SEE: FORGOTTEN REALMS FANTASY ADVENTURE

MECHANICAL SKY (Donald Moffitt)

1. *Crescent in the sky.* (1990)
2. *A gathering of stars.* (1990)

MECKLER'S BIBLIOGRAPHIES ON SCIENCE FICTION, FANTASY, AND HORROR (various authors)

1.   *PKD: A Philip K. Dick bibliography, rev. ed.* [Daniel J. H. Levack]. (1988)
2.   *Dune master: a Frank Herbert bibliography.* [Daniel J. H. Levack]. (1988)
3.   *Gothic fiction: a master list of twentieth century criticism and research.* [Frederick S. Frank]. (1988)

MED SERVICE (Murray Leinster)

1.   *The mutant weapon.* (1959)
2.   *This world is taboo.* (1961)
3.   *Doctor to the stars* (1964)
4.   *S.O.S. from three worlds.* (1967)
1-3. *The Med series.* (1983)

MEG MURRY (Madeleine L'Engle)

1.   *A wrinkle in time.* (1962)
2.   *A wind in the door.* (1973)
3.   *A swiftly tilting planet.* (1978)
4.   *Many waters.* (1986)
5.   *An acceptable time.* (1989)

MEGAN (Betsy Gould Hearne)

1.   *South star.* (1977)
2.   *Home.* (1979)

MELDE (Lucy Cullyford Babbitt)

1.   *The oval amulet.* (1985)
2.   *Children of the Maker.* (1988)

MELLONIA—SEE: ANCIENT HISTORY

MEMORY, SORROW & THORN (Tad Williams)

1.   *The dragonbone chair.* (1988)
2.   *Stone of farewell.* (1990)

MERLIN SERIES (Mary Stewart)

1.   *The crystal cave.* (1970)
2.   *The hollow hills.* (1973)
3.   *The last enchantment.* (1979)
4.   *The wicked day.* (1983)
1-3. *Mary Stewart's Merlin trilogy.* (1980)

MEROVINGEN NIGHTS (C. J. Cherryh)

1.   *Angel with the sword.* (1985/1986)
1A. *Festival moon.* (1987)
2.   *Fever season.* (1987)
3.   *Troubled waters.* (1988)
4.   *Smuggler's gold.* (1988)
5.   *Divine right.* (1989)
6.   *Flood tide.* (1990)
7.   *Endgame.* (1991)

MESMERIAN ANNALS (Allan W. Eckert)

1.   *The dark green tunnel.* (1984)
2.   *The wand: the return to Mesmeria.* (1985)

MESSENGER (Monica Dickens)

1.   *The messenger.* (1985)
2.   *Ballad of Favour.* (1985)
3.   *The haunting of Bellamy 4.* (1986)

MESSENGER CHRONICLES (James Patrick Kelly)

1.   *Planet of whispers.* (1984)
2.   *Look into the sun.* (1989)

MESSIAH (Anthony Storey)

1.   *The rector.* (1970)
2.   *The centre holds.* (1973)
3.   *The saviour: a novel.* (1978)

MESSIAH STONE (Martin Caidin)

1.   *The Messiah Stone.* (1986)
2.   *Dark messiah.* (1990)

METEORITE (Anne Mason)

1.   *The dancing meteorite.* (1984)
2.   *The stolen law.* (1986)

METZADA (Joel Rosenberg)

1.   *Ties of blood and silver.* (1984)
2.   *Emile and the Dutchman.* (1986)
3.   *Not for glory.* (1988)
4.   *Hero.* (1990)

MICHAEL KANE (Michael Moorcock)

1.   *Warriors of Mars.* (1965)
1A. *The city of the beast.* (1970)
2.   *Blades of Mars.* (1965)
2A. *The lord of the spiders* (1971)
3.   *Barbarians of Mars.* (1965)
3A. *The masters of the pit.* (1971)
1-3. *Warrior of Mars.* (1981)

MICHAEL PERRIN (Greg Bear)

1.   *The infinity concerto.* (1984)
2.   *The Serpent Mage.* (1986)

MICRO ADVENTURE (various authors)

1.   *Space attack.* [Eileen Buckholtz & Ruth Glick]. (1984)
2.   *Jungle quest.* [Megan Stine & H. William Stine]. (1984)
3.   *Million dollar gamble.* [Chassie L. West]. (1984)
4.   *Time trap.* [Jean M. Favors]. (1984)
5.   *Mindbenders.* [Eileen Buckholtz & Ruth Glick]. (1984)
6.   *Robot race.* [David Anthony Kraft]. (1984)
7.   *Doom stalker.* [Ruth Glick & Eileen Buckholtz]. (1985)
8.   *The big freeze.* [Jean M. Favors]. (1985)
9.   *Dead ringer.* [Chassie L. West]. (1985)
10. *Spellbound.* [Megan Stine & H. William Stine]. (1985)

MICROKID MYSTERY (various authors)

1.   *The great gradepoint mystery.* [Barbara Bartholomew]. (1983)
2.   *The fox's lair.* [Ian McMahan]. (1983)

3? *Lake Fear.* [Ian McMahan]. (1985)
4? *The lost forest.* [Ian McMahan]. (1985)

MICRONAUTS (Gordon Williams)

1. *The micronauts.* (1977)
2. *The microcolony.* (1979)
2A. *Micronaut world.* (1981)
3. *Revolt of the micronauts.* (1981)

MIDDLE-EARTH QUEST/TOLKIEN QUEST (various authors)

1. *Night of the Nazgul.* [John David Ruemmler]. (1985)
2. *The legend of Weathertop.* [Heike Kubasch]. (1985)
3. *Rescue in Mirkwood.* [Gerald Lientz]. (1986)
4. *Treason at Helms Deep.* [Kevin Barrett & Saul Peters]. (1988)
5. *A spy in Isengard* [Terry K. Amthor]. (1988)

MIKLEJOHN & LEIDL (Kate Wilhelm)

1. *The Hamlet trap.* (1987)
2. *The dark door.* (1988)
3. *Smart house.* (1989)
4. *Sweet, sweet poison.* (1990)

MILFORD SERIES: POPULAR WRITERS OF TODAY (various authors)

1. *Robert A. Heinlein: stranger in his own land.* [George Edgar Slusser]. (1976)
1A. *Robert A. Heinlein: stranger in his own land, second edition.* [George Edgar Slusser]. (1977)
2. *Alistair MacLean: The key is fear.* [Robert A. Lee]. (1976)
3. *The farthest shores of Ursula K. Le Guin.* [George Edgar Slusser]. (1976)
4. *The Bradbury chronicles.* [George Edgar Slusser]. (1977)
5. *John D. MacDonald and the Colorful World of Travis McGee.* [Frank D. Campbell Jr.]. (1977)
6. *Harlan Ellison: unrepentant harlequin.* [George Edgar Slusser]. (1977)
7. *Kurt Vonnegut: the gospel from outer space (or, Yes we have no nirvanas.* [Clark Mayo]. (1977)
8. *The space odysseys of Arthur C. Clarke.* [George Edgar Slusser]. (1977)
9. *Aldiss unbound: the science fiction of Brian W. Aldiss.* [Richard Mathews]. (1977)
10. *The Delany intersection: Samuel R. Delany considered as a writer of semi-precious words.* [George Edgar Slusser]. (1977)
11. *The classic years of Robert A. Heinlein.* [George Edgar Slusser]. (1977)
12. *The dream quest of H. P. Lovecraft.* [Darrell Schweitzer]. (1978)
13. *Worlds beyond the world: The fantastic vision of William Morris.* [Richard Mathews]. (1978)
15. *Lightning from a clear sky: Tolkien, the Trilogy, and the Silmarillion.* [Richard Mathews]. (1978)
16. *David Lodge: How far can you go?.* [Merrit Moseley]. (1991)
17. *Conan's world and Robert E. Howard.* [Darrell Schweitzer]. (1978)
18. *Against time's arrow: the high crusade of Poul Anderson.* [Sandra Miesel]. (1978)
19. *The clockwork universe of Anthony Burgess.* [Richard Mathews]. (1978)
20. *The haunted man: the strange genius of David Lindsay.* [Colin Wilson]. (1979)

21. *Colin Wilson: the outsider and beyond.* [Clifford P. Bendau]. (1979)
22. *A poetry of force and darkness: The fiction of John Hawkes.* [Eliot Berry]. (1979)
23. *Science fiction voices #1: interviews with science fiction writers.* [Darrell Schweitzer]. (1979)
24. *A clash of symbols: the triumph of James Blish.* [Brian M. Stableford]. (1979)
25. *Science fiction voices #2: interviews with science fiction writers.* [Jeffrey M. Elliot]. (1979)
26. *Earth is the alien planet: J. G. Ballard's four-dimensional nightmare.* [David Pringle]. (1979)
27. *Literary voices #1.* [Jeffrey M. Elliot]. (1980)
28. *The rainbow quest of Thomas Pynchon.* [Douglas A. Mackey]. (1980)
29. *Science fiction voices #3: interviews with science fiction writers.* [Jeffrey M. Elliot]. (1980)
30. *Still worlds collide: Philip Wylie and the end of the American dream.* [Clifford P. Bendau]. (1980)
31. *Fantasy voices: interviews with American fantasy writers.* [Jeffrey M. Elliot]. (1982)
32. *Masters of science fiction: essays on six science fiction authors.* [Brian M. Stableford]. (1981)
33. *Science fiction voices [#4]: interviews with modern science fiction writers.* [Jeffrey M. Elliot]. (1982)
34. *Anti-Sartre, with an essay on Camus.* [Colin Wilson]. (1981)
35. *Science fiction voices #5: interviews with American science fiction writers of the golden age.* [Darrell Schweitzer]. (1981)
36. *From here to absurdity: the moral battlefields of Joseph Heller.* [Stephen W. Potts]. (1982)
37. *Pulp voices; or, Science fiction voices #6: interviews with pulp magazine writers and editors.* [Jeffrey M. Elliot]. (1983)
38. *The magic labyrinth of Philip José Farmer.* [Edgar L. Chapman]. (1984)
39. *Interviews with Britain's angry young men.* [Dale Salwak]. (1984)
40. *Demon prince: the dissonant worlds of Jack Vance.* [Jack Rawlins]. (1986)
41. *George Orwell's guide through Hell: a psychological study of 1984.* [Robert Plank]. (1986)
42. *D. H. Lawrence; The poet who was not wrong.* [Douglas A. Mackey]. (1986)
45. *Hugo Gernsback, father of modern science fiction, with essays on Frank Herbert and Bram Stoker.* [Mark Siegel]. (1988)
46. *The magic that works: John W. Campbell and the American response to technology.* [Albert I. Berger]. (1992)
47. *Jerzy Kosinski: the literature of violation.* [Welch D. Everman]. (1991)
50. *The second Marxian invasion: the fiction of the Strugatsky Brothers.* [Stephen W. Potts]. (1991)
52. *At Wolfe's door: the Nero Wolfe novels of Rex Stout.* [J. Kenneth Van Dover]. (1990)

MIND (Wilanne Schneider Belden)

1. *Mind-call.* (1981)
2. *Mind-hold.* (1987)
3. *Mind-find.* (1988)

MIND MASTERS (John F. Rossmann)

1. *The mind masters.* (1974)
2. *Shamballah.* (1975)
3. *The door.* (1975)
4. *Amazons.* [as IAN ROSS]. (1976)

5.   *Recycled souls.* [as IAN ROSS]. (1976)

MINDKILLER (Spider Robinson)

1.   *Mindkiller.* (1982)
2.   *Time pressure.* (1987)

MINDSLIP (Michael Elder)

1.   *Mindslip.* (1976)
2.   *Mindquest.* (1978)

MINERVAN EXPERIMENT (James P. Hogan)

1.   *Inherit the stars.* (1977)
2.   *The gentle giants of Ganymede.* (1978)
3.   *Giants' star.* (1981)
4.   *Entoverse.* (1991)
1-3. *The Minervan experiment.* (1981)
1-3. *The giants novels.* (1991)

MINNIFIELD (J. N. Williamson)

1.   *Ghost mansion.* (1981)
2.   *Horror mansion.* (1982)

MINOTAUR—SEE: ANCIENT HISTORY

MINSTREL ORFEO—SEE: WARHAMMER

MISS BIANCA (Margery Sharp)

1.   *The rescuers.* (1959)
2.   *Miss Bianca.* (1962)
3.   *The turret.* (1963)
4.   *Miss Bianca in the salt mines.* (1966)
5.   *Miss Bianca in the Orient.* (1970)
6.   *Miss Bianca in the Antarctic.* (1971)
7.   *Miss Bianca and the bridesmaid.* (1972)
8.   *Bernard the brave.* (1977)
9.   *Bernard into battle.* (1978)

Associated Title

The Rescuers Downunder. [A. L. Singer]. (1990)

MISS PICKERELL (Ellen MacGregor & [with Dora Pantell].

1.   *Miss Pickerell goes to Mars.* (1951)
2.   *Miss Pickerell and the geiger counter.* (1953)
3.   *Miss Pickerell goes undersea.* (1953)
4.   *Miss Pickerell goes to the Arctic.* (1954)
5.   *Miss Pickerell on the Moon.* [with Dora Pantell]. (1965)
6.   *Miss Pickerell goes on a dig.* [with Dora Pantell]. (1966)
7.   *Miss Pickerell harvests the sea.* [with Dora Pantell]. (1968)
8.   *Miss Pickerell and the weather satellite.* [with Dora Pantell]. (1971)
9.   *Miss Pickerell meets Mr. H.U.M.* [with Dora Pantell]. (1974)
10. *Miss Pickerell takes the bull by the horns.* [with Dora Pantell]. (1976)
11. *Miss Pickerell to the earthquake rescue.* [with Dora Pantell]. (1977)
12. *Miss Pickerell and the supertanker.* [with Dora Pantell]. (1978)

13. *Miss Pickerell tackles the energy crisis.* [with Dora Pantell]. (1980)
14. *Miss Pickerell on the trail.* [with Dora Pantell]. (1982)
15. *Miss Pickerell and the blue whales.* [with Dora Pantell]. (1983)
16. *Miss Pickerell and the war of the computers.* [Dora Pantell]. (1984)
17. *Miss Pickerell and the lost world.* [Dora Pantell]. (1986)

MISSION EARTH (L. Ron Hubbard)

1.   *The invaders plan.* (1985)
2.   *Black genesis, fortress of evil.* (1986)
3.   *The enemy within.* (1986)
4.   *An alien affair.* (1986)
5.   *Fortune of fear.* (1986)
6.   *Death quest.* (1987)
7.   *Voyage of vengeance.* (1987)
8.   *Disaster.* (1987)
9.   *Villainy victorious.* (1987)
10. *The doomed planet.* (1987)

MITHGARIAN SERIES (Dennis L. McKiernan)

IRON TOWER TRILOGY

1.   *The dark tide.* (1984)
2.   *Shadows of doom.* (1984)
3.   *The Darkest Day.* (1984)

SILVER CALL DUOLOGY

1.   *Trek to Kraggen-Cor.* (1986)
2.   *The Drega path.* (1986)

MOLT BROTHER (Jacqueline Lichtenberg)

1.   *Molt brother.* (1982)
2.   *City of a million legends.* (1985)

MONGO (George C. Chesbro)

1.   *Shadow of a broken man.* (1977)
2.   *The city of whispering stone.* (1978)
3.   *An affair of sorcerers.* (1979)
4.   *The beasts of Valhalla.* (1985)
5.   *Two songs this archangel sings.* (1986)
6.   *The cold smell of sacred stone.* (1988)
7.   *Second horseman out of Eden.* (1989)
8.   *The language of cannibals.* (1990)
9.   *In the house of secret enemies.* (1990)
10. *The fear in yesterday's rings.* (1991)

VEIL KENDRY SERIES

1.   *Veil.* (1986)
2.   *Jungle of steel & stone.* (1988)

MONSTER HUNTERS (Nancy Garden)

1.   *Mystery of the night raiders.* (1987)
2.   *Mystery of the midnight menace.* (1988)
3.   *Mystery of the secret marks.* (1989)

MONSTROUS REGIMENT (Storm Constantine)

1.   *The monstrous regiment.* (1990)
2.   *Aleph.* (1991)

MOON CHALICE QUEST (Catherine Darby)

1. *Whisper down the moon.* (1977)
2. *Frost on the moon.* (1977)
3. *The flaunting moon.* (1977)
4. *Sing me a moon.* (1977)
5. *Cobweb across the moon.* (1978)
6. *Moon in Pisces.* (1978)

MOON SINGER (Andre Norton)

1. *Moon of three rings.* (1966)
2. *Exiles of the stars.* (1971)
3. *Flight in Yiktor.* (1986)
4. *Dare to go a-hunting.* (1990)

MOONHEART (Charles de Lint)

1. *Moonheart: a romance.* (1984)
2. *Ascian in rose.* (1987)
3. *Westlin wind.* (1989)
4. *Ghostwood.* (1990)

MOONSHAE TRILOGY—SEE: FORGOTTEN REALMS FANTASY ADVENTURE

MORDANT'S NEED (Stephen R. Donaldson)

1. *The mirror of her dreams.* (1986)
2. *A man rides through.* (1987)

MORGAINE—SEE: CHRONICLES OF MORGAINE

MORGANA SHEE—SEE: SOLSTICE

MORIGU (Mark C. Perry)

1. *The desecration.* (1986)
2. *The dead.* (1990)

MORK & MINDY (various authors)

1. *Mork & Mindy.* [Ralph Church]. (1979)
2. *The incredible shrinking Mork.* [Robin S. Wagner]. (1980)

Associated Title

Mork & Mindy. [Paul D. Schneck]. (1980)

MORPHODITE TRILOGY (M. A. Foster)

1. *The Morphodite.* (1981)
2. *Transformer.* (1983)
3. *Preserver.* (1985)

MORROW (H. M. Hoover)

1. *Children of Morrow.* (1973)
2. *Treasures of Morrow.* (1976)

MORTORIO (Eric Burgess & Arthur Friggens)

1. *Mortorio.* (1973)
2. *Mortorio two.* (1975)

MOSTLY GHOSTS (Mary Anderson)

1. *The haunting of Hillcrest.* (1987)
2. *The Leipzig vampire.* (1987)

3. *Terror under the tent.* (1987)
4. *The three spirits of Vandermeer Manor.* (1987)

MOTH-KIN (Kathy Kennedy Tapp)

1. *Moth-kin magic.* (1983)
2. *Flight of the moth-kin.* (1987)
3. *The Scorpio ghosts and the black hole gang.* (1987)
3A. *The ghostmobile.* (1988)

MOTTO EXCELSIOR (V. C. De Vere)

1. *The motto excelsior.* (1988)
2. *The motto excelsior, books II-IV.* (1988)
3. *The motto excelsior, books V-VIII.* (1990)
1. *The idea: the Motto excelsior, books I-VI.* [as ROGER MASON]. (1991)
2. *The idea: the Motto excelsior, books VII-XII.* [as ROGER MASON]. (1991)

MOUSEHAVEN MANOR (Mary DeBall Kwitz)

1. *Shadow over Mousehaven Manor.* (1989)
2. *The bell tolls at Mousehaven Manor.* (1991)

MR BROWSER—SEE: THE BRAIN SHARPENERS

MR. MERLIN (William Rotsler)

1. *Mr. Merlin, episode 1.* (1981)
2. *Mr. Merlin, episode 2.* (1981)

MUTANT (Karen Haber)

1. *The mutant season.* [with Robert Silverberg]. (1989)
2. *The mutant prime.* (1990)

MUTANTS (Isidore Haiblum)

1. *The mutants are coming.* (1984)
2. *Out of sync.* (1990)

MUTANTS AMOK (various authors as MARK GRANT)

1. *Mutants amok.* [David Bischoff]. (1991)
2. *Mutant hell.* [David Bischoff]. (1991)
3. *Rebel attack.* [David Bischoff]. (1991)
4. *Holocaust horror.* [David Bischoff]. (1991)
5. *Christmas slaughter.* [Bruce King]. (1991)

MY NAME IS PARIS (Elizabeth Howard)

1. *Mystery of the Metro.* (1987)
2. *Mystery of the magician.* (1987)
3. *The scent of mystery.* (1987)

MY TEACHER IS AN ALIEN (Bruce Coville)

1. *My teacher is an alien.* (1989)
2. *My teacher fried my brains.* (1991)
3. *My teacher glows in the dark.* (1991)

MYRA MORGANA (Adriana DeBolt/Christopher Dane)

1. *The crystal of power.* (1980)
2. *The galactic arena / by Christopher Dane.* (1981)

MYSTIC REBEL (Ryder Syvertsen)

1. *Mystic rebel.* (1988)

2.   *The dancing dead.* (1988)
3.   *Darkness descends.* (1988)
4.   *Temple of dark destiny.* (1989)
5.   *Cave of the master.* (1990)
6.   *Fortress of forbidden destiny.* (1991)

MYTHAGO (Robert Holdstock)

1.   *Mythago Wood.* (1984)
2.   *Lavondyss: journey to an unknown region.* (1988)

MYTHOLOGY (Jody Lynn Nye)

1.   *Mythology 101.* (1990)
2.   *Mythology abroad.* (1991)

NAME TO CONJURE WITH (Donald Aamodt)

1.   *A name to conjure with.* (1989)
2.   *A troubling along the border.* (1991)

NAPHAR (Sharon Baker)

1.   *Quarreling, they met the dragon.* (1984)
2.   *Journey to Membliar.* (1987)
3.   *Burning tears of Sassurum.* (1988)

NARNIA SOLO GAMES (various authors)

1.   *Return to Deathwater.* [Curtis Norris]. (1988)
2.   *The sorceress and the book of spells.* [Anne E. Schraff]. (1988)
3.   *Leap of the lion.* [Curtis Norris]. (1988)
4.   *The lost crowns of Cair Paravel.* [Gerald Lientz]. (1988)
5.   *Return of the white witch.* [Rob Bell]. (1988)

NATHAN BRAZIL—SEE: WELL WORLD

NATIVE TONGUE (Suzette Haden Elgin)

1.   *Native tongue.* (1984)
2.   *The Judas rose.* (1987)

NAVIGATOR (Jayge Carr)

1.   *Navigator's sindrome.* (1983)
2.   *The treasure in the heart of the maze.* (1985)
3.   *Rabelaisian reprise.* (1988)

NECROSCOPE (Brian Lumley)

1.   *Necroscope.* (1982)
2.   *Wamphyri!* (1988)
2A. *Vamphyri!* (1989)
3.   *The source.* (1989)
4.   *Deadspeak.* (1990)
5.   *Deadspawn.* (1991)

NEDAO (Ru Emerson)

1.   *To the haunted mountains.* (1987)
2.   *In the caves of exile.* (1988)
3.   *On the seas of destiny.* (1989)

NEEDLE (Hal Clement)

1.   *Needle.* (1950)
1A. *From outer space.* (1957)
2.   *Through the eye of a needle.* (1978)

NELSON MALONE (Louise Hawes)

1.   *Nelson Malone meets the man from Mush-Nut.* (1986)
2.   *Nelson Malone saves Flight 942.* (1988)

NEUROMANCER (William Gibson)

1.   *Neuromancer.* (1984)
2.   *Count Zero.* (1986)
3.   *Mona Lisa overdrive.* (1988)

NEVERYON (Samuel R. Delany)

1.   *Tales of Nevèrÿon.* (1979)
2.   *Neveryóna; or, The tale of signs and cities: some informal remarks toward the modular calculus, part four.* (1983)
3.   *Flight from Nevèrÿon.* (1985)
4.   *The bridge of lost desire.* (1987)
4A. *Return to Nevèrÿon.* (1989)

NEW ADVENTURES OF FRANKENSTEIN—SEE: FRANKENSTEIN

NEW SPRINGTIME (Robert Silverberg)

1.   *At winter's end.* (1988)
1A. *Winter's end.* (1990)
2.   *The queen of springtime.* (1989)
2A. *The new springtime.* (1990)

NEW WORLD (James Kahn)

1.   *World enough, and time.* (1980)
2.   *Time's dark laughter.* (1982)
3.   *Timefall.* (1987)

NEW YORK BY KNIGHT (Esther M. Friesner)

1.   *New York by knight.* (1986)
2.   *Elf defense.* (1988)
3.   *Sphynxes wild.* (1989)

NEWEDEN (Stephenu Leigh)

1.   *Slow fall to dawn.* (1981)
2.   *Dance of the hag.* (1983)
3.   *A quiet of stone.* (1984)

NEWHOME (Marta Randall)

1.   *Journey.* (1978)
2.   *Dangerous games.* (1980)

NEXT WAVE (various authors)

1.   *Red genesis.* [S. C. Sykes]. (1991)
2.   *Alien tongue.* [Stephen Leigh]. (1991)

NICK OF TIME (George Alec Effinger)

1.   *The nick of time.* (1985)
2.   *The bird of time.* (1986)

NIGHT DATE (Edward Lee as PHILIP STRAKER)

1.   *Night date.* (1982)
2.   *Night lust.* (1982)

NIGHT WARRIORS (Graham Masterton)

1. *Night warriors.* (1986)
2. *Death dream.* (1988)
3. *Night plague.* (1991)

NIGHTHUNTER (Robert Holdstock as ROBERT FAULCON)

1. *The stalking.* (1983)
1A. *Night hunter.* (1987)
2. *The talisman.* (1983)
3. *The ghost dance.* (1983)
4. *The shrine.* (1984)
5. *The hexing.* (1984)
6. *The labyrinth.* (1987)
1-2. *The stalking.* (1987)
3-4. *The ghost dance.* (1987)
5 6. *The hexing and The labyrinth.* (1989)

NIGHTMARE ON ELM STREET (various authors)

1-3. *Nightmares on Elm Street, parts 1, 2, 3: the continuing story: a novel.* [Jeffrey Cooper]. (1987)
4-5. *Nightmares on Elm Street, part 4: The dream master; part 5: The dream child: a novel.* [Joseph Locke]. (1989)

Associated Titles

The Nightmare on Elm Street companion: the official guide to America's favorite fiend. [Jeffrey Cooper]. (1987)
Nightmares on Elm Street: Freddy Krueger's seven sweetest dreams. [Martin H. Greenberg]. (1991)

NIGHT-THREADS (Ru Emerson)

1. *The calling of the three.* (1990)
2. *The two in hiding.* (1991)

NIGHTWORLD (David Bischoff)

1. *Nightworld.* (1979)
2. *Vampires of nightworld.* (1981)

NI-LACH (Marcia J. Bennett)

1. *Where the Ni-lach.* (1983)
2. *Shadow singer.* (1984)
3. *Beyond the Draak's Teeth.* (1986)
4. *Seeking the dream brother.* (1989)

NILS JÄRNHAN (John Dalmas)

1. *The yngling.* (1971/1984)
2. *Homecoming.* (1984)

NIMH (various authors)

1. *Mrs. Frisby and the rats of NIMH.* [Robert C. O'Brien]. ()
1A. *The secret of NIMH.* [Robert C. O'Brien]. (1982)
2. *Rasco and the rats of NIMH.* [Jane Leslie Conly]. (1986)
3. *RT, Margaret, and the rats of NIMH.* [Jane Leslie Conly]. (1990)

NINJA MASTER (Richard S. Meyers as WADE BARKER)

Year of the Ninja Master

1. *Dragon rising: the year of the Ninja Master: Spring.* (1985)
2. *Lion's fire: the year of the Ninja Master: Summer.* (1985)
3. *Serpent's eye: the year of the Ninja Master: Autumn.* (1985)
4. *Phoenix sword: the year of the Ninja Master: Winter.* (1986)

War of the Ninja Master

1. *The kohga ritual.* (1988)
2. *The shibo discipline.* (1988)
3. *The himitsu attack.* (1988)
4. *The zakka slaughter.* (1988)

NINTENDO ADVENTURE BOOKS (various authors)

1. *Double trouble.* [Clyde Bosco]. (1991)
2. *Leaping lizards.* [Clyde Bosco]. (1991)
3. *Monster mix-up.* [Bill McCay]. (1991)
4. *Koopa capers.* [Bill McCay]. (1991)
5. *Pipe down!* [Clyde Bosco]. (1991)
6. *Doors to doom.* [Bill McCay]. (1991)
7. *Dinosaur dilemma.* [Clyde Bosco]. (1991)
8. *Flown the Koopa.* [Matt Wayne]. (1991)
9. *The crystal trap.* [Matt Wayne]. (1991)
10. *The shadow prince.* [Matt Wayne]. (1991)
11. *Unjust desserts.* [Matt Wayne]. (1991)
12. *Brain drain.* [Matt Wayne]. (1991)

NITA & KIT (Diane Duane)

1. *So you want to be a wizard?* (1983)
2. *Deep wizardry.* (1985)
3. *High wizardry.* (1990)
1-3. *Support your local wizard.* (1990)

THE NOMAD OF TIME—SEE: OSWALD BASTABLE

NOOSE OF LIGHT (Seamus Cullen)

1. *A noose of light.* (1986)
2. *The sultan's turret.* (1986)

NORBY (Isaac Asimov & Janet Jeppson Asimov)

1. *Norby, the mixed-up robot.* (1983)
2. *Norby's other secret.* (1984)
3. *Norby and the lost princess.* (1985)
4. *Norby and the invaders.* (1985)
5. *Norby and the queen's necklace.* (1986)
6. *Norby finds a villain.* (1987)
7. *Norby down to Earth.* (1989)
8. *Norby and Yobo's great adventure.* (1989)
9. *Norby and the oldest dragon.* (1990)
10. *Norby and the court jester.* (1991)
1-2. *The Norby chronicles.* (1986)
3-4. *Norby: robot for hire.* (1987)
5-6. *Norby through space and time.* (1988)

NOREN (Sylvia Louise Engdahl)

1. *This star shall abide.* (1972)
2. *Beyond the Tomorrow Mountains.* (1973)
3. *The doors of the universe.* (1981)

NORGIL (Walter B. Gibson)

1. *Norgil the magician.* (1977)
2. *Norgil: more tales of prestidigitection.* (1979)

NORTH AMERICAN CONFEDERACY (L. Neil Smith)

1. *Tom Paine Maru.* (1984)
2. *The Gallatin divergence.* (1985)
3. *Brightsuit MacBear.* (1988)

NORTHWORLD (David Drake)

1. *Northworld.* (1990)
2. *Vengeance.* (1991)

NOSTRADAMUS (Andrew Laurance)

1. *Premonitions of an inherited mind.* (1979)
1A. *The premonition.* (1991)
2. *The link.* (1980)
3. *The embryo.* (1980)
3A. *The unborn.* (1991)

NOT QUITE HUMAN (Seth McEvoy)

1. *Batteries not included.* (1985)
2. *All geared up.* (1985)
3. *A bug in the system.* (1985)
4. *Reckless robot.* (1986)
5. *Terror at play.* (1986)
6. *Killer robot.* (1986)

NOVARIA—SEE: JORIAN

NUALA (Katharine Eliska Kimbriel)

1. *Fire sanctuary: a novel.* (1986)
2. *Fires of Nuala.* (1988)
3. *Hidden fires.* (1991)

NUCLEAR TRILOGY (B. Wongar)

1. *Walg.* (1983)
2. *Karan.* (1985)
3. *Gabo Djara.* (1987)

NULL-A (A. E. van Vogt)

1. *The world of null-A.* (1948)
2. *The pawns of null-A.* (1956)
3. *Null-A three.* (1985)

THE OBERNEWTYN CHRONICLES (Isobelle Carmody)

1. *Obernewtyn.* (1987)
2. *The farseekers.* (1990)
3. *Scatterlings.* (1991)

OCEAN (Gregory Benford)

1. *In the ocean of night: a novel.* (1977)
2. *Across the sea of suns.* (1984)
2A. *Across the sea of suns.* (1987)
3. *Deeper than the darkness.* (1970)
3A. *The stars in shroud.* (1978)

ODAN THE HALF-GOD (Kenneth Bulmer as MANNING NORVIL)

1. *Dream chariots.* (1977)
2. *Whetted bronze.* (1978)
3. *Crown of the sword god.* (1980)

ODD JOBS (Ron Goulart)

1. *Odd job #101, and other future crimes and intrigues.* (1974)
2. *Calling Dr. Patchwork.* (1978)
3. *Big bang.* (1982)
4. *Brainz, Inc.* (1985)

ODIN (T. Ernesto Bethancourt)

1. *The mortal instruments.* (1977)
2. *Instruments of darkness.* (1977)

OFF SEASON (Jack Ketchum)

1. *Off season.* (1980)
2. *Offspring.* (1991)

OIL-SEEKER (Michael Elder)

1. *Oil-seeker.* (1977)
2. *Oil-planet.* (1978)

OLD ONES (Anthony Horowitz)

1. *The Devil's Door-Bell.* (1983)
2. *The night of the scorpion.* (1984)
3. *The Silver Citadel.* (1986)

OMARAN SAGA (Adrian Cole)

1. *A place among the fallen.* (1986)
2. *Throne of fools.* (1987)
3. *The king of light and shadows.* (1988)
4. *The gods in anger.* (1988)

OMEGA POINT (George Zebrowski)

1. *Ashes and stars.* (1977)
2. [Not separately published]
3. [Not separately published]
1-3. *The Omega point trilogy.* (1983)

OMEGA SUB (various authors as J. D. CAMERON)

1. *Omega sub.* [Michael Jahn]. (1991)
2. *Command decision.* [David Robbins]. (1991)
3. *City of fear.* [Michael Jahn]. (1991)
4. *Blood tide.* [David Robbins]. (1991)

OMEN (various authors)

1. *The omen.* [David Seltzer]. (1976)
2. *Damien.* [Joseph Howard]. (1978)
3. *The final conflict.* [Gordon McGill]. (1980)
4. *Armageddon 2000.* [Gordon McGill]. (1982)
5. *The abomination.* [Gordon McGill]. (1985)

OMINA (Donald S. Rowland as ROLAND STARR)

1. *Operation Omina.* (1970)
2. *Omina uncharted.* (1974)
3. *Time factor.* (1975)
4. *Return from Omina.* (1976)

OMNI ODYSSEYS (various authors)

1.   *Astropilots*. [Laura J. Mixon]. (1987)
1A. *Astro pilots*. [Laura J. Mixon]. (1987)
2.   *Space Station ICE-3*. [Bruce Coville]. (1987)
2A. *Murder in orbit*. [Bruce Coville]. (1987)
3.   *Skyborn*. [Marcia Kruchten]. (1988)
3A. *Skytorn*. [Marcia Kruchten]. (1988)

OMNIVORE: ORN (Piers Anthony)

1.   *Omnivore*. (1968)
2.   *Orn*. (1970)
3.   *OX*. (1976)
1-3. *Of man and mantra: a trilogy*. (1986)

OMRI (Lynne Reid Banks)

1.   *The Indian in the cupboard*. (1980)
2.   *Return of the Indian*. (1986)
3.   *The secret of the Indian*. (1989)

THE ONCE & FUTURE KING (T. H. White)

1.   *The sword in the stone*. (1938)
2.   *The witch in the wood*. (1939)
3.   *The ill-made knight*. (1940)
5.   *The book of Merlyn: the unpublished conclusion to The once and future king*. (1977)
1-4. *The once and future king*. (1958)

OPAR SERIES—SEE: HADON OF ANCIENT OPAR

OPERATION MISFIT (E. Hoffmann Price)

1.   *Operation misfit*. (1980)
2.   *Operation longlife*. (1983)
3.   *Operation exile*. (1986)
4.   *Operation Isis*. (1987)

OPERATION STARHAWKS (Jay D. Blakeney as SEAN DALTON)

1.   *Space hawks*. (1990)
2.   *Code name Peregrine*. (1990)
3.   *Beyond the void*. (1991)
4.   *The Rostma lure*. (1991)
5.   *Destination: mutiny*. (1991)

OPERATION TITAN (Dilwyn Horvat)

1.   *Operation Titan*. (198?)
2.   *Assault on Omega 4*. (1986)

ORANGE COUNTY (Kim Stanley Robinson)

1.   *The wild shore*. (1984)
2.   *The gold coast*. (1988)
3.   *Pacific edge*. (1990)

ORBITAL DECAY (Allen Steele)

1.   *Orbital decay*. (1989)
2.   *Lunar descent*. (1991)

ORBITSVILLE (Bob Shaw)

1.   *Orbitsville*. (1975)
2.   *Orbitsville departure*. (1983)
3.   *Orbitsville judgement*. (1990)

ORGANIC FUTURE (Thomas A. Easton)

1.   *Sparrowhawk*. (1990)
2.   *Greenhouse*. (1991)

ORIGIN OF DRAGONREALM (Richard A. Knaak)

1.   *The shrouded realm*. (1991)
2.   *Children of the drake*. (1991)

ORION (Ben Bova)

1.   *Orion*. (1984)
2.   *Vengeance of Orion*. (1988)
3.   *Orion in the dying time*. (1990)

ORION (Rosemary Harris)

1.   *Quest for Orion*. (1978)
2.   *Tower of the stars*. (1980)

ORN—SEE: OMNIVORE

ORON (David C. Smith)

1.   *Oron*. (1978)
2.   *The sorcerer's shadow*. (1978)
3.   *Mosutha's magic: Oron*. (1982)
4.   *The valley of Ogrum*. (1982)
5.   *The ghost army*. (1983)

ORTHE (Mary Gentle)

1.   *Golden witchbreed*. (1983)
2.   *Ancient light*. (1987)

OSCAR NOODLEMAN (Stephen Manes)

1.   *That game from outer space*. (1983)
2.   *The Oscar J. Noodleman television network*. (1984)
3.   *Chicken trek*. (1987)

OSWALD BASTABLE (Michael Moorcock)

1.   *The Warlord of the air*. (1971)
2.   *The Land Leviathan*. (1974)
3.   *The steel tsar*. (1981)
1-3. *The nomad of time*. (1982)

OTHERS (Margaret Wander Bonnano)

1.   *The others*. (1990)
2.   *Otherwhere*. (1991)

OUT OF THIS WORLD—SEE: MAX

OUTRIDER (Robert Tine as RICHARD HARDING)

1.   *The outrider*. (1984)
2.   *Fire and ice*. (1984)
3.   *Blood highway*. (1984)
4.   *Bay City burnout*. (1985)
5.   *Built to kill*. (1985)

OVERLOAD (Bob Ham)

1.   *Personal war*. (1989)
2.   *The wrath*. (1989)
3.   *Highway warriors*. (1989)

4.   *Tennessee terror.* (1989)
5.   *Atlanta burn.* (1990)
6.   *Nebraska nightmare.* (1990)
7.   *Rolling vengeance.* (1990)
8.   *Ozark payback.* (1991)
9.   *Huntsville horror.* (1991)
10. *Michigan madness.* (1991)
11. *Alabama bloodbath.* (1991)
12. *Vegas gamble.* (1991)

OVERSOUL SEVEN (Jane Roberts)

1.   *The education of Oversoul Seven.* (1973)
2.   *The further education of Oversoul Seven.* (1979)
3.   *Oversoul Seven and the Museum of Time.* (1984)

OWL (Robert Forward)

1.   *The owl.* (1984)
2.   *Scarlet serenade.* (1990)

OXRUN STATION (Charles L. Grant)

Nightmare seasons. (1982)
The bloodwind. (1982)
The dark cry of the moon. (1985)
The grave. (1981)
The hour of the Oxrun dead. (1977)
The last call of mourning. (1979)
The long night of the grave. (1986)
The orchard. (1986)
The soft whisper of the dead. (1982)
The sound of midnight. (1978)

OZ SEQUELS (various authors)

The autocrats of Oz. [Jon Michael Suter]. (1976)
The Orange Knight of Oz. [Jon Michael Suter]. (1976)
A barnstormer in Oz; or, A rationalization and extrapolation of the split-level continuum. [Philip José Farmer]. (1982)
Return to Oz: a novel. [Joan D. Vinge]. (1985)
1.   *Dorothy of Oz.* [Roger S. Baum]. (1989)
2.   *The Rewolf of Oz.* [Roger S. Baum]. (1990)
3.   *The SillyOZbuls of Oz.* [Roger S. Baum]. (1991)

OZARK FANTASY TRILOGY (Suzette Haden Elgin)

1.   *Twelve fair kingdoms.* (1981)
2.   *The Grand Jubilee.* (1981)
3.   *And then there'll be fireworks.* (1981)
1-3. *The Ozark trilogy.* (1982)

PAGANS TRILOGY (Richard Herley)

1.   *The stone arrow.* (1978)
2.   *The Flint Lord.* (1981)
3.   *The earth goddess.* (1984)
1-3. *The pagans.* (1986)

PAN SAGITTARIUS—SEE: CLAUDINE ST. CYR

PANDORA (Frank Herbert & Bill Ransom)

1.   *Destination: void.* [By Herbert alone]. (1966/1978)
2.   *The Jesus incident.* (1979)
3.   *The Lazarus effect.* (1983)
4.   *The Ascension factor.* (1988)

PANDORA (Kathryn Lance)

1.   *Pandora's genes.* (1985)
2.   *Pandora's children.* (1986)

PANGAIA (Nigel Firth)

1.   *Jormundgand.* (1986)
2.   *Dragon.* (1987)
3.   *Olympiad.* (1988)

PANGUR BAN (Fay Sampson)

1.   *Pangur Ban the white cat.* (1983)
2.   *Finnglas of the horses.* (1985)
3.   *Finnglas and the stones of choosing.* (1986)
4.   *Shape-shifter: the naming of Pangur Ban.* (1988)
5.   *The Serpent of Senargad.* (1989)
6.   *The white horse is running.* (1990)

PAPA SCHIMMELHORN (Reginald Bretnor)

1.   *The Schimmelhorn file.* (1979)
2.   *Schimmelhorn's gold.* (1986)

PARATIME POLICE (H. Beam Piper and others)

1.   *Lord Kalvan of otherwhen.* LORD KALVAN #1. (1965)
1A. *Gunpowder god.* LORD KALVAN #1. (1978)
2.   *Paratime.* (1981)
3.   *Great Kings' War.* LORD KALVAN #2. [John F. Carr & Roland Green]. (1985)

PARATWA SAGA (Christopher Hinz)

1.   *Liege-killer.* (1987)
2.   *Ash Ock.* (1989)
3.   *The Paratwa.* (1991)

PARRIC FAMILY (Charles L. Grant)

1.   *Shadow of Alpha.* (1976)
2.   *Ascension.* (1977)
3.   *Legion.* (1979)

PARSINA SAGA (Stephen Goldin)

1.   *Shrine of the desert mage.* (1988)
2.   *The storyteller and the Jann.* (1988)
3.   *Crystals of air and water.* (1989)

PATTERAN TRILOGY (Patricia Wendorf)

1.   *Larksleve.* (1985)
2.   *Blanche.* (1986)
3.   *Bye bye blackbird.* (1987)

PATTERNIST (Octavia E. Butler)

1.   *Patternmaster.* (1976)
2.   *Mind of my mind.* (1977)
3.   *Survivor.* (1978)
4.   *Wild seed.* (1980)
5.   *Clay's ark.* (1984)

PEACE COMPANY (Roland Green)

1.   *Peace Company.* (1985)
2.   *These green foreign hills.* (1987)

3. *The mountain walks.* (1989)

PEGASUS (Anne McCaffrey)

1. *To ride Pegasus.* (1973)
2. *Pegasus in flight.* (1990)
1-2. *The wings of Pegasus.* (1991)

PELBAR CYCLE (Paul O. Williams)

1. *The breaking of Northwall.* (1981)
2. *The ends of the circle.* (1981)
3. *The dome in the forest.* (1981)
4. *The fall of the shell.* (1982)
5. *An ambush of shadows.* (1983)
6. *The song of the axe.* (1984)
7. *The sword of forbearance.* (1985)

PELMEN (Robert Don Hughes)

1. *The prophet of Lamath.* (1979)
2. *The wizard in waiting.* (1982)
3. *The power and the prophet.* (1985)

PENDRAGON CYCLE (Stephen Lawhead)

1. *Taliesen.* (1987)
2. *Merlin.* (1988)
3. *Arthur.* (1989)

PENNY SPRING & TOBY GLENDOWER SERIES (Petronelle Marguerite Mary Cook as MARGOT ARNOLD)

Death of a voodoo doll. (1982)
Death on the dragon's tongue. (1982)

PENTECOST (W. J. Corbett)

1. *The song of Pentecost.* (1982)
2. *Pentecost and the chosen one.* (1984)
3. *Pentecost of Lickey Top.* (1987)

THE PEOPLE (Zenna Henderson)

1. *The book of the People.* (1961)
2. *The People: no different flesh.* (1966)
1-2. *The People collection.* (1991).

PEOPLE IN THE PICTURE (Haydn Middleton)

1. *The people in the picture.* (1987)
2. *The collapsing castle.* (1990)

PEOPLE OF THE WOLF (Kathleen O'Neal Gear & W. Michael Gear)

1. *People of the wolf.* (1990)
2. *People of the fire.* (1991)

PEREGRINE (Avram Davidson)

1. *Peregrine: primus.* (1971)
2. *Peregrine: secundus.* (1981)

PEREGRINE CONNECTION (Ruth Glick & Eileen Buckholtz as REBECCA YORK)

1. *Tales of the falcon.* (1986)
2. *Flight of the raven.* (1986)
3. *In search of the dove.* (1986)

PERELANDRA: RANSOM (C. S. Lewis)

1. *Out of the silent planet.* (1938)
2. *Perelandra.* (1943)
3. *That hideous strength.* (1945)
1-3. *The cosmic trilogy.* (1990)

PERILOUS QUEST FOR LYONESSE (Antony Swithin)

1. *Princes of Sandastre.* (1990)
2. *The lords of the Stoney Mountains.* (1991)

PERN: DRAGONRIDERS OF PERN (Anne McCaffrey)

1. *Dragonflight.* (1968)
2. *Dragonquest.* (1971)
3. *The white dragon.* (1978)
4. *Dragonsong.* HARPER HALL #1. (1976)
5. *Dragonsinger.* HARPER HALL #2. (1977)
6. *Dragondrums.* HARPER HALL #3. (1979)
7. *Moreta, dragonlady of Pern.* (1983)
8. *Nerilka's story.* (1986)
9. *Dragonsdawn.* (1988)
10. *The renegades of Pern.* (1989)
11. *All the weyrs of Pern.* (1991)
1-3. *The Dragonriders of Pern.* (1978)
1-3. *The Harper Hall of Pern.* (1984)

Associated Titles

A time when: being a tale of young Lord Jaxom, his white dragon Ruth, and various fire-lizards. (1975)
The girl who heard dragons. (1985)
Dragonharper: a Crossroads adventure in the world of Anne McCaffrey's Pern. [Jody Lynn Nye]. (1987)
Dragonfire: a Crossroads adventure in the world of Anne McCaffrey's Pern. [Jody Lynn Nye]. (1988)
Rescue run. (1991)

PERRY RHODAN (various authors)

1-60. [See the 1979 edition of this bibliography]
61. *Death waits in semispace.* [Kurt Mahr]. (1975)
62. *The last days of Atlantis.* [K. H. Scheer]. (1975)
63. *The Tigris leaps.* [Kurt Brand]. (1975)
64. *The ambassadors from Aurigel.* [Kurt Mahr]. (1975)
65. *Renegades of the future.* [Kurt Mahr]. (1975)
66. *The horror.* [William Voltz]. (1975)
67. *Crimson universe.* [K. H. Scheer]. (1975)
68. *Under the stars of Druufon.* [Walter Ernsting as CLARK DARLTON]. (1975)
69. *The bonds of eternity.* [Walter Ernsting as CLARK DARLTON]. (1975)
70. *Thora's sacrifice.* [Kurt Brand]. (1975)
71. *The atom hell of Grautier.* [Kurt Mahr]. (1975)
72. *Caves of the Druufs.* [Kurt Mahr]. (1975)
73. *Spaceship of ancestors.* [Walter Ernsting as CLARK DARLTON]. (1975)
74. *Checkmate: universe.* [Kurt Mahr]. (1975)
75. *Planet Topide, please reply!* [Kurt Brand]. (1975)
76. *Recruits for Arkon.* [Walter Ernsting as CLARK DARLTON]. (1975)
77. *Conflict center: Naator.* [Walter Ernsting as CLARK DARLTON]. (1975)
78. *Power key.* [K. H. Scheer]. (1975)
79. *The sleepers.* [William Voltz]. (1975)
80. *The Columbus affair.* [K. H. Scheer]. (1975)
81. *Pucky's greatest hour.* [Kurt Brand]. (1975)

82. *Atlan in danger.* [Kurt Brand]. (1975)
83. *Ernst Ellert returns!* [Walter Ernsting as CLARK DARLTON]. (1975)
84. *Secret mission: Moluk.* [William Voltz]. (1975)
85. *Enemy in the dark.* [Kurt Mahr]. (1975)
86. *Blazing sun.* [Walter Ernsting as CLARK DARLTON]. (1976)
87. *The starless realm.* [Walter Ernsting as CLARK DARLTON]. (1976)
88. *The mystery of the Anti.* [K. H. Scheer]. (1976)
89. *Power's price.* [Kurt Brand]. (1976)
90. *Unleashed powers.* [Kurt Brand]. (1976)
91. *Friend to mankind.* [William Voltz]. (1976)
92. *The target star.* [K. H. Scheer]. (1976)
93. *Vagabond of space.* [Walter Ernsting as CLARK DARLTON]. (1976)
94. *Action: Division 3.* [Kurt Mahr]. (1976)
95. *The plasma monster.* [Kurt Mahr]. (1976)
96. *Horn: green.* [William Voltz]. (1976)
97. *Phantom fleet.* [Walter Ernsting as CLARK DARLTON]. (1976)
98. *The idol from Passa.* [Kurt Mahr]. (1976)
99. *The blue system.* [K. H. Scheer]. (1976)
100. *Desert of death's domain.* [Kurt Mahr]. (1976)
101. *Blockade: Lepso.* [Kurt Brand]. (1976)
102. *Spoor of the Antis.* [William Voltz]. (1976)
103. *False front.* [Walter Ernsting as CLARK DARLTON]. (1976)
104. *The man with two faces.* [Kurt Brand]. (1976)
105. *Wonderflower of Utik.* [Kurt Mahr]. (1976)
106. *Caller from eternity.* [Kurt Brand]. (1976)
107. *The emperor and the monster.* [William Voltz]. (1977)
108. *Duel under the double sun.* [K. H. Scheer]. (1977)
109. *The stolen spacefleet.* [Walter Ernsting as CLARK DARLTON]. (1977)
110. *Sgt. Robot.* [Kurt Mahr]. (1977)
111. *Seeds of ruin.* [William Voltz]. (1977)
112. *Planet Mechanica.* [K. H. Scheer]. (1977)
113. *Heritage of the lizard people.* [Walter Ernsting as CLARK DARLTON]. (1977)
114. *Death's demand.* [Kurt Mahr]. (1977)
115. *Saboteurs in A-1.* [Kurt Brand]. (1977)
116. *The psycho duel.* [William Voltz]. (1977)
117. *Savior of the empire.* [K. H. Scheer]. (1977)
118. *The shadows attack.* [Walter Ernsting as CLARK DARLTON]. (1977)
119. *Between the galaxies.* [Kurt Mahr]. (1978)
120. *Killers from hyperspace.* [William Voltz]. (1978)
121. *Atom fire on Mechanica.* [Walter Ernsting as Clark Darlton]. (1978)
122. *Volunteers for Frago.* [Kurt Brand]. (1978)
123. *Fortress in time.* [Kurt Mahr]. (1978)
124. *The sinister power.* [Kurt Brand]. (1978)
125. *Robots, bombs, and mutants.* (1979)
126. *The guns of Everblack.* [K. H. Scheer]. (1979)
127. *Sentinels of solitude.* [Walter Ernsting as CLARK DARLTON]. (1979)
128. *The beasts below.* [Kurt Mahr]. (1979)
129. *Blitzkrieg galactica.* [Kurt Brand]. (1979)
130. *Peril unlimited.* [Kurt Brand]. (1979)
131. *World without mercy.* [William Voltz]. (1979)
132. *Deadmen shouldn't die.* [Walter Ernsting as CLARK DARLTON]. (1979)
133. *Station of the invisibles.* [Kurt Mahr]. (1979)
134. *Agents of destruction.* [Kurt Brand]. (1979)
135. *Humans keep out!* [William Voltz]. (1979)
136. *The robot invitation.* [K. H. Scheer]. (1979)
137. *The phantom horde.* [Walter Ernsting as CLARK DARLTON]. (1979)

Unnumbered Titles

In the center of the galaxy. [Walter Ernsting as Clark Darlton]. (1978)
Menace of atomigeddon. [Kurt Mahr]. (1977)
Robot threat: New York. [W. W. Shols]. (1977)
The wasp men attack. [W. W. Shols]. (1977)

PETER PROUD (Max Ehrlich)

1. *The reincarnation of Peter Proud.* (1974)
2. *Reincarnation in Venice.* (1979)

PHANTOM VALLEY (Kathryn Lance as LYNN BEACH)

1. *The evil one.* (1991)
2. *The dark.* (1991)

PHILIP JOSE FARMER'S THE DUNGEON (various authors)

1. *The black tower.* [Richard A. Lupoff]. (1988)
2. *The dark abyss.* [Bruce Coville]. (1989)
3. *The valley of thunder.* [Charles de Lint]. (1989)
4. *The lake of fire.* [Robin W. Bailey]. (1989)
5. *The hidden city.* [Charles de Lint]. (1990)
6. *The final battle.* [Richard A. Lupoff]. (1990)

PHOENIX (David Alexander)

1. *Dark messiah.* (1987)
2. *Ground zero.* (1987)
3. *Death quest.* (1988)
4. *Metalstorm.* (1988)
5. *Whirlwind.* (1988)

PHOENIX LEGACY (M. K. Wren)

1. *The sword of the Lamb.* (1981)
2. *Shadow of the swan.* (1981)
3. *House of the wolf.* (1981)

PHOTINUS (John James)

1. *Votan.* (1966)
2. *Not for all the gold in Ireland.* (1968)
3. *Men went to Cattraeth.* (1969)

PHOTON (David Peters)

1. *For the glory.* (1987)
2. *High stakes.* (1987)
3. *In search of MOM.* (1987)
4. *This is your life, Bhodi Li.* (1987)
5. *Exile.* (1987)
6. *Skin deep.* (1988)

Associated Title

Thieves of light. [Michael P. Kube-McDowell as MICHAEL HUDSON]. (1987)

PICK-A-PATH (various authors)

1. *The dandee diamond mystery.* [Jane O'Connor & Joyce Milton]. (1982)
2. *The roller coaster ghost.* [Fran Manushkin]. (1983)
3. *The great baseball championship.* [Richard Wenk]. (1983)

4. *The amazing bubblegum caper*. [Richard Wenk]. (1983)
5. *The super trail bike race*. [Richard Wenk]. (1983)
6. *Mystery at Mockingbird Manor*. [Laurie Pascal & Jamie Pascal]. (1983)
7. *The fantastic journey of the space shuttle Astra*. [B. B. Hiller]. (1984)
8. *The magic top mystery*. [Jane O'Connor & Jim O'Connor]. (1984)
9. *Jungle adventure*. [Nora Logan]. (1984)
10. *The mystery of the missing mummy*. [Kate McMullan]. (1984)
11. *Dinosaur adventure*. [Nora Logan]. (1984)
12. *The ballarina mystery*. [Jamie Pascal & Laurie Pascal]. (1984)
13. *The secret of 13*. [B. B. Hiller]. (1984)
14. *RIM, the rebel robot*. [Nora Logan]. (1984)
15. *The Hot Dog Gang caper*. [B. B. Hiller & Neil W. Hiller]. (1985)
16. [unknown title]
17. *Murf the monster*. [Nora Logan]. (1984)

PIERS ANTHONY'S WORLDS OF CHTHON—SEE: CHTHON

PIG (Karen A. Brush)

1. *The pig, the prince, & the unicorn*. (1987)
2. *The demon pig*. (1991)

PIG PLANTAGENET (Allen Andrews)

1. *The Pig Plantagenet*. (1980)
2. *Castle Crespin*. (1982)

PILGRIM (Fred Saberhagen)

1. *Pyramids*. (1987)
2. *After the fact*. (1988)

PINEAPPLE PLACE (Anne Lindbergh)

1. *The people in Pineapple Place*. (1982)
2. *The prisoner of Pineapple Place*. (1988)

PINK PIG (C. S. Adler)

1. *Goodbye, Pink Pig*. (1985)
2. *Help, Pink Pig*. (1990)

PIT DRAGONS (Jane Yolen)

1. *Dragon's blood*. (1982)
2. *Heart's blood*. (1984)
3. *A sending of dragons*. (1987)

PLANET BUILDERS (various authors as ROBYN TALLIS)

1. *Mountain of stolen dreams*. [Bruce Coville]. (1988)
2. *Night of ghosts and lightning*. [Debra Doyle & James D. Macdonald]. (1989)
3. *Rebel from Alphorion*. [Sherwood Smith]. (1989)
4. *Visions from the sea*. [Sherwood Smith]. (1989)
5. *Zero-sum games*. [Debra Doyle & James D. Macdonald]. (1989)
6. *Night of two new moons*. [Bruce Coville]. (1989)
7. *Children of the storm*. [Mary Frances Zambreno]. (1989)
8. *Horrorvid*. [Jymn Magon]. (1989)
9. *Giants of Elenna*. [Sherwood Smith]. (1989)

10. *Fire in the sky*. [Sherwood Smith]. (1989)

PLANET OF ADVENTURE (Jack Vance)

1. *City of the Chasch*. (1968)
2. *Servants of the Wankh*. (1969)
3. *The Dirdir*. (1969)
4. *The Pnume*. (1970)
1-4. *The planet of adventure omnibus*. (1985)

PLANET OF THE APES (various authors)

1. *Planet of the apes*. [Pierre Boullc]. (1963)

MOVIE SERIES

2. *Beneath the planet of the apes*. [Michael Avallonc]. (1970)
3. *Escape from the planet of the apes*. [Jerry Pournelle]. (1974)
4. *Conquest of the planet of the apes*. [John Jakes]. (1974)
5. *Battle for the planet of the apes*. [David Jerrold]. (1973)

TELEVISION SERIES (George Alec Effinger)

1. *Man, the fugitive*. (1974)
2. *Escape to tomorrow*. (1975)
3. *Journey into terror*. (1975)
4. *Lord of the apes*. (1976)

RETURN TO THE PLANET OF THE APES
(various authors as WILLIAM ARROW)

1. *Visions from nowhere*. [William Rotsler]. (1976)
2. *Escape from Terror* [Donald J. Pfeil]. (1976)
3. *Man, the hunted animal*. [William Rotsler]. (1976)

PLANET OF THE DAMNED (Harry Harrison)

1. *Planet of the damned*. (1962)
1A. *Sense of obligation*. (1967)
2. *Planet of no return*. (1981)

PLANET PIRATES (Anne McCaffrey with various authors)

1. *Sassinak*. [with Elizabeth Moon]. (1990)
2. *The death of sleep*. [with Jody Lynn Nye]. (1990)
3. *Generation warriors*. [with Elizabeth Moon]. (1991)

PLANETARY AGENT (Mack Reynolds)

1. *Planetary Agent X*. (1965)
2. *Dawnsman planet*. (1966)
3. *The rival Rigellians*. (1967)
4. *Code duello*. (1968)
5. *Section G: United Planets*. (1976)
1,3 *The rival Rigellians; Planetary Agent X*. (1974)

PLANETFALL (Arthur Byron Cover)

1. *Planetfall*. (1988)
2. *Stationfall*. (1989)

THE PLANT (Stephen King)

1. *The plant: the opening segment of an ongoing work*. (1982)
2. *The plant, part 2*. (1983)

3. *The plant, part 3.* (1985)

PLANT THAT ATE DIRTY SOCKS (Nancy McArthur)

1. *The plant that ate dirty socks.* (1988)
2. *The return of the plant that ate dirty socks.* (1990)

PLOT-IT-YOURSELF/PLOT YOUR OWN HORROR STORIES
(Hilary Milton)

PLOT YOUR OWN HORROR STORIES

1. *Craven house horrors.* (1982)
2. *Nightmare store.* (1982)
3. *Space-age terrors!* (1983)
3A. *Space age terrors!* (1984)
4. *Horror hotel!* (1983)
4A. *Grand hotel of horror.* (1984)

PLOT-IT-YOURSELF HORROR STORIES

5. *Escape from high doom.* (1984)
6. *Fun house terrors!* (1984)
7. *Museum of the living dead.* (1985)
7A. *Dining with dinosaurs.* (1985)
8. *Dungeon demons.* (1985)

PLOT YOUR OWN HORROR STORIES—SEE: PLOT-IT-YOURSELF HORROR STORIES

POCKETS (William Sanders as WILL SUNDOWN)

1. *Pockets of resistance.* (1990)
2. *The hellbound train.* (1990)

POLESOTECHNIC LEAGUE—SEE: FUTURE HISTORY

POLTERGEIST (James Kahn)

1. *Poltergeist.* (1982)
2. *Poltergeist II: The other side.* (1986)

POSSESSED (Ronald Powe)

1. *Possessed.* (1989)
2. *Possessed II: the sequel.* (1990)

POWERS OF LIGHT (Kathleen O'Neal Gear as KATHLEEN
M. O'NEAL)

1. *An abyss of light.* (1990)
2. *Treasure of light.* (1990)
3. *Redemption of light.* (1991)

PREDATOR (various authors)

1. *Predator: a novel.* [Paul Monette]. (1987)
2. *Predator 2: a novel.* [Simon Hawke]. (1990)

PRESIDENTIAL TRILOGY (Raymond Hawkey)

1. *Wild card.* [with Roger Bingham]. (1988)
2. *Side-effect.* (1979)
3. *It.* (1983)
3A. *End stage.* (1988)

THE PRESIDENT'S DAUGHTER (Ellen Emerson White)

1. *The president's daughter.* (1984)
2. *White House autumn.* (1985)

THE PRINCE IN WAITING (John Christopher)

1. *The Prince in Waiting.* (1970)
2. *Beyond the Burning Lands.* (1971)
3. *The sword of the spirits.* (1972)
1-3. *The prince in waiting trilogy.* (1983)

PRINCE OF SHADOWS (Gary Chalk & Joe Dever)

1. *Mean streets.* (1988)
2. *Creatures from the depths.* (1989)

PRINCE OF STARS IN THE CAVERN OF TIME (Ian Dennis)

1. *Bagdad.* (1985)
2. *The prince of stars.* (1987)
1-2. *The prince of stars in the cavern of time.* (1989)

PRINCE ZARKON—SEE: ZARKON, LORD OF THE UN-KNOWN

THE PRISONER (various authors)

1. *The prisoner.* [Thomas M. Disch]. (1969)
2. *Number Two.* [David McDaniel]. (1969)
2A. *The Prisoner: Who is Number Two?* [David Mc-Daniel]. (1982)
3. *A day in the life.* [Hank Stine]. (1970)

PRISONER OF DREAMS (Karen Ripley)

1. *Prisoner of dreams.* (1989)
2. *The tenth class.* (1991)

PRIVATE SCHOOL (Charles L. Grant as STEVEN CHARLES)

1. *Nightmare session.* (1986)
2. *Academy of terror.* (1986)
3. *Witch's eye.* (1986)
4. *Skeleton key.* (1986)
5. *The enemy within.* (1987)
6. *The last alien.* (1987)

PROBE (Carole Nelson Douglas)

1. *Probe.* (1985)
2. *Counterprobe.* (1988)

**PROCEEDINGS OF THE J. LLOYD EATON CONFERENCE ON
SCIENCE FICTION AND FANTASY LITERATURE** (George
Edgar Slusser & others)

1. *Bridges to science fiction.* [with George R. Guffey &
    Mark Rose]. (1980)
2. *Bridges to fantasy.* [with Eric S. Rabkin & Robert
    Scholes]. (1982)
3. *Coordinates: placing science fiction and fantasy.*
    [with Eric S. Rabkin & Robert Scholes]. (1983)
4. *Shadows of the magic lamp: fantasy and science fic-
    tion in films.* [with Eric S. Rabkin]. (1985)
5. *Hard science fiction.* [with Eric S. Rabkin]. (1986)
6. *Storm warnings: science fiction confronts the future.*
    [with Eric S. Rabkin & Colin Greenland]. (1987)
7. *Aliens: the anthropology of science fiction.* [with
    Eric S. Rabkin]. (1987)
8. *Intersections: fantasy and science fiction.* [with Eric
    S. Rabkin]. (1987)
9. *Mindscapes: the geographies of imagined worlds.*
    [with Eric S. Rabkin]. (1989)

PROCURATOR (Kirk Mitchell)

1. *Procurator.* (1984)
2. *New barbarians.* (1986)
3. *Cry republic.* (1989)

PROJEKT SAUCER (W. A. Harbinson)

1. *Inception.* (1991)
2. *Genesis.* (1980)

PROTECTOR (Irwin Zacharia)

1. *Brotherhood of evil.* (1982)
2. *Princess of darkness.* (1982)
3. *Reddy or not.* (1982)
4. *Three to get Reddy.* (1982)

PROTEUS (Charles Sheffield)

1. *Sight of Proteus.* (1978)
2. *Proteus unbound.* (1989)
1-2. *Proteus manifest.* (1989)

PRYDAIN Chronicles (Lloyd Alexander)

1. *The Book of Three.* (1964)
2. *The Black Cauldron.* (1965)
3. *The Castle of Llyr.* (1966)
4. *Taran Wanderer.* (1967)
5. *The High King.* (1968)
1-3. *The first chronicles of Prydain.* (1986)
1-5. *The Prydain chronicles.* (1991)
4-5. *The second chronicles of Prydain.* (1986)

Associated titles

The foundling, and other tales of Prydain. (1973)

PSI PATROL (Betty Anne Crawford as various authors)

1. *Sal's book.* [as SAL LIQUORI]. (1985)
2. *Hendra's book.* [as HENDRA BENOIT]. (1985)
3. *Max's book.* [as MAXWELL HURLEY]. (1985)

PSI-MAN (David Peters)

1. *Psi-Man.* (1990)
2. *Deathscape.* (1991)
3. *Main Street D.O.A.* (1991)
4. *The chaos kid.* (1991)
5. *Stalker.* (1991)

PSION (Joan D. Vinge)

1. *Psion.* (1982)
2. *Catspaw.* (1988)
2A. *Cats paw.* (1989)
1-2. *Alien blood: Psion; Catspaw.* (1988)

PSYCH (Brian Lumley)

1. *Psychomech.* (1984)
2. *Psychosphere.* (1984)
3. *Psychamok.* (1985)

PSYCHODROME (Simon Hawke)

1. *Psychodrome.* (1987)
2. *The shapechanger scenario.* (1988)

PSYCHOTECHNIC LEAGUE (Poul Anderson)

1. *The Psychotechnic League.* (1981)
2. *Cold victory.* (1982)
3. *Starship.* (1982)

PULP CLASSICS (various authors)

1. *Gangland's doom: the Shadow of the pulps.* [Frank Eisgruber Jr.]. (1974)
2. *Python men of the lost city.* [Chester Hawk]. (1974)
3. *Revelry in Hell.* [Robert Weinberg]. (1974)
4. *Brand of the metal maiden.* [Brant House]. (1974)
5. *The Moon man.* [Robert Weinberg]. (1974)
6. *Dr. Satan.* [Paul Ernst and Basil Wells]. (1974)
7. *America's Secret Service ace.* [Nick Carr]. (1974)
8. *The case of the six coffins.* [Robert J. Hogan]. (1975)
9. *The mystery of the dragon's shadow.* [Donald E. Keyhoe]. (1975)
10. *The Angel.* [Robert Weinberg]. (1975)
11. *The city condemned to Hell.* [Craig Randolph]. (1975)
12. *Satan's incubators.* [Craig Randolph]. (1975)
13. *Death orchids, & other bizarre tales.* [Robert Weinberg]. (1976)
14. *The green lama.* [Kendell Foster Crossen & Frederick C. Davis]. (1976)
15. *The football racketeers.* [Clifford Goodrich]. (1977)
16. *Breathless island.* [Wallace Brooker]. (1977)
17. *The red shadow.* [Robert J. Hogan]. (1977)
18. *The flying spy.* [Nick Carr]. (1978)
19. *12 must die.* [Zorro]. (1979)
20. *The emperor of death.* [Robert Weinberg]. (1979)
21. *The death dealers.* [Robert Weinberg]. (1980)
22. *Secret Agent X: a history.* [Will Murray & Tom Johnson]. (1980)

Q (Trevor Hoyle)

1. *Seeking the mythical future.* (1977)
2. *Through the eye of time.* (1977)
3. *The gods look down.* (1978)

QHE (William Bloom as W. W.)

1. *The taming power.* (1974)
2. *White fire.* (1974)
3. *The riches.* (1975)
4. *The prophets of evil.* (1976)

QUANTUM LEAP (Julie Robitaille)

1. *The beginning.* (1990)
2. *The ghost and the gumshoe.* (1990)

QUEEN'S QUARTER (Midori Snyder)

1. *New moon.* (1989)
2. *Sadar's keep.* (1990)

QUEST (Frances Mary Hendry)

1. *Quest for a kelpie.* (1986)
2. *Quest for a maid.* (1988)
3. *Quest for a babe.* (1990)

QUEST FOR THE WHITE DUCK (Charles L. Grant as LI-ONEL FENN)

1. *Blood river down.* (1986)
2. *Web of defeat.* (1987)
3. *Agnes day.* (1987)

QUESTIONER TRILOGY (Dennis Schmidt)

1. *Labyrinth.* (1989)
2. *City of crystal shadow.* (1990)
3. *Dark paradise.* (1990)

QUINTARA MARATHON (Jack L. Chalker)

1. *The demons at Rainbow Bridge.* (1989)
2. *The run to Chaos Keep.* (1991)
3. *The ninety trillion Fausts.* (1991)

RACK (Laurence James)

1. *Earth lies sleeping.* (1974)
2. *War on Aleph.* (1974)
3. *Backflash.* (1975)
4. *Planet of the blind.* (1975)
5. *New life for old.* (1975)

RACK THE HEALER (Zach Hughes)

1. *The book of Rack the Healer.* (1973)
2. *Thunderworld.* (1982)

RADIX TETRAD (A. A. Attanasio)

1. *Radix.* (1981)
2. *In other worlds.* (1984)
3. *Arc of the dream.* (1986)
4. *The last legends of Earth.* (1989)

RAJAN (Tim Lukeman)

1. *Rajan.* (1979)
2. *Koren.* (1981)

RAMA (Arthur C. Clarke)

1. *Rendezvous with Rama.* (1973)
1A. *Rendezvous with Rama.* [with David Fickling]. (1979)
2. *Rama II.* [with Gentry Lee]. (1989)
3. *The garden of Rama.* [with Gentry Lee]. (1991)

RAMON AND MORGAN (Mike McQuay)

1. *Pure blood.* (1985)
2. *Mother Earth.* (1985)

RANDY KNOWLES (Hans Holzer)

1. *The Red Chindvit conspiracy.* (1970)
2. *The alchemy deception.* (1973)
3. *The unicorn.* (1976)

RANSOM—SEE: PERELANDRA

RATHA (Clare Bell)

1. *Ratha's creature.* (1983)
2. *Clan ground.* (1984)
3. *Ratha and Thistle-Chaser.* (1990)

RATS (James Herbert)

1. *The rats.* (1974)
1A. *Deadly eyes.* (1983)
2. *Lair.* (1979)
3. *Domain.* (1984)

RAUM (Carl Sherrell)

1. *Raum.* (1977)
2. *Skraelings.* (1987)

RAVEN (Robert Holdstock & Angus Wells as RICHARD KIRK)

1. *Raven, swordmistress of chaos.* (1978)
2. *A time of ghosts.* (1978)
3. *The frozen god.* (1978)
4. *Lords of the shadows.* (1979)
5. *A time of dying.* (1979)

RAVENLOFT (various authors)

1. *Vampire of the mists.* [Christie Golden]. (1991)
2. *Knight of the black rose.* [James Lowder]. (1991)

REALTIME (Vernor Vinge)

1. *The peace war.* (1984)
2. *Marooned in realtime.* (1986)
1-2. *Across realtime.* (1986/1991)

REBEL ANGELS (Robertson Davies)

1. *The rebel angels.* (1981)
2. *What's bred in the bone.* (1985)
3. *The lyre of Orpheus.* (1988)

REBEL DYNASTY—SEE: RISSA KERGUELEN

RED DWARF (Rob Grant & Doug Naylor as GRANT NAYLOR)

1. *Red dwarf.* (1989)
2. *Better than life.* (1990)

RED MOON (Marion Zimmer Bradley & Paul Edwin Zimmer)

1. *Hunters of the Red Moon.* (1973)
2. *The survivors.* (1979)

RED SONJA (David C. Smith & Richard L. Tierney)

1. *The ring of Ikribu.* (1981)
2. *Demon night.* (1982)
3. *When Hell laughs.* (1982)
4. *Endithor's daughter.* (1982)
5. *Against the prince of Hell.* (1983)
6. *Star of doom.* (1983)

REDWALL (Brian Jacques)

1. *Mossflower.* (1988)
2. *Redwall.* (1986)
3. *Mattimeo.* (1989)
4. *Mariel of Redwall.* (1991)
1-3. *The Redwall trilogy.* (1991)

REFERENCE PUBLICATION IN SCIENCE FICTION (various authors)

Index to science fiction anthologies and collections. [William G. Contento]. (1978)
Index to stories in thematic anthologies of science fiction. [L. W. Currey & Martin H. Greenberg & Marshall Tymn & Joseph D. Olander]. (1978)
British and American utopian literature, 1516-(1975): an annotated bibliography. [Lyman Tower Sargent]. (1979)
Uranian worlds: a reader's guide to alternative sexuality in science fiction and fantasy. [Eric Garber & Lyn Paleo]. (1983)
Index to science fiction anthologies and collections, (1977)-(1983). [William G. Contento]. (1984)

REGIMENT (John Dalmas)

1. *The regiment.* (1987)
2. *The white regiment.* (1990)
3. *The Kalif's war.* (1991)

REHUMANIZATION OF JADE DARCY (Stephen Goldin & Mary Mason)

1. *Jade Darcy and the affair of honor.* (1988)
2. *Jade Darcy and the zen pirates.* (1990)

REINDEER MOON (Elizabeth Marshall Thomas)

1. *Reindeer moon.* (1987)
2. *The animal wife.* (1990)

REINDEER PEOPLE (Megan Lindholm)

1. *The reindeer people.* (1988)
2. *Wolf's brother.* (1988)
1-2. *A saga of the reindeer people.* (1988)

RELUCTANT VAMPIRE (Eric Morecambe)

1. *The reluctant vampire.* (1982)
2. *The vampire's revenge.* (1983)

REMEMBER (Robert Cornett & Kevin Randle)

1. *Remember the Alamo!* (1980)
2. *Remember Gettysburg!* (1988)
3. *Remember the Little Bighorn!* (1990)

RENTAGHOST (Hugh Morgan)

1. *Rentaghost unlimited.* (1982)
2. *Rentaghost enterprises.* (1984)
3. *Rentaghost rules.* (1985)

THE RESCUERS—SEE: MISS BIANCA

RETIEF SERIES (Keith Laumer)

1. *Envoy to new worlds.* (1963)
1A. *Retief: envoy to new worlds.* (1987)
2. *Galactic diplomat.* (1965)
3. *Retief's war.* (1966)
4. *Retief and the warlords* (1968)
5. *Retief: ambassador to space.* (1969)
6. *Retief's ransom.* (1971)
6A. *Retief and the Pangalactic Pageant of Pulchritude.* (1986)

7. *Retief of the CDT.* (1971)
8. *Retief: Emissary to the stars.* (1975)
9. *Retief: Diplomat at arms.* (1982)
10 *Retief to the rescue.* (1983)
11. *The return of Retief.* (1984)
12. *Retief in the ruins.* (1986)
13. *Reward for Retief.* (1989)
1,6. *Retief unbound.* (1979)

Associated Title

Retief at large. (1978)

RETURN TO THE PLANET OF THE APES—SEE: PLANET OF THE APES

REX BADER—SEE: LAGRANGIA

RHADA (Alfred Coppel as ROBERT CHAM GILMAN)

1. *The Warlock of Rhada.* (1985)
2. *The Rebel of Rhada.* (1968)
3. *The navigator of Rhada.* (1969)
4. *The Starkahn of Rhada.* (1970)

RICHARD BLADE (various authors as JEFFREY LORD)

1. *The bronze axe.* [Manning Lee Stokes]. (1969)
2. *The jade warrior.* [Manning Lee Stokes]. (1969)
3. *Jewel of Tharn.* [Manning Lee Stokes]. (1969)
4. *Slave of Sarma.* [Manning Lee Stokes]. (1969)
5. *Liberator of Jedd.* [Manning Lee Stokes]. (1971)
6. *Monster of the maze.* [Manning Lee Stokes]. (1972)
7. *Pearl of Patmos.* [Manning Lee Stokes]. (1973)
8. *Undying world.* [Manning Lee Stokes]. (1973)
9. *Kingdom of Royth.* [Roland Green]. (1974)
10. *Ice dragon.* [Roland Green]. (1974)
11. *Dimension of dreams.* [Roland Green]. (1974)
12. *King of Zunga.* [Roland Green]. (1975)
13. *The golden steed.* [Roland Green]. (1975)
14. *The temples of Ayocan.* [Roland Green]. (1975)
15. *The towers of Melnon.* [Roland Green]. (1975)
16. *The crystal seas.* [Roland Green]. (1975)
17. *The mountains of Brega.* [Roland Green]. (1976)
18. *Warlords of Gaikon.* [Roland Green]. (1976)
19. *Looters of Tharn.* [Roland Green]. (1976)
20. *Guardians of the coral throne.* [Roland Green]. (1976)
21. *Champion of the gods.* [Roland Green]. (1976)
22. *The forests of Gleor.* [Roland Green]. (1977)
23. *Empire of blood.* [Roland Green]. (1977)
24. *The dragons of Englor.* [Roland Green]. (1977)
25. *The Torian pearls.* [Roland Green]. (1977)
26. *City of the living dead.* [Roland Green]. (1978)
27. *Master of the Hashomi.* [Roland Green]. (1978)
28. *Wizard of Rentoro.* [Roland Green]. (1978)
29. *Treasure of the stars.* [Roland Green]. (1978)
30. *Dimension of horror.* [Ray Faraday Nelson]. (1979)
31. *Gladiators of Hapanu.* [Roland Green]. (1979)
32. *Pirates of Gohar.* [Roland Green]. (1979)
33. *Killer plants of Binaark.* [Roland Green]. (1980)
34. *The ruins of Kaldac.* [Roland Green]. (1981)
35. *The Lords of the Crimson River.* [Roland Green]. (1981)
36. *Return to Kaldak.* [Roland Green]. (1983)
37. *Warriors of Latan.* [Roland Green]. (1984)

RICK BRANT SCIENCE-ADVENTURE STORIES (John Blaine)

1. *The rocket's shadow.* (1947)
2. *The lost city.* (1947)
3. *Sea gold.* (1947)
4. *100 fathoms under.* (1947)
5. *The whispering box mystery.* (1948)
6. *The phantom shark.* (1949)
7. *Smugglers' Reef.* (1950)
8. *The Caves of Fear.* (1951)
9. *Stairway to danger.* (1952)
10. *The golden skull.* (1954)
11. *The wailing octopus.* (1956)
12. *The electronic mind reader.* (1957)
13. *The Scarlet Lake mystery.* (1958)
14. *The pirates of Shan.* (1958)
15. *The blue ghost mystery.* (1960)
16. *The Egyptian cat mystery.* (1961)
17. *The flaming mountain.* (1962)
18. *The flying stingaree.* (1963)
19. *The ruby ray mystery.* (1964)
20. *The veiled raiders.* (1965)
21. *Rocket jumper.* (1966)
22. *The deadly Dutchman.* (1967)
23. *Danger below!* (1968)
24. *The magic talisman.* (1990)

RIFKIND SERIES (Lynn Abbey)

1. *Daughter of the bright moon.* (1979)
2. *The Black Flame.* (1980)

Associated Title

Warhorn: a Crossroads adventure in the world of Lynn Abbey's Rifkind, daughter of the bright moon. [Dana Kramer]. (1987)

RIFTWAR SAGA (Raymond E. Feist)

1. *Magician.* (1982)
1A. *Magician: apprentice.* (1986)
1B. *Magician: master.* (1986)
2. *Silverthorn.* (1985)
3. *A darkness at Sethanon.* (1986)
4. *Prince of the blood.* (1989)

RIG WARRIOR (William W. Johnstone)

1. *Rig warrior.* (1987)
2. *Wheels of death.* (1988)
3. *Eighteen-wheel avenger.* (1988)

RIM SERIES—SEE: GRIMES SERIES

RINGS OF THE MASTER (Jack L. Chalker)

1. *Lords of the middle dark.* (1986)
2. *Pirates of the thunder.* (1987)
3. *Warriors of the storm.* (1987)
4. *Masks of the martyrs.* (1988)

RINGWORLD—SEE: KNOWN SPACE

RISSA KERGUELEN (F. M. Busby)

Originally published in two parts in 1976, reprinted as one volume in 1977, and further reprinted in 1984 as three volumes.

1. *Rissa Kerguelen.* (1976)
2. *The long view.* (1976)

1-2. *Rissa Kerguelen.* (1977)

1A. *Young Rissa.* (1984)
2A. *Rissa and Tregare.* (1984)
3A. *The long view.* (1984)

BRAN TREGARE SERIES

1. *Star rebel.* (1984)
2. *The alien debt.* (1984)
3. *Rebel's quest.* (1985)
4. *Rebel's seed.* (1986)
1-2. *The rebel dynasty, volume 1: Star rebel; Rebel's quest.* (1987)
3-4. *The rebel dynasty, volume 2: The alien debt; Rebel's seed.* (1988)

RIVERWORLD (Philip José Farmer)

1. *To your scattered bodies go.* (1971)
2. *The fabulous Riverboat.* (1971)
3. *The dark design.* (1977)
4. *The magic labyrinth.* (1980)
5. *Gods of Riverworld.* (1983)

Associated Title

River of eternity. (1983)

ROADBLASTER (Paul Hofrichter)

1. *Hell ride.* (1987)
2. *Death ride.* (1988)
3. *Blood fire.* (1988)

ROBBY HOENIG (Gordon R. Dickson)

1. *Secret under the sea.* (1960)
2. *Secret under Antartica.* (1963)
3. *Secret under the Caribbean.* (1964)
1-3. *Secrets of the deep.* (1985)

ROBERT SILVERBERG'S TIME TOURS (various authors)

1. *The Robin Hood ambush.* [William F. Wu]. (1990)
2. *Glory's end.* [Scott Ciencin as NICK BARON]. (1990)
3. *Timecrime, Inc.* [Debra Doyle & James D. Macdonald]. (1991)
4. *The dinosaur trackers.* [Tim Sullivan & Arthur Byron Cover & John Gregory Betancourt as THOMAS SHADWELL]. (1991)
5. *The Pirate paradox.* [Scott Ciencin as NICK BARON & Greg Cox]. (1991)
6. *Caesar's time legions.* [John Gregory Betancourt as JEREMY KINGSTON]. (1991)

ROBIN OF SHERWOOD (various authors)

1. *Robin of Sherwood and the hounds of Lucifer.* [Robin May]. (1985)
2. *The hooded man.* [Anthony Horowitz]. (1986)
3. *The sword of the templar.* [Richard Carpenter]. (1987)
4. *The time of the wolf.* [Paul Mason]. (1988)

ROBOCOP (Ed Naha)

1. *Robocop.* (1987)
2. *Robocop 2.* (1990)

ROBOT CITY—SEE: ISAAC ASIMOV'S ROBOT CITY

ROBOT SERIES [LIJE BALEY] (Isaac Asimov) **SEE ALSO: FOUNDATION**

ROBOT SERIES

1. *I, robot.* (1950)
2. *The caves of steel.* (1954)
3. *The naked sun.* (1957)
4. *The rest of the robots.* (1964). [Includes *The caves of steel, The naked sun*, and misc. stories]
5. *The complete robot.* (1982)
6. *The robots of dawn.* (1983)
7. *Robots and empire.* (1985)

ROBOT COLLECTIONS

Eight stories from The rest of the robots. (1966) [A retitling of *The rest of the robots*, but excludes the two novels]
Robot dreams. (1986)
Robot visions. (1990)
The robot collection: the robot novels. (1983). [Includes *The caves of steel; The naked sun; The complete robot*].

LIJE BALEY & R. DANEEL OLIVAW

1. *The caves of steel.* (1954)
2. *The naked sun.* (1957)
3. *The robots of dawn.* (1983)
4. *Robots and empire.* (1985)
1-2. *The robot novels; The caves of steel; The naked sun.* (1972)
1-2. *The rest of the robots.* (1964). [Includes *The caves of steel, The naked sun*, and misc. stories]
1-3. *The robot novels.* (1988). [Not the same as 1972 book of the same title; includes *The caves of steel; The naked sun; The robots of Dawn*].

ROBOTECH (Brian Daley & James Luceno as JACK MCKINNEY)

1. *Genesis.* (1987)
2. *Battle cry.* (1987)
3. *Homecoming.* (1987)
4. *Battlehymn.* (1987)
5. *Force of arms.* (1987)
6. *Doomsday.* (1987)
7. *Southern cross.* (1987)
8. *Metal fire.* (1987)
9. *The final nightmare.* (1987)
10. *Invid invasion.* (1987)
11. *Metamorphosis.* (1987)
12. *Symphony of light.* (1987)
13. *The end of the circle.* (1990)

ROBOTS—SEE: ROBOT SERIES

ROBOTS & ALIENS—SEE: ISAAC ASIMOV'S ROBOT CITY

RODERICK (John Sladek)

1. *Roderick; or, The education of a young machine.* (1980)
2. *Roderick at random; or, Further education of a young machine.* (1983)

ROGER RABBIT (Gary K. Wolf)

1. *Who censored Roger Rabbit?* (1981)
2. *Who p-p-plugged Roger Rabbit?* (1991)

Associated Title

1. *Who framed Roger Rabbit?* [Martin Noble]. (1988)

ROGER ZELAZNY'S ALIEN SPEEDWAY (various authors)

1. *Clypsis.* [Jeffrey A. Carver]. (1987)
2. *Pitfall.* [Thomas Wylde]. (1988)
3. *The web.* [Thomas Wylde]. (1988)

RO-LAN (Mike Sirota)

1. *Master of Boranga.* (1980)
2. *The shrouded walls of Boranga.* (1980)
3. *Journey to Mesharra.* (1980)
4. *The demons of Zammar.* (1981)

ROSE OF THE PROPHET (Margaret Weis & Tracy Hickman)

1. *The will of the wanderer.* (1989)
2. *The paladin of the night.* (1989)
3. *The prophet of Akhran.* (1989)

ROSEMARY (Jane Louise Curry)

1. *Parsley Sage, Rosemary, & time.* (1975)
2. *The magical cupboard.* (1976)

ROSINANTE (Alexis A. Gilliland)

1. *The revolution from Rosinante.* (1981)
2. *Long shot for Rosinante.* (1981)
3. *The pirates of Rosinante.* (1982)

RULERS OF HYLOR (Cherry Wilder)

1. *A princess of the Chameln.* (1984)
2. *Yorath the wolf.* (1984)
3. *The summer's king.* (1986)

RUNESTAFF—SEE: HISTORY OF THE RUNESTAFF

RUNESWORD (various authors)

1. *Outcasts.* [Clayton Emery]. (1990)
2. *Skryling's blade.* [Rose Estes & Tom Wham]. (1990)
3. *The dreamstone.* [J. F. Rivkin]. (1991)
4. *Horrible humes.* [Stephen Billias]. (1991)
5. *Dark divide.* [Mark Acres]. (1991)

RUNNING (Elizabeth Levy)

1. *Running out of time.* (1980)
2. *Running out of magic with Houdini.* (1981)

RUSALKA (C. J. Cherryh)

1. *Rusalka.* (1989)

2. *Chernevog.* (1990)
3. *Yvgenie.* (1991)

RUSSIAN QUARTET (D. M. Thomas)

1. *Ararat.* (1983)
2. *Swallow.* (1984)
3. *Sphinx.* (1986)
4. *Summit.* (1987)

SABAT (Guy N. Smith)

1. *The graveyard vultures.* (1982)
2. *The blood merchants.* (1982)
3. *Cannibal cult.* (1982)
4. *The druid connection.* (1983)

SABAZEL (Lillian Stewart Carl)

1. *Sabazel.* (1985)
2. *The winter king.* (1986)
3. *Shadow dancers.* (1987)

SACRED STONES SERIES (Moyra Caldecott)

1. *The tall stones.* (1977)
2. *The Temple of the Sun.* (1977)
3. *Shadow on the stones.* (1978)
4. *The silver vortex.* (1987)
1-3. *Guardians of the tall stones: the sacred stones trilogy.* (1986)

SAGA OF CUCKOO (Frederik Pohl & Jack Williamson)

1. *Farthest star.* (1975)
2. *Wall around a star.* (1983)
1-2. *The saga of Cuckoo.* (1983?)

SAGA OF LOST LANDS (Rose Estes)

1. *Blood of the tiger.* (1987)
2. *Brother to the lion.* (1988)
3. *Spirit of the hawk.* (1988)

SAGA OF PLIOCENE EXILE (Julian May)

1. *The Many-Colored Land.* (1981)
2. *The golden torc.* (1982)
3. *The nonborn king.* (1983)
4. *The adversary.* (1984)
1-2. *The Many-colored Land; The golden torc.* (1982)
3-4. *The bonborn king; The adversary.* (1984)

Associated Title

Brede's tale. (1982)

GALACTIC MILIEU

1. *Intervention: a root tale to the Galactic milieu and a vinculum between it and the Saga of Pliocene exile.* (1987)
1A. *The surveillance.* (1988)
1B. *The metaconcert.* (1988)

SAGA OF THE HOUSE OF EIGIN (Justin Leiber)

1. *The sword and the Eye.* (1985)
2. *The sword and the tower.* (1986)

SAGA OF THE PHENWICK WOMEN (John M. Kimbro as KATHERYN KIMBROUGH)

1. *Augusta, the first.* (1975)
2. *Jane, the courageous.* (1975)
3. *Margaret, the faithful.* (1975)
4. *Patricia, the beautiful.* (1975)
5. *Rachel, the possessed.* (1975)
6. *Susannah, the righteous.* (1975)
7. *Rebecca, the mysterious.* (1975)
8. *Joanne, the unpredictable.* (1976)
9. *Olivia, the tormented.* (1976)
10. *Harriet, the haunted.* (1976)
11. *Nancy, the daring.* (1976)
12. *Marcia, the innocent.* (1976)
13. *Kate, the curious.* (1976)
14. *Ilene, the superstitious.* (1977)
15. *Millijoy, the determined.* (1977)
16. *Barbara, the valiant.* (1977)
17. *Ruth, the unsuspecting.* (1977)
18. *Ophelia, the anxious.* (1977)
19. *Dorothy, the terrified.* (1977)
20. *Ann, the gentle.* (1978)
21. *Nellie, the obvious.* (1978)
22. *Isabelle, the frantic.* (1978)
23. *Evelyn, the ambitious.* (1978)
24. *Louise, the restless.* (1978)
25. *Polly, the worried.* (1979)
26. *Yvonne, the confident.* (1979)
27. *Joyce, the beloved.* (1979)
28. *Augusta, the second.* (1979)
29. *Carol, the pursued.* (1979)
30. *Katherine, the returned.* (1980)
31. *Peggy, the concerned.* (1980)
32. *Olga, the disillusioned.* (1980)
33. *Phyllis, the cautious.* (1980)
34. *Ursala, the proud.* (1980)
35. *Letitia, the dreamer.* (1981)
36. *Alexandria, the ambivalent.* (1981)
37. *Romula, the dedicated.* (1981)
38. *Laura, the imperiled.* (1981)
39. *Iris, the bewitched.* (1982)
40. *Belinda, the impatient.* (1982)

SAGA OF THORGRIM (Gerald Earl Bailey)

1. *Sword of the Nurlingas.* (1979)
2. *The sword of Poyana.* (1979)

SAGAMORE (Kara Dalkey)

1. *The curse of Sagamore.* (1986)
2. *The sword of Sagamore.* (1989)

SAGARD THE BARBARIAN (Flint Dille & Gary Gygax)

1. *The ice dragon.* (1985)
2. *The green Hydra.* (1985)
3. *The Crimson Sea.* (1985)
4. *The fire demon.* (1986)

SAGAS OF THE DEMONSPAWN (J. H. Brennan)

1. *Fire wolf.* (1984)
2. *The crypts of terror.* (1984)
3. *Ancient evil.* (1985)
4?. *Demonstration.* (1985)

SAINT-GERMAIN (Chelsea Quinn Yarbro)

1. *Hôtel Transylvania.* (1978)
2. *The palace.* (1978)
3. *Blood games.* (1979)
4. *Path of the eclipse.* (1981)
5. *Tempting fate.* (1982)
6. *The Saint-Germain chronicles.* (1983)
7. *Out of the house of life.* (1990)
8. *The spider glass.* (1991)

SAKAELAND (Ganpat)

1. *Harilek.* (1923)
2. *Wrexham's romance.* (1935)
1-2. *Adventures in Sakaeland.* (1978)

SAM MCCADE (William C. Dietz)

1. *War world.* (1986)
2. *Imperial bounty.* (1988)
3. *Alien bounty.* (1990)
4. *McCade's bounty.* (1990)

SAM SPACE (William F. Nolan)

1. *Space for hire.* (1971)
2. *Look out for Space.* (1985)

SAMANTHA SLADE (Susan Smith)

1. *Samantha Slade, monster-sitter.* (1987)
1A. *Monster-sitter.* (1989)
2. *Confessions of a teenage frog.* (1987)
3. *Our friend, public nuisance #1.* (1987)
4. *The terrors of rock and roll.* (1988)

SAMARKAND (Graham Diamond)

1. *Samarkand.* (1980)
2. *Samarkand dawn.* (1981)

SAMUEL WALTON (Roger J. Green)

1. *The fear of Samuel Walton.* (1984)
2. *The lengthening shadow.* (1986)

SAMURAI CAT (Mark E. Rogers)

1. *The adventures of Samurai Cat.* (1984)
2. *More adventures of Samurai Cat.* (1986)
3. *Samurai Cat in the real world.* (1989)
4. *The sword of Samurai Cat.* (1991)

SAND CHILD (Tahar Ben Jelloun)

1. *The sand child.* (1987)
2. *The sacred night.* (1989)

SAND WARS (Rhondi Vilott as CHARLES INGRID)

1. *Solar kill.* (1987)
2. *Lasertown blues.* (1988)
3. *Celestial hit list.* (1988)
4. *Alien salute.* (1989)
5. *Return fire.* (1989)
6. *Challenge met.* (1990)

SANDWRITER (Monica Hughes)

1. *Sandwriter.* (1985)
2. *The promise.* (1989)

SATURNALIA (Grant Callin)

1. *Saturnalia.* (1986)
2. *A lion on Tharthee.* (1987)

SAVAGE EMPIRE (Jean Lorrah and others)

1. *Savage Empire.* (1981)
2. *Dragon Lord of the savage empire.* (1982)
3. *Captives of the Savage Empire.* (1984)
4. *Flight to the Savage Empire.* [with Winston A. Howlett]. (1986)
5. *Sorcerers of the frozen isles.* (1986)
6. *Wulfston's odyssey.* [with Winston A. Howlett]. (1987)
7. *Empress unborn.* (1988)

SCANNERS (various authors)

1. *Scanners.* [Leon Whiteson]. (1981)
1A. *David Cronenberg's Scanners.* [Leon Whiteson]. (1981)
2. *Scanners II: the new order.* [Janus Kimball]. (1991)

SCHRODINGER'S CAT (Robert Anton Wilson)

1. *The universe next door.* (1979)
2. *The trick top hat.* (1981)
3. *The homing pigeons.* (1981)
1-3. *Schrödinger's cat trilogy.* (1988)

SCIENCE FICTION ANTHOLOGY—SEE: ISAAC ASIMOV'S SCIENCE FICTION ANTHOLOGY

SCIENCE FICTION BIBLIOGRAPHIES (various authors)

1. *The first editions of Andre Norton.* [David G. Turner]. (1974)
2. *The first editions of Philip Jose Farmer.* [Lawrence J. Knapp]. (1976)

SCIENCE FICTION IN OLD SAN FRANCISCO (various authors)

1. *Science fiction in old San Francisco, volume I: history of the movement from 1854 to 1890.* [Sam Moskowitz]. (1980)
2. *Into the sun, & other stories.* [Robert Duncan Milne]. (1980)

SCORPIO (Alex McDonough)

1. *Scorpio.* (1990)
2. *Scorpio rising.* (1990)
3. *Scorpio descending.* (1991)
4. *Dragon's blood.* (1991)

SCORPION (Michael R. Linaker)

1. *Scorpion.* (1981)
2. *Scorpion: Second generation.* (1982)

SCOTT SAUNDERS (Patrick Moore)

1. *Spy in space.* (1977)
2. *Planet of fear.* (1977)
3. *The moon raiders.* (1978)

4. *Killer comet.* (1978)
5. *The terror star.* (1979)
6. *The secret of the black hole.* (1980)

SEA KING (Nancy Springer)

1. *Madbond.* (1987)
2. *Mindbond.* (1987)
3. *Godbond.* (1988)

SECOND STAR (Dana Stabenow)

1. *Second star.* (1991)
2. *A handful of stars.* (1991)

SECRET BOOKS OF PARADYS (Tanith Lee)

1. *The book of the damned.* (1988)
2. *The book of the beast.* (1988)
3. *The book of the dead.* (1991)
1-2. *The secret books of Paradys I & II.* (1991)

SECRET COUNTRY (Pamela Dean)

1. *The Secret Country.* (1985)
2. *The Hidden Land.* (1986)
3. *The whim of the dragon.* (1989)

SECRET FILES OF DAKOTA KING (Jake MacKenzie)

1. *Operation Black Fang.* (1987)
2. *The haunted city of gold.* (1987)
3. *Two-wheeled terror.* (1988)
4. *The ghost of the lost mine.* (1988)

SECRET OF THE UNICORN QUEEN (various authors)

1. *Swept away.* [Josepha Sherman]. (1988)
2. *Sun blind.* [Gwen Hansen]. (1988)
3. *Final test.* [Dory Perlman]. (1988)
4. *Into the dream.* [Suzanne Weyn]. (1989)
5. *The dark gods.* [Josepha Sherman]. (1989)
6. *Moonspell.* [Gwen Hansen]. (1989)

SECRET WINDOW (Betty Ren Wright)

1. *The secret window.* (1982)
2. *A ghost in the window.* (1987)

SECRETS OF POWER (Robert N. Charrette)

1. *Shadowrun: Never deal with a dragon.* (1990)
2. *Choose your enemies carefully.* (1991)
3. *Find your own truth.* (1991)

SECTOR GENERAL (James White)

1. *Hospital station.* (1962)
2. *Star surgeon.* (1963)
3. *Major operation.* (1971)
4. *Ambulance ship.* (1979)
5. *Sector General.* (1983)
6. *Star healer.* (1985)
7. *Code blue—emergency.* (1987)

SEED (Edmund Plante)

1. *Seed of evil.* (1988)
2. *Garden of evil.* (1988)

SEEDS OF WAR (Robert Cornett & Kevin Randle)

1. *Seeds of war.* (1986)
2. *The Aldebaran campaign.* (1988)
3. *The Aquarian attack.* (1989)

SEEKING SWORD (Jaan Kangilaski)

1. *The Seeking Sword.* (1977)
2. *Hands of glory.* (1981)

SEETEE (Jack Williamson)

1. *Seetee ship* (1951)
2. *Seetee shock.* (1950)
1-2. *Seetee ship/Seetee shock.* (1972)
1-2. *Seetee.* (1979)

SENSITIVES (Herbert Burkholz)

1. *The sensitives.* (1987)
2. *Strange bedfellows.* (1988)

SENTIENCE (Terry A. Adams)

1. *Sentience: a novel of first contact.* (1986)
2. *The master of chaos.* (1989)

SENTINEL (Jeffrey Konvitz)

1. *The sentinel.* (1974)
2. *The guardian.* (1979)
2A. *The apocalypse.* (1979)

SENTINELS (Brian Daley & James Luceno as JACK MCKINNEY)

1. *The devil's hand.* (1988)
2. *Dark powers.* (1988)
3. *Death dance.* 1988)
4. *World killers.* (1988)
5. *Rubicon.* (1988)

SEPARATION (Richard Rohmer)

1. *Exodus/UK.* (1975)
2. *Separation.* (1976)
3. *Separation two.* (1981)

SERVANTS OF ARK (Julia Smith & Mark Smith as JONATHAN WYLIE)

1. *The first named.* (1987)
2. *The centre of the circle.* (1987)
2A. *The center of the circle.* (1988)
3. *The mage-born child.* (1988)

SEVEN CITADELS (Geraldine Harris)

1. *Prince of the Godborn.* (1982)
2. *The children of the wind.* (1982)
3. *The dead kingdom.* (1983)
4. *The seventh gate.* (1983)

SEVEN WORLDS (Mary Caraker)

1. *Seven worlds.* (1986)
2. *The snows of Jaspre.* (1989)

SEVENTH CARRIER (Peter Albano)

1. *The seventh carrier.* (1983)
2. *The second voyage of the seventh carrier.* (1986)
3. *Return of the seventh carrier.* (1987)
4. *Quest of the seventh carrier.* (1989)
5. *Attack of the seventh carrier.* (1989)
6. *Trial of the seventh carrier.* (1990)

SEVENTH SWORD (Dave Duncan)

1. *The reluctant swordsman.* (1988)
2. *The coming of wisdom.* (1988)
3. *The destiny of the sword.* (1988)

SHADITH'S QUEST—SEE: DIADEM

SHADOW (Walter B. Gibson as MAXWELL GRANT)

1. *The living Shadow.* (1974)
2. *The black master.* (1974)
3. *The mobsmen on the spot.* (1974)
4. *Hands in the dark.* (1975)
5. *Double Z.* (1975)
6. *The crime cult.* (1975)
7. *The red menace.* (1975)
8. *Mox.* (1975)
9. *The Romanoff jewels.* (1975)
10. *The Silent Seven.* (1975)
11. *Kings of crime.* (1976)
12. *Shadowed millions.* (1976)
13. *Green Eyes.* (1977)
14. *The creeping death.* (1977)
15. *Gray Fist.* (1977)
16. *The Shadow's shadow.* (1977)
17. *Fingers of death.* (1977)
18. *Murder trail.* (1977)
19. *Zemba.* (1977)
20. *Charg, monster.* (1977)
21. *The wealth seeker.* (1978)
22. *The silent death.* (1978)
23. *The Death Giver.* (1978)

Associated Titles

The crime oracle; and, The teeth of the dragon: two adventures of the Shadow. (1975)
The Shadow: The mask of Mephisto & Murder by magic. (1975)
The Shadow: A quarter of eight & The freak show murders. (1978)
The Shadow: Crime over Casco & The Mother Goose murders. (1979)
The Shadow: Jade dragon & House of ghosts. (1981)
The Shadow and the Golden Master. (1984)

SHAI (Daniel Walther)

1. *The book of Shai.* (1984)
2. *Shai's destiny.* (1985)

SHANNARA (Terry Brooks)

1. *The sword of Shannara.* (1977)
2. *The Elfstones of Shannara.* (1982)
3. *The wishsong of Shannara.* (1985)
4. *The scions of Shannara.* (1990)
5. *The druid of Shannara.* (1991)

SHAPER EXILE (Sheila Finch)

1. *The garden of the shaped.* (1987/1988)
2. *Shaper's legacy.* (1989)
3. *Shaping the dawn.* (1989)

SHATTERED (Kate Green)

1. *Shattered moon.* (1986)
2. *Night angel.* (1989)

SHATTERED WORLD (Michael Reaves)

1. *The shattered world.* (1984)
2. *The burning realm.* (1988)

SHE SEQUELS (various authors)

Journey to the flame. [Richard Monaco]. (1985)
The vengeance of She. [Peter Tremayne]. (1978)
Sherlock Holmes on the roof of the world. [Thos. Kent Miller]. (1987)

SHERLOCK HOLMES SEQUELS (various authors)

The earthquake machine. [Austin Mitchelson & Nicholas Utechin]. (1976)
Exit Sherlock Holmes: the great detective's final days. [Robert Lee Hall]. (1977)
The case of the philosophers' ring. [Randall Collins as DR. JOHN H. WATSON]. (1978)
1. *Sherlock Holmes vs. Dracula; or, The adventure of the sanguinary count.* [Loren D. Estleman as DR. JOHN H. WATSON]. (1978)
2. *Dr. Jekyll and Mr. Holmes.* [Loren D. Estleman as DR. JOHN H. WATSON]. (1979)
The adventures of the ectoplasmic man. [Daniel Stashower]. (1985)
Sherlock Holmes on the roof of the world. [Thos. Kent Miller]. (1987)
Sherlock Holmes in The adventure of the ancient gods. [Ralph E. Vaughan]. (1990)

SHIMMER AND THORN (Laurence Yep)

1. *Dragon of the lost sea.* (1982)
2. *Dragon steel.* (1985)
3. *Dragon cauldron.* (1991)

SHIP THAT SAILED THE TIME STREAM (G. C. Edmondson)

1. *The ship that sailed the time stream.* (1965/1978)
2. *To sail the century sea.* (1981)

SHIVA (J. H. Brennan)

1. *Shiva.* (1989)
2. *The crone.* (1990)
2A. *Shiva accused.* (1991)

SHORT STORY HARDBACKS (various authors)

1. *Losers' night.* [Poul Anderson]. (1991)
2. *A case of painter's ear.* [John Brunner]. (1991)
3. *Xolotl.* [Robert Sheckley]. (1991)
4. *The cutter.* [Edward Bryant]. (1991)
5. *The girl who fell into the sky.* [Kate Wilhelm]. (1991)
6. *Yours truly, Jack the Ripper.* [Robert Bloch]. (1991)

7. *The steel valentine.* [Joe R. Lansdale]. (1991)
8. *The doors of his face, the lamps of his mouth.* [Roger Zelazny]. (1991)
9. *More than the sum of his parts.* [Joe Haldeman]. (1991)
10. *The spider glass.* [Chelsea Quinn Yarbro]. (1991)
11. *Uncle Dobbin's parrot fair.* [Charles de Lint]. (1991)
12. *Dinosaurs.* [Walter Jon Williams]. (1991)
13. *The dark country.* [Dennis Etchison]. (1991)
14. *The sword and the stone.* [Jane Yolen]. (1991)
15. *Piecework.* [David Brin]. (1991)
16. *Sedalia.* [David J. Schow]. (1991)
17. *Twilight time.* [Lewis Shiner]. (1991)
18. *The war of the roses.* [Karen Joy Fowler]. (1991)
19. *Where the summer ends.* [Karl Edward Wagner]. (1991)
20. *Daisy, in the sun.* [Connie Willis]. (1991)
21. *The peacemaker.* [Gardner Dozois]. (1991)
22. *The hero as werwolf.* [Gene Wolfe]. (1991)
24. *The pear-shaped man.* [George R. R. Martin]. (1991)

SHORT STORY PAPERBACKS (various authors)

1. *Losers' night.* [Poul Anderson]. (1991)
2. *A case of painter's ear.* [John Brunner]. (1991)
3. *Xolotl.* [Robert Sheckley]. (1991)
4. *All the clocks are melting.* [Bruce Boston]. (1991)
5. *Blossoms.* [Kim Antieau]. (1991)
6. *Ecce hominid.* [Esther M. Friesner]. (1991)
7. *A case of mistaken identity.* [L. Timmel Duchamp]. (1991)
8. *The cutter.* [Edward Bryant]. (1991)
9. *The girl who fell into the sky.* [Kate Wilhelm]. (1991)
10. *Yours truly, Jack the Ripper.* [Robert Bloch]. (1991)
11. *The steel valentine.* [Joe R. Lansdale]. (1991)
12. *The quickening.* [Michael Bishop]. (1991)
13. *The doors of his face, the lamps of his mouth.* [Roger Zelzany]. (1991)
14. *More than the sum of his parts.* [Joe Haldeman]. (1991)
15. *No way street.* [Bruce Clemence]. (1991)
16. *The spider glass.* [Chelsea Quinn Yarbro]. (1991)
17. *Uncle Dobbin's parrot fair.* [Charles de Lint]. (1991)
18. *Dinosaurs.* [Walter Jon Williams]. (1991)
19. *Listening to Brahms.* [Suzy McKee Charnas]. (1991)
20. *Black air.* [Kim Stanley Robinson]. (1991)
21. *The dark country.* [Dennis Etchison]. (1991)
22. *Journey to the goat star.* [Brian W. Aldiss]. (1991)
23. *Piecework.* [David Brin]. (1991)
24. *I remember, I remember...* [Mary Caraker]. (1991)
25. *Sedalia.* [David J. Schow]. (1991)
26. *Slumming in Voodooland.* [Brian Stableford]. (1991)
27. *The sword and the stone.* [Jane Yolen]. (1991)
28. *The war of the roses.* [Karen Joy Fowler]. (1991)
29. *The cat with the tulip face.* [A. R. Morlan]. (1991)
30. *Twilight time.* [Lewis Shiner]. (1991)
31. *Where the summer ends.* [Karl Edward Wagner]. (1991)
32. *Into gold.* [Tanith Lee]. (1991)
33. *Daisy, in the sun.* [Connie Willis]. (1991)
34. *Inuit.* [M. Shayne Bell]. (1991)
35. *The shade of Lo Man Gong.* [William F. Wu]. (1991)
36. *Buckets.* [F. Paul Wilson]. (1991)
37. *The pear-shaped man.* [George R. R. Martin]. (1991)

38. *The evening and the morning and the night.* [Octavia E. Butler]. (1991)
39. *The peacemaker.* [Gardner Dozois]. (1991)
40. *The hero as werwolf.* [Gene Wolfe]. (1991)

SIDHE: LUGH (Kenneth C. Flint)

1. *The riders of the Sidhe.* (1984)
2. *Champions of the Sidhe.* (1984)
3. *Master of the Sidhe.* (1985)

SIDHE LEGENDS

1. *The hound of Culain.* (1986)

SIDNEY (Brian Herbert)

1. *Sidney's comet.* (1983)
2. *The garbage chronicles.* (1985)

SILENCE LEIGH (Melissa Scott)

1. *Five-twelfths of Heaven.* (1985)
2. *Silence in solitude.* (1986)
3. *The empress of Earth.* (1987)
1-3. *The roads of Heaven.* (1988)

SILISTRA (Janet Morris)

1. *High couch of Silistra (returning creation).* (1977)
1A. *Returning creation.* (1984)
2. *The golden sword.* (1977)
3. *Wind from the abyss.* (1978)
4. *The carnelian throne.* (1979)

SILVER BRUMBIES (Elyne Mitchell)

1. *The silver Brumby.* (1958)
2. *Silver Brumby's daughter.* (1960)
3. *Silver Brumbies of the south.* (1965)
4. *Silver brumby kingdom.* (1966)
5. *Silver brumby whirlwind.* (1973)

SILVER CALL DUOLOGY—SEE: MITHGARIAN SERIES

SILVER JOHN (Manly Wade Wellman)

1. *Who fears the devil?* (1963)
1A. *John the balladeer.* (1988)
2. *The old gods waken.* (1979)
3. *After dark.* (1980)
4. *The lost and the lurking.* (1981)
5. *The hanging stones.* (1982)
6. *The voice of the mountain.* (1984)

SILVERGLASS (J. F. Rivkin)

1. *Silverglass.* (1986)
2. *Web of wind.* (1987)
3. *Witch of Rhostshyl.* (1989),
4. *Silverglass: Mistress of ambiguities.* (1991)

SILVERLOCK (John Myers Myers)

1. *Silverlock.* (1949)
2. *The moon's fire-eating daughter.* (1981)

SIME/GEN SERIES [HOUSE OF ZEOR] (Jacqueline Lichtenberg & Jean Lorrah)

1. *House of Zeor.* [Jacqueline Lichtenberg]. (1974)
2. *Unto Zeor, forever.* [Jacqueline Lichtenberg]. (1978)
3. *First channel.* [Jacqueline Lichtenberg & Jean Lorrah]. (1980)
4. *Mahogany trinrose.* [Jacqueline Lichtenberg]. (1981)
5. *Channel's destiny.* [[Jacqueline Lichtenberg & Jean Lorrah]. (1982)
6. *RenSime.* [Jacqueline Lichtenberg]. (1984)
7. *Ambrov Keon.* [Jean Lorrah]. (1986)
8. *Zelerod's doom.* [Jacqueline Lichtenberg & Jean Lorrah]. (1986)

SIMON & SALLY (Terrance Dicks)

1. *Cry vampire!* (1981)
2. *War of the witches.* (1983)

SIMON ARK (Edward D. Hoch)

1. *The judges of Hades, and other Simon Ark stories.* (1971)
2. *City of Brass.* (1971)
3. *The quests of Simon Ark.* (1984)

SIMON BLACKSTONE—SEE: CHANGELING TRILOGY

SINBAD (Kin Platt)

1. *Sinbad and me.* (1966)
2. *The mystery of the witch who wouldn't.* (1969)
3. *The ghost of Hellsfire Street.* (1980)

SIMEON (Peter Tatc)

1. *The thinking seat.* (1969)
2. *Moon on an iron meadow.* (1974)
3. *Faces in the flames.* (1976)

SINGREALE CHRONICLES (Calvin Miller)

1. *Guardians of the Singreale.* (1982)
2. *Star riders of Ren.* (1983)
3. *War of the Moonrhymes.* (1984)

SIPSTRASSI TALES (David A. Gemmell)

1. *Wolf in shadow.* (1987)
2. *Ghost king.* (1988)
3. *Last sword of power.* (1988)
4. *The last guardian.* (1989)

SISCOE & BLOCK (Isidore Haiblum)

1. *The identity plunderers.* (1984)
2. *The hand of Ganz.* (1985)

SIX KINGDOMS (Bruce Fergusson)

1. *The shadow of his wings.* (1987)
2. *The mace of souls.* (1989)

SIX MILLION DOLLAR MAN (STEVE AUSTIN) (Martin Caidin and others)

By Martin Caidin

1. *Cyborg.* (1972)
2. *Operation Nuke.* (1973)
3. *High crystal.* (1974)
4. *Cyborg IV.* (1975)

Warner Books Series

1. *Wine, women, and war.* [Mike Jahn]. (1975)
2. *Solid gold kidnapping.* [Evan Richards]. (1975)
3. *Cyborg IV.*
4. *Pilot error: a novel.* [Jay Barbree]. (1975)
5. *The rescue of Athena One.* [Mike Jahn]. (1975)

Berkley Books Series

1. *The secret of Bigfoot Pass.* [Mike Jahn]. (1976)
2. *International incidents.* [Mike Jahn]. (1977)

SIXTH PERCEPTION (Dan Morgan)

1. *The new minds.* (1967)
2. *The several minds.* (1969)
3. *Mind trap.* (1970)
4. *The country of the mind.* (1975)

SKEEN (Jo Clayton)

1. *Skeen's leap.* (1986)
2. *Skeen's return.* (1987)
3. *Skeen's search.* (1987)

SKEEVE (Robert Lynn Asprin)

1. *Another fine myth....* (1978)
2. *Myth conceptions* (1980)
3. *Myth directions* (1982)
4. *Hit or myth* (1983)
5. *Myth-ing persons* (1984)
6. *Little myth marker* (1985)
7. *M.Y.T.H. Inc. link.* (1986)
8. *Myth-nomers and im-pervections.* (1987)
9. *M.Y.T.H. Inc. in action.* (1990)
1-4. *Myth adventures.* (1984)
5-7. *Myth alliances.* (1987)

SKIFFY (William Mayne)

1. *Skiffy.* (1972)
2. *Skiffy and the twin planets.* (1982)

SKIPJACK (Simon Lang)

1. *All the gods of Eisernon.* (1973)
2. *The elluvon gift.* (1975)

SKULL-FACE (Robert E. Howard)

1. *Skull-face, and others.* (1946)
1A. *Skull-face omnibus.* (1974)
2. *The return of Skull-Face.* [with Richard A. Lupoff]. (1977)

SKY LORDS (John Brosnan)

1. *The sky lords: a novel.* (1988)
2. *War of the sky lords.* (1989)
3. *The fall of the sky lords.* (1991)

SKYRIDER (Melisa C. Michaels)

1. *Skirmish.* (1985)
2. *First battle.* (1985)
3. *Last war.* (1986)
4. *Pirate prince.* (1987)
5. *Floater factor.* (1988)

SKYROCKET STEELE (Ron Goulart)

1. *Skyrocket Steele.* (1980)
2. *Skyrocket Steele conquers the universe, and other media tales.* (1990)

SKYWAY TRILOGY (John DeChancie)

1. *Starrigger.* (1983)
2. *Red limit freeway.* (1984)
3. *Paradox alley.* (1987)

SLIPPERY JIM DiGRIZ—SEE: THE STAINLESS STEEL RAT

SLITHER (John Halkin)

1. *Slither.* (1980)
2. *Slime.* (1984)
3. *Squelch.* (1985)

SLUGS (Shaun Hutson)

1. *Slugs.* (1982)
2. *Breeding ground.* (1985)

SNAKE OIL WARS (Parke Godwin)

1. *Waiting for the galactic bus.* (1988)
2. *The snake oil wars; or, Scheherazade Ginsberg strikes again.* (1989)

SNARKOUT BOYS (Daniel M. Pinkwater)

1. *The Snarkout boys & the avocado of death.* (1982)
2. *The Snarkout boys and the Baconburg horror.* (1984)

SNOW QUEEN CYCLE (Joan D. Vinge)

1. *The Snow queen.* (1980)
2. *World's end.* (1984)
3. *The Summer queen.* (1991)

SNOW SPIDER (Jenny Nimmo)

1. *Snow spider.* (1986)
2. *Emlyn's moon.* (1987)
2A. *Orchard of the crescent moon.* (1989)
3. *The chestnut spider.* (1989)

SNOW-EYES (Stephanie A. Smith)

1. *Snow-Eyes.* (1985)
2. *The boy who was thrown away.* (1987)

SOFTWARE (Rudy Rucker)

1. *Software.* (1982)
2. *Wetware.* (1988)

SOLITUDE TRILOGY (Parke Godwin & Marvin Kaye)

1. *The masters of solitude.* (1978)
2. *Wintermind.* (1982)
3. [never published]

SOLOMON KANE (Robert E. Howard)

1. *Skulls in the stars.* (1978)
2. *The hills of the dead.* (1979)

SOLSTICE: MORGANA SHEE (L. J. Smith)

1. *The night of the solstice.* (1987)
2. *Heart of valor.* (1990)

SONG (Thorarinn Gunnarsson)

1. *Song of the dwarves.* (1988)
2. *Revenge of the Valkyrie.* (1989)

A SONG CALLED YOUTH (John Shirley)

1. *Eclipse.* (1985)
2. *Eclipse penumbra.* (1988)
3. *Eclipse corona.* (1990)

SONG OF EARTH—SEE: GREATAWAY

SONG OF NAGA TEOT (Heather Gladney)

1. *Teot's war.* (1987)
2. *Blood storm.* (1989)

SONG OF THE LIONESS (Tamora Pierce)

1. *Alanna: the first adventure.* (1983)
2. *In the hand of the goddess.* (1984)
3. *The woman who rides like a man.* (1986)
4. *Lioness rampant.* (1988)

SONGKILLER SAGA (Elizabeth Scarborough)

1. *Phantom banjo.* (1991)
2. *Picking the ballad's bones.* (1991)

SORCERER (Paula Volsky)

1. *The sorcerer's lady.* (1986)
2. *The sorcerer's heir.* (1988)
3. *The sorcerer's curse.* (1989)

SORCERER'S SON (Phyllis Eisenstein)

1. *Sorcerer's son.* (1979)
2. *The crystal palace.* (1988)

SORCERY! (Steve Jackson)

1. *The Shamutanti Hills.* (1984)
2. *Kharé-cityport of traps.* (1984)
3. *The seven serpents.* (1984)
4. *The crown of kings.* (1985)

Associated Title

The sorcery spell book. (1983)

SORCERY HALL (Suzy McKee Charnas)

1. *The bronze king.* (1985)

2. *The silver glove.* (1988)
3. *The golden thread.* (1989)

SOUL DRINKER—SEE: DRINKER OF SOULS

SOUL OF THE ROBOT (Barrington J. Bayley)

1. *Soul of the robot.* (1974)
2. *The rod of light.* (1984)

SOUL RIDER (Jack L. Chalker)

1. *Spirits of Flux & Anchor.* (1984)
2. *Empires of Flux & Anchor.* (1984)
3. *Masters of Flux & Anchor.* (1985)
4. *The birth of Flux & Anchor.* (1985)
5. *Children of Flux & Anchor.* (1986)

SPACE: 1999 (various authors)

Year One

1. *Breakaway.* [E. C. Tubb]. (1975)
2. *Moon odyssey* [Douglas Mason as JOHN RANKINE]. (1975)
3. *Phoenix of Megaron.* [Douglas Mason as JOHN RANKINE]. (1975)
4. *Collision course.* [E. C. Tubb]. (1975)
5. *Lunar attack.* [Douglas Mason as JOHN RANKINE]. (1975)
6. *Astral quest.* [Douglas Mason as JOHN RANKINE]. (1975)
7. *Alien seed.* [E. C. Tubb]. (1976)
8. *Android planet.* [Douglas Mason as JOHN RANKINE]. (1976)
9. *Rogue planet.* [E. C. Tubb]. (1976)
10. *Earthfall.* [E. C. Tubb]. (1977)

Year Two

1. *Planets of peril.* [Michael Butterworth]. (1977)
2. *Mind-breaks of space.* [[Michael Butterworth with J. Jeff Jones]. (1977)
3. *The space-jackers.* [Michael Butterworth]. (1977)
4. *The psychomorph.* [Michael Butterworth]. (1977)
5. *The time fighters.* [Michael Butterworth]. (1977)

SPACE ANGEL (John Maddox Roberts)

1. *Space Angel.* (1979)
2. *Spacer: window of the mind.* (1988)

SPACE CADETS (R. L. Stine)

1. *Jerks-in-training.* (1991)
2. *Losers in space.* (1991)
3. *Bozos on patrol.* (1992)

SPACE DEMONS (Gillian Rubinstein)

1. *Space demons.* (1986)
2. *Skymaze.* (1989)

SPACE EXPRESS COMPANY (Franz Harkon)

1. *Space pirates.* [as Astron Del Martia]. (1951)
2. *Spawn of space.* (1951)
3. *Interstellar espionage.* [as Astron Del Martia]. (1952)

SPACE HAWKS (Edward Packard)

1. *Faster than light.* (1991)
2. *Alien invaders.* (1991)
3. *Space fortress.* (1991)
4. *The comet masters.* (1991)

SPACE MAVERICKS (Michael K. Kring)

1. *The space mavericks.* (1980)
2. *Children of the night.* (1981)

SPACE MERCHANTS (Frederik Pohl)

1. *The space merchants.* [with C. M. Kornbluth]. (1953)
2. *The merchants' war.* (1984)
1-2. *Venus, Inc.* [with C. M. Kornbluth]. (1985)

SPACE POLICE (Leo P. Kelley)

1. *Prison satellite.* (1979)
2. *Worlds apart.* (1979)
3. *Earth Two.* (1979)
4. *Backward in time.* (1979)
5. *Sunworld.* (1979)
6. *Death sentence.* (1979)

Associated Title

Space police: teacher's guide. (1979)

SPACEACHE (Snoo Wilson)

1. *Spaceache.* (1984)
2. *Inside Babel.* (1985)

SPACEBREAD (Steve Senn)

1. *Spacebread.* (1981)
2. *Born of flame.* (1982)

SPACEWAYS (Andrew J. Offutt with various authors as JOHN CLEVE)

1. *Of alien bondage.* (1982)
2. *Corundum's woman.* (1982)
3. *Escape from Macho.* (1982)
4. *Satana enslaved.* (1982)
5. *Master of Misfit.* (1982)
6. *Purrfect plunder.* (1982)
7. *The manhuntress.* (1982)
8. *Under twin suns.* (1982)
9. *In quest of Qalara.* (1983)
10. *The yoke of Shen.* (1983)
11. *The Iceworld Connection.* (1983)
12. *Star slaver.* (1983)
13. *Jonuta rising!* (1983)
14. *Assignment: Hellhole.* (1983)
15. *Starship Sapphire.* (1984)
16. *The planet murderer.* (1984)
17. *The Carnadyne Horde.* (1984)
18. *Race across the stars.* (1984)
19. *King of the slavers.* (1985)

SPECIALIST (Wilfred McNeilly as ERROL LECALE)

1. *The tigerman of Terrahpur.* (1973)
2. *Castledoom.* (1974)
3. *The severed hand.* (1974)

4. *The death box.* (1974)
5. *Zombie.* (1975)
6. *Blood of my blood.* (1975)

SPECTROS (Logan Winters)

1. *Silverado.* (1981)
2. *Hunt the beast down.* (1981)
3. *Natchez.* (1981)
4. *The silver canyon.* (1981)

SPELLSINGER (Alan Dean Foster)

1. *Spellsinger.* (1983)
2. *The hour of the gate.* (1984)
3. *The day of the dissonance.* (1984)
4. *The moment of the magician.* (1984)
5. *The paths of the perambulator.* (1985)
6. *The time of the tranference.* (1986)
7. *Spellsinger's scherzo.* (1987)
1-2. *Spellsinger at the gate.* (1983)
1-3. *Season of the spellsong.* (1985)

SPIDER (W. Michael Gear)

0. *The artifact.* [A prequel]. (1990)
1. *The warriors of spider.* (1988)
2. *The way of spider.* (1989)
3. *The web of spider.* (1989)

THE SPIDER (GRANT STOCKBRIDGE)

FIRST SERIES

1. *Death reign of the vampire king.* (1975)
2. *Hordes of the red butcher.* (1975)
3. *The city destroyer.* (1975)
4. *Death and the Spider.* (1975)

SECOND SERIES

1. *Satan's death blast: the Spider thriller.* (1984)
2. *Corpse cargo: the Spider thriller.* (1985)

THIRD SERIES

The Spider, master of men! (1991)

SPIDER WORLD (Colin Wilson)

1. *The tower.* (1987)
1A. *The desert.* (1988)
1B. *The tower.* (1989)
1C. *The fortress.* (1989)
2. *The delta.* (1987)

SPIDERMAN—SEE: MARVEL SUPERHEROES

SQUED (Richard Miller)

1. *SQUED.* (1989)
2. *Sowboy.* (1991)

STACY—ADVENTURES OF THE EMPIRE PRINCESS—SEE: THE HAVEN

THE STAINLESS STEEL RAT (Harry Harrison)

1. *The Stainless Steel Rat.* (1961)
2. *The Stainless Steel Rat's revenge.* (1970)

3. *The Stainless Steel Rat saves the world.* (1972)
4. *The Stainless Steel Rat wants you.* (1978)
5. *The Stainless Steel Rat for president.* (1982)
6. *A Stainless Steel Rat is born.* (1985)
7. *The Stainless Steel Rat gets drafted.* (1987)
1-3. *The adventures of the Stainless Steel Rat: The Stainless Steel Rat; The Stainless Steel Rat's revenge; The Stainless Steel Rat saves the world.* (1977)

Associated Title

You can be The Stainless Steel Rat: an interactive game book. (1985)

STAIRWAY TO FOREVER (Robert Adams)

1. *Stairway to forever.* (1988)
2. *Monsters and magicians.* (1989)

STAR CHALLENGE (Christopher Black)

1. *Planets in peril.* (1984)
2. *The android invasion.* (1984)
3. *The cosmic funhouse.* (1984)
4. *The exploding suns.* (1984)
5. *Galactic raiders.* (1984)
6. *The weird zone.* (1984)
7. *Dimension of doom.* (1985)
8. *The lost planet.* (1985)
9. *Moons of mystery.* (1985)
10. *The haunted planet.* (1985)

STAR COLONY (Keith Laumer and others)

1. *Star colony.* (1981)
2. *Combat command in the world of Keith Laumer's Star colony: The omega rebellion.* [Troy Denning]. (1987)

STAR COMMANDOS (P. M. Griffin)

1. *Star Commandos.* (1986)
2. *Colony in peril.* (1987)
3. *Mission underground.* (1988)
4. *Death planet.* (1989)
5. *Mind slaver.* (1990)
6. *Return to war.* (1990)
7. *Fire planet.* (1990)
8. *Jungle assault.* (1991)
9. *Call to arms.* (1991)

STAR FALL (David Bischoff)

1. *Star Fall.* (1980)
2. *Star spring.* (1982)

STAR HAWKS (Ron Goulart)

1. *Star Hawks: Empire 99.* (1980)
2. *The cyborg king.* (1981)

STAR HOUNDS (David Bischoff)

1. *The infinite battle.* (1985)
2. *Galactic warriors.* (1985)
3. *The macrocosmic conflict.* (1986)

STAR JAM PACK (Brian Earnshaw)

1. *Starclipper and the song wars.* (1985)
2. *Starclipper on the snowstone.* (1986)
3. *Starclipper and the galactic final.* (1987)

STAR KA'ATS (Andre Norton & Dorothy Madlee)

1. *Star Ka'at.* (1976)
2. *Star Ka'at world.* (1978)
3. *Star Ka'ats and the plant people.* (1979)
4. *Star Ka'ats and the winged warriors.* (1981)

STAR KINGS (Edmond Hamilton)

1. *The Star Kings.* (1949)
2. *Return to the stars.* (1970)
1-2. *Chronicles of the Star Kings.* (1986)

STAR MAN (Stuart J. Byrne)

1. *Star man.* (1969)
1-5. *Star man 1 5.* (1979)
6-11. *Star man 6-11.* (1980)

STAR OF THE GUARDIANS (Margaret Weis)

1. *The lost king.* (1990)
2. *King's test.* (1990)
3. *King's sacrifice.* (1991)

STAR PIRATES (Chris Evans as NATHAN ELLIOTT)

1. *Kidnap in space.* (1987)
2. *Plague moon.* (1987)
3. *Treasure planet.* (1987)

STAR QUEST (Terrance Dicks)

1. *Spacejack!* (1978)
2. *Roboworld.* (1979)
3. *Terrorsaur!* (1981)

STAR REQUIEM (Adrian Cole)

1. *Mother of storms.* (1989)
2. *Thief of dreams.* (1989)
3. *Warlord of Heaven.* (1990)
4. *Labyrinth of worlds.* (1990)

STAR TREK (various authors)

BANTAM BOOKS SERIES (James Blish)
(Novelizations of the TV Series)

1. *Star Trek.* (1967)
1A. *Star Trek 1.* (1975)
2. *Star Trek 2.* (1968)
3. *Star Trek 3.* (1969)
4. *Star Trek 4.* (1971)
5. *Star Trek 5.* (1972)
6. *Star Trek 6.* (1972)
7. *Star Trek 7.* (1972)
8. *Star Trek 8.* (1972)
9. *Star Trek 9.* (1973)
10. *Star Trek 10.* (1974)
11. *Star Trek 11.* (1975)
11A. *Day of the dove.* (1985)
12. *Star Trek 12.* [With J. A. Lawrence]. (1977)

13. *Mudd's angels.* [With J. A. Lawrence (uncredited)]. (1978)
2, 3, 8. *The Star Trek reader.* (1976)
1, 4, 9. *The Star Trek reader II.* (1977)
5, 6, 7. *The Star Trek reader III.* (1977)
10, 11. *The Star Trek reader IV* (Also includes *Spock Must Die!*). (1978)

Star Trek #1-12 Reorganized

Star Trek: the classic episodes 1. [with J. A. Lawrence]. (1991)
Star Trek: the classic episodes 2. (1991)
Star Trek: the classic episodes 3. [with J. A. Lawrence]. (1991)

Other Bantam Star Trek Books (Unnumbered)

Spock must die! [James Blish]. (1970)
Spock, messiah! [Theodore R. Cogswell & Charles A. Spano, Jr.]. (1976)
Star Trek: the new voyages. [Myrna Culbreath & Sondra Marshak]. (1976)
Planet of Judgment. [Joe Haldeman]. (1977)
The price of the phoenix. [Myrna Culbreath & Sondra Marshak]. (1977)
Star Trek: the new voyages 2. [Myrna Culbreath & Sondra Marshak]. (1978)
The starless world. [Gordon Eklund]. (1978)
Vulcan! [Kathleen Sky]. (1978)
Devil world. [Gordon Eklund]. (1979)
World without end: a Star Trek novel. [Joe Haldeman]. (1979)
The fate of the phoenix. [Myrna Culbreath & Sondra Marshak]. (1979)
Trek to madworld: a Star Trek novel. [Stephen Goldin]. (1979)
The galactic whirlpool: a Star Trek novel. [David Gerrold]. (1980)
Perry's planet. [Jack C. Haldeman II]. (1980)
Death's angel: a Star Trek novel. [Kathleen Sky]. (1981)

STAR TREK LOGS (Alan Dean Foster)
(Novelization of the Animated TV Series)

1. *Star Trek, log one.* (1974)
2. *Star Trek, log two.* (1974)
3. *Star Trek, log three.* (1975)
4. *Star Trek, log four.* (1975)
5. *Star Trek, log five.* (1975)
6. *Star Trek, log six.* (1976)
7. *Star Trek, log seven.* (1976)
8. *Star Trek, log eight.* (1976)
9. *Star Trek, log nine.* (1977)
10. *Star Trek, log ten.* (1978)

POCKET BOOKS SERIES (various authors)

1. *Star Trek: The motion picture.* [Gene Roddenberry]. STAR TREK I. (1979)
2. *The entropy effect.* [Vonda N. McIntyre]. (1981)
3. *The Klingon gambit.* [Robert E. Vardeman]. (1981)
4. *The covenant of the crown.* [Howard Weinstein]. (1981)
5. *The Prometheus design.* [Myrna Culbreath & Sondra Marshak]. (1982)
6. *The abode of life.* [G. Harry Stine as LEE CORREY]. (1982)

7. *Star Trek, The wrath of Khan: a novel.* [Vonda N. McIntyre]. STAR TREK II. (1982)
8. *Black fire.* [Sonni Cooper]. 1983)
9. *Triangle.* [Myrna Culbreath & Sondra Marshak]. (1983)
10. *Web of the Romulans.* [M. S. Murdock]. (1983)
11. *Yesterday's son.* [A. C. Crispin]. (1983)
12. *Mutiny on the Enterprise.* [Robert E. Vardeman]. (1983)
13. *The wounded sky.* [Diane Duane]. (1983)
14. *The Trellisane confrontation.* [David Dvorkin]. (1984)
15. *Corona.* [Greg Bear]. (1984)
16. *The final reflection.* [John M. Ford]. (1984)
17. *Star Trek III, The search for Spock: a Star Trek novel.* [Vonda N. McIntyre]. STAR TREK III. (1984)
18. *My enemy, my ally.* [Diane Duane]. (1984)
19. *The tears of the Singers.* [Melinda M. Snodgrass]. (1984)
20. *The Vulcan Academy murders.* [Jean Lorrah]. (1984)
21. *Uhura's song.* [Janet Kagan]. (1985)
22. *Shadow lord.* [Laurence Yep]. (1985)
23. *Ishmael.* [Barbara Hambly]. (1985)
24. *Killing time.* [Della Van Hise]. (1985)
25. *Dwellers in the crucible.* [Margaret Wander Bonanno]. (1985)
26. *Pawns and symbols.* [Majliss Larson]. (1985)
27. *Mindshadow.* [J. M. Dillard]. (1986)
28. *Crisis on Centaurus.* [Brad Ferguson]. (1986)
29. *Dreadnought!* [Diane Carey]. DREADNOUGHT #1. (1986)
30. *Demons.* [J. M. Dillard]. (1986)
31. *Battlestations!* [Diane Carey]. DREADNOUGHT #2. (1986)
32. *Chain of attack.* [Gene DeWeese]. (1987)
33. *Deep domain.* [Howard Weinstein]. (1987)
34. *Dreams of the raven.* [Carmen Carter]. (1987)
35. *The Romulan way.* [Diane Duane & Peter Morwood]. (1987)
36. *How much for just the planet?* [John M. Ford]. (1987)
37. *Bloodthirst.* [J. M. Dillard]. (1987)
38. *The IDIC epidemic.* [Jean Lorrah]. (1988)
39. *Time for yesterday.* [A. C. Crispin]. (1988)
40. *Timetrap.* [David Dvorkin]. (1988)
41. *The three-minute universe.* (1988)
42. *Memory Prime.* [Garfield Reeves-Stevens & Judith Reeves-Stevens]. (1988)
43. *The final nexus.* [Gene DeWeese]. (1988)
44. *Vulcan's glory.* [D. C. Fontana]. (1989)
45. *Double, double.* [Michael Jan Friedman]. (1989)
46. *The cry of the Onlies.* [Judy Klass]. (1989)
47. *The Kobayashi Maru.* [Julia Ecklar]. (1989)
48. *Rules of engagement.* [Peter Morwood]. (1990)
49. *The pandora principle.* [Carolyn Clowes]. (1990)
50. *Doctor's orders.* [Diane Duane]. (1990)
51. *Enemy unseen.* [V. E. Mitchell]. (1990)
52. *Home is the hunter* [Dana Kramer]. (1990)
53. *Ghost walker.* [Barbara Hambly]. (1991)
54. *A flag full of stars.* [Brad Ferguson]. (1991)
55. *Renegade.* [Gene DeWeese]. (1991)
56. *Legacy.* [Michael Jan Friedman]. (1991)
57. *The rift.* [Peter David]. (1991)

STAR TREK MOTION PICTURE NOVELIZATIONS

1. *Star Trek: The motion picture.* [Gene Roddenberry]. (1979)

2. *Star Trek, The wrath of Khan.* [Vonda N. McIntyre]. (1982)
3. *Star Trek III, The search for Spock.* [Vonda N. McIntyre]. (1984)
4. *Star Trek IV, The voyage home.* [Vonda N. McIntyre]. (1986)
4. *Star Trek IV, the voyage home.* [Peter Lerangis]. (1986)
5. *Star Trek V, the final frontier.* [J. M. Dillard]. (1989)

Other Pocket Books Star Trek Novels (Unnumbered)

Demons. [J. M. Dillard]. (1986)
Enterprise: the first adventure. [Vonda N. McIntyre]. (1986)
The Romulan way. [Peter Morwood & Diane Duane]. (1987)
Strangers from the sky. [Margaret Wander Bonanno]. (1987)
Final frontier. [Diane Carey]. (1988)
Spock's world: a novel. [Diane Duane]. (1988)
The lost years. [J. M. Dillard]. (1989)
Prime directive. [Garfield Reeves-Stevens & Judith Reeves-Stevens]. (1990)

STAR TREK FAN FICTION

Alternative: the epilog to Orion. [Gerry Downs]. (1976)
Full moon rising. [Jean Lorrah]. (1976)
Jean Lorrah's Sarek collection. [Jean Lorrah]. ()
The night of the twin moons. [Jean Lorrah]. 1976
Enterprise incidents 2: stories. [Sheila Clark]. (1977)
As new wine. [Meg Wright]. (1979)
Epilogue, part 1. [Jean Lorrah]. (1979)
Epilogue, part 2. [Jean Lorrah]. (1979)
Night visions. [Carol Frisbie & Susan James]. (1979)
The perfect object. [Mindy Glazer]. (1979)
Something hidden. [Sheila Clark]. (1979)
Tomorrow is another day. [Lesley Coles]. (1979)
The web of Selagor. [Simone Mason]. (1979)
The wheel turns. [Valerie Piacentini]. (1979)
Wine of Calvoro. [Valerie Piacentini]. (1979)
Beyond shattered illusions. [Carmen Dexter]. (1980)
Companion: the rest of the story. [Pamela Rose]. (1980)
The wheel of fate. [Sheila Clark *with* Valerie Piacentini]. (1980)
The rack; &, All the king's horses, all the king's men. [J. Emily Vance]. (1981?)
The tribe of Jen-Wae. [Meg Wright]. (1981)
Weaver of dreams. [Pam Baddeley]. (1981)
Acceptance. [Vicki Richards]. (1982)
The displaced. [Lois Welling]. (1982?)
The female of the species is more deadly than the male. [Meg Wright]. (1982)
Home is where the heart is. [Vicki Richards]. (1982)
The third verdict. [Beverly C. Zuk]. (1982)
Time is, time was, time yet to be: (inscription on an old sun-dial). [Janet Stewart]. (1982)
Transition. [Lois Welling]. (1982)
T'Zad'U, part 2. [D. Dubois & K. S. T'Lan]. (1982)
Closer than a brother. [Meg Wright]. (1983)
Continuum. [Lois Welling]. (1983)
The reality barrier. [Donna Jadis]. (1983)
Something lost. [Sheila Clark]. (1983)

When heroes die: a starchild's quest. [Joyce Tullock]. (1983)
When the sun shines. [Karen Hayden]. (1983)
When two worlds collide. [Janice Pitkethley]. (1983)
The world of difference. [Lesley Coles]. (1983)
Enterprise: log entries 60. [anonymous]. (1984)
Fall of night. [Pam Baddeley]. (1984)
Know thine enemy. [Lyn Viviers]. (1984)
The mark of Cain. [Pam Baddeley]. (1984)
1942: from starship to Lancaster. [Jackie Regan]. (1984)
Stars or dust. [C. E. Roush]. (1984)
Friendship and duty. [Doris Schulze]. (1985)
A human kind of learning. [Karen Hayden & Vicki Richards]. (1985)
Tender expressions. [Wendy Montgomery]. (1985)
Spinner of nightmares. [Pam Baddeley]. (1986)
Blood of others. [Lyn Viviers]. (1988)
Crystal clear. [Doris Schulze & Irene Wohlfahrt]. (1988?)
Fallen angel. [Lyn Viviers]. (1990)

STAR TREK TIE-INS

Star Trek: the motion picture make-your-own costume book. [Lynn Edelman Schnurnberger]. (1979)
Star Trek II biographies. [William Rotsler]. (1982)
Star Trek II: Distress call. [William Rotsler]. (1982)
Star Trek II short stories. [William Rotsler]. (1982)
Star Trek III short stories. [William Rotsler]. (1984)
Star Trek III, the search for Spock storybook. [Larry Weinberg]. (1984)
Star Trek III: The Vulcan treasure. [William Rotsler]. (1984)
Star Trek: Voyage to adventure. [Michael J. Dodge]. (1984)
Star Trek: Phaser fight. [Barbara Siegel & Scott Siegel]. (1986)

STAR TREK—THE NEXT GENERATION

1. *Ghost ship.* [Diane Carey]. (1988)
2. *The peacekeepers.* [Gene DeWeese]. (1988)
3. *The children of Hamlin.* [Carmen Carter]. (1988)
4. *Survivors.* [Jean Lorrah]. (1989)
5. *Strike zone.* [Peter David]. (1989)
6. *Power hungry.* [Howard Weinstein]. (1989)
7. *Masks.* [John Vornholt]. (1989)
8. *The captain's honor.* [Daniel Dvorkin & David Dvorkin]. (1989)
9. *A call to darkness.* [Michael Jan Friedman]. (1989)
10. *A rock and a hard place.* [Peter David]. (1990)
11. *Gulliver's fugitives.* [Keith Sharee]. (1990)
12. *Doomsday world.* [Carmen Carter & Michael Jan Friedman & Peter David & Robert Greenberger]. (1990)
13. *The eyes of the beholder.* [A. C. Crispin]. (1990)
14. *Exiles.* [Howard Weinstein]. (1990)
15. *Fortune's light.* [Michael Jan Friedman]. (1991)
16. *Contamination.* [John Vornholt]. (1991)
17. *Boogeymen.* [Mel Gilden]. (1991)
18. *Q-in-law.* [Peter David]. (1991)
19. *Perchance to dream.* [Howard Weinstein]. (1991)

Unnumbered Titles

Encounter at Farpoint. [David Gerrold]. (1987)
Star Trek the next generation officer's manual. [John Terra & Rick Stuart]. (1988)
Metamorphosis. [Jean Lorrah]. (1990),

Reunion. [Michael Jan Friedman]. (1991)
Vendetta: the giant novel. [Peter David]. (1991)
Unification: a novel. [Jeri Taylor]. (1991)

STAR TREK PARODIES

Up your asteroid! a science fiction farce. [Robert Reginald as C. EVERETT COOPER]. (1977)
The Doctor and the Enterprise. (DOCTOR WHO series). [Jean Airey]. (1986)
Star wreck: the generation gap: the spacy spoof that dares to boldly go where nobody wanted to go before. [Leah Rewolinski]. (1989)

STAR WARS (various authors)

1. *Star wars: from the adventures of Luke Skywalker.* [George Lucas]. (1976)
2. *Star wars: The Empire strikes back.* [Donald F. Glut]. (1980)
3. *Star wars: Return of the Jedi.* [James Kahn]. (1983)
1-3. *The Star Wars trilogy.* [George Lucas & James Kahn & Donald F. Glut]. (1987)

STAR WARS STORYBOOKS

1. *The Star Wars storybook.* [Geraldine Richelson]. (1978)
2. *Star Wars, the empire strikes back storybook.* [Shep Steneman]. (1980)
3. *Star Wars, Return of the Jedi: the storybook based on the movie.* [Joan D. Vinge]. (1983)
1-3. *Star wars—the first ten years—storybook trilogy: the storybook based on the movies.* [Geraldine Richelson & Shep Steneman & Joan D. Vinge]. (1987)

HAN SOLO SERIES (Brian Daley)

1. *Han Solo at Star's End, from the adventures of Luke Skywalker.* (1979)
2. *Han Solo's revenge, from the adventures of Luke Skywalker.* (1979)
3. *Han Solo and the lost legacy: from the adventures of Luke Skywalker.* [Brian Daley]. (1980)

LANDO CALRISSIAN SERIES (L. Neil Smith)

1. *Lando Calrissian and the Mindharp of Sharu: a novel.* (1983)
2. *Lando Calrissian and the Flamewind of Oseon: a novel.* (1983)
3. *Lando Calrissian and the Starcave of ThonBoka: a novel.* (1983)

SECOND STAR WARS SERIES (Timothy Zahn)

1. *Heir to the empire.* (1991)

OTHER STAR WARS FICTION

Splinter of the mind's eye, from the adventures of Luke Skywalker. [Alan Dean Foster]. (1978)
Esper! [Cary A. Bucar]. (1981?)
Knight of shadows. [Karen Osman]. (1982)
The Empire strikes back. [Larry Weinberg]. (1985)
Star Wars: adaptation. [Larry Weinberg]. (1985)
Wicket and the dandelion warriors: an Ewok adventure. [Larry Weinberg]. (1985)

The ring, the witch, and the crystal: an Ewok adventure, based on the television movie Ewoks. [Cathy East Dubowski]. (1986)

STAR WARS PARODIES

Space nymph/Orgy in orbit. [Dustin Lasser as TRAVES TEA]. (1980)

STAR WARS TIE-INS

Star Wars: the roleplaying game. [Greg Costikyan]. (1987)

STARBRIDGE (A. C. Crispin)

1. *StarBridge, book one.* (1989)
2. *Silent dances.* [*with* Kathleen O'Malley]. (1990)
3. *Shadow world.* [*with* Jannean Elliott]. (1991)

STARBRIDGE CHRONICLES (Paul Park)

1. *Soldiers of paradise.* (1987)
2. *Sugar rain.* (1989)
3. *The cult of loving kindness.* (1991)
1-2. *The sugar festival.* (1989)

STARCATS (Phyllis Gotlieb)

1. *A judgment of dragons.* (1980)
2. *Emperor, swords, pentacles.* (1982)
3. *The kingdom of the cats.* (1985)

STARCHILD TRILOGY (Frederik Pohl & Jack Williamson)

1. *The Reefs of Space.* (1964)
2. *Starchild.* (1965)
3. *Rogue star.* (1969)
1-3. *The starchild trilogy.* (1977)

STARCRUISER SHENANDOAH (Roland Green)

1. *Squadron alert* (1989)
2. *Division of the spoils* (1990)
3. *The sum of things.* (1991)

STARDANCE (Jeanne Robinson & Spider Robinson)

1. *Stardance.* (1979)
2. *Starseed.* (1991)

STARDUST (Stephen Tall)

1. *The Stardust voyages.* (1975)
2. *The ramsgate paradox.* (1976)

STARFARERS (Vonda N. McIntyre)

1. *Starfarers.* (1989)
2. *Transition.* (1990)

STARFISHERS TRILOGY (Glen Cook)

1. *Shadowline.* (1982)
2. *Starfishers.* (1982)
3. *Stars' End.* (1982)

STARHOUNDS—SEE: STAR HOUNDS

STARHUNTERS (David Drake)

1. *Men hunting things.* (1988)
2. *Things hunting men.* (1988)
3. *Bluebloods.* (1990)

STARKADDER (Bernard King)

1. *Starkadder.* (1985)
2. *Vargr-moon.* (1986)
3. *Death-blinder.* (1988)

STARMONT FACSIMILE FICTION (various authors)
[missing numbers are not yet published]

1. *Theodore Roscoe's A grave must be deep.* [Theodore Roscoe]. (1989)
2. *Theodore Roscoe's Z is for zombie.* (1989)
3. *Toughest in the legion.* [Theodore Roscoe]. (1989)
6. *Secret of the earth star, and others.* [Henry Kuttner]. (1991)
12. *Worlds within worlds: four classic Argosy tales of science fiction.* [Thaddeus Dikty as anonymous editor]. (1991)
13. *Red twilight; World's end: two classic novels from Argosy.* [Victor Rousseau & Harl Vincent]. (1991)
14. *The monster of the lagoon.* [George F. Worts]. (1991)

STARMONT POPULAR CULTURE STUDIES (various authors)
[missing numbers are not yet published]

1. *The weirds: a facsimile selection of fiction from the era of the shudder pulps.* [Sheldon Jaffery]. (1987)
2. *The corpse maker.* [Hugh B. Cave]. (1988)
3. *The western pulp hero: an investigation into the psyche of an American legend.* [Nick Carr]. (1990)
6. *Pulp man's odyssey: the Hugh B. Cave story.* [Audrey Parente]. (1988)
8. *The super feds: A facsimile selection of dynamic G-man stories from the 1930s.* [Don Hutchison]. (1988)
9. *It's raining corpses in Chinatown.* [Don Hutchison]. (1991)
13. *Pulpmaster: The Theodore Roscoe story.* [Audrey Parente]. (1992)
16. *The devil's notebook: collected epigrams and pensées of Clark Ashton Smith.* [Clark Ashton Smith]. (1990)

STARMONT POPULAR FICTION (various authors)
[missing numbers are not yet published]

0. *Far below, and other horrors.* [Robert Weinberg]. (1986)
1. *Seven men.* [Theodore Roscoe]. (1988)
2. *The eighth green man (and other strange folk).* [Robert Weinberg]. (1989)
4. *We are all legends.* [Darrell Schweitzer]. (1988)
5. *The shattered goddess.* [Darrell Schweitzer]. (1988)

STARMONT PULP & DIME NOVEL STUDIES (various authors)

1. *Gangland's doom: The Shadow of the pulps.* [Frank Eisgruber]. (1985)
2. *America's Secret Service ace: The Operator 5 story.* [Nick Carr]. (1985)
3. *The flying spy: a history of G-8.* [Nick Carr]. (1989)
4. *Robert Kenneth Jones' The lure of Adventure.* [Robert Kenneth Jones]. (1989)

SERIES INDEX

STAR-PILOT GRAINGER (Brian M. Stableford)

1. *The Halcyon Drift.* (1972)
2. *Rhapsody in black.* (1973)
3. *Promised land.* (1974)
4. *The paradise game.* (1974)
5. *The Fenris device.* (1974)
6. *Swan song.* (1975)

STARQUEST (Gregory J. Smith)

1. *Captive planet.* (1986)
2. *Operation master planet.* (1986)

STARR FAMILY ADVENTURES (G. P. Jordan)

1. *The Milky Way run.* (1985)
2. *Extraterrestrial cover up.* (1986)

STARSHIP ORPHEUS (Symon Jade)

1. *Starship Orpheus #1: [Return from the dead].* (1982)
2. *Cosmic carnage.* (1983)
3. *Alter evil.* (1983)

STARSHIP TROOPERS (Robert A. Heinlein and others)

1. *Starship troopers.* (1959)
2. *Combat command in the world of Robert A. Heinlein's Starship troopers: Shines the name.* [Mark Acres]. (1987)

STARSTORMERS (Nicholas Fisk)

1. *Starstormers.* (1980)
2. *Sunburst.* (1980)
3. *Catfang.* (1981)
4. *Evil eye.* (1982)
5. *Volcano.* (1983)

STARWOLF (Edmond Hamilton)

1. *The weapon from beyond.* (1967)
2. *The Closed Worlds.* (1968)
3. *World of the Starwolves.* (1968)
1-3. *Starwolf.* (1982)

STARWOLVES (Thorarinn Gunnarsson)

1. *The starwolves.* (1988)
2. *Battle of the ring.* (1989)
3. *Tactical error.* (1991)

STEELE (Simon Hawke as J. D. MASTERS)

1. *Steele.* (1989)
2. *Cold Steele.* (1989)
3. *Killer Steele.* (1990)
4. *Jagged Steele.* (1990)
5. *Renegade Steele.* (1990)
6. *Target Steele.* (1990)
7. *Fugitive Steele.* [S. L. Hunter]. (1991)
8. *Molten Steele.* [S. L. Hunter]. (1991)

STEELEYE (Saul Dunn)

1. *The coming of Steeleye.* (1976)
2. *The Wideways.* (1976)
3. *Waterspace.* (1976)

STEFAN & EVONN (Margaret Cooper)

1. *Solution: escape.* (1980)
2. *Code name: Clone.* (1982)

STEN (Chris Bunch & Allan Cole)

1. *Sten.* (1982)
2. *The wolf worlds.* (1984)
3. *The court of a thousand suns.* (1986)
4. *Fleet of the damned.* (1988)
5. *Revenge of the damned.* (1989)
6. *The return of the emperor.* (1990)

STERLING O'BLIVION (Jody Scott)

1. *Passing for human.* (1977)
2. *I, vampire.* (1984)

STEVE AUSTIN—SEE: THE SIX MILLION DOLLAR MAN

STONER MCTAVISH (Sarah Dreher)

1. *Stoner McTavish.* (1985)
2. *Something shady.* (1986)
3. *Gray magic.* (1987)
4. *A captive in time.* (1990)

STORIES OF SIX WORLDS (Cherith Baldry)

1. *The book and the phoenix.* (1989)
1A. *A rush of golden wings.* (1991)
2. *Hostage of the sea.* (1990)

STORIES OF THE REALM (Phil Allcock)

1. *The will of Dargan.* (1989)
2. *In search of the golden sceptre.* (1991)

STORM LORD—SEE: WARS OF VIS

STORMLANDS (John Maddox Roberts)

1. *The islander.* (1990)
2. *The black shields.* (1991)

STORY OF THE GARDENER (Phillip Mann)

1. *Master of Paxwax.* (1986)
2. *The fall of the families.* (1987)

STORYTRAILS (Allen Sharp)

The haunters of Marsh Hall: can you find the secret of the ghostly guardian? (1982)
The stone of Badda: can you face the deadly guardians of Otherworld? (1982)
Terror in the fourth dimension: can you return from a 2000 year journey through time? (1982)
The deadly trap: caught up in the web of a strange prophecy, can you avoid the trap? (1983)
The evil of Mr. Happiness: can you defeat the schemes of a criminal mastermind? (1983)
Night of the comet: can you destroy the giants from the sea? (1983)
The tomb of Amenosis: can you stop a war, solve a riddle as old as Genesis? (1983)
Return of the undead: can you destroy the vampire of Valdah? (1984)

The eye of Heaven: can you save the victim of a web of mystery? (1985)
The hands of Pablo Santos. (1985)
The second conquest: can you change the world's future? (1985)
The dark awakening: can you destroy an ancient sorcery? (1986)
The island of the walking dead: can you save the victim of a terrifying revenge? (1986)
The wolf with no tail: can you discover Kutzka's ancient secret? (1987)

STRANGE OCCURRENCE SQUAD (Richard Laymon)

The beast. (1986)
The night creature. (1986)
The return. (1986)
Thin air. (1986)

STRIKE FIGHTERS (Tom Willard)

1. *Strike fighters.* (1990)
2. *Strike fighters #2.* (1990)
3. *War chariot.* (1990)
4. *Sudden fury.* (1991)
5. *Red dancer.* (1991)

STRYKER (David F. Nighbert)

1. *Timelapse.* (1988)
2. *The clouds of Magellan.* (1991)

STUDIES IN SPECULATIVE FICTION (various authors)

1. *Feminist futures: contemporary women's speculative fiction.* [Natalie M. Rosinsky]. (1984)
2. *Ray Bradbury and the poetics of reverie: fantasy, science fiction, and the reader.* [William F. Touponce]. (1984)
3. *The scientific world view in dystopia.* [Alexandra Aldridge]. (1984)
4. *Approaches to the fiction of Ursula K. Le Guin.* [James W. Bittner]. (1984)
5. *Utopia: the psychology of a cultural fantasy.* [David Bleich]. (1984)
6. *Biological themes in modern science fiction.* [Helen N. Parker]. (1984)
7. *Red stars: political aspects of Soviet science fiction.* [Patrick L. McGuire]. (1985)
8. *Scientific attitudes in Mary Shelley's Frankenstein.* [Samuel Holmes Vasbinder]. (1984)
9. *The novels of Philip K. Dick.* [Kim Stanley Robinson]. (1984)
10. *The politics of fantasy: C. S. Lewis and J. R. R. Tolkien.* [Lee D. Rossi]. (1984)
11. *The unified ring: narrative art and the science-fiction novel.* [Frank Sadler]. (1984)
12. *Science, myth, and the fictional creation of alien worlds.* [Albert Wendland. (1985)
13. *Italo Calvino: metamorphoses of fantasy.* [Albert Howard Carter III]. (1987)
14. *The monster in the mirror: gender and the sentimental/gothic myth in Frankenstein.* [Mary K. Patterson Thornburg]. (1987)
15. *Specter or delusion? the supernatural in gothic fiction.* [Margaret L. Carter]. (1987)
16. *Le Guin and identity in contemporary fiction.* [Bernard Selinger]. (1988)
17. *Counterings: utopian dialectics in contemporary contexts.* [Kingsley Widner]. (1988)

18. *Sanity plea: schizophrenia in the novels of Kurt Vonnegut.* [Lawrence R. Broer]. (1989)
19. *Dracula: the vampire and the critics.* [Margaret L. Carter]. (1988)
20. *Redefining the American gothic: from Wieland to Day of the dead.* [Louis S. Gross]. (1989)
21. *The vampire in literature: a critical bibliography.* [Margaret L. Carter]. (1989)

SUBSPACE EXPLORERS (E. E. Smith and others)

1. *Subspace explorers.* (1965)
2. *Subspace encounter.* [with Lloyd Arthur Eshbach]. (1983)

SUN WOLF (Barbara Hambly)

1. *The Ladies of Mandrigyn.* (1984)
2. *The Witches of Wenshar.* (1987)
3. *The dark hand of magic.* (1990)
1-2. *The unschooled wizard.* (1987)

SUNGLASSES (Nancy A. Collins)

1. *Sunglasses after dark.* (1989)
2. *Tempter.* (1990)

SUN'S END (Richard A. Lupoff)

1. *Sun's end.* (1984)
2. *Galaxy's end.* (1988)

SUNSET WARRIOR (Eric Van Lustbader)

1. *The sunset warrior.* (1977)
2. *Shallows of night.* (1978)
3. *Dai-San.* (1978)
4. *Beneath an opal moon.* (1980)

SUNSTONE SCROLLS (Sydney J. Van Scyoc)

1. *Darkchild.* (1982)
2. *Bluesong.* (1983)
3. *Starsilk.* (1984)
1-3. *Daughters of the sunstone.* (1985)

SUPER ENDLESS QUEST ADVENTURE GAMEBOOK—SEE: ADVANCED DUNGEONS & DRAGONS ADVENTURE GAMEBOOK

SUPER POWERS WHICH WAY BOOKS—SEE: WHICH WAY BOOKS—SUPER POWERS

SUPERMAN (various authors)

Superman: Last son of Krypton. [Elliot S. Maggin]. (1978)
Superman: Miracle Monday. [Elliot S. Maggin]. (1981)
Superman (the movie). [Gary Libman]. (1983)
Superman III. [William Kotzwinkle]. (1983)
Superman IV. [B. B. Hiller]. (1987)
Superman IV. [Nancy E. Krulik]. (1987)

Associated Titles

Superman, serial to cereal. [Gary H. Grossman]. (1976)
The making of Superman, the movie. [David Michael Petrou]. (1978)

Superman's maze challenge. [Vladimir Koziakin]. (1978)

Daily planet: a world of news every day! (*Superman II* tie-in). [Stephanie Spinner]. (1981)

DC Comics presents: Superman II, the movie magazine. [Michael Fleisher & Joe Orlando]. (1981)

Superman, the man of steel. [Andrew Helfer]. (1983)

Superman and Spider-Man. [Edward Gross]. (1986)

The Superman files. [James Van Hise]. (1986)

Superman IV, the quest for peace: the official poster magazine. [David McDonnell]. (1987)

Superman at fifty: the persistence of a legend. [Dennis Dooley & Gary Engle]. (1987)

It's a bird—it's a plane—no, it's the television adventures of Superman. [James Van Hise]. (1989)

SURVIVAL 2000 (James McPhee)

1. *Blood quest.* (1991)
2. *Renegade war.* (1991)
3. *Frozen fire.* (1991),

SURVIVALIST (Jerry Ahern)

1. *Total war.* (1981)
2. *The nightmare begins.* (1981)
3. *The quest.* (1981)
4. *The doomsayer.* (1981)
5. *The web.* (1983)
6. *The savage horde.* (1983)
7. *The prophet.* (1984)
8. *The end is coming.* (1984)
9. *Earth fire.* (1984)
10. *The awakening.* (1984)
11. *The reprisal.* (1985)
12. *The rebellion.* (1985)
13. *Pursuit.* (1986)
14. *The terror.* (1987)
15. *Overlord.* (1987)
16. *The arsenal.* (1988)
17. *The ordeal.* (1988)
18. *The struggle.* (1989)
19. *Final rain.* (1989)
20. *Firestorm.* (1990)
21. *To end all war.* (1990)
22. *Brutal conquest.* (1991)

Unnumbered titles

Mid-wake. (1988)
The legend. (1991)

SURVIVORS (various authors)

1. *Survivors.* [Terry Nation]. (1976)
2. *Genesis of a hero.* [John Eyers]. (1977)

SUSAN SHAW (Edward Ormondroyd)

1. *Time at the top.* (1963)
2 *All in good time.* (1975)

SWAMP THING (various authors)

FIRST SERIES

1. *Swamp Thing.* [David Houston & Len Wein]. (1982)

2. *The return of Swamp Thing: a novel.* [David Peters as PETER DAVID]. (1989)

SECOND SERIES

1. *Swamp Thing.* [Martin Cannon]. (1987)
2. *Green mansions.* [Martin Cannon]. (1987)
3. *Swamp Thing finale.* [James Van Hise]. (1987)

SWORD & CIRCLET: KENDRIC & IRISSA (Carole Nelson Douglas)

1. *Keepers of Edanvant* [KENDRIC & IRISSA #3]. (1987)
2. *Heir of Reingarth.* (1988).
3. *Seven of swords.* (1989)

KENDRIC & IRISSA

1. *Six of Swords.* (1982)
2. *Exiles of the Rynth.* (1984)
3. *Keepers of Edanvant.* [SWORD & CIRCLET #1]. (1987)

SWORD AND THE DREAM (Janice Elliott)

1. *The king awakes.* (1987)
2. *The empty throne.* (1988)

SWORD OF KNOWLEDGE (C. J. Cherryh)

1. *A dirge for Sabis.* [with Leslie Fish]. (1989)
2. *Wizard spawn.* [with Nancy Asire]. (1989)
3. *Reap the whirlwind.* [with Mercedes Lackey]. (1989)

SwordQuest series (Bill Fawcett)

Quest for the unicorn's horn. (1985)
Quest for the dragon's eye. (1985)
Quest for the Demon Gate. (1986)
Quest for the elf king. (1987)

SWORDS OF RAEMLLYN (Geo. W. Proctor & Robert E. Vardeman)

1. *To demons bound.* (1985)
2. *A yoke of magic.* (1985)
3. *Blood fountain.* (1985)
4. *Death's acolyte.* (1986)
5. *The beasts of the mist.* (1986)
6. *For crown and kingdom.* (1987)

SYMPHONY TRILOGY (Calvin Miller)

1. *A requiem of love.* (1989)
2. *A symphony in sand.* (1990)

T-CITY TRILOGY (Mark Adlard)

1. *Interface.* (1971)
2. *Volteface.* (1972)
3. *Multiface.* (1975)

TAASH (Ellen Kindt McKenzie)

1. *Taash and the jesters.* (1968)
2. *Kashka.* (1987)

TAIN (Gregory Frost)

1. *Tain.* (1986)
2. *Remscéla.* (1988)

TAKERS (Jerry Ahern & Sharon Ahern)

1. *The takers.* (1984)
2. *River of gold.* (1985)

TALE OF KRISPOS—SEE: VIDESSOS CYCLE

TALENTS (Douglas Hill)

1. *Blade of the poisoner.* (1987)
2. *Master of fiends.* (1987)

TALES FROM THE FLAT EARTH (Tanith Lee)

1. *Night's master.* (1978)
2. *Death's master.* (1979)
3. *Delusion's master.* (1981)
4. *Delirium's Mistress.* (1986)
5. *Night's sorceries.* (1987)
1-3. *Tales from the Flat Earth: The lords of darkness.* (1987)
4-5. *Tales from the Flat Earth: Night's daughter.* (1987)

TALES FROM THE LAND OF ERIN (Michael Scott)

1. *A bright enchantment.* (1985)
2. *A golden dream.* (1985)
3. *A silver wish.* (1985)

TALES OF CLAVERING GRANGE (R. Chetwynd-Hayes)

Tales of darkness. (1981)
The king's ghost. (1985)
retitled: *The grange.* (1985)
Ghosts from the mist of time (1985)
Tales of the hidden world. (1988)
The haunted grange. (1988)

TALES OF GOM IN THE LEGENDS OF ULM (Grace Chetwin)

1. *Gom on Windy Mountain.* (1986)
2. *The riddle and the rune* (1987)
3. *The crystal stair.* (1988)
4. *The starstone.* (1989)

TALES OF THE BARD (Michael Scott)

1. *Magician's law.* (1987)
2. *Demon's law.* (1988)
3. *Death's law.* (1989)

TALES OF THE CONCORDAT (Jefferson P. Swycaffer)

1. *The empire's legacy.* (1988)
2. *Voyage of the planetslayer.* (1988)
3. *Revolt and rebirth.* (1988)

TALES OF THE CONTINUING TIME (Daniel Keys Moran)

1. *Emerald eyes.* (1988)
2. *The long run.* (1989)

TALES OF THE GALACTIC MIDWAY (Mike Resnick)

1. *Sideshow.* (1982)

2. *The three-legged hootch dancer.* (1983)
3. *The wild alien tamer.* (1983)
4. *The best rootin' tootin' shootin' gunslinger in the whole damned galaxy.* (1983)

TALES OF THE PRIMAL LAND (Brian Lumley)

1. *The house of Cthulhu.* (1984)
2. *Tarra Khash: Hrossak!* (1991)
3. *Sorcery in Shad.* (1991)

TALES OF THE VELVET COMET (Mike Resnick)

1. *Eros ascending.* (1984)
2. *Eros at zenith.* (1984)
3. *Eros descending.* (1985)
4. *Eros at nadir.* (1986)

TALES OF THE WEREWOLF CLAN (H. Warner Munn)

1. *The werewolf of Ponkert.* (1958)
2. *In the tomb of the bishop.* (1979)
3. *The master goes home.* (1980)

TALES OF TOMORROW (David Houston)

1. *Invaders at ground zero.* (1981)
2. *Red dust.* (1981)
3. *Substance X.* (1981)
4. *Ice from space.* (1982)

TANGLED WEBS (Steve Mudd)

1. *Tangled webs.* (1989)
2. *The planet beyond.* (1990)

TANKWAR (Larry Steelbaugh)

1. *Tankwar.* (1990)
2. *Fireball.* (1990)
3. *Firestorm.* (1991)
4. *Firebrand.* (1991)

TAROT (Piers Anthony)

1. *God of Tarot.* (1979)
2. *Vision of Tarot.* (1980)
3. *Faith of Tarot.* (1980)
1-3. *Tarot.* (1987)

TARTARUS (William Greenleaf)

1. *The Tartarus incident.* (1983)
2. *Starjacked!* (1987)

TARZAN SEQUELS (various authors)

For a complete list of the Edgar Rice Burroughs Tarzan stories, see the 1979 volume of this bibliography.

Tarzan and the lightning man. [William Gilmour]. (1963)
Tarzan at Mars' core. [Edward Hirschman]. (1977)
Tarzan, king of the apes. [Edgar Rice Burroughs with Joan D. Vinge]. (1983)
Tarzan and the tower of diamonds. [Richard Reinsmith]. (1985)
Tarzan and the well of slaves. (ENDLESS QUEST #26). [Douglas Niles]. (1985)

Tarzan of the apes: four volumes in one. [Edgar Rice Burroughs]. (1988)

Associated Titles

Jungle scenes of Tarzan. (art) [Zdenek Burian] (1973)
Tarzan encyclopedia. [John Harwood & Allan Howard]. (1975)
Tarzan and the classics. [Erling B. Holtsmark]. (1979)
Tarzan and tradition: classic myth in popular literature. [Erling B. Holtsmark]. (1981)
Burroughs dictionary. [George T. McWhorter]. (1987)

TED QUANTRILL (Dean Ing)

1. *Systemic shock.* (1981)
2. *Single combat.* (1983)
3. *Wild country.* (1985)

TEE-BO SERIES (Mary Burg Whitcomb)

1. *Tee-Bo the incredible talking dog on the trail of the persnickety prowler.* (1975)
2. *Tee-Bo the incredible talking dog leads the way in the great hort hunt.* (1978)

TEEN WITCH (Megan Barnes)

1. *Lucky 13.* (1988)
2. *Be careful what you wish for.* (1988)
3. *Gone with the witch.* (1989)
4. *Witch switch.* (1989)

TEENAGE MUTANT NINJA TURTLES (Dave Morris)

Teenage mutant ninja turtles. [B. B. Hiller]. (1990)
Buried treasure. (1990)
Red herrings. (1990)
Six-guns and shurikens. (1990)
Sky-high. (1990)

Associated Titles

The official teenage mutant ninja turtles treasury. [Stanley Wiater]. (1991)
Teenage mutant ninja turtles knitting book. [Joy Gammon]. (1990)
The unauthorized Teenage Mutant Ninja Turtles quiz book: an unofficial trivia guide to America's hottest phenomenon. [Jeff Rovin]. (1990)

TEGNE (Richard La Plante)

1. *Warlord of Zendow.* (1988)
2. *The killing blow.* (1990)

TEKUMEL (M. A. R. Barker)

1. *The man of gold.* (1984)
2. *Flamesong.* (1985)

TEKWAR (William Shatner)

1. *TekWar.* (1989)
2. *TekLords.* (1991)
3. *TekLab.* (1991)

TELZEY SERIES—SEE: THE HUB

TEMPLE STREET (JUDITH SPEARING)

1. *Ghosts who went to school.* (1966)
2. *The museum house ghosts.* (1969)

TEMPUS—SEE: THIEVES' WORLD

TERMINATOR (various authors)

1. *The Terminator.* [Randall Frakes & W. H. Wisher]. (1985)
2. *T2: Terminator 2: Judgment day.* [Randall Frakes]. (1991)

British novelization

1. *The Terminator.* [Shaun Hutson]. (1984)

Associated Titles

The making of T2, Terminator 2: Judgment day. [Don Shay & Jody Duncan]. (1991)
Terminator 2: Judgment day: the book of the film: an illustrated screenplay. [James Cameron & William Wisher]. (1991)

TERRA MAGICA (Lin Carter)

1. *Kesrick.* (1982)
2. *Dragonrouge.* (1984)
3. *Mandricardo.* (1987)
4. *Callipygia.* (1988)

TERRAPLANE (Jack Womack)

1. *Ambient.* (1987)
2. *Terraplane.* (1988)
3. *Heathern.* (1990)

TERRILIAN (Sharon Green)

1. *The warrior within.* (1982)
2. *The warrior enchanted.* (1983)
3. *The warrior rearmed.* (1984)
4. *The warrior challenged.* (1986)
5. *The warrior victorious.* (1988)

THERE WILL BE WAR (Jerry Pournelle & John F. Carr)

1. *There will be war.* (1983)
2. *Men of war.* (1984)
3. *Blood and iron.* (1984)
4. *Day of the tyrant.* (1985)
5. *Warrior.* (1986)
6. *Guns of darkness.* (1987)
7. *Call to battle.* (1988)
8. *Armageddon!* (1989)
9. *After armageddon.* (1990)

THESE LAWLESS WORLDS (Sharon Jarvis & Ellen M. Kozak as JARROD COMSTOCK)

1. *The love machine.* (1984)
2. *Scales of justice.* (1984)

SERIES INDEX

THIEVES' WORLD (Robert Lynn Asprin)

1. *Thieves' world* (1979)
2. *Tales from the Vulgar Unicorn.* (1980)
3. *Shadows of Sanctuary.* (1981)
4. *Storm season.* (1982)
5. *The face of chaos.* [with Lynn Abbey]. (1983)
6. *Wings of omen.* [with Lynn Abbey]. (1984)
7. *The dead of winter.* [with Lynn Abbey]. (1985)
8. *Soul of the city.* [with Lynn Abbey]. (1986),
9. *Blood ties.* [with Lynn Abbey]. (1986)
10. *Aftermath.* [with Lynn Abbey]. (1987)
11. *Uneasy alliances.* [with Lynn Abbey]. (1988)
12. *Stealers' sky.* [with Lynn Abbey]. (1989)
1-3. *Sanctuary.* (1982)
4-6. *Cross-currents.* [with Lynn Abbey]. (1984)
7-9. *The shattered sphere.* [with Lynn Abbey]. (1986)
10-12. *The price of victory.* [with Lynn Abbey] (1990)

Associated Titles

Jamie the Red [Gordon R. Dickson & Roland Green]. (1984)
Lythande. [Marion Zimmer Bradley]. (1986)
Shadowspawn. [Andrew J. Offutt]. (1987)
Dagger. [David Drake]. (1988)

TEMPUS SERIES (Janet Morris)

1. *Beyond Sanctuary.* (1985)
2. *Beyond the veil.* (1985)
3. *Beyond Wizardwall.* (1986)
4. *Tempus.* (1987)
5. *City at the edge of time.* [with Chris Morris]. (1988)
6. *Tempus unbound.* [with Chris Morris]. (1989)
7. *Storm seed.* [with Chris Morris]. (1990)

THIRD WORLD WAR (John Hackett)

1. *The third world war: a future history (August (1985).* (1978)
2. *The third world war: the untold story.* (1982)

Associated Titles

Team Yankee: a novel of World War III. [Harold W. Coyle]. (1987) [A sequel to Hackett's novel]
Alternative Third World War, (1985)-2035: a personal history. [William Jackson]. (1987)

THIRD WORLD WAR NOVELS (various authors)

World War III. [John Stanley]. (1976)
World War III: a novelization. [Harold King, *as* BRIAN HARRIS] (1982)

THIRST (Guy N. Smith)

1. *Thirst.* (1980)
2. *The plague.* (1987)

THLASSA MEY (Dennis McCarty)

1. *Flight to Thlassa Mey.* (1986)
2. *Warriors of Thlassa Mey.* (1987)
3. *Lords of Thlassa Mey.* (1989)
4. *Across the Thlassa Mey.* (1991)

THOMAS COVENANT THE UNBELIEVER (Stephen R. Donaldson)

The First Chronicles

1. *Lord Foul's bane.* (1977)
2. *The Illearth war.* (1977)
3. *The power that preserves.* (1977)
1-3. *The first chronicles of Thomas Covenant the Unbeliever.* (1983)

The Second Chronicles

1. *The wounded land.* (1980)
2. *The one tree.* (1982)
3. *White gold wielder.* (1983)

Associated Titles

Gilden fire. (1981)

THRANX SERIES (Alan Dean Foster)

1. *Nor crystal tears.* (1982)
2. *Midworld.* (1975)
3. *Icerigger.* (1974)
4. *Mission to Moulokin.* (1979)
5. *The deluge drivers.* (1987)
6. *Voyage to the city of the dead.* (1984)
7. *Sentenced to Prism.* (1985)

THREE DAMOSELS (Vera Chapman)

1. *The green knight.* (1975)
2   *The king's damosel.* (1976)
3. *King Arthur's daughter.* (1976)
1-3. *The three damosels.* (1978)

THRONE TRILOGY (Artemis OakGrove)

1. *The raging peace.* (1984)
2. *Dreams of vengeance.* (1985)
3. *Throne of council.* (1986)

THUNDERCATS SERIES (H. William Stine & Megan Stine)

The Thundercats and the ghost warrior. (1985)
The Thundercats and the snowmen of Hook Mountain. (1985)
The spear of Azzura. (1986)

THYRI (Michael D. Weaver)

1. *Wolf-dreams.* (1987)
2. *Nightreaver.* (1988)
3. *Bloodfang.* (1989)
1-3. *Wolf-dreams.* (1989)

TIGER & DEL (Jennifer Roberson)

1. *Sword-dancer.* (1986)
2. *Sword-singer.* (1988)
3. *Sword-maker.* (1989)
4. *Sword-breaker.* (1991)

TIME GATE (Robert Silverberg)

1. *Time gate.* (1989)
2. *Dangerous interfaces.* (1990)

TIME KEEPER (Barbara Bartholomew)

1. *The time keeper.* (1985)
2. *Child of tomorrow.* (1985)
3. *When dreams cease to dream.* (1985)

TIME MACHINE (various authors)

1. *Secret of the knights.* [Jim Gasperini]. (1984)
2. *Search for dinosaurs.* [David Bischoff]. (1984)
3. *Sword of the samurai.* [Steve Perry & Michael Reaves]. (1984)
4. *Sail with pirates.* [Jim Gasperini]. (1984)
5. *Civil War secret agent.* [Steve Perry]. (1984)
6. *The rings of Saturn.* [Arthur Byron Cover]. (1985)
7. *Ice age explorer.* [Dougal Dixon]. (1985)
8. *The mystery of Atlantis.* [Jim Gasperini]. (1985)
9. *Wild west rider.* [Stephen Overholser]. (1985)
10. *American revolutionary.* [Arthur Byron Cover]. (1985)
11. *Mission to World War II.* [Marc Kornblatt & Susan Nanus]. (1986)
12. *Search for the Nile.* [Robert W. Walker]. (1986)
13. *Secret of the royal treasure.* [Carol Gaskin]. (1986)
14. *Blade of the guillotine.* [Arthur Byron Cover]. (1986)
15. *Flame of the Inquisition.* [Marc Kornblatt]. (1986)
16. *Quest for the cities of gold.* [Richard Glatzer]. (1987)
17. *Scotland Yard detective.* [Seymour V. Reit]. (1987)
18. *Sword of Caesar.* [Bruce Stevenson & Robin Stevenson]. (1987)
19. *Death mask of Pancho Villa.* [Carol Gaskin & George Guthridge]. (1987)
20. *Bound for Australia.* [Nancy Bailey]. (1987)
21. *Caravan to China.* [Carol Gaskin]. (1987)
22. *The last of the dinosaurs.* [Peter Lerangis]. (1988)
23. *Quest for King Arthur.* [Ruth Ashby]. (1988)
24. *World War I flying ace.* [Richard Mueller]. (1988)

Time Machine special edition

(25) *World War II code breaker.* [Peter Lerangis]. (1989)

TIME MACHINE SEQUELS (various authors)

The Original Novel

The time machine. [H. G. Wells]. (1895)

Sequels and Parodies

The return of the time machine. [Egon Friedell]. (1972)
The Space Machine: a scientific romance. [Christopher Priest]. (1976)
Morlock night. [K. W. Jeter]. (1979)
The man who loved Morlocks: a sequel to The time machine as narrated by The Time Traveller. [David J. Lake]. (1981)
Time machine II. [Joe Morhaim & George Pal]. (1981)

TIME MASTER TRILOGY (Louise Cooper)

1. *The initiate.* (1985)
2. *The outcast.* (1986)
3. *The master.* (1987)

TIME PATROL (Poul Anderson)

1. *Guardians of time.* (1960)
2. *Time Patrolman.* 1983)
3. *The year of the ransom.* (1988)
4. *The shield of time.* (1990)
1-2. *Annals of the Time Patrol.* (1984)
1-3. *Time Patrol.* (1991)

TIME POLICE (Warren Norwood)

1. *Vanished.* (1988)
2. *Trapped!* (1989)
3. *Stranded.* [with Mel Odom]. (1989)

TIME ROPE (Robert Leeson)

1. *Time rope.* (1986)
2. *Three against the world.* (1986)
3. *At war with tomorrow.* (1986)
4. *The metro gangs attack.* (1986)

TIME TOURS—SEE: ROBERT SILVERBERG'S TIME TOURS

TIME TRAVELER (various authors)

1. *Voyage with Columbus.* [Seymour V. Reit]. (1986)
2. *The legend of Hiawatha.* [Carol Gaskin]. (1986)
3. *The first settlers.* [Carol Gaskin]. (1987)
4. *The amazing Ben Franklin.* [Peter Lerangis]. (1987)
5. *Paul Revere and the Boston Tea Party.* [Mark Kornblatt]. (1987)
6. *George Washington and the Constitution.* [Ellen Frankel]. (1987)

TIME TRILOGY (Margaret J. Anderson)

1. *In the keep of time.* (1977)
2. *In the circle of time.* (1979)
3. *The mists of time.* (1984)

TIME WARRIOR (Matthew J. Costello)

1. *Time of the fox.* (1990)
2. *Hour of the scorpion.* (1991)

TIME WARRIORS (David North)

1. *Fuse point.* (1991)
2. *Forbidden region.* (1991)
3. *The guardian strikes.* (1991)

TIMEBINDERS (Ray Nelson)

1. *The Prometheus man: a Nrobook.* (1982)
2. *The revolt of the unemployables.* (1978)

TIMELINER (Richard C. Meredith)

1. *At the narrow passage.* (1973)
2. *No brother, no friend.* (1976)
3. *Vestiges of time.* (1978)

TIMEQUEST (William G. Tedford)

1. *Rashanyn dark.* (1981)
2. *Hydrabyss red.* (1981)
3. *Nemydia Deep.* (1981)

TIMEWARS (Simon Hawke)

1. *The Ivanhoe gambit.* (1984)
2. *The timekeeper conspiracy.* (1984)
3. *The Pimpernel plot.* (1984)
4. *The Zenda vendetta.* (1985)
5. *The Nautilus sanction.* (1985)
6. *The Khyber connection.* (1986)
7. *The Argonaut affair.* (1987)
8. *The Dracula caper.* (1988)
9. *The Lilliput legion.* (1989)
10. *The hellfire rebellion.* (1990)
11. *The Cleopatra crisis.* (1990)
12. *The six-gun solution.* (1991)

TIMOTHY, ELLEN & MELINDA (Margaret Storey)

1. *Timothy and the two witches.* (1967}
2. *A quarrel of witches.* (1970)
3. *The sleeping witch.* 1971
4. *A war of wizards.* (1976)
5. *The double wizard.* (1979)

TINIEBLAS TRILOGY (R. M. Koster)

1. *The prince.* (1972)
2. *The dissertation.* (1975)
3. *Mandragon.* (1979)

TITANS (Patrick H. Adkins)

1. *Lord of the crooked paths.* (1987)
2. *Master of the fearful depths.* (1989)
3. *Sons of the titans.* (1990)

TITUS CROW (Brian Lumley)

1. *The burrowers beneath.* (1974)
2. *The transition of Titus Crow.* (1975/1991)
3. *The clock of dreams.* (1978)
4. *Spawn of the winds.* (1978)
5. *In the moons of Borea.* (1979)
6. *The Compleat Crow.* (1987)

TNT (Doug Masters)

1. *TNT.* (1985)
2. *The Beast.* (1985)
3. *Spiral of death.* (1985)
4. *The Devil's Claw.* (1985)
5. *Killer angel.* (1986)
6. *Ritual of blood.* (1986)

TO THE STARS (Harry Harrison)

1. *Homeworld.* (1980)
2. *Wheelworld.* (1981)
3. *Starworld.* (1981)
1-3. *To the stars.* (1981)

TOLKIEN QUEST—SEE: MIDDLE-EARTH QUEST

TOM HUMBOLDT (Delia Huddy)

1. *Time piper.* (1976)
2. *The Humboldt effect.* (1982

TOM "RED CLAY" (Rebecca Ore)

1. *Becoming alien.* (1988)

2. *Being alien.* (1989)
3. *Human to human.* (1990)

TOM SWIFT SERIES

FIRST SERIES

See the 1979 edition of this bibliography for a complete list of the original Tom Swift books.

TOM SWIFT JR. [SECOND SERIES]
(various authors as VICTOR APPLETON II)

1. *Tom Swift and his flying lab.* [William Dougherty]. (1954)
2. *Tom Swift and his jetmarine.* [John Almquist]. (1954)
3. *Tom Swift and his rocket ship.* [John Almquist]. (1954)
4. *Tom Swift and his giant robot.* [Richard Sklar]. (1954)
5. *Tom Swift and his atomic earth blaster.* [Jim Lawrence]. (1954)
5A. *Tom Swift and his sky wheel.* [Jim Lawrence]. (1977)
6. *Tom Swift and his outpost in space.* [By Jim Lawrence]. (1955)
7. *Tom Swift and his diving seacopter.* [Jim Lawrence]. (1956)
8. *Tom Swift in the caves of nuclear fire.* [Thomas Mulvey]. (1956)
9. *Tom Swift on the phantom satellite.* [Jim Lawrence]. (1957)
10. *Tom Swift and his ultrasonic cycloplane.* [Jim Lawrence]. (1957)
11. *Tom Swift and his deep-sea hydrodome.* [Jim Lawrence]. (1958)
12. *Tom Swift in the race to the Moon.* [Jim Lawrence]. (1958)
13. *Tom Swift and his space solartron.* [Jim Lawrence]. (1958)
14. *Tom Swift and his electronic retroscope.* [Jim Lawrence]. (1959)
14A. *Tom Swift in the jungle of the Mayas.* [Jim Lawrence]. (1972)
15. *Tom Swift and his spectromarine selector.* [Jim Lawrence]. (1960)
15A. *Tom Swift and the city of gold.* [[Jim Lawrence]. (1972)
16. *Tom Swift and the cosmic astronauts.* [Jim Lawrence]. (1960)
17. *Tom Swift and the visitor from Planet X.* [Jim Lawrence]. (1961)
18. *Tom Swift and the electric hydrolung.* [Jim Lawrence]. (1961)
19. *Tom Swift and his triphibian atomicar.* [Jim Lawrence]. (1962)
20. *Tom Swift and his megascope space prober.* [Jim Lawrence]. (1962)
21. *Tom Swift and the asteroid pirates.* [Jim Lawrence]. (1963)
22. *Tom Swift and his repelatron skyway.* [Jim Lawrence]. (1963)
23. *Tom Swift and his aquatomic tracker.* [Jim Lawrence]. (1964)
24. *Tom Swift and his 3-D telejector.* [Jim Lawrence]. (1964)
25. *Tom Swift and his polar-ray dynasphere.* [Jim Lawrence]. (1965)

26. *Tom Swift and his sonic boom trap.* [Jim Lawrence]. (1965)
27. *Tom Swift and his subocean geotron.* [Jim Lawrence]. (1966)
28. *Tom Swift and the mystery comet.* [Jim Lawrence]. (1966)
29. *Tom Swift and the captive planetoid.* [Jim Lawrence]. (1967)
30. *Tom Swift and his G-force inverter.* [Jim Lawrence]. (1968)
31. *Tom Swift and his Dyna-4 capsule.* [Richard McKenna]. (1969)
32. *Tom Swift and his Cosmotron Express.* [Richard McKenna]. 1970
33. *Tom Swift and the galaxy ghosts.* [Richard McKenna]. (1971)

THIRD SERIES (various authors as VICTOR APPLETON)

1. *The city in the stars.* [William Rotsler & Sharman DiVono]. (1981)
2. *Terror on the moons of Jupiter.* [William Rotsler & Sharman DiVono]. (1981)
3. *The alien probe.* [William Rotsler & Sharman DiVono]. (1981)
4. *The war in outer space.* [William Rotsler & Sharman DiVono]. (1981)
5. *The astral fortress.* [William Rotsler & Sharman DiVono]. (1981)
6. *The rescue mission.* [William Rotsler & Sharman DiVono]. (1981)
7. *Ark Two.* [Neal Barrett Jr.?]. (1982)
8. *Crater of mystery.* [[Mike McQuay]. (1983)
9. *Gateway to doom.* [Robert E. Vardeman]. (1983)
10. *The invisible force.* [Neal Barrett Jr.?]. (1983)
11. Planet of nightmares. [Mike McQuay]. (1984)

FOURTH SERIES (various authors as VICTOR APPLETON)

1. *The black dragon.* [Bill McCay]. (1991)
2. *The negative zone.* [Bill McCay]. (1991)
3. *Cyborg kickboxer.* [Steven Grant]. (1991)
4. *The DNA disaster.* [F. Gwynplaine MacIntyre]. (1991)
5. *Monster machine.* [James D. Macdonald & Debra Doyle]. (1991)
6. *Aquatech warriors.* [James D. Macdonald & Debra Doyle]. (1991)

TOMOE GOZEN (Jessica Amanda Salmonson)

1. *Tomoe Gozen.* (1981)
2. *The Golden Naginata.* (1982)
3. *Thousand shrine warrior.* (1984)

TOMORROW PEOPLE (Roger Price)

1. *The visitor.* [with Julian R. Gregory]. (1973)
2. *Three in three.* (1974)
3. *Four into three.* (1975)
4. *One law.* (1976)
5. *The lost gods, with Hitler's last secret and The Thargon menace.* (1979)

TOM'S AMAZING MACHINE (Gordon Snell)

1. *Tom's amazing machine.* (1988)
2. *Tom's amazing machine zaps back.* (1989)
3. *Tom's amazing machine takes a trip.* (1990)

TORCH (Roger MacBride Allen)

1. *The torch of honor.* (1985)
2. *Rogue powers.* (1986)

TORG: THE POSSIBILITY WARS (various authors)

1. *Storm knights.* [Bill Slavicsek & C. J. Tramontana]. (1990)
2. *The dark realm.* [Douglas Kaufman]. (1990)
3. *The nightmare dream.* [Jonatha Ariadne Caspian]. (1991)

TORIN (Cherry Wilder)

1. *The luck of Brin's Five.* (1977)
2. *The nearest fire.* (1980)
3. *The tapestry warriors.* (1983)

TORNOR (Elizabeth A. Lynn)

1. *Watchtower.* (1979)
2. *The dancers of Arun.* (1979)

TRACKER (Ron Stillman)

1. *Tracker.* (1990)
2. *Green lightning.* (1990)
3. *Blood money.* (1991)
4. *Black phantom.* (1991)
5. *Firekill.* (1991)
6. *Death hunt.* (1991)

TRANSFORMERS (various authors)

Dinobot war. [Dave Morris]. (1985)
Peril from the stars. [Dave Morris]. (1985)
Highway clash. [Dave Morris]. (1986)
Island of fear. [Dave Morris]. (1986)

TRANSFORMERS, JUNIOR—SEE: FIND YOUR FATE JUNIOR TRANSFORMERS

TRAUMA 2020 (Peter Beere)

1. *Urban prey.* (1984)
2. *The crucifixion squad.* (1984)
3. *Silent slaughter.* (1985)

THE TRAVELER (Ed Naha and John Shirley as D. B. DRUMM)

1. *First, you fight.* [Ed Naha]. (1984)
2. *Kingdom come.* [John Shirley]. (1984)
3. *The stalkers.* [John Shirley]. (1984)
4. *To kill a shadow.* [John Shirley]. (1984)
5. *Road war.* [John Shirley]. (1985)
6. *Border war.* [John Shirley]. (1985)
7. *The road ghost.* [Ed Naha]. (1985)
8. *Terminal road.* [John Shirley]. (1986)
9. *The stalking time.* [Ed Naha]. (1986)
10. *Hell on Earth.* [Ed Naha]. (1986)
11. *The children's crusade.* [Ed Naha]. (1987)
12. *The prey.* [Ed Naha]. (1987)
13. *Ghost dancers.* [Ed Naha]. (1987)

TREDANA TRILOGY (Joyce Ballou Gregorian)

1. *The broken citadel.* (1975)
2. *Castledown.* (1977)

3.   *The great wheel.* (1987)

TREES (Larry Niven)

1.   *The integral trees.* (1984)
2.   *The smoke ring.* (1987)

TRIAD (Richard Rohmer)

1.   *Periscope red.* (1980)
2.   *Triad.* (1982)

TRIANGULUM TRILOGY (Redmond Wallis)

1.   *Starbloom.* (1989)
2.   *The mills of space.* (1989)

TRICKSTER (Zohra Greenhalgh)

1.   *Contrarywise.* (1989)
2.   *Trickster's touch.* (1989)

TRIGON DISUNITY (Michael P. Kube-McDowell)

1.   *Emprise.* (1985)
2.   *Enigma.* (1986)
3.   *Empery.* (1987)

TRIO: REBELS IN THE NEW WORLD (R. A. Montgomery)

1.   *Traitors from within.* (1990)
2.   *Crossing enemy lines.* (1990)
3.   *Almost lost.* (1990)
4.   *The hidden evil.* (1990)
5.   *Escape from China.* (1990)
6.   *Deadly encounter.* (1990)

TROS OF SAMOTHRACE (Talbot Mundy)

Tros of Samothrace. (1934)

Broken into three parts for reprinting:

1.   *Lud of Lunden.* (1976)
2.   *Avenging Liafail.* (1976)
3.   *The Praetor's dungeon.* (1976)

TRUE GAME (Sheri S. Tepper)

1.   *King's Blood Four.* (1983)
2.   *Necromancer Nine.* (1983)
3.   *Wizard's Eleven.* (1984)
1-3. *The true game.* (1985)

JINIAN SERIES

1.   *Jinian Footseer.* (1985)
2.   *Dervish daughter.* (1986)
3.   *Jinian Star-eye.* (1986)

MAVIN MANYSHAPED

1.   *The song of Mavin Manyshaped.* (1985)
2.   *The flight of Mavin Manyshaped.* (1985)
3.   *The search of Mavin Manyshaped.* (1985)

TURBO COWBOYS (various authors as TONY PHILLIPS)

1.   *Jump start.* [Chet Cunningham]. (1988)
2.   *Spin out.* [Chet Cunningham]. (1989)

3.   *Spark fire.* [Chet Cunningham]. (1989)
4.   *Full throttle.* [Chet Cunningham]. (1989)
5.   *Super charge.* [Paul Bagdon]. (1989)
6.   *Rat trap.* [John Read]. (1989)
7.   *Night riders.* [Paul Bagdon]. (1989)
8.   *Speed shift.* [Paul Bagdon]. (1989)
9.   *Duster trouble.* [John Read]. (1989)
10. *City of glass.* [Paul Bagdon]. (1989)

TURQUOISE DRAGON (David Rains Wallace)

1.   *The turquoise dragon.* (1985)
2.   *The vermilion parrot.* (1991)

TWILIGHT SERIES (various authors)

1.   *Deadly sleep.* [Dale Cowan]. (1982)
2.   *The power.* [Betsy Haynes]. (1982)
3.   *The initiation.* [Robert Brunn]. (1982)
4.   *Fatal attraction.* [Imogen Howe]. (1982)
5.   *Blink of the mind.* [Dorothy Brenner Francis]. (1982)
6.   *Voices in the dark.* [James Haynes]. (1982)
7.   *Play to live.* [Charles Veley]. (1982)
8.   *Blood red roses.* [Sarah Armstrong]. (1982)
9.   *Demon tree.* [Colin Daniel]. (1983)
10. *The avenging spirit.* [E. Stevenson]. (1983)
11. *Nightmare lake.* [Carl Laymon]. (1983)
12. *The twisted room.* [Janeet Patton Smith]. (1983)
13. *Vicious circle.* [Imogen Howe]. (1983)
14. *Footprints of the dead.* [Jay Callahan]. (1983)
15. *Spirits & spells.* [Bruce Coville]. (1983)
16. *Drawing the dead.* [Neil Selden]. (1983)
17. *Storm child.* [Susan Netter]. (1983)
18. *Watery grave.* [Joseph Trainor]. (1983)
19. *Dance of death.* [Lou Kassem]. (1984)
20. *Family crypt.* [Joseph Trainor]. (1984)
21. *Evil on the bayou.* [Richie Tankersley Cusick]. (1984)
22. *The haunted dollhouse.* [Susan Blake]. (1984)
23. *The warning.* [Amanda Byron]. (1985)
24. *Amulet of doom.* [Bruce Coville]. (1985)
25. *A deadly rhyme.* [Gloria Gonzalez]. (1986)
26. *Scavenger's hunt.* [Arthur Bicknell]. (1987)

TWILIGHT OF THE GODS (Dennis Schmidt)

1.   *The first name.* (1985)
2.   *Groa's other eye.* (1986)
3.   *Three trumps sounding.* (1988)

TWILIGHT ZONE (Rod Serling)

1.   *Stories from The twilight zone.* (1960)
2.   *More stories from The twilight zone.* (1961)
3.   *New stories from The twilight zone.* (1962)
1-3. *Stories from The Twilight zone.* (1986)
     From The twilight zone. (1970?)

TWIN PLANETS (Richard A. Lupoff)

1.   *Circumpolar!* (1984)
2.   *Countersolar!* (1987)

TWISTAPLOT (various authors)

1.   *The time raider.* [R. L. Stine]. (1982)
2.   *The train of terror.* [Louise Munro Foley]. (1982)
3.   *The formula for trouble.* [Megan Stine & H. William Stine]. (1983)

4. *Golden sword of Dragonwalk*. [R. L. Stine]. (1983)
5. *The sinister studios of KESP-TV*. [Louise Munro Foley]. (1983)
6. *Crash landing!* [Arthur Roth]. (1983)
7. *The video avenger*. [Douglas Colligan]. (1983)
8. *Race into the past*. [Megan Stine & H. William Stine]. (1983)
9. *Horrors of the haunted museum*. [R. L. Stine]. (1983)
10. *Mission of the secret spy squad*. [Ruth Glick & Eileen Buckholtz]. (1984)
11. *Camp-out on Danger Mountain*. [B. B. Hiller]. (1984)
12. *Journey to Vernico 5*. [Megan Stine & H. William Stine]. (1984)
13. *Midnight at monster mansion*. [Steven Otfinoski]. (1984)
14. *Instant millionaire*. [R. L. Stine]. (1984)
15. *Spellcaster*. [Katy Brown]. (1984)
16. *Secrets of the lost island*. [Kathryn Lance as LYNN BEACH]. (1984)
17. *Ghost riders of Goldspur*. [Scott Siegel & Barbara Siegel]. (1985)
18. *Calling outer space*. [Jean Nugent]. (1985)

UFO CONSPIRACY (David Bischoff)

1. *Abduction*. (1990)
2. *Deception*. (1991)
3. *Revelation*. (1991)

ULTIMATUM (Richard Rohmer)

1. *Ultimatum*. (1973)
2. *Exxoneration*. (1974)

UNBALANCED EARTH TRILOGY (Mark Smith & Julia Smith as JONATHAN WYLIE)

1. *Dreams of stone*. (1989)
2. *The lightless kingdom*. (1989)
3. *The age of chaos*. (1989)

UNCLE ALBERT (Russell Stannard)

1. *The time and space of Uncle Albert*. (1989)
2. *Black holes and Uncle Albert*. (1991)

UNICORN & DRAGON (Lynn Abbey)

1. *Unicorn & dragon*. (1987)
2. *Conquest*. (1988)
2A. *The green man*. (1989)

UNICORN QUEST (John Lee)

1. *The unicorn quest*. (1986)
2. *The unicorn dilemma*. (1988)
3. *The unicorn solution*. (1991)

U.S.S.A. (various authors)

1. *U.S.S.A., book 1*. [Tom De Haven]. (1987)
2. *U.S.S.A., book 2*. [S. N. Lewitt]. (1987)
3. *U.S.S.A., book 3*. [S. C. Sykes]. (1987)
4. *U.S.S.A., book 4*. [S. N. Lewitt]. (1987)

Unrelated Titles

U.S.S.A.: a novel. [James Frey]. (1987)

U.S.S.A. [David Madsen]. (1989)

V (various authors)

1. *V.* [A. C. Crispin]. (1984)
2. *East Coast crisis*. [A. C. Crispin & Howard Weinstein]. (1984)
3. *The pursuit of Diana*. [Allen Wold]. (1984)
4. *The Chicago conversion*. [Geo. W. Proctor]. (1985)
5. *The Florida project*. [Tim Sullivan]. (1985)
6. *Prisoners and pawns*. [Howard Weinstein]. (1985)
7. *The alien swordmaster*. [Somtow Sucharitkul]. (1985)
8. *The crivit experiment*. [Allen Wold]. (1985)
9. *The New England resistance*. [Tim Sullivan]. (1985)
10. *Death tide*. [A. C. Crispin & Deborah A. Marshall]. (1985)
11. *The Texas run*. [Geo. W. Proctor]. (1985)

Unnumbered Novels

To conquer the throne. [Tim Sullivan]. (1987)
Path to conquest. [Howard Weinstein]. (1987)
Symphony of terror. [Somtow Sucharitkul]. (1988)
The Oregon invasion. [Jayne Tannehill]. (1988)
Below the threshold. [Allen Wold]. (1988)

Associated Titles

The arrival. [James Van Hise]. (1986)
They're back. [Edward Gross]. (1986)
Conclusion. [Edward Gross]. (1986)
A new beginning. [Edward Gross]. (1986)

VAGABONDS (Colin Dann)

1. *King of the vagabonds*. (1987)
2. *The city vagabonds*. (1991)

VAMPIRE DIARIES (L. J. Smith)

1. *The awakening*. (1991)
2. *The struggle*. (1991)
3. *The fury*. (1991)

VAMPIRE FILES (P. N. Elrod)

1. *Bloodlist*. (1990)
2. *Lifeblood*. (1990)
3. *Bloodcircle*. (1990)
4. *Art in the blood*. (1991)
5. *Fire in the blood*. (1991)

VAMPIRELLA (Ron Goulart)

1. *Bloodstalk*. (1975)
2. *On alien wings*. (1975)
3. *Deadwalk*. (1976)
4. *Blood wedding*. (1976)
5. *Deathgame*. (1976)
6. *Snakegod*. (1976)

VAMPIRES (Jeffrey N. McMahan)

1. *Somewhere in the night*. (1989)
2. *Vampires anonymous*. (1991)

THE VANG (Christopher Rowley)

1. *Starhammer*. (1986)

2. *The military form.* (1988)
3. *The battlemaster.* (1990)

VARAYAN MEMOIR (Rick Shelley)

1. *Son of the hero.* (1990)
2. *The hero of Varay.* (1991)

VCR TIME MACHINE (Susan Pfeffer)

1. *Rewind to yesterday.* (1988)
2. *Future forward.* (1989)

VECTOR (Rob Swigart)

1. *Vector.* (1986)
2. *Toxin.* (1989)

VEIL KENDRY—SEE: MONGO

VENDETTA (M. S. Murdock)

1. *Vendetta.* (1987)
2. *Dynteryx.* (1988)

VENTURER TWELVE (John Kippax)

1. *Thunder of stars.* (1968)
2. *Seed of stars.* (1972)
3. *The neutral stars.* (1973)
4. *Where no stars guide.* (1975)

VENUS TRILOGY (Pamela Sargent)

1. *Venus of dreams.* (1986)
2. *Venus of shadows.* (1988)

VESPER HOLLY (Lloyd Alexander)

1. *The Illyrian adventure.* (1986)
2. *The El Dorado adventure.* (1987)
3. *The Drackenberg adventure.* (1988)
4. *The Jedera adventure.* (1989)
5. *The Philadelphia adventure.* (1990)

VIAGENS—SEE: KRISHNA

VICTIM (Robert Sheckley)

1. *The 10th victim.* (1965)
2. *Victim prime.* (1987)
3. *Hunter/victim.* (1988)

VIDAR (Michael Jan Friedman)

1. *The hammer and the horn.* (1985)
2. *The seekers and the sword.* (1985)
3. *The fortress and the fire.* (1988)

VIDESSOS CYCLE (Harry Turtledove)

1. *The misplaced legion.* (1987)
2. *An Emperor for the legion.* (1987)
3. *The Legion of Videssos.* (1987)
4. *Swords of the legion.* (1987)
5. *A world of difference.* (1990)

TALE OF KRISPOS

1. *Krispos rising.* (1991)

2. *Krispos of Videssos.* (1991)

VIRGIL MAGUS (Avram Davidson)

1. *The Phoenix and the mirror.* (1969)
2. *Virgil in Averno.* (1987)

VIRICONIUM (M. John Harrison)

1. *The pastel city.* (1971)
2. *A storm of wings.* (1980)
3. *In Viriconium.* (1982)
3A. *The floating gods.* (1983)
4. *Viriconium nights.* (1984/1985)
3-4. *Viriconium.* (1988)

VISION (Judith Merkle Riley)

1. *A vision of light.* (1989)
2. *In pursuit of the green lion.* (1990)

VISION OF BEASTS (Jack Lovejoy)

1. *Creation descending.* (1984)
2. *The second kingdom.* (1984)
3. *The Brotherhood of Diablo.* (1985)

VLAD THE DRAC (Ann Jungman)

1. *Vlad the Drac.* (1982)
2. *Vlad the Drac returns.* (1984)
3. *Vlad the Drac superstar.* (1985)
4. *Vlad the Drac vampire.* (1988)
5. *Vlad the Drac down under.* (1989)

VORKOSIGAN (Lois McMaster Bujold)

1. *Borders of infinity.* (1989)
2. *The Vor game.* (1990)
3. *Brothers in arms.* (1989)
4. *Barrayar.* (1991)
1-2. *Vorkosigan's game.* (1990)

VOWS AND HONOR (Mercedes Lackey)

1. *The oathbound.* (1988)
2. *Oathbreakers.* (1989)

VOYAGERS (Ben Bova)

1. *Voyagers.* (1981)
2. *The alien within.* (1986)
3. *Star brothers.* (1990)

WALK IN THE DARK (Spedding)

1. *The road and the hills.* (1986)
2. *A cloud over water.* (1988)
3. *Streets of the city.* (1988)

WALK TO THE END OF THE WORLD (Suzy McKee Charnas)

1. *Walk to the end of the world.* (1974)
2. *Motherlines.* (1978)

WANDERING JEW (various authors)

The wandering Jew. [Eugène Sue]. (1844)

The Wandering Jew: an account of his last adventures, with an appendix of selected memoirs. [S. D. P. Clough]. (1983)
The wandering Jew. [Stefan Heym]. (1984)
Tales of the wandering Jew. [Brian M. Stableford]. (1991)

WANDOR (Roland Green)

1. *Wandor's ride.* (1973)
2. *Wandor's journey.* (1975)
3. *Wandor's voyage.* (1979)
4. *Wandor's flight.* (1981)

WAR AGAINST THE CHTORR (David Gerrold)

1. *A matter for men.* (1983/1989)
2. *A day for damnation.* (1984/1989)
3. *A rage for revenge.* (1989)
1-2. *The war against the Chtorr: Invasion.* (1984)

WAR OF POWERS (Robert E. Vardeman & Victor Milán)

1. *The Sundered Realm.* (1980)
2. *The city in the glacier.* (1980)
3. *The Destiny Stone.* (1980)
4. *The Fallen Ones.* (1982)
5. *In the shadow of Omizantrim.* (1982)
6. *Demon of the Dark Ones.* (1982)
1-3. *The war of powers.* (1984)
4-6. *Istu awakened.* (1985)

WAR OF THE DRAGONS (Dave Smeds)

1. *The sorcery within.* (1985)
2. *The schemes of dragons.* (1989)

WAR OF THE GODS ON EARTH (Andrew J. Offutt)

1. *The iron lords.* (1979)
2. *Shadows out of Hell.* (1980)
3. *The Lady of the Snowmist.* (1983)

WAR OF THE NINJA MASTER—SEE: NINJA MASTER

WAR OF THE WIZARDS (Andrew J. Offutt & Richard K. Lyon)

1. *Demon in the mirror.* (1978)
2. *The Eyes of Sarsis.* (1980)
3. *Web of the spider.* (1981)

WAR OF THE WORLDS SEQUELS (H. G. Wells and others)

The war of the worlds. (1898)
Sherlock Holmes's war of the worlds. (1975)

WAR SURPLUS (Lawrence Watt-Evans)

1. *The Cyborg and the sorcerers.* (1982)
2. *The wizard and the war machine.* (1987)

WAR WORLD (Jerry Pournelle)

1. *The burning eye.* [with John F. Carr & Roland Green]. (1988)
2. *Death's head rebellion.* (1990)
3. *Sauron dominion.* [with John F. Carr]. (1991)

WAR YEARS (Bill Fawcett)

1. *The far stars war.* (1990)
2. *The siege of Arista.* (1991)
3. *The Jupiter war.* (1991)

WARBOTS (G. Harry Stine)

1. *Warbots.* (1988)
2. *Operation Steel Band.* (1988)
3. *The Bastaard rebellion.* (1988)
4. *Sierra Madre.* (1988)
5. *Operation High Dragon.* (1989)
6. *The lost battalion.* (1989)
7. *Operation iron fist.* (1989)
8. *Force of arms.* (1990)
9. *Blood siege.* (1990)
10. *Guts and glory.* (1991)

WARCHILD (Richard Bowes)

1. *Warchild.* (1986)
2. *Goblin market.* (1988)

WARHAMMER (various authors)

Drachenfels. [Kim Newman as JACK YEOVIL]. (1989)
Ignorant armies. [David Pringle]. (1989)
Wolf riders. [David Pringle]. (1989)
Red thirst. [David Pringle]. (1990)
Beasts in velvet. [Kim Newman as Jack Yeovil]. (1991)

MINSTREL ORFEO (Brian Stableford as BRIAN CRAIG)

1. *Zaragoz.* (1989)
2. *Plague demon.* (1990)
3. *Storm warriors.* (1991)

KONRAD TRILOGY (David S. Garnett as DAVID FERRING)

1. *Konrad.* (1990)
2. *Shadowbreed.* (1991)
3. *Warblade.* [not yet published]

WARHAMMER 40,000 (David Pringle & Neal Jones)

Deathwing. [David Pringle & Neal Jones]. (1990)
Inquisitor. INQUISITION WAR #1. [Ian Watson]. (1990)

WARLORD (various authors as JASON FROST)

1. *The Warlord.* [Raymond Obstfeld]. (1983)
2. *The cutthroat.* [Raymond Obstfeld]. (1984)
3. *Badland.* [Raymond Obstfeld]. (1984)
4. *Prisonland.* [Raymond Obstfeld]. (1985)
5. *Terminal island.* [Raymond Obstfeld]. (1985)
6. *Killer's keep.* [Rich Rainey]. (1987)

THE WARP (Neil Oram)

1. *The storm's howling through Tiflis.* (1980)
2. *Lemmings on the edge.* (1981)
3. *The balustrade paradox.* (1982)

WARRIOR OF VENGEANCE (Ron Renauld as ROSS ANTON COE)

1. *Sorcerer's blood.* (1982)

2.   *Trails of peril.* (1982)

WARS OF THE WELL—SEE: WELL WORLD

WARS OF VIS (Tanith Lee)

1.   *The Storm Lord.* (1976)
2.   *Anackire.* (1983)
3.   *The white serpent.* (1988)
1-2. *The wars of Vis.* (1984)

WASTEWORLD (James Barton)

1.   *Aftermath.* (1983)
2.   *Resurrection.* (1983)
3.   *Angels.* (1984)
4.   *My way.* (1984)

WATCHERS (Stuart Gordon)

1.   *Achon!* (1987)
2.   *The hidden world.* (1988)
3.   *The mask.* (1990)

WATCHERS OF SPACE (Nancy Etchemendy)

1.   *The watchers of space.* (1980)
2.   *The crystal city.* (1985)

WATCHMAN CHRONICLES (D. G. Finlay)

1.   *Watchman.* (1984)
2.   *The grey regard.* (1985)
3.   *Deadly relations.* (1986)
4.   *Graven image.* (1987)
1-4. *The killing glance.* (1989)

WAY OF THE TIGER (Mark Smith & Jamie Thomson)

1.   *Avenger!* (1985)
2.   *Assassin!* (1985)
3.   *Usurper!* (1985)
4.   *Overlord!* (1986)
5.   *Warbringer!* (1986)
6.   *Inferno!* (1987)

WEAPONS OF CHAOS (Robert E. Vardeman)

1.   *Echoes of chaos.* (1986)
2.   *Equations of chaos.* (1987)
3.   *Colors of chaos.* (1988)
1-3. *Weapons of chaos.* (1989)

WEETZIE BAT (Francesca Lia Block)

1.   *Weetzie Bat.* (1989)
2.   *Witch baby.* (1991)

WEIRD HEROES (various authors)

1.   *Weird heroes.* [Byron Preiss]. (1975)
2.   *Weird heroes, volume 2.* [Byron Preiss]. (1975)
3.   *Quest of the Gypsy: a novel.* [Ron Goulart]. (1976)
4.   *Nightshade.* [Tappan King & Beth Meacham]. (1976)
5.   *Phoenix.* [Ted White & Marv Wolfman]. (1977)
6.   *Weird heroes, volume six.* [Byron Preiss]. (1977)
7.   *Eye of the vulture.* [Ron Goulart]. (1977)
8.   *Weird heroes, volume eight.* [Byron Preiss]. (1977)

WEIRD MENACE CLASSICS (various authors)

1.   *The corpse factory.* [Robert Weinberg]. (1977)
2.   *Satan's roadhouse.* [Robert Weinberg]. (1977)
3.   *The chair where terror sat.* [Robert Weinberg]. (1977)
4.   *Devils in the dark.* [Robert Weinberg]. (1979)
5.   *Slaves of the blood wolves.* [Robert Weinberg]. (1979)
6.   *The dance of the skeletons.* [Robert Weinberg]. (1980)

WELL WORLD (NATHAN BRAZIL SERIES) (Jack L. Chalker)

1.   *Midnight at the Well of Souls.* (1977)
2.   *Exiles of the Well of Souls.* (1978)
3.   *Quest for the Well of Souls.* (1978)
4.   *The return of Nathan Brazil.* (1980)
5.   *Twilight at the Well of Souls.* (1980)

WELLS OF YTHAN (Marc Alexander)

1.   *Ancient dreams.* (1988)
2.   *Magic casements.* (1989)
3.   *Shadow realm.* (1991)

WEREWOLF (Guy N. Smith)

1.   *Werewolf by moonlight.* (1974)
2.   *Return of the werewolf.* (1977)
3.   *The son of the werewolf.* (1978)

WEREWOLF'S TALE (Richard Jaccoma)

1.   *The werewolf's tale.* (1988)
2.   *The werewolf's revenge.* (1991)

WEREWOLVES (Brian M. Stableford)

1.   *The werewolves of London.* (1989)
2.   *The angel of pain.* (1991)

WESTMARK (Lloyd Alexander)

1.   *Westmark.* (1981)
2.   *The Kestrel.* (1982)
3.   *The beggar queen.* (1984)

WESTRIA (Diana L. Paxson)

1.   *Lady of light.* (1982)
2.   *Lady of darkness.* (1983)
3.   *Silverhair the wanderer.* (1986)
4.   *The earthstone.* (1987)
5.   *The sea star.* (1988)
6.   *The wind crystal.* (1990)
1-2. *Lady of light, lady of darkness.* (1990)
1-2. *The mistress of the jewels.* (1991)

WHAT MIGHT HAVE BEEN? (Martin H. Greenberg & Gregory Benford)

1.   *Alternate empires.* (1989)
2.   *Alternate heroes.* (1990)
3.   *Alternate wars.* (1991)

WHEEL OF TIME (Robert Jordan)

1.   *The eye of the world.* (1990)

2. *The great hunt.* (1990)
3. *The dragon reborn.* (1991)

WHICH WAY BOOKS (various authors)

1. *The castle of no return.* [R. G. Austin]. (1982)
2. *Vampires, spies, and alien beings.* [R. G. Austin]. (1982)
3. *The spell of the black raven.* [R. G. Austin]. (1982)
4. *Famous and rich.* [R. G. Austin]. (1982)
5. *Lost in a strange land.* [R. G. Austin]. (1982)
6. *Sugarcane Island.* [Edward Packard].(1982)
7. *Curse of the sunken treasure.* [R. G. Austin]. (1982)
8. *Cosmic encounters.* [R. G. Austin]. (1982)
9. *Creatures of the dark.* [R. G. Austin]. (1982)
10. *Invasion of the black slime, and other tales of horror.* [R. G. Austin]. (1983)
11. *Space raiders and the planet of doom.* [Stephen Mooser]. (1983)
12. *Trapped in the black box.* [R. G. Austin]. (1983)
13. *Starship warrior.* [Stephen Mooser]. (1984)
14. *Poltergeists, ghosts, and psychic encounters.* [R. G. Austin]. (1984)
15. *Star Trek: Voyage to adventure.* [Michael J. Dodge]. (1984)
16. *The shadow stealers.* [R. G. Austin]. (1984)
17. *Invasion of the mutants.* [Stephen Mooser]. (1985)
18. *Islands of terror.* [R. G. Austin]. (1985)
19. *Nightmare planet.* [Stephen Mooser]. (1985)
20. *Mind bandits.* [Stephen Mooser]. (1985)
21. *Ten-ton monster.* [R. G. Austin]. (1985)
22. *The champ of TV wrestling.* [Barbara Siegel & Scott Siegel]. (1986)
23. *Monster express.* [Stephen Mooser]. (1986)
24. *Star Trek: Phaser fight.* [Barbara Siegel & Scott Siegel]. (1986)

WHICH WAY—SUPER POWERS BOOKS

1. *Superman: The man of steel.* [Andrew Helfer]. (1983)
2. *Supergirl: The girl of steel.* [Andrew Helfer]. (1984)
3. *Justice League of America.* [Robert Loren Fleming]. (1984)
4. *Batman: The doomsday prophecy.* [Richard Wenk]. (1986)

WHITE CROW (Mary Gentle)

1. *Rats and gargoyles.* (1990)
2. *The architecture of desire.* (1991)

WHITE WOLF (Trish Reinius)

1. *The Planet of Tears.* (1979)
2. *Power of the white wolf.* (1985)

WHITFIELD (William W. Johnstone)

1. *The devil's kiss.* (1980)
2. *The devil's heart.* (1983)
3. *The devil's touch.* (1984)
4. *The devil's cat.* (1987)

WILD CARD RUN (Sara Stamey)

1. *Wild card run.* (1987)
2. *Win, lose, draw.* (1988)
3. *Double blind.* (1990)

WILD CARDS (George R. R. Martin)

1. *Wild cards.* (1986)
2. *Aces high.* (1987)
3. *Jokers wild.* (1987)
4. *Aces abroad.* (1988)
5. *Down & dirty.* (1988)
6. *Ace in the hole.* [with Melinda M. Snodgrass]. (1990)
7. *Dead man's hand.* [with John J. Miller & Melinda M. Snodgrass]. (1990)
8. *One-eyed jacks.* [with Melinda M. Snodgrass]. (1991)
9. *Jokertown shuffle.* [with Melinda M. Snodgrass]. (1991)

WILD TALENTS (Ron Goulart)

1. *A talent for the invisible.* (1973)
2. *Hello, Lemuria, hello.* (1979)

WILDERNESS OF FOUR—SEE: CIRCLE OF LIGHT

WILKES THE WIZARD (Jackie Webb)

1. *Wilkes the wizard.* (1985)
2. *Wilkes the wizard and the S.P.A.M.* (1986)

WILLOW WOOD SPRINGS (Terry Ellis)

1. *Legend of Willow Springs.* (1989)
2. *Explorers of Willow Springs.* (1989)
3. *Invasion of Willow Springs.* (1989)

WIN BEAR (L. Neil Smith)

1. *The Probability Broach.* (1980)
2. *The Venus belt.* (1981)
3. *The Nagasaki vector.* (1983)

WIND DANCERS (R. M. Meluch)

1. *Wind dancers.* (1981)
2. *Wind child.* (1982)

WINDAMEIR CIRCLE—SEE: CIRCLE OF LIGHT

WINDHOVER TAPES (Warren Norwood)

1. *An image of voices.* (1982)
2. *Flexing the warp.* (1983)
3. *Fize of the Gabriel Ratchets.* (1983)
4. *Planet of flowers.* (1984)

WINDOW ON YESTERDAY (Joan Hohl)

1. *Window on yesterday.* (1988)
2. *Window on today.* (1989)
3. *Window on tomorrow.* (1989)

WINDROSE (Barbara Hambly)

1. *The silent tower.* (1986)
2. *The silicon mage.* (1988)
1-2. *Darkmage.* (1988)

WINDSINGERS (Megan Lindholm)

1. *Harpy's flight.* (1983)
2. *The Windsingers.* (1984)

3. *The Limbreth Gate.* (1984)
4. *Luck of the wheels.* (1989)
1-3. *The Windsingers.* (1986)

WINGED ASSASSIN (Catherine Cooke)

1. *The winged assassin.* (1987)
2. *Realm of the gods.* (1988)
3. *The crimson goddess.* (1989)

WINGMAN (Mack Maloney)

1. *Wingman.* (1987)
2. *The circle war.* (1987)
3. *The Lucifer crusade.* (1987)
4. *Thunder in the East.* (1988)
5. *The twisted cross.* (1989)
6. *The final storm.* (1989)
7. *Freedom express.* (1990)
8. *Skyfire.* (1990)
9. *Return from the inferno.* (1991)

WINTER (Pamela F. Service)

1. *Winter of magic's return.* (1985)
2. *Tomorrow's magic.* (1987)

WINTER KING'S WAR (Susan Dexter)

1. *The Ring of Allaire.* (1981)
2. *The Sword of Calandra.* (1985)
3. *The Mountains of Channadran.* (1986)

WINTER OF THE WORLD (Michael Scott Rohan)

1. *The anvil of ice.* (1986)
2. *The forge in the forest.* (1987)
3. *The hammer of the sun.* (1988)

WINTER WORLD (C. J. Mills)

1. *Winter world.* (1988)
2. *Egil's book.* (1991)
3. *Kit's book.* (1991)

WIRRUN—SEE: BOOK OF WIRRUM

WISE CHILD (Monica Furlong)

1. *Wise child.* (1987)
2. *A year and a day.* (1990)
2A. *Juniper.* (1991)

WITCH (Phyllis Reynolds Naylor)

1. *Witch's sister.* (1975)
2. *Witch water.* (1977)
3. *The witch herself.* (1978)
4. *The witch's eye.* (1990)
5. *Witch weed.* (1991)

WITCH FINDER (Brian Ball)

1. *The mark of the beast.* (1976)
2. *The evil at Monteine.* (1977)

WITCH MOUNTAIN (Alexander Key)

1. *Escape to Witch Mountain.* (1968)
2. *Return from Witch Mountain.* (1978)

WITCH WORLD SERIES (Andre Norton and others)

1. *Witch world.* ESTCARP #1. (1963)
2. *Web of the witch world.* ESTCARP #2. (1964)
3. *Three against the witch world.* ESTCARP #3. (1965)
4. *Year of the unicorn.* HIGH HALLACK #3. (1965)
5. *Warlock of the witch world.* ESTCARP #4. (1967)
6. *Sorceress of the witch world.* ESTCARP #5. (1968)
7. *The crystal gryphon.* HIGH HALLACK #1. (1972)
8. *Spell of the witch world.* HIGH HALLACK #2. (1972)
9. *The jargoon pard.* HIGH HALLACK #4. (1974)
10. *Trey of swords.* (1977)
11. *Zarsthor's bane.* (1978)
12. *Lore of the Witch World.* (1980)
13. *Gryphon in glory.* HIGH HALLACK #5. (1981)
14. *Horn Crown.* (1981)
15. *'Ware Hawk.* (1983)
16. *Were-Wrath.* (1984)
17. *Gryphon's eyrie.* HIGH HALLACK #6. [With A. C. Crispin]. (1984)
18. *Serpent's tooth.* (1987)
19. *The gate of the cat.* (1987)
20. *Four from Witch World.* (1989)
21. *The turning: Storms of victory.* [With P. M. Griffin]. (1991)

WITCHES (James Laurence as JAMES DARKE)

1. *The prisoner.* (1983)
2. *The trial.* (1983)
3. *The torture.* (1983)
4. *The escape.* (1984)
5. [title unknown].
6. [title unknown].
7. *The feud.* (1986)
8. *The plague.* (1986)

WITCHFINDER—SEE: WITCH FINDER

WIZARD (Simon Hawke)

1. *The wizard of 4th Street.* (1987)
2. *The wizard of Whitechapel.* (1988)
3. *The wizard of Sunset Strip.* (1989)
4. *The wizard of Rue Morgue.* (1990)
5. *The samurai wizard.* (1991)
6. *The wizard of Santa Fe.* (1991)
7. *The 9 lives of Catseye Gomez.* (1991)

WIZARD CRYSTAL (Tanya Huff)

1. *Child of the grove.* (1988)
2. *The last wizard.* (1989)

WIZARD WAR CHRONICLES—SEE: CHRONICLES OF AN AGE OF DARKNESS

WIZARD'S BANE (Rick Cook)

1. *Wizard's bane.* (1989)
2. *The wizardry compiled.* (1990)
3. *The wizardry cursed.* (1991)

WIZARD'S WAR—SEE: WORLD OF ALFAR

WIZARDS, WARLOCKS & YOU (various authors)

1. *The forest of twisted dreams.* [R. L. Stine]. (1984)
2. *The siege of the dragonriders.* [R. L. Stine as ERIC AFFABEE]. (1984)
3. *Who kidnapped Princess Saralinda?* [H. William Stine & Megan Stine]. (1984)
4. *Ghost knights of Camelot.* [David Anthony Kraft]. (1984)
5. *The haunted castle of Ravencurse.* [Kathryn Lance as LYNN BEACH]. (1985)
6. *Revenge of the falcon knight.* [Scott Siegel]. (1985)
7. *Challenge of the Wolf Knight.* [R. L. Stine]. (1985)
8. *Conquest of the Time Master.* [Kathryn Lance as LYNN BEACH]. (1985)
9. *The Dragon Queen's revenge.* [R. L. Stine as ERIC AFFABEE]. (1986)
10. *Tournament for terror.* [H. William Stine & Megan Stine]. (1986)
11. *The imposter king.* [H. William Stine & Megan Stine]. (1986)
12. *The Scarlet Shield of Shalimar.* [Barbara Siegel & Scott Siegel]. (1986)
13. *Cavern of the Phantoms.* [R. L. Stine]. (1986)
14. *Carnival of demons.* [William Sno]. (1986)
15. *Invaders from Darkland.* [Kathryn Lance as LYNN BEACH]. (1986)
16. *Attack on the King.* [R. L. Stine as ERIC AFFABEE]. (1986)
17. *Conquest of the barbarians.* [H. William Stine & Megan Stine]. (1986)
18. *The warrior women of Weymouth.* [Barbara Siegel & Scott Siegel]. (1986)

WIZENBEAK (Alexis A. Gilliland)

1. *Wizenbeak.* (1986)
2. *The shadow Shaia.* (1990)

WOLFWALKER (Tara K. Harper)

1. *Wolfwalker.* (1990)
2. *Shadow leader.* (1991)

WOODWORLD (Garry Kilworth)

1. *The wizard of Woodworld.* (1987)
2. *The voyage of the Vigilance.* (1988)

WORKS OF M. P. SHIEL (various authors)

1. *The Empress of the Earth (1898); The purple cloud, (1901); "Some short stories": offprints of the original editions.* [M. P. Shiel]. (1979)
2-3. *The works of M. P. Shiel updated: a study in bibliography, including "About myself," by M. P. Shiel, 1865-1947 (new revised version), with a new appendix on Louis Tracy (1863-1928).* [A. Reynolds Morse]. (1980)

WORLD DIONYSUS

Margaret Priestley Titles

1. *The ring of fortune.* (1948)
2. *The three queens.* (1950)
3. *Tomay is loyal.* (1951)

Meriol Trevor Titles

1. *The forest and the kingdom.* (1949)
2. *Hunt the king, hide the fox.* (1950)
3. *The fires and the stars.* (1951)

WORLD IN AMBER (A. Orr)

1. *The world in Amber.* (1985)
2. *In the ice king's palace.* (1986)

WORLD OF ALFAR (Elizabeth Boyer)

1. *The sword and the satchel.* (1980)
2. *The elves and the otterskin.* (1981)
3. *The thrall and the dragon's heart.* (1982)
4. *The wizard and the warlord.* (1983)

WIZARD'S WAR

1. *The troll's grindstone.* (1986)
2. *The curse of Slagfid.* (1989)
3. *The dragon's carbuncle.* (1990)
4. *Lord of chaos.* (1991)

WORLD OF LONE WOLF—SEE: LONE WOLF

WORLD OF O (Maurice Gee)

1. *The halfmen of O.* (1982)
2. *The priests of Ferris.* (1984)
3. *Motherstone.* (1985)

WORLD OF TIERS (Philip José Farmer)

1. *The maker of universes.* (1965)
2. *The gates of creation.* (1966)
3. *A private cosmos.* (1968)
4. *Behind the walls of Terra.* (1970)
5. *The lavalite world.* (1977)
1-5. *The world of tiers.* (1981)
1-3. *World of tiers 1.* (1986)
4-5. *World of tiers 2.* (1986)

WORLDS (Joe Haldeman)

1. *Worlds.* (1981)
2. *Worlds apart.* (1983)

WORLDS OF CHTHON—SEE: CHTHON

WORLDS OF POWER (various authors)

1. *Worlds of power: Blaster master: a novel based on the best-selling game by Sunsoft.* [A. L. Singer]. (1990)
2. *Worlds of power: Metal gear: a novel based on the best-selling game by Ultragames.* [Alexander Frost]. (1990)
3. *Worlds of power: Ninja garden: a novel based on the best-selling game by Tecmo.* [A. L. Singer]. (1990)
4. *Worlds of power: Castlevania II: Simon's quest: a novel based on the best-selling game by Konami.* [Christopher Howell]. (1990)
5. *Worlds of power: Wizards & warriors: a novel based on the best-selling game by Acclaim.* [Ellen Miles]. (1990)
6. *Worlds of power: Bionic commando: a novel based on the best-selling game by CAPCOM.* [J. B. Stamper]. (1991)

7. *Worlds of power: Infiltrator: a novel based on the best-selling game by MINDSCAPE.* [A. L. Singer]. (1991)
8. *Worlds of power: Before Shadowgate: the exciting prequel to the game created by ICOM Simulations, Inc.* [Ellen Miles]. (1990)

Unnumbered Titles

Worlds of power: Mega man 2: a novel based on the best-selling game by CAPCOM. [Ellen Miles]. (1990)
Worlds of power: Bases loaded II, second season: a n based on the best-selling game by Jaleco. [A. L. Singer]. (1991)

WORTHING CHRONICLES (Orson Scott Card)

Capitol. (1979)
Hot sleep. (1979)
The Worthing chronicle. (1983)
The Worthing saga. (1990)

WW III (Ian Slater)

1. *WW III.* (1990)
2. *World in flames.* (1991)

WWIII: BEHIND THE LINES (James B. Adair & Gordon Rottman)

1. *Target Texas.* (1990)
2. *Target nuke.* (1990)
3. *Target Iran.* (1991)

WYND FAMILY (Stephen Krensky)

1. *The dragon circle.* (1977)
2. *The witching hour.* (1981)
3. *A ghostly business.* (1984)

WYNDCLIFFE (Louise Lawrence)

1. *The Wyndcliffe.* (1974)
2. *Sing and scatter daisies.* (1977)

XANTH (Piers Anthony)

1. *A spell for Chameleon.* (1977)
2. *The source of magic.* (1979)
3. *Castle Roogna.* (1979)
4. *Centaur Aisle.* (1982)
5. *Ogre, ogre.* (1982)
6. *Night mare.* (1983)
7. *Dragon on a pedestal.* (1983)
8. *Crewel lye: a caustic yarn.* (1985)
9. *Golem in the gears.* (1986)
10. *Vale of the vole.* (1987)
11. *Heaven cent.* (1988)
12. *The man from Mundania.* (1989)
13. *Isle of view.* (1990)
14. *Question quest.* (1991)
1-3. *The magic of Xanth.* (1981)

Associated Titles

Encyclopedia of Xanth: a Crossroads adventure in the world of Piers Anthony's Xanth. [Jody Lynn Nye]. (1987)

Ghost of a chance: a Crossroads adventure in the world of Piers Anthony's Xanth. [Jody Lynn Nye]. (1988)

XENOGENESIS (Octavia E. Butler)

1. *Dawn.* (1987)
2. *Adulthood rites.* (1988)
3. *Imago.* (1989)
1-3. *Xenogenesis.* (1989)

XORANDOR (Christine Brooke-Rose)

1. *Xorandor.* (1986)
2. *Verbivore.* (1990)

XUMA—SEE: BREAKOUT

YESTERDAY AND TOMORROW (T. Ernesto Bethancourt)

1. *Tune in yesterday.* (1978)
2. *The tomorrow connection.* (1984)

YOLANDA (Dominique Verseau)

1. *Yolanda, The girl from erosphere.* (1975)
2. *Slaves of space.* (1976)

YORK TRILOGY (Phyllis Reynolds Naylor)

1. *Shadows on the wall.* (1980)
2. *Faces in the water.* (1981)
3. *Footprints at the window.* (1981)

YOUNG ASTRONAUTS (various authors as RICK NORTH)

1. *The young astronauts.* (1990)
2. *Ready for blastoff!* (1990)
3. *Space blazers.* (1990)
4. *Destination Mars.* (1991)
5. *Space pioneers.* (1991)
6. *Citizens of Mars.* (1991)

YOUR AMAZING ADVENTURES (Richard Brightfield)

1. *The castle of doom.* (1984)
2. *Island of fear.* (1984)
3. *Terror under the Earth.* (1984)
4. *The dragonmaster.* (1985)
5. *Revenge of the dragonmaster.* (1985)
6. *Battle of the dragons.* (1986)

ZANDRA (William Rotsler)

1. *Zandra.* (1978)
2. *The far frontier.* (1980)
3. *The hidden worlds of Zandra.* (1983)

ZARATHUSTRA TRILOGY (John Brunner)

1. *Castaways' world.* (1963)
1A. *Polymath.* (1974)
2. *Secret agent of Terra.* (1962)
2A. *The avengers of Carrig.* (1969)
3. *The repairmen of Cyclops.* (1965)
1-3. *Victims of the nova.* (1989)

ZARKON, LORD OF THE UNKNOWN (Lin Carter)

1. *Zarkon, Lord of the Unknown, in The nemesis of evil, a case from the files of Omega.* (1975)
1A. *The nemesis of evil.* (1978)
2. *Zarkon, Lord of the Unknown, in Invisible death, a case from the files of Omega.* (1975)
2A. *Zarkon, Lord of the Unknown and his Omega Crew: Invisible death.* (1978)
3. *Zarkon, Lord of the Unknown, in The volcano ogre, a case from the files of Omega.* (1976)
3A. *Zarkon, Lord of the Unknown and his Omega Crew: The volcano ogre.* (1978)
4. *Zarkon, Lord of the Unknown, in The Earth-shaker, a case from the files of Omega.* (1982)
5. *Horror wears blue.* (1987)

ZIAX II (John Morressy)

1. *The humans of Ziax II.* (1974)
2. *The drought on Ziax II.* (1978)
1-2. *The drought on Ziax II; and, The humans of Ziax II.* (1978)

THE ZONE (James Rouch)

1. *Hard target.* (1980)
2. *Blind fire.* (1980)
3. *Hunter killer.* (1981)
4. *Sky strike.* (1981)
5. *Overkill.* (1982)
6. *Plague bomb.* (1986)
7. *Killing ground.* (1988)
8. *Civilian slaughter.* (1989)
9. *Body count.* (1990)

ZOOT MARLOWE (Mel Gilden)

1. *Surfing samurai robots.* (1988)
2. *Hawaiian U.F.O. aliens.* (1991)
3. *Tubular android superheroes.* (1991)

ZORACHUS (Mark E. Rogers)

1. *Zorachus.* (1986)
2. *The nightmare of God.* (1988)

ZORK (S. Eric Meretzky)

1. *The forces of Krill.* (1983)
2. *The Malifestro quest.* (1983)
3. *The cavern of doom.* (1983)
4. *Conquest at Quendor.* (1984)

ZORK TIE-INS (various authors)

The Zork chronicles. [George Alec Effinger]. (1990)
The lost city of Zork. [Robin W. Bailey]. (1991)

ADDENDUM

FORGOTTEN FANTASY LIBRARY (various authors)

1. *The story of the glittering plain.* [William Morris]. (1973)
2. *Eric Brighteyes.* [H. Rider Haggard]. (1974). [Cover title reads: *The saga of Eric Brighteyes*]
3. *The food of death: fifty-one tales.* [Lord Dunsany]. (1974)
4. *The haunted woman.* [David Lindsay]. (1975)
5. *Aladore.* [Henry Newbolt]. (1975)
6. *She and Allan.* [H. Rider Haggard]. (1975)
7. *Gerfalcon.* [Leslie Barringer]. (1976)
8. *Golden wings, and other stories.* [William Morris]. (1976)
9. *Joris of the Rock.* [Leslie Barringer]. (1976)
10. *Heart of the world.* [H. Rider Haggard]. (1976)
11. *The wonderful adventures of Phra the Phoenician.* [Edwin Lester Arnold]. (1977)
12. *Child Christopher and Goldilind the fair.* [William Morris]. (1977)
13. *Shy leopardess.* [Leslie Barringer]. (1977)
14. *Ayesha: the return of She.* [H. Rider Haggard]. (1977)
15. *The fates of the princes of Dyfed.* [Kenneth Morris]. (1978)
16. *A tale of the House of the Wolfings.* [William Morris]. (1978)
17. *Under the sunset.* [Bram Stoker]. (1978)
18. *Allan Quatermain.* [H. Rider Haggard]. (1978)
19. *The roots of the mountains.* [William Morris]. (1979)
20. *Nada the Lily.* [H. Rider Haggard]. (1979)
21. *Jaufry the knight and the fair Brunissende.* [Jaufré]. (1979)
22. *The spirit of Bambatse.* [H. Rider Haggard]. (1979)
23. *When the birds fly south.* [Stanton A. Coblentz]. (1980)
24. *Allan's wife, with hunter Quatermain's story, A tale of three lions, and Long odds.* [H. Rider Haggard]. (1980)

DOUBLES INDEX

TOR DOUBLES

0. *The other sky* / by Keith Laumer. 1985, 170 p.
    The house in November / by Keith Laumer.
    1985, 79 p.
    [Issued as a pattern volume.]

1. *A meeting with Medusa* / by Arthur C. Clarke.
    1988, 67 p.
    Green Mars / by Kim Stanley Robinson. 1988,
    113 p.

2. *Hardfought* / by Greg Bear. 1988, 97 p.
    Cascade Point / by Timothy Zahn. 1988, 82 p.

3. *Born with the dead* / by Robert Silverberg.
    1988, 96 p.
    The saliva tree / by Brian W. Aldiss. 1988, 87
    p.

4. *Tango Charlie and Foxtrot Romeo* / by John
    Varley. 1989, 101 p.
    The star pit / by Samuel R. Delany. 1989, 82 p.

5. *No truce with kings* / by Poul Anderson. 1989,
    104 p.
    Ship of shadows / by Fritz Leiber. 1989, 77 p.

6. *Enemy mine* / by Barry B. Longyear. 1989, 90
    p.
    Another orphan / by John Kessel. 1989, 60 p.

7. *Screwtop* / by Vonda N. McIntyre. 1989, 79 p.
    The girl who was plugged in / by James Tiptree
    Jr. 1989, 57 p.

8. *The nemesis from Terra* / by Leigh Brackett.
    1989, 107 p.
    Battle for the stars / by Edmond Hamilton.
    1989, 141 p.

9. *The ugly little boy* / by Isaac Asimov. 1989, 60
    p.
    The [widget], the [wadget], and boff / by
    Theodore Sturgeon. 1989, 123 p.

10. *Sailing to Byzantium* / by Robert Silverberg.
    1989, 99 p.
    Seven American nights / by Gene Wolfe. 1989,
    84 p.

11. *Houston, Houston, do you read?* / by James
    Tiptree, Jr. 1989, 92 p.
    Souls / by Joanna Russ. 1989, 84 p.

12. *He who shapes* / by Roger Zelazny. 1989, 107
    p.
    The infinity box / by Kate Wilhelm. 1989, 76 p.

13. *The blind geometer* / by Kim Stanley Robinson.
    1989, 141 p.

The new Atlantis / by Ursula K. Le Guin. 1989,
42 p.

14. *The Saturn game* / by Poul Anderson. 1989, 85
    p.
    Iceborn / by Gregory Benford & Paul A.
    Carter. 1989, 96 p.

15. *The last castle* / by Jack Vance. 1989, 101 p.
    Nightwings / by Robert Silverberg. 1989, 81 p.

16. *The color of Neanderthal eyes* / by James Tip-
    tree, Jr. 1990, 76 p.
    And strange at Ecbatan the trees / by Michael
    Bishop. 1990, 133 p.

17. *Divide and rule* / by L. Sprague de Camp.
    1990, 94 p.
    The sword of Rhiannon / by Leigh Brackett.
    1990, 136 p.

18. *In another country* / by Robert Silverberg.
    1990, [200] p.
    Vintage season / by C. L. Moore. 1990, [200]
    p.

19. *Ill met in Lankhmar* / by Fritz Leiber. 1990,
    104 p.
    The fair in Emain Macha / by Charles de Lint.
    1990, 104 p.

20. *The pugnacious peacemaker* / by Harry Turtle-
    dove. 1990, [185] p.
    The wheels of if / by L. Sprague de Camp.
    1990, [185] p.

21. *Home is the hangman* / by Roger Zelazny.
    1990, 96 p.
    *We, in some strange power's employ, move on a
    rigorous line* / by Samuel R. Delany. 1990,
    84 p.

22. *Thieves' carnival* / by Karen Haber. 1990, [187]
    p.
    The jewel of Bas / by Leigh Brackett. 1990,
    [187] p.

23. *Riding the torch* / by Norman Spinrad. 1990,
    114 p.
    Tin soldier / by Joan D. Vinge. 1990, 68 p.

24. *The graveyard heart* / by Roger Zelazny. 1990,
    [187] p.
    Elegy for angels and dogs / by Walter Jon
    Williams. 1990, [187] p.

25. *Fugue state* / by John M. Ford. 1990, 121 p.
    The death of Doctor Island / by Gene Wolfe.
    1990, 62 p.

26. *Press enter ▇* / by John Varley. 1990, 98 p.
    Hawksbill Station / by Robert Silverberg. 1990,
    86 p.

27. *Eye for eye* / by Orson Scott Card. 1990, [186]
    p.
    The tunesmith / by Lloyd Biggle Jr. 1990, [186]
    p.

28. *A short, sharp shock* / by Kim Stanley Robin-
    son. 1990, [216] p.
    The dragon masters / by Jack Vance. 1990,
    [216] p.

29. *Nanoware time* / by Ian Watson. 1990, [188] p.
    The persistence of vision / by John Varley.
    1990, [188] p.

30. *The longest voyage* / by Poul Anderson. 1990,
    [241] p.
    Slow lightning / by Steven Popkes. 1990, [241]
    p.

31. *Naked to the stars* / by Gordon R. Dickson.
    1990, [282] p.
    The alien way / by Gordon R. Dickson. 1990,
    [282] p.

32. *Run for the stars* / by Harlan Ellison. 1991,
    [184] p.
    Echoes of thunder / by Jack Dann & Jack C.
    Haldeman II. 1991, [184] p.

33. *Bwana* / by Mike Resnick. 1991, [179] p.
    Bully! / by Mike Resnick. 1991, [179] p.

34. *Rule golden* / by Damon Knight. 1991, [188] p.
    Double meaning / by Damon Knight. 1991,
    [188] p.

35. *Silent thunder* / by Dean Ing. 1991, [120] p.
    Universe / by Robert A. Heinlein. 1991, [120]
    p.

36. *Conjure wife* / by Fritz Leiber. 1991, [347] p.
    Our lady of darkness / by Fritz Leiber. 1991,
    [347] p.

OTHER DOUBLES

AXOLOTL PRESS

1. *The way down the hill* / by Tim Powers. 1986, vii+31 p.
   The pink of fading neon / by James P. Blaylock. 1986, vi+8 p.

2. *Trilobyte* / by Edward Bryant. 1987, iii+27 p.
   The shadow on the doorstep / by James P. Blaylock. 1987, iv+14 p.

3. *Two views of a cave painting; and, The idol's eye* / by James P. Blaylock. 1988, iv+16+22 p.
   Escape from Kathmandu / by Kim Stanley Robinson. 1988, 75 p.

BINARY STAR SERIES
(Dell Books)
Anonymously edited by James Frenkel

1. *Binary star no. 1: Destiny times three* / Fritz Leiber ; *Riding the torch* / Norman Spinrad. 1978, 251 p.

2. *Binary star no. 2: The twilight river* / Gordon Eklund ; *The tery* / F. Paul Wilson. 1979, 268 p.

3. *Binary star no. 3: Dr. Scofflaw* / Ron Goulart ; *Outerworld* / Isidore Haiblum. 1979, 303 p.

4. *Binary star no. 4: Legacy* / Joan D. Vinge ; *The Janus equation* / Steven G. Spruill. 1980, 287 p.

5. *Binary star no. 5: Nightflyers* / George R. R. Martin ; *True names* / Vernor Vinge. 1981, 239 p.

DRUMM BOOKLETS

23. *Adventures in the space trade* / by Richard Wilson. 1986, 20 p.
    A Richard Wilson checklist / by Chris Drumm. 1986, 16 p.

25. *J. T. McIntosh: memoir* / by Ian Covell. 1987, 32 (for both).
    J. T. McIntosh bibliography / by Ian Covell.

GRIMES DOUBLES (Ace Books)
By A. Bertram Chandler

1. *The road to the rim ; The Hard way up.* 1978, 340 p.

2. *The inheritors ; Gateway to never.* 1978, 377 p.

3. *The dark dimensions ; The Rim gods.* 1978, 406 p.

4. *Into the alternate universe ; Contraband from otherspace.* 1979, 309 p.

5. *The commodore at sea ; Spartan planet.* 1979, 374 p.

NESFA PRESS

Up to the sky in ships / by A. Bertram Chandler. 1982, iv+94 p.
In and out of quandry / by Lee Hoffman. 1982, iv+63 p.

Between two worlds / by Terry Carr. 1986, vi+68 p.
Messages found in an oxygen bottle / by Bob Shaw. 1986, iv+103 p.

SCHOLASTIC BOOK SERVICES

The drought on Ziax II / by John Morressy. 1978, 55 p.
The humans of Ziax II / by John Morressy. 1978, 49 p.

STARMONT HOUSE

Red twilight; World's end: two classic novels from Argosy / by Harl Vincent & Victor Rousseau. 1991, vi+123 p.

AWARDS INDEX

THE BRAM STOKER AWARDS
(Horror Writers of America)

1987 (1988)
Novel—(tie) *Misery*, by Stephen King; *Swan Song*, by Robert McCammon
First Novel—*The Manse*, by Lisa Cantrell
Novelette—(tie) "The Pear-Shaped Man," by George R. R. Martin; "The Boy Who Came Back from the Dead," by Alan Rodgers
Short Story—"The Deep End," by Robert McCammon
Collection—*The Essential Ellison*, by Harlan Ellison
Nonfiction—*Mary Shelley*, by Muriel Spark
Life Achievement—Fritz Leiber, Frank Belknap Long, and Clifford D. Simak

1988 (1989)
Novel—*The Silence of the Lambs*, by Thomas Harris
First Novel—*The Suiting*, by Kelley Wilde
Novelette—"Orange Is for Anguish, Blue for Insanity," by David Morrell
Short Story—"The Night They Missed the Horror Show," by Joe R. Lansdale
Collection—*Charles Beaumont: Selected Stories*, by Charles Beaumont, edited by Roger Anker
Life Achievement—Ray Bradbury; Ronald Chetwynd-Hayes

1989 (1990)
Novel—*Carrion Comfort*, by Dan Simmons
First Novel—*Sunglasses After Dark*, by Nancy Collins
Novella/Novelette—"On the Far Side of the Cadillac Desert with Dead Folks," by Joe R. Lansdale
Short Story—"Eat Me," by Robert R. McCammon
Collection—*Richard Matheson: Collected Stories*, by Richard Matheson
Nonfiction—(tie) *Harlan Ellison's Watching*, by Harlan Ellison; *Horror: 100 Best Books*, edited by Stephen Jones and Kim Newman

1990 (1991)
Novel—*Mine*, by Robert R. McCammon
First Novel—*The Revelation*, by Bentley Little
Novella/Novelette—"Stephen," by Elizabeth Massie
Short Story—"The Calling," by David B. Silva
Collection—*Four Past Midnight*, by Stephen King
Nonfiction—*Dark Dreamers: Conversations with the Masters of Horror*, by Stanley Wiater
Life Achievement—Hugh B. Cave; Richard Matheson

1991 (1992)
Novel—*Boy's Life*, by Robert R. McCammon
First Novel—(tie) *The Cipher*, by Kathe Koja; *Prodigal*, by Melanie Tem
Novelette—"The Beautiful Uncut Hair of Graves," by David Morrell
Short Story—"Lady Madonna," by Nancy Holder
Collection—*Prayers to Broken Stones*, by Dan Simmons
Non-Fiction—*Shadows in Eden*, by Stephen Jones

THE HUGO AWARDS

1952 (1953)
Number One Fan Personality—Forrest J Ackerman
Novel—*The Demolished Man*, by Alfred Bester
Professional Magazine—(tie) *Galaxy Science Fiction*,
  Horace L. Gold, ed.; *Astounding Science Fiction*,
  John W. Campbell, Jr., ed.
Cover Artist—(tie) Ed Emshwiller; Hannes Bok
New Author/Artist—Philip José Farmer
Interior Illustrator—Virgil Finlay
Excellence in Fact Articles—Willy Ley

1953 (1954)—no awards

1954 (1955)
Novel—*They'd Rather Be Right*, by Frank Riley and
  Mark Clifton
Novelette—"The Darfstellar," by Walter M. Miller, Jr.
Short Story—"Allamagoosa," by Eric Frank Russell
Professional Magazine—*Astounding Science Fiction*,
  John W. Campbell, Jr., ed.
Illustrator—Frank Kelly Freas
Amateur Publication—*Fantasy Times*, James V. Taurasi
  and Ray van Houten, eds.
Special Plaque—Sam Moskowitz for *The Immortal Storm*
Best Unpublished Story—"Sven," by Lou Tabakow

1955 (1956)
Novel—*Double Star*, by Robert A. Heinlein
Novelette—"Exploration Team," by Murray Leinster
Short Story—"The Star," by Arthur C. Clarke
Feature Writer—Willy Ley
Professional Magazine—*Astounding Science Fiction*,
  John W. Campbell, Jr., ed.
Illustrator—Frank Kelly Freas
New Author—Robert Silverberg
Amateur Publication—*Inside and Science Fiction Advertiser*, Ron Smith, ed.
Critic—Damon Knight

1956 (1957)
American Professional Magazine—*Astounding Science
  Fiction*, John W. Campbell, Jr., ed.
British Professional Magazine—*New Worlds*, Edward J.
  Carnell, ed.
Amateur Publication—*Science Fiction Times*, James V.
  Taurasi, Ray van Houten, and Frank Prieto, eds.

1957 (1958)
Novel—*The Big Time*, by Fritz Leiber
Short Story—"Or All the Seas With Oysters," by Avram
  Davidson
Professional Magazine—*The Magazine of Fantasy and
  Science Fiction*, Anthony Boucher, ed.
Illustrator—Frank Kelly Freas
Motion Picture—*The Incredible Shrinking Man*, Richard
  Matheson, screenwriter
Most Outstanding Actifan—Walter A. Willis

1958 (1959)
Novel—*A Case of Conscience*, by James Blish
Novelette—"The Big Front Yard," by Clifford D. Simak
Short Story—"The Hell-Bound Train," by Robert Bloch
Illustrator—Frank Kelly Freas
Professional Magazine—*The Magazine of Fantasy and
  Science Fiction*, Anthony Boucher and Robert P.
  Mills, eds.
Amateur Publication—*Fanac*, Terry Carr and Ron Ellik,
  eds.
New Author—No award; Brian W. Aldiss received a
  plaque as runner-up

1959 (1960)
Novel—*Starship Troopers*, by Robert A. Heinlein
Short Fiction—"Flowers for Algernon," by Daniel Keyes
Professional Magazine—*The Magazine of Fantasy and
  Science Fiction*, Robert P. Mills, ed.
Amateur Publication—*Cry of the Nameless*, F. M.
  Busby, ed.
Illustrator—Ed Emshwiller
Dramatic Presentation—*The Twilight Zone*, created [and
  mostly written] by Rod Serling
Special Award—Hugo Gernsback, as "The Father of
  Magazine Science Fiction"

1960 (1961)
Novel—*A Canticle for Leibowitz*, by Walter M. Miller,
  Jr.
Short Story—"The Longest Voyage," by Poul Anderson
Professional Magazine—*Analog Science Fiction/Science
  Fact*, John W. Campbell, Jr., ed.
Amateur Publication—*Who Killed Science Fiction?* Earl
  Kemp, ed.
Illustrator—Ed Emshwiller
Dramatic Presentation—*The Twilight Zone*, created by
  Rod Serling

1961 (1962)
Novel—*Stranger in a Strange Land*, by Robert A. Heinlein
Short Fiction—The "Hothouse" series, by Brian W.
  Aldiss
Professional Magazine—*Analog Science Fiction/Science
  Fact*, John W. Campbell, Jr., ed.
Amateur Magazine—*Warhoon*, Richard Bergeron, ed.
Professional Artist—Ed Emshwiller
Dramatic Presentation—*The Twilight Zone*, created by
  Rod Serling
Special Plaque—Cele Goldsmith, for editing *Amazing
  Stories* and *Fantastic Stories*
Special Plaque—Donald Tuck, for *The Handbook of Science Fiction*

1962 (1963)
Novel—*The Man in the High Castle*, by Philip K. Dick
Short Fiction—"The Dragon Masters," by Jack Vance
Dramatic Presentation—No award

Professional Magazine—*The Magazine of Fantasy and Science Fiction*, Robert P. Mills and Avram David-son, eds.
Amateur Magazine—*Xero*, Richard Lupoff, ed.
Professional Artist—Roy G. Krenkel
Special Plaque—P. Schuyler Miller, for "The Reference Library" column in *Analog Science Fiction/Science Fact*
Special Plaque—Isaac Asimov, for his distinguished contributions to the field of science fiction

1963 (1964)
Novel—*Way Station*, by Clifford D. Simak [the original winning magazine serialization title was *Here Gather the Stars*]
Short Fiction—"No Truce With Kings," by Poul Ander-son
Professional Magazine—*Analog Science Fiction/Science Fact*, John W. Campbell, Jr., ed.
Professional Artist—Ed Emshwiller
Publisher—Ace Books, Donald A.Wollheim, ed.
Amateur Publication—*Amra*, George Scithers, ed.

1964 (1965)
Novel—*The Wanderer*, by Fritz Leiber
Short Fiction—"Soldier, Ask Not," by Gordon R. Dick-son
Professional Magazine—*Analog Science Fiction/Science Fact*, John W. Campbell, Jr., ed.
Professional Artist—John Schoenherr
Publisher—Ballantine Books, Ian and Betty Ballantine, eds.
Amateur Publication—*Yandro*, Robert and Juanita Coul-son, eds.
Dramatic Presentation—*Doctor Strangelove*, screenplay by Stanley Kubrick and Peter George

1965 (1966)
Novel—(tie) *And Call Me Conrad* [aka *The Dream Mas-ter*], by Roger Zelazny; *Dune*, by Frank Herbert
Short Fiction—"'Repent, Harlequin,' said the Ticktock-man," by Harlan Ellison
Professional Magazine—*Worlds of If*, Frederik Pohl, ed.
Professional Artist—Frank Frazetta
Amateur Magazine—*ERB-dom*, Camille Cazadessus, ed.
Best All-time Series—*The Foundation Trilogy*, by Isaac Asimov

1966 (1967)
Novel—*The Moon Is a Harsh Mistress*, by Robert A. Heinlein
Novelette—"The Last Castle," by Jack Vance
Short Story—"Neutron Star," by Larry Niven
Professional Magazine—*Worlds of If*, Frederik Pohl, ed.
Professional Artist—Jack Gaughan
Dramatic Presentation—"The Menagerie" episode of *Star Trek*, teleplay by Gene Roddenberry
Amateur Publication—*Niekas*, Ed Meskys and Felice Rolfe, eds.
Fan Artist—Jack Gaughan
Fan Writer—Alexei Panshin
Special Plaque—CBS-TV, for *The 21st Century*

1967 (1968)
Novel—*Lord of Light*, by Roger Zelazny
Novella—(tie) "Weyr Search," by Anne McCaffrey; "Riders of the Purple Wage," by Philip José Farmer
Novelette—"Gonna Roll Them Bones," by Fritz Leiber
Short Story—"I Have No Mouth, and I Must Scream," by Harlan Ellison

Dramatic Presentation—"City at the Edge of Forever," an episode of *Star Trek*, teleplay by Harlan Ellison
Professional Magazine—*Worlds of If*, Frederik Pohl, ed.
Amateur Publication—*Amra*, George Scithers, ed.
Professional Artist—Jack Gaughan
Fan Writer—George Barr
Fan Artist—Ted White
Special Plaque—Harlan Ellison, for *Dangerous Visions*
Special Plaque—Gene Roddenberry, for *Star Trek*

1968 (1969)
Novel—*Stand on Zanzibar*, by John Brunner
Novella—"Nightwings," by Robert Silverberg
Novelette—"The Sharing of Flesh," by Poul Anderson
Short Story—"The Beast That Shouted Love at the Heart of the World," by Harlan Ellison
Dramatic Presentation—*2001: A Space Odyssey*, screenplay by Arthur C. Clarke and Stanley Kubrick
Professional Magazine—*The Magazine of Fantasy and Science Fiction*, Edward L. Ferman, ed.
Professional Artist—Jack Gaughan
Amateur Publication—*Psychotic* [aka *Science Fiction Review*], Richard E. Geis, ed.
Fan Writer—Harry Warner, Jr.
Fan Artist—Vaughn Bodé
Special Award—Neil Armstrong, Edwin Aldrin, and Michael Collins, for "The Best Moon Landing Ever"

1969 (1970)
Novel—*The Left Hand of Darkness*, by Ursula K. Le Guin
Novella—"Ship of Shadows," by Fritz Leiber
Short Story—"Time Considered as a Helix of Semi-Pre-cious Stones," by Samuel R. Delany
Dramatic Presentation—TV coverage of the Apollo XI flight
Professional Magazine—*The Magazine of Fantasy and Science Fiction*, Edward L. Ferman, ed.
Professional Artist—Frank Kelly Freas
Amateur Magazine—*Science Fiction Review*, Richard E. Geis, ed.
Fan Writer—Wilson Tucker
Fan Artist—Tim Kirk

1970 (1971)
Novel—*Ringworld*, by Larry Niven
Novella—"Ill Met in Lankhmar," by Fritz Leiber
Short Story—"Slow Sculpture," by Theodore Sturgeon
Dramatic Presentation—No award
Professional Artist—Leo and Diane Dillon
Professional Magazine—*The Magazine of Fantasy and Science Fiction*, Edward L. Ferman, ed.
Amateur Magazine—*Locus*, Charles and Dena Brown, eds.
Fan Writer—Richard E. Geis
Fan Artist—Alicia Austin

1971 (1972)
Novel—*To Your Scattered Bodies Go*, by Philip José Farmer
Novella—"The Queen of Air and Darkness," by Poul Anderson
Short Story—"Inconstant Moon," by Larry Niven
Dramatic Presentation—*A Clockwork Orange*, screen-play by Anthony Burgess and Stanley Kubrick
Amateur Magazine—*Locus*, Charles and Dena Brown, eds.
Professional Magazine—*The Magazine of Fantasy and Science Fiction*, Edward L. Ferman, ed.
Professional Artist—Frank Kelly Freas

Fan Writer—Harry Warner, Jr.
Fan Artist—Tim Kirk
Special Plaque—Club du Livre d'Anticipation (France), for excellence in book production
Special Plaque—Harlan Ellison, for *Again, Dangerous Visions*
Special Plaque—*Nueva Dimensión* (Spain), for excellence in magazine production

1972 (1973)
Novel—*The Gods Themselves*, by Isaac Asimov
Novella—"The Word for World Is Forest," by Ursula K. Le Guin
Novelette—"Goat Song," by Poul Anderson
Short Story—(tie) "Eurema's Dam," by R. A. Lafferty; "The Meeting," by Frederik Pohl and C. M. Kornbluth
Dramatic Presentation—*Slaughterhouse 5*, screenplay by Kurt Vonnegut, Jr.
Editor—Ben Bova
Fanzine—*Energumen*, Michael and Susan Glicksohn, eds.
Fan Writer—Terry Carr
Fan Artist—Tim Kirk
Special Plaque—Pierre Versins, for his *Encyclopédie de l'Utopie et de la Science Fiction*
Campbell Award—Jerry Pournelle

1973 (1974)
Novel—*Rendezvous with Rama*, by Arthur C. Clarke
Novella—"The Girl Who Was Plugged in," by James Tiptree, Jr.
Short Story—"The Ones Who Walk Away from Omelas," by Ursula K. Le Guin
Professional Editor—Ben Bova
Professional Artist—Frank Kelly Freas
Dramatic Presentation—*Sleeper*, screenplay by Woody Allen
Fanzine—(tie) *Algol*, Andrew Porter, ed.; *Alien Critic*, Richard E. Geis, ed.
Fan Writer—Susan Wood
Fan Artist—Tim Kirk
Special Hugo—Chesley Bonestell
Campbell Award—(tie) Spider Robinson; Lisa Tuttle
Gandalf Award (Grand Master)—J. R. R. Tolkien

1974 (1975)
Novel—*The Dispossessed*, by Ursula K. Le Guin
Novella—"A Song for Lya," by George R. R. Martin
Novelette—"Adrift, Just Off the Islets of Langerhans...," by Harlan Ellison
Short Story—"The Hole Man," by Larry Niven
Professional Editor—Ben Bova
Professional Artist—Frank Kelly Freas
Dramatic Presentation—*Young Frankenstein*, screenplay by Mel Brooks and Gene Wilder
Fanzine—*Alien Critic*, Richard E. Geis, ed.
Fan Writer—Richard E. Geis
Fan Artist—William Rotsler
Special Plaque—Donald A. Wollheim, as "The Fan Who Has Done Everything"
Special Plaque—Walt Lee, for *The Reference Guide to Fantastic Films*
Campbell Award—P. J. Plauger
Gandalf Award (Grand Master)—Fritz Leiber

1975 (1976)
Novel—*The Forever War*, by Joe Haldeman
Novella—"Home Is the Hangman," by Roger Zelazny
Novelette—"Borderland of Sol," by Larry Niven

Short Story—"Catch That Zeppelin," by Fritz Leiber
Dramatic Presentation—*A Boy and His Dog*, screenplay by L. Q. Jones based on the story by Harlan Ellison
Fanzine—*Locus*, Charles and Dena Brown, eds.
Professional Editor—Ben Bova
Professional Artist—Frank Kelly Freas
Fan Writer—Richard E. Geis
Fan Artist—Tim Kirk
Campbell Award—Tom Reamy
Gandalf Award (Grand Master)—L. Sprague de Camp

1976 (1977)
Novel—*Where Late the Sweet Birds Sang*, by Kate Wilhelm
Novella—(tie) "Houston, Houston, Do You Read?" by James Tiptree, Jr.; "By Any Other Name," by Spider Robinson
Novelette—"The Bicentennial Man," by Isaac Asimov
Short Story—"Tricentennial," by Joe Haldeman
Dramatic Presentation—No award
Fanzine—*Science Fiction Review*, Richard E. Geis, ed.
Professional Artist—Rick Sternbach
Professional Editor—Ben Bova
Fan Writer—(tie) Susan Wood; Richard E. Geis
Fan Artist—Phil Foglio
Special Plaque—George Lucas, for *Star Wars*
Campbell Award—C. J. Cherryh
Gandalf Award (Grand Master)—Andre Norton

1977 (1978)
Novel—*Gateway*, by Frederik Pohl
Novella—"Stardance," by Spider and Jeanne Robinson
Novelette—"Eyes of Amber," by Joan D. Vinge
Short Story—"Jeffty Is Five," by Harlan Ellison
Dramatic Presentation—*Star Wars*, screenplay by George Lucas
Professional Artist—Rick Sternbach
Professional Editor—George Scithers
Fanzine—*Locus*, Charles and Dena Brown, eds.
Fan Writer—Richard E. Geis
Fan Artist—Phil Foglio
Campbell Award—Orson Scott Card
Gandalf Award (Grand Master)—Poul Anderson
Gandalf Award (Fantasy Novel)—*The Silmarillion*, by J. R. R. Tolkien

1978 (1979)
Novel—*Dreamsnake*, by Vonda N. McIntyre
Novella—"The Persistence of Vision," by John Varley
Novelette—"Hunter's Moon," by Poul Anderson
Short Story—"Cassandra," by C. J. Cherryh
Dramatic Presentation—*Superman*, screenplay by Mario Puzo, David Newman, Leslie Newman, and Robert Benton
Professional Artist—Vincent DiFate
Professional Editor—Ben Bova
Fanzine—*Science Fiction Review*, Richard E. Geis, ed.
Fan Writer—Bob Shaw
Fan Artist—William Rotsler
Campbell Award—Stephen R. Donaldson
Gandalf Award (Grand Master)—Ursula K. Le Guin
Gandalf Award (Fantasy Novel)—*The White Dragon*, by Anne McCaffrey

1979 (1980)
Novel—*The Fountains of Paradise*, by Arthur C. Clarke
Novella—"Enemy Mine," by Barry B. Longyear
Novelette—"Sandkings," by George R. R. Martin
Short Story—"The Way of Cross and Dragon," by George R. R. Martin

Nonfiction—*The Science Fiction Encyclopedia*, Peter Nicholls and John Clute, eds.
Dramatic Presentation—*Alien*, screenplay by Dan O'Bannon and Ronald Shusett
Professional Artist—Michael Whelan
Professional Editor—George Scithers
Fanzine—*Locus*, Charles N. Brown, ed.
Fan Writer—Bob Shaw
Fan Artist—Alexis Gilliland
Campbell Award—Barry B. Longyear
Gandalf Award (Grand Master)—Ray Bradbury

1980 (1981)
Novel—*The Snow Queen*, by Joan D. Vinge
Novella—"Lost Dorsai," by Gordon R. Dickson
Novelette—"The Cloak and the Staff," by Gordon R. Dickson
Short Story—"Grotto of the Dancing Deer," by Clifford D. Simak
Nonfiction—*Cosmos*, by Carl Sagan
Professional Editor—Edward L. Ferman
Professional Artist—Michael Whelan
Fanzine—*Locus*, Charles N. Brown, ed.
Fan Writer—Susan Wood [posthumous]
Fan Artist—Victoria Poyser
Dramatic Presentation—*The Empire Strikes Back*, screenplay by George Lucas, Leigh Brackett, and Lawrence Kasdan
Campbell Award—Somtow Sucharitkul (S. P. Somtow)
Gandalf Award (Grand Master)—C. L. Moore

1981 (1982)
Novel—*Downbelow Station*, by C. J. Cherryh
Novella—"The Saturn Game," by Poul Anderson
Novelette—"Unicorn Variation," by Roger Zelazny
Short Story—"The Pusher," by John Varley
Nonfiction—*Danse Macabre*, by Stephen King
Dramatic Presentation—*Raiders of the Lost Ark*, screenplay by Lawrence Kasdan
Professional Editor—Edward L. Ferman
Professional Artist—Michael Whelan
Fanzine—*Locus*, Charles N. Brown, ed.
Fan Writer—Richard E. Geis
Fan Artist—Victoria Poyser
Campbell Award—Alexis Gilliland
Special Award—Mike Glyer, for "Keeping the fan in fanzine publishing"

1982 (1983)
Novel—*Foundation's Edge*, by Isaac Asimov
Novella—"Souls," by Joanna Russ
Novelette—"Fire Watch," by Connie Willis
Short Story—"Melancholy Elephants," by Spider Robinson
Nonfiction—*Isaac Asimov: The Foundations of Science Fiction*, by James E. Gunn
Dramatic Presentation—*Blade Runner*, screenplay by Hampton Fancher and David Peoples
Professional Editor—Edward L. Ferman
Professional Artist—Michael Whelan
Fanzine—*Locus*, Charles N. Brown, ed.
Fan Writer—Richard E. Geis
Fan Artist—Alexis Gilliland
Campbell Award—Paul O. Williams

1983 (1984)
Novel—*Startide Rising*, by David Brin
Novella—"Cascade Point," by Timothy Zahn
Novelette—"Blood Music," by Greg Bear
Short Story—"Speech Sounds," by Octavia E. Butler

Nonfiction—*Encyclopedia of Science Fiction and Fantasy, Vol. 3*, by Donald Tuck
Dramatic Presentation—*Return of the Jedi*, screenplay by George Lucas and Lawrence Kasdan
Professional Editor—Shawna McCarthy
Professional Artist—Michael Whelan
Semiprozine—*Locus*, Charles N. Brown, ed.
Fanzine—*File 770*, Mike Glyer, ed.
Fan Writer—Mike Glyer
Fan Artist—Alexis Gilliland
Campbell Award—R. A. MacAvoy
Special Award—Robert Bloch
Special Award—Larry Shaw

1984 (1985)
Novel—*Neuromancer*, by William Gibson
Novella—"Press ENTER ▮," by John Varley
Novelette—"Bloodchild," by Octavia E. Butler
Short Story—"The Crystal Spheres," by David Brin
Nonfiction—*Wonder's Child: My Life in Science Fiction*, by Jack Williamson
Dramatic Presentation—*2010*, screenplay by Arthur C. Clarke
Professional Editor—Terry Carr
Professional Artist—Michael Whelan
Semiprozine—*Locus*, Charles N. Brown, ed.
Fanzine—*File 770*, Mike Glyer, ed.
Fan Writer—Dave Langford
Fan Artist—Alexis Gilliland
Campbell Award—Lucius Shepard

1985 (1986)
Novel—*Ender's Game*, by Orson Scott Card
Novella—"Twenty-Four Views of Mt. Fuji, by Hokusai," by Roger Zelazny
Novelette—"Paladin of the Lost Hour," by Harlan Ellison
Short Story—"Fermi and Frost," by Frederik Pohl
Nonfiction—*Science Made Stupid*, by Tom Weller
Dramatic Presentation—*Back to the Future*, screenplay by Robert Zemeckis and Bob Gale
Professional Editor—Judy-Lynn del Rey [posthumous; refused by Lester del Rey]
Professional Artist—Michael Whelan
Semiprozine—*Locus*, Charles N. Brown, ed.
Fanzine—*Lan's Lantern*, George Laskowski, ed.
Fan Writer—Mike Glyer
Fan Artist—Joan Hanke-Woods
Campbell Award—Melissa Scott

1986 (1987)
Novel—*Speaker for the Dead*, by Orson Scott Card
Novella—"Gilgamesh in the Outback," by Robert Silverberg
Novelette—"Permafrost," by Roger Zelazny
Short Story—"Tangents," by Greg Bear
Nonfiction—*Trillion Year Spree*, by Brian W. Aldiss and David Wingrove
Dramatic Presentation—*Aliens*, screenplay by James Cameron
Professional Editor—Terry Carr [posthumous]
Professional Artist—Jim Burns
Semiprozine—*Locus*, Charles N. Brown, ed.
Fanzine—*Ansible*, Dave Langford, ed.
Fan Writer—Dave Langford
Fan Artist—Brad Foster
Campbell Award—Karen Joy Fowler

1987 (1988)
Novel—*The Uplift War*, by David Brin
Novella—"Eye for Eye," by Orson Scott Card

Novelette—"Buffalo Gals, Won't You Come Out Tonight," by Ursula K. Le Guin
Short Story—"Why I Left Harry's All-Night Hamburgers," by Lawrence Watt-Evans
Nonfiction—*Michael Whelan's Works of Wonder*, by Michael Whelan
Semiprozine—*Locus*, Charles N. Brown, ed.
Other Forms—*Watchmen*, by Alan Moore and Dave Gibbons
Dramatic Presentation—*The Princess Bride*, screenplay by William Goldman, from his novel
Professional Artist—Michael Whelan
Professional Editor—Gardner Dozois
Fanzine—*Texas SF Inquirer*, Pat Mueller, ed.
Fan Writer—Mike Glyer
Fan Artist—Brad Foster
Campbell Award—Judith Moffett
Special Award—The SF Oral History Association

1988 (1989)
Novel—*Cyteen*, by C. J. Cherryh
Novella—"The Last of the Winnebagos," by Connie Willis
Novelette—"Schrödinger's Kitten," by George Alec Effinger
Short Story—"Kirinyaga," by Mike Resnick
Nonfiction—*The Motion of Light in Water*, by Samuel R. Delany
Dramatic Presentation—*Who Framed Roger Rabbit?*, screenplay by Jeffrey Price and Peter S. Seaman
Semiprozine—*Locus*, Charles N. Brown, ed.
Professional Editor—Gardner Dozois
Professional Artist—Michael Whelan
Fanzine—*File 770*, Mike Glyer, ed.
Fan Writer—David Langford
Fan Artist—(tie) Diana Gallagher Wu; Brad Foster
Campbell Award—Michaela Roessner
Special Award—SF Lovers Digest (Computer Network)
Special Award—Alex Schomburg

1989 (1990)
Novel—*Hyperion*, by Dan Simmons
Novella—"The Mountains of Mourning," by Lois McMaster Bujold
Novelette—"Enter a Soldier. Later: Enter Another," by Robert Silverberg
Short Story—"Boobs," by Suzy McKee Charnas
Dramatic Presentation—*Indiana Jones and the Last Crusade*, screenplay by Jeffrey Boam, based on a story by George Lucas
Nonfiction—*The World Beyond the Hill*, by Alexei and Cory Panshin
Professional Editor—Gardner Dozois
Professional Artist—Don Maitz
Semiprozine—*Locus*, Charles N. Brown, ed.
Fan Writer—Dave Langford
Fan Artist—Stu Shiffman
Fanzine—*The Mad 3 Party*, Leslie Turek, ed.
Campbell Award—Kristine Kathryn Rusch
Original Artwork [not a Hugo Award]—Don Maitz, for *Rimrunners*, by C. J. Cherryh

1990 (1991)
Novel—*The Vor Game*, by Lois McMaster Bujold
Novella—"The Hemingway Hoax," by Joe Haldeman
Novelette—"The Manamouki," by Mike Resnick
Short Story—"Bears Discover Fire," by Terry Bisson
Dramatic Presentation—*Edward Scissorhands*
Nonfiction—*How to Write Science Fiction and Fantasy*, by Orson Scott Card

Professional Editor—Gardner Dozois
Professional Artist—Michael Whelan
Semiprozine—*Locus*, Charles N. Brown, ed.
Fan Writer—Dave Langford
Fan Artist—Teddy Harvia
Fanzine—*Lan's Lantern*, George Laskowski, ed.
Campbell Award—Julia Ecklar
Special Award—Andrew Porter, for excellence in editing *Science Fiction Chronicle*
Special Award [not a Hugo Award]—Elst Weinstein, as Best Hoax, for keeping humor alive in fandom

1991 (1992)
Novel—*Barrayar*, by Lois McMaster Bujold
Novella—"Beggars in Spain," by Nancy Kruss
Novelette—"Gold," by Isaac Asimov
Short Story—"A Walk in the Sun," by Geoffrey Landis
Dramatic Presentation—*Terminator 2*
Nonfiction—*The World of Charles Addams*, by Charles Addams
Professional Editor—Gardner Dozois
Professional Artist—Michael Whelan
Semiprozine—*Locus*, Charles N. Brown, ed.
Fan Writer—Dave Langford
Fan Artist—Brad Foster
Fanzine—*Mimosa*, Nick and Dickie Lynch, eds.
Campbell Award—Ted Chiang
Original Artwork—*Snow Queen*, by Michael Whelan

THE INTERNATIONAL FANTASY AWARDS

1949/50 (1951)
Fiction—*Earth Abides*, by George R. Stewart
Nonfiction—*The Conquest of Space*, by Willy Ley and
   Chesley Bonestell

1951 (1952)
Fiction—*Fancies and Goodnights*, by John Collier
2nd—*The Day of the Triffids*, by John Wyndham
3rd—*The Illustrated Man*, by Ray Bradbury

Nonfiction—*The Exploration of Space*, by Arthur C.
   Clarke
2nd—*Dragons in Amber*, by Willy Ley
3rd—*Rockets, Jets, Guided Missiles and Spaceships*, by
   Jack Coggins and Fletcher Pratt

1952 (1953)
Fiction—*City*, by Clifford D. Simak
2nd—*Takeoff*, by Cyril M. Kornbluth
3rd—*Player Piano*, by Kurt Vonnegut, Jr.

Nonfiction—*Lands Beyond*, by Willy Ley and L. Sprague
   de Camp

1953 (1954)
Fiction—*More Than Human*, by Theodore Sturgeon
2nd—*The Demolished Man*, by Alfred Bester

1954 (1955)
Fiction—*A Mirror for Observers*, by Edgar Pangborn
2nd—*Mission of Gravity*, by Hal Clement

1955 (1956)—No award

1956 (1957)
Fiction—*The Lord of the Rings Trilogy*, by J. R. R.
   Tolkien
Awards discontinued.

THE J. LLOYD EATON AWARDS
(For Best Nonfiction Book of the Year)

1976/77 (1979)—*The Creation of Tomorrow: Fifty Years of Magazine Science Fiction*, by Paul A. Carter

1978 (1980)—*Future Tense: The Cinema of Science Fiction*, by John Brosnan

1979 (1981)—*The Known and the Unknown: The Iconography of Science Fiction*, by Gary K. Wolfe

1980 (1982)—*Robert A. Heinlein: America As Science Fiction*, by H. Bruce Franklin

1981 (1983)—*Alien Encounters*, by Mark Rose

1982 (1984)—*The Logic of Fantasy*, by John Huntington

1983 (1985)—*The Entropy Exhibition*, by Colin Greenland

1984 (1986)—*Fantasy and Mimesis*, by Kathryn Hume

1985 (1987)—(tie) *Some Kind of Paradise*, by Thomas D. Clareson; *Scientific Romance in Britain*, by Brian Stableford

1986 (1988)—*Trillion Year Spree*, by Brian W. Aldiss and David Wingrove; **Lifetime Achievement**—Reginald Bretnor

1987 (1989)—*Origins of Futuristic Fiction*, by Paul K. Alkon

1988 (1990)—*Jules Verne Rediscovered*, by Arthur B. Evans

1989 (1991)—*Science Fiction, Fantasy & Horror 1988*, by Charles N. Brown, William G. Contento, and Hal W. Hall

1990 (1992)—*The last frontier: imagining other worlds, from the Copernican revolution to modern science fiction*, by Karl S. Guthke; **Lifetime Achievement**—James Gunn

THE JOHN W. CAMPBELL JR. MEMORIAL AWARDS

1972 (1973)—*Beyond Apollo*, by Barry N. Malzberg

1973 (1974)—(tie) *Rendezvous with Rama*, by Arthur C. Clarke; *Malevil*, by Robert Merle; **Special Award**—*The Cosmic Connection*, by Carl Sagan

1974 (1975)—*Flow My Tears, the Policeman Said*, by Philip K. Dick

1975 (1976)—No award; **Special Award**—*The Year of the Quiet Sun* (1970), by Wilson Tucker

1976 (1977)—*The Alteration*, by Kingsley Amis

1977 (1978)—*Gateway*, by Frederik Pohl

1978 (1979)—*Gloriana*, by Michael Moorcock

1979 (1980)—*On Wings of Song*, by Thomas M. Disch

1980 (1981)—*Timescape*, by Gregory Benford

1981 (1982)—*Riddley Walker*, by Russell Hoban

1982 (1983)—*Helliconia: Spring*, by Brian W. Aldiss

1983 (1984)—*The Citadel of the Autarch*, by Gene Wolfe

1984 (1985)—*The Years of the City*, by Frederik Pohl

1985 (1986)—*The Postman*, by David Brin

1986 (1987)—*A Door into Ocean*, by Jean Slonczewski

1987 (1988)—*Lincoln's Dreams*, by Connie Willis

1988 (1989)—*Islands in the Net*, by Bruce Sterling

1989 (1990)—*The Child Garden*, by Geoff Ryman

1990 (1991)—*Pacific Edge*, by Kim Stanley Robinson

1991 (1992)—*Buddy Holly Is Alive and Well*, by Bradley Denton

THE *LOCUS* AWARDS

1970 (1971)
Novel—*Ringworld*, by Larry Niven
Short Fiction—"The Region Between," by Harlan Ellison
Anthology/Collection—*Science Fiction Hall of Fame, Vol. 1*, Robert Silverberg, ed.
Magazine—*The Magazine of Fantasy and Science Fiction*, Edward L. Ferman, ed.
Fanzine—*Locus*, Charles and Dena Brown, eds.
Single Issue of Fanzine—*Locus #70*, Charles and Dena Brown, eds.
Paperback Cover Illustrator—Leo and Diane Dillon
Fan Writer—Harry Warner, Jr.
Fan Artist—(tie) Alicia Austin; William Rotsler
Fan Critic—Ted Pauls

1971 (1972)
Novel—*The Lathe of Heaven*, by Ursula K. Le Guin
Short Fiction—"The Queen of Air and Darkness," by Poul Anderson
Original Anthology/Collection—*Universe 1*, Terry Carr, ed.
Reprint Anthology/Collection—*World's Best Science Fiction: 1971*, Donald A. Wollheim and Terry Carr, eds.
Publisher—Ballantine Books, Betty Ballantine, ed.
Magazine—*The Magazine of Fantasy and Science Fiction*, Edward L. Ferman, ed.
Paperback Artist—Gene Szafran
Fanzine—*Locus*, Charles and Dena Brown, eds.
Fan Writer—Charles N. Brown
Fan Artist—William Rotsler
Convention—Noreascon

1972 (1973)
Novel—*The Gods Themselves*, by Isaac Asimov
Novella—"The Gold at the Starbow's End," by Frederik Pohl
Short Fiction—"Basilisk," by Harlan Ellison
Reprint Anthology/Collection—*The Best Science Fiction of the Year: 1972*, Terry Carr, ed.
Original Anthology/Collection—*Again, Dangerous Visions*, Harlan Ellison, ed.
Magazine—*The Magazine of Fantasy and Science Fiction*, Edward L. Ferman, ed.
Publisher—Ballantine Books, Betty Ballantine and Judy-Lynn del Rey, eds.
Professional Artist—Frank Kelly Freas
Fanzine—*Locus*, Charles and Dena Brown, eds.
Fan Artist—Tim Kirk
Fan Critic—Richard E. Geis

1973 (1974)
Novel—*Rendezvous with Rama*, by Arthur C. Clarke
Novella—"The Death of Doctor Island," by Gene Wolfe
Short Fiction—"The Deathbird," by Harlan Ellison
Original Anthology/Collection—*Astounding*, Harry Harrison, ed.

Reprint Anthology/Collection—*The Best Science of the Year: 1973*, Terry Carr, ed.
Magazine—*The Magazine of Fantasy and Science Fiction*, Edward L. Ferman, ed.
Publisher—Ballantine Books, Betty Ballantine and Judy-Lynn del Rey, eds.
Professional Artist—Frank Kelly Freas
Fanzine—*Locus*, Charles and Dena Brown, eds.
Fan Artist—Tim Kirk
Fan Critic—Richard E. Geis

1974 (1975)
Novel—*The Dispossessed*, by Ursula K. Le Guin
Novella—"Born with the Dead," by Robert Silverberg
Novelette—"Adrift, Just Off the Islets of Langerhans...," by Harlan Ellison
Short Story—"The Day Before the Revolution," by Ursula K. Le Guin
Magazine—*The Magazine of Fantasy and Science Fiction*, Edward L. Ferman, ed.
Publisher—Ballantine Books, Judy-Lynn del Rey, ed.
Original Anthology/Collection—*Universe 4*, Terry Carr, ed.
Reprint Anthology/Collection—*Before the Golden Age*, Isaac Asimov, ed.
Professional Artist—Frank Kelly Freas
All-Time Best Novel—*Dune*, by Frank Herbert
Fanzine—*Outworlds*, Bill Bowers, ed.
Fan Artist—Tim Kirk
Fan Critic—P. Schuyler Miller

1975 (1976)
Novel—*The Forever War*, by Joe Haldeman
Novella—"The Storms of Windhaven," by George R. R. Martin and Lisa Tuttle
Novelette—"The New Atlantis," by Ursula K. Le Guin
Short Story—"Croatoan," by Harlan Ellison
Anthology—*Epoch*, Roger Elwood and Robert Silverberg, eds.
Collection—*The Wind's Twelve Quarters*, by Ursula K. Le Guin
Associational Item—*Alternate Worlds*, by James E. Gunn
Magazine—*The Magazine of Fantasy and Science Fiction*, Edward L. Ferman, ed.
Hardcover Publisher—Science Fiction Book Club
Paperback Publisher—Ballantine Books, Judy-Lynn del Rey, ed.
Professional Artist—Rick Sternbach
Fan Critic—Richard E. Geis
Fanzine—*Locus*, Charles and Dena Brown, eds.

1976 (1977)
Novel—*Where Late the Sweet Birds Sang*, by Kate Wilhelm
Novella—"The Samurai and the Willows," by Michael Bishop
Novelette—"The Bicentennial Man," by Isaac Asimov

Short Story—"Tricentennial," by Joe Haldeman
Collection—*A Song for Lya*, by George R. R. Martin
Reprint Anthology—*The Best Science Fiction of the Year #5*, Terry Carr, ed.
Original Anthology—*Stellar #2*, Judy-Lynn del Rey, ed.
Publisher—Ballantine Books, Judy-Lynn del Rey, ed.
Magazine—*The Magazine of Fantasy and Science Fiction*, Edward L. Ferman, ed.
Professional Artist—Rick Sternbach
Fanzine—*Locus*, Charles and Dena Brown, eds.
Fan Critic—Spider Robinson
Best All-time Author—Robert A. Heinlein
Special Award—John Varley
Special Award—Peter Weston, for *Andromeda*

1977 (1978)
SF Novel—*Gateway*, by Frederik Pohl
Novella—"Stardance," by Spider and Jeanne Robinson
Short Fiction—"Jeffty Is Five," by Harlan Ellison
Fantasy Novel—*The Silmarillion*, by J. R. R. Tolkien
Publisher—Ballantine/Del Rey Books, Judy-Lynn del Rey, ed.
Magazine—*The Magazine of Fantasy and Science Fiction*, Edward L. Ferman, ed.

1978 (1979)
Novel—*Dreamsnake*, by Vonda N. McIntyre
Novella—"The Persistence of Vision," by John Varley
Novelette—"The Barbie Murders," by John Varley
Short Story—"Count the Clock That Tells Time," by Harlan Ellison

1979 (1980)
SF Novel—*Titan*, by John Varley
Fantasy Novel—*Harpist in the Wind*, by Patricia McKillip
Novella—"Enemy Mine," by Barry B. Longyear
Novelette—"Sandkings," by George R. R. Martin
Short Story—"The Way of Cross and Dragon," by George R. R. Martin
Anthology—*Universe 9*, Terry Carr, ed.
Collection—*Convergent Series*, by Larry Niven
Art Book—*Barlowe's Guide to the Extraterrestrials*, by Wayne Barlowe and Ian Summers and Beth Meacham
Magazine—*The Magazine of Fantasy and Science Fiction*, Edward L. Ferman, ed.
Publisher—Ballantine/Del Rey Books, Judy-Lynn and Lester del Rey, eds.
Professional Artist—Michael Whelan
Nonfiction—*The Science Fiction Encyclopedia*, Peter Nicholls and John Clute, eds.

1980 (1981)
SF Novel—*The Snow Queen*, by Joan D. Vinge
Fantasy Novel—*Lord Valentine's Castle*, by Robert Silverberg
First Novel—*Dragon's Egg*, by Robert L. Forward
Novella—"Nightflyers," by George R. R. Martin
Novelette—"The Brave Little Toaster," by Thomas M. Disch
Short Story—"Grotto of the Dancing Deer," by Clifford D. Simak
Anthology—*The Magazine of Fantasy and Science Fiction: A 30-Year Retrospective*, Edward L. Ferman, ed.
Collection—*The Barbie Murders*, by John Varley
Nonfiction—*In Joy Still Felt*, by Isaac Asimov
Professional Artist—Michael Whelan
Magazine—*The Magazine of Fantasy and Science Fiction*, Edward L. Ferman, ed.

Publisher—Ballantine/Del Rey Books, Judy-Lynn and Lester del Rey, eds.

1981 (1982)
SF Novel—*The Many Colored Land*, by Julian May
Fantasy Novel—*The Claw of the Conciliator*, by Gene Wolfe
First Novel—*Starship & Haiku*, by S. P. Somtow (Somtow Sucharitkul)
Novella—"Blue Champagne," by John Varley
Novelette—"Guardians," by George R. R. Martin
Short Story—"The Pusher," by John Varley
Anthology—*Shadows of Sanctuary*, Robert Asprin, ed.
Collection—*Sandkings*, by George R. R. Martin
Nonfiction—*Danse Macabre*, by Stephen King
Professional Artist—Michael Whelan
Magazine—*The Magazine of Fantasy and Science Fiction*, Edward L. Ferman, ed.
Publisher—Pocket/Timescape Books, David G. Hartwell, ed.

1982 (1983)
SF Novel—*Foundation's Edge*, by Isaac Asimov
Fantasy Novel—*The Sword of the Lictor*, by Gene Wolfe
First Novel—*Courtship Rite*, by Donald Kingsbury
Novella—"Souls," by Joanna Russ
Novelette—"Djinn, No Chaser," by Harlan Ellison
Short Story—"Sur," by Ursula K. Le Guin
Anthology—*The Best Science Fiction of the Year #11*, Terry Carr, ed.
Collection—*The Compass Rose*, by Ursula K. Le Guin
Nonfiction—*The Engines of the Night*, by Barry N. Malzberg
Professional Artist—Michael Whelan
Magazine—*Locus*, Charles N. Brown, ed.
Publisher—Pocket/Timescape Books, David Hartwell, ed.

1983 (1984)
SF Novel—*Startide Rising*, by David Brin
Fantasy Novel—*The Mists of Avalon*, by Marion Zimmer Bradley
First Novel—*Tea with the Black Dragon*, by R. A. MacAvoy
Novella—"Her Habiline Husband," by Michael Bishop
Novelette—"The Monkey Treatment," by George R. R. Martin
Short Story—"Beyond the Dead Reef," by James Tiptree
Nonfiction—*Dream Makers, Volume 2*, Charles Platt, ed.
Collection—*Unicorn Variations*, by Roger Zelazny
Anthology—*The Best Science Fiction of the Year #12*, Terry Carr, ed.
Professional Artist—Michael Whelan
Magazine—*Locus*, Charles N. Brown, ed.
Publisher—Ballantine/Del Rey Books, Judy-Lynn and Lester del Rey, eds.

1984 (1985)
SF Novel—*The Integral Trees*, by Larry Niven
Fantasy Novel—*Job: A Comedy of Justice*, by Robert A. Heinlein
First Novel—*The Wild Shore*, by Kim Stanley Robinson
Novella—"Press ENTER ■," by John Varley
Novelette—"Bloodchild," by Octavia E. Butler
Short Story—"Salvador," by Lucius Shepard
Nonfiction—*Sleepless Nights in the Procrustean Bed: Essays*, by Harlan Ellison, edited by Marty Clark
Collection—*The Ghost Light*, by Fritz Leiber
Anthology—*Light Years and Dark*, Michael Bishop, ed.
Professional Artist—Michael Whelan

Magazine—*Locus*, Charles N. Brown, ed.
Publisher—Ballantine/Del Rey Books, Judy-Lynn and Lester del Rey, eds.

1985 (1986)
SF Novel—*The Postman*, by David Brin
Fantasy Novel—*Trumps of Doom*, by Roger Zelazny
First Novel—*Contact*, by Carl Sagan
Novella—"The Only Neat Thing to Do," by James Tiptree
Novelette—"Paladin of the Lost Ark," by Harlan Ellison
Short Story—"With Virgil Oddum at the East Pole," by Harlan Ellison
Nonfiction—*Benchmarks: Galaxy Bookshelf*, by Algis Budrys
Collection—*Skeleton Crew*, by Stephen King
Anthology—*Medea: Harlan's World*, Harlan Ellison, ed.
Professional Artist—Michael Whelan
Magazine—*Locus*, Charles N. Brown, ed.
Publisher—Ballantine/Del Rey Books

1986 (1987)
SF Novel—*Speaker for the Dead*, by Orson Scott Card
Fantasy Novel—*Soldier of the Mist*, by Gene Wolfe
First Novel—*The Hercules Text*, by Jack McDevitt
Novella—"R and R," by Lucius Shepard
Novelette—"Thor Meets Captain America," by David Brin
Short Story—"Robot Dreams," by Isaac Asimov
Nonfiction—*Trillion Year Spree*, by Brian W. Aldiss and David Wingrove
Collection—*Blue Champagne*, by John Varley
Anthology—*The Year's Best Science Fiction, Third Annual Collection*, Gardner Dozois, ed.
Professional Artist—Michael Whelan
Magazine—*The Magazine of Fantasy and Science Fiction*, Edward L. Ferman, ed.
Publisher—Ballantine/Del Rey Books

1987 (1988)
SF Novel—*The Uplift War*, by David Brin
Fantasy Novel—*Seventh Son*, by Orson Scott Card
First Novel—*War for the Oaks*, by Emma Bull
Novella—"The Secret Sharer," by Robert Silverberg
Novelette—"Rachel in Love," by Pat Murphy
Short Story—"Angel," by Pat Cadigan
Nonfiction—*Watchmen*, by Alan Moore and Dave Gibbons
Collection—*The Jaguar Hunter*, by Lucius Shepard
Anthology—*The Year's Best Science Fiction, Fourth Annual Collection*, Gardner Dozois, ed.
Professional Artist—Michael Whelan
Magazine—*The Magazine of Fantasy and Science Fiction*, Edward L. Ferman, ed.
Publisher—Tor Books
All-Time Author—Robert A. Heinlein
1980's Author—David Brin

1988 (1989)
SF Novel—*Cyteen*, by C. J. Cherryh
Fantasy Novel—*Red Prophet*, by Orson Scott Card
Horror Novel—*Those Who Hunt the Night*, by Barbara Hambly
First Novel—*Desolation Road*, by Ian McDonald
Novella—"The Scalehunter's Beautiful Daughter," by Lucius Shepard
Novelette—"The Function of Dream Sleep," by Harlan Ellison
Short Story—"Eidolons," by Harlan Ellison
Nonfiction—*First Maitz*, by Don Maitz

Anthology—*Full Spectrum*, Lou Aronica and Shawna McCarthy, eds.
Collection—*Angry Candy*, by Harlan Ellison
Editor—Gardner Dozois
Artist—Michael Whelan
Publisher—Tor/St. Martin's Books
Magazine—*Isaac Asimov's Science Fiction Magazine*, Shawna McCarthy, ed.

1989 (1990)
SF Novel—*Hyperion*, by Dan Simmons
Fantasy Novel—*Prentice Alvin*, by Orson Scott Card
Horror Novel—*Carrion Comfort*, by Dan Simmons
First Novel—*Orbital Decay*, by Allen Steele
Novella—"The Father of Stones," by Lucius Shepard
Novelette—"Dogwalker," by Orson Scott Card
Short Story—"Lost Boys," by Orson Scott Card
Nonfiction—*Grumbles From the Grave*, by Robert A. Heinlein, edited by Virginia Heinlein [posthumous]
Anthology—*The Year's Best SF, Sixth Annual Collection*, Gardner Dozois, ed.
Collection—*Patterns*, by Pat Cadigan
Magazine—*Isaac Asimov's Science Fiction Magazine*
Editor—Gardner Dozois
Artist—Michael Whelan
Publisher—Tor/St. Martin's Books

1990 (1991)
SF Novel—*The Fall of Hyperion*, by Dan Simmons
Fantasy Novel—*Tehanu: The Last Book of Earthsea*, by Ursula K. Le Guin
Horror/Dark Fantasy Novel—*The Witching Hour*, by Anne Rice
First Novel—*In the Country of the Blind*, by Michael F. Flynn
Novella—"A Short, Sharp Shock," by Kim Stanley Robinson
Novelette—"Entropy's Bed at Midnight," by Dan Simmons
Short Story—"Bears Discover Fire," by Terry Bisson
Nonfiction—*SFWA Handbook*, Kristine Kathryn Rusch and Dean Wesley Smith, eds.
Anthology—*The Year's Best SF, Seventh Annual Collection*, Gardner Dozois, ed.
Collection—*Maps in a Mirror*, by Orson Scott Card
Magazine—*Isaac Asimov's Science Fiction Magazine*
Editor—Gardner Dozois
Artist—Michael Whelan
Publisher—Tor/St. Martin's Press Books

1991 (1992)
SF Novel—*Barrayar*, by Lois McMaster Bujold
Fantasy Novel—*Beauty*, by Sheri S. Tepper
Horror/Dark Fantasy Novel—*Summer of Night*, by Dan Simmons
First Novel—*The Cipher*, by Kathe Koje
Novella—"The Gallery of His Dreams," by Kristine Kathryn Rusch
Novelette—"All Dracula's Children," by Dan Simmons
Short Story—"Buffalo," by John Kessel
Nonfiction—*Science Fiction: The Early Years*, by Everett F. Bleiler
Anthology—*Full Spectrum 3*, Lou Aronica, Amy Stout, Betsy Mitchell, eds.
Collection—*Night of the Cooters: More Neat Stories*, by Howard Waldrop
Magazine—*Isaac Asimov's Science Fiction Magazine*
Editor—Gardner Dozois
Artist—Michael Whelan
Publisher—Tor/St. Martin's Press Books

THE MILFORD AWARDS
(For Lifetime Contributions to the Publishing and Editing of Science Fiction and Fantasy Literature)

1980—Donald A. Wollheim
1981—Robert Silverberg
1982—Judy-Lynn del Rey; Lester del Rey
1983—Terry Carr
1984—Edward L. Ferman
1985—Thaddeus E. Dikty
1986—Harlan Ellison
1987—H. L. Gold
1988—Lloyd Arthur Eshbach
1989—Martin Harry Greenberg
1990—David G. Hartwell
1991—Judith Merril
1992—Betty Ballantine; Ian Ballantine

THE NEBULA AWARDS
(Science Fiction and Fantasy Writers of America)

1965 (1966)
Novel—*Dune*, by Frank Herbert
Novella—(tie) "He Who Shapes," by Roger Zelazny; "The Saliva Tree," by Brian W. Aldiss
Novelette—"The Doors of His Face, the Lamps of His Mouth," by Roger Zelazny
Short Story—"'Repent, Harlequin,' said the Ticktockman," by Harlan Ellison

1966 (1967)
Novel—(tie) *Babel-17*, by Samuel R. Delany; *Flowers for Algernon*, by Daniel Keyes
Novella—"The Last Castle," by Jack Vance
Novelette—"Call Him Lord," by Gordon R. Dickson
Short Story—"The Secret Place," by Richard McKenna [posthumous]

1967 (1968)
Novel—*The Einstein Intersection*, by Samuel R. Delany
Novella—"Behold the Man," by Michael Moorcock
Novelette—"Gonna Roll Them Bones," by Fritz Leiber
Short Story—"Aye, and Gomorrah," by Samuel R. Delany

1968 (1969)
Novel—*Rite of Passage*, by Alexei Panshin
Novella—"Dragon Rider," by Anne McCaffrey
Novelette—"Mother to the World," by Richard Wilson
Short Story—"The Planners," by Kate Wilhelm

1969 (1970)
Novel—*The Left Hand of Darkness*, by Ursula K. Le Guin
Novella—"A Boy and His Dog," by Harlan Ellison
Novelette—"Time Considered As a Helix of Semi-Precious Stones," by Samuel R. Delany
Short Story—"Passengers," by Robert Silverberg

1970 (1971)
Novel—*Ringworld*, by Larry Niven
Novella—"Ill Met in Lankhmar," by Fritz Leiber
Novelette—"Slow Sculpture," by Theodore Sturgeon
Short Story—No award

1971 (1972)
Novel—*A Time of Change*, by Robert Silverberg
Novella—"The Missing Man," by Katherine MacLean
Novelette—"The Queen of Air and Darkness," by Poul Anderson
Short Story—"Good News from the Vatican," by Robert Silverberg

1972 (1973)
Novel—*The Gods Themselves*, by Isaac Asimov
Novella—"A Meeting with Medusa," by Arthur C. Clarke
Novelette—"Goat Song," by Poul Anderson

Short Story—"When It Changed," by Joanna Russ

1973 (1974)
Novel—*Rendezvous with Rama*, by Arthur C. Clarke
Novella—"The Death of Dr. Island," by Gene Wolfe
Novelette—"Of Mist, and Grass, and Sand," by Vonda N. McIntyre
Short Story—"Love Is the Plan, the Plan Is Death," by James Tiptree, Jr.
Dramatic Presentation—*Soylent Green*, screenplay by Stanley Greenberg

1974 (1975)
Novel—*The Dispossessed*, by Ursula K. Le Guin
Novella—"Born with the Dead," by Robert Silverberg
Novelette—"The Stars Are Gods," by Gregory Benford
Short Story—"The Day Before the Revolution," by Ursula K. Le Guin
Dramatic Presentation—*Sleeper*, screenplay by Woody Allen
Grand Master—Robert A. Heinlein

1975 (1976)
Novel—*The Forever War*, by Joe Haldeman
Novella—"Home Is the Hangman," by Roger Zelazny
Novelette—"San Diego Lightfoot Sue," by Tom Reamy
Short Story—"Catch That Zeppelin," by Fritz Leiber
Dramatic Presentation—*Young Frankenstein*, by Mel Brooks and Gene Wilder
Grand Master—Jack Williamson
Special Plaque—George Pal, for his work in films

1976 (1977)
Novel—*Man Plus*, by Frederik Pohl
Novella—"Houston, Houston, Do You Read?," by James Tiptree, Jr.
Novelette—"The Bicentennial Man," by Isaac Asimov
Short Story—"A Crowd of Shadows," by Charles L. Grant
Dramatic Presentation—No award
Grand Master—Clifford D. Simak

1977 (1978)
Novel—*Gateway*, by Frederik Pohl
Novella—"Stardance," by Spider and Jeanne Robinson
Novelette—"The Screwfly Solution," by Racoona Sheldon (James Tiptree, Jr.)
Short Story—"Jeffty Is Five," by Harlan Ellison
Special Plaque—George Lucas, for *Star Wars*

1978 (1979)
Novel—*Dreamsnake*, by Vonda N. McIntyre
Novella—"The Persistence of Vision," by John Varley
Novelette—"A Glow of Candles, a Unicorn's Eye," by Charles L. Grant
Short Story—"Stone," by Edward Bryant
Grand Master—L. Sprague de Camp

1979 (1980)
Novel—*The Fountains of Paradise*, by Arthur C. Clarke
Novella—"Enemy Mine," by Barry B. Longyear
Novelette—"Sandkings," by George R. R. Martin
Short Story—"giANTS," by Edward Bryant

1980 (1981)
Novel—*Timescape*, by Gregory Benford
Novella—"Unicorn Tapestry," by Suzy McKee Charnas
Novelette—"The Ugly Chickens," by Howard Waldrop
Short Story—"Grotto of the Dancing Deer," by Clifford D. Simak
Grand Master—Fritz Leiber

1981 (1982)
Novel—*The Claw of the Conciliator*, by Gene Wolfe
Novella—"The Saturn Game," by Poul Anderson
Novelette—"The Quickening," by Michael Bishop
Short Story—"The Bone Flute," by Lisa Tuttle [refused]

1982 (1983)
Novel—*No Enemy But Time*, by Michael Bishop
Novella—"Another Orphan," by John Kessel
Novelette—"The Watch," by Connie Willis
Short Story—"A Letter From the Clearys," by Connie Willis

1983 (1984)
Novel—*Startide Rising*, by David Brin
Novella—"Hardfought," by Greg Bear
Novelette—"Blood Music," by Greg Bear
Short Story—"The Peacemaker," by Gardner Dozois
Grand Master—Andre Norton

1984 (1985)
Novel—*Neuromancer*, by William Gibson
Novella—"Press Enter ■," by John Varley
Novelette—"Bloodchild," by Octavia E. Butler
Short Story—"Morning Child," by Gardner Dozois
Special Award—Ian and Betty Ballantine, for outstanding contributions to science fiction publishing

1985 (1986)
Novel—*Ender's Game*, by Orson Scott Card
Novella—"Sailing to Byzantium," by Robert Silverberg
Novelette—"Portraits of His Children," by George R. R. Martin
Short Story—"Out of All Them Bright Stars," by Nancy Kress
Grand Master—Arthur C. Clarke

1986 (1987)
Novel—*Speaker for the Dead*, by Orson Scott Card
Novella—"R and R," by Lucius Shepard
Novelette—"The Girl Who Fell into the Sky," by Kate Wilhelm
Short Story—"Tangents," by Greg Bear
Grand Master—Isaac Asimov

1987 (1988)
Novel—*The Falling Woman*, by Pat Murphy
Novella—"The Blind Geometer," by Kim Stanley Robinson
Novelette—"Rachel In Love," by Pat Murphy
Short Story—"Forever Yours, Anna," by Kate Wilhelm
Grand Master—Alfred Bester [posthumous]

1988 (1989)
Novel—*Falling Free*, by Lois McMaster Bujold

Novella—"The Last of the Winnebagos," by Connie Willis
Novelette—"Schrödinger's Kitten," by George Alec Effinger
Short Story—"Bible Stories for Adults, #17: The Deluge," by James Morrow
Grand Master—Ray Bradbury

1989 (1990)
Novel—*The Healer's War*, by Elizabeth Ann Scarborough
Novella—"The Mountains of Mourning," by Lois McMaster Bujold
Novelette—"At the Rialto," by Connie Willis
Short Story—"Ripples in the Dirac Sea," by Geoffrey A. Landis

1990 (1991)
Novel—*Tehanu: The Last Book of Earthsea*, by Ursula K. Le Guin
Novella—"The Hemingway Hoax," by Joe Haldeman
Novelette—"Tower of Babylon," by Ted Chiang
Short Story—"Bears Discover Fire," by Terry Bisson
Grand Master—Lester del Rey

1991 (1992)
Novel—*Stations of the Tide*, by Michael Swanwick
Novella—"Beggars in Spain," by Nancy Kress
Novelette—"Guide Dog," by Mike Conner
Short Story—"Ma Qui," by Alan Brennert

THE PILGRIM AWARDS
(For Lifetime Contributions to the Scholarship of Science Fiction and Fantasy Literature)

1970—J. O. Bailey
1971—Marjorie Hope Nicholson
1972—Julius Kagarlitski [Yulii Kagarlitskii]
1973—Jack Williamson
1974—I. F. Clarke
1975—Damon Knight
1976—James E. Gunn
1977—Thomas D. Clareson
1978—Brian W. Aldiss
1979—Darko Suvin
1980—Peter Nicholls
1981—Sam Moskowitz
1982—Neil Barron
1983—H. Bruce Franklin
1984—Everett F. Bleiler
1985—Samuel R. Delany
1986—George E. Slusser
1987—Gary K. Wolfe
1988—Joanna Russ
1989—Ursula K. Le Guin
1990—Marshall B. Tymn
1991—Pierre Versins
1992—Mark R. Hillegas

THE *SCIENCE FICTION CHRONICLE* AWARDS

1981 (1982)
Novel—*The Claw of the Conciliator*, by Gene Wolfe
Novella—"In the Western Tradition," by Phyllis Eisenstein
Novelette—"Mummer Kiss," by Michael Swanwick
Short Story—"The Pusher," by John Varley
Editor—Edward L. Ferman
Artist—Michael Whelan
Dramatic Presentation—*Raiders of the Lost Ark*, screenplay by Lawrence Kasdan
Fanzine—*Science Fiction Chronicle*, Andrew Porter, ed.
Fan Writer—Richard E. Geis
Fan Artist (Fanzines)—Alexis Gilliland
Fan Artist (Conventions)—Victoria Poyser
Convention—Denvention 2

1982 (1983)
Novel—*The Sword of the Lictor*, by Gene Wolfe
Novella—"Souls," by Joanna Russ
Novelette—"Fire Watch," by Connie Willis
Short Story—"Petra," by Greg Bear
Editor—Edward L. Ferman
Artist—Michael Whelan
Dramatic Presentation—*Blade Runner*, screenplay by Hampton Fancher and David Peoples
Fanzine—*File 770*, Mike Glyer, ed.
Fan Artist (Fanzines)—Alexis Gilliland
Fan Artist (Conventions)—No award
Semiprozine—*Science Fiction Chronicle*, Andrew Porter, ed.
Convention—World Fantasy Convention 1982

1983 (1984)
Novel—*The Anubis Gates*, by Tim Powers
Novella—"Her Habiline Husband," by Michael Bishop
Novelette—"Black Air," by Kim Stanley Robinson
Short Story—"The Peacemaker," by Gardner Dozois
Editor (Magazines)—Edward L. Ferman
Editor (Books)—David Hartwell
Artist—Michael Whelan
Fanzine—*File 770*, Mike Glyer, ed.
Fan Writer—Richard E. Geis
Fan Artist—Alexis Gilliland
Semiprozine—*Science Fiction Chronicle*, Andrew I. Porter, ed.
Cover (Books)—Ace Books, Gene Mydlowski, art ed.
Cover (Magazines)—*Analog*, Ralph Rubino, art ed.
Most Attractive Female Writer—Tanith Lee
Most Attractive Male Writer—(tie) Harlan Ellison; Thomas Monteleone
Most Attractive Female Artist—Dawn Wilson
Most Attractive Male Artist—Don Maitz
Most Attractive Female Editor—Susan Allison
Most Attractive Male Editor—David Hartwell
Most Attractive Female Fan—Tess Kissinger
Most Attractive Male Fan—Jean Gonzalez
Best Buns (Either Gender)—Douglas E. Winter

1984 (1985)
Novel—*Neuromancer*, by William Gibson
Novella—"Press ENTER ▮," by John Varley
Novelette—"Bloodchild," by Octavia E. Butler
Short Story—"Salvador," by Lucius Shepard
Editor (Magazines)—Edward L. Ferman
Editor (Books)—Terry Carr
Artist—Michael Whelan
Dramatic Presentation—*2010: Odyssey Two*, screenplay by Peter Hyams
Fanzine—*File 770*, Mike Glyer, ed.
Fan Writer—Richard E. Geis
Fan Artist—Brad Foster
Semiprozine—*Science Fiction Chronicle*, Andrew Porter, ed.

1985 (1986)
Novel—*Ender's Game*, by Orson Scott Card
Novella—"The Only Neat Thing to Do," by James Tiptree, Jr.
Novelette—"Paper Dragons," by James P. Blaylock
Short Story—"Portraits of His Children," by George R. R. Martin
Editor (Magazines)—Shawna McCarthy
Editor (Books)—Judy-Lynn del Rey
Artist—Michael Whelan
Dramatic Presentation—*Back to the Future*, screenplay by Robert Zemeckis and Bob Gale
Fanzine—*File 770*, Mike Glyer, ed.
Fan Writer—Richard E. Geis
Fan Artist—Brad Foster
Semiprozine—*Science Fiction Chronicle*, Andrew Porter, ed.

1986 (1987)
Novel—*Speaker for the Dead*, by Orson Scott Card
Novella—"R and R," by Lucius Shepard
Novelette—"Aymara," by Lucius Shepard
Short Story—"Pretty Boy Crossover," by Pat Cadigan
Editor (Magazines)—Gardner Dozois
Editor (Books)—David Hartwell
Artist—Michael Whelan
Dramatic Presentation—*Aliens*, James Cameron, Writer and Director
Fanzine—*Ansible*, Dave Langford, ed.
Fan Writer—Dave Langford
Fan Artist—Brad Foster
Semiprozine—*Science Fiction Chronicle*, Andrew Porter, ed.

1987 (1988)
Novel—*The Urth of the New Sun*, by Gene Wolfe
Novella—"The Secret Sharer," by Robert Silverberg
Novelette—"The Evening and the Morning and the Night," by Octavia E. Butler
Short Story—"The Circular Library of Stones," by Carol Emshwiller
Editor (Magazines)—Gardner Dozois

Editor (Books)—David Hartwell
Artist—Michael Whelan
Dramatic Presentation—*The Princess Bride*, screenplay by William Goldman
Fanzine—*Izzard*, Patrick and Teresa Nielsen Hayden, eds.
Fan Writer—Teresa Nielsen Hayden
Fan Artist—Arthur "ATom" Thompson
Semiprozine—*Science Fiction Chronicle*, Andrew Porter, ed.

1988 (1989)
Novel—*Cyteen*, by C. J. Cherryh
Novella—"Last of the Winnebagos," by Connie Willis
Novelette—"Schrödinger's Kitten," by George Alec Effinger
Short Story—"Kirinyaga," by Mike Resnick
Dramatic Presentation—*Who Framed Roger Rabbit?*, screenplay by Jeffrey Price and Peter S. Seaman
Artist—Don Maitz
Editor (Magazines)—Edward L. Ferman
Editor (Books)—David Hartwell
Semiprozine—*Science Fiction Chronicle*, Andrew Porter, ed.
Fanzine—*Fosfax*, Timothy Lane, ed.
Fan Writer—Mike Glyer
Fan Artist—Brad Foster

1989 (1990)
Novel—*A Fire in the Sun*, by George Alec Effinger
Novella—"The Mountains of Mourning," by Lois McMaster Bujold
Novelette—"For I Have Touched the Sky," by Mike Resnick
Short Story—"Dori Bangs," by Bruce Sterling
Dramatic Presentation—*Field of Dreams*
Artist—Tom Canty
Editor (Magazines)—Gardner Dozois
Editor (Books)—Beth Meacham
Semiprozine—*Science Fiction Chronicle*, Andrew Porter, ed.
Fanzine—*Lan's Lantern*, George Laskowski, ed.
Fan Writer—Dave Langford
Fan Artist—Teddy Harvia

1990 (1991)
Novel—*The Fall of Hyperion*, by Dan Simmons
Novella—"Bully!" by Mike Resnick
Novelette—"The Manamouki," by Mike Resnick
Short Story—"Bears Discover Fire," by Terry Bisson
Dramatic Presentation—*Total Recall*
Artist—Michael Whelan
Editor (Magazines)—Edward Ferman
Editor (Books)—Ellen Datlow
Semiprozine—*Science Fiction Chronicle*, Andrew Porter, ed.
Fanzine—*Lan's Lantern*, George Laskowski, ed.
Fan Writer—Dave Langford
Fan Artist—Teddy Harvia

1991 (1992)
Novel—*Stations of the Tide*, by Michael Swanwick
Novella—"Beggars in Spain," by Nancy Kress
Novelette—"Gate of Faces," by Ray Aldridge
Short Story—"Vinland the Dream," by Kim Stanley Robinson
Dramatic Presentation—*Terminator 2*
Artist—Michael Whelan
Editor (Magazines)—Gardner Dozois
Editor (Books)—Ellen Datlow

Semiprozine—*Science Fiction Chronicle*, Andrew Porter, ed.
Fanzine—*Ansible*, Dave Langford, ed.
Fan Writer—Dave Langford
Fan Artist—Teddy Harvia

THE WORLD FANTASY AWARDS

1973/74 (1975)
Novel—*The Forgotten Beasts of Eld*, by Patricia A. McKillip
Short Fiction—"Pages From a Young Girl's Diary," by Robert Aickman
Single Author Collection/Anthology—*Worse Things Waiting*, by Manly Wade Wellman
Artist—Lee Brown Coye
Lifetime Achievement—Robert Bloch
Special Award (Professional)—Ian and Betty Ballantine, for publishing excellence
Special Award (Nonprofessional)—Stuart David Schiff, for *Whispers*

1975 (1976)
Novel—*Bid Time Return*, by Richard Matheson
Short Fiction—"Belsen Express," by Fritz Leiber
Single Author Collection/Anthology—*The Enquiries of Dr. Esterhazy*, by Avram Davidson
Artist—Frank Frazetta
Lifetime Achievement—Fritz Leiber
Special Award (Professional)—Donald M. Grant, for publishing excellence
Special Award (Nonprofessional)—Carcosa Publishers

1976 (1977)
Novel—*Doctor Rat*, by William Kotzwinkle
Short Fiction—"There's a Long, Long Trail A-Winding," by Russell Kirk
Single Author Collection/Anthology—*Frights*, edited by Kirby McCauley
Artist—Roger Dean
Lifetime Achievement—Ray Bradbury
Special Award (Professional)—Alternate World Recordings
Special Award (Nonprofessional)—Stuart David Schiff, for *Whispers*

1977 (1978)
Novel—*Our Lady of Darkness*, by Fritz Leiber
Short Fiction—"The Chimney," by Ramsey Campbell
Single Author Collection/Anthology—*Murgunstrumm and Others*, by Hugh B. Cave
Artist—Lee Brown Coye
Lifetime Achievement—Frank Belknap Long
Special Award (Professional)—Everett F. Bleiler
Special Award (Nonprofessional)—Robert Weinberg

1978 (1979)
Novel—*Gloriana*, by Michael Moorcock
Short Fiction—"Naples," by Avram Davidson
Single Author Collection/Anthology—*Shadows*, by Charles L. Grant
Artist—Alicia Austin; Dale Enzenbacher
Lifetime Achievement—Jorge Luis Borges
Special Award (Professional)—Edward L. Ferman, for *The Magazine of Fantasy & Science Fiction*
Special Award (Nonprofessional)—Donald H. Tuck

Special Award—Kirby McCauley, for starting the World Fantasy Convention

1979 (1980)
Novel—*Watchtower*, by Elizabeth A. Lynn
Short Fiction—(tie) "The Woman Who Loved the Moon," by Elizabeth A. Lynn; "Mackintosh Willy," by Ramsey Campbell
Single Author Collection/Anthology—*Amazons!*, by Jessica Amanda Salmonson
Artist—Don Maitz
Lifetime Achievement—Manly Wade Wellman
Special Award (Professional)—Donald M. Grant, for publishing excellence
Special Award (Nonprofessional)—Paul C. Allen

1980 (1981)
Novel—*The Shadow of the Torturer*, by Gene Wolfe
Short Fiction—"The Ugly Chickens," by Howard Waldrop
Single Author Collection/Anthology—*Dark Forces*, edited by Kirby McCauley
Artist—Michael Whelan
Lifetime Achievement—C. L. Moore
Special Award (Professional)—Donald A. Wollheim
Special Award (Nonprofessional)—Pat Cadigan and Arnold Fenner
Special Award—Gahan Wilson

1981 (1982)
Novel—*Little, Big*, by John Crowley
Novella—"The Fire When It Comes," by Parke Godwin
Short Story—(tie) "The Dark Country," by Dennis Etchison; "Do the Dead Sing?," by Stephen King
Anthology/Collection—*Elsewhere*, Terri Windling and Mark Allan Arnold, eds.
Artist—Michael Whelan
Lifetime Achievement—Italo Calvino
Special Award (Professional)—Edward L. Ferman, for editing *The Magazine of Fantasy & Science Fiction*
Special Award (Nonprofessional)—Paul Allen and Robert Collins, for *Fantasy Newsletter*
Special Award—Roy G. Krenkel
Special Award—Joseph Payne Brennan

1982 (1983)
Novel—*Nifft the Lean*, by Michael Shea
Novella—(tie) "Beyond All Measure," by Karl Edward Wagner; "Confess the Seasons," by Charles L. Grant
Short Story—"The Gorgon," by Tanith Lee
Anthology/Collection—*Nightmare Seasons*, by Charles L. Grant
Artist—Michael Whelan
Lifetime Achievement—Roald Dahl
Special Award (Professional)—Donald M. Grant, for publishing excellence
Special Award (Nonprofessional)—Stuart David Schiff, for *Whispers*

Special Award—Arkham House Publishers

1983 (1984)
Novel—*The Dragon Waiting*, by John M. Ford
Novella—"Black Air," by Kim Stanley Robinson
Short Story—"Elle est Trois (La Mort)," by Tanith Lee
Anthology/Collection—*High Spirits*, by Robinson Davies
Artist—Steve Gervais
Lifetime Achievement—L. Sprague de Camp, E. Hoffmann Price, Donald Wandrei [refused], Richard Matheson, Jack Vance
Special Award (Professional)—Ian and Betty Ballantine, Joy Chant, George Sharp, and David Larking for *The High Kings*
Special Award (Nonprofessional)—Stephen Jones and David Sutton for *Fantasy Tales*
Special Award—Donald M. Grant

1984 (1985)
Novel—(tie) *Mythago Wood*, by Robert Holdstock; *Bridge of Birds*, by Barry Hughart
Novella—"The Unconquered Country," by Geoff Ryman
Short Story—(tie) "Still Life With Scorpion," by Scott Baker; "The Bones Wizard," by Alan Ryan
Anthology/Collection—*Books of Blood, Vols. 1-3*, by Clive Barker
Artist—Edward Gorey
Lifetime Achievement—Theodore Sturgeon
Special Award (Professional)—Chris van Allsburg, for *The Mysteries of Harris Burdick*
Special Award (Nonprofessional)—Stuart David Schiff, for *Whispers*
Special Award—Evangeline Walton

1985 (1986)
Novel—*Song of Kali*, by Dan Simmons
Novella—"Nadelman's God," by T. E. D. Klein
Short Story—"Paper Dragons," by James P. Blaylock
Anthology/Collection—*Imaginary Lands*, by Robin McKinley
Artist—Jeff Jones; Thomas Canty
Lifetime Achievement—Avram Davidson
Special Award (Professional)—Pat LoBrutto
Special Award (Nonprofessional)—Douglas E. Winter
Special Award—Donald A. Wollheim

1986 (1987)
Novel—*Perfume*, by Patrick Suskind
Novella—"Hatrack River," by Orson Scott Card
Short Story—"Red Light," by David J. Schow
Anthology/Collection—*Tales of the Quintana Roo*, by James Tiptree, Jr.
Artist—Robert Gould
Lifetime Achievement—Jack Finney
Special Award (Professional)—Jane Yolen
Special Award (Nonprofessional)—Jeff Conner; W. Paul Ganley
Special Award—Andre Norton

1987 (1988)
Novel—*Replay*, by Ken Grimwood
Novella—"Buffalo Gals, Won't You Come Out Tonight," by Ursula K. Le Guin
Short Story—"Friend's Best Man," by Jonathan Carroll
Anthology/Collection—*The Jaguar Hunter*, by Lucius Shepard
Artist—J. K. Potter
Lifetime Achievement—Everett F. Bleiler
Special Award (Professional)—David G. Hartwell

Special Award (Nonprofessional)—David B. Silva, for *The Horror Show*; Robert and Nancy Garcia, for *American Fantasy*

1988 (1989)
Novel—*Koko*, by Peter Straub
Novella—"The Skin Trade," by George R. R. Martin
Short Story—"Winter Solstice, Camelot Station," by John M. Ford
Collection—(tie) *Storeys from the Old Hotel*, by Gene Wolfe; *Angry Candy*, by Harlan Ellison
Anthology—*The Year's Best Fantasy: First Annual Collection*, Ellen Datlow and Terri Windling, eds.
Artist—Edward Gorey
Lifetime Achievement—Evangeline Walton
Special Award (Professional)—Terri Windling; Robert Weinberg
Special Award (Nonprofessional)—Kristine Kathryn Rusch and Dean Wesley Smith, for *Pulphouse*

1989 (1990)
Novel—*Lyonesse: Madouc*, by Jack Vance
Novella—"Great Work of Time," by John Crowley
Short Fiction—"The Illusionist," by Steven Millhauser
Collection—*Richard Matheson: Collected Stories*, by Richard Matheson
Anthology—*The Year's Best Fantasy: Second Annual Collection*, Ellen Datlow and Terri Windling, eds.
Artist—Thomas Canty
Lifetime Achievement—R. A. Lafferty
Special Award (Professional)—Mark V. Ziesing, for Mark V. Ziesing Publications
Special Award (Nonprofessional)—Peggy Nadramia, for editing *Grue Magazine*

1990 (1991)
Novel—(tie) *Only Begotten Daughter*, by James Morrow; *Thomas the Rhymer*, by Ellen Kushner
Novella—"Bones," by Pat Murphy
Short Fiction—"A Midsummer Night's Dream," by Neil Gaiman and Charles Vess
Collection—*The Start of the End of It All and Other Stories*, by Carol Emshwiller
Anthology—*Best New Horror*, Stephen Jones and Ramsey Campbell, eds.
Artist—Dave McKean
Lifetime Achievement—Ray Russell
Special Award (Professional)—Arnie Fenner
Special Award (Nonprofessional)—Richard Chizmar, for editing *Cemetery Dance*

ABOUT THE AUTHOR

ROBERT REGINALD (Michael Burgess) has been a librarian at California State University, San Bernardino since 1970. A native of Fukuoka, Japan, he obtained his A.B. at Gonzaga University in Spokane, Washington (1969), and his M.S. in L.S. at the University of Southern California (1970). His first reference book, *Stella Nova*, the direct bibliographical ancestor of *Science Fiction and Fantasy Literature*, was the result of a senior Honor's project at Gonzaga, being compiled at the age of twenty. It was published under the name R. Reginald because, he says, "my own name had already been appropriated by the late historical novelist Noel Gerson." Since this auspicious beginning he has written or edited sixty-five books (through 1992), assembled four reprint series for Arno Press, edited three journals, and managed two publishing companies. At Cal State, he has successively worked as Periodicals Librarian, Assistant Bibliographer, and (currently) Chief Cataloger; he was promoted to full professor in 1984. His biography appears in *Who's Who in America, Contemporary Authors*, and sixty other sources.

BOOKS BY ROBERT REGINALD

Stella Nova: The Contemporary Science Fiction Authors (1970)
Cumulative Paperback Index, 1939-1959 (1973)
Contemporary Science Fiction Authors, First Edition (1975)
Ancestral Voices: An Anthology of Early Science Fiction, with Douglas Menville (1975)
The Attempted Assassination of John F. Kennedy: A Political Fantasy (1976)
Alistair MacLean: The Key Is Fear, by Robert A. Lee (ed., 1976)
Ancient Hauntings, with Douglas Menville (1976)
Phantasmagoria, with Douglas Menville (1976)
R.I.P.: Five Stories of the Supernatural, with Douglas Menville (1976)
The Spectre Bridegroom & Other Horrors, with Douglas Menville (1976)
Up Your Asteroid! A Science Fiction Farce (1977)
John D. MacDonald and the Colorful World of Travis McGee, by Frank D. Campbell Jr. (ed., 1977)
Things To Come: An Illustrated History of the Science Fiction Film, with Douglas Menville (1977)
Dreamers of Dreams: An Anthology of Fantasy, with Douglas Menville (1978)
King Solomon's Children: Some Parodies of H. Rider Haggard, with Douglas Menville (1978)
They: Three Parodies of H. Rider Haggard's She, with Douglas Menville (1978)
Worlds of Never: Three Fantastic Novels, with Douglas Menville (1978)
Science Fiction and Fantasy Literature: A Checklist, 1700-1974, with Contemporary Science Fiction Authors II (1979)
Science Fiction and Fantasy Book Review, with Neil Barron (1980)
The Paperback Price Guide No. 1, with Kevin Hancer (1980)
Science Fiction and Fantasy Awards (1981)
The Holy Grail Revealed: The Real Secret of Rennes-le-Château, by Patricia and Lionel Fanthorpe (ed., 1982)
If J.F.K. Had Lived: A Political Scenario, with Jeffrey M. Elliot (1982)
Candle for Poland: 469 Days of Solidarity, by Leszek Szymanski (ed., 1982)
The Paperback Price Guide No. 2, with Kevin Hancer (1982)
The House of the Burgesses (1983)
The Wickizer Annals, with Mary A. Burgess (1983)
Tempest in a Teapot: The Falkland Islands War, with Jeffrey M. Elliot (1983)
A Guide to Science Fiction & Fantasy in the Library of Congress Classification Scheme (1984)
The Work of Jeffrey M. Elliot: An Annotated Bibliography & Guide (1984)
The Work of R. Reginald: An Annotated Bibliography & Guide, (1985)
The Work of Julian May: An Annotated Bibliography & Guide, with Thaddeus Dikty (1985)
Lords Temporal & Lords Spiritual: A Chronological Checklist of the Popes, Patriarchs, Katholikoi, and Independent Archbishops and Metropolitans of the Monarchical Autocephalous Bishops of the Christian East and West (1985)

Futurevisions: The New Golden Age of the Science Fiction Film, with Douglas Menville and Mary A. Burgess (1985)

The Work of Bruce McAllister: An Annotated Bibliography & Guide, by David Ray Bourquin (ed., 1985)

The Work of Charles Beaumont: An Annotated Bibliography & Guide, by William F. Nolan (ed., 1986)

The Work of George Zebrowski: An Annotated Bibliography & Guide, with Jeffrey M. Elliot (1986)

The Work of Bruce McAllister: An Annotated Bibliography & Guide, Rev. Ed., by David Ray Bourquin (ed., 1986)

Mystery & Detective Fiction in the Library of Congress Classification Scheme (1987)

A Guide to Science Fiction & Fantasy in the Library of Congress Classification Scheme, 2nd Ed. (1988)

Western Fiction in the Library of Congress Classification Scheme, with Beverly A. Ryan (1988)

California Ranchos: Patented Private Land Grants Listed by County, by Burgess McK. Shumway (ed., 1988)

The Work of William F. Nolan: An Annotated Bibliography & Guide, with James Hopkins (1988)

The Arms Control, Disarmament, and Military Security Dictionary, with Jeffrey M. Elliot (1989)

The Work of Colin Wilson: An Annotated Bibliography & Guide, by Colin Stanley (ed., 1989)

The Work of Chad Oliver: An Annotated Bibliography & Guide, by Hal W. Hall (ed., 1989)

The Work of Ross Rocklynne: An Annotated Bibliography & Guide, by Douglas Menville (ed., 1989)

The Work of Ian Watson: An Annotated Bibliography & Guide, by Douglas A. Mackey (ed., 1989)

The Work of Reginald Bretnor: An Annotated Bibliography & Guide, by Scott Alan Burgess (ed., 1989)

The Work of Pamela Sargent: An Annotated Bibliography & Guide, by Jeffrey M. Elliot (ed., 1990)

The Work of Jack Dann: An Annotated Bibliography & Guide, by Jeffrey M. Elliot (ed., 1990)

Hancer's Price Guide to Paperback Books, with Kevin Hancer (1990)

The Work of George Zebrowski: An Annotated Bibliography & Guide, 2nd Ed., with Jeffrey M. Elliot (1990)

To Kill or Not to Kill: Thoughts on Capital Punishment, by Rep. William L. Clay, Sr. (ed., 1990)

The Work of Charles Beaumont: An Annotated Bibliography & Guide, 2nd Ed., by William F. Nolan (ed., 1990)

The Work of Dean Ing: An Annotated Bibliography & Guide, by Scott Alan Burgess (ed., 1990)

The Work of Louis L'Amour: An Annotated Bibliography & Guide, by Hal W. Hall (ed., 1991)

The Trilemma of World Oil Politics, by Sheikh R. Ali and Jeffrey M. Elliot (ed., 1991)

Reginald's Science Fiction and Fantasy Awards, 2nd Ed., with Daryl F. Mallett (1991)

The Work of Robert Reginald: An Annotated Bibliography & Guide, 2nd Ed. (1992)

Reference Guide to Science Fiction, Fantasy, and Horror (1992)

The Work of Brian W. Aldiss: An Annotated Bibliography & Guide, by Margaret Aldiss (ed., 1992)

Science Fiction and Fantasy Literature, 1975-1991 (1992)

Reginald's Science Fiction and Fantasy Awards, 3rd Ed., with Daryl F. Mallett (1992)

Lords Temporal & Lords Spiritual: A Chronological Checklist of the Popes, Patriarchs, Katholikoi, and Independent Archbishops and Metropolitans of the Monarchical Autocephalous Bishops of the Christian East and West, 2nd Ed. (1992)

The Work of Katherine Kurtz: An Annotated Bibliography & Guide (1992)